Copyright © Macmillan London Limited 1984, 1985, 1986, Macmillan Press
Limited, 1987, 1988, 1989, 1990, 1991, 1992, Pan Macmillan 1993, 1994;
Macmillan General Books 1995, 1996, 1997, 1998, 1999

All rights reserved. No reproduction, copy or transmission of this publication
may be made without written permission. No paragraph of this publication
may be reproduced, copied or transmitted save with written permission or in
accordance with the provisions of the Copyright, Designs and Patents Act
1988, or under the terms of any licence permitting limited copying issued
by the Copyright Licensing Agency, 90 Tottenham Court Road, London
W1P 9HE. Any person who does any unauthorised act in relation to this
publication may be liable to criminal prosecution and civil claims for damages.

This edition published 1999 by Macmillan
an imprint of Macmillan Publishers Limited
25 Eccleston Place, London SW1W 9NH

British Library Cataloguing in Publication Data
A CIP catalogue record for this book is available from the British Library

ISBN 0–333–725719 (Hardback)
ISBN 0–333–765990 (Paper laminate case)

Note
Whilst every care has been taken in compiling the information contained in
this book, the Publishers, Editor and Sponsors accept no responsibility for
any errors or omissions.

Correspondence
Letters on editorial matters should be addressed to:
The Editor, Royal & Ancient Golfer's Handbook
Macmillan General Books
25 Eccleston Place,
London SW1W 9NF

Enquiries about despatch, invoicing and commercial matters should be
addressed to:
Customer Services Department
Macmillan Press Limited
Houndmills
Basingstoke
Hampshire RG21 2XS

Advertising
Enquiries about advertising space in this book should be addressed to:
Communications Management International
Chiltern House
120 Eskdale Avenue
Chesham
Buckinghamshire HP5 3BD

Cover photograph of Mark O'Meara © Phil Sheldon

Typeset by Heronwood Press, Medstead, Hampshire

Printed by Mackays of Chatham plc, Chatham, Kent

Contents

Foreword *Renton Laidlaw*	9
The Captain of the R&A, 1998–99	11
The Year in Review *Renton Laidlaw*	13
O'Meara Tops 1998 List of Outstanding Players *Renton Laidlaw*	17
Women's Golf *Lewine Mair*	29
The Amateurs *Mark Garrod*	33
What the Players Had to Say During the 1998 Majors	35
Playing by the Rules – Tricky Decisions of 1998 *Keith Mackie*	38
The Ladies' Golf Union – the Year in Review *Julie Hall*	40
R&A Venues and Dates for Championships, 1999–2002	41
Future Venues and Dates for the US Major Championships	42
Schedules for the 1999 Season	43

Part I The Major Championships

The Open Golf Championship	54
The US Open Championship	64
The Masters	72
US PGA Championship	79
Men's Major Title Table	87
Weetabix Women's British Open Championship	88
US Women's Open Championship	95
McDonald's LPGA Championship	103
Nabisco Dinah Shore	110
Du Maurier Classic	117
Women's Major Title Table	124

Part II Men's Professional Tournaments

Index	126
Official World Golf Ranking, 1998	128
European Tour (1998 and Past Results)	130
European Challenge Tour, 1998	150
European Senior Tour, 1998	152
US PGA Tour, 1998	155
US Senior PGA Tour, 1998	166
US Nike Tour	170
Japan Tour	172
Asian PGA Omega Tour	174
Asian Tour	175

Experience the De Vere difference.

Those accustomed to playing the finest championship courses in beautiful surroundings will recognise the De Vere

difference instantly. The De Vere difference is in the detail. Enjoy championship golf designed to challenge yet inspire, including Slaley Hall in Northumberland, host to the PGA European Tour, and The Belfry in Warwickshire, host of the Ryder Cup for an unprecedented fourth time. Play through spectacular landscapes, from the stunning scenery of Loch Lomond to the beauty of Lincoln's finest parkland at Belton Woods. And afterwards, relax in the nineteenth or refresh yourself in superb leisure clubs before dining in elegance, from The Park restaurant at Blackpool to The Georgian restaurant at Cameron House, overlooking Loch Lomond.

Where exhilaration awaits on every fairway. Experience the De Vere difference.

Golf breaks from £82.50.
For more information call 01925 639499.
QUOTING REFERENCE GROY 1

Hotels of character, run with pride.

P.O. Box 333, The Malt Building,
Greenalls Avenue, Warrington, Cheshire WA4 6HL.
*Prices correct at time of going to press and based on per person per night.

From Seve's 10th at The Belfry to the Sleeping Giant at Slaley Hall.

From Greenalls Hotels and Leisure

Vodacom South African PGA Tour	176
South American PGA Tour	178
Australasian Tour	179
Other International Events – Individual and Team	180
British National and Regional Championships	197
Overseas National Championships (1989–98)	205

Part III Women's Professional Events

Index	210
Ping Leaderboard World Ranking, 1998	211
European LPGA Tour	212
US LPGA Tour	216
Japan LPGA Tour	223
Australasian LPGA Tour	225
International Team Events	226
Professional Women's Overseas Championships	230

Part IV Men's Amateur Events

Index	234
National and International Amateur Championships	235
Other Men's Amateur Tournaments	265
Regional Amateur Championships	281
Overseas Amateur Championships	288

Part V Women's Amateur Events

Index	292
National and International Tournaments	293
Other Women's Amateur Tournaments	314
Regional Amateur Championships	315
Overseas Amateur Championships	321

Part VI Junior Events

Index	324
Boys' and Youths' Tournaments	325
Girls' and Junior Women's Tournaments	335
Golf Foundation Events	341

Part VII: Awards

	346

Part VIII Who's Who in Golf

British Isles Players	350
Overseas Players	382
British Isles International Players, Professional Men	404
British Isles International Players, Amateur Men	411
British Isles International Players, Amateur Women	429
Association of Golf Writers	442

Part IX Guide to Golfing Services and Places to Stay in the British Isles and Ireland

Buyer's Guide	444
Golf Club Facilities	470
Golfing Hotel Compendium	484
Index of Advertisers	522

Part X Clubs and Courses in the British Isles and Europe

1999 Centenary Clubs	526
Golf Clubs and Courses in the British Isles and Europe	
Explanation of details and abbreviations	527
Great Britain and Ireland county index	528
List of new entries/Stop Press, Great Britain and Ireland	529
Clubs and courses:	
England	530
Ireland	663
Scotland	687
Wales	721
Regional index of clubs and courses in continental Europe	733

Part XI The Government of the Game

The Royal & Ancient Golf Club of St Andrews	820
Other Governing Bodies	826
Championship and International Match Conditions	831
Golf Associations	835
Addresses of Golfing Organisations Worldwide	838

Part XII Golf History

The Championships of Great Britain	850
Famous Players of the Past	854
Interesting Facts and Unusual Incidents	870
Record Scoring	898

General Index	907

PRO-PLAY

the best choice for course planners and yardage books in golf today.

Club Secretaries and Professionals, boost your profits with a PRO-PLAY course planner. Our superbly presented, laser-measured yardage books generate additional revenues and profits for golf clubs which stock them. We custom-design a yardage book you can sell in number, then we keep you stocked *Sale or Return*.
Send for sample books and details of our simple, no-cost, no-risk system. Phone of fax:-
+ 44 (0) 1788 54 39 64

PO Box 1286, Rugby CV21 1YX, United Kingdom.

RHOD McEWAN
GOLF BOOKS

Specialist dealer in rare, second-hand and out-of-print golf books.

I offer a prompt valuation and full advisory service.

Always looking to purchase collections or single volumes.

Member of the Antiquarian Booksellers Association.

Free catalogue available.

Glengarden, Ballater
Aberdeenshire, AB35 5UB
Tel: 013397 55429 • Fax: 013397 55995

Original SCHOTTEN *Trophies*

Enhance the thrill and enjoyment of winning with a special and collectable keepsake.

Exquisite Hand Crafted Trophies from The Schotten Collection

Visit our Website at http://www.schotten.com
or for a brochure contact us at
109 High Street, Burford, Oxfordshire OX18 4RH
Tel: 01993 822302 Fax: 01993 822055

DEREK BURRIDGE
WHOLESALE LIMITED
(Established 1960)

OFFICIAL TROPHY SUPPLIERS TO
THE ENGLISH GOLF UNION

■ UNBEATABLE *PRICES*
■ UNBEATABLE *VARIETY*
■ UNBEATABLE *QUALITY*
■ UNBEATABLE *SERVICE*

Before you buy prizes for your next golf Day make sure you are familiar with the DEREK BURRIDGE RANGE.

FOR ALL YOUR PRESENTATION AWARDS AT **TRADE TERMS** VISIT OUR SHOWROOMS AND WORKSHOP OR PHONE FOR OUR LATEST BROCHURES.

AWARDS HOUSE, UNIT 15, THE METRO CENTRE,
SPRINGFIELD ROAD, HAYES, MIDDLESEX UB4 0LE
TEL: 0181-569 0123 FAX: 0181-569 0111

THE BEST CLUB IN THE WORLD

Stoke Poges Golf Club has great pleasure in announcing the completion of its multi-million pound refurbishment restoring the glorious Grade I Palladian Mansion and the 300 acre estate to its former glory. The Club was established in 1908, its course was designed by the most influential golf architect in history, Harry Shapland Colt. Hailed as one of the most important events in golf, Stoke Poges opened a further 9 holes in August 1998. This recreated the original 27 hole course designed by Colt in 1908. Thus providing the opportunity to apply for new memberships for the first time in 90 years. Annual 7 day individual membership is only £1,750 inc. VAT.

• Championship Golf Course • 8 Private Rooms for Conferences or Entertaining •
• 21 Bedrooms • Corporate Golf Days • FREE Shuttle Service to and from Heathrow •

Stoke Park, Park Road, Stoke Poges, Buckinghamshire, SL2 4PG
Telephone: 01753 717171   Email: info@stokepark.co.uk
Facsimile: 01753 717181   http://www.stokepark.co.uk

Foreword

Renton Laidlaw

Renton Laidlaw

Regular subscribers to *The Golfer's Handbook* will notice one or two changes to this latest edition of a publication which first hit the bookshelves at the end of the last century. The changes, which will continue into next year's edition, are designed to improve its value as a reference book and to make it more reader friendly.

In this edition and in future editions, current tournament results will not be divorced from past results. Now the past winners appear immediately before the 1998 winners and, in many cases, with the names and scores of the players who finished second and third. With the addition of a new, more detailed index it is hoped that those seeking information in this section will find it easier to track down the information they require.

Yet this is just one aspect of the modernisation of golf's most popular reference book. All the regular sections remain but some will, in future, be repositioned in a more logical way.

The Clubs and Courses section, supervised by the ever-diligent Jan Bennett, has been expanded and will continue to be improved and enhanced. The hotel guide is more comprehensive and, as always, I am indebted to Alan Elliott for his work in the biographies section, which will be even more extensive in future editions. Judy Williams supervised the results section with her son Roddy.

Lewine Mair's review of the year in women's golf and Mark Garrod's in-depth look at the amateur scene are now regular features, but in this edition Keith Mackie, who is responsible for the Royal & Ancient's members' newsletter, highlights the talking points on the rules front. This will become a regular annual feature, as will the article highlighting the working of the Ladies' Golf Union, which has its headquarters not far from that of the Royal & Ancient Golf Club in St Andrews.

The *Golfer's Handbook* will no longer carry automatically the rules of golf or the handicapping system used in women's golf, but both are readily available in separate booklets available free from the R&A and the LGU, respectively. In the year following the four-yearly review by the R&A and USGA, however, the rules will be printed in full with the changes highlighted.

Enjoy your golf in 1999.

H.M.T. PLASTICS LTD

Fairway House, 31A Framfield Road,
Uckfield, East Sussex TN22 5AH
Tel: (01825) 769393 Fax: (01825) 769494

Round, pear-shaped, shield and sunrise bag tags.
Annually renewable year stickers.
All available in a variety of colours.
Prices and samples sent on request.

European Golf Machinery

BUCKLESHAM, IPSWICH,
SUFFOLK IP10 0DN

MANUFACTURERS OF GOLF RANGE EQUIPMENT

* Lightweight "Poly Pikka" Ball Collectors
* Range Ball Dispensers
* Manual or Semi-Auto Ball Washers
* Kawasaki ATV's and Mule Low Ground Pressure Trucks adapted for range of use
* Elevators, Trailers, Target Nets, Mats and Balls
* After Sales Service and Part Exchanges

Suppliers of ball collectors to I.M.G. European Tour from 1991-1998 **Kawasaki**

Ask for details of our special promotion.
*Exclusive **diesel engined** Mule utility vehicle*
TEL: (01473) 659815   FAX: (01473) 659045
QUALITY BRITISH PRODUCTS

The National Golf Show
golf live '99
"Everything for the perfect round under one roof"

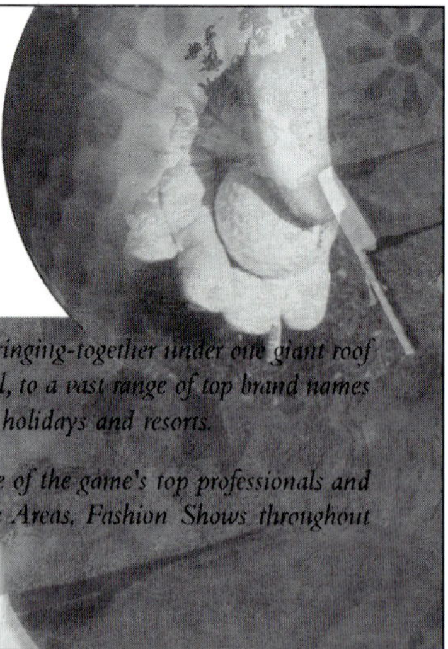

golf live '99, a major consumer showpiece event, will pioneer the bringing-together under one giant roof everything of interest to golfers, from golfing equipment and apparel, to a vast range of top brand names in the leisure, health and fashion industries, to the best in golfing holidays and resorts.

golf live '99 will be honoured with personal attendances from some of the game's top professionals and other golfing celebrities, and will include State-of-the-art Feature Areas, Fashion Shows throughout each day, Competitions and Free Prize Draws.

The golfing extravaganza of the year!

Tickets available in advance £8.00 • On the day £12.00
Under 16's No charge with adult
For further information contact 0181 373 7756

London • Wembley Exhibition Centre • 23rd-25th July 1999
10.00am - 7.00pm Friday & Saturday • 10.00am - 6.00pm Sunday

The Captain of the Royal and Ancient Golf Club of St Andrews

John Charles Beharrell

Forty-two years after he became the youngest winner of the Amateur Championship, John Charles Beharrell assumed his duties last September as Captain of the Royal and Ancient Golf Club of St Andrews. Since that day at Royal Troon in 1956 when, just a year after he had played for England at senior and junior level, he took the Amateur title against Leslie Taylor, only two other 18-year-olds have been successful: South African Bobby Cole in 1966 and Spaniard Sergio Garcia with his win over Craig Williams at Muirfield last year.

Mr Beharrell's home club is Little Aston and he is an honorary member at Edgbaston, Blackwell and Handsworth. He has been a member of the R&A since 1956 and is currently playing off 5. He is a keen historian of the game and enjoys playing with hickory clubs. He has served on four R&A committees: the Championship Committee, the Rules of Golf Committee, the Amateur Status Committee and the Implements and Ball Committee. He has been involved in golf administration at club, county, regional and national level.

John Beharrell is married to the former Veronica Anstey, who was in a winning Curtis Cup side in 1956. A former Australian and New Zealand women's champion, she played international golf for England between 1955 and 1957 and captained the side in 1961. They have a daughter, two sons and seven grandchildren. Having retired as managing director of an international trade finance company in 1990, John Beharrell has turned gardening, one of his hobbies, into a horticultural business which he runs with his sons, both of whom are qualified chartered surveyors.

Although he is vice-president of the Artisan Golfing Association and is much concerned about the welfare of the artisan, it is perhaps logical that he would choose, during his term of office, to publicise and encourage support of junior golf at all levels – national, regional, county and club. 'We need more youngsters to take up golf in the light of a worrying statistic

which shows that 25% fewer people under 25 took up golf in the past five years. Much is being done by the Golf Foundation to introduce golf to children at school but it does not appear that the message is getting through to those youngsters whose parents do not play the game,' says Beharrell. He applauds the Royal and Ancient Golf Club's decision to give youngsters free admission to the Open each year.

Mr Beharrell supports junior golf and in particular the Golf Foundation, which currently organises tuition for children in over 2000 schools and institutions and cooperates with local councils in the provision of Starter Centres for all juniors. A target of 350 of these centres is likely to be met within two years, which should bring 100,000 more young players into the game. The Foundation is a non-profit-making organisation, but currently fewer than 1000 of Britain's 2500 clubs make any contribution. Perhaps that number will have increased by the end of captain Beharrell's term of office. While appreciating that the game must be advanced into the 21st century, he is strong in his view that tradition and etiquette must be maintained.

PRO-PLAY — the best choice for course planners and yardage books in golf today.

Club Secretaries and Professionals, boost your profits with a **PRO-PLAY** course planner. Our superbly presented, laser-measured yardage books generate additional revenues and profits for golf clubs which stock them. We custom-design a yardage book you can sell in number, then we keep you stocked *Sale or Return*.
Send for sample books and details of our simple, no-cost, no-risk system. Phone of fax:-

+ 44 (0) 1788 54 39 64

PO Box 1286, Rugby CV21 1YX,
United Kingdom.

GOLF TROPHY SPECIALISTS
Societies - Clubs - Secretaries Professionals

All discounted

Export Worldwide

Quality and Service at affordable prices

Call for free colour brochure brand new for 1999

- ■ **Hole in One Awards**
- ■ **Antique Replicas**
- ■ **Pewter Gifts**
- ■ **Print Golf Clocks**
- ■ **Silverware**
- ■ **Logo Balls**
- ■ **Float Bronze Figures**
- ■ **Engraving**
- ■ **Cups and Awards**
- ■ **Replica Clubs**
- ■ **Leather Accessories**
- ■ **Crystal Golf Clubs**

BIRKDALE PROMOTIONS
97 Old Watford Road, Bricket Wood,
Nr. St Albans, Hertfordshire AL2 3UN.
Tel: 01923 671225 Fax: 01923 662522

Complete and Professional Survey and Measurement Service

strokesaver
GOLF'S No1 DISTANCE GUIDE

ABBEY MILL BUSINESS CENTRE
PAISLEY PA1 1TJ   SCOTLAND
Tel: 0141 848 1199 Fax: 0141 887 1642

3 Drayton Avenue, Ealing, London W13 0LE.

Would you buy a luxury car and its back up if it cost the same as a small economy car? Yes? Well read on.

- Melex electric & petrol golf buggies at **unbeatable** prices, and we mean **unbeatable**!
- UK-wide service and parts back up.
- Finance terms to suit.
- Accessories for housing and transportation.

WHY SETTLE FOR LESS WHEN YOU CAN HAVE THE BEST!!

TELEPHONE: 0181-997 4885
FAX: 0181-997 4825
e-mail: ChipnChubLtd@BTinternet.com

The Year in Review

Renton Laidlaw

It was the year that Mark O'Meara, after 56 attempts at winning a major, won two – the first American to do so in the same season since Tom Watson took the US and British Open titles in 1982, and only the tenth since the war. O'Meara's first triumph came at Augusta, where he rolled in a 20-footer across the last green to become a member of that exclusive group of golfers who have birdied the last hole to earn a Green Jacket. He then edged out fellow-American, Japan Tour regular, Brian Watts, in the four-hole play-off for the Open at a stormy Royal Birkdale. With a 32nd place finish in the US Open and fourth place in the US PGA, O'Meara became the first player to win $1 million in prize money from the four Grand Slam events. His double major triumph earned him Golfer of the Year honours in the US, ahead of David Duval, who, after taking several seasons to learn how to win, did so dramatically – winning four times on the US Tour in 1998 to boost his victories tally to seven in 12 months.

Americans in the money

O'Meara had edged out Duval and former winner Fred Couples at Augusta but, despite winning $1,786,699, he finished seventh on the US money list, behind Duval who amassed $2,591,031. That was $270,914 less than the money banked by golf's most successful over-50s golfer Hale Irwin, who played 22 events on the US Senior Tour, won seven times, had six second-place finishes, came third twice, fourth three times and fifth twice. Irwin set a new average score record of 68.59. Since turning Senior he has finished in the top three in 44 of 80 starts. No one dominated a world circuit as effectively as Irwin, though his old rival Gil Morgan won two Senior majors and also topped $2 million in earnings.

Payne Stewart, a double major winner in his own right, has come close to winning the US Open on two other occasions only to be thwarted twice by his bogeyman Lee Janzen. The first time was at Baltusrol in 1993, when Janzen, equalling Jack Nicklaus' 72-hole low score record, pipped him by two shots. In 1998 the venue was the Olympic Club in San Francisco, where Stewart played impressively but ended in the supporting role again to the 1995 Players' champion.

At Sahalee in Seattle later in the year, golf's most ardent practiser, Fijian Vijay Singh, earned the reward he deserved by winning the US PGA Championship. Steve Stricker, Steve Elkington and Mark O'Meara, trying to equal Ben Hogan's record of three majors in one season, challenged for a time on the final day, but the Fijian held firm to take his first major.

The Europeans

In Europe, Lee Westwood won four times and came within a whisker of ending Colin Montgomerie's reign as European No. 1, but like many others since 1993 he must wait another year. Yet Westwood's performances in 1998 merited his being named Golfer of the Year. Not only did he shoot 15 under par to win the Freeport McDermott Classic in New Orleans, 40 under par for European victories in the Deutsche Bank – SAP Tournament Players' Championship and the National Car Rental English Open in successive weeks, and land further first prize cheques impressively at Loch Lomond and at Royal Zoute in Belgium, but he also went to Japan and won the Taheiyo Masters for the third successive year and then followed that up by successfully defending his Dunlop Phoenix Open title. That triumph was his seventh in 30 events and his 13th in his three years as a professional – it might have been 14 but he lost the play-off for the Malaysian Open in early summer to Ed Fryatt.

Westwood is justifiably the leader of the younger European Tour set which includes Darren Clarke (winner of the Benson & Hedges International and Volvo Masters), Andrew Coltart, Patrik Sjoland, Thomas Bjorn, Stephen Allan, Stephen Leaney and David Carter, all of whom finished in the top 16 in the end of the season money list.

Despite his individual successes, however, Westwood could not quite match Montgomerie's amazing consistency. The Scotsman's strong finish to the season, in which he won two of the last four events he played in, more than made up for

the disappointment of not winning that elusive first major and of experiencing his first slump, a mini one, when he temporarily lost form on the greens. He solved the problem by enlisting the help of short-game guru Dave Pelz, and late in the season called in long-time coach Bill Ferguson to sort out some niggling swing problems.

Another top coach, David Leadbetter, hit the headlines when he parted company, not all that amicably, with one of his star pupils, Nick Faldo, whose troubles off the course hardly helped him find top form on it. For Faldo it was a disappointing season, but the desire is still there. A first win for England in partnership with David Carter in the World Cup of Golf in New Zealand and a fourth-place finish in the late season Australian Open at Royal Adelaide is indicative perhaps that he has not yet finished collecting titles.

Seniors

If Hale Irwin dominated senior golf in America, Tommy Horton remained top dog in Europe for the third year running. Having retired this year from his post as golf professional at Royal Jersey, Horton is happy to concentrate his efforts on the expanding European circuit, even if some other former European Tour stars are winning or coming close to winning bigger money on the Stateside Senior Tour – notably Hugh Baiocchi, Brian Barnes (who scored his first US Senior Tour success in 1998), Vicente Fernandez and José Maria Canizares.

The Senior circuits on both sides of the Atlantic have given older golfers the opportunity to maintain their competitive edge at a time when, in days gone by, they would have long since retired from all but regional competitions. Significantly, in Europe, evergreen Neil Coles, who has now won in five different decades and still possesses one of the best swings in golf, and battling Welshman Brian Huggett may be in their early 60s but are still competing with the intensity that has always been a mark of their golf in the past 40 years. Huggett won twice, including the Senior British Open for the first time, and Coles picked up one first-prize cheque.

Australasia

Globetrotting Scot Andrew Coltart was top earner on the Australasian circuit, clinching that top spot the week he scored his first victory on the European Tour in Qatar, one of the Tour's two Middle East stops.

Yet, for Australians, the main story of the year featured their most successful modern era superstar, Greg Norman. After missing the half-way cut at the Masters in Augusta, where he played in pain because of a damaged right shoulder, 'The Shark' took six months off to have corrective surgery. Some felt he might retire to concentrate on his massive business interests, but he never lost the urge to return to competitive action and had recovered sufficiently to return to win his own Shark Shoot-out with Steve Elkington.

Team events

Norman also played an inspirational part in the resounding success at Royal Melbourne of the International side against the Americans in the Presidents' Cup, the Ryder Cup-style match held in alternate years to the more established fixture. The International side, led brilliantly by five-times Open champion Peter Thomson, won in convincing manner by nine points. The result, following two Ryder Cup defeats by the Europeans, came as a major shock to the men led by Jack Nicklaus, who curiously put his big guns out late on the final day when he badly needed points. That meant that the showcase match between Woods and Norman, which Woods won on the last green, had less emphasis on the overall result than it might have had.

The American women professionals, however, won their Solheim Cup match against Europe at Muirfield Village. The match made headlines for the quality of the golf on both sides and, rather more unfortunately, for some over-enthusiastic partisanship by some of the American players. Europe's Laura Davies felt that the always-intense Dottie Pepper acted unfairly at the end of one Saturday foursomes by her histrionics before the opposition had holed out. Davies called Pepper's action unprofessional and reported the incident to American team captain Judy Rankin, who did not accept her player had been rude but apologised anyway for the incident, arguing it had been the result of the intense emotion of the moment.

Great Britain & Ireland's club professionals were also well beaten by the Americans in the biennial PGA Cup, and the amateur women lost the Curtis Cup 10—8. The women pulled out of the World Team Championship for the Espirito Santo Trophy in Chile because of a political situation involving both countries and former Chilean president Pinochet, but, despite security warnings, the men did go and, captained by Peter McEvoy, were victorious in the Eisenhower Trophy, beating the Australians, the defending champions, into second place. Gary Wolstenholme, Luke Donald, Lorne Kelly and Paddy Gribben shot 852 to win by four. Australia's Kim Felton took the individual title.

America's amateur ladies Jenny Chuasiriporn, Kellee Booth and Brenda Corrie Kuehn were duly successful by a whopping 21 shots in the Espirito

Santo Trophy, with Miss Chuasiriporn waltzing away with the individual title by shooting four sub-par rounds. Earlier in the year, Thai-American Chuasiriporn had come close to becoming only the second amateur winner of the US Women's Open title but, after holing from 50 feet across the green on the last at Blackwolf Run to force a first-ever all-Asian 18-hole play-off with Se Ri Pak, it was the Korean golfer who came out top after two more extra holes.

The women break records

Se Ri Pak had already won the McDonald's LPGA title and, in winning the national crown, she, like O'Meara and Morgan, had won two majors in a year – but in her rookie year. It was Pak, winner of four events on the US Women's Tour overall, who shot the low and historic round of the year – a 10-under-par 61 *en route* to victory in the Jamie Farr Kroger Classic – and who won the First Union Betsy King Classic without dropping a shot in 72 holes.

Pak, sponsored by Korean electronics company Samsung, attracted most of the attention during the season in America, but the top earner at the end of the day despite winning no majors in 1998, was Sweden's own 'Miss Consistency' Annika Sörenstam, who wrote her own piece of golfing history by shooting an average score for the season of 69.99 – the first time in the history of the Tour a golfer has averaged a score under 70.

In Europe, the somewhat truncated fixture list saw Helen Alfredsson finish in top spot, and what had been a difficult season ended on a happy note when Marie Laure di Lorenzi led her side, helped by the use of some forward tees, to an honourable draw with Europe's senior men in their annual fixture. With a new chief executive now appointed, there is hope that the Women's Tour in Europe will thrive as it heads towards the millenium

Notable

The year was notable for a number of things, not least Sam Torrance notching up his 600th European Tour appearance in the Linde German Masters. He has played nearly 100 more events than his nearest rival on Tour and, though he did get the Canon award for the best shot of the season (which went to Miguel Angel Jimenez' chip-in at the last to beat, among others, David Duval and Mark O'Meara at the Trophée Lancôme), the popular Scot had every right to claim his 7-wood second shot uphill and into the teeth of the wind at the 17th in the Peugeot French Open at Golf National was a masterpiece of judgement and timing. It finished just a foot away and, with the help of a birdie at a hole few managed to par in the conditions, the second oldest man in the field went on to win for the first time in two and a half years. 'I'm fit and strong and young at heart and I feel I have a few more victories in me before I'm 50,' said the 41-year-old. Torrance missed out on Ryder Cup duty at Valderrama in 1997, but his aim is to make the European side which will face the Americans at the Country Club, Brookline, in 1999. Even if he does not make it – and teetotaller Torrance will not entertain such a thought – he will at least have a role this time, acting as a lieutenant to Mark James who will captain Europe against Ben Crenshaw's line-up.

It was the year Tiger Woods, who won only once in the US but had 13 top ten finishes and remained the main crowdpuller and sponsors' favourite, parted company with Hughes Norton, a top IMG manager who has not had the best of luck with his clients, which in the past have included Greg Norman and Curtis Strange.

Phil Mickelson made history by winning the longest event in US Tour history, the rain-interrupted AT&T Championship, three rounds of which were played in January and the final round on August 17th.

During the year, Casey Martin, who because of a permanent leg problem was allowed to use an electric cart after winning his historic court case against the Tour, started the season encouragingly with victory in the first Nike event, but it ended with his having to return to the Tour school.

In Europe, Greg Chalmers from Australia, playing in the National Car Rental English Open, needed a par, par finish to shoot an elusive first ever 59, but bogeyed the last two holes for 61.

In 1998, Michael Bonallack, five times British and English amateur champion and Secretary of the Royal & Ancient Golf Club of St Andrews deservedly received a knighthood for his services to golf as both a competitor and administrator. Sir Michael is only the second golfer to be knighted. (Henry Cotton was the first.)

Losses

To end on a sad note, golf lost several notables during the year including Gardner Dickinson, a fearsome opponent, and Dr Cary Middlecoff; but the saddest story involved Stuart Appleby, who lost his wife Renay in a bizarre accident *en route* to a second honeymoon in Paris after the Open. They were a team on and off the course. An excellent golfer in her own right, Renay had often caddied for her husband who, at season's end, knew how proud she would have been of him as he challenged strongly for the Australian Open title, played his part brilliantly in the International team's President's Cup success and won the Coolum Classic at a venue they both loved.

CENTENARY CLUBS
1999

WE WOULD LIKE TO EXTEND OUR WARMEST WISHES TO THE FOLLOWING CLUBS IN THEIR CENTENARY YEAR.

Oxford City Golf Club
Hilltop Road, Oxford OX4 1PF
Tel: 01865 242158

Oxford City Golf Club is part of Southfield Golf Club Ltd as is Oxford University G.C. and also Oxford Ladies G.C.

Formed in 1899 on Cowley Marsh, Oxford City Golf Club moved to the Southfield Estate together with Oxford University 76 years ago. The famous course designer, Harry Colt, had constructed a new course incorporating some holes of the original James Braid layout. The course is typical of Harry Colt with each hole both different and intimidating. The 12th hole was once described by the renowned TV commentator and former University golfer, Henry Longhurst, as *"....one of the best holes in English golf"*. In the 1920s the Football Association commissioned the Crown Silversmith to make a new trophy to replace the F.A. cup. they made three, one of which now adorns the club's trophy cabinet, having been presented in 1926 by William Morris (Lord Nuffield), to celebrate his 27 years as President of the Oxford City Golf Club.

Prestwick St Cuthbert Golf Club
East Road, Prestwick, Ayrshire KA9 2SX.
Tel: 01292 477101
Fax: 01292 671730

Prestwick St Cuthbert Golf Club was founded in 1899 originally as a 9-hole course, converting to 18 holes in 1907. The club moved to its present position in 1963 due to the expansion of Prestwick Airport. The course, which while close to the sea, is parkland and was designed by John R Stutt Ltd. It is a good test of golf at 6133 yards, par 71, with an interesting mixture of 11 par 4s.

O'Meara Tops 1998 List of Outstanding Players

Renton Laidlaw

Mark O'Meara

For Mark O'Meara it was the year to dream about. The 41-year-old golfer, whose best performances in 56 attempts to win a major had been one top 10 in The Masters, and two top 10s in each of the US Open, the British Open and the US PGA Championships, surprised the world of golf by taking two majors in the space of 15 weeks, with perhaps a little help from golfing phenomenon Tiger Woods.

The two golfers live close to each other in Florida and play practice rounds together. O'Meara's experience and calm approach has proved invaluable in helping Woods cope with the pressure of being the Tour's superstar, expected to perform every time he tees up. But playing regularly with Woods benefitted O'Meara, the quiet unassuming family man, as well. O'Meara gained a new confidence that he could achieve golfing greatness. In 1998, he reached new heights of competitive achievement to become the oldest player in modern times to win two majors in one season. He joined an exclusive club: Jack Nicklaus and Ben Hogan were both 40 when they won multiple major victories in 1980 and 1953.

Nobody rated him a potential winner when he teed up at Augusta in April last year. No champion had ever won for the first time having had 13 previous attempts. There was nothing on his record round the famous National course that indicated O'Meara would even be a challenger, but that week he putted like a magician on the most frighteningly fast greens in world golf. Five behind after the first and second rounds, O'Meara narrowed the gap between him and front-runner and former winner Fred Couples to two with a round to go, then produced a winning 67 with a finish of which to be justifiably proud. He birdied three of the last four holes, holing a slick cross-green 20-footer on the last to edge out Couples and David Duval who were anticipating a play-off.

O'Meara was only the fifth player to birdie the last to win – Sandy Lyle, Gary Player, Arnold Palmer and Art Wall Jr were the others – and only

Mark O'Meara wins The Masters at his 14th attempt.

the third after Palmer and Wall to birdie the last two to win a Green Jacket. It was appropriate that Tiger, the winner the previous year, was the man who put the Jacket on his shoulders. He calls O'Meara the big brother he never had, but the relationship has benefitted the older player as well. It has given him a sharper edge to his golf. 'I am a better player because I understand my game better now,' O'Meara says. 'Now my game matches my personality. Now I know I can be me and win any tournament I enter.'

If his record coming into the Open in July was unimpressive – six missed cuts in his eight previous appearances – O'Meara at least knew and had won a European Tour event over the challenging

Royal Birkdale course. What surprised him last July was the weather. Gales gusting at times to 40 mph blew away the title hopes of many, but O'Meara stuck to his task and ended 72 holes tied with Japanese Tour regular Brian Watts, who nearly snatched victory in dramatic fashion at the last with a bunker recovery from a cruelly difficult lie which finished inches from the hole. Tiger Woods missed out on the four-hole play-off by a shot despite finishing with three birdies in the last four, but in the end O'Meara triumphed in the Championship he loves. 'Victory is unbelievable,' he said, adding: 'I cannot put my finger on it, but this Championship has always been special to me. Winning The Masters earlier this year helped me handle the pressure this week. I hung in there. I was relaxed and remained calm. I'm pretty impressed with myself.'

He deserved to be and, a few weeks later, he challenged strongly for a third major to equal Ben Hogan's 1953 record, beating par three times, matching it once and finishing joint fourth behind winner Vijay Singh in the US PGA Championship. Twelve times players have come to the final major of the year with the chance to match Hogan's three major wins in a season. All have failed but nobody came closer to winning that elusive third title than O'Meara.

Yet his fabulous season was not over yet. He and Woods came to Wentworth for the Cisco World Matchplay Championship, Tiger for the first time. There were traffic jams and huge crowds to watch high-quality golf round a super test in an event which must never be allowed to become a victim of golf's new World Championships circuit. Mark McCormack, who had the brainwave to start the event back in 1964, can be justifiably proud of what he has achieved with this tournament. Come Sunday, there were just two players left and, helped by a shrewdly worked out draw and seeding, it was the fairy-tale final featuring Woods and O'Meara, two friends each as determined as the other to win the highly respected title. Woods was three up at lunch, lost four out of the first six holes in the afternoon, then grabbed the lead again with birdies around the turn. Yet, just as he had at Augusta and at Royal Birkdale, O'Meara produced some of his best golf on the back nine again to catch and pass his 22-year-old rival. The crucial hole was the 16th in the afternoon, where O'Meara came out of a bunker to 15 feet and holed for par and Woods three putted from 12 feet. O'Meara was ahead and stayed in front to the end.

'There is no way I could ever have dreamed what has happened to me this year,' he said in his final press conference as if he expected to wake up and find it had all been a fantasy.

Woods gave his friend and mentor the final accolade when he said: 'I am very happy for him. I have always said he has never been given the credit for being the great player he is. Now he is getting his just dues.'

It really was Mark O'Meara's year.

Lee Westwood

In 1998 Lee Westwood, in only his third year as a professional, underlined his potential as an international star. Whoever was going to pip Colin Montgomerie, No. 1 for a remarkable sixth time in a row, for the two top European golf awards knew his achievements needed to be extra special. Westwood met the strict criteria and filled the bill ideally. He easily triumphed in the poll held annually by golf writers as the player who had done most for European golf during the year, and Montgomerie was among the first to congratulate him.

Modestly, because his family upbringing has assured Westwood has his feet firmly planted on the ground, the young Englishman suggested that his back-to-back wins in Japan late in the year may well have tipped the balance his way. Maybe he did not end the season as European No. 1, nor score a glorious fairy-tale victory in the Million Dollar Challenge at Sun City in South Africa despite leading going into the final day, but his overall performance during the year, the quality of his play and, just as importantly, his demeanour were impressive.

Like Montgomerie, a major win is now his most immediate goal. Since turning professional after an amateur career which saw him miss out on Walker Cup honours and only just squeeze into the English international side, Westwood has just got better and better. Helped immensely in his bid to find extra distance off the tee without losing any of his through-the-green consistency by inspirational coach Peter Cowen, himself a former player, Westwood remains loyal, too, to the man who helped him in the early years – Worksop professional John King. It was King who taught him the basics of a good swing when, as a teenager, Westwood decided that it was no longer fun to caddie for his father, a headmaster in a local school. It was take up fishing or concentrate on golf, and Westwood, a young man who knows his own mind and is being shrewdly managed by another former player, Andrew 'Chubby' Chandler, made the correct decision.

Earlier season performances had indicated that young professional Westwood was in a different class to some of the other youngsters on Tour. He had a solid, reliable game, a perfect,

Europe's newest star Lee Westwood (here holding the English Open Trophy) won seven times on three continents.

There has been for some time now great rivalry between him and Ulsterman Darren Clarke, so his 61-66 over the weekend, which earned him the Deutsche Bank – SAP Open Tournament Players Championship of Europe at Clarke's expense, was particularly pleasing.

Maintaining that form the following week and landing the National Car Rental English Open – he was 40 under par for eight successive rounds at Gut Kaden and Hanbury Manor – made up for his having lost a play-off earlier in the year to Ed Fryatt in that Malaysian Open.

His next, equally rewarding, success came in the curiously named Standard Life Loch Lomond – the old Loch Lomond Invitational played on the course Tom Weiskopf designed and built.

Late in the year, Westwood's fourth win came at the Belgacom Open at Royal Zoute after a play-off with Frederik Jacobsen – a victory that made his late run for No. 1 spot in Europe more exciting. Westwood just lost out, dropping away on the final day after hitting three balls out of bounds and running up an 8 at the short 14th on a much improved Montecastillo course at Jerez in the Volvo Masters. In the end, he finished third in the money list behind Montgomerie and Volvo Masters winner Clarke.

He may have been bitterly disappointed not to have deposed Montgomerie, but it did not take Westwood long to bounce back. He flew to Japan, won the Taiheyo Masters in the shadow of Mount Fuji for the third successive time and then picked up his second Dunlop Phoenix title the following week, again with Clarke as runner-up.

Westwood, who achieved his goal of getting into the world's top 10 in 1998 – he finished the year in eighth spot – has new goals for 1999. 'I'd like to make it into the top five this year with an eye on becoming No. 1 somewhere along the way. Obviously I should like to play well in the majors because victories in the Grand Slam events are what matter. I need to win a few.' Who would dare suggest, taking his 1998 form as a guide, that Westwood will not end up a multiple major winner like Ballesteros and Faldo.

In the close season, such as it is for the globe-trotting stars these days, he married Andrew Coltart's sister Laurae and, as a result, took some time off from playing golf. He deserved the break. When he re-emerges refreshed and enthusiastic on the competitive scene he will hope to peak during majors' weeks. In 1998, he won the week before The Masters, the week before the US Open and the week before the Open. Just a little adjustment to that form timetable is required to help him take his golf game to a new level.

nearly always unflappable, temperament for the big occasion and the ardent desire, like Seve Ballesteros and Nick Faldo before him, to win. In addition, he is blessed with that valuable quality of being able, in a flash, to put behind him the memory of any slack or destructive shots or the disappointment when a well-hit putt does not drop because it has hit a spike mark. That in itself is an important asset.

When the season began, he had already won in Scandinavia, in Malaysia (where he has a golf club endorsement), in Japan twice and in England, but in 1998 he played so well he charged into the top 10 in world golf with the help of seven international successes. 'All the best players have a proven record in different countries and that was what I wanted to establish quickly,' he told journalists at the end of the year. 'It is difficult to pick out one victory above another, but winning for the first time in America on the Jack Nicklaus-designed English Turn course at the Freeport-McDermott event was big for me. It got me recognised in the US.' In fact, he was reasonably well known anyway, because all European Tour events are beamed these days to 25 million homes in the United States by The Golf Channel.

Vijay Singh

Fourteen years ago, at a low point in his eventful career, Vijay Singh, the tall Fijian with the elegant swing, had given up, albeit reluctantly, playing tournament golf. To make ends meet he had taken a club job, far off the beaten track, in steamy Borneo. In those far-off days, when his only golfing pleasure was hitting balls in strength-sapping 100° Fahrenheit temperatures each day, he may could only dream that some time in the future he might find himself playing with distinction on the US Tour and winning a Grand Slam title.

In 1994, he turned the first part of that distant dream into reality when, having sharpened up his game in Europe, he earned his US Tour card, and four years later completed the job by winning the 80th US PGA Championship. He won his first major – there may well be more – impressively enough from determined Steve Stricker at Sahalee in Seattle, watched proudly by his Malaysian-born wife Ardena and eight-year-old son Qass. That week, golf's most assiduous practiser became an even bigger hero back in Fiji. Golf is not a major sport in the islands where Rugby Union football is most popular, but the small Pacific country is mightily proud of what 35-year-old Singh, truly a world star, has done to put the island on the golfing map. After all, in Fiji international stars in any sport are thin on the ground, even if this one seldom finds himself back home these days.

In some respects it is appropriate that a golfer who is a world traveller extraordinaire these days should have learned his golf at the airport course in the Fijian capital, Suva. Singh's father, Mohan, was an airport worker who had access to the course, and when he played, Vijay often caddied for him. It was the most natural thing in the world that, having shown an unusual talent for the game, he should consider making it his career. Singh has seen his fair share of airports over the years as he goes about learning the trade with disciplined dedication. Glance at his *curriculum vitae* and what impresses instantly is the number of countries in which he has won tournaments in the past 12 years. Take Europe: in England he ended Ernie Els' run of successes by beating the South African in the 1997 World Matchplay Championship at Wentworth, but he has won, too, in France, Spain and Germany, where he was victorious in the national Open in 1993 by 11 shots. Africa has also been a happy hunting ground for him, with victories in Morocco, South Africa, the Ivory Coast, Zimbabwe and Nigeria, where he proved as adept at putting on browns (a mixture of oil and sand) as on grass greens. He has won in Malaysia and, of course, America, where he has won seven times in the past four years – it

Vijay Singh at the US PGA Championship, Sahalee, 1998.

© Phil Sheldon

might have been eight had he not lost a play-off to the fast-finishing Hal Sutton in the season-ending Tour Championship after leading for four days at East Lake in Atlanta.

On reflection, it was almost inevitable that someway down the line Singh would win a major. His game, modelled on that of Tom Weiskopf from instruction pieces in old magazines, was good enough, his work-rate impressive and his commitment unquestioned. At most events he is usually last to leave the practice ground as he diligently continues to groove his swing to ensure that under pressure it does not break down. During those lonely months in the jungles of Borneo, Singh, who had had his problems in the past as a Tour player in Asia and Australia, gained genuine respect for the game and all it represents in terms of individual courage, integrity and discipline. When, finally, he had clinched victory and seen the limpit-like Stricker off at the cruelly tight Sahalee with its punishing rough, there was genuine respect for him from his colleagues on Tour. 'He has had an enormously difficult road to pick up that trophy,' said Steve Elkington, who got to know him in his early years on the Australian Tour. 'He will be a great champion.'

Tiger Woods had led after the first day in Seattle, but Singh had taken the lead at the halfway stage with rounds of 70 and 66, stayed in front with a 67 on the third day and rounded off his two-stroke win with a final round 69, not without its almost mandatory slice of luck. At the par 5 11th hole on the final day, Singh, normally so straight through the green, sent his second shot crashing into the trees beside the green only to see it rebound onto the green. At the 14th he hooked a wedge 130 yards round some trees and onto the green. It bent 50 yards in the air! Leading by just one shot from Stricker with two to play, Singh came out of sand and holed from 18 feet for a par 3 at the 17th. The American, also bunkered, had left himself with a 12-foot putt on the same line, but missed.

During the week, Singh had only one three-putt on Sahalee's testing undulating greens, but maybe that is not so surprising. Earlier in the year he had reverted, on his wife's advice, to the left-hand-below-right style he used when he first started playing. Encouraged by his Scottish caddie, Dave Renwick, to work harder on his putting, Singh reaped the benefits.

Renwick, from East Calder, a small village outside Edinburgh, had won major titles with José Maria Olazábal at Augusta in 1994 and Steve Elkington in the US PGA Championship at Riviera in 1995. He is one of the most experienced caddies in the business, and Singh generously paid tribute to the part Renwick had played in his success. 'I could not have done this without him,' he said. 'We talked about a lot of things out there and he kept me calm and kept me focussed. He helped me concentrate.'

In majors, big-hitting Singh's best of five previous top ten finishes had been fourth in the 1994 US PGA Championship. In 1998, the 6ft 2 ins tall Fijian, who some say has practised even harder over the years than Ben Hogan in his heyday, broke through. Now he is no longer one of the best players around never to have won a major.

David Duval

If Lee Westwood has become Europe's most prolific winner in recent times, David Duval fits the bill perfectly in America, albeit with one major difference. While Westwood has won in eight different countries, Duval has yet to take a title away from his home Tour. But that is not to downgrade his remarkable achievements. He may have taken some time to learn how to win – 86 tournaments to be exact – but when he had mastered the knack, the 26-year-old bachelor certainly enjoyed himself.

At the end of the 1997 season he had achieved what few have on Tour by winning three events in a row – the Michelob Championship, the Walt Disney World/Oldsmobile Classic and the Tour Championship. In 1998, he won the Tucson Chrysler Classic, the Shell Houston Open NEC World Series, and when he successfully defended the Michelob Championship he had notched up his fourth victory of the season and scored his seventh win in a remarkable 12 months – the most prolific performance since Tom Watson was to be seen picking up cheques with amazing regularity between May 1979 and May 1980. In that golden period for the five-times Open champion, Watson won eight titles and picked up $600,000. Duval's seven wins in 12 months earned him $3,733,400.

Duval continued his remarkable form by winning the first two events in which he played in 1999. He won in Hawaii by nine shots and then took the Bob Hope Desert Classic with a dramatic last round 59 – only the third ever recorded on the PGA Tour. He had 11 birdies and an eagle at the 543 yard last hole, where he hit a 5-iron to six feet. He was out in 31 but home in 28 to match the scores recorded by Al Geiberger in the 1977 Danny Thomas Memphis Classic

Four-times winner David Duval was America's top earner but missed out on Golfer of the Year.

and by Chip Beck in the 1991 Las Vegas Invitational. Duval's was the first last round 59, which enabled him to come from seven behind Fred Funk to win by a shot from Steve Pate. 'I have lots of goals,' he said. 'What I want now is to win the majors.' You can be sure he will start favourite in most if he continues to produce the form he showed in Hawaii and Palm Springs: form that enabled him to earn over a million dollars in two weeks with a 52-under-par nine-round score.

Only nine players since 1960 have won three titles or more in consecutive years – Jack Nicklaus and Arnold Palmer (that was to be expected), Billy Casper, Raymond Floyd, Tom Watson, Lee Trevino, Johnny Miller and Nick Price. Duval admitted it gave him 'a funny feeling' to join that list. Yet his philosphy regarding records is coldly clinical and may be a result of his less than arrogant assessment of his own ability. 'I don't bother with records. All that I'm interested in is being the best golfer on Sunday night at whatever tournament I've been playing in. It matters to me only that I am the best golfer on the week.'

At the end of the 1998 season, Duval, with his quartet of title successes and seven more top 10 finishes, topped the money list in the States with a Tour record $2.59 million, which, in normal circumstances, might have earned him Player of the Year recognition had Mark O'Meara not won two majors and the Cisco World Matchplay Championship. Still, Duval was philosophical about the situation. 'Maybe I deserve a nod for what I did, but do I deserve Player of the Year?' he asked pressmen. 'I'd have to think about that.' There was no bitterness and why should there have been?

Despite his triumphs, Duval has not attracted much additional sponsorship – perhaps because he is a somewhat remote figure on the golf course, hiding behind wraparound dark glasses which give him a rather sinister look. For a time he also favoured a small goatee beard, which many felt added even more unfavourably to his image, but that has gone and a more friendly Duval is emerging. He is dealing with fans more sympathetically and is learning to appreciate the role the press play week in, week out.

He may not yet have won a major, although he came desperately close at last year's Masters. Despite three-putting the 16th, Duval shot a closing 67 and was leading, with Fred Couples in the clubhouse, when Mark O'Meara coolly trundled in his 20-footer to win the title with a closing birdie. Had there been a play-off and had Duval won, he might well have ended the season with over $3 million in prize money. Typically, in the moment of defeat Duval was generous in his comments. 'I thought my 67 would have been good enough to win, but it wasn't. Mark has done a lot of good things for golf and has been a good friend to all we younger players on Tour.' He even found time to praise six-times Masters champion Jack Nicklaus who, at 58, finished joint sixth. 'We could hear the roars from his gallery all over the course. His was an amazing performance.'

In the other majors, he finished seventh in the US Open, 11th in the Open, again behind O'Meara, but missed the cut at the US PGA Championship. He has still to win abroad, although he came close at last year's Trophée Lancôme, won by Miguel Angel Jiménez. Duval, who had hit his tee shot into the water to the right of the last green at the short 18th on the third day, amazed the gallery by doing the same on the final day when well in contention. With that, his chance was gone. Nevertheless, the talented Duval, whose 69.13 made him No. 1 on the US stroke averages, is on the threshold of what could turn out to be a wonderful international career.

Se Ri Pak

Most rookie golfers on any professional Tour hope to score a victory in their first year. Se Ri Pak, the South Korean, won four times but, even more amazingly, included two majors in her quartet of successes. She did not finish top earner and did not have the low-scoring average for the year, but her wins in the McDonald PGA Championship, the first major in which she had ever played, and her dramatic extra-holes victory over Jenny Chuasiriporn in the US Open, only her second major, did enough to detract attention from the continuing excellent form of the ever-consistent Annika Sorenstam, fiery Dottie Pepper, Donna Andrews, Karrie Webb Laura Davies, Juli Inkster, Liselotte Neumann and the rest.

In short, Se Ri Pak was a revelation in 1998, and in the process gave her country, saddled with massive money problems after having to receive an $85 million loan from the International Monetary Fund, something to cheer about. South Korean President Dae Jung Kim called Pak 'a hero of this era and our hope', and the South Korean ambassador to the United States said that Se Ri Pak produced the best news of the year for the country.

Yet it was not just in the majors that she shone. The 61 she shot in the second round of the Jamie Farr Kroger Classic, after having changed to a heavier putter following an overnight putting lesson from her father, a former Korean amateur champion, was the lowest score in LPGA history. After adding 63 and 66, her 72-hole total of

South Korea's Se Ri Pak won two major titles in her rookie year.

23-under-par 261 was the lowest ever on Tour and it tied the under par record for 72 holes. Her 36-hole total of 124 for the second and third rounds was a record, and her 54-hole total of 190 for the last three rounds was too. Se Ri Pak was magical, and there was another first for her too – a more personal one. After she had beaten fellow 20-year-old and top amateur Jenny Chuasiriporn at the 92nd hole of the US Women's Open, she cried, she claimed, for the first time in her life. Chuasiriporn had been attempting to become only the second amateur to win the US Women's Open – Catherine Lacoste did so in 1967 – but she finally lost out to Pak at the second sudden-death hole, after they had finished their 18-hole play-off still tied. Ironically, Pak had survived a visit to the water at the last hole in the 18-hole play-off, but Chuasiriporn also bogeyed to lose the chance of victory. Two extra holes later it was all over, and Pak had become the youngest woman ever to win America's national title and the youngest ever to win two majors in a year. It was little wonder this golfing tigress has been dubbed the 'female Tiger Woods'.

At the end of the season, Pak had made $872,170 to finish second on the US Tour money list behind Sörenstam, who topped the million mark by $92,748 dollars and earned the Rolex Player of the Year Award. The Award is decided differently from the men's or Pak's two major wins might have tipped the balance her way. At any rate, she was Rolex Rookie of the Year, amassing 1,428 points – a staggering 900 more than second - best rookie Janice Moodie.

When she returned to South Korea late in the year, she received a heroine's welcome but it had been a tiring year and it proved to be an exhausting week. After flying for 21 hours from Orlando via New York and Anchorage to Seoul, she launched herself into a frenetic schedule of parades, autograph sessions, television interviews, press conferences, dinners and, of course, she was required to play golf. *Golf World* magazine reported that her schedule was so gruelling that she had to change clothes four times on one particularly hectic day. It was hardly surprising, therefore, that she had to withdraw after two rounds of the Korean Ladies Professional Golfers' Championship because of exhaustion and a bad cold. Medical experts said that she was suffering from a high fever, throat pain and muscle ache brought on by fatigue, jet lag and exposure to rain and cold. She had to cancel a visit to the Blue House, official residence of the South Korean President, where she was to receive a medal of honour for her wonderful performances during the year.

So impressed were her sponsors Samsung with her, that they readily renegotiated her ten-year contract to one of shorter duration but tripled her $1 million-a-year staff fee!

There were signs, too, that she was loosening up and beginning to smile more. Her manager Steven Sung-Yong Kil, explained in mid-summer that her severe manner was a result of having been educated in Confucianism, a discipline that teaches you not to talk or to show emotional reaction if you do well. 'She will learn to smile more as time goes by.'

Before the end of the year, Kil's services had been dispensed with and, in another surprise move, Pak moved away from coach David Leadbetter to join up with Tiger Woods in Butch Harmon's coaching group.

Leadbetter, who earlier in the year had lost Nick Faldo, a long-time client, was not amused when she told reporters that the break-up was because she needed more freedom. 'He is a busy man and I sometimes had to wait for him because of his schedule. I need someone around who can check my swing every day if need be and I need to be able to call on a chipping and putting expert whenever I need to, which I can do when not contracted to one coach.'

She is so single-minded about her golf that

she has even decided not to return in the close season to her parents in Korea, but to remain in Florida with her older sister. 'Now I want to focus on my golf game. I do not want anyone around me right now. I have to make my own choices, find myself in order to make myself a stronger and better player.' Newcomer Se Ri Pak means business.

Sergio Garcia

Spain's newest golfing sensation, Sergio Garcia, achieved one of his golfing ambitions when he won the Amateur Championship with a 7 and 6 victory over 20-year-old Welshman Craig Williams at rain-lashed Muirfield last summer. Now the golfer, dubbed 'El Niño' because of his explosive performances, has his eyes set on an Open Championship victory sooner rather than later.

Likely to turn professional after The Masters in Augusta this April, 18-year-old Garcia from Castellon, and with an unprecedented handicap of plus 5.3, came close to becoming the first golfer since Bob Dickson in 1967 to complete the transatlantic double but, having beaten defending champion Matt Kuchar in the quarter-finals by 2 and 1, he lost in the semi-final of the American Championship to 44-year-old re-instated amateur Tom McKnight, who in turn lost to Hank Kuehne in the final.

Kuehne's older brother was a finalist in 1994 and his sister Kelli won the US Girls and was twice women's champion. Hank and Kelli Kuehne are the only brother and sister to win the national titles.

Golfweek, the US golf magazine, and Titleist operate an amateur ranking during the year, and although the likeable Garcia played in only three of the points-counting events – the two amateur championships and the World Amateur Team Championship, where he finished seventh in the individual behind winner Australian Kim Felton – he still finished well ahead of second-placed Kuchar in the table.

When the Spanish youngster teed it up with the professionals he did not do too badly. He had tied 19th in the Nike Tour's Monterey Open earlier in the year, then was third when he played the Nike Greensboro Classic in June. On the European Tour he finished 12th behind Colin Montgomerie in the British One-2-One Masters, 18th in the Trophée Lancôme behind fellow Spaniard Miguel Angel Jiménez, 29th in the Open at Royal Birkdale, and made the cut in the four other Tour events in which he played – the Peugeot Spanish Open, Murphy's Irish Open, the Turespana Masters and the Standard Life sponsored event at Loch Lomond.

Teenager Sergio Garcia won the British Amateur Championship and made the last four in the US Amateur.

How different from the form shown on Tour by Justin Rose, another candidate for top amateur spot in 1998 after his great fourth-place finish in the Open behind Mark O'Meara. Rose's holed third shot from the rough, rated by most pundits as the best by any amateur in any major competition during the year, was his last as an amateur. Sadly, having turned professional (some say rather too early), he missed the cut in the seven events he played on the European Tour and then missed earning a card at the European Tour School. Rose was never under any illusion that the transfer from amateur to professional would not be a tough one.

There is a bright future on the horizon for Rose, but his one performance at the Open was overshadowed by Garcia's more solid portfolio. The Spaniard has much to live up to but he has already shown he has the game and the temperament to be a huge success as a professional. Frankly, I cannot wait to see how well he will do, encouraged by the fact that he has the support of both Seve Ballesteros and José Maria Olazábal, to whom he is regularly likened. That in itself is a mark of his potential.

Let us welcome you to
WOODHALL SPA

Visit the National Golf Centre at Woodhall Spa, home of the English Golf Union, and play golf on the world-famous Hotchkin Course, voted 29th best course in the world by *Golf Magazine of America;* or the new Donald Steel designed Bracken Course – just as challenging but with a character all of its own.

We offer • Extensive practice facilities including a 20 bay driving range • Wide choice of catering for small and large groups • Coaching packages for all standards of golfer • Tailor made packages for corporate and society days • Large well stocked golf shop • Pitch and putt course set in beautiful surroundings.

ENGLISH GOLF UNION, THE NATIONAL GOLF CENTRE, THE BROADWAY, WOODHALL SPA, LINCOLNSHIRE LN10 6PU.
Tel: 01526 352511 Fax: 01526 354020.
E-mail: flint@englishgolfunion.org WEB: http//www.englishgolfunion.org

---

- 18 HOLE PARKLAND CHAMPIONSHIP GOLF COURSE - PAR 71
- BEAUFORT, IS LOCATED CLOSE TO THE TOURISM MECCA OF KILLARNEY.
- STONE-BUILT CLUBHOUSE OFFERS A TRADITIONAL AND WARM ATMOSPHERE
- SOCIETIES, GROUPS AND VISITORS WELCOME 7 DAYS
- ELECTRIC BUGGIES, TROLLEYS, CLUBS AND CADDIES FOR HIRE
- GOLF TUITION BY ARRANGEMENT
- GOLF SHOP
- BAR FOOD AND SNACKS ALL DAY

KILLARNEY: 10KM   KERRY AIRPORT: 20KM
CORK AIRPORT: 50K

**Churchtown, Beaufort, Killarney, Co Kerry, Ireland.
Tel: +353 64 44440
Fax: +353 64 44752**

THE FRIENDLIEST COURSE IN
KERRY - JUDGE FOR YOURSELF

The ethos of the Sun Longest Day Challenge is for golfers to have fun, test their stamina, and help the less fortunate in society.

If your club is looking for a unique and novel way to raise money for your favourite charity this summer, then why not stage a 72 hole challenge at your club. In every club there will be a number of golfers - it does not matter if it is only a few - who will be prepared to 'take up the challenge' and play at least 72 holes in a day. With members and friends supporting them, considerable sums can be raised.

IF YOU ARE INTERESTED, OR WOULD LIKE MORE INFORMATION, PLEASE CALL OUR HELPLINE ON **01428 741333**

CENTENARY CLUBS
1999

Nairn Dunbar Golf Club,
Lochloy Road, Nairn IV12 5AE

Clubhouse & Secretary Tel: 01667 452741   Fax: 01667 456897

Situated on the shores of the Moray Firth, the Nairn Dunbar golf course, founded in 1899, is a highly rated Scottish links championship course representing a very formidable challenge with its gorse and whin lined fairways. Renowned for its excellent condition and friendly reception to visitors, it is the chosen venue in 1999 for the Northern Open Professional Championship, the Scottish Ladies Amateur Stroke Play and the Scottish Boys Strokeplay. Nairn Dunbar will also be hosting much of the 1999 Walker Cup associate golf.

Three new holes were introduced in 1994 to enhance the overall layout. The new 9th hole, a par 5, is cut into a silver birch wood, with a testing dog-leg, par 4, 10th separated by a winding waterway. The 11th is a short but tricky par 3. With these changes the course now measures 6720 yards, par 72, SSS 73.

A spacious new clubhouse was officially opened in May 1998 by Sir Michael Bonallack OBE. Facilities include an extensive lounge/bar and dining room, a golfers' lounge/bar with TV and pool, visitors' locker room as well as a junior lounge with TV and pool. Catering is available from full Scottish breakfast to evening meals with bar snacks available throughout the day.

Your day at Nairn Dunbar will be a memorable one

When in Somerset...

...treat yourself to a stay at the Burnham and Berrow Golf Club. Championship links golf course and accommodation at the Dormy House from £62 per night including breakfast and Green Fees.

St. Christophers Way
Burnham on Sea TA8 2PE
Telephone 01278 785760

OLD CONNA GOLF CLUB
Ferndale Road, Bray, Co Wicklow, Ireland.
Tel: +353 1 282 6055 & 6766
Fax: +353 1 282 5611

"The Garden of Ireland"

Testing parkland course with spectacular views of the Irish Sea and Wicklow mountains and only two miles from the town of Bray.

18-hole 6,550 yards SSS 72

**Green fees: Weekdays £27.50:
Saturday & Sundays £40.00.**

**Specific Early Bird rate £17.00 before 9.30am
Monday to Friday.**

Full catering facilities and club professional available.

EDMONDSTOWN GOLF CLUB
Edmondstown Road, Rathfarnham, Dublin 16, Ireland.
Tel: +353 1 493 1082 • Fax: +353 1 493 3152

Edmondstown Golf Club is situated amongst the most delightful surroundings on the foothills of the Dublin mountains, and only 11km (7 miles) from Dublin's City centre.

A testing parkland course, it lends itself to the golfer who desires a socially enjoyable round of golf on a well-maintained and manicured golf course.

THE DORMY HOUSE

Ideal for small parties wishing to play the Championship Course.
Accommodation for men only for a minimum stay of 2 nights.

*For terms and reservations please contact -
The Assistant Secretary*

**Royal Lytham & St. Annes Golf Club
Links Gate, Lytham St. Annes, Lancs. FY8 3LQ
Tel: (01253) 724206 Fax: (01253) 780946**

BUSHEY HALL GOLF CLUB
Bushey, Hertfordshire WD2 2EP

Established 1890, Bushey Hall is the oldest
golf course in Hertfordshire
A full 18-hole tree-lined parkland course
open to visitors seven days a week
For Tee-Times ring (01923) 225802
Societies welcome weekdays
Membership available

Tel: (01923) 222253 Fax: (01923) 229759

HARROGATE GOLF CLUB

One of the oldest courses in Yorkshire, it is,
indisputably one of the most attractive and best. It
has a fine tradition of welcoming visitors to its
colonial style clubhouse.
Chef cuisine, good Stewardship, Resident,
Tournament and Teaching Pro's combine with
management to provide excellent facilities for
all golfers.

**Forest Lane Head, Harrogate,
North Yorkshire HG2 7TF
Tel 01423 862999**

Ballater Golf Club Founded 1892

Picture a corner of Scotland with a delightful warmth of welcome, together with breathtaking scenery and an interesting and challenging golf course and you have discovered Ballater.
Situated on the north bank of the River Dee 42 miles west of Aberdeen, Ballater is surrounded by hills with names such as Craigendarroch, Pannannich, The Coyles of Muick and Craigcoillich enough to stir the blood of any hill walker. From these peaks the scenery is second to none and indeed Queen Victoria thought so highly of this area that she purchased Balmoral Castle a mere 8 miles up river from Ballater. The Royal family return here still on an annual pilgrimage for their summer vacation.
Apart from the golf course Ballater has much to offer the visitor. For the sporting enthusiasts there are bowls, tennis and putting at the golf club. Fishing can be arranged on the river for salmon or in one of the many highland lochs nearby for trout. There is also a gliding club nearby.
The golf course itself is arguably the most scenic in Scotland. It is a slightly undulating, medium length course situated in the heart of Royal Deeside. A delightful golfing experience which is enjoyed by golfers of all calibre and age group. Indeed, Ballater Golf Course is a real "Hidden Gem" or is it "A Jewel in the Crown of Royal Deeside?"

**Victoria Road, Ballater AB35 5QX
Tel: 013397 55567 & 55057**

"A Hidden Gem"

Women's Golf: Se Ri Pak Sets New Records in Rookie Year

Lewine Mair Golf Correspondent, *The Daily Telegraph*

If 1997 was the Year of the Tiger, 1998 was the year when Se Ri Pak reignited the women's game. Aged 20, a year younger than Woods when he had his *annus mirabilis*, Pak won two majors – the McDonald's LPGA and the US Open – along with two other US Tour events, and in one of those, the Jamie Farr Kruger Classic, her winning tally included a record-breaking 61.

When she came to Europe, where the women's professional Tour had been in the doldrums, Pak's entry for the Weetabix British Women's Open at Royal Lytham and St Annes did more than any junior initiative to encourage young girls come and watch her play. Not that too many were begging to be exposed to the same rigorous training. Se Ri's father's methods allegedly included night-time trips to a cemetery where he would regale his offspring with ghost stories by way of toughening her up.

However, the Pak training was not enough to prepare her for the spookily shrill winds at Lytham. In a week when Laura Davies failed to make the half-way cut, Pak returned scores of 78-74-79-77 to finish in joint 34th place.

Sherri Steinhauer, despite an 81, came out on top at the Weetabix. She finished a shot ahead of Sophie Gustafson and Brandie Burton in the middle of what was a spectacular all-American run.

Americans triumph in team events

Prior to the Weetabix, America won back the Curtis Cup for the first time since 1990. After Steinhauer's triumph on these shores, she was a member of the American professional side which defeated Europe for a fourth time in five starts in the Solheim Cup. In the Curtis Cup, the score was 10–8 to the Americans; in the Solheim Cup, the result was America 16, Europe 12.

In the case of the Curtis Cup at the Minikahda Club in Minneapolis, the final scoreline was flattering to the visitors. The Americans were ahead 7½–4½ after the penultimate series – so they needed just two points from the last six matches to win. They got those from Kellee Booth in the top match and Brenda Corrie Kuehn, who was playing directly behind.

Se Ri Pak set a new US Tour record with her 61 in the Jamie Farr Kruger Classic.

© Phil Sheldon

Only after the match had been won did Great Britain and Ireland come in with a series of results to remind us that the winners were by no means as far ahead of their rivals as people had begun to suspect.

However, the Americans were better on the greens, making almost three times as many putts in the ten-foot-and-over bracket as the opposition.

Putting was a problem for the visitors, although Rebecca Hudson, the 19-year-old Yorkshire woman, distinguished herself by collecting two and a half points from three starts. She halved her single first afternoon against Jenny Chuasiriporn, the player who had lost earlier in the year to Pak in a play-off for the US Women's Open. Karen Stupples, who defeated Carol Semple Thompson at the 18th on the second afternoon at Minikahda, said that she had been thrown by the severity of the slopes: 'I'd never come across such severe slopes before. . . . Sometimes you had to aim almost in the opposite direction for the ball to come round.' In the foursomes, where Great Britain and

Ireland won just two of the six points on offer, it seemed that there was too much conferring over putts. Indeed, one member of the Ladies' Golf Union suggested that they were having 'committee meetings' on the greens. More than once, a player could not get an uninterrupted look at the potential putting line she needed, so eager was she to make way for her partner and caddie to have their chance to weigh things up.

Nor were the foursomes a strong point in the Solheim Cup at Muirfield Village.

By the end of the first two days, the European professionals were trailing 10½–5½. Then, as in the Curtis Cup, there was a marked European revival in the last singles series. On this occasion, the visitors came close to inflicting real damage as they collected each of the first four points.

Davies won the top match against Pat Hurst, with no shot finer, albeit not one of her best, than the one she hit to the last green after the American was in trouble on the right. 'The shot was pathetic, even puny, but it did the business,' said a relieved Davies later. After a summer of missed putts, she then got down in two from 25 feet for the winning par which put the first of Europe's last day points on the board.

Helen Alfredsson, playing second, was magnificent in defeating Juli Inkster by 2 and 1 in the second game; while Annika Sörenstam, who had been below her best over the first two days, had a ruthlessly efficient 2 and 1 victory over Donna Andrews. Lotta Neumann, who had lost each of her first three matches, was two down after six holes against Brandie Burton but blossomed under the pressure to win on the home green.

The other European points belonged to Marie Laure de Lorenzi and Lisa Hackney, the latter whipping Betsy King to the tune of 6 and 5.

'We left ourselves with too much to do but we went out with a lot of pride in the singles and acquitted ourselves well,' said Pia Nilsson, the European captain.

At much the same time, Davies made the point that the match had tightened up to a degree where people should stop suggesting that the Solheim Cup should be between America and the Rest of the World in order to bring in players such as Karrie Webb of Australia and Se Ri Pak.

Confidence restored

Over the winter, Alison Nicholas emerged as the key figure in the women's tour search for a new chairman-cum-executive director. Nicholas, who received an MBE for her services to the women's game, helped to sift through the 70 or so applications, none of whom adequately filled the bill. In the circumstances, Nicholas and the committee wisely decided that John Mort, a tournament official with accountancy qualifications, should be asked to take temporary control. He never pretended that he knew how to 'sell' the women professionals but, over the season, this quietly efficient and unassuming man succeeded in restoring confidence in the women's operation. The hope is that the 1999 circuit will mirror that new confidence now that a new chief executive is in place. Tim Howland of the European Sports Group, whose sister companies run the commercial side of the Asian and Australian Tours, is now at the helm.

Helen Alfredsson won the Order of Merit in Europe, while her compatriot Annika Sörenstam succeeded in heading the American money list. Meanwhile, from the ranks of the British players doing duty in the States, the Scottish duo of Janice Moodie and Mhairi McKay deserve a mention for some grand achievements in their rookie season. But for the phenomenal Pak, Moodie would have dominated the Rookie of the Year lists for most of the season. McKay demonstrated her class by tieing for seventh place in the US Women's Open.

Moodie and McKay joined the US tour after highly successful careers on the British amateur scene followed by college educations in the States. Moodie attended San José State, while McKay was the first British player, man or woman, to win a golf scholarship to Stanford.

Awards

There are plenty more British girls currently endeavouring to take much the same route but Kim Andrew, the leading British amateur in 1998, is not among them: she sees herself as an out-and-out amateur. Last year, Andrew (née Rostron), won the British Women's Championship at Little Aston and the inaugural English Order of Merit. These twin triumphs contributed to her winning the *Daily Telegraph*'s Golfer of the Year Award.

Meanwhile, the Joyce Wethered award went to Liza Walters, who was a runner-up to Elaine Ratcliffe in the English Championship. If Walters, 18, needed any consolation for missing out on a place in the Curtis Cup, it came in the shape of a win in the English Girls' Championship which was played in the same week.

On the senior scene, Angela Uzielli won the British Women's Senior Championship, but it was Valerie Hassett from County Clare who emerged from the season with unarguably the best of the GB&I results to be recorded on American soil in 1998. The Irish golfer, who was playing in the US Senior Championship as part of 'a dream tour' of Canada and the United States, reached the final of the event at the Golden Horseshoe GC in Williamsburg. She lost to Canada's Gayle Borthwick at the 15th in the 18-hole final, but the ensuing excitement captured to perfection what the late Sir Henry Cotton used to say about golf. Namely, that the best thing about it is that it was a game for everyone – all ages, both sexes.

THE ROYAL DUBLIN GOLF CLUB

North Bull Island, Dollymount, Dublin 3, Ireland.
Tel: +353 1 833 6346 Fax +353 1 833 6504

The Royal Dublin Golf Club is Ireland's second oldest golf club and one of the country's premier sporting theatres.

Royal Dublin provides visiting players with a combination of a superb championship links and a degree of hospitality that mirrors its historic development.

Rest Bay, Porthcawl, Mid Glamorgan CF36 3UW

Royal Porthcawl Golf Club is unlike most link's courses, its magnificent setting sloping down towards the Bristol Channel gives the golfer a view of the sea from every hole.
This Championship golf course is one of the finest tests of golf, a course where one plays every club in the bag, it changes direction frequently so that the player is always being tested by the wind.
With its excellent Dormy accommodation available for small groups, this world class golf club is able to offer the discerning golfer the perfect golfing break.
Visitors to Royal Porthcawl are assured of three things, a warm welcome, challenging golf and a stay to remember.

Telephone 01656 782251 Fax: 01656 771687

THE SAND MOOR GOLF CLUB

Sand Moor, described as the finest example of a golfing paradise being created out of a barren moor, was developed with the assistance of Dr Alister Mackenzie. The course, an excellent challenge of golf, provides magnificent views of the surrounding countryside. Major extensions and refurbishment of the Clubhouse during the winter of 1996/7 have improved still further the quality of the facilities available. Yorkshire Champions on 22 occasions, Sand Moor was English Champion Club in 1994 and 1995, and runner-up in 1996. Its members included Amateur Champions Alex Kyle (1939) and Iain Pyman (1993), together with English Champion, Stuart Cage (1992).

Alwoodley Lane, Leeds LS17 7DJ
0113 268 5180

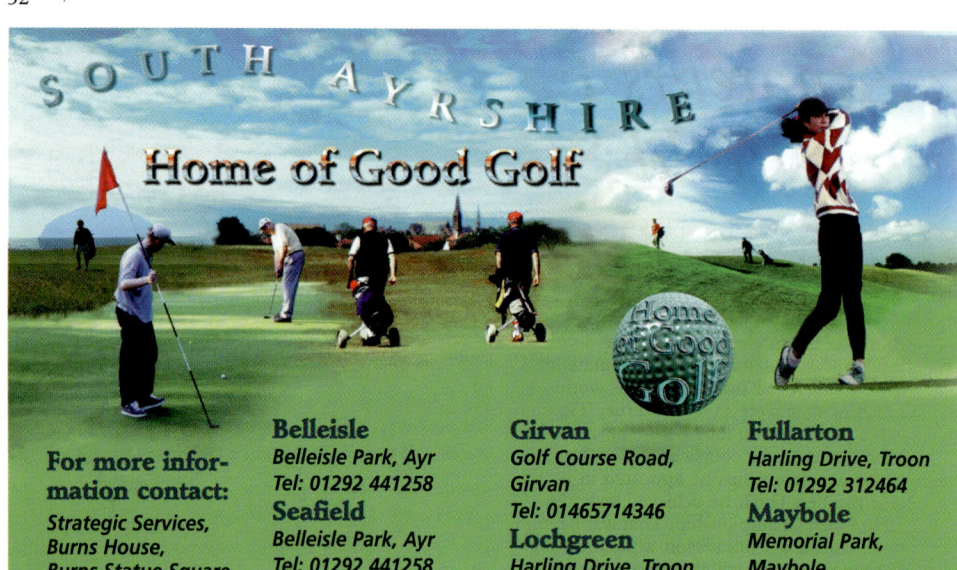

For more information contact:
Strategic Services,
Burns House,
Burns Statue Square,
Ayr, KA7 1UT
Tel: 01292 616255
Fax: 01292 616161

Belleisle
Belleisle Park, Ayr
Tel: 01292 441258
Seafield
Belleisle Park, Ayr
Tel: 01292 441258
Dalmilling
Westwood Avenue,
Ayr
Tel: 01292 263893

Girvan
Golf Course Road,
Girvan
Tel: 01465714346
Lochgreen
Harling Drive, Troon
Tel: 01292 312464
Darley
Harling Drive, Troon
Tel: 01292 312464

Fullarton
Harling Drive, Troon
Tel: 01292 312464
Maybole
Memorial Park,
Maybole
Tel: 01655 889770

Ballyboughal, Co Dublin, Ireland.
Tel: +353 1 843 3406/7
Fax: +353 1 843 3002

Parkland course featuring water hazards and lakes at 5-holes and also the longest par 5 in Ireland at 639 yards (14th-hole).
Convivial atmosphere together with complete restaurant and bar facilties.
Green fees: Weekdays - £18.00 Weekends - £23.00

PENRITH GOLF CLUB Penrith (1890)

Secretary: D Noble
Professional: G Key
18 holes L 6026 yds SSS 69
Visitors welcome Mon-Fri 9.15 am onwards
Weekends 10.06 & 3.00 pm
Fees £20 D£25 Weekends £25

Penrith course is 107 years old and lies half a mile east of Penrith, and provides panoramic views to the Lakeland Hills. We are easily accessible from junction 41 on the M6 motorway. Visitors are very welcome.

Salkeld Road, Penrith, Cumbria CA11 8SG
Tel: 01768 891919

Amateurs Force Recognition on World Stage

Mark Garrod   Golf Correspondent, Press Association

Rarely in the modern age – an age dominated by the professional game – have amateurs forced themselves to be noticed on the world stage as much as they were in 1998. True, Tiger Woods was a phenomenon long before he started to earn his millions on the course and off it, but in the six major championships he appeared in as an amateur the best finish he achieved was 22nd at the 1996 Open Championship. That was beaten three times during a 1998 season which, for other performances as well, will live long in the memory.

Matt Kuchar, Woods's little-known successor as American amateur champion, followed a superb 21st place in The Masters tournament with a 14th position at the US Open on his 20th birthday. But even Kuchar would concede that pride of place had to go to 17-year-old Justin Rose for what he produced in the Open Championship at Royal Birkdale. Three years after hitting the headlines for winning one of the regional qualifying events for the Open and 11 months after becoming the youngest player ever to appear in the Walker Cup, Rose achieved international celebrity status with a stunning joint fourth place, the best by an amateur in the Championship since American Frank Stranahan's joint runner-up finish at Carnoustie in 1953.

On the windswept Southport links, the fresh-faced Hampshire teenager, whose cheery nature instantly endeared him to the watching millions in exactly the same way as Kuchar's ever-present smile had, made the most of the chance he had earned for himself by qualifying in even more testing conditions over the adjoining Hillside course. After an opening 72, Rose equalled the lowest round ever by an amateur in the Open the next day with a 66 and at halfway was in joint second place with Woods and Nick Price, a single stroke behind American Brian Watts.

As the wind strengthened on the Saturday, Woods, the world no. 1, and Price, the 1994 champion, scored 77 and 80 respectively, but Rose battled his way to a 75 to remain in the hunt three behind Watts, and his closing 69, completed in fairytale fashion when he holed a 45-yard pitch shot for a birdie on the last, left him a mere two shots away from the play-off in which Mark O'Meara defeated Watts for his second major of the season.

Peter McEvoy (centre) captained the winning Great Britian and Ireland side in the Eisenhower Trophy.

Despite his tender years, Rose found the temptation to turn professional at that moment too great to resist. Many would have preferred to see him stay amateur a while longer – as Kuchar did – and when he missed the halfway cut in his first eight tournaments in the paid ranks and failed to win a card at the European tour qualifying school, all under the glare of publicity, one had to wonder if the chosen path was the right one. Other special talents had found the transition hard before him, but Rose had made such a name for himself in one never-to-be-forgotten week that more opportunities are bound to come his way.

One of the tournaments he missed out on with his decision was the Eisenhower Trophy World Team Championship in Chile – yet even without him Great Britain and Ireland achieved only their fourth victory in the event and their first outside Europe following successes in Italy in 1964, Portugal in 1976 and Sweden in 1988.

A week earlier, Britain and Ireland's women

had withdrawn from their world championship, also in Santiago, over fears for their safety following the arrest in London of former Chilean leader General Augusto Pinochet. But Gary Wolstenholme, Luke Donald, Paddy Gribben and Lorne Kelly travelled with non-playing captain Peter McEvoy after receiving assurances, and how glad they were that they did.

All but Ulsterman Gribben had been part of the team three months earlier which suffered its first loss to the Continent of Europe in the St Andrews Trophy for 16 years (Europe won 14–10 in Milan), so few people were predicting a triumph. In South America, joint second with a round to play, three behind Finland, Wolstenholme scored a flawless 67, Kelly a 70 and Donald a 71, enabling the side to discard Gribben's 72 and run out winners by four over holders Australia, whose Kim Felton won the individual title by two from Finn Mikko Ilonen. 'It was a fantastic performance on the last day with the pressure on,' said a proud McEvoy, individual champion himself in Britain and Ireland's 1988 victory. Pre-tournament favourites America managed only seventh place, their seven over par total of 865 being 13 more than Britain and Ireland's aggregate.

With Nick Dougherty, Jamie Elson, Adam Frayne and David Griffiths winning the World Junior Team Championship for England in Japan earlier in the season, Andrew Smith the Doug Sanders world junior crown and Scotland's Steven O'Hara the British Boys' Championship, there appears no shortage of players with the potential to step into Rose's shoes.

El Niño

Nobody can argue, however, that the amateur who continues to show most promise is Sergio Garcia, the Spaniard already bestowed with the nickname of 'El Niño'. European amateur champion at 15 and British Boys' champion at 17, Garcia became at 18 years and four months one of the youngest-ever winners of the Amateur championship. He very nearly added the United States amateur title as well and survived the halfway cut in all seven European tour events he played – including the Open, where he finished 28th.

The Amateur was staged on the majestic Muirfield links, and Garcia, qualifying for the matchplay stages in joint fourth place, did not have to go beyond the 16th hole until he faced leading qualifier Mark Hilton in the semi-finals. The 6ft 7in Sussex player was two down with two to play, but took the match to the 23rd before losing and a relieved Garcia showed no mercy against Welshman Craig Williams in the final, triumphing seven and six.

In the US Amateur later in the summer, Garcia beat Kuchar two and one in an eagerly awaited quarter-final, only to go down three and one at the next hurdle to former professional Tom McKnight, who in turn lost in the final by two and one to Hank Kuehne, whose sister Kelli was twice American and once British women's champion and whose brother Trip lost to Woods in the 1994 final.

Hilton's brave effort to topple Garcia followed his victory in the Berkshire Trophy, while on the same day at the Lytham Trophy Kelly had to go to a play-off to beat defending champion and Walker Cup international Graham Rankin and England's Graeme Storm.

Most promising

The English Amateur Strokeplay Championship, otherwise known as the Brabazon Trophy, was won in style at Formby by Sweden's Peter Hansson. The 20-year-old's closing seven-foot birdie putt was his fourth in the last six holes and his 67 gave him a one-under-par total of 287 and a one-stroke winning margin over Irishman Brian Omelia.

Gribben's place in the victorious Eisenhower Trophy team owed much to his success in the European Amateur Championship in Bordeaux – Williams was a runner-up again – while Donald and Wolstenholme were instrumental in England's sixth successive, but very narrow, win in the home internationals at Royal Porthcawl. Philip Rowe's singles win over Irishman David Jones from three down with six to play was the all-important one and earlier in the week England, for whom 38-year-old Wolstenholme was making his 100th appearance to join an exclusive club whose only previous members are McEvoy and Sir Michael Bonallack, had achieved a first for the event by winning all 10 singles against Wales – and that after losing the foursomes 4–1.

Rankin gained compensation for losing the Lytham Trophy by becoming Scottish amateur champion, while the Irish title went to Michael Howey, the Welsh to Mark Pilkington and the English to Mark Sanders.

The impact that amateurs had during the season was felt further afield as well. In South Korea, 16-year-old schoolboy Kim Dae-Sub spectacularly won an event on the Asian Omega Tour, overcoming an opening 76 to win the Kolon Sports Korean Open by five strokes with a ten-under-par total of 278.

But maybe, even with all that Garcia, Rose, Kuchar and Kim achieved, it was a performance at Woodhall Spa that was the most remarkable. In a 36-hole stableford competition to decide the English Golf Union's champion handicap golfer of the year, 13-handicapper Gary Boyd from Northamptonshire scored 32 points in the first round, then 40 in the second to win by one. A total of 78 players, mostly adults, took part, but the new champion was just 11 years old. Remember the name.

What The Players Had to Say During the 1998 Majors

The Masters

I'm walking down the seventh fairway and people are yelling: 'You'd better look out for Jack' and it wasn't even funny. What he did is better than what Mark O'Meara did, better than what I did, better than David Duval. Fred Couples about 58-year-old Jack Nicklaus who finished joint sixth, just four behind the winner.

If a 21-year-old kid went at it like I've been, he'd be begging to go into the woods for a while to relax. 85-year-old Sam Snead who came out of hospital where he had been treated for circulation problems caused by fatigue to take his usual place as one of the honorary starters and hit a 220 yards drive.

I did not realise I was so sentimental. I haven't had that happen to me very often. Six-times Masters winner Jack Nicklaus after choking on his words at his acceptance speech for the plaque placed in his honour at Augusta

I think we were all hoping that it would be a once-in-a-lifetime thing. Colin Montgomerie about the possibility of Tiger Woods dominating The Masters after his spectacular 1997 victory. In 1998 Woods finished joint eighth.

The aim each year is to make the cut. I know where to hit the ball. The problem is doing it. 66-year-old Gay Brewer after shooting 72 – just one shot worse than defending champion Tiger Woods in the first round. He is the oldest man to shoot par at The Masters but he missed the cut after a second round 86.

The competitor in me says 'Jack, I don't care what age you are and who's out in front. You're a competitor who can still play and win.' That may not be realistic but that is the way I have to think or else there is no sense in being here, right? Jack Nicklaus.

If I win tomorrow I'll quit. That's a promise. I will never play another competitive round of golf. How could you top winning The Masters at 58. Jack Nicklaus going into the final round two off the lead.

I need an ambulance. Two-times Masters winner Ben Crenshaw after an opening 83. He missed the half-way cut.

To shoot a second round 72 at 62 was a thrill for me. Gary Player, a three-times Masters winner, who became the oldest man to make the cut at Augusta.

Let's play as if we were in the final group. Jack Nicklaus to Ernie Els on Sunday.

Although I still don't feel like I putt well enough to win round here, I feel I can win if I get everything right. Colin Montgomerie

Friends of mine have always said I had a good chance here. I did not hit the ball as well as I would have liked to this week but I stayed in the game mentally and emotionally. That's what sets this one apart from all the others. Mark O'Meara.

Being around Tiger so much was a huge positive for Mark, Tiger loved Augusta and some of that rubbed off on Mark. Hank Haney, Mark O'Meara's coach. Woods and O'Meara are near neighbours in Florida.

It did not get away from me. It took a birdie putt on the last green to beat me. David Duval, who finished runner-up to the man he described as one of the best putters in the game.

Everyone was looking at Fred and David and forgot about Mark. Boom, he sneaks in and wins. Tiger Woods.

The US Open

I cannot think of a much better way to spend my birthday. Matt Kuchar, the US Amateur champion, who finished joint 14th on his 20th birthday.

I hit six fairways today, Lee hit 12. I hit nine greens today, Lee hit 14. Bingo. That's why I didn't win. Payne Stewart after the final round when he shot 74 to lose by a shot to Janzen who closed with 68.

It is incredible the way the USGA can limit the scoring. There was not one pin position that was a gift out there today. Colin Montgomerie after a second round 74.

I came to the US Open expecting nothing to be fair. It is a test of wills to find out who overcomes adversity best and who has the most patience. Winner Lee Janzen.

It's embarrassing. I mean the USGA should go out there and hit putts and see how diabolical it is. Fred Couples, who finished joint 53rd, about the second round pin positions.

People get aggressive and tend to crowd in and it can get pretty ugly out there. Adults are even knocking over kids to get autographs. Tiger Woods.

I'm happy with everything but my putting. I'm so close it is ridiculous. Nick Faldo who missed the half-way cut.

Nick has always been a great putter and the greatest holer-out ever. Now he is not making the birdie putts and missing short ones for par. It's tough and you really feel for him because he has just as much desire as ever. David Leadbetter about Nick Faldo.

My physiotherapist says that the golf swing is not bad for the back but all the travelling is. ... I've been travelling all over the place, and sitting in an aeroplane is not the most comfortable place for me. Injured Ernie Els who played but never once broke par in defence of his title.

You have to be patient and play boring golf. Ernie Els on how to play the Olympic Club.

I'll admit I was almost crying when they gave me that ovation on the first tee. Casey Martin, who was allowed to use a traditional golf cart up to 30 yards from the green after two smaller carts could not cope with the hills at Olympic. Martin, who suffers from a degenerative circulatory problem in his right leg, finished tied 23rd.

Having won majors with Sandy Lyle and Seve Ballesteros I know he could do nothing but help me. The first two weeks he worked for me at the Scottish and British Opens I did not understand a word he said but he's a great caddie. Winner Lee Janzen on Dave Musgrove who gave up his job as a draughtsman at the Rolls-Royce factory to become a caddie.

The Open

I play my best golf when I relax. Colin Montgomerie who missed the half-way cut by one.

I almost saw myself as Jack Nicklaus for some silly reason. Every time he walks up the 18th, he gets a standing ovation. Seventeen-year-old amateur Justin Rose, who finished joint fourth.

We have to keep reminding ourselves that it is just a game but it can get pretty frustrating. Defending champion Justin Leonard, who finished with 69 after making the half-way cut on the mark.

I would have thought the R&A would have made the course a little bit easier today - 82 of the world's best professional golfers can't break par. Something's amiss. Nick Price after nobody broke par on the third day and only Katsuyoshi Tomori equalled it.

I don't think anyone recognised me. Brian Watts who lost the play-off to O'Meara.

If you are going to put your name with the greatest players of all time, this is one tournament you have to win. US Open champion Lee Janzen, who finished 11 shots behind winner O'Meara.

Tiger Woods will win The Open one day – no question. Five-times winner Tom Watson, who missed the half-way cut.

I'm winning a major every day I wake up. John Daly the 1996 champion and a recovering alcoholic.

Royal Birkdale just beats you to death. David Duval who finished joint 11th.

My parents have been tremendously supportive throughout and my girlfriend helped keep me calm through the worst times when I kept missing cuts. Raymond Russell, who had missed 12 out of 14 cuts before finishing joint fourth in the Open.

This course is a very special place for my family and myself. I came here in 1987 and won the Lawrence Batley International, and now I have won the most special championship there is. Mark O'Meara.

The Open is my favourite event. You cannot get anything more special. I love playing in front of an Open crowd because they are the most knowledgeable in the world. There is no roar like an Open roar. Jesper Parnevik, who has been second twice and fourth once since 1994.

This is the oldest and probably the greatest tournament in the world, one I would dearly like to win and it's the one I probably get most excited about. Davis Love III, who was eighth in 1998.

I have to admit the courses are a bit easier in Japan than overseas. Royal Birkdale is the toughest I have ever played. Shigeki Maruyama who shot 292.

Someone asked if it was a two-club wind. I would say it was a bit more. In practice, Tiger Woods hits a 9-iron 157 yards but on the 150-yard 7th he had to use a 3-iron today. Mark O'Meara about the wind on the third day.

I'd rather not be here. I play because I am contracted to do so by my sponsors. I have a five-year deal but I will not be at St Andrews in 2000 because I don't like the place. My grandmother's Scottish and must be turning in her grave but I don't see much of a golf course there. Scott Hoch who missed the half-way cut.

I think the security is justified. I do not know how many guys out there get death threats but I do. Tiger Woods, who had four security guards with him all week.

There's less pressure than there was when I started as a professional. I now forget the media and do not read a word about me. I do not need to read someone else's perspective on what I am going through. Tiger Woods, who came up a shot shy of the play-off.

I took my driver, 5-iron and putter out with me for a quick practice on Monday and by the ninth I had lost the six balls I had with me. The course was not unplayable but it was very difficult. Tom Lehman.

I was pretty impressed with myself. I was so relaxed and pretty calm. I think having won The Masters earlier in the year helped me cope with the pressure here. I hung in. Winning the title is a tremendous honour. Mark O'Meara.

US PGA Championship

That guy has torn up more practice tees. He can hit drivers and practice balls for hours. I don't even know if Mr Hogan practised as hard as Vijay does. I'd be surprised if he did. Twice US PGA champion Nick Price about 1998 winner Vijay Singh.

He will be a great champion. He has had an enormously difficult road to pick up this trophy. Steve Elkington, third at Sahalee, about winner Vijay Singh.

I never expected it to happen like this. I've practised so hard for this. It is a dream come true. Winner Vijay Singh.

You've got to be honest with yourself as a caddie. You cannot be a 'yes' man. At the end of the day your player hits the ball but you've got to have him in the right frame of mind. Dave Renwick, US PGA champion Vijay Singh's Scottish caddie.

I don't have a very good record in the majors lately. I'm not happy. I know time is running out but I still think there are enough good swings there. Tom Watson who missed the cut at Sahalee after playing only two rounds at Augusta, Olympic and Royal Birkdale.

It would have been a tremendous honour to go alongside Ben Hogan's name but it was not meant to be. It is not easy winning out here on Tour, let alone another major. Mark O'Meara, the Masters and Open champion, who finished joint fourth in the US PGA Championship when trying to equal Ben Hogan's record of winning three majors in a season.

I was struggling with my swing and fighting some thoughts – I'm not going to lie about that but I hung in there and I am proud of myself for doing that. Steve Stricker on his last day performance at Sahalee, where he finished runner-up to Vijay Singh.

Back in 1985 I was in Asia hitting balls and practising in 100 degree heat and trying to think what I would do next. My wife and I have come a long way from those days. I never thought about coming to America, let alone winning a golf tournament in the US. Winner Vijay Singh, who was a club professional in Borneo in the mid-80s.

It was a lot of fun but it was a long week. Everyone was screaming for me and I would never say I did not have a good time but I knew that my work that week would be cut out for me. Fred Couples on playing in the Championship in Seattle, his home town.

Quite frankly it was a miracle I shot what I shot the last two rounds, the way I was hitting the ball. Tiger Woods after shooting 70-71 over the weekend to finish in a share of tenth spot, eight behind winner Singh.

We all got frustrated at times because Sahalee is a tricky course. You have to be patient. Defending champion Davis Love III, who finished joint seventh in his bid to be the first to win the title in back-to-back years since Denny Shute in 1937.

Playing by the Rules – Tricky Decisions of 1998

Keith Mackie

By an odd coincidence both Open Champion Mark O'Meara and US Open Champion Lee Janzen came within seconds of having penalty strokes added to their winning scores during the 1998 majors. Janzen's case was relatively straightforward; O'Meara's rather more complicated.

In San Francisco, Janzen pushed a 4-wood tee shot to the right of the Olympic Club's fifth hole during the final round. Spectators said that they could see the ball caught in a tree, but after a brief search Janzen started the long walk back to play a second tee shot under a one-stroke penalty. Before he reached the tee his original ball fell out of the tree and with a few seconds of the five minutes allowed under the Rules of Golf to spare he returned to the spot and identified the ball as his.

If he had struck another ball from the tee, that would automatically have become the ball in play and that second stroke and the penalty shot accompanying it would have been added to his score. With a few seconds grace he avoided that situation and in a remarkable turnaround he regained the fairway, hit his approach over the green and chipped in for a less-than-standard par four. Janzen subsequently won the US Open title by a single shot from Payne Stewart.

The lucky

O'Meara's flirtation with the lost ball rule came at Royal Birkdale's sixth hole in the third round. His second shot to the sixth hole was swept away on the wind into heavy rough to the right of the green. Several balls were found but not O'Meara's, and before his allotted five minutes had expired he headed back down the fairway to put another ball into play. He was stopped in his tracks by a shout from those still searching by the green. Within the five-minute period his ball had been found. But by the time he reached the spot and identified it as his, the stop-watch had ticked on beyond the official limit.

Match referee Michael Lunt, a former Walker Cup player and member of the R&A Championship Committee, called for a second opinion from R&A Rules Secretary David Rickman, who ruled that the ball had been found within the specified time and was therefore not lost.

By this time O'Meara's ball had been picked up by the spectator who had found it, believing it was no longer in play. The eventual champion was allowed to drop the ball as close to the spot where it had been found as possible. The first attempt rolled more than two club lengths from where it struck the ground and the second rolled nearer the hole. Finally, O'Meara was allowed to place the ball and he completed the hole in a one-over-par five, eventually winning the championship after a four-hole play-off with fellow American Brian Watts.

The lost ball procedure which was called into action on both sides of the Atlantic is Rule 27-1. It states that a ball is lost if it is not found or identified as his by the player within five minutes after the player's side or his or their caddies have begun to search for it.

Both the R&A and the USGA have been considering the wording of this rule and feel that as long as the ball is found within the five-minute period it can be identified beyond that strict limitation.

The not so lucky

While Janzen and O'Meara came out on the right side of the law, Brian Barnes was not so lucky in the US Senior Open at the Riviera Country Club in Los Angeles. His final round 69 left him tied for fourth place behind Hale Irwin. Without the two-shot penalty he picked up on the 11th green he would have been joint runner-up. Asked by fellow competitor José Maria Canizares to move his ball marker to one side, Barnes failed to replace his ball in the correct place when it was his turn to play and incurred the penalty.

Suggestions that the player who asks for the marker to be moved should incur the penalty if it is not correctly replaced are unlikely to win any support from the rule makers at the R&A and USGA.

Many players have their own safety checks to ensure they don't fall foul of Rule 20-7 in this way. Some of those who use a coin as a marker will always put it heads up. If asked to move the marker to one side they will turn it over so the tails side gives them a mental jolt. Others will put the ball in the opposite pocket to normal while they wait their turn to putt out.

When he won the 1957 Open at St Andrews, Bobby Locke moved his ball on the final green to

avoid a fellow competitors' line and then holed his short putt to win from the wrong spot. The error was not noticed until some time later, but the R&A ruled that he had gained no advantage and his winning three-stroke margin over Peter Thomson was allowed to stand.

The luckiest?

Perhaps the luckiest man of the 1998 season was *Sunday Telegraph* golf correspondent Derek Lawrenson. His 198-yard three-iron hole-in-one during a celebrity pro-am won him a £189,000 Lamborghini, yet it left him in a state of golfing limbo. Having decided to accept the prize he immediately forfeited his amateur status. This means that he can no longer hold an official handicap or take part in amateur competitions, for the Rules of Amateur Status limit prizes in a one-round event to a maximum of £200.

R&A fear abuses

'The danger of taking a more lenient attitude towards hole-in-one prizes is that it would almost certainly lead to a proliferation of such prizes, with the hole-in-one competition becoming more important than the main event,' says the R&A. 'In addition, the high financial incentive to win such a prize may well give rise to abuses of the Rules of Play in a game which currently benefits from being largely self-regulating.'

LGU Members Prepare to Face Overseas Challengers

Julie Hall (Secretary of the Ladies' Golf Union)

As the Ladies' Golf Union looks back over the 1998 season, several thoughts come to mind, in particular the poor, windy, wet conditions of the Championships, continental dominance in the Girls' Championship and the Strokeplay Championship, and the number of questions and queries regarding the new handicapping system which was implemented on 1st February 1998.

The early part of the season was a time for our Great Britain and Ireland players to impress the selectors in order to gain a place on the Curtis Cup Team. But the continental players were strong – the Helen Holm Scottish Open Amateur was won by Karen Margrethe Juul from Denmark and the St Rule Trophy by Nuria Clau from Spain. By June the British and Irish players had a great deal at stake. The Ladies' Amateur Championship was played in poor weather conditions, but in the end Kim Rostron of Clitheroe prevailed, defeating Gwladys Nocera of France in the final.

The Curtis Cup team was selected and at the end of July, the team, LGU officials and many supporters travelled to Minneapolis for the biennial match. The overall result was a close win for the United States but the match was played in great spirit and the GB&I players put up a fine defence on American soil.

Continental players dominate

At home preparations were under way for the Girls' Championship at Holyhead Golf Club. With an ever-increasing field featuring international players (we were delighted to welcome two Russian competitors from the Moscow Country Club to their first Championship in Britain), it was Spain's Maria Beautell, smiling her way through the Championship, who triumphed over Miriam Nagl of Germany in the final.

The Weetabix Women's British Open Championship was played at Royal Lytham & St Anne's in August. The weather conditions did not assist low scoring, but the strong crosswind and heavy rough caused by the wet conditions over such a long period did produce a terrific test of skill and ball control. Sherri Steinhauer of the US lifted the coveted trophy to become the 1998 Champion, producing some brilliant golf for a 69 in the last round.

Meanwhile at Mullingar Golf Club the Girls' Internationals were being played on Irish soil for the first time. Scotland won and Ireland produced a fine performance to be runners-up.

Stirling was the venue for the Strokeplay Championship. Again the weather conditions were difficult and again the continental players dominated. Nienke Nijenhuis of the Netherlands won, with Becky Morgan of Wales just one shot behind.

For the Home International matches Burnham and Berrow provided a fine test of golf and England won all three matches to retain the trophy for the seventh consecutive time.

The Senior Ladies' Championship, played at Powfoot at the end of September, produced a very cosmopolitan field with players from the four home countries, Europe, the United States and Canada, but Britain's Angela Uzielli, producing some excellent golf over the delightful links, proved herself the champion.

Looking forward to the next season

As the 1999 season approaches, we look forward to hosting the Vagliano Trophy at North Berwick in July. In August, the Great Britain team will compete in the Commonwealth Tournament in Vancouver, Canada, and we hope that the women will regain the trophy won by Australia in Sydney four years ago.

The Ladies' Golf Union is again fortunate to have superb venues for the 1999 British championships and international matches. With the Amateur Championship being staged at Royal Birkdale, the competitors will have extra incentive to get their name on the Championship Cup. The Girls' Championship and Girls' International matches will be held at High Post Golf Club in Wiltshire. This will be our first visit to High Post, which we are sure will prove a fine test of golf. The Strokeplay Championship travels north to Huddersfield where the 1994 Home Internationals were played. The Home Internationals though will be played at Royal Dornoch at the end of September. For the final event of the year, we travel to Malone in Belfast for the Seniors' Championship, and with our ever-increasing number of challengers from overseas we are hoping for a great deal of support.

R&A Venues and Dates for Championships, 1999–2002

	1999	2000	2001	2002
The Amateur Championship	31 May–5 June R. County Down/ Kilkeel	5–10 June R. Liverpool/ Wallasey	4–9 June Prestwick/ Kilmarnock Barassie	3–8 July R. Porthcawl/ Pyle & Kenfig
The Open Championship	15–18 July Carnoustie	20–23 July St Andrews	19–22 July R. Lytham & St Annes	18–21 July Muirfield
(Final Qualifying)	11–12 July Downfield Monifieth Links Montrose Links Panmure	16–17 July Ladybank Leven Links Lundin Scotscraig	15–16 July St Anne's Old Links Fairhaven Southport & Ainsdale Hillside	14–15 July Gullane No. 1 Luffness New North Berwick Dunbar
The Seniors' Open Amateur Championship	4–6 August Frilford Heath (Red and Green)	9–11 August Gullane Nos 1 & 2	8–10 August Royal Portrush (Dunluce and Valley)	7–9 August Woodhall Spa
The Boys' Home Internationals	4–6 August Conwy	9–11 August Portmarnock	8–10 August Moortown	7–9 August Blairgowrie Lansdowne
The Boys' Amateur Ch'p	9–14 August R. St David's	14–19 August Hillside	13–18 August Ganton	12–17 August Carnoustie
British Mid-Amateur Ch'p	11–15 August Walton Heath	16–20 August Royal Troon	15–19 August Seaton Carew	14–18 August Formby
The Walker Cup	11–12 September Nairn		11–12 August Ocean Forest, Sea Island, Georgia	
The St Andrews Trophy		30 June–1 July Turnberry		30–31 August TBA, Europe
The Jacques Leglise Trophy	27–28 August Burnham & Berrow	1–2 September Turnberry	31 Aug–1 Sept TBA, Europe	30–31 August TBA, Europe
The Eisenhower Trophy		31 Aug–3 Sept Berlin, Germany		TBA TBA, Malaysia

Future Venues and Dates for the US Major Championships and the Ryder Cup

	The Masters	The US Open	US PGA Championship
1999	**8–11 April** Augusta National, Augusta, Georgia	**17–20 June** Pinehurst No. 2, Pinehurst, North Carolina	**12–15 August** Medinah, Chicago
2000	**6–9 April** Augusta National, Augusta, Georgia	**15–18 June** Pebble Beach, Monterey California	**17–20 August** Valhalla, Louisville, Kentucky
2001	**5–8 April** Augusta National, Augusta, Georgia	**14–17 June** Southern HIlls, Oklahoma	**16–19 August** Atlanta, Georgia
2002	**11–14 April** Augusta National, Augusta, Georgia	**13–16 June** Bethpage SP, New York	**15–18 August** Hazeltine National, Massachusetts

The US Masters normally begins on the Thursday following the first Sunday in April.

The US Open Championship normally commences on the Thursday following the second Sunday in June.

The US PGA Championship normally commences on the second Thursday in August.

Ryder Cup

1999 at The Country Club, Brookline, Massachusetts on 24–26 September.

2001 at The Belfry, Sutton Coldfield, West Midlands on 28–30 September.

2003 at Oakland Hills Country Club, Birmingham, Michigan

2005 at The K Club, County Kildare, Ireland

2007 at Valhalla Golf Club, Louisville, Kentucky

2009 *Not yet decided*

2011 at Medinah Country Club, Illinois

Schedules for the 1999 Season

PGA European Tour

January
14–17 Alfred Dunhill South African PGA, Houghton GC, Johannesburg
21–24 South African Open, Stellenbosch, Cape Town
28–31 Heineken Classic, The Vines Resort, Perth, Australia

February
4–7 Benson & Hedges Malaysian Open, Kuala Lumpur, Malaysia
11–14 Dubai Classic, Dubai Desert Creek Golf & Yacht Club
17–20 Qatar Masters, Doha GC
25–28 *World Golf Championship (WGC) Andersen Consulting Matchplay Ch'p*, La Costa Resort, Carlsbad, USA

March
4–7 Portuguese Algarve Open, Le Meridien, Penina
11–14 Turespaña Masters Open Andalucia, Parador Malaga del Golf
25–28 Madeira Island Open, Santo da Serra

April
8–11 **US Masters**, Augusta National, USA
15–18 Estoril Open, Penha Longa
22–25 Peugeot Open de España, El Prat, Barcelona
29–2 Fiat and Fila Italian Open, Circolo Golf, Turin

May
6–9 Novotel Perrier Open de France, Golf du Medoc, Bordeaux
13–16 Benson & Hedges International, The Oxfordshire, Thame
21–24 Deutsche Bank/SAP Open – TPC of Europe, St Leon Rot, Heidelberg
28–31 Volvo PGA Ch'p, Wentworth Club, Surrey

June
3–6 English Open, Marriott Hanbury Manor, Ware
10–13 German Open, Sporting Club, Berlin
17–20 **US Open**, Pinehurst No 2, NC
17–20 Moroccan Open, Golf Royal d'Agadir
24–27 Compaq European Grand Prix, De Vere Slaley Hall, Northumberland

July
1–4 Murphy's Irish Open, Druid's Glen, Dublin
7–10 Standard Life Loch Lomond, Loch Lomond, Glasgow
15–18 **Open Championship**, Carnoustie
22–25 TNT Dutch Open, Hilversum GC, Amsterdam
30–2 Smurfit European Open, The K Club, Dublin

August
5–8 Volvo Scandinavian Masters, Barseback G&CC, Malmo
12–15 **US PGA Championship**, Medinah CC, Chicago
19–22 BMW International Open München, Nord-Eichenried GC, Munich
26–29 *WGC NEC Invitational*, Firestone CC, Ohio, USA

September
2–5 Canon European Masters, Crans-Sur-Sierre, Switzerland
9–12 British Masters, Woburn, Bucks
16–19 Trophée Lancôme, St-Nom-La Breteche, Paris
24–26 The 33rd Ryder Cup, The Country Club, Brookline, Massachusetts
30–3 Linde German Masters, Gut Lärchenhof, Cologne

October
7–10 *Alfred Dunhill Cup*, St Andrews, Fife
14–17 *Cisco World Matchplay Ch'p*, Wentworth Club, Surrey
21–24 Belgacom Open, Royal Zoute, Belgium
28–31 Volvo Masters, Montecastillo, Jerez, Spain

November
4–7 *WGC American Express Strokeplay Ch'p*, Valderrama, Spain
11–14 Johnnie Walker Classic, Ta Shee G&CC, Taiwan
18–21 *World Cup of Golf*, Mines Resort & GC, Kuala Lumpur, Malaysia
18–23 Qualifying School Finals, San Roque and Sotogrande, Spain

Bold type indicates a major; light italics a European Tour approved event; bold italics a World Ch'p event

United States PGA Tour

January 1999
7–10 Mercedes Championship, Plantation Course, Kapalua, HA
14–17 Sony Open, Waialae CC, Honolulu, HA
20–24 Bob Hope Chrysler Classic, Indian Wells, CA
28–31 Phoenix Open, TPC of Scottsdale, AZ

February
4–7 AT&T Pebble Beach National Pro-Am, Pebble Beach, CA
11–14 Buick Invitational, Torrey Pines GC, La Jolla, CA
18–21 Nissan Open, Riviera CC, Pacific Palisades, CA
24–28 *WGC Andersen Consulting Matchplay*, La Costa Resort, Carlsbad, CA
24–28 Tucson Open Omni Tucson, National Resort, Tucson, AZ

March
3–7 Doral-Ryder Open, Doral Resort & CC, Miami, FL
11–14 Honda Classic, TPC at Heron Bay, Coral Springs, FL
18–21 Bay Hill Invitational, Bay Hill GC, Orlando, FL
25–28 The Players' Championship, TPC at Sawgrass, Ponte Vedra Beach, FL

April
1–4 BellSouth Classic, TPC at Sugarloaf, Duluth, GA
8–11 **US Masters**, Augusta National GC, Augusta, GA
15–18 MCI Classic, Harbor Town, Hilton Head Island, SC
22–25 Great Greensboro Chrysler Classic, Forest Oaks CC, Greensboro, NC
29–2 Shell Houston Open, TPC at The Woodlands, The Woodlands, TX

May
6–9 Entergy Classic, English Turn G&CC, New Orleans, LA
13–16 GTE Byron Nelson Classic, TPC at Four Seasons, Cottonwood Valley CC, Irwing, TX
20–23 MasterCard Colonial, Colonial CC, Fort Worth, TX
27–30 Kemper Open, TPC at Avenel, Potomac, MD

June
3–6 Memorial Tournament, Muirfield Village GC, Dublin, OH
10–13 FedEx St Jude Classic, TPC at Southwind, Memphis, TN
17–20 **US Open**, Pinehurst No. 2, Pinehurst Resort & CC, NC
24–27 Buick Classic, Westchester CC, Rye, NY

July
1–4 Motorola Western Open, Cog Hill G&CC, Lemont, IL
8–11 Greater Milwaukee Open, Brown Deer GC, Milwaukee, WI
15–18 **The Open**, Carnoustie, Scotland
15–18 Southwestern Farm Bureau Classic, Annandale GC, Madison, MA
22–25 John Deere Classic, Oakwood CC, Coal Valley, IL
29–1 Canon Greater Hartford Open, TPC at River Highlands, Cromwell, CN

August
5–8 Buick Open, Warwick Hills G&CC, Grand Blanc, MS
12–15 **US PGA Ch'p**, Medinah CC, IL
19–22 The Sprint International, Castle Pines GC, Castle Rock, CO
26–29 *WGC-NEC Invitational*, Firestone CC, Akron, OH
26–29 Reno-Tahoe Open, Montreux G&CC, Reno, NV

September
2–5 Air Canada Ch'p, Northview G&CC, Surrey, BC, Canada
9–12 Bell Canadian Open, Glen Abbey GC, Oakville, Ontario, Canada
16–19 BC Open, En-Joie GC, Endicott, NY
23–26 Westin Texas Open, LaCantera GC, San Antonio, TX
24–26 Ryder Cup, The Country Club, Brookline, MA
30–3 Buick Challenge, Callaway Gardens, Pine Mountain, GA

October
7–10 Michelob Championship, Kingsmill GC, Williamsburg, VA
13–17 Las Vegas International, TPC at Summerlin, Las Vegas, NV
21–24 Walt Disney Classic, Magnolia & Palm GC, Lake Buena Vista, FL
28–31 The Tour Championship, Champions GC, Cypress Creek, Houston, TX

November
4–7 *WGC American Express Ch'p*, Valderrama GC, Sotogrande, Spain
12–14 *Franklin Templeton Shark Shoot-out*, Sherwood CC, Thousand Oaks, CA
18–21 *World Cup of Golf*, The Mines Resort, Kuala Lumpur, Malaysia
27–28 *Skins Game*, La Quinta, CA

December
2–5 *JC Penney Classic*, Westin Innisbrook Resort, Clearwater, FL
10–12 *Diners Club Matches*, TBA
18–19 *Wendy's Three Tour Challenge*, Lake Las Vegas Resort, Henderson, NV

Bold type indicates a major; light italics a European Tour approved event; bold italics a World Ch'p event

Japanese Tour

March
11–14 Token Corporation Cup, Kedoin GC, Kagoshima
18–21 Dydo-Drinco Shizouka Open, Shizuoka CC, Shizuoka
25–28 KSB Open, Tojigaoka Marine Hills, Okayama

April
1–4 Descente Classic Munsingwear Cup, Taiheiyo Club, Chiba
15–18 Tsuruya Open, Sports Shinko CC, Hyogo
22–25 Kirin Open, Ibaragi GC, Ibaragi
29–2 Chunichi Crowns, Nagoya GC, Aichi

May
6–9 Fuji Sankei Classic, Kawana Hotel, Shizuoka
13–16 Japan PGA Championship, Twin Fields GC, Ishikawa
20–23 Ube Kosan Open, Ube CC, Yamaguchi
27–30 Mitsubishi Galant Tournament, Lake Green GC, Gifu

June
3–6 JCB Classic Sendai, Omotezao Kokusai GC, Miyagi
10–13 Sapporo Tokyu Open, Sapporo Kokusai CC, Hokkaido
17–20 Yomiuri Open, Yomiuri CC, Hyogo
24–27 Mizuno Open, Setonaikai GC, Okayama

July
1–4 PGA Philanthropy, Fuji Country Syuga Club, Gifu
8–11 Yonex Open Hiroshima, Hiroshima CC

July *continued*
22–25 Aiful Cup, Ajigasawa Kogen GC, Aomori
29–1 NST Niigata Open, TBA

August
19–22 Sanko Grand SummerChampionship, Sanko 72 CC, Gunma
26–29 KBC Augusta, Keya GC, Fukuoka

September
2–5 JPGA Matchplay, Nidom Classic Course, Hokkaido
9–12 Suntory Open, Subu CC, Chiba
16–19 ANA Open, Sapporo GC, Hokkaido
23–26 Gene Sarazen Junior Classic, Junior Classic CC, Tochigi
30–3 Japan Open, Otaru CC, Hokkaido

October
7–10 Tokai Classic, Miyoshi CC, Aichi
14–17 Nikkei Cup Nakamura, Fuji Country Dejima Club, Ibaragi
21–2 Bridgestone Open, Sodegaura CC, Chiba
28–31 Philip Morris Championship, ABC GC, Hyogo

November
4–7 Acom International, TBA
11–14 Sumitomo Visa Taiheiyo Masters, Taiheiyo Club, Shizuoka
18–21 Dunlop Phoenix Tournament, Phoenix CC, Miyazaki
25–28 Casio World Open, Ibusuki GC, Kagoshima

December
2–5 Japan Series JT Cup, Tokyo Yomiuri CC, Tokyo
9–12 Okinawa Open, Daikyo CC, Okinawa

US Nike Tour

January
7–10 South Florida Open, Palm-Aire CC, Pompano Beach, FL
14–17 Lakeland Classic, Grasslands G&CC, Lakeland, FL

February
4–7 Florida Classic, Gainesville CC, Gainesville, FL
18–21 Mississippi Gulf Coast Open, The Oaks GC, Pass Christian, MS

March
4–7 Greater Austin Open, The Hills CC, Austin, TX
18–21 Monterrey Open, Club Campestre, Monterrey, MX
25–28 Louisiana Open, Le Triomphe CC, Broussard, LA

April
15–18 Shreveport Open, Southern Trace CC, Shreveport, LA
21–24 South Carolina Classic, CC of South Carolina, Florence, SC
29–2 Upstate Classic, Verdae Greens GC, Greenville SC

May
6–9 Caroline Classic, Raleigh CC, Raleigh, NC
13–16 Dominion Open, The Dominion Club, Richmond, VA.
20–23 Knoxville Open, Fox Den CC, Knoxville, TN

June
10–13 Cleveland Open, Quail Hollow Resort, Concord, OH
17–20 Dayton Open, GC at Yankee Trace, Dayton, OH

June *continued*
24–27 Lehigh Valley Open, Center Valley Club, Allentown, PA

July
1–4 Hershey Open, CC of Hershey (East), Hershey, PA
7–10 Greensboro Open, Sedgefield CC, Greensboro, NC
22–25 Wichita Open, Missouri Bluffs GC, St Louis, MO
29–1 Dakota Dunes Open, Dakota Dunes CC, Dakota Dunes, SD

August
5–8 Omaha Classic, The Champions Club, Omaha, NE
12–15 Ozarks Open, Highland Springs CC, Springfield, MO
19–22 Fort Smith Classic, Hardscrabble CC, Fort Smith, Arkansas
26–29 Permian Basin Open, Mission Dorado CC, Odessa, TX

September
2–5 Utah Classic, Willow Creek CC, Salt Lake City, UT
9–12 Tri-Cities Open, Meadow Springs CC, Tri-Cities, WA
16–19 Boise Open, Hillcrest CC, Boise, Idaho
23–26 Oregon Classic, Shadow Hills CC, Eugene, OR
30–3 San Jose Open, Almaden CC, San Jose, CA

October
7–10 Inland Empire Open, Moreno Valley Ranch GC, CA
21–24 Tour Championship, Robert Trent Jones Golf Trail, AL

Bold type indicates a Senior Tour major

European Challenge Tour

March
11–14 Tusker Kenya Open, Muthaiga GC, Kenya
25–27 OKI Telepizza Challenge, Golf del Guadiana, Spain

April
29–2 Challenge d'España, Castellón, Spain

May
13–16 BIL Luxembourg Open, Kikuoka G&CC, Luxembourg
13–16 Is Molas Challenge, Is Molas, Sardinia, Italy
20–23 Open dei Tessali, Riva dei Tessali, Italy
27–30 Challenge de Sablé, Sablé Solesmes, France

June
10–13 NCC Open, Söderåsens GC, Sweden
17–20 CLOSED EVENT WEEK
24–27 Diners Club Austrian Open, Millstäter See GC, Austria

July
1–4 Open des Volcans, Golf des Volcans, France
2–4 # Neuchâtel Open Golf Trophy, Neuchâtel GC, Switzerland
8–11 Volvo Finnish Open, Espoo Golf, Finland
15–18 BTC Slovenian Open, Bled GC, Slovenia
15–18 # Rolex Trophy, Golf Club de Genève, Switzerland
22–25 Interlaken Open, Interlaken GC, Switzerland
29–1 Finnish Masters, Masters GC, Finland

August
5–8 Challenge Tour Championship, Bowood G&CC, Wiltshire, England
12–15 Moscow Country Club Russian Open, Moscow G&CC, Russia
19–22 Norwegian Open, Sorknes GC, Norway
31–3 Formby Hall Challenge, Formby Hall GC, England

September
2–5 Öhrlings Swedish Matchplay, Kristianstads GC, Sweden
8–11 Warsaw Golf Open, Warsaw Golf International, Poland
14–17 Qualifying School – First Stage, The Wynyard Club, Five Lakes Hotel & CC, Woodbury Park G&CC, Chart Hills GC, Carden Park GC
23–26 Open Galea, Golf de Neguri, Bilbao, Spain
30–3 Telia Grand Prix, Ljunghusens GC, Sweden

October
6–9 San Paolo Vita Open, Margara GC, Italy
14–17 Challenge de France, Golf Disneyland, Paris, France
21–24 Challenge Tour Grand Final, TBA
26–29 Qualifying School – Second Stage, Pals GC, Emporda GC, Peralada GC

November
17–22 European Tour Qualifying School Finals, San Roque Club and Real Club de Golf Sotogrande, Spain

 # Invitational event

Asian PGA Tour
Provisional schedule

January
10 Pre-qualifying School, Tanjung Puteri Golf Resort, Malaysia
17 Qualifying School, Tanjung Puteri Golf Resort, Malaysia
31 London Myanmar Open, Yangan City Golf Resort, Myanmar

February
7 *Benson & Hedges Malaysian Open*, Saujana G&CC, Kuala Lumpur

March
14 Wills Indian Open, Royal Calcutta GC

April
18 Macau Open, Macau G&CC
25 Kirin Open, Ibaraki GC, Japan

May
2 **Maekyung Daks Open**, Nam Seoul GC, South Korea
9 Guam Open, Leo Palace Resort, Manenggon Hills
16 Tianjin Open, Tianjin Warner International GC, China
23 Volvo China Open, Shanghai Silport GC
30 Philippine Open, Manila Southwoods

July
4 Beijing Open, Course TBC, China

August
1 Asian Nations Cup, The Mines Resort, Malaysia
22 Ericsson Singapore Open, Singapore
29 Volvo Masters, Kota Parmat G&CC, Malaysia

September
5 Mercedes Benz Taiwan Open, Sunrise G&CC, Taiwan
12 Mercuries Masters, Taiwan (Not APGA)
19 **Kolon Korean Open**, Seoul CC, S. Korea
26 † Satelindo Indonesia Open, Indonesia

October
3 Ericsson Classic, Formosa First CC, Taiwan
17 Lexus International, Thailand
24 † Pakistan Masters, Karachi GC
31 Hero Honda Masters, Delhi GC, India

November
7 Fedex PGA Championship, Raffles CC, Singapore
14 *Johnnie Walker Classic*, Ta Shee G&CC, Taiwan
21 World Cup, The Mines Resort, Malaysia
28 Hong Kong Open, Hong Kong GC

December
5 Thailand Open, Thana City G&CC
12 Omega PGA Ch'p, Course TBC, China

European PGA Senior Tour

May
7–9 Beko Classic, Klassis G&CC, Turkey
14–16 AIB Irish Seniors' Open, Mount Juliet
29–31 Philips PFA Golf Classic, Marriott Meon Valley Hotel & CC, England

June
4–6 Montecastillo Seniors' Grand Prix, Montecastillo GC, Spain
11–13 Jersey Seniors' Open, La Moye GC
24–26 Lawrence Batley Seniors', Huddersfield GC, England

July
8–10 Elf Seniors' Open, Pau GC, France
22–25 Senior British Open, Royal Portrush GC, N. Ireland
30–1 Wentworth Senior Masters, Edinburgh Course, Wentworth GC, England

August
6–8 Bad Ragaz PGA Seniors' Open, Bad Ragaz GC, Switzerland

August *continued*
13–15 De Vere Hotels Seniors' Classic, Ferndown GC, England
20–22 Golden Charter PGA Scottish Seniors' Open, Marriott Dalmahoy Hotel & CC, Scotland
27–30 The Belfry PGA Seniors' Championship, PGA National, England

September
9–11 Zepter Monte Carlo Pro-Celebrity Championship, Monte Carlo GC
17–19 Ordina Trophy, Prise d'Eau GC, Holland

October
8–10 Greek Seniors' Open, Glyfada GC
22–24 Senior Tournament of Champions, Buckinghamshire GC, England

November
19–21 Praia D'el Rey European Cup, Praia D'el Rey GC, Portugal

Bold type indicates a special approved event; italic type a joint European Tour event; † event to be confirmed

US PGA Senior Tour

January
21–24   MasterCard Championship, Hualalai GC, HA
28–31   *Senior Skins Game*, Mauna Lani Resort, HA

February
4–7   Royal Caribbean Classic, Crandon Park GC, Key Biscayne, FL
11–14   American Express Invitational, TPC at Prestancia, Sarasota, FL
18–21   GTE Classic TPC at Tampa Bay, Lutz, FL
25–28   ACE Group Classic, Bay Colony GC, Naples, FL

March
4–7   **Senior Slam**, Cabo Real, Cabo San Lucas, MX
11–14   Toshiba Senior Classic, Newport Beach CC, Newport Beach, CA
18–21   Liberty Mutual Legends of Golf, Slammer/Squire courses, St Augustine, FL
25–28   Emerald Coast Classic, The Moors GC, Milton, FL

April
1–4   **The Tradition**, Desert Mountain, Scottsdale, AZ
15–18   **PGA Seniors' Championship**, Champion Course, PGA National GC, Palm Beach Gardens, FL
22–25   The Home Depot Invitational, TPC at Piper Glen, Charlotte, NC

May
6–9   Nationwide Championship, Golf Club of Georgia, Alpharetta, Atlanta, GA
13–16   Las Vegas Senior Classic, TPC at Summerlin, Las Vegas, NV
20–23   Bell Atlantic Classic, Hartefield National, Avondale, PA
27–30   Boone Valley Classic, Boone Valley GC, Augusta, MO

June
3–6   Cadillac NFL Golf Classic, Upper Montclair CC, Clifton, NJ
10–13   BellSouth Senior Classic, Springhouse GC, Nashville, TN
17–20   Southwestern Bell Dominion, Dominion CC, San Antonio, TX

June *continued*
24–27   **Ford Senior Players' Championship**, TPC of Michigan, Dearborn, MI

July
1–4   Slate Farm Senior Classic, Hobbit's Glen GC, Columbia, MD
8–11   **US Senior Open**, Des Moines G&CC, Des Moines, IO
15–18   Ameritech Senior Open, Kemper Lakes, Long Grove, IL
22–25   Caldwell Banker/Burner Classic, Bunker Hills GC, Coon Rapids, MN
29–1   Utah Showdown Park, Meadows CC, Park City, UT

August
5–8   Lightpath Long Island Classic, Meadow Brook GC, Jericho, NJ
12–15   Foremost Insurance Championship, Egypt Valley CC, Ada, Mississippi
19–22   BankBoston Classic, Nashawtuc CC, Concord, MA
26–29   AT&T Canada Senior Open, Richelieu Valley GC, Montreal, Canada

September
2–5   Kansas City Classic, Tiffany Greens GC, Kansas City
9–12   Comfort Classic, Brickyard Crossing, Indianapolis, IN
16–19   Bank One Championship, Bent Tree CC, Dallas, TX
23–26   Kroger Senior Classic, Kings Island Golf Center, Mason, Cincinnati
30–3   Vantage Championship, Tanglewood Park, Winston-Salem, NC

October
7–10   The Transamerica, Silverado Resort Napa, CA
14–17   Raley's Gold Rush, Serrano CC, El Dorado Hills, Sacramento, CA
21–24   EMC Kaanapali Classic, Kaanapali (North), Maui, HA
28–31   Pacific Bell Senior Classic, The Wilshire CC, Los Angeles, CA

November
4–7   **Ingersoll-Rand Senior Tour Ch'p**, TPC at Myrtle Beach, SC
11–14   Senior Matchplay Challenge, Hyatt Dorado Beach, Dorado, Puerto Rico

Bold type indicates a Senior Tour major

United States LPGA Tour

January
15–17 HealthSouth Inaugural Grand Cypress, Orlando, FL
21–24 Naples LPGA Memorial, Pelican Strand, Naples, FL
27–30 The Office Depot Championship, Ibis G&CC, West Palm Beach, FL

February
12–14 Los Angeles Women's Championship, Oakmont CC, Glendale, CA
18–20 Hawaiian Open, Kapolei, Oahu, HA
25–28 Australian Masters, Royal Pines, Ashmore, Queensland

March
11–14 Welch's/Circle K Championship, Randolph North, Tucson, AZ
18–21 Standard Register PING, Moon Valley CC, Phoenix, AZ
25–28 **Nabisco Dinah Shore**, Mission Hills CC, Rancho Mirage, CA

April
1–4 Longs Drugs Challenge, Twelve Bridges GC, Lincoln, CA
23–25 Chick-fil-A Charity Championship, Eagles Landing CC, Stockbridge, GA
29–2 City of Hope Myrtle Beach Classic, Wachesaw Plantation East GC, Murrells Inlet, SC

May
6–9 Titleholders by Mercury LPGA International, Daytona Beach, FL
14–16 Sara Lee Classic, Hermitage GC, Old Hickory, TN
20–23 Phillips Invitational/Harvey Penick, Onion Creek, Austin, TX
27–30 LPGA Corning Classic, Corning CC, Corning, NY

June
3–6 **US Women's Open**, Old Waverley GC, West Point, MS
10–13 Wegmens Rochester International, Locust Hill CC, Pittsford, NY
18–20 ShopRite LPGA Classic, Marriott Seaview (Bay), Atlantic City, NJ
24–27 **McDonald's LPGA Championship**, DuPont CC, Wilmington, DE

July
1–4 Jamie Farr Kroger Classic, Highland Meadows GC, Sylvania, OH
8–11 Michelob Light Classic, Forest Hill CC, St Louis, MO
15–11 Japan Airlines Big Apple Classic, Wykagyl CC, New Rochelle, NY
23–25 Giant Eagles LPGA Classic, Avalon Lakes, Warren, OH
29–1 **du Maurier Classic**, Priddis Greens G&CC, Calgary, Alberta, Canada

August
5–8 Boston LPGA Classic, Pleasant Valley CC, Sutton, Massachusetts
12–15 **Weetabix Women's British Open**, Woburn G&CC, Milton Keynes, England
20–22 Firstar LPGA Classic, North Beavercreek CC, OH
26–29 Oldsmobile Classic, Walnut Hills CC, East Lansing, MI

September
4–6 State Farm Rail Classic, The Rail CC, Springfield, IL
9–12 Samsung World Championship, TBA
16–19 SAFECO Classic, Meridian Valley CC, Kent, WA
23–26 The Safeway LPGA Championship, Columbia Edgewater CC, Portland, OR
30–3 Columbus LPGA Classic, New Albany CC, New Albany, OH

October
7–10 First Union Betsy King Classic, Berkleigh CC, Kutztown, PN
14–17 Lifetime's AFLAC Tournament of Champions, Robert Trent Jones Golf Trail, AL
29–31 Nichirei International, TBA, Japan
TBA Gillette Tour Challenge

November
5–7 LPGA Mizuno Classic, Kansai, Japan
11–14 PageNet Championship, TBA

December
2–5 JC Penney Classic, Westin Innisbrook, Clearwater, FL
9–12 Diners Club Matches, TBA
18–19 Wendy's Three Tour Challenge, Las Vegas Resort, Henderson, NV

European LPGA Tour

Schedule not available

Bold Type indicates a major

British and European Men's and Boys' Amateur Tournaments

March
17–21 Portuguese Amateur Ch'p, Praia d'El Rey
25–28 Sherry's International Champions Cup, Sotogrande, Spain

April
1–5 French Boys Ch'p, Massane
14–18 French Amateur Ch'p, venue TBC

May
1–2 Lytham Trophy, Royal Lytham & St Annes
1–2 Berkshire Trophy, The Berkshire
14–16 Irish Amateur Open Ch'p, Royal Dublin
14–16 English Open Strokeplay (Brabazon Trophy), Moortown
29–30 Welsh Open Youth Ch'p, Rhuddlan
31–5 British Amateur Ch'p, Royal Co. Down & Kilkeel, N. Ireland

June
3–5 International European Mid-Amateur, GC Grand-Ducal, Luxembourg
10–12 Coupe Murat, Chantilly
12–13 Scottish Strokeplay Ch'p, St Andrews Old & Jubilee
12–13 Polish Open Amateur Ch'p, Amber Baltic GC (Miedzyzdroje)
17–19 International European Seniors Ch'p, Ascona GC, Switzerland
18–20 Welsh Open Strokeplay Ch'p, Northop
19–20 Scottish Youths Strokeplay Ch'p, Crieff & Auchterarder
24–25 Irish Youths Amateur Open Ch'p, Cork
29–3 European Men's Team Ch'p, Amateur, Monticello GC, Italy

July
3–5 North of England Youths, Middlesborough
5–10 European Senior Golf Associations' Team Ch'p, GC Fontana/Oberwaltersdorf Austria GC, Ebreichsdorf
7–11 Luxembourg Amateur Ch'p, GC Grand-Ducal
6–10 Boys European Team Ch'p, Upsala GC, Sweden
11–12 Open Ch'p Final Qualifying, Downfield, Monifieth, Montrose, Panmure

July *continued*
16–18 Russian Amateur Ch'p, Moscow CC
20–22 English Boys (under 18) Amateur Strokeplay Ch'p (Carris Trophy), High Post
26–31 **English Amateur Ch'p**, St Mellion
27–29 European Young Masters Ch'p, I Roveri GC, Italy
29–1 Czech Amateur Ch'p, Mariánské Lázne

August
3–4 Polish Junior Open Ch'p, Amber Baltic GC (Miedzyzdroje)
4–6 British Seniors' Ch'p, Frilford Heath
6–8 Finnish Amateur Ch'p, Helsinki GC
6–8 Swiss Amateur Ch'p, Montreux GC
9–14 British Boys Ch'p, Royal St. David's
11–15 British Mid-Amateur Ch'p (over 25s), Walton Heath
14–15 English Golf Union Gold Medal, Woodhall Spa
17–18 Doug Sanders World Boys Tournament European Qualifyings for Boys and Girls, Aberdeen, Scotland
18–21 European Amateur Ch'p, Celtic Manor, Wales
20–22 English Open Over-35s Strokeplay, Little Aston
20–23 Doug Sanders' World Tournament Final, Aberdeen, Scotland
24–28 Belgian Juniors Ch'p, Royal GC de Belgique
27–29 Hungarian Open Amateur Ch'p, TBC
28 *Golf Weekly/Illustrated* Gold Vase, Walton Heath

September
2–5 German Amateur Ch'p, Scharmützelsee, Bad Saarow
2–5 Slovenian Amateur Ch'p, G&CC Bled
8–12 Spanish Junior Ch'p, La Coruña
11–12 Walker Cup, Nairn, Scotland
15–19 Italian International Amateur Ch'p, Milano GC
22–24 Home Internationals, Royal County Down, Newcastle, N. Ireland
30–3 Hellenic Amateur Ch'p, Glyfada GC of Athens

October
1–3 English County Finals, Seaton Carew
27–30 European Club Cup (Albacom Trophy), Parco de'Medici GC, Italy

US Men's Amateur Championship
16–22 August at Pebble Beach Golf Links, Pebble Beach, California

British and European Women's and Girls' Amateur championships

March
3–7 Spanish Ladies' Amateur Ch'p, Real Club Pineda (Sevilla)
     Spanish Amateur Ch'p, Real Golf Sevilla (Sevilla)
17–21 Portuguese Ladies' Amateur Ch'p, Praia d'El Rey

April
1–5 French Lady Juniors Ch'p, Saint-Cloud
24–25 Scottish Ladies' Open Strokeplay Ch'p, Troon

May
12–16 French Ladies' Amateur Ch'p, St Germain
18–22 English Ladies' Closed Ch'p, Ganton, East Yorks
18–22 Irish Ladies' Closed Ch'p, Carlow GC
18–22 Scottish Ladies' Closed Ch'p, Nairn, Dunbar
18–22 Welsh Ladies' Closed Ch'p, Conwy GC
21–24 Austrian Ladies' Amateur Ch'p, GC Schloss Schönborn
     Austrian Amateur Ch'p, GC Schloss Schönborn
24–25 Helen Holm Scottish Open Strokeplay, Portland and Royal Troon

June
8–12 Ladies' British Open Amateur Ch'p, Royal Birkdale
26–27 Welsh Ladies' Open Strokeplay Ch'p, Celtic Manor G&CC

July
6–10 Ladies' European Team Ch'p, St Germain, France
6–10 Girls European Team Ch'p, Katinkulta GC, Finland
7–11 Luxembourg Ladies' Amateur Ch'p, GC Grand-Ducal
16–18 Russian Ladies' Amateur Ch'p, Moscow CC
23–24 Vagliano Trophy, North Berwick, Scotland

July continued
24–25 Irish Ladies' Open Strokeplay Ch'p, Waterford Castle GC
29–1 Czech Ladies' Amateur Ch'p, Mariánské Lázne

August
3–7 Girls' British Open Amateur Ch'p, High Post
6–8 Finnish Ladies' Amateur Ch'p, Helsinki GC
6–8 Swiss Ladies' Amateur Ch'p, Montreux GC
11–14 English Ladies' Open Intermediate Ch'p, Woodbury Park G&CC
17–18 Doug Sanders World Boys Tournament European Qualifyings for Boys and Girls, Aberdeen, Scotland
18–20 Ladies' British Open Amateur Strokeplay Ch'p, Huddersfield
20–23 Doug Sanders' World Tournament Final, Aberdeen, Scotland
24–28 Belgian Lady Juniors Ch'p, Royal GC de Belgique
25–28 International European Ladies' Ch'p, Karlovy Vary GC, Czech Republic

September
2–5 German Ladies' Amateur Ch'p, Sporting GC, Berlin
2–5 Slovenian Ladies' Amateur Ch'p, G&CC Bled
8–12 Spanish Lady Juniors Ch'p, La Coruña
15–19 Italian International Ladies Amateur Ch'p, Milano GC
24–26 French Ladies' Strokeplay Ch'p, Morfontaine
30–3 Hellenic Ladies' Amateur Ch'p, Glyfada GC of Athens

October
5–8 European Senior Women's Golf Assocations' Team Ch'p, Castelgondolfo, Italy

US Women's Amateur Championship
9–14 August at Bitmore Forest Country Club, Asheville, North Carolina

PART I

The Major Championships

The Open	54
US Open	64
The Masters	72
US PGA	79
Men's Major Title Table	87
Weetabix British Open	88
US Women's Open	95
McDonald's LPGA	103
Nabisco Dinah Shore	110
du Maurier Classic	117
Women's Major Title Table	124

The Open Championship

127th Open Championship *at Royal Birkdale* (7018 yds, Par 70)

Prize money: £1,750,000. Entries: 2,336. Regional qualifying courses: Beau Desert, Blackmoor, Burnham & Berrow, Carlisle, Copt Heath, County Louth, Coxmoor, Glenbervie, Hankley Common, Moortown, Northamptonshire County, Ormskirk, Romford, South Herts, Stockport and Wildernesse. Final qualifying courses: Hesketh, Hillside, Southport & Ainsdale and West Lancashire. Final field comprised 151 players, of whom 78, including three amateurs, made the half-way cut on 146 or better.

Pos	Name	Score	Prize Money £
1	Mark O'Meara (US)*	72-68-72-68—280	300000
2	Brian Watts (US)	68-69-73-70—280	188000
*O'Meara won four-hole play-off			
3	Tiger Woods (US)	65-73-77-66—281	135000
4	Jim Furyk (US)	70-70-73-70—282	76666
	Jesper Parnevik (Swe)	68-72-72-70—282	76666
	Raymond Russell (Sco)	68-73-75-66—282	76666
	Justin Rose (Am) (Eng)	72-66-75-69—282	
7	Davis Love III (US)	67-73-77-68—285	49500
8	Thomas Björn (Den)	68-71-76-71—286	40850
	Costantino Rocca (It)	72-74-70-70—286	40850
10	John Huston (US)	65-77-73-72—287	33333
	Brad Faxon (US)	67-74-74-72—287	33333
	David Duval (US)	70-71-75-71—287	33333
13	Gordon Brand Jr (Sco)	71-70-76-71—288	29000
14	Peter Baker (Eng)	69-72-77-71—289	23650
	Greg Turner (NZ)	68-75-75-71—289	23650
	José Maria Olazábal (Sp)	73-72-75-69—289	23650
	Des Smyth (Ire)	74-69-75-71—289	23650
18	Curtis Strange (US)	73-73-74-70—290	17220
	Vijay Singh (Fij)	67-74-78-71—290	17220
	Sandy Lyle (Sco)	71-72-75-72—290	17220
	Robert Allenby (Aus)	67-76-78-69—290	17220
	Mark James (Eng)	71-74-74-71—290	17220
23	Sam Torrance (Sco)	69-77-75-70—291	12480
	Bob Estes (US)	72-70-76-73—291	12480
	Stephen Ames (T&T)	68-72-79-72—291	12480
	Peter O'Malley (Aus)	71-71-78-71—291	12480
	Lee Janzen (US)	72-69-80-70—291	12480
28	Scott Dunlap (US)	72-69-80-71—292	10030
	Nick Price (Zim)	66-72-82-72—292	10030
	Shigeki Maruyama (Jpn)	70-73-75-74—292	10030
	Loren Roberts (US)	66-76-76-74—292	10030
	Ernie Els (SA)	72-74-74-72—292	10030
	Sergio Garcia (Am) (Sp)	69-75-76-72—292	
33	Mark Calcavecchia (US)	69-77-76-71—293	8900
	Santiago Luna (Sp)	70-72-80-71—293	8900
	Sven Strüver (Ger)	75-70-80-68—293	8900

Pos	Name	Score	Prize Money £
36	Patrik Sjöland (Swe)	72-72-77-73—294	8350
	Joakim Haeggman (Swe)	71-74-78-71—294	8350
	Philip Walton (Ire)	68-76-74-76—294	8350
	Naomichi Ozaki (Jpn)	72-73-76-73—294	8350
	Tom Kite (US)	72-69-79-74—295	8350
	Steen Tinning (Den)	69-76-77-72—294	8350
42	Katsuyoshi Tomori (Jpn)	75-71-70-79—295	7581
	David Howell (Eng)	68-77-79-71—295	7581
	David Frost (SA)	72-73-78-72—295	7581
	Rodger Davis (Aus)	76-70-78-71—295	7581
	David Carter (Eng)	71-75-76-73—295	7581
	Nick Faldo (Eng)	72-73-75-75—295	7581
	Payne Stewart (US)	71-71-78-75—295	7581
	Andrew Coltart (Sco)	68-77-75-75—295	7581
50	Steve Stricker (US)	70-72-80-74—296	6860
	Bill Mayfair (US)	72-73-77-74—296	6860
	Brandt Jobe (US)	70-73-82-71—296	6860
	Larry Mize (US)	70-75-79-72—296	6860
	Frankie Minoza (Phil)	69-75-76-76—296	6860
55	Trevor Dodds (Nam)	73-71-81-72—297	6264
	Eduardo Romero (Arg)	71-70-79-77—297	6264
	Steven Jones (US)	73-72-79-73—297	6264
	Justin Leonard (US)	73-73-82-69—297	6264
	Ignacio Garrido (Sp)	71-74-80-72—297	6264
	Ian Woosnam (Wal)	72-74-76-75—297	6264
	Greg Chalmers (Aus)	71-75-77-74—297	6264
62	Lee Westwood (Eng)	71-71-78-78—298	5975
	Carlos Daniel Franco (Para)	71-73-76-78—298	5975
64	Stewart Cink (US)	71-73-83-72—299	5800
	Mark Brooks (US)	71-73-75-80—299	5800
	Michael Campbell (NZ)	73-73-80-73—299	5800
	Fred Couples (US)	66-74-78-81—299	5800
	Michael Long (NZ)	70-74-78-77—299	5800
	Didier De Vooght (Am) (Bel)	70-76-80-73—299	
69	Andrew Clapp (Eng)	72-74-81-73—300	5650
70	Gary Evans (Eng)	69-74-84-74—301	5600
71	Bob May (US)	70-73-85-75—303	5550
72	Andrew McLardy (SA)	72-74-80-78—304	5500
73	Fredrik Jacobson (Swe)	67-78-81-79—305	5450
74	Kazuhiko Hosokawa (Jpn)	72-73-81-80—306	5400
75	Robert Giles (Ire)	72-74-83-78—307	5350
76	Phil Mickelson (US)	71-74-85-78—308	5300
77	Andrew Oldcorn (Sco)	75-71-84-79—309	5250
78	Dudley Hart (US)	73-72-85-80—310	5200

The following players missed the half-way cut

Pos	Name	Score	Pos	Name	Score
79	Barry Lane (Eng)	72-75—147	91	Seve Ballesteros (Sp)	73-75—148
	Keiichiro Fukabori (Jpn)	70-77—147		Toru Taniguchi (Jpn)	71-77—148
	Colin Montgomerie (Sco)	73-74—147		Darren Clarke (N.Ire)	73-75—148
	Bob Tway (US)	68-79—147	91T	Peter Mitchell (Eng)	76-72—148
	Tony Johnstone (Zim)	73-74—147		Joe Durant (US)	74-74—148
	Paul McGinley (Ire)	72-75—147		Yoshinori Mizumaki (Jpn)	71-77—148
	Carl Suneson (Eng)	77-70—147		Glen Day (US)	75-73—148
	Thomas Levet (Fr)	72-75—147		Peter Senior (Aus)	71-77—148
	Brian Davis (Eng)	72-75—147		Simon McCarthy (Am)	73-75—148
	Jeff Maggert (US)	73-74—147	99	Tom Watson (US)	73-76—149
	Phillip Price (Wal)	72-75—147		JP Hayes (US)	70-79—149
	Craig Parry (Aus)	73-74—147		Paul Azinger (US)	76-73—149

127th Open Championship *continued*

Pos	Name	Score
99T	Padraig Harrington (Ire)	73-76—149
	Gary Brown (Eng)	74-75—149
	Grant Dodd (Aus)	70-79—149
	Bernhard Langer (Ger)	74-75—149
	Derrick Cooper (Eng)	72-77—149
	Paul Lawrie (Sco)	73-76—149
	Richard Bland (Eng)	71-78—149
109	Jean Louis Guepy (Fr)	74-76—150
	Scott Hoch (US)	73-77—150
	Corey Pavin (US)	74-76—150
	Per-Ulrik Johansson (Swe)	74-76—150
	Kyoung-Ju Choi (Kor)	70-80—150
	Lee Jones (Eng)	77-73—150
	Retief Goosen (SA)	74-76—150
	Tom Lehman (US)	71-79—150
	David Shacklady (Eng)	76-74—150
	John Lovell (Eng)	72-78—150
	Matt Kuchar (US) (Am)	75-75—150
119	Mark McNulty (Zim)	73-78—151
	Fredrik Henge (Swe)	75-76—151
	Skip Kendall (US)	74-77—151
	Stephen Leaney (Aus)	75-76—151
	John Daly (US)	73-78—151
	Gary Player (SA)	77-74—151
	Matthew McGuire (Eng)	74-77—151
126	Stephen Allan (Aus)	72-80—152
126T	Ross Drummond (Sco)	74-78—152
	Steven Young (Sco)	74-78—152
	Howard Clark (Eng)	73-79—152
130	Andrew Magee (US)	75-78—153
	Russell Claydon (Eng)	74-79—153
	Frank Nobilo (NZ)	76-77—153
133	Robert Karlsson (Swe)	72-82—154
	Ben Crenshaw (US)	76-78—154
	Graham Spring (Ire)	74-80—154
	Steve Alker (NZ)	73-81—154
	Mats Hallberg (Swe)	77-77—154
	Daren Lee (Eng)	76-78—154
	Steven Armstrong (Sco)	76-78—154
140	Toru Suzuki (Jpn)	78-77—155
	Mark Litton (Eng)	75-80—155
142	Stuart Appleby (Aus)	76-80—156
	Greig Hutcheon (Sco)	73-83—156
	Gary Orr (Sco)	78-78—156
	Bradley Dredge (Wal)	78-78—156
146	Scott Henderson (Sco)	77-80—157
147	Peter Hedblom (Swe)	76-82—158
148	Jeff Remesy (Fr)	77-82—159
149	Miguel Angel Jiménez (Sp)	73 Dis
	Steve Elkington (Aus)	75 Ret'd
	Francis Howley (Ire)	78 W/D

1997 Open Championship *at Royal Troon* (7079 yds, Par 71)

Prize money: £1,586,300. Entries: 2,133. Regional qualifying courses: Beau Desert, Burnham & Berrow, Carlisle, Copt Heath, Coxmoor, Glenbervie, Hankley Common, Moortown, North Hants, Romford, South Herts, Sundridge Park, Wilmslow. Final qualifying courses: Irvine Bogside, Glasgow Gailes, Kilmarnock Barassie, Western Gailes. 156 players took part, 70 (including 1 amateur) qualified for final 36 holes.

Pos	Name	Score	Prize £
1	J Leonard (US)	69-66-72-65—272	250000
2	D Clarke (N.Ire)	67-66-71-71—275	150000
	J Parnevik (Swe)	70-66-66-73—275	150000
4	J Furyk (US)	67-72-70-70—279	90000
5	S Ames (T&T)	74-69-66-71—280	62500
	P Harrington (Ire)	75-69-69-67—280	62500
7	F Couples (US)	69-68-70-74—281	40666
	E Romero (Arg)	74-68-67-72—281	40666
	P O'Malley (Aus)	73-70-70-68—281	40666
10	R Goosen (SA)	75-69-70-68—282	24300
	L Westwood (Eng)	73-70-67-72—282	24300
	T Watson (US)	71-70-70-71—282	24300
	M Calcavecchia (US)	74-67-72-69—282	24300
	R Allenby (Aus)	76-68-66-72—282	24300
	S Maruyama (Jpn)	74-69-70-69—282	24300
	T Kite (US)	72-67-74-69—282	24300
	D Love III (US)	70-71-74-67—282	24300
	E Els (SA)	75-69-69-69—282	24300
	F Nobilo (NZ)	74-72-68-68—282	24300
20	JM Olazábal (Sp)	75-68-73-67—283	14500
	M James (Eng)	76-67-70-70—283	14500
	B Faxon (US)	77-67-72-67—283	14500
	S Appleby (Aus)	72-72-68-71—283	14500
24	P Lonard (Aus)	72-70-69-73—284	10362
	C Montgomerie (Sco)	76-69-69-70—284	10362
	I Woosnam (Wal)	71-73-69-71—284	10362
	D A Russell (Eng)	75-72-68-69—284	10362
	T Woods (US)	72-74-64-74—284	10362
	T Lehman (US)	74-72-72-66—284	10362
	J Haas (US)	71-70-73-70—284	10362
	P Mickelson (US)	76-68-69-71—284	10362
32	M McNulty (Zim)	78-67-72-68—285	8750
33	J Lomas (Eng)	72-71-69-74—286	8283
	D Duval (US)	73-69-73-71—286	8283
	R Davis (Aus)	73-73-70-70—286	8283
36	A Magee (US)	70-75-72-70—287	7950
	G Norman (Aus)	69-73-70-75—287	7950

Other Totals: R Russell (Sco), M O'Meara (US), J Kernohan (US), M Bradley (US), B Langer (Ger), V Singh (Fij) 288; J Coceres (Arg), D Tapping (Eng), C Strange (US), J Kelly (US) 289; S Jones (US), J Payne (Eng), R Boxall (Eng) 290; A Cabrera (Arg), J Maggert (US), W Riley (Aus), P Senior (Aus), C Pavin (US), P Mitchell (Eng), N Faldo (Eng), G Turner (NZ) 291; P Stewart (US) 292; J Nicklaus (US), B Howard (Am) (Sco) 293; T Purtzer (US), J Spence (Eng), S Stricker (US), P Teravainen (US) 294; P McGinley (Ire), P-U Johansson (Swe), G Clark (Eng) 295; T Tolles (US) 296; B Andrade (US) 298.

1996 Open Championship at Royal Lytham & St Annes (6892 yds, Par 71)

Prize money: £1,400,000. Entries: 1,918. Regional qualifying courses: Beau Desert, Burnham & Berrow, Carlisle, Copt Heath, Coxmoor, Glenbervie, Hankley Common, Moortown, North Hants, Romford, South Herts, Sundridge Park, Wilmslow. Final qualifying courses: Fairhaven, Formby, St Anne's Old Links, Southport & Ainsdale. Qualified for final 36 holes: 77 (including 1 amateur).

Pos	Name	Score	Prize £	Pos	Name	Score	Prize £
1	T Lehman (US)	67-67-64-73—271	200000	18T	R Mediate (US)	69-70-69-72—280	15500
2	M McCumber (US)	67-69-71-66—273	125000	22	M James (Eng)	70-68-75-68—281	11875
	E Els (SA)	68-67-71-67—273	125000		J Haas (US)	70-72-71-68—281	11875
4	N Faldo (Eng)	68-68-68-70—274	75000		T Woods (Am) (US)	75-66-70-70—281	
5	J Maggert (US)	69-70-72-65—276	50000		C Mason (Eng)	68-70-70-73—281	11875
	M Brooks (US)	67-70-68-71—276	50000		S Stricker (US)	71-70-66-74—281	11875
7	P Hedblom (Swe)	70-65-75-67—277	35000	27	B Crenshaw (US)	73-68-71-70—282	9525
	G Norman (Aus)	71-68-71-67—277	35000		T Kite (US)	77-66-69-70—282	9525
	G Turner (NZ)	72-69-68-68—277	35000		P Broadhurst (Eng)	65-72-74-71—282	9525
	F Couples (US)	67-70-69-71—277	35000		C Pavin (US)	70-66-74-72—282	9525
11	A Cejka (Ger)	73-67-71-67—278	27000		P Mitchell (Eng)	71-68-71-72—282	9525
	D Clarke (N.Ire)	70-68-69-71—278	27000		F Nobilo (NZ)	70-72-68-72—282	9525
	V Singh (Fij)	69-67-69-73—278	27000	33	E Romero (Arg)	70-71-75-67—283	7843
14	M McNulty (Zim)	69-71-70-69—279	20250		T Tolles (US)	73-70-71-69—283	7843
	D Duval (US)	76-67-66-70—279	20250		S Simpson (US)	71-69-73-70—283	7843
	P McGinley (Ire)	69-65-74-71—279	20250		E Darcy (Ire)	73-69-71-70—283	7843
	S Maruyama (Jpn)	68-70-69-72—279	20250		D Gilford (Eng)	71-67-71-74—283	7843
18	M Welch (Eng)	71-68-73-68—280	15500		M O'Meara (US)	67-69-72-75—283	7843
	P Harrington (Ire)	68-68-73-71—280	15500		H Tanaka (Jpn)	67-71-70-75—283	7843
	L Roberts (US)	67-65-72-72—280	15500		B Faxon (US)	67-73-68-75—283	7843

Other Totals: M Calcavecchia (US), P Mickelson (US), K Eriksson (Swe), D Frost (SA) 284; C Stadler (US), B Mayfair (US), P Jacobsen (US), T Hamilton (Can), B Hughes (Aus), P Stewart (US), R Boxall (Eng), J Nicklaus (US), N Price (Zim), J Furyk (US), J Parnevik (Swe) 285; J Payne (Eng), S Lyle (Sco), R Allenby (Aus), S Ames (T&T) 286; M Jonzon (Swe), DA Weibring (US), J Sluman (US), B Barnes (Sco) 287; C Suneson (Eng), C Rocca (It), G Law (Sco) 288; DA Russell (Eng), B Ogle (Aus), J Daly (US) 289; H Clark (Eng) 290; B Charles (NZ) 291; D Hospital (Sp), R Todd (Can), C Strange (US), R Chapman (Eng) 292; R Goosen (SA) 293; A Langenaeken (Bel) 298.

1995 Open Championship at St Andrews (6933 yds, Par 72)

Prize money: £1,250,000. Entries: 1,836. Regional qualifying courses: Beau Desert, Blackwell, Glenbervie, Hankley Common, Lanark, Moortown, North Hants, Romford, Sherwood Forest, South Herts, Sundridge, Wilmslow. Final qualifying courses: Ladybank, Leven Links, Lundin, Scotscraig. Qualified for final 36 holes: 103 (including 4 amateurs).

Pos	Name	Score	Prize £	Pos	Name	Score	Prize £
1	J Daly (US)*	67-71-73-71—282	125000	20	P Mitchell (Eng)	73-74-71-70—288	13500
2	C Rocca (It)	69-70-70-73—282	100000		D Duval (US)	71-75-70-72—288	13500

Daly won four-hole play-off

					A Coltart (Sco)	70-74-71-73—288	13500
3	S Bottomley (Eng)	70-72-72-69—283	65666		B Lane (Eng)	72-73-68-75—288	13500
	M Brooks (US)	70-69-73-71—283	65666	24	L Janzen (US)	73-73-71-72—289	10316
	M Campbell (NZ)	71-71-65-76—283	65666		S Webster (Am) (Eng)	70-72-74-73—289	
6	V Singh (Fij)	68-72-73-71—284	40500		B Langer (Ger)	72-71-73-73—289	10316
	S Elkington (Aus)	72-69-69-74—284	40500		J Parnevik (Swe)	75-71-70-73—289	10316
8	M James (Eng)	72-75-68-70—285	33333		M Calcavecchia (US)	71-72-72-74—289	10316
	B Estes (US)	72-70-71-72—285	33333		B Glasson (US)	68-74-72-75—289	10316
	C Pavin (US)	69-70-72-74—285	33333		K Tomori (Jpn)	70-68-73-78—289	10316
11	P Stewart (US)	72-68-75-71—286	26000	31	R Drummond (Sco)	74-68-77-71—290	8122
	B Ogle (Aus)	73-69-71-73—286	26000		JM Olazábal (Sp)	72-72-74-72—290	8122
	S Torrance (Sco)	71-70-74-71—286	26000		D Frost (SA)	72-72-74-72—290	8122
	E Els (SA)	71-68-72-75—286	26000		H Sasaki (Jpn)	74-71-72-73—290	8122
15	G Norman (Aus)	71-74-72-70—287	18200		J Huston (US)	71-74-72-73—290	8122
	R Allenby (Aus)	71-74-71-71—287	18200		P Jacobsen (US)	71-76-70-73—290	8122
	B Crenshaw (US)	67-72-76-72—287	18200		D Clarke (N.Ire)	69-77-70-74—290	8122
	P-U Johansson (Swe)	69-78-68-72—287	18200		D Feherty (N.Ire)	68-75-71-76—290	8122
	B Faxon (US)	71-67-75-74—287	18200		T Watson (US)	67-76-70-77—290	8122

Other Totals: S Ballesteros (Sp), W Bennett (Eng), P Mickelson (US), M McNulty (Zim), N Faldo (Eng), B Watts (US), G Sherry (Am) (Sco), J Cook (US), N Price (Zim), I Woosnam (Wal), A Forsbrand (Swe), M O'Meara (US), T Nakajima (Jpn), B Claar (US), K Green (US) 292; J Gallagher (US), P O'Malley (Aus), R Claydon (Eng) 293; P Senior (Aus), P Broadhurst (Eng), D Cooper (Eng), E Herrera (Col), T Kite (US), P Lawrie (Sco), M Gates (Eng), R Floyd (US), J Leonard (US), D Gilford (Eng) 294; P Baker (Eng), J Maggert (US), J Lomas (Eng), F Nobilo (NZ), G Player (SA), O Karlsson (Swe), M Hallberg (Swe), S Hoch (US), G Hallberg (US), J Rivero (Sp), T Woods (Am) (US) 295.

1994 Open Championship *at Turnberry* (6957 yds, Par 70)

Prize money: £1,100,000. Entries 1,701. Regional qualifying courses: Blackwell, Glenbervie, Hankley Common, Lanark, Moortown, North Hants, Orsett, Sherwood Forest, South Herts, Sundridge Park, Wilmslow. Final qualifying courses: Glasgow Gailes, Irvine Bogside, Kilmarnock Barassie, Western Gailes. Qualified for final 36 holes: 81 (including 1 amateur). Non-qualifiers after 36 holes with scores of 143 or more: 75 (71 professionals, 4 amateurs)

Pos	Name	Score	Prize £	Pos	Name	Score	Prize £
1	N Price (Zim)	69-66-67-66—268	110000	20	M Brooks (US)	74-64-71-68—277	12500
2	J Parnevik (Swe)	68-66-68-67—269	88000		V Singh (Fij)	70-68-69-70—277	12500
3	F Zoeller (US)	71-66-64-70—271	74000		G Turner (NZ)	65-71-70-71—277	12500
4	A Forsbrand (Swe)	72-71-66-64—273	50666		P Senior (Aus)	68-71-67-71—277	12500
	M James (Eng)	72-67-66-68—273	50666	24	B Estes (US)	72-68-72-66—278	7972
	D Feherty (N.Ire)	68-69-66-70—273	50666		T Price (Aus)	74-65-71-68—278	7972
7	B Faxon (US)	69-65-67-73—274	36000		P Lawrie (Sco)	71-69-70-68—278	7972
8	N Faldo (Eng)	75-66-70-64—275	30000		J Maggert (US)	69-74-67-68—278	7972
	T Kite (US)	71-69-66-69—275	30000		T Lehman (US)	70-69-70-69—278	7972
	C Montgomerie (Sco)	72-69-65-69—275	30000		E Els (SA)	69-69-69-71—278	7972
11	R Claydon (Eng)	72-71-68-65—276	19333		M Springer (US)	72-67-68-71—278	7972
	M McNulty (Zim)	71-70-68-67—276	19333		L Roberts (US)	68-69-69-72—278	7972
	F Nobilo (NZ)	69-67-72-68—276	19333		P Jacobsen (US)	69-70-67-72—278	7972
	J Lomas (Eng)	66-70-72-68—276	19333		C Stadler (US)	71-69-66-72—278	7972
	M Calcavecchia (US)	71-70-67-68—276	19333		A Coltart (Sco)	71-69-66-72—278	7972
	G Norman (Aus)	71-67-69-69—276	19333	35	M Davis (Eng)	75-68-69-67—279	6700
	L Mize (US)	73-69-64-70—276	19333		L Janzen (US)	74-69-69-67—279	6700
	T Watson (US)	68-65-69-74—276	19333		G Evans (Eng)	69-69-73-68—279	6700
	R Rafferty (N.Ire)	71-66-65-74—276	19333				

Other Totals: D Gilford (Eng), D Hospital (Sp), JM Olazabal (Sp), S Ballesteros (Sp), B Marchbank (Eng), D Clarke (N.Ire) 280; J Van De Velde (Fr), D Love III (US), M Ozaki (Jpn) 280; J Gallagher Jr (US), D Edwards (US), G Kraft (US), H Twitty (US) 281; D Frost (SA), M Lanner (Swe), K Tomori (Jpn), T Watanabe (US), P Baker (Eng), J Cook (US), T Nakajima (Jpn), B Watts (US), R McFarlane (Eng) 283; G Brand Jr (Sco), H Meshiai (Jpn), B Langer (Ger), C O'Connor Jr (Ire), P-U Johansson (Swe), R Allenby (Aus), W Grady (Aus) 284; S Elkington (Aus), M Roe (Eng), L Clements (US), C Mason (Eng), R Alvarez (Arg) 285; W Bennett (Am) (GB), W Riley (Aus) 286; A Lyle (Sco) 287; C Ronald (Eng), C Gillies (Eng) 288; B Crenshaw (US), C Parry (Aus), J Haeggman (Swe) 289; N Henning (SA) 291; J Daly (US) 292.

1993 Open Championship *at Royal St George's* (6860 yds, Par 70)

Prize money: £1,017,000. Entries 1,827. Regional qualifying courses: Beau Desert, Blackwell, Coxmoor, Hankley Park, Lanark, Langley Park, North Hants, Orsett, Sherwood Forest, South Herts, Sundridge Park, Wilmslow. Final qualifying courses: Littlestone, North Foreland, Prince's and Royal Cinque Ports. Qualified for final 36 holes: 78 (77 professionals, 1 amateur). Non-qualifiers after 36 holes: 78 (73 professionals, 5 amateurs) with scores of 144 and above.

Pos	Name	Score	Prize £	Pos	Name	Score	Prize £
1	G Norman (Aus)	66-68-69-64—267	100000	14T	T Kite (US)	72-70-68-68—278	15214
2	N Faldo (Eng)	69-63-70-67—269	80000	21	H Clark (Eng)	67-72-70-70—279	10000
3	B Langer (Ger)	67-66-70-67—270	67000		J Parnevik (Swe)	68-74-68-69—279	10000
4	C Pavin (US)	68-66-68-70—272	50500		P Baker (Eng)	70-67-74-68—279	10000
	P Senior (Aus)	66-69-70-67—272	50500	24	R Davis (Aus)	68-71-71-70—280	8400
6	N Price (Zim)	68-70-67-69—274	33166		D Frost (SA)	69-73-70-68—280	8400
	E Els (SA)	68-69-69-68—274	33166		M Roe (Eng)	70-71-73-66—280	8400
	P Lawrie (Sco)	72-68-69-65—274	33166	27	L Mize (US)	67-69-74-71—281	7225
9	W Grady (Aus)	74-68-64-69—275	25500		S Ballesteros (Spa)	68-73-69-71—281	7225
	F Couples (US)	68-66-72-69—275	25500		M James (Eng)	70-70-70-71—281	7225
	S Simpson (US)	68-70-71-66—275	25500		D Smyth (Ire)	67-74-70-70—281	7225
12	P Stewart (US)	71-72-70-63—276	21500		Y Mizumaki (Jpn)	69-69-73-70—281	7225
13	B Lane (Eng)	70-68-71-68—277	20500		M Mackenzie (Eng)	72-71-71-67—281	7225
14	J Daly (US)	71-66-70-71—278	15214		I Pyman (Am) (Eng)	68-72-70-71—281	
	F Zoeller (US)	66-70-71-71—278	15214	34	H Twitty (US)	71-71-67-73—282	6180
	G Morgan (US)	70-68-70-70—278	15214		R Floyd (US)	70-72-67-73—282	6180
	J Rivero (Sp)	68-73-67-70—278	15214		W Westner (SA)	67-73-72-70—282	6180
	M McNulty (Zim)	67-71-71-69—278	15214		P Broadhurst (Eng)	71-69-74-68—282	6180
	M Calcavecchia (US)	66-73-71-68—278	15214		J Van de Velde (Fr)	75-67-73-67—282	6180

Other Totals: D Clarke (N.Ire), C O'Connor Jr (Ire), A Sorensen (Den), D Waldorf (US), P Moloney (Aus), G Turner (NZ), C Mason (Eng), A Magee (US), R Mediate (US) 283; L Janzen (US), S Elkington (Aus), J Huston (US) 284; J Sewell (Eng), M Pinero (Sp), F Nobilo (NZ), S Torrance (Sco), MA Jimenez (Sp), I Woosnam (Wal), S Ames (T&T), I Garbutt (Eng) 285; C Parry (Aus), T Lehman (US), V Singh (Fij), P Azinger (US) 286; J Spence (Eng), O Karlsson (Swe), R Drummond (Eng) 287; T Pernice (US), W Guy (Eng), J Cook (US), M Sunesson (Swe) 288; I Baker-Finch (Aus), T Purtzer (US), M Miller (Eng) 289; M Harwood (Aus), P Mitchell (Eng), P Fowler (Aus), D Forsman (US) 290; M Krantz (Swe) 292; R Willison (Eng) 293.

1992 Open Championship at Muirfield (6970 yds, Par 71)

Prize money: £950,000. Entries 1,666. Regional qualifying courses: Beau Desert, Blackwell, Coxmoor, Glenbervie, Lanark, North Hants, Orsett, Sherwood Forest, South Herts, Sundridge Park, Wilmslow. Final qualifying courses: Dunbar, Gullane, Luffness New, North Berwick. Qualified for final 36 holes: 75 (74 professionals, 1 amateur). Non-qualifiers after 36 holes: 81 (77 professionals, 4 amateurs) with scores of 143 and above.

Pos	Name	Score	Prize £	Pos	Name	Score	Prize £
1	N Faldo (Eng)	66-64-69-73—272	95000	19T	I Baker-Finch (Aus)	71-71-72-68—282	11066
2	J Cook (US)	66-67-70-70—273	75000		T Kite (US)	70-69-71-72—282	11066
3	JM Olazábal (Sp)	70-67-69-68—274	64000	22	P Mitchell (Eng)	69-71-72-71—283	8950
4	S Pate (US)	64-70-69-73—276	53000		P Lawrie (Sco)	70-72-68-73—283	8950
5	D Hammond (US)	70-65-70-74—279	30071		T Purtzer (US)	68-69-75-71—283	8950
	A Magee (US)	67-72-70-70—279	30071	25	B Andrade (US)	69-71-70-74—284	7700
	E Els (SA)	66-69-70-74—279	30071		D Waldorf (US)	69-70-73-72—284	7700
	I Woosnam (Wal)	65-73-70-71—279	30071		P Senior (Aus)	70-69-70-75—284	7700
	G Brand Jr (Sco)	65-68-72-74—279	30071	28	M Calcavecchia (US)	69-71-73-72—285	6658
	M Mackenzie (Chile)	71-67-70-71—279	30071		M McNulty (Zim)	71-70-70-74—285	6658
	R Karlsson (Swe)	70-68-70-71—279	30071		J Mudd (US)	71-69-74-71—285	6658
12	J Spence (Eng)	71-68-70-71—280	17383		C Parry (Aus)	67-71-76-71—285	6658
	C Beck (US)	71-68-67-74—280	17383		R Cochran (US)	71-68-72-74—285	6658
	R Floyd (US)	64-71-73-72—280	17383		M Lanner (Swe)	72-68-71-74—285	6658
	A Lyle (Sco)	68-70-70-72—280	17383	34	A Forsbrand (Swe)	70-72-70-74—286	5760
	M O'Meara (US)	71-68-72-69—280	17383		C Pavin (US)	69-74-73-70—286	5760
	L Rinker (US)	69-68-70-73—280	17383		P Stewart (US)	70-73-71-72—286	5760
18	G Norman (Aus)	71-72-70-68—281	13200		S Elkington (US)	68-70-75-73—286	5760
19	H Irwin (US)	70-73-67-72—282	11066		T Johnstone (Zim)	72-71-74-69—286	5760

Other Totals: DW Basson (SA), L Janzen (US), L Trevino (US), S Richardson (Eng), W Grady (Aus), R Rafferty (Ire) 287; M Harwood (Aus), L Wadkins (US), J Coceres (Arg), R Mediate (US), C Mann (Aus), B Marchbank (Eng) 288; R Mackay (Aus), V Singh (Fij), N Price (Zim), B Lane (Eng) 289; C Rocca (It), D Feherty (N.Ire), M Brooks (US), O Vincent III (US) 290; P Azinger (US), B Langer (Ger), W Riley (Aus), W Guy (Eng), M Clayton (Aus) 291; C Stadler (US), R Chapman (Eng), D Mijovic (Can), H Buhrmann (SA) 292; P-U Johansson (Swe), P O'Malley (Aus), A Sherborne (Eng), J Robson (Eng), D Lee (Eng) 293; F Funk (US) 294; P Mayo (Eng) 295; J Daly (US) 298.

1991 Open Championship at Royal Birkdale (6940 yds, Par 70)

Prize money: £900,000. Entries 1,496. Regional qualifying courses: Beau Desert, Blackwell, Deer Park, Hankley Common, Langley Park, Ormskirk, Orsett, Sherwood Forest, South Herts. Final qualifying courses: Hesketh, Hillside, Southport & Ainsdale, West Lancashire. Qualified for final 36 holes: 113 (111 professionals, 2 amateurs). Non-qualifiers after 36 holes: 43 (37 professionals, 6 amateurs) with scores of 149 and above.

Pos	Name	Score	Prize £	Pos	Name	Score	Prize £
1	I Baker-Finch (Aus)	71-71-64-66—272	90000	17T	C Beck (US)	67-78-70-66—281	10055
2	M Harwood (Aus)	68-70-69-67—274	70000		I Woosnam (Wal)	70-72-69-70—281	10055
3	M O'Meara (US)	71-68-67-69—275	55000		P Broadhurst (Eng)	71-73-68-69—281	10055
	F Couples (US)	72-69-70-64—275	55000		M Mouland (Wal)	68-74-68-71—281	10055
5	J Mudd (US)	72-70-72-63—277	34166		A Sherborne (Eng)	73-70-68-70—281	10055
	E Darcy (Ire)	73-68-66-70—277	34166		P Senior (Aus)	74-67-71-69—281	10055
	B Tway (US)	75-66-70-66—277	34166	26	C Montgomerie (Sco)	71-69-71-71—282	6750
8	C Parry (Aus)	71-70-69-68—278	27500		M Reid (US)	68-71-70-73—282	6750
9	G Norman (Aus)	74-68-71-66—279	22833		W Grady (Aus)	69-70-73-70—282	6750
	B Langer (Ger)	71-71-70-67—279	22833		T Watson (US)	69-72-72-69—282	6750
	S Ballesteros (Sp)	66-73-69-71—279	22833		E Romero (Arg)	70-73-68-71—282	6750
12	M Sunesson (Swe)	72-73-68-67—280	17100		M James (Eng)	72-68-70-72—282	6750
	D Williams (Eng)	74-71-68-67—280	17100	32	G Hallberg (US)	68-70-73-72—283	5633
	V Singh (Fij)	71-69-69-71—280	17100		P Stewart (US)	72-72-71-68—283	5633
	R Davis (Aus)	70-71-73-66—280	17100		S Richardson (Eng)	74-70-72-67—283	5633
	R Chapman (Eng)	74-66-71-69—280	17100		G Brand Jr (Sco)	71-72-69-71—283	5633
17	L Trevino (US)	71-72-71-67—281	10055		M Miller (Sco)	73-74-67-69—283	5633
	B Lane (Eng)	68-72-71-70—281	10055		C O'Connor Jr (Ire)	72-71-71-69—283	5633
	N Faldo (Eng)	68-75-70-68—281	10055				

Other Totals: C Strange (US), A Forsbrand (Swe), P O'Malley (Aus), N Henke (US), M Poxon (Eng), J Payne (Am) (Eng) 284; G Marsh (Aus), R Gamez (US), T Kite (US), S Elkington (Aus), F Allem (SA), S Torrance (Sco), C Rocca (It), D Love III (US), D Smyth (Ire), J Spence (Eng), J Nicklaus (US), N Price (Zim), D Hammond (US) 285; G Levenson (SA), A Magee (US), H Irwin (US), S Simpson (US), T Simpson (US), J Rivero (Sp), G Player (SA) 286; MA Martin (Sp), JD Blake (US), M McLean (Eng), A Oldcorn (Sco), M McNulty (Zim), S Jones (US), S Pate (US), G Morgan (US), D Clarke (N.Ire) 287.

1990 Open Championship *at St Andrews* (6933 yds, Par 72)

Prize money: £825,000. Entries 1,707. Regional qualifying courses: Blackwell, Deer Park, Hankley Common, Langley Park, Ormskirk, Orsett, Sherwood Forest, South Herts. Final qualifying courses: Ladybank, Leven Links, Lundin, Panmure, Scotscraig. Qualified for final 36 holes: 72 (all professionals). Non-qualifiers after 36 holes: 84 (80 professionals and 4 amateurs) with scores of 144 and above.

Pos	Name	Score	Prize £	Pos	Name	Score	Prize £
1	N Faldo (Eng)	67-65-67-71—270	85000	16T	P Jacobsen (US)	68-70-70-73—281	11150
2	M McNulty (Zim)	74-68-68-65—275	60000		F Nobilo (NZ)	72-67-68-74—281	11150
	P Stewart (US)	68-68-68-71—275	60000	22	E Darcy (Ire)	71-71-72-68—282	7933
4	I Woosnam (Wal)	68-69-70-69—276	40000		C Parry (Aus)	68-68-69-77—282	7933
	J Mudd (US)	72-66-72-66—276	40000		J Spence (Eng)	72-65-73-72—282	7933
6	I Baker-Finch (Aus)	68-72-64-73—277	28500	25	N Price (Zim)	70-67-71-75—283	6383
	G Norman (Aus)	66-66-76-69—277	28500		F Couples (US)	71-70-70-72—283	6383
8	S Pate (US)	70-68-72-69—279	22000		C O'Connor Jr (Ire)	68-72-71-72—283	6383
	C Pavin (US)	71-69-68-71—279	22000		L Trevino (US)	69-70-73-71—283	6383
	D Hammond (US)	70-71-68-70—279	22000		J Rivero (Sp)	70-70-70-73—283	6383
	D Graham (Aus)	72-71-70-66—279	22000		J Sluman (US)	72-70-70-71—283	6383
12	V Singh (Fij)	70-69-72-69—280	16375	31	B Norton (US)	71-72-68-73—284	5125
	T Simpson (US)	70-69-69-72—280	16375		L Mize (US)	71-72-70-71—284	5125
	R Gamez (US)	70-72-67-71—280	16375		R Rafferty (N.Ire)	70-71-73-70—284	5125
	P Broadhurst (Eng)	74-69-63-74—280	16375		B Crenshaw (US)	74-69-68-73—284	5125
16	M Roe (Eng)	71-70-72-68—281	11150		M McCumber (US)	69-74-69-72—284	5125
	S Jones (US)	72-67-72-70—281	11150		M James (Eng)	73-69-70-72—284	5125
	A Lyle (Sco)	72-70-67-72—281	11150		V Fernandez (Arg)	72-67-69-76—284	5125
	JM Olazábal (Sp)	71-67-71-72—281	11150		G Powers (US)	73-68-69-74—284	5125

Other Totals: D Cooper (Eng), N Ozaki (Jpn), D Pooley (US), M Hulbert (US), M Reid (US), A North (US), S Simpson (US), R Floyd (US), S Torrance (Sco) 285; M O'Meara (US), C Montgomerie (Sco), B Langer (Ger), P Fowler (Aus), P Azinger (US) 286; H Irwin (US), E Romero (Arg), J Bland (SA), M Allen (US) 287; D Ray (Eng), A Sorensen (Den), B McCallister (US), J Rutledge (Can), D Mijovic (US), M Clayton (Aus) 288; M Poxon (Eng), P Baker (Eng), J Nicklaus (US), R Chapman (Eng), D Canipe (US) 289; J Berendt (Arg), D Feherty (N.Ire) 290; A Saavedra (Arg) 291; M Mackenzie (Eng) 292; JM Canizares (Sp) 296.

1989 Open Championship *at Royal Troon* (7907 yds, Par 72)

Prize money: £750,000. Entries 1,481. Regional qualifying courses: Glenbervie, Hankley Common, Langley Park, Lindrick, Little Aston, Ormskirk, Porters Park, South Herts. Final qualifying courses: Glasgow Gailes, Irvine (Bogside), Kilmarnock (Barassie), Western Gailes. Qualified for final 36 holes: 80 (78 professionals, 2 amateurs). Non-qualifiers after 36 holes: 76 (68 professionals, 8 amateurs) with scores of 147 and above.

Pos	Name	Score	Prize £	Pos	Name	Score	Prize £
1	M Calcavecchia (US)*	71-68-68-68—275	80000	19T	D Cooper (Eng)	69-70-76-68—283	8575
2	W Grady (Aus)	68-67-69-71—275	55000		T Kite (US)	70-74-67-72—283	8575
	G Norman (Aus)	69-70-72-64—275	55000		D Pooley (US)	73-70-69-71—283	8575
Calcavecchia won four-hole play-off				23	V Singh (Fij)	71-73-69-71—284	6733
4	T Watson (US)	69-68-68-72—277	40000		D Love III (US)	72-70-73-69—284	6733
5	J Mudd (US)	73-67-68-70—278	30000		JM Olazábal (Sp)	68-72-69-75—284	6733
6	F Couples (US)	68-71-68-72—279	26000	26	S Bennett (Eng)	75-69-68-73—285	5800
	D Feherty (N.Ire)	71-67-69-72—279	26000		L Wadkins (US)	72-70-69-74—285	5800
8	E Romero (Arg)	68-70-75-67—280	21000		C Beck (US)	75-69-68-73—285	5800
	P Azinger (US)	68-73-67-72—280	21000		S Simpson (US)	73-66-72-74—285	5800
	P Stewart (US)	72-65-69-74—280	21000	30	J Hawkes (SA)	75-67-69-75—286	4711
11	N Faldo (Eng)	71-71-70-69—281	17000		G Koch (US)	72-71-74-69—286	4711
	M McNulty (Zim)	75-70-70-66—281	17000		J Nicklaus (US)	74-71-71-70—286	4711
13	P Walton (Ire)	69-74-69-70—282	13000		P Jacobsen (US)	71-74-71-70—286	4711
	H Clark (Eng)	72-68-72-70—282	13000		B Marchbank (Sco)	69-74-73-70—286	4711
	S Pate (US)	69-70-70-73—282	13000		M Martin (Sp)	68-73-73-72—286	4711
	R Chapman (Eng)	76-68-67-71—282	13000		I Baker-Finch (Aus)	72-69-70-75—286	4711
	M James (Eng)	69-70-71-72—282	13000		M Ozaki (Jpn)	71-73-70-72—286	4711
	C Stadler (US)	73-69-69-71—282	13000		M Davis (Eng)	77-68-67-74—286	4711
19	L Mize (US)	71-74-66-72—283	8575				

Other Totals: M Harwood (Aus), T Armour III (US), J Woodland (Aus) 287; M O'Meara (US), L Trevino (US), R Floyd (US), J Rivero (Sp) 288; M McCumber (US), A Lyle (Sco), N Ozaki (Jpn) 289; J Miller (US), I Woosnam (Wal), C O'Connor Jr (Ire) 290; B Ogle (Aus), M Roe (Eng), T Ozaki (Jpn), M Allen (US), T Johnstone (Zim), E Dussart (Fra), R Boxall (Eng), G Sauers (US), B Crenshaw (US) 291; C Strange (US), D Graham (Aus), K Green (US), P Hoad (Eng), B Tway (US), R Rafferty (Ire), M Reid (US), W Stephens (Eng) 292; L Carbonetti (Arg), A Stephen (Eng), R Claydon (Am) (Eng) 293; C Gillies (Eng) 294; B Faxon (US), P Teravainen (US) 295; E Aubrey (US) 296; M Sludds (Ire) 297; S Ballesteros (Sp), R Karlsson (Am) (Swe) 299; G Levenson (SA) 301; B Langer (Ger) 309.

OPEN CHAMPIONSHIP HISTORY

The Belt

Year	Winner	Score	Venue	Entrants
1860	W Park, Musselburgh	174	Prestwick	8
1861	T Morris Sr, Prestwick	163	Prestwick	12
1862	T Morris Sr, Prestwick	163	Prestwick	6
1863	W Park, Musselburgh	168	Prestwick	14
1864	T Morris Sr, Prestwick	167	Prestwick	6
1865	A Strath, St Andrews	162	Prestwick	10
1866	W Park, Musselburgh	169	Prestwick	12
1867	T Morris Sr, St Andrews	170	Prestwick	10
1868	T Morris Jr, St Andrews	157	Prestwick	10
1869	T Morris Jr, St Andrews	154	Prestwick	8
1870	T Morris Jr, St Andrews	149	Prestwick	17

Having been won thrice in succession by young Tom Morris, the Belt became his property. The Championship was held in abeyance for one year. From 1872 the present cup was offered for annual competition.

The Claret Jug

Year	Winner	Score	Venue	Entrants
1872	T Morris Jr, St Andrews	166	Prestwick	8
1873	T Kidd, St Andrews	179	St Andrews	26
1874	M Park, Musselburgh	159	Musselburgh	32
1875	W Park, Musselburgh	166	Prestwick	18
1876	B Martin, St Andrews	176	St Andrews	34
(D Strath tied but refused to play off)				
1877	J Anderson, St Andrews	160	Musselburgh	24
1878	J Anderson, St Andrews	157	Prestwick	26
1879	J Anderson, St Andrews	169	St Andrews	46
1880	B Ferguson, Musselburgh	162	Musselburgh	30
1881	B Ferguson, Musselburgh	170	Prestwick	22
1882	B Ferguson, Musselburgh	171	St Andrews	40
1883	W Fernie, Dumfries	159	Musselburgh	41
(After a tie with B Ferguson, Musselburgh)				
1884	J Simpson, Carnoustie	160	Prestwick	30
1885	B Martin, St Andrews	171	St Andrews	51
1886	D Brown, Musselburgh	157	Musselburgh	46
1887	W Park Jr, Musselburgh	161	Prestwick	36
1888	J Burns, Warwick	171	St Andrews	53
1889	W Park Jr, Musselburgh	155	Musselburgh	42
(After a tie with A Kirkaldy)				
1890	J Ball, Royal Liverpool (Am)	164	Prestwick	40
1891	H Kirkaldy, St Andrews	166	St Andrews	82

After 1891 the competition was extended to 72 holes and for the first time entry money was imposed

1892	H Hilton, Royal Liverpool (Am)	305	Muirfield	66
1893	W Auchterlonie, St Andrews	322	Prestwick	72
1894	J Taylor, Winchester	326	Sandwich, R St George's	94
1895	J Taylor, Winchester	322	St Andrews	73
1896	H Vardon, Ganton	316	Muirfield	64
(Vardon won a 36 hole play-off after a tie with a score of 157 to Taylor's 161)				
1897	H Hilton, Royal Liverpool (Am)	314	Hoylake, R Liverpool	86
1898	H Vardon, Ganton	307	Prestwick	78
1899	H Vardon, Ganton	310	Sandwich, R St George's	98
1900	J Taylor, Mid-Surrey	309	St Andrews	81
1901	J Braid, Romford	309	Muirfield	101
1902	A Herd, Huddersfield	307	Hoylake, R Liverpool	112
1903	H Vardon, Totteridge	300	Prestwick	127
1904	J White, Sunningdale	296	Sandwich, R St George's	144
1905	J Braid, Walton Heath	318	St Andrews	152

continued

Open Championship Claret Jug winners history *continued*

Year	Winner	Score	Venue	Qual	Ents
1906	J Braid, Walton Heath	300	Muirfield	183	
1907	A Massy, La Boulie	312	Hoylake, R Liverpool	193	
1908	J Braid, Walton Heath	291	Prestwick	180	
1909	J Taylor, Mid-Surrey	295	Deal, R Cinque Ports	204	
1910	J Braid, Walton Heath	299	St Andrews	210	
1911	H Vardon, Totteridge	303	Sandwich, R St George's	226	

(After a tie with A Massy. The tie was over 36 holes, but Massy picked up at the 35th hole before holing out. He had taken 148 for 34 holes, and when Vardon holed out at the 35th hole his score was 143.)

Year	Winner	Score	Venue	Qual	Ents
1912	E Ray, Oxhey	295	Muirfield	215	
1913	J Taylor, Mid-Surrey	304	Hoylake, R Liverpool	269	
1914	H Vardon, Totteridge	306	Prestwick	194	
1915–19	*No Championship owing to the Great War*				
1920	G Duncan, Hanger Hill	303	Deal, R Cinque Ports	81	190
1921	J Hutchison, Glenview, Chicago	296	St Andrews	85	158

(After a tie with R Wethered (Am). Play-off scores: Hutchison 150; Wethered 159.)

Year	Winner	Score	Venue	Qual	Ents
1922	W Hagen, Detroit, USA	300	Sandwich, R St George's	80	225
1923	A Havers, Coombe Hill	295	Troon	88	222
1924	W Hagen, Detroit, USA	301	Hoylake, R Liverpool	86	277
1925	J Barnes, USA	300	Prestwick	83	200
1926	R Jones, USA (Am)	291	R Lytham and St Annes	117	293
1927	R Jones, USA (Am)	285	St Andrews	108	207
1928	W Hagen, USA	292	Sandwich, R St George's	113	271
1929	W Hagen, USA	292	Muirfield	109	242
1930	R Jones, USA (Am)	291	Hoylake, R Liverpool	112	296
1931	T Armour, USA	296	Carnoustie	109	215
1932	G Sarazen, USA	283	Sandwich, Prince's	110	224
1933	D Shute, USA	292	St Andrews	117	287

(After a tie with C Wood, USA. Play-off scores: Shute 149; Wood 154.)

Year	Winner	Score	Venue	Qual	Ents
1934	T Cotton, Waterloo, Belgium	283	Sandwich, R St George's	101	312
1935	A Perry, Leatherhead	283	Muirfield	109	264
1936	A Padgham, Sundridge Park	287	Hoylake, R Liverpool	107	286
1937	T Cotton, Ashridge	290	Carnoustie	141	258
1938	R Whitcombe, Parkstone	295	Sandwich, R St George's	120	268
1939	R Burton, Sale	290	St Andrews	129	254
1940–45	*No Championship owing to Second World War*				
1946	S Snead, USA	290	St Andrews	100	225
1947	F Daly, Balmoral	293	Hoylake, R Liverpool	100	263
1948	T Cotton, Royal Mid-Surrey	284	Muirfield	97	272
1949	A Locke, South Africa	283	Sandwich, R St George's	96	224

(After a tie with H Bradshaw, Kilcroney. Play-off scores: Locke 135; Bradshaw 147.)

Year	Winner	Score	Venue	Qual	Ents
1950	A Locke, South Africa	279	Troon	93	262
1951	M Faulkner, England	285	R Portrush	98	180
1952	A Locke, South Africa	287	R Lytham and St Annes	96	275
1953	B Hogan, USA	282	Carnoustie	91	196
1954	P Thomson, Australia	283	Birkdale	97	349
1955	P Thomson, Australia	281	St Andrews	94	301
1956	P Thomson, Australia	286	Hoylake, R Liverpool	96	360
1957	A Locke, South Africa	279	St Andrews	96	282
1958	P Thomson, Australia	278	R Lytham and St Annes	96	362

(After a tie with D Thomas, Sudbury. Play-off scores: Thomson 139; Thomas 143.)

Year	Winner	Score	Venue	Qual	Ents
1959	G Player, South Africa	284	Muirfield	90	285
1960	K Nagle, Australia	278	St Andrews	74	410
1961	A Palmer, USA	284	Birkdale	101	364
1962	A Palmer, USA	276	Troon	119	379
1963	R Charles, New Zealand	277	R Lytham and St Annes	119	261

(After a tie with P Rodgers, USA. Play-off scores: Charles 140; Rodgers 148)

Year	Winner	Score	Venue	Qual	Ents
1964	T Lema, USA	279	St Andrews	119	327
1965	P Thomson, Australia	285	R Birkdale	130	372
1966	J Nicklaus, USA	282	Muirfield	130	310
1967	R De Vicenzo, Argentina	278	Hoylake, R Liverpool	130	326
1968	G Player, South Africa	289	Carnoustie	130	309
1969	A Jacklin, England	280	R Lytham and St Annes	129	424
1970	J Nicklaus, USA	283	St Andrews	134	468

(After a tie with Doug Sanders, USA. Play-off scores: Nicklaus 72; Sanders 73.)

Year	Winner	Score	Venue	Qual	Ents
1971	L Trevino, USA	278	R Birkdale	150	528
1972	L Trevino, USA	278	Muirfield	150	570
1973	T Weiskopf, USA	276	Troon	150	569
1974	G Player, South Africa	282	R Lytham and St Annes	150	679

Year	Winner	Score	Venue	Qual	Ents
1975	T Watson, USA	279	Carnoustie	150	629
(After a tie with J Newton, Australia. Play-off scores: Watson 71; Newton 72.)					
1976	J Miller, USA	279	R Birkdale	150	719
1977	T Watson, USA	268	Turnberry	150	730
1978	J Nicklaus, USA	281	St Andrews	150	788
1979	S Ballesteros, Spain	283	R Lytham and St Annes	150	885
1980	T Watson, USA	271	Muirfield	151	994
1981	B Rogers, USA	276	Sandwich, R St George's	153	971
1982	T Watson, USA	284	R Troon	176	1,121
1983	T Watson, USA	275	R Birkdale	151	1,107
1984	S Ballesteros, Spain	276	St Andrews		1,413
1985	A Lyle, Scotland	282	Sandwich, R St George's	149	1,361
1986	G Norman, Australia	280	Turnberry	152	1,347
1987	N Faldo, England	279	Muirfield	153	1,407
1988	S Ballesteros, Spain	273	R Lytham and St Annes	153	1,393
1989	M Calcavecchia, USA	275	R Troon	156	1,481
(Calcavecchia won a four-hole play-off after a tie with W Grady, Australia, and G Norman, Australia.)					
1990	N Faldo, England	270	St Andrews	152	1,707
1991	I Baker-Finch, Australia	272	R Birkdale	156	1,496
1992	N Faldo, England	272	Muirfield	156	1,666
1993	G Norman, Australia	267	Sandwich, R St George's	156	1,827
1994	N Price, Zimbabwe	268	Turnberry	156	1,701
1995	J Daly, USA	282	St Andrews	159	1,836
(Daly won a four-hole play-off after a tie with C Rocca, Italy)					
1996	T Lehman, USA	271	R Lytham and St Annes	156	1,918
1997	J Leonard, USA	272	R Troon	156	2,133
1998	M O'Meara, USA	280	R Birkdale	152	2,336

(O'Meara won a four-hole play-off after a tie with B Watts, USA)

The US Open Championship

98th US Open at *The Olympic Club, San Francisco* (6797 yds, Par 70)

Prize money: $3,000,000. Entries: 7,117. Final field: 154, of whom 60, including one amateur, made the half-way cut on 147 or better.

Pos	Name	Score	Prize Money $
1	Lee Janzen	73-66-73-68—280	535000
2	Payne Stewart	66-71-70-74—281	315000
3	Bob Tway	68-70-73-73—284	201730
4	Nick Price (Zim)	73-68-71-73—285	140597
5	Steve Stricker	73-71-69-73—286	107392
	Tom Lehman	68-75-68-75—286	107392
7	David Duval	75-68-75-69—287	83794
	Lee Westwood (Eng)	72-74-70-71—287	83794
	Jeff Maggert	69-69-75-74—287	83794
10	Jeff Sluman	72-74-74-68—288	64490
	Phil Mickelson	71-73-74-70—288	64490
	Stuart Appleby (Aus)	73-74-70-71—288	64490
	Stewart Cink	73-68-73-74—288	64490
14	Paul Azinger	75-72-77-65—289	52214
	Jesper Parnevik (Swe)	69-74-76-70—289	52214
	Matt Kuchar (Am)	70-69-76-74—289	
	Jim Furyk	74-73-68-74—289	52214
18	Colin Montgomerie (Sco)	70-74-77-69—290	41833
	Loren Roberts	71-76-71-72—290	41833
	Frank Lickliter II	73-71-72-74—290	41833
	José Maria Olazábal (Sp)	68-77-71-74—290	41833
	Tiger Woods	74-72-71-73—290	41833
23	Casey Martin	74-71-74-72—291	34043
	Glen Day	73-72-71-75—291	34043
25	DA Weibring	72-72-75-73—292	25640
	Per-Ulrik Johansson (Swe)	71-75-73-73—292	25640
	Eduardo Romero (Arg)	72-70-76-74—292	25640
	Chris Perry	74-71-72-75—292	25640
	Vijay Singh (Fij)	73-72-73-74—292	25640
	Thomas Björn (Den)	72-75-70-75—292	25640
	Mark Carnevale	67-73-74-78—292	25640
32	Mark O'Meara	70-76-78-69—293	18372
	Padraig Harrington (Ire)	73-72-76-72—293	18372
	Bruce Zabriski	74-71-74-74—293	18372
	Steve Pate	72-75-73-73—293	18372
	John Huston	73-72-72-76—293	18372
	Joe Durant	68-73-76-76—293	18372
	Chris DiMarco	71-71-74-77—293	18372
	Lee Porter	72-67-76-78—293	18372
40	Justin Leonard	71-75-77-71—294	15155
	Scott McCarron	72-73-77-72—294	15155
	Frank Nobilo (NZ)	76-67-76-75—294	15155

Players are of American nationality unless stated

Pos	Name	Score	Prize Money $
43	Darren Clarke (N.Ire)	74-72-77-72—295	12537
	Joey Sindelar	71-75-75-74—295	12537
	Tom Kite	70-75-76-74—295	12537
	Joe Acosta Jr	73-72-76-74—295	12537
	Olin Browne	73-70-77-75—295	12537
	Jack Nicklaus	73-74-73-75—295	12537
49	Ernie Els (SA)	75-70-75-76—296	9711
	Mike Reid	76-70-73-77—296	9711
	Brad Faxon	73-68-76-79—296	9711
	Scott Verplank	74-72-73-77—296	9711
53	Fred Couples	72-75-79-71—297	8531
	Tim Herron	75-72-77-73—297	8531
	James Johnston	74-73-79-71—297	8531
	John Daly	69-75-75-78—297	8531
57	Mark Brooks	75-71-76-76—298	8030
58	Scott Simpson	72-71-78-79—300	7844
59	Rocky Walcher	77-70-77-79—303	7696
60	Tom Sipula	75-71-78-81—305	7549

The following players missed the cut

61	Billy Andrade	74-74—148	105T	Tim Straub	74-78—152
	John Cook	75-73—148		Tom Sutter	79-73—152
	Brad Fabel	75-73—148		Vaughn Taylor	76-76—152
	Gene Fieger	76-72—148		Kirk Triplett	73-79—152
	Brent Geiberger	71-77—148	112	Mike Brisky	74-79—153
	Derek Gilchrist	74-74—148		Brandel Chamblee	76-77—153
	Retief Goosen (SA)	74-74—148		Jason Gore	77-76—153
	Jay Haas	76-72—148		Pete Jordan	81-72—153
	Hale Irwin	80-68—148		Bernhard Langer (Ger)	75-78—153
	Patrick Lee	72-76—148		Davis Love III	78-75—153
	Andrew Magee	70-78—148		Mike Small	76-77—153
	Corey Pavin	76-72—148		Kevin Sutherland	77-76—153
	Paul Simson (Am)	76-72—148		Garrett Willis	83-70—153
	Grant Waite	77-71—148	121	Jason Allen	76-78—154
	Tom Watson	73-75—148		Shane Bertsch	77-77—154
76	Michael Baird	75-74—149		Jim Estes	77-77—154
	David Eger (Am)	78-71—149		Ignacio Garrido (Sp)	76-78—154
	Nick Faldo (Eng)	77-72—149		Robert Karlsson	78-76—154
	Edward Fryatt	73-76—149		Martin Lonardi	76-78—154
	Gary Hallberg	77-72—149		Perry Moss	76-78—154
	Scott Hoch	74-75—149		Perry Parker	75-79—154
	Steve Jones	72-77—149		Costantino Rocca (It)	71-83—154
	Chris Kaufman	77-72—149	130	Chip Beck	78-77—155
	Doug Martin	74-75—149		Rick Gehr	73-82—155
	Jumbo Ozaki (Jpn)	78-71—149		Ted Oh	74-81—155
	Paul Stankowski	76-73—149		Ryan Palmer	82-83—155
	Omar Uresti	78-71—149		Curtis Strange	77-78—155
	Kevin Wentworth	76-73—149		Wes Weston	79-76—155
89	Mark Calcavecchia	74-76—150	136	Guy Boros	77-79—156
	Christian Chernock	73-77—150		Chris Tidland	76-80—156
	Trevor Dodds (Nam)	74-76—150		Rick Todd	80-76—156
	Steve Elkington (Aus)	77-73—150	139	Michael Burke Jr	81-76—157
	Jimmy Green	76-74—150		Gary March	76-81—157
	David Kirkpatrick	78-72—150	141	Joel Kribel	83-75—158
	David Ogrin	70-80—150		Jeff Thorsen	77-81—158
	Sam Randolph	80-70—150		Brett Wetterich	78-80—158
	Clarence Rose	75-75—150	144	Garrett Larson	80-79—159
	Phil Tataurangi	77-73—150		Ken Peyre-Ferry	80-79—159
	Mark Wilson	74-76—150	146	Ben Crenshaw	82-78—160
	Willie Wood	74-76—150		Howard Twitty	79-81—160
101	Grant Clough	78-73—151	148	Jimmy Johnston	84-78—162
	Don Pooley	74-77—151		Alan Morin	80-82—162
	Ian Woosnam (Wal)	72-79—151		Rene Rangel	82-80—162
	Fuzzy Zoeller	75-76—151	151	Jeff McMillian	82-81—163
105	Robert Deruntz	75-77—152	152	Tom Anderson	84-80—164
	Graham Marsh	75-77—152	153	Adrian Stills	85-81—166
	Dick Mast	76-76—152	154	Richard Ames	86-81—167

Players are of American nationality unless stated

1997 US Open at Congressional CC, Bethesda, Maryland (7213 yds, Par 70)

Prize money: $2,600,000. Entries: 7,013

Pos	Name	Score	Prize $	Pos	Name	Score	Prize $
1	E Els (SA)	71-67-69-69—276	465000	19T	P Stankowski	75-70-68-73—286	31915
2	C Montgomerie (Sco)	65-76-67-69—277	275000		H Sutton	66-73-73-74—286	31915
3	T Lehman	67-70-68-73—278	172828	24	L Mattiace	71-75-73-68—287	24173
4	J Maggert	73-66-68-74—281	120454		E Fryatt	72-73-73-69—287	24173
5	B Tway	71-71-70-70—282	79875		S Dunlap	75-66-75-71—287	24173
	O Browne	71-71-69-71—282	79875		S Elkington (Aus)	75-68-72-72—287	24173
	J Furyk	74-68-69-71—282	79875	28	P Goydos	73-72-74-69—288	17443
	J Haas	73-69-68-72—282	79875		P Azinger	72-72-74-70—288	17443
	T Tolles	74-67-69-72—282	79875		P Stewart	71-73-73-71—288	17443
10	S McCarron	73-71-69-70—283	56949		M McNulty (Zim)	67-73-75-73—288	17443
	S Hoch	71-68-72-72—283	56949		H Kase	68-73-73-74—288	17443
	D Ogrin	70-69-71-73—283	56949		F Zoeller	72-73-69-74—288	17443
13	L Roberts	72-69-72-71—284	47348		K Gibson	72-69-72-75—288	17443
	S Cink	71-67-74-72—284	47348		J Sluman	69-72-72-75—288	17443
	B Andrade	75-67-69-73—284	47348	36	J Leonard	69-72-78-70—289	13483
16	B Hughes (Aus)	75-71-69-70—285	40086		G Waite	72-74-72-71—289	13483
	JM Olazábal (Sp)	71-71-72-71—285	40086		S Stricker	66-76-75-72—289	13483
	D Love III	75-70-69-71—285	40086		M O'Meara	73-73-71-72—289	13483
19	N Price (Zim)	71-74-71-70—286	31915		S Appleby (Aus)	71-75-70-73—289	13483
	L Westwood (Eng)	71-71-73-71—286	31915		F Nobilo (NZ)	71-74-70-74—289	13483
	T Woods	74-67-73-72—286	31915		J Cook	72-71-71-75—289	13483

Other players who made the cut: D Clarke (N.Ire), P Mickelson, F Funk, C Perry, C Parry (Aus) 290; J Parnevik (Swe), D Duval, N Faldo (Eng) 291; D White 292; L Janzen, J Nicklaus, H Irwin, F Couples, P Teravainen, P Broadhurst (Eng) 293; L Mize, C Rose 294; C Smith, D Waldorf, R Butcher, S Jones 295; T Watson 296; D Schreyer, B Crenshaw, B Faxon 297; T Kite, M Hulbert, G Kraft, J Morse, S Ames (T&T), T Björn (Den) 298; J Green 299; R Wylie, A Coltart (Sco) 300; D Mast, G Towne, V Singh (Fij), P Parker, D Hammond 301; J Ferenz 303; M Dawson 304; S Adams 306.

1996 US Open at Oakland Hills, Birmingham, Michigan (6990 yds, Par 70)

Prize money: $2,400,000. Entries: 5,925

Pos	Name	Score	Prize $	Pos	Name	Score	Prize $
1	S Jones	74-66-69-69—278	425000	16T	S Cink	69-73-70-73—285	33188
2	D Love III	71-69-70-69—279	204801		S Torrance (Sco)	71-69-71-74—285	33188
	T Lehman	71-72-65-71—279	204801	23	B Bryant	73-71-74-68—286	23806
4	J Morse	68-74-68-70—280	111235		P Jacobsen	71-74-70-71—286	23806
5	E Els (SA)	72-67-72-70—281	84964		B Andrade	72-69-72-73—286	23806
	J Furyk	72-69-70-70—281	84964		W Austin	67-72-72-75—286	23806
7	S Hoch	73-71-71-67—282	66294	27	C Strange	74-73-71-69—287	17809
	V Singh (Fij)	71-72-70-69—282	66294		P Jordan	71-74-72-70—287	17809
	K Green	73-67-72-70—282	66294		J Nicklaus	72-74-69-72—287	17809
10	L Janzen	68-75-71-69—283	52591		P Stewart	67-71-76-73—287	17809
	G Norman (Aus)	73-66-74-70—283	52591		J Daly	72-69-73-73—287	17809
	C Montgomerie (Sco)	70-72-69-72—283	52591	32	M Swartz	72-72-74-70—288	14070
13	D Forsman	72-71-70-71—284	43725		T Purtzer	76-71-71-70—288	14070
	T Watson	70-71-71-72—284	43725		B Mayfair	72-71-74-71—288	14070
	F Nobilo (NZ)	69-71-70-74—284	43725		B Ogle (Aus)	70-75-72-71—288	14070
16	N Faldo (Eng)	72-71-72-70—285	33188		S Gotsche	72-70-74-72—288	14070
	D Begganio	69-72-72-72—285	33188		M Campbell (NZ)	70-73-73-72—288	14070
	M Brooks	76-68-69-72—285	33188		A Forsbrand (Swe)	74-71-71-72—288	14070
	M O'Meara	72-73-68-72—285	33188		S Murphy	71-75-68-74—288	14070
	J Cook	70-71-71-73—285	33188				

Other players who made the cut: L Parsons, JL Lucas, B Ford, S Simpson, W Riley (Aus), S Elkington (Aus), T Tolles, C Pavin, K Triplett, L Roberts 289; W Westner (SA), B Gilder, K Perry, J Sluman, J Gullion, H Irwin, A Cejka (Ger), M Bradley, K Gibson, J Leonard 290; S Stricker, S Lowery, B Porter, W Murchison, R Leen (Am), D Gilford (Eng), D Harrington 291; D Duval, A Morse, P Azinger, F Linkliter II, M Ozaki (Jpn), C Rocca (It), W Grady (Aus), D Ogrin, P O'Malley (Aus), C Byrum, J Gallagher Jr, B Tway 292; T Kuehne (Am), M Christie, I Woosnam (Wal) 293; T Woods (Am), J Huston, K Jones, S Kendall, S McCarron, T Kite, B Faxon, N Lancaster 294; C Parry (Aus), J Sanchez, J O'Keefe, J Haas 295; A Rodriguez, T Pernice Jr, P Mickelson 296; J Maggert, J Thorpe, B McCallister (Aus), P Walton (Ire) 297; O Uresti, O Browne 298; G Trevisonno 299; M Wiebe 300; S Scott (Am), R Yokota (Jpn) 301; M Burke Jr 302; S Kelly 309.

Players are of American nationality unless stated

1995 US Open at Shinnecock Hills, New York (6944 yd, Par 70)

Prize money: $2,000,000. Entries: 6,001

Pos	Name	Score	Prize $	Pos	Name	Score	Prize $
1	C Pavin	72-69-71-68—280	350000	21T	B Ogle (Aus)	71-75-72-69—287	20085
2	G Norman (Aus)	68-67-74-73—282	207000		P Jordan	74-71-71-71—287	20085
3	T Lehman	70-72-67-74—283	131974		B Andrade	72-69-74-72—287	20085
4	N Lancaster	70-72-77-65—284	66633		S Verplank	72-69-71-75—287	20085
	J Maggert	69-72-77-66—284	66633		I Woosnam (Wal)	72-71-69-75—287	20085
	B Glasson	69-70-76-69—284	66633	28	C Montgomerie (Sco)	71-74-75-68—288	13912
	J Haas	70-73-72-69—284	66633		MA Jimenez (Sp)	72-72-75-69—288	13912
	D Love III	72-68-73-71—284	66633		M Hulbert	74-72-72-70—288	13912
	P Mickelson	68-70-72-74—284	66633		M Ozaki (Jpn)	69-68-80-71—288	13912
10	F Nobilo (NZ)	72-72-70-71—285	44184		S Simpson	67-75-74-72—288	13912
	V Singh (Fij)	70-71-72-72—285	44184		D Duval	70-73-73-72—288	13912
	B Tway	69-69-72-75—285	44184		JM Olazábal (Sp)	73-70-72-73—288	13912
13	M McCumber	70-71-77-68—286	30934		G Hallberg	70-76-69-73—288	13912
	D Waldorf	72-70-75-69—286	30934	36	B Porter	73-70-79-67—289	9812
	Brad Bryant	71-75-70-70—286	30934		R Floyd	74-72-76-67—289	9812
	J Sluman	72-69-74-71—286	30934		H Sutton	71-74-76-68—289	9812
	M Roe (Eng)	71-69-74-72—286	30934		C Strange	70-72-76-71—289	9812
	L Janzen	70-72-72-72—286	30934		G Boros	73-71-74-71—289	9812
	N Price (Zim)	66-73-73-74—286	30934		S Elkington (Aus)	72-73-73-71—289	9812
	S Stricker	71-70-71-74—286	30934		C Byrum	70-70-76-73—289	9812
21	F Zoeller	69-74-76-68—287	20085		B Langer (Ger)	74-67-74-74—289	9812
	P Stewart	74-71-73-69—287	20085				

Other players who made the cut: B Lane (Eng) 290; J McGovern, C Pena, O Uresti, J Daly, N Faldo (Eng), B Hughes 291; B Burns, E Romero (Arg), T Tryba, P Jacobsen, M Gogel 292; B Faxon, T Watson, C Perry, S Lowery, S Hoch, G Bruckner 293; J Gallagher, J Cook, B Jobe, D Edwards, P Goydos 294; T Kite, M Brisky, T Armour III 295; J Connelly 296; B Crenshaw, J Maginnes 297; J Gullion 301.

1994 US Open at Oakmont, Pennsylvania (6946 yds, Par 71)

Prize money: $1,700,000. Entries: 6,010

Pos	Name	Score	Prize $	Pos	Name	Score	Prize $
1	E Els (SA)*	69-71-66-73—279	320000	18T	S Ballesteros (Sp)	72-72-70-73—287	22477
2	L Roberts	76-69-64-70—279	141828		H Irwin	69-69-71-78—287	22477
	C Montgomerie (Sco)	71-65-73-70—279	141828	21	S Torrance (Sco)	72-71-76-69—288	19464
Els won at second sudden-death play-off hole against Roberts after both shot 74 in 18-hole play-off. Montgomerie shot 78.					S Pate	74-66-71-77—288	19464
				23	B Langer (Ger)	72-72-73-72—289	17223
4	C Strange	70-70-70-72—282	75728		K Triplett	70-71-71-77—289	17223
5	J Cook	73-65-73-71—282	61318	25	M Springer	74-72-73-71—290	14705
6	C Dennis	71-71-70-71—283	49485		C Parry (Aus)	78-68-71-73—290	14705
	G Norman (Aus)	71-71-69-72—283	49485		C Beck	73-73-70-74—290	14705
	T Watson	68-73-68-74—283	49485	28	D Love III	74-72-74-72—292	11514
9	D Waldorf	74-68-73-69—284	37179		J Furyk	74-69-74-75—292	11514
	J Maggert	71-68-76-69—284	37179		L Clements	73-71-73-75—292	11514
	J Sluman	72-69-72-71—284	37179		J Nicklaus	69-70-77-76—292	11514
	F Nobilo (NZ)	69-71-68-76—284	37179		M Ozaki (Jpn)	70-73-69-80—292	11514
13	J McGovern	73-69-74-69—285	29767	33	M Carnevale	75-72-76-70—293	9578
	S Hoch	72-72-70-71—285	29767		T Lehman	77-68-73-75—293	9578
	D Edwards	73-65-75-72—285	29767		F Allen	73-70-74-76—293	9578
16	F Couples	72-76-69-74—286	25899		T Kite	73-71-72-77—293	9578
	S Lowery	71-71-68-76—286	25899		B Crenshaw	71-74-70-78—293	9578
18	S Verplank	70-72-75-70—287	22477		B Faxon	73-69-71-80—293	9578

Other players who made the cut: B Hughes, P Baker (Eng), G Brand Jr (Sco), B Jobe 294; F Quinn Jr 295; P Goydos, F Funk, D Walsworth 296; T Dunlavey, O Browne, B Lane (Eng), M Emery, D Bergano, J Gallagher Jr, W Levi, P Mickelson 297; T Armour III, H Royer III, S Simpson 298; S Richardson (Eng), F Zoeller 299; D Rummells, D Martin 301; E Humenik, M Smith, M Aubrey 302.

Players are of American nationality unless stated

1993 US Open at Baltusrol, Springfield, NJ (7155 yds, Par 70)
Prize money: $1,600,000. Entries: 5,905

Pos	Name	Score	Prize $	Pos	Name	Score	Prize $
1	L Janzen	67-67-69-69—272	290000	16T	F Couples	68-71-71-71—281	21576
2	P Stewart	70-66-68-70—274	145000		M Standly	70-69-70-72—281	21576
3	C Parry (Aus)	66-74-69-68—277	78556	19	B McCallister	68-73-73-68—282	18071
	P Azinger	71-68-69-69—277	78556		D Forsman	73-71-70-68—282	18071
5	S Hoch	66-72-72-68—278	48730		C Pavin	68-69-75-70—282	18071
	T Watson	70-66-73-69—278	48730		T Lehman	71-70-71-70—282	18071
7	E Els (SA)	71-73-68-67—279	35481		S Pate	70-71-71-70—282	18071
	R Floyd	68-73-70-68—279	35481		I Baker-Finch (Aus)	70-70-70-72—282	18071
	N Henke	72-71-67-69—279	35481	25	C Strange	73-68-75-67—283	14531
	F Funk	70-72-67-70—279	35481		J Ozaki (Jap)	70-70-74-69—283	14531
11	L Roberts	70-70-71-69—280	26249		R Mediate	68-72-73-70—283	14531
	J Sluman	71-71-69-69—280	26249		C Beck	72-68-72-71—283	14531
	J Adams	70-70-69-71—280	26249		K Perry	74-70-68-71—283	14531
	D Edwards	70-72-66-72—280	26249		M Calcavecchia	70-70-71-72—283	14531
	N Price (Zim)	71-66-70-73—280	26249		J Cook	75-66-70-72—283	14531
16	B Lane (Eng)	74-68-70-69—281	21576		W Levi	71-69-69-74—283	14531

Other players who made the cut: S Lowery, C Montgomerie (Sco), B Gilder, J Ozaki (Jpn), G Twiggs, B Andrade, L Rinker, J Daly, C Stadler, R Allenby (Aus), D Love III, S Elkington (Aus), M Donald 284; S Simpson, M Brooks, M McCumber, B Claar, R Fehr, L Nelson 285; K Triplett, I Woosnam (Wal), F Allem (SA), V Heafner, E Kirby, M Christie, K Clearwater, A Lyle (Sco), B Estes, J Maggert 286; M Hulbert, H Irwin, M Smith, A Knoll, J Edwards, JD Blake, 287; F Zoeller, S Gotsche, J Leonard (Am), B Faxon 288; J Nicklaus, N Faldo (Eng), G Waite, P Jordan, D Waldorf, 289; M Wiebe, T Johnstone (Zim), J Haas, B Thompson, 290; W Grady (Aus), T Schulz 291; S Stricker 292; S Flesch 294; D Weaver, J Flannery 295; R Wrenn 297; R Gamez 298.

1992 US Open at Pebble Beach, Monterey, California (6809 yds, Par 72)
Prize money: $1,500,000. Entries: 6,244

Pos	Name	Score	Prize $	Pos	Name	Score	Prize $
1	T Kite	71-72-70-72—285	275000	17	T Tyner	74-72-78-70—294	18069
2	J Sluman	73-74-69-71—287	137500		W Grady (Aus)	74-66-81-73—294	18069
3	C Montgomerie (Sco)	70-71-77-70—288	84245		F Couples	72-70-78-74—294	18069
4	N Faldo (Eng)	70-76-68-77—291	54924		W Wood	70-75-75-74—294	18069
	N Price (Zim)	71-72-77-71—291	54924		A Magee	77-69-72-76—294	18069
6	I Woosnam (Wal)	72-72-69-79—292	32315		A Dillard	68-70-79-77—294	18069
	JD Blake	70-74-75-73—292	32315	23	B Bryant	71-76-75-73—295	13906
	B Gilder	73-70-75-74—292	32315		B Mayfair	74-73-75-73—295	13906
	B Andrade	72-74-72-74—292	32315		C Strange	67-78-76-74—295	13906
	M Hulbert	74-73-70-75—292	32315		J Haas	70-77-74-74—295	13906
	T Lehman	69-72-74-77—292	32315		J Kane	73-71-76-75—295	13906
	J Sindelar	74-72-68-78—292	32315		B Langer (Ger)	73-72-75-75—295	13906
13	M McCumber	70-76-73-74—293	22531		D Hammond	73-73-73-76—295	13906
	J Cook	72-72-74-75—293	22531		J Ozaki (Jpn)	77-70-72-76—295	13906
	I Baker-Finch(Aus)	74-71-72-76—293	22531		D Hart	76-71-71-77—295	13906
	G Morgan	66-69-77-81—293	22531		S Ballesteros (Sp)	71-76-69-79—295	13906

Other players who made the cut: F Funk, J Delsing, C Parry (Aus), R Cochran, A Forsbrand, T Purtzer, M Calcavecchia, R Zokol (Can), P Azinger, C Stadler, M McNulty (Zim) 296; D Pooley, D Pruitt, B Estes, R Floyd, R Mediate, G Hallberg, M Brooks 297; S Gump, A Lyle (Sco), H Irwin, B Wolcott, T Schulz, P Stewart 298; D Donovan, D Waldorf, J Gallagher Jr 299; D Love III, D Forsman 300; M Smith 301; P Jacobsen 302; G Twiggs, S Simpson 303; K Triplett 305.

Players are of American nationality unless stated

1991 US Open at Hazeltine National, Chaska, Minnesota (7149 yds Par 72)
Prize money: $1,300,000. Entries: 6,063

Pos	Name	Score	Prize $	Pos	Name	Score	Prize $
1	P Stewart*	67-70-73-72—282	235000	19	BR Brown	73-71-77-71—292	14166
2	S Simpson	70-68-72-72—282	117500		P Persons	70-75-75-72—292	14166
*Stewart won 18 hole play-off					M Brooks	73-73-73-73—292	14166
3	L Nelson	73-72-72-68—285	62754		T Sieckmann	74-70-74-74—292	14166
	F Couples	70-70-75-70—285	62574		J Cook	76-70-72-74—292	14166
5	F Zoeller	72-73-74-67—286	41542		C Stadler	71-69-77-75—292	14166
6	S Hoch	69-71-74-73—287	36090		N Price (Zim)	74-69-71-78—292	14166
7	N Henke	67-71-77-73—288	32176	26	T Simpson	73-72-76-72—293	11711
8	R Floyd	73-72-76-68—289	26958		M Reid	74-72-74-73—293	11711
	JM Olazábal (Sp)	73-71-75-70—289	26958		B Tway	75-69-75-74—293	11711
	C Pavin	71-67-79-72—289	26958		J Mudd	71-70-77-75—293	11711
11	DA Weibring	76-71-75-68—290	20909		R Fehr	74-69-73-77—293	11711
	D Love III	70-76-73-71—290	20909	31	D Rummells	72-73-77-72—294	10133
	J Gallagher Jr	70-72-75-73—290	20909		E Humenik	72-70-78-74—294	10133
	C Parry (Aus)	70-73-73-74—290	20909		C Perry	72-73-75-74—294	10133
	H Irwin	71-75-70-74—290	20909		P Jacobsen	72-73-74-75—294	10133
16	T Watson	73-71-77-70—291	17186		L Ten Broeck	72-73-74-75—294	10133
	N Faldo (Eng)	72-74-73-72—291	17186		B Kamm	69-73-73-79—294—10133
	A Lyle (Sco)	72-70-74-75—291—17186					

Other players who made the cut: T Purtzer, M Calcavecchia, B Mayfair, K Clearwater, T Kite, B Gardner, A North 295; I Baker-Finch (Aus), J Hallet 296; R Davis, J Nicklaus, B McCallister 297; S Pate, M Harwood, W Levi, L Roberts 298; L Rinker, J Inman 299; P Mickelson (Am) 300; L Mize, S Gotsche, S Elkington (Aus), I Woosnam (Wal) 300; D Graham 302; S Utley 303; J Adams 304; T Snodgrass, L Wadkins, W Grady (Aus) 305.

1990 US Open at Medinah, Chicago Illinois (7195 yds, Par 72)
Prize money: $1,200,000. Entries: 6,198

Pos	Name	Score	Prize	Pos	Name	Score	Prize $
1	H Irwin*	69-70-74-67—280	180000	14T	S Simpson	66-73-73-73—285	15712
2	M Donald	67-70-72-71—280	108000		L Mize	72-70-69-74—285	15712
*Irwin won at first extra hole after tied 18-hole play-off					J Sluman	66-70-74-75—285	15712
3	N Faldo (Eng)	72-72-68-69—281	56878		L Nelson	74-67-69-75—285	15712
	BR Brown	69-71-69-72—281	56878	21	S Elkington (Aus)	73-71-73-69—286	12843
5	G Norman (Aus)	72-73-69-69—283	33271		I Woosnam (Wal)	70-70-74-72—286	12843
	T Simpson	66-69-75-73—283	33271		C Strange	73-70-68-75—286	12843
	M Brooks	68-70-72-73—283	33271	24	M Ozaki (Jpn)	73-72-74-68—287	11308
8	S Jones	67-76-74-67—284	22236		W Heintzelman	70-75-74-68—287	11308
	C Stadler	71-72-70-71—284	22236		C Pavin	74-70-73-70—287	11308
	S Hoch	70-73-69-72—284	22236		B Tuten	74-70-72-71—287	11308
	T Sieckmann	74-70-68-72—284	22236		P Azinger	72-72-69-74—287	11308
	JM Olazábal (Sp)	73-69-70-72—284	22236	29	P Mickelson (Am)	74-71-71-72—288	
	F Zoeller	73-70-68-73—284	22236		C Beck	71-71-73-73—288	10022
14	J Benepe	72-70-73-70—285	15712		M Hulberts	76-66-71-75—288	10022
	J Huston	68-72-73-72—285	15712		B Claar	70-71-71-76—288	10022
	J Inman	72-71-70-72—285	15712				

Other players who made the cut: T Byrum, K Triplett, B Lohr, I Aoki (Jpn), D Frost (SA), B Tway, S Pate, B Wadkins, S Ballesteros (Sp), J Nicklaus, J Gallagher Jr, T Schulz, M Reid 289; C Parry (Aus) 290; D Barr, M McCumber, R Thompson, D Rummells 291; R Stewart, B Glasson, A North, G Twiggs, L Wadkins 292; T Kite, B McCallister (Aus), D Duval (Am) 293; B Gilder, G Morgan 293; S Verplank, R Garnez 294; R Rafferty (N.Ire) 296; D Graham 298; H Twitty 299; B Faxon 301; ME Smith 308; R Wylie 308.

Players are of American nationality unless stated

1989 US Open at Oak Hill CC, Rochester, NY (6902 yds, Par 70)

Prize money: $1,490,089. Entries: 5,786

Pos	Name	Score	Prize $	Pos	Name	Score	Prize $
1	C Strange	71-64-73-70—278	200000	13T	P Stewart	66-75-72-71—284	15634
2	C Beck	71-69-71-68—279	67823	18	JD Blake	66-71-72-76—285	13013
	M McCumber	70-68-72-69—279	67823		N Faldo (Eng)	68-72-73-72—285	13013
	I Woosnam (Wal)	70-68-73-68—279	67823		D Frost (SA)	73-72-70-70—285	13013
5	B Claar	71-72-68-69—280	34345	21	F Couples	74-71-67-74—286	11306
6	J Ozaki (Jpn)	70-71-68-72—281	28220		S Elkington (Aus)	70-70-78-68—286	11306
	S Simpson	67-70-69-75—281	28220		B Glasson	73-70-70-73—286	11306
8	P Jacobsen	71-70-71-70—282	24307		N Henke	75-69-72-70—286	11306
9	P Azinger	71-72-70-70—283	19968		DA Weibring	70-74-73-69—286	11306
	H Green	69-72-74-68—283	19968	26	R Floyd	68-74-74-71—287	9983
	T Kite	67-69-69-78—283	19968		D Pooley	74-69-71-73—287	9983
	JM Olazábal (Sp)	69-72-70-72—283	19968		R Wrenn	74-71-73-69—287	9983
13	S Hoch	70-72-70-72—284	15634	29	E Aubrey	69-73-73-73—288	9006
	M Lye	71-69-72-72—284	15634		D Pohl	71-71-73-73—288	9006
	L Nelson	68-73-68-75—284	15634		H Sutton	69-75-72-72—288	9006
	T Pernice Jr	67-75-68-74—284	15634		S Taylor	69-71-76-72—288	9006

Other players who made the cut: I Aoki (Jpn), B Faxon, D Forsman, E Kirby, D Love III, B Mayfair, L Mize, G Norman (Aus), J Sindelar, M Wiebe 289; S Ballesteros (Sp), C Dennis, J Nicklaus 290; K Green, S Jones, J Mahaffey, T Watson, R Zokol (Can) 291; J Mudd, S Pate, T Sieckmann 292; R Black, W Heintzelman, H Irwin, D Ogrin, C Perry 293; B Langer (Ger), C Rose 294; M Calcavecchia, D Graham 295; D Halldorson, T Sills, G Lesher (Am) 296; B Wadkins 297; E Humenik, D Pruitt 298; J Daly, D Weaver 300; K Beck 301.

US OPEN CHAMPIONSHIP HISTORY

Year	Winner	Runner-up	Venue	By
1894	W Dunn	W Campbell	St Andrews, NY	2 holes

After 1894 decided by stroke play

Year	Winner	Venue	Score
1895	HJ Rawlins	Newport	173
1896	J Foulis	Southampton	152
1897	J Lloyd	Wheaton, IL	162
1898	F Herd	Shinnecock Hills	328

72 holes played from 1898

Year	Winner	Venue	Score
1899	W Smith	Baltimore	315
1900	H Vardon (Eng)	Wheaton, IL	313
1901	W Anderson	Myopia, MA	315
1902	L Auchterlonie	Garden City	305
1903	W Anderson	Baltusrol	307
1904	W Anderson	Glenview	304
1905	W Anderson	Myopia, MA	335
1906	A Smith	Onwentsia	291
1907	A Ross	Chestnut Hill, PA	302
1908	F McLeod	Myopia, MA	322
1909	G Sargent	Englewood, NJ	290
1910	A Smith	Philadelphia	289

(After a tie with J McDermott and M Smith)

1911	J McDermott	Wheaton, IL	307
1912	J McDermott	Buffalo, NY	294
1913	F Ouimet (Am)	Brookline, MA	304

(After a tie with H Vardon and E Ray)

1914	W Hagen	Midlothian	297
1915	J Travers (Am)	Baltusrol	290
1916	C Evans (Am)	Minneapolis	286
1917-18	*No Championship*		
1919	W Hagen	Braeburn	301
1920	E Ray (Eng)	Inverness	295

Year	Winner	Venue	Score
1921	J Barnes	Washington	289
1922	G Sarazen	Glencoe	288
1923	R Jones Jr (Am)	Inwood, LI	295

(After a tie with R Cruikshank. Play-off: Jones 76, Cruikshank 78)

1924	C Walker	Oakland Hills	297
1925	W MacFarlane	Worcester	291
1926	R Jones Jr (Am)	Scioto	293
1927	T Armour	Oakmont	301

(After a tie with H Cooper. Play-off: Armour 76, Cooper 79)

| 1928 | J Farrell | Olympia Fields | 294 |

(After a tie with R Jones Jr. Play-off: Farrell 143; Jones 144)

| 1929 | R Jones Jr (Am) | Winged Foot, NY | 294 |

(After a tie with A Espinosa. Play-off: Jones 141, Espinosa 164)

| 1930 | R Jones Jr (Am) | Interlachen | 287 |
| 1931 | B Burke | Inverness | 292 |

(After a tie with G von Elm. Play-off: Burke 149-148, von Elm 149-149)

1932	G Sarazen	Fresh Meadow	286
1933	J Goodman (Am)	North Shore	287
1934	O Dutra	Merion	293
1935	S Parks	Oakmont	299
1936	T Manero	Springfield	282
1937	R Guldahl	Oakland Hills	281
1938	R Guldahl	Cherry Hills	284
1939	B Nelson	Philadelphia	284

(After a tie with C Wood and D Shute)

| 1940 | W Lawson Little | Canterbury, OH | 287 |

(After a tie with G Sarazen. Play-off: Little 70; Sarazen 73)

| 1941 | C Wood | Fort Worth, TX | 284 |

Players are of American nationality unless stated

The US Open Championship

Year	Winner	Venue	Score
1942–45	*No Championship*		
1946	L Mangrum	Canterbury	284

(After a tie with B Nelson and V Ghezzie)

Year	Winner	Venue	Score
1947	L Worsham	St Louis	282

(After a tie with S Snead. Play-off: Worsham 69, Snead 70)

Year	Winner	Venue	Score
1948	B Hogan	Los Angeles	276
1949	Dr C Middlecoff	Medinah, IL	286
1950	B Hogan	Merion, PA	287

(After a tie with L Mangrum and G Fazio. Play-off: Hogan 69, Mangrum 73, Fazio 75)

Year	Winner	Venue	Score
1951	B Hogan	Oakland Hills, MI	287
1952	J Boros	Dallas, TX	281
1953	B Hogan	Oakmont	283
1954	E Furgol	Baltusrol	284
1955	J Fleck	San Francisco	287

(After a tie with B Hogan. Play-off: Fleck 69, Hogan 72)

Year	Winner	Venue	Score
1956	Dr C Middlecoff	Rochester, NY	281
1957	D Mayer	Inverness	282

(After a tie with Dr C Middlecoff. Play-off: Mayer 72, Middlecoff 79)

Year	Winner	Venue	Score
1958	T Bolt	Tulsa, OK	283
1959	W Casper	Winged Foot, NY	282
1960	A Palmer	Denver, CO	280
1961	G Littler	Birmingham, MI	281
1962	J Nicklaus	Oakmont	283

(After a tie with A Palmer. Play-off: Nicklaus 71, Palmer 74)

Year	Winner	Venue	Score
1963	J Boros	Brookline, MA	293

(After a tie. Play-off: J Boros 70, J Cupit 73, A Palmer 76)

Year	Winner	Venue	Score
1964	K Venturi	Washington	278
1965	G Player (SA)	St Louis, MO	282

(After a tie with K Nagle. Play-off: Player 71, Nagle 74)

Year	Winner	Venue	Score
1966	W Casper	San Francisco	278

(After a tie with A Palmer. Play-off: Casper 69, Palmer 73)

Year	Winner	Venue	Score
1967	J Nicklaus	Baltusrol	275
1968	L Trevino	Rochester, NY	275
1969	O Moody	Houston, TX	281
1970	A Jacklin (Eng)	Hazeltine, MN	281
1971	L Trevino	Merion, PA	280

(After a tie with J Nicklaus. Play-off: Trevino 68, Nicklaus 71)

Year	Winner	Venue	Score
1972	J Nicklaus	Pebble Beach	290
1973	J Miller	Oakmont, PA	279
1974	H Irwin	Winged Foot, NY	287
1975	L Graham	Medinah, IL	287

(After a tie with Mahaffey. Play-off: Graham 71, Mahaffey 73)

Year	Winner	Venue	Score
1976	J Pate	Atlanta, GA	277
1977	H Green	Southern Hills, Tulsa	278
1978	A North	Cherry Hills	285
1979	H Irwin	Inverness, OH	284
1980	J Nicklaus	Baltusrol	272
1981	D Graham (Aus)	Merion, PA	273
1982	T Watson	Pebble Beach	282
1983	L Nelson	Oakmont, PA	280
1984	F Zoeller	Winged Foot	276

(After a tie with G Norman. Play-off: Zoeller 67, Norman 75)

Year	Winner	Venue	Score
1985	A North	Oakland Hills, MI	279
1986	R Floyd	Shinnecock Hills, NY	279
1987	S Simpson	Olympic, San Francisco	277
1988	C Strange	Brookline, MA	278

(After a tie with N Faldo. Play-off: Strange 71, Faldo 75)

Year	Winner	Venue	Score
1989	C Strange	Rochester, NY	278
1990	H Irwin	Medinah	280

(After a tie with M Donald won at 1st extra hole after 18-hole play-off tie)

Year	Winner	Venue	Score
1991	P Stewart	Hazeltine, MN	282
1992	T Kite	Pebble Beach, FL	285
1993	L Janzen	Baltusrol	272
1994	E Els (SA)	Oakmont, PA	279
1995	C Pavin	Shinnecock Hills, NY	280
1996	S Jones	Oakland Hills, MI	278
1997	E Els (SA)	Congressional, Bethesda	276
1998	L Janzen	Olympic, San Francisco	280

Players are of American nationality unless stated

The Masters

62nd US Masters *at Augusta National GC, Georgia.* (6925 yds, Par 72)

Prize money: $3,200,000. Final field comprised 88 players, of whom 44, including one amateur, made the half-way cut on 150 or better

Pos	Name	Score	Prize Money $
1	Mark O'Meara	74-70-68-67—279	576000
2	David Duval	71-68-74-67—280	281600
	Fred Couples	69-70-71-70—280	281600
4	Jim Furyk	76-70-67-68—281	153600
5	Paul Azinger	71-72-69-70—282	128000
6	Jack Nicklaus	73-72-70-68—283	111200
	David Toms	75-72-72-64—283	111200
8	Darren Clarke (N. Ire)	76-73-67-69—285	89600
	Justin Leonard	74-73-69-69—285	89600
	Colin Montgomerie (Sco)	71-75-69-70—285	89600
	Tiger Woods	71-72-72-70—285	89600
12	Jay Haas	72-71-71-72—286	64800
	Per-Ulrik Johansson (Swe)	74-75-67-70—286	64800
	Phil Mickelson	74-69-69-74—286	64800
	José Maria Olazábal (Sp)	70-73-71-72—286	64800
16	Mark Calcavecchia	74-74-69-70—287	48000
	Ernie Els (SA)	75-70-70-72—287	48000
	Scott Hoch	70-71-73-73—287	48000
	Ian Woosnam (Wal)	74-71-72-70—287	48000
	Scott McCarron	73-71-72-71—287	48000
21	Willie Wood	74-74-70-70—288	38400
	Matt Kucher (Am)	72-76-68-72—288	
23	Stewart Cink	74-76-69-70—289	33280
	John Huston	77-71-70-71—289	33280
	Jeff Maggert	72-73-72-72—289	33280
26	David Frost (SA)	72-73-74-71—290	26133
	Steve Jones	75-70-75-70—290	26133
	Brad Faxon	73-74-71-72—290	26133
29	Michael Bradley	73-74-72-72—291	23680
30	Steve Elkington (Aus)	75-75-71-71—292	22720
31	Andrew Magee	74-72-74-73—293	21280
	Jesper Parnevik (Swe)	75-73-73-72—293	21280
33	Lee Janzen	76-74-72-72—294	18112
	Fuzzy Zoeller	71-74-75-74—294	18112
	Phil Blackmar	71-78-75-70—294	18112
	John Daly	77-71-71-75—294	18112
	Davis Love III	74-75-67-78—294	18112
38	Tom Kite	73-74-74-74—295	15680
39	Bernhard Langer (Ger)	75-73-74-74—296	14720
	Paul Stankowski	70-80-72-74—296	14720
41	Corey Pavin	73-77-72-75—297	13440
	Craig Stadler	79-68-73-77—297	13440

Players are of American nationality unless stated

Pos	Name	Score	Prize Money $
43	John Cook	75-73-74-76—298	12480
44	Lee Westwood (Eng)	74-76-72-78—300	11840
	Joel Kribel (Am)	74-76-76-75—301	
46	Gary Player (SA)	77-72-78-75—302	11200

The following players missed the half-way cut:

Pos	Name	Score	Pos	Name	Score
47	Nick Faldo (Eng)	72-79—151	65T	Jeff Sluman	78-76—154
	Ray Floyd	74-77—151	69	Ben Crenshaw	83-72—155
	Tim Herron	76-75—151		David Ogrin	77-78—155
	Billy Mayfair	76-75—151	71	Tom Lehman	80-76—156
	Nick Price (Zim)	75-76—151		Vijay Singh (Fij)	76-80—156
	Tom Watson	78-73—151		Mark Brooks	80-76—156
	Billy Ray Brown	76-75—151	74	Seve Ballesteros (Sp)	78-79—157
	Retief Goosen (SA)	74-77—151		Fred Funk	79-78—157
	Sandy Lyle (Sco)	74-77—151		Gabriel Hjertstedt (Swe)	79-78—157
	Tommy Tolles	75-76—151		Scott Simpson	79-78—157
57	Olin Browne	72-80—152		Ignacio Garrido (Sp)	85-72—157
	Larry Mize	73-79—152		Craig Watson (Am) (Sco)	79-78—157
	Jumbo Ozaki (Jpn)	75-77—152	80	Gay Brewer	72-86—158
	Bob Tway	74-78—152		Tim Clark	80-78—158
61	Billy Andrade	75-78—153	82	Tommy Aaron	81-79—160
	Bradley Hughes (Aus)	75-78—153		Ken Bakst	82-78—160
	Frank Nobilo (NZ)	75-78—153	84	Bill Glasson	82-79—161
	Costantino Rocca (It)	81-72—153	85	Charles Coody	79-85—164
65	Stuart Appleby (Aus)	77-77—154	86	Arnold Palmer	79-87—166
	Shigeki Maruyama (Jpn)	74-80—154	87	Billy Casper	81-86—167
	Greg Norman (Aus)	76-78—154	88	Doug Ford	

1997 US Masters *at Augusta* (6925 yds, Par 72)

Prize money: $2,500,000. Entries: 86, of whom 46 made the half-way cut.

Pos	Name	Score	Prize $	Pos	Name	Score	Prize $
1	T Woods	70-66-65-69—270	486000	24	N Price (Zim)	71-71-75-74—291	24840
2	T Kite	77-69-66-70—282	291600		L Westwood (Eng)	77-71-73-70—291	24840
3	T Tolles	72-72-72-67—283	183600	26	L Janzen	72-73-74-73—292	21195
4	T Watson	75-68-69-72—284	129600		C Stadler	77-72-71-72—292	21195
5	C Rocca (It)	71-69-70-75—285	102600	28	P Azinger	69-73-77-74—293	19575
	P Stankowski	68-74-69-74—285	102600		J Furyk	74-75-72-72—293	19575
7	F Couples	72-69-73-72—286	78570	30	S McCarron	77-71-72-74—294	17145
	B Langer (Ger)	72-72-74-68—286	78570		L Mize	79-69-74-72—294	17145
	J Leonard	76-69-71-70—286	78570		C Montgomerie (Sco)	72-67-74-81—294	17145
	D Love III	72-71-72-71—286	78570		M O'Meara	75-74-70-75—294	17145
	J Sluman	74-67-72-73—286	78570	34	A Lyle (Sco)	73-73-74-75—295	14918
12	S Elkington (Aus)	76-72-72-67—287	52920		F Zoeller	75-73-69-78—295	14918
	P-U Johansson (Swe)	72-73-73-69—287	52920	36	D Waldorf	74-75-72-75—296	13905
	T Lehman	73-76-69-69—287	52920	37	D Frost (SA)	74-71-73-79—297	13230
	JM Olazábal (Sp)	71-70-74-72—287	52920	38	S Hoch	79-68-73-78—298	12690
	W Wood	72-76-71-68—287	52920	39	J Nicklaus	77-70-74-78—299	11610
17	M Calcavecchia	74-73-72-69—288	39150		S Torrance (Sco)	75-73-73-78—299	11610
	E Els (SA)	73-70-71-74—288	39150		I Woosnam (Wal)	77-68-75-79—299	11610
	F Funk	73-74-69-72—288	39150	42	M Ozaki (Jpn)	74-74-74-78—300	10530
	V Singh (Fij)	75-74-69-70—288	39150	43	C Pavin	75-74-78-74—301	9720
21	S Appleby (Aus)	72-76-70-71—289	30240		C Rose	73-75-79-74—301	9720
	J Huston	67-77-75-70—289	30240	45	B Crenshaw	75-73-74-80—302	8910
	J Parnevik (Swe)	73-72-71-73—289	30240	46	F Nobilo (NZ)	76-72-74-81—303	8370

Players are of American nationality unless stated

1996 US Masters *at Augusta* (6925 yds, Par 72)

Prize money: $2,500,000. Entries: 92, of whom 44 made the half-way cut.

Pos	Name	Score	Prize $	Pos	Name	Score	Prize $
1	N Faldo (Eng)	69-67-73-67—276	450000	23	L Mize	75-71-77-68—291	25000
2	G Norman (Aus)	63-69-71-78—281	270000		L Roberts	71-73-72-75—291	25000
3	P Mickelson	65-73-72-72—282	170000	25	R Floyd	70-74-77-71—292	21000
4	F Nobilo (NZ)	71-71-72-69—283	120000		B Faxon	69-77-72-74—292	21000
5	S Hoch	67-73-73-71—284	95000	27	B Estes	71-71-79-72—293	18900
	D Waldorf	72-71-69-72—284	95000		J Leonard	72-74-75-72—293	18900
7	D Love III	72-71-74-68—285	77933	29	J Furyk	75-70-78-71—294	15571
	J Maggert	71-73-72-69—285	77933		J Gallagher Jr	70-76-77-71—294	15571
	C Pavin	75-66-73-71—285	77933		H Irwin	74-71-77-72—294	15571
10	S McCarron	70-70-72-74—286	65000		S Simpson	69-76-76-73—294	15571
	D Frost (SA)	70-68-74-74—286	65000		C Stadler	73-72-71-78—294	15571
12	B Tway	67-72-76-72—287	52500		J Daly	71-74-71-78—294	15571
	L Janzen	68-71-75-73—287	52500		I Woosnam (Wal)	72-69-73-80—294	15571
	E Els (SA)	71-71-72-73—287	52500	36	F Funk	71-72-76-76—295	12333
15	F Couples	78-68-71-71—288	43750		J Haas	70-73-75-77—295	12333
	M Calcavecchia	71-73-71-73—288	43750		B Langer (Ger)	75-70-72-78—295	12333
17	J Huston	71-71-71-76—289	40000	39	C Montgomerie (Sco)	72-74-75-75—296	11050
18	P Azinger	70-74-76-70—290	32600		V Singh (Fij)	69-71-74-82—296	11050
	M O'Meara	72-71-75-72—290	32600	41	S Lowery (Sco)	71-74-75-77—297	10050
	T Lehman	75-70-72-73—290	32600		J Nicklaus	70-73-76-78—297	10050
	N Price (Zim)	71-75-70-74—290	32600	43	S Ballesteros (Sp)	73-73-77-76—299	9300
	D Duval	73-72-69-76—290	32600	44	A Cejka (Ger)	73-71-78-80—302	8800

1995 US Masters *at Augusta* (6905 yds, Par 72)

Prize money: $2,132,000. Entries: 86, of whom 47 made the half-way cut.

Pos	Name	Score	Prize $	Pos	Name	Score	Prize $
1	B Crenshaw	70-67-69-68—274	396000	24T	D Edwards	69-73-73-71—286	18260
2	D Love III	69-69-71-66—275	237600		L Roberts	72-69-72-73—286	18260
3	J Haas	71-64-72-70—277	127600		N Faldo (Eng)	70-70-71-75—286	18260
	G Norman (Aus)	73-68-68-68—277	127600		D Waldorf	74-69-67-76—286	18260
5	S Elkington (Aus)	73-67-67-72—279	83600	29	B Estes	73-70-76-68—287	15300
	D Frost (SA)	66-71-71-71—279	83600		M Ozaki (Jpn)	70-74-70-73—287	15300
7	S Hoch	69-67-71-73—280	70950	31	B Lietzke	72-71-71-74—288	13325
	P Mickelson	66-71-70-73—280	70950		P Jacobsen	72-73-69-74—288	13325
9	C Strange	72-71-65-73—281	63800		B Langer (Ger)	71-69-73-75—288	13325
10	F Couples	71-69-67-75—282	57200		M O'Meara	68-72-71-77—288	13325
	B Henninger	70-68-68-76—282	57200	35	D Forsman	71-74-74-71—290	10840
12	K Perry	73-70-71-69—283	48400		W Grady (Aus)	69-73-74-74—290	10840
	L Janzen	69-69-74-71—283	48400		J Nicklaus	67-78-70-75—290	10840
14	JM Olazábal (Spa)	66-74-72-72—284	39600		C Beck	68-76-69-77—290	10840
	T Watson	73-70-69-72—284	39600		M McCumber	73-69-69-79—290	10840
	H Irwin	69-72-71-72—284	39600	40	T Lehman	71-72-74-75—292	9500
17	C Montgomerie (Sco)	71-69-76-69—285	28786	41	M Calcavecchia	70-72-78-73—293	8567
	P Azinger	70-72-73-70—285	28786		T Woods (Am)	72-72-77-72—293	
	B Faxon	76-69-69-71—285	28786		J Sluman	73-72-71-77—293	8567
	I Woosnam (Wal)	69-72-71-73—285	28786		P Stewart	71-72-72-78—293	
	R Floyd	71-70-70-74—285	28786	45	S Ballesteros (Sp)	75-68-78-75—296	7500
	C Pavin	67-71-72-75—285	28786		J Daly	75-69-71-81—296	
	J Huston	70-66-72-77—285	28786	47	R Fehr	76-69-69-83—297	6800
24	D Gilford (Eng)	67-73-75-71—286	18260				

Players are of American nationality unless stated

1994 US Masters at *Augusta* (6905 yds, Par 72)

Prize money: $1,960,000. Entries: 86, of whom 51 made the half-way cut.

Pos	Name	Score	Prize $	Pos	Name	Score	Prize $
1	JM Olazábal (Sp)	74-67-69-69—279	360000	27	S Simpson	74-74-73-73—294	14800
2	T Lehman	70-70-69-72—281	216000		V Singh (Fij)	70-75-74-75—294	14800
3	L Mize	68-71-72-71—282	136000		C Strange	74-70-75-75—294	14800
4	T Kite	69-72-71-71—283	96000	30	L Janzen	75-71-76-73—295	13300
5	J Haas	72-72-72-69—285	73000		C Parry (Aus)	75-74-73-73—295	13300
	J McGovern	72-70-71-72—285	73000	32	N Faldo (Eng)	76-73-73-74—296	12400
	L Roberts	75-68-72-70—285	73000	33	R Cochran	71-74-74-79—297	11500
8	E Els (SA)	74-67-74-71—286	60000		S Torrance (Sco)	76-73-74-74—297	11500
	C Pavin	71-72-73-70—286	60000	35	D Frost (SA)	74-71-75-78—298	10300
10	I Baker-Finch (Aus)	71-71-71-74—287	50000		N Price (Zim)	74-73-74-77—298	10300
	R Floyd	70-74-71-72—287	50000		F Zoeller	74-72-74-78—298	10300
	J Huston	72-72-74-69—287	50000	38	F Allem (SA)	69-77-76-77—299	9000
13	T Watson	70-71-73-74—288	42000		F Funk	79-70-75-75—299	9000
14	D Forsman	74-66-76-73—289	38000		A Lyle (Sco)	75-73-78-73—299	9000
15	C Beck	71-71-78-71—291	34000	41	W Grady (Aus)	74-73-73-80—300	7400
	B Faxon	71-73-73-74—291	34000		A Magee	74-74-76-76—300	7400
	M O'Meara	75-70-76-70—291	34000		H Meshiai (Jpn)	71-71-80-78—300	7400
18	S Ballesteros (Sp)	70-76-75-71—292	24343		C Rocca (It)	79-70-78-73—300	7400
	B Crenshaw	74-73-73-72—292	24343		M Standly	77-69-79-75—300	7400
	D Edwards	73-72-77-72—292	24343	46	J Cook	77-72-77-75—301	6000
	B Glasson	72-73-75-72—292	24343		I Woosnam (Wal)	76-73-77-75—301	6000
	H Irwin	73-68-79-72—292	24343	48	J Daly	76-73-77-78—304	5250
	G Norman (Aus)	70-70-75-77—292	24343		H Twitty	73-76-74-81—304	5250
	L Wadkins	73-74-73-72—292	24343	50	J Maggert	75-73-82-75—305	5000
25	B Langer (Ger)	74-74-72-73—293	16800		J Harris (Am)	72-76-80-77—305	
	J Sluman	74-75-71-73—293	16800				

1993 US Masters at *Augusta* (6905 yds, Par 72)

Prize money: $1,705,700. Entries: 90, of whom 61 made the half-way cut.

Pos	Name	Score	Prize $	Pos	Name	Score	Prize $
1	B Langer (Ger)	68-70-69-70—277	306000	31T	A Magee	75-69-70-76—290	10533
2	C Beck	72-67-72-70—281	183600		G Norman (Aus)	74-68-71-77—290	10533
3	T Lehman	67-75-73-68—283	81600	34	G Sauers	74-71-75-71—291	8975
	J Daly	70-71-73-69—283	81600		B Gilder	69-76-75-71—291	8975
	S Elkington (Aus)	71-70-71-71—283	81600		P Mickelson	72-71-75-73—291	8975
	L Wadkins	69-72-71-71—283	81600		C Stadler	73-74-69-75—291	8975
7	JM Olazabal (Sp)	70-72-74-68—284	54850	38	J Haas	70-73-75-74—292	8000
	D Forsman	69-69-73-73—284	54850	39	N Faldo (Eng)	71-76-79-67—293	6817
9	P Stewart	74-70-72-69—285	47600		T Schulz	69-76-76-72—293	6817
	B Faxon	71-70-72-72—285	47600		D Waldorf	72-75-73-73—293	6817
11	A Forsbrand (Swe)	71-74-75-66—286	34850		K Clearwater	74-70-75-74—293	6817
	S Ballesteros (Sp)	74-70-71-71—286	34850		J Cook	76-67-75-75—293	6817
	C Pavin	67-75-71-72—286	34850		L Janzen	67-73-76-77—293	6817
	S Simpson	72-71-71-72—286	34850	45	M Ozaki (Jpn)	75-71-77-71—294	4940
	R Floyd	68-71-74-73—286	34850		N Ozaki (Jpn)	74-70-78-72—294	4940
	F Zoeller	76-67-71-73—286	34850		T Watson	71-75-75-73—294	4940
17	I Woosnam (Wal)	71-74-73-69—287	24650		JD Blake	71-74-73-76—294	4940
	M Calcavecchia	71-70-74-72—287	24650		C Parry (Aus)	69-72-75-78—294	4940
	H Twitty	70-71-73-73—287	24650	50	C Morgan	72-74-72-77—295	4250
	J Sluman	71-72-71-73—287	24650		B Ogle (Aus)	70-74-71-80—295	4250
21	M O'Meara	75-69-73-71—288	17000	52	D Peoples	71-73-78-74—296	4050
	F Couples	72-70-74-72—288	17000		C Montgomerie (Sco)	71-72-78-75—296	4050
	L Mize	67-74-74-73—288	17000	54	I Baker-Finch (Aus)	73-72-73-80—298	3900
	A Lyle (Sco)	73-71-71-73—288	17000		D Edwards	73-73-76-76—298	3900
	J Maggert	70-67-75-76—288	17000		D Love III	73-72-76-77—298	3900
	R Cochran	70-69-73-76—288	17000	57	D Coody	74-72-75-78—299	3800
27	J Nicklaus	67-75-76-71—289	12350		G Hallberg	72-74-78-75—299	3800
	H Irwin	74-69-74-72—289	12350	59	J Huston	68-74-84-75—301	3800
	J Sindelar	72-69-76-72—289	12350	60	G Player (SA)	71-76-75-80—302	3700
	N Henke	76-69-73-71—289	12350	61	B Andrade	73-74-80-76—303	3700
31	B Lietzke	74-71-71-74—290	10533				

Players are of American nationality unless stated

1992 US Masters at *Augusta* (6905 yds, Par 72)

Prize money: $1,500,000. Entries: 83, of whom 63 made the half-way cut.

Pos	Name	Score	Prize $	Pos	Name	Score	Prize $
1	F Couples	69-67-69-70—275	270000	31T	S Richardson (Eng)	69-75-70-71—285	8717
2	R Floyd	69-68-69-71—277	162000		C Strange	73-72-71-69—285	8717
3	C Pavin	72-71-68-67—278	102000		P Azinger	70-73-70-72—285	8717
4	J Sluman	65-74-70-71—280	66000		M Calcavecchia	73-72-75-65—285	8717
	M O'Meara	74-67-69-70—280	66000	37	C Montgomerie (Sco)	72-71-73-70—286	6800
6	S Pate	73-71-70-67—281	43829		S Elkington	69-71-74-72—286	6800
	N Henke	70-71-70-70—281	43829		M McCumber	72-70-76-68—286	6800
	I Baker-Finch (Aus)	70-69-68-74—281	43829		A Lyle (Sco)	72-69-70-75—286	6800
	N Price (Zim)	70-71-67-73—281	43829		R Mediate	70-73-70-73—286	6800
	G Norman (Aus)	70-70-73-68—281	43829	42	B Gilder	72-71-73-71—287	5450
	L Mize	73-69-71-68—281	43829		J Nicklaus	69-75-69-74—287	5450
	T Schulz	68-69-72-72—281	43829		JM Olazábal (Sp)	76-69-72-70—287	5450
13	D Pruitt	75-68-70-69—282	26500		B Mayfair	71-71-72-73—287	5450
	W Grady (Aus)	68-75-71-68—282	26500	46	B Crenshaw	72-71-71-74—288	4700
	S Simpson	70-71-71-70—282	26500	47	H Irwin	72-70-72-75—289	4400
	B Leitzke	69-72-68-73—282	26500	48	B McCallister	71-71-76-72—290	3933
	N Faldo (Eng)	71-72-68-71—282	26500		L Wadkins	65-75-76-74—290	3933
	C Parry (Aus)	69-66-69-78—282	26500		T Watson	73-70-76-71—290	3933
19	BR Brown	70-74-70-69—283	17550	51	G Archer	74-69-76-72—291	3700
	A Magee	73-70-70-70—283	17550	52	F Allem (SA)	69-71-78-74—292	3550
	M Hulbert	68-74-71-70—283	17550		D Feherty (N.Ire)	73-72-77-70—292	3550
	I Woosnam (Wal)	69-66-73-75—283	17550	54	B Andrade	73-71-73-76—293	3440
	F Zoeller	71-70-73-69—283	17550		J Cook	72-73-71-77—293	3440
	J Daly	71-71-73-68—283	17550		L Janzen	74-71-74-74—293	3440
25	B Fleisher	73-70-72-69—284	11467		T Aaron	76-69-77-71—293	3440
	J Huston	69-73-70-60—284	11467		D Peoples	73-71-72-77—293	3440
	C Stadler	70-71-70-73—284	11467	59	M Zerman (Am)	70-71-76-77—294	
	J Gallagher Jr	74-68-71-71—284	11467		S Ballesteros (Sp)	75-68-70-81—294	3300
	D Love III	68-72-72-72—284	11467	61	P Jacobsen	72-70-77-76—295	3300
	D A Weibring	71-68-72-73—284	11467		T Purtzer	76-69-75-75—295	3300
31	B Langer (Ger)	69-73-69-74—285	8717	63	R Davis (Aus)	77-68-77-79—301	3200
	B Faxon	71-71-69-74—285	8717				

1991 US Masters at *Augusta* (6905 yds, Par 72)

Prize money: $1,347,700. Entries: 87, of whom 57 made the half-way cut.

Pos	Name	Score	Prize $	Pos	Name	Score	Prize $
1	I Woosnam (Wal)	72-66-67-72—277	243000	29T	J Huston	73-72-71-70—286	9200
2	JM Olazábal (Sp)	68-71-69-70—278	145800		M Hatalsky	71-72-70-73—286	9200
3	T Watson	68-68-70-73—279	64800	32	D Frost (SA)	71-73-71-72—287	8000
	S Pate	72-73-69-65—279	64800		B Langer (Ger)	71-68-74-74—287	8000
	B Crenshaw	70-73-68-68—279	64800		W Levi	69-73-70-75—287	8000
	L Wadkins	67-71-70-71—279	64800	35	M McNulty (Zim)	67-72-74-75—288	6371
7	J Mudd	70-70-71-69—280	42100		M Brooks	69-72-74-73—288	6371
	I Baker-Finch (Aus)	71-70-70-70—280	42100		S Hoch	72-70-73-73—288	6371
	A Magee	70-72-68-70—280	42100		K Green	70-74-71-73—288	6371
10	H Irwin	70-70-75-66—281	35150		M Ozaki (Jpn)	68-77-69-74—288	6371
	T Nakajima (Jpn)	74-71-67-69—281	35150		F Couples	68-73-72-75—288	6371
12	B Mayfair	72-72-72-66—282	26500		J Nicklaus	68-72-72-76—288	6371
	M Calcavecchia	70-68-77-76—282	26500	42	D Hammond	71-72-73-73—289	4875
	F Zoeller	70-70-75-67—282	26500		D Love III	72-72-71-74—289	4875
	C Stadler	70-72-71-60—282	26500		C Strange	71-72-74-72—289	4875
	N Faldo (Eng)	72-73-67-70—282	26500		BR Brown	73-74-65-77—289	4875
17	J Gallagher Jr	67-71-74-71—283	18920	46	P Mickelson (Am)	74-69-73-74—290	
	M McCumber	67-71-73-72—283	18920		J Sindelar	72-70-70-78—290	4050
	P Jacobsen	73-70-68-72—283	18920		D Pooley	72-71-69-78—290	4050
	R Floyd	71-68-71-73—283	18920	49	L Trevino	71-71-72-77—291	3533
	L Mize	72-71-66-74—283	18920		T Aaron	74-70-74-73—291	3533
22	S Ballesteros (Sp)	75-70-69-70—284	12960		N Price (Zim)	74-72-73-72—291	3533
	S Elkington (Aus)	72-69-74-69—284	12960	52	P Azinger	72-73-67-80—292	3300
	R Mediate	72-69-71-72—284	12960	53	B Tennyson	73-78-67-75—293	3200
	C Pavin	73-70-69-72—284	12960		N Henke	77-73-71-72—293	3200
	S Simpson	69-73-69-73—284	12960	55	L Nelson	75-74-69-76—294	3100
27	M O'Meara	74-68-72-71—285	10200	56	T Kite	71-71-75-78—295	3100
	JD Blake	74-72-68-71—285	10200	57	M Zerman (Am)	71-71-77-80—299	
29	J Sluman	71-71-72-72—286	9200				

Players are of American nationality unless stated

1990 US Masters at Augusta (6905 yds, Par 72)

Prize money: $1,237,300. Entries: 85, of whom 49 made the half-way cut.

Pos	Name	Score	Prize $	Pos	Name	Score	Prize $
1	N Faldo* (Eng)	71-72-66-69—278	225000	24T	D Hammond	71-74-75-71—291	11000
2	R Floyd	70-68-68-72—278	135000		G Player (SA)	73-74-68-76—291	11000
*Faldo beat Floyd at second hole of sudden-death play-off				27	W Grady (Aus)	72-75-72-73—292	9267
3	J Huston	66-74-68-75—283	72500		A North	71-73-77-71—292	9267
	L Wadkins	72-73-70-68—283	72500		J Sluman	78-68-75-71—292	9267
5	F Couples	74-69-72-69—284	50000	30	P Jacobsen	67-75-76-75—293	8133
6	J Nicklaus	72-70-69-74—285	45000		J Mudd	74-70-73-76—293	8133
7	S Ballesteros (Sp)	74-73-68-71—286	35150		I Woosnam (Wal)	72-75-70-76—293	8133
	B Britton	68-74-71-73—286	35150	33	A Bean	76-72-74-72—294	7100
	B Langer (Ger)	70-73-69-74—286	35150		B Glasson	70-75-76-73—294	7100
	S Simpson	74-71-68-73—286	35150		N Ozaki (Jpn)	75-73-74-72—294	7100
	C Strange	70-73-71-72—286	35150	36	M McCumber	74-74-76-71—295	6133
	T Watson	77-71-67-71—286	35150		P Stewart	71-73-77-74—295	6133
13	JM Olazábal (Sp)	72-73-68-74—287	26300		B Tway	72-76-73-74—295	6133
14	B Crenshaw	72-74-73-69—288	20650	39	C Beck	72-74-75-75—296	5500
	S Hoch	71-68-73-76—288	20650		M Lye	75-73-73-75—296	5500
	T Kite	75-73-66-74—288	20650		C Patton (Am)	71-73-74-78—296	
	L Mize	70-76-71-71—288	20650	42	J Mahaffey	72-74-75-76—297	4867
	R Rafferty (N.Ire)	72-74-69-73—288	20650		D Pooley	73-73-72-79—297	4867
	C Stadler	72-70-74-72—288	20650		P Senior (Aus)	72-75-73-77—297	4867
20	M Calcavecchia	74-73-73-69—289	15100	45	M Hulbert	71-71-77-79—298	4250
	S Jones	77-69-72-71—289	15100		T Purtzer	71-77-76-74—298	4250
	F Zoeller	72-74-73-70—289	15100	47	M Donald	64-82-77-76—299	3900
23	M Ozaki (Jpn)	70-71-77-72—290	13000	48	L Nelson	74-73-79-74—300	3600
24	L Trevino	78-69-72-72—291	11000	49	G Archer	70-74-82-75—301	3400

1989 US Masters at Augusta (6905 yds, Par 72)

Prize money: $1,109,600. Entries: 85, of whom 52 made the half-way cut.

Pos	Name	Score	Prize $	Pos	Name	Score	Prize $
1	N Faldo* (Eng)	68-73-77-65—283	200000	26T	L Mize	72-77-69-75—293	8240
2	S Hoch	69-74-71-69—283	120000		S Pate	76-75-74-68—293	8240
*Faldo beat Hoch at second-hole of sudden-death play-off					L Wadkins	76-71-73-73—293	8240
3	G Norman (Aus)	74-75-68-67—284	64450		F Zoeller	76-74-69-74—293	8240
	B Crenshaw	71-72-70-71—284	64450	31	M Calcavecchia	74-72-74-74—294	6900
5	S Ballesteros (Sp)	71-72-73-69—285	44400		S Jones	74-73-80-67—294	6900
6	M Reid	72-71-71-72—286	40000		D Rummells	74-74-75-71—294	6900
7	J Mudd	73-76-72-66—287	37200	34	H Green	74-75-76-71—296	6000
8	J Sluman	74-72-74-68—288	32200		P Jacobsen	74-73-78-71—296	6000
	JM Olazábal (Sp)	77-73-70-68—288	32200		B Lietzke	74-75-79-68—296	6000
	C Beck	74-76-70-68—288	32200	37	B Gilder	75-74-77-71—297	5400
11	F Couples	72-76-74-67—289	25567	38	T Aaron	74-76-72-76—298	4900
	K Green	74-69-73-73—289	25567		C Coody	76-74-76-72—298	4900
	M O'Meara	74-71-72-72—289	25567		R Floyd	76-75-73-74—298	4900
14	P Azinger	75-75-69-71—290	19450		S Simpson	72-77-72-77—298	4900
	D Pooley	70-77-76-67—290	19450	42	D Pohl	72-74-78-75—299	4300
	T Watson	72-73-74-71—290	19450	43	G Archer	75-75-75-75—300	3900
	I Woosnam (Wal)	74-76-71-69—290	19450		M McCumber	72-75-81-72—300	3900
18	D Frost (SA)	76-72-73-70—291	14000		G Twiggs	75-76-79-70—300	3900
	T Kite	72-72-72-75—291	14000	46	J Haas	73-77-79-72—301	3125
	J Nicklaus	73-74-73-71—291	14000		B Lohr	75-76-77-73—301	3125
	J Ozaki (Jpn)	71-75-73-72—291	14000		M Sullivan	76-74-73-78—301	3125
	C Strange	74-71-74-72—291	14000		DA Weibring	72-79-74-76—301	3125
	L Trevino	67-74-81-69—291	14000	50	C Pavin	74-74-78-76—302	2800
24	T Purtzer	71-76-73-72—292	10250	51	A Bean	70-80-77-77—304	2700
	P Stewart	73-75-74-70—292	10250	52	TC Chen (Tai)	71-75-76-84—306	2600
26	B Langer	74-75-71-73—293	8240				

Players are of American nationality unless stated

The Masters History

Year	Winner	Score	Year	Winner	Score
1934	H Smith	284	1968	R Goalby	277
1935	G Sarazen	282	1969	G Archer	281
1936	H Smith	285	1970	W Casper*	279
1937	B Nelson	283	1971	C Coody	279
1938	H Picard	285	1972	J Nicklaus	286
1939	R Guldahl	279	1973	T Aaron	283
1940	J Demaret	280	1974	G Player (SA)	278
1941	C Wood	280	1975	J Nicklaus	276
1942	B Nelson*	280	1976	R Floyd	271
1946	H Keiser	282	1977	T Watson	276
1947	J Demaret	281	1978	G Player (SA)	277
1948	C Harmon	279	1979	F Zoeller*	280
1949	S Snead	283	1980	S Ballesteros (Sp)	275
1950	J Demaret	282	1981	T Watson	280
1951	B Hogan	280	1982	C Stadler*	284
1952	S Snead*	286	1983	S Ballesteros (Sp)	280
1953	B Hogan	274	1984	B Crenshaw	277
1954	S Snead	289	1985	B Langer (Ger)	282
1955	C Middlecoff	279	1986	J Nicklaus	279
1956	J Burke	289	1987	L Mize*	285
1957	D Ford	283	1988	A Lyle (Sco)	281
1958	A Palmer	284	1989	N Faldo (Eng)*	283
1959	A Wall	284	1990	N Faldo (Eng)*	278
1960	A Palmer	282	1991	I Woosnam (Wal)	277
1961	G Player (SA)	280	1992	F Couples	275
1962	A Palmer*	280	1993	B Langer (Ger)	277
1963	J Nicklaus	286	1994	JM Olazabal (Sp)	279
1964	A Palmer	276	1995	B Crenshaw	274
1965	J Nicklaus	271	1996	N Faldo (Eng)	276
1966	J Nicklaus	288	1997	T Woods	270
1967	G Brewer	280	1998	M O'Meara	279

* Winner after play-off

Players are of American nationality unless stated

US PGA Championship

80th US PGA Championship at *Sahalee, Seattle* (6906 yds, Par 70)
Prize money: $3,000,000. Final field comprised 150, of whom 75 made the half-way cut on 145 or better.

Pos	Name	Score	Prize Money $
1	Vijay Singh (Fij)	70-66-67-68—271	540000
2	Steve Stricker	69-68-66-70—273	324000
3	Steve Elkington (Aus)	69-69-69-67—274	204000
4	Frank Lickliter	68-71-69-68—276	118000
	Mark O'Meara	69-70-69-68—276	118000
	Nick Price (Zim)	70-73-68-65—276	118000
7	Billy Mayfair	73-67-67-70—277	89500
	Davis Love III	70-68-69-70—277	89500
9	John Cook	71-68-70-69—278	80000
10	Kenny Perry	69-72-70-68—279	69000
	Tiger Woods	66-72-70-71—279	69000
	Skip Kendall	72-68-68-71—279	69000
13	Brad Faxon	70-68-74-68—280	46000
	Fred Couples	74-71-67-68—280	46000
	Bob Tway	69-76-67-68—280	46000
	Paul Azinger	68-73-70-69—280	46000
	Bill Glasson	68-74-69-69—280	46000
	Steve Flesch	75-69-67-69—280	46000
	John Huston	70-71-68-71—280	46000
	Robert Allenby (Aus)	72-68-69-71—280	46000
21	Ernie Els (SA)	72-72-71-66—281	32000
	Andrew Magee	70-68-72-71—281	32000
23	Per-Ulrik Johansson (Swe)	69-74-71-68—282	26000
	Fred Funk	70-71-71-70—282	26000
	Scott Gump	68-69-72-73—282	26000
	Greg Kraft	71-73-65-73—282	26000
27	Jeff Sluman	71-73-70-69—283	20500
	Hal Sutton	72-68-72-71—283	20500
29	Glen Day	68-71-75-70—284	17100
	Tom Lehman	71-71-70-72—284	17100
	Ian Woosnam (Wal)	70-75-67-72—284	17100
	Lee Rinker	70-70-71-73—284	17100
	Scott Hoch	72-69-70-73—284	17100
34	Phil Mickelson	70-70-78-67—285	14250
	Bob Estes	68-76-69-72—285	14250
	Paul Goydos	70-70-72-73—285	14250
	Russ Cochran	69-71-70-75—285	14250
38	Craig Stadler	69-74-71-72—286	12750
	Duffy Waldorf	74-70-70-72—286	12750
40	Joey Sindelar	71-71-75-70—287	11250
	Jay Haas	72-73-73-69—287	11250
	Joe Durant	75-68-74-70—287	11250
	Carlos Franco (Para)	71-70-73-73—287	11250

Players are of American nationality unless stated

80th US PGA Championship *continued*

Pos	Name	Score	Prize Money $
44	Joe Ozaki (Jpn)	73-71-75-69—288	7990
	Jeff Maggert	71-73-73-71—288	7990
	Steve Lowery	76-69-72-71—288	7990
	David Ogrin	73-72-71-72—288	7990
	Kevin Sutherland	74-71-71-72—288	7990
	Colin Montgomerie (Sco)	70-67-77-74—288	7990
	PH Horgan III	71-71-72-74—288	7990
	Mark Calcavecchia	70-73-71-74—288	7990
	Dudley Hart	70-75-69-74—288	7990
	Billy Andrade	68-77-68-75—288	7990
54	Nick Faldo (Eng)	73-71-72-73—289	6550
	Scott Verplank	71-71-71-76—289	6550
56	Ted Tryba	70-74-76-70—290	6175
	Mark Brooks	72-73-72-73—290	6175
	Brian Watts	72-73-72-73—290	6175
	Jim Carter	71-73-72-74—290	6175
	David Frost (SA)	70-69-76-75—290	6175
	Jay Don Blake	70-72-73-75—290	6175
62	Trevor Dodds (Nam)	69-75-75-72—291	5900
	Tom Byrum	72-71-74-74—291	5900
	Olin Browne	73-71-71-76—291	5900
65	Robert Karlsson (Swe)	71-73-75-73—292	5750
	Shigeki Maruyama (Jpn)	68-77-73-74—292	5750
	Loren Roberts	72-71-74-75—292	5750
68	Stephen Leaney (Aus)	72-70-72-79—293	5650
69	Andrew Coltart (Sco)	70-75-75-74—294	5600
70	David Sutherland	77-68-77-73—295	5550
71	Brent Geiberger	73-70-79-74—296	5450
	Craig Parry (Aus)	70-75-74-77—296	5450
	Brad Fabel	73-72-73-78—296	5450
74	Chris Perry	73-71-75-78—297	5350
75	Tim Herron	73-70-79-76—298	5300

The following players missed the halfway cut:

76	R Thompson	73-73—146
	L Mize	75-71—146
	P Stankowski	72-74—146
	J Parnevik (Swe)	70-76—146
	L Mattiace	71-75—146
	B Crenshaw	70-76—146
	J Furyk	72-74—146
83	R Mediate	75-72—147
	C Rocca (It)	73-74—147
	G Fieger	74-73—147
	T Armour III	78-69—147
	S Cink	73-74—147
	J Leonard	70-77—147
	M Wiebe	75-72—147
	S McCarron	69-78—147
	R Goosen (SA)	69-78—147
	H Frazar	69-78—147
93	S Simpson	70-78—148
	E Romero (Arg)	70-78—148
	G Chalmers	75-73—148
	J Ozaki (Jpn)	74-74—148
	T Björn (Den)	75-73—148
	B Jobe	70-78—148
	I Garrido (Sp)	73-75—148
	M Mielke	74-74—148
93T	E Terasa	72-76—148
	M Burke Jr	75-73—148
	D Toms	72-76—148
	T Watson	72-76—148
	L Janzen	76-72—148
	C Dennis	73-75—148
107	S Keppler	73-76—149
	J Overton	77-72—149
	JM Olazábal (Sp)	75-74—149
	R Gaus	72-77—149
111	L Westwood (Eng)	74-76—150
	T Kite	73-77—150
	S Appleby (Aus)	77-73—150
	K Stauffer	74-76—150
	J Schuman	71-79—150
	JP Hayes	74-76—150
	N Lancaster	75-75—150
	P Stewart	76-74—150
	C Pavin	71-79—150
	K Triplett	73-77—150
121	B Boyd	77-74—151
	R McDougal	77-74—151
	S Pate	72-79—151
	B Ford	72-79—151
125	J Daly	80-72—152
125T	R Damron	74-78—152
	T Tolles	80-72—152
	G Turner	72-80—152
	S Williams	78-74—152
130	F Nobilo (NZ)	75-78—153
	B Zabriski	79-74—153
	P Lonard	72-81—153
	P Sjöland (Swe)	74-79—153
134	J Thomsen	78-76—154
	P Blackmar	79-75—154
	TM Smith	77-77—154
	D Duval	76-78—154
	G Hjertstedt (Swe)	76-78—154
139	K Kimball	80-75—155
140	C Tucker	78-78—156
141	A Geiberger	81-77—158
	W Grady (Aus)	76-82—158
	B Groff	84-74—158
	W Frantz	81-77—158
	G Waite	79-79—158
146	R Stelten	78-81—159
	K Schall	79-80—159
	J Lankford	78-81—159
149	P Earnest	85-82—167

Players are of American nationality unless stated

1997 US PGA Championship *at Winged Foot CC, New York*
(6987 yds, Par 70) Prize money: $2,600,000. Entries 150, of whom 77 made the half-way cut.

Pos	Name	Score	Prize $	Pos	Name	Score	Prize $
1	D Love III	66-71-66-66—269	470000	13T	B Tway	68-75-72-69—284	35100
2	J Leonard	68-70-65-71—274	280000		M O'Meara	69-73-75-67—284	35100
3	J Maggert	69-69-73-65—276	175000	23	M Calcavecchia	71-74-73-67—285	22500
4	L Janzen	69-67-74-69—279	125000		B Langer (Ger)	73-71-72-69—285	22500
5	T Kite	68-71-71-70—280	105000		D Martin	69-75-74-67—285	22500
6	P Blackmar	70-68-74-69—281	85000		S Maruyama (Jpn)	68-70-74-73—285	22500
	J Furyk	69-72-72-68—281	85000		K Perry	73-68-73-71—285	22500
	S Hoch	71-72-68-70—281	85000		J Cook	71-71-74-69—285	22500
9	T Byrum	69-73-70-70—282	70000	29	P Azinger	68-73-71-74—286	13625
10	T Lehman	69-72-72-70—283	60000		R Black	76-69-71-70—286	13625
	S McCarron	74-71-67-71—283	60000		F Couples	71-67-73-75—286	13625
	J Sindelar	72-71-71-69—283	60000		J Daly	66-73-77-70—286	13625
13	D Duval	70-70-71-73—284	35100		P Goydos	70-72-71-73—286	13625
	T Herron	72-73-68-71—284	35100		H Irwin	73-70-71-72—286	13625
	C Montgomerie (Sco)	74-71-67-72—284	35100		P Mickelson	69-69-73-75—286	13625
	G Norman (Aus)	68-71-74-71—284	35100		F Nobilo (NZ)	72-73-67-74—286	13625
	N Price (Zim)	72-70-70-72—284	35100		D Pooley	72-74-70-70—286	13625
	V Singh (Fij)	73-66-76-69—284	35100		P Stewart	70-70-72-74—286	13625
	T Tolles	75-70-73-66—284	35100		L Westwood (Eng)	74-68-71-73—286	13625
	K Triplett	73-70-71-70—284	35100		T Woods	70-70-71-75—286	13625

Other Totals: I Garrido (Sp), S Jones, D Ogrin, E Romero (Arg) 287; T Björn (Den), S Elkington (Aus), J Parnevik (Swe), S Torrance (Sco) 288; R Allenby (Aus), B Henninger, C Perry, L Roberts 289; O Browne, E Els (SA), B Mayfair, T Smith, C Stadler 290; S Lowery, L Mize, L Wadkins 291; S Appleby (Aus), J Haas, R Cochran, F Funk, R Goosen (SA), L Rinker 292; P Jacobsen, P-U Johansson (Swe), P Stankowski 293; C Franco (Para) 294; M Bradley, Y Kaneko (Jpn), L Nelson, C Rocca (It) 295; A Magee 296; P Jordan, K Sutherland 297.

1996 US PGA Championship *at Valhalla, Louisville, Kentucky*
(7144 yds, Par 72) Prize money: $2,400,000. Entries: 150, of whom 87 made the half-way cut.

Pos	Name	Score	Prize $	Pos	Name	Score	Prize $
1	M Brooks*	68-70-69-70—277	430000	17T	D Edwards	69-71-72-70—282	27285
2	K Perry	66-72-71-68—277	260000		J Furyk	70-70-73-69—282	27285
Brooks won play-off at extra hole					G Norman (Aus)	68-72-69-73—282	27285
3	S Elkington (Aus)	67-74-67-70—278	140000	24	E Aubrey	69-74-72-68—283	21500
	T Tolles	69-71-67-71—278	140000		M Jimenez (Sp)	71-71-71-70—283	21500
5	J Leonard	71-66-72-70—279	86666	26	F Funk	73-69-73-69—284	18000
	J Parnevik (Swe)	73-67-69-70—279	86666		M O'Meara	71-70-74-69—284	18000
	V Singh (Fij)	69-69-69-72—279	86666		C Pavin	71-74-70-69—284	18000
8	L Janzen	68-71-71-70—280	57500		C Strange	73-70-68-73—284	18000
	P-U Johansson (Swe)	73-72-66-69—280	57500		S Stricker	73-72-72-67—284	18000
	P Mickelson	67-67-74-72—280	57500	31	P Azinger	70-75-71-69—285	13000
	L Mize	71-70-69-70—280	57500		M Bradley	73-72-70-70—285	13000
	F Nobilo (NZ)	69-72-71-68—280	57500		P Burke	71-72-69-73—285	13000
	N Price (Zim)	68-71-69-72—280	57500		J Haas	72-71-69-73—285	13000
14	M Brisky	71-69-69-72—281	39000		T Herron	71-73-68-73—285	13000
	T Lehman	71-71-69-70—281	39000	36	M Calcavecchia	70-74-70-72—286	9050
	J Sindelar	73-72-69-67—281	39000		R Mediate	71-72-67-76—286	9050
17	B Faxon	72-68-73-69—282	27285		D Ogrin	75-70-68-73—286	9050
	T Watson	69-71-73-69—282	27285		I Woosnam (Wal)	68-72-75-71—286	9050
	D A Weibring	71-73-71-67—282	27285		F Zoeller	76-67-72-71—286	9050
	R Cochran	68-72-65-77—282	27285				

Other Totals: G Day, D Duval, G Morgan, J Morse 287; J Sluman, F Couples 287; P Blackmar, J Cook, S McCarron, P Stankowski, B Watts 288; J Adams, B Boyd, A Cejka (Ger), J Gallagher Jr, L Rinker, C Rocca (It), N Lancaster, B Mayfair, T Nakajima (Jpn) 289; E Els (SA), D Forsman, S Hoch, M Wiebe 290; N Faldo (Eng), W Grady (Aus), C Parry (Aus), W Wood 291; W Austin, B Crenshaw, N Henke, P Stewart 292; P Goydos, J Maggert 293; M Dawson 294; B Langer (Ger) 295; J Edwards 296; S Higashi (Jpn), S Ingraham 297; H Clark (Eng), J Reeves 298.

Players are of American nationality unless stated

1995 US PGA Championship at Riviera, Los Angeles
(6956 yds, Par 71) Prize money: $2,000,000. Entries: 150, of whom 72 made the half-way cut.

Pos	Name	Score	Prize $	Pos	Name	Score	Prize $
1	S Elkington (Aus)*	68-67-68-64—267	360000	20	G Norman (Aus)	66-69-70-72—277	21000
2	C Montgomerie (Sco)	68-67-67-65—267	216000		J Parnevik (Swe)	69-69-70-69—277	21000
*Elkington won at first play-off hole					D Waldorf	69-69-67-72—277	21000
3	E Els (SA)	66-65-66-72—269	116000	23	W Austin	70-70-70-68—278	15500
	J Maggert	66-69-65-69—269	116000		N Henke	68-73-67-70—278	15500
5	B Faxon	70-67-71-63—271	80000		P Jacobsen	69-67-71-71—278	15500
6	B Estes	69-68-68-68—273	68500		L Janzen	66-70-72-70—278	15500
	M O'Meara	64-67-69-73—273	68500		B Lietzke	73-68-67-70—278	15500
8	J Haas	69-71-64-70—274	50000		B Mayfair	68-68-72-70—278	15500
	J Leonard	68-66-70-70—274	50000		S Stricker	75-64-69-70—278	15500
	S Lowery	69-68-68-69—274	50000		S Torrance (Sco)	69-69-69-71—278	15500
	J Sluman	69-67-68-70—274	50000	31	P Azinger	70-70-72-67—279	8906
	C Stadler	71-66-66-71—274	50000		M Brooks	67-74-69-69—279	8906
13	J Furyk	68-70-69-68—275	33750		F Couples	70-69-74-66—279	8906
	MA Jimenez (Sp)	69-69-67-70—275	33750		N Faldo (Eng)	69-73-70-67—279	8906
	P Stewart	69-70-69-67—275	33750		G Morgan	66-73-74-66—279	8906
	K Triplett	71-69-68-67—275	33750		JM Olazábal (Sp)	72-66-70-71—279	8906
17	M Campbell (NZ)	71-65-71-69—276	26000		Joe Ozaki (Jpn)	71-70-65-73—279	8906
	C Rocca (It)	70-69-68-69—276	26000		DA Weibring	74-68-69-68—279	8906
	C Strange	72-68-68-68—276	26000				

Other Totals: L Clements, F Funk, A Lyle (Sco) 280; N Price (Zim), P Walton (Eng) 280; C Beck, B Crenshaw, J Gallagher Jr, G Sauers, P Senior (Aus) 281; J Adams, B Claar, R Freeman, Jumbo Ozaki (Jpn), K Perry 282; M Bradley, H Irwin, T Kite, S Simpson 283; E Dougherty, P-U Johansson (Swe), S Pate, L Roberts, T Watson 284; B Lane (Eng), M Sullivan, L Wadkins 285; D Pruitt 286; D Frost (SA), J Nicklaus 287; F Zoeller 288; B Kamm 289; C Byrum, W Defrancesco 291.

1994 US PGA Championship at Southern Hills, Tulsa, Oklahoma
(6834 yds, Par 70) Prize money: $1,750,000. Entries: 151, of whom 76 made the half-way cut.

Pos	Name	Score	Prize $	Pos	Name	Score	Prize $
1	N Price (Zim)	67-65-70-67—269	310000	19T	M McCumber	73-70-71-68—282	18666
2	C Pavin	70-67-69-69—275	160000		F Zoeller	69-71-72-70—282	18666
3	P Mickelson	68-71-67-70—276	110000		B Glasson	71-73-68-70—282	18666
4	N Faldo (Eng)	73-67-71-66—277	76666		C Strange	73-71-68-70—282	18666
	G Norman (Aus)	71-69-67-70—277	76666		C Parry (Aus)	70-69-70-73—282	18666
	J Cook	71-67-69-70—277	76666	25	B Lane (Eng)	70-73-68-72—283	13000
7	S Elkington (Aus)	73-70-66-69—278	57500		B Langer (Ger)	73-71-67-72—283	13000
7T	JM Olazábal (Sp)	72-66-70-70—278	57500		D Frost (SA)	71-69-70-73—283	13000
9	I Woosnam (Wal)	68-72-73-66—279	41000		E Els (SA)	68-71-69-75—283	13000
	T Kite	72-68-69-70—279	41000		J Sluman	70-72-66-75—283	13000
	T Watson	69-72-67-71—279	41000	30	B Faxon	72-73-73-66—284	8458
	L Roberts	69-72-67-71—279	41000		W Grady (Aus)	75-68-71-70—284	8458
	B Crenshaw	70-67-70-72—279	41000		B Boyd	72-71-70-71—284	8458
14	J Haas	71-66-68-75—280	32000		L Clements	74-70-69-71—284	8458
15	K Triplett	71-69-71-70—281	27000		S Torrance (Sco)	69-75-69-71—284	8458
	L Mize	72-72-67-70—281	27000		R Zokol (Can)	77-67-67-73—284	8458
	M McNulty (Zim)	72-68-70-71—281	27000	36	C Beck	72-70-72-71—285	7000
	G Day	70-69-70-72—281	27000		B McAllister	74-64-75-72—285	7000
19	C Stadler	70-70-74-68—282	18666		C Montgomerie (Sco)	67-76-70-72—285	7000

Other Totals: F Couples, B Mayfair, G Morgan, T Lehman, H Irwin 286; N Lancaster, D Edwards, D Gilford (Eng) 287; B Andrade, F Allem (SA), B Estes, A Magee, F Nobilo (NZ), G Kraft, J Ozaki (Jpn), DA Weibring 288; D Hart, F Funk, H Sutton, T Dolby, K Perry, M Springer 289; R Floyd, T Nakajima (Jpn), R McDougal, L Wadkins, B Fleisher 290; L Janzen, JD Blake, P Stewart, J Inman, T Smith 291; D Hammond, P Senior (Aus) 292; A Lyle (Sco), D Pride 297; B Henninger, H Meshiai (Jpn) 298.

Players are of American nationality unless stated

1993 US PGA Championship *at Inverness, Toledo, Ohio*
(6982 yds, Par 71) Prize money: $1,700,000. Entries: 151, of whom 74 made the half-way cut.

Pos	Name	Score	Prize $	Pos	Name	Score	Prize $
1	P Azinger*	69-66-69-68—272	300000	22	G Sauers	68-74-70-69—281	14500
2	G Norman (Aus)	68-68-67-69—272	155000		F Nobilo (NZ)	69-66-74-72—281	14500
	Azinger won at second play-off hole				L Janzen	70-68-71-72—281	14500
3	N Faldo (Eng)	68-68-69-68—273	105000		I Woosnam (Wal)	70-71-68-72—281	14500
4	V Singh (Fij)	68-63-73-70—274	90000		G Twiggs	70-69-70-72—281	14500
5	T Watson	69-65-70-72—276	75000		J McGovern	71-67-69-74—281	14500
6	S Hoch	74-68-68-67—277	47812	28	P Jacobsen	71-67-76-72—282	10166
	N Henke	72-70-67-68—277	47812		B Mayfair	68-73-70-71—282	10166
	P Mickelson	67-71-69-70—277	47812		L Roberts	67-67-77-68—282	10166
	J Cook	72-66-68-71—277	47812	31	M Calcavecchia	68-70-77-68—283	7057
	S Simpson	64-70-71-72—277	47812		M McCumber	67-72-75-69—283	7057
	D Hart	66-68-71-72—277	47812		D Love III	70-72-72-69—283	7057
	B Estes	69-66-69-73—277	47812		S Ingraham	74-69-71-69—283	7057
	H Irwin	68-69-67-73—277	47812		F Zoeller	72-70-71-70—283	7057
14	B Fleisher	69-74-67-68—278	25000		N Price (Zim)	74-66-72-71—283	7057
	R Zokol (Can)	66-71-71-70—278	25000		T Wargo	71-71-70-71—283	7057
	S Elkington (Aus)	67-66-74-71—278	25000		F Allem (SA)	70-71-70-72—283	7057
	G Hallberg	70-69-68-71—278	25000		M Hulbert	67-72-72-72—283	7057
	B Faxon	70-70-65-73—278	25000		H Sutton	69-69-73-72—283	7057
	L Wadkins	65-68-71-74—278	25000		C Parry (Aus)	70-73-68-72—283	7057
20	E Romero (Arg)	67-67-74-71—279	18500		F Couples	70-68-71-74—283	7057
	J Haas	69-68-70-72—279	18500		W Levi	69-73-66-75—283	7057

Other Totals: F Funk, DA Weibring, R Cochran, J Huston, D Forsman, P Stewart, J Ozaki (Jpn) 284; A Magee, J Daly, J Maggert, H Green, P Senior (Aus) 285; L Nelson, J M Olazábal (Sp), T Kite, R Fehr, A Lyle (Sco) 286; M Allen, J Sluman, B Crenshaw, D Hammond, M Standly 287; I Baker-Finch (Aus) 288; M Wiebe 289; B Ford, R Mediate 290; S Pate 292; K Burton, B Lane (Eng) 294; B Borowicz 295; J Adams 296.

1992 US PGA Championship *at Bellerive, St Louis, Missouri*
(7148 yds, Par 71) Prize money: $1,400,000. Entries: 151, of whom 85 made the half-way cut.

Pos	Name	Score	Prize $	Pos	Name	Score	Prize $
1	N Price (Zim)	70-70-68-70—278	280000	21	T Purtzer	72-72-74-70—288	14000
2	N Faldo (Eng)	68-70-76-67—281	101250		L Janzen	74-71-72-71—288	14000
	J Gallagher Jr	72-66-72-71—281	101250		B Britton	70-77-70-71—288	14000
	J Cook	71-72-67-71—281	101250		F Couples	69-73-73-73—288	14000
	G Sauers	67-69-70-75—281	101250		T Kite	73-73-69-73—288	14000
6	J Maggert	71-72-65-74—282	60000		T Nakajima (Jpn)	71-75-69-73—288	14000
7	R Cochran	69-69-76-69—283	52500		G Morgan	71-69-73-75—288	14000
	D Forsman	70-73-70-70—283	52500	28	N Ozaki (Jpn)	76-72-74-67—289	9000
9	D Waldorf	74-73-68-69—284	40000		M Hulbert	74-74-70-71—289	9000
	A Forsbrand (Swe)	73-71-70-70—284	40000		T Wargo	72-72-73-72—289	9000
	B Claar	68-73-73-70—284	40000		P Jacobsen	73-71-72-73—289	9000
12	J Sluman	73-71-72-69—285	30166		L Nelson	72-68-75-74—289	9000
	C Pavin	71-73-70-71—285	30166	33	B Fabel	72-76-74-68—290	7000
	B Andrade	72-71-70-72—285	30166		D Love III	77-71-70-72—290	7000
15	B Faxon	72-69-75-70—286	24000		B Fleisher	70-72-75-73—290	7000
	G Norman (Aus)	71-74-71-70—286	24000		F Nobilo (NZ)	69-74-74-73—290	7000
	M Brooks	71-72-68-75—286	24000		C Montgomerie (Sco)	72-76-69-73—290	7000
18	J Huston	73-75-71-68—287	19000		D Pruitt	73-70-73-74—290	7000
	R Fehr	74-73-71-69—287	19000		P Azinger	72-73-68-77—290	7000
	S Elkington (Aus)	74-70-71-72—287	19000				

Other Totals: D Edwards, M James, BR Brown, L Mize, F Allem (SA), B Langer (Ger), L Wadkins, R Mediate 291; P Senior (Aus), B Bryant, S Pate, M Calcavecchia, V Singh (Fij), C Stadler, S Richardson, R Floyd 292; J Sindelar, L Rinker 293; A Magee, K Clearwater, B Tway, G Hallberg 293; J Overton, B McCallister, J Haas, T Watson 294; J Kane, H Irwin, R Mackay 295; P Stewart, I Baker-Finch (Aus), D Peoples, T Schulz 296; B Lietzke, D Frost (SA), B Crenshaw 298; D Blake, B Estes, S Veriato 300; T Smith, R Gamez, S Gump 303; J Daly 304; H Perry 305; N Lancaster, K McDonald 307.

Players are of American nationality unless stated

1991 US PGA Championship *at Crooked Stick, Carmel, Indiana*

(7289 yds, Par 72) Prize money: $1,400,000. Entries: 151, of whom 77 made the half-way cut.

Pos	Name	Score	Prize $	Pos	Name	Score	Prize $
1	J Daly	69-67-69-71—276	230000	16T	N Faldo (Eng)	70-69-71-76—286	17000
2	B Lietzke	68-69-72-70—279	140000	23	M Hulbert	72-72-73-70—287	11500
3	J Gallagher Jr	70-72-72-67—281	95000		J Nicklaus	71-72-73-71—287	11500
4	K Knox	67-71-70-74—282	75000		C Beck	73-73-70-71—287	11500
5	S Richardson (Eng)	70-72-72-69—283	60000		S Ballesteros (Sp)	71-72-71-73—287	11500
	B Gilder	73-70-67-73—283	60000	27	L Roberts	72-74-72-70—288	8150
7	D Feherty (N.Ire)	71-74-71-68—284	38000		F Couples	74-67-76-71—288	8150
	R Floyd	69-74-72-69—284	38000		J Hallet	69-74-73-72—288	8150
	S Pate	70-75-70-69—284	38000		M McNulty (Zim)	75-71-69-73—288	8150
	H Sutton	74-67-72-71—284	38000		R Fehr	70-73-71-74—288	8150
	J Huston	70-72-70-72—284	38000	32	D Tewell	75-72-74-68—289	6000
	C Stadler	68-71-69-76—284	38000		M Calcavecchia	70-74-73-72—289	6000
13	J D Blake	75-70-72-68—285	24000		D Edwards	71-75-71-72—289	6000
	P Stewart	74-70-71-70—285	24000		S Elkington (Aus)	74-68-74-73—289	6000
	A Magee	69-73-68-75—285	24000		G Norman (Aus)	70-74-72-73—289	6000
16	H Twitty	70-71-75-70—286	17000		D Love III	72-72-72-73—289	6000
	W Levi	73-71-72-70—286	17000		T Purtzer	69-76-71-73—289	6000
	R Mediate	71-71-73-71—286	17000		C Pavin	72-73-71-73—289	6000
	G Morgan	70-71-74-71—286	17000		D Forsman	73-74-68-74—289	6000
	A Lyle (Sco)	68-75-71-72—286	17000		B Andrade	73-74-68-74—289	6000
	K Green	68-73-71-74—286	17000				

Other Totals: C Parry (Aus), S Hoch, L Wadkins, E Dougherty, W Grady (Aus) 290; K Clearwater, B Faxon, D Frost (SA), I Woosnam (Wal) 291; T Kite, E Romero (Arg), T Sieckmann, D Graham (Aus), M McCumber 292; B McCallister, L Miller, N Henke, F Funk 293; D Barr, J Sluman 294; B Wolcott, J Sindelar, G Sauers 295; S Williams, B Tway, D Pruitt, M Wiebe 296; D Peoples, D Hepler, L Nelson 297; P Blackmar, B R Brown, H Irwin, D Pooley 298; K Perry 300.

1990 US PGA Championship *at Shoal Creek, Birmingham, Alabama*

(7145 yds, Par 72) Prize money: $1,350,000. Entries: 152, of whom 74 made the half-way cut.

Pos	Name	Score	Prize $	Pos	Name	Score	Prize $
1	W Grady (Aus)	72-67-72-71—282	225000	19T	B McCallister	75-73-74-73—295	14000
2	F Couples	69-71-73-72—285	135000		G Norman (Aus)	77-69-76-73—295	14000
3	G Morgan	77-72-65-72—286	90000		M O'Meara	69-76-79-71—295	14000
4	B Britton	72-74-72-71—289	73500		T Watson	74-71-77-73—295	14000
5	C Beck	71-70-78-71—290	51666		M Wiebe	74-73-75-73—295	14000
	B Mayfair	70-71-75-74—290	51666	26	M Brooks	78-69-73-76—296	8650
	L Roberts	73-71-70-76—290	51666		P Jacobsen	74-75-71-76—296	8650
8	M McNulty (Zim)	74-72-75-71—292	34375		C Perry	75-74-72-75—296	8650
	D Pooley	75-74-71-72—292	34375		R Stewart	73-73-75-75—296	8650
	T Simpson	71-73-75-73—292	34375		B Tennyson	71-77-71-77—296	8650
	P Stewart	71-72-76-73—292	34375	31	P Azinger	76-70-74-77—297	6500
12	H Irwin	77-72-70-74—283	27000		B Crenshaw	74-70-78-75—297	6500
	L Mize	72-68-76-77—293	27000		D Frost (SA)	76-74-69-78—297	6500
14	B Andrade	75-72-74-73—294	20600		S Pate	71-75-71-80—297	6500
	M Hatalsky	73-78-71-72—294	20600		T Purtzer	74-74-77-72—297	6500
	JM Olazábal (Sp)	73-77-72-72—294	20600		D Rummells	73-73-77-74—297	6500
	C Pavin	73-75-72-74—294	20600		J Sluman	74-74-73-76—297	6500
	F Zoeller	72-71-76-75—294	20600		S Verplank	70-76-73-78—297	6500
19	B Boyd	74-74-71-76—295	14000		I Woosnam (Wal)	74-75-70-78—297	6500
	N Faldo (Eng)	71-75-80-69—295	14000				

Other Totals: I Aoki (Jpn), T Kite, D Love III, J Mahaffey, C Parry (Aus) 298; A Magee, S Rachels, M Reid, B Tway 299; S Hoch, M McCumber, K Perry, H Sutton, R Floyd, R Gamez, M Hulbert, S Utley 300; I Baker-Finch (Aus), B Gilder, J Huston, D Peoples, C Stadler 301; P Senior (Aus) 302; J Delsing, D Hammond, N Price (Zim) 303; D Graham (Aus), S Simpson, B Wadkins 304; J Blair, E Fiori, C Hungate, R Mediate, M Ozaki (Jpn) 305; B Ford 306.

Players are of American nationality unless stated

1989 US PGA Championship *at Kemper Lakes GC, Hawthorn, Illinois*
(7197 yds, Par 72) Prize money: $1,200,000. Entries: 150, of whom 70 made the half-way cut.

Pos	Name	Score	Prize $	Pos	Name	Score	Prize $
1	P Stewart	74-66-69-67—276	200000	17T	B McCallister	71-72-70-70—283	15000
2	A Bean	70-67-74-66—277	83333		L Mize	73-71-68-71—283	15000
	M Reid	66-67-70-74—277	83333		C Perry	67-70-70-76—283	15000
	C Strange	70-68-70-69—277	83333	24	T Armour	70-69-73-72—284	10000
5	D Rummells	68-69-69-72—278	45000		D Pohl	71-69-74-70—284	10000
6	I Woosnam (Wal)	68-70-70-71—279	40000		J Sluman	75-70-69-70—284	10000
7	S Hoch	69-69-69-73—280	36250	27	M Hulbert	70-71-72-72—285	7535
	C Stadler	71-64-72-73—280	36250		J Nicklaus	68-72-73-72—285	7535
9	N Faldo (Eng)	70-73-69-69—281	30000		H Twitty	72-71-68-74—285	7535
	E Fiori	70-67-75-69—281	30000		D Frost (SA)	70-74-69-72—285	7535
	T Watson	67-69-74-71—281	30000		P Jacobsen	70-70-73-72—285	7535
12	S Ballesteros (Sp)	72-70-66-74—282	21900		T Simpson	69-70-73-73—285	7535
	J Gallagher Jr	73-69-68-72—282	21900		B Tennyson	71-69-72-73—285	7535
	G Norman (Aus)	74-71-67-70—282	21900	34	I Baker-Finch (Aus)	74-68-70-74—286	5750
	M Sullivan	76-66-67-73—282	21900		C Beck	73-71-69-73—286	5750
	M Wiebe	71-70-69-72—282	21900		B Gilder	72-72-74-68—286	5750
17	I Aoki (Jpn)	72-71-65-75—283	15000		Tm Kite	67-73-72-74—286	5750
	B Crenshaw	68-72-72-71—283	15000		D Pooley	70-71-72-73—286	5750
	B Gardner	72-71-70-70—283	15000		L Roberts	69-71-72-74—286	5750
	D Love III	73-69-72-69—283	15000		L Thompson	66-69-73-78—286	5750

Other Totals: B Britton, D Edwards, S Elkington (Aus), B Lohr, S Pate, R Floyd, W Grady (Aus), B Lietzke, L Nelson, N Price (Zim), S Jones, K Perry, P Blackmar, T Purtzer, C Rose, S Simpson, D Tewell, B Bryant, A North, G Sauers, G Koch, B Langer (Ger), A Palmer, G Twiggs, M McCumber, H Green, J Mudd, D Stockton, R Black, C Byrum 307.

US PGA Championship History

Year	Winner	Runner-up	Venue	By
1916	J Barnes	J Hutchison	Siwanoy	1 hole
1919	J Barnes	F McLeod	Engineers' Club	6 and 5
1920	J Hutchison	D Edgar	Flossmoor	1 hole
1921	W Hagen	J Barnes	Inwood Club	3 and 2
1922	G Sarazen	E French	Oakmont	4 and 3
1923	G Sarazen	W Hagen	Pelham	38th hole
1924	W Hagen	J Barnes	French Lick	2 holes
1925	W Hagen	W Mehlhorn	Olympic Fields	6 and 4
1926	W Hagen	L Diegel	Salisbury	4 and 3
1927	W Hagen	J Turnesa	Dallas, TX	1 hole
1928	L Diegel	A Espinosa	Five Farms	6 and 5
1929	L Diegel	J Farrell	Hill Crest	6 and 4
1930	T Armour	G Sarazen	Fresh Meadow	1 hole
1931	T Creavy	D Shute	Wannamoisett	2 and 1
1932	O Dutra	F Walsh	St Paul, MN	4 and 3
1933	G Sarazen	W Goggin	Milwaukee	5 and 4
1934	P Runyan	C Wood	Buffalo	38th hole
1935	J Revolta	T Armour	Oklahoma	5 and 4
1936	D Shute	J Thomson	Pinehurst	3 and 2
1937	D Shute	H McSpaden	Pittsburgh	37th hole
1938	P Runyan	S Snead	Shawnee	8 and 7
1939	H Picard	B Nelson	Pomonok	37th hole
1940	B Nelson	S Snead	Hershey, PA	1 hole
1941	V Ghezzie	B Nelson	Denver, CO	38th hole
1942	S Snead	J Turnesa	Atlantic City, NJ	2 and 1
1943	*No Championship*			
1944	B Hamilton	B Nelson	Spokane, WA	1 hole
1945	B Nelson	S Byrd	Dayton, OH	4 and 3
1946	B Hogan	E Oliver	Portland	6 and 4
1947	J Ferrier	C Harbert	Detroit	2 and 1
1948	B Hogan	M Turnesa	Norwood Hills	7 and 6
1949	S Snead	J Palmer	Richmond, VA	3 and 2	*continued*

Players are of American nationality unless stated

United States PGA Championship History *continued*

Year	Winner	Runner-up	Venue	By
1950	C Harper	H Williams	Scioto, OH	4 and 3
1951	S Snead	W Burkemo	Oakmont, PA	7 and 6
1953	W Burkemo	F Lorza	Birmingham, MI	2 and 1
1954	C Harbert	W Burkemo	St Paul, MN	4 and 3
1955	D Ford	C Middlecoff	Detroit	4 and 3
1956	J Burke	T Kroll	Boston	3 and 2
1957	L Hebert	D Finsterwald	Miami Valley, Dayton	3 and 1

Changed to strokeplay

Year	Winner	Venue	Score	Year	Winner	Venue	Score
1958	D Finsterwald	Llanerch, PA	276	1979	D Graham (Aus)*	Oakland Hills, MI	272
1959	B Rosburg	Minneapolis, MN	277	1980	J Nicklaus	Oak Hill, NY	274
1960	J Hebert	Firestone, Akron, OH	281	1981	L Nelson	Atlanta, GA	273
1961	J Barber*	Olympia Fields, IL	277	1982	R Floyd	Southern Hills, OK	272
1962	G Player (SA)	Aronimink, PA	278	1983	H Sutton	Pacific Palisades, CA	274
1963	J Nicklaus	Dallas, TX	279	1984	L Trevino	Shoal Creek, AL	273
1964	B Nichols	Columbus, OH	271	1985	H Green	Cherry Hills, Denver, CO	278
1965	D Marr	Laurel Valley, PA	280	1986	R Tway	Inverness, Toledo, OH	276
1966	A Geiberger	Firestone, Akron, OH	280	1987	L Nelson*	PGA National, FL	287
1967	D January*	Columbine, CO	281	1988	J Sluman	Oaktree, OK	272
1968	J Boros	Pecan Valley, TX	281	1989	P Stewart	Kemper Lakes, IL	276
1969	R Floyd	Dayton, OH	276	1990	W Grady (Aus)	Shoal Creek, AL	282
1970	D Stockton	Southern Hills, OK	279	1991	J Daly	Crooked Stick, IN	276
1971	J Nicklaus	PGA National, FL	281	1992	N Price (Zim)	Bellerive, MS	278
1972	G Player (SA)	Oakland Hills, MI	281	1993	P Azinger*	Inverness, Toledo, OH	272
1973	J Nicklaus	Canterbury, OH	277	1994	N Price (Zim)	Southern Hills, OK	269
1974	L Trevino	Tanglewood, NC	276	1995	S Elkington (Aus)*	Riviera, LA	267
1975	J Nicklaus	Firestone, Akron, OH	276	1996	M Brooks*	Valhalla, Kentucky	277
1976	D Stockton	Congressional, MD	281	1997	D Love III	Winged Foot, NY	269
1977	L Wadkins*	Pebble Beach, CA	287	1998	V Singh (Fij)	Sahalee, Seattle, WA	271
1978	J Mahaffey*	Oakmont, PA	276				

* *Winner after play-off*

Players are of American nationality unless stated

Men's Major Title Table

Jack Nicklaus  *Bobby Jones*  *Walter Hagen*

	US Open	British Open	PGA	Masters	US Amateur	British Amateur	Total Titles
Jack Nicklaus	4	3	5	6	2	0	20
Bobby Jones	4	3	0	0	5	1	13
Walter Hagen	2	4	5	0	0	0	11
John Ball	0	1	0	0	0	8	9
Ben Hogan	4	1	2	2	0	0	9
Gary Player	1	3	2	3	0	0	9
Arnold Palmer	1	2	0	4	1	0	8
Tom Watson	1	5	0	2	0	0	8
Harold Hilton	0	2	0	0	1	4	7
Gene Sarazen	2	1	3	1	0	0	7
Sam Snead	0	1	3	3	0	0	7
Harry Vardon	1	6	0	0	0	0	7
Lee Trevino	2	2	2	0	0	0	6
Nick Faldo	0	3	0	3	0	0	6

All photographs © Phil Sheldon

Weetabix Women's British Open Championship

1998 Weetabix Ladies' British Open Championship

at Royal Lytham & St Annes (6355 yds, Par 72) Prize money: £575,000

Pos	Name	Score	Prize Money £
1	S Steinhauer	81-72-70-69—292	100000
2	S Gustafson	78-71-74-70—293	50000
	B Burton	71-74-77-71—293	50000
4	J Moodie	75-72-72-75—294	30000
5	K Webb	76-76-71-73—296	25000
6	L Spalding	76-70-75-76—297	17000
	W Ward	76-71-74-76—297	17000
	S Mehra	73-77-71-76—297	17000
	B King	71-77-72-77—297	17000
10	C Nilsmark	77-77-69-75—298	12000
11	T Johnson	72-77-77-73—299	9687
	J Inkster	75-75-76-73—299	9687
	A Sorenstam	75-73-77-74—299	9687
	ML de Lorenzi	79-70-76-74—299	9687
15	M McKay	75-74-75-76—300	8000
16	M Murray	81-76-69-75—301	7300
	D Reid	73-79-73-76—301	7300
	H Wadsworth	79-74-72-76—301	7300
19	H Kobayashi	77-74-75-76—302	6800
20	M Hjorth	82-73-76-72—303	6300
	K Tschetter	79-75-73-76—303	6300
	J Gallacher-Smith	76-74-74-79—303	6300
	K Marshall	79-74-71-79—303	6300
24	D Andrews	81-72-76-75—304	5600
	J Morley	79-74-74-77—304	5600
	P Hurst	76-77-70-81—304	5600
27	C Johnstone-Forbes	78-76-79-72—305	5100
	S Strudwick	75-72-75-83—305	5100
29	C Koch	79-74-76-77—306	4700
	K Saiki	80-76-73-77—306	4700
31	C McCurdy	80-77-75-75—307	4216
	F Dassu	82-72-77-76—307	4216
	A Nicholas	79-72-76-80—307	4216
34	L Fairclough	77-77-78-76—308	3300
	SR Pak	78-74-79-77—308	3300
	W Doolan	83-72-76-77—308	3300
	L Baugh	77-80-74-77—308	3300
	C Dibnah	77-80-74-77—308	3300
	H Dobson	80-71-79-78—308	3300
	C McMillan	76-78-76-78—308	3300
	C Figg-Currier	78-78-74-78—308	3300
	V Odegard	82-73-74-79—308	3300
43	E Klein	82-75-76-76—309	2362
	C Sorenstam	81-76-76-76—309	2362

Women's British Open Championship

Pos	Name	Score	Prize Money £
43T	R Carriedo	80-77-74-78—309	2362
	S Lowe	77-79-72-81—309	2362
47	S Dallongeville	80-76-74-80—310	2050
	L Philo	80-73-74-83—310	2050
49	A Munt	81-71-83-76—311	1808
	C Hall	75-81-77-78—311	1808
	T Fischer	78-73-80-80—311	1808
52	K Pearce	79-77-79-77—312	1500
	L Kane	85-75-78-77—312	1500
	B Whitehead	80-75-79-78—312	1500
	J Forbes	81-76-76-79—312	1500
	D Barnard	79-76-75-82—312	1500
57	I Tinning	80-74-84-75—313	1275
	L Neumann	79-78-74-82—313	1275
59	L Maritz	80-76-80-78—314	1165
	T Barrett	77-79-77-81—314	1165
	H Stacy	82-74-77-81—314	1165
62	R Hakkerainen	75-79-81-81—316	1077
	A Berg	76-81-78-81—316	1077
64	M Hirase	78-77-79-83—317	1025
65	C Johnson	79-74-80-85—318	1000
66	M Spencer-Devlin	82-72-78-87—319	800
67	E Knuth	77-75-85-84—321	800

The following players missed the cut:

68	R Hetherington	84-74—158	95T	L Bemvenuti	80-80—160
	AM Knight	82-76—158		M Burstrom	78-82—160
	K Lunn	82-76—158	104	P Wright	83-78—161
	J Crafter	82-76—158		A Takasu	81-80—161
	A Gottmo	81-77—158		J Lidback	81-80—161
	M McGuire	81-77—158		J Mills	80-81—161
	F Muraguchi	80-78—158		C Louw	79-82—161
	E Esteri	80-78—158	109	J Piers	82-80—162
	L Navarro	80-78—158		K Tebbet	81-81—162
	N Noro	79-79—158		S Waugh	80-82—162
	L Davies	79-79—158	112	L Brooky	85-78—163
	C Flom	79-79—158		M Hedblom	85-78—163
	L Hackney	79-79—158		V Skinner	85-78—163
	F Pike	78-80—158		G Graham	83-80—163
82	S Croce	85-74—159		H Daly-Donofrio	81-82—163
	W Dicks	83-76—159		M Lojdahl	81-82—163
	J Stephenson	82-77—159	118	C Schmitt	87-77—164
	N Murray	81-78—159		X Wunsch	80-84—164
	L Lambert	81-78—159		P Gonzalez Aguirre	80-84—164
	K Robbins	81-78—159	121	N Moult	85-80—165
	H Alfredsson	80-79—159		B Pestana	85-80—165
	S Head	80-79—159		P Grice Whittaker	84-81—165
	K Taylor	80-79—159	124	MJ Rouleau	88-78—166
	C Matthew	79-80—159		K Orum	87-79—166
	D Eggeling	78-81—159		K Poppmeier	84-82—166
	S Farron	77-82—159		S Mendiburu	80-86—166
	M Lunn	76-83—159	128	E Aron-Quelhas	88-79—167
95	S Prosser	83-77—160		R Lautens	84-83—167
	S Cavalleri	83-77—160		N Scranton	84-83—167
	M Estill	82-78—160	131	K Margrethe Juul (Am)	85-84—169
	D Ammaccapane	82-78—160		C Kerr	84-85—169
	P Meunier Lebouc	81-79—160	133	K Albers	92-78—170
	S Dickens	81-79—160	134	D Booker	87-86—173
	K Higo	81-79—160			

1997 Women's British Open Championship
at Sunningdale (6255 yds, Par 72) Prize money: £525,000

Pos	Name	Score	Prize £	Pos	Name	Score	Prize £
1	K Webb	65-70-63-71—269	82500	19T	C Dibnah	72-71-70-73—286	5837
2	R Jones	70-70-66-71—277	52000		A Dibos	71-72-70-73—286	5837
3	A Sorenstam	72-70-69-67—278	36750	23	L Davies	74-73-69-71—287	5300
4	B Burton	73-69-71-67—280	27000		R Hetherington	75-70-71-71—287	5300
5	L Hackney	74-69-67-71—281	20000		K Tschetter	73-70-72-72—287	5300
	C Matthew	70-70-70-71—281	20000	26	E Klein	69-74-70-75—288	5000
7	W Doolan	74-70-68-70—282	14000	27	S Farron	72-75-75-67—289	4475
	T Barrett	70-72-70-70—282	14000		B Whitehead	71-74-77-67—289	4475
9	C Johnson	71-71-73-68—283	11500		J Morley	75-69-76-69—289	4475
10	C Sorenstam	71-70-72-71—284	10100		L Brooky	72-73-72-72—289	4475
	B King	71-72-68-73—284	10100		H Alfredsson	69-76-72-72—289	4475
12	J Lidback	71-74-70-70—285	7414		J Moodie	74-71-71-73—289	4475
	M Hirase	76-65-74-70—285	7414	33	K Lunn	74-71-75-70—290	3875
	L Neumann	68-75-71-71—285	7414		P Hurst	76-72-70-72—290	3875
	J Inkster	69-71-73-72—285	7414		S Cavalleri (Am)	70-73-73-74—290	
	B Mucha	72-67-73-73—285	7414	36	S Maynor	72-74-74-71—291	3650
	H Dobson	73-69-69-74—285	7414	37	S Strudwick	72-74-74-72—292	3350
	K Marshall	70-68-73-74—285	7414		D Richard	71-72-75-74—292	3350
19	C Hj Koch	76-71-71-68—286	5837		G Graham	73-73-71-75—292	3350
	L Lambert	70-73-73-70—286	5837				

Other players who made the cut: M Estill, S Steinhauer, K Parker-Gregory 293; P Meunier Lebouc, A Gottmo, S Prosser, A Fruhwirth, S Waugh 294; M Spencer-Devlin, H Kobayashi, F Dassu 295; T Green, A Yamaoka, T Johnson, E Esterl (Am) 296; S Croce, C Pierce, J Lee, W Dicks 297; M Koch, K Taylor, H Wadsworth, L Fairclough, L Kane, M Murray 298; C Figg-Currier 299; N Moult, D Barnard, S Gustafson 301; S Dallongeville 302.

1996 Women's British Open Championship
at Woburn G&CC, Milton Keynes (6309 yds, Par 73) Prize money: £500,000

Pos	Name	Score	Prize £	Pos	Name	Score	Prize £
1	E Klein	68-66-71-72—277	80000	19T	K Yamazaki	71-70-74-73—288	5675
2	P Hammel	71-70-72-71—284	42500		H Alfredsson	69-76-69-74—288	5675
	A Alcott	72-70-70-72—284	42500		J Lidback	68-73-73-74—288	5675
4	J Geddes	72-73-70-70—285	20416	25	J Morley	72-71-74-72—289	4850
	L Hackney	71-69-73-72—285	20416		K Marshall	71-72-73-73—289	4850
	A Nicholas	68-71-74-72—285	20416		T Abitbol	70-75-70-74—289	4850
7	B Whitehead	76-70-71-69—286	9571		T Barrett	71-74-69-75—289	4850
	D Richard	71-73-71-71—286	9571		M Hjorth	70-70-71-78—289	4850
	ML de Lorenzi	74-72-68-72—286	9571	30	S Gronberg-Whitmore	75-73-71-71—290	4100
	P Bradley	70-75-69-72—286	9571		A Fukushima	74-74-69-73—290	4100
	C Johnson	72-69-73-72—286	9571		C Sorenstam	76-70-71-73—290	4100
	R Jones	69-71-73-73—286	9571		V Goetze	74-70-72-74—290	4100
	T Kerdyk	70-70-72-74—286	9571		J Piers	68-73-72-77—290	4100
14	B Mucha	73-71-74-69—287	6600	35	B Daniel	77-71-71-72—291	3300
	D Eggeling	69-77-71-70—287	6600		C Matthew	71-73-75-72—291	3300
	C Nilsmark	72-76-68-71—287	6600		S Maynor	73-73-71-74—291	3300
	K Webb	69-70-74-74—287	6600		T Fischer	72-71-74-74—291	3300
	A Sorenstam	69-70-73-75—287	6600		D Pepper	71-72-72-76—291	3300
19	D Andrews	80-65-74-69—288	5675		W Doolan	72-74-67-78—291	3300
	L Davies	72-75-71-70—288	5675				
	D Reid	68-74-74-72—288	5675				

Other players who made the cut: H Kobayashi, T Hanson, M Hirase 292; E Knuth, K Parker-Gregory 293; M Mallon, S Strudwick, L Brooky, S Croce, E Orley, L Navarro 294; A-M Knight, P Sterner, S Redman, C Dibnah, P Rigby-Jinglov, M Figueras-Dotti, M Berteotti, C Figg-Currier 295; R Hetherington, J Crafter, B Hackett (Am) 296; R Carriedo, J Forbes, X Wunsch-Ruiz, M Estill 297; S Farwig, J Mcgill, C Hj Koch 298; N Harvey 300; K Weiss 302; M Sutton, K Harada 303.

1995 Women's British Open Championship
at Woburn G&CC, Milton Keynes (6257 yds, Par 73) Prize money: £360,000

Pos	Name	Score	Prize £	Pos	Name	Score	Prize £
1	K Webb	69-70-69-70—278	60000	19T	A Gottmo	70-73-74-74—291	4032
2	J McGill	71-73-71-69—284	30000		B Burton	72-70-74-75—291	4032
	A Sorenstam	70-72-71-71—284	30000	23	R Hetherington	74-76-76-66—292	3710
4	M Berteotti	73-71-71-70—285	14333		J Morley	72-72-74-74—292	3710
	C Pierce	70-70-72-73—285	14333		E Orley	71-73-74-74—292	3710
	V Skinner	74-68-67-76—285	14333	26	V Michaud	76-73-75-69—293	3215
7	S Strudwick	73-68-71-74—286	9500		A Nicholas	73-72-76-72—293	3215
8	ML de Lorenzi	68-74-73-73—288	6937		S Dallongeville	76-72-72-73—293	3215
	W Doolan	73-71-70-74—288	6937		M McGuire	68-78-73-74—293	3215
	N Lopez	71-73-70-74—288	6937		T Fischer	76-66-77-74—293	3215
	L Neumann	67-74-71-76—288	6937		L Hackney	74-74-70-75—293	3215
12	K Tschetter	73-75-74-67—289	4957		L Fairclough	76-68-72-77—293	3215
	C Matthew	74-71-73-71—289	4957		M Lunn	73-67-73-80—293	3215
	V Goetze	73-72-71-73—289	4957	34	M McNamara	76-73-74-71—294	2585
	P Meunier	73-71-71-74—289	4957		T Johnson	75-74-74-71—294	2585
16	J Forbes	69-73-77-71—290	4430		Li Wen-Lin	74-71-75-74—294	2585
	S Prosser	70-74-74-72—290	4430		L West	73-75-71-75—294	2585
	H Kobayashi	72-70-74-74—290	4430		S Waugh	68-75-72-79—294	2585
19	L Brooky	69-74-76-72—291	4032		S Croce	71-71-73-79—294	2585
	K Pearce	74-71-74-72—291	4032				

Other players who made the cut: D Barnard, C Hall, T Hanson, C Hjalmarsson, P Hammel 296; L Davies, LA Mills, S Burnell, P Wright, W Dicks, E Klein, K Peterson-Parker 297; C Duffy, E Knuth 298; A Brighouse, K Orum, J Geddes 298; A Rogers, K Marshall, L Weima, C Eliasson-Wharton, S Gr-Whitmore 299; A Arruti, A Shapcott, T Barrett, K Davies 300; G Stewart, L Dermott (Am) 301; S Moon, D Reid 302; J Soulsby, P Sterner 303; H Hopkins, C Evelyn Louw 304; K Stupples (Am) 305; N Buxton 307.

1994 Women's British Open Championship
at Woburn G&CC, Milton Keynes (6224 yds, Par 73) Prize money: £335,000

Pos	Name	Score	Prize £	Pos	Name	Score	Prize £
1	L Neumann	71-67-70-72—280	52500	17T	E Knuth	78-69-72-73—292	4100
2	D Mochrie	73-66-74-70—283	27250	21	P Wright	68-75-78-72—293	3740
	A Sorenstam	69-75-69-70—283	27250		K Pearce	70-74-75-74—293	3740
4	L Davies	74-66-73-71—284	14625		K Tschetter	68-76-75-74—293	3740
	C Dibnah	75-70-67-72—284	14625	24	K Cockerill	71-77-73-73—294	3425
6	C Figg-Whittaker	69-74-68-74—285	10750		A Alcott	74-74-75-71—294	3425
7	H Alfredsson	71-76-71-68—286	9250		B King	73-74-69-78—294	3425
8	T Hanson	74-73-66-74—287	8000		A Ritzman	69-76-75-74—294	3425
9	S Strudwick	71-71-75-71—288	6250	28	S Moon	72-78-74-71—295	2930
	V Skinner	77-71-66-74—288	6250		A Nicholas	72-73-70-80—295	2930
	C Pierce	70-75-71-72—288	6250		D Reid	76-72-75-72—295	2930
12	H Kobayashi	73-75-69-74—289	5100		M Lunn	73-75-75-72—295	2930
13	S Gautrey	69-74-72-75—290	4800		K Marshall	76-72-75-72—295	2930
14	T Abitbol	76-68-75-72—291	4526		L Fairclough	75-72-72-76—295	2930
	P Grice-Whittaker	77-72-70-72—291	4526		S Redman	74-71-76-74—295	2930
	M McGuire	71-73-78-69—291	4526	35	T Johnson	75-75-72-74—296	2480
17	S Gronberg-Whitmore	71-69-74-78—292	4100		E Orley	73-76-74-73—296	2480
	Li Wen-Lin	73-70-73-76—292	4100		K Albers	75-67-78-76—296	2480
	J Gedes	74-72-72-74—292	4100				

Other players who made the cut: LA Mills, H Person, C Hall, L Navarro, L West 297; T Barrett 298; M Figueras-Dotti, K Orum, W Doolan, T Fischer (Am), J Forbes 299; ML de Lorenzi, C Hjalmarsson, I Maconi 300; X Wunsch-Ruiz, LR Sugg, K Noble 301; F Dassu, M De Boer, G Steward, F Descampe, C Nilsmark, S Prosser, M Spencer-Devlin, S Waugh, H Wadsworth, S Mendiburu, S Robinson 302; N Scranton 303; D Barnard, L Hackney, E Crosby 304; M Hageman 306; B New, M Burstrom, N Moult, M Lawrence Wengler 307; J Lawrence, S Gustafson 309.

1993 Women's British Open Championship
at Woburn G&CC, Milton Keynes (6224 yds, Par 73) Prize money: £300,000

Pos	Name	Score	Prize £	Pos	Name	Score	Prize £
1	K Lunn	71-69-68-67—275	50000	21	J Soulsby	76-75-73-72—296	3685
2	B Burton	75-70-68-70—283	32000		C Figg-Currier	75-75-72-74—296	3685
3	K Marshall	73-71-69-73—286	21000	23	G Stewart	74-75-76-72—297	3505
4	L Wen-Lin	70-71-74-72—287	14350		P Meunier (Am)	73-76-77-71—297	
	J Geddes	76-75-72-64—287	14350		J Morley (Am)	77-74-74-72—297	
6	P Sheehan	75-70-72-72—289	10500		V Michaud	79-73-70-75—297	3505
7	L Davies	69-76-75-70—290	7300	27	T Abitbol	77-74-74-73—298	3145
	ML de Lorenzi	73-77-72-68—290	7300		F Dassu	70-75-75-78—298	3145
	S Strudwick	72-71-73-74—290	7300		X Wunsch-Ruiz	73-79-71-75—298	3145
	C Nilsmark	76-71-74-69—290	7300		D Hanna	74-73-73-78—298	3145
11	A Nicholas	74-73-70-74—291	5400		K Cathrein	74-76-73-75—298	3145
12	T Johnson	72-75-77-69—293	4670		A Gottmo	77-70-74-77—298	3145
	D Reid	76-75-74-68—293	4670		N Buxton (Am)	74-74-74-76—298	
	C Hjalmarsson	77-74-68-74—293	4670	34	L Neumann	74-72-80-73—299	2740
	H Alfredsson	77-71-74-71—293	4670		S Waugh	77-75-74-73—299	2740
16	S Gronberg-Whitmore	76-70-79-69—294	4180		C Hall	75-71-75-78—299	2740
	K Orum	75-72-73-74—294	4180	37	K Espinasse	77-74-74-75—300	2470
	S Gautrey	76-75-69-74—294	4180		F Descampe	75-77-74-74—300	2470
19	C Duffy	75-76-71-73—295	3880		A-C Jonasson (Am)	72-74-78-76—300	
	R Hast	77-71-72-75—295	3880		L Cowan	74-77-75-74—300	2470

Other players who made the cut: C Dibnah, K Weiss, S Dallongeville (Am) 301; S Moon, D Patterson, C Lambert (Am) 302; C Soules 303; L Brooky (Am), V Palli 304; R Lautens, S Van Wyk, MG Estuesta, S Burnell (Am), T Loveys, S Bennett 305; M Sutton (Am), H Wadsworth 306; K Leadbetter 307; D Barnard, C Sorenstam (Am) 309; D Petrizzi 310; M Hageman 311.

1992 Women's British Open Championship
at Woburn G&CC, Milton Keynes (6224 yds, Par 73) Prize money: £300,000

Pos	Name	Score	Prize £	Pos	Name	Score	Prize £
1	P Sheehan	68-72-67—207	50000	20	T Abitbol	72-71-78—221	3550
2	C Dibnah	70-69-71—210	32000		F Dassu	73-77-71—221	3550
3	ML de Lorenzi	71-71-70—212	21000		T Johnson	73-73-75—221	3550
4	L Neumann	69-74-70—213	16000		Li Wen-Lin	74-70-77—221	3550
5	P Rizzo	72-70-72—214	11600		C Hjalmarsson	74-75-72—221	3550
	H Alfredsson	74-72-68—214	11600		C Figg-Currier	71-77-73—221	3550
7	D Mochrie	74-68-73—215	9000		K Marshall	74-73-74—221	3550
8	J Arnold	70-74-72—216	6120	27	C Soules	78-73-71—222	3100
	S Strudwick	75-72-69—216	6120		D Petrizzi	76-72-74—222	3100
	F Descampe	71-73-72—216	6120		S Croce	79-73-70—222	3100
	M Burstrom	72-73-71—216	6120	30	A Shapcott	74-75-74—223	2830
	E Orley	70-75-71—216	6120		L Sugg	76-71-76—223	2830
13	K Davies	75-70-73—218	4560		S Robinson	75-76-72—223	2830
	P Wright	73-76-69—218	4560	33	G Stewart	76-75-73—224	2425
	K Parker	72-74-72—218	4560		K Cornelius	73-77-74—224	2425
16	J Geddes	78-69-72—219	4300		K Lasken	76-74-74—224	2425
17	D Reid	73-73-74—220	4060		LA Mills	74-76-74—224	2425
	A Dibos	75-75-70—220	4060		J Sevil	74-75-75—224	2425
	V Michaud	71-76-73—220	4060		L Hackney	74-74-76—224	2425

Other players who made the cut: L Davies, L Maritz-Atkins, A Nicholas, A Fukushima (Am), H Wadsworth 225; K Douglas, P Smillie, M Lunn, N Hall, S Rule, C Savy, M Hageman 226; C Duffy, S Gronberg, C Nilsmark, K Pearce 227; D Dowling, E Farquharson 228; R Comstock, L Fairclough 229; K Orum 230; S Mendiburu 231; V Marvin 232; J Poseter 235.

1991 Women's British Open Championship
at Woburn G&CC, Milton Keynes (6224 yds, Par 73) Prize money: £150,000

Pos	Name	Score	Prize £	Pos	Name	Score	Prize £
1	P Grice-Whittaker	69-69-77-69—284	25000	20T	K Pearce	76-70-74-75—295	1887
2	D Barnard	73-72-71-71—287	13250	22	K Espinasse	76-75-73-72—296	1752
	H Alfredsson	73-69-76-69—287	13250		P Gonzalez	73-79-72-72—296	1752
4	L Davies	71-74-71-72—288	7175		K Gregg	71-75-74-76—296	1752
	S Croce	75-74-70-69—288	7175		A Fukushima (Am)	73-73-78-72—296	
6	H Wadsworth	68-75-72-74—289	5250		L Fairclough	72-78-77-69—296	1752
7	ML de Lorenzi	73-70-76-71—290	3650	27	D Dowling	72-78-76-71—297	1572
	T Johnson	71-72-76-71—290	3650		D Hutton	72-77-77-71—297	1572
	K Parker	73-69-75-73—290	3650		B New	73-76-75-73—297	1572
	E Orley	75-71-72-72—290	3650		S Prosser	73-77-76-71—297	1572
11	A Nicholas	75-73-70-73—291	2516	31	J Hill	72-74-76-76—298	1392
	K Markette	72-69-77-73—291	2516		L Neumann	79-72-74-73—298	1392
	J Forbes	74-73-71-73—291	2516		N Hall	76-76-71-75—298	1392
14	K Douglas	73-75-71-73—292	2280		M Wooding	72-74-78-74—298	1392
15	R Comstock	71-75-76-71—293	2120	35	L Maritz-Atkins	77-71-77-74—299	1235
	C Soules	74-77-72-70—293	2120		T Luckhurst	76-75-76-72—299	1235
	J Larsen	77-72-72-72—293	2120		L Hackney	73-72-73-81—299	1235
	J Stephenson	74-73-71-75—293	2120	38	C Baker	73-73-79-75—300	1122
19	S Strudwick	69-75-74-76—294	1970		M Spencer-Devlin	72-77-78-73—300	1122
20	F Dassu	73-70-75-77—295	1887		J Hall (Am)	76-76-74-74—300	

Other players who made the cut: T Abitbol, P Smillie, X Wunsch-Ruiz 301; R Bell, P Conley, K Lunn, J Soulsby, D Baldwin 302; S Moon 303; D Clum, J Furby, N Ste-Marie, S Morgan (Am) 304; A Sheard, F Martin 305; E Dahilof 306; R Lautens, S Robinson 307; K Leadbetter, M Walker, C Louw 308; J Germs 310.

1990 Women's British Open Championship
at Woburn G&CC, Milton Keynes (6224 yds, Par 73) Prize money: £130,000

Pos	Name	Score	Prize£	Pos	Name	Score	Prize £
1	H Alfredsson*	70-71-74-73—288	20000	18T	S Strudwick	79-71-71-78—299	1712
2	J Hill	77-74-69-68—288	13200	22	J Connachan	74-75-76-74—300	1570
Alfredsson won at sudden-death play-off				D Hutton	77-76-74-73—300	1570
3	L Davies	75-73-73-70—291	7393		T Luckhurst	74-72-76-78—300	1570
	K Douglas	69-71-75-76—291	7353	25	T Abitbol	74-75-75-77—301	1430
	D Lofland	73-70-75-73—291	7353		D Reid	76-70-77-78—301	1430
6	ML de Lorenzi	72-70-72-79—293	4130		M Sugimoto	76-74-79-72—301	1430
	T Johnson	71-74-73-75—293	4130		T Craik	76-76-75-74—301	1430
	M Blackwelder	73-70-78-72—293	4130	29	A Sheard	72-80-77-73—302	1270
9	D Barnard	75-70-73-76—294	2750		G Stewart	74-73-77-70—302	1270
	A Nicholas	75-75-68-76—294	2750		X Wunsch-Ruiz	72-78-75-77—302	1270
11	P Sinn	70-74-77-74—295	2390		S Shapcott	72-75-76-79—302	1270
12	A Shapcott	73-74-73-76—296	2230		S Bennett (Am)	75-77-78-72—302	
13	C Duffy	76-74-74-73—297	2013	34	S Gronberg	74-78-77-47—303	1150
	Li Wen-Lin	73-69-76-79—297	2013		L Maritz	71-76-76-80—303	1150
	M Estill	77-70-76-74—297	2013	36	K Lasken	74-77-74-79—304	1070
16	T Fernando	74-73-74-72—298	1855		LA Mills	74-75-74-81—304	1070
	A Dibos	76-73-72-77—298	1855	38	J Forbes	80-72-74-79—305	1010
18	J Arnold	79-73-74-73—299	1712		L Fairclough (Am)	73-78-79-75—305	
	C Dibnah	71-81-74-73—299	1712				
	B Huke	76-76-74-73—299	1712				

Other players who made the cut: R Hast, N Lowien, H Andersson, E Dahlof 306; P Grice-Whittaker, C Panton, M Spencer-Devlin, S Morgan (Am) 308; C Mah-Lyford, R Gawthrop, C Scholefield 309; N Kessler 311; M Burton, J Lawrence, A Munt 313; J Morley (Am), J Brown (Am) 314; Julia Hill 315; R Lautens 318; S Moor 324.

1989 Women's British Open Championship

at Ferndown GC, Dorset (5975 yds, Par 73)   Prize money: £120,000

Pos	Name	Score	Prize £	Pos	Name	Score	Prize £
1	J Geddes	67-67-72-68—274	18000	21	T Johnson	72-75-69-73—289	1560
2	F Descampe	73-66-70-67—276	12340		S Strudwick	70-74-69-75—289	1560
3	ML Taya	68-71-67-72—278	8880		K Davies	73-70-72-74—289	1560
4	P Rizzo	71-69-68-71—279	6480	24	N Lowien	71-70-79-70—290	1440
	M Spencer-Devlin	72-69-67-71—279	6480	25	J Connachan	72-75-69-75—291	1290
6	P Conley	70-67-76-67—280	4860		F Dassu	74-72-73-72—291	1290
7	X Wunsch-Ruiz	69-73-72-67—281	4140		S Moon	75-71-77-68—291	1290
8	K Douglas	71-70-71-70—282	3540		A Munt	73-70-73-75—291	1290
9	A Dibos	67-75-72-69—283	3060	29	M Jones	74-75-70-73—292	1110
10	R Bell	71-68-74-72—285	2480		L Neumann	71-72-75-74—292	1110
	M Figueras-Dotti	69-71-72-73—285	2480	31	C Dibnah	69-73-78-73—293	936
	H Alfredsson	73-70-69-73—285	2480		K Espinasse	73-74-71-75—293	936
13	L Maritz	67-74-71-74—286	2160		J Hill	73-77-74-69—293	936
14	L Davis	75-71-69-71—287	1924		J Stratham	72-76-73-72—293	936
	R Hast	73-71-73-70—287	1924		D Kortgaard	72-76-68-77—293	936
	A Nicholas	71-69-71-76—287	1924	36	D Pavish	74-71-74-75—294	750
	M McNamara	73-70-72-72—287	1924		C Soules	72-74-72-75—294	750
	C Scholefield	75-72-71-69—287	1924		D Petrizzi	74-74-71-75—294	750
19	D Dowling	69-76-72-71—288	1710		K Cornelius	73-77-73-71—294	750
	J Furby	71-72-70-75—288	1710		J Morley (Am)	72-75-74-73—294	

Other players who made the cut: J Brown, K Lunn, C Panton, S Little 295; J Arnold, J Howard, G Stewart, A Jones 296; M Thomson, L Fairclough (Am) 297; R Lautens, J Ralls, S Robinson (Am) 298; R Comstock, M Garner, S Gronberg, L Percival, D Reid, K Ericson 299; T Abitbol, C Griffiths, J Rumsey 301; T Hammond, C Waite, T Craik, S Bennett (Am) 302; K Clark 304; M Burton, J Greco, Li Wen-Lin 305.

WOMEN'S BRITISH OPEN HISTORY

Year	Winner	Country	Venue	Score
1976	J Lee Smith	England	Fulford	299
1977	V Saunders	England	Lindrick	306
1978	J Melville	England	Foxhills	310
1979	A Sheard	South Africa	Southport and Ainsdale	301
1980	D Massey	USA	Wentworth (East)	294
1981	D Massey	USA	Northumberland	295
1982	Figueras-Dotti	Spain	Royal Birkdale	296
1983	*Not played*			
1984	A Okamoto	Japan	Woburn	289
1985	B King	USA	Moor Park	300
1986	L Davies	England	Royal Birkdale	283
1987	A Nicholas	England	St Mellion	296
1988	C Dibnah*	Australia	Lindrick	296

* Won play-off after a tie with S Little

1989	J Geddes	USA	Ferndown	274
1990	H Alfredsson*	Sweden	Woburn	288

* Won play-off at fourth extra hole after a tie with J Hill

1991	P Grice-Whittaker	England	Woburn	284
1992	P Sheehan	USA	Woburn	207

Reduced to 54 holes by rain

1993	K Lunn	Australia	Woburn	275
1994	L Neumann	Sweden	Woburn	280
1995	K Webb	Australia	Woburn	278
1996	E Klein	USA	Woburn	277
1997	K Webb	Australia	Sunningdale	269
1998	S Steinhauer	USA	Royal Lytham & St Annes	292

US Women's Open Championship

1998 US Women's Open Championship
at Blackwolf Run, Wisconsin (6412 yds, Par 71). Prize money: $1,500,000

Pos	Name	Score	Prize Money $
1	SR Pak*	69-70-75-76—290	267500
2	J Chuasiriporn (Am)	72-71-75-72—290	

*Se Ri Pak won at second extra hole after both had tied on 18 extra holes

Pos	Name	Score	Prize Money $
3	L Neumann	70-70-75-76—291	157500
4	Danielle Ammaccapane	76-71-74-71—292	77351
	P Hurst	69-75-75-73—292	77351
	C Johnson	72-70-76-74—292	77351
7	S Croce	74-71-76-72—293	46737
	T Green	73-71-76-73—293	46737
	M McKay	72-70-73-78—293	46737
10	T Johnson	73-71-77-73—294	39015
11	L Davies	68-75-78-74—295	34929
	D Pepper	71-71-78-75—295	34929
13	C Koch	72-74-77-73—296	30684
	H Alfredsson	75-75-73-73—296	30684
15	H Stacy	76-68-82-71—297	25871
	A Acker Macosko	74-74-76-73—297	25871
	Dina Ammaccapane	75-70-78-74—297	25871
	B Burton	74-72-77-74—297	25871
19	L Kane	74-72-82-70—298	18998
	J Lidback	71-73-79-75—298	18998
	A Fukushima	72-71-79-76—298	18998
	R Jones	74-74-74-76—298	18998
	W Ward	76-69-75-78—298	18998
	D Andrews	70-75-75-78—298	18998
	L Walters	76-70-74-78—298	18998
26	D Dormann	72-76-79-72—299	12972
	N Scranton	76-72-78-73—299	12972
	M Estill	75-74-76-74—299	12972
	H Dobson	71-75-77-76—299	12972
	L Rinker Graham	75-71-77-76—299	12972
31	K Williams	68-81-79-72—300	10093
	P Hammel	71-79-77-73—300	10093
	B Daniel	77-69-78-76—300	10093
	D Eggeling	71-72-79-78—300	10093
	K Webb	76-73-73-78—300	10093
36	D Coe Jones	71-74-83-73—301	8897
	I Blais (Am)	74-73-78-76—301	
	K Tschetter	75-72-77-77—301	8897
	B Corrie Kuehn (Am)	70-72-80-79—301	
	L Spalding	69-74-78-80—301	8897
41	H Wadsworth	77-71-80-74—302	7709
	E Klein	72-75-80-75—302	7709
	N Bowen	72-74-80-76—302	7709

1998 US Women's Open Championship *continued*

Pos	Name	Score	Prize Money $
41T	A Sorenstam	71-75-79-77—302	7709
	B Mucha	70-74-75-83—302	7709
46	P Bradley	71-77-83-73—304	6525
	P Rizzo	73-73-80-78—304	6525
	P Sinn	77-73-75-79—304	6525
49	K Albers	75-74-79-77—305	5490
	M Redman	74-73-79-79—305	5490
	M Lovander	72-77-77-79—305	5490
	K Booth (Am)	75-73-77-80—305	
	A De Luca	77-73-74-81—305	5490
54	H Kobayashi	74-73-78-81—306	4750
55	ML de Lorenzi	76-74-81-76—307	4623
56	S Lowe	74-75-79-80—308	4505
57	J Stephenson	73-77-82-77—309	4338
	TJ Myers	73-77-80-79—309	4338
59	JJ Robertson (Am)	74-75-81-80—310	
60	C Kerr	74-74-82-81—311	4179
61	K Parker	76-74-85-79—314	4085
62	K Baue	71-76-85-84—316	3990

The following players missed the cut:

63	C Nilsmark	74-77—151	94	S Florin	79-75—154	117T	C Semple Thompson		
	T Barrett	76-75—151		OH Ku	75-79—154		(Am)	76-81—157
	A Finney	73-78—151		S Redman	77-77—154	125	A Fruhwirth	81-77—158
	C McCurdy	77-74—151		L Kean	76-78—154		J Feldott	76-82—158
	J Gallagher			L Hackney	73-81—154		M Kim	79-79—158
	Smith	70-81—151		K Golden	72-82—154		P Liscio	82-76—158
	C Matthew	75-76—151	100	N Fink	77-78—155		S Mehra	84-74—158
	S Steinhauer	76-75—151		K Noble	77-78—155	130	M Bell	77-82—159
	J Egan	72-79—151		K Saiki	78-77—155		J Anschutz	86-73—159
	M Spencer			E Wicoff	75-80—155		M McGann	79-80—159
	Devlin	74-77—151		L DePaulo	75-80—155		V Fergon	78-81—159
72	V Odegard	75-77—152		K Coats	74-81—155		V Derby	
	L Earley	77-75—152		S Hallock	72-83—155		Grimes (Am)	79-80—159
	B Bauer (Am)	73-79—152		C Childs	76-79—155		K Marshall	79-80—159
	C Walker	79-73—152		K Brozer	80-75—155	136	N Lopez	77-83—160
	C Figg-Currier	78-74—152		P Sheehan	75-80—155		Z Grimbeek	79-81—160
	M Morris	77-75—152		C Johnston			M Baena (Am)	79-81—160
	K Robbins	76-76—152		Forbes	80-75—155		S Martin	83-77—160
	B King	73-79—152	111	S Little	77-79—156	140	R Rinaldo (Am)	79-82—161
	J Inkster	75-77—152		J Park	77-79—156		R Burke (Am)	77-84—161
	M Nause	74-78—152		A Alcott	79-77—156	142	N Dalkas (Am)	78-84—162
82	S Dallongeville	75-78—153		A Nicholas	78-78—156		N Ste Marie	79-83—162
	M Mallon	77-76—153		C Hill	80-76—156	144	L Sugg	83-81—164
	L Kreutz	76-77—153		C Coetzee			T Parker	77-87—164
	L Whiteside	77-76—153		Hirst	78-78—156	146	R Wishna	86-82—168
	S Strudwick	80-73—153	117	J Geddes	78-79—157		L Coleman	87-81—168
	S Finnestad	76-77—153		L Brooky	77-80—157		M Newton	
	J Gibson	77-76—153		J Kleiman	80-77—157		(Am)	84-84—168
	M Lunn	74-79—153		A Burks	80-77—157	149	S Horton (Am)	87-86—173
	G Graham	74-79—153		MJ Rouleau	76-81—157		J Hanna	91-82—173
	J Pitcock	74-79—153		C Hannemann				
	J McGill	77-76—153		(Am)	78-79—157			
	K Lindstrom	76-77—153		T Tombs	76-81—157			

1997 US Women's Open Championship

at Pumpkin Ridge GC, Cornelius, OR (6365 yds, Par 71) Prize money: $1,300,000

Pos	Name	Score	Prize $	Pos	Name	Score	Prize $
1	A Nicholas	70-66-67-71—274	232500	21	K Kuehne	72-73-74-67—286	13800
2	N Lopez	69-68-69-69—275	137500		K Weiss	74-72-72-68—286	13800
3	K Robbins	68-69-74-66—277	86708		S Pak	68-74-75-69—286	13800
4	K Webb	73-72-65-68—278	60432		P Hurst	72-74-70-70—286	13800
5	S Croce	72-69-71-67—279	46159		L Bemvenuti	73-71-72-70—286	13800
	L Hackney	71-70-67-71—279	46159		C Pierce	71-71-73-71—286	13800
7	T Green	74-70-71-65—280	37542	27	C Matthew	76-69-70-72—287	10961
	M Redman	74-67-70-69—280	37542	28	S Smyers	71-71-75-71—288	9188
9	P Sheehan	72-71-71-68—282	28769		P Bradley	72-71-73-72—288	9188
	C Johnson	72-68-73-69—282	28769		K Marshall	72-71-73-72—288	9188
	D Coe-Jones	72-67-73-70—282	28769		B King	74-72-69-73—288	9188
	D Andrews	74-71-66-71—282	28769		J Pitcock	71-69-75-73—288	9188
	A Fukushima	71-71-69-71—282	28769	33	D Eggeling	71-74-76-70—291	7392
14	B Burton	73-72-69-70—284	21287		E Makings	72-73-75-71—291	7392
	D Pepper	72-72-70-70—284	21287		V Fergon	72-75-71-73—291	7392
	J Inkster	72-66-76-70—284	21287		M Morris	75-69-74-73—291	7392
	L Neumann	67-70-76-71—284	21287		R Jones	70-74-73-74—291	7392
	D Richard	68-70-73-73—284	21287		P Sinn	70-73-74-74—291	7392
19	T Johnson	69-74-71-71—285	17407		M McGann	73-70-73-75—291	7392
	K Williams	71-71-67-76—285	17407		C Nilsmark	76-70-69-76—291	7392

Other players who made the cut: A Dibos, J McGill 292; N Bowen, M McGeorge, M Mallon, J Lidback, E Wicoff 293; J Stephenson, H Alfredsson, L Kane 294; B Iverson, B Mucha 295; E Klein, J Gallagher-Smith, M Spencer-Devlin 296; T Hanson, S Redman, J Chuasiriporn (Am) 297; D Dormann, N Harvey 298; M Edge, R Walton 299; B Corrie Kuehn (Am) 302; P Dunlap 303.

1996 US Women's Open Championship

at Pine Needles Lodge & GC, Southern Pines, NC (6207 yds, Par 70)
Prize money: $1,200,000

Pos	Name	Score	Prize $	Pos	Name	Score	Prize $
1	A Sorenstam	70-67-69-66—272	212500	19T	B Daniel	69-78-68-72—287	14374
2	K Tschetter	70-74-68-66—278	12500		W Ward	76-68-71-72—287	14374
3	P Bradley	74-70-67-69—280	60372		M Hirase	74-69-69-75—287	14374
	J Geddes	71-69-70-70—280	60372	25	M Hattori	74-71-74-69—288	10482
	B Burton	70-70-69-71—280	60372		K Williams	69-78-69-72—288	10482
6	L Davies	74-68-70-69—281	40077		B Iverson	73-71-71-73—288	10482
7	C Nilsmark	72-73-68-69—282	35995		N Harvey	72-71-69-76—288	10482
8	C Rarick	73-70-72-68—283	29584	29	K Weiss	74-72-73-70—289	8134
	L Neumann	74-69-70-70—283	29584		S Redman	73-73-71-72—289	8134
	V Skinner	74-68-71-70—283	29584		R Jones	71-70-76-72—289	8134
	T Green	72-70-69-72—283	29584		T Kerdyk	73-72-69-75—289	8134
12	J Lidback	70-76-68-70—284	24654		E Klein	71-69-73-76—289	8134
13	A Nicholas	74-70-74-67—285	23243	34	C Pierce	72-75-73-70—290	7294
14	P Sheehan	74-71-72-69—286	19664		J Inkster	74-71-71-74—290	7294
	S Croce	72-70-74-70—286	19664	36	G Graham	72-70-76-73—291	6479
	C Schreyer	74-70-70-72—286	19664		H Kobayashi	77-71-69-74—291	6479
	M Will	71-72-70-73—286	19664		S Steinhauer	72-73-71-75—291	6479
	M Redman	70-73-70-73—286	19664		K Saiki	73-70-73-75—291	6479
19	C Johnston-Forbes	72-75-71-69—287	14374		B Mucha	74-71-70-76—291	6479
	M Mallon	77-68-72-70—287	14374		C Kerr (Am)	73-73-76-69—291	
	K Webb	74-73-68-72—287	14374				

Other players who made the cut: K Albers, C Mockett, J Piers, M McGeorge, M McGann, I Shiotani, J Pitcock 292; J McGill, K Golden, T Johnson 293; Danielle Ammaccapane, C Matthew 294; S Farwig, J Stephenson, M Bell, M Baena (Am) 295; K Robbins, S Turner, C Johnson 296; E Dahllof, N Foust 300.

1995 US Women's Open Championship

at The Broadmoor, Colorado Springs, CO (6398 yds, Par 70) Prize money: $1,000,000

Pos	Name	Score	Prize $	Pos	Name	Score	Prize $
1	A Sorenstam	67-71-72-68—278	175000	21	L Neumann	70-71-75-71—287	11154
2	M Malon	70-69-66-74—279	103500		A Okamoto	70-73-71-73—287	11154
3	B King	72-69-72-67—280	56238		A Ritzman	75-69-69-74—287	11154
	P Bradley	67-71-72-70—280	56238	24	C Hill	74-73-70-71—288	9287
5	L Lindley	70-68-74-69—281	35285		J Pitcock	72-73-72-71—288	9287
	R Jones	69-70-70-72—281	35285		L Davies	72-73-69-74—288	9287
7	T Green	68-70-75-69—282	28009		MB Zimmerman	72-72-68-76—288	9287
	D Coe-Jones	68-70-74-70—282	28009	28	A Fruhwirth	75-72-72-70—289	6841
	J Larsen	68-71-68-75—282	28009		B Burton	72-74-73-70—289	6841
10	M Morris	73-73-70-67—283	22190		N Lopez	72-73-74-70—289	6841
	P Sheehan	70-73-71-69—283	22190		M Hirase	70-74-73-72—289	6841
	V Skinner	68-72-72-71—283	22190		C Walker	69-73-75-72—289	6841
13	D Mochrie	73-70-69-72—284	18007		P Wright	72-73-71-73—289	6841
	K Tschetter	68-74-69-73—284	18007		D Miho Koyama	74-68-73-74—289	6841
	K Robbins	74-68-68-74—284	18007		J Bartholomew	67-71-77-74—289	6841
16	C Johnson	71-70-74-70—285	14454		G Graham	71-72-71-75—289	6841
	J Briles-Hinton	66-72-74-73—285	14454	37	S Strudwick	75-70-73-72—290	5218
	T Abitbol	67-72-72-74—285	14454		J Inkster	72-73-72-73—290	5218
	D Eggeling	70-68-73-74—285	14454		H Stacy	69-72-75-74—290	5218
20	M Redman	70-75-71-70—286	12449				

Other players who made the cut: H Alfredsson, J Dickinson, M McGann, A Dibos, C Hjalmarsson, J Geddes 291; K Peterson-Parker 292; L Kean, M McGeorge, P Hurst, A Nicholas 293; S Turner, J Stephenson, S Lebrun Ingram (Am) 294; K Marshall, E Hayashida, V Goetze 295; K Albers, L Rinker-Graham, M Nause, K Noble, W Ward (Am), K Booth (Am) 296; A Alcott, E Crosby, A Benz, M Will, L Rittenhouse, M Estill, G Park (Am) 297; S Rule, S Maynor, C Keggi 298; B Mucha, A Acker-Macosko 299; M Platt 303; A Munt 306.

1994 US Women's Open Championship

at Indianwood G&CC, Lake Orion, MI (6244 yds, Par 71) Prize money: $850,000

Pos	Name	Score	Prize $	Pos	Name	Score	Prize $
1	P Sheehan	66-71-69-71—277	155000	22T	L Walters	72-73-72-71—288	9011
2	T Green	66-72-69-71—278	85000		S Steinhauer	68-72-74-74—288	9011
3	L Neumann	69-72-71-69—281	47752	25	K Tschetter	71-73-72-73—289	8089
4	T Abitbol	72-68-70-73—283	31132		D Richard	68-74-72-75—289	8089
	A Dibos	69-68-73-73—283	31132		P Bradley	72-69-70-78—289	8089
6	M Mallon	70-72-73-69—284	21486		P Wright	74-65-71-79—289	8089
	A Alcott	71-67-77-69—284	21486	29	K Lunn	72-72-77-69—290	7371
	B King	69-71-72-72—284	21486		V Goetze	71-73-73-73—290	7371
9	K Robbins	71-72-70-72—285	16445	31	D Eggeling	67-73-79-72—291	6929
	D Andrews	67-72-70-76—285	16445		J Carner	69-74-75-73—291	6929
	H Alfredsson	63-69-76-77—285	16445		A Read	68-72-76-75—291	6929
12	L Merten	74-68-75-69—286	12805		C Semple Thompson (Am)	66-75-76-74—291	
	D Mochrie	72-72-71-71—286	12805	35	C Walker	73-73-75-71—292	6048
	L Grimes	72-73-69-72—286	12805		H Vaughn	74-70-76-72—292	6048
	J Dickinson	66-73-73-74—286	12805		K Williams	72-74-72-74—292	6048
	M Estill	69-68-75-74—286	12805		J Geddes	73-72-73-74—292	6048
	L Davies	68-68-75-75—286	12805		D Coe-Jones	73-73-71-75—292	6048
18	M McGann	71-70-77-69—287	10202		N Lopez	73-71-73-75—292	6048
	J Inkster	75-72-69-71—287	10202		M McGeorge	69-73-75-75—292	6048
	B Daniel	69-74-71-73—287	10202		K Monaghan	75-69-72-76—292	6048
	J Pitcock	74-72-67-74—287	10202				
22	S Maynor	73-70-76-69—288	9011				

Other players who made the cut: V Fergon, M Berteotti, E Crosby, M Hirase, B Burton, S Little 293; N Bowen, A Okamoto 294; S Turner, D Dormann, E Klein (Am) 295; J Stephenson, H Kobayashi, N Ramsbottom 296; C Pierce, T Fleming, A Ritzman, M Edge, S LeBrun Ingram (Am) 297; T Kimura, L Kiggens 298; P Sinn, P Dunlap 300; J Sams 303; S McGuire 304

1993 US Women's Open Championship
at *Crooked Stick GC, Carmel, IN* (6311 yds, Par 72) Prize money: $800,000

Pos	Name	Score	Prize $	Pos	Name	Score	Prize $
1	L Merten	71-71-70-68—280	144000	17T	K Tschetter	73-71-69-75—288	9978
	D Andrews	71-70-69-71—281	62431	21	M Mallon	73-72-69-75—289	9061
	H Alfredsson	68-70-69-74—281	62431	22	D Ammaccapane	73-74-73-70—290	8334
4	P Bradley	72-70-68-73—283	29249		A Finney	74-72-73-71—290	8334
	H Kobayashi	71-67-71-74—283	29249		M Redman	75-71-72-72—290	8334
6	P Sheehan	73-71-69-71—284	22379		D Coe-Jones	69-72-76-73—290	8334
7	B King	74-70-72-69—285	17525	26	L West	73-73-73-72—291	6894
	M McGann	70-66-78-71—285	17525		A Miller	73-68-78-72—291	6894
	N Lopez	70-71-70-74—285	17525		L Brower	73-73-72-73—291	6894
	A Okamoto	68-72-71-74—285	17525		J Larsen	76-71-70-74—291	6894
11	L Davies	73-71-69-73—286	13993		A Alcott	70-74-73-74—291	6894
	J Carner	71-69-73-73—286	13993		C Mah-Lyford	73-73-70-75—291	6894
13	T Barrett	73-73-70-71—287	11999		S Hamlin	74-68-73-76—291	6894
	C Johnson	71-75-69-72—287	11999		K Robbins	71-70-74-76—291	6894
	S Steinhauer	73-67-75-72—287	11999		Dina Ammaccapane	71-70-70-80—291	6894
	N Foust	71-71-71-74—287	11999		D Miho Koyama (Am)	70-74-72-75—291	
17	D Mochrie	72-71-74-71—288	9978	36	J Dickinson	74-73-72-73—292	5907
	G Graham	72-73-70-73—288	9978		M Estill	74-70-75-73—292	5907
	B Mucha	75-69-71-73—288	9978		M Berteotti	72-75-70-75—292	5907

Other players who made the cut: Melissa McNamara, C Rarick, E Crosby, D Richard, J Inkster, B Burton 293; M McGeorge, P Wright, F Descampe, N Ramsbottom, L Rittenhouse 294; L Walters, J Geddes, V Goetze 295; A Read, B Daniel 296; B Bunkowsky 297; K Cathrein, J Anschutz 298; K Guadagnino, A Benz, S Ingram (Am) 299; A Munt 301; L Neumann 303; J Myers 305.

1992 US Women's Open Championship
at *Oakmont CC, Oakmont, PA* (6312 yds, Par 71) Prize money: $700,000

Pos	Name	Score	Prize $	Pos	Name	Score	Prize $
1	P Sheehan*	69-72-70-69—280	130000	16T	B King	74-73-73-75—295	8674
2	J Inkster	72-68-71-69—280	65000	22	A Ritzman	74-69-77-76—296	7327
P Sheehan won play-off 72–74					L Walters	74-72-72-78—296	7327
3	D Andrews	69-73-72-70—284	38830		A Benz	73-71-73-79—296	7327
4	M Mallon	73-72-72-70—287	28336	25	K Monaghan	75-72-75-75—297	6578
5	D Coe	71-71-72-74—288	22295		V Fergon	74-73-75-75—297	6578
6	D Mochrie	70-74-72-73—289	17472		R Jones	73-75-73-76—297	6578
	M McGann	72-73-74-70—289	17472		J Dickinson	75-72-74-76—297	6578
	G Graham	72-71-71-75—289	17472	29	A Fukushima	77-72-78-71—298	5643
9	J Geddes	73-70-78-70—291	13372		P Bradley	74-74-78-72—298	5643
	T Green	73-75-70-73—291	13372		M Figueras-Dotti	74-77-74-73—298	5643
	P Wright	70-69-76-76—291	13372		B Mucha	78-71-75-74—298	5643
12	M Edge	73-74-72-73—292	11731		T Barrett	73-75-75-75—298	5643
13	A Alcott	76-74-73-70—293	10887		T Kerdyk	69-77-76-76—298	5643
	H Alfredsson	71-79-72-71—293	10887		N Ramsbottom	69-75-77-77—298	5643
15	L Neumann	76-72-72-74—294	10111	36	S Steinhauer	74-75-76-74—299	4788
16	N Lopez	75-76-71-73—295	8674		M Spencer-Devlin	69-80-76-74—299	4788
	S Strudwick	75-73-74-73—295	8674		J Stephenson	75-71-78-75—299	4788
	M Estill	74-74-73-74—295	8674		S Little	74-74-74-77—299	4788
	Ok-Hee Ku	73-74-74-74—295	8674		K Albers	72-76-74-77—299	4788
	N Foust	73-74-74-74—295	8674		K Tschetter	70-74-76-79—299	4788

Other players who made the cut: S Turner, K Davies, K Skalicky, C Keggi, J Carner, D Eggeling 300; K Peterson-Parker, V Goetze (Am), N Bowen, D Richard, M Murphy, M McNamara, C Johnson 301; K Robbins, L Depaulo 303; J Anschutz, L Rinker-Graham, B Bunkowsky 304; P Sinn, K Saiki 306; C Schreyer 307; A Sorenstam (Am), S Hamlin, C Mackey 308; M Berteotti 313.

1991 US Women's Open Championship

at Colonial CC, Fort Worth, TX (6340 yds, Par 71) Prize money: $600,000

Pos	Name	Score	Prize $
1	M Mallon	70-75-71-67—283	110000
2	P Bradley	69-73-72-71—285	55000
3	A Alcott	75-68-72-71—286	32882
4	L Kean	70-76-71-70—287	23996
5	D Mochrie	73-76-68-71—288	17642
	C Johnson	76-72-68-72—288	17642
7	J Pitcock	70-72-72-75—289	14623
8	K Albers	76-70-71-73—290	12252
	J Anschutz	73-72-72-73—290	12252
	B Burton	75-71-69-75—290	12252
11	B Daniel	74-76-75-66—291	9738
	T Barrett	74-74-72-71—291	9738
	D Massey	72-72-75-72—291	9738
	J Carner	73-72-73-73—291	9738
15	A Lukken	75-76-70-71—292	7665
	P Sheehan	74-75-72-71—292	7665
	L Neumann	74-72-74-72—292	7665
	A Ritzman	72-71-77-72—292	7665
	A Okamoto	76-72-71-73—292	7665
	K Tschetter	77-72-67-76—292	7665
21	C Walker	72-77-47-70—293	6121
	M Edge	75-76-71-71—293	6121
	T Hanson (Am)	75-76-71-71—293	
	C Gerring	76-70-76-71—293	6121
	N Scranton	72-75-73-73—293	6121
	J Dickinson	72-74-74-73—293	6121
	C Keggi	74-72-73-73—293	6121
28	B King	74-78-74-68—294	5323
	V Goetze (Am)	76-75-71-72—294	
	J Geddes	71-74-76-73—294	5323
	A Nicholas	77-72-71-74—294	5323
32	D Eggeling	77-72-75-71—295	4882
	A Benz	73-74-75-73—295	4882
	G Graham	77-72-69-77—295	4882
35	S Palmer	77-75-73-71—296	4660
36	V Fergon	77-75-73-72—297	4330
	D Lofland	72-77-75-73—297	4330
	A Miller	73-73-77-74—297	4330
	B Bunkowsky	81-68-73-75—297	4330
	P Rizzo	74-74-72-77—297	4330

Other players who made the cut: H Stacy, S Lebrun Ingram (Am), M Berteotti 298; K Kennedy, J Stephenson, A Munt, S Little, L Davies 299; C Pierce, A Read, T Green 300; M Figueras-Dotti, M Will, T Tatum 301; M Foyer, Ok-Hee Ku, C Rarick, Danielle Ammaccapane 302; M Bozarth, K Robbins (Am), K Postlewait 303; R Jones, R Weiss (Am), N Daghe 304; C Stacy, C Mueller Riess, M Floyd, M McGeorge, T Hession, B Mucha 305; S Fogleman, P Sinn, M Moore 306; S Sanders 309.

1990 US Women's Open Championship

at Atlanta Athletic Club, Duluth, GA (6298 yds, Par 72) Prize money: $500,000

Pos	Name	Score	Prize $
1	B King	72-71-71-70—284	85000
2	P Sheehan	66-68-75-76—285	42500
3	D Mochrie	74-74-72-66—286	23956
	Dani. Ammaccapane	72-73-70-71—286	23956
5	M Murphy	70-74-69-74—287	15904
6	E Crosby	71-74-73-70—288	12464
	T Green	70-74-73-71—288	12464
	B Daniel	71-71-74-72—288	12464
9	H Stacy	71-72-77-69—289	8533
	M Mallon	71-71-77-70—289	8533
	C Gerring	70-78-70-71—289	8533
	S Turner	74-72-71-72—289	8533
	C Walker	69-75-73-72—289	8533
	A Alcott	72-72-72-73—289	8533
	C Keggi	67-75-73-74—289	8533
16	M McGeorge	72-74-72-72—290	6727
	R Jones	72-70-74-74—290	6727
18	J Carner	73-71-70-77—291	6287
19	A Ritzman	77-70-73-72—292	5424
	D Andrews	75-72-73-72—292	5424
19T	J Anschutz	72-73-74-73—292	5424
	P Bradley	74-70-75-73—292	5424
	N Lopez	68-76-75-73—292	5424
	J Geddes	66-74-79-73—292	5424
	C Rarick	73-74-70-75—292	5424
26	C Figg-Currier	76-72-73-72—293	4623
	B Mucha	74-72-75-72—293	4623
	L Davies	73-73-74-73—293	4623
29	K Postlewait	75-74-75-70—294	4221
	D Massey	70-73-75-76—294	4221
	A Finney	73-73-71-77—294	4221
32	C Morse	73-75-74-73—295	3694
	M Nause	75-71-76-73—295	3694
	A Okamoto	74-74-73-74—295	3694
	H Kobayashi	75-72-73-75—295	3694
	D Richard	74-72-74-75—295	3694
	P Wright	72-74-74-75—295	3694
	N Rubin	71-72-76-76—295	3694
	S Furlong	71-71-77-76—295	3694

Other players who made the cut: J Anderson, N Brown, S Sanders 296; C Marino, H Drew, G Hull, A Nicholas, J Gallagher 297; J Stephenson 298; A Benz, M Blackwelder, K Tschetter, J Britz, J Delk 299; L Neumann, K Cockerill, V Goetze (Am) 300; C Pierce, J Myers (Am) 301; V Fergon 302; K Peterson (Am) 303; D Eggeling 304; K Hughes (Am) 307; N Harvey 311.

1989 US Women's Open Championship

at Indianwood G&CC, Lake Orion, MI (6109 yds, Par 71) Prize money: $450,000

Pos	Name	Score	Prize $	Pos	Name	Score	Prize $
1	B King	67-71-72-68—278	80000	20T	B Daniel	73-73-71-73—290	5392
2	N Lopez	73-70-71-68—282	40000		C Keggi	71-73-73-73—290	5392
3	P Hammel	74-73-69-67—283	24250		L Neumann	71-71-75-73—290	5392
	P Bradley	73-74-68-68—283	24250		K Postlewait	77-70-70-73—290	5392
5	D Mochrie	72-70-75-67—284	15043		D Cusano-Wilkins	71-72-71-76—290	5392
	L Garbacz	71-70-73-70—284	15043	26	S Quinlan	78-71-73-69—291	4680
7	L Davies	73-71-75-66—285	11931		A Alcott	73-71-73-74—291	4680
	V Fergon	72-74-69-70—285	11931		K Shipman	74-69-74-74—291	4680
9	J Geddes	70-72-72-72—286	9974	29	D White	75-73-74-70—292	4172
	C Walker	72-69-71-74—286	9974		C Johnson	73-73-75-71—292	4172
11	A Okamoto	76-72-74-65—287	8304		N Taylor	74-73-73-72—292	4172
	Dani. Ammaccapane	73-70-74-70—287	8304		P Rizzo	77-69-73-73—292	4172
	M Blackwelder	76-68-71-72—287	8304		D Massey	71-72-75-74—292	4172
	M Delorenze Taya	68-74-71-74—287	8304	34	J Rosenthal	80-69-76-69—294	3786
15	K Bauer	72-72-73-71—288	7137		D McHaffie	71-73-80-70—294	3786
	M Figueras-Dotti	74-70-70-74—288	7137		C Rarick	75-73-73-73—294	3786
17	G Hull	74-72-72-71—289	6374	37	A Benz	71-76-76-72—295	3458
	J Carner	76-69-71-73—289	6374		H Stacy	78-70-73-74—295	3458
	P Sheehan	74-67-69-79—289	6374		K Albers	71-73-75-76—295	3457
20	S Furlong	74-75-73-68—290	5392		S Haynie	72-73-74-76—295	3458

Other players who made the cut: L Rittenhouse, Linda Hunt 296; A Finney, K Guadagnino, M McGeorge, P Kirsch, M Will, T Green, A Ritzman 297; V Skinner, L West, A Nicholas 298; N Rubin 299; D Richard, V Goetze (Am) 300; K Monaghan, 301; A Ridgeway, R Walton, R Jones, M McGann, 303; P Wright 304.

US WOMEN'S OPEN HISTORY

Players are of American nationality unless stated

Year	Winner	Venue	By
1946	P Berg	Spokane	5 and 4

Changed to strokeplay

Year	Winner	Venue	Score
1947	B Jamieson	Greensboro	300
1948	B Zaharias	Atlantic City	300
1949	L Suggs	Maryland	291
1950	B Zaharias	Wichita	291
1951	B Rawls	Atlanta	294
1952	L Suggs	Bala, PA	284
1953	B Rawls*	Rochester, NY	302

* *Won play-off after a tie with J Pung*

1954	B Zaharias	Peabody, MA	291
1955	F Crocker	Wichita	299
1956	K Cornelius*	Duluth	302

* *Won play-off after a tie with B McIntire*

1957	B Rawls	Mamaroneck	299
1958	M Wright	Bloomfield Hills, MI	290
1959	M Wright	Pittsburgh, PA	287
1960	B Rawls	Worchester, MA	292
1961	M Wright	Springfield, NJ	293
1962	M Lindstrom	Myrtle Beach	301
1963	M Mills	Kenwood	289
1964	M Wright*	San Diego	290

* *Won play-off after a tie with R Jessen, Seattle*

US Women's Open Championship *continued*

Year	Winner	Venue	Score
1965	C Mann	Northfield, NJ	290
1966	S Spuzich	Hazeltine National, MN	297
1967	C Lacoste (Am) (Fr)	Hot Springs, VA	294
1968	S Berning	Moselem Springs, PA	289
1969	D Caponi	Scenic-Hills	294
1970	D Caponi	Muskogee, OK	287
1971	J Gunderson-Carner	Erie, PA	288
1972	S Berning	Mamaroneck, NY	299
1973	S Berning	Rochester, NY	290
1974	S Haynie	La Grange, IL	295
1975	S Palmer	Northfield, NJ	295
1976	J Carner*	Springfield, PA	292

* *Won play-off after a tie with S Palmer*

1977	H Stacy	Hazeltine, MN	292
1978	H Stacy	Indianapolis	299
1979	J Britz	Brooklawn, CN	284
1980	A Alcott	Richland, TN	280
1981	P Bradley	La Grange, IL	279
1982	J Alex	Del Paso, Sacramento, CA	283
1983	J Stephenson (Aus)	Broken Arrow, OK	290
1984	H Stacy	Salem, MA	290
1985	K Baker	Baltusrol, NJ	280
1986	J Geddes*	NCR	287

* *Won play-off after a tie with S Little*

1987	L Davies (Eng)*	Plainfield	285

* *Won play-off after a tie with J Carner and A Okamoto*

1988	L Neumann (Swe)	Baltimore	277
1989	B King	Indianwood, MI	278
1990	B King	Atlanta Athletic Club, GA	284
1991	M Mallon	Colonial, TX	283
1992	P Sheehan*	Oakmont, PA	280

* *Won play-off after a tie with J Inkster*

1993	L Merton	Crooked Stick	280
1994	P Sheehan	Indianwood, MI	277
1995	A Sorenstam (Swe)	The Broadmore, CO	278
1996	A Sorenstam (Swe)	Pine Needles Lodge, NC	272
1997	A Nicholas (Eng)	Pumpkin Ridge, OR	274
1998	SR Pak (Kor)*	Blackwolf Run, WI	290

* *Won play-off after a tie with J Chuasiriporn (Am)*

McDonald's LPGA Championship

1998 McDonald's LPGA Championship

at Du Pont CC, Wilmington, Delaware (6386 yds, Par 71)

Prize money: $1,300,000

Pos	Name	Score	Prize Money $
1	Se Ri Pak	65-68-72-68—273	195000
2	Donna Andrews	71-67-69-69—276	104666
	Lisa Hackney	70-66-69-71—276	104666
4	Karrie Webb	71-73-67-66—277	62145
	Wendy Ward	71-67-69-70—277	62145
6	Meg Mallon	71-69-68-70—278	39467
	Chris Johnson	69-71-67-71—278	39467
	Emilee Klein	72-67-68-71—278	39467
9	Catrin Nilsmark	69-73-70-67—279	29110
	Kelly Robbins	69-71-68-71—279	29110
11	Joan Pitcock	69-75-70-66—280	23180
	Annette DeLuca	70-70-71-69—280	23180
	Jane Geddes	69-69-70-72—280	23180
14	Tammie Green	72-68-70-71—281	19691
	Lisa Walters	66-69-73-73—281	19691
16	Maria Hjorth	71-70-73-68—282	17402
	Juli Inkster	70-71-69-72—282	17402
18	Michele Redman	70-71-74-68—283	15767
	Carin Koch	71-73-69-70—283	15767
	Cathy Johnston-Forbes	71-70-70-72—283	15767
21	Janice Moodie	75-69-73-67—284	13558
	Helen Dobson	76-70-70-68—284	13558
	Pat Hurst	71-73-68-72—284	13558
	Jenny Lidback	70-73-68-73—284	13558
25	Dana Dormann	71-74-74-66—285	11579
	Michelle McGann	68-74-73-70—285	11579
	Nancy Scranton	73-73-67-72—285	11579
	Susie Redman	68-76-69-72—285	11579
	Dale Eggeling	68-69-74-74—285	11579
30	Wendy Doolan	73-72-71-70—286	9365
	Vickie Odegard	69-74-73-70—286	9365
	Annika Sörenstam	73-71-71-71—286	9365
	Rachel Hetherington	71-71-72-72—296	9365
	Lorie Kane	72-73-68-73—286	9365
	Kris Tschetter	71-71-71-73—286	9365
	Joanne Morley	73-69-69-75—286	9365
37	Sherri Steinhauer	73-73-71-70—287	7093
	Betsy King	71-73-72-71—287	7093
	Muffin Spencer-Devlin	74-71-70-72—287	7093
	Liselotte Neumann	73-69-73-72—287	7093
	Maggie Halpin	73-73-68-73—287	7093
	Michelle Estill	72-70-72-73—287	7093

1998 McDonald's LPGA Championship *continued*

Pos	Name	Score	Prize Money $
37T	Catriona Matthew	74-70-68-75—287	7093
44	Dawn Coe-Jones	71-69-80-68—288	5168
	Sally Little	76-70-73-69—288	5168
	Nancy Lopez	75-71-71-71—288	5168
	Laura Davies	72-73-72-71—288	5168
	Cindy McCurdy	70-74-72-72—288	5168
	Marta Figueras-Dotti	72-72-71-73—288	5168
	Pat Bradley	72-73-67-76—288	5168
51	Cindy Figg-Currier	73-73-74-69—289	3794
	Kim Saiki	69-74-74-72—289	3794
	Barb Mucha	70-74-72-73—289	3794
	Diane Barnard	72-74-69-74—289	3794
	Helen Alfredsson	71-71-73-74—289	3794
56	Eva Dahllof	72-74-72-72—290	3107
	Charlotta Sörenstam	72-72-71-75—290	3107
58	Caroline McMillan	73-72-75-71—291	2499
	Kristi Albers	73-71-76-71—291	2499
	Kris Monaghan	75-69-73-74—291	2499
	Beth Daniel	70-74-73-74—291	2499
	Missie Berteotti	72-70-74-75—291	2499
63	Hollis Stacy	68-78-75-71—292	2028
	Michelle Dobek	72-74-72-74—292	2028
	Penny Hammel	70-73-71-78—292	2028
66	Gail Graham	73-73-73-74—293	1864
	Tracy Hanson	71-73-75-74—293	1864
68	Missie McGeorge	72-74-75-74—295	1733
	Brandie Burton	74-70-76-75—295	1733
70	Jackie Gallagher-Smith	71-75-75-76—297	1603
	Marianne Morris	71-74-76-76—297	1603
72	Heather Daly-Donofrio	68-76-78-76—298	1505

1997 McDonald's LPGA Championship

at Du Pont CC, Wilmington, Delaware (6386 yds, Par 71)   Prize money: $1,200,000

Pos	Name	Score	Prize $
1	C Johnson*	68-73-69-71—281	180000
2	L Lindley	72-69-69-71—281	111711

Johnson won play-off at second extra hole

Pos	Name	Score	Prize $
3	A Sörenstam	70-73-72-67—282	81519
4	L Davies	67-75-74-68—284	57365
	S Steinhauer	68-71-73-72—284	57365
6	G Graham	69-79-71-66—285	38947
	D Coe-Jones	70-75-71-69—285	38947
8	T Johnson	70-73-72-71—286	31400
9	K Webb	71-79-70-67—287	26871
	B Mucha	68-73-72-74—287	26871
11	K Robbins	73-74-74-67—288	20047
	P Bradley	70-75-76-67—288	20047
	B Burton	71-73-76-68—288	20047
	D Dormann	70-73-75-70—288	20047
	J Dickinson	75-72-68-73—288	20047
16	W Doolan	74-72-74-69—289	15397
	L Kane	73-74-71-71—289	15397
	D Andrews	73-71-73-72—289	15397
16T	K Saiki	68-75-69-77—289	15397
20	A Fruhwirth	72-75-73-70—290	13586
	J Wyatt	73-75-71-71—290	13586
22	M Lunn	72-77-75-67—291	12176
	M Mallon	72-76-73-70—291	12176
	T Barrett	69-77-75-70—291	12176
25	D Reid	74-75-73-70—292	10446
	W Ward	72-78-71-71—292	10446
	C Matthew	71-75-75-71—292	10446
	M McGeorge	73-74-73-72—292	10446
	A Dibos	71-76-73-72—292	10446
	C Figg-Currier	71-76-72-73—292	10446
31	S Strudwick	72-74-77-70—293	8423
	M McGann	74-76-71-72—293	8423
	H Dobson	78-72-69-74—293	8423
	K Weiss	73-75-71-74—293	8423
	C Walker	72-74-73-74—293	8423
	N Bowen	73-72-73-75—293	8423

Other players who made the cut: N Lopez, K Monaghan, D Richard, N Ramsbottom, D Pepper, M Edge, M Estill, K Parker-Gregory, B Whitehead 294; A Miller, K Albers, A Finney, K Marshall, J Lidback, M Morris, J Pitcock 295; B King, H Stacy, C Hj Koch, M Berteotti, S Redman, J Inkster 296; MB Zimmerman 297; J McGill, V Goetze-Ackerman, H Kobayashi, J Crafter, R Hetherington, K Peterson-Parker, N Scranton 298; C Mockett, H Alfredsson, Danielle Ammaccapane, J Geddes, D Killeen, A Alcott, J Gallagher-Smith, E Klein 299; M Hirase, M Spencer-Devlin, C Johnston-Forbes, A-M Palli, P Hurst 300; L Walters, V Skinner 301; Vickie Odegard 302.

1996 McDonald's LPGA Championship

at Du Pont CC, Wilmington, Delaware (6386 yds, Par 71)   Prize money: $1,200,000
Rain reduced event to 54 holes

Pos	Name	Score	Prize $	Pos	Name	Score	Prize $
1	L Davies	72-71-70—213	180000	18T	S Steinhauer	74-71-74—219	13080
2	J Piers	72-72-70—214	111711		D Richard	74-70-75—219	13080
3	P Hammel	73-72-70—215	72461		A Benz	73-71-75—219	13080
	J Crafter	75-68-72—215	72461		N Lopez	70-73-76—219	13080
5	J Dickinson	71-74-71—216	37800		K Robbins	69-71-79—219	13080
	J Inkster	70-73-73—216	37800	26	J McGill	76-70-74—220	9744
	S Furlong	70-73-73—216	37800		S Redman	74-72-74—220	9744
	V Skinner	73-69-74—216	37800		D Pepper	70-76-74—220	9744
	H Kobayashi	71-70-75—216	37800		T-J Myers	74-71-75—220	9744
10	M Dobek	72-75-70—217	22342		J Geddes	71-74-75—220	9744
	P Sheehan	72-74-71—217	22342		C Pierce	75-69-76—220	9744
	M Mallon	69-75-73—217	22342		M McGeorge	74-79-76—220	9744
	K Albers	72-71-74—217	22342		B Daniel	72-72-76—220	9744
14	L Kiggens	75-70-73—218	17058	34	B Mucha	76-72-73—221	7366
	B King	72-72-74—218	17058		P Hurst	76-72-73—221	7366
	J Briles-Hinton	73-69-76—218	17058		T Johnson	75-73-73—221	7366
	A Sörenstam	69-73-76—218	17058		C Figg-Currier	73-74-74—221	7366
18	CH Koch	73-74-72—219	13080		L Grimes	74-70-77—221	7366
	K Tschetter	75-71-73—219	13080		E Dahllof	72-72-77—221	7366
	K Marshall	73-73-73—219	13080		R Hood	71-73-77—221	7366

Other players who made the cut: T Kerdyk, A Dibos, M Redman, K Monaghan, K Webb, M McGann, M Hirase, L Neumann, S Croce, T Hanson 222; D Dormann, P Bradley, G Graham, MB Zimmerman, B Whitehead, A Nicholas, M Nause 223; M Lunn, E Klein, S Maynor, S Strudwick, C Johnson 224; L West, D Andrews, B Iverson, B Burton, T Green, K Parker-Gregory 225; K Williams, R Jones, M Dunn 226; M Will, M Berteotti 227; M Morris, C Johnston-Forbes 228; A-M Palli, V Goetze 229; M Spencer-Devlin 231; M Estill 232.

1995 McDonald's LPGA Championship

at Du Pont CC, Wilmington, Delaware (6386 yds, Par 71)   Prize money: $1,200,000

Pos	Name	Score	Prize $	Pos	Name	Score	Prize $
1	K Robbins	66-68-72-68—274	180000	18T	S Redman	73-71-71-71—286	13080
2	L Davies	68-68-69-70—275	111711		L Garbacz	71-71-72-72—286	13080
3	J Larsen	71-68-70-71—280	65416		K Tschetter	73-69-71-73—286	13080
	M Morris	67-71-70-72—280	65416		N Lopez	73-71-68-74—286	13080
	P Sheehan	67-68-72-73—280	65416		C Walker	70-70-72-74—286	13080
6	B Thomas	70-66-73-72—281	38947		A Finney	71-68-70-77—286	13080
	D Mochrie	67-70-71-73—281	38947	26	S Turner	73-74-70-70—287	10626
8	P Bradley	71-70-70-71—282	29890		K Guadagnino	72-73-68-74—287	10626
	T Green	69-72-70-71—282	29890		N Bowen	71-71-71-74—287	10626
10	A Sörenstam	71-71-72-69—283	25362	29	K Williams	72-71-75-70—288	9374
11	K Albers	71-71-72-70—284	20681		M Redman	75-68-72-73—288	9374
	D Eggeling	72-72-68-72—284	20681		J Geddes	71-71-71-75—288	9374
	J Pitcock	75-66-71-72—284	20681		M Estill	72-73-67-76—288	9374
	B King	69-71-72-72—284	20681	33	P Hurst	74-72-74-69—289	7970
15	L Kiggens	70-70-75-70—285	16504		K Peterson-Parker	74-73-71-71—289	7970
	M Mallon	70-72-71-72—285	16504		V Fergon	73-71-74-71—289	7970
	B Mucha	71-69-71-74—285	16504		E Gibson	73-69-74-73—289	7970
18	B Daniel	71-73-72-70—286	13080		R Jones	72-71-68-78—289	7970
	N Scranton	71-75-69-71—286	13080				

Other players who made the cut: J Carner, S Little, J Lidback, R Heiken, L Neumann, H Alfredsson, C Johnson, B Iverson, T Johnson 290; B Coe-Jones, A Nicholas, L Walters, T Kerdyk, J Inkster, M Edge, K Noble, V Skinner 291; A Ritzman, M Berteotti, J Dickinson, C Hill, J Crafter, M Figueras-Dotti 292; C Pierce, M McGeorge, C Johnston-Forbes, H Dobson, MB Zimmerman 293; D Massey, V Goetze, B Scherbak, C Mockett, A Benz 294; C Rarick 295; E Klein, T Hanson 296; J Briles-Hinton 297; E Dahllof 298; S Strudwick 299; L Tatum 300.

1994 McDonald's LPGA Championship

at Du Pont CC, Wilmington, Delaware (6386 yds, Par 71) Prize money: $1,100,000

Pos	Name	Score	Prize $	Pos	Name	Score	Prize $
1	L Davies	70-72-69-68—279	165000	17T	D Andrews	73-76-69-71—289	12257
2	A Ritzman	68-73-71-70—282	102402		B King	74-73-71-71—289	12257
3	E Crosby	76-71-69-67—283	54660		M McGeorge	75-71-70-73—289	12257
	P Bradley	73-73-70-67—283	54660		K Monaghan	72-72-72-73—289	12257
	H Kobayashi	72-73-71-67—283	54660		M Lunn	70-75-70-74—289	12257
	L Neumann	74-73-67-69—283	54660		R Walton	70-70-75-74—289	12257
7	S Steinhauer	75-70-72-68—285	27676	26	J Carner	73-75-74-68—290	9907
	A Alcott	71-75-70-69—285	27676		M McGann	70-76-75-69—290	9907
	B Daniel	72-74-68-71—285	27676	28	J Lidback	73-73-74-71—291	8460
	P Sheehan	72-68-72-73—285	27676		M Berteotti	75-70-75-71—291	8460
11	D Mochrie	68-78-70-70—286	20203		G Graham	73-71-76-71—291	8460
	M Mallon	71-71-69-75—286	20203		B Burton	76-70-73-72—291	8460
13	V Skinner	74-69-72-72—287	18266		A Okamoto	74-72-73-72—291	8460
14	J Inkster	69-76-74-69—288	16051		J Wyatt	72-74-73-72—291	8460
	D Dormann	71-76-71-70—288	16051		T Barrett	73-77-68-73—291	8460
	C Johnson	70-74-73-71—288	16051	35	D Eggeling	76-74-71-71—292	6891
17	B Mucha	73-74-75-67—289	12257		P Dunlap	71-74-75-72—292	6891
	N Bowen	73-75-73-68—289	12257		A Arruti	75-73-71-73—292	6891
	T Green	71-76-74-68—289	12257		H Alfredsson	73-74-71-74—292	6891

Other players who made the cut: J Dickinson, C Schreyer, M Spencer-Devlin, L Kiggens, K Guadagnino, L West 293; H Stacy 294; B Bunkowsky, L Merton, MB Zimmerman 295; M Morris, N Daghe, N Scranton, N Foust, K Tschetter 296; A Finney, L Walters, C Figg-Currier 297; P Sinn, K Noble, P Allen, M Estill, M Figueras-Dotti, J Anschutz 298; J Stephenson, A Benz, C Rarick 299; J Larsen, N Ramsbottom, C Johnston-Forbes, K Saiki, A Miller, C Keggi, M Edge 300; S Hamlin, N Harvey, V Goetze, M Will 301; D Coe-Jones 303; K Marshall 304; L Rinker-Graham, S Biago 305.

1993 Mazda LPGA Championship

at Du Pont CC, Wilmington, Delaware (6398 yds, Par 71) Prize money: $900,000

Pos	Name	Score	Prize $	Pos	Name	Score	Prize $
1	L Davies	66-69-73-69—277	135000	20T	J Inkster	69-74-72-70—285	9747
2	S Steinhauer	69-72-70-67—278	83783		B Burton	74-74-66-71—285	9747
3	H Alfredsson	74-68-70-67—279	54346		J Carner	70-73-69-73—285	9747
	L Merton	68-69-72-70—279	54346	24	P Wright	75-73-70-68—286	8106
5	H Kobayashi	72-71-69-68—280	38494		R Hood	69-71-76-70—286	8106
6	P Bradley	73-70-71-67—281	25814		D Mochrie	70-71-74-71—286	8106
	MB Zimmerman	72-74-65-70—281	25814		D Lofland-Dormann	70-70-72-74—286	8106
	P Sheehan	68-73-70-70—281	25814		R Walton	74-65-72-75—286	8106
	G Graham	66-69-74-72—281	25814		A Dibos	70-71-69-76—286	8106
10	C Johnson	71-74-71-66—282	16756	30	P Sinn	72-75-70-70—287	6781
	N Lopez	73-69-70-70—282	16756		B Thomas	72-73-71-71—287	6781
	V Skinner	70-70-72-70—282	16756		L Kean	73-69-73-72—287	6781
	H Stacy	73-67-70-72—282	16756		M Berteotti	72-67-76-72—287	6781
14	B King	71-67-78-67—283	12793	34	D Coe-Jones	80-68-71-69—288	6090
	A Nicholas	73-74-67-69—283	12793		C Pierce	71-72-73-72—288	6090
	D Eggeling	70-76-68-69—283	12793	36	K Peterson-Parker	74-73-74-68—289	5411
	A Fukushima	72-69-68-74—283	12793		K Robbins	74-71-72-72—289	5411
18	J Dickinson	75-71-71-67—284	11095		L Neumann	71-75-69-74—289	5411
	T Barrett	73-72-71-68—284	11095		L Garbacz	73-69-72-75—289	5411
20	L Walters	69-73-76-67—285	9747				

Other players who made the cut: M Will, B Daniel, N Scranton, M Mallon, D Wilkins 290; N Ramsbottom, M Spencer-Devlin, J Larsen, A Alcott, M Murphy, E Crosby, E Gibson, J Crafter 291; K Albers, D Baldwin, J Briles-Hinton, M McGeorge, T Kerdyk, D Massey 292; T Green, P Rizzo, Dina Ammaccapane, J Pitcock, T-J Myers, C Figg-Currier, K Tschetter, P Dunlap, L Rinker-Graham 293; S Hamlin, D Ammaccapane, K Williams, S Turner 294; M Redman, J Wyatt, T Johnson 295; D Andrews, B Mucha, C Semple Thompson (Am) 296; K Postlewait, L Baugh 297; T Tombs 298; N White, P Hammel 300; J Sams 303.

1992 Mazda LPGA Championship

at Du Pont CC, Wilmington, Delaware (6398 yds, Par 71) Prize money: $750,000
Rain reduced event to 54 holes

Pos	Name	Score	Prize $	Pos	Name	Score	Prize $
1	A Okamoto	67-69-69—205	112500	17T	J Anschutz	72-72-69—213	7928
2	P Bradley	72-70-66—208	53465		D Andrews	72-72-69—213	7928
	D Richard	68-70-70—208	53465		E Gibson	73-70-70—213	7928
	B Burton	73-63-72—208	53465		S Turner	72-70-71—213	7928
5	J Dickinson	70-68-71—209	32079		D McHaffie	72-70-71—213	7928
6	J Geddes	77-65-68—210	24342		N White	71-71-71—213	7928
	D Mochrie	71-70-69—210	24342		F Descampe	75-66-72—213	7928
8	M McGann	74-69-68—211	16888		D Lasker	72-69-72—213	7928
	C Walker	72-70-69—211	16888		A Benz	69-71-73—213	7928
	N Scranton	70-72-69—211	16888	29	J Inkster	75-71-68—214	5371
	N Lopez	67-73-71—211	16888		Ok-Hee Ku	75-69-70—214	5371
12	H Alfredsson	72-71-69—212	11699		J Carner	73-71-70—214	5371
	K Shipman	71-72-69—212	11699		E Crosby	72-71-71—214	5371
	Dani. Ammaccapane	72-70-70—212	11699		T Green	71-72-71—214	5371
	J Crafter	72-69-71—212	11699		M Mackall	74-68-72—214	5371
	C Keggi	70-70-72—212	11699		S McGuire	72-69-73—214	5371
17	M Mallon	74-70-69—213	7928		B Daniel	72-69-73—214	5371
	S Steinhauer	73-71-69—213	7928		M Redman	71-69-74—214	5371
	P Sheehan	72-72-69—213	7928				

Other players who made the cut: M Nause, H Stacy, B King, T Barrett, L Neumann 215; T Kerdyk, N Ramsbottom, M Berteotti, L Davies, K Peterson-Parker 216; D Eggeling, K Robbins, B Pearson, P Sinn, J Briles-Hinton, G Hull, A Miller, L Rinker-Graham, V Fergon, S Hamlin, V Skinner 217; P Hammel, M Edge, B Mucha, P Wright, J Thobois, S Little, K Albers, J Lidback 218; S Palmer, R Hood, K Davies 219; K Postlewait, M Spencer-Devlin, G Graham 221; A Finney 222; A Alcott, A Ritzman, R Walton, M McGeorge 223; K Rogerson 225; L Baugh 230.

1991 Mazda LPGA Championship

at Du Pont CC, Wilmington, Delaware (6398 yds, Par 71) Prize money: $750,000

Pos	Name	Score	Prize $	Pos	Name	Score	Prize $
1	B Daniel	67-71-67-68—273	112500	19T	N Lopez	71-71-68-74—284	8825
2	P Bradley	69-67-70-71—277	60000	21	L Davies	68-69-75-73—285	7899
	S Little	67-69-67-74—277	60000		M Berteotti	70-68-73-74—285	7899
4	M McGann	70-66-72-70—278	35625		C Gerring	69-68-73-75—285	7899
	A Okamoto	70-65-73-70—278	35625	24	L Walters	73-71-74-68—286	6949
6	K Albers	68-70-72-69—279	24187		N Harvey	72-71-72-71—286	6949
	T Green	64-71-72-72—279	24187		T-J Myers	69-74-71-72—286	6949
8	D Mochrie	70-68-70-72—280	19500		D Richard	67-72-74-73—286	6949
9	D Coe	72-71-68-70—281	14133	28	P Sheehan	72-72-73-70—287	6274
	T Johnson	72-69-70-70—281	14133		C Figg-Currier	69-72-71-75—287	6274
	V Fergon	70-70-71-70—281	14133	30	M Mallon	71-71-74-72—288	5724
	J Geddes	71-69-70-71—281	14133		B Bunkowsky	71-73-73-74—288	5724
	M McGeorge	70-68-70-73—281	14133		J Pitcock	70-69-74-75—288	5724
	S Steinhauer	70-68-69-74—281	14133	33	L Adams	69-76-71-73—289	4868
15	S Maynor	70-69-70-73—282	10888		L Neumann	73-71-72-73—289	4868
16	Ok-Hee Ku	73-68-71-71—283	9763		N Scranton	71-73-72-73—289	4868
	C Hill	69-68-74-72—283	9763		J Anderson	72-72-70-75—289	4868
	B King	69-71-68-75—283	9763		S Furlong	71-73-70-75—289	4868
19	C Keggi	68-74-69-73—284	8825		MA Klinchock	71-71-68-79—289	4868

Other players who made the cut: A-M Palli, L Rinker, C Walker, A Benz, N Foust 290; B Pearson, M Nause, D Heinicke-Rauch, D Massey, L Baugh, T Purtzer, H Kobayashi, M Fuller 291; MB Zimmerman, K Shipman, K Monaghan, S Hamlin, M Spencer-Devlin, Danielle Ammaccapane 292; R Jones, K Cockerill, L Kean, A Ritzman 293; A Miller, A Alcott, R Walton 295; V Skinner, M Blackwelder, M Edge, D Lofland, K Postlewait 296; J Briles-Hinton, D White 297; G Graham 298; J Gibson 299; N Bowen 301.

1990 Mazda LPGA Championship

at Du Pont CC, Wilmington, Delaware (6366 yds, Par 71) Prize money: $650,000

Pos	Name	Score	Prize $	Pos	Name	Score	Prize $
1	P Sheehan	70-67-68-70—275	97500	20T	A Ritzman	72-71-73-69—285	6880
2	K Albers	69-73-69-68—279	41438		P Rizzo	73-71-71-70—285	6880
	B King	70-70-70-69—279	41438		D Eggeling	74-72-68-71—285	6880
	C Gerring	69-72-67-71—279	41438		S Turner	69-74-71-71—285	6879
	A Okamoto	70-69-69-71—279	41438	25	C Morse	74-71-73-68—286	5645
6	C Walker	69-71-71-69—280	19608		J Carner	71-74-71-70—286	5645
	J Geddes	68-68-74-70—280	19608		C Johnson	75-70-69-72—286	5645
	B Mucha	68-72-67-73—280	19608		M Nause	70-74-70-72—286	5645
9	P Bradley	70-73-71-67—281	14463		M McGeorge	71-70-72-73—286	5645
	D Richard	68-71-73-69—281	14463		A Finney	73-71-68-74—286	5645
11	D Massey	75-71-66-70—282	11885	31	J Crafter	69-76-73-69—287	4475
	C Hill	72-69-71-70—282	11885		K Postlewait	71-75-70-71—287	4475
13	N Lopez	70-72-73-68—283	9772		P Hammel	72-73-70-72—287	4475
	R Jones	74-69-71-69—283	9772		H Drew	73-71-71-72—287	4475
	B Daniel	74-72-66-71—283	9772		J Anschutz	72-70-72-73—287	4475
	T Green	71-71-70-71—283	9772		C Pierce	70-71-73-73—287	4475
17	D Mochrie	74-69-72-69—284	8147		Dani. Ammaccapane	71-72-70-74—287	4475
	D Lasker	72-74-67-71—284	8147	38	J Briles	73-73-72-70—288	3662
	L Rinker	67-71-72-74—284	8147		C Rarick	73-73-72-70—288	3662
20	S Furlong	72-74-70-69—285	6880		N Brown	70-73-74-71—288	3662

Other players who made the cut: M Blackwelder, T Johnson, TL Carter 289; N Rubin, J Britz, K Cockerill, D McHaffie, M Will, M Berteotti 290; J Anderson, A Benz, C Figg-Currier, M Bozarth, J Inkster, L Walters, P Wright, A Alcott 291; T Kerdyk, K Hanson, M Foyer, M Ward 292; L Davies, P Jordan, M B Zimmerman, M Figueras-Dotti, K Whitworth, K Tschetter 293; V Fergon 294; H Stacy, C Marino, T-J Myers 295; C Johnston 296; L Connelly 299.

1989 Mazda LPGA Championship

at Du Pont CC, Wilmington, Delaware (6385 yds, Par 71) Prize money: $550,000

Pos	Name	Score	Prize $	Pos	Name	Score	Prize $
1	B King	69-65-71-67—272	82500	18T	D Ammaccapane	70-70-70-72—282	6601
2	P Bradley	69-66-71-68—274	44000	21	C Marino	71-70-70-72—283	5672
	S Furlong	66-69-66-73—274	44000		L Rittenhouse	71-71-68-73—283	5672
4	D McHaffie	68-69-69-70—276	28875		C Pierce	71-70-69-73—283	5672
5	A Finney	69-71-69-69—278	19617		S Sanders	68-71-70-74—283	5672
	P Sheehan	69-72-67-70—278	19617	25	D White	74-68-70-72—283	5088
	J Carner	71-70-66-71—278	19617		N Ramsbottom	67-73-70-74—284	5088
8	S Turner	71-69-73-66—279	12925	27	L Garbacz	75-69-71-70—285	4510
	C Walker	73-71-67-68—279	12925		M Bozarth	73-69-73-70—285	4510
	P Rizzo	74-70-66-69—279	12925		C Rarick	70-71-74-70—285	4510
11	T Green	70-73-67-70—280	9420		M McGeorge	70-71-70-74—285	4510
	E Crosby	69-69-72-70—280	9420		A Alcott	69-70-71-75—285	4510
	C Johnson	69-71-69-71—280	9420	32	R Walton	74-72-70-70—286	3699
	B Daniel	70-66-72-72—280	9420		T Kerdyk	72-71-72-71—286	3699
15	A Okamoto	70-74-69-68—281	7518		K Monaghan	71-71-73-71—286	3699
	N Brown	73-68-69-71—281	7518		M Figueras-Dotti	74-71-69-72—286	3699
	M Berteotti	67-70-73-71—281	7518		D Eggeling	72-70-72-72—286	3699
18	J Geddes	71-71-70-70—282	6601		H Stacy	70-72-71-73—286	3699
	V Fergon	70-72-70-70—282	6601				

Other players who made the cut: L Davies, K Albers, C Figg-Currier, L Rinker, R Jones, L Merten, L Neumann, L Baugh, S Quinlan 287; M McGann, P Wright 288; Mei-Chi Cheng, D Massey, M Murphy, K Postlewait 289; M Edge, J Stephenson, C Gowan, B Lauer, L Walters 290; A Benz, C Gerring, V Skinner, J Rosenthal, T Johnson 291; D Coe, C Nakajima 292; K Whitworth, D Richard, S Steinhauer, S Hamlin, M Rodriguez Hardin 293; L Adams 294; C Morse, M Blackwelder 295; H Farr, M Foyer, K Guadagnino, L Connelly, C Johnston 296.

LPGA Championship History

The Championship was known simply as the LPGA Championship from its inauguration in 1955 until 1987. It was sponsored by Mazda from 1988 until 1993 when the sponsorship was taken over by McDonald's.

Players are of American nationality unless stated

Year	Winner	Venue	Score
1955	B Hanson	Orchard Ridge	4 & 3
1956	M Hagg	Forest Lake	291
(After a tie with P Berg)			
1957	L Suggs	Churchill Valley	285
1958	M Wright	Churchill CC	288
1959	B Rawls	Churchill CC	288
1960	M Wright	French Lick	292
1961	M Wright	Stardust	287
1962	J Kimball	Stardust	282
1963	M Wright	Stardust	294
1964	M Mills	Stardust	278
1965	S Haynie	Stardust	279
1966	G Ehret	Stardust	282
1967	K Whitworth	Pleasant Valley	284
1968	S Post	Pleasant Valley	294
(After a tie with K Whitworth)			
1969	B Rawls	Concord	293
1970	S Englehorn	Pleasant Valley	285
(After a tie with K Whitworth)			
1971	K Whitworth	Pleasant Valley	288
1972	K Ahern	Pleasant Valley	293
1973	M Mills	Pleasant Valley	288
1974	S Haynie	Pleasant Valley	288
1875	K Whitworth	Pine Ridge	288
1976	B Burfeindt	Pine Ridge	287
1977	C Higuchi (Jpn)	Bay Tree	279
1978	N Lopez	Kings Island	275
1979	D Caponi	Kings Island	279
1980	S Little (SA)	Kings Island	285
1981	D Caponi	Kings Island	280
1982	J Stephenson (Aus)	Kings Island	279
1983	P Sheehan	Kings Island	279
1984	P Sheehan	Kings Island	272
1985	N Lopez	Kings Island	273
1986	P Bradley	Kings Island	277
1987	J Geddes	Kings Island	275
1988	S Turner	Kings Island	281
1989	B King	Wilmington, Delaware	272
1990	P Sheehan	Wilmington, Delaware	275
1991	B Daniel	Wilmington, Delaware	273
1992	A Okamoto (Jpn)	Wilmington, Delaware	205
(Reduced to 54 holes – bad weather)			
1993	L Davies (Eng)	Wilmington, Delaware	277
1994	L Davies (Eng)	Wilmington, Delaware	275
1995	K Robbins	Wilmington, Delaware	274
1996	L Davies (Eng)	Wilmington, Delaware	213
(Reduced to 54 holes – bad weather)			
1997	C Johnson	Wilmington, Delaware	281
1998	SR Pak (Kor)	Wilmington, Delaware	273

Nabisco Dinah Shore

1998 Nabisco Dinah Shore

at Mission Hills CC, Rancho Mirage, CA (6460 yds, Par 72) Prize money: $1,000,000

Pos	Name	Score	Prize Money $
1	Pat Hurst	69-72-70-71—281	150000
2	Helen Dobson	70-74-71-67—282	93093
3	Laura Davies	75-70-70-68—283	60385
	Helen Alfredsson	70-73-70-70—283	60385
5	Donna Andrews	71-72-71-70—284	38998
	Liselotte Neumann	69-71-71-73—284	38998
7	Annika Sörenstam	76-71-69-70—286	27928
	Karrie Webb	71-72-70-73—286	27928
9	Dottie Pepper	73-72-74-68—287	22393
	Sherri Steinhauer	69-76-71-71—287	22393
11	Amy Fruhwirth	73-71-73-71—288	18438
	Dawn Coe-Jones	70-72-74-72—288	18438
13	Catriona Matthew	75-74-70-70—289	15670
	Penny Hammel	73-72-71-73—289	15670
	Nancy Lopez	71-71-73-74—289	15670
16	Meg Mallon	75-69-76-70—290	13658
	Beth Bauer (Am)	76-70-72-72—290	
18	Lorie Kane	76-71-74-70—291	12147
	Rosie Jones	75-66-78-72—291	12147
	Jo Anne Carner	73-72-73-73—291	12147
	Muffin Spencer-Devlin	72-70-76-73—291	12147
	Lisa Hackney	71-71-73-76—291	12147
23	Grace Park (Am)	77-73-71-71—292	
24	Emilee Klein	76-74-73-70—293	9256
	Juli Inkster	74-75-74-70—293	9256
	Cindy Figg-Currier	74-72-77-70—293	9256
	Becky Iverson	74-72-77-70—293	9256
	Barb Mucha	72-75-74-72—293	9256
	Tammie Green	72-72-76-73—293	9256
	Danielle Ammaccapane	75-73-71-74—293	9256
	Michelle McGann	74-71-72-76—293	9256
	Mayumi Hirase	73-69-73-78—293	9256
33	Hiromi Kobayashi	77-71-77-69—294	6964
	Tina Barrett	76-73-74-71—294	6964
	Maggie Halpin	72-77-74-71—294	6964
	Gail Graham	71-75-74-74—294	6964
	Alison Nicholas	75-70-75-74—294	6964
	Jane Geddes	73-75-71-75—294	6964
	Dana Dormann	73-74-72-75—294	6964
40	Amy Alcott	74-75-75-71—295	5832
	Jan Stephenson	73-74-75-73—295	5832
42	Cindy McCurdy	76-75-75-70—296	4705
	Kim Saiki	72-77-75-72—296	4705
	Jane Crafter	70-79-75-72—296	4705

Pos	Name	Score	Prize Money $
42T	Patty Sheehan	72-76-74-74—296	4705
	Michele Redman	75-73-73-75—296	4705
	Joan Pitcock	73-73-75-75—296	4705
	Pat Bradley	75-71-74-76—296	4705
	Kelly Robbins	72-74-72-78—296	4705
50	Vicki Fergon	75-74-77-71—297	3421
	Deb Richard	73-77-75-72—297	3421
	Dale Eggeling	75-76-72-74—297	3421
	Julie Piers	73-71-79-74—297	3421
	Brandie Burton	71-72-73-81—297	3421
55	Jenny Lidback	76-74-74-74—298	2711
	Mary Beth Zimmerman	76-72-74-76—298	2711
	Kathryn Marshall	73-73-75-77—298	2711
	Lisa Walters	73-74-73-78—298	2711
59	Tina Tombs	75-73-77-74—299	2258
	Rachel Hetherington	68-77-79-75—299	2258
61	Cindy Rarick	77-73-77-73—300	1932
	Betsy King	73-74-79-74—300	1932
	Karen Weiss	75-75-75-75—300	1932
64	Val Skinner	76-72-74-79—301	1731
65	Susie Redman	76-74-78-74—302	1579
	Patti Rizzo	72-76-80-74—302	1579
	Nanci Bowen	76-74-77-75—302	1579
68	Shelley Hamlin	77-72-77-77—303	1454
	Trish Johnson	75-72-76-80—303	1454
70	Marianne Morris	74-76-81-73—304	1378
71	Lisa Kiggens	75-75-75-80—305	1328
72	Beth Daniel	74-73-79-80—306	1278

1997 Nabisco Dinah Shore
at Mission Hills CC, CA (6460 yds, Par 72)   Prize money: $900,000

Pos	Name	Score	Prize $
1	B King	71-67-67-71—276	135000
2	K Tschetter	66-76-66-70—278	83783
3	A Fruhwirth	69-70-68-72—279	54346
	K Robbins	70-67-68-74—279	54346
5	N Bowen	70-74-70-68—282	35097
	L Hackney	70-72-72-68—282	35097
7	T Barrett	70-71-70-72—283	26720
8	MB Zimmerman	75-74-72-63—284	21285
	H Kobayashi	72-69-71-72—284	21285
	A Sörenstam (Am)	70-72-68-74—284	21285
11	M Morris	71-75-72-67—285	15065
	D Andrews	73-71-72-69—285	15065
	J Geddes	68-75-72-70—285	15065
	J Crafter	70-71-72-72—285	15065
	D Pepper	69-70-71-75—285	15065
16	T Green	72-73-71-70—286	10898
	J Inkster	72-74-69-71—286	10898
	M McGann	74-70-71-71—286	10898
	L Neumann	74-71-69-72—286	10898
	P Hurst	74-69-71-72—286	10898
16T	L Davies	70-70-74-72—286	10898
	K Marshall	66-73-73-74—286	10898
23	C Schreyer	72-74-73-68—287	8690
	M Baena (Am)	74-71-73-69—287	
	P Hammel	76-72-67-72—287	8690
	T Johnson	70-72-73-72—287	8690
	N Lopez	70-74-69-74—287	8690
28	B Mucha	71-72-73-72—288	8000
29	K Webb	69-74-71-75—289	7728
30	M Hirase	70-77-72-71—290	6940
	M Estill	72-73-73-72—290	6940
	D Coe-Jones	73-72-72-73—290	6940
	D Richard	68-75-74-73—290	6940
	D Eggeling	68-72-75-75—290	6940
35	J Briles-Hinton	72-76-74-69—291	5668
	C Johnson	75-72-72-72—291	5668
	E Klein	73-74-71-73—291	5668
	A-M Palli	73-74-70-74—291	5668
	H Stacy	72-73-72-74—291	5668
	P Bradley	69-72-73-77—291	5668

Other players who made the cut: A Nicholas, C Walker 292; V Skinner, J Lidback, C Rarick, B Iverson, L Walters 293; S Turner, B Burton, S Steinhauer, K Harada, J Pitcock, V Goetze-Ackerman 294; J Piers, R Hood, H Alfredsson 295; T Hanson, A Finney, A Alcott, K Monaghan 296; N Ramsbottom, R Walton 298; P Sheehan 299; A Okamoto 300; M Spencer-Devlin 301; A Ritzman, TJ Myers 302; B Bunkowsky-Scherbak, A Fukushima, L Kiggens 303; V Fergon, B Whitehead 304; T Kerdyk, A Benz 305.

1996 Nabisco Dinah Shore
at Mission Hills CC, CA (6460 yds, Par 72)   Prize money: $900,000

Pos	Name	Score	Prize $
1	P Sheehan	71-72-67-71—281	135000
2	K Robbins	71-72-71-68—282	64158
	M Mallon	71-70-71-70—282	64158
	A Sorenstam	67-72-73-70—282	64158
5	A Fruhwirth	71-73-68-71—283	32305
	K Webb	72-70-70-71—283	32305
	B Burton	75-67-68-73—283	32305
8	H Stacy	69-71-74-70—284	23550
9	K Tschetter	71-74-70-70—285	21285
10	D Richard	73-71-73-69—286	16212
	L Neumann	73-69-75-69—286	16212
	V Skinner	74-71-71-70—286	16212
	R Jones	72-67-75-72—286	16212
	T Hanson	69-69-74-74—286	16212
15	N Lopez	73-72-73-69—287	12114
	M McGeorge	74-70-74-69—287	12114
	J Pitcock	71-74-71-71—287	12114
	L Davies	72-70-70-75—287	12114
19	M Morris	76-71-71-70—288	10189
	S Farwig	71-73-73-71—288	10189
19T	T Kerdyk	67-72-77-72—288	10189
	J Inkster	70-70-74-74—288	10189
23	P Bradley	73-76-71-69—289	8111
	J Geddes	74-72-74-69—289	8111
	D Andrews	74-70-76-69—289	8111
	A Fukushima	74-68-78-69—289	8111
	A Alcott	68-78-71-72—289	8111
	P Hammel	75-69-73-72—289	8111
	D Pepper	71-71-75-72—289	8111
	N Bowen	76-70-70-73—289	8111
31	B Iverson	76-71-73-70—290	6544
	S Redman	73-75-71-71—290	6544
	A Nicholas	75-72-72-71—290	6544
	H Kobayashi	72-74-72-72—290	6544
35	C Pierce	72-71-75-73—291	5411
	T Johnson	74-72-71-74—291	5411
	D Coe-Jones	72-73-72-74—291	5411
	P Sinn	73-73-70-75—291	5411
	C Schreyer	72-71-73-75—291	5411
	S Little	69-73-71-78—291	5411

Other players who made the cut: C Johnston-Forbes, K Parker-Gregory, N Ramsbottom, R Walton, B Mucha, G Graham, M Nause 292; J Piers, H Alfredsson, A Okamoto, T Barrett, J Wyatt, S Furlong 293; I Shiotani, Leta Lindley, V Fergon, M Redman 294; C Walker, K Marshall, M Estill, K Albers 295; J Dickinson, M McGann, MB Zimmerman, Danielle Ammaccapane, A Ritzman 296; K Shipman, L Rinker-Graham 297; J Crafter 298; A Dibos, A Finney, S Strudwick, P Wright 299; A Benz, K Guadagnino, 301; S Palmer, E Klein 302; J Stephenson 303; J Carner, C Mackey 305.

1995 Nabisco Dinah Shore
at Mission Hills CC, CA (6460 yds, Par 72)   Prize money: $850,000

Pos	Name	Score	Prize $
1	N Bowen	69-75-71-70—285	127500
2	S Redman	75-70-70-71—286	79129
3	B Burton	76-71-71-69—287	42237
	S Turner	72-74-71-70—287	42237
	L Davies	75-69-70-73—287	42237
	N Lopez	74-71-68-74—287	42237
7	C Walker	74-73-69-72—288	23738
	T Green	71-70-70-77—288	23738
9	D Coe-Jones	71-75-71-72—289	20103
10	C Pierce	77-71-73-69—290	17964
11	B King	77-75-71-68—291	14200
	D Mochrie	78-73-70-70—291	14200
	B Mucha	74-74-72-71—291	14200
	S Palmer	72-73-74-72—291	14200
	D Massey	71-75-72-73—291	14200
16	A Dibos	77-74-75-66—292	10056
	S Steinhauer	78-74-72-68—292	10056
	A Nicholas	75-74-73-70—292	10056
16T	P Bradley	74-75-71-72—292	10056
	J Inkster	76-70-73-73—292	10056
	T-J Myers	77-68-73-74—292	10056
	M Estill	72-72-74-74—292	10056
	M Mallon	74-72-71-75—292	10056
24	A Sörenstam	76-74-74-69—293	8040
	M Spencer-Devlin	69-79-74-71—293	8040
	K Albers	76-72-72-73—293	8040
27	J Geddes	76-75-74-69—294	8014
	K Tschetter	75-74-73-72—294	7014
	L West	74-75-71-74—294	7014
	K Robbins	76-67-76-75—294	7014
	B Thomas	79-69-70-76—294	7014
32	D Eggeling	72-78-75-70—295	5859
	C Rarick	74-73-78-70—295	5859
	L Neumann	75-74-74-72—295	5859
	J Larsen	74-76-72-73—295	5859
	K Noble	71-77-71-76—295	5859

Other players who made the cut: C Keggi, V Skinner, H Kobayashi, A Okamoto, N Ramsbottom, L Merten 296; P Sheehan, A Benz, L Walters, MB Zimmerman 297; Danielle Ammaccapane, C Schreyer, A Ritzman, B Daniel, P Jordan 298; R Jones, F Descampe, J Crafter, J Briles-Hinton, M McNamara 299; Jean Zedlitz, M McGann, I Shiotani, T Johnson, C Johnson, P Hammel 300; K Guadagnino, M Figueras-Dotti 301; L Kiggens, C Johnston-Forbes 302; P Sinn 303; A Finney, T Barrett, K Peterson-Parker, S Farwig, C Hill 304; J Stephenson, M Nause, D Andrews 305; M Berteotti 307; J Anschutz 311.

1994 Nabisco Dinah Shore
at Mission Hills CC, CA (6446 yds, Par 72)   Prize money: $700,000

Pos	Name	Score	Prize $	Pos	Name	Score	Prize $
1	D Andrews	70-69-67-70—276	105000	19T	C Keggi	72-73-72-71—288	7204
2	L Davies	70-68-69-70—277	65165		C Johnson	74-73-69-72—288	7204
3	T Green	70-72-69-68—279	47553		P Sheehan	73-71-72-72—288	7204
4	J Stephenson	70-69-70-71—280	36985		D Mochrie	74-73-68-73—288	7204
5	M McGann	70-68-70-73—281	29940		A Okamoto	69-74-72-73—288	7204
6	G Graham	73-71-71-68—283	21251		M McGeorge	72-71-70-75—288	7204
	K Robbins	73-70-69-71—283	21251	28	T Tombs	73-74-72-70—289	5670
	B Burton	73-73-65-72—283	21251		S Turner	72-74-71-72—289	5670
9	H Stacy	72-72-70-70—284	15674		V Skinner	72-72-72-73—289	5670
	N Lopez	68-72-73-71—284	15674		M Berteotti	71-73-72-73—289	5670
11	M Mallon	72-75-69-69—285	12064	32	T-J Myers	76-73-71-70—290	4913
	L Neumann	76-71-68-70—285	12064		H Kobayashi	72-77-71-70—290	4913
	D Dormann	73-71-70-71—285	12064		K Tschetter	73-69-76-72—290	4913
	D Eggeling	71-71-71-72—285	12064		S Steinhauer	76-68-72-74—290	4913
15	K Monaghan	70-76-70-70—286	9862	36	J Larsen	76-70-75-70—291	3949
	V Fergon	69-74-72-71—286	9862		K Albers	77-73-70-71—291	3949
17	L Merten	74-74-71-68—287	8982		C Rarick	72-74-74-71—291	3949
	N Scranton	75-70-69-73—287	8982		D Coe-Jones	74-70-75-72—291	3949
19	B Daniel	76-72-70-70—288	7204		Toshimi Kimura	71-74-73-73—291	3949
	J Geddes	70-77-71-70—288	7204		M Nause	74-71-72-74—291	3949
	P Bradley	71-75-71-71—288	7204		A Miller	68-71-77-75—291	3949

Other players who made the cut: M Spencer-Devlin, E Crosby, Danielle Ammaccapane, D Richard, T Johnson 292; J Crafter, J Carner, K Noble, S Strudwick, H Alfredsson, C Schreyer, J Dickinson, L Kean, B King, L Walters 293; C Figg-Currier, A Alcott 294; S Redman, M McNamara, T Kerdyk, L Garbacz 295; A Ritzman, M Will, R Hood, A Benz 296; M Estill 297; B Mucha, S Little, K Guadagnino 298; S Palmer, C Walker, P Wright 299; E Klein (Am) 300; C Mackey 305; S Farwig 306; A-M Palli 307.

1993 Nabisco Dinah Shore
at Mission Hills CC, CA (6437 yds, Par 72)   Prize money: $700,000

Pos	Name	Score	Prize $	Pos	Name	Score	Prize $
1	H Alfredsson	69-71-72-72—284	105000	19T	N Scranton	73-72-71-75—291	8101
2	A Benz	72-73-71-70—286	49901	22	M McGann	78-70-75-69—292	7237
	T Barrett	70-73-72-71—286	49901		S Barrett	69-77-72-74—292	7237
	B King	71-74-67-74—286	49901	24	L Garbacz	75-75-72-71—293	6304
5	H Stacy	72-74-71-70—287	25126		C Keggi	74-74-73-72—293	6304
	M Berteotti	68-74-73-72—287	25126		Dani. Ammaccapane	69-75-74-75—293	6304
	D Coe-Jones	72-68-72-75—287	25126		C Schreyer	75-70-72-76—293	6304
8	N Lopez	68-72-72-70—288	15762		A-M Palli	70-71-76-76—293	6304
	B Burton	73-73-68-74—288	15762		M Figueras-Dotti	68-72-75-78—293	6304
	T Johnson	74-68-72-74—288	15762	30	D Lofland-Dormann	76-75-75-68—294	4740
	J Crafter	71-72-70-75—288	15762		D Mochrie	77-73-74-70—294	4740
12	P Sheehan	73-70-76-70—289	10625		H Drew	79-70-74-71—294	4740
	D Massey	70-74-74-71—289	10625		V Skinner	73-75-74-72—294	4740
	T Green	72-73-72-72—289	10625		A Finney	70-73-79-72—294	4740
	L Davies	72-72-73-72—289	10625		C Rarick	76-75-70-73—294	4740
	P Wright	74-68-75-72—289	10625		S Turner	73-72-76-73—294	4740
	P Bradley	71-69-75-74—289	10625		T-J Myers	74-73-73-74—294	4740
18	K Monaghan	76-71-74-69—290	8806		J Pitcock	70-72-76-76—294	4740
19	D Andrews	73-74-72-72—291	8101		S Steinhauer	72-74-71-77—294	4740
	K Noble	74-72-70-75—291	8101				

Other players who made the cut: L Neumann, J Carner, P Rizzo, J Inkster, M Will, S Hamlin, K Postlewait, B Mucha, J Stephenson 295; F Descampe, J Dickinson, J Geddes, C Walker, M Mallon, S Little, L Walters 296; A Ritzman, A Alcott, C Figg-Currier, A Miller 297; K Tschetter, D Richard 298; R Jones, M Estill, V Fergon 299; S Redman, S Farwig, L Connelly, L Adams 300; E Crosby, B Daniel 301; N Foust, M Spencer-Devlin, P Jordan, L Merten 302; Marlene Hagge 304; C Johnson, S Palmer, B Pearson 305; A Okamoto 307; S Furlong, V Goetze (Am) 308.

1992 Nabisco Dinah Shore

at Mission Hills CC, CA (6437 yds, Par 72) Prize money: $700,000

Pos	Name	Score	Prize $	Pos	Name	Score	Prize $
1	D Mochrie*	69-71-70-69—279	105000	17T	J Carner	70-72-75-71—288	8517
2	J Inkster	72-68-68-71—279	65165		J Geddes	75-68-73-72—288	8517
*Winner after play-off					P Bradley	73-71-69-75—288	8517
3	B Burton	70-72-71-68—281	42269	22	Dani. Ammaccapane	74-73-70-72—289	7046
	P Sheehan	71-69-69-72—281	42269		S Little	71-75-71-72—289	7046
5	M Mallon	73-69-72-68—282	29940		Ok-Hee Ku	71-73-73-72—289	7046
6	S Steinhauer	72-73-69-70—284	22719		V Fergon	72-72-71-74—289	7046
	D Eggeling	67-78-69-70—284	22719	26	C Marino	70-74-73-73—290	5946
8	K Tschetter	73-71-73-68—285	15778		L Kean	70-71-76-73—290	5946
	P Wright	74-71-71-69—285	15778		C Figg-Currier	73-74-69-74—290	5946
	B Daniel	70-68-76-71—285	15778		B Mucha	73-72-71-74—290	5946
	M McGann	68-74-71-72—285	15778		L Walters	72-72-71-75—290	5946
12	E Crosby	72-70-73-71—286	11335		L Neumann	68-76-71-75—290	5946
	A Okamoto	71-71-72-72—286	11335	32	C Keggi	71-77-72-71—291	4712
	M Spencer-Devlin	73-69-71-73—286	11335		L Rinker	73-72-75-71—291	4712
	J Stephenson	72-72-68-74—286	11335		C Rarick	70-76-73-72—291	4712
16	T Green	70-70-74-73—287	9574		D Coe	71-68-79-73—291	4712
17	K Postlewait	73-74-72-69—288	8517		T Barrett	74-73-70-74—291	4712
	C Johnson	71-71-75-71—288	8517		R Jones	74-71-72-74—291	4712

Other players who made the cut: A Benz, H Stacy, A Miller, MB Zimmerman 292; M Estill, J Coles, M Berteotti 293; A Ritzman, T Johnson, I Shiotani, M McNamara, M Will 294; M McGeorge, C Mackey, M Nause, M Figueras-Dotti, A Fruhwirth (Am) 295; B King 296; T-J Myers, Corrine Dibnah, N Scranton, A-M Palli, B Bunkowsky, D Lofland 297; C Walker 298; M Faulconer, C Hill 300; J Anschutz, H Drew, L Adams 301; V Goetze (Am) 302; P Pulz 304; S LeBrun Ingram (Am) 305; T Purtzer 306.

1991 Nabisco Dinah Shore

at Mission Hills CC, CA (6437 yds, Par 72) Prize money: $600,000

Pos	Name	Score	Prize $	Pos	Name	Score	Prize $
1	A Alcott	67-70-68-68—273	90000	17T	L Baugh	70-72-72-74—288	7254
2	D Mochrie	70-71-71-69—281	55500		E Crosby	72-70-71-75—288	7254
3	P Bradley	70-72-73-67—282	36000	23	R Jones	73-75-70-71—289	5715
	P Sheehan	71-71-70-70—282	36000		L Davies	72-73-73-71—289	5715
5	L Garbacz	73-71-70-70—284	25500		L Kean	75-71-71-72—289	5715
6	C Keggi	72-70-73-70—285	17100		C Johnson	74-71-72-72—289	5715
	A Okamoto	72-68-74-71—285	17100		D Eggeling	71-74-72-72—289	5715
	N Scranton	74-69-70-72—285	17100		L Connelly	73-72-71-73—289	5715
	M Nause	71-72-69-73—285	17100		A Ritzman	72-71-70-76—289	5715
10	Ok-Hee Ku	69-72-73-72—286	12600	30	B Daniel	74-70-76-70—290	4172
11	B King	72-75-71-69—287	9704		C Gerring	73-74-71-72—290	4172
	Dani. Ammaccapane	75-70-71-71—287	9704		J Stephenson	74-70-74-72—290	4172
	A Benz	73-70-73-71—287	9704		J Inkster	72-69-77-72—290	4172
	V Fergon	70-76-69-72—287	9704		D White	72-74-71-73—290	4172
	J Dickinson	71-75-67-74—287	9704		L Neumann	71-73-73-73—290	4172
	T Green	73-71-68-75—287	9704		N Lopez	75-72-69-74—290	4172
17	T Barrett	70-73-74-71—288	7254		M Foyer	73-71-72-74—290	4172
	V Goetze (Am)	71-75-70-72—288			M Mallon	70-76-74-70—290	4172
	S Steinhauer	72-71-72-73—288	7254		D Richard	74-71-70-75—290	4172
	J Geddes	71-71-72-74—288	7254		S Furlong	68-74-77-71—290	4172

Other players who made the cut: K Postlewait, M Figueras-Dotti, C Walker, R Walton, B Mucha 291; S Turner, M Will 292; L Merten 293; P Hurst (Am), H Alfredsson, C Morse, K Rogerson, M Ward 294; K Albers, B Bunkowsky, C Mackey, L Rinker, C Marino 295; M Berteotti 296; M Edge, C Johnston, V Skinner, J Anderson 297; S Palmer, J Pitcock, H Drew 298; J Briles-Hinton, P Rizzo 300; K Guadagnino, C Rarick 301; M Spencer-Devlin 304; B Lauer 307.

1990 Nabisco Dinah Shore
at Mission Hills CC, CA (6441 yds, Par 72)   Prize money: $600,000

Pos	Name	Score	Prize $	Pos	Name	Score	Prize $
1	B King	69-70-69-75—283	90000	23	J Anderson	72-77-71-73—293	5487
2	S Furlong	74-73-70-68—285	42000		C Marino	73-75-72-73—293	5487
	K Postlewait	73-72-68-72—285	42000		M Berteotti	71-74-72-76—293	5487
4	C Rarick	72-72-72-70—286	28000		L Adams	77-67-72-77—293	5487
5	C Walker	74-72-67-74—287	24000	27	C Morse	76-71-75-72—294	4795
6	A Okamoto	73-72-72-71—288	17217		Dani. Ammaccapane	79-70-71-74—294	4795
	B Daniel	71-73-72-72—288	17217		L Garbacz	72-74-74-74—294	4795
	R Jones	72-71-71-74—288	17216		P Wright	74-71-74-75—294	4795
9	P Bradley	74-73-69-73—289	12699	31	D Massey	72-78-73-72—295	4225
	M Mallon	74-72-70-73—289	12698		J Carner	75-72-70-78—295	4224
11	D Mochrie	71-76-72-71—290	9209		C Reynolds	72-74-70-79—295	4224
	D Richard	74-71-74-71—290	9209	34	M Edge	78-69-78-71—296	3306
	J Inkster	70-75-74-71—290	9209		C Johnson	77-72-74-73—296	3306
	J Briles	73-72-73-72—290	9209		D Coe	76-73-74-73—296	3306
	P Sheehan	76-73-68-73—290	9209		J Crafter	72-76-75-73—296	3306
	E Crosby	73-71-73-73—290	9209		S Hamlin	74-73-75-74—296	3306
17	D White	75-70-73-73—291	7021		J Coles	73-73-75-75—296	3306
	A Benz	71-73-74-73—291	7021		J Geddes	77-73-70-76—296	3306
	D Eggeling	72-75-69-75—291	7021		A Alcott	72-73-75-76—296	3306
	M Ward	72-72-71-76—291	7021		L Rittenhouse	67-78-74-77—296	3306
21	V Skinner	74-74-76-68—292	6165		P Hammel	73-76-67-80—296	3306
	P Rizzo	72-76-72-72—292	6165				

Other players who made the cut: J Anschutz, L Davies, S Little, J Dickinson, M McGeorge, M Foyer, A-M Palli 297; S Sanders, L Rinker, V Fergon 298; S Palmer, M Figueras-Dotti, L Merten, K Peterson (Am) 299; M Blackwelders, N Brown, T Barrett, M Nause, C Gerring 300; T-J Myers, R Walton, C Hill 301; Ok-Hee Ku, C Keggi 302; A Finney, M Spencer-Devlin 303; J Pitcock 305; D Caponi 309; A Sander (Am) 312; D McHaffie 315.

1989 Nabisco Dinah Shore
at Mission Hills CC, CA (6441 yds, Par 72)   Prize money: $500,000

Pos	Name	Score	Prize $	Pos	Name	Score	Prize $
1	J Inkster	66-69-73-71—279	80000	18T	A Ritzman	72-74-72-73—291	5352
2	T Green	72-68-75-69—284	34000	23	P Sheehan	73-72-74-73—292	4455
	J Carner	71-71-71-71—284	34000		D Massey	74-72-72-74—292	4455
4	B King	73-75-68-71—287	19750		A Finney	74-71-73-74—292	4454
	J Rosenthal	69-72-72-74—287	19750		L Neumann	69-73-76-74—292	4454
6	P Bradley	70-75-75-68—288	12511	27	M Nause	72-78-75-68—293	3962
	A Benz	74-74-71-69—288	12511		C Rarick	71-73-73-76—293	3962
	C Morse	72-72-73-71—288	12511		L Garbacz	69-74-73-77—293	3962
	J Coles	72-70-73-73—288	12511	30	K Postlewait	73-76-75-70—294	3684
	B Daniel	69-70-76-73—288	12511	31	M Blackwelder	75-75-70-75—295	3314
11	K Guadagnino	76-71-72-70—289	7960		H Stacy	75-73-73-74—295	3314
	C Walker	73-74-69-73—289	7960		P Hammel	71-76-73-75—295	3314
	Dani. Ammaccapane	72-69-74-74—289	7960		C Mackey	72-74-73-75—295	3313
	L Adams	74-70-69-76—289	7960		L Rinker	74-70-74-77—295	3313
15	P Rizzo	77-73-71-69—290	6357	36	A Nicholas	73-74-79-70—296	2677
	M McGeorge	76-70-72-72—290	6357		C Johnston	76-75-73-72—296	2677
	D Eggeling	68-73-75-74—290	6357		S Steinhauer	74-74-76-72—296	2676
18	N Lopez	72-75-73-71—291	5353		M Spencer-Devlin	71-76-76-73—296	2676
	V Skinner	74-74-71-71—291	5353		C Chillemi	77-71-74-74—296	2676
	S Turner	71-73-75-72—291	5352		Ok-Hee Ku	72-72-77-75—296	2676
	S Haynie	74-74-70-73—291	5352				

Other players who made the cut: L Davies, J Anderson, J Stephenson, D Richard, K Whitworth, K Young 297; K Albers, ML de Taya, S Little 298; A-M Palli, C Semple Thompson (Am), M Figueras-Dotti, S Quinlan, B Lauer 299; S Furlong, M Edge 300; S Palmer, J Geddes, H Farr 301; P Sinn (Am) 302; P Jordan, A Alcott, J Briles, J Crafter 303; D Mochrie, M Berteotti 304; J Dickinson, L Merten 305; T-J Myers, D Coe 306; B Thomas 307; J Washam 308; M Bozarth 309.

Nabisco Dinah Shore History

This event was inaugurated in 1972 as the Colgate Dinah Shore and continued to be sponsored by Colgate until 1981. Nabisco took over the sponsorship in 1982; and the Nabisco Dinah Shore was designated a Major Championship in 1983. Mission Hills CC, Rancho Mirage, California, is the event's permanent venue.

Players are of American nationality unless stated

Year	Winner	Score	Year	Winner	Score
1972	J Blalock	213	1986	P Bradley	280
1973	M Wright	284	1987	B King*	283
1974	J Prentice	289		* Won play-off after a tie with P Sheehan	
1975	S Palmer	283	1988	A Alcott	274
1976	J Rankin	285	1989	J Inkster	279
1977	K Whitworth	289	1990	B King	283
1978	S Post	283	1991	A Alcott	273
1979	S Post	276	1992	D Mochrie*	279
1980	D Caponi	275		* Won play-off after a tie with J Inkster	
1981	N Lopez	277	1993	H Alfredsson (Swe)	284
1982	S Little	278	1994	D Andrews	276
1983	A Alcott	282	1995	N Bowen	285
1984	J Inkster*	280	1996	P Sheehan	281
	* Won play-off after a tie with P Bradley		1997	B King	276
1985	A Miller	278	1998	P Hurst	281

du Maurier Classic

1998 du Maurier Classic

at Essex G&CC, Ontario (6359 yds, Par 72) Prize money: $1,200,000

Pos	Name	Score	Prize Money $
1	Brandie Burton	68-64-66-72—270	180000
2	Annika Sörenstam	68-66-67-70—271	111711
3	Betsy King	64-69-70-72—275	81519
4	Gail Graham	70-70-68-68—276	44804
	Dawn Coe-Jones	67-70-69-70—276	44804
	Deb Richard	67-69-70-70—276	44804
	Michelle Estill	69-69-66-72—276	44804
	Meg Mallon	65-69-67-75—276	44804
9	Sherri Steinhauer	70-71-69-67—277	26871
	Hiromi Kobayashi	68-70-66-73—277	26871
11	Tammie Green	66-69-74-69—278	21335
	Alicia Dibos	68-68-69-73—278	21335
	Pat Hurst	67-65-71-75—278	21335
14	Juli Inkster	74-68-68-69—279	15624
	Catriona Matthew	68-68-74-69—279	15624
	Michele Redman	70-70-69-70—279	15624
	Charlotta Sörenstam	69-69-71-70—279	15624
	Karrie Webb	69-69-69-72—279	15624
	Allison Finney	70-67-70-72—279	15624
	Dottie Pepper	66-70-71-72—279	15624
	Dana Dormann	68-68-70-73—279	15624
22	Penny Hammel	73-68-69-70—280	11774
	Sally Little	67-74-69-70—280	11774
	Donna Andrews	70-70-68-72—280	11774
	Rosie Jones	67-73-66-74—280	11774
	Laura Davies	69-67-70-74—280	11774
27	Nancy Lopez	69-72-72-68—281	9566
	Hollis Stacy	71-69-72-69—281	9566
	Lisa Kiggens	71-71-68-71—281	9566
	Smriti Mehra	68-69-72-72—281	9566
	Marta Figueras-Dotti	68-71-68-74—281	9566
	Chris Johnson	66-72-69-74—281	9566
	Mardi Lunn	68-68-70-75—281	9566
34	Mayumi Hirase	69-70-74-69—282	7366
	Shani Waugh	70-68-73-71—282	7366
	Mhairi McKay	70-71-69-72—282	7366
	Emilee Klein	66-71-72-73—282	7366
	Helen Alfredsson	70-66-73-73—282	7366
	Wendy Ward	68-69-71-74—282	7366
	Lisa Hackney	66-71-71-74—282	7366
41	Dina Ammaccapane	70-70-75-68—283	5434
	Kristi Albers	71-69-71-71—283	5434
	Maria Hjorth	70-71-71-71—283	5434
	Tina Barrett	67-69-76-71—283	5434
	Se Ri Pak	69-70-71-73—283	5434

1998 du Maurier Classic *continued*

Pos	Name	Score	Prize Money $
41T	Becky Iverson	69-66-75-73—283	5434
	Jenny Lidback	67-70-70-76—283	5434
48	Karen Weiss	71-71-71-71—284	3924
	Liselotte Neumann	74-66-73-71—284	3924
	Terry-Jo Myers	70-70-73-71—284	3924
	Cathy Johnston-Forbes	71-70-71-72—284	3924
	Danielle Ammaccapane	69-67-75-73—284	3924
	Diane Barnard	69-69-72-74—284	3924
54	Cristie Kerr	70-72-72-71—285	2897
	Martha Nause	69-71-73-72—285	2897
	Liz Earley	67-71-73-74—285	2897
	Kris Tschetter	71-67-72-75—285	2897
	Beth Daniel	69-68-71-77—285	2897
59	Patty Sheehan	70-72-73-71—286	2173
	Kim Williams	69-73-73-71—286	2173
	Susie Redman	71-71-72-72—286	2173
	Cindy Flom	69-73-70-74—286	2173
63	Joan Pitcock	69-72-76-70—287	1781
	Vickie Odegard	70-72-73-72—287	1781
	Kathy Guadagnino	68-72-73-74—287	1781
	Carin Koch	68-69-75-75—287	1781
67	Val Skinner	72-69-74-73—288	1539
	Nancy Scranton	70-71-72-75—288	1539
	Marie-Josée Rouleau	67-73-72-76—288	1539
	Wendy Doolan	65-75-70-78—288	1539
71	Moira Dunn	71-68-77-73—289	1358
	Barb Mucha	71-68-76-74—289	1358
73	Nanci Bowen	70-72-74-74—290	1268
	Anna Acker-Macosko	71-70-74-75—290	1268
	Tracy Hanson	72-70-72-76—290	1268
76	Kris Monaghan	70-70-75-77—292	1200

1997 du Maurier Classic *at Glen Abbey GC, Toronto, Canada*

(6267 yds, Par 73) Prize money: $1,200,000

Pos	Name	Score	Prize $
1	C Walker	68-72-73-65—278	180000
2	L Neumann	71-67-73-69—280	111711
3	B King	71-69-72-69—281	72461
	K Robbins	71-65-73-72—281	72461
4	C Figg-Currier	69-74-69-70—282	46797
	J Inkster	70-69-71-72—282	46797
6	E Klein	73-70-71-69—283	33513
	R Jones	69-71-71-72—283	33513
8	L Hackney	73-69-75-67—284	26871
	C Johnson	70-72-72-70—284	26871
10	J Geddes	74-69-74-68—285	21335
	D Andrews	71-69-76-69—285	21335
	B Burton	69-75-66-75—285	21335
13	H Alfredsson	75-70-69-72—286	18114
	T Barrett	71-71-70-74—286	18114
15	R Hetherington	73-72-74-68—287	14197
	K Tschetter	72-73-74-68—287	14197
	H Kobayashi	71-73-72-71—287	14197
	L Davies	73-70-73-71—287	14197
	Dani. Ammaccapane	71-75-69-72—287	14197

Pos	Name	Score	Prize $
15T	D Richard	72-73-70-72—287	14197
	K Saiki	75-69-71-72—287	14197
	W Ward	72-71-72-72—287	14197
23	S Steinhauer	72-73-73-70—288	11351
	T Hanson	72-69-76-71—288	11351
	B Mucha	71-75-70-72—288	11351
26	D Pepper	72-75-73-69—289	10264
	H Dobson	74-69-73-73—289	10264
	K Webb	71-72-70-76—289	10264
29	J Briles-Hinton	77-70-73-70—290	8583
	J Gallagher-Smith	76-69-73-72—290	8583
	J Crafter	70-73-74-73—290	8583
	K Marshall	68-75-74-73—290	8583
	L Kane	74-72-70-74—290	8583
	S Redman	72-72-72-74—290	8583
	M Mallon	74-70-71-75—290	8583
36	M Edge	72-75-73-71—291	6913
	T Green	69-78-70-74—291	6913
	J Lidback	74-71-72-74—291	6913
	N Bowen	73-71-73-74—291	6913

Other players who made the cut: M Nause, C Schreyer, D Dormann, C Matthew, M Redman, M Morris, L Brower, J Pitcock, A Fruhwirth, H Stacy, P Hammel 292; C Sörenstam, C Johnston-Forbes, M McGeorge, A Alcott, V Fergon, K Postlewait, D Reid 293; S Croce, K Monaghan, J Anschutz, K Peterson-Parker, J Stephenson 294; L Walters, N Ramsbottom 295; L Lindley, V Odegard, S Little, C Greatrex, B Whitehead, M Estill, K Parker-Gregory 296; P Liscio 298; A Acker-Macosko 299; C Rarick, M Dunn 300; N Scranton 301.

1996 du Maurier Classic at Edmonton CC, Alberta, Canada
(6324 yds, Par 72) Prize money: $1,000,000

Pos	Name	Score	Prize $	Pos	Name	Score	Prize $
1	L Davies	71-70-70-66—277	150000	23	M Redman	71-74-72-72—289	8861
2	N Lopez	68-71-69-71—279	80513		H Kobayashi	73-71-73-72—289	8861
	K Webb	65-68-74-72—279	80513		L West	72-71-74-72—289	8861
4	M Mallon	72-65-69-74—280	52837		J Crafter	71-72-74-72—289	8861
5	P Hurst	69-70-68-74—281	42772		L Brower	71-74-71-73—289	8861
6	L Neumann	69-74-67-73—283	32456		A Ritzman	71-72-72-74—289	8861
	A Sörenstam	71-70-69-73—283	32456		K Marshall	69-72-74-74—289	8861
8	K Postlewait	72-68-70-74—284	24909		M Estill	75-69-69-76—289	8861
	D Dormann	69-70-71-74—284	24909		N Bowen	70-72-69-78—289	8861
10	A Fruhwirth	70-71-71-73—285	20128	32	R Hood	73-72-74-71—290	7019
	R Jones	70-71-68-76—285	20128		G Graham	73-71-72-74—290	7019
12	C Matthew	71-73-72-70—286	14808		B Whitehead	72-71-72-75—290	7019
	C Greatrex	74-69-71-72—286	14808		W Doolan	70-72-72-76—290	7019
	J Inkster	73-72-68-73—286	14808	36	M McGeorge	76-71-73-71—291	5529
	E Klein	71-73-69-73—286	14808		H Stacy	73-73-74-71—291	5529
	B Mucha	68-74-71-73—286	14808		M Berteotti	74-70-75-72—291	5529
	M Figueras-Dotti	70-71-72-73—286	14808		Dani. Ammaccapane	75-72-71-73—291	5529
	V Skinner	71-72-69-74—286	14808		B Daniel	72-73-73-73—291	5529
19	J Dickinson	73-70-73-71—287	11574		L Kane	70-71-77-73—291	5529
	J Stephenson	73-71-70-73—287	11574		A Alcott	76-71-69-75—291	5529
	J Pitcock	73-67-71-76—287	11574		C Figg-Currier	70-73-73-75—291	5529
22	M McNamara	69-74-71-74—288	10567				

Other players who made the cut: T Green, V Goetze, C Johnson, T Kerdyk, MB Zimmerman 292; C Pierce, K Tschetter, K Weiss, P Wright 293; P Bradley, W Ward, C Nilsmark 294; D Coe-Jones, K Williams, K Shipman, J Lidback, J Geddes, S Strudwick 295; A Dibos, P Hammel, K Albers, A Benz, D Lee, B Bunkowsky Scherbak, C Schreyer 296; M Nause, N Harvey, E Gibson, J Anschutz, K Monaghan 297; J McGill 298; M Morris 299; A-M Palli, K Bauer 300; S Furlong, A Miller 301; T Hanson 304.

1995 du Maurier Classic at Beaconsfield GC, Pointe-Claire, Quebec, Canada
(6261 yds, Par 72) Prize money: $1,000,000

Pos	Name	Score	Prize $	Pos	Name	Score	Prize $
1	J Lidback	71-69-68-72—280	150000	18T	H Kobayashi	76-70-72-72—290	11859
2	L Neumann	71-66-72-72—281	93093		D Dormann	74-72-72-72—290	11859
3	J Inkster	72-71-70-70—283	67933	22	C Rarick	73-72-75-71—291	10180
4	T Green	75-71-68-70—284	52837		T Kerdyk	76-72-71-72—291	10180
5	B King	76-70-67-72—285	38998		P Jordan	72-72-74-73—291	10180
	J Geddes	71-73-69-72—285	38998	25	M Redman	75-75-75-67—292	8442
7	M Estill	73-77-69-67—286	27928		A Fruhwirth	77-72-75-68—292	8442
	L Rinker Graham	71-71-70-74—286	27928		K Marshall	74-75-73-70—292	8442
9	H Alfredsson	75-70-70-71—287	21314		E Crosby	73-72-76-71—292	8442
	Dani. Ammaccapane	76-71-68-72—287	21314		J Larsen	76-72-72-72—292	8442
	H Stacy	73-73-69-72—287	21314		P Hurst	73-72-74-73—292	8442
12	D Mochrie	74-72-69-72—288	16136		B Scherbak	73-74-70-75—292	8442
	M Mallon	73-72-73-70—288	16136		P Sheehan	66-77-74-75—292	8442
	V Skinner	74-72-71-71—288	16136	33	A Finney	76-74-72-71—293	6801
	K Tschetter	75-70-71-72—288	16136		G Graham	74-73-73-73—293	6801
16	R Jones	79-70-73-67—289	13369		A Alcott	75-73-71-74—293	6801
	J Pitcock	76-70-69-74—289	13369		C Pierce	72-76-70-75—293	6801
18	E Klein	79-71-69-71—290	11859		MA Lapointe (Am)	72-78-72-71—293	
	C Schreyer	73-74-72-71—290	11859				

Other players who made the cut: MB Zimmerman, J Briles-Hinton, M McNamara, R Walton, J Stephenson, A Dibos, P Wright, M Edge 294; M Bell, L Tatum, A Sörenstam, D Eggeling, B Daniel, A Benz, D Andrews 295; V Goetze, M Platt, T Hanson, L Lindley, V Fergon, B Burton, R Heiken, P Sinn 296; J Anschutz, M Berteotti, B Mucha, S Farwig, L Biehl, M Figueras-Dotti 297; C Hill, K Coats, L Kane, J Crafter, E Gibson 298; T Barrett 300; L McFadden-Shephard, N White-Brophy 301.

1994 du Maurier Classic at Ottawa Hunt &GC, Ottawa, Ontario, Canada
(6400 yds, Par 72) Prize money: $800,000

Pos	Name	Score	Prize $	Pos	Name	Score	Prize $
1	M Nause	65-71-72-71—279	120000	16T	J Lidback	70-72-71-74—287	9862
2	M McGann	66-71-71-72—280	74474		A Dibos	71-71-70-75—287	9862
3	L Neumann	70-67-71-73—281	54346	22	S Little	74-72-73-69—288	7348
4	J Geddes	74-67-70-72—283	34888		M Berteotti	70-72-73-73—288	7348
	M Mallon	70-72-68-73—283	34888		B Burton	71-74-69-74—288	7348
	B King	67-69-74-73—283	34888		B Bunkowsky	74-69-71-74—288	7348
7	D Coe-Jones	72-70-71-71—284	20128		K Williams	67-74-73-74—288	7348
	M Morris	69-72-70-73—284	20128		K Lunn	70-73-70-75—288	7348
	J Dickinson	72-68-70-74—284	20128		A Sorenstam	72-67-73-76—288	7348
	K Robbins	66-70-73-75—284	20128		N Lopez	67-70-75-76—288	7348
11	V Fergon	72-68-75-70—285	14223		LA Mills	66-72-70-80—288	7348
	S Steinhauer	68-72-73-72—285	14223	31	T Barrett	71-75-72-71—289	5514
	P Sheehan	71-71-68-75—285	14223		L Walters	73-72-73-71—289	5514
14	A Alcott	73-70-72-71—286	12076		A Miller	72-71-74-72—289	5514
	D Mochrie	67-74-72-73—286	12076		M Redman	72-72-73-72—289	5514
16	J Crafter	71-74-75-67—287	9862		H Alfredsson	71-73-71-74—289	5514
	P Dunlap	72-69-75-71—287	9862		R Walton	73-67-72-77—289	5514
	A Ritzman	76-70-68-73—287	9862		J Wyatt	69-72-69-79—289	5514
	R Jones	73-70-70-74—287	9862				

Other players who made the cut: J Sams, G Graham, L West, M Estill, L Davies 290; M Edge, L Garbacz, S Maynor, M McGeorge 291; D Richard, C Johnson, C Hill, C Pierce, D Eggeling 292; M Will, B Mucha, P Bradley, A Benz, M Figueras-Dotti 293; L Kiggens, J Pitcock, F Descampe, C Walker, S Turner 294; H Kobayashi, M Lunn 295; V Goetze, K Peterson-Parker, L Merten, J Stephenson, H Drew, N Scranton 296; K Albers, P Wright 297; C Johnston-Forbes, T Abitbol 298; P Hammel 299; D Massey 300.

1993 du Maurier Classic at London Hunt &CC, London, Ontario, Canada
(6331 yds, Par 72) Prize money: $800,000

Pos	Name	Score	Prize $	Pos	Name	Score	Prize $
1	B Burton*	71-70-66-70—277	120000	21	C Rarick	73-73-70-70—286	8302
2	B King	65-70-71-71—277	74474		N Harvey	75-70-71-70—286	8302
*Burton won sudden-death play-off					A Benz	73-70-71-72—286	8302
3	D Coe-Jones	64-74-72-68—278	54346		J Lidback	70-73-68-75—286	8302
4	D Mochrie	68-69-71-71—279	42269	25	R Jones	69-71-77-70—287	7084
5	K Monaghan	72-71-71-66—280	31198		D Eggeling	70-73-73-71—287	7084
	V Fergon	67-73-68-72—280	31198		K Albers	70-72-72-73—287	7084
7	D Lofland-Dormann	68-68-73-72—281	23751		M McGann	67-74-72-74—287	7084
8	H Alfredsson	70-70-72-70—282	19926		A Alcott	70-70-73-74—287	7084
	K Guadagnino	69-69-70-74—282	19926	30	K Robbins	76-71-72-69—288	5317
10	Dani. Ammaccapane	72-72-73-66—283	14894		L Connelly	76-71-71-70—288	5317
	S Steinhauer	73-69-71-70—283	14894		J Anschutz	73-74-71-70—288	5317
	J Dickinson	70-71-71-71—283	14894		A Dibos	73-71-73-71—288	5317
	C Johnson	71-69-72-71—283	14894		D Andrews	73-71-72-72—288	5317
14	G Graham	71-72-72-69—284	11674		S Farwig	71-73-72-72—288	5317
	T Green	69-73-72-70—284	11674		M McGeorge	72-73-70-73—288	5317
	L West	72-72-69-71—284	11674		H Kobayashi	73-72-69-74—288	5317
17	T Barrett	74-72-70-69—285	9862		L Merten	75-69-70-74—288	5317
	D Richard	72-74-70-69—285	9862		K Williams	70-73-71-74—288	5317
	S Little	72-69-69-75—285	9862		R Hood	71-70-73-74—288	5317
	B Daniel	69-70-68-78—285	9862				

Other players who made the cut: J Crafter 289; N Foust, C Pierce, L Walters, M Nause, C Walker, M Spencer-Devlin, A Finney, Dina Ammaccapane, MB Zimmerman, M Morris 290; E Gibson, K Lunn, J Larsen, H Stacy, S Croce, D Baldwin, J Inkster 291; J Stephenson, T Abitbol, C Schreyer, M Will, M McNamara 292; E Crosby, M Mallon, K Peterson-Parker, B Bunkowsky, C Figg-Currier 293; L Garbacz, N Ramsbottom 294; M Faulconer, J Carner, T-J Myers 295; J Pitcock, T Kerdyk, Jean Zedlitz 296; J Sams, M Mackall 298; L Earley 299; S Barrett 300.

1992 du Maurier Classic at St Charles CC, Winnipeg, Manitoba, Canada
(6527 yds, Par 72) Prize money: $700,000

Pos	Name	Score	Prize $	Pos	Name	Score	Prize $
1	S Steinhauer	67-73-67-70—277	105000	20T	L Neumann	74-69-72-72—287	7467
2	J Dickinson	70-71-67-71—279	65165		M Estill	69-73-73-72—287	7467
3	J Inkster	70-69-73-68—280	47553		M Edge	72-69-74-72—287	7467
4	E Gibson	71-73-74-65—283	36985	25	A Ritzman	76-68-74-70—288	6446
5	S Hamlin	74-68-75-67—284	29940		A-M Palli	70-75-72-71—288	6446
6	T Barrett	74-71-70-70—285	17269		J Geddes	72-73-70-73—288	6446
	D Andrews	73-69-72-71—285	17269	28	C Walker	74-71-74-70—289	5608
	B Mucha	71-71-72-71—285	17269		L Rinker-Graham	76-70-72-71—289	5608
	K Albers	70-68-75-72—285	17269		H Alfredsson	73-73-72-71—289	5608
	C Keggi	73-71-68-73—285	17269		B King	67-77-72-73—289	5608
	F Descampe	71-71-70-73—285	17269		D Coe	70-73-72-74—289	5608
	T Green	70-71-70-74—285	17269	33	K Postlewait	73-73-77-67—290	4333
13	P Wright	72-74-73-67—286	9848		Dani. Ammaccapane	72-73-75-70—290	4333
	C Rarick	70-76-73-67—286	9848		C Schreyer	72-72-74-72—290	4333
	P Sheehan	70-74-72-70—286	9848		J Anschutz	71-72-75-72—290	4333
	M Mackall	67-74-75-70—286	9848		H Stacy	70-72-76-72—290	4333
	K Robbins	67-72-76-71—286	9848		A Read	72-75-70-73—290	4333
	K Williams	70-72-72-72—286	9848		C Hill	71-74-72-73—290	4333
	M Mallon	67-73-72-74—286	9848		K Saiki	72-69-76-73—290	4333
20	L Davies	72-72-74-69—287	7467		A Benz	73-71-72-74—290	4333
	D Mochrie	72-72-71-72—287	7467				

Other players who made the cut: J Stephenson, D Massey 291; D Eggeling, G Hull, C Johnson, M Will, N Scranton, B Bunkowsky 292; V Skinner, L Merten, M Figueras-Dotti, R Jones, L Brower, D Lofland 293; M Morris, N LeRoux 294; L Walters, L Alderete, D Lasker, V Fergon, R Walton 295; K Noble, T Fleming, S Little, M Spencer-Devlin 296; M McGann, A Finney 297; N Rubin 300; K Mundinger, B Pearson, C Mackey 301.

1991 du Maurier Classic at Vancouver GC, Coquitlam, British Columbia, Canada
(6421 yds, Par 72) Prize money: $700,000

Pos	Name	Score	Prize $	Pos	Name	Score	Prize $
1	N Scranton	72-75-64-68—279	105000	19	S Maynor	74-73-73-69—289	7875
2	D Massey	67-70-72-73—282	64750		L Neumann	72-72-75-70—289	7875
3	L Davies	71-71-71-71—284	37916		E Gibson	73-73-71-72—289	7875
	T Johnson	67-71-73-73—284	37916		D Lasker	74-70-70-75—289	7875
	P Wright	72-69-69-74—284	37916	23	P Bradley	76-72-72-70—290	6587
6	D Coe	68-77-71-70—286	17966		M Mallon	71-73-75-71—290	6587
	V Fergon	72-72-72-70—286	17966		K Rogerson	72-76-72-70—290	6587
	C Pierce	70-73-71-72—286	17966		T Green	75-72-71-72—290	6587
	B King	71-71-72-72—286	17966		C Figg-Currier	70-73-73-74—290	6587
	D Mochrie	69-69-74-74—286	17966	28	K Postlewait	69-76-78-68—291	5537
	R Jones	71-71-69-75—286	17966		J Anderson	74-73-72-72—291	5537
12	D Richard	72-71-74-70—287	11550		A Benz	72-75-72-72—291	5537
	K Albers	69-74-73-71—287	11550		S Little	73-76-69-73—291	5537
	B Burton	71-71-72-73—287	11550		H Kobayashi	71-75-72-73—291	5537
15	J Pitcock	75-74-68-71—288	9362	33	A Ritzman	71-74-76-71—292	4795
	M Figueras-Dotti	71-74-72-71—288	9362		J Dickinson	75-70-72-75—292	4795
	J Geddes	69-77-70-72—288	9362		N White	73-71-73-75—292	4795
	K Davies	74-70-71-73—288	9362				

Other players who made the cut: C Johnson, Ok-Hee Ku, S Furlong, M Berteotti, T Barrett, E Crosby, J Inkster, C Schreyer 293; T Purtzer, M Edge, C Hill, A Alcott, P Sinn, M McGann, S Steinhauer, J Wyatt, M McGeorge, L Merten, D Andrews, C Mackey, L Rinker 295; J Crafter, J Anschutz, A Munt, K Monaghan, Danielle Ammaccapane, N Bowen, M Nause, B Pearson 295; Nicky LeRoux, K Cockerill, N Ramsbottom, T-J Myers 296; T Kerdyk, A-M Palli, M McNamara, J Carner, G Hull 297; R Walton, C Teno, S Sanders 298; S Redman, H Stacy 299; K Mundinger, L Walters 303.

1990 du Maurier Classic at Westmount G&CC, Kitchener, Ontario, Canada
(6420 yds, Par 72) Prize money: $600,000

Pos	Name	Score	Prize $	Pos	Name	Score	Prize $
1	C Johnston	65-70-70-71—276	90000	19T	S Steinhauer	71-72-72-74—289	6750
2	P Sheehan	69-70-70-69—278	55500		M McGeorge	74-70-67-78—289	6750
3	B Daniel	74-66-71-70—281	40500	23	C Rarick	73-73-72-72—290	5738
4	L Neumann	68-72-70-72—282	31500		Dani. Ammaccapane	75-69-74-72—290	5738
5	M Berteotti	74-68-69-72—283	25500		L Kean	72-72-74-72—290	5738
6	G Hull	70-68-76-70—284	19350		N Foust	70-75-72-73—290	5738
	J Anschutz	70-72-70-72—284	19350	27	TL Carter	69-74-73-75—291	5010
8	P Bradley	73-69-70-73—285	14850		D Mochrie	72-71-72-76—291	5010
	P Rizzo	67-69-73-76—285	14850		S Sanders	70-70-75-76—291	5010
10	J Geddes	72-67-74-73—286	12000		L Baugh	71-75-68-77—291	5010
	B King	70-72-70-74—286	12000	31	A Okamoto	74-73-75-70—292	3885
12	J Anderson	70-75-73-69—287	9300		H Kobayahsi	73-73-75-71—292	3885
	D White	72-73-71-71—287	9300		D Massey	76-71-73-72—292	3885
	T Green	73-70-73-71—287	9300		K Shipman	73-67-80-72—292	3885
	V Fergon	69-73-73-72—287	9300		C Figg-Currier	75-72-72-73—292	3885
	A Benz	73-70-71-73—287	9300		V Skinner	76-72-70-74—292	3885
17	S Turner	74-70-72-72—288	7650		J Briles	72-74-72-74—292	3885
	D Richard	69-71-74-74—288	7650		S Palmer	73-71-73-75—292	3885
19	C Keggi	74-70-75-70—289	6750		L Rittenhouse	71-76-78-77—292	3885
	D Coe	72-70-76-71—289	6750		J Britz	71-70-74-77—292	3885

Other players who made the cut: M Ward, Ok-Hee Ku, A Ritzman, C Hill, K Tschetter, C Johnson, S Ertl, T Purtzer 293; P Hammel, K Cockerill, C Sherk, K Rogerson, K Postlewait, D Lasker, H Drew, J Crafter 294; M Nause, B Thomas, M Edge, L Walters 295; C Gerring, C Walker, R Jones, M Moore 296; D Eggeling, L Merten 297; M McNamara, H Stacy, M Figueras-Dotti, P Wright, P Jordan, K Monaghan 298; L Hurlbut, B Lauer 299; T Tatum, A Finney, J Lidback, A Lukken, T Johnson, R Walton 300; MC Cheng 301; K Hanson 303.

1989 du Maurier Classic at Beaconsfield GC, Pointe Claire, Quebec, Canada
(6261 yds, Par 72) Prize money: $600,000

Pos	Name	Score	Prize $	Pos	Name	Score	Prize $
1	T Green	68-69-70-72—279	90000	21	K Rogerson	75-71-71-71—288	6310
2	P Bradley	69-75-69-67—280	48000		M Blackwelder	73-72-70-73—288	6310
	B King	67-69-74-70—280	48000		A Ritzman	69-75-70-74—288	6310
4	P Sheehan	69-74-69-69—281	26000	24	M Bozarth	72-74-73-70—289	5550
	A Alcott	70-70-72-69—281	26000		D White	72-73-74-70—289	5550
	P Hammel	71-71-68-71—281	26000		A Okamoto	73-71-71-74—289	5550
7	N Brown	70-74-70-68—282	16650		H Stacy	69-72-69-79—289	5550
	B Daniel	71-69-71-71—282	16650	28	T Kerdyk	75-69-77-69—290	4508
9	N Lopez	72-67-72-72—283	14100		S Redman	74-73-72-71—290	4508
10	D Coe	71-73-73-67—284	10740		R Walton	72-75-72-71—290	4508
	N Foust	75-73-68-68—284	10740		K Cockerill	73-73-72-72—290	4508
	J Carner	73-71-72-68—284	10740		M Rodriguez Hardin	75-70-72-73—290	4507
	C Walker	71-70-73-70—284	10740		T Johnson	75-72-69-74—290	4507
	J Geddes	69-71-70-74—284	10740		S Furlong	73-72-71-74—290	4507
15	A Benz	71-73-71-70—285	8400		C Rarick	73-71-71-75—290	4507
	C Reynolds	71-72-71-71—285	8400	36	L Merten	73-74-73-71—291	3585
17	L Davies	71-69-72-74—286	7800		Ok-Hee Ku	74-72-74-71—291	3585
18	D Mochrie	74-70-72-71—287	7200		L Adams	69-77-72-73—291	3585
	P Rizzo	73-68-75-71—287	7200		S Turner	72-71-70-78—291	3585
	J Rosenthal	72-71-70-74—287	7200				

Other players who made the cut: D Heinicke-Rauch, K Guadagnino, T Barrett, K Whitworth, K Albers, C Pierce 292; R Jones, S Thomas, H Farr, C Schreyer, S Haynie, D McHaffie, D Richard 293; H Drew, B Mucha, L Hurlbut, C Mackey, C Gerring, V Fergon 294; M Mallon, A Finney, M Nause, B Thomas, B Bunkowsky, C Morse 295; C Marino, J Briles, L Walters, S Spuzich, C Figg-Currier 296; V Skinner, K Young, S Ertl, J Crafter, J Anderson 297; C Chillemi 298; S Palmer, M Will 299; R Hood 300; M Ward 301.

DU MAURIER CLASSIC HISTORY

The Du Maurier Classic was inaugurated in 1973 and designated a Major Championship in 1979.

Players are of American nationality unless stated.

Year	Winner	Venue	Score
1973	J Bourassa*	Montreal GC, Montreal	214
Won play-off after a tie with S Haynie, J Rankin			
1974	CJ Callison	Candiac GC, Montreal	208
1975	J Carner*	St George's CC, Toronto	214
Won play-off after a tie with C Mann			
1976	D Caponi*	Cedar Brae G&CC, Toronto	212
Won play-off after a tie with J Rankin			
1977	J Rankin	Lachute G&CC, Montreal	214
1978	J Carner	St. George's CC, Toronto	278
1979	A Alcott	Richelieu Valley CC, Montreal	285
1980	P Bradley	St George's CC, Toronto	277
1981	J Stephenson (Aus)	Summerlea CC, Dorian, Quebec	278
1982	S Haynie	St George's CC, Toronto	280
1983	H Stacy	Beaconsfield CC, Montreal	277
1984	J Inkster	St. George's CC, Toronto	279
1985	P Bradley	Beaconsfield CC, Montreal	278
1986	P Bradley*	Board of Trade CC, Toronto	276
Won play-off after a tie with A Okamoto			
1987	J Rosenthal	Islesmere GC, Laval, Quebec	272
1988	S Little (SA)	Vancouver GC, Coquitlam, BC	279
1989	T Green	Beaconsfield GC, Montreal	279
1990	C Johnston	Westmount G&CC, Kitchener, Ontario	276
1991	N Scranton	Vancouver GC, Coquitlam, BC	279
1992	S Steinhauer	St Charles CC, Winnipeg, Manitoba	277
1993	B Burton*	London H&CC, Ontario	277
Won play-off after a tie with B King			
1994	M Nause	Ottawa Hunt Club, Ontario	279
1995	J Lidback	Beaconsfield CC, Montreal	280
1996	L Davies (Eng)	Edmonton CC, Edmonton, Alberta	277
1997	C Walker	Glen Abbey GC, Toronto	278
1998	B Burton	Essex G&CC, Ontario	270

Women's Major Title Table

Mickey Wright

Jo Anne Carner

Betsy King

	US Open	LPGA	*du Maurier	†Dinah Shore	British Open	US Amateur	British Amateur	Total titles
Mickey Wright	4	4	0	0	0	0	0	8
Jo Anne Carner	2	0	0	0	0	5	0	7
Betsy King	2	1	0	3	1	0	0	7
Pat Bradley	1	1	3	1	0	0	0	6
Betsy Rawls	4	2	0	0	0	0	0	6
Glenna Collett Vare	0	0	0	0	0	6	0	6
Juli Inkster	0	0	1	2	0	3	0	6
Louise Suggs	2	1	0	0	0	1	1	5
Babe Zaharias	3	0	0	0	0	1	1	5
Amy Alcott	1	0	1	3	0	0	0	5
Laura Davies	1	2	1	0	1	0	0	5

* *Designated a major championship in 1979* † *Designated a major championship in 1983*

All photographs © Phil Sheldon

PART II
Men's Professional Tournaments

Index on pages 126–27

Index – Men's Professional Tournaments and Events

Official World Golf Ranking, 1998, Top 80	**128**
European Tour, 1998 & Past Results	**130**
Volvo Ranking	130
Career Money List	131
Tour Statistics	132
Tour Results (1998 and past results)	133
Johnnie Walker Classic	133
Heineken Classic	133
South African Open	133
Alfred Dunhill South African PGA	133
Dubai Desert Classic	134
Qatar Masters	134
Moroccan Open	134
Portuguese Open	134
Cannes Open	135
Peugeot Open de España	135
Italian Open	136
Turespaña Masters Open Baleares	137
Benson & Hedges International Open	137
Volvo PGA Championship	137
Deutsche Bank – SAP Open TPC of Europe	139
National Car Rental English Open	139
Madeira Island Open	139
Peugeot Open de France	140
Murphy's Irish Open	140
Standard Life Loch Lomond	141
TNT Dutch Open	142
Volvo Scandinavian Masters	142
German Open	143
Smurfit European Open	143
BMW International Open	144
Canon European Masters	144
One-2-One British Masters	145
Trophée Lancôme	145
Linde German Masters	146
Belgacom Open	146
Alfred Dunhill Cup	147
Cisco World Matchplay	147
Open Novotel Perrier	148
Volvo Masters	148
European Tour Qualifying School	148
European Challenge Tour, 1998	**148**
Final Ranking	150
Tour Results	150
European Senior Tour, 1998	**150**
Final Ranking	152
Career Money List	153
Tour Results	153
Senior Tour Qualifying School	154
US PGA Tour, 1998	**155**
Final Ranking	155
Career Money List	156
Tour Statistics	157
Tour Results	158
Mercedes Championship	158
Bob Hope Chrysler Classic	158
Phoenix Open	158
AT&T Pebble Beach National Pro-Am	158
Buick Invitational	158
United Airlines Hawaiian Open	158
Tucson Chrysler Classic	159
Nissan Open	159
Doral-Ryder Open	159
Honda Classic	159
Bay Hill Invitational	159
The Players Championship	159
Freeport-McDermott Classic	159
MCI Classic	160
Greater Greensboro Chrysler Classic	160
Shell Houston Open	160
BellSouth Classic	160
GTE Byron Nelson Classic	160
MasterCard Colonial	160
Memorial Tournament	161
Kemper Open	161
Buick Classic	161
Motorola Western Open	161
Canon Greater Hartford Open	161
Quad City Classic	161
Deposit Guaranty Golf Classic	162
CVS Charity Classic	162
FedEx St Jude Classic	162
Buick Open	162
Sprint International	162
NEC World Series of Golf	162
Greater Vancouver Open	163
Greater Milwaukee Open	163
Bell Canadian Open	163
BC Open	163
Westin Texas Open	163
Buick Challenge	163
Michelob Championship	163

European Tour 127

Las Vegas Invitational	164
National Car Rental Classic	164
The Tour Championship	164
ADDITIONAL UNOFFICIAL EVENTS	164
TOUR QUALIFYING SCHOOL	165

US Senior Tour, 1998 — *165*
FINAL RANKING	166
CAREER MONEY LIST	166
TOUR STATISTICS	167
TOUR RESULTS	168
US SENIOR TOUR QUALIFYING SCHOOL	169

US Nike Tour, 1998 — *170*
FINAL RANKING	170
TOUR RESULTS	171

Japan PGA Tour, 1998 — *172*
FINAL RANKING	172
TOUR RESULTS	172

Omega (Asian PGA) Tour, 1998 — *174*
FINAL RANKING	174
TOUR RESULTS	174

Asian Tour, 1998 — *175*
TOUR RESULTS	175

Vodacom South African Tour, 1998 — *176*
FINAL RANKING	176
TOUR RESULTS	176

South American Tour, 1998 — *178*
FINAL RANKING	178
TOUR RESULTS	178

Australasian Tour, 1998–99 — *179*
TOUR RANKING	179
TOUR RESULTS	179

Additional International Events — *180*
Andersen Consulting World Championship of Golf	180
Hassan II Trophy	180
Million Dollar Challenge	180
Subaru Sarazen World Open Championship	181
TEAM EVENTS	181
Great Britain & Ireland v USA	181
The Ryder Cup	181
Ryder Cup – Individual Records	187
PGA Cup	191
President's Cup	192
World Cup of Golf	193
Alfred Dunhill Cup	196

British National and Regional Championships — *197*
NATIONAL CHAMPIONSHIPS	
PGA Assistants' Championship	197
PGA Seniors Championship	197
Club Professionals' Championship	197
Irish PGA Championship	198
Irish Club Professionals' Championship	198
Scottish Assistants' Championship	199
Scottish PGA Matchplay Championship	199
Scottish Professionals' Championship	199
Welsh Professionals' Championship	200

REGIONAL CHAMPIONSHIPS	200
Derbyshire Professionals'	200
Devon Open	200
East Anglian Open	200
East Region PGA	200
Essex Open	200
Essex Professionals'	200
Glasgow Matchplay	201
Glasgow Strokeplay	201
Hampshire PGA	201
Hampshire Matchplay	201
Hampshire, Isle of Wight and Channel Islands Open	201
Herts Professionals'	201
Kent Open	201
Kent Professionals'	201
Lancashire Open	201
Leicestershire and Rutland Open	201
Lincolnshire Open	201
Middlesex Open	201
Midland Masters	202
Midland Professionals' Matchplay	202
Midland Professionals' Strokeplay	202
Midland Seniors'	202
Norfolk Open	202
Norfolk Professionals'	202
Northern Region PGA	202
Northern Open	202
Nottinghamshire Open	202
South of Scotland	202
South West PGA	202
Southern Assistants'	202
Southern Assistants' Matchplay	203
Southern Professionals'	203
Staffordshire Open	203
Staffordshire and Shropshire Strokeplay	203
Suffolk Open	203
Suffolk Professionals'	203
Sunderland of Scotland Masters	203
Sussex Open	203
Ulster Professionals'	203
Warwickshire Open	203
Warwickshire Professionals' Matchplay	203
Warwickshire Professionals' Strokeplay	203
West Region PGA	204
Hills Wiltshire Pro Champ	204
Worcestershire Open	204
Worcestershire Strokeplay	204
Yorkshire Professionals'	204

Overseas National Championships — *205*

Official World Golf Ranking, 1998, Top 80

Lee Westwood, with seven international victories – three more than any other player, had the highest 'net gain' in World Ranking points through 1998 to move up from 23rd to 8th in the final 1998 ranking list. Four of Lee's victories came on his 'home Tour' in Europe, two in successive weeks in Japan and one on the US PGA Tour.

Of the 12 players who moved into the World Top 50 during the year, three US players had 'comeback' years on the US PGA Tour – John Huston (141st to 10th on PGA Tour Money List), Hal Sutton (54th to 5th on PGA Tour Money List) and Scott Verplank (1997 PGA Tour Qualifying Tournament winner to 18th on 1998 Money List) had the greatest 'net gain' in World Ranking points.

Outside the Top 50, Steve Flesch, US PGA Tour Rookie with $777,186 in earnings, and Patrik Sjöland, who had his maiden victory and finished No. 5 on the European Tour, had the greatest 'net gain' in World Ranking points.

David Duval, the US PGA Tour No. 1 with four victories, just edged out World No. 1 Tiger Woods and double 1998 Major winner Mark O'Meara as the highest average points earner for the year based on World Ranking points gained in 1998 only.

Position 1998	1997	Name	Country	Points Average	Total Points	No. of Events	96/97 Total	96/97 Minus	1998 Plus
1	(2)	Tiger Woods	US	12.30	566	46	452	-264	378
2	(10)	Mark O'Meara	US	10.43	532	51	383	-259	408
3	(12)	David Duval	US	9.67	532	55	364	-226	394
4	(5)	Davis Love III	US	9.43	481	51	482	-309	308
5	(4)	Ernie Els	SA	9.18	505	55	554	-357	308
6	(3)	Nick Price	Zim	8.98	458	51	437	-257	278
7	(7)	Colin Montgomerie	Sco	8.91	508	57	489	-329	348
8	(23)	Lee Westwood	Eng	8.65	536	62	342	-208	402
9	(15)	Vijay Singh	Fij	8.51	502	59	366	-230	366
10	(6)	Phil Mickelson	US	7.76	396	51	419	-293	270
11	(20)	Fred Couples	US	7.65	306	40	235	-179	250
12	(22)	Jim Furyk	US	7.23	412	57	326	-198	284
13	(8)	'Jumbo' Ozaki	Jpn	6.77	318	47	346	-230	202
14	(18)	Jesper Parnevik	Swe	6.47	330	51	285	-171	216
15	(11)	Justin Leonard	US	6.42	385	60	413	-252	224
16	(16)	Steve Elkington	Aus	6.18	247	40	266	-159	140
17	(36)	Darren Clarke	N.Ire	5.72	326	57	219	-137	244
18	(1)	Greg Norman	Aus	5.65	243	43	517	-326	52
19	(37)	Brian Watts	US	5.23	251	48	182	-119	188
20	(13)	Scott Hoch	US	5.22	287	55	377	-246	156
21	(28)	Mark Calcavecchia	US	5.19	301	58	265	-164	200
22	(9)	Tom Lehman	US	5.08	264	52	425	-305	144
23	(34)	Lee Janzen	US	5.02	276	55	212	-132	196
24	(19)	Tom Watson	US	4.75	190	40	219	-151	122
25	(42)	José M Olazábal	Sp	4.62	245	53	146	-73	172

Official World Golf Ranking   129

Position		Name	Country	Points Average	Total Points	No. of Events	96/97 Total	96/97 Minus	1998 Plus
26	(43)	Steve Stricker	US	4.60	198	43	145	-135	188
27	(47)	Payne Stewart	US	4.49	220	49	167	-115	168
28	(21)	Bernhard Langer	Ger	4.45	227	51	264	-155	118
29	(140)	John Huston	US	4.40	251	57	69	-58	240
30	(=44)	Stuart Appleby	Aus	4.29	253	59	207	-108	154
31	(29)	Jeff Maggert	US	4.25	217	51	232	-157	142
32	(35)	John Cook	US	4.25	238	56	207	-135	166
33	(49)	Bob Tway	US	4.09	225	55	152	-105	178
34	(96)	Hal Sutton	US	4.00	236	59	95	-55	196
35	(24)	Steve Jones	US	3.61	184	51	297	-201	88
36	(66)	Brandt Jobe	US	3.60	162	45	104	-64	122
37	(25)	Ian Woosnam	Wal	3.44	172	50	268	-186	90
38	(56)	Jeff Sluman	US	3.38	213	63	178	-121	156
39	(59)	Carlos Franco	Par	3.36	148	44	111	-69	106
40	(14)	Brad Faxon	US	3.36	178	53	313	-201	66
41	(73)	Thomas Björn	Den	3.33	163	49	120	-79	122
42	(119)	Billy Mayfair	US	3.30	198	60	83	-59	174
43	(33)	Shigeki Maruyama	Jpn	3.27	196	60	237	-145	104
44	(148)	Glen Day	US	3.25	185	57	70	-51	166
45	(130)	Bob Estes	US	3.16	161	51	64	-39	136
46	(55)	Stewart Cink	US	3.10	192	62	145	-79	126
47	(27)	Loren Roberts	US	3.08	148	48	244	-158	62
48	(72)	Andrew Magee	US	3.05	180	59	129	-79	130
49	(41)	Bill Glasson	US	3.05	122	40	139	-73	56
50	(=346)	Scott Verplank	US	3.00	150	50	16	-12	146
51	(133)	Patrik Sjöland	Swe	2.89	159	55	67	-40	132
52	(69)	Frankie Minoza	Phi	2.83	133	47	107	-72	98
53	(40)	Craig Parry	Aus	2.80	165	59	227	-146	84
54	(125)	Miguel A Jimenez	Sp	2.75	151	55	75	-56	132
55	(68)	Fred Funk	US	2.74	192	70	159	-113	146
56	(46)	'Joe' Ozaki	Jpn	2.74	178	65	206	-130	102
57	(17)	Nick Faldo	Eng	2.70	119	44	277	-200	42
58	(137)	Stephen Leaney	Aus	2.67	131	49	51	-30	110
59	(79)	Dudley Hart	US	2.62	144	55	99	-65	110
60	(26)	Frank Nobilo	NZ	2.57	131	51	256	-169	44
61	(54)	Eduardo Romero	Arg	2.56	105	41	122	-75	58
62	(107)	Paul Azinger	US	2.52	106	42	65	-43	84
63	(53)	Michael Bradley	US	2.51	123	49	151	-112	84
64	(48)	Per-Ulrik Johansson	Swe	2.50	105	42	141	-88	52
65	(39)	Craig Stadler	US	2.44	105	43	151	-98	52
66	(83)	Peter O'Malley	Aus	2.41	140	58	112	-68	96
67	(80)	Robert Karlsson	Swe	2.38	112	47	86	-46	72
68	(=171)	Greg Chalmers	Aus	2.38	119	50	54	-35	100
69	(84)	Andrew Coltart	Sco	2.36	151	64	118	-85	118
70	(77)	Greg Turner	NZ	2.34	110	47	100	-64	74
71	(101)	David Toms	US	2.30	124	54	90	-52	86
72	(57)	Jay Haas	US	2.29	112	49	136	-92	68
73	(30)	Mark McNulty	Zim	2.28	91	40	169	-126	48
74	(=388)	Steve Flesch	US	2.22	109	49	13	-12	108
75	(=44)	Scott McCarron	US	2.22	122	55	184	-112	50
76	(221)	Steve Pate	US	2.16	119	55	38	-19	100
77	(31)	Paul Stankowski	US	2.14	122	57	229	-151	44
78	(63)	Billy Andrade	US	2.12	127	60	144	-91	74
79	(126)	Brandel Chamblee	US	2.08	108	52	72	-48	84
80	(193)	Hidemichi Tanaka	Jpn	2.06	134	65	61	-47	120

European Tour – 1998 and Past Results

1998 VOLVO RANKING

Pos	Name	Prize Money £	Pos	Name	Prize Money £
1	Colin Montgomerie (Sco)	993077	51	Peter Lonard (Aus)	136453
2	Darren Clarke (N.Ire)	902867	52	Ian Garbutt (Eng)	133991
3	Lee Westwood (Eng)	814386	53	Mark Roe (Eng)	126149
4	Miguel Angel Jiménez (Sp)	518819	54	Paolo Quirici (Swi)	124731
5	Patrik Sjöland (Swe)	500136	55	Per-Ulrik Johansson (Swe)	123206
6	Thomas Björn (Den)	470798	56	Olle Karlsson (Swe)	122501
7	José Maria Olazábal (Sp)	449132	57	Roger Wessels (SA)	121453
8	Ernie Els (SA)	433884	58	Mark James (Eng)	121351
9	Andrew Coltart (Sco)	388816	59	Mats Lanner (Swe)	113023
10	Mathias Grönberg (Swe)	358779	60	Tony Johnstone (Zim)	111268
11	Stephen Leaney (Aus)	310643	61	Mats Hallberg (Swe)	111095
12	Peter Baker (Eng)	307163	62	Paul Lawrie (Sco)	107099
13	Sven Strüver (Ger)	293208	63	Raymond Russell (Sco)	102276
14	Sam Torrance (Sco)	286807	64	Philip Walton (Ire)	101465
15	Phillip Price (Wal)	283885	65	Jim Payne (Eng)	100296
16	Stephen Allan (Aus)	267743	66	José Coceres (Arg)	96957
17	Robert Karlsson (Swe)	267285	67	Joakim Haeggman (Swe)	93989
18	Bernhard Langer (Ger)	262347	68	Scott Henderson (Sco)	93964
19	David Carter (Eng)	244424	69	Thomas Levet (Fr)	93674
20	Ian Woosnam (Wal)	237570	70	Dennis Edlund (Swe)	91803
21	Eduardo Romero (Arg)	234148	71	Michael Jonzon (Swe)	91510
22	Russell Claydon (Eng)	233913	72	Bob May (US)	91342
23	Jarmo Sandelin (Swe)	231375	73	Dean Robertson (Sco)	90062
24	Costantino Rocca (It)	220759	74	José Rivero (Sp)	89526
25	Greg Chalmers (Aus)	220672	75	Fredrik Jacobson (Swe)	88440
26	Jean Van de Velde (Fr)	214163	76	Peter Senior (Aus)	87764
27	Greg Turner (NZ)	210977	77	Derrick Cooper (Eng)	87342
28	Gary Orr (Sco)	209516	78	Andrew Sherborne (Eng)	86548
29	Padraig Harrington (Ire)	208013	79	Brian Davis (Eng)	82654
30	Paul McGinley (Ire)	201970	80	Mark Mouland (Wal)	82214
31	Santiago Luna (Sp)	201624	81	Michael Campbell (NZ)	81797
32	David Howell (Eng)	199040	82	Nick Faldo (Eng)	78178
33	Retief Goosen (SA)	191249	83	Andrew Beal (Eng)	77195
34	Alex Cejka (Ger)	184673	84	Michael Long (NZ)	77136
35	Paul Broadhurst (Eng)	181839	85	Andrew Oldcorn (Sco)	75549
36	Peter O'Malley (Aus)	172448	86	Jonathan Lomas (Eng)	75466
37	Steve Webster (Eng)	170871	87	Marc Farry (Fr)	74845
38	Peter Mitchell (Eng)	167536	88	Raphaël Jacquelin (Fr)	74844
39	Gordon Brand Jr (Sco)	167500	89	Greg Owen (Eng)	73940
40	Ignacio Garrido (Sp)	166866	90	Anthony Wall (Eng)	73494
41	Craig Hainline (US)	165792	91	Steen Tinning (Den)	72153
42	Pierre Fulke (Swe)	160418	92	Fabrice Tarnaud (Fr)	70778
43	Jamie Spence (Eng)	158612	93	Olivier Edmond (Fr)	69269
44	Robert Allenby (Aus)	152413	94	Gary Evans (Eng)	67767
45	Angel Cabrera (Arg)	150792	95	Paul Eales (Eng)	65708
46	Thomas Gögele (Ger)	150041	96	Daniel Chopra (Swe)	65700
47	Katsuyoshi Tomori (Jpn)	149789	97	Per Haugsrud (Nor)	64953
48	David Gilford (Eng)	149569	98	Mark Davis (Eng)	63779
49	Massimo Florioli (It)	137384	99	Rolf Muntz (Hol)	63583
50	Van Phillips (Eng)	136768	100	Roger Chapman (Eng)	63312

Career Money List (at end 1998)

Pos	Name	Prize Money £	Pos	Name	Prize Money £
1	Colin Montgomerie (Sco)	7 831 681	51	Jean Van de Velde (Fr)	1 385 886
2	Bernhard Langer (Ger)	6 322 509	52	Peter Senior (Aus)	1 372 231
3	Ian Woosnam (Wal)	5 762 799	53	Robert Karlsson (Swe)	1 365 264
4	Nick Faldo (Eng)	5 349 842	54	Carl Mason (Eng)	1 363 991
5	Seve Ballesteros (Sp)	4 593 503	55	Russell Claydon (Eng)	1 354 007
6	Sam Torrance (Sco)	4 338 155	56	Craig Parry (Aus)	1 342 637
7	José Maria Olazábal (Sp)	4 056 785	57	Nick Price (Zim)	1 294 560
8	Ernie Els (SA)	3 500 055	58	José Maria Cañizares (Sp)	1 284 560
9	Mark McNulty (Zim)	3 270 643	59	Mats Lanner (Swe)	1 278 432
10	Costantino Rocca (It)	2 954 854	60	Wayne Westner (SA)	1 201 090
11	Mark James (Eng)	2 952 673	61	Wayne Riley (Aus)	1 195 872
12	Darren Clarke (N.Ire)	2 937 523	62	Mark Mouland (Wal)	1 188 814
13	Barry Lane (Eng)	2 876 572	63	Sven Strüver (Ger)	1 163 000
14	Ronan Rafferty (N.Ire)	2 690 927	64	Richard Boxall (Eng)	1 103 245
15	Gordon Brand Jr (Sco)	2 678 730	65	Mike Harwood (Aus)	1 085 360
16	Anders Forsbrand (Swe)	2 575 086	66	Thomas Björn (Den)	1 083 858
17	Miguel Angel Jiménez (Sp)	2 562 982	67	Padraig Harrington (Ire)	1 082 438
18	Sandy Lyle (Sco)	2 558 177	68	Christy O'Connor Jr (Ire)	1 081 337
19	Fred Couples (US)	2 537 911	69	Santiago Luna (Sp)	1 080 613
20	Vijay Singh (Fij)	2 440 074	70	Ignacio Garrido (Sp)	1 080 331
21	Frank Nobilo (NZ)	2 438 838	71	Phillip Price (Wal)	1 076 406
22	Lee Westwood (Eng)	2 269 054	72	Derrick Cooper (Eng)	1 041 820
23	Eduardo Romero (Arg)	2 238 511	73	David Frost (SA)	1 039 384
24	Rodger Davis (Aus)	2 134 667	74	Peter Fowler (Aus)	1 014 878
25	Per-Ulrik Johansson (Swe)	2 090 808	75	José Coceres (Arg)	1 014 455
26	David Gilford (Eng)	2 072 600	76	Alex Cejka (Ger)	1 007 918
27	Howard Clark (Eng)	2 066 164	77	Andrew Sherborne (Eng)	999 933
28	José Rivero (Sp)	2 029 379	78	Vicente Fernandez (Arg)	990 970
29	Greg Norman (Aus)	1 969 277	79	Patrik Sjöland (Swe)	979 470
30	Peter Baker (Eng)	1 915 735	80	Gordon J Brand (Eng)	967 584
31	Paul Broadhurst (Eng)	1 865 757	81	Mark O'Meara (US)	928 707
32	Tony Johnstone (Zim)	1 807 317	82	Gary Orr (Sco)	904 275
33	Jesper Parnevik (Swe)	1 765 439	83	John Bland (SA)	859 339
34	Mark Roe (Eng)	1 663 903	84	Payne Stewart (US)	855 321
35	David Feherty (N.Ire)	1 662 387	85	Jarmo Sandelin (Swe)	838 059
36	Robert Allenby (Aus)	1 621 753	86	Mark Davis (Eng)	830 091
37	Steven Richardson (Eng)	1 608 583	87	Paul Lawrie (Sco)	815 566
38	Peter Mitchell (Eng)	1 604 887	88	Jim Payne (Eng)	812 192
39	Greg Turner (NZ)	1 596 633	89	Mathias Grönberg (Swe)	807 584
40	Philip Walton (Ire)	1 560 381	90	Manuel Piñero (Sp)	800 845
41	Eamonn Darcy (Ire)	1 557 917	91	Stephen Ames (T&T)	799 228
42	Des Smyth (Ire)	1 522 953	92	Paul Curry (Eng)	796 740
43	Retief Goosen (SA)	1 499 662	93	Ross McFarlane (Eng)	786 836
44	Jamie Spence (Eng)	1 476 607	94	Andrew Oldcorn (Sco)	773 310
45	Andrew Coltart (Sco)	1 418 999	95	Mark Calcavecchia (US)	757 117
46	Miguel Angel Martin (Sp)	1 414 736	96	Paul Way (Eng)	753 051
47	Roger Chapman (Eng)	1 407 940	97	Brett Ogle (Aus)	727 657
48	Paul McGinley (Ire)	1 404 859	98	Ross Drummond (Sco)	719 963
49	Peter O'Malley (Aus)	1 399 166	99	Raymond Russell (Sco)	719 457
50	Joakim Haeggman (Swe)	1 395 710	100	Jonathan Lomas (Eng)	702 324

1998 Tour Statistics

Stroke averages

Pos	Name	Avg
1	Darren Clarke (N.Ire)	69.45
2	Colin Montgomerie (Sco)	69.66
3	Lee Westwood (Eng)	69.85
4	Ernie Els (RSA)	69.89
5	José Maria Olazábal (Sp)	70.25
6	Bernhard Langer (Ger)	70.50
7	Miguel Angel Jiménez (Sp)	70.57
8	Patrik Sjöland (Swe)	70.59
9	Thomas Björn (Den)	70.64
10	Greg Turner (NZ)	70.67
11	Sam Torrance (Sco)	70.80
12	Andrew Coltart (Sco)	70.81
13	Peter O'Malley (Aus)	70.86
14	Paul McGinley (Ire)	70.88
15	Robert Karlsson (Swe)	70.89
16	Nick Faldo (Eng)	70.90
	Peter Baker (Eng)	70.90
18	Alex Cejka (Ger)	70.96
19	Eduardo Romero (Arg)	71.00
	Ian Woosnam (Wal)	71.00
	David Gilford (Eng)	71.00
22	Retief Goosen (RSA)	71.02
23	Jean Van de Velde (Fr)	71.04
24	Peter Mitchell (Eng)	71.05
25	Gordon Brand Jr (Sco)	71.08

Driving accuracy

Pos	Name	%
1	Pierre Fulke (Swe)	75.5
2	David Gilford (Eng)	74.5
3	Michele Reale (It)	74.2
	Adam Hunter (Sco)	74.2
5	Stephen Bennett (Eng)	74.0
	Miguel Angel Jiménez (Sp)	74.0
7	Colin Montgomerie (Sco)	72.6
	Van Phillips (Eng)	72.6
9	Paul Eales (Eng)	72.4
10	Lee Westwood (Eng)	72.2

Driving distance

Pos	Name	Yds
1	Emanuele Canonica (It)	295.8
2	Angel Cabrera (Arg)	289.4
3	Ernie Els (SA)	285.2
4	Steve Webster (Eng)	283.1
5	Carl Suneson (Sp)	282.2
6	Darren Clarke (N.Ire)	280.8
7	Paolo Quirici (Swi)	280.6
8	Colin Montgomerie (Sco)	279.2
9	Santiago Luna (Sp)	278.9
10	Ignacio Garrido (Sp)	278.6

Sand saves

Pos	Name	%
1	Tony Johnstone (Zim)	79.1
2	Philip Walton (Ire)	77.5
3	Joakim Haeggman (Swe)	77.3
4	Olle Karlsson (Swe)	73.5
5	John Bickerton (Eng)	72.9
6	Ignacio Garrido (Sp)	72.2
7	Stephen Bennett (Eng)	72.0
8	Stephen Allan (Aus)	71.1
	Angel Cabrera (Arg)	71.1
10	Bernhard Langer (Ger)	71.0

Greens in regulation

Pos	Name	%
1	Alex Cejka (Ger)	78.2
2	Colin Montgomerie (Sco)	76.6
3	Darren Clarke (N.Ire)	76.2
4	Peter Baker (Eng)	75.8
5	Miguel Angel Jiménez (Sp)	75.4
6	Peter O'Malley (Aus)	75.1
7	Andrew Coltart (Sco)	74.8
8	Bob May (US)	74.5
9	Ian Garbutt (Eng)	74.3
10	Lee Westwood (Eng)	74.0

Average putts per round

Pos	Name	Avg
1	Seve Ballesteros (Sp)	28.0
2	Jay Townsend (US)	28.4
3	Padraig Harrington (Ire)	28.6
	Andrew Beal (Eng)	28.6
5	Russell Claydon (Eng)	28.7
6	Paul Lawrie (Sco)	28.8
	Daniel Chopra (Swe)	28.8
	Gordon Brand Jr (Sco)	28.8
9	Paul Broadhurst (Eng)	28.9
10	Robert Karlsson (Swe)	29.0
	Greg Turner (NZ)	29.0

Putts per greens in regulation

Pos	Name	Avg
1	Seve Ballesteros (Sp)	1.7358
2	Darren Clarke (N.Ire)	1.7363
3	Robert Karlsson (Swe)	1.7429
4	Gordon Brand Jr (Sco)	1.7463
5	Padraig Harrington (Ire)	1.7484
6	Russell Claydon (Eng)	1.7490
7	Jay Townsend (US)	1.7495
8	Paul Broadhurst (Eng)	1.7498
9	Bernhard Langer (Ger)	1.7500
10	Greg Chalmers (Aus)	1.7534

Tour Results (in chronological order)

Johnnie Walker Classic

Pos	Name	Venue	Score
1993	N Faldo	Singapore Island	269
1994	G Norman	Blue Canyon, Phuket	277
1995	F Couples	Orchard GC, Manila	277
1996	I Woosnam*	Tanah Merah, Singapore	272
1997	E Els	Hope Island, Queensland	278

1998 at Blue Canyon CC, Phuket, Thailand

Pos	Name	Score	Prize Money £
1	Tiger Woods (US)*	72-71-71-65—279	133330
2	Ernie Els (SA)	67-65-74-73—279	88880
3	Retief Goosen (SA)	71-71-69-69—280	50070

Heineken Classic *at The Vines, Perth*

Pos	Name	Score
1996	I Woosnam	277
1997	M A Martin	273

1998

Pos	Name	Score	Prize Money £
1	Thomas Björn (Den)	70-68-68-74—280	108935
2	Ian Woosnam (Wal)	66-69-70-76—281	61732
3	Ernie Els (SA)	70-71-70-71—282	28975
	José Maria Olazábal (Sp)	67-72-68-75—282	28975
	Padraig Harrington (Ire)	74-71-71-66—282	28975
	Peter Baker (Eng)	73-71-67-71—282	28975

South African Open

Pos	Name	Venue	Score
1997	V Singh	Glendower CC	270

1998 at Durban Country Club

Pos	Name	Score	Prize Money £
1	Ernie Els (SA)	64-72-68-69—273	71465
2	David Frost (SA)	68-66-71-71—276	52015
3	Patrik Sjöland (Swe)	69-74-68-69—280	31300

Alfred Dunhill South African PGA

Year	Winner	Venue	Score
1995	E Els	Wanderers Club	271
1996	S Strüver	Houghton GC	202 (54 holes)
1997	N Price	Houghton GC	269

1998 at Houghton GC, Johannesburg

Pos	Name	Score	Prize Money £
1	Tony Johnstone (Zim)	68-64-67-72—271	64130
2	Ernie Els (SA)	69-69-66-69—273	46698
3	Retief Goosen (SA)	71-70-69-65—275	24018
	Nick Price (Zim)	71-67-69-68—275	24018

* *Winner after play-off*

Dubai Desert Classic
at Emirates GC, United Arab Emirates

Year	Winner	Score	Year	Winner	Score
1989	M James*	277	1994	E Els	268
1990	E Darcy	276	1995	F Couples	268
1991	*Not played*		1996	C Montgomerie	270
1992	S Ballesteros*	272	1997	R Green	272
1993	W Westner	274			

1998

Pos	Name	Score	Prize Money £
1	José Maria Olazábal (Sp)	69-67-65-68—269	130000
2	Stephen Allan (Aus)	67-70-67-68—272	85000
3	Robert Karlsson (Swe)	66-65-67-75—273	43500
	Ernie Els (SA)	71-63-67-72—273	43500

Qatar Masters *at Doha Golf Club*

1998

Pos	Name	Score	Prize Money £
1	Andrew Coltart (Sco)	68-70-65-67—270	101006
2	Patrik Sjöland (Swe)	70-66-67-69—272	52636
	Andrew Sherborne (Eng)	69-64-68-71—272	52636

Moroccan Open

Year	Winner	Venue	Score
1987	H Clark	Dar-es-Salam	284
1992	D Gilford*	Dar-es-Salam	287
1993	D Gilford	Golf Royal d'Agadir	279
1994	A Forsbrand	Golf Royal d'Agadir	276
1995	M James	Golf Royal d'Agadir	275
1996	P Hedblom	Dar-es-Salam	281
1997	C Whitelaw	Golf Royal d'Agadir	277

1998 *at Golf Royal d'Agadir*

Pos	Name	Score	Prize Money £
1	Stephen Leaney (Aus)	68-67-69-67—271	58330
2	Robert Karlsson (Swe)	70-71-67-71—279	38880
3	Mathias Grönberg (Swe)	67-74-67-74—282	21910

Portuguese Open

Year	Winner	Venue	Score	Year	Winner	Venue	Score
1953	EC Brown	Estoril	260	1969	R Sota	Estoril	270
1954	A Miguel	Estoril	263	1970	R Sota	Estoril	274
1955	F van Donck	Estoril	267	1971	L Platts	Estoril	277
1956	A Miguel	Estoril	268	1972	G Garrido	Estoril	196 (54)
1958	P Alliss	Estoril	264	1973	J Benito*	Estoril	294
1959	S Miguel	Estoril	265	1974	BGC Huggett	Estoril	272
1960	K Bousfield	Estoril	268	1975	H Underwood	Penina	292
1961	K Bousfield	Estoril	263	1976	S Balbuena	Quinta do Lago	283
1962	A Angelini	Estoril	269	1977	M Ramos	Penina	287
1963	R Sota	Estoril	204 (54)	1978	H Clark	Penina	291
1964	A Miguel	Estoril	279	1979	B Barnes	Vilamoura	287
1966	A Angelini	Estoril	273	1982	S Torrance	Penina	207 (54)
1967	A Gallardo	Estoril	214 (54)	1983	S Torrance	Troia	286
1968	M Faulkner	Estoril	273	1984	A Johnstone	Quinta do Lago	274

* *Winner after play-off*

Portuguese Open *continued*

Year	Winner	Venue	Score	Year	Winner	Venue	Score
1985	W Humphreys	Quinta do Lago	279	1992	R Rafferty	Vila Sol	273
1986	M McNulty	Quinta do Lago	270	1993	D Gilford*	Vila Sol	275
1987	R Lee	Estoril	195 (54)	1994	P Price	Penha Longa	278
1988	M Harwood	Quinta do Lago	280	1995	A Hunter*	Penha Longa	277
1989	C Montgomerie	Quinta do Lago	264	1996	W Riley	Aroeira	271
1990	M McLean	Quinta do Lago	274	1997	M Jonzon	Aroeira	269
1991	S Richardson	Estela	283				

1998 *at Le Meridien Penina, Algarve*

Pos	Name	Score	Prize Money £
1	Peter Mitchell (Eng)	67-70-67-70—274	58330
2	Jarmo Sandelin (Swe)	73-71-64-67—275	30395
	David Gilford (Eng)	70-67-70-68—275	30395

Cannes Open

Year	Winner	Venue	Score	Year	Winner	Venue	Score
1984	D Frost	Mougin	280	1991	D Feherty	Mougin	275
1985	R Lee*	Mougin	280	1992	A Forsbrand	Mougin	273
1986	J Bland	Mougin	276	1993	R Davis*	Mougin	271
1987	S Ballesteros	Mougin	275	1994	I Woosnam	Mougin	271
1988	M McNulty	Mougin	279	1995	A Bossert	Royal Mougins	132 (36)
1989	P Broadhurst	Mougin	207 (54)	1996	R Russell	Royal Mougins	272
1990	M McNulty	Mougin	280	1997	S Cage	Royal Mougins	270

1998 *at Royal Mougins, Cannes*

Pos	Name	Score	Prize Money £
1	Thomas Levet (Fr)	69-71-65-73—278	50000
2	Greg Turner (NZ)	70-73-67-69—279	22370
	Phillip Price (Wal)	74-66-72-67—279	22370
	Sven Strüver (Ger)	69-72-69-69—279	22370

Peugeot Open de España

Year	Winner	Venue	Score	Year	Winner	Venue	Score
1912	A Massy	Polo GC, Madrid		1950	A Cerda	Cedana	
1916	A de la Torre	Puerta de Hierro		1951	M Provencio	Puerta de Hierro	281
1917	A de la Torre	Puerta de Hierro		1952	M Faulkner	Puerta de Hierro	275
1919	A de la Torre	Puerta de Hierro		1953	M Faulkner	Puerta de Hierro	
1921	E Lafitte	Puerta de Hierro		1954	S Miguel	Puerta de Hierro	268
1923	A de la Torre	Puerta de Hierro		1955	H de Lamaze (Am)	Puerta de Hierro	271
1925	A de la Torre	Puerta de Hierro		1956	P Alliss	El Prat	285
1926	J Bernardino	Puerta de Hierro		1957	M Faulkner	Club de Campo	283
1927	A Massy	Puerta de Hierro		1958	P Alliss	Puerta de Hierro	268
1928	A Massy	Puerta de Hierro		1959	P Thomson	El Prat	286
1929	E Lafitte	Puerta de Hierro		1960	S Miguel	Club de Campo	286
1930	J Bernardino	Puerta de Hierro		1961	A Miguel	Puerta de Hierro	267
1932	G Gonzalez	Puerta de Hierro		1963	R Sota	El Prat	287
1933	G Gonzalez	Puerta de Hierro		1964	A Miguel	Tenerife	272
1934	J Bernardino	Puerta de Hierro		1966	R de Vicenzo	Sotogrande	279
1935	A de la Torre	Puerta de Hierro		1967	S Miguel	Sant Cugat	265
1941	M Provencio	Puerta de Hierro	283	1968	R Shaw	La Galea	286
1942	G Gonzalez	Sant Cugat	264	1969	J Garaialde	RACE, Madrid	283
1943	M Provencio	Puerta de Hierro	286	1970	A Gallardo	Nueva Andalucia	284
1944	N Sagardia	Pedrena		1971	D Hayes	El Prat	275
1945	C Celles	Puerta de Hierro	274	1972	A Garrido*	Pals	293
1946	M Morcillo	Pedrena	281	1973	N Coles	La Manga	282
1947	M Gonzalez (Am)	Puerta de Hierro	272	1974	J Heard	La Manga	279
1948	M Morcillo	Negun	268	1975	A Palmer	La Manga	283
1949	M Morcillo	Puerta de Hierro	280	1976	E Polland	La Manga	282

* *Winner after play-off*

Peugeot Open de España *continued*

Year	Winner	Venue	Score	Year	Winner	Venue	Score
1977	B Gallacher	La Manga	277	1988	M James	Pedrena	262
1978	B Barnes	El Prat	276	1989	B Langer	El Saler	281
1979	D Hayes	Torrequebrada	278	1990	R Davis	Club de Campo	277
1980	E Polland	Escorpion	276	1991	E Romero*	Club de Campo	275
1981	S Ballesteros	El Prat	273	1992	A Sherborne	RACE	271
1982	S Torrance	Club de Campo	273	1993	J Haeggman	RACE	275
1983	E Darcy	Las Brisas	277	1994	C Montgomerie	Club de Campo	277
1984	B Langer	El Saler	275	1995	S Ballesteros	Club de Campo	274
1985	S Ballesteros	Vallromanos	266	1996	P Harrington	Club de Campo	272
1986	H Clark	La Moraleja	272	1997	M James*	Golf La Moraleja II	277
1987	N Faldo	Las Brisas	286				

1998 at *El Prat, Barcelona*

Pos	Name	Score	Prize Money £
1	Thomas Björn (Den)	68-67-66-66—267	91660
2	Greg Chalmers (Aus)	64-66-69-69—268	47765
	José Maria Olazábal (Sp)	66-71-64-67—268	47765

Italian Open

36 holes only played 1925–34.

Year	Winner	Venue	Score	Year	Winner	Venue	Score
1925	F Pasquali	Stresa	154	1961	R Sota	Garlenda	282
1926	A Boyer	Stresa	147	1972	N Wood	Villa d'Este	271
1927	P Alliss	Stresa	145	1973	A Jacklin	Rome	284
1928	A Boyer	Villa d'Este	145	1974	P Oosterhuis	Venice	249 (63)
1929	R Golias	Villa d'Este	143	1975	W Casper	Monticello	286
1930	A Boyer	Villa d'Este	140	1976	B Dassu	Is Molas	280
1931	A Boyer	Villa d'Este	141	1977	A Gallardo*	Monticello	286
1932	A Boomer	Villa d'Este	143	1978	D Hayes	Pevero	293
1934	N Nutley	San Remo	132	1979	B Barnes*	Monticello	281
1935	P Alliss	San Remo	262	1980	M Mannelli	Rome	276
1936	H Cotton	Sestriere	268	1981	J M Cañizares*	Milan	280
1937	M Dallemagne	San Remo	276	1982	M James	Is Molas	280
1938	F van Donck	Villa d'Este	276	1983	B Langer*	Ugolino	271
1947	F van Donck	San Remo	263	1984	A Lyle	Milan	277
1948	A Casera	San Remo	267	1985	M Piñero	Molinetto	267
1949	H Hassanein	Villa d'Este	263	1986	D Feherty*	Albarella, Venice	270
1950	U Grappasonni	Rome	281	1987	S Torrance*	Monticello	271
1951	J Adams	Milan	289	1988	G Norman	Monticello	270
1952	E Brown	Milan	273	1989	R Rafferty	Monticello	273
1953	F van Donck	Villa d'Este	267	1990	R Boxall	Milan	267
1954	U Grappasonni	Villa d'Este	272	1991	C Parry	Castelconturbia	279
1955	F van Donck	Venice	287	1992	A Lyle	Monticello	270
1956	A Cerda	Milan	284	1993	G Turner	Modena	267
1957	H Henning	Villa d'Este	273	1994	E Romero	Marco Simone	272
1958	P Alliss	Varese	282	1995	S Torrance	Le Rovedine	269
1959	P Thomson	Villa d'Este	269	1996	J Payne	Bergamo GC	275
1960	B Wilkes	Venice	285	1997	B Langer	Gardagolf	273

1998 at *Castelconturbia, Milan* (Rain reduced event to 54 holes)

Pos	Name	Score	Prize Money £
1	Patrik Sjöland (Swe)	64-65-66—195 (54)	81853
2	José Maria Olazábal (Sp)	68-65-65—198	42655
	Joakim Haeggman (Swe)	67-68-63—198	42655

* *Winner after play-off*

Turespaña Masters Open Baleares

Year	Winner	Venue	Score	Year	Winner	Venue	Score
1992	V Singh	Malaga	277	1995	A Cejka	Islantilla	278
1993	A Oldcorn	Novo Sancti Petri	285	1996	D Borrego*	El Saler	271
1994	C Mason	Montecastillo	278	1997	J M Olazábal	Campo de Golf	272

1998 *at Santa Ponsa I, Mallorca*

Pos	Name	Score	Prize Money £
1	Miguel Angel Jiménez (Sp)	69-68-70-72—279	58330
2	Miguel Angel Martin (Sp)	67-72-70-72—281	38880
3	Paul McGinley (Ire)	71-73-67-71—282	19705
	Katsuyoshi Tomori (Jpn)	74-67-73-68—282	19705

Benson and Hedges International Open

Year	Winner	Venue	Score	Year	Winner	Venue	Score
1971	A Jacklin*	Fulford	279	1985	A Lyle	Fulford	274
1972	J Newton	Fulford	281	1986	M James*	Fulford	274
1973	V Baker	Fulford	276	1987	N Ratcliffe	Fulford	275
1974	P Toussaint*	Fulford	276	1988	P Baker*	Fulford	271
1975	V Fernandez	Fulford	266	1989	G Brand Jr	Fulford	272
1976	G Marsh	Fulford	272	1990	JM Olazábal	St Mellion	279
1977	A Garrido	Fulford	280	1991	B Langer	St Mellion	286
1978	L Trevino*	Fulford	274	1992	P Senior*	St Mellion	287
1979	M Bembridge	St Mellion	272	1993	P Broadhurst	St Mellion	276
1980	G Marsh	Fulford	272	1994	S Ballesteros	St Mellion	281
1981	T Weiskopf	Fulford	272	1995	P O'Malley	St Mellion	280
1982	G Norman	Fulford	283	1996	S Ames	The Oxfordshire	283
1983	J Bland	Fulford	273	1997	B Langer	The Oxfordshire	276
1984	S Torrance	Fulford	270				

1998 *at The Oxfordshire GC, Thame, Oxfordshire*

Pos	Name	Score	Prize Money £
1	Darren Clarke (N.Ire)	70-69-67-67—273	125000
2	Santiago Luna (Sp)	69-71-69-67—276	83320
3	Thomas Björn (Den)	68-74-68-67—277	42220
	Massimo Florioli (It)	68-67-71-71—277	42220

Volvo PGA Championship

Year	Winner	Venue	Score	Year	Winner	Venue	Score
1955	K Bousfield	Pannal	277	1977	M Piñero	R St George's	283
1956	CH Ward	Maesdu	282	1978	N Faldo	R Birkdale	278
1957	P Alliss	Maesdu	286	1979	V Fernandez	St Andrews	288
1958	H Bradshaw	Llandudno	287	1980	N Faldo	R St George's	283
1959	DJ Rees	Ashburnham	283	1981	N Faldo	Ganton	274
1960	AF Stickley	Coventry	247 (63)	1982	A Jacklin*	Hillside	284
1961	BJ Bamford	R Mid-Surrey	266	1983	S Ballesteros	R St George's	278
1962	P Alliss	Little Aston	287	1984	H Clark	Wentworth Club	204 (54)
1963	PJ Butler	R Birkdale	306	1985	P Way*	Wentworth Club	282
1964	AG Grubb	Western Gailes	287	1986	R Davis*	Wentworth Club	281
1965	P Alliss	Prince's	286	1987	B Langer	Wentworth Club	270
1966	G Wolstenholme	Saunton	278	1988	I Woosnam	Wentworth Club	274
1967	BGC Huggett	Thorndon Park	271	1989	N Faldo	Wentworth Club	272
1967	ME Gregson	Hunstanton	275	1990	M Harwood	Wentworth Club	271
1968	PM Townsend	R Mid-Surrey	275	1991	S Ballesteros*	Wentworth Club	271
1968	D Talbot	Dunbar	276	1992	T Johnstone	Wentworth Club	272
1969	B Gallacher	Ashburnham	293	1993	B Langer	Wentworth Club	274
1972	A Jacklin	Wentworth Club	279	1994	JM Olazábal	Wentworth Club	271
1973	P Oosterhuis	Wentworth Club	280	1995	B Langer	Wentworth Club	279
1974	M Bembridge	Wentworth Club	278	1996	C Rocca	Wentworth Club	274
1975	A Palmer	R St George's	285	1997	I Woosnam	Wentworth Club	275
1976	NC Coles*	R St George's	280				

* *Winner after play-off*

1998 Volvo PGA Championship *at Wentworth Club, Virginia Water, Surrey*

Pos	Name	Score	Prize Money £
1	Colin Montgomerie (Sco)	70-70-65-69—274	200000
2	Patrik Sjöland (Swe)	72-71-66-66—275	89433
	Ernie Els (SA)	69-69-68-69—275	89433
	Gary Orr (Sco)	70-69-68-68—275	89433
5	Dean Robertson (Sco)	70-69-67-70—276	37160
	Peter Lonard (Aus)	72-65-71-68—276	37160
	Andrew Coltart (Sco)	72-66-70-68—276	37160
	Thomas Björn (Den)	70-69-69-68—276	37160
	Mats Hallberg (Swe)	68-69-69-70—276	37160
10	Paul McGinley (Ire)	72-69-68-68—277	24000
11	Philip Price (Wal)	71-72-68-67—278	20100
	Gordon Brand Jr (Sco)	71-69-72-66—278	20100
	David Gilford (Eng)	70-69-68-71—278	20100
	Padraig Harrington (Ire)	70-69-69-70—278	20100
15	Costantino Rocca (It)	71-70-70-68—279	17600
16	Lee Westwood (Eng)	71-71-69-69—280	15564
	Sam Torrance (Sco)	70-71-71-68—280	15564
	Stephen Leaney (Aus)	69-73-71-67—280	15564
	José Maria Olazábal (Sp)	72-71-70-67—280	15564
	Jean Van de Velde (Fr)	71-71-69-69—280	15564
21	Seve Ballesteros (Sp)	72-71-65-73—281	12780
	Robert Karlsson (Swe)	71-71-71-68—281	12780
	Massimo Florioli (It)	75-68-67-71—281	12780
	David Howell (Eng)	68-71-71-71—281	12780
	Wayne Westner (SA)	73-69-68-71—281	12780
	Per-Ulrik Johansson (Swe)	70-71-72-68—281	12780
	Rodger Davis (Aus)	73-69-69-70—281	12780
	Van Phillips (Eng)	70-73-68-70—281	12780
29	Jose Coceres (Arg)	73-69-68-72—282	10620
	Darren Clarke (N.Ire)	71-68-75-68—282	10620
	Bernhard Langer (Ger)	69-70-72-71—282	10620
	Domingo Hospital (Sp)	69-69-74-70—282	10620
33	Fabrice Tarnaud (Fr)	73-69-72-69—283	9480
	Greg Turner (NZ)	70-68-70-75—283	9480
	Michael Jonzon (Swe)	66-70-72-75—283	9480
	Roger Wessels (SA)	71-71-71-70—283	9480
37	Mark McNulty (Zim)	69-72-72-71—284	8520
	Peter Senior (Aus)	72-70-69-73—284	8520
	Mark Roe (Eng)	71-71-69-73—284	8520
	Tony Johnstone (Zim)	69-73-73-69—284	8520
41	Clinton Whitelaw (SA)	69-74-72-70—285	6960
	Peter Baker (Eng)	74-69-73-69—285	6960
	Russell Claydon (Eng)	71-72-70-72—285	6960
	Katsyumo Tomori (Jpn)	70-70-72-73—285	6960
	Malcolm Mackenzie (Eng)	68-71-74-72—285	6960
	Jonathan Lomas (Eng)	71-71-71-72—285	6960
	Santiago Luna (Sp)	71-71-73-70—285	6960
	Thomas Gögele (Ger)	71-71-72-71—285	6960
	Denis Edlund (Swe)	71-71-74-69—285	6960
50	Mark James (Eng)	69-73-69-75—286	5400
	Brian Davis (Eng)	67-75-72-72—286	5400
	Rolf Muntz (Hol)	72-71-71-72—286	5400
	Andrew Sherborne (Eng)	71-70-74-71—286	5400
54	Ian Woosnam (Wal)	73-70-74-70—287	4320
	Sven Strüver (Ger)	73-69-75-70—287	4320
	Eduardo Romero (Arg)	70-72-70-75—287	4320
	Andrew Lyle (Sco)	69-74-72-72—287	4320
	Peter Hedblom (Swe)	70-70-75-72—287	4320
59	Carl Watts (Eng)	71-69-71-77—288	3660
	Chris Van Der Velde (Hol)	68-75-76-69—288	3660
61	Raymond Burns (N.Ire)	70-72-74-73—289	3480
62	Howard Clark (Eng)	70-73-74-73—290	3360
63	Diego Borrego (Sp)	71-72-74-76—293	3240
64	Steven Richardson (Eng)	70-73-74-78—295	3060
	David Tapping (Eng)	69-74-78-74—295	3060

Deutsche Bank – SAP Open TPC of Europe

Year	Winner	Venue	Score	Year	Winner	Venue	Score
1977	N Coles	Foxhills	288	1986	I Woosnam	The Belfry	277
1978	B Waites	Foxhills	286	1987	Not played		
1979	M King	Moor Park	281	1988	Not played		
1980	B Gallacher	Moortown	268	1989	C Montgomerie	Quinta do Lago	264
1981	B Barnes*	Dalmahoy	276	1990	M McLean	Quinta do Lago	274
1982	N Faldo	Notts	270	1995	B Langer	Gut Kaden	270
1983	B Langer	St Mellion	269	1996	F Nobilo	Gut Kaden	270
1984	J Gonzalez*	St Mellion	265	1997	R McFarlane	Gut Kaden	282
1985	Not played						

1998 *at Gut Kaden, Hamburg*

Pos	Name	Score	Prize Money £
1	Lee Westwood (Eng)	69-69-61-66—265	183340
2	Darren Clarke (N.Ire)	67-66-65-68—266	122210
3	Mark O'Meara (US)	67-69-63-70—269	68860

National Car Rental English Open

Year	Winner	Venue	Score	Year	Winner	Venue	Score
1979	S Ballesteros	The Belfry	286	1991	D Gilford	The Belfry	278
1980	M Piñero	The Belfry	286	1992	V Fernandez	The Belfry	283
1981	R Davis	The Belfry	283	1993	I Woosnam	Forest of Arden	269
1982	G Norman	The Belfry	279	1994	C Montgomerie	Forest of Arden	274
1983	H Baiocchi*	The Belfry	279	1995	P Walton*	Forest of Arden	274
1988	H Clark	Royal Birkdale	279	1996	R Allenby	Forest of Arden	278
1990	M James*	The Belfry	284	1997	P-U Johansson	Hanbury Manor	269

1998 *at Marriott Hanbury Manor, Ware*

Pos	Name	Score	Prize Money £
1	Lee Westwood (Eng)	68-68-67-68—271	108330
2	Greg Chalmers (Aus)	70-73-61-69—273	56450
	Olle Karlsson (Swe)	70-70-67-66—273	56450

Madeira Island Open

Year	Winner	Venue	Score
1993	M James	Campo de Golf da Madeira	281
1994	M Lanner	Campo de Golf da Madeira	206 (54)
1995	S Luna	Campo de Golf da Madeira	272
1996	J Sandelin	Campo de Golf da Madeira	279
1997	P Mitchell	Santo de Serra GC	204 (54)

1998 *at Santo da Serra GC*

Pos	Name	Score	Prize Money £
1	Mats Lanner (Swe)	70-66-68-73—277	50000
2	Stephen Scahill (NZ)	72-61-69-76—278	33330
3	Andrew Beal (Eng)	71-68-67-73—279	18780

* *Winner after play-off*

Peugeot Open de France

Year	Winner	Venue	Score	Year	Winner	Venue	Score
1906	A Massy	La Boulie	292	1958	F van Donck	St Germain	276
1907	A Massy	La Boulie	294	1959	DC Thomas	La Boulie	276
1908	JH Taylor	La Boulie	300	1960	R de Vicenzo	St Cloud	275
1909	JH Taylor	La Boulie	290	1961	KDG Nagle	La Boulie	271
1910	J Braid	La Boulie	298	1962	A Murray	St Germain	274
1911	A Massy	La Boulie	284	1963	B Devlin	St Cloud	273
1912	J Gassiat	La Boulie	284	1964	R de Vicenzo	Chantilly	272
1913	G Duncan	Chantilly	304	1965	R Sota	St Nom-la-Breteche	268
1914	JD Edgar	Le Touquet	284	1966	DJ Hutchinson	La Boulie	274
1920	W Hagen	La Boulie	298	1967	BJ Hunt	St Germain	271
1921	A Boomer	Le Touquet	284	1968	PJ Butler	St Cloud	272
1922	A Boomer	La Boulie	284	1969	J Garaialde	St Nom-la-Breteche	277
1923	J Ockenden	Dieppe	284	1970	D Graham	Chantaco	268
1924	CJH Tolley (Am)	La Boulie	290	1971	Lu Liang Huan	Biarritz	262
1925	A Massy	Chantilly	291	1972	B Jaeckel*	Biarritz & La Nivelle	265
1926	A Boomer	St Cloud	280	1973	P Oosterhuis	La Boulie	280
1927	G Duncan	St Germain	290	1974	P Oosterhuis	Chantilly	284
1928	CJH Tolley (Am)	La Boulie	283	1975	B Barnes	La Boulie	281
1929	A Boomer	Fourqueux	283	1976	V Tshabalaia	Le Touquet	272
1930	ER Whitcombe	Dieppe	282	1977	S Ballesteros	Le Touquet	282
1931	A Boomer	Deauville	291	1978	D Hayes	La Baule	269
1932	AJ Lacey	St Cloud	296	1979	B Gallacher	Lyons	284
1933	B Gadd	Chantilly	283	1980	G Norman	St Cloud	268
1934	SF Brews	Dieppe	284	1981	A Lyle	St Germain	270
1935	SF Brews	Le Touquet	292	1982	S Ballesteros	St Nom-la-Breteche	278
1936	M Dallemagne	St Germain	277	1983	N Faldo*	La Boulie	277
1937	M Dallemagne	St Cloud	278	1984	B Langer	St Cloud	270
1938	M Dallemagne	Fourqueux	282	1985	S Ballesteros	St Germain	263
1939	M Pose	Le Touquet	285	1986	S Ballesteros	La Boulie	269
1946	TH Cotton	St Cloud	269	1987	J Rivero	St Cloud	269
1947	TH Cotton	Chantilly	285	1988	N Faldo	Chantilly	274
1948	F Cavalo	St Cloud	287	1989	N Faldo	Chantilly	273
1949	U Grappasonni	St Germain	275	1990	P Walton*	Chantilly	275
1950	R de Vicenzo	Chantilly	279	1991	E Romero	National GC	281
1951	H Hassanein	St Cloud	278	1992	MA Martin	National GC	276
1952	AD Locke	St Germain	268	1993	C Rocca*	National GC	273
1953	AD Locke	La Boulie	276	1994	M Roe	National GC	274
1954	F van Donck	St Cloud	275	1995	P Broadhurst	National GC	274
1955	B Nelson	La Boulie	271	1996	R Allenby*	National GC	272
1956	A Miguel	Deauville	277	1997	R Goosen	National GC	271
1957	F van Donck	St Cloud	266				

1998 *at Le Golf National, Paris*

Pos	Name	Score	Prize Money £
1	Sam Torrance (Sco)	64-70-72-70—276	83330
2	Massimo Florioli (It)	69-67-75-67—278	33262
	Olivier Edmond (Fr)	70-70-71-67—278	33262
	Bernhard Langer (Ger)	71-70-68-69—278	33262
	Matthew Goggin (Aus)	69-70-69-70—278	33262

Murphy's Irish Open

Year	Winner	Venue	Score	Year	Winner	Venue	Score
1927	G Duncan	Portmarnock	312	1938	A Locke	Portmarnock	292
1928	E Whitcombe	Newcastle	288	1939	A Lees	Newcastle	287
1929	A Mitchell	Portmarnock	309	1946	F Daly	Portmarnock	288
1930	C Whitcombe	Portrush	289	1947	H Bradshaw	Portrush	290
1931	E Kenyon	Royal Dublin	291	1948	D Rees	Portmarnock	295
1932	A Padgham	Cork	283	1949	H Bradshaw	Belvoir Park	286
1933	E Kenyon	Malone	286	1950	H Pickworth	Royal Dublin	287
1934	S Easterbrook	Portmarnock	284	1953	E Brown	Belvoir Park	272
1935	E Whitcombe	Newcastle	292	1975	C O'Connor Jr	Woodbrook	275
1936	R Whitcombe	Royal Dublin	281	1976	B Crenshaw	Portmarnock	284
1937	B Gadd	Portrush	284	1977	H Green	Portmarnock	283

* *Winner after play-off*

Year	Winner	Venue	Score	Year	Winner	Venue	Score
1978	K Brown	Portmarnock	281	1988	I Woosnam	Portmarnock	278
1979	M James	Portmarnock	282	1989	I Woosnam*	Portmarnock	278
1980	M James	Portmarnock	284	1990	JM Olazábal	Portmarnock	282
1981	S Torrance	Portmarnock	276	1991	N Faldo	Killarney	283
1982	J O'Leary	Portmarnock	287	1992	N Faldo*	Killarney	274
1983	S Ballesteros	Royal Dublin	271	1993	N Faldo*	Mount Juliet	276
1984	B Langer	Royal Dublin	267	1994	B Langer	Mount Juliet	275
1985	S Ballesteros*	Royal Dublin	278	1995	S Torrance*	Mount Juliet	277
1986	S Ballesteros	Portmarnock	285	1996	C Montgomerie	Druid's Glen	279
1987	B Langer	Portmarnock	269	1997	C Montgomerie	Druid's Glen	269

1998 at Druid's Glen, Dublin

Pos	Name	Score	Prize Money £
1	David Carter (Eng)*	68-72-67-71—278	159991
2	Colin Montgomerie (Sco)	65-74-71-68—278	106631

Carter won at first hole of play-off

3	Peter Baker (Eng)	69-75-66-70—280	53996
	John McHenry (Ire)	70-68-70-72—280	53996

Standard Life Loch Lomond

at Loch Lomond, Glasgow, Scotland

Year	Winner	Score
1996	T Björn	277
1997	T Lehman	265

1998

Pos	Name	Score	Prize Money £
1	Lee Westwood (Eng)	69-69-68-70—276	141660
2	Ian Woosnam (Wal)	67-73-74-66—280	51180
	Eduardo Romero (Arg)	71-70-71-68—280	51180
	Robert Allenby (Aus)	72-72-68-68—280	51180
	David Howell (Eng)	68-71-70-71—280	51180
	Dennis Edlund (Swe)	70-69-67-74—280	51180

The Open Championship

Past results and fuller details in *Part I The Majors*

1998 at Royal Birkdale, Southport

Pos	Name	Score	Prize Money £
1	Mark O'Meara (US)*	72-68-72-68—280	300000
2	Brian Watts (US)	68-69-73-70—280	188000

O'Meara won after four-hole play-off

3	Tiger Woods (US)	65-73-77-66—281	135000

* *Winner after play-off*

TNT Dutch Open

Year	Winner	Venue	Score	Year	Winner	Venue	Score
1919	D Oosterveer	The Hague	158	1962	BGC Huggett	Hilversumsche	274
1920	H Burrows	Kennemer	155	1963	R Waltman	Wassenaar	279
1921	H Burrows	Domburg	151	1964	S Sewgolum	Eindhoven	275
1922	G Pannell	Noordwijk	160	1965	A Miguel	Breda	278
1923	H Burrows	Hilversumsche	153	1966	R Sota	Kennemer	276
1924	A Boomer	The Hague	138	1967	P Townsend	The Hague	282
1925	A Boomer	The Hague	144	1968	J Cockin	Hilversumsche	292
1926	A Boomer	The Hague	151	1969	G Wolstenholme	Utrecht	277
1927	P Boomer	The Hague	147	1970	V Fernandez	Eindhoven	279
1928	ER Whitcombe	The Hague	141	1971	R Sota	Kennemer	277
1929	JJ Taylor	Hilversumsche	153	1972	J Newton	The Hague	277
1930	J Oosterveer	The Hague	152	1973	D McClelland	The Hague	279
1931	F Dyer	Kennemer	145	1974	B Barnes	Hilversumsche	211 (54)
1932	A Boyer	The Hague	137	1975	H Baiocchi	Hilversumsche	279
1933	M Dallemagne	Kennemer	143	1976	S Ballesteros	Kennemer	275
1934	SF Brews	Utrecht	286	1977	R Byman	Kennemer	278
1935	SF Brews	Kennemer	275	1978	R Byman	Noordwijkse	21 (54)
1936	F van Donck	Hilversumsche	285	1979	G Marsh	Noordwijkse	285
1937	F van Donck	Utrecht	286	1980	S Ballesteros	Hilversumsche	280
1938	AH Padgham	The Hague	281	1981	H Henning	The Hague	280
1939	AD Locke	Kennemer	281	1982	P Way	Utrecht	276
1946	F van Donck	Hilversumsche	290	1983	K Brown	Kennemer	274
1947	G Ruhl	Eindhoven	290	1984	B Langer	Rosendaelsche	275
1948	C Denny	Hilversumsche	290	1985	G Marsh	Noordwijkse	282
1949	J Adams	The Hague	294	1986	S Ballesteros	Noordwijkse	271 (70)
1950	R de Vicenzo	Breda	269	1987	G Brand Jr	Hilversumsche	272
1951	F van Donck	Kennemer	281	1988	M Mouland	Hilversumsche	274
1952	C Denny	Hilversumsche	284	1989	JM Olazábal*	Kennemer	277
1953	F van Donck	Eindhoven	286	1990	S McAllister	Kennemer	274
1954	U Grappasonni	The Hague	295	1991	P Stewart	Noordwijkse	267
1955	A Angelini	Kennemer	280	1992	B Langer*	Noordwijkse	277
1956	A Cerda	Eindhoven	277	1993	C Montgomerie	Noordwijkse	281
1957	J Jacobs	Hilversumsche	284	1994	MA Jiménez	Hilversumsche	270
1958	D Thomas	Kennemer	277	1995	S Hoch	Hilversumsche	269
1959	S Sewgolum	The Hague	283	1996	M McNulty	Hilversumsche	266
1960	S Sewgolum	Eindhoven	280	1997	S Strüver	Hilversumsche	266
1961	BBS Wilkes	Kennemer	279				

1998 at *Hilversumsche GC, Hilversum*

Pos	Name	Score	Prize Money £
1	Stephen Leaney (Aus)	66-63-70-67—266	133330
2	Darren Clarke (N.Ire)	68-69-67-63—267	88880
3	Lee Westwood (Eng)	63-66-72-67—268	45035
	Nick Price (Zim)	68-65-69-66—268	45035

Volvo Scandinavian Masters

Year	Winner	Venue	Score	Year	Winner	Venue	Score
1991	C Montgomerie	Drottningholm	270	1995	J Parnevik	Barsebäck	270
1992	N Faldo	Barsebäck	277	1996	L Westwood	Forsgården	281
1993	P Baker*	Forsgårdens	278	1997	J Haeggman	Barsebäck	270
1994	V Singh	Drottningholm	268				

1998 at *Kungsängen Golf Club, Stockholm*

Pos	Name	Score	Prize Money £
1	Jesper Parnevik (Swe)	67-65-71-70—273	133330
2	Darren Clarke (N.Ire)	67-70-68-71—276	88880
3	Stephen Field (Eng)	70-68-70-69—277	50070

★ *Winner after play-off*

German Open

Year	Winner	Venue	Score	Year	Winner	Venue	Score
1911	H Vardon	Baden-Baden	279	1967	D Swaelens	Krefeld	273
1912	JH Taylor	Baden-Baden	279	1968	B Franklin	Cologne	265
1926	P Alliss	Berlin	284	1969	J Garaialde	Frankfurt	272
1927	P Alliss	Berlin	288	1970	J Garaialde	Krefeld	276
1928	P Alliss	Berlin	280	1971	NC Coles	Bremen	279
1929	P Alliss	Berlin	285	1972	G Marsh	Frankfurt	271
1930	A Boyer	Baden-Baden	266	1973	F Abreu	Hubblerath	276
1931	R Golias	Berlin	298	1974	S Owen*	Krefeld	276
1932	A Boyer	Bad Ems	282	1975	M Bembridge	Bremen	285
1933	P Allis	Bad Ems	284	1976	S Hobday	Frankfurt	266
1934	AH Padgham	Bad Ems	285	1977	T Britz	Dusseldorf	275
1935	A Boyer	Bad Ems	280	1978	S Ballesteros	Cologne	268
1936	A Boyer	Berlin	291	1979	A Jacklin	Frankfurt	277
1937	TH Cotton	Bad Ems	274	1980	M McNulty	Berlin	280
1938	TH Cotton	Frankfurt	285	1981	B Langer	Hamburg	272
1939	TH Cotton	Bad Ems	280	1982	B Langer*	Stuttgart	279
1951	A Cerda	Hamburg	286	1983	C Pavin	Cologne	275
1952	A Cerda	Hamburg	283	1984	W Grady	Frankfurt	268
1953	F van Donck	Frankfurt	271	1985	B Langer	Garstedt	183 (54)
1954	AD Locke	Krefeld	277	1986	B Langer*	Hubblerath	273
1955	K Bousfield	Hamburg	279	1987	M McNulty	Frankfurt	259
1956	F van Donck	Frankfurt	271	1988	S Ballesteros	Frankfurt	263
1957	H Weetman	Cologne	279	1989	C Parry*	Frankfurt	266
1958	F de Luca	Krefeld	275	1990	M McNulty	Hubblerath	270
1959	K Bousfield	Hamburg	271	1991	M McNulty*	Hubblerath	273
1960	PW Thomson	Cologne	281	1992	V Singh	Hubblerath	262
1961	BJ Hunt	Krefeld	272	1993	B Langer	Hubblerath	269
1962	R Verwey	Hamburg	276	1994	C Montgomerie	Hubblerath	269
1963	BGC Huggett	Cologne	278	1995	C Montgomerie	Nippenburg	268
1964	R de Vicenzo	Krefeld	275	1996	I Woosnam	Nippenburg	193 (54)
1965	HR Henning	Hamburg	274	1997	I Garrido	Nippenburg	271
1966	R Stanton	Frankfurt	274				

1998 *at Sporting Club, Berlin*

Pos	Name	Score	Prize Money £
1	Stephen Allan (Aus)	72-71-68-69—280	116660
2	Steve Webster (Eng)	69-73-69-70—281	46557
	Mark Roe (Eng)	71-69-69-71—281	46557
	Ignacio Garrido (Sp)	67-72-68-74—281	46557
	Padraig Harrington (Ire)	73-69-70-69—281	46557

Smurfit European Open

Year	Winner	Venue	Score	Year	Winner	Venue	Score
1978	B Wadkins*	Walton Heath	283	1988	I Woosnam	Sunningdale	260
1979	A Lyle	Turnberry	275	1989	A Murray	Walton Heath	277
1980	T Kite	Walton Heath	284	1990	P Senior	Sunningdale	267
1981	G Marsh	Royal Liverpool	275	1991	M Harwood	Walton Heath	277
1982	M Piñero	Sunningdale	266	1992	N Faldo	Sunningdale	262
1983	L Aoki	Sunningdale	274	1993	G Brand Jr	E. Sussex National	275
1984	G Brand Jr	Sunningdale	270	1994	D Gilford	E. Sussex National	275
1985	B Langer	Sunningdale	269	1995	B Langer*	The K Club	280
1986	G Norman*	Sunningdale	269	1996	P-U Johansson	The K Club	277
1987	P Way	Walton Heath	279	1997	P-U Johansson	The K Club	267

1998 *at The K Club, Dublin*

Pos	Name	Score	Prize Money £
1	Marthias Grönberg (Swe)	68-71-67-69—275	208300
2	Miguel Angel Jiménez (Sp)	73-72-71-69—285	108562
	Phillip Price (Wal)	72-74-68-71—285	108562

* *Winner after play-off*

BMW International Open

Year	Winner	Venue	Score	Year	Winner	Venue	Score
1989	D Feherty	Golfplatz, Munich	269	1994	M McNulty	St Eurach L&GC	274
1990	P Azinger*	Golfplatz, Munich	277	1995	F Nobilo	St Eurach L&GC	272
1991	A Lyle	Golfplatz, Munich	268	1996	M Farry	St Eurach L&GC	132 (36)
1992	P Azinger*	Golfplatz, Munich	266	1997	R Karlsson	GC München Nord Eichenried	264
1993	P Fowler	Golfplatz, Munich	267				

1998 *at Golfclub München Nord-Eichenried, Munich*

Pos	Name	Score	Prize Money £
1	Russell Claydon (Eng)	66-72-64-68—270	141660
2	Jamie Spence (Eng)	68-71-66-66—271	94440
3	Thomas Gögele (Ger)	65-71-67-69—272	53210

Canon European Masters *at Crans-sur-Sierre*

Year	Winner	Venue	Score	Year	Winner	Venue	Score
1923	A Ross	Engen	149	1967	R Vines		272
1924	P Boomer	Engen	150	1968	R Bernardini		272
1925	A Ross	Engen	148	1969	R Bernardini		277
1926	A Ross	Lucerne	145	1970	G Marsh		274
1929	A Wilson	Lucerne	142	1971	PM Townsend		270
1930	A Boyer	Samedan	150	1972	G Marsh		270
1931	M Dallemagne	Lucerne	145	1973	H Baiocchi		278
1934	A Boyer	Lausanne	133	1974	RJ Charles		275
1935	A Boyer	Lausanne	137	1975	D Hayes		273
1936	F Francis (Am)	Lausanne	134	1976	M Piñero		274
1937	M Dallemagne	Samedan	138	1977	S Ballesteros		273
1938	J Saubaber	Zumikon	139	1978	S Ballesteros		272
1939	F Cavalo	Crans-sur-Sierre	273	1979	H Baiocchi		275
1948	U Grappasonni		285	1980	N Price		267
1949	M Dallemagne		270	1981	M Piñero*		277
1950	A Casera		276	1982	I Woosnam*		272
1951	EC Brown		267	1983	N Faldo*		268
1952	U Grappasonni		267	1984	J Anderson		261
1953	F van Donck		267	1985	C Stadler		267
1954	AD Locke		276	1986	JM Olazábal		262
1955	F van Donck		277	1987	A Forsbrand		263
1956	DJ Rees		278	1988	C Moody		268
1957	A Angelini		270	1989	S Ballesteros		266
1958	K Bousfield		272	1990	R Rafferty		267
1959	DJ Rees		274	1991	J Hawkes		268
1960	H Henning		270	1992	J Spence*		271
1961	KDG Nagle		268	1993	B Lane		270
1962	RJ Charles*		272	1994	E Romero		266
1963	DJ Rees*		278	1995	M Grönberg		270
1964	HR Henning		276	1996	C Montgomerie		260
1965	HR Henning		208 (54)	1997	C Rocca		266
1966	A Angelini		271				

1998

Pos	Name	Score	Prize Money £
1	Sven Strüver (Ger)*	69-63-65-66—263	133330
2	Patrik Sjöland (Swe)	65-66-62-70—263	88880

* *Strüver won at second hole of play-off*

3	Darren Clarke (N.Ire)	64-68-66-67—265	50070

---

* *Winner after play-off*

One-2-One British Masters

Year	Winner	Venue	Score	Year	Winner	Venue	Score
1946T	AD Locke	Stoneham	286	1971	M Bembridge	St Pierre	273
	J Adams			1972	R J Charles	Northumberland	277
1947	A Lees	Little Aston	283	1973	A Jacklin	St Pierre	272
1948	N Von Nida	Sunningdale	272	1974	B Gallacher*	St Pierre	282
1949	C Ward	St. Andrews	290	1975	B Gallacher	Ganton	289
1950	D Rees	Hoylake	281	1976	B Dassu	St Pierre	271
1951	M Faulkner	Wentworth Club	281	1977	G Hunt*	Lindrick	291
1952	H Weetman	Mere	281	1978	T Horton	St Pierre	279
1953	H Bradshaw	Sunningdale	272	1979	G Marsh	Woburn	283
1954	AD Locke	Prince's	291	1980	B Langer	St Pierre	270
1955	H Bradshaw	Little Aston	277	1981	G Norman	Woburn	273
1956	C O'Connor	Prestwick	277	1982	G Norman	St Pierre	267
1957	E Brown	Hollinwell	275	1983	L Woosnam	St Pierre	269
1958	H Weetman	Little Aston	276	1985	L Trevino	Woburn	278
1959	C O'Connor	Portmarnock	276	1986	S Ballesteros	Woburn	275
1960	J Hitchcock	Sunningdale	275	1987	M McNulty	Woburn	274
1961	P Thomson	Porthcawl	284	1988	A Lyle	Woburn	273
1962	D Rees	Wentworth Club	278	1989	N Faldo	Woburn	267
1963	B Hunt	Little Aston	282	1990	M James	Woburn	270
1964	C Legrange	Royal Birkdale	288	1991	S Ballesteros	Woburn	275
1965	B Hunt	Portmarnock	283	1992	C O'Connor Jr*	Woburn	270
1966	N Coles	Lindrick	278	1993	P Baker	Woburn	266
1967	A Jacklin	R St George's	274	1994	I Woosnam	Woburn	271
1968	P Thomson	Sunningdale	274	1995	S Torrance	Collingtree Park	270
1969	C Legrange	Little Aston	281	1996	R Allenby*	Collingtree Park	284
1970	B Huggett	R Lytham & St Annes	293	1997	G Turner	Forest of Arden	275

1998 *at Marriott Forest of Arden, Coventry*

Pos	Name	Score	Prize Money £
1	Colin Montgomerie (Sco)	70-72-70-69—281	125000
2	Pierre Fulke (Swe)	71-72-72-67—282	65130
	Eduardo Romero (Arg)	70-69-75-68—282	65130

Trophée Lancôme *at Saint-Nom-La-Bretèche*

Year	Winner	Score	Year	Winner	Score
1970	A Jacklin	206 (54)	1985	N Price*	275
1971	A Palmer	202 (54)	1986T	S Ballesteros*	274
1972	T Aaron	279		B Langer*	
1973	J Miller	277	1987	I Woosnam	264
1974	W Casper	283	1988	S Ballesteros	269
1975	G Player	278	1989	E Romero	266
1976	S Ballesteros	283	1990	JM Olazábal	269
1977	G Marsh*	273	1991	F Nobilo	267
1978	L Trevino	272	1992	M Roe	267
1979	J Miller	281	1993	I Woosnam	267
1980	L Trevino	280	1994	V Singh	263
1981	D Graham	280	1995	C Montgomerie	269
1982	D Graham	276	1996	J Parnevik	268
1983	S Ballesteros	269	1997	M O'Meara	271
1984	A Lyle*	278			

1998

Pos	Name	Score	Prize Money £
1	Miguel Angel Jiménez (Sp)	67-70-67-69—273	133330
2	Greg Turner (NZ)	67-71-68-69—275	53207
	Jarmo Sandelin (Swe)	68-74-70-63—275	53207
	Mark O'Meara (US)	70-67-69-69—275	53207
	David Duval (US)	69-72-67-67—275	53207

★ *Winner after play-off*

Linde German Masters

Year	Winner	Venue	Score	Year	Winner	Venue	Score
1987	A Lyle*	Stuttgart	278	1993	S Richardson	Stuttgart	271
1988	JM Olazábal	Stuttgart	279	1994	S Ballesteros*	Motzener See	270
1989	B Langer	Stuttgart	276	1995	A Forsbrand	Motzener See	264
1990	S Torrance	Stuttgart	272	1996	D Clarke	Motzener See	264
1991	B Langer*	Stuttgart	275	1997	B Langer	Berliner G & CG	267
1992	B Lane	Stuttgart	272				

1998 *at Gut Lärchenhof, Cologne*

Pos	Name	Score	Prize Money £
1	Colin Montgomerie (Sco)	65-68-66-67—266	166660
2	Robert Karlsson (Swe)	68-65-69-65—267	86850
	Vijay Singh (Fij)	65-67-69-66—267	86850

Belgacom Open

Year	Winner	Venue	Score	Year	Winner	Venue	Score
1910	A Massy	Brussels	139	1947	F van Donck	Spa	283
1911	CH Mayo	Brussels	144	1948	WS Forrester	Brussels	288
1912	G Duncan	Brussels	144	1949	J Adams	Spa	283
1913	T Ball	Lombartzyde	154	1950	R de Vicenzo	Le Zoute	282
1914	T Ball	Antwerp	144	1951	A Pelissier	Ghent	279
1920	R Jones	Le Zoute	154	1952	A Cerda	Spa	286
1921	E Lafitte	Brussels	145	1953	F van Donck	Waterloo	270
1922	A Boomer	Brussels	150	1954	DJ Rees	Antwerp	287
1923	P Boomer	Brussels	143	1955	DC Thomas	Spa	290
1924	W Hagen	Le Zoute	142	1956	F van Donck	Ghent	269
1925	E Lafitte	Antwerp	145	1957	BJ Hunt*	Ghent	280
1926	A Boomer	Le Zoute	137	1958	K Bousfield	Ravenstein	271
1927	M Dallemagne	Le Zoute	140	1978	N Ratcliffe	Brussels	280
1928	A Tingey Jr	Brussels	293	1979	G Levenson	Waterloo	279
1929	S F Brews	Antwerp	300	1987	E Darcy	Waterloo	200 (54)
1930	TH Cotton	Brussels	281	1988	JM Olazabal	Bercuit, Brussels	269
1931	A Lacey	Spa	301	1989	GJ Brand	Royal Waterloo	273
1932	A Lacey	Brussels	291	1990	O Sellberg	Royal Waterloo	272
1933	A Boyer	Spa	282	1991	P-U Johansson*	Royal Waterloo	276
1934	TH Cotton	Waterloo	279	1992	MA Jiménez	Royal Zoute	274
1935	W J Branch	Brussels	283	1993	D Clarke	Royal Zoute	270
1936	A Boyer	Spa	285	1994	N Faldo*	Royal Zoute	279
1937	M Dallemagne	Le Zoute	285	1995	Not played		
1938	TH Cotton	Waterloo	277	1996	Not played		
1939	F van Donck	Spa	291	1997	Not played		
1946	F van Donck	Waterloo	289				

1998 *at Royal Zoute, Belgium*

Pos	Name	Score	Prize Money £
1	Lee Westwood (Eng)*	67-68-67-66—268	66660
2	Fredrik Jacobson (Swe)	65-67-69-67—268	44440

* Westwood won at first hole of play-off

Pos	Name	Score	Prize Money £
3	Robert Karlsson (Swe)	64-72-68-66—270	22520
	Greg Turner (NZ)	64-70-67-69—270	22520

* Winner after play-off

Alfred Dunhill Cup (Instituted 1985 at St Andrews)
For fuller details see page 194

Year	Winner	Runner-up	Year	Winner	Runner-up
1986	Australia	Japan	1992	England	Scotland
1987	England	Scotland	1993	USA	England
1988	Ireland	Australia	1994	Canada	USA
1989	USA	Japan	1995	Scotland	Zimbabwe
1990	Ireland	England	1996	USA	New Zealand
1991	Sweden	South Africa	1997	South Africa	Sweden

1998 at The Old Course, St Andrews, Fife

Semi-Finals
Spain beat USA 2–1
 MA Jimenez (75) lost to J Daly (73)
 S Luna (71) beat T Woods (72)
 JM Olazábal (72) beat M O'Meara (76)

South Africa beat Australia 2–1
 D Frost (72) beat C Parry (78)
 R Goosen (71) beat S Appleby (74)
 E Els (73) lost to S Elkington (72)

Final
South Africa beat Spain 3–0
 R Goosen (72) beat S Luna (73)
 D Frost (76) beat MA Jimenez (78)
 E Els beat (75) JM Olazábal (77)

World Matchplay Championship
Cisco took over sponsorship from Toyota in 1998.

Year	Winner	Runner-up	By	Year	Winner	Runner-up	By
1964	A Palmer	N Coles	2 and 1	1981	S Ballesteros	B Crenshaw	1 hole
1965	G Player	P Thomson	3 and 2	1982	S Ballesteros	A Lyle	37th hole
1966	G Player	J Nicklaus	6 and 4	1983	G Norman	N Faldo	3 and 2
1967	A Palmer	P Thomson	1 hole	1984	S Ballesteros	B Langer	2 and 1
1968	G Player	R Charles	1 hole	1985	S Ballesteros	B Langer	6 and 5
1969	R Charles	G Littler	37th hole	1986	G Norman	A Lyle	2 and 1
1970	J Nicklaus	L Trevino	2 and 1	1987	I Woosnam	A Lyle	1 hole
1971	G Player	J Nicklaus	5 and 4	1988	A Lyle	N Faldo	2 and 1
1972	T Weiskopf	L Trevino	4 and 3	1989	N Faldo	I Woosnam	1 hole
1973	G Player	G Marsh	40th hole	1990	I Woosnam	M McNulty	4 and 2
1974	H Irwin	G Player	3 and 1	1991	S Ballesteros	N Price	3 and 2
1975	H Irwin	A Geiberger	4 and 2	1992	N Faldo	J Sluman	8 and 7
1976	D Graham	H Irwin	38th hole	1993	C Pavin	N Faldo	1 hole
1977	G Marsh	R Floyd	5 and 3	1994	E Els	C Montgomerie	4 and 2
1978	I Aoki	S Owen	3 and 2	1995	E Els	S Elkington	2 and 1
1979	W Rogers	I Aoki	1 hole	1996	E Els	V Singh	3 and 2
1980	G Norman	A Lyle	1 hole	1997	V Singh	E Els	1 hole

1998 at West Course, Wentworth, Surrey
Total prize money: £640,000

First Round
Patrick Sjöland beat Steve Stricker 1 hole
Colin Montgomerie beat Thomas Björn 4 and 3
Lee Westwood beat Stuart Appleby 8 and 7
Ian Woosnam beat Darren Clarke 4 and 3

Second Round
Vijay Singh beat Patrik Sjöland 7 and 6
Mark O'Meara beat Colin Montgomerie 5 and 4
Lee Westwood beat Ernie Els 2 and 1
Tiger Woods beat Ian Woosnam at 37th hole

Semi-Finals
Mark O'Meara beat Vijay Singh 11 and 10
Tiger Woods beat Lee Westwood 5 and 4

Final
Mark O'Meara beat Tiger Woods by 1 hole
(O'Meara received £170,000, Woods £90,000)

Open Novotel Perrier

1998 *at Golf du Médoc, Bordeaux, France*

Pos	Name	Score	Prize Money £
1	Jarmo Sandelin/Olle Karlsson (Swe)	62-68-63-136–329	35000 each
2	Richard Boxall/Derrick Cooper (Eng)	65-69-65-133–332	25000 each
3	Seve Ballesteros/Miguel A Jiménez (Sp)	64-69-67-134–334	17500 each

Volvo Masters

Year	Winner	Venue	Score	Year	Winner	Venue	Score
1988	N Faldo	Valderrama	284	1993	C Montgomerie	Valderrama	274
1989	R Rafferty	Valderrama	282	1994	B Langer	Valderrama	276
1990	M Harwood	Valderrama	286	1995	A Cejka	Valderrama	282
1991	R Davis	Valderrama	280	1996	M McNulty	Valderrama	276
1992	A Lyle	Valderrama	287	1997	L Westwood	Montecastillo	200 (54)

1998 *at Montecastillo, Jerez, Spain*

Pos	Name	Score	Prize Money £
1	Darren Clarke (N.Ire)	67-73-68-63—271	166000
2	Andrew Coltart (Sco)	69-73-65-66—273	110000
3	Colin Montgomerie (Sco)	70-67-69-68—274	63000

TOUR QUALIFYING SCHOOL

at San Roque Club & Sotogrande, Spain

The following players won tour cards for 1999:

Pos	Name	Score	Prize Money £
1	Ross Drummond (Sco)	70-67-69-73-74-72–425	8500
2	Henrik Nyström (Swe)	66-71-74-70-68-76–425	8500
3	Anders Hansen (Den)	73-72-70-72-68-72–427	5000
4	Jesus Arruti (Sp)	71-72-70-75-71-70–429	3500
5	Pedro Linhart (Sp)	72-73-72-68-73-71–429	3500
6	Robert-Jan Derksen (Hol)	70-71-70-73-74-71–429	3500
7	Juan Quiros (Sp)	71-72-69-72-73-73–430	2700
8	Andrew McLardy (SA)	72-70-73-70-70-76–431	2350
9	Jean Pierre Cixous (Fr)	70-73-71-71-70-76–431	2350
10	Stephen Dodd (Wal)	74-76-68-71-69-74–432	2000
11	Diego Borrego (Sp)	74-71-69-71-72-75–432	2000
12	Francis Valera (Sp)	66-73-67-75-76-75–432	2000
13	Alberto Binaghi (It)	71-71-71-69-74-76–432	2000
14	Emanuele Canonica (It)	75-66-65-75-75-76–432	2000
15	Stephen Bennett (Eng)	77-71-69-73-73-70–433	1562
16	Mark Pilkington (Wal)	73-72-70-74-72-72–433	1562
17	Robert Lee (Eng)	76-70-70-71-69-77–433	1562
18	Marcello Santi (It)	74-72-68-70-69-80–433	1562
19	Tomas Jesus Munoz (Sp)	74-73-71-71-74-71–434	1300
20	Märten Olander (Swe)	76-77-71-68-68-74–434	1300
21	Geoff Ogilvy (Aus)	69-71-76-72-72-74–434	1300
22	Carlos Rodiles (Sp)	68-72-69-76-75-74–434	1300
23	Andrew Raitt (Eng)	77-73-73-66-70-75–434	1300
24	Richard Boxall (Eng)	74-72-73-69-76-71–435	1110
25	Christian Cévaer (Fr)	75-74-68-71-75-72–435	1110

Pos	Name	Score	Prize Money £
26	Nick O'Hern (Aus)	76-71-72-72-68-76–435	1110
27	Michele Reale (It)	73-72-73-75-73-70–436	1006
28	Mac O'Grady (US)	75-74-75-67-74-71–436	1006
29	Gary Emerson (Eng)	75-74-70-72-72-73–436	1006
30	Kalle Brink (Swe)	72-74-71-74-72-73–436	1006
31	Steven Richardson (Eng)	73-70-72-75-73-73–436	1006
32	R Neil Roderick (Wal)	77-69-69-74-72-75–436	1006
33	Andrew Bonhomme (Aus)	67-75-71-74-74-75–436	1006
34	Henrik Bjornstad (Nor)	73-71-70-75-71-76–436	1006
35	Jeremy Robinson (Eng)	75-69-72-75-73-73–437	970
36	Ian Hutchings (Eng)	72-68-71-76-73-77–437	970
37	Stephane Talbot (Can)	73-69-71-73-74-77–437	970
38	Johan Ryström (Swe)	74-69-72-72-72-78–437	970

European Challenge Tour, 1998

FINAL RANKING

The top 15 earned European Tour Cards

Pos	Name	Prize Money £	Pos	Name	Prize Money £
1	Warren Bennett (Eng)	81052	26	Marten Olander (Swe)	18007
2	Per Nyman (Swe)	37196	27	Raimo Sjöberg (Swe)	17524
3	Massimo Scarpa (It)	35523	28	Robert Lee (Eng)	15985
4	Roger Winchester (Eng)	33796	29	David Park (Wal)	15467
5	Ricardo Gonzalez (Arg)	33159	30	Morten Backhausen (Den)	15174
6	John Bickerton (Eng)	30205	31	Markus Brier (Au)	14764
7	John Mellor (Eng)	30015	32	Francisco Valera (Sp)	14162
8	Fredrik Lindgren (Swe)	28864	33	Fredrik Larsson (Swe)	13859
9	John Senden (Aus)	28769	34	Christian Cevaer (Fr)	13754
10	Soren Hansen (Den)	27984	35	Anders Hansen (Den)	13750
11	Max Anglert (Swe)	27522	36	Euan Little (Sco)	13131
12	Jorge Berendt (Arg)	27194	37	Henrik Bjornstad (Nor)	12735
13	Christopher Hanell (Swe)	26884	38	Alvaro Salto (Sp)	12599
14	Stephen Gallacher (Sco)	26673	39	Jos Carriles (Sp)	12591
15	Darren Lee (Eng)	26133	40	Pauli Hughes (Fin)	12242
			41	Johan Ryström (Swe)	12057
16	Kevin Carissimi (US)	24890	42	Magnus Persson (Swe)	12053
17	Scott Watson (Eng)	23627	43	Antoine Lebouc (Fr)	11480
18	José Manuel Lara (Sp)	22343	44	Jesus Maria Arruti (Sp)	10727
19	Marc Pendaries (Fr)	22109	45	Benoit Telleria (Fr)	10627
20	Marcello Santi (It)	21729	46	Elliot Boult (NZ)	10586
21	Thomas Nielsen (Nor)	21673	47	Frédéric Cupillard (Fr)	10460
22	Jeremy Robinson (Eng)	21567	48	Brian Nelson (US)	10292
23	David R Jones (Eng)	18764	49	Pehr Magnebrant (Swe)	9389
24	Mikael Lundberg (Swe)	18732	50	Stephen Scahill (NZ)	9225
25	Gary Emerson (Eng)	18213			

TOUR RESULTS

Tournament	Venue	Winner	Score
Open de Côte d'Ivoire	Ivoire GC, Abidjan	John Mellor (Eng)	281 (-7)
Tusker Kenya Open	Muthaiga, Nairobi	Ricardo Gonzalez (Arg)	272 (-12)
Is Molas Challenge	Is Molas, Sardinia	Magnus Persson (Swe)	283 (-5)
Rimini International Open	Rimini GC, Italy	Massimo Scarpa (It)	278(-10)
Albarella International Open	Albarella, Venice	Fredrik Lindgren (Swe)	267 (-21)
3rd Modena Classic	Modena G&CC, Italy	Marc Pendaries (Fr)	270 (-18)
Challenge de France	Sable Solesmes	Warren Bennett (Eng)	272 (-16)

European Challenge Tour

Tournament	Venue	Winner	Score
KB Golf Challenge	Praha Karlstein, Czech Republic	Stephen Gallacher (Sco)	270 (-14)
Diners Club Austrian Open	Milstätter See	Kevin Carissimi (US)	269 (-11)
NCC Open	Soderasens GC, Sweden	Johan Ryström (Swe)	276 (-8)
Lancia Golf Pokal§	Germany	Alex Cejka (Ger)	202 (-17)
Fontana Open§	Austria	Uli Weinhandl (Aust)	288 (par)
Championship de France Professional	France	Jean Van de Velde (Fr)	267 (-21)
Omnium National Ch'p§ Lloyd Italico	Italy	Massimo Scarpa (It)	270 (-18)
Osmanli Bankasi Klassis Turkish Open	Klassis	Thomas Nielsen (Nor)	273 (-11)
Open dei Tessali	Tessali, Italy	Pehr Magnebrant (Swe)	276 (-8)
Mastercard Challenge	Princes, England	Robert Lee (Eng)	277 (-11)
Audi Quattro Trophy	Bad Abbach, Germany	Marcello Santi (It)	269 (-19)
BTC Slovenian Open	Bled	Warren Bennett (Eng)	270 (-22)
Volvo Finnish Open	Espoo	Christian Cévaër (Fr)	280 (-8)
Open des Volcans	Volcans, France	Warren Bennett (Eng)	277 (-11)
Rolex Trophy†	Geneva, Switzerland	David H Park (Wal)	276 (-12)
Interlaken Open	Interlaken, Switzerland	John Senden (Aus)	263 (-25)
Challenge Tour Championship	East Sussex, England	Warren Bennett (Eng)	276 (-12)
Finnish Masters	Masters, Espoo	Massimo Scarpa (It)	271 (-17)
Moscow CC Russian Open	Russia	Warren Bennett (Eng)	270 (-18)
Denmark Closed Event§	Denmark	Ben Tinning (Den)	212 (-1)
Netcom Norwegian Open	Borre	Gary Emerson (Eng)	275 (-17)
Navision Open Championship	Himmerland, Denmark	Søren Hansen (Den)	206 (-10)
Ohrlings Swedish Matchplay	Varbergs GC	Kevin Carissimi (US)	
Open de Strasbourg– La Wantzenau	France	John Senden (Aus)	276 (-12)
Warsaw Golf Open	Poland	José Manuel Lara (Sp)	273 (-11)
Eulen Open Galea	Neguri, Bilbao, Spain	Alvaro Salto (Sp)	280 (-8)
Telia Grand Prix	Ljunghusens GC, Sweden	Mats Lanner (Swe)	284 (par)
San Paolo Vita Open	Margara GC, Italy	Roger Winchester (Eng)	272 (-16)
Challenge Tour Grand Final	GC de Belas, Portugal	Jorge Berendt (Arg)	275 (-13)

§ *Closed event*   † *Invitational event*

Men's Professional Tournaments

European Senior Tour, 1998

Final Ranking

Pos	Name	Prize Money £	Pos	Name	Prize Money £
1	Tommy Horton (Eng)	127656	51	Lloyd Monroe (US)	10725
2	Brian Huggett (Wal)	102382	52	Joe Carr (US)	10365
3	Eddie Polland (N.Ire)	92145	53	Steve Wild (Eng)	9637
4	David Jones (N.Ire)	74133	54	Tienie Britz (SA)	9286
5	Noel Ratcliffe (Aus)	69528	55	Harry Flatman (Eng)	8976
6	Jim Rhodes (Eng)	64021	56	Guy Hunt (Eng)	8734
7	Bobby Verwey (SA)	62595	57	Chick Evans (US)	8489
8	Neil Coles (Eng)	58663	58	Jan Bjornsson (Swe)	8440
9	Denis O'Sullivan (Ire)	54990	59	DeRay Simon (US)	7759
10	Brian Waites (Eng)	54515	60	David Snell (Eng)	7381
11	Antonio Garrido (Sp)	54271	61	Bernard Hunt (Eng)	7177
12	Bob Lendzion (US)	54165	62	Agim Bardha (US)	7015
13	Malcolm Gregson (Eng)	54023	63	Roger Fidler (Eng)	6417
14	Maurice Bembridge (Eng)	53414	64	Graham Burroughs (Eng)	6359
15	John Garner (Eng)	48134	65	Don McCart (Sco)	6216
16	David Huish (Sco)	45271	66	Dr Arthur Spring (Ire)	5994
17	Paul Leonard (N.Ire)	44976	67	Bill Lockie (Sco)	5928
18	Bill Hardwick (Can)	43640	68	Kenny Stevenson (N.Ire)	5874
19	Bill Brask (US)	43621	69	Roger Stern (US)	5489
20	Terry Gale (Aus)	43495	70	Andrew Brooks (Sco)	5157
21	John Fourie (SA)	42025	71	Stewart Adwick (Eng)	4741
22	Renato Campagnoli (It)	40784	72	Bryan Carter (Eng)	4460
23	Barry Sandry (Eng)	38622	73	Gordon Gray (Sco)	4229
24	David Creamer (Eng)	37686	74	Glenn MacDonald (Can)	4117
25	Joe McDermott (Ire)	36689	75	Michael Murphy (Ire)	4108
26	Liam Higgins (Ire)	36074	76	Javier Viladomiu (Sp)	3997
27	Michael Slater (Eng)	35340	77	Jan Dorrestein (Hol)	3584
28	Norman Wood (Sco)	32522	78	Hiro Tahara (Jpn)	3535
29	Ian Richardson (Eng)	28429	79	José Maria Roca (Sp)	3513
30	Alberto Croce (It)	27272	80	Roberto Bernardini (It)	3455
31	David Oakley (US)	26492	81	Francisco Abreu (Sp)	3382
32	Bob Shearer (Aus)	26014	82	Terry Kendall (NZ)	3375
33	John Morgan (Eng)	25906	83	Tommy Halpin (Ire)	3176
34	Craig Defoy (Wal)	24986	84	Peter Butler (Eng)	3173
35	Jay Dolan III (US)	23932	85	Randall Vines (Aus)	3080
36	Peter Townsend (Eng)	23579	86	Hugh Jackson (N.Ire)	3070
37	Tony Jacklin (Eng)	21306	87	Gerolamo Delfino (It)	2690
38	JR Delich (US)	20770	88	Hugh Boyle (Ire)	2535
39	Snell Lancaster (US)	19215	89	David Talbot (Eng)	2185
40	Arnold O'Connor (Ire)	18649	90	Kenneth Magnusson (Swe)	2130
41	Hugh Inggs (SA)	18273	91	Skip Pratt (USA)	2082
42	José Cabo (Sp)	18062	92	Ossie Gartenmaier (Aut)	1895
43	Doug Dalziel (US)	16714	93	Alan Hall (Eng)	1847
44	Geoff Parslow (Aus)	16008	94	Hedley Muscroft (Eng)	1605
45	Iain Clark (Sco)	14363	95	Sooky Maharaj (T&T)	1585
46	Gordon Parkhill (N.Ire)	13820	96	Matt McCrorie (Sco)	1512
47	Bob Menne (US)	13352	97	Sid Denham (Eng)	1182
48	Christy O'Connor Jr (Ire)	12285	98	Adam Whiston (Ire)	1161
49	John Hudson (Eng)	10861	99	Fred Whitfield (Eng)	1148
50	TR Jones (US)	10810	100	John Lister (NZ)	1132

Career Money List

Pos	Name	Prize Money £	Pos	Name	Prize Money £
1	Tommy Horton	614892	26	Hugh Inggs	93607
2	Brian Huggett	329348	27	Terry Gale	92043
3	Neil Coles	312335	28	Chick Evans	91098
4	Brian Waites	265458	29	Vincent Tshabalala	82734
5	Antonio Garrido	240465	30	Bill Hardwick	80842
6	Malcolm Gregson	239617	31	Tony Grubb	79457
7	Bobby Verwey	227176	32	David Snell	77530
8	Noel Ratcliffe	225342	33	Doug Dalziel	76660
9	John Morgan	223946	34	DeRay Simon	76158
10	Gary Player	217581	35	Michael Murphy	74731
11	Bob Charles	203535	36	David Oakley	73922
12	John Fourie	184304	37	John Garner	70651
13	Renato Campagnoli	172443	38	Ian Richardson	70467
14	Liam Higgins	161379	39	Roger Fidler	68322
15	Maurice Bembridge	156908	40	Tom Wargo	63670
16	Brian Barnes	149698	41	Norman Wood	61409
17	Jim Rhodes	143194	42	Harry Flatman	59962
18	David Creamer	133665	43	Hugh Boyle	58559
19	Alberto Croce	132162	44	Bernard Hunt	58443
20	David Huish	126721	45	Jose Maria Roca	57719
21	Eddie Polland	118956	46	Tienie Britz	56188
22	David Jones	110867	47	Randall Vines	55066
23	Peter Butler	107527	48	Denis O'Sullivan	54990
24	David Butler	100858	49	Joe Carr	54750
25	Paul Leonard	95303	50	Snell Lancaster	54376

Tour Results

Tournament	Venue	Winner	Score
El Bosque Senior Open	El Bosque GC, Spain	Tommy Horton (Eng)	201 (-15)
Beko Classic	Gloria Golf Resort, Turkey	Robert L Lendzion (US)	211 (-5)
AIB Irish Senior Open	Woodbrook GC	Joe McDermott (Ire)	208 (-8)
Phillips PFA Golf Classic	Marriott Meon Valley Hotel & CC, England	Neil Coles (Eng)	203 (-13)
Jersey Seniors Open	La Moye GC	Bob Shearer (Aus)	211 (-5)
De Vere Hotels Senior Classic	Belton Woods GC, England	Tommy Horton (Eng)	211 (-5)
Ryder Senior Classic	Welcombe Hotel, England	Bill Hardwick (Can)	202 (-8)
Swedish Seniors	Fägelbro GC	Maurice Bembridge (Eng)	209 (-4)
Lawrence Batley Seniors'	Huddersfield GC, England	Bobby Verwey (SA)	210 (-3)
Credit Suisse Private Banking Senior Open	Bad Ragaz GC, Switzerland	Bobby Verwey (SA)	200 (-10)
Schroder Senior Masters	Wentworth GC, England	Brian Huggett (Wal)	209 (-7)
Senior British Open	R. Portrush GC, N. Ireland	Brian Huggett (Wal)	283 (-5)
West of Ireland Seniors' Ch'p	East Clare GC	John Morgan (Eng)	205 (-8)
The Belfry PGA Seniors' Ch'p	PGA National, England	Tommy Horton (Eng)	277 (-11)
Golden Charter PGA Scottish Seniors' Open Ch'p	Marriott Dalmahoy Hotel & CC	David Huish (Sco)	273 (-15)
Efteling European Trophy	Efteling Golf Park, Holland	Paul Leonard (N.Ire)	204 (-12)
Elf Senior Open	Pau GC, France	Brian Waites (Eng)	195 (-12)
Is Molas Senior Open	Is Molas GC, Sardinia	Malcolm Gregson (Eng)	209 (-7)
Senior Tournament of Champions	Buckinghamshire GC, England	John Garner (Eng)	139 (-5) (36 holes)

Senior Tour Qualifying School

at Hardelot GC, France

The following players won Tour cards for 1999:

Pos	Name	Score
1	Doug Robb (Can)	75-61-73-74–283
2	Gordon MacDonald (Am) (Sco)	74-61-73-75–283
3	Raymond Carrasco (US)	74-64-73-76–287
4	Trevor Downing (Aus)	71-63-77-77–288
5	Agim Bardha (US)	65-76-69-78–288
6	Fritz Gambetta (US)	64-73-73-78–288
7	Kenny Stevenson (N.Ire)	66-74-73-76–289
8	John McTear (Sco)	67-76-71-76–290
9	Alan Tapie (US)	75-60-79-76–290
10	Jerry Bruner (US)	62-79-68-81–290
11	Francisco Abreu (Sp)	74-64-78-74–290
12	Volker Krajewski (US)	58-78-80-75–291
13	Ross Metherell (Aus)	72-65-78-76–291
14	Jay Horton (US)	64-78-71-78–291
15	Jan Dorrestein (Hol)	66-73-74-78–291
16	Gordon Gray (Sco)	80-63-79-70–292
17	Gordon Parkhill (N.Ire)	63-79-77-73–292
18	Thomas Persson (Swe)	70-75-72-75–292
19	Sid Denham (Eng)	63-72-79-78–292
20	Tommy Price (US)	75-63-74-80–292

US PGA Tour, 1998

Final Ranking

Pos	Name	Prize Money $	Pos	Name	Prize Money $
1	David Duval	2591031	51	JP Hayes	555272
2	Vijay Singh	2238998	52	Tommy Armour III	554650
3	Jim Furyk	2054334	53	Dudley Hart	553729
4	Tiger Woods	1841117	54	Tim Herron	525373
5	Hal Sutton	1838740	55	Tom Pernice Jr	520400
6	Phil Mickelson	1837246	56	Jay Haas	514453
7	Mark O'Meara	1786699	57	Bob Friend	492189
8	Justin Leonard	1671823	58	Kenny Perry	487551
9	Fred Couples	1650389	59	Kirk Triplett	472145
10	John Huston	1544110	60	Loren Roberts	467285
11	Davis Love III	1541152	61	Joey Sindelar	466797
12	Mark Calcavecchia	1368554	62	Larry Mize	464294
13	Steve Stricker	1313948	63	Harrison Frazar	461633
14	Jesper Parnevik	1290822	64	Scott Simpson	449777
15	Glen Day	1283416	65	Nolan Henke	444561
16	Billy Mayfair	1281685	66	Kevin Sutherland	444429
17	Scott Hoch	1237053	67	Ted Tryba	421786
18	Scott Verplank	1223436	68	Len Mattiace	418416
19	Payne Stewart	1193996	69	Scott McCarron	414247
20	Lee Janzen	1155314	70	Steve Lowery	409940
21	Jeff Sluman	1148375	71	Jim Carter	407184
22	John Cook	1145511	72	Jay Don Blake	405305
23	Fred Funk	1121988	73	Scott Gump	402092
24	Bob Tway	1073447	74	Brad Faxon	401496
25	Tom Lehman	1033673	75	Clark Dennis	401440
26	Nick Price	1019404	76	Willie Wood	397110
27	Jeff Maggert	992964	77	John Daly	393740
28	Bob Estes	987930	78	Rocco Mediate	389996
29	Tom Watson	976585	79	Bruce Lietzke	377188
30	Andrew Magee	964302	80	Bradley Hughes	370767
31	Stewart Cink	833648	81	Robert Damron	370211
32	Skip Kendall	796564	82	Paul Goydos	368413
33	Trevor Dodds	791340	83	Stephen Ames	357859
34	Steve Pate	782504	84	Bill Glasson	353222
35	Steve Flesch	777185	85	Craig Stadler	350091
36	Ernie Els	763783	86	Neal Lancaster	346563
37	Brandel Chamblee	755936	87	Jerry Kelly	340144
38	Steve Jones	741544	88	Mike Hulbert	335954
39	Chris Perry	730171	89	Phil Tataurangi	335821
40	Stuart Appleby	717962	90	Brian Watts	335735
41	Billy Andrade	705434	91	Russ Cochran	332889
42	Steve Elkington	695775	92	Peter Jacobsen	327336
43	Joe Durant	651803	93	Esteban Toledo	327244
44	David Toms	635073	94	Greg Kraft	326571
45	Frank Lickliter	600847	95	Lee Porter	325415
46	Lee Westwood	599586	96	Paul Stankowski	322036
47	Olin Browne	590240	97	Colin Montgomerie	321823
48	Michael Bradley	576501	98	Craig Parry	312710
49	Brent Geiberger	573098	99	Dan Forsman	312058
50	Paul Azinger	568233	100	Barry Cheesman	310535

CAREER MONEY LIST (at end 1998)

Pos	Name	Prize Money $	Pos	Name	Prize Money $
1	Greg Norman	11 936 443	51	Tiger Woods	4 698 544
2	Fred Couples	10 535 876	52	Fred Funk	4 684 274
3	Tom Kite	10 447 472	53	Steve Jones	4 640 723
4	Mark O'Meara	10 293 473	54	Wayne Levi	4 634 518
5	Davis Love III	10 012 134	55	Bill Glasson	4 560 029
6	Nick Price	9 813 834	56	Kenny Perry	4 526 783
7	Payne Stewart	9 659 058	57	Nick Faldo	4 522 963
8	Tom Watson	9 283 862	58	Joey Sindelar	4 512 493
9	Scott Hoch	9 136 303	59	Ernie Els	4 500 017
10	Mark Calcavecchia	8 981 485	60	DA Weibring	4 342 195
11	Corey Pavin	8 298 841	61	David Edwards	4 237 596
12	Paul Azinger	8 019 642	62	Billy Andrade	4 119 484
13	John Cook	7 254 627	63	Dan Forsman	3 965 441
14	Curtis Strange	7 226 587	64	Tom Purtzer	3 910 659
15	Craig Stadler	7 220 968	65	John Mahaffey	3 876 852
16	Ben Crenshaw	7 075 996	66	Mike Reid	3 857 161
17	Steve Elkington	7 023 912	67	Larry Nelson	3 827 401
18	Hal Sutton	6 972 978	68	Russ Cochran	3 804 292
19	Phil Mickelson	6 964 977	69	Bob Estes	3 789 454
20	Jay Haas	6 906 099	70	Mike Hulbert	3 766 359
21	Tom Lehman	6 676 673	71	Steve Stricker	3 694 374
22	Lee Janzen	6 493 245	72	Ken Green	3 585 926
23	David Frost	6 475 440	73	Lee Trevino	3 478 328
24	David Duval	6 406 041	74	Rocco Mediate	3 473 010
25	Jeff Sluman	6 293 739	75	Duffy Waldorf	3 465 995
26	Lanny Wadkins	6 282 248	76	Brad Bryant	3 432 069
27	Bruce Lietzke	6 257 272	77	Rick Fehr	3 417 333
28	Brad Faxon	6 244 115	78	Andy Bean	3 408 512
29	Vijay Singh	6 226 556	79	Jay Don Blake	3 408 107
30	Loren Roberts	6 091 388	80	Tim Simpson	3 406 017
31	Chip Beck	6 005 490	81	Gene Sauers	3 290 841
32	Bob Tway	5 949 395	82	Jesper Parnevik	3 268 949
33	Hale Irwin	5 907 550	83	Don Pooley	3 266 681
34	Fuzzy Zoeller	5 706 218	84	Blaine McCallister	3 227 141
35	Jack Nicklaus	5 691 673	85	Nolan Henke	3 177 407
36	Scott Simpson	5 659 927	86	Kirk Triplett	3 087 712
37	Larry Mize	5 614 010	87	Mark Wiebe	3 083 312
38	John Huston	5 611 195	88	Dan Pohl	3 033 203
39	Jeff Maggert	5 403 996	89	Donnie Hammond	3 032 825
40	Billy Mayfair	5 349 481	90	Bob Gilder	2 951 820
41	Ray Floyd	5 300 595	91	Steve Lowery	2 866 716
42	Peter Jacobsen	5 297 028	92	Phil Blackmar	2 866 652
43	Mark McCumber	5 290 798	93	Jodie Mudd	2 806 955
44	Gil Morgan	5 259 164	94	Bobby Wadkins	2 791 859
45	Jim Gallagher Jr	5 227 376	95	Scott Verplank	2 752 219
46	Jim Furyk	5 184 747	96	Johnny Miller	2 747 484
47	Mark Brooks	5 169 581	97	Howard Twitty	2 713 551
48	Justin Leonard	5 091 701	98	David Ogrin	2 648 405
49	Andrew Magee	4 883 387	99	Doug Tewell	2 640 391
50	Steve Pate	4 715 935	100	Hubert Green	2 591 959

TOUR STATISTICS

Stroke averages

Pos	Name	Avg
1	David Duval	69.13
2	Tiger Woods	69.21
3	Davis Love III	69.41
4	Jim Furyk	69.50
5	Mark O'Meara	69.63
6	Nick Price	69.64
7	John Huston	69.65
8	Ernie Els	69.71
9	Jesper Parnevik	69.82
10	Vijay Singh	69.85
11	Fred Couples	69.87
12	Steve Stricker	69.89
13	Bob Tway	69.92
14T	Scott Hoch	69.93
	Payne Stewart	69.93
16	Hal Sutton	70.05
17	Scott Verplank	70.06
18	Glen Day	70.08
19	Mark Calcavecchia	70.11
20	Justin Leonard	70.12
21	Tom Lehman	70.15
22	Lee Janzen	70.19
23	Stewart Cink	70.21
24	Jeff Maggert	70.24
25T	Steve Jones	70.25
	Loren Roberts	70.25

Driving accuracy
(Percentage of fairways in regulation)

Pos	Name	%
1	Bruce Fleisher	81.4
2	Larry Mize	80.4
3	Jeff Maggert	78.7
4	Hal Sutton	78.6
5	Tim Loustalot	78.5
6	Joe Durant	78.4
7	Fred Funk	78.1
8T	Scott Gump	78.0
	Lee Porter	78.0
10	Tom Byrum	77.7

Driving distance (Average yards per drive)

Pos	Name	Yds
1	John Daly	299.4
2	Tiger Woods	296.3
3	Harrison Frazar	289.8
4T	Fred Couples	289.1
	Scott McCarron	289.1
6	David Duval	286.8
7	Barry Cheesman	284.1
8	Vance Veazey	283.9
9	Phil Mickelson	283.4
10	Kelly Gibson	283.0

Sand saves

Pos	Name	%
1	Keith Fergus	71.0
2	Len Mattiace	69.8
3	Kirk Triplett	66.7
4	Fuzzy Zoeller	64.9
5	Justin Leonard	64.4
6	Craig Parry	63.0
7T	Stewart Cink	62.9
	Steve Stricker	62.9
9	Billy Mayfair	62.7
10	Esteban Toledo	61.5

Greens in regulation

Pos	Name	%
1	Hal Sutton	71.3
2	Tom Lehman	71.1
3	Dan Forsman	70.7
4T	David Duval	70.5
	Steve Flesch	70.5
6	Steve Jones	70.1
7	Mark Calcavecchia	69.7
8	Kirk Triplett	69.5
9	Bradley Hughes	69.4
10	Duffy Waldorf	69.2

Putts per greens in regulation

Pos	Name	Avg
1	Rick Fehr	1.722
2	Stewart Cink	1.724
3	Davis Love III	1.728
4	John Huston	1.730
5T	David Duval	1.732
	Dave Stockton Jr	1.732
7	Steve Stricker	1.740
8	RW Eaks	1.744
9	Jim Furyk	1.745
10T	Chris Perry	1.746
	Loren Roberts	1.746

TOUR RESULTS (in chronological order)

Players are of American nationality unless stated

Mercedes Championships
La Costa Resort, Carlsbad, CA

1	Phil Mickelson	68-67-68-68—271	$306000
2	Mark O'Meara	71-70-67-64—272	149600
	Tiger Woods	72-67-69-64—272	149600

Bob Hope Chrysler Classic
Indian Wells, Bermuda Dunes, La Quinta, Indian Wells, CA

1	Fred Couples*	64-70-66-66-66—332	$414000
2	Bruce Lietzke	65-65-71-62-69—332	248400
3	Andrew Magee	63-68-64-68-70—333	156400

Phoenix Open
TPC of Scottsdale, Scottsdale, AZ

1	Jesper Parnevik (Swe)	68-68-66-67—269	$450000
2	Tommy Armour III	68-70-70-64—272	165000
	Brent Geiberger	64-70-72-66—272	165000
	Steve Pate	69-69-70-64—272	165000
	Tom Watson	68-70-68-66—272	165000

AT&T Pebble Beach National Pro-Am
Spyglass Hill GC, Poppy Hills, Pebble Beach, CA

1	Phil Mickelson	65-70-67—202	$450000
2	Tom Pernice Jr	67-60-67—203	270000
3	Paul Azinger	67-69-68—204	130000
	Jim Furyk	69-67-68—204	130000
	JP Hayes	70-67-67—204	130000

Buick Invitational
Torrey Pines GC, South Course, North Course, LaJolla, CA

1	Scott Simpson*	69-71-64—204	$378000
2	Skip Kendall	71-63-70—204	226800
3	Davis Love III	62-73-70—205	109200
	Kevin Sutherland	68-67-70—205	109200
	Tiger Woods	71-66-68—205	109200

United Airlines Hawaiian Open
Waialae Country Club, Honolulu, HI

1	John Huston	63-65-66-66—260	$324000
2	Tom Watson	67-64-70-66—267	194400
3	Trevor Dodds (Nam)	65-70-65-68—268	122400

* Winner after play-off

Tucson Chrysler Classic
Tucson National Golf Resort, Tucson, AZ

1	David Duval	66-62-68-73—269	$360000
2	Justin Leonard	65-70-68-70—273	176000
	David Toms	70-67-68-68—273	176000

Nissan Open
Valencia Country Club, Valencia, CA

1	Billy Mayfair*	65-71-69-67—272	$378000
2	Tiger Woods	68-73-65-66—272	226800
3	Stephen Ames (T&T)	66-71-70-68—275	142800

Doral-Ryder Open
Doral Resort & Country Club, Miami, FL

1	Michael Bradley	71-66-70-71—278	$360000
2	John Huston	70-69-73-67—279	176000
	Billy Mayfair	72-70-68-69—279	176000

Honda Classic
TPC at Heron Bay, Coral Springs, FL

1	Mark Calcavecchia	70-67-68-65—270	$324000
2	Vijay Singh (Fij)	70-68-68-67—273	194400
3	Colin Montgomerie (Sco)	69-69-71-66—275	122400

Bay Hill Invitational
Bay Hill Club & Lodge, Orlando, FL

1	Ernie Els (SA)	67-69-65-73—274	$360000
2	Bob Estes	69-71-67-71—278	176000
	Jeff Maggert	70-71-69-68—278	176000

The Players Championship
TPC at Sawgrass, Ponte Vedra Beach, FL

1	Justin Leonard	72-69-70-67—278	$720000
2	Glen Day	66-73-70-71—280	352000
	Tom Lehman	72-70-70-68—280	352000

Freeport-McDermott Classic
English Turn Golf & Country Club, New Orleans, LA

1	Lee Westwood (Eng)	69-68-67-69—273	$306000
2	Steve Flesch	66-68-71-71—276	183600
3	Jim Carter	68-69-71-71—279	81600
	Mark Wiebe	69-68-71-71—279	81600
	Glen Day	64-75-69-71—279	81600
	Steve Lowery	72-66-70-71—279	81600

*Winner after play-off

The Masters
Augusta National GC, Georgia
(Fuller details in Part I The Majors, page 72)

1	Mark O'Meara	74-70-68-67—279	$576000
2	David Duval	71-68-74-67—280	281600
	Fred Couples	69-70-71-70—280	281600

MCI Classic
Harbour Town Golf Links, Hilton Head Island, SC

1	Davis Love III	67-68-66-65—266	$342000
2	Glen Day	67-67-72-67—273	205200
3	Payne Stewart	69-71-64-72—276	110200
	Phil Mickelson	67-71-65-73—276	110200

Greater Greensboro Chrysler Classic
Forest Oaks Country Club, Greensboro, NC

1	Trevor Dodds (Nam)*	68-69-70-69—276	$396000
2	Scott Verplank	67-71-66-72—276	237600
3	Bob Estes	67-65-72-73—277	149600

Shell Houston Open
TPC at The Woodlands, The Woodlands, TX

1	David Duval	69-70-73-64—276	$360000
2	Jeff Maggert	71-71-64-71—277	216000
3	Fred Couples	72-68-70-68—278	136000

BellSouth Classic
TPC at Sugarloaf, Duluth, GA

1	Tiger Woods	69-67-63-72—271	$324000
2	Jay Don Blake	67-68-67-70—272	194400
3	Steve Flesch	66-71-68-69—274	104400
	Esteban Toledo (Mex)	66-75-66-67—274	104400

GTE Byron Nelson Classic
TPC at Las Colinas, Cottonwood Valley, Irving, TX

1	John Cook	66-68-66-65—265	$450000
2	Fred Couples	66-67-63-72—268	186666
	Hal Sutton	66-65-68-69—268	186666
	Harrison Frazar	64-68-66-70—268	186666

MasterCard Colonial
Colonial Country Club, Ft Worth, TX

1	Tom Watson	68-66-65-66—265	$414000
2	Jim Furyk	66-67-66-68—267	248400
3	Jeff Sluman	67-67-66-69—269	156400

*Winner after play-off

Memorial Tournament
Muirfield Village Golf Club, Dublin, OH

1	Fred Couples	68-67-67-69—271	$396000
2	Andrew Magee	67-71-68-69—275	237600
3	David Duval	74-66-67-69—276	149600

Kemper Open
TPC at Avenel Potomac, MD

1	Stuart Appleby (Aus)	70-63-69-72—274	$360000
2	Scott Hoch	69-68-68-70—275	216000
3	Clark Dennis	70-65-70-73—278	90200
	Brad Fabel	69-66-70-73—278	90200
	Fred Funk	64-66-71-77—278	90200
	Mark O'Meara	68-70-71-69—278	90200
	Tommy Tolles	70-68-66-74—278	90200

Buick Classic
Westchester Country Club, Rye, NY

1	JP Hayes	66-67-68—201	$324000
2	Jim Furyk	70-63-68—201	194400
3	Tom Lehman	67-72-65—204	122400

US Open
The Olympic Club, San Francisco, CA
(Fuller details in Part I The Majors)

1	Lee Janzen	73-66-73-68—280	$535000
2	Payne Stewart	66-71-70-74—281	315000
3	Bob Tway	68-70-73-73—284	201730

Motorola Western Open
Cog Hill Golf & Country Club, Lemont, IL

1	Joe Durant	68-67-70-66—271	$396000
2	Vijay Singh (Fij)	68-68-65-72—273	237600
3	Dudley Hart	74-70-70-63—277	127600
	Lee Janzen	68-69-69-71—277	127600

Canon Greater Hartford Open
TPC at River Highlands, Cromwell, CT

1	Olin Browne	67-66-66-67—266	$360000
2	Stewart Cink	67-65-67-67—266	176000
	Larry Mize	68-63-66-69—266	176000

Quad City Classic
Oakwood Country Club, Coal Valley, IL

1	Steve Jones	64-65-68-66—263	$279000
2	Scott Gump	65-67-64-68—264	167400
3	Kenny Perry	65-65-67-68—265	105400

Deposit Guaranty Golf Classic
Annandale Golf Club, Madison, MS

1	Fred Funk	69-64-69-68—270	$216000
2	Paul Goydos	66-66-72-68—272	89600
	Franklin Langham	67-67-70-68—272	89600
	Tim Loustalot	69-69-68-66—272	89600

CVS Charity Classic
Pleasant Valley Country Club, Sutton, MA

1	Steve Pate	70-65-67-67—269	$270000
2	Scott Hoch	68-68-69-65—270	132000
	Bradley Hughes (Aus)	68-69-67-66—270	132000

FedEx St Jude Classic
TPC at Southwind, Memphis, TN

1	Nick Price (Zim)*	65-67-70-66—268	$324000
2	Jeff Sluman	70-67-66-65—268	194400
3	Glen Day	69-64-72-65—270	122400

Buick Open
Warwick Hills Golf & Country Club, Grand Blanc, MI

1	Billy Mayfair	70-69-65-67—271	$324000
2	Scott Verplank	71-67-71-64—273	194400
3	Andrew Magee	69-71-70-64—274	122400

US PGA Championship
Sahalee, Seattle, Washington

(Fuller details in *Part I The Majors*)

1	Vijay Singh (Fij)	70-66-67-68—271	$540000
2	Steve Stricker	69-68-66-70—273	324000
3	Steve Elkington (Aus)	69-69-69-67—274	204000

Sprint International
Castle Pines Golf Club, Castle Rock, CO

1	Vijay Singh	47 pts	$360000
2	Phil Mickelson	41 pts	176000
	Willie Wood	41 pts	176000

NEC World Series of Golf
Firestone CC, Akron, OH

1	David Duval	69-66-66-68—269	$405000
2	Phil Mickelson	66-71-66-68—271	243000
3	Davis Love III	71-69-67-65—272	153000

*Winner after play-off

Greater Vancouver Open
Northview Golf & Country Club, Surrey, BC, Canada

1	Brandel Chamblee	67-64-68-66—265	$360000
2	Payne Stewart	64-69-65-70—268	216000
3	Lee Porter	67-67-71-66—271	136000

Greater Milwaukee Open
Brown Deer Park Golf Course, Milwaukee, WI

1	Jeff Sluman	68-66-63-68—265	$324000
2	Steve Stricker	68-63-67-68—266	194400
3	Mark Calcavecchia	66-64-69-69—268	93600
	Nolan Henke	70-62-67-69—268	93600
	Chris Perry	68-62-67-71—268	93600

Bell Canadian Open
Glen Abbey Golf Course, Oakville, Ontario

1	Billy Andrade*	68-69-69-69—275	$396000
2	Bob Friend	69-67-68-71—275	237600
3	Mike Hulbert	72-70-66-68—276	149600

BC Open
En-Joie Golf Club, Endicott, NY

1	Chris Perry	67-70-69-67—273	$270000
2	Peter Jacobsen	68-70-71-67—276	162000
3	Nolan Henke	69-69-67-72—277	102000

Westin Texas Open
LaCantera Golf Club, San Antonio, TX

1	Hal Sutton	67-68-67-68—270	$306000
2	Jay Haas	70-69-64-68—271	149600
	Justin Leonard	67-67-69-68—271	149600

Buick Challenge
Callaway Gardens Resort, Pine Mountain, GA

1	Steve Elkington (Aus)	66-70-66-65—267	$270000
2	Fred Funk	63-67-68-69—267	162000
3	Bill Glasson	69-65-65-69—268	102000

Michelob Championship
Kingsmill GC, Williamsburg

1	David Duval	65-67-68-68—268	$342000
2	Phil Tataurangi (NZ)	65-68-69-69—271	205200
3	Barry Cheesman	69-68-69-66—272	129200

★Winner after play-off

Las Vegas Invitational
TPC at Summerlin/Desert Inn GC, Las Vegas, NV

1	Jim Furyk	67-68-69-63-68—335	$360000
2	Mark Calcavecchia	65-71-69-65-66—336	216000
3	Scott Verplank	67-68-69-67-67—338	136000

National Car Rental Classic
at Walt Disney World Resort

1	John Huston	67-70-69-66—272	$360000
2	Davis Love III	73-64-65-71—273	216000
3	Brent Geiberger	72-70-68-65—275	136000

The Tour Championship
East Lake GC, Atlanta, GA

1	Hal Sutton	69-67-68-70—274	$720000
2	Vijay Singh (Fij)	63-70-70-71—274	432000
3	Jim Furyk	67-68-69-71—275	234000
	Jesper Parnevik (Swe)	70-70-67-68—275	234000

ADDITIONAL UNOFFICIAL EVENTS

Tournament	Venue	Winner	Score
Subaru Sarazen World Open *See page 181 for details*	Chateau Elan, Atlanta, GA	Dudley Hart	272 (-16)
Franklin Templeton Shoot-out	Sherwood CC, Thousand Oaks	Greg Norman and Steve Elkington	189 (-27)
Won at third hole of play-off after a tie with Peter Jacobsen and John Cook			
JC Penney Classic	Westin Innisbrook Resort, FL	Steve Pate and Meg Mellon	255 (-29)
Wendy's Three-Tour Challenge	Lake Las Vegas Resort	PGA Senior Tour	
PGA Grand Slam of Golf *Woods received $400000*	Poipu Bay Resort, Kauai, HA	Tiger Woods	
Skins Game *O'Meara received $430000*	Rancho La Quinta	Mark O'Meara	

Players are of American nationality unless stated

US Tour Qualifying School

at La Quinta, CA

The following 41 players won Tour Cards for 1999:

Pos	Name	Score	Prize Money $
1	Mike Weir	75-65-66-68-70-64—408	50000
2	Jonathan Kaye	65-71-64-69-72-70—411	37500
3	Deane Pappas (SA)	73-67-68-68-66-69—411	37500
4	Dave Stockton	67-69-70-70-69-67—412	26875
5	Pete Jordan	66-72-68-67-70-69—412	26875
6	Greg Chalmers (Aus)	66-69-67-69-71-70—412	26875
7	Geoffrey Sisk	67-74-69-67-65-70—412	26875
8	Mike Brisky	67-71-70-68-70-67—413	25000
9	Rich Beem	69-68-70-71-69-66—413	25000
10	Cameron Beckman	71-74-66-66-68-68—413	25000
11	Brent Schwarzrock	66-69-68-68-73-70—414	25000
12	PH Horgan	68-70-72-71-67-67—415	25000
13	Briny Baird	71-66-68-68-70-72—415	25000
14	John Elliott	73-68-67-69-70-69—416	25000
15	Ted Purdy	65-67-73-72-68-71—416	25000
16	Rick Fehr	62-71-70-67-72-74—416	25000
17	Alan Bratton	69-70-72-70-69-67—417	25000
18	Charles Warren III	68-71-69-70-70-69—417	25000
19	Robert Allenby (Aus)	71-70-69-68-69-70—417	25000
20	Chris Couch	69-70-67-68-71-72—417	25000
21	Bo Van Pelt	73-70-67-70-65-72—417	25000
22	Craig Barlow	67-70-69-70-68-73—417	25000
23	Katsumasa Miyamoto (Jpn)	67-73-71-69-71-67—418	25000
24	Jeff Brehaut	73-70-68-67-71-69—418	25000
25	Ty Armstrong	71-67-73-67-68-72—418	25000
26	Steve Jurgensen	69-69-72-72-68-70—420	25000
27	Jay Delsing	68-69-69-69-73-72—420	25000
28	Jay Williamson	72-73-66-71-66-72—420	25000
29	Chris Smith	66-71-69-67-72-75—420	25000
30	Chris Riley	74-70-71-71-66-68—420	25000
31	Danny Briggs	71-71-69-71-70-69—421	25000
32	Dicky Pride	72-66-70-73-69-71—421	25000
33	David Seawell	67-72-71-69-74-68—421	25000
34	Brian Gay	64-70-73-71-68-75—421	25000
35	Carlos Franco (Para)	68-75-71-69-66-73—422	25000
36	Tim Loustalot	69-66-68-70-76-73—422	25000
37	Scott Dunlap	65-73-68-71-72-73—422	25000
38	Clarence Rose	68-68-70-73-69-74—422	25000
39	Perry Moss	67-71-68-69-71-76—422	25000
40	Rory Sabbatini	69-71-76-69-70-67—422	25000
41	Kent Jones	70-71-71-75-64-71—422	25000

Players are of American nationality unless stated

US Senior Tour, 1998

Final Ranking

Pos	Name	Prize Money $	Pos	Name	Prize Money $
1	Hale Irwin	2861945	26	Joe Inman	653902
2	Gil Morgan	2179047	27	Jim Albus	643380
3	Larry Nelson	1442476	28	JC Snead	612307
4	Jay Sigel	1403912	29	Jim Dent	610729
5	Hugh Baiocchi	1183959	30	Bob Murphy	569398
6	Jim Colbert	1122413	31	Dale Douglass	569293
7	Dana Quigley	1103882	32	Brian Barnes	531561
8	Bruce Summerhays	1098942	33	Bob Dickson	513815
9	Isao Aoki	1042200	34	Walter Morgan	497913
10	Dave Stockton	1040524	35	Frank Conner	492634
11	Jose Maria Canizares	1025425	36	Tom Jenkins	455212
12	Vicente Fernandez	996338	37	Gary Player	455206
13	David Graham	945300	38	David Lundstrom	451979
14	Leonard Thompson	927753	39	Bob Eastwood	440163
15	John Jacobs	799654	40	John Morgan	427392
16	Mike McCullough	741735	41	Bobby Stroble	426574
17	Bob Duval	734573	42	Dave Eichelberger	417153
18	Lee Trevino	716366	43	Gibby Gilbert	416584
19	Ray Floyd	702472	44	Ed Dougherty	412679
20	Terry Dill	701210	45	Bob Charles	402284
21	Hubert Green	689303	46	Bud Allin	391224
22	Tom Wargo	679579	47	Tom Shaw	371921
23	Walter Hall	668700	48	Simon Hobday	370581
24	Graham Marsh	664432	49	John Mahaffey	365233
25	George Archer	660076	50	Kermit Zarley	357978

Career Money List

Pos	Name	Prize Money $	Pos	Name	Prize Money $
1	Jim Colbert	8249 210	14	Jay Sigel	4995 067
2	Lee Trevino	8165 927	15	Gary Player	4933 813
3	Dave Stockton	7676 552	16	Bruce Crampton	4642 684
4	Bob Charles	7646 958	17	JC Snead	4635 818
5	Hale Irwin	7620 253	18	Gil Morgan	4496 948
6	Mike Hill	6611 263	19	Jim Albus	4487 178
7	George Archer	6332 067	20	Al Geiberger	4414 145
8	Ray Floyd	6282 742	21	Tom Wargo	4350 004
9	Chi Chi Rodriguez	6184 587	22	Graham Marsh	4159 051
10	Isao Aoki	6172 337	23	Miller Barber	3879 890
11	Jim Dent	6103 239	24	Rocky Thompson	3802 281
12	Dale Douglass	5709 925	25	Gibby Gilbert	3674 771
13	Bob Murphy	5188 326	26	Harold Henning	3618 712

Pos	Name	Prize Money $	Pos	Name	Prize Money $
27	Simon Hobday	3 602 947	39	Walter Morgan	2 735 258
28	Charles Coody	3 543 057	40	Dave Eichelberger	2 703 941
29	Jimmy Powell	3 488 137	41	Don Bies	2 683 536
30	Kermit Zarley	3 324 813	42	Jack Nicklaus	2 588 903
31	Orville Moody	3 311 522	43	Larry Laoretti	2 549 716
32	Don January	3 216 777	44	Tom Shaw	2 508 811
33	Jack Kiefer	3 188 395	45	Jim Ferree	2 461 477
34	Bruce Summerhays	3 075 136	46	Tommy Aaron	2 413 882
35	John Bland	3 034 312	47	Butch Baird	2 397 269
36	Walter Zembriski	2 952 458	48	David Graham	2 390 295
37	Terry Dill	2 855 644	49	Dave Hill	2 360 583
38	Dewitt Weaver Jr	2 737 027	50	Vicente Fernandez	2 291 503

TOUR STATISTICS

Stroke averages

Pos	Name	Avg
1	Hale Irwin	68.59
2	Gil Morgan	69.46
3	Larry Nelson	69.87
4	Dave Stockton	70.49
5	Vicente Fernandez	70.51
6	Isao Aoki	70.54
7	Jay Sigel	70.55
8	José Maria Cañizares	70.60
9	David Graham	70.81
10T	Jim Colbert	70.84
	Ray Floyd	70.84

Driving accuracy

Pos	Name	%
1	Calvin Peete	80.4
2	Bob E Smith	79.9
3	Hale Irwin	79.6
4	John Bland	78.3
5	Hubert Green	78.1
6	Bruce Crampton	77.0
7	Bob Murphy	75.3
8T	Hugh Baiocchi	74.6
	Mike Hill	74.6
10	Gary Player	74.4

Driving distance (Average yards per drive)

Pos	Name	Yds
1	John Jacobs	284.9
2	Ray Arinno	281.9
3	Bob Duval	280.1
4	Hank Cooper	279.4
5	Terry Dill	278.8
6	Jay Sigel	278.3
7	David Graham	277.6
8	Gil Morgan	277.4
9	John Schroeder	275.9
10	Brian Barnes	274.6

Putting leaders (Average putts per hole)

Pos	Name	Avg
1	Hale Irwin	1.700
2	Dave Stockton	1.740
3	Isao Aoki	1.746
4	Larry Nelson	1.748
5	Gil Morgan	1.752
6	Vicente Fernandez	1.755
7	Hubert Green	1.762
8	Dana Quigley	1.763
9T	George Archer	1.766
	John Schroeder	1.766

Sand saves

Pos	Name	%
1	José Maria Cañizares	64.4
2	Vicente Fernandez	60.2
3	Hubert Green	58.1
4	Lee Trevino	57.6
5	Bob Duval	57.0
6	Gary Player	56.8
7	Hugh Baiocchi	56.4
8T	Simon Hobday	56.1
	Hale Irwin	56.1
10	Jim Colbert	55.6

Greens in regulation

Pos	Name	%
1	Hale Irwin	76.4
2	John Mahaffey	74.8
3	Gil Morgan	73.5
4	Jay Sigel	72.3
5	Brian Barnes	71.6
6	Hugh Baiocchi	70.8
7	Larry Nelson	70.5
8	Ed Dougherty	70.4
9	David Graham	70.2
10	Isao Aoki	70.1

Tour Results

Tournament	Venue	Winner	Score
MasterCard Championship	Hualalai GC, Kailua-Kona, HI	Gil Morgan	195
Senior Skins Game	Mauna Lani Resort	Raymond Floyd	
Royal Caribbean Classic	Crandon Park GC, Key Biscayne, FL	David Graham*	202
LG Championship	Bay Colony GC, Naples, FL	Gil Morgan	210
GTE Classic	TPC of Tampa Bay, Lutz, FL	Jim Albus	207
American Express Invitational	TPC of Prestancia, Sarasota, FL	Larry Nelson	203
Senior Slam	Cabo del Sol GC, Los Cabos, Mexico	Gil Morgan	134
Toshiba Senior Classic	Newport Beach CC, CA	Hale Irwin	200
Liberty Mutual Legends of Golf	GC of Amelia Island at Summer Beach, FL	Charles Coody/ Dale Douglass*	192
Southwestern Bell Dominion	The Dominion, San Antonio, TX	Lee Trevino	205
The Tradition presented by Countrywide	Desert Mountain, Scottsdale, AZ	Gil Morgan	276
PGA Seniors' Championship	PGA National, Palm Beach, FL	Hale Irwin	275
Las Vegas Senior Classic by TruGreen-ChemLawn	TPC at The Canyons, Las Vegas, NV	Hale Irwin	281
Bruno's Memorial Classic	Greystone GC, Birmingham, AL	Hubert Green	203
Home Depot Invitational	TPC at Piper Glen, Charlotte, NC	Jim Dent*	207
St Luke's Classic	Loch Lloyd CC, Belton, MO	Larry Ziegler	208
Bell Atlantic Classic	Hartefeld National, Avondale, PA	Jay Sigel*	205
Pittsburgh Senior Classic	Sewickley Heights GC, Sewickley, PA	Larry Nelson	204
Nationwide Championship	GC of Georgia, Alpharetta, GA	John Jacobs	206
BellSouth Senior Classic at Opryland	Springhouse GC, Nashville, TN	Isao Aoki	198
AT&T Canada Senior Open	Glencoe G&CC, Calgary, Canada	Brian Barnes	277
Cadillac NFL Golf Classic	Upper Montclair CC, Clifton, NJ	Bob Dickson*	207
State Farm Senior Classic	Hobbit's Glen, Columbia, MD	Bruce Summerhays	206
Ford Senior Players Ch'p	TPC of Michigan Darborn, MI	Gil Morgan	267
Ameritech Senior Open	Kemper Lakes, Long Grove, IL	Hale Irwin	201
US Senior Open	Riviera CC, Pacific Palisades, CA	Hale Irwin	285
Utah Showdown	Park Meadows CC, Park City, UT	Gil Morgan	200
Burnet Senior Classic	Bunker Hills, Coon Rapids, MN	Leonard Thompson*	134
First of America Classic	Egypt Valley CC, Grand Rapids, MI	George Archer	199
Northville Long Island Classic	Meadow Brook Club, Jericho, NY	Gary Player	204
BankBoston Classic	Nashawtuc CC, Concord, MA	Hale Irwin	201
Emerald Coast Classic	The Moors GC, Milton, FL	Dana Quigley	200
Comfort Classic	Brickyard Crossing, Indianapolis, IN	Hugh Baiocchi	196
Kroger Senior Classic	GC at Kings Island, Mason, OH	Hugh Baiocchi*	133
Boone Valley Classic	Boone Valley GC, Augusta, MO	Larry Nelson	200
Vantage Championship	Tanglewood Park, Clemmons, NC	Gil Morgan	198
The Transamerica	Silverado Resort, Napa, CA	Jim Colbert	205
Raley's Gold Rush Classic	Serrano CC, El Dorado Hills, CA	Dana Quigley	203
Hyatt Regency Kaanapali Classic	Kaanapali GC, Lahaina, HA	Jay Sigel	201
Pacific Bell Senior Classic	The Wilshire CC, Los Angeles, CA	Joe Inman	202
Energizer Senior Tour Ch'p	The Dunes, Myrtle Beach, SC	Hale Irwin	274
Senior Matchplay Ch'p	Bighorn GC, Palm Desert, CA	Hale Irwin	6 and 4

Winner after play-off

US Senior Tour Qualifying School

at Grenelefe Golf Resort, Haines City, FL

The top eight players receive a full Tour Card for 1999 and the next eight players receive conditional playing privileges.

Pos	Name	Score	Prize Money $
1	Allen Doyle	67-70-71-67—275	30000
2	Bruce Fleisher	69-69-70-70—278	19000
3	Tom McGinnis	70-69-72-71—282	13000
4	Alberto Giannone	67-69-72-74—282	13000
5	Barney Thompson	69-72-73-69—283	10000
6	Jim Thorpe	67-76-72-69—284	7500
7	Howard Twitty	68-71-74-71—284	7500
8	Fred Gibson	71-71-69-74—285	6000
9	Mike Malone	75-68-73-70—286	5500
10	Noel Ratcliffe	72-73-74-68—287	4475
11	Jesse Patino	72-72-73-70—287	4475
12	Buzz Thomas	73-73-69-72—287	4475
13	Jim Barker	69-72-73-73—287	4475
14	Tony Peterson	70-74-73-71—288	3467
15	Gary McCord	72-73-72-71—288	3467
16	Hiro Kazami	73-72-71-72—288	3467

US Nike Tour, 1998

Final Ranking

Pos	Name	Events	Prize $	Pos	Name	Events	Prize $
1	Bob Burns	23	178664	51	Stiles Mitchell	27	47049
2	Robin Freeman	20	169389	52	Brian Tennyson	21	46515
3	Joe Ogilvie	30	157813	53	Sam Randolph	23	42677
4	Eric Booker	23	153526	54	Chris Starkjohann	13	42581
5	John Maginnes	20	145210	55	Paul Claxton	28	42296
6	Dennis Paulson	26	145065	56	Rob McKelvey	18	42213
7	Charles Raulerson	28	142976	57	Vance Veazey	3	41681
8	Woody Austin	23	140955	58	Jeff Barlow	17	39730
9	Mika Sposa	28	140139	59	Danny Briggs	22	39682
10	Notah Begay III	22	136289	60	Charlie Rymer	22	38544
11	Jimmy Green	26	131942	61	Joey Gullion	27	37843
12	Sean Murphy	27	130030	62	Kevin Johnson	27	36881
13	Emlyn Aubrey	26	129967	63	Steve Flesch	1	34050
14	Tom Scherrer	26	129134	64	Craig Perks	21	33613
15	Doug Dunakey	25	128052	65	Brent Schwarzrock	24	33535
16	Matt Gogel	26	119899	66	Paul Gow	24	32433
17	John Wilson	21	112010	67	Michael Walton	26	32107
18	Jay Williamson	28	110921	68	Rocky Walcher	27	31871
19	Chris Zambri	27	108511	69	JL Lewis	3	31819
20	Brian Bateman	26	107590	70	Jaxon Brigman	24	31412
21	Gene Sauers	18	104721	71	Ty Armstrong	23	29059
22	Ryan Howison	27	100477	72	Chris Couch	25	28349
23	Michael Clark	26	99128	73	Kevin Riley	25	28000
24	Jeff Gove	28	96502	74	Jason Gore	18	27378
25	Deane Pappas	27	92317	75	Keith Fergus	9	26875
26	Eric Johnson	25	91598	76	Adam Spring	28	26833
27	Craig Bowden	29	86954	77	Charlie Wi	13	26571
28	Pat Bates	27	85991	78	Bruce Vaughan	13	26550
29	Casey Martin	22	81937	79	Dave Schreyer	25	24736
30	Greg Lesher	27	79523	80	Brian Gay	23	24591
31	Jeff Julian	25	78736	81	Patrick Lee	27	24481
32	David Berganio Jr	20	76969	82	Garrett Willis	11	24130
33	Mark Hensby	25	75359	83	Anthony Rodriguez	18	23828
34	Don Walsworth	27	74364	84	Chris M Anderson	28	23824
35	Chris Riley	24	74239	85	Tom R Shaw	24	23762
36	Perry Moss	25	73900	86	Craig A Spence	9	23724
37	John Elliott	29	72449	87	Jay C Davis	25	22793
38	Geoffrey Sisk	28	71849	88	Chris Stutts	26	22691
39	John Kernohan	29	71145	89	Michael Muehr	26	22687
40	Carl Paulson	30	69628	90	Dick Mast	11	22007
41	Mike Sullivan	20	67548	91	Steve Hart	22	21890
42	Michael Allen	21	67482	92	Gary Rusnak	23	21465
43	Anthony Painter	17	67291	93	Karl Zoller	19	21318
44	Craig Kanada	25	64423	94	Robert Floyd	28	20529
45	Scott Dunlap	21	64159	95	Esteban Toledo	2	18750
46	Marco Gortana	26	63006	96	Ron Whittaker	12	18734
47	Joey Snyder III	29	61533	97	Bob Sowards	28	18700
48	Steve Lamontagne	25	59880	98	Steve Haskins	25	18010
49	Don Reese	26	55860	99	JC Anderson	21	17447
50	Jeff Brehaut	27	52853	100	Curt Byrum	15	17313

Tour Results

Tournament	Venue	Winner	Score
MorganLakeland Classic	Grasslands GC, Lakeland, FL	Casey Martin	269
South Florida Classic	Palm-Aire CC, Pompano Beach, FL	Eric Johnson	267
Greater Austin Open	The Hills CC Austin, TX	Michael Allen	280
Mexico City Open	*Event cancelled*		
Monterrey Open	Club Campestre Monterrey, Mexico	Joe Ogilvie	274
Louisiana Open	Le Triomphe CC, Broussard, LA	John Wilson	274
Shreveport Open	Southern Trace CC, Shreveport, PA	Vance Veazey*	280
Upstate Classic	Verdae Greens GC, Greenville, SC	Tom Scherrer	200
Huntsville Open	Hampton Cove GC, Huntsville, AL	Dennis Paulson*	279
South Carolina Classic	CC of S Carolina, Florence, SC	Gene Sauers	280
Carolina Classic	Raleigh CC, Raleigh, NC	Brian Bateman	266
Dominion Open	Dominion Club, Glen Allen, VA	Bob Burns	274
Knoxville Open	Three Ridges GC, Knoxville, TN	Robin Freeman*	270
Miami Valley Open	Heatherwoode GC, Springboro, OH	Craig Bowden	264
Cleveland Open	Quail Hollow Resort, Concord, OH	Doug Dunakey	270
Lehigh Valley Open	Center Valley Club, Center Valley, PA	Eric Booker*	271
Greensboro Open	Sedgefield CC, Greensboro, NC	Joe Ogilvie	266
Hershey Open	CC of Hershey (East), Hershey, PA	Michael Clark	273
St Louis Golf Classic	Missouri Bluffs GC, St Charles, MO	Chris Starkjohann	263
Wichita Open	Willowbend GC, Wichita, KS	Emlyn Aubrey	265
Dakota Dunes Open	Dakota Dunes CC, Dakota Dunes, SD	John Maginnes*	274
Omaha Classic	Champions Club, Omaha, NE	Matt Gogel*	271
Ozarks Open	Highland Springs CC, Springfield, MO	Anthony Painter	267
Fort Smith Classic	Hardscrabble CC, Fort Smith AR	Mark Hensby	260
Permian Basin Open	Mission Dorado CC, Odessa, TX	Stiles Mitchell*	276
Tri-Cities Open	Meadow Springs CC, Richland, WA	Matt Gogel*	276
Boise Open	Hillcrest CC, Boise, ID	Mike Sposa	265
Oregan Classic	Shadow Hills CC, Junction City, OR	Charles Raulerson	272
San Jose Open	Almaden CC, San José, CA	Robin Freeman*	272
Inland Empire Open	Moreno Valley Ranch GC, Moreno Valley, CA	Charles Raulerson	268
Nike Tour Championship	Robert Trent Jones Trail, Magnolia Grove, Mobile, AL	Bob Burns	283

* *Winner after play-off*

Japan PGA Tour, 1998

Ranking

Pos	Name	Prize Money ¥	Pos	Name	Prize Money ¥
1	Jumbo Ozaki	179 662 740	14	Kazuhiko Hosokawa	58 472 304
2	Brian Watts (US)	132 014 990	15	Kenichiro Fukabori	56 220 182
3	Hidemichi Tanaka	103 941 437	16	Hajime Meshiai	54 866 597
4	Brandt Jobe (US)	97 566 406	17	Joe Ozaki	53 853 954
5	Katsumasa Miyamoto	93 580 618	18	Toru Taniguchi	49 515 691
6	Carlos Franco (Par)	92 569 038	19	Nobuhito Sato	48 045 128
7	Shigeki Maruyama	86 422 421	20	Eduardo Herrera (Col)	47 809 590
8	Frankie Minoza (Phi)	74 102 769	21	Yoshinori Mizumaki	44 989 934
9	Kaname Yokoo	74 090 419	22	Shingo Katayama	44 807 900
10	Lee Westwood (Eng)	72 000 000	23	Nobumitsu Yuhara	43 993 660
11	Toshimitsu Izawa	63 295 563	24	Satoshi Higashi	42 367 831
12	Toru Suzuki	63 252 358	25	Tateo Ozaki	40 661 307
13	Katsunori Kuwabara	62 661 761			

Tour Results

Tournament	Venue	Winner	Score
Token Corporation Cup	Kedoin GC, Kagoshima	Hajime Meshiai	272 (-16)
Dydo Drinco Shizuoka Open	Shizuoka CC, Shizuoka	Eduardo Herrera	203 (-13)
Just System KSB Open	Ayutaki CC, Kagawa	Carlos Franco	267 (-17)
Descente Classic	Taiheiyo Club, Chiba	Dinesh Chand	271 (-17)
Tsuruya Open	Sports Shinko CC, Hyogo	Katsumasa Miyamoto	271 (-17)
Kirin Open	Ibaragi GC, Ibaragi	Frankie Minoza	279 (-5)
Chunichi Crowns	Nagoya GC, Aichi	Davis Love III	269 (-11)
Fuji Sankei Classic	Kawana Hotel GC, Shizuoka	Carlos Franco	275 (-9)
JPGA Championship	Grandage GC, Nara	Brandt Jobe	280 (-8)
Ube Kosan Open	Ube CC, Yamaguchi	Brandt Jobe	271 (-17)
Mitsubishi Galant Trn	Tosa CC, Kochi	Toru Taniguchi	268 (-16)
JCB Classic Sendai	Omotezao Kokusai GC, Miyagi	Yoshinori Mizumaki	270 (-14)
Sapporo Tokyu Open	Sapporo Kokusai CC, Hokkaido	Toru Suzuki	272 (-16)
Yomiuri Open	Yomiuri CC, Hyogo	Brian Watts	134 (-10)
Mizuno Open	Sentonaikai GC, Okayama	Brandt Jobe*	275 (-13)
PGA Philanthropy	Shirosui GC, Gunma	Shigeki Maruyama	264 (-20)
Yonex Open Hiroshima	Hiroshima CC, Hiroshima	Jumbo Ozaki	270 (-18)
Aiful Cup	Aomori GC, Aomori	Hidemichi Tanaka	273 (-15)

* Winner after play-off

Tournament	Venue	Winner	Score
NST Niigata Open	Forest GC, Niigata	Masayuki Kawamura	268 (-20)
Sanko Grand Summer Ch'p	Sanko 72 CC, Gunma	Shingo Katayama*	274 (-14)
KBC Augusta	Keya GC, Fukuoka	Jumbo Ozaki	275 (-13)
Japan Matchplay	Nidom Classic Course, Hokkaido	Katsunori Kuwabara	1 up
Suntory Open	Narashino CC, Chiba	Mamoru Osanai	274 (-10)
ANA Open	Sapporo GC, Hokkaido	Kenichiro Fukabori	279 (-9)
Gene Sarazen Junior Classic	Rope Club, Tochigi	Todd Hamilton	270 (-18)
Japan Open	Oarai GC, Ibaragi	Hidemichi Tanaka	283 (-5)
Tokai Classic	Miyoshi CC, Aichi	Toshimitsu Izawa	277 (-11)
Nikkei Cup	Fuji Country Dejima Club, Ibaragi	Mitsutaka Kusakabe	280 (-8)
Bridgestone Open	Sodegaura CC, Chiba	Nobuhito Sato*	275 (-13)
Philip Morris Championship	ABC GC, Hyogo	Jumbo Ozaki	275 (-13)
Acom International	Seve Ballesteros GC, Fukushima	Kaname Yokoo	46 pts
Sumitomo VISA Taiheiyo Masters	Taiheiyo Club, Shizuoka	Lee Westwood	275 (-13)
Dunlop Phoenix Tournament	Phoenix CC, Miyazaki	Lee Westwood	271 (-13)
Casio World Open	Ibusuki GC, Kagoshima	Brian Watts*	274 (-14)
Golf Nippon Series JT Cup	Tokyo Yomiuri CC, Tokyo	Katsumasa Miyamoto*	275 (-5)
Okinawa Open	Daikyo CC, Okinawa	Hidemichi Tanaka	273 (-11)

Winner after play-off

Omega Tour, 1998
(now known as Asian PGA Tour)

Final Ranking

Pos	Name	Prize Money $	Pos	Name	Prize Money $
1	Kang Wook-soon (Kor)	150771	14	James Kingston (SA)	57972
2	Ed Fryatt (Eng)	139447	15	Eric Meeks (US)	57555
3	Shaun Micheel (US)	124502	16	Choi Kyung-ju (Kor)	57422
4	Chris Williams (Eng)	124043	17	Rob Huxtable (US)	55613
5	Nico Van Rensburg (SA)	89368	18	Zhang Lian-Wei (PRC)	55311
6	Jerry Smith (US)	87541	19	Fran Quinn (US)	54556
7	Boonchu Ruangkit (Thai)	83534	20	Taimur Hussain (Pak)	54378
8	Lu Wen-Teh (Tai)	73216	21	Ted Purdy (US)	54216
9	Gerry Norquist (US)	69403	22	Jyoti Randhawa (Ind)	52128
10	Hendrik Buhrmann (SA)	65762	23	Satoshi Oide (Jpn)	51937
11	Chawalit Plaphol (Tha)	63135	24	Firoz Ali (Ind)	51695
12	Carlos Espinosa (Mex)	61849	25	Eric Rustand (US)	51243
13	Takeshi Ohyama (Jpn)	59042			

Career Money List

Pos	Name	Prize Money $	Pos	Name	Prize Money $
1	Kang Wook-Soon (Kor)	453500	9	Prayed Markseng (Thai)	273565
2	Boonchu Ruangkit (Thai)	419659	10	Thammanoon Sriroj (Thai))	273376
3	Gerry Norquist (US)	368484	11	Rob Willis (Aus)	257875
4	Jeev Milkha Singh (Ind)	364461	12	Zaw Moe (Myn)	244728
5	Mike Cunning (US)	351569	13	Clay Devers (US)	240299
6	Craig Kamps (SA)	321855	14	Park Nam-Sin (S. Kor)	239713
7	Nico Van Rensburg (SA)	314484	15	Lin Keng-Chi (Tai)	216144
8	Lu Wen-Teh (Tai)	275949			

Tour Results

Tournament	Venue	Winner	Score
Pre-tour Qualifying School	Johor Baru, Malaysia	Christian Chernock	268
London Myanmar Open	Bagan Golf Club, Myanmar	Taimur Hussain	280 (-8)
Classic Indian Open	Royal Calcutta GC	Firoz Ali	274 (-14)
China Orient Masters	Orient G&CC, Xiamen	Chawalit Plaphol	278 (-10)
Volvo China Open	Shanghai Sunisland IC, China	Ed Fryatt	269 (-19)
Macau Open	Macau G&CC, Macau	Satoshi Oide	283 (-1)

Tournament	Venue	Winner	Score
Guam Open	Leo Palace Resort, Manenggon Hills, Guam	Jerry Smith	272 (-16)
Fila Open	Tae Young CC, Seoul, Korea	Robert Huxtable	276 (-12)
Sabah Masters	Shan Shui G&CC, Malaysia	Simon Yates	278 (-10)
Volvo Masters of Malaysia	Kelab Golf Sultan Abdul Aziz Shah, Malaysia	Chris Williams	279 (-9)
Ericsson Singapore Open	Safra Resort & Country Club	Shaun Micheel	272 (-16)
Kolon Sports Korean Open	Seoul CC, Korea	Kim Dae-sub (Am)	278 (-10)
Kuala Lumpur Open	The Mines Resort, Malaysia	Nico Van Rensburg	278 (-6)
Fedex PGA Championship	Raffles CC, Singapore	Chris Williams	277 (-11)
Ericsson Classic	Formosa First GC, Taiwan	Lu Wen-Teh	280 (-8)
Hero Honda Masters	Delhi GC, Delhi, India	Jyoti Randhawa	275 (-13)
Thailand Open	Thana City GC, Thailand	James Kingston	272 (-16)
Hong Kong Open	Hong Kong GC, Fanling	Kang Wook-Soon	272 (-12)
Omega PGA Championship	Clearwater Bay G&CC, HK	Kang Wook-Soon	263 (-17)
Volvo Asian Matchplay Ch'p	Mission Hills GC, China	Gerry Norquist	2 and 1
Hugo Boss Foursomes	Mission Hills GC, China	Jim Routledge and Chawalit Plaphol	

Asian Tour, 1998

TOUR RESULTS

Tournament	Venue	Winner	Score
Ericsson 13th Philippine Masters	Passay City, Manila	Firoz Minoza	
Benson & Hedges Malaysian Open	Saujana G&CC, Kuala Lumpur	Lee Westwood	278
Rolex Masters	Singapore Island CC, Singapore	F Minoza	273
Classic Indian Open	Royal Calcutta GC, Calcutta	Firoz Ali	274
83rd Ericsson Philippines Open	Riviera G&CC	Frankie Minoza	278
Kirin Open Golf Championship	Ibaraki, Japan	Firoz Minoza	279
17th Maekyung LG Fashion Open	Lake Side CC, Seoul, Korea	Scott Rowe	204

Vodacom South African Tour, 1998–99

The tour year begins in April and ends in March of the following year.

Final Ranking 1999

Pos	Name	Prize R	Pos	Name	Prize R
1	David Frost	1189761	26	Francis Quinn Jr (US)	133804
2	Scott Dunlap (US)	885792	27	Andrew McLardy	126984
	Ernie Els	773741	28	Bobby Lincoln	125830
3	Richard Kaplan	525151		Nick Price	117300
4	Desvonde Botes	410598	29	Clinton Whitelaw	100274
5	Ashley Roestoff	367725	30	Hennie Walters	97176
6	Hennie Otto	359068	31	Alan McLean	94686
7	Mark McNulty (Zim)	358395	32	Sean Ludgater	94098
8	Marc Cayeux (Eng)	350555	33	Brett Liddle	93777
9	Chris Davison	336648	34	Ian Hutchings	92810
10	Steve van Vuuren	321836	35	Grant Muller	91766
11	Nic Henning	283659	36	Don Gammon	91670
12	Sammy Daniels	256815	37	Roger Wessels	87851
13	Justin Hobday	253871	38	James Loughnane (Ire)	84901
14	Dean van Staden	220932	39	Titch Moore	84477
15	Andre Cruse	217471	40	Kevin Stone	80309
16	James Kingston	194538	41	Bradley Davison	75652
17	Marco Gortana	192519	42	Adilson da Silva (Bra)	75367
18	Tjaart van der Walt	180954	43	Michael Archer (Eng)	73689
19	Nico van Rensburg	175064	44	Wimpie Botha	73347
20	Warren Abery	173545	45	Chris Williams (Eng)	72774
21	Bruce Vaughan (US)	153184	46	Mark Murless	70586
22	Brenden Pappas	145347	47	Wayne Bradley	70412
23	Bradford Vaughan	144678	48	Des Terblanche	65896
24	Darren Fichardt	139321	49	Robbie Stewart	65857
25	Wellie Coetsee	139171	50	Callie Swart	65588

Tour Results

Tournament	Venue	Winner	Score
Vodacom Series: Western Cape	Rondebosch GC Capetown	Alan McLean	201 (-15)
Kalahari Classic	Sishen GC, Sishen, Northern Cape	Andrew McLardy	205 (-11)
Pietersburg Classic	Pietersburg Golf Club	Desvonde Botes	197 (-19)
Vodacom Series: Eastern Cape	Humewood GC, Port Elizabeth	Sammy Daniels	207 (-9)
Vodacom Series: Kwazulu/Natal	Durban	Keith Horne	204 (-12)

Tournament	Venue	Winner	Score
Vodacom Series: Mpumalanga	White River GC, White River/Mpumalanga Province	Callie Swart	202 (-11)
Royal Swazi Sun Classic	Royal Swazi Sun CC, Ezulwini Valley	Justin Hobday	207 (-9)
PGA Cup	Germiston GC, Johannesburg	Johan Krugel Gavin Levenson	120 (-24)
Bearing Man Highveld Classic	Witbank GC, Witbank	Wayne Bradley	202 (-14)
Vodacom Series: Free State	Schoeman Park GC, Bloemfontein	Gary Matthews	205 (-11)
FNB Botswana Open	Gaborone GC, Gaborone	Justin Hobday	201 (-12)
Phalaborwa Mafunyane Trophy	Hans Merensky GC, Phalabora	Sammy Daniels	199 (-17)
Vodacom Series: Gauteng	Royal Johannesburg GC, Johannesburg	Brenden Pappas	202 (-11)
FNB Namibia Open	Windhoek CC, Windhoek	Ashley Roestoff	203 (-10)
Platinum Classic	Mooinooi GC, Mooinooi NW Province	Bobby Lincoln	202 (-14)
Zambia Open	Lusaka GC, Lusaka, Zambia	Marc Cayeux	273 (-11)
Zimbabwe Open	Harare, Zimbabwe	Nick Price	271 (-17)
Alfred Dunhill PGA Ch'p[†]	Houghton GC, Johannesburg	Ernie Els	273 (-15)
South African Open[†]	Stellenbosch GC, Cape Province	David Frost	279 (-5)
Vodacom Players Ch'p	Royal Durban CC, Durban	Chris Davison	275 (-13)
Dimension Data Pro-Am	Gary Player CC/Lost City GC, Sun City	Scott Dunlap	273 (-15)
South African Masters	Oppenheimer GC, Welkom, Free State	Desvonde Botes	269 (-19)
Stenham Royal Swazi Sun Open	Royal Swazi Sun CC, Mbabane, Swaziland	Marc Cayeux	266 (-22)
Million Dollar Challenge	Gary Player CC, Sun City	Nick Price	273 (-15)

[†] *Joint ventures with the European Tour*

South American Tour, 1998

Final Ranking

Pos	Name	Prize $	Pos	Name	Prize $
1	Raul Fretes (Par)	101088	15	Pedro Martinez (Par)	14770
#	Angel Cabrera (Arg)	39250	16	Esteban Isasi (Par)	13871
2	Scott Dunlap (US)	35034	17	Jorge Berendt (Arg)	13854
3	Gustavo Mendoza (Col)	33723	#	Miguel Martinez (Ven)	13680
#	Eduardo Romero (Arg)	33114	#	Blaine McCallister (US)	13600
4	Angel Franco (Par)	27230	18	Ron Wuenche (US)	13235
5	Tim Hegna (US)	25983	#	David Frost (SA)	12284
6	Sebastian Fernandez (Arg)	25161	#	Dudley Hart (US)	12284
7	Roberto Coceres (Arg)	25081	#	Craig Stadler (US)	12284
#	Gustavo Rojas (Arg)	23684	19	Philip Jonas (Can)	12283
8	Claudio Muskus (Ven)	21600	20	Rodolfo Gonzalez (Arg)	12090
9	Shawn Savage (US)	19029	21	Rob Moss (US)	10730
10	David Morland (Can)	18713	22	Henrik Stensson (Swe)	10500
11	Jeffrey Schimd (US)	17847	23	Jose Cantero (Arg)	9676
12	Armando Saavedra (Arg)	16913	24	Miguel Guzman (Arg)	9616
13	Stuart Hendley (Can)	16316	25	Ricardo Montenegro (Arg)	8076
14	Mauricio Molina (Arg)	15690			

Tour Results

Tournament	Venue	Winner	Score
TPG Open	Guataparo CC, Valencia	Claudio Muskus	272
Peru Open	Los Incas CC, Lima	Scott Dunlap	275
City of La Plata Open	La Plata GC, La Plata, Argentina	Roberto Coceros	205
Litoral Open	Rosario GC, Rosario, Argentina	Tim Hegna	272
Torneo de Maestros	Olivos GC, Buenos Aires	Raul Fretes	271
JPGA Argentina	Club Metropolitan, Buenos Aires	Jeffrey Schmidt	270
Abierto de Las Delicias	Las Delicias GC, Cordoba, Argentina	Sebastian Fernandez	274
93rd Republic of Argentina Open	Jockey Club, Buenos Aires	Raul Fretes	271

 # Players who are not South American Tour members are unplaced

Australasian Tour, 1998-99

The Tour begins in October and ends in March of the following year. Order of Merit is based on events played, with one, the Tour Championship, remaining.

ANZ Order of Merit

Players are of Australian nationality unless stated

Pos	Name	Prize Aus$	Pos	Name	Prize Aus$
1	Jarrod Moseley	321498	26	David Smail (NZ)	61712
2	Rodney Pampling	265557	27	Tim Elliott	60363
3	Craig Spence	264160	28	Richard Backwell	60059
4	Peter Lonard	223574	29	John Senden	58195
5	Michael Long (NZ)	219880	30	Justin Cooper	57450
6	Craig Parry	197800	31	Nick O'Hern	56934
7	Stephen Leaney	171482	32	Peter McWhinney	55526
8	Peter O'Malley	170238	33	Wayne Riley	54866
9	Peter Senior	165620	34	Robert Stephens	54303
10	Michael Campbell (NZ)	126833	35	Paul Devenport (NZ)	52650
11	Anthony Painter	104928	36	Marcus Cain	50673
12	Terry Price	103943	37	Raymond Russell (Sco)	50007
13	Matthew Lane (NZ)	101465	38	Robin Byrd (US)	47260
14	Stuart Bouvier	97200	39	Wayne Smith	42801
15	Geoff Ogilvy	88052	40	Todd Demsey (US)	42467
16	Lucas Parsons	84908	41	Robert Willis	40865
17	Stephen Allan	77550	42	Rodger Davis	37522
18	Kenny Druce	76085	43	Shane Robinson	37451
19	Tony Carolan	73163	44	Wayne Grady	36770
20	Jean-Louis Guepy (Fr)	70880	45	Chris Gray	36670
21	Stephen Scahill (NZ)	68124	46	Gavin Coles	36604
22	Paul Gow	66815	47	Scott Laycock	34204
23	Brett Partridge	64005	48	Ian Leggatt	34101
24	David McKenzie	62727	49	Andre Stolz	33474
25	Bradley King	62490	50	Anthony Edwards	31549

Tour Results

Tournament	Venue	Winner	Score
Ford Open	Kooyunga GC	Stuart Bouvier	282 (-6)
MasterCard PGA	NSW GC	David Howell (Eng)	275 (-13)
ANZ Players Championship	Royal Queensland GC, Brisbane	Stephen Leaney	275 (-13)
Holden Australian Open	Royal Adelaide GC	Greg Chalmers	288 (par)
Coolum Classic	Hyatt Coolum Resort, Queensland	Stuart Appleby	271 (-17)
Smokefree Victorian Open	Victoria GC, Melbourne	Ken Druce	275 (-13)
Heineken Classic†	Vines Resort, Perth	Jarrod Moseley	274 (-14)
GN Holden International	The Lakes, Sydney	Michael Long (NZ)	283 (-5)
Ericsson Masters	Huntingdale GC, Melbourne	Craig Spence	276 (-16)
Canon Challenge	Terrey Hills G&CC	Rod Pampling	270 (-18)

† *Joint venture with the European Tour*

Other International Events

INDIVIDUAL

Andersen Consulting World Championship of Golf

Year	Winner
1995	Barry Lane (Eng) beat David Frost (SA) one hole
1996	Greg Norman (Aus) beat Scott Hoch (US) two holes

1997 Total prize money: $3,500,000 **World Finals** at *Grayhawk GC, Scottsdale, AZ*

Regional Finals
International	E Els beat S Elkington 1 hole
Japan	H Meshiai beat K Hosokawa 1 hole
USA	D Love III beat P Mickelson at 20th hole
Europe	C Montgomerie beat C Rocca 5 and 4

World Semi-Finals: D Love III beat H Meshiai 1 hole; C Montgomerie beat E Els 3 and 2

Final: C Montgomerie beat D Love III 2 up
(Montgomerie received $1 million, Love $500000, Els $350000, Meshiai $300000)

Hassan II Trophy *at Golf de Dar-es-Salaam, Rabat, Morocco*

1998

Pos	Name	Score	Prize Money $
1	S Luna*	71-67-70-69—277	100000
* Luna won at first hole after play-off			
2	T Pernice	72-69-69-67—277	
3	S Jones	71-68-70-69—278	
	S Ames	71-71-66-70—278	

Million Dollar Challenge

at Sun City, Bophutatswana, South Africa (7597 yds, Par 72)

Year	Winner	Score	Year	Winner	Score	Year	Winner	Score
1982 (Jan)	J Miller	277	1987	I Woosnam	274	1993	N Price	264
1982 (Dec)	R Floyd	280	1988	F Allem	278	1994	N Faldo	272
1983	S Ballesteros	274	1989	D Frost	276	1995	C Pavin	276
1984	S Ballesteros	279	1990	D Frost	284	1996	C Montgomerie	274
1985	B Langer	278	1991	B Langer	272	1997	N Price	275
1986	M McNulty	282	1992	D Frost	276			

1998 Prize money: $2,570,000

Pos	Name	Score	Prize Money $
1	Nick Price*	67-68-72-66—273	1000000
* Price won at fifth extra hole of play-off			
2	Tiger Woods	72-68-67-66—273	250000
3	Justin Leonard	69-68-68-69—274	200000

Subaru Sarazen World Open Championship

Year	Winner	Score	Year	Winner	Score
1994	E Els	273	1996	F Nobilo	272
1995	F Nobilo	208	1997	M Calcavecchia	272

1998 at *Chateau Elan, Atlanta* (6993 yds, Par 72) Prize money: $2,000,000

Pos	Name	Score	Prize Money $
1	D Hart	72-69-62-69—272	360000
2	B Tway	66-70-66-74—276	210000
3	B Langer	68-72-69-68—277	124000

TEAM EVENTS

Great Britain & Ireland v USA

Year		GB&I		USA		Venue
1921 (June 6)	Foursomes Singles	4 6½	10½	1 3½	4½	Gleneagles
1926 (June 4–5)	Foursomes Singles	5 8½	13½	0 1½	1½	Wentworth

The Ryder Cup (Instituted 1927)

Year		GB&I		USA		Venue
1927 (June 3–4)	Foursomes Singles	1 1½	2½	3 6½	9½	Worcester, Mass
1929 (May 26–27)	Foursomes Singles	1½ 5½	7	2½ 2½	5	Moortown
1931 (Nov 5–6)	Foursomes Singles	1 2	3	3 6	9	Columbus, Ohio
1933 (June 26–27)	Foursomes Singles	2½ 4	6½	1½ 4	5½	Southport and Ainsdale
1935 (Sept 28–29)	Foursomes Singles	1 2	3	3 6	9	Ridgewood, NJ
1937 (June 29–30)	Foursomes Singles	1½ 2½	4	2½ 5½	8	Southport and Ainsdale
1947 (Nov 1–2)	Foursomes Singles	0 1	1	4 7	11	Portland, Oregon
1949 (Sept 16–17)	Foursomes Singles	3 2	5	1 6	7	Ganton
1951 (Nov 2 and 4)	Foursomes Singles	1 1½	2½	3 6½	9½	Pinehurst, N Carolina
1953 (Oct 2–3)	Foursomes Singles	1 4½	5½	3 3½	6½	Wentworth
1955 (Nov 5–6)	Foursomes Singles	1 3	4	3 5	8	Palm Springs, California
1957 (Oct 4–5)	Foursomes Singles	1 6½	7½	3 1½	4½	Lindrick
1959 (Nov 6–7)	Foursomes Singles	1½ 2	3½	2½ 6	8½	Eldorado, California
1961 (Oct 13–14)	Foursomes Singles	2 7½	9½	6 8½	14½	R Lytham and St Annes

From 1963 Fourball matches were played in the afternoon of the first two days

| 1963 (Oct 11–13) | Foursomes
Fourball
Singles | 2
2
5 | 9 | 6
6
11 | 23 | Atlanta, Georgia |

Ryder Cup *continued*

Year		GB&I		USA		Venue
1965	Foursomes	4		4		
(Oct 7–9)	Fourball	3	12½	5	19½	R Birkdale
	Singles	5½		10½		
1967	Foursomes	2½		5½		
(Oct 20–22)	Fourball	½	8½	7½	23½	Houston, Texas
	Singles	5½		10½		
1969	Foursomes	4½		3½		
(Oct 18–20)	Fourball	3½	16	4½	16	R Birkdale
	Singles	8		8		
1971	Foursomes	4½		3½		
(Sept 16–18)	Fourball	1½	13½	6½	18½	St Louis, Missouri
	Singles	7½		8½		
1973	Foursomes	4½		3½		
(Sept 20–22)	Fourball	3½	13	4½	19	Muirfield
	Singles	5		11		
1975	Foursomes	1		7		
(Sept 19–21)	Fourball	2½	11	5½	21	Laurel Valley, Pennsylvania
	Singles	7½		8½		
1977	Foursomes	1½		3½		
(Sept 15–17)	Fourball	1	7½	4	12½	R Lytham and St Annes
	Singles	5		5		

From 1979 players from the Continent of Europe also became available for selection

Year		Europe		USA		Venue
1979	Foursomes	4½		3½		
(Sept 14–16)	Fourball	3	11	5	17	Greenbrier, WVa
	Singles	3½		8½		
1981	Foursomes	2		6		
(Sept 18–20)	Fourball	3½	9½	4½	18½	Walton Heath
	Singles	4		8		
1983	Foursomes	4		4		
(Oct 14–16)	Fourball	4	13½	4	14½	PGA National, Florida
	Singles	5½		6½		
1985	Foursomes	4		4		
(Sept 13–15)	Fourball	5	16½	3	11½	The Belfry
	Singles	7½		4½		
1987	Foursomes	4½		3½		
(Sept 13–15)	Fourball	6	15	2	13	Muirfield Village, Ohio
	Singles	4½		7½		

1989 at The Belfry, Sutton Coldfield, on 22nd, 23rd and 24th September, 1989
(Non-playing Captains: A Jacklin, Europe; R Floyd, USA)

Europe		USA	
First Day – Foursomes			
N Faldo and I Woosnam (halved)	½	T Kite and C Strange (halved)	½
H Clark and M James	0	L Wadkins and P Stewart (1 hole)	1
S Ballesteros and JM Olazábal (halved)	½	T Watson and C Beck (halved)	½
B Langer and R Rafferty	0	M Calcavecchia and K Green (2 and 1)	1
	1		3
Fourball			
S Torrance and G Brand Jr (1 hole)	1	C Strange and P Azinger	0
H Clark and M James (3 and 2)	1	F Couples and L Wadkins	0
N Faldo and I Woosnam (2 holes)	1	M Calcavecchia and M McCumber	0
S Ballesteros and JM Olazábal (6 and 5)	1	T Watson and M O'Meara	0
	4		0

Match position: Europe 5, USA 3

Second Day – Foursomes

I Woosnam and N Faldo (3 and 2)	1	L Wadkins and P Stewart	0
G Brand Jr and S Torrance	0	C Beck and P Azinger (4 and 3)	1
C O'Connor Jr and R Rafferty	0	M Calcavecchia and K Green (3 and 2)	1
S Ballesteros and JM Olazábal (1 hole)	1	T Kite and C Strange	0
	2		2

Fourball

N Faldo and I Woosnam	0	C Beck and P Azinger (2 and 1)	1
B Langer and JM Canizares	0	T Kite and M McCumber (2 and 1)	1
H Clark and M James (1 hole)	1	P Stewart and C Strange	0
S Ballesteros and JM Olazábal (4 and 2)	1	M Calcavecchia and K Green	0
	2		2

Match position: Europe 9, USA 7

Third Day – Singles

S Ballesteros	0	P Azinger (1 hole)	1
B Langer	0	C Beck (3 and 2)	1
JM Olazábal (1 hole)	1	P Stewart	0
R Rafferty (1 hole)	1	M Calcavecchia	0
H Clark	0	T Kite (8 and 7)	1
M James (3 and 2)	1	M O'Meara	0
C O'Connor Jr (1 hole)	1	F Couples	0
JM Canizares (1 hole)	1	K Green	0
G Brand Jr	0	M McCumber (1 hole)	1
S Torrance	0	T Watson (3 and 2)	1
N Faldo	0	L Wadkins (1 hole)	1
I Woosnam	0	C Strange (2 holes)	1
	5		7

Result: Europe 14, USA 14

1991 *at Kiawah Island, South Carolina, on 27th, 28th and 29th September, 1991*
Non-playing captains: D Stockton, USA; B Gallacher, Europe.

Europe   **USA**

First Day – Foursomes

S Ballesteros and JM Olazábal (2 and 1)	1	P Azinger and C Beck	0
B Langer and M James	0	R Floyd and F Couples (2 and 1)	1
D Gilford and C Montgomerie	0	L Wadkins and H Irwin (4 and 2)	1
N Faldo and I Woosnam	0	P Stewart and M Calcavecchia (1 hole)	1
	1		3

Fourball

S Torrance and D Feherty	½	L Wadkins and M O'Meara	½
S Ballesteros and JM Olazábal (2 and 1)	1	P Azinger and C Beck	0
S Richardson and M James (5 and 4)	1	C Pavin and M Calcavecchia	0
N Faldo and I Woosnam	0	R Floyd and F Couples (5 and 3)	1
	2½		1½

Match position: Europe 3½, USA 4½

Second Day – Foursomes

S Torrance and D Feherty	0	H Irwin and L Wadkins (4 and 2)	1
M James and S Richardson	0	M Calcavecchia and P Stewart (1 hole)	1
N Faldo and D Gilford	0	P Azinger and M O'Meara (7 and 6)	1
S Ballesteros and JM Olazábal (3 and 2)	1	F Couples and R Floyd	0
	1		3

Fourball

I Woosnam and P Broadhurst (2 and 1)	1	P Azinger and H Irwin	0
B Langer and C Montgomerie (2 and 1)	1	S Pate and C Pavin	0
M James and S Richardson (3 and 1)	1	L Wadkins and W Levi	0
S Ballesteros and JM Olazábal	½	F Couples and P Stewart	½
	3½		½

Match position: Europe 8, USA 8

1991 Ryder Cup *continued*

Third Day – Singles

N Faldo (2 holes)	1	R Floyd	0
D Feherty (2 and 1)	1	P Stewart	0
C Montgomerie	½	M Calcavecchia	½
JM Olazábal	0	P Azinger (2 holes)	1
S Richardson	0	C Pavin (2 and 1)	1
S Ballesteros (3 and 2)	1	W Levi	0
I Woosnam	0	C Beck (3 and 1)	1
P Broadhurst (3 and 1)	1	M O'Meara	0
S Torrance	0	F Couples (3 and 2)	1
M James	0	L Wadkins (3 and 2)	1
B Langer	½	H Irwin	½
D Gilford (withdrawn)	½	S Pate (withdrawn – injured)	½
	5½		6½

Result: USA 14½, Europe 13½

1993 at The Belfry, Sutton Coldfield, on 24th, 25th and 26th September, 1993

Non-playing captains: B Gallacher, Europe; T Watson, USA.

Europe   USA

First Day – Foursomes

S Torrance and M James	0	L Wadkins and C Pavin (4 and 3)	1
I Woosnam and B Langer (7 and 5)	1	P Azinger and P Stewart	0
S Ballesteros and JM Olazábal	0	T Kite and D Love III (2 and 1)	1
N Faldo and C Montgomerie (4 and 3)	1	R Floyd and F Couples	0
	2		2

Fourball

I Woosnam and P Baker (1 hole)	1	J Gallagher Jr and L Janzen	0
B Lane and B Langer	0	L Wadkins and C Pavin (4 and 2)	1
N Faldo and C Montgomerie	½	P Azinger and F Couples	½
S Ballesteros and JM Olazábal (4 and 3)	1	T Kite and D Love III	0
	2½		1½

Match position: Europe 4½, USA 3½

Second Day – Foursomes

N Faldo and C Montgomerie (3 and 2)	1	L Wadkins and C Pavin	0
B Langer and I Woosnam (2 and 1)	1	F Couples and P Azinger	0
P Baker and B Lane	0	R Floyd and P Stewart (3 and 2)	1
S Ballesteros and JM Olazábal (2 and 1)	1	T Kite and D Love III	0
	3		1

Fourball

N Faldo and C Montgomerie	0	C Beck and J Cook (2 holes)	1
M James and C Rocca	0	C Pavin and J Gallagher Jr (5 and 4)	1
I Woosnam and P Baker (6 and 5)	1	F Couples and P Azinger	0
JM Olazábal and J Haeggman	0	R Floyd and P Stewart (2 and 1)	1
	1		3

Match position: Europe 8½, USA 7½

Third Day – Singles

I Woosnam	½	F Couples	½
B Lane	0	C Beck (1 hole)	1
C Montgomerie (1 hole)	1	L Janzen	0
P Baker (2 holes)	1	C Pavin	0
J Haeggman (1 hole)	1	J Cook	0
S Torrance (withdrawn at start of day)	½	L Wadkins (withdrawn at start of day)	½
M James	0	P Stewart (3 and 2)	1
C Rocca	0	D Love III (1 hole)	1
S Ballesteros	0	J Gallagher Jr (3 and 2)	1
JM Olazábal	0	R Floyd (2 holes)	1
B Langer	0	T Kite (5 and 3)	1
N Faldo	½	P Azinger	½
	4½		7½

Result: Europe 13, USA 15

1995 *at Oak Hill, Rochester, New York, on 22nd, 23rd and 24th September, 1995*

Non-playing captains: L Wadkins, USA; B Gallacher, Europe

Europe

USA

First Day – Foursomes

N Faldo and C Montgomerie	0	C Pavin and T Lehman (1 hole)	1
S Torrance and C Rocca (3 and 2)	1	J Haas and F Couples	0
H Clark and M James	0	D Love III and J Maggert (4 and 3)	1
B Langer and P-U Johansson (1 hole)	1	B Crenshaw and C Strange	0
	2		2

Fourball

D Gilford and S Ballesteros (4 and 3)	1	B Faxon and P Jacobsen	0
S Torrance and C Rocca	0	J Maggert and L Roberts (6 and 5)	1
N Faldo and C Montgomerie	0	F Couples and D Love III (3 and 2)	1
B Langer and P-U Johansson	0	C Pavin and P Mickelson (6 and 4)	1
	1		3

Match position: Europe 3, USA 5

Second Day – Foursomes

N Faldo and C Montgomerie (4 and 2)	1	J Haas and C Strange	0
S Torrance and C Rocca (6 and 5)	1	D Love III and J Maggert	0
I Woosnam and P Walton	0	L Roberts and P Jacobsen (1 hole)	1
B Langer and D Gilford (4 and 3)	1	C Pavin and L Roberts	0
	3		1

Fourball

S Torrance and C Montgomerie	0	B Faxon and F Couples (4 and 2)	1
I Woosnam and C Rocca (3 and 2)	1	D Love III and B Crenshaw	0
S Ballesteros and D Gilford	0	J Haas and P Mickelson (3 and 2)	1
N Faldo and B Langer	0	C Pavin and L Roberts (1 hole)	1
	1		3

Match position: Europe 7, USA 9

Third Day – Singles

S Ballesteros	0	T Lehman (4 and 3)	1
H Clark (1 hole)	1	P Jacobsen	0
M James (4 and 3)	1	J Maggert	0
I Woosnam	½	F Couples	½
C Rocca	0	D Love III (3 and 2)	1
D Gilford (1 hole)	1	B Faxon	0
C Montgomerie (3 and 1)	1	B Crenshaw	0
N Faldo (1 hole)	1	C Strange	0
S Torrance (2 and 1)	1	L Roberts	0
B Langer	0	C Pavin (3 and 2)	1
P Walton (1 hole)	1	J Haas	0
P-U Johansson	0	P Mickelson (2 and 1)	1
	7½		4½

Result: Europe 14½, USA 13½

1997 Ryder Cup at Valderrama, Spain on 26th, 27th and 28th September, 1997

Non-playing captains: S Ballesteros, Europe; T Kite, USA

Europe		USA	
First Day – Fourball			
JM Olazábal and C Rocca (1 hole)	1	D Love III and P Mickelson	0
N Faldo and L Westwood	0	F Couples and B Faxon (1 hole)	1
J Parnevik and P-U Johansson (1 hole)	1	T Lehman and J Furyk	0
C Montgomerie and B Langer	0	T Woods and M O'Meara (3 and 2)	1
	2		2
Foursomes			
C Rocca and JM Olazábal	0	S Hoch and L Janzen (1 hole)	1
B Langer and C Montgomerie (5 and 3)	1	M O'Meara and T Woods	0
N Faldo and L Westwood (3 and 2)	1	J Leonard and J Maggert	0
J Parnevik and I Garrido	½	T Lehman and P Mickelson	½
	2½		1½

Match position: Europe 4½, USA 3½

Second Day – Fourball			
C Montgomerie and D Clarke (1 hole)	1	F Couples and D Love III	0
I Woosnam and T Bjorn (2 and 1)	1	J Leonard and B Faxon	0
N Faldo and L Westwood (2 and 1)	1	T Woods and M O'Meara	0
JM Olazábal and I Garrido	½	P Mickelson and T Lehman	½
	3½		½
Foursomes			
C Montgomerie and B Langer (1 hole)	1	L Janzen and J Furyk	0
N Faldo and L Westwood	0	S Hoch and J Maggert (2 and 1)	1
J Parnevik and I Garrido	½	J Leonard and T Woods	½
JM Olazábal and C Rocca (5 and 4)	1	D Love III and F Couples	0
	2½		1½

Match position: Europe 10½, USA 5½

Third Day – Singles			
I Woosnam	0	F Couples (8 and 7)	1
P-U Johansson (3 and 2)	1	D Love III	0
C Rocca (4 and 2)	1	T Woods	0
T Bjorn	½	J Leonard	½
D Clarke	0	P Mickelson (2 and 1)	1
J Parnevik	0	M O'Meara (5 and 4)	1
JM Olazábal	0	L Janzen (1 hole)	1
B Langer (2 and 1)	1	B Faxon	0
L Westwood	0	J Maggert (3 and 2)	1
C Montgomerie	½	S Hoch	½
N Faldo	0	J Furyk (3 and 2)	1
I Garrido	0	T Lehman (7 and 6)	1
	4		8

Result: Europe 14½, USA 13½

Ryder Cup – INDIVIDUAL RECORDS

Matches were contested as Great Britain v USA from 1927–71; as Great Britain & Ireland v USA from 1973–77; and as Europe v USA from 1979. Bold type indicates captain; non-playing in brackets.

Europe

Name	Year	Played	Won	Lost	Halved
Jimmy Adams	*1939-47-49-51-53	7	2	5	0
Percy Alliss	1929-33-35-37	6	3	2	1
Peter Alliss	1953-57-59-61-63-65-67-69	30	10	15	5
Laurie Ayton	1949	0	0	0	0
Peter Baker	1993	4	3	1	0
Severiano Ballesteros (Sp)	1979-83-85-87-89-91-93-95-(97)	37	20	12	5
Harry Bannerman	1971	5	2	2	1
Brian Barnes	1969-71-73-75-77-79	25	10	14	1
Maurice Bembridge	1969-71-73-75	16	5	8	3
Thomas Björn (Den)	1997	2	1	0	1
Aubrey Boomer	1927-29	4	2	2	0
Ken Bousfield	1949-51-55-57-59-61	10	5	5	0
Hugh Boyle	1967	3	0	3	0
Harry Bradshaw	1953-55-57	5	2	2	1
Gordon J Brand	1983	1	0	1	0
Gordon Brand Jr	1987-89	7	2	4	1
Paul Broadhurst	1991	2	2	0	0
Eric Brown	1953-55-57-59-(**69**)-(**71**)	8	4	4	0
Ken Brown	1977-79-83-85-87	13	4	9	0
Stewart Burns	1929	0	0	0	0
Dick Burton	1935-37-*39-49	5	2	3	0
Jack Busson	1935	2	0	2	0
Peter Butler	1965-69-71-73	14	3	9	2
José Maria Canizares (Sp)	1981-83-85-89	11	5	4	2
Alex Caygill	1969	1	0	0	1
Clive Clark	1973	1	0	1	0
Howard Clark	1977-81-85-87-89-95	15	7	7	1
Darren Clarke	1997	2	1	1	0
Neil Coles	1961-63-65-67-69-71-73-77	40	12	21	7
Archie Compston	1927-29-31	6	1	4	1
Henry Cotton	1929-37-*39-47-(**53**)	6	2	4	0
Bill Cox	1935-37	3	0	2	1
Allan Dailey	1933	0	0	0	0
Fred Daly	1947-49-51-53	8	3	4	1
Eamonn Darcy	1975-77-81-87	11	1	8	2
William Davies	1931-33	4	2	2	0
Peter Dawson	1977	3	1	2	0
Norman Drew	1959	1	0	0	1
George Duncan	1927-**29**-31	5	2	3	0
Syd Easterbrook	1931-**33**	3	2	1	0
Nick Faldo	1977-79-81-83-85-87-89-91-93-95-97	46	23	19	4
John Fallon	1955-(**63**)	1	1	0	0
Max Faulkner	1947-49-51-53-57	8	1	7	0
David Feherty	1991	3	1	1	1
George Gadd	1927	0	0	0	0
Bernard Gallacher	1969-71-73-75-77-79-81-83-(**91**)-(**93**)-(**95**)	31	13	13	5
John Garner	1971-73	1	0	1	0
Antonio Garrido (Sp)	1979	5	1	4	0
Ignacio Garrido (Sp)	1997	4	0	1	3
David Gilford	1991-95	6	3	3	0
Eric Green	1947	0	0	0	0
Malcolm Gregson	1967	4	0	4	0
Joakim Haeggman (Swe)	1993	2	1	1	0
Tom Haliburton	1961-63	6	0	6	0
Jack Hargreaves	1951	0	0	0	0
Arthur Havers	1927-31-33	6	3	3	0
Jimmy Hitchcock	1965	3	0	3	0
Bert Hodson	1931	1	0	1	0
Reg Horne	1947	0	0	0	0
Tommy Horton	1975-77	8	1	6	1
Brian Huggett	1963-67-69-71-73-75-(**77**)	25	9	10	6
Bernard Hunt	1953-57-59-61-63-65-67-69-(**73**)-(**75**)	28	6	16	6
Geoffrey Hunt	1963	3	0	3	0
Guy Hunt	1975	3	0	2	1
Tony Jacklin	1967-69-71-73-75-77-79-(**83**)-(**85**)-(**87**)-(**89**)	35	13	14	8

* In 1939 a GB&I team was named but the match was not played because of the Second World War.

Ryder Cup European Individual Records *continued*

Name	Year	Played	Won	Lost	Halved
John Jacobs	1955-(79)-(81)	2	2	0	0
Mark James	1977-79-81-89-91-93-95	24	8	15	1
Edward Jarman	1935	1	0	1	0
Per-Ulrik Johansson (Swe)	1995-97	5	3	2	0
Herbert Jolly	1927	2	0	2	0
Michael King	1979	1	0	1	0
Sam King	1937-*39-47-49	5	1	3	1
Arthur Lacey	1933-37-(51)	3	0	3	0
Barry Lane	1993	3	0	3	0
Bernhard Langer (Ger)	1981-83-85-87-89-91-93-95-97	38	18	15	5
Arthur Lees	1947-49-51-55	8	4	4	0
Sandy Lyle	1979-81-83-85-87	18	7	9	2
Jimmy Martin	1965	1	0	1	0
Peter Mills	1957-59	1	1	0	0
Abe Mitchell	1929-31-33	6	4	2	0
Ralph Moffitt	1961	1	0	1	0
Colin Montgomerie	1991-93-95-97	18	9	6	3
Christy O'Connor, Jr	1975-89	4	1	3	0
Christy O'Connor, Sr	1955-57-59-61-63-65-67-69-71-73	36	11	21	4
José Maria Olazábal (Sp)	1987-89-91-93-97	25	14	8	3
John O'Leary	1975	4	0	4	0
Peter Oosterhuis	1971-73-75-77-79-81	28	14	11	3
Alf Padgham	1933-35-37-*39	6	0	6	0
John Panton	1951-53-61	5	0	5	0
Jesper Parnevik (Swe)	1997	4	1	1	2
Alf Perry	1933-35-37	4	0	3	1
Manuel Pinero (Sp)	1981-85	9	6	3	0
Lionel Platts	1965	5	1	2	2
Eddie Polland	1973	2	0	2	0
Ronan Rafferty	1989	3	1	2	0
Ted Ray	1927	2	0	2	0
Dai Rees	1937-*39-47-49-51-53-55-57-59-61-(67)	18	7	10	1
Steven Richardson	1991	4	2	2	0
José Rivero (Sp)	1985-87	5	2	3	0
Fred Robson	1927-29-31	6	2	4	0
Costantino Rocca (It)	1993-95-97	11	6	5	0
Syd Scott	1955	2	0	2	0
Des Smyth	1979-81	7	2	5	0
Dave Thomas	1959-63-65-67	18	3	10	5
Sam Torrance	1981-83-85-87-89-91-93-95	27	7	15	5
Peter Townsend	1969-71	11	3	8	0
Brian Waites	1983	4	1	3	0
Philip Walton	1995	2	1	1	0
Charlie Ward	1947-49-51	6	1	5	0
Paul Way	1983-85	9	6	2	1
Harry Weetman	1951-53-55-57-59-61-63-(65)	15	2	11	2
Lee Westwood	1997	5	2	3	0
Charles Whitcombe	1927-29-31-33-35-37-*39-(49)	9	3	2	4
Ernest Whitcombe	1929-31-35	6	1	4	1
Reg Whitcombe	1935-*39	1	0	1	0
George Will	1963-65-67	15	2	11	2
Norman Wood	1975	3	1	2	0
Ian Woosnam	1983-85-87-89-91-93-95-97	31	14	12	5

United States of America

Name	Year	Played	Won	Lost	Halved
Tommy Aaron	1969-73	6	1	4	1
Skip Alexander	1949-51	2	1	1	0
Paul Azinger	1989-91-93	14	5	7	2
Jerry Barber	1955-**61**	5	1	4	0
Miller Barber	1969-71	7	1	4	2
Herman Barron	1947	1	1	0	0
Andy Bean	1979-87	6	4	2	0
Frank Beard	1969-71	8	2	3	3
Chip Beck	1989-91-93	9	6	2	1
Homero Blancas	1973	4	2	1	1
Tommy Bolt	1955-57	4	3	1	0
Julius Boros	1959-63-65-67	16	9	3	4

* In 1939 a GB&I team was named but the match was not played because of the Second World War.

Name	Year	Played	Won	Lost	Halved
Gay Brewer	1967-73	9	5	3	1
Billy Burke	1931-33	3	3	0	0
Jack Burke	1951-53-55-57-59-(73)	8	7	1	0
Walter Burkemo	1953	1	0	1	0
Mark Calcavecchia	1987-89-91	11	5	5	1
Billy Casper	1961-63-65-67-69-71-73-75-(79)	37	20	10	7
Bill Collins	1961	3	1	2	0
Charles Coody	1971	3	0	2	1
John Cook	1993	2	1	1	0
Fred Couples	1989-91-93-95-97	20	7	9	4
Wilfred Cox	1931	2	2	0	0
Ben Crenshaw	1981-83-87-95	12	3	8	1
Jimmy Demaret	*1941-47-49-51	6	6	0	0
Gardner Dickinson	1967-71	10	9	1	0
Leo Diegel	1927-29-31-33	6	3	3	0
Dale Douglass	1969	2	0	2	0
Dave Douglas	1953	2	1	0	1
Ed Dudley	1929-33-37	4	3	1	0
Olin Dutra	1933-35	4	1	3	0
Lee Elder	1979	4	1	3	0
Al Espinosa	1927-29-31	4	2	1	1
Johnny Farrell	1927-29-31	6	3	2	1
Brad Faxon	1995-97	6	2	4	0
Dow Finsterwald	1957-59-61-63-(77)	13	9	3	1
Ray Floyd	1969-75-77-81-83-85-(89)-91-93	31	12	16	3
Doug Ford	1955-57-59-61	9	4	4	1
Ed Furgol	1957	1	0	1	0
Marty Furgol	1955	1	0	1	0
Jim Furyk	1997	3	1	2	0
Jim Gallagher Jr	1993	3	2	1	0
Al Geiberger	1967-75	9	5	1	3
Vic Ghezzi	*1939-*41	0	0	0	0
Bob Gilder	1983	4	2	2	0
Bob Goalby	1963	5	3	1	1
Johnny Golden	1927-29	3	3	0	0
Lou Graham	1973-75-77	9	5	3	1
Hubert Green	1977-79-85	7	4	3	0
Ken Green	1989	4	2	2	0
Ralph Guldahl	1937-*39	2	2	0	0
Fred Haas, Jr	1953	1	0	1	0
Jay Haas	1983-95	8	3	4	1
Walter Hagen	**1927-29-31-33-35-(37)**	9	7	1	1
Bob Hamilton	1949	2	0	2	0
Chick Harbert	1949-55	2	2	0	0
Chandler Harper	1955	1	0	1	0
Dutch (EJ) Harrison	1947-49-51	3	2	1	0
Fred Hawkins	1957	2	1	1	0
Mark Hayes	1979	3	1	2	0
Clayton Heafner	1949-51	4	3	0	1
Jay Hebert	1959-61-(71)	4	2	1	1
Lionel Hebert	1957	1	0	1	0
Dave Hill	1969-73-77	9	6	3	0
Jimmy Hines	*1939	0	0	0	0
Scott Hoch	1997	3	2	0	1
Ben Hogan	*1941-47-(49)-51-(67)	3	3	0	0
Hale Irwin	1975-77-79-81-91	20	13	5	2
Tommy Jacobs	1965	4	3	1	0
Peter Jacobsen	1985-95	6	2	4	0
Don January	1965-77	7	2	3	2
Lee Janzen	1993-97	5	2	3	0
Herman Keiser	1947	1	0	1	0
Tom Kite	1979-81-83-85-87-89-93-(97)	28	15	9	4
Ted Kroll	1953-55-57	4	3	1	0
Ky Laffoon	1935	1	0	1	0
Tom Lehman	1995-97	7	3	2	2
Tony Lema	1963-65	11	8	1	2
Justin Leonard	1997	4	0	2	2
Wayne Levi	1991	2	0	2	0
Bruce Lietzke	1981	3	0	2	1
Gene Littler	1961-63-65-67-69-71-75	27	14	5	8
Davis Love III	1993-95-97	13	5	8	0
Jeff Maggert	1995-97	7	4	3	0
John Mahaffey	1979	3	1	2	0

US teams were selected in 1939 and 1941, but did not play because of the Second World War.

Ryder Cup American Individual Records *continued*

Name	Year	Played	Won	Lost	Halved
Mark McCumber	1989	3	2	1	0
Jerry McGee	1977	2	1	1	0
Harold McSpaden	*1939-*41	0	0	0	0
Tony Manero	1937	2	1	1	0
Lloyd Mangrum	*1941-47-49-51-53	8	6	2	0
Dave Marr	1965-(81)	6	4	2	0
Billy Maxwell	1963	4	4	0	0
Dick Mayer	1957	2	1	0	1
Bill Mehlhorn	1927	2	1	1	0
Dick Metz	*1939	0	0	0	0
Phil Mickelson	1995-97	7	4	1	2
Cary Middlecoff	1953-55-59	6	2	3	1
Johnny Miller	1975-81	6	2	2	2
Larry Mize	1987	4	1	1	2
Gil Morgan	1979-83	6	1	2	3
Bob Murphy	1975	4	2	1	1
Byron Nelson	1937-*39-*41-47-(65)	4	3	1	0
Larry Nelson	1979-81-87	13	9	3	1
Bobby Nichols	1967	5	4	0	1
Jack Nicklaus	1969-71-73-75-77-81-(83)-(87)	28	17	8	3
Andy North	1985	3	0	3	0
Ed Oliver	1947-51-53	5	3	2	0
Mark O'Meara	1985-89-91-97	12	4	7	1
Arnold Palmer	1961-**63**-65-67-71-73-(75)	32	22	8	2
Johnny Palmer	1949	2	0	2	0
Sam Parks	1935	1	0	0	1
Jerry Pate	1981	4	2	2	0
Steve Pate	1991	1	0	1	0
Corey Pavin	1991-93-95	8	5	3	0
Calvin Peete	1983-85	7	4	2	1
Henry Picard	1935-37-*39	4	3	1	0
Dan Pohl	1987	3	1	2	0
Johnny Pott	1963-65-67	7	5	2	0
Dave Ragan	1963	4	2	1	1
Henry Ransom	1951	1	0	1	0
Johnny Revolta	1935-37	3	2	1	0
Loren Roberts	1995	4	3	1	0
Chi Chi Rodriguez	1973	2	0	1	1
Bill Rogers	1981	4	1	2	1
Bob Rosburg	1959	2	2	0	0
Mason Rudolph	1971	3	1	1	1
Paul Runyan	1933-35-*39	4	2	2	0
Doug Sanders	1967	5	2	3	0
Gene Sarazen	1927-29-31-33-35-37-*41	12	7	2	3
Densmore Shute	1931-33-37	6	2	2	2
Dan Sikes	1969	3	2	1	0
Scott Simpson	1987	2	1	1	0
Horton Smith	1929-31-33-35-37-*39-*41	4	3	0	1
JC Snead	1971-73-75	11	9	2	0
Sam Snead	1937-*39-*41-47-49-51-53-55-**59**-(**69**)	13	10	2	1
Ed Sneed	1977	2	1	0	1
Mike Souchak	1959-61	6	5	1	0
Craig Stadler	1983-85	8	4	2	2
Payne Stewart	1987-89-91-93	16	7	8	1
Ken Still	1969	3	1	2	0
Dave Stockton	1971-77-(**91**)	5	3	1	1
Curtis Strange	1983-85-87-89-95	20	6	12	2
Hal Sutton	1985-87	9	3	3	3
Lee Trevino	1969-71-73-75-79-81-(85)	30	17	7	6
Jim Turnesa	1953	1	1	0	0
Joe Turnesa	1927-29	4	1	2	1
Ken Venturi	1965	4	1	3	0
Lanny Wadkins	1977-79-83-85-87-89-91-93-(95)	33	20	11	2
Art Wall, Jnr	1957-59-61	6	4	2	0
Al Watrous	1927-29	3	2	1	0
Tom Watson	1977-81-83-89-(93)	15	10	4	1
Tom Weiskopf	1973-75	10	7	2	1
Craig Wood	1931-33-35-*41	4	1	3	0
Tiger Woods	1997	5	1	3	1
Lew Worsham	1947	2	2	0	0
Fuzzy Zoeller	1979-83-85	10	1	8	1

* *US teams were selected in 1939 and 1941, but did not play because of the Second World War.*

PGA Cup (Instituted 1973)
Great Britain and Ireland Club Professionals *v* United States Club Professionals

Year	Winner	Venue	Result	Year	Winner	Venue	Result
1973	USA	Pinehurst, USA	13–3	1983	GB&I	Muirfield	14½–6½
1974	USA	Pinehurst, USA	11½–4½	1984	GB&I	Turnberry	12½–8½
1975	USA	Hillside	9½–6½				
1976	USA	Moortown	9½–6½	*Played alternate years from 1984*			
1977	Halved	Miss Hills, USA	8½–8½	1986	USA	Knollwood	16–9
1978	GB&I	St Mellion	10½–6½	1988	USA	The Belfry	15½–10½
1979	GB&I	Castletown	12½–4½	1990	USA	Kiawah Island, SC	19–7
1980	USA	Oak Tree	15–6	1992	USA	K Club, Ireland	15–11
1981	Halved	Turnberry, Isle	10½–10½	1994	USA	Palm Beach, Florida	15–11
1982	USA	Knoxville, TN	13–7	1996	Halved	Gleneagles	13–13

1998 at The Broadmoor, West Course, Colorado Springs, Colorado, USA

Non-playing captains: T Addis III, USA; C Defoy, GB&I

USA   GB&I

First Day – **Foursomes**

G Fieger and B Zabriski (3 and 1)	1	B Rimmer and P Wesselingh	0
J Overton and J Lankford (2 and 1)	1	P Simpson and M Jones	0
D Kestner and B Guas (2 and 1)	1	A George and S Bennett	0
R McDougal and M Burke Jr	½	R Weir and J Greaves	½
	3½		½

Fourball

G Fieger and B Zabriski (5 and 4)	1	B Rimmer and P Wesselingh	0
J Overton and J Lankford (1 hole)	1	P Simpson and M Jones	0
C Tucker and M Mielke	0	A George and S Bennett (3 and 2)	1
D Kestner and M Burke Jr (3 and 2)	1	J Greaves and K Dickens	0
	3		1

Match position: USA 6½, GB&I 1½

Second Day – **Foursomes**

G Fieger and B Zabriski (1 hole)	1	A George and S Bennett	0
D Kestner and R McDougal (4 and 2)	1	R Weir and J Greaves	0
B Guas and C Tucker (2 and 1)	1	B Rimmer and M Macara	0
M Burke Jr and M Mielke (2 and 1)	1	P Simpson and M Jones	0
	4		0

Fourball

J Overton and J Lankford	0	K Dickens and P Wesselingh (3 and 2)	1
G Fieger and D Kestner	0	R Weir and J Greaves (3 and 1)	1
B Guas and C Tucker (3 and 1)	1	A George and S Bennett	0
R McDougal and M Mielke	0	P Simpson and B Rimmer (3 and 2)	1
	1		3

Match position: USA 11½, GB&I 4½

continued

1998 PGA Cup continued

Third Day – Singles

G Fieger	0	R Weir (1 hole)	1
B Zabriski	0	S Bennett (5 and 3)	1
C Tucker (2 holes)	1	J Greaves	0
J Overton	½	P Simpson	½
B Guas	½	P Wesselingh	½
J Lankford	0	B Rimmer (2 and 1)	1
M Burke Jr (2 and 1)	1	A George	0
R McDougal	½	R Dickens	½
D Kestner (1 hole)	1	M Jones	0
M Mielke (4 and 3)	1	M Macara	0
	5½		4½

Result: USA 17, GB&I 9

President's Cup (Instituted 1994)

Year	Winner	Venue	Result
1994	USA	Lake Manassas, Virginia	20–12
1996	USA	Lake Manassas, Virginia	16½–15½

1998 at Royal Melbourne, Australia

Non-playing captains: Peter Thomson, International Team; Jack Nicklaus, USA

International Team   **USA**

First Day – Fourball

G Norman and S Elkington (2 and 1)	1	M O'Meara and J Furyk	0
S Maruyama and J Ozaki (4 and 3)	1	M Calcavecchia and J Huston	0
E Els and N Price	½	D Duval and P Mickelson	½
C Parry and C Franco	0	F Couples and D Love III (1 hole)	1
S Appleby and V Singh (2 and 1)	1	J Leonard and T Woods	0
	3½		1½

Foursomes

F Nobilo and G Turner (1 hole)	1	M O'Meara and D Duval	0
G Norman and S Elkington (2 holes)	1	J Furyk and J Huston	0
S Maruyama and C Parry (3 and 2)	1	L Janzen and S Hoch	0
E Els and V Singh	0	T Woods and F Couples (5 and 4)	1
S Appleby and N Price	½	D Love III and J Leonard	½
	3½		1½

Match position: International 7, USA 3

Second Day – Fourball

F Nobilo and G Turner	0	M O'Meara and S Hoch (1 hole)	1
E Els and V Singh (1 hole)	1	T Woods and J Huston	0
S Maruyama and J Ozaki (3 and 2)	1	D Duval and P Mickelson	0
N Price and C Franco	0	L Janzen and M Calcavecchia (3 and 2)	1
G Norman and S Elkington (2 and 1)	1	F Couples and D Love III	0
	3		2

Foursomes

F Nobilo and G Turner (2 holes)	1	D Love III and J Leonard	0
G Norman and S Elkington	½	L Janzen and M Calcavecchia	½
S Maruyama and C Parry (1 hole)	1	T Woods and F Couples	0
S Appleby and N Price (1 hole)	1	D Duval and P Mickelson	0
E Els and V Singh (6 and 4)	1	S Hoch and J Furyk	0
	4½		½

Match position: International 14½, USA 5½

Third Day – Singles

C Parry (5 and 3)	1	J Leonard	0
N Price (2 and 1)	1	D Duval	0
F Nobilo	0	J Furyk (4 and 2)	1
C Franco	½	P Mickelson	½
S Maruyama (3 and 2)	1	J Huston	0
J Ozaki	0	S Hoch (4 and 3)	1
G Turner	½	M Calcavecchia	½
S Elkington	½	L Janzen	½
E Els (1 hole)	1	D Love III	0
V Singh	½	F Couples	½
G Norman	0	T Woods (1 hole)	1
S Appleby	0	M O'Meara (1 hole)	1
	6		6

Result: International Team 20½, USA 11½

World Cup of Golf (Known as the Canada Cup until 1966)

Year	Winner	Runners-up	Venue	Score
1953	Argentina	Canada	Montreal	287
	(A Cerda and R De Vincenzo)	(S Leonard and B Kerr)		
	(Individual: A Cerda, Argentina, 140)			
1954	Australia	Argentina	Laval-Sur-Lac	556
	(P Thomson and K Nagle)	(A Cerda and R De Vincenzo)		
1955	United States	Australia	Washington	560
	(C Harbert and E Furgol)	(P Thomson and K Nagle)		
	(Individual: E Furgol, USA, after a play-off with P Thomson and F van Donck, 279)			
1956	United States	South Africa	Wentworth	567
	(B Hogan and S Snead)	(A Locke and G Player)		
	(Individual: B Hogan, USA, 277)			
1957	Japan	United States	Tokyo	557
	(T Nakamura and K Ono)	(S Snead and J Demaret)		
	(Individual: T Nakamura, Japan, 274)			
1958	Ireland	Spain	Mexico City	579
	(H Bradshaw and C O'Connor)	(A Miguel and S Miguel)		
	(Individual: A Miguel, Spain, after a play-off with H Bradshaw, 286)			
1959	Australia	United States	Melbourne	563
	(P Thomson and K Nagle)	(S Snead and C Middlecoff)		
	(Individual: S Leonard, Canada, 275, after a tie with P Thomson, Australia)			
1960	United States	England	Portmarnock	565
	(S Snead and A Palmer)	(H Weetman and B Hunt)		
	(Individual: F van Donck, Belgium, 279)			
1961	United States	Australia	Puerto Rico	560
	(S Snead and J Demaret)	(P Thomson and K Nagle)		
	(Individual: S Snead, USA, 272)			
1962	United States	Argentina	Buenos Aires	557
	(S Snead and A Palmer)	(F de Luca and R De Vicenzo)		
	(Individual: R De Vincenzo, Argentina, 276)			
1963	United States	Spain	St Nom-La-Bretèche	482
	(A Palmer and J Nicklaus)	(S Miguel and R Sota)		
	(Individual: J Nicklaus, USA, 237 [63 holes])			

continued

World Cup of Golf *continued*

Year	Winner	Runners-up	Venue	Score
1964	United States (A Palmer and J Nicklaus) (Individual: J Nicklaus, USA, 276)	Argentina (R De Vicenzo and L Ruiz)	Maui, Hawaii	554
1965	South Africa (G Player and H Henning) (Individual: G Player, South Africa, 281)	Spain (A Miguel and R Sota)	Madrid	571
1966	United States (J Nicklaus and A Palmer) (Individual: G Knudson, Canada, and H Sugimoto, Japan, each 272; Knudson won play-off)	South Africa (G Player and H Henning)	Tokyo	548
1967	United States (J Nicklaus and A Palmer) (Individual: A Palmer, USA, 276)	New Zealand (R Charles and W Godfrey)	Mexico City	557
1968	Canada (A Balding and G Knudson) (Individual: A Balding, Canada, 274)	United States (J Boros and L Trevino)	Olgiata, Rome	569
1969	United States (O Moody and L Trevino) (Individual: L Trevino, USA, 275)	Japan (T Kono and H Yasuda)	Singapore	552
1970	Australia (B Devlin and D Graham) (Individual: R De Vicenzo, Argentina, 269)	Argentina (R De Vicenzo and V Fernandez)	Buenos Aires	545
1971	United States (J Nicklaus and L Trevino) (Individual: J Nicklaus, USA, 271)	South Africa (H Henning and G Player)	Palm Beach, Florida	555
1972	Taiwan (H Min-Nan and LL Huan) (Individual: H Min-Nan, Taiwan, 217 [3 rounds only])	Japan (T Kono and T Murakami)	Melbourne	438
1973	United States (J Nicklaus and J Miller) (Individual: J Miller, USA, 277)	South Africa (G Player and H Baiocchi)	Marbella, Spain	558
1974	South Africa (R Cole and D Hayes) (Individual: R Cole, South Africa, 271)	Japan (I Aoki and M Ozaki)	Caracas	554
1975	United States (J Miller and L Graham) (Individual: J Miller, USA, 275)	Taiwan (H Min-Nan and KC Hsiung)	Bangkok	554
1976	Spain (S Ballesteros and M Pinero) (Individual: EP Acosta, Mexico, 282)	United States (J Pate and D Stockton)	Palm Springs	574
1977	Spain (S Ballesteros and A Garrido) (Individual: G Player, South Africa, 289)	Philippines (R Lavares and B Arda)	Manilla, Philippines	591
1978	United States (J Mahaffey and A North) (Individual: J Mahaffey, USA, 281)	Australia (G Norman and W Grady)	Hawaii	564
1979	United States (J Mahaffey and H Irwin) (Individual: H Irwin, USA, 285)	Scotland (A Lyle and K Brown)	Glyfada, Greece	575
1980	Canada (D Halldorson and J Nelford) (Individual: A Lyle, Scotland, 282)	Scotland (A Lyle and S Martin)	Bogota	572
1981	*Not played*			
1982	Spain (M Pinero and JM Canizares) (Individual: M Pinero, Spain, 281)	United States (B Gilder and B Clampett)	Acapulco	563
1983	United States (R Caldwell and J Cook) (Individual: D Barr, Canada, 276)	Canada (D Barr and J Anderson)	Pondok Inah, Jakarta	565
1984	Spain (JM Canizares and J Rivero) (Individual: JM Canizares, Spain, 205. Played over 54 holes due to storm)	Scotland (S Torrance and G Brand, Jr)	Olgiata, Rome	414
1985	Canada (D Halidorson and D Barr) (Individual: H Clark, England, 272)	England (H Clark and P Way)	La Quinta, Calif.	559
1986	*Not played*			
1987	Wales (won play-off) (I Woosnam and D Llewelyn) (Individual: I Woosnam, Wales, 274)	Scotland (S Torrance and A Lyle)	Kapalua, Hawaii	574
1988	United States (B Crenshaw and M McCumber) (Individual: B Crenshaw, USA, 275)	Japan (T Ozaki and M Ozaki)	Royal Melbourne, Australia	560

Year	Winner	Runners-up	Venue	Score
1989	Australia (P Fowler and W Grady) (Individual: P Fowler. Played over 36 holes due to storms.)	Spain (JM Olazábal and JM Canizares)	Las Brisas, Spain	
1990	Germany (B Langer and T Giedeon) (Individual: P Stewart, USA, 271)	T England (M James and R Boxall) Ireland (R Rafferty and D Feherty)	Grand Cypress Resort, Orlando, Florida	556
1991	Sweden (A Forsbrand and P-U Johansson) (Individual: I Woosnam, Wales, 273)	Wales (I Woosnam and P Price)	La Querce, Rome	563
1992	USA (F Couples and D Love III) (Individual: B Ogle, Australia, 270 after a tie with I Woosnam, Wales)	Sweden (A Forsbrand and P-U Johansson)	La Moraleja II, Madrid, Spain	548
1993	USA (F Couples and D Love III) (Individual: B Langer, Germany, 272)	Zimbabwe (N Price and M McNulty)	Lake Nona, Orlando, FL	556
1994	USA (F Couples and D Love III) (Individual: F Couples, USA, 265)	Zimbabwe (M McNulty and T Johnstone)	Dorado Beach, Puerto Rico	536
1995	USA (F Couples and D Love III) (Individual: D Love III, USA, 267)	Australia (B Ogle and R Allenby)	Mission Hills, Shenzhen, China	543
1996	South Africa (E Els and W Westner) (Individual: E Els, S. Africa, 272)	USA (T Lehman and S Jones)	Erinvale, Cape Town South Africa	547
1997	Ireland (P Harrington and P McGinley) (Individual: C Montgomerie, Scotland, 266)	Scotland (C Montgomerie and R Russell)	Kiawah Island, SC	545

1998 – The 44th World Cup of Golf
at Gulf Harbour, Auckland, New Zealand (6876 yds, Par 72) Prize money: $1,500,000

1	ENGLAND (568)		
	David Carter	73-71-76-68—288	
	Nick Faldo	68-70-73-69—280	$200000 each
2	ITALY (570)		
	Costantino Rocca	65-74-71-70—280	
	Massimo Florioli	74-77-71-68—290	$100000 each
3	USA (571)		
	John Daly	70-77-77-68—292	
	Scott Verplank	70-72-74-63—279	$50833 each
	SCOTLAND (571)		
	Colin Montgomerie	72-69-75-68—284	
	Andrew Coltart	70-74-77-66—287	$50833 each
	ARGENTINA (571)		
	Angel Cabrera	69-71-71-73—284	
	Ricardo Gonzalez	73-74-72-68—287	$50833 each

International Trophy (Individual leading scores)

1	Scott Verplank (US)	279	$100000
2	Costantino Rocca (It)	280	37500
	Nick Faldo (Eng)	280	37500

Alfred Dunhill Cup (Instituted 1985 *at St Andrews*)

Year	Winner	Runner-up	Score
1985	Australia	USA	3–0
	(G Norman, G Marsh, D Graham)	(M O'Meara, R Floyd, C Strange)	
1986	Australia	Japan	3–0
	(R Davis, D Graham, G Norman)	(T Ozaki, N Ozaki, T Nakajima)	
1987	England	Scotland	2–1
	(N Faldo, G Brand, H Clark)	(S Lyle, S Torrance, G Brand Jr)	
1988	Ireland	Australia	2–1
	(D Smyth, R Rafferty, E Darcy)	(R Davis, D Graham, G Norman)	
1989	USA	Japan	3½–2½
	(M Calcavecchia, T Kite, C Strange)	(H Meshiai, N Ozaki, K Suzuki)	
1990	Ireland	England	3½–2½
	(P Walton, R Rafferty, D Feherty)	(M James, R Boxall, H Clark)	
1991	Sweden	South Africa	2–1
	(A Forsbrand, P-U Johansson, M Lanner)	(J Bland, D Frost, G Player)	
1992	England	Scotland	2–0
	(S Richardson, J Spence, D Gilford)	(G Brand Jr, C Montgomerie, S Lyle)	
1993	USA	England	2–1
	(P Stewart, F Couples, J Daly)	(M James, N Faldo, P Baker)	
1994	Canada	USA	2–1
	(D Barr, R Gibson, R Stewart)	(T Kite, C Strange, F Couples)	
1995	Scotland	Zimbabwe	2–1
	(A Coltart, C Montgomerie, S Torrance)	(T Johnstone, M McNulty, N Price)	
1996	USA	New Zealand	2–1
	(M O'Meara, P Mickelson, S Stricker)	(F Nobilo, G Turner, G Waite)	
1997	South Africa	Sweden	2–1
	(R Goosen, D Frost, E Els)	(J Parnevik, P-U Johansson, J Haeggman)	

1998 *at The Old Course, St Andrews, Fife*

Group 1
Sweden beat Japan	3–0
USA beat England	3–0
USA beat Japan	3–0
Sweden beat England	3–0
USA beat Sweden	2–0
England beat Japan	3–0

Group 2
Scotland beat China	2–1
Spain beat Ireland	2–1
Spain beat China	2–1
Scotland beat Ireland	2–1
Spain beat Scotland	2–1
Ireland beat China	3–0

Group 3
New Zealand lost to Korea	1–2
Australia beat Argentina	3–0
New Zealand beat Argentina	2–1
Australia beat Korea	3–0
Argentina beat Korea	2–1
Australia lost to New Zealand	1–2

Group 4
South Africa beat France	3–0
Zimbabwe beat Germany	3–0
Zimbabwe lost to France	1–2
South Africa lost to Germany	1–2
Germany beat France	2–1
Zimbabwe lost to South Africa	1–2

Semi-Finals

Spain beat USA 2–1
  MA Jimenez (75) lost to J Daly (73)
  S Luna (71) beat T Woods (72)
  JM Olazábal (72) beat M O'Meara (76)

South Africa beat Australia 2–1
  D Frost (72) beat C Parry (78)
  R Goosen (71) beat S Appleby (74)
  E Els (73) lost to S Elkington (72)

Final

South Africa beat Spain 3–0
  R Goosen (72) beat S Luna (73)
  D Frost (76) beat MA Jimenez (78)
  E Els beat (75) JM Olazábal (77)

British National and Regional Championships

NATIONAL CHAMPIONSHIPS

PGA Assistants' Championship

Year	Winner	Venue	Score	Year	Winner	Venue	Score
1984	G Weir	Coombe Hill	286	1991	S Wood	Wentworth	288
1985	G Coles	Coombe Hill	284	1992	P Mayo	E Sussex National	285
1986	J Brennand	Sand Moor	280	1993	C Everett	Oaklands	280
1987	J Hawksworth	Coombe Hill	282	1994	M Plummer	Burnham & Berrow	278
1988	J Oates	Coventry	284	1995	I Sparkes	The Warwickshire	285
1989	C Brooks	Hillside	291	1996	S Purves	Moor Allerton	281
1990	A Ashton	Hillside	213 (54)	1997	P Sefton	De Vere, Blackpool	273

1998 *at Bearwood Lakes*
1. Andrew Raitt 280
2. Simon Khan 281
3. Ian Harrison 283

PGA Seniors' Championship

Year	Winner	Venue	Score	Year	Winner	Venue	Score
1970	M Faulkner	Longniddry	288	1984	E Jones	Stratford-upon-Avon	280
1971	K Nagle	Elie	269	1985	N Coles	Pannal, Harrogate	284
1972	K Bousfield	Longniddry	291	1986	N Coles	Mere, Cheshire	276
1973	K Nagle	Elie	270	1987	N Coles	Turnberry	279
1974	E Lester	Lundin	282	1988	P Thomson	North Berwick	287
1975	K Nagle	Longniddry	268	1989	N Coles	West Hill	277
1976	C O'Connor	Cambridgeshire Hotel	284	1990	B Waites	Brough	269
1977	C O'Connor	Cambridgeshire Hotel	288	1991	B Waites	Wollaton Park	277
1978	P Skerritt	Cambridgeshire Hotel	288	1992	T Horton	R Dublin	290
1979	C O'Connor	Cambridgeshire Hotel	280	1993	B Huggett	Sunningdale	204 *(54 holes)*
1980	P Skerritt	Gleneagles Hotel	286	1994	J Morgan	Sunningdale	203
1981	C O'Connor	North Berwick	287	1995	J Morgan	Sunningdale	204
1982	C O'Connor	Longniddry	285	1996	T Gale	The Belfry	284
1983	C O'Connor	Burnham and Berrow	277	1997	W Hall	The Belfry	277

1998 *at PGA National, The Belfry, Sutton Coldfield*
1. Tommy Horton 277
2. Jim Rhodes 279
   Renato Campagnoli 279

Club Professionals' Championship

Year	Winner	Venue	Score	Year	Winner	Venue	Score
1973	DN Sewell	Calcot Park	276	1978	D Jones	Pannal	281
1974	WB Murray	Calcot Park	275	1979	D Jones	Pannal	278
1975	DN Sewell	Calcot Park	276	1980	D Jagger	Turnberry	286
1976	WJ Ferguson	Moortown	283	1981	M Steadman	Woburn	289
1977	D Huish	Notts	284	1982	D Durnian	Hill Valley	285

Club Professionals' Championship *continued*

Year	Winner	Venue	Score	Year	Winner	Venue	Score
1983	J Farmer	Heaton Park	270	1991	W McGill	King's Lynn	285
1984	D Durnian	Bolton Old Links	278	1992	J Hoskison	St Pierre	275
1985	R Mann	The Belfry	291	1993	C Hall	Coventry	274
1986	D Huish	R Birkdale	278	1994	D Jones	North Berwick	278
1987	R Weir	Sandiway	273	1995	P Carman	West Hill	269
1988	R Weir	Harlech	269	1996	B Longmuir	Co Louth	280
1989	B Barnes	Sandwich, Prince's	280	1997	B Rimmer	Northop	268
1990	A Webster	Carnoustie	292				

1998 *at Royal St David's*

1	Michael Jones	280
2	Paul Simpson	281
	Michael Macara	281

Irish PGA Championship

Year	Winner	Venue	Score	Year	Winner	Venue	Score
1960	C O'Connor	Warrenpoint	271	1979	D Smyth	Dollymount	215 (54)
1961	C O'Connor	Lahinch	280	1980	D Feherty	Dollymount	283
1962	C O'Connor	Bangor	264	1981	D Jones	Woodbrook	283
1963	C O'Connor	Little Island	271	1982	D Feherty	Woodbrook	287
1964	E Jones	Knock	279	1983	L Higgins	Woodbrook	275
1965	C O'Connor	Mullingar	283	1984	M Sludds	Skerries	277
1966	C O'Connor	Warrenpoint	269	1985	D Smyth	Co Louth	204 (54)
1967	H Boyle	Tullamore	214 (54)	1986	D Smyth	Waterville	282
1968	C Greene	Knock	282	1987	P Walton	Co Louth	144 (36)
1969	J Martin	Dundalk	268	1988	E Darcy	Castle, Dublin	269
1970	H Jackson	Massareene	283	1989	P Walton	Castle, Dublin	266
1971	C O'Connor	Galway	278	1990	D Smyth	Woodbrook	271
1972	J Kinsella	Bundoran	289	1991	P Walton	Woodbrook	277
1973	J Kinsella	Limerick	284	1992	E Darcy	K Club	285
1974	E Polland	Portstewart	277	1993	M Sludds	K Club	285
1975	C O'Connor	Carlow	275	1994	D Clarke	Galway Bay	285
1976	P McGuirk	Waterville	291	1995	P Walton	Belvoir Park	273
1977	P Skerritt	Woodbrook	281	1996	D Smyth	Slieve Russell GC	281
1978	C O'Connor	Dollymount	286	1997	P McGinley	Fota Island	285

1998 *at Powerscourt GC* (54 holes due to bad weather)

1	P Harrington*	216
2	M Bannon	216
	D Smyth	216
	F Howley	216

Irish Club Professionals' Championship

Year	Winner	Venue	Score
1993	D Mooney	Royal Tara	208
1994	K O'Donnell	Knockanally	216
1995	D Jones	Fota Island	145
1996	B McGovern	Headfort	140
1997	N Manchip	Mount Wolseley	141

1998 *at Nuremore Hotel G&GC*

1	L Robinson	140
2	D Walker	142
	D Mooney	142
	B McGovern	142
	M Allan	142
	J Langan	142

* *Winner after play-off*

Scottish Assistants' Championship

Year	Winner	Venue	Score	Year	Winner	Venue	Score
1980	F Mann	Dunbar	294	1990	P Lawrie	Cruden Bay	279
1981	M Brown	West Kilbride	290	1991	G Hume	Kilmarnock Barassie	299
1982	R Collinson	West Kilbride	294	1992	E McIntosh	Turnberry Hotel	266
1983	A Webster	Stirling	285	1993	J Wither	Alloa	280
1984	C Elliott	Stirling	285	1994	S Henderson	Newmacher	283
1985	C Elliott	Falkirk Tryst	284	1995	A Tait	Newmacher	276
1986	P Helsby	Erskine	295	1996	S Thompson	Newmacher	278
1987	C Innes	Hilton Park	284	1997	M Hastie	Balbirnie Park	275
1988	G Collinson	Turnberry	289				
1989	C Brooks	Windyhill	282				

1998 at Balbirnie Park, Markinch
1. D Orr — 272
2. D Drysdale — 277
3. F Cromarty — 278

Scottish PGA Matchplay Championship

Year	Winner	Venue	Year	Winner	Venue
1990	J Chillas	North Berwick	1995	S Thompson	Glasgow Gailes
1991	I Young	North Berwick	1996	A Taitt	Gleneagles
1992	*Not played*		1997	D Thompson	Turnberry
1993	*Not played*		1998	*Not played*	
1994	*Not played*				

Scottish Professionals' Championship

Year	Winner	Venue	Score	Year	Winner	Venue	Score
1965	EC Brown	Forfar	271	1981	B Barnes	Dalmahoy	275
1966T	EC Brown	Cruden Bay	137 (36)	1982	B Barnes	Dalmahoy	286
	J Panton			1983	B Gallacher	Dalmahoy	276
1967	H Bannerman	Montrose	279	1984	I Young	Dalmahoy	276
1968	EC Brown	Monktonhall	286	1985	S Torrance	Dalmahoy	277
1969	G Cunningham	Machrihanish	284	1986	R Drummond	Glenbervie	270
1970	RDBM Shade	Montrose	276	1987	R Drummond	Glenbervie	268
1971	NJ Gallacher	Lundin Links	282	1988	S Stephen	Haggs Castle	283
1972	H Bannerman	Strathaven	268	1989	R Drummond	Monktonhall	274
1973	BJ Gallacher	Kings Links	276	1990	R Drummond	Deer Park	278
1974	BJ Gallacher	Drumpellier	276	1991	S Torrance	Erskine	274
1975	D Huish	Duddingston	279	1992	P Lawrie	Cardross	273
1976	J Chillas	Haggs Castle	286	1993	S Torrance	Dalmahoy	269
1977	BJ Gallacher	Barnton	282	1994	A Coltart	Dalmahoy	281
1978	S Torrance	Strathaven	269	1995	C Gillies	Dalmahoy	278
1979	AWB Lyle	Glasgow Gailes	274	1996	B Marchbank	Dalmahoy	276
1980	S Torrance	East Kilbride	273	1997	G Law	Downfield	284

1998 at Newmacher GC
1. C Gillies — 273
2. A Tait — 275
3. B Marchbank — 276
   S McGregor — 276
   A Raitt — 276

Welsh Professionals' Championship

Year	Winner	Venue	Score	Year	Winner	Venue	Score
1960	RH Kemp, Jr	Llandudno	288	1979	*Cancelled*		
1961	S Mouland	Southerndown	286	1980	A Griffiths	Cardiff	139
1962	S Mouland	Porthcawl	302	1981	C DeFoy	Cardiff	139
1963	H Gould	Wrexham	291	1982	C DeFoy	Cardiff	137
1964	B Bielby	Tenby	297	1983	S Cox	Cardiff	136
1965	S Mouland	Penarth	281	1984	K Jones	Cardiff	135
1966	S Mouland	Conway	281	1985	D Llewellyn	Whitchurch	132
1967	S Mouland	Pyle and Kenfig	219 (54)	1986	P Parkin	Whitchurch	142
1968	RJ Davies	Southerndown	292	1987	A Dodman	Cardiff	132
1969	S Mouland	Llandudno	277	1988	I Woosnam	Cardiff	137
1970	W Evans	Tredegar Park	289	1989	K Jones	Royal Porthcawl	140
1971	J Buckley	St Pierre	291	1990	P Mayo	Fairwood Park	136
1972	J Buckley	Porthcawl	298	1991	P Mayo	Fairwood Park	138
1973	A Griffiths	Newport	289	1992	C Evans	Asburnham	142
1974	M Hughes	Cardiff	284	1993	P Price	Caerphilly	138
1975	C DeFoy	Whitchurch	285	1994	M Plummer	Northop	133
1976	S Cox	Radyr	284	1995	S Dodd	Northop	139
1977	C DeFoy	Glamorganshire	135	1996	M Stanford	Northop	137
1978	BCC Huggett	Whitchurch	145	1997	M Ellis	Vale of Glamorgan	139

1998 at *Vale of Glamorgan*

1	L Bond	69
2	R Dinsdale	70
3	S Bebb	71

REGIONAL CHAMPIONSHIPS

Derbyhire Professionals'

Year	Winner	Year	Winner
1989	N Hallam	1994	D Stafford
1990	M Deeley	1995	A Carnall
1991	W Bird	1996	C Cross
1992	J Proctor	1997	A Carnall
1993	K Cross	1998	J Mellor

Devon Open

Year	Winner	Year	Winner
1989	D Sheppard	1994	I Higgins
1990	G Tomkinson	1995	B Austin
1991	R Troake	1996	J Langmead
1992	R Troake	1997	J Langmead
1993T	D Sheppard	1998	D Sheppard
	T McSherry		

East Anglian Open

Year	Winner	Year	Winner
1989	R Mitchell	1994	R Mann
1990	N Wichelow	1995	N Brown
1991	M Mackenzie	1996	N Brown
1992	L Fickling	1997	I Poulter
1993	A George	1998	P Curry

East Region PGA

Year	Winner
1995	L Fickling
1996	T Charnley
1997	R Mann
1998	T Charnley

Essex Open

Year	Winner	Year	Winner
1989	H Flatman	1994	D Jones
1990	G Burrows	1995	J Robson
1991	R Joyce	1996	S Khan
1992	C Platts	1997	V Cox
1993	A Blackburn	1998	J Robson

Essex Professionals'

Year	Winner	Year	Winner
1989	C Williams	1994	V Cox
1990	C Cox	1995	M Stokes
1991	S Cipa	1996	P Joiner
1992	P Barham	1997	M Stokes
1993	T Wheals	1998	G Carter

Glasgow Matchplay

Year	Winner	Year	Winner
1989	L McLaughlin	1994	C Kelly
1990	C Barrowman	1995	C Kelly
1991	C Barrowman	1996	M Loftus
1992	C Barrowman	1997	G Lamond
1993	M Pairman	1998	I Mackie

Glasgow Strokeplay

Year	Winner	Year	Winner
1989	G Shaw	1994	G Crawford
1990	H Kemp	1995	D Lamond
1991	C Barrowman	1996	A Forsyth
1992	G Crawford	1997	J Finnigan
1993	CE Watson	1998	M Loftus

Hampshire PGA

Year	Winner	Year	Winner
1989	J Coles	1994	G Hughes
1990	S Watson	1995	I Benson
1991	J Hay	1996	R Bland
1992	I Benson	1997	J Lovell
1993	R Edwards	1998	G Hughes

Hampshire Matchplay

Year	Winner	Year	Winner
1989	I Young	1994	M Wheeler
1990	K Bowden	1995	M Wheeler
1991	S Ward	1996	J Le Roux
1992	J Hay	1997	D Harris
1993	K Saunders	1998	D Harris

Hampshire, Isle of Wight and Channel Islands Open

Year	Winner	Year	Winner
1989	J Coles	1994	R Bland
1990	R Watkins	1995	R Bland
1991	R Adams	1996	G Hughes
1992	I Benson	1997	M Blackey
1993	R Bland	1998	R Bland

Herts Professionals'

Year	Winner	Year	Winner
1989	N Lawrence	1995	N Brown
1990	N Brown	1996	R Hurd
1991	L Jones	1997	P Winston
1992	P Cherry	1998T	R Mitchell
1993	L Jones		I Parker
1994T	N Brown		
	D Tapping		

Kent Open

Year	Winner	Year	Winner
1989	R Cameron	1994	T Berry
1990	S Barr	1995	T Milford
1991	S Wood	1996	S Green
1992	S Barr	1997	S Page
1993	N Haynes	1998	D Parris

Kent Professionals'

Year	Winner	Year	Winner
1989	P Lyons	1994	M Lawrence
1990	R Cameron	1995	T Poole
1991	R Cameron	1996	A Butterfield
1992	M Lawrence	1997	P Lyons
1993	R Cameron	1998	T Milford

Lancashire Open

Year	Winner	Year	Winner
1989	M Jones	1994	A Lancaster
1990	P Allan	1995	G Furey
1991	G Furey	1996	G Furey
1992	S Townend	1997	G Furey
1993	L Edwards	1998	J Cheetham

Leicestershire and Rutland Open

Year	Winner	Year	Winner
1989	R Adams	1994	J Herbert
1990	R Larratt	1995	I Lyner
1991	CM Harries	1996	D Gibson
1992	Not played	1997	N Bland
1993	P Frith	1998	J Caylis (Am)

Lincolnshire Open

Year	Winner	Year	Winner
1989	A Hare	1994	S Brewer
1990	A Butler (Am)	1995	S Cox
1991	J Payne (Am)	1996	S Bennett
1992	P Streeter (Am)	1997	M King
1993	S Bennett	1998	M King

Middlesex Open

Year	Winner	Year	Winner
1989	L Fickling	1994	N Wichelow
1990	R Willison (Am)	1995	N Wichelow
1991	R Willison (Am)	1996	C Austin (Am)
1992	GA Homewood	1997	L Fickling
1993	GA Homewood	1998	T Sheaff

Midland Masters

Year	Winner	Year	Winner
1989	C Haycock	1994	C Hall
1990	J King	1995	J Higgins
1991	S Rose	1996	Not played
1992	C Hall	1997	Not played
1993	Not played	1998	Not played

Midland Professionals' Matchplay

Year	Winner	Year	Winner
1989	K Hayward	1994	N Turley
1990	G Farr	1995	D Eddiford
1991	B Waites	1996	S Bennett
1992	J Higgins	1997	J Higgins
1993	C Clark	1998	J Robinson

Midland Professionals' Strokeplay

Year	Winner	Year	Winner
1989	J Higgins	1994	P Baker
1990	G Stafford	1995	S Rose
1991	K Dickens	1996	DJ Russell
1992	J Higgins	1997	J Higgins
1993	P Baker	1998	S Webster

Midland Seniors'

Year	Winner	Year	Winner
1989	RG Hiatt	1995	T Squires
1990	A Harrison	1996	JC Thomas
1991	DS Kirkland	1997T	EW Hammond
1992	A Guest		C Moir
1993	J Humphries		MA Smith
1994	G Pope	1998	I Clark

Norfolk Open

Year	Winner	Year	Winner
1989	M Few	1994	J Hill
1990	A Brydon	1995	M Barrett
1991	I Hardy	1996	M Barrett
1992	C Green	1997	N Lythgoe
1993	A Collison	1998	R Wilson

Norfolk Professionals'

Year	Winner	Year	Winner
1989	M Few	1994	A Collison
1990	M Few	1995	P Briggs
1991	A Collison	1996	P Bower
1992	A Collison	1997	T Varney
1993	A Collison	1998	R Wilson

Northern Region PGA

Year	Winner	Year	Winner
1989	S Bottomley	1994	P Wesselingh
1990	J Morgan	1995	G Furey
1991	H Selby-Green	1996	S Townend
1992	P Cowen	1997	G Furey
1993	C Smiley	1998	P Carman

Northern Open

Year	Winner	Year	Winner
1989	C Brooks	1994	K Stables
1990	C Brooks	1995	J Higgins
1991	C Cassells	1996	S Henderson
1992	P Smith	1997	D Thomson
1993	K Stables	1998	L James

Nottinghamshire Open

Year	Winner	Year	Winner
1989	P Hinton	1994	J King
1990	C Hall	1995	J King
1991	C Jepson	1996	D McJannet
1992	J King	1997	R Ellis
1993	J King	1998	P Wheatcroft

South of Scotland

Year	Winner	Year	Winner
1989	V Reid	1994	I Reid
1990	B Kerr	1995	B Scott
1991	J Power	1996	E Little
1992	J Wright	1997	I Brotherston
1993	D Wallis	1998	Not played

South West PGA

Year	Winner	Year	Winner
1994	G Emerson	1997	M Stanford
1995	G Howell	1998	S Little
1996	M Stanford		

Southern Assistants'

Year	Winner	Year	Winner
1989	J Sewell	1994	M Wheeler
1990	Not played	1995	P Lyons
1991	G Orr	1996	D Parris
1992	G Orr	1997	A Lovelace
1993	R Edwards	1998	D Parris

Southern Assistants' Matchplay

Year	Winner	Year	Winner
1989	Not played	1994	M Groombridge
1990	G Orr	1995	M Groombridge
1991	I Roper	1996	A Butterfield
1992	G McQuitty	1997	B Hodkin
1993	N Gorman	1998	B Hodkin

Southern Professionals'

Year	Winner	Year	Winner
1989	W Grant	1994	R Edwards
1990	Not played	1995	P Sefton
1991	J Hoskison	1996	P Hughes
1992	J Hoskison	1997	P Sherman
1993	G Smith	1998	P Simpson

Staffordshire Open

Year	Winner	Year	Winner
1989	M Passmore	1994	D Scott
1990	J Rhodes	1995	I Proverbs
1991	M McGuire	1996	B Rimmer
1992	J Rhodes	1997	A Roger
1993	M McGuire	1998	R Peace

Staffordshire and Shropshire Strokeplay

Year	Winner	Year	Winner
1989	J Higgins	1994	J Rhodes
1990	G Farr	1995	B Stevens
1991	M Knight	1996	J Higgins
1992	S Russell	1997	R Fisher
1993	J Rhodes	1998	A Feriday

Suffolk Open

Year	Winner	Year	Winner
1989	M Elsworthy	1994	L Patterson
1990	S Crosby (Am)	1995	R Mann
1991	R Mann	1996	S McPherson
1992	R Mann	1997	P Wilby
1993	R Mann	1998	J Wright

Suffolk Professionals'

Year	Winner	Year	Winner
1989	S Whymark	1995	R Mann
1990	R Mann	1996	T Cooper
1991	K Golding	1997T	A Lucas
1992	R Mann		C Jenkins
1993	K Golding	1998	S MacPherson
1994	L Patterson		

Sunderland of Scotland Masters

Year	Winner	Year	Winner
1989	C Maltman	1994	R Weir
1990		1995	M Jones
1991	G Orr	1996	C Ronald
1992	K Walker	1997	L Vennet
1993	A Oldcorn	1998	M Miller*

Sussex Open

Year	Winner	Year	Winner
1989	M Groombridge (Am)	1994	K Hinton
		1995	J Blamires
1990	Not played	1996	K Macdonald
1991	J Pinsent	1997	K Macdonald
1992	P Harrison	1998	J Doherty (Am)
1993	N Burke		

Ulster Professionals'

Year	Winner	Year	Winner
1989	D Feherty	1994	P Russell
1990	J Heggarty	1995	R Burns
1991	D Carson	1996	J Heggarty
1992	D Clarke	1997	D Mooney
1993	D Jones	1998	D Mooney

Warwickshire Open

Year	Winner	Year	Winner
1989	A Allen (Am)	1994	D White
1990	M Biddle (Am)	1995	C Dowling
1991	A Allen (Am)	1996	P Chalkley
1992	P Chalkley	1997	D Barton
1993	A Bownes	1998	SJ Walker

Warwickshire Professionals' Matchplay

Year	Winner	Year	Winner
1989	T Rouse	1994	C Wicketts
1990	N McEwan	1995	J Cook
1991	D Quinn	1996	C Phillips
1992	C Harrison	1997	L Bashford
1993	A Bands	1998	Match postponed

Warwickshire Professionals' Strokeplay

Year	Winner	Year	Winner
1989	T Rouse	1994	S Webster (Am)
1990	N McEwan	1995	J Cook
1991	M Jennings	1996	S Edwards
1992	A Allen	1997	C Phillips
1993	G Marston	1998	J Corns*

*Winner after play-off

West Region PGA

Year	Winner	Year	Winner
1989	G Laing	1994	S Little
1990	P Price	1995	M Thompson
1991	S Dodd	1996	M McEwan
1992	M Thomas	1997	M Thompson
1993	P Mayo	1998	J Taylor

Worcestershire Strokeplay

Year	Winner	Year	Winner
1989	K Hayward	1994	C Clark
1990	K Hayward	1995	I Clark
1991	L Bashford	1996	F Clark
1992	R Cameron	1997	I Clark
1993	F Clark	1998	D Eddiford

Hills Wiltshire Pro Champ

Year	Winner	Year	Winner
1989	G Emerson	1994	S Robertson
1990	G Clough	1995	G Laing
1991	A Beal	1996	B Sandry
1992	G Emerson	1997	M Smith
1993T	G Emerson	1998	R Blake
	D Ray		

Yorkshire Professionals'

Year	Winner	Year	Winner
1989	D Stirling	1994	L Turner
1990	D Stirling	1995	R Golding
1991	S Elliott	1996	N Ludwell
1992	L Turner	1997	S Robinson
1993	A Nicholson	1998	G Brown

Worcestershire Open

Year	Winner	Year	Winner
1989	K Hayward	1994	S Edwards
1990	J Bickerton	1995	C Clark
1991	MC Reynard	1996	D Clee
1992	A Robinson	1997	P Scarrett
1993	P Scarrett	1998	D Eddiford*

* *Winner after play-off*

Overseas National Championships

(Excluding European Tour or Affiliated Events)

Argentine Open

Year	Winner	Year	Winner
1989	E Romero	1994	M O'Meara
1990	V Fernandez	1995	M Calcavecchia
1991	JD Blake	1996	P Martinez
1992	C Stadler	1997	J Furyk
1993	M Calcavecchia	1998	R Fretes

Australian Open

Year	Winner	Score
1978	J Nicklaus	284
1979	J Newton	288
1980	G Norman	284
1981	W Rogers	282
1982	B Shearer	287
1983	P Fowler	285
1984	T Watson	281
1985	G Norman	212 *(54 holes only – rain)*
1986	R Davis	278
1987	G Norman	273
1988	M Calcavecchia	269
1989	P Senior	271
1990	J Morse	283
1991	W Riley	285
1992	S Elkington	280
1993	B Faxon	275
1994	R Allenby	280
1995	G Norman	278
1996	G Norman	280
1997	L Westwood	274
1998	G Chalmers	288

Australian PGA

Year	Winner	Year	Winner
1989	P Senior	1994	A Coltart
1990	B Ogle	1995	*Not played*
1991	W Grady	1996	P Tataurangi
1992	C Parry	1997	A Coltart
1993	I Baker-Finch	1998	D Howell

Austrian Open

Year	Winner	Year	Winner
1990	B Langer	1995	A Cejka
1991	B Davis	1996	P McGinley
1992	P Mitchell	1997	E Simsek
1993	R Rafferty	1998	K Carissimi
1994	M Davis		

Canadian Open

Year	Winner	Year	Winner
1978	B Lietzke	1989	S Jones
1979	L Trevino	1990	W Levi
1980	B Gilder	1991	N Price
1981	P Oosterhuis	1992	G Norman
1982	B Lietzke	1993	D Frost
1983	J Cook	1994	N Price
1984	G Norman	1995	M O'Meara
1985	C Strange	1996	D Hart
1986	B Murphy	1997	S Jones
1987	C Strange	1998	B Andrade
1988	K Green		

Côte d'Ivoire Open

Year	Winner	Year	Winner
1991	D Llewellyn	1995	*Not played*
1992	M Bescanceny	1996	M Florioli
1993	*Not played*	1997	K Storegaard
1994	W Bradley	1998	J Mellor

German PGA

Year	Winner	Year	Winner
1989	T Giedeon	1994	S Yates
1990	S Strüver	1995	D O'Flynn
1991	T Giedeon	1996	E Simsek
1992	M Pyatt	1997	E Simsek
1993	W Linnenfelser	1998	F Lubenau

Hong Kong Open

Year	Winner	Year	Winner
1989	B Claar	1994	D Frost
1990	K Green	1995	G Webb
1991	B Langer	1996	G Webb
1992	T Watson	1997	F Nobilo
1993	B Watts	1998	WS Kang

India Open

Year	Winner	Year	Winner
1989	R Bouchard	1994	E Aubrey
1990	A Debusk	1995	J Rutledge
1991	A Sher	1996	H Shirakata
1992	S Ginn	1997	E Fryatt
1993	A Sher	1998	A Firoz

Malaysian Open

Year	Winner	Year	Winner
1989	J Maggert	1994	J Haeggman
1990	G Day	1995	C Devers
1991	R Gibson	1996	S Flesch
1992	V Singh	1997	L Westwood
1993	G Norquist	1998	E Fryatt

Italian Professionals'

Year	Winner	Year	Winner
1989	C Rocca	1994	G Cali
1990	M Mannelli	1995	E Bolognesi
1991	A Canessa	1996	L Gallardo
1992	M Reale	1997	M Florioli
1993	G Cali	1998	M Scarpa

Mauritius Open

Year	Winner
1994	M McLean
1995	M Santi
1996	P Golding
1997	G Sherry
1998	R Davis

Japan Open

Year	Winner	Year	Winner
1989	M Ozaki	1994	M Ozaki
1990	T Nakajima	1995	T Izwa
1991	T Nakajima	1996	P Teravainen
1992	M Ozaki	1997	C Parry
1993	S Okuda	1998	H Tanaka

Mexican Open

Year	Winner	Year	Winner
1993	T Sieckmann	1996	S Cink
1994	C Perry	1997	F Nobilo
1995	J Cook	1998	E Romero

Japan Professionals'

Year	Winner	Year	Winner
1989	M Ozaki	1994	H Goda
1990	H Kase	1995	H Sasaki
1991	O Masashi	1996	M Ozaki
1992	M Kuramoto	1997	S Maruyama
1993	M Ozaki	1998	B Jobe

New Zealand Open

Year	Winner	Year	Winner
1989	G Turner	1994	C Jones
1990	*Not played*	1995	L Parsons
1991	R Davis	1996	M Long
1992	G Waite	1997	G Turner
1993	P Fowler	1998	G Turner

Kenya Open

Year	Winner	Year	Winner
1989	D Jones	1994	P Carman
1990	C O'Connor Jr	1995	J Lee
1991	J Robinson	1996	M Miller
1992	A Bossert	1997	J Berendt
1993	C Maltman	1998	R Gonzalez

Nigerian Open

Year	Winner	Year	Winner
1989	V Singh	1994	E Korblah
1990	W Stephens	1995	L Lasisi
1991	J Lebbie	1996	*Not played*
1992	J Lebbie	1997	*Not played*
1993	G Manson	1998	*Not played*

Korea Open

Year	Winner	Year	Winner
1989	Chul Sang Cho	1994	M Cunning
1990	L Kang-Sun	1995	B Jobe
1991	Choi Sang Ho	1996	Choi Kyung-Ju
1992	T Hamilton	1997	K Jong-Duck
1993	Y Kun Han	1998	DS Kim (Am)

Singapore Open

Year	Winner	Year	Winner
1989	C-S Lu	1994	KH Han
1990	A Fernando	1995	S Conran
1991	J Kay	1996	J Kernohan
1992	B Israelson	1997	Z Moe
1993	P Maloney	1998	S Micheel

South African PGA

Year	Winner	Year	Winner
1989	A Johnstone	1994	D Frost
1990	F Allem	1995	E Els
1991	R Wessels	1996	S Struver
1992	E Els	1997	N Price
1993	M McNulty	1998	T Johnstone

Swedish Professionals'

Year	Winner	Year	Winner
1989	L Hederström	1994	A Mednick
1990	A Mednick	1995	D Edlund
1991	J Ryström	1996	M Anglert
1992	S Bottomley	1997	M Krantz
1993	N Fasth	1998	U Gustaffson

Swedish Open International Strokeplay

Year	Winner	Year	Winner
1989	A Gillner	1994	E Carlberg
1990	J Parnevik	1995	D Edlund
1991	J Sewell	1996	K Väinölä
1992	J Haeggman	1997	J Rask
1993	D Chopra	1998	J Ryström

Swedish Open *(Closed 1984–9)*

Year	Winner	Year	Winner
1989	M Grankvist	1994	P Nyman
1990	E O'Connell	1995	P Thorn
1991	M Gronberg	1996	A Mednick
1992	J Cantero	1997	R Sjöberg
1993	P Haugsrud	1998	K Carrissimi

Thailand Open

Year	Winner
1997	C Chernock
1998	J Kingston

Zambian Open

Year	Winner	Year	Winner
1989	C Maltman	1994	*Not played*
1990	GJ Brand	1995	*Not played*
1991	DR Jones	1996	D Botes
1992	J Robinson	1997	*Not played*
1993	P Harrison	1998	M Cayeux

Zimbabwe Open

Year	Winner	Year	Winner
1991	K Waters	1995	N Price
1992	M McNulty	1996	N Price
1993	*Not played*	1997	M McNulty
1994	C Williams	1998	H Alberts

PART III

Women's Professional Tournaments

Index on page 210

Index – Women's Professional Tournaments

Ping World Ranking for Women's Professional Golf, 1998 211

European LPGA Tour, 1998 212
  FINAL RANKING 212
  TOUR RESULTS 213
    Evian Masters 213
    Ladies' Austrian Open 213
    Chrysler Open 213
    Ladies' German Open 213
    McDonald's WPGA Championship of Europe 213
    Weetabix Women's British Open 213
    Compaq Open 214
    Donegal Ladies' Irish Open 214
    Air France Madame Opn 214
    Marrakesh Palmeraie Open 214
  TOUR QUALIFYING SCHOOL 214

US LPGA Tour, 1998 216
  FINAL RANKING 216
  TOUR RESULTS 217
    HealthSouth Inaugural 217
    The Office Depot Tournament 217
    Los Angeles Championship 217
    1998 Cup Noodles Hawaiian Ladies' Open 217
    Australian Ladies' Masters 217
    Welch's/Circle K Championship 217
    Standard Register Ping 218
    Nabisco Dinah Shore 218
    Longs Drugs Challenge 218
    City of Hope Myrtle Beach Classic 218
    Chick-Fil-A Charity Championship 218
    Mercury Titleholders Championship 218
    Sara Lee Classic 218
    McDonald's LPGA Championship 219
    LPGA Corning Classic 219
    Wegmans Rochester International 219
    Michelob Light Classic 219
    Oldsmobile Classic 219
    Friendly's Classic 219
    Shoprite LPGA Classic 219
    US Women's Open 220
    Jamie Farr Kroger Classic 220
    Jal Big Apple Classic 220
    Giant Eagle LPGA Classic 220
    Du Maurier Classic 220
    Starbank LPGA Classic 220
    Rainbow Foods LPGA Classic 220
    State Farm Rail Classic 221
    Safeway LPGA 221
    Safeco Classic 221
    First Union Betsy King Classic 221
    Aflac Tournament of Champions 221
    Samsung World Championship of Women's Golf 221
    Japan Classic 221
    PageNet Tour Championship 222
  TOUR QUALIFYING SCHOOL 222

Japan LPGA Tour, 1998 223
  FINAL RANKING 223
  TOUR RESULTS 223

International Team Events – Professional Women 225
  Solheim Cup 225
  Solheim Cup - Individual Records 228
  European Women v Senior Men 229

Professional Women's Overseas Championships 230

Ping Leaderboard – World Ranking for Women's Professional Golf, 1998

Pos	Name	Points	Pos	Name	Points
1	Annika Sorenstam	487.24	51	Michele Redman	55.92
2	Karrie Webb	337.28	52	Kris Tschetter	55.75
3	Laura Davies	250.95	53	Karen Lunn	55.38
4	Kelly Robbins	242.54	54	Jane Geddes	55.25
5	Donna Andrews	241.84	55	Mayumi Murai	54.10
6	Helen Alfredsson	231.52	56	Loraine Lambert	53.58
7	Juli Inkster	221.20	57	Carin Hj Koch	52.43
8	Liselotte Neumann	218.32	58	Deb Richard	51.71
9	Meg Mallon	191.87	59	Helen Dobson	51.18
10	Dottie Pepper	180.96	60	Gail Graham	50.53
11	Brandie Burton	178.97	61	Natsuko Noro	50.19
12	Pat Hurst	176.88	62	Marnie McGuire	49.77
13	Lorie Kane	173.07	63	Shani Waugh	49.75
14	Hiromi Kobayashi	172.95	64	Catriona Matthew	48.96
15	Chris Johnson	167.16	65	Patricia Meunier-Lebouc	48.80
16	Tammie Green	144.45	66	Yuri Fudoh	48.75
17	Se Ri Pak	138.79	67	Lora Fairclough	48.24
18	Rosie Jones	137.95	68	Pernilla Sterner	47.35
19	Lisa Hackney	125.96	69	Dawn Coe-Jones	46.45
20	Danielle Ammaccapane	116.32	70	Pearl Sinn	45.83
21	Akiko Fukushima	115.37	71	Nayoko Yoshikawa	45.42
22	Trish Johnson	114.85	72	Terry-Jo Myers	45.25
23	Sherri Steinhauer	114.18	73	Penny Hammel	44.66
24	Betsy King	114.12	74	Wendy Doolan	44.13
25	Sophie Gustafson	114.10	75	Fumiko Muraguchi	43.73
26	Alison Nicholas	112.33	76	Akemi Yamaoka	42.99
27	Ok-Hee Ku	111.07	77	Jenny Lidback	42.96
28	Kaori Harada	103.51	78	Kumiko Hiyoshi	42.69
29	Tina Barrett	100.79		Tracy Hanson	42.69
30	Michiko Hattori	92.16	80	Raquel Carriedo-Tomas	42.25
31	Nancy Lopez	90.84	81	Aki Takamura	41.67
32	Barb Mucha	89.51	82	Joanne Morley	41.50
33	Michelle McGann	88.42	83	Aiko Takasu	40.50
34	Cindy Figg-Currier	86.52	84	Young-Me Lee	40.00
35	Charlotta Sorenstam	84.20		Hiromi Takamura	40.00
36	Wendy Ward	83.49	86	Colleen Walker	39.46
37	Marie Laure de Lorenzi	83.22	87	Ae-Sook Kim	38.76
38	Emilee Klein	81.48	88	Cindy Schreyer	38.20
39	Maria Hjorth	80.16	89	Iben Tinning	36.00
40	Michelle Estill	71.55	90	Laura Philo	35.67
41	Lisa Walters	71.50	91	Diane Barnard	34.88
42	Kaori Higo	70.78	92	Alicia Dibos	34.83
43	Dale Eggeling	67.75	93	Karen Weiss	34.17
44	Kim Saiki	66.75	94	Janice Moodie	34.16
45	Dana Dormann	65.54	95	Yu-Chen Huang	33.58
46	Patty Sheehan	65.09	96	Man-Soo Kim	33.50
47	Catrin Nilsmark	63.66	97	Leta Lindley	33.33
48	Amy Fruhwirth	62.88	98	Chieko Nishida	33.17
49	Woo-Soon Ko	61.85	99	Kathryn Marshall	32.95
50	Rachel Hetherington	56.88	100	Wendy Dicks	32.80

European LPGA Tour, 1998

Final Ranking

Pos	1997	Name	Prize £	Pos	1997	Name	Prize £
1	(2)	Helen Alfredsson	125975	51		Ana Sanchez Torreblanca	9751
2	(45)	Sophie Gustafson	103443	52	(81)	Claire Duffy	9128
3	(10)	Maria Hjorth	77733	53	(63)	Mette Hageman	8278
4	(9)	Trish Johnson	73190	54	(30)	Anna Berg	8211
5	(4)	Laura Davies	70918	55		Silvia Cavalleri	8177
6		Catriona Matthew	59747	56	(70)	Katharina Poppmeier	8141
7		Catrin Nilsmark	52544	57	(18)	Natascha Fink	8103
8	(1)	Alison Nicholas	47412	58		Ludivine Kreutz	7913
9	(14)	Lora Fairclough	37575	59	(48)	Catherine Schmitt	7712
10	(3)	Marie-Laure de Lorenzi	36021	60	(42)	Valerie Michaud	7428
11	(29)	Karen Pearce	32530	61	(104)	Aideen Rogers	7365
12	(37)	Raquel Carriedo	28086	62	(86)	Regine Lautens	7345
13	(7)	Joanne Morley	27753	63	(52)	Nicola Moult	7185
14		Laura Philo	26573	64	(24)	Susan Farron	6926
15		Mhairi McKay	25978	65	(90)	Karolina Andersson	6711
16	(17)	Shani Waugh	25913	66	(56)	Samantha Head	6576
17	(54)	Johanna Head	25568	67	(26)	Valerie Van Ryckeghem	6352
18	(62)	Iben Tinning	24996	68	(107)	Malin Burstrom	5757
19		Carin Koch	22679	69	(69)	Marlene Hedblom	5578
20	(38)	Diane Barnard	22205	70	(97)	Lisa Educate	5446
21	(27)	Wendy Dicks	21688	71	(84)	Marie-Thérèse Pistolet-Boselli	5250
22	(44)	Stephanie Dallongeville	20498	72	(115)	Tracy Eakin	4792
23	(6)	Patricia Meunier Lebouc	19388	73	(91)	Lotte Greve	4791
24	(22)	Asa Gottmo	19208	74	(67)	Mia Lojdahl	4788
25		Charlotta Sörenstam	19057	75	(43)	Barbara Pestana	4711
26		Kathryn Marshall	18760	76	(65)	Caryn Louw	4289
27		Lynnette Brooky	18190	77	(25)	Laura Navarro	4157
28		Lisa Hackney	18185	78		Nina Karlsson	4105
29	(15)	Helen Wadsworth	16914	79	(50)	Debbie Dowling	3973
30	(55)	Myra Murray	16190	80		Alison Munt	3943
31	(8)	Anne-Marie Knight	15743	81		Elisabeth Aron-Quelhas	3925
32	(31)	Corinne Dibnah	15640	82	(57)	Vibeke Stensrud	3818
33	(20)	Pernilla Sterner	15346	83	(78)	Marie-Josee Rouleau	3651
34	(72)	Caroline Hall	14921	84	(68)	Tracey Craik	3619
35	(12)	Laurette Maritz	14804	85	(66)	Anna Radford	3350
36	(28)	Dale Reid	14744	86	(83)	Marina Arruti	3219
37	(74)	Sandrine Mendiburu	14550	87	(98)	Sofie Eriksson	3066
38	(11)	Joanne Mills	14102	88	(64)	Xonia Wunsch-Ruiz	3061
39	(16)	Loraine Lambert	13987	89	(41)	Gillian Stewart	3034
40	(35)	Tina Fischer	13609	90	(19)	Karina Orum	3027
41	(5)	Karen Lunn	13436	91	(21)	Mandy Sutton	2990
42	(60)	Estefania Knuth	13428	92		Eva Engstrom	2937
43	(34)	Federica Dassu	13427	93		Ana Larraneta	2921
44	(39)	Julie Forbes	12557	94	(79)	Janet Soulsby	2700
45	(23)	Sally Prosser	12123	95	(75)	Kristel Mourgue d'Algue	2613
46	(118)	Elisabeth Esterl	11603	96	(40)	Martina Koch	2599
47	(32)	Jane Leary	11555	97		Riikka Hakkarainen	2333
48		Sofia Gronberg	11058	98	(71)	Sara Forster	2239
49	(53)	Kirsty Taylor	10660	99	(95)	Katharina Larsson	1962
50	(33)	Fiona Pike	10207	100	(46)	Amaia Arruti	1850

Tour Results (in chronological order)

Evian Masters
at Royal Golf Club, Evian, France

1	H Alfredsson	70-69-73-65—277	£75000
2	M Hjorth	69-70-72-70—281	50625
3	T Johnson	70-70-69-73—282	30950
	A Nicholas	70-70-71-71—282	30950

Ladies' Austrian Open
at Steiermarkischer GC Nurhof, Austria

1	L Brooky	64-70-69—203	£12000
2	T Johnson	70-66-68—204	8120
3	F Dassu	69-69-67—205	4028
	L Davies	68-66-71—205	4028
	E Knuth	70-66-69—205	4028
	L Philo	67-69-69—205	4028

Chrysler Open
at Sjögärde GC, Frillesås, Sweden

1	L Davies	72-71-71-70—284	£18750
2	T Johnson	73-76-71-70—290	10718
	R Carriedo	71-74-72-73—290	10718

Ladies' German Open
at Marriott Hotel, Treudelberg

1	L Fairclough	67-71-70-74—282	£15000
2	S Dallongeville	71-73-68-73—285	8575
	J Morley	74-70-71-70—285	8575

McDonald's WPGA Championship of Europe
at Gleneagles Hotel (King's Course)

1	C Matthew	71-69-67-69—276	£45000
2	H Alfredsson	72-68-70-71—281	25725
	L Davies	72-69-68-72—281	25725

Weetabix Women's British Open
(Full details of this Championship are included in *Part 1 The Majors*).

at Royal Lytham & St. Annes

1	S Steinhauer	81-72-70-69—292	£100000
2	S Gustafson	78-71-74-70—293	50000
	B Burton	71-74-77-71—293	50000

Compaq Open
at Barseback, Sweden

1	A Sörenstam	70-71-71-67—279	£45000
2	C Nilsmark	72-73-72-72—289	22550
	J Head	71-70-74-74—289	22550
	H Alfredsson	75-69-70-75—289	22550

Donegal Ladies' Irish Open
at Ballyliffin GC, Co Donegal, Ireland

1	S Gustafson	68-78-68—214	Punts 12900
2	I Tinning	73-73-68—214	8729
3	A Gottmo	70-78-70—218	6020

Air France Madame Open
at New Golf de Deauville, Deauville

1	P Meunier-Lebouc	69-67-72—208	£9450
2	M Hjorth	71-68-70—209	6394
3	D Barnard	74-68-69—211	4410

Marrakesh Palmeraie Open
at Palmeraie Golf Palace, Marrakesh, Morocco

1	Sophie Gustafson	66-67-68—201	£12000
2	Marie-Laure de Lorenzi	69-68-72—209	8000
3	Wendy Dicks	67-74-69—210	5600

TOUR QUALIFYING SCHOOL

at Aroeira, Portugal

The top 41 players earned full ELPGA tour cards for 1999:

Pos	Name	Score	Prize £
1	Christine Greatrex	71-69-72-70—282	1100
2	Elaine Ratcliffe	75-73-74-74—296	800
3	Marisa Baena	74-73-72-78—297	750
4	Judith Van Hagen	80-76-69-74—299	600
5	Kirsty Thomas	79-74-76-71—300	450
6	Sonia Helene Bauer	79-71-75-77—302	350
7	Lara Tadiotto	75-80-71-77—303	275
8	Susanne Westling	76-76-78-74—304	250
9	Karin Ross	74-77-79-74—304	225
10	Emma Fields	75-75-79-75—304	200
11	Ana Larraneta	80-74-74-76—304	
12	Tracey Lipp	78-77-77-73—305	
13	Esther Poburski	80-75-75-75—305	
14	Riikka Hakkarainen	74-73-83-75—305	
15	Sarah Gallagher	74-75-80-76—305	
16	Zoe Grimbeek	78-79-71-77—305	
17	Caroline Grady	78-80-72-76—306	
18	Linda Ericsson	78-77-74-77—306	

Pos	Name	Score
19	Joanne Oliver	76-75-74-81—306
20	Karen Stupples	77-79-75-76—307
21	Jenny Park	80-79-71-77—307
22	Barbara Hackett	81-76-77-74—308
23	Therese Hjertstedt	77-81-73-77—308
24	Sara Eklund	81-77-74-77—309
25	Tina Poulton	81-83-73-73—310
26	Odile Roux	77-82-76-75—310
27	Sandra Fischer	81-74-78-77—310
28	Lisa Dermott	79-75-75-81—310
29	Marjan De Boer	83-79-75-75—312
30	Susan Moorcraft	75-83-79-75—312
31	Josefin Stalvant	80-77-78-77—312
32	Bettina Herrmann-Bensinger	80-78-76-78—312
33	Sara Melin	79-79-76-78—312
34	Virginie Roques	80-76-75-81—312
35	Katie Tebbet	82-80-77-74—313
36	Amaia Arruti	81-82-74-76—313
37	Marion Verspieren	80-76-78-79—313
38	Erica Steen	77-79-77-80—313
39	Caroline Diethelm	75-81-79-79—314
40	Suzanne Dickens	77-79-78-80—314
41	Rachel Kirkwood	78-80-75-81—314

US LPGA Tour, 1998

Final Order of Merit

Pos	Name	Prize Money $	Pos	Name	Prize Money $
1	Annika Sörenstam	1092748	51	Dina Ammaccapane	142442
2	Se Ri Pak	872170	52	Gail Graham	141623
3	Donna Andrews	715428	53	Cathy Johnston-Forbes	141020
4	Karrie Webb	704477	54	Tracy Hanson	139427
5	Liselotte Neumann	665069	55	Catrin Nilsmark	137505
6	Juli Inkster	656012	56	Maria Hjorth	133943
7	Brandie Burton	652084	57	Kristi Albers	128734
8	Pat Hurst	612329	58	Alicia Dibos	127256
9	Meg Mallon	593458	59	Beth Daniel	124853
10	Dottie Pepper	539792	60	Deb Richard	122764
11	Laura Davies	517547	61	Nancy Scranton	122432
12	Lorie Kane	508249	62	Jackie Gallagher-Smith	122425
13	Danielle Ammaccapane	482564	63	Catriona Matthew	118157
14	Helen Alfredsson	471859	64	Stefania Croce	114534
15	Hiromi Kobayashi	460311	65	Jane Geddes	109259
16	Sherri Steinhauer	452282	66	Mayumi Hirase	107760
17	Kelly Robbins	442932	67	Kris Tschetter	104837
18	Rosie Jones	395241	68	Anna Acker-Macosko	103593
19	Chris Johnson	365710	69	Luciana Bemvenuti	103365
20	Wendy Ward	342495	70	Susie Redman	101702
21	Tammie Green	338884	71	Smriti Mehra	100760
22	Michelle Estill	334337	72	Wendy Doolan	98742
23	Emilee Klein	326975	73	Lisa Keggens	90020
24	Lisa Hackney	324018	74	Cristie Kerr	88613
25	Lisa Walters	308933	75	Moira Dunn	88442
26	Barb Mucha	307644	76	Caroline McMillan	85915
27	Betsy King	307069	77	Jane Crafter	85431
28	Tina Barrett	282989	78	Leta Lindley	85413
29	Dana Dormann	279828	79	Eva Dahllof	85225
30	Dale Eggeling	277217	80	Mhairi McKay	84694
31	Charlotta Sörenstam	261207	81	Trish Johnson	83440
32	Cindy Figg-Currier	229200	82	Suzanne Strudwick	82073
33	Helen Dobson	216144	83	Sophie Gustafson	81915
34	Jenny Lidback	215430	84	Alison Nicholas	80609
35	Carin Koch	207432	85	Sara Sanders	80401
36	Janice Moodie	205126	86	Leslie Spalding	78118
37	Pearl Sinn	201988	87	Becky Iverson	77884
38	Rachel Hetherington	200455	88	Cindy Flom	75143
39	Dawn Coe-Jones	192735	89	Karen Weiss	73826
40	Penny Hammel	191291	90	Robin Walton	73550
41	Kim Saiki	174873	91	Mardi Lunn	72114
42	Cindy McCurdy	167767	92	Vicki Fergon	70794
43	Michele Redman	156950	93	Nanci Bowen	70379
44	Amy Fruhwirth	156065	94	Muffin Spencer-Devlin	67360
45	Michelle McGann	152280	95	Jan Stephenson	65861
46	Nancy Lopez	151169	96	Stephanie Lowe	65814
47	Hollis Stacy	150420	97	Julie Piers	65061
48	Vickie Odegard	150154	98	Marianne Morris	64862
49	Joan Pitcock	149000	99	Kris Monaghan	60520
50	Patty Sheehan	143771	100	Annette DeLuca	59698

Tour Results (in chronological order)

Players are of American nationality unless stated

HealthSouth Inaugural
at Grand Cypress Resort, Orlando

1	Kelly Robbins	76-67-66—209	$90000
2	Meg Mallon	71-71-69—211	55855
3	Patty Sheehan	71-72-69—212	40759

The Office Depot Tournament
at Ibis G&CC - The Legend Course, West Palm Beach, Florida

1	Helen Alfredsson (Swe)	68-71-67-71—277	$90000
2	Liselotte Neumann (Swe)	70-70-71-68—279	55855
3	Kelly Robbins	72-70-73-67—282	27414
	Michelle McGann	72-68-75-67—282	27414
	Tracy Hanson	70-73-69-70—282	27414
	Pat Hurst	67-75-67-73—282	27414
	Wendy Ward	69-68-71-74—282	27414

Los Angeles Championship
at Oakmont CC, Glendale, California

1	Dale Eggeling*	72-69—141	$97500
2	Hiromi Kobayashi (Jpn)	67-74—141	60510
3	Cindy Schreyer	72-70—142	35433
	Karrie Webb (Aus)	72-70—142	35433
	E Crosby	70-72—142	35433

1998 Cup Noodles Hawaiian Ladies' Open
at Kapolei GC, Kapolei

1	Wendy Ward	65-69-70—204	$97500
2	Dana Dormann	66-66-72—204	60510
3	Laura Davies (Eng)	68-68-69—205	44156

Australian Ladies' Masters
at Royal Pines Resort, Queensland

1	Karrie Webb (Aus)	69-69-64-70—272	$105000
2	HS Park	70-68-71-68—277	56359
	Annika Sörenstam	69-68-70-70—277	56359

Welch's/Circle K Championship
at Randolph North, Arizona

1	Helen Alfredsson (Swe)	68-64-70-72—274	$75000
2	Liselotte Neumann (Swe)	71-69-67-68—275	40256
	Dana Dormann	70-68-68-69—275	40256

* *Winner after play-off*

Standard Register Ping
at Moon Valley, Arizona

1	Liselotte Neumann (Swe)*	69-67-69-74—279	$127500
2	Rosie Jones	70-72-67-70—279	79129
3	Cathy Johnston-Forbes	71-71-69-69—280	57743

Nabisco Dinah Shore
at Mission Hills, Rancho Mirage, California

1	Pat Hurst	68-72-70-71—281	$150000
2	H Dobson (Eng)	70-74-71-67—282	93093
3	Laura Davies (Eng)	75-70-70-68—283	60385
	Helen Alfredsson (Swe)	70-73-70-70—283	60385

Fuller details of this event are included in *Part I The Majors*

Longs Drugs Challenge
at Twelve Bridges GC, Lincoln

1	Donna Andrews	70-69-70-69—278	$90000
2	Carin Koch	66-70-73-70—279	55855
3	Annika Sörenstam (Swe)	73-73-66-70—282	40759

City of Hope Myrtle Beach Classic
at Wachesaw East GC

1	Karrie Webb (Aus)	68-66-68-67—269	$90000
2	Meg Mallon	62-73-68-69—272	55855
3	Dottie Pepper	73-68-68-64—273	40759

Chick-Fil-A Charity Championship
at Eagles Landing CC, Georgia

1	Liselotte Neumann (Swe)	67-65-60—202	$105000
2	Lorie Kane	70-68-67—205	56359
	Dottie Pepper	68-68-69—205	56359

Mercury Titleholders Championship
at LPGA International, Daytona Beach

1	Danielle Ammaccapane	70-68-67-71—276	$150000
2	Michelle Estill	68-71-69-69—277	93093
3	Annika Sörenstam (Swe)	67-69-69-73—278	67933

Sara Lee Classic
at Hermitage GC, Old Hickory, Tenn.

1	Barb Mucha*	67-69-69—205	$112500
2	Donna Andrews	65-73-67—205	53465
	Nancy Lopez	66-71-68—205	53465
	Jenny Lidback	72-63-70—205	53465

*Winner after play-off

McDonald's LPGA Championship
at DuPont CC, Delaware

1	Se Ri Pak (S.Kor)	65-68-72-68—273	$195000
2	Donna Andrews	71-67-69-69—276	104666
	Lisa Hackney (Eng)	70-66-69-71—276	104666

Fuller details of this event are included in Part I The Majors

LPGA Corning Classic
at Corning CC, New York

1	Tammie Green	67-70-66-65—268	$105000
2	Emilee Klein	71-69-68-67—275	56359
	Brandie Burton	68-66-71-70—275	56359

Wegmans Rochester International
at Locust Hill, New York

1	Rosie Jones	74-69-64-72—279	$105000
2	Juli Inkster	71-68-74-68—281	65165
3	Hollis Stacy	74-67-71-70—282	47553

Michelob Light Classic
at Forest Hills, Missori

1	Annika Sörenstam (Swe)*	67-73-68—208	$90000
2	Donna Andrews	72-66-70—208	55855
3	S Hallock	74-68-69—211	40759

Oldsmobile Classic
at Walnut Hills CC, Michigan

1	Lisa Walters	67-67-65-66—265	$97500
2	Donna Andrews	64-68-72-67—271	60510
3	Karrie Webb (Aus)	66-70-69-67—272	44156

Friendly's Classic
at Crestview, Massachussetts

1	Amy Fruhwirth	69-71-68-72—280	$90000
2	Charlotta Sörenstam (Swe)	69-70-73-70—282	48307
3	Kim Saiki (Jpn)	72-71-67-71—282	48307

Shoprite LPGA Classic
at Marriott Seaview Resort, Atlantic City

1	A Sörenstam (Swe)	66-65-65—196	$150000
2	Juli Inkster	67-66-67—200	93093
3	Lorie Kane	69-67-67—203	67933

*Winner after play-off

US Women's Open
at Blackwolf Run, Wisconsin

1	Se Ri Pak (S.Kor)	69-70-75-76—290	$267500
2	J Chuasiriporn (Am)	72-71-75-72—290	
3	Liselotte Neumann (Swe)	70-70-75-76—291	157500

Fuller details of this event are included in the *Part I The Majors*

Jamie Farr Kroger Classic
at Highland Meadows GC, Ohio

1	Se Ri Pak (S.Kor)	71-61-63-66—261	$120000
2	Lisa Hackney (Eng)	69-68-68-65—270	74474
3	Karrie Webb (Aus)	67-70-67-67—271	54346

Jal Big Apple Classic
at Wykagyl CC, New York

1	Annika Sörenstam (Swe)	67-66-65-67—265	$116250
2	J Pitcock	70-67-70-66—273	72147
3	Michelle Estill	71-68-65-71—275	52648

Giant Eagle LPGA Classic
at Avalon Lakes, Ohio

1	Se Ri Pak (S.Kor)	65-69-67—201	$120000
2	Dottie Pepper	67-64-71—202	74474
3	Robn Walton	69-70-64—203	54346

du Maurier Classic
at Essex G&CC, Ontario

1	Brandie Burton	68-64-66-72—270	$180000
2	Annika Sörenstam (Swe)	68-66-67-70—271	111711
3	Betsy King	64-69-70-72—275	81519

Fuller details of this event are included in *Part I The Majors*

Starbank LPGA Classic
at Country Club of the North, Ohio

1	Meg Mallon*	64-67-68—199	$90000
2	Dottie Pepper	63-70-66—199	55855
3	Donna Andrews	67-65-68—200	40759

Rainbow Foods LPGA Classic
at Rush Creek GC, Minnesota

1	Hiromi Kobayashi* (Jpn)	69-68-69—206	$90000
2	Tracy Hanson	67-70-69—206	55855
3	Meg Mallon	71-69-67—207	36230
	Michelle Estill	65-71-71—207	36230

* *Winner after play-off*

State Farm Rail Classic
The Rail Golf Course, Springfield, Illinois

1	Pearl Sinn	69-66-65—200	$105000
2	Michele Redman	70-63-68—201	65165
3	Tammie Green	66-67-69—202	47553

Safeway LPGA
at Columbia Edgewater CC, Oregon

1	Danielle Ammaccapane	65-67-72—204	$90000
2	Emilee Klein	68-67-70—205	55855
3	Dina Ammaccapane	71-70-66—207	40759

Safeco Classic
at Meridian Valley CC, Washington

1	Annika Sörenstam (Swe)	68-70-67-68—273	$90000
2	Laura Davies (Eng)	69-71-70-68—278	48307
	Patty Sheehan	71-66-67-74—278	48307

First Union Betsy King Classic
at Berkleigh CC, Pennsylvania

1	Rachel Hetherington	69-66-70-69—274	$97500
2	Annika Sörenstam (Swe)	71-69-68-66—274	60510
3	Beth Daniel	67-69-70-71—277	44156

Aflac Tournament of Champions
at Grand National, Alabama

1	Kelly Robbins	66-73-67-70—276	$122000
2	Juli Inkster	67-73-71-69—280	75500
3	Sherri Steinhauer	70-70-70-71—281	54250

Samsung World Championship of Women's Golf
at Tierra del Sol G&CC, The Villages, Florida

1	Juli Inkster	70-73-66-66—275	$137000
2	Annika Sörenstam	69-73-66-70—278	78500
3	Dottie Pepper	69-70-71-72—282	44750
	Brandie Burton	70-72-71-69—282	44750

Japan Classic
at Musashigoaka CC, Hanno, Japan

1	Hiromi Kobayashi (Jpn)	68-68-69—205	$120000
2	Tina Barrett	64-75-66—205	74474
3	Lorie Kane	70-64-73—207	54346

PageNet Tour Championship
at Desert Inn, Las Vegas, Nevada

1	Laura Davies (Eng)	66-67-75-69—277	$215000
2	Brandie Burton	69-74-71-67—281	86000
	Karrie Webb (Aus)	70-69-74-68—281	86000
	Pat Hurst	74-69-68-70—281	86000

Tour Qualifying School
at LPGA International, Daytona Beach, Florida

The top 24 players earned full exempt cards for the 1999 tour:

Pos	Name	Score	Prize $
1	Shani Waugh	70-72-67-68—277	2750
	AJ Fathorne	67-70-69-71—277	2750
3	Marianne Morris	69-66-69-74—278	2400
4	Karen Lunn	70-71-70-69—280	2300
5	Akiko Fukushima	73-68-71-69—281	2150
	Shelley Wendels	69-69-67-76—281	2150
7	Marnie McGuire	73-68-71-70—282	2000
8	Kristi Coats	71-71-73-68—283	1500
	Lori Atsedes	68-72-73-70—283	1500
	Angie Ridgeway	70-71-70-72—283	1500
11	Jill McGill Giangiorgi	66-75-70-73—284	1000
12	Denise Killeen	74-72-71-68—285	750
	Nicole Jeray	69-74-72-70—285	750
	Mi-Hyun Kim	69-73-71-72—285	750
	Jean Bartholomew	69-73-71-72—285	750
16	Patti Liscio	78-70-69-69—286	
	Ashli Bunch	70-74-70-72—286	
	Elizabeth Makings	68-73-73-72—286	
19	Kate Golden	72-75-68-72—287	
20	Sue Thomas	73-70-76-69—288	
	Laura Philo	73-73-72-70—288	
	Diane Barnard	74-70-73-71—288	
	Nadine Ash	69-72-74-73—288	
24	Asa Gottmo	73-72-70-74—289	

Japan LPGA Tour, 1998

Final Ranking

Players are of Japanese nationality unless stated

Pos	Name	Prize ¥	Pos	Name	Prize ¥
1	Michiko Hattori	81570423	14	Mayumi Murai	31845400
2	Kaori Harada	68443639	15	Yuri Kawanami	31778920
3	Ok-Hee Ku (Kor)	66123215	16	Aki Nakano	31231708
4	Kaori Higo	61160877	17	Hiromi Takamura	30775977
5	Akiko Fukushima	57225025	18	Woo-Soon Ko (Kor)	29858912
6	Natsuko Noro	48669180	19	Aiko Takasu	29478800
7	Huang-Yu Chen (Tai)	46047738	20	Man-Soo Kim (Kor)	27074961
8	Young-Me Lee (Kor)	42475641	21	Fumiko Muraguchi	26551405
9	Fuki Kido	41797400	22	Akemi Yamaoka	25353916
10	Yuri Fudo	40027445	23	Eiko Hatsuno	25204683
11	Aki Takamura	34516895	24	Marnie McGuire (NZ)	24876533
12	Nayoko Yoshikawa	32715688	25	Michie Ohba	24420200
13	Ae-Sook Kim (Kor)	32580347			

Tour Results

Tournament	Venue	Winner	Score
Daikin Orchid Ladies'	Ryukyu GC, Okinawa	Ae-Sook Kim	211 (−5)
Saishunkan Ladies'	Kumamoto Airport CC, Kumamoto	Michiko Hattori	215 (−1)
Yellow Hat Tokyo Ladies' Open	Wakasu Golf Links, Tokyo	Akemi Yamaoka	212 (−4)
Kenshoen Ladies' Dohgo	Dohgo GC, Ehime	Chihiro Furukawa	207 (−9)
Glory Queens Cup	Shishido GC, Ibaragi	Kaori Harada	215 (−1)
Nasu Ogawa Ladies' Tournament	Nasu Ogawa GC, Tochigi	Michiko Hattori	216 (par)
Katokichi Queens Tournament	Sakaide CC, Kagawa	Tamayo Ueda	216 (par)
Gunze Cup World Ladies'	Tokyo Yomiuri CC, Tokyo	Liselotte Neumann	282 (−6)
Yakult Ladies' Golf Tournament	Fukuoka Kokusai CC, Fukuoka	Aiko Takasu	213 (−3)
Chukyo TV Bridgestone Open	Kasugai CC, Aichi	Ok-Hee Ku	213 (−3)
Toto Motors Ladies' Tournament	Toto Hannoh CC, Saitama	Young-Me Lee	208 (−8)
Resort Trust Ladies'	Maple Point Club, Yamanashi	Kaori Harada	207 (−9)

continued

Japan LPGA Tour results *continued*

Tournament	Venue	Winner	Score
We Love Kobe Suntory Open	Arima Royal GC, Hyogo	Marnie McGuire	283 (-5)
Dunlop Twin Lakes Ladies' Open	The Cypress GC, Hyogo	Huang-Yu Chen	213 (-3)
Japan Women's Open	Miyoshi CC, Aichi	Natsuko Noro	286 (-2)
Toyo Suisan Ladies' Hokkaido	Kosaido Sapporo CC, Hokkaido	Michie Oba	210 (-6)
Sumitomo Visa Taiheiyo Club Ladies'	Taiheiyo Club Gotembe, Shizuoka	Aki Nakano	208 (-8)
Golf 5 Ladies'	Mizunami CC, Gifu	Akiko Fukushima	208 (-8)
Mizuno Ladies' Tournament	Asahi Kokusai Tojo CC, Hyogo	Fuki Kido	281 (-7)
NEC Karuizawa 72 Tournament	Karuizawa 72 Golf, Nagano	Yuka Irie	204 (-12)
New Caterpillar Mitsubishi Ladies'	Dai Hakone CC, Kanagawa	Kyoko Ono	216 (-3)
Goyo Kensetsu Ladies' Cup	Nomozaki GC, Nagasaki	Harumi Sakagami	209 (-7)
Fuji Sankei Ladies' Classic	Fuji Sakura CC, Yamanashi	Masako Ishihara	213 (par)
JLPGA Championship	Miho GC, Ibaragi	Michiko Hattori	290 (+2)
Yukijirushi Ladies' Tokai Classic	Ryosen GC, Mie	Kaori Higo	207 (-9)
Miyagi TV Cup	Hananomori GC, Miyagi	Akiko Fukushima	208 (+8)
Kosaido Ladies' Golf Cup	Chiba Kosaido CC, Chiba	Mayumi Murai	213 (-3)
Takara World Invitational	Caledonian GC, Chiba	Aki Takamura	211 (-5)
Fujitsu Ladies'	Tokyu Seven Hundred Club, Chiba	Kaori Higo	211 (-5)
Hisako Higuchi Kibun Classic	Greenbriar West Village, Fukushima	Michiko Hattori	212 (-4)
Nichirei International	Tsukuba CC, Ibaragi	US LPGA team	65 (Jpn 72)
LPGA Japan Classic	Musashigoaka GC, Saitama	Hiromi Kobayashi	205 (-11)
Ito-En Ladies' Golf Tournament	Great Island Club, Chiba	Michiko Hattori	197 (-19)
Daiohseishi Elleair Ladies' Open	Elleair GC, Matsuyama, Ehime	Chikayo Yamazaki	210 (-6)
Japan LPGA Meiji Nyugyo Cup	Hibiscus GC, Miyazaki	Young-Me Lee	274 (-14)

International Team Events

Solheim Cup

1990 *at Lake Nona GC, Florida, 16th–18th November*
Captains: Mickey Walker, Europe; Kathy Whitworth, US

Europe		USA	
***First Day* – Foursomes**			
L Davies and A Nicholas (2 and 1)	1	P Bradley and N Lopez	0
P Wright and L Neumann	0	C Gerring and D Mochrie (6 and 5)	1
D Reid and H Alfredsson	0	P Sheehan and R Jones (6 and 5)	1
T Johnson and ML de Lorenzi	0	B Daniel and B King (5 and 4)	1
	1		3
***Second Day* – Fourball**			
T Johnson and ML de Lorenzi	0	P Sheehan and R Jones (2 and 1)	1
D Reid and H Alfredsson	0	P Bradley and N Lopez (2 and 1)	1
L Davies and A Nicholas	0	B King and B Daniel (4 and 3)	1
L Neumann and P Wright (4 and 2)	1	C Gerring and D Mochrie	0
	1		3
***Third Day* – Singles**			
H Alfredsson	0	C Gerring (4 and 3)	1
L Davies (3 and 2)	1	R Jones	0
A Nicholas	0	N Lopez (6 and 4)	1
P Wright	½	B King	½
L Neumann	0	B Daniel (7 and 6)	1
D Reid (2 and 1)	1	P Sheehan	0
ML de Lorenzi	0	D Mochrie (4 and 2)	1
T Johnson	0	P Bradley (8 and 7)	1
	2½		5½

Result: USA 11½, Europe 4½

1992 *at Dalmahoy on 2nd–4th October*
Captains: Mickey Walker, Europe; Kathy Whitworth, US. Vice-captain: Alice Miller, US

Europe		USA	
***First Day* – Foursomes**			
L Davies and A Nicholas (1 hole)	1	B King and B Daniel	0
L Neumann and H Alfredsson (2 and 1)	1	P Bradley and D Mochrie	0
F Descampe and T Johnson	0	D Ammaccapane and M Mallon (1 hole)	1
D Reid and P Wright	½	P Sheehan and J Inkster	½
	2½		1½
***Second Day* – Fourball**			
L Davies and A Nicholas (1 hole)	1	P Sheehan and J Inkster	0
T Johnson and F Descampe	½	B Burton and D Richard	½
P Wright and D Reid	0	M Mallon and B King (1 hole)	1
H Alfredsson and L Neumann	½	P Bradley and D Mochrie	½
	2		2

1992 Solheim Cup *continued*

Europe
Third Day – Singles

L Davies (4 and 2)	1
H Alfredsson (4 and 3)	1
T Johnson (2 and 1)	1
A Nicholas	0
F Descampe	0
P Wright (4 and 3)	1
C Nilsmark (3 and 2)	1
K Douglas	0
L Neumann (2 and 1)	1
D Reid (3 and 2)	1
	7

USA

B Burton	0
D Ammaccapane	0
P Sheehan	0
J Inkster (3 and 2)	1
B Daniel (2 and 1)	1
P Bradley	0
M Mallon	0
D Richard (7 and 6)	1
B King	0
D Mochrie	0
	3

Result: Europe 11½, United States 6½

1994 *at the Greenbrier, West Virginia, 21st–23rd October*

Captains: Mickey Walker, Europe; Jo Anne Carner, US

Europe
First Day – Foursomes

H Alfredsson and L Neumann	0
C Nilsmark and A Sorenstam (1 hole)	1
L Fairclough and D Reid (2 and 1)	1
L Davies and A Nicholas (2 holes)	1
T Johnson and P Wright	0
	3

Second Day – Fourball

L Davies and A Nicholas	0
C Nilsmark and A Sorenstam	0
L Fairclough and D Reid (4 and 3)	1
T Johnson and P Wright	0
H Alfredsson and L Neumann (1 hole)	1
	2

Third Day – Singles

H Alfredsson (2 and 1)	1
C Nilsmark	0
T Johnson	0
L Fairclough	0
P Wright	0
A Nicholas (3 and 2)	1
L Davies	0
A Sorenstam	0
D Reid	0
L Neumann	0
	2

USA

B Burton and D Mochrie (3 and 2)	1
B Daniel and M Mallon	0
T Green and K Robbins	0
D Andrews and B King	0
P Sheehan and S Steinhauer (2 holes)	1
	2

B Burton and D Mochrie (2 and 1)	1
B Daniel and M Mallon (6 and 5)	1
T Green and K Robbins	0
D Andrews and B King (3 and 2)	1
P Sheehan and S Steinhauer	0
	3

B King	0
D Mochrie (6 and 5)	1
B Daniel (1 hole)	1
K Robbins (4 and 2)	1
M Mallon (1 hole)	1
P Sheehan	0
B Burton (1 hole)	1
T Green (3 and 2)	1
S Steinhauer (2 holes)	1
D Andrews (3 and 2)	1
	8

Result: United States 13, Europe 7

1996 *at St Pierre, Chepstow, 20th–22nd September*

Captains: Mickey Walker, Europe; Judy Rankin, US

Europe
First Day – Foursomes

A Sorenstam and C Nilsmark	½
L Davies and A Nicholas	0
ML de Lorenzi and D Reid	0
H Alfredsson and L Neumann	0
	½

USA

K Robbins and M McGann	½
P Sheehan and R Jones (1 hole)	1
B Daniel and V Skinner (1 hole)	1
D Pepper and B Burton (2 and 1)	1
	3½

Solheim Cup

Fourball

L Davies and T Johnson (6 and 5)	1	K Robbins and P Bradley	0
A Sorenstam and K Marshall (1 hole)	1	V Skinner and J Geddes	0
L Neumann and C Nilsmark	0	D Pepper and B King (1 hole)	1
H Alfredsson and A Nicholas	½	M Mallon and B Daniel	½
	2½		1½

***Second Day* – Foursomes**

L Davies and T Johnson (4 and 3)	1	P Sheehan and R Jones	0
A Sorenstam and C Nilsmark (1 hole)	1	D Pepper and B Burton	0
L Neumann and K Marshall	½	M Mallon and J Geddes	½
ML de Lorenzi amd H Alfredsson (4 and 3)	1	K Robbins and M McGann	0
	3½		½

Fourball

L Davies and L Hackney (6 and 5)	1	B Daniel and V Skinner	0
A Sorenstam and T Johnson	½	M McGann and M Mallon	½
ML de Lorenzi and J Morley	0	K Robbins and B King (2 and 1)	1
C Nilsmark and L Neumann (2 and 1)	1	P Sheehan and J Geddes	0
	2½		1½

***Third Day* – Singles**

A Sorenstam (2 and 1)	1	P Bradley	0
K Marshall	0	V Skinner (2 and 1)	1
L Davies	0	M McGann (3 and 2)	1
L Neumann	½	B Daniel	½
L Hackney	0	B Burton (1 hole)	1
T Johnson	0	D Pepper (3 and 2)	1
A Nicholas	½	K Robbins	½
ML de Lorenzi	0	B King (6 and 4)	1
J Morley	0	R Jones (5 and 4)	1
D Reid	0	J Geddes (2 holes)	1
C Nilsmark	0	P Sheehan (2 and 1)	1
H Alfredsson	0	M Mallon (4 and 2)	1
	2		10

Result: USA 17, Europe 11

1998 *at Muirfield Village, Dublin, Ohio, 18th–20th September*

Non-playing Captains: Pia Nilsson, Europe; Judy Rankin, US

Europe		USA	

***First Day* – Foursomes**

L Davies and T Johnson	0	D Pepper and J Inkster (3 and 1)	1
H Alfredsson and A Nicholas	0	M Mallon and B Burton (3 and 1)	1
L Hackney and L Neumann	0	K Robbins and P Hurst (1 hole)	1
A Sorenstam and C Matthew (3 and 2)	1	D Andrews and T Green	0
	1		3

Fourball

L Davies and C Sorenstam	½	B King and C Johnson	½
L Hackney and S Gustafson	0	P Hurst and R Jones (7 and 5)	1
H Alfredsson and ML de Lorenzi (2 and 1)	1	K Robbins and S Steinhauer	0
A Sorenstam and C Nilsmark	0	D Pepper and B Burton (2 holes)	1
	1½		2½

Match position: Europe 2½, USA 5½

***Second Day* – Foursomes**

A Sorenstam and C Matthew	0	D Andrews and S Steinhauer (3 and 2)	1
L Davies and C Sorenstam (3 and 2)	1	M Mallon and B Burton	0
H Alfredsson and ML de Lorenzi	0	D Pepper and J Inkster (1 hole)	1
L Neumann and C Nilsmark	0	K Robbins and P Hurst (1 hole)	1
	1		3

continued

1998 Solheim Cup *continued*

Fourball

A Sorenstam and C Nilsmark (5 and 3)	1	B King and R Jones	0	
L Davies and L Hackney (2 holes)	1	C Johnson and T Green	0	
H Alfredsson and ML de Lorenzi	0	D Andrews and S Steinhauer (4 and 3)	1	
L Neumann and C Sorenstam	0	M Mallon and J Inkster (2 and 1)	1	
	2		2	

Match position: Europe 5½, USA 10½

Third Day – Singles

Laura Davies (1 hole)	1	Pat Hurst	0
Helen Alfredsson (2 and 1)	1	Juli Inkster	0
Annika Sorenstam (2 and 1)	1	Donna Andrews	0
Liselotte Neumann (1 hole)	1	Brandie Burton	0
Trish Johnson	0	Dottie Pepper (3 and 2)	1
Charlotta Sorenstam	0	Kelly Robbins (2 and 1)	1
Marie Laure de Lorenzi (1 hole)	1	Chris Johnson	0
Catrin Nilsmark	0	Rosie Jones (6 and 4)	1
Alison Nicholas	0	Tammie Green (1 hole)	1
Catriona Matthew	0	Sheri Steinhauer (3 and 2)	1
Lisa Hackney (6 and 5)	1	Betsy King	0
Sophie Gustafson	½	Meg Mallon	½
	6½		5½

Result: Europe 12, USA 16

Solheim Cup – INDIVIDUAL RECORDS

Brackets indicate non-playing captain

Europe

Name		Year	Played	Won	Lost	Halved
Helen Alfredsson	Swe	1990-92-94-96-98	18	7	9	2
Laura Davies	Eng	1990-92-94-96-98	19	12	6	1
Florence Descampe	Bel	1992	3	0	2	1
Kitrina Douglas	Eng	1992	1	0	1	0
Lora Fairclough	Eng	1994	3	2	1	0
Sophie Gustafson	Swe	1998	2	0	1	1
Lisa Hackney	Eng	1996-98	6	3	3	0
Trish Johnson	Eng	1990-92-94-96-98	15	3	10	2
Marie Laure de Lorenzi	Fra	1990-96-98	11	3	8	0
Kathryn Marshall	Sco	1996	3	1	1	1
Catriona Matthew	Sco	1998	3	1	2	0
Joanne Morley	Eng	1996	2	0	2	0
Liselotte Neumann	Swe	1990-92-94-96-98	18	6	9	3
Alison Nicholas	Eng	1990-92-94-96-98	14	5	7	2
Catrin Nilsmark	Swe	1992-94-96-98	13	5	7	1
Pia Nilsson	Swe	(1998)	0	0	0	0
Dale Reid	Sco	1990-92-94-96	11	4	6	1
Annika Sorenstam	Swe	1994-96-98	13	7	4	2
Charlotta Sorenstam	Swe	1998	4	1	2	1
Mickey Walker	Eng	(1990)-(92)-(94)-(96)	0	0	0	0
Pam Wright	Sco	1990-92-94	6	1	4	1

United States

Name	Year	Played	Won	Lost	Halved
Danielle Ammacapane	1992	2	1	1	0
Donna Andrews	1994-98	7	4	3	0
Pat Bradley	1990-92-96	8	2	5	1
Brandie Burton	1992-94-96-98	11	7	3	1

Name	Year	Played	Won	Lost	Halved
Jo Anne Carner	(1994)	0	0	0	0
Beth Daniel	1990-92-94-96	12	7	3	2
Jane Geddes	1996	4	1	2	1
Cathy Gerring	1990	3	2	1	0
Tammie Green	1994-98	6	2	4	0
Pat Hurst	1998	4	3	1	0
Juli Inkster	1992-98	7	4	2	1
Chris Johnson	1998	3	0	2	1
Rosie Jones	1990-96-98	9	6	3	0
Betsy King	1990-92-94-96-98	15	7	6	2
Nancy Lopez	1990	3	2	1	0
Michelle McGann	1996	4	1	1	2
Meg Mallon	1992-94-96-98	14	7	3	4
Alice Miller	(1992)*	0	0	0	0
Dottie Pepper	1990-92-94-96-98	17	12	4	1
Judy Rankin	(1996)-(98)	0	0	0	0
Deb Richard	1992	2	1	0	1
Kelly Robbins	1994-96-98	12	5	5	2
Patty Sheehan	1990-92-94-96	13	5	7	1
Val Skinner	1996	4	2	2	0
Sherri Steinhauer	1994-98	7	5	2	0
Kathy Whitworth	(1990)-(92)*	0	0	0	0

Praia d'el Rey European Cup

(European LPGA Women *v* European Senior Tour Men) *at Praia d'el Rey, Portugal*

Captains: Marie Laure de Lorenzi and Tommy Horton

ELPGA | European Seniors

Foursomes
T Johnson and K Lunn	0	E Polland and C O'Connor Jr (3 and 2)	1
A Nicholas and ML de Lorenzi	0	B Verwey and D O'Sullivan (3 and 2)	1
M Hjorth and L Fairclough (1 hole)	1	B Waites and B Huggett	0
C Matthew and Mhairi McKay (2 and 1)	1	D Jones and J Rhodes	0
S Gustafson and C Nilsmark (1 hole)	1	N Coles and T Horton	0
	3		2

Fourball
S Gustafson and C Nilsmark	0	E Polland and D Jones (1 hole)	1
K Lunn and T Johnson	½	D O'Sullivan and B Verwey	½
L Fairclough and M Hjorth	0	N Coles and J Rhodes (4 and 3)	1
A Nicholas and ML de Lorenzi	0	B Waites and B Huggett (1 hole)	1
M McKay and C Matthew	0	C O'Connor Jr and T Horton (4 and 3)	1
	½		4½

Match position: ELPGA 3½, Seniors 6½

Singles
Sophie Gustafson (4 and 3)	1	Denis O'Sullivan	0
Trish Johnson (2 and 1)	1	Brian Waites	0
Catriona Matthew (4 and 2)	1	Bobby Verwey	0
Karen Lunn (3 and 2)	1	Jim Rhodes	0
Catrin Nilsmark	½	Brian Huggett	½
Alison Nicholas	0	Neil Coles (2 and 1)	1
Lora Fairclough	0	David Jones (2 and 1)	1
Maria Hjorth (5 and 4)	1	Eddie Polland	0
Mhairi McKay	0	Christy O'Connor Jr (5 and 4)	1
Marie Laure de Lorenzi (4 and 2)	1	Tommy Horton	0
	6½		3½

Result: ELPGA 10, Seniors 10

Professional Women's Overseas Championships

Australian Ladies' Masters

Year	Winner
1998	K Webb

AAMI Australian Women's Open

Year	Winner
1995	L Neumann
1996	C Matthew
1997	J Crafter
1998	M McGuire

Austrian Ladies' Open

Year	Winner
1994	F Descampe
1995	A Sorenstam
1996	M Koch
1997	*Not played*
1998	L Brooky

French Ladies' Open

Year	Winner	Year	Winner
1989	S Strudwick	1994	J Forbes
1990	*Not played*	1995	L Kreutz
1991	S Strudwick	1996	L Rolner
1992	*Not played*	1997	K Lunn
1993	*Not played*	1998	*Not played*

German Ladies' Open
(Became Hennessy Cup in 1993)

Year	Winner	Year	Winner
1989	A Nicholas	1994	L Neumann
1990	A Okamoto	1995	A Sorenstam
1991	F Descampe	1996	H Alfredsson
1992	*Not played*	1997	L Davies
1993	L Neumann	1998	L Fairclough

German Ladies' PGA Close

Year	Winner	Year	Winner
1989	D Franz	1994	F Fehlauer
1990	D Franz	1995	F Fehlauer
1991	S Lehmeier	1996	M Koch
1992	S Lehmeier	1997	F Fehlauer
1993	S Lehmeier	1998	D Chudzinski

Italian Ladies' Open

Year	Winner	Year	Winner
1989	X Wunsch-Ruiz	1994	C Dibnah
1990	F Descampe	1995	D Booker
1991	C Dibnah	1996	L Davies
1992	L Davies	1997	V Van Ryckegham
1993	A Arruti	1998	*Not played*

Malaysian Women's Open

Year	Winner	Year	Winner
1989	N Terazawa	1994	J-S Won
1990	C Nishida	1995	C Dibnah
1991	C Nishida	1996	C Dibnah
1992	C Nishida	1997	P Rigby-Jinglov
1993	S Prosser	1998	S Mendiburu

Swedish Ladies' Open

Year	Winner	Year	Winner
1989	P Nilsson	1994	L Neumann
1990	J Allmark	1995	M Löjdahl
1991	L Ericsson	1996	A Berg
1992	C Hjalmarsson	1997	C Nilsmark
1993	M Hjorth	1998	H Koch

TAKE THE FAMILY FOR A WALK ROUND THE WOODS.

Five hundred years of golfing history, and a great day out are waiting to be discovered at the British Golf Museum—with the latest Philips CD-i and touch-screen displays as your guide. Find out the secrets of the royal, the ancient, and the modern game and its players. Then finish the round at our gift shop.

British Golf Museum
St Andrews

WINNER OF SEVEN MAJOR AWARDS

The British Golf Museum,
Bruce Embankment, St Andrews, Fife KY16 9AB. Telephone: 01334 478880.

PART IV
Men's Amateur Tournaments

Index on page 234

Index – Men's Amateur Events

National and International Amateur Championships

Amateur Championship	235
103rd Amateur Championship	236
British Seniors' Open Amateur Championship	237
British Mid-Amateur Championship	238
English Amateur Championship	238
English Open Amateur Strokeplay Championship (Brabazon Trophy)	239
English Seniors' Amateur Championship	240
English Open Mid-Amateur Championship (Logan Trophy)	240
English County Champions' Tournament	240
Irish Amateur Championship	241
Irish Seniors' Open Amateur Championship	242
Scottish Amateur Championship	242
Scottish Open Amateur Strokeplay Championship	243
Scottish Senior Championship	244
Scottish Champion of Champions	244
Scottish Mid-Amateur Championship	244
Welsh Amateur Championship	245
Welsh Amateur Strokeplay Championship	246
Welsh Seniors' Amateur Championship	246
Welsh Mid-Amateur Championship	246
Welsh Champions of Champions	247
European Amateur Championship	247
European Seniors' Championship	247
Europen Mid-Amateur Championship	247

TEAM EVENTS	248
United States v Great Britain & Ireland	248
The Walker Cup	248
Walker Cup - Individual Records	252
Eisenhower Trophy (World Amateur Team Championship)	259
European Amateur Team Championship	259
European Club Cup	260
St Andrews Trophy	260
England v France	261

Home Internationals	262
English County Championship	263
English Club Championship	263
All-Ireland Inter-County	264
Scottish Club Championship	264
Scottish Area Team Championship	264
Scottish Foursomes Tournament (Glasgow Evening Times Trophy)	264
Welsh Inter-Counties Championship	264

Other Men's Amateur Tournaments **265**

Aberconwy Trophy	265
The Antlers	265
Berkhamsted Trophy	266
Berkshire Trophy	266
Burhill Family Foursomes	267
Cameron Corbett Vase	267
Craigmillar Park Open	268
John Cross Bowl	268
Duncan Putter	269
Fathers and Sons Foursomes	269
Frame Trophy	269
Golf Illustrated Gold Vase	270
Grafton Morrish Trophy	270
Halford-Hewitt Cup	270
Hampshire Hog	270
King George V Coronation Cup	272
Lagonda Trophy	272
Leven Gold Medal	272
Lytham Trophy	273
Oxford v Cambridge Varsity Match	273
Oxford and Cambridge Golfing Society for the President's Putter	274
Prince of Wales Challenge Cup	275
Rosebery Challenge Cup	275
St Andrews Links Trophy	276
St David's Gold Cross	276
St George's Grand Challenge Cup	277
Selborne Salver	277
Sunningdale Foursomes	278
Tennant Cup	278
Tillman Trophy	279
Trubshaw Cup	279
Worplesdon Mixed Foursomes	280

Regional Amateur Championships **281**

Overseas Amateur Championships **288**

National and International Amateur Championships

Amateur Championship

Year	Winner	Runner-up	Venue	By	Ent
1885	A MacFie	H Hutchinson	Hoylake, R Liverpool	7 and 6	44
1886	H Hutchinson	H Lamb	St Andrews	7 and 6	42
1887	H Hutchinson	J Ball	Hoylake, R Liverpool	1 hole	33
1888	J Ball	J Laidlay	Prestwick	5 and 4	38
1889	J Laidlay	L Melville	St Andrews	2 and 1	40
1890	J Ball	J Laidlay	Hoylake, R Liverpool	4 and 3	44
1891	J Laidlay	H Hilton	St Andrews	20th hole	50
1892	J Ball	H Hilton	Sandwich, R St George's	3 and 1	45
1893	P Anderson	J Laidlay	Prestwick	1 hole	44
1894	J Ball	S Fergusson	Hoylake, R Liverpool	1 hole	64
1895	L Melville	J Ball	St Andrews	19th hole	68

From 1896 36 holes played

Year	Winner	Runner-up	Venue	By	Ent
1896	F Tait	H Hilton	Sandwich, R St George's	8 and 7	64
1897	A Allan	J Robb	Muirfield	4 and 2	74
1898	F Tait	S Fergusson	Hoylake, R Liverpool	7 and 5	77
1899	J Ball	F Tait	Prestwick	37th hole	101
1900	H Hilton	J Robb	Sandwich, R St George's	8 and 7	68
1901	H Hilton	J Low	St Andrews	1 hole	116
1902	C Hutchings	S Fry	Hoylake, R Liverpool	1 hole	114
1903	R Maxwell	H Hutchinson	Muirfield	7 and 5	142
1904	W Travis (US)	E Blackwell	Sandwich, R St George's	4 and 3	104
1905	A Barry	Hon O Scott	Prestwick	3 and 2	148
1906	J Robb	C Lingen	Hoylake, R Liverpool	4 and 3	166
1907	J Ball	C Palmer	St Andrews	6 and 4	200
1908	E Lassen	H Taylor	Sandwich, R St George's	7 and 6	197
1909	R Maxwell	Capt C Hutchison	Muirfield	1 hole	170
1910	J Ball	C Aylmer	Hoylake, R Liverpool	10 and 9	160
1911	H Hilton	E Lassen	Prestwick	4 and 3	146
1912	J Ball	A Mitchell	Westward Ho!, R North Devon	38th hole	134
1913	H Hilton	R Harris	St Andrews	6 and 5	198
1914	J Jenkins	C Hezlet	Sandwich, R St George's	3 and 2	232

1915–19 *No Championship owing to the Great War*

Year	Winner	Runner-up	Venue	By	Ent
1920	C Tolley	R Gardner (US)	Muirfield	37th hole	165
1921	W Hunter	A Graham	Hoylake, R Liverpool	12 and 11	223
1922	E Holderness	J Caven	Prestwick	1 hole	252
1923	R Wethered	R Harris	Deal, R Cinque Ports	7 and 6	209
1924	E Holderness	E Storey	St Andrews	3 and 2	201
1925	R Harris	K Fradgley	Westward Ho!, R North Devon	13 and 12	151
1926	J Sweetser (US)	A Simpson	Muirfield	6 and 5	216
1927	Dr W Tweddell	D Landale	Hoylake, R Liverpool	7 and 6	197
1928	T Perkins	R Wethered	Prestwick	6 and 4	220
1929	C Tolley	J Smith	Sandwich, R St George's	4 and 3	253
1930	R Jones (US)	R Wethered	St Andrews	7 and 6	271
1931	E Smith	J De Forest	Westward Ho!, R North Devon	1 hole	171
1932	J De Forest	E Fiddian	Muirfield	3 and 1	235
1933	Hon M Scott	T Bourn	Hoylake, R Liverpool	4 and 3	269
1934	W Lawson Little (US)	J Wallace	Prestwick	14 and 13	225
1935	W Lawson Little (US)	Dr W Tweddell	R Lytham and St Annes	1 hole	232
1936	H Thomson	J Ferrier (Aus)	St Andrews	2 holes	283
1937	R Sweeney Jr (US)	L Munn	Sandwich, R St George's	3 and 2	223
1938	C Yates (US)	R Ewing	Troon	3 and 2	241

continued

Amateur Championship *continued*

Year	Winner	Runner-up	Venue	By	Ent
1939	A Kyle	A Duncan	Hoylake, R Liverpool	2 and 1	167
1940–45	*Suspended during Second World War*				
1946	J Bruen	R Sweeny (US)	Birkdale	4 and 3	263
1947	W Turnesa (US)	R Chapman (US)	Carnoustie	3 and 2	200
1948	F Stranahan (US)	C Stowe	Sandwich, R St George's	5 and 4	168
1949	S McCready	W Turnesa (US)	Portmarnock	2 and 1	204
1950	F Stranahan (US)	R Chapman (US)	St Andrews	8 and 6	324
1951	R Chapman (US)	C Coe (US)	R Porthcawl	5 and 4	192
1952	E Ward (US)	F Stranahan (US)	Prestwick	6 and 5	286
1953	J Carr	E Harvie Ward (US)	Hoylake, R Liverpool	2 holes	279
1954	D Bachli (Aus)	W Campbell (US)	Muirfield	2 and 1	286
1955	J Conrad (US)	A Slater	R Lytham and St Annes	3 and 2	240
1956	J Beharrell	L Taylor	Troon	5 and 4	200
1957	R Reid Jack	H Ridgley (US)	Formby	2 and 1	200
In 1956 and 1957 the Quarter Finals, Semi-Finals and Final were played over 36 holes					
1958	J Carr	A Thirlwell	St Andrews	3 and 2	488
In 1958, Semi-Finals and Final only were played over 36 holes					
1959	D Beman (US)	W Hyndman (US)	Sandwich, R St George's	3 and 2	362
1960	J Carr	R Cochran (US)	R Portrush	8 and 7	183
1961	M Bonallack	J Walker	Turnberry	6 and 4	250
1962	R Davies (US)	J Povall	Hoylake, R Liverpool	1 hole	256
1963	M Lunt	J Blackwell	St Andrews	2 and 1	256
1964	G Clark	M Lunt	Ganton	39th hole	220
1965	M Bonallack	C Clark	R Porthcawl	2 and 1	176
1966	R Cole (SA)	R Shade	Carnoustie (18 holes)	3 and 2	206
1967	R Dickson (US)	R Cerrudo (US)	Formby	2 and 1	
1968	M Bonallack	J Carr	Troon	7 and 6	249
1969	M Bonallack	W Hyndman (US)	Hoylake, R Liverpool	3 and 2	245
1970	M Bonallack	W Hyndman (US)	Newcastle, R Co Down	8 and 7	256
1971	S Melnyk (US)	J Simons (US)	Carnoustie	3 and 2	256
1972	T Homer	A Thirlwell	Sandwich, R St George's	4 and 3	253
1973	R Siderowf (US)	P Moody	R Porthcawl	5 and 3	222
1974	T Homer	J Gabrielsen (US)	Muirfield	2 holes	330
1975	M Giles (US)	M James	Hoylake, R Liverpool	8 and 7	206
1976	R Siderowf (US)	J Davies	St Andrews	37th hole	289
1977	P McEvoy	H Campbell	Ganton	5 and 4	235
1978	P McEvoy	P McKellar	R Troon	4 and 3	353
1979	J Sigel (US)	S Hoch (US)	Hillside	3 and 2	285
1980	D Evans	D Suddards (SA)	R Porthcawl	4 and 3	265
1981	P Ploujoux (Fr)	J Hirsch (US)	St Andrews	4 and 2	256
1982	M Thompson	A Stubbs	Deal, R Cinque Ports	4 and 3	245
1983	A Parkin	J Holtgrieve (US)	Turnberry	5 and 4	288
1984	JM Olazábal (Sp)	C Montgomerie	Formby	5 and 4	291
1985	G McGimpsey	G Homewood	R Dornoch	8 and 7	457
1986	D Curry	G Birtwell	R Lytham and St Annes	11 and 9	427
1987	P Mayo	P McEvoy	Prestwick	3 and 1	373
1988	C Hardin (Swe)	B Fouchee (SA)	R Porthcawl	1 hole	391
1989	S Dodd	C Cassells	R Birkdale	5 and 3	378
1990	R Muntz (Neth)	A Macara	Muirfield	7 and 6	510
1991	G Wolstenholme	B May (US)	Gsanton	8 and 6	345
1992	S Dundas	B Dredge	Carnoustie	7 and 6	364
1993	I Pyman	P Page	R Portrush	37th hole	279
1994	L James	G Sherry	Nairn	2 and 1	288
1995	G Sherry	M Reynard	Hoylake, R Liverpool	7 and 6	288
1996	W Bladon	R Beames	Turnberry	1 hole	288
1997	C Watson	T Immelman	R St Georges, R Cinque Ports	3 and 2	369
1998	S Garcia	C Williams	Muirfield	7 and 6	288

103rd Amateur Championship at *Muirfield* (288 entrants from 25 countries played in the 36-hole qualifying competition, 66 of whom qualified on 148 or better for the matchplay stage)

First Round
S Sheehan beat T Cochrane 5 and 4

Second Round
M Hilton beat J Powell 2 holes
R Quiros beat A Farmer 2 holes

Second Round *continued*
G Rankin beat A Grenier 1 hole
S Wittkop beat R Fenwick 4 and 2
G Havret beat D Yates 5 and 3
T Immelmann beat R Haag 3 and 2
R Gerwin beat S Davis at 19th

Second Round *continued*
J Bunch beat J Rose 1 hole
M Harris beat P McKechnie 3 and 2
A Wainwright beat R Hoit 1 hole
K Wallbank beat O David 1 hole
K Ferrie beat L Kelly 5 and 4
M Side beat P Rowe 2 and 1
M Loftus beat I Goroneskoul at 20th
S McCarthy beat L Cederqvist 3 and 2
S Garcia beat S Branger 7 and 5
G Ogilvy beat G Storm 2 and 1
J Wahlstedt beat S Williams 3 and 1
N Pimm beat J Fanagan 2 and 1
G Maly beat S Dyson 1 hole
J Olver beat W Bryson at 19th
C Williams beat S Mackenzie 4 and 3
C Ravetto beat T Dier 2 holes
R Vera beat R Oosthuizen 3 and 2
B Mason beat M King 1 hole
M Thomson beat R Gillot 2 and 1
C Rodgers beat J Herbert 1 hole
E Gibstein beat E Wilson 4 and 3
P Hansson beat U Van Den Berg at 19th
M Illonen beat U Kaltenberger 3 and 1
C Elliot beat L Storm 3 and 2
B Omelia beat S Sheehan at 19th

Third Round
Hilton beat Quiros 2 and 1
Rankin beat Wittkop 4 and 2
Immelmann beat Havret 5 and 3
Bunch beat Gerwin at 19th
Wainwright beat Harris 1 hole
Ferrie beat Wallbank 1 hole
Side beat Loftus at 20th
Garcia beat McCarthy 4 and 3
Ogilvy beat Wahlstedt 4 and 3
Pimm beat Maly 1 hole
Williams beat Olver 2 holes
Vera beat Ravetto at 22nd
Mason beat Thomas 2 and 1
Rodgers beat Gibstein 5 and 3
Hansson beat Illonen 8 and 7
Omelia beat Elliot 2 and 1

Fourth Round
Hilton beat Rankin 1 hole
Immelman beat Bunch 2 and 1
Wainwright beat Ferrie 1 hole
Garcia beat Side 3 and 2
Ogilvy beat Pimm 5 and 3
Williams beat Vera 3 and 1
Mason beat Rodgers 2 and 1
Hansson beat Omelia 2 holes

Quarter Finals
Hilton beat Immelman 2 and 1
Garcia beat Wainwright 5 and 4
Williams beat Ogilvy 4 and 3
Mason beat Hansson 1 hole

Semi-Finals
Garcia beat Hilton at 23rd
Williams beat Mason 3 and 2

Final
Garcia beat Williams 7 and 6

British Seniors' Open Amateur Championship

Year	Winner	Venue	Score	Year	Winner	Venue	Score
1969	R Pattinson	Formby	154	1984	JC Owens (US)	Western Gailes	222
1970	K Bamber	Prestwick	150	1985	D Morey (US)	Hesketh	223
1971	GH Pickard	Deal, R Cinque Ports; Sandwich, R St George's	150	1986	AN Sturrock	Panmure	229
				1987	B Soyars (US)	Deal, R Cinque Ports	226
1972	TC Hartley	St Andrews	147	1988	CW Green	Barnton, Edinburgh	221
1973	JT Jones	Longniddry	142	1989	CW Green	Moortown, Alwoodley	226
1974	MA Ivor-Jones	Moortown	149	1990	CW Green	The Berkshire	207
1975	HJ Roberts	Turnberry	138	1991	CW Green	Prestwick	219
1976	WM Crichton	Berkshire	149	1992	C Hartland	Purdis Heath	221
1977	Dr TE Donaldson	Panmure	228	1993	CW Green	R Aberdeen, Murcar	150
1978	RJ White	Formby	225	1994	CW Green	Formby, Southport & Ainsdale	223
1979	RJ White	Harlech, R St David's	226				
1980	JM Cannon	Prestwick St Nicholas	218	1995	G Steel	Hankley Common	218
1981	T Branton	Hoylake, R Liverpool	227	1996	J Hirsch	Blairgowrie	210
1982	RL Glading	Blairgowrie	218	1997	G Bradley (US)	Sherwood Forest	216
1983	AJ Swann (US)	Walton Heath	222				

1998 *at Western Gailes and Glasgow Gailes*
1 D Lane   73-73-75—221
2 W Shean   75-76-76—227
3 H Mackeown   77-74-77—228

British Mid-Amateur Championship

Year	Winner	Runner-up	Venue
1995	G Wolstenholme	S Vale	Sunningdale
1996	G Wolstenholme	G Steel	Hillside, Lancs
1997	S Philipson	G Thomson	Prestwick

1998 *at Ganton*

Semi-Finals
G Wolstenholme beat J Longcake 1 hole
S Twynholm beat A Jackson 5 and 4

Final
G Wolstenholme beat S Twynholm at 19th hole

English Amateur Championship

Year	Winner	Runner-up	Venue	By
1925	TF Ellison	S Robinson	Hoylake, R Liverpool	1 hole
1926	TF Ellison	Sq Ldr CH Hayward	Walton Heath	6 and 4
1927	TP Perkins	JB Beddard	Little Aston	2 and 1
1928	JA Stout	TP Perkins	R Lytham and St Annes	3 and 2
1929	W Sutton	EB Tipping	Northumberland	3 and 2
1930	TA Bourn	CE Hardman	Burhham	3 and 2
1931	LG Crawley	W Sutton	Hunstanton	1 hole
1932	EW Fiddian	AS Bradshaw	Sandwich, R St George's	1 hole
1933	J Woollam	TA Bourn	Ganton	4 and 3
1934	S Lunt	LG Crawley	Formby	37th hole
1935	J Woollam	EW Fiddian	Hollinwell	2 and 1
1936	HG Bentley	JDA Langley	Deal	5 and 4
1937	JJ Pennink	LG Crawley	Saunton	6 and 5
1938	JJ Pennink	SE Banks	Moortown	2 and 1
1939	AL Bentley	W Sutton	R Birkdale	5 and 4
1946	IR Patey	K Thom	Mid-Surrey	5 and 4
1947	GH Micklem	C Stow	Ganton	1 hole
1948	AGB Helm	HJR Roberts	Little Aston	2 and 1
1949	RJ White	C Stowe	Formby	5 and 4
1950	JDA Langley	IR Patey	Deal	1 hole
1951	GP Roberts	H Bennett	Hunstanton	39th hole
1952	E Millward	TJ Shorrock	Burnham and Berrow	2 holes
1953	GH Micklem	RJ White	R Birkdale	2 and 1
1954	A Thirlwell	HG Bentley	Sandwich, R St George's	2 and 1
1955	A Thirlwell	M Burgess	Ganton	7 and 6
1956	GB Wolstenholme	H Bennett	R Lytham and St Annes	1 hole
1957	A Walker	G Whitehead	Hoylake, R Liverpool	4 and 3
1958	DN Sewell	DA Procter	Walton Heath	8 and 7
1959	GB Wolstenholme	MF Bonallack	Formby	1 hole
1960	DN Sewell	MJ Christmas	Hunstanton	41st hole
1961	I Caldwell	GJ Clark	Wentworth	37th hole
1962	MF Bonallack	MSR Lunt	Moortown	2 and 1
1963	MF Bonallack	A Thirlwell	Burnham and Berrow	4 and 3
1964	Dr D Marsh	R Foster	Hollinwell	1 hole
1965	MF Bonallack	CA Clark	Berkshire	3 and 2
1966	MSR Lunt	DJ Millensted	R Lytham and St Annes	3 and 2
1967	MF Bonallack	GE Hyde	Woodhall Spa	4 and 2
1968	MF Bonallack	PD Kelley	Ganton	12 and 11
1969	JH Cook	P Dawson	Sandwich, R St George's	6 and 4
1970	Dr D Marsh	SG Birtwell	R Birkdale	6 and 4
1971	W Humphreys	JC Davies	Burnham and Berrow	9 and 8
1972	H Ashby	R Revell	Northumberland	5 and 4
1973	H Ashby	SC Mason	Formby	5 and 4
1974	M James	JA Watts	Woodhall Spa	6 and 5
1975	N Faldo	D Eccleston	R Lytham and St Annes	6 and 4
1976	P Deeble	JC Davies	Ganton	3 and 1
1977	TR Shingler	J Mayell	Walton Heath	4 and 3
1978	P Downes	P Hoad	R Birkdale	1 hole
1979	R Chapman	A Carman	Sandwich, R St George's	6 and 5
1980	P Deeble	P McEvoy	Moortown	4 and 3

Year	Winner	Runner-up	Venue	By
1981	D Blakeman	A Stubbs	Burnham and Berrow	3 and 1
1982	A Oldcorn	I Bradshaw	Hoylake, R Liverpool	4 and 3
1983	G Laurence	A Brewer	Wentworth	7 and 6
1984	D Gilford	M Gerrard	Woodhall Spa	4 and 3
1985	R Winchester	P Robinson	Little Aston	1 hole
1986	J Langmead	B White	Hillside	2 and 1
1987	K Weeks	R Eggo	Frilford Heath	37th hole
1988	R Claydon	D Curry	R Birkdale	38th hole
1989	S Richardson	R Eggo	Sandwich, R St George's	2 and 1
1990	I Garbutt	G Evans	Woodhall Spa	8 and 7
1991	R Willison	M Pullan	Formby	10 and 8
1992	S Cage	R Hutt	Deal	3 and 2
1993	D Fisher	R Bland	Saunton	3 and 1
1994	M Foster	A Johnson	Moortown	8 and 7
1995	M Foster	S Jarman	Hunstanton	6 and 5
1996	S Webster	D Lucas	Hollinwell	6 and 4
1997	A Wainwright	P Rowe	Hoylake, R Liverpool	2 and 1

1998 at *Woodhall Spa*

Quarter Finals
N Ridewood beat D Errington 2 and 1
S Gorry beat B Taylor 3 and 2
R Smithies beat B Mason 5 and 4
M Sanders beat C Roake 3 and 2

Semi-Finals
M Sanders beat R Smithies 1 hole
S Gorry beat N Ridewood 2 and 1

Final
M Sanders beat S Gorry 6 and 5

English Open Amateur Strokeplay Championship (Brabazon Trophy)

Year	Winner	Venue	Score	Year	Winner	Venue	Score
1957	D Sewell	Moortown	287	1979	D Long	Little Aston	291
1958	AH Perowne	Birkdale	289	1980T	R Rafferty		
1959	D Sewell	Hollinwell	300		P McEvoy	Hunstanton	293
1960	GB Wolstenholme	Ganton	286	1981	P Way	Hillside	292
1961	RDBM Shade	Hoylake, R Liverpool	284	1982	P Downes	Woburn	299
1962	A Slater	Woodhall Spa	209	1983	C Banks	Hollinwell	294
1963	RDBM Shade	R Birkdale	306	1984	M Davis	Deal, R Cinque Ports	286
1964	MF Bonallack	Deal, R Cinque Ports	290	1985T	R Roper		
1965T	CA Clark	Formby	289		P Baker	Seaton Carew	296
	DJ Millensted			1986	R Kaplan	Sunningdale	286
	MJ Burgess			1987	JG Robinson	Ganton	287
1966	PM Townsend	Hunstanton	282	1988	R Eggo	Saunton	289
1967	RDBM Shade	Saunton	299	1989T	C Rivett		
1968	MF Bonallack	Walton Heath	210		RN Roderick	Hoylake, R Liverpool	293
1969T	R Foster			1990T	O Edmond		
	MF Bonallack	Moortown	290		G Evans	Burnham and Berrow	287
1970	R Foster	Little Aston	287	1991T	G Evans		
1971	MF Bonallack	Hillside	294		M Pullan	Hunstanton	284
1972	PH Moody	Hoylake, R Liverpool	296	1992	I Garrido	Notts	280
1973	R Revell	Hunstanton	294	1993	D Fisher	Stoneham	277
1974	N Sundelson	Moortown	291	1994	G Harris	Little Aston	280
1975	A Lyle	Hollinwell	298	1995T	M Foster		
1976	P Hedges	Saunton	294		CS Edwards	Hillside	283
1977	A Lyle	Hoylake, R Liverpool	293	1996	P Fenton	R St Georges	297
1978	G Brand Jr	Woodhall Spa	289	1997	D Park	Saunton	271

1998 at *Formby*

1	P Hansson	71-74-75-67—287
2	B Omelia	74-71-72-71—288
3	S Dyson	73-71-71-74—289

English Seniors' Amateur Championship

Year	Winner	Venue	Score	Year	Winner	Venue	Score
1981	CR Spalding	Copt Heath	152	1991	W Williams	Gerrards Cross, Denham	217
1982	JL Whitworth	Lindrick	152	1992	B Cawthray	Fulford	223
1983	B Cawthray	Ross-on-Wye	154	1993	G Edwards	John O'Gaunt	221
1984	RL Glading	Thetford	150	1994T	G Steel	Parkstone &	
1985	JR Marriott	Bristol and Clifton	153		F Jones	Broadstone	72§
1986	R Hiatt	Northants County	153	1995	H Hopkinson	Copt Heath	226
1987	I Caldwell	North Hants, Fleet	72	1996T	G Edwards		
(Curtailed due to bad weather)					B Berney	West Lancs	224
1988	G Edwards	Bromborough	222	1997	D Lane	West Hill & Woking	215
1989	G Clark	West Sussex	212				
1990	N Paul	Enville, Bridgnorth	217				

1998 *at Saunton*

1	J Marks	74-75-68—217
2	D Lane	73-69-76—218
3	B Berney	75-71-77—223
	R Smethurst	76-74-73—223

English Open Mid-Amateur Championship (Logan Trophy)

Year	Winner	Venue	Score	Year	Winner	Venue	Score
1988	P McEvoy	Little Aston	284	1994T	I Richardson		
1989	A Mew	Moortown	290		A McLure	Trentham	217
1990	A Mew	Wentworth	214	1995	C Banks	Seacroft	222
1991	I Richardson	West Lancashire	223	1996	C Banks	Pannal, Harrogate	222
1992	A Mew	King's Lynn	222	1997	C Banks	Stockport	211
1993	R Godley	Southport & Ainsdale	210				

1998 *at Broadstone*

1	S East	69-75-72—216
2	R Jones	71-72-74—217
3	A Mew	77-74-71—222
	K Weeks	76-72-74—222

English County Champions' Tournament

(Formerly President's Bowl)

Year	Winner	Year	Winner
1962 T	G Edwards, Cheshire	1980	D Lane, Berks, Bucks and Oxon
	A Thirwell, Northumberland	1981	M Kelly, Yorks
1963 T	M Burgess, Sussex/R Foster, Yorks	1982	P Deeble, Northumberland
1964	M Attenborough, Kent	1983	N Chesses, Warwickshire
1965	M Lees, Lincs	1984 T	N Briggs, Herts/P McEvoy, Warwickshire
1966	R Stephenson, Middx	1985	P Robinson, Herts
1967	P Benka, Surrey	1986	A Gelsthorpe, Yorks
1968	G Hyde, Sussex	1987 T	F George, Berks, Bucks & Oxon
1969	A Holmes, Herts		D Fay, Surrey
1970	M King, Berks, Bucks and Oxon	1988	R Claydon, Cambridge
1971	M Lee, Yorks	1989	R Willison, Middlesex
1972	P Berry, Glos	1990 T	P Streeter, Lincs/R Sloman, Kent
1973	A Chandler, Lancs	1991	T Allen, Warwickshire
1974 T	G Hyde, Sussex/A Lyle, Shrops & Hereford	1992	L Westwood, Notts
1975	N Faldo, Herts	1993	R Walker, Durham
1976	R Brown, Devon	1994	G Wolstenholme, Glos
1977	M Walls, Cumbria	1995	S Webster, Warwickshire
1978	I Simpson, Notts	1996T	J Herbert, Leics/G Wolstenholme, Glos
1979	N Burch, Essex	1997	J Herbert, Leicestershire & Rutland

1998 English County Champions' Tournament at Woodhall Spa

1	G Wolstenholme (Leics)	67-71—138
2	C Hudson (Hants)	71-72—143
3	G Keate (Northants)	73-74—147

Irish Amateur Championship

Year	Winner	Runner-up	Venue	By
1960	M Edwards	N Fogarty	Portstewart	6 and 5
1961	D Sheahan	J Brown	Rosses Point	5 and 4
1962	M Edwards	J Harrington	Baltray	42nd hole
1963	JB Carr	EC O'Brien	Killarney	2 and 1
1964	JB Carr	A McDade	Co Down	6 and 5
1965	JB Carr	T Craddock	Rosses Point	3 and 2
1966	D Sheahan	J Faith	Dollymount	3 and 2
1967	JB Carr	PD Flaherty	Lahinch	1 hole
1968	M O'Brien	F McCarroll	Portrush	2 and 1
1969	V Nevin	J O'Leary	Co Sligo	1 hole
1970	D Sheahan	M Bloom	Grange	2 holes
1971	P Kane	M O'Brien	Ballybunion	3 and 2
1972	K Stevenson	B Hoey	Co Down	2 and 1
1973	RKM Pollin	RM Staunton	Rosses Point	1 hole
1974	R Kane	M Gannon	Portmarnock	5 and 4
1975	MD O'Brien	JA Bryan	Cork	5 and 4
1976	D Brannigan	D O'Sullivan	Portrush	2 holes
1977	M Gannon	A Hayes	Westport	19th hole
1978	M Morris	T Cleary	Carlow	1 hole
1979	J Harrington	MA Gannon	Ballybunion	2 and 1
1980	R Rafferty	MJ Bannon	Co Down	8 and 7
1981	D Brannigan	F McMenamin	Co Sligo	19th hole
1982	P Walton	B Smyth	Woodbrook	7 and 6
1983	T Corridan	E Power	Killarney	2 holes
1984	CB Hoey	L McNamara	Malone	20th hole
1985	D O'Sullivan	D Branigan	Westport	1 hole
1986	J McHenry	P Rayfus	Dublin	4 and 3
1987	E Power	JP Fitzgerald	Tranmore	2 holes
1988	G McGimpsey	D Mulholland	Portrush	2 and 1
1989	P McGinley	N Goulding	Rosses Point	3 and 2
1990	D Clarke	P Harrington	Baltray	3 and 2
1991	G McNeill	N Goulding	Ballybunion	3 and 1
1992	G Murphy	JP Fitzgerald	Portstewart	2 and 1
1993	E Power	D Higgins	Enniscrone	3 and 2
1994	D Higgins	P Harrington	Portmarnock	20th hole
1995	P Harrington	D Coughlan	Lahinch	3 and 2
1996	P Lawrie	G McGimpsey	Royal Co Down	3 and 2
1997	K Kearney	P Lawrie	Fota Island	5 and 4

1998 at *The Island Golf Club*

Quarter Finals
E Power beat M McGinley 7 and 6
G Cullen beat B Ronan at 20th
M Hoey beat R Symes 1 hole
B Omelia beat D Coyle 2 and 1

Semi-Finals
E Power beat G Cullen 2 holes
B Omelia beat M Hoey 1 hole

Final
E Power beat B Omelia 1 hole

Irish Seniors' Open Amateur Championship

Year	Winner	Venue	Score	Year	Winner	Venue	Score
1980	GN Fogarty	Galway	144	1989	B McCrea	Royal Belfast	150
1981	GN Fogarty	Bundoran	149	1990	C Hartland	Cork	149
1982	J Murray	Douglas	141	1991	C Hartland	Mullingar	147
1983	F Sharpe	Courtown	153	1992	C Hartland	Athlone	145
1984	J Boston	Connemara	147	1993	P Breen	Bangor	147
1985	J Boston	Newcastle	155	1994	B Buckley	Tramore	151
1986	J Coey	Waterford	141	1995	B Hoey	Dundalk	151
1987	J Murray	Castleroy	150	1996	E Condren	Oughterard	148
1988	WB Buckley	Westport	154	1997	B Wilson	Knock, Belfast	152

1998 *at Thurles Golf Club*

1	J Harrington	74-75—149
2	T J Semple	76-75—151
3	K Rogers	74-77—151

Scottish Amateur Championship

Year	Winner	Runner-up	Venue	By
1922	J Wilson	E Blackwell	St Andrews	19th hole
1923	TM Burrell	Dr A McCallum	Troon	1 hole
1924	WW Mackenzie	W Tulloch	Aberdeen	3 and 2
1925	JT Dobson	W Mackenzie	Muirfield	3 and 2
1926	WJ Guild	SO Shepherd	Leven	2 and 1
1927	A Jamieson Jr	Rev D Rutherford	Gailes	22nd hole
1928	WW Mackenzie	W Dodds	Muirfield	5 and 3
1929	JT Bookless	J Dawson	Aberdeen	5 and 4
1930	K Greig	T Wallace	Carnoustie	9 and 8
1931	J Wilson	A Jamieson Jr	Prestwick	2 and 1
1932	J McLean	K Greig	Dunbar	5 and 4
1933	J McLean	KC Forbes	Aberdeen	6 and 4
1934	J McLean	W Campbell	Western Gailes	3 and 1
1935	H Thomson	J McLean	St Andrews	2 and 1
1936	ED Hamilton	R Neill	Carnoustie	1 hole
1937	H McInally	K Patrick	Barassie	6 and 5
1938	ED Hamilton	R Rutherford	Muirfield	4 and 2
1939	H McInally	H Thomson	Prestwick	6 and 5
1946	EC Brown	R Rutherford	Carnoustie	3 and 2
1947	H McInally	J Pressley	Glasgow Gailes	10 and 8
1948	AS Flockhart	G Taylor	Balgownie, Aberdeen	7 and 6
1949	R Wright	H McInally	Muirfield	1 hole
1950	WC Gibson	D Blair	Prestwick	2 and 1
1951	JM Dykes	J Wilson	St Andrews	4 and 2
1952	FG Dewar	J Wilson	Carnoustie	4 and 3
1953	DA Blair	J McKay	Western Gailes	3 and 1
1954	JW Draper	W Gray	Nairn	4 and 3
1955	RR Jack	AC Miller	Muirfield	2 and 1
1956	Dr FWG Deighton	A MacGregor	Troon	8 and 7
1957	JS Montgomerie	J Burnside	Balgownie	2 and 1
1958	WD Smith	I Harris	Prestwick	6 and 5
1959	Dr FWG Deighton	R Murray	St Andrews	6 and 5
1960	JR Young	S Saddler	Carnoustie	5 and 3
1961	J Walker	ST Murray	Western Gailes	4 and 3
1962	SWT Murray	R Shade	Muirfield	2 and 1
1963	RDBM Shade	N Henderson	Troon	4 and 3
1964	RDBM Shade	J McBeath	Nairn	8 and 7
1965	RDBM Shade	G Cosh	St Andrews	4 and 2
1966	RDBM Shade	C Strachan	Western Gailes	9 and 8
1967	RDBM Shade	A Murphy	Carnoustie	5 and 4
1968	GB Cosh	R Renfrew	Muirfield	4 and 3
1969	JM Cannon	A Hall	Troon	6 and 4
1970	CW Green	H Stewart	Balgownie, Aberdeen	1 hole
1971	S Stephen	C Green	St Andrews	3 and 2
1972	HB Stuart	A Pirie	Prestwick	3 and 1
1973	IC Hutcheon	A Brodie	Carnoustie	3 and 2
1974	GH Murray	A Pirie	Western Gailes	2 and 1

National Amateur Championships 243

Year	Winner	Runner-up	Venue	By	
1975	D Greig	G Murray	Montrose	7 and 6	
1976	GH Murray	H Stuart	St Andrews	6 and 5	
1977	A Brodie	P McKellar	Troon	1 hole	
1978	IA Carslaw	J Cuddihy	Downfield	7 and 6	
1979	K Macintosh	P McKellar	Prestwick	5 and 4	
1980	D Jamieson	C Green	Balgownie, Aberdeen	2 and 1	*(18)*
1981	C Dalgleish	A Thomson	Western Gailes	7 and 6	
1982	CW Green	G McGregor	Carnoustie	1 hole	
1983	CW Green	J Huggan	Gullane	1 hole	
1984	A Moir	K Buchan	Renfrew	3 and 3	
1985	D Carrick	D James	Southerness	4 and 2	
1986	C Brooks	A Thomson	Monifieth	3 and 2	
1987	C Montgomerie	A Watt	Nairn	9 and 8	
1988	J Milligan	A Colthart	Barassie	1 hole	
1989	A Thomson	A Tait	Moray	1 hole	
1990	C Everett	M Thomson	Gullane	7 and 5	
1991	G Lowson	L Salariya	Downfield	4 and 3	
1992	S Gallacher	D Kirkpatrick	Glasgow Gailes	37th hole	
1993	D Robertson	R Russell	R Dornoch	2 holes	
1994	H McKibben	A Reid	Renfrew	39th hole	
1995	S Mackenzie	H McKibben	Southerness	8 and 7	
1996	M Brooks	A Turnbull	Dunbar	7 and 6	
1997	C Hislop	S Cairns	Carnoustie	5 and 3	

1998 *at Prestwick*

Quarter Finals
M Donaldson beat C Watson 1 hole
A Thomson beat A Laing at the 22nd
T Cochrane beat C Heap 4 and 2
G Rankin beat B Main 2 and 1

Semi-Finals
M Donaldson beat A Thomson at the 20th
G Rankin beat T Cochrane 8 and 7

Final
G Rankin beat M Donaldson 6 and 5

Scottish Open Amateur Strokeplay Championship

Year	Winner		Score	
1967	BJ Gallacher	Muirfield and Gullane	291	
1968	RDBM Shade	Prestwick and Prestwick St Nicholas	282	
1969	JS Macdonald	Carnoustie and Monifieth	288	
1970	D Hayes	Glasgow Gailes and Barassie	275	
1971	IC Hutcheon	Leven and Lundin Links	277	
1972	BN Nicholas	Dalmahoy and Ratho Park	290	
1973 T	DM Robertson/GJ Clark	Dunbar and North Berwick	284	
1974	IC Hutcheon	Blairgowrie and Alyth	283	
1975	CW Green	Nairn and Nairn Dunbar	295	
1976	S Martin	Monifieth and Carnoustie	299	
1977	PJ McKellar	Muirfield and Gullane	299	
1978	AR Taylor	Keir and Cawder	281	
1979	IC Hutcheon	Lansdowne and Rosemount	286	
1980	G Brand Jr	Musselburgh and R Musselburgh	207	*(54 holes)*
1981	F Walton	Erskine and Renfrew	287	
1982	C Macgregor	Downfield and Camperdown	287	
1983	C Murray	Irvine	291	
1984	CW Green	Blairgowrie	287	
1985	C Montgomerie	Dunbar	274	
1986	KH Walker	Carnoustie	289	
1987	D Carrick	Lundin Links	282	
1988	S Easingwood	Cathkin Braes	277	
1989	F Illouz	Blairgowrie	281	
1990	G Hay	R Aberdeen	133	*(36 holes)*
1991	A Coltart	Renfrew	291	
1992	D Robertson	Mortonhall	281	*continued*

Scottish Open Amateur Strokeplay Championship *continued*

Year	Winner		Score
1993	A Reid	St Andrews	289
1994	D Downie	Letham Grange	288
1995	S Gallacher	Paisley	284
1996	A Forsyth	Cardross	279
1997	DB Howard	Monifieth and Panmure	271

1998 *at Moray GC and Elgin GC*

1	L Kelly	74-65-64-72—275
2	S Carmichael	70-66-71-74—281
3	E Forbes	73-71-67-72—283

Scottish Senior Championship

Year	Winner	Venue	Score	Year	Winner	Venue	Score
1978 T	JM Cannon	Glasgow Killermont	149	1986	RL Glading	Royal Burgess	153
	GR Carmichael			1987	I Hornsby	Glasgow Killermont	145
1979	A Sinclair	Glasgow Killermont	143	1988	J Hayes	Royal Burgess	143
1980	JM Cannon	Royal Burgess	149	1989	AS Mayer	Glasgow Killermont	
1981 T	IR Harris	Glasgow Killermont	146	1990	G Hartland	Royal Burgess	146
	Dr J Hastings			1991	CW Green	Glasgow Killermont	140
	AN Sturrock			1992	G Clark	Royal Burgess	148
1982 T	JM Cannon	Royal Burgess	143	1993	J Maclean	Glasgow Killermont	141
	J Niven			1994	DM Laurie	Ladybank	149
1983	WD Smith	Glasgow Killermont	145	1995	CW Green	Glasgow	141
1984	A Sinclair	Royal Burgess	148	1996	CW Green	Western Gailes	146
1985	AN Sturrock	Glasgow Killermont	143	1997	CW Green	Glasgow Killermont	137

1998 *at Ladybank*

1	C Green	74-72—146
2	M Niven	71-75—146
3	N Grant	71-76—147

Scottish Champion of Champions

Year	Winner	Year	Winner	Year	Winner
1970	A Horne	1980	I Hutcheon	1990	J Milligan
1971	D Black	1981	I Hutcheon	1991	G Hay
1972	R Strachan	1982	G Macgregor	1992	D Robertson
1973	*Not held*	1983	D Carrick	1993	R Russell
1974	M Niven	1984	S Stephen	1994	G Sherry
1975	A Brodie	1985	I Brotherston	1995	S Gallacher
1976	A Brodie	1986	I Hutcheon	1996	M Brooks
1977	V Reid	1987	G Shaw	1997	G Rankin
1978	D Greig	1988	I Hutcheon		
1979	B Marchbank	1989	J Milligan		

1998 *at Leven*

1	G Rankin	73-67-71-68—279
2	J Rose	76-69-70-70—285
3	E Forbes	75-71-71-72—289

Scottish Mid-Amateur Championship

1998 *at Blairgowrie*

Semi-Final	**Final**
G Campbell beat E Moir 5 and 4	G Campbell beat G Hay 5 and 4
G Hay beat H Thompson 3 and 2	

Welsh Amateur Championship

Year	Winner	Runner-up	Venue	By
1934	SB Roberts	GS Noon	Prestatyn	4 and 3
1935	R Chapman	GS Noon	Tenby	1 hole
1936	RM de Lloyd	G Wallis	Aberdovey	1 hole
1937	DH Lewis	R Glossop	Porthcawl	2 holes
1938	AA Duncan	SB Roberts	Rhyl	2 and 1
1946	JV Moody	A Marshman	Porthcawl	9 and 8
1947	SB Roberts	G Breen Turner	Harlech	8 and 7
1948	AA Duncan	SB Roberts	Porthcawl	2 and 1
1949	AD Evans	MA Jones	Aberdovey	2 and 1
1950	JL Morgan	DJ Bonnell	Southerndown	9 and 7
1951	JL Morgan	WI Tucker	Harlech	3 and 2
1952	AA Duncan	JL Morgan	Ashburnham	4 and 3
1953	SB Roberts	D Pearson	Prestatyn	5 and 3
1954	AA Duncan	K Thomas	Tenby	6 and 5
1955	TJ Davies	P Dunn	Harlech	38th hole
1956	A Lockley	WI Tucker	Southerndown	2 and 1
1957	ES Mills	H Griffiths	Harlech	2 and 1
1958	HC Squirrell	AD Lake	Conway	4 and 3
1959	HC Squirrell	N Rees	Porthcawl	8 and 7
1960	HC Squirrell	P Richards	Aberdovey	2 and 1
1961	AD Evans	J Toye	Ashburnham	3 and 2
1962	J Povall	HC Squirrell	Harlech	3 and 2
1963	WI Tucker	J Povall	Southerndown	4 and 3
1964	HC Squirrell	WI Tucker	Harlech	1 hole
1965	HC Squirrell	G Clay	Porthcawl	6 and 4
1966	WI Tucker	EN Davies	Aberdovey	6 and 5
1967	JK Povall	WI Tucker	Asburnham	3 and 2
1968	J Buckley	J Povall	Conway	8 and 7
1969	JL Toye	EN Davies	Porthcawl	1 hole
1970	EN Davies	J Povall	Harlech	1 hole
1971	CT Brown	HC Squirrell	Southerndown	6 and 5
1972	EN Davies	JL Toye	Prestatyn	40th hole
1973	D McLean	T Holder	Ashburnham	6 and 4
1974	S Cox	EN Davies	Caernarvonshire	3 and 2
1975	JL Toye	WI Tucker	Porthcawl	5 and 4
1976	MPD Adams	WI Tucker	Harlech	6 and 5
1977	D Stevens	JKD Povall	Southerndown	3 and 2
1978	D McLean	A Ingram	Caernarvonshire	11 and 10
1979	TJ Melia	MS Roper	Ashburnham	5 and 4
1980	DL Stevens	G Clement	Prestatyn	10 and 9
1981	S Jones	C Davies	Porthcawl	5 and 3
1982	D Wood	C Davies	Harlech	8 and 7
1983	JR Jones	AP Parkin	Southerndown	2 holes
1984	JR Jones	A Llyr	Prestatyn	1 hole
1985	ED Jones	MA Macara	Ashburnham	2 and 1
1986	C Rees	B Knight	Conwy	1 hole
1987	PM Mayo	DK Wood	Porthcawl	2 holes
1988	K Jones	RN Roderick	Harlech	40th hole
1989	S Dodd	K Jones	Tenby	2 and 1
1990	A Barnett	A Jones	Prestatyn	1 hole
1991	S Pardoe	S Jones	Ashburnham	7 and 5
1992	H Roberts	R Johnson	Pyle & Kenfig	3 and 2
1993	B Dredge	M Ellis	Southerndown	3 and 1
1994	C Evans	M Smith	Royal Porthcawl	5 and 4
1995	G Houston	C Evans	R St David's	3 and 2
1996	Y Taylor	DH Park	Ashburnham	3 and 2
1997	JR Donaldson	M Pilkington	Pyle & Kenfig	5 and 4

1998 *at Prestatyn*

Quarter Finals
I Campbell beat M Griffiths 4 and 3
M Pilkington beat S Roberts 2 and 1
NB Edwards beat G James 2 and 1
K Sullivan beat PJ Hunt at 20th

Semi-Finals
K Sullivan beat NB Edwards 1 up
M Pilkington beat I Campbell at 20th

Final
M Pilkington beat K Sullivan 2 and 1

Welsh Amateur Strokeplay Championship

Year	Winner	Venue	Score	Year	Winner	Venue	Score
1967	EN Davies	Harlech	295	1983	G Davies	Aberdovey	287
1968	JA Buckley	Harlech	294	1984	RN Roderick	Newport	292
1969	DL Stevens	Tenby	288	1985	MA Macara	Harlech	291
1970	JK Povall	Newport	292	1986	M Calvert	Pyle & Kenfig	299
1971T	EN Davies	Harlech	296	1987	MA Macara	Llandudno (Maesdu)	290
	JL Toye			1988	RN Roderick	Tenby	283
1972	JR Jones	Pyle & Kenfig	299	1989	SC Dodd	Conwy	304
1973	JR Jones	Llandudno (Maesdu)	300	*Open event since 1990*			
1974	JL Toye	Tenby	307				
1975	D McLean	Wrexham	288	1990	G Houston	Pyle & Kenfig	288
1976	WI Tucker	Newport	282	1991	A Jones	R Porthcawl	290
1977	JA Buckley	Prestatyn	302	1992	AJ Barnett	R St David's	278
1978	HJ Evans	Pyle & Kenfig	300	1993	M Macara	Maesdu	280
1979	D McLean	Holyhead	289	1994	N Van Hootegem	St Pierre	290
1980	TJ Melia	Tenby	291	1995	M Peet	Prestatyn	282
1981	D Evans	Wrexham	270	1996	M Blackey	Tenby	276
1982	JR Jones	Cradoc	287	1997	G Wolstenholme	Conwy	286

1998 *at Southerndown*

1	DAJ Patrick	71-71-69-69—279
2	L Kelly	69-68-73-72—282
3	B Lamb	65-74-73-71—283
	L Donald	68-71-72-72—283
	P Rowe	66-71-72-74—283

Welsh Seniors' Amateur Championship

Year	Winner	Venue	Score	Year	Winner	Venue	Score
1975	A Marshman	Aberdovey	77 (18)	1987	WS Gronow	Aberdovey	146
1976	AD Evans	Aberdovey	156	1988	NA Lycett	Aberdovey	150
1977	AE Lockley	Aberdovey	154	1989	WI Tucker	Aberdovey	160
1978	AE Lockley	Aberdovey	75 (18)	1990	I Hughes	Aberdovey	159
1979	CR Morgan	Aberdovey	158	1991	RO Ward	Aberdovey	155
1980	ES Mills	Aberdovey	152	1992	I Hughes	Aberdovey	150
1981	T Branton	Aberdovey	153	1993	G Perks	Aberdovey	149
1982	WI Tucker	Aberdovey	147	1994T	G Perks/I Hughes/A Prytherch	Aberdovey	157
1983	WS Gronow	Aberdovey	153	1995	I Hughes	Aberdovey	147
1984	WI Tucker	Aberdovey	150	1996	G Isaac	Aberdovey	152
1985	NA Lycett	Aberdovey	149	1997	I Hughes	Aberdovey	148
1986	E Mills	Aberdovey	154				

1998 *at Aberdovey*

1	D Reidford	76-82—158
2	B Sandford	79-80—159
	EG Evans	79-80—159
	RM Edwards	79-80—159
	J Evans	76-83—159

Welsh Mid-Amateur Championship

1998 *at Pennard GC*

1	M Skinner	76-73-69—218
2	C Rowe	76-75-73—224
3	R Maliphant	77-73-75—225

Welsh Champion of Champions
1998 *at Cradoc GC*

1	M Gwyther (Morlais Castle)	145
2	T Need (Celtic Manor)	148
3	L Bannister (Brecon)	148

European Amateur Championship

Year	Winner	Venue	Year	Winner	Venue
1986	A Haglund (Swe)	Eindhoven, Netherlands	1994	S Gallacher (Sco)	Aura, Finland
1988	D Ecob (Aus)	Falkenstein, Germany	1995	S Garcia (Sp)	El Prat, Spain
1990	K Erikson (Swe)	Aalborg, Denmark	1996	D Olsson (Swe)	Karlstad, Sweden
1991	J Payne (Eng)	Hillside, England	1997	D de Vooght (Bel)	Domaine Imperial, Switzerland
1992	M Scarpa (It)	Le Querce, Italy			
1993	M Backhausen (Den)	Dalmahoy, Scotland			

1998 *at Golf du Medoc, France*

1	P Gribben (Ire)	274
2	C Williams (Wal)	276
	G Wolstenholme (Eng)	276

European Seniors' Championship
1998 *at Ascona, Switzerland*

1	D Lane (Eng)	213
2	J Sanchez (Sp)	218
3	HJ Ecklebe (Ger)	221

European Mid-Amateur Championship
1998 *at Roma GC, Italy*

1	Victor Grande (Sp)	215
2	Miguel Preysler (Sp)	218
	Per Anders Winge (Swe)	218

Team Events

United States *v* Great Britain & Ireland *(Unofficial)*

Year		Great Britain		USA		Venue
1921 (May 21)	Foursomes Singles	0 3	3	4 5	9	Hoylake

The Walker Cup *(Instituted 1922)*

Year		GB&I		USA		Venue
1922 (August 29)	Foursomes Singles	1 3	4	3 5	8	Long Island, NY
1923 (May 18–19)	Foursomes Singles	3 2½	5½	1 5½	6½	St Andrews
1924 (Sept 12–13)	Foursomes Singles	1 2	3	3 6	9	Garden City, NY
1926 (June 2–3)	Foursomes Singles	1 4½	5½	3 3½	6½	St Andrews
1928 (Aug 30–31)	Foursomes Singles	0 1	1	4 7	11	Chicago
1930 (May 15–16)	Foursomes Singles	1 1	2	3 7	10	Sandwich
1932 (Sept 1–2)	Foursomes Singles	0 2½	2½	4 5½	9½	Brookline, Massachusetts
1934 (May 11–12)	Foursomes Singles	1 1½	2½	3 6½	9½	St Andrews
1936 (Sept 2–3)	Foursomes Singles	1 ½	1½	3 7½	10½	Pine Valley, NJ
1938 (June 3–4)	Foursomes Singles	2½ 5	7½	1½ 3	4½	St Andrews
1947 (May 16–17)	Foursomes Singles	2 2	4	2 6	8	St Andrews
1949 (Aug 19–20)	Foursomes Singles	1 1	2	3 7	10	Winged Foot, NY
1951 (May 11–12)	Foursomes Singles	1 3½	4½	3 4½	7½	Royal Birkdale
1953 (Sept 4–5)	Foursomes Singles	1 2	3	3 6	9	Kittansett, Massachusetts
1955 (May 20–21)	Foursomes Singles	0 2	2	4 6	10	St Andrews
1957 (Sept 1–2)	Foursomes Singles	1½ 2	3½	2½ 6	8½	Minikahda
1959 (May 15–16)	Foursomes Singles	0 3	3	4 5	9	Muirfield
1961 (Sept 1–2)	Foursomes Singles	0 1	1	4 7	11	Seattle, Washington

From 1963 Foursomes and Singles matches were played on both days, each match over 18 holes.

1963 (May 24–25)	Foursomes Singles	1 7	8	6 6	12	Turnberry
1965 (Sept 3–4)	Foursomes Singles	4 7	11	3 8	11	Baltimore, Maryland
1967 (May 15–20)	Foursomes Singles	3 4	7	4 9	13	Sandwich

Year		GB&I		USA		Venue
1969 (Aug 22–23)	Foursomes Singles	3 5	8	3 7	10	Milwaukee, Wisconsin
1971 (May 26–27)	Foursomes Singles	5½ 7½	13	2½ 8½	11	St Andrews
1973 (Aug 24–25)	Foursomes Singles	1 9	10	7 7	14	Brookline, Massachusetts
1975 (May 28–29)	Foursomes Singles	3 5½	8½	5 10½	15½	St Andrews
1977 (Aug 26–27)	Foursomes Singles	3 5	8	5 11	16	Shinnecock Hills, NY
1979 (May 30–31)	Foursomes Singles	4 4½	8½	4 11½	15½	Muirfield
1981 (Aug 28–29)	Foursomes Singles	4 5	9	4 11	15	Cypress Point
1983 (May 25–26)	Foursomes Singles	4½ 6	10½	3½ 10	13½	Hoylake
1985 (Aug 21–22)	Foursomes Singles	3 8	11	5 8	13	Pine Valley, NJ
1987 (May 27–28)	Foursomes Singles	1 6½	7½	7 9½	16½	Sunningdale

1989 at Peachtree, Atlanta, 16th and 17th August

Great Britain and Ireland   USA

First Day – Foursomes

R Claydon and D Prosser	0	R Gamez and D Martin (3 and 2)	1
S Dodd and G McGimpsey	½	D Yates and P Mickelson	½
P McEvoy and E O'Connell (6 and 5)	1	G Lesher and J Sigel	0
J Milligan and A Hare (2 and 1)	1	D Eger and K Johnson	0
	2½		1½

Singles

J Milligan	0	R Gamez (7 and 6)	1
R Claydon (5 and 4)	1	D Martin	0
S Dodd	½	E Meeks	½
E O'Connell (5 and 4)	1	R Howe	0
P McEvoy (2 and 1)	1	D Yates	0
G McGimpsey	0	P Mickelson (4 and 2)	1
C Cassells (1 hole)	1	G Lesher	0
RN Roderick	½	J Sigel	½
	5		3

Match position: GB&I 7½, USA 4½

Second Day – Foursomes

P McEvoy and E O'Connell	½	R Gamez and D Martin	½
R Claydon and C Cassells (3 and 2)	1	J Sigel and G Lesher	0
J Milligan and A Hare (2 and 1)	1	D Eger and K Johnson	0
G McGimpsey and S Dodd (2 and 1)	1	P Mickelson and D Yates	0
	3½		½

Singles

S Dodd	0	R Gamez (1 hole)	1
A Hare	½	D Martin	½
R Claydon	0	G Lesher (3 and 2)	1
P McEvoy	0	D Yates (4 and 3)	1
E O'Connell	½	P Mickelson	½
RN Roderick	0	D Eger (4 and 2)	1
C Cassells	0	GK Johnson (4 and 2)	1
J Milligan	½	J Sigel	½
	1½		6½

Result: Great Britain and Ireland 12½, USA 11½

1991 Walker Cup at Portmarnock, Dublin, 5th and 6th September

Great Britain and Ireland

First Day – Foursomes
J Milligan and G Hay	0
J Payne and G Evans	0
G McGimpsey and R Willison	0
P McGinley and P Harrington	0
	0

USA

P Mickelson and B May (5 and 3)	1
D Duval and M Sposa (1 hole)	1
M Voges and D Eger (1 hole)	1
J Sigel and A Doyle (2 and 1)	1
	4

Singles

A Coltart	0	P Mickelson (4 and 3)	1
J Payne (2 and 1)	1	F Langham	0
G Evans (2 and 1)	1	D Duval	0
R Willison	0	B May (2 and 1)	1
G McGimpsey (1 hole)	1	M Sposa	0
P McGinley	0	A Doyle (6 and 4)	1
G Hay (1 hole)	1	T Scherrer	0
L White	0	J Sigel (4 and 3)	1
	4		4

Match position: GB&I 4, USA 8

Second Day – Foursomes
J Milligan and G McGimpsey (2 and 1)	1	M Voges and D Eger	0
J Payne and R Willison	0	D Duval and M Sposa (1 hole)	1
G Evans and A Coltart (4 and 3)	1	F Langham and T Scherrer	0
L White and P McGinley (1 hole)	1	P Mickelson and B May	0
	3		1

Singles

J Milligan	0	P Mickelson (1 hole)	1
J Payne (3 and 1)	1	A Doyle	0
G Evans	0	F Langham (4 and 2)	1
A Coltart (1 hole)	1	J Sigel	0
R Willison (3 and 2)	1	T Scherrer	0
P Harrington	0	D Eger (3 and 2)	1
G McGimpsey	0	B May (4 and 3)	1
G Hay	0	M Voges (3 and 1)	1
	3		5

Result: Great Britain and Ireland 10, USA 14

1993 at Interlachen, Edina, Minnesota, on 18th and 19th August

Match shortened because of rain and flooding

Great Britain and Ireland

First Day – Singles
I Pyman	0	A Doyle (1 hole)	1
M Stanford (3 and 2)	1	D Berganio	0
D Robertson (3 and 2)	1	J Sigel	0
S Cage	½	K Mitchum	½
P Harrington	0	T Herron (1 hole)	1
P Page	0	D Yates (2 and 1)	1
R Russell	0	T Demsey (2 and 1)	1
R Burns	0	J Leonard (4 and 3)	1
V Phillips (2 and 1)	1	B Gay	0
B Dredge	0	J Harris (4 and 3)	1
	3½		6½

Match position: GB&I 3½, USA 6½

Second Day – Foursomes
I Pyman and S Cage	0	A Doyle and J Leonard (4 and 3)	1
M Stanford and P Harrington	0	D Berganio and T Demsey (3 and 2)	1
B Dredge and V Phillips	0	J Sigel and K Mitchum (3 and 2)	1
R Russsell and D Robertson	0	J Harris and T Herron (1 hole)	1
	0		4

Singles

D Robertson	0	A Doyle (4 and 3)	1
I Pyman	0	J Harris (3 and 2)	1
S Cage	0	D Yates (2 and 1)	1
P Harrington	½	B Gay	½
P Page	0	J Sigel (5 and 4)	1
V Phillips	0	T Herron (3 and 2)	1
R Russell	0	K Mitchum (4 and 2)	1
R Burns (1 hole)	1	D Berganio	0
B Dredge	0	T Demsey (3 and 2)	1
M Stanford	0	J Leonard (5 and 4)	1
	1½		8½

Result: Great Britain and Ireland 5, USA 19

1995 *at Royal Porthcawl, Wales, on 9th and 10th September*

Great Britain and Ireland   **USA**

First Day – **Foursomes**

G Sherry and S Gallacher	0	J Harris and T Woods (4 and 3)	1
M Foster and D Howell	½	A Bratton and C Riley	½
G Rankin and B Howard	0	N Begay and T Jackson (4 and 3)	1
P Harrington and J Fanagan (5 and 3)	1	K Cox and T Kuehne	0
	1½		2½

Singles

G Sherry (3 and 2)	1	N Begay	0
L James	0	K Cox (1 hole)	1
M Foster (4 and 3)	1	B Marucci	0
S Gallacher (4 and 3)	1	T Jackson	0
P Harrington (2 holes)	1	J Courville	0
B Howard	½	A Bratton	½
G Rankin	0	J Harris (1 hole)	1
G Wolstenholme (1 hole)	1	T Woods	0
	5½		2½

Match position: GB&I 7, USA 5

Second Day – **Foursomes**

G Sherry and S Gallacher	0	A Bratton and C Riley (4 and 2)	1
D Howell and M Foster (3 and 2)	1	K Cox and T Kuehne	0
G Wolstenholme and L James	0	B Marucci and J Courville (6 and 5)	1
P Harrington and J Fanagan (2 and 1)	1	J Harris and T Woods	0
	2		2

Singles

G Sherry (2 holes)	1	C Riley	0
D Howell (2 and 1)	1	N Begay	0
S Gallacher (3 and 2)	1	T Kuehne	0
J Fanagan (3 and 2)	1	J Courville	0
B Howard	½	T Jackson	½
M Foster	½	B Marucci	½
P Harrington	0	J Harris (3 and 2)	1
G Wolstenholme	0	T Woods (4 and 3)	1
	5		3

Result: Great Britain and Ireland 14, USA 10

1997 Walker Cup *at Quaker Ridge, New York, on 9th and 10th August*

Great Britain and Ireland   USA

First Day – Foursomes

B Howard and S Young	0	B Elder and J Kribel (4 and 3)	1
J Rose and M Brooks	0	J Courville and B Marucci (5 and 4)	1
G Wolstenholme and K Nolan	0	J Gore and J Harris (6 and 4)	1
R Coughlan and D Park	0	R Leen and C Wollmann (1 hole)	1
	0		4

Singles

S Young (5 and 4)	1	D Delcher	0
C Watson (1 hole)	1	S Scott	0
B Howard	0	B Elder (5 and 4)	1
J Rose (1 hole)	1	J Kribel	0
K Nolan	0	R Leen (3 and 2)	1
G Rankin	0	J Gore (3 and 2)	1
R Coughlan	½	C Wollmann	½
G Wolstenholme	0	J Harris (1 hole)	1
	3½		4½

Match position: GB&I 3½, USA 8½

Day Two – Foursomes

S Young and C Watson	0	J Harris and B Elder (3 and 2)	1
B Howard and G Rankin	0	J Courville and B Marucci (5 and 4)	1
R Coughlan and D Park	0	D Delcher and S Scott (1 hole)	1
G Wolstenholme and J Rose (2 and 1)	1	R Leen and C Wollmann	0
	1		3

Singles

S Young (2 and 1)	1	J Kribel	0
C Watson	½	J Gore	½
J Rose	0	J Courville (3 and 2)	1
K Nolan	0	B Elder (2 and 1)	1
M Brooks	0	J Harris (6 and 5)	1
D Park	0	B Marucci (4 and 3)	1
G Wolstenholme	0	D Delcher (2 and 1)	1
R Coughlan	0	S Scott (2 and 1)	1
	1½		6½

Result: Great Britain and Ireland 6, USA 18

Walker Cup – INDIVIDUAL RECORDS

Notes: Bold type indicates captain; in brackets, did not play
* indicates players who have also played in the Ryder Cup

Great Britain and Ireland

Name		Year	Played	Won	Lost	Halved
MF Attenborough	Eng	1967	2	0	2	0
CC Aylmer	Eng	1922	2	1	1	0
*P Baker	Eng	1985	3	2	1	0
JB Beck	Eng	1928-(38)-(47)	1	0	1	0
PJ Benka	Eng	1969	4	2	1	1
HG Bentley	Eng	1934-36-38	4	0	2	2
DA Blair	Scot	1955-61	4	1	3	0
C Bloice	Scot	1985	3	0	2	1
MF Bonallack	Eng	1957-59-61-63-65-67-**69**-**71**-**73**	25	8	14	3
*G Brand	Scot	1979	3	0	3	0
OC Bristowe	Eng	(1923)-24	1	0	1	0
A Brodie	Scot	1977-79	8	5	2	1
A Brooks	Scot	1969	3	2	0	1

Name		Year	Played	Won	Lost	Halved
M Brooks	Scot	1997	2	0	2	0
C Brown	Wales	**1995**-(97)	0	0	0	0
Hon WGE Brownlow	Eng	1926	2	0	2	0
J Bruen	Ire	1938-49-51	5	0	4	1
JA Buckley	Wales	1979	1	0	1	0
J Burke	Ire	1932	2	0	1	1
R Burns	Ire	1993	2	1	1	0
AF Bussell	Scot	1957	2	1	1	0
S Cage	Eng	1993	3	0	2	1
I Caldwell	Eng	1951-55	4	1	2	1
W Campbell	Scot	1930	2	0	2	0
JB Carr	Ire	1947-49-51-53-55-57-59-61-63-**(65)**-67	20	5	14	1
RJ Carr	Ire	1971	4	3	0	1
DG Carrick	Scot	1983-87	5	0	5	0
IA Carslaw	Scot	1979	3	1	1	1
C Cassells	Eng	1989	3	2	1	0
JR Cater	Scot	1955	1	0	1	0
J Caven	Scot	1922	2	0	2	0
BHG Chapman	Eng	1961	1	0	1	0
R Chapman	Eng	1981	4	3	1	0
MJ Christmas	Eng	1961-63	3	1	2	0
*CA Clark	Eng	1965	4	2	0	2
GJ Clark	Eng	1965	1	0	1	0
*HK Clark	Eng	1973	3	1	1	1
R Claydon	Eng	1989	4	2	2	0
A Coltart	Scot	1991	3	2	1	0
GB Cosh	Scot	1965	4	3	1	0
R Coughlan	Ire	1997	4	0	3	1
T Craddock	Ire	1967-69	6	2	3	1
LG Crawley	Eng	1932-34-38-47	6	3	3	0
B Critchley	Eng	1969	4	1	1	2
D Curry	Eng	1987	4	1	3	0
CR Dalgleish	Scot	1981	3	1	2	0
B Darwin	Eng	1922	2	1	1	0
JC Davies	Eng	1973-75-77-79	13	3	8	2
P Deeble	Eng	1977-81	5	1	4	0
FWG Deighton	Scot	(1951)-57	2	0	2	0
SC Dodd	Wales	1989	4	1	1	2
B Dredge	Wales	1993	3	0	3	0
*NV Drew	Ire	1953	1	0	1	0
AA Duncan	Wales	**(1953)**	0	0	0	0
JM Dykes	Scot	1936	2	0	1	1
R Eggo	Eng	1987	2	0	2	0
D Evans	Wales	1981	3	1	1	1
G Evans	Eng	1991	4	2	2	0
RC Ewing	Ire	1936-38-47-49-51-55	10	1	7	2
GRD Eyles	Eng	1975	4	2	2	0
J Fanagan	Ire	1995	3	3	0	0
EW Fiddian	Eng	1932-34	4	0	4	0
J de Forest	Eng	1932	1	0	1	0
M Foster	Eng	1995	4	2	0	2
R Foster	Eng	1965-67-69-71-73-**(79)**-**(81)**	17	2	13	2
DW Frame	Eng	1961	1	0	1	0
S Gallacher	Scot	1995	4	2	2	0
*D Gilford	Eng	1985	1	0	1	0
P Girvan	Scot	1987	3	0	3	0
G Godwin	Eng	1979-81	7	2	4	1
CW Green	Scot	1963-69-71-73-75-**(83)**-**(85)**	17	4	10	3
RH Hardman	Eng	1928	1	0	1	0
A Hare	Eng	1989	3	2	2	0
P Harrington	Ire	1991-93-95	9	3	5	1
R Harris	Scot	**(1922)**-23-26	4	1	3	0
RW Hartley	Eng	1930-32	4	0	4	0
WL Hartley	Eng	1932	2	0	2	0
J Hawksworth	Eng	1985	4	2	1	1
G Hay	Scot	1991	3	1	2	0
P Hedges	Eng	1973-75	5	0	2	3
CO Hezlet	Ire	1924-26-28	6	0	5	1
GA Hill	Eng	1936-**(55)**	2	0	1	1
Sir EWE Holderness	Eng	1923-26-30	6	2	4	0

* *Players who have also played in the Ryder Cup*

Walker Cup Individual Records *continued*

Name		Year	Played	Won	Lost	Halved
TWB Homer	Eng	1973	3	0	3	0
CVL Hooman	Eng	1922-23	3	†1	2	†0
WL Hope	Scot	1923-24-28	5	1	4	0
DB Howard	Scot	1995-97	6	0	4	2
D Howell	Eng	1995	3	2	0	1
G Huddy	Eng	1961	1	0	1	0
W Humphreys	Eng	1971	3	2	1	0
IC Hutcheon	Scot	1975-77-79-81	15	5	8	2
RR Jack	Scot	1957-59	4	2	2	0
L James	Eng	1995	2	0	2	0
*M James	Eng	1975	4	3	1	0
A Jamieson, Jr	Scot	1926	2	1	1	0
MJ Kelley	Eng	1977-79	7	3	3	1
SD Keppler	Eng	1983	4	0	3	1
*MG King	Eng	1969-73	7	1	5	1
AT Kyle	Scot	1938-47-51	5	2	3	0
DH Kyle	Scot	1924	1	0	1	0
JA Lang	Scot	(1930)	0	0	0	0
JDA Langley	Eng	1936-51-53	6	0	5	1
CD Lawrie	Scot	(1961)-(63)	0	0	0	0
ME Lewis	Eng	1983	1	0	1	0
PB Lucas	Eng	(1936)-47-(49)	2	1	1	0
MSR Lunt	Eng	1959-61-63-65	11	2	8	1
*AWB Lyle	Scot	1977	3	0	3	0
AR McCallum	Scot	1928	1	0	1	0
SM McCready	Ire	1949-51	3	0	3	0
JS Macdonald	Scot	1971	3	1	1	1
P McEvoy	Eng	1977-79-81-85-89	18	5	11	2
G McGimpsey	Ire	1985-89-91	11	4	5	2
P McGinley	Ire	1991	3	1	2	0
G Macgregor	Scot	1971-75-83-85-87	14	5	8	1
RC MacGregor	Scot	1953	2	0	2	0
J McHenry	Ire	1987	4	2	2	0
P McKellar	Scot	1977	1	0	1	0
WW Mackenzie	Scot	1922-23	3	1	2	0
SL McKinlay	Scot	1934	2	0	2	0
J McLean	Scot	1934-36	4	1	3	0
EA McRuvie	Scot	1932-34	4	1	2	1
JFD Madeley	Ire	1963	2	0	1	1
LS Mann	Scot	1983	4	2	1	1
B Marchbank	Scot	1979	4	2	2	0
GC Marks	Eng	1969-71-(87)-(89)	6	2	4	0
DM Marsh	Eng	(1959)-71-(73)-(75)	3	2	1	0
GNC Martin	Ire	1928	1	0	1	0
S Martin	Scot	1977	4	2	2	0
P Mayo	Wales	1985-87	4	0	3	1
GH Micklem	Eng	1947-49-53-55-(57)-(59)	6	1	5	0
DJ Millensted	Eng	1967	2	1	1	0
JW Milligan	Scot	1989-91	7	3	3	1
EB Millward	Eng	(1949)-55	2	0	2	0
WTG Milne	Scot	1973	4	2	2	0
*CS Montgomerie	Scot	1985-87	8	2	5	1
JL Morgan	Wales	1951-53-55	6	2	4	0
P Mulcare	Ire	1975	3	2	1	0
GH Murray	Scot	1977	2	1	1	0
SWT Murray	Scot	1963	4	2	2	0
WA Murray	Scot	1923-24-(26)	4	1	3	0
K Nolan	Ire	1997	3	0	3	0
E O'Connell	Ire	1989	4	2	0	2
A Oldcorn	Eng	1983	4	4	0	0
*PA Oosterhuis	Eng	1967	4	1	2	1
R Oppenheimer	Eng	(1951)	0	0	0	0
P Page	Eng	1993	2	0	2	0
D Park	Wales	1997	3	0	3	0
P Parkin	Wales	1983	3	2	1	0
J Payne	Eng	1991	4	2	2	0
JJF Pennink	Eng	1938	2	1	1	0
TP Perkins	Eng	1928	2	0	2	0

* *Players who have also played in the Ryder Cup*

Name		Year	Played	Won	Lost	Halved
AH Perowne	Eng	1949-53-59	4	0	4	0
GB Peters	Scot	1936-38	4	2	1	1
V Phillips	Eng	1993	3	1	2	0
AD Pierse	Ire	1983	3	0	2	1
AK Pirie	Scot	1967	3	0	2	1
MA Poxon	Eng	1975	2	0	2	0
D Prosser	Eng	1989	1	0	1	2
I Pyman	Eng	1993	3	0	3	0
*R Rafferty	Ire	1981	4	2	2	0
G Rankin	Scot	1995-97	4	0	4	0
D Robertson	Scot	1993	3	1	2	0
J Robinson	Eng	1987	4	2	2	0
RN Roderick	Wales	1989	2	0	1	1
J Rose	Eng	1997	4	2	2	0
R Russell	Scot	1993	3	0	3	0
AC Saddler	Scot	1963-65-67-(77)	10	3	5	2
Hon M Scott	Eng	1924-**34**	4	2	2	0
R Scott, Jr	Scot	1924	1	1	0	0
PF Scrutton	Eng	1955-57	3	0	3	0
DN Sewell	Eng	1957-59	4	1	3	0
RDBM Shade	Scot	1961-63-65-67	14	6	6	2
G Shaw	Scot	1987	4	1	2	1
DB Sheahan	Ire	1963	4	2	2	0
AE Shepperson	Eng	1957-59	3	1	1	1
G Sherry	Scot	1995	4	2	2	0
AF Simpson	Scot	(1926)	0	0	0	0
JN Smith	Scot	1930	2	0	2	0
WD Smith	Scot	1959	1	0	1	0
M Stanford	Eng	1993	3	1	2	0
AR Stephen	Scot	1985	4	2	1	1
EF Storey	Eng	1924-26-28	6	1	5	0
JA Stout	Eng	1930-32	4	0	3	1
C Stowe	Eng	1938-47	4	2	2	0
HB Stuart	Scot	1971-73-75	10	4	6	0
A Thirlwell	Eng	1957	1	0	1	0
KG Thom	Eng	1949	2	0	2	0
MS Thompson	Eng	1983	3	1	2	0
H Thomson	Scot	1936-38	4	2	2	0
CJH Tolley	Eng	1922-23-**24**-26-30-34	12	4	8	0
TA Torrance	Scot	1924-28-30-**32**-34	9	3	5	1
WB Torrance	Scot	1922	2	0	2	0
*PM Townsend	Eng	1965	4	3	1	0
LP Tupling	Eng	1969	2	1	1	0
W Tweddell	Eng	**1928**-(**36**)	2	0	2	0
J Walker	Scot	1961	2	0	2	0
*P Walton	Ire	1981-83	8	6	2	0
C Watson	Scot	1997	3	1	1	1
*P Way	Eng	1981	4	2	2	0
RH Wethered	Eng	1922-23-26-**30**-34	9	5	3	1
L White	Eng	1991	2	1	1	0
RJ White	Eng	1947-49-51-53-55	10	6	3	1
R Willison	Eng	1991	4	1	3	0
J Wilson	Scot	1923	2	2	0	0
JC Wilson	Scot	1947-53	4	0	4	0
GB Wolstenholme	Eng	1957-59	4	1	2	1
GP Wolstenholme	Eng	1995-97	7	2	5	0
S Young	Scot	1997	4	2	2	0

United States of America

Name	Year	Played	Won	Lost	Halved
*TD Aaron	1959	2	1	1	0
B Alexander	1987	3	2	1	0
DC Allen	1965-67	6	0	4	2
B Andrade	1987	4	2	2	0
ES Andrews	1961	1	1	0	0
D Ballenger	1973	1	1	0	0

† *In 1922 Hooman beat Sweetser at the 37th – on all other occasions halved matches have counted as such.*
* *Players who have also played in the Ryder Cup*

Walker Cup Individual Records *continued*

Name	Year	Played	Won	Lost	Halved
R Baxter, jr	1957	2	2	0	0
N Begay III	1995	3	1	2	0
DR Beman	1959-61-63-65	11	7	2	2
D Berganio	1993	3	1	2	0
RE Billows	1938-49	4	2	2	0
SE Bishop	1947-49	3	2	1	0
AS Blum	1957	1	0	1	0
J Bohmann	1969	3	1	2	0
M Brannan	1977	3	1	2	0
A Bratton	1995	3	1	0	2
GF Burns	1975	3	2	1	0
C Burroughs	1985	3	1	2	0
AE Campbell	1936	2	2	0	0
JE Campbell	1957	1	0	1	0
WC Campbell	1951-53-(55)-57-65-67-71-75	18	11	4	3
RJ Cerrudo	1967	4	1	1	2
RD Chapman	1947-51-53	5	3	2	0
D Cherry	1953-55-61	5	5	0	0
D Clarke	1979	3	2	0	1
RE Cochran	1961	1	1	0	0
CR Coe	1949-51-53-(57)-59-61-63	13	7	4	2
R Commans	1981	3	1	1	1
JW Conrad	1955	2	1	1	0
J Courville Jr	1995-97	6	4	2	0
K Cox	1995	3	1	2	0
N Crosby	1983	2	1	1	0
BH Cudd	1955	2	2	0	0
RD Davies	1963	2	0	2	0
JW Dawson	1949	2	2	0	0
D Delcher	1997	3	2	1	0
T Demsey	1993	3	3	0	0
RB Dickson	1967	3	3	0	0
A Doyle	1991-93	6	5	1	0
GT Dunlap Jr	1932-34-36	5	3	1	1
D Duval	1991	3	2	1	0
D Edwards	1973	4	4	0	0
HC Egan	1934	1	1	0	0
D Eger	1991	3	2	1	0
HC Eger	1989	3	1	2	0
D Eichelberger	1965	3	1	2	0
B Elder	1997	4	4	0	0
J Ellis	1973	3	2	1	0
W Emery	1936	2	1	0	1
C Evans Jr	1922-24-28	5	3	2	0
J Farquhar	1971	3	1	2	0
*B Faxon	1983	4	3	1	0
R Fehr	1983	4	2	1	1
JW Fischer	1934-36-38-(65)	4	3	0	1
D Fischesser	1979	3	1	2	0
MA Fleckman	1967	2	0	2	0
B Fleisher	1969	4	0	2	2
J Fought	1977	4	4	0	0
WC Fownes Jr	**1922-24**	3	1	2	0
F Fuhrer	1981	3	2	1	0
JR Gabrielsen	1977-(81)-(91)	3	1	2	0
R Gamez	1989	4	3	0	1
RA Gardner	1922-23-24-26	8	6	2	0
RW Gardner	1961-63	5	4	0	1
B Gay	1993	2	0	1	1
M Giles	1969-71-73-75	15	8	2	5
HL Givan	1936	1	0	0	1
JG Goodman	1934-36-38	6	4	2	0
J Gore	1997	3	2	0	1
M Gove	1979	3	2	1	0
J Grace	1975	3	2	1	0
JA Grant	1967	2	2	0	0
AD Gray Jr	1963-65-67-(**95**)-(**97**)	12	5	6	1
JP Guilford	1922-24-26	6	4	2	0

* *Players who have also played in the Ryder Cup*

Name	Year	Played	Won	Lost	Halved
W Gunn	1926-28	4	4	0	0
*F Haas Jr	1938	2	0	2	0
*J Haas	1975	3	3	0	0
J Haas	1985	3	1	2	0
G Hallberg	1977	3	1	2	0
GS Hamer Jr	(1947)	0	0	0	0
J Harris	1993-95-97	11	10	1	0
LE Harris Jr	1963	4	3	1	0
V Heafner	1977	3	3	0	0
SD Herron	1923	2	0	2	0
T Herron	1993	3	3	0	0
*S Hoch	1979	4	4	0	0
W Hoffer	1983	2	1	1	0
J Holtgrieve	1979-81-83	10	6	4	0
JM Hopkins	1965	3	0	2	1
R Howe	1989	1	0	1	0
W Howell	1932	1	1	0	0
W Hyndman	1957-59-61-69-71	9	6	1	2
J Inman	1969	2	2	0	0
JG Jackson	1953-55	3	3	0	0
T Jackson	1995	3	1	1	1
K Johnson	1989	3	1	2	0
HR Johnston	1923-24-28-30	6	5	1	0
RT Jones Jr	1922-24-26-**28-30**	10	9	1	0
AF Kammer	1947	2	1	1	0
M Killian	1973	3	1	2	0
C Kite	1987	3	2	1	0
*TO Kite	1971	4	2	1	1
RE Knepper	(1922)	0	0	0	0
RW Knowles	1951	1	1	0	0
G Koch	1973-75	7	4	1	2
CR Kocsis	1938-49-57	5	2	2	1
J Kribel	1997	3	1	2	0
T Kuehne	1995	3	0	3	0
F Langham	1991	3	1	2	0
R Leen	1997	3	2	1	0
*J Leonard	1993	3	3	0	0
G Lesher	1989	4	1	3	0
B Lewis Jr	1981-83-85-87	14	10	4	0
JW Lewis	1967	4	3	1	0
WL Little Jr	1934	2	2	0	0
*GA Littler	1953	2	2	0	0
B Loeffler	1987	3	2	1	0
*D Love	1985	3	2	0	1
MJ McCarthy Jr	(1928)-32	1	1	0	0
BN McCormick	1949	1	1	0	0
JB McHale	1949-51	3	2	0	1
RR Mackenzie	1926-28-30	6	5	1	0
MR Marston	1922-23-24-34	8	5	3	0
D Martin	1989	4	1	1	2
B Marucci	1995-97	6	4	1	1
L Mattiace	1987	3	2	1	0
R May	1991	4	3	1	0
B Mayfair	1987	3	3	0	0
E Meeks	1989	1	0	0	1
SN Melnyk	1969-71	7	3	3	1
*P Mickelson	1989-91	8	4	2	2
AL Miller	1969-71	8	4	3	1
L Miller	1977	4	4	0	0
K Mitchum	1993	3	2	0	1
DK Moe	1930-32	3	3	0	0
B Montgomery	1987	2	2	0	0
G Moody	1979	3	1	2	0
GT Moreland	1932-34	4	4	0	0
D Morey	1955-65	4	1	3	0
J Mudd	1981	3	3	0	0
*RJ Murphy	1967	4	1	2	1
JF Neville	1923	1	0	1	0
*JW Nicklaus	1959-61	4	4	0	0
LW Oehmig	(1977)	0	0	0	0

* *Players who have also played in the Ryder Cup*

Walker Cup Individual Records *continued*

Name	Year	Played	Won	Lost	Halved
FD Ouimet	1922-23-24-26-30-**32-34**-(36)-(38)-(47)-(49)	16	9	5	2
HD Paddock Jr	1951	1	0	0	1
*J Pate	1975	4	0	4	0
WJ Patton	1955-57-59-63-65-(69)	14	11	3	0
*C Pavin	1981	3	2	0	1
M Peck	1979	3	1	1	1
M Pfeil	1973	4	2	1	1
M Podolak	1985	2	1	0	1
SL Quick	1947	2	1	1	0
S Randolph	1985	4	2	1	1
J Rassett	1981	3	3	0	0
F Ridley	1977-(87)-(89)	3	2	1	0
RH Riegel	1947-49	4	4	0	0
C Riley	1995	3	1	1	1
H Robbins Jr	1957	2	0	1	1
*W Rogers	1973	2	1	1	0
GV Rotan	1923	2	1	1	0
*EM Rudolph	1957	2	1	0	1
B Sander	1977	3	0	3	0
T Scherrer	1991	3	0	3	0
S Scott	1997	3	2	1	0
CH Seaver	1932	2	2	0	0
RL Siderowf	1969-73-75-77-(**79**)	14	4	8	2
J Sigel	1977-79-81-**83**-85-87-89-91-93	33	18	10	5
RH Sikes	1963	3	1	2	0
JB Simons	1971	2	0	2	0
*S Simpson	1977	3	3	0	0
CB Smith	1961-63	2	0	1	1
R Smith	1936-38	4	2	2	0
R Sonnier	1985	3	0	2	1
J Sorensen	1987	3	1	1	1
M Sposa	1991	3	2	1	0
*C Stadler	1975	3	3	0	0
FR Stranahan	1947-49-51	6	3	2	1
*C Strange	1975	4	3	0	1
*H Sutton	1979-81	7	2	4	1
JW Sweetser	1922-23-24-26-28-32-(67)-(73)	12	7	†4	†1
FM Taylor	1957-59-61	4	4	0	0
D Tentis	1983	2	0	1	1
RS Tufts	(**1963**)	0	0	0	0
WP Turnesa	1947-49-**51**	6	3	3	0
B Tuten	1983	2	1	1	0
EM Tutweiler	1965-67	6	5	1	0
ER Updegraff	1963-65-69-(**75**)	7	3	3	1
S Urzetta	1951-53	4	4	0	0
K Venturi	1953	2	2	0	0
S Verplank	1985	4	3	0	1
M Voges	1991	3	2	1	0
GJ Voigt	1930-32-36	5	2	2	1
G Von Elm	1926-28-30	6	4	1	1
D von Tacky	1981	3	1	2	0
*JL Wadkins	1969-71	7	3	4	0
D Waldorf	1985	3	1	2	0
EH Ward	1953-55-59	6	6	0	0
MH Ward	1938-47	4	2	2	0
M West	1973-79	6	2	3	1
J Westland	1932-34-53-(**61**)	5	3	0	2
HW Wettlaufer	1959	2	2	0	0
E White	1936	2	2	0	0
OF Willing	1923-24-30	4	4	0	0
JM Winters Jr	(**1971**)	0	0	0	0
C Wollman	1997	3	1	1	1
W Wood	1983	4	1	2	1
*T Woods	1995	4	2	2	0
FJ Wright	1923	1	1	0	0
CR Yates	1936-38-(**53**)	4	3	0	1
D Yates	1989-93	6	3	2	1
RL Yost	1955	2	2	0	0

† In 1922 Hooman beat Sweetser at the 37th – on all other occasions halved matches have counted as such.
* Players who have also played in the Ryder Cup

World Amateur Team Championship for the Eisenhower Trophy

Year	Winners	Runners-up	Venue	Score
1958	Australia	United States	St Andrews	918

(After a tie, Australia won the play-off by two strokes: Australia 222, United States 224)

Year	Winners	Runners-up	Venue	Score
1960	United States	Australia	Ardmore, USA	834
1962	United States	Canada	Kawana, Japan	854
1964	Great Britain & Ireland	Canada	Olgiata, Rome	895
1966	Australia	United States	Mexico City	877
1968	United States	Great Britain & Ireland	Melbourne	868
1970	United States	New Zealand	Madrid	857
1972	United States	Australia	Buenos Aires	865
1974	United States	Japan	Dominican Rep.	888
1976	Great Britain & Ireland	Japan	Penina, Portugal	892
1978	United States	Canada	Fiji	873
1980	United States	South Africa	Pinehurst, USA	848
1982	United States	Sweden	Lausanne	859
1984	Japan	United States	Hong Kong	870
1986	Canada	United States	Caracas, Venezuela	860
1988	Great Britain & Ireland	United States	Ullva, Sweden	882
1990	Sweden	New Zealand	Christchurch, New Zealand	879
1992	New Zealand	United States	Capilano, Canada	823
1994	United States	Great Britain & Ireland	Paris, France	838
1996	Australia	Sweden	Manila, Philippines	838

1998 *at Los Leones/La Dehesa, Chile*

1	Great Britain & Ireland		852
	L Donald	70-70-69-71—280	
	G Wolstenholme	70-71-74-67—282	
	L Kelly	77-77-72-70—296	
	P Gribben	71-78-76-72—297	
2	Australia		856

Individual winner: K Felton (Aust) 70-67-69-69—275

European Amateur Team Championship

Year	Winner	Second	Venue
1959	Sweden		
1961	Sweden	England	Brussels, Belgium
1963	England	Sweden	Falsterbo, Sweden
1965	Ireland	Scotland	St George's, England
1967	Ireland	France	Turin, Italy
1969	England	W Germany	Hamburg, W Germany
1971	England	Scotland	Lausanne, Switzerland
1973	England	Scotland	Penina, Portugal
1975	Scotland	Italy	Killarney, Ireland
1977	Scotland	Sweden	The Haagsche, Holland
1979	England	Wales	Esbjerg, Denmark
1981	England	Scotland	St Andrews, Scotland
1983	Ireland	Spain	Chantilly, France
1985	Scotland	Sweden	Halmstad, Sweden
1987	Ireland	England	Murhof, Austria
1989	England	Scotland	Royal Porthcawl
1991	England	Italy	Puerta de Hierro
1993	Wales	England	Marianske Lasne, Czech Republic
1995	Scotland	England	Royal Antwerp, Belgium
1997	Spain	Scotland	Portmarnock

European Club Cup

Year	Winner	Venue	Year	Winner	Venue
1975	Club de Campo, Spain	Club de Campo	1987	Puerto de Hierro, Spain	Aloha
1976	Växjö Golfklub, Sweden	El Prat	1988	Brokenhurst Manor, England	Aloha
1977	Chantilly, France	RC Belgique	1989	Ealing, England	Aloha
1978	Hamburger, Germany	Deauville	1990	Ealing, England	Aloha
1979	Hamburger, Germany	Santa Ponsa	1991	Club de Golf Terramar, Spain	La Quinta
1980	Limerick, Ireland	Santa Ponsa	1992	Hillerod, Denmark	La Quinta
1981	El Prat, Spain	Aloha	1993	Lahden, Finland	La Quinta
1982	El Prat, Spain	Aloha	1994	Kilmarnock, Scotland	Vilamoura
1983	Rapallo, Italy	Aloha	1995	Racing C de France, France	Vilamoura
1984	Hamburger, Germany	Aloha	1996	Racing C de France, France	Vilamoura
1985	El Prat, Spain	Aloha	1997	Racing C de France, France	Parco de Medici
1986	Hamburger, Germany	Aloha			

1998 at Parco de Medici

1	Aalborg, Denmark	560
2	Racing Club de France	565
3	Cork, Ireland	581

Leading Individual Scores

1	T Norret (Den)	64-67-73-71—275
2	C Ravetto (Fr)	69-74-70-69—282
3	AH Madsen (Den)	68-72-72-74—286
	U Kaltenberger (Aus)	70-70-67-79—286

St Andrews Trophy (Great Britain & Ireland v Continent of Europe) *Match instituted 1956, trophy presented 1962*

Year	Winner	Venue	Result
1956	Great Britain & Ireland	Wentworth	12½–2½
1958	Great Britain & Ireland	St Cloud, France	10–5
1960	Great Britain & Ireland	Walton Heath	13–5
1962	Great Britain & Ireland	Halmstead, Sweden	18–12
1964	Great Britain & Ireland	Muirfield	23–7
1966	Great Britain & Ireland	Bilbao, Spain	19½–10½
1968	Great Britain & Ireland	Portmarnock	20–10
1970	Great Britain & Ireland	La Zoute, Belgium	17½–12½
1972	Great Britain & Ireland	Berkshire	19½–10½
1974	Continent of Europe	Punta Ala, Italy	16–14
1976	Great Britain & Ireland	St Andrews	18½–11½
1978	Great Britain & Ireland	Bremen, Germany	20½–9½
1980	Great Britain & Ireland	Sandwich, R St George's	19½–10½
1982	Continent of Europe	Rosendaelsche, Netherlands	14–10
1984	Great Britain & Ireland	Taunton, Devon	13–11
1986	Great Britain & Ireland	Halmstead, Sweden	14½–9½
1988	Great Britain & Ireland	St Andrews	15½–8½
1990	Great Britain & Ireland	El Saler, Spain	13–11
1992	Great Britain & Ireland	R Cinque Ports	14–10
1994	Great Britain & Ireland	Chantilly, France	14–10
1996	Great Britain & Ireland	Woodhall Spa	16–8

1998 at Villa d'Este, Italy

Continent of Europe		**Great Britain & Ireland**	
First Day – **Foursomes**			
C Aronson and M Thannhauser (6 and 4)	1	G Wolstenholme and G Rankin	0
O David and C Ravetto (4 and 2)	1	L Kelly and C Watson	0
S Maio and R Quiros	0	B Omelia and C Williams (1 hole)	1
P Hansson and H Stenson	0	S Dyson and L Donald (2 and 1)	1
	2		2

Singles

C Aronson	0	G Rankin (5 and 4)	1
M Thannhauser (2 and 1)	1	L Kelly	0
P Kyllianen (1 hole)	1	G Wolstenholme	0
C Ravetto	½	D Patrick	½
O David (4 and 3)	1	C Williams	0
R Quiros	½	S Dyson	½
H Stenson	0	L Donald (3 and 1)	1
P Hansson (7 and 6)	1	C Watson	0
	5		3

Match position: Europe 7, GB&I 5

Day Two **– Foursomes**

P Hansson and H Stenson (4 and 3)	1	G Rankin and C Watson	0
C Aronson and M Thannhauser	0	L Kelly and G Wolstenholme (3 and 1)	1
O David and C Ravetto (1 hole)	1	D Dyson and L Donald	0
S Maio and R Quiros	0	B Omelia and C Williams (5 and 4)	1
	2		2

Singles

P Hansson	½	G Rankin	½
H Stenson	0	L Kelly (1 hole)	1
C Aronson	½	S Dyson	½
C Ravetto (2 and 1)	1	C Williams	0
M Thannhauser (1 hole)	1	B Omelia	0
P Kyllianen (2 and 1)	1	D Patrick	0
O David (3 and 2)	1	L Donald	0
R Quiros	0	G Wolstenholme (1 hole)	1
	5		3

Result: Europe 14, Great Britain and Ireland 10

England *v* France

1998 *at Les Bordes, France*

France   **England**

First Day **– Foursomes**

O David and A Grenier (3 and 1)	1	G Wolstenholme and J Rose	0
G Havret and JM de Polo	0	C Edwards and G Storm (1 hole)	1
S Branger and J Thalamy (2 holes)	1	B Mason and S Dyson	0
D Montesi and C Ravetto (4 and 3)	1	M Reynard and P Rowe	0
	3		1

Singles

F Stolear	0	J Rose (1 hole)	1
O David	½	G Storm	½
JM de Polo (5 and 4)	1	G Wolstenholme	0
A Grenier	0	S Dyson (1 hole)	1
D Montesi (2 and 1)	1	A Wainwright	0
S Branger (3 and 2)	1	M Reynard	0
G Havret	½	C Edwards	½
C Ravetto (3 and 2)	1	P Rowe	0
	5		3

Match position: France 8, England 4

continued

England v France continued

Day Two – Foursomes

O David and A Grenier	0	C Edwards and G Storm (1 hole)	1
G Havret and JM de Polo	0	J Rose and G Wolstenholme (1 hole)	1
D Montesi and C Ravetto (2 and 1)	1	S Dyson and B Mason	0
S Branger and J Thalamy (6 and 5)	1	M Reynard and P Rowe	0
	2		**2**

Singles

O David	0	J Rose (1 hole)	1
F Stolear	0	G Wolstenholme (1 hole)	1
JM de Polo (5 and 4)	1	G Storm	0
D Montesi	½	C Edwards	½
S Branger	0	P Rowe (4 and 3)	1
G Havret	0	S Dyson (2 and 1)	1
J Thalamy (2 and 1)	1	A Wainwright	0
C Ravetto	0	B Mason (4 and 3)	1
	2½		**5½**

Result: France 12½, England 11½

Home Internationals

Year	Winner
1932	Scotland
1933	Scotland
1934	Scotland
1935T	England/Ireland/Scotland
1936	Scotland
1937	Scotland
1938	England
1939–46	No Internationals held
1947	England
1948	England
1949	England
1950	Ireland
1951T	Ireland and Scotland
1952	Scotland
1953	Scotland
1954	England
1955	Ireland
1956	Scotland
1957	England
1958	England
1959T	England/Ireland/Scotland
1960	England
1961	Scotland
1962T	England/Ireland/Scotland
1963T	England/Ireland/Scotland
1964	England
1965	England
1966	England
1967	Scotland
1968	England
1969	England
1970	Scotland
1971	Scotland
1972T	Scotland/England
1973	England
1974	England
1975	Scotland
1976	Scotland
1977	England
1978	England
1979	No Internationals held
1980	England
1981	Scotland
1982	Scotland
1983	Ireland
1984	England
1985	England
1986	Scotland
1987	Ireland
1988	England
1989	England
1990	Ireland

1991 at Rosses Point

Ireland halved with Wales	7½ matches each
Scotland beat England	9½ matches to 5½
Ireland beat England	11 matches to 4
Wales beat Scotland	8 matches to 7
England beat Wales	9 matches to 6
Ireland beat Scotland	10 matches to 5

Winners: Ireland

1992 at Prestwick

Ireland halved with England	7½ matches each
Scotland beat Wales	8 matches to 7
Ireland beat Wales	11 matches to 4
England beat Scotland	11½ matches to 3½
England beat Wales	8½ matches to 6½
Ireland beat Scotland	12½ matches to 2½

Winners: England and Ireland tied

1993 at Hoylake

England beat Scotland	8 matches to 7
Wales beat Ireland	8½ matches to 6½
England beat Ireland	9½ matches to 5½
Wales halved with Scotland	7½ matches each
Ireland beat Scotland	8½ matches to 6½
England halved with Wales	7½ matches each

Winners: England

1994 at Ashburnham, Dyfed

England beat Scotland	9½ matches to 5½
Ireland beat Wales	10½ matches to 4½
England beat Wales	10 matches to 5
Ireland beat Scotland	11 matches to 4
Scotland beat Wales	8 matches to 7
England beat Ireland	9 matches to 6

Winners: England

Home Internationals *continued*

1995 *at Royal Portrush, Co Antrim*

Ireland beat Scotland	8½ matches to 6½
Wales beat England	8½ matches to 6½
Scotland beat Wales	11 matches to 4
England beat Ireland	9 matches to 6
Ireland beat Wales	10 matches to 5
England beat Scotland	9½ matches to 5½

Winners: England beat Ireland on countback 25 wins to 24½

1996 *at Moray, Scotland*

England beat Wales	9 matches to 6
Ireland beat Scotland	8½ matches to 6½
England halved with Scotland	7½ matches each
Ireland beat Wales	9½ matches to 5½
England beat Ireland	10 matches to 5
Scotland beat Wales	9 matches to 6

Winners: England

1997 *at Burnham & Berrow*

England beat Wales	10½ matches to 4½
Ireland beat Scotland	10½ matches to 4½
England beat Scotland	10½ matches to 4½
Ireland beat Wales	8½ matches to 6½
England halved with Ireland	7½ matches to 7½
Scotland beat Wales	9 matches to 6

Winners: England

1998 *at Royal Porthcawl*

Ireland beat Scotland	11 matches to 4
England beat Wales	11 matches to 4
Ireland halved with Wales	7½ matches each
England beat Scotland	9 matches to 6
England beat Ireland	8 matches to 7
Wales beat Scotland	11½ matches to 3½

Winners: England

English County Championship

Year	Winner	Year	Winner	Year	Winner
1928	Warwickshire	1956	Staffordshire	1978	Kent
1929	Lancashire	1957	Surrey	1979	Gloucestershire
1930	Lancashire	1958	Surrey	1980	Surrey
1931	Yorkshire	1959	Northumberland	1981	Surrey
1932	Surrey	1961	Lancashire	1982	Yorkshire
1933	Yorkshire	1962	Northumberland	1983	Berks, Bucks, Oxon
1934	Worcestershire	1963	Yorkshire	1984	Yorkshire
1935	Worcestershire	1964	Northumberland	1985T	Devon/Hertfordshire
1936	Surrey	1965	Northumberland	1986	Hertfordshire
1937	Lancashire	1966	Surrey	1987	Yorkshire
1938	Staffordshire	1967	Lancashire	1988	Warwickshire
1939	Worcestershire	1968	Surrey	1989	Middlesex
1947	Staffordshire	1969	Berks, Bucks, Oxon	1990	Warwickshire
1948	Staffordshire	1970	Gloucestershire	1991	Middlesex
1949	Lancashire	1971	Staffordshire	1992	Dorset
1950	*Not played*	1972	Berks, Bucks, Oxon	1993	Yorkshire
1951	Lancashire	1973	Yorkshire	1994	Middlesex
1952	Yorkshire	1974	Lincolnshire	1995	Lancashire
1953	Yorkshire	1975	Staffordshire	1996	Hampshire
1954	Cheshire	1976	Warwickshire	1997	Yorkshire
1955	Yorkshire	1977	Warwickshire		

1998 *at Stoneham*

Devon beat Berks, Bucks & Oxon 5½–3½
Yorkshire beat Staffordshire 5–4
Berks, Bucks & Oxon beat Staffordshire 5½–3½
Yorkshire beat Devon 8–1
Devon beat Staffordshire 5–4
Yorkshire beat Berks, Bucks & Oxon 7½–1½

Result: 1 Yorkshire, 2 Devon, 3 Berks, Bucks, & Oxon, 4 Staffordshire

English Club Championship

Year	Winner	Venue	Year	Winner	Venue
1989	Ealing	Southport and Ainsdale	1994	Sandmoor	Coxmoor
1990	Ealing	Goring and Streatley	1995	Sandmoor	Ipswich
1991	Trentham	Porters Park	1996	Hartlepool	Frilford Heath
1992	Bristol & Clifton	South Staffs	1997	Royal Mid-Surrey	Sandiway
1993	Worksop	Rotherham			

continued

English Club Championship *continued*

1998 *at Northumberland*

1	Moor Park (S Waller, J Ambridge, J Conteh)	287
2	Royal Mid-Surrey (C Rodgers, M Booker, R Rea)	288
3	Newquay (I Veale, M Lock, I Atkinson)	289

All-Ireland Inter-County Championship

Year	Winner	Runner-up	Venue	Score
1995	Down	Waterford	Rosslare	3½–1½
1996	Down	Dublin	Co Sligo	4–1
197	Cork	Wicklow	Doneghal	4–1

1998 *at Lahinch*

Semi-Finals
Kerry beat Sligo 3½–1½
Dublin beat Derry 3½–1½

Final
Dublin beat Kerry 4–1

Scottish Club Championship

1998 *at Boat-of-Garten*

1	Turriff	282
2	Rothesay	284
3	Pitlochry	286
	Mortonhall	286
	Dumfries & County	286

Scottish Area Team Championship

Year	Winner	Year	Winner
1989	Lanarkshire	1994	Lothians
1990	North East	1995	North
1991	Glasgow	1996	Renfrewshire
1992	North East	1997	Lothians
1993	Lothians	1998	Lanarkshire

Scottish Foursomes Tournament – *Glasgow Evening Times* Trophy

Year	Winner	Year	Winner
1989	Cochrane Leith	1994	Standard Life
1990	Dunblane New	1995	Ratho Park
1991	Irvine Ravenspark	1996	Cardross
1992	Cochrane Castle	1997	Cardross
1993	Baberton	1998	Haggs Castle beat Pitreavie 3 and 2

Welsh Inter-Counties Championship

1998 *at Borth & Ynyslas*

1	Glamorgan
2	Flintshire
3	Anglesey

Other Men's Amateur Tournaments

Aberconwy Trophy (Inaugurated 1976) at Conwy/Llandudno (Maesdu), Gwynedd

Year	Winner	Year	Winner	Year	Winner
1976	JR Jones	1984	D McLean	1992	MJ Ellis
1977	EN Davies	1985	MA Macara	1993	S Wilkinson
1978	MG Mouland	1986	JR Berry	1994	G Marsden
1979	JM Morrow	1987	M Sheppard	1995	S Andrew
1980	JM Morrow	1988	MG Hughes	1996	R Williams
1981	D Evans	1989	JN Lee	1997	I Campbell
1982	G Tuttle	1990	S Wilkinson		
1983	GH Brown	1991	S Wilkinson		

1998

1	J Donaldson	254 (54)
2	A Delves	260
3	C Davies	263

The Antlers (Inaugurated 1933) at Royal Mid-Surrey

Year	Winner	Score	Year	Winner	Score
1933	TFB Law and PWL Risdon	147	1969T	JC Davies and W Humphreys	146
1934	GA Hill and HS Malik	153		RD Watson-Jones and LOM Smith	
1935	EF Storey and Sir WS Worthington Evans	152	1970	JB Carr and R Carr	142
1936	HG Bentley and F Francis	144	1971	I Mosey and I Gradwell	144
1937	LG Crawley and C Stowe	145	1972	MJ Kelley and W Smith	144
1938	RW Hartley and PWL Risdon	149	1973	DOJ Albutt and P Flaherty	148
1939	LG Crawley and H Thomson	148	1974	BF Critchley and MC Hughesdon	140
1940–47	*Not played due to Second World War*		1975	JC Davies and PJ Davies	140
1948	RC Quilter and E Bromley-Davenport	151	1976	JK Tate and P Deeble	144
1949	LG Crawley and JC Wilson	143	1977	JC Davies and PJ Davies	141
1950	L Gracey and I Caldwell	151	1978	R Chapman and R Fish	148
1951	LG Crawley and JC Wilson	147	1979	N Roche and D Williams	143
1952T	Major DA Blair and GH Micklem	145	1980	G Coles and M Johnson	148
	LG Crawley and JC Wilson		1981	R Boxall and R Chapman	143
1953	D Wilson and G Simmons	148	1982	IA Carslaw and J Huggan	139
1954	JR Thornhill and PF Scrutton	147	1983	N Fox and G Lashford	147
1955	G Evans and D Sewell	147	1984	M Palmer and M Belsham	147
1956	GH Micklem and AF Bussell	141	1985	S Blight and R Wilkins	143
1957	Major DA Blair and CD Lawrie	138	1986	M Gerrard and B White	146
1958	D Sewell and G Evans	143	1987	IA Carslaw and J Huggan	141
1959	HC Squirrell and P Dunn	146	1988	A Raitt and P Thornley	143
1960	MSR Lunt and JC Behrrell	139	1989	A Howard and R Hunter	146
1961	HC Squirrell and P Dunn	145	1990	AC Livesey and RG Payne	143
1962	AW Holmes and JM Leach	142	1991	WM Hopkinson and MR Cook	143
1963	RC Pickering and MJ Cooper	146	1992	J C Davies and P J Davies	148
1964	MF Bonallack and Dr DM Marsh	145	1993	M Benka and S Seman	138
1965	MSR Lunt and DE Rodway	146	1994	D Cowap and J Brant	142
1966	PD Kelley and Dr DM Marsh	144	1995	R Neill and G Evans	141
1967	Play abandoned		1996	I Tottingham and R Harris	144
1968	H Broadbent and G Birtwell	144	1997	S Kay and R Peacock	143
1969T	SR Warrin and JH Cook	146			
	J Povall and K Dabson				

continued

The Antlers *continued*
1998
1	G and B Willman	142
2	S Seman and M Benka	145
3	T Marwick and C Hudson	146

Berkhamsted Trophy (Inaugurated 1960)

Year	Winner	Score	Year	Winner	Score	Year	Winner	Score
1960	HC Squirrell	150	1973	SC Mason	141	1986	P McEvoy	144
1961	DW Frame	147	1974	P Fisher	144	1987	F George	141
1962	DG Neech	149	1975	PG Deeble	147	1988	J Cowgill	146
1963	HC Squirrell	149	1976	JC Davies	144	1989	J Payne	142
1964	PD Flaherty	149	1977	A Lyle	144	1990	J Barnes	144
1965	LF Millar	153	1978	JC Davies	146	1991	G Homewood	141
1966	P Townsend	150	1979	JC Davies	147	1992	P Page	141
1967	DJ Millensted	150	1980	R Knott	143	1993	S Burnell	143
1968	PD Flaherty	144	1981	P Dennett	146	1994	M Treleaven	140
1969	MM Niven	149	1982	DG Lane	148	1995	J Crampton	142
1970	R Hunter	145	1983	J Hawksworth	146	1996	L Donald	139
1971	A Millar	144	1984	R Willison	139	1997	P Streeter	143
1972	C Cieslewicz	148	1985	F George	144			

1998
1	G Storm	69
2	P Rowe	70
	N Pimm	71

Berkshire Trophy (Inaugurated 1946) *at The Berkshire*

Year	Winner	Score	Year	Winner	Score	Year	Winner	Score
1946	R Sweeney	148	1963	DW Frame	289	1981	D Blakeman	280
1947	PB Lucas	298	1964	R Foster	281	1982	SD Keppler	278
1948	LG Crawley	301	1965	MF Bonallack	278	1983	S Hamer	288
1949	PB Lucas	300	1966	P Oosterhuis	287	1984	JL Plaxton	276
1950	PF Scrutton	296	1967	DJ Millensted	283	1985	P McEvoy	279
1951	PF Scrutton	301	1968	MF Bonallack	273	1986	R Muscroft	280
1952	PF Scrutton	286	1969	JC Davies	278	1987	J Robinson	275
1953	JL Morgan	289	1970	MF Bonallack	274	1988	R Claydon	276
1954T	Ft Lt K Hall	303	1971T	MF Bonallack	277	1989	J Metcalfe	272
	E Bromley-Davenport			J Davies		1990	J O'Shea	271
1955	GH Micklem	282	1972	DP Davidson	280	1991	J Bickerton	280
1956	GB Wolstenholme	285	1973	PJ Hedges	278	1992	V Phillips	274
1957	MF Bonalbck	291	1974	J Downie	280	1993	V Phillips	271
1958T	GB Wolstennolme	284	1975	N Faldo	281	1994T	J Knight	274
	AH Perowne		1976	PJ Hedges	284		A Marshall	
1959	JB Carr	279	1977	A Lyle	279	1995	G Harris	275
1960	GB Wolstenholme	276	1978	PJ Hedges	281	1996	G Wolstenholme	274
1961	MF Bonallack	275	1979	D Williams	274	1997	G Wolstenholme	275
1962	SC Saddler	279	1980	P Downes	280			

1998
1	M Hilton	70-72-71-71—284
2	M Side	69-71-74-71—285
	J Doherty	71-69-75-70—285

Burhill Family Foursomes (Inaugurated 1937) at Burhill, Surrey

Year	Winners	Year	Winners
1937	Captain JR Stroyan and Miss S Stroyan	1971	PHA Brownrigg and Miss D Brownrigg
1938	W Price and Miss E Price	1972	Mrs S Grant and NJ Grant
1939–1946	*No competition*	1973	MV Blake and Miss B Blake
1947	Mrs GH Brooks and PJ Brooks	1974	Mrs NR Bailhache and WJ Bailhache
1948	W Price and Miss E Price	1975	Mrs PR Williams and PM Williams
1949	Mrs EC Pepper and W Pepper	1976	Mrs D Gotla and C Gotla
1950	A Forbes Ilsley and Miss J Ilsley	1977	Mrs J Maudsley and C Maudsley
1951	Major E Loxley Land and Miss J Land	1978	Mrs H Calderwood and WR Calderwood
1952	CHV Elliot and Miss S Elliott	1979	Dr AG Wells and Miss E Wells
1953	JC Hubbard and Miss A Hubbard	1980	JL Hall and Miss Cynthia Hall
1954	JC Hubbard and Miss A Hubbard	1981	Mrs J Fox and N Fox
1955	Mrs HP Thornhill and JR Thornhill	1982	Mrs J Fox and N Fox
1956	Mrs HP Thornhill and JR Thornhill	1983	Mrs J Rowe and D Rowe
1957	CH Young and Mrs PBK Gracey	1984	Mrs JS Gilbert and AS Gilbert
1958	Mrs HM Winckley and JB Winckley	1985	Mrs MM Pollitt and R Pollitt
1959	Jack and Anna van Zwanenberg	1986	Mrs J Maudesley and C Maudesley
1960	Mrs M Kippax and JM Kippax	1987	Mrs A Croft and M Croft
1961	Mrs R Sutherland Pilch and J Sutherland Pilch	1988	Mrs V Hargreaves and R Hargreaves
1962	JC Hubbard and Miss Trudi Hubbard	1989	Mrs J Lawson and P Lawson
1963	GA Rowan-Robinson and Miss 'Pooh' Rowan Robinson	1990	Mrs M Maisey and S Maisey
		1991	Mrs M Pollitt and R Pollitt
1964	Mrs P Todhunter and T Todhunter	1992	R Stocks and Miss Joanna Stocks
1965	Mrs WT Warrin and SR Warrin	1993	Mrs M Bartlett and Jerome Bartlett
1966	Mrs WT Warrin and SR Warrin	1994	MJ Toole and Miss SJ Toole
1967	Mrs WT Warrin and SR Warrin	1995	Mrs G Warner and R Warner
1968	Mrs CHP Trollope and Nigel Trollope	1996	Mrs AP Croft and MC Croft
1969	Mrs EPP D'A Walton and JF Walton	1997	Mrs J Clink and T Clink
1970	JF Young and Miss EJ Young		

1998
Final: MJ Toole and Miss SJ Toole beat A Cox and Miss A Cox 7 and 5

Cameron Corbett Vase (Inaugurated 1897) at Haggs Castle, Glasgow

Year	Winner	Year	Winner	Year	Winner
1897	AF Duncan	1928	SL McKinlay	1960	J Mackenzie
1898	AF Duncan	1929	D McBride	1961	GB Cosh
1899	W Laidlaw	1930	HM Dickson	1962	JH Richmond
1900	GH Hutcheson	1931	HM Dickson	1963	JA Davidson
1901	G Fox Jr	1932	W Stringer	1964	IA MacCaskill
1902	AF Duncan	1933	W Tulloch	1965	H Frazer
1903	G Fox Jr	1934	JM Dykes	1966	D Black
1904	R Bone	1935	H Thomson	1967	JRW Walkinshaw
1905	R Bone	1936	J Gray	1968	CW Green
1906	W Gemmill	1937	Tl Craig Jr	1969	A Brooks
1907	G Wilkie	1938	JS Logan	1970T	J McTear
1908	AF Duncan	1939	A Steel		D Hayes
1909	EB Tipping	1940–41	*No competition*	1971	G Macgregor
1910	JH Irons	1942	AC Taylor	1972	HB Stuart
1911	G Morris	1943–45	*No competition*	1973	MJ Miller
1912	R Scott Jr	1946	JS Montgomerie	1974	M Rae
1913	R Scott Jr	1947	W Maclaren	1975	D Barclay Howard
1914	D Martin	1948	J Pressley	1976	GH Murray
1915–18	*Not played due to First World War*	1949	GB Peters	1977	MJ Miller
		1950	J Gray	1978	GH Murray
1919	HR Orr	1951	GB Peters	1979	KW Macintosh
1920	DJ Murray Campbell	1952	J Stewart Thomson	1980	IA Carslaw
1921	HM Dickson	1953	J Orr	1981	GH Murray
1922	WS Macfarlane	1954	JR Cater	1982	GH Murray
1923	JO Stevenson	1955	RC Macgregor	1983	AS Oldcorn
1924	JO Stevenson	1956	RC Macgregor	1984	D Barclay Howard
1925	A Jamieson Jr	1957	I Rennie	1985	J McDonald
1926	G Chapple	1958	DH Reid		
1927	RS Rodger	1959	AS Kerr		*continued*

Cameron Corbett Vase *continued*

Year	Winner	Year	Winner	Score	Year	Winner	Score
1986	JW Milligan	1990	D Robertson	290	1994	J Hodson	280
1987	J Semple	1991	K Gallacher	281	1995	D Barclay Howard	268
1988	C Everett	1992	D Kirkpatrick	284	1996	C Watson	282
1989	AG Tait	1993	R Russell	278	1997	C Watson	268

1998 (reduced to 36 holes)

1	E Wilson	69-71—140
2	S McGavin	71-70—141
3	RA Clark	68-74—142

Craigmillar Park Open *at Craigmillar Park, Edinburgh*

Year	Winner	Year	Winner
1991	N Walton	1995	C Watson
1992	S Knowles	1996	G Tough
1993	R Russell	1997	C Hislop
1994	B Collier		

1998

1	G Rankin	70-35-67-70—242
2	E Forbes	65-38-74-67—244
3	D Patrick	71-34-71-71—247

(Second round curtailed due to heavy snow)

John Cross Bowl (Inaugurated 1957) *at Worplesdon, Surrey*

Year	Winner	Year	Winner	Year	Winner
1957	DW Frame	1971	PBQ Drayson	1985	M Devetta
1958	G Evans	1972	AR Kerr	1986	C Rotheroe
1959	G Evans	1973	DW Frame	1987	B White
1960	DW Frame	1974	RPF Brown	1988	B White
1961	DW Frame	1975	BJ Winteridge	1989	KG Jones
1962	DW Frame	1976	DW Frame	1990	D Lee
1963	PO Green	1977	DW Frame	1991	P Sefton
1964	RL Glading	1978	RPF Brown	1992	R Watts
1965	P Townsend	1979	JG Bennett	1993	J Collier
1966	P Townsend	1980	JG Bennett	1994	P Benka
1967	MJ Burgess	1981	ME Johnson	1995	M Galway
1968	PJ Benka	1982	R Boxall	1996	B Barham
1969	DW Frame	1983	DG Lane	1997	C Banks
1970	P Dawson	1984	I Gray		

1998 (reduced to one round due to bad weather)

1	J Wormald	69
2	R Fenwick	70
	B Porter	70

Duncan Putter (Inaugurated 1959) *at Southerndown, Bridgend, Glamorgan*

Year	Winner	Score	Year	Winner	Score	Year	Winner	Score
1959	G Huddy	301	1972	P Berry (3 rounds)	230	1984	JP Price	284
1960	Wl Tucker	289	1973	JKD Povall	299	1985	P McEvoy	299
1961T	G Huddy	295	1974	S Cox	302	1986	D Wood	300
	WI Tucker		1975	JG Jermine	295	1987	P McEvoy	278
1962	EN Davies	297	1976T	Wl Tucker	286	1988	S Dodd	290
1963	Wl Tucker	296		H Stott		1989	RN Roderick	280
1964	JL Toye	293	1977	H Stott	295	1990	R Willison	311
1965	P Townsend	305	1978	P McEvoy	295	1991	R Willison	267
1966	MF Attenborough	291	1979	HJ Evans	292	1992	R Dinsdale	213
1967	D Millensted	297	1980	P McEvoy	296	1993	M Thomson	289
1968	JL Morgan	299	1981T	R Chapman	294	1994	G Wolstenholme	226
1969	Wl Tucker	304		PG Way		1995	B Dredge	293
1970	JL Toye	305	1982	D McLean	283	1996	G Wolstenholme	291
1971	W Humphreys	295	1983	JG Jermine	297	1997	M Pilkington	283

1998

1	M King	74-74-72-71—291
2	M Pilkington	77-70-73-72—292
3	N Edwards	77-73-73-72—295

Fathers and Sons Foursomes *at West Hill, Surrey*

Year	Winner	Score	Year	Winner	Score
1991	DM and WK Laing		1995	J and D Niven	
1992	JA and R Piggott		1996	MJ and J Hickey	
1993	B and R Groce		1997	DR and M Baxter	
1994	RJ and P Hill				

1998

Semi-Finals
TWG and R Betts beat AR and R Guest-Gornall 1 hole
SF and P Brown beat BM and B Clarke 2 and 1

Final
SF and P Brown beat TWG and R Betts 3 and 1

Frame Trophy (Inaugurated 1986) *at Worplesdon, Surrey*

Year	Winner	Score	Year	Winner	Score	Year	Winner	Score
1988	DW Frame	229	1992	DW Frame	223	1996	DG Lane	217
1989	JRW Walkinshaw	219	1993	DW Frame	216	1997	B Turner	226
1990	WJ Williams	224	1994	DG Lane	222			
1991	DB Sheahan	223	1995	M Christmas	223			

1998

1	DG Lane	211
2	MH Dixon	218
3	NH Barnes	223

Golf Illustrated **Gold Vase** (Inaugurated 1909)

Year	Winner	Year	Winner	Year	Winner
1909	CK Hutchison	1948	RD Chapman	1973	J Davies
1910	Abe Mitchell	1949	RJ White	1974	P Hedges
1911	R Harris	1950	AW Whyte	1975	MF Bonallack
1912	R Harris	1951	JB Carr	1976	A Brodie
1913	Abe Mitchell	1952	JDA Langley	1977	J Davies
1914	H Hilton	1953	JDA Langley	1978	P Thomas
1919	D Darwin	1954	H Ridgeley	1979	KJ Miller
1920	DS Crowther	1955	Major DA Blair	1980	G Brand Jr
1921	M Seymour	1956	Major DA Blair	1981	P Garner
1922	WA Murray	1957	G Wolstenholme	1982	I Carslaw
1923	CJH Tolley	1958	M Lunt	1983	S Keppler
1924	CC Aylmer	1959	A Bussell	1984	JV Marks
1925	JB Beck	1960	D Sewell	1985	M Davis
1926T	CJH Tolley/TA Torrance	1961T	DJ Harrison/	1986	R Eggo
1927	RH Wethered		MF Bonallack	1987	D Lane
1928	CJH Tolley	1962	BHG Chapman	1988	M Turner
1929	D Grant	1963	RH Mummery	1989	G Wolstenholme
1930	RT Jones (US)	1964	D Moffat	1990	A Rogers
1931	WA Murray	1965	C Clark	1991	R Scott
1932	RW Hartley	1966	PM Townsend	1992	P Page
1933	RW Hartley	1967T	RA Durrant/	1993T	C Challen/V Phillips
1934	WL Hartley		MF Bonallack	1994	S Burnell
1935	J Thomas	1968	MF Bonallack	1995	A Wall
1936	J Ferrier	1969T	MF Bonallack/J Hayes	1996	*Not played*
1937	R Sweeney	1970	D Harrison	1997	M James
1938	CJ Anderson	1971	MF Bonallack/H Ashby		
1939	SB Robert	1972T	DP Davidson/R Hunter		

1998
For the first time in the tournament's history there was an 18-hole play-off following a five-way tie:

Pos	Name	Score	Play-off score
1	Rupert Rea (Royal Mid-Surrey)	73-74—147	70
2	Steven Barwick (East Berkshire)	75-72—147	74
3	Mark Side (Shirley Park)	73-74—147	75
4	Michael Reynard (Moseley)	75-72—147	78
5	Adam Gee (Leatherhead)	74-73—147	85

Grafton Morrish Trophy (Inaugurated 1963)

Year	Winner	Year	Winner	Year	Winner
1963	Tonbridge	1975	Oundle	1987	Harrow
1964	Tonbridge	1976	Charterhouse	1988	Robert Gordon's
1965	Charterhouse	1977	Haileybury	1989	Tonbridge
1966	Charterhouse	1978	Charterhouse	1990	Clifton
1967	Charterhouse	1979	Harrow	1991	Repton
1968	Wellington	1980	Charterhouse	1992	Charterhouse
1969	Sedbergh	1981	Charterhouse	1993	Malvern
1970	Sedbergh	1982	Marlborough	1994	George Heriot's
1971	Dulwich	1983	Wellington	1995	Repton
1972	Sedbergh	1984	Sedbergh	1996	Coventry
1973	Pangbourne	1985	Warwick	1997	George Heriot's
1974	Millfield	1986	Tonbridge		

1998 *at Hunstanton and Brancaster*

Semi-Finals
Solihull beat Repton 2–1
George Heriot's beat Coventry 2–1

Final
Solihull beat George Heriot's 2–1

Halford-Hewitt Cup (Inaugurated 1924)

Year	Winner	Year	Winner	Year	Winner
1924	Eton	1953	Harrow	1976	Merchiston
1925	Eton	1954	Rugby	1977	Watsons
1926	Eton	1955	Eton	1978	Harrow
1927	Harrow	1956	Eton	1979	Stowe
1928	Eton	1957	Watsons	1980	Shrewsbury
1929	Harrow	1958	Harrow	1981	Watsons
1930	Charterhouse	1959	Wellington	1982	Charterhouse
1931	Harrow	1960	Rossall	1983	Charterhouse
1932	Charterhouse	1961	Rossall	1984	Charterhouse
1933	Rugby	1962	Oundle	1985	Harrow
1934	Charterhouse	1963	Repton	1986	Repton
1935	Charterhouse	1964	Fettes	1987	Merchiston
1936	Charterhouse	1965	Rugby	1988	Stowe
1937	Charterhouse	1966	Charterhouse	1989	Eton
1938	Marlborough	1967	Eton	1990	Tonbridge
1939	Charterhouse	1968	Eton	1991	Shrewsbury
1940–46 *No competition*		1969	Eton	1992	Tonbridge
1947	Harrow	1970	Merchiston	1993	Shrewsbury
1948	Winchester	1971	Charterhouse	1994	Tonbridge
1949	Charterhouse	1972	Marlborough	1995	Harrow
1950	Rugby	1973	Rossall	1996	Radley
1951	Rugby	1974	Charterhouse	1997	Oundle
1952	Harrow	1975	Harrow		

1998 *at Deal*
Semi-Final
Charterhouse beat Clifton 3½–1½
Tonbridge beat Harrow 3½–1½

Final
Charterhouse beat Tonbridge 3–2

Hampshire Hog (Inaugurated 1957)

Year	Winner	Year	Winner	Year	Winner
1957	MF Bonallack	1971	DW Frarne	1985	A Clapp
1958	PF Scrutton	1972	R Revell	1986	R Eggo
1959	Col AA Duncan	1973	SC Mason	1987	A Rogers
1960	MF Attenborough	1974	TJ Giles	1988	S Richardson
1961	HC Squirrell	1975	HAN Stott	1989	P McEvoy
1962	FD Physick	1976	MC Hughesdon	1990	J Metcalfe
1963	Sqn Ldr WE McCrea	1977	AWB Lyle	1991	M Welch
1964	DF Wilkie	1978	GF Godwin	1992	S Graham
1965	T Koch de Gooreynd	1979	MF Bonallack	1993	D Hamilton
1966	Maj DA Blair	1980	RA Durrant	1994	B Ingleby
1967	Maj DA Blair	1981	G Brand Jr	1995	J Rose
1968	MJ Burgess	1982	A Sherborne	1996	R Tate
1969	B Critchley	1983	I Gray	1997	G Wolstenholme
1970	Maj DA Blair	1984	J Hawksworth		

1998
1   P Rowe   67-67—134
2   S Dyson   69-66—135
3   G Storm   68-70—138

King George V Coronation Cup *at Porters Park, Herts.*

Year	Winner		Year	Winner		Year	Winner	
1990	C Boal	141	1993	D Hamilton	134	1996	N Swaffield	134
1991	S Hoffman	142	1994	S Webster	146	1997	J Knight	136
1992	R Watts	141	1995	S Jarvis	140			

1998

1	M King	65
2	S Standing	67
3	D Hastings	70
	R Rea	70

Lagonda Trophy (Inaugurated 1975) *at Camberley Heath; from 1990 at Gog Magog*

Year	Winner		Year	Winner		Year	Winner
1975	WJ Reid		1983	I Sparkes		1991	J Cook
1976	JC Davies		1984	M Davis		1992	L Westwood
1977	WS Gronow		1985	J Robinson		1993	L James
1978	JC Davies		1986	D Cilford		1994	S Webster
1979	JC Bennett		1987	DG Lane		1995	P Nelson
1980	P McEvoy		1988	R Claydon		1996	S Collingwood
1981	N Mitchell		1989	T Spence		1997	L Donald
1982	A Sherborne		1990	L Parsons			

1998

1	K Ferrie	71-64-67-71—273
2	C Rodgers	68-70-68-68—274
3	J Harris	71-68-70-66—275
	R McEvoy	72-64-69-70—275

Leven Gold Medal (Inaugurated 1870) *at Leven Links, Fife*

Year	Winner	Score	Year	Winner	Score	Year	Winner	Score
1870	J Elder	85	1899	G Wilkie Jr	78	1931	A Dunsire	71
1871	R Wallace	91	1900	W Henderson	78	1932	J Ballingall	72
1872	P Anderson	91	1901	R Simpson	76	1933	CA Danks	73
1873	R Armit	95	1902	J Bell	76	1934	EA McRuvie	67
1874	D Campbell	93	1903	W Henderson	76	1935	EG Stoddart	71
1875	AM Ross	90	1904	W Henderson	77	1936	GA Buist	73
1876	AM Ross	88	1905	G Wilkie	76	1937	JY Strachan	75
1877	J Wilkie	88	1906	G Wilkie	78	1938	S Macdonald	71
1878	R Wallace	90	1907	M Goodwillie	73	1939	D Jamieson	72
1879	C Anderson	89	1908	W Henderson	77	1940–45	*No competition*	
1880	C Anderson	89	1909	W Henderson	77	1946	EA McRuvie	77
1881	J Foggo	91	1910	W Whyte	76	1947	JE Young	74
1882	J Wilkie	89	1911	G Wilkie	73	1948	J Imrie	77
1883	J Foggo	86	1912	G Wilkie	73	1949	WM Ogg	76
1884	C Anderson	89	1913	W Whyte	73	1950	E McRuvie	77
1885	R Adam	84	1914	GB Rattray	76	1951	J Imrie	72
1886	R Adam	87	1915–18	*No competition*		1952	HVS Thomson	69
1887	J Foggo	81	1919	G Wilkie	77	1953	O Rolland	70
1888	DA Leitch	86	1920	JJ Smith	76	1954	JW Draper	73
1889	R Adam	81	1921	GV Donaldson	77	1955	JW Draper	72
1890	W Marshall	80	1922	SO Shepperd	72	1956	R Dishart	72
1891	DM Jackson	80	1923	GV Donaldson	73	1957	I Pearson	72
1892	Col DW Mackinnon	85	1924	JN Smith	76	1958	W McIntyre	71
1893	HS Colt	79	1925	A Robertson	73	1959	W Moyes	71
1894	J Bell Jr	82	1926	T Ainslie	75	1960	T Taylor	69
1895	C Wllkie Jr	80	1927	EA McRuvie	72	1961	A Cunningham	69
1896	J Bell Jr	78	1928	EA McRuvie	70	1962	W Moyes	71
1897	J Bell Jr	79	1929	EA McRuvie	72	1963	W Moyes	68
1898	G Wilkie Jr	82	1930	EA McRuvie	68	1964	A Cunningham	68

Other Men's Amateur Tournaments

Year	Winner	Score	Year	Winner	Score	Year	Winner	Score
1965	PG Buchanan	71	1974	P Smith	282	1987	G Macgregor	271
			1975	HB Stuart	286	1988	CE Everett	280
Two rounds played from 1966			1976	IC Hutcheon	266	1989	AJ Coltart	280
1966	GM Rutherford	144	1977	IC Hutcheon	289	1990	CE Everett	280
1967	AO Maxwell	140	1978	R Wallace	287	1991	GA Lowson	284
1968	A Cunningham	140	1979	B Marchbank	274	1992	D Robertson	279
			1980	J Huggan	279	1993	L Westwood	276
Four rounds played from 1966			1981	IC Hutcheon	282	1994	B Howard	265
1969	P Smith	284	1982	IC Hutcheon	272	1995	S Mackenzie	273
1970	JC Farmer	277	1983	J Huggan	274	1996	M Eliasson	267
1971	J Scott Macdonald	207	1984	S Stephen	278	1997	S Carmichael	278
1972	J Rankine	282	1985	AD Turnbull	281			
1973	S Stephen	288	1986	P-U Johansson	275			

1998

1	G Rankin	67-68-64-69—268
2	L Kelly	66-69-68-70—273
3	A Farmer	67-71-71-66—275

Lytham Trophy (Inaugurated 1965) at Royal Lytham & St Annes

Year	Winner	Score	Year	Winner	Score	Year	Winner	Score
1965T	MF Bonallack	295	1973T	SG Birtwell		1986	S McKenna	297
	CA Clark		1974	CW Green	291	1987	D Wood	293
1966	PM Townsend	290	1975	G Macgregor	299	1988	P Broadhurst	296
1967	R Foster	296	1976	MJ Kelley	292	1989	N Williamson	286
1968	R Foster	286	1977	P Deeble	296	1990	G Evans	291
1969T	T Craddock	290	1978	B Marchbank	288	1991	G Evans	284
	SG Birtwell		1979	P McEvoy	279	1992	S Cage	294
1970T	JC Farmer	296	1980	IC Hutcheon	293	1993	T McLure	292
	CW Green		1981	R Chapman	221	1994	W Bennett	285
	GC Marks		1982	MF Sludds	306	1995	S Gallacher	281
1971	W Humphreys	292	1983	S McAllister	299	1996	M Carver	284
1972	MF Bonallack	281	1984	J Hawksworth	289	1997	G Rankin	279
1973T	MG King	292	1985	L Macnamara	144			

1998

1	L Kelly*	73-69-72-74—288
2	G Storm	73-67-73-75—288
	G Rankin	67-72-73-75—288

Oxford v Cambridge Varsity Match (Inaugurated 1878)

Year	Winner	Venue	Year	Winner	Venue
1878	Oxford	Wimbledon	1897	Cambridge	Sandwich
1879	Cambridge	Wimbledon	1898	Cambridge	Sandwich
1880	Oxford	Wimbledon	1899	Oxford	Sandwich
1881	*Not played*		1900	Oxford	Sandwich
1882	Cambridge	Wimbledon	1901	Oxford	Sandwich
1883	Oxford	Wimbledon	1902	Oxford	Sandwich
1884	Oxford	Wimbledon	1903	Oxford	Sandwich
1885	Oxford	Wimbledon	1904	Oxford	Woking
1886	Oxford	Wimbledon	1905	Cambridge	Sunningdale
1887	Cambridge	Wimbledon	1906	Cambridge	Hoylake
1888	Cambridge	Wimbledon	1907	Cambridge	Hoylake
1889	Oxford	Wimbledon	*After 1907 the result was arrived at by matches won*		
1890	Cambridge	Wimbledon			
1891	Cambridge	Wimbledon	1908	Cambridge	Sunningdale
1892	Cambridge	Wrlmbledon	1909	Oxford	St George's, Sandwich
1893	Cambridge	Wimbledon	1910	Cambridge	Hoylake
1894	Oxford	Sandwich	1911	Oxford	Rye
1895	Cambridge	Sandwich	1912	Halved	Prince's,
1896	Halved	Wimbledon	1913	Halved	Hoylake

* *Winner after play-off*

Oxford v Cambridge Varsity Match *continued*

Year	Winner	Venue	Year	Winner	Venue
1914	Oxford	Rye	1960	Cambridge	R Lytham & St Annes
1915–19	*No competitions due to First World War*		1961	Oxford	Sandwich, R St George's
1920	Cambridge	Sunningdale	1962	Halved	Hunstanton
1921	Oxford	Hoylake	1963	Cambridge	R Birkdale
1922	Cambridge	Prince's, Sandwich	1964	Oxford	Rye
1923	Oxford	Rye	1965	Cambridge	Sandwich, R St George's
1924	Cambridge	Hoylake	1966	Cambridge	Hunstanton
1925	Oxford	Hunstanton	1967	Cambridge	Rye
1926	Cambridge	Burnham and Berrow	1968	Cambridge	Porthcawl
1927	Cambridge	Hoylake	1969	Cambridge	Formby
1928	Cambridge	Prince's, Sandwich	1970	Halved	Sandwich, R St George's
1929	Cambridge	Rye	1971	Oxford	Rye
1930	Oxford	Hoylake	1972	Cambridge	Formby
1931	Oxford	Prince's, Sandwich	1973	Oxford	Saunton
1932	Oxford	Lytham St Annes	1974	Cambridge	Ganton
1933	Cambridge	Prince's, Sandwich	1975	Cambridge	Hoylake
1934	Oxford	Formby	1976	Cambridge	Woodhall Spa
1935	Cambridge	Burnham and Berrow	1977	Cambridge	Porthcawl
1936	Cambridge	Hoylake	1978	Oxford	Rye
1937	Cambridge	Prince's, Sandwich	1979	Oxford	Harlech
1938	Cambridge	Westward Ho!	1980	Oxford	Hoylake
1939	Cambridge	St George's, Sandwich	1981	Cambridge	Formby
1940–45	*No competitions due to Second World War*		1982	Cambridge	Hunstanton
1946	Cambridge	R Lytham & St Annes	1983	Cambridge	Sandwich, R St George's
1947	Oxford	Rye	1984	Cambridge	Sunningdale
1948	Oxford	Sandwich, R St George's	1985	Oxford	Rye
1949	Cambridge	Hoylake	1986	Oxford	Ganton
1950	Oxford	R Lytham & St Annes	1987	Cambridge	Formby
1951	Cambridge	Rye	1988	Cambridge	Royal Porthcawl
1952	Cambridge	Rye	1989	Cambridge	Rye
1953	Cambridge	Rye	1990	Cambridge	Muirfield
1954	Cambridge	Rye	1991	Cambridge	Sandwich, R St George's
1955	Cambridge	Rye	1992	Oxford	R Cinque Ports
1956	Oxford	Formby	1993	Oxford	R Liverpool
1957	Oxford	Sandwich, R St George's	1994	Oxford	Rye
1958	Cambridge	Rye	1995	Oxford	R Lytham & St Annes
1959	Cambridge	Burnham & Berrow	1996	Oxford	R West Norfolk
			1997	Oxford	R St Georges

1998
Cambridge beat Oxford 9–6

Oxford and Cambridge Golfing Society for the President's Putter (Inaugurated 1920) *at Rye*

Year	Winner	Year	Winner	Year	Winner
1920	EWE Holderness	1939	JOH Greenly	1965	WJ Uzielli
1921	EWE Holderness	1940–46	*No competition*	1966	MF Attenborough
1922	EWE Holderness	1947	LG Crawley	1967	JR Midgley
1923	EWE Holderness	1948	Major AA Duncan	1968	AWJ Holmes
1924	B Darwin	1949	PB Lucas	1969	P Moody
1925	HD Gillies	1950	DHR Martin	1970	DMA Steel
1926T	EF Storey	1951	LG Crawley	1971	GT Duncan
	RH Wethered	1952	LG Crawley	1972	P Moody
1927	RH Wethered	1953	GH Micklem	1973	AD Swanston
1928	RH Wethered	1954	G Huddy	1974	R Biggs
1929	Sir EWE Holderness	1955	G Huddy	1975	CJ Weight
1930	TA Bourn	1956	GT Duncan	1976	MJ Reece
1931	AG Pearson	1957	AE Shepperson	1977	AWJ Holmes
1932	LG Crawley	1958	Lt-Col AA Duncan	1978	MJ Reece
1933	AJ Peech	1959	ID Wheater	1979	*Cancelled due to snow*
1934	DHR Martin	1960	JME Anderson	1980	S Melville
1935	RH Wethered	1961	ID Wheater	1981	AWJ Holmes
1936	RH Wethered	1962	MF Attenborough	1982	DMA Steel
1937	JB Beck	1963	JG Blackwell	1983	ER Dexter
1938	CJH Tolley	1964	DMA Steel	1984	A Edmond

Year	Winner	Year	Winner	Year	Winner
1985	ER Dexter	1990	G Woollett	1995	A Woolnough
1986	J Caplan	1991	B Ingleby	1996	C Rotheroe
1987	CD Meacher	1992	M Cox	1997	C Rotheroe
1988	G Woollett	1993	C Weight		
1989	M Froggatt	1994	S Seman		

1998

Quarter Finals
R Randall beat S Ellis 1 hole
J Warman beat N Burke 4 and 3
M Williamson beat C Nevill 1 hole
N Pabari beat P Hill 4 and 3

Semi-Finals
J Warman beat R Randall 2 and 1
N Pabari beat M Williamson 4 and 3

Final
N Pabari beat J Warman 2 and 1

Prince of Wales Challenge Cup (Inaugurated 1927) *at Royal Cinque Ports*

Year	Winner	Score	Year	Winner	Score	Year	Winner	Score
1928	D Grant	142	1958T	KR Mackenzie	158	1979	GF Godwin	148
1929	NR Reeves	153		BAF Belmore		1980T	GM Dunsire	149
1930	R Harris	156	1959	D Johnstone	149		B Nicholson	
1931	RW Hartley	149	1960	CG Moore	162	1981	JM Baldwin	146
1932	EN Layton	151	1961	RH Bazell	151	1982	SG Homewood	145
1933	JB Nash	148	1962	Dr J Pittar	145	1983	M Davis	141
1934	R Sweeney	304	1963	Sq Ldr WE McCrea	155	1984T	F Wood	146
1935	HG Bentley	301	1964	NA Paul	153.		DH Niven	
1936	LOM Munn	301	1965T	NA Paul	150	1985	RJ Tickner	141
1937	DHR Martin	291		VE Barton		1986	JM Baldwin	149
1938	EA Head	291	1966	P Townsend	150	1987	S Finch	148
1939–46	*No competition*		1967	MF Bonallack	141	1988	MP Palmer	144
1947	PB Lucas	154	1968T	NA Paul	144	1989T	T Lloyd	146
1948	Capt DA Blair	151		GC Marks			NA Farrell	
1949	C Stowe	142	1969	MF Attenborough	152	1990T	G Homewood	
1950	I Caldwell	151	1970	J Butterworth	153		BS Ingleby	145
1951	I Caldwell	151	1971	VE Barton	147	1991	S Pardoe	152
1952	I Caldwell	150	1972	PJ Hedges	162	1992	L Westwood	160
1953	JG Blackwell	159	1973	PJ Hedges	138	1993	ML Welch	143
1954	DLW Woon	143	1974	PJ Hedges	146	1994	I Hardy	149
1955T	C Taylor	153	1975	JC Davies	150	1995	L Ferris	152
	GT Duncan		1976	MJ Inglis	162	1996	J Maddock	142
1956	PF Scrutton	151	1977	PJ Hedges	154	1997	J Carter	154
1957	*No competition*		1978	ER Dexter	145			

1998

1	G Woodman	73-71—144
2	P Langford	78-70—148
	K Staunton	75-73—148

Rosebery Challenge Cup (Inaugurated 1933) *at Ashridge*

Year	Winner	Year	Winner	Year	Winner
1933	GA Hill	1953	R Pattinson	1965	EJ Wiggs
1934	JS Rowell	1954	C Ostler	1966	A Holmes
1935	PB Lucas	1955	D Gray	1967	A Holmes
1936	LG Crawley	1956	W Cmdr CH Beamish	1968	A Holmes
1937	JO Levinson	1957	GH Foster	1969	A Holmes
1938	AS Anderson	1958	JT Anderson	1970	PW Bent
1939	AS Anderson	1959	RW Acton	1971	AW Holmes
1940–48	*No competition*	1960	EJ Wiggs	1972	AW Holmes
1949	AA McNair	1961	KT Warren	1973	AJ Mason
1950	RAR Black	1962	PR Johnston	1974	G Stradling
1951	JW Taylor	1963	CA Murray	1975	JA Watts
1952	R Pattinson	1964	A Millar		

continued

Rosebery Challenge Cup *continued*

Year	Winner	Year	Winner	Year	Winner
1976	G Stradling	1984	DG Lane	1992	R Harris
1977	J Ambridge	1985	P Wharton	1993	M Hooper
1978	RJ Bevan	1986	JE Ambridge	1994	P Wilkins
1979	JB Berney	1987	HA Wilkerson	1995	P Wilkins
1980	JA Watts	1988	N Leconte	1996	J Kemp
1981	RY Mitchell	1989	C Slattery	1997	L Watcham
1982	DG Lane	1990	C Tingey		
1983	N Briggs	1991	M Thompson		

1998
1	S Vinnicombe	71-72—143
2	C Boal	76-68—144
3	B Connelly	68-75—144

St Andrews Links Trophy *at St Andrews*

Year	Winner	Year	Winner
1990	S Bouvier	1994	B Howard
1991	R Willison	1995	G Rankin
1992	C Watson	1996	B Howard
1993	G Hay	1997	J Rose

1998
1	C Watson	70-63-71-72—276
2	S Dyson	68-70-71-69—278
3	D Patrick	71-64-73-73—281

St David's Gold Cross (Inaugurated 1930) *at Royal St David's, Gwynedd*

Year	Winner	Year	Winner	Year	Winner
1930	GC Stokoe	1956	W Cdr CH Beamish	1977	JA Fagan
1931	EW Fiddian	1957	CD Lawrie	1978	S Wild
1932	Dr W Tweddell	1958	GB Turner	1979	MA Smith
1933	IS Thomas	1959	MSR Lunt	1980	CP Hodgkinson
1934	SB Roberts	1960	LJ Ranells	1981	G Broadbent
1935	IS Thomas	1961	MSR Lunt	1982	MW Calvert
1936	RMW Pritchard	1962	PD Kelley	1983	RD James
1937	IS Thomas	1963	JKD Povall	1984	RJ Green
1938	SB Roberts	1964	MSR Lunt	1985	KH Williams
1939	IS Thomas	1965	MSR Lunt	1986	RN Roderick
1940–45	*No competition*	1966	MSR Lunt	1987	SR Andrew
1946	SB Roberts	1967	MSR Lunt	1988	MW Calvert
1947	G Mills	1968	AW Holmes	1989	AJ Barnett
1948	CH Eaves	1969	AJ Thomson	1990	MA Macara
1949	SB Roberts	1970	AJ Thomson	1991	RJ Dinsdale
1950	DMG Sutherland	1971	A Smith	1992	B Dredge
1951	JL Morgan	1972	EN Davies	1993	B Dredge
1952	SB Roberts	1973	RD James	1994	C Evans
1953	S Lunt	1974	GC Marks	1995	M Skinner
1954	GB Turner	1975	CP Hodgkinson	1996	L Harpin
1955	JL Morgan	1976	JR Jones	1997	M Pilkington

1998
1	L Harpin	289
2	S Merrill	291
3	A Smith	292

St George's Grand Challenge Cup (Inaugurated 1888)
at Royal St. George's

Year	Winner	Score	Year	Winner	Score	Year	Winner	Score
1888	J Ball	180	1926	Maj CO Hezlet	158	1966	P Townsend	148
1889	J Ball	169	1927	WL Hartley	153	1967	Maj DA Blair	154
1890	J Ball	175	1928	D Grant	146	1968	MF Bonallack	142
1891	J Ball	174	1929	TA Torrance	148	1969	PJ Benka	150
1892	FA Fairlie	167	1930	RW Hartley	148	1970	PJ Hedges	150
1893	HH Hilton	165	1931	WL Hartley	149	1971	EJS Garrett	143
1894	HH Hilton	167	1932	HG Bentley	151	1972	JC Davies	149
1895	E Blackwell	176	1933	JB Beck	151	1973	JC Davies	141
1896	FG Tait	165	1934	AGS Penman	153	1974	JC Davies	140
1897	CE Hambro	162	1935	Maj WHH Aitken	158	1975	JC Davies	147
1898	FG Tait	163	1936	DHR Martin	150	1976	JC Davies	158
1899	FG Tait	155	1937	DHR Martin	144	1977	JC Davies	154
1900	R Maxwell	155	1938	JJF Pennink	142	1978	C Phillips	145
1901	SH Fry	165	1939	AA McNair	153	1979	CF Godwin	146
1902	H Castle	162	1940–46	*No competition*		1980	J Simmance	150
1903	CK Hutchison	158	1947	PB Lucas	147	1981	MF Bonallack	151
1904	J Craham Jr	154	1948	M Gonzalez	144	1982	SJ Wood	145
1905	R Harris	154	1949	PF Scrutton	143	1983	R Willison	155
1906	S Mure Fergusson	155	1950	E Bromley-Davenport	148	1984	SJ Wood	142
1907	CE Dick	161	1951	PF Strutton	142	1985	SJ Wood	144
1908	AC Lincoln	157	1952	GH Micklem	148	1986	RC Claydon	143
1909	SH Fry	153	1953	Maj DA Blair	148	1987	MR Coodwin	147
1910	Capt CK Hutchison	157	1954	H Berwick (Aus)	141	1988	T Ryan	143
1911	E Martin Smith	148	1955	PF Scrutton	150	1989	S Green	149
1912	Hon Michel Scott	146	1956	DAC Marr	148	1990	P Sullivan	144
1913	HD Gillies	153	1957	PF Scrutton	148	1991	D Fisher	141
1914	J Grahm Jr	146	1958	PF Scrutton	144	1992	L Westwood	146
1915–19	*No competition*		1959	J Nicklaus (US)	149	1993	P Sefton	137
1920	R Harris	162	1960	JG Blackwell	152	1994	M Welch	142
1921	WB Torrance	154	1961	Sq Ldr WE McCrea	143	1995	J Harris	142
1922	WI Hunter	156	1962	Sq Ldr WE McCrea	145	1996	M Brooks	137
1923	F Ouimet (US)	153	1963	Sq Ldr WE McCrea	150	1997	*Abandoned due to rain*	
1924	RH Wethered	149	1964	Maj DA Blair	153			
1925	D Grant	149	1965	MF Bonallack	144			

1998
1	C Gold	74-71—145
2	G Woodman	72-74—146
3	D Holmes	75-73—148
	D Jeal	72-76—148

Selborne Salver (Inauguarated 1976) *at Blackmoor*

Year	Winner	Year	Winner	Year	Winner
1976	A Miller	1984	D Curry	1992	M Treleaven
1977	CS Mitchell	1985	SM Bottomley	1993	M Welch
1978	GM Brand	1986	TE Clarke	1994	W Bennett
1979	P McEvoy	1987	A Clapp	1995	S Drummond
1980	P McEvoy	1988	NE Holman	1996	J Knight
1981	A Sherborne	1989	M Stamford	1997	R Binney
1982	IA Cray	1990	J Metcalfe		
1983	DG Lane	1991	J Payne		

1998
1	M Side	70-66—136
2	A Wainwright	72-67—139
3	S Dyson	71-69—140

Sunningdale Foursomes (Inaugurated 1934) *at Sunningdale*

Year	Winners	Year	Winners
1934	Miss D Fishwick and EN Layton	1970	R Barrell and Miss A Willard
1935	Miss J Wethered and JSF Morrison	1971	A Bird and H Flatman
1936	Miss J Wethered and JSF Morrison	1972	JC Davies and MG King
1937	AS Anderson and Dai Rees	1973	J Putt and Miss M Everard
1938	Miss P Barton and Alf Padgham	1974	PJ Butler and CA Clark
1939	C Rissik and EWH Kenyon	1975	*Cancelled due to snow*
1940-47	*Not played due to Second World War*	1976	CA Clark and M Hughesdon
1948	Miss Wanda Morgan and Sam King	1977	GN Hunt and D Matthew
1949	RG French and SS Field	1978	GA Caygill and Miss J Greenhalgh
1950	M Faulkner and J Knipe	1979	G Will and R Chapman
1951	Miss J Donald and TB Haliburton	1980	NC Coles and D McClelland
1952	PF Scrutton and Alan Waters	1981	A Lyddon and G Brand Jr
1953	Miss J Donald and TB Haliburton	1982	Miss MA McKenna and Miss M Madill
1954	PF Scrutton and Alan Waters	1983	J Davies and M Devetta
1955	W Sharp and SS Scott	1984	Miss M McKenna and Miss M Madill
1956	G Knipe and DC Smalldon	1985	J O'Leary and S Torrance
1957	BGC Huggett and R Whitehead	1986	R Rafferty and R Chapman
1958	Miss J Donald and Peter Alliss	1987	I Mosey and W Humphreys
1959	MF Bonallack and D Sewell	1988	SC Mason and A Chandler
1960	Miss B McCorkindale and MJ Moir	1989	AD Hare and R Claydon
1961	Mrs J Anderson and Peter Alliss	1990	Miss D Reid and Miss C Dibnah
1962	ER Whitehead and NC Coles	1991	J Robinson and W Henry
1963	L Platts and D Snell	1992	R Boxall and D Cooper
1964	B Critchley and R Hunter	1993	A Beal and L James
1965	Mrs AD Spearman and T Fisher	1994	S Webster and A Wall
1966	RRW Davenport and A Walker	1995	D Cooper and R Boxall
1967	NC Coles and K Warren	1996	L Donald and M O'Connor
1968	JC Davies and W Humphreys	1997	Mrs J Hall and Miss H Wadsworth
1969	P Oosterhuis and PJ Benka		

1998

Quarter Finals
R Chapman and K Will beat G Emerson and N Tokely 3 and 2
R Hodgkinson and P Carr beat S Barwick and G Woodman 5 and 4
D Fisher and W Bennett beat O Lindsay and B Pile 2 and 1
R Hurd and L Jones beat R Misra and M Aubrey-Fletcher 1 hole

Semi-Finals
R Hodgkinson and P Carr beat R Chapman and K Will 3 and 2
D Fisher and W Bennett beat R Hurd and L Jones 3 and 2

Final
D Fisher and W Bennett beat R Hodgkinson and P Carr 4 and 3

Tennant Cup (Inaugurated 1880)

This trophy was presented by Sir Charles Tennant to the Glasgow Club in 1880 and is the oldest open amateur stroke play competition in the world. It has been a 72-hole competition since 1986.

Year	Winner	Year	Winner	Year	Winner
1880	AW Smith	1894	W Doleman	1908	R Carson
1881	AW Smith	1895	JA Shaw	1909	WS Colville
1882	AM Ross	1896	J Thomson	1910	R Andrew
1883	J Kirk	1897	D Bone	1911	WS Colville
1884	W Doleman	1898	R Bone	1912	R Scott Jr
1885	TR Lamb	1899	W Hunter	1913	SO Shepherd
1886	D Bone	1900	JG Macfarlane	1914	John Caven
1887	JR Motion	1901	R Bone	1915–19	*No competition*
1888	D Bone	1902	CB Macfarlane	1920	G Lockhart
1889	W Milne	1903	CB Macfarlane	1921	R Scott Jr
1890	W Marshll	1904	WS Colville	1922	WD Macleod
1891	D Bone	1905	TW Robb	1923	FW Baldie
1892	D Bone	1906	JG Macfarlane	1924	J Barrie Cooper
1893	W Doleman	1907	R Andrew	1925	R Scott Jr

Year	Winner	Year	Winner	Year	Winner
1926	W Tulloch	1954	H McInally	1977	S Martin
1927	W Tulloch	1955	LG Taylor	1978	IA Carslaw
1928	A Jamieson Jr	1956	JM Dykes	1979	G Hay
1929	R Scott Jr	1957	LG Taylor	1980	Allan Brodie
1930	JE Dawson	1958	Dr FWG Deighton	1981	G MacDonald
1931	GNS Tweedale	1959	JF Milligan	1982	LS Mann
1932	SL McInlay	1960	Dr FWG Deighton	1983	C Dalgleish
1933	H Thomson	1961	R Reid Jack	1984	E Wilson
1934	K Lindsay Jr	1962	WS Jack	1985	CJ Brooks
1935	JM Dykes Jr	1963	SWT Murray	1986	PG Girvan
1936	JNW Dall	1964	Dr FWG Deighton	1987	J Rasmussen
1937	WS McCleod	1965	J Scott Cochran	1988	C Dalgleish
1938	A Jamieson Jr	1966	AH Hall	1989	DG Carrick
1939	GB Peters	1967	BJ Gallacher	1990	C Everett
1940–45	*No competition*	1968	CW Green	1991	C Everett
1946	JB Stevenson	1969	J Scott Cochran	1992	D Robertson
1947	JC Wilson	1970	CW Green	1993	D Robertson
1948	J Wallace	1971	Andrew Brodie	1994	G Rankin
1949	W Irvine	1972	Allan Brodie	1995	S Gallacher
1950	JW Mill	1973	PJ Smith	1996	G Rankin
1951	WS McCleod	1974	D McCart	1997	C Hislop
1952	GT Black	1975	CW Green		
1953	AD Gray	1976	IC Hutcheon		

1998

1	G Rankin	70-66-64-68—268
2	P McKechnie	63-69-74-66—272
3	L Rhind	70-71-64-69—274

Tillman Trophy

Year	Winner	Year	Winner
1988	E Els	1993	C Nowicki
1989	J Cook	1994	*Not played*
1990	M Wiggett	1995	P Stuart
1991	A Tillman	1996	S Wakefield
1992	D Probert	1997	M Searle

1998 *at Prince's*

1	R Blaxhill	70-71-77-71—289
2	J Little	74-71-71-74—290
	R McEvoy	77-74-69-70—290

Trubshaw Cup (Inaugurated 1989) *at Ashburnham & Tenby, Dyfed*

Year	Winner	Year	Winner
1989	MA Macara	1994	C Evans
1990	TSM Wilkinson	1995	B Dredge
1991	S Pardoe	1996	M Ellis
1992	B Dredge	1997	M Pilkington
1993	B Dredge		

1998

1	M Pilkington	64-72-74-74—284
2	O Pughe	71-75-75-76—297
3	N Edwards	78-73-74-76—301

Worplesdon Mixed Foursomes (Inaugurated 1921) at Worplesdon, Surrey

Year	Winner	Year	Winner
1921	Miss Helme and TA Torrance	1963	Mrs G Valentine and JE Behrend
1922	Miss Joyce Wethered and R Wethered	1964	Mrs G Valentine and JE Behrend
1923	Miss Joyce Wethered and CJ Tolley	1965	Mrs G Valentine and JE Behrend
1924	Miss SR Fowler and EN Layton	1966	Mrs C Barclay and DJ Miller
1925	Miss Cecil Leitch and E Esmond	1967	JF Gancedo and Mlle C Lacoste
1926	Mlle de la Chaume and R Wethered	1968	JD van Heel and Miss Dinah Oxley
1927	Miss Joyce Wethered and CJH Tolley	1969	Mrs R Ferguson and Alistair Wilson
1928	Miss Joyce Wethered and JSF Morrison	1970	Miss R Roberts and RL Glading
1929	Miss M Gourlay and Maj CO Hezlet	1971	Mrs D Frearson and A Smith
1930	Miss M Gourlay and Maj CO Hezlet	1972	Miss B Le Garreres and CA Strang
1931	Miss J Wethered and Hon M Scott	1973	Miss T Perkins and RJ Evans
1932	Miss J Wethered and RH Oppenheimer	1974	Mrs S Birley and RL Glading
1933	Miss J Wethered and B Darwin beat	1975	Mr and Mrs JR Thornhill
1934	Miss M Gourlay and TA Torrance	1976	Mrs B Lewis and J Caplan
1935,	Miss G and J Craddock-Hartopp	1977	Mrs D Henson and J Caplan
1936	Miss J Wethered and Hon T Coke	1978	Miss T Perkins and R Thomas
1937	Mrs Heppel and LG Crawley	1979	Miss J Melville and A Melville
1938	Mrs MR Garon and EF Storey	1980	Mrs L Bayman and I Boyd
1939–45	*Not played due to First World War*	1981	Mrs J Nicholsen and MN Stern
1946	Miss J Gordon and AA Duncan	1982	Miss B New and K Dobson
1947	Miss J Gordon and AA Duncan	1983	Miss B New and K Dobson
1948	Miss W Morgan and EF Storey	1984	Mrs L Bayman and MC Hughesdon
1949	Miss F Stephens and LG Crawley	1985	Mrs H Kaye and D Longmuir
1950	Miss F Stephens and LG Crawley	1986	Miss P Johnson and RN Roderick
1951	Mrs AC Barclay and G Evans	1987	Miss J Nicholson and B White
1952	Mrs RT Peel and GW Mackie	1988	Mme A Larrezac and JJ Caplan
1953	Miss J Gordon and G Knipe	1989	Miss J Kershaw and M Kershaw
1954	Miss F Stephens and WA Slark	1990	Miss S Keogh and A Rodgers
1955	Miss P Garvey and PF Scrutton	1991	J Rhodes and C Banks
1956	Mrs L Abrahams and Maj WD Henderson	1992	D Henson and B Turner
1957	Mrs B Singleton and WD Smith	1993	A Macdonald and S Skeldon
1958	Mr and Mrs M Bonallack	1994	Mr and Mrs K Quinn
1959	Miss J Robertson and I Wright	1995	Mrs C Caldwell and P Carr
1960	Miss B Jackson and MJ Burgess	1996	Miss L Walters and M Naylor
1961	Mrs R Smith and B Critchley	1997	Miss K Burton and G Wolstenholme
1962	Viscomtesse de Saint Sauveur and DW Frame		

1998
Miss K Burton and J Smith beat C Bushell and C Rotheroe 5 and 4

Regional Amateur Championships

Anglesey Amateur

Year	Winner	Year	Winner
1989	M Robinson	1994	J Campbell
1990	D McLean	1995	D McLean
1991	J Campbell	1996	A Williams
1992	D McLean	1997	M Perdue
1993	M Perdue	1998	EO Jones

Angus Amateur

Year	Winner	Year	Winner
1989	IC Hutcheon	1994	E Wilson
1990	JA Watt	1995	J Rae
1991	W Taylor	1996	G Bell
1992	D Downie	1997	P Cunningham
1993	G Tough	1998	E Ramsay

Argyll and Bute Amateur

Year	Winner	Year	Winner
1989	G Tyre	1994	G Bolton
1990	G Reynolds	1995	G Tyre
1991	G Bolton	1996	L Kelly
1992	G Bolton	1997	S Campbell
1993	G Tyre-Cole	1998	J Sharp

Ayrshire Amateur

Year	Winner	Year	Winner
1989	D Hawthorn	1994	G Lawrie
1990	R Crawford	1995	A Gourlay
1991	JA Thomson	1996	G Lawrie
1992	G Lawrie	1997	G Fox
1993	G Sherry	1998	I Robertson

Bedfordshire Amateur

Year	Winner	Year	Winner
1989	C Staroscik	1994	J Kemp
1990	D Charlton	1995	I Tottingham
1991	M Wharton	1996	M Wharton
1992	L Watcham	1997	K Kemp
1993	C Beard	1998	M Wharton

Berks, Bucks and Oxfordshire Amateur

Year	Winner	Year	Winner
1989	H Bareham	1994	D Fisher
1990	S Barwick	1995	D Lane
1991	VL Phillips	1996	J Carlsen
1992	VL Phillips	1997	L Donald
1993	R Walton	1998	L Donald

Border Golfers' Association Amateur

Year	Winner	Year	Winner
1989	A Turnbull	1994	M Thomson
1990	M Thomson	1995	M Thomson
1991	A Turnbull	1996	D Ballantyne
1992	M Thomson	1997	W Simpson
1993	D Valentine	1998	D Ballantyne

Caernarfonshire and District Amateur

Year	Winner	Year	Winner
1989	W Jones	1994	D McLean
1990	D McLean	1995	S Pritchard
1991	J Dabecki	1996	A Williams
1992	D McLean	1997	Not played
1993	E Jones	1998	A Clishem

Caernarfonshire Amateur Cup

Year	Winner	Year	Winner
1989	M Sheppard	1994	J Dabecki
1990	I Jones	1995	J Dabecki
1991	R Williams	1996	M Pilkington
1992	MA Macara	1997	Not played
1993	L Harpin	1998	M Pilkington

Cambridgeshire Amateur

Year	Winner	Year	Winner
1989	B Jackson	1994	A Emery
1990	G Stevenson	1995	S Jarvis
1991	M Seaton	1996	P Rains
1992	LG Yearn	1997	O Cousins
1993	LG Yearn	1998	L Yearn

Central England Open Men's Foursomes

Year	Winners
1991	S Cox and P Birkin
1992	Not played
1993	S Macpherson and N Meadows
1994	C Banks and J Hemphrey
1995	L Walker and P Huddlestone
1996	L Toyne and S Caswell
1997	G Shaw and C Radford
1998	L Walker and P Huddlestone

Channel Islands Amateur

Year	Winner	Year	Winner
1989	TA Gray	1994	C Chevalier
1990	TA Gray	1995	C Chevalier
1991	R Eggo	1996	R Eggo
1992	C Chevalier	1997	R Williamson
1993	B Eggo	1998	DA Rowlinson

Cheshire Amateur

Year	Winner	Year	Winner
1989	P Bailey	1994	J Hodgson
1990	J Berry	1995	C Smethurst
1991	D Bathgate	1996	D Vaughan
1992	A Hill	1997	N Pabari
1993	J Hodgson	1998	J Donaldson

Clackmannanshire Amateur

Year	Winner	Year	Winner
1989	J Gullen	1994	P McLeod
1990	P MacLeod	1995	I Ross
1991	AJ Watson	1996	R Stewart
1992	G Kennedy	1997	G Bowie
1993	S Horne	1998	B Stewart

Cornwall Amateur

Year	Winner	Year	Winner
1989	C Phillips	1994	R Binney
1990	M Edmunds	1995	M Lock
1991	I Veale	1996	I Veale
1992	P Clayton	1997	P Darlington
1993	C Phillips	1998	I Atkinson

Cumbria Amateur (Formerly Cumberland and Westmorland Amateur)

Year	Winner	Year	Winner
1989	G Winter	1994	B Story
1990	G Winter	1995	N Mitchell
1991	G Winter	1996	R Secular
1992	A Greenbank	1997	G Watson
1993	R Secular	1998	P Jack

Derbyshire Amateur

Year	Winner	Year	Winner
1989	P Eastwood	1994	J Feeney
1990	R Fletcher	1995	G Shaw
1991	J Feeney	1996	J Feeney
1992	J Feeney	1997	AS Humpston
1993	G Shaw	1998	L Walley

Devon Amateur

Year	Winner	Year	Winner
1989	R Barrow	1994	M Crossfield
1990	G Milne	1995	A Capping
1991	A Richards	1996	D Eva
1992	D Lewis	1997	G Ruth
1993	R Goodey	1998	S Pike

Dorset Amateur

Year	Winner	Year	Winner
1989	A Lawrence	1994	M Davies
1990	P McMullen	1995	M Davies
1991	A Lawrence	1996	A Lawrence
1992	L James	1997	J Baldwin
1993	A Lawrence	1998	J Pounder

Dunbartonshire Amateur

Year	Winner	Year	Winner
1989	D Shaw	1994	D Carrick
1990	J Kinloch	1995	T McKeown
1991	T McKeown	1996	K MacNair
1992	D Shaw	1997	S Carmichael
1993	F Jardine	1998	S Carmichael

Dunbartonshire Amateur Matchplay

Year	Winner	Year	Winner
1989	C Stewart	1994	F Hutchison
1990	D Shaw	1995	F Jardine
1991	F Jardine	1996	A Leitch
1992	R Blair	1997	S McLeitch
1993	F Jardine	1998	G Murphy

Durham Amateur

Year	Winner	Year	Winner
1989	G Bell	1994	J Kennedy
1990	R Walker	1995	A McLure
1991	C Kilgour	1996	S Ord
1992	A McLure	1997	J Dryden
1993	R Walker	1998	C Hamilton

East of Ireland Open Amateur

Year	Winner	Year	Winner
1989	D Clarke	1994	G McGimpsey
1990	D O'Sullivan	1995	D Brannigan
1991	P Hogan	1996	N Fox
1992	R Burns	1997	S Quinlivan
1993	R Burns	1998	G McGimpsey

East of Scotland Open Amateur Strokeplay

Year	Winner	Year	Winner
1989	K Hird	1994	A Reid
1990	G Lawrie	1995	G Davidson
1991	R Clark	1996	C Hislop
1992	ST Knowles	1997	S Meiklejohn
1993	S Meiklejohn	1998	B Lamb

Essex Amateur

Year	Winner	Year	Winner
1989	V Cox	1994	R Coles
1990	Null and void	1995	D Salisbury
1991	D Lee	1996	G Clark
1992	D Lee	1997	B Taylor
1993	R Coles	1998	B Taylor

Fife Amateur

Year	Winner	Year	Winner
1989	D Spriddle	1994	C MacDougall
1990	D Spriddle	1995	D Paton
1991	GD McNab	1996	B Erskine
1992	N Urquhart	1997	S Meiklejohn
1993	DA Paton	1998	J Bunch

Glamorgan Amateur

Year	Winner	Year	Winner
1989	B Knight	1994	N Edwards
1990	P Bloomfield	1995	S Roberts
1991	R Maliphant	1996	N Edwards
1992	CM Rees	1997	Y Taylor
1993	M Stimson	1998	C Williams

Gloucestershire Amateur

Year	Winner	Year	Winner
1989	R Broad	1994	G Wolstenholme
1990	D Hares	1995	T Smith
1991	J Webber	1996	G Wolstenholme
1992	G Wolstenholme	1997	M Unwin
1993	G Wolstenholme	1998	TP Smith

Gwent Amateur (Formerly Monmouthshire Amateur)

Year	Winner	Year	Winner
1989	P Glyn	1994	B Dredge
1990	M Hayward	1995	C Dinsdale
1991	E Foster	1996	M Hayward
1992	CN Evans	1997	R Price
1993	A Harray	1998	N Povall

Hampshire, Isle of Wight and Channel Islands Amateur

Year	Winner	Year	Winner
1989	M Smith	1994	R Bland
1990	M Wiggett	1995	M Le Mesurier
1991	AD Mew	1996	M Blackey
1992	C Chevalier	1997	S Stanley
1993	M Blackey	1998	C Hudson

Herts Amateur

Year	Winner	Year	Winner
1989	S Hankin	1994	G Maly
1990	N Leconte	1995	H Steel
1991	M Peake	1996	S Little
1992	S Burnell	1997	C Duke
1993	S Burnell	1998	R Conway-Lye

Isle of Man Amateur

Year	Winner	Year	Winner
1989	G Ashe	1994	R Sayle
1990	M Pugh	1995	G Wilson
1991	GK Gelling	1996	G Wilson
1992	G Wilson	1997	P McMullan
1993	G Wilson	1998	P McMullan

Kent Amateur

Year	Winner	Year	Winner
1989	S Green	1994	B Barham
1990	R Sloman	1995	T Milford
1991	P Oliver	1996	B Barham
1992	P Sherman	1997	D Ottoway
1993	G Brown	1998	D Ottoway

Lanarkshire Amateur

Year	Winner	Year	Winner
1989	J Taylor	1994	W Bryson
1990	G Shanks	1995	K Nisbet
1991	D Blair	1996	K Ralston
1992	W Bryson	1997	W Bryson
1993	D Brown	1998	R Hishelwood

Lancashire Amateur

Year	Winner	Year	Winner
1989	R Bardsley	1994	K Wallbank
1990	T Foster	1995	G Boardman
1991	GS Lacy	1996	G Boardman
1992	R Hutt	1997	D Johnson
1993	G Helsby	1998	P Wiliams

Leicestershire and Rutland Amateur

Year	Winner	Year	Winner
1989	J Cayless	1994	I Lyner
1990	D Gibson	1995	P Frith
1991	D Gibson	1996	J Herbert
1992	D Gibson	1997	J Herbert
1993	P Frith	1998	G Wolstenholme

Lincolnshire Amateur

Year	Winner	Year	Winner
1989	J Payne	1994	J Crampton
1990	P Streeter	1995	J Crampton
1991	J Payne	1996	P Streeter
1992	P Streeter	1997	P Streeter
1993	J Crampton	1998	A White

Lothians Amateur

Year	Winner	Year	Winner
1989	K Hastings	1994	S Smith
1990	S Middleton	1995	S Smith
1991	C MacPhail	1996	N Shillinglaw
1992	C MacPhail	1997	K Nicholson
1993	S Smith	1998	K Nicholson

Middlesex Amateur

Year	Winner	Year	Winner
1989	R Willison	1994	W Bennett
1990	A Rogers	1995	G Clark
1991	J O'Shea	1996	S Kay
1992	WJ Bennett	1997	C Austin
1993	GA Homewood	1998	R Varney

Midland Open Amateur

Year	Winner	Year	Winner
1989	J Cook	1994	D Howell
1990	J Bickerton	1995	G Harris
1991	P Sefton	1996	M Carver
1992	M McGuire	1997	P Streeter
1993	N Williamson	1998	L Donald

Norfolk Amateur

Year	Winner	Year	Winner
1989	N Williamson	1994	J Durrant
1990	P Little	1995	I Ellis
1991	CJ Lamb	1996	P Little
1992	A Marshall	1997	G Price
1993	DA Edwards	1998	CJ Lamb

Northamptonshire Amateur

Year	Winner	Year	Winner
1989	N Goodman	1994	A Print
1990	A Print	1995	A Lord
1991	S McDonald	1996	I Dallas
1992	AJ Wilson	1997	P Langrish-Smith
1993	S McIlwain	1998	G Keates

North of Ireland Open Amateur

Year	Winner	Year	Winner
1989	N Anderson	1994	N Ludwell
1990	D Clarke	1995	F Nolan
1991	G McGimpsey	1996	M McGinley
1992	G McGimpsey	1997	M Sinclair
1993	G McGimpsey	1998	IP Gribben

North of Scotland Open Amateur Strokeplay

Year	Winner	Year	Winner
1989	G Hickman	1994	E Forbes
1990	S McIntosh	1995	R Beames
1991	S Henderson	1996	C Dunan
1992	K Buchan	1997	G Crawford
1993	D Downie	1998	C Taylor

Northumberland Amateur

Year	Winner	Year	Winner
1989	J Metcalfe	1994	S Twynholm
1990	K Fairbairn	1995	M Hall
1991	K Fairbairn	1996	K Cademy-Taylor
1992	S Philipson	1997	D Clark
1993	P Taylor	1998	J McCallum

Nottinghamshire Amateur

Year	Winner	Year	Winner
1989	P Shaw	1994	D Lucas
1990	L White	1995	H Hopkinson
1991	L White	1996	D McJannet
1992	L Westwood	1997	O Wilson
1993	L Westwood	1998	AJ Liddle

South of Scotland Amateur

Year	Winner	Year	Winner
1989	V Reid	1994	I Reid
1990	B Kerr	1995	B Scott
1991	J Power	1996	E Little
1992	J Wright	1997	I Brotherston
1993	D Wallis	1998	D Sutton

Perth and Kinross Amateur Strokeplay

Year	Winner	Year	Winner
1989	A Campbell	1994	E Lindsay
1990	G Smith	1995	S Herd
1991	D Robertson	1996	M Rose
1992	B Grieve	1997	N Macdonald
1993	T McLevy	1998	K Grant

South-Western Counties Amateur

Year	Winner	Year	Winner
1989	K Jones	1994	A Lawrence
1990	S Amor	1995	S McCarthy
1991	P McMullen	1996	D Marsh
1992	S Edgley	1997	S McCarthy
1993	B Sandry	1998	S McCarthy

Renfrewshire Amateur

Year	Winner	Year	Winner
1989	R Clark	1994	M Carmichael
1990	R Clark	1995	R Adam
1991	R Clark	1996	S Nicol
1992	G Urquhart	1997	D Owens
1993	R Clark	1998	A McKay

Staffordshire Amateur

Year	Winner	Year	Winner
1989	C Poxon	1994	R Mayfield
1990	P Sweetsur	1995	T Ryder
1991	M McGuire	1996	R Parkes
1992	M McGuire	1997	SD Wakefield
1993	C Poxon	1998	KD Hale

Shropshire and Herefordshire Amateur

Year	Winner	Year	Winner
1989	M Welch	1994	M Welch
1990	M Welch	1995	D Park
1991	M Welch	1996	D Harris
1992	M Welch	1997	K Preece
1993	M Welch	1998	O Pughe

Stirlingshire Amateur Strokeplay

Year	Winner	Year	Winner
1989	S Russell	1994	K McArthur
1990	K Goodwin	1995	K Brunton
1991	K Goodwin	1996	G McDonald
1992	H Anderson	1997	A Ellison
1993	D Smith	1998	JR Johnson

Somerset Amateur

Year	Winner	Year	Winner
1989	C Edwards	1994	C Edwards
1990	C Edwards	1995	B Whittock
1991	C Edwards	1996	D Dixon
1992	C Edwards	1997	R Swords
1993	C Edwards	1998	J Morgan

Suffolk Amateur

Year	Winner	Year	Winner
1989	M Turner	1994	J Maddock
1990	J Booth	1995	D Quinney
1991	N Meadows	1996	J Keely
1992	P Buckle	1997	J Maddock
1993	J Maddock	1998	J Wright

South of Ireland Open Amateur

Year	Winner	Year	Winner
1989	S Keenan	1994	D Higgins
1990	D Clarke	1995	J Fanagan
1991	P McGinley	1996	A Morrow
1992	L MacNamara	1997	P Collier
1993	P Sheehan	1998	J Foster

Surrey Amateur

Year	Winner	Year	Winner
1989	T Lloyd	1994	M Ellis
1990	J Good	1995	A Wall
1991	A Tillman	1996	M Palmer
1992	A Wall	1997	T Paterson
1993	A Raitt	1998	C Rodgers

Sussex Amateur

Year	Winner	Year	Winner
1989	P Hurring	1994	P Clevely
1990	D Arnold	1995	M Allen
1991	R Lowles	1996	M Harris
1992	M Galway	1997	M Harris
1993	M Galway	1998	M Harris

Warwickshire Amateur

Year	Winner	Year	Winner
1989	J Cook	1994	N Connolly
1990	J Cook	1995	S Webster
1991	A Allen	1996	A Carey
1992	G Lord	1997	T Whitehouse
1993	G Marston	1998	T Whitehouse

West of England Open Amateur Championship

(Inaugurated 1912) *at Burnham & Berrow*

Year	Winner	Year	Winner
1912	RA Riddell	1961	JM Leach
1913	Hon M Scott	1962	Sq Ldr WE McCrea
1914–18	*No competition*		
1919	Hon M Scott	1963	KT Warren
1920	Hon D Scott	1964	DC Allen
1921	CVL Hooman	1965	DE Jones
1922	Hon M Scott	1966	A Forrester
1923	D Grant	1967	A Forrester
1924	D Grant	1968	SR Warrin
1925	D Grant	1969	SR Warrin
1926	K Whetstone	1970	C Ball
1927	GC Brooks	1971	G Irlam
1928	JA Pierson	1972	JA Bloxham
1929	DE Landale	1973	SC Mason
1930	RH de Montmorency	1974	CS Mitchell
		1975	MR Lovett
1931	DR Howard	1976	*No competition*
1932	R Straker	1977	AR Dunlop
1933	DM Anderson	1978	R Broad
1934	Hon M Scott	1979	N Burch
1935	JJF Pennink	1980	JM Durbin
1936	PH White	1981	M Mouland
1937	O Austreng	1982	M Higgins
1938	HJ Roberts	1983	C Peacock
1939–45	*No competition*	1984	GB Hickman
1946	JH Neal	1985	AC Nash
1947	WF Wise	1986	J Bennett
1948	WF Wise	1987	D Rosier
1949	J Payne	1988	N Holman
1950	EB Millward	1989	N Holman
1951	J Payne	1990	I West
1952	EB Millward	1991	S Amor
1953	F Griffin	1992	K Baker
1954	EB Millward	1993	D Haines
1955	SJ Fox	1994	A Emery
1956	SJ Fox	1995	A March
1957	D Gardner	1996	M Carver
1958	AJN Young	1997	SJ Martin
1959	DM Woolmer	1998	D Dixon
1960	AW Holmes		

West of England Open Amateur Strokeplay Championship (Inaugurated 1968)

Year	Winner	Year	Winner
1968	PJ Yeo	1984	A Sherborne
1969	A Forrester	1985	P McEvoy
1970	PJ Yeo	1986	P Baker
1971	P Berry	1987	G Wolstenholme
1972	P Berry	1988	M Evans
1973	SC Mason	1989	AD Hare
1974	R Abbott	1990	J Payne
1975	BG Steer	1991	S Amor
1976	R Abbott	1992	M Stanford
1977	P McEvoy	1993	P Trew
1978	JG Bennett	1994	C Nowicki
1979	R Kane	1995	C Clark
1980	P McEvoy	1996	R Wiggins
1981	N Taee	1997	M Reynard
1982	MP Higgins	1998	C Edwards
1983	P McEvoy		

West of Ireland Open Amateur

Year	Winner	Year	Winner
1989	P McInerney	1994	P Harrington
1990	N Goulding	1995	E Brady
1991	N Goulding	1996	G McGimpsey
1992	K Kearney	1997	J Fanagan
1993	G McGimpsey	1998	N Fox

West of Scotland Close Amateur

Year	Winner	Year	Winner
1989	G Lawrie	1994	A Forsyth
1990	B Smith	1995	D Howard
1991	W Bryson	1996	A Forsyth
1992	D Robertson	1997	*Not played*
1993	R Weir	1998	*Not played*

West of Scotland Open Amateur

Year	Winner	Year	Winner
1989	A Elliot	1994	J Hodgson
1990	S Knowles	1995	G Rankin
1991	A Coltart	1996	C Hislop
1992	S Henderson	1997	C Hislop
1993	B Howard	1998	L Kelly

Wigtownshire Amateur

Year	Winner	Year	Winner
1989	D Taylor	1994	K Hardie
1990	R Burns	1995	R O'Keefe
1991	G Sharp	1996	E Little
1992	R O'Keefe	1997	R Shaw
1993	K Hardie	1998	R Shaw

Wiltshire Amateur

Year	Winner	Year	Winner
1989	A Burch	1994	R Searle
1990	N Williams	1995	N Mumford
1991	R White	1996	A Mutch
1992	D Howell	1997	P Bicknell
1993	RE Searle	1998	P Bicknell

Worcestershire Amateur

Year	Winner	Year	Winner
1989	S Braithwaite	1994	R Sadler
1990	D Eddiford	1995	M Reynard
1991	J Bickerton	1996	M Reynard
1992	M Reynard	1997	S Braithwaite
1993	M Reynard	1998	D Glover

Yorkshire Amateur

Year	Winner	Year	Winner
1989	G Harland	1994	P Wood
1990	P Wood	1995	J Ellis
1991	ML Pullan	1996	R Jones
1992	ID Pyman	1997	R Jones
1993	J Healey	1998	S Tarplett

Yorkshire Amateur Strokeplay

Year	Winner	Year	Winner
1989	S East	1995T	N Gibson
1990	L Walker		J Hepworth
1991	D Delaney	1996	N Emmerson
1992	J Docker	1997	A Wright
1993	J Roberts	1998T	M Bugg
1994	N Ludwell		R Hodgkinson

Overseas Amateur Championships

Argentine Amateur

Year	Winner
1996	C Alvarez Jr
1997	J Pablo Abbatge
1998	J Nicolosi
1997	K Felton
1998	B Rumford

Australian Amateur

Year	Winner	Year	Winner
1989	S Conran	1994	W Bennett
1990	C Gray	1995	M Coggin
1991	L Parsons	1996	D Gleeson
1992	M Campbell	1997	K Felton
1993	GJ Chalmers	1998	B Rumford

Austrian Amateur Open

Year	Winner	Year	Winner
1989	U Zilg	1994	J-J Wolff
1990	A Peterskovsky	1995	J Gruere
1991	D Vanbegin	1996	T Biermann
1992	H-C Winkler	1997	C Bausek
1993	N Zitny	1998	M Tannhäuser

Canadian Amateur

Year	Winner	Year	Winner
1989	P Major	1994	W Sye
1990	W Sye	1995	G Willis
1991	J Kraemer	1996	R McMillan
1992	D Ritchie	1997	D Goehring
1993	G Simpson	1998	C Matthew

Czechoslovak Open Amateur

Year	Winner	Year	Winner
1989	A Krag	1994	F Mansson
1990	J Janda	1995	R Chudoba
1991	J Kunšta	1996	M Ettl
1992	R Chudoba	1997	U Paulsen (Aust)
1993	R Pientka	1998	CC Prader (Aust)

Danish Amateur Strokeplay

Year	Winner	Year	Winner
1989	R Budde	1994	AR Hansen
1990	T Bjørn	1995	N Roerbaek-Peterson
1991	T Svendsen	1996	C Moelholm
1992	AR Hansen	1997	S Hansen
1993	N Roerbaek-Peterson	1998	M Jorgensen

French Amateur

Year	Winner	Year	Winner
1989	C Cevaer	1994	L Pargade
1990	O Edmond	1995	R Eyraud
1991	F Cupillard	1996	S Fabrice
1992	N Joakimides	1997	G Havret
1993	M Dieu	1998	G Havret

German Open Amateur

Year	Winner	Year	Winner
1989	J Steenkamer	1995	M Brier
1991	JE Schapmann	1996	G Ogilvy
1992	M Zerman	1997	H Forster
1993	JE Schapmann	1998	T Dier
1994	JE Schapmann		

German Close Amateur

Year	Winner	Year	Winner
1989	HG Reiter	1994	JE Schapmann
1990	M vom Hagen	1995	B Schlichting
1991	T Himmel	1996	F Lubenau
1992	T Himmel	1997	T Schuster
1993	T Himmel	1998	T Schuster

Italian Open Amateur

Year	Winner	Year	Winner
1989	R Victor	1994	D Dupin
1990	M Tadini	1995	R Paolillo
1991	D Borrego	1996	H Stenson
1992	*Not played*	1997	R Quiros
1993	J Kjaerbye	1998	K Baraka

Italian Close Amateur

Year	Winner	Year	Winner
1989	G Ferrero	1994	N Bisazza
1990	M Aragnetti	1995	A Napoleoni
1991	M Santi	1996	A Napoleoni
1992	F Pustetto	1997	A Napoleoni
1993	F Crotti	1998	A Maestroni

Japan Amateur

Year	Winner	Year	Winner
1989	K Oie	1994	S Sugimoto
1990	Y Kuramoto	1995	S Sugimoto
1991	K Miyamoto	1996	H Hoshino
1992	K Yonekura	1997	H Chia-Yuh
1993	K Yonekura	1998	H Hoshino

New Zealand Amateur

Year	Winner	Year	Winner
1989	L Peterson	1994	P Fitzgibbon
1990	M Long	1995	S Bittle
1991	L Parsons	1996	D Somervaille
1992	R Lee	1997	C Johns
1993	P Tataurangi	1998	B MacDonald

Nordic Amateur

(Team event since 1993; previously Scandinavian Amateur Open)

Year	Winner	Year	Winner
1989	P-U Johansson	1994	*Not played*
1990	P Magnebrandt	1995	Sweden
1991	M Olander	1996	*Not played*
1992	P Sterner	1997	Sweden
1993	Sweden	1998	*Not played*

Portuguese Open Amateur

Year	Winner	Year	Winner
1989	S Bjorn	1994	M Backhausen
1990	R Oliveira	1995	G D'Hollander
1991	*Not played*	1996	M Lehtinen
1992	K Ekjord	1997	
1993	A Townhill	1998	P Kylliainen

Portuguese Close Amateur

Year	Winner	Year	Winner
1989	A Castelo	1994	J Correia
1990	J Granja	1995	M Coelho
1991	J Carvalhosa	1996	S Corte-Real
1992	A Castelo	1997	S Castro Ferreira
1993	J Carvalhosa	1998	S Castro Ferreira

South African Amateur

Year	Winner	Year	Winner
1989	C Rivett	1994	B Vaughn
1990	R Goosen	1995	W Abery
1991	D Botes	1996	T Moore
1992	B Davison	1997	T Immelman
1993	L Chitengwa	1998	J Hugo

South African Amateur Strokeplay

Year	Winner	Year	Winner
1989	E Els	1994	N Homann
1990	P Pascoe	1995	M Murles
1991	N Henning	1996	T Moore
1992	J Nelson	1997	U Van den Berg
1993	D Kinnear	1998	T Immelman

Spanish Open Amateur

Year	Winner	Year	Winner
1989	E Giraud	1994	J Healey
1990	D Clarke	1995	B Muir
1991	TJ Muñoz	1996	JM Lara
1992	M Stanford	1997	M Lafeber
1993	F Stolear	1998	S Garcia

Spanish Close Amateur

Year	Winner	Year	Winner
1989	T Muñoz	1994	F Valera
1990	G de la Riva	1995	F Cisa
1991	D Borrego	1996	R Gonzalez
1992	A Prat	1997	S Garcia
1993	JA Vizcaya	1998	A Mata

Swiss Open Amateur

Year	Winner	Year	Winner
1989	M Frank	1994	M Brier
1990	M Santi	1995	A Langenaeken
1991	J Wade	1996	F Luca
1992	T Gottstein	1997	M Lafeber
1993	N Zitny	1998	G Birch

Swiss Close Amateur

Year	Winner	Year	Winner
1989	M Frank	1994	M Chatelain
1990	T Gottstein	1995	M Velan
1991	M Frank	1996	N Sulzer
1992	J Ciola	1997	M Chatelain
1993	J Ciola	1998	J Lee

United States Amateur Championship

Year	Winner	Runner-up	Venue	By
1946	SE Bishop	S Quick	Baltusrol	37th hole
1947	RH Riegel	J Dawson	Pebble Beach	2 and 1
1948	WP Turnesa	R Billows	Memphis, TN	2 and 1
1949	C Coe	R King	Rochester, NY	11 and 10
1950	S Urzetta	FR Stranahan	Minneapolis	39th hole
1951	WJ Maxwell	J Cagliardi	Saucon Valley, PA	4 and 3
1952	J Westland	A Mengert	Seattle	3 and 2
1953	G Littler	D Morey	Oklahoma City	1 hole
1954	A Palmer	R Sweeney	Detroit, MI	1 hole
1955	E Harvie Ward	W Hyndman	Richmond, VA	9 and 8
1956	E Harvie Ward	C Kocsis	Lake Forest, IL	5 and 4
1957	H Robbins	Dr F Taylor	Brookline	5 and 4
1958	C Coe	T Aaron	San Francisco	5 and 4
1959	J Nicklaus	C Coe	Broadmoor	1 hole
1960	DR Beman	R Gardner	St Louis, MO	6 and 4
1961	J Nicklaus	D Wysong	Pebble Beach	8 and 6
1962	LE Harris, Jr	D Gray	Pinehurst	1 hole
1963	DR Beman	D Sikes	Des Moines	2 and 1
1964	W Campbell	E Tutweiler	Canterbury, OH	1 hole

Changed to strokeplay

Year	Winner	Venue	Score
1965	R Murphy	Tulsa, OK	291
1966	G Cowan	Ardmore, PA	285
1967	R Dickson	Colorado	285
1968	B Fleisher	Columbus	284
1969	S Melnyk	Oakmont	286
1970	L Wadkins	Portland	280
1971	G Cowan	Wilmington	280
1972	M Giles	Charlotte, NC	285

Reverted to matchplay

Year	Winner	Runner-up	Venue	By
1973	C Stadler	D Strawn	Inverness, OH	6 and 5
1974	J Pate	J Grace	Ridgewood, NJ	2 and 1
1975	F Ridley	K Fergus	Richmond, VA	2 holes
1976	B Sander	P Moore	Bel-Air	8 and 6
1977	J Fought	D Fischesser	Aronimonk, Pa	9 and 8
1978	J Cook	S Hoch	Plainfield, NJ	5 and 4
1979	M O'Meara	J Cook	Canterbury, OH	8 and 7
1980	H Sutton	B Lewis	North Carolina	9 and 8
1981	N Crosby	B Lyndley	San Francisco	37th hole
1982	J Sigel	D Tolley	The Country Club, Brookline	8 and 7
1983	J Sigel	C Perry	North Shore, Chicago	8 and 7
1984	S Verplank	S Randolph	Oak Tree, OK	4 and 3
1985	S Randolph	P Persons	Montclair, NJ	1 hole
1986	S Alexander	C Kite	Shoal Creek	5 and 3
1987	W Mayfair	E Rebmann	Jupiter Hills, FL	4 and 3
1988	E Meeks	D Yates	Hot Springs, VA	7 and 6
1989	C Patton	D Green	Merion, PA	3 and 1
1990	P Mickelson	M Zerman	Cherry Hills, CO	5 and 4
1991	M Voges	M Zerman	Honours Course, TN	7 and 6
1992	J Leonard	T Scherrer	Muirfield Village, OH	8 and 7
1993	J Harris	D Ellis	Champions, Houston	5 and 3
1994	T Woods	T Kuehne	Sawgrass	2 holes
1995	T Woods	G Marucci	Newport, Long Island, NY	2 holes
1996	T Woods	S Scott	Pumpkin Ridge, OR	38th hole
1997	M Kuchar	J Kribel	Cog Hill, Lemont, IL	2 and 1

1998 *at Oak Hill, Rochester, New York*

Quarter Finals
T McKnight beat S Knapp 5 and 3
S Garcia beat M Kuchar 2 and 1
B Lunde beat L Mahan 5 and 4
H Kuehne beat B Molder 5 and 4

Semi-Finals
McKnight beat Garcia 3 and 1
Kuehne beat Lunde 6 and 5

Final
H Kuehne beat T McKnight 2 and 1

PART V

Women's Amateur Tournaments

Index on page 292

Index – Women's Amateur Tournaments

Women's National and International Amateur Events	***293***
Ladies' British Amateur Championship	293
Ladies' British Open Amateur Strokeplay Championship	295
Senior Ladies' British Amateur Strokeplay Championship	295
English Ladies' Amateur Championship	295
English Ladies' Strokeplay Championship	296
English Ladies' Under-23 Championship	297
English Ladies' Senior Strokeplay Championship	297
English Senior Ladies' Matchplay Championship	297
English Ladies' Intermediate Championship	298
Irish Ladies' Close Amateur Championship	298
Irish Ladies' Amateur Strokeplay Championship	299
Irish Senior Ladies' Amateur Championship	299
Scottish Ladies' Close Amateur Championship	299
Scottish Ladies' Open Strokeplay Championship (Helen Holm Trophy)	300
Scottish Senior Ladies' Amateur Championship	301
Welsh Ladies' Amateur Championship	301
Welsh Ladies' Open Amateur Strokeplay Championship	302
Welsh Senior Ladies' Championship	302
Ladies' European Open Amateur Championship	302
TEAM EVENTS	303
Great Britain & Ireland v USA for the Curtis Cup	303
Curtis Cup Individual Records	306
Women's World Amateur Team Ch'p (Espirito Santo Trophy)	310
Commonwealth Tournament	311
Women's European Amateur Team Championship	311
Vagliano Trophy – Great Britain & Ireland v Europe	311
Women's Home Internationals	312
England and Wales Ladies' County Championship	313
Scotland Ladies' County Championship	313
Scotland Ladies' Foursomes	313
Welsh Ladies' Team Championship	313
Other Women's Amateur Events	***314***
Astor Salver	314
Bridget Jackson Bowl	314
Hampshire Rose	314
Mothers and Daughters Foursomes	314
St Rule Trophy	314
Women's Regional Amateur Championships	***315***
Women's Amateur Championships Overseas	***321***

National and International Tournaments

Ladies' British Amateur Championship

Year	Winner	Runner-up	Venue	By
1893	Lady Margaret Scott	Miss I Pearson	St Annes	7 and 5
1894	Lady Margaret Scott	Miss I Pearson	Littlestone	3 and 2
1895	Lady Margaret Scott	Miss E Lythgoe	Portrush	5 and 4
1896	Miss Pascoe	Miss L Thomson	Hoylake, R Liverpool	3 and 2
1897	Miss EC Orr	Miss Orr	Gullane	4 and 2
1898	Miss L Thomson	Miss EC Neville	Yarmouth	7 and 5
1899	Miss M Hezlet	Miss Magill	Newcastle Co Down	2 and 1
1900	Miss Adair	Miss Neville	Westward Ho!, R North Devon	6 and 5
1901	Miss Graham	Miss Adair	Aberdovey	3 and 1
1902	Miss M Hezlet	Miss E Neville	Deal	19th hole
1903	Miss Adair	Miss F Walker-Leigh	Portrush	4 and 3
1904	Miss L Dod	Miss M Hezlet	Troon	1 hole
1905	Miss B Thompson	Miss ME Stuart	Cromer	3 and 2
1906	Mrs Kennon	Miss B Thompson	Burnham	4 and 3
1907	Miss M Hezlet	Miss F Hezlet	Newcastle Co Down	2 and 1
1908	Miss M Titterton	Miss D Campbell	St Andrews	19th hole
1909	Miss D Campbell	Miss F Hezlet	Birkdale	4 and 3
1910	Miss Grant Suttie	Miss L Moore	Westward Ho!, R North Devon	6 and 4
1911	Miss D Campbell	Miss V Hezlet	Portrush	3 and 2
1912	Miss G Ravenscroft	Miss S Temple	Turnberry	3 and 2

(Final played over 36 holes after 1912)

Year	Winner	Runner-up	Venue	By
1913	Miss M Dodd	Miss Chubb	St Annes	8 and 6
1914	Miss C Leitch	Miss G Ravenscroft	Hunstanton	2 and 1

1915–18 *No Championship owing to the Great War*
1919 *Should have been played at Burnham in October, but abandoned owing to railway strike*

Year	Winner	Runner-up	Venue	By
1920	Miss C Leitch	Miss M Griffiths	Newcastle Co Down	7 and 6
1921	Miss C Leitch	Miss J Wethered	Turnberry	4 and 3
1922	Miss J Wethered	Miss C Leitch	Prince's, Sandwich, R St George's	9 and 7
1923	Miss D Chambers	Miss A Macbeth	Burnham, Somerset	2 holes
1924	Miss J Wethered	Mrs Cautley	Portrush	7 and 6
1925	Miss J Wethered	Miss C Leitch	Troon	37th hole
1926	Miss C Leitch	Mrs Garon	Harlech	8 and 7
1927	Miss Thion de la Chaume (Fr)	Miss Pearson	Newcastle Co Down	5 and 4
1928	Miss N Le Blan (Fr)	Miss S Marshall	Hunstanton	3 and 2
1929	Miss J Wethered	Miss G Collett (US)	St Andrews	3 and 1
1930	Miss D Fishwick	Miss G Collett (US)	Formby	4 and 3
1931	Miss E Wilson	Miss W Morgan	Portmarnock	7 and 6
1932	Miss E Wilson	Miss CPR Montgomery	Saunton	7 and 6
1933	Miss E Wilson	Miss D Plumpton	Gleneagles	5 and 4
1934	Mrs AM Holm	Miss P Barton	Porthcawl	6 and 5
1935	Miss W Morgan	Miss P Barton	Newcastle Co Down	3 and 2
1936	Miss P Barton	Miss B Newell	Southport and Ainsdale	5 and 3
1937	Miss J Anderson	Miss D Park	Turnberry	6 and 4
1938	Mrs AM Holm	Miss E Corlett	Burnham	4 and 3
1939	Miss P Barton	Mrs T Marks	Portrush	2 and 1

1940–45 *No Championship owing to Second World War*

Year	Winner	Runner-up	Venue	By
1946	GW Hetherington	P Garvey	Hunstanton	1 hole
1947	B Zaharias (US)	J Gordon	Gullane	5 and 4
1948	L Suggs (US)	J Donald	Lytham St Annes	1 hole
1949	F Stephens	V Reddan	Harlech	5 and 4
1950	Vicomtesse de Saint Sauveur (Fr)	J Valentine	Newcastle Co Down	3 and 2

continued

Ladies' British Amateur Championship *continued*

Year	Winner	Runner-up	Venue	By
1951	PJ MacCann	F Stephens	Broadstone	4 and 3
1952	M Paterson	F Stephens	Troon	39th hole
1953	M Stewart (Can)	P Garvey	Porthcawl	7 and 6
1954	F Stephens	E Price	Ganton	4 and 3
1955	J Valentine	B Romack (US)	Portrush	7 and 6
1956	M Smith (US)	M Janssen (US)	Sunningdale	8 and 7
1957	P Garvey	J Valentine	Gleneagles	4 and 3
1958	J Valentine	E Price	Hunstanton	1 hole
1959	E Price	B McCorkindale	Ascot	37th hole
1960	B McIntyre (US)	P Garvey	Harlech	4 and 2
1961	M Spearman	DJ Robb	Carnoustie	7 and 6
1962	M Spearman	A Bonallack	Birkdale	1 hole
1963	B Varangot (Fr)	P Garvey	Newcastle Co Down	3 and 1
1964	C Sorenson (US)	BAB Jackson	Sandwich, Prince's, R St George's	37th hole
1965	B Varangot (Fr)	IC Robertson	St Andrews	4 and 3
1966	E Chadwick	V Saunders	Ganton	3 and 2
1967	E Chadwick	M Everard	Harlech	1 hole
1968	B Varangot (Fr)	C Rubin (Fr)	Walton Heath	20th hole
1969	C Lacoste (Fr)	A Irvin	Portrush	1 hole
1970	D Oxley	IC Robertson	Gullane	1 hole
1971	M Walker	B Huke	Alwoodley	3 and 1
1972	M Walker	C Rubin (Fr)	Hunstanton	2 holes
1973	A Irvin	M Walker	Carnoustie	3 and 2
1974	C Semple (US)	A Bonallack	Porthcawl	2 and 1
1975	N Syms (US)	S Cadden	St Andrews	3 and 2
1976	C Panton	A Sheard	Silloth	1 hole
1977	A Uzielli	V Marvin	Hillside	6 and 5
1978	E Kennedy (Aus)	J Greenhalgh	Notts	1 hole
1979	M Madill	J Lock (Aus)	Nairn	2 and 1
1980	A Quast (US)	L Wollin (Swe)	Woodhall Spa	3 and 1
1981	IC Robertson	W Aitken	Conway	20th hole
1982	K Douglas	G Stewart	Walton Heath	4 and 2
1983	J Thornhill	R Lautens (Switz)	Silloth	4 and 2
1984	J Rosenthal (US)	J Brown	Royal Troon	4 and 3
1985	L Beman (Ire)	C Waite	Ganton	1 hole
1986	McGuire (NZ)	L Briars (Aus)	West Sussex	2 and 1
1987	J Collingham	S Shapcott	Harlech	19th hole
1988	J Furby	J Wade	Deal	4 and 3
1989	H Dobson	E Farquharson	Hoylake, R Liverpool	6 and 5
1990	J Hall	H Wadsworth	Dunbar	3 and 2
1991	V Michaud (Fr)	W Doolan (Aus)	Pannal	3 and 2
1992	P Pedersen (Den)	J Morley	Saunton	1 hole
1993	C Lambert	K Speak	R Lytham	3 and 2
1994	E Duggleby	C Mourgue d'Algue	Newport	3 and 1
1995	J Hall	K Mourgue d'Algue	R Portrush	3 and 2
1996	K Kuehne (US)	B Morgan	R Liverpool	5 and 3
1997	A Rose	M McKay	Cruden Bay	4 and 3

1998 *at Little Aston*

Quarter Finals
H Monaghan beat C Dowling 5 and 4
G Nocera beat S Arricau 1 hole
K Rostron beat V Roques 3 and 2
F Brown beat C Kuld at 19th

Semi-Finals
G Nocera beat H Monaghan 3 and 2
K Rostron beat F Brown 2 and 1

Final
K Rostron beat C Nocera 3 and 2

Ladies' British Open Amateur Strokeplay Championship

Year	Winner	Venue	Score	Year	Winner	Venue	Score
1969	A Irvin	Gosforth Park	295	1984	C Waite	Caernarvonshire	295
1970	M Everard	Birkdale	313	1985	IC Robertson	Formby	300
1971	IC Robertson	Ayr Belleisle	302	1986	C Hourihane	Blairgowrie	291
1972	IC Robertson	Silloth	296	1987	L Bayman	Ipswich	297
1973	A Stant	Purdis Heath	298	1988	K Mitchell	Porthcawl	317
1974	J Greenhalgh	Seaton Carew	302	1989	H Dobson	Southerness	298
1975	J Greenhalgh	Gosforth Park	298	1990	V Thomas	Strathaven	287
1976	J Lee Smith	Fulford	299	1991	J Morley	Long Ashton	297
1977	M Everard	Lindrick	306	1992	J Hockley	Frilford Heath	287
1978	J Melville	Foxhills	310	1993	J Hall	Gullane	290
1979	M McKenna	Moseley	305	1994	K Speak	Woodhall Spa	297
1980	M Mahill	Brancepeth Castle	304	1995	MJ Pons (Sp)	Princes	289
1981	J Soulsby	Norwich	300	1996	C Kuld (Den)	Conwy (Caernarvonshire)	289
1982	J Connachan	Downfield	294	1997	KM Juul (Den)	Silloth-on-Solway	293
1983	A Nicholas	Moortown	292				

1998 *at Stirling*

1	N Nijenhuis	71-76-75-75—297
2	B Morgan	73-77-76-72—298
3	S Beautell	76-75-70-79—300

Senior Ladies' British Amateur Strokeplay Championship

Year	Winner	Venue	Score	Year	Winner	Venue	Score
1981	BM King	Formby	159	1990	A Uzielli	Harrogate	153
1982	P Riddiford	Ilkley	161	1991	A Uzielli	Ladybank	154
1983	M Birtwistle	Troon Portland	167	1992	A Uzielli	Stratford-upon-Avon	148
1984	O Semelaigne	Woodbridge	152	1993	J Thornhill	Ashburnham	151
1985	Dr G Costello	Prestatyn	158	1994	D Williams	Nottingham	154
1986	P Riddiford	Longniddry	154	1995	A Uzielli	Blairgowrie	152
1987	O Semelaigne	Copt Heath	152	1996	V Hassett	Pyle & Kenfig	236
1988	C Bailey	Littlestone	156	1997	T Wiesner (US)	Frilford Heath	231
1989	C Bailey	Wrexham	149				

1998 *at Powfoot*

1	A Uzielli	227
2	V Hassett	234

English Ladies' Amateur Championship

Year	Winner	Runner-up	Venue	By
1960	M Nichol	A Bonallack	Burnham	3 and 1
1961	R Porter	P Reece	Littlestone	2 holes
1962	J Roberts	A Bonallack	Woodhall Spa	3 and 1
1963	A Bonallack	E Chadwick	Liphook	7 and 6
1964	M Spearman	M Everard	R Lytham and St Annes	6 and 5
1965	R Porter	C Cheetham	Whittington Barracks	6 and 5
1966	J Greenhalgh	JC Holmes	Hayling Island	3 and 1
1967	A Irwin	A Pickard	Alwoodley	3 and 2
1968	S Barber	D Oxley	Hunstanton	5 and 4
1969	B Dixon	M Wenyon	Burnham and Berrow	6 and 4
1970	D Oxley	S Barber	Rye	3 and 2
1971	D Oxley	S Barber	Hoylake	5 and 4
1972	M Everard	A Bonallack	Woodhall Spa	2 and 1
1973	M Walker	C Le Feuvre	Broadstone	6 and 5
1974	A Irvin	J Thornhill	Sunningdale	1 hole
1975	B Huke	L Harrold	R Birkdale	2 and 1
1976	L Harrold	A Uzielli	Hollinwell	3 and 2
1977	V Marvin	M Everard	Burnham and Berrow	1 hole
1978	V Marvin	R Porter	West Sussex	2 and 1

continued

English Ladies' Amateur Championship *continued*

Year	Winner	Runner-up	Venue	By
1979	J Greenhalgh	S Hedges	Hoylake	2 and 1
1980	B New	J Walker	Aldeburgh	3 and 2
1981	D Christison	S Cohen	Cotswold Hills	2 holes
1982	J Walter	C Nelson	Brancepeth Castle	4 and 3
1983	L Bayman	C Mackintosh	Hayling Island	4 and 3
1984	C Waite	L Bayman	Hunstanton	3 and 2
1985	P Johnson	L Bayman	Ferndown	1 hole
1986	J Thornhill	S Shapcott	Sandwich, Princes	3 and 1
1987	J Furby	M King	Alwoodley	4 and 3
1988	J Wade	S Shapcott	Little Aston	19th hole
1989	H Dobson	S Morgan	Burnham and Berrow	4 and 3
1990	A Uzielli	L Fletcher	Rye	2 and 1
1991	N Buxton	K Stupples	Sheringham	2 holes
1992	C Hall	J Hockley	St Annes Old Links	1 hole
1993	N Buxton	S Burnell	St Enodoc	2 and 1
1994	J Hall	S Sharpe	The Berkshire	1 hole
1995	J Hall	E Ratcliffe	Ipswich	2 and 1
1996	J Hockley	L Educate	Silloth	4 and 3
1997	K Rostron	K Burton	Saunton	4 and 2

1998 *at Walton Heath*

Quarter Finals
E Ratcliffe beat K Rostron 4 and 3
K Stupples beat C Court 3 and 2
S Heath beat K Knowles 4 and 3
L Walters beat K Fisher

Semi-Finals
E Ratcliffe beat K Stupples 1 hole
L Walters beat S Heath 3 and 2

Final
E Ratcliffe beat L Walters at 19th

English Ladies' Strokeplay Championship

Year	Winner	Venue	Score	Year	Winner	Venue	Score
1984	P Grice	Moor Park	300	1991	J Morley	Ganton	301
1985	P Johnson	Northants County	301	1992	J Morley	Littlestone	289
1986	S Shapcott	Broadstone	301	1993	J Hall	King's Norton	298
1987	J Wade	Northumberland	296	1994	F Brown	Ferndown	289
1988	S Prosser	Wentworth	297	1995	L Walton	Hallamshire	289
1989	S Robinson	Notts	302	1996	S Gallagher	Little Aston	290
1990	K Tebbet	Saunton	299	1997	L Tupholme	Hankley Common	293

1998 *at Broadstone*

1	E Duggleby	74-76-81-75—306
2	L Meredith	74-77-81-75—307
3	L Walters	77-80-79-72—308
	G Simpson	76-78-80-74—308

English Ladies' Under-23 Championship

Year	Winner	Venue	Score	Year	Winner	Venue	Score
1978	S Bamford	Caldy	228	1988	J Wade	Wentworth	299
1979	B Cooper	Coxmoor	223	1989	A Shapcott	Notts Ladies	302
1980	B Cooper	Porters Park	226	1990	K Tebbet	Saunton	299
1981	J Soulsby	Willesley Park	220	1991	J Hockley	Saunton	303
1982	M Gallagher	High Post	221	1992	N Buxton	Littlestone	292
1983	P Grice	Hallamshire	219	1993	R Millington	King's Norton	302
1984	P Johnson	Moor Park	300	1994	F Brown	Ferndown	289
1985	P Johnson	Northants County	301	1995	E Fields	Hallamshire	297
1986	S Shapcott	Broadstone	301	1996	R Hudson	Little Aston	299
1987	J Wade	Northumberland	296	1997	R Bailey	Hankley Common	306

1998 *at Broadstone*

1	L Meredith	307
2	L Walters	308
3	G Simpson	308

English Ladies' Senior Strokeplay Championship

Year	Winner	Venue	Score	Year	Winner	Venue	Score
1988	A Thompson	Wentworth	158	1993	A Uzielli	Hunstanton	150
1989	C Bailey	Notts Ladies	163	1994	S Bassindale	Littlestone	163
1990	A Thompson	Fairhaven	162	1995	V Morgan	Tandridge	151
1991	C Bailey	Burnham and Berrow	155	1996	A Uzielli	Royal North Devon	153
1992	A Thompson	Pleasington	154	1997	A Thompson	Formby Ladies	152

1998 *at Royal Liverpool*

1	E Boatman	78-76—154
2	L McCombe	77-78—155
3	S Westall	77-79—156

English Ladies' Senior Matchplay Championship

Year	Venue	Winner	Runner-up
1994	Whitting Heath	E Annison	S Bassindale
1995	R Ashdown Forest	A Thompson	G Palmer
1996	Lindrick	R Farrow	V Morgan
1997	S Winchester	G Palmer	C Means

1998 *at West Sussex*

Quarter Finals
E McCombe beat S Donald 4 and 2
S Westall beat S Hedges 3 and 2
J Thornhill beat S Timberlake 3 and 2
H Kaye beat R Watters 3 and 2

Semi-Finals
E McCombe beat S Westall 3 and 2
J Thornhill beat H Kaye 4 and 3

Final
E McCombe beat J Thornhill 1 hole

English Ladies' Intermediate Championship

Year	Winner	Venue	Score	Year	Winner	Venue	Score
1982	J Rhodes	Headingley	19th hole	1990	L Fletcher	Whitley Bay	7 and 6
1983	L Davies	Worksop	2 and 1	1991	J Morley	West Lancashire	6 and 5
1984	P Grice	Whittington Barracks	3 and 2	1992	K Speak	South Staffs	3 and 1
1985	S Lowe	Caldy	2 and 1	1993	K Speak	Seascale	2 and 1
1986	S Moorcroft	Hexham	6 and 5	1994	J Oliver	Beaconsfield	2 up
1987	J Wade	Sheringham	2 and 1	1995	K Smith	Clitheroe	5 and 4
1988	S Morgan	Enville, Staffs	20th hole	1996	R Bailey	Sandiway	3 and 2
1989	L Fairclough	Warrington	4 and 3	1997	K Smith	Abbotsley	2 and 1

1998 *at Hornsea*

Quarter Finals
K Fisher beat K McKenna at 22nd
D Rushworth beat S Coverley 5 and 4
J Lamb beat L Tupholme 4 and 3
L Meredith beat C George 4 and 3

Semi-Finals
D Rushworth beat K Fisher 5 and 4
J Lamb beat L Meredith 4 and 3

Final
J Lamb beat D Rushworth 1 hole

Irish Ladies' Close Amateur Championship

Year	Winner	Runner-up	Venue	By
1960	P Garvey	PG McGann	Cork	5 and 3
1961	K McCann	A Sweeney	Newcastle	5 and 3
1962	P Garvey	M Earner	Baltray	7 and 6
1963	P Garvey	E Barnett	Killarney	9 and 7
1964	Z Fallon	P O'Sullivan	Portrush	37th hole
1965	E Purcell	P O'Sullivan	Mullingar	3 and 2
1966	E Bradshaw	P O'Sullivan	Rosslare	3 and 2
1967	G Brandom	P O'Sullivan	Castlerock	3 and 2
1968	E Bradshaw	M McKenna	Lahinch	3 and 2
1969	M McKenna	C Hickey	Ballybunion	3 and 2
1970	P Garvey	M Earner	Portrush	2 and 1
1971	E Bradshaw	M Mooney	Baltray	3 and 1
1972	M McKenna	I Butler	Killarney	5 and 4
1973	M Mooney	M McKenna	Bundoran	2 and 1
1974	M McKenna	V Singleton	Lahinch	3 and 2
1975	M Gorry	E Bradshaw	Tramore	1 hole
1976	C Nesbitt	M McKenna	Rosses Point	20th hole
1977	M McKenna	R Hegarty	Ballybunion	2 holes
1978	M Gorry	I Butler	Grange	4 and 3
1979	M McKenna	C Nesbitt	Donegal	6 and 5
1980	C Nesbitt	C Hourihane	Lahinch	1 hole
1981	M McKenna	M Kenny	Laytown & Bettystown	1 hole
1982	M McKenna	M Madill	Portrush	2 and 1
1983	C Hourihane	V Hassett	Cork	6 and 4
1984	C Hourihane	M Madill	Rosses Point	19th hole
1985	C Hourihane	M McKenna	Waterville	4 and 3
1986	T O'Reilly	E Higgins	Castlerock	4 and 3
1987	C Hourihane	C Hickey	Lahinch	5 and 4
1988	L Bolton	E Higgins	Tramore	2 and 1
1989	M McKenna	C Wickham	West Port	19th hole
1990	ER McDaid	L Callan	The Island	2 and 1
1991	C Hourihane	E McDaid	Ballybunion	1 hole
1992	ER Power	C Hourihane	Co. Louth	1 hole
1993	E Higgins	A Rogers	R Belfast	2 and 1
1994	L Webb	H Kavanagh	Rosses Point	20th hole
1995	ER Power	S O'Brien-Kenney	Cork	1 hole
1996	B Hackett	L Behan	Tullamore	3 and 2
1997	S Fanagan	ER Power	Enniscrone	4 and 3

1998 Irish Ladies' Close Amateur Championship at *Clandeboye GC*

Quarter Finals
P Gorman beat S O'Brien (*née* Fanagan) 1 hole
O Purfield beat Y Cassidy 2 holes
L Behan beat N Moore at 20th
M McEvoy beat A Coffey 2 holes

Semi-Finals
O Purfield beat P Gorman 3 and 2
L Behan beat M McEvoy 3 and 2

Final
L Behan beat O Purfield at 19th hole

Irish Ladies' Amateur Strokeplay Championship

Year	Winner	Venue	Score
1993	T Eakin	Milltown	293
1994	H Kavanagh	Milltown	286
1995	N Quigg	Grange	300
1996	ER Power	Grange	218
1997	Y Cassidy	Waterford Castle	217

1998 at *Waterford Castle*

1	S O'Brien	141
2	L Behan	147
3	E Dowdall	148

(Reduced to 36 holes due to bad weather)

Irish Senior Ladies' Amateur Championship at *Athlone*

Year	Winner	Score	Year	Winner	Score
1991	C Hickey	77	1995	A Gaynor	81
1992	C Hickey	79	1996	M Stuart	81
1993	G Costello	81	1997	M O'Donnell	85
1994	G Costello	80			

1998 *(Reduced to 36 holes due to bad weather)*

1	M Moran	78
2	R Fanagan	79

Scottish Ladies' Close Amateur Championship

Year	Winner	Runner-up	Venue	By
1960	JS Robertson	DT Sommerville	Turnberry	2 and 1
1961	JS Wright (*née* Robertson)	AM Lurie	St Andrews	1 hole
1962	JB Lawrence	C Draper	R Dornoch	5 and 4
1963	JB Lawrence	IC Robertson	Troon	2 and 1
1964	JB Lawrence	SM Reid	Gullane	5 and 3
1965	IC Robertson	JB Lawrence	Nairn	5 and 4
1966	IC Robertson	M Fowler	Machrihanish	2 and 1
1967	J Hastings	A Laing	North Berwick	5 and 3
1968	J Smith	J Rennie	Carnoustie	10 and 9
1969	JH Anderson	K Lackie	West Kilbride	5 and 4
1970	A Laing	IC Robertson	Dunbar	1 hole
1971	IC Robertson	A Ferguson	R Dornoch	3 and 2
1972	IC Robertson	CJ Lugton	Machrihanish	5 and 3
1973	I Wright	Dr AJ Wilson	St Andrews	2 holes

continued

Scottish Ladies' Amateur Championship *continued*

Year	Winner	Runner-up	Venue	By
1974	Dr AJ Wilson	K Lackie	Nairn	22nd hole
1975	LA Hope	JW Smith	Elie	1 hole
1976	S Needham	T Walker	Machrihanish	3 and 2
1977	CJ Lugton	M Thomson	R Dornoch	1 hole
1978	IC Robertson	JW Smith	Prestwick	2 holes
1979	G Stewart	LA Hope	Gullane	2 and 1
1980	IC Robertson	F Anderson	Carnoustie	1 hole
1981	A Gemmill	W Aitken	Stranraer	2 and 1
1982	J Connachan	P Wright	R Troon	19th hole
1983	G Stewart	F Anderson	North Berwick	3 and 1
1984	G Stewart	A Gemmill	R Dornoch	3 and 2
1985	A Gemmill	D Thomson	Barassie	2 and 1
1986	IC Robertson	L Hope	St Andrews	3 and 2
1987	F Anderson	C Middleton	Nairn	4 and 3
1988	S Lawson	F Anderson	Southerness	3 and 1
1989	J Huggon	L Anderson	Lossiemouth	5 and 4
1990	E Farquharson	S Huggan	Machrihanish	3 and 2
1991	C Lambert	F Anderson	Carnoustie	3 and 2
1992	J Moody	E Farquharson	R Aberdeen	2 and 1 *d*
1993	C Lambert	M McKay	Prestwick St Nicholas	5 and 4
1994	C Matthew	V Melvin	Gullane	1 hole
1995	H Monaghan	S McMaster	Portpatrick	21st hole
1996	A Laing	A Rose	R Dornoch	1 hole
1997	A Rose	H Monaghan	W Kilbride	3 and 2

1998 *at North Berwick*

Quarter Finals
P Mackay beat C Hargan 2 and 1
E Moffat beat K Marshall 2 and 1
V Laing beat J Smith 6 and 4
C Agnew beat E Farquharson-Black 1 hole

Semi-Finals
E Moffat beat P Mackay 3 and 2
C Agnew beat V Laing 3 and 2

Final
E Moffat beat C Agnew 4 and 3

Scottish Ladies' Open Strokeplay Championship (Helen Holm Trophy)

Year	Winner	Year	Winner
1988	E Farquharson	1993	J Hall
1989	S Robinson	1994	K Tebbet
1990	C Lambert	1995	M Hjorth
1991	J Hall	1996	J Hockley
1992	M McKay	1997	K Rostron

1998 *at Royal Troon*

1 K-M Juul Esbjerg 71-79-75—225
2 A Coffey   76-73-78—227
3 F Brown   75-76-77—228

Scottish Senior Ladies' Amateur Championship

Year	Winner
1997	A Wilson
1998	I McIntosh

Welsh Ladies' Amateur Championship

Year	Winner	Runner-up	Venue	By
1960	M Barron	E Brown	Tenby	8 and 6
1961	M Oliver	N Sneddon	Aberdovey	5 and 4
1962	M Oliver	P Roberts	Radyr	4 and 2
1963	P Roberts	N Sneddon	Harlech	7 and 5
1964	M Oliver	M Wright	Southerndown	1 hole
1965	M Wright	E Brown	Prestatyn	3 and 2
1966	A Hughes	P Roberts	Ashburnham	5 and 4
1967	M Wright	C Phipps	Harlech	21st hole
1968	S Hales	M Wright	Porthcawl	3 and 2
1969	P Roberts	A Hughes	Caernarvonshire	3 and 2
1970	A Briggs	J Morris	Newport	19th hole
1971	A Briggs	EN Davies	Harlech	2 and 1
1972	A Hughes	J Rogers	Tenby	3 and 2
1973	A Briggs	J John	Holyhead	3 and 2
1974	A Briggs	Dr H Lyall	Ashburnham	3 and 2
1975	A Johnson (née Hughes)	K Rawlings	Prestatyn	1 hole
1976	T Perkins	A Johnson	Porthcawl	4 and 2
1977	T Perkins	P Whitley	Aberdovey	5 and 4
1978	P Light	A Briggs	Newport	2 and 1
1979	V Rawlings	A Briggs	Caernarvonshire	2 holes
1980	M Rawlings	A Briggs	Tenby	2 and 1
1981	M Rawlings	A Briggs	Harlech	5 and 3
1982	V Thomas (née Rawlings)	M Rawlings	Ashburnham	7 and 6
1983	V Thomas	T Thomas (née Perkins)	Llandudno	1 hole
1984	S Roberts	K Davies	Newport	5 and 4
1985	V Thomas	S Jump	Prestatyn	1 hole
1986	V Thomas	L Isherwood	Porthcawl	7 and 6
1987	V Thomas	S Roberts	Aberdovey	3 and 1
1988	S Roberts	F Connor	Tenby	4 and 2
1989	H Lawson	V Thomas	Conwy	2 and 1
1990	S Roberts	H Wadsworth	Ashburnham	3 and 2
1991	V Thomas	H Lawson	R St David's	4 and 3
1992	J Foster	S Boyes	Newport	4 and 3
1993	A Donne	V Thomas	Abergele & Pensarn	19th hole
1994	V Thomas	L Dermott	Royal Porthcawl	19th hole
1995	L Dermott	K Stark	Aberdovey	19th hole
1996	L Dermott	V Thomas	Tenby	4 and 3
1997	E Pilgrim	L Davis	Northop	4 and 2

1998 *at Ashburnham*

Quarter Finals
R Morgan beat D Richards 3 and 1
S Mountford beat B Jones 4 and 3
L Davis beat R Brewerton 2 and 1
H Lawson beat C Joyce 2 holes

Semi-Finals
R Morgan beat S Mountford 7 and 6
L Davis beat H Lawson 1 hole

Final
L Davis beat R Morgan 1 hole

Welsh Ladies' Open Amateur Strokeplay Championship

Year	Winner	Venue	Score	Year	Winner	Venue	Score
1981	V Thomas	Aberdovey	224	1990	L Hackney	Newport	218
1982	V Thomas	Aberdovey	225	1991	M Sutton	R Porthcawl	224
1983	J Thornhill	Aberdovey	239	1992	C Lambert	R Porthcawl	218
1984	L Davies	Aberdovey	230	1993	J Hall	Newport	221
1985	C Swallow	Aberdovey	219	1994	A Rose	Newport	217
1986	H Wadsworth	Aberdovey	223	1995	F Brown	Newport	221
1987	S Shapcott	Newport	225	1996	E Duggleby	Whitchurch	223
1988	S Shapcott	Newport	218	1997	K Edwards	Whitchurch	216
1989	V Thomas	Newport	220				

1998 *at Rolls of Monmouth*
1	G Simpson	75-75—150
2	C Court	76-76—152
3	J Lamb	78-76—154

Welsh Senior Ladies' Championship

Year	Winner	Venue	Score	Year	Winner	Venue	Score
1990	E Higgs	Vale of Llangollen	171	1994	C Thomas	Llandudno	163
1991	H Lyall	Pyle and Kenfig	160	1995	C Thomas	Tredegar Park	157
1992	P Morgan	Cardigan	83	1996	C Thomas	Vale of Llangollen	157
1993	P Morgan	Pwllheli	157	1997	C Thomas	Fairwood Park	160

1998 *at Padeswood*
1	C Thomas	163
2	J White	171

Ladies' European Open Amateur Championship

Year	Winner	Venue	Score
1995	M Hjorth	Germany	284
1996	S Cavalleri	Denmark	288
1997	S Cavalleri	Formby	297

1998 *at Noordwijkse, Netherlands*
1	G Sergas (It)	295
2	S Sandolo (It)	298
3	R Hudson (Eng)	299
	R Fowler (NZ)	299

Team Events

Great Britain & Ireland v USA for the Curtis Cup

Year		GB&I		USA		Venue
1932	Foursomes	0	3½	3	5½	Wentworth
	Singles	3½		2½		
1934	Foursomes	1½	2½	1½	6½	Chevy Chase
	Singles	1		5		
1936	Foursomes	1½	4½	1½	4½	Gleneagles
	Singles	3		3		
1938	Foursomes	2½	3½	½	5½	Essex County Club
	Singles	1		5		
1948	Foursomes	1	2½	2	6½	Birkdale
	Singles	1½		4½		
1950	Foursomes	1	1½	2	7½	Buffalo
	Singles	½		5½		
1952	Foursomes	2	5	1	4	Muirfield
	Singles	3		3		
1954	Foursomes	0	3	3	6	Merion
	Singles	3		3		
1956	Foursomes	1	5	2	4	Sandwich, Prince's
	Singles	4		2		
1958	Foursomes	2	4½	1	4½	Brae Burn GC
	Singles	2½		3½		
1960	Foursomes	1	2½	2	6½	Lindrick
	Singles	1½		4½		
1962	Foursomes	0	1	3	8	Colorado Springs
	Singles	1		5		
1964	Foursomes	3½	7½	2½	10½	Porthcawl
	Singles	4		8		
1966	Foursomes	1½	5	4½	13	Hot Springs
	Singles	3½		8½		
1968	Foursomes	2½	7½	3½	10½	Newcastle, Co Down
	Singles	5		7		
1970	Foursomes	2½	6½	3½	11½	Brae Burn, USA
	Singles	4		8		
1972	Foursomes	3½	8	2½	10	Western Gailes
	Singles	4½		7½		
1974	Foursomes	2½	5	3½	13	San Francisco, California
	Singles	2½		9½		
1976	Foursomes	2	6½	4	11½	R Lytham and St Annes
	Singles	4½		7½		
1978	Foursomes	2½	6	3½	12	Apawamis, NY
	Singles	3½		8½		
1980	Foursomes	1	5	5	13	St Pierre
	Singles	4		8		
1982	Foursomes	1½	3½	4½	14½	Denver, Colorado
	Singles	2		10		
1984	Foursomes	3	8½	3	9½	Muirfield
	Singles	5½		6½		
1986	Foursomes	5½	13	½	5	Prairie Dunes, Kansas
	Singles	7½		4½		
1988	Foursomes	4½	11	1½	7	Royal St George's
	Singles	6½		5½		

continued

1990 Curtis Cup *at Somerset Hills, New Jersey, 28th–29th July*

Great Britain and Ireland | USA

First Day – **Foursomes**

H Dobson and C Lambert	0	V Goetze and A Sander (4 and 3)	1
J Hall and K Imrie (2 and 1)	1	K Noble and M Platt	0
E Farquharson and H Wadsworth	0	C Semple-Thompson and R Weiss (3 and 1)	1
	1		2

Singles

J Hall (2 and 1)	1	V Goetze	0
K Imrie	0	K Peterson (3 and 2)	1
E Farquharson	0	B Burton (3 and 1)	1
L Fletcher	0	R Weiss (4 and 3)	1
C Lambert	0	K Noble (1 hole)	1
V Thomas (1 hole)	1	C Semple-Thompson	0
	2		4

Match position: GB&I 3, USA 6

Second Day – **Foursomes**

J Hall and K Imrie	0	V Goetze and A Sander (4 and 3)	1
C Lambert and H Dobson (1 hole)	1	K Noble and M Platt	0
E Farquharson and H Wadsworth	0	K Peterson and B Burton (5 and 4)	1
	1		2

Singles

H Dobson	0	V Goetze (4 and 3)	1
C Lambert	0	B Burton (4 and 3)	1
K Imrie	0	K Peterson (1 hole)	1
J Hall	0	K Noble (2 holes)	1
E Farquharson	0	R Weiss (2 and 1)	1
V Thomas	0	C Semple-Thompson (3 and 1)	1
	0		6

Result: Great Britain and Ireland 4, United States 14

1992 *at Royal Liverpool, Hoylake, on 5th–6th June*

Great Britain and Ireland | USA

First Day – **Foursomes**

J Hall and C Hall	½	A Fruhwirth and V Goetze	½
V Thomas and C Lambert (2 and 1)	1	L Shannon and S Lebrun Ingram	0
J Morley and C Hourihane (2 and 1)	1	T Hanson and C Semple Thompson	0
	2½		½

Singles

J Morley	½	A Fruhwirth	½
J Hall	0	V Goetze (3 and 2)	1
E Farquharson (2 and 1)	1	R Weiss	0
N Buxton	0	M Lang (2 holes)	1
C Lambert (3 and 2)	1	C Semple Thompson	0
C Hall (6 and 5)	1	L Shannon	0
	3½		2½

Match position: GB&I 6, USA 3

Second Day – **Foursomes**

J Hall and C Hall	½	A Fruhwirth and V Goetze	½
C Hourihane and J Morley	½	M Lang and R Weiss	½
C Lambert and V Thomas	0	T Hanson and C Semple Thompson (3 and 2)	1
	1		2

Second Day – **Singles**

J Morley (2 and 1)	1	A Fruhwirth	0
C Lambert (6 and 5)	1	T Hanson	0
E Farquharson	0	S Lebrun Ingram (2 and 1)	1
V Thomas	0	L Shannon (2 and 1)	1
C Hourihane	0	M Lang (2 and 1)	1
C Hall (1 hole)	1	V Goetze	0
	3		3

Result: Great Britain and Ireland 10, United States 8

1994 at The Honors Course, Ooltewah, Chattanooga, Tennessee, on 30th–31st July 1994

Great Britain and Ireland		USA	
First Day – Foursomes			
C Matthew and J Moodie	½	J McGill and S Lebrun Ingram	½
M McKay and K Speak	0	C Semple Thompson and E Klein (7 and 5)	1
J Hall and L Walton (6 and 5)	1	W Kaupp and E Port	0
	1½		1½
Singles			
J Hall	½	J McGill	½
J Moodie	0	E Klein (3 and 2)	1
L Walton (1 hole)	1	W Ward	0
M McKinlay	0	C Semple Thompson (2 and 1)	1
M McKay	0	E Port (2 and 1)	1
C Matthew (1 hole)	1	S Sparks	0
	2½		3½

Match position: GB&I 4, USA 5

Second Day – Foursomes			
J Hall and L Walton (2 and 1)	1	J McGill and S Lebrun Ingram	0
M McKinlay and ER Power	0	C Semple Thompson and E Klein (4 and 2)	1
C Matthew and J Moodie (3 and 2)	1	W Ward and S Sparks	0
	2		1
Singles			
J Hall	0	J McGill (4 and 3)	1
C Matthew (2 and 1)	1	E Klein	0
M McKay	0	E Port (7 and 5)	1
M McKinlay (3 and 2)	1	W Kaupp	0
L Walton	0	W Ward (4 and 3)	1
J Moodie (2 holes)	1	C Semple Thompson	0
	3		3

Result: Great Britain and Ireland 9, United States 9

1996 at Killarney, Ireland, on 21st–22nd June

Great Britain and Ireland		USA	
First Day – Foursomes			
J Hall and L Educate	0	E Port and K Kuehne (2 and 1)	1
A Rose and L Dermott (3 and 1)	1	M Jemsek and B Corrie Kuehn	0
J Moodie and M McKay	½	C Kerr and C Semple Thompson	½
	1½		1½
Singles			
J Hall	0	S Lebrun Ingram (4 and 2)	1
K Stupples (3 and 2)	1	K Booth	0
A Rose (5 and 4)	1	B Corrie Kuehn	0
E Ratcliff	½	M Jemsek	½
M McKay (1 hole)	1	C Kerr	0
J Moodie (3 and 1)	1	C Semple Thompson	0
	4½		1½

Match position: GB&I 6, USA 3

Second Day – Foursomes			
J Moodie and M McKay (3 and 2)	1	K Booth and S Lebrun Ingram	0
A Rose and L Dermott (2 and 1)	1	M Jemsek and B Corrie Kuehn	0
J Hall and L Educate	0	E Port and K Kuehne (1 hole)	1
	2		1
Singles			
J Hall	0	C Kerr (1 hole)	1
E Ratcliffe (3 and 1)	1	S Lebrun Ingram	0
K Stupples	0	K Booth (3 and 2)	1
A Rose (6 and 5)	1	E Port	0
M McKay	½	C Semple Thompson	½
J Moodie (2 and 1)	1	K Kuehne	0
	3½		2½

Result: Great Britain and Ireland 11½, United States 6½

1998 Curtis Cup at Minikhada, Minnesota, on 1st–2nd August

Great Britain and Ireland

First Day – **Foursomes**

K Rostron and E Ratcliffe (1 hole)	1	
F Brown and K Stupples	0	
A Rose and B Morgan	0	
	1	

Singles

K Rostron	0
A Rose	0
R Hudson	½
H Monaghan	0
B Morgan (2 and 1)	1
E Ratcliffe (3 and 2)	1
	2½

Match position: GB&I 3½, USA 5½

Second Day – **Foursomes**

A Rose and B Morgan	0
F Brown and R Hudson (2 holes)	1
K Rostron and E Ratcliffe	0
	1

Singles

K Rostron	0
B Morgan	0
K Stupples (1 hole)	1
R Hudson (2 and 1)	1
F Brown (1 hole)	1
E Ratcife	½
	3½

USA

B Bauer and J Chuasiriporn	0
B Corrie Kuehn and K Booth (2 and 1)	1
V Derby-Grimes and R Burke (3 and 2)	1
	2

Singles

K Booth (2 and 1)	1
B Corrie Kuehn (3 and 2)	1
J Chuasiriporn	½
B Bauer (5 and 3)	1
JJ Robertson	0
C Semple Thompson	0
	3½

Foursomes

B Corrie Kuehn and K Booth (6 and 5)	1
J Chuasiriporn and B Bauer	0
V Derby-Grimes and R Burke (2 and 1)	1
	2

Singles

K Booth (2 and 1)	1
B Corrie Kuehn (2 and 1)	1
C Semple Thompson	0
R Burke	0
JJ Robertson	0
V Derby-Grimes	½
	2½

Result: Great Britain and Ireland 8, United States 10

Curtis Cup INDIVIDUAL RECORDS

Bold print: captain; bold print in brackets: non-playing captain
Maiden name in parentheses, former surname in square brackets

Great Britain and Ireland

Name		Year	Played	Won	Lost	Halved
Jean Anderson (Donald)	Scot	1948	6	3	3	0
Diane Bailey [Frearson] (Robb)	Eng	1962-72-**(84)**-**(86)**-**(88)**	5	2	2	1
Sally Barber (Bonallack)	Eng	1962	1	0	1	0
Pam Barton	Eng	1934-36	4	0	3	1
Linda Bayman	Eng	1988	4	2	1	1
Baba Beck (Pym)	Ire	**(1954)**	0	0	0	0
Charlotte Beddows [Watson] (Stevenson)	Scot	1932	1	0	1	0
Lilian Behan	Ire	1986	4	3	1	0
Veronica Beharrell (Anstey)	Eng	1956	1	0	1	0
Pam Benka (Tredinnick)	Eng	1966-68	4	0	3	1
Jeanne Bisgood	Eng	1950-52-54-**(70)**	4	1	3	0
Elizabeth Boatman (Collis)	Eng	**(1992)**-**(94)**	0	0	0	0
Zara Bolton (Davis)	Eng	1948-**(56)**-**(66)**-**(68)**	2	0	2	0
Angela Bonallack (Ward)	Eng	1956-58-60-62-64-66	15	6	8	1
Fiona Brown	Eng	1998	3	2	1	0
Ita Butler (Burke)	Ire	1966-**(96)**	3	2	1	0
Nicola Buxton	Eng	1992	1	0	1	0
Lady Katherine Cairns	Eng	**(1952)**	0	0	0	0
Carole Caldwell (Redford)	Eng	1978-80	5	0	3	2
Doris Chambers	Eng	**(1934)**-**(36)**-**(48)**	0	0	0	0
Carol Comboy (Grott)	Eng	**(1978)**-**(80)**	0	0	0	0
Jane Connachan	Scot	1980-82	5	0	5	0
Elsie Corlett	Eng	1932-38-**(64)**	3	1	2	0
Diana Critchley (Fishwick)	Eng	1932-34-**(50)**	3	1	2	0

Name		Year	Played	Won	Lost	Halved
Karen Davies	Wales	1986-88	7	4	1	2
Laura Davies	Eng	1984	2	1	1	0
Lisa Dermott	Wales	1996	2	2	0	0
Helen Dobson	Eng	1990	3	1	2	0
Kitrina Douglas	Eng	1982	4	0	3	1
Marjorie Draper [Peel] (Thomas)	Scot	1954	1	0	1	0
Lisa Educate (Walton)	Eng	1994-96	6	3	3	0
Mary Everard	Eng	1970-72-74-78	15	6	7	2
Elaine Farquharson	Scot	1990-92	6	1	5	0
Daisy Ferguson	Ire	(1958)	0	0	0	0
Marjory Ferguson (Fowler)	Scot	1966	1	0	1	0
Elizabeth Price Fisher (Price)	Eng	1950-52-54-56-58-60	12	7	4	1
Linzi Fletcher	Eng	1990	1	0	1	0
Maureen Garner (Madill)	Ire	1980	4	0	3	1
Marjorie Ross Garon	Eng	1936	2	1	0	1
Maureen Garrett (Ruttle)	Eng	1948-(60)	2	0	2	0
Philomena Garvey	Ire	1948-50-52-54-56-60	11	2	8	1
Carol Gibbs (Le Feuvre)	Eng	1974	3	0	3	0
Jacqueline Gordon	Eng	1948	2	1	1	0
Molly Gourlay	Eng	1932-34	4	0	2	2
Julia Greenhalgh	Eng	1964-70-74-76-78	17	6	7	4
Penny Grice-Whittaker (Grice)	Eng	1984	4	2	1	1
Caroline Hall	Eng	1992	4	2	0	2
Julie Hall (Wade)	Eng	1988-90-92-94-96	19	6	10	3
Marley Harris [Spearman] (Baker)	Eng	1960-62-64	6	2	2	2
Dorothea Hastings (Sommerville)	Scot	1958	0	0	0	0
Lady Heathcoat-Amory (Joyce Wethered)	Eng	**1932**	2	1	1	0
Dinah Henson (Oxley)	Eng	1968-70-72-76	11	3	6	2
Helen Holm (Gray)	Scot	1936-38-48	5	3	2	0
Claire Hourihane	Ire	1984-86-88-90-92	8	3	3	2
Ann Howard (Phillips)	Eng	1956-68	2	0	2	0
Rebecca Hudson	Eng	1998	3	2	0	1
Beverley Huke	Eng	1972	2	0	2	0
Kathryn Imrie	Scot	1990	4	1	3	0
Ann Irvin	Eng	1962-68-70-76	12	4	7	1
Bridget Jackson	Eng	1958-64-68	8	1	6	1
Patricia Johnson	Eng	1986	4	4	0	0
Susan Langridge (Armitage)	Eng	1964-66	6	0	5	1
Joan Lawrence	Scot	1964	2	0	2	0
Shirley Lawson	Scot	1988	2	1	1	0
Wilma Leburn (Aitken)	Scot	1982	2	0	2	0
Jenny Lee Smith	Eng	1974-76	3	0	3	0
Kathryn Lumb (Phillips)	Eng	1970-72	2	1	1	0
Mhairi McKay	Scot	1994-96	7	2	3	2
Mary McKenna	Ire	1970-72-74-76-78-80-82-84-86	30	10	16	4
Myra McKinlay	Scot	1994	3	1	2	0
Suzanne McMahon (Cadden)	Scot	1976	4	0	4	0
Sheila Maher (Vaughan)	Eng	1962-64	4	1	2	1
Vanessa Marvin	Eng	1978	3	1	2	0
Catriona Matthew (Lambert)	Scot	1990-92-94	12	7	4	1
Moira Milton (Paterson)	Scot	1952	2	1	1	0
Hilary Monaghan	Scot	1998	1	0	1	0
Janice Moodie	Scot	1994-96	8	5	1	2
Becky Morgan	Wales	1998	4	1	3	0
Wanda Morgan	Eng	1932-34-36	6	0	5	1
Joanne Morley	Eng	1992	4	2	0	2
Beverley New	Eng	1984	4	1	3	0
Maire O'Donnell	Ire	(1982)	0	0	0	0
Margaret Pickard (Nichol)	Eng	1968-70	5	2	3	0
Diana Plumpton	Eng	1934	2	1	1	0
Elizabeth Pook (Chadwick)	Eng	1966	4	1	3	0
Doris Porter (Park)	Scot	1932	1	0	1	0
Eileen Rose Power (McDaid)	Ire	1994	1	0	1	0
Elaine Ratcliffe	Eng	1996-98	6	3	1	2
Clarrie Reddan (Tiernan)	Ire	1938-48	3	2	1	0
Joan Rennie (Hastings)	Scot	1966	2	0	1	1
Maureen Richmond (Walker)	Scot	1974	4	2	2	0
Jean Roberts	Eng	1962	1	0	1	0
Belle Robertson (McCorkindale)	Scot	1960-66-68-70-72-(74)-(76)-82-86	24	5	12	7

continued

Curtis Cup Individual Records *continued*

Name		Year	Played	Won	Lost	Halved
Claire Robinson (Nesbitt)	Ire	1980	3	0	1	2
Alison Rose	Scot	1996-98	7	4	3	0
Kim Rostron	Eng	1998	4	1	3	0
Vivien Saunders	Eng	1968	4	1	2	1
Susan Shapcott	Eng	1988	4	3	1	0
Linda Simpson (Moore)	Eng	1980	3	1	1	1
Ruth Slark (Porter)	Eng	1960-62-64	7	3	3	1
Anne Smith [Stant] (Willard)	Eng	1976	1	0	1	0
Frances Smith (Stephens)	Eng	1950-52-54-56-58-60-(62)-(72)	11	7	3	1
Janet Soulsby	Eng	1982	4	1	2	1
Kirsty Speak	Eng	1994	1	0	1	0
Gillian Stewart	Scot	1980-82	4	1	3	0
Karen Stupples	Eng	1996-98	4	2	2	0
Tegwen Thomas (Perkins)	Wales	1974-76-78-80	14	4	8	2
Vicki Thomas (Rawlings)	Wales	1982-84-86-88-90-92	13	6	5	2
Muriel Thomson	Scot	1978	3	2	1	0
Jill Thornhill	Eng	1984-86-88	12	6	2	4
Angela Uzielli (Carrick)	Eng	1978	1	0	1	0
Jessie Valentine (Anderson)	Scot	1936-38-50-52-54-56-58	13	4	9	0
Helen Wadsworth	Wales	1990	2	0	2	0
Claire Waite	Eng	1984	4	2	2	0
Mickey Walker	Eng	1972-74	4	3	0	1
Pat Walker	Ire	1934-36-38	6	2	3	1
Verona Wallace-Williamson	Scot	(1938)	0	0	0	0
Nan Wardlaw (Baird)	Scot	1938	1	0	1	0
Enid Wilson	Eng	1932	2	1	1	0
Janette Wright (Robertson)	Scot	1954-56-58-60	8	3	5	0
Phyllis Wylie (Wade)	Eng	1938	1	0	0	1

United States of America

Name	Year	Played	Won	Lost	Halved
Roberta Albers	1968	2	1	0	1
Danielle Ammaccapane	1986	3	0	3	0
Kathy Baker	1982	4	3	0	1
Barbara Barrow	1976	2	1	0	1
Beth Barry	1972-74	5	3	1	1
Beth Bauer	1998	3	1	2	0
Larua Baugh	1972	4	2	1	1
Judy Bell	1960-62-(86)-(88)	2	1	1	0
Peggy Kirk Bell (Kirk)	1950	2	1	1	0
Amy Benz	1982	3	2	1	0
Patty Berg	1936-38	4	1	2	1
Barbara Fay Boddie (White)	1964-66	8	7	0	1
Jane Booth (Bastanchury)	1970-72-74	12	9	3	0
Kellee Booth	1996-98	7	5	2	0
Mary Budke	1974	3	2	1	0
Robin Burke	1998	3	2	1	0
Brandie Burton	1990	3	3	0	0
Jo Anne Carner (Gunderson)	1958-60-62-64	10	6	3	1
Lori Castillo	1980	3	2	1	0
Leona Cheney (Pressler)	1932-34-36	6	5	1	0
Sis Choate	(1974)	0	0	0	0
Jenny Chuasiriporn	1998	3	0	2	1
Peggy Conley	1964-68	6	3	1	2
Mary Ann Cook (Downey)	1956	2	1	1	0
Patricia Cornett	1978-88	4	1	2	1
Brenda Corrie Kuehn	1996-98	7	4	3	0
Jean Crawford (Ashley)	1962-66-68-(72)	8	6	2	0
Clifford Ann Creed	1962	2	2	0	0
Grace Cronin (Lenczyk)	1948-50	3	2	1	0
Carolyn Cudone	1956-(70)	1	1	0	0
Beth Daniel	1976-78	8	7	1	0
Virginia Dennehy	(1958)	0	0	0	0
Virginia Derby-Grimes	1998	3	2	0	1
Mary Lou Dill	1968	3	1	1	1
Alice Dye	1970	2	1	0	1

Name	Year	Played	Won	Lost	Halved
Heather Farr	1984	3	2	1	0
Jane Fassinger	1970	1	0	1	0
Mary Lena Faulk	1954	2	1	1	0
Carol Sorensen Flenniken (Sorensen)	1964-66	8	6	1	1
Edith Flippin (Quier)	(1954)-(56)	0	0	0	0
Amy Fruhwirth	1992	4	0	1	3
Kim Gardner	1986	3	1	1	1
Charlotte Glutting	1934-36-38	5	3	1	1
Vicki Goetze	1990-92	8	4	2	2
Brenda Goldsmith	1978-80	4	2	2	0
Aniela Goldthwaite	1934-(52)	1	0	1	0
Joanne Goodwin	1960	2	1	1	0
Mary Hafeman	1980	2	1	0	1
Shelley Hamkin	1968-70	8	3	3	2
Penny Hammel	1984	3	1	1	1
Nancy Hammer (Hager)	1970	2	1	1	0
Cathy Hanlon	1982	3	2	1	0
Beverley Hanson	1950	2	2	0	0
Tracy Hanson	1992	3	1	2	0
Patricia Harbottle (Lesser)	1954-56	3	2	1	0
Helen Hawes	(1964)	0	0	0	0
Kathryn Hemphill	1938	1	0	0	1
Helen Hicks	1932	2	1	1	0
Carolyn Hill	1978	2	0	0	2
Cindy Hill	1970-74-76-78	14	5	6	3
Opel Hill	1932-34-36	6	2	3	1
Marion Hollins	(1932)	0	0	0	0
Dana Howe	1984	3	1	1	1
Juli Inkster	1982	4	4	0	0
Maria Jemsek	1996	3	0	2	1
Ann Casey Johnstone	1958-60-62	4	3	1	0
Mae Murray Jones (Murray)	1952	1	0	1	0
Wendy Kaupp	1994	2	0	2	0
Caroline Keggi	1988	3	0	2	1
Tracy Kerdyk	1988	4	2	1	1
Cristie Kerr	1996	3	1	1	1
Kandi Kessler	1986	3	1	1	1
Dorothy Kielty	1948-50	4	4	0	0
Dorothy Kirby	1948-50-52-54	7	4	3	0
Martha Kirouac (Wilkinson)	1970-72	8	5	3	0
Emilee Klein	1994	4	3	1	0
Nancy Knight (Lopez)	1976	2	2	0	0
Kelli Kuehne	1996	3	2	1	0
Martha Lang	1992-(96)	3	2	0	1
Bonnie Lauer	1974	4	2	2	0
Sarah Le Brun Ingram	1992-94-96	7	2	4	1
Marjorie Lindsay	1952	2	1	1	0
Patricia Lucey (O'Sullivan)	1952	1	0	1	0
Mari McDougall	1982	2	2	0	0
Jill McGill	1994	4	1	1	2
Barbara McIntire	1958-60-62-64-66-72-(76)	16	6	6	4
Lucile Mann (Robinson)	1934	1	0	1	0
Debbie Massey	1974-76	5	5	0	0
Marion Miley	1938	2	1	0	1
Dottie Mochrie (Pepper)	1986	3	0	2	1
Evelyn Monsted	(1968)	0	0	0	0
Terri Moody	1980	2	1	0	1
Karen Noble	1990	4	2	2	0
Judith Oliver	1978-80-82-(92)	8	5	1	2
Maureen Orcutt	1932-34-36-38	8	5	3	0
Joanne Pacillo	1984	3	1	1	1
Estelle Page (Lawson)	1938-48	4	3	1	0
Katie Peterson	1990	3	3	0	0
Margaret Platt	1990	2	0	2	0
Frances Pond (Stebbins)	(1938)	0	0	0	0
Ellen Port	1994-96	6	4	2	0
Dorothy Germain Porter	1950-(66)	2	1	0	1
Phyllis Preuss	1962-64-66-68-70-(84)	15	10	4	1
Betty Probasco	(1982)	0	0	0	0
Mildred Prunaret	(1960)	0	0	0	0

continued

Curtis Cup Individual Records *continued*

Name	Year	Played	Won	Lost	Halved
Polly Riley	1948-50-52-54-56-58-(62)	10	5	5	0
Jo Jo Robertson	1998	2	0	2	0
Barbara Romack	1954-56-58	5	3	2	0
Jody Rosenthal	1984	3	2	0	1
Anne Sander [Welts] [Decker] (Quast)	1958-60-62-66-68-74-84-90	22	11	7	4
Cindy Scholefield	1988	3	0	3	0
Cindy Schreyer	1986	3	1	2	0
Kathleen McCarthy Scrivner (McCarthy)	1986-88	6	2	3	1
Carol Semple Thompson	1974-76-80-82-90-92-94-96-**98**	29	13	12	4
Leslie Shannon	1986-88-90-92	9	1	6	2
Patty Sheehan	1980	4	4	0	0
Pearl Sinn	1988	2	1	1	0
Grace De Moss Smith (De Moss)	1952-54	3	1	2	0
Lancy Smith	1972-78-80-82-84-(**94**)	16	7	5	4
Margaret Smith	1956	2	2	0	0
Stephanie Sparks	1994	2	0	2	0
Hollis Stacy	1972	2	0	1	1
Claire Stancik (Doran)	1952-54	4	4	0	0
Judy Street (Eller)	1960	2	2	0	0
Louise Suggs	1948	2	0	1	1
Nancy Roth Syms (Roth)	1964-66-76-(**80**)	9	3	5	1
Noreen Uihlein	1978	3	1	1	1
Virginia Van Wie	1932-34	4	3	0	1
Glenna Collett Vare (Collett)	1932-(**34**)-**36**-38-48-(**50**)	7	4	2	1
Wendy Ward	1994	3	1	2	0
Jane Weiss (Nelson)	1956	1	0	1	0
Robin Weiss	1990-92	5	3	1	1
Donna White (Horton)	1976	2	2	0	0
Mary Anne Widman	1984	3	2	1	0
Kimberley Williams	1986	3	0	3	0
Helen Sigel Wilson (Sigel)	1950-66-(**78**)	2	0	2	0
Joyce Ziske	1954	1	0	1	0

Women's World Amateur Team Championship for the Espirito Santo Trophy

Year	Winners	Runners-up	Venue	Score
1964	France	United States	St Germain	588
1966	United States	Canada	Mexico	580
1968	United States	Australia	Melbourne	616
1970	United States	France	Madrid	598
1972	United States	France	Buenos Aires	583
1974	United States	GB&I, South Africa	Dominican Republic	620
1976	United States	France	Vilamoura, Portugal	605
1978	Australia	Canada	Fiji	596
1980	United States	Australia	Pinehurst, USA	588
1982	United States	New Zealand	Geneva, Switzerland	579
1984	United States	France	Hong Kong	585
1986	Spain	France	Caracas, Venezuela	580
1988	United States	Sweden	Drottningholm, Sweden	587
1990	United States	New Zealand	Christchurch, New Zealand	585
1992	Spain	GB&I	Vancouver, Canada	588
1994	United States	Korea	Paris, France	569
1996	Korea	Italy	Manila, Philippines	438

1998 *at Santiago, Chile*
Discarded scores in brackets

```
1     UNITED STATES       143-134-139-142—558
      J Chuasiriporn       71- 65- 69- 71
      K Booth              72-(70)- 70- 71
      B Corrie Kuehn      (74)- 69-(74)-(76)
```

2T	ITALY	153-143-143-140—579
	G Sergas	(79)-70- 69- 74
	F Piovano	78-(74)-(75)- 66
	S Sandolo	75- 73- 74- (75)
	GERMANY	149-141-145-144—579
	M Eberl	72- 68- 75- 73
	N Stillig	77- 73-(78)- 71
	M Nagl	(79)-(76)-70-(76)

Leading Individual Scores

1	J Chuasiriporn (US)	276
2	K Booth (US)	283
3	M Eberl (Ger)	288

Commonwealth Tournament (Instituted 1959, played every four years)

Year	Winner	Venue	Year	Winner	Venue
1959	Great Britain	St Andrews	1983	Australia	Glendale, Edmonton, Canada
1963	Great Britain	Royal Melbourne, Australia	1987	Canada	Christchurch, New Zealand
1967	Great Britain	Ancaster, Ontario, Canada	1991	Great Britain	Northumberland, England
1971	Great Britain	Hamilton, New Zealand	1995	Australia	Royal Sydney, Australia
1975	Great Britain	Ganton, England			
1979	Canada	Lake Karrinup, Perth, Australia			

Womens' European Amateur Team Championship

Year	Winner	Second	Venue	Year	Winner	Second	Venue
1967	England	France	Penina, Portugal	1983	Ireland	England	Waterloo, Belgium
1969	France	England	Tylosand, Sweden	1985	England	Italy	Stavanger, Norway
1971	England	France	Ganton, England	1987	Sweden	Wales	Turnberry, Scotland
1973	England	France	Brussels, Belgium	1989	France	England	Pals, Spain
1975	France	Spain	Paris, France	1991	England	Sweden	Wentworth, England
1977	England	Spain	Sotogrande, Spain	1993	England	Spain	Royal Haagshe
1979	Ireland	Germany	Hermitage, Ireland	1995	Spain	Scotland	Milan, Italy
1981	Sweden	France	Troia, Portugal	1997	Sweden	Scotland	Nordcenter, Finland

Vagliano Trophy – Great Britain & Ireland v Europe

Played for biennially between teams of women amateur golfers representing the British Isles and Europe. (From 1947–57 was played between the British Isles and France.)

Year	Winner	Result	Venue
1959	Great Britain & Ireland	12–3	Wentworth
1961	Great Britain & Ireland	8–7	Villa d'Este
1963	Great Britain & Ireland	20–10	Muirfield
1965	Continent of Europe	17–13	Cologne
1967	Continent of Europe	15½–14½	R Lytham and St Annes
1969	Continent of Europe	16–14	Chantilly
1971	Great Britain & Ireland	17½–12½	Worplesdon
1973	Great Britain & Ireland	20–10	Eindhoven
1975	Great Britain & Ireland	13½–10½	Muirfield
1977	Great Britain & Ireland	15½–8½	Malmo
1979	Halved	12–12	R Porthcawl
1981	Continent of Europe	14–10	P de Hierro
1983	Great Britain & Ireland	14–10	Woodhall Spa
1985	Great Britain & Ireland	14–10	Hamburg
1987	Great Britain & Ireland	15–9	The Berkshire
1989	Great Britain & Ireland	14½–9½	Venice
1991	Great Britain & Ireland	13½–10½	Nairn
1993	Great Britain & Ireland	13½–10½	Morfontaine
1995	Continent of Europe	14–10	Ganton
1997	Continent of Europe	14–10	Halmstad

Women's Home Internationals

Year	Winner	Venue	Year	Winner	Venue
1948	England	R Lytham and St Annes	1971	England	Longniddry
1949	Scotland	Harlech	1972	England	R Lytham and St Annes
1950	Scotland	Newcastle Co Down	1973	England	Harlech
1951	Scotland	Broadstone	1974T	England/Scotland/Ireland	Sandwich, Princes
1952	Scotland	Troon			
1953	England	Porthcawl	1975	England	Newport
1954T	England/Scotland	Ganton, Scotland	1976	England	Troon
1955	England	Western Gailes	1977	England	Cork
1956	Scotland	Sunningdale	1978	England	Moortown
1957	Scotland	Troon	1979T	Scotland/Ireland	Harlech
1958	England	Hunstanton	1980	Ireland	Cruden Bay
1959	England	Hoylake	1981	Scotland	Portmarnock
1960	England	Gullane	1982	England	Burnham and Barrow
1961	Scotland	Portmarnock	1983	*Matches abandoned due to weather*	
1962	Scotland	Porthcawl	1984	England	Gullane
1963	England	Formby	1985	England	Waterville
1964	England	Troon	1986	Ireland	Whittington Barracks
1965	England	Portrush	1987	England	Ashburnham
1966	England	Woodhall Spa	1988	Scotland	Barassie
1967	England	Sunningdale	1989	England	Westport
1968	England	Porthcawl	1990	Scotland	Hunstanton
1969T	England/Scotland	Western Gailes	1991	Scotland	Aberdovey
1970	England	Killarney			

1992 at Hamilton, Lanarkshire

Ireland beat Wales	5½ matches to 2½
England halved with Scotland	4 matches each
Scotland beat Wales	6 matches to 3
England beat Ireland	8 matches to 1
Scotland beat Ireland	6 matches to 3
England beat Wales	7½ matches to 1½

Result: England 2½; Scotland 2½; Ireland 1; Wales 0

1993 at Hermitage, Dublin

England beat Wales	7 matches to 2
Scotland beat Ireland	5 matches to 4
England beat Ireland	5½ matches to 3½
Scotland beat Wales	7 matches to 2
England beat Scotland	5½ matches to 3½
Ireland beat Wales	7 matches to 2

Result: England 3; Scotland 2; Ireland 1; Wales 0

1994 at Huddersfield, Yorkshire

England beat Ireland	6½ matches to 2½
Scotland beat Wales	8½ matches to ½
England beat Wales	8 matches to 1
Scotland halved with Ireland	4½ matches to 4½
England beat Scotland	6 matches to 3
Ireland beat Wales	5½ matches to 3½

Result: England 3; Scotland 1½; Ireland 1½; Wales 0

1995 at Wrexham, Clwyd

England beat Scotland	6 matches to 3
Ireland halved with Wales	4½ matches to 4½
Ireland beat Scotland	5 matches to 4
Wales beat England	5 matches to 4
England beat Ireland	9 matches to 0
Scotland beat Wales	5 matches to 4

Result: England 2; Wales 1½; Ireland 1½; Scotland 1

1996 at Longniddry

Scotland beat Ireland	5½ matches to 3½
England beat Wales	6 matches to 3
Scotland beat Wales	5 matches to 4
England beat Ireland	6 matches to 3
England beat Scotland	5 matches to 4
Ireland beat Wales	5½ matches to 3½

Result: England 3; Scotland 2; Ireland 1; Wales 0

1997 at Lahinch, Ireland

Ireland beat Wales	6½ matches to 2½
England beat Scotland	6½ matches to 2½
England beat Ireland	6 matches to 3
Scotland beat Wales	5½ matches to 3½
England beat Wales	5 matches to 4
Ireland beat Scotland	7 matches to 2

Result: England 3; Ireland 2; Scotland 1; Wales 0

1998 at Burnham & Berrow

Ireland beat Wales	6 matches to 3
England beat Scotland	6 matches to 3
England beat Ireland	5 matches to 4
Ireland halved with Scotland	4½ matches to 4½
England beat Wales	6½ matches to 2½
Scotland halved with Wales	4½ matches to 4½

Result: England 3; Ireland 1½; Scotland 1; Wales ½

England and Wales Ladies' County Championship

Year	Winner	Year	Winner	Year	Winner
1908	Lancashire	1948	Yorkshire	1974	Surrey
1909	Surrey	1949	Surrey	1975	Glamorgan
1910	Cheshire	1950	Yorkshire	1976	Staffordshire
1911	Cheshire	1951	Lancashire	1977	Essex
1912	Cheshire	1952	Lancashire	1978	Glamorgan
1913	Surrey	1953	Surrey	1979	Essex
1920	Middlesex	1954	Warwickshire	1980	Lancashire
1921	Surrey	1955	Surrey	1981	Glamorgan
1922	Surrey	1956	Kent	1982	Surrey
1923	Surrey	1957	Middlesex	1983	Surrey
1924	Surrey	1958	Lancashire	1984	Surrey/Yorkshire
1925	Surrey	1959	Middlesex	1985	Surrey
1926	Surrey	1960	Lancashire	1986	Glamorgan
1927	Yorkshire	1961	Middlesex	1987	Lancashire
1928	Cheshire	1962	Staffordshire	1988	Surrey
1929	Yorkshire	1963	Warwickshire	1989	Cheshire
1930	Surrey	1964	Lancashire	1990	Cheshire
1931	Middlesex	1965	Staffordshire	1991	Glamorgan
1932	Cheshire	1966	Lancashire	1992	Hampshire
1933	Yorkshire	1967	Lancashire	1993	Lancashire
1934	Surrey	1968	Surrey	1994	Staffordshire
1935	Essex	1969	Lancashire	1995	Hampshire
1936	Surrey	1970	Yorkshire	1996	Cheshire
1937	Surrey	1971	Kent	1997	Surrey
1938	Lancashire	1972	Kent		
1947	Surrey	1973	Northumberland		

1998 *at Ulverton*
1 Yorkshire 2 Surrey 3 Devon 4 Worcestershire

Scottish Ladies' County Championship

Year	Winner	Year	Winner
1989	Lanarkshire	1994	East Lothian
1990	East Lothian	1995	Fife
1991	East Lothian	1996	East Lothian
1992	Dunbartonshire & Argyll	1997	Dunbartonshire & Argyll
1993	Gullane	1998	East Lothian

Scottish Ladies' Foursomes

Year	Winner	Year	Winner
1989	Gullane	1994	Turnberry
1990	Gullane	1995	Gullane
1991	West of Scotland Girls' Golf Assoc.	1996	Hilton Park
		1997	Stirling
1992	Haggs Castle	1998	Prestonfield
1993	North Berwick		

Welsh Ladies' Team Championship

Year	Winner	Year	Winner
1989	Llandudno (Maesdu)	1993	Pennard
		1994	St Pierre
1990	Llandudno (Maesdu)	1995	R. St Davids
		1996	R. St Davids
1991	Wenvoe Castle	1997	St Pierre
1992	Whitchurch	1998	Wrexham

Other Women's Amateur Tournaments

Astor Salver (Inaugurated 1951)

Year	Winner	Year	Winner
1988	J Thornhill	1994	S Lambert
1989	S Sutton	1995	J Oliver
1990T	J Hall/J Morley	1996	S Gallagher
1991	EJ Smith	1997	J Lamb
1992	L Walton	1998	R Morgan
1993	S Lambert		

Bridget Jackson Bowl at Handsworth

Year	Winner	Year	Winner
1991	F Edmond	1995	K Stupples
1992	F Brown	1996	R Hudson
1993	S Morgan	1997	K Macintosh
1994	K Speak	1998	C Dowling

Hampshire Rose (Inaugurated 1973) at North Hants

Year	Winner	Year	Winner
1989	A MacDonald	1994T	K Shepherd/K Egford
1990	S Keogh	1995	J Oliver
1991	K Egford	1996	K Stupples
1992	A Uzielli	1997	S Sanderson
1993	C Hourihane	1998	C Court

Mothers and Daughters Foursomes
at Royal Mid-Surrey

Year	Winner	Year	Winner
1991	Mrs P Carrick and Mrs A Uzielli	1996T	Mrs A Uzielli and Miss C Uzielli
1992	Mrs P Carrick and Mrs A Uzielli		Mrs E Boatman and Miss A Boatman
1993	Mrs P Carrick and Mrs A Uzielli		Mrs S Lines and Miss K Lines
1994	Mrs P Carrick and Mrs A Uzielli	1997	Mrs S Lines and Miss K Lines
1995T	Mrs P Carrick and Mrs A Uzielli	1998	Mrs H Joyce and Miss C Joyce
	Mrs P Huntley and Miss J Huntley		

St Rule Trophy at St Andrews

Year	Winner	Score	Year	Winner	Score
1990	A Sörenstam	228	1995	M Hjorth	220
1991	A Rose	237	1996	A Laing	227
1992	M Wright	222	1997	K Rostron	217
1993	C Lambert	215	1998	N Clau[†]	154 (36)
1994	C Matthew	217			

[†] *At 16 years, the youngest ever winner*

Women's Regional Amateur Championships

Aberdeenshire Ladies'

Year	Winner	Year	Winner
1989	J Forbes	1994	C Hunter
1990	E Farquharson	1995	J Matthews
1991	C Middleton	1996	S Wood
1992	R MacLennan	1997	K Moggach
1993	G Penny	1998	L Urquhart

Angus Ladies'

Year	Winner	Year	Winner
1989	C Hope	1994	M Summers
1990	K Sutherland	1995	K Sutherland
1991	M Summers	1996	S Simpson
1992	M Summers	1997	S Raitt
1993	M Summers	1998	L Fenton

Ayrshire Ladies'

Year	Winner	Year	Winner
1989	A Gemmill	1994	A Gemmill
1990	C Gibson	1995	R Kennedy
1991	A Gemmill	1996	A Gemmill
1992	C Gibson	1997	A Gemmill
1993	M Wilson	1998	S Lambie

Bedfordshire Ladies'

Year	Winner	Year	Winner
1989	T Gale	1994	T Gale
1990	C Cummings	1995	A Bradley
1991	E James	1996	C Hoskin
1992	S Cormack	1997	J Faris
1993	S Cormack	1998	S Cormack

Berkshire Ladies'

Year	Winner	Year	Winner
1989	L Walton	1994	J Guntrip
1990	A Uzielli	1995	A Uzielli
1991	A Uzielli	1996	S Sanderson
1992	J Guntrip	1997	L Meredith
1993	A Uzielli	1998	S Sanderson

Border Counties Ladies'

Year	Winner	Year	Winner
1989	A Fleming	1994	W Wells
1990	J Anderson	1995	A Fleming
1991	J Anderson	1996	K Inkpen
1992	J Anderson	1997	J Anderson
1993	D Turnbull	1998	A Hunter

Bucks Ladies'

Year	Winner	Year	Winner
1989	C Hourihane	1994	P Williamson
1990	C Watson	1995	C Dowling
1991	C Watson	1996	C Watson
1992	C Watson	1997	C Watson
1993	C Watson	1998	C Watson

Caernarfonshire and Anglesey Ladies'

Year	Winner	Year	Winner
1989	S Roberts	1994	C Thomas
1990	S Roberts	1995	L Davies
1991	Not played	1996	L Davies
1992	S Turner	1997	F Vaughan-Thomas
1993	A Lewis	1998	F Vaughan-Thomas

Cambridgeshire and Hunts Ladies'

Year	Winner	Year	Winner
1989	J Hatcher	1994	T Eakin
1990	J Walter	1995	P Parker
1991	J Walter	1996	J Walter
1992	T Eakin	1997	J Walter
1993	T Eakin	1998	J Walter

Channel Islands Ladies'

Year	Winner	Year	Winner
1989	L Cummins	1994	L Cummins
1990	L Cummins	1995	M Chamberlayne
1991	L Cummins	1996	J Deeley
1992	V Bougourd	1997	J Deeley
1993	L Cummins	1998	J Deeley

Cheshire Ladies'

Year	Winner	Year	Winner
1989	J Morley	1994	F Brown
1990	J Morley	1995	E Ratcliffe
1991	F Brown	1996	L Dermott
1992	J Morley	1997	E Ratcliffe
1993	J Morley	1998	E Ratcliffe

Cornwall Ladies'

Year	Winner	Year	Winner
1989	S Currie	1994	E Fields
1990	S Currie	1995	L Simpson
1991	S Currie	1996	L Simpson
1992	G Fields	1997	L Simpson
1993	J Ryder	1998	G Dowling

Cumbria Ladies'

Year	Winner	Year	Winner
1989	S Tuck	1994	J Currie
1990	S Tuck	1995	J Viles
1991	J Currie	1996	R Bruce
1992	J Currie	1997	J Blaydes
1993	J Currie	1998	A Wood

Denbighshire and Flintshire Ladies'

Year	Winner	Year	Winner
1989	S Thomas	1994	A Donne
1990	L Dermott	1995	S Lovatt
1991	B Jones	1996	B Jones
1992	B Jones	1997	R Brewerton
1993	S Lovatt	1998	B Jones

Derbyshire Ladies'

Year	Winner	Year	Winner
1989	D Andrews	1994	L Walters
1990	D Andrews	1995	L Holmes
1991	L Holmes	1996	L Shaw
1992	L Holmes	1997	L Walters
1993	L Holmes	1998	L Shaw

Devon Ladies'

Year	Winner	Year	Winner
1989	S Germain	1994	K Tebbet
1990	V Holloway	1995	J Roberts
1991	K Tebbet	1996	R Cirin
1992	K Tebbet	1997	J Roberts
1993	K Tebbet	1998	C Copping

Dorset Ladies'

Year	Winner	Year	Winner
1989	T Loveys	1994	W Russell
1990	T Loveys	1995	A Monk
1991	H Davidson	1996	C Brown
1992	S Lowe	1997	A Monk
1993	S Sanderson	1998	A Monk

Dumfriesshire Ladies'

Year	Winner	Year	Winner
1989	D Douglas	1994	F Watson
1990	L Armstrong	1995	D Douglas
1991	M Morrison	1996	C Adamson
1992	D Douglas	1997	L Wells
1993	G Adamson	1998	D MacDonald

Dunbartonshire and Argyll Ladies'

Year	Winner	Year	Winner
1989	M McKinlay	1994	V Melvin
1990	M McKinlay	1995	A Laing
1991	M McKinlay	1996	V Melvin
1992	J Moodie	1997	K Burns
1993	M McKinlay	1998	A Laing

Durham Ladies'

Year	Winner	Year	Winner
1989	L Still	1994	P Dobson
1990	B Mansfield	1995	K Lee
1991	P Dobson	1996	A Dobson
1992	L Still	1997	K Lee
1993	L Keers	1998	P Dobson

East Anglian Ladies'

Year	Winner	Year	Winner
1989	W Fryer	1994	T Eakin
1990	J Sheldrick	1995	S Little
1991	J Walter	1996	C O'Grady
1992	T Eakin	1997	T Williamson
1993	T Eakin	1998	C Grady

East Lothian Ladies'

Year	Winner	Year	Winner
1989	C Lugton	1994	C Matthew
1990	C Lambert	1995	H Monaghan
1991	S Spiewak	1996	H Monaghan
1992	C Lambert	1997	S McMaster
1993	S McMester	1998	S McEwan

Eastern Division Ladies' (Scotland)

Year	Winner	Year	Winner
1989	H Rose	1994	J Ford
1990	A Hendry	1995	L Nicholson
1991	C Lambert	1996	H Monaghan
1992	J Ford	1997	S Grant
1993	A Rose	1998	F Lockhart

Essex Ladies'

Year	Winner	Year	Winner
1989	A MacDonald	1994	T Wilson
1990	S Bennett	1995	G Scase
1991	M King	1996	G Scase
1992	F Edmond	1997	S Barber
1993	T Poulton	1998	M Williams

Fife County Ladies'

Year	Winner	Year	Winner
1989	J Ford	1994	L Bennett
1990	J Lawrence	1995	K Milne
1991	C McDonald	1996	E Moffat
1992	A Watson	1997	J Hall
1993	K Milne	1998	K Milne

Galloway Ladies'

Year	Winner	Year	Winner
1989	F Rennie	1994	C Meldrum
1990	F Rennie	1995	T Dodds
1991	M Wright	1996	A Cairns
1992	C Meldrum	1997	S McMurtrie
1993	H Nesbit	1998	S McMurtrie

Glamorgan County Ladies'

Year	Winner	Year	Winner
1989	V Thomas	1994	V Thomas
1990	A Perriam	1995	J Thomas
1991	V Thomas	1996	V Thomas
1992	J Foster	1997	V Thomas
1993	V Thomas	1998	P Chugg

Gloucestershire Ladies'

Year	Winner	Year	Winner
1989	S Elliott	1994	K Hamilton
1990	M Mayes	1995	N Sutton
1991	C Hall	1996	J Clingan
1992	C Hall	1997	C Lipscombe
1993	C Hamilton	1998	C Lipscombe

Hampshire Ladies'

Year	Winner	Year	Winner
1989	S Pickles	1994	K Egford
1990	A MacDonald	1995	H Wheeler
1991	H Wheeler	1996	C Stirling
1992	A MacDonald	1997	H Wheeler
1993	K Egford	1998	E Weekes

Herts Ladies'

Year	Winner	Year	Winner
1989	H Kaye	1994	J Oliver
1990	S Alison	1995	J Oliver
1991	A Magee	1996	K Evans
1992	S Alison	1997	K Evans
1993	C Hawkes	1998	M Allen

Isle of Wight Ladies'

Year	Winner	Year	Winner
1989	M Ankers	1994	J Hurd
1990	M Ankers	1995	J Hurd
1991	M Ankers	1996	M Ankers
1992	G Fahy	1997	M Ankers
1993	M Ankers	1998	L Morris

Kent Ladies'

Year	Winner	Year	Winner
1989	S Sutton	1994	M Sutton
1990	H Wadsworth	1995	C Caldwell
1991	H Wadsworth	1996	K Stupples
1992	C Caldwell	1997	S Butchers
1993	M Sutton	1998	K Stupples

Lanarkshire Ladies' County

Year	Winner	Year	Winner
1989	K Dallas	1994	J Gardner
1990	A Hendry	1995	R Rankin
1991	A Hendry	1996	A Prentice
1992	F McKay	1997	L Lloyd
1993	M Hughes	1998	F Prior

Lancashire Ladies'

Year	Winner	Year	Winner
1989	C Blackshaw	1994	G Nutter
1990	L Fairclough	1995	G Nutter
1991	A Baines	1996	A Murray
1992	J Collingham	1997	G Nutter
1993	K Rostron	1998	A Murray

Leicestershire and Rutland Ladies'

Year	Winner	Year	Winner
1989	M Page	1994	M Page
1990	R Reed	1995	C Gay
1991	A Jenno	1996	H Lowe
1992	H Summ	1997	J Morris
1993	M Page	1998	C Gay

Lincolnshire Ladies'

Year	Winner	Year	Winner
1989	H Dobson	1994	S Brook
1990	A Johns	1995	A Thompson
1991	A Thompson	1996	M Willerton
1992	R Jones	1997	A Thompson
1993	R Broughton	1998	M Willerton

London Ladies' Foursomes

Year	Winner	Year	Winner
1988	Harpenden	1994	Knebworth
1989	Walton Heath	1995	The Berkshire
1990	Stoke Poges	1996	The Berkshire
1991	Stoke Poges	1997	The Berkshire
1992	Chelmsford	1998	The Berkshire
1993	Knebworth		

Middlesex Ladies'

Year	Winner	Year	Winner
1989	S Keogh	1994	M Henderson
1990	S Keogh	1995	J Sadler
1991	J Dannhauser	1996	P Ramchand
1992	J Sadler	1997	J Barnett
1993	L Housman	1998	J Sadler

Midland Ladies'

Year	Winner	Year	Winner
1989	R Bolas	1994	J Morris
1990	J Hockley	1995	K Edwards
1991	R Millington	1996	S Gallagher
1992	R Bolas	1997	R Bailey
1993	R Bolas	1998	N Lawrenson

Midlothian Ladies'

Year	Winner	Year	Winner
1989	E Bruce	1994	E Bruce
1990	E Jack	1995	P Silver
1991	E Bruce	1996	M Quigley
1992	K Marshall	1997	P Silver
1993	E Bruce	1998	V Laing

Mid-Wales Ladies'

Year	Winner	Year	Winner
1989	S Wilson	1994	G Gibb
1990	P Morgan	1995	J James
1991	T Gittens	1996	L Davies
1992	P Morgan	1997	K Humphries
1993	A Owen	1998	A Hubbard

Monmouthshire Ladies'

Year	Winner	Year	Winner
1989	B Chambers	1994	E Pilgrim
1990	W Wood	1995	E Pilgrim
1991	W Wood	1996	C Waite
1992	R Morgan	1997	S O'Sullivan
1993	S Musto	1998	S O'Sullivan

Norfolk Ladies'

Year	Winner	Year	Winner
1989	T Keeley	1994	J Wilkerson
1990	T Ireland	1995	J Wilkerson
1991	T Williamson	1996	C Grady
1992	T Williamson	1997	T Williamson
1993	T Williamson	1998	T Williamson

Northamptonshire Ladies'

Year	Winner	Year	Winner
1989	C Gibbs	1994	S Sharpe
1990	C Gibbs	1995	S Sharpe
1991	C Gibbs	1996	S Carter
1992	G Gibbs	1997	S Carter
1993	S Sharpe	1998	C Gibbs

Northern Counties (Scotland) Ladies'

Year	Winner	Year	Winner
1989	E Fiskin	1994	L Roxburgh
1990	F McKay	1995	F McKay
1991	M Vass	1996	F McLennan
1992	I Shannon	1997	E Vass
1993	S Alexander	1998	L Vass

Northern Women's (ELGA)

Year	Winner	Year	Winner
1989	L Fletcher	1994	G Nutter
1990	L Fairclough	1995	K Rostron
1991	C White	1996	K Rostron
1992	G Simpson	1997	G Nutter
1993	A Brighouse	1998	R Lomas

Northern Women's Counties Championship

Year	Winner	Year	Winner
1993	Lancashire	1996	Lancashire
1994	Lancashire	1997	Lancashire
1995	Cheshire	1998	Yorkshire

Northern Division Ladies' (Scotland)

Year	Winner	Year	Winner
1989	S Wood	1994	J Matthews
1990	K Imrie	1995	J Harrison
1991	C Middleton	1996	J Harrison
1992	S Alexander	1997	C Hunter
1993	S Alexander	1998	J Tough

Northumberland Ladies'

Year	Winner	Year	Winner
1989	D Glenn	1994	D Glenn
1990	L Fletcher	1995	H Wilson
1991	C Hall	1996	C Hall
1992	C Hall	1997	C Hall
1993	H Wilson	1998	C Hall

Nottinghamshire Ladies'

Year	Winner	Year	Winner
1989	A Peters	1994	G Palmer
1990	L Broughton	1995	G Palmer
1991	L Broughton	1996	L Wright
1992	S Bishop	1997	J Collingham
1993	L Rayner	1998	J Collingham

Oxfordshire Ladies'

Year	Winner	Year	Winner
1989	L King	1994	L King
1990	N Sparks	1995	L King
1991	L King	1996	L King
1992	L King	1997	L King
1993	N Sparks	1998	N Woolford

Perth and Kinross Ladies'

Year	Winner	Year	Winner
1989	A Sharp	1994	C Dunbar
1990	S Mailer	1995	F Farquharson
1991	I Shannon	1996	E Wilson
1992	S Mailer	1997	N Harding
1993	E Wilson	1998	J Yellowlees

Renfrewshire County Ladies'

Year	Winner	Year	Winner
1989	D Jackson	1994	C Agnew
1990	D Jackson	1995	D Jackson
1991	D Jackson	1996	D Jackson
1992	D Jackson	1997	L Robertson
1993	K Fitzgerald	1998	K Fitzgerald

Shropshire Ladies'

Year	Winner	Year	Winner
1989	C Gauge	1994	A Johnson
1990	J Marvell	1995	B Smith
1991	A Johnson	1996	B Smith
1992	A Johnson	1997	S Heath
1993	A Johnson	1998	L Archer

Somerset Ladies'

Year	Winner	Year	Winner
1989	K Nicholls	1994	S Burnell
1990	K Nicholls	1995	L Wixon
1991	S Whiting	1996	L Wixon
1992	C Whiting	1997	L Wixon
1993	R Murr	1998	G Pritchard

South-Eastern Ladies'

Year	Winner	Year	Winner
1989	A MacDonald	1994	K Egford
1990	A MacDonald	1995	K Smith
1991	K Egford	1996	J Oliver
1992	A MacDonald	1997	L Evans
1993	K Smith	1998	A Waller

Southern Division Ladies' (Scotland)

Year	Winner	Year	Winner
1989	F Rennie	1994	D Douglas
1990	F Rennie	1995	J Anderson
1991	J Anderson	1996	D Douglas
1992	D Douglas	1997	J Anderson
1993	C Meldrum	1998	D MacDonald

South of Scotland Ladies'

Year	Winner	Year	Winner
1989	M Wright	1994	F Rennie
1990	M Wright	1995	C Meldrum
1991	F Rennie	1996	S McMurtrie
1992	M Wilson	1997	J Anderson
1993	D Douglas	1998	D Sutton

South-Western Women's

Year	Winner	Year	Winner
1989	C Hall	1994	R Morgan
1990	V Thomas	1995	E Fields
1991	V Thomas	1996	B Morgan
1992	C Hall	1997	E Pilgrim
1993	E Fields	1998	C Lipscombe

Warwickshire Ladies'

Year	Winner	Year	Winner
1989	S Morgan	1994	S Westhall
1990	S Morgan	1995	S Westhall
1991	S Morgan	1996	C Dowling
1992	N Moutt	1997	C Dowling
1993	S Morgan	1998	C Dowling

Staffordshire Ladies'

Year	Winner	Year	Winner
1989	R Bolas	1994	S Gallagher
1990	R Bolas	1995	K Edwards
1991	R Bolas	1996	S Gallagher
1992	P Hale	1997	K Edwards
1993	R Bolas	1998	K Edwards

Western Division Ladies' (Scotland)

Year	Winner	Year	Winner
1989	K Dallas	1994	V Melvin
1990	S Spiewak	1995	A Hendry
1991	J Moodie	1996	K Fitzgerald
1992	M McKinlay	1997	C Malcolm
1993	J Moodie	1998	A Laing

Stirling and Clackmannan County Ladies'

Year	Winner	Year	Winner
1989	J Abernethy	1994	H Stirling
1990	A Rose	1995	S Grant
1991	A Rose	1996	H Hume
1992	A Rose	1997	S Grant
1993	H Stirling	1998	L Kenny

Wiltshire Ladies'

Year	Winner	Year	Winner
1989	J Lawrence	1994	S Sutton
1990	M Johnston	1995	J Lamb
1991	S Sutton	1996	J Lamb
1992	S Sutton	1997	J Lamb
1993	V Hanks	1998	W Martin

Suffolk Ladies'

Year	Winner	Year	Winner
1989	J Hall	1994	J Hockley
1990	J Hall	1995	J Hall
1991	J Hall	1996	J Hockley
1992	J Hall	1997	L Wright
1993	J Hall	1998	J Hockley

Worcestershire Ladies'

Year	Winner	Year	Winner
1989	L Waring	1994	N Lawrenson
1990	J Deeley	1995	S Tufnall
1991	L Jones	1996	N Lawrenson
1992	L Montgomery	1997	N Lawrenson
1993	L Jones	1998	N Lawrenson

Surrey Ladies'

Year	Winner	Year	Winner
1989	J Thornhill	1994	S Lambert
1990	W Wooldridge	1995	J Thornhill
1991	J Thornhill	1996	L McGowan
1992	J Thornhill	1997	J Thornhill
1993	S Lambert	1998	K Burton

Yorkshire Ladies'

Year	Winner	Year	Winner
1989	K Firth	1994	N Buxton
1990	N Buxton	1995	R Hudson
1991	N Buxton	1996	J Aldersley
1992	N Buxton	1997	R Hudson
1993	N Buxton	1998	R Hudson

Sussex Ladies'

Year	Winner	Year	Winner
1989	M Cornelius	1994	J Head
1990	M Cornelius	1995	Z Steel
1991	K Mitchell	1996	C Court
1992	J Head	1997	C Court
1993	C Titcomb	1998	J Galway

Women's Amateur Championships Overseas

Australian Ladies' Amateur

Year	Winner	Year	Winner
1989	J Higgins	1994	T McKinnon
1990	J Shearwood	1995	J Hall (GB)
1991	L Briers	1996	D Linnertson
1992	J Leary	1997	M Ellis
1993	A-M Knight	1998	M Ellis

Austrian Ladies' Amateur

Year	Winner	Year	Winner
1989	K Poppmeier	1994	M Fischer
1990	A Rast	1995	A Heuser
1991	L Navarro	1996	E Poburski
1992	K Poppmeier	1997	T Schneeberger
1993	N Fink	1998	C Kuld

Canadian Ladies' Open Amateur

Year	Winner	Year	Winner
1989	C Damphouse	1994	A Robertson
1990	S Lebrun	1995	T Lipp
1991	A Moore	1996	MA Lapointe
1992	MJ Rouleau	1997	AJ Eathorne
1993	MA Lapointe	1998	K Qually

Czechoslovak Ladies' Open Amateur

Year	Winner	Year	Winner
1989	A Kugelmüller	1994	L Křenková
1990	A Kugelmüller	1995	G Teissingová
1991	L Křenková	1996	G Teissingová
1992	L Křenková	1997	G Teissingová
1993	H Dvorská	1998	P Kvídová

Danish Ladies' Strokeplay

Year	Winner	Year	Winner
1989	M Brandt Anderson	1994	C Faaborg
		1995	I Tinning
1990	P Carlson	1996	C Kuld
1991	I Tinning	1997	KM Juul
1992	I Tinning	1998	H Gram
1993	A Östberg		

French Ladies' Amateur

Year	Winner	Year	Winner
1989	C Bourtayre	1994	C Mourgue d'Algue
1990	C Bourson	1995	A Vincent
1991	V Michaud	1996	C Morgue d'Algue
1992	P Mennier	1997	M Monnet
1993	S Louapre-Pfeiffer	1998	A Thevenin

German Ladies' Open Amateur

Year	Winner	Year	Winner
1989	M Fischer	1994	AC Jonasson
1990		1995	C Schmitt
1991	E Knuth	1996	M Neggers
1992	A Heuser	1997	M Eberl
1993	M Koch	1998	G Sergas

New Zealand Ladies' Amateur

Year	Winner	Year	Winner
1989	W Sook	1994	JA Atkin
1990	L Brooky	1995	G Scott
1991	A Stott	1996	L Aldridge
1992	L Lambert	1997	J Oliver
1993	L Brooky	1998	A Parsons

Portuguese Ladies' Open

Year	Winner	Year	Winner
1989	S Clauset	1994	S Dallongeville
1990	S Navarro	1995	ML de Lorenzi
1991	T Abecassis	1996	F Rossary
1992	L Navarro	1997	A Belen Sanchez
1993	M Arruti	1998	V Roques

Spanish Ladies' Open Amateur

Year	Winner	Year	Winner
1989	I Calogero	1994	AC Jonasson
1990	D Bourson	1995	M Jorth
1991	C Quintarelli	1996	J Hall
1992	J Hall	1997	K Icher
1993	C Lambert	1998	F Brown

Swedish Ladies' Open Amateur Strokeplay

Year	Winner	Year	Winner
1989	S Norberg	1994	P Rigby
1990	M Bjurö	1995	M Löjdahl
1991	A Sörenstam	1996	P Rigby-Jinglov
1992	C Sörenstam	1997	M Tveit
1993	D Reid	1998	S Jelander

Swiss Ladies' Open Amateur

Year	Winner	Year	Winner
1989	V Pamard	1994	A Nistri
1990	M Hagemann	1995	M Alsuguren
1991	M Hagemann	1996	M Alsuguren
1992	M Alsuguren	1997	A Gasser
1993	N Fink	1998	S Sandolo

United States Ladies' Amateur Championship

Year	Winner	Runner-up	Venue	By
1960	J Gunderson	J Ashley	Tulsa, OK	6 and 5
1961	A Quast	P Preuss	Tacoma	14 and 13
1962	J Gunderson	A Baker	Rochester, NY	9 and 8
1963	A Quast	P Conley	Williamstown	2 and 1
1964	B McIntyre	J Gunderson	Prairie Dunes, KA	3 and 2
1965	J Ashley	A Quast	Denver	5 and 4
1966	J Carner	JD Streit	Pittsburgh	41st hole
1967	L Dill	J Ashley	Annandale, Pasadena	5 and 4
1968	J Carner	A Quast	Birmingham, MI	5 and 4
1969	C Lacoste (Fra)	S Hamlin	Las Colinas, TX	3 and 2
1970	M Wilkinson	C Hill	Darien, CN	3 and 2
1971	L Baugh	B Barry	Atlanta, GA	1 hole
1972	M Budke	C Hill	St Louis, MO	5 and 4
1973	C Semple	A Quast	Montclair, NJ	1 hole
1974	C Hill	C Semple	Broadmoor, Seattle	5 and 4
1975	B Daniel	D Horton	Brae Burn, MA	3 and 2
1976	D Horton	M Bretton	Del Paso, CA	2 and 1
1977	B Daniel	C Sherk	Cincinnati	3 and 1
1978	C Sherk	J Oliver	Sunnybrook, PA	4 and 3
1979	C Hill	P Sheehan	Memphis, TN	7 and 6
1980	J Inkster	P Rizzo	Prairie Dunes, KA	2 holes
1981	J Inkster	L Coggan (Aus)	Portland, OR	1 hole
1982	J Inkster	C Hanton	Colorado Springs	4 and 3
1983	J Pacillo	S Quinlan	Canoe Brook, NJ	2 and 1
1984	D Richard	K Williams	Broadmoor, Seattle	37th hole
1985	M Hattori (Jpn)	C Stacy	Pittsburgh, PA	5 and 4
1986	K Cockerill	K McCarthy	Pasatiempo, CA	9 and 7
1987	K Cockerill	T Kerdyk	Barrington, RI	3 and 2
1988	P Sinn	K Noble	Minikahde, MN	6 and 5
1989	V Goetze	B Burton	Pinehurst, NC	4 and 3
1990	P Hurst	S Davis	Canoe Brook, NJ	37th hole
1991	A Fruhwirth	H Voorhees	Prairie Dunes	5 and 4
1992	V Goetze	A Sörenstam (Swe)	Kemper Lakes	1 hole
1993	J McGill	S Ingram	San Diego	1 hole
1994	W Ward	J McGill	Hot Springs, VA	2 and 1
1995	K Kuehne	A-M Knight	Brookline	4 and 2
1996	K Kuehne	M Baena	Lincoln, Nebraska	2 and 1
1997	S Cavalleri	R Burke	Brae Burn, MA	5 and 4

1998 *at Blackwolf Run GC, Kohler, Wisconsin*
Quarter Finals
J Chuasiriporn beat A Stanford 4 and 3
B Miller beat N Dalkas 3 and 1
G Park beat E Ratcliffe 2 and 1
M Newton beat S Keever 3 and 2

Semi-Finals
J Chuasiriporn beat B Miller at 21st hole
G Park beat M Newton

Final
G Park beat J Chuasiriporn 7 and 6

PART VI
Junior Tournaments and Events

Index on page 324

Index – Junior Tournaments and Events

Boys' and Youths' Tournaments	325
Boys' Amateur Championship	325
English Boys' Strokeplay Championship	326
English Boys' Under-16 Championship (McGregor Trophy)	327
IMSL Boys' Championship	327
Irish Youth's Open Amateur Championship	327
Scottish Boys' Championship	327
Scottish Boys' Strokeplay Championship	328
Scottish Boys' Under-16 Strokeplay Championship	329
Scottish Youths' Strokeplay Championship	329
Welsh Boys' Championship	329
Welsh Boys' Under-15 Championship	330
Welsh Open Youths' Championship	330
Peter McEvoy Trophy	330
Doug Sanders World Junior Championship	331
Nick Faldo Junior Series	331
Midland Boys' Amateur Championship	331
TEAM EVENTS	
World Junior Team Championship	331
European Boys' Team Championship	331
European Youths' Team Championship	332
Great Britain & Ireland *v* Continent of Europe (Jacques L'Eglise Trophy)	332
Boys' Home Internationals (R&A Trophy)	333
English Boys' County Finals	334
Scottish Boys' Team Championship	334
Girls' Tournaments	335
Girls' British Open Championship	335
English Girls' Championship	336
Irish Girls' Championship	336
Scottish Ladies' Junior Open Strokeplay Championship	337
Scottish Girls' Close Championship	338
Welsh Girls' Championship	338
Nick Faldo Junior Series	339
TEAM EVENTS	
European Lady Juniors' Team Championship	339
Girls' Home International (Stroyan Cup)	340
Golf Foundation Age Goup Championships	341
Boys	341
Girls	342
Duke of York Trophy Winners	343
Golf Foundation Team Championship for Schools for the R&A Trophy	343
PGA European Tour Trophy	343
Golf Foundation Award Winners	344

Boys' and Youths' Tournaments

Boys' Amateur Championship

Year	Winner	Runner-up	Venue	By
1921	ADD Mathieson	GH Lintott	Ascot	37th hole
1922	HS Mitchell	W Greenfield	Ascot	4 and 2
1923	ADD Mathieson	HS Mitchell	Dunbar	3 and 2
1924	RW Peattie	P Manuevrier	Coombe Hill	2 holes
1925	RW Peattie	A McNair	Barnton	4 and 3
1926	EA McRuvie	CW Timmis	Coombe Hill	1 hole
1927	EW Fiddian	K Forbes	Barnton	4 and 2
1928	S Scheftel	A Dobbie	Formby	6 and 5
1929	J Lindsay	J Scott-Riddell	Barnton	6 and 4
1930	J Lindsay	J Todd	Fulwell	9 and 8
1931	H Thomson	F McGloin	Killermont	5 and 4
1932	IS MacDonald	LA Hardie	R Lytham and St Annes	2 and 1
1933	PB Lucas	W McLachlan	Carnoustie	3 and 2
1934	RS Burles	FB Allpass	Moortown	12 and 10
1935	JDA Langley	R Norris	Balgownie, Aberdeen	6 and 5
1936	J Bruen	W Innes	Birkdale	11 and 9
1937	IM Roberts	J Stewart	Bruntsfield	8 and 7
1938	W Smeaton	T Snowball	Moor Park	3 and 2
1939	SB Williamson	KG Thom	Carnoustie	4 and 2
1940-45	Suspended during War			
1946	AFD MacGregor	DF Dunstan	Bruntsfield	7 and 5
1947	J Armour	I Caldwell	Hoylake	5 and 4
1948	JD Pritchett	DH Reid	Barasssie	37th hole
1949	H MacAnespie	NV Drew	St Andrews	3 and 2
1950	J Glover	I Young	R Lytham and St Annes	2 and 1
1951	N Dunn	MSR Lunt	Prestwick	6 and 5
1952	M Bonallack	AE Shepperson	Formby	37th hole
1953	AE Shepperson	AT Booth	Dunbar	6 and 4
1954	AF Bussell	K Warren	Hoylake	38th hole
1955	SC Wilson	BJK Aitken	Barassie	39th hole
1956	JF Ferguson	CW Cole	Sunningdale	2 and 1
1957	D Ball	J Wilson	Carnoustie	2 and 1
1958	R Braddon	IM Stungo	Moortown	4 and 3
1959	AR Murphy	EM Shamash	Pollok	3 and 1
1960	P Cros	PO Green	Olton	5 and 3
1961	FS Morris	C Clark	Dalmahoy	3 and 2
1962	PM Townsend	DC Penman	R Mid-Surrey	1 hole
1963	AHC Soutar	DI Rigby	Prestwick	2 and 1
1964	PM Townsend	RD Gray	Formby	9 and 8
1965	GR Milne	DK Midgley	Gullane	4 and 2
1966	A Phillips	A Muller	Moortown	12 and 11
1967	LP Tupling	SC Evans	Western Gailes	4 and 2
1968	SC Evans	K Dabson	St Annes Old Links	3 and 2
1969	M Foster	M Gray	Dunbar	37th hole
1970	ID Gradwell	JE Murray	Hillside	1 hole
1971	H Clark	G Harvey	Barassie	6 and 5
1972	G Harvey	R Newsome	Moortown	7 and 5
1973	DM Robertson	S Betti	Blairgowrie	5 and 3
1974	TR Shannon	A Lyle	Hoylake	10 and 9
1975	B Marchbank	A Lyle	Bruntsfield	1 hole
1976	M Mouland	G Hargreaves	Sunningdale	6 and 5
1977	I Ford	CR Dalgleish	Downfield	1 hole

continued

Boys' Amateur Championship *continued*

Year	Winner	Runner-up	Venue	By
1978	S Keppler	M Stokes	Seaton Carew	3 and 2
1979	R Rafferty	D Ray	Barassie	6 and 5
1980	D Muscroft	A Llyr	Formby	7 and 6
1981	J Lopez	R Weedon	Gullane	4 and 3
1982	M Grieve	G Hickman	Burnham and Barrow	37th hole
1983	JM Olazabal	M Pendaries	Glenbervie	6 and 5
1984	L Vannett	A Mednick	Royal Porthcawl	2 and 1
1985	J Cook	W Henry	Barnton	5 and 4
1986	L Walker	G King	Seaton Carew	5 and 4
1987	C O'Carrol	P Olsson	Barassie	3 and 1
1988	S Pardoe	D Haines	Formby	3 and 2
1989	C Watts	C Fraser	Nairn	5 and 3
1990	M Welch	M Ellis	Hunstanton	3 and 1
1991	F Valera	R Walton	Montrose	4 and 3
1992	L Westerberg	T Biermann	R Mid-Surrey	3 and 2
1993	D Howell	V Gustavsson	Glenbervie	3 and 1
1994	C Smith	C Rodgers	Little Aston	2 and 1
1995	S Young	S Walker	Dunbar	7 and 6
1996	K Ferrie	M Pilkington	Littlestone	2 and 1
1997	S Garcia	R Jones	Saunton	6 and 5

1998 *at Ladybank*

Quarter Finals
O Wilson beat D Jones 1 hole
S Reale beat B Hume 6 and 5
S O'Hara beat T Tuovinen 5 and 4
R Coulson beat R Costello 6 and 5

Semi-Finals
S O'Hara beat R Coulson 2 and 1
S Reale beat O Wilson 7 and 6

Final
S O'Hara beat S Reale 1 hole

English Boys' Strokeplay Championship (formerly Carris Trophy)

Year	Winner	Score	Year	Winner	Score	Year	Winner	Score
1935	R Upex	75 (18)	1960	PM Baxter	150	1979	P Hammond	288
1936	JDA Langley	152	1961	DJ Miller	143	1980	MP McLean	290
1937	RJ White	149	1962	FS Morris	145	1981	D Gilford	290
1938	IP Garrow	147	1963	EJ Threlfall	147	1982	M Jarvis	298
1939	CW Warren	149	1964	PM Townsend	148	1983	P Baker	288
1946	AH Perowne	158	1965	G McKay	145	1984	J Coe	283
1947	I Caldwell	159	1966	A Black	151	1985	P Baker	286
1948	I Caldwell	152	1967	RF Brown	147	1986	G Evans	292
1949	PB Hine	148	1968	P Dawson	149	1987	D Bathgate	289
1950	J Glover	144	1969	ID Gradwell	150	1988	P Page	284
1951	I Young	154	1970	MF Foster	146	1989	I Garbutt	285
1952	N Thygesen	150	1971	RJ Evans	146	1990	M Welch	276
1953	N Johnson	148	1972	L Donovan	143	1991	I Pyman	284
1954	K Warren	149	1973	S Hadfield	148	1992	M Foster	286
1955	ID Wheater	151	1974	KJ Brown	304	1993	J Harris	285
1956	G Maisey	141	1975	A Lyle	270	1994	R Duck	280
1957	G Maisey	145	1976	H Stott	285	1995	J Rose	266
1958	J Hamilton	149	1977	R Mugglestone	293	1996	G Storm	281
1959	RT Walker	152	1978	J Plaxton	144	1997	D Griffiths	283

1998 *at Whittington Heath, Lichfield*

1	S Godfrey	72-76-68-70—286
2	S Robinson	72-74-70-75—291
	D Porter	72-74-70-75—291

English Boys' Under-16 Championship (McGregor Trophy)

Year	Winner	Score
1994	G Storm	291
1995	J Rose	287
1996	E Molinari	291
1997	R Paolillo	285

1998 *at Radcliffe on Trent*

1	M Y Ali	66-70-71-73—280
2	N Dougherty	70-68-73-73—284
3	D Porter	72-72-69-73—286

IMSL (Irish) Boys' Championship

Year	Winner	Runner Up	Venue	Score
1990	R Burns		Kilkenny	213
1991	R Coughlan	R Burns	Thurles	207
1992	J O'Sullivan	D Dunne	Atholone	210
1993	H Armstrong	C McMonagle/P Byrne	Warrenpoint	222
1994	P Byrne	R Leonard/A Thomas	Nenagh	209
1995	L Dalton	M McGreedy	Mullingar	222
1996	M Campbell	L Dalton	Galway	213
1997	M Hoey	D Jones	Galway	217

1998 *at Youghal, Cork*

1	D Jones	74-72-68—214
2	D O'Connor	71-76-68—215
	J Clarke	71-73-71—215

Irish Youths' Open Amateur Championship

Year	Winner	Venue	Score	Year	Winner	Venue	Score
1980	J McHenry	Clandeboye	296	1989	A Mathers	Athlone	280
1981	J McHenry	Westport	303	1990	D Errity	Dundalk	293
1982	K O'Donnell	Mullingar	286	1991	R Coughlan	Lahinch	288
1983	P Murphy	Cork	287	1992	K Nolan	Clandeboye	275
1984	JC Morris	Bangor	292	1993	CD Hislop	Co Sligo	279
1985	J McHenry	Co Sligo	287	1994	B O'Melia	Tullamore	272
1986	JC Morris	Carlow	280	1995	S Young	Ballybunion	286
1987	C Everett	Killarney	300	1996	S Young	Royal Portrush	291
1988	P McGinley	Malone	283	1997	N Howley	Galway	284

1998 *at Headfort*

1	A Murray	70-74-69-68—281
2	D Jones	68-68-71-74—281
3	M Merkes	75-68-70-72—285

Scottish Boys' Championship

Year	Winner	Runner-up	Venue	By
1960	L Carver	S Wilson	North Berwick	6 and 5
1961	K Thomson	G Wilson	North Berwick	10 and 8
1962	HF Urquhart	S MacDonald	North Berwick	3 and 2
1963	FS Morris	I Clark	North Berwick	9 and 8
1964	WR Lockie	MD Cleghorn	North Berwick	1 hole
1965	RL Penman	J Wood	North Berwick	9 and 8
1966	J McTear	DG Greig	North Berwick	4 and 3
1967	DG Greig	I Cannon	North Berwick	2 and 1
1968	RD Weir	M Grubb	North Berwick	6 and 4

continued

Scottish Boys' Championship *continued*

Year	Winner	Runner-up	Venue	By
1969	RP Fyfe	IP Doig	North Berwick	4 and 2
1970	S Stephen	M Henry	North Berwick	38th hole
1971	JE Murray	AA Mackay	North Berwick	4 and 3
1972	DM Robertson	G Cairns	North Berwick	9 and 8
1973	R Watson	H Alexander	North Berwick	8 and 7
1974	DM Robertson	J Cuddihy	North Berwick	6 and 5
1975	A Brown	J Cuddihy	North Berwick	6 and 4
1976	B Marchbank	J Cuddihy	Dunbar	2 and 1
1977	JS Taylor	GJ Webster	Dunbar	3 and 2
1978	J Huggan	KW Stables	Dunbar	2 and 1
1979	DR Weir	S Morrison	West Kilbride	5 and 3
1980	R Gregan	AJ Currie	Dunbar	2 and 1
1981	C Stewart	G Mellon	Dunbar	3 and 2
1982	A Smith	J White	Dunbar	39th hole
1983	C Gillies	C Innes	Dunbar	38th hole
1984	K Buchan	L Vannet	Dunbar	2 and 1
1985	AD McQueen	FJ McCulloch	Dunbar	1 hole
1986	AG Tait	EA McIntosh	Dunbar	6 and 5
1987	AJ Coltart	SJ Bannerman	Dunbar	37th hole
1988	CA Fraser	F Clark	Dunbar	9 and 8
1989	M King	D Brolls	Dunbar	8 and 7
1990	B Collier	D Keeney	West Kilbride	2 and 1
1991	C Hislop	R Thorton	West Kilbride	11 and 9
1992	A Reid	A Forsyth	West Kilbride	2 and 1
1993	S Young	A Campbell	West Kilbride	4 and 2
1994	S Young	E Little	Dunbar	2 and 1
1995	S Young	M Donaldson	R Aberdeen	7 and 6
1996	S Whiteford	I McLaughlin	West Kilbride	3 and 2
1997	M Donaldson	L Rhind	Dunbar	1 hole

1998 *at Murcar*

Quarter Finals
D Sutton beat N Lockie 4 and 3
L Harper beat J Rae 1 hole
S O'Hara beat S Reekie 4 and 3
C Campbell beat S Rennie 3 and 2

Semi-Finals
D Sutton beat L Harper 5 and 3
S O'Hara beat C Campbell 1 hole

Final
S O'Hara beat D Sutton 2 holes

Scottish Boys' Strokeplay Championship

Year	Winner	Venue	Score	Year	Winner	Venue	Score
1970	D Chillas	Carnoustie	298	1984	K Walker	Carnoustie	280
1971	JE Murray	Lanark	274	1985	G Matthew	Baberton	297
1972	S Martin	Montrose	280	1986	G Cassells	Edzell	294
1973	S Martin	Barnton	284	1987	C Ronald	Lanark	287
1974	PW Gallacher	Lundin Links	290	1988	M Urquhart	Dumfries and County	280
1975	A Webster	Kilmarnock Barassie	286	1989	C Fraser	Stirling	282
1976	A Webster	Forfar	292	1990	N Archibald	Monifieth	292
1977T	J Huggan	Renfrew	303	1991	S Gallacher	Crieff	280
	L Mann			1992	S Gallacher	Monifieth	288
1978	R Fraser	Arbroath	283	1993	J Bunch	Powfoot	292
1979	L Mann	Stirling	289	1994	S Young	Drumpellier	288
1980	ASK Glen	Forfar	288	1995	C Lee	Arbroath	284
1981	J Gullen	Bellshill	296	1996	M Brown	Dullatur	286
1982	D Purdie	Monifieth	296	1997	L Rhind	Downfield	287
1983	L Vannet	Barassie	286				

1998 *at Burntisland*

1	G Holland	70-72-71-68—281
2	S Rennie	74-69-71-70—284
3	S Kuczerepa	75-69-67-73—284

Scottish Boys' Under-16 Strokeplay Championship

Year	Winner	Venue	Score	Year	Winner	Venue	Score
1990	G Davidson	W Linton	148	1994	S Fraser	Crieff	142
1991	D Patrick	R Musselburgh	152	1995	C Campbell	Shotts	73 (18)
1992	Not played			1996	P Whiteford	Bothwell	143
1993	S Lamond	Old Ranfurly	150	1997	D Inglis	Glenbervie	139

1998 *at Braehead*
1. D Inglis — 71-68—139
2. J Doherty — 71-74—145
   C MacDonald — 71-74—145

Scottish Youths' Strokeplay Championship

Year	Winner	Venue	Score	Year	Winner	Venue	Score
1979	A Oldcorn	Dalmahoy	217	1989	J Mackenzie	Longniddry	281
1980	G Brand, Jr	Monifieth & Ashludie	281	1990	S Bannerman	Portpatrick & Stranraer	213
1981	S Campbell	Cawder and Keir	279	1991	D Robertson	Hilton Park	273
1982	LS Mann	Leven and Scoonie	270	1992	R Russell	Nairn	296
1983	A Moir	Mortonhall	284	1993	CD Hislop	West Kilbride	284
1984	B Shields	Eastwood, Renfrew	280	1994	S Gallacher	Crieff	275
1985	H Kemp	East Kilbride	282	1995	E Little	Irvine, Ayr	280
1986	A Mednick	Cawder	282	1996	E Little	Stranraer & Portpatrick	280
1987	K Walker	Bogside	291	1997	S Young	Cawder	269
1988	P McGinley	Ladybank & Glenrothes	281				

1998 *at Bruntsfield Links and Royal Burgess*
1. T Rice* — 70-70-69-78—287
2. S O'Hara — 69-72-73-73—287
3. P McKechnie — 71-68-77-72—288

Welsh Boys' Championship

Year	Winner	Runner-up	Venue	By
1960	C Gilford	JL Toye	Llandrindod Wells	5 and 4
1961	AR Porter	JL Toye	Llandrindod Wells	3 and 2
1962	RC Waddilove	W Wadrup	Harlech	20th hole
1963	G Matthews	R Witchell	Penarth	6 and 5
1964	D Lloyd	M Walters	Conway	2 and 1
1965	G Matthews	DG Lloyd	Wenvoe Castle	7 and 6
1966	J Buckley	DP Owen	Holyhead	4 and 2
1967	J Buckley	DL Stevens	Glamorganshire	2 and 1
1968	J Buckley	C Brown	Maesdu	1 hole
1969	K Dabson	P Light	Glamorganshire	5 and 3
1970	P Tadman	A Morgan	Conway	2 and 1
1971	R Jenkins	TJ Melia	Ashburnham	3 and 2
1972	MG Chugg	RM Jones	Wrexham	3 and 2
1973	R Tate	N Duncan	Penarth	2 and 1
1974	D Williams	S Lewis	Llandudno	5 and 4
1975	G Davies	PG Garrett	Glamorganshire	20th hole
1976	JM Morrow	MG Mouland	Caernarvonshire	1 hole
1977	JM Morrow	MG Mouland	Glamorganshire	2 and 1
1978	JM Morrow	A Laking	Harlech	2 and 1
1979	P Mayo	M Hayward	Penarth	24th hole
1980	A Llyr	DK Wood	Llandudno (Maesdu)	2 and 1
1981	M Evans	P Webborn	Pontypool	5 and 4
1982	CM Rees	KH Williams	Prestatyn	2 holes
1983	MA Macara	RN Roderick	Radyr	1 hole
1984	GA Macara	D Bagg	Llandudno	1 hole
1985	B Macfarlane	R Herbert	Cardiff	1 hole
1986	C O'Carroll	GA Macara	Rhuddlan	1 hole

continued

* *Winner after play-off*

Welsh Boys' Championship *continued*

Year	Winner	Runner-up	Venue	By
1987	SJ Edwards	A Herbert	Abergavenny	19th hole
1988	C Platt	P Murphy	Holyhead	2 and 1
1989	R Johnson	RL Evans	Southerndown	2 holes
1990	M Ellis	C Sheppard	Llandudno (Maesdu)	3 and 2
1991	B Dredge	A Cooper	Tenby	2 and 1
1992	Y Taylor	J Pugh	Wrexham	1 hole
1993	R Davies	S Raybould	Pyle and Kenfig	3 and 2
1994	R Peet	K Sullivan	Abergele & Pensarn	7 and 6
1995	M Palmer	O Pughe	Newport	4 and 3
1996	A Smith	M Griffiths	Borth & Ynyslas	at 19th hole
1997	A Lee	I Campbell	Glamorganshire	4 and 3

1998 *at Llandudno*

Quarter Finals
D Price beat G Bennett 2 and 1
B Lee beat A Brown 3 and 2
M Hearne beat M Serpell 1 hole
MJ Setterfield beat J Knight 3 and 2

Semi-Finals
D Price beat B Lee 7 and 6
M Setterfield beat M Hearne 5 and 4

Final
M Setterfield beat D Price 3 and 2

Welsh Boys' Under-15 Championship

1998 *at Aberdare*

1	BM Briscoe	152

Welsh Open Youths' Championship

1998 *at Carmarthen*

1	M Hearne	294

Peter McEvoy Trophy *at Copt Heath*

Year	Winner	Year	Winner
1988	P Sefton	1993	S Webster
1989	D Bathgate	1994	J Harris
1990	P Sherman	1995	C Duke
1991	L Westwood	1996	M Pilkington
1992	B Davis	1997	P Rowe

1998

1	J Rose	75-69-71—215
2	D Griffiths	72-76-68—216
3	J Elson	74-72-71—217

Doug Sanders World Junior Championship
at Newmachar, Aberdeen

Year	Winner	Score	Year	Winner	Score
1990	M Welch (Eng)	276	1994	S Webster (Eng)	275
1991	D Chopra (India)	281	1995	D Gleeson (Aus)	302
1992	F Jacobsen (Swe)	276	1996	M Eibe-Hastrup	281
1993	G Morales (Venezuela)	272	1997	A Scott (Aus)	281

1998

1	A Smith (Eng)	292
2	C Villegas (Colombia)	294
3	J O'Sullivan (Aus)	296

Nick Faldo Junior Series
1998 *at Loch Lomond*

1	G Hyde	66-72—138

Midland Boys' Amateur Championship

Year	Winner	Year	Winner
1989	M Wilson	1995	C Richardson
1990	ML Welch	1996T	S Walker
1991	S Drummond		K Cliffe
1992	S Drummond	1997	K Hale
1993	S Webster	1998	E Vernon
1994	R Duck		

TEAM EVENTS

World Junior Team Championship

Year	Winner	Score
1995	USA	643
1996	Japan	625
1997	USA	864

1998 *at Asahi Kokusai Toyjo G&CC, Toyjo, Japan*

1	England	874
2	Japan	880
3	USA	893

European Boys' Team Championship

Year	Winner	Venue	Year	Winner	Venue
1980	Spain	El Prat GC, Barcelona	1987	Scotland	Chantilly GC, France
1981	England	Olgiata GC, Rome	1988	France	Renfrew GC, Scotland
1982	Italy	Frankfurt GC, Germany	1989	England	Lyckoma, Sweden
1983	Sweden	Helsinki GC, Finland	1990	Spain	Reykjavik, Iceland
1984	Scotland	R St George's, England	1991	Sweden	Oslo, Norway
1985	England	Troia GC, Portugal	1992	Scotland	Conwy, Wales
1986	England	Turin GC, Italy			

continued

European Boys' Team Championship *continued*

Year	Winner	Venue	Year	Winner	Venue
1993	Sweden	Ascona, Switzerland	1996	Spain	Gut Murstatten, Austria
1994	England	Vilamoura, Portugal	1997	Spain	Bled G&CC, Slovenia
1995	England	Woodhall Spa			

1998 *at Gullane, Scotland*
Final
Ireland beat Scotland 4–3

Final Ranking: 1 Ireland, 2 Scotland, 3 England, 4 Italy

European Youths' Team Championship

Year	Winner	Runner-up	Venue
1990	Italy	Sweden	Turin, Italy
1992	Sweden	England	Helsinki, Finland
1994	Ireland	Sweden	Esbjerg, Denmark
1996	Scotland	Spain	Madeira

1998 *at Royal Waterloo Club, Belgium*
Final
Wales beat Sweden 4–3

Final Ranking: 1 Wales, 2 Sweden, 3 Finland, 4 Scotland

Great Britain & Ireland *v* Continent of Europe (Jacques L'Eglise Trophy)

Year	Winner	Result	Venue	Year	Winner	Result	Venue
1958	GB&I	11½–½	Moortown	1983	GB&I	6½–5½	Glenbervie
1959	GB&I	7–2	Pollok	1984	GB&I	6½–5½	Porthcawl
1960	GB&I	8–7	Olton	1985	GB&I	7½–4½	Barnton
1961	GB&I	11–4	Dalmahoy	1986	Europe	8½–3½	Seaton Carew
1962	GB&I	11–4	Mid-Surrey	1987	GB&I	7½–4½	Barassie
1963	GB&I	12–3	Prestwick	1988	GB&I	5½–2½	Formby
1964	GB&I	12–1	Formby	1989	GB&I	7½–4½	Nairn
1965	GB&I	12–1	Gullane	1990	GB&I	10–2	Hunstanton
1966	GB&I	10–2	Moortown	1991	GB&I	6½–5½	Montrose
1967–76	*Not played*			1992	GB&I	8–7	Royal Mid-Surrey
1977	Europe	7–6	Downfield	1993	GB&I	8–7	Glenbervie
1978	Europe	7–6	Seaton Carew	1994	GB&I	12½–2½	Little Aston
1979	GB&I	9½–2½	Barassie	1995	GB&I	9–6	Dunbar
1980	GB&I	7–5	Formby	1996	Europe	13–11	Woodhall Spa
1981	GB&I	8–4	Gullane	1997	Europe	12½–11½	Aberdeen
1982	GB&I	11–1	Burnham & Berrow				

1998 *at Villa d'Este, Italy*

Continent of Europe   **Great Britain & Ireland**

Day One – Foursomes

R Paolillo and E Molinari (3 and 2)	1	D Griffiths and A Frayne	0
R Vera and M Kurhonen	0	I Campbell and S O'Hara (1 hole)	1
N Colsaerts and P Celhay	0	R Symes and J Kehoe (4 and 3)	1
S Reale and M Jorgensen	0	D Jones and N Dougherty (4 and 3)	1
	1		3

Singles

R Ballesteros	0	S O'Hara (3 and 2)	1
E Molinari	0	D Griffiths (4 and 3)	1
R Paolillo (3 and 2)	1	R Symes	0
M Kurhonen (1 hole)	1	J MacDougall	0
P Celhay	½	N Dougherty	½
R Vera	0	A Frayne (4 and 3)	1
N Colsaerts	0	I Campbell (1 hole)	1
S Reale (1 hole)	1	D Jones	0
	3½		4½

Match position: Europe 4½, GB&I 7½

Day Two – **Foursomes**

S Reale and P Celhay	½	D Griffiths and A Frayne	½
R Paolillo and E Molinari (3 and 2)	1	I Campbell and S O'Hara	0
M Kurhonen and N Colsaerts (3 and 2)	1	R Symes and J Kehoe	0
R Vera and R Ballesteros	0	D Jones and N Dougherty (3 and 2)	1
	2½		1½

Singles

R Paolillo	0	S O'Hara (1 hole)	1
M Jorgensen	0	D Griffiths (6 and 5)	1
M Kurhonen (1 hole)	1	A Frayne	0
S Reale	0	J MacDougall (1 hole)	1
R Ballesteros	0	N Dougherty (2 and 1)	1
P Celhay (3 and 2)	1	J Kehoe	0
N Colsaerts (2 and 1)	1	I Campbell	0
R Vera	0	D Jones (3 and 2)	1
	3		5

Result: Europe 10, Great Britain and Ireland 14

Boy's Home Internationals (R&A Trophy) (Instituted 1985)

Year	Winner	Venue
1985T	England/Ireland	Barnton
1986	Ireland	Seaton Carew
1987	Scotland	Barassie
1988	England	Formby
1989	England	Nairn
1990	Scotland	Hunstanton
1991	England	Montrose
1992T	Wales/Scotland	R Mid-Surrey
1993	England	Glenbervie
1994	England	Little Aston
1995	Scotland	Dunbar
1996	England	Littlestone
1997	Ireland	R North Devon

1998 *at St. Andrews*

England beat Wales	12–3
Scotland beat Ireland	9½–5½
England beat Ireland	9½–5½
Scotland beat Wales	10–5
England beat Scotland	9½–5½
Ireland beat Wales	11½–3½

Result: 1 England, 2 Scotland, 3 Ireland, 4 Wales

English Boys' County Finals
1998 *at Delamere Forest*

1	Cheshire
2	Berks, Bucks & Oxon
3	Warwicks
4	Somerset

Scottish Boys' Team Championship
1998 *at Cowglen*

1	Ayrshire	356
2	Lothians	361
3	Dunbartonshire	363

Girls' and Junior Ladies' Tournaments

Girls' British Open Championship

Year	Winner	Runner-up	Venue	By
1960	S Clarke	AL Irvin	Barassie	2 and 1
1961	D Robb	J Roberts	Beaconsfield	3 and 2
1962	S McLaren-Smith	A Murphy	Foxton Hall	2 and 1
1963	D Oxley	B Whitehead	Gullane	2 and 1
1964	P Tredinnick	K Cumming	Camberley Heath	2 and 1
1965	A Willard	A Ward	Formby	3 and 2
1966	J Hutton	D Oxley	Troon Portland	20th hole
1967	P Burrows	J Hutton	Liphook	2 and 1
1968	C Wallace	C Reybroeck	Leven	4 and 3
1969	J de Witt Puyt	C Reybroeck	Ilkley	2 and 1
1970	C Le Feuvre	Michelle Walker	North Wales	2 and 1
1971	J Mark	Maureen Walker	North Berwick	4 and 3
1972	Maureen Walker	S Cadden	Norwich	2 and 1
1973	AM Palli	N Jeanson	Northamptonshire	2 and 1
1974	R Barry	T Perkins	Dunbar	1 hole
1975	S Cadden	L Isherwood	Henbury	4 and 3
1976	G Stewart	S Rowlands	Pyle and Kenfig	5 and 4
1977	W Aitken	S Bamford	Formby Ladies	2 and 1
1978	M L de Lorenzi	D Glenn	Largs	2 and 1
1979	S Lapaire	P Smilie	Edgbaston	19th hole
1980	J Connachan	L Bolton	Wrexham	2 holes
1981	J Connachan	P Grice	Woodbridge	20th hole
1982	C Waite	M Mackie	Edzell	6 and 5
1983	E Orley	A Walters	Leeds	7 and 6
1984	C Swallow	E Farquharson	Maesdu	1 hole
1985	S Shapcott	E Farquharson	Hesketh	3 and 1
1986	S Croce	S Bennett	West Kilbride	5 and 4
1987	H Dobson	S Croce	Barnham Broom	19th hole
1988	A Macdonald	J Posener	Pyle and Kenfig	3 and 2
1989	M McKinlay	S Eriksson	Carlisle	19th hole
1990	S Cavalleri	E Valera	Penrith	5 and 4
1991	M Hjorth	J Moodie	Whitchurch	3 and 2
1992	M McKay	L Navarro	Northamptonshire	2 holes
1993	M McKay	A Vincent	Helensburgh	4 and 3
1994	A Vincent	R Hudson	Gog Magog	1 up
1995	A Lemoine	J Krantz	Northop Park	3 and 2
1996	M Monnet	C Laurens	Formby	4 and 3
1997	C Laurens	M Nagl	West Kilbride	2 and 1

1998 *at Holyhead*

Quarter Finals
A Walker beat V Laing 1 hole
M Nagl beat L Moffat at 19th
S Petterson beat P Murphy 6 and 4
M Beautell beat M Estrada 2 holes

Semi-Finals
M Nagl beat A Walker 3 and 2
M Beautell beat S Petterson at 19th

Final
M Beautell beat M Nagl 4 and 3

English Girls' Championship

Year	Winner	Runner-up	Venue	By
1964	S Ward	P Tredinnick	Wollaton Park	2 and 1
1965	D Oxley	A Payne	Edgbaston	2 holes
1966	B Whitehead	D Oxley	Woodbridge	1 hole
1967	A Willard	G Holloway	Burhill	1 hole
1968	K Phillips	C le Feuvre	Harrogate	6 and 5
1969	C le Feuvre	K Phillips	Hawkstone Park	2 and 1
1970	C le Feuvre	M Walker	High Post	2 and 1
1971	C Eckersley	J Stevens	Liphook	4 and 3
1972	C Barker	R Kelly	Trentham	4 and 3
1973	S Parker	S Thurston	Lincoln	19th hole
1974	C Langford	L Harrold	Knowle	2 and 1
1975	M Burton	R Barry	Formby	6 and 5
1976	H Latham	D Park	Moseley	3 and 2
1977	S Bamford	S Jolly	Chelmsford	21st hole
1978	P Smillie	J Smith	Willesley Park	3 and 2
1979	L Moore	P Barry	Cirencester	1 hole
1980	P Smillie	J Soulsby	Kedleston Park	3 and 2
1981	J Soulsby	C Waite	Worksop	7 and 5
1982	C Waite	P Grice	Wilmslow	3 and 2
1983	P Grice	K Mitchell	West Surrey	2 and 1
1984	C Swallow	S Duhig	Bath	3 and 1
1985	L Fairclough	K Mitchell	Coventry	6 and 5
1986	S Shapcott	N Way	Huddersfield	7 and 6
1987	S Shapcott	S Morgan	Sandy Lodge	1 hole
1988	H Dobson	S Shapcott	Long Ashton	1 hole
1989	H Dobson	A MacDonald	Edgbaston	3 and 1
1990	C Hall	J Hockley	Bolton Old Links	20th hole
1991	N Buxton	C Hall	Knole Park	2 and 1
1992	F Brown	L Nicholson	Finham Park	2 and 1
1993	G Simpson	L Wixon	Cotswold Hills	7 and 5
1994	K Hamilton	S Forster	Whitley Bay	3 and 2
1995	R Hudson	G Nutter	Porters Park	2 and 1
1996	R Hudson	D Rushworth	Bedford	8 and 6
1997	S McKevitt	C Ritson	Kingsdown	3 and 2

1998 *at Harrogate*

Quarter Finals
S Heath beat K Dobson 8 and 7
L Walters beat E Brede 2 and 1
M Allen beat F More 6 and 5
K Lawton beat S Hassan 1 hole

Semi-Finals
L Walters beat S Heath 3 and 2
K Lawton beat M Allen 1 hole

Final
L Walters beat K Lawton 5 and 4

Irish Girls' Championship

Year	Winner	Runner-up	Venue	By
1961	M Coburn	C McAuley	Portrush	6 and 5
1962	P Boyd	P Atkinson	Elm Park	4 and 3
1963	P Atkinson	C Scarlett	Donaghadee	8 and 7
1964	C Scarlett	A Maher	Milltown	6 and 5
1965	V Singleton	P McKenzie	Ballycastle	7 and 6
1966	M McConnell	D Hulme	Dun Laoghaire	3 and 2
1967	M McConnell	C Wallace	Portrush	6 and 5
1968	C Wallace	A McCoy	Louth	3 and 1
1969	EA McGregor	M Sheenan	Knock	6 and 5
1970	EA McGregor	J Mark	Greystones	3 and 2
1971	J Mark	C Nesbitt	Belfast	3 and 2

Girls' and Junior Ladies' Tournaments

Year	Winner	Runner-up	Venue	By
1972	P Smyth	M Governey	Elm Park	1 hole
1973	M Governey	R Hegarty	Mullingar	3 and 1
1974	R Hegarty	M Irvine	Castletroy	2 holes
1975	M Irvine	P Wickham	Carlow	2 and 1
1976	P Wickham	R Hegarty	Castle	5 and 3
1977	A Ferguson	R Walsh	Birr	3 and 2
1978	C Wickham	B Gleeson	Killarney	1 hole
1979	L Bolton	B Gleeson	Milltown	3 and 2
1980	B Gleeson	L Bolton	Kilkenny	5 and 3
1981	B Gleeson	E Lynn	Donegal	1 hole
1982	D Langan	S Lynn	Headfort	5 and 4
1983	E McDaid	S Lynn	Ennis	20th hole
1984	S Sheehan	L Tormey	Thurles	6 and 4
1985	S Sheehan	D Hanna	Laytown/Bettystown	5 and 4
1986	D Mahon	T Eakin	Mallow	4 and 3
1987	V Greevy	B Ryan	Galway	8 and 7
1988	L McCool	P Gorman	Courtown	3 and 2
1989	A Rogers	R MacGuigan	Athlone	2 and 1
1990	G Doran	L McCool	Royal Portrush	3 and 1
1991	A Rogers	D Powell	Mallow	2 and 1
1992	M McGreevy	N Gorman	Kilkenny	2 and 1
1993	M McGreevy	E Dowdall	Strandhill	2 and 1
1994	A O'Leary	D Doyle	Mullingar	23rd hole
1995	P Murphy	G Hegarty	Douglas	5 and 4
1996	P Murphy	C Smyth	Warren Point	2 holes
1997	J Gannon	C Coughlan	Lay/Bettystown	3 and 2

1998 *at Galway*
Semi-Finals
P Murphy beat M Riordan 3 and 2
C Coughlan beat A Burke 4 and 2

Final
P Murphy beat C Coughlan 5 and 4

Scottish Ladies' Junior Open Strokeplay Championship

Year	Winner	Venue	Year	Winner	Venue
1960	J Greenhalgh	Ranfurly Castle	1980	J Connachan	Kirkcaldy
1961	D Robb	Whitecraigs	1981	K Douglas	Downfield
1962	S Armitage	Dalmahoy	1982	J Rhodes	Dumfries & Galloway
1963	A Irvin	Dumfries	1983	S Lawson	Largs
1964	M Nuttall	Dalmahoy	1984	S Lawson	Dunbar
1965	I Wylie	Carnoustie	1985	K Imrie	Ballater
1966	J Smith	Douglas Park	1986	K Imrie	Dumfries and County
1967	J Bourassa	Dunbar	1987	K Imrie	Douglas Park
1968	K Phillips	Dumfries	1988	C Lambert	Baberton
1969	K Phillips	Prestonfield	1989	C Lambert	Dunblane New
1970	B Huke	Leven	1990	J Moodie	Royal Troon
1971	B Huke	Dalmahoy	1991	C Macdonald	Alyth
1972	L Hope	Troon, Portland	1992	L McCool	North Berwick
1973	G Cadden	Edzell	1993	J Moodie	Dumfries and County
1974	S Lambie	Stranraer	1994	C Agnew	Dumfries and County
1975	S Cadden	Lanark	1995	R Hakkarainen (Fin)	Lanark
1976	S Cadden	Prestonfield	1996	L Moffat	Auchterarder
1977	S Cadden	Edzell	1997	L Nicholson	Stranraer
1978	J Connachan	Peebles	1998	V Laing	Duff House Royal
1979	A Gemmill	Troon, Portland			

Scottish Girls' Close Championship

Year	Winner	Runner-up	Venue	By
1960	J Hastings	A Lurie	Kilmacolm	6 and 4
1961	I Wylie	W Clark	Murrayfield	3 and 1
1962	I Wylie	U Burnet	West Kilbride	3 and 1
1963	M Norval	S MacDonald	Carnoustie	6 and 4
1964	JW Smith	C Workman	West Kilbride	2 and 1
1965	JW Smith	I Walker	Leven	7 and 5
1966	J Hutton	F Jamieson	Arbroath	2 holes
1967	J Hutton	K Lackie	West Kilbride	4 and 2
1968	M Dewar	J Crawford	Dalmahoy	2 holes
1969	C Panton	A Coutts	Edzell	23rd hole
1970	M Walker	L Bennett	Largs	3 and 2
1971	M Walker	S Kennedy	Edzell	1 hole
1972	G Cadden	C Panton	Stirling	3 and 2
1973	M Walker	M Thomson	Cowal, Dunoon	1 hole
1974	S Cadden	D Reid	Arbroath	3 and 1
1975	W Aitken	S Cadden	Leven	1 hole
1976	S Cadden	D Mitchell	Dumfries and County	4 and 2
1977	W Aitken	G Wilson	West Kilbride	2 holes
1978	J Connachan	D Mitchell	Stirling	7 and 5
1979	J Connachan	G Wilson	Dunbar	3 and 1
1980	J Connachan	P Wright	Dumfries and County	21st hole
1981	D Thomson	P Wright	Barassie	2 and 1
1982	S Lawson	D Thomson	Montrose	1 hole
1983	K Imrie	D Martin	Leven	2 and 1
1984	T Craik	D Jackson	Peebles	3 and 2
1985	E Farquharson	E Moffat	West Kilbride	2 holes
1986	C Lambert	F McKay	Nairn	4 and 3
1987	S Little	L Moretti	Stirling	3 and 2
1988	J Jenkins	F McKay	Dumfries and County	4 and 3
1989	J Moodie	V Melvin	Kilmacolm	19th hole
1990	M McKay	J Moodie	Duff House Royal	3 and 2
1991	J Moodie	M McKay	Leven Links	5 and 4
1992	M McKay	L Nicholson	Powfoot	2 and 1
1993	C Agnew	H Stirling	Baberton	19th hole
1994	C Nicholson	L Moffat	Deeside	3 and 1
1995	L Moffat	F Lockhart	Paisley	2 and 1
1996	V Laing	C Hunter	Peebles	5 and 4
1997	V Laing	A Walker	Dunfermline	5 and 4

1998 *at Kilmarnock Barassie*
Semi-Finals
L Moffat beat L Kerry 5 and 4
V Laing beat S Laing 4 and 3

Final
V Laing beat L Moffat at 21st hole

Welsh Girls' Championship

Year	Winner	Runner-up	Venue	By
1960	A Hughes	D Wilson	Llandrindod Wells	6 and 4
1961	J Morris	S Kelly	North Wales	3 and 2
1962	J Morris	P Morgan	Southerndown	4 and 3
1963	A Hughes	A Brown	Conway	8 and 7
1964	A Hughes	M Leigh	Holyhead	5 and 3
1965	A Hughes	A Reardon-Hughes	Swansea Bay	19th hole
1966	S Hales	J Rogers	Prestatyn	1 hole
1967	E Wilkie	L Humphreys	Pyle and Kenfig	1 hole
1968	L Morris	J Rogers	Portmadoc	1 hole
1969	L Morris	L Humphreys	Wenvoe Castle	5 and 3
1970	T Perkins	P Light	Rhuddlan	2 and 1
1971	P Light	P Whitley	Glamorganshire	4 and 3
1972	P Whitley	P Light	Llandudno (Maesdu)	2 and 1
1973	V Rawlings	T Perkins	Whitchurch	19th hole
1974	L Isherwood	S Rowlands	Wrexham	4 and 3
1975	L Isherwood	S Rowlands	Swansea Bay	1 hole

Year	Winner	Runner-up	Venue	By
1976	K Rawlings	C Parry	Rhuddlan	5 and 4
1977	S Rowlands	D Taylor	Clyne	7 and 5
1978	S Rowlands	G Rees	Abergele	3 and 2
1979	M Rawlings	J Richards	St Mellons	19th hole
1980	K Davies	M Rawlings	Vale of Llangollen	19th hole
1981	M Rawlings	F Connor	Radyr	4 and 3
1982	K Davies	K Beckett	Wrexham	6 and 5
1983	N Wesley	J Foster	Whitchurch	4 and 2
1984	J Foster	J Evans	Pwllheli	6 and 5
1985	J Foster	S Caley	Langland Bay	6 and 5
1986	J Foster	L Dermott	Holyhead	3 and 2
1987	J Lloyd	S Bibbs	Cardiff	2 and 1
1988	L Dermott	A Perriam	Builth Wells	2 holes
1989	L Dermott	N Stroud	Carmarthen	4 and 2
1990	L Dermott	N Stroud	Padeswood and Buckley	6 and 4
1991	S Boyes	R Morgan	Clyne	3 and 1
1992	B Jones	S Musto	Rhuddlan	2 and 1
1993	K Stark	S Tudor-Jones	Radyr	3 and 2
1994	K Stark	J Evans	Wrexham	4 and 3
1995	E Pilgrim	L Davis	Borth and Ynyslas	2 holes
1996	K Stark	S Bourne	Monmouth	4 and 3
1997	R Brewerton	K Stark	Perhos	19th hole
1998	B Brewerton	L Archer	Old Padeswood	3 and 1

Nick Faldo Junior Series

1998 *at Loch Lomond*

1	K Phillips	78-76—154

Team Events

European Lady Juniors' Team Championship

Year	Winner	Second	Venue
1990	Sweden	England	Shannon, Ireland
1992	Spain	Sweden	St Nom-la-Breteche, France
1994	Sweden	France	Gutenhof, Vienna, Austria
1996	France	Spain	Nairn, Scotland

1998 *at Oslo, Norway*

Quarter Finals
Sweden beat Germany   4–3
Italy beat France   5–2
England beat Denmark   5½–1½
Spain beat Scotland   4–3

Semi-Finals
Italy beat Sweden   4–3
Spain beat England   4½–2½

Final
Spain beat Italy   5–2

Girls' Home Internationals (Stroyan Cup)

Year	Winner	Venue	Year	Winner	Venue
1966	Scotland	Troon (Portland)	1982	England	Edzell
1967	England	Liphook	1983	England	Alwoodley
1968	England	Leven	1984	Scotland	Llandudno (Maesdu)
1969	England	Ilkley	1985	England	Hesketh GC
1970	England	North Wales	1986	England	West Kilbride
1971	England	North Berwick	1987	England	Barnham Broom
1972	Scotland	Royal Norwich	1988	England	Pyle and Kenfig
1973	Scotland	Northamptonshire County	1989	England	Carlisle
1974	England	Dunbar	1990	England	Penrith
1975	England	Henbury	1991	England	Whitchurch
1976	Scotland	Pyle and Kenfig	1992	Scotland	Moseley
1977	England	Formby Ladies	1993	Scotland	Helensburgh
1978	England	Largs	1994	Scotland	Gog Magog
1979	England	Edgbaston	1995	England	Northop
1980	England	Wrexham	1996	England	Formby
1981	England	Woodbridge	1997	England	Forfar

1998 *at Mullingar, Ireland*

England beat Scotland 5–4
Wales halved with Ireland 4½–4½
England halved with Wales 4½–4½
Scotland beat Ireland 8½–½

Result: 1 England   2 Wales and Scotland   3 Ireland

Golf Foundation Events

AGE GROUP CHAMPIONSHIPS
at Patshull Park, Shropshire

Boys

Year	Under 16	Under 15	Under 14
1987	I Garbutt (Wheatley)	L Westwood (Worksop)	N Heron (Ashridge)
1988	L Westwood (Worksop)	B Collier (Callander)	S Pigott (West Malling)
1989	K Harrison (Cottesmore)	C Lane (Kingsthorpe)	G Harris (Broome Manor)
1990	C Lane (Kingsthorpe)	G Harris (Broome Manor)	P Collier (Limerick)
1991	G Harris (Broome Manor)	C Richardson (Burghley Park)	J Bajcer (Church Stretton)
1992	C Leach (Gillingham)	S Walker (Walmley)	D Kirton (Worksop)
1993	K Godfrey (St Enodoc)	S Young (Seascale)	J Rose (North Hants)
1994	A Smith (Rhondda)	T Hilton (Lewes)	A Smith (Enville)
1995	G Legg (Enmore Park)	S Robinson (Seaton Carew)	D Inglis (Glencorse)
1996	S Fromant (Orsett)	D Skinns (Canwick Park)	C Smith (Cotgrave Place)
1997	M Stam (Royal Liverpool)	G Lockerbie (Keswick)	S Robinson (Thames Ditton)

Year	Under 13
1987	M Neil (Stirling)
1988	P Drew (Worthing)
1989	A Cooper (Taymouth Castle)
1990	S Walker (Boldmere)
1991	N Rossin (John O'Gaunt)
1992	D Main (Moray)
1993	S Godfrey (St Enodoc)
1994	D Tarbotton (Hull)
1995	D Porter (Wellow)
1996	J Maxwell (Muckhart)
1997	J Turner (Newmarket Links)

1998

Under 16

Darren Rix (Malton & Norton)	72-75—147
Craig Stevenson (Whittington Heath)	74-74—148
Tom Gooding (Baildon)	79-73—152
Jamie Wood (Ashford, Kent)	79-74—153
Marc Kynes (Old Conna)	75-79—154
William Bowe (Workington)	78-79—157
Stephen Lewton (Woburn)	78-79—157

Under 15

Michael Skelton (Hunley Hall)	73-78—151
Christopher Clarke (Wath)	74-79—153
Robert Taylor (Cardross)	77-78—155
Christopher Yeomans (Tilsworth)	81-75—156
William Shucksmith (Sand Moor)	78-78—156
Sam Wright (Oakmere Park)	81-77—158

Boys Age Group Championships *continued*

Under 14
Lee Shepherd (Cleckheaton & District)	79-74—153
Jack Budgen (East Sussex National)	76-79—155
Bobby Wallace (Canmore)	79-79—158
James Ruth (Tavistock)	80-79—159
Neil Brennan (Dunmurry)	79-80—159
Gregg Morgan (Belmont)	78-81—159
Jamie Moul (Stoke by Nayland)	76-83—159

Under 13
Christopher Paisley (Stocksfield)	80-84—164
Samuel Hufton (Copt Heath)	86-85—171
Mark Coppell (Woodcote Park)	89-86—175
Jack Stevenson (Torrington)	87-88—175
Daniel Hewitt (Alsager)	86-90—176
Martyn Hamer (Castle Hawk)	91-88—179

Girls

Year	Under 17	Under 16	Under 15
1987		L Walton (Calcot Park)	N Buxton (Woodsome Hall)
1988		V Melvin (Clydebank & District)	J Williamson (Hadley Wood)
1989		S Boyes (Wenvoe Castle)	N Gorman (Balmoral)
1990		T Poulton (Boyce Hill)	V Hanks (Broome Manor)
1991		G Simpson (Cleckheaton & District)	D Doyle (Lahinch)
1992		H Stirling (Bridge of Allan)	G Nutter (Prestwich)
1993		K Wrigglesworth (Hornsea)	R Hudson (Wheatley)
1994		L Meredith (Wentworth)	L Moffat (W. Kilbride)
1995	R Hudson (Wheatley)	L Moffat (W. Kilbride)	V Laing (Musselburgh)
1996	K Fisher (Leyland)	F More (Lindrick)	L Archer (Lilleshall Hall)
1997	V Laing (Musselburgh)	R Bell (Northcliff)	L Kenney (Pitreavie)

Year	Under 14	Under 13
1987	L Tupholme (Northcliffe)	M McKay (Turnberry)
1988	M McKay (Turnberry)	
1989	V Hanks (Broome Manor)	
1990	K Wrigglesworth (Hornsea)	
1991	E Wilcock (Sherwood Forest)	
1992	R Hudson (Wheatley)	
1993	L Walters (Ormonde Fields)	
1994	V Laing (Musselburgh)	

1998

Under 17
Joanne Pritchard (Tredegar Park)	81-82—163
Emma Brown (West Wilts)	83-81—164
Rachel Esplin (Goring & Streatley)	80-85—165
Emily Lowther (Roseberry Grange)	88-80—168
Sarah Gallagher (Claremorris)	85-85—170
Katie Parsley (Royal Liverpool)	83-87—170
Claudine Beaver (Royal Lytham & St Annes)	77-93—170

Under 16
Laura Archer (Lilleshall Hall)	78-80—158
Claire Harrison (Chesterfield)	85-85—170
Maria Dunne (Skerries)	85-87—172
Rebecca Rowlands (Cosby)	89-84—173
Clare Queen (Drumpellier)	92-85—177
Sarah Anyan (Greetham Valley)	89-94—183

Under 15

Alexandra Marshall (Burghley Park)	85-82—167
Heather MacRae (Callander)	88-87—175
Laura Eastwood (Yelverton)	86-90—176
Dawn Dewar (Monifieth)	90-90—180
Niamh Doggett (Co Louth)	92-89—181
Emma McBride (Upton by Chester)	94-88—182

Duke of York Trophy Winners (for best 36-hole aggregate)

Year	Boys	Girls
1991	Gary Harris (Broome Manor)	Georgina Simpson (Cleckheaton)
1992	Christopher Leach (Gillingham)	Heather Stirling (Bridge of Allan)
1993	Kristian Godfrey (St Enodoc)	Katy Wrigglesworth (Hornsea)
1994	Alex Smith (Rhondda)	Lisa Meredith (Wentworth)
1995	Gavin Legg (Enmore Park)	Rebecca Hudson (Wheatley)
1996	Stuart Fromant (Orsett)	Fame More (Lindrick)
1997	Marcus Stam (Royal Liverpool)	Louise Kenney (Pitreavie)
1998	Darren Rix (Malton & Norton)	Laura Archer (Lilleshall Hall)

Golf Foundation Schools' Team Championship (for the R&A Trophy)

Year	Winner	Country	Venue
1987	Klippans Gymnasieskola	Sweden	Foxhills
1988	Klippans Gymnasieskola	Sweden	Sunningdale
1989	Marks Gymnasium	Sweden	St Andrews
1990	Lycée Bellevue	France	St Andrews
1991	Lycée Bellevue	France	Sunningdale
1992	Lycée Bellevue	France	St Andrews
1993	Lycée Bellevue	France	Gleneagles
1994	Lycée Bellevue	France	St Andrews
1995	Kelvin Grove High School	Australia	Sunningdale
1996	Welkom Gymnasium	South Africa	Blairgowrie
1997	Lycée Bellevue	France	Loch Lomond

1998 *at Sunningdale Golf Club*

1st South Africa
Damelin College, Randburg

Gareth Botha (Scr)	76-73—149
Wesley Botha (Scr)	73-73—146
Tyrone van Aswegen (Scr)	73-78—151
	446

2nd Australia
St Patrick's College, New South Wales

Stephen Carroll (2)	78-74—152
Adam Firmani (2)	75-66—141
Adam Trent (4)	78-76—154
	447

3rd England
Kenilworth School, Warwickshire

Jamie Elson (1)	69-69—138
Daniel Howe (4)	71-76—147
Richard Logue (4)	89-75—164
	449

4th New Zealand
Auckland Grammar School, Auckland

Bradley Heaven (1)	77-70—147
Douglas Batty (2)	77-74—151
Clarke Osborne (2)	77-75—152
	450

PGA European Tour Trophy

Jamie Elson, England   69-69—138

Golf Foundation Award Winners

Year	Winner	Club
1982	Lindsey Anderson	Tain
1983	Nigel Osborne Clarke	Shirehampton
1984	Wayne Henry	Redbourn
1985	David Grantham	Hull
1986	Matthew Stanford	Saltford
1987	Jane Marchant	Whittington Barracks
1988	*Boys:* Ian Garbutt	Wheatley
	Girls: Lisa Dermott	St Melyd
1989	*Boys:* Lee Westwood	Worksop
	Girls: Lynn McCool	Strabane
1990	*Boys:* Keith Law	Forfar
	Girls: Mhairi McKay	Turnberry
1991	*Boys:* Gary Harris	Broome Manor
	Girls: Nicola Buxton	Woodsome Hall
1992	*Boys:* Shaun Devenney	Strabane
	Girls: Mhairi McKay	Turnberry
1993	*Boys:* Craig Williams	Greigiau
	Girls: Georgina Simpson	Cleckheaton & Dist
1994	*Boys:* Denny Lucas	Worksop
	Girls: Rebecca Hudson	Wheatley
1995	*Boys:* Justin Rose	North Hants
	Girls: Rebecca Hudson	Wheatley
1996	*Boys:* Mark Pilkington	Nefyn & District GC and Pwllheli
	Girls: Fame More	Chesterfield GC and Lindrick GC
1997	*Boys:* Nicholas Dougherty	Shaw Hill, Lancs
	Girls: Rebecca Brewerton	Abergele & Pensarn
1998	*Not yet decided*	

PART VII
Awards

Awards

Association of Golf Writers' Trophy

Awarded to the man or woman who, in the opinion of golf writers, has done most for golf during the year

1951 Max Faulkner
1952 Miss Elizabeth Price
1953 Joe Carr
1954 Mrs Roy Smith (Miss Frances Stephens)
1955 Ladies' Golf Union's Touring Team
1956 John Beharrell
1957 Dai Rees
1958 Harry Bradshaw
1959 Eric Brown
1960 Sir Stuart Goodwin (sponsor of international golf)
1961 Commdr Charles Roe (ex-hon secretary, PGA)
1962 Mrs Marley Spearman, British Ladies' Champion 1961–1962
1963 Michael Lunt, Amateur Champion, 1963
1964 Great Britain & Ireland Eisenhower Trophy Team
1965 Gerald Micklem, golf administrator, President, English Golf Union
1966 Ronnie Shade
1967 John Panton
1968 Michael Bonallack
1969 Tony Jacklin
1970 Tony Jacklin
1971 Great Britain & Ireland Walker Cup Team
1972 Miss Michelle Walker
1973 Peter Oosterhuis
1974 Peter Oosterhuis
1975 Golf Foundation
1976 Great Britain & Ireland Eisenhower Trophy Team
1977 Christy O'Connor
1978 Peter McEvoy
1979 Severiano Ballesteros
1980 Sandy Lyle
1981 Bernhard Langer
1982 Gordon Brand Jr
1983 Nick Faldo
1984 Severiano Ballesteros
1985 European Ryder Cup Team
1986 Great Britain and Ireland Curtis Cup Team
1987 European Ryder Cup Team
1988 Sandy Lyle
1989 Great Britain & Ireland Walker Cup Team
1990 Nick Faldo
1991 Severiano Ballesteros
1992 European Solheim Cup Team
1993 Bernhard Langer
1994 Laura Davies
1995 European Ryder Cup Team
1996 Colin Montgomerie
1997 Alison Nicholas
1998 Lee Westwood

Harry Vardon Trophy

Awarded to the PGA member heading the Order of Merit at the end of the season

Year	Winner	Year	Winner	Year	Winner
1937	Charles Whitcombe	1961	Christy O'Connor	1980	Sandy Lyle
1938	Henry Cotton	1962	Christy O'Connor	1981	Bernhard Langer
1939	Roger Whitcombe	1963	Neil Coles	1982	Greg Norman
1940–45	In abeyance	1964	Peter Alliss	1983	Nick Faldo
1946	Bobby Locke	1965	Bernard Hunt	1984	Bernhard Langer
1947	Norman Von Nida	1966	Peter Alliss	1985	Sandy Lyle
1948	Charlie Ward	1967	Malcolm Gregson	1986	Severiano Ballesteros
1949	Charlie Ward	1968	Brian Huggett	1987	Ian Woosnam
1950	Bobby Locke	1969	Bernard Gallacher	1988	Severiano Ballesteros
1951	John Panton	1970	Neil Coles	1989	Ronan Rafferty
1952	Harry Weetman	1971	Peter Oosterhuis	1990	Ian Woosnam
1953	Flory van Donck	1972	Peter Oosterhuis	1991	Severiano Ballesteros
1954	Bobby Locke	1973	Peter Oosterhuis	1992	Nick Faldo
1955	Dai Rees	1974	Peter Oosterhuis	1993	Colin Montgomerie
1956	Harry Weetman	1975	Dale Hayes	1994	Colin Montgomerie
1957	Eric Brown	1976	Severiano Ballesteros	1995	Colin Montgomerie
1958	Bernard Hunt	1977	Severiano Ballesteros	1996	Colin Montgomerie
1959	Dai Rees	1978	Severiano Ballesteros	1997	Colin Montgomerie
1960	Bernard Hunt	1979	Sandy Lyle	1998	Colin Montgomerie

Sir Henry Cotton European Rookie of the Year

1960	Tommy Goodwin	1980	Paul Hoad
1961	Alex Caygill	1981	Jeremy Bennett
1962	No Award	1982	Gordon Brand Jr
1963	Tony Jacklin	1983	Grant Turner
1964	No Award	1984	Philip Parkin
1966	Robin Liddle	1985	Paul Thomas
1967	No Award	1986	José Maria Olazabal
1968	Bernard Gallacher	1987	Peter Baker
1969	Peter Oosterhuis	1988	Colin Montgomerie
1970	Stuart Brown	1989	Paul Broadhurst
1971	David Llewellyn	1990	Russell Claydon
1972	Sam Torrance	1991	Per-Ulrik Johansson
1973	Philip Elson	1992	Jim Payne
1974	Carl Mason	1993	Gary Orr
1975	No Award	1994	Jonathan Lomas
1976	Mark James	1995	Jarmo Sandelin
1977	Nick Faldo	1996	Thomas Bjorn
1978	Sandy Lyle	1997	Scott Henderson
1979	Mike Miller	1998	Olivier Edmond

Daily Telegraph Woman Golfer of the Year

1982	Jane Connachan	1992	GB&I Curtis Cup Team, Captain Liz Boatman
1983	Jill Thornhill		
1984	Gillian Stewart and Claire Waite		
		1993	Catriona Lambert and Julie Hall
1985	Belle Robertson		
1986	GB&I Curtis Cup Team	1994	GB&I Curtis Cup Team, Captain Liz Boatman
1987	Linda Bayman		
1988	GB&I Curtis Cup Team	1995	Julie Hall
		1996	GB&I Curtis Cup Team
1989	Helen Dobson		
1990	Angela Uzielli	1997	Alison Rose
1991	Joanne Morley	1998	Kim Andrew

Jack Nicklaus US PGA Player of the Year

1990	Wayne Levi	1995	Greg Norman
1991	Fred Couples	1996	Tom Lehman
1992	Fred Couples	1997	Tiger Woods
1993	Nick Price	1998	Mark O'Meara
1994	Nick Price		

Arnold Palmer Award

Awarded to the US PGA Tour leading money-winner

1981	Tom Kite	1990	Greg Norman
1982	Craig Stadler	1991	Corey Pavin
1983	Hal Sutton	1992	Fred Couples
1984	Tom Watson	1993	Nick Price
1985	Curtis Strange	1994	Nick Price
1986	Greg Norman	1995	Greg Norman
1987	Paul Azinger	1996	Tom Lehman
1988	Curtis Strange	1997	Tiger Woods
1989	Tom Kite	1998	David Duval

Bobby Jones Award

Awarded by USGA for distinguished sportsmanship in golf

1955	Francis Ouimet	1978	Bob Hope and Bing Crosby
1956	Bill Campbell		
1957	Babe Zaharias	1979	Tom Kite
1958	Margaret Curtis	1980	Charles Yates
1959	Findlay Douglas	1981	JoAnne Carner
1960	Charles Evans Jr	1982	Billy Joe Patton
1961	Joe Carr	1983	Maureen Garrett
1962	Horton-Smith	1984	Jay Sigel
1963	Patty Berg	1985	Fuzzy Zoeller
1964	Charles Coe	1986	Jess W Sweetser
1965	Mrs Edwin Vare	1987	Tom Watson
1966	Gary Player	1988	Isaac B Grainger
1967	Richard Tufts	1989	Chi-Chi Rodriquez
1968	Robert Dickson	1990	Peggy Kirk Bell
1969	Gerald Micklem	1991	Ben Grenshaw
1970	Roberto De Vicenzo	1992	Gene Sarazen
1971	Arnold Palmer	1993	PJ Boatwright Jr
1972	Michael Bonallack	1994	Lewis Oehmig
1973	Gene Littler	1995	Herbert Warren Wind
1974	Byron Nelson		
1975	Jack Nicklaus	1996	Betsy Rawls
1976	Ben Hogan	1997	Fred Brand
1977	Joseph C Dey	1998	Ed Updegraff

The US Vardon Trophy

The award is made to the member of the US PGA who completes 60 rounds or more, with the lowest scoring average over the calendar year.

1948	Ben Hogan	1974	Lee Trevino
1949	Sam Snead	1975	Bruce Crampton
1950	Sam Snead	1976	Don January
1951	Lloyd Mangrum	1977	Tom Watson
1952	Jack Burke	1978	Tom Watson
1953	Lloyd Mangrum	1979	Tom Watson
1954	Ed Harrison	1980	Lee Trevino
1955	Sam Snead	1981	Tom Kite
1956	Cary Middlecoff	1982	Tom Kite
1957	Dow Finsterwald	1983	Ray Floyd
1958	Bob Rosburg	1984	Calvin Peete
1959	Art Wall	1985	Don Pooley
1960	Billy Casper	1986	Scott Hoch
1961	Arnold Palmer	1987	Dan Pohl
1962	Arnold Palmer	1988	Chip Beck
1963	Billy Casper	1989	Greg Norman
1964	Arnold Palmer	1990	Greg Norman
1965	Billy Casper	1991	Fred Couples
1966	Billy Casper	1992	Fred Couples
1967	Arnold Palmer	1993	Nick Price
1968	Billy Casper	1994	Greg Norman
1969	Dave Hill	1995	Steve Elkington
1970	Lee Trevino	1996	Tom Lehman
1971	Lee Trevino	1997	Nick Price
1972	Lee Trevino	1998	David Duval
1973	Bruce Crampton		

US PGA Player of the Year Award

1948	Ben Hogan	1974	Johnny Miller
1949	Sam Snead	1975	Jack Nicklaus
1950	Ben Hogan	1976	Jack Nicklaus
1951	Ben Hogan	1977	Tom Watson
1952	Julius Boros	1978	Tom Watson
1953	Ben Hogan	1979	Tom Watson
1954	Ed Furgol	1980	Tom Watson
1955	Doug Ford	1981	Bill Rogers
1956	Jack Burke	1982	Tom Watson
1957	Dick Mayer	1983	Hal Sutton
1958	Dow Finsterwald	1984	Tom Watson
1959	Art Wall	1985	Lanny Wadkins
1960	Arnold Palmer	1986	Bob Tway
1961	Jerry Barner	1987	Paul Azinger
1962	Arnold Palmer	1988	Curtis Strange
1963	Julius Boros	1989	Tom Kite
1964	Ken Venturi	1990	Nick Faldo
1965	Dave Marr	1991	Corey Pavin
1966	Billy Casper	1992	Fred Couples
1967	Jack Nicklaus	1993	Nick Price
1968	*not awarded*	1994	Nick Price
1969	Orville Moody	1995	Greg Norman
1970	Billy Casper	1996	Tom Lehman
1971	Lee Trevino	1997	Tiger Woods
1972	Jack Nicklaus	1998	Mark O'Meara
1973	Jack Nicklaus		

US PGA Tour Rookie of the Year

1990	Robert Games	1995	Woody Austin
1991	John Daly	1996	Tiger Woods
1992	Mark Carnevale	1997	Stewart Cink
1993	Vijay Singh	1998	Steve Flesch
1994	Ernie Els		

US LPGA Gatorade Rookie of the Year

1980	Myra Van Hoose
1981	Patty Sheehan
1982	Patti Rizzo
1983	Stephanie Farwig
1984	Juli Inkster
1985	Penny Hammel
1986	Jody Rosenthal
1987	Tammie Green
1988	Liselotte Neumann (Swi)
1989	Pamela Wright (Sco)
1990	Hiromi Kobayashi (Jpn)
1991	Brandie Burton
1992	Helen Alfredsson (Swe)
1993	Suzanne Strudwick (Eng)
1994	Annika Sörenstam (Swe)
1995	Pat Hurst
1996	Karrie Webb (Aus)
1997	Lisa Hackney (Eng)

US LPGA Rolex Player of the Year

1980	Beth Daniel	1990	Beth Daniel
1981	Jo Anne Carner	1991	Pat Bradley
1982	Jo Anne Carner	1992	Dottie Mochrie
1983	Patty Sheehan	1993	Betsy King
1984	Betsy King	1994	Beth Daniel
1985	Nancy Lopez	1995	Annika Sörenstam
1986	Pat Bradley	1996	Laura Davies
1987	Ayako Okamoto	1997	Annika Sörenstam
1988	Nancy Lopez	1998	Annika Sörenstam
1989	Betsy King		

US LPGA Vare Trophy

		Scoring average
1980	Amy Alcott	71.51
1981	Jo Anne Carner	71.75
1982	Jo Anne Carner	71.49
1983	Jo Anne Carner	71.41
1984	Patty Sheehan	71.40
1985	Nancy Lopez	70.73
1986	Pat Bradley	71.10
1987	Betsy King	71.14
1988	Colleen Walker	71.26
1989	Beth Daniel	70.38
1990	Beth Daniel	70.54
1991	Pat Bradley	70.66
1992	Dottie Mochrie	70.80
1993	Nancy Lopez	70.83
1994	Beth Daniel	70.90
1995	Annika Sörenstam	71.00
1996	Annika Sörenstam	70.47
1997	Karrie Webb	70.01
1998	Annika Sörenstam	69.99

Vivien Saunders Trophy

Awarded to the Women Professional Golfers' European Tour winner of the strokeplay averages

		Scoring average
1991	Alison Nicholas	71.71
1992	Laura Davies	70.35
1993	Laura Davies	71.63
1994	Liselotte Neumann	69.56
1995	Annika Sörenstam	69.75
1996	Marie Laure de Lorenzi	71.39
1997	Marie Laure de Lorenzi	72.20
1998	Laura Davies	71.96

Joyce Wethered Trophy

Awarded to the outstanding amateur under the age of 25

1994	Janice Moodie
1995	Rebecca Hudson
1996	Mhairi McKay
1997	Rebecca Hudson
1998	Liza Walters

PART VIII
Who's Who in Golf

Compiled by Alan Elliott

British Isles Players

Abbreviations used

Cls Club membership
Maj The Open, US Open, USPGA, US Masters (men) Ladies British Open, US Women's Open, USLPGA (ladies)
Chp Amateur Championship or Ladies British Open Amateur (or, within text, any championship)
Nat The player's national championship
Trn Tournament(s)
Oth Other national championship or tournament
Reg Regional tournaments
Int International team appearances
Eur European Tour or general European tournament(s)
US Tournament(s) in United States or Canada
RoW Tournament(s) in the rest of the world
Cha Challenge Tour
Sen Senior(s)
Jun Junior
Mis Miscellaneous information
r/u runner up
s/f semi-finalist
tied A lost play-off after first place tie
Eur(L) T Ch European (Ladies) Amateur Team Championship

Captaincy is indicated by the year printed in bold type; years in bold type within brackets indicate non-playing captain.

Aitken, Wilma See **Leburn**

Alliss, Peter
Born Berlin on 28th February, 1931. Turned Professional 1946
PROFESSIONAL
Eur Spanish Open 1956-58. Italian Open, Portuguese Open 1958.
Trn Daks 1954; Dunlop 1955; PGA Close 1957; Dunlop 1959; Sprite 1960 (shared). PGA Close 1962; Daks 1963 (shared); Swallow-Penfold, Esso Golden 1964; PGA Close, Jeyes 1965; Martini (shared), Rediffusion 1966; Agfa-Gevaert 1967; Piccadilly 1969; Sunningdale Foursomes 1958-61; Wentworth Pro-Am Foursomes 1959
Oth British Assistants 1952
RoW Brazilian Open 1961
Reg West of England Open Professional 1956-58-62-66

Int Ryder Cup 1953-57-59-61-63-65-67-69; UK v Europe 1954-55-56; England in World Cup 1954-55-57-58-59-61-62-64-66-67; Home International **1967**
Mis Vardon Trophy 1964-66; PGA Captain 1962-87; Author, TV commentator. Golf course architect.
AMATEUR
Jun Int England Boys 1946

Anderson, Fiona
Born Perth on 24th August, 1954
Cls Blairgowrie
Nat Scottish Ladies Amateur 1987. r/u 1980-83-88
Reg North of Scotland Ladies 1977. Scottish Universities Champion 1975
Int Vagliano Trophy 1987. Scotland (Home Int) 1977-79-80-81-83-84-86-87-88-89-90-91-92; Eur(L) T Ch 1979-83-87-91

Anderson, Jessie *See* **Valentine**

Andrew, Kim (*née* Rostron)
Born 12th February, 1974
- **Cls** Clitheroe
- **Chp** Ladies British Open Amateur 1998
- **Nat** English Ladies, Scottish Ladies Stroke Play 1997
- **Trn** Formby Leveret 1995; St Rule Trophy 1997
- **Reg** Lancashire Ladies 1993; Northern Ladies 1995-96
- **Int** Curtis Cup 1998; Vagliano Trophy 1997; England (Home Int) 1996-97-98; Eur(L) T CH 1997
- **Jun** English Girls 1991-92

Anstey, Veronica *See* **Beharrell**

Attenborough, Michael F
Born Britford, nr Salisbury in October, 1939
- **Cls** Chislehurst, Royal St George's, Royal & Ancient
- **Oth** Scandinavian Amateur 1965
- **Trn** Hampshire Hog 1960. President's Putter 1962-66. County Champion of Champions 1964. Duncan Putter 1966. Prince of Wales Challenge Cup 1969
- **Reg** Kent Amateur 1963-64-65
- **Int** Walker Cup 1967. GB *v* Europe 1966-68. England (Home Int) 1964-66-67-68; Eur T Ch 1967
- **Mis** Captain of Royal & Ancient 1989/90

Bailey, Diane, MBE [Frearson], (*née* Robb)
Born Wolverhampton on 31st August, 1943
- **Cls** Enville (Hon), Reigate Heath, Betchworth Park
- **Chp** British Ladies Amateur r/u 1961
- **Trn** Worplesdon Mixed Foursomes 1971. Avia Foursomes 1972
- **Reg** Staffordshire Ladies 1961. Lincolnshire Ladies 1966-67. Midland Ladies 1966
- **Int** Curtis Cup 1962-72-(**84**)-(**86**)-(**88**). Vagliano Trophy 1961-(**83**)-(**85**). Espirito Santo 1968. England (Home Int) 1961-62-71. Commonwealth Team Ch (**1983**).
- **Mis** Surrey Ladies County Captain 1981-2
- **Jun** British Girls 1961. Scottish Girls Open Stroke Play 1959-61
- **Int** England Girls 1957-61

Baker, Peter
Born Shifnal on 7th October, 1967. Turned Professional 1986
PROFESSIONAL
- **Eur** Benson & Hedges International 1988; Dunhill British Masters, Scandinavian Masters 1993
- **Oth** UAP U25 European Open 1990; Midland Professional Chp 1993-94; Tournoi Perrier de Paris 1994
- **Int** Ryder Cup 1993; England in Dunhill Cup 1993(r/u)-98
- **Mis** Rookie of the Year 1987

AMATEUR
- **Nat** English Open Amateur Stroke Play 1985 (shared)
- **Reg** Shropshire & Herefordshire Amateur 1983-84-85
- **Trn** Tillman Trophy 1985
- **Int** Walker Cup 1985; GBI *v* Europe 1986; England (Home Int) 1985
- **Jun** Carris Trophy 1983-85

Bannerman, Harry
Born Aberdeen on 5th March, 1942. Turned Professional 1965
PROFESSIONAL
- **Oth** Scottish Professional 1967-72. Northern Scottish Open 1967-69-72. East of Scotland PGA Match Play 1969. Scottish Coca Cola 1976
- **Int** Ryder Cup 1971. Scotland in World Cup 1967-72; in Double Diamond 1972-74
- **Mis** Frank Moran Trophy 1972

AMATEUR
- **Reg** North of Scotland Stroke Play 1962; North-East Scotland Stroke Play 1963-64-65
- **Jun Int** Scottish Boys 1959

Barber, Sally (*née* Bonallack)
Born Chigwell, Essex on 9th April, 1938. Turned Professional 1979. Reinstated Amateur 1982
AMATEUR
- **Cls** Thorpe Hall, Thorndon Park, Hunstanton (Hon), Killarney (Hon)
- **Nat** English Ladies Amateur 1968; r/u 1970-71
- **Oth** German Ladies 1958
- **Trn** Astor Salver 1972; Avia Foursomes 1976
- **Reg** Essex Ladies 1958-59-60-61-62-63-66-67-70-71; London Foursomes 1984
- **Int** Curtis Cup 1962; Vagliano Trophy 1961-69; England (Home Int) 1960-61-62-63-68-70-72-77-(**78**) Eur(L) T Ch 1969-71. CW (**1995**)

Barnes, Brian
Born Addington, Surrey on 3rd June, 1945. Turned Professional 1964
PROFESSIONAL
- **Eur** Agfacolor 1969; Martini International 1972; Dutch Open 1974; French Open 1975; Sun Alliance PGA Match Play 1976; Spanish Open, Greater Manchester Open 1978; Italian Open, Portuguese Open 1979; Tournament Players Chp 1981
- **Oth** Scottish Professional 1981-82; Coca Cola Young Professionals 1969; East of Scotland Professional 1975; Northern Scottish Open 1978; PGA Club Professional Chp 1989
- **RoW** Flame Lily (Rhodesia) 1967; Australian Masters 1970; Zambian Open 1979-81; Kenya Open 1981
- **Sen** Senior British Open 1995-96; US AT&T Canada Senior Open 1998
- **Int** Ryder Cup 1969-71-73-75-77-79; Hennessy–Cognac Cup 1974-76-78-80; *v* South Africa; Scotland in World Cup 1974-75-76-77; in Double Diamond 1972-73-74-75-76-77; in PGA Cup 1990

AMATEUR
- **Reg** Somerset Amateur 1964; South Western Counties Amateur 1964
- **Jun** British Youths 1964
- **Int** English Youths 1964

Bayman, Linda (née Denison-Pender)
Born 10th June, 1948
- **Nat** English Ladies Amateur 1983; Ladies British Amateur Stroke Play 1987
- **Trn** Avia Foursomes 1969-71-73-79-80; Worplesdon Mixed Foursomes 1980-84; Astor Salver 1983-84; Critchley Salver 1984
- **Reg** Kent Ladies 1968-72-73-78
- **Int** Curtis Cup 1988; Vagliano Trophy 1971-73-85-87; Espirito Santo 1988; England (Home Int) 1971-72-73-83-84-85-87-88-95; Eur(L) T Ch 1983-85-87-(97)
- **Jun** Kent Girls 1966
- **Mis** Avia Woman Golfer of the Year 1987; Doris Chambers Trophy 1987-88-89; Angus Trophy 1987-89

Behan, Lillian
Born Co Kildare on 12th January, 1965. Turned Professional 1986
AMATEUR
- **Chp** Ladies British Open Amateur 1985
- **Nat** Irish Ladies 1998
- **Trn** The Curragh Scratch Cup 1986
- **Int** Curtis Cup 1986; Vagliano Trophy 1985; Ireland (Home Int) 1984-85-86-98; Eur(L) T Ch 1985

Beharrell, John Charles
Born Solihull, Warwickshire on 2nd May, 1938
- **Cls** Royal & Ancient, Edgbaston, Aldeburgh. Hon member of Little Aston, Blackwell, Handsworth
- **Chp** Amateur Champion 1956
- **Trn** Antlers Royal Mid-Surrey 1960.
- **Reg** Central England Mixed Foursomes 1956-57-75
- **Int** GB v Europe 1956; v Professionals 1956. England (Home Int) 1956
- **Jun Int** English Boy 1955
- **Mis** Captain of Royal and Ancient 1998/99

Beharrell, Veronica (née Anstey)
Born Birmingham on 14th January, 1935
- **Cls** Edgbaston (Hon), Little Aston
- **Oth** Australian Ladies, New Zealand Ladies 1955; Victoria Ladies Open 1955
- **Reg** Warwickshire Ladies 1955-56-57-58-60-71-72-75; Central England Mixed Foursomes 1957-75
- **Int** Curtis Cup 1956. England (Home Int) 1955-56-58-(61)
- **Jun Int** English Girls 1953

Benka, Peter
Born London on 18th September, 1946
- **Cls** Addington, West Sussex
- **Nat** Scottish Open Amateur Stroke Play r/u 1969
- **Oth** Dutch Amateur 1972
- **Trn** County Champion of Champions 1967; Sunningdale Foursomes 1969; St George's Challenge Cup 1969. Mullingar Trophy 1970; St George's Hill Trophy 1971-75; John Cross Bowl 1994
- **Reg** Surrey Amateur 1967-68
- **Int** Walker Cup 1969; GBI v Europe 1970; England (Home Int) 1967-68-69-70; Eur T Ch 1969
- **Jun** British Youths 1967-68
- **Int** Boys 1964; Youths 1966-67-68

Bennett, Warren
Born Ruislip on 20th August, 1971. Turned Professional 1994
- **Maj** Open: leading amateur 1994
PROFESSIONAL
- **Cha** Dutch Challenge Open 1995; Challenge Eulen Open Galea 1997; BTC Slovenian Open, Open de Volcans, Challenge de France, Challenge Tour Chp, Moscow CC Russian Open 1998
AMATEUR
- **Nat** English Open Amateur Stroke Play (Brabazon) r/u 1994
- **Oth** Australian Centennial Amateur 1994; International Team Chp Sydney
- **Trn** St Andrews Links Trophy r/u 1994. Selborne Salver; Lytham Trophy 1994.
- **Reg** Middlesex Chp 1994
- **Int** GBI v Europe 1994; Eisenhower Trophy 1994; England (Home Int) 1992-93-94; v France 1994
- **Jun Int** English Youths 1991-92; British Youths 1992

Bisgood, Jeanne, CBE
Born Richmond, Surrey on 11th August, 1923
- **Cls** Parkstone (Hon)
- **Nat** English Ladies 1951-53-57
- **Oth** Swedish Ladies 1952; Italian Ladies, German Ladies 1953; Portuguese Ladies 1954; Norwegian Ladies 1955.
- **Trn** Astor Salver 1951-52-53; Roehampton Gold Cup 1951-52-53. Daily Graphic Cup 1945-51
- **Reg** South Eastern Ladies 1950-52; Surrey Ladies 1951-53-69
- **Int** Curtis Cup 1950-52-54-(70); England (Home Int) 1949-50-51-52-53-54-56-58

Bladon, Warren
Born Coventry on 4th May, 1966
- **Cls** Kenilworth
- **Chp** Amateur Champion 1996
- **Trn** Guinness Open 1984, 1993
- **Reg** Warwickshire Champion 1985
- **Int** GBI v Europe 1996; England (Home Int) 1996

Boatman, Elizabeth (née Collis)
Born 7th April, 1944
- **Nat** English Ladies s/f 1974
- **Reg** Essex Ladies 1964-65-69-80-83
- **Int** England (Home Int) 1974-80-(84)-(85)-(90)-(91); Eur(L) T Ch (1985)-(87)-(91); (GBI) Commonwealth Trn (1987)-(91); Vagliano Trophy (1987); Curtis Cup (1992)-(94)
- **Mis** Chairman ELGA 1989

Bonallack, Sir Michael Francis, Kt, OBE
Born Chigwell on 31st December, 1934
- **Cls** Thorpe Hall, Pine Valley, Elie.
- **Maj** Leading Amateur in Open 1968-71
- **Chp** Amateur Champion 1961-65-68-69-70; s/f 1958-72-77

Nat	English Amateur 1962-63-65-67-68; r/u 1959; English Open Amateur Stroke Play 1964-68-69 (tied)-71; r/u 1959-66-67
Trn	Berkshire Trophy 1957-61-65-68-70-71 (shared); Hampshire Hog 1957-79; Worplesdon Mixed Foursomes 1958; Sunningdale Foursomes 1959; Golf Illustrated Golf Vase 1961 (shared)-67 (shared)-68-69 (shared)-71-75; Scrutton Jug 1961-64-66-68-70-71; Lytham Trophy 1965 (shared)-72; Antlers Royal Mid-Surrey 1964; St George's Challenge Cup 1965-68-81; Prince of Wales Challenge Cup 1967
Reg	Essex Amateur 1954-57-59-60-61-63-64-68-69-70-72; Essex Open 1969; East Anglian Open 1973
Int	Walker Cup 1957-59-61-63-65-67-**69-71**-73; GB Commonwealth Team 1959-63-**67-71**-(**75**); Eisenhower Trophy 1960-62-64-66-**68** (individual winner, shared)-**70-72**; v Professionals 1957-58-59-60; v Europe 1958-60-62-64-66-68-70-72. England (Home Int) 1957 to 72-74 (**1962** to **67**); Eur T Ch 1959-61-63-65-67-69-71
Jun	British Boys 1952
Mis	AGW Trophy 1968; Bobby Jones Award 1972; PGA Chairman 1976 to 1981; Chairman Golf Foundation 1977; President English Golf Union 1982. Best equal individual score Eisenhower Trophy 1968. Chairman Royal & Ancient Selection Committee 1975 to 1979. Donald Ross Award 1991. Gerald Micklem Award 1991. Ambassador of Golf Award 1995. Secretary to Royal & Ancient since 1983

Bonallack, Angela (Lady Bonallack) (née Ward)
Born Birchington on 7th April, 1937

Cls	Prince's, Thorpe Hall, St Rule
Chp	Ladies British Open Amateur r/u 1962-74
Nat	English Ladies 1958-63, r/u 1960-62-72. British Ladies r/u 1962-74
Oth	Swedish Ladies, German Ladies 1955; Scandinavian Ladies 1956; Portuguese Ladies 1957
Trn	Astor Salver 1957-58-60-61-66; Worplesdon Mixed Foursomes 1958; Kayser-Bondor Foursomes 1958 (shared); Astor Prince's 1968; Avia Foursomes 1976; Roehampton Gold Cup 1980.
Reg	Essex Ladies 1968-69-73-74-76-77-78-82; South East Ladies 1957-65; Kent Ladies' 1955-56-58
Int	Curtis Cup 1956-58-60-62-64-66. Vagliano Trophy 1959-61-63. England (Home Int) 1956 to 1964; 1966-72
Jun	British Girls 1955
Mis	Leading amateur Colgate European Ladies' Open 1975-76

Bousfield, Kenneth
Born Marston Moor on 2nd October, 1919. Turned Professional 1938

Eur	German Open 1955-59. Swiss Open, Belgian Open 1958; Portuguese Open 1960-61
Trn	News Chronicle 1951; PGA Match Play 1955. PGA Close 1955; Yorkshire Evening News 1956 (shared); Dunlop 1957. Sprite 1959. Irish Hospitals 1960 (shared); Swallow-Penfold 1961. Maritime Foursomes (with G Low) 1957; Lord Derby Trn (Formby) 1959; Ryder Cup Re-Union Foursomes (A Caygill) 1964.

British Isles Players 353

Oth	Gleneagles Pro-Am 1964. Surrey Open 1951, 1975; Surrey Match Play 1967
Reg	Southern England Professional 1951-57-74. Pringle Seniors 1972
Int	Ryder Cup 1949-51-55-57-59-61; England in World Cup 1956-57

Brand, Gordon J
Born Cambridge on 6th August, 1955. Turned Professional 1976
PROFESSIONAL

Maj	Open r/u 1986
Eur	Volvo Belgian Open 1989
RoW	Ivory Coast Open 1981; Nigerian Open 1983; Nigerian Open, Ivory Coast Open 1986; Zimbabwe Open 1987; Ivory Coast Open 1988; Zambian Open 1990
Int	Ryder Cup 1983; Nissan Cup 1986; England in World Cup 1983; Dunhill Cup 1986-87 (winners)
Mis	Tooting Bec Cup 1981-86; Braid-Taylor Memorial Medal 1986; Headed Safari Tour Order of Merit 1983, 1986, 1987

AMATEUR

Int	GBI v Europe 1976; England (Home Int) 1976

Brand, Gordon Jr
Born Burntisland, Fife on 19th August, 1958. Turned Professional 1981

Cls	Hon member of Woodhall Spa, Knowle

PROFESSIONAL

Eur	Coral Classic, Bob Hope British Classic 1982; Celtic International, Panasonic European Open 1984; KLM Dutch Open, Scandinavian Enterprise Open 1987; Benson & Hedges International 1989; GA European Open 1993
RoW	South Australian Open 1988
Oth	PGA Qualifying School winner 1981
Int	Ryder Cup 1987-89; Nissan Cup 1985; Kirin Cup 1988; Four Tours World Chp 1989; Scotland in World Cup 1984-85-88-89-90-92-94; in Dunhill Cup 1985-86-87 (r/u)-88-89-91-92(r/u)-93-94-97.
Mis	Rookie of the Year 1982; AGW Trophy 1982

AMATEUR

Nat	English Open Amateur Stroke Play 1978; Scottish Open Amateur Stroke Play 1980
Oth	Swedish Open Amateur Stroke Play 1979; Portuguese Amateur 1981
Trn	Golf Illustrated Gold Vase 1980; Sunningdale Foursomes 1981
Reg	Gloucestershire Amateur 1977; South-Western Counties Amateur 1977-78
Int	Walker Cup 1979; Eisenhower Trophy 1978-80; GB v Europe 1978-80; Scotland (Home Int) 1978-80; v England 1979; v Italy 1979; v France 1980-81; v Belgium 1980; Eur T Ch 1979
Jun	British Youths 1979; Scottish Youths 1980
Int	Youths 1977-78-79

Briggs, Audrey (née Brown)
Born Kent on 31st January, 1945

Cls	Royal Liverpool
Nat	Welsh Ladies 1970-71-73-74, r/u 1978-79-80-81
Reg	Sussex Ladies 1969. Cheshire Ladies 1971-73-76-80-81. North of England Ladies 1976
Int	Vagliano Trophy 1971-73. Wales (Home Int) 1969 to 84, Eur(L) T Ch 1969-71-73-75-77-79-81-83; Fiat Trophy 1978-79-80

For list of abbreviations see page 350

Broadhurst, Paul
Born Staffordshire on 14th August, 1965. Turned Professional 1988
Maj Leading amateur in Open 1988
PROFESSIONAL
Eur Crédit Lyonnais Cannes Open 1989; Motorola Classic 1990; European Pro-Celebrity 1991; B&H International Open 1993; Open de France 1995
Int Ryder Cup 1991. England in Dunhill Cup 1991; World Cup 1995-97. Four Tours World Chp 1991
Mis Rookie of the Year 1989; Tooting Bec Cup 1990
AMATEUR
Trn Lytham Trophy 1988
Int (GBI) *v* Europe 1988. England (Home Int) 1986-87

Brodie, Allan
Born Glasgow on 25th September, 1947
Cls Balmore (Hon), Glasgow
Chp Amateur s/f 1976
Nat Scottish Amateur 1977; r/u 1973. Scottish Open Amateur Stroke Play r/u 1970
Trn Tennant Cup 1972-80; *Golf Illustrated* Gold Vase 1976
Reg West of Scotland Open Amateur 1974; Dunbartonshire Amateur Stroke Play 1975-76
Int Walker Cup 1977-79; Eisenhower Trophy 1978; GBI *v* Europe 1974-76-78-80; Scotland (Home Int) 1970-72-73-74-75-76-77-78-80; Eur T Ch 1973-77-79; *v* Belgium, Spain 1977; *v* France 1978; *v* England, Italy 1979
Jun Int Youths 1966-67

Brown, Audrey *See* Briggs

Brown, Kenneth
Born Harpenden, Herts on 9th January, 1957. Turned Professional 1974
Eur Carrolls Irish Open 1978; KLM Dutch Open 1983; Glasgow Classic 1984; Four Stars Pro-Celebrity 1985
US Southern Open 1987
RoW Kenya Open 1983
Oth Hertfordshire Open 1975
Int Ryder Cup 1977-79-83-85-87; Hennessy-Cognac Cup 1978-84; Kirin Cup 1987. Scotland: Double Diamond 1977; World Cup 1977-78-79-83
Mis Tooting Bec Cup 1980
Jun Carris Trophy 1974
Int Boys 1974

Burke, Ita *See* Butler

Bussell, Alan Francis
Born Glasgow on 25th February, 1937
Cls Whitecraigs (Hon), Coxmoor (Hon), Chevin
Chp Amateur s/f 1957
Trn Antlers Royal Mid-Surrey 1956. *Golf Illustrated* Gold Vase 1959
Reg Nottinghamshire Amateur 1959-60-62-63-64-68-69. Nottinghamshire Open 1960-62. Nottinghamshire Match Play 1960-62. Renfrewshire Amateur 1955

Int Walker Cup 1957. GB *v* Europe 1956-62; *v* Professionals 1956-57-59. Scotland (Home Int) 1956-57-58-61; *v* Scandinavia 1956-60
Jun British Boys 1954. Boy International 1954. British Youths 1956. Youth International 1954-55-56

Butler, Ita (*née* Burke)
Born Nenagh, Co Tipperary
Cls Hon member of Elm Park, Killarney, Woodbrook, Nenagh
Nat Irish Ladies r/u 1972-78
Reg Leinster Ladies three times. Munster and Midland Ladies twice
Int Curtis Cup 1966-96. World Team Championship 1966-(94). Vagliano Trophy 1965-(91)-(93). Ireland (World Cup) 1964; (Home Int) 1962-63-64-65-66-68-71-72-73-76-77-78-79; Eur T Ch 1967; Fiat Trophy 1978

Butler, Peter J
Born Birmingham on 25th March, 1932. Turned Professional 1948
Cls French Open 1968. Colombian Open 1975
Trn Swallow-Penfold 1959. Yorkshire Evening News 1962; PGA Close 1963. Bowmaker 1963-67. Cox Moore 1964. PGA Match Play r/u 1964-75. Martini 1965. Piccadilly 1965-67. Penfold, Wills 1968. RTV 1969. Classic International 1971. Sumrie 1974 Evian International 1963. Grand Bahama Invitation Open 1971-72
Reg Midland Open 1956-58-60-65-69. Midland Professional 1961.
Sen Lawrence Batley Seniors 1993
Oth Gleneagles Pro-Am 1963. Sunningdale Foursomes 1974
Int Ryder Cup 1965-69-71-73. England in World Cup. 1969-70-73. England in Double Diamond 1971-72-76. GBI *v* Europe 1976. PGA Cup 1978-79-81-82-84
Mis Equal lowest round in British events of 61. Second in Order of Merit 1968. PGA Captain 1972

Buxton, Nicola
Born 9th March, 1973
Cls Woodsome Hall
Nat English Ladies 1991-93; English Ladies Stroke Play r/u 1992; English U-23 and U-21 Stroke Play 1992
Oth Portuguese Women's Open r/u 1994
Trn Critchley Salver 1991
Reg Yorkshire Ladies 1989-90-91
Int Curtis Cup 1992; Vagliano Trophy 1991-93; England (Home Int) 1991-92-93; Eur(L) T Ch 1991
Jun English Girls 1991

Cadden, Suzanne *See* McMahon

Caldwell, Ian
Born Streatham on 17th May, 1930
Cls Royal & Ancient, Sunningdale, Walton Heath
Nat English Amateur 1961

For list of abbreviations see page 350

Trn	Prince of Wales Challenge Cup 1950-51-52. Boyd Quaich 1954.
Reg	Surrey Amateur 1961
Int	Walker Cup 1951-55. GB Commonwealth Team 1954. GBI *v* Europe 1955. England (Home Int) 1950-51-52-53-54-55-56-57-61
Jun	Carris Trophy 1947-48

Caldwell, Carole *(née* Redford)

Born Kingston, Surrey on 23rd April, 1949

Cls	Canterbury (Hon)
Trn	Newmark-Avia International 1973. Roehampton Gold Cup 1973-75-78; Hampshire Rose 1973, 1984; Avia Foursomes 1974; Critchley Salver 1974; Canadian Ladies Foursomes 1978; London Foursomes 1984
Oth	Portuguese Ladies 1980
Reg	South Eastern Ladies 1973-78. Kent Ladies 1970-75-77-86. Berkshire Ladies 1982
Int	Curtis Cup 1978-80; Vagliano Trophy 1973; England (Home Int) 1973-78-79-80
Mis	Playing captain of LGU U-23 team to tour Canada 1973. Lost at 27th hole in first round of American Ladies Amateur 1978

Carr, Joseph B

Born Dublin on 18th February, 1922

Cls	Sutton (Hon)
Maj	Leading Amateur in Open 1956-58
Chp	Amateur Champion 1953-58-60, r/u 1968 s/f 1952-54.
Nat	Irish Amateur 1954-57-63-64-65-67, r/u 1951-59. Irish Open Amateur 1946-50-54-56, r/u 1947-48-51; US Amateur s/f 1961
Trn	*Golf Illustrated* Gold Vase 1951. Gleneagles Saxone 1955. Berkshire Trophy 1959. Formby Hare 1962. Mullingar Trophy 1963. Antlers Royal Mid-Surrey 1970
Reg	South of Ireland Open Amateur 1948-66-69. East of Ireland Open Amateur 1941-43-45-46-48-56-57-58-60-61-64-69. West of Ireland Open Amateur 1946-47-48-51-53-54-56-58-60-61-62-66
Int	Walker Cup 1947-49-51-53-55-57-59-61-**63**-(**65**)-67. GBI *v* Europe 1954-56-**64-66**-68. Eisenhower Trophy 1958-60-(**64**)-(**66**). Ireland (Home Int) 1947 to 1969 Eur T Ch 1965-67-69
Mis	AGW Trophy 1953. Bobby Jones Award 1961. Walter Hagen Award 1967. Captain of Royal & Ancient 1991/92

Carrick, David

Born Glasgow on 28th January, 1957

Nat	Scottish Amateur 1985. Scottish Open Amateur Stroke Play 1987
Trn	Scottish Champion of Champions 1983. Glasgow Amateur 1980-81
Reg	Dunbartonshire Amateur 1979-80-82-83
Int	Walker Cup 1983-87. GBI *v* Europe 1986. Scotland (Home Int) 1981 to 1989; *v* Italy 1988; *v* France 1989; Eur T Ch 1989; *v* West Germany 1987
Mis	Braid Panton Trophy 1987

Chadwick, Elizabeth *See* Pook

Chapman, Roger

Born in Nakuru, Kenya on 1st May, 1959. Turned Professional 1981

PROFESSIONAL
RoW	Zimbabwe Open 1988
Trn	Sunningdale Open Foursomes 1986
Mis	Tooting Bec Cup 1991(shared)

AMATEUR
Nat	English Amateur 1979
Trn	Duncan Putter (shared), Lytham Trophy 1981; Sunningdale Open Foursomes 1979
Int	Walker Cup 1981; GBI *v* Europe 1980; England (Home Int) 1980-81; Eur T Ch 1981

Christmas, Martin J

Born 1939

Cls	West Sussex, Addington
Chp	Amateur s/f 1961-64-65
Nat	English Amateur r/u 1960. English Open Amateur Stroke Play r/u 1960
Trn	Gleneagles Pro-Am 1961. Wentworth Pro-Am Foursomes 1962
Oth	Belgian Open Amateur 1976
Reg	Sussex Amateur 1962
Int	Walker Cup 1961-63. Eisenhower Trophy 1962. GBI *v* Europe 1960-62-64. England (Home Int) 1960-61-62-63-64

Clark, Clive Anthony

Born Winchester, Hants on 27th June, 1945. Turned Professional 1965

PROFESSIONAL
Maj	Open (tied) 3rd 1967 (leading British player)
Trn	Danish Open 1966; Bowmaker Agfa-Gevaert 1968; John Player Trophy 1970; Sumrie 1974
Int	Ryder Cup 1973

AMATEUR
Chp	Amateur r/u 1965
Nat	English Amateur r/u 1965. English Open Amateur Stroke Play 1965 (tied)
Trn	Lytham Trophy 1965 (tied). *Golf Illustrated* Gold Vase, Scrutton Jug 1965
Oth	Sunningdale Foursomes 1974-76
Int	Walker Cup 1965. GBI *v* Europe 1964. England (Home Int) 1964-65
Mis	Braid-Taylor Memorial Medal 1967; TV commentator. Golf course architect

Clark, Howard K

Born Leeds on 26th August, 1954. Turned Professional October 1973

PROFESSIONAL
Eur	Portuguese Open, Madrid Open 1978; Cepsa Madrid Open, Whyte & Mackay PGA Chp 1984; Jersey Open, Glasgow Open 1985; Cepsa Madrid Open, Peugeot Spanish Open 1986; Moroccan Open, PLM Open 1987; English Open 1988
Oth	U-25 TPD 1976
Int	Ryder Cup 1977-81-85-87-89-95; Nissan Cup 1985-86; Hennessy-Cognac Cup 1978-84; England in World Cup 1978-84-85 (individual winner)-87; Dunhill Cup 1985-86-87 (winners)-89-90(r/u)-94-95

AMATEUR
Chp	Amateur s/f 1973
Reg	Yorkshire Amateur 1973

Int Walker Cup 1973; England (Home Int) 1973
Jun British Boys 1971
Int Boys 1969-71; Youths 1971-72-73

Clarke, Darren
Born Dungannon on 14th August, 1968. Turned Professional 1990
PROFESSIONAL
Maj Open r/u 1997
Eur Alfred Dunhill Open 1993; Linde German Masters 1996; B&H International Open, Volvo Masters 1998
Int Ireland in World Cup 1994-95-96; Dunhill Cup 1994-95-96-98
AMATEUR
Nat Irish Amateur 1990; Spanish Open Amateur 1990
Int Ireland (Home Int) 1987-89; (GBI) v Europe 1990

Claydon, Russell
Born on 19th November, 1965. Turned Professional 1989
Maj Leading amateur in Open 1989
PROFESSIONAL
Eur BMW International Open 1998
Int England: Dunhill Cup 1997
Mis Rookie of the Year 1990
AMATEUR
Nat English Amateur 1988
RoW Australian Masters r/u 1989
Trn St George's Challenge Cup 1986; Berkshire Trophy, County Champion of Champions 1988; St Andrews Links Trophy 1989; Sunningdale Open Foursomes 1989
Reg Cambridge Amateur 1987-88
Oth UAP U-25 European Open r/u 1988
Int Walker Cup 1989; England (Home Int) 1988 Eur T Ch 1989

Coles, Neil, MBE
Born London on 26th September, 1934. Turned Professional 1950
Maj Open 3rd 1961; r/u 1973; leading British player 1975 (7th)
Eur German Open 1971. Spanish Open 1973
Trn Ballantine 1961. Service Service 1962. Daks 1963 (tied)-64-70-71 (tied). Martini 1963 (tied). Engadine Open 1963. Bowmaker 1964-70. PGA Match Play 1964-65-73, r/u 1966-72-78. Carrolls 1965-71. Pringle, Dunlop Masters 1966. Sumrie 1970-73. Shell BP Italy, Walworth Aloyco Italy 1970; Penfold 1971. Sunbeam 1972. Wills 1974. Penfold PGA 1976. Tournament Players' Championship 1977. Sanyo Open 1982
Oth British Assistants 1956. Sunningdale Foursomes 1962-67-80. Wentworth Pro-Am Foursomes 1963-70. Southern England Professionals 1970
Int Ryder Cup 1961-63-65-67-69-71-73-77. England in World Cup 1963-68. England in Double Diamond 1971-73-75-76-77. Hennessy-Cognac Cup 1974-76-78-80. (Sen) European Cup 1998
Sen Seniors British Open 1987. PGA Seniors Chp 1985-86-87-89. Geneva Seniors Open 1991.

Collingtree Homes Senior Classic 1992. Gary Player Seniors Classic 1993. Collingtree Seniors 1995. Ryder Collingtree Classic 1997. Philips PFA Classic 1998
Mis Harry Vardon Trophy 1963-70. Second in Order of Merit 1987. Chairman PGA European Tour. Golf course architect.

Collingham, Janet (*née* Melville)
Born Barrow-in-Furness on 16th March, 1958
Cls Notts Ladies
Chp Ladies British Open Amateur 1987
Nat Ladies British Open Amateur Stroke Play 1978
Trn Worplesdon Mixed Foursomes 1979. Northern Foursomes 1977-78. Mary McCalley Trophy 1980
Reg Highland Open 1978. Midland Ladies 1986. Lancashire Champion 1983-86. Notts Ladies 1998
Int Vagliano Trophy 1979-87. England (Home Int) 1978-79-81-84-86-87-92; Eur(L) T Ch 1979. Girls International 1976-(**81**)
Mis Varsity Athlete in golf at Florida International University 1980-81; Duncan Salver 1978

Collis, Elizabeth *See* Boatman

Coltart, Andrew John
Born Dumfries on 12th May, 1970. Turned Professional 1991
Cls Thornhill
PROFESSIONAL
Eur Qatar Masters 1998
RoW Australian PGA 1994-97
Oth Scottish Professional 1994
Int Scotland: Dunhill Cup 1994-95(winners)-96-98. World Cup 1994-95-96-98
Mis ANZ Tour Order of Merit Winner 1998
AMATEUR
Nat Scottish Amateur r/u 1988; Scottish Open Amateur Stroke Play 1991
Trn Leven Gold Medal 1989
Reg West of Scotland 1991
Int Walker Cup 1991. Eisenhower Trophy 1990; GBI v Europe 1990. Scotland (Home Int) 1988-89-90; Eur T Ch 1989-91; Nixdorf Nations Cup 1990; v Sweden, Italy 1990
Oth Leone de San Marco 1990
Jun British Youths r/u 1989-90; Scottish Boys 1987

Cosh, Gordon B
Born Glasgow on 26th March, 1939
Cls Troon, Royal Aberdeen, Bruntsfield Links. Hon member of Cowglen, Killarney
Nat Scottish Amateur 1968, r/u 1965. Scottish Open Amateur Stroke Play r/u 1968
Trn Newlands Trophy 1980
Reg West of Scotland Amateur 1961-64-65-66. Glasgow County Match Play 1965-66. Glasgow Amateur 1969. Glasgow County Stroke Play 1972-74
Int Walker Cup 1965. Eisenhower Trophy 1966-68. GB Commonwealth Team 1967. GBI v Europe 1966-68. Scotland (Home Int) 1964-65-66-67-68-69; Eur T Ch 1965-**69**
Jun Int Youths 1959-60

Craddock, Tom
Born Malahide on 16th December, 1931
- **Cls** Malahide, Donabate, Sutton, The Island Malahide, Malone, Woodbrook, Mullingar, Carlow, Howth, Tara, Killarney
- **Nat** Irish Amateur 1959, r/u 1965. Irish Open Amateur 1958
- **Trn** Lytham Trophy 1969
- **Reg** East of Ireland Open Amateur 1959-65-66
- **Int** Walker Cup 1967-69. Ireland (Home Int) 1955-56-57-58-59-60-65-66-67-69; Eur T Ch 1967-71

Critchley, Bruce
Born 9th December, 1942
- **Cls** Sunningdale, Killarney (Hon)
- **Chp** Amateur s/f 1970
- **Trn** Worplesdon Mixed Foursomes 1961. Sunningdale Foursomes 1964. Hampshire Hog 1969. Antlers Royal Mid-Surrey 1974
- **Reg** Surrey Amateur 1969
- **Int** Walker Cup 1969. GBI v Europe 1970. England (Home Int) 1962-69-70; Eur T Ch 1969
- **Mis** TV commentator. Co-founder annual match between former Ryder Cup v Walker Cup Players

Curry, David H
Born 6th July, 1963. Turned Professional 1988
- **Chp** Amateur Champion 1986
- **Trn** Selborne Salver 1984
- **Int** (GBI) Walker Cup 1987, Eisenhower Trophy 1986, v Europe 1986-88. England (Home Int) 1984-86-87, v France 1988

Dalgleish, Colin R
Born Glasgow on 24th September, 1960
- **Cls** Helensburgh (Hon), Millstone Mills (Hon)
- **Nat** Scottish Amateur 1981
- **Trn** Tennant Cup 1983-88
- **RoW** East of India Amateur 1981. Indian Amateur r/u 1981. Lake Macquarie International Stroke-Play Champion (Australia) 1983
- **Oth** Scottish Universities Champion 1983
- **Int** Walker Cup 1981. Scotland (Home Int) 1981-82-83; v France 1982; Eur T Ch 1981-83. GB v Europe 1982. Europe v South America 1982. Scottish Captain 1994-95-96
- **Jun** International Junior Masters 1977. Belgian Junior Championship 1980. British Boys r/u 1977. British Youths r/u 1979-82. Boy International 1976-77-78. Youth International 1979-80-81-82

Darcy, Eamonn
Born Delgany on 7th August, 1952. Turned Professional 1969
- **Eur** Spanish Open 1983; Belgian Open 1987; Desert Classic 1990
- **Trn** Sumrie 1976-78. Greater Manchester Open 1977
- **RoW** Air New Zealand Open 1980. Cock o' the North Open 1981. Kenya Open 1982. Mufulira Open 1984. West Lakes Classic (Aus) 1981
- **Oth** Irish Dunlop 1976. Cacharel World Under-25 1976. Irish Match Play 1981
- **Int** Ryder Cup 1975-77-81-87. Ireland in Double Diamond 1975-76-77. Ireland in World Cup 1976-77-83-84-85-87-91. GBI v Europe 1976; v South Africa 1976. Hennessy-Cognac Cup 1976-84. Dunhill Cup 1987-88 (winners)-91
- **Mis** Second in Order of Merit 1976; Tooting Bec Cup 1980(shared)-1991(shared); Braid Taylor Memorial Medal 1991

Davies, John C
Born London on 14th February, 1948
- **Cls** Mid-Surrey, Sunningdale, Royal Cinque Ports, Killarney
- **Chp** Amateur r/u 1976.
- **Nat** English Amateur r/u 1971-76. English Open Amateur Stroke Play r/u 1977
- **Trn** Berkshire Trophy 1969-71 (tied). Royal St George's Challenge Cup 1972-73-74-75-76-77. Sunningdale Foursomes 1968-72. Antlers Royal Mid-Surrey 1969-75-77. Golf Illustrated Gold Vase 1973-77. Prince of Wales Cup 1975. Berkhamsted Trophy 1976-78-79
- **Oth** Second equal in South African Open Amateur Stroke Play 1974
- **Reg** Surrey Amateur 1971-72-77
- **Int** Walker Cup 1973-75-77-79. Eisenhower Trophy 1974-76 (winners). GBI v Europe 1972-74-76-78; England (Home Int) 1969-70-71-72-73-74-78; Eur T Ch 1973-75-77
- **Mis** Member of European Team to tour South Africa 1974

Davies, Karen L
Born 19th June, 1965. Turned Professional 1988
PROFESSIONAL
- **Int** Sunrise Cup 1992

AMATEUR
- **Oth** Florida State Tournament 1985. South-Eastern USA Championship 1985
- **Int** Curtis Cup 1986-88. Wales (Home Int) 1981-82-83 (Eur L U-22) 1981-82-83-84-85-86; Eur(L) T Ch 1987, Commonwealth Team 1987
- **Jun** Welsh Girls 1980-82

Davies, Laura, MBE
Born Coventry on 5th October, 1963. Turned Professional 1985
- **Maj** Ladies British Open 1986; r/u 1987. US Women's Open 1987; McDonald's LPGA 1994-96; Du Maurier Classic 1996

PROFESSIONAL
- **Eur** Belgian Ladies Open 1985; McEwan's Wirral Classic, Greater Manchester Tournament, Ladies Spanish Open 1986; Italian Open 1987; Italian Open, Ford Ladies Classic, Biarritz Ladies Open 1988; Laing Charity Ladies Classic 1989; AGF Biarritz Ladies Open 1990; Valextra Classic 1991; European Ladies Open, Ladies English Open, BMW Ladies Italian Open 1992; Ladies English Open 1993; Ladies Irish Open, Ladies Scottish Open 1994; Evian Masters, Irish Holidays Open, Welsh Open, English Open 1995; Evian Masters, English Open, Open de Sicilia 1996; Danish Open, Hennessy Cup 1997; Chrysler Open 1998

For list of abbreviations see page 350

US Tucson Open, Toledo Classic 1988; Lady Keystone Open 1989; Inamori Classic 1991; McDonald's Chp 1993; Standard Register Ping, Sara Lee Classic 1994; Standard Register Ping, Chick-fil-A Charity Chp 1995; Standard Register Ping, du Maurier Classic, Star Bank LPGA Classic 1996; Standard Register Ping 1997; JCPenney Skins Game, LPGA Tour Chp 1998
RoW Itoki Classic (Jpn) 1989-95; Australian Ladies' Masters 1993-94, Thailand Open 1993-94; Itoen Ladies (Jpn) 1994-95
Int Solheim Cup 1990-92-94-96-98; Sunrise Cup 1992; (for LPGA) Nichirei International 1993
Mis Rookie of the Year 1985. Order of Merit winner 1985-86-92-96. Hon. Member of WPGET 1993. Top of LPGA Money List 1994. Ping No. 1 1994. AGW Trophy 1994. American Golf Writers LPGA Player of the Year 1994-96. Rolex Player of the Year 1996. Vivien Saunders Trophy 1992-93
AMATEUR
Nat Welsh Open Stroke Play 1984
Oth English Intermediate 1983
Trn London Foursomes 1981
Reg South-Eastern Champion 1983-84
Int Curtis Cup 1984; Vilmorin Cup 1984; England (Home Int) 1983-84
Jun Surrey Girls 1982

Deeble, Peter George
Born Alnwick on 27th February, 1954
Cls Alnmouth, Alnwick, Hon member of Ponteland, Hexham, Rothbury, Washington, Tynedale
Nat English Amateur 1976-80
Trn Antlers Royal Mid-Surrey 1976. Lytham Trophy 1977. Berkhamsted Trophy 1975. County Champion of Champions 1982
Reg Northumberland Amateur 1975-82-83. Northumberland Stroke Play 1973-75-77-78-79. Northumberland and Durham Open 1976
Int Walker Cup 1977-81. GBI v Europe 1978. Europe v South America 1980. GB in Colombian International 1978. England (Home Int) 1975-76-77-78-80-81-83; Eur T Ch 1979-81; v Scotland 1979; v France 1982. England in Fiat Trophy 1980
Jun Int Boys 1970-71. Youths 1973-75-76

Deighton, Dr FWG
Born Glasgow on 21st May, 1927
Cls Royal & Ancient, Western Gailes, Elie, Glasgow, Hilton Park (Hon), North Hants
Nat Scottish Amateur 1956-59
Trn Edward Trophy 1954. Gleneagles Silver Tassie 1956. Tennant Cup 1958-60-64
Oth Boyd Quaich 1947 (tied). Royal & Ancient Silver Cross 1953-60-63-70-73. Royal Medal 1956-59-61-63-66-73. Glennie Medal 1956-58-59-60-66-70-73
Reg West of Scotland Amateur 1959. Dunbartonshire Amateur 1949-50-53-54. Glasgow Amateur 1951-55
Int Walker Cup 1951-57. GB Commonwealth Team 1954-59. GBI v Professionals 1956-57. Scotland (Home Int) 1950-52-53-56-58-59-60; v South Africa 1954; v New Zealand 1954; v Scandinavia 1956
Mis Member of British Touring Team to South Africa 1952

Dobson, Helen
Born Skegness on 25th February, 1971. Turned Professional 1990
PROFESSIONAL
Eur BMW European Masters 1993
US LPGA: State Farm Rail Classic 1993
Int Union Cup 1994
AMATEUR
Chp Ladies British Open Amateur 1989
Nat Ladies British Open Amateur Stroke Play 1989; English Ladies 1989
Trn Wentworth Scratch Trophy, Bridget Jackson Bowl 1989
Oth World Fourball (with Elaine Farquharson) 1989
Int Curtis Cup 1990; Vagliano Trophy 1989; England (Home Int) 1987-88-89; Eur(L) T Ch 1989
Jun British Girls 1987; English Girls 1988-89
Jun Int English Girls 1988
Mis Duncan Salver 1989. Avia Woman Golfer of the Year 1989

Dodd, Stephen
Born Cardiff on 15th July, 1966. Turned Professional 1990
PROFESSIONAL
Eur Memorial Olivier Barras 1991; Bank of Austria Open 1992
Reg West Region PGA 1991. Welsh PGA 1995
AMATEUR
Chp Amateur Champion 1989
Nat Welsh Amateur 1989
Trn Silver Dragon, WI Tucker Trophy 1987; Duncan Putter, Carad Trophy, Cardiff Feathers, Golden Lamp 1988
Int Walker Cup 1989; Wales (Home Int) 1985-87-88-89, Eur T Ch 1987

Douglas, Kitrina
Born Bristol on 6th September, 1960. Turned Professional 1984
Maj Ladies British Open 3rd 1990
PROFESSIONAL
Eur Ford Classic, Swedish Ladies Open, Rookie of the Year 1984; Mitsubishi Colt Cars, Jersey Open 1986; Hennessy-Cognac Ladies Cup 1987; St Moritz Ladies Classic, Godiva European Masters 1989; English Open 1991; BMW European Masters 1992
Int Solheim Cup 1992
Mis Rookie of the Year 1984
AMATEUR
Chp British Ladies 1982
Oth Portuguese Champion 1983
Trn Critchley Salver 1983
Reg Gloucestershire Champion 1980-81-82-83-84
Int Curtis Cup 1982. Vagliano Trophy 1983. England (Home Int) 1981-82. Eur(L) T Ch 1983
Jun Scottish Girls Stroke-Play 1981

Dowling, Claire (née Hourihane)
Born 18th February, 1958
Cls Woodbrook
Nat Irish Ladies 1983-84-85-87-91; r/u 1980. British Ladies Stroke Play 1986; r/u 1990
Trn South Atlantic (USA) 1983; Hampshire Rose 1986; Critchley Salver 1990

Reg	South Ireland Cup 1977; Leinster Ladies 1980
Int	Curtis Cup 1984-86-88-90-92; Vagliano Trophy 1981-83-85-87-89-91; Espirito Santo 1986-90; Ireland (Home Int) 1979 to 1992, **1996**; Eur(L) T Ch 1981-83-85-87-89-**97**

Dowling, Deborah

Born Wimbledon on 26th July, 1962. Turned Professional 1981

PROFESSIONAL
Eur	Jersey Open, Woodhall Hills Trn 1983; Portuguese Ladies Open 1985; Eastleigh Classic, Laing Ladies Classic 1986; Bloor Homes Eastleigh Classic 1989
RoW	Singapore Open 1996
Int	Union Cup 1994

AMATEUR
Reg	Surrey Champion 1980
Int	England (Home Int) 1981, Eur(L) T Ch 1981

Dredge, Bradley

Born Gwent, Wales on 6th July, 1973. Turned Professional 1995

PROFESSIONAL
Oth	Klassis Turkish Open 1997

AMATEUR
Chp	Amateur r/u 1992
Nat	European Amateur r/u 1992
Trn	St David's Gold Cross 1992; Welsh Trn of Champions 1994; Duncan Putter, Trubshaw Cup 1995
Int	Walker Cup 1993; (GB) Eisenhower Trophy 1992, v Europe 1994; Wales (Home Int) 1992-93-94-95; Eur T Ch 1995
Jun	Welsh Boys 1991

Drew, Norman Vico

Born Belfast on 25th May, 1932. Turned Professional 1958

PROFESSIONAL
Trn	Yorkshire Evening News, Irish Dunlop 1959
Oth	Irish Professional 1959; Ulster Professional 1966-72
Int	Ryder Cup 1959; Ireland in World Cup 1960-61

AMATEUR
Nat	Irish Open Amateur 1952-53
Reg	North of Ireland Open Amateur 1950-52; East of Ireland Open Amateur 1952
Int	Walker Cup 1953; Ireland (Home Int) 1952-53

Dundas, Stephen

Born Glasgow on 20th December, 1973

Cls	Haggs Castle
Chp	Amateur Champion 1992
Nat	Scottish Amateur s/f 1992
Int	Scotland (Home Int) 1992-93
Jun	Glasgow Boys Stroke Play, Match Play 1988-89; West of Scotland Boys 1988
Jun Int	Scotland Boys **1989**

Educate, Lisa *(née Walton)*

Born 17th June, 1972

Cls	Calcot Park
Nat	English Women's Stroke Play U-18 Award 1989; Welsh Ladies' Stroke Play U-21 1991

Trn	Todd Bowl 1990; Sunningdale Gold Vase 1989; Pleasington Putter 1991; Ping Lady Sun Dial Collegiate Trn 1991
Int	Curtis Cup 1994-96; Espirito Santo 1994; Vagliano Trophy 1993-95; CW 1995; England (Home Int) 1991-94-95; Eur(L) T Ch 1993-95
Jun Int	English Girls 1988-89-90

Evans, Albert David

Born Newton, Brecon, Wales on 28th August, 1911

Cls	Royal & Ancient, Royal Porthcawl. Hon member of Brecon, Ross-on-Wye, Hereford, Worcestershire, Builth Wells, Pennard, Monmouth, Killarney
Chp	Welsh Amateur 1949-61
Reg	Herefordshire Amateur 1938-46-49-51-53-54-55-59-60-61-62. Breconshire Amateur 1929-31-32-33-34-37
Int	Wales (Home Int) 1931-32-33-34-35-38-39-47-48-49-50-51-52-53-54-55-56-**60-61-62-63-64-65**; v Australia 1954
Mis	Walker Cup Selector 1964-75

Evans, Duncan

Born Crewe on 23rd January, 1959

Cls	Hon member of Leek, Conway, Holyhead, Royal Porthcawl, Westwood
Chp	Amateur Champion 1980
Nat	Welsh Amateur Stroke Play Championship 1981, r/u 1980
Reg	Staffordshire Amateur 1979. Aberconwy Trophy 1981
Int	Walker Cup 1981. GBI v Europe, Europe v South America 1980. Wales (Home Int) 1978-80; v Ireland 1979; in Fiat Trophy 1980. Eur T Ch 1981
Jun Int	Youths 1980

Evans, Gary

Born Rustington on 22nd February, 1969. Turned Professional 1991

Cls	Worthing
Nat	English Amateur r/u 1990; English Open Amateur Stroke Play 1990-91
Trn	Lytham Trophy 1990-91; St Andrews Trophy r/u 1991
Int	Walker Cup 1991; Eisenhower Trophy 1990; England (Home Int) 1990; Eur T Ch 1991
Jun Int	British Youths 1989; English Youths 1989; English Boys 1986

Everard, Mrs D Mary

Born Sheffield on 8th October, 1942

Cls	Hallamshire (Hon), Woodhall Spa (Hon), Kilton Forest (Hon), Lindrick
Maj	Ladies British Open r/u 1977
Chp	Ladies British Open Amateur r/u 1967
Nat	Ladies British Open Amateur Stroke Play 1970-77, r/u 1971-73; English Ladies 1972, r/u 1964-77
Trn	Astor Salver 1967-68-78. Hovis Ladies 1967. Roehampton Gold Cup 1970. Sunningdale Foursomes 1973. Hoylake Mixed Foursomes 1965-67-71-76. Avia Foursomes 1978
Reg	North of England Ladies 1972. Yorkshire Ladies 1964-67-72-73-77

For list of abbreviations see page 350

Int	Curtis Cup 1970-72-74-78. Vagliano Trophy 1967-69-71-73. GB Commonwealth Team 1971. World Team Championship 1968-72-78, England (Home Int) 1964-67-70-72-73-77-78; Eur(L) T Ch 1967-71-73-77
Mis	Member of British team to tour Australia 1973. Captain English team to tour Kenya 1973

Faldo, Nicholas Alexander, MBE
Born Welwyn Garden City on 18th July, 1957. Turned Professional 1976
PROFESSIONAL

Maj	Open Champion 1987-90-92, r/u 1993; 3rd 1988; US Open r/u 1988 (tied) 3rd 1990; US Masters 1989-90-96; US PGA r/u 1992; 3rd 1993
Eur	Colgate PGA 1978; Sun Alliance PGA 1980; Sun Alliance 1981; Haig Whisky TPC 1982; French Open, Martini Int'l, Lawrence Batley Int'l, Car Care Plan Int'l, Ebel Swiss Open European Masters 1983; Car Care Plan Int'l 1984; Peugeot Spanish Open 1987; Peugeot French Open, Volvo Masters 1988; Volvo PGA, Dunhill British Masters, Peugeot French Open, Suntory World Match Play 1989; Carrolls Irish Open 1991; Carrolls Irish Open, Scandinavian Masters, GA European Open, Toyota World Match Play 1992; Johnnie Walker Classic, Carrolls Irish Open 1993; Alfred Dunhill Open 1994
US	Heritage Classic 1984; Doral–Ryder Open 1995; Nissan Open 1997
RoW	ICL Int'l 1979; Johnnie Walker Asian Classic 1990; Johnnie Walker World Chp 1992; Million Dollar Challenge 1994
Oth	Skol Lager 1977
Int	Ryder Cup 1977-79-81-83-85-87-89-91-93-95-97; Nissan Cup 1986; Kirin Cup 1987-88; Hennessy-Cognac Cup 1978-80-82-84; England in World Cup 1977-91-98 (winners); in Double Diamond 1977; in Dunhill Cup 1985-86-87 (winners)-88-91-93(r/u); Four Tours Chp 1990
Mis	Rookie of the Year 1977; Harry Vardon Trophy 1983-92; AGW Trophy 1983-90; Braid-Taylor Memorial Medal 1983-84-87-88-90; BBC Sports Personality of the Year 1989; US PGA Player of the Year 1990; Tooting Bec Cup 1992. World Golf Hall of Fame 1997

AMATEUR

Nat	English Amateur 1975
Trn	Berkshire Trophy, Scrutton Jug, County Champion of Champions 1975
Reg	Hertfordshire Amateur 1975
Oth	South African GU Special Stroke Chp 1975
Int	GB Commonwealth Trn 1975; England (Home Int) 1975
Jun	British Youths 1975
Int	Boys 1974; Youths 1975

Farquharson-Black, Elaine
Born Aberdeen on 21st March, 1968. Turned Professional 1992. Reinstated Amateur

Cls	Deeside

PROFESSIONAL

Int	Union Cup 1994

AMATEUR

Chp	Ladies British Open Amateur r/u 1989
Nat	Scottish Ladies 1990
Oth	World Fourball (with Helen Dobson) 1989
Trn	Helen Holm Trophy 1987

Reg	Aberdeenshire Ladies 1983-86-87
Int	Curtis Cup 1990-92; Vagliano Trophy 1989-91; Commonwealth Trn 1991; Scotland (Home Int) 1987-88-89-90-91-97-98; Eur(L) T Ch 1989-91
Jun	British Girls r/u 1984-85; Scottish Girls 1985
Int	Scottish Girls 1982-84-85; Eur Jun(L) T Ch 1986-88

Faulkner, Max
Born Bexhill, Sussex on 29th July, 1916. Turned Professional June 1933

Maj	Open Champion 1951
Eur	Spanish Open 1952-53-57. Portuguese Open 1968
Trn	Dunlop Southport 1946. Dunlop 1949-52. Penfold Foursomes 1949. Lotus 1949. Dunlop Masters 1951. PGA Match Play 1953. Irish Hospitals 1959
Reg	West of England Open Professional 1947. Southern England Professional 1964.
Oth	Sunningdale Open Foursomes 1964; Pringle Seniors 1968-70
Int	Ryder Cup 1947-49-51-53-57; PGA Cup 1975

Feherty, David
Born in Bangor, NI on 13th August, 1958. Turned Professional 1976

Eur	Italian Open, Bells Scottish Open 1986; BMW International Open 1989; Cannes Open 1991; Iberia Madrid Open 1992
RoW	ICL International 1984; Lexington PGA 1988; Bells Cup (SA) 1992
Int	Ryder Cup 1991. Ireland: Dunhill Cup 1986-90 (winners) -91-93; World Cup 1990; Four Tours World Chp 1990-91
Mis	Braid-Taylor Memorial Medal 1989

Ferguson, Marjory *(née Fowler)*
Born North Berwick on 15th May, 1937

Cls	North Berwick, Gullane, Killarney (Hon)
Nat	Scottish Ladies r/u 1966-71
Oth	Portuguese Ladies 1960
Reg	East of Scotland Ladies 1959-60-62-75. East Lothian Ladies 1957-58-59-60-61-62-63-64-66-67-69-74-81
Int	Curtis Cup 1966. Vagliano Trophy 1965. Scotland (Home Int) 1959-62-63-64-65-66-67-69-70; Eur(L) T Ch 1965-67-71

Le Feuvre, Carol *See* Gibbs

Fiddian, Eric Westwood
Born Stourbridge on 28th March, 1910

Cls	Stourbridge, Handsworth, Lindrick
Chp	Amateur r/u 1932
Nat	English Amateur 1932, r/u 1935. Irish Open Amateur r/u 1933
Reg	Worcestershire Amateur 1928-30-50. Midland Counties 1931
Int	Walker Cup 1932-34. England (Home Int) 1929-30-31-32-33-34-35
Jun	Boys 1927
Int	English Boys 1926-27
Mis	Had two holes-in-one in the Final of 1933 Irish Open Amateur

For list of abbreviations see page 350

Fletcher, Linzi
Born on 21st January, 1968
Cls   Alnmouth
Nat   English Ladies r/u 1990; English Womens Intermediate 1990
Trn   Critchley Salver 1989; Wentworth Scratch Trophy 1990
Int   Curtis Cup 1990; GB Commonwealth Trn 1991; England (Home Int) 1989-90; Eur(L) T Ch 1991

Forster, Dorothy *See* Humphreys

Foster, Mark B
Born Worksop on 1st August, 1975. Turned Professional 1996
Cls   Worksop; Hunstanton (Hon)
Nat   English Amateur 1994-95; English Open Amateur Stroke Play 1995
Reg   Midland Counties Champion 1994
Int   Walker Cup 1995; England (Home Int) 1994-95; v Spain 1995; Eur T Ch 1995
Jun   Carris Trophy 1992; European Youths 1994
Jun Int   English Boys 1991-92-**93**; British Boys 1992; British Youths 1994
Mis   McEvoy Trophy r/u 1993

Foster, Rodney
Born Shipley, Yorkshire on 13th October, 1941
Cls   Royal & Ancient, Hon member of Bradford, Halifax, Leeds, West Bowling, Ilkley, East Bierley
Chp   Amateur s/f 1962-65
Nat   English Amateur r/u 1964. English Open Amateur Stroke Play 1969 (tied)-70, r/u 1965
Trn   Berkshire Trophy 1964. Lytham Trophy 1967-68. County Champion of Champions 1963 (tied)
Reg   Yorkshire Amateur 1963-64-65-67-70
Int   Walker Cup 1965-67-69-71-73-(**79**). GBI v Europe 1964-66-68-70-(**80**). Eisenhower Trophy 1964-70-(**80**). GB Commonwealth Team 1967-71. England (Home Int) 1963-64-66-67-68-69-70-71-72-(**76**)-(**77**)-(**78**); Eur T Ch 1963-65-67-69-71-73-(77)
Jun Int   Boys 1958. Youths 1959

Fowler, Marjory *See* Ferguson

Frearson, Diane *See* Bailey

Gallacher, Bernard, OBE
Born Bathgate on 9th February, 1949. Turned Professional 1967
PROFESSIONAL
Eur   Spanish Open 1977; French Open 1979
Trn   Schweppes, Wills 1969; Martini International 1971; Carrolls International, Dunlop Masters 1974; Dunlop Masters 1975; Tournament Players Chp 1980; Greater Manchester Open 1981; Martini International; Jersey Open 1982; Jersey Open 1984
Oth   Scottish Professional 1971-73-74-77; Coca-Cola Young Professionals 1973
RoW   Zambia Eagle Open, Zambia Cock o' the North 1969; Mufulira Open 1970
Int   Ryder Cup 1969-71-73-75-77-79-81-83-(**91**)-(**93**)-(**95**); Hennessy-Cognac Cup 1974-78-82-84; Scotland in World Cup 1969-71-74-82-83; in Double Diamond 1971-72-73-74-75-76-77; v South Africa 1976
Mis   Rookie of the Year 1968; Harry Vardon Trophy 1969 (then youngest winner); Scottish Sportsman of the Year 1969; Frank Moran Trophy 1973
AMATEUR
Nat   Scottish Open Amateur Stroke Play 1967
Int   Scotland (Home Int) 1967
Jun Int   Boys 1965-66

Gallacher, Stephen
Born Dechmont on 1 November, 1974. Turned Professional 1996
PROFESSIONAL
Cha   KB Golf Challenge 1998
AMATEUR
Chp   Amateur: leading qualifier 1994
Nat   Scottish Amateur 1992; European Individual Amateur 1994; Scottish Amateur Stroke Play 1995
Reg   Lothians Stroke Play 1992
Trn   Scottish Champion of Champions, Tennant Cup, Lytham Trophy 1995
Int   Walker Cup 1995; World Cup 1994; Scotland (Home Int) 1992-93-94-95; v Italy, v Spain 1994; v Sweden, v France 1995; Eur T Ch 1993-95; Eisenhower Trophy 1994
Jun   Scottish Boys Chp 1991-92; Scottish Youths Chp 1994
Jun Int   Scottish Boys 1991-92; British Boys 1992; Scottish Youths 1992-93-94; British Youths 1994

Garrett, Maureen (née Ruttle)
Born 22nd August, 1922
Oth   French Ladies 1964
Int   Curtis Cup **1960**. England (Home Int) **1960**. Vagliano Trophy **1961**
Mis   LGU President 1982-85. Bobby Jones Award 1983

Garvey, Philomena K
Born Drogheda, Co Louth on 26th April, 1927. Turned Professional 1964, subsequently reinstated Amateur
Cls   Co Down, Co Louth, Portrush, Milltown
Chp   British Ladies 1957, r/u 1946-53-60-63
Nat   Irish Ladies 1946-47-48-50-51-53-54-55-57-58-59-60-62-63-70
Trn   Worplesdon Mixed Foursomes 1955
Reg   Munster Ladies 1951
Int   Curtis Cup 1948-50-52-54-56-60. GBI v France 1949-51-53-55; vBelgium 1951-53. Vagliano Trophy 1959-63. Ireland (Home Int) 1947-48-49-50-51-52-53-54-55-56-59-60-61-62-63-69; v Australia 1950
Mis   Quarter-finalist US Ladies 1950

Gibbs, Carol (née Le Feuvre)
Born Jersey on 18th October, 1951
Cls   Jersey, Lee-on-the-Solent
Nat   English Ladies r/u 1973
Oth   Dutch Ladies 1972

Trn	Avia Foursomes 1974
Reg	Jersey Ladies 1966-67-68. Hampshire Ladies 1970-71-72-73-74-76. South-Eastern Ladies 1974
Int	Curtis Cup 1974. Vagliano Trophy 1973. England (Home Int) 1971-72-73-74; Eur(L) T Ch 1973
Jun	English Girls 1969-70. British Girls 1970
Int	English Girls 1968-69-70
Mis	Member of LGU Team to tour Australia 1973, and Under-25 team to tour Canada 1973

Gilford, David
Born 14th September, 1965. Turned Professional 1986
PROFESSIONAL
Eur	Johnnie Walker International 1990; English Open 1991; Moroccan Open 1992-93; Portuguese Open 1993; Open de Tenerife, European Open 1994
RoW	Tobago International 1992
Oth	Silvermere Satellite Trophy 1987
Int	Ryder Cup 1991-95. (England) Dunhill Cup 1992(winners). World Cup 1992-93

AMATEUR
Nat	English Amateur 1984
Trn	Lagonda Trophy 1986
Int	Walker Cup 1985. GBI v Europe 1986. England (Home Int) 1983-84-85; Eisenhower Trophy 1984.
Jun	British Youths 1986. Carris Trophy 1981

Glover, John
Born Belfast on 3rd March, 1933
Cls	Killarney (Hon), New Club, St Andrews
Trn	Formby Hare 1963
Oth	British Universities 1954-55
Reg	Lancashire Amateur 1970
Int	Ireland (Home Int) 1951-52-53-55-59-60-62-70
Jun	Boy Champion 1950. Carris Trophy 1950
Mis	Secretary Royal & Ancient Rules of Golf Committee 1980-95

Green, Charles Wilson, OBE
Born Dumbarton on 2nd August, 1932
Cls	Dumbarton, Cardross, Helensburgh
Maj	Leading amateur in Open 1962
Nat	Scottish Amateur 1970-82-83, r/u 1971-80. Scottish Open Amateur Stroke Play 1975, 1984, r/u 1967-83. British Seniors 1988-89-90-91, r/u 1992-96. Scottish Seniors 1991-95-96
Trn	Lytham Trophy 1970 (tied)-74. Eden Tournament 1959. Tennant Cup 1968-70-75. Edward Trophy 1968-73-74-75
Reg	West of Scotland Amateur 1962-70-79. Dunbartonshire Amateur 1960-67-68-73-77. Dunbartonshire Match Play 1965-67-69-71-74. Glasgow Amateur 1979
Int	Walker Cup 1963-69-71-73-75-(**83**)-(**85**); GBI v Scandinavia 1962; v Europe 1962-66-68-70-72-74-76. Eisenhower Trophy 1970-72-84-86. GB Commonwealth Team 1971. Scotland (Home Int) 1961 to 1965; 1967 to 1978; **1980**; v Australia 1964, Eur T Ch 1965-67-69-71-73-75-77-**79**-81-83; v Belgium 1973-75-77-78; v Spain 1977; v Italy 1979; v England 1979
Mis	Frank Moran Trophy 1974. British Selector 1980. Scottish Sports Photographer Award 1983

Greenhalgh, Julia *See* Merrill

Gregson, Malcolm Edward
Born Leicester on 15th August, 1943. Turned Professional 1961
Trn	Schweppes 1967. RTV 1967. Daks 1967-68. Martini 1967 (tied). Sumrie 1972
RoW	Zambia Cock o' the North 1974. Gambian Open 1981
Oth	Pannal Foursomes 1964. British Assistants 1964
Int	Ryder Cup 1967. England in World Cup 1967. GBI v France 1966. Sumrie 1972 England in Double Diamond 1975. (Sen) European Cup 1997
Mis	Harry Vardon Trophy 1967
Am	Boy International 1959-60

Grice-Whittaker, Penny
Born Sheffield on 11th September, 1964. Turned Professional 1985
PROFESSIONAL
Maj	Women's British Open 1991
Eur	Belgian Open 1986; Longines Classic 1991

AMATEUR
Nat	English Intermediate Champion 1984; English Stroke Play 1984; English Ladies U-23 Chp 1983
Reg	Yorkshire Champion 1981-82-83. Northern Foursomes 1984
Int	Curtis Cup 1984. England (Home Int) 1983-84. Eur(L) T Ch 1983. Vilmorin Trophy 1984. Espirito Santo 1984
Jun	English Girls 1983

Hackney, Lisa
Born Stoke-on-Trent on 24th September, 1967. Turned Professional 1991
PROFESSIONAL
Eur	Welsh Open 1996
RoW	Indonesian Open 1995
Int	Solheim Cup 1996-98; (for LPGA) Nichirei International 1997-98
Mis	Gatorade Rookie of the Year 1997; Kosaido Asian Order of Merit 1995

AMATEUR
Int	England (Home Int) 1990

Hall, Caroline
Born 4th November, 1973. Turned Professional 1992
PROFESSIONAL
Eur	Ladies Danish Open 1995
Int	Union Cup 1994

AMATEUR
Chp	Ladies British Open Amateur s/f 1991
Nat	English Ladies Under-18 Stroke Play 1991; English Ladies 1992
Trn	Frilford Heath Scratch Cup 1990; Cotswold Hills Gold Vase 1990-91
Reg	Gloucestershire Ladies 1991
Int	Curtis Cup 1992; Vagliano Trophy 1991; England (Home Int) 1991-92; Eur(L) T Ch 1991
Jun	English Girls 1990, r/u 1991

For list of abbreviations see page 350

Hall, Julie (née Wade)
Born Ipswich on 10th March, 1967
- **Cls** Ladybank, Felixstowe Ferry
- **Chp** Ladies British Open Amateur 1990-95
- **Nat** English Ladies Intermediate 1987; English Ladies Stroke Play 1987-93; English Ladies 1988-94-95; British Ladies Amateur Stroke Play 1988(r/u)-93; Welsh Women's Open Stroke Play 1993
- **Oth** World Fourball Chp (with Helen Wadsworth) 1987; Australian Women's Amateur 1995; Spanish Ladies Open Amateur 1992-96
- **Reg** Suffolk Chp 7 times; Suffolk Stroke Play 10 times. Fife Chp 1997
- **Trn** Critchley Salver 1988; Astor Salver 1990; Helen Holm Trophy 1991-93; Wentworth Scratch Cup 1993; Hermitage Scratch Cup 1994; Sunningdale Foursomes (with Helen Wadsworth) 1997
- **Int** Curtis Cup 1988-90-92-94-96; England (Home Int) 1987 to 1995, Eur(L) T Ch 1987-89-91-93-95; GBI Espirito Santo 1988-90-94, Vagliano Trophy 1989-91-93-95; Commonwealth Trn 1991-95
- **Mis** Winner of the Doris Chambers Trophy, the Angus Trophy and *The Daily Telegraph* Woman Golfer of the Year Trophy 1993 (shared). *The Daily Telegraph* Woman Golfer of the Year 1995. Secretary of the LGU 1996.

Harrington, Padraig
Born Dublin on 31st August, 1971. Turned Professional 1995
PROFESSIONAL
- **Eur** Open de España 1996
- **Int** Ireland in Dunhill Cup 1996-97-98; World Cup 1996-97 (winners)-98

AMATEUR
- **Nat** Irish Open Amateur 1995; Irish Close Amateur r/u 1990-94-95
- **Oth** Sherry Cup 1991
- **Int** Walker Cup 1991-93-95. Ireland (Home Int) 1990-91-92-95; Eur T Ch 1991-95. GBI v Europe 1992-94
- **Jun Int** GBI Youths 1990-91; Boys 1988-89; Ireland Youths 1990-91; Boys 1987-88-89

Harris, Marley [Spearman]
Born on 11th January, 1928
- **Cls** Sudbury
- **Chp** British Ladies 1961-62
- **Nat** English Ladies 1964
- **Trn** Spalding Ladies 1956; Worplesdon Mixed Foursomes r/u 1956-64; Kayser-Bondor Foursomes 1958 (tied); London Ladies Foursomes 1960; Astor Salver 1964-65; Astor Princes' Trophy 1964-65; Sunningdale Foursomes, Casa Pupo Foursomes, Roehampton Gold Cup, Hovis Ladies 1965
- **RoW** New Zealand Ladies Stroke Play 1963
- **Reg** Middlesex Ladies 1955-56-57-58-59-61-64-65. South-East Ladies 1956-58-61
- **Int** Curtis Cup 1960-62-64. Vagliano Trophy 1959-61. GB Commonwealth Trn 1959-63. England (Home Int) 1955 to 65
- **Mis** AGW Trophy 1962. Non-playing captain English Team European Team Championship 1971

Hay, Garry
Born Perth on 27th August, 1959
- **Cls** Hilton Park, Downfield
- **Nat** Scottish Amateur Stroke Play 1990, r/u 1980
- **Trn** Tennant Cup 1979. Scottish Champion of Champions 1991; St Andrews Links Trophy 1993
- **Int** Walker Cup 1991. Scotland (Home Int) 1980-88-90-91-92; v England 1979; v Belgium 1980; v France 1980-82-89-91-93; v Italy 1988-92-94; v Sweden 1992; v Spain 1994. GBI v Europe 1980
- **Jun** British Youths 1980

Hedges, Peter J
Born 30th March, 1947
- **Cls** Langley Park (Hon), Royal Cinque Ports, Addington, Wildernesse, Royal & Ancient
- **Nat** English Open Amateur Stroke Play 1976
- **Trn** Royal St George's Challenge Cup 1970. Prince of Wales Challenge Cup 1972-73-74-77. Berkshire Trophy 1973-76-78. *Golf Illustrated* Gold Vase 1974. Scrutton Jug 1976
- **Reg** Kent Amateur 1968-71-79. Kent Open 1970-74
- **Int** Walker Cup 1973-75. GBI v Europe 1974-76 Eisenhower Trophy 1974. England (Home Int) 1970-73-74-75-76-77-78-82; Eur T Ch 1973-75-77
- **Jun** Youth International 1968
- **Mis** Member of European Team to tour South Africa 1974

Henson, Dinah (née Oxley)
Born Dorking on 17th October, 1948
- **Cls** Hon member of West Byfleet, Killarney, Fairfield, USA
- **Chp** British Ladies 1970.
- **Nat** English Ladies 1970-71, r/u 1968. British Ladies Stroke Play r/u 1969
- **Trn** Wills Ladies 1969-70-71. Worplesdon Mixed Foursomes 1968-77. Newmark International 1975 (tied)-77
- **Reg** Surrey Ladies 1967-70-71-76
- **Int** Curtis Cup 1968-70-72-76. Vagliano Trophy 1967-69-71. Espirito Santo 1970. GB Commonwealth Trn 1967-71. England (Home Int) 1967-68-69-70-75-76-77-78; Eur(L) T Ch 1971-77
- **Jun** British Girls 1963. English Girls 1965. French Girls 1969. Girl International 1964-65-66
- **Mis** Daks Woman Golfer of the Year 1970. Leading Amateur Colgate European Ladies Open 1974

Hetherington, Jean (née McClure) See Holmes

Holmes, Jean [Hetherington] (née McClure)
Born Wanstead, Essex on 17th August, 1923
- **Cls** Wanstead, Hunstanton, Thorndon Park
- **Chp** British Ladies 1946, r/u 1958.
- **Nat** English Ladies r/u 1966
- **Reg** Nottinghamshire Ladies 1949-50-51. Essex Ladies 1956-57
- **Int** England (Home Int) 1957-66-(67)

For list of abbreviations see page 350

Homer, Trevor Walter Brian
Born Bloxwich on 8th September, 1943. Turned Professional July 1974. Reinstated as Amateur in 1978
- **Chp** Amateur Champion 1972-74
- **Trn** Leicestershire Fox 1972. Harlech Gold Cross 1970
- **Int** Walker Cup 1973. Eisenhower Trophy 1972. GBI v Europe 1972. England (Home Int) 1972-73; Eur T Ch 1973

Horton, Tommy
Born St Helens, on 16th June, 1941. Turned Professional 1957
- **Trn** RTV 1968. PGA Match Play 1970. Gallaher Ulster 1971. Piccadilly 1972. Penfold 1974. Uniroyal International 1976. Dunlop Masters 1978
- **RoW** South African Open 1970. Nigerian Open 1973. Zambian Open 1977. Tobago Open 1975. Gambian Open 1975
- **Sen** Forte PGA Sen Chp 1992; Shell Scottish Sen, Collingtree Sen, Zurich Lexus Trophy 1993; Irish Sen Masters, St Pierre Sen Classic 1994; De Vere Hotels Sen Classic, Sen Club Pro Chp 1995; Castle Royal European Sen Classic, Stella Sen Open, Northern Electric Sen, The Players Chp 1996; Turkish Sen Open, Irish Sen Open, Jersey Sen Open, Scottish Sen Open, Clubhaus Sen Classic, Sen Trn of Champions 1997; El Bosque Sen Open, De Vere Hotels Sen Classic, Belfry PGA Sen Chp 1998
- **Int** Ryder Cup 1975-77. GBI v France 1966. England in World Cup 1976. England in Double Diamond 1971-74-75-76-77. GBI v Europe 1974-76. (Sen) European Cup **1997-98**
- **Mis** Second in Order of Merit 1967. PGA Captain 1978; Braid-Taylor Memorial Medal 1976-77; Sen Order of Merit winner (John Jacobs Trophy) 1993-96-97-98

Hourihane, Claire *See* Dowling

Howard, D Barclay
Born Johnstone on 27th January, 1953
- **Cls** Cochrane Castle
- **Maj** Leading Amateur in Open Chp 1997
- **Nat** Scottish Amateur sf 1971, 1994; Scottish Strokeplay 1997, r/u 1979; European Amateur r/u 1996
- **Trn** St Andrews Links Trophy 1994-96; Leven Gold Medal 1994; Cameron Corbett Vase 1975-84-95
- **Reg** West of Scotland Strokeplay 1980-93; Glasgow Open 1996
- **Int** Walker Cup 1995-97; Eisenhower Trophy 1996; GBI v Europe 1980-94-96; Scotland (Home Int) 1980-81-82-83-93-94-95-96; v Belgium 1980; v France 1980-81-83-95-97; v Italy 1984-94; v Sweden 1995-97; Eur T Ch 1981-95-97; v Spain 1996
- **Jun** Scottish Boys 1969-70; Scottish Youths 1971-72-73-74; British Youths 1971-72-73-74
- **Mis** Scottish Order of Merit winner 1994-96.

Huggan, Shirley Margaret (*née* Lawson)
Born Glasgow on 16th September, 1964
- **Cls** Eastwood, Rock Ridge, USA
- **Nat** Scottish Ladies Amateur 1988-89 r/u 1990; Taunton Trophy 1987
- **Reg** West of Scotland Ladies 1986-88; Renfrewshire Ladies 1985-86-87-88
- **Int** Curtis Cup 1988; Scotland (Home Int) 1985-86-87-88-89; Eur(L) T Ch 1985-87-89; GBI Vagliano Trophy 1989
- **Jun** Scottish Girls 1982; Scottish Girls Stroke Play 1983-84; r/u 1982-85
- **Int** Girls 1980-81-82

Huggett, Brian George Charles, MBE
Born Porthcawl on 18th November, 1936. Turned Professional 1951
- **Maj** Open r/u 1965. 3rd 1962
- **Eur** Dutch Open 1962. German Open 1963. Portuguese Open 1974
- **Trn** Cox-Moore 1963. Smart-Weston 1965. Sumrie 1968-72. PGA Close 1967. Martini 1967 (tied)-68. Shell Winter Tournament 1967-68. PGA Match Play 1968, r/u 1977. Daks 1969-71 (tied). Bowmaker 1969 (tied). Carrolls 1970. Dunlop Masters 1970. British Airways-Avis 1978
- **RoW** Singapore International 1962. Algarve Open 1970
- **Sen** Anvil Sen Classic, Northern Electric Sen 1992; Northern Electric Sen, Forte PGA Sen 1993; Spanish Sen Open 1994; Windsor Sen Masters, Scottish Sen Open 1995; Schroder Sen Masters, Sen British Open 1998
- **Oth** Sunningdale Foursomes 1957. British Assistants 1958. Gleneagles Pro-Am 1961-65. Turnberry Pro-Am 1968. Welsh Professional 1978
- **Reg** East Anglian Open 1962-67
- **Int** Ryder Cup 1963-67-69-71-73-75-(77). Wales in World Cup 1963-64-65-68-69-70-71-76-79. Wales in Double Diamond 1971-72-73-74-75-76-77. GBI v Europe 1974-**78**. (Sen) European Cup 1998
- **Mis** Vardon Trophy 1968

Huke, Beverly Joan Mary
Born Great Yarmouth on 10th May, 1951. Turned Professional 1978
- **Cls** Cotswold Hills (Hon), Windmill Hill (Hon), Leighton Buzzard, Panmure Barry
- **Chp** British Ladies r/u 1971
- **Nat** English Ladies 1975
- **Eur** Carlsberg (Ballater) 1979. Carlsberg (Rosemount) 1980. NABS Pro-Am 1st Pro Individual 1981. Brickendon Grange and Stourbridge Pro-Am 1983; Lark Valley Classic 1983 (shared); White Horse Whisky Challenge Trophy 1983. Trusthouse Forte Classic 1985. German Ladies Open 1984. Wester Volkswagen Classic 1986
- **Trn** Roehampton Gold Cup 1971. Renfrew Rose Bowl 1976-77-78. Helen Holm Trophy 1977
- **Reg** Gloucestershire Ladies 1972. Angus Ladies 1976
- **Int** Curtis Cup 1972. Vagliano Trophy 1971-75. England (Home Int) 1971-72-75-76-77; Eur(L) T Ch 1975-77
- **Jun** Scottish Girls Open Stroke Play 1970-71. Girl International 1966-67-68
- **Mis** Chairman WPGET 1988

Humphreys, Dorothy (*née* Forster)
Lisburn, Co Antrim on 7th May, 1927
- **Cls** Troon Ladies; Balmoral (Hon), Clandeboye (Hon)
- **Nat** Irish Ladies 1952, r/u 1951
- **Reg** Leinster Ladies 1951; Ulster Ladies 1952-53-57

Int GB Commonwealth Team 1953; GB v France, Belgium 1953. Ireland (Home Int) 1950-51-52-53-55-56-57

Hunt, Bernard John, MBE

Born Atherstone on 2nd February, 1930. Turned Professional 1946
Maj Open 3rd 1960; leading British player (4th) 1964
Eur Belgian Open 1957; German Open 1961; French Open 1967
Trn Spalding, Goodwin Foursomes, Gleneagles-Saxone 1953; Goodwin Foursomes 1954; Irish Hospitals 1956; Bowmaker 1958 (shared); Martini, Daks 1961; Carrolls, Swallow-Penfold, Smart-Weston, Gevacolour, Dunlop Masters 1963; Rediffusion 1964; Dunlop Masters, Gallaher Ulster 1965; Piccadilly 1966; Gallaher Ulster 1967; Penfold, Sumrie, Agfacolor 1970; Wills 1971; Sumrie 1973
Reg Southern England Professional 1959-60-62-67; West of England Open Professional 1960-61
Oth British Assistants 1953; Algarve Open, BP Italy 1969
RoW Egyptian Open 1956; Brazilian Open 1962
Int Ryder Cup 1953-57-59-61-63-65-67-69-(73)-(75); England in World Cup 1958-59-60-62-63-64-68; in Double Diamond 1971-72-73
Mis Harry Vardon Trophy 1958-60-65. PGA Captain 1966

Hutcheon, Ian C

Born Monifieth, Angus on 22nd February, 1942
Cls Monifieth (Hon), Grange and Dundee (Hon)
Nat Scottish Amateur 1973. Scottish Open Amateur Stroke Play 1971-74-79
Trn Tennant Cup 1976; Lytham Trophy 1980; Scottish Champion of Champions 1980-81-86-88; Leven Gold Medal 1981-82
Oth North of Spain Stroke Play 1972
Reg Scottish Central District Amateur 1972. Angus Match Play 1965-70-72. Angus Stroke Play 1968-71-72-74. North of Scotland District Amateur Stroke Play 1975-76-82
Int GBI v Europe 1974-76. Eisenhower Trophy 1974-76 (winners and joint winning individual)-80. Scotland (Home Int) 1971-72-73-74-75-76-77-78-80; Eur T Ch 1973-75-77-79-81; v Spain 1972-77; v Belgium 1973-75-77-78-80; v France 1978-80-81; v Italy 1979; in Fiat Trophy 1979. GBI in Dominican International 1973. Walker Cup 1975-77-79-81. GBI in Colombian International 1975. GB Commonwealth Trn 1975
Mis Frank Moran Trophy 1976

Imrie, Kathryn *See* Marshall

Irvin, Ann Lesley

Born 11th April, 1943
Cls Lytham (Hon), Lytham Green Drive (Hon)
Chp British Ladies 1973, r/u 1969
Nat English Ladies 1967-74. British Ladies Stroke Play 1969
Trn Roehampton Gold Cup 1967-68-69-72-76. Hovis Ladies 1966-68-70. Avia Foursomes 1968
Reg Northern Ladies 1963-64. Lancashire Ladies 1965-67-69-71-72-74. Northern Foursomes Championship 1973

Int Curtis Cup 1962-68-70-76. Vagliano Trophy 1961-63-65-67-69-71-73-75. GB Commonwealth Trn 1967-75. England (Home Int) 1962-63-65-67-68-69-70-71-72-73-75; Eur(L) T Ch 1965-67-69-71-73-75
Jun French Girls 1963
Int Girls 1960-61; British Girls 1961
Mis Daks Woman Golfer of the Year 1968-69. Captain of British Team to tour Australia 1973. Lancashire 1981. County Captain 1979. England Junior Captain. 1981-82. International Selector 1981-82. England Selector 1981-82. County Selector and Junior Organiser

Jack, Robert Reid

Born Cumbernauld on 17th January, 1924
Cls Dullatur
Maj Leading Amateur in Open 1959
Chp Amateur Champion 1957
Nat Scottish Amateur 1955
Trn Edward Trophy 1959. Tennant Cup 1961
Oth Royal & Ancient Royal Medal 1965-67. Silver Cross 1956-66. Glennie Medal 1965
Reg Glasgow Amateur 1953-54-58. Dunbartonshire Match Play 1949
Int Walker Cup 1957-59. Eisenhower Trophy 1958. GB Commonwealth Trn 1959. GBI v Europe 1956. Scotland (Home Int) 1950-51-54-55-56-57-58-59-61; vScandinavia 1956-58

Jacklin, Tony, CBE

Born Scunthorpe on 7th July, 1944. Turned Professional 1962
PROFESSIONAL
Maj Open 1969, 3rd 1971-72; US Open 1970
Eur Blaxnit 1966; Pringle, Dunlop Masters 1967; Wills, Lancôme Trophy 1970; Benson & Hedges Festival 1971; Viyella PGA Close 1972; Dunlop Masters, Italian Open 1973; Scandinavian Enterprise Open 1974; Kerrygold International Classic 1976; German Open 1979; Jersey Open 1981; Sun Alliance PGA 1982
Oth British Assistants 1964; English Professional 1977
US Greater Jacksonville Open 1968-72
RoW Kimberley 1966 (shared); Forest Products, New Zealand, New Zealand PGA 1967; Dunlop International Australia 1972; Los Lagartos Open 1973-74; Venezuelan Open 1979
Sen US Tour: First of America Classic 1994; Franklin Quest 1995
Int Ryder Cup 1967-69-71-73-75-77-79-(83)-(85)-(87)-(89); Hennessy-Cognac 1976; England in World Cup 1966-70-71-72; in Double Diamond 1972-73-74-76-77
Mis Rookie of the Year 1963; Hon Life President PGA; first British player since Harry Vardon to hold Open and US Open simultaneously; Braid-Taylor Memorial Medal 1969-70-71-72
AMATEUR
Reg Lincolnshire Open 1961

Jackson, Barbara Amy Bridget

Born Birmingham on 10th July, 1936
Cls Royal St David's, Edgbaston. Hon member of Handsworth, Hunstanton, Killarney
Chp British Ladies r/u 1964.
Nat English Ladies 1956, r/u 1958

For list of abbreviations see page 350

Trn	Fairway and Hazard Foursomes 1954. Kayser Bondor Foursomes 1962. Avia Foursomes 1967. Worplesdon Mixed Foursomes 1960. Astor Prince's 1963
Oth	German Ladies 1956. Canadian Ladies 1967
Reg	Midland Ladies 1954-56-57-58-59-60-69. Staffordshire Ladies 1954-56-57-58-59-63-64-67-69-76
Int	Curtis Cup 1958-64-68. Vagliano Trophy 1959-63-65-67-(73)-(75). GB Commonwealth Team 1959-67. GBI v Belgium 1957; v France 1957. Espirito Santo 1964. England (Home Int) 1955-56-57-58-59-63-64-65-66-(73)-(74); Eur(L) T Ch (1975), v France 1964-66
Jun	British Girls 1954
Mis	LGU International Selector 1983. English and GBI Selector 1983 to 1988. Chairman of English Ladies Association 1970-71

Jacobs, John Robert Maurice

Born Lindrick, Yorkshire on 14th March, 1925. Turned Professional 1947

Eur	Dutch Open 1957
RoW	South African Match Play 1957
Int	Ryder Cup 1955-(79)-(81). GBI v Continent 1954-55-58
Mis	Former PGA Tournament Director-General. TV commentator. Coach to many international teams

James, Lee

Born Poole on 27th January, 1973. Turned Professional 1995

PROFESSIONAL

Cha	Challenge First Modena Classic Open 1996

AMATEUR

Chp	Amateur Champion 1994
Nat	European Amateur r/u 1994
Int	Walker Cup 1995; GBI v Europe 1994; World Cup 1994; England (Home Int) 1993-94-95; v France 1994; v Spain 1995; Eur T Ch 1995

James, Mark H

Born Manchester on 28th October, 1953. Turned Professional 1975

PROFESSIONAL

Maj	Open 3rd 1981
Eur	Sun Alliance Match Play 1978; Welsh Classic, Carroll's Irish Open 1979; Carroll's Irish Open, Italian Open 1980; Tunisian Open 1983; GSI Open 1985; Benson & Hedges International 1986; Peugeot Spanish Open 1988; Karl Litten Desert Classic, AGF Open, NM English Open 1989; Dunhill British Masters, English Open 1990; Madeira Island Open, Open de Canarias 1993; Moroccan Open 1995; Open de España 1997
RoW	Lusaka Open 1977; Sao Paulo Open 1981; South African TPC 1988
Int	Ryder Cup 1977-79-81-89-91-93-95; Hennessy-Cognac 1976-78-80-82 (individual winner)-84; World Cup 1978-79-82-84-87-88-90-93-97; Dunhill Cup 1988-89-90(r/u)-93(r/u)-95-97; Kirin Cup 1988; Four Tours World Chp 1989-90
Mis	Tooting Bec Cup 1976; Braid-Taylor Memorial Medal 1976-79-81; Rookie of the Year 1976; Captain-elect Ryder Cup 1999

AMATEUR

Chp	Amateur r/u 1975
Nat	English Amateur 1974
Trn	Leicestershire Fox 1974
Int	Walker Cup 1975; England (Home Int) 1974-75; Eur T Ch 1975
Jun Int	(England) Boys 1971; Youths 1974-75

Johnson, Patricia (Trish)

Born Bristol on 17th January, 1966. Turned Professional 1987

PROFESSIONAL

Eur	McEwan's Wirral Classic, Bloor Homes Eastleigh Classic, Woolmark Match Play 1987; Hennessy Cup, Bloor Homes Eastleigh Classic, European Open, Longines Classic 1990; Spanish Classic 1992; European Open, French Open 1996
US	LPGA Qualifying School 1987; Las Vegas LPGA, Atlanta Women's Chp 1993; Fieldcrest Cannon Classic 1996
Int	Solheim Cup 1990-92-94-96-98; Sunrise Cup 1992 (individual winner); European Cup 1997-98; (for LPGA) Nichirei International 1993
Mis	Rookie of the Year 1987. Woolmark Order of Merit leader 1990

AMATEUR

Nat	English Ladies 1985. English Ladies Stroke Play 1985
Trn	Roehampton Gold Cup 1986
Reg	South-Western Ladies 1984
Int	Curtis Cup 1986; Espirito Santo 1986; Vagliano Trophy 1985; England (Home Int) 1984-85-86; Eur(L) T Ch 1985
Jun	Devon Girls 1982

Jones, John Roger

Born Old Colwyn, Denbighshire on 14th June, 1944

Cls	Langland Bay (Hon)
Nat	Welsh Amateur Stroke Play 1972-73-82, r/u 1983. Welsh Amateur 1983
Trn	Harlech Gold Cross 1976
Reg	Denbighshire Amateur 1969-71. Caernarfonshire and Anglesey Amateur 1970 (tied)-72-74-75. Glamorgan Amateur 1977-79. North Wales Amateur 1976. Carmarthenshire Amateur 1979-80. Landsdowne Trophy (Channel League) Stroke Play 1979-80-83
Int	Wales (Home Int) 1970-72-73-77-78-80-81-82-83; Eur T Ch 1973-79-81-83; v Denmark 1976-80; v Ireland 1979; v Switzerland 1980; v Spain 1980; in Asian Team Championship 1979

Kelley, Michael John

Born Scarborough on 6th February, 1945

Cls	Ganton, Hon member of Scarborough North Cliff, Bridlington, Bradford
Trn	Lytham Trophy 1976. Antlers Royal Mid-Surrey 1972
Reg	Yorkshire Amateur 1969-74-81. Yorkshire Open 1969-75. Champion of Champions 1981
Int	Walker Cup 1977-79. Eisenhower Trophy 1976 (winners). GBI v Europe 1976-78-82; GBI in Colombian International 1978. England (Home Int) 1974-75-76-77-78-80-81-82-88; Eur T Ch 1977-79; v France 1982
Jun Int	Boys 1962. Youths 1965-66

For list of abbreviations see page 350

King, Michael
Born London on 15th February, 1950. Turned Professional 1974
PROFESSIONAL
Eur   Tournament Players Chp 1979
Int   Ryder Cup 1979; England in World Cup 1979
AMATEUR
Trn   St George's Hill Trophy 1970; County Champion of Champions 1970; Sunningdale Foursomes 1972; Lytham Trophy 1973 (shared)
Reg   Berks, Bucks & Oxon Amateur 1968-69-70-73-74; Berks, Bucks & Oxon Open 1968-73
Int   Walker Cup 1969-73; GB Commonwealth Trn 1971; v Europe 1972; England (Home Int) 1971-72-73; Eur T Ch 1971-73

King, Samuel Leonard
Born Sevenoaks, Kent on 27th March, 1911
Maj   Open 3rd 1939
Trn   Daily Mail 1937. Yorkshire Evening News 1944-49
Oth   British Assistants 1933. Dunlop-Southern 1936-37. Sunningdale Foursomes 1948. Teachers Senior 1961-62
Int   Ryder Cup 1937-47-49. England 1934-36-37-38

Lambert, Catriona *See* **Matthew**

Lane, Barry
Born Hayes, Middlesex on 21st June, 1960. Turned Professional 1976
Eur   Equity & Law Challenge 1987; Scottish Open 1988; Mercedes German Masters 1992; European Masters 1993; Open de Baleares 1994
RoW   Jamaica Open 1983
Oth   Andersen Consulting World Chp 1995
Int   Ryder Cup 1993; (England) Dunhill Cup 1988-94-95-96; World Cup 1988-94

Lawrence, Joan B
Born Kinghorn, Fife on 20th April, 1930
Cls   Honorary member of Dunfermline, Aberdour, Killarney
Chp   Scottish Ladies 1962-63-64, r/u 1965. Scottish Veteran Ladies Champion 1982
Reg   East of Scotland Ladies 1971-72. Fife Ladies fifteen times winner 1953-90
Int   Curtis Cup 1964. World Team Champion 1964. GB Commonwealth Trn 1971. Vagliano Trophy 1963-65. Scotland (Home Int) 1959 to 70-(77); Eur(L) T Ch 1965-67-**69**-71-(77)
Jun   Girl International 1949
Mis   LGU International Selector 1973-74-75-76-80-81-82-83. Treasurer Scottish Ladies Golfing Association from 1980. Chairman LGU Executive 1989

Leburn, Wilma *(née* Aitken)
Born 24th January, 1959
Trn   Helen Holm Trophy 1978-80-82. Avia Foursomes 1982
Reg   West of Scotland 1978-80-81. Renfrewshire Champion 1978-79-80-81-82

Int   Curtis Cup 1982. Vagliano Trophy 1981-83. Scotland (Home Int) 1978-79-80-81-82-83. Vilmorin Cup 1979. Eur(L) T Ch 1979-81-83
Jun   Scottish Girls 1975-77. West of Scotland Girls 1977. British Girls 1977
Int   Scottish Girls 1975-77-78

Lee-Smith, Jenny
Born Newcastle-upon-Tyne on 2nd December, 1948. Turned Professional 1977
Maj   Ladies British Open 1976 (as amateur)
PROFESSIONAL
Eur   Carlsberg 1979; Carlsberg, Robert Windsor Trn, Volvo Swedish International, Manchester Evening News Classic 1980; Sports Space Trn, McEwan's Lager Welsh Classic, Lambert & Butler Match Play 1981; Ford Classic 1982; British Olivetti 1984
Mis   Order of Merit winner 1981-82
AMATEUR
Nat   Ladies British Open Amateur Stroke Play 1976
Trn   Wills Match Play 1974; Newmark 1976; Hoylake Mixed Foursomes 1969
Reg   Northumberland Ladies 1972-73-74
Int   Curtis Cup 1974-76; Espirito Santo 1976; GB Commonwealth Trn 1975; Colombian International 1975; England (Home Int) 1973-74-75-76; Eur(L) T Ch 1975
Mis   Daks Woman Golfer of the Year 1976

Lumb, Kathryn *(née* Phillips)
Born Bradford on 24th February, 1952
Cls   Hon member of Bradford, West Bowling, Killarney, Filton
Reg   Central England Mixed Foursomes 1966-70. Yorkshire Ladies 1968-69
Int   Curtis Cup 1970-72. Vagliano Trophy 1969-71. England (Home Int) 1968-69-70-71; Eur(L) T Ch 1969
Jun   English Girls 1968. Scottish Girls Open Stroke Play 1968-69. French Girls 1970
Int   Girls 1967-68-69

Lunt, Michael Stanley Randle
Born Birmingham on 20th May, 1935
Cls   Royal & Ancient, Walton Heath, St Enodoc, Hon. mem. of Blackwell, Royal St David's, Moseley, Edgbaston, Stourbridge, Willesley Park, Kibworth, Handsworth, King's Norton, Dudley
Chp   Amateur Champion 1963, r/u 1964
Nat   English Amateur 1966, r/u 1962. English Open Amateur Stroke Play r/u 1961
Trn   Golf Illustrated Gold Vase 1958, Harlech Gold Cross 1959-61-64-65-66-67. Leicestershire Fox 1966
Reg   Midland Counties Amateur 1960-62
Int   Walker Cup 1959-61-62-65. Eisenhower Trophy 1964 GB Commonwealth Team 1963. England (Home Int) 1956-57-58-59-60-62-63-64-66-(72)-(**73**)-(74)-(75). Eur T Ch (**1973**)-(75)
Jun   Boy International 1949-50-51-52
Mis   AGW Trophy 1963. President Midland Counties Golf Association 1978 to 1980

For list of abbreviations see page 350

Lyle, Alexander Walter Barr (Sandy), MBE

Born Shrewsbury on 9th February, 1958. Turned Professional 1977

PROFESSIONAL
- **Maj** Open Champion 1985. US Masters 1988
- **Eur** Jersey Open, Scandinavian Enterprise Open, European Open 1979; Coral Classic 1980; French Open, Lawrence Batley International 1981; Lawrence Batley International 1982; Madrid Open 1983; Italian Open, Lancôme Trophy 1984; Benson & Hedges International 1985; German Masters 1987; Dunhill British Masters, Suntory World Match Play 1988; BMW International Open 1991; Italian Open, Volvo Masters 1992
- **US** Greater Greensboro Open 1986; Tournament Players Championship 1987; Phoenix Open, Greater Greensboro Open 1988
- **Oth** PGA Qualifying School winner 1977; Scottish Professional Chp 1979
- **RoW** Nigerian Open 1978; Casio World Open, Kapalua International (Hawaii) 1984
- **Int** Ryder Cup 1979-81-83-85-87; Nissan Cup 1985-86, Kirin Cup 1987-88; Hennessy-Cognac Cup 1980-84; Scotland in World Cup 1979-80 (Individual Winner) -87(r/u); Dunhill Cup 1985-86-87 (r/u)-88-89-90-92(r/u)
- **Mis** Rookie of the Year 1978; Harry Vardon Trophy 1979-80-85; AGW Trophy 1980-88; Tooting Bec Cup 1982-88; Braid-Taylor Memorial Medal 1985; Frank Moran Trophy 1985

AMATEUR
- **Nat** English Open Amateur Stroke Play 1975-77
- **Trn** County Champion of Champions 1974; Hampshire Hog, Berkshire Trophy, Scrutton Jug, Berkhamsted Trophy 1977
- **Reg** Midland Amateur, Shropshire & Herefordshire Amateur 1974; Midland Open 1975; Shropshire & Herefordshire Amateur 1976
- **Int** Walker Cup 1977; GB Commonwealth Trn 1975; GBI v Europe 1976; England (Home Int) 1975-76-77, Eur T Ch 1977
- **Jun** Carris Trophy 1975; British Youths 1977; r/u British Boys 1974-75
- **Int** Boys 1972-73-74-75
- **Mis** In 1975 represented England in Boy, Youth and Full Internationals

McCann, Catherine (née Smye)

Born Clonmel, Co Tipperary in 1922

- **Cls** Tullamore
- **Chp** British Ladies 1951
- **Nat** Irish Ladies 1949-61, r/u 1947-52-57-60
- **Reg** Munster Ladies 1958, Irish Midland Ladies 1952-57-58
- **Int** Curtis Cup 1952. Ireland (Home Int) 1947-48-49-50-51-52-53-54-56-57-58-60-61-62; v New Zealand 1953; v Canada 1953

McClure, Jean See Holmes

McCorkindale, Isabella
See **Robertson**

McEvoy, Peter

Born London on 22nd March, 1953

- **Cls** Copt Heath (Hon), R&A
- **Maj** Open leading amateur 1978-79
- **Chp** Amateur Champion 1977-78, r/u 1987
- **Nat** English Open Amateur Stroke Play 1980 (tied), r/u 1978. English Amateur r/u 1980
- **Trn** Duncan Putter 1978-80-87; Scrutton Jug 1978-80-85; Lytham Trophy 1978; Selborne Salver 1979-80; Leicestershire Fox 1976; Lagonda Trophy 1980; Berkshire Trophy 1985; County Champion of Champions 1984 (shared); Berkhamsted Trophy 1986; Hampshire Hog 1989
- **Oth** British Universities Stroke Play 1973
- **Reg** Warwickshire Match Play 1975-81; Warwickshire Amateur 1974-76-77-80-84; Warwickshire Open 1973-74; West of England Open Amateur Stroke Play 1977-80-83-85; Midland Open Amateur Stroke Play 1978; Midland Scratch Cup (Ireland) 1982-83-84-88
- **Int** Walker Cup 1977-79-81-85-89; Eisenhower Trophy 1978-80-84-86-88(winners) (leading individual)-**98**(winners); GBI v Europe 1978-80-82-84-86-88; England (Home Int) 1976-77-78-80-81-82-83-84-85-86-87-88-89-91; v Scotland 1979; Eur T Ch 1977-79-81-83-85-87-89; in Fiat Trophy 1980; v France 1982-84-86-88-90; v Spain 1985-87-89. England Captain 1995
- **Jun** Youth International 1974
- **Mis** Only British amateur to complete 72 holes in US Masters (1978); AGW Trophy 1978; most capped England player

McGimpsey, Garth M

Born 17th July, 1955

- **Cls** Bangor, Royal Portrush, Royal Co Down
- **Chp** Amateur Champion 1985, s/f 1989
- **Nat** Irish Amateur 1985-88
- **Reg** North of Ireland 1978-84-91-92, West of Ireland 1984-88-96, East of Ireland 1988-94, r/u 1979-80
- **Int** Walker Cup 1985-89-91. GBI v Europe 1984-86-88-92. Eisenhower Trophy 1984-86-88 (winners). Ireland (Home Int) 1978; 1980 to 1998. Eur T Ch 1981-89-91-95-97
- **Mis** Irish long-driving champion 1977; UK long-driving champion 1979

McGinley, Paul

Born Dublin on 16th December, 1966. Turned Professional 1991

PROFESSIONAL
- **Eur** Höhe Brücke Open 1996; Oki Pro-Am 1997
- **Oth** UAP U-25 European Open 1991
- **Int** (Ireland) Dunhill Cup 1993-96-97-98; World Cup 1993-97 (winners)-98

AMATEUR
- **Nat** Irish Amateur 1989
- **Reg** South of Ireland 1991
- **Oth** Long Beach Open 1990
- **Int** Walker Cup 1991; Ireland (Home Int) 1989-90
- **Jun** Irish Youths, Scottish Youths 1988

For list of abbreviations see page 350

Macgregor, George
Born Edinburgh on 19th August, 1944
Cls Glencorse, Killarney (Hon), West Linton (Hon)
Nat Scottish Open Amateur Stroke Play 1982 r/u 1975-79-80
Trn Lytham Trophy 1975. Leven Gold Medal 1987
Reg Lothians Amateur 1968. South-East Scotland Amateur 1972-75-79-80-81. East of Scotland Open Amateur 1979-82
Int Walker Cup 1971-75-83-85-87-(**91**). Eisenhower Trophy 1982. GBI *v* Europe 1970-74-84. GB Commonwealth Trn 1971-75. Scotland (Home Int) 1969-70-71-72-73-74-75-76-80-81-82-83-84-85-86-87; Eur T Ch 1971-73-75-81-83-85-87; *v* Belgium 1973-75-80; *v* England 1979; *v* France 1981-82; Scotland *v* Sweden 1983
Jun Int Youths 1964-65-66
Mis Leading Amateur Wills PGA Open 1970-71; Chairman of R&A Selection Committee

McKay, Mhairi
Born Glasgow on 18th April, 1975. Turned Professional 1997
PROFESSIONAL
Int European Cup 1998
AMATEUR
Nat British Ladies Stroke Play U-23 (Duncan Salver), U-21 (Dinwiddy Trophy) 1993; Scottish Ladies 1993(r/u); Scottish U-21 Stroke Play 1991(r/u)-92-93
Trn Mackie Bowl 1991-93; Helen Holm Trophy 1992; Riccarton Rosebowl 1993-96
Int Curtis Cup 1994-96; Espirito Santo 1996; Vagliano Trophy 1993-95-97; Commonwealth Trn 1995; Scotland (Home Int) 1991-92-93-94-96; Eur(L) T Ch 1993-95
Jun British Girls 1992-93; Scottish Girls 1990-91(r/u)-92; Belgian Junior 1992
Jun Int Scottish Girls 1989-90-91-92-93; Jun Eur 1990-92-94-96
Mis *Daily Telegraph* Junior Golfer of the Year 1991. Golf scholarship to Stanford University. Angus Trophy 1996. Joyce Wethered Trophy 1996

McKenna, Mary A
Born Dublin on 29th April, 1949
Cls Donabate
Nat British Ladies Open Amateur Stroke Play 1979, r/u 1976. Irish Ladies 1969-72-74-77-79-81-82-89, r/u 1968-73-76. Irish Women's Close Ch 1981
Trn Dorothy Grey Stroke Play 1970-71-73. Players No 6 Cup 1971-72-74. Avia Foursomes 1977-84-86. Hermitage Scratch Cup 1975-79
Reg South of Ireland Scratch Cup 1973-74-76-79
Int Curtis Cup 1970-72-74-76-78-80-82-84-86. Vagliano Trophy 1969-71-73-75-77-79-81-85-87-(**95**). Espirito Santo 1970-74-76-**86**; Ireland (Home Int) 1968 to 1991; Eur(L) T Ch 1969-71-73-75-77-79-81-83-85-87; in Fiat Trophy 1979
Mis S/f US Women's Western 1972, Broadmoor Trn 1972 and US Women's Amateur 1980. Captain of LGU Touring Team to South Africa 1974. Leading Amateur Colgate European LPGA 1977 (tied)-79. Daks Woman Golfer of the Year 1979. Smyth Salver 1984. Taunton Trophy 1976

McLean, David
Born Holyhead on 30th January, 1947
Cls Holyhead, Baron Hill, Killarney
Nat Welsh Amateur 1973-78. Welsh Amateur Stroke Play 1975-79
Trn Duncan Putter 1982
Reg North Wales Amateur 1971-75-77-81. Caernarfonshire Amateur 1966-68-69-70 (tied)-77-79-81-82. Anglesey Amateur 1965-67-68-69-70-72-73-74-76-78-79-80-81-82
Int Wales (Home Int) 1968 to 78, 80 to 83, 85-86-88; Eur T Ch 1975-77-79-81-83; *v* France 1975-76; *v* Denmark 1976-80-82; *v* Ireland 1979; *v* Spain 1980; *v* Austria 1982; *v* Switzerland 1980-82; in Fiat Trophy 1978-79; in Asian Team Chp 1979

McMahon, Suzanne *(née Cadden)*
Born Old Kilpatrick, Dunbartonshire on 8th October, 1957
Cls Troon
Chp British Ladies r/u 1975. British Ladies Stroke Play r/u 1975
Nat Scottish Ladies Foursomes 1972
Reg Dunbartonshire Ladies 1976-77-79
Int Curtis Cup 1976. Vagliano Trophy 1975. Scotland (Home Int) 1974-75-76-77-79; Eur(L) T Ch 1975
Jun Scottish Girls 1974-76. Scottish Girls Open Stroke Play 1976-77. British Girls 1975. Girl International 1972-73-74-75-76. World Junior Championship 1973
Mis Daks Woman Golfer of the Year 1975

Madill, Maureen
Born Coleraine, Co Derry on 1st February, 1958. Turned Professional 1986
Chp Ladies British Amateur 1979
Nat Ladies British Open Amateur Stroke Play 1980. Irish Foursomes 1980
Maj Avia Foursomes 1980-85.
Reg North-West Scratch Cup 1978. Ulster Ladies 1980
Int Curtis Cup 1980. Espirito Santo 1980; Vagliano Trophy 1979-81-85. GB Commonwealth Trn 1979. Ireland (Home Int) 1978-79-80-81-82-83; Eur(L) T Ch 1979-81-83
Jun Int Girls 1972-73-74-75-76

Marks, Geoffrey C
Born Hanley, Stoke-on-Trent, in November, 1938
Cls Hon member of Trentham, Trentham Park, Greenway Hall, Killarney, Walsall, Newcastle, Trevose, Stone. Royal & Ancient
Chp Amateur s/f 1968-75
Nat English Open Amateur Stroke Play r/u 1973-75
Trn Scrutton Jug 1967. Prince of Wales Challenge Cup 1968. Leicestershire Fox 1968. Lytham Trophy 1970 (tied). Harlech Gold Cup 1974. Homer Salver 1977
Reg Midland Amateur 1967. Staffordshire Amateur 1959-60-63-66-67-68-69-73
Int Walker Cup 1969-71-**87**. Eisenhower Trophy 1970. England (Home Int) 1963-67-68-69-70-71-74-75-(**80**)-(**81**)-(**82**)-(**83**); Eur T Ch 1967-69-71-75. GB Commonwealth Trn 1975. GBI in Colombian International 1975

For list of abbreviations see page 350

Jun Int Boys 1955-56. Youths 1957-58-59-60
Mis England Selector 1980-81-82-83 (chairman); R&A Selection Committee (chairman) 1989-93. President English Golf Union 1995

Marsh, Dr David Max
Born Southport on 29th April, 1934
Cls Royal & Ancient, Hon member of Southport & Ainsdale, Ormskirk, West Lancashire, Worlington & Newmarket, Hillside, Clitheroe, Whalley
Nat English Amateur 1964-70
Trn Antlers Royal Mid-Surrey 1964-66. Formby Hare 1968. Boyd Quaich 1957
Int Walker Cup 1959-71-(73)-(75); GBI v Europe 1958-(72)-(74). GBI v Professionals 1959. England (Home Int) 1956-57-58-59-60-64-65-66-**68**-**69**-**70**-**71**-72; Eur T Ch 1971
Jun Int Boys 1951
Mis EGU Selector 1974. British Selector 1975. Chairman R & A Selection Committee 1979-83. President EGU 1987. Captain of R & A 1990/91

Marshall, Kathryn *(née Imrie)*
Born Southend on 8th June, 1967. Turned Professional 1990
Maj Ladies British Open 3rd 1993; leading amateur 1988 (Smyth Salver)
PROFESSIONAL
US Toledo Classic 1995
Int Solheim Cup 1996; European Cup 1997
AMATEUR
Trn St Rule Trophy 1985; Riccarton Rosebowl 1985; Roehampton Gold Cup 1990
Reg Highland Open 1985; North of Scotland Ladies Amateur 1988-90; Northern Counties Ladies Open Stroke Play 1986-87-88-89; Angus Ladies 1982-83-84-85
Int Curtis Cup 1990; Vagliano Trophy 1989; Scotland (Home Int) 1984-88-89; Eur(L) T Ch 1987-89
Mis Taunton Trophy 1986; winner of two NCAA events whilst at University of Arizona (1985-89); Doris Chambers Trophy, Angus Trophy 1990
Jun Scottish Girls Open Stroke Play 1985-86-87

Marvin, Vanessa Price
Born Cosford on 30th December, 1954. Turned Professional 1978
PROFESSIONAL
Eur Carlsberg Trn 1979
AMATEUR
Chp British Ladies Amateur r/u 1977
Nat English Ladies Amateur 1977-78.
Trn Hampshire Rose 1975-78 (tied). Roehampton Gold Cup 1976. Newmark-Avia 1978
Reg Yorkshire Ladies 1975-78. North of England Ladies 1975
Int Curtis Cup 1978. Vagliano Trophy 1977. England (Home Int) 1977-78; Eur(L) T Ch 1977; in Fiat Trophy 1978
Mis Leading amateur Colgate European LPGA 1977. Daks Woman Golfer of the Year 1978

Matthew, Catriona *(née Lambert)*
Born on 25th August, 1969. Turned Professional 1994
PROFESSIONAL
Eur McDonald's Chp of Europe 1998
RoW Australian Ladies Open 1996
Int Solheim Cup 1998; European Cup 1998
AMATEUR
Chp British Ladies 1993
Nat Scottish Ladies 1991-93-94. Welsh Women's Open Stroke Play 1992
Trn Roehampton Gold Cup 1989; Helen Holm Trophy 1990; British Universities Women's Chp 1990; St Rule Trophy, Ness Trophy 1993; Astor Salver 1994
Int Curtis Cup 1990-92-94; Espirito Santo 1992; Vagliano Trophy 1989-91-93; Commonwealth Trn 1991; Scotland (Home Int) 1989-90-91-92-93; Eur(L) T Ch 1989-91
Jun Scottish Girls 1986; Scottish Girls Open Stroke Play 1988-89, r/u 1987

Matthews, Tegwen [Thomas] *(née Perkins)*
Born Cardiff on 2nd October, 1955
Cls Wenvoe Castle, Porthcawl, Pennard
Nat Welsh Ladies Amateur 1976-77. Welsh Ladies Open Amateur Stroke Play 1980. British Ladies Amateur Stroke Play r/u 1974
Trn Wills Match Play 1973. Avia Foursomes 1977; Worplesdon Mixed Foursomes 1973-78
Reg South-Western Ladies 1973-74-76. Glamorganshire Ladies 1972-74-75-77-78-80-81-83
Int Curtis Cup 1974-76-78-80. Vagliano Trophy 1973-75-77-79. Espirito Santo 1974. GB Commonwealth Trn 1975-79. GBI: Colombian Int. 1977-79. Wales (Home Int) 1972 to 84; Eur(L) T Ch 1975-77-79-81-83; in Fiat Trophy 1978
Jun Welsh Girls 1970.
Int Girls 1970-71-72-73
Mis Dinwiddy Trophy 1973-74. 1974: in LGU Team touring SA; first Welsh player in Curtis Cup team; Taunton Trophy. 1976: first Welsh woman player to win all matches in Home Ints; Daks Woman Golfer of the Year (joint). Duncan Salver 1974-76

Merrill, Julia *(née Greenhalgh)*
Born Bolton on 6th January, 1941
Cls Pleasington (Hon), Killarney, Ganton, Hermitage
Chp Ladies British Open Amateur r/u 1978
Nat British Ladies Stroke Play 1974-75. Runner-up British English Ladies 1966-79. Welsh Ladies Open Amateur Stroke Play 1977
Trn Astor Salver 1969-79. Hermitage Cup, Hampshire Rose 1977. Sunningdale Foursomes 1978
Oth New Zealand Ladies 1963
Reg Lancashire Ladies 1961-62-66-68-73-75-76-77-78; Northern Ladies 1961-62
Int Curtis Cup 1964-70-74-76-78. Vagliano Trophy 1961-65-75-77. GB Commonwealth Trn 1963-75. Espirito Santo **1970**-74-78. England (Home Int) 1960-61-63-66-69-70-71-76-77-78; Eur(L) T Ch 1971-75-77-79
Jun Scottish Girls Open Stroke Play 1960. Girl International 1957-58-59
Mis Leading Amateur (4th) in Australian Wills Ladies Open Stroke Play 1974. Daks Woman Golfer of the Year 1974. Taunton Trophy 1975-77. Doris Chambers Trophy 1977

For list of abbreviations see page 350

Milligan, James W
Born Irvine on 15th June, 1963
- **Cls** Kilmarnock (Barassie)
- **Nat** Scottish Amateur 1988
- **Trn** Scottish Champion of Champions 1989-90
- **Int** Walker Cup 1989-91; Scotland (Home Int) 1986-87-88-89-90-91-92; v West Germany 1987; v Italy 1988-90; v Sweden 1990-92; Eur T Ch 1989-91; GBI v Europe 1988-90-92; Eisenhower Trophy 1988 (winners)-90
- **Jun** Scottish Youths 1984

Milton, Moira (née Paterson)
Born 18th December, 1923
- **Cls** Turnhouse, Gullane (Hon), Lenzie, Maccauvlei
- **Chp** British Ladies 1952
- **Nat** Scottish Ladies r/u 1951
- **Reg** Dunbartonshire Ladies 1949. Midlothian Ladies 1962
- **Int** Curtis Cup 1952. GBI v France 1949-50; vBelgium 1950; Scotland (Home Int) 1949-50-51-52; v Australia 1951; v South Africa 1951; Eur(L) T Ch (**1973**)
- **Mis** Member of LGU Team to South Africa 1951

Montgomerie, Colin S, MBE
Born Glasgow on 23rd June, 1963. Turned Professional 1987
PROFESSIONAL
- **Maj** US Open r/u 1994-97, 3rd 1992; USPGA r/u 1995 (tied)
- **Eur** Portuguese Open 1989; Scandinavian Masters 1991; Dutch Open, Volvo Masters 1993; Open de España, English Open, German Open 1994; German Open, Trophée Lancôme 1995; Dubai Desert Classic, Irish Open, European Masters 1996; Andersen Consulting Eur Chp, Compaq Eur Grand Prix, Murphy's Irish Open 1997; Volvo PGA Chp, One2One British Masters, Linde German Masters 1998
- **RoW** Nedbank Million Dollar Challenge 1996; King Hussein II Trophy, Andersen Consulting World Cup 1997
- **Int** Ryder Cup 1991-93-95-97; Scotland in Dunhill Cup 1988-91-92(r/u)-93-94-95(winners)-96-97-98; in World Cup 1988-91-92-93-97 (r/u, individual winner)-98; Four Tours World Chp 1991
- **Mis** Rookie of the Year 1988; Harry Vardon Trophy 1993-94-95-96-97-98; Johnnie Walker Golfer of the Year 1995-96-97; AGW Trophy 1996

AMATEUR
- **Chp** Amateur r/u 1984
- **Nat** Scottish Open Amateur Stroke Play 1985; Scottish Amateur 1987
- **Int** Walker Cup 1985-87; Eisenhower Trophy 1984-86; GBI v Europe 1986; Scotland (Home Int) 1984-85-86 Eur T Ch 1985; v Sweden 1984-86; v France 1985

Montgomerie, John Speir
Born Cambuslang on 7th August, 1913
- **Cls** Royal & Ancient, Cambuslang, Kilmarnock (Barassie), Pollok
- **Nat** Scottish Amateur 1957
- **Reg** Lanarkshire Amateur 1951-54

- **Int** Scotland (Home Int) 1957-(**62**)-(**63**); v Scandinavia 1958
- **Mis** Non-playing captain Scottish Team Eur T Ch 1965. Walker Cup Selector 1957 to 1965. President Scottish Golf Union 1965-66

Moodie, Janice
Born 31st May, 1973. Turned Professional 1997
PROFESSIONAL
- **Int** Nichirei Int 1998

AMATEUR
- **Nat** British Ladies Stroke Play r/u 1991; winner U-23 (Duncan Salver) and U-21 (Dinwiddy Trophy) 1990-91; Scottish Ladies 1992; Scottish U-21 Stroke Play 1990-93
- **Trn** Munross Trophy, Mary McCallay Trophy; Inverness Stroke Play 1993
- **Reg** West of Scotland Ladies 1991
- **Int** Curtis Cup 1994-96; Vagliano Trophy 1993-95-97; Espirito Santo 1996; Commonwealth Trn 1995; Scotland (Home Int) 1990-91-92; Eur(L) T Ch 1991-93-95-97
- **Jun** Scottish Girls 1989-90(r/u)-91; British Girls s/f 1989-91
- **Jun Int** Scottish Girls 1989-90 (r/u)-91; Eur Jun(L) T Ch 1990-92
- **Mis** Doris Chambers Trophy, Angus Trophy 1993; Wilson PGA Junior Chp 1990. Currently a golf scholar at San José State University. Joyce Wethered Trophy 1994

Morley, Joanne
Born 30th December, 1966. Turned Professional 1994
- **Cls** Sale
- **Maj** Leading Amateur in Women's British Open (Smyth Salver) 1989-93

PROFESSIONAL
- **Eur** Ladies German Open 1996; European Cup 1997
- **Int** Solheim Cup 1996; Union Cup 1994

AMATEUR
- **Nat** Ladies British Amateur r/u 1992; Ladies British Amateur Stroke Play 1991; English Ladies Close Amateur Stroke Play 1991-92, r/u 1990; English Intermediate 1991
- **Trn** St Rule Trophy 1987; Wentworth Scratch Cup 1988(tied); Avia Foursomes (with L Fairclough) 1989; Astor Salver 1990
- **Int** Curtis Cup 1992; Vagliano Trophy 1991-93; Espirito Santo 1992; England (Home Int) 1990-91-92-93; Eur(L) T Ch 1991
- **Mis** Taunton Trophy 1991; Daily Telegraph Woman Golfer of the Year 1991

Nesbitt, Claire See Robinson

New, Beverley Jayne
Born Bristol on 30th July, 1960. Turned Professional 1984
PROFESSIONAL
- **Eur** Broadway Group Wirral Classic 1988
- **RoW** Thailand Ladies Open 1987; Malaysian Ladies Open 1988

AMATEUR
- **Nat** English Ladies 1980; Welsh Ladies Stroke Play r/u 1979

For list of abbreviations see page 350

Trn	Hampshire Rose 1980; WPGA United Friendly Insurance Trn, Worplesdon Mixed Foursomes 1982; Roehampton Gold Cup, Worplesdon Mixed Foursomes, Martin Bowl 1983
Reg	Somerset Ladies 1979-80-81-82-83; Bristol & District Open 1983
Int	Curtis Cup 1984; Vagliano Trophy 1983; England (Home Int) 1980-81-82-83; Eur(L) T Ch 1981-83; Fiat Trophy 1980
Mis	Doris Chambers Trophy 1983

Nichol, Margaret See Pickard

Nicholas, Alison, MBE
Born Gibraltar on 6th March, 1962. Turned Professional 1984

PROFESSIONAL
Maj	Ladies British Open 1987, 3rd 1988; US Women's Open 1997
Eur	Laing Charity Classic 1987; Variety Club Classic, British Olivetti, Guernsey Open 1988; Lufthansa German Open, Gislaved Open 1989; Variety Club Classic 1990; Open de Paris 1992; Scottish Open 1995; Guardian Irish Holidays Open 1996
US	Corning Classic, Ping-Cellular One Chp 1995
RoW	Malaysian Open, Western Open (Aus) 1992
Int	Solheim Cup 1990-92-94-96-98; (for LPGA) Nichirei International 1995-97; European Cup 1997-98
Mis	Vivien Saunders Trophy 1991. Order of Merit winner 1997. AGW Award 1997

AMATEUR
Nat	Ladies British Open Amateur Stroke Play 1983
Reg	Yorkshire Ladies 1984; Northern Foursomes 1983
Jun	North of England Girls 1982-83
Mis	Taunton Trophy 1983; Duncan Salver 1983

O'Connor, Christy
Born Galway on 21st December, 1924

Maj	Open r/u 1965, 3rd 1958-61
Trn	Swallow-Penfold 1955. Dunlop Masters 1956-59. Spalding 1956 (tied). PGA Match Play 1957. Daks 1959. Ballantine 1960. Irish Hospitals 1960-62. Carling-Caledonian 1961. Martini 1963 (tied)-64. Jeyes 1964. Carrolls 1964-66-67-72. Senior Service 1965; Gallaher Ulster 1966-68-69. Alcan International 1968 (tied). Bowmaker 1970. John Player Classic 1970
Oth	Ulster Professional 1953-54. Irish Professional 1958-60-61-62-63-65-66-71-75-77. Irish Dunlop 1962-65-66-67. Gleneagles Pro-Am 1962. Southern Ireland Professional 1969-76. Sean Connery Pro-Am 1970
Sen	PGA Seniors 1976-77-79-81-82-83. World Seniors 1976-77
Int	Ryder Cup 1955-57-59-61-63-65-67-69-71-73. GBI v Commonwealth 1956. Ireland in World Cup 1956-57-58 (winners) -59-60-61-62-63-64-66-67-68-69-71-75. Ireland in Double Diamond 1971-72-73-74-75-76-77
Mis	Harry Vardon Trophy 1961-62. Second in order of Merit 1964 (equal)-65-66-69-70. AGW Trophy 1977

O'Connor, Christy, Jr
Born Galway on 19th August, 1948. Turned Professional 1965

Maj	Open 3rd 1985
Eur	Martini 1975 (tied). Carrolls Irish Open 1975. Sumrie 1976-78. Jersey European Airways Open 1989. Dunhill British Masters 1992
Oth	Irish Dunlop 1974. Carrolls Irish Match Play 1975-77
RoW	Zambian Open 1974. Kenya Open 1990
Int	Ryder Cup 1975-89. Ireland in Double Diamond 1972-74-76-77. Ireland in World Cup 1974-75-78-85-89-92. Hennessy-Cognac 1974-84. GBI v South Africa 1976. Dunhill Cup 1985-89-92. (Sen) European Cup 1998
Mis	Braid Taylor Memorial Medal 1976-83. Tooting Bec Cup 1985

O'Leary, John E
Born Dublin on 19th August, 1949. Turned Professional 1970

PROFESSIONAL
Trn	Sumrie 1975. Greater Manchester Open 1976. Carrolls Irish Open 1982; Irish Dunlop 1972
RoW	Holiday Inns (Swaziland) 1975
Int	Ryder Cup 1975; Ireland in World Cup 1972-80-82; Ireland in Double Diamond 1972-73-74-75-76-77; GBI v Europe 1976-78-82

AMATEUR
Reg	South of Ireland Amateur 1970.
Int	Ireland (Home Int) 1969-70; Eur T Ch 1969
Jun Int	Youths 1970

Oosterhuis, Peter A
Born London on 3rd May, 1948. Turned Professional November 1968

PROFESSIONAL
Maj	Open r/u 1974-82; leading British player 1975 (7th), 1978 (6th) US Masters 3rd 1973
Eur	Agfacolor, Sunbeam Pro-Am, Piccadilly 1971; Penfold 1972; French Open, Piccadilly, Viyella PGA 1973; French Open, Italian Open 1974
US	Canadian Open 1981
RoW	General Motors South Africa 1970; Transvaal Open, Schoeman Park, Rhodesian Dunlop Masters 1971; Glen Anil Classic 1972; Rothman's Match Play South Africa, Maracaibo Open 1973; El Paraiso Open 1974
Oth	Sunningdale Foursomes 1969; Coca-Cola Young Professionals 1970-72
Reg	Southern England Professional 1971
Int	Ryder Cup 1971-73-75-77-79-81; Hennessy-Cognac 1974; England in World Cup 1971-73, in Double Diamond 1973-74
Mis	Rookie of the Year 1969; Harry Vardon Trophy 1971-72-73-74; AGW Trophy 1973-74

AMATEUR
Trn	Berkshire Trophy 1966
Int	Walker Cup 1967; Eisenhower Trophy 1968; England (Home Int) 1966-67-68
Jun	British Youths 1966
Int	Boys 1964-65; Youths 1966-67-68

For list of abbreviations see page 350

O'Sullivan, Dr William M
Born Killarney on 13th March, 1911
- **Cls** Waterville, Killarney (Hon), Dooks (Hon), Tralee (Hon), Muskerry (Hon), Cork (Hon), Ballybunion (Hon)
- **Chp** Irish Open Amateur 1949, r/u 1936-53. Irish Amateur r/u 1940
- **Int** Ireland (Home Int) 1934-35-36-37-38-47-48-49-50-51-53-54. President Golfing Union of Ireland 1959-60

Oxley, Dinah See Henson

Panton-Lewis, Catherine Rita
Born Bridge of Allan, Stirlingshire on 14th June, 1955. Turned Professional 1978
- **Cls** Glenbervie (Hon), Pitlochry (Hon), Silloth (Hon), South Herts

PROFESSIONAL
- **Eur** Carlsberg Tournament 1979. State Express Ladies Ch'p 1979. Elizabeth Ann Classic 1980. European Ladies Champion 1981. Moben Kitchens Classic 1982. Qualified for USLPGA Tour, January 1983. Smirnoff Irish Classic, UBM Northern Classic 1983, Dunham Forest Pro-Am 1983. McEwans Wirral Caldy Classic 1985. Delsjö Open 1985. Portuguese Open 1986-87. Scottish Open 1988
- **Int** Union Cup 1994
- **Mis** Order of Merit winner 1979

AMATEUR
- **Chp** Ladies British Open Amateur 1976
- **Reg** East of Scotland Ladies 1976
- **Int** Espirito Santo 1976. Vagliano Trophy 1977. Scotland (Home Int) 1972-73-76-77-78; Eur(L) T Ch 1973-77
- **Jun** Scottish Girls 1969. Girl Int 1969-70-71-72-73
- **Mis** Scottish Sportswoman of the Year 1976. Member of LGU under-25 team to tour Canada 1973

Panton, John, MBE
Born Pitlochry, Perthshire on 9th October, 1916. Turned Professional 1935
- **Maj** Leading British player in 1956 Open (5th)
- **Trn** Silver King 1950. Daks 1951. North-British-Harrogate 1952. Goodwin Foursomes 1952. Yorkshire Evening News 1954. PGA Match Play 1956, r/u 1968
- **Eur** Woodlawn Invitation Open (Germany) 1958-59-60
- **Oth** West of Scotland Professional 1947-48-52-54-55-61-63. Scottish Professional 1948-49-50-51-54-55-59-66 (tied). Northern Open 1948-51-52-56-59-60-62. West of Scotland PGA Match Play 1954-55-56-64. Goodwin Foursomes 1952. Gleneagles-Saxone 1956
- **Sen** Pringle Seniors 1967-69. World Seniors 1967
- **Int** Ryder Cup 1951-53-61. Scotland in World Cup 1955-56-57-58-59-60-62-63-64-65-66-68
- **Mis** Harry Vardon Trophy 1951. AGW Trophy 1967. Hon Professional to Royal & Ancient from 1988

Parkin, Philip
Born Doncaster on 12th December, 1961. Turned Professional 1984
PROFESSIONAL
- **Reg** Welsh PGA 1986

- **Int** Wales in World Cup 1984-89; Dunhill Cup 1985-86-87-89-90-91; Hennessy-Cognac Cup 1984
- **Mis** Rookie of the Year 1984. Commentator for Sky TV

AMATEUR
- **Chp** Amateur Champion 1983
- **Int** Walker Cup 1983. Wales (Home Int) 1980-81-82.
- **Jun** British Youths 1982

Paterson, Moira See Milton

Payne, Jim
Born Louth, Lincolnshire on 17th April, 1970. Turned Professional 1991
PROFESSIONAL
- **Maj** Leading Amateur in Open 1991
- **Eur** Open de Baleares 1993; Italian Open 1996
- **Int** World Cup 1996

AMATEUR
- **Trn** Berkhamsted Trophy 1989; Selborne Salver 1991
- **Oth** Greek Amateur 1989, European Amateur 1991
- **Reg** West of England Stroke Play 1990
- **Int** Walker Cup 1991; England (Home Int) 1989-90; Eur T Ch 1991; GBI v Europe 1990
- **Jun** British Youths 1991
- **Int** English Youths 1989-90-91
- **Mis** PGA European Rookie of the Year 1992

Perkins, Tegwen See Matthews

Perowne, Arthur Herbert
Born Norwich on 21st February, 1930
- **Cls** Royal Norwich, Hunstanton, West Norfolk
- **Chp** English Open Amateur Stroke Play 1958
- **Oth** Swedish Amateur 1974
- **Trn** Berkshire Trophy 1958 (tied)
- **Reg** East Anglia Open 1952. Norfolk Amateur 1948-51-52-53-54-55-56-57-58-60-61. Norfolk Open 1964
- **Int** Walker Cup 1949-53-59. Eisenhower Trophy 1958. GBI v Denmark 1955; v Professionals 1956-58. England (Home Int) 1947-48-49-50-51-53-54-55-57; v France 1950-54-56-59; v Sweden 1947; v Denmark 1947
- **Jun** Carris Trophy 1946
- **Int** Boys 1946

Phillips, Kathryn See Lumb

Pickard, Margaret (née Nichol)
Born 25th April, 1938
- **Cls** Alnmouth (Hon)
- **Nat** English Ladies 1960, r/u 1957-67
- **Reg** Northern Ladies 1957-58. Northumberland Ladies 1956-57-58-61-62-64-65-66-67-69-70-71-76-77-82
- **Int** Curtis Cup 1968-70. Vagliano Trophy 1959-61-67. England (Home Int) 1957-58-59-60-61-67-69-(83). Eur(L) T Ch (1983)

Pook, Elizabeth (née Chadwick)
Born Inverness on 4th April, 1943
- **Cls** Bramall Park (Hon), Anglesey (Rhosneigr)
- **Chp** British Ladies 1966-67.
- **Nat** English Ladies r/u 1963. Italian Ladies r/u 1967

For list of abbreviations see page 350

Reg	Central England Mixed Foursomes 1962-63-64 North of England Ladies 1965-66-67. Cheshire Ladies 1963-64-65-66-67
Trn	Avia Foursomes (with C Lacoste) r/u 1967
Int	Curtis Cup 1966. GB Commonwealth 1967. GBI v Europe 1963-67. England (Home Int) 1963-65-66-67; Eur(L) T Ch 1967; v France 1965
Jun	Girl International 1961

Porter, Ruth *See* **Slark**

Price Fisher, Elizabeth

Born London on 17th January, 1923. Turned Professional 1968, reinstated as Amateur 1971

Cls	Hankley Common, Farnham, Berkshire
Chp	British Ladies 1959, r/u 1954-58
Nat	English Ladies r/u 1947-54-55
Oth	Danish Ladies 1952. Portuguese Ladies 1964
Trn	Spalding Ladies 1955-59. Astor Salver 1955-56-59. Fairway and Hazard Foursomes 1954-60. Kayser Bondor Foursomes 1958 (tied). Roehampton Gold Cup 1960. Central England Mixed Foursomes 1971-76-82
Reg	South Eastern Ladies 1955-59-60-69. Surrey Ladies 1954-55-56-57-58-59-60
Int	Curtis Cup 1950-52-54-56-58-60. Vagliano Trophy 1959. GBI v Canada 1950-54-58; v France 1953-55-57; v Belgium 1953-55-57. GB Commonwealth Team 1955-59. England (Home Int) 1948-51-52-53-54-55-56-57-58-59-60
Mis	AGW Trophy 1952

Pyman, Iain

Born Whitby on 3rd March, 1973

Cls	Sand Moor
Maj	Open Chp 1993; leading amateur 1993
Chp	Amateur Champion 1993
Trn	Formby Hare 1992
Oth	Top amateur in NSW Open (Aus)
Reg	Yorkshire champion 1992
Int	GBI Walker Cup 1993; England (Home Int) 1993
Jun	Carris Trophy 1991; Yorkshire Youths 1993
Jun Int	GBI Boys 1991; England Boys 1991

Rafferty, Ronan

Born Newry on 13th January, 1964. Turned Professional 1981

PROFESSIONAL

Eur	Equity & Law Challenge 1988; Lancia Italian Open, Scandinavian Enterprise Open, Volvo Masters 1989; PLM Open, Swiss Open 1990; Portuguese Open 1992; Austrian Open 1993
RoW	Venezuelan Open 1982; South Australian Open, New Zealand Open 1987; Australian Match Play 1988; Coca-Cola Classic (Aus) 1990; Daikyo Palm Meadow (Aus) 1992
Int	Ryder Cup 1989; Kirin Cup 1988; Four Tours World Chp 1989-90-91; GBI v Australia 1988; Hennessy-Cognac 1984; Ireland in World Cup 1983-84-87-88-91-92-93; Dunhill Cup 1986-87-88(winners)-89-90(winners)-91-92-93-95
Mis	Harry Vardon Trophy 1989

AMATEUR

Nat	Irish Amateur 1980; English Amateur Open Stroke Play 1980(tied)
Int	Walker Cup 1981; Eisenhower Trophy 1980; GBI v Europe 1980; Ireland (Home Int) 1980; v Wales 1979; v France, Germany, Sweden 1980; Fiat Trophy 1980; Eur T Ch 1981
Jun	British Boys 1979; Irish Youths 1979; Ulster Youths 1979
Int	Boys 1978-79; Youths 1979-80

Rankin, Graham

Born 18 January, 1966

Cls	Palacerigg
Nat	Scottish Amateur 1998
Trn	St Andrews Links Trophy 1995; Lytham Trophy 1997; Tennant Cup 1998
Int	Walker Cup 1995-97; Scotland (Home Int) 1994-95-97-98; Eur T Ch 1995(winners)-1997; v Sweden 1995-97; v France 1995-97; v Spain 1996
Mis	J&B Order of Merit 1997-98

Rawlings, Vicki *See* **Thomas**

Redford, Carole *See* **Caldwell**

Reid, Dale

Born Ladybank, Fife on 20th March, 1959. Turned Professional 1979

PROFESSIONAL

Eur	Carlsberg (Coventry) 1980. Carlsberg (Gleneagles), Moben Kitchens 1981. Guernsey Open 1982. United Friendly, International Classic 1983. Caldy Classic 1983. UBM Classic, JS Bloor Classic 1984. Ulster Volkswagen Classic, Brend Hotels International 1985. British Olivetti 1986. Volmac Open, European Open, Bowring Scottish Open, Volkswagen Classic 1987. European Open, Toshiba Players Chp 1988. Haninge Open 1990. Ford Ladies Classic, Eastleigh Classic 1997
Oth	Sunningdale Foursomes (with C. Dibnah) 1990
Int	Solheim Cup 1990-92-94-96; Sunrise Cup 1992; Union Cup 1994
Mis	Order of Merit winner 1984-87; first Honorary Member of WPGET 1991

AMATEUR

Int	Scotland (Home Int) 1978
Jun	Fife Girls 1973-75
Jun Int	Scottish Girls International 1974-75-76-77

Richardson, Steven

Born Windsor on 24th July, 1966. Turned Professional 1989

PROFESSIONAL

Eur	Girona Open, Portuguese Open 1991; German Masters 1993
Int	Ryder Cup 1991; England in Dunhill Cup 1991-92(winners); World Cup 1991-92; Four Tours World Chp 1991

AMATEUR

Nat	English Amateur 1989
Int	England (Home Int) 1986-87-88

Robb, Diane *See* **Bailey**

For list of abbreviations see page 350

Robertson, Dean
Born Sarnia, Canada on 11th July, 1970. Turned Professional 1993
Cls Cochrane Castle
PROFESSIONAL
Trn HIS Assistants 1994
AMATEUR
Nat Scottish Amateur Stroke Play 1993, r/u 1993
Trn Scottish Champion of Champions 1992; Tennant Cup 1992-93; Leven Gold Medal 1992
Int GBI Walker Cup 1993; vEurope 1992; Eisenhower Trophy 1992; Scotland (Home Int) 1991-92-93; v Sweden 1992, v Italy 1992
Mis Scottish Golfer of the Year 1992

Robertson, Isabella (Belle), MBE
Born Southend, Argyll, on 11th April, 1936
Cls Dunaverty (Hon)
Maj Ladies British Open: leading amateur (Smyth Salver); r/u 1980-81
Chp Ladies British Open Amateur 1981, r/u 1959-65-70
Nat Ladies British Open Amateur Stroke Play 1971-72-85; Scottish Ladies 1965-66-71-72-78-80; r/u 1959-63-70
Oth New Zealand Ladies Match Play 1971
Trn Sunningdale Foursomes 1960; Avia Foursomes 1972-81-84-86; Helen Holm Trophy 1973-79-86; Players No 6 Cup 1973-76; Roehampton Gold Cup 1978 (tied)-79-81-82
Reg West of Scotland Ladies 1957-64-66-69; Dunbartonshire Ladies 1958 to 1963, 1965-66-68-69-78
Sen US Women's Amateur Seniors r/u 1991
Int Curtis Cup 1960-66-68-70-72-(74)-(76)-82-86; Vagliano Trophy 1959-63-65-69-71-81; Espirito Santo 1964-66-**68**-72-80-82; GB Commonwealth Trn 1971-(75); Scotland (Home Int) 1958 to 1966, 69-72-73-78-80-81-82 Eur(L) T Ch 1965-**67**-69-71-73-81-83; Fiat Trophy 1978-80
Mis Daks Woman Golfer of the Year 1971-81; Frank Moran Trophy 1971; leading qualifier US Ladies Amateur 1978; Scottish Sportswoman of the Year 1968-71-78-81; Avia Woman Golfer of the Year 1985

Robertson, Janette *See* Wright

Rose, Alison
Born Stirling on 18th June, 1968
Cls Stirling
Chp Ladies' British Open Amateur 1997
Nat Welsh Open Amateur Stroke Play 1994; Scottish Ladies 1997, r/u 1996
Reg East of Scotland Ladies 1988-90-93; Stirlingshire Ladies 1990-91-92
Trn St Rule Trophy 1991; Mary McCallay Trophy 1995
Int Curtis Cup 1996-98; Vagliano Trophy 1995-97; Commonwealth Trn 1995. Scotland (Home Int) 1990 to 1998; Eur(L) T Ch 1991-93-95-97
Jun Int Jun Eur(L) T Ch 1988
Mis Order of Merit winner 1994-96. Taunton Trophy 1996

Rose, Justin Peter
Born Johannesburg, South Africa on 30 July, 1980. Turned Professional after Open 1998
Maj Leading amateur in Open 1998
Trn Carris Trophy, Malcolm Reid Salver, Hampshire Hog 1995; St Andrews Links Trophy 1997; Peter McEvoy Trophy 1998
Int Walker Cup 1997; England (Home Int) 1996; Eur T Ch 1997; v Spain 1997; Eur Men v Asia Pacific 1998

Rostron, Kim *See* Andrew

Russell, Raymond
Born Edinburgh on 26th July, 1972. Turned Professional 1993
PROFESSIONAL
Eur Cannes Open 1996
Int Scotland in Dunhill Cup 1996-97; World Cup 1997 (r/u)
AMATEUR
Int Walker Cup 1993; Scotland (Home Int) 1992-93; Eur T Ch 1993
Jun Scottish Youths 1992

Saddler, AC (Sandy)
Born Forfar, Angus on 11th August, 1935
Cls Forfar, Carnoustie
Nat Scottish Amateur r/u 1960
Trn Berkshire Trophy 1962
Int Walker Cup 1963-65-67-(77); Eisenhower Trophy 1962-(76) (winners)-78; GB Commonwealth Trn 1959-63-67; v Europe 1960-62-66-(76)-(78); v Professionals 1959-61. Scotland (Home Int) 1959-60-61-62-63-65-(74)-(75)-(76)-(77); Eur T Ch (1975)-(77)

Saunders, Vivien Inez
Born Sutton on 24th November, 1946. Turned Professional 1969
PROFESSIONAL
Maj Ladies British Open 1977
Trn Avia Foursomes 1978; Keighley Trophy 1981; British Car Auctions 1980
US 1969 First European to qualify for LPGA tour
RoW Schweppes-Tarax Open (Australia), Chrysler Open (Australia) 1973
Mis Founder WPGA & Chairman 1978-79
AMATEUR
Chp Ladies British Open Amateur r/u 1966
Trn Avia Foursomes 1967
Int Curtis Cup 1968; Vagliano Trophy 1967; GB Commonwealth Team 1967; England (Home Int) 1967-68 Eur(L) T Ch 1967; v France 1966-67
Jun Int Girls 1964-65-66-67

Sewell, Douglas
Born Woking on 19th November, 1929. Turned Professional 1960
PROFESSIONAL
Trn Martini International 1970 (shared); Wentworth Pro-Am Foursomes 1968
Reg West of England Open Professional 1968-70
Int PGA Cup 1973-74-75

AMATEUR
Nat English Amateur 1958-60; English Open Amateur Stroke-Play 1957-59
Trn Scrutton Jug 1959; *Golf Illustrated* Gold Vase 1960; Sunningdale Foursomes 1959
Reg Surrey Amateur 1954-56-58
Int Walker Cup 1957-59; Eisenhower Trophy 1960; GB Commonwealth Trn 1959; England (Home Int) 1956-57-58-59-60

Sheahan, Dr David B
Born Southsea, England on 25th February, 1940
Cls Grange
Nat Irish Amateur 1961-66-70
Trn Jeyes Professional 1962 (as an Amateur); Frame Trophy 1991
Oth Boyd Quaich 1962
Int Walker Cup 1963. GBI *v* Europe 1962-64. Ireland (Home Int) 1961-62-63-64-65-66-67-70; Eur T Ch 1965-67 (winners both times)

Shepperson, AE
Born Sutton-in-Ashfield on 8th April, 1936
Cls Coxmoor (Hon), Notts
Nat English Open Amateur Stroke Play r/u 1958-62
Trn President's Putter 1957
Reg Nottinghamshire Amateur 1955-58-61-65. Nottinghamshire Open 1955-58
Int Walker Cup 1957-59. England (Home Int) 1956-57-58-59-60-62
Jun British Boys 1953

Sherry, Gordon
Born Kilmarnock on 8th April, 1974
Cls Kilmarnock Barassie
Chp Amateur Champion 1995; r/u 1994
Nat Scottish Amateur sf 1994; European Amateur r/u 1994
Trn St Andrews Links r/u 1995; Edward Trophy 1993-94; Scottish Champion of Champions 1994; Boyd Quaich 1993
Reg Ayrshire Matchplay 1992; Ayrshire Strokeplay 1993; Scotland South-East District 1994
Oth Scottish Universities Champion 1993; European Club Cup Champion 1994
Int Walker Cup 1995; Eisenhower Trophy 1994; GBI *v* Europe 1994; Scotland (Home Int) 1993-94-95; *v* France 1993-95; *v* Spain 1994; *v* Sweden 1995; Eur T Ch 1995
Jun Int European Youths, Scottish Youths 1994; European Boys (Champions) 1992; Scottish Boys (Champions) 1992
Mis Scottish Amateur Golfer of the Year 1995

Sinclair, Alexander, OBE
Born West Kilbride, Ayrshire on 6th July, 1920
Cls Royal & Ancient, Honorary member of West Kilbride, Drumpellier, Bothwell Castle, Royal Troon
Trn Newlands Trophy 1950
Oth Royal & Ancient Silver Cross 1972. Royal Medal 1977. Scottish Open Amateur Seniors 1979
Reg West of Scotland Amateur 1950. Lanarkshire Amateur 1952-59-61. Glasgow Amateur 1961
Int Scotland (Home Int) 1950-(**66**)-(**67**). Eur T Ch (**1967**)
Mis Chairman R & A Selection Committee from 1969 to 1975. Leading Amateur (joint second) in Northern Open 1948. President Scottish Golf Union 1976-78. Frank Moran Trophy 1978. Chairman R & A Amateur Status Committee 1979-81. President European Golf Association 1981-82-83. Captain of R&A 1988/89. President of Golf Foundation from 1990

Slark, Ruth (née Porter)
Born Chesterfield on 6th May, 1939
Cls Long Ashton (Hon), Bath, Burnham and Berrow, Reigate Heath, Walton Heath
Nat English Ladies 1959-61-65, r/u 1978
Oth Australian Ladies r/u 1963
Trn Astor Prince's 1961. Fairway and Hazard Foursomes 1958. Roehampton Gold Cup 1963. Astor Salver 1962-63. Hovis Ladies 1966 (tied). Avia Foursomes 1968
Reg South Western Ladies 1956-57-60-61-62-64-65-66-67-69-72-77-79. Gloucestershire Ladies 1957-59-61-62-63-64-66-67-69-73-74-75-76-77
Int Curtis Cup 1960-62-64. Vagliano Trophy 1959-61-65. GB Commonwealth Team 1963. Espirito Santo 1964-66. England (Home Int) 1959-60-61-62-64-65-66-68-75-78; Eur(L) T Ch 1965
Jun British Girls 1956. Scottish Girls Open Stroke Play 1958. Girls International 1955-56-57
Mis Taunton Trophy 1978

Smith, William Dickson
Born Glasgow on 2nd February, 1918
Cls Prestwick (Hon), Royal & Ancient, Royal Troon, Selkirk (Hon), Southerness, Gullane
Maj Leading amateur (5th) in Open 1957
Nat Scottish Amateur 1958. Scottish Senior Open Amateur 1983
Oth Indian Open Amateur 1945. Portuguese Open Amateur 1967-70.
Trn Worplesdon Mixed Foursomes 1957. Royal & Ancient Royal Medal 1971
Reg Border Amateur 1949-51-57-63. Dumfriesshire Amateur 1956
Int Walker Cup 1959. GBI *v* Europe 1958. Scotland (Home Int) 1957-58-59-60-63-(83); *v* Scandinavia 1958-60

Smye, Catherine *See* McCann

Smyth, Des
Born Drogheda on 12th February, 1953. Turned Professional 1973
PROFESSIONAL
Trn PGA Match Play 1979. Newcastle Brown 900, Greater Manchester Open 1980. Coral Classic 1981. Sanyo Open 1983. Jersey Open 1988. Madrid Open 1993
Oth Irish PGA 1979-90. Carrolls Irish Match Play, Irish Dunlop 1980. Irish Masters 1994.
Int Ryder Cup 1979-81. Ireland in World Cup 1979-80-82-83-88-89. Hennessy-Cognac Cup 1980-82-84. Dunhill Cup 1985-86-87-88 (winners)
AMATEUR
Int Ireland (Home Int) 1972-73; Eur T Ch 1973

Speak, Kirsty
Born on 18th June, 1971
- **Cls** Clitheroe
- **Chp** British Ladies r/u 1993
- **Nat** English Intermediate 1990(r/u)-92-93; British Ladies Stroke Play 1994
- **Trn** Pleasington Putter 1990; Bridget Jackson Bowl 1994; Wentworth Scratch 1994
- **Oth** World Student Chp 1992
- **Int** Curtis Cup 1994; Vagliano Trophy 1993; Espirito Santo 1994; England (Home Int) 1993-94; Eur(L) T Ch 1993

Spearman, Marley *See* Harris

Squirrell, Hew Crawford
Born Cardiff on 15th August, 1932
- **Cls** Hon member of Cardiff, Moseley, Killarney
- **Nat** Welsh Amateur 1958-59-60-64-65, r/u 1962-71
- **Trn** Antlers Royal Mid-Surrey 1959-61. Hampshire Hog 1961. Berkhamsted Trophy 1960-63. Boyd Quaich 1955
- **Reg** Glamorgan Amateur 1959-65. Herts Amateur 1963-73
- **Int** Wales (Home Int) 1955-56-57-58-59-60-61-62-63-64-65-66-67-68-**69**-**70**-**71**-73-74-75; Eur T Ch 1965-67-69-71-75; v France 1975
- **Mis** Deputy-Director Golf Foundation

Stephen, Alexander R (Sandy)
Born St Andrews on 8th January, 1954. Turned Professional 1985
- **Cls** Lundin (Hon), Muckhart (Hon), Broomieknowe

PROFESSIONAL
- **Trn** Scottish Professional Chp 1988

AMATEUR
- **Nat** Scottish Amateur 1971
- **Trn** Scottish Champion of Champions 1984. Leven Gold Medal 1984
- **Reg** North of Scotland Open Amateur 1972-77. Fife Amateur 1973. Lothians Amateur 1978; East of Scotland Open Amateur 1974-77-83-84. West of Scotland Open Amateur 1975
- **Int** Walker Cup 1985. GBI v Europe 1972. Scotland (Home Int) 1971-72-73-74-75-76-77-84-85; Eur T Ch 1975-85; v Spain 1974; v Belgium 1975-77-78
- **Jun** Scottish Boys 1970.
- **Int** Boys 1970-71. Youths 1972-73-74-75
- **Mis** Finished third in World Boys International Trophy (USA) 1970

Stewart, Gillian
Born Inverness on 21st October, 1958. Turned Professional 1985
- **Cls** Inverness (Hon), Nairn

PROFESSIONAL
- **Eur** IBM European Open 1984 (as amateur). Ford Ladies Classic 1985-87
- **Int** Union Cup 1994

AMATEUR
- **Nat** Scottish Ladies 1979-83-84. Ladies British Open Amateur r/u 1982
- **Trn** Helen Holm Trophy 1981-84
- **Reg** Northern Counties Ladies 1976-78-82. North of Scotland Ladies 1975-78-80-82-83
- **Int** Curtis Cup 1980-82. GB Commonwealth Team 1979-83. Vagliano Trophy 1979-81-83. Espirito Santo 1982-84. Scotland (Home Int) 1979-80-81-82-83-84; Eur(L) T Ch 1979-81-83
- **Jun** British Girls 1976. Scottish U-19 Stroke Play Champion 1975
- **Int** Girls 1975-76-77
- **Mis** Member of Scottish team which won the 1980 European Junior Team Championship. Avia Woman Golfer of the Year 1984

Stuart, Hugh Bannerman
Born Forres on 27th June, 1942
- **Cls** Forres (Hon), Murcar (Hon)
- **Chp** Amateur s/f 1974
- **Nat** Scottish Amateur 1972, r/u 1970-76
- **Reg** North of Scotland Amateur 1967-74. Moray Amateur 1960. Nairnshire Amateur 1966
- **Int** Walker Cup 1971-73-75; GB Commonwealth Trn 1971; Eisenhower Trophy 1972; GBI v Europe 1968-72-74. Scotland (Home Int) 1967-68-70-71-72-73-74-76; Eur T Ch 1969-71-73-75; v Belgium 1973-75
- **Jun** Scottish Boys 1959
- **Int** Boys 1959
- **Mis** Won all his matches in 1971 Walker Cup. In European Team touring South Africa 1974

Thirlwell, Alan
Born 8th August, 1928
- **Cls** Gosforth, Formby
- **Chp** Amateur r/u 1958-72
- **Nat** English Amateur 1954-55, r/u 1963. English Open Amateur Stroke Play r/u 1964
- **Trn** County Champion of Champions 1962. Wentworth Pro-Am Foursomes 1960-61-68
- **Reg** Northumberland Amateur 1952-55-62-64. Northumberland and Durham Open 1960
- **Int** Walker Cup 1957. GB Commonwealth Trn 1954-63. GBI v Europe 1956-58; v Denmark 1955; v Professionals 1963. England (Home Int) 1951-52-54-55-56-57-58-59-63-64; v France 1954-56-59
- **Mis** Canadian Amateur s/f 1957. EGU Selector 1974 to 1977. Secretary CONGU

Thomas, David C
Born Newcastle-upon-Tyne on 16th August, 1934. Turned Professional 1949
- **Maj** Open r/u 1958 (tied), r/u 1966
- **Eur** Belgian Open 1955. Dutch Open 1958. French Open 1959
- **Trn** Esso Golden 1961 (tied)-62-66. PGA Matchplay, Olgiata Trophy (Rome) 1963. Silentnight 1965 (tied). Penfold-Swallow, Jeyes 1966. Penfold 1968 (tied). Graham Textiles 1969. Pains-Wessex 1969
- **RoW** Caltex (NZ) 1958-59
- **Oth** British Assistants 1955. Wentworth Pro-Am Foursomes 1960-61
- **Int** Ryder Cup 1959-63-65-67. Wales in World Cup 1957-58-59-60-61-62-63-66-67-69-70. Wales in Double Diamond 1972-73
- **Mis** Won qualifying competition for US Open 1964

For list of abbreviations see page 350

Thomas, Vicki (née Rawlings)
Born Northampton on 27th October, 1954
- **Cls** Pennard
- **Maj** Leading Amateur in Women's British Open (Smyth Salver) 1986
- **Nat** Welsh Ladies Amateur 1979-82-83-85-86-87-91-94; British Ladies Amateur Stroke Play 1990, r/u 1979. Welsh Ladies Open Stroke Play 1981-82-89, r/u 1980
- **Trn** Roehampton Gold Cup 1983-85. Cotswold Gold Vase 1983. Keithley Trophy 1983. Sunningdale Foursomes 1989. Welsh Trn of Champions 1991-94
- **Reg** Glamorganshire Ladies 1970-71-79; Women's South-West Chp 1991
- **Oth** Women's Greek Amateur Stroke Play 1991
- **Int** Curtis Cup 1982-84-86-88-90-92; GB Commonwealth Trn 1979-83-87-91; Vagliano Trophy 1979-83-85-87-89-91; Espirito Santo 1990; Wales (Home Int) 1971 to 1998; Eur(L) T Ch 1973-75-77-79-81-83-87-91
- **Jun** Welsh Girls 1973
- **Int** Girls 1969-70-71-72-73
- **Mis** Taunton Trophy 1979

Thomson, Muriel
Born Aberdeen on 12th December, 1954. Turned Professional 1979
PROFESSIONAL
- **Eur** Carlsberg, Viscount Double Glazing, Barnham Broom 1980; Elizabeth Ann Classic 1981; Guernsey Open, Sands International 1984; Laing Classic 1985; Irish Open, Ford Classic 1986
- **Mis** Order of Merit winner 1980-83; Frank Moran Trophy 1981

AMATEUR
- **Nat** Scottish Ladies r/u 1977
- **Trn** Helen Holm Trophy 1975-76; Canadian Ladies Foursomes 1978
- **Reg** North of Scotland Ladies 1973-74; Aberdeenshire Ladies 1977
- **Int** Curtis Cup 1978; Vagliano Trophy 1977; Espirito Santo 1978; GBI in Colombian International 1979; Scotland (Home Int) 1974-75-76-77-78; Eur(L) T Ch 1975-77

Thornhill, Jill
Born 18th August, 1942
- **Cls** Walton Heath, Silloth-on-Solway
- **Chp** Ladies British Open Amateur 1983
- **Nat** English Ladies 1986, r/u 1974. Ladies British Open Amateur Stroke Play r/u 1987
- **Trn** Avia Foursomes 1970-83. Astor Salver 1972-75. Newmark International 1974. Worplesdon Mixed Foursomes 1975. Hampshire Rose 1982-87
- **Eur** Belgian Ladies 1967
- **Reg** South Eastern Ladies 1964-64-85. Surrey Ladies 1962-64-65-73-74-77-78-81-82-83-84
- **Int** Curtis Cup 1984-86-88-(**90**). Vagliano Trophy 1965-83-85-87-(**90**). England (Home Int) 1964-65-74-82-83-84-85-86 -87-88. Commonwealth Trn 1983; Eur(L) T Ch 1983
- **Sen** British Ladies Seniors 1993, r/u 1994
- **Mis** Doris Chambers Trophy 1986. Avia Woman Golfer of the Year 1983

Torrance, Sam
Born Largs, Ayrshire on 24th August, 1953. Turned Professional 1970
PROFESSIONAL
- **Eur** Piccadilly Medal, Martini International 1976; Carrolls Irish Open 1981; Spanish Open, Portuguese Open 1982; Scandinavian Enterprise and Portuguese Opens 1983; Tunisian and Sanyo Opens, Benson & Hedges International 1984; Monte Carlo Open 1985; Lancia Italian Open 1987; German Masters 1990; Jersey Open 1991; Kronenbourg, Catalan and Honda Opens 1993; Italian and Irish Opens, British Masters 1995; Peugeot Open de France 1998
- **Oth** U-25 Match Play 1972; Scottish Uniroyal 1975; Scottish Professional 1978-80-91-93
- **RoW** Zambian Open 1975; Colombian Open 1979; Australian PGA 1980
- **Int** Ryder Cup 1981-83-85-87-89-91-93-95; Hennessy-Cognac Cup 1976-80-82-84; Nissan Cup 1985; Four Tours World Chp 1991; Scotland in World Cup 1976-78-82-84-85-87-89-90-91-93-95; Double Diamond 1973-76-77; Dunhill Cup 1985-86-87-89-90-91-93-95(winners)
- **Mis** Rookie of the Year 1972; Tooting Bec Cup 1984

AMATEUR
- **Jun Int** Scottish Boys 1970

Townsend, Peter Michael Paul
Born Cambridge on 16th September, 1946. Turned Professional 1966
PROFESSIONAL
- **Eur** Dutch Open 1967; Swiss Open, Carrolls Irish Match Play 1971; Carrolls Irish Match Play 1976; Irish Dunlop 1977
- **Oth** PGA Close, Coca-Cola Young Professionals 1968
- **US** Chesterfield 1968
- **RoW** Western Australia Open 1968; Caracas Open 1969; Walworth Aloyco 1971; Los Lagaratos Open 1972; ICL International (SA) 1975; Moroccan Grand Prix, Los Lagaratos, Caribbean and Zambian Opens 1978; Laurent Perrier 1981
- **Int** Ryder Cup 1969-71; Hennessy-Cognac 1974; England in World Cup 1969-74; in Double Diamond 1971-72-74
- **Mis** Captain PGA 1984

AMATEUR
- **Nat** English Open Amateur Stroke Play 1966
- **Trn** Duncan Putter 1965; Mullingar Trophy 1965-66; Lytham Trophy 1966; *Golf Illustrated* Vase 1966; Prince of Wales Challenge Cup 1966; St George's Challenge Cup 1966; Berkhamsted Trophy 1966
- **Reg** Herts Amateur 1964
- **Int** Walker Cup 1965; Eisenhower Trophy 1966; GBI v Europe 1966; England (Home Int) 1965-66
- **Jun** British Boys 1962-64; British Youths 1965
- **Int** Boys 1961-62-63-64; Youths 1965

Tucker, William Iestyn
Born Nantyglo, Monmouth on 9th December, 1926
- **Cls** Monmouthshire, Brecon, Killarney, Morlais Castle, Tredegar and Rhymney, Pontynewydd, Llantrisant, Radyr, Whitehall
- **Nat** Welsh Amateur 1933-36, r/u 1951-56-64-67-75-76. Welsh Amateur Stroke Play 1976
- **Trn** Duncan Putter 1960-61 (tied)-63-69-76

Reg Monmouthshire Amateur 1949, 1952 to 63, 1967-69-74. Gwent Amateur 1976
Int Wales (Home Int) 1949 to 72, 1974-75; Eur T Ch 1965-67-69-75; *v* Australia 1953; *v* France 1975. Captain Welsh Team 1966-67-68

Uzielli, Angela (née Carrick)
Born Swanton Morley, Norfolk on 1st February, 1940
Cls Berkshire (Hon),
Chp British Ladies Open Amateur 1977.
Nat English Ladies 1990, r/u 1976
Trn Astor Salver 1971-73 (tied)-77-81. Roehampton Gold Cup 1977. Avia Foursomes 1982. Hampshire Rose 1985
Reg Berkshire Ladies 1976-77-78-79-80-81-83
Int Curtis Cup 1978. Vagliano Trophy 1977. England (Home Int) 1976-77-78-90; Eur(L) T Ch 1977
Sen British Ladies Seniors 1990-91-92-95, r/u 1993-96
Mis Daks Woman Golfer of the Year 1977; *Daily Telegraph* Woman Golfer of the Year 1990

Valentine, Jessie, MBE (née Anderson)
Born Perth on 18th March, 1915. Turned Professional 1960
Cls Honorary member of Craigie Hill, St Rule, Hunstanton, Blairgowrie, Murrayshall
Chp British Ladies 1937-55-58, r/u 1950-57
Nat Scottish Ladies 1938-39-51-53-55-56, r/u 1934-54
Oth New Zealand Ladies 1935. French Ladies 1936
Trn Spalding Ladies 1957. Kayser Bondor Foursomes 1959-61. Worplesdon Mixed Foursomes 1963-64-65
Reg East of Scotland Ladies 1936-38-39-50
Int Curtis Cup 1936-38-50-52-54-56-58. GBI *v* France 1935-36-38-39-47-49-51-55; *v* Belgium 1949-51-54-55; *v* Canada 1938-50. GB Commonwealth Trn 1953-55-(59). Scotland (Home Int) 1934-35-36-37-38-39-47-49-50-51-52-53-54-55-56-57-58
Jun British Girls 1933
Mis Canadian Ladies s/f 1938. Member of LGU Team to Australia and New Zealand 1935. Frank Moran Trophy 1967

Vaughan, Sheila See Maher

Wade, Julie See Hall

Wadsworth, Helen Elizabeth
Born on the Gower, Swansea on 7th April, 1964. Turned Professional 1991
PROFESSIONAL
Eur BMW European Masters 1994
Int Sunrise Cup 1992
Mis Rookie of the Year 1991
AMATEUR
Chp British Ladies Open Amateur r/u 1990 s/f 1988
Nat Welsh Ladies Open Amateur Stroke Play 1986. Welsh Ladies r/u 1990
Oth World Fourball Chp with Julie Hall 1987
Trn Astor Salver, Wentworth Scratch Trophy 1985; Sunningdale Foursomes (with Julie Hall) 1997

Reg Kent Ladies 1990
Int Curtis Cup 1990. Wales (Home Int) 1987-88-89-90; Eur(L) T Ch 1985-87-89
Jun South-East Girls 1981
Int Wales (Jun Eur T Ch) 1983
Mis Leading amateur, Ladies European Open 1990. Taunton Trophy 1990

Waites, Brian J
Born Bolton on 1st March, 1940. Turned Professional 1957
Eur Tournament Players' Championship 1978. Car Care Plan International 1982
RoW Kenya Open 1980. Mufulira Open (Zambia) 1980-82. Cock o' the North (Zambia) Open 1985
Oth National ProAm Chp 1979
Reg Midland Open 1971-76-81. Midland Professional Stroke Play 1972-77-78-79. Midland Professional Match Play 1972-73-74.
Sen PGA Sen 1990-91; D-Day Sen Open 1994; Northern Electric Sen 1995; Crédit Suisse Sen Open 1997; Elf Sen Open 1998
Int Ryder Cup 1983; PGA Cup 1973-75-76-77-78-90; GBI *v* Europe 1980; Hennessy-Cognac Cup 1984; England in World Cup 1980-82-83; (Sen) European Cup 1997-98

Walker, Carole Michelle (Mickey), OBE
Born Alwoodley, nr Leeds on 17th December, 1952. Turned Professional 1973
PROFESSIONAL
Maj Ladies British Open r/u 1979
Eur Carlsberg 1979; Lambert & Butler Match Play 1980; Carlsberg 1981; Sands International 1983; Baume-Mercier Classic, Lorne Stewart Match Play 1984
Oth Sunningdale Foursomes 1982
Int Solheim Cup (1990)-(92)-(94)-(96)
AMATEUR
Chp Ladies British Open Amateur 1971-72; r/u 1973
Nat Ladies British Open Amateur Stroke Play r/u 1972; English Ladies 1973
Oth Portuguese Ladies Amateur, US Trans-Mississippi 1972; Spanish Ladies Amateur 1973
Trn Hovis Ladies 1972
Int Curtis Cup 1972-74; GB Commonwealth Trn 1971; Espirito Santo 1971; Vagliano Trophy 1971; England (Home Int) 1970-72 Eur(L) T Ch 1971-73
Jun French Girls U-22 Open 1971
Int English Girls 1969-70-71
Mis AGW Trophy 1972; Daks Women Golfer of the Year 1972; Duncan Salver 1972

Walton, Lisa See Educate

Walton, Philip
Born Dublin on 28th March, 1962. Turned Professional 1983
PROFESSIONAL
Eur French Open 1990, Open Catalonia, English Open 1995
Trn Irish Professional 1989-91
Int Ryder Cup 1995; Ireland in World Cup 1995; Dunhill Cup 1989-90 (winners)-92-94-95

For list of abbreviations see page 350

AMATEUR
Nat   Scottish Open Amateur Stroke Play 1981. Irish Amateur 1982
Int   Walker Cup 1981-83; Eisenhower Trophy 1982. Ireland (Home Int) 1980-81; Eur T Ch 1981

Ward, Angela See Bonallack

Ward, Charles Harold
Born Birmingham on 16th September, 1911
Maj   Open 3rd 1948-51, leading British player (4th) 1946
Trn   *Daily Mail* Victory 1945. Silver King (tied), Yorkshire Evening News 1948. Spalding, North British-Harrogate, Dunlop Masters 1949. *Daily Mail* 1950. Dunlop, Lotus 1951. PGA Close 1956
Oth   West of England Open Professional 1937. *Daily Telegraph* Pro-Am 1947-48. Midland Professional 1933-34-50-53-55-63. Midland Open 1949-51-52-54-57
Int   Ryder Cup 1947-49-51
Mis   Vardon Trophy 1948-49

Watson, Craig
Born Glasgow on 1st August 1966
Cls   East Renfrewshire
Chp   Amateur Champion 1997
Nat   Scottish Amateur s/f 1996; Scottish Mid-Amateur 1994
Trn   St Andrews Links Trophy 1992; Cameron-Corbett Vase 1996-97
Int   Walker Cup 1997; Scotland (Home Int) 1991-92-94-95-96-97-98; Eur T Ch 1997

Way, Paul
Born Kingsbury, Middlesex on 12th March, 1963. Turned Professional 1981
PROFESSIONAL
Eur   KLM Dutch Open 1982. Whyte & McKay PGA 1985. European Open 1987
RoW   South African Charity Classic 1985
Int   Ryder Cup 1983-85. England in World Cup 1985. Dunhill Cup 1985
AMATEUR
Nat   English Open Amateur Stroke Play 1981
Int   Walker Cup 1981. England (Home Int) 1981; Eur T Ch 1981

Westwood, Lee
Born Worksop on 24th April, 1973. Turned Professional 1993
PROFESSIONAL
Eur   Scandinavian Masters, Volvo Masters 1997; Open TPC of Europe, English Open, Loch Lomond Invitational, Belgacom Open 1998
US   Freeport McDermott Classic 1998
RoW   Taiheiyo Masters 1996-97-98; Malaysian Open, Australian Open 1997; Dunlop Phoenix 1998
Int   Ryder Cup 1997; England in Dunhill Cup 1996-97-98
Mis   AGW Trophy 1998
AMATEUR
Trn   Peter McEvoy Trophy 1991; Lagonda Trophy 1992; Leven Gold Medal 1993
Int   England (Home Int) 1993
Jun   British Youths 1993

White, Ronald James
Born Wallasey on 9th April, 1921
Cls   Hon member of Royal Birkdale, Woolton, Buxton and High Peak, Killarney
Nat   English Amateur 1949 r/u, 1953. English Open Amateur Stroke Play 1950-51
Trn   *Golf Illustrated* Gold Vase 1949. *Daily Telegraph* Pro-Am 1947-49
Sen   British Seniors Open Amateur 1978-79
Reg   Lancashire Amateur 1948
Int   Walker Cup 1947-49-51-53-55. England (Home Int) 1947-48-49-53; France 1947-48
Jun   Carris Trophy 1937
Int   Boys 1936-37-38

Whitlock, Susan See Hedges

Wolstenholme, Gary Peter
Born Egham, Surrey on 21st August, 1960
Cls   Bristol & Clifton, The Leicestershire, Scarborough North Cliff, County Sligo, Kilworth Springs
Chp   Amateur Champion 1991
Nat   British Mid-Amateur 1995, 1996
Oth   Chinese Amateur 1993, Emirates Amateur 1995, Finnish Amateur 1996
Trn   Berkshire Trophy 1996; Duncan Putter 1994-96; Gloucestershire County Champion 1992-93-94-96; Leicestershire Matchplay Champion 1984-85-86-88; Leicestershire Silver Fox 1984-85-89; Leicestershire Spring Tournament 1986, *Golf Illustrated* Gold Vase 1989; Ealing Open 1990; Bristol Open 1990-93; City & County Strokeplay 1994-95; Ross Scratch Trophy 1993; Long Ashton Vase 1990-92-93; Failand Cup 1989-90-91-93; John Cheatle Open Scratch Foursomes 1987-88-89-90
Reg   English Counties Champion of Champions 1994-96; West of England Strokeplay 1987; Midland Open (Amateur) 1986; Midland Closed Strokeplay 1986; West Midland Amateur 1987
Int   Walker Cup 1995-97; Eisenhower Trophy 1996-98(winners). GBI v Europe 1992-94-96; England (Home Int) 1988 to 1998; v France 1988-90-92-94; v Spain 1989-91-93-95; Eur T Ch 1995-97
Mis   Cameron Trophy 1984-86-89; Duchess Salver 1990-92-93; Scrutton Jug 1996; Leading Amateur B&H Int 1993

Woosnam, Ian, MBE
Born Oswestry on 2nd March, 1958. Turned Professional 1976
PROFESSIONAL
Maj   Open 3rd 1986; US Open r/u 1989; US Masters 1991
Eur   Swiss Open 1982; Silk Cut Masters 1983; Scandinavian Enterprise Open 1984; Lawrence Batley TPC 1986; Jersey Open, Cepsa Madrid Open, Bell's Scottish Open, Lancôme Trophy, Suntory World Match Play 1987; Volvo PGA, Carrolls Irish Open, Panasonic European Open 1988; Carrolls Irish Open 1989; Mediterranean Open, Monte Carlo Open, Bell's Scottish Open, Suntory World Match Play, Epson Grand Prix

For list of abbreviations see page 350

1990; Mediterranean Open, Monte Carlo Open 1991; Monte Carlo Open 1992; English Open, Lancôme Trophy 1993; Cannes Open, Dunhill British Masters 1994; Johnnie Walker Classic, Heineken Classic, Scottish Open, German Open 1996; Volvo PGA Chp 1997
US USF&G Classic, Grand Slam of Golf 1991
Oth *News of the World* U-23 Match Play 1979; Cacharel U-25 Chp 1982
RoW Zambian Open 1985; Kenya Open 1986; Hong Kong Open 1987; Heineken Classic (ANZ) 1996; Hyundai Motors Open 1997
Reg Welsh PGA 1988
Int Ryder Cup 1983-85-87-89-91-93-95-97; Nissan Cup 1985-86; Kirin Cup 1987; Four Tours World Chp 1989-90; GBI *v* Australia 1988; Hennessy-Cognac Cup 1982-84; Wales in World Cup 1980-82-83-84-85-87 (winners; also individual winner)-90-91 (r/u; individual winner)-92-93-96-97-98; in Dunhill Cup 1985-86-87-88-89-90-91-93-95
Mis Harry Vardon Trophy 1987-90
AMATEUR
Reg Shropshire & Herefordshire Amateur 1975

Wright, Janette (*née* Robertson)
Born Glasgow on 7th January, 1935
Cls Honorary member of Lenzie, Troon, Cruden Bay, Aboyne, St Rule
Nat Scottish Ladies 1959-60-61-73, r/u 1958
Trn Kayser Bondor Foursomes 1958 (tied)-61. Worplesdon Mixed Foursomes 1959
Reg North of Scotland Ladies 1970. Lanarkshire Ladies 1954-55-56-57-58-59. West of Scotland Ladies 1956-58-59
Int Curtis Cup 1954-56-58-60. Vagliano Trophy 1959-61. GBI *v* France 1957; *v* Belgium 1957; *v* Canada 1954. GB Commonwealth Team 1959. Scotland (Home Int) 1952-53-54-55-56-57-58-59-60-61-63-65-66-67-73-(**78**)-(**79**)-(**80**). Eur(L) T Ch 1965-73-(**79**)
Jun British Girls 1950.
Int Girls 1950-51-52-53

Wright, Pamela
Born Aboyne on 26th June, 1964. Turned Professional 1988
PROFESSIONAL
Int Europe Solheim Cup 1990-92-94; Scotland Sunrise Cup 1992
Mis Gatorade Rookie of the Year 1989
AMATEUR
Nat British U-18 Stroke Play 1981; British Ladies Stroke Play r/u 1981; Scottish Ladies Junior Stroke Play r/u 1980; Scottish Ladies r/u 1982; Scottish Ladies Stroke Play 1985
Reg North of Scotland Ladies 1984
Int GBI Vagliano 1981; Scotland (Home Int) 1981 to 1984; Eur(L) T Ch 1987
Jun Scottish Girls r/u 1980-81
Mis All-American 1987-88; Collegiate Player of the Year 1988

Overseas Players

Aaron, Tommy
Born Gainesville, Georgia, USA on 22nd February, 1937. Turned Professional 1961
PROFESSIONAL
Maj   US Masters 1973; USPGA r/u 1972
Eur   Lancôme Trophy 1972
US   Canadian Open 1969; Georgia-Pacific Atlanta Golf Classic 1970
Sen   Kaanapali Classic 1992
Int   Ryder Cup 1969-73
AMATEUR
Nat   US Amateur r/u 1958
Int   Walker Cup 1959

Alcott, Amy
Born Kansas City, Missouri, USA on 22nd February, 1956. Turned Professional 1975
PROFESSIONAL
Maj   Du Maurier Classic 1979; Nabisco Dinah Shore 1983-88-91; US Women's Open 1980, 3rd 1984-91; USLPGA r/u 1988;
US   29 LPGA wins 1975 to 1992
Mis   Gatorade Rookie of the Year 1975; Vare Trophy, *Golf Magazine* Player of the Year 1980; Founders Cup 1986
AMATEUR
Jun   USGA Girls 1973

Alfredsson, Helen
Born Göteborg on 9th April, 1965. Turned Professional 1989
Maj   Ladies British Open 1990, r/u 1991; US Women's Open 3rd, Nabisco Dinah Shore 1993
PROFESSIONAL
Eur   Hennessy Ladies Cup, Trophée Coconut Skol, Benson & Hedges Trophy (with A Forsbrand 1991; Hennessy Ladies Cup 1992; Evian Masters 1994; Hennessy Ladies Cup 1996; McDonald's WPGA Chp of Europe 1997; Evian Masters 1998
US   The Office Depot, Welch's/Circle K Chp 1998
RoW   Queensland Women's Open, Ellair Open (Japan) 1991; Itoki Classic 1992; Itoen Ladies 1997
Int   Solheim Cup 1990-92-94-96-98; Sunrise Cup 1990 (winners)-92(winners); (for LPGA) Nichirei International 1993-95
Mis   Rookie of the Year 1989; Gatorade Rookie of the Year 1992
AMATEUR
Nat   Swedish Ladies 1986-87-88; Swedish Ladies Open Stroke Play 1988

Int   Sweden Eur(L) T Ch 1983-85-87 (winners) Espirito Santo 1988(r/u)

Allenby, Robert
Born Melbourne on 12th July, 1971. Turned Professional 1992
PROFESSIONAL
Eur   Honda Open 1994; English Open, Open de France, British Masters 1996
RoW   Johnnie Walker Classic 1992; Players Chp (ANZ) 1993; Australian Open 1994; Heineken Classic (ANZ) 1995
Oth   Perak Masters (Malaysia) 1992
Int   President's Cup 1996; World Cup r/u 1995; Dunhill Cup 1997
AMATEUR
Reg   Victorian Amateur 1990

Aoki, Isao
Born Abiko, Chiba, Japan on 31st August, 1942. Turned Professional 1964
Eur   World Match Play Chp 1978. European Open 1983
US   Hawaiian Open 1983
RoW   Japan PGA 1973-81-86; Japan Open 1983-87; Dunlop Jap International 1987; Tokai Classic, Casio World Open, Coca Cola Classic (Aust) 1989; Mitsubishi Gallant 1990-92; Casio World Open 1992
Sen   US Tour Nationwide Chp 1992; Bank One Sen Classic, Brickyard Crossing Chp 1994; American Express Grand Slam, Bank of Boston Sen Golf Classic 1995; BellSouth Classic, Kroger Sen Classic 1996; Emerald Coast Classic 1997; BellSouth Classic 1998
Int   Japan *v* US 1982-83-84. Dunhill Cup 1985. Nissan Cup 1985. Kirin Cup 1987-88

Azinger, Paul William
Born Holyoke, Massachusetts, USA on 6th January, 1960. Turned Professional 1981
Maj   Open r/u 1987; US Open 3rd 1993; USPGA 1993, r/u 1988
Eur   BMW International Open 1990-92
US   1987-three; 1988-one; 1989-one; 1990-one; 1991-one; 1992-one (Tour Chp); 1993-two (Memorial Trn, New England Classic)
Int   Ryder Cup 1989-91-93. World Cup 1989
Mis   USPGA Player of the Year 1987

For list of abbreviations see page 350

Baiocchi, Hugh
Born Johannesburg, South Africa on 17th August, 1946. Turned Professional 1971
PROFESSIONAL
Eur Swiss Open 1973; Dutch Open 1975; Scandinavian Enterprise Open 1976; PGA Match Play 1977; Swiss Open 1979; State Express Classic 1983
RoW South African Open 1978; South African PGA 1980; Western Province Open, SA International Classic 1973; Transvaal Open 1974-76; Rhodesian Dunlop Masters, Swaziland Holiday Inns, 1976; Zimbabwe Open, Vaal Reefs Open 1980; Twee Jongegezellen Masters 1989
Sen Pittsburgh Sen Classic 1997
Int South Africa in World Cup 1973-77-79; Hennessy-Cognac Cup 1982
Mis Captain SA PGA 1978-79
AMATEUR
Nat South African Amateur 1970
Oth Brazilian Amateur 1968

Baker, Kathy
Born Albany, New York, USA on 20th March, 1961. Turned Professional 1983.
PROFESSIONAL
Maj US Women's Open 1985
AMATEUR
Int Curtis Cup 1982; Espirito Santo 1982 (winners)

Baker-Finch, Ian
Born Nambour, Queensland, Australia on 24th October, 1960. Turned Professional 1979
Maj Open Champion 1991
Eur Scandinavian Open 1985
US Colonial National Invitation 1989
RoW New Zealand Open 1983; Australian Match Play 1987; Australian Masters 1988; Western Australian Open, NSW Open, Queensland PGA 1984; Victoria Open 1985; *Golf Digest* 1987; Pocarisweat Open 1988; Vines Classic 1992; Australian PGA 1993
Int Nissan Cup 1986; Kirin Cup 1987-88; Four Tours World Chp 1990(winners)-91; Dunhill Cup 1992

Ballesteros, Severiano
Born Pedreña, Spain on 9th April, 1957. Turned Professional 1974
Maj Open Champion 1979-84-88; r/u 1976. US Open 3rd 1987. US Masters 1980-83 r/u 1985-87; 3rd 1982
Eur Dutch Open, Lancôme Trophy 1976; French Open, Uniroyal International, Swiss Open 1977; Martini International, German Open, Scandinavian Enterprise Open, Swiss Open 1978; English Classic 1979; Madrid Open, Martini International, Dutch Open 1980; Scandinavian Enterprise Open, Spanish Open, Suntory World Match Play 1981; Madrid Open, French Open, Suntory World Match Play 1982; Sun Alliance PGA, Irish Open, Lancôme Trophy 1983. Suntory World Match Play 1984; Irish Open, French Open, Sanyo Open, Spanish Open, Suntory World Match Play 1985; British Masters, Irish Open, Monte Carlo Open, French Open, Dutch Open, Lancôme Trophy (shared) 1986; Suze Open 1987; Open de Baleares, Scandinavian Enterprise Open, German Open, Lancôme Trophy 1988. Cepsa Madrid Open; Epson Grand Prix; Ebel European Masters-Swiss Open 1989; Open de Baleares 1990. Volvo PGA, Dunhill British Masters, Toyota World Match Play 1991; Dubai Desert Classic, Open de Baleares 1992; Benson & Hedges International Open, German Masters 1994; Tournoi Perrier de Paris, Open de España 1995
US Greater Greensboro Open 1978; Westchester Classic 1983-88; USF&G Classic 1985
RoW Japanese Open, Dunlop Phoenix , Otago Classic 1977; Japanese Open, Kenya Open 1978; Dunlop Phoenix, Australian PGA 1981; Visa Taiheiyo Masters 1988; Chunichi Crowns 1991
Int Ryder Cup 1979-83-85-87-89-91-93-95-(**97**); Hennessy-Cognac Cup 1976-78; Spain in World Cup 1975-76(winners)-77(winners)-91; Dunhill Cup 1985-86-88
Mis Harry Vardon Trophy 1976-77-78-86-88-91; AGW Trophy 1979-84-91; Ritz Club Golfer of the Year 1988-91; World Golf Hall of Fame 1997

Barber, Miller
Born Shreveport, Louisiana, USA on 31st March, 1931. Turned Professional 1958
US 11 wins 1964 to 1978
Sen US Seniors PGA 1981. US Seniors Open 1982-84-85. US Sen Tour 24 wins 1981-89
Int Ryder Cup 1969-71

Beck, Chip
Born Fayetteville, North Carolina, USA on 12th September, 1956. Turned Professional 1978
Maj US Open r/u 1986-89; US Masters r/u 1993
US Los Angeles Open, USF & G Classic 1988; Buick Open 1990; Freeport Classic 1992
Int Ryder Cup 1989-91-93, Dunhill Cup 1988
Mis Vardon Trophy 1988

Beman, Deane R
Born Washington, DC, USA on 22nd April, 1938. Turned Professional 1987.
Maj US Open r/u 1969, leading amateur 1962
PROFESSIONAL
US Texas Open 1969; Greater Milwaukee Open; Quad Cities Open 1972; Shrine-Robinson Classic 1973
Mis Commissioner of US PGA Tour since 1974; Herb Graffis Award 1987
AMATEUR
Chp Amateur Champion 1960
Nat US Amateur 1960-63, r/u 1966
Reg Eastern Amateur 1960-61-63-64
Int Walker Cup 1959-61-63-65; Eisenhower Trophy 1960(winners)-62(winners)-64-66(r/u)

Berg, Patty
Born Minneapolis, USA on 13th February, 1918. Turned Professional 1940 (Founder member of LPGA)
PROFESSIONAL
Maj US Women's Open 1946, r/u 1957
US 57 LPGA wins 1941-62 Western Open 1941-48-51-55-57-58; Titleholders Chp 1948-53-55-57)
Mis Leading money winner 1954-55-57; Bobby Jones Award 1963; Ben Hogan Award 1975; first President of USLPGA; LPGA Hall of Fame 1951; World Golf Hall of Fame 1974; Founder's Cup 1981; Old Tom Morris Award 1986
AMATEUR
Nat US Ladies Amateur 1938
Reg Western Amateur 1938
Trn 29 amateur wins 1934-40
Int Curtis Cup 1936-38

Bevione, Isa *See* Goldschmid

Björn, Thomas
Born Silkeborg, Denmark on 18th February, 1971. Turned Professional 1993
PROFESSIONAL
Eur Loch Lomond Invitational 1996; Heineken Classic, Peugeot Open de España 1998
Oth Challenge Himmerland Open, Interlaken Open, Esbjerg Danish Closed, Coca-Cola Open 1995
Int Ryder Cup 1997; World Cup 1996-97
Mis Rookie of the Year 1996. First Dane to play in Ryder Cup
AMATEUR
Nat Danish Amateur 1990-91

Bradley, Pat
Born Westford, Massachusetts, USA on 24th March, 1951. Turned Professional 1974
Maj US Women's Open 1981, r/u 1991, 3rd 1989; USLPGA 1986 r/u 1991, 3rd 1984-85-94; Du Maurier Classic 1980-85-86; Nabisco Dinah Shore 1986
US 32 LPGA wins 1976 to 1996
RoW Colgate Far East Open 1975; JC Penney Classic 1978-89
Int Solheim Cup 1990-92-96
Mis Rolex Player of the Year 1986-91; Vare Trophy 1986-91; Mazda-LPGA Series 1983-86; *Golf Magazine* Player of the Year 1986; Ben Hogan, Powell Award 1991; LPGA Hall of Fame 1991

Brooks, Mark
Born Fort Worth, Texas, USA on 25th March, 1961. Turned Professional 1983
Maj Open 3rd 1995; USPGA 1996
US Greater Hartford Open 1988; Greater Greensboro Open, Greater Milwaukee Open 1991; Kemper Open 1994; Bob Hope Chrysler Classic, Shell Houston Open 1996
Int President's Cup 1996

Burke, Jack, Jr
Born Fort Worth, Texas, USA in January, 1923. Turned Professional 1940
Maj USPGA 1956; US Masters 1956, r/u 1952
US 15 wins 1950 to 1963

Int Ryder Cup 1951-53-55-57-59-(73)
Mis USPGA Player of the Year 1956

Calcavecchia, Mark
Born Laurel, Nebraska, USA on 12th June, 1960. Turned Professional 1981
Maj Open Champion 1989; US Masters r/u 1988
US WSW Golf Classic 1986 Honda Classic 1987, Bank of Boston Classic 1988; Phoenix Open, Nissan Los Angeles Open 1989; Phoenix Open 1992; BellSouth Classic 1995; Greater Vancouver Open 1997; Honda Classic 1998
RoW Australian Open 1988; Argentine Open 1993
Oth Subaru Sarazen World Open 1997
Int Ryder Cup 1987-89-91; Dunhill Cup 1989 (winners)-90; Kirin Cup 1987; Four Tours World Chp 1990; President's Cup 1998

Campbell, William Cammack
Born West Virginia, USA on 5th May, 1923
Chp Amateur r/u 1954
Nat US Amateur 1964
Oth Canadian Amateur r/u 1952-54-65; Mexican Amateur 1956
Reg North & South Amateur 1950-53-57-67. Tam O'Shanter World Amateur 1948-49. Ontario Amateur 1967
Sen USGA Seniors 1979-80. US Seniors Open r/u 1980
Int Walker Cup 1951-53-55-57-65-67-71-75. Eisenhower Trophy 1964-(68)
Mis Bobby Jones Award 1956. President USGA 1983. Captain R&A 1987/88. Old Tom Morris Award 1991; World Golf Hall of Fame 1990

Canizares, José Maria
Born Madrid on 18th February, 1947. Turned Professional 1967
Eur Lancia D'Oro 1972; Avis Jersey Open; Bob Hope British Classic 1980; Italian Open 1981; Bob Hope British Classic 1983; Benson & Hedges Trophy (with Tania Abitbol) 1990; Roma Masters 1992
RoW Kenya Open 1984
Int Ryder Cup 1981-83-85-89; Hennessy-Cognac Cup 1974-76-78-80-82-84; Spain in World Cup 1974-80-82(winners)-83-84(winners, individual winner)-85-87-89; Dunhill Cup 1985-87-89-90; Double Diamond 1974; (Sen) European Cup 1997

Caponi, Donna
Born Detroit, Michigan, USA on 29th January, 1945. Turned Professional 1965
Maj US Women's Open 1969-70. USLPGA 1979-81
Eur Colgate European Open 1975
US 24 LPGA wins 1969 to 1981
Mis *LA Times* Woman Golfer of the Year 1970; Mickey Wright Award 1980-81

Carner, JoAnne (*née* Gunderson)
Born Kirkland, Washington, USA on 4th April, 1939. Turned Professional 1970
PROFESSIONAL
Maj US Women's Open 1971-76, r/u 1975-78-82-83-87 (tied); USLPGA r/u 1974-82

For list of abbreviations see page 350

US	42 LPGA wins 1970 to 85
RoW	Australian Ladies Open 1975
Int	Solheim Cup (**1994**)
Mis	Rolex Player of the Year 1974-81-82; Vare Trophy 1974-75-81-82-83; Gatorade Rookie of the Year 1970; *Golf Magazine* Player of the Year 1974-81-82; LPGA Hall of Fame 1982; World Golf Hall of Fame 1985; Bobby Jones Award 1981; Mickey Wright Award 1974-82

AMATEUR

Nat	US Ladies Amateur 1957-60-62-66-68, r/u 1956-64
Trn	LPGA Burdine's Invitational 1969 (as amateur)
Reg	Western Ladies Open Amateur 1959
Int	Curtis Cup 1958-60-62-64
Jun	US Girls 1956

Casper, Billy

Born in San Diego, California, USA on 24th June, 1931. Turned Professional 1954

Maj	US Open 1959-66; USPGA r/u 1958-65-71; US Masters 1970, r/u 1969
Eur	Lancôme Trophy 1974; Italian Open 1975
Oth	Alcan Golfer of the Year 1969; Lancia D'Oro 1974
US	51 wins 1956 to 1975; Canadian Open 1967
RoW	Brazilian Open 1959-60; Moroccan Grand Prix 1973-75; Mexican Open 1977
Sen	US: 9 wins 1982-89. US Senior Open 1983
Int	Ryder Cup 1961-63-65-67-69-71-73-75-(**79**)
Mis	Vardon Trophy 1960-63-65-66-68; leading money winner 1966-68. USPGA Player of the Year 1966-70; Byron Nelson Award 1966-68-70. World Golf Hall of Fame 1978; USPGA Hall of Fame 1982

Cavalleri, Silvia

Born Milan, Italy on 10th October, 1972. Turned Professional 1997

Cls	Milan
Chp	US Ladies Amateur 1997
Nat	European Ladies Chp 1996-97; World Chp (Individual) 1996
Jun	Italian National Junior Chp 1985-87-90-92-93; Italian Girls 1987-89-90; British Girls 1990
Int	Italy Eur(L)T Ch 1997

Cejka, Alexander

Born Marienbad on 2nd December, 1970. Turned Professional 1989

Eur	Open Andalucia, Hohe Brucke Open, Volvo Masters 1995
Oth	Czech Open 1990-92; Audi Quattro Open 1991-93; KB Golf Challenge 1997; Lancia Golf Pokal 1998
Int	Germany in Dunhill Cup 1994-95-97-98; World Cup 1996-97

Charles, Robert J (Bob)

Born Carterton, New Zealand on 14th March, 1936. Turned Profesional 1960

PROFESSIONAL

Maj	Open Champion 1963, r/u 1968-69; US Open 3rd 1964-70; USPGA r/u 1968
Eur	Bowmaker 1961; Engadine Open, Swiss Open, Daks 1962; Piccadilly World Match Play 1969, r/u 1968; John Player Classic, Dunlop Masters 1972; Scandinavian Enterprise Open 1973; Swiss Open 1974
US	4 wins 1963 to 1974; Canadian Open 1968
RoW	New Zealand Open 1954 (as amateur)-66-70-73, r/u 1974; New Zealand Professional 1961-79-80; 17 other trn wins in New Zealand 1961-78; South African Open 1973
Sen	Volvo Seniors British Open 1989-93; US Sen Tour 22 wins 1986-94; Japan Sen 3 wins
Int	New Zealand in World Cup 1962 to 1968, 1971-72; Dunhill Cup 1985-86
Mis	First New Zealander and first left-handed player to win the Open

AMATEUR

Int	Eisenhower Trophy 1960

Coe, Charles R

Born Oklahoma City, USA on 26th October, 1923

Maj	US Masters r/u 1961
Chp	Amateur r/u 1951
Nat	US Amateur 1949-58; r/u 1959
Reg	Western Amateur 1950
Int	Walker Cup 1949-51-53-(**57**)-59-61-63. Eisenhower Trophy 1960
Mis	Bobby Jones Award 1964

Cole, Robert

Born Springs, South Africa on 11th May, 1948. Turned Professional 1966

PROFESSIONAL

Maj	Open 3rd 1975
US	Buick Open 1977
RoW	South African Open 1974-80; Dunlop Masters (SA) 1969; Natal Open 1969-70-72; Cape Classic 1970; Transvaal Open 1972; Rhodesian Masters 1972; Vavasseur (SA) 1974
Int	South Africa in World Cup 1969-74 (winners, individual winner)-76

AMATEUR

Chp	Amateur 1966
Nat	English Open Amateur Stroke Play r/u 1966
Trn	*Golf Illustrated* Gold Vase 1966 (shared)
Int	Eisenhower Trophy 1966

Cook, John

Born Toledo, Ohio, USA on 2nd October, 1957. Turned Professional 1979

PROFESSIONAL

Maj	Open r/u 1992; USPGA r/u 1992
US	Bing Crosby National ProAm 1981; Canadian Open 1983; The International 1987; Bob Hope Chrysler Classic, Hawaiian Open, Las Vegas Invitational 1992; St Jude Classic, CVS Charity Classic 1996; Bob Hope Chrysler Classic 1997; GTE Byron Nelson Classic 1998
RoW	Sao Paulo–Brazilian Open 1982; Mexican Open 1995
Int	Ryder Cup 1993; World Cup 1983

AMATEUR

Nat	US Amateur 1978
Int	US World Cup 1979
Jun	World Juniors 1974
Mis	All-American 1977-78-79

For list of abbreviations see page 350

Couples, Fred
Born Seattle, Washington, USA on 3rd October, 1959. Turned Professional 1980
- **Maj** Open 3rd 1991; US Open leading amateur 1978, 3rd 1991; US Masters 1992; USPGA r/u 1990, 3rd 1982
- **Eur** Dubai Desert Classic, Johnnie Walker Classic 1995
- **US** 15 wins 1983-98 (Bob Hope Chrysler Classic, Memorial Trn 1998)
- **RoW** Tournoi Perrier de Paris, Johnnie Walker World Chp 1991-95
- **Int** Ryder Cup 1989-91-93-95-97; Four Tours World Chp 1990(individual winner)-91; Dunhill Cup 1991-92-93(winners)-94(r/u); World Cup 1992(winners)-93(winners)-94(winners, individual winner)-95(winners); President's Cup 1994-96-98
- **Mis** Vardon Trophy 1991-92; USPGA Player of the Year 1991-92; Arnold Palmer Award 1992

Crenshaw, Ben
Born Austin, Texas, USA on 11th January, 1952. Turned Professional 1973
PROFESSIONAL
- **Maj** Open r/u 1978-79, 3rd 1980; US Open leading amateur 1970, 3rd 1975; USPGA r/u 1979; US Masters 1984-95, r/u 1976-83, 3rd 1989-91
- **Eur** Carrolls Irish Open 1976
- **US** 19 wins 1973 to 1996
- **RoW** Australian Open r/u 1978; Mexican Open 1982
- **Oth** Grand Slam of Golf 1995
- **Int** Ryder Cup 1981-83-87-95; US in World Cup 1972-87-88(winners, individual winner); Kirin Cup 1988
- **Mis** Rookie of the Year 1974; Byron Nelson Award 1976; William Richardson Award 1989; Bobby Jones Award 1991; US Ryder Cup Captain-elect 1999

AMATEUR
- **Trn** NCAA Chp 1971-72(shared)-73
- **Int** Eisenhower Trophy 1972(winners)

Daly, John
Born Sacramento, California, USA on 28th April, 1966. Turned Professional 1984
- **Maj** Open Champion 1995; US Masters 3rd 1993; USPGA 1991

PROFESSIONAL
- **US** BC Open 1992; BellSouth Classic 1994
- **Oth** Ben Hogan Utah Classic 1990; Missouri Open 1987
- **Int** Dunhill Cup 1993(winners)-98; World Cup 1998
- **Mis** USPGA Rookie of the Year 1991

AMATEUR
- **Reg** Missouri and Arkansas State Amateur 1983-84

Daniel, Beth
Born Charleston, South Carolina, USA on 14th October, 1956. Turned Professional October, 1978
- **Maj** USLPGA 1990, r/u 1984

PROFESSIONAL
- **US** 32 LPGA wins 1979 to 1995 (Ping Welch's Chp 1995)
- **RoW** World Ladies Championship (Japan) 1979
- **Oth** JC Penney Classic (with D Love III) 1994-95
- **Int** Solheim Cup 1990-92-94-96; Nichirei Int 1995
- **Mis** USLPGA Rookie of the Year 1979; USLPGA leading money winner 1980; Rolex Player of the Year 1980-90-94; Vare Trophy 1989-90-94; Order of Merit winner 1990; Mickey Wright Award 1990-94

AMATEUR
- **Nat** US Ladies Amateur 1975-77
- **Int** Curtis Cup 1976-78

Davies, Richard
Born USA on 29th October, 1930
- **Maj** US Open leading amateur 1963
- **Chp** Amateur Champion 1962
- **Int** Walker Cup 1963

Davis, Rodger
Born Sydney, New South Wales, Australia on 18th May, 1951. Turned Professional 1974
- **Maj** Open r/u 1987
- **Eur** State Express Classic 1981; Whyte & Mackay PGA 1986; Wang Four Stars 1988; Spanish Open, Wang Four Stars 1990; Volvo Masters 1991; Cannes Open 1993
- **RoW** Australian Open 1986; New Zealand Open 1986-91; South Australia Open 1978; Victoria Open 1979; New South Wales Open 1989; Palm Meadows Cup 1990; Sanctuary Cove Classic 1991-92
- **Int** World Cup 1985-87-91-93; Dunhill Cup 1986 (winners)-87-88-90-92; Nissan Cup 1986; Kirin Cup 1987-88, Four Tours World Chp 1990 (winners)-91

Decker, Anne *See* Sander

Descampe, Florence
Born Belgium on 1st June, 1969. Turned Professional 1988
PROFESSIONAL
- **Eur** Danish Ladies Open 1988; Valextra Classic, Italian Open, Woolmark Ladies Match Play 1990; Ladies German Open 1991; Ladies Austrian Open 1994
- **US** McCall's LPGA Classic 1992
- **Int** Solheim Cup 1992

AMATEUR
- **Nat** European Amateur 1988; Belgian Ladies Match Play 1987
- **Jun** Belgian Junior Champion 1987

Dibnah, Corinne
Born Brisbane, Australia on 29th July, 1962. Turned Professional 1984
- **Maj** Women's British Open 1988, r/u 1992

PROFESSIONAL
- **Eur** 12 WPGET wins 1986-92 (Ladies Italian Open 1994)
- **RoW** Indonesian Open, Malaysian JAL Open 1996
- **Oth** Sunningdale Foursomes (with Dale Reid) 1990
- **Int** Sunrise Cup 1992
- **Mis** Woolmark Order of Merit winner 1991

AMATEUR
- **Nat** Australian Ladies 1981. New Zealand Ladies 1983
- **Int** Commonwealth Tournament 1983 (winners)

For list of abbreviations see page 350

Dickson, Robert B
Born McAlester, Oklahoma, USA on 25th January, 1944. Turned Professional 1968
PROFESSIONAL
US 2 wins 1968-73
AMATEUR
Chp Amateur Champion 1967
Nat US Amateur 1967
Int Walker Cup 1967
Mis One of only four to win British and US Amateur titles in the same year. Bobby Jones Award 1968.

Duval, David
Born Jacksonville, Fl, USA on 9th November, 1971. Turned Professional 1993
PROFESSIONAL
US Michelob Chp, Walt Disney Classic, The Tour Chp 1997; Tucson Chrysler Classic, Shell Houston Open, NEC World Series, Michelob Chp 1998
Oth Nike Wichita Open, Nike Tour Chp 1993
Int President's Cup 1996-98
AMATEUR
Int Walker Cup 1991

Elkington, Steve
Born Inverell, Australia on 8th December, 1962. Turned Professional 1985
PROFESSIONAL
Maj US Masters 3rd 1993; USPGA 1995; 3rd 1996
US Greater Greensboro Open 1990; Trn Players Chp 1991; Infiniti Trn of Champions 1992; Buick Southern Open 1994; Mercedes Chp 1995; Doral-Ryder Open 1997; Buick Challenge 1998
RoW Australian Open 1992
Int President's Cup 1994-96-98; Dunhill Cup 1994-95-96-97-98; World Cup 1994
Mis Vardon Trophy 1995
AMATEUR
Nat Australia-New Zealand Amateur 1980; Australian Amateur 1981
Jun Doug Sanders Jun World Chp 1981
Mis All-American 1984-85

Els, Ernie
Born Johannesburg on 17th October, 1969. Turned Professional 1989
PROFESSIONAL
Maj Open r/u 1996; US Open 1994-97; USPGA 3rd 1995
Eur Dubai Desert Classic, Toyota World Match Play Chp 1994-95-96; Lexington PGA 1995; Johnnie Walker Classic 1997; SA Open 1998
US Sarazen World Open 1994; Byron Nelson Classic 1995; Buick Classic 1996-97; Andersen Consulting Int Chp 1997; Bay Hill Invitational 1998
RoW SA Open, SA Masters (Jpn), SAPGA, Swazi Sun Classic, Goodyear Classic, SA Trn Players Chp 1992; Dunlop Phoenix 1993; Johnnie Walker World Chp 1994; SA Bells Cup, SA PGA 1995
Int SA in Dunhill Cup 1992-93-94-95-96-97(winners)-98 (winners); World Cup 1992-93-96 (winners, individual winner)-97; Alfred Dunhill Challenge 1995; President's Cup 1996-98
Mis USPGA Rookie of the Year 1994. Hon Member of PGA Tour 1998

AMATEUR
Nat SA Amateur 1986; SA Amateur Strokeplay 1989
Trn Tillman Trophy 1988

Faxon, Brad
Born Oceanport, NJ, USA on 1st August, 1961. Turned Professional 1983
PROFESSIONAL
US Provident Classic 1986; Buick Open 1991; New England Classic, The Invitational 1992; Freeport-McDermott Classic 1997
RoW Australian Open 1993
Oth Fred Meyer Challenge (with G Norman) 1995-96
Int Ryder Cup 1995-97
AMATEUR
Int Walker Cup 1983

Fernandez, Vicente
Born Corrientes, Argentina on 5th May, 1946. Turned Professional 1964
Eur Dutch Open 1970; Benson & Hedges 1975; Colgate PGA 1979; Tenerife Open 1990; English Open 1992
RoW Argentine Open 1968-69-81-90; Maracaibo Open 1972; Brazil Open 1977-83-84
Sen US Burnet Seniors Classic 1996; Bank One Classic 1997
Int World Cup 1970-72-78-84-85. Dunhill Cup 1986-88-89

Finsterwald, Dow
Born Athens, Ohio, USA on 6th September, 1929. Turned Professional 1951
Maj US Open 3rd 1960; USPGA 1958; r/u 1957; US Masters r/u 1962 (tied), 3rd, 1960
US 11 wins 1955 to 1963; Canadian Open 1956
Int Ryder Cup 1957-59-61-63-(77)
Mis Vardon Trophy 1957; USPGA Player of the Year 1958

Floyd, Ray
Born Fort Bragg, North Carolina, USA on 4th September, 1942. Turned Professional 1961
Maj Open r/u 1978; 3rd 1981; US Open 1986; US Masters 1976, r/u 1985-90-92; USPGA 1969-82, r/u 1976
US 22 wins 1963 to 1994
RoW Brazilian Open 1978; Daiwa KBC Augusta Open (Japan) 1991
Sen US Tour 16 wins 1992-96 (Senior Tour Chp 1992-94); USPGA Seniors Chp 1995; Senior Players Chp 1996
Int Ryder Cup 1969-75-77-83-(**89**)-91-93. Dunhill Cup 1985-86. Nissan Cup 1985
Mis Rookie of the Year 1963. Vardon Trophy 1983. World Golf Hall of Fame 1989.

Ford, Doug
Born West Haven, Connecticut, USA on 6th August, 1922. Turned Professional 1949
Maj US Masters 1957; r/u 1958. USPGA 1955
US 15 wins 1955 to 1962; Canadian Open 1959-63
Sen 1987-one
Int Ryder Cup 1955-57-59-61
Mis USPGA Player of the Year 1955

For list of abbreviations see page 350

Forsbrand, Anders
Born Filipstad, Sweden on 1st April, 1961. Turned Professional 1981
PROFESSIONAL
Eur   Ebel European Masters–Swiss Open 1987; Open di Firenze, Benson & Hedges Trophy (with H Alfredsson) 1991; Open di Firenze, Cannes Open, Equity & Law Challenge 1992; Moroccan Open 1994; German Masters 1995
Oth   Swedish PGA 1982; Open Novotel Perrier (with M Jonzon) 1997
Int   Hennessy-Cognac Cup 1984; Kirin Cup 1984; World Cup 1984-85-88-91(winners)-92-93; Dunhill Cup 1985-86-87-88-91(winners)-92-94

Frost, David
Born Cape Town, South Africa on 11th September, 1959
Eur   Cannes Open 1984
RoW   South African Open 1986; Million Dollar Challenge 1989-90-92; Dunlop Phoenix Open 1992; Lexington PGA, Hong Kong Open 1994
US   1988-two; 1989-one; 1990-one; 1992-one; 1993-two; 1994-one; 1997-one (MasterCard Colonial)
Int   South Africa in Dunhill Cup 1991(r/u)-92-94-95-97(winners)-98(winners); President's Cup 1994-96; Alfred Dunhill Challenge 1995; World Cup 1998

Furyk, Jim
Born West Chester, PA, USA on 12th May, 1970. Turned Professional 1992
US   Las Vegas Invitational 1995-98; Hawaiian Open 1996
RoW   Argentine Open 1997
Oth   Nike Mississippi Gulf Coast Classic 1993
Int   Ryder Cup 1997; President's Cup 1998

Garcia, Sergio Garcia Fernandez
Born Castellón on 9th January, 1980
Chp   Amateur Champion 1998
Nat   French Amateur, Spanish Amateur 1997
Trn   Eur Amateur Masters 1997-98; Puerta de Hierro Cup, Canarias Chp, International King of Spain Cup, Jacksonville Junior 1998
Oth   Catalonian Open 1997
Int   Spain Eur T Ch 1997; Eisenhower Trophy 1998
Jun   British Boys 1997
Mis   Leading amateur in Lancôme Trophy 1997

Garrido, Ignacio
Born Madrid, Spain on 27th March, 1972. Turned Professional 1993
PROFESSIONAL
Eur   Volvo German Open 1997
RoW   Hassan II Trophy 1996
Oth   Challenge AGF (Fr), Spanish PGA 1993; Cepsa APG 1996
Int   Ryder Cup 1997; Spain in Dunhill Cup 1997; World Cup 1996-97
Mis   His father played in first European Ryder Cup in 1979
AMATEUR
Nat   English Open Amateur Strokeplay (Brabazon) 1992

Geddes, Jane
Born Huntingdon, New York, USA on 5th February, 1960. Turned Professional 1983
Maj   Ladies British Open 1989; US Women's Open 1986; USLPGA 1987
US   Boston Five Classic 1986; Women's Kemper Open, GNA Glendale Federal Classic, Toledo Classic, Boston Five Classic 1987; Jamaica Classic, Atlantic City Classic 1991; Oldsmobile Classic 1993; Chicago Challenge 1994
RoW   Australian Women's Masters 1990-92
Int   Solheim Cup 1996; Sunrise Cup 1992; Nichirei Int 1993-95-96-97

Giles, Marvin
Maj   US Open leading amateur 1973
Chp   Amateur Champion 1975
Nat   US Amateur Champion 1972, r/u 1967-68-69
Int   Walker Cup 1969-71-73-75. Eisenhower Trophy (winners) 1968-70-72

Goldschmid, Isa (née Bevione)
Born Italy
Nat   Italian Ladies' Close 1947-51-53-54-55-56-57-58-59-60-61-62-63-64-65-66-67-69-71-73-74. Italian Ladies' Open 1952-57-58-60-61-63-64-67-68-69
Oth   Spanish Ladies 1952. French Ladies 1975
Trn   Kayser Bondor 1963
Int   Vagliano Trophy 1959-61-63-65-67-69-71-73-(77) Eur v United States 1968. Italy in Espirito Santo 1964-66-68-70-72

Grady, Wayne
Born Brisbane, Queensland, Australia on 26th July, 1957. Turned Professional 1978
Maj   Open r/u 1989 (tied); USPGA 1990
Eur   German Open 1984
US   Westchester Classic 1989
RoW   Australia PGA 1991; West Lakes Classic (Aus) 1978
Int   Australia in World Cup 1978-83-89 (winners); Nissan Cup 1985; Four Tours Chp 1990 (winners); Dunhill Cup 1989-90-91; Alfred Dunhill Challenge 1995

Graham, David
Born Windsor, Tasmania on 23rd May, 1946. Turned Professional 1962
Maj   Open 3rd 1985; US Open 1981; USPGA 1979
Eur   French Open 1970; Piccadilly World Match Play 1976; Lancôme Trophy 1982
US   6 wins 1972-83
RoW   Australian Open 1977, r/u 1972; Australian Wills Masters 1975; Thailand Open, Victoria Open, Tasmanian Open, Yomiuri Open 1970; Caracas Open, Japanese Airlines 1971; Chunichi Crowns (Japan) 1976; West Lakes Classic (Aust), New Zealand Open 1979; Queensland Open 1987
Sen   Southwestern Bell Dominion, GTE Classic, Comfort Classic 1997
Int   President's Cup 1994

For list of abbreviations see page 350

Graham, Lou
Born Nashville, Tennessee, USA on 7th January, 1938. Turned Professional 1962
- **Maj** US Open 1975; r/u 1977
- **US** 1967-one. 1972-one. 1979-three.
- **Int** Ryder Cup 1973-75-77. World Cup 1975(winners)

Green, Hubert
Born Birmingham, Alabama, USA on 18th December, 1946. Turned Professional 1970
- **Maj** US Open 1977. US Masters r/u 1978. US PGA 1985
- **Eur** Carrolls Irish Open 1977
- **US** 16 wins 1971 to 1984
- **RoW** Dunlop Phoenix (Japan) 1975
- **Int** Ryder Cup 1977-79-85. USA in World Cup 1977
- **Mis** Rookie of the Year 1971

Guadagnino, Kathy *See* Baker

Gunderson, JoAnne *See* Carner

Haas, Jay
Born St Louis, MO, USA on 2nd December, 1953. Turned Professional 1976
PROFESSIONAL
- **Maj** US Masters 3rd 1995
- **US** 9 wins 1978 to 1993
- **RoW** Mexican Open 1991
- **Int** Ryder Cup 1983-95; President's Cup 1994

AMATEUR
- **Int** Walker Cup 1975

Haeggman, Joakim
Born Kalmar, Sweden on 28th August, 1969. Turned Professional 1989
- **Eur** Peugeot Open d'España 1993
- **RoW** Malaysian Open 1994
- **Oth** Wermland Open 1990; SI/Compaq Open 1992
- **Int** Ryder Cup1993; Sweden in Dunhill Cup 1993-94-97 (r/u); World Cup 1993-94-97
- **Mis** First Swede to play for Europe in Ryder Cup

Harper, Chandler
Born Portsmouth, Virginia, USA on 10th March, 1914. Turned Professional 1934
- **Maj** USPGA 1950
- **US** Won over 20 tournaments. Ten times Virginia Open Champion.
- **Sen** National Seniors 1965 World Senior Professional, USPGA Seniors 1968.
- **Int** Ryder Cup 1955
- **Mis** Elected to USPGA Hall of Fame 1969. In 1941 scored round of 58 (29-29) on 6100 yards, Portsmouth, Virginia

Harris, John
Born Edina, Minnesota, USA in 1952
- **Chp** US Amateur 1993; qf 1995
- **Int** Walker Cup 1993-95-97; Eisenhower Trophy 1994

Harwood, Mike
Born Sydney, NSW, Australia on 8th January, 1959 Turned Professional 1979
- **Maj** Open r/u 1991
- **Eur** Portuguese Open 1988; PLM Open 1989; Volvo PGA, Volvo Masters 1990; European Open 1991
- **RoW** Australian PGA 1986; Fijian Open, Pacific Harbour Open 1984; South Australian Open 1990.
- **Int** Australia in World Cup1984; Dunhill Cup 1991; Four Tours World Chp 1991

Hayes, Dale
Born Pretoria, South Africa on 1st July, 1952. Turned Professional 1970
PROFESSIONAL
- **Eur** Spanish Open 1971; Swiss Open 1975; Italian Open, French Open 1978; Spanish Open 1979
- **Oth** Coca-Cola Young Professionals 1974; PGA U-25 1975
- **RoW** South African Open 1976, leading amateur 1969; South African PGA 1974-75-76; 12 wins in Southern Africa 1970-76; Brazilian Open 1970; Bogota Open 1979
- **Int** South Africa in World Cup 1974(winners)-76
- **Mis** Accles & Pollock Award 1973; Harry Vardon Trophy 1975

AMATEUR
- **Nat** South African Amateur Stroke Play 1969-70
- **Oth** English Open Amateur Stroke Play r/u 1969; German Amateur 1969; Scottish Open Amateur Stroke Play 1970
- **Trn** *Golf Illustrated* Gold Vase 1969 (shared)
- **Int** Eisenhower Trophy 1970(r/u individual)
- **Jun** World Junior Chp 1969

Haynie, Sandra
Born Fort Worth, Texas, USA on 4th June 1943. Turned Professional 1961
- **Maj** US Open 1965-74, r/u 1963-70-82; USLPGA 1974, r/u 1975-83; Du Maurier Classic 1982
- **US** 42 LPGA wins 1962-82
- **Mis** Rolex Player of the Year 1970; LPGA Hall of Fame 1977

Henning, Harold
Born Johannesburg, South Africa on 3rd October, 1934. Turned Professional 1953
- **Maj** Open 3rd 1960-70.
- **Trn** Daks 1958 (tied). *Yorkshire Evening News* 1958 (tied). Spalding 1959 (tied). Sprite 1960. Pringle 1964
- **Nat** South African Open 1957-62. South African PGA 1965-66-67-72
- **Eur** Italian Open 1957. Swiss Open 1960-64. Danish Open 1960-64-65. German Open 1965.
- **RoW** Malaysian Open 1966
- **US** 2 wins 1966-70
- **Sen** US Liberty Mutual Legends 1993
- **Oth** Transvaal Open 1957. Natal Open 1957. Western Province Open 1957-59. Cock o' the North 1959. Engadine Open 1966. South African International Classic 1972. ICL International (SA) 1980
- **Int** South Africa in World Cup 1957-58-59-61-65 (winners)-66-67-69-70-71

Hjörth, Maria
Born Sweden on 15th October, 1973. Turned Professional 1996
PROFESSIONAL
Int   European Cup 1997-98
AMATEUR
Oth   Finnish Ladies, Norwegian Ladies 1990; Spanish Open 1995; Eur Women's Individual Chp 1995; Sherry Cup 1995
Trn   St Rule Trophy, Helen Holm Trophy 1995; R&A Bursars' Trn 1995
Int   Vagliano Trophy 1995; Sweden in Espirito Santo 1994; Eur(L) T Ch 1995
Mis   Swedish Order of Merit 1991. Golf bursary at University of Stirling

Hoch, Scott
Born Raleigh, NC, USA on 24th November, 1955. Turned Professional 1979
PROFESSIONAL
Maj   US Masters r/u 1989; US PGA 3rd 1987
Eur   Dutch Open 1995
US   8 wins 1980 to 1997 (Greater Milwaukee Open 1997)
RoW   Pacific Masters, Casio World Open 1982-86; Korean Open 1990-91
Oth   Andersen Consulting US Chp 1996
Int   Ryder Cup 1997; President's Cup 1994-96-98
Mis   Vardon Trophy 1986
AMATEUR
Int   Walker Cup 1979; Eisenhower Trophy 1978

Hyndman, William III
Born 25th December, 1915
Chp   Amateur r/u 1959-69-70
Nat   US Amateur r/u 1955
Sen   US Seniors 1973
Int   Walker Cup 1957-59-61-71. Eisenhower Trophy 1958-**60**

Inkster, Juli
Born Santa Cruz, California, USA on 24th June, 1960. Turned Professional 1983
PROFESSIONAL
Maj   Du Maurier Classic 1984; Nabisco Dinah Shore 1984-89; US Women's Open r/u 1992
US   15 wins 1983 to 1992 (JAL Big Apple Classic, 1992)
Int   Solheim Cup 1992
Mis   Gatorade Rookie of the Year 1984
AMATEUR
Nat   US Ladies Amateur 1980-81-82
Int   Curtis Cup 1982; World Cup 1980-82

Irwin, Hale
Born Joplin, Montana, USA on 3rd June, 1945. Turned Professional 1968
Maj   Open r/u 1983; US Open 1974-79-90, 3rd 1975
Eur   Piccadilly World Match Play 1974-75
US   20 wins 1971 to 1994 (MCI Heritage Classic 1994)
RoW   Australian PGA 1978. South African PGA 1978. Bridgestone 1981
Sen   US Ameritech Senior Open, Vantage Chp 1995;

American Express Invitational, USPGA Seniors Chp 1996; MasterCard Chp, LG Chp, USPGA Seniors Chp, Las Vegas Sen Classic, Burnet Sen Classic, Bank Boston Classic, Boone Valley Classic, Vantage Chp 1997
Int   Ryder Cup 1975-77-79-81-91. USA in World Cup 1974-79 (winners, individual winner); President's Cup 1994
Mis   World Golf Hall of Fame 1992

Jacobsen, Peter
Born Portland, Oregon, USA on 4th March, 1954. Turned Professional 1976
PROFESSIONAL
US   Buick-Goodwrench Open 1980; Greater Hartford Open, Colonial National Invitation 1984; Bob Hope Chrysler Classic 1990; AT&T Pebble Beach Pro-Am, Buick Invitational of California 1995
RoW   Western Australia Open 1979
Oth   Oregon Open, North California Open 1976
Int   Ryder Cup 1985-95
AMATEUR
Mis   All-American 1974-76

January, Don
Born Plainview, Texas, USA on 20th November, 1929. Turned Professional 1955
Maj   USPGA 1967; r/u 1961-76
US   11 wins 1956 to 1976
Sen   US Sen Tour 22 wins 1980-87
Int   Ryder Cup 1965-67

Janzen, Lee
Born Austin, MN, USA on 28th August, 1964. Turned Professional 1986
Maj   US Open 1993-98
US   Northern Telecom Open 1992; Phoenix Open 1993; Buick Classic 1994; The Players Chp, Kemper Open, The Sprint International 1995
Int   Ryder Cup 1993-97; Dunhill Cup 1995; President's Cup 1998
Mis   All-American 1985-86

Jiménez, Miguel Angel
Born Malaga on 5th January, 1964. Turned Professional 1982
Eur   PIAGET Open 1992; Heineken Dutch Open 1994; Turespaña Masters 1998
Oth   Open de Lyon 1988; B&H Trophy 1989 (with Xonia Wunsch-Ruiz)
Int   Spain in Dunhill Cup 1990-92-93-94-95-96-98; World Cup 1990-92-93-94

Johansson, Per-Ulrik
Born Uppsala, Sweden on 6th December, 1966. Turned Professional 1990
PROFESSIONAL
Eur   Renault Belgian Open 1991; Czech Open 1994; European Open 1996; English Open, European Open 1997
Int   Ryder Cup 1995-97; Sweden in World Cup 1991(winners); Dunhill Cup 1991(winners)-92-95-97(r/u)-98
Mis   Sir Henry Cotton Rookie of the Year 1991

For list of abbreviations see page 350

AMATEUR
Trn Leven Gold Medal 1986
Mis Arizona State University Team 1990

Jones, Steve
Born Artesia, New Mexico, USA on 27th December, 1958. Turned Professional 1981
Maj US Open 1996
US AT&T Pebble Beach National Pro-Am 1988; MONY Trn of Champions, Bob Hope Chrysler Classic, Canadian Open 1989; Phoenix Open, Bell Canadian Open 1997; Quad City Classic 1998
Int World Cup 1996 (r/u)
Mis Bike accident in 1991 caused him to miss three years of golf play

King, Betsy
Born Reading, Pennsylvania, USA on 13th August, 1955. Turned Professional 1977
Maj British Open 1985, r/u 1984; US Open 1989-90, 3rd 1986; USLPGA 1992, r/u 1987; Nabisco Dinah Shore 1987-90-97
US 31 LPGA wins 1984 to 1997
Int Solheim Cup 1990-92-94-96; Nichirei Int 1998
Mis *Golf Magazine* Player of the Year 1984-89; Founder's Cup 1989; Rolex Player of the Year 1984-89-93; Vare Trophy 1987; LPGA Hall of Fame 1995

Kite, Tom
Born Austin, Texas, USA on 9th December, 1949. Turned Professional 1972
PROFESSIONAL
Maj Open r/u 1978; US Open 1992; US Masters r/u 1983-86-97, 3rd 1977
US 19 wins 1976 to 1993 (Bob Hope Classic, Los Angeles Open 1993)
RoW Auckland Classic (NZ) 1974
Oth Oki Pro-Am 1996
Int Ryder Cup 1979-81-83-85-87-89-93-(**97**); Kirin Cup 1987(individual winner); Dunhill Cup 1989 (winners)-90-92-94(r/u); World Cup 1984-85
Mis Rookie of the Year 1973; Vardon Trophy 1981-82; Arnold Palmer Award 1981-89; Bobby Jones Award 1979; Golf Writers Player of the Year 1981; USPGA Player of the Year 1989.
AMATEUR
Chp Amateur s/f 1971
Nat US Amateur r/u 1970
Trn NCAA Chp 1972(shared)
Int Walker Cup 1971; Eisenhower Trophy 1970 (winners)

Klein, Emilee
Born Santa Monica, California, USA on 11th June, 1974. Turned Professional 1994
PROFESSIONAL
Maj Weetabix Women's British Open 1996, LPGA Ping Welch's Chp 1996
Int Nichirei Int 1998
AMATEUR
Reg Californian Women's Amateur 1989-92
Oth NCAA Chp 1994
Jun US Girls 1991
Int Curtis Cup 1994

Knight, Nancy *See* Lopez

Kuchar, Matt
Born Lake Mary, Fl on 21st June, 1978
Maj Leading Amateur in US Masters, US Open 1998
Chp US Amateur 1997
Int Einsenhower Trophy 1998

Kuehne, Kelli
Born Texas, USA in 1978
Maj Ladies British Amateur 1996; US Women's Amateur 1995-96
Jun US Girls 1994
Int Curtis Cup 1996; Espirito Santo 1996

Lacoste, Catherine *See* Prado

Langer, Bernhard
Born Anhausen, Germany on 27th August, 1957. Turned Professional 1972
Maj Open r/u 1981-84, 3rd 1985-86-93; US Masters 1985-93
Eur Dunlop Masters 1980; German Open, Bob Hope Classic 1981; German Open 1982; Italian Open, Glasgow Golf Classic, St Mellion TPC 1983; French, Dutch, Irish and Spanish Opens 1984; German and European Opens 1985; Lancôme Trophy(shared), German Open 1986; Whyte & Mackay PGA, Irish Open 1987; Epson Grand Prix 1988; Peugeot Spanish Open, German Masters 1989; Cepsa Madrid and Austrian Opens 1990; B&H International Open, German Masters 1991; Dutch and Honda Opens 1992; Volvo PGA, German Open 1993; Murphy's Irish Open, Volvo Masters 1994; Volvo PGA Chp, Deutsche Bank Open – TPC of Europe, European Open 1995; Italian Open, B&H International Open, Czech Open, German Masters 1997
Oth German Close Professional, Cacherel U-25 Chp 1979; Belgian Classic 1987
US Sea Pines Heritage Classic 1985
RoW Colombian Open 1980; Johnnie Walker Trn, Casio World Open 1983; Australian Masters 1985; Hong Kong Open, Million Dollar Challenge 1991; Hong Kong Alfred Dunhill Masters 1996; Argentine Masters 1997
Int Ryder Cup 1981-83-85-87-89-91-93-95-97; Hennessy-Cognac Cup 1976-78-80-**82**; Germany in World Cup 1976-77-78-79-80-90 (winners)-91-92-93 (individual winner)-94-96; Four Tours World Chp 1989-90; Nissan Cup 1985-86; Kirin Cup 1987; Dunhill Cup 1992-94
Mis Harry Vardon Trophy 1981-84; AGW Trophy 1981-93. Ritz Club Trophy 1985; PGAET Golfer of the Year 1993

Lehman, Tom
Born Austin, Minnesota, USA on 7th March, 1959. Turned Professional 1982
Maj Open Champion 1996; US Open r/u 1996, 3rd 1997; US Masters 3rd 1993, r/u 1994
Eur Loch Lomond World Invitational 1997
US Memorial Trn 1994; Colonial 1995; The Tour Chp 1996
RoW Casio World Open 1993

For list of abbreviations see page 350

Oth	Grand Slam of Golf 1996
Int	Ryder Cup 1995-97; President's Cup 1994; World Cup 1996 (r/u)
Mis	Ben Hogan Player of the Year 1991; Vardon Trophy 1996

Leonard, Justin
Born Dallas, TX, USA on 15th June, 1972. Turned Professional 1994
PROFESSIONAL
Maj	Open Champion 1997; USPGA r/u 1997
US	Buick Open 1996; Kemper Open 1997; Players Cup 1998
Int	Ryder Cup 1997; President's Cup 1996-98; USA in World Cup 1997

AMATEUR
| Nat | US Amateur 1992 |
| Int | Walker Cup 1993; Eisenhower Trophy 1992 |

Littler, Gene
Born San Diego, California, USA on 21st July, 1930. Turned Professional 1954
PROFESSIONAL
Maj	US Open 1961, r/u 1954; USPGA r/u 1977; US Masters r/u 1970(tied)
US	26 wins 1955 to 1977; Canadian Open 1965
RoW	Taiheiyo Pacific Masters 1974-75; Australian Masters 1980; Yellow Pages (SA) 1977
Sen	1987-two
Int	Ryder Cup 1961-63-65-67-69-71-75
Mis	Byron Nelson Award 1959; Bobby Jones Award, Ben Hogan Award 1973; USPGA Hall of Fame 1982; World Golf Hall of Fame 1990

AMATEUR
| Nat | US Amateur 1953 |
| Int | Walker Cup 1953 |

Lopez, Nancy
Born Torrance, California, USA on 6th January, 1957. Turned Professional July, 1977
| Maj | US Women's Open r/u 1975 (leading amateur)-77-89-97; US LPGA 1978-85-89 |

PROFESSIONAL
Eur	Colgate European 1978-79
US	48 LPGA wins 1978 to 1997 (Chick-Fil-A Charity Chp 1997)
RoW	Colgate Far East 1978
Int	Solheim Cup 1990
Mis	Rolex Player of the Year 1978-79-85-88; Vare Trophy 1978-79-85; Mazda-LPGA Series 1985; Gatorade Rookie of the Year 1978; Powell Award 1987; *Golf Magazine* Player of the Year 1978-79-85; LPGA Hall of Fame 1987; World Golf Hall of Fame 1989

AMATEUR
Oth	Mexican Ladies Amateur 1975
Int	Curtis Cup 1976; Espirito Santo 1976 (winners)
Jun	US Girls 1972-74

de Lorenzi, Marie-Laure
Born Biarritz, France on 21st January, 1961. Turned Professional 1986
PROFESSIONAL
Maj	Women's British Open (3rd) 1989-92
Eur	BMW Ladies German Open, Belgian Ladies Godiva Open 1987; French Open, Volmac Open, Hennessy Ladies Cup, Gothenburg Ladies Open, Laing Charity Classic, Woolmark Match Play Chp, Qualitair Ladies Spanish Open, Benson & Hedges Trophy (with M McNulty) 1988; Ford Ladies Classic, Hennessy Ladies Cup, BMW Ladies Classic 1989; Ford Ladies Classic 1990; Var Open de France Féminin 1993; Spanish Open 1994; Ladies Open Costa Azul, Staatsloterij Dutch Open, French Ladies Open 1995; Swiss Open 1997
Int	Solheim Cup 1990-96-98; Sunrise Cup 1992; European Cup 1997-98
Mis	Woolmark Order of Merit winner 1988-89. Vivien Saunders Trophy 1996

AMATEUR
Nat	French Close Chp 1983
Oth	Spanish Ladies 1978-80-83; South African Ladies', South African Ladies' Stroke Play 1981
Int	France Eur(L) T Ch 1977-83; Vagliano Trophy 1983
Jun	French Girls 1976; British Girls 1978
Mis	Doris Chambers Trophy 1982-85; Angus Trophy 1980

Love III, Davis
Born Charlotte, NC, USA on 13th April, 1964. Turned Professional 1985
PROFESSIONAL
Maj	US Open r/u 1996; USPGA 1997
US	Heritage Classic 1987-91-92; The International 1990; Trn Players Chp, Greater Greensboro Open, Kapalua International 1992; Infiniti Trn of Champions, Las Vegas Invitational 1993; Freeport McMoran Classic 1995; Buick Invitational 1996; Andersen Consulting US, Buick Challenge, Lincoln-Mercury Kapalua International 1997; MCI Classic 1998
Oth	JC Penney Classic (with B Daniel) 1994-95
Int	(US) Ryder Cup 1993-95-97; Dunhill Cup 1992-93; World Cup 1992(winners)-93(winners)-94(winners)-95(winners, individual winner)-97; President's Cup 1994-98

AMATEUR
| Int | Walker Cup 1985 |

Lunn, Karen
Born Sydney, Australia on 21st March, 1966. Turned Professional 1985
PROFESSIONAL
Maj	Ladies British Open 1993
Eur	Borlange Ladies Open 1986; European Masters 1988-90; Slovenian Open 1992; AmEx Tour Players Classic, French Open 1997
RoW	Thailand Ladies Open 1988; Daikyo Challenge 1990
Int	European Cup 1997-98
Mis	Spalding Order of Merit winner 1993

AMATEUR
Reg	Queensland Ladies Amateur, Victoria Ladies Match Play, South Australian Ladies Stroke Play 1984
Jun	NSW Junior, Australian Schoolgirls 1982; Queensland Junior 1984
Int	NSW Juniors 1981-85

McIntire, Barbara
| Maj | US Women's Open r/u 1956 |
| Chp | Ladies British Amateur 1960 |

For list of abbreviations see page 350

Nat US Ladies Amateur 1959-64
Int Curtis Cup 1958-60-62-64-66-72

McNulty, Mark
Born Zimbabwe on 25th October, 1953. Turned Professional 1977
Maj Open r/u 1990
Eur Greater Manchester Open 1979; German Open 1980; Portuguese Open 1986; German Open, 4 Stars Pro-Celebrity, Dunhill Masters 1987; Cannes Open, Benson & Hedges Trophy (with Marie-Laure de Lorenzi) 1988; Torres Monte Carlo Open 1989; Cannes Open, German Open 1990-91, BMW Int'l Open 1994; Dimension Data Pro-Am, Dutch Open, Volvo Masters 1996
RoW SA Open 1987, SA Masters 1982-86-97; 25 wins 1980 to 1997; Malay Open 1980; Zimbabwe Open 1992-96
Int (Zimbabwe) Dunhill Cup 1993-94-95-96-97-98; World Cup 1993(r/u)-94(r/u)-95-96-97-98; President's Cup 1994-96; Alfred Dunhill Challenge 1995

Maggert, Jeff
Born Columbia, MO, USA on 20th February, 1964. Turned Professional 1986
Maj USPGA 3rd 1995-97
US Walt Disney World Classic 1993
RoW Malaysian Open 1989; Vines Classic (ANZ) 1990
Oth Nike Knoxville Open, Buffalo Open 1990
Int Ryder Cup 1995-97; President's Cup 1994

Mallon, Meg
Born Natick, Maryland, USA on 14th April, 1963. Turned Professional 1986.
Maj US Women's Open 1991; US LPGA 1991
PROFESSIONAL
US Oldsmobile Classic, Trophée-Urban World Chp 1991; Ping Welch's Chp, Sara Lee Classic 1993; Hawaiian Ladies Open, Sara Lee Classic 1996; Star Bank LPGA Classic 1998
RoW Daikyo World Chp 1991;
Int Solheim Cup 1992-94-96; Sunrise Cup 1992; Nichirei International 1995
AMATEUR
Oth Michigan Ladies Amateur 1983

Marsh, Graham, MBE
Born Kalgoorlie, Western Australia on 14th January, 1944. Turned Professional 1968
Eur Swiss Open 1970; German Open 1972; Sunbeam Electric 1973; Benson & Hedges International 1976; Colgate World Match Play, Lancôme Trophy 1977; Dutch Open, Dunlop Masters 1979; Benson & Hedges International 1980; European Open 1981; Dutch Open 1985
US 1977-one
RoW Watties Open (NZ) 1970; Indian Open, Spalding Masters (NZ) 1971; Indian Open, Thailand Open 1973; Malaysian Open 1974; Malaysian Open 1975; Western Australian Open 1976; 17 wins in Japan 1972-81; Sapporo-Tokyu Open (Jpn) 1989; Tokai Classic 1990
Sen US: Bruno's Memorial Classic 1995; Paine Webber Invitational 1996; Nationwide Chp, US Sen Open 1997

Int Dunhill Cup 1985(winners); Nissan Cup 1986; Kirin Cup 1987; Four Tours World Chp 1991
Mis USPGA Rookie of the Year 1977; Australian Sportsman of the Year 1977

Massey, Debbie
Born Grosse Pointe, Michigan, USA on 5th November, 1950. Turned Professional 1977.
Maj Ladies British Open 1980-81; US Women's Open leading amateur 1974; USLPGA 3rd 1983
PROFESSIONAL
US Mizuno Japan Classic 1977; Wheeling Classic 1979; Mazda Japan Classic 1990
Mis Gatorade Rookie of the Year 1977
AMATEUR
Oth Canadian Ladies Amateur 1974-75-76
Reg Western Amateur 1972-75; Eastern Amateur 1975
Int Curtis Cup 1974-76; Espirito Santo 1976
Mis Doris Chambers Trophy, Angus Trophy 1976

Mayfair, Billy
Born Phoenix, Arizona, USA on 6th August, 1966. Turned Professional 1988
PROFESSIONAL
US Greater Milwaukee Open 1993; Motorola Western Open, The Tour Chp 1995; Nissan Open, Buick Open 1998
Int Four Tours World Chp 1991
AMATEUR
Nat US Amateur 1987
Oth US Public Links 1986; Arizona Stroke Play Chp 1985-87
Int Walker Cup 1987

Melnyk, Steve
Born Brunswick, Georgia, USA on 26th February, 1947. Turned Professional 1971
AMATEUR
Maj Leading amateur Open and US Masters 1970
Chp Amateur Champion 1971
Nat US Amateur 1969
Reg Western Amateur 1969. Eastern Amateur 1970
Int Walker Cup 1969-71
Mis US Amateur Golfer of the Year 1969

Mickelson, Phil
Born Arizona, USA. Turned Professional 1991
Maj Leading amateur in US Open 1991, US Masters 3rd 1996; USPGA 3rd 1994
PROFESSIONAL
US Tucson Open 1991 (as amateur); Buick Invitational of California, The International 1993; Mercedes Chp 1994; Northern Telecom Open 1995; Nortel Open, Phoenix Open, Byron Nelson Classic, NEC World Series 1996; Bay Hill Invitational, Sprint International 1997; Mercedes Chp, AT&T Pebble Beach National Pro-Am 1998
Int Ryder Cup 1995-97; President's Cup 1994-96-98; Dunhill Cup 1996 (winners)-97
AMATEUR
Nat US Amateur 1990
Oth NCAA Chp 1989-90-92
Int Walker Cup 1989-91
Mis Plays left-handed

For list of abbreviations see page 350

Miller, Johnny Lawrence
Born San Francisco, USA on 29th April, 1947. Turned Professional 1969
- **Maj** Open Champion 1976, r/u 1973, 3rd 1975; US Open 1973, leading amateur 1966; US Masters r/u 1971-75
- **Eur** Lancôme Trophy 1973-79
- **US** 24 wins 1971 to 1994 (AT&T Pebble Beach 1994)
- **RoW** Dunlop Phoenix International (Jpn) 1974. Otago Classic (NZ) 1972
- **Int** Ryder Cup 1975-81; World Cup 1973 (winners; individual winner)-75 (winners, individual winner)-80; v Japan 1983
- **Mis** USPGA Player of the Year 1974. US leading money winner 1974

Mize, Larry Hogan
Born Augusta, Georgia, USA on 23rd September, 1958. Turned Professional 1980
- **Maj** US Masters 1987; 3rd 1994
- **US** Memphis Classic 1983; Northern Telecom Open, Buick Open 1993
- **RoW** Casio World Open (Jpn) 1988; Dunlop Phoenix Open 1989-90; Johnnie Walker World Chp 1993
- **Int** Ryder Cup 1987

Muntz, Rolf
Born Voorschoten, Netherlands on 26th March, 1969. Turned Professional 1993
PROFESSIONAL
- **Oth** Nedcar Open, Neuchatel Open 1994; Nedcar National Open, Challenge Changeurs 1995

AMATEUR
- **Chp** Amateur Champion 1990
- **Nat** Dutch Open Amateur 1989
- **Trn** Lancôme Trophy 1988-89
- **Int** Europe v GBI 1990-92; Dutch National Team 1989-90
- **Jun** Dutch Junior Match Play, Dutch Junior Stroke Play 1989; Dutch International Junior Open 1989
- **Int** Dutch Boys 1986-87

Nagle, Kelvin DG
Born North Sydney, Australia on 21st December, 1920. Turned Professional 1946
- **Maj** Open Champion 1960, r/u 1962; US Open r/u 1965 (tied)
- **Eur** Irish Hospitals, Dunlop, French Open 1961. Bowmaker 1962-65. Esso Golden 1963-67
- **US** Canadian Open 1964
- **RoW** Australian Open 1959. Australian Professional 1949-54-58-59-65-68. New Zealand Professional 1957-58-60-70-73-74-75. New Zealand Open 1957-58-62-64-67-68-69. New Zealand BP 1968; Caltex 1969, Garden City, 1969, Otago Charity Classic 1970-76. Stars Travel 1970. In Australia: West End 1968-72-74, New South Wales Open 1968. Victoria Open 1969, NBN Newcastle 1970, New South Wales Professional 1971, South Coast Open 1975, Western Australia PGA 1977
- **Sen** World Seniors 1971-75; British Seniors 1971-73-75(winners)
- **Int** Australia in World Cup 1954(winners) 55-58-59-(winners)-60-61-62-65-66
- **Mis** Honorary Member of Royal & Ancient.

Nakajima, Tsuneyuki
Born Kiryu City, Gumma, Japan on 20th October, 1954. Turned Professional 1975
- **Maj** USPGA 3rd 1988
- **RoW** Japan Amateur 1973. Japan Open 1985-86-90-91. Japan PGA 1983-84-86-92; 23 wins 1984 to 1995 (Fuji Sankei Classic 1995)
- **Int** Dunhill Cup 1986. Nissan Cup 1986(individual winner). Kirin Cup 1987-88. World Cup 1996

Nelson, Byron
Born Fort Worth, Texas, USA on 4th February, 1912. Turned Professional 1932
- **Maj** US Open 1939; r/u 1946; USPGA 1940-45, r/u 1939-41-44; US Masters 1937-42, r/u 1941-47
- **Eur** French Open 1955
- **US** 54 wins 1935-one 1936-one 1937-two 1938-two 1939-three 1940-two 1941-three 1942-three 1944-six 1945-fifteen 1946-five
- **Int** Ryder Cup 1937-47
- **Mis** Vardon Trophy 1939; leading money winner 1944-45; USPGA Hall of Fame 1953; World Golf Hall of Fame 1974; Bobby Jones Award 1974; 11 consecutive tour wins March-August 1945, and 18 for the year

Nelson, Larry Gene
Born Fort Payne, Alabama, USA on 10th September, 1947. Turned Professional 1971
- **Maj** US Open 1983, 3rd 1991; USPGA 1981-87
- **US** 4 wins 1979 to 1988
- **RoW** Suntory Open (Japan) 1989; Dunlop Phoenix Open (Japan) 1991
- **Int** Ryder Cup 1979-81-87

Neumann, Liselotte
Born Finspang, Sweden on 20th May, 1966. Turned Professional 1985
PROFESSIONAL
- **Maj** Weetabix Women's British Open 1994; US Women's Open 1988, 3rd 1995; USLPGA r/u 1986-92, 3rd 1994
- **Eur** 10 wins 1985 to 1995 (Trygg Hansa Open 1995)
- **US** Mazda Japan Classic 1991; Minnesota LPGA Classic, GHP Heartland Classic 1994; Chrysler Plymouth Trn of Champions, Ping Welch's Chp, Edina Realty LPGA Classic 1996; Welch's Chp, Toray Japan Queens Cup 1997; Standard Register Ping, Chick-fil-A Chp 1998
- **RoW** Singapore Open 1987; Takara Invitational (Jpn) 1993
- **Int** Solheim Cup 1990-92-94-96-98; Sunrise Cup 1992(winners, individual winner); (for LPGA) Nichirei International 1995-96-97
- **Mis** Gatorade Rookie of the Year 1988. Vivien Saunders Trophy 1994

AMATEUR
- **Nat** Swedish Ladies Open 1982-83; Swedish Ladies Match Play 1983
- **Int** Sweden (Eur(L) T Ch) 1983. Espirito Santo 1982-84; Vagliano Trophy 1983

For list of abbreviations see page 350

Newton, Jack
Born Sydney, Australia on 30th January, 1950.
Turned Professional 1969
- **Maj** Open r/u 1975 (tied); US Masters r/u 1980
- **Nat** Australian Open 1979
- **Eur** Benson & Hedges Festival, Dutch Open 1972; Benson & Hedges PGA Match Play 1974; Sumrie 1975
- **US** 1978-one
- **RoW** City of Auckland Classic (NZ) 1972. Amoco Forbes (Aust) 1972. Nigerian Open 1974. Cock o' the North (Zambia) 1976. Mufulira Open 1976. New South Wales Open 1976-79
- **Mis** Seriously injured on tarmac by aeroplane propeller accident 1983

Nicklaus, Jack William
Born Columbus, Ohio, USA on 21st January, 1940.
Turned Professional 1961
- **Maj** Open Champion 1966-70-78, r/u 1964-67-68-72-76-77-79, 3rd 1963-74-75; US Open 1962-67-72-80, r/u 1960 (leading am)-68-71(tied)-82, leading am (4th) 1961; USPGA 1963-71-73-75-80, r/u 1964-65-74-83, 3rd 1967-77; US Masters 1963-65-66-72-75-86, r/u 1964-71-77-81, 3rd 1973-76

PROFESSIONAL
- **Eur** Piccadilly World Match Play 1970, r/u 1966-71
- **US** 71 wins 1962-84; World Series 1962-63-67-70-76
- **RoW** Australian Open 1964-68-71-75-76-78; Dunlop International (Aust) 1971; Indonesian Open 1994
- **Sen** US Sen Tour 10 wins 1990-96 (US Senior Open, USPGA Seniors 1991; US Seniors Open 1993)
- **Int** Ryder Cup 1969-71-73-75-77-81-(**83**)-(**87**); World Cup 1963(winners, individual winner)-64(winners, individual winner)-65-66(winners)-67(winners)-71(winners, individual winner)-73(winners); President's Cup (**1998**)
- **Mis** Rookie of the Year 1962; USPGA Player of the Year 1967-72-73-75-76; leading money winner 1964-65-67-71-72-73-75-76; Byron Nelson Award 1964-65-67-72-73; Bobby Jones Award 1975; Walter Hagen Award 1980; World Golf Hall of Fame 1974; US Sportsman of the Year 1978; Card Walker Award 1983; Honorary Member of Royal & Ancient

AMATEUR
- **Nat** US Amateur 1959-61
- **Trn** NCAA Chp 1961
- **Int** Walker Cup 1959-61; Eisenhower Trophy 1960(winners, individual winner)

Nobilo, Frank
Born Auckland, New Zealand on 14th May, 1960.
Turned Professional 1979
PROFESSIONAL
- **Eur** PLM Open 1988; Lancôme Trophy 1991; Open Mediterrania 1993; BMW International Open 1995; Deutsche Bank TPC of Europe 1996
- **US** Greater Greensboro Classic 1997
- **RoW** New South Wales PGA 1982; New Zealand PGA 1985-87; Indonesian Open 1994; Hong Kong Open 1997
- **Oth** New Zealand U-25 Stroke Play 1979; Sarazen World Open 1995-96

- **Int** New Zealand in World Cup 1982-87-88-90-93-94-95-98; Dunhill Cup 1985-86-87-89-90-92-94-95-96-97-98; President's Cup 1994-96-98; Alfred Dunhill Challenge 1995
- **Mis** Rookie of the Year 1981

AMATEUR
- **Nat** New Zealand Amateur 1978

Norman, Greg
Born Mt Isa, Queensland, Australia on 10th February, 1955. Turned Professional 1976
- **Maj** Open Champion 1986-93, r/u 1989(tied); US Open r/u 1984(tied), r/u 1995; USPGA 1986(r/u)-93(tied); US Masters r/u 1986-1987(tied)-96, 3rd 1989-95
- **Eur** Martini 1977; Martini 1979; Scandinavian Enterprise Open, French Open, Suntory World Match Play 1980; Martini, Dunlop Masters 1981; Dunlop Masters, Benson & Hedges Int, State Express Classic 1982; Suntory World Match Play 1983; European Open, Suntory World Match Play 1986; Italian Open 1988; Johnnie Walker Classic 1994
- **US** Kemper Open, Canadian Open 1984; Panasonic-Las Vegas Invitational, Kemper Open 1986; MCI Heritage Classic 1988; The International, Greater Milwaukee Open 1989; Doral Ryder Open 1990; Canadian Open 1992; Doral Ryder Open 1993; The Players Chp 1994; Memorial Trn, Greater Hartford Open, NEC World Series 1995; Doral Ryder Open 1996; FedEx St Jude Classic, NEC World Series 1997
- **RoW** Australian Open 1980-85-95-96; Australian Masters 1984-87-89-90; Australian PGA 1984-85; Australian TPC 1988-89; West Lakes Classic (Aus) 1976; South Seas Classic (Fiji), NSW Open 1978; Hong Kong Open 1979; NSW Open, Hong Kong Open 1983; Victoria Open 1984; NSW, Queensland, South Australian and Western Australian Opens 1986; ESP Open, Palm Meadows Cup 1988; Chunichi Crowns 1989; Taiheiyo Masters 1993; Ford Open 1996
- **Oth** Andersen Consulting World Chp 1996
- **Int** Australia in World Cup 1976-78; Dunhill Cup 1985(winners)-1986(winners)-87-88-89-90-92-94-95-96; Nissan Cup 1985-86, Kirin Cup 1987; test match *v* GBI 1988; Alfred Dunhill Challenge 1995; President's Cup 1996-98
- **Mis** Harry Vardon Trophy 1982; Arnold Palmer Award 1986-90; Mary Bea Porter Award 1988; Vardon Trophy 1989-90-94; Sony Ranking No 1 1995-96-97

North, Andy
Born Thorp, Wisconsin, USA on 9th March, 1950.
Turned Professional 1972
- **Maj** US Open 1978-85
- **US** 1 win 1977
- **Int** US in World Cup 1978
- **Mis** ESPN commentator

Okamoto, Ayako
Born Hiroshima, Japan on 2nd April, 1951. Turned Professional 1976
- **Maj** Ladies British Open 1984; US Women's Open r/u 1987 (tied), 3rd 1986; USLPGA r/u 1989-91, 3rd 1986-87-88

For list of abbreviations see page 350

Eur	German Open 1990
US	17 wins 1982 to 1992
RoW	Japan Women's Open 1993-97; Itoen Ladies (Jpn) 1993
Int	Nichirei International 1996
Mis	Rolex Player of the Year 1987; Mazda-LPGA Series 1984-87

Olazábal, José Maria

Born Fuenterrabia, Spain on 5th February, 1966. Turned Professional 1985

Maj	Open 3rd 1992; US Masters 1994, 1991(r/u)
PROFESSIONAL	
Eur	Ebel European Masters -Swiss Open, Sanyo Open 1986; Volvo Belgian Open, German Masters 1988; Tenerife Open, KLM Dutch Open 1989; Benson & Hedges International, Carrolls Irish Open, Lancôme Trophy 1990; Catalonia Open, Epson Grand Prix 1991; Open de Tenerife, Open Mediterrania 1992; Turespaña Open Mediterrania, Volvo PGA Chp 1994; Tournoi Perrier de Paris 1995; Turespaña Masters 1997; Dubai Desert Classic 1998
US	NEC World Series 1990-94; Wild Coast Skins Game 1990; The International 1991
RoW	Japanese Masters 1989
Int	Ryder Cup 1987-89-91-93-97; Kirin Cup 1987; Spain in Dunhill Cup 1986-87-88-89-92-98; Four Tours World Chp 1989; World Cup 1989.
Mis	PGA Qualifying School winner 1985
AMATEUR	
Chp	Amateur Champion 1984
Nat	Spanish Open Amateur 1983
Oth	Italian Open Amateur 1983
Jun	British Boys 1983; Belgian International Youths Chp 1984; British Youths 1985

O'Meara, Mark

Born Goldsboro, North Carolina, USA on 13th January, 1957. Turned Professional 1980

PROFESSIONAL	
Maj	Open Champion 1998; 3rd 1985-91; US Open 3rd 1988; US Masters 1998
Eur	Lawrence Batley International 1987; Trophée Lancôme 1997; World Match Play 1998
US	Greater Milwaukee Open 1984; Bing Crosby Pro-Am, Hawaiian Open 1985; AT&T Pebble Beach National Pro-Am 1989-90; Texas Open 1990; Walt Disney World Classic 1991; AT&T Pebble Beach National Pro-Am 1992; Canadian Open, Honda Classic 1995; Mercedes Chp, Greater Greensboro Open 1996; AT&T Pebble Beach National Pro-Am, Buick Invitational 1997
RoW	Kapalua International, Fuji Sankei Classic (Jap) 1985; Australian Masters 1986
Int	Ryder Cup 1985-89-91-97; Nissan Cup 1985; Dunhill Cup 1985-86-87-96 (winners)-97-98; US v Japan 1984; President's Cup 1996-98
Mis	Rookie of the Year 1981
AMATEUR	
Nat	US Amateur 1979
Oth	Mexican Amateur 1979

Ozaki, Masashi 'Jumbo'

Born Kaiman Town, Tokushima, Japan on 24th January, 1947. Turned Professional 1980

RoW	Japan Open 1974-88-89-94; Japan PGA 1971-74-89-91-93; Japan Match Play 1989; Japan Tour 78 wins 1984 to 1997
Oth	Dunlop International Open (Asa) 1992
Int	Nissan Cup 1986; Kirin Cup 1987; Four Tours World Chp 1989; President's Cup 1996

Pak, Se Ri,

Born Daejeon, Korea on 28th September, 1977. Turned Professional 1996

PROFESSIONAL	
Maj	US Women's Open 1998; USLPGA 1998
US	Jamie Farr Kroger Classic, Giant Eagle Classic 1998
Oth	In 1996-97 in KLPGA played 14 events, won 6, runner-up 7
AMATEUR	
Mis	Won 30 tournaments in Korea

Palmer, Arnold

Born Latrobe, Pennsylvania, USA on 10th September, 1929. Turned Professional 1954

PROFESSIONAL	
Maj	Open Champion 1961-62, r/u 1960; US Open 1960, r/u 1962-63(tied)-66(tied)-67, 3rd 1972; USPGA r/u 1964-68-70; US Masters 1958-60-62-64, r/u 1961-65, 3rd 1959
Eur	Piccadilly World Match Play 1964-67; Lancôme Trophy 1971; Penfold PGA, Spanish Open 1975
US	61 wins 1956-four 1957-four 1958-two 1959-three 1960-six 1961-five 1962-six 1963-seven 1964-one 1965-one 1966-four 1967-four 1968-two 1969-two 1970-one 1971-four 1973-one. Canadian Open 1955; Canadian PGA 1980
RoW	Australian Open 1966
Int	Ryder Cup 1961-63-65-67-71-73-(75); World Cup 1960-62-63-64-66-67 (winners each year; individual winner 1967); President's Cup **1996**
Mis	USPGA Player of the Year 1960-62; Vardon Trophy 1961-62-64-67; leading money winner 1958-60-62-63; Byron Nelson Award 1957-60-61-62-63; World Golf Hall of Fame 1974; USPGA Hall of Fame 1980; Bobby Jones Award 1971; William Richardson Award 1970; Walter Hagen Award 1981; Old Tom Morris Award 1983; Honorary Member of Royal & Ancient
AMATEUR	
Nat	US Amateur 1954

Parnevik, Jesper

Born Danderyd, Stockholm on 7th March, 1965. Turned Professional 1986

PROFESSIONAL	
Maj	Open r/u 1994-97
Eur	Bell's Scottish Open 1993; Volvo Scandinavian Masters 1995; Trophée Lancôme 1996; Volvo Scandinavian Masters 1998
US	Phoenix Open 1998
Oth	Ramlosa Trophy, Odense Open, Open Passing Shot 1988; SI/Compaq Open 1990

Parry, Craig
Born Sunshine, Victoria, Australia on 12th January, 1966. Turned Professional 1985
- **Maj** US Open 3rd 1993
- **Eur** Wang Four Stars National Pro-Celebrity, German Open 1989; Italian Open, Scottish Open 1991
- **US** Canadian TPC 1987
- **RoW** Australian Masters, Australian PGA 1992; NSW Open, South Australian PGA 1987; Bridgestone Open 1989; NSW Open 1992; Australian Masters 1994; Greg Norman Holden Classic 1995; Australian Masters 1996; Japan Open 1997; Schweppes Coolum Classic 1997; Indonesia Open 1997
- **Int** Kirin Cup 1988; Four Tours World Chp 1990(winners)-91; Dunhill Cup 1991-93-98; President's Cup 1994-96-98

Pate, Jerry
Born Macon, Georgia, USA on 16th September, 1953. Turned Professional 1975
PROFESSIONAL
- **Maj** US Open 1976; r/u 1979; USPGA 1978; US Masters 3rd 1982
- **US** 4 wins 1977 to 1982; Canadian Open 1976
- **RoW** Taiheiyo Pacific Masters 1976; Brazilian Open 1980
- **Int** Ryder Cup 1981; USA in World Cup 1976
- **Mis** Rookie of the Year 1976

AMATEUR
- **Nat** US Amateur 1974
- **Int** Walker Cup 1975

Pavin, Corey
Born Oxnard, California, USA on 16th November, 1959. Turned Professional 1981
PROFESSIONAL
- **Maj** US Open 1995; US Masters 3rd 1992; USPGA r/u 1994
- **Eur** German Open 1983; Toyota World Match Play 1993
- **US** 13 wins 1984 to 1996 (MasterCard Colonial 1996)
- **RoW** SA PGA 1983; Tokai Classic (Jpn) 1994; Volvo Asian Masters 1995; Nedbank Million Dollar Challenge 1995
- **Int** Ryder Cup 1991-93-95; Nissan Cup 1985; President's Cup 1994-96
- **Mis** USPGA Player of the Year 1991; Arnold Palmer Award 1991

AMATEUR
- **Int** Walker Cup 1981

Pepper, Dottie
Born Saratoga Springs, NY on 17th August, 1965. Turned Professional 1987
PROFESSIONAL
- **Maj** Nabisco Dinah Shore 1992
- **US** Oldsmobile LPGA Classic 1989; Crestar Classic 1990; Nabisco Dinah Shore, Sega Women's Chp, Welch's Classic, Sun Times Challenge 1992; World Chp of Women's Golf 1993; Chrysler-Plymouth Trn of Champions 1994; Ping Welch's Chp; McCall's LPGA Classic 1995; Rochester International, Shoprite LPGA Classic, Friendly's Classic, Safeway LPGA Chp 1996
- **RoW** Tokyo Ladies Open (Jpn) 1989
- **Oth** JC Penney Classic, Wendy's Three-Tour Challenge 1992
- **Int** Solheim Cup 1990-92-94-96-98
- **Mis** Rolex Player of the Year 1992; Vare Trophy 1992

AMATEUR
- **Reg** New York State Champion 1981

Pinero, Manuel
Born Badajoz, Spain on 1st September, 1952. Turned Professional 1968
- **Eur** Madrid Open 1974; Swiss Open 1976; Penfold PGA 1977; English Classic 1980; Madrid Open, Swiss Open 1981; European Open 1982; Cepsa Madrid Open, Italian Open 1985
- **Oth** Spanish Professional 1972-73
- **Int** Ryder Cup 1981-85; Hennessy-Cognac Cup 1974-76-78-80-82; Spain in World Cup 1974-76(winners)-78-79-80-82(winners, individual winner)-83-85-88; Dunhill Cup 1985

Player, Gary
Born Johannesburg, South Africa on 1st November, 1935. Turned Professional 1953
- **Maj** Open Champion 1959-68-74, 3rd 1967; US Open 1965, r/u 1958-79; USPGA 1962-72, r/u 1969; US Masters 1961-74-78, r/u 1962(tied)-65, 3rd 1970
- **Eur** Dunlop 1956; Piccadilly World Match Play 1965-66-68-71-73; Ibergolf European Chp 1974; Lancôme Trophy 1975
- **US** 21 wins 1958-78; World Series 1965-68-72
- **RoW** South African Open 1956-60-65-66-67-68-69-72-75-76-77-79-81; South African PGA 1968-79-81; South African Masters 1959-60-64-67-71-72-73-74-76(2)-79; Australian Open 1958-62-63-65-69-70-74; Australian PGA 1957; Brazilian Open 1972-74; Chile Open 1980; Ivory Coast Open 1980; Transvaal Open 1959-60-62-66; Natal Open 1958-60-66-68; Western Province Open 1968-71-72; General Motors (SA) 1971-75-76; Rothmans Match Play (SA) 1973; Int Classic (SA) 1974; ICL Int (SA) 1977; Johannesburg Int, Sun City Classic 1979; Wills Masters (Aust) 1968; Dunlop Int (Aus) 1970; Japan Airlines Open 1972
- **Sen** USPGA Senior Open 1987-88; Senior TPC 1987; Volvo Seniors British Open 1988-90-97; US Sen Tour 18 wins 1985 to 1995 (Bank One Classic 1995); Irish Sen Masters 1993; Shell Wentworth Senior Masters 1997
- **Int** South Africa in World Cup 1956-57-58-59-60-62-63-64-65(winners, individual winner) -66-67-68-71-72-73-77(individual winner); Dunhill Cup 1991 (r/u)
- **Mis** US leading money winner 1961; Bobby Jones Award 1966; World Golf Hall of Fame 1974; William Richardson Award 1976; SA PGA captain 1977, president 1978; Honorary member of the R&A

For list of abbreviations see page 350

Ploujoux, Philippe
Born La Bouille, Seine Maritime, France on 20th February, 1955
- **Chp** Amateur Champion 1981
- **Nat** French Amateur Close Match Play 1977
- **Oth** International Moroccan Stroke Play 1977
- **Int** Continental Team (St Andrews Trophy-5 times (including winners 1982), Continental Youth Team-4 times. Represented France more than 50 times
- **Jun** French Youths Match Play 1972-73-74-75-76. French Boys 1969-70

Prado, Catherine (*née* Lacoste)
Born Paris on 27th June, 1945
- **Maj** US Women's Open 1967
- **Chp** Ladies British Open Amateur 1969
- **Nat** French Ladies Open Amateur 1967-69-70-72. French Ladies Close Amateur 1968-69
- **Oth** US Ladies' Amateur 1969; Spanish Ladies Amateur 1969-72-76
- **Reg** Western Ladies Amateur 1968
- **Trn** Astor Princes' 1966; Worplesdon Foursomes 1967; Hovis 1969
- **Int** Espirito Santo 1964 (winners, individual winner)-68 (individual winner)
- **Mis** Doris Chambers Trophy 1967-69; First amateur, first non-American and youngest player at that time to win the US Women's Open

Price, Nick
Born Durban, South Africa on 28th January, 1957. Turned Professional 1977
- **Maj** Open Champion 1994, r/u 1982-1988; US PGA 1992-94
- **Eur** Swiss Open 1980; Lancôme Trophy 1985
- **US** World Series 1983; Byron Nelson Classic, Canadian Open 1991; Texas Open 1992; Players Chp, Greater Hartford Open, Sprint Western Open, St Jude Classic 1993; Honda Classic, SouthWestern Bell Colonial, Motorola Western Open, Canadian Open 1994; MCI Classic 1997; FedEx St Jude Classic 998
- **RoW** South African Masters 1980; Vaal Reefs Open (SA) 1982; ICL International (SA) 1985-93; South Australian Open 1989; Hassan II Trophy (Morocco) 1995; Zimbabwe Open, Nedbank Million Dollar Challenge 1997-98; Dimension Data Pro-Am, South African PGA 1997
- **Int** Zimbabwe in Dunhill Cup 1993-94-95-96-97-98; World Cup 1993 (r/u); President's Cup 1994-96-98; Alfred Dunhill Challenge 1995
- **Mis** Arnold Palmer Award and USPGA Player of the Year 1993-94; Vardon Trophy 1993-97 Sony Ranking No. 1 1994

Quast, Anne See Sander

Rawls, Betsy
Born Spartanburg, South Carolina, USA on 4th May, 1928. Turned Professional 1951
- **Maj** US Women's Open 1951-53-57-60, r/u 50(as amateur)-61; USLPGA 1959-69
- **US** 55 LPGA wins 1951 to 1972 (incl Western Open 1952-59)
- **Mis** Vare Trophy 1959; LPGA Hall of Fame 1960; World Golf Hall of Fame 1987; Patty Berg Award 1980; Bobby Jones Award 1996

Rivero, José
Born Spain on 20th September, 1955. Turned Professional 1973
- **Eur** Lawrence Batley International 1984. French Open 1987. Monte Carlo Open 1988. Open de Catalonia 1992
- **Int** Ryder Cup 1985-87. World Cup 1984 (winners)-87-88-90-91-93-94. Dunhill Cup 1986-87-88-90-91-92-94 Kirin Cup 1988

Roberts, Loren
Born San Luis Obispo, California, USA on 24th June, 1955. Turned Professional 1975
- **Maj** US Open r/u 1994
- **US** Nestle Invitational 1994-95; MCI Classic, Greater Milwaukee Open 1996; CVS Charity Classic 1997
- **Int** President's Cup 1994; Ryder Cup 1995

Rocca, Costantino
Born Bergamo, Italy on 4th December, 1956. Turned Professional 1981
- **Maj** Open r/u (tied) 1995
- **Eur** Open du Grand Lyon, Peugeot Open de France 1993; Volvo PGA 1996; Canon European Masters 1997
- **Oth** Rolex ProAm (Swi) 1988
- **Int** Ryder Cup 1993-95-97; Italy in World Cup 1993-94-95-98 (runners-up)
- **Mis** First Italian to play for Europe in the Ryder Cup

Rogers, William Charles (Bill)
Born Waco, Texas, USA on 10th September, 1951. Turned Professional 1974
PROFESSIONAL
- **Maj** Open Champion 1981; US Open r/u 1981, 3rd 1982
- **Eur** Suntory World Match Play 1979
- **US** 1978-one, 1981-three, 1983-one
- **Oth** Pacific Masters 1977
- **RoW** Suntory Open (Jap) 1980; NSW Open, Australian Open, Suntory Open (Jap) 1981
- **Int** Ryder Cup 1981
- **Mis** USPGA Player of the Year 1981

AMATEUR
- **Int** Walker Cup 1973

Romero, Eduardo
Born Cordoba, Argentina on 12th July, 1954. Turned Professional 1982
- **Eur** Lancôme Trophy 1989; Volvo Open di Firenze 1990; Spanish Open, French Open 1991; Italian Open, European Masters 1994
- **RoW** Argentine Open 1989; Argentine PGA 1983-86; Chile Open 1984-86
- **Int** Argentina in Dunhill Cup 1988-89-90-95-97-98; World Cup 1983-84-87-88-91-93-94-95

Rosenthal, Jody
Born Minneapolis, Minnesota, USA on 18th October, 1962. Turned Professional 1985
PROFESSIONAL
US   United Virginia Bank Classic, du Maurier Classic 1987
Mis   Gatorade Rookie of the Year 1986
AMATEUR
Chp   Ladies British Open Amateur 1984
Int   Curtis Cup 1984; Espirito Santo 1984(winners)

St Sauveur, Vicomtesse de *See* Segard

Sander, Anne [Welts] [Decker] (*née* Quast)
Chp   Ladies British Open Amateur 1980.
Nat   US Ladies Amateur 1958-61-63, r/u 1965-68-73
Int   Curtis Cup 1958-60-62-66-68-74-84-90; Espirito Santo 1966(winners)-68(winners)
Mis   Doris Chambers Trophy 1973-74; Angus Trophy 1974

Sarazen, Gene
Born Harrison, New York, USA on 27th February, 1902. Turned Professional 1920
Maj   Open Champion 1932, r/u 1928, 3rd 1931-33; US Open 1922-32, r/u 1934-40; USPGA 1922-23-33, r/u 1930; US Masters 1935
Eur   North of England Professional 1923
US   1922-one 1925-one 1927-two 1928-two 1930-two 1935-one 1936-one 1937-two 1938-one 1939-one 1941-one; USPGA Seniors 1954-58
RoW   Australian Open 1936
Int   Ryder Cup 1927-29-31-33-35-37
Mis   PGA Hall of Fame 1940; World Golf Hall of Fame 1974; William Richardson Award 1966; Old Tom Morris Award 1988; Bobby Jones Award 1992; one of the few to win the Open and the US Open in the same year; Honorary Member of the Royal & Ancient

Segard, Mme Patrick [De St Sauveur]
(*née* Lally Vagliano)
Chp   British Ladies 1950.
Trn   Worplesdon Foursomes 1962. Avia Foursomes 1966. Kayser-Bondor Foursomes 1960
Nat   French Ladies' Open 1948-50-51-52. French Ladies' Close 1939-46-49-50-51-54
Oth   Swiss Ladies 1949-65. Luxembourg Ladies 1949. Italian Ladies 1949-51. Spanish Ladies 1951
Int   France 1937-38-39-47-48-49-50-51-52-53-54-55-56-57-58-59-60-61-62-63-64-65-70. Vagliano Trophy **1959-61**-63-65-(**75**)
Jun   British Girls 1937
Mis   Chairman of The Women's Committee of World Amateur Golf Council 1964 to 1972

Semple Thompson, Carol
Chp   British Ladies 1974.
Nat   US Ladies' Amateur 1973
Trn   Newmark International 1975 (tied), r/u 1974
Int   Curtis Cup 1974-76-80-82-90-92-94-96-98. World Team Championship 1974(winners)-80 (winners)

Senior, Peter
Born Singapore on 31st July, 1959. Turned Professional 1978
Eur   PLM Open 1986; Monte Carlo Open 1987; Panasonic European Open 1990; Benson & Hedges International Open 1992
RoW   New South Wales PGA, Rich River Classic, (South Australian Open) 1979; Queensland Open, New South Wales PGA 1984; Queensland PGA 1987; Australian Open, Australian PGA 1989; Johnnie Walker Classic 1989-91; Australian Masters 1991; Bridgestone Open (Jpn) 1992; Vines Classic, Chunichi Crowns (Jpn) 1993; Canon Challenge 1994; Dunlop Open (Jpn), Australian Masters 1995; Holden Classic, Canon Challenge 1996-97
Int   Australia in Dunhill Cup 1987. Kirin Cup 1987; World Cup 1988-90. Four Tours World Chp 1990 (winners); President's Cup 1994-96

Sheehan, Patty
Born Middlebury, Vermont, USA on 27th October, 1956. Turned Professional 1980
PROFESSIONAL
Maj   Women's British Open 1992-94; US Women's Open 1992-94, r/u 1983-88-90; USLPGA 1983-84-93, r/u 1986; Nabisco Dinah Shore 1996
US   33 LPGA wins 1981 to 1996
Int   Solheim Cup 1990-92-94-96
Mis   Gatorade Rookie of the Year 1981; Rolex Player of the Year 1983; Vare Trophy 1984; Founders Cup 1985; LPGA Hall of Fame 1993
AMATEUR
Nat   US Ladies' Amateur r/u 1979
Int   Curtis Cup 1980

Siderowf, Dick
Maj   US Open leading amateur 1968
Chp   Amateur Champion 1973-76
Oth   Canadian Amateur 1971
Int   Walker Cup 1969-73-75-77-(**79**). Eisenhower Trophy 1968-76

Sigel, Jay
Born Narberth, PA, USA on 13th November, 1943. Turned Professional 1993
PROFESSIONAL
Sen   US Tour GTE West Classic 1994; Bruno's Memorial Classic, Kroger Senior Classic 1997
AMATEUR
Maj   US Open leading amateur 1984; US Masters leading amateur 1981-82-88
Chp   Amateur Champion 1979
Nat   US Amateur 1982-83
Int   Walker Cup 1977-79-81-**83**-85-87-89-91-93
Mis   Most wins (18) in Walker Cup matches; Bobby Jones Award 1984

Simpson, Scott William
Born San Diego, California, USA on 17th September, 1955. Turned Professional 1977
PROFESSIONAL
Maj   US Open 1987, r/u 1991 (tied)
US   1980-one. 1984-one. 1987-one (Greater Greensboro Open); BellSouth Atlanta Classic 1989; Buick Invitational 1998

RoW	1984-two wins (Chunichi Crowns, Dunlop Phoenix)
Int	Ryder Cup 1987. Kirin Cup 1987

AMATEUR

Trn	NCAA Chp 1976-77

Singh, Vijay

Born Lautoka, Fiji on 22nd February, 1963. Turned Professional 1982

Maj	US PGA 1998
Eur	Volvo Open 1989; El Bosque Open 1990; Open de Andalucia, German Open 1992; Scandinavian Masters, Trophée Lancôme 1994; South African Open, Toyota World Match Play Chp 1997
US	Buick Classic 1993; Phoenix Open, Buick Classic 1995; Memorial Trn, Buick Open 1997; Sprint International 1998
RoW	Malay PGA 1984; Nigerian Open, Swedish PGA 1988; Zimbabwe Open, Nigerian Open, Ivory Coast Open 1989; Hassan Trophy (Morocco) 1991; Malaysian Open 1992; Bell's Cup (SA) 1993; President's Cup 1994; Johnnie Walker Super Tour 1998
Int	Alfred Dunhill Challenge 1995; President's Cup 1996-98
Mis	USPGA Rookie of the Year 1993

Snead, Samuel Jackson

Born Hot Springs, Virginia, USA on 27th May, 1912. Turned Professional 1934

Maj	Open Champion 1946; US Open r/u 1937-47-49-53; USPGA 1942-49-51, r/u 1938-40, 3rd 1974; US Masters 1949-52-54, r/u 1939-57
US	84 wins 1936 to 1965; Canadian Open 1938-40-41
Sen	USPGA Seniors 1964-65-67-70-72-73 World Senior Professional 1964-65-70-72-73
Int	Ryder Cup 1937-47-49-51-53-55-59-(69); USA in World Cup 1954-56-57-58-59-60-61-62; (winners 56-60-61-62; individual winner 1961)
Mis	US leading money winner 1938-49-50. USPGA Player of the Year 1949. Oldest professional to win a Tour event in 1965. Unofficially credited with 164 victories (including 84 official USPGA tournaments) in his long career of which full details are not available. Finished second equal in a 1974 USPGA tournament aged 61 and third equal in the 1974 USPGA Chp aged 62. 24 holes-in-one

Sörenstam, Annika

Born Stockholm, Sweden on 9th October, 1970. Turned Professional 1992

PROFESSIONAL

Maj	British Women's Open r/u 1994; 3rd 1995; US Women's Open 1995-96
Eur	OVB Damen Open, Hennessy Cup 1995; Trygg-Hansa Open 1996; Compaq Open 1997; Compaq Open 1998
US	LPGA GHP Heartland Classic, World Chp of Women's Golf 1995; Betsy King Classic, World Chp of Women's Golf 1996; Trn of Champions, Hawaiian Ladies Open, Long's Drugs Challenge, Michelob Light Classic, Betsy King Classic, ITT Tour Chp 1997; Michelob Light Classic, ShopRite Classic, JAL Big Apple Classic, Safeco Classic 1998

RoW	Holden Australian Open 1994
Int	Solheim Cup 1994-96-98
Mis	Rookie of the Year 1993; LPGA Rookie of the Year 1994; Rolex Player of the Year 1995-97; Vare Trophy 1995-96-98; Leading Money Winner Vivien Saunders Trophy 1995; Mickey Wright Award 1995-97; Ping World Ranking No 1 1998

AMATEUR

Nat	US Women's Amateur r/u 1992
Int	Espirito Santo 1992 (individual winner); Swedish Ladies 1987 to 1992; NCAA All-American 1991-92

Stacy, Hollis

Born Savannah, Georgia, USA on 16th March, 1954. Turned Professional 1974

PROFESSIONAL

Maj	US Women's Open 1977-78-84; r/u 1980; Du Maurier Classic 1983
US	14 wins 1977 to 1985

AMATEUR

Int	Curtis Cup 1972
Jun	US Girls 1969-70-71

Stadler, Craig

Born San Diego, California, USA on 2nd June, 1953. Turned Professional 1975

PROFESSIONAL

Maj	US Masters 1982, 3rd 1988
Eur	Scandinavian Enterprise Open 1990
US	12 wins 1980-96 (Nissan Open 1996)
RoW	Argentine Open 1992
Int	Ryder Cup 1983-85
Mis	Arnold Palmer Award 1982

AMATEUR

Nat	US Amateur 1973
Int	Walker Cup 1975

Steinhauer, Sherri

Born Madison, Wisconsin, USA on 27th December, 1962. Turned Professional 1985

Maj	Ladies British Open 1998; Leading amateur in US Women's Open 1983; Du Maurier Classic 1992
US	Sprint Chp 1994
Int	Solheim Cup 1994-98; Nichirei Int 1998

Stephenson, Jan

Born Sydney, NSW, Australia on 22nd December, 1951. Turned Professional 1973

Maj	Du Maurier Classic 1981; LPGA 1982; US Women's Open 1983
Nat	Australian Ladies Open 1973-77
US	13 wins 1976 to 1986; 1987-two
Int	Sunrise Cup 1992
Mis	Gatorade Rookie of the Year 1974

Stewart, Payne

Born Springfield, Missouri, USA on 30th January, 1957. Turned Professional 1979

Maj	Open r/u 1985-90; US Open 1991, r/u 1993; USPGA 1989
Eur	Dutch Open 1991

For list of abbreviations see page 350

US 9 wins 1982-95 (Shell Houston Open 1995)
RoW Indian Open, Indonesian Open 1981; Tweed Head Classic (Aust) 1982; Jun Classic (Jpn) 1985
Int Ryder Cup 1987-89-91-93; Nissan Cup 1986; Kirin Cup 1988; Four Tours World Chp 1990; World Cup 1990 (individual winner); Dunhill Cup 1993 (winners)

Stockton, Dave
Born San Bernardino, California, USA on 2nd November, 1941. Turned Professional 1964
Maj US Open r/u 1978. USPGA 1970-76. US Masters r/u 1974.
US 1967-two wins; 1968-two; 1971-one; 1973-one; 1974-three; 1967 to 1974-nine
Sen 14 wins 1991 to 1997; US Senior Players Chp 1992; US Seniors Open 1996
Int Ryder Cup 1971-77-(**91**). World Cup 1970-76

Stranahan, Frank R
Born Toledo, Ohio, USA on 5th August, 1922. Turned Professional 1954
PROFESSIONAL
Maj Open r/u 1947-53, leading amateur 1947-49-50-51-53
US 1955-one, 1958-one
AMATEUR
Chp Amateur 1948-50, r/u 1952
Nat US Amateur r/u 1950
Oth Mexican Amateur 1946-48-51; Canadian Amateur 1947-48
Reg North & South Amateur 1946-49-52; Western Amateur 1946-49-51-53; Tam o' Shanter All-American Amateur 1948-49-50-51-52-53; Tam o' Shanter World Amateur 1950-51-52-53-54
Int Walker Cup 1947-49-51

Strange, Curtis
Born Norfolk, Virginia, USA on 20th January, 1955. Turned Professional 1976
PROFESSIONAL
Maj US Open 1988-89, 3rd 1984; USPGA r/u 1989; US Masters r/u 1985
Oth Canadian Open 1985-87
US 14 wins 1979 to 1988
RoW Palm Meadows Cup (Aus) 1989
Int Ryder Cup 1983-85-87-89-95. Dunhill Cup 1985-87-88-89 (winners)-90-91-94(r/u). Nissan Cup 1985. Kirin Cup 1987-88
Mis Arnold Palmer Award 1985-87. USPGA Player of the Year 1988
AMATEUR
Int Walker Cup 1975; Eisenhower Trophy 1974

Streit, Marlene Stewart
Born Cereal, Alberta, Canada on 9th March, 1934
Chp Ladies British Amateur 1953
Nat Canadian Ladies Open 1951-54-55-56-58-59-63-68-72-73. Canadian Ladies Close 1951 to 1957, 1963-68
Oth US Ladies Amateur 1956; r/u 1966. Australian Ladies 1963

Reg Ontario Provincial 1951-56-57-58. US North and South Ladies 1956
Int Canadian Commonwealth Team 1959-63-**79**
Mis Canadian Athlete of the Year 1951-53-56. Canadian Woman Athlete of the Year 1951-53-56-60-63

Stricker, Steve
Born Edgerton, Wisconsin, USA on 23rd February, 1967. Turned Professional 1990
US Kemper Open, Motorola Western Open 1996
Oth Victoria Open (Canada) 1990; Canadian PGA 1993
Int Dunhill Cup 1996 (winners)

Suggs, Louise
Born Atlanta, Georgia, USA on 7th September, 1923. Turned Professional 1948
PROFESSIONAL
Maj US Women's Open 1949-52, r/u 1951-55-58-59-63; USLPGA 1957, r/u 1955-60-61-63
US 50 LPGA wins 1949 to 1962 (incl Titleholders Chp 1946(as amateur)-54-56-59; Western Open 1946-47(both as amateur)-49-53
Mis Leading money winner 1953-60; Vare Trophy 1957; LPGA Hall of Fame 1951; World Golf Hall of Fame 1979. Founder Member of the LPGA
AMATEUR
Chp British Ladies 1948
Nat US Ladies Amateur 1947
Int Curtis Cup 1948

Sutton, Hal
Born Shreveport, Louisiana, USA on 28th April, 1958. Turned Professional 1981
Maj USPGA 1983
US 10 wins 1982-98 (La Cantera Texas Open Tour Chp 1998)
Int Ryder Cup 1985-87; Nissan Cup 1986; v Japan 1983
Mis Arnold Palmer Award 1983; Golf Writers Player of the Year 1983; USPGA Player of the Year 1983
AMATEUR
Nat US Amateur 1980
Int Walker Cup 1979-81

Thomson, Peter W, CBE
Born Melbourne, Australia on 23rd August, 1929. Turned Professional 1949
Maj Open Champion 1954-55-56-58-65, r/u 1952-53-57, 3rd 1969
Eur PGA Match Play 1954; *Yorkshire Evening News* 1957; Dunlop, Daks(shared) 1958; Italian Open, Spanish Open 1959; German Open, *Yorkshire Evening News*, Bowmaker, Daks 1960; PGA Match Play, *Yorkshire Evening News*, Esso Golden(shared), Dunlop Masters 1961; Martini International, Piccadilly 1962; Daks 1965; PGA Match Play 1966; Alcan International, PGA Match Play, Esso Golden(tied) 1967; Dunlop Masters 1968; Martini International 1970(shared); Wills 1972
US 1956-one, 1957-one

For list of abbreviations see page 350

RoW	Australian Open 1951-67-72, r/u 1950, leading amateur 1948; Australian Professional 1967; New Zealand Open 1950-51-53-55-59-60-61-65-71; New Zealand Professional 1953; Hong Kong Open 1960-65-67; India Open 1963-76; Philippines Open 1964; New Zealand Caltex 1967; Victorian Open 1973
Sen	PGA Seniors Chp 1988
Int	Australia in World Cup 1953-54(winners)-55-56-67-59(winners)-60-61-62-65-69; President's Cup **(1996)-(1998)**
Mis	World Golf Hall of Fame 1988. Honorary Member of Royal & Ancient

Trevino, Lee
Born Dallas, Texas, USA on 1st December, 1939. Turned Professional 1961

Maj	Open Champion 1971-72, r/u 1980, 3rd 1970; US Open 1968-71; USPGA 1974-84, r/u 1985
Eur	Benson & Hedges International, Lancôme Trophy 1978; Lancôme Trophy 1980; Dunhill British Masters 1985
US	27 wins: 1968-one, 1969-one, 1970-two, 1971-three, 1972-three, 1973-two, 1974-one, 1975-one, 1976-one, 1978-one, 1980-three, 1981-one; World Series 1974; Canadian Open 1971-77-79; Canadian PGA 1979-83
RoW	Chrysler Classic (Aust) 1973; Mexican Open 1975; Moroccan Grand Prix 1977
Sen	US Sen Tour 27 wins 1990 to 1996; USPGA Senior Open 1990; USPGA Seniors Chp 1992-94; Fuji Electric Grand Slam (Jpn) 1993
Int	Ryder Cup 1969-71-73-75-79-81-(**85**); World Cup 1968-69(winners, individual winner) -70-71(winners) -74
Mis	Rookie of the Year 1967; leading money winner 1970; USPGA Player of the Year 1971; Vardon Trophy 1970-71-72-74-80; Byron Nelson Award 1971; Ben Hogan Award 1981; World Golf Hall of Fame 1981; William Richardson Award 1985

Vagliano, Lally *See* Segard

Varangot, Brigitte
Born Biarritz, France on 1st May, 1940

Chp	Ladies British Open Amateur 1963-65-68
Nat	French Ladies Open Amateur 1961-62-64-65-66-73, r/u 1960-63-67-70; French Ladies Close Amateur 1959-61-63-70
Oth	Italian Ladies 1970
Trn	Kayser-Bondor Foursomes; Casa Pupo Foursomes 1965; Avia Foursomes 1966-73
Int	France in Vagliano Trophy 1959-61-63-65-69-71; Espirito Santo 1964(winners)-66-68-70-72-74

De Vicenzo, Roberto
Born Buenos Aires, Argentina on 14th April, 1923. Turned Professional 1938

Maj	Open Champion 1967, r/u 1950, 3rd 1948-49-56-60-64-69; US Masters r/u 1968
Eur	Belgian Open, Dutch Open, French Open 1950; French Open 1960; French Open, German Open 1964; Spanish Open 1966
US	1951-two 1953-one 1957-two 1966-one
RoW	Argentine Open 1944-49-51-52-58-65-67-70-74; Argentine Professional 1944-45-47-48-49-51-52; Chile Open 1946; Colombia Open 1947; Uruguay Open 1949; Mexican Open 1951; Panama Open 1952; Mexican Open 1953; Jamaican Open 1956; Brazilian Open, Jamaican Open 1957; Brazilian Open 1960-63-64; Bogota Open 1969; Panama Open, Brazilian Open, Caracas Open 1973; Panama Open 1974
Sen	USPGA Seniors 1974; World Senior Professional 1974; Legends of Golf 1979; US Senior Open 1980
Int	Argentina in World Cup 1953(winners) -54-55-62(individual winner) -63-64-65-66-68-69-70 (individual winner) -71-72-73-74; Mexico in World Cup 1956-59-60-61
Mis	Bobby Jones Award 1970; William Richardson Award 1971; Walter Hagen Award 1979; USPGA Hall of Fame 1979; World Golf Hall of Fame 1989; Honorary Member of the R&A.

Wadkins, Lanny
Born Richmond, Virginia, USA on 5th December, 1949. Turned Professional 1971

PROFESSIONAL

Maj	US Open r/u 1986; USPGA 1977, r/u 1982-84-87, 3rd 1973; US Masters 3rd 1990-91-93
US	20 wins 1972 to 1991; World Series 1977, r/u 1990; Greater Hartford Open 1992
RoW	Victoria PGA (Aust) 1978
Int	Ryder Cup 1977-79-83-85-87-89-91-93-(**95**); World Cup 1977-84-85; *v* Japan 1982-83; Nissan Cup 1985; Kirin Cup 1987; Four Tours World Chp 1991
Mis	USPGA Player of the Year 1985; Rookie of the Year 1972

AMATEUR

Nat	US Amateur 1970
Reg	Western Amateur 1970; Southern Amateur 1968-70; Eastern Amateur 1969
Int	Walker Cup 1969-71; Eisenhower Trophy 1970(winners)

Ward, Harvie
Born Tarboro, North Carolina, USA in 1926. Turned Professional 1973

Chp	Amateur Champion 1952; r/u 1953
Nat	US Amateur 1955-56
Oth	Canadian Amateur 1964
Trn	NCAA Chp 1949
Reg	North and South Amateur 1948
Int	Walker Cup 1953-55-59

Watson, Tom
Born Kansas City, Missouri, USA on 4th September, 1949. Turned Professional 1971

Maj	Open Champion 1975-77-80-82-83, r/u 1984; US Open 1982, r/u 1983-87, 3rd 1980; USPGA r/u 1978; US Masters 1977-81, r/u 1978-79-84, 3rd 1991
US	33 wins: 1974-one, 1975-one, 1977-three, 1978-five, 1979-five, 1980-five, 1981-four, 1982-two, 1984-three, 1987-one, 1996-one , 1998-one (MasterCard Colonial). World Series 1975-80
RoW	Phoenix Open (Jpn) 1980; Hong Kong Open 1992; Dunlop Phoenix (Jpn) 1997
Int	Ryder Cup 1977-81-83-89-(93); *v* Japan 1982-84

Mis Vardon Trophy 1977-78-79; leading money winner 1977-78-79-80-84; USPGA Player of the Year 1977-78-79-80-82-84; Bobby Jones Award 1986; World Golf Hall of Fame 1988; William Richardson Award 1991; Old Tom Morris Award 1991

Webb, Karrie
Born Ayr, Queensland on 21st December, 1974. Turned Professional 1994
PROFESSIONAL
Maj British Women's Open 1995-97
US HealthSouth Inaugural, Sprint Titleholders Chp, Safeco Classic 1996; Komen International, Safeco Classic 1997; Australian Ladies Masters, City of Hope Myrtle Beach Classic 1998
Int Nichirei International 1996
Mis Rookie of the Year 1995; Gatorade Rookie of the Year 1996; Mickey Wright Award 1996; Vare Trophy 1997
AMATEUR
Nat Australian Stroke Play 1994
Oth Queensland, New South Wales and Victoria Stroke Play 1994

Weiskopf, Tom
Born Massillon, Ohio, USA on 9th November, 1942. Turned Professional 1964
Maj Open Champion 1973; US Open r/u 1976; 3rd 1973-77; USPGA 3rd 1975; US Masters r/u 1969-72-74-75
Eur Piccadilly World Match Play 1972
US 1968-two, 1971-two, 1972-one, 1973-three, 1975-one, 1977-one, 1978-one, 1982-one; World Series 1973; Canadian Open 1973-75
RoW South African PGA 1973; Argentine Open 1979
Sen US Tour Franklin Quest Chp 1994; US Seniors Open 1995; SBC Dominion Seniors, Pittsburgh Senior Classic 1996
Int Ryder Cup 1973-75; USA in World Cup 1972

Welts, Anne *See* Sander

Whitworth, Kathy
Born Monahans, Texas, USA on 27th September, 1939. Turned Professional 1959
Maj Titleholder's Chp 1965-66; Western Open 1967; US Open r/u 1971; USLPGA 1967-71-75, r/u 1968-70
US 88 LPGA wins 1962-85
Int Solheim Cup (**1990**)-(**92**)
Mis Rolex Player of the Year 1966-67-68-69-71-72-73. Vare Trophy 1965-66-67-69-70-71-72. William Richardson Award 1986; Woman Athlete of the Year 1965-66; LPGA Hall of Fame; World Golf Hall of Fame 1982; Powell Award 1986; Patty Berg Award 1987

Woods, Eldrick 'Tiger'
Born Cypress, CA, USA on 30th December, 1975. Turned Professional 1996
PROFESSIONAL
Maj US Masters 1997
Eur Johnnie Walker Classic 1998
US Las Vegas Invitational, Walt Disney World/Oldsmobile Classic 1996; Mercedes Chp, Byron Nelson Classic, Motorola Western Open 1997; BellSouth Classic 1998
Int Ryder Cup 1997; Dunhill Cup 1998; President's Cup 1998
Mis Rolex Player of the Year 1996; USPGA Player of the Year 1997; World Ranking No 1 1998
AMATEUR
Nat US amateur 1994-95-96
Reg Western amateur, Pacific North West amateur 1994
Int Walker Cup 1995; Eisenhower Trophy 1994
Jun USGA Junior National Chp 1991-92-93
Jun Int Rolex Junior All American 1990-91-92-93
Mis Nine holes in 48 at age 3; won Junior World Trns in 1984-85-88-89; *Golf Digest* Player of the Year 1991-92; *Golf World* Player of the Year 1993. Entered Stanford University 1994

Wright, Mary Kathryn (Mickey)
Born San Diego, California, USA on 14th February, 1935. Turned Professional 1954
Maj US Open 1958-59-61-64, r/u 1968, leading amateur 1954; USLPGA 1958-60-61-63, r/u 1964-66; Titleholders Chp 1961-62; Western Open 1962-63-66
US 82 LPGA wins 1956-73 (13 wins in 1963)
Mis Leading money winner 1961-62-63-64; Vare Trophy 1960-61-62-63-64; LPGA Hall of Fame 1964; World Golf Hall of Fame 1976; Woman Athlete of the Year 1963-64

Yates, Charles Richard
Born Atlanta, Georgia, USA on 9th September, 1913
Maj US Masters leading amateur 1934-39-40
Chp Amateur Champion 1938
Reg Western Amateur 1935.
Int Walker Cup 1936-38-(**53**)
Mis Bobby Jones Award 1980

Zoeller, Frank Urban (Fuzzy)
Born New Albany, Indiana, USA on 11th November, 1951. Turned Professional 1973
Maj US Open 1984, 3rd 1994; USPGA r/u 1981; US Masters 1979
US 1979-two, 1983-two, 1985-one, 1986-three
Int Ryder Cup 1979-83-85
Mis Bobby Jones Award 1985. Ben Hogan Award 1986

For list of abbreviations see page 350

British Isles International Players, Professional Men

Captaincy is indicated by the year printed in bold type

Adams, J
(Scotland): v England 1932-33-34-35-36-37-38; v Wales 1937-38; v Ireland 1937-38. (GBI): Ryder Cup 1947-49-51-53

Affleck, P
(Wales): Dunhill Cup 1995-96

Ainslie, T
(Scotland): v Ireland 1936

Alliss, Percy
(England): v Scotland 1932-33-34-35-36-37; v Ireland 1932-38; v Wales 1938. (GBI): v France 1929; Ryder Cup 1929-31-33-35-37

Alliss, Peter
(England): Canada Cup 1954-55-57-58-59-61-62-64-66; World Cup 1967. (GBI): Ryder Cup 1953-57-59-61-63-65-67-69

Anderson, Joe
(Scotland): v Ireland 1932

Anderson, W
(Scotland): v Ireland 1936; v England 1937; v Wales 1937

Ayton, LB
(Scotland): v England 1910-12-13-33-34

Ayton, JB, jr
(Scotland): v England 1937. (GBI): Ryder Cup 1949

Baker, P
(England): Dunhill Cup 1993 (r/u)-98. (Eur): Ryder Cup 1993

Ballantine, J
(Scotland): v England 1932-36

Ballingall, J
(Scotland): v England 1938; Ireland 1938; v Wales 1938

Bamford, BJ
(England): Canada Cup 1961

Bannerman, H
(Scotland): World Cup 1967-72. (GBI): Ryder Cup 1971

Barber, T
(England): v Ireland 1932-33

Barnes, BW
(Scotland): World Cup 1974-75-76-77. (GBI): Ryder Cup 1969-71-73-75-77-79; v Europe 1974-76-78-80; v South Africa 1976

Batley, JB
(England): v Scotland 1912

Beck, AG
(England): v Wales 1938; v Ireland 1938

Bembridge, M
(England): World Cup 1974-75. (GBI): Ryder Cup 1969-71-73-75; v South Africa 1976. (Sen) European Cup 1997

Boomer, A
(England): (GBI): v America 1926; Ryder Cup 1927-29

Bousfield, K
(England): Canada Cup 1956-57. (GBI): Ryder Cup 1949-51-55-57-59-61

Boxall, R
(England): Dunhill Cup 1990; World Cup 1990

Boyle, HF
(Ireland): World Cup 1967. (GBI): Ryder Cup 1967

Bradshaw, H
(Ireland): Canada Cup 1954-55-57-58-59; v Scotland 1937-38; v Wales 1937; v England 1938. (GBI): Ryder Cup 1953-55-57

Braid, J
(Scotland): v England 1903-04-05-06-07-09-10-12. (GBI): v America 1921

Branch, WJ
(England): v Scotland 1936

Brand, G, jr
(Scotland): World Cup 1984-85-88-89-90-92-94; Dunhill Cup 1985-86-87-88-89-91-92-93-94-97; (Eur): Nissan Cup 1985; Kirin Cup 1988; Four Tours World Chp 1989; (GBI): Ryder Cup 1987-89; v Australia 1988

Brand, GJ
(England): World Cup 1983; Dunhill Cup 1986-87 (winners). (GBI): Ryder Cup 1983; (Eur) Nissan Cup 1986

Broadhurst, P
(England): Dunhill Cup 1991; World Cup 1997. (Eur) Ryder Cup 1991; Four Tours World Chp 1991-95

Brown, EC
(Scotland): Canada Cup 1954-55-56-57-58-59-60-61-62-65-66; World Cup 1987-68. (GBI): Ryder Cup 1953-55-57-59

Brown, K
(Scotland): World Cup 1977-78-79-83. (GBI): Ryder Cup 1977-79-83-85-87; v Europe 1978; (Eur) Kirin Cup 1987

Burns, S
(Scotland): v England 1932. (GBI): Ryder Cup 1929

Burton, J
(England): v Ireland 1933

Burton, R
(England): v Scotland 1935-36-37-38; v Ireland 1938; v Wales 1938. (GBI): Ryder Cup 1935-37-49

Busson, JH
(England): v Scotland 1938

Busson, JJ
(England): *v* Scotland 1934-35-36-37. (GBI): Ryder Cup 1935

Butler, PJ
(England): World Cup 1969-70-73. (GBI): Ryder Cup 1965-69-71-73; *v* Europe 1976

Callum, WS
(Scotland): *v* Ireland 1935

Campbell, J
(Scotland): *v* Ireland 1936

Carrol, LJ
(Ireland): *v* Scotland 1937-38; *v* Wales 1937; *v* England 1938

Carter, D
(England): Dunhill Cup 1998; World Cup 1998 (winners)

Cassidy, D
(Ireland): *v* Scotland 1936-37; *v* Wales 1937

Cassidy, J
(Ireland): *v* England 1933; *v* Scotland 1934-35

Cawsey, GH
(England): *v* Scotland 1906-07

Caygill, GA
(England): (GBI): Ryder Cup 1969

Clark, C
(England): (GBI): Ryder Cup 1973

Clark, HK
(England): World Cup 1978-84-85-87; Dunhill Cup 1985-86-87 (winners)-89-90(r/u)-94-95. (GBI): Ryder Cup 1977-81-85-87-89-95; *v* Australia 1988; *v* Europe 1978-84. (Eur): Nissan Cup 1985

Clarke, D
(Ireland): Dunhill Cup 1994-95-96-97-98; World Cup 1994-95-96. (GBI): Ryder Cup 1997

Claydon, R
(England): Dunhill Cup 1997

Coles, NC
(England): Canada Cup 1963; World Cup 1968. (GBI): Ryder Cup 1961-63-65-67-69-71-73-77; *v* Europe 1974-76-78-80

Collinge, T
(England): *v* Scotland 1937

Collins, JF
(England): *v* Scotland 1903-04

Coltart, A
(Scotland): Dunhill Cup 1994-95 (winners) -96-98; World Cup 1994-95-96-98

Coltart, F
(Scotland): *v* England 1909

Compston, A
(England): *v* Scotland 1932-35; *v* Ireland 1932. (GBI): *v* America 1926, Ryder Cup 1927-29-31; *v* France 1929

Cotton, TH
(England): (GBI): Ryder Cup 1929-37-47; *v* France 1929

Cox, S
(Wales): World Cup 1975

Cox, WJ
(England): *v* Scotland 1935-36-37. (GBI): Ryder Cup 1935-37

Curtis, D
(England): *v* Scotland 1934-38; *v* Ireland 1938; *v* Wales 1938

Dabson, K
(Wales): World Cup 1972

Dailey, A
(Scotland): *v* England 1932-33-34-35-36-38; *v* Ireland 1938; *v* Wales 1938. (GBI): Ryder Cup 1933

Daly, F
(Ireland): *v* Scotland 1936-37-38; *v* England 1938; *v* Wales 1937; Canada Cup 1954-55. (GBI): Ryder Cup 1947-49-51-53

Darcy, E
(Ireland): World Cup 1976-77-83-84-85-87; Dunhill Cup 1987-88(winners) -91. (GBI): Ryder Cup 1975-77-81-87; *v* Europe 1976-84; *v* South Africa 1976

Davies, R
(Wales): World Cup 1968

Davies, WH
(England): *v* Scotland 1932-33; *v* Ireland 1932-33. (GBI): Ryder Cup 1931-33

Davis, W
(Scotland): *v* Ireland 1933-34-35-36-37-38; *v* England 1937-38; *v* Wales 1937-38

Dawson, P
(England): World Cup 1977. (GBI): Ryder Cup 1977

De Foy, CB
(Wales): World Cup 1971-73-74-75-76-77-78

Denny, CS
(England): *v* Scotland 1936

Dobson, T
(Scotland): *v* England 1932-33-34-35-36-37; *v* Ireland 1932-33-34-35-36-37-38; *v* Wales 1937-38

Don, W
(Scotland): *v* Ireland 1935-36

Donaldson, J
(Scotland): *v* England 1932-35-38; *v* Ireland 1937; *v* Wales 1937

Dornan, R
(Scotland): *v* Ireland 1932

Drew, NV
(Ireland): Canada Cup 1960-61. (GBI): Ryder Cup 1959

Duncan, G
(Scotland): *v* England 1906-07-09-10-12-13-32-34-35-36-37. (GBI): *v* America 1921-26, Ryder Cup 1927-29-31

Durnian, D
(England): World Cup 1989; Dunhill Cup 1989

Durward, JG
(Scotland): *v* Ireland 1934; *v* England 1937

Easterbrook, S
(England): *v* Scotland 1932-33-34-35-38; *v* Ireland 1933. (GBI): Ryder Cup 1931-33

Edgar, J
(Ireland): *v* Scotland 1938

Fairweather, S
(Ireland): *v* England 1932; *v* Scotland 1933. (Scotland): *v* England 1933-35-36; *v* Ireland 1938; *v* Wales 1938

Faldo, NA
(England): World Cup 1977-91-98 (winners); Dunhill Cup 1985-86-87 (winners) -88-91-93 (r/u). (GBI): Ryder Cup 1977-79-81-83-85-87-89-91-93-95-97; *v* Europe 1978-80-82-84; *v* Rest of World 1982. (Eur) Nissan Cup 1986. Kirin Cup 1987; Four Tours World Chp 1990

Fallon, J
(Scotland): *v* England 1936-37-38; *v* Ireland 1937-38; *v* Wales 1937-38. (GBI): Ryder Cup 1955

Faulkner, M
(England): (GBI): Ryder Cup 1947-49-51-53-57

Feherty, D
(Ireland): World Cup 1990; Dunhill Cup 1985-86-90(winners) -91-93; (Eur): Ryder Cup 1991; Four Tours World Chp 1990-91

Fenton, WB
(Scotland): *v* England 1932; *v* Ireland 1932-33

Fernie, TR
(Scotland): v England 1910-12-13-33

Foster, M
(England): World Cup 1976. (GBI): v Europe 1976

Gadd, B
(England): v Scotland 1933-35-38; v Ireland 1933-38; v Wales 1938

Gadd, G
(England): (GBI): v America 1926, Ryder Cup 1927

Gallacher, BJ
(Scotland): World Cup 1969-71-74-82-83. (GBI): Ryder Cup 1969-71-73-75-77-79-81-83-**91-93-95**; v Europe 1974-78-82-84; v South Africa 1976; v Rest of World 1982

Garner, JR
(England): (GBI): Ryder Cup 1971-73

Gaudin, PJ
(England): v Scotland 1905-06-07-09-12-13

Gilford, D
(England): World Cup 1992-93; Dunhill Cup 1992(winners); (Eur): Ryder Cup 1991-95

Good, G
(Scotland): v England 1934-36

Gould, H
(Wales): Canada Cup 1954-55

Gow, A
(Scotland): v England 1912

Grabham, C
(Wales): v England 1938; v Scotland 1938

Grant, T
(Scotland): v England 1913

Gray, E
(England): v Scotland 1904-05-07

Green, E
(England): (GBI): Ryder Cup 1947

Green, T
(England): v Scotland 1935. (Wales): v Scotland 1937-38; v Ireland 1937; v England 1938

Greene, C
(Ireland): Canada Cup 1965

Gregson, M
(England): World Cup 1967. (GBI): Ryder Cup 1967. (Sen) European Cup 1997

Haliburton, TB
(Scotland): v Ireland 1935-36-38; v England 1938; v Wales 1938; Canada Cup 1954. (GBI): Ryder Cup 1961-63

Hamill, J
(Ireland): v Scotland 1933-34-35; v England 1932-33

Hargreaves, J
(England): (GBI): Ryder Cup 1951

Harrington, P
(Ireland): Dunhill Cup 1996-97-98; World Cup 1996-97 (winners)-98

Hastings, W
(Scotland): England 1937-38; v Wales 1937-38; v Ireland 1937-38

Havers, AG
(England): v Scotland 1932-33-34; v Ireland 1932-33. (GBI): v America 1921-26, Ryder Cup 1927-31-33; v France 1929

Healing, SF
(Wales): v Scotland 1938

Hepburn, J
(Scotland): v England 1903-05-06-07-09-10-12-13

Herd, A
(Scotland): v England 1903-04-05-06-09-10-12-13-32

Hill, EF
(Wales): v Scotland 1937-38; v Ireland 1937; v England 1938

Hitchcock, J
(England): (GBI): Ryder Cup 1965

Hodson, B
(England): v Ireland 1933. (Wales): v Scotland 1937-38;v Ireland 1937; v England 1938. (GBI): Ryder Cup 1931

Holley, W
(Ireland): v Scotland 1933-34-35-36-38; v England 1932-33-38

Horne, R
(England): (GBI): Ryder Cup 1947

Horton, T
(England): World Cup 1976. (GBI): v Europe 1974-76; Ryder Cup 1975-77. (Sen) European Cup 1997

Houston, D
(Scotland): v Ireland 1934

Huggett, BGC
(Wales): Canada Cup 1963-64-65; World Cup 1968-69-70-71-76-79. (GBI): Ryder Cup 1963-67-69-71-73-75; v Europe 1974-78

Huish, D
(Scotland): World Cup 1973

Hunt, BJ
(England): Canada Cup 1958-59-60-62-63-64; World Cup 1968. (GBI): Ryder Cup 1953-57-59-61-63-65-67-69

Hunt, GL
(England): World Cup 1972-75. (GBI): v Europe 1974; Ryder Cup 1975

Hunt, Geoffrey M
(England): (GBI): Ryder Cup 1963

Hunter, W
(Scotland): v England 1906-07-09-10

Hutton, GC
(Scotland): v Ireland 1936-37; v England 1937-38; v Wales 1937

Ingram, D
(Scotland): World Cup 1973

Jacklin, A
(England): Canada Cup 1966; World Cup 1970-71-72. (GBI): Ryder Cup 1967-69-71-73-75-77-79-**83-85-87-89**; v Europe 1976-82; v Rest of World 1982

Jackson, H
(Ireland): World Cup 1970-71

Jacobs, JRM
(England): (GBI): Ryder Cup 1955

Jagger, D
(England): (GBI): v Europe 1976

James, G
(Wales): v Scotland 1937; v Ireland 1937

James, MH
(England): World Cup 1978-79-82-84-87-88-93-97; Dunhill Cup 1988-89-90(r/u)-93(r/u)-95-97. (GBI): Ryder Cup 1977-79-81-89-91-93-95; v Europe 1978-80-82; v Rest of World 1982; v Australia 1988; (Eur): Kirin Cup 1988; Four Tours World Chp 1989-90

Jarman, EW
(England): v Scotland 1935. (GBI): Ryder Cup 1935

Job, N
(England): (GBI): v Europe 1980

Jolly, HC
(England): (GBI): v America 1926, Ryder Cup 1927; v France 1929

Jones, DC
(Wales): v Scotland 1937-38; v Ireland 1937; v England 1938

Jones, E
(Ireland): Canada Cup 1965

Jones, R
(England): v Scotland 1903-04-05-06-07-09-10-12-13

Jones, T
(Wales): v Scotland 1936; v Ireland 1937; v England 1938

Kenyon, EWH
(England): v Scotland 1932; v Ireland 1932

King, M
(England): World Cup 1979. (GBI): Ryder Cup 1979

King, SL
(England): v Scotland 1934-36-37-38; v Wales 1938; v Ireland 1938. (GBI): Ryder Cup 1937-47-49

Kinsella, J
(Ireland): World Cup 1968-69-72-73

Kinsella, W
(Ireland): v Scotland 1937-38; v England 1938

Knight, G
(Scotland): v England 1937

Lacey, AJ
(England): v Scotland 1932-33-34-36-37-38; v Ireland 1932-33-38; v Wales 1938. (GBI): Ryder Cup 1933-37

Laidlaw, W
(Scotland): v England 1935-36-38; v Ireland 1937; v Wales 1937

Lane, B
(England): World Cup 1988-94; Dunhill Cup 1988-94-95-96. (Eur): Ryder Cup 1993

Lawrie, P
(Scotland): World Cup 1996

Lees, A
(England): v Scotland 1938; v Wales 1938; v Ireland 1938. (GBI): Ryder Cup 1947-49-51-55

Llewellyn, D
(Wales): World Cup 1974-85-87 (winners)-88; Dunhill Cup 1985-88. (GBI): v Europe 1984

Lloyd, F
(Wales): v Scotland 1937-38; v Ireland 1937; v England 1938

Lockhart, G
(Scotland): v Ireland 1934-35

Lomas, J
(England): Dunhill Cup 1996

Lyle, AWB
(Scotland): World Cup 1979-80-87; Dunhill Cup 1985-86-87-88-89-90-92. (GBI): Ryder Cup 1979-81-83-85-87; v Europe 1980-82-84; v Rest of World 1982; v Australia 1988. (Eur): Nissan Cup 1985-86; Kirin Cup 1987.

McCartney, J
(Ireland): v Scotland 1932-33-34-35-36-37-38; v England 1932-33-38; v Wales 1937

McCulloch, D
(Scotland): v England 1932-33-34-35-36-37; v Ireland 1932-33-34-35

McDermott, M
(Ireland): v England 1932; v Scotland 1932

McDowall, J
(Scotland): v England 1932-33-34-35-36; v Ireland 1933-34-35-36

McEwan, P
(Scotland): v England 1907

McGinley, P
(Ireland): Dunhill Cup 1993-94-96-97-98; World Cup 1993-94-97(winners)-98

McIntosh, G
(Scotland): v England 1938; v Ireland 1938; v Wales 1938

McKenna, J
(Ireland): v Scotland 1936-37-38; v Wales 1937-38; v England 1938

McKenna, R
(Ireland): v Scotland 1933-35; v England 1933

McMillan, J
(Scotland): v England 1933-34-35; v Ireland 1933-34

McMinn, W
(Scotland): v England 1932-33-34

McNeill, H
(Ireland): v England 1932

Mahon, PJ
(Ireland): v Scotland 1932-33-34-35-36-37-38; v Wales 1937-38; v England 1932-33-38

Martin, J
(Ireland): Canada Cup 1962-63-64-66; World Cup 1970. (GBI): Ryder Cup 1965

Martin, S
(Scotland): World Cup 1980

Mason, SC
(England): World Cup 1980. (GBI): v Europe 1980

Mayo, CH
(England): v Scotland 1907-09-10-12-13

Mayo, P
(Wales): Dunhill Cup 1993

Mills, RP
(England): (GBI): Ryder Cup 1957

Mitchell, A
(England): v Scotland 1932-33-34. (GBI): v America 1921-26, Ryder Cup 1929-31-33

Mitchell, P
(England): World Cup 1996

Moffitt, R
(England): (GBI): Ryder Cup 1961

Montgomerie, C
(Scotland): World Cup 1988-91-92-93-97(individual winner)-98; Dunhill Cup 1988-91-92-93-94-95(winners)-96-97-98. (Eur): Ryder Cup 1991-93-95-97; Four Tours World Chp 1991

Mouland, M
(Wales): World Cup 1988-89-90-92-93-95-96; Dunhill Cup 1986-87-88-89-93-95-96. (Eur): Kirin Cup 1988.

Mouland, S
(Wales): Canada Cup 1965-66; World Cup 1967

O'Brien, W
(Ireland): v Scotland 1934-36-37; v Wales 1937

Ockenden, J
(England): (GBI): v America 1921

O'Connor, C
(Ireland): Canada Cup 1956-57-58-59-60-61-62-63-64-66; World Cup 1967-68-69-71-73. (GBI): Ryder Cup 1955-57-59-61-63-65-67-69-71-73

O'Connor, C, jr
(Ireland): World Cup 1974-75-78-85-89-92; Dunhill Cup 1985-89-92. (GBI): Ryder Cup 1975-89; v Europe 1974-84; v South Africa 1976

O'Connor, P
(Ireland): v Scotland 1932-33-34-35-36; v England 1932-33

Oke, WG
(England): v Scotland 1932

O'Leary, JE
(Ireland): World Cup 1972-80-82. (GBI): Ryder Cup 1975; v Europe 1976-78-82; v Rest of World 1982

O'Neill, J
(Ireland): *v* England 1933

O'Neill, M
(Ireland): *v* Scotland 1933-34; *v* England 1933

Oosterhuis, PA
(England): World Cup 1971. (GBI): Ryder Cup 1971-73-75-77-79-81; *v* Europe 1974

Orr, G
(Scotland): Dunhill Cup 1998

Padgham, AH
(England): *v* Scotland 1932-33-34-35-36-37-38; *v* Ireland 1932-33-38; *v* Wales 1938. (GBI): Ryder Cup 1933-35-37

Panton, J
(Scotland): Canada Cup 1955-56-57-58-59-60-61-62-63-64-65-66; World Cup 1968. (GBI): Ryder Cup 1951-53-61

Park, J
(Scotland): *v* England 1909

Parkin, P
(Wales): World Cup 1984-89; Dunhill Cup 1985-86-87-89-90-91. (GBI): *v* Europe 1984

Patterson, E
(Ireland): *v* Scotland 1933-34-35-36; *v* England 1933; *v* Wales 1937

Payne, J
(England): World Cup 1996

Perry, A
(England); *v* Ireland 1932; *v* Scotland 1933-36-38. (GBI): Ryder Cup 1933-35-37

Pickett, C
(Wales): *v* Scotland 1937-38; *v* Ireland 1937; *v* England 1938

Platts, L
(Wales): (GBI): Ryder Cup 1965

Polland, E
(Ireland): World Cup 1973-74-76-77-78-79. (GBI): Ryder Cup 1973; *v* Europe 1974-76-78-80; *v* South Ryder Cup 1976

Pope, CW
(Ireland): *v* England 1932; *v* Scotland 1932

Price, P
(Wales): Dunhill Cup 1991-96; World Cup 1994-95-97-98

Rafferty, R
(Ireland): World Cup 1983-84-87-88-90-91-92-93; Dunhill Cup 1986-87-88(winners)-89-90(winners)-91-92-93-95. (GBI): *v* Europe 1984; *v* Australia 1988. (Eur): Ryder Cup 1989; Kirin Cup 1988; Four Tours World Chp 1989-90-91

Rainford, P
(England): *v* Scotland 1903-07

Ray, E
(England): *v* Scotland 1903-04-05-06-07-09-10-12-13. (GBI): *v* America 1921-26, Ryder Cup 1927

Rees, DJ
(Wales): *v* Scotland 1937-38; *v* Ireland 1937; England 1938; Canada Cup 1954-56-57-58-59-60-61-62-64. (GBI): Ryder Cup 1937-47-49-51-53-55-57-59-61

Reid, W
(England): *v* Scotland 1906-07

Renouf, TG
(England): *v* Scotland 1903-04-05-10-13

Richardson, S
(England): Dunhill Cup 1991-92(winners); World Cup 1992. (Eur): Ryder Cup 1991; Four Tours World Chp 1991

Ritchie, WL
(Scotland): *v* England 1913

Robertson, F
(Scotland): *v* Ireland 1933; *v* England 1938

Robertson, P
(Scotland): *v* England 1932; *v* Ireland 1932-34

Robson, F
(England): *v* Scotland 1909-10. (GBI): *v* America 1926, Ryder Cup 1927-29-31

Roe, M
(England): World Cup 1989-94-95; Dunhill Cup 1994

Rowe, AJ
(England): *v* Scotland 1903-06-07

Russell, R
(Scotland): Dunhill Cup 1996-97; World Cup 1997

Sayers, B, jr
(Scotland): *v* England 1906-07-09

Scott, SS
(England): (GBI): Ryder Cup 1955

Seymour, M
(England): *v* Scotland 1932-33; *v* Ireland 1932-33. (Scotland): *v* Ireland 1932

Shade, RDBM
(Scotland): World Cup 1970-71-72

Sherlock, JG
(England): *v* Scotland 1903-04-05-06-07-09-10-12-13. (GBI): *v* America 1921

Simpson, A
(Scotland): *v* England 1904

Smalldon, D
(Wales): Canada Cup 1955-56

Smith, CR
(Scotland): *v* England 1903-04-07-09-13

Smith, GE
(Scotland): *v* Ireland 1932

Smyth, D
(Ireland): World Cup 1979-80-82-83-88-89; Dunhill Cup 1985-86-87-88 (winners). (GBI): Ryder Cup 1979-81; *v* Europe 1980-82-84; *v* Rest of World 1982

Snell, D
(England): Canada Cup 1965

Spark, W
(Scotland): *v* Ireland 1933-35-37; *v* England 1935; *v* Wales 1937

Spence, J
(England): Dunhill Cup 1992 (winners)

Stevenson, P
(Ireland): *v* Scotland 1933-34-35-36-38; *v* England 1933-38

Sutton, M
(England): Canada Cup 1955

Taylor, JH
(England): *v* Scotland 1903-04-05-06-07-09-10-12-13 (GBI): *v* America 1921

Taylor, JJ
(England): *v* Scotland 1937

Taylor, Josh
(England): *v* Scotland 1913. (GBI): *v* America 1921

Thomas, DC
(Wales): Canada Cup 1957-58-59-60-61-62-63-66; World Cup 1967-69-70. (GBI): Ryder Cup 1959-63-65-67

Thompson, R
(Scotland): *v* England 1903-04-05-06-07-09-10-12

Tingey, A
(England): *v* Scotland 1903-05

Torrance, S
(Scotland): World Cup 1976-78-82-84-85-87-89-90-93-95; Dunhill

Cup 1985-86-87-89-90-91-93-95 (winners). (GBI): *v* Europe 1976-78-80-82-84; Ryder Cup 1981-83-85-87-89-91-93-95; *v* Rest of World 1982. (Eur): Nissan Cup 1985; Four Tours World Chp 1991

Townsend, P
(England): World Cup 1969-74. (GBI): Ryder Cup 1969-71; *v* Europe 1974

Twine, WT
(England): *v* Ireland 1932

Vardon, H
(England): (GBI): *v* America 1921

Vaughan, DI
(Wales): World Cup 1972-73-77-78-79-80

Waites, BJ
(England): World Cup 1980-82-83. (GBI): *v* Europe 1980-82-84; *v* Rest of World 1982; Ryder Cup 1983. (Sen) European Cup 1997

Walker, RT
(Scotland): Canada Cup 1964

Wallace, L
(Ireland): *v* England 1932; *v* Scotland 1932

Walton P
(Ireland): Dunhill Cup 1989-90 (winners)-92-94-95; World Cup 1995. (Eur): Ryder Cup 1995

Ward, CH
(England): *v* Ireland 1932. (GBI): Ryder Cup 1947-49-51

Watt, T
(Scotland): *v* England 1907

Watt, W
(Scotland): *v* England 1912-13

Way, P
(England): Dunhill Cup 1985; World Cup 1985. (GBI): Ryder Cup 1983-85

Weetman, H
(England): Canada Cup 1954-56-60. (GBI): Ryder Cup 1951-53-55-57-59-61-63

Westwood, L
(England): Dunhill Cup 1996-97-98. (GBI): Ryder Cup 1997

Whitcombe, CA
(England): *v* Scotland 1932-33-34-35-36-37-38; *v* Ireland 1933. (GBI): Ryder Cup 1927-29-31-33-35-37; *v* France 1929

Whitcombe, EE
(England): *v* Scotland 1938; *v* Wales 1938; *v* Ireland 1938

Whitcombe, ER
(England): *v* Scotland 1932; *v* Ireland 1933. (GBI): *v* America 1926, Ryder Cup 1929-31-35; *v* France 1929

Whitcombe, RA
(England): *v* Scotland 1933-34-35-36-37-38. (GBI): Ryder Cup 1935

White, J
(Scotland): *v* England 1903-04-05-06-07-09-12-13

Wilcock, P
(England): World Cup 1973

Will, G
(Scotland): Canada Cup 1963; World Cup 1969-70. (GBI): Ryder Cup 1963-65-67

Williams, K
(Wales): *v* Scotland 1937-38; *v* Ireland 1937; *v* England 1938

Williamson, T
(England): *v* Scotland 1904-05-06-07-09-10-12-13

Wilson, RG
(England): *v* Scotland 1913

Wilson, T
(Scotland): *v* England 1933-34; *v* Ireland 1932-33-34

Wolstenholme, GB
(England): Canada Cup 1965

Wood, N
(Scotland): World Cup 1975. (GBI): Ryder Cup 1975

Woosnam, I
(Wales): World Cup 1980-82-83-84-85-87 (winners)-90-91-92-93-94-96-97-98; Dunhill Cup 1985-86-87-88-89-90-91-93-95. (GBI): *v* Europe 1982-84; *v* Rest of World 1982. Ryder Cup 1983-85-87-89-91-93-95-97; *v* Australia 1988. (Eur): Nissan Cup 1985-86. Kirin Cup 1987; Four Tours World Chp 1989-90

British Isles International Players, Amateur Men

Abbreviations:

CW — Commonwealth Tournament (Team from UK)
Eur T Ch — played in European Team Championship for home country
Home Int — played in Home International matches

Adams, MPD
(Wales): Home Int 1969-70-71-72-75-76-77; Eur T Ch 1971

Aitken, AR
(Scotland): v England 1906-07-08

Alexander, DW
(Scotland): Home Int 1958; v Scandinavia 1958

Allison, A
(Ireland): v England 1928; v Scotland 1929

Anderson, N
(Ireland): Home Int 1985-86-87-88-89-90-93. Eur T Ch 1989. (GBI): v Europe 1988

Anderson, RB
(Scotland): v Scandinavia 1960-62; Home Int 1962-63

Andrew, R
(Scotland): v England 1905-06-07-08-09-10

Armour, A
(Scotland): v England 1922

Armour, TD
(GBI): v America 1921

Ashby, H
(England): Home Int 1972-73-74. (GBI): Dominican Int 1973. (GBI): v Europe 1974

Atkinson, HN
(Wales): v Ireland 1913

Attenborough, M
(England): Home Int 1964-66-67-68; Eur T Ch 1967. (GBI): Walker Cup 1967; v Europe 1966-68

Aylmer, CC
(England): v Scotland 1911-22-23-24. (GBI): v America 1921, Walker Cup 1922

Babington, A
(Ireland): v Wales 1913

Baker, P
(England): Home Int 1985. (GBI): Walker Cup 1985; v Europe 1986

Baker, RN
(Ireland): Home Int 1975

Ball, J
(England): v Scotland 1902-03-04-05-06-07-08-09-10-11-12

Bamford, JL
(Ireland): Home Int 1954-56

Banks, C
(England): Home Int 1983

Banks, SE
(England): Home Int 1934-38

Bannerman, SJ
(Scotland): Home Int 1988; v Sweden 1990

Bardsley, R
(England): Home Int 1987; v France 1988

Barker, HH
(England): v Scotland 1907

Barnett, A
(Wales): Home Int 1989-90-91; Eur T Chp 1991

Barrie, GC
(Scotland): Home Int 1981-83; v Sweden 1983

Barry, AG
(England): v Scotland 1906-07

Bathgate, D
(England): Home Int 1990

Bayliss, RP
(England): v Ireland 1929; Home Int 1933-34

Bayne, PWGA
(Wales): Home Int 1949

Beames, R
(Scotland): Home Int 1995-96; v Spain 1996; v France, Sweden 1997; (GBI) v Europe 1996

Beamish, CH
(Ireland): Home Int 1950-51-53-56

Beck, JB
(England): v Scotland 1926-30; Home Int 1933. (GBI): Walker Cup 1928-38 (Captain) -47 (Captain)

Beddard, JB
(England): v Wales/Ireland 1925; v Ireland 1929; v Scotland 1927-28-29

Beharrell, JC
(England): Home Int 1956

Bell, HE
(Ireland): v Wales 1930; Home Int 1932

Bell, RK
(England): Home Int 1947

Benka, PJ
(England): Home Int 1967-68-69-70; Eur T Ch 1969. (GBI): Walker Cup 1969; v Europe 1970

Bennett, H
(England): Home Int 1948-49-51

Bennett, S
(England): v Scotland 1979

Bennett, W
(England): Home Int 1992-93-94; v France 1994. (GBI) v Europe 1994; Eisenhower Trophy 1994

Bentley, AL
(England): Home Int 1936-37; v France 1937-39

Bentley, HG
(England): v Ireland 1931; v Scotland 1931. Home Int 1932-33-34-35-36-37-38-47; v France 1934-35-36-37-39-54. (GBI): Walker Cup 1934-36-38

Berry, P
(England): Home Int 1972. (GBI): v Europe 1972

Bevan, RJ
(Wales): Home Int 1964-65-66-67-73-74

Beveridge, HW
(Scotland): v England 1908

Birnie, J
(Scotland): v Ireland 1927

Birtwell, SG
(England): Home Int 1968-70-73

Black, D
(Scotland): Home Int 1966-67

Black, FC
(Scotland): Home Int 1962-64-65-66-68; v Scandinavia 1962; Eur T Ch 1965-67. (GBI): v Europe 1966

Black, GT
(Scotland): Home Int 1952-53; v South Africa 1954

Black, JL
(Wales): Home Int 1932-33-34-35-36

Black, WC
(Scotland): Home Int 1964-65

Blackey, M
(England): v France 1994-96; v Spain 1995; Home Int 1995-96-97; Eur T Ch 1997

Blackwell, EBH
(Scotland): v England 1902-04-05-06-07-09-10-12-23-24-25

Bladon, W
(England): Home Int 1996; (GBI) v Europe 1996

Blair, DA
(Scotland): Home Int 1948-49-51-52-53-55-56-57; v Scandinavia 1956-58-62. (GBI): Walker Cup 1955-61; CW 1954

Blakeman, D
(England): Home Int 1981; v France 1982

Bland, R
(England): Home Int 1994-95; v Spain 1995

Bloice, C
(Scotland): Home Int 1985-86; v France 1985; Eur T Ch 1985; v Italy 1986; v Sweden 1986. (GBI): Walker Cup 1985

Bloxham, JA
(England): Home Int 1966

Blyth, AD
(Scotland): v England 1904

Bonallack, MF
(England): Home Int 1957-58-59-60-61-62-63-64-65-66-67-68-69-70-71-72-73-74; Eur T Ch 1969-71. (GBI): Walker Cup 1957-59-61-63-65-67-**69**-71-73; v Europe 1958-62-64-66-68-70-72; CW 1959-63-67-71; Eisenhower Trophy 1960-62-64-66-68-70-72

Bonnell, DJ
(Wales): Home Int 1949-50-51

Bookless, JT
(Scotland): v England 1930-31; v Ireland 1930; v Wales 1931

Bottomley, S
(England): Home Int 1986

Bourn, TA
(England): v Ireland 1928; v Scotland 1930; Home Int 1933-34; v France 1934. (GBI): v Australia 1934

Bowen, J
(Ireland): Home Int 1961

Bowman, TH
(England): Home Int 1932

Boxall, R
(England): Home Int 1980-81-82; v France 1982

Boyd, HA
(Ireland): v Wales 1913-23

Bradshaw, AS
(England): Home Int 1932

Bradshaw, EI
(England): v Scotland 1979; Eur T Ch 1979

Brady, E
(Ireland): Home Int 1995-98

Braid, HM
(Scotland): v England 1922-23

Bramston, JAT
(England): v Scotland 1902

Brand, GJ
(England): Home Int 1976. (GBI) v Europe 1976

Brand Jr, G
(Scotland): Home Int 1978-80; v England 1979; Eur T Ch 1979; v Italy 1979; v Belgium 1980; v France 1980-81. (GBI): Walker Cup 1979; v Europe 1978-80; Eisenhower Trophy 1978-80

Branigan, D
(Ireland): Home Int 1975-76-77-80-81-82-86; Eur T Ch 1977-81; v West Germany, France, Sweden 1976

Bretherton, CF
(England): v Scotland 1922-23-24-25; v Wales/Ireland 1925

Briscoe, A
(Ireland): v England 1928-29-30-31; v Scotland 1929-30-31; v Wales 1929-30-31; Home Int 1932-33-38

Bristowe, OC
(GBI): Walker Cup 1923-24

Broad, RD
(Wales): v Ireland 1979; Home Int 1980-81-82-84; Eur T Ch 1981

Broadhurst, P
(England): Home Int 1986-87; v France 1988. (GBI) v Europe 1988

Brock, J
(Scotland) v Ireland 1929; Home Int 1932

Brodie, Allan
(Scotland): Home Int 1970-72-73-74-75-76-77-78-80; Eur T Ch 1973-77-79; v England 1979; v Italy 1979; v Belgium 1977; v Spain 1977; v France 1978. (GBI): Walker Cup 1977-79; v Europe 1974-76-78-80; Eisenhower Trophy 1978

Brodie, Andrew
(Scotland): Home Int 1968-69; v Spain 1974

Bromley-Davenport, E
(England): Home Int 1938-51

Brooks, A
(Scotland): Home Int 1968-69; Eur T Ch 1969. (GBI): Walker Cup 1969

Brooks, CJ
(Scotland): Home Int 1984-85; v Sweden 1984-86; v Italy 1986. (GBI): v Europe 1986

Brooks, M
(Scotland): v Austria 1994; Home Int 1995-96; v Spain 1996; v France, Sweden 1997; Eur T Ch 1997. (GBI) Walker Cup 1997; v Europe 1996; Eisenhower Trophy 1996

Brotherston, IR
(Scotland): Home Int 1984-85; v France 1985; Eur T Ch 1985

Brough, S
(England): Home Int 1952-55-59-60; v France 1952-60. (GBI): v Europe 1960

Brown, CT
(Wales): Home Int 1970-71-72-73-74-75-77-78-80-**88**; Eur T Ch 1973; v Denmark 1977-80; v Ireland 1979; v Switzerland, Spain 1980; (GBI) v Walker Cup **1995**; v Europe **1996**

Brown, D
(Wales): v Ireland 1923-30-31; v England 1925; v Scotland 1931

Brown, JC
(Ireland): Home Int 1933-34-35-36-37-38-48-52-53

Brownlow, Hon WGE
(GBI): Walker Cup 1926

Bruen, J
(Ireland): Home Int 1937-38-49-50. (GBI): Walker Cup 1938-49-51

Bryson, WS
(Scotland): Home Int 1991-92-93; v Sweden 1992; v Italy 1992; v France 1993; v Spain 1994

Bucher, AMM
(Scotland): Home Int 1954-55-56; v Scandinavia 1956

Buckley, JA
(Wales): Home Int 1967-68-69-76-77-78; Eur T Ch 1967-69; v Denmark 1976-77. (GBI): Walker Cup 1979

Burch, N
(England): Home Int 1974

Burgess, MJ
(England): Home Int 1963-64-67; Eur T Ch 1967

Burke, J
(Ireland): v England 1929-30-31; v Wales 1929-30-31; v Scotland 1930-31; Home Int 1932-33-34-35-36-37-38-47-48-49. (GBI): Walker Cup 1932

Burns, M
(Ireland): Home Int 1973-75-83

Burns, R
(Ireland): Home Int 1991-92. (GBI): Walker Cup 1993; v Europe 1992; Eisenhower Trophy 1992

Burnside, J
(Scotland): Home Int 1956-57

Burrell, TM
(Scotland): v England 1924

Bussell, AF
(Scotland): Home Int 1956-57-58-61; v Scandinavia 1956-60. (GBI): Walker Cup 1957; v Europe 1956-62

Butterworth, JR
(England): v France 1954

Cage, S
(England): Home Int 1992. (GBI): Walker Cup 1993

Cairnes, HM
(Ireland): v Wales 1913-25; v England 1904; v Scotland 1904-27

Cairns, S
(Scotland): Home Int 1997

Caldwell, I
(England): Home Int 1950-51-52-53-54-55-56-57-58-59-61; v France 1950. (GBI): Walker Cup 1951-55

Calvert, M
(Wales): Home Int 1983-84-86-87-89-91

Cameron, D
(Scotland): Home Int 1938-51

Campbell, A
(Wales): Home Int 1996-97

Campbell, Bart, Sir Guy C
(Scotland): v England 1909-10-11

Campbell, HM
(Scotland): Home Int 1962-64-68; v Scandinavia 1962; v Australia 1964; Eur T Ch 1965-**79**. (GBI): v Europe 1964

Campbell, I
(Wales): Home Int 1998

Campbell, JGS
(Scotland): Home Int 1947-48

Campbell, W
(Scotland): v Ireland 1927-28-29-30-31; v England 1928-29-30-31; v Wales 1931; Home Int 1933-34-35-36. (GBI): Walker Cup 1930

Cannon, JHS
(England): v Ireland/Wales 1925

Cannon, JM
(Scotland): Home Int 1969; v Spain 1974

Carman, A
(England): v Scotland 1979; Home Int 1980

Carmichael, S
(Scotland): Home Int 1998

Carr, FC
(England): v Scotland 1911

Carr, JB
(Ireland): Home Int 1947 to 1969; Eur T Ch 1965-67-69. (GBI): Walker Cup 1947-49-51-53-55-57-59-61-63-**65-67**; v Europe 1954-56-64-66-68; Eisenhower Trophy 1958-60

Carr, JJ
(Ireland): Home Int 1981-82-83

Carr, JP
(Wales): v Ireland 1913

Carr, JR
(Ireland): v Wales 1930-31; v England 1931; Home Int 1933

Carr, R
(Ireland): Home Int 1970-71; Eur T Ch 1971; (GBI): Walker Cup 1971

Carrgill, PM
(England): Home Int 1978

Carrick, DG
(Scotland): Home Int 1981 to 1989; v West Germany 1987; v Italy 1984-86-88; v France 1987-89; v Sweden 1983-84-86; Eur T Ch 1987-**89-91**. (GBI): Walker Cup 1983-87; v Europe 1986

Carroll, CA
(Ireland): v Wales 1924

Carroll, JP
(Ireland): Home Int 1948-49-50-51-62

Carroll, W
(Ireland): v Wales 1913-23-24-25; v England 1925; v Scotland 1929; Home Int 1932

Carslaw, IA
(Scotland): Home Int 1976-77-78-80-81; Eur T Ch 1977-79; v England 1979; v Italy 1979; v Spain 1977; v Belgium 1978; v France 1978-83. (GBI): Walker Cup 1979; v Europe 1978

Carver, M
(England): Home Int 1996; Eur T Ch 1997

Carvill, J
(Ireland): Home Int 1989; Eur T Ch 1989. (GBI): v Europe 1990

Cashell, BG
(Ireland): Home Int 1978; v France, West Germany, Sweden 1978

Cassells, C
(England): Home Int 1989

Castle, H
(England): v Scotland 1903-04

Cater, JR
(Scotland): Home Int 1952-53-54-55-56; v South Africa 1954; v Scandinavia 1956. (GBI): Walker Cup 1955

Caul, P
(Ireland): Home Int 1968-69-71-72-73-74-75

Caven, J
(Scotland): *v* England 1926.
(GBI): Walker Cup 1922

Chapman, BHG
(England): Home Int 1961-62.
(GBI): Walker Cup 1961;
v Europe 1962

Chapman, JA
(Wales): *v* Ireland 1923-29-30-31;
v Scotland 1931; *v* England 1925

Chapman, R
(Wales): *v* Ireland 1929; Home Int 1932-34-35-36

Chapman, R
(England): *v* Scotland 1979; Home Int 1980-81; Eur T Ch 1981. (GBI): Walker Cup 1981; *v* Europe 1980

Charles, WB
(Wales): *v* Ireland 1924

Chillas, D
(Scotland): Home Int 1971

Christmas, MJ
(England): Home Int 1960-61-62-63-64. (GBI): Walker Cup 1961-63; *v* Europe 1962-64; Eisenhower Trophy 1962

Clark, CA
(England): Home Int 1964.
(GBI): Walker Cup 1965;
v Europe 1964

Clark, G
(England): Home Int 1995

Clark, GJ
(England): Home Int 1961-64-66-67-68-71. (GBI): Walker Cup 1965; *v* Europe 1964-66

Clark, HK
(England): Home Int 1973.
(GBI): Walker Cup 1973

Clark, MD
(Wales): *v* Ireland 1947

Clarke, D
(Ireland): Home Int 1987-89;
(GBI): *v* Europe 1990

Clay, G
(Wales): Home Int 1962

Claydon, R
(England): Home Int 1988; Eur T Ch 1989: (GBI): Walker Cup 1989

Cleary, T
(Ireland): Home Int 1976-77-78-82-83-84-85-86; *v* Wales 1979; *v* France, West Germany, Sweden 1976

Clement, G
(Wales): *v* Ireland 1979

Cochran, JS
(Scotland): Home Int 1966

Collier, B
(Scotland): Home Int 1994;
v Austria 1994

Colt, HS
(England): *v* Scotland 1908

Coltart, A
(Scotland): Home Int 1988-89-90;
Eur T Ch 1989-91; *v* Sweden 1990;
v Italy 1990; Nixdorf Nations Cup 1990; *v* France 1991. (GBI):
Walker Cup 1991; *v* Europe 1990;
Eisenhower Trophy 1990

Cook, J
(England): Home Int 1989-90

Cook, JH
(England): Home Int 1969

Corcoran, DK
(Ireland): Home Int 1972-73; Eur T Ch 1973

Corridan, T
(Ireland): Home Int 1983-84-91-92

Cosh, GB
(Scotland): Home Int 1964-65-66-67-68-69; Eur T Ch 1965-69 (Captain). (GBI): Walker Cup 1965; *v* Europe 1966-68; CW 1967; Eisenhower Trophy 1966-68

Coughlan, R
(Ireland): Home Int 1991-94. (GBI): Walker Cup 1997; Eur T Ch 1997

Coulter, JG
(Wales): Home Int 1951-52

Coutts, FJ
(Scotland): Home Int 1980-81-82;
Eur T Ch 1981-83; *v* France 1981-82-83

Cox, S
(Wales): Home Int 1970-71-72-73-74; Eur T Ch 1971-73

Crabbe, JL
(Ireland): *v* Wales 1925; *v* Scotland 1927-28

Craddock, T
(Ireland): Home Int 1955-56-57-58-59-60-67-68-69-70; Eur T Ch 1971. (GBI): Walker Cup 1967-69

Craigan, RM
(Ireland): Home Int 1963-64

Crawford, DR
(Scotland): Home Int 1990-91; Eur T Ch 1991; *v* France 1991

Crawley, LG
(England): *v* Ireland 1931;
v Scotland 1931; Home Int 1932-33-34-36-37-38-47-48-49-54-55;
v France 1936-37-38-49.
(GBI): Walker Cup 1932-34-38-47

Critchley, B
(England): Home Int 1962-69-70;
Eur T Ch 1969. (GBI): Walker Cup 1969; *v* Europe 1970

Crosbie, GF
(Ireland): Home Int 1953-55-56-57-**88**

Crowley, M
(Ireland): *v* England 1928-29-30-31;
v Wales l929-31; *v* Scotland 1929-30-31; Home Int 1932

Cuddihy, J
(Scotland): Home Int 1977-78

Curry, DH
(England): Home Int 1984-86-87;
v France 1988. (GBI): Walker Cup 1987; *v* Europe 1986-88;
Eisenhower Trophy 1986

Dalgleish, CR
(Scotland): Home Int 1981-82-83-89-**95**; *v* France 1982; Eur T Ch 1981-83-**93-95**; Nixdorf Nations Cup 1989. (GBI): Walker Cup 1981; *v* Europe 1982

Darwin, B
(England): *v* Scotland 1902-04-05-08-09-10-23-24. (GBI): Walker Cup 1922

Davies, EN
(Wales): Home Int 1959-60-61-62-63-64-65-66-67-68-69-70-71-72-73-74; Eur T Ch 1969-71-73

Davies, FE
(Ireland): *v* Wales 1923

Davies, G
(Wales): *v* Denmark 1977; Home Int 1981-82-83

Davies, HE
(Wales): Home Int 1933-34-36

Davies, JC
(England): Home Int 1969-71-72-73-74-78; Eur T Ch 1973-75-77.
(GBI): Walker Cup 1973-75-77-79;
v Europe 1972-74-76-78;
Eisenhower Trophy 1974-76 (winners)

Davies, M
(England): Home Int 1984-85

Davies, TJ
(Wales): Home Int 1954-55-56-57-58-58-60

Davison, C
(England): Home Int 1989

Dawson, JE
(Scotland): v Ireland 1927-29-30-31; v England 1930-31; v Wales 1931; Home Int 1932-33-34-37

Dawson, M
(Scotland): Home Int 1963-65-66

Dawson, P
(England): Home Int 1969

De Bendern, Count J (John de Forest)
(England): v Scotland, Ireland 1931. (GBI): Walker Cup 1932

Deboys, A
(Scotland): Home Int 1956-59-60; v Scandinavia 1960

Deeble, P
(England): Home Int 1975-76-77-78-80-81-83-84; v France 1982; v Scotland 1979; Eur T Ch 1979-81. (GBI): Walker Cup 1977-81; v Europe 1978; Colombian Int 1978

Deighton, FWG
(Scotland): Home Int 1950-52-53-56-58-59-60; v South Africa 1954; v New Zealand 1954; v Scandinavia 1956. (GBI): Walker Cup 1951-57; CW 1954-59

Denholm, RB
(Scotland): v Ireland 1927-29-31; v Wales 1931; v England 1931; Home Int 1932-33-34

Dewar, FG
(Scotland): Home Int 1952-53-55; v South Africa 1954; Eur T Ch **1971-73**

Dick, CE
(Scotland): v England 1902-03-04-05-09-12

Dickson, HM
(Scotland): v Ireland 1929-31

Dickson, JR
(Ireland): Eur T Ch 1977; Home Int 1980

Dinsdale, R
(Wales): Home Int 1991-92-93

Disley, A
(Wales): Home Int 1976-77-78; v Denmark 1977; v Ireland 1979

Dodd, SC
(Wales):Home Int 1985-87-88-89. (GBI): Walker Cup 1989

Donald, L
(England): Home Int 1996-97-98; v France 1996. (GBI) Eisenhower Trophy 1998 (winners)

Donaldson, J
(Wales): Home Int 1996-97-98; Eur T Ch 1997

Donellan, B
(Ireland): Home Int 1952

Dowie, A
(Scotland): Home Int 1949

Downes, P
(England): Home Int 1976-77-78-80-81-82; Eur T Ch 1977-79-81. (GBI): v Europe 1980

Downie, D
(Scotland): Home Int 1993-94; v Italy 1994; v Spain 1994; v Sweden 1995; v France 1995

Downie, JJ
(England): Home Int 1974

Draper, JW
(Scotland): Home Int 1954

Dredge, B
(Wales): Home Int 1992-93-94-95; Eur T Ch 1995. (GBI): Walker Cup 1993; Eisenhower Trophy 1992; v Europe 1994

Drew, NV
(Ireland): Home Int 1952-53. (GBI): Walker Cup 1953

Drummond, S
(England): Home Int 1995

Duck, R
(England): Home Int 1997

Duffy, I
(Wales): Home Int 1975

Duncan, AA
(Wales): Home Int 1933-34-36-38-47-48-49-50-51-52-53-54-55-56-57-58-59. (GBI): Walker Cup **1953**

Duncan, GT
(Wales): Home Int 1952-53-54-55-56-57-58

Duncan, J, jr
(Wales): v Ireland 1913

Duncan, J
(Ireland): Home Int 1959-60-61

Dundas, S
(Scotland): Home Int 1992-93

Dunn, NW
(England): v Ireland 1928

Dunn, P
(Wales): Home Int 1957-58-59-60-61-62-63-65-66

Dunne, D
(Ireland): Home Int 1997

Dunne, E
(Ireland): Home Int 1973-74-76-77; v Wales 1979; Eur T Ch 1975

Durrant, RA
(England): Home Int 1967; Eur T Ch 1967

Dykes, JM
(Scotland): Home Int 1934-35-36-48-49-51. (GBI): Walker Cup 1936

Dyson, S
(England): Home Int 1998

Easingwood, SR
(Scotland): Home Int 1986-87-88-90; v Italy 1988-90; v France 1987-89; Eur T Ch 1989

Eaves, CH
(Wales): Home Int 1935-36-38-47-48-49

Edwards, B
(Ireland): Home Int 1961-62-64-65-66-67-68-69-73

Edwards, CS
(England): Home Int 1991-92-93-94-95-97-98; v France 1992-94-96; v Spain 1993-95; Eur T Ch 1995

Edwards, M
(Ireland): Home Int 1956-57-58-60-61-62

Edwards, N
(Wales): Home Int 1995-96-97-98; Eur T Ch 1997

Edwards, S
(Wales): Home Int 1992

Edwards, TH
(Wales): Home Int 1947

Egan, TW
(Ireland): Home Int 1952-53-59-60-62-67-68; Eur T Ch 1967-69

Eggo, R
(England): Home Int 1986-87-88-89-90; v France 1988. (GBI): Walker Cup 1987; v Europe 1988

Elliot, A
(Scotland): Home Int 1989; v France 1989; Eur T Ch 1989

Elliot, C
(Scotland): Home Int 1982; v France 1983

Elliot, IA
(Ireland): Home Int 1975-77-78; Eur T Ch 1975, v France, West Germany, Sweden 1978

Ellis, HC
(England): v Scotland 1902-12

Ellis, M
(Wales): Home Int 1992-93-94-95-96; (GBI): v Europe 1996

Ellison, TF
(England): v Scotland 1922-25-26-27

Emerson, T
(Wales): Home Int 1932

Emery, G
(Wales): v Ireland 1925; Home Int 1933-36-38

Errity, D
(Ireland): Home Int 1990

Evans, AD
(Wales): v Scotland 1931-35; v Ireland 1931; Home Int 1932-33-34-35-38-47-49-50-51-52-53-54-55-56-61

Evans, C
(Wales): Home Int 1990-91-92-93-94-95; Eur T Ch 1995

Evans, Duncan
(Wales): Home Int 1978-80-81; v Ireland 1979; Eur T Ch 1981. (GBI) Walker Cup 1981; v Europe 1980

Evans, G
(England): Home Int 1961

Evans, G
(England): Home Int 1990; Eur T Ch 1991. (GBI) Walker Cup 1991; Eisenhower Trophy 1990

Evans, HJ
(Wales): Home Int 1976-77-78-80-81-84-85-87-88; v France 1976; v Denmark 1977-80; v Ireland 1979; Eur T Ch 1979-81; v Switzerland, Spain 1980

Evans, M Gear
(Wales): v Ireland 1930-31; v Scotland 1931

Everett, C
(Scotland): Home Int 1988-89-90; v Italy 1988-90; v France 1988-89-91; Eur T Ch 1989-91; Nixdorf Nations Cup 1989-90; v Sweden 1990

Ewing, RC
(Ireland): Home Int 1934-35-36-37-38-47-48-49-50-51-53-54-55-56-57-58. (GBI) Walker Cup 1936-38-47-49-51-55

Eyles, GR
(England): Home Int 1974-75; Eur T Ch 1975. (GBI) Walker Cup 1975; v Europe 1974; Eisenhower Trophy 1974

Fairbairn, KA
(England): Home Int 1988

Fairchild, CEL
(Wales): v Ireland 1923; v England 1925

Fairchild, LJ
(Wales): v Ireland 1924

Fairlie, WE
(Scotland): v England 1912

Faldo, N
(England): Home Int 1975. (GBI): CW 1975

Fanagan, J
(Ireland): Home Int 1989 to 1997; Eur T Ch 1995-97. (GBI): Walker Cup 1995; v Europe 1992-96

Farmer, A
(Scotland): Home Int 1997

Farmer, JC
(Scotland): Home Int 1970

Fenton, P
(England): Home Int 1996

Ferguson, M
(Ireland): Home Int 1952

Ferguson, WJ
(Ireland): Home Int 1952-54-55-58-59-61

Fergusson, S Mure
(Scotland): v England 1902-03-04

Ferrie, K
(England): Home Int 1998

French, WF
(Ireland): v Scotland 1929; Home Int 1932

Fiddian, EW
(England): v Scotland 1929-30-31; v Ireland 1929-30-31; Home Int 1932-33-34-35; v France 1934. (GBI): Walker Cup 1932-34

Fisher, D
(England): Home Int 1993-94; v France 1994. (GBI): v Europe 1994

Fitzgibbon, JF
(Ireland): Home Int 1955-56-57

Fitzsimmons, J
(Ireland): Home Int 1938-47-48

Flaherty, JA
(Ireland): Home Int 1934-35-36-37

Flaherty, PD
(Ireland): Home Int 1967; Eur T Ch 1967-69

Fleming, J
(Scotland): Home Int 1987

Fleury, RA
(Ireland): Home Int 1974

Flockhart, AS
(Scotland): Home Int 1948-49

Fogarty, GN
(Ireland): Home Int 1956-58-63-64-67

Fogg, HN
(England): Home Int 1933

Forbes, E
(Scotland): Home Int 1996-98; v Italy 1996; v France, Sweden 1997

Forsyth, A
(Scotland): Home Int 1996; v Italy 1996; v France, Sweden 1997; Eur T Ch 1997

Foster, J
(Ireland): Home Int 1998

Foster, M
(England): Home Int 1994-95; v Spain 1995; Eur T Ch 1995. (GBI): Walker Cup 1995

Foster, MF
(England): Home Int 1973

Foster, R
(England): Home Int 1963-64-66-67-68-69-70-71-72; Eur T Ch 1967-69-71-73. (GBI): Walker Cup 1965-67-69-71-73-79-81; v Europe 1964-66-68-70; CW 1967-71; Eisenhower Trophy 1964-70-80(Captain)

Fowler, WH
(England): v Scotland 1903-04-05

Fox, G
(Scotland): Home Int 1997-98

Fox, N
(Ireland): Home Int 1996-97-98; Eur T Ch 1997

Fox, SJ
(England): Home Int 1956-57-58

Frame, DW
(England): Home Int 1958-59-60-61-62-63. (GBI): Walker Cup 1961

Francis, F
(England): Home Int 1936; v France 1935-36

Frazier, K
(England): Home Int 1938

Froggatt, P
(Ireland): Home Int 1957

Fry, SH
(England): v Scotland 1902-03-04-05-06-07-09

Gairdner, JR
(Scotland): v England 1902

Gallacher, BJ
(Scotland): Home Int 1967

Gallacher, S
(Scotland): Home Int 1992-93-94-95; v Italy 1994; v Spain 1994; v Sweden 1995; v France 1995; Eur T Ch 1993-95. (GBI): Walker Cup 1995; Eisenhower Trophy 1994

Galloway, RF
(Scotland): Home Int 1957-58-59; v Scandinavia 1958

Gannon, MA
(Ireland): Home Int 1973-74-77-78-80-81-83-84-87-88-89-90; v France, West Germany, Sweden 1978-80; Eur T Ch 1979-81-89. (GBI): v Europe 1974-78

Garbutt, I
(England): Home Int 1990-91-92; Eur T Ch 1991; v France 1992. (GBI): v Europe 1992

Garner, PF
(England): Home Int 1977-78-80; v Scotland 1979

Garnet, LG
(England): v France 1934. (GBI): v Australia 1934

Garson, R
(Scotland): v Ireland 1927-28-29

Gent, J
(England): v Ireland 1930; Home Int 1938

Gibb, C
(Scotland): v England 1927; v Ireland 1928

Gibson, WC
(Scotland): Home Int 1950-51

Gilford, CF
(Wales): Home Int 1963-64-65-66-67

Gilford, D
(England): Home Int 1983-84-85. (GBI): Walker Cup 1985; v Europe 1986; Eisenhower Trophy 1984

Gill, WJ
(Ireland): v Wales 1931; Home Int 1932-33-34-35-36-37

Gillies, HD
(England): v Scotland 1908-25-26-27

Girvan, P
(Scotland): Home Int 1986; West Germany 1987; Eur T Ch 1987. (GBI): Walker Cup 1987

Glossop, R
(Wales): Home Int 1935-37-38-47

Glover, J
(Ireland): Home Int 1951-52-53-55-59-60-70

Godwin, G
(England): Home Int 1976-77-78-80-81; v Scotland 1979; v France 1982; Eur T Ch 1979-81. (GBI): Walker Cup 1979-81

Goulding, N
(Ireland): Home Int 1988-89-90-91-92; Eur T Ch 1991

Graham, AJ
(Scotland): v England 1925

Graham, J
(Scotland): v England 1902-03-04-05-06-07-08-09-10-11

Graham, JSS
(Ireland): Home Int 1938-50-51

Gray, CD
(England): Home Int 1932

Green, CW
(Scotland): Home Int 1961 to 1978; Eur T Ch 1965-67-69-71-73-75-77-79-**81-83**; v Scandinavia 1962; v Australia 1964; v Belgium 1973-75-77-78; v Spain 1977; v Italy 1979; v England 1979. (GBI): Walker Cup 1963-69-71-73-75-**83-85**; v Europe 1962-66-68-70-72-74-76; CW 1971; Eisenhower Trophy 1970-72-**84-86**

Green, HB
(England): v Scotland 1979

Green, PO
(England): Home Int 1961-62-63. (GBI): CW 1963

Greene, R
(Ireland): Home Int 1933

Greig, DG
(Scotland): Home Int 1972-73-75. (GBI): CW 1975

Greig, K
(Scotland): Home Int 1933

Gribben, P
(Ireland): Home Int 1997-98. (GBI) Eisenhower Trophy 1998 (winners)

Griffiths, HGB
(Wales): v Ireland 1923-24-25

Griffiths, HS
(Wales): v England 1958

Griffiths, JA
(Wales): Home Int 1933

Guerin, M
(Ireland): Home Int 1961-62-63

Guild, WJ
(Scotland): v England 1925-27-28; v Ireland 1927-28

Hales, JP
(Wales): v Scotland 1963

Hall, A
(Wales): Home Int 1994

Hall, AH
(Scotland): Home Int 1962-66-69

Hall, D
(Wales): Home Int 1932-37

Hall, K
(Wales): Home Int 1955-59

Hambro, AV
(England): v Scotland 1905-08-09-10-22

Hamilton, CJ
(Wales): v Ireland 1913

Hamilton, ED
(Scotland): Home Int 1936-37-38

Hamer, S
(England): Home Int 1983-84

Hanway, M
(Ireland): Home Int 1971-74

Hardman, RH
(England): v Scotland 1927-28. (GBI): Walker Cup 1928

Hare, A
(England): Home Int 1988; Eur T Ch 1989. (GBI) Walker Cup 1989

Hare, WCD
(Scotland): Home Int 1953; v New Zealand 1954

Harpin, L
(Wales): Home Int 1996-98

Harrhy, A
(Wales): Home Int 1988-89-95

Harrington, J
(Ireland): Home Int 1960-61-74-75-76; Eur T Ch 1975; v Wales 1979

Harrington, P
(Ireland): Home Int 1990-91-92-93-94-95; Eur T Ch 1991-95. (GBI): Walker Cup 1991-93-95; v Europe 1992-94

Harris, D
(Wales): Home Int 1997

Harris, G
(England): Home Int 1994; v Spain 1995; Eur T Ch 1995

Harris, IR
(Scotland): Home Int 1955-56-58-59

Harris, M
(England): Home Int 1998

Harris, R
(Scotland): v England 1905-08-10-11-12-22-23-24-25-26-27-28 (GBI): Walker Cup **1922-23-26**

Harrison, JW
(Wales): Home Int 1937-50

Hartley, RW
(England): v Scotland 1926-27-28-29-30-31; v Ireland 1928-29-30-31; Home Int 1933-34-35. (GBI): Walker Cup 1930-32

Hartley, WL
(England): v Ireland/Wales 1925; v Scotland 1927-31; v Ireland 1928-31; Home Int 1932-33; v France 1935.(GBI): Walker Cup 1932

Hassall, JE
(England): v Scotland 1923; v Ireland/Wales 1925

Hastings, JL
(Scotland): Home Int 1957-58; v Scandinavia 1958

Hawksworth, J
(England): Home Int 1984-85. (GBI): Walker Cup 1985

Hay, G
(Scotland): v England 1979; Home Int 1980-88-90-91-92; v Belgium 1980; v France 1980-82-89-91-92; v Italy 1988-92-94; v Sweden 1992; v Spain 1994; Eur T Ch 1991-93. (GBI): v Europe 1980; Walker Cup 1991

Hay, J
(Scotland): Home Int 1972

Hayes, JA
(Ireland): Home Int 1977

Hayward, CH
(England): v Scotland 1925; v Ireland 1928

Healy, TM
(Ireland): v Scotland 1931; v England 1931

Heather, D
(Ireland): Home Int 1976; v France, West Germany, Sweden 1976

Hedges, PJ
(England): Home Int 1970-73-74-75-76-77-78-82-83; Eur T Ch 1973-75-77. (GBI): Walker Cup 1973-75; v Europe 1974-76; Eisenhower Trophy 1996

Hegarty, J
(Ireland): Home Int 1975

Hegarty, TD
(Ireland): Home Int 1957

Helm, AGB
(England): Home Int 1948

Henderson, J
(Ireland): v Wales 1923

Henderson, N
(Scotland): Home Int 1963-64

Henriques, GLQ
(England): v Ireland 1930

Henry, W
(England): Home Int 1987; v France 1988

Herlihy, B
(Ireland): Home Int 1950

Herne, KTC
(Wales): v Ireland 1913

Heverin, AJ
(Ireland): Home Int 1978; v France, West Germany, Sweden 1978

Hezlet, CO
(Ireland): v Wales 1923-25-27-29-31; v Scotland 1927-28-29-30-31; v England 1929-30-31. (GBI): Walker Cup 1924-26-28; v South Africa 1927

Higgins, D
(Ireland): Home Int 1993-94

Higgins, L
(Ireland): Home Int 1968-70-71

Hill, GA
(England): Home Int 1936-37. (GBI): Walker Cup 1936-**55**

Hilton, HH
(England): v Scotland 1902-03-04-05-06-07-09-10-11-12

Hird, K
(Scotland): Home Int 1987-88-89; Nixdorf Nations Cup 1989; v Italy 1990

Hislop, C
(Scotland): Home Int 1994-96; v Austria 1994; v Italy 1996

Hoad, PGJ
(England): Home Int 1978; v Scotland 1979

Hodgson, C
(England): v Scotland 1924

Hodgson, J
(England): Home Int 1994

Hoey, TBC
(Ireland): Home Int 1970-71-72-73-77-84; Eur T Ch 1971-77

Hogan, P
(Ireland): Home Int 1985-86-87-88; Eur T Ch 1991

Holderness, Sir EWE
(England): v Scotland 1922-23-24-25-26-28. (GBI): v America 1921; Walker Cup 1923-26-30

Holmes, AW
(England): Home Int 1962

Homer, TWB
(England): Home Int 1972-73; Eur T Ch 1973. (GBI): Walker Cup 1973; v Europe 1972; Eisenhower Trophy 1972

Homewood, G
(England): Home Int 1985-91; Eur T Ch 1991

Hooman, CVL
(England): v Scotland 1910-22. (GBI): Walker Cup 1922-23

Hope, WL
(Scotland): v England 1923-25-26-27-28-29. (GBI): Walker Cup 1923-24-28

Horne, A
(Scotland): Home Int 1971

Horne, S
(Scotland): Home Int 1997-98

Hosie, JR
(Scotland): Home Int 1936

Houston, G
(Wales): Home Int 1990-91-92-93-94-95; Eur T Ch 1991-95

Howard, DB
(Scotland): v England 1979; Home Int 1980-81-82-83-93-94-95-96; v Belgium 1980; v France 1980-81-83-95-97; v Italy 1984-94; v Spain 1994-96; v Sweden 1995-97. Eur T Ch 1981-95-97. (GBI): Walker Cup 1995-97; v Europe 1980-94-96; Eisenhower Trophy 1996

Howell, D
(England): Home Int 1994-95; v Spain 1995; Eur T Ch 1995. (GBI) Walker Cup 1995

Howell, HR
(Wales): v Ireland 1923-24-25-29-30-31; v England 1925; v Scotland 1931; Home Int 1932-34-35-36-37-38-47

Howell, H Logan
(Wales): v Ireland 1925

Huddy, G
(England): Home Int 1960-61-62. (GBI): Walker Cup 1961

Huggan, J
(Scotland): Home Int 1981-82-83-84; v France 1982-83; v Sweden 1983; v Italy 1984; Eur T Ch 1981

Hughes, I
(Wales): Home Int 1954-55-56

Hulme, WJ
(Ireland): Home Int 1955-56-57

Humphrey, JG
(Wales): v Ireland 1925

Humphreys, AR
(Ireland): v England 1957

Humphreys, DI
(Wales): Home Int 1972

Humphreys, W
(England): Home Int 1970-71; Eur T Ch 1971. (GBI): Walker Cup 1971; v Europe 1970

Hunter, NM
(Scotland): v England 1903-12

Hunter, R
(Scotland): Home Int 1996

Hunter, WI
(Scotland): v England 1922

Hutcheon, I
(Scotland): Home Int 1971-72-73-74-75-76-77-78-80; v Belgium 1973-75-77-78-80; v Spain 1977; v France 1978-80-81; v Italy 1979; v Sweden 1983; Eur T Ch 1973-75-77-79-81. (GBI): Walker Cup 1975-77-79-81; v Europe 1974-76; Eisenhower Trophy 1974-76 (winners)-80; CW 1975; Dominican Int 1973; Colombian Int 1975

Hutchings, C
(England): v Scotland 1902

Hutchinson, HG
(England): v Scotland 1902-03-04-06-07-09

Hutchison, CK
(Scotland): v England 1904-05-06-07-08-09-10-11-12

Hutt, R
(England): Home Int 1991-92-93

Hutton, R
(Ireland): Home Int 1991

Hyde, GE
(England): Home Int 1967-68

Illingworth, G
(England): v Scotland 1929; v France 1937

Inglis, MJ
(England): Home Int 1977

Isitt, GH
(Wales): v Ireland 1923

Jack, RR
(Scotland): Home Int 1950-51-54-55-56-57-58-59-61; v New Zealand 1954; v Scandinavia 1956-58. (GBI): Walker Cup 1957-59; v Europe 1956; Eisenhower Trophy 1958; CW 1959

Jack, WS
(Scotland): Home Int 1955

Jacob, NE
(Wales): Home Int 1932-33-34-35-36

James, D
(Scotland): Home Int 1985

James, L
(England): Home Int 1993-94-95; v France 1994; v Spain 1995; Eur T Ch 1995. (GBI): Walker Cup 1995; v Europe 1994; Eisenhower Trophy 1994

James, M
(England): Home Int 1974-75; Eur T Ch 1975. (GBI): Walker Cup 1975

James, RD
(England): Home Int 1974-75

Jameson, JF
(Ireland): v Wales 1913-24

Jamieson, A, jr
(Scotland): v England 1927-28-31; v Ireland 1928-31; v Wales 1931; Home Int 1932-33-36-37. (GBI): Walker Cup 1926

Jamieson, D
(Scotland): Home Int 1980

Jenkins, JLC
(Scotland): v England 1908-12-22-24-26-28; v Ireland 1928. (GBI): v America 1921

Jermine, JG
(Wales): Home Int 1972-73-74-75-76-82; Eur T Ch 1975-77; v France 1975

Jobson, RH
(England): v Ireland 1928

Johnson, R
(Wales): Home Int 1990-92-93-94; Eur T Ch 1991. (GBI) v Europe 1994

Johnson, TWG
(Ireland): v England 1929

Johnstone, JW
(Scotland): Home Int 1970-71

Jones, A
(Wales): Home Int 1989-90; Eur T Ch 1991

Jones, D
(Ireland): Home Int 1998

Jones, DK
(Wales): Home Int 1973

Jones, EO
(Wales): Home Int 1983-85-86

Jones, JG Parry
(Wales): Home Int 1959-60

Jones, JL
(Wales): Home Int 1933-34-36

Jones, JR
(Wales): Home Int 1970-72-73-77-78-80-81-82-83-84-85; Eur T Ch 1973-79-81; v Denmark 1976-80; v Ireland 1979; v Switzerland, Spain 1980; v Ireland 1979

Jones, JW
(England): Home Int 1948-49-50-51-52-54-55

Jones, KG
(Wales): Home Int 1988

Jones, MA
(Wales): Home Int 1947-48-49-50-51-53-54-57

Jones, Malcolm F
(Wales): Home Int 1933

Jones, SP
(Wales): Home Int 1981-82-83-84-85-86-88-89-91-93

Kane, RM
(Ireland): Home Int 1967-68-71-72-74-78; Eur T Ch 1971-79; v Wales 1979. (GBI): v Europe 1974

Kearney, K
(Ireland): Home Int 1988-89-90-92-94-95-97-98

Keenan, S
(Ireland): Home Int 1989

Kelleher, WA
(Ireland): Home Int 1962

Kelley, MJ
(England): Home Int 1974-75-76-77-78-80-81-82-**88**; v France 1982; Eur T Ch 1977-79. (GBI): Walker Cup 1977-79; v Europe 1976-78; Eisenhower Trophy 1976 (winners); Colombian Int 1978

Kelley, PD
(England): Home Int 1965-66-68

Kelly, L
(Scotland): Home Int 1997-98. (GBI) Eisenhower Trophy 1998 (winners)

Kelly, NS
(Ireland): Home Int 1966

Keppler, SD
(England): Home Int 1982-83; v France 1982. (GBI): Walker Cup 1983

Kilduff, AJ
(Ireland): v Scotland 1928

Killey, GC
(Scotland): v Ireland 1928

King, M
(England): Home Int 1969-70-71-72-73; Eur T Ch 1971-73 (GBI): Walker Cup 1969-73; v Europe 1970-72; CW 1971

Kirkpatrick, D
(Scotland): Home Int 1992; v France 1993; Eur T Ch 1993

Kissock, B
(Ireland): Home Int 1961-62-74-76; v France, Germany, Sweden 1978

Kitchin, JE
(England): v France 1949

Knight, B
(Wales): Home Int 1986

Knight, J
(England): v France 1996

Knipe, RG
(Wales): Home Int 1953-54-55-56

Knowles, ST
(Scotland): Home Int 1990-91-92; v France 1991

Knowles, WR
(Wales): v England 1948

Kyle, AT
(Scotland): Home Int 1938-47-49-50-51-52-53. (GBI): Walker Cup 1938-47-51; v South Africa 1952

Kyle, DH
(Scotland): v England 1924-30. (GBI): Walker Cup 1924

Kyle, EP
(Scotland): v England 1925

Laidlay, JE
(Scotland): v England 1902-03-04-05-06-07-08-09-10-11

Lake, AD
(Wales): Home Int 1958

Lang, JA
(Scotland): v England 1929-31; v Ireland 1929-30-31; v Wales 1931. (GBI): Walker Cup 1930

Langley, JDA
(England): Home Int 1950-51-52-53; v France 1950. (GBI): Walker Cup 1936-51-53

Langmead, J
(England): Home Int 1986

Lassen, EA
(England): v Scotland 1909-10-11-12

Last, CN
(Wales): Home Int 1975

Laurence, C
(England): Home Int 1983-84-85

Lawrie, CD
(Scotland): Home Int 1949-50-55-56-57-58; v Sweden 1950; v Scandinavia 1956-58. (GBI): Walker Cup **1961-63**; v South Africa 1952; v Europe **1960-62**; Eisenhower Trophy **1960-62**

Lawrie, GA
(Scotland): Home Int 1990-91; Eur T Ch 1991

Lawrie P
(Ireland): Home Int 1996; Eur T Ch 1997

Layton, EN
(England): v Scotland 1922-23-26; v Ireland/Wales 1925

Lee, IGF
(Scotland): Home Int 1958-59-60-61-62; v Scandinavia 1960

Lee, JN
(Wales): Home Int 1988-89; Eur T Ch 1991

Lee, M
(England): Home Int 1950

Lee, MG
(England): Home Int 1965

Lehane, N
(Ireland): Home Int 1976; v France, West Germany, Sweden 1976

Lewis, DH
(Wales): Home Int 1935-36-37-38

Lewis, DR
(Wales): v Ireland 1925-29-30-31; v Scotland 1931; Home Int 1932-34

Lewis, ME
(England): Home Int 1980-81-82; v France 1982. (GBI): Walker Cup 1983

Lewis, R Cofe
(Wales): v Ireland 1925

Leyden, PJ
(Ireland): Home Int 1953-55-56-57-59

Lincoln, AC
(England): v Scotland 1907

Lindsay, J
(Scotland): Home Int 1933-34-35-36

Little, E
(Scotland): v Italy 1996

Lloyd, HM
(Wales): v Ireland 1913

Lloyd, RM de
(Wales): v Scotland 1931; v Ireland 1931; Home Int 1932-33-34-35-36-37-38-47-48

Llyr, A
(Wales): Home Int 1984-85

Lockhart, G
(Scotland): v England 1911-12

Lockley, AE
(Wales): Home Int 1956-57-58-62

Logan, GW
(England): Home Int 1973

Long, D
(Ireland): Home Int 1973-74-80-81-82-83-84; v Wales 1979; Eur T Ch 1979

Low, AJ
(Scotland): Home Int 1964-65; Eur T Ch 1965; v Australia 1964

Low, JL
(Scotland): v England 1904

Lowdon, CJ
(Scotland): v Ireland 1927

Lowe, A
(Ireland): v Wales 1924; v England 1925-28; v Scotland 1927-28

Lowson, AG
(Scotland): Home Int 1989-90-91-97; v Sweden 1990-92; v Italy 1992

Lucas, D
(England): Home Int 1996

Lucas, PB
(England): Home Int 1936-48-49; v France 1936. (GBI): Walker Cup 1936-47-**49**

Ludwell, N
(England): Home Int 1991; v France 1992

Lunt, MSR
(England): Home Int 1956-57-58-59-60-62-63-64-66. (GBI): Walker Cup 1959-61-63-65; v Europe 1964; CW 1963; Eisenhower Trophy 1964

Lunt, S
(England): Home Int 1932-33-34-35; v France 1934-35-39

Lygate, M
(Scotland): Home Int 1970-75-**88**;
Eur T Ch 1971-**85-87**

Lyle, AWB
(England): Home Int 1975-76-77;
Eur T Ch 1977. (GBI): Walker Cup
1977; CW 1975; v Europe 1976

Lynn, D
(England): Home Int 1995

Lyon, JS
(England): Home Int 1937-38

Lyons, P
(Ireland): Home Int 1986

McAllister, SD
(Scotland): Home Int 1983;
v Sweden 1983; Eur T Ch 1983

Macara, MA
(Wales): Home Int 1983-84-85-87-89-90-91-92-93

McArthur, W
(Scotland): Home Int 1952-54;
v South Africa 1954

McBeath, J
(Scotland): Home Int 1964

McBride, D
(Scotland): Home Int 1932

McCallum, AR
(Scotland): v England 1929.
(GBI): Walker Cup 1928

McCarrol, F
(Ireland): Home Int 1968-69

McCart, DM
(Scotland): Home Int 1977-78;
v Belgium 1978; v France 1978

McCarthy, L
(Ireland): Home Int 1953-54-55-56

McCarthy, S
(England): Home Int 1998

McConnell, FP
(Ireland): v Wales 1929-30-31;
v England 1929-30-31;v Scotland
1930-31; Home Int 1934

McConnell, RM
(Ireland): v Wales 1924-25-29-30-31; v England 1925-28-29-30-31;
v Scotland 1927-28-29-31; Home
Int 1934-35-36-37

McConnell, WG
(Ireland): v England 1925

McCormack, JD
(Ireland): v Wales 1913-24;
v England 1928, Home Int 1932-33-34-35-36-37

McCormick, A
(Ireland): Home Int 1997-98

McCrea, WE
(Ireland): Home Int 1965-66-67;
Eur T Ch 1965

McCready, SM
(Ireland): Home Int 1947-49-50-52-54. (GBI): Walker Cup 1949-51

McDaid, B
(Ireland): v Wales 1979

MacDonald, GK
(Scotland): Home Int 1978-81-82;
v England 1979; v France 1981-82-83

McDonald, H
(Scotland): Home Int 1970

Macdonald, JS
(Scotland): Home Int 1969-70-71-72; v Belgium 1973; Eur T Ch
1971. (GBI): Walker Cup 1971;
v Europe 1970

McEvoy, P
(England): Home Int 1976-77-78-80-81-83-84-85-86-87-88-89-91,
94 to 97; v Scotland 1979; v France
1982-88-92; Eur T Ch 1977-79-81-89; (GBI): Walker Cup 1977-79-81-85-89; v Europe 1978-80-86-88;
Eisenhower Trophy 1978-80-84-86-88 (winners)

Macfarlane, CB
(Scotland): v England 1912

McGimpsey, G
(Ireland): Home Int 1978 and 1980
to 1998; v Wales 1979; Eur T Ch
1981-89-91-95-97. (GBI): Walker
Cup 1985-89-91; v Europe 1986-88-90-92; Eisenhower Trophy
1984-86-88 (winners)

McGinley, M
(Ireland): Home Int 1996

McGinley, P
(Ireland): Home Int 1989-90;
Eur T Ch 1991. (GBI): Walker
Cup 1991

Macgregor, A
(Scotland): v Scandinavia 1956

Macgregor, G
(Scotland): Home Int 1969 to
1976, 1980 to 1987; v Belgium
1973-75-80; v England 1979;
v Sweden 1983-84-86; v Italy 1984-86; v France 1981-82-85-87; Eur T
Ch 1971-73-75-81-83-85-87.
(GBI): Walker Cup 1971-75-83-85-87-**91-93**; v Europe 1970-74-84;
CW 1971-75; Eisenhower Trophy
1982

MacGregor, RC
(Scotland): Home Int 1951-52-53-54; v New Zealand 1954. (GBI):
Walker Cup 1953

McGuire, M
(England): Home Int 1992

McHenry, J
(Ireland): Home Int 1985-86.
(GBI): Walker Cup 1987

McInally, H
(Scotland): Home Int 1937-47-48

McInally, RH
(Ireland): Home Int 1949-51

McIntosh, EA
(Scotland): Home Int 1989

Macintosh, KW
(Scotland): v England 1979; Home
Int 1980; v France 1980; v Belgium
1980. (GBI): v Europe 1980

McKay, G
(Scotland): Home Int 1969

McKay, JR
(Scotland): Home Int 1950-51-52-54; v New Zealand 1954

McKechnie, P
(Scotland): Home Int 1998

McKellar, PJ
(Scotland): Home Int 1976-77-78;
v Belgium 1978; v France 1978;
v England 1979. (GBI): Walker
Cup 1977; v Europe 1978

Mackenzie, F
(Scotland): v England 1902-03

MacKenzie, S
(Scotland): Home Int 1990-93-94-95-96-97-98; v Italy 1994; v Spain
1994-96; v France, Sweden 1997

Mackenzie, WW
(Scotland): v England 1923-26-27-29; v Ireland 1930. (GBI): Walker
Cup 1922-23

Mackeown, HN
(Ireland): Home Int 1973; Eur T
Ch 1973

McKibbin, H
(Scotland): Home Int 1994-95;
v Sweden 1995; v France 1995; Eur
T Ch 1995; v Spain 1996

Mackie, GW
(Scotland): Home Int 1948-50

McKinlay, SL
(Scotland): v England 1929-30-31;
v Ireland 1930; v Wales 1931;
Home Int 1932-33-35-37-47.
(GBI): Walker Cup 1934

McKinna, RA
(Scotland): Home Int 1938

McKinnon, A
(Scotland): Home Int 1947-52

McLean, D
(Wales): Home Int 1968-69-70-71-72-73-74-75-76-77-78-80-81-82-83-85-86-88-90; Eur T Ch 1975-77-79-81; v France 1975-76; v Denmark 1976-80; v Ireland 1979; v Switzerland, Spain 1980

McLean, J
(Scotland): Home Int 1932-33-34-35-36. (GBI): Walker Cup 1934-36; v Australia 1934

McLeod, AE
(Scotland): Home Int 1937-38

McLeod, WS
(Scotland): Home Int 1935-37-38-47-48-49-50-51; v Sweden 1950

McMenamin, E
(Ireland): Home Int 1981

McMullan, C
(Ireland): Home Int 1933-34-35

McNair, AA
(Scotland): v Ireland 1929

MacNamara, L
(Ireland): Home Int 1977-83-84-85-86-87-88-89-90-91-92; Eur T Ch 1977-91

McNeill, G
(Ireland): Home Int 1991-93

McRuvie, EA
(Scotland): v England 1929-30-31; v Ireland 1930-31; v Wales 1931; Home Int 1932-33-34-35-36. (GBI): Walker Cup 1932-34

McTear, J
(Scotland): Home Int 1971

Madeley, JFD
(Ireland): Home Int 1959-60-61-62-63-64. (GBI): Walker Cup 1963; v Europe 1962

Mahon, RJ
(Ireland): Home Int 1938-52-54-55

Maliphant, FR
(Wales): Home Int 1932

Malone, B
(Ireland): Home Int 1959-64-69-71-75; Eur T Ch 1971-75

Manford, GC
(Scotland): v England 1922-23

Manley, N
(Ireland): v Wales 1924; v England 1928; v Scotland 1927-28

Mann, LS
(Scotland): Home Int 1982-83; v Sweden 1983; Eur T Ch 1983. (GBI): Walker Cup 1983

Marchbank, B
(Scotland): Home Int 1978; v Italy 1979; Eur T Ch 1979. (GBI): Walker Cup 1979; v Europe 1976-78; Eisenhower Trophy 1978

Marks, GC
(England): Home Int 1963-67-68-69-70-71-74-75-82; Eur T Ch 1967-69-71-75; v France **1982**. (GBI): Walker Cup 1969-71-**87-89**; v Europe 1968-70; Eisenhower Trophy 1970; CW 1975; Colombian Int 1975.

Marren, JM
(Ireland): v Wales 1925

Marsden, G
(Wales): Home Int 1994

Marsh, DM
(England): Home Int 1956-57-58-59-60-64-66-68-69-70-71-72; Eur T Ch 1971. (GBI): Walker Cup 1959-71-**73**-75; v Europe 1958

Marshman, A
(Wales): Home Int 1952

Marston, CC
(Wales): v Ireland 1929-30-31; v Scotland 1931

Martin, DHR
(England): Home Int 1938; v France 1934-49

Martin, GNC
(Ireland): v Wales 1923-29; v Scotland 1928-29-30; v England 1929-30. (GBI): Walker Cup 1928

Martin, S
(Scotland): Home Int 1975-76-77; Eur T Ch 1977; v Belgium 1977; v Spain 1977. (GBI): Walker Cup 1977; v Europe 1976; Eisenhower Trophy 1976 (winners)

Mason, B
(England): Home Int 1998

Mason, SC
(England): Home Int 1973

Mathias-Thomas, FEL
(Wales): v Ireland 1924-25

Matthews, RL
(Wales): Home Int 1935-37

Maxwell, R
(Scotland): v England 1902-03-04-05-06-07-09-10

Mayo, PM
(Wales): Home Int 1982-87. (GBI): Walker Cup 1985-87

Meharg, W
(Ireland): Home Int 1957

Melia, TJ
(Wales): Home Int 1976-77-78-80-81-82; v Ireland 1979; Eur T Ch 1977-79; v Denmark 1976-80; v Switzerland, Spain 1980

Mellin, GL
(England): v Scotland 1922

Melville, LM Balfour
(Scotland): v England 1902-03

Melville, TE
(Scotland): Home Int 1974

Menzies, A
(Scotland): v England 1925

Metcalfe, J
(England): Home Int 1989. (GBI) v Europe 1990

Micklem, GH
(England): Home Int 1947-48-49-50-51-52-53-54-55. (GBI): Walker Cup 1947-49-53-55-**57-59**; Eisenhower Trophy **1958**

Mill, JW
(Scotland): Home Int 1953-54

Millensted, DJ
(England): Home Int 1966; Eur T Ch 1967. (GBI): Walker Cup 1967; CW 1967

Miller, AC
(Scotland): Home Int 1954-55

Miller, MJ
(Scotland): Home Int 1974-75-77-78; v Belgium 1978; v France 1978

Milligan, JW
(Scotland): Home Int 1986-87-88-89-90-91-92; v West Germany 1987; v Italy 1988-90-92; v France 1987-89-91; Eur T Ch 1987-89-91; Nixdorf Nations Cup 1989; v Sweden 1986-90-92. (GBI): Walker Cup 1989-91; Eisenhower Trophy 1988(winners)-90; v Europe 1988-92

Mills, ES
(Wales): Home Int 1957

Millward, EB
(England): Home Int 1950-52-53-54-55. (GBI): Walker Cup 1949-55

Milne, WTG
(Scotland): Home Int 1972-73; Eur T Ch 1973; v Belgium 1973. (GBI): Walker Cup 1973

Mitchell, A
(England): v Scotland 1910-11-12

Mitchell, CS
(England): Home Int 1975-76-78

Mitchell, FH
(England): v Scotland 1906-07-08

Mitchell, JWH
(Wales): Home Int 1964-65-66

Moffat, DM
(England): Home Int 1961-63-67; v France 1959-60

Moir, A
(Scotland): Home Int 1983-84; v Sweden 1984; v Italy 1984; v France 1985; Eur T Ch 1985. (GBI): v Europe 1984

Montgomerie, CS
(Scotland): Home Int 1984-85-86; v West Germany 1987; v Sweden 1984-86; v Italy 1984; v France 1985; Eur T Ch 1985-87. (GBI): Walker Cup 1985-87; v Europe 1986; Eisenhower Trophy 1984-86

Montgomerie, JS
(Scotland): Home Int 1957; v Scandinavia 1958; Eur T Ch 1965

Montmorency, RH de
(England): v Scotland 1908; v Wales/Ireland 1925; v South Africa 1927. (GBI): v America 1921

Moody, JV
(Wales): Home Int 1947-48-49-51-56-58-59-60-61

Moody, PH
(England): Home Int 1971-72. (GBI): v Europe 1972

Moore, GJ
(Ireland): v England 1928; v Wales 1929

Morgan, JL
(Wales): 1948-49-50-51-52-53-54-55-56-57-58-59-60-61-62-64-68. (GBI): Walker Cup 1951-53-55

Morris, FS
(Scotland): Home Int 1963

Morris, JC
(Ireland): Home Int 1993-94-95-96-97-98; Eur T Ch 1995

Morris, MF
(Ireland): Home Int 1978-80-82-83-84; v Wales 1979; Eur T Ch 1979; v France, W. Germany, Sweden 1980

Morris, R
(Wales): Home Int 1983-86-87

Morris, TS
(Wales): v Ireland 1924-29-30

Morrison, JH
(Scotland): v Scandinavia 1960

Morrison, JSF
(England): v Ireland 1930

Morrow, AJC
(Ireland): Home Int 1975-83-92-93-96-97

Morrow, JM
(Wales): v Ireland 1979; Home Int 1980-81; Eur T Ch 1979-81; v Denmark 1980, v Switzerland 1980, v Spain 1980

Mosey, IJ
(England): Home Int 1971

Moss, AV
(Wales): Home Int 1965-66-68

Mouland, MG
(Wales): Home Int 1978-81; v Ireland 1979; Eur T Ch 1979

Moxon, GA
(Wales): v Ireland 1929-30

Mulcare, P
(Ireland): Home Int 1968-69-70-71-72-74-78-80; v France, West Germany, Sweden 1978-80; Eur T Ch 1975-79. (GBI): Walker Cup 1975; v Europe 1972

Mulholland, D
(Ireland): Home Int 1988

Munn, E
(Ireland): v Wales 1913-23-24; v Scotland 1927

Munn, L
(Ireland): v Wales 1913-23-24; Home Int 1936-37

Munro, RAG
(Scotland): Home Int 1960

Murdoch, D
(Scotland): Home Int 1964

Murphy, AR
(Scotland): Home Int 1961-67

Murphy, G
(Ireland): Home Int 1992-93-94-95; Eur T Ch 1995

Murphy, P
(Ireland): Home Int 1985-86

Murray, GH
(Scotland): Home Int 1973-74-75-76-77-78-83; v Spain 1974-77; v Belgium 1975-77; Eur T Ch 1975-77. (GBI): Walker Cup 1977; v Europe 1978

Murray, P
(Ireland): Home Int 1995-96

Murray, SWT
(Scotland): Home Int 1959-60-61-62-63; v Scandinavia 1960. (GBI): Walker Cup 1963; v Europe 1958-62

Murray, WA
(Scotland): v England 1923-24-25-26-27. (GBI): Walker Cup 1923-24

Murray, WB
(Scotland): Home Int 1967-68-69; Eur T Ch 1969

Muscroft, R
(England): Home Int 1986

Nash A
(England): Home Int 1988-89

Neech, DG
(England): Home Int 1961

Neill, JH
(Ireland): Home Int 1938-47-48-49

Neill, R
(Scotland): Home Int 1936

Nelson, P
(England): v France 1996

Nestor, JM
(Ireland): Home Int 1962-63-64

Nevin, V
(Ireland): Home Int 1960-63-65-67-69-72; Eur T Ch 1967-69-73

Newey, AS
(England): Home Int 1932

Newman, JE
(Wales): Home Int 1932

Newton, H
(Wales): v Ireland 1929

Nicholson, J
(Ireland): Home Int 1932

Nolan, K
(Ireland): Home Int 1992-93-94-95-96; Eur T Ch 1995-97. (GBI): Walker Cup 1997; v Europe 1996; Eisenhower Trophy 1996

Noon, GS
(Wales): Home Int 1935-36-37

Noon, J
(Scotland): Home Int 1987

O'Boyle, P
(Ireland): Eur T Ch 1977

O'Brien, MD
(Ireland): Home Int 1968-69-70-71-72-75-76-77; Eur T Ch 1971; v France, West Germany, Sweden 1976

O'Carroll, C
(Wales): Home Int 1989-90-91-92-93; Eur T Ch 1991

O'Connell, A
(Ireland): Home Int 1967-70-71

O'Connell, E
(Ireland): Home Int 1985; Eur T Ch 1989. (GBI): Walker Cup 1989; v Europe 1988; Eisenhower Trophy 1988 (winners)

O'Leary, JE
(Ireland): Home Int 1969-70; Eur T Ch 1969

O'Neill, JJ
(Ireland): Home Int 1968

O'Rourke, P
(Ireland): Home Int 1980-81-82-84-85

O'Sullivan, DF
(Ireland): Home Int 1976-85-86-87-91; Eur T Ch 1977

O'Sullivan, WM
(Ireland): Home Int 1934-35-36-37-38-47-48-49-50-51-53-54

Oldcorn, A
(England): Home Int 1982-83. (GBI): Walker Cup 1983; Eisenhower Trophy 1982

Omelia, B
(Ireland): Home Int 1994-95-96-97

Oosterhuis, PA
(England): Home Int 1966-67-68. (GBI): Walker Cup 1967; v Europe 1968; Eisenhower Trophy 1968

Oppenheimer, RH
(England): v Ireland 1928-29-30; v Scotland 1930. (GBI): Walker Cup **1957**

Osgood, TH
(Scotland): v England 1925

Owen, JB
(Wales): Home Int 1971

Owens, GF
(Wales): Home Int 1960-61

Ownes, GH
(Ireland): Home Int 1935-37-38-47

Page, P
(England): Home Int 1993. (GBI): Walker Cup 1993

Palferman, H
(Wales): Home Int 1950-53

Palmer, DJ
(England): Home Int 1962-63

Palmer, M
(Wales): Home Int 1998

Pardoe, S
(Wales): Home Int 1991

Parfitt, RWM
(Wales): v Ireland 1924

Park, D
(Wales): Home Int 1994-95-96-97; Eur T Ch 1995-97. (GBI) Walker Cup 1997

Parkin, AP
(Wales): Home Int 1980-81-82. (GBI): Walker Cup 1983

Parry, JR
(Wales): Home Int 1966-75-76-77; v France 1976

Patey, IR
(England): Home Int 1952; v France 1948-49-50

Paton, DA
(Scotland): Home Int 1991

Patrick, D
(Scotland): Home Int 1997-98

Patrick, KG
(Scotland): Home Int 1937

Patterson, AH
(Ireland): v Wales 1913

Pattinson, R
(England): Home Int 1949

Payne, J
(England): Home Int 1950-51

Payne, J
(England): Home Int 1989-90; Eur T Ch 1991. (GBI): Walker Cup 1991; v Europe 1990

Pearson, AG
(GBI): v South Africa 1927

Pearson, MJ
(England): Home Int 1951-52

Pease, JWB (later Lord Wardington)
(England): v Scotland 1903-04-05-06

Peet, M
(Wales): Home Int 1995-96

Pennink, JJF
(England): Home Int 1937-38-47; v France 1937-38-39. (GBI): Walker Cup 1938

Perkins, TP
(England): v Scotland 1927-28-29. (GBI): Walker Cup 1928

Perowne, AH
(England): Home Int 1947-48-49-50-51-53-54-55-57. (GBI): Walker Cup 1949-53-59; Eisenhower Trophy 1958

Peters, GB
(Scotland): Home Int 1934-35-36-37-38. (GBI): Walker Cup 1936-38

Peters, JL
(Wales): Home Int 1987-88-89

Philipson, S
(England): Home Int 1997

Phillips, LA
(Wales): v Ireland 1913

Phillips, V
(GBI): Walker Cup 1993

Pierse, AD
(Ireland): Home Int 1976-77-78-80-81-82-83-84-85-87-88; v Wales 1979; v France, West Germany, Sweden 1980; Eur T Ch 1981. (GBI): Walker Cup 1983; v Europe 1980; Eisenhower Trophy 1982

Pilkington, M
(Wales): Home Int 1997-98; Eur T Ch 1997

Pinch, AG
(Wales): Home Int 1969

Pirie, AK
(Scotland): Home Int 1966 to 1975; Eur T Ch 1967-69; v Belgium 1973-75; v Spain 1974. (GBI): Walker Cup 1967; v Europe 1970

Plaxton, J
(England): Home Int 1983-84

Pollin, RKM
(Ireland): Home Int 1971; Eur T Ch 1973

Pollock, VA
(England): v Scotland 1908

Povall, J
(Wales): Home Int 1960-61-62-63-65-66-67-68-69-70-71-72-73-74-75-76-77; Eur T Ch 1967-69-71-73-75-77; v France 1975-76; v Denmark 1976. (GBI): v Europe 1962

Powell, WA
(England): v Scotland 1923-24; v Wales/Ireland 1925

Power, E
(Ireland): Home Int 1987-88-93-94-95-97-98

Power, M
(Ireland): Home Int 1947-48-49-50-51-52-54

Poxon, MA
(England): Home Int 1975-76; Eur T Ch 1975. (GBI): Walker Cup 1975

Pressdee, RNG
(Wales): Home Int 1958-59-60-61-62

Pressley, J
(Scotland): Home Int 1947-48-49

Price, JP
(Wales): Home Int 1986-87-88

Price, R
(Wales): Home Int 1994-96-97

Prosser, D
(England): Eur T Ch 1989

Pugh, O
(Wales): Home Int 1997-98

Pugh, RS
(Wales): v Ireland 1923-24-29

Pullan, M
(England): Home Int 1991-92

Purcell, J
(Ireland): Home Int 1973

Pyman, I
(England): Home Int 1993. (GBI): Walker Cup 1993

Raeside, A
(Scotland): v Ireland 1929

Rafferty, R
(Ireland): v Wales 1979; Home Int 1980-81; v France, West Germany, Sweden 1980; Eur T Ch 1981. (GBI): Walker Cup 1981; v Europe 1980; Eisenhower Trophy 1980

Rainey, WHE
(Ireland): Home Int 1962

Rankin, G
(Scotland): Home Int 1994-95-97-98; v Sweden 1995-97; v France 1995-97; Eur T Ch 1995-97; v Spain 1996. (GBI): Walker Cup 1995-97

Rawlinson, D
(England): Home Int 1949-50-52-53

Ray, D
(England): Home Int 1982; v France 1982

Rayfus, P
(Ireland): Home Int 1986-87-88

Reade, HE
(Ireland): v Wales 1913

Reddan, B
(Ireland): Home Int 1987

Rees, CN
(Wales): Home Int 1986-88-89-91-92-94-95-96-97

Rees, DA
(Wales): Home Int 1961-62-63-64

Reid, A
(Scotland): Home Int 1993-94-95; Eur T Ch 1993-95; v Spain 1994; v Italy 1994; v France 1995

Renfrew, RL
(Scotland): Home Int 1964

Renwick, G, jr
(Wales): v Ireland 1923

Revell, RP
(England): Home Int 1972-73; Eur T Ch 1973

Reynard, M
(England): Home Int 1996-97; v France 1996

Ricardo, W
(Wales); v Ireland 1930-31; v Scotland 1931

Rice, JH
(Ireland): Home Int 1947-52

Rice-Jones, L
(Wales): v Ireland 1924

Richards, PM
(Wales): Home Int 1960-61-62-63-71

Richardson, S
(England): Home Int 1986-87-88

Risdon, PWL
(England): Home Int 1935-36

Robb, J, jr
(Scotland): v England 1902-03-05-06-07

Robb, WM
(Scotland): Home Int 1935

Roberts, AT
(Scotland): v Ireland 1931

Roberts, GP
(England): Home Int 1951-53; v France 1949

Roberts, GW
(Scotland): Home Int 1937-38

Roberts, H
(Wales): Home Int 1992-93

Roberts, HJ
(England): Home Int 1947-48-53

Roberts, J
(Wales): Home Int 1937

Roberts, S
(Wales): Home Int 1998

Roberts, SB
(Wales): Home Int 1932-33-34-35-37-38-47-48-49-50-51-52-53-54

Roberts, WJ
(Wales): Home Int 1948-49-50-51-52-53-54

Robertson, A
(England): Home Int 1986-87; v France 1988

Robertson, CW
(Ireland): v Wales 1930; v Scotland 1930

Robertson, D
(Scotland): Home Int 1991-92-93; v Sweden 1992; v Italy 1992; v France 1993; Eur T Ch 1993. (GBI): Walker Cup 1993; v Europe 1992; Eisenhower Trophy 1992

Robertson, DM
(Scotland): Home Int 1973-74; v Spain 1974

Robertson-Durham, JA
(Scotland): v England 1911

Robinson, J
(England): v Ireland 1928

Robinson, J
(England): Home Int 1986. (GBI): Walker Cup 1987

Robinson, S
(England): v Scotland 1925; v Ireland 1928-29-30

Roderick, RN
(Wales): Home Int 1983-84-85-86-87-88. (GBI) v Europe 1988. (GBI): Walker Cup 1989

Rogers, A
(England): Home Int 1991; v France 1992

Rolfe, B
(Wales): Home Int 1963-65

Roobottom, EL
(Wales): Home Int 1967

Roper, HS
(England): v Ireland 1931; v Scotland 1931

Roper, MS
(Wales): v Ireland 1979

Roper, R
(England): Home Int 1984-85-86-87

Rose, J
(England): Home Int 1997; Eur T Ch 1997. (GBI) Walker Cup 1997

Rothwell, J
(England): Home Int 1947-48

Rowe, P
(England): Home Int 1997-98

Russell, R
(Scotland): Home Int 1992-93; v France 1993; Eur T Ch 1993. (GBI): Walker Cup 1993

Rutherford, DS
(Scotland): *v* Ireland 1929

Rutherford, R
(Scotland): Home Int 1938-47

Saddler, AC
(Scotland): Home Int 1959-60-61-62-63-64-66; *v* Scandinavia 1962; Eur T Ch 1965-67-(75)-(77). (GBI): Walker Cup 1963-65-67-77; *v* Europe 1960-62-64-66; CW 1959-63-67; Eisenhower Trophy 1962-76(winners)

Sanders, M
(England): Home Int 1998

Sandywell, A
(England): Home Int 1990; Eur T Ch 1991

Scannel, BJ
(Ireland): Home Int 1947-48-49-50-51-53-54

Scott, KB
(England): Home Int 1937-38; *v* France 1938

Scott, Hon M
(England): *v* Scotland 1911-12-23-24-25-26. (GBI): Walker Cup 1924-34 (Captain); *v* Australia 1934

Scott, Hon O
(England): *v* Scotland 1902-05-06

Scott, R, jr
(Scotland): *v* England 1924-28. (GBI): Walker Cup 1924

Scott, WGF
(Scotland): *v* Ireland 1927

Scratton, EWHB
(England): *v* Scotland 1912

Scroggie: FH
(Scotland): *v* England 1910

Scrutton, PF
(England): Home Int 1950-55. (GBI): Walker Cup 1955-57

Sewell, D
(England): Home Int 1956-57-58-59-60. (GBI): Walker Cup 1957-59; CW 1959; Eisenhower Trophy 1960

Shade, RDBM
(Scotland): Home Int 1957, 1960 to 1968; *v* Scandinavia 1960-62; Eur T Ch 1965-67. (GBI): Walker Cup 1961-63-65-67; *v* Europe 1962-64-66-68; Eisenhower Trophy 1962-64-66-68; CW 1963-67; *v* Australia 1964

Shaw, G
(Scotland): Home Int 1984-86-87-88-90; *v* West Germany 1987;
v Sweden 1984; *v* France 1987; Eur T Ch 1987. (GBI): Walker Cup 1987

Sheals, HS
(Ireland): *v* Wales 1929; *v* England 1929-30-31; *v* Scotland 1930; Home Int 1932-33

Sheahan, D
(Ireland): Home Int 1961-62-63-64-65-66-67-70. (GBI): Walker Cup 1963; *v* Europe 1962-64-67

Sheppard, M
(Wales): Home Int 1990

Shepperson, AE
(England): Home Int 1956-57-58-59-60-62. (GBI): Walker Cup 1957-59

Sherborne, A
(England): Home Int 1982-83-84

Sherry, G
(Scotland): Home Int 1993-94-95; *v* France 1993-95; *v* Spain 1994; *v* Sweden 1995; Eur T Ch 1995. (GBI): Walker Cup 1995; *v* Europe 1994; Eisenhower Trophy 1994

Shields, B
(Scotland):Home Int 1986

Shingler, TR
(England): Home Int 1977

Shorrock, TJ
(England): *v* France 1952

Simcox, R
(Ireland): *v* Wales 1930-31; *v* Scotland 1930-31; *v* England 1931; Home Int 1932-33-34-35-36-38

Simpson, AF
(Scotland): *v* Ireland 1928; *v* England 1927

Simpson, JG
(Scotland): *v* England 1906-07-08-09-11-12-22-24-26. (GBI): *v* America 1921

Sinclair, A
(Scotland): Home Int 1950; Eur T Ch 1967 (Captain)

Slark, WA
(England): Home Int 1957

Slater, A
(England): Home Int 1955-62

Slattery, B
(Ireland): Home Int 1947-48

Sludds, MF
(Ireland): Home Int 1982

Smith, A
(Wales): Home Int 1998

Smith, Eric M
(England): *v* Ireland 1931; *v* Scotland 1931

Smith, Everard
(England): *v* Scotland 1908-09-10-12

Smith, GF
(England): *v* Scotland 1902-03

Smith, JN
(Scotland): *v* Ireland 1928-30-31; *v* England 1929-30-31; *v* Wales 1931; Home Int 1932-33-34. (GBI): Walker Cup 1930

Smith, JR
(England): Home Int 1932

Smith, LOM
(England): Home Int 1963

Smith, M
(Wales): Home Int 1993-94-95-96-97; Eur T Ch 1995-97

Smith, S
(Scotland): *v* Austria 1994

Smith, VH
(Wales): *v* Ireland 1924-25

Smith, W
(England): Home Int 1972. (GBI): *v* Europe 1972

Smith, WD
(Scotland): Home Int 1957-58-59-60-63; *v* Scandinavia 1958-60. (GBI): Walker Cup 1959; *v* Europe 1958

Smyth, D
(Ireland): Home Int 1972-73; Eur T Ch 1973

Smyth, DW
(Ireland): *v* Wales 1923-30; *v* England 1930; *v* Scotland 1931; Home Int 1933

Smyth, HB
(Ireland): Home Int 1974-75-76-78; Eur T Ch 1975-79; *v* France, West Germany, Sweden 1976. (GBI): *v* Europe 1976

Smyth, V
(Ireland): Home Int 1981-82

Snowdon, J
(England): Home Int 1934

Soulby, DEB
(Ireland): *v* Wales 1929-30; *v* England 1929-30; *v* Scotland 1929-30

Spiller, EF
(Ireland): *v* Wales 1924; *v* England 1928; *v* Scotland 1928-29

Spring, G
(Ireland): Home Int 1996

Squirrell, HC
(Wales): Home Int 1955 to 1971, 1973 to 1975; Eur T Ch 1967-69-71-75; v France 1975

Stanford, M
(England): Home Int 1991-92-93; v France 1992. (GBI): Walker Cup 1993; v Europe 1992; Eisenhower Trophy 1992

Staunton, R
(Ireland): Home Int 1964-65-72; Eur T Ch 1973

Steel, DMA
(England): Home Int 1970

Stephen, AR
(Scotland): Home Int 1971-72-73-74-75-76-77-84-85; Eur T Ch 1975-85; v France 1985; v Spain 1974; v Belgium 1975-77-78. (GBI): Walker Cup 1985; v Europe 1972

Stevens, DI
(Wales): Home Int 1968-69-70-74-75-76-77-78-80-82; Eur T Ch 1969-77; v France 1976; v Denmark 1977

Stevens, LB
(England): v Scotland 1912

Stevenson, A
(Scotland): Home Int 1949

Stevenson, JB
(Scotland): v Ireland 1931; Home Int 1932-38-47-49-50-51

Stevenson, JF
(Ireland): v Wales 1923-24; v England 1925

Stevenson, K
(Ireland): Home Int 1972

Stockdale, B
(England): Home Int 1964-65

Stoker, K
(Wales): v Ireland 1923-24

Stokoe, GC
(Wales): v England 1925; v Ireland 1929-30

Storey, EF
(England): v Scotland 1924-25-26-27-28-30; Home Int 1936; v France 1936. (GBI): Walker Cup 1924-26-28

Stott, HAN
(England): Home Int 1976-77

Stout, JA
(England): v Scotland 1928-29-30-31; v Ireland 1929-31. (GBI): Walker Cup 1930-32

Stowe, C
(England): Home Int 1935-36-37-38-47-49-54; v France 1938-39-49. (GBI): Walker Cup 1938-47

Strachan, CJL
(Scotland): Home Int 1965-66-67; Eur T Ch 1967

Straker, R
(England): Home Int 1932

Streeter, P
(England): Home Int 1992; v France 1994-96

Stuart, HB
(Scotland): Home Int 1967-68-69-70-71-72-73-74-76; Eur T Ch 1969-71-73-75; v Belgium 1973-75. (GBI): Walker Cup 1971-73-75; v Europe 1968-72-74; CW 1971; Eisenhower Trophy 1972

Stuart, JE
(Scotland): Home Int 1959

Stubbs, AK
(England): Home Int 1982

Sullivan, K
(Wales): Home Int 1998

Suneson, C
(England): Home Int 1988; Eur T Ch 1989

Sutherland, DMG
(England): Home Int 1947

Sutton, W
(England): v Scotland 1929-31; v Ireland 1929-30-31

Symonds, A
(Wales): v Ireland 1925

Taggart, J
(Ireland): Home Int 1953

Tait, AG
(Scotland): Home Int 1987-88-89; Nixdorf Nations Cup 1989

Tate, JK
(England): Home Int 1954-55-56

Taylor, GN
(Scotland): Home Int 1948

Taylor, HE
(England): v Scotland 1911

Taylor, JS
(Scotland): v England 1979; Home Int 1980; v Belgium 1980; v France 1980

Taylor, LG
(Scotland): Home Int 1955-56

Taylor, TPD
(Wales): Home Int 1963

Taylor, Y
(Wales): Home Int 1995-96-97; Eur T Ch 1995-97

Thirlwell, A
(England): Home Int 1951-52-54-55-56-57-58-63-64. (GBI): Walker Cup 1957; v Europe 1956-58-64; CW 1953-64

Thirsk, TJ
(England): v Ireland 1929; Home Int 1933-34-35-36-37-38; v France 1935-36-37-38-39

Thom, KG
(England): Home Int 1947-48-49-53. (GBI): Walker Cup 1949

Thomas, I
(England): Home Int 1933

Thomas, KR
(Wales): Home Int 1951-52

Thompson, ASG
(England): Home Int 1935-37

Thompson, MS
(England): Home Int 1982. (GBI): Walker Cup 1983

Thomson, AP
(Scotland): Home Int 1970; Eur T Ch 1971

Thomson, G
(Scotland): Home Int 1996

Thomson, H
(Scotland): Home Int 1934-35-36-37-38. (GBI): Walker Cup 1936-38

Thomson, JA
(Scotland): Home Int 1981-82-83-84-85-86-87-88-89-91-92; Eur T Ch 1983; v West Germany 1987; v Italy 1984-86-88-90; v Sweden 1990

Thomson, M
(Scotland): Home Int 1998

Thorburn, K
(Scotland): v England 1928; v Ireland 1927

Timbey, JC
(Ireland): v Scotland 1928-31; v Wales 1931

Timmis, CW
(England): v Ireland 1930; Home Int. 1936-37

Tipping, EB
(England): v Ireland 1930

Tipple, ER
(England): v Ireland 1928-29; Home Int 1932

Tolley, CJH
(England): v Scotland 1922-23-24-25-26-27-28-29-30; Home Int

1936-37-38; *v* Ireland/Wales 1925; *v* France 1938. (GBI): *v* America 1921, Walker Cup 1922-23-24 (Captain) -26-30-34; *v* South Africa 1927

Tooth, EA
(Wales): *v* Ireland 1913

Torrance, TA
(Scotland): *v* England 1922-23-25-26-28-29-30; Home Int 1933. (GBI): Walker Cup 1924-28-30-**32**-**34**

Torrance, WB
(Scotland): *v* England 1922-23-24-26-27-28-30; *v* Ireland 1928-29-30. (GBI): Walker Cup 1922

Townsend, PM
(England): Home Int 1965-66. (GBI): Walker Cup 1965; *v* Europe 1966; Eisenhower Trophy 1966

Toye, JL
(Wales): Home Int 1963-64-65-66-67-69-70-71-72-73-74-76-78; Eur T Ch 1971-73-75-77; *v* France 1975

Tredinnick, SV
(England): Home Int 1950

Tucker, WI
(Wales): Home Int 1949 to 1972, 1974-75; Eur T Ch 1967-69-75; *v* France 1975

Tulloch, W
(Scotland): *v* England 1927-29-30-31; *v* Ireland 1930-31; *v* Wales 1931; Home Int 1932

Tupling, LP
(England): Home Int 1969; Eur T Ch 1969. (GBI): Walker Cup 1969

Turnbull, A
(Scotland): Home Int 1995-96-97; *v* France 1995; *v* Spain 1996

Turnbull, CH
(Wales): *v* Ireland 1913-25

Turner, A
(England): Home Int 1952

Turner, GB
(Wales): Home Int 1947-48-49-50-51-52-55-56

Tweddell, W
(England): *v* Scotland 1928-29-30; Home Int 1935.(GBI): Walker Cup **1928-36**

Twynholm, S
(Scotland): Home Int 1990. Nixdorf Nations Cup 1990

Urquhart, M
(Scotland): Home Int 1993; *v* Italy 1996

Vannet, L
(Scotland): Home Int 1984

Waddell, G
(Ireland): *v* Wales 1925

Wainwright, A
(England): Home Int 1997

Walker, J
(Scotland): Home Int 1954-55-57-58-60-61-62-63; *v* Scandinavia 1958-62. (GBI): Walker Cup 1961; *v* Europe 1958-60

Walker, KH
(Scotland): Home Int 1985-86

Walker, MS
(England): *v* Ireland/Wales 1925

Walker, RS
(Scotland): Home Int 1935-36

Wallbank, K
(England): Home Int 1996-97; *v* France 1996

Wallis, G
(Wales): Home Int 1934-36-37-38

Walls, MPD
(Ireland): Home Int 1980-81-85

Walters, EM
(Wales): Home Int 1967-68-69; Eur T Ch 1969

Walton, AR
(England): Home Int 1934-35

Walton, P
(Ireland): *v* Wales 1979: Home Int 1980-81; *v* France, Germany, Sweden 1980; Eur T Ch 1981. (GBI): Walker Cup 1981-83; Eisenhower Trophy 1982

Warren, KT
(England): Home Int 1962

Watson, CR
(Scotland): Home Int 1991-92-94-95-96-97-98; *v* Sweden 1992-97; *v* Italy 1992; *v* Austria 1994; *v* Spain 1996; *v* France 1997; Eur T Ch 1997. (GBI) Walker Cup 1997

Watt, AW
(Scotland): Home Int 1987

Watts, C
(England): Home Int 1991-92; *v* France 1992

Way, P
(England): Home Int 1981; Eur T Ch 1981. (GBI): Walker Cup 1981.

Webster, AJ
(Scotland): Home Int 1978

Webster, F
(Ireland): Home Int 1949

Webster, S
(England): Home Int 1995-96; Eur T Ch 1997

Weeks, K
(England): Home Int 1987-88; *v* France 1988

Welch, L
(Ireland): Home Int 1936

Welch, M
(England): Home Int 1993-94; *v* France 1994

Wemyss, DS
(Scotland): Home Int 1937

Werner, LE
(Ireland): *v* Wales 1925

West, CH
(Ireland): *v* England 1928; Home Int 1932

Westwood, L
(England): Home Int 1993

Wethered, RH
(England): *v* Scotland 1922-23-24-25-26-27-28-29-30. (GBI): *v* America 1921, Walker Cup 1922-23-26-**30**-34

White, L
(England): Home Int 1990; Eur T Ch 1991. (GBI): Walker Cup 1991

White, RJ
(England): Home Int 1947-48-49-53-54. (GBI): Walker Cup 1947-49-51-53-55

Whyte, AW
(Scotland): Home Int 1934

Wiggett, M
(England): Home Int 1990

Wiggins, R
(England): Home Int 1996; Eur T Ch 1997. (GBI): *v* Europe 1996

Wight, R
(Scotland): *v* Sweden 1950

Wilkie, DF
(Scotland): Home Int 1962-63-65-67-68

Wilkie, G
(Scotland): *v* England 1911

Wilkie, GT
(Wales): Home Int 1938

Wilkinson, S
(Wales): Home Int 1990-91

Willcox, FS
(Wales): *v* Scotland 1931; *v* Ireland 1931

Williams, C
(Wales): Home Int 1998

Williams, DF
(England): v Scotland 1979

Williams KH
(Wales): Home Int 1983-84-85-86-87

Williams, PG
(Wales): v Ireland 1925

Williamson, SB
(Scotland): Home Int 1947-48-49-51-52

Willison, R
(England): Home Int 1988-89-90; Eur T Ch 1989-91. (GBI): Walker Cup 1991; v Europe 1990. Eisenhower Trophy 1990

Wills, M
(Wales): Home Int 1990

Wilson, E
(Scotland): Home Int 1985

Wilson, J
(Scotland): v England 1922-23-24-26; v Ireland 1932. (GBI): Walker Cup 1923

Wilson, JC
(Scotland): Home Int 1947-48-49-51-52-53; v Sweden 1950; v New Zealand 1954. (GBI): Walker Cup 1947-53; v South Africa 1954; CW 1954

Wilson, P
(Scotland): Home Int 1976; Belgium 1977

Winchester, R
(England): Home Int 1985-87-89

Winfield, HB
(Wales): v Ireland 1913

Winter, G
(England): Home Int 1991

Wise, WS
(England): Home Int 1947

Wolstenholme, GB
(England): Home Int 1953-55-56-57-58-59-60 (GBI): Walker Cup 1957-59; Eisenhower Trophy 1958-60; CW 1959

Wolstenholme, GP
(England): Home Int 1988 to 1998; v France 1988-92-94; v Spain 1989-91-95; Eur T Ch 1995-97. (GBI): Walker Cup 1995-97; v Europe 1992-94; Eisenhower Trophy 1996-98 (winners)

Wood, DK
(Wales): Home Int 1982-83-84-85-86-87

Woollam, J
(England): Home Int 1933-34-35; v France 1935

Woolley, FA
(England): v Scotland 1910-11-12

Woosnam, I
(Wales): v France 1976

Worthington, JS
(England): v Scotland 1905

Wright, I
(Scotland): Home Int 1958-59-60-61; v Scandinavia 1960-62

Yeo, J
(England): Home 1971

Young, D
(Ireland): Home Int 1969-70-77

Young, ID
(Scotland): Home Int 1981-82; v France 1982. (GBI): v Europe 1982

Young, JR
(Scotland): Home Int 1960-61-65; v Scandinavia 1960. (GB): v Europe 1960

Young, S
(Scotland): Home Int 1996; v Italy 1996; Eur T Ch 1997. (GBI) Walker Cup 1997

Zacharias, JP
(England): Home Int 1935

Zoete, HW de
(England): v Scotland 1903-04-06-07

British Isles International Players, Amateur Women

Abbreviations
CW   Commonwealth Tournament (Team from UK)
Eur(L) T Ch   played in European Ladies Amateur Team Championship
Home Int   played in Home International matches
Captaincy is indicated by the year printed in bold type
Previous surnames are shown in brackets.

Agnew, C
(Scotland): Home Int 1995

Aitken, E (Young)
(Scotland): Home Int 1954

Alexander, M
(Ireland): Home Int 1920-21-22-30

Allen, F
(England): Home Int 1952

Allington Hughes, Miss
(Wales): Home Int 1908-09-10-12-14-22-25

Anderson, E
(Scotland): Home Int 1910-11-12-21-25

Anderson, F
(Scotland): Home Int 1977-79-80-81-83-84-86-87-88-89-90-91-92; Eur(L) T Ch 1979-83-87-91. (GBI): Vagliano Trophy 1987

Anderson, H
(Scotland): Home Int 1964-65-68-69-70-71; Eur(L) T Ch 1969. (GBI): Vagliano Trophy 1969

Anderson, J (Donald)
(Scotland): Home Int 1947-48-49-50-51-52-53. (GBI): Curtis Cup 1948-50-52

Anderson, L.
(Scotland): Home Int 1986-87-88-89; Eur(L) T Ch 1987-89

Anderson, VH
(Scotland): Home Int 1907

Andrew, K
(England): Home Int 1996-97; Eur(L) T Ch 1997. (GBI): Curtis Cup 1998; Vagliano Trophy 1997

Arbuthnot, M
(Ireland): Home Int 1921

Archer, A (Rampton)
(England): Home Int **1968**

Armstrong, M
(Ireland): Home Int 1906

Ashcombe, Lady
(Wales): Home Int 1950-51-52-53-54

Aubertin, Mrs
(Wales): Home Int 1908-09-10

Bailey, D [Frearson] (Robb)
(England): Home Int 1961-62-71; Eur(L) T Ch 1968-**93**. (GBI): Curtis Cup 1962-72-**84-86-88**; Vagliano Trophy 1961-**83-85**; CW 1983

Baker, J
(Wales): Home Int 1990

Bald, J
(Scotland): Home Int 1968-69-71; Eur(L) T Ch 1969

Barber, S (Bonallack)
(England): Home Int 1960-61-62-68-70-72-77-**78**; Eur(L) T Ch 1969-71. (GBI): Curtis Cup 1962; Vagliano Trophy 1961-63-69; CW **1995**; Espirito Santo **1996**

Barclay, C (Brisbane)
(Scotland): Home Int 1953-61-68

Bargh Etherington, B (Whitehead)
(England): Home Int 1974

Barlow, Mrs
(Ireland): Home Int 1921

Barron, M
(Wales): Home Int 1929-30-31-34-35-36-37-38-39-47-48-49-50-51-52-53-54-55-56-57-58-60-61-62-63

Barry, L
(England): Home Int 1911-12-13-14

Barry, P
(England): Home Int 1982

Barton, P
(England): Home Int 1935-36-37-38-39. (GBI): Curtis Cup 1934-36

Bastin, G
(England): Home Int 1920-21-22-23-24-25

Bayliss, Mrs
(Wales): Home Int 1921

Bayman, L (Denison Pender)
(England): Home Int 1971-72-73-83-84-85-87-**88**-**95-96**; Eur(L) T Ch 1985-87-89-**97**. (GBI): Curtis Cup 1988; Vagliano Trophy 1971-85-87; Espirito Santo 1988

Baynes, Mrs CE
(Scotland): Home Int 1921-22

Beck, B (Pim)
(Ireland): Home Int 1930-31-32-33-34-36-37-47-**48**-49-50-51-52-53-54-55-56-58-59-61

Beckett, J
(Ireland): Home Int 1962-66-67-68; Eur(L) T Ch 1967

Beddows, C [Watson] (Stevenson)
(Scotland): Home Int 1913-14-21-22-23-27-29-30-31-32-33-34-35-36-37-39-47-48-49-50-51. (GBI): Curtis Cup 1932

Behan, L
(Ireland): Home Int 1984-85-86-96-98. (GBI): Curtis Cup 1986; Vagliano Trophy 1985

Beharrell, V (Anstey)
(England): Home Int 1955-56-57-61. (GBI): Curtis Cup 1956

Benka, P (Tredinnick)
(England): Home Int 1967. (GBI): Curtis Cup 1966-68; Vagliano Trophy 1967

Bennett, L
(Scotland): Home Int 1977-80-81

Benton, MH
(Scotland): Home Int 1914

Biggs, A (Whittaker)
(England): (GBI): Vagliano Trophy 1959

Birmingham, M
(Ireland): Home Int 1967

Bisgood, J
(England) Home Int 1949-50-51-52-53-54-56-58. (GBI): Curtis Cup 1950-52-54-**70**

Blair, N (Menzies)
(Scotland): Home Int 1955

Blake, Miss
(Ireland): Home Int 1931-32-34-35-36

Blaymire, J
(England): Home Int 1971-88-**89**

Bloodworth, D (Lewis)
(Wales): Home Int 1954-55-56-57-60

Boatman, EA (Collis)
(England): Home Int 1974-80-**84-85-90-91**; Eur(L) T Ch **1985-87**. (GBI): Curtis Cup **1992-94**; CW **1987-91**

Bolas, R
(England): Home Int 1992

Bolton, Z (Bonner Davis)
(England): Home Int 1939-48-49-50-51-**55**-56. (GBI): Curtis Cup 1948-**56-66-68-94**; CW 1967

Bonallack, A (Ward)
(England): Home Int 1956-57-58-59-60-61-62-63-64-**65**-66-72. (GBI): Curtis Cup 1956-58-60-62-64-66; Vagliano Trophy 1959-61-63

Bostock, M
(England): Home Int **1954**

Bourn, Mrs
(England): Home Int 1909-12

Bowhill, M (Robertson-Durham)
(Scotland): Home Int 1936-37-38

Boyd, J
(Ireland): Home Int 1912-13-14

Boyes, S
(Wales): Home Int 1992

Bradley, K (Rawlings)
(Wales): Home Int 1975-76-77-78-79-82-83

Bradshaw, E
(Ireland): Home Int 1964-66-67-68-69-70-71-74-75-**80-81**; Eur(L) T Ch 1969-71-75. (GBI): Vagliano Trophy 1969-71

Brandom, G
(Ireland): Home Int 1965-66-67-68; Eur(L) T Ch 1967. (GBI): Vagliano Trophy 1967

Brearley, M
(Wales): Home Int 1937-38

Brennan, R (Hegarty)
(Ireland): Home Int 1974-75-76-77-78-79-81

Brewerton, R
(Wales): Home Int 1997-98

Brice, Mrs
(Ireland): Home Int 1948

Bridges, Mrs
(Wales): Home Int 1933-38-39

Briggs, A (Brown)
(Wales): Home Int 1969-70-71-72-73-74-75-76-77-78-79-80-**81-82-83**-84-**93**; Eur(L) T Ch 1971-75. (GBI): Vagliano Trophy 1971-75

Brinton, Mrs
(Ireland): Home Int 1922

Bromley-Davenport, I (Rieben)
(Wales): Home Int 1932-33-34-35-36-48-50-51-52-53-54-55-56

Brook, D
(Wales): Home Int 1913

Brooks, E
(Ireland): Home Int 1953-54-56

Broun, JG
(Scotland): Home Int 1905-06-07-21

Brown, B
(Ireland): Home Int 1960

Brown, E (Jones)
(Wales): Home Int 1947-48-49-50-52-53-57-58-59-60-61-62-63-64-65-66-68-69-70

Brown, F
(England): Home Int 1994-96-97-98; Eur(L) T Ch 1997; (GBI) Curtis Cup 1998

Brown, Mrs FW (Gilroy)
(Scotland): Home Int 1905-06-07-08-09-10-11-13-21

Brown, J
(Wales): Home Int 1960-61-62-64-65; Eur(L) T Ch 1965-69

Brown, J
(England): Home Int 1984

Brown, TWL
(Scotland): Home Int 1924-25

Brown, Mrs
(Wales): Home Int 1924-25-27

Brownlow, Miss
(Ireland): Home Int 1923

Bryan-Smith, S
(Wales): Home Int 1947-48-49-50-51-52-56

Burnell, S
(England): Home Int 1993; Eur(L) T Ch 1993

Burrell, Mrs
(Wales): Home Int 1939

Burton, H (Mitchell)
(Scotland): Home Int 1931-55-56-**59**. (GBI): Vagliano Trophy 1961

Burton, M
(England): Eur(L) T Ch 1997

Burton, M
(England): Home Int 1975-76

Butler, I (Burke)
(Ireland): Home Int 1962-63-64-65-66-68-70-71-72-73-76-77-78-79-**86-87**; Eur(L) T Ch 1967. (GBI): Curtis Cup 1966-**96**; Vagliano Trophy 1965; Espirito Santo 1964-66

Buxton, N
(England): Home Int 1991-92-93; Eur LT Ch 1991-93. (GBI): Curtis Cup 1992; Vagliano Trophy 1991-93

Byrne, A (Sweeney)
(Ireland): Home Int 1959-60-61-62-63-**90-91**

Cadden, G
(Scotland): Home Int 1974-75-**95-96**; Eur(L) T Ch **1997**. (GBI) Vagliano Trophy **1997**

Cairns, Lady Katherine
(England): Home Int 1947-48-50-51-52-53-54. (GBI): Curtis Cup **1952**

Caldwell, C (Redford)
(England): Home Int 1973-78-79-80. (GBI): Curtis Cup 1978-80; Vagliano Trophy 1973

Callen, L
(Ireland): Home Int 1990

Campbell, J (Burnett)
(Scotland): Home Int 1960

Cann, M (Nuttall)
(England): Home Int 1966

Carrick, P (Bullard)
(England): Home Int 1939-47

Caryl, M
(Wales): Home Int 1929

Casement, M (Harrison)
(Ireland): Home Int 1909-10-11-12-13-14

Cassidy, Y
(Ireland): Home Int 1994-95

Cautley, B (Hawtrey)
(England): Home Int 1912-13-14-22-23-24-25-27

Chambers, D
(England): Home Int 1906-07-09-10-11-12-20-24-25. (GBI): Curtis Cup **1934-36-38**

Christison, D
(England): Home Int 1981

Chugg, P (Light)
(Wales): Home Int 1973-74-75-76-77-78-86-87-88-96; Eur(L) T Ch 1975-87

Clark, G (Atkinson)
(England): Home Int 1955

Clarke, Mrs ML
(England): Home Int 1933-35

Clarke, P
(England): Home Int 1981

Clarke, Mrs
(Ireland): Home Int 1922

Clarkson, H (Reynolds)
(Wales): Home Int 1935-38-39

Clay, E
(Wales): Home Int 1912

Clement, V
(England): Home Int 1932-34-35

Close, M (Wenyon)
(England): Home Int 1968-69; Eur(L) T Ch 1969. (GBI): Vagliano Trophy 1969

Coats, Mrs G
(Scotland): Home Int 1931-32-33-34

Cochrane, K
(Scotland): Home Int 1924-25-28-29-30

Coffey, A
(Ireland): Home Int 1995-96-97-98; Eur(L) T Ch 1997

Cole, C
(Wales): Home Int 1998

Collett, P
(England): Home Int 1910

Collingham, J (Melville)
(England): Home Int 1978-79-81-84-86-87-92; Eur(L) T Ch 1989. (GBI): Vagliano Trophy 1979-87; CW 1987

Colquhoun, H
(Ireland): Home Int 1959-60-61-63

Comboy, C (Grott)
(England): Home Int **1975-76**. (GBI): Curtis Cup **1978-80**; Vagliano Trophy **1977-1979**; Espirito Santo **1978**; CW 1979

Connachan, J
(Scotland): Home Int 1979-80-81-82-83. (GBI): Curtis Cup 1980-82; Vagliano Trophy 1981-83; Espirito Santo 1980-82; CW 1983

Coote, Miss
(Ireland): Home Int 1925-28-29

Copley, K (Lackie)
(Scotland): Home Int 1974-75

Corlett, E
(England): Home Int 1927-29-30-31-32-33-35-36-37-38-39.(GBI): Curtis Cup 1932-38-**64**

Costello, G
(Ireland): Home Int 1973-**84-85**

Cotton, S (German)
(England): Home Int 1967-68; Eur(L) T Ch 1967. (GBI): Vagliano Trophy 1967

Couper, M
(Scotland): Home Int 1929-34-35-36-37-39-56

Cowley, Lady
(Wales): Home Int 1907-09

Cox, Margaret
(Wales): Home Int 1924-25

Cox, Nell
(Wales): Home Int 1954

Craik, T
(Scotland): Home Int 1988

Cramsie, F (Hezlet)
(Ireland): Home Int 1905-06-07-08-09-10-13-20-24

Crawford, I (Wylie)
(Scotland): Home Int 1970-71-72

Cresswell, K (Stuart)
(Scotland): Home Int 1909-10-11-12-14

Critchley, D (Fishwick)
(England): Home Int 1930-31-32-33-35-36-47. (GBI): Curtis Cup 1932-34-**50**

Croft, A
(England): Home Int 1927

Cross, M
(Wales): Home Int 1922

Cruickshank, DM (Jenkins)
(Scotland): Home Int 1910-11-12

Crummack, Miss
(England): Home Int 1909

Cuming, Mrs
(Ireland): Home Int 1910

Cunninghame, S
(Wales): Home Int 1922-25-29-31

Cuthell, R (Adair)
(Ireland): Home Int 1908

Dampney, S
(Wales): Home Int 1924-25-27-28-29-30

David, Mrs
(Wales): Home Int 1908

Davidson, B (Inglis)
(Scotland): Home Int 1928

Davies, K
(Wales): Home Int 1981-82-83; Eur(L) T Ch 1987. (GBI): Curtis Cup 1986-88; Vagliano Trophy 1987; CW 1987

Davies, L
(England): Home Int 1983-84. (GBI): Curtis Cup 1984; CW 1987

Davies, P (Griffiths)
(Wales): Home Int 1965-66-67-68-70-71-73; Eur(L) T Ch 1971

Davis, L
(Wales): Home Int 1997-98; Eur(L) T Ch 1997

Deacon, Mrs
(Wales): Home Int 1912-14

Denny, A (Barrett)
(England): Home Int 1951

Dering, Mrs
(Ireland): Home Int 1923

Dermott, L
(Wales): Home Int 1987-88-89-91-92-93-94-95-96; Eur(L) T Ch 1991-93. (GBI): Curtis Cup 1996

Dickson, M
(Ireland): Home Int 1909

Dobson, H
(England): Home Int 1987-88-89; Eur(L) T Ch 1989. (GBI): Curtis Cup 1990; Vagliano Trophy 1989

Dod, L
(England): Home Int 1905

Donne, A
(Wales): Home Int 1993-94; Eur(L) T Ch 1993

Douglas, K
(England): Home Int 1981-82-83. (GBI): Curtis Cup 1982; Vagliano Trophy 1983

Dowdall, E
(Ireland): Home Int 1997-98

Dowling, C (Hourihane)
(Ireland): Home Int 1979 to 1992; Eur(L) T Ch 1981-83-85-87-89-**97**. (GBI):Curtis Cup 1984-86-88-90-92; Vagliano Trophy 1981-83-85-87-89-91; Espirito Santo 1986-90

Dowling, D
(England): Home Int 1979

Draper, M [Peel] (Thomas)
(Scotland): Home Int 1929-34-38-49-50-51-52-53-**54-55**-56-57-58-**61**-62. (GBI): Curtis Cup 1954; Vagliano Trophy **1963**

Duggleby, E
(England): Home Int 1994-95-96; Eur(L) T Ch 1995. (GBI): Vagliano Trophy 1995

Duncan, B
(Wales): Home Int 1907-08-09-10-12

Duncan, M
(Wales): Home Int 1922-23-28-34

Duncan, MJ (Wood)
(Scotland): Home Int 1925-27-28-39

Durlacher, Mrs
(Ireland): Home Int 1905-06-07-08-09-10-14

Durrant, B [Green] (Lowe)
(England): Home Int 1954

Dwyer, Mrs
(Ireland): 1928

Eakin, P (James)
(Ireland): Home Int 1967

Eakin, T
(Ireland): Home Int 1990-91-92-93-94; Eur(L) T Ch 1993

Earner, M
(Ireland): Home Int 1960-61-62-63-70

Edmond, F (Macdonald)
(England): Home Int 1991; Eur LT Ch 1991. (GBI): Vagliano Trophy 1991

Educate, L (Walton)
(England): Home Int 1991-94-95; Eur(L) T Ch 1993-95. (GBI): Curtis Cup 1994-96; Vagliano Trophy 1993-95; CW 1995

Edwards, E
(Wales): Home Int 1949-50

Edwards, J
(Wales): Home Int 1932-33-34-36-37

Edwards, J (Morris)
(Wales): Home Int 1962-63-66-67-68-69-70-77-**78**-79; Eur(L) T Ch 1967-69-**93**

Egford, K
(England): Home Int 1992-94

Ellis, E
(Ireland): Home Int 1932-35-37-38

Ellis Griffiths (Mrs)
(Wales): Home Int 1907-08-09-12-13

Emery, MJ
(Wales): Home Int 1928-29-30-31-32-33-34-35-36-37-38-47

Evans, H
(England): Home Int 1908

Evans, N
(Wales): Home Int 1908-09-10-13

Evans, N
(Wales): Home Int 1996-97-98; Eur(L) T Ch 1997

Everard, M
(England): Home Int 1964-67-69-70-72-73-77-78; Eur(L) T Ch 1967-71-77. (GBI): Curtis Cup 1970-72-74-78; Vagliano Trophy 1967-69-71-73; Espirito Santo 1968-72-78; CW 1971

Fairclough, L
(England): Home Int 1988-89-90; Eur(L) T Ch 1989. (GBI): Vagliano Trophy 1989

Falconer, V (Lamb)
(Scotland): Home Int 1932-36-37-47-48-49-50-51-52-53-54-55-56

Farie-Anderson, J
(Scotland): Home Int 1924

Farquharson-Black, E
(Scotland): Home Int 1987-88-89-90-91-97-98; Eur(L) T Ch 1989-91. (GBI): Curtis Cup 1990-92; Vagliano Trophy 1989-91; CW 1991

Ferguson, A
(Ireland): Home Int 1989

Ferguson, D
(Ireland): Home Int 1927-28-29-30-31-32-34-35-36-37-38-**61**. (GBI): Curtis Cup **1958**

Ferguson, M (Fowler)
(Scotland): Home Int 1959-62-63-64-65-66-67-69-70-85; Eur(L) T Ch 1965-67-71. (GBI): Curtis Cup 1966; Vagliano Trophy 1965

Ferguson R (Ogden)
(England): Home Int 1957

Fields, E
(England): Home Int 1995-96

Fisher, K
(England): Home Int 1998

Fitzgibbon, M
(Ireland): Home Int 1920-21-29-30-31-32-33

FitzPatrick, O (Heskin)
(Ireland): Home Int 1967

Fletcher, L
(England): Home Int 1989-90; Eur (L)T Ch 1991. (GBI): Curtis Cup 1990; CW 1991

Fletcher, P (Sherlock)
(Ireland): Home Int 1932-34-35-36-38-39-54-55-**66**

Forbes, J
(Scotland): Home Int 1985-86-87-88-89; Eur(L) T Ch 1987-89

Ford, J
(Scotland): Home Int 1993-94-95

Foster, C
(England): Home Int 1905-06-09

Fowler, J
(England): Home Int 1928

Franklin Thomas, E
(Wales): Home Int 1909

Freeguard, C
(Wales): Home Int 1927

Furby, J
(England): Home Int 1987-88; Eur(L) T Ch 1987

Fyshe, M
(England): Home Int 1938

Gallagher, S
(Scotland): Home Int 1983-84

Gardiner, A
(Ireland): Home Int 1927-29

Garfield Evans, PR (Whittaker)
(Wales): Home Int 1948-49-50-51-52-53-54-**55**-**56**-**57**-**58**

Garon, MR
(England): Home Int 1927-28-32-33-34-36-37-38. (GBI): Curtis Cup 1936

Garrett, M (Ruttle)
(England): Home Int 1947-48-50-53-**59**-**60**-**63**. (GBI): Curtis Cup 1948-**60**; Vagliano Trophy 1959

Garvey, P
(Ireland): Home Int 1947-48-49-50-51-52-53-**54**-56-57-**58**-**59**-**60**-61-62-63-68-69. (GBI): Curtis Cup 1948-50-52-54-56-60; Vagliano Trophy 1959-63

Gaynor, Z (Fallon)
(Ireland): Home Int 1952-53-54-55-56-57-58-59-60-61-62-63-64-65-68-69-70-**72**. (GBI): Espirito Santo 1964

Gear Evans, A
(Wales): Home Int 1932-33-34

Gee, Hon. J (Hives)
(England): Home Int 1950-51-52

Gemmill, A
(Scotland): Home Int 1981-82-84-85-86-87-88-89-91-**97**

Gethin Griffith, S
(Wales): Home Int 1914-22-23-24-28-29-30-31-35

Gibb, M (Titterton)
(England): Home Int 1906-07-08-10-12

Gibbs, C (Le Feuvre)
(England): Home Int 1971-72-73-74. (GBI): Curtis Cup 1974; Vagliano Trophy 1973

Gibbs, S
(Wales): Home Int 1933-34-39

Gildea, Miss
(Ireland): Home Int 1936-37-38-39

Glendinning, D
(Ireland): Home Int 1937-54

Glennie, H
(Scotland): Home Int 1959

Glover, A
(Scotland): Home Int 1905-06-08-09-12

Gold, N
(England): Home Int 1929-31-32

Gordon, J
(England): Home Int 1947-48-49-52-53. (GBI): Curtis Cup 1948

Gorman, S
(Ireland): Home Int 1976-79-80-81-82-**92**-**93**; Eur(L) T Ch **1993**

Gorry, Mary
(Ireland): Home Int 1971-72-73-74-75-76-77-78-79-80-88-**89**; Eur(L) T Ch 1971-75. (GBI): Vagliano Trophy 1977

Gotto, Mrs C
(Ireland): Home Int 1923

Gotto, Mrs L
(Ireland): Home Int 1920

Gourlay, M
(England): Home Int 1923-24-27-28-29-30-32-33-34-38-**57**. (GBI): Curtis Cup 1932-34

Gow, J
(Scotland): Home Int 1923-24-27-28

Graham, MA
(Scotland): Home Int 1905-06

Graham, N
(Ireland): Home Int 1908-09-10-12

Granger Harrison, Mrs
(Scotland): Home Int 1922

Grant-Suttie, E
(Scotland): Home Int 1908-10-11-14-22-23

Grant-Suttie, R
(Scotland): Home Int 1914

Green, B (Pockett)
(England): Home Int 1939

Grice-Whittaker, P (Grice)
(England): Home Int 1983-84. (GBI): Curtis Cup 1984; Espirito Santo 1984

Griffith, W
(Wales): Home Int 1981

Griffiths, M
(England): Home Int 1920-21

Greenlees, E
(Scotland): Home Int 1924

Greenlees, Y
(Scotland): Home Int 1928-30-31-33-34-35-38

Guadella, E (Leitch)
(England): Home Int 1908-10-20-21-22-27-28-29-30-33

Gubbins, Miss
(Ireland): Home Int 1905

Hackett, B
(Ireland): Home Int 1993-94-96

Hackney, L
(England): Home Int 1990

Haig, J (Mathias Thomas)
(Wales): Home Int 1938-39

Hall, C
(England): Home Int 1991-92; Eur LT Ch 1991. (GBI): Curtis Cup 1992; Vagliano Trophy 1991

Hall, CM
(England): Home Int 1985

Hall, J (Wade)
(England): Home Int 1987 to 1995; Eur(L) T Ch 1987-89-91-93-95. (GBI): Curtis Cup 1988-90-92-94-96; Espirito Santo 1988-90-94; Vagliano Trophy 1989-91-93-95; CW 1991-95

Hall, Mrs
(Ireland): Home Int 1927-30

Hamilton, S (McKinven)
(Scotland): Home Int 1965

Hambro, W (Martin Smith)
(England): Home Int 1914

Hamilton, J
(England): Home Int 1937-38-39

Hammond, T
(England): Home Int 1985

Hampson, M
(England): Home Int 1954

Hanna, D
(Ireland): Home Int 1987-88

Harrington, D
(Ireland): Home Int 1923

Harris, M [Spearman]
(England): Home Int 1955-56-57-58-59-60-61-62-63-64-65; Eur(L) T Ch 1965-71. (GBI): Curtis Cup 1960-62-64; Vagliano Trophy 1959-61-65; Espirito Santo 1964

Harrold, L
(England): Home Int 1974-75-76

Hartill, D
(England): Home Int 1923

Hartley, E
(England): Home Int **1964**

Hartley, R
(Wales): Home Int 1958-59-62

Hastings, D (Sommerville)
(Scotland): Home Int 1955-56-57-58-59-60-61-62-63. (GBI): Curtis Cup 1958; Vagliano Trophy 1963

Hay, J (Pelham Burn)
(Scotland): Home Int 1959

Hayter, J (Yuille)
(England): Home Int 1956

Hazlett, VP
(Ireland): Home Int 1956

Healy, B (Gleeson)
(Ireland): Home Int 1980-82

Heathcoat-Amory, Lady (Joyce Wethered)
(England): Home Int 1921-22-23-24-25-29. (GBI): Curtis Cup 1932

Hedges, S (Whitlock)
(England): Home Int 1979. (GBI): Vagliano Trophy 1979; CW 1979

Hedley Hill, Miss
(Wales): Home Int 1922

Hegarty, G
(Ireland): Home Int 1955-56-64

Helme, E
(England): Home Int 1911-12-13-20

Heming Johnson, G
(England): Home Int 1909-11-13

Henson, D (Oxley)
(England): Home Int 1967-68-69-70-75-76-77-78; Eur(L) T Ch 1971-77. (GBI): Curtis Cup 1968-70-72-76; Vagliano Trophy 1967-69-71; Espirito Santo 1970; CW 1967-71

Heskin, A
(Ireland): Home Int 1968-69-70-72-75-77-82-83

Hetherington, Mrs (Gittens)
(England): Home Int 1909

Hewett, G
(Ireland): Home Int 1923-24

Hezlet, Mrs
(Ireland): Home Int 1910

Hickey, C
(Ireland): Home Int 1969-75-76

Higgins, E
(Ireland): Home Int 1981 to 1988, 1991 to 1996; Eur(L) T Ch 1987-93

Hill, J
(England): Home Int 1986

Hill, Mrs
(Wales): Home Int 1924

Hockley, J
(England): Home Int 1991-92-93-96. (GBI): Espirito Santo 1992; Vagliano Trophy 1993

Hodge, S (Shapcott)
(England): Home Int 1986-88;
Eur(L) T Ch 1987. (GBI): Curtis Cup 1988; Vagliano Trophy 1987; CW 1987; Espirito Santo 1988

Hodgson, M
(England): Home Int 1939

Holland, I (Hurst)
(Ireland): Home Int 1958

Holm, H (Gray)
(Scotland): Home Int 1932-33-34-35-36-37-38-47-48-50-51-55-57. (GBI): Curtis Cup 1936-38-48

Holmes, A
(England): Home Int 1931

Holmes, J [Hetherington] (McClure)
(England): Home Int 1957-66-67

Hooman, EM [Gavin]
(England): Home Int 1910-11

Hope, LA
(Scotland): Home Int 1975-76-80-84-85-86-87-88-89-90

Hort, K
(Wales): Home Int 1929

Howard, A (Phillips)
(England): Home Int 1953-54-55-56-57-58-79-80. (GBI): Curtis Cup 1956-58

Hudson, R
(England): Home Int 1996-97-98; Eur(L) T Ch 1997.
(GBI): Curtis Cup 1998, Vagliano Trophy 1997

Huggan, S (Lawson)
(Scotland): Home Int 1985-86-87-88-89; Eur(L) T Ch 1985-87-89. (GBI): Curtis Cup 1988, Vagliano Trophy 1989

Hughes, J
(Wales): Home Int 1967-71-88-89; Eur(L) T 1971

Hughes, Miss
(Wales): Home Int 1907

Huke, B
(England): Home Int 1971-72-75-76-77. (GBI): Curtis Cup 1972; Vagliano Trophy 1975

Hulton, V (Hezlet)
(Ireland): Home Int 1905-07-09-10-11-12-20-21

Humphreys, A (Coulman)
(Wales): Home Int 1969-70-71

Humphreys, D (Forster)
(Ireland): Home Int 1951-52-53-55-57

Hunter, D (Tucker)
(England): Home Int 1905

Hurd, D [Howe] (Campbell)
(Scotland): Home Int 1905-06-08-09-11-28-30

Hurst, Mrs
(Wales): Home Int 1921-22-23-25-27-28

Hyland, B
(Ireland): Home Int 1964-65-66

Inghram, E (Lever)
(Wales): Home Int 1947-48-49-50-51-52-53-54-55-56-57-58-64-65

Irvin, A
(England): Home Int 1962-63-65-67-68-69-70-71-72-73-75; Eur(L) T Ch 1965-67-69-71. (GBI): Curtis Cup 1962-68-70-76; Vagliano Trophy 1961-63-65-67-69-71-73-75; Espirito Santo 1982; CW 1967-75

Irvine, Miss
(Wales): Home Int 1930

Isaac, Mrs
(Wales): Home Int 1924

Isherwood, L
(Wales): Home Int 1972-76-77-78-80-86-88-89-90-91

Jack, E (Philip)
(Scotland): Home Int 1962-63-64-81-82

Jackson, B
(Ireland): Home Int 1937-38-39-50

Jackson, B
(England): Home Int 1955-56-57-58-59-63-64-65-66-73-74. (GBI): Curtis Cup 1958-64-68; Vagliano Trophy 1959-63-65-67-73-75; Espirito Santo 1964; CW 1959-67

Jackson, D
(Scotland): Home Int 1990

Jackson, Mrs H
(Ireland): Home Int 1921

Jackson, J
(Ireland): Home Int 1912-13-14-20-21-22-23-24-25-27-28-29-30

Jackson, Mrs L
(Ireland): Home Int 1910-12-14-20-22-25

Jameson, S (Tobin)
(Ireland): Home Int 1913-14-20-24-25-27

Jenkin, B
(Wales): Home Int 1959

Jenkins, J (Owen)
(Wales): Home Int 1953-56

John, J
(Wales): Home Int 1974

Johns, A
(England): Home Int 1987-88-89

Johnson, A (Hughes)
(Wales): Home Int 1964, 1966 to 1976, 1978-79-85-**95**; Eur(L) T Ch 1965-67-69-71

Johnson, J (Roberts)
(Wales): Home Int 1955

Johnson, M
(England): Home Int 1934-35

Johnson, PM
(England): Home Int 1984-85-86; Eur(L) T Ch 1985. (GBI): Curtis Cup 1986; Vagliano Trophy 1985; Espirito Santo 1986

Johnson, R
(Wales): Home Int 1955

Jones, A (Gwyther)
(Wales): Home Int 1959

Jones, B
(Wales): Home Int 1994-95-96-98; Eur(L) T Ch 1993

Jones, K
(Wales): Home Int **1959-60-61**

Jones, M (De Lloyd)
(Wales): Home Int 1951

Jones, Mrs
(Wales): Home Int 1932-35

Justice, M
(Wales): Home Int 1931-32

Kavanagh, H
(Ireland): Home Int 1993-94-95-97-98; Eur(L) T Ch 1997. (GBI): Vagliano Trophy 1995

Kaye, H (Williamson)
(England): Home Int **1986-87**

Keenan, D
(Ireland): Home Int 1989

Keiller, G [Style]
(England): Home Int 1948-49-52

Kelway Bamber, Mrs
(Scotland): Home Int 1923-27-33

Kennedy, D (Fowler)
(England): Home Int 1923-24-25-27-28-29

Kennion, Mrs (Kenyon Stow)
(England) Home Int 1910

Kerr, J
(Scotland): Home Int 1947-48-49-54

Kidd, Mrs
(Ireland): Home Int 1934-37

King Mrs
(Ireland): Home Int 1923-25-27-29

Kinloch, Miss
(Scotland): Home Int 1913-14

Kirkwood, Mrs
(Ireland): Home Int 1955

Knight, Mrs
(Scotland): Home Int 1922

Kyle, B [Rhodes] (Norris)
(England): Home Int 1937-38-39-48-49

Kyle, E
(Scotland): Home Int 1909-10

Laing, A
(Scotland): Home Int 1966-67-70-71-**73-74**; Eur(L) T Ch 1967. (GBI): Vagliano Trophy 1967

Laing, A
(Scotland): Home Int 1995-96-97-98; Eur(L) T Ch 1997

Laing, V
(Scotland): Home Int 1997-98

Lamb, J
(England): Home Int 1998

Lambert, S (Cohen)
(England): Home Int 1979-80-93-94-95; Eur(L) T Ch 1995. (GBI): Vagliano Trophy 1979-95

Lambie, S
(Scotland): Home Int 1976

Laming Evans, Mrs
(Wales): Home Int 1922-23

Langford, Mrs
(Wales): Home Int 1937

Langridge, S (Armitage)
(England): Home Int 1963-64-65-66; Eur(L) T Ch 1965. (GBI): Curtis Cup 1964-66; Vagliano Trophy 1963-65

Large, P (Davies)
(England): Home Int 1951-52-**81-82**

Larkin, C (McAuley)
(Ireland): Home Int 1966-67-68-69-70-71-72; Eur(L) T Ch 1971

Latchford, B
(Ireland): Home Int 1931-33

Latham Hall, E (Chubb)
(England): Home Int 1928

Lauder, G
(Ireland): Home Int 1911

Lauder, R
(Ireland): Home Int 1911

Lawrence, JB
(Scotland): Home Int 1959-60-61-62-63-64-65-66-67-68-69-70-77; Eur(L) T Ch 1965-67-69-71. (GBI): Curtis Cup 1964; Vagliano Trophy 1963-65; Espirito Santo 1964; CW 1971

Lawson, H
(Wales): Home Int 1989-90-91-92-97-98; Eur(L) T Ch 1991-93-97

Lebrun, W (Aitken)
(Scotland): Home Int 1978-79-80-81-82-83-85. (GBI): Curtis Cup 1982; Vagliano Trophy 1981-83

Leaver, B
(Wales): Home Int 1912-14-21

Lee Smith, J
(England): Home Int 1973-74-75-76. (GBI): Curtis Cup 1974-76; Espirito Santo 1976; CW 1975

Leete, Mrs IG
(Scotland): Home Int 1933

Leitch, C
(England): Home Int 1910-11-12-13-14-20-21-22-24-25-27-28

Leitch, M
(England): Home Int 1912-14

Little, S
(Scotland): Home Int 1993

Llewellyn, Miss
(Wales): Home Int 1912-13-14-21-22-23

Lloyd, J
(Wales): Home Int 1988

Lloyd, P
(Wales): Home Int 1935-36

Lloyd Davies, VH
(Wales): Home Int 1913

Lloyd Roberts, V
(Wales): Home Int 1907-08-10

Lloyd Williams, Miss
(Wales): Home Int 1909-10-12-14

Lobbett, P
(England): Home Int 1922-24-27-29-30

Lovatt, S
(Wales): Home Int 1994-95

Lowry, Mrs
(Ireland): Home Int 1947

Luckin, B (Cooper)
(England): Home Int 1980

Lugton, C
(Scotland): Home Int 1968-72-73-75-**76**-77-78-80

Lumb, K (Phillips)
(England): Home Int 1968-69-70-71; Eur(L) T Ch 1969. (GBI): Curtis Cup 1972; Vagliano Trophy 1969-71

Lyons, T (Ross Steen)
(England): Home Int 1959. (GBI): Vagliano Trophy 1959

MacAndrew, F
(Scotland): Home Int 1913-14

Macbeth, M (Dodd)
(England): Home Int 1913-14-20-21-22-23-24-25

MacCann, K
(Ireland): Home Int 1984-85-86

MacCann, K (Smye)
(Ireland): Home Int 1947-48-49-50-51-52-53-54-56-57-58-60-61-62-64-**65**

McCarthy, A
(Ireland): Home Int 1951-52

McCarthy, D
(Ireland): Home Int 1988-90-91-95; Eur(L) T Ch 1993

McCool, L
(Ireland): Home Int 1993

McCulloch, J
(Scotland): Home Int 1921-22-23-24-27-29-30-31-32-33-35-**60**

McDaid, E (O'Grady)
(Ireland): Home Int 1959

Macdonald, F
(England): Home Int 1990

Macdonald, K
(Scotland): Home Int 1928-29

MacGeach, C
(Ireland): Home Int 1938-39-48-49-50

McGreevy, M
(Ireland): Home Int 1996-97-98; Eur(L) T Ch 1997

McGreevy, V
(Ireland): Home Int 1987-90-92

McIntosh, B (Dixon)
(England): Home Int 1969-70; Eur(L) T Ch 1969. (GBI): Vagliano Trophy 1969

MacIntosh, I
(Scotland): Home Int **1991-92-93**; Eur(L) T Ch **1993**

McIntyre, J
(England): Home Int 1949-54

McKay, F
(Scotland): Home Int 1992-93-94; Eur(L) T Ch 1993

McKay, M
(Scotland): Home Int 1991-93-94-96; Eur(L) T Ch 1993-95. (GBI): Curtis Cup 1994-96; Vagliano Trophy 1993-95-97; CW 1995; Espirito Santo 1996

MacKean, Mrs
(Wales): Home Int 1938-39-47

McKenna, M
(Ireland): Home Int 1968 to 1991-93; Eur(L) T Ch 1969-71-75-87. (GBI): Curtis Cup 1970-72-74-76-78-80-82-84-86; Vagliano Trophy 1969-71-73-75-77-79-81-85-87-**95**; Espirito Santo 1970-74-76-**86**-**90**

Mackenzie, A
(Scotland): Home Int 1921

McKinlay, M
(Scotland): Home Int 1990-92-93; Eur(L) T Ch 1993. (GBI): Curtis Cup 1994

McLarty, E
(Scotland): Home Int **1966-67-68**

McMahon, S (Cadden)
(Scotland): Home Int 1974-75-76-77-79. (GBI): Curtis Cup 1976; Vagliano Trophy 1975

McMaster, S
(Scotland): Home Int 1994-95-96-97; Eur(L) T Ch 1995-97

McNair, W
(England): Home Int 1921

McNeil, K
(Scotland): Home Int **1969-70**

McNeile, CL
(Ireland): Home Int 1906

McQuillan, Y
(Ireland): Home Int 1985-86

MacTier, Mrs
(Wales): Home Int 1927

Madeley, M (Coburn)
(Ireland): Home Int 1964-69; Eur(L) T Ch 1969

Madill, M
(Ireland): Home Int 1978-79-80-81-82-83-84-85. (GBI): Curtis Cup 1980; Vagliano Trophy 1979-81-85; Espirito Santo 1980; CW 1979

Madill, Mrs
(Ireland): Home Int 1920-24-25-27-28-29-33

Magee, A-M
(Wales): Home Int 1991-92-93-94

Magill, J
(Ireland): Home Int 1907-11-13

Maher, S (Vaughan)
(England): Home Int 1960-61-62-63-64. (GBI): Curtis Cup 1962-64; Vagliano Trophy 1961; CW 1963

Mahon, D
(Ireland): Home Int 1989-90

Main, M (Farquhar)
(Scotland): Home Int 1950-51

Maitland, M
(Scotland): Home Int 1905-06-08-12-13

Mallam, Mrs S
(Ireland): Home Int 1922-23

Margan, T
(Ireland): Home Int 1998

Marks, Mrs T
(Ireland): Home Int 1950

Marks, Mrs
(Ireland): Home Int 1930-31-33-35

Marley, MV
(Wales): Home Int 1921-22-23-30-37

Marr, H (Cameron)
(Scotland): Home Int 1927-28-29-30-31

Marshall, K (Imrie)
(Scotland): Home Int 1984-85-89. Eur(L) T Ch 1987-89. (GBI): Curtis Cup 1990; Vagliano Trophy 1989

Martin, P [Whitworth Jones] (Low)
(Wales): Home Int 1948-50-56-59-60-61

Marvin, V
(England): Home Int 1977-78; Eur(L) T Ch 1977. (GBI): Curtis Cup 1978; Vagliano Trophy 1977

Mason, Mrs
(Wales): Home Int 1923

Mather, H
(Scotland): Home Int 1905-09-12-13-14

Matthew, C (Lambert)
(Scotland): Home Int 1989-90-91-92-93; Eur(L) T Ch 1989-91-93. (GBI): Curtis Cup 1990-92-94; Vagliano Trophy 1989-91-93; Espirito Santo 1992; CW 1991

British Isles International Players, Amateur Women

Matthews, T [Thomas] (Perkins)
(Wales): Home Int 1972-73-74-75-76-77-78-79-80-81-82-83-84; Eur(L) T Ch 1975. (GBI): Curtis Cup 1974-76-78-80; Vagliano Trophy 1973-75-77-79; Espirito Santo 1974; CW 1975-79

Mellis, Mrs
(Scotland): Home Int 1924-27

Melvin, V
(Scotland): Home Int 1994-96

Menton, D
(Ireland): Home Int 1949

Menzies, M
(Scotland): Home Int **1962**

Merrill, J (Greenhalgh)
(England): Home Int 1960-61-63-66-69-70-71-75-76-77-78; Eur(L) T Ch 1971-77. (GBI): Curtis Cup 1964-70-74-76-78; Vagliano Trophy 1961-65-75-77; Espirito Santo 1970-**74**-78; CW 1963

Millar, D
(Ireland): Home Int 1928

Milligan, J (Mark)
(Ireland): Home Int 1971-72-73

Mills, I
(Wales): Home Int 1935-36-37-39-47-48

Milton, M (Paterson)
(Scotland): Home Int 1948-49-50-51-52. (GBI): Curtis Cup 1952

Mitchell, J
(Ireland): Home Int 1930

Moffat, L
(Scotland): Home Int 1996-98

Monaghan, H
(Scotland): Home Int 1995-96-97-98; Eur(L) T Ch 1997. (GBI): Curtis Cup 1998

Moodie, J
(Scotland): Home Int 1990-91-92; Eur(L) T Ch 1991-93-95-97. (GBI): Curtis Cup 1994-96; Vagliano Trophy 1993-95-97; Espirito Santo 1996; CW 1995

Mooney, M
(Ireland): Home Int 1972-73; Eur(L) T Ch 1971. (GBI): Vagliano Trophy 1973

Moorcroft, S
(England): Home Int 1985-86; Eur(L) T Ch 1985-87

Moore, S
(Ireland): Home Int 1937-38-39-47-48-49-**68**

Moran, V (Singleton)
(Ireland): Home Int 1970-71-73-74-75; Eur(L) T Ch 1971-75

Morant, E
(England): Home Int 1906-10

Morgan, R
(Wales): Home Int 1996-97-98; Eur(L) T Ch 1997. (GBI): Curtis Cup 1998; Vagliano Trophy 1997

Morgan, S
(England): Home Int 1989; Eur(L) T Ch 1989

Morgan, W
(England): Home Int 1931-32-33-34-35-36-37. (GBI): Curtis Cup 32-34-36

Morgan, Miss
(Wales): Home Int 1912-13-14

Moriarty, M (Irvine)
(Ireland): Home Int 1979

Morley, J
(England): Home Int 1990-91-92-93; Eur(L) T Ch 1991-93. (GBI): Curtis Cup 1992; Vagliano Trophy 1991-93; Espirito Santo 1992

Morris, L (Moore)
(England): Home Int 1912-13

Morris, Mrs de B
(Ireland): Home Int 1933

Morrison, G (Cheetham)
(England): Home Int 1965-**69**. (GBI): Vagliano Trophy 1965

Morrison, G (Cradock-Hartopp)
(England): Home Int 1936

Mountford, S
(Wales): Home Int 1989-90-91-92; Eur(L) T Ch 1991

Murray, Rachel
(Ireland): Home Int 1952

Murray, S (Jolly)
(England): Home Int 1976

Musgrove, Mrs
(Wales): Home Int 1923-24

Myles, M
(Scotland): Home Int 1955-57-59-60-67

Neill-Fraser, M
(Scotland): Home Int 1905-06-07-08-09-10-11-12-13-14

Nes, K (Garnham)
(England): Home Int 1931-32-33-36-37-38-39

Nevile, E
(England): Home Int 1905-06-08-10

New, B
(England): Home Int 1980-81-82-83. (GBI): Curtis Cup 1984; Vagliano Trophy 1983

Newell, B
(England): Home Int 1936

Newman, L
(Wales): Home Int 1927-31

Newton, B (Brown)
(England): Home Int 1930-33-34-35-36-37

Nicholls, M
(Wales): Home Int **1962**

Nicholson, J (Hutton)
(Scotland): Home Int 1969-70; Eur(L) T Ch 1971. (GBI): CW 1971

Nicholson, L
(Scotland): Home Int 1994-95-96-97-98; Eur(L) T Ch 1995-97

Nicholson, Mrs WH
(Scotland): Home Int 1910-13

Nimmo, H
(Scotland): Home Int 1936-38-39

Norris, J (Smith)
(Scotland): Home Int 1966-67-68-69-70-71-72-75-76-77-78-79-**83**-**84**; Eur(L) T Ch 1971. (GBI): Vagliano Trophy 1977

Norwell, I (Watt)
(Scotland): Home Int 1954

Nutting, P (Jameson)
(Ireland): Home Int 1927-28

O'Brien, A
(Ireland): Home Int 1969

O'Brien, S (Fanagan)
(Ireland): Home Int 1995-96-97-98; Eur L T Ch 1997

O'Brien Kenney, S
(Ireland): Home Int 1977-78-83-84-85-86

O'Donnell, M
(Ireland): Home Int 1974-77 -**78**-**79** Eur(L) T Ch **1980**. (GBI): Curtis Cup 1982; Vagliano Trophy **1981**

O'Donohoe, A
(Ireland): Home Int 1948-49-50-51-53-**73**-**74**

O'Hare, S
(Ireland): Home Int 1921-22

O'Reilly, T (Moran)
(Ireland): Home Int 1977-78-86-88-**95**; Eur(L) T Ch 1987

O'Sullivan, A
(Ireland): Home Int 1982-83-84-92-94-95-96; Eur(L) T Ch 1993-97

O'Sullivan, P
(Ireland): Home Int 1950-51-52-53-54-55-56-57-58-59-60-63-64-65-66-67-**69-70-71**; Eur(L) T Ch **1971**

Oliver, J
(England): Home Int 1995

Oliver, M (Jones)
(Wales): Home Int 1955-60-61-62-63-64-65-66. (GBI): Espirito Santo 1964

Ormsby, Miss
(Ireland): Home Int 1909-10-11

Orr, P (Boyd)
(Ireland): Home Int 1971

Orr, Mrs
(Wales): Home Int 1924

Owen, E
(Wales): Home Int 1947

Panton-Lewis, C (Panton)
(Scotland): Home Int 1972-73-76-77-78. (GBI): Vagliano Trophy 1977; Espirito Santo 1976

Park, Mrs
(Scotland): Home Int 1952

Parker, S
(England): Home Int 1973

Patey, Mrs
(Scotland): Home Int 1922-23

Pearson, D
(England): Home Int 1928-29-30-31-32-34

Percy, G (Mitchell)
(Scotland): Home Int 1927-28-30-31

Perriam, A
(Wales): Home Int 1988-90-91-92; Eur(L) T Ch 1991

Phelips, M
(Wales): Home Int 1913-14-21

Phillips, ME
(England): Home Int 1905

Phillips, Mrs
(Wales): Home Int 1921

Pickard, M (Nichol)
(England): Home Int 1958-59-60-61-67-69-**83**. (GBI): Curtis Cup 1968-70; Vagliano Trophy 1959-61-67

Pilgrim, E
(Wales): Home Int 1995-97; Eur(L) T Ch 1997

Pim, Mrs
(Ireland): Home Int 1908

Pook, E (Chadwick)
(England): Home Int 1963-65-66-67; Eur(L) T Ch 1967.(GBI): Curtis Cup 1966; Vagliano Trophy 1963-67; CW 1967

Porter, D (Park)
(Scotland): Home Int 1922-25-27-29-30-31-32-33-34-35-37-38-47-48. (GBI): Curtis Cup 1932

Porter, M (Lazenby)
(England): Home Int 1931-32

Powell, M
(Wales): Home Int 1908-09-10-12

Power, ER (McDaid)
(Ireland): Home Int 1987 to 1997; Eur(L) T Ch 1987-93-97. (GBI): Curtis Cup 1994; Vagliano Trophy 1995-97

Price, M (Greaves)
(England): Home Int 1956(Captain)

Price Fisher, E (Price)
(England): Home Int 1948-51-52-53-54-55-56-57-58-59-60. (GBI): Curtis Cup 1950-52-54-56-58-60; Vagliano Trophy 1959; CW 1959

Proctor, Mrs
(Wales): Home Int 1907

Provis, I (Kyle)
(Scotland): Home Int 1910-11

Purcell, E
(Ireland): Home Int 1965-66-67-72-73

Purfield, O
(Ireland): Home Int 1998

Purvis-Russell-Montgomery, C
(Scotland): Home Int 1921-22-23-25-28-29-30-31-32-33-34-35-36-37-38-39-47-48-49-50-52

Pyman, B
(Wales): Home Int 1925-28-29-30-32-33-34-35-36-37-38

Rabbidge, R
(England): Home Int 1931

Ratcliffe, E
(England): Home Int 1995-96-97; Eur(L) T Ch 1995-97. (GBI): Curtis Cup 1998; Espirito Santo 1996; Vagliano Trophy 1997

Rawlings, M
(Wales): Home Int 1979-80-81-83-84-85-86-87. (GBI): Vagliano Trophy 1981

Rawlinson, T (Walker)
(Scotland): Home Int 1970-71-73-76. (GBI): Vagliano Trophy 1973

Read, P
(England): Home Int 1922

Reddan, C (Tiernan)
(Ireland): Home Int 1935-36-38-39-47-48-49. (GBI): Curtis Cup 1938-48

Reddan, MV
(Ireland): Home Int 1955

Reece, P (Millington)
(England): Home Int 1966(Captain)

Rees, G
(Wales): Home Int 1981

Rees, MB
(Wales): Home Int 1927-31

Reid, A (Lurie)
(Scotland) Home Int 1960-61-62-63-64-66. (GBI): Vagliano Trophy 1961

Reid, A (Kyle)
(Scotland): Home Int 1923-24-25

Reid, D
(Scotland): Home Int 1978-79

Remer, H
(England): Home Int 1909

Rennie, J (Hastings)
(Scotland): Home Int 1961-65-66-67-71-72; Eur(L) T Ch 1967. (GBI): Curtis Cup 1966; Vagliano Trophy 1961-67

Rhys, J
(Wales): Home Int 1979

Rice, J
(Ireland): Home Int 1924-27-29

Richards, D
(Wales): Home Int 1994-95-96

Richards, J
(Wales): Home Int 1980-82-83-85

Richards, S
(Wales): Home Int 1967

Richardson, Mrs
(England): Home Int 1907-09

Richmond, M (Walker)
(Scotland): Home Int 1972-73-74-75-77-78. (GBI): Curtis Cup 1974; Vagliano Trophy 1975

Rieben, Mrs
(Wales): Home Int 1927-28-29-30-31-32-33

Rigby, F (Macbeth)
(Scotland): Home Int 1912-13

Ritchie, C (Park)
(Scotland): Home Int 1939-47-48-51-52-53-**64**

Roberts, B
(Wales): Home Int **1984-85-86**

Roberts, E (Pentony)
(Ireland): Home Int 1932-33-34-35-36-39

Roberts, E (Barnett)
(Ireland): Home Int 1961-62-63-64-65; Eur(L) T Ch 1964

Roberts, G
(Wales): Home Int 1949-52-53-54

Roberts, M (Brown)
(Scotland): Home Int **1965**. (GBI): Espirito Santo 1964

Roberts, P
(Wales): Home Int 1950-51-53-55-56-57-58-59-60-61-62-63-**64-65-66-67**-68-69-70; Eur(L) T Ch 1965-67-69. (GBI): Espirito Santo 1964

Roberts, S
(Wales): Home Int 1983-84-85-86-87-88-89-90; Eur(L) T Ch 1983-87

Robertson, B (McCorkindale)
(Scotland): Home Int 1958-59-60-61-62-63-64-65-66-69-72-73-78-80-81-82-84 -85-86; Eur(L) T Ch 1965-**67**-69-71. (GBI): Curtis Cup 1960-66-68-70-72-74-**76**-82-86; Vagliano Trophy 1959-63-69-71-81-85; CW 1971-**75**; Espirito Santo 1964-66-**68**-72-80-82

Robertson, D
(Scotland): Home Int 1907

Robertson, E
(Scotland): Home Int 1924

Robertson, G
(Scotland): Home Int 1907-08-09

Robinson, C (Nesbitt)
(Ireland): Home Int 1974-75-76-77-78-79-80-81. (GBI): Curtis Cup 1980; Vagliano Trophy 1979

Robinson, R (Bayly)
(Ireland): Home Int 1947-56-57

Robinson, S
(England): Home Int 1989

Roche, Mrs
(Ireland): Home Int 1922

Rogers, A
(Ireland): Home Int 1992-93; Eur(L) T Ch 1993

Rogers, J
(Wales): Home Int 1972

Rose, A
(Scotland): Home Int 1990 to 1998; Eur(L) T Ch 1991-93-95-97. (GBI): Curtis Cup 1996-98; Vagliano Trophy 1995-97; CW 1995

Roskrow, M
(England): Home Int 1948-50

Ross, M (Hezlet)
(Ireland): Home Int 1905-06-07-08-11-12

Roxburgh, L
(Scotland): Home Int 1993-94-95

Roy, S (Needham)
(Scotland): Home Int 1969-71-72-73-74-75-76-83. (GBI): Vagliano Trophy 1973-75

Rudgard, G
(England): Home Int 1931-32-50-51-52

Rusack, J
(Scotland): Home Int 1908

Sabine, D (Plumpton)
(England): Home Int 1934-35. (GBI): Curtis Cup 1934

Saunders, V
(England): Home Int 1967-68; Eur(L) T Ch 1967. (GBI): Curtis Cup 1968; Vagliano Trophy 1967; CW 1967

Scott Chard, Mrs
(Wales) Home Int 1928-30

Seddon, N
(Wales): Home Int 1962-63-74 -**75-76**

Selkirk, H
(Wales): Home Int 1925-28

Shapcott, A
(England): Home Int 1989

Shaw, P
(Wales): Home Int 1913

Sheldon, A
(Wales): Home Int 1981

Sheppard, E (Pears)
(England): Home Int 1947

Simpson, L (Moore)
(England): Home Int 1979-80

Singleton, B (Henderson)
(Scotland): Home Int 1939-52-53-54-55-56-57-58-60-61-62-63-64-65

Slade, Lady
(Ireland): Home Int 1906

Slark, R (Porter)
(England): Home Int 1959-60-61-62-64-65-66-68-78; Eur(L) T Ch 1965; Espirito Santo 1964. (GBI): Curtis Cup 1960-62-64; Vagliano Trophy 1959-61-65; Espirito Santo 19**66**; CW 1963

Slocombe, E (Davies)
(Wales): Home Int 1974-75

Smalley, Mrs A
(Wales): Home Int 1924-25-31-32-33-34

Smillie, P
(England): Home Int 1985-86

Smith, A [Stant] (Willard)
(England): Home Int 1974-75-76. (GBI): Curtis Cup 1976; Vagliano Trophy 1975; CW 1959-63

Smith, E
(England): Home Int 1991

Smith, F (Stephens)
(England): Home Int 1947-48-49-50-51-52-53-54-55-59-**62-71-72** (GBI): Curtis Cup 1950-52-54-56-58-60-**(62)-(72)**; Vagliano Trophy 1959-71; CW 1959-63

Smith, K
(England): Home Int 1997-98

Smith, Mrs L
(Ireland): Home Int 1913-14-21-22-23-25

Smythe, M
(Ireland): Home Int 1947-48-49-50-51-52-53-54-55-56-58-59-**62**

Sowter, Mrs
(Wales): Home Int 1923

Speak, K
(England): Home Int 1993-94; Eur(L) T Ch 1993. (GBI): Curtis Cup 1994; Vagliano Trophy 1993; Espirito Santo 1994

Speir, M
(Scotland): Home Int 1957-64-68-**71-72**

Stark, K
(Wales): Home Int 1995-96

Starrett, L (Malone)
(Ireland): Home Int 1975-76-77-78-80

Stavert, M
(Scotland): Home Int 1979

Steel, Mrs DC
(Scotland): Home Int 1925

Steel, E
(England): Home Int 1905-06-07-08-11

Stewart, G
(Scotland): Home Int 1979-80-81-82-83-84; Eur(L) T Ch 1982-84. (GBI): Curtis Cup 1980-82; Vagliano Trophy 1979-81-83; CW 1979-83

Stewart, L (Scraggie)
(Scotland): Home Int 1921-22-23

Stocker, J
(England): Home Int 1922-23

Stockton, Mrs
(Wales): Home Int 1949

Storry, Mrs
(Wales): Home Int 1910-14

Stroud, N
(Wales): Home Int 1989

Stuart, M
(Ireland): Home Int 1905-07-08

Stuart-French, Miss
(Ireland): Home Int 1922

Stupples, K
(England): Home Int 1995-96-97-98; Eur(L) T Ch 1995-97. (GBI): Curtis Cup 1996-98; Vagliano Trophy 1997

Sugden, J (Machin)
(England): Home Int 1953-54-55

Summers, M (Mackie)
(Scotland): Home Int 1986

Sumpter, Mrs
(England): Home Int 1907-08-12-14-24

Sutherland Pilch, R (Barton)
(England): Home Int 1947-49-50-58(Captain)

Swallow, C
(England): Home Int 1985; Eur(L) T Ch 1985

Sweeney, L
(Ireland): Home Int 1991

Tamworth, Mrs
(England): Home Int 1908

Taylor, I
(Ireland): Home Int 1930

Teacher, F
(Scotland): Home Int 1908-09-11-12-13

Tebbet, K
(England): Home Int 1990-94

Temple, S
(England): Home Int 1913-14

Temple Dobell, G (Ravenscroft)
(England): Home Int 1911-12-13-14-20-21-25-30

Thomas, C (Phipps)
(Wales): Home Int 1959-63-64-65-66-67-68-69-70-71-72-73-76-77-80

Thomas, I
(Wales): Home Int 1910

Thomas, J (Foster)
(Wales): Home Int 1984-85-86-87-92-93-95; Eur(L) T Ch 1987-89-91-93

Thomas, O
(Wales): Home Int 1921

Thomas, S (Rowlands)
(Wales): Home Int 1977-82-84-85

Thomas, V (Rawlings)
(Wales): Home Int 1971 to 1998; Eur(L) T Ch 1973-75-77-79-81-83-87-91-97. (GBI): Curtis Cup 1982-84-86-88-90; Vagliano Trophy 1979-83 -85-87-89-91; CW 1979-83-87-91. Espirito Santo 1990

Thompson, M
(Wales): Home Int 1937-38-39

Thompson, M (Wallis)
(England): Home Int 1948-49

Thompson, M
(Scotland): Home Int 1949

Thomson, D
(Scotland): Home Int 1982-83-85-87

Thomson, M
(Scotland): Home Int 1907

Thomson, M
(Scotland): Home Int 1974-75-76-77-78; Eur(L) T Ch 1978. (GBI): Curtis Cup 1978; Vagliano Trophy 1977

Thornhill, J (Woodside)
(England): Home Int 1965-74-82-83-84-85-86-87-88; Eur(L) T Ch 1965-85-87. (GBI): Curtis Cup 1984-86-88; Vagliano Trophy 1965-83-85-87-**89**; CW 1983-87

Thornhill, Miss
(Ireland): Home Int 1924-25

Thornton, Mrs
(Ireland): Home Int 1924

Todd, Mrs
(Ireland): Home Int 1931-32-34-35-36

Thomlinson, J [Evans] (Roberts)
(England): Home Int 1962-64. (GBI): Curtis Cup 1962; Vagliano Trophy 1963

Treharne, A [Mills]
(Wales): Home Int 1952-61

Turner, B
(England): Home Int 1908

Turner, S (Jump)
(Wales): Home Int 1982-84-85-86-91-93

Tynte, V
(Ireland): Home Int 1905-06-08-09-11-12-13-14

Uzielli, A (Carrick)
(England): Home Int 1976-77-78-90-**92-93**; Eur(L) T Ch 1977. (GBI): Curtis Cup 1978; Vagliano Trophy 1977

Valentine, J (Anderson)
(Scotland): Home Int 1934-35-36-37-38-39-47-49-50-51-52-53-54-55-**56**-57-58. (GBI): Curtis Cup 1938-48-50-52-54-56-58; CW 1959

Valentine, P (Whitley)
(Wales): Home Int 1973-74-75-77-78-79-80-**90**

Veitch, F
(Scotland): Home Int 1912

Wadsworth, H
(Wales): Home Int 1987-88-89-90; Eur(L) T Ch 1987-90. (GBI): Curtis Cup 1990

Waite, C
(England): Home Int 1981-82-83-84, Eur(L) T Ch 1985. (GBI): Curtis Cup 1984; Vagliano Trophy 1983; Espirito Santo 1984; CW 1983

Wakelin, H
(Wales): Home Int 1955

Walker, B (Thompson)
(England): Home Int 1905-06-07-08-09-11

Walker, M
(England): Home Int 1970-72; Eur(L) T Ch 1971. (GBI): Curtis Cup 1972; Vagliano Trophy 1971; CW 1971

Walker, P
(Ireland): Home Int 1928-29-30-31-32-33-34-35-36-37-38-39-48. (GBI): Curtis Cup 1934-36-38

Walker-Leigh, F
(Ireland): Home Int 1907-08-09-11-12-13-14

Wallace-Williamson, V
(Scotland): Home Int 1932. (GBI): Curtis Cup **1938**

Walsh, R
(Ireland): Home Int 1987

Walter, J
(England): Home Int 1974-79-80-82-86

Walters, L
(England): Home Int 1998

Wardlaw, N (Baird)
(Scotland): Home Int 1932-35-36-37-38-39-47-48. (GBI): Curtis Cup 1938

Watson, C (Nelson)
(England): Home Int 1982

Webb, L (Bolton)
(Ireland): Home Int 1981-82-88-89-91-92-94

Webster, S (Hales)
(Wales): Home Int 1968-69-72-91(Captain)

Wesley, N
(Wales): Home Int 1986

Westall, S (Maudsley)
(England): Home Int 1973

Weston, R
(Wales): Home Int 1927

Whieldon, Miss
(Wales): Home Int 1908

Wickham, C
(Ireland): Home Int 1983-89

Wickham, P
(Ireland): Home Int 1976-83-87; Eur(L) T Ch 1987

Williams, M
(Wales): Home Int 1936

Williamson, C (Barker)
(England): Home Int 1979-80-81

Willock-Pollen, G
(England): Home Int 1907

Wilson, A
(Scotland): Home Int 1973-74-85 (Captain)

Wilson, E
(England): Home Int 1928-29-30. (GBI): Curtis Cup 1932

Wilson, Mrs
(Ireland): Home Int 1931

Wilson Jones, D
(Wales): Home Int 1952

Winn, J
(England): Home Int 1920-21-23-25

Wooldridge, W (Shaw)
(Scotland): Home Int 1982

Wragg, M
(England): Home Int 1929

Wright, J (Robertson)
(Scotland): Home Int 1952-53-54-55-56-57-58-59-60-61-63-65-67-73-**78-79-80-86**; Eur(L) T Ch 1965. (GBI): Curtis Cup 1954-56-58-60; Vagliano Trophy 1959-61-63; CW 1959

Wright, M
(Scotland): Home Int 1990-91-92; Eur(L) T Ch 1991

Wright, N (Cook)
(Wales): Home Int 1938-47-48-49-51-52-53-54-57-58-59-60-62-63-64-66-67-68-**71-72-73**; Eur(L) T Ch 1965-71. (GBI): Espirito Santo 1964

Wright, P
(Scotland): Home Int 1981-82-83-84; Eur(L) T Ch 1987. (GBI): Vagliano Trophy 1981

Wylie, P (Wade)
(England): Home Int 1934-35-36-37-38-47. (GBI): Curtis Cup 1938

Association of Golf Writers

Adamson, Tony
Aitken, Michael
(L) Baker, John E
Ballantine, John
Birtill, David *Manchester Evening News*
Bisher, Firman *Atlanta Journal*
Blackstock, Dixon
Blighton, Bill
Blomqvist, Jan *Golf Digest Sverige*
Bolze, Gerd A
Booth, Alan
Bowden, Ken
Britten, Mike
(H) Butler, Frank
Callander, Colin *Golf Monthly*
Campbell, Malcolm
Carter, Jane *Women and Golf*
Chapman, Jeremy *The Sporting Life*
Clark, Bill *Sunday Mirror*, Belfast
Clough, Frank
Corrigan, Peter
Creighton, Brian Reuters
Crockett, Scott
Dabell, Norman
Davies, Bob *Wolverhampton Express and Star*
Davies, David *The Guardian*
Davies, Patricia
Dempster, Martin
Donald, Peter
Ebbinge, Jan B
(L) Edwards, Leslie
Elliott, Bill
Ellison, Stanley
Farquharson, Colin
Farrell, Andrew *The Independent*
Fenton, John
Ferrier, Bob
Figar, Jose
Adesport, Madrid
Frederick, Adrian
Garrod, Mark Press Association
Gilleece, Dermot *The Irish Times*
Glover, Tim *Daily Express*
Godsiff, Peter
Goodner, Ross
Green, Bob
Green, Robert
Grimsley, Will
Hamilton, David
Harding, Colin *Hampshire Golf*
Hardy, Martin
Haslam, Peter *Golf World*
Hedley, Alan *The Journal*, Newcastle-upon-Tyne
Hennessy, John
Hermann, Philippe *Tribune de Geneva*
Herron, Allan *The People*
Higgs, Peter *Mail on Sunday*
Hopkins, John *The Times*
Howard, Jock *Golf World*
(L) Huggins, Percy
Ingham, John
Jacobs, Raymond
Jansen, Anders *Svensk Golf*
Jenkins, Dan
Kahn, Elizabeth
Kelly, Jeff *Andalucia Golf*
Lafaurie, André-Jean
Laidlaw, Renton *Golfer's Handbook*
Lawrenson, Derek *Sunday Telegraph*
Leitao, Jaoá Morais *Pluripress*
(L) Lincoln, Stanley
MacCullum, Scott
McDonnell, Michael *Daily Mail*
Mackie, Keith
Macniven, Ian
MacVicar, Jock *Daily Express*
Magowan, Jack *Belfast Telegraph*
Mair, Norman
Mair, Lewine *Daily Telegraph*
Maitland, Bobby
Mancinelli, Piero *Parliamo di Golf*, Milan
Masters, Peter *Golf World*
Mearing, Paddy
Moody, John
Mossop, James
Mulqueen, Charles *Cork Examiner*
Nicol, Alister
Oakley, John
Ortega, Jesús Ruiz *Golf*, Madrid
Ostermann, Ted
Pargeter, John
Pastor, Nuria *La Vanguardia*, Barcelona
Pinner, John
(H) Place, Tom
(H) Platts, Mitchell
Plumridge, Chris
Potter, Bryan
Price Fisher, Elizabeth
Ramsey, Tom, *News International, Australia*
Redmond, John
Reece, John K
Reid, Philip *Irish Times*
Riach, Ian
Richardson, Gordon
Robertson, Bill *Today's Golfer*
Robertson, Jack
Rodrigo, Robert (Bob Rodney)
Roseforte, Tim
Ross, John
Ruddy, Pat *Golfers Companion*
(L) Ryde, Peter
St John, Lauren *Sunday Times*
(L) Scatchard, Charles
Scott, Graham
Seitz, Nick
Severino, Dick, *Golf Features Service*, San Diego
Simmons, Richard
Simpson, Gordon, *Daily Record*
Skelton, Ronald
Smart, Chris, *Mid-Glamorgan Press Agency*
Smith, Colm *Irish Independent*
Somers, Robert
Spander, Art
Spink, Alex
(L) Steel, Donald
Stenson, Tony *Daily Mirror*
Stobbs, John
Tait, Alistair *Golf Monthly*
(H) Thornberry, Henry W
Trillo Amores, Isabel
(H) Ullyett, Roy
Van Esbeck, Edmund
Ward, Barry E
Webb, Mel
Whitbread, John S *Surrey Herald*
White, Gordon S
Wilson, Mark
Wind, Herbert Warren
Wood, Ian
Wright, Ben
Zachrisson, Goran

(L) = Life member   (H) = Honorary member

PART IX

Guide to Golfing Services and Places to Stay in the British Isles and Ireland

Buyer's Guide to Good Golfing and Golf Course Maintenance

This compact but informative guide to manufacturers and organisations offering services to golf clubs and individual golfers includes a wide number of categories, from services to personal accessories and golfing equipment to golf course maintenance.

AFTER-DINNER SPEAKERS
ANTIQUES
ARCHITECTS & CONSULTANTS
AWARDS, PRIZES & TROPHIES
BADGES & TIES
BAG/MEMBERSHIP TAGS
BAGS/GOLF ACCESSORIES
BALL MANUFACTURERS/SUPPLIERS
BOOKSELLERS & PUBLISHERS
CARTS, TROLLEYS & BUGGIES
CHARITY ORGANISATIONS
CLOTHING/GOLFWEAR
CLUB MANAGEMENT CONSULTANTS
CLUB MANUFACTURERS
CLUBHOUSE FURNISHINGS & EQUIPMENT
COMPUTER SYSTEMS
CORPORATE GIFTS & EVENTS
COURSE MEASUREMENT
DISTRIBUTORS & WHOLESALERS
DRIVING RANGE & PRACTICE EQUIPMENT
EDUCATION/TRAINING & TEACHING AIDS
ELECTRONIC POINT-OF-SALE
EXHIBITIONS
GIFTS & NOVELTIES
GOLF COURSE CONSTRUCTION & UPGRADING
GOLF COURSE DESIGN CONSULTANTS
GOLF COURSE DISTANCE GUIDES
GOLF COURSE MAINTENANCE & UPGRADING
GOLF COURSE PLANNERS
GOLF COURSE YARDAGE BOOKS
GOLF DEVELOPMENT/MANAGEMENT & MAINTENANCE
GOLF FITNESS CONSULTANT
GOLF GRIPS & SHAFTS

GOLF HOLIDAYS/ TOUR OPERATORS HOME & ABROAD
GOLFING AIDS/PRACTICE EQUIPMENT
GOVERNING BODIES
GREEN KEEPING & DRIVING RANGE VEHICLES
INSURANCE
IRRIGATION EQUIPMENT/DESIGN & INSTALLATION
JEWELLERY
LOCKER MANUFACTURERS
MAIL ORDER
PERSONAL EQUIPMENT & ACCESSORIES
PERSONALISED PRODUCTS
PICTURES & PRINTS
PRACTICE NETTING/CAGES
PROMOTION/PUBLICITY
PROPERTY CONSULTANTS
PUTTER MANUFACTURERS
RANGE BALL MANUFACTURERS
RECRUITMENT CONSULTANTS
REMOTE CONTROLLED TROLLEYS
SCORECARDS & PLANNERS
SHOE ACCESSORIES
SIGNS & MARKERS
SIMULATORS/ANALYSERS
SYNTHETIC SURFACES
TEE SIGNS
THERMAL WEAR
TOWELS
TUITION
UMBRELLAS
VIDEOS
WATER STORAGE/TANKS
WEATHERWEAR
WINTER-ALL-WEATHER TEE MATS

AFTER-DINNER SPEAKERS

Antique Golf
with Robert Thomson
10 Glasgow Road, Paisley PA1 3QG.
Tel 0141-889 1860 Fax 0141-889 1880

e-mail:robert@antiquegolf.com
Website:www.antiquegolf.com
The History of Golf with Robert Thomson: Robert speaks in a light hearted manner and illustrates this by handing to the audience antique golf clubs, balls and memorabilia. His talk would normally last 20 minutes - then he does a question and answer session. Ideal for small groups.

ANTIQUES

Antique Golf
10 Glasgow Road, Paisley PA1 3QG.
Tel 0141-889 1860 Fax 0141-889 1880

e-mail:robert@antiquegolf.com
Website:www.antiquegolf.com
The most extensive range of antique golf clubs and memorabilia in the world. All clubs drawn from the period 1840 to 1920. We supply individual collectors, golf clubs, and the corporate marketplace. For a preview ask for our catalogue or view our website.

Schotten Trophies
- Manfred Schotten Antiques
109 High Street, Burford,
Oxfordshire OX18 4RH.
Tel (01993) 822302 Fax (01993) 822055

http.//www.schotten.com
Exquisite hand crafted trophies in traditional style, designed, manufactured and hand finished in our own workshop by craftsmen using solid woods, brass and bronze. Also available are golf antiques, clubs, novelty items, desk sets etc, and golf club furnishings. (See advertisement page 7 for further details.)

ARCHITECTS & CONSULTANTS

British Institute
of Golf Course Architects
Merrist Wood House, Worplesdon,
Guildford, Surrey GU3 3PE.
Tel (01483) 884036 Fax (01483) 884037

Professional Institute of qualified golf course architects officially recognised by the Royal & Ancient and English Golf Union.

Chris Stanton
Golf Course Architect,
Chartered Town Planner
14 Shaw Wood Close,
North End,
Durham DH1 4LZ.
Tel 0191-384 3771 Fax 0191-333 6293

Ideally placed to address sensitive development issues. Since the early 1970s, Chris Stanton has demonstrated his commitment to golf architecture, whilst still in full-time planning employment, by designing/directly supervising construction of new golf courses, comprehensive course/hole renovation; greens rebuilt to USGA specification and major grant-aided tree planting programmes.

Christy O'Connor Jnr, Ltd
Weir House,
Kilcolgan,
Galway, Ireland.
Tel +353 91 796475 Fax +353 91 796476

Golf course architect and course re-modelling. Built 20 golf courses in Ireland and Europe. Ryder Cup and World Cup player.

David Hemstock Associates
Golf Course Architects & Consultants
Suite 4a,
Northmill, Bridgefoot,
Belper, Derbyshire DE56 1YD.
Tel (01773) 827115 Fax (01773) 821284
e-mail: David_Hemstock@golf-design.demon/co.uk
website: www.golf-design.demon.co.uk
40 projects since 1991, from championship-quality new to total re-modelling of existing; Europe to China. Design and documentation, project and maintenance management, clubhouse design, through the qualified and experienced team of David Hemstock, BSc IEng., Les Watts, B.Arch., and Geoff Porter, NDH.

David Williams Golf Design
27 Prince's Drive,
Colwyn Bay,
North Wales LL29 8HT.
Tel (01492) 533818 Fax (01492) 533012

Golf course architects and project managers. Fully integrated service *from conception through construction to completion.* Over a dozen 18-hole courses built in Britain within last five years. Full member of British Institute of Golf Course Architects (BIGCA).

Gaunt & Marnoch Ltd
- Golf Course Architects
5 Frederick's Place,
Old Jewry,
London EC2R 8AB.
Tel 0171-726 6645 Fax 0171-726 6646
'Hilltop', Lakeside, Bakewell DE45 1GN.
Tel (01629) 815453 Fax (01629) 815170

e-mail: jonathan@gauntandmarnoch.com
steve@gauntand marnoch.com
Website:www.gauntandmarnoch.com
Gaunt & Marnoch Limited provides top quality, cost-conscious and environmentally sympathetic golf course development. Broad and flexible service offered, including reconstruction works and course extensions. The practice is committed to better golf through good design. Please call for more information.

Greens of Scotland
**Cruickshank Building,
Craibstone Estate,
Bucksburn, Aberdeen AB21 9TR.
Tel (01224) 711106 Fax (01224) 714591**

An international golf course consultancy providing specialist skills for feasibility studies, planning, course design, buildings design, course construction, project management and turf agronomy. Our project range covers alterations, renovations, driving ranges and new courses.

J Hamilton Stutt BSc FRSA
**Golf Course Architect
12 Bingham Avenue,
Poole, Dorset BH14 8NE.
Tel (01202) 708406**

Founder member of the British Institute of Golf Course Architects (BIGCA). One of Europe's most experienced golf course architects. Personal attention throughout to each new project.

John Greasley Ltd
**Ashfield House,
1154 Melton Road,
Syston, Leicester LE7 2HB.
Tel 0116-269 6766 Fax 0116-269 6866**

John Greasley established his company in 1984 and has specialised in the construction of new courses, along with alterations, improvements and refurbishment on existing ones. Works have been completed on some of the countries oldest and most prestigious courses.

Mercator International
**Golf Design & Development
Contact: Tel +44 (0) 171 584 8877**

e-mail:info@mercator.co.uk
Golf Course Architecture; Golf Real Estate & Resort Masterplanning; Golf Development Business Planning, Marketing and Operational Management. European Management and Marketing operations are conducted in JV partnership with the National Golf Company of Florida. The Golf Course Architecture Department offers a choice of Mercator Design or Gary Player Signature Design, both under lead architect Guy Hockley, MA Hons Phil BIGCA. Mercator operates throughout Europe and the Middle East with offices in London and Italy.

Patrick F Merrigan BAgr Sc MBIGCA
**Golf Course Architect,
Agronomist & Consultant
PO Box 119, Cork, Ireland.
Tel +353 21 353613 Fax +353 21 354153**

e-mail:merriganp@tinet.ie
Member British Institute Golf Course Architects (BIGCA). Personal 'hands on' service and commitment. Feasibility studies, masterplanning, re-modelling. World class rated courses include, eg Old Head, Slieve Russell Tulfarris, Woodenbridge. International portfolio.

Robin Hiseman
Golf Course Design
**Berrymeadow Cottage,
No 4, West Cairnbeg, Laurencekirk,
Aberdeenshire AB30 1SR.
Tel/Fax (01561) 320827**

e-mail:robin@hisemangolf.freeserve.co.uk
Scotland's only BIGCA qualified golf course architect. Considerable experience and specialist skills in feasibility studies, planning, course design, tender documentation and construction supervisor for new golf courses, or re-modelling projects. All work personally controlled.

Ronnie Lumsden
**Golf Course Architect & Course Management Consultany
14E Church Hill, Edinburgh EH10 4BQ.
Tel/Fax 0131-447 1052**

Graduate member of the British Institute of Golf Course Architects (BIGCA), and qualified in course management. A comprehensive design service and advice on improving the quality and condition of your course.

Simon Gidman International Golf Course Architects
Wychwood House,
43 Shipton Road,
Ascott Under Wychwood, Oxon OX7 6AG.
Tel (01993) 830441 Fax (01993) 831860

A full member of the British Institute of Golf Course Architects (BIGCA), Simon Gidman has been involved with some 50 projects in Europe and throughout the world. The company also specialises in preparing reports and studies for the restoration and upgrading of existing golf courses.

Swan Golf Designs Ltd
Telfords Barn,
Willingale, Ongar,
Essex CM5 0QF.
Tel (01277) 896229 Fax (01277) 896300

e-mail:SwanGolfDesigns@btinternet.com
Professional golf course architects with traditional values, offering initial appraisals, conceptual designs, detailed design work and construction management. Specialising in improvements of existing golf courses, extensions, re-design of greens and tees etc, including restorations of classic old courses.

York & Martin
39 Salisbury Street,
Fordingbridge, Hampshire SP6 1AB.
Tel (01425) 652087 Fax (01425) 652476

e-mail:yorkmartinl@compuserve.com
Independent irrigation consultants providing objective advice on all irrigation related matters including water souring, existing system evaluation, system designs and specifications, project supervision etc. Operating throughout the UK and mainland Europe.

AWARDS, PRIZES & TROPHIES

Birkdale Promotions
97 Old Watford Road, Bricket Wood,
Nr St Albans, Hertfordshire AL2 3UN.
Tel (01923) 671225 Fax (01923) 662522

An exclusive range of bronze figurines, silverplated golf trophies, shields, antique replica plaques all suitable for clubs, societies and corporate events. Our in-house engraving enables each to be personalised to your specification and delivery can be made to any address worldwide. Please call for our free colour brochure and price list. (See advertisement page 12 for further details.)

Chorley & Saunders Golf Art
Chequers End,
Chequers Lane,
Preston Village,
Hitchin, Hertfordshire SG4 7TY.
Tel/Fax (01462) 440277

Richard Chorley, England's premier golf artist. Private Commissions. Original oil paintings, drawings and limited edition prints. Prints signed by the artist, numbered and embossed. Collection of classic courses and golfing greats. Ideal corporate and captain's prizes gifts.

Derek Burridge (Wholesale) Ltd
Awards House,
Unit 15,
The Metro Centre,
Springfield Road,
Hayes, Middlesex UB4 0LE.
Tel 0181-569 0123 Fax 0181-569 0111

The country's leading suppliers of golf prizes. We offer a vast range of silverplate, crystal, china, clocks, leather goods and sporting trophies, all at trade prices. Glass and silverplate in-house engraving service. Next day delivery throughout the UK. Call for brochure. (See advertisement page 7 for further details.)

Galloway Glass
New Abbey Road,
Beeswing,
by Dumfries DG2 8ED.
Tel/Fax (01387) 760643

e-mail: mcc@gallowayglass.demon.co.uk
website: www.dmcsoft.com/scotplay
Specialist plain and cut crystal suppliers and engravers. Many innovative golfing gift ideas through our Muirfield collection and our St Andrews collection. Personalisation our speciality. Ask for our catalogue along with club and reseller pricelists.

Grandison Golf Gallery
25 Hyndland Road,
Glasgow G12 9UZ.
Tel/Fax 0141-339 9438

Finest quality limited edition prints of the world's premier golfing venues by award-winning artist William Grandison. Gifts and prizes of distinction for the discerning golfer. Free catalogue available.

Schotten Trophies - Manfred Schotten Antiques
109 High Street,
Burford,
Oxfordshire OX18 4RH.
Tel (01993) 822302 Fax (01993) 822055

http://www.schotten.com

Exquisite hand crafted trophies in traditional style, designed, manufactured and hand finished in our own workshop by crafstmen using solid woods, brass and bronze. Also available are golf antiques, clubs, novelty items, desk sets etc, and golf club furnishings. (See advertisement page 7 for further details.)

Solent Souvenirs Ltd
Hamble Bank,
40 Newtown Road, Warsash,
Southampton, Hampshire SO31 9FZ.
Tel (01489) 577985 Fax (01489) 577886

Britain's premier supplier of specialised golf jewellery and quality gifts. Many items designed and manufactured exclusively for us and unobtainable elsewhere. Replace that traditional trophy with an elegant prize which will be both useful and cherished. Most items delivered overnight.

BADGES & TIES

Elizabeth Parker
The Charles Parker Building,
Midland Road,
Higham Ferrers,
Northamptonshire NN10 8DN.
Tel (01933) 418099 Fax (01933) 358058

e-mail: liziparker@compserve.com

Gold and silver wire hand embroidered blazer badges and silk or polyester ties all produced to your own club logo. Also suppliers of ties, badges, cuff links, key rings and blazer buttons. Quotations and artwork supplied by return.

BAG/MEMBERSHIP TAGS

H M T Plastics Ltd
Fairway House, 31A Framfield Road,
Uckfield, East Sussex TN22 5AH.
Tel (01825) 769393 Fax (01825) 769494

Bag tags supplied in nine colours either round, pear shaped maxi or sunrise to accommodate club logo, from a choice of six print colours. Adhesive year stickers available in choice of nine colours and sold separately. (See advertisement page 10 for further details.)

BAGS/GOLF ACCESSORIES

Glenscot Golf Ltd
Osborne Court,
Thelwall New Road,
Warrington, Cheshire WA4 2LS.
Tel (01925) 861740 Fax (01925) 861750

e-mail: Glenscotgo@aol.com

Glenscot Golf are manufacturers and distributors of the Seal brand of component golf equipment. All of which is made to measure up to your exact specifications. This is completed by a full range of quality golf bags.

Hymax Products (UK) Ltd
Unit 19
Team Valley Business Centre,
Earlsway Team Valley,
Gateshead NE11 0RG.
Tel 0191-491 1138 Fax 0191-487 1911

e-mail:Info@Hymax.co.uk
website: www.hymax.co.uk

Manufacturers of golf accessories and corporate gift packs. Unique and innovative British made goods. *Gifts that the golfer uses.*

P B Sports
Oakmont House, Unit 8, Waterloo Avenue,
Chelmsley Wood Industrial Estate,
Birmingham B37 6QQ.
Tel 0121-770 2240 Fax 0121-770 7575

Manufacturers of on-course golf bags, golf accessories and personalised products for golf clubs and corporate days.

Prosimmon Golf (UK) Ltd
21 Monkspath Business Park,
Highlands Road,
Shirley, Solihull, West Midlands B90 4NZ.
Tel 0121-744 9551 Fax 0121-744 9541

Manufacturers of Premium golf clubs, bags and rainwear including the *Icon* range of golf clubs featuring the revolutionary *Torsionally Tuned* graphite and steel shafts. Designers of unique *Matchplay* custom programme.

Rogue Golf Company Ltd
The Downs Farm, Reigate Road,
Ewell, Surrey KT17 3BY.
Tel 0181-786 8896 Fax 0181-394 1895

Manufacture and supply of innovative golf equipment including metalwoods, irons, bags and accessories. The range incorporates a fresh, youthfull image combined with high quality products sourced predominantly from USA.

Sun Mountain Sports
c/o Golf Products Ltd
The Downs Farm, Reigate Road,
Ewell, Surrey KT17 3BY.
Tel 0181-786 8896 Fax 0181-394 1895

Distribution of a superb range of American made golf bags including innovative, lightweight stand and carry bags, as well as new trolley bag offerings. One of the world's leading suppliers of golf bags and related products.

Transline Tiger Golf
5 Bridgwater Court, Weston Super Mare,
North Somerset BS24 9AY.
Tel (01934) 642214 Fax (01934) 642004
e-mail:tigerben@compuserve.com

Sole manufacturers and registered owners of all Transline Tiger, Tigercub and Westcoast products. Woods, irons, bags, putters - plus Tiger accessories. Chairman: Roger Bennett. Secretary: Sandra Bennett.

BALL MANUFACTURERS/SUPPLIERS

Dimensions in Sport Ltd
First Floor, Woodcock House,
Gibbard Mews, High Street,
Wimbledon Village, London SW19 5BY.
Tel 0181-947 6555 Fax 0181-947 5544

Dimensions in Sport are the UK and European distributors for PRECEPT golf balls. The high Performance range of PRECEPT MC golf balls is endorsed by, amongst others, Nick Faldo, Nick Price, Lee Janzen and Stuart Appleby.

S T E L - Golf Division
Unit T, Lympne Industrial Park,
Hythe, Kent CT21 4LR.
Tel +44 (0) 1303 265777
Fax +44 (0) 1303 265054

Manufacturing and marketing of *Thommo* golf balls endorsed by Peter Thomson, five time British Open champion. New - The *Thommo* titanium series for extra distance, spin and superb feel. Specialised in corporate logo balls and undertakes contract manufacturing and driving range balls.

Wilson Sporting Goods Co Ltd
1 Tanners Yard, London Road,
Bagshot, Surrey GU19 5HD.
Tel (01294) 316200 Fax (01294) 316255

Wilson manufactures and supplies a full range of 'Game Improvement' products for the average golfer. Wilson has taken technological advancement to the next level, with the launch of the Fat Shaft woods and irons, and the Staff Titanium golf bag range. Fat Shaft technology features a 36% wider tip diameter than a traditional skinny shaft, this gives the club greater stability through impact on off-centre hits. This gives the average golfer deadly accuracy and remarkable distance. The Staff titanium golf ball range, now features the revolutionary straight distance ball, which has less spin than a conventional ball. The reduced spin makes the ball fly straighter by eliminating the harmful side-spin which causes hooks and slices.

BOOKSELLERS & PUBLISHERS

Rhod McEwan Golf Books
Glengarden, Ballater,
Aberdeenshire AB35 5UB.
Tel (013397) 55429 Fax (013397) 55995

Rare and out of print golf books. Catalogue available on request. Publisher of golf titles. We are always looking to purchase golf books in any quantity. (See advertisement page 7 for further details.)

Steve Schofield Golf Books
29 Nichols Way, Wetherby,
West Yorkshire LS22 6AD.
Tel/Fax (01937) 581276
e-mail: steve@golfbooks.u-net.com

Classic golf books for sale, new, old and antiquarian. Books on golf history, architecture, biography, club and ball collecting and instruction. Free catalogue on request.

CARTS, TROLLEYS & BUGGIES

A La Carts
Beechwood, Bakeham Lane,
Englefield Green TW20 9TU.
Tel/Fax (01784) 472982

Manufacturers and distributors of single and two-seat golf buggies. Also special-purpose vehicles. New and reconditioned.

Chip 'N' Chub (Melex) Ltd
3 Drayton Avenue, Ealing,
London W13 0LE.
Tel 0181-997 4885 Fax 0181-997 4825
e-mail: ChipnChubLtd@BTinternet.com

Sales and hire of new and used Melex golf and utility cars to include full after-sales service UK wide, with full stocks of all spares. Demo and

continued over

loan vehicles available and all finance packages subject to status. (See advertisement page 12 for further details.)

Middlemore Ltd
**Valley Road Works,
Sedgley, Dudley,
West Midlands DY3 1TS.
Tel (01902) 673360 Fax (01902) 880783**

Manufacturers of *Electra Caddie 'Classic'* and *Compact* one piece foldaway powered trolleys, 4-wheel single seater *Rydeon '2000'* buggy that you load in the boot of your car! Our mission - Break Par not your back!

Patterson Products
**Unit 6,
Fordwater Trading Estate,
Ford Road,
Chertsey, Surrey KT16 8HG.
Tel (01932) 570016 Fax (01932) 570084**

Manufacturers and retailers of the *Trio* single-seat, transportable golf cart. Major suppliers and consultants to Handigolf, a charity for the severely disabled golfer. The *Trio* is now in its 12th year, with over 3,000 happy users.

Yamaha Motor (UK) Ltd
**Sopwith Drive,
Brooklands,
Weybridge, Surrey KT13 0UZ.
Tel (01932) 358000 Fax (01932) 358030**

Suppliers of petrol and electric golf cars for clubs and individuals. Fleet contracts with optional purchase and lease schemes, full maintenance and service support. On and off-course utility vehicles, multi-passenger cars and beverage units.

CHARITY ORGANISATIONS

Sun Longest Day Challenge - The Marathon of Golf
**Campbell Park,
Fernhurst Road,
Millard, Nr Liphook GU30 7LU.
Tel (01428) 741233**

The *Challenge* offers golfers of every ability the chance to put something back into the community and have fun doing so. The object is to play 72 holes on or about the *Longest Day of the Year - June 21*, and by your efforts raise money to help your favoured charity. For details call our Helpline 01428 741333. (See advertisement page 24 for further details.)

CLOTHING/GOLFWEAR

Sunderland of Scotland Ltd
**PO Box 14, Glasgow G2 1ER.
Tel 0141-552 3261 Fax 0141-552 8518**

www.sunderlandgolf.com
Sunderland of Scotland manufacture high quality golf rainwear in Scotland. All rainsuits are tour tested and guaranteed waterproof and breathable, a variety of fabrics including Goretex being used. Sunderlands also manufacture the famous Sunderland Original Weatherbeater and Classic Windproof Pullover. Official supplier to PGA, PGAE, LPGA, ELPGA and St Andrews Links Trust.

CLUB MANAGEMENT CONSULTANTS

Mercator International
**Golf Design & Development
Contact: Tel +44 (0) 171 584 8877**

e-mail:info@mercator.co.uk
Golf Course Architecture; Golf Real Estate & Resort Masterplanning; Golf Development Business Planning, Marketing and Operational Management. European Management and Marketing operations are conducted in JV partnership with the National Golf Company of Florida. The Golf Course Architecture Department offers a choice of Mercator Design or Gary Player Signature Design, both under lead Guy Hockley, MA Hons Phil BIGCA. Mercator operates throughout Europe and the Middle East with offices in London and Italy.

CLUB MANUFACTURERS

Aldila UK
**12 Heather Road, Binley Woods,
Coventry CV3 2DE.
Tel/Fax (01203) 545651**

World's leading manufacturer of graphite golf shafts, including Tour Grade series, Clubmaker series, Value series, Speciality series, Classic series and G Loomis shafts.

Bronty Golf Co Ltd
**81A Bradford Road, Stanningley,
Pudsey, West Yorkshire LS28 6AT.
Tel 0113-257 7266 Fax 0113-257 0771**

e-mail:sales@brontygolf.com
Website:www.brontygolf.co.uk
Manufacturers of high quality British made custom golf clubs, putters and specialist clubs. Authentic replicas and hickory shafted putters etc.

Callaway Golf Europe Ltd
Units A27 Barwell Business Park,
Leatherhead Road, Chessington,
Surrey KT9 2NY.
Tel 0181-391 0111

Manufacturer of golf clubs and accessories. Callaway Golf is now the distributor for Odyssey Golf.

Cleveland Golf UK
4 Orchard Hill,
Windlesham,
Surrey GU20 6DB.
Tel (01276) 479087 Fax (01276) 451865

Manufacturers of golfs most popular wedges. Consistently rated the No 1 wedge on the US and European PGA Tours. Cleveland Golf also manufacture Tour Action irons, woods, putters and accessories. The Tour Action range has something for everyone, with models for the very low handicap player, to game improvement sets for the beginner. The Tour Action range is available for both men and women.

Dimensions in Sport Ltd
First Floor, Woodcock House,
Gibbard Mews, High Street,
Wimbledon Village, London SW19 5BY.
Tel 0181-947 6555 Fax 0181-947 5544

Dimensions in Sport are the UK distributors for *Adams Tight Lie* golf clubs. A range of easy to hit Fairway woods designed to enable you to take the difficult to hit long irons out of your bag, and thus improve your score. *Tight Lies* are endorsed by six-time Major winner Nick Faldo.

Glenscot Golf Ltd
Osborne Court, Thelwall New Road,
Warrington, Cheshire WA4 2LS.
Tel (01925) 861740 Fax (01925) 861750

e-mail: Glenscotgo@aol.com
Glenscot Golf are manufacturers and distributors of the Seal brand of component golf equipment. All of which is made to measure up to your exact specifications. This is completed by a full range of quality golf bags.

Prosimmon Golf (UK) Ltd
21 Monkspath Business Park,
Highlands Road, Shirley, Solihull,
West Midlands B90 4NZ.
Tel 0121-744 9551 Fax 0121-744 9541

Manufacturers of Premium golf clubs, bags and rainwear including the *Icon* range of golf clubs featuring the revolutionary *Torsionally Tuned* graphite and steel shafts. Designers of unique *Matchplay* custom programme.

Rogue Golf Company Ltd
The Downs Farm, Reigate Road,
Ewell, Surrey KT17 3BY.
Tel 0181-786 8896 Fax 0181-394 1895

Manufacture and supply of innovative golf equipment including metalwoods, irons, bags and accessories. The range incorporates a fresh, youthfull image combined with high quality products sourced predominently from USA.

Transline Tiger Golf
5 Bridgwater Court, Weston Super Mare,
North Somerset BS24 9AY.
Tel (01934) 642214 Fax (01934) 642004

e-mail:tigerben@compuserve.com
Sole manufacturers and registered owners of all Transline Tiger, Tigercub and Westcoast products. Woods, irons, bags, putters - plus Tiger accessories. Chairman: Roger Bennett. Secretary: Sandra Bennett.

True Temper UK/Europe
c/o Tucker Fasteners
Walsall Road, Birmingham B42 1BP.
Tel 0121-331 2276 Fax 0121-331 2286

Golf shaft manufacturer both steel and graphite. In 1998 achieved over 120 Tournament wins on PGA Tours. Dynamic Gold used by leading players. Sensicore continues to grow in usage by both Tournament players and amateurs.

Wilson Sporting Goods Co Ltd
1 Tanners Yard,
London Road,
Bagshot, Surrey GU19 5HD.
Tel (01294) 316200 Fax (01294) 316255

Wilson manufactures and supplies a full range of 'Game Improvement' products for the average golfer. Wilson has taken technological advancement to the next level, with the launch of the Fat Shaft woods and irons, and the Staff Titanium golf bag range. Fat Shaft technology features a 36% wider tip diameter than a traditional skinny shaft, this gives the club greater stability through impact on off-centre hits. This gives the average golfer deadly accuracy and remarkable distance. The Staff titanium golf ball range, now features the revolutionary straight distance ball which has less spin than a conventional ball. The reduced spin makes the ball fly straighter by eliminating the harmful side-spin which causes hooks and slices.

Yonex UK Ltd
Yonex House,
74 Wood Lane,
White City,
London W12 7RH.
Tel 0181-742 9777 Fax 0181-742 9612

Manufacturer and distributor of Yonex premium golf equipment. The range includes the highest quality titanium woods and irons, all with graphite shafts. The world's number one left-hander, Phil Mickelson, plays and endorse Yonex equipment.

CLUBHOUSE FURNISHINGS & EQUIPMENT

Club Class Cabinets
Quality Row House,
1 Purdeys Industrial Estate,
Purdeys Way,
Rochford, Essex SS4 1ND.
Tel (01702) 209500 Fax (01702) 209530

Golf Club Class locker room furniture specialist. Modular standard ranges or purpose built to your specified design. Free survey and quotation service

Links Leisure
Unit 22,
Civic Industrial Park,
Whitchurch,
Shropshire SY13 ITT.
Tel (01948) 663002 Fax (01948) 666381

Website: http://www.web-marketing.co.uk/linksleisure
The latest addition to the Links Leisure range is the GRC Litter Bin. This is supplied with or without a lid, can be painted any colour and can be supplied with either your club logo or sponsor board. Uses a standard plastic bag to assist with disposal of rubbish.

Schotten Trophies
- Manfred Schotten Antiques
109 High Street,
Burford,
Oxfordshire OX18 4RH.
Tel (01993) 822302 Fax (01993) 822055

http://www.schotten.com
Exquisite hand crafted trophies in traditional style, designed, manufactured and hand finished in our own workshop by craftmen using solid woods, brass and bronze. Also available are golf antiques, clubs, novelty items, desk sets etc, and golf club furnishings. (See advertisement page 7 for further details.)

COMPUTER SYSTEMS

Euro Systems Projects (ESP)
Europa House,
8 Kimpton Link Business Park,
Kimpton Road, Sutton, Surrey SM3 9PF.
Tel 0181-641 7216 Fax 0181-641 3179

ESP is universally recognised as the UK's market leader for integrated point-of-sale and management systems. GOLFMASTER has been specifically designed for both the golf professional and the golf club, and encompasses all aspects encountered when running a successful and profitable golf operation.

CORPORATE GIFTS & EVENTS

Hymax Products (UK) Ltd
Unit 19 Team Valley Business Centre,
Earlsway Team Valley,
Gateshead NE11 0RG.
Tel 0191-491 1138 Fax 0191-487 1911

e-mail: Info@Hymax.co.uk
website: www.hymax.co.uk
Manufacturers of golf accessories and corporate gift packs. Unique and innovative British made goods. *Gifts that the golfer uses.*

COURSE MEASUREMENT

Eagle Promotions Ltd
Eagle House, 1 Clearway Court,
139-141 Croydon Road, Caterham,
Surrey CR3 6PF.
Tel (01883) 344244 Fax (01883) 341777

Eagle Promotions offer a comprehensive range of products from certified course measurement and tee signs through to scorecards, yardage books, green fee tickets, members' tags, event and leader boards, honours boards, clubhouse and general course signage. For further information please contact Philip McInley on 01883 344244.

Strokesport
Abbey Mill Business Centre,
Paisley PA1 1TJ.
Tel 0141-848 1199 Fax 0141-887 1642

Measurement and survey to professional standard. Certification accepted by National Golf unions. Leading specialists in course measurement. We are also publishers of **Strokesaver Distance Guides** which are recognised as the most accurate and useful golf course management aids worldwide.

continued over

Strokesaver provides professionals and clubs with a constant profit centre. (See advertisement page 12 for further details.)

Vickers Sports Optics
Unit 9, 35 Revenge Road,
Lordswood, Kent ME5 8DW.
Tel (01634) 201284 Fax (01634) 201286

Bushnells Yardage *ProTM* 400 instantaneously measures distances up to 400 yards with incredible accuracy (± 1 yard). Know whether - you can reach the green in one - clear the water or bunker - it's safe to hit or how far I have driven/hit the ball.

DISTRIBUTORS & WHOLESALERS

Aldila UK
12 Heather Road,
Binley Woods,
Coventry CV3 2DE.
Tel/Fax (01203) 545651

Aldila Golf equipment distributors: Diamond Golf Ltd, 4/5 Rudford Industrial Estate, Ford Road, Arundel BN18 0BS Tel (01903) 726999 Fax (01903) 726998; Golfsmith (Europe) Ltd, Leewood Business Park, Upton Road, Huntingdon PE17 5XQ Tel (01480) 891909 Fax (01480) 891836; Regal Golf Corporation, Golf House, Broad Lane, Bradford, West Yorkshire Tel (01274) 664289 Fax (01274) 656040.

Cleveland Golf UK
4 Orchard Hill, Windlesham,
Surrey GU20 6DB.
Tel (01276) 479087 Fax (01276) 451865

Manufacturers of golfs most popular wedges. Consistently rated the No 1 wedge on the US and European PGA Tours. Cleveland Golf also manufacture Tour Action irons, woods, putters and accessories. The Tour Action range has something for everyone, with models for the very low handicap player, to game improvement sets for the beginner. The Tour Action range is available for both men and women.

Eaton Ltd - Golf Pride Grips
Units 1 & 2 The Stirling Centre,
Northfields Industrial Estate,
Market Deeping,
Nr Peterborough PE6 8EQ.
Tel (01778) 341555 Fax (01778) 344025

Manufacturers of golf grips for over 50 years, they have been the leader in golf grip technology and the leader in rubber and cord grip sales for both professional and amateur players alike.

Sun Mountain Sports
c/o Golf Products Ltd
The Downs Farm,
Reigate Road,
Ewell, Surrey KT17 3BY.
Tel 0181-786 8896 Fax 0181-394 1895

Distribution of a superb range of American made golf bags including innovative, lightweight stand and carry bags as well as new trolley bag offerings. One of the world's leading suppliers of golf bags and related products.

Yonex UK Ltd
Yonex House,
74 Wood Lane,
White City, London W12 7RH.
Tel 0181-742 9777 Fax 0181-742 9612

Manufacturer and distributor of Yonex premium golf equipment. The range includes the highest quality titanium woods and irons, all with graphite shafts. The world's number one left-hander, Phil Mickelson, plays and endorse Yonex equipment.

DRIVING RANGE & PRACTICE EQUIPMENT

Driving Force Leisure Europe Ltd - Epic Golf
Badcock House,
Unit 11a, Dolphin Park,
Castle Road, Eurolink Industrial Centre,
Sittingbourne, Kent ME10 3RL.
Tel (01795) 427333 Fax (01795) 425222

Manufacturers of golf driving range equipment including Epic ball dispensers, ball pickers, ball washers, conveyor and ancillary products. Easy Picker Europe are the UK sole distributor for Astroturf range mats and golf surfaces, together with winter tees, walkways and putting surfaces.

European Golf Machinery
Street Garage,
Bucklesham,
Ipswich, Suffolk IP10 0DN.
Tel (01473) 659815 Fax (01473) 659045

Manufacturers of driving range equipment including golf ball collectors, dispensers, ball washers and elevators. Kawasaki ATV and Mule Distributors. Exclusive diesel engined Mule utility vehicle. (See advertisement page 10 for further details.)

Golftek (UK) Ltd
Curtis Road, Dorking, Surrey RH4 1XD.
Tel (01306) 741888 Fax (01306) 877888

Distributor of the world's best golf swing, club fitting analyser and three dimensional golf simulator, as on TV. Distributor of the best *digitised video* system available. Sports coach as well as video teaching systems. Europe's largest manufacturer of golf mats, portarange nets and cage nets.

Grassform Ltd
**3 Cricketers Row, Herongate,
Brentwood, Essex CM13 3QA.**
Tel (01277) 812973 Fax (01277) 812972

Grassform Limited undertakes all types of golf course projects. From new build to reconstruction of tees, greens and bunkers. We also install land drainage systems, sand banding, lakes, water features, footpaths, buggy paths and driving ranges. For further information please contact Mark Dunning.

Range Servant UK Ltd
**Hempstead Road, Hunton Bridge,
Watford, Hertfordshire WD1 3NJ.**
Tel/Fax (01923) 263777

Manufacture and market golf range and practice ground equipment. Golf ball dispensers, golf ball washers, golf ball collectors, play mats for ranges and practice grounds - winter tee mats a speciality, range balls and baskets.

Tildenet Ltd
Hartcliffe Way, Bristol BS3 5RJ.
Tel 0117-966 9684 Fax 0117-923 1251

Supply and installation of the ultimate netting based solutions for the world of golf. Including perimeter safety netting, practice nets to cater for professionals, warm-up tees, advanced players and beginners. Anti-ball plugging netting, target nets, target greens anti-dazzle netting. And for the greenkeeper - grass growth acceleration technology and bunker membrane.

EDUCATION/TRAINING & TEACHING AIDS

Brian P Jennings
**42 Grange Wood, Rathfarnham,
Dublin 16, Ireland.**
Tel +353 1 494 6433 Fax +353 1 493 9295

Brian P Jennings, fitness consultant to the Cobra European Golf Academy. In-club presentation on *'The Physical and Mental Approach to Golf'* by appointment. Also golf preparation training schedules by mail, fax and/ or voice mail.

Chartex Products International Ltd
**20 Grasmere,
Liden,
Swindon, Wiltshire SN3 6LE.**
Tel (01793) 530880 Fax (01793) 491035

Golf Fitness Programmes - *Keeping Fit for Better Golf* is a new, unique programme of exercises designed to help improve stamina, suppleness and strength for enhanced control and greater distance. The 36-page book, plus the warm-up stretching booklet is supplemented with two thera-band rubber tubes for progressive strength training. Endorsed by the PGA of Europe.

Golf Projects Ltd
**The Lodge,
East Sussex National Golf Club,
Uckfield,
East Sussex TN22 5ES.**
Tel (01825) 880250 Fax (01825) 880251

Distributors of hi-tech golf teaching and entertainment systems including the Astar digital video teaching system and Deadsolid simulators and analysers.

ELECTRONIC POINT-OF-SALE

Euro Systems Projects (ESP)
**Europa House,
8 Kimpton Link Business Park,
Kimpton Road,
Sutton, Surrey SM3 9PF.**
Tel 0181-641 7216 Fax 0181-641 3179

ESP is universally recognised as the UK's market leader for integrated point-of-sale and management systems. GOLFMASTER has been specifically designed for both the golf professional and the golf club, and encompasses all aspects encountered when running a successful and profitable golf operation.

EXHIBITIONS

Exclusive Media Events Ltd
Tel 0181-373 7756 Fax 0181-373 7759

(See advertisement page 10 for further details.)

GIFTS & NOVELTIES

Antique Golf
10 Glasgow Road, Paisley PA1 3QG.
Tel 0141-889 1860 Fax 0141-889 1880

e-mail:robert@antiquegolf.com
Wesite:www.antiquegolf.com
The most extensive range of antique golf clubs and memorabilia in the world. All clubs drawn from the period 1840 to 1920. We supply individual collectors, golf clubs, and the corporate marketplace. For a preview ask for our catalogue or view our website.

Birkdale Promotions
97 Old Watford Road, Bricket Wood,
Nr St Albans, Hertfordshire AL2 3UN.
Tel (01923) 671225 Fax (01923) 662522

An exclusive range of bronze figuerines, silverplated golf trophies, shields, antique replica plaques all suitable for clubs, societies and corporate events. Our in-house engraving enables each to be personalised to your specification and delivery can be made to any address worldwide. Please call for our free colour brochure and price list. (See advertisement page 12 for further details.)

Derek Burridge (Wholesale) Ltd
Awards House, Unit 15, The Metro Centre,
Springfield Road,
Hayes, Middlesex UB4 0LE.
Tel 0181-569 0123 Fax 0181-569 0111

The country's leading suppliers of golf prizes. We offer a vast range of silverplate, crystal, china, clocks, leather goods and sporting trophies, all at trade prices. Glass and silverplate in-house engraving service. Next day delivery throughout the UK. Call for brochure. (See advertisement page 7 for further details.)

Schotten Trophies
- Manfred Schotten Antiques
109 High Street, Burford,
Oxfordshire OX18 4RH.
Tel (01993) 822302 Fax (01993) 822055

http.//www.schotten.com
Exquisite hand crafted trophies in traditional style, designed, manufactured and hand finished in our own workshop by craftsmen using solid woods, brass and bronze. Also available are golf antiques, clubs, novelty items, desk sets etc, and golf club furnishings. (See advertisement page 7 for further details.)

GOLF COURSE CONSTRUCTION & UPGRADING

M J Abbott Ltd
Bratch Lane,
Dinton,
Salisbury,
Wiltshire SP3 5EB.
Tel (01722) 716361 Fax (01722) 716828

M J Abbott Limited offer a range of specialist services to the golf and leisure industry. Recognised as one of Britain's leading companies offering Rain Bird irrigation systems. Land drainage, golf course construction and maintenance are all undertaken by experienced employees utilising the company's own specially adapted machinery.

Chris Stanton
Golf Course Architect,
Chartered Town Planner
14 Shaw Wood Close,
North End,
Durham DH1 4LZ.
Tel 0191-384 3771 Fax 0191-333 6293

Ideally placed to address sensitive development issues. Since the early 1970s, Chris Stanton has demonstrated his commitment to golf architecture, whilst still in full-time planning employment, by designing/directly supervising construction of new golf courses, comprehensive course/hole renovation; greens rebuilt to USGA specification and major grant-aided tree planting programmes.

Christy O'Connor Jnr, Ltd
Weir House,
Kilcolgan,
Galway, Ireland.
Tel +353 91 796475 Fax +353 91 796476

Golf course architect and course re-modelling. Built 20 golf courses in Ireland and Europe. Ryder Cup and World Cup player.

C J Collins Construction Ltd
Bridge Farm House, Cuckfield Road,
Burgess Hill, West Sussex RH15 8RE.
Tel (01444) 242993 Fax (01444) 247318

The UK's foremost constructor of golf courses and the English Golf Union's appointed contractors. Nationally respected for complete new courses and highly acclaimed for remodelling and upgrading works with existing clubs. Member of BAGCC. Driving range consultancy and construction.

David Hemstock Associates
Golf Course Architects & Consultants
Suite 4a,
Northmill, Bridgefoot,
Belper, Derbyshire DE56 1YD.
Tel (01773) 827115 Fax (01773) 821284

e-mail: David_Hemstock@golf-design.demon/co.uk
website: www.golf-design.demon.co.uk
40 projects since 1991, from championship-quality new to total re-modelling of existing; Europe to China. Design and documentation, project and maintenance management, clubhouse design, through the qualified and experienced team of David Hemstock, BSc IEng., Les Watts, B.Arch., and Geoff Porter, NDH.

David Williams Golf Design
27 Prince's Drive,
Colwyn Bay,
North Wales LL29 8HT.
Tel (01492) 533818 Fax (01492) 533012

Colf course architects and project managers. Fully integrated service *from conception through construction to completion*. Over a dozen 18-hole courses built in Britain within last five years. Full member of British Institute of Golf Course Architects (BIGCA).

Dura-Sport Ltd
- Synthetic Surfaces for Golf
Unit 12, Cornwall Business Centre,
Cornwall Road,
South Wigston, Leicestershire LE18 4XH.
Tel 0116-277 0899 Fax 0116-277 0433

e-mail:durasport@easynet.co.uk
Sure Step patented pathway solutions
True Pace patented putting surfaces
Natural Impact patented target greens
Winter Teeing Areas. Miniature Golf Course design and construction. Please call for further discussion and/or a consultation.

Fox Contracting (Owmby) Ltd
Caenby Hall, Caenby Corner,
Market Rasen LN8 2BU.
Tel (01673) 878444 Fax (01673) 878644

e-mail: office@fox-group.co.uk
Fox Contracting (Owmby) Limited - The contracting division of the Fox group of companies was founded early 1991. Since its formation the company has successfully completed many new developments together with completing upgrading and redevelopment works on existing courses.

Gaunt & Marnoch Ltd
- Golf Course Architects
5 Frederick's Place,
Old Jewry,
London EC2R 8AB.
Tel 0171-726 6645 Fax 0171-726 6646
'Hilltop', Lakeside, Bakewell DE45 1GN.
Tel (01629) 815453 Fax (01629) 815170

e-mail: jonathan@gauntandmarnoch.com
steve@gauntand marnoch.com
Website:www.gauntandmarnoch.com
Gaunt & Marnoch Limited provides top quality, cost-conscious and environmentally sympathetic golf course development. Broad and flexible service offered, including reconstruction works and course extensions. The practice is committed to better golf through good design. Please call for more information.

Grassform Ltd
3 Cricketers Row,
Herongate,
Brentwood, Essex CM13 3QA.
Tel (01277) 812973 Fax (01277) 812972

Grassform Limited undertakes all types of golf course projects. From new build to reconstruction of tees, greens and bunkers. We also install land drainage systems, sand banding, lakes, water features, footpaths, buggy paths and driving ranges. For further information please contact Mark Dunning.

Greens of Scotland
Cruickshank Building,
Craibstone Estate,
Bucksburn, Aberdeen AB21 9TR.
Tel (01224) 711106 Fax (01224) 714591

An international golf course consultancy providing specialist skills for feasibility studies, planning, course design, buildings design, course construction, project management and turf agronomy. Our project range covers alterations, renovations, driving ranges and new courses.

Land Unit Construction Ltd
Hanslope,
Milton Keynes,
Buckinghamshire MK19 7BX.
Tel (01908) 510414 Fax (01908) 511056

We have the knowledge and experience gained over 20 years in golf course construction and constantly work with many of the country's leading golf course architects to provide clients with unparalleled quality of service.

P S D Agronomy Ltd
42 Garstang Road,
Preston,
Lancashire PR1 1NA.
Tel (01772) 884450 Fax (01772) 884445

A specialist team of golf course agronomists working throughout the UK and Europe. Whether building a new course, extending an existing one or just making the best of what you have - we have the technical expertise to help.

Patrick F Merrigan BAgr Sc MBIGCA
Golf Course Architect,
Agronomist & Consultant
PO Box 119,
Cork, Ireland.
Tel +353 21 353613 Fax +353 21 354153

e-mail:merriganp@tinet.ie
Member British Institute Golf Course Architects (BIGCA). Personal 'hands on' service and commitment. Feasibility studies, masterplanning, re-modelling. World class rated courses include, eg Old Head, Slieve Russell Tulfarris, Woodenbridge. International portfolio.

Robin Hiseman Golf Course Design
Berrymeadow Cottage,
No 4, West Cairnbeg,
Laurencekirk,
Aberdeenshire AB30 1SR.
Tel/Fax (01561) 320827

e-mail:robin@hisemangolf.freeserve.co.uk
Scotland's only BIGCA qualified golf course architect. Considerable experience and specialist skills in feasibility studies, planning, course design, tender documentation and construction supervisor for new golf courses, or re-modelling projects. All work personally controlled.

Ronnie Lumsden
Golf Course Architect & Course Management Consultancy
14E Church Hill,
Edinburgh EH10 4BQ.
Tel/Fax 0131-447 1052

Graduate member of the British Institute of Golf Course Architects (BIGCA), and qualified in course management. A comprehensive design service and advice on improving the quality and condition of your course.

Ryder Golf Services
50 Gally Hill Road,
Church Crookham,
Hampshire GU13 0QF.
Tel (01252) 617542 Fax (01252) 812082

Specialist consultancy providing advanced CAD services to architects, contractors, developers and clubs for: Feasibility studies; planning applications; course design and re-design; construction cost planning; environmental impact analysis; contract drawings; bills of quantities, 3D visualisations.

Simon Gidman International Golf Course Architects
Wychwood House,
43 Shipton Road,
Ascott Under Wychwood, Oxon OX7 6AG.
Tel (01993) 830441 Fax (01993) 831860

A full member of the British Institute of Golf Course Architects (BIGCA), Simon Gidman has been involved with some 50 projects in Europe and throughout the world. The company also specialises in preparing reports and studies for the restoration and upgrading of existing golf courses.

Swan Golf Designs Ltd
Telfords Barn, Willingale,
Ongar, Essex CM5 0QF.
Tel (01277) 896229 Fax (01277) 896300

e-mail:SwanGolfDesigns@btinternet.com
Professional golf course architects with traditional values, offering initial appraisals, conceptual designs, detailed design work and construction management. Specialising in improvements of existing golf courses, extensions, re-design of greens and tees etc, including restorations of classic old courses.

GOLF COURSE DESIGN CONSULTANTS

Fox Contracting (Owmby) Ltd
Caenby Hall,
Caenby Corner,
Market Rasen LN8 2BU.
Tel (01673) 878444 Fax (01673) 878644

e-mail: office@fox-group.co.uk
Fox Contracting (Owmby) Limited - The contracting division of the Fox group of companies was founded early 1991. Since its formation the company has successfully completed many new developments together with completing upgrading and redevelopment works on existing courses.

Grassform Ltd
3 Cricketers Row, Herongate,
Brentwood, Essex CM13 3QA.
Tel (01277) 812973 Fax (01277) 812972

Grassform Limited undertakes all types of golf course projects. From new build to re-construction of tees, greens and bunkers. We also install land drainage systems, sand banding, lakes, water features, footpaths, buggy paths and driving ranges. For further information please contact Mark Dunning.

P S D Agronomy Ltd
42 Garstang Road, Preston,
Lancashire PR1 1NA.
Tel (01772) 884450 Fax (01772) 884445

A specialist team of golf course agronomists working throughout the UK and Europe. Whether building a new course, extending an existing one or just making the best of what you have - we have the technical expertise to help.

Ryder Golf Services
50 Gally Hill Road,
Church Crookham, Hampshire GU13 0QF.
Tel (01252) 617542 Fax (01252) 812082

Specialist consultancy providing advanced CAD services to architects, contractors, developers and clubs for: Feasibility studies; planning applications; course design and re-design; construction cost planning; environmental impact analysis; contract drawings; bills of quantities, 3D visualisations.

GOLF COURSE DISTANCE GUIDES

Kevin Randell Media & Marketing
PO Box 1286, Rugby CV21 1YX.
Tel/Fax +44 (0) 1788 543964

The choice for profitable, laser-measured yardage booklets. We custom-design the presentation and content, to ensure your club has the exact course planner it needs. Supplied on a *sale or return* basis means no cost outlay, no bulky quantities of stock, no unsold copies, no financial risk - just profit. (See advertisement on page 7 and 12 for further details.)

Strokesport
Abbey Mill Business Centre,
Paisley PA1 1TJ.
Tel 0141-848 1199 Fax 0141-887 1642

We are publishers of *Strokesaver Distance Guides* which are recognised as the most accurate and useful golf course management aids worldwide. *Strokesaver* provides professionals and clubs with a constant profit centre. Course Measurement - Measurement and survey to professional standard. Certification accepted by National Golf unions. Leading specialists in course measurement. (See advertisement page 12 for further details.)

Vickers Sports Optics
Unit 9, 35 Revenge Road,
Lordswood, Kent ME5 8DW.
Tel (01634) 201284 Fax (01634) 201286

Bushnells Yardage *ProTM* 400 instantaneously measures distances up to 400 yards with incredible accuracy ($\pm$ 1 yard). Know whether - you can reach the green in one - clear the water or bunker - it's safe to hit or how far I have driven/hit the ball.

GOLF COURSE MAINTENANCE & UPGRADING

Dura-Sport Ltd
- Synthetic Surfaces for Golf
Unit 12, Cornwall Business Centre,
Cornwall Road, South Wigston,
Leicestershire LE18 4XH.
Tel 0116-277 0899 Fax 0116-277 0433

e-mail: durasport@easynet.co.uk
Sure Step patented pathway solutions
True Pace patented putting surfaces
Natural Impact patented target greens
Winter Teeing Areas. Miniature Golf Course design and construction. Please call for further discussion and/or a consultation.

European Golf Machinery
Street Garage, Bucklesham,
Ipswich, Suffolk IP10 0DN.
Tel (01473) 659815 Fax (01473) 659045

Manufacturers of driving range equipment including golf ball collectors, dispensers, ball washers and elevators. Kawasaki ATV and Mule Distributors. Exclusive diesel engined Mule utility vehicle. (See advertisement page 10 for further details.)

Grassform Ltd
3 Cricketers Row, Herongate,
Brentwood, Essex CM13 3QA.
Tel (01277) 812973 Fax (01277) 812972

Grassform Limited undertakes all types of golf course projects. From new build to reconstruction of tees, greens and bunkers. We also install land drainage systems, sand banding,

lakes, water features, footpaths, buggy paths and driving ranges. For further information please contact Mark Dunning.

John Greasley Ltd
Ashfield House,
1154 Melton Road,
Syston, Leicester LE7 2HB.
Tel 0116-269 6766 Fax 0116-269 6866

John Greasley established his company in 1984 and has specialised in the construction of new courses, along with alterations, improvements and refurbishment on existing ones. Works have been completed on some of the countries oldest and most prestigious courses.

Land Unit Construction Ltd
Hanslope, Milton Keynes,
Buckinghamshire MK19 7BX.
Tel (01908) 510414 Fax (01908) 511056

We have the knowledge and experience gained over 20 years in golf course construction and constantly work with many of the country's leading golf course architects to provide clients with unparalleled quality of service.

Toro Commercial Products
Lely (UK) Ltd
Station Road, St Neots, Huntingdon,
Cambridgeshire PE19 1QH.
Tel (01480) 476971 Fax (01480) 216167
e-mail:toro.sales@lely.co.uk

Toro offer an extensive range of professional turf maintenance equipment which includes: greens mowers, fairway mowers, triplex mowers, rotary mowers, aeration and utility vehicles. *Toro* manufacture to an exceptionally high quality and give unrivalled quality of cut.

GOLF COURSE PLANNERS

D G P Marketing Ltd
Persimmon House, 33 Lord Street, Leigh,
Lancashire WN7 1BY.
Tel (01942) 684001 Fax (01942) 684002
e-mail:enquiries@sports-publications.co.uk
Website:http://www.sports-publications.co.uk

FREE SCORECARDS AND PLANNERS - DGP Marketing offer a totally new concept to providing clubs with scorecards/planners. All products are in full colour and in many cases totally free, (numerous layouts available). Call us today for fast response and guaranteed satisfaction. We'll take the worry/costs away. Contact Graeme or Nigel 01942 684001.

Kevin Randell Media & Marketing
PO Box 1286, Rugby CV21 1YX.
Tel/Fax +44 (0) 1788 543964

The choice for profitable, laser-measured yardage booklets. We custom-design the presentation and content, to ensure your club has the exact course planner it needs. Supplied on a *sale or return* basis means no cost outlay, no bulky quantities of stock, no unsold copies, no financial risk - just profit. (See advertisement on page 7 and 12 for further details.)

GOLF COURSE YARDAGE BOOKS

Kevin Randell Media & Marketing
PO Box 1286, Rugby CV21 1YX.
Tel/Fax +44 (0) 1788 543964

The choice for profitable, laser-measured yardage booklets. We custom-design the presentation and content, to ensure your club has the exact course planner it needs. Supplied on a *sale or return* basis means no cost outlay, no bulky quantities of stock, no unsold copies, no financial risk - just profit. (See advertisement on page 7 and 12 for further details.)

GOLF DEVELOPMENT/MANAGEMENT & MAINTENANCE

Barrelfield Golf Ltd
302 Ewell Road, Surbiton,
Surrey KT6 7AQ.
Tel 0181-390 6566 Fax 0181-390 8830

Barrelfield Golf Limited has an unrivalled track record in the development, marketing, management and maintenance of profitable golf clubs in Britain. Other services include feasibility studies and arranging finance. For further information contact Melvin Thomas 0181-390 6566.

Mercator International
Golf Design & Development
Contact: Tel +44 (0) 171 584 8877
e-mail:info@mercator.co.uk

Golf Course Architecture; Golf Real Estate & Resort Masterplanning; Golf Development Business Planning, Marketing and Operational Management. European Management and Marketing operations are conducted in JV partnership with the National Golf Company of Florida. The Golf Course Architecture Department offers a choice of Mercator Design or Gary Player Signature Design, both under lead Guy Hockley, MA Hons Phil BIGCA.

continued over

GOLF FITNESS CONSULTANT

Brian P Jennings
42 Grange Wood, Rathfarnham,
Dublin 16, Ireland.
Tel +353 1 494 6433 Fax +353 1 493 9295

Brian P Jennings, fitness consultant to the Cobra European Golf Academy. In-club presentation on *'The Physical and Mental Approach to Golf'* by appointment. Also golf preparation training schedules by mail, fax and/or voice mail.

GOLF GRIPS & SHAFTS

Eaton Ltd - Golf Pride Grips
Units 1 & 2 The Stirling Centre,
Northfields Industrial Estate,
Market Deeping,
Nr Peterborough PE6 8EQ.
Tel (01778) 341555 Fax (01778) 344025

Manufacturers of golf grips for over 50 years, they have been the leader in golf grip technology and the leader in rubber and cord grip sales for both professional and amateur players alike.

True Temper UK/Europe
c/o Tucker Fasteners
Walsall Road, Birmingham B42 1BP.
Tel 0121-331 2276 Fax 0121-331 2286

Golf shaft manufacturer both steel and graphite. In 1998 achieved over 120 Tournament wins on PGA Tours. Dynamic Gold used by leading players. Sensicore continues to grow in usage by both Tournament players and amateurs.

GOLF HOLIDAYS/ TOUR OPERATORS - HOME & ABROAD

3D Golf plc
3D House, Ayr KA8 8HH.
Tel 0800 333 323 or 01292 263331
or 07000 3D Golf Fax (01292) 293033
e-mail:sales@3dgolf.co.uk
website: www.3dgolf.co.uk

UK's largest golf holiday company. For over 20 years we have given the British golfer *'The best Golf Holiday Deals in the Business'* to Spain, Portugal, France, Ireland and the USA.

Mercator operates throughout Europe and the Middle East with offices in London and Italy.

GOLFING AIDS/PRACTICE EQUIPMENT

Pan European (Golf) 1973 (PEP)
Old Mill Works, High Street,
Maldon, Essex CM9 5EH.
Tel/Fax (01621) 851700

Products include a wide range of practice nets and mats for beginners through to professionals. We also make a commercial range of nets and mats for clubs, stores and leisure centres. Worldwide export sales our speciality.

Smart Golf UK
PO Box 220, Southport,
Merseyside PR8 26H.
Tel (01704) 575575 Fax (01704) 575566

Suppliers of the most realistic and accurate indoor golf simulators in the world, together with swing analysis systems. Smart Golf is the acknowledged expert in the creation of profitable installations and has a proven track record.

GOVERNING BODIES

English Golf Union (EGU)
The National Golf Centre, The Broadway,
Woodhall Spa, Lincolnshire LN10 6PU.
Tel (01526) 352511 Fax (01526) 354020

e-mail: flint@englishgolfunion.org
http://www.englishgolfunion.org

The governing body for mens' amateur golf in England on behalf of its members, promotes the game and offers to them the facilities of the National Golf Centre. A major new initiative is the scheme enabling casual golfers access to an EGU handicap. (See advertisement page 24 for further details.)

GREEN KEEPING & DRIVING RANGE VEHICLES

Toro Commercial Products
Lely (UK) Ltd
Station Road, St Neots, Huntingdon,
Cambridgeshire PE19 1QH.
Tel (01480) 476971 Fax (01480) 216167

e-mail:toro.sales@lely.co.uk

Toro offer an extensive range of professional turf maintenance equipment which includes: greens mowers, fairway mowers, triplex mowers, rotary mowers, aeration and utility vehicles. *Toro* manufacture to an exceptionally high quality and give unrivalled quality of cut.

INSURANCE

Golfplan
International Golf & Travel Insurance
Redcliffe House, Whitehouse Street,
Bristol BS3 4AU.
Tel 0117-963 6198 Fax 0117-923 1058

e-mail: golfplan@dial.pipex.com
Golfplan, endorsed by the PGA, is Europe's largest specialist golf insurance provider. A Golfplan policy covers individual golfers against personal liability; accidental damage to third party property; golf equipment; personal effects; equipment hire charges; tournament entry fees; membership fees; personal accident; Hole-in-One; free legal advice. Contact your professional or call Golfplan quoting Ref: GHB3.

IRRIGATION EQUIPMENT, DESIGN & INSTALLATION

M J Abbott Ltd
Bratch Lane, Dinton, Salisbury,
Wiltshire SP3 5EB.
Tel (01722) 716361 Fax (01722) 716828

M J Abbott Limited offer a range of specialist services to the golf and leisure industry. Recognised as one of Britain's leading companies offering Rain Bird irrigation systems. Land drainage, golf course construction and maintenance are all undertaken by experienced employees utilising the company's own specially adapted machinery.

British Overhead Irrigation Ltd
Upper Halliford Green,
Shepperton Middlesex TW17 8SB.
Tel (01932) 788301 Fax (01932) 780437

Established 75 years, British Overhead Irrigation provide a complete professional, independent golf course irrigation engineering service - design, installation, upgrading and maintenance. Also manufacture *Wizard* fairway self-travelling sprinklers and sectional covers for circular butyl-lined water storage tanks.

I S S Aquaturf Systems Ltd
Unit 18, Downton Industrial Estate,
Batten Road, Downton,
Salisbury, Wiltshire SP5 3HU.
Tel (01725) 513880 Fax (01725) 513003

ISS Aquaturf Systems Limited are master dealers for *Hunter Industries* operating throughout southern England in the design, supply and installation of automatic pop-up irrigation systems for golf courses. The company has been in business for 20 years and specialises in providing quality systems at competitive prices.

Landline Ltd
1 Bluebridge Industrial Estate,
Halstead, Essex CO9 2EX.
Tel (01787) 476699 Fax (01787) 472507

Supply and install impermeable waterproof liners to water features, irrigation reservoirs and ponds. A technical advisory service is available for all aspects of liner installation. We offer customers a professional and complete service, backed by almost 20 years of practical experience of a specialised industry.

Ocmis Irrigation (UK) Ltd
Head Office: Higher Burrow, Kingsbury,
Martock, Somerset TA12 6BU.
Tel (01460) 241939 Fax (01460) 242198

Scotland: Broadmeadow, Harburn,
West Calder, West Lothian EH55 8RT.
Tel 0131-220 2102 Fax 0131-220 6122

Ocmis Irrigation offer the complete irrigation service including the design, supply and installation of Rain Bird, Buckner and Hunter irrigation systems. Complete after-sales service and full maintenance and service contracts for all types and makes of irrigation systems.

York & Martin
39 Salisbury Street,
Fordingbridge, Hampshire SP6 1AB.
Tel (01425) 652087 Fax (01425) 652476

e-mail:yorkmartinl@compuserve.com
Independent irrigation consultants providing objective advice on all irrigation related matters including water souring, existing system evaluation, system designs and specifications, project supervision etc. Operating throughout the UK and mainland Europe.

JEWELLERY

Solent Souvenirs Ltd
Hamble Bank, 40 Newtown Road, Warsash,
Southampton, Hampshire SO31 9FZ.
Tel (01489) 577985 Fax (01489) 577886

Britain's premier supplier of specialised golf jewellery and quality gifts. Many items designed and manufactured exclusively for us and unobtainable elsewhere. Replace that traditional trophy with an elegant prize which will be both useful and cherished. Most items delivered overnight.

LOCKER MANUFACTURERS

Club Class Cabinets
Quality Row House,
1 Purdeys Industrial Estate,
Purdeys Way,
Rochford, Essex SS4 1ND.
Tel (01702) 209500 Fax (01702) 209530

Golf Club Class locker room furniture specialist. Modular standard ranges or purpose built to your specified design. Free survey and quotation service

MAIL ORDER

Birkdale Promotions
97 Old Watford Road,
Bricket Wood,
Nr St Albans,
Hertfordshire AL2 3UN.
Tel (01923) 671225 Fax (01923) 662522

An exclusive range of bronze figurines, silverplated golf trophies, shields, antique replica plaques all suitable for clubs, societies and corporate events. Our in-house engraving enables each to be personalised to your specification and delivery can be made to any address worldwide. Please call for our free colour brochure and price list. (See advertisement page 12 for further details.)

Solent Souvenirs Ltd
Hamble Bank,
40 Newtown Road,
Warsash,
Southampton, Hampshire SO31 9FZ.
Tel (01489) 577985 Fax (01489) 577886

Britain's premier supplier of specialised golf jewellery and quality gifts. Many items designed and manufactured exclusively for us and unobtainable elsewhere. Replace that traditional trophy with an elegant prize which will be both useful and cherished. Most items delivered overnight.

Steve Schofield Golf Books
29 Nichols Way,
Wetherby,
West Yorkshire LS22 6AD.
Tel/Fax (01937) 581276

e-mail: steve@golfbooks.u-net.com
Classic golf books for sale, new, old and antiquarian. Books on golf history, architecture, biography, club and ball collecting and instruction. Free catalogue on request.

PERSONAL EQUIPMENT & ACCESSORIES

Cleveland Golf UK
4 Orchard Hill,
Windlesham,
Surrey GU20 6DB.
Tel (01276) 479087 Fax (01276) 451865

Manufacturers of golfs most popular wedges. Consistently rated the No 1 wedge on the US and European PGA Tours. Cleveland Golf also manufacture Tour Action irons, woods, putters and accessories. The Tour Action range has something for everyone, with models for the very low handicap player, to game improvement sets for the beginner. The Tour Action range is available for both men and women.

Rogue Golf Company Ltd
The Downs Farm,
Reigate Road,
Ewell, Surrey KT17 3BY.
Tel 0181- 786 8896 Fax 0181-394 1895

Manufacture and supply of innovative golf equipment including metalwoods, irons, bags and accessories. The range incorporates a fresh, youthfull image combined with high quality products sourced predominently from USA.

Softspikes®
Distributed by:
The Grassroots Golf Company Ltd
Unit C17,
Wem Industrial Estate,
Soulton Road,
Wem, Shropshire SY4 5SD.
Tel (01939) 235711 Fax (01939) 235722

e-mail:sales@softspikes.co.uk
The world's No 1 plastic alternative to metal spikes. We offer a complete programme to golf courses wishing to ban the use of metal spikes, and nationwide distribution servicing retail outlets.

PERSONALISED PRODUCTS

Brollies Limited
45 Allerton Road,
Woolton Village, Liverpool L25 7AL.
Tel 0151-421 0250 Fax 0151-421 0091

Brollies Limited carry a comprehensive range in best quality British made Hoyland and Fox Frame umbrellas. Also available seat sticks, twinbrellas, garden parasols, imported double ribbed golf umbrellas and golf ball retrievers. All printed or unprinted.

Derek Burridge (Wholesale) Ltd
Awards House,
Unit 15,
The Metro Centre,
Springfield Road,
Hayes, Middlesex UB4 0LE.
Tel 0181-569 0123 Fax 0181-569 0111

The country's leading suppliers of golf prizes. We offer a vast range of silverplate, crystal, china, clocks, leather goods and sporting trophies, all at trade prices. Glass and silverplate in-house engraving service. Next day delivery throughout the UK. Call for brochure. (See advertisement page 7 for further details).

Elizabeth Parker
The Charles Parker Building,
Midland Road,
Higham Ferrers,
Northamptonshire NN10 8DN.
Tel (01933) 418099 Fax (01933) 358058

e-mail: liziparker@compserve.com
Gold and silver wire hand embroidered blazer badges and silk or polyester ties all produced to your own club logo. Also suppliers of ties, badges, cuff links, key rings and blazer buttons. Quotations and artwork supplied by return.

Galloway Glass
New Abbey Road,
Beeswing,
by Dumfries DG2 8ED.
Tel/Fax (01387) 760643

e-mail: mcc@gallowayglass.demon.co.uk
website: www.dmcsoft.com/scotplay
Specialist plain and cut crystal suppliers and engravers. Many innovative golfing gift ideas through our Muirfield collection and our St Andrews collection. Personalisation our speciality. Ask for our catalogue along with club and reseller pricelists.

H M T Plastics Ltd
Fairway House,
31A Framfield Road,
Uckfield,
East Sussex TN22 5AH.
Tel (01825) 769393 Fax (01825) 769494

Bag tags supplied in nine colours either round, pear shaped maxi or sunrise to accommodate club logo, from a choice of six print colours. Adhesive year sticker available in choice of nine colours and sold separately. (See advertisement page 10 for further details.)

The Highland Connection
38 Watt Road, Glasgow G52 4RW.
Tel 0141-882 8340 Fax 0141-882 7090

The Highland Connection supply the golf professionals at the best known golf clubs throughout the UK, with their own distinctive woven golf towels made in Glasgow, Scotland. Embroidered towels in various quantities also available.

P B Sports
Oakmont House, Unit 8, Waterloo Avenue,
Chelmsley Wood Industrial Estate,
Birmingham B37 6QQ.
Tel 0121-770 2240 Fax 0121-770 7575

Manufacturers of on-course golf bags, golf accessories and personalised products for golf clubs and corporate days.

PICTURES & PRINTS

Chorley & Saunders Golf Art
Chequers End, Chequers Lane,
Preston Village, Hitchin,
Hertfordshire SG4 7TY.
Tel/Fax (01462) 440277

Richard Chorley, England's premier golf artist. Private Commissions. Original oil paintings, drawings and limited edition prints. Prints signed by the artist, numbered and embossed. Collection of classic courses and golfing greats. Ideal corporate and captain's prizes gifts.

Grandison Golf Gallery
25 Hyndland Road, Glasgow G12 9UZ.
Tel/Fax 0141-339 9438

Finest quality limited edition prints of the world's premier golfing venues by award-winning artist William Grandison. Gifts and prizes of distinction for the discerning golfer. Free catalogue available.

PRACTICE NETTING/CAGES

Golftek (UK) Ltd
Curtis Road, Dorking, Surrey RH4 1XD.
Tel (01306) 741888 Fax (01306) 877888

Distributor of the world's best golf swing, club fitting analyser and three dimensional golf simulator, as on TV. Distributor of the best *digitised video* system available. Sports coach as well as video teaching systems. Europe's largest manufacturer of golf mats, portarange nets and cage nets.

Pan European (Golf) 1973 (PEP)
Old Mill Works,
High Street,
Maldon, Essex CM9 5EH.
Tel/Fax (01621) 851700

Products include a wide range of practice nets and mats for beginners through to professionals. We also make a commercial range of nets and mats for clubs, stores and leisure centres. Worldwide export sales our speciality.

Tildenet Ltd
Hartcliffe Way,
Bristol BS3 5RJ.
Tel 0117-966 9684 Fax 0117-923 1251

Supply and installation of the ultimate netting based solutions for the world of golf. Including perimeter safety netting, practice nets to cater for professionals, warm-up tees, advanced players and beginners. Anti-ball plugging netting, target nets, target greens anti-dazzle netting. And for the greenkeeper - grass growth acceleration technology and bunker membrane.

PROMOTION/PUBLICITY

Exclusive Media Events Ltd
Tel 0181-373 7756 Fax 0181-373 7759
(See advertisement page 10 for further details.)

The Highland Connection
38 Watt Road,
Glasgow G52 4RW.
Tel 0141-882 8340 Fax 0141-882 7090

The Highland Connection supply the golf professionals at the best known golf clubs throughout the UK, with their own distinctive woven golf towels made in Glasgow, Scotland. Embroidered towels in various quantities also available.

PROPERTY CONSULTANTS

Edward Symmons Hotel & Leisure
11-14 Grafton Street,
London W1X 3LA.
Tel 0171-344 4500 Fax 0171-344 4555

Consultant surveyors providing specialist property advice to the golf and leisure industry. Established track record in sales, valuations, acquisitions, development appraisals, rating and feasibility studies throughout the UK and Europe.

PUTTER MANUFACTURERS

Bronty Golf Co Ltd
81A Bradford Road,
Stanningley,
Pudsey, West Yorkshire LS28 6AT.
Tel 0113-257 7266 Fax 0113-257 0771
e-mail:sales@brontygolf.com
Website:www.brontygolf.co.uk

Manufacturers of high quality British made custom golf clubs, putters and specialist clubs. Authentic replicas and hickory shafted putters etc.

Callaway Golf UK Ltd
Units A27 Barwell Business Park,
Leatherhead Road,
Chessington,
Surrey KT9 2NY.
Tel 0181-391 0111

Manufacturer of golf clubs and accessories. Callaway Golf is now the distributor for Odyssey Golf.

RANGE BALL MANUFACTURERS

S T E L - Golf Division
Unit T, Lympne Industrial Park,
Hythe, Kent CT21 4LR.
Tel +44 (0) 1303 265777
Fax +44 (0) 1303 265054

Manufacturing and marketing of *Thommo* golf balls endorsed by Peter Thomson, five time British Open champion. New - The *Thommo* titanium series for extra distance, spin and superb feel. Specialised in corporate logo balls and undertakes contract manufacturing and driving range balls.

RECRUITMENT CONSULTANTS

Golf Search - The Golfing Recruitment Specialists
Argyle House, Dee Road,
Richmond-on-Thames, Surrey TW9 2JN.
Tel 0181-334 1125 Fax 0181-334 1112

Golf Search has years of recruitment experience and the largest database of golf management personnel in Europe. We carry out comprehensive interviews, psychometric tests and reference checks on all short-listed candidates. The professional service provided offers exceptional value for money. Please phone for further information.

REMOTE CONTROLLED TROLLEYS

Middlemore Ltd
Valley Road Works,
Sedgley, Dudley,
West Midlands DY3 1TS.
Tel (01902) 673360 Fax (01902) 880783

Distributors of the world's foremost remote controlled powered golf trolley - the *Lectronic Kaddy Phoenix*. There is no other all aluminium remote controlled unit loaded with features this model has to offer. Test drive one today. Our mission - Break Par not your back!

SCORECARDS & PLANNERS

D G P Marketing Ltd
Persimmon House, 33 Lord Street,
Leigh, Lancashire WN7 1BY.
Tel (01942) 684001 Fax (01942) 684002

e-mail:enquiries@sports-publications.co.uk
Website:http://www.sports-publications.co.uk
FREE SCORECARDS AND PLANNERS - DGP Marketing offer a totally new concept to providing clubs with scorecards/planners. All products are in full colour and in many cases totally free, (numerous layouts available). Call us today for fast response and guaranteed satisfaction. We'll take the worry/costs away. Contact Graeme or Nigel 01942 684001.

Eagle Promotions Ltd
Eagle House,
1 Clearway Court, 139-141 Croydon Road,
Caterham, Surrey CR3 6PF.
Tel (01883) 344244 Fax (01883) 341777

Eagle Promotions offer a comprehensive range of products from certified course measurement and tee signs through to scorecards, yardage books, green fee tickets, members' tags, event and leader boards, honours boards, clubhouse and general course signage. For further information please contact Philip McInley on 01883 344244.

SHOE ACCESSORIES

Softspikes®
Distributed by:
The Grassroots Golf Company Ltd
Unit C17, Wem Industrial Estate,
Soulton Road, Wem, Shropshire SY4 5SD.
Tel (01939) 235711 Fax (01939) 235722

e-mail:sales@softspikes.co.uk
The world's No 1 plastic alternative to metal spikes. We offer a complete programme to golf courses wishing to ban the use of metal spikes, and nationwide distribution servicing retail outlets.

SIGNS & MARKERS

Alpha Signs
23 Henham Road,
Debden Green,
Saffron Walden, Essex CB11 3NA.
Tel (01279) 850555

Specialising in the manufacture of high quality golf signs. Our comprehensive range includes tee-signs, directional and interior signage in many materials. All signs custom designed to suit the individual course. Ask for our 1999 brochure.

Links Leisure
Unit 22,
Civic Industrial Park,
Whitchurch, Shropshire SY13 1TT.
Tel (01948) 663002 Fax (01948) 666381

Website:http://www.web-marketing.co.uk/linksleisure
Cast from strong durable GRC the Pro-Tee golf signs come in three sizes and are designed to suit the individual course. They can be painted to six standard colours and supplied with a variety of stands.

SIMULATORS/ANALYSERS

Golf Projects Ltd
The Lodge,
East Sussex National Golf Club,
Uckfield, East Sussex TN22 5ES.
Tel (01825) 880250 Fax (01825) 880251

Distributors of hi-tech golf teaching and entertainment systems including the Astar digital video teaching system and Deadsolid simulators and analysers.

Golftek (UK) Ltd
Curtis Road,
Dorking,
Surrey RH4 1XD.
Tel (01306) 741888 Fax (01306) 877888

Distributor of the world's best golf swing, club fitting analyser and three dimensional golf simulator, as on TV. Distributor of the best *digitised video* system available. Sports coach as well as video teaching systems. Europe's largest manufcturer of golf mats, portarange nets and cage nets.

Smart Golf UK
PO Box 220,
Southport, Merseyside PR8 26H.
Tel (01704) 575575 Fax (01704) 575566

Suppliers of the most realistic and accurate indoor golf simulators in the world, together with swing analysis systems. Smart Golf is the acknowledged expert in the creation of profitable installations and has a proven track record.

SYNTHETIC SURFACES

Dura-Sport Ltd
- Synthetic Surfaces for Golf
Unit 12,
Cornwall Business Centre,
Cornwall Road,
South Wigston, Leicestershire LE18 4XH.
Tel 0116-277 0899 Fax 0116-277 0433

e-mail: durasport@easynet.co.uk
Sure Step patented pathway solutions
True Pace patented putting surfaces
Natural Impact patented target greens
Winter Teeing Areas. Miniature Golf Course design and construction. Please call for further discussion and/or a consultation.

TEE SIGNS

Alpha Signs
23 Henham Road, Debden Green,
Saffron Walden, Essex CB11 3NA.
Tel (01279) 850555

Specialising in the manufacture of high quality golf signs. Our comprehensive range includes tee-signs, directional and interior signage in many materials. All signs custom designed to suit the individual course. Ask for our 1999 brochure.

Eagle Promotions Ltd
Eagle House,
1 Clearway Court,
139-141 Croydon Road,
Caterham, Surrey CR3 6PF.
Tel (01883) 344244 Fax (01883) 341777

Eagle Promotions offer a comprehensive range of products from certified course measurement and tee signs through to scorecards, yardage books, green fee tickets, members' tags, event and leader boards, honours boards, clubhouse and general course signage. For further information please contact Philip McInley on 01883 344244.

THERMAL WEAR

Mycoal Warm Packs Ltd
Unit 1,
Imperial Park,
Empress Road,
Southampton SO14 0JW.
Tel (01703) 211068 Fax (01703) 231398

Suppliers and manufacturers of the ever popular handwarmers and thermo-mittens. All enquiries welcomed. Nothing too small or too large.

TOWELS

The Highland Connection
38 Watt Road,
Glasgow G52 4RW.
Tel 0141-882 8340 Fax 0141-882 7090

The Highland Connection supply the golf professionals at the best known golf clubs throughout the UK, with their own distinctive woven golf towels made in Glasgow, Scotland. Embroidered towels in various quantities also available.

TUITION

Barnham Broom Hotel
- Peter Ballingall Golf School
Honingham Road,
Barnham Broom,
Norwich, Norfolk NR9 4DD.
Tel (01603) 759393 Fax (01603) 758224

Voted best school in UK in *Golf Monthly* survey. A range of three or four day courses offers the perfect solution to those who seek to improve their skills. Small classes ensure progress is made. Video instructions available.

Beaufort Golf Course
Churchtown,
Beaufort,
Killarney,
Co Kerry, Ireland.
Tel +353 64 44440 Fax +353 64 44752

A traditional Kerry welcome awaits you at the *Friendliest Course in Kerry*. Challenging 18-hole par 71 championship course, buggies and caddies for hire, excellent golf shop, bar food and snacks. Tuition can be arranged with our golf professional. Societies and groups welcome. (See advertisement page 24 for further details.)

Borth and Ynyslas Golf Club
Borth,
Ceredigion SY24 5JS.
Tel (01970) 871202
e-mail:secretary@borthgc.u-net.com

18-holes links course adjoining Borth beach. Humps and hollows provide great variation, although the topography and springy turf make for easy walking. Professional's shop, practice area, modern clubhouse with bar and catering. Tuition available.

Cannington Golf Course
Cannington College,
Cannington,
Bridgwater,
Somerset TA5 2LS.
Tel/Fax (01278) 655050

Designed by Martin Hawtree of Oxford and built to highest international specifications in 1992 by Brian D Pierson Ltd under the consultancy of top agronomists Jim Arthur and Gordon Child. Together they have produced arguably the best 9-hole golf course in the west of England. With its *'Links-Like'* appearance, in high summer the subtle contours make for a testing round of golf for the scratch golfer, yet are receptive for the beginner with its wide open spaces, at 2,929 yards par 34. Beating par will take skill and courage.

Rodway Hill Golf Course
Newent Road,
Highnam,
Gloucestershire GL2 8DN.
Tel (01452) 384222 Fax (01989) 766450

An 18-hole pay and play par 70 course two miles south west of Gloucester, with panoramic views of the Cotswolds. It has a well stocked shop, practice and teaching facilities. Hire kit available. Societies welcome.

UMBRELLAS

Brollies Limited
45 Allerton Road,
Woolton Village,
Liverpool L25 7AL.
Tel 0151-421 0250 Fax 0151-421 0091

Brollies Limited carry a comprehensive range in best quality British made Hoyland and Fox Frame umbrellas. Also available seat sticks, twinbrellas, garden parasols, imported double ribbed golf umbrellas and golf ball retrievers. All printed or unprinted.

VIDEOS

Barnham Broom Hotel - Peter Ballingall Golf School
Honingham Road,
Barnham Broom,
Norwich, Norfolk NR9 4DD.
Tel (01603) 759393 Fax (01603) 758224

Voted best school in UK in *Golf Monthly* survey. A range of three or four day courses offers the perfect solution to those who seek to improve their skills. Small classes ensure progress is made. Video instructions available.

WATER STORAGE/TANKS

British Overhead Irrigation Ltd
Upper Halliford Green,
Shepperton,
Middlesex TW17 8SB.
Tel (01932) 788301 Fax (01932) 780437

Established 75 years, British Overhead Irrigation provide a complete professional, independent golf course irrigation engineering service - design, installation, upgrading and maintenance. Also manufacture *Wizard* fairway self-travelling sprinklers and sectional covers for circular butyl-lined water storage tanks.

I S S Aquaturf Systems Ltd
Unit 18, Downton Industrial Estate,
Batten Road, Downton,
Salisbury, Wiltshire SP5 3HU.
Tel (01725) 513880 Fax (01725) 513003

ISS Aquaturf Systems Limited are master dealers for *Hunter Industries* operating throughout southern England in the design, supply and installation of automatic pop-up irrigation systems for golf courses. The company has been in business for 20 years and specialises in providing quality systems at competitive prices.

Landline Ltd
1 Bluebridge Industrial Estate,
Halstead,
Essex CO9 2EX.
Tel (01787) 476699 Fax (01787) 472507

Supply and install impermeable waterproof liners to water features, irrigation reservoirs and ponds. A technical advisory service is available for all aspects of liner installation. We offer customers a professional and complete service, backed by almost 20 years of practical experience of a specialised industry.

Ocmis Irrigation (UK) Ltd
Head Office: Higher Burrow, Kingsbury, Martock, Somerset TA12 6BU.
Tel (01460) 241939 Fax (01460) 242198

Scotland: Broadmeadow, Harburn, West Calder, West Lothian EH55 8RT.
Tel 0131-220 2102 Fax 0131-220 6122

Ocmis Irrigation offer the complete irrigation service including the design, supply and installation of Rain Bird, Buckner and Hunter irrigation systems. Complete after-sales service and full maintenance and service contracts for all types and makes of irrigation systems.

WEATHERWEAR

Mycoal Warm Packs Ltd
Unit 1, Imperial Park, Empress Road, Southampton SO14 0JW.
Tel (01703) 211068 Fax (01703) 231398

Suppliers and manufacturers of the ever popular handwarmers and thermo-mittens. All enquiries welcomed. Nothing too small or too large.

Sunderland of Scotland Ltd
PO Box 14, Glasgow G2 1ER.
Tel 0141-552 3261 Fax 0141-552 8518

www.sunderlandgolf.com
Sunderland of Scotland manufacture high quality golf rainwear in Scotland. All rainsuits are tour tested and guaranteed waterproof and breathable, a variety of fabrics including Goretex being used. Sunderlands also manufacture the famous Sunderland Original Weatherbeater and Classic Windproof Pullover. Official supplier to PGA, PGAE, LPGA, ELPGA and St Andrews Links Trust.

WINTER-ALL-WEATHER TEE MATS

Driving Force Leisure Europe Ltd - Epic Golf
Badcock House, Unit 11a, Dolphin Park, Castle Road, Eurolink Industrial Centre, Sittingbourne, Kent ME10 3RL.
Tel (01795) 427333 Fax (01795) 425222

Manufacturers of golf driving range equipment including Epic ball dispensers, ball pickers, ball washers, conveyor and ancillary products. Easy Picker Europe are the UK sole distributor for Astroturf range mats and golf surfaces, together with winter tees, walkways and putting surfaces.

Links Leisure
Unit 22, Civic Industrial Park, Whitchurch, Shropshire SY13 ITT.
Tel (01948) 663002 Fax (01948) 666381

Website:http://www.web-marketing.co.uk/linksleisure
The Pro-Tee all-weather golf mat gives the golfer a flat, solid surface on which to stand. Couple this with the unique tee peg retention slot and the Pro-Tee gives the ideal substitute for the natural grass surface. The Pro-Tee is supplied in three sizes, 1.5m x 1.0m, 2.0m x 1.0m and 1.5m x 1.5m, the first two having three replaceable grass sections.

Range Servant UK Ltd
Hempstead Road, Hunton Bridge, Watford, Hertfordshire WD1 3NJ.
Tel/Fax (01923) 263777

Manufacture and market golf range and practice ground equipment. Golf ball dispensers, golf ball washers, golf ball collectors, play mats for ranges and practice grounds - winter tee mats a speciality, range balls and baskets.

British Golf Museum
St Andrews

HEROIC
SURPRISING
STRIKING
HISTORIC

you can't miss this

Bruce Embankment, St Andrews, Fife KY16 9AB Telephone 01334 478880. Fax 01334 473306.
1999 Opening Times Summer Hours: Easter to Mid October • 9.30am - 5.30pm Open 7 days
Winter Hours: 11am - 3pm Closed Tuesday & Wednesday.

Golf Club Facilities

This section, included for the first time in 1992, lists clubs which can offer hotel accommodation, and hotels which have their own golf facilties. They are able to provide for society or corporate days, and in some instances offer an extensive range of other sports and leisure activities. A sub-section also includes driving ranges, practice grounds and leisure complexes

Abbotsley Golf Hotel
Eynesbury Hardwicke, St Neots, Cambridgeshire PE19 4XN.
Tel (01480) 474000 Fax (01480) 471018

Friendly country house hotel set amidst two 18-hole courses. *Golf Monthly* "The Abbotsley course - the design is a revelation. The presentation superb." Award-winning gardens; relaxed atmosphere. Home of Vivien Saunders golf schools.

Aldwark Manor Hotel Golf & Country Club
Aldwark, Alne, York, West Yorkshire YO61 1UF.
Tel:(Hotel) (01347) 838146
(Golf) (01347) 838353 Fax (01347) 838867

Aldwark Manor extends a warm welcome to everyone. Situated in the Vale of York is a 6,171 yard par 71 golf course, laid out in easy walking parkland with the river Ure meandering beside a number of fairways. The ideal venue for your society or company golf day. (See advertisement page 501 for further details.)

Alverton Manor Country House Hotel
Tregolls Road, Truro, Cornwall TR1 1ZQ.
Tel (01872) 276633 Fax (01872) 2222989

AA/RAC 3-Star; Award-Winning 2-AA Rosettes Restaurant; Johansen's Guide: West Country Tourist Board 4-Crown Highly Commended; *Best Loved Hotels of the World.* Cornwall's premier house hotel in the cathedral city of Truro. A former convent dating from c1700. Quietly set in six acres of terraced grounds and centrally situated for all Cornish golf courses. Golfing breaks at our own splendid parkland course. (See advertisement page 489 for further details.)

Ashdown Forest Golf Hotel
Chapel Lane, Forest Row, East Sussex RH18 5BB.
Tel (01342) 824866 Fax (01342) 824869

e-mail:reservations@ashgolf.demon.co.uk
website: http://www.ashgolf.demon.co.uk
Newly refurbished hotel with 19 en suite bedrooms, large function room, conference facilities, restaurant and two bars. The hotel operates the Royal Ashdown Forest Golf Club West Course, 18-holes, 5,606 yards SSS 67. Several other courses incorporated in residential golf breaks. (See advertisement page 495 for further details.)

Ayr - Scotland
For information on accommodation available in South Ayrshire whilst playing at one or more of the many courses in the *Heart of Scotland's Golf Country* as detailed in the advertisement on page 32. Contact the Ayrshire and Arran Tourist Board on 01292 616255.

Ballater Golf Club
Victoria Road, Ballater AB35 5QX.
Tel (013397) 55567 Fax (013397) 55057

The most scenic golf course in Scotland, slightly undulating, medium length course situated in the heart of Royal Deeside. A delightful golfing experience which is enjoyed by golfers of all calibre. Situated 42 miles west of Aberdeen with Balmoral Castle a mere eight miles up river. (See advertisement page 28 for further details.)

Golf Club Facilities

Barnham Broom Hotel
Golf • Conference • Leisure
Honingham Road, Barnham Broom,
Norwich, Norfolk NR9 4DD.
Tel (01603) 759393 Fax (01603) 758224

EETB 4-Crown. East Anglia's finest conference and leisure centre lies in 250 acres of countryside. 53 fully equipped bedrooms include family rooms, served by Flints restaurant and sports snack bar. Four squash courts, snooker, heated indoor swimming pool and spa jets, tennis and 36-hole golf. *Golfing Getaways* from £25. Professional tuition available. (See advertisement page 497 for further details.)

Beaufort Golf Course
Churchtown, Beaufort, Killarney,
Co Kerry, Ireland.
Tel +353 64 44440 Fax +353 64 44752

A traditional Kerry welcome awaits you at *the Friendliest Course in Kerry*. Challenging 18-hole par 71 championship course, buggies and caddies for hire, excellent golf shop, bar food and snacks. Tuition can be arranged with our golf professional. Societies and groups welcome. (See advertisement page 24 for further details.)

The Belfry
Wishaw, North Warwickshire B76 9PR.
Tel (01675) 470033 Fax (01675) 470256

The Belfry, venue for three Ryder Cup Matches and a unique fourth returning in 2001, is one of Europe's foremost business, golf and leisure resorts. Top class facilities includes 324 4-Star bedrooms, five restaurants, eight bars and Bel Air nightclub. Leisure facilities include gym, indoor pool, sauna, snooker and beautician to name but a few. Three golf courses including The Brabazon, PGA National and Derby courses. Floodlit driving range and putting green, largest on-course golf leisure and life style shop in Europe. (De Vere Hotel Group - see advertisement page 499 for further details.)

Belleisle Golf Course
Belleisle Park, Ayr.
c/o South Ayrshire Council, Burns House,
Burns Statue Square, Ayr KA7 1UT.
Tel (01292) 616269/616270

18-holes, length of course 6,431 yards SSS 72. For advance reservations telephone (01292) 441258. Practice area, caddy cars, catering and bar facilities are available. Visitors welcome all week. Professional David Gemmell (01292) 441314. (See advertisement page 32 for further details.)

Belmont Lodge & Golf Course
Belmont,
Hereford HR2 9SA.
Tel (01432) 352666 Fax (01432) 358090

18-hole golf course running along the beautiful Wye Valley with a 30-bedroomed hotel on-site. Other facilities include bar, restaurant, fishing, bowling, tennis and snooker. Only a mile and a half from Hereford City centre.

Borth and Ynyslas Golf Club
Borth, Ceredigion SY24 5JS.
Tel (01970) 871202

e-mail:secretary@borthgc.u-net.com
18 holes links course adjoining Borth beach. Humps and hollows provide great variation, although the topography and springy turf make for easy walking. Professional's shop, practice area, modern clubhouse with bar and catering. Tuition available.

Botley Park Hotel
Golf & Country Club
Winchester Road, Boorley Green,
Botley, Hampshire SO3 2UA.
Tel (01489) 780888 Fax (01489) 789242

Set in 176 acres of rolling Hampshire countryside, this 4-Star hotel has 100 en suite bedrooms, superb restaurant, extensive leisure facilities and its own picturesque and challenging 18-hole par 70 golf course and driving range. (See advertisement page 497 for further details).

Bryn Morfydd Golf Hotel
Llanrhaeadr, Nr Denbigh,
Denbighshire LL16 4NP.
Tel (01745) 890280 Fax (01745) 890488

Situated in the beautiful Vale of Clwyd, North Wales. The hotel is surrounded by its own two golf courses. A 3-Star hotel with excellent accommodation and restaurant facilities. Special golfing rates available. (See advertisement page 511 for further details.)

Burnham & Berrow Golf Club
St Cristopher's Way,
Burnham-on-Sea, Somerset TA8 2PE.
Tel (01278) 785760

18-hole championship links golf course and 9-hole course. Dormy accommodation available. (See advertisement page 27 for further details.)

Bushey Hall Golf Club
Bushey Hall Drive,
Bushey,
Hertfordshire WD2 2EP.
Tel (01923) 222253 Fax (01923) 229759
Pro Shop: Tel (01923) 225802

www.golfclubuk.co.uk
Established in 1890 Bushey Hall Golf Club has one of the oldest and best established courses in Hertfordshire. Facilities include a fully equipped pro shop, practice net, clubhouse restaurant and bar. Open for membership. Pay as you play operated. (See advertisement page 28 for further details.)

Cally Palace Hotel
Gatehouse of Fleet DG7 2DL.
Tel (01557) 814341 Fax (01557) 814522

This award-winning 4-Star country mansion has its own exclusive par 70, 18-hole golf course sculpted perfectly into the surrounding 150 acres of mature parkland. Other facilities include fishing loch and leisure complex.

Cambridgeshire Moat House Hotel
Bar Hill,
Cambridge CB3 8EU.
Tel (01954) 780098 Fax (01954) 780010

18-hole championship golf course set in 134 acres of parkland. Golf professional David Vernon. Newly built clubhouse and golf shop. 99 en suite bedrooms. Extensive leisure facilities. five miles north of Cambridge on A14. Visitors welcome.

Cannington Golf Course
Cannington College,
Cannington,
Bridgwater, Somerset TA5 2LS.
Tel/Fax (01278) 655050

Designed by Martin Hawtree of Oxford and built to highest international specifications in 1992 by Brian D Pierson Limited under the consultancy of top agronomists Jim Arthur and Gordon Child. Together they have produced arguably the best 9-hole golf course in the west of England. With its 'Links-Like' appearance, in high summer the subtle contours make for a testing round of golf for the scratch golfer, yet are receptive for the beginner with its wide open spaces, at 2,929 yards par 34. Beating par will take skill and courage.

Carden Park Hotel Golf Resort & Spa
Nr Chester,
Cheshire CH3 9DQ.
Tel (01829) 731000 Fax (01829) 731032

Set in 750-acres of beautiful Cheshire countryside near Chester. A true golf resort with two 18-hole golf courses - the mature Cheshire course and the new Nicklaus course, the 9-hole par 3 Azalea course and Europe's first Jack Nicklaus Residential Golf School. The superb AA/RAC 4-Star hotel also has an extensive spa and there are many other leisure facilities on the estate. For further information and a brochure call Liz Mole on 01829 731000. (See advertisement page 501 for further details.)

Castletown Golf Links Hotel
Derbyhaven,
Castletown,
Isle of Man IM9 1UA.
Tel (01624) 822201 Fax (01624) 625535

Situated on our own peninsula, our championship golf course of 6,700 yards, with all holes having sea views, is a real test of links golf. The hotel facilities are of a luxurious 3-Star standard.

Cave Castle Golf Hotel
South Cave, Brough,
East Yorkshire HU15 2EU.
Tel (01430) 421286 Fax (01430) 421118

Superb manor house in 160 acres of parkland situated at foot of the Wolds. Five minutes from M62 motorway link and fifteen minutes from Hull. 25 en suite bedrooms with restaurant, function and conference facilities. Own 18-hole golf course 6,524 yards SSS 71. Golf breaks, societies and non-members welcome.

China Fleet Country Club
Saltash,
Cornwall PL12 6LJ.
Tel (01752) 848668 Fax (01752) 848456

Situated in 180 acres of Cornish countryside, 40 self-catering 4- and 6-berth apartments, 18-hole par 72 golf, 28-bay driving range, pool, health suite, gymnasium, racket sports, bars, restaurant and coffee shop. (See advertisement page 493 for further details.)

Cottesmore Golf & Country Club
Buchan Hill,
Pease Pottage,
Crawley, West Sussex RH11 9AT.
Tel (01293) 528256 Fax (01293) 522819

12 en suite bedrooms overlooking peaceful undulating Sussex countryside. Guests can enjoy two full 18-hole mature golf courses, tennis, squash, indoor pool, spa bath, steam room, sauna and gymnasium. Ten minutes from Gatwick, one mile from the Pease Pottage exit (Junction 11) off the M23.

Courtown Golf Club
Kiltennel, Gorey,
Co Wexford, Ireland.
Tel +353 55 25166 Fax +353 55 25553

This 18-hole heavily wooded parkland course features four challenging par 3's and three long par 5's. The variety (no two holes are alike) and excellence of this course is matched by its luxurious clubhouse and bar and catering facilities.

Dale Hill Hotel
Ticehurst, Wadhurst,
East Sussex TN5 7DQ.
Tel (01580) 200112

Highly commended luxurious hotel situated in an area of outstanding national beauty, with health club and highly acclaimed 18-hole golf course. New Ian Woosnam championship course opened to rave reviews in September, 1997.

Dalmilling Golf Course
Westwood Avenue, Ayr.
c/o South Ayrshire Council, Burns House, Burns Statue Square, Ayr KA7 1UT.
Tel (01292) 616269/616270

18-holes, length of course 5,724 yards SSS 68. For advance reservations telephone (01292) 263893. Practice area, caddy cars, catering and bar facilities available. Visitors welcome all week. Professional Philip Cheyney (01292) 263893. (See advertisement page 32 for further details.)

Darley Golf Course
Harling Drive, Troon KA10 6NF.
c/o South Ayrshire Council, Burns House, Burns Statue Square, Ayr KA7 1UT.
Tel (01292) 616269/616270

18-holes, length of course 6,501 yards SSS 72. For advance reservations telephone (01292) 312464. Practice area, caddy cars, catering and bar facilities are available. Visitors welcome all week. Professional Gordon McKinley (01292) 315566. (See advertisement page 32 for further details.)

De Vere Belton Woods
Belton,
Nr Grantham,
Lincolnshire NG32 2LN.
Tel (01476) 593200 Fax (01476) 514399

A magnificent hotel, golf and leisure resort set in 475 acres of glorious countryside. Two challenging 18-hole championship golf courses, 9-hole course, driving range, putting green and extensive leisure facilities. 136 bedrooms.
(De Vere Hotel Group - see advertisement page 4 for further details.)

De Vere Cameron House
Loch Lomond,
Dunbartonshire G83 8QZ.
Tel (01389) 755565 Fax (01389) 759522

4-Star. Ancestral home of the Smollett family and 18th-century historian and novelist Tobias, Cameron House is a magnificent award-winning hotel with one of the finest views in the world, overlooking Loch Lomond. Set in its own estate, including a mile of loch shoreline and 108 acres of lawns, gardens, a 9-hole golf course, and mature woodland. Cameron House even has its own motor cruiser. Other facilities include 96 luxury en suite bedrooms, superb leisure club with indoor pool, sauna, steam room and solarium and three different restaurants serving exquisite cuisine.
(De Vere Hotel Group - see advertisement page 4 for further details.)

De Vere Hotel Blackpool
East Park Drive,
Blackpool, Lancashire FY3 8LL.
Tel (01253) 838866 Fax (01253) 798800

De Vere Hotel Blackpool adds a touch of 4-Star elegance to one of Europe's most popular tourist destinations. Extensive facilities include: 164 bedrooms, first class restaurant, five bars, six conference rooms, indoor swimming pool, 18-bay floodlit driving range and an 18-hole championship golf course designed by Peter Alliss and Clive Clark. The course regularly hosts corporate golf and society days and was the recent venue for both the PGA Northern Championship and Reebok PGA and Lancashire Open. (De Vere Hotel Group - see advertisement page 4 for further details.)

De Vere Mottram Hall
Wilmslow Road,
Mottram St Andrew,
Prestbury, Cheshire SK10 4QT.
Tel (01625) 828135 Fax (01625) 828950

Mottram Hall is an elegant 18th-century Georgian building, set in secluded parkland with delightful ornamental gardens and lake. The 4-Star hotel has 132 luxury bedrooms, conference facilities for up to 275 guests, a superb leisure club, and 18-hole championship golf course designed by international golf architect Dave Thomas. Leisure facilities include spacious swimming pool, spa, saunas and steam rooms, fully equipped gym - even a full sized soccer pitch utilised by European football champions, Germany, who stayed here in 1996. (De Vere Hotel Group - see advertisement page 4 for further details.)

De Vere Oulton Hall
Rothwell Lane,
Oulton, Leeds LS26 8HN.
Tel 0113-282 1000 Fax 0113-282 0066

This elegant 5-Star Yorkshire hotel complete with 19th-century style formal gardens, is situated adjacent to the Oulton Park Golf Club where guests have the choice of either 18- or 9-hole courses set in spectacular countryside. Facilities also include a 22-bay driving range. 152 luxury bedrooms. Leisure club featuring indoor pool, sauna, steam room and two superb restaurants. (De Vere Hotel Group - see advertisement page 4 for further details.)

De Vere Slaley Hall
Slale, Hexham,
Northumberland NE47 0BY.
Tel (01434) 673350 Fax (01434) 673962

Set in 1000 acres of prime Northumberland countryside yet only 30 minutes' drive from the provincial capital of Newcastle upon Tyne, Slaley Hall is one of the UK's finest golf resorts. The Edwardian stately home has been integrated into a luxury 139 bedroom hotel with a range of facilities including a leisure club with 20 metre pool and gym, health and beauty spa; extensive function suites and Fairways Restaurant. The Dave Thomas designed championship course is a regular venue on the PGA European Tour and it has earned the reputation as one of Britain's most scenic and challenging courses. A second championship course will open in April 1999. (De Vere Hotel Group - see advertisement page 4 for further details.)

De Vere The Dormy
New Road,
Ferndown, Dorset BH22 8ES.
Tel (01202) 872121 Fax (01202) 895388

4-Star. Set in 12 acres of delightful landscaped gardens on the edge of the beautiful New Forest, The Dormy is a friendly, country-style hotel with excellent leisure facilities including indoor heated pool, sauna, steam room and solarium, superb restaurants and bars and a health and beauty studio ideal for relaxation and pampering. Adjacent to the hotel is the famous Ferndown golf club, which has a championship 18-hole course and a testing President's 9-hole course with 18 tees. There are 20 golf courses within 20 minutes of the hotel. (De Vere Hotel Group - see advertisement page 4 for further details.)

Donnington Grove Country Club Golf Hotel & Conference Centre
Grove Road,
Donnington,
Newbury, Berkshire RG14 2LA.
Tel (01635) 581000 Fax (01635) 552259

18-hole parkland/moorland championship course designed by Dave Thomas. The clubhouse and hotel are located within a beautifully renovated 18th-century gothic mansion. This will provide an ideal setting for your society, company golf day or conference stay.

Dromoland Castle
Newmarket-on-Fergus,
Co Clare, Ireland.
Tel +353 61 368444 Fax +353 61 368498

Dromoland Castle is a magnificent renaissance castle on 375 acres of parkland. It offers the highest accommodation standards, and award-winning restaurant. Activities include golf, clay pigeon shooting, horseriding and fishing, we also have a fully equipped health centre. The castle is located eight miles from Shannon International Airport in County Clare.

Druids Glen Golf Club
Newtownmountkennedy,
Co Wicklow, Ireland.
Tel +353 1 287 3600 Fax +353 1 287 3699

Druids Glen has been the venue for the Irish Open 1996, 1997, 1998 and again for 1999. Facilities include an 18-hole championship golf course, 3-hole teaching academy, practice ground and sumptuously converted 18th-century clubhouse with full bar and dining facilities.

Golf Club Facilities

Drumoig Golf Club & Hotel
Drumoig,
Leuchars,
St Andrews, Fife KY16 0BE.
Tel (01382) 541800 Fax (01382) 542211

Superb new golf hotel only ten minutes from St Andrews. 24 fully equipped en suite lodge bedrooms, well stocked bar, lounge and à la carte restaurant. Own 18-hole tournament standard golf course. Ideally located for touring Fife, Tayside and Perthshire.

East Dorset Golf Club
Bere Regis,
Dorset BH20 7NT.
Tel (01929) 472244 Fax (01929) 471294

e-mail: edgc@golf.co.uk www.golf.co.uk/edgc
Hawtree design. 7,027 yards SSS 75 with the record of 66. Other tees available! The course features all-the-year-round greens protected by large bunkers with water coming into play on several holes. A flat terrain in Hardy country overlooking Purbeck Hills. Attractive and challenging 9-hole woodland course, surrounded by rhododendrons. Provides all-round golfing opportunities. Packages includes accommodation, meals and all golf. (See Hotel Compendium entry.)

Edmondstown Golf Club
Rathfarnham,
Dublin 16,
Ireland.
Tel +353 1 493 1082 Fax +353 1 493 3152

Edmondstown Golf Club is situated amongst the most delightful surroundings on the foothills of the Dublin mountains, and only seven miles from Dublin City centre. A testing parkland course - it lends itself to the golfer who desires a socially enjoyable round of golf - on a well maintained and manicured golf course. (See advertisement page 27 for further details.)

Faithlegg House Hotel
Waterford, Ireland. *(OPENING SPRING 1999.)*
Tel +353 51 38200 Fax +353 1 8730194

e-mail: sales@towerhotelgroup.ie
Faithlegg House Hotel is a 4-Star 18th-century house hotel situated beside Faithlegg golf course, and provides 14 magnificent rooms. A discreet extension will provide a further 68 rooms. With full health and fitness facilities, as well as the 18-hole championship course, it is the ideal place to take a relaxing break. Call for our *Tee Time in Ireland* golf brochure. *(TOWER HOTEL GROUP.)*

Farthingstone Hotel & Golf Course
Farthingstone, Towcester,
Northamptonshire NN12 8HA.
Tel (01327) 361291 Fax (01327) 361645

Set in glorious wooded countryside, just 90 minutes outside London. Farthingstone Hotel offers 16 superb en suite rooms, a challenging 18-hole golf course, squash court, full size snooker tables, and a carvery restaurant. Highly competitive tariffs.

Fullarton Golf Course
Harling Drive, Troon KA10 6NF.
c/o South Ayrshire Council, Burns House,
Burns Statue Square, Ayr KA7 1UT.
Tel (01292) 616269/616270

18-holes, length of course 4,919 yards SSS 63. For advance reservations telephone (01292) 312464. Practice area, caddy cars, catering and bar facilities are available. Visitors are welcome all week. Professional Gordon McKinley (01292) 315566. (See advertisement page 32 for further details.)

Gainsborough Golf Club
Thonock, Gainsborough,
Lincolnshire DN21 1PZ.
Tel (01427) 613088 Fax (01427) 810172

The Karsten Lakes championship course, designed by Neil Coles, MBE, is part of a 36-hole complex set amongst undulating Lincolnshire parkland. The two courses are complemented with a 4-Star clubhouse offering restaurant and conference facilities. Society and corporate golf parties welcome.

Gatton Manor Hotel Golf & Country Club Ltd
Ockley, Nr Dorking, Surrey RH5 5PQ.
Tel (01306) 627555

Set amidst its own 18-hole golf course in 200 acres of parklands and lakes, situated between London and the south coast, in the heart of the Surrey countryside. Superb all en suite accommodation overlooking the golf course and grounds. À la carte restaurants, large lounge bar, conference suites, gym and health club.

Girvan Golf Course
Golf Course Road, Girvan.
c/o South Ayrshire Council, Burns House,
Burns Statue Square, Ayr KA7 1UT.
Tel (01292) 616269/616270

18-holes, length of course 5,095 yards SSS 64. For advance reservations telephone (01465)

continued over

714346. Practice area, trolleys available for hire, catering and bar facilities available. Visitors welcome all week. (See advertisement page 32 for further details.)

The Golf Club - Thorpeness
**Thorpeness, Nr Aldeburgh,
Suffolk IP16 4NH.**
Tel (01728) 452176 Fax (01728) 453868

One of East Anglia's finest and most challenging 18-hole courses. Handicap certificate required, advisable to book in advance. Accommodation, bars, restaurant, golf shop, tennis courts and course set adjacent to picturesque coastal village on Suffolk Heritage coast. (See advertisement page 492 for further details.)

Gosforth Park Golfing Complex
**(Parklands Golf Course)
High Gosforth Park,
Newcastle-upon-Tyne NE3 5HQ.**
Tel 0191-236 4480

The complex has an 18-hole golf course, 45-bay two tier floodlit driving range, 9-hole pitch and putt course and putting green. Also pro shop, bar and restaurant. Open to non-members.

The Grange & Links Hotel
**Sea Lane, Sandilands, Sutton-on-Sea,
Lincolnshire LN12 2RA.**
Tel (01507) 441334 Fax (01507) 443033

3-Star 30-bedroom hotel with own 18-hole links course. Two tennis courts, snooker and ballroom. Award-winning hotel renowned for superb cuisine, friendliness, comfort and service.

Harrogate Golf Club
**Forest Lane Head, Harrogate,
North Yorkshire HG2 7TF.**
Tel (01423) 862999

A long established 18-hole golf course set amongst mature trees formerly part of the Forest of Knaresborough. Visitors are assured of a warm reception in the extensively refurbished clubhouse and restaurant. (See advertisement page 28 for further details.)

Hawkstone Park Hotel
**Weston-under-Redcastle,
Shrewsbury, Shropshire SY4 5UY.**
Tel (01939) 200611 Fax (01939) 200311

Hawkstone Park Hotel with its 65 en suite bedrooms, has been accommodating golfing visitors since 1920. This tradition is enhanced by our 5-Star golfing facilities, including two championship courses and extensive up-to-date teaching services and practice areas.

Hollywood Lakes Golf Club
**Ballyboughal,
Co Dublin, Ireland.**
Tel +353 1 843 3406/7 Fax +353 1 843 3002

Parkland course featuring water hazards and lakes at 5 holes and also the longest par 5 in Ireland at 630 yards (14th hole). Green fees weekday £18.00; weekend £23.00. (See advertisement page 32 for details.)

Holyhead Golf Club
**Lon Garreg Fawr,
Trearddur Bay,
Anglesey LL65 2YG.**
Tel/Fax (01407) 763279

Comfortable twin-bedded accommodation is available at the Holyhead Golf Club, with all meals provided in the club restaurant. Enjoy excellent golf on heathland course with spectaculor view to Snowdonia. Reservations ring 01407 763279.

Horsted Place Hotel
**Little Horsted,
Uckfield,
East Sussex TN22 5ES.**
*Tel (01825) 750581 Fax (01825) 750459
Club Tel/Fax (01825) 880088
Fax (01825) 880066*

Combine Victorian elegance and luxury at Horsted Place Hotel with exceptional golf on one of the two spectacular courses at East Sussex National Golf Club. If you require golf tuition there is a superb golf academy which has its own three hole course. Experience for yourself challenging golf and exceptional accommodation in beautiful surroundings. (See advertisement page 495 for further details.)

Howth Golf Club
**St Fintan's,
Carrickbrack Road,
Sutton,
Dublin 13, Ireland.**
Tel +353 1 832 3055 Fax +353 1 832 1793

Howth Golf Club is a long established parkland course located within ten miles of Dublin City centre and Dublin airport. The club boasts a fine clubhouse and enjoys panoramic views of land and sea scapes.

Ingon Manor Golf & Country Club
Ingon Lane,
Snitterfield,
Nr Stratford upon Avon,
Warwickshire CV37 0QE.
Tel (01789) 731857 Fax (01789) 731657

Located two miles from Stratford, close to the A46. Par 72, 18-hole golf course 6,554 yards white tees, 6,091 yards yellow tees. Driving range and practice area. All day bar and catering. Accommodation available.

The Island Golf Club
Corballis, Donabate, Co Dublin, Ireland.
Tel +353 1 843 6462 Fax +353 1 843 6860

Continuing a tradition of links golf since its inception in 1890. The magnificent splendour and solitude associated with the Island, is highlighted by undulating fairways rolling through majestic sand dunes.

The K Club
At Straffan, Co Kildare, Ireland.
Tel +353 1 601 7300 Fax +353 1 601 7399

Located 30 minutes from Dublin. Arnold Palmer designed 18-hole championship golf course, clubhouse, practice area and driving range. Resident golf professional Ernie Jones. Home to The Smurfit European Open since September 1995 until the year 2000. Hotel AA 5-Red Stars. Fishing, health club and sports centre with indoor and outdoor tennis. (See advertisement page 512 for further details.)

Kenwick Park Hotel
Kenwick Park,
Louth, Lincolnshire LN11 8NR.
Tel (01507) 608806 Fax (01507) 608027

The Kenwick estate boasts magnificent settings for hotel, top class leisure club and superb golf course, comprising many tree lined fairways and water features. A relaxing retreat for golfers and their families.

La Grande Mare Hotel Golf Club
La Grande Mare,
Vazon, Castel, Guernsey.
*Tel (01481) 56576 & 53544
Fax (01481) 55194*

www: lgm.guernsey.net
Beautifully appointed luxury hotel with 18-hole golf course playing off 14 greens. Professional shop and tuition on-site. First class, well priced restaurant. 2-AA Rosettes. Beachside location. Golfing breaks catered for.

Letham Grange
Colliston, by Arbroath DD11 4RL.
Tel (01241) 890373 Fax (01241) 890725

42-bedrooms, Victorian mansion with 36-holes of superb golf. First class facilities set in the heartland of golf. Company/society golf outings/breaks welcome. (See advertisement page 505 for further details.)

Linden Hall Golf Club
Longhorsley, Morpeth,
Northumberland NE65 8XF.
Tel (01670) 788050 Fax (01670) 788544

Linden Hall Golf Club is located within the grounds of Linden Hall Hotel, a 4-Star luxury country house hotel. The 18-hole, 6,809 yard SSS 73 golf course, recently voted one of the ten best new golf courses built in the British Isles since 1996 by *Golf World*, is set within mature woodland, rolling parkland with established burns and lakes amidst a stunning backdrop of the Cheviot hills and Northumbrian coastline.

Lochgreen Golf Course
Harling Drive, Troon KA10 6NF.
c/o South Ayrshire Council, Burns House, Burns Statue Square, Ayr KA7 1UT.
Tel (01292) 616269/616270

18-holes, length of course 6,822 yards SSS 73. For advance reservations telephone (01292) 312464. Practice area, caddy cars and catering facilities are available. Visitors are welcome all week. Professional Gordon McKinley (01292) 315566. (See advertisement page 32 for further details.)

Machrie Hotel & Golf Links Course
Port Ellen, Isle of Islay, Argyll PA42 7AN.
Tel (01496) 302310 Fax (01496) 302404

Play a hidden gem of a course. Traditional 18-hole championship links course situated on the doorstep of the Machrie Hotel. Superior and standard accommodation, excellent food and friendly service. Self-catering and golf packages also available.

Mannings Heath Golf Club
Fullers, Hammerpond Road,
Mannings Heath, Horsham,
West Sussex RH13 6PH.
Tel (01403) 210228 Fax (01403) 270974

Mannings Heath Golf Club was founded in 1905. With two *18-hole championship courses*

continued over

providing a challenging test to the discerning golfer. 'Fullers', the family mansion has been tastefully restored to provide first class clubhouse facilities for all our clients. Overnight accommodation available at South Lodge Hotel nearby. (See advertisement page 497 for further details.)

Maybole Golf Course
Memorial Park, Maybole.
  c/o South Ayrshire Council, Burns House, Burns Statue Square, Ayr KA7 1UT.
Tel (01655) 889770

9-holes, length of course 2,635 yards SSS 33. For advance reservations telephone (01655) 889770. Trolleys available for hire. Visitors welcome all week. (See advertisement page 32 for further details.)

Mentmore Golf & Country Club
Mentmore,
Nr Leighton Buzzard,
Bedfordshire LU7 0UA.
Tel (01296) 662020 Fax (01296) 662592

Two 18-hole championship golf courses. Rothschild Course par 72, 6,763 yards. Rosebery Course par 72, 6,777 yards. Practice range. Restaurant, swimming pool, sauna, jacuzzi and steam room. Leisure club and tennis courts.

Mersey Valley Golf Club (1995)
Warrington Road,
Bold Heath,
Widnes, Cheshire WA8 3XL.
Tel/Fax 0151-424 6060

Conference facilities, corporate golf days and memberships, societies and visitors welcome. Buggy hire. We specialise in corporate golf days - easy walking course. 20 minutes from Liverpool and Manchester, two miles from junction 7, on the M62. Superb bar and catering facilities.

Mount Juliet
Thomastown,
Co Kilkenny,
Ireland.
Tel +353 56 73000 Fax +353 56 73019

Deluxe accommodation in the elegant Mount Juliet House or the informal Hunters Yard. Ireland's premier sporting estate offers guests on-site fishing, horseriding, tennis, stylish leisure centre, David Leadbetter Golf Academy. Home of the Irish Open, 1993, 1994 and 1995.

Nailcote Hall Hotel
Nailcote Lane,
Berkswell,
Warwickshire CV7 7DE.
Tel (01203) 466174 Fax (01203) 470720

www.nailcotehall.co.uk
Home of the British Professional Short Course.
Delightful and challenging championship 9-hole par 3 course designed to test any golfers short game. Set in the grounds of this 17th-century black and white Jacobean country house hotel, used by Cromwell in the English Civil War.

Nairn Dunbar Golf Club
Lochloy Road,
Nairn IV12 5AE
Tel 01667 452741 Fax 01667456 897

Championship course, 6,720 yards, par 72. Highly rated Scottish links course. New clubhouse opened 1998. Extensive lounge/bar and dining room, golfers' bar, junior lounge, visitors' locker room, full restaurant facilities available all day in season. Visitors and golf groups all welcome. Resident PGA teaching Professional, fully stocked golf shop. Golf carts, trolleys and club hire. Practice facilities. Situated in Nairn. Good range of hotel accommodation. Nairn Dunbar Golf Club celebrates its centenary during 1999.

North Shore Hotel Golf Club & Course
North Shore Road,
Skegness P62S 1DN.
Tel (01754) 763298 Fax (01754) 761902

A mature and challenging 18-hole part parkland and part links course with sea views on the edge of Skegness. Good all year round climate. Rarely closed in winter with no winter greens. Rarely closed bars, superb bar food and à la carte restaurant. 33 bedrooms available.

Northop Country Park Golf Club
Northop,
Flintshire CH7 6WA.
Tel (01352) 840440 Fax (01352) 840445

John Jacob's designed par 72, 18-hole championship course in 247 acres of mature parkland. Driving range, pratice greens and pro shop plus two all-weather tennis courts, gym and sauna. Award-winning restaurant. Overnight accommodation available at nearby St David's Park Hotel five minutes away. (See advertisement page 501 for further details.)

Old Conna Golf Club
Ferndale Road, Bray, Co Wicklow, Ireland.
Tel +353 1 282 6055 & 6766
Fax +353 1 282 5611

The Garden of Ireland - Testing parkland course with spectacular views of the Irish sea and Wicklow mountains. Two miles from the town of Bray. 18-hole 6,550 yards SSS 72. Green fees: Weekdays £27.50; Saturday/Sunday £40.00. Special *Early Bird* rate £17.00 before 9.30am Monday to Friday. Full catering facilities. Club professional available. (See advertisement page 27 for further details.)

Old Course Hotel - St Andrews Golf Resort & Spa
St Andrews, Fife KY16 9SP.
Tel (01334) 474371 Fax (01334) 477668

This luxury 125-bedroom hotel overlooks the 17th Road Hole of the Old Course and is a five minute walk to the beach and town. Facilities include health spa with swimming pool, whirlpool, fitness room and full range of massage and beauty treatments. The hotel now has its own championship golf course, the Duke's Course. Open to non-residents, with residents enjoying guaranteed tee-times and reduced green fees.

Parknasilla Great Southern Hotel
Parknasilla, Sneen, Co Kerry, Ireland.
Tel +353 64 45122 Fax +353 64 45323

Parknasilla Great Southern is one of Ireland's best loved hotels. Set in 300 acres of its own grounds it has extensive leisure facilities as well as its own private 9-hole golf course. Overlooking Kenmare Bay, this Victorian hotel is truly in a world of its own.

Patshull Park Hotel Golf & Country Club
Pattingham, Shropshire WV6 7HR.
Tel (01902) 700100 Fax (01902) 700874

Parkland, lakeside 18-hole championship John Jacobs' designed course in grounds of the Earl of Dartmouth estate. Corporate, society and residential packages. 49 en suite bedrooms, swimming pool, leisure centre, gymnasium, fishing. Restaurant and Bunkers coffee shop.

Penrith Golf Club
Salkeld Road, Penrith, Cumbria CA11 8SG.
Tel (01768) 891919

The club, which is 108 years old, is easily accessible from junction 41 on the M6 motorway and lies half a mile east of Penrith, enjoying panoramic views to the Lakeland hills. Visitors are very welcome to play this excellent course. (See advertisement page 32 for further details.)

Portmarnock Hotel & Golf Links
Strand Road, Portmarnock,
Co Dublin, Ireland.
Tel +353 1 846 0611 Fax +353 1 846 2442

This prestigious new development is located 15 minutes from Dublin airport and 25 minutes from the city centre. The hotel's 18-hole golf links was designed by Bernard Langer and is the only PGA European Tour course in Ireland.

Radisson Roe Park Hotel & Golf Resort
Roe Park, Limavady,
Co Londonderry BT49 9LB.
Tel (015047) 22222 Fax (015047) 22313

Northern Ireland's first golf and leisure resort featuring 64 luxurious bedrooms, O'Cahan's bar, Coach House Brasserie, Courtyard Restaurant, Fairways Leisure Club and the Eden Health and Beauty Salon. 18-hole championship parkland course, driving range, putting green and golf shop.

Raemoir House Hotel
Raemoir, Banchory,
Aberdeen AB31 4ED.
Tel (01330) 824884 Fax (01330) 822171

AA 3-Star 76%; 2-Rosettes Cuisine; RAC 3-Star; Michelin; Good Hotel Guide; Johansens. Magnificent mansion set in 3,500 acres of parkland and forest in Royal Deeside, including a splendid short 9-hole par 3 course. 'Perfect for Practice', also croquet and tennis court. Many excellent varied courses within 30 minutes. Aberdeen airport 20 minutes. Unbeatable terms from £94.00 per person for 3 days to include 3 full days golf. (See advertisement page 509 for further details.)

Ramside Hall Hotel & Golf Club
Carrville, Durham DH1 1TD.
Tel 0191-386 5282 Fax 0191-386 0399

Set in 220 acres on the outskirts of the cathedral city of Durham and surrounded by a stimulating 27-hole golf course. 3-Star; 4-Crown Highly Commended. 80 luxury bedrooms, restaurant, grill room and carvery. Conference and banqueting facilities. Superb floodlit driving range and practice areas. (See advertisement page 503 for further details.)

Rodway Hill Golf Course
Newent Road,
Highnam,
Gloucestershire GL2 8DN.
Tel (01452) 384222 Fax (01989) 766450

An 18-hole pay and play par 70 course two miles south west of Gloucester, with panoramic views of the Cotswolds. It has a well stocked shop, practice and teaching facilities. Hire kit available. Societies welcome.

The Roxburghe Hotel & Golf Course
Kelso,
Roxburghshire TD5 8JZ.
Tel (01573) 450331 Fax (01573) 450611

22-bedroom hotel owned by the Duke and Duchess of Roxburghe. Luxury accommodation, superb cuisine. The 18-hole championship standard Roxburghe golf course, designed by Dave Thomas, surrounds the hotel.

The Royal Dublin Golf Club
North Bull Island,
Dollymount,
Dublin 3, Ireland.
Tel +353 1 833 6346 Fax +353 1 833 6504

The Royal Dublin Golf Club is Ireland's second oldest golf club and one of the country's premier sporting theatres. Royal Dublin provides visiting players with a combination of a superb championship links and a degree of hospitality that mirrors its historic development. (See advertisement page 31 for further details.)

Royal Lytham & St Anne's Golf Club
Links Gate,
Lytham St Anne's,
Lancashire FY8 3LQ.
Tel (01253) 724206 Fax (01253) 780946

Ideal for small parties wishing to play the championship course. Accommodation for men only. Apply to the assistant secretary. (See advertisement page 27 for further details.)

Royal Porthcawl Golf Club
Rest Bay,
Porthcawl,
Mid Glamorgan CF36 3UW.
Tel (01656) 782251 Fax (01656) 771687

Luxury dormy accommodation for parties of up to twelve persons. Apply to the secretary. (See advertisement page 31 for further details.)

Rudding Park Golf
Rudding Park, Harrogate,
North Yorkshire HG3 1DJ.
Tel (01423) 872100 Fax: (01423) 873011

Superb floodlit driving range and golf academy. Complete the golf experience on our 18-hole, par 72 parkland course. Corporate and society bookings welcome. (See advertisement page 499 for further details.)

Rusacks Hotel Golf Club
Pilmour Links, St Andrews, Fife KY16 9JQ.
Tel (01334) 474321 Fax (01334) 477896
Golf Club Tel/Fax (01334) 479176

Rusacks Hotel, overlooking the first and last fairways of the Old Course, provides outstanding facilities for golfers. The Rusacks Golf Club, situated within the hotel, offers guests a full golf booking service, lockers, sauna, solarium, club bar and golf shop. Voted one of the *Top Ten Golf Hotels in the World*.

Sand Moor Golf Club
Alwoodley Lane, Leeds LS17 7DJ.
Tel 0113-268 5180

A golfing paradise created out of a barren moor, with magnificent views of the surrounding countryside. The course is an excellent challenge of golf. Refurbishment of the clubhouse during 1997 has improved still further the quality of facilities available. (See advertisement page 31 for further details.)

Seafield Golf Course
Belleisle Park, Ayr.
c/o South Ayrshire Council, Burns House,
Burns Statue Square, Ayr KA7 1UT.
Tel (01292) 616269/616270

18-holes, length of course 5,498 yards SSS 66. For advance reservations telephone (01292) 441258. Practice area, caddy cars, catering and bar facilities available. Visitors welcome all week. Professional David Gemmell (01292) 441314. (See advertisement page 32 for further details.)

Seaford Golf Club
East Blatchington, Seaford,
East Sussex BN25 2JD.
Tel (01323) 892442

The Dormy House provides comfortable accommodation for 20 guests in 10 twin-bedded en suite bedrooms on the first floor of the clubhouse, and two single rooms in our bungalow annexe. For latest brochure ring 01323 892442.

Golf Club Facilities

Shannon Oaks Hotel & Country Club
Portumna,
Co Galway, Ireland.
Tel +353 509 41777 Fax +353 509 41357

The Shannon Oaks Hotel and Country Club offers extensive golf, leisure and conference facilities with our 5-Star leisure club and 18-hole parkland golf course adjacent.

The Silverwood Golf Hotel
Kiln Road,
Lurgan, Craigavon BT66 6NF.
Tel (01762) 327722 Fax (01762) 325290

The hotel lies within a complex of an 18-hole golf course, putting courses, driving range, gym and a certified ski slope. Also available - game and coarse fishing, sailing, winter skiing, windsurfing, bird and wildlife reserve and parascending. (See advertisement page 520 for further details.)

The Slieve Russell Hotel Golf & Country Club
Ballyconnell, Co Cavan, Ireland.
Tel +353 49 9526444 Fax +353 49 9526474

Located only two hours' drive from both Dublin and Belfast, the Slieve Russell is a complete resort with its 5-Star leisure facilities, championship 18-hole golf course. 151 superbly appointed bedrooms and a selection of restaurants and bars. Conference and banqueting suites - The *Perfect* location for business or pleasure.

The Springs Hotel
Wallingford Road,
North Stoke,
Wallingford, Oxon OX10 6BE.
Tel (01491) 836687 Fax (01491) 836877

Situated twix Oxford and Henley this Tudor-style country house offers, 30 en suite luxurious rooms, AA-2 Rosette restaurant, outdoor swimming pool and an 18-hole par 72 golf course. Your comfort and well-being are our priority. (See advertisement page 495 for further details.)

St Helen's Bay Golf & Country Club
St Helens, Kilrane, Rosslare Harbour,
Co Wexford, Ireland.
Tel +353 53 33234 Fax +353 53 33803

Superbly located championship 18-hole golf course, which has blended the best of parkland characteristics with a finish that is true links and plenty of difficulty. Luxury on-site accommodation together with tennis courts, leisure room and sauna. Full bar and catering facilities available in the clubhouse. Situated only five minutes from Rosslare ferryport. Green fee and society-friendly, playable all year.

The St Pierre Park Hotel
Rohais,
St Peter Port,
Guernsey GYI 1FD.
Tel (01481) 728282 Fax (01481) 712041

This 4-Star hotel offers extensive leisure facilities including a 9-hole par 3 golf course, designed by Tony Jacklin. Three tennis courts and a health suite with heated indoor swimming pool, spa bath, saunas, steam rooms, solaria and exercise room.

Stakis Puckrup Hall Hotel & Golf Club
Puckrup, Tewkesbury,
Gloucestershire GL20 6EL.
Tel (01684) 296200 Fax (01684) 850788

If golf is your chosen sport, Stakis Puckrup Hall is an excellent choice. Established trees, lakes and parkland play host to a challenging and beautifully tended par 70 championship course, situated between the Cotswold and Malvern hills. New clubhouse opens Spring 1999. (See advertisement page 489 for further details.)

Stocks Hotel Golf & Country Club
Stocks Road,
Aldbury,
Nr Tring, Hertfordshire HP23 5RX.
Tel (01442) 851341 Fax (01442) 851253

A championship 18-hole all-weather golf course, PGA Game Improvement Centre. Chipping and putting greens, practice fairway. Full stocked professional shop. 18 bedrooms, two restaurants, riding stables, full leisure facilities, conference rooms.

Stoke Poges Golf Club
Park Road,
Stoke Poges,
Buckinghamshire SL2 4PG.
Tel (01753) 717170 Fax (01753) 717181

Golf Club of the Year 1996. The ultimate venue for both corporate and social entertaining (six conference rooms, three restaurants and 21 bedrooms). Providing outstanding service and cuisine in unique surroundings close to London and Heathrow. (See advertisement page 8 for further details.)

Sweetwoods Park Golf Club
Cowden,
Edenbridge, Kent TN8 7JN.
Tel (01342) 850729 Fax (01342) 850866

Situated two miles west of Edenbridge off junction 6 of the M25. Simply the best value in golf around. Excellent 18-holes 6,512 yards par 72 course and floodlit driving range. AccoMarriott Goodwood Park

Telford Golf & Country Club
Great Hay,
Sutton Hill,
Telford, Shropshire TF7 4DT.
Tel (01952) 429977 Fax (01952) 586602

Overlooking the Ironbridge Gorge, the hotel offers its own 18-hole championship course. Floodlit driving range and practice areas. The extensive leisure facilities include squash courts, swimming pool, gymnasium, snooker, whirlpool, sauna and steam rooms. Resident masseur.

Tewkesbury Park Hotel Country Club Resort
Lincoln Green Lane,
Tewkesbury,
Gloucestershire GL20 7DN.
Tel (01684) 295405 Fax (01684) 292386

This 78-bedroom hotel with modern facilities is surrounded by its own 18-hole golf course. It also offers indoor heated swimming pool, jacuzzi, sauna, solarium, squash courts, floodlit tennis courts, extensive gym facilities and dance studio. Health and beauty treatments are also available, on a pre-booked basis. (See advertisement page 8 for further details.)

Trevose Golf & Country Club
Constantine Bay,
Padstow,
North Cornwall PL28 8JB.
Tel (01841) 520208 Fax (01841) 521057

e-mail: @trevose-gc.co.uk
http://www.trevose-gc.co.uk
Trevose offers not only great golf (championship 18-hole course, a 9-hole full length (3,100 yards) par 35 plus a 9-hole short course) but also a first class clubhouse and restaurant, three hard all-weather tennis courts, a heated outdoor swimming pool in the summer, a games room for the kids and a boutique. Accommodation is available in bungalows, chalets, luxury flats and dormy suites. Send for our detailed coloured brochure. Open all the year.

Turnberry Hotel Golf Courses & Spa
Ayrshire KA26 9LT.
Tel (01655) 331000 Fax (01655) 331706

One of the world's finest luxury hotel, golf and spa resorts. Edwardian country house overlooking its own Ailsa and Arran championship courses. The Ailsa is ranked 16th in the world and was the venue for the 1994 Open Championship.

Welbeck Manor & Sparkwell Golf Course
Blacklands, Sparkwell,
Plymouth, Devon PL7 5DF.
Tel/Fax (01752) 837219

A testing 9-hole, pay as you play course and also a par 3 course, set in 60 acres of parkland. Facilities include a well equipped golf shop, excellent hotel accommodation, restaurant and bar. Open to the public. Golf societies welcome.

Welcombe Hotel & Golf Course
Warwick Road, Stratford-upon-Avon,
Warwickshire CV37 0NR.
Tel (01789) 295252 Fax (01789) 414666
Corporate Golf Office:
Tel/Fax (01789) 262665

A 4-Star Jacobean-style mansion house hotel with private 18-hole championship golf course set in 157 acres of wooded parkland with picturesque lakes. Corporate golf and green fees most welcome.

West Waterford Golf & Country Club
West Waterford Golf Club
Dungarvan, Co Waterford, Ireland.
Tel +353 58 43216 & 41475
Fax +353 58 44343

Featured in 1996 by *Golf World - In Golfing Gems of Ireland*. A new golfing experience and wonderful welcome awaits you at the West Waterford golf club. Excellent self-catering bungalow available, situated on the course along the 18th fairway.

Westport Golf Club
Carrowholly, Westport, Co Mayo, Ireland
Tel +353 98 28262 Fax +353 98 27217

Westport Golf Club is recognised as a prestigious venue and has hosted both the Ladies Home Internationals in 1989, and the Irish Amateur Close Championship on three occasions, most recently in 1997.

Whitefields Hotel Golf & Country Club
Coventry Road,
Thurlaston,
Nr Rugby, Warwickshire CV23 9JR.
Tel (01788) 521800 Fax (01788) 521695

18-hole course 6,223 yards. Driving range, putting green 18. Four conference rooms. 33 en suite rooms. Bars and à la carte restaurant. Societies welcome seven days. Call the secretary on 01788 815555. Reservations 01788 521800.

Woodbury Park Golf & Country Club
Woodbury Castle,
Woodbury,
Exeter, Devon EX5 1JJ.
Tel (01395) 233382 Fax (01395) 233384

Luxury 55-bedroom hotel with five superb lodges. The Nigel Mansell owned resort encompasses 27 holes, including the Oaks championship course, in addition to extensive leisure facilities. The ideal venue for your golfing break.

DRIVING RANGES

The Burgess Hill Golf Academy
Cuckfield Road, Burgess Hill,
West Sussex RH15 8RE.
Tel (01444) 258585

New 24-bay, undercover, floodlit driving range and comprehensive practice facilities. Superb new 9-hole par 3 golf course. Open seven days a week, 7am to 10pm. PGA professionals for lessons and pro shop for all your golfing requirements.

Carden Park Hotel Golf Resort & Spa
Nr Chester, Cheshire CH3 9DQ.
Tel (01829) 731000 Fax (01829) 731032

Set in 750-acres of beautiful Cheshire countryside near Chester. A true golf resort with two 18-hole golf courses - the mature Cheshire course and the new Nicklaus course, the 9-hole par 3 Azalea course and Europe's first Jack Nicklaus Residential Golf School. The superb AA/RAC 4-Star hotel also has an extensive spa and there are many other leisure facilities on the estate. For further information and a brochure call Liz Mole on 01829 731000 (See advertisement page 501 for further details.)

Gainsborough Golf Club
Thonock, Gainsborough,
Lincolnshire DN21 1PZ.
Tel (01427) 613088 Fax (01427) 810172

The Karsten Lakes championship course, designed by Neil Coles, MBE, is part of a 36-hole complex set amongst undulating Lincolnshire parkland. The two courses are complemented wit h a 4-Star clubhouse ofering restaurant and conference facilities. Society and corporate golf parties welcome.

Gosforth Park Golfing Complex
(Parklands Golf Course)
High Gosforth Park,
Newcastle-upon-Tyne NE3 5HQ.
Tel 0191-236 4480

The complex has an 18-hole golf course, 45-bay two tier floodlit driving range, 9-hole pitch and putt course and putting green. Also pro shop, bar and restaurant. Open to non-members.

The K Club
At Straffan, Co Kildare, Ireland.
Tel +353 1 601 7300 Fax +353 1 601 7399
e-mail: *golf@kclub.ie http://www.kclub.ie*

Located 30 minutes from Dublin. Arnold Palmer designed 18-hole championship golf course, clubhouse, practice area and driving range. Resident golf professional Ernie Jones. Home to The Smurfit European Open since September 1995 until the year 2000. Hotel AA 5-Red Stars. Fishing, health club and sports centre with indoor and outdoor tennis. (See advertise-ment page 512 for further details.)

Rudding Park Golf
Rudding Park, Harrogate,
North Yorkshire HG3 1DJ.
Tel (01423) 872100 Fax: (01423) 873011

Superb floodlit driving range and golf academy. Complete the golf experience on our 18-hole, par 72 parkland course. Corporate and society bookings welcome. (See advertisement page 499 for further details.)

Telford Golf & Country Club
Great Hay, Sutton Hill,
Telford, Shropshire TF7 4DT.
Tel (01952) 429977 Fax (01952) 586602

Overlooking the Ironbridge Gorge, the hotel offers its own 18-hole championship course. Floodlit driving range and practice areas. Extensive leisure facilities include squash courts, swimming pool, gymnasium, snooker, whirlpool, sauna/steam rooms and resident masseur.

Choose from among the best Hotels in the British Isles & Ireland

SOUTH LODGE HOTEL, West Sussex

Golfing Hotel Compendium

The Golfing Hotel Compendium is a comprehensive source of information for golfers wishing to find the most comfortable place to stay at or close to some of the finest courses in the country. This section has been compiled from the premier hotels, guest houses and self-catering facilities in the British Isles which include golf among their many attractions.

If readers wish especially to recommend an establishment which is not listed in this section of the Royal & Ancient Golfer's Handbook the editors will be happy to be advised.

ENGLAND

South West

Alverton Manor Country House Hotel
Tregolls Road, Truro, Cornwall TR1 1ZQ.
Tel (01872) 276633 Fax (01872) 2222989

AA/RAC 3-Star; Award-Winning 2-AA Rosettes Restaurant; *Johansen's Guide*; West Country Tourist Board 4-Crown Highly Commended; *Best Loved Hotels of the World*. Cornwall's premier house hotel in the cathedral city of Truro. A former convent dating from c1700. Quietly set in six acres of terraced grounds and centrally situated for all Cornish golf courses. Golfing breaks at our own splendid parkland course. (See advertisement page 489 for further details.)

Berry Head Hotel
Berry Head Road, Brixham,
Devon TQ5 9AJ.
Tel (01803) 853225 Fax (01803) 882084

AA 3-Star; ETB 4-Crown Commended. In an area of outstanding natural beauty the Berry Head Hotel is surrounded by six acres of secluded grounds and yet only a short walk from the fishing port of Brixham. All bedrooms en suite with full facilities. Private functions and seminars catered for. Walking, sailing and angling all available locally. Golf can be arranged at Churston Golf Club only three miles away. Indoor heated swimming pool.

Burnham & Berrow Golf Club
The Dormy,
St Cristopher's Way,
Burnham-on-Sea, Somerset TA8 2PE.
Tel (01278) 785760

18-hole championship links golf course and 9-hole course. Dormy accommodation available. (See advertisement page 27 for further details.)

China Fleet Country Club
Saltash, Cornwall PL12 6LJ.
Tel (01752) 848668 Fax (01752) 848456

Situated in 180 acres of Cornish countryside, 40 self-catering 4- and 6-berth apartments, 18-hole par 72 golf, 28-bay driving range, pool, health suite, gymnasium, racket sports, bars, restaurant and coffe shop. (See advertisement page 493 for further details.)

De Vere The Dormy
New Road, Ferndown, Dorset BH22 8ES.
Tel (01202) 872121 Fax (01202) 895388

4-Star. Set in 12 acres of delightful landscaped gardens on the edge of the beautiful New Forest, The Dormy is a friendly, country-style hotel with excellent leisure facilities including -

continued over

indoor heated pool, sauna, steam room and solarium, superb restaurants and bars and a health and beauty studio ideal for relaxation and pampering. Adjacent to the hotel is the famous Ferndown golf club, which has a championship 18-hole course and a testing President's 9-hole course with 18 tees. There are 20 golf courses within 20 minutes of the hotel. (De Vere Hotel Group - see advertisement 485 for further details.)

The Duke of Cornwall Hotel
Millbay Road,
Plymouth, Devon PL1 3LG.
Tel (01752) 266256 Fax (01752) 600062

3-Star Victorian style city centre hotel. 70 en suite bedrooms with every modern comfort. Awarded AA 2-Rosettes for food and service. Conference and banqueting facilities for up to 300 delegates. Friendly and professional staff. Easily accessible from all routes.

East Dorset Golf Club
Bere Regis,
Dorset BH20 7NT.
Tel (01929) 472244 Fax (01929) 471294

e-mail: edgc@golf.co.uk Web: www.golf.co.uk/edgc
3-Crown Commended golf lodge. 18-hole lakeland and 9-hole woodland courses. Floodlit covered driving range. Reputation for personal service. Excellent English cuisine. 12-twin and 4-double rooms, en suite, usual facilities. Own lounge and games room. Two hours from London. In Hardy countryside overlooking the Purbeck Hills.

Fircroft Hotel
Owls Road, Bournemouth BH5 1AE.
Tel (01202) 309771 Fax (01202) 395644

The hotel is situated close to sea and shops with many superb golf courses in the area. Fine restaurant with choice of menus. Large car park. Late bar. Free use of leisure club 9am to 6pm, with indoor pool, jacuzzi, sauna steam room and gym.

Golf View Hotel
Headland Road,
Newquay, Cornwall TR7 1HN.
Tel/Fax (01637) 875082

An outstanding family run hotel overlooking Newquay golf course and Newquay's world famous Fistral beach (150 yards from the hotel). Most rooms en suite. Own car park. Reduced green fees on most local courses. Special party rates.

Hannafore Point Hotel
Marine Parade,
West Looe,
Cornwall PL13 2DG.
Tel (01503) 263273 Fax (01503) 263272

Situated overlooking Looe Bay at waters edge. Comfortable en suite bedrooms, superb cuisine and fine wines. Excellent indoor leisure facilities. Special arrangements for golf at Looe Bin Down and St Austell.

Headland House
Headland Road,
Carbis Bay,
St Ives, Cornwall TR26 2NS.
Tel/Fax (01736) 796647

Family run Victorian house with spectacular views over St Ive's Bay. Excellent, comfortable accommodation at an affordable price. Just one mile for West Cornwall golf club and ideally situated for many Cornish golf courses. Ample parking.

The Lordleaze Hotel
Forton Road,
Chard, Somerset TA20 2HW.
Tel (01460) 61066 Fax (01460) 66468

AA 3-Star. Conveniently located, ten minutes from the 18-hole par 71 Windwhistle golf club with squash courts. Good, friendly and efficient service and food. 16 en suite bedrooms.

The Mount
Northdown Road,
Bideford,
Devon EX39 3LP.
Tel (01237) 473748

Charming Georgian licensed guest house near the centre of Bideford. Private garden, car parking. All rooms en suite with colour TV. Only five minutes' drive to Royal North Devon golf club. Golf packages available. B&B from £22.00 per person per night.

Penventon Hotel
Redruth,
Cornwall TR15 1TE.
Tel (01209) 214141 Fax (01209) 219164

AA 3-Star Rosette. Large country house hotel, parkland setting, central for six courses. Superior restaurant, resident pianists, three bars, nightclub, indoor pool complex, sauna, jacuzzi, robes provided, masseuse, hairdresser. Special bargain rates all year. Colour brochures. A Cornish welcome awaits you. Open all year.

Pines Hotel
**Burlington Road, Swanage,
Dorset BH19 1LT.**
Tel (01929) 425211

50-bedroom family run 3-Star hotel. All bedrooms have private bathroom, telephone and colour TV. One and a half miles from Isle of Purbeck golf club. Within easy reach of all Dorset courses.

Polurrian Hotel
**Mullion, Lizard Peninsula,
Helston, Cornwall TR12 7EN.**
Tel (01326) 240421 Fax (01326) 240083

AA 3-Star; ETB 4-Crown Highly Commended. Every comfort and warmest of welcomes awaits you at the Polurrian Hotel. Set in an enchanting position overlooking its own private cove, this is the ideal location for walking or just relaxing. Superb leisure facilities including gym, sauna, solarium, tennis, indoor and outdoor pools, play areas and registered crèche. Golf can be arranged at Mullion golf club just two miles away.

Riversford Hotel
Limers Lane, Bideford, Devon EX39 2RG.
Tel (01237) 474239 Fax (01237) 421661

Peace and tranquility in gardens beside the river Torridge. A relaxing retreat after a day on the fairways of North Devon. Excellent food, a flexible lounge bar and comfortable en suite bedrooms. Concessionary golf at North Devon only five minutes from hotel.

The Sea & Horses Hotel
**Seafront, Alexandra Terrace,
Penzance, Cornwall TR18 4NX.**
Tel (01736) 361961 Fax (01736) 330499

Golf should always be played this way. Fabulous courses, majestic seascapes and the knowledge of wonderful hospitality at and beyond the 19th hole. Enjoy the very best of golf alongside the joys of Atlantic Cornwall.

Sherborne Lodge Hotel
**Torrs Park, Ilfracombe,
North Devon EX34 8AY.**
Tel (01271) 862297 Fax (01271) 865520

Small friendly family run hotel offering excellent value for money. Conveniently situated for Saunton, Ilfracombe and Royal North Devon golf courses. Driving range and 9-hole course at Morthoe. Fully licensed. Secure parking. Drying facilities.

The Slipway Hotel
**The Harbour Front, Port Isaac,
Cornwall PL29 3RH.**
Tel/Fax (01208) 880264

Set in the heart of this beautiful old fishing village the Slipway is the ideal base for a Cornish holiday and is situated within easy striking distance of sailing facilities at Rock and several excellent golf courses including the championship course of St Enodoc.

Stakis Puckrup Hall Hotel & Golf Club
**Puckrup, Tewkesbury,
Gloucestershire GL20 6EL.**
Tel (01684) 296200 Fax (01684) 850788

If golf is your chosen sport, Stakis Puckrup Hall is an excellent choice. Established trees, lakes and parkland play host to a challenging and beautifully tended par 70 championship course, situated between the Cotswold and Malvern hills. New clubhouse opens 1999. (See advertisement page 489 for further details.)

Tewkesbury Park Hotel Country Club Resort
**Lincoln Green Lane, Tewkesbury,
Gloucestershire GL20 7DN.**
Tel (01684) 295405 Fax (01684) 292386

This 78-bedroom hotel with modern facilities is surrounded by its own 18-hole golf course. It also offers indoor heated swimming pool, jacuzzi, sauna, solarium, squash courts, floodlit tennis courts, extensive gym facilities and dance studio. Health and beauty treatments are also available, on a pre-booked basis. (See advertisement page 493 for further details.)

Trevose Golf & Country Club
**Constantine Bay, Padstow,
North Cornwall PL28 8JB.**
Tel (01841) 520208 Fax (01841) 521057

e-mail: @trevose-gc.co.uk
website: http://www.trevose-gc.co.uk

Trevose offers not only great golf (championship 18-hole course, a 9-hole full length (3,100 yards) par 35 plus a 9-hole short course) but also a first class clubhouse and restaurant, three hard all-weather tennis courts, a heated outdoor swimming pool in the summer, a games room for the kids and a boutique. Accommodation is available in bungalows, chalets, luxury flats and dormy suites. Send for our detailed full colour brochure. Open all the year.

Welbeck Manor & Sparkwell Golf Course
Blacklands,
Sparkwell,
Plymouth, Devon PL7 5DF.
Tel/Fax (01752) 837219

A testing 9-hole, pay as you play course and also a par 3 course, set in 60 acres of parkland. Facilities include a well equipped golf shop, excellent hotel accommodation, restaurant and bar. Open to the public. Golf societies welcome.

Woodbury Park Golf & Country Club
Woodbury Castle,
Woodbury,
Exeter, Devon EX5 1JJ.
Tel (01395) 233382 Fax (01395) 233384

Luxury 55-bedroom hotel with five superb lodges. The Nigel Mansell owned resort encompasses 27 holes, including the Oaks championship course, in addition to extensive leisure facilities. The ideal venue for your golfing break.

Yeoldon House Hotel
Durrant Lane, Northam,
Bideford, Devon EX39 2RL.
Tel (01237) 474400 Fax (01237) 476618

Play the oldest course in England: Royal North Devon. We take pride in our excellent cuisine and fine wines. Our rooms are comfortable and perfect to rest those well golfed bones. Societies and parties of any number welcome. ETB 4-Crown Highly Commended. £40-£50 Single, £70-£90 Double. (See advertisement page 489 for further details.)

South East

Ashdown Forest Golf Hotel
Chapel Lane,
Forest Row,
East Sussex RH18 5BB.
Tel (01342) 824866 Fax (01342) 824869

e-mail: reservations@ashgolf.demon.co.uk
website: http://www.ashgolf.demon.co.uk
Newly refurbished hotel with 19 en suite bedrooms, large function room, conference facilities, restaurant and two bars.The hotel operates the Royal Ashdown Forest Golf Club West Course. Several other courses incorporated in residential golf breaks. (See advertisement page 495 for further details.)

Botley Park Hotel Golf & Country Club
Winchester Road, Boorley Green,
Botley, Hampshire SO3 2UA.
Tel (01489) 780888 Fax (01489) 789242

Set in 176 acres of rolling Hampshire countryside, this 4-Star hotel has 100 en suite bedrooms, superb restaurant, extensive leisure facilities and its own picturesque and challenging 18-hole par 70 golf course and driving range. (See advertisement page 497 for further details).

Cottesmore Golf & Country Club
Buchan Hill, Pease Pottage,
Crawley, West Sussex RH11 9AT.
Tel (01293) 528256 Fax (01293) 522819

12 en suite bedrooms overlooking peaceful undulating Sussex countryside. Guests can enjoy two full 18-hole mature golf courses, tennis, squash, indoor pool, spa bath, steam room, sauna and gymnasium. Ten minutes from Gatwick, one mile from the Pease Pottage exit (Junction 11) off the M23.

Dale Hill Hotel
Ticehurst, Wadhurst,
East Sussex TN5 7DQ.
Tel (01580) 200112

Highly commended luxurious hotel situated in an area of outstanding national beauty, with health club and highly acclaimed 18-hole golf course. New Ian Woosnam championship course opened to rave reviews in September, 1997.

Donnington Grove Country Club Golf Hotel & Conference Centre
Grove Road, Donnington,
Newbury, Berkshire RG14 2LA.
Tel (01635) 581000 Fax (01635) 552259

18-hole parkland/moorland championship course designed by Dave Thomas. The clubhouse and hotel are located within a beautifully renovated 18th-century gothic mansion. This will provide an ideal setting for your society, company golf day or conference stay.

Farringford Hotel
Bedbury Lane, Freshwater Bay,
Isle of White PO40 9PE.
Tel (01983) 752500 Fax (01983) 756515

Country house hotel set in 33 acres, Farringford offers en suite bedrooms or self-

continued over

489

YEOLDON HOUSE HOTEL AND RESTAURANT

AA 2-Star 75%

Durrant Lane, Northam, Bideford, Devon. EX39 2RL.
Tel: (01237) 474400 Fax: (01237) 476618.

Tee off to Seven of the countries finest and most historic golf courses. The renowned Championship Royal North Devon (5 mins) is a wonderful course to enjoy or test your golfing skills. Beginners and experienced players welcome. Beautifully situated overlooking estuary and unspoilt countryside. Your comfort is our concern. To achieve this we provide the finest food and quality wines, with friendly staff who are eager to make your stay enjoyable, and homely, individually decorated en-suite bedrooms you won't want to leave.

Sue & Kevin Jelley. Hosts and Resident Proprietors.

Alverton Manor

Tregolls Road, Truro, Cornwall, England TR1 1ZQ

Set in picturesque and peaceful gardens, close to Truro City centre, Alverton Manor is a superb base from which to enjoy the many fine golf courses throughout the county of Cornwall. The hotel's own course within the historic Killiow estate located in over 400 acres of splendid rolling parkland is approximately five minutes away by car.

Our two-day golfing breaks including golf fees at two of our preferred 18-hole courses, start from £154.00 pp B&B.

AA 3-Star
2 Rosettes
RAC 3-Star

- 34 LUXURY EN-SUITE BEDROOMS
- 2-7 DAY GOLFING BREAKS
- CORPORATE HOSPITALITY DAYS
- EQUIPMENT HIRE
- 8-BAY FLOODLIT DRIVING RANGE
- GOLF SIMULATOR

PLAY FOUR TOP USA COURSES WITHOUT THE AIR FAIR, OR PRACTISE YOUR SWING ON OUR ADVANCE GOLF COURSE SIMULATOR

For further information on our exclusive golfing breaks please contact Reception, Tel: 00 44 (0)1872 276633

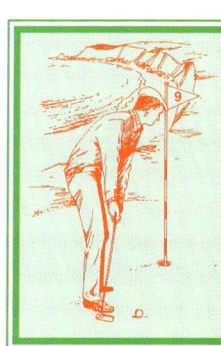

MAKE YOUR CHOICE FROM AMONG SOME OF THE BEST HOTELS IN THE UNITED KINGDOM AND IRELAND

STAKIS PUCKRUP HALL HOTEL & GOLF CLUB

Puckrup, Tewkesbury, Gloucestershire GL20 6EL.
Tel: (01684) 296200 Fax: (01684) 850788

If golf is your chosen sport then Stakis Puckrup Hall is the perfect choice. Situated in over 140 acres of secluded wood and parkland between the Cotswold and Malvern Hills, established trees, lakes and parkland play host to a challenging and beautifully tended par 70, 18-hole Championship course, ideal for the discerning player. 112 well appointed en suite bedrooms - conference facilities for up to 200 delegates. As well as golf enjoy the superb leisure club including a fully equipped gym, pool complex, steam room, sun beds and beauty salon.

NEW CLUBHOUSE
OPENS SPRING 1999

catering cottages. 9-hole golf course free to residents. Swimming, tennis, croquet, putting, snooker etc. Excellent food. Dinner dance every Saturday.

The Flackley Ash Hotel
Peasmarsh, Rye, East Sussex TN31 6YH.
Tel (01797) 230651 Fax (01797) 230510

3-Star Georgian country house hotel set in beautiful grounds with croquet lawn. Indoor swimming pool, whirlpool spa, saunas, mini-gym and 'beautique'. Extensive wine list, a friendly welcome and an AA Rosette for our food.

Gatton Manor Hotel Golf & Country Club
Ockley, Nr Dorking, Surrey RH5 5PQ.
Tel (01306) 627555

Set amidst its own 18-hole golf course in 200 acres of parklands and lakes, situated between London and the south coast, in the heart of the Surrey countryside. Superb all en suite accommodation overlooking the golf course and grounds. À la carte restaurants, large lounge bar, conference suites, gym and health club.

Horsted Place Hotel
**Little Horsted, Uckfield,
East Sussex TN22 5ES.**
Tel (01825) 750581 Fax (01825) 750459
Club Tel (01825) 880088
Fax (01825) 880066

Combine Victorian elegance and luxury at Horsted Place Hotel with exceptional golf on one of the two spectacular courses at East Sussex National Golf Club. If you require golf tuition there is a superb golf academy which has its own three hole course. Experience for yourself challenging golf and exceptional accommodation in beautiful surroundings. (See advertisement page 495 for further details.)

Lansdowne Hotel
**King Edward's Parade, Eastbourne,
East Sussex BN21 4EE.**
Tel (01323) 725174 Fax (01323) 739721

RAC/AA 3-Star. Play 36 holes a day on choice of seven courses; we book your tee-off time. Two nights with green fees, light lunch at club and use of our drying room. 1 April to 31 May, £146; 1 June to 30 September, £156; 1 October to 31 December, £140; 1 January to 28 February, £135; 1 to 31 March, £145. Extra days pro rata. (See advertisement page 493 for further details.

Marriott Goodwood Park Hotel & Country Club
**Goodwood, Chichester,
West Sussex PO18 0QB.**
Tel (01243) 775537 Fax (01243) 520120

Country club hotel set in the 12,000-acre Goodwood Estate, the ancestral home of the Duke of Richmond. The 18-hole golf course is all you would expect of *Marriott*. A fairly generous course getting harder as you reach the turn - you'll need to be at the top of your game! Golf range and practice area. Complimentary leisure facilties. *Marriott Hotel Group.*

Marriott Hanbury Manor Hotel & Country Club
Ware, Hertfordshire SG12 0SD.
Tel (01920) 487722 Fax (01920) 487692

5-Star country resort set in 200 acres of beautiful parkland, yet only 25 miles north of central London and 15 minutes from the M25.The 18-hole championship golf course (1998 ALAMO English Open) offers a real challenge to any level of player. Three award-winning restaurants and 96 deluxe bedrooms. Ten conference rooms. Complimentary leisure facilities.
Marriott Hotel Group.

Marriott Meon Valley Hotel & Country Club
**Sandy Lane, Shedfield,
Nr Southampton, Hampshire SO32 2HQ.**
Tel (01329) 833455 Fax (01329) 834411

Set in 225 acres of beautiful Hampshire parkland and easily reached by the M27 and M3, the hotel offers excellent accommodation. The 18-hole championship Meon course, host to the Philips PGA Seniors European Tour Classic, provides a real challenge. The picturesque 9-hole Valley course offers the same challenge. Ideal for a morning round and can be played twice. Complimentary leisure facilities. *Marriott Hotel Group.*

Marriott Tudor Park Hotel & Country Club
**Ashford Road, Bearsted,
Maidstone, Kent ME14 4NQ.**
Tel (01622) 734334 Fax (01622) 735360

Situated in the Garden of England, Tudor Park is set in a 220-acre former deer park and offers excellent accommodation. Less than half an hour from London and minutes from the M20, this is the ideal base for that special golf event. Designed by Donald Steel, each of the 18-holes

exhibits its own distinctive personality. Complimentary leisure facilities. *Marriott Hotel Group.*

Seaford - The Dormy House
**Seaford Golf Club,
East Blatchington,
Seaford, East Sussex BN25 2JD.
Tel (01323) 892442**

The Dormy House provides comfortable accommodation for 20 guests in 10 twin-bedded en suit bedrooms on the first floor of the clubhouse, and two single rooms in our bungalow annexe. For latest brochure ring 01323 892442.

South Lodge Hotel
**Brighton Road,
Lower Beeding,
Nr Horsham, West Sussex RH13 6PS.
Tel (01403) 891711 Fax (01403) 891766**
e-mail: *inquiries@southlodgehotel.dial.iql.co.uk*
http://www.southlodgehotel.co.uk
South Lodge Hotel is a fine Victorian country house set in 93 acres of secluded wooded parkland with views over the South Downs. Golf at our two spectacular 18-hole championship courses at Mannings Heath Golf Club. Enjoy tennis, croquet, petanque, putting or snooker. (See advertisement page 497 for further details.)

The Springs Hotel
**Wallingford Road,
North Stoke,
Wallingford, Oxon OX10 6BE.
Tel (01491) 836687 Fax (01491) 836877**

Situated twix Oxford and Henley this Tudor-style country house offers, 30 en suite luxurious rooms, AA-2 Rosette restaurant, outdoor swimming pool and an 18-hole par 72 golf course. Your comfort and well-being are our priority. (See advertisement page 497 for further details.)

Stocks Hotel Golf & Country Club
**Stocks Road,
Aldbury, Nr Tring,
Hertfordshire HP23 5RX.
Tel (01442) 851341 Fax (01442) 851253**

A championship 18-hole all-weather golf course, PGA Game Improvement Centre. Chipping and putting greens, practice fairway. Full stocked professional shop. 18 bedrooms, two restaurants, riding stables, full leisure facilities, conference rooms.

Sweetwoods Park Golf Club
**Cowden,
Edenbridge,
Kent TN8 7JN.
Tel (01342) 850729 Fax (01342) 850866**

Situated two miles west of Edenbridge off junction 6 of the M25. Simply the best value in golf around. Excellent 18-holes 6,512 yards par 72 course and floodlit driving range. Accommodation and corporate membership available.

East Anglia

Abbotsley Golf Hotel
**Eynesbury Hardwicke,
St Neots,
Cambridgeshire PE19 4XN.
Tel (01480) 474000 Fax (01480) 471018**

Friendly country house hotel set amidst two 18-hole courses. *Golf Monthly* "The Abbotsley course - the design is a revelation. The presentation superb." Award-winning gardens; relaxed atmosphere. Home of Vivien Saunders golf schools.

Barnham Broom Hotel
**Golf • Conference • Leisure
Honingham Road,
Barnham Broom,
Norwich, Norfolk NR9 4DD.
Tel (01603) 759393 Fax (01603) 758224**

EETB 4-Crown. East Anglia's finest conference and leisure centre lies in 250 acres of countryside. 53 fully equipped bedrooms include family rooms, served by Flints restaurant and sports snack bar. Four squash courts, snooker, heated indoor swimming pool and spa jets, tennis and 36-hole golf. *Golfing Getaways* from £125. Professional tution available. (See advertisement page 497 for further details.)

Bay Leaf Guest House
**10 Saint Peters Road,
Sheringham,
Norfolk NR26 8QY.
Tel/Fax (01263) 823779**

Charming Victorian licensed guest house situated in an area of outstanding beauty. Comfortable, en suite bedrooms with TV and courtesy tray. B&B with full generous English breakfast. Superb seaside courses only minutes away make this an ideal golfing base.

Beaumaris Hotel
15 South Street,
Sheringham,
Norfolk NR26 8LL.
Tel (01263) 822370 Fax (01263) 821421

Established and run by the same family for 50 years with a reputation for personal service and excellent English cuisine. 22 en suite bedrooms. AA 2-Star Ashley Courtenay Recommended; EATB 4-Crown Commended. Three minutes' walk Sheringham's exhilerating cliff top golf course.

Cambridgeshire Moat House Hotel
Bar Hill,
Cambridge CB3 8EU.
Tel (01954) 780098 Fax (01954) 780010

18-hole championship golf course set in 134 acres of parkland. Golf professional David Vernon. Newly built clubhouse and golf shop. 99 en suite bedrooms. Extensive leisure facilities. five miles north of Cambridge on A14. Visitors welcome.

Tel: 01728 452176
Fax: 01728 453868

THORPENESS
GOLF CLUB & HOTEL LTD.

Mature and challenging 18-hole heathland course set in Suffolk coastal countryside. Good all year round climate. Fully irrigated in the Summer, rarely closed in the Winter.

HANDICAP CERTIFICATE MANDATORY

Traditional clubhouse with bars and restaurant 30 bedrooms with twin and double accommodation Well stocked Golf Shop, green fees and lessons available.

Seven tennis courts adjacent to the beach

Ideal venue for individuals or societies. Two hours from London. One hour from port of Harwich.

**The Golf Club
Thorpeness
Nr Aldeburgh Suffolk IP16 4NH**

Fieldview Guest House
West Barsham Road,
East Barsham,
North Norfolk NR21 OAR.
Tel (01328) 820083

e-mail: fieldview@csl.com
Tranquil village location overlooking fields. Friendly welcoming atmosphere, substantial breakfast. Come and go as you please. All rooms include TV, tea/coffee-making facilities, hairdryer. No smoking. No pets. £20.00 per person per night.

The Golf Club - Thorpeness
Thorpeness,
Nr Aldeburgh, Suffolk IP16 4NH.
Tel (01728) 452176 Fax (01728) 453868

One of East Anglia's finest and most challenging 18-hole courses. Handicap certificate required, advisable to book in advance. Accommodation, bars, restaurant, golf shop, tennis courts and course set adjacent to picturesque coastal village on Suffolk Heritage coast. (See advertisement page 492 for further details.)

Oaklands Hotel
89 Yarmouth Road, Thorpe St Andrew,
Norwich NR7 OHH.
Tel (01603) 434471 Fax (01603) 700318

RAC 3-Star hotel set in its own grounds overlooking the Yare Valley river. It is situated within easy reach of several local golf clubs, and is renowned for its excellent food, wine and service.

Virginia Court Hotel
Cliff Avenue, Cromer, Norfolk NR27 0AN.
Tel (01263) 512398 Fax (01263) 515529

Originally built as 'Cromer Clubhouse' in 1899 and converted to a hotel late in the 1920s. Now offering en suite bedrooms, the Billet Bar, Raffles Coffee Lounge, plus pleasant restaurant offering superb menus. Royal Cromer and other good courses nearby.

Wentworth Hotel
Wentworth Road, Aldeburgh,
Suffolk IP15 5BD.
Tel (01728) 452312 Fax (01728) 454343

Country house hotel with sea views. 38 bedrooms all with colour TV, radio and teamaker. Two comfortable lounges, cosy bar, log fires and antique furniture. Our restaurant specialises in local, fresh produce and seafood.

7 courses to choose from!
Any two days from 1st April 1999 to 31st March 2000

The break includes 2 days free golf (up to 36 holes each day) accommodation, a newspaper *(except Sunday)*, full English breakfast, a light lunch at the golf club with a 4 course dinner and coffee at the hotel.

The cost of your break is from
1 April - 31 May, £146;
1 June - 30 September, £156;
1 October - 31 December, £140;
1 January - 28 February 2000, £135; 1 March - 31 March 2000, £145.

Extra days pro rata. Guaranteed tee-off times. Handicap certificates required. You may, subject to availability, play a selection of 7 clubs (all 18-hole) in this lovely area. AA *"Courtesy & Care"* award 1992. Please write or telephone for our golfing break folder.

Lansdowne Hotel RAC***AA
King Edward's Parade, Eastbourne BN21 4EE.
Tel: (01323) 725174 Fax: (01323) 739721

Best Western

TEWKESBURY PARK HOTEL
Country Club Resort

Tewkesbury Park Hotel, Golf and Country Club is set amidst a classic rural landscape with the 5th hole overlooking the famous Tewkesbury Abbey.
This 18 hole, 6533 yds, par 73 course, recognised by the PGA, provides wooded areas and water early in your round, but the later holes offer some welcome relief with spacious fairways. The hotel is friendly and relaxed and provides the atmosphere for relaxation after a competitive day. The superb dining facilities, well appointed accommodation and extensive leisure facilities adds the final touch to any event.

**Full corporate and society packages are available.
Call 01684 295405 for further details.**

LINCOLN GREEN LANE, TEWKESBURY, GLOUCESTERSHIRE
GL20 7DN. FAX: 01684 292386

China Fleet
Your Favourite Golf Club

Golf Breaks

- 72 hole championship standard course
- 28 bay floodlit driving range
- Well stocked golf shop
- Superb self catering apartments
- Excellent Bars and Restaurant
- Wide range of leisure activities including indoor swimming pool
- Health & Fitness Suites
- Easy access to all main routes

In 180 acres of Beautiful Rolling Cornish Countryside by the River Tamar

Special society days and mid-week packages

BREAKS FROM £52.50 Per person

Call on 01752 854657

China Fleet Country Club, Saltash, Cornwall PL12 6LJ.
Tel: (01752) 848668 Fax: (01752) 848456
E-mail: sales@china-fleet.co.uk Web Site: www.china-fleet.co.uk

White Horse Hotel - Leiston
Station Road,
Leiston, Suffolk IP16 4HD.
Tel (01728) 830694 Fax (01728) 833105

Close to three excellent courses in the heart of Suffolk Heritage coast. Friendly bars, excellent food, 12 rooms, 11 en suite, all with TV and telephone. Bargain weekend breaks all year.

White Horse Inn - Cromer
West Street,
Cromer, Norfolk NR27 9DS.
Tel (01263) 512275

What a load of balls! See Norfolk's biggest collection of golf balls at this original coaching inn. Just off town centre, the inn is run by a couple of golfing nuts. *Babs the Bandit* and *Gary the Groove*. Everything is great - the accommodation, food, drink and weekend entertainment. Free parking. Call us on 01263 512275.

Northamptonshire

Farthingstone Hotel & Golf Course
Farthingstone,
Towcester,
Northamptonshire NN12 8HA.
Tel (01327) 361291 Fax (01327) 361645

Set in glorious wooded countryside, just 90 minutes outside London. Farthingstone Hotel offers 16 superb en suite rooms, a challenging 18-hole golf course, squash court, full size snooker tables, and a carvery restaurant. Highly competitive tariffs.

East Midlands

De Vere Belton Woods
Belton,
Nr Grantham,
Lincolnshire NG32 2LN.
Tel (01476) 593200 Fax (01476) 514399

A magnificent hotel, golf and leisure resort set in 475 acres of glorious countryside. Two challenging 18-hole championship golf courses, 9-hole course, driving range, putting green and extensive leisure facilities. 136 bedrooms. (De Vere Hotel Group - see advertisement page 4 for further details.)

Dower House Hotel
Manor Estate,
Woodhall Spa,
Lincolnshire LN10 6PY.
Tel (01526) 352588 Fax (01526) 352588

Situated within the Manor Estate the Dower House overlooks the new Woodhall 18-hole golf course. The hotel is renowned for food and wine. 3-Crown Commended. Golfing parties' tariff available.

The Grange & Links Hotel
Sea Lane,
Sandilands, Sutton-on-Sea,
Lincolnshire LN12 2RA.
Tel (01507) 441334 Fax (01507) 443033

3-Star 30-bedroom hotel with own 18-hole links course. Two tennis courts, snooker and ballroom. Award-winning hotel renowned for superb cuisine, friendliness, comfort and service.

Kenwick Park Hotel
Kenwick Park, Louth,
Lincolnshire LN11 8NR.
Tel (01507) 608806 Fax (01507) 608027

The Kenwick estate boasts magnificent settings for hotel, top class leisure club and superb golf course, comprising many tree lined fairways and water features. A relaxing retreat for golfers and their families.

North Shore Hotel Golf Club & Course
North Shore Road,
Skegness PE25 1DN.
Tel (01754) 763298 Fax (01754) 761902

A mature and challenging 18-hole part parkland and part links course with sea views on the edge of Skegness. Good all year round climate. Rarely closed in winter with no winter greens. Rarely closed bars, superb bar food and à la carte restaurant. 33 bedrooms available.

Petwood Hotel
Woodhall Spa,
Lincolnshire LN10 6QF.
Tel (01526) 352411 Fax (01526) 353473

Built at the turn of the century, this traditional country house is set in a 30-acre estate, close to Woodhall Spa's championship golf course. 47 en suite bedrooms. Snooker, croquet and putting. Popular restaurant specialising in local produce.

495

HORSTED PLACE HOTEL — EAST SUSSEX NATIONAL GOLF CLUB

setting the standard

Where else can you combine the grand luxury of a Victorian stately home with the excellence of two championship courses set in 1100 acres of majestic countryside? Only at the Horsted Place Hotel and East Sussex National Golf Club.

for more details call now on
01825 880088

East Sussex National, Little Horsted, Uckfield, East Sussex TN22 5ES

Golf Tours of Sussex

ASHDOWN FOREST GOLF HOTEL
Ideal Centre

- 2 Championship courses on site
- 14 courses within 20 minutes' drive
- 19 ensuite rooms
- Renowned à la carte restaurant
- Societies welcome - 7 days

Chapel Lane, Forest Row, East Sussex RH18 5BB
Tel: 01342 824866 Fax: 01342 824869
Email: enquiries@ashgolf.co.uk
Internet: http://www.ashgolf.co.uk

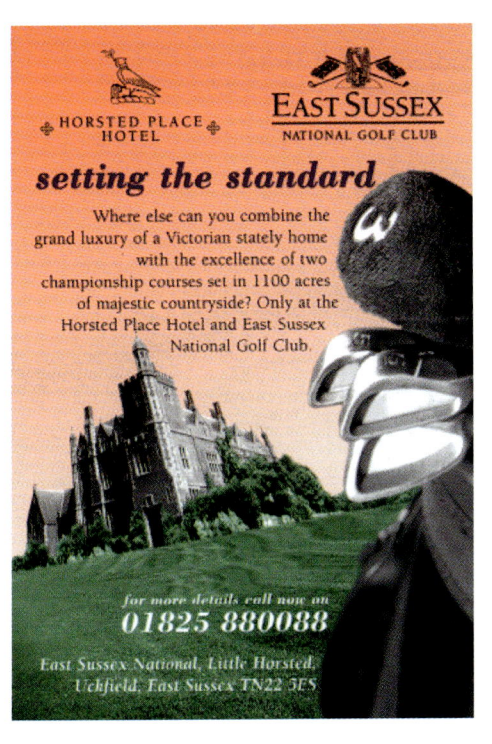

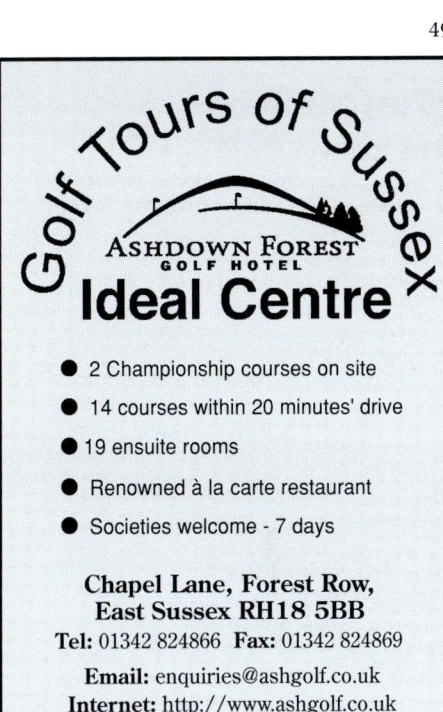

The Springs Hotel & Golf Club

"Your comfort and well-being are our priority"

Idyllic luxury is a fine example of this Victorian Tudor-style country house hotel. Built in 1874 with superb views overlooking the lake, infinite pains in choosing decor and furnishings have been taken to preserve the ambience but at the same time achieving the highest standards of modern comfort. The Brian Huggett-designed 18-hole 6,470 yards Par 72 course is a challenge to golfers of every standard. The clubhouse offers spike bar, restaurant, lounge, meeting room, well equipped changing rooms and pro-shop.

Private parties and conferences catered for.

**Wallingford Road,
North Stoke,
Wallingford,
Oxfordshire OX10 6BE**

Tel: (01491) 836687 Fax: (01491) 836877
e-mail: SpringsUK@aol.com

AA 2-Rosette Restaurant
AA/RAC 3 Star
RAC Awards of Merit

West Midlands

The Belfry
Wishaw, North Warwickshire B76 9PR.
Tel (01675) 470033 Fax (01675) 470256

The Belfry, venue for three Ryder Cup Matches and a unique fourth returning in 2001, is one of Europe's foremost business, golf and leisure resorts. Top class facilities includes 324 4-Star bedrooms, five restaurants, eight bars and Bel Air nightclub. Leisure facilities include gym, indoor pool, sauna, snooker and beautician to name but a few. Three golf courses including The Brabazon, PGA National and Derby courses. Floodlit driving range and putting green, largest on-course golf leisure and lifestyle shop in Europe. (De Vere Hotel Group - see advertisement page 499 for further details.

The Chequers Inn
Fladbury, Nr Pershore,
Worcestershire WR10 2PZ.
Tel (01386) 860276 Fax (01386) 861286

A 14th-century inn containing cosy beamed restaurant and bar with magnificent open fire. Situated between Evesham and Pershore on the edge of the Cotswolds. Golf breaks include four days golf at different courses and three nights dinner, bed and breakfast.

Ingon Manor Golf & Country Club
Ingon Lane, Snitterfield,
Nr Stratford upon Avon,
Warwickshire CV37 0QE.
Tel (01789) 731857 Fax (01789) 731657

Located two miles from Stratford, close to the A46. Par 72, 18-hole golf course 6,554 yards white tees, 6,091 yards yellow tees. Driving range and practice area. All day bar and catering. Accommodation available.

Marriott Forest of Arden Hotel & Country Club
Maxstoke Lane, Meriden,
Warwickshire CV7 7HR.
Tel (01676) 522335 Fax (01676) 523711

Set in 10,000 acres of Warwickshire countryside, the Forest of Arden, host to the 1998 One-2-One British Masters, offers some of Britain's best golfing alongside first class accommodation, leisure and conference facilities. Choice of the Aylesford course and the championship Arden course provides an enjoyable challenge for golfers of all abilities. Complimentary leisure facilities. *Marriott Group.*

Nailcote Hall Hotel
Nailcote Lane, Berkswell,
Warwickshire CV7 7DE.
Tel (01203) 466174 Fax (01203) 470720
www.nailcotehall.co.uk

Home of the British Professional Short Course. Delightful and challenging championship 9-hole par 3 course designed to test any golfers short game. Set in the grounds of this 17th-century black and white Jacobean country house hotel, used by Cromwell in the English Civil War.

Patshull Park Hotel Golf & Country Club
Pattingham, Shropshire WV6 7HR.
Tel (01902) 700100 Fax (01902) 700874

Parkland, lakeside 18-hole championship John Jacobs' designed course in grounds of the Earl of Dartmouth estate. Corporate, society and residential packages. 49 en suite bedrooms, swimming pool, leisure centre, gymnasium, fishing. Restaurant and Bunkers coffee shop.

Telford Golf & Country Club
Great Hay, Sutton Hill, Telford,
Shropshire TF7 4DT.
Tel (01952) 429977 Fax (01952) 586602

Overlooking the Ironbridge Gorge, the hotel offers its own 18-hole championship course. Floodlit driving range and practice areas. The extensive leisure facilities include squash courts, swimming pool, gymnasium, snooker, whirlpool, sauna/steam rooms. Resident masseur.

Welcombe Hotel & Golf Course
Warwick Road, Stratford-upon-Avon,
Warwickshire CV37 0NR.
Tel (01789) 295252 Fax (01789) 414666
Corporate Golf Office:
Tel/Fax (01789) 262665

A 4-Star Jacobean-style mansion house hotel with private 18-hole championship golf course set in 157 acres of wooded parkland with picturesque lakes. Corporate golf and green fees most welcome.

Whitefields Hotel Golf & Country Club
Coventry Road, Thurlaston, Nr Rugby,
Warwickshire CV23 9JR.
Tel (01788) 521800 Fax (01788) 521695

18-hole course 6,223 yards. Driving range, putting green 18. Four conference rooms. 33 en suite rooms. Bars and à la carte restaurant.

BOTLEY PARK HOTEL
GOLF & COUNTRY CLUB
Winchester Road, Boorley Green, Botley,
Hampshire SO3 2UA

★★★★ STAR

Beautifully set in 176 acres of the rolling Hampshire countryside the Botley Park offers comfort and excellent service to all guests. Enjoy superb cuisine in our excellent restaurant.
100 beautifully placed bedrooms, all en suite with colour TV and tea-coffee-making facilities. Club members and residents' leisure bar serving food all day.
Indoor pool, jacuzzi, gym, sauna, steam room and solaria. Two indoor squash courts. 3 all-weather tennis courts and our challenging 18-hole par 70 golf course and driving range practice area.

TEL: (01489) 780888   FAX: (01489) 789242

SOUTH LODGE HOTEL is a fine Victorian country house set in 93 acres of secluded wooded parkland with views over the South Downs. Delicious cuisine by Chef Lewis Hamblet, using local game and fish, with soft fruits and herbs from the hotel's own walled garden. Superbly appointed bedrooms and suites, each individually decorated in true country house style. Enjoy tennis, croquet, petanque, putting, snooker or

golf at our two spectacular 18-hole championship courses at Mannings Heath Golf Club (established 1905).

South Lodge is the perfect location for London and the south coast and for many famous gardens and national properties in the area.

For further information on our GOLFING BREAK PACKAGES please contact:

SOUTH LODGE HOTEL
Brighton Road, Lower Beeding,
Nr Horsham, W Sussex RH13 6PS.
Tel: (01403) 891711 Fax: (01403) 891766
E-mail: inquiries@southlodgehotel.dial.iql.co.uk
http://www.southlodgehotel.co.uk

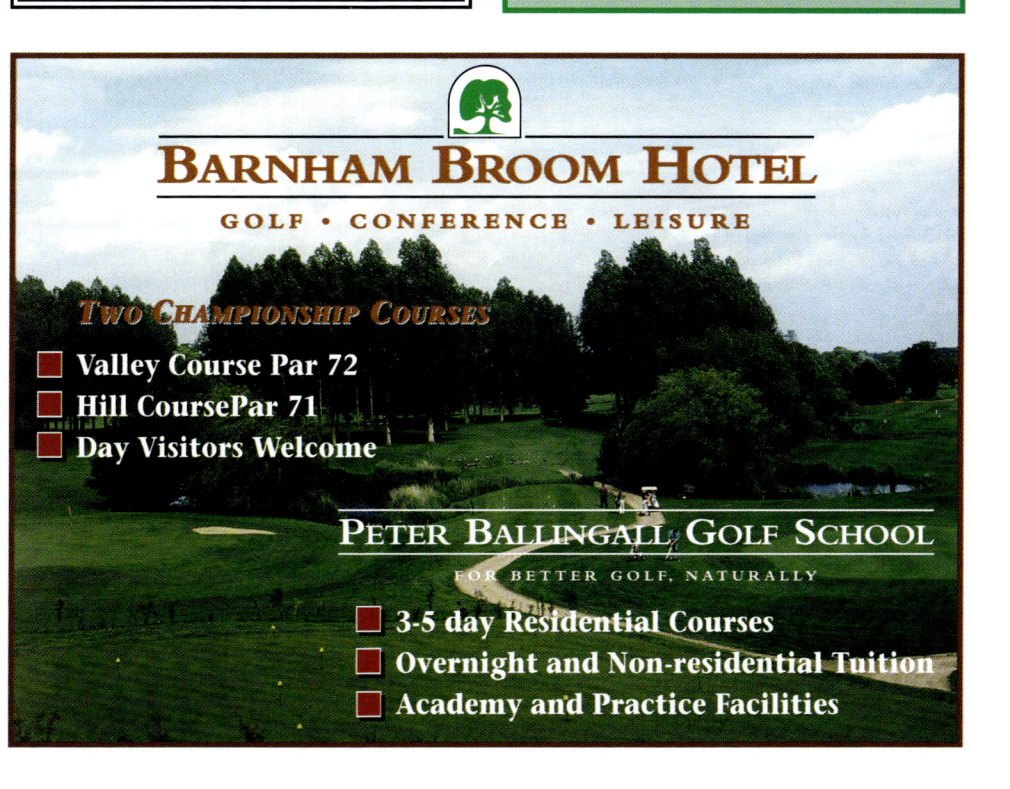

BARNHAM BROOM HOTEL
GOLF • CONFERENCE • LEISURE

TWO CHAMPIONSHIP COURSES

- Valley Course Par 72
- Hill Course Par 71
- Day Visitors Welcome

PETER BALLINGALL GOLF SCHOOL
FOR BETTER GOLF, NATURALLY

- 3-5 day Residential Courses
- Overnight and Non-residential Tuition
- Academy and Practice Facilities

Societies welcome seven days. Call the secretary on 01788 815555. Reservations 01788 521800.

Yorkshire & Humberside

Aldwark Manor Hotel
Golf & Country Club
Aldwark, Alne, York, Yorkshire YO61 1UF.
(Hotel) Tel (01347) 838146
(Golf) Tel (01347) 838353
Fax (01347) 838867

This fully restored Victorian manor offers its guests all modern facilities with superb food, wine and country location to complement the 18-hole par 71 parkland course, which holds many surprises for our visitors. Open all year round to non-residents. Twelve miles from York and Harrogate on the river Ure. (See advertisement page 501 for further details.)

Cave Castle Golf Hotel
South Cave, Brough,
East Yorkshire HU15 2EU.
Tel (01430) 421286 Fax (01430) 421118

Superb manor house in 160 acres of parkland situated at foot of the Wolds. Five minutes from M62 motorway link and fifteen minutes from Hull. 25 en suite bedrooms with restaurant, function and conference facilities. Own 18-hole golf course 6,524 yards SSS 71. Golf breaks, societies and non-members welcome.

Central Hotel - Scarborough
1-3 The Crescent, Scarborough,
Yorkshire YO11 2PW.
Tel (01723) 365766 Fax (01723) 367433

Refurbished, elegant Georgian hotel in town centre. Own car park. 30 fully equipped en suite rooms. Public bar. Food served from 12 noon to midnight every day. Pool table. Lift to all floors. Five golf courses within 20 mile radius.

De Vere Oulton Hall
Rothwell Lane, Oulton, Leeds LS26 8HN.
Tel 0113-282 1000 Fax 0113-282 0066

This elegant 5-Star Yorkshire hotel complete with 19th-century style formal gardens, is situated adjacent to the Oulton Park Golf Club where guests have the choice of either 18- or 9-hole courses set in spectacular countryside. Facilities also include a 22-bay driving range. 152 luxury bedrooms. Leisure club featuring indoor pool, sauna, steam room and two superb restaurants. (De Vere Hotel Group - see advertisement page 4 for details.)

Hotel Majestic - Scarborough
57 Northstead Manor Drive,
Scarborough,
North Yorkshire YO12 6AG.
Tel/Fax (01723) 363806

Privately owned hotel overlooking Peasholm Park. Minutes from Northcliffe golf course. All 19 bedrooms have en suite, double glazed, fully centrally heated. Cocktail bar. Draught beers. Golf parties welcomed. Flexible evening dinner times can be arranged.

Marriott Hollins Hall
Hotel & Country Club
Hollins Hill,
Baildon, Shipley,
West Yorkshire BD17 7QW.
Tel (01274) 530053 Fax (01274) 530187

An exceptionally attractive hotel built in Elizabethan style in the 19th-century. Magnificent views over the stunning Aire Valley and yet only minutes from Leeds and Bradford city centres. A new classically designed 18-hole 6,698 yards course, due to open in Spring 1999, is set in natural heathland and is both majestic and challenging to USPGA specifications. Complimentary leisure facilities. *Marriott Hotel Group.*

Rudding Park Hotel
Follifoot, Harrogate,
North Yorkshire HG3 1JH.
Tel (01423) 871350 Fax (01423) 872286

Rudding Park, situated two and half miles south of Harrogate, is the ideal venue for the discerning golfer. It offers a contemporary 4-Star AA/RAC hotel as well as an 18-hole, par 72 parkland golf course. (See advertisement page 499 for further details.)

Sea Brink Hotel
3 The Beach,
Filey,
North Yorkshire YO14 9LA.
Tel (01723) 513257 Fax (01723) 514139

ETB 3-Crown Commended; AA/RAC 2-Star. Traditional seafront hotel overlooking beautiful Filey Bay. 9 en suite rooms, many with sea views. Centrally heated, colour TV, telephone, clock radio and hospitality tray. Licensed restaurant and coffee shop. Five golf courses nearby including Ganton.

499

Rudding Park
*Follifoot, Harrogate,
North Yorkshire HG3 1JH*

A COMPLETE GOLFING EXPERIENCE

YORKSHIRE'S PREMIER PARKLAND COURSE

CORPORATE & SOCIETY DAYS WELCOME

18 HOLE PARKLAND COURSE

PGA TEACHING ACADEMY

FLOODLIT DRIVING RANGE

FRIENDLY CLUBHOUSE

WELL STOCKED SHOP

AA/RAC 4-STAR HOTEL

REGENCY PERIOD CONFERENCE & BANQUETING VENUE

RUDDING PARK GOLF
Tel: 01423 872100
Fax: 01423 873011

RUDDING PARK HOTEL
Tel: 01423 871350
Fax: 01423 872286

YORKSHIRE'S HOTEL, GOLF & CONFERENCE RESORT

The Belfry

A 'BREATH OF FRESH AIR'

In the Heart of England

The Belfry is considered to be the best located business, golf and leisure resort in the UK, set in 500 acres of beautiful North Warwickshire countryside and minutes from Birmingham International Airport, the NEC and the M42.

- Famous venue of three Ryder Cup Matches.
- 324 bedrooms and fully equipped leisure club.
- 21 conference and meeting rooms.
- 3 golf courses, including the world famous Brabazon.
- 5 restaurants, 8 bars and Bel Air Nightclub, all open to the public.
- The largest on-course golf, leisure and lifestyle shop in Europe.

RYDER CUP VENUE 2001

THE BELFRY WISHAW NORTH WARWICKSHIRE B76 9PR TELEPHONE 01675 470033 FACSIMILE 01675 470256
E-MAIL belfry@airtime.co.uk

North West

The Allerdale Court Hotel
Market Place, Cockermouth,
Cumbria CA13 9NQ.
Tel (01900) 823654 Fax (01900) 823033

3-Crown Commended. Excellent restaurant, 24 en suite rooms, well stocked 19th hole. Two miles from Cockermouth golf club and near to Keswick and Silloth courses. Good value package deals for groups, societies and individuals.

Carden Park Hotel Golf Resort & Spa
Nr Chester, Cheshire CH3 9DQ.
Tel (01829) 731000 Fax (01829) 731032

Set in 750-acres of beautiful Cheshire countryside near Chester. A true golf resort with two 18-hole golf courses - the mature Cheshire course and the new Nicklaus course, the 9-hole par 3 Azalea course and Europe's first Jack Nicklaus Residential Golf School. The superb AA/RAC 4-Star hotel also has an extensive spa and there are many other leisure facilities on the estate. For further information and a brochure call Liz Mole on 01829 731000. (See advertisement page 501 for further details.)

Clifton Arms Hotel
West Beach, Lytham, Lancashire FY8 5QJ.
Tel (01253) 739898 Fax (01253) 730657

The Clifton Arms Hotel is set in the picturesque town of Lytham, overlooking Lytham Green and seafront. Ideally situated for all local golf courses, including Royal Lytham, Fairhaven, Greendrive and Old Links.

Crimond Hotel
28 Knowsley Road, Southport PR9 0HN.
Tel (01704) 536456 Fax (01704) 548643

4-Crown rated hotel with 17 bedrooms en suite. Heated indoor swimming pool and jacuzzi. Fully licensed with excellent cuisine. Ideally located within 12 golf courses within half an hour's drive.

De Vere Hotel Blackpool
East Park Drive, Blackpool,
Lancashire FY3 8LL.
Tel (01253) 838866 Fax (01253) 798800

De Vere Hotel Blackpool adds a touch of 4-Star elegance to one of Europe's most popular tourist destinations. Extensive facilities include: 164 bedrooms, first class restaurant, five bars, six conference rooms, indoor swimming pool, 18-bay floodlit driving range and an 18-hole championship golf course designed by Peter Alliss and Clive Clark. The course regularly hosts corporate golf and society days and was the recent venue for both the PGA Northern Championship and Reebok PGA and Lancashire Open. (De Vere Hotel Group - see advertisement page 4 for further details.)

De Vere Mottram Hall
Wilmslow Road,
Mottram St Andrew,
Prestbury, Cheshire SK10 4QT.
Tel (01625) 828135 Fax (01625) 828950

Mottram Hall is an elegant 18th-century Georgian building, set in secluded parkland with delightful ornamental gardens and lake. The 4-Star hotel has 132 luxury bedrooms, conference facilities for up to 275 guests, a superb leisure club, and 18-hole championship golf course designed by international golf architect Dave Thomas. Leisure facilities include spacious swimming pool, spa, saunas and steam rooms, fully equipped gym - even a full sized soccer pitch utilised by European football champions, Germany, who stayed here in 1966. (De Vere Hotel Group - see advertisement page 4 for further details.)

The Dormy House
Royal Lytham & St Anne's Golf Club
Links Gate,
Lytham St Anne's,
Lancashire FY8 3LQ.
Tel (01253) 724206 Fax (01253) 780946

Ideal for small parties wishing to play the championship course. Accommodation for men only. Apply to the assistant secretary. (See advertisement page 27 for further details.)

The Fishermans Arms Hotel
The Coast Road,
Baycliff,
Ulverston, Cumbria LA12 9RJ.
Tel (01229) 869267

Family run hotel built and styled in 1930's decor. Overlooking Morecombe Bay the ever changing real ales and good food add to the warm and welcoming atmosphere of the establishment. Nearest hotel to the Ulverston course.

St. David's Park Hotel Golf Club

EXCELLENCE *in* BUSINESS, GOLF *and* LEISURE

St. David's Park Hotel and Northop Country Park Golf Club offer luxury accommodation and superb facilities second to none, including our *championship 18 hole golf course, swimming pool, tennis courts, pro-shop, gymnasium and renowned restaurants.*

for further information please
TELEPHONE:
01244 520800
St. David's Park, Ewloe, Nr. Chester, Flintshire, CH5 3YB.

CARDEN PARK HOTEL, GOLF RESORT & SPA
NEAR CHESTER, CHESHIRE CH3 9DQ

Only 30 minutes from the M6 and 45 minutes from Manchester Airport, Carden Park is set in 750 acres of beautiful Cheshire countryside near the historical old city of Chester.

A truly complete golf resort with two 18 hole golf courses - the mature Cheshire Course and the new Nicklaus Course, the 9 hole par 3 Azalea Course and the magnificent Jack Nicklaus Residential Golf School - the first in Europe.

The superb AA/RAC **** Hotel and luxurious clubhouse offer a range of dining options, and there is an extensive Spa as well as many other leisure facilities on the Estate.

For further information and a brochure please call Liz Mole on
01829 731000

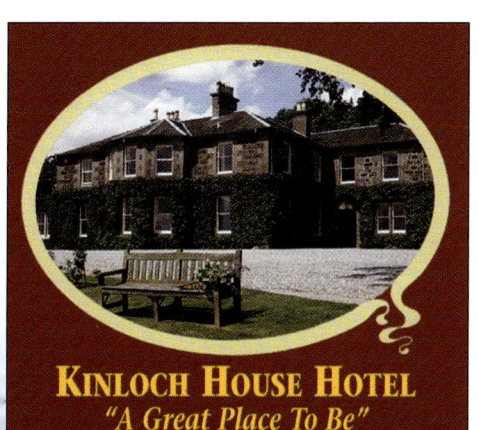

KINLOCH HOUSE HOTEL
"A Great Place To Be"

Built in 1840, and in the same ownership since 1981, Kinloch House is set in 25 acres of wooded parkland, and is a fine example of a Scottish country house. All rooms and suites traditionally furnished to the highest standard and fully en suite. One of the top dining venues in Scotland complemented by the choice of an extensive wine list.

We offer an almost unique proposition for golfers. 35 courses within an hour's drive. Planning of rounds and tee-times all taken care of.
Health and fitness includes sauna, steam room, spa, exercise pool and gym.

Tel: (01250) 884237
Fax: (01250) 884333
by Blairgowrie, Perthshire PH10 6SG

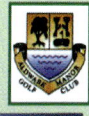

ALDWARK MANOR
HOTEL GOLF & COUNTRY CLUB

This fully restored Victorian manor offers its guests all modern facilities with superb food, wine and country location to complement the 18-hole par 71 parkland course, which holds many surprises for our visitors. Open all year round to non-residents. Twelve miles from York and Harrogate on the river Ure.

★ **28 Individually designed bedrooms**
★ **Excellent dining facilities**
★ **Full bar facilities**

For further information and reservations please telephone
(01347) 838146 (Hotel) 838353 (Golf)
Fax (01347) 838867
Aldwark, Alne, York YO61 1UF

The George Hotel – Penrith
**Devonshire Street, Penrith,
Cumbria CA11 7SU.
Tel (01768) 862696 Fax (01768) 868223**

Privately owned hotel. All rooms with private facilities, TV, direct dial telephone, hospitality tray, radio and baby listening system. Private car park. Double or twin room from £58.00. Single room from £42.75inclusive of VAT and full English breakfast.

Llyndir Hall Hotel
**Llyndir Lane, Rossett,
Nr Chester LL12 0AY.
Tel (01244) 571648 Fax (01244) 571258**

Set in peaceful countryside six miles from the historic city of Chester. AA 3-Star hotel with leisure facilities. 38 bedrooms all en suite with satellite TV. Formal dining and Redwoods Brasserie. Located close to many superb golf courses.

Marriott Manchester Hotel & Country Club
**Worsley Park, Worsley,
Manchester M28 2QT.
Tel 0161-975 2000 Fax 0161-799 6341**

The hotel is set in the historic 200-acre Worsley Park and yet only seven miles from Manchester City centre. The 6,638 yards golf course with strategic positioning of pot bunkers and water hazards provides an exciting challenge to golfers of all abilities. With PGA professionals on hand, group clinics and video services available we can guarantee your golf event will be a huge success. Complimentary leisure facilities. *Marriott Hotel Group.*

Martin Lane Farmhouse Holiday Cottages
**Martin Lane, Burscough,
Nr Southport, Lancashire L40 8JH.
Tel/Fax (01704) 893527**

e-mail: Martinlanefarmhouse@btinternet.com
Our comfortable, first class cottages are the ideal base for a relaxed golfing holiday. Over 20 golf courses within a 15 mile radius ranging from easy walking parkland to testing links. Catering can be arranged if required.

Metropole Hotel
**3 Portland Street, Southport,
Merseyside PR8 1LL.
Tel (01704) 536836 Fax (01704) 549041**

RAC/AA 2-Star hotel. Centrally situated and close to Royal Birkdale and other championship courses. Fully licensed - late bar facilities for residents. Full size snooker table. Reduced rates for golfers. Golfing proprietors will assist with tee reservations.

Pheasant Inn
**Casterton,
Kirkby Lonsdale,
Cumbria LA6 2RX.
Tel/Fax (015242) 71230**

18th-century residential inn adjacent to the 18-hole Kirkby Lonsdale and 9-hole Casterton golf courses. Comfortable en suite bedrooms. Cask ales, excellent wine list. *Good Pub Guide* recommended. Only ten minutes from the M6 motorway.

The Prince of Wales Hotel
**Lord Street,
Southport,
Merseyside PR8 1JS.
Tel (01704) 536688 Fax (01704) 543922**

Since 1876 the Prince of Wales Hotel has been the premier hotel in Southport - the Golfers' Paradise. Used as the base for the Ryder Cup and British Open over the years, the hotel provides quality 4-Star accommodation. 103 rooms, two restaurants and bars. We are able to arrange tee-times at any of the twelve courses in the area including Royal Birkdale. The hotel, located centrally in Southport, offers free car parking.

The Royal Hotel – Kirkby Lonsdale
**Market Place,
Kirkby Lonsdale,
Cumbria LA6 2AE
Tel (015242) 71217 Fax (015242) 72228**

Situated in the main square The Royal is a fine old building. With 17 en suite and 4 non-en suite bedrooms. Ideal for party groups. With two bars, dining room, lounge - and three real log fires.

St David's Park Hotel
**St David's Park,
Ewloe, Nr Chester, Flintshire CH5 3YB.
Tel (01244) 520800 Fax (01244) 520930**

AA 4-Star hotel with extensive leisure facilities, including gym and swimming pool. 145 bedrooms and suites, excellent restaurant. Northop Country Park Golf Club only five minutes away, and Carden Park Golf Resort 20 minutes. Special golf packages available. (See advertisement page 501 for further details.)

TILLMOUTH PARK
COUNTRY HOUSE HOTEL

Hotel of the year 1997

Tillmouth Park, a superb Baronial Country House, was built by the renowned architect Charles Barry in 1882 using stones from nearby Twizel Castle. Sit in its Galleried Lounge and you'll feel yourself relax into a more leisured bygone age. Set in 15 acres of secluded parkland, high above the river Till, Tillmouth Park boasts 14 individual styled en-suite bedrooms, AA award-winning cuisine and is the ultimate venue for peace and tranquility. Only nine miles from the A1 at Berwick-upon-Tweed, at the gateway to the Borders, Tillmouth Park makes an ideal base from which to enjoy world-class golf without the crowds. 18 golf courses within a 50 mile radius of the hotel. Elegant private lounge and dining facilities for groups.

For further information contact Tillmouth Park Country House Hotel, Cornhill-on-Tweed, Northumberland TD12 4UU.
Tel: (01890) 882255 Fax: (01890) 882540

AA-72% ❀ Rosette Award • ETB 4-Crown Highly Commended

Ramside Hall Hotel & GOLF CLUB

3-Star, 4-Crown Highly Commended

THE NORTH EAST'S PREMIER PRIVATELY OWNED HOTEL
— WITH GOLF —

This marvellous 80-bedroom hotel, renowned for its popular bars and good food has 27 holes of golf with a magnificent driving range and practice areas which opened in April 1996.

FOR DETAILS OF THE NORTH EAST'S BEST KEPT SECRET

Ramside Hall Hotel
Carrville, Durham DH1 1TD.
Tel: 0191-386 5282
Fax: 0191-386 0399

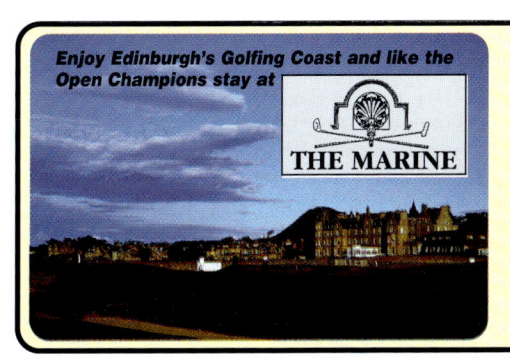

See pages 479 & 504 for more details

Enjoy Edinburgh's Golfing Coast and like the Open Champions stay at

THE MARINE

Play Muirfield, Gullane, North Berwick, Whitekirk, Dunbar, Longniddry, Royal Musselburgh, Kilspindie and a dozen other first class courses within a few minutes of the hotel. With 83 bedrooms which offer the best 3-Star food, service and facilities in the county and we overlook the golf course and the beach.

The Marine Hotel, Cromwell Road, North Berwick EH39 4LZ.
Tel: 01620 892406 Fax 01620 894480

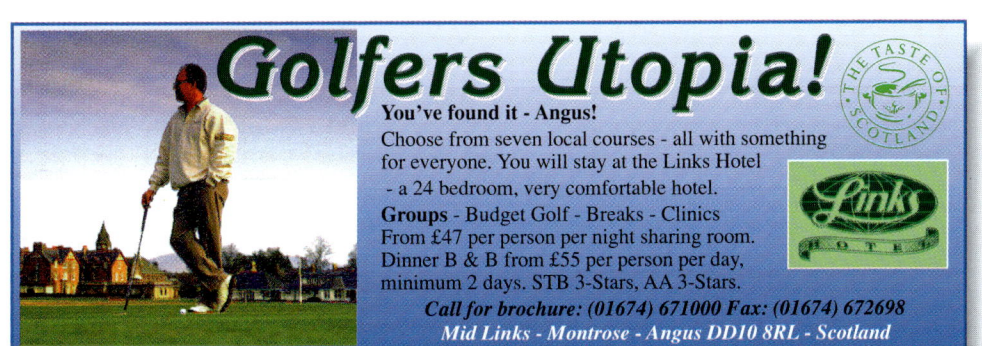

Golfers Utopia!

THE TASTE OF SCOTLAND

You've found it - Angus!
Choose from seven local courses - all with something for everyone. You will stay at the Links Hotel - a 24 bedroom, very comfortable hotel.
Groups - Budget Golf - Breaks - Clinics
From £47 per person per night sharing room. Dinner B & B from £55 per person per day, minimum 2 days. STB 3-Stars, AA 3-Stars.

Links HOTEL

Call for brochure: (01674) 671000 Fax: (01674) 672698
Mid Links - Montrose - Angus DD10 8RL - Scotland

The Stanley Arms
Calderbridge, Seascale,
Cumbria CA20 1DN.
Tel (01946) 841235 Fax (01946) 841759

Former coaching inn ideally situated for west Cumbrian golf courses. Private salmon and sea trout fishing in grounds. 12 en suite bedrooms.

Isle of Man

Castletown Golf Links Hotel
Derbyhaven, Castletown,
Isle of Man IM9 1UA.
Tel (01624) 822201 Fax (01624) 625535

Situated on our own peninsula, our championship golf course of 6,700 yards, with all holes having sea views, is a real test of links golf. Hotel facilities are of a luxurious 3-Star standard.

North East

De Vere Slaley Hall
Slale, Hexham,
Northumberland NE47 0BY.
Tel (01434) 673350 Fax (01434) 673962

Set in 1000 acres of prime Northumberland countryside yet only 30 minutes' drive from the provincial capital of Newcastle upon Tyne, Slaley Hall is one of the UK's finest golf resorts. The Edwardian stately home has been integrated into a luxury 139 bedroom hotel with a range of facilities including a leisure club with 20 metre pool and gym, health and beauty spa: extensive function suites and Fairways Restaurant. The Dave Thomas designed championship course is a regular venue on the PGA European Tour and it has earned the reputation as one of Britain's most scenic and challenging courses. A second championship course will open in April 1999. (De Vere Hotel Group - see advertisement page 4 for further details.)

Linden Hall Golf Club
Longhorsley, Morpeth,
Northumberland NE65 8XF.
Tel (01670) 788050 Fax (01670) 788544

Linden Hall Golf Club is located within the grounds of Linden Hall Hotel, a 4-Star luxury country house hotel. The 18-hole, 6,809 yard SSS 73 golf course, recently voted one of the ten best new golf courses built in the British Isles since 1996 by *Golf World*, is set within mature woodland, rolling parkland with established burns and lakes amidst a stunning backdrop of the Cheviot hills and Northumbrian coastline.

Ramside Hall Hotel & Golf Club
Carrville, Durham DH1 1TD.
Tel 0191-386 5282 Fax 0191-386 0399

Set in 220 acres on the outskirts of the cathedral city of Durham and surrounded by a stimulating 27-hole golf course. 3-Star; 4-Crown Highly Commended. 80 luxury bedrooms, restaurant, grill room and carvery. Conference and banqueting facilities. Superb floodlit driving range and practice areas. (See advertisement page 503 for further details.)

Tillmouth Park Country House Hotel
Cornhill-on-Tweed,
Northumberland TD12 4UU.
Tel (01890) 882255 Fax (01890) 882540

AA 76%; AA Rosette Award: ETB 4-Crown Highly Commended; Les Routiers Hotel of the Year 1997. Magnificent award-winning secluded Victorian mansion. Perfect venue for world class golf, without crowds, in the English and Scottish Borders. 18 golf courses within 50 mile radius. Elegant private lounge and dining facilities for groups. (See advertisement page 503 for further details.)

White Swan Hotel
Bondgate Within, Alnwick,
Northumberland NE66 1TD.
Tel (01665) 602109 Fax (01665) 504100

AA 3-Star 17th-century coaching inn. Over ten courses within 25 miles. Packages arranged, tee-times booked. Spectacular coastline. Also racing breaks. Visit our magnificent Olympic suite from the Titanic's sister ship.

SCOTLAND

Scottish Borders

Castle Hotel - Coldstream
11 High Street, Coldstream,
Berwickshire TD12 4AP.
Tel/Fax (01890) 882830

Small family run hotel offering en suite accommodation 400 metres from Hirsel Golf Club, Kelso club eight miles, Berwick club fourteen miles. Public bar open all day. B&B £25 per person.

Letham Grange Resort
& Golf Courses

Set in 350 acres of mature woodland estate, Letham Grange offers luxurious accommodation, the finest of international cuisine, and the best of Scottish hospitality. 36 holes of magnificent golf! Widely acclaimed as one of the premier courses in Scotland, the Championship standard Old Course is both scenic and dramatic - with water playing a major role. The New Course, although slightly shorter, offers golfers a more relaxed and less arduous round. However, it can be deceptive! Situated in the heartland of golf, Letham Grange is the ideal base - the leading hotel in 'Carnoustie Country'

For your golfing holiday, or a pleasant day's golf, contact us now for further information.

SPECIAL EAGLE GOLF BREAKS AND SOCIETY PACKAGES

Colliston by Arbroath DD11 4RL Tel: (01241) 890373 Fax: (01241) 890725

RCI

KILCONQUHAR CASTLE ESTATE

INTERVAL INTERNATIONAL.
THE QUALITY VACATION EXCHANGE NETWORK

Scotland's Premier Holiday Resort

Nestling in over 100 acres of woodlands and manicured gardens and just one hours drive to the cultural city of Edinburgh

If you're... looking for a unique holiday experience with...

... superb luxurious accommodation of 2-, 3- and 4-bedroom villas and castle suites ...

... with quaint local fishing villages ...

... horse riding available, golf nearby, indoor heated swimming pool and ...

... situated in the "Glorious Kingdom of Fife", Scotland with St Andrews close by – "The Home of Golf"...

Well... you've found it!

Kilconquhar with it's 12th century castle offers memorable quality holidays 365 days a year, exacting standards with excellent facilities, this ancestral home of *"Robert the Bruce"* offers guests the *'magic'* you've been looking for including fine dining in the Lindsay Room.

Save up to £100.00 per weeks holiday on all bookings made for 1999 prior to 31 March 1999 (subject to availability).

Call our Reservations now on 01333 340501
to receive a complimentary holiday video and brochure.

Ask about our late break offers for that well deserved Golfing Holiday!
Prices available on request.

County Hotel - Selkirk
3-5 High Street, Selkirk TD7 4BZ.
Tel/Fax (01750) 21233

16th-century coaching inn. All rooms en suite. Excellent menu and wine list at reasonable prices. *Freedom of the Fairways* 3-5 day passport. 19 courses within 25 miles. Cost per round £7.00 approximately.

Cross Keys Inn
Ettrickbridge, Selkirk TD7 5JN.
Tel/Fax (01750) 52224

Surrounded by several scenic courses, set in the heart of the Scottish Borders, this small family run 17th-century coaching inn offers 5 en suite rooms and 5 self-catering cottages. Price per person sharing from three nights B&B including golf £125.00, five nights £200.

Kingsknowes Hotel
1 Selkirk Road, Galashiels TD1 3HY.
Tel (01896) 758375 Fax (01896) 750377

AA/RAC 3-Star; STB 4-Crown. Owned and run by golfing family who can book and organise your golf. Beautifully situated and centrally located. Excellent bedrooms, cuisine and service.

The Marine Hotel
Cromwell Road,
North Berwick,
East Lothian EH39 4LZ.
Tel (01620) 892406 Fax (01620) 894480

Superb 83-bedroom sporting hotel overlooking the North Berwick West Links with fabulous sea and golfing views. Home-from-home for many of the world's top golfers and famed for friendly service and traditional value for money holidays. For non-golfers there is swimming, tennis and snooker. Families, individuals and golfing parties enjoy the relaxed atmosphere of this all-year-round holiday hotel. Special seasonal leisure breaks and holiday rates. (See advertisement page 503 for further details.)

The Roxburghe Hotel & Golf Course
Kelso,
Roxburghshire TD5 8JZ.
Tel (01573) 450331 Fax (01573) 450611

22-bedroom hotel owned by the Duke and Duchess of Roxburghe. Luxury accommodation, superb cuisine. The 18-hole championship standard Roxburghe golf course, designed by Dave Thomas, surrounds the hotel.

Tweeddale Arms Hotel
High Street, Gifford,
East Lothian EH41 4QU.
Tel (01620) 810240 Fax (01620) 810488

Situated in the conservation village of Gifford eighteen miles from Edinburgh. We have eighteen of the finest golf courses to cater for everyone, from novice to champion, all within 20 minutes of the hotel. In addition to the excellent amenities and outstanding personal service the hotel offers warmth and hospitality in the true Scottish tradition.

South

Auchen Castle Hotel
Beattock, Moffat,
Dumfries-shire DG10 9SH.
Tel (01683) 300407 Fax (01683) 300667

This beautiful mansion, just off the A74, is convenient to Moffat, Lockerbie, Dumfries and Powfoot golf courses. The excellent restaurant, elegant rooms, private trout loch and gardens, all make for an ideal golfing break.

Cally Palace Hotel
Gatehouse of Fleet DG7 2DL.
Tel (01557) 814341 Fax (01557) 814522

This award-winning 4-Star country mansion has its own exclusive par 70, 18-hole golf course sculpted perfectly into the surrounding 150 acres of mature parkland. Other facilities include fishing loch and leisure complex.

Clonyard House Hotel
Colvend, Dalbeattie, Kirkshire DG5 4QW.
Tel (01556) 630372 Fax (01556) 630422

Family run country hotel in quiet grounds. Excellent restaurant, also informal meals in our lively bar. Ground floor rooms with facilities including direct dial telephone. Five golf courses within a ten mile radius, including Southerness. Double room £32.50 per person. Special rates for golfing parties.

Douglas Arms Hotel
King Street, Castle Douglas,
Kirkcudbrightshire DG7 1DB.
Tel (01556) 502231 Fax (01556) 504000

Situated at the centre of Galloway and with over 20 courses within one hour's drive, the hotel has 24 en suite bedrooms, a popular restaurant and two friendly bars. Private and secure car parking.

507

Dalmunzie House Hotel
the hotel in the hills

This family-run country house hotel has 17 bedrooms, 16 with private bathrooms, traditional Scottish cooking, open fires and personal service. On the doorstep is our own 9-hole golf course, and within an hour's drive are some of Scotland's finest courses.

For a brochure, please contact
Alexandra and Simon Winton,
Dalmunzie House Hotel,
Spittal O' Glenshee, Blairgowrie, Perthshire,
Scotland PH10 7QG.

Tel: Glenshee (01250) 885224 Fax: (01250) 885225

**AA • TASTE OF SCOTLAND
STB 3-STAR • AA ONE ROSETTE

PARK HOTEL
40 Coupar Angus Road,
Dundee DD2 3HY.

Tel:
01382 610691

Fax:
01382 612633

COMMENDED

■ Conveniently situated, within easy access of city centre and roads to Edinburgh and Aberdeen.

■ 11 comfortable bedrooms all with private facilities, TV and direct dial telephone.

■ Quality food served throughout the day.

■ Ideal venue for functions and meetings.

■ The perfect base from which to visit the excellent golf courses in the area.

For details call 01382 610691

CULLODEN HOUSE
MILTON OF CULLODEN, INVERNESS IV2 7BZ

*E*asy access and a short drive to Royal Dornoch, Nairn and 28 other golf courses. This STB/AA 4-Star historical Georgian country house, originally a Jacobean Castle dating back to Bonnie Prince Charlie, sits in 40 acres of tranquil parkland with lawns large enough for helicopters or a marquee for wedding celebrations. Only minutes from Dalcross airport and Inverness.

ON-SITE OR ON-COURSE
PGA INSTRUCTION/TOUR.

Tel 0800-980-4561
Fax (01463) 792181
USA Toll-free Fax 0044-1-800-3737987

Central & East

Balbirnie House Hotel
**Balbirnie Park, Markinch,
by Glenrothes, Fife KY7 6NE.
Tel (01592) 610066 Fax (01592) 610529**

Balbirnie is an elegant 18th-century mansion in a 416 acre park. AA 4-Red Star; 5-Crown Deluxe STB with 30 rooms/suites. Ideally located for Ladybank, St Andrews, Carnoustie. Balbirnie Park Golf Course within the Park.

Chapelbank House Hotel
**69 East High Street, Forfar DD8 2EP.
Tel (01307) 463151 Fax (01307) 461922**

An attractive farmhouse with a renowned restaurant serving à la carte lunch and table d hôte dinner. The 4 rooms are all en suite with colour TV, tea/coffee-making facilities, trouser press, hairdryer and telephone. Ten minutes drive from Forfar golf club and within easy travelling distance of Kirriemuir, Carnoustie and Alych golf clubs. Family run, friendly 4-Star hotel.

Crusoe Hotel
**2 Main Street, Lower Largo, Fife KY8 6BT.
Tel (01333) 320759 Fax (01333) 320865**

The Crusoe Hotel is ideally situated at the village harbour, and most bedrooms have superb views overlooking Largo Bay. In this historic setting you will find excellent cuisine and comfortable accommodation. Discount given for groups of eight plus.

Dalmunzie House Hotel
**Spittal O'Glenshee,
Blairgowrie,
Perthshire PH10 7QG.
Tel (01250) 885224 Fax (01250) 885225**

Set in the Highlands with our own 9-hole course. This friendly country house offers an ideal base for a golfing holiday with excellent local courses at Blairgowrie, Pitlochry, Alyth and many more. AA Rosette for food. (See advertisement page 507 for further details.)

De Vere Cameron House
**Loch Lomond,
Dunbartonshire G83 8QZ.
Tel (01389) 755565 Fax (01389) 759522**

4-Star. Ancestral home of the Smollett family and 18th-century historian and novelist Tobias, Cameron House is a magnificent award-winning hotel with one of the finest views in the world, overlooking Loch Lomond. Set in its own estate, including a mile of loch shoreline and 108 acres of lawns, gardens, a 9-hole golf course, and mature woodland. Cameron House even has its own motor cruiser. Other facilities include 96 luxury en suite bedrooms, a superb leisure club with indoor pool, sauna, steam room and solarium and three different restaurants serving exquisite cuisine. (De Vere Hotel Group - see advertisement page 4 for further details.)

Drumoig Golf Club & Hotel
**Drumoig, Leuchars,
St Andrews,
Fife KY16 0BE.
Tel (01382) 541800 Fax (01382) 542211**

Superb new golf hotel only ten minutes from St Andrews. 24 fully equipped en suite lodge bedrooms, well stocked bar, lounge and à la carte restaurant. Own 18-hole tournament standard golf course. Ideally located for touring Fife, Tayside and Perthshire.

Goldenstones Hotel
**Queens Road, Dunbar,
East Lothian EH42 1LG.
Tel (01368) 862356 Fax (01368) 865644**

STB 3-Crown. We can arrange tee-times for you at some of the finest Scottish golf courses, including Muirfield, Dunbar and North Berwick. There are nineteen superb courses all within half an hour of the hotel. £27.00 B&B.

Golf Hotel - North Berwick
**34 Dirleton Avenue,
North Berwick,
East Lothian EH39 4BH.
Tel (01620) 892202 Fax (01620) 892290**

Family run hotel ideal for golfers wishing to play any of East Lothian's eighteen courses. Starting times arranged. Lounge bar, TV lounge, all rooms with private bathroom and colour TV.

Gynack Villa
**High Street,
Kingussie,
Inverness-shire PH21 1HS.
Tel (01540) 661038**

Friendly family run B&B offering excellent accommodation. 5 bedrooms, 2 with en suite. The charming village of Kingussie has a superb golf course with outstanding scenery and five delightful courses nearby. Highly competitive rates.

509

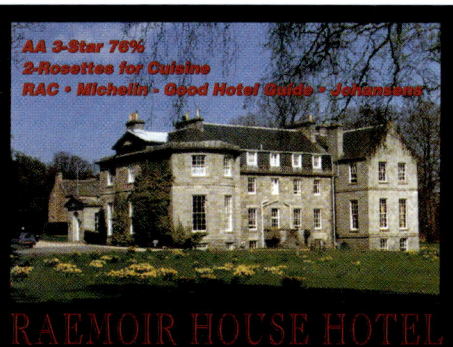

AA 3-Star 76%
2-Rosettes for Cuisine
RAC • Michelin - Good Hotel Guide - Johansens

RAEMOIR HOUSE HOTEL
– ROYAL DEESIDE –

Raemoir, a magnificent mansion, set in 3,500 acres of parkland and forest in Royal Deeside, including a splendid short 9-hole Par 3 course - "Perfect for Practice" - also croquet and tennis court.

Inside, a wonderful welcome, profusions of antiques, paintings, flowers and blazing fires, divine food created by one of Scotland's best young chefs.

Many excellent varied courses within 30 minutes. Aberdeen Airport 20 minutes. Unbeatable terms from £94.00 per person for three days and to include three full days golf.

**Raemoir House Hotel,
Raemoir, Banchory, Aberdeen AB31 4ED.
Tel: (01330) 824884 Fax: (01330) 822171**

PATIO HOTEL
★ ★ ★ ★

Less than five minutes from the famous Royal Aberdeen Golf Club, the Patio Hotel can boast 20 golf courses within 30 minutes' drive. Scotland's premier driving range and largest golf superstore is two minutes' drive from the hotel.
124 beautifully appointed double and twin rooms, some with stunning sea views. Indulge in delicious freshly prepared meals served in one of our award-winning restaurants or a light lunch in our Cafe bar. Complimentary membership of Breakers' Leisure Club with indoor pool, saunas, Turkish steam and spa baths, solarium, treatment room and fully equipped gym.

STB 4-Star Highly Commended   AA 4-Star and Rosette
BEACH BOULEVARD, ABERDEEN AB24 5EF
TEL: 01224 633339 • FAX: 01224 638833

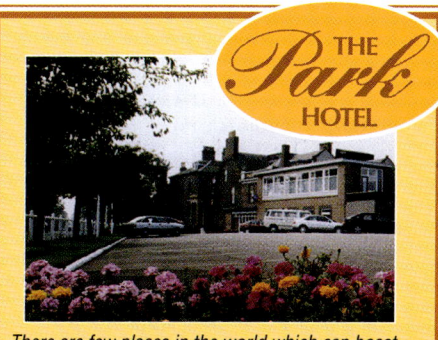

THE *Park* HOTEL

There are few places in the world which can boast such a varied collection of classic golf courses as you will discover in close proximity to the historical seaside town of Montrose.
The Links at Montrose, a qualifying course for the 1999 Open at Carnoustie (20 miles) is an excellent test of golf.
The family owned 3-Star Park Hotel has 53 en-suite bedrooms and offers superb food in both its refurbished Parkers Brasserie and Cedar Restaurant. Special tailor made golf packages can be arranged to include the **Best of Golf** in Angus.

**The Park Hotel, John Street, Montrose DD10 8RJ.
Tel: 01674 673415   Fax: 01674 677091
e-mail: recep@parkhotel-mont.demon.co.uk**

JOHNSTOUNBURN HOUSE HOTEL
HUMBIE, EAST LOTHIAN EH36 5PL.
Tel: 01875 833696   Fax: 01875 833626

The definitive statement of traditional Scottish hospitality - fine food and drink, warmth and comfort. Set in a 300 acre estate beside the Lammermuir hills, 30 minutes from both Edinburgh city centre and East Lothian's finest links courses, Johnstounburn dates from 1625, and retains the character of its proud heritage. Facilities include 20 bedrooms with private bathrooms, satellite television, exquisite wood panneled public rooms, a 350 yard practice ground surrounded by gardens, lawns and parkland. We welcome your enquiry.

Hazelbank Hotel
28 The Scores,
St Andrews, Fife KY16 9AS.
Tel (01334) 72466

Situated 400 yards from R&A Clubhouse overlooking St Andrews Bay this family run hotel offers quality accommodation (STB 3-Crown Commended) at affordable prices. All rooms en suite. Rates 1999 £25 - £48 per person B&B, double/twin.

Horse Shoe Inn
Eddleston, Peebles EH45 8QP.
Tel (01721) 730225 & 730306
Fax (01721) 730268

Website: http://business.virgin.net horseshoe.inn/index.htm
Traditional country inn, good food, wine and ale. Half hour south of Edinburgh. Golf, fishing, hunting, shooting, walking, cycling, ornethology, antiquities and historic houses.

Johnstounburn House Hotel
Humbie, East Lothian EH36 5PL.
Tel (01875) 833696 Fax (01875) 833626

Magnificent 17th-century house set on its own estate. 20 bedrooms, each with private facilities. 30 minutes from East Lothian's championship courses. Edinburgh City and airport. STB AA/ RAC 3-Star. Exclusive use available. (See advertisement page 509 for further details.)

Kilconquhar Castle Estate & Country Club
Kilconquhar, Elie, Leven, Fife KY9 1EZ.
Tel (01333) 340501 Fax (01333) 340239

A world renowned resort just ten miles from St Andrews with 1/2/3 and 4-bedroomed luxury villas nestling in over 100 acres of woodland and gardens, including driving range. Excellent cuisine, leisure facilities, indoor heated pool, horse riding and golf holidays arranged. (See advertisement page 505 for further details.)

Kinloch House Hotel
by Blairgowrie, Perthshire PH10 6SG.
Tel (01250) 884237 Fax: (01250) 884333

Kinloch House offers an almost unique proposition for golfers. 35 courses within an hour's drive, planning of rounds and booking of tee-times, sportsman's room with every facility and the best of Scottish hospitality. In-house health and fitness centre. AA 3-Red Star; 3-Rosette; STB 5-Star. (See advertisement page 501 for further details.)

Letham Grange
Colliston,
by Arbroath DD11 4RL.
Tel (01241) 890373 Fax (01241) 890725

The Leading Hotel in Carnoustie Country.
42-bedrooms, Victorian mansion, with 36-holes of superb golf. First class facilities set in the heartland of golf. Company/society golf outings/ breaks welcome. (See advertisement page 505 for further details.)

The Links Hotel - Montrose
Mid Links, Montrose DD10 8RL.
Tel (01674) 671000 Fax (01674) 672698

STB 3-Star; AA 3-Star. Use the hotel as a base to enjoy the pleasures of Angus, sandy beaches, golf courses, Glen Esk, House of Dun, Montrose Basin Nature Reserve, local museum distillery, and Glamis Castle. (See advertisement page 503 for further details.)

Loch Monzievaird Chalets
Ochtertyre, Crieff, Perthshire PH7 4JR.
Tel (01764) 652586 Fax (01764) 652555

The beautiful grounds at Loch Monzievaird, are hidden away one mile from Crieff. Our Norwegian and Danish chalets are laid out amongst ancient oak, beech and scots pine. 20 golf courses within half an hour's drive!

Marriott Dalmahoy Hotel & Country Club
Kirknewton, Nr Edinburgh,
Midlothian EH27 8EB.
Tel 0131-333 1845 Fax 0131-333 1433

Set in over 1,000 acres of fine Scottish woodland in the shadow of the Pentland Hills, Dalmahoy offers something special for every golfer. A regular European tour venue, only seven miles from Edinburgh. Choice of two outstanding courses - East Championship Course and the West Course. 4-Star hotel with 215 bedrooms and excellent conference facilities. Complimentary leisure facilities.
Marriott Hotel Group.

Navitie Guest House
Nr Loch Leven, Lochgelly, Fife KY5 8LR.
Tel (01592) 860295 Fax (01592) 869769

10-bedroom house set in four acres. Quiet location, private parking. All rooms en suite, centrally heated, tea/coffee making facilities, TV in all rooms. Sauna. Guests' lounge with log fire. Over 100 golf courses from a two to 30 minutes' drive! STB 3-Crown Commended.

COUNTY HOTEL

Wellington Square
Ayr, South Ayrshire KA7 1EY.

STAY AND PLAY

AT THE COUNTY HOTEL WITH A CHOICE OF 30 COURSES WITHIN A TEN MILE RADIUS COMPLEMENTED BY NO LESS THAN 30 MALT WHISKIES IN THE BAR! WELL APPOINTED EN-SUITE BEDROOMS ALL WITH TV AND TELEPHONE. EXCELLENT FOOD FROM BAR SNACKS TO FINE DINING. IDEAL LOCATION FOR PRESTWICK, BELLEISLE AND TROON COURSES. WE WELCOME YOUR ENQUIRY FOR CLUB OR GROUP RATES.

CALL
01292 263368 OR FAX **01292 282781**

Cadmore Lodge

HOTEL, RESTAURANT & COUNTRY CLUB
TENBURY WELLS, WORCESTERSHIRE

Idyllic lakeside setting in a private estate, perfect venue for weddings, conferences and private functions. Our own 9-hole golf course Par 68 5132 yards SSS65 on the Estate. Indoor 16 metre pool and leisure facilities. Two excellent fishing lakes - fly and coarse fishing - bowls and tennis.
Warm welcoming ambiance and log fires in winter. 14 en-suite bedrooms. Excellent cuisine prepared with imagination and flair using only fresh local produce.

SPECIAL 2-DAY GOLF AND FISHING BREAKS CAN BE ARRANGED.

CALL US, WE ARE WELL WORTH A VISIT!
01584 810044

The Templar Lodge

COME TO GULLANE **AND BY DAY** PLAY MUIRFIELD, GULLANE, ROYAL MUSSELBURGH AND THE OLDEST COURSE IN THE WORLD - MUSSELBURGH LINKS
Tel: **(01620) 842275**
Fax: **(01620) 842970**

PLAY ST ANDREWS, THE BELFRY, TROON NORTH OR VALDERAMA **BY NIGHT**.
STAY AT TEMPLAR LODGE, A 5-STAR EXPERIENCE AT A 3-STAR PRICE

For further information visit our website at http://come.to/templarlodge
e-mail: templodge@aol.com

Originally a twelfth century fortified house, Templar Lodge retains a character all of its own. From the ancient stonework in the dining room, through the library to the magnificent original Georgian panelling in the music room, you'll find yourself enveloped in the warm ambiance of a more tranquil time.

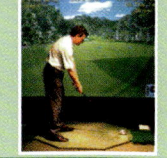

GULLANE, NEAR EDINBURGH, SCOTLAND
EH31 2AS

BRYN MORFYDD GOLF HOTEL

Situated in the beautiful Vale of Clwyd in North Wales with panoramic views of the Clwydian Range, the Bryn Morfydd Golf Hotel is surrounded by its own 2 golf courses - the 18-hole Par 70 Dukes Course plus the Peter Alliss-designed Par 3 Duchess Course.

SPECIAL GOLFING RATES

DINNER, BED & BREAKFAST AND GOLF
DAILY RATE: £51.00
WEEKEND RATE: £56.00
GOLF SOCIETY day packages
FROM £20 PP INCLUSIVE OF MEALS AND 27 HOLES

The Bryn Morfydd Hotel, Llanrhaeadr, Denbighshire LL16 4NP
Tel: 01745 890280 Fax: 01745 890488

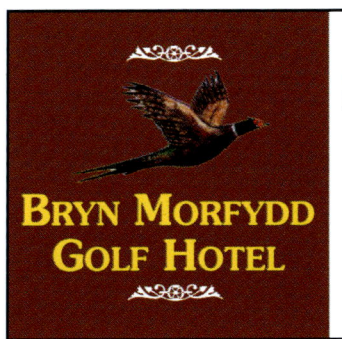

Tan Lan Hotel

**Great Ormes Road, West Shore,
Llandudno, North Wales LL30 2AR**

- One of the top rated AA 2-Star hotels in Llandudno
- 17 en suite bedrooms
- Excellent wholesome food featuring 5-course dinner
- Well stocked bar and comfortable lounges
- Two 18-hole golf courses only quarter of a mile away
- Ample parking
- Group discounts available

For more details please call:
Tel: (01492) 860221 • Fax: (01492) 870219

The Royal Sportsman Hotel
(3 crowns)

131 HIGH STREET,
PORTHMADOG, GWYNEDD,
NORTH WALES LL49 9HA.
TEL: +44 (0)1766 512015
FAX: +44 (0)1766 512490

http://www.royalsportsman.co.uk
e-mail:enquiries@royalsportsman.co.uk

Charming town centre hotel in Porthmadog with 28 en suite rooms. 4-Star service and cuisine. Private garage, Tavern bar and special inclusive H/B golf packages inclusive of green fees and arranged tee times. Five courses within 30 minutes of hotel.

THE K CLUB

• AT STRAFFAN • COUNTY KILDARE • IRELAND •
TEL: +353 1 601 7200   FAX: +353 1 601 7299

HOME TO THE SMURFIT EUROPEAN OPEN TO THE YEAR 2000.

Ireland's only 5 Red Star hotel graded by the Automobile Association, is surrounded by the fairways of the golf club, offers sumptuous accommodation with each room boasting its own individuality and decorated to the very highest standards. There are also exquisitely appointed courtyard suites.

The resort is ideal, be it for business or pleasure, and is a multi-facility sporting paradise where everyone can enjoy the 18-hole championship course designed by Arnold Palmer, practice area and driving range.

River and lake fishing. Indoor/outdoor tennis and full health and leisure club. Clay target shooting.

Old Course Hotel - St Andrews Golf Resort & Spa
St Andrews, Fife KY16 9SP.
Tel (01334) 474371 Fax (01334) 477668

This luxury 125-bedroom hotel overlooks the 17th Road Hole of the Old Course and is a five minute walk to the beach and town. Facilities include health spa with swimming pool, whirlpool, fitness room and full range of massage and beauty treatments. The hotel now has its own championship golf course, the Duke's Course. Open to non-residents, with residents enjoying guaranteed tee-times and reduced green fees.

The Old Manse Guest House
136 Main Street, Newmills,
By Culross, Fife KY12 8SX.
Tel (01383) 880150 Fax (01383) 880323

STB 2-Star Commended. Overlooking the Forth, ample parking. Edinburgh and St Andrews within easy reach. 6 bedrooms, 3 with en suite, all with TV, tea/coffee facilities. Rooms £16 - £22 B&B.

The Park Hotel - Dundee
Coupar Angus Road, Dundee DD2 3HY.
Tel (01382) 610691 Fax (01382) 612633

4-Crown Commended. Small hotel with 12 bedrooms, personally run with excellent standards at budget prices. Restaurant and function facilities. (See advertisement page 507 for further details.)

The Park Hotel - Montrose
John Street, Montrose, Angus DD10 8RJ.
Tel (01674) 673415 Fax (01674) 677091

Family owned 3-Star 59-bedroom hotel, quietly situated yet close to town centre. Golf, tennis and all sports and leisure facilities. Recently refurbished brasserie bar and restaurant offering quality, variety and exceptional value for money. Superb golf packages tailor-made to your requirements, including Montrose Medal, Carnoustie, Letham Grange and Edzell. (See advertisement page 509 for further details.)

Rusacks Hotel Golf Club
Pilmour Links, St Andrews, Fife KY16 9JQ.
Tel (01334) 474321 Fax (01334) 477896
Golf Club Tel/Fax (01334) 479176

Rusacks Hotel, overlooking the first and last fairways of the Old Course, provides outstanding facilities for golfers. The Rusacks Golf Club, situated within the hotel, offers guests a full golf booking service, lockers, sauna, solarium, club bar and golf shop. Voted one of the *Top Ten Golf Hotels in the World*.

The Scores Hotel
St Andrews,
Fife, KY16 9BB.
Tel (01334) 472451 Fax (01334) 473947

Overlooking the Royal & Ancient clubhouse and first tee of the Old Course, this famous golfers 3-Star hotel enjoys a commanding position with panoramic views over one of Scotland's most beautiful bays. The Scorecard bar offers a fascinating collection of golf memorabilia, including a comprehensive collection of the actual players' scorecards from *The Open* and *Dunhill Cups*. A stay at the Scores Hotel is part of the *St Andrews Experience*.

St Andrews Golf Hotel
St Andrews,
Fife KY16 9AS.
Tel (01334) 472611 Fax (01334) 472188

AA 3-Star and Rossette; STB 4-Crown Deluxe. Most comfortable, traditional Scottish hotel (all bedrooms en suite). Fine restaurant. Extensive cellar. On the seafront 220 yards from the 'Old Course'. Let us arrange your golf in Scotland.

Templar Lodge Hotel
Gullane, Nr Edinburgh EH31 2AS.
Tel (01620) 842275 Fax (01620) 842970

Website: http://come.to/templarlodge
e-mail: templodge@aol.com
The hotel has been refurbished to a high standard and will incorporate the Sanctuary Leisure Complex due to open in Spring 1999. The hotel is surrounded by golf courses. Five within the village, including Gullane No's 1, 2 and 3, Muirfield (host to the Open), and Luffness. Musselburgh Links said to be the oldest course in the country is also within easy access. (See advertisement page 511 for further details.)

Woodland Holidays
Kincaple Lodge,
St Andrews,
Fife KY16 9SH.
Tel/Fax (01334) 850217

Nine Scandinavian lodges in peaceful country setting, looking towards golf courses in St Andrews. Lodges are well equipped including bed linen, electric blankets and towels. Ample car parking. Open all year. Tennis court. Home cooking available. Groups welcome.

Highlands, Islands & North

Corrour House Hotel
Inverdruie, Aviemore PH22 1QH.
Tel (01479) 810220 Fax (01479) 811500

A lovely country house hotel with charm and character, set in four acres of garden and woodland with spectacular views of the Cairngorm mountains. Where golfing guests return year after year to enjoy superb comfort, food and wines. Set in the heart of Strathspey, half a mile from Aviemore with six delightful courses nearby. Recommended by leading hotel guides. STB 4-Star; *Taste of Scotland.*

Covenanters' Inn
Auldearn, Nairn IV12 5TG.
Tel (01667) 452456 Fax (01667) 453583

Family run inn with over 25 courses within one hour's drive. All bedrooms en suite. Single-storey throughout. Dine in the Eren restaurant or Kiln lounge bar. Inverness airport eight miles, Aberdeen airport 70 miles.

Culloden House
Milton of Culloden, Inverness IV2 7BZ.
Tel 0800 980 4561 Fax (01463) 792181
USA Toll-free Fax 0044-1-800-3737987

Easy to access and a short drive to Royal Dornoch, Nairn and 28 other golf courses. This STB/AA 4-Star historical Georgian country house sits in 40 acres of tranquil parkland only minutes from Dalcross airport and Inverness. On-site or on-course PGA instruction/tour. (See advertisement page 507 for details.)

Dochlaggie
Boat of Garten, Inverness-shire PH24 3BU.
Tel (01479) 831242

Dochlaggie is a comfortable farmhouse offering B&B accommodation one mile from Boat of Garten golf course and driving range. Self-catering house to sleep 5 persons situated right by the Boat of Garten course.

Dornoch Castle
Dornoch, Sutherland IV25 3SD.
Tel (01862) 810216 Fax (01862) 810981

Formerly a bishop's palace, the hotel has 17 bedrooms. The panelled cocktail bar, elegant lounge and Bishop's Room restaurant overlook historic Dornoch Cathedral. Superb food and wines.

Kingsmills Hotel
Culcabock Road, Inverness IV2 3LP.
Tel (01463) 237166 Fax (01463) 225208

Overlooking Inverness golf club and centrally located for Royal Dornoch and the Nairn golf clubs, this 4-Star luxurious Swallow hotel offers purpose-built GOLF VILLAS and extensive leisure facilities with a 3-hole pitch and putt course.

Machrie Hotel & Golf Links Course
Port Ellen, Isle of Islay, Argyll PA42 7AN.
Tel (01496) 302310 Fax (01496) 302404

Play a hidden gem of a course. Traditional 18-hole championship links course situated on the doorstep of the Machrie Hotel. Superior and standard accommodation, excellent food and friendly service. Self-catering and golf packages also available.

Patio Hotel
Beach Boulevard, Aberdeen AB24 5EF.
Tel (01224) 633339 Fax (01224) 638833

Luxury 4-Star hotel with 124 en suite rooms. Two restaurants and leisure facilities. Situated close to Royal Aberdeen golf course with eight other courses within easy driving from the hotel. (See advertisement page 509 for further details.)

Raemoir House Hotel
Raemoir, Banchory, Aberdeen AB31 4ED.
Tel (01330) 824884 Fax (01330) 822171

Magnificent mansion set in 3,500 acres of parkland and forest in Royal Deeside, including a splendid short 9-hole par 3 course. 'Perfect for Practice', also croquet and tennis court. Many excellent varied courses within 30 minutes. Aberdeen airport 20 minutes. Unbeatable terms from £94.00 per person for 3 days to include 3 full days golf. (See advertisement page 509 for further details.)

Ramleh Hotel & Fingal's Restaurant
**2 Academy Street, Nairn,
Inverness-shire IV12 4RJ.**
Tel (01667) 453551 Fax (01667) 456577

1994 Les Routiers British Restaurant of the Year. George and Carol Woodhouse offer a warm welcome to their 10-bedroomed hotel and renowned restaurant. Close to both of Nairn's championship courses, many more within 30 miles. Beautiful beaches, whisky and castle trails.

The Royal Hotel - Fortrose
Fortrose, Ross-shire IV10 8SU.
Tel (01381) 620236

Friendly Highland hotel 20 minutes from Inverness. 15 well appointed bedrooms, large lounge, two bars, dining room serving a wide menu including traditional Scottish home cooking. 12 golf courses including Nairn and Royal Dornoch within three quarters of an hour's drive.

West

Carlton Toby Hotel
187 Ayr Road, Prestwick,
Ayrshire KA9 1TP.
Tel (01292) 476811 Fax (01292) 673712

Recently refurbished, the Carlton Toby Hotel is set in its own grounds. Ideally located for Ayr, Prestwick and Troon centres. Two minutes' walk from Centrum Ice Arena. All rooms are en suite, have tea/coffee-making facilities, Sky TV, hairdryer and telephone.

County Hotel - Ayr
Wellington Square, Ayr KA7 1EY.
Tel (01292) 263368 Fax (01292) 282781

Superb golf in the south west coast of Scotland, and a friendly family run hotel offering full facilities including residents' bar with a choice of 30 malt whiskies. Bar snacks to fine dining available. Pay and Stay Golf - ask for group rates. (See advertisement page 511)

Cowans Farm Guesthouse
Kirkgunzeon, Dumfries DG2 8JY.
Tel (01387) 760284

This Place Near to Heaven wrote a guest. Idyllic location close to Dumfries and Dalbeattie with 20 courses within 20 miles. Our own fishing lochs. All rooms ground floor, en suite in converted barns. Home cooking.

Dunduff House
Dunduff Farm, Dunure, Ayr KA7 4LH.
Tel (01292) 500225 Fax (01292) 500222

Situated on the edge of Dunure overlooking Arran and Firth of Clyde. Golf courses include Royal Troon, Turnberry and many more interesting courses. All rooms have TV, radio, tea-making facilities, wash hand basin. Two double rooms have en suite facilities. STB 4-Star; STB Highly Commended 2-Crown; AA Selected 4-Q. Self-catering cottage available sleeps four.

Fairfield House Hotel
12 Fairfield Road, Ayr KA7 2AR.
Tel (01292) 267461 Fax (01292) 261456

The 4-Star Fairfield House with its 2-Rosettes for food is simply the most luxurious hotel of its type in the area, with a well deserved reputation for comfort and fine dining. Local courses include Turnberry and Royal Troon.

Langley Bank Guest House
39 Carrick Road,
Ayr KA7 2RD.
Tel (01292) 264246 Fax (01292) 282628

Langley Bank is an elegantly refurbished Victorian house offering quality accommodation at affordable prices. Centrally situated and in close proximity to all local golf courses. En suite facilities, direct dial telephone. Private car park.

Marriott Breadsall Priory Hotel & Country Club
Moor Road, Morley,
Nr Derby, Derbyshire DE7 6DL.
Tel (01332) 832235 Fax (01332) 833509

A 13th-century mansion replete with battlements, set in 400 acres with stunning views. Breadsall Priory offers two superb golf courses and excellent accommodation. The 18-hole Priory course winds through undulating parkland and needs a fair degree of accuracy. In complete contrast the Moorland course is set deep in the heart of typical Derbyshire landscape. Complimentary leisure facilities. *Marriott Hotel Group.*

South Beach Hotel
South Beach,
Troon, Ayrshire KA10 6EG.
Tel (01292) 312033 Fax (01292) 318438

3-Star RAC and STB privately owned hotel facing the sea. Golfers' paradise, fifteen courses within easy reach. Royal Troon being most famous. 34 bedrooms all en suite. Golf can be arranged. Friendly atmosphere.

Turnberry Hotel Golf Courses & Spa
Ayrshire KA26 9LT.
Tel (01655) 331000 Fax (01655) 331706

One of the world's finest luxury hotel, golf and spa resorts. Edwardian country house overlooking its own Ailsa and Arran championship courses. The Ailsa is ranked 16th in the world and was the venue for the 1994 Open Championship.

West End Hotel
West Bay, Dunoon PA23 7HU.
Tel (01369) 702907 Fax (01369) 706266

website: http://www.westendhotel.com
Family run, fully licensed hotel. Single and twin rooms available. Very attractive rates for golfing parties. Five minutes from the superb Cowal championship course.

WALES

Welsh Borders

Belmont Lodge & Golf Course
**Belmont,
Hereford HR2 9SA.**
Tel (01432) 352666 Fax (01432) 358090

18-hole golf course running along the beautiful Wye Valley with a 30-bedroomed hotel on-site. Other facilities include bar, restaurant, fishing, bowling, tennis and snooker. Only a mile and a half from Hereford City centre.

Cadmore Lodge Hotel
**St Michaels,
Tenbury Wells,
Worcestershire WR15 8TQ.**
Tel/Fax (01584) 810044

A warm welcome awaits at Cadmore Lodge Hotel. Excellent cuisine from chefs with imagination and flair. 9-hole golf course par 68 SSS 65 (18 holes). Two fishing lakes for trout and course fishing. Indoor swimming pool, with spa, steam room and cardio-vascular equipment. (See advertisement page 511 for further details.)

Hawkstone Park Hotel
**Weston-under-Redcastle,
Shrewsbury, Shropshire SY4 5UY.**
Tel (01939) 200611 Fax (01939) 200311

Hawkstone Park Hotel with its 65 en suite bedrooms, has been accommodating golfing visitors since 1920. This tradition is enhanced by our 5-Star golfing facilities, including two championship courses and extensive up-to-date teaching services and practice areas.

The Talbot Hotel
**West Street, Leominster,
Herefordshire HR6 8EP.**
Tel (01568) 616347 Fax (01568) 614880

A privately owned town centre hotel, parts of which date from the 15th-century, is to be found in the small, ancient market town of Leominster. Good food and friendly staff with comfortable surroundings help to make your golfing break enjoyable. Courses of preference and tee-off times arranged for your society/party at nearby recommended courses of Leominster, Herefordshire, Kington, Upper Sapey, Ludlow and Belmont. Two days golf plus DB&B £148 inclusive.

North

Bryn Morfydd Golf Hotel
**Llanrhaeadr,
Nr Denbigh,
Denbighshire LL16 4NP.**
Tel (01745) 890280 Fax (01745) 890488

Situated in the beautiful Vale of Clwyd, North Wales. The hotel is surrounded by its own two golf courses. A 3-Star hotel with excellent accommodation and restaurant facilities. Special golfing rates available. (See advertisement page 511 for further details.)

Caeau Capel Hotel
**Nefyn,
Gwynedd LL53 6EB.**
Tel (01758) 720240

WTB 3-Star family run hotel. Home cooking. Comfortable en suite rooms. Golf arranged at any of our five local courses. Discounts available on green fees. Please telephone for further details.

Holyhead Golf Club
**Lon Garreg Fawr, Trearddur Bay,
Anglesey LL65 2YG.**
Tel/Fax (01407) 763279

Comfortable twin-bedded accommodation is available at the Holyhead Golf Club, with all meals provided in the club restaurant. Enjoy excellent golf on heathland course with spectaculor view to Snowdonia. Reservations ring 01407 763279.

Imperial Hotel - Llandudno
**The Promenade,
Llandudno,
Gwynedd LL30 1AP.**
Tel (01492) 877466 Fax (01492) 878043

100-bedroomed hotel with extensive leisure facilities including 45' indoor swimming pool. Ideally situated for all North Wales' golf courses. Award-winning restaurant and private dining room for up to 30 available.

The Links Hotel - Conwy
Conwy Road,
Llandudno, Conwy,
Gwynedd LL30 1PN.
Tel (01492) 879180

A small, family run hotel/public house, situated near the premier courses in the area. The hotel is close to the town's amenities and its own huge car park.

Royal Sportsman Hotel
131 High Street,
Porthmadog,
Gwynedd LL49 9HA.
Tel (01766) 512015 Fax (01766) 512490
e-mail: enquiries@royalsportsman.co.uk
htpp://www.royalsportsman.co.uk

Charming town centre hotel in Porthmadog with 28 en suite rooms. 4-Star service and cuisine. Private garage, Tavern bar and special inclusive half board golf packages inclusive of green fees and arranged tee times. Five courses within 30 minutes of hotel. (See advertisement page 512 for further details.)

Tan Lan Hotel
Great Ormes Road, West Shore,
Llandudno, North Wales LL30 2AR.
Tel (01492) 860221 Fax (01492) 870219

One of the top rated AA-2 Star hotels in Llandudno representing excellent value for money. Only a quarter of a mile from Maesdu and North Wales golf clubs. Tee-off times can be arranged on your behalf. (See advertisement page 512 for further details.)

The West Arms Hotel
Llanarmon Dyffryn Ceiriog,
Nr Llangollen, Clwyd LL20 7LD.
Tel (01691) 600665 Fax (01691) 600622

16th-century hotel with award-winning cuisine and in close proximity to golf clubs at Llangollen, Chirk, Oswestry, Mile End (Oswestry) and Llanymynech. The hotel is set in an idyllic location and also offers many other country pursuits.

South & South West

The Court Hotel
Lamphey, Pembroke,
Pembrokeshire SA71 5NT.
Tel (01646) 672273 Fax (01646) 672480

One of Wales' leading country hotels. Deluxe bedrooms, superb leisure centre, swimming pool, jacuzzi, gym, sauna and floodlit tennis. Special arrangements with Tenby, South Pembrokeshire, Trefloyne and Haverfordwest golf clubs. Excellent food and wine -local produce. A Best Western Hotel.

The Crown at Wintebrook
Whitebrook,
Monmouth,
Monmouthshire NP5 4TX.
Tel (01600) 860254 Fax (01600) 860607

Award-winning restaurant with 10 en suite bedrooms situated in idyllic wooded valley. Seven golf courses within 20 minutes. Featured in The Good Food Guide, Good Hotel Guide, Egon Ronay etc. AA 3-Rosettes. Special breaks.

The Dormy
Royal Porthcawl Golf Club
Rest Bay,
Porthcawl,
Mid Glamorgan CF36 3UW.
Tel (01656) 782251 Fax (01656) 771687

Luxury dormy accommodation for parties of up to twelve persons. Apply to the secretary. (See advertisement page 31 for further details.)

Great House Restaurant & Hotel
High Street,
Laleston, Bridgend CF32 0HP.
Tel (01656) 657644 Fax (01656) 668892

4-Crown deluxe hotel in a 15th-century manor house in a village location. Award-winning restaurant. Within 15 minutes of several prestigious golf courses, including Royal Porthcawl. Personally supervised by the owner.

Marriott St Pierre Hotel & Country Club
St Pierre Park,
Chepstow,
Monmouthshire NP6 6YA.
Tel (01291) 625261 Fax (01291) 629975

The St Pierre is a hotel of international calibre, easily reached by motorway. Set in 400 acres of exceptional parkland, the hotel offers excellent accommodation and boasts two superb golf courses. The championship Old Course, host to the 1996 Solheim Cup, has staged more professional tournaments than virtually any other venue. The Mathern course. slightly shorter and equally scenic. Complimentary leisure facilities. *Marriott Hotel Group.*

CHANNEL ISLANDS

La Grande Mare Hotel Golf Club
La Grande Mare, Vazon, Castel, Guernsey.
Tel (01481) 56576 & 53544
Fax (01481) 55194

www: lgm.guernsey.net
Beautifully appointed luxury hotel with 18-hole golf course playing off 14 greens. Professional shop and tuition on-site. First class, well priced restaurant. 2-AA Rosettes. Beachside location. Golfing breaks catered for.

Les Arches Hotel
Archirondel, Gorey, St Martin,
Jersey JE3 6DR.
Tel (01534) 853839 Fax (01534) 856660

3-Star hotel overlooking France. Private access to beach. All rooms en suite with TV. One and a half miles from Royal Jersey Golf Club. Swimming pool, garden, tennis court, golf net, sauna, mini-gym and bars. Restaurant. Bed and breakfast rates from £29. Special discount for golfers.

The Moorings Hotel & Restaurant
Gorey Pier, Gorey, Jersey JE3 6EW.
Tel (01534) 853633 Fax (01534) 857618

3-Star intimate and luxurious 17-bedroom hotel overlooking the quaint Gorey harbour and the sandy bay of Grouville. Half a mile from the Royal Jersey golf club. Renowned for its superb food, seafood a speciality. Open all year. Special rates for golfers at any time.

The St Pierre Park Hotel
Rohais, St Peter Port, Guernsey GYI 1FD.
Tel (01481) 728282 Fax (01481) 712041

This 4-Star hotel offers extensive leisure facilities including a 9-hole par 3 golf course, designed by Tony Jacklin. Three tennis courts and a health suite with heated indoor swimming pool, spa bath, saunas, steam rooms, solaria and exercise room.

NORTHERN IRELAND

Beach House Hotel
61 Beach Road, Portballintrae,
Co Antrim BT57 8RT.
Tel (012657) 31214 Fax (012657) 31664
e-mail: info@beachhousehotel.com
www: beachhousehotel.com
With spectacular views of Scotland and Donegal, our seafront hotel is close to Old Bushmills Distillery and the Giant's Causeway. Central to six links courses including Royal Portrush, and is renowned for good food, accommodation and family hospitality.

The Beeches Country House
10 Dunadry Road,
Dunadry,
Antrim BT41 2RR.
Tel (01849) 433161 Fax (01849) 432227

'Grade A' guest house on A6 at Dunadry. Private, quiet accommodation. All rooms en suite, with central heating, tea/coffee-making facilities, colour TV, telephone, trouser press etc. Taste of Ulster award. No smoking. Secure parking. French and German. Golf at Masserene three miles, Stakis Park two miles, Ballyclare six miles.

Glassdrumman Lodge
85 Mill Road,
Annalong,
Co Down BT34 4RH.
Tel (013967) 68451 Fax (013967) 67041

Nestling in the Mourne mountains is this 10-bedroomed country house where comfort and hospitality go hand in hand. The dining room is well acclaimed for serving good local produce grown\ mainly on the farm and gardens.

The Portaferry Hotel
The Strand,
Portaferry,
Co Down BT22 1PE.
Tel (012477) 28231 Fax (012477) 28999

With eight golf courses, including Royal County Down, within 30 minutes' drive, this AA 3-Star hotel with 2-Rosettes for cuisine, is the ideal base for your golfing holiday. Idyllic setting. Member *Ireland's Blue Book*.

Radisson Roe Park Hotel & Golf Resort
Roe Park,
Limavady,
Co Londonderry BT49 9LB.
Tel (015047) 22222 Fax (015047) 22313

Northern Ireland's first golf and leisure resort featuring 64 luxurious bedrooms, O'Cahan's bar, Coach House Brasserie, Courtyard Restaurant, Fairways Leisure Club and the Eden Health and Beauty Salon. 18-hole championship parkland course, driving range, putting green and golf shop.

The Silverwood Golf Hotel
**Kiln Road,
Lurgan, Craigavon BT66 6NF.
Tel (01762) 327722 Fax (01762) 325290**

The hotel lies within a complex of an 18-hole golf course, putting courses, driving range, gym and a certified ski slope. Also available - game and coarse fishing, sailing, winter skiing, windsurfing, bird and wildlife reserve and parascending. (See advertisement page 520 for further details.)

EIRE

Abbee House B&B
**22 Waterloo Road,
Ballsbridge,
Dublin 4, Ireland.
+353 1 660 1488 Fax +353 1 667 7224**

Quality bed and breakfast accommodation in this listed period residence in the heart of Georgian Dublin. Close to most Dublin attractions, shopping and business centre. All rooms en suite. Private parking.

Ballymaloe House
**Shanagarry, Midleton,
Co Cork, Ireland.
+353 21 652531 Fax +353 21 652021**

e-mail: bmaloe@iol.ie
Large family farmhouse, set in 400 acres, only two miles from the coast. The highly recommended food is also served at the Crawford Art Gallery in Cork, and the Allen family also run the *Ballymaloe Cookery School* in Shanagarry. There is an excellent craft shop on the premises. Just 20 minutes from Fota, Youghal and East Cork golf clubs, and 90 minutes from the Old Head club in Kinsale. An ideal golfing base.)

Castlerosse Hotel
**Killarney,
Co Kerry, Ireland.
Tel +353 64 31144 Fax +353 64 31031**

e-mail: castler@iol.ie
Castlerosse Hotel, a 3-Star hotel on the lakeside between golf course and National Park, one mile from Killarney town centre. Magnificent views of lakes and mountains from the restaurant and panoramic bar. Leisure and fitness facilities, including 20 metre swimming pool and two floodlit tennis courts. Call for our *Tee Time in Ireland* golf brochure. *(Tower Hotel Group.)*

Castletroy Park Hotel
**Dublin Road, Limerick, Ireland.
Tel +353 61 335566 Fax +353 61 331117**

e-mail: sales@castletroy-park.ie
Url. http://www.castletroy-park.ie
The Castletroy Park Hotel lies at the heart of the south west of Ireland. The region boasts over 23 golf courses, including the renowned Ballybunion course, all within an hour's drive of the hotel.

Dingle Skellig Hotel
**Dingle, Co Kerry, Ireland.
Tel +353 66 9151144 Fax +353 66 9151501**

110 bedrooms, luxurious health and leisure club and conference centre. Restaurant overlooking Dingle Bay, Blaskets bar, private dining facilities and drying room. Guaranteed tee-times and discounted green fees at Dingle's 18-hole links course. Individuals, societies and groups welcome.

Dromoland Castle
**Newmarket-on-Fergus, Co Clare, Ireland.
Tel +353 61 368444 Fax +353 61 368498**

Dromoland Castle is a magnificent renaissance castle on 375 acres of parkland. It offers the highest accommodation standards, and award-winning restaurant. Activities include golf, clay pigeon shooting, horseriding and fishing, we also have a fully equipped health centre. The castle is located eight miles from Shannon International Airport in County Clare.

Dromquinna Manor Hotel
**Kenmare, Co Kerry, Ireland.
Tel +353 64 41657 Fax +353 64 41791**

Beautiful Victorian manor 40-acre estate. Breathtaking sea, mountain and river views. Ring of Kerry *Tiger* course two minutes. Kenmare, Waterville and Killarney courses within 45 minutes. Riding, tennis, guided walks, own fishing launch. Marina.

Faithlegg House Hotel
Waterford, Ireland. *(OPENING SPRING 1999.)*
Tel +353 51 38200 Fax +353 1 8730194

e-mail: sales@towerhotelgroup.ie
Faithlegg House Hotel is a 4-Star 18th-century house hotel situated beside Faithlegg golf course, and provides 14 magnificent rooms. A discreet extension will provide a further 68 rooms. With full health and fitness facilities, as well as the 18-hole championship course, it is the ideal place to take a relaxing break. Call for our *Tee Time in Ireland* golf brochure. *(Tower Hotel Group.)*

Ferrycarrig Hotel
Ferrycarrig Bridge, Wexford, Ireland.
Tel +353 53 20999 Fax +353 53 20982

The hotel boasts one of the most inspiring locations of any hotel in Ireland with fabulous views over river Slaney Estuary. Facilities include 90 bedrooms and suites. AA 2-Rosette waterfront restaurants, fabulous health and fitness club, 20 metre pool. *Part owners of St Helen's Bay Golf Club.*

Hotel Europe
Killarney, Co Kerry, Ireland.
Tel +353 64 31900 Fax +353 64 32118

Overlooking the famous lakes of Killarney, adjacent to Killeen, Mahony's Point golf courses, the Hotel Europe is within easy reach of Beaufort, Dunloe, Killorglin, Ross, Dooks, Ballybunion, Tralee and Waterville. Other facilities include 25 metre swimming pool, sauna, gymnasium, free horseriding with our own string of Haflinger horses, free indoor tennis courts and billiards. Fishing and boating on the lakes of Killarney.

Hotel Rosslare
Rosslare Harbour, Co Wexford, Ireland.
+353 53 33110 Fax +353 53 33386

This grade A 3-Star hotel stands on a magnificent clifftop position overlooking Rosslare Bay. Rosslare Harbour's oldest hotel is steeped in history. Recalled in the Portholes Bar Maritime Museum. *The hotel is part owner of St Helen's Bay Golf and Country Club.*

Hunter's Hotel
Rathnew, Co Wicklow, Ireland.
Tel +353 404 40106 Fax +353 404 40338

270 year old coaching inn run by the same family for the past 170 years. Ideal centre for golf holidays. Sixteen 18-hole courses within half an hour, nearest three minute's drive away.

Jurys Hotel Waterford
Ferrybank, Waterford, Ireland.
Tel +353 51 832111 Fax +353 51 832863

Situated on 38 acres of parkland and overlooking Waterford City, this hotel has 98 luxurious bedrooms. Facilities include an extensive leisure centre, bar and restaurant. There are six 18-hole courses within a ten mile radius.

Jurys Inn Limerick
Lower Marlow Street, Limerick, Ireland.
Tel +353 61 207000 Fax +353 61 400966

Prime city centre location hotel with 151 new bedrooms that can accommodate three adults or two adults and two children for £51.00 per room per night. Close to famous golf courses of Ballybunion and Lahinch

Kathleen's Country House
Madam's Height, Tralee Road, Killarney, Co Kerry, Ireland.
Tel +353 64 32810 Fax +353 64 32340

Kathleen's is a charming private hotel, 5-Q AA registered; 4-Star ITB; 1993 award-winning *RAC Guesthouse of the Year*. 17 delightful bedrooms furnished in antique pine with private bathroom, orthopaedic beds, telephone, TV/radio, tea/coffee-making facilities, hairdryer. Ideal golfing base for Killarney, Tralee, Waterville, Dooks and Ballybunion.

The Kildare Hotel & Country Club
At Straffan, Co Kildare, Ireland.
Tel +353 1 601 7200 Fax +353 1 601 7299

Located 30 minutes from Dublin. Arnold Palmer designed 18-hole championship golf course, clubhouse, practice area and driving range. Resident golf professional Ernie Jones. Home to The Smurfit European Open since September 1995 until the year 2000. Hotel AA

SILVERWOOD GOLF HOTEL & Country Club
Best Western

SILVERWOOD GOLF CENTRE ON SITE
18 Hole Parkland Course
9 Hole Par 3 Course
Driving Range Floodlit

WEEKEND GOLF PACKAGES
(Thursday to Sunday inclusive)
1 Day Special 1 Bed & Breakfast 1 Evening Meal Plus 1 Day's Golf £40 per person sharing.

3 Day Special 3 Bed & Breakfast 3 Evening Meals Plus 3 Days' Golf £110 per person sharing.

KILN ROAD, LURGAN,
CO ARMAGH BT66 6NF
Tel: (01762) 327722
Fax: (01762) 325290
R of I: (08 01762) 327722

5-Red Stars. Fishing, health club and sports centre with indoor and outdoor tennis. (See advertisement page 512 for further details.)

Killarney Heights Hotel
Cork Road,
Killarney, Co Kerry, Ireland.
Tel +353 64 31158 Fax +353 64 35198

e-mail: khh@iol.ie
This family owned 71-bedroom hotel, opened 1996, is located only a few miles from Killarney, Tralee, Ballybunion and Waterville golf clubs. Other major visitor attractions are Ring of Kerry, Killarney's lakes and mountains and panoramic scenery.

Limerick Inn Hotel
Ennis Road,
Limerick, Ireland.
Tel +353 61 326666 Fax +353 61 326281

The Limerick Inn is located in the heart of Ireland's lovely Shannonside. All 153 bedrooms have private bathroom, direct dial telephone, radio and TV. The hotel has a modern health and leisure centre and full conference facilities.

Mount Juliet
Thomastown, Co Kilkenny, Ireland.
Tel +353 56 73000 Fax +353 56 73019

Deluxe accommodation in the elegant Mount Juliet House or the informal Hunters Yard. Ireland's premier sporting estate offers guests on-site fishing, horseriding, tennis, stylish leisure centre, David Leadbetter Golf Academy. Home of the Irish Open, 1993, 1994 and 1995.

Parknasilla Great Southern Hotel
Parknasilla, Sneen, Co Kerry, Ireland.
Tel +353 64 45122 Fax +353 64 45323

Parknasilla Great Southern is one of Ireland's best loved hotels. Set in 300 acres of its own grounds it has extensive leisure facilities as well as its own private 9-hole golf course. Overlooking Kenmare Bay, this Victorian hotel is truly in a world of its own.

Portmarnock Hotel & Golf Links
Strand Road,
Portmarnock, Co Dublin, Ireland.
Tel +353 1 846 0611 Fax +353 1 846 2442

This prestigious new development is located 15 minutes from Dublin airport and 25 minutes from the city centre. The hotel's 18-hole golf links was designed by Bernard Langer and is the only PGA European Tour course in Ireland.

Randles Court Clarion Hotel
Muckross Road, Killarney,
Co Kerry, Ireland.
Tel +353 64 35333 Fax +353 64 35206

Johansen's recommended for 1999, luxury 4-Star Deluxe hotel. Five minutes' walk from the town centre. Killarney championship courses closeby and within easy access to Ballybunion, Waterville, Old Head, Tralee and Dooks. Elegant country house with open log fires, antique furniture and period paintings. Dine in our Checkers restaurant or Court dining room. 49 luxuriously, spacious en suite bedrooms. A warm and friendly welcome awaits you.

Shannon Oaks Hotel & Country Club
Portumna, Co Galway, Ireland.
Tel +353 509 41777 Fax +353 509 41357

The Shannon Oaks Hotel and Country Club offers extensive golf, leisure and conference facilities with our 5-Star leisure club and 18-hole parkland golf course adjacent.

The Slieve Russell Hotel Golf & Country Club
Ballyconnell, Co Cavan, Ireland.
Tel +353 49 9526444 Fax +353 49 9526474

Located only two hours' drive from both Dublin and Belfast, the Slieve Russell is a complete resort with its 5-Star leisure facilities, championship 18-hole golf course. 151 superbly appointed bedrooms and a selection of restaurants and bars. Conference and banqueting suites - The *Perfect* location for business or pleasure.

Smyth Village Hotel
Feakle, Co Clare, Ireland.
Ten +353 61 924000 Fax +353 61 924244

Smyth's Hotel is just ten minutes from East Clare golf club, venue for the PGA Seniors Tour. 4-Star bedrooms. Gourmet food. Special all-inclusive rates. True Irish hospitality. Just 40 minutes from Shannon airport.

St Helen's Bay Golf & Country Club
St Helens, Kilrane, Rosslare Harbour,
Co Wexford, Ireland.
Tel +353 53 33234 Fax +353 53 33803

Luxury on-site accommodation together with tennis courts, leisure room and sauna. Full bar/catering facilities available in the clubhouse. Superbly located championship 18-hole golf

course, which has blended the best of parkland characteristics with a finish that is true links and plenty of difficulty. Situated only five minutes from Rosslare ferryport. Green fee and society friendly, playable all year round.

Tinakilly Country House & Restaurant
Rathnew, Wicklow, Co Wicklow, Ireland.
Tel +353 404 69274 Fax +353 404 67806

4-Star ITB; RAC Blue Ribbon; AA Red Star and a Small Luxury Hotel of the World. Renowned for splendid fresh food in elegant Victorian surroundings, Tinakilly is situated in seven acres of gardens and has 53 bedrooms, mostly junior suites with sea views. 29 miles from Dublin, eight miles from Druid's Glen, home of the 1996/97/1998 Irish Open, and locally, The European Club, Blainroe, Woodenbridge, Wicklow and Delgany. Don't miss Powerscourt Gardens, Glendalough, Wicklow mountains and Ballykissangel! Special golf brochure available.

Tower Hotel & Leisure Centre - Waterford
The Mall, Waterford, Ireland.
Tel +353 51 875801 Fax +353 51 870129

e-mail: towerw@iol.ie
The Tower Hotel is a 3-Star hotel situated in the heart of Waterford City with 141 en suite bedrooms. All rooms have multi-channel TV and direct dial telephone. Leisure centre and 20 metre pool, easy access to numerous championship golf courses. Call for our *Tee Time in Ireland* golf brochure. *(Tower Hotel Group.)*

Tower Hotel - Sligo
Quay Street, Sligo, Ireland.
Tel +353 71 44000 Fax +353 71 46888

e-mail: towersl@iol.ie
The Tower Hotel and 'Links' Bar is a 3-Star hotel and is hugely popular with locals and visitors alike. The hotel offers a relaxed atmosphere and is the perfect place to unwind and enjoy a drink. Championship golf courses nearby include Rosses Point, Enniscrone and Bundoran. Call for our *Tee Time in Ireland* golf brochure. *(Tower Hotel Group.)*

West Waterford Golf & Country Club
West Waterford Golf Club Dungarvan, Co Waterford, Ireland.
Tel +353 58 43216 & 41475
Fax +353 58 44343

Featured in 1996 by *Golf World* - In *Golfing Gems of Ireland*. A new golfing experience and wonderful welcome awaits you at the West Waterford golf club. Excellent self-catering bungalow available, situated on the course along the 18th fairway.

Index of Advertisers

Aldwark Manor Hotel Golf & Country Club	501	The Kildare Hotel & Country Club	512
Alverton Manor Country House Hotel	489	Kinloch House Hotel	501
Ashdown Forest Golf Hotel	495		
		Lansdowne Hotel	493
Ballater Golf Club	28	Letham Grange	505
Barnham Broom Hotel	497	The Links Hotel - Montrose	503
Beaufort Golf Course	24		
The Belfry	499	The Marine Hotel	503
Birkdale Promotions	12		
Botley Park Hotel Golf & Country Club	497	Northop Country Park Golf Club	501
Bryn Morfydd Golf Hotel	511		
Burnham & Berrow Golf Club	27	Old Conna Golf Club	27
Bushey Hall Golf Club	28		
		The Park Hotel - Dundee	507
Cadmore Lodge Hotel	511	The Park Hotel - Montrose	509
Carden Park Hotel Golf Resort & Spa	501		
China Fleet Country Club	493	Patio Hotel	509
Chip 'N' Chub (Melex) Ltd	12	Penrith Golf Club	32
County Hotel - Ayr	511		
Culloden House	507	Raemoir House Hotel	509
		Ramside Hall Hotel & Golf Club	503
Dalmunzie House Hotel	507	Rhod McEwan Golf Books	7
De Vere Hotels	4	The Royal Dublin Golf Club	31
De Vere Belton Woods	494	Royal Lytham & St Anne's Golf Club	27
De Vere Cameron House	508	Royal Porthcawl Golf Club - The Dormy	31
De Vere The Dormy	485	Royal Sportsman Hotel	512
De Vere Hotel Blackpool	500	Rudding Park Golf Club	499
De Vere Mottram Hall	500	Rudding Park Hotel	499
De Vere Oulton Hall	498		
De Vere Slaley Hall	504	Sand Moor Golf Club	31
Derek Burridge (Wholesale) Ltd	7	Schotten Trophies - Manfred Schotten Antiques	7
		The Silverwood Golf Hotel	520
Edmondstown Golf Club	27	South Ayrshire Golf	32
English Golf Union (EGU)	24	South Lodge Hotel	497
European Golf Machinery	10	The Springs Hotel	495
Exclusive Media Events Ltd (Golflive'99)	10	St David's Park Hotel	501
		Stakis Puckrup Hall Hotel & Golf Club	489
The Golf Club - Thorpeness	492	Stoke Poges Golf Club	8
		Strokesport	12
H M T Plastics Ltd	10	Sun Longest Day Challenge	24
Harrogate Golf Club	28		
Hollywood Lakes Golf Club	32	Tan Lan Hotel	512
Horsted Place Hotel	495	Templar Lodge Hotel	511
Johnstounburn House Hotel	509	Tewkesbury Park Hotel Country Club Resort	493
		Tillmouth Park Country House Hotel	503
The K Club	512		
Kevin Randell Media & Marketing	7/12	Yeoldon House Hotel	489
Kilconquhar Castle Estate & Country Club	505		

PART X

Clubs and Courses in the British Isles and Europe

Compiled by Jan Bennett

1999 Centenary Clubs

The following clubs celebrate their centenaries in 1999:

England
Bakewell
Beccles
East Herts
North Downs
Ormskirk
Orsett
Porters Park
South Herts

Ireland
Carlow
Donaghadee
Rathfarnham

Scotland
Caledonian
Cruden Bay
Nairn Dunbar
Prestwick St Cuthbert
St Boswells
Tillicoultry

Wales
Rhos-on-Sea

Golf Clubs and Courses in the British Isles and Europe

How to use this section

1. Geographical divisions

In England, Ireland and Wales, clubs are listed in alphabetical order within counties. Listing is generally under geographical county, and sometimes under the county of affiliation.

In Scotland, counties are generally grouped under recognised administrative regions.

European clubs are listed in alphabetical order by country, and grouped under regional headings. In some areas, only 18-hole courses are included.

All clubs and courses are listed in the general index at the back of the book.

2. Club details

After the name of the club is the date of foundation (where available).

Courses are private unless otherwise stated. Many public courses have members' clubs which play over them; information on these clubs can be obtained from the course concerned.

The address is the postal address of each club or course. If the postal county is different from the one under which the club or course is listed, it will be shown in the address.

Tel: club telephone number general use.

Mem: total number of playing members. The number of lady members (L) and juniors (J) is sometimes shown separately.

Sec/Pro: telephone numbers for Secretaries and Professionals are shown if different from the club telephone number.

Holes: course length refers to medal tee yardages whenever possible.

Recs: Professional, Amateur and Ladies' Course Records.

V'tors: playing opportunities and restrictions for unaccompanied visitors.

Fees: green fees are quoted for visitors if they are permitted to play unaccompanied by a member. The basic cost per round or per day (D) is shown first, then, in brackets, the cost of a weekend and/or Bank Holiday round. Weekly (W) and monthly (M) are sometimes shown. *Green fees quoted are the most up to date supplied by each club.*

Loc: general location of course.

Mis: other golf facilities.

Arch: course architect/designer.

3. Abbreviations

WD Weekdays.
WE Weekends.
BH Bank Holidays.
U   Unrestricted.
M   With a member, ie casual visitors are not allowed. Only visitors playing with a member are permitted on the days stated.
H   Handicap certificate required.
I   Introduction, ie visitors are permitted on the days stated if they have a letter of introduction from their own club or their own club's membership card.
XL No ladies allowed on the days stated.
NA No visitors allowed.
SOC Recognised Golfing Societies welcome if previous arrangements made with secretary.
CR Course Rating (Europe)
SR Slope Rating (Europe)

The following information is as up to date as possible at the time of going to press. For the accuracy of this information we are indebted to the club secretaries who supply the details, but we are always pleased to be notified of any inaccuracies.

GREAT BRITAIN AND IRELAND COUNTY INDEX

England

Bedfordshire 530
Berkshire 531
Buckinghamshire 534
Cambridgeshire 537
Channel Islands 539
Cheshire 539
Cornwall 544
Cumbria 547
Derbyshire 549
Devon 551
Dorset 554
Durham 557
Essex 559
Gloucestershire 564
Hampshire 567
Herefordshire 572
Hertfordshire 573
Isle of Man 577
Isle of Wight 578
Kent 578
Lancashire 585
Leicestershire 591
Lincolnshire 593
London (list of clubs) 597
Manchester 597
Merseyside 599
Middlesex 601
Norfolk 604
Northamptonshire 607
Northumberland 609
Nottinghamshire 611
Oxfordshire 613
Rutland 615
Shropshire 615
Somerset 617
Staffordshire 620
Suffolk 623
Surrey 626
Sussex (East) 634
Sussex (West) 636
Tyne & Wear 639
Warwickshire 641
Wiltshire 644
Worcestershire 646
Yorkshire (East) 649
Yorkshire (North) 651
Yorkshire (South) 654
Yorkshire (West) 656

Scotland

Aberdeenshire 687
  Aberdeen Clubs 689
  Aberdeen Courses 690
Angus 690
  Carnoustie Clubs 692
  Carnoustie Courses 692
Argyll & Bute 692
Ayrshire 694
Borders 696
Clackmannanshire 698
Dumfries & Galloway 698
Dunbartonshire 700
Fife 701
  St Andrews Clubs 703
  St Andrews Courses 704
Glasgow 704
Highland
  Caithness & Sutherland 706
  Inverness 706
  Orkney & Shetland 708
  West Coast 708
Lanarkshire 709
Lothians
  East Lothian 711
  Midlothian 712
  West Lothian 714
Moray 715
Perth & Kinross 716
Renfrewshire 718
Stirlingshire 719

Ireland

Co Antrim 663
Co Armagh 664
Belfast 665
Co Carlow 665
Co Cavan 666
Co Clare 666
Co Cork 667
Co Donegal 669
Co Down 670
Co Dublin 672
Dublin City 674
Co Fermanagh 675
Co Galway 675
Co Kerry 676
Co Kildare 677
Co Kilkenny 678
Co Laois 678
Co Leitrim 679
Co Limerick 679
Co Londonderry 679
Co Longford 680
Co Louth 680
Co Mayo 680
Co Meath 681
Co Monaghan 682
Co Offaly 682
Co Roscommon 682
Co Sligo 683
Co Tipperary 683
Co Tyrone 684
Co Waterford 684
Co Westmeath 685
Co Wexford 685
Co Wicklow 686

Wales

Cardiganshire 721
Carmarthenshire 721
Conwy 721
Denbighshire 722
Flintshire 723
Gwynedd 723
Isle of Anglesey 724
Mid Glamorgan 725
Monmouthshire 726
Pembrokeshire 728
Powys 728
South Glamorgan 729
West Glamorgan 730
Wrexham 731

LIST OF NEW ENTRIES IN 1999

England

Bedfordshire
Bedford

Berkshire
Deanwood Park

Cheshire
Aldersey Green
Vale Royal Abbey

Dorset
Canford Magna

Essex
The Priors

Hampshire
Petersfield Sussex Road
Somerley Park

Kent
Westerham

Lancashire
Pennington

Lincolnshire
Humberston Park
Market Rasen
  Racecourse
Martin Moor
Pottergate
Tetney

Merseyside
Formby Hall

Northamptonshire
Brampton Heath

Northumberland
Longhirst Hall

Nottinghamshire
Rufford Park

Shropshire
Aqualate

Wiltshire
Rushmore Park

Worcestershire
Ravenmeadow

Yorkshire (West)
Cookridge Hall

Wales

Carmarthenshire
Glyn Abbey

Isle of Anglesey
Henllys Hall

Monmouthshire
Raglan Parc

West Glamorgan
Gower

Wrexham
Clays Farm

Ireland

Co Antrim
Antrim
Galgorm Castle

Co Dublin
Turvey

Co Galway
Curra West

Co Kildare
Newbridge

Co Kilkenny
Mountain View

Scotland

Argyll & Bute
Taynuilt

East Lothian
Castle Park

Midlothian
King's Acre
Vogrie

Stop Press

England

Pennington
Pennington Country Park, St Helens Road, Leigh WN7 3PB
Tel (01942) 682852
Mem 136
Sec AT Wilson
Pro T Kershaw
Holes 9 L 5698 yds Par 70 SSS 69
Recs Am–62 D Belch (1998)
V'tors U
Fees £4 (£4.50)
Loc 1/2 mile off A580, on Leigh bypass

Ireland

Mountain View
Kiltorcan, Ballyhale
Tel (056) 68122
Fax (056) 24655
Holes 9 L 5025 m Par 70
V'tors U
Fees £11 (£11)
Loc 12 miles S of Kilkenny
Mis Driving range. Pitch & putt
Arch John O'Sullivan

England

Bedfordshire

Aspley Guise & Woburn Sands (1914)
West Hill, Aspley Guise, Milton Keynes MK17 8DX
- **Tel** (01908) 582264
- **Fax** (01908) 582974
- **Mem** 560
- **Sec** B Hunt (01908) 583596
- **Pro** D Marsden (01908) 582974
- **Holes** 18 L 6079 yds Par 71 SSS 70
- **Recs** Am–67 M Wharton
  Pro–68 P Webster
- **V'tors** WD–H WE/BH–MH SOC–Wed & Fri
- **Fees** £23 D–£29
- **Loc** 2 miles W of M1 Junction 13
- **Arch** Herd/Sandow

Aylesbury Vale (1991)
Wing, Leighton Buzzard LU7 0UJ
- **Tel** (01525) 240196
- **Fax** (01525) 240848
- **Mem** 600
- **Sec** C Wright (Sec/Mgr)
- **Pro** C Skeet (01525) 240197
- **Holes** 18 L 6612 yds Par 72 SSS 72
- **Recs** Am–69 C Beesley (1997)
  Pro–69 D Armor (1993)
- **V'tors** WD–U WE–U phone first SOC–WD
- **Fees** £12
- **Loc** 3 miles W of Leighton Buzzard on Wing-Stewkley road
- **Mis** Driving range
- **Arch** Sq Ldr Don Wright

Beadlow Manor Hotel G&CC (1973)
Beadlow, Shefford SG17 5PH
- **Tel** (01525) 860800
- **Fax** (01525) 861345
- **Mem** 700
- **Sec** R Tommey (01525) 843398
- **Pro** P Hetherington (01525) 861292
- **Holes** 18 L 6238 yds SSS 71
  18 L 6042 yds SSS 70
- **Recs** Am–71 C Skinner
  Pro–66 L Fickling
- **V'tors** U H SOC
- **Fees** On application
- **Loc** 2 miles W of Shefford on A507
- **Mis** Driving range

Bedford (1999)
Carnoustie Drive, Great Denham, Biddenham MK40 4BF
- **Tel** (01234) 320022
- **Fax** (01234) 320023
- **Pro** Z Thompson, J Richardson
- **Holes** 18 L 6560 yds Par 72

Bedford & County (1912)
Green Lane, Clapham, Bedford MK41 6ET
- **Tel** (01234) 352617
- **Fax** (01234) 357195
- **Mem** 600
- **Sec** RP Walker (Mgr), D Sinfield
- **Pro** R Tattersall (01234) 359189
- **Holes** 18 L 6399 yds SSS 70
- **Recs** Am–66 C Allen (1980),
  SD Folbigg (1990),
  D West (1996)
  Pro–66 M King (1978)
  Ladies–69 R Hudson (1996)
- **V'tors** WD–U H WE–M SOC
- **Fees** D–£30
- **Loc** 2 miles NW of Bedford on A6

Bedfordshire (1891)
Bromham Rd, Biddenham, Bedford MK40 4AF
- **Tel** (01234) 261669
- **Fax** (01234) 261669
- **Mem** 600
- **Sec** CD Carrington (Gen Mgr)
- **Pro** P Saunders (01234) 353653
- **Holes** 18 L 6305 yds SSS 70
- **Recs** Am–63 JC Kemp
  Pro–65 K Warren
- **V'tors** WD–U (phone first) WE–M before noon SOC–WD
- **Fees** On application
- **Loc** 2 miles NW of Bedford (A428)

Chalgrave Manor
Dunstable Road, Chalgrave, Toddington LU5 6JN
- **Tel** (01525) 876556
- **Fax** (01525) 876556
- **Mem** 450
- **Sec** S Rumball
- **Pro** M Brewer (01525) 876554
- **Holes** 18 L 6382 yds Par 72 SSS 70
- **Recs** Am–69 M Parrett (1995)
  Pro–69 M Brewer (1994)
- **V'tors** U SOC–WD
- **Fees** £10 (£15)
- **Loc** 2 miles W of M1 Junction 12 on A5120
- **Mis** Practice range
- **Arch** Mike Palmer

Colmworth (1992)
New Road, Colmworth MK44 2NV
- **Tel** (01234) 378181
- **Fax** (01234) 376235
- **Mem** 350
- **Sec** P Watmough (01234) 266636
- **Pro** S Bryden (01234) 378822
- **Holes** 18 L 6420 yds Par 70 SSS 71
- **V'tors** U SOC
- **Loc** 6 miles N of Bedford, off Kimbolton road
- **Arch** John Glasgow

Colworth (1985)
Unilever Research, Sharnbrook, Bedford MK44 1LQ
- **Tel** (01234) 222076
- **Mem** 405
- **Sec** S Pound
- **Holes** 9 L 2626 yds Par 68 SSS 66
- **Recs** Am–69 W Young (1997)
- **V'tors** M
- **Fees** D–£6.50
- **Loc** Sharnbrook, 10 miles N of Bedford, off A6

Dunstable Downs (1907)
Whipsnade Road, Dunstable LU6 2NB
- **Tel** (01582) 604472
- **Fax** (01582) 478700
- **Mem** 640
- **Sec** DH Mear
- **Pro** M Weldon (01582) 662806
- **Holes** 18 L 6255 yds SSS 70
- **Recs** Am–64 J Todd (1989)
  Pro–64 K Golding (1992)
- **V'tors** WD–H WE–M SOC–WD exc Wed
- **Fees** £25 D–£35
- **Loc** 2 miles SW of Dunstable on B4541. M1 Junction 11
- **Arch** James Braid

Griffin (1985)
Chaul End Road, Caddington LU1 4AX
- **Tel** (01582) 415573
- **Fax** (01582) 415314
- **Mem** 500
- **Sec** Mrs J Johnson
- **Pro** None
- **Holes** 18 L 6240 yds Par 71 SSS 70
- **Recs** Am–63 M Ecart (1993)
- **V'tors** WD–U WE/BH–phone first SOC
- **Fees** D–£13 (£16)
- **Loc** 3 miles W of Luton on A505 between Dunstable and Caddington. M1 Junction 11

John O'Gaunt (1948)
Sutton Park, Sandy, Biggleswade SG19 2LY
- **Tel** (01767) 260360
- **Fax** (01767) 262834
- **Mem** 1450
- **Sec** J Keight
- **Pro** P Round (01767) 260094

For list of abbreviations see page 527

Holes John O'Gaunt 18 L 6513 yds
       SSS 71; Carthagena 18 L
       5869 yds SSS 69
Recs   Am–64 N Wharton
       Pro–67 SC Evans
V'tors H–phone first SOC–WD
Fees   £45 (£50)
Loc   3 miles NE of Biggleswade on
       B1040
Arch   Hawtree

Leighton Buzzard (1925)
Plantation Road, Leighton Buzzard LU7 7JF
Tel   (01525) 373811/373812
Mem   650
Sec   J Burchell (01525) 373811
Pro   L Scarbrow (01525) 372143
Holes 18 L 6101 yds SSS 70
Recs   Am–66 S Wells (1993)
       Pro–66 N Brown (1997)
V'tors WD exc Tues–U H
       WE/BH–MH
Fees   £20 D–£27
Loc   Heath and Reach, 1 mile N of
       Leighton Buzzard. M1
       Junction 12

Lyshott Heath (1980)
Ampthill MK45 2JB
Tel   (01525) 840252
Fax   (01525) 406249
Mem   380
Sec   DC Cooke
Pro   D Armor (01525) 402269
Holes 18 L 7051 yds SSS 73
Recs   Am–70 S Cherry
       Pro–68 D Armor
V'tors WD–U exc Thurs WE–NA
       before 2pm
Fees   £18 (£30)
Loc   4 miles from M1 Junctions 12
       or 13 on A507
Arch   W Sutherland

Mount Pleasant (1992)
Pay and play
Station Road, Lower Stondon, Henlow SG16 6JL
Tel   (01462) 850999
Fax   (01462) 850257
Mem   300
Sec   D Simkins (Prop)
Pro   M Roberts (01462) 850999
Holes 9 L 6003 yds Par 70 SSS 69
V'tors U SOC–WD
Fees   9 holes–£7 (£9)
       18 holes–£12 (£16)
Loc   4 miles N of Hitchin, off A600
Arch   Derek Young

Mowsbury (1975)
Public
Kimbolton Road, Bedford MK41 8DQ
Tel   (01234) 216374/771041
Mem   611
Sec   LW Allan
Pro   M Summers
Holes 18 L 6514 yds SSS 71
Recs   Am–64
       Pro–66

V'tors U
Fees   £7.50 (£9.50)
Loc   2 miles N of Bedford on B660
Mis   Driving range
Arch   Hawtree

Pavenham Park (1994)
Pavenham, Bedford MK43 7PE
Tel   (01234) 822202
Fax   (01234) 826602
Mem   700
Sec   M Rizzi
Pro   ZL Thompson
Holes 18 L 6353 yds SSS 71
V'tors WD–U WE–M SOC–WD
Fees   £19
Loc   4 miles NW of Bedford on A6
Arch   Zac Thompson

RAF Henlow (1985)
RAF Henlow Camp, Henlow SG16 6DN
Tel   (01462) 851515 Ext 7083
Fax   (01462) 851515 Ext 7687
Mem   250
Sec   CJ Harwood (01462) 851515
       (Ext 7769)
Pro   Beverley Huke
       (01908) 310247
Holes 9 L 5618 yds SSS 67
Recs   Am–68 R Shimwell (1995)
V'tors M
Fees   D–£5
Loc   3 miles SE of Shefford
       on A600

South Beds (1892)
Warden Hill Road, Luton LU2 7AA
Tel   (01582) 591209
Fax   (01582) 495381
Mem   850
Sec   CAI Gyford (01582) 591500
Pro   E Cogle (01582) 591209
Holes Galley 18 L 6332 yds SSS 71
       Warden 9 L 4954 yds SSS 64
Recs   Am–64 I Tottingham (1993)
V'tors Galley WD–U (Ladies
       Day-Tues) WE/BH–H exc
       comp days–NA SOC
       Warden–U
Fees   Galley £19 D–£29 (£26
       D–£38) Warden £7 (£10)
Loc   3 miles N of Luton, E of A6

Stockwood Park (1973)
Public
Stockwood Park, London Rd, Luton LU1 4LX
Tel   (01582) 413704
Fax   (01582) 481001
Mem   900
Sec   Mrs B McMillan
Pro   G McCarthy
Holes 18 L 6049 yds SSS 69
Recs   Am–67 D Smith (1993)
       Pro–66 T Minshall
V'tors U
Fees   £8.15 (£10.75)
Loc   1 mile S of Luton on A6. M1
       Junction 10
Mis   Driving range

Tilsworth (1972)
Pay and play
Dunstable Rd, Tilsworth, Dunstable LU7 9PU
Tel   (01525) 210721/210722
Fax   (01525) 210465
Mem   370
Sec   A Cant
Pro   N Webb (Mgr)
Holes 18 L 5303 yds Par 69 SSS 66
Recs   Am–68 J Howells
       Pro–65 N Webb
V'tors U SOC
Fees   £10 (£12)
Loc   2 miles N of Dunstable (A5)
Mis   Driving range

Wyboston Lakes (1978)
Public
Wyboston Lakes, Wyboston MK44 3AL
Tel   (01480) 223004
Fax   (01480) 407330
Mem   300
Sec   B Chinn (Mgr)
Pro   P Ashwell (01480) 223004
Holes 18 L 5995 yds Par 70 SSS 69
Recs   Am–69
       Pro–64 P Ashwell
V'tors WD–U WE–booking SOC
Fees   £11 (£15)
Loc   S of St Neots, off A1 and
       St Neots bypass
Mis   Driving range
Arch   Neil Ockden

Berkshire

Bearwood (1986)
Mole Road, Sindlesham, Wokingham RG41 5DB
Tel   (0118) 976 1330
Fax   (0118) 977 2687
Mem   500
Sec   BFC Tustin (Mgr)
       (0118) 976 0060
Pro   (0118) 976 0156
Holes 9 L 5614 yds SSS 68
Recs   Am–66 D Primrose (1996)
       Pro–66 JB Tustin (1995)
V'tors WD–H before 4pm –M after
       4pm WE/BH–M
Fees   18 holes–£18 9 holes–£10
Loc   1 mile SW of Winnersh, on
       B3030. M4 Junction 10

Bearwood Lakes (1996)
Bearwood Road, Sindlesham RG41 4SJ
Tel   (0118) 979 7900
Fax   (0118) 979 2911
Mem   750
Sec   S Evans (Gen Mgr)
Pro   E Inglis (0118) 978 3030
Holes 18 L 6800 yds Par 72 SSS 72
V'tors M H
Fees   £25 (£30)
Loc   1 mile S of M4 Junction 10,
       between Wokingham and
       Sindlesham
Arch   Martin Hawtree

For list of abbreviations see page 527

Berkshire

The Berkshire (1928)
Swinley Road, Ascot SL5 8AY
- **Tel** (01344) 621495
- **Mem** 935
- **Sec** Lt Col JCF Hunt (01344) 621496
- **Pro** P Anderson (01344) 622351
- **Holes** Red 18 L 6369 yds SSS 71
  Blue 18 L 6260 yds SSS 71
- **V'tors** WD–I WE/BH–M
- **Fees** On application
- **Loc** 3 miles from Ascot on A332
- **Arch** Herbert Fowler

Bird Hills (1985)
Public
Drift Road, Hawthorn Hill, Maidenhead SL6 3ST
- **Tel** (01628) 771030/75588/26035
- **Fax** (01628) 31023
- **Sec** A Kibblewhite
- **Pro** S Kelly, C Cowie
- **Holes** 18 L 6212 yds SSS 69
  Pro–65 S Kelly (1988)
- **V'tors** U SOC–WD
- **Fees** On application
- **Loc** 4 miles S of Maidenhead on A330
- **Mis** Floodlit driving range

Blue Mountain Golf Centre (1993)
Pay and play
Wood Lane, Binfield RG42 4EX
- **Tel** (01344) 300220
- **Fax** (01344) 360960
- **Mem** 1200
- **Pro** N Dainton
- **Holes** 18 L 6097 yds SSS 70
- **Recs** Am–69 C Challen (1993)
  Pro–63 P Simpson
- **V'tors** U SOC
- **Loc** 1 mile W of Bracknell on B3408. M4 Junction 10
- **Mis** Driving range. Golf Academy

Calcot Park (1930)
Bath Road, Calcot, Reading RG31 7RN
- **Tel** (0118) 942 7124
- **Fax** (0118) 945 3373
- **Mem** 750
- **Sec** T Harris
- **Pro** IJ Campbell (0118) 942 7797
- **Holes** 18 L 6283 yds SSS 70
- **Recs** Am–65 R Walton (1994)
  Pro–63 C Defoy (1983)
  Ladies–69 L Walton (1992)
- **V'tors** WD–I H WE/BH–M SOC
- **Fees** On application
- **Loc** 3 miles W of Reading on A4. M4 Junction 12
- **Arch** HS Colt

Castle Royle (1994)
Knowl Hill, Reading RG10 9XA
- **Tel** (01628) 829252
- **Sec** B Lee, G Payne (Props)
- **Pro** P Stanwick
- **Holes** 18 L 6700 yds Par 72
- **V'tors** M

Fees
£35 (£45)
- **Loc** 2 miles W of Maidenhead (A4). M4 Junction 8/9
- **Arch** Neil Coles

Datchet (1890)
Buccleuch Road, Datchet SL3 9BP
- **Tel** (01753) 543887 (Clubhouse)
- **Fax** (01753) 541872
- **Mem** 210 50(L) 25(J)
- **Sec** Mrs S Thompson (01753) 541872
- **Holes** 9 L 5978 yds SSS 69
- **Recs** Am–66 S McKee (1996)
  Pro–63 N Wood (1979)
- **V'tors** WD–U before 3pm –M after 3pm WE–M SOC
- **Fees** £16 D–£24
- **Loc** Slough, Windsor 2 miles

Deanwood Park (1995)
Pay and play
Stockcross, Newbury RG20 8JS
- **Tel** (01635) 48772
- **Fax** (01635) 48772
- **Mem** 212
- **Sec** J Bowness
- **Pro** D Tunn
- **Holes** 9 L 4230 yds Par 64 SSS 61
- **Recs** Am–63 J Bowness (1997)
- **V'tors** U
- **Fees** £12 (£15)
- **Loc** 2 miles W of Newbury (B4000)
- **Mis** Practice range

Donnington Grove CC
Donnington, Newbury RG13 2LA
- **Tel** (01635) 581000
- **Fax** (01635) 552259
- **Mem** 250
- **Sec** E Tanaka (Mgr)
- **Pro** G Williams
- **Holes** 18 L 7050 yds Par 72 SSS 74
- **V'tors** U SOC–WD/BH
- **Fees** £20 D–£30 (£30 D–£45)
- **Loc** NW of Newbury, off old Oxford road (B4494) or A4. M4 Junction 13
- **Arch** Dave Thomas

Donnington Valley (1985)
Old Oxford Road, Donnington, Newbury RG14 3AG
- **Tel** (01635) 32488
- **Fax** (01635) 569481
- **Mem** 500
- **Sec** LC Storey
- **Pro** E Lainchbury
- **Holes** 18 L 4029 yds SSS 60
- **V'tors** U
- **Fees** On application
- **Loc** N of Newbury, off old Oxford road

Downshire (1973)
Public
Easthampstead Park, Wokingham RG11 3DH
- **Tel** (01344) 302030
- **Fax** (01344) 301020

- **Sec** DM Coles
- **Pro** W Humphreys
- **Holes** 18 L 6382 yds SSS 70
- **Recs** Am–67 T Smith
  Pro–66 M King
- **V'tors** U SOC
- **Fees** £12.50 (£15.50)
- **Loc** Off Nine Mile Ride
- **Mis** Driving range. Pitch & putt

East Berkshire (1903)
Ravenswood Ave, Crowthorne RG45 6BD
- **Tel** (01344) 772041
- **Fax** (01344) 777378
- **Mem** 700
- **Sec** JF Stocker
- **Pro** A Roe (01344) 774112
- **Holes** 18 L 6345 yds SSS 70
- **Recs** Am–64 J Brant (1992)
- **V'tors** WD–H WE/BH–M SOC
- **Fees** £37
- **Loc** Nr Crowthorne Station
- **Arch** P Paxton

Goring & Streatley (1895)
Rectory Road, Streatley-on-Thames RG8 9QA
- **Tel** (01491) 872688
- **Fax** (01491) 875224
- **Mem** 740 115(L) 50(J)
- **Sec** I McColl (Sec/Mgr) (01491) 873229
- **Pro** R Mason (01491) 873715
- **Holes** 18 L 6320 yds SSS 70
- **Recs** Am–65 DG Lane
  Pro–62 P Simpson
- **V'tors** WD–U WE/BH–M SOC–WD
- **Fees** £22 D–£30 (£25 D–£40)
- **Loc** 10 miles NW of Reading on A417
- **Arch** Tom Dunne

Hennerton (1992)
Crazies Hill Road, Wargrave RG10 8LT
- **Tel** (0118) 940 1000/4778
- **Fax** (0118) 940 1042
- **Mem** 500
- **Sec** PJ Hearn
- **Pro** W Farrow (0118) 940 4778
- **Holes** 9 L 2730 yds SSS 34
- **Recs** Am–66 C Pilbrow (1994)
- **V'tors** WD–U WE–pm only SOC
- **Fees** 18 holes–£15 (£18)
  9 holes–£10 (£14)
- **Loc** Between Maidenhead and Reading (A4/A321)
- **Mis** Driving range
- **Arch** Dion Beard

Hurst (1979)
Public
Sandford Lane, Hurst, Wokingham RG10 0SQ
- **Tel** (01734) 344355
- **Sec** AG Poncia (Hon)
- **Pro** P Watson
- **Holes** 9 L 3015 yds SSS 70
- **Fees** On application
- **Loc** Reading 5 miles. Wokingham 3 miles

For list of abbreviations see page 527

Maidenhead (1896)
Shoppenhangers Road, Maidenhead SL6 2PZ
Tel (01628) 624693
Mem 600
Sec TP Jackson
Pro S Geary (01628) 624067
Holes 18 L 6360 yds SSS 70
Recs Am–S Maynard (1992)
Pro–64 AN Walker,
G Wolstenholme
V'tors WD–H Fri–M after noon WE–M
Fees D–£35
Loc Off A308, nr Maidenhead Station

Mapledurham (1992)
Mapledurham, Reading RG4 7UD
Tel (0118) 946 3353
Fax (0118) 946 3363
Mem 400
Sec D Burton
Pro S O'Keefe
Holes 18 L 5625 yds SSS 69
Recs Am–67 A Brash (1996)
Pro–64 D Burton (1995)
V'tors U
Fees £14 (£17)
Loc 4 miles NW of Reading, off A4074
Arch MRM Sandow

Mill Ride (1990)
Mill Ride, Ascot SL5 8LT
Tel (01344) 886777
Fax (01344) 886820
Mem 300
Sec G Irvine (Gen Mgr)
Pro M Palmer
Holes 18 L 6752 yds SSS 72
Recs Am–68 G Weeks (1992)
Pro–64 G Houston
V'tors H SOC
Fees On application
Loc 2 miles W of Ascot
Mis www.mill-ride.com
Arch Donald Steel

Newbury & Crookham (1873)
Bury's Bank Road, Greenham Common, Newbury RG19 8BZ
Tel (01635) 40035
Fax (01635) 40045
Mem 626
Sec Mrs JR Hearsey
Pro DW Harris (01635) 31201
Holes 18 L 5940 yds SSS 68
Recs Am–63 G Woodham (1996)
Pro–64 M Squire (1997)
V'tors WD–U H WE–M (recognised club members)
Fees £20
Loc 2 miles SE of Newbury

Newbury Racecourse (1994)
The Racecourse, Newbury RG14 7NZ
Tel (01635) 551464
Fax (01635) 528254

Mem 300
Sec P Henderson (01635) 580784
Pro N Mitchell (01635) 551464
Holes 18 L 6311 yds Par 70 SSS 70
Recs Am–69 E Richardson (1996)
V'tors U SOC
Fees £13 (£17)
Loc 4 miles S of M4 Junction 13 on A34
Mis Driving range

Reading (1910)
17 Kidmore End Road, Emmer Green, Reading RG4 8SG
Tel (0118) 947 2169
Fax (0118) 946 4468
Mem 725
Sec R Harris (0118) 947 2909
Pro AR Wild (0118) 947 6116
Holes 18 L 6212 yds SSS 70
Recs Am–66 B Smith
Pro–64 TP Morrison
V'tors Mon–Thurs–UH Fri/WE/BH–M SOC–Tues–Thurs
Fees £30
Loc 2 miles N of Reading, off Peppard Road (B481)
Arch James Braid

Royal Ascot (1887)
Winkfield Road, Ascot SL5 7LJ
Tel (01344) 625175
Fax (01344) 872330
Mem 600
Sec NCW Barker
Pro A White (01344) 624656
Holes 18 L 5716 yds SSS 68
Recs Am–65 M Milne,
G Woodman, J Johnson
Pro–67 B Lane
V'tors M SOC
Fees On application
Loc On Ascot Heath, inside Ascot racecourse. Windsor 4 miles
Arch JH Taylor

The Royal Household (1901)
Buckingham Palace, London SW1A 1AA
Tel (0171) 930 4832
Fax (0171) 839 5950
Mem 200
Sec A Barrett
Holes 9 L 4560 yds SSS 62
V'tors Strictly by invitation
Loc Home Park, Windsor Castle
Arch Muir Ferguson

Sand Martins (1993)
Finchampstead Road, Wokingham RG11 3RQ
Tel (0118) 979 2711
Fax (0118) 977 0282
Mem 820
Sec AJ Hall
Pro AJ Hall (0118) 977 0265
Holes 18 L 6204 yds Par 70 SSS 70
Recs Am–69 L Gauthier (1997)
Pro–64 I Mosey (1997)

V'tors WD–U WE–NA SOC
Fees £22
Loc 1 mile S of Wokingham. M4 Junction 10
Mis Driving range
Arch ET Fox

Sonning (1911)
Duffield Road, Sonning, Reading RG4 6GJ
Tel (0118) 969 3332
Fax (0118) 944 8409
Mem 700
Sec AJ Tanner
Pro RT McDougall (0118) 969 2910
Holes 18 L 6366 yds SSS 70
Recs Am–65 J Lush
Pro–65 B Lane
V'tors WD–H WE–M
Fees On application
Loc 1½ miles E of A329(M). S of A4, nr Sonning

Sulham Valley (1992)
Pincents Lane, Calcot, Reading RG3 5UQ
Tel (01734) 305959
Fax (01734) 305002
Mem 700
Sec To be appointed
Pro Tina Tetley
Holes 18 L 6121 yds Par 71
V'tors U SOC
Fees £20 (£25)
Loc M4 Junction 12, 1 mile

Swinley Forest (1909)
Coronation Road, Ascot SL9 5LE
Tel (01344) 620197
Fax (01344) 874733
Mem 310
Sec IL Pearce (01344) 874979
Pro RC Parker (01344) 874811
Holes 18 L 6045 yds Par 69 SSS 70
Recs Am–65 IL Pearce
Pro–62 R Chapman
V'tors M
Fees £65
Loc S of Ascot
Arch HS Colt

Temple (1909)
Henley Road, Hurley, Maidenhead SL6 5LH
Tel (01628) 824795
Fax (01628) 828119
Mem 450
Sec KGM Adderley (01628) 824795
Pro J Whiteley (01628) 824254
Holes 18 L 6232 yds SSS 70
Recs Am–63 S Hodsdon
V'tors WD–H WE/BH–M SOC
Fees £30 (£35)
Loc Between Maidenhead and Henley on A4130. M4 Junction 8/9. M40 Junction 4
Arch Willie Park Jr

For list of abbreviations see page 527

West Berkshire (1975)
Chaddleworth, Newbury RG20 7DU
Tel (01488) 638574
Mem 500
Sec Mrs CM Clayton
Pro P Simpson (01488) 638851
Holes 18 L 7059 yds SSS 74
Recs Am–71 D Murphy (1993)
Pro–65 W Grant (1994)
Ladies–75 D Edwards (1995)
V'tors WD–U WE–M SOC–WD
Fees £20 D–£28
Loc Off A338 to Wantage. M4 Junction 14

Winter Hill (1976)
Grange Lane, Cookham SL6 9RP
Tel (01628) 527613
Fax (01628) 527613
Mem 800
Sec JE Hoskings
Pro R Frost (01628) 527610
Holes 18 L 6408 yds SSS 71
Recs Am–63 J Ackland-Snow (1996)
V'tors WD–U WE–M SOC
Fees £25
Loc Maidenhead 3 miles
Arch Charles Lawrie

Buckinghamshire

Abbey Hill (1975)
Monks Way, Two Mile Ash, Milton Keynes MK8 8AA
Tel (01908) 563845
Mem 500
Sec Mrs L Bentley
Pro G Woodham
Holes 18 L 6193 yds SSS 69
Par 3 course
Recs Am–67 T Mernagh
Pro–67 S Roche
V'tors U
Fees On application
Loc 2 miles S of Stony Stratford
Mis Driving range

Aylesbury Golf Centre (1992)
Public
Hulcott Lane, Bierton HP22 5GA
Tel (01296) 393644
Sec K Partington (Mgr)
Pro M Kierstenson
Holes 18 L 5965 yds SSS 69
V'tors U
Fees £10
Loc 1 mile N of Aylesbury on A418
Mis Driving range
Arch TS Benwell

Beaconsfield (1914)
Seer Green, Beaconsfield HP9 2UR
Tel (01494) 676545
Fax (01494) 681148
Mem 850
Sec RE Thomas
Pro M Brothers (01494) 676616
Holes 18 L 6493 yds Par 72 SSS 71
Recs Am–66 D Haines
Pro–63 E Murray
V'tors WD–H WE–M SOC
Fees £30 D–£40
Loc 2 miles E of Beaconsfield. M40 Junction 2
Mis Driving range
Arch HS Colt

Buckingham (1914)
Tingewick Road, Buckingham MK18 4AE
Tel (01280) 813282 (Clubhouse)
Fax (01280) 821812
Mem 680
Sec T Gates (Gen Mgr) (01280) 815566
Pro T Gates (01280) 815210
Holes 18 L 6082 yds SSS 69
Recs Am–67 S Impey (1993)
Pro–67 S Watson (1990)
V'tors WD–U WE–M SOC–Tues & Thurs
Fees £28
Loc 2 miles SW of Buckingham on A421

The Buckinghamshire (1992)
Denham Court, Denham Court Drive, Denham UB9 5BG
Tel (01895) 835777
Fax (01895) 835210
Mem 650
Sec W Kirby (Mgr)
Pro J O'Leary
Holes 18 L 6880 yds SSS 72
Recs Am–70 P Kilgour
Pro–70 G Lee
V'tors I or M SOC–WD exc Fri
Fees £70 (£80)
Loc Off A40(M). M25 Junction 16b/M40 Junction 1
Mis Driving range (Members)
Arch John Jacobs

Burnham Beeches (1891)
Green Lane, Burnham, Slough SL1 8EG
Tel (01628) 661150
Fax (01628) 668968
Mem 670
Sec AJ Buckner (Mgr) (01628) 661448
Pro R Bolton (01628) 661661
Holes 18 L 6449 yds SSS 71
Recs Am–66 LC Donald
Pro–64 H Flatman
V'tors WD–I WE/BH–M H
Fees £30 D–£45
Loc 4 miles W of Slough

Chalfont Park (1994)
Three Households, Chalfont St Giles HP8 4LW
Tel (01494) 876293
Mem 720
Sec P Jackson (Golf Dir)
Pro P Howson
Holes 18 L 5300 yds SSS 68
V'tors U SOC–WD
Fees £18
Loc 3 miles N of M40 Junction 2
Arch Jonathan Gaunt

Chartridge Park (1989)
Chartridge, Chesham HP5 2TF
Tel (01494) 791772
Fax (01494) 786462
Mem 700
Sec Mr & Mrs P Gibbins
Pro P Gibbins
Holes 18 L 5516 yds SSS 66
Recs Am–64 S Richards (1997)
Pro–67 P Gibbins (1995)
Ladies Pro–68 L Davies (1997)
V'tors U SOC
Fees £20 (£25)
Loc 2 miles NW of Chesham. 9 miles W of M25 Junction 18
Arch John Jacobs

Chesham & Ley Hill (1900)
Ley Hill, Chesham HP5 1UZ
Tel (01494) 784541
Fax (01494) 785806
Mem 422
Sec B Durand
Holes 9 L 5240 yds SSS 66
Recs Am–62 GA Knowes (1994)
Pro–65 M Lovegrove (1986)
V'tors WD–U exc Wed am–NA & Tues–M after 3pm WE/BH–M SOC–Thurs only
Fees On application
Loc Chesham 2 miles
Mis Course closed Sun after 2pm from 1st Apr-30th Sept

Chiltern Forest
Aston Hill, Halton, Aylesbury HP22 5NQ
Tel (01296) 631267
Fax (01296) 631267
Mem 600
Sec S Thornton (01296) 631267
Pro A Lavers (01296) 631817
Holes 18 L 5765 yds SSS 70
Recs Am–65 S Welfare (1997)
Pro–64 I Mosey, M Booth (1997)
V'tors WD–U WE–M SOC
Fees £18 D–£23
Loc 5 miles SE of Aylesbury, off A4011

Denham (1910)
Tilehouse Lane, Denham UB9 5DE
Tel (01895) 832022
Fax (01895) 835340
Mem 800
Sec MJ Miller
Pro S Campbell (01895) 832801
Holes 18 L 6456 yds SSS 71
Recs Am–66 DMA Steel (1975)
V'tors Mon–Thurs–I H Fri–Sun/BH–M
Fees £36 D–£52
Loc 2 miles NW of Uxbridge
Arch HS Colt

For list of abbreviations see page 527

Buckinghamshire 535

Ellesborough (1906)
Butlers Cross, Aylesbury HP17 0TZ
- **Tel** (01296) 622114
- **Fax** (01296) 622114
- **Mem** 700
- **Sec** PMJ York (Gen Mgr)
- **Pro** M Squire (01296) 623126
- **Holes** 18 L 6283 yds SSS 71
- **Recs** Am–64 C Roake
  Pro–66 T Ashton
- **V'tors** WE/BH–M WD–I or H
  SOC–Wed & Thurs only
- **Fees** On application
- **Loc** 1 mile W of Wendover

Farnham Park (1974)
Public
Park Road, Stoke Poges, Slough SL2 4PJ
- **Tel** (01753) 643332
- **Mem** 600
- **Sec** Mrs M Brooker (01753) 647065
- **Pro** P Warner
- **Holes** 18 L 6172 yds SSS 71
- **Recs** Am–66 P Robshaw
  Pro–68 T Bowers
- **V'tors** U
- **Fees** £9 (£12)
- **Loc** 2 miles N of Slough
- **Arch** Hawtree

Flackwell Heath (1905)
Treadaway Road, Flackwell Heath, High Wycombe HP10 9PE
- **Tel** (01628) 520027
- **Fax** (01628) 530040
- **Mem** 750
- **Sec** Pamela Morgan (01628) 520929
- **Pro** P Watson (01628) 523017
- **Holes** 18 L 6207 yds SSS 70
- **Recs** Am–63 PJ Collett
  Pro–64 M Booth
- **V'tors** WD–U WE–M
  SOC–Wed & Thurs
- **Fees** £30
- **Loc** Between High Wycombe and Beaconsfield, off A40. M40 Junction 3/4

Gerrards Cross (1934)
Chalfont Park, Gerrards Cross SL9 0QA
- **Tel** (01753) 883263
- **Fax** (01753) 883593
- **Mem** 725
- **Sec** Inger Perkins
- **Pro** M Barr (01753) 885300
- **Holes** 18 L 6212 yds SSS 70
- **Recs** Am–64 R Gill (1997)
  Pro–63 AP Barr
- **V'tors** WD–H WE/BH–M SOC
- **Fees** £32 D–£44
- **Loc** 1 mile from Station, off A313

Harewood Downs (1908)
Cokes Lane, Chalfont St Giles HP8 4TA
- **Tel** (01494) 762308
- **Fax** (01494) 766869
- **Mem** 700
- **Sec** Wg Cdr MR Cannon (01494) 762184

- **Pro** GC Morris (01494) 764102
- **Holes** 18 L 5958 yds SSS 69
- **Recs** Am–65 AL Parsons
  Pro–65 JM Hume
- **V'tors** WD–H WE/BH–H XL before noon SOC
- **Fees** £27 (£33)
- **Loc** 2 miles E of Amersham, off A413

Harleyford (1996)
Harleyford Estate, Henley Road, Marlow SL7 2SP
- **Tel** (01628) 402300
- **Fax** (01628) 478434
- **Mem** 850
- **Sec** R Eades (Mgr) (01628) 402338
- **Pro** A Barr (01628) 402300
- **Holes** 18 L 6604 yds Par 72 SSS 72
- **V'tors** U H
- **Fees** £40 (£60)
- **Loc** 1 mile W of Marlow on A4155
- **Mis** Driving range
- **Arch** Donald Steel

Hazlemere G&CC (1982)
Penn Road, Hazlemere, High Wycombe HP15 7LR
- **Tel** (01494) 714722
- **Fax** (01494) 713914
- **Mem** 850
- **Sec** DE Hudson
- **Pro** A McKay, P Harrison (01494) 718298
- **Holes** 18 L 5855 yds SSS 68
- **Recs** Am–65 N Bennett (1995)
  Pro–62 M Booth (1994)
- **V'tors** WD–U WE–booking req SOC–WD
- **Fees** £26 (£40)
- **Loc** 3 miles NE of High Wycombe on B474
- **Arch** Terry Murray

Iver (1983)
Hollow Hill Lane, Iver SL0 0JJ
- **Tel** (01753) 655615
- **Fax** (01753) 654225
- **Mem** 500
- **Sec** G Noble
- **Pro** K Teschner
- **Holes** 9 L 6300 yds SSS 72
- **Recs** Am–68 D Sargood (1990)
- **V'tors** U SOC
- **Fees** 18 holes–£11 (£14.50)
  9 holes–£6 (£7.50)
- **Loc** 1/2 mile from Langley station, off Langley Park Road. M4 Junction 5, 2 miles

Ivinghoe (1967)
Wellcroft, Ivinghoe, Leighton Buzzard LU7 9EF
- **Tel** (01296) 668696
- **Fax** (01296) 662755
- **Mem** 250
- **Sec** Mrs SE Garrad (0296) 662478
- **Pro** PW Garrad (01296) 668696
- **Holes** 9 L 4508 yds SSS 62
- **Recs** Am–61 J Dillon (1984)
  Pro–57 M Flitney (1994)

- **V'tors** WD–U WE–U after 8am SOC
- **Fees** 18 holes–£7 (£8)
  9 holes–£5
- **Loc** 3 miles N of Tring. M1 Junction 11, 5 miles
- **Arch** R Garrad

Lambourne (1992)
Dropmore Road, Burnham SL1 8NF
- **Tel** (01628) 666755
- **Fax** (01628) 663301
- **Mem** 600
- **Sec** W Sheffield
- **Pro** D Hart (Golf Dir) (01628) 662936
- **Holes** 18 L 6771 yds SSS 73
- **Recs** Am–70 C Challen
  Pro–67 P Robshaw
- **V'tors** H or I
- **Fees** £38 (£48)
- **Loc** 1 mile N of Burnham. M40 Junction 2. M4 Junction 7
- **Arch** Donald Steel

Little Chalfont (1981)
Lodge Lane, Little Chalfont, Amersham HP8 4AJ
- **Tel** (01494) 764877
- **Fax** (01494) 762860
- **Mem** 260
- **Sec** JM Dunne
- **Pro** B Woodhouse (01494) 762942
- **Holes** 9 L 5852 yds SSS 68
- **Recs** Am–76 D Brown
  Pro–65 S Parker
- **V'tors** U SOC
- **Fees** On application
- **Loc** Chalfont & Latimer Station 1/2 mile
- **Arch** JM Dunne

Mentmore G&CC (1992)
Mentmore, Leighton Buzzard LU7 0UA
- **Tel** (01296) 662020
- **Fax** (01296) 662592
- **Mem** 1100
- **Sec** M Fallows (Man Dir)
- **Pro** P Elson
- **Holes** Rothschild 18 L 6777 yds SSS 72; Rosebery 18 L 6850 yds SSS 73
- **V'tors** WD–H WE/BH–H by appointment SOC
- **Fees** £30 D–£45
- **Loc** 4 miles S of Leighton Buzzard
- **Mis** Driving range
- **Arch** Bob Sandow

Princes Risborough (1990)
Lee Road, Saunderton Lee, Princes Risborough HP27 9NX
- **Tel** (01844) 346989 (Clubhouse)
- **Fax** (01844) 274938
- **Mem** 400
- **Sec** JF Tubb (Man Dir)
- **Pro** (01844) 274567
- **Holes** 9 L 5440 yds Par 68 SSS 66
- **Recs** Am–67 J Murray (1997)
  Pro–62 M Booth (1994)
- **V'tors** U SOC

For list of abbreviations see page 527

Buckinghamshire

Fees £14 (£18)
Loc 7 miles NW of High Wycombe on A4010
Arch Guy Hunt

Richings Park G&CC (1996)
North Park, Iver SL0 9DL
Tel (01753) 655352
Fax (01753) 655409
Mem 650
Sec S Hodsdon (Mgr) (01753) 655370
Pro M Heys (01753) 655352
Holes 18 L 6094 yds Par 70 SSS 69
V'tors WD–U WE–M
Fees £17
Loc Nr M4 Junction 5
Mis Driving range
Arch Alan Higgins

Silverstone (1992)
Pay and play
Silverstone Road, Stowe, Buckingham MK18 5LH
Tel (01280) 850005
Fax (01280) 850156
Mem 570
Sec DG Allen
Pro R Holt
Holes 18 L 6213 yds SSS 71
V'tors U–booking advisable SOC–WD
Fees £11 (£15)
Loc Opposite Silverstone Race Circuit, N of Buckingham
Mis Driving range
Arch David Snell

Stoke Poges (1908)
Park Road, Stoke Poges SL2 4PG
Tel (01753) 717171
Fax (01753) 717181
Mem 750
Pro D Woodward
Holes 18 L 6721 yds SSS 72
9 L 3074 yds
V'tors U
Fees £65 D–£95 W–£150
Loc 2 miles N of Slough
Arch HS Colt

Stowe (1974)
Stowe, Buckingham MK18 5EH
Mem 300
Sec Mrs CM Shaw (01280) 813650
Holes 9 L 4573 yds SSS 63
V'tors WD/WE 8am–1pm & after 7pm–M; School holidays–M SOC
Fees On application
Loc M1 Junction 16. 4 miles NW of Buckingham

Thorney Park (1992)
Thorney Mill Lane, Iver SL0 9AL
Tel (01895) 422095
Fax (01895) 431207
Mem 200
Sec L Grundon

Pro A Killing
Holes 9 L 3000 yds SSS 34
Recs Am–S Walker
V'tors U SOC
Fees 9 holes–£7 (£9)
18 holes–£10 (£13)
Loc 3 miles N of M4 Junction 5 (B470)
Mis Practice range
Arch S Adby

Three Locks (1992)
Great Brickhill, Milton Keynes MK17 9BH
Tel (01525) 270470
Fax (01525) 270470
Mem 300
Sec P Critchley
Holes 18 L 6025 yds Par 70 SSS 68
Recs Am–67 G Tarbox (1995)
V'tors U SOC exc Sun
Fees £12.50 (£14.50)
Loc N of Leighton Buzzard on A4146. M1 Junction 14
Arch MRM Sandow

Wavendon Golf Centre (1990)
Lower End Road, Wavendon, Milton Keynes MK17 8DA
Tel (01908) 281811
Fax (01908) 281257
Mem 250
Sec J Droke
Pro G Iron
Holes 18 L 5460 yds Par 67 SSS 66
9 hole Par 3 course
V'tors U SOC
Fees £10 (£14)
Loc 2 miles W of M1 Junction 13
Mis Floodlit driving range

Weston Turville (1973)
New Road, Weston Turville, Aylesbury HP22 5QT
Tel (01296) 424084
Fax (01296) 395376
Mem 600
Sec BJ Hill
Pro G George (01296) 425949
Holes 18 L 6008 yds SSS 69
Recs Am–68 P Jackson
V'tors U
Fees £20 (£25)
Loc 1½ miles SE of Aylesbury

Wexham Park (1979)
Pay and play
Wexham Street, Wexham, Slough SL3 6ND
Tel (01753) 663271
Fax (01753) 663210
Mem 850
Sec B Foyster
Pro D Morgan (01753) 663425
Holes 18 L 5323 yds SSS 66
Green 9 L 2283 yds SSS 32
Red 9 L 2851 yds SSS 34
V'tors U SOC–WD/Sat & Sun pm
Fees 18 hole:£11 (£14.50)
9 hole:£6 (£7.50)

Loc 2 miles N of Slough
Mis Driving range
Arch David Morgan

Whiteleaf (1904)
Whiteleaf, Princes Risborough HP27 0LY
Tel (01844) 343097/274058
Mem 300
Sec Mrs F Ward
Pro KS Ward (01844) 345472
Holes 9 L 5391 yds SSS 66
Recs Am–66 GE Oates
Pro–63 MM Caines
V'tors WD–U WE–M SOC
Fees £18
Loc Princes Risborough 2 miles

Windmill Hill (1972)
Public
Tattenhoe Lane, Bletchley, Milton Keynes MK3 7RB
Tel (01908) 648149 (Clubhouse)
Fax (01908) 271478
Mem 450
Sec Mrs PM Long
Pro C Clingan (01908) 378623
Holes 18 L 6773 yds SSS 72
Recs Am–69 RJ Long
Pro–66 C Defoy
V'tors U SOC
Fees £8.50 (£11.85)
Loc 4 miles from M1 Junction 14, on A421
Mis Floodlit driving range
Arch Henry Cotton

Woburn (1976)
Bow Brickhill, Milton Keynes MK17 9LJ
Tel (01908) 370756
Fax (01908) 378436
Sec E Bullock (Man Dir)
Glenna Beasley (Sec)
Pro L Blacklock (01908) 647987
Holes Duke's 18 L 6973 yds SSS 74
Duchess 18 L 6651 yds SSS 72
Recs Duke's Pro–63 P Baker, I Woosnam
Ladies Pro–64 J Geddes
Duchess Ladies Pro–67 S Waugh
V'tors WD–H (by arrangement) WE–M
Fees By arrangement
Loc ½ mile E of A5. 4 miles W of M1 Junction 13
Arch Charles Lawrie (Duke's)

Wycombe Heights (1991)
Public
Rayners Avenue, Loudwater, High Wycombe HP10 9SW
Tel (01494) 816686
Fax (01494) 816728
Mem 1200
Sec P Talbot (01494) 813185
Pro A Bishop (01494) 812862
Holes 18 L 6300 yds Par 70 SSS 72
18 hole Par 3 course
V'tors U SOC
Fees £11 (£14.95)

For list of abbreviations see page 527

Loc	½ mile from M40 Junction 3, on A40 to Wycombe
Mis	Driving range
Arch	John Jacobs

Cambridgeshire

Abbotsley (1986)

Eynesbury Hardwicke, St Neots PE19 4XN

Tel	(01480) 210033/474000
Fax	(01480) 471018
Mem	550
Sec	Fiona Ellis
Pro	R Jessup
Holes	18 L 6311 yds SSS 72
Recs	Am–70 H Watts (1997) Pro–69 S Whymark (1984)
V'tors	WD/BH–U WE–M before 2.30pm –U after 2.30pm SOC
Fees	£25 (£30)
Loc	2 miles SE of St Neots on B1046. M11 Junction 13 (A428)

Abbotsley Cromwell

Pay and play
Eynesbury Hardwicke, St Neots PE19 4XN

Tel	(01480) 215153
Fax	(01480) 403280
Mem	250
Sec	Shonah Wakefield
Pro	Denise Hastings
Holes	18 L 6087 yds SSS 69
V'tors	U SOC
Fees	£12 (£15)
Loc	2 miles SE of St Neots on B1046. M11 Junction 13 (A428)
Mis	Floodlit driving range

Bourn (1991)

Toft Road, Bourn, Cambridge CB3 7TT

Tel	(01954) 718057
Fax	(01954) 718908
Pro	C Watson (01954) 718958
Holes	18 L 6417 yds SSS 71
Recs	Am–68 A Stubbs (1996) Pro–67 P Dimmock
V'tors	U SOC–WD
Fees	On application
Loc	8 miles W of Cambridge, off B1046. M11 Junction 12

Brampton Park (1991)

Buckden Road, Brampton, Huntingdon PE18 8NF

Tel	(01480) 434700
Fax	(01480) 411145
Mem	650
Sec	MN Staveley (Gen Mgr)
Pro	A Currie (01480) 434705
Holes	18 L 6300 yds SSS 72
Recs	Am–66 R Beadles (1998) Pro–64 (1998) Ladies–67 P Parker (1995)
V'tors	U

Fees	£25 (D–£35)
Loc	3 miles W of Huntingdon, off A1/A604
Arch	Simon Gidman

Cambridge

Station Road, Longstanton, Cambridge CB4 5DR

Tel	(01954) 789388
Mem	300
Sec	K Green
Pro	G Huggett
Holes	18 L 6736 yds Par 72 SSS 74
V'tors	U SOC
Fees	£9 (£12)
Loc	5 miles NW of Cambridge, off A14 (B1050)
Mis	Floodlit driving range

Cambridge Meridian

Comberton Road, Toft, Cambridge CB3 7RY

Tel	(01223) 264700
Fax	(01223) 264701
Mem	610
Sec	J Allen (Sec/Mgr)
Pro	M Clemons (01223) 264702
Holes	18 L 6651 yds Par 73 SSS 72
Recs	Am–72 G Hopkinson (1994)
V'tors	U SOC
Fees	£18 (£20)
Loc	3 miles SW of Cambridge on B1046. M11 Junction 12
Arch	Alliss/Clark

Cambridgeshire Moat House (1974)

Bar Hill, Cambridge CB3 8EU

Tel	(01954) 780555
Fax	(01954) 780010
Mem	550
Sec	D Hefferland
Pro	D Vernon (01954) 780098
Holes	18 L 6734 yds SSS 72
Recs	Am–68 P Way Pro–68 P Townsend
V'tors	U SOC
Fees	£15 D–£25 (£30)
Loc	5 miles NW of Cambridge on A14

Elton Furze (1993)

Bullock Road, Haddon, Peterborough PE7 3TT

Tel	(01832) 280189
Fax	(01832) 280299
Mem	440
Sec	Angela Hyde
Pro	F Kiddie (01832) 280614
Holes	18 L 6289 yds SSS 70
Recs	Am–67 E Couduit (1996) Pro–69 F Kiddie (1994)
V'tors	WD–phone in advance SOC
Fees	On application
Loc	4 miles W of Peterborough on old A605
Mis	Driving range
Arch	Roger Fitton

Ely City (1961)

Cambridge Road, Ely CB7 4HX

Tel	(01353) 662751
Fax	(01353) 668636
Mem	950
Sec	MS Hoare (Mgr)
Pro	A George (01353) 663317 (Touring Pro H Baiocchi)
Holes	18 L 6627 yds SSS 72
Recs	Am–66 L Yearn Pro–66 L Trevino Ladies Am–71 K Miller Ladies Pro–68 B Lunsford
V'tors	WD–H WE–H SOC–Tues–Fri
Fees	£28 (£34)
Loc	12 miles N of Cambridge
Arch	Henry Cotton

Girton (1936)

Dodford Lane, Girton CB3 0QE

Tel	(01223) 276169
Fax	(01223) 277150
Mem	800
Sec	Miss VM Webb
Pro	S Thomson (01223) 276991
Holes	18 L 6080 yds SSS 69
Recs	Am–66 O Cousins (1997) Ladies–72 J Walter (1993)
V'tors	WD–U WE/BH–M SOC–WD
Fees	£16
Loc	3 miles N of Cambridge (A14)

The Gog Magog (1901)

Shelford Bottom, Cambridge CB2 4AB

Tel	(01223) 247626
Fax	(01223) 414990
Mem	1200
Sec	I Skellern
Pro	I Bamborough (01223) 246058
Holes	Old 18 L 6398 yds SSS 70; Wandlebury 18 L 6754 yds SSS 73
Recs	Am–64 RW Guy, MT Seaton, DWG Woods, L James, R Claydon, M Landrum, T Milford, J Cook Pro–60 J Boast Ladies–69 J Hockley
V'tors	WD–I or H WE/BH–M SOC–WD exc Wed
Fees	£35 D–£42
Loc	2 miles S of Cambridge on A1307 (A604)
Arch	Hawtree

Hemingford Abbots (1991)

New Farm Lodge, Cambridge Road, Hemingford Abbots PE18 9HQ

Tel	(01480) 495000
Fax	(01480) 496149
Mem	410
Sec	BJ Smith
Pro	B Mylward (01480) 492939
Holes	9 L 5468 yds SSS 68
V'tors	WD–U WE–M before 1pm –U after 1pm
Fees	On application
Loc	2 miles S of Huntingdon on A604
Mis	Floodlit driving range

For list of abbreviations see page 527

Cambridgeshire

Heydon Grange G&CC (1994)
Heydon, Royston SG8 7NS
Tel (01763) 208988
Fax (01763) 208926
Mem 200
Sec AJ Swatton
Pro S Smith
Holes 18 L 6512 yds SSS 72
9 L 3249 yds SSS 36
V'tors U SOC
Fees £15 (£20)
Loc 4 miles E of Royston on A505. M11 Junction 10
Arch Cameron Sinclair

Lakeside Lodge (1992)
Fen Road, Pidley, Huntingdon PE17 3DD
Tel (01487) 740540
Fax (01487) 740852
Mem 550
Sec Mrs J Hopkins
Pro S Waterman (01487) 741541
Holes 18 L 6865 yds SSS 73
9 L 2601 yds SSS 33
V'tors U SOC
Fees £10 (£16)
Loc 4 miles N of St Ives on B1040
Mis Driving range
Arch A Headley

Malton (1993)
Malton Lane, Meldreth, Royston SG8 6PE
Tel (01763) 262200
Fax (01763) 262209
Mem 450
Sec A Boyce (01638) 751222
Pro None
Holes 18 L 6708 yds Par 72 SSS 72
V'tors U SOC–exc WE–NA before 11am
Fees £10 (£12)
Loc 8 miles SW of Cambridge, off A10. 5 miles SW of M11 Junction 11
Mis Driving range
Arch Bruce Critchley

March (1922)
Frogs Abbey, Grange Rd, March PE15 0YH
Tel (01354) 652364
Mem 400
Sec Lt Cdr LE Taylor RN
Pro J Hadland
Holes 9 L 6210 yds SSS 70
Recs Am–67 JW Kisby, J Greenall
V'tors H SOC–WD
Fees £17
Loc 18 miles E of Peterborough on A141

Old Nene G&CC (1992)
Muchwood Lane, Bodsey, Ramsey PE17 1XQ
Tel (01487) 813519
Mem 200
Sec PB Cade

Pro S Mills (01487) 710122
Holes 9 L 5605 yds SSS 68
Recs Am–R Dale (1995)
V'tors U SOC
Fees 18 holes–£10 (£15)
9 holes–£7 (£10)
Loc 1 mile N of Ramsey, towards Ramsey Mereside
Mis Driving range
Arch Richard Edrich

Orton Meadows (1987)
Public
Ham Lane, Peterborough PE2 0UU
Tel (01733) 237478
Mem 600
Sec Mrs S Ramsay (01733) 234769
Pro N Grant, J Mitchell
Holes 18 L 5800 yds SSS 68
Recs Am–68 J Wood (1997)
Pro–69 J Mitchell (1996)
Ladies–71 C McCulloch (1997)
V'tors U–phone Pro
Fees £9.80 (£12.50)
Loc 2 miles SW of Peterborough on old A605
Mis 12 hole pitch & putt
Arch D & R Fitton

Peterborough Milton (1937)
Milton Ferry, Peterborough PE6 7AG
Tel (01733) 380204
Fax (01733) 380489
Mem 850
Sec Mrs D Adams (01733) 380489
Pro M Gallagher (01733) 380793
Holes 18 L 6462 yds SSS 72
Recs Am–66 M Peacock (1995)
Pro–62 S Bennett (1996)
V'tors WD–U WE–M SOC
Fees £20 (£25)
Loc 4 miles W of Peterborough on A47
Arch James Braid

Ramsey (1964)
4 Abbey Terrace, Ramsey, Huntingdon PE17 1DD
Tel (01487) 812600
Fax (01487) 815746
Mem 750
Sec RAR Hill
Pro S Scott (01487) 813022
Holes 18 L 6163 yds Par 71 SSS 70
Recs Am–65 S Train (1996)
Pro–66 R Robertson (1994)
V'tors WD–H WE/BH–M SOC
Fees £25
Loc 12 miles SE of Peterborough
Arch J Hamilton Stutt

St Ives (1923)
St Ives, Huntingdon PE17 4RS
Tel (01480) 64459
Fax (01480) 468392
Mem 385

Sec BE Dunn (01480) 468392
Pro D Glasby (01480) 466067
Holes 9 L 6100 yds SSS 69
Recs Am–67 Fl-Lt CJB Murdoch
Pro–61 P Alliss
V'tors WD–U H WE–M
Fees £20
Loc 5 miles E of Huntingdon

St Neot's (1890)
Crosshall Road, St Neot's PE19 4AE
Tel (01480) 472363
Fax (01480) 472363
Mem 600
Sec AR Peck (Mgr) (01480) 472363
Pro G Bithrey (01480) 476513
Holes 18 L 6074 yds SSS 69
Recs Am–65 O Cousins
Pro–65 M Gallagher, H Flatman
V'tors WD–H WE–M
Fees On application
Loc By A1/B1048 Junction

Thorney Golf Centre (1991)
Public
English Drove, Thorney, Peterborough PE6 0TJ
Tel (01733) 270570
Fax (01733) 270842
Sec Jane Hind
Pro M Templeman
Holes Fen 18 L 6104 yds SSS 69
Lakes 18 L 6402 yds SSS 71
9 hole Par 3 course
Recs Fen Am–71 M Perkins (1992)
Pro–66 M Templeman (1993)
Lakes Am–66 I Whittingham (1997)
Pro–69 J Darroch (1996), P Streeter (1998)
V'tors Lakes WD–U SOC WE–M
Fees Fen £6.50 (£8.50) Lakes £11 (£17.50)
Loc 8 miles E of Peterborough, off A47
Mis Floodlit driving range
Arch A Dow

Thorpe Wood (1975)
Public
Nene Parkway, Peterborough PE3 6SE
Tel (01733) 267701
Fax (01733) 332774
Sec R Palmer
Pro D Fitton, R Fitton
Holes 18 L 7086 yds SSS 74
Recs Am–68 S Fitton (1998)
Pro–71 R Fitton (1986)
Ladies–72 S Sharpe (1992)
V'tors U–booking required SOC–WD
Fees £9.80 (£12.50)
Loc 3 miles W of Peterborough, on A47
Arch Alliss/Thomas

For list of abbreviations see page 527

Channel Islands

Alderney
Route des Carrieres, Alderney GY9 3YD
Tel (01481) 822835
Fax (01481) 823609
Mem 320
Sec HCA Armstrong
 (01481) 822057
Pro None
Holes 9 L 5006 yds Par 64 SSS 63
Recs Am–65 M Hugman
V'tors U SOC
Fees £12.50 (£17.50)
Loc 1 mile E of St Anne

La Grande Mare (1994)
Vazon Bay, Castel, Guernsey GY5 7LL
Tel (01481) 55313
Fax (01481) 55194
Mem 650
Sec J Vermeulen (01481) 53544
Pro M Groves (01481) 53432
Holes 18 L 5112 yds SSS 66
Recs Am–63 I Thomas (1997)
V'tors U–booking necessary SOC
Fees D–£25 (£28)
Loc Vazon Bay, W coast of Guernsey
Mis www.LGM.Guernsey.net
Arch Hawtree

Les Mielles G&CC
(1994)
St Ouens Bay, Jersey
Tel (01534) 482787
Fax (01534) 485414
Email lmgolfcc@itl.net
 www.lesmielles.com
Mem 1500
Sec J Le Brun (Golf Dir)
Pro L Elstone
Holes 18 L 5705 yds Par 70
 Driving range
Recs Am–65 D Carey
 Pro–61 I Woosnam
V'tors H or Green Card SOC–WD
 SOC–WE after 12 noon
Fees £20.50 (£23.50)
Loc Five Mile Road, St Ouens Bay
Arch Le Brun/Whitehead

La Moye (1902)
La Moye, St Brelade, Jersey JE3 8GQ
Tel (01534) 743401,
 (01534) 747166 (Bookings)
Fax (01534) 747289
Mem 1350
Sec CHM Greetham
Pro M Deeley (01534) 743130
Holes 18 L 6664 yds SSS 72
Recs Am–68 T Gray (1996)
 Pro–62 G Brand Jr
V'tors I H SOC–9.30–11am and
 2.30–4pm WE–after 2.30pm
Fees £40 D–£60 (£45) W–£180
Loc 2 miles from Jersey Airport
Mis Driving range
Arch James Braid

Les Ormes (1996)
Pay and play
Mont à la Brune, St Brelade, Jersey JE3 8FL
Tel (01534) 499077/44464
Fax (01534) 499122
Mem 600
Sec G Stubbs (01534) 44464
Pro A Chamberlain
 (01534) 499077
Holes 9 L 5018 yds Par 66 SSS 65
V'tors U SOC
Fees 9 holes–£12 (£14)
 18 holes–£19 (£22)
Loc Mont à la Brune, nr Airport
Mis Driving range

Royal Guernsey (1890)
L'Ancresse, Guernsey GY3 5BY
Tel (01481) 47022
Fax (01481) 43960
Mem 1520
Sec M de Laune (Club Mgr)
 R Eggo (Golf Mgr)
Pro N Wood (01481) 45070
Holes 18 L 6215 yds SSS 70
Recs Am–64 R Eggo (1986)
 Pro–64 P Cunningham
V'tors WD–H WE–M
Fees £34
Loc 3 miles N of St Peter Port
Mis Driving range

Royal Jersey (1878)
Grouville, Jersey JE3 9BD
Tel (01534) 854416
Fax (01534) 854684
Mem 1300
Sec RC Leader
Pro T Horton (01534) 852234
Holes 18 L 6059 yds SSS 70
Recs Am–64 R Harrop (1989)
 Pro–64 P Le Chevalier (1988)
V'tors WD–H after 10am WE/BH–H
 after 2.30pm
Fees £40 (£40)
Loc 4 miles E of St Helier

St Clements (1925)
Public
St Clements, Jersey JE2 6QN
Tel (01534) 821938
Pro R Marks
Holes 9 L 3972 yds SSS 61
Recs Am–61 T Gray, B McCarthy
V'tors U exc Sun am–NA
Fees On application
Loc 1 mile E of St Helier

St Pierre Park
Rohais, St Peter Port, Guernsey GY1 1FD
Tel (01481) 727039
Mem 290
Pro R Corbet (Mgr)
Holes 9 hole Par 3 course
V'tors U SOC
Fees 18 holes–£15 (£17)
Loc 1 mile W of St Peter Port
Mis Driving range
Arch Tony Jacklin

Cheshire

Alder Root (1993)
Alder Root Lane, Winwick, Warrington WA2 8RZ
Tel (01925) 291919
Fax (01925) 291919
Mem 450
Sec E Lander
Pro T Yarwood (01925) 291932
Holes 10 L 5820 yds Par 69 SSS 68
Recs Am–67 I Dallimore (1996)
V'tors WD–U SOC
Fees £16 (£18)
Loc 4 miles N of Warrington
 (A49). M6 Junction 22. M62 Junction 9
Arch Millington/Lander

Alderley Edge (1907)
Brook Lane, Alderley Edge SK9 7RU
Tel (01625) 585583
Mem 212 90(L) 40(J) 40(5)
Sec JBD Page
Pro P Bowring (01625) 584493
Holes 9 L 5823 yds SSS 68
Recs Am–62 RF Brindle (1993)
 Pro–63 MJ Slater (1994)
V'tors M or H SOC
Fees £18 (£22)
Loc 12 miles S of Manchester

Aldersey Green
Aldersey, Chester CH3 9EH
Tel (01829) 782157
Sec S Bradbury
Pro S Bradbury
Holes 18 L 6150 yds Par 70
V'tors U SOC
Fees £12 (£15)
Loc 8 miles S of Chester, off A41

Altrincham Municipal
(1893)
Public
Stockport Road, Timperley, Altrincham WA15 7LP
Tel (0161) 928 0761
Mem 276
Sec S Feltham
Pro S Partington
Holes 18 L 6204 yds Par 71 SSS 69
Recs Am–67
 Pro–67
V'tors U
Fees £8.40 (£10)
Loc 1 mile W of Altrincham (A560)
Mis Driving range

Alvaston Hall (1992)
Middlewich Road, Nantwich CW5 6PD
Tel (01270) 624341
Mem 296
Sec RH Llewellyn
 (01270) 626268
Pro K Valentine
Holes 9 L 3708 yds Par 64 SSS 59

For list of abbreviations see page 527

540 Cheshire

Recs Am–64 MJ Conroy (1995)
V'tors U
Fees £10 (£10)
Loc 11 miles W of M6 Junction 18 on A530
Mis Driving range
Arch K Valentine

Antrobus
Foggs Lane, Antrobus, Northwich CW9 6JQ
Tel (01925) 730890
Fax (01925) 730100
Mem 550
Sec Miss C Axford
Pro P Farrance (01925) 730900
Holes 18 L 6220 yds Par 72 SSS 72
V'tors H SOC
Fees £18 (£20)
Loc Nr M56 Junction 10, on A559 to Northwich
Mis Driving range
Arch M Slater

Ashton-on-Mersey (1897)
Church Lane, Sale M33 5QQ
Tel (0161) 973 3220
Mem 180 70(L) 40(J)
Sec DE McMahon (0161) 976 4390
Pro MJ Williams (0161) 962 3727
Holes 9 L 3073 yds SSS 69
Recs Am–66 P Bolton (1997) Pro–67 R Williamson, D Cooper, MJ Williams
V'tors WD–U H exc Tues–NA before 3pm WE–M
Fees £18
Loc 5 miles W of Manchester. M60 Junction 7, 1½ miles

Astbury (1922)
Peel Lane, Astbury, Congleton CW12 4RE
Tel (01260) 272772 (Clubhouse)
Mem 700
Sec C Radley (01260) 279139
Pro A Salt (01260) 298663
Holes 18 L 6296 yds SSS 70
Recs Am–61 IA Jones (1996) Pro–69 I Mosey (1979)
V'tors WD–H or M WE–M SOC–Thurs only
Fees £25 SOC–£20
Loc 1 mile S of Congleton, off A34

Birchwood (1979)
Kelvin Close, Birchwood, Warrington WA3 7PB
Tel (01925) 818819
Fax (01925) 822403
Mem 745
Sec A Harper
Pro P McEwan (01925) 816574
Holes 18 L 6727 yds Par 71 SSS 73
Recs Am–67 A Stokes (1997) Pro–65 P Affleck
V'tors U SOC–Mon/Wed/Thurs

Fees £18 D–£26 (£34)
Loc M62 Junction 11, 2 miles. Signs to 'Science Park North'
Arch TJA Macauley

Bramall Park (1894)
20 Manor Road, Bramhall, Stockport SK7 3LY
Tel (0161) 485 3119 (Clubhouse)
Fax (0161) 485 7101
Mem 715
Sec IR McNeill (0161) 485 7101
Pro M Proffit (0161) 485 2205
Holes 18 L 6214 yds SSS 70
Recs Am–65 SM Hughes (1993) Pro–63 D Cooper (1984)
V'tors I
Fees £25 (£35)
Loc 8 miles S of Manchester (A5102)

Bramhall (1905)
Ladythorn Road, Bramhall, Stockport SK7 2EY
Tel (0161) 439 4057
Fax (0161) 439 0264
Mem 300 155(L) 85(J)
Sec BJ Cluley (Hon) (0161) 439 6092
Pro R Green (0161) 439 1171
Holes 18 L 6300 yds SSS 70
Recs Am–63 G Bradley (1994) Pro–66 I Higby (1987)
V'tors U exc Thurs SOC–Wed
Fees £25 D–£29 (£32 D–£39)
Loc S of Stockport, off A5102

Carden Park (1993)
Carden, Broxton, Chester CH3 9DQ
Tel (01829) 731600
Fax (01829) 731636
Mem 234
Sec D Nutter, D Llewelyn
Pro D Williams (01829) 731500
Holes Cheshire 18 L 6564 yds SSS 73; Nicklaus 18 L 7010 yds Par 72; 9 hole Par 3 course
Recs Am–74 J Clorley (1995) Pro–67 S Edwards (1996)
V'tors H SOC
Fees £30 (£30)
Loc 10 miles S of Chester on A534
Mis Golf Academy. Driving range
Arch Alan Higgins

Cheadle (1885)
Shiers Drive, Cheadle Road, Cheadle SK8 1HW
Tel (0161) 428 2160
Mem 350
Sec RS Lee (0161) 491 4452
Pro S Booth (0161) 428 9878
Holes 9 L 5006 yds SSS 65
Recs Am–63 PS Griffiths (1991)
V'tors H or I exc Tues & Sat–NA SOC
Fees £18 (£22.50)
Loc 1 mile S of Cheadle. M63 Junction 11, 2 miles

Chester (1901)
Curzon Park, Chester CH4 8AR
Tel (01244) 675130
Fax (01244) 676667
Mem 840
Sec VFC Wood (01244) 677760
Pro G Parton (01244) 671185
Holes 18 L 6508 yds SSS 71
Recs Am–66 R Howell Pro–66 D Screeton
V'tors U H SOC
Fees £23 (£28)
Loc Chester 1 mile

Congleton (1898)
Biddulph Road, Congleton CW12 3LZ
Tel (01260) 273540
Mem 440
Sec FW Griffiths
Pro JA Colclough (01260) 271083
Holes 12 L 5103 yds Par 68 SSS 65
Recs Am–60 M Griffiths (1989) Pro–59 N Coles (1968)
V'tors U H SOC
Fees £20
Loc 1½ miles E of Congleton on A527

Crewe (1911)
Fields Road, Haslington, Crewe CW1 5TB
Tel (01270) 584227 (Steward)
Fax (01270) 584099
Mem 628
Sec Ms PM Stratton (01270) 584099
Pro M Booker (01270) 585032
Holes 18 L 6424 yds SSS 71
Recs Am–65 CR Smethurst (1995) Pro–65 M Brunton (1994)
V'tors WD–U WE/BH–M SOC
Fees £27 After 1pm–£22
Loc 2 miles NE of Crewe Station, off A534. 5 miles W of M6 Junction 17

Davenport (1913)
Worth Hall, Middlewood Road, Poynton, Stockport SK12 1TS
Tel (01625) 876951
Fax (01625) 877489
Mem 650
Sec DE Jacks
Pro D Norcott (01625) 877319
Holes 18 L 6027 yds SSS 69
Recs Am–64 R Lauder Pro–67 B Evans
V'tors U exc Sat–NA SOC–Tues & Thurs
Fees £27 (£32)
Loc 5 miles S of Stockport

Delamere Forest (1910)
Station Road, Delamere, Northwich CW8 2JE
Tel (01606) 883264
Fax (01606) 883800
Mem 400
Sec TG Owen (01606) 883800
Pro EB Jones (01606) 883307

For list of abbreviations see page 527

Holes 18 L 6328 yds SSS 70	**Pro** D Yates	**Sec** JR Smith (0161) 442 8054
Recs Am–65 J Brown	**Holes** 18 L 6432 yds SSS 71	**Pro** SJ Marsh (0161) 432 0846
Pro–63 M Bembridge	**Recs** Am–66 A Waterhouse	**Holes** 18 L 5968 yds SSS 69
V'tors WD–U WE–2 ball only SOC	Pro–67 B Evans, A Caygill	**Recs** Am–66 D Howarth
Fees £30 D–£45 (£35)	**V'tors** WD–U WE–arrange with Pro	Pro–66 D Cooper
Loc 10 miles E of Chester, off	SOC–WD	**V'tors** U SOC
B5152	**Fees** £5.60 (£6.50)	**Fees** £23 (£31)
Arch Herbert Fowler	**Loc** 9 miles N of Chester on A41	**Loc** 2 miles from M63 Junction 12, off A5145

Disley (1889)
Stanley Hall Lane, Disley, Stockport SK12 2JX
Tel (01663) 762071
Mem 500
Pro AG Esplin (01663) 762884
Holes 18 L 5990 yds SSS 69
Recs Am–63 P Leadbetter (1998)
Pro–63 B Charles
V'tors WD–U exc Thurs WE/BH–M
Fees £25 (£30)
Loc 6 miles S of Stockport on A6

Dukinfield (1913)
Yew Tree Lane, Dukinfield SK16 5DB
Tel (0161) 338 2340
Mem 300 80(L) 65(J)
Sec L Holmes (0161) 366 0542
Pro J Lowe
Holes 18 L 5203 yds SSS 66
Recs Am–7 C Kenworthy
V'tors WD–U exc Wed pm WE–M SOC
Fees £16.50
Loc 6 miles E of Manchester

Dunham Forest G&CC (1961)
Oldfield Lane, Altrincham WA14 4TY
Tel (0161) 928 2605
Fax (0161) 929 8975
Mem 600
Sec Mrs S Klaus
Pro I Wrigley (0161) 928 2727
Holes 18 L 6636 yds SSS 72
V'tors WD–U WE/BH–M SOC exc 12–1pm
Fees £35 (£40)
Loc 1 mile SW of Altrincham

Eaton (1965)
Guy Lane, Waverton, Chester CH3 7PH
Tel (01244) 335885
Fax (01244) 335782
Mem 550
Sec GC Parry
Pro N Dunroe (01244) 335826
Holes 18 L 6562 yds SSS 71
Recs Am–69 M Picton (1994)
V'tors H SOC–WD
Fees On application
Loc 3 miles SE of Chester, off A41
Arch Donald Steel

Ellesmere Port (1971)
Public
Chester Road, Childer Thornton, South Wirral L66 1QF
Tel (0151) 339 7689
Mem 350
Sec P Walker

Frodsham (1990)
Simons Lane, Frodsham WA6 6HE
Tel (01928) 732159
Fax (01928) 734070
Mem 550
Sec EI Roylance
Pro G Tonge (01928) 739442
Holes 18 L 6298 yds SSS 70
Recs Am–65 J Thompson (1998)
V'tors WD/BH–U WE–M SOC–WD
Fees £30
Loc 9 miles NE of Chester (A56). M56 Junction 12, 3 miles
Arch John Day

Gatley (1911)
Waterfall Farm, Styal Road, Heald Green, Cheadle SK8 3TW
Tel (0161) 437 2091
Mem 400
Sec CB Hamnett
Pro S Reeves (0161) 436 2830
Holes 9 L 5934 yds SSS 68
Recs Am–67 M Hoyland
Pro–63 C Timperley
V'tors WD exc Tues–arrange with Sec WE/Tues–NA
Fees £20
Loc 7 miles S of Manchester. Manchester Airport 2 miles

Hale (1903)
Rappax Road, Hale WA15 0NU
Tel (0161) 980 4225
Mem 350
Sec JT Goodman
Pro A Bickerdike (0161) 904 0835
Holes 9 L 5780 yds SSS 68
Recs Am–66 PF Veitch
Pro–65 D Durnian
V'tors WD–U exc Thurs–NA before 5pm WE/BH–M SOC
Fees D–£20
Loc 2 miles SE of Altrincham

Hazel Grove (1912)
Hazel Grove, Stockport SK7 6LU
Tel (0161) 483 3217
Mem 550
Sec HAG Carlisle (0161) 483 3978
Pro ME Hill (0161) 483 7272
Holes 18 L 6263 yds SSS 71
Recs Am–66 MJ Rogers
V'tors U
Fees On application
Loc 3 miles S of Stockport (A6)

Heaton Moor (1892)
Mauldeth Road, Heaton Mersey, Stockport SK4 3NX
Tel (0161) 432 2134
Mem 550

Helsby (1901)
Tower's Lane, Helsby, Warrington WA6 0JB
Tel (01928) 722021
Mem 600
Sec JI Buckley
Pro M Jones (01928) 725457
Holes 18 L 6229 yds SSS 70
Recs Am–69 D Stallard
Pro–68 I Wright
V'tors H WE–NA
SOC–Tues & Thurs
Fees £22
Loc 1 mile SE of M56 Junction 14, off Primrose Lane
Arch James Braid

Heyrose (1990)
Budworth Road, Tabley, Knutsford WA16 0HY
Tel (01565) 733664/733623
Fax (01565) 733664
Mem 700
Sec C Stewart (01565) 733664
Pro M Redrup (01565) 734267
Holes 18 L 6515 yds SSS 71
Pro–68
Fees £19 (£24)
Loc 3 miles W of Knutsford, off Pickmere Lane. M6 Junction 19

Houldsworth (1910)
Houldsworth Park, Houldsworth Street, Reddish, Stockport SK5 6BN
Tel (0161) 442 9611
Fax (0161) 442 1712
Mem 625
Sec SW Zielinski (0161) 442 1712
Pro D Naylor (0161) 442 1714
Holes 18 L 6209 yds Par 71 SSS 70
Recs Am–67 R Arnold
Pro–63 D Vaughan
V'tors U SOC
Fees £20 (£25)
Loc 4 miles S of Manchester

Knights Grange (1983)
Public
Grange Lane, Winsford CW7 2PT
Tel (01606) 552780
Sec Mrs P Littler (Mgr)
Pro G Moore (01606) 75476
Holes 9 L 5720 yds SSS 68
V'tors U SOC
Fees 18 holes–£3.50 (£5.10)
9 holes–£2.70 (£3.95)
Loc Knights Grange Sports Complex

For list of abbreviations see page 527

Knutsford (1891)
Mereheath Lane, Knutsford WA16 6HS
Tel **(01565) 633355**
Mem 250
Sec JM Long
Pro A Gillies
Holes 9 L 6288 yds SSS 70
Recs Am–65 B Stockdale
 Pro–65 D Cooper
V'tors H exc Wed–NA SOC
Fees £25 (£30)
Loc Knutsford ½ mile

Leigh (1906)
Kenyon Hall, Culcheth, Warrington WA3 4BG
Tel **(01925) 763130**
Fax (01925) 765097
Mem 700
Sec PF Saunders (01925) 762943
Pro A Baguley (01925) 762013
Holes 18 L 5892 yds SSS 68
Recs Am–63 WN Denton (1997)
 Pro–65 A Baguley (1997)
V'tors U H SOC
Fees £26 (£33)
Loc 5 miles NE of Warrington
Arch James Braid

Lymm (1907)
Whitbarrow Road, Lymm WA13 9AN
Tel **(01925) 752177**
Fax (01925) 755020
Mem 400 100(L) 75(J) 50(5)
Sec S Nash (01925) 755020
Pro S McCarthy (01925) 755054
Holes 18 L 6304 yds SSS 70
Recs Am–68 CN Brown (1987)
 Pro–69 S Lyle (1987)
V'tors WD–H WE–M SOC–Wed
Fees £22 (£30)
Loc 5 miles SE of Warrington. M6 Junction 20

Macclesfield (1889)
The Hollins, Macclesfield SK11 7EA
Tel **(01625) 423227**
Fax (01625) 260061
Mem 600
Sec DJ English (01625) 615845
Pro T Taylor (01625) 616952
Holes 18 L 5769 yds SSS 68
Recs Am–66 J Donaldson
V'tors WD/BH–H WE–M SOC–WD
Fees £20 (£25)
Loc SE edge of Macclesfield
Arch Hawtree

Malkins Bank (1980)
Public
Malkins Bank, Sandbach CW11 4XN
Tel **(01270) 765931**
Fax (01270) 764730
Pro D Wheeler
Holes 18 L 6071 yds SSS 69
Recs Am–65 J Parry (1994)
V'tors U SOC
Fees £7.75 (£8.85)
Loc 2 miles S of Sandbach via A534/A533. M6 Junction 17

Marple (1892)
Barnsfold Road, Hawk Green, Marple, Stockport SK6 7EL
Tel **(0161) 427 2311**
Fax (0161) 427 1125
Mem 435 100(L) 60(J)
Sec MR Baguley
 (0161) 427 1125
Pro D Myers (0161) 427 1195
Holes 18 L 5552 yds SSS 67
Recs Am–66 T Christie (1984)
 Pro–64 I Spencer (1995)
V'tors WD–U exc Thurs–NA
 WE/BH–M SOC
Fees £20 (£30)
Loc 2 miles from High Lane North, off A6

Mellor & Townscliffe (1894)
Tarden, Gibb Lane, Mellor, Stockport SK6 5NA
Tel **(0161) 427 9700 (Clubhouse)**
Mem 700
Sec G Lee (0161) 427 2208
Pro G Broadley
 (0161) 427 5759
Holes 18 L 5925 yds SSS 69
Recs Am–68 GD Williams (1988),
 MG Senior, AJH Ellis (1992)
 Pro–64 MJ Slater (1977)
V'tors WD–U WE–M SOC
Fees £20 (£27.50)
Loc 7 miles SE of Stockport, off A626

Mere G&CC (1934)
Chester Road, Mere, Knutsford WA16 6LJ
Tel **(01565) 830155**
Fax (01565) 830713
Mem 375 200(L) 40(J)
Sec WG Squires,
 Karen Bucksey
Pro P Eyre (01565) 830219
Holes 18 L 6817 yds SSS 73
Recs Am–65 S Andrew (1996)
 Pro–64 D Clarke (1995)
V'tors WE/BH–M Wed & Fri–M
 Mon/Tues/Thurs–H SOC
Fees D–£60
Loc 1 mile E of M6 Junction 19. 2 miles W of M56 Junction 7
Mis Driving range–members and green fees only
Arch James Braid

Mersey Valley (1995)
Warrington Road, Bold Heath, Widnes WA8 3XL
Tel **(0151) 424 6060**
Fax (0151) 424 6060
Mem 550
Sec A Rigby
Pro A Stevenson
Holes 18 L 6300 yds SSS 70
V'tors U
Fees £15 (£20)
Loc M62 Junction 7, 2 miles
Arch RMR Bush

Mottram Hall Hotel (1991)
Wilmslow Road, Mottram St Andrew, Prestbury SK10 4QT
Tel **(01625) 828135**
Fax (01625) 829284
Mem 500
Sec D Goodwin
Pro T Rastall
Holes 18 L 7006 yds SSS 74
Recs Pro–66 J Matthews (1991)
V'tors U H
Fees £39 (£44)
Loc 4 miles SE of Wilmslow
Arch Dave Thomas

Portal G&CC (1992)
Cobblers Cross Lane, Tarporley CW6 0DJ
Tel **(01829) 733933**
Fax (01829) 733928
Mem 250
Sec D Wills (Golf Dir)
Pro M Slater
Holes 18 L 7037 yds SSS 73
Recs Pro–67 D Clare, D Wills,
 D Cooper
V'tors U H SOC
Fees £40
Loc 11 miles SE of Chester on A51. M6 Junctions 16 or 19
Mis Driving range
Arch Donald Steel

Portal Premier (1990)
Forest Road, Tarporley CW6 0JA
Tel **(01829) 733884**
Fax (01829) 733666
Mem 550
Sec K Brain (Golf Dir)
Pro Miss J Statham (01829) 733703
Holes 18 L 6508 yds SSS 71
Recs Am–67 P Mayoh
 Pro–69 B Rimmer
V'tors U SOC–WD
Fees £30 (£35)
Loc 1 mile N of Tarporley on A49 Warrington road
Mis Driving range
Arch Tim Rouse

Poulton Park (1980)
Dig Lane, Cinnamon Brow WA2 0SH
Tel **(01925) 812034/822802**
Fax (01925) 822802
Mem 360
Sec K Berry
Pro D Newing (01925) 825220
Holes 9 L 4978 metres SSS 66
Recs Am–64 I Quirk
V'tors WD–NA 5–6pm WE–NA 12–2pm
Fees £18 (£19)
Loc Off Crab Lane, Fearnhead

Prestbury (1920)
Macclesfield Road, Prestbury, Macclesfield SK10 4BJ
Tel **(01625) 829388**
Fax (01625) 828241

Mem 725
Sec Dianne Bradley
 (01625) 828241
Pro N Summerfield
 (01625) 828242
Holes 18 L 6359 yds SSS 71
Recs Am–64 P Bolton
 Pro–67 D Brunton
V'tors WD–I WE–M SOC–Thurs
Fees £38
Loc 2 miles NW of Macclesfield
Arch HS Colt

Pryors Hayes (1993)
Willington Road, Oscroft, Tarvin CH3 8NL
Tel (01829) 741250
Fax (01829) 741250
Mem 600
Sec T Berrisford
Pro N Rothe (01829) 740140
Holes 18 L 6074 yds Par 69 SSS 69
Recs Am–69 D Amitage (1997)
V'tors U SOC
Fees £15 (£20)
Loc 5 miles E of Chester
Arch Day

Queens Park (1985)
Public
Queens Park Drive, Crewe CW2 7SB
Tel (01270) 666724
Mem 250
Sec KF Lear (01270) 628352
Pro R Johnson
Holes 9 L 4920 yds SSS 64
Recs Am–66 S Thompson
V'tors WD–U WE–U after 12 noon
 SOC
Fees £5 (£7)
Loc 2 miles from Crewe, off
 Victoria Avenue

Reaseheath (1987)
Reaseheath College, Reaseheath, Nantwich CW5 6DF
Tel (01270) 625131
Fax (01270) 625665
Mem 400
Sec GM Oakes (Hon)
Holes 9 L 3726 yds SSS 58
V'tors M SOC–WD
Fees £5
Loc 2 miles NW of Nantwich on
 College campus
Arch D Mortram

Reddish Vale (1912)
Southcliffe Road, Reddish, Stockport SK5 7EE
Tel (0161) 480 2359
Fax (0161) 477 8242
Mem 600
Sec D Edwards
Pro RE Freeman (0161) 480 3824
Holes 18 L 6086 yds SSS 69
Recs Am–64 KR Gorton, D Young
 Pro–67 R Williamson,
 P Cheetham, D Fletcher
V'tors WD–U exc 12.30–1.30pm–M
 WE–M SOC–WD

Fees £22
Loc 1 mile NNE of Stockport
Arch Dr A Mackenzie

Ringway (1909)
Hale Mount, Hale Barns, Altrincham WA15 8SW
Tel (0161) 904 9609
Mem 345 165(L) 41(J)
Sec D Wright (0161) 980 2630
Pro N Ryan (0161) 980 8432
Holes 18 L 6494 yds SSS 71
Recs Am–67 RE Preston, S Brown,
 P Runciman
 Pro–66 M Hollingworth
V'tors Tues–NA before 3pm Fri–M
 Sun–NA before 11am SOC
Fees £28 (£34)
Loc 8 miles S of Manchester, off
 M56 Junction 6 (A538)

Romiley (1897)
Goosehouse Green, Romiley, Stockport SK6 4LJ
Tel (0161) 430 2392
Mem 700
Sec P Trafford
Pro G Butler (0161) 430 7122
Holes 18 L 6454 yds Par 70 SSS 71
Recs Am–67 CC Harrison
 Pro–67 D Roberts
V'tors U SOC
Fees £24 (£33)
Loc Station 3/4 mile (B6104)

Runcorn (1909)
Clifton Road, Runcorn WA7 4SU
Tel (01928) 572093 (Members)
Fax (01928) 574214
Mem 375 80(L) 80(J)
Sec WB Reading (01928) 574214
Pro A Franklin (01928) 564791
Holes 18 L 6035 yds SSS 69
Recs Am–58 L Kopanski (1995)
V'tors WD–U H exc comp days
 WE–M SOC
Fees £18
Loc Runcorn (A557). M56
 Junction 12

St Michaels Jubilee (1977)
Public
Dundalk Road, Widnes WA8 8BS
Tel (0151) 424 6230
Mem 200
Sec KB Stevenson
Pro R Bilton (01295) 65241
Holes 18 L 5612 yds SSS 67
Recs Am–67 I O'Connor (1989)
V'tors U
Fees On application
Loc Widnes

Sale (1913)
Sale Lodge, Golf Road, Sale M33 2XU
Tel (0161) 973 3404
Fax (0161) 962 4217
Mem 600
Sec JH Prow (Gen Mgr)
 (0161) 973 1638

Pro M Stewart
 (0161) 973 1730
Holes 18 L 6351 yds SSS 70
Recs Am–61 C Wetton
 Pro–65 D Brunton
V'tors U SOC–WD
Fees £28 (£33)
Loc N boundary of Sale. M60
 Junction 8

Sandbach (1895)
Middlewich Road, Sandbach CW11 1FH
Tel (01270) 762117
Mem 240 115(L) 50(J)
Sec JM Pegg
Holes 9 L 5598 yds SSS 67
Recs Am–63 DN Hughes
V'tors WD–U WE/BH–M
Fees D–£16
Loc 1 mile W of Sandbach (A533).
 M6 Junction 17

Sandiway (1921)
Chester Road, Sandiway CW8 2DJ
Tel (01606) 883247
Fax (01606) 888548
Mem 730
Sec MC Gilyeat
Pro W Laird (01606) 883180
Holes 18 L 6435 yds SSS 72
Recs Am–67 G Stewart (1997)
 Pro–65 D Huish (1987)
V'tors II SOC
Fees £35 (£40)
Loc 15 miles E of Chester
 on A556
Arch Ted Ray

Shrigley Hall (1989)
Shrigley Park, Pott Shrigley, Macclesfield SK10 5SB
Tel (01625) 575757
Fax (01625) 573323
Mem 400
Sec G Hay
Pro GA Ogden
 (01625) 575626
Holes 18 L 6281 yds SSS 71
Recs Am–69 J Murphy (1995)
 Pro–67 D Durnian (1995)
V'tors H SOC
Fees £25 (£30
Loc 5 miles NE of Macclesfield,
 off A523. M6 Junction 18
Arch Donald Steel

Stamford (1901)
Oakfield House, Huddersfield Road, Stalybridge SK15 3PY
Tel (01457) 832126
Mem 500
Sec BD Matthews
Pro B Badger (01457) 834829
Holes 18 L 5701 yds SSS 68
Recs Am–68 A Derry
V'tors WD–U WE comp days–after
 2.30pm SOC–WD
Fees On application
Loc NE boundary of Stalybridge
 on B6175

Cheshire 543

For list of abbreviations see page 527

Stockport (1906)
Offerton Road, Offerton, Stockport SK2 5HL
Tel (0161) 427 2001 (Members)
Fax (0161) 449 8293
Mem 510
Sec JE Flanagan (0161) 427 8369
Pro M Peel (0161) 427 2421
Holes 18 L 6326 yds SSS 71
Recs Am–67 JR Whittaker,
S Fraser-Thompson,
SM Hughes, P Pearse
Pro–66 E Lester
Ladies–68 RA Hughes
V'tors SOC–WD
Fees £35 (£45)
Loc 4 miles SE of Stockport on A627

Styal (1994)
Station Road, Styal SK9 4JN
Tel (01625) 531359
Fax (01625) 530063
Mem 650
Sec W Higham (01625) 530063
Pro G Traynor (01625) 530063
Holes 18 L 6301 yds Par 71 SSS 70
V'tors U SOC
Fees £12 (£16)
Loc 2 miles from M56 Junction 5
Mis Floodlit driving range
Arch T Holmes

The Tytherington Club (1986)
Macclesfield SK10 2JP
Tel (01625) 434562
Fax (01625) 430882
Mem 800
Sec To be appointed
Pro J Foss
Holes 18 L 6737 yds SSS 73
Recs Am–68 J Hodgson
Pro–71 P Affleck, L Turner
Ladies Pro–63 L Davies
V'tors U H SOC–WD
Fees £28 D–£35 (£34 D–£45)
Loc N of Macclesfield (A523)
Mis Driving range
Arch Thomas/Dawson

Upton-by-Chester (1934)
Upton Lane, Chester CH2 1EE
Tel (01244) 381183
Fax (01244) 376955
Mem 750
Sec F Hopley
Pro PA Gardner (01244) 381333
Holes 18 L 5850 yds SSS 68
Recs Am–62 J Davies
Pro–66 A Perry
V'tors U SOC–WD
Fees £20 (£25)
Loc Off Liverpool road, near 'Frog' PH

Vale Royal Abbey (1998)
Whitegate, Northwich CW8 2BA
Tel (01606) 301291
Fax (01606) 301414
Mem 450
Sec WG Squires
Pro RJ Welsby (01606) 301702
Holes 18 holes Par 71 SSS 71
V'tors M–by invitation only
Fees £15 (£20)
Loc Whitegate, 2 miles W of Hartford, off A556
Arch Simon Gidman

Vicars Cross (1939)
Tarvin Road, Great Barrow, Chester CH3 7HN
Tel (01244) 335174
Fax (01244) 335686
Mem 800
Sec Mrs K Hunt
Pro JA Forsythe (01244) 335595
Holes 18 L 6243 yds SSS 70
V'tors U SOC–Tues & Thurs
Fees £25 (£25)
Loc 3 miles E of Chester on A51
Arch E Parr

Walton Hall (1972)
Public
Warrington Road, Higher Walton, Warrington WA4 5LU
Tel (01925) 266775
Mem 350
Sec I England
Pro J Jackson (01925) 263061
Holes 18 L 6843 yds Par 72 SSS 73
Recs Am–70 R Davies (1988)
V'tors U SOC
Fees £6.50 (£8)
Loc 2 miles S of Warrington. M56 Junctions 10/11
Arch Dave Thomas

Warrington (1903)
Hill Warren, Appleton WA4 5HR
Tel (01925) 261620
Fax (01925) 265933
Mem 875
Sec NF Morrall (01925) 261775
Pro R Mackay (01925) 265431
Holes 18 L 6305 yds SSS 70
Recs Am–66 JR Bennett
Pro–65 EG Lester
V'tors U SOC–Wed
Fees On application
Loc 3 miles S of Warrington

Werneth Low (1912)
Werneth Low Road, Gee Cross, Hyde SK14 3AF
Tel (0161) 368 2503
Mem 315 60(L) 40(J)
Sec R Clapham (0161) 366 0837
Pro T Bacchus (0161) 367 9376
Holes 11 L 6113 yds Par 70 SSS 69
Recs Am–67 S Madden
Pro–57 D Cooper
V'tors U exc Sun–NA Sat/BH–M SOC
Fees £18
Loc 2 miles SE of Hyde, nr Gee Cross. M67 Junction 4
Arch Peter Campbell

Widnes (1924)
Highfield Road, Widnes WA8 7DT
Tel (0151) 424 2440
Fax (0151) 495 2849
Mem 600
Sec MM Cresswell (0151) 424 2995
Pro J O'Brien (0151) 420 7467
Holes 18 L 5729 yds SSS 68
Recs Am–64 F Whitfield (1990)
Pro–64 A Murray (1976)
V'tors WD–U WE–H NA on comp days SOC–Thurs
Fees £20 (£33)
Loc Station ½ mile

Wilmslow (1889)
Great Warford, Mobberley, Knutsford WA16 7AY
Tel (01565) 872148
Fax (01565) 872172
Mem 780
Sec Mrs MI Padfield
Pro J Nowicki (01565) 873620
Holes 18 L 6607 yds SSS 72
Recs Am–66 C Nowicki (1995)
Pro–62 C Corrigan (1994)
V'tors U H exc Wed–NA before 3pm
Fees £40 (£50)
Loc 3 miles W of Alderley Edge

Cornwall

Bowood Park (1992)
Valley Truckle, Lanteglos, Camelford PL32 9RT
Tel (01840) 213017
Fax (01840) 212622
Mem 300
Pro R Jenkins
Holes 18 L 6692 yds SSS 72
V'tors H (phone first) SOC
Fees £23 (£25)
Loc 2 miles SW of Camelford, off A39, on to B3266
Mis Driving range

Bude & North Cornwall (1891)
Burn View, Bude EX23 8DA
Tel (01288) 352006
Fax (01288) 356855
Mem 500 220(L) 60(J)
Sec PK Brown
Pro J Yeo
Holes 18 L 6057 yds SSS 70
Recs Am–65 S Rickard
Pro–67 B Austin
Ladies–73 S Currie
V'tors WD–H 9.30–12.30pm, 2–5pm and after 6.30pm WE–restricted SOC
Fees £20 D–£28 (£25)
Loc Bude town centre

Budock Vean Hotel (1922)
Falmouth TR11 5LG
Tel (01326) 252102
Fax (01326) 250892

For list of abbreviations see page 527

Mem 150
Sec JP Loughnan
Pro A Ramsden (Golf Mgr)
Holes 9 L 5153 yds SSS 65
Recs Am–61 RJ Sadler
 Pro–64 D Short
V'tors H
Fees D–£18 (D–£20)
Loc Falmouth 5 miles
Arch James Braid

Cape Cornwall G&CC

(1990)
St Just, Penzance TR19 7NL
Tel (01736) 788611
Fax (01736) 788611
Mem 450
Sec M Waters
Pro D Knapp (01736) 788867
Holes 18 L 5650 yds SSS 68
V'tors WD/Sat–U Sun–NA before noon SOC
Fees £20 (£20)
Loc 1 mile W of St Just. 8 miles W of Penzance, off A3071
Arch R Hamilton

Carlyon Bay (1926)

Carlyon Bay, St Austell PL25 3RD
Tel (01726) 814250
Fax (01726) 814250
Mem 500
Sec Y Lister, P Clemo
Pro M Rowe (01726) 814228
Holes 18 L 6560 yds SSS 71
Recs Am–68 A Nash
 Pro–65 N Coles
V'tors U–book with Pro
Fees £29
Loc 2 miles E of St Austell
Arch J Hamilton Stutt

China Fleet CC (1991)

Saltash PL12 6LJ
Tel (01752) 848668
Fax (01752) 848456
Mem 600
Sec DW O'Sullivan
Pro RA Moore
Holes 18 L 6551 yds SSS 72
Recs Am–69 I Ashenden (1993)
V'tors H–by arrangement SOC
Fees On application
Loc 1 mile from Tamar Bridge, off A38
Mis Floodlit driving range
Arch Martin Hawtree

Culdrose

Royal Naval Air Station, Culdrose
Tel (01326) 574121 Ext 2413
Mem 173
Sec VC Williams (Hon) (01326) 572540
Holes 18 L 6432 yds Par 72 SSS 71
Recs Am–74 P McDonald
V'tors M–play restricted to WE and evenings
Fees D–£5 (D–£5)
Loc Culdrose, 1 mile S of Helston on A3083

Falmouth (1894)

Swanpool Road, Falmouth TR11 5BQ
Tel (01326) 311262/314296
Fax (01326) 317783
Mem 500
Sec R Wooldridge
Pro B Patterson (Golf Dir)
Holes 18 L 5937 yds Par 71 SSS 70
V'tors U H SOC
Fees £20 D–£26
Loc ¼ mile W of Swanpool Beach
Mis Driving range

Isles of Scilly (1904)

St Mary's, Isles of Scilly TR21 0NF
Tel (01720) 422692
Fax (01720) 422049
Mem 130
Sec S Watt
Holes 9 L 6001 yds SSS 69
Recs Am–70 M Twynham
 Pro–66 G Ryall, P Evans
V'tors WD–U Sun–M
Fees £16
Loc Hughtown 1½ miles
Arch Horace Hutchinson

Killiow Park (1987)

Killiow, Kea, Truro TR3 6AG
Tel (01872) 270246
Fax (01872) 240915
Mem 500
Sec D Pratt, J Penrose (Prop)
Holes 18 L 3946 yds Par 62
V'tors WD–U WE–NA before 9.30am
Fees £12.50
Loc 2½ miles S of Truro, off A39
Mis Driving range

Lanhydrock (1991)

Lostwithiel Road, Bodmin PL30 5AQ
Tel (01208) 73600
Fax (01208) 77325
Mem 400
Sec G Bond (Gen Mgr)
Pro J Broadway
Holes 18 L 6100 yds Par 70 SSS 70
Recs Am–66 R Binney (1996)
 Pro–65 A Nash (1996)
V'tors U SOC
Fees On application
Loc 1 mile S of Bodmin, off B3268
Mis Driving range
Arch J Hamilton Stutt

Launceston (1927)

St Stephen, Launceston PL15 8HF
Tel (01566) 773442
Fax (01566) 777506
Mem 900
Sec BJ Grant
Pro J Tozer
Holes 18 L 6407 yds SSS 71
Recs Am–67 C Phillips (1987)
 Pro–64 S Little (1989)
V'tors WD–U H WE–NA SOC
Fees £24
Loc 1 mile N of Launceston, off Bude road
Arch J Hamilton Stutt

Looe (1933)

Bin Down, Looe PL13 1PX
Tel (01503) 240239
Fax (01503) 240864
Mem 600
Sec G Bond (Gen Mgr)
Pro A MacDonald
Holes 18 L 5940 yds SSS 68
Recs Am–64 I Veale (1993)
V'tors U SOC
Fees On application
Loc 3 miles E of Looe
Arch Harry Vardon

Lostwithiel G&CC (1990)

Lower Polscoe, Lostwithiel PL22 0HQ
Tel (01208) 873550
Fax (01208) 873479
Mem 350
Sec D Higman
Pro T Nash (01208) 873822
Holes 18 L 5984 yds Par 72
Recs Am–67 C Sears
 Pro–70 M Hammond (1990)
V'tors H SOC
Fees £20 (£23)
Loc ½ mile E of Lostwithiel, off A390
Mis Driving range
Arch Stuart Wood

Merlin (1991)

Mawgan Porth, Newquay TR8 4DN
Tel (01841) 540222
Fax (01841) 541031
Sec Mrs M Oliver
Holes 18 L 5227 yds SSS 67
V'tors U SOC
Fees 18 holes–£12 9 holes–£9
Loc 4 miles N of Newquay
Mis Driving range
Arch Ross Oliver

Mullion (1895)

Cury, Helston TR12 7BP
Tel (01326) 240685
Mem 700
Sec G Fitter
Pro P Blundell (01326) 241176
Holes 18 L 6037 yds SSS 70
V'tors H (restricted comp days and open days) SOC–WD
Fees £20 W–£70
Loc 6 miles S of Helston
Arch W Sich

Newquay (1890)

Tower Road, Newquay TR7 1LT
Tel (01637) 872091
Fax (01637) 874066
Mem 600
Sec G Binney (01637) 874354
Pro M Bevan (01637) 874830
Holes 18 L 6161 yds SSS 69
Recs Am–63 R Binney (1998)
 Pro–63 D Haines (1994)
V'tors WD/Sat–H Sun–H SOC
Fees £20 (£22) W–£80
Loc Newquay town centre
Arch HS Colt

For list of abbreviations see page 527

Perranporth (1927)
Budnic Hill, Perranporth TR6 0AB
Tel (01872) 572454
Mem 600
Sec SJ Brooking (01872) 573701
Pro DC Mitchell (01872) 572317
Holes 18 L 6286 yds SSS 72
Recs Am–62 P Trew (1993)
Pro–65 T Nash (1998)
V'tors WD–U WE–H SOC
Fees D–£20 (D–£25)
Loc ½ mile NW of Perranporth
Arch James Braid

Praa Sands (1971)
Praa Sands, Penzance TR20 9TQ
Tel (01736) 763445
Fax (01736) 763399
Mem 300
Sec D & K Phillips (Props)
Holes 9 L 4122 yds Par 62 SSS 60
Recs Am–59 P Lorys (1981)
V'tors U exc Sun am
Fees £14.50 D–£20
Loc 7 miles E of Penzance on A394 Penzance-Helston road
Arch RA Hamilton

St Austell (1912)
Tregongeeves, St Austell PL26 7DS
Tel (01726) 74756
Mem 780
Sec K Trahair
Pro T Pitts (01726) 68621
Holes 18 L 5981 yds SSS 69
Recs Am–67 AC Nash
Pro–64 AC Nash (1993)
V'tors SOC exc comp days
Fees On application
Loc 1½ miles W of St Austell

St Enodoc (1890)
Rock, Wadebridge PL27 6LD
Tel (01208) 863216
Fax (01208) 862976
Mem 1360
Sec Col L Guy OBE
Pro NJ Williams (01208) 862402
Holes Church 18 L 6207 yds SSS 70
Holywell 18 L 4165 yds SSS 61
Recs Am–64 D Griffiths
Pro–67 Dai Rees
V'tors Church H–max 24 SOC
Holywell–U
Fees Church £35 (£40) Holywell £15 (£15)
Loc 6 miles NW of Wadebridge
Arch James Braid

St Kew (1993)
Pay and play
St Kew Highway, Wadebridge, Bodmin PL30 3EF
Tel (01208) 841500
Fax (01208) 841500
Mem 250
Sec MC Cole
Pro N Rogers
Holes 9 L 4543 yds SSS 62
Recs Pro–63
V'tors U SOC
Fees 9 holes–£8.50 18 holes–£13
Loc 2½ miles N of Wadebridge on A39
Mis Covered driving range
Arch David Derry

St Mellion Hotel G&CC (1976)
St Mellion, Saltash PL12 6SD
Tel (01579) 351351
Fax (01579) 350537
Mem 850
Sec Fiona Walker (Golf Mgr)
Pro D Moon, A Milton
Holes Old 18 L 5782 yds SSS 68
Nicklaus 18 L 6651 yds SSS 72
Recs Nicklaus Am–66 N Tull
Nicklaus Pro–63 C Mason
V'tors U H SOC
Fees From £16
Loc Tamar Bridge, 5 miles NW of Saltash
Mis Driving range for members and visitors
Arch Hamilton Stutt/Nicklaus

Tehidy Park (1922)
Camborne TR14 0HH
Tel (01209) 842208
Fax (01209) 843680
Mem 1000
Sec R Parker
Pro J Dumbreck (01209) 842914
Holes 18 L 6241 yds SSS 71
Recs Am–67 N Rogers (1989)
Pro–62 S Little (1998)
V'tors H
Fees £22 (£27)
Loc 3 miles N of Camborne

Tregenna Castle Hotel (1982)
St Ives TR26 2DE
Tel (01736) 795254 Ext 121
Mem 297
Sec J Goodman
Holes 18 L 3549 yds SSS 57
Recs Am–62 G Thomas (1989)
Pro–54 L Knapp (1986)
V'tors U SOC
Fees On application
Loc St Ives 1 mile, off A3074

Treloy (1991)
Treloy, Newquay TR7 4JN
Tel (01637) 878554
Mem 145
Sec J Reid
Holes 9 L 2143 yds SSS 31
V'tors U SOC
Fees 18 holes–£12.50
9 holes–£8
Loc 2 miles E of Newquay on A3059
Arch MRM Sandow

Trethorne
Kennards House, Launceston PL15 8QE
Tel (01566) 86324
Fax (01566) 86903
Mem 600
Sec M Davey
Pro C Kaminski
Holes 18 holes Par 71
V'tors U
Fees £16 (£17)
Loc 2 miles SW of Launceston (A30)
Mis Driving range
Arch Frank Frayn

Trevose (1924)
Constantine Bay, Padstow PL28 8JB
Tel (01841) 520208
Fax (01841) 521057
Mem 960
Sec P Gammon (Prop)
PW O'Shea (Sec/Mgr)
Pro G Alliss (01841) 520261
Holes 18 L 6608 yds SSS 72
9 L 3031 yds SSS 35
9 L 1367 yds SSS 29
Recs Am–67 C Phillips
Pro–66 N Burch
Ladies–70 L Simpson
V'tors H SOC
Fees On application
Loc 4 miles W of Padstow
Mis 3 & 4 ball times restricted (phone first)
Arch HS Colt

Truro (1937)
Treliske, Truro TR1 3LG
Tel (01872) 272640
Fax (01872) 278684
Mem 900
Sec HWD Leicester (Sec/Mgr) (01872) 278684
Pro NK Bicknell (01872) 276595
Holes 18 L 5347 yds SSS 66
Recs Am–61 AJ Ring
Pro–60 Nash
V'tors U H SOC
Fees £18 (£22)
Loc 2 miles W of Truro on A390
Arch Colt/Alison/Morrison

West Cornwall (1889)
Lelant, St Ives TR26 3DZ
Tel (01736) 753401
Fax (01736) 753401
Mem 825
Sec MC Lack
Pro P Atherton (01736) 753177
Holes 18 L 5884 yds SSS 69
Recs Am–63 P Rowe
Pro–64 G Emerson
V'tors H
Fees £20 (£25)
Loc 2 miles E of St Ives

For list of abbreviations see page 527

Whitsand Bay Hotel
(1909)
Portwrinkle, Torpoint PL11 3BU
Tel (01503) 230470 (Clubhouse)
Fax (01503) 230329
Mem 400
Sec GG Dyer (01503) 230164
Pro S Poole (01503) 230778
Holes 18 L 5885 yds SSS 68
Recs Am–62 GG Dyer (1981)
 Pro–62 M Faulkner (1948)
V'tors U SOC
Fees £15 (£17.50)
Loc 6 miles W of Plymouth
Arch Willie Fernie

Cumbria

Alston Moor (1906)
The Hermitage, Alston CA9 3DB
Tel (01434) 381675
Mem 170
Sec H Robinson (01434) 381354
Holes 10 L 5380 yds SSS 66
Recs Am–S Embleton (1995)
V'tors U SOC
Fees D–£9 (D–£11)
Loc 2 miles S of Alston on B6277

Appleby (1903)
Brackenber Moor, Appleby CA16 6LP
Tel (017683) 51432
Mem 834
Sec D Metcalfe (Hon)
Pro P Jenkinson
 (017683) 52922
Holes 18 L 5901 yds SSS 68
Recs Am–62 G Dougherty (1998)
 Pro–69 SS Scott
V'tors U H
Fees £16 (£20)
Loc 2 miles SE of Appleby. ½ mile N of A66
Arch Willie Fernie

Barrow (1921)
Rakesmoor Lane, Hawcoat, Barrow-in-Furness LA14 4QB
Tel (01229) 825444
Mem 535 125(L) 69(J)
Sec J Slater (Hon)
Pro J McLeod (01229) 832121
Holes 18 L 6184 yds SSS 70
Recs Am–66 NL Brooks,
 P McNulty (1994)
 Ladies–68 J McCall (1984)
V'tors U H Ladies Day–Fri SOC
Fees £15 W–£60
Loc 2 miles E of Barrow, off A590

Brampton (Talkin Tarn) (1907)
Brampton CA8 1HN
Tel (016977) 2255
Mem 775
Sec IJ Meldrum (01228) 23155
Pro S Harrison (016977) 2000
Holes 18 L 6407 yds Par 72 SSS 71

Recs Am–66 R Secular (1993),
 R Richardson (1995)
 Ladies–71 L Fletcher (1989)
V'tors U
Fees D–£20 (D–£23)
Loc B6413, 1 mile SE of Brampton
Arch James Braid

Brayton Park (1986)
Pay and play
Lakeside Inn, Brayton Park, Aspatria CA5 3TD
Tel (016973) 20840
Mem 110
Sec D MacLaren
Holes 9 L 2521 yds SSS 65
V'tors U
Fees 9 holes–£5 (£6)
 18 holes–£7 (£8)
Loc 1 mile N of Aspatria. 10 miles N of Cockermouth
Mis Driving range

Carlisle (1908)
Aglionby, Carlisle CA4 8AG
Tel (01228) 513029
Fax (01228) 513303
Mem 735
Sec C Ward (Mgr)
Pro (01228) 513241
Holes 18 L 6278 yds SSS 70
Recs Am–63 C Hislop (1995)
 Pro–63 M Archer (1993)
V'tors WD–U exc Tues–NA Sat–NA Sun–restricted
 SOC–Mon/Wed/Fri
Fees £22 D–£33 (£30 D–£40)
Loc ¼ mile E of M6 Junction 43, on A69
Arch Mackenzie Ross

Carus Green (1996)
Pay and play
Burneside Road, Kendal LA9 6EB
Tel (01539) 721097
Fax (01539) 721097
Mem 250
Sec G Corrie
Pro None
Holes 18 L 5642 yds Par 70 SSS 68
V'tors U SOC
Fees £9 (£9)
Loc 1 mile N of Kendal on Burneside Road

Casterton
Sedbergh Road, Casterton, Carnforth LA6 2LA
Tel (015242) 71592
Fax (015242) 74387
Mem 300
Sec J & E Makinson (Props)
Pro R Williamson
Holes 9 L 3015 yds Par 35
Recs Am–63 A Burton (1995)
V'tors U SOC
Fees £9 (£12)
Loc 1 mile NE of Kirkby Lonsdale on A683. M6 Junction 36, 6 miles
Arch Will Adamson

Cockermouth (1896)
Embleton, Cockermouth CA13 9SG
Tel (017687) 76223/76941
Fax (017687) 76941
Mem 539
Sec RD Pollard (01900) 822650
Pro None
Holes 18 L 5496 yds SSS 67
Recs Am–62 DL Bragg
V'tors WD–U before 3.30pm exc Wed Sun–NA before 11am and 2–3.15pm SOC
Fees £15 (£20)
Loc 4 miles E of Cockermouth
Arch James Braid

Dalston Hall (1990)
Dalston Hall, Dalston, Carlisle CA5 7JX
Tel (01228) 710165
Mem 270
Sec Jane Simpson
Holes 9 L 2700 yds SSS 67
V'tors U
Fees 9 holes–£5 (£6.50)
 18 holes–£9 (£12)
Loc 5 miles SW of Carlisle on B5299. 6 miles W of M6 Junction 42

The Dunnerholme (1905)
Duddon Road, Askam-in-Furness LA16 7AW
Tel (01229) 462675
Mem 440
Sec Mrs ME Tyson
 (01229) 581400
Holes 10 L 6162 yds SSS 70
Recs Am–68 H Bayliff
 Pro–70 JB Ball
V'tors U
Fees £12 (£15)
Loc 6 miles N of Barrow on A595

Eden (1992)
Crosby-on-Eden, Carlisle CA6 4RA
Tel (01228) 573003
Fax (01228) 818435
Mem 700
Pro S Harrison (01228) 573003
Holes 18 L 6368 yds SSS 72
Recs Am–64 C Hislop (1997)
V'tors U SOC
Fees £20 (£25)
Loc 5 miles NE of Carlisle, off A689. M6 Junction 44
Mis Driving range

Furness (1872)
Walney Island, Barrow-in-Furness LA14 3LN
Tel (01229) 471232
Mem 625
Sec WT French
Pro None
Holes 18 L 6363 yds SSS 71
Recs Am–65 M Day (1996)
 Pro–65 A Chandler,
 GJ Brand (1984)
V'tors H SOC
Fees £17 (£17)
Loc Walney Island

For list of abbreviations see page 527

Grange Fell (1952)
*Fell Road, Grange-over-Sands
LA11 6HB*
Tel (015395) 32536
Mem 300
Sec JB Asplin (015395) 32021
Holes 9 L 4826 metres SSS 66
Recs Am–65 D Airey (1996)
Pro–66 F Robinson
V'tors U
Fees £12 (£17)
Loc W of Grange-over-Sands, towards Cartmel

Grange-over-Sands (1919)
*Meathop Road, Grange-over-Sands
LA11 6QX*
Tel (015395) 33180
Fax (015395) 33754
Mem 430 170(L) 40(J)
Sec JR Green (015395) 33754
Pro S Sumner-Roberts (015395) 35937
Holes 18 L 5938 yds SSS 69
Recs Am–67 DA Shepherd
Pro–67 G Cuthbert
V'tors H SOC
Fees £18 D–£24 (£24 D–£28)
Loc E of Grange, off B5277

Haltwhistle (1967)
*Wallend Farm, Greenhead, Carlisle
CA6 7HN*
Tel (01697) 747367
Fax (01434) 344000
Mem 300
Sec JD Gilbertson (Hon)
Pro None
Holes 18 L 5522 yds Par 69 SSS 69
V'tors U SOC
Fees D–£12 (£15)
Loc 3 miles W of Haltwhistle on A69
Arch Andrew Mair

Kendal (1891)
The Heights, Kendal LA9 4PQ
Tel (01539) 724079 (Clubhouse), (01539) 723499 (Bookings)
Mem 731
Sec I Grant, R Maunder (Mgr) (01539) 733708
Pro D Turner (01539) 723499
Holes 18 L 5691 yds SSS 68
V'tors U H SOC
Fees £20 (£25)
Loc 1 mile NW of Kendal

Keswick (1978)
Threlkeld Hall, Keswick CA12 4SX
Tel (017687) 79324, (017687) 79010 (Bookings)
Mem 900
Sec JV Simpson
Pro C Hamilton (017687) 79010
Holes 18 L 6225 yds SSS 72
Recs Am–68 G Watson (1997)
Pro–69 I Clark (1984)
V'tors U H–book with Pro SOC

Fees D–£18 (£23)
Loc 4 miles E of Keswick (A66)
Arch E Brown

Kirkby Lonsdale
*Scaleber Lane, Barbon, Carnforth
LA6 2LJ*
Mem 600 50(J)
Sec G Hall (015242) 76365
Pro C Barrett (015242) 76366
Holes 18 L 6482 yds SSS 71
V'tors U SOC
Fees £18 (£22)
Loc 3 miles N of Kirkby Lonsdale, off A683
Arch W Squires

Maryport (1905)
Bankend, Maryport CA15 6PA
Tel (01900) 812605
Mem 380
Sec A Carlton (01900) 822680
Holes 18 L 6088 yds SSS 70
Recs Am–70 D Roberts (1989)
V'tors U SOC
Fees D–£15 (£20)
Loc 1 mile N of Maryport, off B5300

Penrith (1890)
Salkeld Road, Penrith CA11 8SG
Tel (01768) 891919/865429
Mem 750
Sec D Noble (01768) 891919
Pro G Key (01768) 891919
Holes 18 L 6026 yds SSS 69
Recs Am–63 JD Dockar
Pro–61 J Metcalfe
V'tors WD–H WE/BH–H 10.06–11.30am & after 3pm
Fees £20 D–£25 (£25 D–£30)
Loc ½ mile E of Penrith

St Bees (1931)
*Rhoda Grove, Rheda, Frizington
CA26 3TE*
Tel (01946) 812105/824300 (Clubhouse)
Mem 375
Sec JB Campbell
Holes 9 L 5122 yds SSS 65
Recs Am–62 D Cooper
V'tors U
Fees £10 (£12)
Loc 4 miles S of Whitehaven

Seascale (1893)
Seascale CA20 1QL
Tel (019467) 28202/28800
Fax (019467) 28202
Mem 650
Sec C Taylor (019467) 28202
Pro J Graham
Holes 18 L 6416 yds Par 71 SSS 71
Recs Am–66 J Graham (1995), S Young (1996)
Pro–65 MF Studds (1992)
V'tors U SOC
Fees £20 D–£25 (£25 D–£30)
Loc 15 miles S of Whitehaven
Arch Campbell/Lowe

Sedbergh (1896)
*Catholes-Abbot Holme, Sedbergh
LA10 5SS*
Tel (015396) 21551
Fax (015396) 20993
Mem 350
Sec AD Lord (015396) 20993
Pro J Garner
Holes 9 L 5588 yds Par 70 SSS 68
Recs Am–66 A Pickering (1996)
Pro–66 P Walker (1995)
V'tors U–phone in advance SOC H
Fees £14 D–£20 (£18 D–£25)
Loc 1 mile S of Sedbergh on Dent road. M6 Junction 37, 5 miles
Arch WG Squires

Silecroft (1903)
Silecroft, Millom LA18 4AG
Tel (01229) 774250
Mem 300
Sec DLA MacLardie (01229) 774342
Pro None
Holes 9 L 5877 yds Par 68 SSS 68
Recs Am–66 A Leece (1996)
Ladies–71 J Currie (1995)
V'tors WD–U WE/BH–restricted
Fees £15 (£15)
Loc 3 miles W of Millom

Silloth-on-Solway (1892)
Silloth, Carlisle CA5 4BL
Tel (016973) 31304
Fax (016973) 31782
Mem 800
Sec JG Proudlock
Pro A Mackenzie (016973) 32404
Holes 18 L 6614 yds SSS 73
Recs Am–65 J Longcake
V'tors U H–booking advisable SOC
Fees D–£25
Loc 22 miles W of Carlisle (B5302). M6 Junction 43
Arch Willie Park Jr

Silverdale (1906)
*Red Bridge Lane, Silverdale, Carnforth
LA5 0SP*
Tel (01524) 701300
Mem 500
Sec PJ Watts (01524) 702074
Holes 12 L 5559 yds Par 69 SSS 67
V'tors U exc Sun (Summer)–M
Fees £15 (£18)
Loc 3 miles NW of Carnforth, by Silverdale Station

Stony Holme (1974)
*Public
St Aidan's Road, Carlisle CA7 1LS*
Tel (01228) 34856
Sec DJ Daley (01228) 75641
Pro S Ling
Holes 18 L 5775 yds Par 69 SSS 68
Recs Am–64
V'tors U SOC
Fees On application
Loc 1 mile E of Carlisle, off A69. M6 Junction 43
Arch Frank Pennink

For list of abbreviations see page 527

Ulverston (1895)
Bardsea Park, Ulverston LA12 9QJ
Tel (01229) 582824
Mem 745
Sec JW Wood
Pro MR Smith (01229) 582806
Holes 18 L 6201 yds SSS 70
Recs Am–64 AJ Edwards (1997)
Pro–63 A Pickering (1998)
V'tors H or I SOC
Fees £25 D–£30 (£30 D–£35) Summer £14 D–£18 (£18 D–£22) Winter
Loc 1½ miles SW of Ulverston on A5087
Arch Herd/Colt

Windermere (1891)
Cleabarrow, Windermere LA23 3NB
Tel (015394) 43123
Fax (015394) 43123
Mem 700
Sec KR Moffat
Pro WSM Rooke (015394) 43550
Holes 18 L 5132 yds SSS 65
V'tors H SOC
Fees £24 (£28)
Loc 1½ miles E of Bowness
Arch George Lowe

Workington (1893)
Branthwaite Road, Workington CA14 4SS
Tel (01900) 603460/67818
Mem 600 110(L) 85(J)
Sec MWStG Addison
Pro A Drabble
Holes 18 L 6252 yds SSS 70
Recs Am–65 A Drabble
V'tors H SOC
Fees £15 (£18)
Loc 2 miles SE of Workington
Arch James Braid

Derbyshire

Alfreton (1892)
Oakerthorpe, Alfreton DE55 7LH
Tel (01773) 832070
Mem 300
Sec E Brown
Pro J Mellor (01773) 831901
Holes 11 L 5393 yds SSS 66
Recs Am–60 R Surgey (1995)
Pro–65 J Smith
V'tors WD–U H before 4.30pm –M after 4.30pm WE–M SOC H
Fees £16
Loc W of Alfreton (A38). M1 Junction 28

Allestree Park (1949)
Public
Allestree Hall, Allestree, Derby DE22 2EU
Tel (01332) 550616
Sec G Rawson (01332) 552971
Pro A Carnell
Holes 18 L 5749 yds SSS 68
Recs Am–66 A Oates
V'tors WD–U WE–booking req SOC
Fees On application
Loc 2 miles N of Derby on A6

Ashbourne (1886)
Wyaston Road, Ashbourne DE6 2NR
Tel (01335) 342078
Mem 600
Sec RG Lowe (01335) 343457
Holes 18 L 6402 yds SSS 71
V'tors U SOC
Fees £20 (£25)
Loc 1½ miles SW of Ashbourne
Arch David Hemstock

Bakewell (1899)
Station Road, Bakewell DE4 1GB
Tel (01629) 812307
Mem 305 67(L) 25(J)
Sec F Parker
Pro None
Holes 9 L 5240 yds SSS 66
Recs Am–63 W Hudson
V'tors WD–U WE/BH–by arrangement SOC
Fees £15 (£20)
Loc ½ mile NE of Bakewell and A6

Blue Circle (1985)
Cement Works, Hope S33 2RP
Tel (01433) 622315
Mem 154
Sec DS Smith
Holes 9 L 5350 yds SSS 66
Recs Am–69 B Harper
V'tors M
Loc Hope Valley

Bondhay (1991)
Bondhay Lane, Whitwell, Worksop S80 3EH
Tel (01909) 723608
Fax (01909) 720226
Mem 470
Sec H Hardisty
Pro M Bell
Holes 18 L 6785 yds Par 72
9 hole course
Recs Pro–70 M Ramsden
V'tors U SOC
Fees £20 (£25)
Loc 2 miles E of M1 Junction 30, off A619
Mis Driving range
Arch Donald Steel

Brailsford
Pools Head Lane, Brailsford DE6 3BU
Tel (01335) 360096
Mem 46
Sec D Garrett
Pro WD McCarthy, RG Brown
Holes 9 L 3148 yds Par 36 SSS 35
V'tors U SOC
Fees £7.50 (£10)
Loc On A52 between Derby and Ashbourne
Mis Driving range

Breadsall Priory Hotel G&CC (1976)
Moor Road, Morley, Derby DE7 6DL
Tel (01332) 832235
Fax (01332) 833509
Mem 900
Sec G Moran (Gen Mgr)
Pro A Smith (01332) 834425
Holes 18 L 6201 yds SSS 70
18 L 6028 yds SSS 69
Recs Am–66 A Thomas
Pro–66 M Glynn, DJ Russell
V'tors WD–U SOC–WD only
Fees £25–£35
Loc Morley, 5 miles N of Derby (A61)

Burton-on-Trent (1894)
43 Ashby Road East, Burton-on-Trent DE15 0PS
Tel (01283) 568708 (Clubhouse)
Fax (01283) 544551
Mem 600
Sec D Hartley (01283) 544551
Pro G Stafford (01283) 562240
Holes 18 L 6579 yds SSS 71
Recs Am–67 DI Clarke, M Grundy
Pro–65 C Hall (1994)
V'tors I H WD–NA before 9am or 1–2pm SOC
Fees £27 (£34)
Loc 3 miles E of Burton on A511
Arch HS Colt

Buxton & High Peak (1887)
Townend, Buxton SK17 7EN
Tel (01298) 23453
Fax (01298) 26333
Mem 450
Sec JW Critchley
Pro G Brown (01298) 23112
Holes 18 L 5954 yds SSS 69
Recs Am–66 P Anderson, P Norton
Pro–63 N Hallam
V'tors U
Fees £20 (£25)
Loc NE boundary of Buxton (A6)

Carsington Water (1994)
Pay and play
Carsington, Wirksworth
Tel (01629) 85650
Mem 300
Sec GWR Coleman (Mgr) (01403) 784864
Pro To be appointed
Holes 9 L 6000yds SSS
V'tors U SOC
Fees On application
Loc 8 miles NE of Ashbourne, off B5035
Arch John Ludlow

Cavendish (1925)
Gadley Lane, Buxton SK17 6XD
Tel (01298) 23494
Fax (01298) 23494
Mem 600
Sec JD Rushton (01298) 79708

For list of abbreviations see page 527

Pro P Hunstone (01298) 25052
Holes 18 L 5833 yds SSS 68
Recs Am–64 I Menzies (1992)
Pro–63 I Buckley (1988)
V'tors U H SOC–by prior arrangement with Pro
Fees £25 (£35)
Loc 3/4 mile W of Buxton Station. St John's Road (A53)
Arch Dr A Mackenzie

Chapel-en-le-Frith (1905)
The Cockyard, Manchester Road, Chapel-en-le-Frith SK23 9UH
Tel (01298) 812118
Fax (01298) 814990
Mem 640
Sec J Hilton (01298) 813943
Pro DJ Cullen (01298) 812118
Holes 18 L 6054 yds SSS 69
Recs Am–67 D Buckle (1996)
Pro–67 J Line (1996)
V'tors U
Fees £22 (£30)
Loc 13 miles SE of Stockport, off A6 (B5470)

Chesterfield (1897)
Walton, Chesterfield S42 7LA
Tel (01246) 279256
Fax (01246) 276622
Mem 590
Sec DA Peacock
Pro M McLean (01246) 276297
Holes 18 L 6247 yds SSS 70
Recs Am–65 I Wyatt
Pro–66 K Nagle, B Hutchison
V'tors WD–U H WE–M SOC
Fees £25–£34
Loc 2 miles SW of Chesterfield on A263

Chesterfield Municipal
(1934)
Public
Murray House, Crow Lane, Chesterfield S41 0EQ
Tel (01246) 273887,
(01246) 239500 (Bookings)
Sec J Hearnshaw
Pro C Weatherhead
(01246) 203960
Holes 18 L 6013 yds SSS 69
9 hole course
Recs Pro–71 K Moss
V'tors U
Fees On application
Loc 1/4 mile past Chesterfield station
Mis Pitch & putt

Chevin (1894)
Duffield, Derby DE56 4EE
Tel (01332) 841864
Fax (01332) 841864
Mem 500 100(L) 80(J) 70(5D)
Sec JA Milner
Pro W Bird (01332) 841112
Holes 18 L 6057 yds SSS 69
Recs Am–64 P Gration (1997)
Pro–64 A Hare (1991)

V'tors WD–U WE–M SOC–WD
Fees £27
Loc 5 miles N of Derby on A6

Derby Sinfin (1923)
Public
Wilmore Road, Sinfin, Derby DE24 9HD
Tel (01332) 766323
Sec P Davidson
Pro J Siddons (01332) 766462
Holes 18 L 6163 yds SSS 69
Recs Am–67 DT James, KS Taylor
Pro–68 C Henderson
V'tors U SOC
Fees On application
Loc 1 mile S of Derby, off A52

Erewash Valley (1905)
Stanton-by-Dale, Ilkeston DE7 4QR
Tel (0115) 932 3258
Fax (0115) 932 2984
Mem 575
Sec JA Beckett (0115) 932 2984
Pro MJ Ronan (0115) 932 4667
Holes 18 L 6492 yds SSS 71
Recs Am–67 R Claydon (1988), A Dalton (1993)
Pro–68 MJ Ronan (1981)
V'tors WE/BH–NA before noon SOC–WD
Fees £22 D–£27 (D–£27)
Loc 10 miles E of Derby, off A52. M1 Junction 25, 3 miles

Glossop & District (1894)
Sheffield Road, Glossop SK13 7PU
Tel (01457) 865247 (Clubhouse)
Mem 250
Sec DM Pridham
Pro D Marsh (01457) 853117
Holes 11 L 5800 yds SSS 68
Recs Am–64 MA Boothroyd
Pro–68 S Sewgolum
V'tors U SOC
Fees £15 (£20)
Loc 1 mile E of Glossop, off A57

Grassmoor Golf Centre
Pay and play
North Wingfield Road, Grassmoor, Chesterfield S42 5EA
Tel (01246) 856044
Fax (01246) 853933
Mem 310
Sec H Chester
Pro P Goldthorpe
Holes 18 L 5721 yds Par 69
Recs Am–70 D Hill, C Bryan
Pro–64 P Goldthorpe
V'tors U SOC
Fees £10 (£12)
Loc 2 miles S of Chesterfield on B6038. M1 Junction 29, 3 miles
Mis Floodlit driving range
Arch Hawtree

Horsley Lodge (1992)
Smalley Mill Road, Horsley DE21 5BL
Tel (01332) 780838
Fax (01332) 781118
Mem 600

Sec G Johnson
Pro P Kent (01332) 780838
Holes 18 L 6336 yds SSS 70
Recs Am–70 S Hughes (1995)
V'tors U H
Fees On application
Loc 4 miles NE of Derby. M1 Junction 28
Mis Driving range
Arch GM White

Ilkeston (1929)
Public
Peewit West End Drive, Ilkeston DE7 5GH
Tel (0115) 930 4550
Mem 100
Sec M Ogden (0115) 944 2304
Pro None
Holes 9 L 4116 yds Par 62 SSS 60
Recs Am–62 (1996)
V'tors U SOC–WD
Fees On application
Loc 1/2 mile E of Ilkeston

Kedleston Park (1947)
Kedleston, Quarndon, Derby DE22 5JD
Tel (01332) 840035
Fax (01332) 842329
Mem 797
Sec K Wilson
Pro DJ Russell (01332) 841685
Holes 18 L 6585 yds SSS 71
Recs Am–64 JP Feeney
Pro–65 K Waters
V'tors WD–H
Fees £27 (£35)
Loc 4 miles N of Derby. National Trust signs to Kedleston Hall
Arch James Braid

Matlock (1907)
Chesterfield Road, Matlock Moor, Matlock DE4 5LZ
Tel (01629) 582191
Mem 496 78(L) 55(J)
Sec AJ Box
Pro M Whithorn (01629) 584934
Holes 18 L 5804 yds SSS 68
Recs Am–64 N Furniss
Pro–65 W Bird
V'tors WD–U exc
12.30–1.30pm–NA
WE/BH–M SOC–WD
Fees D–£25
Loc 1 1/2 miles NE of Matlock (A632)

Maywood (1990)
Rushy Lane, Risley, Derby DE7 3ST
Tel (0115) 939 2306
Mem 500
Sec P Moon (Prop)
Pro (0115) 949 0043
Holes 18 L 6424 yds SSS 71
Recs Am–74 M Thomson (1995)
V'tors WD–U before 4pm WE–NA SOC
Fees £15 (£20)
Loc Between Nottingham and Derby. M1 Junction 25

For list of abbreviations see page 527

Mickleover (1923)
Uttoxeter Road, Mickleover DE3 5AD
Tel   (01332) 513339 (Clubhouse)
Mem 800
Sec   D Rodgers (01332) 512092
Pro   T Coxon (01332) 518662
Holes 18 L 5708 yds SSS 68
Recs   Am–62 D Bartlett
       Pro–63 A Skingle
V'tors U SOC–Tues & Thurs
Fees   £22 (£25)
Loc   3 miles W of Derby
      on A516/B5020

New Mills (1907)
Shaw Marsh, New Mills, High Peak SK22 4QE
Tel   (01663) 743485
Mem 350
Sec   P Jenkinson (01663) 744305
Pro   S James (01663) 746161
Holes 9 L 5633 yds SSS 67
Recs   Am–65 T Jones
       Pro–64 E Litchfield
V'tors WD–U WE–M SOC
Fees   On application
Loc   8 miles SE of Stockport

Ormonde Fields (1906)
Nottingham Road, Codnor, Ripley DE5 9RG
Tel   (01773) 742987
Mem 660
Sec   K Constable
Pro   P Buttifant
Holes 18 L 6504 yds SSS 72
Recs   Am–71 N Ratcliffe (1998)
       Pro–69 S Rose (1998)
V'tors U SOC
Fees   On application
Loc   A610 Ripley to Nottingham road. M1 Junction 26, 5 miles
Arch John Fearn

Pastures (1969)
Pastures Hospital, Mickleover DE3 5DQ
Tel   (01332) 521074
Mem 320
Sec   S McWilliams
Holes 9 L 5095 yds SSS 65
Recs   Am–62 C Whyatt (1989)
V'tors M SOC–WD
Loc   4 miles W of Derby
Arch JF Pennink

Shirland (1977)
Lower Delves, Shirland DE5 6AU
Tel   (01773) 834935
Mem 350
Sec   G Brassington (01246) 852816
Pro   NB Hallam (01773) 834345
Holes 18 L 6072 yds SSS 70
Recs   Am–67 R Skingle (1990)
       Pro–67 NB Hallam (1998)
V'tors WD–U WE–U after 3pm SOC
Fees   £15 (£20) (1998)
Loc   1 mile N of Alfreton, off A61 by Shirland Church

Sickleholme (1898)
Bamford, Sheffield S33 0BH
Tel   (01433) 651306
Mem 250 100(L) 72(J)
Sec   PH Taylor (Mgr)
Pro   PH Taylor
Holes 18 L 6064 yds SSS 69
Recs   Am–63 IL Fletcher,
       DRM Kinsey
       Pro–65 AP Highfield
V'tors U exc Wed am
Fees   £26 (£32)
Loc   W of Sheffield, between Hathersage and Hope (A625)

Stanedge (1934)
Walton Hay Farm, Chesterfield S45 0LW
Tel   (01246) 566156
Mem 300
Sec   W Tyzack (01246) 276568
Holes 9 L 5786 yds SSS 68
V'tors WD–U before 2pm –M after 2pm Sat–M Sun–NA before 4pm –M after 4pm
Fees   £15
Loc   5 miles SW of Chesterfield, off B5057

Devon

Ashbury (1991)
Fowley Cross, Okehampton EX20 4NL
Tel   (01837) 55453
Fax   (01837) 55468
Mem 50
Sec   DJ Fensom
Pro   R Cade
Holes 18 L 5536 yds SSS 67
       18 L 5623 yds SSS 67
       18 hole Par 3 course
V'tors U
Fees   £12 (£15)
Loc   4 miles W of Okehampton, off A3079
Arch DJ Fensom

Axe Cliff (1894)
Squires Lane, Axmouth, Seaton EX12 4AB
Tel   (01297) 24371
Mem 400
Sec   Mrs H Kenworthy
Pro   M Dack (01297) 21754
Holes 18 L 5969 yds SSS 70
Recs   Am–64 P Raven
V'tors U H SOC
Fees   £20 (£22)
Loc   Nr Yacht Club at Axmouth Bridge

Bigbury (1923)
Bigbury, Kingsbridge TQ7 4BB
Tel   (01548) 810207
Mem 850
Sec   BJ Perry (01548) 810557
Pro   S Lloyd (01548) 810412
Holes 18 L 6076 yds SSS 69
Recs   Am–65 CS Yeoman
       Pro–65 R Tuddenham, S Little

V'tors I H SOC
Fees   D–£24 (£26)
Loc   15 miles SE of Plymouth

Chulmleigh (1976)
Leigh Road, Chulmleigh EX18 7BL
Tel   (01769) 580519
Fax   (01769) 580519
Mem 100
Sec   HM Meadows
Holes Summer 18 L 1450 yds SSS 54
       Winter 9 L 2309 yds SSS 54
Recs   Am–49 A Robarts (1998)
       Pro–48 M Blackwell (1992)
V'tors U
Fees   £6.50 D–£12
Loc   1 mile N of A377 at Chulmleigh
Arch John Goodban

Churston (1890)
Churston, Brixham TQ5 0LA
Tel   (01803) 842218
Fax   (01803) 845738
Mem 750
Sec   KP Loosemore (01803) 842751
Pro   N Holman (01803) 843442
Holes 18 L 6208 yds SSS 70
Recs   Am–64 RHP Knott (1989)
       Pro–64 J Langmead (1995)
       Ladies–70 S Guthrie (1995)
V'tors H exc Tues am–NA SOC–Mon/Thurs/Fri
Fees   £25 (£30)
Loc   5 miles S of Torquay
Arch HS Colt

Dainton Park (1993)
Totnes Road, Ipplepen, Newton Abbot TQ12 5TN
Tel   (01803) 813812
Fax   (01803) 813390
Mem 600
Sec   M Penlington
Pro   M Tyson
Holes 18 L 6210 yds SSS 70
Recs   Am–70 A Davies (1995)
V'tors U SOC
Fees   £15 (£18)
Loc   2 miles S of Newton Abbot on A381
Mis   Driving range
Arch Adrian Stiff

Dartmouth G&CC (1992)
Blackawton, Totnes TQ9 7DE
Tel   (01803) 712686
Fax   (01803) 712628
Mem 800
Sec   S Butterfield
Pro   J Fullard (01803) 712650
Holes Ch'ship 18 L 7191 yds SSS 74
       Club 9 L 2583 yds SSS 33
V'tors WD–U phone first WE–H SOC
Fees   Ch'ship £25 (£35) Club £10
Loc   4 miles NE of Dartmouth on A3122
Mis   Driving range
Arch Jeremy Pern

For list of abbreviations see page 527

Dinnaton (1989)
Ivybridge PL21 9HU
Tel (01752) 892512/892452
Fax (01752) 698334
Mem 300
Sec B Rimes
Pro D Ridyard (01752) 691288
Holes 9 L 4100 yds SSS 59
9 hole course Par 64
Recs Am–66 P Tuckwell (1996)
V'tors U SOC
Fees D–£10 (D–£12.50)
Loc 12 miles SE of Plymouth, off A38/B3213
Arch Pink/Cotton

Downes Crediton (1976)
Hookway, Crediton EX17 3PT
Tel (01363) 773991
Fax (01363) 775060
Mem 700
Sec Mrs G Mullins, PT Lee (01363) 773025
Pro H Finch (01363) 774464
Holes 18 L 5934 yds Par 70 SSS 68
V'tors H SOC
Fees £20 (£25)
Loc 2 miles S of Crediton, off A377

East Devon (1902)
North View Road, Budleigh Salterton EX9 6DQ
Tel (01395) 442018
Fax (01395) 445547
Mem 850
Sec (01395) 443370
Pro T Underwood (01395) 445195
Holes 18 L 6214 yds SSS 70
Recs Am–65 R Winchester (1987), R Martin (1992)
Pro–64 G Ryall (1990)
V'tors H SOC–Thurs only
Fees £27 (£35)
Loc 12 miles SE of Exeter

Elfordleigh Hotel G&CC (1932)
Colebrook, Plympton, Plymouth PL7 5EB
Tel (01752) 336428
Fax (01752) 344581
Mem 400
Sec Mrs P Parfitt (01752) 348425
Holes 9 L 5664 yds SSS 67
Recs Am–65 A Moon (1992)
V'tors H–phone first
Fees £15 (£20)
Loc 4 miles E of Plymouth
Arch JH Taylor

Exeter G&CC (1895)
Countess Wear, Exeter EX2 7AE
Tel (01392) 874139
Fax (01392) 874139
Mem 850
Sec KJ Ham (Golf Mgr)
Pro M Rowett (01392) 875028
Holes 18 L 6000 yds SSS 69
Recs Am–63 G Milne (1988), D Turnbull (1995)
Pro–62 I Sparks (1990)
V'tors WD–U WE–I SOC–Thurs
Fees D–£26 (D–£26)
Loc 4 miles SE of Exeter
Arch James Braid

Fingle Glen (1992)
Tedburn St Mary, Exeter EX6 6AF
Tel (01647) 61817
Fax (01647) 61135
Mem 450
Sec P Miliffe
Pro S Gould
Holes 9 L 2466 yds SSS 63
Recs Am–61 J Hoskins (1998)
Pro–63 R Troake (1992)
V'tors U SOC
Fees 18 holes–£10 (£14)
9 holes–£7 (£8)
Loc 5 miles W of Exeter on A30
Mis Driving range

Hartland Forest G&CC (1980)
East Yagland, Woolsery, Bideford EX39 5RA
Tel (01237) 431442
Fax (01237) 431734
Mem 130
Sec A Cartwright
Pro None
Holes 18 L 6015 yds Par 71 SSS 69
V'tors U SOC
Fees £20
Loc 6 miles S of Clovelly, off A39
Arch Alan Cartwright

Hele Park Golf Centre
Pay and play
Ashburton Road, Newton Abbot TQ12 6JN
Tel (01626) 336060
Fax (01626) 332661
Mem 300
Sec W Stanbury (01626) 336060
Pro J Langmead
Holes 9 L 2584 yds SSS 65
Recs Am–64 J Beare (1996)
V'tors U SOC
Fees £13 (£14.50)
Loc W of Newton Abbot on A383
Mis Driving range
Arch M Craig

Holsworthy (1937)
Kilatree, Holsworthy EX22 6LP
Tel (01409) 253177
Fax (01409) 253177
Mem 650
Sec B Megson
Pro S Chapman (01409) 254771
Holes 18 L 6062 yds SSS 69
Recs Am–64 G Webb (1995)
Pro–68 D Shepperd, A Cave (1998)
V'tors WD–U Sun–U after 2.30pm
Fees £20 (£25)
Loc 1 mile W of Holsworthy.
7 miles E of Bude (A3072)

Honiton (1896)
Middlehills, Honiton EX14 8TR
Tel (01404) 44422
Fax (01404) 46383
Mem 800
Sec JL Carter
Pro A Cave (01404) 42943
Holes 18 L 5902 yds SSS 68
Recs Am–67 A March (1992), K Harper (1996)
Pro–66 B Dredge, J Langmead (1996)
Ladies–74 J Easterbrook (1995)
V'tors U (recognised club member) SOC
Fees On application
Loc 2 miles S of Honiton

Hurdwick (1990)
Tavistock Hamlets, Tavistock PL19 8PZ
Tel (01822) 612746
Mem 175
Sec Maj RW Cullen (Mgr)
Holes 18 L 5217 yds Par 68
V'tors U SOC
Fees £14 (£14)
Loc 1 mile N of Tavistock, on Brentor Church road
Arch Hawtree/Bartlett

Ilfracombe (1892)
Hele Bay, Ilfracombe EX34 9RT
Tel (01271) 862176
Fax (01271) 867731
Mem 648
Sec BSR Warren
Pro D Hoare (01271) 863328
Holes 18 L 5893 yds SSS 69
Recs Am–66 PA Boot (1993), P Redmore (1996)
V'tors H SOC WD–NA 12–2pm WE/BH–U after 10am –NA 12–2pm
Fees £19 (£20) 5D–£75
Loc 2 miles E of Ilfracombe, towards Combe Martin
Arch TK Weir

Libbaton (1990)
High Bickington, Umberleigh EX37 9BS
Tel (01769) 560269
Mem 475
Sec JH Brough
Pro JN Phillips (01769) 560167
Holes 18 L 6494 yds SSS 72
Recs Am–67 S Herniman (1995)
V'tors U SOC
Fees £15 (£18)
Loc 1 mile S of High Bickington on B3217. M5 Junction 27
Mis Floodlit driving range

Manor House Hotel (1929)
Moretonhampstead TQ13 8RE
Tel (01647) 440998
Fax (01647) 440961
Mem 250

For list of abbreviations see page 527

Sec R Lewis
Pro R Lewis
Holes 18 L 6016 yds SSS 69
Recs Am–68 G Milne (1989)
Pro–65 G Emerson (1985)
V'tors U H SOC
Fees £25 (£32)
Loc 15 miles SW of Exeter on B3212. M5 Junction 31
Arch JF Abercromby

Mortehoe & Woolacombe (1992)
Easewell, Mortehoe, Ilfracombe EX34 7EH
Tel (01271) 870225
Mem 225
Sec M Wilkinson (01271) 870745
Holes 9 L 4852 yds SSS 63
Recs Am–66 D Huxtable (1997)
V'tors U
Fees 9 holes–£6 18 holes–£10
Loc E of Mortehoe village
Arch David Hoare

Newton Abbot (1930)
Newton Abbot TQ12 6QQ
Tel (01626) 352460
Fax (01626) 330210
Mem 886
Sec R King
Pro M Craig (01626) 362078
Holes 18 L 5862 yds SSS 68
Recs Am–63 M Pym (1989)
Pro–67 B Barnes (1977)
V'tors H SOC–Thurs
Fees D–£22
Loc Stover, 3 miles N of Newton Abbot on A382
Arch James Braid

Okehampton (1913)
Okehampton EX20 1EF
Tel (01837) 52113
Fax (01837) 52734
Mem 500
Sec CS Hicks
Pro S Jefferies (01837) 53541
Holes 18 L 5243 yds SSS 67
Recs Am–65 D File Jr (1997)
Pro–H Finch
V'tors H SOC
Fees On application
Loc S boundary of Okehampton
Arch JH Taylor

Padbrook Park (1992)
Pay and play
Cullompton EX15 1RU
Tel (01884) 38286
Fax (01804) 34259
Mem 450
Sec R Chard (Mgr)
Pro S Adwick (01884) 820805
Holes 9 L 6108 yds SSS 70
V'tors U SOC–WD
Fees 18 holes–£10 (£16)
9 holes–£7 (£8)
Loc 10 miles E of Exeter. M5 Junction 28, 1 mile
Arch Bob Sandow

Portmore Golf Park (1997)
Pay and play
Landkey Road, Barnstaple EX32 9LB
Tel (01271) 378378
Fax (01271) 378378
Mem 60
Sec C Webber
Pro S Gould, G Ross
Holes 9 L 3176 yds Par 54
V'tors U
Fees 9 holes–£7 (£8)
18 holes–£10 (£12)
Loc 1 mile E of Barnstaple, off A361
Mis Floodlit driving range
Arch Hawtree

Royal North Devon (1864)
Golf Links Road, Westward Ho! EX39 1HD
Tel (01237) 473824 (Clubhouse)
Fax (01237) 423456
Mem 1100
Sec R Fowler (01237) 473817
Pro I Higgins (01237) 477598
Holes 18 L 6653 yds SSS 72
Recs Am–66 D Boughey,
S McCarthy (1995)
Pro–66 P Dawson,
KDG Nagle, MF Foster
Ladies–69 P Johnson
V'tors U H
Fees £28 D–£34 (£34 D–£40)
Loc 2 miles N of Bideford (A39)
Mis Golf Museum
Arch Tom Morris

Saunton (1897)
Saunton, Braunton EX33 1LG
Tel (01271) 812436
Fax (01271) 814241
Mem 1250
Sec TC Reynolds
Pro AT Mackenzie (01271) 812013
Holes East 18 L 6729 yds SSS 73
West 18 L 6403 yds SSS 71
Recs East Am–65 M Treleaven (1993), DH Park, G Ogilvy (1997); Pro–66 J Taylor
West Am–68 PH Watts (1991)
Pro–67 JP Langmead (1996)
V'tors U H SOC
Fees £40 D–£60 (£50 D–£75)
Loc 6 miles W of Barnstaple
Arch Fowler/Pennink

Sidmouth (1889)
Cotmaton Road, Sidmouth EX10 8SX
Tel (01395) 513023
Fax (01395) 514661
Mem 850
Sec IM Smith (01395) 513451
Pro G Tapper (01395) 516407
Holes 18 L 5068 yds SSS 65
Recs Am–59 N Winchester
Pro–62 J Robinson
V'tors U SOC
Fees £20 (£20)
Loc ½ mile W of Sidmouth.
12 miles SE of M5 Junction 30
Arch JH Taylor

Sparkwell (1993)
Pay and play
Sparkwell, Plymouth PL7 5DF
Tel (01752) 837219
Fax (01752) 837219
Mem 108
Sec G Adamson
Pro None
Holes 9 L 5772 yds SSS 68
V'tors U SOC
Fees 18 holes–£10 (£12)
9 holes–£6 (£7)
Loc 8 miles NE of Plymouth. A38 Plympton Junction
Mis 9 hole pitch & putt
Arch J Gabb

Staddon Heights (1904)
Plymstock, Plymouth PL9 9SP
Tel (01752) 402475
Fax (01752) 401998
Mem 740
Sec K Bravant
Pro I Marshall (01752) 492630
Holes 18 L 5845 yds SSS 70
Recs Am–66 G Box
Pro–62 J Cowgill
V'tors WE–H SOC–WD
Fees D–£18 (D–£22)
Loc SE Plymouth, via Plymstock

Tavistock (1890)
Down Road, Tavistock PL19 9AQ
Tel (01822) 612049
Fax (01822) 612344
Mem 700
Sec R Vandenbergh (01822) 612344
Pro D Rehaag (01822) 612316
Holes 18 L 6250 yds SSS 70
Recs Am–66 MG Symons (1981)
Pro–69 S Chadwick,
N Bicknell
Ladies–72 D Gosling (1989),
E Fields (1991)
V'tors U SOC–WD
Fees £18 (£23)
Loc Whitchurch Down

Teign Valley (1995)
Christow, Exeter EX6 7PA
Tel (01647) 253026
Fax (01647) 253026
Mem 300
Sec Sue Pearman
Pro R Stephenson (01647) 253127
Holes 18 L 5913 yds Par 70 SSS 68
V'tors U SOC
Fees £12 (£16)
Loc SW of Exeter, via A38 (B3193)
Arch Peter Nicholson

Teignmouth (1924)
Exeter Road, Teignmouth TQ14 9NY
Tel (01626) 773614
Fax (01626) 777070
Mem 900
Sec D Holloway (01626) 777070
Pro P Ward (01626) 772894

For list of abbreviations see page 527

Holes 18 L 6227 yds SSS 70
Recs Am–65 JH Laidler (1980)
Pro–66 P Millhouse (1987)
V'tors WD–H (recognised club member) WE–by appointment SOC–WD
Fees £22 (£25)
Loc 2 miles N of Teignmouth on B3192
Arch Dr A Mackenzie

Thurlestone (1897)
Thurlestone, Kingsbridge TQ7 3NZ
Tel (01548) 560405
Fax (01548) 560405
Mem 770
Sec R Marston
Pro P Laugher (01548) 560715
Holes 18 L 6340 yds Par 71 SSS 70
Recs Am–65 D Eva (1995)
Pro–67 PJ Yeo (1975)
V'tors I or H
Fees £26 W–£100
Loc 5 miles W of Kingsbridge, off A379
Arch HS Colt

Tiverton (1932)
Post Hill, Tiverton EX16 4NE
Tel (01884) 252114 (Clubhouse)
Fax (01884) 252187
Mem 600 130(L) 45(J)
Sec T Pond (Sec/Mgr) (01884) 252187
Pro D Sheppard (01884) 254836
Holes 18 L 6236 yds SSS 71
Recs Am–65 SC Waddington (1977)
Pro–67 D Sheppard (1997)
Ladies–70 C Trew (1977)
V'tors H
Fees On application
Loc 5 miles W of M5 Junction 27. 1½ miles E of Tiverton on B3391
Arch Braid/Cotton

Torquay (1910)
Petitor Road, St Marychurch, Torquay TQ1 4QF
Tel (01803) 327471
Fax (01803) 316116
Mem 800
Sec BG Long (01803) 314591
Pro M Ruth (01803) 329113
Holes 18 L 6198 yds Par 69 SSS 70
Recs Am–63 AD Stubbs (1996)
Pro–65 G Emerson (1992)
V'tors H SOC
Fees £20 (£25)
Loc 2 miles N of Torquay

Torrington (1895)
Weare Trees, Torrington EX38 7EZ
Tel (01805) 622229
Fax (01805) 622514
Mem 440
Sec GSC Green (Hon)
Pro None
Holes 9 L 4429 yds Par 64 SSS 63
Recs Am–58 DL George
V'tors U exc Sun am–NA SOC

Fees D–£12
Loc 1 mile W of Torrington on Weare Gifford road

Warren (1892)
Dawlish Warren EX7 0NF
Tel (01626) 862255
Fax (01626) 888005
Mem 600
Sec D Daniell
Pro AJ Naldrett (01626) 864002
Holes 18 L 5968 yds SSS 69
Recs Am–65 J Langmead (1987)
V'tors H SOC–Mon/Wed/Fri
Fees £21.50 (£24.50)
Loc 1½ miles E of Dawlish

Waterbridge (1992)
Pay and play
Down St Mary, Crediton EX17 5LG
Tel (01363) 85111
Sec CA Petherick
Pro D Ridyard
Holes 9 L 1955 yds Par 32
V'tors U
Fees 18 holes–£10 (£12)
9 holes–£6 (£7)
Loc 1 mile N of Copplestone on A377
Arch David Taylor

Woodbury Park (1992)
Woodbury Castle, Woodbury EX5 1JJ
Tel (01395) 233382
Fax (01395) 233384
Mem 720
Sec PJ Flavin
Pro A Richards
Holes 18 L 6707 yds SSS 72
9 L 4582 yds SSS 62
Recs Am–67 G Harper
Pro–67 G Norman (1995),
F Nobilo (1996)
V'tors U
Fees 18 hole:£35 9 hole:£9
Loc 10 miles E of Exeter on A3052. M5 Junction 30, 6 miles
Mis Driving range
Arch J Hamilton Stutt

Wrangaton (1895)
Golf Links Road, Wrangaton, South Brent TQ10 9HJ
Tel (01364) 73229
Fax (01364) 73229
Mem 790
Sec G Williams
Pro A Whitehead (01364) 72161
Holes 18 L 6083 yds SSS 69
Recs Am–66 D Marsh (1996)
V'tors H SOC
Fees £18 (£24)
Loc Dartmoor, 3 miles E of Ivybridge
Arch Donald Steel

Yelverton (1904)
Golf Links Road, Yelverton PL20 6BN
Tel (01822) 852824
Fax (01822) 852824

Mem 600
Sec HS Fleming (01822) 852824
Pro T McSherry (01822) 853593
Holes 18 L 6351 yds Par 71 SSS 72
Recs Am–67 MJ Lavers (1998)
Pro–63 I Harrison (1998)
V'tors H SOC
Fees D–£30 (£40)
Loc 6 miles N of Plymouth on A386
Arch Herbert Fowler

Dorset

The Ashley Wood (1896)
Wimborne Road, Blandford Forum DT11 9HN
Tel (01258) 452253
Fax (01258) 450590
Mem 670
Sec P Lillford
Pro S Taylor
Holes 18 L 6276 yds Par 70 SSS 70
Recs Am–66 S Sanger (1996)
Pro–67 S Taylor (1996)
V'tors WD–U WE–H
Fees Phone in advance
Loc 1½ miles SE of Blandford on B3082
Arch Patrick Tallack

Bournemouth & Meyrick Park (1890)
Pay and play
Central Drive, Meyrick Park, Bournemouth BH2 6LH
Tel (01202) 290307,
(01202) 290862 (Bookings)
Mem 400
Pro L Thompson
Holes 18 L 5637 yds Par 69
Recs Am–63
Pro–62 D Ray (1994)
V'tors U
Fees £11 (£12)
Loc ½ mile behind Town Hall, Bournemouth
Arch Dunn(1894)/Colt(1925)

Bridport & West Dorset (1891)
East Cliff, West Bay, Bridport DT6 4EP
Tel (01308) 421095/422597
Fax (01308) 421095
Mem 700
Sec PJ Ridler (01308) 421095
Pro D Parsons (01308) 421491
Holes 18 L 6028 yds SSS 69
Recs Am–61 M Rees (1990)
Pro–66 S Bishop (1980),
R Crockford (1983)
V'tors WD/Sat–U after 9.30am
Sun–U after 1pm SOC
Fees £22 After 2pm–£16
Loc 2 miles S of Bridport at West Bay
Mis 9 hole pitch & putt course (Summer)

For list of abbreviations see page 527

Broadstone (1898)
*Wentworth Drive, Broadstone
BH18 8DQ*
Tel (01202) 692595
Fax (01202) 692595
Mem 650
Sec C Robinson
Pro N Tokely (01202) 692835
Holes 18 L 6315 yds SSS 70
Recs Am–66 JH Nash (1988),
LS James (1992), LG Orchard (1997), A Mew (1998)
Pro–63 S Little, G Emerson (1998)
V'tors WD–H after 9.30am
WE/BH–restricted SOC–WD
Fees £25
Loc 4 miles N of Poole, off A349
Arch Dunn(1898)/Colt(1925)

The Bulbury Club (1989)
Bulbury Lane, Lytchett Matravers, Poole BH16 6EP
Tel (01929) 459574
Fax (01929) 459000
Mem 400
Sec IG Brooks
Pro N Gravelle
Holes 18 L 6313 yds Par 72 SSS 70
Recs Pro–63 D Read (1991)
V'tors U SOC–WD
Fees £20
Loc 3 miles NW of Poole, off A35

Came Down (1896)
Came Down, Dorchester DT2 8NR
Tel (01305) 812531
Fax (01305) 813494
Mem 700
Sec DE Matthews (Mgr) (01305) 813494
Pro D Holmes (01305) 812670
Holes 18 L 6244 yds SSS 71
Recs Am–66 A Louden (1993)
Pro–63 S Robertson (1997)
V'tors H Sun am–NA SOC
Fees £22 (£27.50)
Loc 2 miles S of Dorchester
Arch Taylor/Colt

Canford Magna
*Knighton Lane, Wimborne
BH21 3AS*
Tel (01202) 593901
Fax (01202) 592550
Mem 1400
Sec D Riddle (01202) 592505
Pro M Thompson (01202) 592555
Holes Parkland 18 L 6495 yds Par 71 SSS 71; Riverside 18 L 6231 yds Par 70 SSS 70
Recs Riverside Am–68 M Fletcher
Pro–66 I Harrison
Fees £16 (£19.50)
Loc 2 miles E of Wimborne on A341
Mis Driving range
Arch Howard Swann

Canford School
*Canford School, Wimborne
BH21 3AD*
Tel (01202) 841254
Fax (01202) 881009
Mem 420
Sec C Jervis BEd
Holes 9 L 5918 yds SSS 68
Recs Am–69 J Lovett (1996), J Davidson (1998)
V'tors M SOC
Fees £8
Loc 2 miles SE of Wimborne, off A341
Arch P Boult

Chedington Court (1991)
South Perrott, Beaminster DT8 3HU
Tel (01935) 891413
Fax (01935) 891217
Mem 360
Sec D Astill (Man Dir)
Holes 18 L 5950 yds SSS 69
V'tors U SOC
Fees £16 (£20)
Loc 4 miles SE of Crewkerne on A356
Arch Chapman/Hemstock/Steel

Christchurch (1977)
*Barrack Road, Iford, Christchurch
BH23 2BA*
Tel (01202) 473817
Mem 300
Sec ME Harvey
Pro PL Troth
Holes 9 L 4330 yds SSS 61
Recs Am–62 S Cailes
V'tors U
Fees £7
Loc Bournemouth/Christchurch boundary
Mis Driving range

Crane Valley (1992)
The Clubhouse, Verwood BH31 7LE
Tel (01202) 814088
Fax (01202) 813407
Mem 600
Sec A Blackwell (Gen Mgr)
Pro P Cannings
Holes 18 L 6421 yds SSS 71
9 L 2030 yds SSS 60
Recs Am–70 A Ross (1996)
Pro–66 G Ryall (1996)
V'tors H SOC 9 hole–U
Fees 18 hole:£20 (£30)
9 hole:£5.50 (£6.50)
Loc Nr Ringwood, off B3081
Verwood-Cranborne road
Mis Floodlit driving range
Arch Donald Steel

Dorset Heights (1990)
*Belchalwell, Blandford Forum
DT11 0EG*
Tel (01258) 861386
Fax (01258) 860900
Mem 350
Sec Mrs J Burton, RBM Moore (Dir)
Pro A Stuart
Holes 18 L 6500 yds SSS 71
V'tors U SOC
Fees £12 (£15)
Loc Between Okeford Fitzpaine and Ibberton

Dudsbury (1992)
*64 Christchurch Road, Ferndown
BH22 8ST*
Tel (01202) 593499
Fax (01202) 594555
Sec GH Legg
Pro R Tuddenham (01202) 594488
Holes 18 L 6765 yds Par 71 SSS 73
Recs Am–68 C Jessup (1997), G Legg (1998)
Pro–R Davis (1998)
V'tors U
Fees On application
Loc 3 miles N of Bournemouth (B3073)
Mis Driving range. Academy course
Arch Donald Steel

East Dorset (1978)
Bere Regis, Wareham BH20 7NT
Tel (01929) 472244
Fax (01929) 471294
Mem 620
Sec BR Lee (Gen Mgr)
Pro D Honan
Holes Lakeland 18 L 7027 yds SSS 75; Woodland 18 L 4887 yds SSS 64
Recs Am–71 L James (1992)
Pro–66 R Dinsdale (1998)
V'tors Lakeland–H SOC
Woodland–U
Fees Lakeland–£29 (£34)
Woodland–£19 (£21)
Loc 5 miles S of Bere Regis, off Wool road
Mis Driving range
Arch Martin Hawtree

Ferndown (1923)
*119 Golf Links Road, Ferndown
BH22 8BU*
Tel (01202) 874602
Fax (01202) 873926
Mem 700
Sec E Robertson (Mgr) (01202) 874602
Pro IAB Parker (01202) 873825
Holes 18 L 6452 yds SSS 71
9 L 5604 yds SSS 68
Recs Old Am–65 JP Baldwin, A Sandeman
Pro–68 DN Sewell
President's Am–65 SW Findlay
Pro–68 DN Sewell
V'tors WD–H after 9.30am
SOC–Tues & Fri
Fees Old: £42 (£50)
President's: £15 (£20)
Loc 6 miles N of Bournemouth
Arch Harold Hilton

For list of abbreviations see page 527

Ferndown Forest (1993)
Forest Links Road, Ferndown BH22 9QE
Tel (01202) 876096
Fax (01202) 894095
Mem 360
Sec M Kitson (Golf Dir)
Pro K Spurgeon
Holes 18 L 5200 yds Par 67
V'tors U
Fees £9 (£11)
Loc 5 miles N of Bournemouth. N of Ferndown Bypass
Mis Floodlit driving range
Arch Hunt/Grafham

Halstock (1988)
Pay and play
Common Lane, Halstock BA22 9SF
Tel (01935) 891689
Fax (01935) 891839
Mem 200
Sec LR Church (Mgr)
Holes 18 L 4351 yds Par 65 SSS 61
Recs Am–61 R Glover (1997)
V'tors U SOC
Fees £10 (£12)
Loc 6 miles S of Yeovil, off A37
Mis Driving range

Highcliffe Castle (1913)
107 Lymington Road, Highcliffe-on-Sea, Christchurch BH23 4LA
Tel (01425) 272953
Fax (01425) 272210
Mem 350 100(L) 50(J)
Sec BE Savery (01425) 272210
Holes 18 L 4776 yds Par 64 SSS 63
Recs Am–58 S Jenkins (1986) Pro–59 M Butcher (1988)
V'tors H SOC
Fees £20 (£30)
Loc 8 miles E of Bournemouth

Isle of Purbeck (1892)
Studland BH19 3AB
Tel (01929) 450361
Fax (01929) 450501
Mem 400
Sec Mrs J Robinson (Man Dir)
Pro I Brake (01929) 450354
Holes 18 L 6283 yds SSS 71 9 L 2022 yds SSS 30
Recs Am–67 N Holman Pro–72 K Sparkes
V'tors U SOC
Fees £27.50 D–£36.50 (£35 D–£45)
Loc 3 miles N of Swanage on B3351. Ferry from Sandbanks to Studland
Arch HS Colt

Knighton Heath (1976)
Francis Avenue, West Howe, Bournemouth BH11 8NX
Tel (01202) 572633
Fax (01202) 590774
Mem 700
Sec R Bestwick
Pro Miss J Miles (01202) 578275
Holes 18 L 6084 yds SSS 69
Recs Am–64 H McCann (1990), N Tanswell (1991) Pro–64 A Beal (1990) Ladies–69 J Brown (1990)
V'tors WD–H after 9.30am WE–M
Fees On application
Loc 3 miles N of Poole, at junction of A348/A3049

Lyme Regis (1893)
Timber Hill, Lyme Regis DT7 3HQ
Tel (01297) 442963, (01297) 442043 (Steward)
Mem 750
Sec RSF McWhinney (01297) 442963
Pro A Black (01297) 443822
Holes 18 L 6283 yds SSS 70
Recs Am–67 MR Searle, D Gee (1996) Pro–68 D Honan
V'tors H WD–U after 9.30am (2.30pm Thurs) Sun–U after noon SOC
Fees £20 After 2pm–£17
Loc Between Lyme Regis and Charmouth, off A3502/A35

Lyons Gate (1991)
Lyons Gate Farm, Lyons Gate, Dorchester DT2 7AZ
Tel (01300) 345239
Mem 80
Sec NW Pires
Holes 9 L 1943 yds SSS 30
V'tors U SOC
Fees 18 holes–£8.50 9 holes–£5
Loc Middle Marsh, 12 miles N of Dorchester (A352)
Arch Ken Abel

Moors Valley (1989)
Public
Horton Road, Ringwood BH24 2ET
Tel (01425) 480448
Fax (01425) 480799
Mem 310
Sec D Meharg
Pro M Torrens (01425) 479776
Holes 18 L 6270 yds SSS 70 4-hole short course
Recs Am–74 P Cutmore Ladies–67 A Dean
V'tors U
Fees On application
Loc 4 miles SW of Ringwood, off A31
Mis Driving range

Parkstone (1910)
Links Road, Parkstone, Poole BH14 9QS
Tel (01202) 707138
Fax (01202) 706027
Mem 500 160(L) 50(J)
Sec AS Kinnear
Pro A Peach (01202) 708092
Holes 18 L 6250 yds SSS 70
Recs Am–65 DSL Cook, RA Latham, T Spence Pro–63 P Alliss
V'tors H WD–NA before 9.30am and 12.30–2.10pm WE–NA before 9.45am and 12.30–2.30pm
Fees £33 D–£44 (£45 D–£55)
Loc 3 miles W of Bournemouth, off A35
Arch W Park Jr/Braid

Queens Park (1905)
Public
Queens Park West Drive, Queens Park, Bournemouth BH8 9BY
Tel (01202) 302611/396198 (Bookings)
Mem 520
Sec MJ Poole (01202) 302611
Pro R Hill (01202) 396817
Holes 18 L 6305 yds SSS 70
Recs Am–69 M Butcher Pro–66 A Caygill, H Boyle
V'tors U SOC
Fees £12.80
Loc 2 miles NE of Bournemouth
Mis Closed Sun pm

Riversmeet Par Three
Stony Lane South, Christchurch BH23 1HW
Tel (01202) 477987
Fax (01202) 470853
Mem 250
Sec N Williams
Holes 18 L 1650 yds Par 54
V'tors U
Fees On application
Loc 2 miles W of Bournemouth

Sherborne (1894)
Clatcombe, Sherborne DT9 4RN
Tel (01935) 812475
Fax (01935) 814218
Sec Mrs JMC Guy (01935) 814431
Pro S Wright (01935) 812274
Holes 18 L 5882 yds Par 70 SSS 68
Recs Am–62 AW Lawrence (1997) Pro–64 K Spurgeon, R Davis (1997)
V'tors H
Fees £25 (£30)
Loc 1 mile N of Sherborne, off B3145

Solent Meads Par Three
Public
Rolls Drive, Hengistbury Head, Bournemouth
Tel (01202) 420795
Holes 18 L 2325 yds Par 54
V'tors U
Fees On application
Loc Hengistbury Head, S of Christchurch
Mis Driving range

For list of abbreviations see page 527

Sturminster Marshall (1992)
Moor Lane, Sturminster Marshall BH21 4AH
Tel (01258) 858444
Fax (01258) 858262
Mem 490
Sec DR Holdsworth
Pro G Howell
Holes 9 L 4882 yds SSS 65
Recs Am–68
V'tors U SOC
Fees 18 holes–£11
9 holes–£8
Loc 8 miles N of Poole on A350
Arch John Sharkey

Wareham (1908)
Sandford Road, Wareham BH20 4DH
Tel (01929) 554147
Fax (01929) 554147
Mem 550
Sec Maj MA Bartlett
Holes 18 L 5603 yds SSS 67
Recs Am–66 K Knott (1993)
V'tors WD–H 9.30am–5pm SOC WE–M
Fees £20
Loc N of railway station, on A351
Arch C Whitcombe

Weymouth (1876)
Links Road, Weymouth DT4 0PF
Tel (01305) 773981
Fax (01305) 788029
Mem 750
Sec BR Chatham
Pro D Lochrie (01305) 773997
Holes 18 L 5981 yds SSS 69
Recs Am–63 MJ Watson (1987)
Pro–60 G Emerson (1993)
Ladies–72 T Loveys (1988)
V'tors H SOC–WD
Fees £22 (£28)
Loc 1 mile from town centre (A354), off Manor roundabout
Arch Braid/Hamilton Stutt

Durham

Barnard Castle (1898)
Harmire Road, Barnard Castle DL12 8QN
Tel (01833) 638255
Mem 700
Sec WC Raine
Pro D Pearce
Holes 18 L 6406 yds SSS 71
Recs Am–68 C Hamilton (1995)
Pro–66 D Curry (1995)
V'tors U SOC
Fees £18 D–£26 (£25 D–£32)
Loc N boundary of Barnard Castle on B6278

Beamish Park (1950)
Beamish, Stanley DH9 0RH
Tel (0191) 370 1382
Fax (0191) 370 2937
Mem 520
Sec B Bradley
Pro C Cole (0191) 370 1984
Holes 18 L 6205 yds SSS 70
Recs Am–64 D Vest
V'tors WD/Sat–U before 4pm Sun–NA SOC
Fees £16 (£24)
Loc Beamish, nr Stanley
Arch Henry Cotton

Billingham (1967)
Sandy Lane, Billingham TS22 5NA
Tel (01642) 554494/533816
Fax (01642) 533816
Mem 850
Sec EI Douglas (01642) 533816
Pro M Ure (01642) 557060
Holes 18 L 6404 yds SSS 71
Recs Am–66 S Twynholm (1993)
Pro–63 M Maith (1993)
V'tors WD–H after 9am WE/BH–H after 10am SOC
Fees D–£20 (£33)
Loc W boundary of Billingham by A19, E of bypass
Arch Frank Pennink

Bishop Auckland (1894)
High Plains, Durham Road, Bishop Auckland DL14 8DL
Tel (01388) 602198
Mem 860
Sec G Thatcher (01388) 663648
Pro D Skiffington (01388) 661618
Holes 18 L 6420 yds SSS 71
Recs Am–64 G Border (1994)
Pro–65 P Harrison
V'tors H (closed Good Friday and Christmas Day)
Fees £20 D–£24 (£26)
Loc ½ mile NE of Bishop Auckland
Arch James Kay

Blackwell Grange (1930)
Briar Close, Blackwell, Darlington DL3 8QX
Tel (01325) 464464
Fax (01325) 464458
Mem 650
Sec PB Burkill (Hon) (01325) 464458
Pro R Givens (01325) 462088
Holes 18 L 5621 yds SSS 67
Recs Am–63 GE Johnson
Pro–63 M Gregson
V'tors U exc Wed 11am–2.30pm–NA Sat–booking req Sun-restricted SOC
Fees £20 D–£25 (£30)
Loc 1 mile S of Darlington on A66
Arch Frank Pennink

Brancepeth Castle (1924)
Brancepeth Village, Durham DH7 8EA
Tel (0191) 378 0075
Fax (0191) 378 3835
Mem 768 118(L) 74(J)
Sec K Stewart
Pro D Howdon (0191) 378 0183
Holes 18 L 6415 yds SSS 71
Recs Am–64 G Boardman (1992)
Pro–64 B Rumney (1990)
V'tors SOC–WD WE–NA
Fees £24 (£30)
Loc 5 miles W of Durham on A690
Arch HS Colt

Castle Eden & Peterlee (1927)
Castle Eden, Hartlepool TS27 4SS
Tel (01429) 836220
Mem 650
Sec D Livingston (01429) 836510
Pro G Laidlaw (01429) 836689
Holes 18 L 6262 yds SSS 70
Recs Am–65 D Nichols (1998)
Pro–66 P Harrison (1995)
V'tors U
Fees £22 (£30)
Loc 2 miles S of Peterlee
Arch Henry Cotton

Chester-Le-Street (1908)
Lumley Park, Chester-Le-Street DH3 4NS
Tel (0191) 388 3218
Fax (0191) 388 1220
Mem 435 130(L) 90(J)
Sec B Forster
Pro D Fletcher (0191) 389 0157
Holes 18 L 6437 yds SSS 71
Recs Am–67 J Goss
V'tors WD–H after 9.30am –NA 12–1pm WE–NA before 10.30am or 12–2pm
Fees £20 (£25)
Loc E of Chester-Le-Street
Arch JH Taylor

Consett & District (1911)
Elmfield Road, Consett DH8 5NN
Tel (01207) 502186
Fax (01207) 505060
Mem 650
Sec B Bromley (01207) 521190
Pro C Dilley (01207) 580210
Holes 18 L 6020 yds SSS 69
Recs Am–63 J Kennedy (1996)
V'tors WD–U SOC–exc Sat
Fees £17 (£25)
Loc 14 miles N of Durham on A691
Arch Harry Vardon

Crook (1919)
Low Job's Hill, Crook DL15 9AA
Tel (01388) 762429/767926
Mem 450
Sec R Hoggarth
Pro None
Holes 18 L 6102 yds SSS 70

For list of abbreviations see page 527

Recs Am–68 D Hanlon
Pro–64 K Fairbairn
V'tors U SOC
Fees £18 (£25)
Loc ½ mile E of Crook (A689)

Darlington (1908)
Haughton Grange, Darlington DL1 3JD
Tel **(01325) 355324**
Fax (01325) 488126
Mem 764
Sec L Cossins
Pro (01325) 484198
Holes 18 L 6270 yds SSS 70
Recs Am–67 J Howson
V'tors WD–U from 10am–12 & 2–4pm WE–M
Fees £20 D–£29
Loc Off Salters Lane, NE of Darlington

Dinsdale Spa (1910)
Middleton St George, Darlington DL2 1DW
Tel **(01325) 332222**
Fax (01325) 332222
Mem 875
Sec DW Corcoran (01325) 332297
Pro N Metcalfe (01325) 332515
Holes 18 L 6090 yds Par 71 SSS 69
Recs Am–65 MJ Howe (1995)
Pro–65 M Joseph (1995)
V'tors WD–U exc Tues–NA WE–M
Fees D–£20
Loc 5 miles SE of Darlington

Durham City (1887)
Littleburn, Langley Moor, Durham DH7 8HL
Tel **(0191) 378 0069**
Fax (0191) 378 4265
Mem 750
Sec LTI Wilson (0191) 386 0200
Pro S Corbally (0191) 378 0029
Holes 18 L 6326 yds SSS 70
Recs Am–66
V'tors WD–U SOC
Fees £22 (£30)
Loc 1½ miles W of Durham, off A690
Arch CC Stanton

Eaglescliffe (1914)
Yarm Road, Eaglescliffe, Stockton-on-Tees TS16 0DQ
Tel **(01642) 780098**
Mem 835
Sec AH Painter (01642) 780238
Pro P Bradley (01642) 790122
Holes 18 L 6275 yds SSS 70
Recs Am–63 CM Hoggart (1993)
Pro–65 N Gilkes (1993)
V'tors U SOC
Fees £24 (£30)
Loc 3 miles S of Stockton-on-Tees on A135

Hartlepool (1906)
Hart Warren, Hartlepool TS24 9QF
Tel **(01429) 274398**
Fax (01429) 274129
Mem 700
Sec LG Gordon (01429) 261723
Pro ME Cole (01429) 267473
Holes 18 L 6255 yds SSS 70
Recs Am–62 G Storm (1997)
Pro–65 J Harrison, D Curry
V'tors WD–U SOC
Fees £20 (£30)
Loc N boundary of Hartlepool

Hobson Municipal (1978)
Public
Hobson, Burnopfield, Newcastle-upon-Tyne NE16 6BZ
Tel **(01207) 271605**
Sec RJ Handrick
Pro J Ord
Holes 18 L 6403 yds SSS 71
V'tors U SOC
Fees £12 (£15)
Loc Between Gateshead and Consett on A692

Knotty Hill Golf Centre (1992)
Pay and play
Sedgefield, Stockton-on-Tees TS21 2BB
Tel **(01740) 620320**
Fax (01740) 622227
Sec D Craggs (Mgr)
Holes 18 L 6517 yds Par 72 SSS 71
9 hole course
V'tors U SOC
Fees £12 (£12)
Loc 1 mile N of Sedgefield on A177. A1(M) Junction 60, 2 miles
Mis Floodlit driving range
Arch Chris Stanton

Mount Oswald (1924)
South Road, Durham City DH1 3TQ
Tel **(0191) 386 7527**
Fax (0191) 386 0975
Mem 120
Sec SE Reeve
Holes 18 L 6009 yds SSS 69
Recs Am–64 J Mee (1986)
Pro–66 J Mathews (1984)
V'tors U SOC
Fees Mon–Thurs £11 D–£19
Fri/WE–£12.50 D–£22
Loc SW of Durham on A177

Norton (1989)
Pay and play
Junction Road, Norton, Stockton-on-Tees TS20 1SU
Tel **(01642) 676385**
Fax (01642) 608467
Holes 18 L 5870 yds SSS 71
V'tors U SOC
Fees £9 (£10)
Loc 1 mile E of A177 on B1274
Arch Tim Harper

Oakleaf Golf Complex (1993)
Pay and play
School Aycliffe Lane, Newton Aycliffe DL5 6QZ
Tel **(01325) 310820**
Fax (01325) 300873
Sec A Bailey (Mgr) (01325) 300700
Pro C Burgess
Holes 18 L 5334 yds SSS 66
V'tors WD–U WE–booking req
Fees £6 (£7)
Loc 1 mile W of Aycliffe on A6072, from A68
Mis Floodlit driving range

Ramside (1995)
Ramside Hall Hotel, Carrville, Durham DH1 1TD
Tel **(0191) 386 9514**
Fax (0191) 386 9519
Mem 300
Sec TI Flowers
Pro R Lister (0191) 386 9514
Holes 27 holes: 6217-6851 yds SSS 70-73
Recs Pro–66 MW Forster (1998)
V'tors U SOC
Fees £27 (£33)
Loc 2 miles NE of Durham on A690. A1(M) Junction 62
Mis Driving range. Golf Academy
Arch J Gaunt

Roseberry Grange (1986)
Public
Grange Villa, Chester-Le-Street DH2 3NF
Tel **(0191) 370 0670**
Mem 500
Sec R McDermott (Hon)
Pro A Hartley (0191) 370 0660
Holes 18 L 5892 yds SSS 68
Recs Am–66 D Brolls (1989), D Matthews (1994)
Pro–65 B Rumney (1988)
V'tors U SOC
Fees £10 (£12)
Loc 3 miles W of Chester-Le-Street on A693
Mis Driving range

Ryhope (1992)
Public
Leechmere Way, Hollycarrside, Ryhope, Sunderland SR2 0DH
Tel **(0191) 523 7333**
Fax (0191) 521 3811
Mem 300
Sec A Brown
Pro None
Holes 18 L 4601 yds SSS 65
Recs Am–67 JA Nelson, A Hall
V'tors U
Fees £6 (£6)
Loc 2 miles SW of Sunderland, off A1018
Arch Jonathan Gaunt

Seaham (1911)
Shrewsbury Street, Dawdon, Seaham SR7 7RD
Tel (0191) 581 2354
Mem 550
Sec V Smith (0191) 581 1268
Pro T Jenkins (0191) 513 0837
Holes 18 L 5972 yds SSS 69
Recs Am–63 C Walton (1993)
V'tors U SOC
Fees On application
Loc Dawdon, 2 miles NE of A19

Seaton Carew (1874)
Tees Road, Hartlepool TS25 1DE
Tel (01429) 266249/261040
Mem 650
Sec PR Wilson (01429) 261473
Pro W Hector
Holes Old 18 L 6613 yds SSS 72
Brabazon 18 L 6855 yds SSS 73
Recs Old Am–66 MJ Kelley, B Popple
Pro–66 N Bell
Brabazon Am–66 ID Garbutt
V'tors U SOC
Fees £27 (£38)
Loc Hartlepool 2 miles
Arch Dr A Mackenzie

South Moor (1923)
The Middles, Craghead, Stanley DH9 6AG
Tel (01207) 232848/283525
Fax (01207) 284616
Mem 650
Sec B Davison (0191) 388 4523
Pro S Cowell (01207) 283525
Holes 18 L 6445 yds Par 72 SSS 71
Recs Am–66 G Wearmouth (1991)
Pro–67 LP Tupling (1980)
Ladies–70 PA Dobson (1987)
V'tors WD–H WE/BH–M SOC–WD/Sat
Fees £14 (£25)
Loc 8 miles NW of Durham
Arch Dr A Mackenzie

Stressholme (1976)
Public
Snipe Lane, Darlington DL2 2SA
Tel (01325) 461002
Fax (01325) 351826
Sec R Taylor
Pro M Watkins, D Patterson
Holes 18 L 6511 yds SSS 71
Recs Am–69 S Aitken
Pro–64 N Coles
V'tors U
Fees On application
Loc 2 miles S of Darlington on A66
Mis Floodlit driving range

Woodham G&CC (1983)
Burnhill Way, Newton Aycliffe DH5 4PM
Tel (01325) 320574
Fax (01325) 315254
Mem 610
Sec JD Jenkinson
Pro E Wilson
Holes 18 L 6770 yds SSS 72
Recs Am–68 L McCavanagh
Pro–67 M Ure
V'tors WD–U WE/BH–booking SOC
Fees £15 D–£20 (£24)
Loc 1 mile N of Newton Aycliffe
Arch J Hamilton Stutt

The Wynyard
Wellington Drive, Wynyard Park, Billingham TS22 5QJ
Tel (01740) 644399
Fax (01740) 644592
Sec Lynne Lowther (Mgr)
Pro A Oliphant
Holes 18 holes Par 72 SSS 73
Recs Am–66 N Emmerson (1997)
Pro–63 O Edmond (1997)
V'tors M SOC–H
Fees On application
Loc 5 miles E of Sedgefield, between A1 and A19
Mis Floodlit driving range
Arch Hawtree

Essex

Abridge G&CC (1964)
Epping Lane, Stapleford Tawney RM4 1ST
Tel (01708) 688396
Fax (01708) 688550
Mem 650
Sec G Winckless (01708) 688396
Pro S Layton (01708) 688333
Holes 18 L 6703 yds SSS 72
Recs Am–67 R Curtis
Pro–68 D Feherty
V'tors WD–H WE/BH–NA
Fees £30
Loc Theydon Bois/Epping Stations 3 miles
Arch Henry Cotton

Ballards Gore G&CC (1980)
Gore Road, Canewdon, Rochford SS4 2DA
Tel (01702) 258917
Mem 600
Sec NG Patient
Pro A Curry (01702) 258924
Holes 18 L 7062 yds SSS 74
V'tors WD–U WE–M after 12.30pm (summer) 11.30am (winter) SOC
Fees £16 D–£22
Loc 1 1/2 miles NE of Rochford

Basildon (1967)
Public
Clayhill Lane, Sparrow's Hearne, Basildon SS16 5JP
Tel (01268) 533297
Fax (01268) 533849
Mem 400
Sec AM Burch
Pro W Paterson (01268) 533532
Holes 18 L 6236 yds Par 72 SSS 70
Recs Am–70 S Rooney (1997)
Pro–67 J Fryatt (1996)
V'tors U SOC
Fees £9 (£15)
Loc 1 mile S of Basildon, off A176 at Kingswood roundabout

Belfairs (1926)
Public
Eastwood Road North, Leigh-on-Sea SS9 4LR
Tel (01702) 525345 (Starter)
Pro M Foreman (01702) 520202
Holes 18 L 5802 yds SSS 68
V'tors WD–U exc Thurs am. Booking necessary
Fees £11 (£16)
Loc Between A127 and A13

Belhus Park (1972)
Pay and play
Belhus Park, South Ockendon RM15 4QR
Tel (01708) 854260
Mem 280
Sec DA Faust
Pro G Lunn
Holes 18 L 5188 yds SSS 68
Recs Am–67 D Cordery (1997)
Pro–63 R Joyce
V'tors U
Fees £9 (£13.50)
Loc 1 mile N of A13/M25 Dartford Tunnel
Mis Floodlit driving range

Bentley G&CC (1972)
Ongar Road, Brentwood CM15 9SS
Tel (01277) 373179
Fax (01277) 375097
Mem 550
Sec JA Vivers
Pro N Garrett (01277) 372933
Holes 18 L 6709 yds SSS 72
Recs Am–71 J Moody (1987)
Pro–69 S Cipa (1988), B Smith (1988)
V'tors WD–UH WE–M after noon BH–after 11am SOC–WD
Fees £21 D–£28
Loc 18 miles E of London. M25 Junction 28, 3 miles

Benton Hall (1993)
Wickham Hill, Witham CM8 3LH
Tel (01376) 502454
Fax (01376) 521050
Sec B Major (Mgr)
Holes 18 L 6570 yds SSS 72
9 hole Par 3 course
V'tors U SOC–WD
Fees £25–£30
Loc Witham, 8 miles NE of Chelmsford, off A12
Mis Driving range
Arch Walker/Cox

For list of abbreviations see page 527

Essex

Birch Grove (1970)
Layer Road, Colchester CO2 0HS
Tel (01206) 734276
Mem 250
Sec Mrs M Marston
Holes 9 L 4108 yds SSS 60
Recs Am–58 A Green (1993)
V'tors U exc Sun–U after 1pm SOC
Fees D–£10
Loc 3 miles S of Colchester on B1026

Boyce Hill (1921)
Vicarage Hill, Benfleet SS7 1PD
Tel (01268) 793625
Fax (01268) 750497
Mem 600
Sec PD Keeble
Pro G Burroughs (01268) 752565
Holes 18 L 5956 yds SSS 68
Recs Am–64 N Perrin
 Pro–61 G Burroughs
V'tors WD–UH WE/BH–MH SOC–Thurs only
Fees D–£25
Loc 4 miles W of Southend
Arch James Braid

Braintree (1891)
Kings Lane, Stisted, Braintree CM7 8DA
Tel (01376) 346079
Fax (01376) 331216
Mem 700
Sec MND Robinson
Pro T Parcell (01376) 343465
Holes 18 L 6161 yds SSS 69
Recs Am–65 M Hawes, M Davis
 Pro–65 P Golding
V'tors WD–U exc Fri–H Sat/BH–H Sun–NA SOC
Fees £25 (£40)
Loc 1 mile E of Braintree, off A120 towards Stisted
Arch Hawtree

Braxted Park (1953)
Braxted Park, Witham CM8 3EN
Tel (01376) 572372
Fax (01621) 892840
Mem 83
Sec M Woollett
Pro M Woollett
Holes 9 L 2940 yds Par 70 SSS 68
V'tors WD–U SOC–WD
Fees 18 holes–£12 9 holes–£9
Loc 1½ miles off A12, nr Kelvedon
Arch Sir Allen Clark

Bunsay Downs (1982)
Public
Little Baddow Road, Woodham Walter, Maldon CM9 6RW
Tel (01245) 412648/412369
Sec MFL Durham
Pro Mickey Walker (01245) 414662
Holes 9 L 2913 yds SSS 68
 9 hole Par 3 course
V'tors WD–U WE/BH–book in advance SOC–WD
Fees On application
Loc 7 miles E of Chelmsford, off A414
Mis Indoor driving range

Burnham-on-Crouch (1923)
Ferry Road, Creeksea, Burnham-on-Crouch CM0 8PQ
Tel (01621) 782282/785508
Fax (01621) 782282
Mem 600
Sec LR Posner
Pro K Smith, S Caroy (01621) 786280
Holes 18 L 6056 yds SSS 69
Recs Am–66 D Clarke (1966)
 Pro–64 FJ Winser
V'tors WD–H WE/BH–M
Fees £22
Loc 1½ miles W of Burnham
Arch D Swan

The Burstead (1995)
Tye Common Road, Little Burstead, Billericay CM12 9SS
Tel (01277) 631171
Fax (01277) 632766
Mem 900
Sec L Mence
Pro K Bridges
Holes 18 L 6150 yds SSS 69
V'tors WD–U H
Fees £18
Loc 2 miles S of Billericay, off A176
Arch Patrick Tallack

Canons Brook (1962)
Elizabeth Way, Harlow CM19 5BE
Tel (01279) 421482
Fax (01279) 626393
Mem 800
Sec Mrs SJ Langton
Pro A McGinn (01279) 418357
Holes 18 L 6763 yds SSS 73
Recs Am–68 H Cornick
 Pro–65 G Burroughs
V'tors WD–U WE/BH–M
Fees £20 D–£27
Loc 25 miles N of London
Arch Henry Cotton

Castle Point (1988)
Public
Waterside Farm, Somnes Avenue, Canvey Island SS8 9FG
Tel (01268) 510830
Mem 240
Sec Mrs D Archer (01268) 696298
Pro M Utteridge (01268) 510830
Holes 18 L 6153 yds SSS 69
Recs Am–67 C Ledger (1997)
V'tors U SOC
Fees £9 (£13)
Loc On A130 to Canvey Island, off A13 Eastbound
Mis Driving range
Arch Golf Landscapes

Channels (1974)
Belsteads Farm Lane, Little Waltham, Chelmsford CM3 3PT
Tel (01245) 440005
Fax (01245) 442032
Mem 650
Sec AM Squire
Pro IB Sinclair (01245) 441056
Holes 18 L 6402 yds Par 71 SSS 71
 18 L 4779 yds Par 67 SSS 63
Recs Am–67 P Wilson (1998)
V'tors WD–U WE–M SOC
Fees £25 D–£35
Loc 3 miles NE of Chelmsford on A130
Mis Pitch & putt course. Driving range

Chelmsford (1893)
Widford, Chelmsford CM2 9AP
Tel (01245) 250555
Fax (01245) 256483
Mem 650
Sec A Johnson (01245) 256483
Pro GD Bailey (01245) 257079
Holes 18 L 5981 yds SSS 69
Recs Am–66 B Hilsdon
 Pro–65 C Platts
V'tors WD–H WE/BH–M SOC
Fees £27 D–£36
Loc Off A1016 at Widford roundabout
Arch HS Colt

Chigwell (1925)
High Road, Chigwell IG7 5BH
Tel (0181) 500 2059
Fax (0181) 501 3410
Mem 700
Sec RH Danzey
Pro R Beard (0181) 500 2384
Holes 18 L 6279 yds SSS 70
Recs Am–66 AM Ronald, JM Bint (1991)
 Pro–66 H Flatman
V'tors WD–H WE/BH–M
Fees £35 D–£45
Loc 13 miles NE of London (A113)
Arch Hawtree/Taylor

Clacton (1892)
West Road, Clacton-on-Sea CO15 1AJ
Tel (01255) 424331
Fax (01255) 424602
Mem 650
Sec H Lucas (01255) 421919
Pro SJ Levermore (01255) 426304
Holes 18 L 6532 yds SSS 71
Recs Am–68 D Lee, A Wenn, D Robertson
 Pro–65 R Wheeler
V'tors H WE/BH–H after 11am SOC
Fees £20 (£30)
Loc On sea front

Colchester (1909)
Braiswick, Colchester CO4 5AU
Tel (01206) 853396
Fax (01206) 852698
Mem 633

For list of abbreviations see page 527

Sec   T Peck
Pro   M Angel (01206) 853920
Holes   18 L 6301 yds SSS 70
Recs   Am–63 B Booth
         Pro–64 V Cox
V'tors   WD–H WE/BH–NA SOC
Fees   £20 D–£25 (£30)
Loc   ¾ mile NW of Colchester
         North Station, towards West
         Berholt on B1508
Arch   James Braid

Colne Valley   (1991)
Station Road, Earls Colne CO6 2LT
Tel   (01787) 224233/224343
Fax   (01787) 224126
Mem   500
Sec   J Martin (Mgr)
         (01787) 224343
Pro   S Clark (01787) 224233
Holes   18 L 6301 yds SSS 70
Recs   Pro–68 M Deal (1995)
V'tors   WD–U WE/BH–after
         10.30am SOC–WD
Fees   £16 (£21)
Loc   12 miles W of Colchester
         (A604)
Arch   Howard Swann

Crondon Park   (1994)
Stock Road, Stock CM4 9DP
Tel   (01277) 841115
Fax   (01277) 841356
Mem   875
Sec   J Lancaster
Pro   M Herbert
Holes   18 L 6585 yds SSS 71
         9 hole course
V'tors   WD–U WE–M SOC–WD
Fees   £17 (£25)
Loc   5 miles S of Chelmsford on
         B1007. M25 Junction 28
Mis   Driving range
Arch   Martin Gillett

Elsenham Golf Centre
(1997)
Hall Road, Elsenham, Bishop's Stortford CM22 6DH
Tel   (01279) 812865
Fax   (01279) 816970
Sec   O McKenna (Prop)
Pro   O McKenna
Holes   9 L 5854 yds Par 70
V'tors   U
Fees   9 holes–£10 (£12)
         18 holes–£14 (£16)
Loc   Off M11, by Stansted Airport
Mis   Driving range

Epping Forest G&CC
(1994)
Woolston Manor, Abridge Road, Chigwell IG7 6BX
Tel   (0181) 500 2549
Fax   (0181) 501 5452
Mem   650
Sec   M Williamson (Golf Dir)
         (0181) 501 7614
Pro   C Stephenson (0181) 559 8272

Holes   18 L 6408 yds SSS 71
Recs   Am–67 D Williams (1996)
         Pro–66 I Ellis
V'tors   H SOC–WD
Fees   £28 (£38)
Loc   1 mile from M11 Junction 5
Mis   Floodlit driving range
Arch   Neil Coles

Essex G&CC   (1990)
Earls Colne, Colchester CO6 2NS
Tel   (01787) 224466
Fax   (01787) 224410
Mem   600
Sec   DJ Clark
Pro   M Spooner
Holes   18 L 6982 yds Par 73
         9 L 2771 yds Par 34
Recs   Am–69 (1995)
         Pro–68 P Joiner (1996)
V'tors   U SOC–WD
Fees   £20 (£25)
Loc   2 miles N of A120 at
         Coggeshall on B1024
Mis   Floodlit driving range.
Arch   Reg Plumbridge

The Essex Golf Complex
(1993)
Pay and play
Garon Park, Eastern Avenue, Southend-on-Sea SS9 4PT
Tel   (01702) 601701
Fax   (01702) 601033
Mem   700
Sec   Mrs J Jacom
Pro   G Jacom
Holes   18 L 6237 yds SSS 70
         9 hole Par 3 course
Recs   Am–67 A Gregory (1995), J
         Tann (1996)
V'tors   U SOC
Fees   £14.70 (£19.25)
Loc   E side of Southend-on-Sea.
         M25 Junction 29
Mis   Floodlit driving range
Arch   Walker/Cox

Fairlop Waters   (1987)
Public
Forest Road, Barkingside, Ilford IG6 3JA
Tel   (0181) 500 9911
Mem   135
Sec   L Quinn
Pro   B Preston (0181) 501 1881
Holes   18 L 6288 yds SSS 72
         9 hole Par 3 course
V'tors   U
Fees   £7.50 (£11)
Loc   2 miles from S end of M11, by
         Fairlop underground station
Mis   Driving range

Five Lakes Hotel G&CC
(1974)
Colchester Road, Tolleshunt Knights, Maldon CM9 8HX
Tel   (01621) 868888
Fax   (01621) 869196

Mem   600
Pro   G Carter
Holes   Links 18 L 6250 yds SSS 70
         Lakes 18 L 6765 yds SSS 72
Recs   Links Am–68 D Wilks (1991)
         Pro–68 K Ashdown (1988)
         Lakes Pro–63 E Dussart
         (1992)
V'tors   U BH–U after 1pm SOC
Fees   Links £18 (£25) Lakes £25
         (£33)
Loc   8 miles S of Colchester, off
         B1026
Mis   Driving range
Arch   Neil Coles

Forrester Park   (1975)
Beckingham Road, Great Totham, Maldon CM9 8EA
Tel   (01621) 891406
Fax   (01621) 891406
Mem   900
Sec   T Forrester-Muir
Pro   G Pike (01621) 893456
Holes   18 L 6073 yds SSS 69
Recs   Am–68 K Chamberlain
         (1997)
V'tors   WD–U WE–NA before noon
         SOC–WD
Fees   £18 (£20)
Loc   3 miles NE of Maldon on
         B1022
Arch   Everett/Forrester-Muir

Frinton   (1895)
1 The Esplanade, Frinton-on-Sea CO13 9EP
Tel   (01255) 674618
Fax   (01255) 674618
Mem   850
Sec   Lt Col RW Attrill
Pro   P Taggart (01255) 671618
Holes   18 L 6259 yds SSS 70
         9 L 2508 yds SSS 33
Recs   Am–67 IA Quick
         Pro–64 A Raitt
V'tors   18 hole:H WE/BH–NA before
         11.30am SOC
Fees   18 hole:D–£25; 9 hole:£10
Loc   18 miles E of Colchester
Arch   W Park Jr/HS Colt

Gosfield Lake   (1986)
The Manor House, Gosfield, Halstead CO9 1SE
Tel   (01787) 474747
Fax   (01787) 476044
Mem   630
Sec   JA O'Shea (Sec/Mgr)
Pro   R Wheeler (01787) 474488
Holes   Lakes 18 L 6756 yds SSS 72;
         Meadows 9 L 4180 yds Par 66
Recs   Lakes Am–68 S Bearman
         (1993)
V'tors   Lakes WD–H WE(pm)–H by
         arrangement SOC;
         Meadows–U
Fees   Lakes D–£25
         Meadows D–£10
Loc   7 miles N of Braintree
         (A1017)
Arch   Sir H Cotton/Swann

For list of abbreviations see page 527

Hainault Forest (1912)
Public
Romford Road, Chigwell Row
IG7 4QW
Tel (0181) 500 2131 (Caddy Master), (0181) 500 2097 (Clubhouse)
Mem 630
Sec Mrs V Crinks (0181) 500 0385
Pro CS Hope (0181) 500 2131
Holes No 1 18 L 5754 yds SSS 67
No 2 18 L 6600 yds SSS 71
Recs No 1 Am–65 TG Patmore
Pro–65 AE Frost
No 2 Am–68 S Middleton
Pro–68 AE Frost
V'tors U
Fees On application
Loc Hog Hill, Redbridge

Hanover G&CC (1991)
Hullbridge Road, Rayleigh SS6 9QS
Tel (01702) 232377
Fax (01702) 231811
Mem 700
Sec T Harrold
Pro A Blackburn
Holes Georgian 18 L 6669 yds SSS 72; Regency 18 L 3700 yds SSS 58
Recs Am –74 A Wheeler, T Brown (1996)
Pro–69 A Blackburn (1996)
V'tors Georgian:WD–H WE–M SOC Regency:U SOC
Fees Georgian £25 D–£35
Regency £11.75 (£14.10)
Loc 3 miles NW of Southend
Arch Reg Plumbridge

Hartswood (1967)
Public
King George's Playing Fields, Brentwood CM14 5AE
Tel (01277) 214830 (Bookings)
Fax (01277) 218850
Mem 400
Sec M Freeman (01227) 218850
Pro S Cole (01277) 218714
Holes 18 L 6192 yds SSS 70
Recs Am–70 A Cornell
Pro–64 M Sharman
V'tors WD–U after 1pm SOC
Fees On application
Loc E of Brentwood on A128

Harwich & Dovercourt (1906)
Station Road, Parkeston, Harwich CO12 4NZ
Tel (01255) 503616
Mem 400
Sec JA Eldridge
Holes 9 L 2950 yds SSS 69
V'tors WD–U SOC
Fees On application
Loc A120 to roundabout to Harwich Port, course entrance 20 yds on LHS

Ilford (1907)
Wanstead Park Road, Ilford IG1 3TR
Tel (0181) 554 2930
Fax (0181) 554 0822
Mem 500
Sec FLK Clapp
Pro S Dowsett (0181) 554 0094
Holes 18 L 5299 yds SSS 66
Recs Am–63 P Happe (1990)
Pro–64 B Huggett, A Campbell
V'tors WD–U WE–phone Pro SOC
Fees £16 (£20)
Loc S end of M11, off A406

Langdon Hills (1991)
Lower Dunton Road, Bulphan RM14 3TY
Tel (01268) 548444/544300
Fax (01268) 490084
Mem 700
Sec B Hardie
Pro T Moncur, P Wernham
Holes 27 holes:
Langdon 9 L 3132 yds Par 35
Bulphan 9 L 3372 yds Par 37
Horndon 9 L 3054 yds Par 36
Recs Am–67 S McAnally
V'tors U SOC
Fees £11 (£12)
Loc SW of Basildon between A127 and A13. M25 Junction 29, 8 miles
Mis Floodlit driving range
Arch MRM Sandow

Loughton (1981)
Public
Clays Lane, Debden Green, Loughton IG10 2RZ
Tel (0181) 502 2923
Mem 190
Sec A Day
Pro S Layton
Holes 9 L 4735 yds SSS 62
V'tors U–booking required SOC
Fees 18 holes–£8 (£10)
9 holes–£5 (£6)
Loc M25 Junction 26

Maldon (1891)
Beeleigh Langford, Maldon CM9 6LL
Tel (01621) 853212
Mem 400
Sec GR Bezant
Holes 9 L 6253 yds SSS 70
Recs Am–71 R Byford
Pro–67 S Levermore
V'tors WD–U H WE–M SOC
Fees £15 D–£20
Loc 3 miles NW of Maldon on B1019

Maylands (1936)
Harold Park, Romford RM3 0AZ
Tel (017083) 42055
Fax (017083) 73080
Mem 600
Sec (017083) 73080
Pro JS Hopkin (017083) 46606

Holes 18 L 6351 yds SSS 70
Recs Am–65 I Moore (1995)
Pro–67 H Flatman
V'tors WD–I WE/BH–M SOC
Fees £20 (£30)
Loc 2 miles E of Romford on A12. M25 Junction 28, 1 mile
Arch HS Colt

Nazeing (1992)
Middle Street, Nazeing EN9 2LW
Tel (01992) 893798/893915
Fax (01992) 893882
Mem 350
Sec J Speller (01992) 893915
Pro R Green (01992) 893798
Holes 18 L 6598 yds SSS 71
Recs Am–68 M Hales (1994)
Pro–65 P Barham (1995)
V'tors WD–H WE/BH–H after 11am SOC
Fees £20 (£28)
Loc 3 miles SW of Harlow. M11 Junction 7
Mis Open air driving range
Arch Martin Gillett

North Weald (1996)
Rayley Lane, North Weald, Epping CM16 6AR
Tel (01992) 522118
Fax (01992) 522881
Mem 500
Sec PH Newson
Pro M Janes (01992) 524725
Holes 18 L 6311 yds Par 71 SSS 70
V'tors H SOC–WD
Fees £20 (£27.50)
Loc 1½ miles E of M11 Junction 7 on A414
Mis Driving range
Arch David Williams

Orsett (1899)
Brentwood Road, Orsett RM16 3DS
Tel (01375) 891352
Fax (01375) 892471
Mem 800
Sec TN Collingwood
Pro P Joiner (01375) 891797
Holes 18 L 6614 yds SSS 72
Recs Am–68 S Fromant, M Jennings (1989)
Pro–68 K Lunt
V'tors WD–H SOC–WD exc Thurs
Fees £22.50–£32.50
Loc 4 miles NE of Grays on A128. M25 Junction 30/31
Arch James Braid

The Priors (1992)
Horseman's Side, Tysea Hill, Stapleford Abbotts RM4 1JU
Tel (01708) 381108, (01708) 373344 (Bookings)
Fax (01708) 386345
Sec D Eagle (Gen Mgr)
Pro J Stanion
Holes 18 L 5720 yds SSS 68
Recs Am–66 S Harris (1998)
V'tors U SOC

For list of abbreviations see page 527

Fees £11–£15
Loc 3 miles N of Romford. M25 Junction 28
Arch Howard Swann

Regiment Way Golf Centre (1995)
Pay and play
Back Lane, Little Waltham, Chelmsford CM3 3PR
Tel   (01245) 361100
Sec   R Pamphilon
Pro   D Marsh
Holes 9 L 4760 yds Par 65 SSS 64
V'tors U
Fees 9 holes–£8 18 holes–£12
Loc   3 miles NE of Chelmsford (A130)
Mis   Floodlit driving range

Risebridge (1972)
Pay and play
Risebridge Chase, Lower Bedfords Road, Romford RM1 4DG
Tel   (01708) 741429
Mem   275
Sec   J Alexander
Pro   P Jennings
Holes 18 L 6280 yds SSS 70
      9 hole Par 3 course
Recs Am–67 B Reeve (1979),
      D Girdlestone (1985)
V'tors U
Fees £8.45 (£10.50)
Loc   2 miles from M25 Junction 28, off A12
Arch F Hawtree

Rochford Hundred (1893)
Rochford Hall, Hall Road, Rochford SS4 1NW
Tel   (01702) 544302
Fax   (01702) 541343
Mem   340 150(L) 60(J)
Sec   AH Bondfield
Pro   GS Hill
Holes 18 L 6256 yds SSS 70
Recs Am–65 DK Wood
      Pro–65 C Tucker
V'tors WD–U H WE–M
Fees On application
Loc   4 miles N of Southend-on-Sea
Arch James Braid

Romford (1894)
Heath Drive, Gidea Park, Romford RM2 5QB
Tel   (01708) 740007 (Members)
Fax   (01708) 752157
Mem   680
Sec   Mrs H Robinson (01708) 740986
Pro   H Flatman (01708) 749393
Holes 18 L 6395 yds SSS 70
Recs Am–66 D Girdlestone
      Pro–D Jones
      Ladies–72 M Knights
V'tors WD–I WE–NA SOC
Fees £25 D–£35

Loc   1 mile E of Romford. 3 miles W of M25 Junction 29
Arch HS Colt

Royal Epping Forest (1888)
Public
Forest Approach, Station Road, Chingford, London E4 7AZ
Tel   (0181) 529 6407
Fax   (0181) 559 4664
Mem   300 50(L) 25(J)
Sec   Mrs P Runciman (0181) 529 2195
Pro   J Francis (0181) 529 5708
Holes 18 L 6220 yds SSS 70
Recs Am–68 A Johns
      Pro–65 R Gowers
V'tors U–booking necessary SOC
Fees £9.80 (£13.40)
Loc   Nr Chingford station
Mis   Red coats or trousers compulsory

Saffron Walden (1919)
Windmill Hill, Saffron Walden CB10 1BX
Tel   (01799) 522689
Fax   (01799) 522786
Mem   950
Sec   DH Smith (Mgr) (01799) 522786
Pro   P Davis (01799) 527728
Holes 18 L 6606 yds SSS 72
Recs Am–65 J Dickinson (1997)
      Pro–63 L Fickling (1991)
V'tors WD–U H WE/BH–M SOC
Fees £30
Loc   Saffron Walden, on B184

South Essex G&CC
Herongate, Brentwood CM13 3LW
Tel   (01277) 811289
Fax   (01277) 811304
Mem   650
Sec   S Cipa (Golf Dir)
Pro   S Cipa
Holes 18 L 6851 yds Par 72 SSS 73
      9 L 3102 yds Par 35
Recs Am–70 M Lloyd (1997)
      Pro–68 M Davis (1997)
V'tors U SOC–WD/WE pm
Fees £15 (£25)
Loc   4 miles E of M25 Junction 29 (A127/A128)
Mis   Driving range. Golf Academy
Arch Reg Plumbridge

St Cleres
St Cleres Hall, Stanford-le-Hope SS17 0LX
Tel   (01375) 673007
Mem   500
Sec   D Wood
Pro   D Wood (01375) 361565
Holes 18 holes Par 72 SSS 71
V'tors U H SOC
Fees £15 (£20)
Loc   5 miles E of M25 Junction 30/31 (A130)
Arch Adrian Stiff

Stapleford Abbotts (1989)
Horseman's Side, Tysea Hill, Stapleford Abbotts RM4 1JU
Tel   (01708) 381108
Fax   (01708) 386345
Mem   750
Sec   D Eagle (Gen Mgr)
Pro   J Stanion (01708) 381108
Holes 18 L 6501 yds SSS 71
      9 hole Par 3 course
Recs Am–66 B Galbraith, S Harris (1998)
      Pro–66 D Eagle (1994)
V'tors WD–U WE–H SOC
Fees £25–£45
Loc   3 miles N of Romford. M25 Junction 28
Arch Howard Swann

Stock Brook Manor (1992)
Queen's Park Avenue, Stock, Billericay CM12 0SP
Tel   (01277) 653616
Fax   (01277) 633063
Mem   750
Sec   K Roe (Dir)
Pro   K Merry
Holes 18 L 6728 yds SSS 72
      9 L 2977 yds SSS 69
Recs Am–69 D Wilson (1995)
      Pro–66 K Merry (1995)
V'tors H–booking necessary
Fees £25 (£30)
Loc   5 miles S of Chelmsford on B1007
Mis   Driving range. Par 3 course
Arch Martin Gillett

Theydon Bois (1897)
Theydon Bois, Epping CM16 4EH
Tel   (01992) 813054
Fax   (01992) 813054
Mem   600
Sec   RS Blower
Pro   RJ Hall (01992) 812460
Holes 18 L 5480 yds SSS 68
Recs Am–63 B Taylor (1997)
      Pro–64 R Joyce (1989)
V'tors Thurs am–restricted H SOC WE–M
Fees £23 After 2pm–£20
Loc   1 mile S of Epping. M25 Junction 26
Arch James Braid

Thorndon Park (1920)
Ingrave, Brentwood CM13 3RH
Tel   (01277) 810345
Fax   (01277) 810645
Mem   450 140(L) 60(J)
Sec   JE Leggitt
Pro   BV White (01277) 810736
Holes 18 L 6492 yds SSS 71
Recs Am–66 MES Davis
      Pro–65 BJ Hunt, B Waites
V'tors WD–I WE/BH–M
Fees £35 D–£50
Loc   2 miles SE of Brentwood on A128
Arch HS Colt

For list of abbreviations see page 527

Thorpe Hall (1907)
Thorpe Hall Avenue, Thorpe Bay SS1 3AT
Tel (01702) 582205
Fax (01702) 582205
Mem 1000
Sec RM O'Hara
Pro WJ McColl (01702) 588195
Holes 18 L 6286 yds SSS 71
Recs Am–64 S Feltham (1995)
Pro–66 C Laurence (1993)
V'tors WD–H
Fees On application
Loc E of Southend-on-Sea

Three Rivers (1973)
Stow Road, Purleigh, Chelmsford CM3 6RR
Tel (01621) 828631
Fax (01621) 828060
Mem 700
Sec P Davidson (Gen Mgr)
Pro To be appointed
Holes 18 L 6609 yds Par 73 SSS 71
18 L 4637 yds Par 65
V'tors WD–U WE/BH–U after 10.30am SOC
Fees £19 (£22)
Loc Cold Norton, 5 miles S of Maldon
Mis Driving range
Arch Hawtree

Toot Hill (1991)
School Road, Toot Hill, Ongar CM5 9PU
Tel (01277) 365747
Fax (01277) 364509
Mem 400
Sec Mrs Cameron
Pro M Bishop
Holes 18 L 6013 yds SSS 70
V'tors H SOC–WD
Fees £25
Loc 2 miles W of Ongar
Mis Practice range
Arch Martin Gillett

Top Meadow (1986)
Fen Lane, North Ockendon RM14 3PR
Tel (01708) 852239 (Clubhouse)
Sec D Stock
Pro P King (01708) 859545
Holes 18 L 6227 yds Par 72
V'tors WD–U WE–M SOC
Fees £12
Loc N Ockendon, off B186
Mis Driving range

Towerlands (1985)
Panfield Road, Braintree CM7 5BJ
Tel (01376) 326802
Fax (01376) 552487
Mem 325
Sec R Crane
Pro (01376) 347951
Holes 9 L 5559 yds Par 68
V'tors WD–U WE–U after 12.30pm SOC
Fees 18 holes–£10 (£12) 9 holes–£8
Loc 1 mile NW of Braintree (B1053)
Mis Practice range

Upminster (1928)
114 Hall Lane, Upminster RM14 1AU
Tel (01708) 222788
Fax (01708) 222788
Mem 1040
Sec J Collantine
Pro N Carr (01708) 220000
Holes 18 L 6076 yds SSS 69
Recs Am–66 A Emery, N Leonard
V'tors WD–U H exc Tues am Ladies Day WE/BH–NA SOC
Fees £25 D–£30
Loc Station 3/4 mile

Wanstead (1893)
Wanstead, London E11 2LW
Tel (0181) 989 0604
Fax (0181) 532 9138
Mem 650
Sec K Jones (0181) 989 3938
Pro D Hawkins (0181) 989 9876
Holes 18 L 6262 yds SSS 69
Recs Am–62 P Sullivan
Pro–64 N Coles, P Brown
V'tors WD–H WE/BH–M
Fees D–£28
Loc Off A12, nr Wanstead station
Arch James Braid

Warley Park (1975)
Magpie Lane, Little Warley, Brentwood CM13 3DX
Tel (01277) 224891
Fax (01277) 200679
Mem 800
Sec K Regan
Pro J Groat (01277) 200441
Holes 27 hole course
Recs Am–65 M Cox (1996)
V'tors WD–H
Fees £25
Loc 2 miles S of Brentwood. M25 Junction 29
Arch Reg Plumbridge

Warren (1932)
Woodham Walter, Maldon CM9 6RW
Tel (01245) 223258/223198
Fax (01245) 223989
Mem 800
Sec MFL Durham (01245) 223258
Pro Mickey Walker OBE (01245) 224662
Holes 18 L 6211 yds SSS 69
Recs Am–65 M Robarts (1990)
Pro–66 H Flatman
V'tors WD–H WE–M SOC
Fees £30 D–£35
Loc 7 miles E of Chelmsford, off A414
Mis Golf Academy (01245) 223198

Weald Park (1994)
Coxtie Green Road, South Weald, Brentwood CM14 5RJ
Tel (01277) 375101
Fax (01277) 374888
Mem 600
Sec June Mackison (Gen Mgr)
Pro (01277) 375484

Holes 18 L 6612 yds SSS 72
Recs Am–68 D Mackison (1995), R Gold, A Gibson (1996)
Pro–65 P Barham (1994)
V'tors U–booking necessary
Fees £18 (£21)
Loc 3 miles from M25 Junction 28 (A1023)
Arch Reg Plumbridge

West Essex (1900)
Bury Road, Sewardstonebury, Chingford, London E4 7QL
Tel (0181) 529 7558
Fax (0181) 524 7870
Mem 630
Sec D Wilson
Pro R Joyce (0181) 529 4367
Holes 18 L 6289 yds SSS 70
Recs Am–64 G Stowe (1996)
Pro–63 G Burroughs
V'tors WD–U H WE/BH–M H SOC–Mon/Wed/Fri
Fees £28 D–£35
Loc 2 miles N of Chingford BR station. M25 Junction 26
Mis Driving range
Arch James Braid

Woodford (1890)
2, Sunset Avenue, Woodford Green IG8 0ST
Tel (0181) 504 0553/4254
Fax (0181) 504 3330
Mem 430
Sec GJ Cousins (0181) 504 3330
Pro A Johns (0181) 504 4254
Holes 9 L 5867 yds SSS 68
Recs Am–69 M Everitt, R Piper, P Blaxill, MG Smith
Pro–66 C Platts, L Jones
V'tors WD–U exc Tues am–NA Sat–M Sun–NA before noon SOC
Fees £10–£15
Loc 11 miles NE of London
Mis Major item of red clothing to be worn on course
Arch Tom Dunn

Gloucestershire

Brickhampton Court
Cheltenham Road, Churchdown GL2 9QF
Tel (01452) 859444
Fax (01452) 859333
Sec R East (Gen Mgr)
Pro D Finch
Holes Spa 18 L 6449 yds Par 71 SSS 71
Glevum 9 L 1859 yds Par 31
V'tors U SOC
Fees £16 D–£25 (£22.50 D–£30)
Loc Between Cheltenham and Gloucester on B4063. M5 Junction 11, 3 miles
Mis Floodlit driving range
Arch Simon Gidman

For list of abbreviations see page 527

Gloucestershire

Bristol & Clifton (1891)
Beggar Bush Lane, Failand, Clifton, Bristol BS8 3TH
Tel (01275) 393474/393117
Fax (01275) 394611
Mem 800
Sec RC Bennett (01275) 393474
Pro P Mawson (01275) 393031
Holes 18 L 6316 yds SSS 70
Recs Am–65 G Wolstenholme Pro–64 P Oosterhuis
V'tors WD–UH WE/BH–MH
Fees On request
Loc 2 miles W of suspension bridge. 4 miles S of M5 Junction 19

Broadway (1895)
Willersey Hill, Broadway, Worcs WR12 7LG
Tel (01386) 858997
Fax (01386) 858643
Mem 500 160(L) 70(J)
Sec B Carnie (Sec/Mgr) (01386) 853683
Pro M Freeman (01386) 853275
Holes 18 L 6216 yds SSS 70
Recs Am–65 M Dove Pro–66 D Steele, R Adams
V'tors H exc Sat–M SOC
Fees £27 (£33)
Loc 1½ miles E of Broadway (A44)
Arch James Braid

Canons Court (1982)
Bradley Green, Wotton-under-Edge GL12 7PN
Tel (01453) 843128
Fax (01453) 844151
Mem 300
Sec AR Webb (Gen Mgr)
Pro None
Holes 9 L 5323 yds SSS 68
Recs Am–61 J Harvie (1998)
V'tors U
Fees £8 (£10)
Loc 3 miles E of M5 Junction 14, off B4058

Chipping Sodbury
Chipping Sodbury, Bristol BS17 6PU
Tel (01454) 312024 (Members), (01454) 315822 Catering
Fax (01454) 319042
Mem 750
Sec D Bird (01454) 319042
Pro M Watts (01454) 314087
Holes New 18 L 6912 yds SSS 73 Old 9 L 6194 yds SSS 69
Recs New Am–66 D Wood (1988) Pro–65 B Austin (1993)
V'tors WD–U WE–pm only Sat/Sun am–XL SOC
Fees New £20 (£25) Old £4 (£5)
Loc 12 miles NE of Bristol. M4 Junction 18, 5 miles. M5 Junction 14, 9 miles.
Arch Fred Hawtree

Cirencester (1893)
Cheltenham Road, Bagendon, Cirencester GL7 7BH
Tel (01285) 653939
Fax (01285) 650665
Mem 800
Sec IA Gray (01285) 652465
Pro P Garratt (01285) 656124
Holes 18 L 6055 yds Par 70 SSS 69
Recs Am–65 G Bennett
V'tors H SOC–WD
Fees £20 (£25)
Loc 1½ miles N of Cirencester on A435
Arch James Braid

Cleeve Hill (1976)
Pay and play
Cleeve Hill, Cheltenham GL52 3PW
Tel (01242) 672025
Sec S Gilman (Mgr)
Pro (01242) 672592
Holes 18 L 6444 yds SSS 71
V'tors U exc Sat 11–3pm/Sun am–NA SOC
Fees £8 (£10)
Loc 3 miles N of Cheltenham on A46 to Winchcombe
Mis Tee booking 7 days in advance

Cotswold Edge (1980)
Upper Rushmire, Wotton-under-Edge GL12 7PT
Tel (01453) 844167
Fax (01453) 845120
Mem 800
Sec NJ Newman
Pro DJ Gosling (01453) 844398
Holes 18 L 5816 yds SSS 69
Recs Am–68 J Lathom-Sharp (1989) Pro–65 J Taylor (1998) Ladies–70 M Mayes (1995)
V'tors WD–U WE–M SOC
Fees £15
Loc 2 miles NE of Wotton-under-Edge on B4058 Tetbury road. M5 Junction 14

Cotswold Hills (1902)
Ullenwood, Cheltenham GL53 9QT
Tel (01242) 573210
Fax (01242) 515264
Mem 450
Sec A O'Reilly (01242) 515264
Pro N Boland (01242) 515263
Holes 18 L 6716 yds SSS 72
Recs Am–67 G Wolstenholme (1992); Pro–67 J Loughnane, S Little (1992)
V'tors I (recognised club members) SOC
Fees £24 (£30)
Loc 3 miles S of Cheltenham
Arch MD Little

Filton (1909)
Golf Course Lane, Bristol BS34 7QS
Tel (0117) 969 2021
Fax (0117) 931 4359
Mem 800
Sec M Burns (0117) 969 4169
Pro JCN Lumb (0117) 969 4158
Holes 18 L 6312 yds SSS 70
Recs Am–66 J Kitchen Pro–68 RH Evans
V'tors WD–U WE/BH–M SOC–WD
Fees £20 £25
Loc 4 miles N of Bristol
Arch Hawtree

Forest Hills (1992)
Mile End Road, Coleford GL16 7BY
Tel (01594) 810620
Mem 400
Sec PC Burston (01594) 810620
Pro None
Holes 18 L 5724 yds SSS 68
Recs Am–P Gibson (1995)
V'tors U SOC
Fees £13 (£15)
Loc 1 mile W of Coleford (B4028)
Arch Adrian Stiff

Forest of Dean (1973)
Lords Hill, Coleford GL16 8BD
Tel (01594) 832583
Fax (01594) 832584
Mem 500
Sec Mrs J Sandalls
Pro J Hansel (01594) 833689
Holes 18 L 5682 yds SSS 67
V'tors U SOC
Fees £18.50
Loc ½ mile SE of Coleford on Parkend road. M50, 10 miles
Arch John Day

Gloucester Hotel (1976)
Matson Lane, Gloucester GL4 9EA
Tel (01452) 525653
Mem 750
Sec P Darnell
Pro P Darnell (01452) 411311
Holes 18 L 6127 yds SSS 69 9 L 1980 yds SSS 27
Recs Am–68 J Wallace Pro–65 P Darnell
V'tors U
Fees £19 (£25)
Loc 2 miles S of Gloucester, off Painswick road. M5 Junction 11
Mis Driving range

Henbury (1891)
Westbury-on-Trym, Bristol BS10 7QB
Tel (0117) 950 0660
Fax (0117) 959 1928
Mem 760
Sec RH White (0117) 950 0044
Pro N Riley (0117) 950 2121
Holes 18 L 6007 yds SSS 70
Recs Am–68 R Broad Pro–65 P Simpson
V'tors WD–H WE–M SOC–Tues & Fri
Fees £21
Loc 3 miles N of Bristol, off A4018. M5 Junction 17

For list of abbreviations see page 527

Kendleshire
Henfield Road, Coalpit Heath, Bristol BS17 2XG
Tel (0117) 956 7007
Fax (0117) 957 3433
Mem 750
Sec P Murphy
Pro P Barrington
  (0117) 956 7000
Holes 18 L 6500 yds Par 70 SSS 71
Recs Am–73
  Pro–66 S Little
V'tors H SOC
Fees £20 (£40)
Loc 1 mile NE of Bristol. M32 Junction 1
Mis Driving range. Golf Academy
Arch Adrian Stiff

Knowle (1905)
Fairway, West Town Lane, Brislington, Bristol BS4 5DF
Tel (0117) 977 6341
Fax (0117) 972 0615
Mem 700
Sec Mrs JD King
  (0117) 977 0660
Pro GM Brand
  (0117) 977 9193
Holes 18 L 6016 yds SSS 69
Recs Am–61 MR Jeffery (1994)
  Pro–64 S Brown
V'tors WD exc Thurs–H WE/BH–H SOC–Thurs
Fees £22 D–£27 (£27 D–£32)
Loc Brislington Hill, 3 miles S of Bristol, off A4
Arch JH Taylor

Lilley Brook (1922)
Cirencester Road, Charlton Kings, Cheltenham GL53 8EG
Tel (01242) 526785
Fax (01242) 256880
Mem 700
Sec K Skeen
Pro F Hadden (01242) 525201
Holes 18 L 6226 yds SSS 70
Recs Am–64 B Mitten (1987)
  Pro–61 S Little (1996)
V'tors WD–H or I (recognised club members) WE–M SOC–WD
Fees £25 D–£30 (£30 D–£35)
Loc 3 miles SE of Cheltenham on A435

Long Ashton (1893)
Clarken Coombe, Long Ashton, Bristol BS41 9DW
Tel (01275) 392229
Fax (01275) 394235
Mem 750
Sec (01275) 392316
Pro DP Scanlan (01275) 392265
Holes 18 L 6077 yds SSS 70
Recs Am–66 G Wolstenholme
  Pro–66 K Aitken, A Sherborne, A Oldcorn, D Sheppard
V'tors WD–U H WE/BH–I H SOC–Wed

Fees £28
Loc 3 miles S of Bristol on B3128
Arch JH Taylor

Lydney (1909)
Lakeside Avenue, Lydney GL15 5QA
Tel (01594) 842614
Mem 300
Sec DA Barnard (01594) 843940
Holes 9 L 5382 yds SSS 66
Recs Am–63 MA Barnard (1988)
  Pro–68 F Goulding
V'tors WD–U WE/BH–M SOC
Fees £10
Loc 20 miles SW of Gloucester, off A48

Mangotsfield (1975)
Carsons Road, Mangotsfield, Bristol BS17 3LW
Tel (0117) 956 5501
Mem 600
Sec C Main
Pro C Trewin
Holes 18 L 5337 yds SSS 66
Recs Am–63 N Pillinger (1990)
  Ladies–77 P Chapman (1988)
V'tors U
Fees On application
Loc 6 miles NE of Bristol

Minchinhampton (1889)
Minchinhampton, Stroud GL6 9BE
Tel (01453) 832642 (Old),
  (01453) 833840 (New)
Fax (01453) 835703
Mem 1860
Sec DT Calvert (01453) 833866
Pro C Steele (01453) 833860
Holes Old 18 L 6019 yds SSS 69;
  Avening 18 L 6279 yds SSS 70; Cherington 18 L 6320 yds SSS 70
Recs Old Am–67 PH Fisher, L Scott
  Pro–67 RA Brown
  Avening Am–67 R Broad
  Pro–66 K Spurgeon
  Cherington Am–66 S Rose
V'tors H SOC
Fees Old–£10 (£13) New–£26 (£30)
Loc Old–3 miles E of Stroud.
  New–5 miles E of Stroud
Arch Old:R Wilson. Avening:F Hawtree. Cherington:M Hawtree

Naunton Downs (1993)
Naunton, Cheltenham GL54 3AE
Tel (01451) 850090
Fax (01451) 850091
Mem 900
Sec ND Powell (Golf Dir)
Pro ND Powell (01451) 850092
Holes 18 L 6078 yds Par 71 SSS 69
Recs Am–73 D Devine
V'tors U–by arrangement
Fees £19.95
Loc 5 miles SW of Stow-on-the-Wold, off B4068
Arch Jacob Pott

Painswick (1891)
Painswick, Stroud GL6 6TL
Tel (01452) 812180
Mem 430
Sec AB Layton-Smith
Pro None
Holes 18 L 4780 yds SSS 65
Recs Am–61 B Hill
V'tors WD/Sat–U Sun–M SOC
Fees £15 Sat–£20
Loc ½ mile N of Painswick on A46
Arch David Brown

Rodway (1991)
Pay and play
Highnam GL2 8DN
Tel (01452) 384222
Fax (01989) 766450
Mem 350
Sec S Williams
Pro T Grubb
Holes 18 L 5860 yds SSS 68
Recs Am–72
V'tors U SOC
Fees 18 holes–£8 (£10)
  9 holes–£5 (£6)
Loc 2 miles W of Gloucester (B4215)
Arch J Gabb

Sherdons Golf Centre (1993)
Pay and play
Manor Farm, Tredington, Tewkesbury GL20 7BP
Tel (01684) 274782
Fax (01684) 275358
Mem 300
Sec R Chatham
Pro P Clark
Holes 9 L 2654 yds Par 34 SSS 66
V'tors U
Fees 18 holes–£9 (£12)
  9 holes–£5.50 (£7.50)
Loc 2 miles S of Tewkesbury, off A38
Mis Driving range

Shirehampton Park (1907)
Park Hill, Shirehampton, Bristol BS11 0UL
Tel (0117) 982 3059
Fax (0117) 982 2083
Mem 600
Sec GW Rees (0117) 982 2083
Pro B Ellis (0117) 982 2488
Holes 18 L 5430 yds SSS 67
Recs Am–63 PM Fisher (1995)
V'tors WD–H WE–M SOC
Fees £18 (£25)
Loc 2 miles E of M5 Junction 18, on B4054

Stakis Puckrup Hall Hotel (1992)
Puckrup, Tewkesbury GL20 6EL
Tel (01684) 296200/271591
Fax (01684) 850788
Mem 500
Sec Mrs C Sandyford-Sykes
Pro K Pickett

For list of abbreviations see page 527

Holes 18 L 6189 yds SSS 70
Recs Am–66 G Spring (1998)
Pro–66 G Ryall (1997)
V'tors WD–H SOC WE–residents
Fees £25 (£30)
Loc 2 miles N of Tewkesbury on A38. M50 Junction 1. M5 Junction 8
Arch Simon Gidman

Stinchcombe Hill (1889)
Stinchcombe Hill, Dursley GL11 6AQ
Tel (01453) 542015
Fax (01453) 549545
Mem 550
Sec GL Davies
Pro P Bushell (01453) 543878
Holes 18 L 5734 yds SSS 68
Recs Am–63 TP Smith (1992)
Pro–64 I Bolt (1984)
V'tors U–phone Pro SOC
Fees £20 (£25)
Loc 1 mile W of Dursley
Arch A Hoare

Tewkesbury Park Hotel (1976)
Lincoln Green Lane, Tewkesbury GL20 7DN
Tel (01684) 295405
Fax (01684) 292386
Mem 710
Sec RS Nichol (01684) 299452
Pro R Taylor (01684) 294892
Holes 18 L 6533 yds SSS 72
6 hole Par 3 course
Recs Am–67 A Soutar (1995)
Pro–68 D Ray (1996)
V'tors WD–U H SOC–WD
WE–residential SOC only
Fees £25 (£30)
Loc ½ mile S of Tewkesbury on A38. M5 Junction 9, 2 miles

Thornbury Golf Centre (1992)
Bristol Road, Thornbury
Tel (01454) 281144
Fax (01454) 281177
Mem 400
Sec I Gibson
Pro S Hubbard
Holes 18 L 6154 yds SSS 69 Par 71
18 L 2195 yds Par 54
Recs Am–70 A Gilbert (1996), D Booth (1998)
Pro–68 G Orr (1994)
V'tors U SOC–WD
Fees £14 (£16)
Loc 10 miles N of Bristol, off A38
Mis Driving range
Arch Hawtree

Tracy Park (1976)
Tracy Park, Bath Road, Wick, Bristol BS15 5RN
Tel (0117) 937 2251
Fax (0117) 937 4288
Mem 950
Sec G Packer (Course Dir)
Pro R Berry (0117) 937 3521

Holes 27 holes:
Avon L 6423 yds SSS 71
Bristol L 6430 yds SSS 71
Cotswold L 6189 yds SSS 69
Recs Am–65 S Pugh
Pro–64 P Pring
V'tors U–phone first SOC
Fees £28 (£35)
Loc 3 miles NW of Bath, off A420. M4 Junction 18
Mis Driving range. Extension to 36 holes Spring 1999

Westonbirt (1971)
Westonbirt, Tetbury GL8 8QG
Tel (01666) 880242
Mem 200
Sec Bursar, Westonbirt School
Holes 9 L 4504 yds SSS 61
Recs Am–62 S Dunlop
V'tors U SOC–WD
Fees On application
Loc 3 miles S of Tetbury, off A433

Woodlands G&CC (1989)
Pay and play
Woodlands Lane, Almondsbury, Bristol BS12 4JZ
Tel (01454) 619319
Fax (01454) 619397
Sec J Seymour
Holes 18 L 6100 yds SSS 70
V'tors U SOC
Fees £12 (£15)
Loc Nr M5 Junction 16
Arch Cliff Chapman

Woodspring G&CC (1994)
Yanley Lane, Long Ashton, Bristol BS41 9LR
Tel (01275) 394378
Fax (01275) 394473
Sec M Pierce (Gen Mgr)
Pro N Beer
Holes 27 holes: 6209-6587 yds Par 71-71 SSS 70-71
V'tors W–H SOC
Fees £25 (£28.50)
Loc 2 miles S of Bristol on A38.
Mis Floodlit driving range
Arch Allis/Clark

Hampshire

Alresford (1890)
Cheriton Road, Alresford SO24 0PN
Tel (01962) 733746
Fax (01962) 736040
Mem 720
Sec Mrs J Ellerker
Pro M Scott (01962) 733998
Holes 18 L 5905 yds Par 69 SSS 68
Recs Am–67 G Richardson (1994)
Pro–64 J Barnes (1996)
V'tors U H WE–after noon SOC
Fees £23 D–£35 (£40)
Loc 1 mile S of Alresford on B3046
Arch Scott Webb Young

Alton (1908)
Old Odiham Road, Alton GU34 4BU
Tel (01420) 82042
Mem 370
Sec P Brown
Pro P Brown (01420) 86518
Holes 9 L 5744 yds SSS 68
Recs Am–64 R Lamport (1993)
Pro–62 R Edwards (1993)
V'tors WD–U WE–H or M SOC–WD
Fees 18 holes–£12 D–£16
9 holes–£7.50
Loc 2 miles N of Alton. 6 miles S of Odiham, off B3349
Arch James Braid

Ampfield Par Three (1963)
Winchester Road, Ampfield, Romsey SO51 9BQ
Tel (01794) 368480
Mem 500
Sec Mrs S Baker
Pro R Benfield (01794) 368750
Holes 18 L 2478 yds SSS 53
Recs Am–49 R Bailey
Pro–49 A Timms
V'tors WD–U WE/BH–H (phone first) SOC
Fees £9 (£15.50)
Loc 5 miles E of Romsey on A31
Arch Henry Cotton

Andover (1907)
51 Winchester Road, Andover SP10 2EF
Tel (01264) 323980
Mem 460 70(L) 30(J)
Sec Mrs L Brearley (01264) 358040
Pro D Lawrence (01264) 324151
Holes 9 L 6096 yds SSS 69
Recs Am–65 V Rusher (1993)
Pro–64 I Young (1991)
V'tors U H SOC–Mon–Wed
Fees £10 (£22)
Loc ½ mile S of Andover on A3057
Arch JH Taylor

Army (1883)
Laffans Road, Aldershot GU11 2HF
Tel (01252) 336776
Fax (01252) 337562
Mem 700
Sec Maj (Retd) JWG Douglass (01252) 337272
Pro G Cowley (01252) 336722
Holes 18 L 6579 yds SSS 71
Recs Am–67 M Rollason
Pro–67 I Benson
V'tors WD–H–contact Sec/Mgr SOC
Fees Special rates for Forces
Loc Between Aldershot and Farnborough

Barton-on-Sea (1897)
Milford Road, New Milton BH25 5PP
Tel (01425) 615308
Fax (01425) 621457
Mem 950

For list of abbreviations see page 527

Sec	N Hallam-Jones	
Pro	P Coombs (01425) 611210	
Holes	27 holes: L 6289–6505 yds Par 72	
Recs	Am–65 K Smith (1997) Pro–65 J Le Roux (1997)	
V'tors	H NA before 9am SOC–WD exc Tues	
Fees	D–£27.50 (D–£32.50)	
Loc	1 mile from New Milton, off B3058. M27 Junction 1	
Arch	J Hamilton Stutt	

Basingstoke (1928)

Kempshott Park, Basingstoke RG23 7LL

Tel	(01256) 465990
Fax	(01256) 331793
Mem	700
Sec	WA Jefford
Pro	G Shoesmith (01256) 351332
Holes	18 L 6350 yds SSS 70
Recs	Am–66 C Humphrey (1996) Pro–63 G Hughes (1996)
V'tors	WD–H WE–M SOC–Wed & Thurs
Fees	£25 D–£35
Loc	3 miles W of Basingstoke on A30. M3 Junction 7
Arch	James Braid

Bishopswood (1978)

Bishopswood Lane, Tadley, Basingstoke RG26 4AT

Tel	(0118) 981 2200/5213
Fax	(0118) 940 8606
Mem	400
Sec	MW Phillips (Mgr) (0118) 940 8600
Pro	S Ward
Holes	9 L 6474 yds SSS 71
Recs	Am–69 C Wilkins (1987) Pro–66 P Bryden (1992)
V'tors	WD–U WE–M SOC
Fees	£15
Loc	6 miles N of Basingstoke, off A340
Mis	Floodlit driving range
Arch	Blake/Phillips

Blackmoor (1913)

Whitehill, Bordon GU35 9EH

Tel	(01420) 472775/475461
Fax	(01420) 487666
Mem	680 100(L) 70(J)
Sec	Mrs C Tupper
Pro	S Clay (01420) 472345
Holes	18 L 6213 yds SSS 70
Recs	Am–65 J Shaw, P Tupper (1998) Pro–64 R Dickman (1990)
V'tors	H WE–NA
Fees	£33 D–£45
Loc	½ mile W of Whitehill on A325
Arch	HS Colt

Blacknest (1993)

Frith End, Binsted GU34 4QL

Tel	(01420) 22888
Fax	(01420) 22001
Mem	600
Sec	GD Lawson

Pro	I Benson
Holes	18 L 5858 yds SSS 69 9 hole Par 3 course
V'tors	U SOC
Fees	£14 (£16) (1997)
Loc	7 miles SW of Farnham, off A325
Mis	Driving range

Botley Park Hotel G&CC (1989)

Winchester Road, Boorley Green, Botley SO3 2UA

Tel	(01489) 780888 Ext 451
Fax	(01489) 789242
Mem	700
Sec	Miss M Johnstone
Pro	T Barter (01489) 789771
Holes	18 L 6341 yds SSS 70
Recs	Am–67 D Lawrence (1996) Pro–G Stubbington (1995)
V'tors	H SOC
Fees	£30
Loc	6 miles E of Southampton on B3354. M27 Junction 7. 8 miles SE of M3 Junction 11
Mis	Driving range
Arch	Potterton/Murray

Bramshaw (1880)

Brook, Lyndhurst SO43 7HE

Tel	(01703) 813433
Fax	(01703) 813958
Mem	1400
Sec	RD Tingey
Pro	C Bonner (01703) 813434
Holes	Forest 18 L 5774 yds SSS 68 Manor 18 L 6517 yds SSS 71
Recs	Forest Am–66 S Edwards Pro–65 R Tuddenham Manor Am–66 M LeMesurier Pro–65 G Stubbington
V'tors	WD–U H WE–M
Fees	Forest–£21 Manor–£27
Loc	10 miles SW of Southampton. M27 Junction 1, 1 mile

Brokenhurst Manor (1919)

Sway Road, Brockenhurst SO42 7SG

Tel	(01590) 623332
Fax	(01590) 624140
Mem	800
Sec	PE Clifford
Pro	J Lovell (01590) 623092
Holes	18 L 6222 yds SSS 70
Recs	Am–63 R Bland, J Rose Pro–64 N Tokely
V'tors	WD–H after 9.30am NA–Tues–Ladies' Day SOC
Fees	£30 D–£40 (£55)
Loc	1 mile SW of Brockenhurst on B3055
Arch	HS Colt

Burley (1905)

Burley, Ringwood BH24 4BB

Tel	(01425) 402431
Fax	(01425) 402431
Mem	520
Sec	GJ Stride
Holes	9 L 6149 yds Par 71 SSS 69

Recs	Am–68 AS Elliott (1991), M Geisler, P Brine (1997)
V'tors	U H
Fees	£15 (£18) W–£75
Loc	4 miles SE of Ringwood

Cams Hall Estate (1993)

Portchester Road, Fareham PO16 8UP

Tel	(01329) 827222
Fax	(01329) 827111
Mem	950
Sec	R Griffiths (Sec/Mgr)
Pro	J Neve (01329) 837732
Holes	27 L 6244-6477 yds SSS 70–71
Recs	Am–69 J Oxford (1994)
V'tors	U SOC
Fees	£19 (£25)
Loc	8 miles W of Portsmouth. M27 Junction 11
Arch	Alliss/Clarke

Chilworth (1989)

Main Road, Chilworth, Southampton SO16 7JP

Tel	(01703) 740544
Fax	(01703) 733166
Sec	Mrs E Garner
Pro	J Barnes
Holes	18 L 5740 yds SSS 69 Pro–65 J Barnes (1997)
V'tors	U
Fees	£12 (£15)
Loc	Between Romsey and Southampton on A27
Mis	Floodlit driving range

Corhampton (1891)

Corhampton, Southampton SO32 3LP

Tel	(01489) 877279
Fax	(01489) 877680
Mem	750
Sec	RE Jones
Pro	I Roper (01489) 877638
Holes	18 L 6444 yds SSS 71
Recs	Am–66 R Edwards (1988), A Clotworthy (1992) Pro–64 MD Jarvis (1991), G Stubbington (1992)
V'tors	WD–U H WE/BH–M SOC–Mons & Thurs
Fees	£21 D–£31
Loc	9 miles S of Winchester

Dibden Golf Centre (1974)

Public
Main Road, Dibden, Southampton SO45 5TB

Tel	(01703) 845596
Fax	(01703) 845596
Mem	700
Sec	Mrs J Lock (Hon)
Pro	A Bridge (01703) 845596
Holes	18 L 5986 yds SSS 69 9 hole course
Recs	Am–63 R Bland (1992) Pro–63 I Young (1988)
V'tors	U
Fees	£10 D–£18 (£12)

For list of abbreviations see page 527

Hampshire 569

Loc	10 miles W of Southampton, off A326 at Dibden roundabout
Mis	Floodlit driving range

Dummer (1993)
Dummer, Basingstoke RG25 2AR
Tel	(01256) 397888
Fax	(01256) 397889
Mem	750
Sec	K Dandridge
Pro	G Stubbington
Holes	18 L 6513 yds SSS 71
Recs	Am–68 R Aldred
	Pro–64 K Saunders, R Adams
V'tors	WD–U
Fees	£25
Loc	7 miles SW of Basingstoke. M3 Junction 7
Arch	Alliss/Clark

Dunwood Manor (1969)
Danes Road, Awbridge, Romsey SO51 0GF
Tel	(01794) 340549
Fax	(01794) 341215
Mem	700
Sec	JR Basford
Pro	H Teschner (01794) 340663
Holes	18 L 5755 yds SSS 69
Recs	Am–69 D Harris
	Pro–61 G Stubbington
V'tors	WE/BH–restricted SOC–WD
Fees	£22 (£30)
Loc	Romsey 4 miles, off A27

Fleetlands (1961)
Fareham Road, Gosport PO13 0AW
Tel	(01705) 544492
Mem	120
Sec	A Eade (01705) 544384
Holes	9 L 4852 yds SSS 64
Recs	Am–67 M Squibb, D Edmunds
	Pro–68 K Jackson
V'tors	M at all times
Loc	2 miles S of Fareham on A32 Gosport road. M27 Junction 12

Fleming Park (1973)
Public
Fleming Park, Magpie Lane, Eastleigh SO50 9LH
Tel	(01703) 612797
Sec	A Wheavil
Pro	C Strickett
Holes	18 L 4436 yds SSS 62
Recs	Am–62 D Cox (1989)
	Pro–61 J Hay
V'tors	U SOC–WD
Fees	On application
Loc	6 miles N of Southampton

Furzeley (1993)
Pay and play
Furzeley Road, Denmead PO7 6TX
Tel	(01705) 231180
Fax	(01705) 231180
Sec	Jackie Cushion
Pro	D Brown

Holes	18 L 4363 yds Par 62 SSS 61
V'tors	U SOC
Fees	£11.50
Loc	2 miles NW of Waterlooville

Gosport & Stokes Bay (1885)
Fort Road, Haslar, Gosport PO12 2AT
Tel	(01705) 581625
Fax	(01705) 527941
Mem	450
Sec	SP Hillary (01705) 527941
Holes	9 L 5957 yds SSS 69
Recs	Am–69 M Stubley (1986)
	Pro–65 P Dawson (1985)
V'tors	U exc Sun–NA SOC–Mon/Wed/Fri
Fees	£15 (£20)
Loc	S boundary of Gosport

Great Salterns (1914)
Public
Portsmouth Golf Centre, Burrfields Road, Portsmouth PO3 5HH
Tel	(01705) 664549
Fax	(01705) 650525
Pro	T Healy
Holes	18 L 5970 yds SSS 68
V'tors	U SOC
Fees	£11
Loc	1 mile off M27 on A2030
Mis	Driving range

The Hampshire
Winchester Road, Goodworth Clatford, Andover SP11 7TB
Tel	(01264) 357555
Fax	(01264) 356606
Mem	735
Sec	T Fiducia
Pro	P Smith, J Slade
Holes	18 L 6376 yds Par 9 hole Par 3 course
Recs	Am–69 A Lewis
	Pro–65 G Stubbington
V'tors	U SOC
Fees	£15 (£25)
Loc	1 mile SW of Andover (A3057)
Mis	Covered driving range
Arch	T Fiducia

Hartley Wintney (1891)
London Road, Hartley Wintney, Basingstoke RG27 8PT
Tel	(01252) 842214
Fax	(01252) 842214
Mem	410
Sec	BD Powell (01252) 844211
Pro	M Smith (01252) 843779
Holes	9 L 6096 yds SSS 69
Recs	Am–70 M Wild
	Pro–63 R Lewington
V'tors	Wed–Ladies Day WE/BH–restricted SOC–Tues & Thurs
Fees	£17 (£20)
Loc	A30 between Camberley and Basingstoke
Mis	Extension to 18 holes–Spring 2000

Hayling (1883)
Links Lane, Hayling Island PO11 0BX
Tel	(01705) 463712/463777
Fax	(01705) 464446
Mem	800
Sec	CJ Cavill (01705) 464446
Pro	R Gadd (01705) 464491
Holes	18 L 6521 yds SSS 71
Recs	Am–65 EJ Tambling (1993)
	Pro–66 F Gilbride (1971)
V'tors	H WE/BH–after 10am SOC–Tues & Wed
Fees	£28 (£38)
Loc	5 miles S of Havant on A3023
Arch	Taylor(1905)/Simpson(1933)

Hockley (1915)
Twyford, Winchester SO21 1PL
Tel	(01962) 713165
Fax	(01962) 713612
Mem	750
Sec	Mrs L Dyer
Pro	T Lane (01962) 713678
Holes	18 L 6336 yds SSS 70
Recs	Am–66
	Pro–64
V'tors	U H SOC
Fees	On application
Loc	2 miles S of Winchester on B3335
Arch	James Braid

Leckford (1929)
Leckford, Stockbridge SO20 6JS
Tel	(01264) 810320
Fax	(01264) 810439
Mem	400
Sec	J Wood
Pro	T Ashton (01264) 338175
Holes	Old 9 L 3251 yds SSS 71
	New 9 L 2281 yds SSS 62
V'tors	M
Fees	£10 (£14)
Loc	5 miles W of Andover

Lee-on-the-Solent (1905)
Brune Lane, Lee-on-the-Solent PO13 9PB
Tel	(01705) 550207
Fax	(01705) 554233
Mem	715
Sec	P Clash (Mgr) (01705) 551170
Pro	J Richardson (01705) 551181
Holes	18 L 5959 yds SSS 69
Recs	Am–66 S Richardson
	Pro–63 R Edwards (1993)
V'tors	WD–U H WE–M H SOC–Thurs
Fees	D–£30 (£35)
Loc	3 miles S of Fareham. M27 Junction 11

Liphook (1922)
Liphook GU30 7EH
Tel	(01428) 723271/723785
Fax	(01428) 724853
Email	Liphookgolfclub@BTInternet.com
Mem	700

For list of abbreviations see page 527

Hampshire

Sec	Maj JB Morgan MBE (01428) 723785
Pro	I Large
Holes	18 L 6167 yds SSS 70
Recs	Am–66 M Blackey, R Eggo Pro–66 TR Pinner
V'tors	I H (max 24) Sun–NA before 1pm SOC
Fees	£30 D–£40 (£40 D–£50)
Loc	1 mile S of Liphook on B2070 (old A3)
Arch	ACG Groome

Marriott Meon Valley Hotel (1977)

Sandy Lane, Shedfield, Southampton SO32 2HQ

Tel	(01329) 833455
Fax	(01329) 834411
Mem	850
Sec	S Coney (Gen Mgr) GF McMenemy (Golf Dir)
Pro	J Stirling
Holes	18 L 6519 yds SSS 71 9 L 2885 yds SSS 68
Recs	Am–66 R Tate (1996) Pro–67 J Garner (1987)
V'tors	H SOC
Fees	18 hole:£30 (£40) 9 hole:£15
Loc	2 miles NW of Wickham. N off A334
Arch	J Hamilton Stutt

New Forest (1888)

Southampton Road, Lyndhurst SO43 7BU

Tel	(01703) 282752
Mem	750
Sec	Mrs B Shaw, R Macdonald (Prop) (01703) 282484
Pro	D Harris
Holes	18 L 5742 yds SSS 68
Recs	Am–64 A Hindmarch (1993) Pro–64 D Harris (1998)
V'tors	U exc Sun am SOC–WD
Fees	£12
Loc	8 miles W of Southampton on A35

North Hants (1904)

Minley Road, Fleet GU13 8RE

Tel	(01252) 616443
Fax	(01252) 811627
Mem	550
Sec	IR Goodliffe
Pro	S Porter (01252) 616655
Holes	18 L 6257 yds Par 69 SSS 70
Recs	Am–65 JP Rose (1995), B Mason (1997) Pro–65 LR Booth, GM Hughes (1994) Ladies–65 A MacDonald, C Caldwell (1990)
V'tors	WD–H by prior arrangement WE/BH–MH SOC–Tues & Wed
Fees	On application
Loc	3 miles W of Farnborough on B3013. M3 Junction 4A
Arch	James Braid

Old Thorns (1982)

Pay and play
Longmoor Road, Griggs Green, Liphook GU30 7PE

Tel	(01428) 724555
Fax	(01428) 725036
Sec	GM Jones (Gen Mgr)
Pro	P Loxley
Holes	18 L 6533 yds SSS 71
Recs	Pro–69 I Aoki (1982)
V'tors	U SOC
Fees	£35 (£45)
Loc	Griggs Green exit off A3
Mis	Driving range
Arch	Cdr John Harris

Otterbourne Golf Centre (1995)

Poles Lane, Otterbourne, Winchester SO21 1DZ

Tel	(01962) 775225
Fax	(01962) 775398
Sec	Mrs E Garner
Holes	9 L 1939 yds Par
V'tors	U
Fees	£4 (£5)
Loc	On A31 between Otterbourne and Hursley
Mis	Driving range

Park (1995)

Pay and play
Avington, Winchester SO21 1DA

Tel	(01962) 779945 (Clubhouse)
Fax	(01962) 779955
Mem	300
Sec	R Stent (Prop) (01962) 779955
Pro	None
Holes	9 L 1949 yds Par 61 SSS 59
V'tors	U SOC
Fees	9 holes–£6.50 (£9.75) 18 holes–£9.50 (£14.25)
Loc	4 miles E of Winchester. M3 Junction 9

Paultons Golf Centre

Pay and play
Old Salisbury Road, Ower, Romsey SO51 6AN

Tel	(01703) 813992
Fax	(01703) 813993
Sec	R Park (Golf Dir)
Pro	(01703) 814626
Holes	18 L 6238 yds SSS 71 9 hole Academy course
Recs	Am–65 M Williamson
V'tors	U SOC
Fees	18 holes–£15 (£20) 9 holes–£5
Loc	Nr M27 Junction 2, at Ower
Mis	Driving range

Petersfield (1892)

Tankerdale Lane, Liss GU33 7QY

Tel	(01730) 895165
Fax	(01730) 894713
Mem	730
Sec	RR Hine
Pro	G Hughes (01730) 895216

Holes	18 L 6400 yds Par 72 SSS 71
Recs	Am–70 M Bailey Pro–66 K Saunders
V'tors	WD–U WE/BH–NA before noon SOC–Mon/Wed/Fri
Fees	£25 (£30)
Loc	Off A3, between Liss and Midhurst
Arch	Hawtree

Petersfield Sussex Road

Pay and play
Sussex Road, Petersfield

Tel	(01730) 267732
Sec	RR Hine
Pro	G Hughes
Holes	9 L 3005 yds
V'tors	U
Fees	9 holes–£6 (£7) 18 holes–£10 (£12)
Loc	Petersfield

Portsmouth (1926)

Public
Crookhorn Lane, Widley, Waterlooville PO7 5QL

Tel	(01705) 372210
Fax	(01705) 200766
Mem	650
Sec	D Houlihan (01705) 201827
Pro	J Banting (01705) 372210
Holes	18 L 6139 yds SSS 70
V'tors	U SOC–arrange with Pro
Fees	£8.80–£11.50
Loc	1 mile N of Portsmouth, on B2177

Romsey (1900)

Nursling, Southampton SO16 0XW

Tel	(01703) 732218
Fax	(01703) 741036
Mem	825
Sec	P Hargraves (01703) 734637
Pro	M Desmond (01703) 736673
Holes	18 L 5752 yds SSS 68
Recs	Am–65 J Archer (1990) Pro–64 J Slade (1985)
V'tors	WD–H WE/BH–M H
Fees	£22 D–£28
Loc	2 miles SE of Romsey on A3057. M27/M271 Junction 3

Rowlands Castle (1902)

Links Lane, Rowlands Castle PO9 6AE

Tel	(01705) 412216
Mem	800 150(L) 50(J)
Sec	KD Fisher (01705) 412784
Pro	P Klepacz (01705) 412785
Holes	18 L 6618 yds Par 72 SSS 72
Recs	Am–69 S Martin (1995) Pro–66 M Gregson (1974) Ladies–73 A Wheble (1994)
V'tors	WD–U H exc Wed am–restricted WE–phone first Sat–M SOC–Tues & Thurs
Fees	£25 (£30)
Loc	9 miles S of Petersfield, off A3(M). 3 miles N of Havant
Arch	HS Colt

For list of abbreviations see page 527

Royal Winchester (1888)
Sarum Road, Winchester SO22 5QE
Tel (01962) 852462
Fax (01962) 865048
Mem 750
Sec D Thomson (Mgr)
Pro S Hunter (01962) 862473
Holes 18 L 6204 yds SSS 70
Recs Am–65 P Arnold
Pro–67 B Lane, D Feherty,
K Bowden, I Roper
V'tors WD–U H WE/BH–M
SOC–Mon/Tues/Wed
Fees On application
Loc W of Winchester. M3
Junction 11

Sandford Springs (1988)
Wolverton, Tadley RG26 5RT
Tel (01635) 297881
Fax (01635) 298065
Mem 700
Sec G Tipple, K Brake (Man Dir)
Pro G Edmunds (01635) 297883
Holes 27 L 6100 yds SSS 70
Recs Am–65 J Knight
Pro–66 A Dillon
V'tors WD–prior booking WE–M
SOC–WD
Fees £23 D–£29
Loc 8 miles NW of Basingstoke
on A339
Arch Hawtree

Somerley Park (1995)
Somerley, Ringwood BH24 3PL
Tel (01425) 461496
Mem 169
Sec J Staley, R Curtis (Props)
Pro J Waring (01202) 821703
Holes 9 L 2155 yds Par 33 SSS 62
V'tors M SOC
Fees £10
Loc 5 miles W of Ringwood
Mis Driving range
Arch John Jacobs OBE

South Winchester
Romsey Road, Winchester SO22 5QW
Tel (01962) 877800
Fax (01962) 877900
Mem 875
Sec S Wright (Gen Mgr)
Pro R Adams (01962) 840469
Holes 18 L 7086 yds SSS 74
Recs Am–66 A New
Pro–68 R Adams, R Bland
Ladies–70 C Quinn
V'tors M SOC
Loc S side of Winchester
Arch Thomas/Alliss

Southampton Municipal (1935)
Public
Golf Course Road, Bassett, Southampton SO16 7AY
Tel (01703) 768407
Pro J Cave

Holes 18 L 6218 yds SSS 70
9 L 2391 yds SSS 33
Recs Am–64 P Dedman
Pro–62 SW Murray
V'tors U
Fees On application
Loc 2 miles N of Southampton

Southwick Park (1977)
Pinsley Drive, Southwick PO17 6EL
Tel (01705) 380131
Mem 650 80(L)
Sec NW Price
Pro J Green (01705) 380442
Holes 18 L 5972 yds SSS 69
Recs Am–67 R Edwards, R Berry
Pro–64 G Hughes
V'tors WD–U before 11am only
SOC–Tues
Fees On application. Service
Personnel reduced rate
Loc 5 miles N of Portsmouth,
off B2177

Southwood (1977)
Public
Ively Road, Farnborough GU14 0LJ
Tel (01252) 548700
Sec R Hammond
Pro R Hammond
Holes 18 L 5738 yds SSS 68
Recs Am–64 P McDonnell
(1998)
Pro–61 R Edwards
V'tors U
Fees £12.50 (£15)
Loc 1 mile W of Farnborough,
off A325
Arch M Hawtree

Stoneham (1908)
Monks Wood Close, Bassett, Southampton SO16 3TT
Tel (01703) 768151
Fax (01703) 766320
Mem 800
Sec AL Bray (Mgr)
(01703) 769272
Pro I Young (01703) 768397
Holes 18 L 6310 yds SSS 70
Recs Am–63 M Blackey
Pro–63 J Martin
V'tors U SOC–Mon/Thurs/Fri
Fees £29 D–£36 (£40)
Loc 2 miles N of Southampton
on A27
Arch Willie Park

Test Valley (1992)
Micheldever Road, Overton, Basingstoke RG25 3DS
Tel (01256) 771737
Mem 550
Sec RV Gardiner (Mgr)
(01256) 770916
Pro A Briggs (01256) 771737
Holes 18 L 6883 yds SSS 73
Pro–66 D Wyborn (1995)
V'tors U SOC
Fees £14 (£20)

Loc 2 miles S of Overton on
Micheldever road. M3
Junction 8
Arch Wright/Darcy

Tournerbury Golf Centre (1993)
Pay and play
Tournerbury Road, Hayling Island PO11 9DL
Tel (01705) 462266
Pro R Brown
Holes 9 L 2956 yds SSS 35
V'tors U SOC
Fees 9 holes–£6.80 (£7.80)
Loc E coast of Hayling Island.
3 miles S of Havant
Mis Driving range

Tylney Park (1973)
Rotherwick, Basingstoke RG27 9AY
Tel (01256) 762079
Fax (01256) 763079
Mem 700
Sec MR Alcock
Pro C de Bruin (Mgr)
Holes 18 L 6108 yds SSS 69
Recs Am–65 J Shaw
Pro–68 S Watson (1988)
V'tors WD–U WE–M or H SOC
Fees On application
Loc 2 miles NW of Hook. M3
Junction 5

Waterlooville (1907)
Cherry Tree Ave, Cowplain, Waterlooville PO8 8AP
Tel (01705) 263388
Fax (01705) 347513
Mem 800
Sec D Nairne
Pro J Hay (01705) 256911
Holes 18 L 6602 yds SSS 72
Recs Am–67 M Blackey (1997)
Pro–64 P Hughes (1996)
Ladies–71 K Smith (1992)
V'tors WD/WE–M H (Sun am–XL) SOC
Fees £25 D–£30
Loc 10 miles N of Portsmouth
on A3
Arch Henry Cotton

Wellow (1991)
Ryedown Lane, East Wellow, Romsey SO51 6BD
Tel (01794) 322872
Fax (01794) 323832
Mem 550
Sec Mrs C Gurd
Pro N Bratley (01794) 323833
Holes 27 L 6000 yds SSS 70
Recs Am–68 A Hemington (1994)
Pro–69 M Mills (1994)
V'tors U SOC–WD
Fees £16 (£19)
Loc 2 miles W of Romsey. M27
Junction 2, via A36
Arch W Wiltshire

For list of abbreviations see page 527

Hampshire

Weybrook Park (1971)
Rooksdown Lane, Basingstoke RG24 9NT
Tel (01256) 320347
Fax (01256) 812973
Mem 600
Sec GE Carpenter
Pro A Dillon (01256) 333232
Holes 18 L 6468 yds SSS 71
V'tors WD–U WE–contact Mgr SOC
Fees £17.50 (£22.50)
Loc 1½ miles N of Basingstoke

Wickham Park
Titchfield Lane, Wickham, Fareham PO17 5PJ
Tel (01329) 833342
Fax (01329) 834798
Sec T Hill (Mgr)
Pro T Hill
Holes 18 L 6022 yds Par 70 SSS 69
Recs Am–71 J Houghton (1996)
V'tors U SOC
Fees £9.50 (£12.50)
Loc 2 miles N of Fareham
Arch Jon Payn

Worldham Park (1993)
Pay and play
Cakers Lane, Worldham, Alton GU34 3AG
Tel (01420) 543151/544606
Mem 500
Sec MJ Vanner
Pro J Le Roux (01420) 543151
Holes 18 L 6500 yds SSS 71
Recs Am–68 P Bemrose
V'tors WD–U WE–U after 11am SOC–WD
Fees £11 (£13)
Loc ½ mile E of Alton on B3004 to Bordon
Mis Driving range
Arch Troth/Whidborne

Herefordshire

Belmont Lodge (1983)
Belmont, Hereford HR2 9SA
Tel (01432) 352666
Fax (01432) 358090
Mem 500
Sec T Thomas
Pro M Welsh (01432) 352717
Holes 18 L 6511 yds SSS 71
Recs Am–71 N Dulson
Pro–66 S Edwards
V'tors U SOC
Fees On application
Loc 1½ miles S of Hereford on A465
Arch B Sandow

Burghill Valley (1991)
Tillington Road, Burghill, Hereford HR4 7RW
Tel (01432) 760456
Fax (01432) 761654
Sec K Smith (Mgr)
Pro N Clarke (01432) 760808
Holes 18 L 6239 yds SSS 70
Recs Am–69
Pro–67
V'tors U SOC
Fees £18 (£25)
Loc 3 miles N of Hereford, off A4110

Cadmore Lodge (1990)
Pay and play
Berrington Green, Tenbury Wells, Worcester WR15 8TQ
Tel (01584) 810044
Mem 150
Sec RV Farr
Pro None
Holes 9 L 5129 yds Par 68 SSS 65
V'tors U
Fees D–£10 (D–£14)
Loc 2 miles S of Tenbury Wells on A4112

Hereford Municipal (1983)
Public
Holmer Road, Hereford HR4 9UD
Tel (01432) 344376
Fax (01432) 266281
Sec G Evans
Pro P Brookes (01432) 344376
Holes 9 L 3060 yds Par 70 SSS 69
V'tors U SOC
Fees 18 holes–£6 (£7.50)
9 holes–£4 (£6)
Loc Hereford Leisure Centre, A49 Leominster road

Herefordshire (1896)
Raven's Causeway, Wormsley, Hereford HR4 8LY
Tel (01432) 830219
Mem 500 75(L) 85(J)
Sec RW Dando (Hon)
Pro D Hemming (01432) 830465
Holes 18 L 6069 yds SSS 69
Recs Am–63 D Park (1993)
Pro–61 B Barnes
V'tors U–phone first SOC
Fees £17 D–£22 (£20 D–£28)
Loc 6 miles NW of Hereford
PRO SHOP 01432830465

Kington (1926)
Bradnor Hill, Kington HR5 3RE
Tel (01544) 230340
Fax (01544) 340270
Mem 500
Sec GR Wictome (01544) 340270
Pro D Oliver (01544) 231520
Holes 18 L 5840 yds SSS 68
Recs Am–65 K Alexander
V'tors WE–NA before 10.15am–restricted 1.30-2.45pm SOC
Fees £13 D–£16 (£16 D–£20)
Loc 1 mile N of Kington
Arch CK Hutchinson

Leominster (1967)
Ford Bridge, Leominster HR6 0LE
Tel (01568) 612863 (Clubhouse)
Fax (01568) 610055
Mem 550
Sec JA Ashcroft (01568) 610055
Pro A Ferriday (01568) 611402
Holes 18 L 6029 yds SSS 69
Recs Am–69 D Francis (1992)
Pro–71 F Clark (1992)
V'tors U SOC
Fees £15.50 D–£19 (£22 D–£25)
Loc 3 miles S of Leominster on A49 (Leominster By-pass)
Arch R Sandow

Ross-on-Wye (1903)
Two Park, Gorsley, Ross-on-Wye HR9 7UT
Tel (01989) 720267
Fax (01989) 720212
Mem 760
Sec NG Ovens
Pro N Catchpole (01989) 720439
Holes 18 L 6500 yds Par 72 SSS 73
Recs Am–69 D Powell (1994)
Pro–68 J Peters (1994)
Ladies–69 E Fields (1994)
V'tors U SOC–Wed-Fri (min 16 players)
Fees £32–£40 SOC–£28–£36
Loc 5 miles N of Ross-on-Wye, by M50 Junction 3
Mis Parkland driving range
Arch CK Cotton

Sapey (1991)
Upper Sapey, Worcester WR6 6XT
Tel (01886) 853288
Fax (01886) 853485
Mem 500
Sec Miss L Stevenson
Pro C Knowles
Holes 18 L 5885 yds SSS 69
Recs Am–64 E Deasey (1994)
Pro–63 K Craggs (1994)
V'tors WD–U WE–NA before 10am SOC
Fees £16 D–£22 (£24 D–£30)
Loc 6 miles N of Bromyard on B4203. M5 Junction 5

South Herefordshire (1992)
Twin Lakes, Upton Bishop, Ross-on-Wye HR9 7UA
Tel (01989) 780535
Fax (01989) 740611
Mem 300
Sec RLA Lee (Mgr)
Pro E Litchfield
Holes 18 L 6672 yds Par 71 SSS 72
9 hole Par 3 course
Recs Am–71 A Rock (1995)
V'tors U SOC
Fees £15 (£18)
Loc 3 miles NE of Ross-on-Wye. M50 Junction 4
Mis Floodlit driving range
Arch John Day

For list of abbreviations see page 527

Hertfordshire

Aldenham G&CC (1975)
Church Lane, Aldenham, Watford
WD2 8AL
Tel (01923) 853929
Fax (01923) 858472
Mem 560
Sec Mrs J Phillips
Pro (01923) 857889
Holes 18 L 6500 yds SSS 71
9 L 2350 yds
Recs Am–67 P Wharton (1987)
Pro–69 B Charles (1982)
V'tors U
Fees £25 (£30)
Loc 3 miles E of Watford, off B462. M1 Junction 5

Aldwickbury Park (1995)
Piggottshill Lane, Wheathampstead Road, Harpenden AL5 1AB
Tel (01582) 765112
Fax (01582) 760113
Mem 700
Sec A Knott
Pro D Germeney (01582) 760112
Holes 18 L 6032 yds Par 71 SSS 69
9 hole Par 3 course
V'tors WD–U booking necessary
WE–U after 1pm SOC–WD
Fees £20 (£26)
Loc E of Harpenden on Wheathampstead road. M1 Junction 9. A1(M) Junction 4
Arch Gillett/Brown

Arkley (1909)
Rowley Green Road, Barnet EN5 3HL
Tel (0181) 449 0394
Mem 350
Sec J Hardie
Pro M Porter (0181) 440 8473
Holes 9 L 6045 yds SSS 69
Recs Am–67 D Wiggins
Pro–63 LV Baker
V'tors WD–U WE–M SOC–Wed–Fri
Fees £20
Loc NW of Barnet, off A1(M)
Arch James Braid

Ashridge (1932)
Little Gaddesden, Berkhamsted
HP4 1LY
Tel (01442) 842244
Fax (01442) 843770
Mem 700
Sec MS Silver
Pro A Ainsworth (01442) 842307
Holes 18 L 6547 yds SSS 71
Recs Am–63 J Kemp (1996)
Pro–66 JRM Jacobs
V'tors WD only–phone Sec
Fees On application
Loc 5 miles N of Berkhamsted on B4506
Arch Campbell/Hutchison/Hotchkin

Barkway Park (1992)
Nuthampstead Road, Barkway, Royston
SG8 8EN
Tel (01763) 849070
Mem 250
Sec Mrs V Sadler
Pro S James (01763) 848215
Holes 18 L 6997 yds SSS 74
V'tors U
Fees £15 (£20)
Loc 5 miles SE of Royston, on B1368
Arch Vivien Saunders

Batchwood Hall (1935)
Pay and play
Batchwood Drive, St Albans AL3 5XA
Tel (01727) 833349
Fax (01582) 793215
Mem 425
Sec BR Mercer
Pro J Thomson
Holes 18 L 6487 yds SSS 71
Recs Am–67 D Tapping (1991)
Pro–62 PP Wynne
V'tors WD–U WE–NA before 10am
Fees £9 (£11)
Loc NW of St Albans on A5081. 5 miles S of M1 Junction 9
Arch JH Taylor

Batchworth Park (1996)
London Road, Rickmansworth WD3 1JS
Tel (01923) 714922
Fax (01923) 710200
Mem 750
Sec M Clarke (Gen Mgr)
Pro R Whitehead, M Arnold
Holes 18 L 6723 yds Par 72 SSS 72
V'tors M
Fees NA
Loc 1 mile SE of Rickmansworth on A404. M25 Junction 18
Mis Indoor Academy. Practice range
Arch Dave Thomas

Berkhamsted (1890)
The Common, Berkhamsted HP4 2QB
Tel (01442) 865832
Fax (01442) 863730
Mem 450 120(L) 50(J)
Sec CD Hextall
Pro BJ Proudfoot (01442) 865851
Holes 18 L 6605 yds Par 71 SSS 72
Recs Am–64 N Leconte (1986)
Pro–69 S Proudfoot (1987)
V'tors U H WE–M before 11.30am SOC–Wed & Fri
Fees £25 (£35)
Loc 1 mile N of Berkhamsted. M25 Junction 21 (A41). M1 Junction 8
Arch HS Colt/James Braid

Bishop's Stortford (1910)
Dunmow Road, Bishop's Stortford
CM23 5HP
Tel (01279) 654715
Fax (01279) 655215
Mem 900

Sec B Collins
Pro V Duncan (01279) 651324
Holes 18 L 6404 yds SSS 71
Recs Am–69 I Hardie (1997)
Pro–66 M Stokes (1997)
Ladies–71 A Smithet (1997)
V'tors WD–U WE–M SOC–WD exc Tues
Fees £22 D–£32
Loc E of Bishop's Stortford on A1250. M11 Junction 8, ¼ mile
Arch James Braid

Boxmoor (1890)
18 Box Lane, Hemel Hempstead
HP2 0DJ
Tel (01442) 242434 (Clubhouse)
Mem 290
Sec P Lavis (01442) 397999
Pro None
Holes 9 L 4854 yds SSS 64
Recs Am–62 G Linton
V'tors U exc Sun–NA
Fees £10 Sat–£15
Loc 1 mile W of Hemel Hempstead on B4505 to Chesham

Brickendon Grange (1964)
Brickendon, Hertford SG13 8PD
Tel (01992) 511258
Fax (01992) 511411
Mem 650
Sec RH Owens
Pro (01992) 511218
Holes 18 L 6325 yds SSS 70
Recs Am–66 M Payne (1998)
Pro–67 S James, K Robson (1985)
V'tors WD–U H WE/BH–M SOC
Fees On application
Loc Bayford, 3 miles S of Hertford

Bridgedown (1994)
St Albans Road, Barnet EN5 4RE
Tel (0181) 440 4120
Fax (0181) 440 4009
Mem 400
Pro D Beal
Holes 18 L 6626 yds Par 72 SSS 72
V'tors By appointment
Fees £13 (£15)
Loc 1 mile S of South Mimms on A1081. M25 Junction 23
Arch Howard Swann

Briggens House Hotel (1988)
Briggens Park, Stanstead Road,
Stanstead Abbotts SG12 8LD
Tel (01279) 793742
Fax (01279) 793685
Mem 200
Sec A Battle (Mgr)
Holes 9 L 5825 yds SSS 69
V'tors U SOC
Fees £10.50 (£15)
Loc 4 miles E of Hertford, off A414

For list of abbreviations see page 527

Brocket Hall (1992)
Welwyn AL8 7XG
Tel (01707) 390055
Fax (01707) 390052
Mem 580
Pro K Wood (01707) 390063
Holes Melbourne 18 L 6584 yds SSS 72; Palmerston 18 L 6925 yds SSS 73
Recs Am–68 Ujlaki (1994)
Pro–65 K Wood (1994)
V'tors M H
Fees £40 (£50)
Loc On B653 to Wheathampstead. A1(M) Junction 4
Mis Driving range. Golf Academy
Arch Melbourne: Clark/Alliss
Palmerston: Steel

Brookmans Park (1930)
Brookmans Park, Hatfield AL9 7AT
Tel (01707) 652487
Fax (01707) 661851
Mem 775
Sec PA Gill
Pro I Jelley (01707) 652468
Holes 18 L 6473 yds SSS 71
Recs Am–66 P Embleton (1990)
Pro–66 I Jelley (1990)
V'tors WD–UH WE/BH–M SOC
Fees £27
Loc 3 miles S of Hatfield, off A1000
Arch Hawtree/Taylor

Bushey G&CC (1980)
High Street, Bushey WD2 1BJ
Tel (0181) 950 2283
Fax (0181) 386 1181
Mem 600
Sec D Hourihan
Pro M Lovegrove (0181) 950 2215
Holes 9 L 3000 yds SSS 69
Recs Pro–67
V'tors WD–before 6pm WE/BH–after 2pm Wed–closed SOC–WD exc Wed
Fees 18 holes–£10 (14)
9 holes–£7 (£9)
Loc 2 miles S of Watford on A4008
Mis Driving range

Bushey Hall (1890)
Pay and play
Bushey Hall Drive, Bushey WD2 2EP
Tel (01923) 222253
Fax (01923) 229759
Mem 400
Sec JK Smith
Pro K Wickham (01923) 225802
Holes 18 L 6099 yds SSS 69
Recs Am–66 M Bowen (1990), S Clement (1992)
Pro–65 N Brown (1992), J Pinsent (1994)
V'tors U SOC–WD
Fees £10 (£17)
Loc 1 mile SE of Watford. M1 Junction 5

Chadwell Springs (1974)
Hertford Road, Ware SG12 9LE
Tel (01920) 463647
Mem 350
Sec M Scott (01920) 461447
Pro M Wall (01920) 462075
Holes 9 L 3021 yds SSS 69
V'tors WD–U WE–M
Fees £20
Loc Between Ware and Hertford on A119

Chesfield Downs (1991)
Pay and play
Jack's Hill, Graveley, Stevenage SG4 7EQ
Tel (01462) 482929
Fax (01462) 482930
Mem 550
Sec D Burridge
Pro Jane Fernley
Holes 18 L 6646 yds SSS 72
9 holes Par 3 course
V'tors U SOC
Fees 18 hole:£14.25 (£21)
9 hole:£3.50 (£4.50)
Loc B197, N of Stevenage. A1(M) Junctions 8 or 9
Mis Driving range
Arch Jonathan Gaunt

Cheshunt (1976)
Public
Park Lane, Cheshunt EN7 6QD
Tel (01992) 29777
Mem 480
Sec JG Duncan
Pro A Traynor (01992) 24009
Holes 18 L 6608 yds SSS 71
Recs Am–65 S Blight (1986)
V'tors U-booking required
Fees £9.50 (£12)
Loc Off A10 at Church Lane, Cheshunt. M25 Junction 25, 3 miles
Arch Hawtree

Chorleywood (1890)
Common Road, Chorleywood WD3 5LN
Tel (01923) 282009
Fax (01923) 286739
Mem 220 55(L) 40(J)
Sec BF Cable MBE
Pro RM Mandeville
Holes 9 L 2838 yds SSS 67
Recs Am–65 N Leconte (1990)
Pro–61 M Squires (1991)
V'tors WD–U exc Tues am WE–U after 11.30am SOC
Fees £16 (£20)
Loc 3 miles N of Rickmansworth, off A404. M25 Junction 18

Danesbury Park (1992)
Codicote Road, Welwyn AL6 9SD
Tel (01438) 840100
Fax (01727) 846109
Mem 300
Sec D Snowdon

Pro G Aris
Holes 9 L 4150 yds SSS 60
V'tors M SOC–WD
Loc ¾ mile from A1(M) Junction 6 on B656 Hitchin road
Arch Derek Snowdon

Dyrham Park CC (1963)
Galley Lane, Barnet EN5 4RA
Tel (0181) 440 3361
Fax (0181) 441 9836
Mem 600
Sec K Sutton
Pro W Large (0181) 440 3904
Holes 18 L 6422 yds SSS 71
Recs Am–67 D Zartz (1991)
Pro–65 P Elson (1978)
V'tors M SOC–Wed
Loc 10 miles N of London, W off A1
Arch CK Cotton

East Herts (1899)
Hamels Park, Buntingford SG9 9NA
Tel (01920) 821923
Fax (01920) 823700
Mem 700
Sec C Wilkinson (01920) 821978
Pro SM Bryan (01920) 821922
Holes 18 L 6456 yds SSS 71
Recs Am–66 D Hamilton
Pro–64 R Joyce
V'tors WD–H exc Wed–NA before 1pm WE–M
Fees On application
Loc ¼ mile N of Puckeridge on A10

Elstree (1984)
Watling Street, Elstree WD6 3AA
Tel (0181) 953 6115
Fax (0181) 207 6390
Mem 600
Sec K Ellis
Pro M Warwick
Holes 18 L 6100 yds SSS 69
Recs Am–68 C Woodcock (1987)
V'tors U SOC
Fees On application
Loc A5183, 1 mile N of Elstree. M1 Junction 4
Mis Floodlit driving range

Forest Hills (1994)
Newgate Street, Newgate Street Village SG13 8EW
Tel (01707) 876825
Fax (01707) 876825
Mem 170
Sec C Easton
Pro C Easton
Holes 9 L 3220 yds Par 72 SSS 71
Recs Am–72 N Brooks (1996)
V'tors WD–U WE/BH–by arrangement
Fees £15 (£20)
Loc 3 miles W of Cheshunt. M25 Junction 25
Arch Mel Flannagan

Great Hadham (1993)
Great Hadham Road, Bishop's Stortford SG10 6JE
Tel (01279) 843558
Fax (01279) 842122
Mem 700
Sec C Day
Pro K Lunt (01279) 843888
Holes 18 L 6854 yds Par 72 SSS 73
Recs Am–68 D Kitteridge (1996)
V'tors WD–U WE/BH–NA before 12 noon SOC
Fees £18 (£25)
Loc 3 miles SW of Bishops Stortford (B1004). M11 Junction 8
Mis Driving range

Hadley Wood (1922)
Beech Hill, Hadley Wood, Barnet EN4 0JJ
Tel (0181) 449 4328
Fax (0181) 364 8633
Mem 635
Sec CS Silcox (Gen Mgr)
Pro P Jones (0181) 449 3285
Holes 18 L 6457 yds SSS 71
Recs Am–67 C Holton (1983), N Leconte (1989)
Pro–67 P Elson (1980)
V'tors WD–H WE/BH–M SOC
Fees On application
Loc 10 miles N of London, off A111 between Potters Bar and Cockfosters. 2 miles S of M25 Junction 24
Mis Practice range
Arch Dr A Mackenzie

Hanbury Manor (1990)
Ware SG12 0SD
Tel (01920) 487722
Fax (01920) 487692
Mem 600
Sec M Newey
Pro P Blaze
Holes 18 L 7016 yds SSS 74
V'tors M H
Loc 8 miles N of M25 Junction 25 on A10
Arch Jack Nicklaus Jr

Harpenden (1894)
Hammonds End, Harpenden AL5 2AX
Tel (01582) 712580
Fax (01582) 712725
Mem 800
Sec J Newton
Pro P Cherry (01582) 767124
Holes 18 L 6381 yds SSS 70
Recs Am–67 B Bulmer (1987), D Ramsay (1995)
Pro–65 J Sewell (1994)
V'tors WD–U exc Thurs WE/BH–M SOC–WD exc Thurs
Fees £24 D–£34
Loc 6 miles N of St Albans on B487
Arch Hawtree/Taylor

Harpenden Common (1931)
East Common, Harpenden AL5 1BL
Tel (01582) 712856
Fax (01582) 715959
Mem 740
Sec RD Parry (01582) 715959
Pro D Fitzsimmons (01582) 460655
Holes 18 L 6214 yds SSS 70
Recs Am–64 T Turner (1998)
V'tors WD–U H WE–M SOC
Fees £25 (£30)
Loc 4 miles N of St Albans, on A1081
Arch K Brown (1995)

Hartsbourne G&CC (1946)
Hartsbourne Avenue, Bushey Heath WD2 1JW
Tel (0181) 950 1133
Fax (0181) 950 5357
Mem 750
Sec Miss S Hobbs
Pro A Cardwell (0181) 950 2836
Holes 18 L 6385 yds SSS 70
9 L 5773 yds SSS 68
Recs Am–66 J Bohn
Pro–62 P Oosterhuis
V'tors NA SOC
Loc 5 miles SE of Watford, off A4008
Arch Hawtree/Taylor

Hatfield London CC (1976)
Pay and play
Bedwell Park, Essendon, Hatfield AL9 6JA
Tel (01707) 642624
Fax (01707) 646187
Mem 308
Sec H Kawashima
Pro N Greer (01707) 650431
Holes 18 L 6880 yds SSS 72
V'tors U SOC
Fees £17 (£32)
Loc 5 miles E of Hatfield on B158. A1(M) Junction 4
Mis 9 hole pitch & putt course
Arch Fred Hawtree

The Hertfordshire (1995)
Pay and play
Broxbournebury Mansion, White Stubbs Lane, Broxbourne EN10 7PY
Tel (01992) 466666
Fax (01992) 470326
Mem 690
Sec J Anderson (Dir)
Pro A Shearn
Holes 18 L 6400 yds Par 70 SSS 70
Recs Pro–64 B Davis (1996)
V'tors U H SOC
Fees £21 (£25)

Loc 8 miles N of M25 Junction 25, off A10
Mis Floodlit driving range
Arch Jack Nicklaus II

Kingsway Golf Centre (1991)
Cambridge Road, Melbourn, Royston SG8 6EY
Tel (01763) 262727
Fax (01763) 263298
Mem 450
Sec Mrs J Trim
Pro Miss D Hastings, R Jessop
Holes 9 L 2500 yds Par 33
9 hole Par 3 course
V'tors U SOC
Fees 9 holes–£5 18 holes–£8
Loc N of Royston on A10
Mis Driving range

Knebworth (1908)
Deards End Lane, Knebworth SG3 6NL
Tel (01438) 812752 (Clubhouse)
Fax (01438) 815216
Mem 1000
Sec M Parsons MBE (01438) 812752
Pro G Parker (01438) 812757
Holes 18 L 6492 yds SSS 71
Recs Am–66 J Phelps (1997)
Pro–66 L Jones (1991)
V'tors WD–U H WE–M SOC–Mon/Tues/Thurs
Fees £30
Loc 1 mile S of Stevenage on B197
Arch Willie Park

Lamerwood (1996)
Codicote Road, Wheathampstead AL4 8GB
Tel (01582) 833013
Fax (01582) 832604
Sec S Takabatake (Prop)
Pro J Coe
Holes 18 L 6953 yds Par 72
V'tors U
Fees £20 (£30)
Loc 5 miles W of A1(M) Junction 4 on B653
Mis Driving range
Arch Campbell Sinclair

Letchworth (1905)
Letchworth Lane, Letchworth SG6 3NQ
Tel (01462) 683203
Fax (01462) 484567
Mem 900
Sec AR Bailey
Pro (01462) 682713
Holes 18 L 6181 yds SSS 69
Recs Am–65 P Tandy
Pro–66 NC Coles
V'tors WD–U WE–M SOC–Wed–Fri
Fees £30
Loc S of Letchworth, off A505. A1(M) Junction 9
Arch Harry Vardon

Hertfordshire 575

Little Hay Golf Complex
(1977)
Pay and play
Box Lane, Bovingdon, Hemel Hempstead HP3 0DQ
Tel (01442) 833798
Pro D Johnson (Golf Dir)
Holes 18 L 6610 yds SSS 72
Recs Pro–69
V'tors U SOC
Fees £11 (£15.50)
Loc 2 miles W of Hemel Hempstead, on B4505 to Chesham
Mis Driving range. Pitch & putt
Arch Hawtree

Manor of Groves G&CC
(1991)
High Wych, Sawbridgeworth CM21 0LA
Tel (01279) 722333
Fax (01279) 726972
Mem 450
Pro C Laurence
Holes 18 L 6280 yds SSS 70
V'tors U SOC
Fees On application
Loc 1 mile N of Harlow
Arch S Sharer

Mid Herts (1892)
Gustard Wood, Wheathampstead AL4 8RS
Tel (01582) 832242
Fax (01582) 832242
Mem 500(M) 125(L)
Sec RJH Jourdan
Pro N Brown (01582) 832788
Holes 18 L 6060 yds SSS 69
Recs Am–67 C Tingey (1990) Pro–63 P Winston (1992)
V'tors WD–UH exc Tues & Wed pm WE/BH–M SOC
Fees On application
Loc 6 miles N of St Albans on B651

Mill Green (1994)
Gypsy Lane, Mill Green, Welwyn Garden City AL7 4TY
Tel (01707) 276900
Fax (01707) 276898
Sec J Tubb (Gen Mgr)
Pro A Hall (01707) 270542
Holes 18 L 6615 yds Par 72 SSS 72 Par 3 course
Recs Pro–64 M Sheppard
V'tors U SOC–WD
Fees Mon–£15 Tues–Fri–£19 (£25)
Loc S of Welwyn Garden City, off A414. A1 Junction 4
Arch Clark/Alliss

Moor Park (1923)
Rickmansworth WD3 1QN
Tel (01923) 773146
Fax (01923) 777109
Mem 1700
Sec JA Davies
Pro L Farmer
Holes High 18 L 6713 yds SSS 72 West 18 L 5823 yds SSS 68
Recs High Am–65 G Harris (1993) Pro–63 B Gallacher (1969) West Am–62 AJ Eisner (1984) Pro–63 AD Locke, A Lees, EE Whitcombe
V'tors WD–H WE/BH–M SOC
Fees On application
Loc 1 mile SE of Rickmansworth, off Batchworth roundabout (A4145). M25 Junction 18, 2 miles
Arch HS Colt

Old Fold Manor (1910)
Old Fold Lane, Hadley Green, Barnet EN5 4QN
Tel (0181) 440 9185
Fax (0181) 441 4863
Mem 520
Sec AW Dickens (Mgr)
Pro G Potter (0181) 440 7488
Holes 18 L 6481 yds SSS 71
Recs Am–66 A Clark Pro–68 SL King
V'tors WD–H WE–M SOC–Thurs & Fri
Fees £20 D–£27
Loc 1 mile N of Barnet on A1000

Oxhey Park
Prestwick Road, South Oxhey, Watford WD1 6DT
Tel (01923) 248312
Mem 210
Sec D McFadden (Mgr)
Holes 9 L 1637 yds Par 58
V'tors U
Fees 9 holes–£6 18 holes–£8
Loc 2 miles SW of Watford. M1 Junction 5
Mis Driving range

Panshanger Golf Complex (1976)
Old Herns Lane, Welwyn Garden City AL7 2ED
Tel (01707) 333312/333350 (Bookings)
Holes 18 L 6167 yds SSS 70 9 hole Par 3 course
Recs Am–71 S Walton (1987) Pro–70 R Green
V'tors U
Fees On application
Loc 2 miles off A1, via B1000 to Hertford

Porters Park (1899)
Shenley Hill, Radlett WD7 7AZ
Tel (01923) 854127
Fax (01923) 855475
Mem 650
Sec PR Phillips (Mgr)
Pro D Gleeson (01923) 854366
Holes 18 L 6313 yds SSS 70
Recs Am–65 CC Boal (1990) Pro–64 P Townsend
V'tors WD–H (phone first) WE/BH–M SOC–Wed & Thurs
Fees £29–£44
Loc E of Radlett on Shenley road

Potters Bar (1923)
Darkes Lane, Potters Bar EN6 1DE
Tel (01707) 652020
Fax (01707) 655051
Mem 550
Sec PK Watson (Mgr)
Pro G Aris (01707) 652987
Holes 18 L 6279 yds SSS 70
Recs Am–66 RR Davis Pro–65 D McClelland
V'tors WD–H WE/BH–M SOC–WD exc Wed
Fees £25 D–£35
Loc 1 mile N of M25 Junction 24, off A1000
Arch James Braid

Redbourn (1970)
Kinsbourne Green Lane, Redbourn, St Albans AL3 7QA
Tel (01582) 793493
Fax (01582) 794362
Sec R Fay
Pro S Hunter
Holes 18 L 6506 yds SSS 71 9 hole Par 3 course
Recs Am–67 R Kosmalski
V'tors WD–U booking necessary WE/BH–H SOC–WD
Fees 18 hole:£18 (£24) 9 hole:£5.50 (£7.50)
Loc 4 miles N of St Albans, off A5. 1 mile S of M1 Junction 9
Mis Target golf range

Rickmansworth (1937)
Public
Moor Lane, Rickmansworth WD3 1QL
Tel (01923) 775278
Mem 250
Sec RA Botham (01494) 763851
Pro A Dobbins (01923) 775278
Holes 18 L 4493 yds SSS 62
Recs Am–63 JC Jackson (1991)
V'tors U
Fees £9 (£13)
Loc ½ mile SE of Rickmansworth, off Batchworth roundabout (A4145). M25 Junction 18, 2 miles
Mis 9 hole pitch & putt course

Royston (1892)
Baldock Road, Royston SG8 5BG
Tel (01763) 242696
Fax (01763) 242696
Mem 750
Sec M Bothamley (01763) 242696
Pro S Clark (01763) 243476
Holes 18 L 6066 yds SSS 69
Recs Am–65 GA Hainsworth Pro–63 B Waites
V'tors WD–U WE/BH–M SOC
Fees £20
Loc SW of Royston on A505

For list of abbreviations see page 527

Sandy Lodge (1910)
Sandy Lodge Lane, Northwood, Middx HA6 2JD
Tel (01923) 825429
Fax (01923) 824319
Mem 700
Sec HE Inman
Pro J Pinsent (01923) 825321
Holes 18 L 6347 yds SSS 71
Recs Am–66 DG Scammell (1992), R Catlin (1994)
  Pro–64 A Jacklin (1977)
V'tors H or M SOC
Fees On application
Loc Adjacent Moor Park Station
Arch Harry Vardon

Shendish Manor (1988)
Pay and play
Shendish House, Apsley, Hemel Hempstead HP3 0AA
Tel (01442) 251806
Fax (01442) 230683
Sec M Thornberry
Holes 18 L 5660 yds Par 70 SSS 68
Recs Am–69 K Swatman (1991)
V'tors U SOC
Fees £15 (£20)
Loc S of Hemel Hempstead, off A41. M25 Junction 20
Arch Cotton/Steel

South Herts (1899)
Links Drive, Totteridge, London N20 8QU
Tel (0181) 445 0117
Fax (0181) 445 7569
Mem 850
Sec PF Wise (0181) 445 2035
Pro RY Mitchell (0181) 445 4633
Holes 18 L 6470 yds SSS 71
  9 L 1581 yds
Recs Am–63 J Little (1998)
  Pro–65 M Litton (1995)
V'tors WD–IH WE/BH–M
Fees On application
Loc Totteridge Lane
Arch Harry Vardon

Stevenage (1980)
Public
Aston Lane, Stevenage SG2 7EL
Tel (01438) 880424
Mem 450
Sec Mrs S Elwin (01438) 880322
Pro S Barker (01438) 880424
Holes 18 L 6451 yds SSS 71
  9 hole Par 3 course
Recs Am–69 T Carter (1990), C Elwin (1992), D Gibson (1995)
  Pro–65 R Green (1989)
V'tors U
Fees £11 (£14)
Loc Off A602 to Hertford. A1(M) Junction 7
Mis Driving range
Arch John Jacobs

Stocks Hotel G&CC (1993)
Stocks Road, Aldbury, Tring HP23 5RX
Tel (01442) 851341
Fax (01442) 851253
Mem 450
Pro PR Lane (Ext 308)
Holes 18 L 7016 yds SSS 74
V'tors H SOC
Fees £30 (£40)
Loc Aldbury, 2 miles E of Tring. A41(T), 2 miles
Arch M Billcliffe

Verulam (1905)
London Road, St Albans AL1 1JG
Tel (01727) 853327
Fax (01727) 812201
Mem 640
Sec AR Crichton-Smith
Pro N Burch (01727) 861401
Holes 18 L 6448 yds Par 72 SSS 71
Recs Am–70 M Witchard (1998)
  Pro–66 P Winston (1998)
V'tors WD–H exc Mon–U WE/BH–M
  SOC–Tues & Thurs
Fees £25 (Mon–£15)
Loc 1 mile SE of St Albans on A1081
Arch Braid/Steel

Welwyn Garden City (1922)
Mannicotts, High Oaks Road, Welwyn Garden City AL8 7BP
Tel (01707) 322722
Fax (01707) 393213
Mem 900
Sec GD Eastwood (Gen Mgr) (01707) 325243
Pro R May (01707) 325525
Holes 18 L 6100 yds SSS 69
Recs Am–64 MJ Deal (1991), D Crilley (1996)
  Pro–63 N Faldo (1998)
V'tors WD–H WE/BH–NA
Fees On application
Loc 1 mile N of Hatfield. A1(M) Junction 4 – B197 to Valley Road
Arch Hawtree

West Herts (1890)
Cassiobury Park, Watford WD1 7SL
Tel (01923) 224264
Fax (01923) 222300
Mem 700
Sec CC Dodman (01923) 236484
Pro CS Gough (01923) 220352
Holes 18 L 6488 yds SSS 71
Recs Am–66 M Hooper (1995)
  Pro–65 R Mann (1995)
  Ladies–73 F Smith (1992)
V'tors WD–U WE/BH–M
  SOC–Wed & Fri
Fees £20 (£30)
Loc Off A412, between Watford and Rickmansworth
Arch Morris/Mackenzie

Whipsnade Park (1974)
Studham Lane, Dagnall HP4 1RH
Tel (01442) 842330
Fax (01442) 842090
Mem 600
Sec Jane Mitchell
Pro M Lewendon
Holes 18 L 6812 yds SSS 72
Recs Am–71 A Calder
  Pro–66 A Clapp
V'tors WD–U WE–M SOC–WD
Fees £22 D–£34
Loc 8 miles N of Hemel Hempstead, off A4147

Whitehill (1990)
Dane End, Ware SG12 0JS
Tel (01920) 438495
Fax (01920) 438891
Mem 700
Sec Mr & Mrs A Smith (Props)
Pro D Ling
Holes 18 L 6636 yds SSS 72
V'tors H–booking necessary
Fees £15 (£18)
Loc 6 miles N of Ware (A10)
Mis Floodlit driving range

Isle of Man

Castletown (1892)
Fort Island, Derbyhaven IM9 1UA
Tel (01624) 822201
Fax (01624) 824633
Mem 400
Sec R Griffiths (Hon)
Pro M Crowe (01624) 822211
Holes 18 L 6716 yds SSS 72
Recs Am–68 WR Ennett
  Pro–65 D Dunk
V'tors U SOC
Fees £22.50 (£27.50)
Loc 1 mile E of Castletown
Arch Mackenzie Ross

Douglas Municipal (1927)
Public
Pulrose Park, Douglas IM2 1AE
Tel (01624) 661558
Pro K Parry
Holes 18 L 5922 yds Par 69 SSS 68
Recs Am–63
V'tors U
Fees £6.30 (£12.50)
Loc Douglas Pier 2 miles
Arch Dr A Mackenzie

King Edward Bay (1893)
Groudle Road, Onchan IM3 2JR
Tel (01624) 620430/673821
Fax (01624) 676794
Mem 400
Sec B Holt (01624) 670977
Pro D Jones (01624) 672709
Holes 18 L 5457 yds SSS 65
Recs Am–63
V'tors U SOC

For list of abbreviations see page 527

Isle of Man

Fees £10 (£12)
Loc 1 mile N of Douglas
Arch Tom Morris (1893 course)

Mount Murray G&CC (1994)
Santon IM4 2HT
Tel (01624) 661111
Fax (01624) 611116
Mem 360
Sec AD Dyson (Ext 3023)
Pro AD Dyson (Ext 3023)
Holes 18 L 6664 yds SSS 72
Recs Am–69 G Wilson (1996)
V'tors U H SOC
Fees £18 (£24)
Loc 3 miles SW of Douglas
Mis Driving range

Peel (1895)
Rheast Lane, Peel IM5 1BG
Tel (01624) 842227
Fax (01624) 843456
Mem 600
Sec Mrs LA Cullen
(01624) 843456
Pro M Crowe
Holes 18 L 5850 yds SSS 69
Recs Am–63 G Kelly
V'tors WD–U WE/BH–NA before 10.30am SOC
Fees £17 (£24)
Loc 10 miles W of Douglas via A1
Arch James Braid

Port St Mary (1936)
Public
Kallow Road, Port St Mary IM9 5EJ
Tel (01624) 834932
Sec T Boyle (Hon)
Pro M Crowe (01624) 822221
Holes 9 L 2711 yds SSS 66
Recs Am–62 A Cain (1994)
V'tors WD–U WE–NA before 10.30am SOC
Fees On application
Loc 6 miles S of Castletown via A5
Arch George Duncan

Ramsey (1891)
Brookfield, Ramsey IM8 2AH
Tel (01624) 813365/812244
Fax (01624) 815833
Mem 700
Sec Mrs J Hignett (01624) 812244
Pro C Wilson (01624) 814736
Holes 18 L 6019 yds SSS 69
Recs Am–65 S Boyd
Pro–64 D Wills
V'tors WD–U after 10am WE–M SOC
Fees £18 (£22)
Loc N of Douglas via A18. W boundary of Ramsey
Arch James Braid

Rowany (1895)
Rowany Drive, Port Erin IM9 6LN
Tel (01624) 834108
Fax (01624) 834108
Mem 600

Sec AJ Laine (Mgr)
(01624) 834072
Holes 18 L 5881 yds SSS 69
Recs Am–65 G Wilson
V'tors U SOC
Fees On application
Loc 6 miles W of Castletown via A5

Isle of Wight

Cowes (1908)
Crossfield Avenue, Cowes PO31 8HN
Tel (01983) 280135 (Clubhouse)
Mem 300
Sec D Weaver (01983) 292303
Holes 9 L 5934 yds SSS 68
Recs Am–66 M Leek, R Greenham
V'tors H Thurs–NA before 3pm (Ladies Day) Fri–NA after 5pm Sun am–NA
Fees £15 (£18)
Loc Nr Cowes High School
Arch J Hamilton Stutt

Freshwater Bay (1894)
Afton Down, Freshwater PO40 9TZ
Tel (01983) 752955
Fax (01983) 756704
Mem 500
Sec JR Copleston
Holes 18 L 5725 yds SSS 68
Recs Am–62 JE Veal (1997)
Pro–66 T Underwood (1981)
V'tors H–NA before 9.30am SOC
Fees £20 (£24)
Loc 400 yds off Military Road (A3055)
Mis www.isle-of-wight.uk.com/golf

Newport (1896)
St George's Down, Shide, Newport PO30 3BA
Tel (01983) 525076
Mem 350
Sec MJ Cunningham
Holes 9 L 5674 yds SSS 68
Recs Am–65 J Burton (1987)
V'tors WD–U exc Wed–NA 12–2.30pm Sat–NA before 3.30pm Sun–NA before noon SOC
Fees £15 (£17.50)
Loc 1 mile SE of Newport
Arch Guy Hunt

Osborne (1903)
Osborne House Estate, East Cowes PO32 6JX
Tel (01983) 295421
Mem 260 90(L)
Sec RS Jones
Holes 9 L 6372 yds SSS 70
V'tors WD–U exc Ladies Day (Tues) 9am–1pm–NA WE–NA before noon SOC
Fees £16 (£19) 5D–£60
Loc S of East Cowes in grounds of Osborne House

Ryde (1921)
Binstead Road, Ryde PO33 3NF
Tel (01983) 614809
Fax (01983) 567418
Mem 450
Sec ARJ Goodall
Pro None
Holes 9 L 5287 yds SSS 66
Recs Am–65 J Thorp
V'tors WD–U exc Wed pm Sun–NA before noon
Fees £15 (£20)
Loc On main Ryde/Newport road
Arch J Hamilton Stutt

Shanklin & Sandown (1900)
Fairway Lake, Sandown PO36 9PR
Tel (01983) 403217
Fax (01983) 403217
Mem 650
Sec AJ Messing
Pro P Hammond (01983) 404424
Holes 18 L 6063 yds SSS 69
Recs Am–65 D McToldridge, K Brochocki
Pro–65 R Wynn
V'tors WD–U WE–NA before noon
Fees £22 (£25) 3D–£55
Loc Off Sandown-Shanklin road at the Fairway in Lake
Arch Cowper/James Braid

Ventnor (1892)
Steephill Down Road, Ventnor PO38 1BP
Tel (01983) 853326
Mem 250
Sec KM Tomes
Holes 12 L 5767 yds Par 70 SSS 68
Recs Am–73 IH Guy
V'tors WD–U exc Ladies Day–Fri Sun–NA before 1pm SOC
Fees On application
Loc NW boundary of Ventnor

Kent

Aquarius (1913)
Marmora Rd, Honor Oak, London SE22 0RY
Tel (0181) 693 1626
Mem 400
Sec S Ridgeway
Pro F Private
Holes 9 L 5246 yds SSS 66
Recs Am–62 R Hare
Pro–63 F Private
V'tors M

Ashford (1903)
Sandyhurst Lane, Ashford TN25 4NT
Tel (01233) 620180
Fax (01233) 622655
Mem 630
Sec AH Story (01233) 622655
Pro H Sherman (01233) 629644
Holes 18 L 6284 yds SSS 70

For list of abbreviations see page 527

Kent 579

Recs Am–69 R Young
Pro–64 P Sherman
V'tors WD–H WE/BH–H SOC
Fees £20 (£30)
Loc Ashford 1½ miles (A20)
Arch Cotton

Austin Lodge (1991)
Eynsford, Swanley DA4 0HU
Tel (01322) 863000
Fax (01322) 862406
Mem 600
Sec S Bevan
Pro P Edwards
Holes 18 L 6600 yds Par 73 SSS 71
Recs Am–68 T Cleary (1998)
Pro–66 N Willis (1995)
V'tors WD–U WE–NA before noon SOC
Fees £16 (£25)
Loc Off A225, nr Eynsford Station. M25 Junction 3, 3 miles
Mis Driving range for members and guests
Arch Peter Bevan

Barnehurst (1903)
Public
Mayplace Road East, Bexley Heath DA7 6JU
Tel (01322) 523746
Fax (01322) 554612
Mem 300
Sec B Davies (01322) 552952
Pro P Tallack (01322) 552952
Holes 9 L 5448 yds SSS 69
Pro–63 S Barr
V'tors U SOC
Fees £5.70 (£9.20)
Loc Between Crayford and Bexleyheath
Arch James Braid

Bearsted (1895)
Ware Street, Bearsted, Maidstone ME14 4PQ
Tel (01622) 738389
Fax (01622) 738198
Mem 780
Sec Mrs LM Siems (01622) 738198
Pro T Simpson (01622) 738024
Holes 18 L 6253 yds SSS 70
Recs Am–66 M Sur (1995)
Pro–67 T Spence (1995)
V'tors WD–I H WE–H M (recognised GC members) SOC
Fees £27 D–£36
Loc 2½ miles E of Maidstone

Beckenham Place Park (1907)
Public
Beckenham Hill Road, Beckenham BR3 2BP
Tel (0181) 650 2292
Fax (0181) 663 1201
Pro H Davies-Thomas
Holes 18 L 5722 yds SSS 68
Recs Am–62 S Champion
Pro–65 T Cotton

V'tors U
Fees £7.60 (£12.40) WE–booking fee
Loc Off A21 on A222

Bexleyheath (1907)
Mount Road, Bexleyheath BR8 7RJ
Tel (0181) 303 6951
Mem 350
Sec SE Squires
Holes 9 L 5239 yds SSS 66
Recs Am–65 D Fillary
V'tors WD–H before 4pm
Fees £20
Loc Station 1 mile

Birchwood Park Golf Centre (1990)
Birchwood Road, Wilmington, Dartford DA2 7HJ
Tel (01322) 660554
Fax (01322) 667283
Mem 450
Sec Julie Smith (Mgr) (01322) 662038
Pro S Cranfield (01322) 615209
Holes 18 L 6364 yds Par 71 SSS 70 9 hole course
Recs Am–63 L Venus (1994)
V'tors U SOC
Fees £15 (£19)
Loc 2 miles S of A2/A2018 Junction
Mis Driving range.
Arch Howard Swann

Boughton (1993)
Pay and play
Brickfield Lane, Boughton, Faversham ME13 9AJ
Tel (01227) 752277
Fax (01227) 752361
Mem 300
Sec S Hall
Pro T Poole
Holes 18 L 6452 yds SSS 71
Recs Am–70 G Houston
Pro–70 T Berry, C Evans
V'tors U SOC–WD
Fees £16 (£22)
Loc NE of Boughton, nr M2/A2 interchange. 6 miles W of Canterbury
Mis Driving range
Arch Philip Sparks

Broke Hill (1993)
Sevenoaks Road, Halstead TN14 7HR
Tel (01959) 533225
Fax (01959) 532880
Sec T Collingwood
Pro C West (01959) 533810
Holes 18 L 6454 yds Par 72 SSS 71
Recs Am–70 S Lloyd (1996)
Pro–69 B Cameron (1997)
V'tors WD–U before 5pm WE–NA
Fees £30
Loc 4 miles S of Bromley on A21. M25 Junction 4
Arch David Williams

Bromley (1948)
Public
Magpie Hall Lane, Bromley BR2 8JF
Tel (0181) 462 7014
Pro A Hodgson
Holes 9 L 5538 yds SSS 66
Recs Am–66 HE Harding, KW Miles
V'tors U
Fees On application
Loc Off Bromley Common (A21)

Broome Park (1981)
Broome Park Estate, Barham, Canterbury CT4 6QX
Tel (01227) 831701
Fax (01227) 831973
Mem 600
Sec RC Cheesworth (Ext 110)
Pro T Britz (01227) 831126
Holes 18 L 6610 yds SSS 72
Recs Am–66 A Roberts (1995)
Pro–66 B Impett (1984)
V'tors H WE–NA before noon SOC–WD
Fees £28 (£32)
Loc M2/A2-A260 Folkestone road, 1½ miles on RH side
Mis Driving range
Arch Donald Steel

Canterbury (1927)
Scotland Hills, Littlebourne Road, Canterbury CT1 1TW
Tel (01227) 453532
Fax (01227) 784277
Mem 650
Sec Mrs P Bates
Pro P Everard (01227) 462865
Holes 18 L 6249 yds SSS 70
Recs Am–65 SP Blake
Pro–64 K Redford
V'tors WD–U H WE–NA before 3pm SOC–Tues & Thurs
Fees £27 D–£36 (£36)
Loc 1 mile E of Canterbury on A257
Arch HS Colt

Chart Hills (1993)
Weeks Lane, Biddenden, Ashford TN27 8JX
Tel (01580) 292222
Fax (01580) 292233
Mem 400
Sec R Hyder (Gen Mgr)
Pro D French (01580) 292148
Holes 18 L 7135 yds SSS 74
Recs Am–65 S Fox
Pro–66 J Cixous
Ladies Am–70 K Smith
Ladies Pro–66 D Reid, C Hjalmarsson
V'tors U exc Sat–NA SOC
Fees On application
Loc 12 miles W of Ashford (A262)
Mis Golf Academy
Arch Nick Faldo

For list of abbreviations see page 527

Chelsfield Lakes Golf Centre (1992)
Pay and play
Court Road, Orpington BR6 9BX
Tel (01689) 896266
Fax (01689) 824577
Mem 650
Sec P Smith (Mgr)
Pro N Lee, B Hodkin
Holes 18 L 6077 yds Par 71 SSS 69
 9 hole Par 3 course
V'tors U–booking required
Fees £15 (£18)
Loc 1 mile from M25 Junction 4 (A224)
Mis Target golf range
Arch MRM Sandow

Cherry Lodge (1969)
Jail Lane, Biggin Hill, Westerham TN16 3AX
Tel (01959) 572250
Fax (01959) 540672
Mem 650
Sec CF Smith
Pro N Child (01959) 572989
Holes 18 L 6652 yds SSS 73
Recs Am–70 K Williams (1996)
 Pro–69 S Barr (1992)
V'tors WD–U WE–M SOC–WD before 3pm
Fees £25 D–£30
Loc 3 miles N of Westerham, off A233
Mis Driving range
Arch John Day

Chestfield (1925)
103 Chestfield Road, Whitstable CT5 3LU
Tel (01227) 794411
Fax (01227) 794454
Mem 692
Sec MA Sutcliffe
Pro J Brotherton
 (01227) 793563
Holes 18 L 6181 yds SSS 70
Recs Am–64 G Pini
 Pro–66 M Campos
V'tors WD–H
Fees On application
Loc 1 mile S of A299 and Chestfield Station

Chislehurst (1894)
Camden Place, Camden Park Road, Chislehurst BR7 5HJ
Tel (0181) 467 3055
Fax (0181) 295 0874
Mem 740
Sec NE Pearson
 (0181) 467 2782
Pro M Lawrence
 (0181) 467 6798
Holes 18 L 5128 yds SSS 65
Recs Am–61 J Murray (1993)
 Pro–61 W Humphrey
V'tors WD–H WE–M SOC
Fees D–£25
Loc M25 Junction 3/A20/A222

Cobtree Manor Park (1984)
Public
Chatham Road, Boxley, Maidstone ME14 3AZ
Tel (01622) 753276
Sec A Ferras
Holes 18 L 5716 yds SSS 68
Recs Am–67 M White (1991)
V'tors WD–U WE/BH–(book 1 wk in advance) SOC–WD
Fees £10 (£18)
Loc 3 miles N of Maidstone on A229
Arch F Hawtree

Corinthian (1987)
Gay Dawn Farm, Fawkham, Dartford DA3 8LZ
Tel (01474) 707559
Mem 400
Sec R Fletton
Pro C McKillop
Holes 9 L 6323 yds Par 72 SSS 70
Recs Am–72 A Walker, G Hesketh (1995)
V'tors WD–U H WE/BH–NA before 1pm SOC
Fees D–£15
Loc 4 miles S of Dartford Tunnel. E of Brands Hatch along Fawkham Valley road

Cray Valley (1972)
Pay and play
Sandy Lane, St Paul's Cray, Orpington BR5 3HY
Tel (01689) 837909
Fax (01689) 891428
Mem 600
Sec J Scappatura (01689) 839677
Pro G Sheriff (01689) 837909
Holes 18 L 5624 yds SSS 67
 9 L 2100 yds SSS 60
V'tors U
Fees £13 (£19)
Loc Off A20 Ruxley roundabout at Sidcup

Darenth Valley (1973)
Pay and play
Station Road, Shoreham, Sevenoaks TN14 7SA
Tel (01959) 522944 (Clubhouse)
Fax (01959) 525089
Sec JR Cooper (Mgr)
Pro S Fotheringham
 (01959) 522922
Holes 18 L 6327 yds Par 72 SSS 71
Recs Am–69 W Leo
 Pro–65 S Wood
V'tors U–booking required SOC
Fees £15 (£20)
Loc 3 miles N of Sevenoaks, off A225

Dartford (1897)
Dartford Heath, Dartford DA1 2TN
Tel (01322) 223516
Mem 600
Sec Mrs MM Gronow

Pro J Gregory (01322) 226409
Holes 18 L 5914 yds Par 69 SSS 69
Recs Am–63 K Will (1997)
 Pro–64 K Saunders (1996)
V'tors WD–I WE–M H
Fees £30
Loc Dartford 2 miles

Deangate Ridge (1972)
Public
Duxcourt Road, Hoo, Rochester ME3 8RZ
Tel (01634) 250537
Mem 560
Sec SP Wright (01634) 255111
Pro R Fox (01634) 251180
Holes 18 L 6300 yds SSS 70
Recs Am–67 L Brookwell (1994)
 Pro–65 N Allen (1990)
V'tors U SOC
Fees On application
Loc 7 miles NE of Rochester on A228. M2, 5 miles
Mis Driving range. Pitch & putt

Edenbridge G&CC (1973)
Crouch House Road, Edenbridge TN8 5LQ
Tel (01732) 867381
Fax (01732) 867029
Mem 800
Sec Mrs M Harris
Pro (01732) 865202
Holes 18 L 6604 yds SSS 72
 18 L 5671 yds SSS 67
 9 hole course
Recs Am–66 ACI Cox
V'tors WD/WE–booking necessary
Fees £20 (£27.50)
Loc 2 miles W of Edenbridge. M25 Junction 6
Mis Floodlit driving range. 9 hole pitch & putt course

Eltham Warren (1890)
Bexley Road, Eltham, London SE9 2PE
Tel (0181) 850 1166
Mem 400
Sec DJ Clare (0181) 850 4477
Pro G Brett (0181) 859 7909
Holes 9 L 5840 yds SSS 68
Recs Am–66 G Janes, D Holmes, RB Hills
 Pro–67 T Spence
V'tors WD–I WE/BH–M SOC–Thurs only
Fees D–£25
Loc ½ mile from Eltham station on A210
Arch James Braid

Etchinghill (1995)
Pay and play
Canterbury Road, Etchinghill CT18 8FA
Tel (01303) 863863
Fax (01303) 863210
Mem 400
Sec D Stodart (Mgr)
Pro C Hodgson (01303) 863966
Holes 18 L 6121 yds Par 70 SSS 69
 9 hole Par 3 course

For list of abbreviations see page 527

Kent 581

Recs Am–65 R Perkins (1997)
       Pro–63 R Dowle (1996)
V'tors U
Fees £15 (£20)
Loc 1 mile N of M20 Junction 12 on B2065
Mis Driving range
Arch John Sturdy

Executive GC Cranbrook (1969)
Golford Road, Cranbrook TN17 4AL
Tel (01580) 712833
Fax (01580) 714274
Sec C Cooper
Pro A Gillard
Holes 18 L 6305 yds SSS 70
Recs Am–67 S Coulter
       Pro–70 S Barr
V'tors WD–U WE/BH–restricted SOC
Fees £23 (£30) (1998)
Loc 15 miles S of Maidstone. M25 Junction 5-A21/A262
Mis Driving range
Arch Cdr J Harris

Faversham (1902)
Belmont Park, Faversham ME13 0HB
Tel (01795) 890561
Fax (01795) 890760
Mem 850
Sec J Edgington
Pro S Rokes (01795) 890275
Holes 18 L 6030 yds Par 70 SSS 69
Recs Am–65 R Chapman (1980)
       Pro–63 T Spence (1995)
V'tors WD–I or H WE–M SOC
Fees £30
Loc Faversham and M2, 2 miles

Gillingham (1908)
Woodlands Road, Gillingham ME7 2AP
Tel (01634) 850999
Fax (01634) 574749
Mem 450 100(L) 50(J)
Sec LP O'Grady (01634) 853017
Pro B Comber (01634) 855862
Holes 18 L 5509 yds SSS 67
Recs Am–62 M Scammell
       Pro–64 P Clark
V'tors WD–I H WE/BH–M
Fees £18 D–£25
Loc A2/M2, 2 miles
Arch Braid/Steel

Hawkhurst (1968)
High Street, Hawkhurst TN18 4JS
Tel (01580) 754074
Fax (01580) 754074
Mem 450
Sec B Morrison (Gen Mgr)
Pro T Collins (01580) 753600
Holes 9 L 5751 yds Par 70 SSS 68
Recs Am–66 R Gerrard
       Pro–68 R Cameron

V'tors WD–U WE–M SOC
Fees 18 holes–£15 (£18)
       9 holes–£10
Loc 14 miles S of Tunbridge Wells on A268

Herne Bay (1895)
Eddington, Herne Bay CT6 7PG
Tel (01227) 374097
Mem 480
Sec B Warren (01227) 373964
Pro S Dordoy (01227) 374727
Holes 18 L 5567 yds SSS 68
V'tors WD–U WE/BH–H after noon SOC–WD
Fees £18 D–£25 (£25)
Loc A299 Thanet road

Hever (1993)
Hever TN8 7NG
Tel (01732) 700771
Fax (01732) 700771
Mem 700
Sec A Chase
Pro R Tinworth
Holes 18 L 7002 yds SSS 75
V'tors H SOC
Fees £29–£45 (£45–£59)
Loc 2 miles E of Edenbridge
Arch Peter Nicholson

High Elms (1969)
Public
High Elms Road, Downe, Orpington BR6 7SZ
Tel (01689) 858175
Sec Mrs P O'Keeffe (Hon)
Pro P Remy
Holes 18 L 6210 yds SSS 70
Recs Am–68 I Farman
V'tors U
Fees On application
Loc Off A21 via Shire Lane

Hythe Imperial (1950)
Prince's Parade, Hythe CT21 6AE
Tel (01303) 267441
Fax (01303) 267554
Mem 445
Sec N Jones (01303) 267554
Pro G Ritchie (01303) 267441
Holes 9 L 5560 yds SSS 67
Recs Am–63 PI Kaye
       Pro–63 G Ritchie
V'tors H SOC
Fees £20
Loc On coast, 4 miles W of Folkestone

Kings Hill (1996)
Kings Hill, West Malling ME19 4AF
Tel (01732) 875040/842121 (Bookings)
Fax (01732) 875019
Mem 430
Sec Margaret Gilbert (Mgr)
Pro D Hudspith (01732) 842121
Holes 18 L 6622 yds Par 72 SSS 72
V'tors WD–U SOC–WD

Fees £25
Loc 3 miles from M20 Junction 4, off A228
Arch David Williams

Knole Park (1924)
Seal Hollow Road, Sevenoaks TN15 0HJ
Tel (01732) 452709
Fax (01732) 463159
Mem 700
Sec PF Lamb (01732) 452150
Pro PE Gill (01732) 451740
Holes 18 L 6249 yds SSS 70
Recs Am–64 RW Seamer
V'tors WD–restricted WE/BH–M H SOC
Fees £32 D–£42
Loc ½ mile from Sevenoaks centre
Arch JF Abercromby

Lamberhurst (1890)
Church Road, Lamberhurst TN3 8DT
Tel (01892) 890241
Fax (01892) 891140
Mem 700
Sec P Gleeson (01892) 890591
Pro BM Impett (01892) 890552
Holes 18 L 6345 yds SSS 70
Recs Am–69 L Ferris
       Pro–65 A Lavers
V'tors WD–U H WE–NA before noon
Fees £22 D–£33 (£36)
Loc 5 miles SE of Tunbridge Wells, off A21

Langley Park (1910)
Barnfield Wood Road, Beckenham BR3 6SZ
Tel (0181) 650 2090
Fax (0181) 658 6310
Mem 650
Sec RK Oakes (0181) 658 6849
Pro C Staff (0181) 650 1863
Holes 18 L 6488 yds SSS 71
Recs Am–66 T Trodd
       Pro–65 P Mitchell (1987), GT Ritchie (1991)
V'tors WD–H WE–M SOC–WD
Fees £35
Loc Bromley South Station 1 mile
Arch JH Taylor

Leeds Castle (1928)
Pay and play
Leeds Castle, Hollingbourne, Maidstone ME17 1PL
Tel (01622) 880467/765400
Fax (01622) 735616
Sec Mrs A Knowlden
Pro None
Holes 9 L 2880 yds Par 33
Recs Pro–30 S Purves
V'tors U SOC–WD
Fees 9 holes–£10 (£11)
Loc 10 miles E of Maidstone (A20). M20 Junction 8, 1 mile
Mis 6-day advance booking
Arch Neil Coles

For list of abbreviations see page 527

Littlestone (1888)
St Andrews Road, Littlestone,
New Romney TN28 8RB
Tel (01797) 362310
Fax (01797) 362740
Email Info@littlestonegolfclub.co.uk
www.littlestonegolfclub.co.uk
Mem 550
Sec Col C Moorhouse
(01797) 363355
Pro S Watkins (01797) 362231
Holes 18 L 6470 yds SSS 72
Recs Am–67 G Godmon (1984),
S Wood (1988), A Stracey
(1995) Pro–65 P Eales,
D Clark, R Green, (1993)
V'tors WD–H WE–by arrangement
SOC
Fees £33 (£45)
Loc 2 miles E of New Romney.
15 miles SE of Ashford
Arch W Laidlaw Purves/
Dr A Mackenzie

The London Golf Club
(1993)
South Ash Manor Estate, Ash,
Sevenoaks TN15 7EN
Tel (01474) 879899
Fax (01474) 879912
Mem 400
Sec J Paulin
Pro G Ryan
Holes Heritage 18 L 7208 yds Par
72 SSS 74; International 18 L
7005 yds Par 72 SSS 74
Recs Heritage Am–68 S Wakefield
(1996) Pro–68 J Nicklaus
(1994)
International Am–71 J Bush
(1996) Pro–66 P Mitchell
(1995)
V'tors M
Fees N/A
Loc Off A20, nr Brands Hatch at
West Kingsdown
Arch Nicklaus/Kirby

Lullingstone Park (1967)
Public
Parkgate Road, Chelsfield, Orpington
BR6 7PX
Tel (01959) 533793
Pro M Watt
Holes 18 L 6779 yds SSS 72
9 L 2445 yds Par 33
Recs Am–71
Pro–69
V'tors U
Fees On application
Loc Off Orpington by-pass
(A224) towards Well Hill.
M25 Junction 4
Mis Driving range. 9 hole
pitch & putt

Lydd
Pay and play
Romney Road, Lydd, Romney Marsh
TN29 9LS
Tel (01797) 320808
Fax (01797) 321482

Email info@lyddgolfclub.co.uk
www.lyddgolfclub.co.uk
Mem 400
Sec BM Evans (Sec/Mgr)
Pro AJ Jones (01797) 321201
Holes 18 L 6517 yds Par 71 SSS 71
Driving range
Recs Am–68 M Cozens (1995)
V'tors U SOC
Fees £15 (£20)
Loc 15 miles SE of Ashford, by
Lydd Airport (B2075). M20
Junction 10
Arch M Smith

Mid Kent (1909)
Singlewell Road, Gravesend DA11 7RB
Tel (01474) 568035
Fax (01474) 564218
Mem 1050
Sec AK McCririck
Pro M Foreman (01474) 332810
Holes 18 L 6218 yds SSS 70
Recs Am–64 S Barker (1995)
Pro–60 K McDonald (1993)
V'tors WD–H WE–M
Fees On application
Loc SE of Gravesend, nr A2
Arch Frank Pennink

Moatlands (1993)
Watermans Lane, Brenchley, Tonbridge
TN12 6ND
Tel (01892) 724400
Fax (01892) 723300
Mem 600
Sec K Wiley
Pro S Wood (01892) 724252
Holes 18 L 7060 yds Par 72 SSS 74
Recs Pro–63 H Stott (1998)
V'tors WD–U H WE–H NA before
noon SOC–WD exc Wed
Fees £29 (£39)
Loc Between Matfield and
Paddock Wood, off B2160
Mis Driving range
Arch T Saito

Nizels (1992)
Nizels Lane, Hildenborough, Tonbridge
TN11 8NX
Tel (01732) 833138
Fax (01732) 833764
Mem 700
Sec A Gemmil
Pro Mrs S Hodge (01732) 838926
Holes 18 L 6408 yds SSS 71
Recs Am–67 R Edwards
V'tors WD–U SOC
Fees £25 D–£35
Loc 4 miles from M25 on B245.
A21 Tonbridge North
Junction
Arch Lennan/Purnell

North Foreland (1903)
Convent Road, Broadstairs, Thanet
CT10 3PU
Tel (01843) 862140
Fax (01843) 862663
Mem 800
Sec BJ Preston

Pro N Hansen (01843) 604471
Holes 18 L 6430 yds SSS 71
18 hole Par 3 course
Recs Am–66 P Walton, A Sheppard
Pro–65 M Lawrence
V'tors WD–H WE–NA am –H pm
Fees £27.50 (£37.50)
Loc B2052, 1½ miles N of
Broadstairs
Arch Fowler/Simpson

Oastpark (1992)
Malling Road, Snodland ME6 5LG
Tel (01634) 242661
Fax (01634) 240744
Mem 300
Sec Anne Green (01634) 242818
Pro D Moreland (01634) 242661
Holes 18 L 6173 yds Par 69 SSS 69
Recs Am–71 D Porthouse (1993)
V'tors U SOC
Fees £10 (£14)
Loc 1 mile E of M20 Junction 4
Mis Driving range

Poult Wood (1974)
Public
Higham Lane, Tonbridge TN11 9QR
Tel (01732) 364039 (Bookings),
(01732) 366180 (Clubhouse)
Mem 520
Sec S Taylor
Pro C Miller
Holes 18 L 5569 yds SSS 67
9 hole course
Recs Am–64 J McIlveney
V'tors U–booking required SOC–WD
Fees £8.60 (£13.20)
Loc 1 mile N of Tonbridge,
off A227
Arch Hawtree

Prince's (1904)
Sandwich Bay, Sandwich CT13 9QB
Tel (01304) 611118
Fax (01304) 612000
Mem 250
Sec WM Howie (Mgr)
Pro D Barbour (01304) 613797
Holes 27 hole course (3 x 9 holes):
Dunes/Himalayas/Shore
Length 6506-6690 yds
Par 71-72 SSS 71-72
Recs Himalayas/Shore
Am–67M Goodwin
Pro–69 M Mannelli
Dunes/Himalayas
Am–69 S Wood
Pro–65 C Hancock
Shore/Dunes Pro–65 J Higgins
V'tors U SOC
Fees £42 D–£50 Sat–£47 D–£55
Sun–£50 D–£55
Loc Sandwich Bay (A256)
Mis Driving range
Arch Morrison/Campbell

Redlibbets
Fawkham, Longfield, Kent DA3 8LY
Tel (01474) 879190
Fax (01474) 879290
Mem 600

For list of abbreviations see page 527

Kent 583

Sec J Potter
Pro R Taylor (01474) 872278
Holes 18 L 6651 yds Par 72
Recs Am–72 A Duffin (1998)
Pro–64 W Westner (1997)
V'tors U SOC
Fees £25
Loc Off A20 between Fawkham and Ash. M20 Junction 2. M25 Junction 3
Arch Jonathan Gaunt

The Ridge (1993)
Chartway Street, East Sutton, Maidstone ME17 3DL
Tel (01622) 844872
Fax (01622) 844168
Mem 650
Sec G Sones
Pro M Rackham (01622) 844243
Holes 18 L 6254 yds SSS 70
V'tors WD–H SOC–Tues & Thurs WE–NA
Fees £18
Loc 3 miles E of Maidstone, off A274. M20 Junction 8
Mis Driving range
Arch Patrick Dawson

Rochester & Cobham Park (1891)
Park Pale, by Rochester ME2 3UL
Tel (01474) 823411
Fax (01474) 824446
Mem 720
Sec Maj JW Irvine (Mgr)
Pro J Blair (01474) 823658
Holes 18 L 6596 yds SSS 71
Recs Am–68 L Brookwell (1998)
Pro–68 P Mitchell (1997)
V'tors WD–U H WE–M before 5pm SOC–Tues & Thurs
Fees £30
Loc 3 miles E of Gravesend exit (A2)
Mis Driving range
Arch D Steel

Romney Warren (1993)
Pay and play
St Andrews Road, Littlestone, New Romney TN28 8RB
Tel (01797) 362231
Fax (01797) 362740
Email am@romneywarrengolfclub.co.uk
www.romneywarrengolfclub.co.uk
Mem 250
Sec E Purkiss (Hon)
Pro S Watkins
Holes 18 L 5126 yds SSS 65
Recs Am–69 C Moorhouse, D Mills
V'tors U SOC
Fees £12 (£17)
Loc 2 miles E of New Romney. 15 miles SE of Ashford
Arch Evans/Lewis

Royal Blackheath (1608)
Court Road, Eltham, London SE9 5AF
Tel (0181) 850 1795
Fax (0181) 859 0150
Mem 700
Sec AG Dunlop
Pro I McGregor (0181) 850 1763
Holes 18 L 6219 yds SSS 70
Recs Am–67 M Leather (1998)
Pro–66 M Lawrence, B Cameron (1993)
V'tors WD–I or H WE/BH–M SOC
Fees £30
Loc 5 miles W of M25 Junction 3
Mis Golf Museum
Arch James Braid

Royal Cinque Ports (1892)
Golf Road, Deal CT14 6RF
Tel (01304) 374007 (Office), (01304) 374328 (Clubhouse)
Fax (01304) 379530
Mem 1000+
Sec CC Hammond (01304) 367856
Pro A Reynolds (01304) 374170
Holes 18 L 6482 yds SSS 71
Recs Am–65 MF Bonallack (1964)
Pro–63 GD Manson (1981)
V'tors WD–I H
Fees On application
Loc A258, N of Deal
Mis Driving range

Royal St George's (1887)
Sandwich CT13 9PB
Tel (01304) 613090
Fax (01304) 611245
Mem 675
Sec GE Watts
Pro A Brooks (01304) 615236
Holes 18 L 6565 yds Par 70 SSS 72
Recs Am–67 H Berwick (1954), JR Harris (1995), M Brooks (1996)
Pro–63 N Faldo, P Stewart (1993)
V'tors WD–I H WE–M SOC–WD
Fees £65 D–£90
Loc 1 mile E of Sandwich
Arch Dr Laidlaw Purves

Ruxley Park (1975)
Pay and play
Sandy Lane, St Paul's Cray, Orpington BR5 3HY
Tel (01689) 871490
Fax (01689) 891428
Mem 500
Sec J Scappatura
Pro A Langoon
Holes 18 L 6027 yds SSS 69
9 hole Par 3 course
V'tors U
Fees £11 (£18)
Loc Off A20 Ruxley roundabout at Sidcup
Mis Floodlit driving range

St Augustines (1907)
Cottington Road, Cliffsend, Ramsgate CT12 5JN
Tel (01843) 590333
Fax (01843) 590444
Mem 650 55(J)
Sec LP Dyke
Pro DB Scott (01843) 590222
Holes 18 L 5197 yds SS 65
Recs Am–64 AD Setterfield
Pro–61 P Mitchell
V'tors H SOC–WD
Fees £21.50 (£23.50)
Loc 2 miles SW of Ramsgate from A253 or A256. Signs to St Augustines Cross
Arch Tom Vardon

Sene Valley (1888)
Sene, Folkestone CT18 8BL
Tel (01303) 268513
Fax (01303) 237513
Mem 650
Sec RW Leaver
Pro N Watson (01303) 268514
Holes 18 L 6215 yds SSS 70
Recs Am–65 J Hamilton
Pro–67 P Moger
V'tors H SOC
Fees £20 (£30)
Loc 2 miles N of Hythe on B2065
Arch Henry Cotton

Sheerness (1906)
Power Station Road, Sheerness ME12 3AE
Tel (01795) 662585
Fax (01795) 666840
Mem 700
Sec AF Jones
Pro D Hawkins (01795) 666840
Holes 18 L 6460 yds SSS 71
Recs Am–66 R Whitington (1996)
V'tors WD–U SOC–Tues–Thurs
Fees £15
Loc 9 miles N of Sittingbourne. M20, M2 or A2 to A249

Shooter's Hill (1903)
Lowood, Eaglesfield Road, London SE18 3DA
Tel (0181) 854 1216
Fax (0181) 854 0469
Mem 310 60(L) 31(J)
Sec S Watt (0181) 854 6368
Pro M Ridge (0181) 854 0073
Holes 18 L 5721 yds SSS 68
Recs Am–63 M Holland (1984)
Pro–62 M Parker (1990)
V'tors WD–I WE/BH–M SOC–Tues & Thurs only
Fees £22 D–£27
Loc Off A207 nr Blackheath

Shortlands (1894)
Meadow Road, Shortlands, Bromley BR2 0PB
Tel (0181) 460 2471
Fax (0181) 460 8828
Mem 525
Sec PW Smeeth (0181) 460 8828

For list of abbreviations see page 527

Pro J Murray (0181) 464 6182
Holes 9 L 5261 yds SSS 66
Recs Am–59 T Coulstock (1990)
Pro–59 N Haynes (1995)
V'tors M
Fees £10
Loc Ravensbourne Ave, Shortlands

Sidcup (1891)
7 Hurst Road, Sidcup DA15 9AE
Tel (0181) 300 2864
Mem 400
Sec K Rawlins (0181) 300 2150
Pro N Willis (0181) 309 0679
Holes 9 L 5722 yds SSS 68
Recs Am–65 M Bennett
Pro–64 D Webb
V'tors WD–H WE/BH–M SOC–WD
Fees £14
Loc On A222. A2/A20, 2 miles

Sittingbourne & Milton Regis (1929)
Wormdale, Newington, Sittingbourne ME9 7PX
Tel (01795) 842261
Fax (01795) 844117
Mem 525 100(L) 50(J)
Sec HDG Wylie
Pro JR Hearn (01795) 842775
Holes 18 L 6291 yds SSS 70
Recs Am–63 PA Stuart (1997)
V'tors WD–H Sat–NA Sun–M
SOC–Tues & Thurs
Fees £20
Loc 1 mile N of M2 Junction 5

Sundridge Park (1901)
Garden Road, Bromley BR1 3NE
Tel (0181) 460 1822
Fax (0181) 289 3050
Mem 1200
Sec R Burden (0181) 460 0278
Pro B Cameron (0181) 460 5540
Holes East 18 L 6538 yds SSS 71
West 18 L 6019 yds SSS 69
Recs East Am–66 J MacNamara (1995)
Pro–63 R Cameron
West Am–64 R Hurd (1993)
Pro–65 R Fidler
V'tors H SOC–WD
Fees £40
Loc 1 mile N of Bromley, by Sundridge Park Station. M25 Junctions 3/4

Tenterden (1905)
Woodchurch Road, Tenterden TN30 7DR
Tel (01580) 763937
Fax (01580) 763937
Mem 650
Sec JM Wilson
Pro A Scullion (01580) 762409
Holes 18 L 6050 yds Par 70 SSS 69
Recs Am–63 R Frape (1998)
Pro–65 R Cameron (1991)
V'tors WD–U WE/BH–M Sun–NA before noon

Fees On application
Loc 1 mile E of Tenterden on B2067

Tudor Park Hotel (1988)
Ashford Road, Bearsted, Maidstone ME14 4NQ
Tel (01622) 734334
Fax (01622) 735360
Mem 750
Sec J Ladbrook
Pro N McNally (01622) 739412
Holes 18 L 6041yds SSS 69
Recs Am–64 D Jessop (1992)
Pro–65 N Haynes (1993)
V'tors H SOC
Fees £25 (£30)
Loc 3 miles E of Maidstone on A20. M20 Junction 8
Arch Donald Steel

Tunbridge Wells (1889)
Langton Road, Tunbridge Wells TN4 8XH
Tel (01892) 523034
Mem 340 98(L) 20(J)
Sec RF Mealing (01892) 536918
Pro M Barton (01892) 541386
Holes 9 L 4725 yds SSS 62
Recs Am–59 EC Chapman
Pro–59 J Humphrey
V'tors U H SOC
Fees £15 D–£20
Loc Tunbridge Wells, next to Spa Hotel

Upchurch River Valley (1991)
Pay and play
Oak Lane, Upchurch, Sittingbourne ME9 7AY
Tel (01634) 360626
Fax (01634) 387784
Mem 550
Sec AJ New (01634) 260594
Pro R Cornwell (01634) 379592
Holes 18 L 6237 yds SSS 70
9 hole Par 3 course
V'tors U SOC–WD
Fees 18 hole:£10.95 (£13.95)
9 hole:£6.75 (£8.45)
Loc 3 miles NE of Rainham, off A2. M2 Junction 4
Mis Floodlit driving range
Arch David Smart

Walmer & Kingsdown (1909)
The Leas, Kingsdown, Deal CT14 8EP
Tel (01304) 373256
Fax (01304) 363017
Mem 627
Sec JP Morgan
Pro M Paget (01304) 363017
Holes 18 L 6437 yds SSS 71
Recs Am–66 P Wilson (1995)
Pro–70 M Lee
V'tors WD–H WE–after noon SOC
Fees D–£28 (£30)
Loc 2½ miles S of Deal on clifftop
Arch James Braid

Weald of Kent (1992)
Pay and play
Maidstone Road, Headcorn TN27 9PT
Tel (01622) 890866
Fax (01622) 891793
Mem 1000
Sec D Etheridge (Mgr)
Holes 18 L 6169 yds SSS 69
V'tors U–booking 3 days in advance SOC
Fees £14.50 (£18.50)
Loc 5 miles S of Maidstone on A274. M20 Junction 8
Arch John Millen

West Kent (1916)
West Hill, Downe, Orpington BR6 7JJ
Tel (01689) 851323
Fax (01689) 858693
Mem 750
Sec N Stone
Pro RS Fidler (01689) 856863
Holes 18 L 6399 yds SSS 70
Recs Am–62 DC Smith (1984)
Pro–65 H Baiocchi (1985)
V'tors WD–H or I–phone to arrange WE/BH–M
Fees On application
Loc 5 miles S of Orpington

West Malling (1974)
Addington, Maidstone ME19 5AR
Tel (01732) 844785
Fax (01732) 844795
Mem 900
Sec MR Ellis
Pro D Lambert
Holes Spitfire 18 L 6142 yds Par 70
Hurricane 18 L 6240 yds Par 70
Recs Spitfire Am–67 S Pigott
Pro–67 H Baiocchi
Hurricane Am–69 S Pigott
V'tors WD–U WE–U H after noon
Fees £20 (£30)
Loc 12 miles W of Maidstone (A20)

Westerham
Valence Park, Brasted Road, Westerham TN16 1LJ
Tel (01959) 563700
Fax (01959) 563787
Mem 800
Pro E Campbell
Holes 18 L 6300 yds Par 72
V'tors WD–U
Fees On application
Loc E of Westerham (A25)
Arch David Williams

Westgate & Birchington (1893)
176, Canterbury Road, Westgate-on-Sea CT8 8LT
Tel (01843) 831115/833905
Mem 325
Sec JM Wood
Pro R Game

Holes 18 L 4889 yds SSS 64
Recs Pro–60 J Hickman
  Ladies–60 M Morgan
V'tors H or I WD–NA before 10am
  WE–NA before 11am SOC
Fees £13 (£15)
Loc 1 mile W of Westgate (A28)

Whitstable & Seasalter
(1910)
*Collingwood Road, Whitstable
CT5 1EB*
Tel **(01227) 272020**
Mem 300
Sec DB Christie
Holes 9 L 5357 yds SSS 63
V'tors WD–U WE–M
Fees On application
Loc 1 mile W of Whitstable

Wildernesse (1890)
Seal, Sevenoaks TN15 0JE
Tel **(01732) 761526**
Mem 700
Sec RA Foster (01732) 761199
Pro CA Walker (01732) 761527
Holes 18 L 6453 yds SSS 72
Recs Am–64 AD Tillman (1991)
  Pro–65 I Grant (1980)
V'tors WD–I H
  SOC–Mon/Thurs/Fri
Fees £32 D–£47
Loc 2 miles E of Sevenoaks (A25).
  M25 Junction 5

Woodlands Manor
(1928)
*Woodlands, Tinkerpot Lane, Sevenoaks
TN15 6AB*
Tel **(01959) 523805**
Mem 650
Sec EF Newman
  (01959) 523806
Pro A Brooks (01959) 524161
Holes 18 L 6000 yds SSS 68
Recs Am–65 N Sherman
  Pro–65 N Coles
V'tors WD–U WE–H NA before
  noon SOC–WD
Fees On application
Loc 4 miles S of M25 Junction 3.
  Off A20 between West
  Kingsdown and Otford
Arch Coles/Lyons

Wrotham Heath (1906)
*Seven Mile Lane Comp, Sevenoaks
TN15 8QZ*
Tel **(01732) 884800**
Mem 424 75(L) 50(J)
Sec LJ Byrne
Pro H Dearden (01732) 883854
Holes 18 L 5954 yds SSS 69
V'tors WD–H WE/BH–M
  SOC–Thurs & Fri
Fees £25 D–£35
Loc 8 miles W of Maidstone on
  B2016. M26/A20 Junction,
  1 mile
Arch Donald Steel

Lancashire

Accrington & District
(1893)
*West End, Oswaldtwistle, Accrington
BB5 4LS*
Tel **(01254) 232734**
Mem 350
Sec JE Pilkington
  (01254) 235070
Pro W Harling (01254) 231091
Holes 18 L 6044 yds SSS 69
Recs Am–64 J Rothwell
V'tors WD/WE–U SOC
Fees On application
Loc 3 miles SW of Accrington

Ashton & Lea (1913)
*Tudor Ave, Blackpool Rd, Lea,
Preston PR4 0XA*
Tel **(01772) 726480**
Fax **(01772) 735762**
Mem 750
Sec T Ashton
  (01772) 735282
Pro M Greenough
  (01772) 720374
Holes 18 L 6370 yds SSS 70
Recs Am–65 K Wallbank (1989)
  Pro–66 J Hawksworth (1988),
  S Townend (1992)
  Ladies–72 L Fairclough (1985)
V'tors U SOC
Fees £22 (£25)
Loc 3 miles W of Preston,
  off A5085. Nr M6, M55 and
  M65
Arch J Steer

Ashton-in-Makerfield
(1902)
*Garswood Park, Liverpool Road,
Ashton-in-Makerfield WN4 0YT*
Tel **(01942) 727267**
Mem 500
Sec JR Hay (01942) 719330
Pro P Allan (01942) 724229
Holes 18 L 6212 yds SSS 70
Recs Am–68 GS Lacy
V'tors WD–U exc Wed WE/BH–M
  SOC
Fees £25
Loc 1 mile W of Ashton-in-
  Makerfield on A58. M6
  Junction 23/24

Ashton-under-Lyne
(1913)
*Gorsey Way, Hurst, Ashton-under-Lyne
OL6 9HT*
Tel **(0161) 330 1537**
Fax **(0161) 330 1537**
Mem 600
Sec D McGee (0161) 339 5394
Pro C Boyle (0161) 308 2095
Holes 18 L 6209 yds SSS 70
Recs Am–67 S Hamer (1992)
V'tors WD–U WE/BH–M SOC
Fees £25
Loc 8 miles E of Manchester

Bacup (1912)
*Maden Road, Bankside Lane, Bacup
OL13 8HN*
Tel **(01706) 873170**
Fax **(01706) 867726**
Mem 396
Sec T Leyland (01706) 879644
Holes 9 L 6008 yds SSS 69
Recs Am–67 M Butcher
V'tors U
Fees On application
Loc Bankside Lane

Baxenden & District
(1913)
*Top o' th' Meadow, Baxenden,
Accrington BB5 2EA*
Tel **(01254) 234555**
Mem 400
Sec N Turner (01706) 225423
Holes 9 L 5702 yds SSS 68
Recs Am–67 N Turner
  Pro–66 C Tobin
V'tors WD–U WE/BH–M
Fees £15
Loc 2 miles SE of Accrington

Beacon Park (1982)
Public
*Beacon Lane, Dalton, Up Holland
WN8 7RU*
Tel **(01695) 627500**
Mem 250
Sec T Harris
Pro R Peters (01695) 622700
Holes 18 L 5927 yds SSS 69
Recs Am–68 D Parkin, I Donaldson
V'tors U–book 6 days in advance
  SOC
Fees On application
Loc Nr Ashurst Beacon and
  M58/M6 Junction 26
Mis Driving range

Blackburn (1894)
Beardwood Brow, Blackburn BB2 7AX
Tel **(01254) 51122**
Fax **(01254) 665578**
Mem 440 90(L) 60(J)
Sec PD Haydock
Pro A Rodwell (01254) 55942
Holes 18 L 6144 yds SSS 70
Recs Am–63 JS Reed (1991)
  Pro–66 M Foster
  Ladies–68 CD Blackshaw
  (1994)
V'tors U SOC–WD
  WE/BH–restricted
Fees £24 (£28)
Loc 1 mile NW of Blackburn
  (A677). M6 Junction 31

Blackpool North Shore
(1904)
Devonshire Road, Blackpool FY2 0RD
Tel **(01253) 351017**
Fax **(01253) 591240**
Mem 980
Sec JM Ogden (01253) 352054
Pro B Ward (01253) 354640

For list of abbreviations see page 527

586 Lancashire

Holes 18 L 6443 yds SSS 71
Recs Am–66 K Wallbank (1995)
Pro–63 C O'Connor
V'tors WD–U WE–restricted SOC
Fees £27.50 (£32.50)
Loc ½ mile E of Queens Promenade (B5124)

Blackpool Park (1925)
Public
North Park Drive, Blackpool FY3 8LS
Tel (01253) 397910
Fax (01253) 397910
Mem 700
Sec D Stones (01253) 397916
Pro B Purdie (01253) 391004
Holes 18 L 6192 yds SSS 69
Recs Am–67 PCooper (1983), D O'Connell (1992)
Pro–68 D Lewis
V'tors U–no telephone booking
Fees £10.50 (£12.50)
Loc 2 miles E of Blackpool, signposted off M55
Mis Tee reservations:Blackpool Borough Council, Town Hall, Talbot Square, Blackpool
Arch Dr A Mackenzie

Bolton (1891)
Lostock Park, Bolton BL6 4AJ
Tel (01204) 843278
Fax (01204) 843067
Mem 600
Sec Mrs HM Stuart (01204) 843067
Pro R Longworth (01204) 843073
Holes 18 L 6237 yds Par 70 SSS 70
Recs Am–66 JB Hope, DE Roocroft, G Boardman
Pro–64 J Wright
V'tors U SOC
Fees £30 D–£36 (£33 D–£40)
Loc 3 miles W of Bolton. M61 Junction 6, 2 miles

Bolton Old Links (1891)
Chorley Old Road, Montserrat, Bolton BL1 5SU
Tel (01204) 840050
Fax (01204) 842307
Mem 600
Sec AW Turner (01204) 842307
Pro P Horridge (01204) 843089
Holes 18 L 6406 yds SSS 72
Recs Am–64 S Kelly (1994)
Pro–64 J Cheetham (1990)
V'tors U H exc comp Sats SOC
Fees £27 (£35)
Loc 3 miles NW of Bolton on B6226
Arch Dr A Mackenzie

Bolton Open Golf
Pay and play
Longsight Park, Longsight Lane, Harwood BL2 4JX
Tel (01204) 597659/309778
Mem 250
Pro CR Loydall (Golf Dir)
Holes 9 hole course

Recs Am–64 S Walsh
V'tors WD–U WE–booking necessary SOC
Fees £6.50 (£8.50)
Loc 3 miles NE of Bolton (A666)
Mis Driving range

Brackley Municipal (1977)
Public
Bullows Road, Little Hulton, Worsley M38 9TR
Tel (0161) 790 6076
Pro S Lomax (Mgr)
Holes 9 L 3003 yds SSS 69
V'tors U
Fees On application
Loc 2 miles NW of Walkden, off A6

Breightmet (1911)
Red Bridge, Ainsworth, Bolton BL2 5PA
Tel (01204) 527381
Mem 200
Sec SP Griffiths
Holes 9 L 6416 yds SSS 71
Recs Am–71 M Durham (1992)
Pro–68 P Alliss (1971)
V'tors WD–H WE–NA SOC–WD
Fees £15 (£18)
Loc 3 miles E of Bolton

Brookdale (1896)
Medlock Road, Woodhouses, Failsworth M35 9WQ
Tel (0161) 681 4534
Fax (0161) 681 4534
Mem 650
Sec W Hilton
Pro T Cupello (0161) 681 2655
Holes 18 L 5841 yds SSS 68
Recs Am–65 G Lever, J Spicer
V'tors WD–U SOC–WD
Fees £20
Loc 5 miles NE of Manchester

Burnley (1905)
Glen View, Burnley BB11 3RW
Tel (01282) 421045
Mem 742
Sec GJ Butterfield (01282) 451281
Pro WP Tye (01282) 455266
Holes 18 L 5911 yds SSS 69
Recs Am–64 GD Haworth
Pro–66 JS Steer
V'tors U SOC
Fees £20 (£25)
Loc Via Manchester Road to Glen View Road

Bury (1890)
Unsworth Hall, Blackford Bridge, Bury BL9 9TJ
Tel (0161) 766 4897
Fax (0161) 796 3480
Mem 750
Sec R Adams
Pro S Crake (0161) 766 2213
Holes 18 L 5927 yds SSS 68

Recs Am–64 PD Hilton
Pro–64 PWT Evans
V'tors H SOC
Fees £26 (£30)
Loc A56, 5 miles N of Manchester. 3 miles N of M62 Junction 17

Castle Hawk (1975)
Chadwick Lane, Castleton, Rochdale OL11 3BY
Tel (01706) 640841
Fax (01706) 860587
Mem 200
Sec J Accleton
Pro M Vipond
Holes 18 L 5398 yds SSS 68
9 L 3158 yds SSS 55
Recs Am–68 S Tyrell
Pro–66 M Vipond
V'tors U SOC
Fees WD/Sat D–£8 Sun D–£10
Loc Castleton Station 1 mile. M62 Junction 20

Chorley (1897)
Hall o' th' Hill, Heath Charnock, Chorley PR6 9HX
Tel (01257) 480263
Fax (01257) 480722
Mem 550
Sec Mrs A Allen
Pro GP Mutch (01257) 481245
Holes 18 L 6240 yds SSS 70
Recs Am–64 WG Bromilow
Pro–65 RN Giles
V'tors WD–I or H WE–NA SOC
Fees On application
Loc 1 mile S of Chorley at junction A6/A673
Arch JA Steer

Clitheroe (1891)
Whalley Road, Clitheroe BB7 1PP
Tel (01200) 422618 (Clubhouse)
Fax (01200) 422292
Mem 700
Sec G Roberts JP (01200) 422292
Pro J Twissell (01200) 424242
Holes 18 L 6326 yds SSS 71
Recs Am–66 P Dwyer
V'tors WD–U H SOC
Fees £33 (£39)
Loc 2 miles S of Clitheroe
Mis Range
Arch James Braid

Colne (1901)
Law Farm, Skipton Old Road, Colne BB8 7EB
Tel (01282) 863391
Mem 328
Sec JT Duerden (Hon)
Pro None
Holes 9 L 5961 yds SSS 69
Recs Am–63 M Brooks
Ladies–66 M Birtwistle
V'tors U exc comp days SOC–WD
Fees £15 (£20)
Loc 1½ miles N of Colne. From end of M65, signs to Keighley and then Lothersdale

For list of abbreviations see page 527

Crompton & Royton (1913)
High Barn, Royton, Oldham
OL2 6RW
Tel (0161) 624 2154
Fax (0161) 624 0986
Mem 620
Sec DG Taylor (0161) 624 0986
G Smith (Mgr)
Pro DA Melling
Holes 18 L 6222 yds SSS 70
Recs Am–65 JA Osbaldeston
Pro–65 D Durnian
V'tors U SOC–WD
Fees £20 (£30)
Loc 3 miles NW of Oldham

Darwen (1893)
Winter Hill, Darwen BB3 0LB
Tel (01254) 701267
Mem 375 70(L) 60(J)
Sec J Kenyon (01254) 704367
Pro W Lennon (01254) 776370
Holes 18 L 5863 yds SSS 68
Recs Am–63 J Grimshaw (1994),
A Durkin (1997)
Pro–65
V'tors U exc Tues & Sat–NA
Fees £20 (£25)
Loc Darwen 1½ miles

Dean Wood (1922)
Lafford Lane, Up Holland, Skelmersdale
WN8 0QZ
Tel (01695) 622219
Fax (01695) 622245
Mem 750
Sec A McGregor
Pro AB Coop
Holes 18 L 6137 yds SSS 70
Recs Am–66 J Dawber (1973),
B Giblin (1992)
V'tors WD–U WE/BH–M SOC
Fees £27 (£30)
Loc 4 miles W of Wigan (A577)
Arch James Braid

Deane (1906)
Off Junction Road, Deane, Bolton
BL3 4NS
Tel (01204) 61944
Mem 490
Sec P Flaxman (01204) 651808
Pro D Martindale
Holes 18 L 5652 yds SSS 67
Recs Am–63 S Simpson
V'tors WD–U WE–restricted
SOC–Tues/Thurs/Fri
Fees £20 (£25)
Loc 2 miles W of Bolton. M61
Junction 5, 1 mile

Dunscar (1908)
Longworth Lane, Bromley Cross, Bolton
BL7 9QY
Tel (01204) 598228
Mem 600
Sec JW Jennings (01204) 303321
Pro G Treadgold (01204) 592992
Holes 18 L 6085 yds Par 71 SSS 69

Recs Am–65 GJW Hastie (1995)
Pro–66 W Slater
V'tors WD–U WE–restricted SOC
Fees £20 (£30)
Loc 3 miles N of Bolton, off A666

Duxbury Park (1975)
Public
Duxbury Hall Road, Duxbury Park,
Chorley PR7 4AS
Tel (01257) 265380
Fax (01257) 241378
Sec R Blease
Pro D Clarke
Holes 18 L 6270 yds SSS 67
Recs Am–69 D Arstall
Pro–66 J Anglada
V'tors U
Fees £6.25 (£8.50)
Loc 1½ miles S of Chorley, off
Wigan Lane

Fairhaven (1895)
Lytham Hall Park, Ansdell, Lytham St
Annes FY8 4JU
Tel (01253) 736741
Fax (01253) 731461
Mem 900
Sec H Fielding
Pro (01253) 736976
Holes 18 L 6883 yds SSS 73
Recs Am–65 SG Birtwell (1967)
Pro–64 J Leonard (1996)
V'tors WD–U WE–NA before 9am
SOC–WD
Fees £33 (£40)
Loc Lytham 2 miles. St Annes 2
miles. M55 Junction 4

Fishwick Hall (1912)
Glenluce Drive, Farringdon Park,
Preston PR1 5TD
Tel (01772) 798300
Fax (01772) 704600
Mem 750
Sec RR Gearing
Pro M Hadfield (01772) 795870
Holes 18 L 6045 yds SSS 69
Recs Am–67 I Lyon (1998)
V'tors Apply to Sec SOC
Fees £24 (£29)
Loc 1 mile E of Preston, nr
junction of A59 and M6
Junction 31

Fleetwood (1932)
Golf House, Princes Way, Fleetwood
FY7 8AF
Tel (01253) 873114 (Clubhouse)
Fax (01253) 773573
Mem 548
Sec R Yates (01253) 773573
Pro S McLaughlin
(01253) 873661
Holes L 18 L 6308 yds SSS 70
Recs Am–67 D Johnson (1994)
Pro–70 S Bennett
V'tors U H exc Tues SOC
Fees £24 (£30)
Loc 1 mile W of Fleetwood
Arch A Steer

Gathurst (1913)
Miles Lane, Shevington, Wigan
WN6 8EW
Tel (01257) 252861 (Clubhouse)
Mem 675
Sec Mrs I Fyffe
(01257) 255235
Pro Shop (01257) 254909
Holes 18 L 6089 yds Par 70 SSS 69
Recs Am–65 S Ainscough
V'tors WD–U before 5pm
WE/BH/Wed–M SOC–WD
Fees £24
Loc 4 miles W of Wigan. 1 mile S
of M6 Junction 27
Arch N Pearson-ADAS

Ghyll (1907)
Ghyll Brow, Barnoldswick, Colne
BB18 6JH
Tel (01282) 842466
Mem 310
Sec JL Gill (01756) 798592
Holes 9 L 5708 yds SSS 68
Recs Am–64 M Boardman (1989)
V'tors U exc Sun–NA
Fees £14 (£18)
Loc 7 miles N of Colne, off A56

Great Harwood (1896)
Harwood Bar, Great Harwood
BB6 7TE
Tel (01254) 884391
Mem 175 60(L) 45(J)
Sec A Garraway
(01254) 886802
Holes 9 L 6413 yds SSS 71
Recs Am–68 J Aspinall
Pro–64 AH Padgham
V'tors U SOC
Fees £13 (£16)
Loc 5 miles NE of Blackburn

Green Haworth (1914)
Green Haworth, Accrington
BB5 3SL
Tel (01254) 237580
Fax (01254) 396176
Mem 225
Sec K Lynch
Holes 9 L 5556 yds SSS 67
Recs Am–66 D Chamberlain
(1996)
V'tors WD–U exc Wed–Ladies only
after 5pm WE/BH–M SOC
Fees On application
Loc Willows Lane

Greenmount (1920)
Greenmount, Bury BL8 4LH
Tel (01204) 883712
Mem 220
Sec J Robinson
Pro J Seed
Holes 9 L 5230 yds SSS 66
Recs Am–63 P Hambleton (1997)
V'tors WD–U exc Tues WE–M
Fees £15
Loc 3 miles N of Bury

For list of abbreviations see page 527

Haigh Hall (1972)
Public
Haigh Hall Country Park, Haigh, Wigan WN2 1PE
Tel (01942) 833337 (Clubhouse)
Fax (01942) 831417 (Pro)
Mem 300
Sec W Fleetwood
Pro I Lee (01942) 831107
Holes 18 L 6423 yds SSS 71
Recs Am–65 G Lacy (1992)
Pro–66 K Waters (1988)
V'tors U
Fees £7 (£9.50)
Loc 2 miles NW of Wigan. M6 Junction 27. M61 Junction 6
Arch Frank Pennink

Harwood (1926)
Springfield, Roading Brook Road, Bolton BL2 4JD
Tel (01204) 522878
Mem 520
Sec D Bamber (01204) 524233
Pro N Dance (01204) 362864
Holes 18 L 5786 yds SSS 69
Recs Am–63 L Irvine
V'tors WD–H WE–M SOC
Fees £20
Loc 4 miles NE of Bolton (B6391)
Arch J Shuttleworth

Heysham (1910)
Trumacar Park, Middleton Road, Heysham, Morecambe LA3 3JH
Tel (01524) 851011
Fax (01524) 853030
Mem 685
Sec FA Bland (Sec/Mgr)
Pro R Dône (01524) 852000
Holes 18 L 6258 yds SSS 70
Recs Am–64 M Murray (1994), DR Hutchinson (1995)
Pro–64 P Walker (1990)
V'tors U H SOC
Fees £19 D–£24 (£29)
Loc 2 miles S of Morecambe. M6 Junction 34, 5 miles
Arch A Herd

Hindley Hall (1905)
Hall Lane, Hindley, Wigan WN2 2SQ
Tel (01942) 525020/523116
Mem 430
Sec GW Gooch (01942) 255131
Pro N Brazell (01942) 255991
Holes 18 L 5913 yds SSS 68
Recs Am–64 NG Hibbs
Pro–65
V'tors U SOC
Fees £20 (£27)
Loc 2 miles S of Wigan. M61 Junction 6

Horwich (1895)
Victoria Road, Horwich BL6 5PH
Tel (01204) 696980
Fax (01942) 205316
Mem 200
Sec C Sherborne
Holes 9 L 5404 yds SSS 67
Recs Am–62 S Southern
V'tors M SOC–WD
Fees £16
Loc 5 miles W of Bolton
Arch George Lowe

Hurlston Hall (1994)
Hurlston Lane, Southport Road, Scarisbrick L40 8JD
Tel (01704) 840400
Fax (01704) 841404
Mem 600
Sec M Atherton
Pro J Esclapez (01704) 841120
Holes 18 L 6746 yds SSS 72
Recs Am–71 J Fisher (1995)
Pro–66 D Shacklady (1996)
V'tors H SOC
Fees £25 (£30)
Loc 2 miles NW of Ormskirk (A570). M58 Junction 3
Mis Floodlit driving range
Arch Donald Steel

Ingol (1981)
Tanterton Hall Road, Ingol, Preston PR2 7BY
Tel (01772) 734556
Mem 700
Sec H Parker
Pro S Laycock
Holes 18 L 5868 yds SSS 68
Recs Am–68
Pro–67
V'tors U SOC–WD
Fees £15 (£25)
Loc 1½ miles NW of Preston (A6). M6 Junction 32

Knott End (1911)
Wyreside, Poulton-le-Fylde FY6 0AA
Tel (01253) 810254 (Clubhouse)
Fax (01253) 810576
Mem 660
Sec A Crossley (01253) 810576
Pro P Walker (01253) 811365
Holes 18 L 5789 yds SSS 68
Recs Am–58 M Davies (1994)
Pro–66 P Harrison (1978)
V'tors WD–U WE/BH–by arrangement SOC–WD
Fees D–£24 (£27)
Loc Over Wyre, 12 miles NE of Blackpool (A588)
Arch James Braid

Lancaster (1932)
Ashton Hall, Ashton-with-Stodday, Lancaster LA2 0AJ
Tel (01524) 752090
Fax (01524) 752742
Mem 530 170(L) 62(J)
Sec KE Butcher (01524) 751247
Pro DE Sutcliffe (01524) 751802
Holes 18 L 6500 yds SSS 71
Recs Am–66 S Andrew
V'tors WD–H SOC–WD
Fees £32
Loc 2 miles S of Lancaster (A588)
Mis Dormy House
Arch James Braid

Lansil (1947)
Caton Road, Lancaster LA4 3PE
Tel (01524) 39269
Mem 450
Sec J Ollerton (01995) 601451
Holes 9 L 5608 yds Par 70 SSS 67
Recs Am–68 DC Whiteway, SM Humpage
V'tors WD–U Sun–U after 1pm
Fees £12 (£12)
Loc A683, 2 miles E of Lancaster

Leyland (1923)
Wigan Road, Leyland PR5 2UD
Tel (01772) 436457
Fax (01772) 436457
Mem 750
Sec J Ross
Pro C Burgess (01772) 423425
Holes 18 L 6123 yds SSS 69
Recs Am–62 J Mann (1991)
Pro–66 T Hastings (1993)
V'tors WD–U WE–M SOC–WD
Fees £25 (1994)
Loc M6 Junction 28, ½ mile

Lobden (1888)
Whitworth, Rochdale OL12 8XJ
Tel (01706) 343228
Fax (01706) 343228
Mem 220
Sec N Danby (01706) 643241
Holes 9 L 5697 yds Par 70 SSS 68
Recs Am–66 C Hardman (1996)
V'tors U
Fees £10 (£15)
Loc 4 miles N of Rochdale

Longridge (1877)
Fell Barn, Jeffrey Hill, Longridge, Preston PR3 2TU
Tel (01772) 783291
Fax (01772) 783022
Mem 700
Sec DC Wensley
Pro S Taylor (01772) 783291
Holes 18 L 5969 yds SSS 69
Recs Am–65 A Taylor (1997)
V'tors U
Fees £15 (£25)
Loc 8 miles NE of Preston, off B6243

Lowes Park (1914)
Hilltop, Lowes Road, Bury BL9 6SU
Tel (0161) 764 1231/763 9503
Fax (0161) 763 9503
Mem 400
Sec J Entwistle
Holes 9 L 6006 yds Par 70 SSS 69
Recs Am–64 M Thornton (1998)
V'tors WD–U exc Wed–NA WE/BH–by arrangement
Fees £17 (£23)
Loc 1 mile NE of Bury, off A56

For list of abbreviations see page 527

Lancashire 589

Lytham Green Drive (1922)
Ballam Road, Lytham FY8 4LE
Tel (01253) 734782
Fax (01253) 731350
Mem 700
Sec R Kershaw (01253) 737390
Pro A Lancaster (01253) 737379
Holes 18 L 6168 yds SSS 69
Recs Am–64 C Rymer (1988)
Pro–64 E Romero (1988)
V'tors WD–U H WE–NA SOC–WD
Fees £25 (£35)

Marland (1928)
Public
Springfield Park, Bolton Road, Rochdale OL11 4RE
Tel (01706) 49801
Fax (01706) 49801
Mem 300
Sec J Wallis
Pro D Wills
Holes 18 L 5237 yds SSS 66
Recs Am–67 C Thornsby (1993)
Pro–67 ME Hill
V'tors WD–U WE–booking necessary
Fees £7 (£8.75)
Loc W of Rochdale (A58). M62 Junctions 19/20, 2 miles

Marsden Park (1969)
Public
Townhouse Road, Nelson BB9 8DG
Tel (01282) 67525
Sec BD Goodwin (01282) 450398
Holes 18 L 5806 yds Par 70 SSS 68
Recs Am–66 A Skelton (1987)
Pro–74 T Gillett
V'tors U SOC
Fees On application
Loc Signposted Walton Lane

Morecambe (1904)
Bare, Morecambe LA4 6AJ
Tel (01524) 418050
Fax (01524) 412841
Mem 1071
Sec Mrs J Atkinson (01524) 412841
Pro S Fletcher (01524) 415596
Holes 18 L 5770 yds SSS 69
Recs Am–64 J Swallow, DP Carney
Pro–63 B Gallacher, P Oosterhuis
V'tors U H SOC
Fees On application
Loc On coast road towards Carnforth (A5105)

Mossock Hall (1996)
Liverpool Road, Bickerstaffe L39 0EE
Tel (01695) 421717
Fax (01695) 424961
Mem 556
Sec K Brain
Pro (01695) 424969
Holes 18 L 6375 yds Par 71 SSS 71
V'tors U exc comp days SOC
Fees £20 (£30)
Loc 4 miles S of Ormskirk
Arch Steve Marnoch

Mytton Fold (1994)
Langho BB6 8AB
Tel (01254) 240662
Fax (01254) 248119
Mem 300
Sec DB Woodburn
Pro G Coope (01254) 240662 Ext 235
Holes 18 L 6217 yds SSS 70
V'tors U SOC
Fees £12 (£15)
Loc 6 miles N of Blackburn, off A59. M6 Junction 31
Arch F Hargreaves

Nelson (1902)
Kings Causeway, Brierfield, Nelson BB9 0EU
Tel (01282) 614583
Fax (01282) 606226
Mem 550
Sec BR Thomason (01282) 611834
Pro N Sumner (01282) 617000
Holes 18 L 5967 yds SSS 69
Recs Am–63 N Nuttley (1995)
Pro–65 H Shoesmith
V'tors WD–U H exc Thurs–NA WE–U exc Sat before 4pm SOC
Fees £25 (£30)
Loc 2 miles N of Burnley

Oldham (1892)
Lees New Road, Oldham OL4 5PN
Tel (0161) 624 4986
Mem 300 45(L) 35(J)
Pro J Peel (0161) 626 8346
Holes 18 L 5045 yds SSS 65
Recs Am–66 D Maloney (1987)
Pro–65 E Smith
V'tors U SOC
Fees On application
Loc Off Oldham-Stalybridge road

Ormskirk (1899)
Cranes Lane, Lathom, Ormskirk L40 5UJ
Tel (01695) 572112
Mem 300
Sec RDJ Lawrence (01695) 572227
Pro J Hammond (01695) 572074
Holes 18 L 6358 yds SSS 70
Recs Am–63 DJ Eccleston
Pro–67 MJ Slater
V'tors I exc Sat–NA SOC
Fees £30 Wed–£35 Sun–£35 D–£40
Loc 2 miles E of Ormskirk

Pennington
See Stop Press on page 529

Penwortham (1908)
Blundell Lane, Penwortham, Preston PR1 0AX
Tel (01772) 743207
Fax (01772) 744630
Mem 700
Sec J Parkinson (01772) 744630

Pro N Marshall (01772) 742345
Holes 18 L 6056 yds SSS 69
Recs Am–62 A Gillespie
Pro–66 W Fletcher
V'tors WD–U WE–no parties
Fees £22 (£28)
Loc 1½ miles W of Preston (A59)

Pleasington (1891)
Pleasington, Blackburn BB2 5JF
Tel (01254) 202177
Fax (01254) 201028
Mem 545
Sec M Trickett
Pro GJ Furey (01254) 201630
Holes 18 L 6445 yds SSS 71
Recs Am–65 J Covill (1992)
Pro–65 D Stirling (1993)
V'tors H
Fees £36 (£42)
Loc 3 miles SW of Blackburn

Poulton-le-Fylde (1982)
Public
Myrtle Farm, Breck Road, Poulton-le-Fylde FY6 7HJ
Tel (01253) 892444
Mem 200
Sec K Hoyle
Pro L Ware
Holes 9 L 2979 yds SSS 69
Recs Am–72 R Walker, L Chenery (1992)
Pro–74 C Mawdesley
V'tors U
Fees On application
Loc 3 miles NE of Blackpool
Mis Indoor driving range

Preston (1892)
Fulwood Hall Lane, Fulwood, Preston PR2 8DD
Tel (01772) 700011
Fax (01772) 794234
Mem 800
Sec DJ Sanders
Pro A Greenbank (01772) 700022
Holes 18 L 6254 yds SSS 70
Recs Am–65 MA Holmes, J Wright
Pro–66 JM Hulme
V'tors WD–U H WE–M SOC–WD
Fees £25 D–£30
Loc 1½ miles W of M6 Junction 32
Arch James Braid

Regent Park (Bolton) (1931)
Public
Links Road, Chorley New Road, Bolton BL6 4AF
Tel (01204) 844170
Mem 260
Sec J Rogers
Pro B Longworth (01204) 842336
Holes 18 L 6221 yds Par 70 SSS 69
Recs Am–62 N Jameson (1995)
Pro–68 L Alamby
V'tors U SOC–WD
Fees £8 (£10)
Loc A673, 3 miles W of Bolton. M61 Junction 6

For list of abbreviations see page 527

Rishton (1927)
Eachill Links, Hawthorn Drive, Rishton BB1 4HG
Tel (01254) 884442
Fax (01254) 51946
Mem 302
Sec T Charnock (Hon)
Holes 9 L 6097 yds SSS 69
Recs Am–68 K Sheridan
 Pro–68 J Matthews
V'tors WD–U WE–M
Fees £12
Loc 3 miles E of Blackburn
Arch Thomas/Alliss

Rochdale (1888)
Edenfield Road, Bagslate, Rochdale OL11 5YR
Tel (01706) 646024 (Clubhouse)
Fax (01706) 643818
Mem 750
Sec (01706) 643818
Pro A Laverty (01706) 522104
Holes 18 L 6031 yds SSS 69
Recs Am–65 SM Lord (1992)
 Pro–65 J Hammond (1989)
V'tors U
Fees £25 (£30)
Loc 3 miles from M62 Junction 20 on A680

Rossendale (1903)
Ewood Lane, Head Haslingden, Rossendale BB4 6LH
Tel (01706) 831339
Fax (01706) 228669
Mem 682
Sec JR Swain
Pro SJ Nicholls (01706) 213616
Holes 18 L 6293 yds SSS 70
Recs Am–64 AG Westwell
 Pro–67 D Screeton
 Ladies–72 J Ruff
V'tors WD/Sun–U Sat–M
Fees £25 (£30)
Loc 7 miles N of Bury, nr end of M66

Royal Lytham & St Annes (1886)
Links Gate, Lytham St Annes FY8 3LQ
Tel (01253) 724206
Fax (01253) 780946
Mem 600
Sec LB Goodwin FCA
Pro E Birchenough (01253) 720094
Holes 18 L 6685 yds SSS 74
Recs Am–66 R Foster, T Craddock
 Pro–64 T Lehman
V'tors WD–I H
Fees £82 (incl lunch)
Loc St Annes 1 mile (A584)
Mis Dormy House

Saddleworth (1904)
Mountain Ash, Uppermill, Oldham OL3 6LT
Tel (01457) 873653
Fax (01457) 820647
Mem 700
Sec AE Gleave
Pro ET Shard
Holes 18 L 5976 yds SSS 69
Recs Am–65 RC Hughes
 Pro–69 M Melling, A Gillies
V'tors U
Fees £23 (£30)
Loc Uppermill, 5 miles E of Oldham
Arch Mackenzie/Leaver

St Annes Old Links (1901)
Highbury Road, Lytham St Annes FY8 2LD
Tel (01253) 723597
Fax (01253) 781506
Mem 945
Sec PW Ray
Pro GG Hardiman (01253) 722432
Holes 18 L 6616 yds SSS 72
Recs Am–66 RD Squire, AC Nash
 Pro–65 R Sailer, T Bjorn, M Florioli, R Boxall
V'tors WD–NA before 9.30am and 12–1.30pm WE/BH–arrange with Sec SOC
Fees £35 (£45)
Loc Between St Annes and Blackpool, off A584
Arch Herd

Shaw Hill Hotel G&CC (1925)
Preston Road, Whittle-le-Woods, Chorley PR6 7PP
Tel (01257) 269221
Fax (01257) 261223
Mem 500
Sec DFW Dimsdale
Pro D Clarke (01257) 279222
Holes 18 L 6318 yds Par 72 SSS 70
Recs Am–66 N Hopwood (1991)
 Pro–69 I Evans (1984)
V'tors WD–U H SOC
Fees £30 (£40)
Loc A6, 1½ miles N of Chorley. M61 Junction 8. M6 Junction 28

Standish Court (1995)
Rectory Lane, Standish, Wigan WN6 0XD
Tel (01257) 425777
Fax (01257) 425888
Mem 500
Sec PC Dawson
Pro T Kershaw
Holes 18 L 5650 yds Par 68 SSS 66
V'tors U SOC
Fees £12 (£16)
Loc M6 Junction 27, 2 miles
Arch Patrick Dawson

Stonyhurst Park (1980)
Stonyhurst, Hurst Green, Blackburn BB6 9QB
Tel (01254) 826478
Mem 315
Sec TA Cooke (01200) 23089
Holes 9 L 5529 yds SSS 66
V'tors WD–phone first WE–M
Fees £12

Loc
5 miles SW of Clitheroe (B6243)
Mis Green fees payable at Bayley Arms, Hurst Green

Towneley (1932)
Public
Towneley Park, Todmorden Road, Burnley BB11 3ED
Tel (01282) 451636
Mem 300
Sec N Clark (01282) 414555
Pro (01282) 38473
Holes 18 L 5811 yds Par 70 SSS 68
 9 hole course
Recs Am–67 T Foster (1990)
 Pro–65 D Whittaker (1985)
V'tors U
Fees £6 (£7)
Loc 1½ miles E of Burnley

Tunshill (1901)
Kiln Lane, Milnrow, Rochdale OL16 3TS
Tel (01706) 342095
Mem 180
Sec D Hardman
Holes 9 L 5743 yds SSS 68
Recs Am–66 D Williams (1994)
V'tors WD–U WE–M SOC
Fees On application
Loc 2 miles E of Rochdale. M62 Junction 21

Turton (1908)
Wood End Farm, Chapeltown Road, Bromley Cross, Bolton BL7 9QH
Tel (01204) 852235
Mem 330 56(L) 51(J)
Sec D Fairclough (01204) 592024
Pro None
Holes 18 L 5901 yds Par 69 SSS 68
Recs Am–70 MJ Rothwell (1997)
V'tors WD–U exc Wed–NA 11.30–2.30pm WE/BH–M SOC
Fees £16 (£20)
Loc 3½ miles N of Bolton

De Vere Blackpool (1993)
Pay and play
East Park Drive, Blackpool FY3 8LL
Tel (01253) 838866/766156
Fax (01253) 798800
Mem 550
Sec DB Smith (Mgr)
Pro D Naughton (01253) 766156
Holes 18 L 6461 yds SSS 71
Recs Am–68
 Pro–67
V'tors U H SOC
Fees £30 (£35)
Loc M55 Junction 4. Follow signs to Blackpool Zoo
Mis Floodlit driving range
Arch Alliss/Clark

Walmersley (1906)
Garrett's Close, Walmersley, Bury BL9 6TE
Tel (0161) 764 1429
Mem 450
Sec RO Goldstein

For list of abbreviations see page 527

Pro	S Crake (0161) 763 9050
Holes	18 L 5341 yds SSS 67
V'tors	WD–U exc Tues–NA Sat–NA Sun–M SOC–Wed–Fri
Fees	D–£20
Loc	2 miles N of Bury (A56). S of M66 Junction 1
Arch	SG Marnoch

Werneth (1909)

Green Lane, Garden Suburb, Oldham OL8 3AZ

Tel	(0161) 624 1190
Mem	400
Sec	JH Barlow
Pro	R Penny
Holes	18 L 5363 yds SSS 66
Recs	Am–63 LF Dooley Pro–63 S Holden
V'tors	WD–U WE–M SOC
Fees	£16.50
Loc	2 miles S of Oldham

Westhoughton (1929)

Long Island, Westhoughton, Bolton BL5 2BR

Tel	(01942) 811085
Fax	(01942) 608958
Mem	230
Sec	F Donohue
Pro	J Seed
Holes	9 L 5834 yds SSS 68
Recs	Am–64 T Woodward
V'tors	WD–U WE/BH–M
Fees	D–£16
Loc	4 miles SW of Bolton on A58

Whalley (1912)

Long Leese Barn, Clerkhill, Whalley, Blackburn BB7 9DR

Tel	(01254) 822236
Mem	325
Sec	JS Dawson (01254) 886313
Pro	H Smith (01254) 824766
Holes	9 L 6258 yds Par 72 SSS 70
Recs	Am–69 J Thompson (1998) Ladies–75 D Dawson (1996)
V'tors	U exc Sat (Apr–Oct) SOC–WD
Fees	£15 (£20)
Loc	7 miles NE of Blackburn

Whittaker (1906)

Littleborough OL5 0LH

Tel	(01706) 378310
Mem	200
Sec	GA Smith (01484) 428546
Holes	9 L 5576 yds SSS 67
Recs	Am–61 D Kernick Pro–65 MT Hoyle
V'tors	WD/Sat–U Sun–NA
Fees	£12 (£16)
Loc	1½ miles N of Littleborough, off A58
Arch	NP Stott

Wigan (1898)

Arley Hall, Haigh, Wigan WN1 2UH

Tel	(01257) 421930
Mem	280

Sec	E Walmsley
Holes	9 L 6058 yds SSS 69
Recs	Am–68 RM Hodson
V'tors	U exc Tues & Sat
Fees	£25 (£30)
Loc	4 miles N of Wigan, off A5106/B5239. M6 Junction 27

Wilpshire (1890)

72 Whalley Road, Wilpshire, Blackburn BB1 9LF

Tel	(01254) 248260
Fax	(01254) 248260
Mem	650
Sec	J Ditchfield
Pro	W Slaven (01254) 249558
Holes	18 L 5911 yds SSS 68
Recs	Am–64 H Green (1975), MJ Savage (1978), PC Livesey (1990) Pro–61 J Hawkesworth (1989)
V'tors	WD–U WE/BH–on request
Fees	£25 (£30)
Loc	3 miles NE of Blackburn, off A666

Leicestershire

Beedles Lake (1993)

Pay and play

170 Broome Lane, East Goscote LE7 3WQ

Tel	(0116) 260 6759
Mem	336
Sec	D Lilley
Pro	SA Byrne
Holes	18 L 6573 yds Par 72 SSS 71
Recs	Am–71
V'tors	U SOC
Fees	£9.50 (£12.50)
Loc	4 miles N of Leicester on B5328, off A46
Mis	Driving range
Arch	D Tucker

Birstall (1901)

Station Road, Birstall, Leicester LE4 3BB

Tel	(0116) 267 4450
Fax	(0116) 267 4322
Mem	430 107(L) 50(J)
Sec	Mrs SE Chilton (0116) 267 4322
Pro	D Clark (0116) 267 5245
Holes	18 L 6222 yds SSS 70
Recs	Am–63 PA Frith, DE Gibson Pro–62 RS Larratt
V'tors	Mon/Wed/Fri–I Other days–M SOC
Fees	£20 D–£25
Loc	3 miles N of Leicester (A6)

Blaby (1991)

Pay and play

Lutterworth Road, Blaby LE8 3DB

Tel	(0116) 278 4804
Pro	B Morris
Holes	9 L 2600 yds SSS 68

V'tors	U
Fees	18 holes–£6 (£8)
Loc	S of Blaby village
Mis	Driving range

Breedon Priory (1990)

Wilson, Derby DE73 1LG

Tel	(01332) 863081
Fax	(01332) 863081
Mem	850
Sec	KM Stevenson
Pro	B Hill
Holes	18 L 5338 yds Par 68 SSS 66
Recs	Am–64 S Marriott (1997) Pro–68 T Coxon (1992)
V'tors	WD–U WE–NA before 2pm (phone first) SOC–WD
Fees	£15.50 (£20.50)
Loc	3½ miles W of M1 Junction 23A on A453
Arch	Snell/Ashton

Charnwood Forest (1890)

Breakback Road, Woodhouse Eaves, Loughborough LE12 8TA

Tel	(01509) 890259
Fax	(01509) 890925
Mem	330
Sec	J Clarke
Holes	9 L 5960 yds SSS 69
Recs	Am–63 D McJannet (1997), A Wainwright (1998) Pro–67 G Coysh (1997)
V'tors	WD–H WE/BH–NA SOC–Wed–Fri
Fees	£15 (£25)
Loc	M1 Junction 23, 3 miles

Cosby (1895)

Chapel Lane, Broughton Road, Cosby, Leicester LE9 1RG

Tel	(0116) 286 4759
Fax	(0116) 286 4484
Mem	690
Sec	GT Kirkpatrick
Pro	M Wing (0116) 284 8275
Holes	18 L 6417 yds Par 71 SSS 71
Recs	Am–67 DE Gibson Pro–69 T Westwood Ladies–74 A Genno
V'tors	WD–U H before 4pm WE/BH–M SOC–WD–H
Fees	£22 D–£26
Loc	½ mile S of Cosby. 7 miles S of Leicester

Enderby (1986)

Public

Mill Lane, Enderby, Leicester LE9 5NW

Tel	(0116) 284 9388
Sec	LJ Speake (0116) 284 1133
Pro	C D'Araujo
Holes	9 L 4356 yds SSS 61
V'tors	U
Fees	18 holes–£5.75 (£7.75)
Loc	Enderby 2 miles. M1 Junction 21

For list of abbreviations see page 527

Glen Gorse (1933)
Glen Road, Oadby, Leicester LE2 4RF
Tel (0116) 271 2226/271 4159
Fax (0116) 271 4159
Mem 360 110(L) 60(J)
Sec M Goodson
  (0116) 271 4159
Pro D Fitzpatrick
  (0116) 271 3748
Holes 18 L 6648 yds SSS 72
Recs Am–69 J Powell (1996)
  Pro–67 G Coysh (1996)
  Ladies–70 M Page (1992)
V'tors WD–U WE/BH–M SOC–WD
Fees £24 D–£28.50
Loc 3 miles S of Leicester on A6

Hinckley (1983)
Leicester Road, Hinckley LE10 3DR
Tel (01455) 615124
Fax (01455) 890841
Mem 650
Pro R Jones (01455) 615014
Holes 18 L 6527 yds SSS 71
Recs Am–65 J Cayless (1996)
  Pro–67 K Dickens (1987)
V'tors WD–U exc Tues Sat–NA before 4pm Sun–M after 11am SOC
Fees £25
Loc NE of Hinckley on A4668

Humberstone Heights (1978)
Public
Gipsy Lane, Leicester LE5 0TB
Tel (0116) 276 1905/3680
Mem 400
Sec Mrs H Cotter
  (0116) 276 3680
Pro J Alcock (0116) 276 4674
Holes 18 L 6343 yds SSS 70
Recs Am–68 S Sansome
  Pro–66 C Hall
V'tors U SOC–WD
Fees On application
Loc 3 miles E of Leicester, off A47
Mis Driving range. Pitch & putt course
Arch Hawtree

Kibworth (1904)
Weir Road, Kibworth Beauchamp, Leicester LE8 0LP
Tel (0116) 279 2301
Fax (0116) 279 2301
Mem 700
Sec PD Ind (Mgr),
  Mrs Y Yeomans
Pro R Larratt
  (0116) 279 2283
Holes 18 L 6312 yds SSS 70
Recs Am–67 EE Feasey,
  C Noble (1991)
  Pro–64 P Broadhurst (1991)
V'tors WD–U WE–M SOC–WD
Fees £23
Loc 9 miles SE of Leicester on A6
Mis Driving range

Kilworth Springs (1993)
South Kilworth Road, North Kilworth, Lutterworth LE17 6HJ
Tel (01858) 575082
Fax (01858) 575078
Mem 514
Sec K Mattock
Pro N Melvin
Holes 18 L 6718 yds SSS 72
V'tors U SOC
Fees £17 (£21)
Loc 4 miles E of M1 Junction 20
Mis Driving range

Kirby Muxloe (1893)
Station Road, Kirby Muxloe, Leicester LE9 2EP
Tel (0116) 239 3107
Fax (0116) 239 3457
Mem 425
Sec H Taylor (Sec/Mgr)
  (0116) 239 3457
Pro B Whipham (0116) 239 2813
Holes 18 L 6279 yds Par 71 SSS 70
Recs Am–66 P Bosworth,
  J Coulthurst (1994)
  Pro–62 J Higgins (1993)
V'tors WD–U before 3.45pm exc Tues–NA WE–Captain's permission only SOC–H
Fees £25 D–£30
Loc 3 miles W of Leicester
Mis Driving range for members and green fees only

Langton Park G&CC (1994)
Langton Hall, Leicester LE16 7TY
Tel (01858) 545374
Fax (01858) 545358
Mem 200
Sec J Window
Holes 18 L 6724 yds SSS 72
V'tors H or I SOC
Fees On application
Loc 12 miles SE of Leicester, off A6. 2 miles N of Market Harborough
Arch Hawtree

Leicestershire (1890)
Evington Lane, Leicester LE5 6DJ
Tel (0116) 273 8825
Fax (0116) 273 8825
Mem 750
Sec JL Adams
Pro JR Turnbull (0116) 273 6730
Holes 18 L 6330 yds SSS 70
Recs Am–64 IR Lyner, DJ Bush
  Pro–63 H Henning, I Mosey,
  S Sherratt
V'tors U H SOC–arrange with Sec or Pro
Fees £24 (£29)
Loc 2 miles E of Leicester

Leicestershire Forest (1991)
Markfield Lane, Botcheston LE9 9FJ
Tel (01455) 824900
Mem 460

Sec
Sec M Fixter
Pro M Wing
Holes 18 L 6111 yds SSS 69
V'tors U–phone first
Fees On application
Loc 6 miles W of Leicester. M1 Junction 22, 4 miles
Mis Driving range
Arch York/Fixter

Lingdale (1967)
Joe Moore's Lane, Woodhouse Eaves, Loughborough LE12 8TF
Tel (01509) 890703
Mem 609
Sec M Green
Pro P Sellears (01509) 890684
Holes 18 L 6545 yds SSS 71
Recs Am–68 R Walker (1994)
  Pro–70 R Larratt (1992)
V'tors U SOC
Fees D–£20 (£23)
Loc 6 miles S of Loughborough. M1 Junction 23, 4 miles

Longcliffe (1905)
Snells Nook Lane, Nanpantan, Loughborough LE11 3YA
Tel (01509) 216321
Mem 650
Sec P Keeling (01509) 239129
Pro I Bailey (01509) 231450
Holes 18 L 6625 yds SSS 72
Recs Am–68 S Critchley
  Pro–67 ID Bailey
V'tors WD–H WE–M
Fees £27
Loc 3 miles SW of Loughborough. M1 Junction 23

Lutterworth (1904)
Lutterworth, Leicester LE17 5HN
Tel (01455) 552532
Fax (01455) 553586
Mem 70
Sec BC Smith
Pro R Tisdall (01455) 557199
Holes 18 L 6226 yds SSS 70
Recs Am–71 M Howkins
V'tors WD–U WE–M SOC–WD
Fees £20 D–£26
Loc By M1 Junction 20 and M6 Junction 1

Market Harborough (1898)
Great Oxendon Road, Market Harborough LE16 8NF
Tel (01858) 463684
Fax (01858) 432906
Mem 560
Sec JR Ingleby (01858) 525688
Pro FJ Baxter (01858) 463684
Holes 18 L 6022 yds Par 70 SSS 69
Recs Am–66 D Musker (1997)
  Pro–63 FJ Baxter (1994)
V'tors WD–U WE–M SOC–WD
Fees £20 D–£25
Loc 1 mile S of Mkt Harborough on A508
Arch Howard Swan

For list of abbreviations see page 527

Melton Mowbray (1925)
Waltham Rd, Thorpe Arnold, Melton Mowbray LE14 4SD
Tel (01664) 562118
Fax (01664) 562118
Mem 575
Sec Mrs EA Sallis
Pro J Hetherington (01664) 569629
Holes 18 L 6222 yds SSS 70
V'tors U H before 3pm –M after 3pm SOC
Fees £17 (£20)
Loc 2 miles NE of Melton Mowbray on A607

Oadby (1974)
Public
Leicester Road Racecourse, Oadby, Leicester LE2 4AB
Tel (0116) 270 9052/270 0215
Pro S Ward (0116) 270 9052
Holes 18 L 6376 yds Par 72 SSS 70
Recs Am–65 S Davis (1988)
Pro–73 C O'Connor Jr
V'tors WD–U WE/BH–book with Pro SOC–WD
Fees £6 (£9)
Loc 2 miles SE of Leicester (A6)

Park Hill (1994)
Park Hill, Seagrave LE12 7NG
Tel (01509) 815454
Fax (01509) 816062
Mem 300
Sec SL Hardy
Pro DC Mee (01509) 815775
Holes 18 L 7219 yds Par 73 SSS 74
V'tors U SOC
Fees £20 D–£28 (£24 D–£36)
Loc 6 miles N of Leicester on A6

Rothley Park (1911)
Westfield Lane, Rothley, Leicester LE7 7LH
Tel (0116) 230 2019
Sec SG Winterton (0116) 230 2809
Pro A Collins (0116) 230 3023
Holes 18 L 6487 yds SSS 71
Recs Am–67 EE Feasey, PJ Askew
Pro–68 PJ Dolan
V'tors WD–H exc Tues–NA WE/BH–NA SOC
Fees £25 D–£30
Loc 6 miles N of Leicester, W of A6

Scraptoft (1928)
Beeby Road, Scraptoft, Leicester LE7 9SJ
Tel (0116) 241 9000
Fax (0116) 241 8863
Mem 563
Sec D Osborn (0116) 241 8863
Pro S Wood (0116) 241 9138
Holes 18 L 6235 yds Par 70 SSS 70
Recs Am–67 L Towers
Pro–66 N Bland (1998)
V'tors WD–U M WE–M SOC–M
Fees £20 D–£25
Loc 3 miles E of Leicester

Six Hills
Pay and play
Six Hills, Melton Mowbray LE14 3PR
Tel (01509) 881225
Mem 85
Sec Mrs J Showler
Pro S Sherratt
Holes 18 L 5758 yds Par 71 SSS 69
V'tors U
Fees £9 (£11)
Loc 10 miles N of leicester, off A46

Ullesthorpe Court Hotel (1976)
Frolesworth Road, Ullesthorpe, Lutterworth LE17 5BZ
Tel (01455) 209023
Fax (01455) 202537
Mem 600
Sec PE Woolley
Pro D Bowring (01455) 209150
Holes 18 L 6650 yds SSS 72
Recs Am–70 M Hodgson
Pro–68
V'tors U SOC–WD
Fees £17 D–£29
Loc 3 miles NW of Lutterworth, off B577

Western Park (1920)
Public
Scudamore Road, Leicester LE3 1UQ
Tel (0116) 287 2339/287 6158
Mem 300
Sec IA Nicholson
Pro BN Whipham (0116) 287 2339
Holes 18 L 6532 yds SSS 71
Recs Am–66 G Jones
V'tors U
Fees On application
Loc 4 miles W of Leicester. M1 Junction 21, 3 miles

Whetstone (1965)
Cambridge Road, Cosby, Leicester LE9 5SH
Tel (0116) 286 1424
Fax (0116) 286 1424
Mem 600
Sec J Collins
Pro N Leatherland, D Raitt
Holes 18 L 5795 yds SSS 68
Recs Am–68 R Fines (1994)
Pro–64 D Raitt (1989)
V'tors U SOC
Fees £10 (£13)
Loc S boundary of Leicester
Mis Driving range
Arch E Callaway

Willesley Park (1921)
Measham Road, Ashby-de-la-Zouch LE65 2PF
Tel (01530) 411532
Mem 600 99(L) 38(J)
Sec RE Brown (01530) 414596
Pro C Hancock (01530) 414820
Holes 18 L 6304 yds SSS 70
Recs Am–64 P Frith, M McGuire (1993); Pro–65 L Jones (1990)

V'tors WD–H WE/BH–H after 9.30am SOC
Fees 308 (£35)
Loc 2 miles S of Ashby on B5006. M1 Junctions 22/23/24. A42(M) Junction 12

Lincolnshire

Ashby Decoy (1936)
Ashby Decoy, Burringham Road, Scunthorpe DN17 2AB
Tel (01724) 842913
Fax (01724) 271708
Mem 520 130(L) 65(J)
Sec KR Ford (01724) 866561
Pro A Miller (01724) 868972
Holes 18 L 6281 yds SSS 71
Recs Am–66 L Day (1997)
Pro–66 G Vickers (1995)
V'tors WD–H Sat–M SOC–WD exc Tues
Fees £18 (£24)
Loc 2 miles SW of Scunthorpe

Belton Park (1890)
Belton Lane, Londonthorpe Road, Grantham NG31 9SH
Tel (01476) 567399
Fax (01476) 592078
Mem 900
Sec T Ireland
Pro B McKee (01476) 563911
Holes 27 holes:
Brownlow L 6420 yds SSS 71;
Ancaster L 6252 yds SSS 70;
Belmont L 6016 yds SSS 69
Recs Am–66 AR Midgley (1991)
Pro–65 S Bennett (1984)
V'tors U H SOC–WD exc Tues
Fees £26 (£32)
Loc 2 miles N of Grantham

Belton Woods Hotel (1991)
Belton, Grantham NG32 2LN
Tel (01476) 593200
Fax (01476) 574847
Mem 350
Sec MJ Carty (01636) 674978
Pro M Forster
Holes Lakes 18 L 6805 yds SSS 73
Woodside 18 L 6835 yds SSS 73; 9 hole Par 3 course
Recs Pro–68 M Ingham
V'tors U SOC
Fees £27 D–£30 (£30 D–£35)
Loc 2 miles N of Grantham on A607 towards Lincoln
Mis Driving range
Arch Cayford

Blankney (1903)
Blankney, Lincoln LN4 3AZ
Tel (01526) 320263
Fax (01526) 322521
Mem 664 138(L) 50(J)
Sec DA Priest
Pro G Bradley (01526) 320202

For list of abbreviations see page 527

594 Lincolnshire

Holes 18 L 6638 yds SSS 73
Recs Am–69 C Wetherall (1998)
      Pro–69 J Cant (1998)
V'tors U H SOC
Fees £20 (£30)
Loc 10 miles SE of Lincoln on B1188
Arch Cameron Sinclair

Boston (1962)
Cowbridge, Horncastle Road, Boston PE22 7EL
Tel (01205) 362306
Fax (01205) 350589
Mem 650 115(L) 60(J)
Sec DE Smith (01205) 350589
Pro TR Squires (01205) 362306
Holes 18 L 6483 yds SSS 71
Recs Am–73 J Woodcock (1993)
     Pro–69 C Jepson (1994)
V'tors WD–U WE/BH–H
Fees £18 (£24)
Loc 2 miles N of Boston on B1183

Boston West (1995)
Pay and play
Hubbert's Bridge, Boston PE20 3QX
Tel (01205) 290670
Fax (01205) 280650
Mem 380
Sec MJ Couture
Holes 9 L 6388 yds Par 72 SSS 70
Recs Am–67 R Owens (1996)
     Pro–65 A Hare (1996)
V'tors U
Fees £5.50 (£6.50)
Loc 2 miles W of Boston on B1192
Mis Floodlit driving range
Arch Michael Zara

Burghley Park (1890)
St Martin's, Stamford PE9 3JX
Tel (01780) 753789
Fax (01780) 753789
Mem 560 140(L) 100(J)
Sec PH Mulligan
Pro G Davies (01780) 762100
Holes 18 L 6236 yds SSS 70
Recs Am–64 I Richardson (1992)
     Pro–70 B Thomson (1990)
V'tors WD–I or H WE/BH–M SOC–WD
Fees £21
Loc 1 mile S of Stamford, off A1 to B1061
Arch Rev JD Day

Canwick Park (1893)
Canwick Park, Washingborough Road, Lincoln LN4 1EF
Tel (01522) 542912/522166
Mem 650
Sec DJ Dixon (01522) 542912
Pro S Williamson (01522) 536870
Holes 18 L 6150 yds SSS 69
Recs Am–65 G Davies (1997)
V'tors WD–U WE–M before 3pm SOC–WD
Fees £15 D–£19 (£19 D–£25)
Loc 1 mile SE of Lincoln
Arch Hawtree

Carholme (1906)
Carholme Road, Lincoln LN1 1SE
Tel (01522) 523725
Fax (01522) 533733
Mem 700
Sec RD Motts
Pro G Leslie (01522) 536811
Holes 18 L 6243 yds Par 71 SSS 70
Recs Am–69 RJ Taylor (1988)
     Ladies–77 J Edmondson (1993)
V'tors WD–U WE–M SOC
Fees On application
Loc Lincoln 1 mile (A57)

Cleethorpes (1894)
Kings Road, Cleethorpes DN35 0PN
Tel (01472) 814060 (Pro)
Mem 750
Sec H Long (01472) 816110
Pro P Davies (01472) 814060
Holes 18 L 6349 yds SSS 70
Recs Am–69 D Burchill (1994)
     Pro–68 H Selby-Green, G Walker
V'tors WD–U exc Wed pm
Fees £20 (£25)
Loc 1 mile S of Cleethorpes

Elsham (1900)
Barton Road, Elsham, Brigg DN20 0LS
Tel (01652) 688382
Fax (01652) 680308
Mem 650
Sec JG Ashton (Mgr) (01652) 680291
Pro S Brewer (01652) 680432
Holes 18 L 6429 yds SSS 71
Recs Am–67 A Hewson (1998)
     Pro–68 HS King (1998)
V'tors WE–M SOC–WD
Fees £24
Loc 5 miles N of Brigg. M180 Junction 5

Forest Pines (1996)
Ermine Street, Brigg DN20 0AQ
Tel (01652) 650756
Fax (01652) 650495
Mem 350
Sec D Edwards (Golf Dir)
Pro D Edwards
Holes 27 holes:6393–6882 yds Par 71–73 SSS 70–73
     Pro–69 M Ulyett
V'tors U SOC
Fees £30 D–£35
Loc M180 Junction 4, on A15 to Scunthorpe
Mis Floodlit driving range
Arch John Morgan

Gainsborough (1894)
Thonock, Gainsborough DN21 1PZ
Tel (01427) 613088
Fax (01427) 810172
Mem 600
Sec D Bowers
Pro S Cooper
Holes 18 L 6266 yds Par 72 SSS 70
     18 L 6724 yds Par 72 SSS 72

Recs Am–66
     Pro–63
V'tors U
Fees £25 D–£35
Loc N of Gainsborough
Mis Floodlit driving range
Arch Neil Coles

Gedney Hill (1991)
Public
West Drove, Gedney End Hill PE12 0NT
Tel (01406) 330922
Mem 400
Sec S McGregor
Pro D Hutton
Holes 18 L 5450 yds SSS 66
Recs Am–67 N Venters
     Pro–66 D Creek (1991)
V'tors U SOC–WD
Fees £6.25 (£10.50)
Loc 4 miles from A47 on B1166
Mis Driving range
Arch C Britton

Grange Park (1992)
Pay and play
Butterwick Road, Messingham, Scunthorpe DN17 3PP
Tel (01724) 762945
Fax (01724) 762851
Sec I Cannon (Mgr)
Holes 13 L 4122 yds SSS 48
     9 hole Par 3 course
V'tors U
Fees £6 (£8)
Loc 5 miles from Scunthorpe. M180 Junction 3
Mis Floodlit driving range
Arch RW Price

Grimsby (1922)
Littlecoates Road, Grimsby DN34 4LU
Tel (01472) 342823 (Clubhouse)
Fax (01472) 342630
Mem 720 150(L) 70(J)
Sec BJ Hoggett (01472) 342630
Pro R Smith (01472) 356981
Holes 18 L 6098 yds Par 70 SSS 69
Recs Am–66 M James
     Pro–66 BJ Hunt
V'tors WD–U Sat pm/Sun am–XL SOC–WD
Fees £20 D–£25 (£25)
Loc 1 mile W of Grimsby, off A46. 1 mile from A180
Arch HS Colt

Hirst Priory
Crowle, Scunthorpe DN17 4BU
Tel (01724) 711619
Mem 400
Sec M Thompson
Holes 18 L 6199 yds Par 71 SSS 69
Recs Am–63
     Pro–67
V'tors U SOC
Fees £13.75 (£17.50)
Loc ¾ mile N of M180 Junction 2, on A161 to Crowle

For list of abbreviations see page 527

Holme Hall (1908)
Holme Lane, Bottesford, Scunthorpe DN16 3RF
Tel (01724) 862078
Fax (01724) 862078
Mem 470 90(L) 50(J)
Sec G Smith
Pro R McKiernan (01724) 851816
Holes 18 L 6475 yds SSS 71
Recs Am–65 K Spencer
Pro–66 B Thompson
V'tors WD–U WE–M H SOC–WD
Fees £20 D–£22
Loc 4 miles SE of Scunthorpe. M180 Junction 4

Horncastle (1990)
West Ashby, Horncastle LN9 5PP
Tel (01507) 526800
Mem 300
Sec RC Chantry
Pro EC Wright
Holes 18 L 5717 yds SSS 70
Recs Am–71 J Page
V'tors U SOC
Fees £10 D–£15
Loc 1 mile N of Horncastle, off A158
Mis Floodlit driving range
Arch EC Wright

Humberston Park
Humberston Avenue, Humberston DN36 4SJ
Tel (01472) 210404
Mem 172
Sec R Bean (01472) 690361
Holes 9 L 3670 yds Par 60 SSS 57
V'tors U exc Wed pm/Thurs am/Sun am SOC
Fees £8 (£10)
Loc Humberston, 3 miles S of Grimsby (A1031)
Arch T Barraclough

Immingham (1975)
St Andrews Lane, Off Church Lane, Immingham DN40 2EU
Tel (01469) 575298
Fax (01469) 577636
Mem 650
Pro N Harding (01469) 575493
Holes 18 L 6215 yds SSS 70
Recs Am–69 C Tuck (1997)
Pro–65 S Bennett
V'tors WD–U Sun–NA before noon SOC–WD
Fees £16 D–£25
Loc N of St Andrew's Church, Immingham
Arch Hawtree/Pennink

Kenwick Park (1992)
Kenwick Hall, Louth LN11 8NY
Tel (01507) 605134
Fax (01507) 606556
Sec PG Shillington
Pro E Sharp (01507) 607161
Holes 18 L 6815 yds Par 72 SSS 73
Recs Am–72 P Spence (1996)
Pro–67 S Bennett (1995)

V'tors U SOC
Fees D–£25 (£35)
Loc 1 mile SE of Louth
Mis Teaching Academy. Driving range
Arch Patrick Tallack

Kingsway (1971)
Public
Kingsway, Scunthorpe DN15 7ER
Tel (01724) 840945
Sec C Mann
Pro C Mann
Holes 9 L 1915 yds SSS 59
V'tors U
Fees On application
Loc ¾ mile W of Scunthorpe, off A18

Kirton Holme (1992)
Pay and play
Holme Road, Kirton Holme, Boston PE20 1SY
Tel (01205) 290669
Mem 360
Sec Mrs T Welberry (01205) 290560
Pro Alison Johns (01205) 369948
Holes 9 L 2884 yds SSS 68
Recs Am–71 R Ellis (1995)
V'tors U SOC–WD
Fees D–£8 (£9)
Loc 3 miles W of Boston, off A52
Arch DW Welberry

Lincoln (1891)
Torksey, Lincoln LN1 2EG
Tel (01427) 718721
Fax (01427) 718721
Mem 700
Sec DB Linton
Pro A Carter (01427) 718273
Holes 18 L 6438 yds SSS 71
Recs Am–66 A Thain, P Taylor
Pro–65 M James
V'tors WD–H SOC
Fees £24 D–£30
Loc 12 miles NW of Lincoln, off A156

Louth (1965)
Crowtree Lane, Louth LN11 9LJ
Tel (01507) 602554
Fax (01507) 603681
Mem 700
Sec M Covey (Mgr), Mrs TL Covey (01507) 603681
Pro AJ Blundell (01507) 604648
Holes 18 L 6424 yds SSS 71
Recs Am–64 D Smith (1991)
Pro–69 C Hall (1989)
V'tors U SOC–WD
Fees £16 D–£22 (£25 D–£30)
Loc W side of Louth

Manor (Laceby) (1992)
Laceby Manor, Laceby, Grimsby DN37 7EA
Tel (01472) 873468
Fax (01472) 276706
Mem 550

Sec Mrs J Mackay, G Mackay (Mgr)
Holes 18 L 6354 yds SSS 70
V'tors U SOC
Fees D–£15 (£22)
Loc 5 miles W of Grimsby at Barton Street (A18)
Arch Nicholson/Rushton

Market Rasen (1912)
Legsby Road, Market Rasen LN8 3DZ
Tel (01673) 842319
Mem 550
Sec JA Brown
Pro AM Chester (01673) 842416
Holes 18 L 6043 yds SSS 69
Recs Am–66 C Osbourne (1990)
Pro–65 S Bennett (1989)
V'tors WD–I WE/BH–M SOC
Fees £18 D–£25
Loc 1 mile E of Market Rasen

Market Rasen Racecourse
Legsby Road, Market Rasen LN8 3EA
Tel (01673) 843434
Fax (01673) 844532
Holes 9 L 2350 yds Par
V'tors U
Fees On application
Loc Market Rasen Racecourse

Martin Moor
Martin Road, Blankney LN4 3BE
Tel (01526) 378243
Mem 170
Holes 9 L 6325 yds Par 72 SSS 70
V'tors U
Fees £7 (£9)
Loc 3 miles E of Metheringham (B1189)
Arch S Harrison

Millfield (1985)
Public
Laughterton, Lincoln LN1 2LB
Tel (01427) 718255/718473
Mem 600
Sec PG Guthrie
Holes 18 L 5973 yds SSS 69
15 L 4300 yds
9 hole Par 3 course
V'tors U
Fees £10
Loc 9 miles W of Lincoln
Mis Driving range

Normanby Hall (1978)
Public
Normanby Park, Scunthorpe DN15 9HU
Tel (01724) 280444 Ext 852 (Bookings)
Mem 800
Sec I Green
Pro C Mann (01724) 720226
Holes 18 L 6548 yds SSS 71
Recs Am–68
Pro–68 N Bundy

596 Lincolnshire

V'tors U SOC–WD
Fees £10 D–£15 (£12)
Loc 5 miles N of Scunthorpe
Arch Hawtree

North Shore (1910)
North Shore Road, Skegness PE25 1DN
Tel (01754) 763298
Fax (01754) 761902
Mem 450
Sec B Howard (01754) 763298
Pro J Cornelius (01754) 764822
Holes 18 L 6254 yds SSS 71
Recs Am–71 G Hunter (1989)
 Pro–69 A Green (1995)
V'tors H SOC–WD
Fees On application
Loc 1 mile N of Skegness
Arch James Braid

Pottergate
Moor Lane, Branston, Lincoln
Tel (01522) 794867
Mem 300
Sec P Woodcock
Pro None
Holes 9 L 5164 yds Par 68 SSS 65
V'tors U
Fees £8 (£8.50)
Loc 3 miles SE of Lincoln (B1188)
Arch WT Bailey

RAF Waddington
Waddington, Lincoln LN5 9NB
Tel (01522) 720271 Ext 7958
Mem 90
Sec D Bennett
Holes 9 L 5519 yds SSS 69
Recs Am–68 T Graham (1987)
V'tors By prior arrangement
Fees On application
Loc 4 miles S of Lincoln (A607)

Sandilands (1900)
Sandilands, Sutton-on-Sea LN12 2RJ
Tel (01507) 441432
Mem 400
Sec D Mumby (01507) 441617
Holes 18 L 5995 yds SSS 69
Recs Am–66 JR Payne
 Pro–63 FG Allott
V'tors U SOC
Fees £15 (£20)
Loc 1 mile S of Sutton-on-Sea, off A52

Seacroft (1895)
Seacroft, Skegness PE25 3AU
Tel (01754) 763020
Fax (01754) 763020
Mem 340 190(L) 90(J)
Sec FA Williams (Sec/Mgr)
Pro R Lawie (01754) 769624
Holes 18 L 6479 yds SSS 71
Recs Am–67 DR Rose
 Pro–67 J Heib (1988)
V'tors WD–U H WE–XL before 11am
Fees £25 (£30)
Loc S boundary of Skegness

Sleaford (1905)
Willoughby Road, South Rauceby, Sleaford NG34 8PL
Tel (01529) 488273
Fax (01529) 488326
Mem 630
Sec TGE Churms
Pro J Wilson (01529) 488644
Holes 18 L 6443 yds SSS 71
Recs Am–65 A Hare (1988)
V'tors U H exc Sun–NA (Winter) SOC–WD
Fees £18 (£25)
Loc 1 mile W of Sleaford on A153
Arch Tom Wlliamson

South Kyme (1990)
Skinners Lane, South Kyme, Lincoln LN4 4AT
Tel (01526) 861113
Fax (01526) 861113
Sec B Overton
Pro P Chamberlain
Holes 18 L 6597 yds SSS 71
Recs Am–71 K Thomson (1998)
 Pro–67 P Streeter (1998)
V'tors U SOC
Fees £12 (£14)
Loc 2 miles from A17 on B1395
Mis 6 hole practice course
Arch Graham Bradley

Spalding (1908)
Surfleet, Spalding PE11 4EA
Tel (01775) 680988
Fax (01775) 680988
Mem 750
Sec BW Walker (01775) 680386
Pro J Spencer (01775) 680474
Holes 18 L 6478 yds SSS 71
Recs Am–62 J Crampton (1996)
 Pro–65 J Spencer
V'tors U H SOC–Tues after 2pm & Thurs
Fees On application
Loc 4 miles N of Spalding, off A16
Arch Spencer/Ward/Price

Stoke Rochford (1924)
Great North Rd, Grantham NG33 5EW
Tel (01476) 530275
Mem 515
Sec JM Butler
Pro A Dow (01476) 530218
Holes 18 L 6252 yds SSS 70
Recs Am–65 A Hare, J Payne, M Wilson; Pro–65 A Dow
V'tors WD–U WE/BH–U after 10.30am
Fees On application
Loc 6 miles S of Grantham (A1)
Arch Maj Hotchkin (1935)

Sudbrook Moor (1991)
Public
Charity Lane, Carlton Scroop, Grantham NG32 3AT
Tel (01400) 250796
Fax (01400) 250796
Sec Judith Hutton

Pro T Hutton (01400) 250796
Holes 9 L 4827 yds Par 66 SSS 64
V'tors U–booking required
Fees D–£5–£6 (D–£7–£9)
Loc Carlton Scroop, 6 miles NE of Grantham (A607)
Arch Tim Hutton

Sutton Bridge (1914)
New Road, Sutton Bridge, Spalding PE12 9RG
Tel (01406) 350323 (Clubhouse)
Mem 340
Sec KC Buckle (01945) 870455
Holes 9 L 5820 yds SSS 68
 Pro–62 CJ Norton
V'tors WD–H WE–NA
Fees £18
Loc 8 miles N of Wisbech (A17)

Tetney
Station Road, Tetney, Grimsby DN36 5HY
Tel (01472) 211644
Fax (01472) 211644
Mem 425
Sec GW Fielding
Pro J Abrams
Holes 18 L 6100 yds Par 71 SSS 69
V'tors U SOC
Fees £10 (£11)
Loc 5 miles S of Grimsby, off A16

Toft Hotel (1988)
Toft, Bourne PE10 0JT
Tel (01778) 590616
Fax (01778) 590264
Mem 500
Pro M Jackson
Holes 18 L 6486 yds Par 72 SSS 71
V'tors U
Fees £12 (£17)
Loc 8 miles from Stamford on A6121
Arch D & R Fitton

Waltham Windmill (1997)
Cheapside, Waltham, Grimsby DN37 0HT
Tel (01472) 824109
Fax (01472) 828391
Mem 450
Sec J Pearce (Mgr)
Pro N Burkitt (01472) 823963
Holes 18 L 6400 yds Par 71 SSS 70
Recs Am–70 M Upton
 Pro–S Bennett (1997)
V'tors WD–U SOC
Fees £18 (£25)
Loc 2 miles S of Grimsby, off A16
Arch Fox/Payne

Woodhall Spa (1905)
Woodhall Spa LN10 6PU
Tel (01526) 351835,
 (01526) 352511 (Bookings)
Fax (01526) 352778
Mem 475
Sec BH Fawcett
Pro CC Elliot (01526) 353229

For list of abbreviations see page 527

Holes Hotchkin 18 L 7047 yds
SSS 75; Bracken 18 L
6735 yds SSS 74
Recs Hotchkin Am–67
G Wolstenholme
V'tors H–booking essential SOC
Fees EGU Members–£30 D–£50
Non–EGU Members–£40
D–£65
Loc 19 miles SE of Lincoln
(B1191)
Mis Driving range. Teaching
Academy (Closed Mon)
Arch Hotchkin/Steel

Woodthorpe Hall (1986)
Woodthorpe, Alford LN13 0DD
Tel (01507) 450294
Fax (01507) 450000
Email secretary@woodthorpehallgolf
club.freeserve.co.uk
www.woodthorpehallgolfclub.
freeserve.co.uk
Mem 300
Sec PC Bell (01507) 450000
Holes 18 L 5140 yds Par 67 SSS 65
Recs Am–68 A Fieldman (1998)
V'tors U SOC
Fees D–£10
Loc 3 miles N of Alford, off
B1373. 8 miles SE of Louth

London clubs

Aquarius (Kent)
Beckenham (Kent)
Bush Hill Park
(Middlesex)
**Central London Golf
Centre** (Surrey)
Chingford (Essex)
Dulwich & Sydenham Hill
(Surrey)
Eltham Warren (Kent)
Finchley (Middlesex)
Hampstead (Middlesex)
Hendon (Middlesex)
Highgate (Middlesex)
Lee Valley (Middlesex)
London Scottish (Surrey)
Mill Hill (Middlesex)
Muswell Hill (Middlesex)
North Middlesex
(Middlesex)
Richmond Park (Surrey)
Roehampton (Essex)
Royal Blackheath (Essex)
Royal Epping Forest
(Essex)

Royal Wimbledon (Surrey)
Shooter's Hill (Essex)
South Herts
(Hertfordshire)
Trent Park (Middlesex)
Wanstead (Essex)
West Essex (Essex)
Wimbledon Common
(Surrey)
Wimbledon Park (Surrey)

Manchester

Blackley (1907)
*Victoria Avenue East, Manchester
M9 7HW*
Tel (0161) 643 2980
Mem 750
Sec CB Leggott
(0161) 654 7770
Pro C Gould (0161) 643 3912
Holes 18 L 6235 yds SSS 70
Recs Am–65 D Royle
Pro–66 J Nixon
V'tors WD–U WE–M SOC–WD exc
Thurs
Fees £24
Loc North Manchester

Chorlton-cum-Hardy
(1902)
*Barlow Hall, Barlow Hall Road,
Manchester M21 7JJ*
Tel (0161) 881 3139
Fax (0161) 881 5830
Mem 800
Sec Mrs K Poole
(0161) 881 5830
Pro D Screeton
(0161) 881 9911
Holes 18 L 5980 yds SSS 69
Recs Am–64 P Bolton
Pro–65 M Turner
V'tors U H SOC–Thurs
Fees £22 (£27)
Loc 4 miles S of Manchester
(A5103/A5145)

Davyhulme Park (1910)
*Gleneagles Road, Davyhulme,
Manchester M41 8SA*
Tel (0161) 748 2260
Fax (0161) 747 4067
Mem 600
Sec GR Swarbrick
Pro D Butler (0161) 748 3931
Holes 18 L 6237 yds SSS 70
Recs Am–67 TF Sharp, B Connor,
D Dunwoodie
Pro–68 KG Geddes, D Rees
V'tors WD–H exc Wed & Fri–NA
Sat–NA Sun–M
SOC–Mon/Tues/Thurs
Fees £24. 27 holes–£30
Loc 7 miles SW of Manchester

Denton (1909)
*Manchester Road, Denton, Manchester
M34 2GG*
Tel (0161) 336 3218
Fax (0161) 336 4751
Mem 686
Sec R Wickham
Pro M Hollingsworth
(0161) 336 2070
Holes 18 L 6496 yds SSS 71
Recs Am–66 R Bardsley (1993)
Pro–65 M Hollingworth
V'tors WD–U WE/BH–NA before
3pm SOC
Fees £25 (£30)
Loc M60 Junction 24, A57 to
Manchester

Didsbury (1891)
*Ford Lane, Northenden, Manchester
M22 4NQ*
Tel (0161) 998 9278
Fax (0161) 998 9278
Mem 760
Sec AL Watson (Mgr)
Pro P Barber (0161) 998 2811
Holes 18 L 6273 yds SSS 70
Recs Am–66 PR Dalby (1991)
Pro–63 P Eales (1995),
D Valentine (1996)
V'tors WD–U H exc
9–10am & 12–1.30pm–NA
WE–U H
10.30–11.30am & after 4pm
Fees £26 (£30)
Loc 6 miles S of Manchester. M63
Junction 9

Ellesmere (1913)
*Old Clough Lane, Worsley, Manchester
M28 7HZ*
Tel (0161) 790 2122
Mem 380 80(L) 75(J)
Sec A Chapman
(0161) 799 0554
Pro T Morley (0161) 790 8591
Holes 18 L 6248 yds SSS 70
Recs Am–67 BA Toone
Pro–68 S Wakefield
V'tors U exc comp days (check with
Pro) SOC–WD
Fees £20 (£24)
Loc 6 miles W of Manchester, nr
junction of M62/A580

Fairfield Golf & Sailing
Club (1892)
*Booth Road, Audenshaw, Manchester
M34 5GA*
Tel (0161) 370 1641
Mem 550
Sec H Jagger (0161) 370 1279
Pro SA Pownell (0161) 370 2292
Holes 18 L 5664 yds SSS 68
Recs Am–65 PW Wrigley, ARS
Pownell
V'tors WD–U WE–NA before noon
SOC–WD
Fees £18 (£24)
Loc 5 miles E of Manchester
on A635

For list of abbreviations see page 527

Flixton (1893)

Church Road, Flixton, Urmston, Manchester M41 6EP

Tel	(0161) 748 2116
Mem	400
Sec	F Baker (0161) 748 3456
Pro	D Proctor (0161) 746 7160
Holes	9 L 6410 yds SSS 71
Recs	Am–66 MJ Wallwork (1995)
	Pro–65 P Reeves (1985)
V'tors	WD–U exc Wed SOC
Fees	£16
Loc	6 miles SW of Manchester on B5213. M63 Junction 6

Great Lever & Farnworth (1911)

Plodder Lane, Farnworth, Bolton BL4 0LQ

Tel	(01204) 656493
Fax	(01204) 656137
Mem	730
Sec	MJ Ivill (01204) 656137
Pro	T Howarth (01204) 656650
Holes	18 L 6064 yds SSS 69
Recs	Am–67 I Johnson (1998)
	Ladies–70 B Hill (1974)
V'tors	H SOC–WD
Fees	£16.50 (£27)
Loc	2 miles S of Bolton. M61 Junction 4

Heaton Park (1912)

Public

Heaton Park, Prestwich, Manchester M25 5SW

Tel	(0161) 798 0295
Sec	V Marcroft
Pro	None
Holes	18 L 5849 yds SSS 68
Recs	Am–66 J Griffiths (1986), S Pilling (1988)
	Pro–65 AP Thomson, B Evans, I Collins, M Gray
V'tors	U SOC
Fees	On application
Loc	North Manchester, via M62 and M66 to Middleton Road

Manchester (1882)

Hopwood Cottage, Rochdale Road, Middleton, Manchester M24 2QP

Tel	(0161) 643 2718, (0161) 643 0023 (Bookings)
Fax	(0161) 643 9174
Mem	700
Sec	KG Flett (0161) 643 3202
Pro	B Connor (0161) 643 2638
Holes	18 L 6450 yds SSS 72
Recs	Am–66 RE Tattersall, M Russell, RB Smithies
	Pro–64 D Lynn, M Stevenson, S Delagrange
V'tors	WD–H WE–NA SOC
Fees	D–£30 (£45)
Loc	7 miles N of Manchester. M62 Junction 20
Mis	Driving range–members and green fees only
Arch	HS Colt

North Manchester (1894)

Rhodes House, Manchester Old Road, Middleton, Manchester M24 4PE

Tel	(0161) 643 9033
Fax	(0161) 643 7775
Mem	600
Sec	D Parkinson
Pro	F Accleton (0161) 643 7094
Holes	18 L 6598 yds SSS 72
Recs	Am–66 J Cheetham
	Pro–66 G Furey
V'tors	U SOC
Fees	£25 (£28)
Loc	5 miles N of Manchester. M62 Junction 18
Arch	A Compston

Northenden (1913)

Palatine Road, Manchester M22 4FR

Tel	(0161) 998 4738
Fax	(0161) 945 5592
Mem	700
Sec	RN Kemp (Sec/Mgr)
Pro	PA Scott
Holes	18 L 6503 yds SSS 71
Recs	Am–67 JEB Waddell
	Pro–64 D Durnian
V'tors	U SOC
Fees	£25 (£30)
Loc	5 miles S of Manchester. M60 Junction 5

Old Manchester (1818)

Tel	(0161) 766 4157
Sec	PT Goodall, 9 Ashbourne Grove, Whitefield M45 7NJ
Holes	Club without a course

Pike Fold (1909)

Cooper Lane, Victoria Avenue, Blackley, Manchester M9 2QQ

Tel	(0161) 740 1136
Mem	300
Sec	H Adams
Pro	None
Holes	9 L 5789 yds SSS 68
Recs	Am–66 P Bradley (1989)
	Pro–66 JE Wiggett
V'tors	WD–U WE/BH–M SOC
Fees	D–£15
Loc	5 miles N of Manchester. M62 Junction 18, 2 miles

Prestwich (1908)

Hilton Lane, Prestwich M25 9XB

Tel	(0161) 773 2544
Mem	500
Sec	WV Trees (0161) 773 4578
Pro	S Wakefield (0161) 773 1404
Holes	18 L 4806 yds SSS 63
Recs	Am–60 J Liwosz
V'tors	WD–H WE–NA before 3pm SOC
Fees	£16 (£18)
Loc	2½ miles N of Manchester, off A56. M63 Junction 17

Stand (1904)

The Dales, Ashbourne Grove, Whitefield, Manchester M45 7NL

Tel	(0161) 766 2388
Fax	(0161) 796 3234
Mem	700
Sec	EB Taylor (0161) 766 3197
Pro	M Dance (0161) 766 2214
Holes	18 L 6411 yds SSS 71
Recs	Am–67 J Seddon (1990)
	Pro–67 PM Eales
V'tors	U SOC–WD
Fees	£25 (£30)
Loc	5 miles N of Manchester. M60 Junction 17
Arch	Alex Herd

Swinton Park (1926)

East Lancashire Road, Swinton, Manchester M27 5LX

Tel	(0161) 794 1785
Fax	(0161) 281 0698
Mem	450 120(L) 50(J)
Sec	A Bowden (0161) 794 0861
Pro	J Wilson (0161) 793 8077
Holes	18 L 6712 yds SSS 72
Recs	Am–66 J Thornley (1984)
	Pro–65 D Wheeler (1992)
V'tors	WD–U WE–M SOC–Tues
Fees	On application
Loc	On A580, 5 miles NW of Manchester

Whitefield (1932)

Higher Lane, Whitefield, Manchester M45 7EZ

Tel	(0161) 766 2728
Fax	(0161) 767 9502
Mem	538
Sec	Mrs A Schofield (0161) 766 2904
Pro	P Reeves (0161) 766 3096
Holes	18 L 6045 yds SSS 69
	18 L 5755 yds SSS 68
V'tors	U SOC–WD
Fees	£25 (£35)
Loc	4 miles N of Manchester. M60 Junction 17

William Wroe (1973)

Public

Pennybridge Lane, Flixton, Manchester M31 3DL

Tel	(0161) 748 8680
Pro	B Parkinson
Holes	18 L 4395 yds SSS 61
Recs	Am–60 C Meadows, D Dunwoodie
V'tors	U–booking necessary
Fees	On application
Loc	6 miles SW of Manchester, by M63 Junction 4

Withington (1892)

243 Palatine Road, West Didsbury, Manchester M20 2UE

Tel	(0161) 445 3912
Mem	340 97(L) 38(J)
Sec	TH Glover (0161) 445 9544
Pro	RJ Ling (0161) 445 4861
Holes	18 L 6410 yds SSS 70

Worsley (1894)
Stableford Avenue, Monton Green, Eccles, Manchester M30 8AP
Tel (0161) 789 4202
Fax (0161) 789 3200
Mem 625
Sec R Pizzey MBE
Pro C Cousins
Holes 18 L 6217 yds SSS 70
Recs Am–65 D Harding (1994)
V'tors I NA–9–9.45am & 12.15–1.30pm
Fees £20
Loc 5 miles W of Manchester

Merseyside

Allerton Municipal (1934)
Public
Allerton Road, Liverpool L18 3JT
Tel (0151) 428 1046
Pro B Large
Holes 18 L 5494 yds SSS 65
 9 hole course
V'tors U SOC
Fees On application
Loc 5 miles S of Liverpool

Arrowe Park (1931)
Public
Arrowe Park, Woodchurch, Birkenhead, Wirral L49 5LW
Tel (0151) 677 1527
Sec K Finlay
Pro C Didsbury
Holes 18 L 6377 yds SSS 70
Recs Am–66 D Ball (1995)
V'tors U
Fees £6 (£6)
Loc 3 miles S of Birkenhead on A552. M53 Junction 3, 1 mile

Bidston (1913)
Bidston Link Road, Wallasey L44 2HR
Tel (0151) 638 3412
Mem 500
Sec JJ Gleeson
Pro S Hubbard (0151) 630 6650
Holes 18 L 6207 yds SSS 70
Recs Am–64 S Earnden (1993)
 Pro–68 JM Hume
V'tors WD–U WE–M SOC
Fees On application
Loc Off Bidston Link Road

Blundells Hill
Blundells Lane, Rainhill L35 6NA
Tel (0151) 430 0100
Fax (01744) 28861
Mem 600
Sec A Roberts

Pro R Burbridge
Holes 18 L 6347 yds Par 71
V'tors U SOC
Fees £20 (£30)
Loc 2 miles SW of St Helens. M62 Junction 7
Arch Steve Marnoch

Bootle (1934)
Dunnings Bridge Road, Litherland L30 2PP
Tel (0151) 928 6196
Mem 400
Sec P Quick (Hon)
Pro A Bradshaw (0151) 928 1371
Holes 18 L 6362 yds SSS 70
Recs Am–64 S Ashcroft
 Pro–69 R Boobyer
V'tors U–book by phone SOC
Fees £6.25 (£7.25)
Loc 5 miles N of Liverpool (A565)
Arch Fred Stevens

Bowring (1913)
Public
Bowring Park, Roby Road, Huyton L36 4HD
Tel (0151) 489 1901
Pro D Weston
Holes 9 L 5592 yds SSS 66
Recs Am–67 G Spurrier
V'tors U
Fees On application
Loc 6 miles N of Liverpool. M62 Junction 5

Brackenwood (1933)
Public
Brackenwood Lane, Bebington, Wirral L63 2LY
Tel (0151) 608 3093
Pro C Disbury
Holes 18 L 6131 yds SSS 69
Recs Am–67 D Charlton
 Pro–64 C Disbury
V'tors U SOC
Fees On application
Loc Nr M53 Junction 4

Bromborough (1904)
Raby Hall Road, Bromborough L63 0NW
Tel (0151) 334 2155
Fax (0151) 334 0303
Mem 800
Sec JT Barraclough (0151) 334 2978
Pro G Berry (0151) 334 4499
Holes 18 L 6603 yds SSS 73
Recs Am–67 J Berry, GM Edwards, GJ Bradley, P Bailey
V'tors U–contact Pro in advance
Fees £28 (£30)
Loc Mid Wirral, M53 Junction 4

Mem 875
Sec TDM Bacon
Pro K Jones (0151) 625 1818
Holes 18 L 6675 yds SSS 73
Recs Am–67 JR Berry
V'tors WD–U exc before 9.30am and from 1–2pm (booking necessary) SOC
Fees On application
Loc 1½ miles S of West Kirby

Childwall (1913)
Naylor's Road, Gateacre, Liverpool L27 2YB
Tel (0151) 487 0654
Fax (0151) 487 0882
Mem 650
Sec KG Jennions (Mgr)
Pro N Parr (0151) 487 9871
Holes 18 L 6425 yds SSS 71
Recs Am–66 M Gamble
V'tors WE/BH/Tues–restricted
Fees £26 (£35)
Loc 7 miles E of Liverpool. M62 Junction 6, 2 miles
Arch James Braid

Eastham Lodge (1973)
117 Ferry Road, Eastham, Wirral L62 0AP
Tel (0151) 327 1483
Fax (0151) 327 3003
Mem 608
Sec CS Camden (0151) 327 3003
Pro R Boobyer (0151) 327 3008
Holes 18 L 5706 yds SSS 68
Recs Am–65 T Whittaker (1998)
V'tors WD–U WE/BH–M SOC–Tues
Fees £22
Loc 6 miles S of Birkenhead, off A41. M53 Junction 5. Signs to Eastham Country Park

Formby (1884)
Golf Road, Formby, Liverpool L37 1LQ
Tel (01704) 872164
Fax (01704) 833028
Mem 600
Sec KR Wilcox
Pro GH Butler (01704) 873090
Holes 18 L 6993 yds SSS 74
Recs Am–66 I Pyman, MJC Hudson
 Pro–65 NC Coles
V'tors WD–I H SOC
Fees £60
Loc By Freshfield Station
Arch Willie Park

Formby Hall
Southport Old Road, Formby L37 0AB
Tel (01704) 875699
Pro D Lloyd
Holes 18 L 6875 yds Par 73
V'tors WD–U SOC
Fees On application
Loc Off Formby bypass
Mis Floodlit driving range

Merseyside

Formby Ladies' (1896)
Formby, Liverpool L37 1YH
Tel (01704) 874127
Sec Mrs M Tasker
 (01704) 873493
Pro C Harrison (01704) 873090
Holes 18 L 5426 yds SSS 71
Recs Am–60 CD Lee
V'tors U–phone first SOC
Fees £30 (£35)
Loc Formby, off A565

Grange Park (1891)
Prescot Road, St Helens WA10 3AD
Tel (01744) 22980 (Members)
Fax (01744) 26318
Mem 730
Sec CV Hadley (01744) 26318
Pro P Roberts (01744) 28785
Holes 18 L 6480 yds SSS 71
Recs Am–65 G Boardman (1989),
 K Wallbank (1995)
 Pro–66 R Ellis (1986)
V'tors I SOC–WD exc Tues
Fees £24 (£36)
Loc 1½ miles W of St Helens
 on A58

Haydock Park (1877)
Golborne Park, Newton Lane, Newton-le-Willows WA12 0HX
Tel (01925) 224389
Fax (01925) 228525
Mem 400 120(L)
Sec JV Smith (01925) 228525
Pro PE Kenwright (01925) 226944
Holes 18 L 6043 yds SSS 69
Recs Am–65 D Pilkington,
 P Boydell, K Sargent,
 P Eckersley
 Pro–61 W Shankland
V'tors H or I SOC–WD exc Tues
Fees £26
Loc 1 mile E of M6 Junction 23

Hesketh (1885)
Cockle Dick's Lane, Cambridge Road, Southport PR9 9QQ
Tel (01704) 530226
Fax (01704) 539250
Mem 650
Sec MG Senior (01704) 536897
Pro J Donoghue (01704) 530050
Holes 18 L 6572 yds SSS 72
Recs Am–67 J Marshall
 Pro–64 D Hayes
V'tors WD–U WE/BH–restricted
 SOC
Fees £35 D–£45 (£50)
Loc 1 mile N of Southport (A565)
Arch JOF Morris

Heswall (1902)
Cottage Lane, Gayton, Heswall, Wirral L60 8PB
Tel (0151) 342 1237
Fax (0151) 342 1237
Mem 902
Sec RJ Butler
Pro AE Thompson
 (0151) 342 7251

Holes 18 L 6492 yds SSS 72
V'tors U H BH–NA
 SOC–Wed & Fri
Fees £35 (£40)
Loc 8 miles NW of Chester
 off A540. M53 Junction 4

Hillside (1909)
Hastings Road, Hillside, Southport PR8 2LU
Tel (01704) 569902
Fax (01704) 563192
Mem 800
Sec JG Graham (01704) 567169
Pro B Seddon (01704) 568360
Holes 18 L 6850 yds SSS 74
Recs Am–67 I Garbutt, J Payne
 Pro–66 M O'Grady, R Craig
V'tors By arrangement with Sec
Fees D–£40 (£50)
Loc Southport

Houghwood
Billinge Hill, Crank Road, Crank, St Helens WA11 8RL
Tel (01744) 894444
Fax (01744) 894754
Mem 630
Sec AJ Martin
Pro P Dickenson (01744) 894444
Holes 18 L 6202 yds SSS 69
Recs Am–69 I Harrison (1997)
V'tors WD–U SOC–WD
Fees £14.50 (£17.50)
Loc 3 miles N of St Helens,
 off A580 (B5201). M6
 Junctions 23 or 26
Arch N Pearson

Hoylake Municipal (1933)
Public
Carr Lane, Hoylake, Wirral L47 4BQ
Tel (0151) 632 2956/4883
 (Bookings)
Sec A Peacock
Pro S Hooton
Holes 18 L 6330 yds SSS 70
Recs Am–67 T Manning (1989)
 Pro–64 T Bennett (1982)
V'tors WD–U WE–phone booking 1
 week in advance SOC
Fees £6
Loc 4 miles W of Birkenhead
Arch James Braid

Huyton & Prescot (1905)
Hurst Park, Huyton Lane, Huyton L36 1UA
Tel (0151) 489 1138
Fax (0151) 489 0797
Mem 700
Sec Mrs S Threlfall
 (0151) 489 3948
Pro GJ Bond (0151) 489 2022
Holes 18 L 5839 yds SSS 68
Recs Am–67
V'tors WD–U WE–H SOC–WD
Fees On application
Loc 7 miles E of Liverpool. 1 mile
 S of Prescot on B5199. M57
 Junction 2

Leasowe (1891)
Leasowe Road, Moreton, Wirral L46 3RD
Tel (0151) 677 5852
Fax (0151) 604 1424
Mem 610
Sec EJ Reeves (Mgr)
Pro AJ Ayre (0151) 678 5460
Holes 18 L 6263 yds SSS 70
Recs Am–63 J Maddocks
V'tors U SOC–H
Fees D–£20 (D–£25)
Loc 1 mile N of Queensway
 Tunnel. M53 Junction 1
Arch John Ball Jr

Lee Park (1954)
Childwall Valley Road, Gateacre, Liverpool L27 3YA
Tel (0151) 487 9861 (Clubhouse)
Mem 550
Sec D Wise (0151) 487 3882
Holes 18 L 6024 yds SSS 69
V'tors SOC
Fees On application
Loc 7 miles SE of Liverpool
 (B5171)

Liverpool Municipal (1967)
Public
Ingoe Lane, Kirkby, Liverpool L32 4SS
Tel (0151) 546 5435
Pro D Weston
Holes 18 L 6571 yds SSS 71
Recs Am–70 J Paton (1986)
 Pro–70
V'tors U WE–booking required SOC
Fees On application
Loc M57 Junction 6 to B5192

Prenton (1905)
Golf Links Road, Prenton, Birkenhead L42 8LW
Tel (0151) 608 1461
Fax (0151) 609 1580
Mem 470 100(L) 51(J)
Sec WFW Disley (0151) 608 1053
Pro R Thompson (0151) 608
 1636
Holes 18 L 6429 yds SSS 71
Recs Am–65 P Langford (1993)
V'tors U SOC–Wed & Fri
Fees £30 (£35)
Loc Outskirts of Birkenhead. M53
 Junction 3

RLGC Village Play (1895)
Hoylake, Wirral L47 4AL
Mem 35
Sec PD Williams (0151) 632 5156
Holes Play over Royal Liverpool

Royal Birkdale (1889)
Waterloo Road, Birkdale, Southport PR8 2LX
Tel (01704) 567920
Fax (01704) 562327
Sec NT Crewe

For list of abbreviations see page 527

Pro RN Bradbeer (01704) 568857
Holes 18 L 6703 yds SSS 73
Recs Am–67 G Hamerton (1995)
Pro–63 J Mudd (1991 Open)
V'tors I H SOC
Fees £90 D–£110 (£110)
Loc 1½ miles S of Southport (A565)
Arch George Lowe

Royal Liverpool (1869)
Meols Drive, Hoylake L47 4AL
Tel (0151) 632 3101/3102
Fax (0151) 632 6737
Email sec@rlgc.u-net.com
www.royal-liverpool-golf.com
Mem 810
Sec Gp Capt CT Moore CBE
Pro J Heggarty (0151) 632 5868
Holes 18 L 7128 yds SSS 76
Recs Am–67 C Nowicki (1993)
Pro–64 B Waites
V'tors H SOC
Fees On application
Loc On A553 from M53 Junction 2

Sherdley Park Municipal
Public
Sherdley Park, St Helens
Tel (01744) 813149
Fax (01744) 817967
Sec B Collins (Mgr)
Pro PR Parkinson
Holes 18 L 5974 yds SSS 69
Recs Am–68 J Greenough
V'tors U SOC
Fees £7 (£8)
Loc 2 miles E of St Helens (A570). M62 Junction 7, 2 miles
Mis Driving range

Southport & Ainsdale
(1907)
Bradshaws Lane, Ainsdale, Southport PR8 3LG
Tel (01704) 578000
Fax (01704) 570896
Mem 462 101(L) 60(J)
Sec NA Wilson (01704) 578000
Pro M Houghton (01704) 577316
Holes 18 L 6612 yds SSS 73
Recs Am–67
Pro–62
V'tors WD–U WE–restricted
Fees £35 D–£45 (£45)
Loc 3 miles S of Southport on A565
Arch James Braid

Southport Municipal
(1914)
Public
Park Road West, Southport PR9 0JS
Tel (01704) 535286
Pro W Fletcher
Holes 18 L 6253 yds SSS 69
Recs Pro–67 W Fletcher (1986)
V'tors U SOC
Fees On application
Loc N end of Southport promenade

Southport Old Links (1926)
Moss Lane, Southport PR9 7QS
Tel (01704) 28207
Mem 450
Sec BE Kenyon
Holes 9 L 6224 yds SSS 71
Recs Am–68 J Robinson
V'tors U exc WE comp days/BH–NA SOC–WD
Fees £18 (£25)
Loc Churchtown, 3 miles NE of Southport

Wallasey (1891)
Bayswater Road, Wallasey L45 8LA
Tel (0151) 639 3630
Fax (0151) 638 8988
Email WallaseyGC@AOL.com
Mem 450 90(L) 50(J)
Sec Mrs LM Dolman (0151) 691 1024
Pro M Adams (0151) 638 3888
Holes 18 L 6607 yds SSS 73
Recs Am–68 P Morgan
Pro–66 P Barber
V'tors H SOC
Fees On application
Loc M53–signs to New Brighton
Arch Tom Morris

Warren (1911)
Public
Grove Road, Wallasey, Wirral L45 0JA
Tel (0151) 639 8323 (Clubhouse)
Pro K Lamb (051) 639 5730
Holes 9 L 5914 yds SSS 68
Recs Am–66 J Hayes
Pro–66 JA MacLachlan
V'tors U
Fees On application
Loc Wallasey

West Derby (1896)
Yew Tree Lane, Liverpool L12 9HQ
Tel (0151) 228 1540
Fax (0151) 259 0505
Mem 550
Sec AP Milne (0151) 254 1034
Pro A Witherup (0151) 220 5478
Holes 18 L 6277 yds SSS 70
Recs Am–65 C Vance
Pro–67 AC Coop
V'tors SOC–WD after 9.30am
Fees £25 (£30)
Loc 2 miles E of Liverpool, off A580–West Derby Junction

West Lancashire (1873)
Blundellsands, Crosby, Liverpool L23 8SZ
Tel (0151) 924 4115
Fax (0151) 931 4448
Mem 700
Sec DD Wilson (0151) 924 1076
Pro T Hastings (0151) 924 5662
Holes 18 L 6767 yds SSS 73
Recs Am–68 J Payne
Pro–66 C Mason

V'tors H SOC–WD exc Tues
Fees £35 D–£50 (£60)
Loc Between Liverpool and Southport, off A565
Arch CK Cotton

Wirral Ladies (1894)
93 Bidston Road, Birkenhead, Wirral L43 6TS
Tel (0151) 652 1255
Fax (0151) 653 4323
Mem 450
Sec Mrs SA Headford
Pro A Law (0151) 652 2468
Holes 18 L 4948 yds SSS 69 (Ladies)
18 L 5185 yds SSS 66 (Men)
Recs Am–71 Miss H Lyall
V'tors U H SOC
Fees £25 (£25)
Loc Birkenhead ½ mile. M53, 2 miles

Woolton (1901)
Doe Park, Speke Road, Woolton, Liverpool L25 7TZ
Tel (0151) 486 1601
Fax (0151) 486 1664
Mem 750
Sec SH King (0151) 486 2298
Pro A Gibson (0151) 486 1298
Holes 18 L 5706 yds SSS 68
Recs Am–63 J Edwards
Pro–66 DJ Rees
V'tors U exc comp days
Fees £20 (£28)
Loc SE Liverpool

Middlesex

Airlinks (1984)
Public
Southall Lane, Hounslow TW5 9PE
Tel (0181) 561 1418
Fax (0181) 813 6284
Sec S Brewster
Pro T Martin
Holes 18 L 6001 yds SSS 69
Recs Am–60 K Dempster
Pro–70 R Critchin (1995)
V'tors U
Fees £10 (£16)
Loc Just off M4 Junction 3
Mis Floodlit driving range
Arch Alliss/Taylor

Ashford Manor (1898)
Fordbridge Road, Ashford TW15 3RT
Tel (01784) 252049
Fax (01784) 420355
Mem 800
Sec DG Seward (01784) 257687
Pro M Finney (01784) 255940
Holes 18 L 6352 yds SSS 70
Recs Am–65 GA Homewood (1989)
Pro–64 D Talbot
V'tors H
Fees £25
Loc Ashford, off A308

Brent Valley (1938)
Public
Church Road, Hanwell, London W7 3BE
Tel (0181) 567 1287 (Bookings)
Mem 195
Sec P Bryant
Pro P Bryant
Holes 18 L 5426 yds SSS 66
Recs Am–62 T Greenwood (1996)
Pro–61 R Green (1988)
V'tors U SOC
Fees On application

Bush Hill Park (1895)
Bush Hill, Winchmore Hill, London N21 2BU
Tel (0181) 360 5738
Fax (0181) 360 5583
Mem 665
Sec IM Kirkwood
Pro A Andrews (0181) 360 4103
Holes 18 L 5825 yds SSS 68
Recs Am–63 PD Lawrence
Pro–63 W McColl
V'tors WD–H WE–M SOC
Fees £24 (£32)
Loc S of Enfield

C & L Country Club (1991)
West End Road, Northolt UB5 6RD
Tel (0181) 845 5662
Holes 9 L 4440 yds SSS 62
V'tors U SOC
Fees £10
Loc A40, opp Northolt Airport
Arch Patrick Tallack

Crews Hill (1920)
Cattlegate Road, Crews Hill, Enfield EN2 8AZ
Tel (0181) 363 0787
Fax (0181) 364 5641
Mem 600
Sec E Hollingsworth (0181) 363 6674
Pro N Wichelow (0181) 366 7422
Holes 18 L 6208 yds SSS 70
Recs Am–68 S Bishop
Pro–65 H Flatman
V'tors WD–I H WE/BH–M SOC
Fees On application
Loc 2½ miles N of Enfield. M25 Junction 24
Arch HS Colt

Ealing (1898)
Perivale Lane, Greenford UB6 8SS
Tel (0181) 997 0937
Fax (0181) 998 0756
Mem 600
Sec Mrs SA Taylor
Pro I Parsons (0181) 997 3959
Holes 18 L 6216 yds SSS 70
Recs Am–64 R Neill, C Challens
Pro–64 R Verwey
V'tors WD–U H WE/BH–M
Fees On application
Loc Marble Arch 6 miles on A40
Arch HS Colt

Enfield (1893)
Old Park Road South, Enfield EN2 7DA
Tel (0181) 363 3970
Fax (0181) 342 0381
Mem 625
Sec NA Challis
Pro L Fickling (0181) 366 4492
Holes 18 L 6154 yds SSS 70
Recs Am–62 T Greenwood
Pro–66 L Fickling
V'tors WD–H WE/BH–M SOC–WD
Fees £25 D–£30
Loc 1 mile NE of Enfield. M25 Junction 24-A1005
Arch James Braid

Finchley (1929)
Nether Court, Frith Lane, London NW7 1PU
Tel (0181) 346 2436
Fax (0181) 343 4205
Mem 550
Sec WD Keene
Pro DM Brown (0181) 346 5086
Holes 18 L 6356 yds SSS 71
Recs Am–65 D Chatterton
Pro–67 T Moore
V'tors WD–U WE–pm only SOC
Fees On application
Loc M1 Junction 2
Arch James Braid

Fulwell (1904)
Wellington Road, Hampton Hill TW12 1JY
Fax (0181) 977 7732
Mem 750
Sec PF Butcher (0181) 977 2733
Pro N Turner (0181) 977 3844
Holes 18 L 6544 yds SSS 71
Recs Am–65 P Wharton (1992)
Pro–63 P Buchan (1982)
V'tors WD–I WE–M SOC
Fees £30 (£35)
Loc Opposite Fulwell Station

Grim's Dyke (1910)
Oxhey Lane, Hatch End, Pinner HA5 4AL
Tel (0181) 428 4093
Fax (0181) 421 5494
Mem 575
Sec DMG Monk (0181) 428 4539
Pro J Rule (0181) 428 7484
Holes 18 L 5600 yds SSS 67
Recs Am–65 J Thornton (1988)
Pro–61 G Kemble (1995)
V'tors WD–U H WE–M SOC exc BH–NA
Fees £20 D–£25
Loc 2 miles NW of Harrow (A4008)
Arch James Braid

Hampstead (1893)
Winnington Road, London N2 0TU
Tel (0181) 455 0203
Fax (0181) 731 6194
Mem 435
Sec ACM Harris
Pro PJ Brown (0181) 455 7089

Holes 9 L 5812 yds SSS 68
Recs Am–66 RDA Smith
Pro–64 A Sheaff
V'tors Phone Pro first SOC
Fees £30 (£35)
Loc 1 mile from Hampstead, nr Spaniards Inn
Arch Tom Dunn

Harrow School (1978)
High Street, Harrow-on-the-Hill HA1 3HW
Mem 440 100(L) 10(J)
Sec PG Dunbar (0181) 869 1253
Holes 9 L 3690 yds SSS 57
Recs Am–58
V'tors M
Loc Harrow School
Arch Donald Steel

Haste Hill (1933)
Public
The Drive, Northwood HA6 1HN
Tel (01923) 825224
Fax (01923) 826485
Mem 250
Sec S Cella
Pro C Smillie
Holes 18 L 5736 yds SSS 68
Recs Am–65 M Stanton
V'tors U SOC
Fees £11.85 (£16.85)
Loc Northwood-Hillingdon

Heath Park (1975)
Stockley Road, West Drayton
Tel (01895) 444232
Fax (01895) 445122
Mem 180
Sec J O'Loughlin (Prop)
Holes 9 L 3800 yds SSS 62
Recs Am–65 P Moor (1994)
V'tors U SOC
Fees 18 holes–£5.50 (£6.50)
Loc Holiday Inn, Heathrow

Hendon (1903)
Ashley Walk, Devonshire Road, London NW7 1DG
Tel (0181) 346 6023
Fax (0181) 343 1974
Mem 560
Sec DE Cooper
Pro S Murray (0181) 346 8990
Holes 18 L 6266 yds SSS 70
Recs Am–68 AL MacLeod
Pro–66 SWT Murray
V'tors WD–U WE/BH–bookings SOC
Fees £28 D–£35 (£35)
Loc M1 Junction 2, by Copthall Sports Centre
Arch HS Colt

Highgate (1904)
Denewood Road, Highgate, London N6 4AH
Tel (0181) 340 1906 (Clubhouse)
Fax (0181) 348 9152
Mem 700
Sec JG Wilson (0181) 340 3745

For list of abbreviations see page 527

Middlesex 603

Pro R Turner (0181) 340 5467
Holes 18 L 5964 yds SSS 69
Recs Am–66 D Kingsman, P Bax, G Clarke, CR Lloyd
Pro–66 I Martin (1987)
V'tors WD–U exc Wed–NA WE/BH–M SOC
Fees £27
Loc Off Sheldon Avenue

Hillingdon (1892)
18 Dorset Way, Hillingdon, Uxbridge UB10 0JR
Tel (01895) 239810
Fax (01895) 233956
Mem 375
Sec KJ Newton (01895) 233956
Pro PCR Smith (01895) 460035
Holes 9 L 5459 yds SSS 67
Recs Am–62 J Hall
Pro–61 N Wichelow
V'tors WD–U exc Thurs 12–4pm WE pm–M H SOC–WD
Fees £15 D–£27
Loc Off Uxbridge Road, opposite St John's Church

Horsenden Hill (1935)
Public
Woodland Rise, Greenford UB6 0RD
Tel (0181) 902 4555
Pro T Martin
Holes 9 L 3264 yds SSS 56
V'tors U
Fees On application
Loc Greenford

Hounslow Heath (1979)
Public
Staines Road, Hounslow TW4 5DS
Tel (0181) 570 5271
Mem 200
Sec G Wakefield
Holes 18 L 5901 yds SSS 68
V'tors WD–U WE–booking essential
Fees £7.70 (£11.20)
Loc Opposite Green Lane, Staines Road (A315)
Arch Fraser

Lee Valley (1973)
Pay and play
Lee Valley Leisure, Picketts Lock Lane, Edmonton, London N9 0AS
Tel (0181) 803 3611
Pro RG Gerken
Holes 18 L 4902 yds SSS 64
V'tors WD–U WE–booking advisable
Fees £10 (£13)
Loc 1 mile N of North Circular Road, Edmonton on Meridian Way
Mis Floodlit driving range

London Golf Centre
(1984)
Public
Ruislip Road, Northolt UB5 6QZ
Tel (0181) 841 6162/845 2332
Fax (0181) 842 2097

Sec JP Clifford (Gen Mgr), N Sturgess
Pro G Newall (0181) 845 3180
Holes 9 L 5838 yds SSS 69
Recs Am–71 D Clark (1990)
Pro–67 J Livesley (1990)
V'tors U SOC
Fees 9 holes–£5 18 holes–£9
Loc Off A40, nr Polish war memorial
Mis Driving range

Mill Hill (1925)
100 Barnet Way, Mill Hill, London NW7 3AL
Tel (0181) 959 2282
Fax (0181) 906 0731
Mem 450
Sec G Mabon (0181) 959 2339
Pro G Harvey (0181) 959 7261
Holes 18 L 6309 yds SSS 70
Recs Am–65 H Aarons
Pro–67 J Hudson
V'tors WD–U H WE/BH–U H after 11.30am SOC–Mon/Wed/Fri
Fees £22.50 (£30)
Loc 3/4 mile N of Apex Corner, nr A1/A41 junction
Arch Abercromby/Colt

Muswell Hill (1893)
Rhodes Avenue, Wood Green, London N22 7UT
Tel (0181) 888 2044
Fax (0181) 889 9380
Mem 600
Sec A Heron (0181) 888 1764
Pro D Wilton (0181) 888 8046
Holes 18 L 6474 yds SSS 71
Recs Am–67 PJ Montague
Pro–65 H Weetman
V'tors WD–U WE–book with Pro SOC
Fees £23 D–£33 (£35)
Loc 1 mile from Bounds Green Station. Central London 7 miles
Arch Braid/Wilson

North Middlesex (1928)
The Manor House, Friern Barnet Lane, Whetstone, London N20 0NL
Tel (0181) 445 1732
Fax (0181) 445 5023
Mem 600
Sec P Marshall (Mgr) (0181) 445 1604
Pro ASR Roberts (0181) 445 3060
Holes 18 L 5625 yds SSS 67
Recs Am–65 M Cohen
Pro–64 S Levermore
V'tors WE/BH–restricted SOC–WD
Fees £22 (£27.50)
Loc 5 miles S of M25 Junction 23, between Barnet and Finchley
Arch Willie Park Jr

Northolt (1991)
Pay and play
Huxley Close, Northolt UB5 5UL
Tel (0181) 841 5550
Mem 250

Sec L Gribben
Pro I Godleman
Holes 9 hole course Par 56 SSS 55
V'tors U SOC
Fees £5
Loc Nr M40 Target roundabout
Mis Driving range

Northwood (1891)
Rickmansworth Road, Northwood HA6 2QW
Tel (01923) 825329
Fax (01923) 840150
Mem 560
Sec D Thompson (01923) 821384
Pro CJ Holdsworth (01923) 820112
Holes 18 L 6553 yds SSS 71
Recs Am–68 JC Haynes (1997)
Pro–67 J Bland (1977)
V'tors WD–H WE/BH–NA SOC
Fees £27 (£35)
Loc 3 miles SE of Rickmansworth (A404)
Arch James Braid

Perivale Park (1932)
Public
Stockdove Way, Argyle Road, Greenford UB6 8EN
Sec GC Taylor
Pro P Bryant (0181) 575 7116
Holes 9 L 5296 yds SSS 65
Recs Am–63 W McWilliams
Pro–63
V'tors U
Fees 9 holes–£4.40 (£6.50) 18 holes–£11.50
Loc 1 mile E of Greenford, off A40

Pinner Hill (1927)
Southview Road, Pinner Hill HA5 3YA
Tel (0181) 866 0963
Fax (0181) 868 4817
Mem 770
Sec RJ Tibbs
Pro M Grieve (0181) 866 2109
Holes 18 L 6266 yds SSS 70
Recs Am–63 SR Warrin
Pro–67 TH Cotton, G Player, T Wilkes, G Low, J Warren
V'tors WD–H exc Wed & Thurs–U Sun/BH–M SOC
Fees £25 (£32) exc Wed & Thurs–£12
Loc 1 mile W from Pinner Green
Arch JH Taylor

Ruislip (1936)
Public
Ickenham Road, Ruislip HA4 7DQ
Tel (01895) 638835
Fax (01923) 822877
Mem 450
Sec BJ Channing (01895) 636963
Pro G Lloyd
Holes 18 L 5702 yds Par 69 SSS 68
Recs Am–64 W Bennet
Pro–65 A George
V'tors U SOC
Fees £10 (£12.50–£15)

For list of abbreviations see page 527

Loc   W Ruislip BR/LTE Station
Mis   Driving range
Arch A Herd

Stanmore (1893)
29 Gordon Avenue, Stanmore
HA7 2RL
Tel   (0181) 954 2599
Mem   590
Sec   AW Schooling
Pro   VR Law (0181) 954 2646
Holes 18 L 5860 yds SSS 68
Recs Am–64 P Hardy (1994)
      Pro–62 V Law (1984)
V'tors WD–H WE/BH–M
      SOC–Wed & Thurs
Fees £25
Loc   Between Stanmore and
      Belmont, off Old Church
      Lane

Stockley Park (1993)
Pay and play
The Clubhouse, Stockley Park, Uxbridge
UB11 1AQ
Tel   (0181) 813 5700/561 6339
      (Bookings)
Fax   (0181) 813 5655
Sec   N Munro
Pro   A Knox
Holes 18 L 6548 yds SSS 71
V'tors U SOC
Fees £23 (£33)
Loc   Heathrow Airport, 2 miles.
      M4 Junction 4, 1 mile
Arch Robert Trent Jones Sr

Strawberry Hill (1900)
Wellesley Road, Strawberry Hill,
Twickenham TW2 5SD
Tel   (0181) 894 1246
Mem   350
Sec   Mrs M King
      (0181) 894 0165
Pro   P Buchan
      (0181) 898 2082
Holes 9 L 2381 yds Par 64 SSS 62
Recs Am–61 RE Heryet
      Pro–59 H Fullicks, R Gerken,
      K Bousfield
V'tors WD–U WE–M XL
Fees £20
Loc   Strawberry Hill Station
Arch JH Taylor

Sudbury (1920)
Bridgewater Road, Wembley
HA0 1AL
Tel   (0181) 902 3713
Fax   (0181) 903 2966
Mem   640
Sec   AJ Poole (Gen Mgr)
Pro   N Jordan (0181) 902 7910
Holes 18 L 6282 yds SSS 70
Recs Am–63 T Greenwood,
      L White
      Pro–65 J Gill
V'tors WD–H WE–M
      SOC–Tues–Fri
Fees On application
Loc   Junction of A4005/A4090

Sunbury (1993)
Pay and play
Charlton Lane, Shepperton TW17 8QA
Tel   (01932) 771414
Fax   (01932) 789300
Mem   350
Sec   R Pilbury (Gen Mgr)
      (01932) 771414
      ML Wadsworth (Hon)
Pro   A Hardaway
      (01932) 772898
Holes 18 L 5540 yds Par 66 SSS 67
      9 L 2607 yds Par 33
V'tors U–phone Pro SOC
Fees £12 (£17)
Loc   SE of Queen Mary Reservoir,
      nr Chalton. M3 Junction 1, 2
      miles
Mis   Floodlit driving range

Trent Park (1973)
Public
Bramley Road, Southgate, London
N14 4UT
Tel   (0181) 366 7432
Fax   (0181) 368 3823
Pro   T Sheaff
Holes 18 L 6008 yds SSS 69
Recs Am–65 M Skinner (1989)
      Pro–64 V Law (1979)
V'tors WD–U SOC WE–NA before
      11am
Fees £10.60 (£13.50)
Loc   Nr Oakwood Tube station
Mis   Driving range

Twickenham (1977)
Pay and play
Staines Road, Twickenham TW2 5JD
Tel   (0181) 783 1698
Fax   (0181) 941 9134
Pro   Suzy Watt (0181) 783 1698
Holes 9 L 6014 yds SSS 69
V'tors U
Fees On application
Loc   2 miles NW of Hampton
      Court, nr end of M3
Mis   Floodlit driving range

Uxbridge (1947)
Public
The Drive, Harefield Place, Uxbridge
UB10 8PA
Tel   (01895) 231169
Fax   (01895) 810262
Pro   P Howard (01895) 237287
Holes 18 L 5711 yds SSS 68
Recs Am–65 A Schyns (1988)
      Pro–64 P Smith (1994)
V'tors U SOC
Fees £10 (£15)
Loc   2 miles N of Uxbridge. B467
      off A40 towards Ruislip

West Middlesex (1891)
Greenford Road, Southall UB1 3EE
Tel   (0181) 574 3450
Fax   (0181) 574 2383
Mem   700
Sec   PJ Furness

Pro   IP Harris (0181) 574 1800
Holes 18 L 6119 yds SSS 69
Recs Am–65 J Walsh
      Pro–64 L Farmer
V'tors WD–U WE–NA
Fees Tues/Thurs/Fri–£15.50
      (£27.50) Mon & Wed–£10
Loc   Junction of Uxbridge Road
      and Greenford Road
Arch James Braid

Whitewebbs (1932)
Public
Beggars Hollow, Clay Hill, Enfield
EN2 9JN
Tel   (0181) 363 2951
Mem   200
Sec   IF Forsyth
Pro   P Garlick (0181) 363 4454
Holes 18 L 5863 yds SSS 68
Recs Am–61 C Smith
      Pro–68 D Lewis
V'tors U
Fees £10 (£12)
Loc   1 mile N of Enfield

Wyke Green (1928)
Syon Lane, Isleworth, Osterley
TW7 5PT
Tel   (0181) 560 8777
Fax   (0181) 569 8390
Mem   700
Sec   JA Knight
Pro   N Smith (0181) 847 0685
Holes 18 L 6242 yds SSS 70
Recs Am–65 MR Johnson
      Pro–64 C DeFoy
V'tors WD–H WE/BH–M SOC
Fees £22.50 D–£27.50 After
      3pm–£16
Loc   ½ mile from Gillette Corner
      (A4)

Norfolk

Barnham Broom Hotel (1977)
Honingham Road, Barnham Broom,
Norwich NR9 4DD
Tel   (01603) 759393 (Hotel),
      (01603) 759552 (Golf Shop)
Fax   (01603) 758224
Mem   500
Sec   P Ballingall (Golf Dir)
      (01603) 759393 Ext 278
Pro   P Ballingall
Holes Valley 18 L 6483 yds Par 72
      SSS 71; Hill 18 L 6538 yds
      Par 71 SSS 71
Recs Valley Am–69 A Elliot
      Pro–65 J Higgins
      Hill Am–71 A Marshall
V'tors I or H SOC
Fees £19 D–£25 (£25 D–£35)
Loc   8 miles SW of Norwich,
      off A47. 4 miles NW of
      Wymondham, off A11
Mis   3 Academy holes
Arch Pennink/Steel

Bawburgh (1978)
Glen Lodge, Marlingford Road, Bawburgh, Norwich NR9 3LU
Tel (01603) 740404
Fax (01603) 740403
Mem 650
Sec I Ladbrooke (Golf Dir), J Barnard
Pro C Potter (01603) 742323
Holes 18 L 6224 yds SSS 70
Recs Am–67 K Parfitt
Pro–67 T Varney, A Hemsley
V'tors U–phone first SOC
Fees £18 (£22)
Loc 2 miles W of Norwich, off A47 Norwich Southern Bypass
Mis Floodlit driving range. Golf Academy
Arch Shaun Manser

Caldecott Hall
Caldecott Hall, Beccles Road, Fritton NR31 9EY
Tel (01493) 488488
Fax (01493) 488561
Mem 600
Sec P Riches
Pro M Snazell
Holes 18 L 6476 yds Par 71 SSS 71
9 hole Par 3 course
V'tors H SOC
Fees £15 (£25)
Loc 5 miles SW of Gt Yarmouth on A413
Mis Floodlit driving range. 9 hole pitch & putt

Costessey Park (1983)
Costessey Park, Costessey, Norwich NR8 5AL
Tel (01603) 746333
Fax (01603) 746185
Mem 600
Sec GC Stangoe
Pro S Cook (01603) 747085
Holes 18 L 5820 yds Par 71 SSS 68
Recs Am–68 S Locke (1998)
V'tors U SOC-WD
Fees On application
Loc 3 miles W of Norwich, off A47 at Round Well PH

Dereham (1934)
Quebec Road, Dereham NR19 2DS
Tel (01362) 695900
Fax (01362) 695904
Mem 390
Sec W Sargeant
Pro R Curtis (01362) 695631
Holes 9 L 6225 yds SSS 70
Recs Am–64 AC Marshall (1995)
Pro–65 M Elsworthy (1986)
V'tors H WE-M
Fees £15 D–£20
Loc Dereham ½ mile

Dunham (1987)
Little Dunham, King's Lynn PE32 2DF
Tel (01328) 701718
Fax (01328) 701906
Mem 250

Sec J Glencross
Pro J Laing (01485) 520076
Holes 9 L 2269 yds SSS 62
V'tors U SOC
Fees £9 (£12)
Loc 4 miles NE of Swaffham, off A47. Signs from Necton
Arch Cecil Denny

Dunston Hall (1994)
Pay and play
Ipswich Road, Dunston, Norwich NR14 8PQ
Tel (01508) 470178
Fax (01508) 471499
Mem 250
Sec J Hillis
Pro P Briggs
Holes 18 L 6200 yds Par 71 SSS 70
V'tors U
Fees £20 (£25)
Loc 5 miles S of Norwich on A140
Mis Driving range
Arch John Glasgow

Eagles (1990)
39 School Road, Tilney All Saints, Kings Lynn PE34 4RS
Tel (01553) 827147
Fax (01553) 829777
Mem 200
Sec D Horn
Pro N Pickerell
Holes 9 L 2142 yds SSS 61
9 hole Par 3 course
V'tors U
Fees 9 holes–£6.50 (£7.50)
Loc 5 miles W of Kings Lynn on A47
Mis Driving range
Arch David Horn

Eaton (1910)
Newmarket Road, Norwich NR4 6SF
Tel (01603) 452881
Fax (01603) 451686
Mem 640 135(L) 70(J)
Sec Mrs LA Bovill (01603) 451686
Pro M Allen (01603) 452478
Holes 18 L 6135 yds SSS 69
Recs Am–64 AK Nichols (1990), M Barrett (1996)
Pro–65 M Spooner (1988)
V'tors H WE–NA before noon SOC-WD
Fees £30 (£40)
Loc S Norwich, off A11

Fakenham (1973)
The Race Course, Fakenham NR21 7NY
Tel (01328) 862867
Mem 510
Sec G Cocker (01328) 855665
Pro C Williams (01328) 863534
Holes 9 L 6174 yds SSS 69
Pro–65 K Golding (1991)
V'tors WD-U WE–NA before noon SOC
Fees £14 (£18)
Loc Fakenham racecourse

Feltwell (1976)
Thor Ave, Wilton Road, Feltwell IP26 4AY
Tel (01842) 827644
Mem 400
Sec PJ Jessop
Pro P Field
Holes 9 L 6260 yds SSS 70
Recs Am–68 S Dupe (1994)
V'tors U SOC-WD
Fees £14 (£22)
Loc 1 mile S of Feltwell on B1112
Mis Former Feltwell aerodrome

Gorleston (1906)
Warren Road, Gorleston, Gt Yarmouth NR31 6JT
Tel (01493) 661911
Mem 900
Sec NP Longbottom (01493) 661911
Pro N Brown (01493) 662103
Holes 18 L 6400 yds SSS 71
Recs Am–68 J Maddock (1981)
Pro–66 R Mann (1991)
V'tors U H SOC
Fees D–£20 (D–£25) W–£85
Loc S of Gorleston, off A12
Arch JH Taylor

Great Yarmouth & Caister (1882)
Beach House, Caister-on-Sea, Gt Yarmouth NR30 5TD
Tel (01493) 720421
Mem 700
Sec HJ Harvey (01493) 728699
Pro J Hill
Holes 18 L 6330 yds SSS 70
Recs Am–65 C Green
Pro–66 E Murray
V'tors WE–NA before noon SOC
Fees £27 (£30)
Loc Caister-on-Sea

Hunstanton (1891)
Golf Course Road, Old Hunstanton PE36 6JQ
Tel (01485) 532811
Fax (01485) 532319
Mem 650 250(L) 60(J)
Sec MT Whybrow
Pro J Carter (01485) 532751
Holes 18 L 6735 yds SSS 72
Recs Am–65 S Robertson (1989)
Pro–65 ME Gregson (1967)
V'tors WD-H after 9.30am WE–H after 10.30am SOC
Fees D–£50 (£60)
Loc 1½ miles NE of Hunstanton
Mis 2-ball play only
Arch George Fernie

King's Lynn (1923)
Castle Rising, King's Lynn PE31 6BD
Tel (01553) 631656
Fax (01553) 631036
Mem 980
Sec GJ Higgins (01553) 631654
Pro C Hanlon (01553) 631655

For list of abbreviations see page 527

Holes 18 L 6646 yds SSS 72
Recs Am–68 J Jones (1993)
Pro–64 P Hinton (1991)
Ladies–75 W Fryer (1989)
V'tors WD–U H WE/BH–NA SOC
Fees £33 (£40)
Loc 4 miles NE of King's Lynn, off A149
Arch Alliss/Thomas

Links Country Park Hotel
West Runton, Cromer NR27 9QH
Tel (01263) 838383
Fax (01263) 838264
Mem 300
Sec CB Abbott
Pro L Patterson (01263) 838215
Holes 9 L 4814 yds SSS 64
Recs Am–64 CJ Lamb (1988)
Pro–65 R Mann, GR Harvey (1987)
V'tors U
Fees £20 (£25)
Loc 3 miles W of Cromer (A149)
Arch JH Taylor

Mattishall (1990)
South Green, Mattishall, Dereham
Tel (01362) 850464
Mem 300
Sec Miss B Todd
Holes 9 L 6218 yds SSS 70
V'tors WD–U WE–U before noon SOC
Fees £8 (£10)
Loc 6 miles E of Dereham (B1063)
Mis 9 hole pitch & putt
Arch BC Todd

Middleton Hall (1989)
Middleton, King's Lynn PE32 1RH
Tel (01553) 841800
Mem 600
Sec J Holland
Pro P Field (01553) 841801
Holes 18 L 6007 yds SSS 69
Recs Am–71 D Woolley
V'tors U SOC
Fees £20 (£25)
Loc 2 miles SE of King's Lynn on A47
Mis Driving range
Arch D Scott

Mundesley (1901)
Links Road, Mundesley NR11 8ES
Tel (01263) 720279
Fax (01263) 720279
Mem 450
Sec P Clarke (Sec/Mgr) (01263) 720095
Pro TG Symmons (01831) 455261
Holes 9 L 5377 yds SSS 66
V'tors WD–U exc Wed 11.30–3.30pm WE–NA before 11.30am
Fees £17.50 (£20)
Loc 7 miles SE of Cromer

The Norfolk G&CC (1993)
Hingham Road, Reymerston, Norwich NR9 4QQ
Tel (01362) 850297
Fax (01362) 850614
Mem 400
Sec C Nunn (Gen Mgr)
Pro Alison Sheard (01362) 850778
Holes 18 L 6603 yds SSS 72
Recs Am–72 J Tavener (1994)
V'tors WD–U before 4pm –M after 4pm WE/BH–NA before noon SOC
Fees £16 (£20)
Loc 14 miles W of Norwich, off B1135 Dereham to Wymondham road
Mis 9 hole pitch & putt course

RAF Marham (1974)
RAF Marham, Kings Lynn PE33 9NP
Mem 353
Sec LS Candlish (01760) 337261 (Ext 7262)
Holes 9 L 5244 yds SSS 66
Recs Am–71
V'tors By prior arrangement–U exc Sun am
Loc 11 miles SE of King's Lynn, nr Narborough
Mis Course situated on MOD land, and may be closed without prior notice

Richmond Park (1990)
Saham Road, Watton IP25 6EA
Tel (01953) 881803
Fax (01953) 881817
Mem 600
Sec Gp Capt E Durham RAF (Rtd)
Pro A Hemsley
Holes 18 L 6300 yds SSS 70
Recs Am–71 D Glenn (1994)
Pro–69 F Kiddie (1995)
V'tors WD–U WE–H before noon SOC
Fees £18 (£24)
Loc ½ mile NW of Watton
Mis Driving range
Arch Scott/Jessup

Royal Cromer (1888)
Overstrand Road, Cromer NR27 0JH
Tel (01263) 512884
Fax (01263) 512884
Mem 700
Sec To be appointed
Pro RJ Page (01263) 512267
Holes 18 L 6508 yds SSS 72
Recs Am–67 T Hurrell (1993)
Pro–69 C Williams,
R Waugh (1991)
V'tors H SOC–WD
Fees D–£33 (D–£40)
Loc 1 mile E of Cromer on B1159
Arch HS Colt/JH Taylor

Royal Norwich (1893)
Drayton High Road, Hellesdon, Norwich NR6 5AH
Tel (01603) 425712
Fax (01603) 417945

Mem 700
Sec J Meggy (Mgr) (01603) 429928
Pro D Futter (01603) 408459
Holes 18 L 6603 yds SSS 72
Recs Am–67 A Barker (1981)
Pro–65 P Whittle (1998)
V'tors WE/BH–restricted SOC
Fees D–£30 (£36)
Loc ½ mile W of Norwich ring road, on Fakenham road
Arch James Braid

Royal West Norfolk (1892)
Brancaster, King's Lynn PE31 8AX
Tel (01485) 210223
Fax (01485) 210087
Mem 760
Sec Maj NA Carrington Smith (01485) 210087
Pro RE Kimber (01485) 210616
Holes 18 L 6428 yds SSS 71
Recs Am–67 AH Perowne
Pro–66 M Elsworthy
V'tors M No fourballs allowed Mid July–mid Sept WE–NA before 10am SOC
Fees £50 (£60)
Loc 7 miles E of Hunstanton on A419
Arch Holcombe Ingleby

Ryston Park (1932)
Ely Road, Denver, Downham Market PE38 0HH
Tel (01366) 382133
Fax (01366) 383834
Mem 320
Sec WJ Flogdell
Pro None
Holes 9 L 6310 yds SSS 70
Recs Am–66 JP Alflatt (1975)
V'tors WD–H WE/BH–M SOC
Fees £15 D–£20
Loc 1 mile S of Downham Market on A10
Arch James Braid

Sheringham (1891)
Sheringham NR26 8HG
Tel (01263) 822038
Fax (01263) 825189
Mem 700
Sec MJ Garrett (01263) 823488
Pro MW Jubb (01263) 822980
Holes 18 L 6464 yds SSS 71
Recs Am–65 J Little (1995)
Pro–66 R Mann (1991)
V'tors WD–U H after 9.30am SOC
Fees £37 (£42)
Loc ½ mile W of Sheringham (A149)
Arch Tom Dunn

Sprowston Park (1980)
Pay and play
Wroxham Road, Sprowston, Norwich NR7 8RP
Tel (01603) 410657
Fax (01603) 788884
Mem 500
Sec G Porter

For list of abbreviations see page 527

Pro G Ireson (01603) 417264
Holes 18 L 5982 yds SSS 70
Recs Am–65 M Frary
Pro–65 N Catchpole
V'tors U SOC
Fees £17 (£21)
Loc 2 miles NE of Norwich on A1151
Mis Floodlit driving range

Swaffham (1922)

Cley Road, Swaffham PE37 8AE
Tel **(01760) 721611**
Mem 500
Sec R Joslin
Pro P Field
Holes 9 L 6252 yds SSS 70
Recs Am–68 G Head
Pro–64 CJ Norton
V'tors WD–U WE–M exc Sun am–NA
Fees £18
Loc 1½ miles SW of Swaffham

Thetford (1912)

Brandon Road, Thetford IP24 3NE
Tel **(01842) 752258 (Clubhouse)**
Fax (01842) 766212
Mem 700
Sec Mrs SA Redpath (01842) 752169
Pro G Kitley (01842) 752662
Holes 18 L 6879 yds SSS 73
Recs Am -66 MP Williamson
Pro–68 C Green
Ladies–74 S Saunders
V'tors WD SOC–Wed–Fri
Fees £32
Loc 2 miles W of Thetford (B1107), off A11 By-pass

Wensum Valley (1990)

Beech Avenue, Taverham, Norwich NR8 6HP
Tel **(01603) 261012**
Fax (01603) 261664
Mem 850
Sec Miss B Todd
Pro P Whittle
Holes 18 L 6000 yds SSS 69
18 L 4862 yds SSS 66
Recs Am–69 P Robson (1993)
Pro–67 M Spooner (1990)
V'tors WD–U H WE–NA before noon SOC
Fees £18 (£18)
Loc 4 miles NW of Norwich on A1067
Mis Floodlit driving range
Arch BC Todd

Weston Park (1993)

Weston Longville, Norwich NR9 5JW
Tel **(01603) 872363**
Fax (01603) 873040
Mem 400
Sec RR Wright (Gen Mgr), DF Cottier
Pro MR Few (01603) 872998
Holes 18 L 6603 yds SSS 72
Recs Am–69 R Brindle (1998)
Pro–72 C Williams (1998)

V'tors WD–U H
Fees £24 (£29)
Loc 7 miles NW of Norwich, off A1067
Arch John Glasgow

Northamptonshire

Brampton Heath

Sandy Lane, Church Brampton NN6 8AX
Tel **(01604) 843939**
Mem 500
Pro R HUdson
Holes 18 L6225 yds Par 71 SSS 70
V'tors U SOC–WD
Fees £12 (£16)
Loc 4 miles N of Northampton between A50 and A428

Cold Ashby (1974)

Stanford Road, Cold Ashby, Northampton NN6 6EP
Tel **(01604) 740548**
Fax (01604) 740548
Mem 600 40(L) 40(J)
Sec DA Croxton (Prop)
Pro S Rose (01604) 740099
Holes 27 L 6308 yds Par 72 SSS 70
Recs Am–69 G Croxton (1997)
Pro–65 J Higgins (1996)
V'tors WD–U WE–U after 12 noon (if booked) SOC
Fees £16 (£19)
Loc 11 miles N of Northampton, nr A5199/A14 Junction 1.
7 miles E of M1 Junction 18
Arch David Croxton

Collingtree Park (1990)

Windingbrook Lane, Northampton NN4 0XN
Tel **(01604) 700000**
Fax (01604) 702600
Mem 900
Sec Miss J Byrne
Pro G Pook
Holes 18 L 6695 yds SSS 72
Recs Am–67 S Bottomley (1993)
Pro–66 M Persson (1994)
Ladies Pro–69 J Hill (1994)
V'tors H SOC
Fees £30 (£40)
Loc ½ mile E of M1 Junction 15
Mis Floodlit driving range
Arch Johnny Miller

Daventry & District (1922)

Norton Road, Daventry NN11 5LS
Tel **(01327) 702829**
Mem 350
Sec J Grainger (01327) 706245
Pro None
Holes 9 L 5812 yds Par 69 SSS 68
V'tors WD–U Sun–NA before 11am SOC–phone Pro
Fees £8 (£10)
Loc 2 miles E of Daventry

Delapre (1976)

Public
Eagle Drive, Nene Valley Way, Northampton NN4 7DU
Tel **(01604) 764036/763957**
Fax (01604) 706378
Mem 1000
Sec JS Corby (01604) 763957
Pro J Corby, J Cuddihy (01604) 764036
Holes 18 L 6293 yds SSS 70
9 L 2146 yds SSS 32
2 x 9 holes Par 3 courses
Recs Am–66 M McNally
V'tors U SOC
Fees £8.50 (£12)
Loc 3 miles from M1 Junction 15, on A508/A45
Mis Pitch & putt. Driving range
Arch Jacobs/Corby

Embankment (1975)

The Embankment, Wellingborough NN8 1LD
Tel **(01933) 228465**
Mem 175
Sec JB Andrew, E Walden (Mgr)
Holes 9 L 3400 yds SSS 56
Recs Am–58
V'tors WD–M
Fees £4
Loc 1 mile SE of Wellingborough
Arch TH Neal

Farthingstone Hotel (1974)

Farthingstone, Towcester NN12 8HA
Tel **(01327) 361291**
Fax (01327) 361645
Mem 400
Sec DC Donaldson (Prop/Mgr)
Pro (01327) 361533
Holes 18 L 6299 yds SSS 70
Recs Am–63 C Lawrence (1996)
Pro–66 D Thorp (1984),
M Gallagher (1985),
K Dickens (1989)
V'tors U SOC
Fees £10 D–£15 (£15 D–£20) SOC–from £10
Loc 4 miles W of A5 on Farthingstone-Everdon road.
M1 Junction 16, 6 miles

Hellidon Lakes Hotel & CC (1991)

Hellidon, Daventry NN11 6LN
Tel **(01327) 62550**
Fax (01327) 62559
Mem 500
Sec J Nicoll
Pro G Wills (01327) 62551
Holes 18 L 6700 yds SSS 72
9 L 5582 yds SSS 67
Recs Am–70 P Hutchinson (1995)
V'tors U H SOC
Fees £15 (£25)
Loc 7 miles SW of Daventry, via A361.
Arch David Snell

For list of abbreviations see page 527

Northamptonshire

Kettering (1891)
Headlands, Kettering NN15 6XA
- **Tel** (01536) 511104
- **Mem** 700 100(L) 50(J)
- **Sec** DG Buckby
- **Pro** K Theobald (01536) 81014
- **Holes** 18 L 6087 yds SSS 69
- **Recs** Am–65 A Draper (1992)
  Pro–64 P Smith (1991)
- **V'tors** WD–U WE/BH–M SOC
- **Fees** D–£24
- **Loc** S boundary of Kettering
- **Arch** Tom Morris

Kingfisher CC
Pay and play
Buckingham Road, Deanshanger, Milton Keynes MK18 6DG
- **Tel** (01908) 562332
- **Fax** (01908) 260857
- **Mem** 200
- **Sec** Maj DM Barraclough (01908) 560217
- **Pro** None
- **Holes** 9 L 5471 yds Par 70 SSS 67
- **V'tors** U SOC
- **Fees** £6.50 (£12.50)
- **Loc** NW of Milton Keynes on A422 to Buckingham
- **Mis** Covered driving range
- **Arch** Donald Steel

Kingsthorpe (1908)
Kingsley Road, Northampton NN2 7BU
- **Tel** (01604) 711173
- **Fax** (01604) 710610
- **Mem** 600
- **Sec** JE Harris (01604) 710610
- **Pro** P Armstrong (01604) 719602
- **Holes** 18 L 5918 yds SSS 69
- **Recs** Am–63 S McDonald
  Pro–64 B Larratt
- **V'tors** WD–U WE/BH–M H SOC–WD
- **Fees** D–£25
- **Loc** 2 miles N of Northampton centre, off A508

Northampton (1893)
Harlestone, Northampton NN7 4EF
- **Tel** (01604) 845102
- **Fax** (01604) 820262
- **Mem** 595 134(L) 65(J)
- **Sec** RL Jones (01604) 845155
- **Pro** K Dickens (01604) 845167
- **Holes** 18 L 6615 yds Par 72 SSS 72
- **Recs** Am–67 GH Keates (1996)
  Pro–67 D Eddiford, J Higgins, A Hare (1995)
  Ladies–73 K Hanwell (1998)
- **V'tors** WD–U H WE–M SOC
- **Fees** £30
- **Loc** 4 miles NW of Northampton, on A428 beyond Harlestone
- **Arch** Donald Steel

Northamptonshire County (1909)
Church Brampton, Northampton NN6 8AZ
- **Tel** (01604) 842170
- **Mem** 650
- **Sec** ME Wadley (01604) 843025
- **Pro** T Rouse (01604) 842226
- **Holes** 18 L 6503 yds SSS 71
- **Recs** Am–65 R Duck (1994)
  Pro–64 J Higgins (1990)
- **V'tors** H SOC
- **Fees** Summer–£40 (£40)
  Winter–£30 (£30)
- **Loc** 5 miles NW of Northampton, off A50
- **Arch** HS Colt

Oundle (1893)
Benefield Road, Oundle PE8 4EZ
- **Tel** (01832) 273267
- **Fax** (01832) 273267
- **Mem** 600
- **Sec** G Brooks (Gen Mgr)
- **Pro** R Keys (01832) 272273
- **Holes** 18 L 6235 yds SSS 70
- **Recs** Am–68
  Pro–67
- **V'tors** WD–U WE–M before 10.30am
  –U after 10.30am SOC
- **Fees** £23 (£31)
- **Loc** 1½ miles W of Oundle on A427

Overstone Park (1994)
Watermark Leisure, Billing Lane, Northampton NN6 0AP
- **Tel** (01604) 647666
- **Fax** (01604) 642635
- **Mem** 450
- **Sec** B Willoughby
- **Pro** B Mudge (01604) 643555
- **Holes** 18 L 6602 yds SSS 72
- **V'tors** M
- **Fees** £14 (£18)
- **Loc** 4 miles E of Northampton, off A45. M1 Junction 15
- **Mis** Driving range
- **Arch** Donald Steel

Priors Hall (1965)
Public
Stamford Road, Weldon, Corby
- **Tel** (01536) 260756
- **Fax** (01536) 260756
- **Mem** 471
- **Sec** T Arnold
- **Pro** G Bradbrook
- **Holes** 18 L 6631 yds SSS 72
- **Recs** Am–72 G Shelton
  Pro–70 RH Kemp
- **V'tors** U SOC–WD
- **Fees** On application
- **Loc** 4 miles E of Corby (A43)
- **Arch** Hawtree

Rushden (1919)
Kimbolton Road, Chelveston, Wellingborough NN9 6AN
- **Tel** (01933) 418511
- **Mem** 350
- **Sec** SP Trayhorn
- **Holes** 10 L 6335 yds Par 71 SSS 70
- **Recs** Am–69
- **V'tors** WD–U exc Wed pm WE/BH–M SOC
- **Fees** £15
- **Loc** On A45, 2 miles E of Higham Ferrers

Staverton Park (1977)
Staverton Park, Staverton, Daventry NN11 6JT
- **Tel** (01327) 302000/302118
- **Fax** (01327) 311428
- **Sec** D Entwhistle (Gen Mgr),
  Mrs A Radford (Sec)
- **Pro** R Mudge (01327) 705506
- **Holes** 18 L 6602 yds SSS 72
- **Recs** Am–67
  Pro–64
- **V'tors** U SOC
- **Fees** On application
- **Loc** 1 mile SW of Daventry, off A425. M1 Junctions 16/18. M40 Junction 11
- **Mis** Driving range

Stoke Albany (1997)
Ashley Road, Stoke Albany, Market Harborough LE16 8PL
- **Tel** (01858) 535208
- **Fax** (01858) 535505
- **Mem** 400
- **Sec** R Want
- **Pro** A Clifford
- **Holes** 18 L 6132 yds Par 71 SSS 69
- **V'tors** U SOC
- **Fees** £12 (£16)
- **Loc** Between Market Harborough and Corby (A427)
- **Arch** Hawtree

Wellingborough (1893)
Harrowden Hall, Great Harrowden, Wellingborough NN9 5AD
- **Tel** (01933) 677234/673022
- **Fax** (01933) 679379
- **Mem** 850
- **Sec** R Tomlin (01933) 677234
- **Pro** D Clifford (01933) 678752
- **Holes** 18 L 6620 yds SSS 72
- **Recs** Am–69 J Campbell (1993)
  Pro–68 M Gallagher (1993)
- **V'tors** WD–U H exc Tues WE–M SOC–WD exc Tues
- **Fees** D–£35
- **Loc** 2 miles N of Wellingborough on A509
- **Arch** Hawtree

Whittlebury Park G&CC (1992)
Whittlebury, Towcester NN12 8XW
- **Tel** (01327) 858092
- **Fax** (01327) 858009
- **Mem** 450
- **Sec** PJ Tomlin
- **Pro** M Leung (01327) 858588
- **Holes** 36 holes: 5000-7000 yds SSS 66-72
- **V'tors** U H SOC
- **Fees** £18 D–£30 (£25 D–£35)
- **Loc** 4 miles S of Towcester on A413
- **Mis** Driving range. Indoor golf centre
- **Arch** Cameron Sinclair

Northumberland

Allendale (1906)
High Studdon, Allenheads Road, Allendale, Hexham NE47 9DH
Mem 140 30(L) 9(J)
Sec Ann Egdell (Hon) (01434) 345005
Holes 9 L 5044 yds SSS 65
V'tors U BH–NA before 2pm SOC
Fees £10
Loc 1½ miles S of Allendale on B6295

Alnmouth (1869)
Foxton Hall, Alnmouth NE66 3BE
Tel (01665) 830231
Fax (01665) 830922
Mem 800
Sec C Jobson
Pro Shop (01665) 830043
Holes 18 L 6484 yds SSS 71
Recs Am–64 IS Ferrie (1996)
V'tors Mon/Tues/Thurs–H (restricted) SOC
Fees £22 D–£29
Loc 5 miles SE of Alnwick
Mis Dormy House
Arch HS Colt

Alnmouth Village (1869)
Marine Road, Alnmouth NE66 2RZ
Tel (01665) 830370
Mem 340
Sec W Maclean (01665) 602096
Holes 9 L 6020 yds SSS 70
Recs Am–63 D Weddell
V'tors H
Fees £15 (£20)
Loc Alnmouth

Alnwick (1907)
Swansfield Park, Alnwick NE66 1AT
Tel (01665) 602632
Mem 500
Sec LE Stewart (01665) 602499
Holes 18 L 6250 yds SSS 70
Recs Am–66 G Ridley (1996)
V'tors U
Fees D–£15 (D–£20)
Loc Alnwick, off A1
Arch Rochester/Rae

Arcot Hall (1909)
Dudley, Cramlington NE23 7QP
Tel (0191) 236 2794
Fax (0191) 217 0370
Mem 660
Sec F Elliott (0191) 236 2794
Pro GM Cant (0191) 236 2794
Holes 18 L 6389 yds SSS 70
Recs Am–65 G Pickup (1990), A Leach, D Caldicott (1994) Pro–64 B Rumney (1997)
V'tors WD–H WE/BH–M SOC
Fees D–£26 (£30) After 3pm–£21
Loc 7 miles N of Newcastle, off A1
Arch James Braid

Bamburgh Castle (1904)
The Club House, 40 The Wynding, Bamburgh NE69 7DE
Tel (01668) 214378
Mem 680
Sec TC Osborne (01668) 214321
Holes 18 L 5621 yds Par 68 SSS 67
Recs Am–64 M Dawson (1994)
V'tors WD–U H WE/BH–M SOC
Fees D–£30 (£35)
Loc 5 miles E of A1, via B1341 or B1342
Arch George Rochester

Bedlingtonshire (1972)
Public
Acorn Bank, Bedlington NE22 5SY
Tel (01670) 822457
Mem 966
Sec E Ramsay
Pro M Webb (01670) 822087
Holes 18 L 6224 metres SSS 73
Recs Am–68 D Gray Pro–64 D Curry
V'tors U
Fees £15 (£20)
Loc 12 miles N of Newcastle (A1068)
Arch Frank Pennink

Belford (1993)
South Road, Belford NE70 7HY
Tel (01668) 213433
Fax (01668) 213919
Mem 300
Sec AM Gilhome
Pro None
Holes 9 L 6304 yds SSS 70
Recs Am–72 MB Turnbull (1995)
V'tors U SOC
Fees On application
Loc 15 miles N of Alnwick, off A1
Mis Driving range
Arch Nigel Williams

Bellingham (1893)
Boggle Hole, Bellingham NE48 2DT
Tel (01434) 220530
Fax (01434) 220160
Mem 630
Sec P Cordiner (01434) 220182
Holes 18 L 6077 yds Par 70 SSS 70
Recs Am–68 S Robinson (1997)
V'tors U SOC
Fees £20 (£25)
Loc 15 miles N of Hexham, off B6320
Mis Driving range
Arch I Wilson

Berwick-upon-Tweed (1890)
Goswick Beal, Berwick-upon-Tweed TD15 2RW
Tel (01289) 387256
Fax (01289) 387256
Mem 550
Sec AE French
Pro P Terras (01289) 387380
Holes 18 L 6449 yds SSS 71

Recs
Am–69 M Hindhaugh (1995) Pro–69 GJ Brand Ladies–72 J Lee-Smith
V'tors WD–U WE–U 10–12 and after 2pm SOC
Fees £20 D–£25 (£25 D–£32)
Loc 5 miles S of Berwick, off A1
Arch James Braid

Blyth (1905)
New Delaval, Blyth NE24 4DB
Tel (01670) 540110
Fax (01670) 540134
Mem 800
Sec L Morpeth
Pro A Brown (01670) 356514
Holes 18 L 6456 yds SSS 71
Recs Am–65 S Brooks (1997)
V'tors WD–U WE/BH–M SOC–WD before 3pm
Fees £18 D–£20
Loc W end of Plessey Road, Blyth

Burgham Park (1994)
Felton, Morpeth NE65 8QP
Tel (01670) 787898
Fax (01670) 787164
Mem 530
Sec J Carr
Pro S McNally (01670) 787978
Holes 18 L 6751 yds SSS 72
Recs Am–68 I Paxton (1997) Pro–67 D Patterson (1998)
V'tors U SOC
Fees On application
Loc 7 miles N of Morpeth on A1
Mis Pitch & putt course
Arch Andrew Mair

Close House (1968)
Close House, Heddon-on-the-Wall, Newcastle-upon-Tyne NE15 0HT
Tel (01661) 852953
Mem 1100
Sec ME Pearse
Holes 18 L 5606 yds SSS 67
Recs Am–61 DJ Craig
V'tors M SOC–WD
Fees SOC D–£18
Loc 9 miles W of Newcastle on A69
Arch Hawtree

Dunstanburgh Castle (1900)
Embleton NE66 3XQ
Tel (01665) 576562
Mem 396
Sec PFC Gilbert (Mgr)
Holes 18 L 6298 yds SSS 70
Recs Am–69
V'tors U
Fees £15 (£20)
Loc 7 miles NE of Alnwick on B1339
Arch James Braid

Hexham (1892)
Spital Park, Hexham NE46 3RZ
Tel (01434) 602057 (Clubhouse)
Fax (01434) 601865
Mem 700

For list of abbreviations see page 527

Sec AN Harris (01434) 603072
Pro MW Forster (01434) 604904
Holes 18 L 6272 yds SSS 70
Recs Am–64 JP Arnott (1994)
Pro–64 D Curry
V'tors U
Fees £25 (£35)
Loc 21 miles W of Newcastle (A69)
Arch Vardon/Caird

Linden Hall (1997)
Longhorsley, Morpeth NE65 8XF
Tel (01670) 788050
Fax (01670) 788544
Mem 250
Sec D Curry (Sec/Mgr)
Pro D Curry (01670) 788050
Holes 18 L 6809 yds Par 72 SSS 73
Recs Pro–68
V'tors H SOC
Fees £25 (£27.50)
Loc 8 miles NW of Morpeth, off A697
Mis Driving range
Arch Jonathan Gaunt

Longhirst Hall (1997)
Longhirst Hall, Longhirst NE61 3LL
Tel (01670) 791505
Fax (01670) 791768
Mem 280
Sec J Boulton (01670) 812442
Pro To be appointed
Holes 18 L 6570 yds Par 72
V'tors U SOC
Fees £16 (£16)
Loc 4 miles NE of Morpeth, via A197/B1337

Magdalene Fields (1903)
Pay and play
Magdalene Fields, Berwick-upon-Tweed TD15 1NE
Tel (01289) 306384
Mem 400
Sec MJ Lynch
Holes 18 L 6407 yds SSS 71
Recs Am–65 J Patterson (1995)
V'tors U SOC
Fees £16 (£18)
Loc Berwick-upon-Tweed 1 mile
Arch Park/Jefferson/Thompson

Matfen Hall (1994)
Matfen, Hexham NE20 0RQ
Tel (01661) 886500
Fax (01661) 886055
Mem 350
Sec D Burton
Pro J Harrison
Holes 18 L 6732 yds Par 72
9 hole Par 3 course
Recs Pro–67 D Curry (1995)
V'tors U
Fees £22 (£25)
Loc 12 miles W of Newcastle, off B6318
Mis Practice range
Arch Mair/James

Morpeth (1907)
The Common, Morpeth NE61 2BT
Tel (01670) 504942
Fax (01670) 504918
Mem 700
Sec KD Cazaly (01670) 504942
Pro MR Jackson (01670) 515675
Holes 18 L 5671 metres SSS 69
Recs Am–65 MD Hall (1995)
Pro–68 T Horton (1976)
V'tors H SOC
Fees £20 (£25)
Loc 1 mile S of Morpeth on A197

Newbiggin (1884)
Newbiggin-by-the-Sea NE64 6DW
Tel (01670) 817344 (Clubhouse)
Fax (01670) 520236
Mem 500
Sec GW Beattie (01670) 852959
Pro M Webb (01670) 817833
Holes 18 L 6452 yds SSS 71
Recs Am–65 J McCallum
Pro–68 K Saint
V'tors U after 10am exc comp days–NA SOC
Fees D–£14 (D–£19)
Loc Newbiggin, nr Church Point

Ponteland (1927)
53 Bell Villas, Ponteland, Newcastle-upon-Tyne NE20 9BD
Tel (01661) 822689
Fax (01661) 860077
Mem 480 170(L) 115(J)
Sec JN Dobson
Pro A Crosby
Holes 18 L 6524 yds SSS 71
Recs Am–65 RJ Wiggins (1997)
Pro–63 B Rumney (1994)
V'tors WD–U WE/BH–M
SOC–Tues & Thurs
Fees £25
Loc 6 miles NW of Newcastle on A696, nr Airport

Prudhoe (1930)
Eastwood Park, Prudhoe-on-Tyne NE42 5DX
Tel (01661) 832466
Mem 450
Sec GB Garratt
Pro J Crawford (01661) 836188
Holes 18 L 5862 yds SSS 68
Recs Am–63 CN Hunter
Pro–65 A Crosby
V'tors WD–U
Fees £20 (£25)
Loc 15 miles W of Newcastle (A695)

Rothbury (1891)
Old Race Course, Rothbury, Morpeth NE65 7TR
Tel (01669) 621271
Mem 348
Sec WT Bathgate (01669) 620718
Pro None
Holes 9 L 5681 yds SSS 67
Recs Am–65 PA Arkle (1996)

V'tors WD–U exc Tues after 4pm & Wed am WE–by arrangement
Fees D–£11 (D–£16)
Loc 15 miles N of Morpeth on A697. W side of Rothbury
Arch JB Radcliffe

Seahouses (1913)
Beadnell Road, Seahouses NE68 7XT
Tel (01665) 720794
Mem 600
Sec JA Stevens (01665) 720809
Holes 18 L 5462 yds SSS 67
Recs Am–64 K Johnston (1993)
V'tors U SOC
Fees £16 (£20)
Loc 14 miles N of Alnwick. 9 miles E of A1 on B1340

Slaley Hall G&CC (1988)
Slaley, Hexham NE47 0BY
Tel (01434) 673350
Fax (01434) 673152
Mem 350
Pro M Stancer (01434) 673154
Holes Hunting 18 L 7021 yds SSS 74; Priestman 18 L 7010 yds SSS 74
Recs Hunting Am–67 G Storm (1998)
Pro–65 C Montgomerie, R Drummond
V'tors U
Fees Hunting: £50 (£60)
Priestman: £45 (£55)
Loc 20 miles W of Newcastle. 7 miles S of Corbridge, off A68
Mis Driving range. Academy
Arch Hunting: Dave Thomas
Priestman: Neil Coles

Stocksfield (1913)
New Ridley, Stocksfield NE43 7RE
Tel (01661) 843041
Fax (01661) 843046
Mem 459 100(L) 75(J)
Sec B Slade
Pro D Mather
Holes 18 L 5978 yds SSS 70
Recs Am–65 AR Paisley
Pro–63 S McKenna
V'tors U SOC–exc Wed & Sat
Fees £20 (£25)
Loc 2 miles S of Stocksfield. 3 miles E of A68
Arch F Pennink

Swarland Hall (1993)
Coast View, Swarland, Morpeth NE65 9JG
Tel (01670) 787940 (Clubhouse)
Sec K Rutter (01670) 787010
Pro D Fletcher (01670) 787010
Holes 18 L 6628 yds SSS 72
V'tors U
Fees £14 (£18)
Loc 8 miles S of Alnwick, 1 mile W of A1

For list of abbreviations see page 527

Tynedale (1908)
Public
Tyne Green, Hexham NE46 3HQ
Tel (01434) 608154
Sec J McDiarmid
Pro Mrs C Brown
Holes 9 L 5706 yds SSS 68
Recs Am–63
V'tors U exc Sun–booking necessary
Fees £10 (£12) (1993)
Loc S side of Hexham

Warkworth (1891)
The Links, Warkworth, Morpeth NE65 0SW
Tel (01665) 711596
Mem 400
Sec JA Gray (01665) 711556
Holes 9 L 5870 yds SSS 68
Recs Am–65 C Shell
V'tors U exc Tues & Sat SOC
Fees D–£12 (D–£20)
Loc 9 miles SE of Alnwick (A1068)
Arch Tom Morris

Wooler (1975)
Dod Law, Doddington, Wooler NE71 6EA
Mem 250
Sec WH Henderson (01668) 281137
Pro None
Holes 9 L 6372 yds SSS 70
Recs Am–72 K Fairbairn, C Renton, M Thompson (1992), S Lowrey (1996)
V'tors U SOC
Fees D–£10 (D–£15)
Loc 3 miles N of Wooler on B6525

Nottinghamshire

Beeston Fields (1923)
Beeston, Nottingham NG9 3DD
Tel (0115) 925 7062
Fax (0115) 925 4280
Mem 525 222(L) 60(J)
Sec J Lewis
Pro A Wardle (0115) 922 0872
Holes 18 L 6404 yds SSS 71
Recs Am–66 P Benson (1984) Pro–65 G Owen (1995)
V'tors U SOC
Fees £20 (£25)
Loc 4 miles W of Nottingham. M1 Junction 25
Arch Tom Williamson

Bulwell Forest (1902)
Public
Hucknall Road, Bulwell, Nottingham NG6 1LQ
Tel (0115) 977 0576
Fax (0115) 976 3172 (Pro)
Mem 400
Sec D Waddilove (Hon)
Pro L Rawlings (0115) 976 3172
Holes 18 L 5746 yds SSS 68
Recs Am–63 J Worthy Pro–62 CD Hall

V'tors U
Fees £11 (£11) Fourball–£32
Loc 4 miles N of Nottingham. M1 Junction 26, 3 miles

Chilwell Manor (1906)
Meadow Lane, Chilwell, Nottingham NG9 5AE
Tel (0115) 925 8958
Fax (0115) 922 0575
Mem 700
Sec RA Westcott
Pro P Wilson (0115) 925 8993
Holes 18 L 6395 yds Par 70 SSS 70
Recs Am–65 P Wheatcroft Pro–65 D Ridley
V'tors U SOC
Fees £18 (£20)
Loc 4 miles W of Nottingham on A6005
Arch Tom Williamson

College Pines (1993)
Worksop College Drive, Sparken Hill, Worksop S80 3AP
Tel (01909) 501431
Mem 550
Sec C Snell (Golf Dir)
Pro C Snell (01909) 501431
Holes 18 L 6663 yds SSS 72
Recs Am–71 W Beeston (1994) Pro–69 B Hunt (1994)
V'tors U–phone first SOC
Fees £12 (£18)
Loc 1 mile SE of Worksop on B6034, off Worksop Bypass
Mis Driving range
Arch David Snell

Cotgrave Place G&CC (1991)
Stragglethorpe NG12 3HB
Tel (0115) 933 3344/933 5500
Mem 400
Sec CC Rathbone
Pro G Towne (0115) 933 4686
Holes 27 L 6560 yds SSS 71-72
V'tors U
Fees £14 (£17)
Loc 4 miles SE of Nottingham, off A52
Mis Driving range
Arch Small/Glasgow

Coxmoor (1913)
Coxmoor Road, Sutton-in-Ashfield NG17 5LF
Tel (01623) 557359
Fax (01623) 557359
Mem 650
Sec N Cockbill
Pro D Ridley (01623) 559906
Holes 18 L 6501 yds SSS 72
Recs Am–65 P Fenton Pro–65 G Owen
V'tors H exc Ladies Day–Tues WE–NA SOC
Fees D–£30
Loc 1 1/2 miles S of Mansfield. 4 miles NE of M1 Junction 27 on A611

Edwalton (1982)
Public
Edwalton, Nottingham NG12 4AS
Tel (0115) 923 4775
Mem 700
Sec Mrs DJ Parkes (Hon)
Pro J Staples
Holes 9 L 3336 yds SSS 36 9 hole Par 3 course
Recs Am–73 Pro–72
V'tors U
Fees On application
Loc 2 miles S of Nottingham (A606)

Kilton Forest (1978)
Public
Blyth Road, Worksop S81 0TL
Tel (01909) 472488
Mem 364
Sec G Lawman (Hon) (01909) 485994
Pro PW Foster (01909) 486563
Holes 18 L 6344 yds Par 72 SSS 71
Recs Am–68 B Hurt (1993) Pro–71 B Hurt (1995)
V'tors WD–U WE–booking necessary SOC
Fees £7.85 (£10.25)
Loc 1 mile NE of Worksop on B6045

Leen Valley Golf Centre (1994)
Pay and play
Wigwam Lane, Hucknall NG15 7TA
Tel (0115) 964 2037
Fax (0115) 964 2724
Mem 670
Sec BR Goodman (Gen Mgr)
Pro J Lines (01623) 422764
Holes 18 L 6233 yds Par 72 SSS 70
Recs Am–70 J Denman (1998)
V'tors U SOC–WD
Fees £9 (£12)
Loc 1/2 mile from Hucknall town centre
Arch Tom Hodgetts

Mansfield Woodhouse (1973)
Public
Mansfield Woodhouse NG19 9EU
Tel (01623) 23521
Sec M Stuart
Pro L Highfield Jr
Holes 9 L 2411 yds SSS 65
Recs Am–67 S Fisher Pro–L Highfield Jr
V'tors U
Fees £3
Loc 2 miles N of Mansfield (A60)

Mapperley (1903)
Central Avenue, Plains Road, Mapperley, Nottingham NG3 5RH
Tel (0115) 955 6672
Mem 650
Sec A Newton

For list of abbreviations see page 527

Pro M Allen (0115) 955 6673
Holes 18 L 6283 yds SSS 70
Recs Am–65 R Eaton (1998)
Pro–69 D Ridley (1990)
V'tors U SOC
Fees £12 D–£15
Loc 3 miles NE of Nottingham, off B684
Arch J Mason

Newark (1901)
Kelwick, Coddington, Newark NG24 2QX
Tel (01636) 626241
Fax (01636) 626497
Mem 600
Sec AW Morgans (01636) 626282
Pro PA Lockley (01636) 626492
Holes 18 L 6421 yds SSS 71
Recs Am–66 J Johnson (1995)
Pro–65 HA Bennett (1995)
Ladies–71 E Glasby (1995)
V'tors H SOC
Fees £22 (£27)
Loc 4 miles E of Newark on A17

Nottingham City (1910)
Public
Lawton Drive, Bulwell, Nottingham NG6 8BL
Tel (0115) 927 8021
Fax (0115) 927 6916
Mem 460
Sec (0115) 927 6916
Pro CR Jepson (0115) 927 2767
Holes 18 L 6218 yds SSS 70
Recs Am–65 D Weir (1994)
Pro–66 T Smart
V'tors WD–U WE–NA before noon SOC
Fees £11 (£11)
Loc 5 miles N of Nottingham. M1 Junction 26

Notts (1887)
Hollinwell, Kirkby-in-Ashfield NG17 7QR
Tel (01623) 753225
Fax (01623) 753655
Mem 500
Sec SFC Goldie
Pro A Thomas (01623) 753087
Holes 18 L 7030 yds Par 72 SSS 74
Recs Am–66 AR Gelsthorpe
Pro–64 J Bland
V'tors WD–H WE/BH–M
Fees On application
Loc 4 miles S of Mansfield on A611. M1 Junction 27
Mis Driving range-green fees only
Arch Willie Park Jr

Oakmere Park (1974)
Oaks Lane, Oxton NG25 0RH
Tel (0115) 965 3545
Fax (0115) 965 5628
Mem 450
Sec D St-John Jones
Pro D St-John Jones
(0115) 965 3545
Holes 18 L 6617 yds SSS 72
9 L 3495 yds SSS 37

Recs Am–69 J Vaughan
Pro–65 J Mellor
V'tors WD–U WE/BH–arrange times with Mgr SOC
Fees 18 hole:£18 (£25)
9 hole:£6 (£8)
Loc 8 miles NE of Nottingham on A614
Mis Floodlit driving range
Arch F Pennink

Radcliffe-on-Trent (1909)
Dewberry Lane, Cropwell Road, Radcliffe-on-Trent NG12 2JH
Tel (0115) 933 3000
Fax (0115) 911 6991
Mem 670
Sec L Wake
Pro R Ellis (0115) 933 2396
Holes 18 L 6381 yds Par 70 SSS 71
Recs Am–64 M Harris (1994)
Pro–66 I Ball (1995)
Ladies–73 M Harris (1983)
V'tors H SOC–Wed only
Fees £23 (£28)
Loc 6 miles E of Nottingham, off A52
Arch Tom Williamson

Ramsdale Park Golf Centre (1992)
Pay and play
Oxton Road, Calverton NG14 6NU
Tel (0115) 965 5600
Fax (0115) 965 4105
Sec B Jenkinson (Mgr)
Pro R Macey
Holes 18 L 6546 yds SSS 71
18 hole Par 3 course
Recs Pro–69 G Orr (1993)
V'tors U SOC–WD
Fees £14 (£16)
Loc 5 miles NE of Nottingham on B6386
Mis Floodlit driving range
Arch Hawtree

Retford (1921)
Brecks Road, Ordsall, Retford DN22 7UA
Tel (01777) 703733
Mem 700
Sec A Harrison (01777) 860682
Pro S Betteridge
Holes 18 L 6370 yds SSS 70
Recs Am–67 PJ Grout (1993)
V'tors WD–U WE–M SOC–WD
Fees £19 D–£23
Loc 2 miles SW of Retford, off A638 or A620. M1 Junction 30

Ruddington Grange (1988)
Wilford Road, Ruddington, Nottingham NG11 6NB
Tel (0115) 984 6141
Fax (0115) 940 5165
Mem 600
Sec A Clowes (Mgr), AR Dessaur
Pro R Simpson (0115) 921 1951

Holes 18 L 6490 yds SSS 72
Recs Am–69 R Curry (1998)
Pro–68 C Hall (1990)
V'tors U H BH–U exc comp days SOC
Fees £D–£15 (£22.50)
Loc 3 miles S of Nottingham

Rufford Park Golf Centre
Rufford Lane, Rufford, Newark NG18 4SY
Tel (01623) 825253
Fax (01623) 825254
Mem 450
Sec Miss J Strange
Pro J Vaughan, J Thompson
Holes 18 L 6173 yds Par 70 SSS 69
Recs Am–69 R Candlin (1998)
Pro–67 P Edwards (1996)
V'tors U–booking necessary SOC–WD/WEpm
Fees £14 D–£20 (£18)
Loc Nr Rufford Abbey on A614. 8 miles S of A1/A614 junction
Mis Floodlit driving range

Rushcliffe (1910)
Stocking Lane, East Leake, Loughborough LE12 5RL
Tel (01509) 852959
Mem 704
Sec DJ Barnes
Pro C Hall (01509) 852701
Holes 18 L 6090 yds SSS 69
V'tors SOC–WD
Fees £24
Loc 9 miles S of Nottingham. M1 Junction 24

Serlby Park (1905)
Serlby, Doncaster DN10 6BA
Tel (01777) 818268
Mem 250
Sec R Wilkinson (01302) 536336
Holes 9 L 5370 yds SSS 66
Recs Am–63 A Pugsley (1988)
Pro–65 M Bembridge (1965)
V'tors M
Loc 12 miles S of Doncaster, between A614 and A638

Sherwood Forest (1895)
Eakring Road, Mansfield NG18 3EW
Tel (01623) 626689
Fax (01623) 420412
Mem 648
Sec K Hall
Pro K Hall (01623) 627403
Holes 18 L 6714 yds SSS 73
Recs Am–67 S Fisher
Pro–64 C Hall
V'tors H SOC–WD
Fees On application to Sec
Loc 2 miles E of Mansfield (A617)
Arch HS Colt/James Braid

Southwell (1993)
Southwell Racecourse, Rolleston, Newark NG25 0TS
Tel (01636) 815394
Fax (01636) 812271

For list of abbreviations see page 527

Mem 400
Sec LI Sear (Mgr)
Pro S Meade (01636) 813706
Holes 18 L 5710 yds Par 71 SSS 68
Recs Am–68 G Barlow (1997)
Pro–63 S Meade (1998)
V'tors U SOC
Fees £15
Loc 6 miles W of Newark on A617. Course adjacent to racetrack
Arch RA Muddle

Springwater (1991)
Pay and play
Moor Lane, Calverton, Nottingham NG14 6FZ
Tel (0115) 965 2129
Mem 300
Sec W Turner (0115) 965 2565
Pro P Wharmsby (0115) 965 2129
Holes 9 L 3203 yds Par 72 SSS 71
Recs Am–69 R Overton (1995)
V'tors U SOC
Fees £9 (£13)
Loc Off A6097 between Lowdham and Oxton
Arch ADAS/McEvoy

Stanton-on-the-Wolds (1906)
Stanton Lane, Keyworth NG12 5BH
Tel (0115) 937 2044
Mem 500 167(L) 100(J)
Sec AR Evans (0115) 937 4885
Pro N Hernon ((0115) 937 2390
Holes 18 L 6437 yds SSS 71
Recs Am–67 CA Banks, PJ Whitt Pro–68 N Turley
V'tors WD–U exc comp days WE–M SOC
Fees D–£20 SOC–£25–£30
Loc 9 miles S of Nottingham

Trent Lock Golf Centre (1991)
Lock Lane, Sawley, Long Eaton NG10 3DD
Tel (0115) 946 4398
Fax (0115) 946 1183
Mem 550
Sec R Bluck
Pro M Taylor
Holes 18 hole course Par 72 SSS 70
V'tors U SOC
Fees £11
Loc S of Long Eaton. M1 Junction 25
Mis Driving range
Arch E McCausland

Wollaton Park (1927)
Wollaton Park, Nottingham NG8 1BT
Tel (0115) 978 7574
Fax (0115) 978 7574
Mem 700
Sec MT Harvey
Pro J Lower (0115) 978 4834
Holes 18 L 6445 yds SSS 71
Recs Am–65 L White
Pro–64 L White
V'tors U SOC

Fees On application
Loc 2 miles SW of Nottingham
Arch T Williamson

Worksop (1914)
Windmill Lane, Worksop S80 2SQ
Tel (01909) 472696
Fax (01909) 477731
Mem 500
Sec GL Lord (01909) 477731
Pro C Weatherhead (01909) 477732
Holes 18 L 6660 yds Par 72 SSS 73
Recs Am–64 P Nelson (1995)
Pro–68 L White (1992)
V'tors WD–H (phone first) WE/BH–M SOC
Fees On application
Loc 1 mile SE of Worksop, off A6034 via by-pass (A57). M1 Junction 30, 9 miles

Oxfordshire

Aspect Park (1988)
Remenham Hill, Henley-on-Thames RG9 3EH
Tel (01491) 578306
Fax (01491) 578306
Mem 600
Sec T Winsland
Pro T Notley (01491) 577562
Holes 18 L 6559 yds Par 72 SSS 71
V'tors WD–U WE–restricted before noon SOC
Fees £20 (£25)
Loc 1 mile E of Henley. M40 Junction 4, 8 miles
Mis Driving range. Pitch & putt
Arch T Winsland

Badgemore Park (1972)
Henley-on-Thames RG9 4NR
Tel (01491) 573667 (Clubhouse)
Fax (01491) 576899
Mem 600
Sec J Connell (Mgr) (01491) 572206
Pro J Dunn (01491) 574175
Holes 18 L 6112 yds SSS 69
Recs Am–67 SJ Mann Pro–65 M Howell
V'tors WD–U WE–pm only SOC–WD
Fees £18 (£26)
Loc 1 mile W of Henley on B290 to Peppard
Arch B Sandow

Banbury Golf Centre (1992)
Aynho Road, Adderbury, Banbury OX17 3NT
Tel (01295) 810419
Fax (01295) 810056
Mem 100
Sec MA Reed (Prop)
Pro Sarah Jarrett (01295) 812880

Holes 27 L 6544 yds Par 71 SSS 71
Recs Am–74 K Moggridge (1996)
Pro–72 G Wills (1994)
V'tors U SOC
Fees £10 (£12)
Loc 6 miles S of Banbury on B4100. M40 Junction 10 or 11
Mis Undergoing reconstruction in 1999
Arch Reed/Payn

Brailes (1992)
Sutton Lane, Lower Brailes, Banbury OX15 5BB
Tel (01608) 685336
Fax (01608) 685205
Mem 430
Sec RAS Malir
Pro M Bendall (01608) 685633
Holes 18 L 6270 yds Par 71 SSS 70
Recs Am–67 A Sheffield (1998)
V'tors U SOC–WD
Fees £18 (£26)
Loc 3 miles E of Shipston-on-Stour on B4035. M40 Junction 11, 10 miles
Arch BA Hull

Burford (1936)
Burford OX18 4JG
Tel (01993) 822583
Mem 710
Sec RP Thompson
Pro N Allen (01993) 822344
Holes 18 L 6414 yds SSS 71
Recs Am–67 DE Giles Pro–67 H Weetman
V'tors WD–H SOC
Fees On application
Loc 19 miles W of Oxford on A40

Carswell CC (1993)
Carswell, Faringdon SN7 8PU
Tel (01367) 870422
Fax (01367) 870592
Mem 300
Sec G Lisi (Prop)
Pro G Robbins
Holes 18 L 6133 yds Par 72
Recs Am–73 I Lewis (1994)
Pro–68 S Defoy (1993), J Nicholas, M Booth (1994)
V'tors U SOC–WD
Fees £15 (£20)
Loc 12 miles W of Oxford on A420
Mis Floodlit driving range

Cherwell Edge (1980)
Chacombe, Banbury OX17 2EN
Tel (01295) 711591
Fax (01295) 712404
Mem 519
Sec RA Beare
Pro J Kingston
Holes 18 L 5947 yds SSS 68
Recs Am–67 K Cole (1995)
Pro–64 M Booth (1995)
Ladies–76 J Lane (1990)
V'tors U SOC–WD
Fees £12 (£16)

For list of abbreviations see page 527

Loc 3 miles E of Banbury on B4525
Mis Driving range

Chesterton (1973)
Chesterton, Bicester OX6 8TE
Tel (01869) 241204
Mem 550
Sec BT Carter
Pro JW Wilkshire (01869) 242023
Holes 18 L 6224 yds SSS 70
Recs Am–68 D Grant (1994)
Pro–68 B Lane (1983)
V'tors U SOC–WD
Fees £12 (£18)
Loc 2 miles SW of Bicester. M40 Junction 9

Chipping Norton (1890)
Southcombe, Chipping Norton OX7 5QH
Tel (01608) 642383
Fax (01608) 645422
Mem 900
Sec S Chislett
Pro D Craik Jr (01608) 643356
Holes 18 L 6280 yds SSS 70
Recs Am–67 A Perrie, J Morewood, A Jones
Pro–62 T Ashton (1996)
V'tors WD–U WE–M
Fees £22
Loc 1 mile E of Chipping Norton on A44

Drayton Park (1992)
Pay and play
Steventon Road, Drayton, Abingdon OX14 2RR
Tel (01235) 550607/528989
Fax (01235) 525731
Mem 600
Sec (01235) 528989
Pro Dinah Masey (01235) 550607
Holes 18 L 6000 yds SSS 67
9 hole Par 3 course
Recs Am–65 O Cooper (1996)
V'tors U SOC
Fees £12 (£15)
Loc 5 miles S of Oxford on A34. M4 Junction 13
Mis Floodlit driving range
Arch Hawtree

Frilford Heath (1908)
Frilford Heath, Abingdon OX13 5NW
Tel (01865) 390864
Fax (01865) 390823
Email reservations@frilfordheath.co.uk
Mem 1200 210(L)
Sec S Styles
Pro DC Craik (01865) 390887
Holes Red 18 L 6884 yds 73
Green 18 L 6006 yds SSS 69
Blue 18 L 6728 yds SSS 72
Recs Red Am–69 J Gallacher (1997)
Green Am–63 K Johnson (1997)
Blue Am–66 J Lawson (1998)

V'tors H SOC
Fees £45 (£60)
Loc 3 miles W of Abingdon on A338
Arch Blue–Simon Gidman

Hadden Hill (1990)
Wallingford Road, Didcot OX11 9BJ
Tel (01235) 510410
Fax (01235) 510410
Mem 420 62(L)
Sec MV Morley
Pro D Halford, A Waters
Holes 18 L 6563 yds SSS 71
Recs Am–65 N Hammond (1995)
V'tors WD–U SOC–WD
Fees £13 (£18)
Loc E of Didcot on A4130
Mis Floodlit driving range
Arch MV Morley

Henley (1908)
Harpsden, Henley-on-Thames RG9 4HG
Tel (01491) 575781
Fax (01491) 412179
Mem 750
Sec AM Chaundy (01491) 575742
Pro M Howell (01491) 575710
Holes 18 L 6329 yds SSS 70
Recs Am–65 D Griffin (1989)
Pro–63 R Lee (1996)
V'tors WD–H WE–M SOC
Fees D–£30
Loc 1 mile S of Henley (A4155)
Arch James Braid

Huntercombe (1901)
Nuffield, Henley-on-Thames RG9 5SL
Tel (01491) 641207
Fax (01491) 642060
Mem 700
Sec Lt Col TJ Hutchison
Pro JB Draycott (01491) 641241
Holes 18 L 6261 yds SSS 70
Recs Am–64 MH Dixon
Pro–63 J Morris
V'tors H–by appointment only SOC–WD
Fees D–£38
Loc 6 miles W of Henley on A4130
Mis Foursomes and singles only
Arch Willie Park Jr

Kirtlington (1995)
Kirtlington OX5 3JY
Tel (01869) 351133
Fax (01869) 331143
Mem 250
Sec P Smith (Sec/Mgr)
Pro P Hughes (01869) 351133
Holes 18 holes Par 70 SSS 69
Recs Am–68 N Woolford (1997)
Pro–68 D Cook (1998)
V'tors U SOC
Fees £15 (£20)
Loc 1 mile from Kirtlington on A4095. M40 Junction 9
Mis Driving range
Arch G Webster

Lyneham (1992)
Lyneham, Chipping Norton OX7 6QQ
Tel (01993) 831841
Fax (01993) 831775
Mem 700
Sec CJT Howkins
Pro R Jefferies
Holes 18 L 6669 yds SSS 72
Recs Am–67 D Yates (1996)
Pro–66 P Saunders (1996), J Dunn (1998)
V'tors U SOC
Fees £16 (£20)
Loc 4 miles W of Chipping Norton, off A361
Mis Driving range
Arch D Carpenter

North Oxford (1907)
Banbury Road, Oxford OX2 8EZ
Tel (01865) 554415
Fax (01865) 515921
Mem 701
Sec GW Pullin (01865) 554924
Pro R Harris (01865) 553977
Holes 18 L 5805 yds SSS 67
Recs Am–62 P Barrow
Pro–62 F George
V'tors WD–U WE–M SOC–WD exc Thurs
Fees On application
Loc 4 miles N of Oxford, off A4260 to Kidlington

The Oxfordshire (1993)
Rycote Lane, Milton Common, Thame OX9 2PU
Tel (01844) 278300
Fax (01844) 278003
Mem 650
Sec M Kayanuma (Gen Mgr)
Pro I Mosey
Holes 18 L 7187 yds SSS 76
Recs Am–68 A Wall (1995)
Pro–65 E Romero (1997)
Ladies Am–73 E Fields (1995), J Oliver (1996)
Pro–64 M-L de Lorenzi (1996)
V'tors M
Fees On application
Loc 1½ miles W of Thame on A329. M40 Junction 7, 2 miles
Mis Driving range
Arch Rees Jones

RAF Benson (1975)
Royal Air Force, Benson
Tel (01491) 837766
Mem 200
Sec Sgt P Hersey RAF (01491) 838091
Holes 9 L 4395 yds Par 63 SSS 61
Recs Am–63 R Mills (1991)
V'tors M
Loc 3½ miles NE of Wallingford

Rye Hill
Milcombe, Banbury OX15 4RU
Tel (01295) 721818
Fax (01295) 720911
Pro L Bond

For list of abbreviations see page 527

Holes 18 L 6569 yds Par 71
V'tors WD–U WE–booking
necessary
Fees £12 (£15)
Loc 5 miles SW of Banbury,
off A361. M40 Junction 11
Mis Academy holes

Southfield (1875)
Hill Top Road, Oxford OX4 1PF
Tel (01865) 242158
Fax (01865) 242158
Mem 700
Sec Sherrol Matthews (Asst)
Pro A Rees (01865) 244258
Holes 18 L 6230 yds SSS 70
Recs Am–66 CM Barrett,
GL Morley
Pro–61 A Rees
V'tors WD–U WE/BH–M H SOC
Fees £24
Loc 2 miles E of Oxford
Arch HS Colt

The Springs (1998)
Wallingford Road, North Stoke,
Wallingford OX10 6BE
Tel (01491) 836687 (Hotel)
Fax (01491) 827312
Mem 550
Sec M Cavilla (01491) 836689
Pro L Atkins (01491) 827310
Holes 18 L 6470 yds Par 72
V'tors By arrangement SOC–WD
Fees £22 (£30)
Loc 2 miles SW of Wallingford on
B4009. M40 Junction 6
Arch Brian Huggett

Studley Wood (1996)
The Straight Mile, Horton-cum-Studley,
Oxford OX33 1BF
Tel (01865) 351144
Fax (01865) 351166
Mem 750
Sec P Fox
Pro T Williams (01865) 351122
Holes 18 L 6711 yds Par 73 SSS 73
Recs Am–70 J Carlsen (1997)
Pro–65 L Stanford (1997)
Ladies–73 L King (1996)
V'tors U SOC
Fees £21 (£30)
Loc 4 miles NE of Oxford. M40
Junction 8
Mis Driving range. Golf academy
Arch Simon Gidman

Tadmarton Heath (1922)
Wigginton, Banbury OX15 5HL
Tel (01608) 737278
Fax (01608) 730548
Mem 600
Sec RE Wackrill
Pro T Jones (01608) 730047
Holes 18 L 5917 yds SSS 69
Recs Am–64 I Manning
Pro–63 G Smith
V'tors WD–H by appointment
WE–M SOC–WD
Fees £28 After 2.30pm–£20

Loc 5 miles SW of Banbury, off
B4035
Arch Maj CJ Hutchison

Waterstock (1994)
Pay and play
Thame Road, Waterstock, Oxford
OX33 1HT
Tel (01844) 338093
Fax (01844) 338036
Mem 500
Sec AJ Wyatt
Pro J Goodman
Holes 18 L 6535 yds Par 73
Recs Am–68 D Watson
V'tors U SOC
Fees £14 (£17)
Loc E of Oxford on A418. M40
Junction 8
Mis Floodlit driving range
Arch Donald Steel

Witney Lakes (1994)
Pay and play
Downs Road, Witney OX8 5SY
Tel (01993) 779000
Fax (01993) 778866
Mem 450
Sec Miss S John (Mgr)
Pro JP Hunt
Holes 18 L 6460 yds SSS 71
Recs Am–71 R Brooks (1998)
Pro–72 S Richardson (1994)
V'tors U
Fees £13 (£18)
Loc 2 miles W of Witney on
B4047
Mis Floodlit driving range
Arch Simon Gidman

Rutland

Greetham Valley (1992)
Greetham, Oakham LE15 7NP
Tel (01780) 460004
Fax (01780) 460623
Mem 900
Sec FE Hinch
Pro J Pengelly (01780) 460666
Holes 18 holes SSS 71
18 holes SSS 68
9 hole Par 3 course
Recs Am–64 T Sweet (1997)
Pro–65 J Pengelly (1997)
V'tors U SOC–WD
Fees £22 (£26)
Loc 5 miles NE of Oakham (B668)
Mis Floodlit driving range

Luffenham Heath (1911)
Ketton, Stamford PE9 3UU
Tel (01780) 720205
Fax (01780) 722416
Mem 555
Sec IF Davenport
Pro I Burnett (01780) 720298
Holes 18 L 6273 yds SSS 70

Recs Am–64 M Welch (1990)
Pro–67 PJ Butler (1959),
RL Moffitt
V'tors U H SOC–WD
Fees £35 (£40)
Loc 5 miles W of Stamford
on A6121
Arch James Braid

RAF Cottesmore (1982)
Oakham, Leicester LE15 7BL
Tel (01572) 812241 Ext 6706
Mem 150
Sec GA Lawrence
Holes 9 L 5622 yds SSS 67
Recs Am–64 P Holiday (1993)
V'tors By arrangement
Fees £8
Loc RAF Cottesmore

RAF North Luffenham (1975)
RAF North Luffenham, Oakham
LE15 8RL
Tel (01780) 720041 Ext 7523
Mem 350 62(L) 25(J)
Sec S Nicholson
Holes 9 L 6048 yds Par 70 SSS 69
Recs Am–71 D Lilley
V'tors U SOC
Fees D–£8
Loc ½ mile from S shore of
Rutland Water

Rutland County (1991)
Great Casterton, Stamford PE9 4AQ
Tel (01780) 460239/460330
Fax (01780) 460437
Sec S Lowe (Golf Dir)
Pro J Darroch
Holes 18 L 6401 yds SSS 71
9 hole Par 3 course
Recs Am–68 (1997)
Pro–64 J Darroch (1993)
V'tors U H SOC
Fees £17.50 (£22.50)
Loc 3 miles N of Stamford on A1
Mis Driving range
Arch Cameron Sinclair

Shropshire

Aqualate
Stafford Road, Newport TF10 9JT
Tel (01952) 811699
Fax (01952) 825343
Mem 120
Sec RG McCartney
Pro K Short
(01952) 402991
Holes 18 L 5659 yds Par 69 SSS 67
V'tors U
Fees On application
Loc 1 mile E of Newport (A518)
Mis Floodlit driving range
Arch MD Simmons

For list of abbreviations see page 527

Arscott (1992)
Arscott, Pontesbury, Shrewsbury SY5 0XP
Tel (01743) 860114
Fax (01743) 860114
Mem 550
Sec T Petersen
Pro I Doran (01743) 860881
Holes 18 L 6112 yds SSS 69
Recs Am–72 R Edwards (1993)
V'tors WD–U WE/BH–M before 2pm SOC
Fees £16 (£20)
Loc 5 miles SW of Shrewsbury, off A488
Arch Martin Hamer

Bridgnorth (1889)
Stanley Lane, Bridgnorth WV16 4SF
Tel (01746) 763315
Fax (01746) 761381
Mem 690
Sec KD Cole (01746) 764179
Pro P Hinton (01746) 762045
Holes 18 L 6638 yds SSS 72
Recs Am–67 C Banks (1985)
Pro–66 P Hinton (1989)
V'tors H SOC
Fees £22 (£28)
Loc 1 mile N of Bridgnorth

Chesterton Valley
Chesterton, Worfield, Bridgnorth WV15 5NX
Tel (01746) 783682
Mem 250
Sec P Hinton
Pro P Hinton
Holes 9 L 3392 yds Par 74 SSS 72
V'tors U–phone first
Fees £6 (£6)
Loc 10 miles W of Wolverhampton on B4176

Church Stretton (1898)
Trevor Hill, Church Stretton SY6 6JH
Tel (01694) 722281
Mem 470
Sec R Broughton (01694) 722633
Pro P Seal (01743) 873751
Holes 18 L 5020 yds SSS 65
Recs Am–62 NJ Evans (1993)
V'tors H WE–NA before 10.30am SOC
Fees £12 (£18)
Loc ½ mile W of Church Stretton, off A49
Arch James Braid

Cleobury Mortimer (1993)
Wyre Common, Cleobury Mortimer DY14 8HQ
Tel (01299) 271112 (Clubhouse)
Fax (01299) 271468
Mem 600
Sec G Pain
Pro G Farr
Holes 27 holes: L 6363 yds Par 69–71 SSS 69–71

Recs Am–67 A Sykes (1997)
Pro–70 T Stevens (1997)
V'tors WD–U H WE–M H SOC
Fees £16.50 (£19.50)
Loc 10 miles SW of Kidderminster on A4117
Mis Driving range

Hawkstone Park (1920)
Weston-under-Redcastle, Shrewsbury SY4 5UY
Tel (01939) 200611
Fax (01939) 200311
Mem 700
Sec KL Brazier
Pro P Wesselingh
Holes Hawkstone 18 L 6491 yds SSS 72; Windmill 18 L 6764 yds SSS 72; Academy 6 holes Par 3 course
Recs Am–65 M Welch
Pro–65 A Jacklin, AWB Lyle
Ladies–71 S Parker
V'tors U
Fees £28 D–£42 (£36 D–£50)
Loc 10 miles S of Whitchurch. 14 miles N of Shrewsbury on A49
Mis Driving range
Arch Braid/Huggett

Hill Valley G&CC (1975)
Terrick Road, Whitchurch SY13 4JZ
Tel (01948) 663584
Fax (01948) 665927
Mem 600
Sec JS Pickering
Pro AR Minshall, CT Burgess
Holes Emerald 18 L 6628 yds Par 73
Sapphire 18 L 4801 yds Par 66
Recs Am–67 M Welch
Pro–64 M Welch, W Milne
V'tors U
Fees Emerald £20 (£25) Sapphire £11 (£15)
Loc 1 mile N of Whitchurch, off A41/A49 Bypass
Mis 6-bay practice range
Arch Alliss/Thomas

Lilleshall Hall (1937)
Abbey Road, Lilleshall, Newport TF10 9AS
Tel (01952) 603840/604776
Fax (01952) 604776
Mem 600
Sec FR Price (01952) 604776
Pro NW Bramall (01952) 604104
Holes 18 L 5789 yds SSS 68
Recs Am–65 P Baker
Pro–70 J Anderson
Ladies–71 L Archer
V'tors WD–U WE–M SOC
Fees £20 (BH–£30)
Loc 3 miles S of Newport between Lilleshall and Sheriffhales. M54 Junction 4
Arch HS Colt

Llanymynech (1933)
Pant, Oswestry SY10 8LB
Tel (01691) 830542
Mem 760

Sec DR Thomas (01691) 830983
Pro A Griffiths (01691) 830879
Holes 18 L 6114 yds Par 70 SSS 69
Recs Am–65 MJ Rooke (1998)
Pro–65 I Woosnam (1983)
V'tors U before 4.30pm –M after 4.30pm SOC–WD
Fees £16 (£20)
Loc 5 miles S of Oswestry on A483

Ludlow (1889)
Bromfield, Ludlow SY8 2BT
Tel (01584) 856285
Mem 550
Sec CR Vane Percy
Pro R Price (01584) 856366
Holes 18 L 6277 yds SSS 70
Recs Am–69 R Rodgers (1996)
Pro–65 P Hinton (1998)
V'tors H SOC–WD
Fees D–£18 (D–£24)
Loc 2 miles N of Ludlow (A49)

Market Drayton (1925)
Sutton, Market Drayton TF9 1LX
Tel (01630) 652266
Fax (01630) 652266
Mem 500
Sec EG Davies
Pro R Clewes
Holes 18 L 6290 yds SSS 71
Recs Am–70 S Thomas (1991)
V'tors WD–U WE–NA
Fees £20
Loc 1 mile S of Market Drayton

Meole Brace (1976)
Public
Meole Brace, Shrewsbury SY2 6QQ
Tel (01743) 364050
Fax (01743) 364050
Pro I Doran
Holes 9 L 2915 yds SSS 68
Recs Am–68 J Mansell
Pro–68 R Cockcroft
V'tors WD–U WE–book in advance
Fees On application
Loc 1 mile S of Shrewsbury. Junction A5/A49

Mile End (1992)
Mile End, Oswestry SY11 4JE
Tel (01691) 671246
Fax (01691) 670580
Sec R Thompson
Pro S Carpenter (01691) 671246
Holes 18 L 6194 yds SSS 69
Recs Am–69 R Farmer, J Seal (1997)
V'tors SOC–WD
Fees £14 D–£20 (£18 D–£25)
Loc 1 mile from Oswestry, off A5
Mis Driving range
Arch Price/Gough

Oswestry (1930)
Aston Park, Oswestry SY11 4JJ
Tel (01691) 610221
Fax (01691) 610535
Mem 880

For list of abbreviations see page 527

Sec A Jennings (01691) 610535
Pro D Skelton (01691) 610448
Holes 18 L 6038 yds SSS 69
Recs Am–62 AL Strange (1978)
Pro–62 DJ Probert (1996)
V'tors M or H SOC–WD
Fees £20 (£28)
Loc 3 miles SE of Oswestry on A5
Arch James Braid

Severn Meadows (1990)
Pay and play
Highley, Bridgnorth WV16 6HZ
Tel (01746) 862212
Mem 190
Sec C Harrison
Pro None
Holes 9 L 5258 yds Par 68 SSS 67
V'tors WD–U WE–booking required
Fees £10 (£12)
Loc 8 miles S of Bridgnorth on B4555

Shifnal (1929)
Decker Hill, Shifnal TF11 8QL
Tel (01952) 460467/460330
Fax (01952) 460330
Mem 500
Sec PW Holden (01952) 460330
Pro J Flanaghan (01952) 460457
Holes 18 L 6422 yds SSS 71
Recs Am–65 C Watts
Pro–64 P Baker
V'tors WD–phone first WE/BH–M
Fees On application
Loc 1 mile NE of Shifnal. M54 Junction 4, 2 miles
Arch Pennink

Shrewsbury (1891)
Condover, Shrewsbury SY5 7BL
Tel (01743) 872976
Fax (01743) 874647
Mem 525 184(L) 70(J)
Sec Mrs SM Kenny (01743) 872977
Pro P Seal (01743) 873751
Holes 18 L 6178 yds Par 70 SSS 69
Recs Am–60 JR Burn
V'tors H SOC
Fees £19 (£24)
Loc 4 miles S of Shrewsbury

The Shropshire (1992)
Pay and play
Muxton, Telford TF2 8PQ
Tel (01952) 677866
Fax (01952) 677844
Mem 500
Sec Lisa Davies
Pro D Bateman
Holes 27 holes: L 6589-6637 yds SSS 70-72
Recs Am–70 R Wheeler (1996)
V'tors U SOC
Fees £15 (£20)
Loc 4 miles NW of Telford (B5060). M54 Junction 4
Mis Floodlit driving range. Pitch & putt course
Arch Martin Hawtree

Telford (1976)
Great Hay, Sutton Heights, Telford TF7 4DT
Tel (01952) 429977
Fax (01952) 586602
Mem 600
Sec I Lucas (Ext 274)
Pro D Thorp (01952) 586052
Holes 18 L 6761 yds SSS 72
Recs Am–66 C Bufton (1986)
Pro–62 D Thorp (1983)
V'tors H SOC
Fees On application
Loc 4 miles SE of Telford, off A442
Mis Driving range
Arch John Harris

Worfield (1991)
Worfield, Bridgnorth WV15 5HE
Tel (01746) 716541
Fax (01746) 716302
Mem 500
Sec W Weaver (Gen Mgr) (01746) 716372
Pro S Russell (01746) 716541
Holes 18 L 6801 yds SSS 73
Recs Am–69 N Doody (1997)
Pro–68 A Ferriday (1998)
V'tors U SOC
Fees £16 (£22)
Loc 7 miles W of Wolverhampton on A454
Arch Gough/Williams

Wrekin (1905)
Wellington, Telford TF6 5BX
Tel (01952) 244032
Fax (01952) 252906
Mem 400 100(L) 90(J)
Sec D Briscoe
Pro K Housden (01952) 223101
Holes 18 L 5657 yds SSS 67
Recs Am–64 S Price, AJ Ford (1993), A Stephenson (1994)
Pro–67 C Holmes
V'tors WD–U before 5pm –M after 5pm SOC
Fees £20 (£28)
Loc Wellington, off B5061

Somerset

Bath (1880)
Sham Castle, North Road, Bath BA2 6JG
Tel (01225) 425182
Fax (01225) 331027
Mem 730
Sec PE Ware (01225) 463834
Pro P Hancox (01225) 466953
Holes 18 L 6442 yds SSS 71
Recs Am–69 CS Edwards (1998)
Pro–66 M McEwan (1997)
V'tors H SOC
Fees £25 (£30)
Loc 1½ miles SE of Bath, off A36
Arch HS Colt

Brean (1973)
Coast Road, Brean, Burnham-on-Sea TA8 2RT
Tel (01278) 751595
Fax (01278) 751595
Mem 400
Sec WS Martin (Hon)
Pro S Spencer (01278) 751570
Holes 18 L 5565 yds SSS 67
Recs Am–69 B Reeves (1963)
V'tors WD–U H WE–pm only SOC–WD
Fees On application
Loc 4 miles N of Burnham-on-Sea. M5 Junction 22, 6 miles

Burnham & Berrow (1890)
St Christopher's Way, Burnham-on-Sea TA8 2PE
Tel (01278) 783137
Fax (01278) 795440
Mem 800
Sec Mrs EL Sloman (01278) 785760
Pro M Crowther-Smith (01278) 784545
Holes 18 L 6606 yds SSS 73
9 L 6332 yds SSS 72
Recs Medal Am–66 SJ Martin
C'ship Am–66 DG Haines (1993)
V'tors I SOC
Fees 18 hole:£38 (£50) 9 hole:£12
Loc 1 mile N of Burnham-on-Sea on B3140
Mis Dormy House

Cannington (1993)
Pay and play
Cannington College, Bridgwater TA5 2LS
Tel (01278) 655050
Fax (01278) 652479
Mem 200
Sec R Macrow (Mgr)
Pro R Macrow
Holes 9 L 2929 yds SSS 68
V'tors U exc Wed eve–restricted
Fees 18 holes–£10 (£12)
9 holes–£6.50 (£7.50)
Loc 4 miles NW of Bridgwater on A39. M5 Junction 24
Arch Hawtree

Clevedon
Castle Road, Clevedon BS21 7AA
Tel (01275) 873140
Fax (01275) 341228
Mem 800
Sec M Heggie (Mgr) (01275) 874057
Pro M Heggie (01275) 874704
Holes 18 L 6042 yds SSS 69
Recs Am–65 N Barker (1995), JE Morgan (1997)
Pro–64 M Plummer (1995)
V'tors WD–U H exc Wed am WE/BH–U H (phone first) SOC
Fees £20 D–£25 (£30)
Loc Off Holly Lane, Walton, Clevedon. M5 Junction 20
Arch JH Taylor

For list of abbreviations see page 527

Enmore Park (1906)
Enmore, Bridgwater TA5 2AN
Tel (01278) 671244 (Members)
Fax (01278) 671481
Mem 780
Sec D Weston
 (01278) 671481
Pro N Wixon
 (01278) 671519
Holes 18 L 6411 yds SSS 71
Recs Am–66 T Lawrence (1990),
 D Dixon Jr (1994)
 Pro–64 R Davis (1994)
 Ladies–70 K Nicholls (1989),
 L Wixon (1994)
V'tors U SOC–WD
Fees £18 (£25)
Loc 3 miles W of Bridgwater,
 off Durleigh road. M5
 Junctions 23/24
Arch Hawtree

Entry Hill (1985)
Public
Entry Hill, Bath BA2 5NA
Tel (01225) 834248
Sec J Sercombe
Pro T Tapley
Holes 9 L 4206 yds SSS 61
Recs Am–63 I Hulley (1992),
 A Peates (1996)
V'tors WD/WE–booking only
Fees 18 holes–£7.85 (£8.95)
 9 holes–£4.95 (£5.60)
Loc 1 mile S of Bath, off A367

Farrington (1992)
Marsh Lane, Farrington Gurney, Bristol BS39 6TS
Tel (01761) 453440 (Clubhouse)
Fax (01761) 241274
Mem 700
Sec Mrs PM Thompson
Pro P Thompson
 (01761) 241787
Holes 18 L 6693 yds Par 72 SSS 72
 9 L 3022 yds Par 54 SSS 53
Recs Am–73 S Ponfield (1997)
 Pro–68 S Little (1997)
V'tors U SOC–WD
Fees 18 hole:£20 (£30)
 9 hole:£7 (£9)
Loc 12 miles S of Bristol (A37)
 10 miles S of Bath (A39)
Mis Floodlit driving range
Arch Peter Thompson

Fosseway CC (1970)
Charlton Lane, Midsomer Norton, Bath BA3 4BD
Tel (01761) 412214
Fax (01761) 418257
Mem 438
Sec RF Jones (Mgr)
Holes 9 L 4608 yds SSS 65
Recs Am–55 M Chedgy (1985)
V'tors WD–U exc Wed–M after 5pm
 WE–NA before 1.30pm
Fees £10 (£12)
Loc 10 miles SW of Bath on A367

Frome Golf Centre (1994)
Pay and play
Critchill Manor, Frome BA11 4LJ
Tel (01373) 453410
Fax (01373) 453410
Mem 300
Sec Mrs S Austin
Pro A Wright
Holes 18 hole course Par 69 SSS 67
V'tors U
Fees £10.50 D–£15
 (£12.50 D–£17)
Loc 12 miles S of Bath
Mis Driving range

Isle of Wedmore (1992)
Lineage, Lascots Hill, Wedmore BS28 4QT
Tel (01934) 712452
Fax (01934) 713696
Mem 560
Sec AC Edwards (01934) 713649
Pro G Coombe (01934) 712452
Holes 18 L 6006 yds Par 70 SSS 69
Recs Am–70 J Body (1994)
 Pro–67 M Watson (1998)
V'tors U SOC–WD
Fees £18 (£22)
Loc 3/4 mile N of Wedmore. M5
 Junction 22
Arch Terry Murray

Kingweston (1983)
(Sec) Mead Run, Compton Street, Compton Dundon, Somerton TA11 6PP
Tel (01458) 43921
Mem 200
Sec JG Willetts
Holes 9 L 4516 yds SSS 62
V'tors M exc Wed & Sat 2–5pm–NA
Fees NA
Loc 1 mile SE of Butleigh. 2 miles
 SE of Glastonbury

Lansdown (1894)
Lansdown, Bath BA1 9BT
Tel (01225) 422138
Fax (01225) 339252
Mem 750
Sec Mrs E Bacon
Pro T Mercer (01225) 420242
Holes 18 L 6316 yds SSS 70
Recs Am–66 VL Phillips (1992)
 Pro–64 D Ray (1995)
V'tors H SOC
Fees £20 (£20)
Loc 2 miles NW of Bath, by
 racecourse. M4 Junction 18, 6
 miles
Arch HS Colt

Long Sutton (1991)
Pay and play
Long Load, Langport TA10 9JU
Tel (01458) 241017
Fax (01458) 241022
Mem 600
Sec GC Bennett
Pro M Blackwell
Holes 18 L 6367 yds SSS 71
Recs Am–70 B Parker
V'tors WD–U WE–booking required
 SOC
Fees £16 (£20)
Loc 3 miles E of Langport
Mis Floodlit driving range
Arch Patrick Dawson

Mendip (1908)
Gurney Slade, Bath BA3 4UT
Tel (01749) 840570
Fax (01749) 841439
Mem 700
Sec BSR Warren
Pro RF Lee (01749) 840793
Holes 18 L 6383 yds SSS 71
Recs Am–65 M Stephens (1992)
 Pro–64 N Blenkarne (1987)
V'tors WD–U WE–H SOC–WD
Fees £20 (£30)
Loc 3 miles N of Shepton Mallet
 (A37)
Arch CK Cotton

Mendip Spring (1992)
Honeyhall Lane, Congresbury BS49 5JT
Tel (01934) 853337/852322
Fax (01934) 853021
Mem 400
Sec I Harrison (Mgr)
Pro J Blackburn, R Moss
Holes 18 L 6334 yds SSS 70
 9 L 4784 yds SSS 66
Recs Am–64 I Harrison
V'tors U
Fees 18 hole:£22 (£29)
 9 hole:£7.50 (£8)
Loc Congresbury. M5 Junction 21.
Mis Driving range
Arch Langholt

Minehead & West Somerset (1882)
The Warren, Minehead TA24 5SJ
Tel (01643) 702057
Fax (01643) 705095
Mem 604
Sec LS Harper
Pro I Read (01643) 704378
Holes 18 L 6228 yds SSS 71
Recs Am–66 M Luckett
 Pro–66 BJ Hunt
V'tors U after 9.30am SOC
Fees £22 (£25) W–£80
Loc E end of sea front

Oake Manor (1993)
Oake, Taunton TA4 1BA
Tel (01823) 461993
Fax (01823) 461995
Mem 600
Sec R Gardner (Golf Mgr)
Pro R Gardner
Holes 18 L 6109 yds Par 70 SSS 69
Recs Am–68 B Downs (1996)
 Pro–65 S Little (1998)
V'tors U–phone first SOC

For list of abbreviations see page 527

Orchardleigh (1996)
From BA11 2PH
Tel (01373) 454200/454206 (Bookings)
Fax (01373) 454202
Mem 500
Sec J Willder (Gen Mgr)
Pro P Green
Holes 18 L 6810 yds Par 72 SSS 73
Recs Am–71 P Chilvers (1996)
Pro–67 N Mitchell (1996)
Ladies–76 C Nicholson (1996)
V'tors WD/BH–U WE–U after 11am SOC
Fees £30 D–£35 (£40)
Loc 2 miles NW of Frome on A362. 12 miles S of Bath
Mis Driving range
Arch Brian Huggett

Puxton Park (1992)
Pay and play
Puxton, Weston-super-Mare BS24 6TA
Tel (01934) 876942
Pro C Ancsell
Holes 18 L 6600 yds Par 72
V'tors U SOC
Fees £8 (£10)
Loc A370, 2 miles E of M5 Junction 21

Saltford (1904)
Golf Club Lane, Saltford, Bristol BS18 3AA
Tel (01225) 873220
Fax (01225) 873525
Mem 650
Sec V Radnedge (01225) 873513
Pro D Millensted (01225) 872043
Holes 18 L 6081 yds SSS 69
Recs Am–64 D Young
Pro–63 S Little
V'tors WD–U SOC–Mon & Thurs
Fees £24
Loc 7 miles SE of Bristol

Stockwood Vale (1991)
Public
Stockwood Lane, Keynsham, Bristol BS18 2ER
Tel (0117) 986 6505
Mem 500
Sec M Edenborough
Pro J Richards
Holes 18 L 6031 yds SSS 71
V'tors U SOC
Fees £12 (£14)
Loc 1 mile SE of Bristol, off A4174
Mis Driving range
Arch Ramsay

Tall Pines (1991)
Cooks Bridle Path, Downside, Backwell, Bristol BS48 3DJ
Tel (01275) 472076
Fax (01275) 474869
Mem 400
Sec T Murray
Pro A Murray
Holes 18 L 6100yds Par 70 SSS 69
V'tors U SOC
Fees £14 (£16)
Loc 8 miles SW of Bristol (A470/A38)
Arch Terry Murray

Taunton & Pickeridge (1892)
Corfe, Taunton TA3 7BY
Tel (01823) 421240
Fax (01823) 421742
Mem 630
Sec GW Sayers (01823) 421537
Pro G Milne (01823) 421790
Holes 18 L 5927 yds SSS 68
Recs Am–63 SN Richards (1992)
Pro–61 M Plummer (1994)
V'tors H SOC
Fees On application
Loc 5 miles S of Taunton on B3170
Arch Hawtree

Taunton Vale (1991)
Creech Heathfield, Taunton TA3 5EY
Tel (01823) 412220
Fax (01823) 413583
Mem 670
Sec DM Kelly
Pro M Keitch (01823) 412880
Holes 18 L 6167 yds Par 70 SSS 69
9 L 2004 yds Par 64 SSS 60
Recs Am–68 M Luckett (1997)
Pro–66 J Palmer (1995)
V'tors U SOC
Fees 18 hole:£15 (£19)
9 hole:£7.50 (£9.50)
Loc 3 miles N of Taunton, off A361. M5 Junctions 24/25
Mis Floodlit driving range
Arch John Pyne

Tickenham (1991)
Clevedon Road, Tickenham, Bristol BS21 6RY
Tel (01275) 856626
Mem 250
Pro A Sutcliffe
Holes 9 L 2000 yds
V'tors U SOC
Fees 18 holes–£9 (£11)
Loc 2 miles E of M5 Junction 20 on B3130, nr Nailsea
Mis Floodlit driving range
Arch Andrew Sutcliffe

Vivary (1928)
Public
Vivary Park, Taunton TA1 3JW
Tel (01823) 289274 (Clubhouse)
Mem 500

Fees £16.50 (£20)
Loc 4 miles W of Taunton, off B3227. M5 Junctions 25/26 onto A38
Mis Driving range. Academy course
Arch Adrian Stiff

Sec G Potter
Pro M Steadman (01823) 333875
Holes 18 L 4620 yds SSS 63
V'tors U SOC–WD
Fees £7.50
Loc Centre of Taunton
Arch Herbert Fowler

Wells (1893)
East Horrington Road, Wells BA5 3DS
Tel (01749) 672868
Fax (01749) 675005
Mem 750
Sec SH Butterfield (Sec/Mgr) (01749) 675005
Pro A Bishop (01749) 679059
Holes 18 L 6015 yds SSS 69
Recs Am–66 M Stevens (1993), B Whittock (1995)
V'tors WD–U WE–H SOC–WD
Fees £18 (£22) Mon–Fri £60
Loc 1½ miles E of Wells, off Radstock road
Mis Floodlit driving range

Weston-super-Mare (1892)
Uphill Road North, Weston-super-Mare BS23 4NQ
Tel (01934) 626968
Fax (01934) 626968
Mem 752
Sec J Keight (01934) 626968
Pro M La Band (01934) 633360
Holes 18 L 6251 yds SSS 70
Recs Am–64 B Porter, S Martin Pro–66 G Ryall
V'tors H SOC
Fees £24 (£35) W–£75
Loc Weston-super-Mare
Arch T Dunn

Wheathill (1993)
Pay and play
Wheathill, Somerton TA11 7HG
Tel (01963) 240667
Fax (01963) 240230
Mem 200
Sec A Lyddon (Sec/Mgr)
Pro A England
Holes 18 L 5362 yds SSS 66
4 hole Par 3 course
Recs Pro–63 J Goymer
V'tors U SOC
Fees £10 (£12)
Loc 3 miles W of Castle Cary on B3153

Windwhistle G&CC (1932)
Cricket St Thomas, Chard TA20 4DG
Tel (01460) 30231
Fax (01460) 30055
Mem 550
Sec IN Dodd
Pro D Driver
Holes 18 L 6470 yds SSS 71
Recs Am–69
V'tors U–phone first SOC
Fees On application

For list of abbreviations see page 527

Loc Windwhistle, 3 miles E of Chard on A30, opp Wildlife Park. M5 Junction 25, 12 miles
Arch JH Taylor/L Fisher

Worlebury (1908)
Monks Hill, Worlebury, Weston-super-Mare BS22 9SX
Tel (01934) 623214
Fax (01934) 625789
Mem 640
Sec MW Penny (01934) 625789
Pro G Marks (01934) 418473
Holes 18 L 5963 yds SSS 69
Recs Am–67 I Heppenstall, P Simmonds (1992) Pro–66 G Marks (1992)
V'tors H SOC–WD
Fees £20 (£30)
Loc 2 miles NE of Weston, off A370
Arch H Vardon

Yeovil (1919)
Sherborne Road, Yeovil BA21 5BW
Tel (01935) 475949 (Clubhouse)
Fax (01935) 411283
Mem 685 165(L) 70(J)
Sec R Wilmott (01935) 422965
Pro G Kite (01935) 473763
Holes 18 L 6144 yds SSS 70
         9 L 4876 yds SSS 65
Recs Am–64 J Pounder (1991) Pro–65 G Laing (1987), R Troake (1989), S Little, G Hampshire (1991)
V'tors WD–U H WE/BH–H (WD/WE–phone Pro) SOC
Fees 18 hole:£25 (£30) 9 hole:£15 (£18)
Loc 1 mile from Yeovil on A30 to Sherborne
Arch Fowler/Alison

Staffordshire

Alsager G&CC (1992)
Audley Road, Alsager, Stoke-on-Trent ST7 2UR
Tel (01270) 875700
Fax (01270) 882207
Mem 660
Sec J Ormes
Holes 18 L 6225 yds SSS 70
Recs Am–67 M Keeling (1998)
V'tors WD–U before 5pm –M after 5pm WE/BH–M SOC
Fees £22
Loc 5 miles W of Crewe. M6 Junction 16

Barlaston (1987)
Meaford Road, Stone ST15 8UX
Tel (01782) 372867
Fax (01782) 372867
Mem 650
Pro I Rogers (01782) 372795
Holes 18 L 5800 yds SSS 68
Recs Am–65 D Lynn (1995)
V'tors WD–U WE–NA before 10am

Fees On application
Loc ½ mile S of Barlaston. M6 Junction 14/15

Beau Desert (1921)
Hazel Slade, Cannock WS12 5PJ
Tel (01543) 422626/422773
Fax (01543) 451137
Mem 500
Sec AJR Fairfield (01543) 422626
Pro B Stevens (01543) 422492
Holes 18 L 6310 yds SSS 71
Recs Am–65 N Isherwood (1995) Pro–64 T Minshall
V'tors WD–U WE–phone in advance BH–NA SOC
Fees £38 (£48)
Loc 4 miles NE of Cannock, off A460

Bloxwich (1924)
Stafford Road, Bloxwich WS3 3PQ
Tel (01922) 405724
Fax (01922) 476593
Mem 595
Sec DA Frost (01922) 476593
Pro RJ Dance
Holes 18 L 6273 yds SSS 71
Recs Am–67 R Fleming Pro–65 J Rhodes
V'tors WD–U WE–M SOC
Fees £25 (£30)
Loc N of Walsall on A34

Branston G&CC (1975)
Burton Road, Branston, Burton-on-Trent DE14 3DP
Tel (01283) 512211
Fax (01283) 566984
Mem 800
Sec G Pyle (Golf Mgr)
Pro S Stiff
Holes 18 L 6647 yds Par 72 SSS 72
Recs Am–70 B Wood Pro–65 C Hislop (1998)
V'tors WD–U WE–M before noon SOC
Fees £28 (£38)
Loc ½ mile S of Burton (A38)
Mis Driving range
Arch G Hamshall

Brocton Hall (1894)
Brocton, Stafford ST17 0TH
Tel (01785) 662627
Fax (01785) 661591
Mem 500
Sec G Ashley (01785) 661901
Pro R Johnson (01785) 661485
Holes 18 L 6095 yds SSS 69
Recs Am–66 P Sutton
V'tors I H SOC
Fees £30 (£35)
Loc 4 miles SE of Stafford, off A34
Arch Harry Vardon

Burslem (1907)
Wood Farm, High Lane, Stoke-on-Trent ST6 7JT
Tel (01782) 837006
Mem 300

Sec FL Barnes (01270) 873692
Holes 9 L 5360 yds SSS 66
Recs Am–64 M Keeling (1988) Pro–66 T Williamson
V'tors WD–U WE–NA
Fees £16
Loc Burslem 2 miles

Calderfields (1983)
Aldridge Road, Walsall WS4 2JS
Tel (01922) 640540 (Clubhouse), (01922) 632243 (Bookings)
Fax (01922) 638787
Mem 550
Sec JE Hampshire
Pro D Williams
Holes 18 L 6636 yds SSS 72
V'tors U SOC
Fees £12
Loc 1 mile N of Walsall (A454). M6 Junction 10
Mis Floodlit driving range

Cannock Park (1993)
Public
Stafford Road, Cannock WS11 2AL
Tel (01543) 578850
Fax (01543) 578850
Mem 270
Sec JN Bradbury (01543) 572800
Pro D Dunk
Holes 18 L 5048 yds SSS 65
V'tors U SOC–WD
Fees £8 (£9)
Loc ½ mile N of Cannock on A34. M6 Junction 11, 2 miles
Arch John Mainland

The Craythorne (1972)
Craythorne Road, Stretton, Burton-on-Trent DE13 0AZ
Tel (01283) 564329
Fax (01283) 511908
Email cray@peach.zee-web.co.uk
Mem 500
Sec AA Wright (Man Dir)
Pro S Hadfield (01283) 533745
Holes 18 L 5255 yds Par 68 SSS 67
Recs Am–66 AA Wright (1997)
V'tors WD–U SOC
Fees £20 (£24)
Loc Stretton, 1½ miles N of Burton. A38/A5121 Junction
Mis Driving range. Pitch & putt course

Dartmouth (1910)
Vale Street, West Bromwich B71 4DW
Tel (0121) 588 2131
Mem 350
Sec CF Wade
Pro G Dean
Holes 9 L 6036 yds SSS 71
Recs Am–66 T Cheese (1991) Pro–70 P Lester
V'tors WD–U WE–M SOC–Tues & Thurs
Fees D–£20
Loc 1 mile from W Bromwich, behind Churchfields High School. Junction M5/M6

Staffordshire 621

Drayton Park (1897)
Drayton Park, Tamworth B78 3TN
Tel (01827) 251139
Fax (01827) 284035
Mem 450
Sec AO Rammell JP
Pro MW Passmore (01827) 251478
Holes 18 L 6414 yds SSS 71
Recs Am–62 M McGuire (1993)
Pro–65 DJ Russell (1987)
V'tors WD–H WE/BH–NA
SOC–Tues & Thurs
Fees R/D–£32
Loc 2 miles S of Tamworth (A4091)
Arch James Braid

Druids Heath (1974)
Stonnall Road, Aldridge WS9 8JZ
Tel (01922) 55595
Mem 577 75(L) 45(J)
Sec PJ Bradford
Pro S Elliott (01922) 59523
Holes 18 L 6659 yds Par 72 SSS 73
Recs Am–69 M Pearce
V'tors WD–U WE–M
Fees £25 (£32)
Loc 6 miles NW of Sutton Coldfield, off A452

Enville (1935)
Highgate Common, Enville, Stourbridge DY7 5BN
Tel (01384) 872074
Fax (01384) 873396
Mem 900
Sec RJ Bannister (Sec/Mgr) (01384) 872074
Pro S Power (01384) 872585
Holes Highgate 18 L 6471 yds SSS 72; Lodge 18 L 6275 yds SSS 70
Recs Highgate Am–67 PJ Randle (1991)
Pro–65 J Stafford (1991)
Lodge Am–67 C Elston (1996)
V'tors WD–U WE/BH–M H SOC
Fees £30–£40
Loc 6 miles W of Stourbridge

Goldenhill (1983)
Public
Mobberley Road, Goldenhill, Stoke-on-Trent ST6 5SS
Tel (01782) 784715
Fax (01782) 775940
Mem 600
Sec P Jones
Pro A Clingan
Holes 18 L 5957 yds SSS 68
V'tors U SOC–book with Pro
Fees £6 (£7)
Loc Between Tunstall and Kidsgrove, off A50

Great Barr (1961)
Chapel Lane, Birmingham B43 7BA
Tel (0121) 357 1232
Mem 600
Sec Mrs HK Devey (0121) 358 4236
Pro R Spragg (0121) 357 5270

Holes 18 L 6459 yds SSS 72
Recs Am–67 CM Lambert, CD Webb
Pro–71 J Higgins
V'tors WD–U WE–I (h'cap max 18) SOC
Fees £25
Loc 6 miles NW of Birmingham. M6 Junction 7

Greenway Hall (1908)
Stockton Brook, Stoke-on-Trent ST9 9LJ
Tel (01782) 503158
Mem 550
Sec A Pedley
Holes 18 L 5676 yds SSS 67
Recs Am–65 A Bailey, A Dathan
V'tors WD–U SOC
Fees £14
Loc 5 miles N of Stoke, off A53

Handsworth (1895)
Sunningdale Close, Handsworth Wood, Birmingham B20 1NP
Tel (0121) 554 3387
Fax (0121) 554 3387
Mem 850
Sec PS Hodnett (Hon)
Pro L Bashford (0121) 523 3594
Holes 18 L 6267 yds SSS 70
Recs Am–65 P Johnson (1994)
Pro–71 HF Boyce
V'tors WD–U WE/BH–M SOC
Fees £30
Loc 3 miles NW of Birmingham. M5 Junction 1. M6 Junction 7

Himley Hall (1980)
Public
Himley Hall Park, Dudley DY3 4DF
Tel (01902) 895207
Mem 300
Sec M Harris
Holes 9 L 3145 yds SSS 36
9 hole short course
Recs Am–65 D Bragg
V'tors WD–U WE/BH–restricted
Fees 18 holes–£8 9 holes–£5.50
Loc Grounds of Himley Hall Park. B4176, off A449
Arch A & K Baker

Ingestre Park (1977)
Ingestre, Stafford ST18 0RE
Tel (01889) 270061
Fax (01889) 270845
Mem 740
Sec CJ Radmore (Mgr) (01889) 270845
Pro D Scullion (01889) 270304
Holes 18 L 6334 yds SSS 70
Recs Am–67 D Hughes (1990)
Pro–68 D Scullion (1982)
Ladies–71 K Edwards (1996)
V'tors WD–H before 3.30pm WE/BH–M SOC–WD exc Wed
Fees £23 D–£28
Loc 6 miles E of Stafford, off Tixall Road. M6 Junctions 13/14
Arch Hawtree

Izaak Walton
Cold Norton, Stone ST15 0NS
Tel (01785) 760900
Mem 425
Sec TT Tyler
Pro J Brown
Holes 18 L 6281 yds SSS 72
Recs Am–72 G Dollochin (1995)
V'tors U SOC
Fees £15 (£20)
Loc 7 miles NW of Stafford on B2056. M6 Junction 14
Mis Driving range

Keele Golf Centre (1973)
Public
Keele Road, Newcastle-under-Lyme ST5 5AB
Tel (01782) 717417
Fax (01782) 712972
Sec GA Bytheway
Pro C Smith
Holes 18 L 5822 metres SSS 70
Recs Am–70 P Rowe
Pro–68 P Rowe
V'tors U
Fees £6.50 (£8.40)
Loc 2 miles W of Newcastle on A525, opposite University. M6 Junction 15
Mis Floodlit driving range
Arch Hawtree

Lakeside (1969)
Rugeley Power Station, Rugeley WS15 1PR
Tel (01889) 575667
Fax (01889) 576412
Mem 550
Sec BJ Cary
Holes 18 L 5478 yds SSS 68
Recs Am–68 S Rodgers
V'tors M
Loc 2 miles SE of Rugeley on A513

Leek (1892)
Big Birchall, Leek ST13 5RE
Tel (01538) 385889
Fax (01538) 384535
Mem 500 100(L) 60(J)
Sec F Cutts (01538) 384779
Pro P Stubbs (01538) 384767
Holes 18 L 6218 yds SSS 70
Recs Am–61 D Evans
Pro–65 P Baker
V'tors U H before 3pm –M after 3pm SOC–Wed only
Fees £24 (£30)
Loc ½ mile S of Leek on A520

Little Aston (1908)
Streetly, Sutton Coldfield B74 3AN
Tel (0121) 353 2066
Fax (0121) 353 2942
Mem 250
Sec NH Russell (0121) 353 2942
Pro J Anderson (0121) 353 0330
Holes 18 L 6670 yds SSS 73
Recs Am–64
Pro–68

For list of abbreviations see page 527

V'tors H–by prior arrangement WE–XL
Fees On application
Loc 4 miles NW of Sutton Coldfield, off A454
Arch Harry Vardon

Manor (Kingstone) (1991)
Leese Hill, Kingstone, Uttoxeter ST14 8QT
Tel (01889) 563234
Mem 280
Sec A Campbell
Holes 9 hole course
V'tors U
Fees £10 (£15)
Loc 4 miles W of Uttoxeter
Mis Driving range
Arch E Anderson

Newcastle-under-Lyme (1908)
Whitmore Road, Newcastle-under-Lyme ST5 2QB
Tel (01782) 616583
Fax (01782) 617006
Mem 575
Sec KP Geddes (Sec/Mgr) (01782) 617006
Pro P Symonds (01782) 618526
Holes 18 L 6317 yds SSS 71
Recs Am–64 MC Keates (1989) Pro–68 A Pauly (1988)
V'tors WD–U H WE/BH–M SOC
Fees On application
Loc 2 miles SW of Newcastle-under-Lyme on A53

Onneley (1968)
Onneley, Crewe, Cheshire CW3 5QF
Tel (01782) 750577
Mem 410
Sec P Ball (01782) 846759
Pro None
Holes 9 L 5584 yds SSS 67
Recs Am–67 D Davenport
V'tors WD–U Sat/BH–M Sun–NA SOC–Mon/Thurs/Fri
Fees £15
Loc 8 miles W of Newcastle, off A525
Arch A Benson

Oxley Park (1914)
Stafford Road, Bushbury, Wolverhampton WV10 6DE
Tel (01902) 420506
Fax (01902) 712241
Mem 550
Sec Mrs K Mann (01902) 425892
Pro LA Burlison (01902) 425445
Holes 18 L 6168 yds SSS 69
Recs Am–67 CD Woolley, MS Roberts (1995) Pro–65 P Weaver (1987)
V'tors U SOC
Fees £25 (£25)
Loc 1 mile N of Wolverhampton, off A449
Arch HS Colt

Parkhall (1989)
Public
Hulme Road, Weston Coyney, Stoke-on-Trent ST3 5BH
Tel (01782) 599584
Sec N Worrall (Mgr) (01831) 456409
Pro A Clingan
Holes 18 L 2335 yds Par 54
Recs Am–53 N Worrall (1991)
V'tors WE–booking necessary SOC
Fees On application
Loc 3 miles E of Stoke. Longton 1 mile

Patshull Park Hotel G&CC (1980)
Pattingham, Wolverhampton WV6 7HR
Tel (01902) 700100/700342
Fax (01902) 700874
Mem 395
Sec K Roberts
Pro J Higgins
Holes 18 L 6412 yds SSS 71
Recs Am–67 S Weir Pro–63 J Higgins
V'tors U H SOC
Fees £22.50 (£27.50)
Loc 7 miles W of Wolverhampton, off A41. M54 Junction 3, 5 miles
Arch John Jacobs

Penn (1908)
Penn Common, Wolverhampton WV4 5JN
Tel (01902) 341142
Mem 650
Sec MH Jones
Pro A Briscoe (01902) 330472
Holes 18 L 6462 yds SSS 71
Recs Am–67 C Upton, M Weston Pro–70 J Rhodes, R Cameron
V'tors WD–U WE–M SOC
Fees £20 (Nov–Feb £15)
Loc 2 miles SW of Wolverhampton, off A449

Perton Park (1990)
Wrottesley Park Road, Perton, Wolverhampton WV6 7HL
Tel (01902) 380103/380073
Fax (01902) 326219
Mem 300
Sec E Greenway (Mgr)
Pro J Harrold (01902) 380073
Holes 18 L 6620 yds SSS 72
V'tors U SOC
Fees £10 (£15)
Loc 6 miles W of Wolverhampton, off A454
Mis Driving range

St Thomas's Priory (1995)
Armitage Lane, Armitage, Rugeley WS15 1ED
Tel (01543) 491116
Fax (01543) 492244
Mem 500
Sec J Bissell

Pro S Berry (01543) 492096
Holes 18 L 5969 yds SSS 70 Pro–67 M McGuire (1997)
V'tors M SOC–WD
Fees On application
Loc 1 mile SE of Rugeley on A513, opp Ash Tree Inn
Arch Paul Mulholland

Sandwell Park (1897)
Birmingham Road, West Bromwich B71 4JJ
Tel (0121) 553 4637
Fax (0121) 525 1651
Mem 600
Sec DA Paterson
Pro N Wylie (0121) 553 4384
Holes 18 L 6468 yds SSS 73
Recs Am–65 J Bromley (1997) Pro–67 F Clark (1994), I Clark (1997), B Larratt (1998)
V'tors WD–U WE–MH SOC–WD
Fees £25–£35
Loc West Bromwich/Birmingham boundary. By M5 Junction 1
Arch HS Colt

Sedgley (1992)
Pay and play
Sandyfields Road, Sedgley, Dudley DY3 3DL
Tel (01902) 880503
Mem 150
Sec JA Cox
Pro G Mercer
Holes 9 L 3150 yds SSS 71
V'tors WD–U WE–booking advised
Fees 9 holes–£5 (£5.50) 18 holes–£7 (£7.50)
Loc ½ mile from Sedgley, off A463 between Dudley and Wolverhampton
Mis Driving range
Arch WG Cox

Seedy Mill (1991)
Elmhurst, Lichfield WS13 3HE
Tel (01543) 417333
Fax (01543) 418098
Mem 1100
Sec J Martin (Gen Mgr)
Pro S Jackson
Holes 18 L 6305 yds SSS 70 9 hole Par 3 course
V'tors U H SOC
Fees On application
Loc 2 miles N of Lichfield on A515
Mis Floodlit driving range
Arch Hawtree

South Staffordshire (1892)
Danescourt Road, Tettenhall, Wolverhampton WV6 9BQ
Tel (01902) 751065
Fax (01902) 741753
Mem 600
Sec JA Macklin
Pro J Rhodes (01902) 754816
Holes 18 L 6513 yds SSS 71

Recs Am–69 IS Guest (1996)
Pro–67 D Gilford (1984)
Ladies–73 A Bullock (1994)
V'tors WD–U WE/BH–M or by arrangement SOC
Fees £34 D–£40 (£47)
Loc 3 miles W of Wolverhampton, off A41
Arch Harry Vardon

Stafford Castle (1907)
Newport Road, Stafford ST16 1BP
Tel (01785) 223821
Mem 440
Sec PJ Ash (Admin)
Holes 9 L 6382 yds Par 71 SSS 70
Recs Am–68 J Campion (1992)
V'tors WD–U WE–after 1pm
Fees £14 (£18)
Loc ½ mile W of Stafford

Stone (1896)
The Fillybrooks, Stone ST15 0NB
Tel (01785) 813103
Mem 314
Sec PR Farley (01785) 284875
Holes 9 L 6299 yds Par 71 SSS 70
Recs Am–68 A Hurst (1991)
Ladies–75 DR Pursell (1995)
V'tors WD–U WE/BH–M SOC–WD
Fees £15
Loc ½ mile W of Stone on A34

Swindon (1976) 897031
Bridgnorth Road, Swindon, Dudley DY3 4PU
Tel (01902) 897031
Fax (01902) 326219
Mem 500
Sec E Greenway (Mgr)
Pro P Lester (01902) 896191
Holes 18 L 6088 yds SSS 69
9 hole Par 3 course
Recs Am–68 N Bennett (1990)
V'tors U SOC–WD
Fees £18 (£27)
Loc 5 miles SW of Wolverhampton on B4176
Mis Driving range

Tamworth (1978)
Public
Eagle Drive, Amington, Tamworth B77 4EG
Tel (01827) 53850
Mem 500
Pro D Scott
Holes 18 L 6695 yds SSS 72
Recs Am–67 CJ Christison
Pro–65 BN Jones
V'tors U SOC–WD
Fees On application
Loc 2½ miles E of Tamworth on B5000. M42, 3 miles

Trentham (1894)
14 Barlaston Old Road, Trentham, Stoke-on-Trent ST4 8HB
Tel (01782) 642347
Mem 680
Sec RN Portas (01782) 658109

Pro S Wilson (01782) 657309
Holes 18 L 6644 yds SSS 72
Recs Am–63 DA Lynn (1995)
Pro–68 D Gilford (1991)
V'tors WD–U H WE/BH–M (or enquire Sec) SOC–WD
Fees £25
Loc 3 miles S of Newcastle, off A34. M6 Junction 15

Trentham Park (1936)
Trentham Park, Stoke-on-Trent ST4 8AE
Tel (01782) 642245
Fax (01782) 658800
Mem 500 100(L) 50(J)
Sec T Berrisford (01782) 658800
Pro B Rimmer (01782) 642125
Holes 18 L 6425 yds SSS 71
Recs Am–67 S Clarke
Pro–68 D Gilford, R Rafferty
V'tors H SOC–Wed & Fri
Fees £22.50 (£30)
Loc 4 miles S of Newcastle on A34. M6 Junction 15, 1 mile

Uttoxeter (1970)
Wood Lane, Uttoxeter ST14 8JR
Tel (01889) 566552
Fax (01889) 567501
Mem 650
Sec R Orme
Pro AD McCandless (01889) 564884
Holes 18 L 5798 yds Par 70 SSS 69
Recs Am–64 B Belcher (1992)
V'tors WD–U WE–by arrangement SOC
Fees £15 D–£22 (£17)
Loc Uttoxeter racecourse ½ mile

Walsall (1907)
Broadway, Walsall WS1 3EY
Tel (01922) 613512
Fax (01922) 616460
Mem 600
Sec E Murray (01922) 613512
Pro R Lambert (01922) 626766
Holes 18 L 6232 yds SSS 70
Recs Am–65 P Brown, S Wakefield (1997)
V'tors WD–U WE–M SOC
Fees £33
Loc 1 mile S of Walsall, off A34. M6 Junction 7
Arch McKenzie

Wergs (1990)
Pay and play
Keepers Lane, Tettenhall WV6 8UA
Tel (01902) 742225
Fax (01902) 744748
Mem 255
Sec Mrs G Parsons
Holes 18 L 6949 yds Par 72 SSS 73
Recs Am–74 T Mathers (1991)
Pro–74 D Prosser (1990)
V'tors U
Fees D–£14 (£18)
Loc 3 miles W of Wolverhampton on A41
Arch CW Moseley

Westwood (1923)
Newcastle Road, Wallbridge, Leek ST13 7AA
Tel (01538) 398385
Fax (01538) 382485
Mem 550
Sec C Plant
Pro N Hyde
Holes 18 L 6207 yds SSS 70
Recs Am–66 M Sales
V'tors U SOC–WD
Fees WD–£18
Loc W boundary of Leek on A53

Whiston Hall (1971)
Whiston, Cheadle ST10 2HZ
Tel (01538) 266260
Mem 500
Sec LC & RM Cliff (Mgr)
Holes 18 L 5742 yds SSS 69
V'tors U SOC
Fees £10
Loc 8 miles NE of Stoke-on-Trent on A52, nr Alton Towers

Whittington Heath (1886)
Tamworth Road, Lichfield WS14 9PW
Tel (01543) 432317 (Admin),
(01543) 432212 (Steward)
Fax (01543) 432317
Mem 670
Sec Mrs JA Burton
Pro AR Sadler (01543) 432261
Holes 18 L 6490 yds SSS 71
V'tors WD–H or I WE/BH + day after–M SOC–Wed & Thurs
Fees £27 D–£36
Loc 2½ miles E of Lichfield on Tamworth road (A51)

Wolstanton (1904)
Dimsdale Old Hall, Hassam Parade, Wolstanton, Newcastle ST5 9DR
Tel (01782) 616995
Mem 625
Sec Mrs VJ Keenan (01782) 622413
Pro S Arnold (01782) 622718
Holes 18 L 5807 yds SSS 68
Recs Am–63 P Sweetsur
Pro–66 CH Ward
V'tors WD–H WE–M SOC–WD
Fees £20
Loc 1½ miles NW of Newcastle (A34)

Suffolk

Aldeburgh (1884)
Aldeburgh IP15 5PE
Tel (01728) 452890
Fax (01728) 452937
Mem 879
Sec IM Simpson
Pro K Preston (01728) 453309
Holes 18 L 6330 yds SSS 71
9 L 2114 yds SSS 64
Recs Am–65 J Lloyd
Pro–67 JM Johnson

For list of abbreviations see page 527

Suffolk

V'tors H SOC
Fees On application
Loc 6 miles E of A12 (A1094)
Arch W Fernie/J Thompson

Beccles (1899)
The Common, Beccles NR34 9BX
Tel (01502) 712244
Mem 150
Sec Mrs LW Allen
(01502) 712479
Holes 9 L 2696 yds SSS 67
Recs Am–65 S Shulver
V'tors WD–U Sun–M SOC
Fees £11 (£13)
Loc 10 miles W of Lowestoft (A146)

Brett Vale
Noakes Road, Raydon, Ipswich IP7 5LR
Tel (01473) 310718
Fax (01473) 312270
Mem 430
Sec JS Reid
Pro R Taylor
Holes 18 L 5847 yds Par 70
Recs Am–71 P Hamblin
Pro–67 R Taylor
V'tors U–booking advisable SOC–WD
Fees £15 (£20)
Loc 10 miles SW of Ipswich, off A12 (B1070)
Mis Golf academy
Arch Howard Swan

Bungay & Waveney Valley (1889)
Outney Common, Bungay NR35 1DS
Tel (01986) 892237
Mem 673
Sec RW Stacey
Pro N Whyte
Holes 18 L 6063 yds SSS 69
Recs Am–64 D Wood
Pro–64 T Spurgeon
V'tors WD–U WE–M SOC–WD
Fees D–£24
Loc ½ mile W of Bungay, on N side of A143
Arch James Braid

Bury St Edmunds (1922)
Tut Hill, Bury St Edmunds IP28 6LG
Tel (01284) 755979
Fax (01284) 763288
Mem 650 180(L)
Sec JC Sayer
Pro M Jillings (01284) 755978
Holes 18 L 6669 yds Par 72 SSS 72
9 L 2217 yds Par 31 SSS 31
Recs Am–68 LH Dodd (1998)
Pro–67 K Golding (1989)
V'tors WD/BH–U WE–M SOC–WD
Fees 18 hole:£24 9 hole:£12 (£14)
Loc 2 miles W of Bury St Edmunds on B1106, off A14
Arch Ted Ray

Cretingham (1984)
Grove Farm, Cretingham, Woodbridge IP13 7BA
Tel (01728) 685275
Fax (01728) 685037
Mem 300
Sec Miss K Coe
Pro N Jackson
Holes 9 L 2260 yds Par 33
Recs Pro–61 T Johnson (1994)
V'tors U SOC
Fees 18 holes–£11 (£13)
Loc 2 miles SE of Earl Soham. 11 miles N of Ipswich
Mis Practice range. Pitch & putt course
Arch J Austin

Diss (1903)
Stuston Common, Diss IP22 4AA
Tel (01379) 641025
Fax (01379) 641025
Mem 750
Sec L Macrow
Pro N Taylor (01379) 644399
Holes 18 L 6238 yds SSS 70
Recs Am–70 T Dawson (1998)
Pro–67 R Curtis (1993)
V'tors WD only
Fees £20
Loc 1 mile SE of Diss, off A140

Felixstowe Ferry (1880)
Ferry Road, Felixstowe IP4 9RY
Tel (01394) 283060
Fax (01394) 273679
Mem 850
Sec N Fisker (01394) 286834
Pro I Macpherson
(01394) 283975
Holes 18 L 6308 yds SSS 70
9 L 2986 yds Par 35
Recs Am–67 S Macpherson (1993)
Pro–65 I Richardson (1979),
L Paterson
V'tors M H WD before 10.30am SOC. 9 hole course–U
Fees £26
Loc 2 miles NE of Felixstowe, towards Felixstowe Ferry
Arch Henry Cotton (1947)

Flempton (1895)
Bury St Edmunds IP28 6HQ
Tel (01284) 728291
Mem 250
Sec JF Taylor
Pro M Jillings
Holes 9 L 6240 yds SSS 70
Recs Am–67 Lt J Reynolds
Pro–69 J Arbon
V'tors WD–H WE/BH–M
Fees £22 D–£28
Loc 4 miles NW of Bury St Edmunds on A1101
Arch JH Taylor

Fynn Valley (1992)
Witnesham, Ipswich IP6 9JA
Tel (01473) 785267
Fax (01473) 785632

Mem 650
Sec AR Tyrrell
Pro G Crane, P Wilby
(01473) 785463
Holes 18 L 5873 yds Par 68 SSS 68
9 hole Par 3 course
Recs Am–69 B Smyth (1998)
Pro–66 A Cotton (1998)
V'tors U exc Sun am SOC
Fees £17 (£24) (1998)
Loc 2 miles N of Ipswich on B1077
Mis Driving range. Course extension Summer 1999
Arch AR Tyrrell

Haverhill (1974)
Coupals Road, Haverhill CB9 7UW
Tel (01440) 761951
Fax (01440) 761951
Mem 600
Sec Mrs J Edwards
Pro S Mayfield (01440) 712628
Holes 18 L 5898 yds SSS 70
Recs Am–66 A Carter (1991),
R Cramsie (1993)
Pro–66 C Cook
V'tors U–phone Pro
SOC–Tues & Thurs
Fees £18 (£22)
Loc 1 mile E of Haverhill, off A1107. Signs to Calford Green
Arch Lawrie/Pilgrim

Hintlesham Hall (1991)
Hintlesham, Ipswich IP8 3NS
Tel (01473) 652761
Fax (01473) 652463
Mem 350
Sec Tina Shannon (Mgr)
Pro A Spink
Holes 18 L 6638 yds SSS 72
Recs Am–67 P McEvoy (1991)
Pro–68 A Lucas (1997)
V'tors WD–U WE–NA before 2pm SOC
Fees £27
Loc 4 miles W of Ipswich on A1071
Arch Hawtree

Ipswich (Purdis Heath) (1895)
Purdis Heath, Bucklesham Road, Ipswich IP3 8UQ
Tel (01473) 727474 (Steward)
Fax (01473) 715236
Mem 740
Sec To be appointed
(01473) 728941
Pro SJ Whymark (01473) 724017
Holes 18 L 6405 yds SSS 71
9 L 1950 yds Par 31
Recs Am–64 JVT Marks
Pro–67 RA Knight
V'tors WD–H SOC 9 hole:U
Fees 18 hole:£35 (£36)
9 hole:£10
Loc 3 miles E of Ipswich
Arch James Braid

For list of abbreviations see page 527

Links (Newmarket) (1902)
Cambridge Road, Newmarket CB8 0TG
- **Tel** (01638) 663000
- **Fax** (01638) 661476
- **Mem** 750
- **Sec** Lt Col MI Botting
- **Pro** J Sharkey (01638) 662395
- **Holes** 18 L 6424 yds SSS 71
- **Recs** Am–66 R Wiseman (1992), M Hartley (1998)
  Pro–64 N Mitchell (1996)
  Ladies–68 T Eakin (1994)
- **V'tors** H exc Sun–M before 11.30am SOC
- **Fees** £28 (£32)
- **Loc** 1 mile SW of Newmarket

Newton Green (1907)
Newton Green, Sudbury CO10 0QN
- **Tel** (01787) 77501
- **Mem** 650
- **Sec** K Mazdon (01787) 377217
- **Pro** T Cooper (01787) 313215
- **Holes** 18 L 5893 yds SSS 69
- **V'tors** WD–U WE–M SOC
- **Fees** £15.50
- **Loc** 4 miles S of Sudbury on A134

Rookery Park (1891)
Carlton Colville, Lowestoft NR33 8HJ
- **Tel** (01502) 560380
- **Fax** (01502) 560380
- **Mem** 1000
- **Sec** DP Kelly
- **Pro** M Elsworthy (01502) 515103
- **Holes** 18 L 6729 yds SSS 72
  9 hole Par 3 course
- **Recs** Am–71 G Long (1985)
  Pro–66 R Mann (1995)
- **V'tors** WD–U Sat/BH–after 11am
  Sun–NA SOC
- **Fees** £25 (£30)
- **Loc** 3 miles W of Lowestoft (A146)

Royal Worlington & Newmarket (1893)
Golf Links Road, Worlington, Bury St Edmunds IP28 8SD
- **Tel** (01638) 712216
- **Fax** (01638) 717787
- **Mem** 310
- **Sec** Maj GWM Hipkin
- **Pro** M Hawkins (01638) 715224
- **Holes** 9 L 6210 yds SSS 70
- **Recs** Am–67 DJ Millensted
  Pro–66 EE Beverley
- **V'tors** I or H–phone first WE–NA
- **Fees** D–£40 After 2pm–£30
- **Loc** 6 miles NE of Newmarket, off A11
- **Arch** Tom Dunn

Rushmere (1927)
Rushmere Heath, Ipswich IP4 5QQ
- **Tel** (01473) 727109
- **Fax** (01473) 725648
- **Mem** 800
- **Sec** PL Coles (01473) 725648
- **Pro** NTJ McNeill (01473) 728076
- **Holes** 18 L 6262 yds SSS 70
- **Recs** Am–66 F Knights (1989), M Turner (1990), M Buck (1998)
  Pro–67 NTJ McNeill (1984), S Beckham (1985)
- **V'tors** WD–H WE/BH–H after 2.30pm
- **Fees** £20
- **Loc** 3 miles E of Ipswich, off Woodbridge road (A1214)

St Helena (1990)
Bramfield Road, Halesworth IP19 9XA
- **Tel** (01986) 875567
- **Fax** (01986) 874565
- **Mem** 400
- **Sec** Mrs RK Ward
- **Pro** PM Heil
- **Holes** 18 L 6580 yds SSS 72
  9 hole course SSS 36
- **Recs** Am–71 N Land (1995)
  Pro–68 PM Heil (1994)
- **V'tors** H SOC
- **Fees** 18 hole:£15 D–£19 (£21)
  9 hole:£7.50
- **Loc** 1 mile S of Halesworth, off A144
- **Mis** Floodlit driving range
- **Arch** JW Johnson

Seckford (1991)
Seckford Hall Road, Great Bealings, Woodbridge IP13 6NT
- **Tel** (01394) 388000
- **Fax** (01394) 382818
- **Mem** 400
- **Sec** J Skinner
- **Pro** J Skinner
- **Holes** 18 L 5328 yds Par 69 SSS 66
- **Recs** Am–66 A Litherland
  Pro–63 J Skinner, S Jay
- **V'tors** U–booking necessary SOC
- **Fees** £15 (£17.50)
- **Loc** SW of Woodbridge, off A12
- **Mis** Driving range
- **Arch** J Johnson

Southwold (1884)
The Common, Southwold IP18 6TB
- **Tel** (01502) 723234
- **Mem** 450
- **Sec** MS Lumsden (01502) 723248
- **Pro** B Allen (01502) 723790
- **Holes** 9 L 6050 yds SSS 69
- **Recs** Am–67 S Fitzgerald
  Pro–65 R Mann
- **V'tors** U (subject to fixtures)
- **Fees** £18 (£22)
- **Loc** 35 miles NE of Ipswich

Stoke-by-Nayland (1972)
Keepers Lane, Leavenheath, Colchester CO6 4PZ
- **Tel** (01206) 262836
- **Fax** (01206) 263556
- **Mem** 1400
- **Pro** K Lovelock (01206) 262769
- **Holes** Gainsborough 18 L 6498 yds SSS 71; Constable 18 L 6544 yds SSS 71

- **Recs** Gainsborough Am–68
  K Browne (1997)
  Pro–67 K Golding (1997)
  Constable Am–66 K Browne (1997)
  Pro–68 J Keely (1998)
- **V'tors** WD–U WE/BH–H after 10am SOC
- **Fees** £20 (£24)
- **Loc** Off A134 Colchester-Sudbury road on B1068
- **Mis** Driving range

Stowmarket (1962)
Lower Road, Onehouse, Stowmarket IP14 3DA
- **Tel** (01449) 736392
- **Fax** (01449) 736826
- **Mem** 600
- **Sec** J Edwards-Hayes (01449) 736473
- **Pro** D Burl
- **Holes** 18 L 6119 yds SSS 69
- **Recs** Am–66 M Darling
  Pro–66 H Flatman
- **V'tors** H SOC–Thurs & Fri
- **Fees** £23 (£29)
- **Loc** 2½ miles SW of Stowmarket
- **Mis** Driving range

The Suffolk G&CC (1974)
St John's Hill Plantation, The Street, Fornham All Saints, Bury St Edmunds IP28 6JQ
- **Tel** (01284) 706777
- **Fax** (01284) 706721
- **Mem** 600
- **Sec** I Dalrymple
- **Pro** S Hall
- **Holes** 18 L 6321 yds SSS 71
- **V'tors** U SOC
- **Fees** £20 (£25)
- **Loc** 2 miles NW of Bury St Edmunds, off B1106

Thorpeness Golf Hotel (1923)
Thorpeness, Leiston IP16 4NH
- **Tel** (01728) 452176
- **Fax** (01728) 453868
- **Mem** 250
- **Sec** NW Griffin
- **Pro** (01728) 454926
- **Holes** 18 L 6271 yds SSS 71
- **Recs** Am–66 J Marks
  Pro–67 K McDonald
- **V'tors** U
- **Fees** On application
- **Loc** 2 miles N of Aldeburgh
- **Arch** James Braid

Ufford Park Hotel (1992)
Yarmouth Road, Ufford, Woodbridge IP12 1QW
- **Tel** (01394) 382836
- **Fax** (01394) 383582
- **Mem** 250
- **Sec** B Tidy
- **Pro** S Robertson
- **Holes** 18 L 6325 yds SSS 71

For list of abbreviations see page 527

626 Suffolk

Recs Am–67 J Maddock
       Pro–67 C Green
V'tors U SOC
Fees   £16 (£20)
Loc   2 miles N of Woodbridge,
       off A12
Mis   Golf Academy
Arch   P Pilgrim

Waldringfield Heath (1983)
Newbourne Road, Waldringfield, Woodbridge IP12 4PT
Tel   (01473) 736768
Fax   (01473) 736436
Mem   640
Sec   LJ McWade
Pro   R Mann, A Lucas
       (01473) 736417
Holes 18 L 6141 yds SSS 69
Recs   Am–70 S Simmonds (1995)
       Pro–67 L Jones,
       A Duffin (1998)
V'tors WD–U WE/BH–M before
       noon SOC–WD
Fees   On application
Loc   3 miles E of Ipswich, off A12
Arch   P Pilgrim

Woodbridge (1893)
Bromeswell Heath, Woodbridge IP12 2PF
Tel   (01394) 382038
Fax   (01394) 382392
Mem   950
Sec   A Theunissen
Pro   A Hubert (01394) 383213
Holes 18 L 6299 yds SSS 70
       9 L 6382 yds SSS 70
Recs   Am–64 JVT Marks (1983)
       Pro–65 F Sunderland (1970)
V'tors WD–H WE/BH–M SOC
Fees   18 hole:£30 9 hole:£15
Loc   2 miles E of Woodbridge
       on A1152 towards Orford
Arch   F Hawtree

Surrey

The Addington (1913)
205 Shirley Church Road, Croydon CR0 5AB
Tel   (0181) 777 1055
Sec   JW Beale
Holes 18 L 6242 yds SSS 71
Recs   Am–66 P Benka
       Pro–68 F Robson
V'tors H SOC–WD
Fees   On application
Loc   E Croydon 2½ miles
Arch   JF Abercromby

Addington Court (1931)
Public
Featherbed Lane, Addington, Croydon CR0 9AA
Tel   (0181) 657 0281
Fax   (0181) 651 0282
Sec   G Cotton

Pro   G Cotton
Holes Old 18 L 5577 yds SSS 67;
       Falconwood 18 L 5513 yds
       SSS 66; Lower 9 L 1812 yds
       SSS 62
Recs   Am–62 S Griffiths (1994)
       Pro–60 W Grant,
       C DeFoy (1992)
V'tors U
Fees   Old: £11.50 (£12.95).
       Falconwood: £9.99 (£11.50)
       9 hole: £6.95
Loc   3 miles E of Croydon
Mis   18 hole pitch & putt course
Arch   F Hawtree Sr

Addington Palace (1923)
Addington Park, Gravel Hill, Addington CR0 5BB
Tel   (0181) 654 3061
Fax   (0181) 655 3632
Mem   700
Sec   LM Dennis-Smither
Pro   R Williams (0181) 654 1786
Holes 18 L 6410 yds SSS 71
Recs   Am–63 R Glading
       Pro–65 AD Locke
V'tors WD–H WE/BH–M
Fees   £30
Loc   2 miles E of Croydon Station

Banstead Downs (1890)
Burdon Lane, Belmont, Sutton SM2 7DD
Tel   (0181) 642 2284
Fax   (0181) 642 5252
Mem   650
Sec   RHA Steele
Pro   R Dickman
       (0181) 642 6884
Holes 18 L 6194 yds SSS 69
Recs   Am–64 P Brittain (1992)
       Pro–64 M Wheeler (1995)
V'tors WD–H WE/BH–M
       SOC–Thurs
Fees   £30 After noon–£20
Loc   1 mile S of Sutton

Barrow Hills (1970)
Longcross, Chertsey KT16 0DS
Tel   (01344) 635770
Mem   320
Sec   RW Routley
       (01932) 848117
Holes 18 L 3090 yds SSS 53
Recs   Am–58 EJ Sewell (1979)
V'tors M
Fees   On application
Loc   4 miles W of Chertsey

Betchworth Park (1911)
Reigate Road, Dorking RH4 1NZ
Tel   (01306) 882052
Fax   (01306) 877462
Mem   725
Sec   B Weeds
Pro   A Tocher (01306) 884334
Holes 18 L 6266 yds SSS 70
Recs   Am–64 M Osborne (1995)
       Pro–65 NC Coles

V'tors WD–by arrangement exc
       Tues & Wed am WE–NA exc
       Sun pm
Fees   £34 (£45)
Loc   1 mile E of Dorking on A25
Arch   HS Colt

Bletchingley (1993)
Church Lane, Bletchingley RH1 4LP
Tel   (01883) 744666
Fax   (01883) 744284
Mem   600
Sec   Mrs N Robinson (Mgr)
Pro   A Dyer (01883) 744848
Holes 18 L 6504 yds Par 72 SSS 71
V'tors WD–U WE–M SOC
Fees   £20 (£28)
Loc   1 mile S of M25 Junction 6
       on A25

Bowenhurst Golf Centre
Mill Lane, Crondall, Farnham GU10 5RP
Tel   (01252) 851695
Fax   (01252) 852039
Mem   202
Sec   GL Corbey
Pro   S Harrison, P Young
       (01252) 851344
Holes 9 L 2007 yds Par 62 SSS 60
V'tors U SOC
Fees   18 holes–£10 (£13)
       9 holes–£6 (£7.50)
Loc   2 miles SW of Farnham
       on A287. M3 Junction 5
Mis   Driving range
Arch   G Finn, N Finn

Bramley (1913)
Bramley, Guildford GU5 0AL
Tel   (01483) 893042
Fax   (01483) 894673
Mem   800
Sec   Ms M Lambert
       (01483) 892696
Pro   G Peddie
       (01483) 893685
Holes 18 L 5990 yds SSS 69
Recs   Am–65 J Jones (1993)
       Pro–63 P Hughes (1994)
V'tors WD–U WE–M SOC–WD
Fees   £27 D–£33
Loc   3 miles S of Guildford
       on A281
Mis   Driving range-members and
       green fees only
Arch   Mayo/Braid

Burhill (1907)
Burwood Road, Walton-on-Thames KT12 4BL
Tel   (01932) 227345
Fax   (01932) 267159
Mem   1100
Sec   G Hogg
Pro   L Johnson (01932) 221729
Holes 18 L 6479 yds SSS 71
Recs   Am–65 SD Clark (1998)
       Pro–65 G Orr (1988)
V'tors WD–H WE/BH–M
Fees   On application

For list of abbreviations see page 527

Surrey

Loc Between Walton-on-Thames and Cobham, off Burwood Road
Mis Game Improvement Centre
Arch Willie Park

Camberley Heath (1913)
Golf Drive, Camberley GU15 1JG
Tel (01276) 23258
Fax (01276) 692505
Mem 725
Sec J Greenwood
Pro G Ralph (01276) 27905
Holes 18 L 6326 yds SSS 71
V'tors WD–H WE–M SOC H
Fees On application
Loc 1½ miles S of Camberley on A325
Arch HS Colt

Central London Golf Centre (1992)
Public
Burntwood Lane, Wandsworth, London SW17 0AT
Tel (0181) 871 2468
Fax (0181) 871 2468
Mem 320
Sec J Robson
Pro J Robson
Holes 9 L 4658 yds SSS 62
V'tors WD–U WE–NA before 12 noon SOC
Fees £6.50 (£8.50)
Loc Off Burntwood Lane SW17
Arch Patrick Tallack

Chessington Golf Centre (1983)
Pay and play
Garrison Lane, Chessington KT9 2LW
Tel (0181) 391 0948
Fax (0181) 397 2068
Mem 120
Sec J Lafferty
Holes 9 L 1400 yds Par 54 SSS 50
Recs Am–60 N Murphy
      Pro–54 R Hunter
V'tors U
Fees £4.50 (£5.40)
Loc Off A243, opp Chessington South Station. M25 Junction 9
Mis Driving range

Chiddingfold (1994)
Petworth Road, Chiddingfold GU8 4SL
Tel (01428) 685888
Fax (01428) 685939
Mem 400
Sec Mrs L Pascolini (Gen Mgr)
     Mrs V Farrow (Admin)
Pro P Creamer
Holes 18 L 5482 yds Par 70 SSS 67
Recs Am–67 D Brown (1995)
      Pro–64 P Creamer (1995)
V'tors U SOC
Fees £15 (£22)
Loc On A283 between Petworth and Guildford
Arch Johnathan Gaunt

Chipstead (1906)
How Lane, Chipstead, Coulsdon CR5 3LN
Tel (01737) 551053
Fax (01737) 555404
Mem 600
Sec SLD Spencer-Skeen (01737) 555781
Pro G Torbett (01737) 554939
Holes 18 L 5450 yds SSS 67
Recs Am–62 T Paterson (1998)
      Pro–64 P Mitchell (1994)
V'tors WD–U WE/BH–M
Fees £25 After 2pm–£20
Loc Nr Chipstead Station

Chobham (1994)
Chobham Road, Knaphill, Woking GU21 2TZ
Tel (01276) 855584
Fax (01276) 855663
Mem 750
Sec D Cross
Pro R Thomas
Holes 18 L 5821 yds Par 69 SSS 68
Recs Am–65 J Rose
      Pro–61 G Harris, R Boxall
V'tors M H–restricted SOC
Fees £24 (£30)
Loc 3 miles E of M3 Junction 3 between Chobham and Knaphill (A3046)
Arch Alliss/Clark

Clandon Regis (1994)
Epsom Road, West Clandon GU4 7TT
Tel (01483) 224888
Fax (01483) 211781
Mem 558
Sec N Caplin
Pro S Lloyd
Holes 18 L 6412 yds Par 72 SSS 71
Recs Am–68 A Booth (1996)
      Pro–65 P Hughes (1995)
V'tors WD–U SOC–WD
Fees £26
Loc 3 miles E of Guildford on A246

Coombe Hill (1911)
Golf Club Drive, Coombe Lane West, Kingston KT2 7DF
Tel (0181) 336 7600
Fax (0181) 336 7601
Mem 553
Sec Mrs C De Foy
Pro C De Foy (0181) 949 3713
Holes 18 L 6303 yds SSS 71
Recs Am–66 C Boal
      Pro–67 B Gallagher
V'tors WD–I or H WE–NA SOC
Fees D–£65
Loc 1 mile W of New Malden on A238
Arch JF Abercromby

Coombe Wood (1904)
George Road, Kingston Hill, Kingston-upon-Thames KT2 7NS
Tel (0181) 942 3828 (Clubhouse)
Fax (0181) 942 0388
Mem 640
Sec PM Urwin (0181) 942 0388
Pro D Butler (0181) 942 6764
Holes 18 L 5299 yds SSS 66
Recs Am–61 M Heath (1997)
      Pro–60 D Butler (1987)
V'tors WD–U H after 9am
      WE/BH–M SOC–WD
Fees On application
Loc 1 mile E of Kingston-upon-Thames, off A3 at Robin Hood roundabout or Coombe junction
Arch Williamson

Coulsdon Manor (1937)
Pay and play
Coulsdon Court Road, Old Coulsdon, Croydon CR5 2LL
Tel (0181) 660 6083
Fax (0181) 668 3118
Pro D Copsey (0181) 660 6083
Holes 18 L 6037 yds SSS 70
Recs Am–66 K Smale
      Pro–66 G Ralph
V'tors U
Fees £13.50 (£16.75)
Loc 5 miles S of Croydon on B2030. M25 Junction 7
Arch HS Colt

Croham Hurst (1911)
Croham Road, South Croydon CR2 7HJ
Tel (0181) 657 5581
Fax (0181) 657 3229
Mem 515 110(L) 50(J)
Sec R Passingham (Mgr)
Pro E Stillwell (0181) 657 7705
Holes 18 L 6286 yds SSS 70
Recs Am–64 CF Staroscik (1991)
      Pro–66 B Firkins
V'tors WD–I WE/BH–M
Fees £33 (£42)
Loc 1 mile from S Croydon. M25 Junction 6-A22-B270-B269

Cuddington (1929)
Banstead Road, Banstead SM7 1RD
Tel (0181) 393 0952
Fax (0181) 786 7025
Mem 760
Sec DM Scott
Pro M Warner (0181) 393 5850
Holes 18 L 6436 yds SSS 71
Recs Am–68 K Hazelden
      Pro–61 J Spence
V'tors WD–I WE–M
Fees £35 (£40)
Loc Nr Banstead Station
Arch HS Colt

Dorking (1897)
Deepdene Avenue, Chart Park, Dorking RH5 4BX
Tel (01306) 886917
Fax (01306) 886917
Mem 420
Sec P Napier (Mgr)
Pro P Napier
Holes 9 L 5163 yds SSS 65
Recs Am–61 R Mann
      Pro–62 A King

For list of abbreviations see page 527

V'tors WD–U WE/BH–M SOC–WD
Fees £12
Loc 1 mile S of Dorking on A24
Arch James Braid

Drift (1976)
The Drift, East Horsley KT24 5HD
Tel (01483) 284641
Fax (01483) 284642
Mem 700
Sec C Rose
Pro J Hagen (01483) 284772
Holes 18 L 6425 yds SSS 72
Recs Am–71 B Rowan
 Pro–71 J Bennett
V'tors WD–U SOC
Fees £30 After 1pm–£20
Loc 2 miles off A3 (B2039). M25 Junction 10

Duke's Dene (1996)
Slines New Road, Woldingham CR3 7HA
Tel (01883) 653501
Fax (01883) 653502
Mem 800
Sec D Sherette (Gen Mgr)
Pro P Thornley (01883) 653501
Holes 18 L 6322 yds Par 71 SSS 70
V'tors U SOC
Fees £25 (£30)
Loc 2½ miles N of M25 Junction 6
Arch Bradford Benz

Dulwich & Sydenham Hill (1894)
Grange Lane, College Road, London SE21 7LH
Tel (0181) 693 3961
Fax (0181) 693 2481
Mem 850
Sec Mrs S Alexander
Pro D Baillie (0181) 693 8491
Holes 18 L 6051 yds SSS 69
Recs Am–64 J Piner
 Pro–63 LF Rowe
V'tors WD–H WE/BH–M SOC
Fees £25

Dunsfold Aerodrome (1965)
Dunsfold Aerodrome, Godalming GU8 4BS
Tel (01483) 265403
Fax (01483) 265670
Mem 270
Sec F Tuck
Pro None
Holes 9 L 6236 yds Par 72 SSS 70
Recs Am–70 R Arkwright (1991)
V'tors M
Fees £6 (£6)
Loc 10 miles S of Guildford, off A281
Arch Sharkey/Hayward

Effingham (1927)
Effingham Crossroads, Effingham KT24 5PZ
Tel (01372) 452203
Fax (01372) 459959
Mem 980
Sec RW Lamb
Pro S Hoatson (01372) 452606
Holes 18 L 6524 yds SSS 71
Recs Am–64 M Feltham (1997)
 Pro–65 B Barnes (1984)
V'tors WD–H WE/BH–M
Fees £35 After 2pm–£27.50
Loc 8 miles N of Guildford on A246
Arch HS Colt

Epsom (1889)
Longdown Lane South, Epsom Downs, Epsom KT17 4JR
Tel (01372) 721666
Fax (01372) 817183
Mem 800
Sec JH Carter FCA
Pro R Goudie (01372) 741867
Holes 18 L 5701 yds SSS 68
Recs Am–68 D Barnett (1994)
 Pro–62 K MacDonald (1996)
V'tors WD–U exc Tues am WE/BH–NA before noon SOC
Fees £22
Loc ¾ mile NE of Epsom Racecourse

Farnham (1896)
The Sands, Farnham GU10 1PX
Tel (01252) 783163
Fax (01252) 781185
Mem 750
Sec Jill Brazill (01252) 782109
Pro G Cowlishaw (01252) 782198
Holes 18 L 6313 yds SSS 70
Recs Am–67 G Walmsley (1988)
 Pro–65 A Lovelace (1998)
V'tors WD–H WE–M SOC–Wed & Thurs
Fees £30 D–£38
Loc 1 mile E of Farnham, off A31

Farnham Park Par Three (1966)
Pay and play
Farnham Park, Farnham GU9 0AU
Tel (01252) 715216
Fax (01252) 718246
Mem 75
Sec P Chapman
Pro P Chapman
Holes 9 L 1163 yds Par 54
Recs Am–50 DW Bryant (1998)
 Pro–56 G Wheeler (1966)
V'tors U
Fees £4 (£4.50)
Loc By Farnham Castle
Arch Henry Cotton

Fernfell G&CC (1985)
Barhatch Lane, Cranleigh GU6 7NG
Tel (01483) 268855
Fax (01483) 267251
Mem 650
Sec M Hale
Pro T Longmuir (01483) 277188
Holes 18 L 5648 yds SSS 67
Recs Am–66 R Edwards (1997)
 Pro–64 A Lovelace (1995)

V'tors WD–U WE/BH–pm only SOC–WD
Fees £23 (£25)
Loc 1 mile from Cranleigh, off A281
Mis Driving range

Foxhills (1975)
Stonehill Road, Ottershaw KT16 0EL
Tel (01932) 872050
Fax (01932) 874762
Mem 975
Sec A Laking (Mgr)
Pro A Good (01932) 873961
Holes 18 L 6680 yds SSS 73
 18 L 6547 yds SSS 72
 9 hole course
Recs Pro–65 P Dawson
V'tors WD–U WE–NA before noon SOC–WD am
Fees £45 D–£65 (£55)
Loc 2 miles SW of Chertsey on B386
Mis Driving range
Arch FW Hawtree

Gatton Manor Hotel G&CC (1969)
Standon Lane, Ockley, Dorking RH5 5PQ
Tel (01306) 627555
Fax (01306) 627713
Mem 250
Sec LC Heath
Pro R Sargent (01306) 627557
Holes 18 L 6653 yds SSS 72
Recs Am–72 J McLaren (1985)
 Pro–73 R Sargent (1985)
V'tors U exc Sun before 1 pm–NA SOC–WD
Fees £21 (£28)
Loc 1½ miles SW of Ockley, off A29. M25 Junction 9, S on A24
Mis Driving range
Arch Henry Cotton

Goal Farm Par Three (1977)
Public
Gole Road, Pirbright GU24 OP2
Tel (01483) 473183/473205
Sec R & J Church (Props)
Holes 9 hole Par 3 course
Recs Am–45 P Wakefield (1991)
V'tors Sat/Thurs un-restricted SOC–WD
Fees £7 (£7.50)
Loc 7 miles NW of Guildford

Guildford (1886)
High Path Road, Merrow, Guildford GU1 2HL
Tel (01483) 563941
Fax (01483) 453228
Mem 600
Sec BJ Green
Pro PG Hollington (01483) 566765
Holes 18 L 6090 yds SSS 70
Recs Am–64 DG Lintott (1989),
 JD Evans (1998)
 Pro–65 M Nichols (1998)

For list of abbreviations see page 527

V'tors WD–U WE–M SOC–WD
Fees £25
Loc 2 miles E of Guildford on A246

Hankley Common (1896)
Tilford, Farnham GU10 2DD
Tel (01252) 792493
Fax (01252) 795699
Mem 700
Sec JSW Scott
Pro P Stow (01252) 793761
Holes 18 L 6438 yds SSS 71
Recs Am–66 J Lee (1987)
Pro–62 H Stott (1988), M Nichols (1994)
V'tors WD–I WE–H at discretion of Sec
Fees £42 (£55)
Loc 3 miles SE of Farnham on Tilford road

Hazelwood Golf Centre
Pay and play
Croysdale Avenue, Green Street, Sunbury-on-Thames TW16 6QU
Tel (01932) 770932
Fax (01932) 770933
Mem 292
Sec J Reed
Pro F Sheridan (01932) 770932
Holes 9 L 5660 yds Par 35 SSS 67
Recs Am 64 C Gough (1997)
V'tors U SOC
Fees £7 (£8.50)
Loc M3 Junction 1, 1 mile
Mis Driving range. Golf academy
Arch Jonathan Gaunt

Hindhead (1904)
Churt Road, Hindhead GU26 6HX
Tel (01428) 604614
Fax (01428) 608508
Mem 500 50(L) 60(J)
Sec PA Owen
Pro N Ogilvy (01428) 604458
Holes 18 L 6356 yds SSS 70
Recs Am–64 M Lassam
Pro–63 A Tillman
V'tors WD–U WE–by arrangement H SOC–Wed & Thurs
Fees £43 (£53)
Loc 1½ miles N of Hindhead on A287. M25 Junction 10, 25 miles

Hoebridge Golf Centre (1982)
Public
Old Woking Road, Old Woking GU22 8JH
Tel (01483) 722611
Fax (01483) 740369
Mem 480
Sec P Dawson (Mgr)
Pro TD Powell
Holes 18 L 6587 yds SSS 71
Inter 9 L 2294 yds Par 33
18 hole Par 3 course
V'tors U
Fees 18 hole:£16 (£18).
Inter:£8.50. Par 3:£7

Loc Between Old Woking and West Byfleet on B382
Mis Floodlit driving range
Arch Jacobs/Hawtree

Home Park (1895)
Hampton Wick, Kingston-upon-Thames KT1 4AD
Tel (0181) 977 6645
Fax (0181) 977 4414
Mem 500
Sec BW O'Farrell
(0181) 977 2423
Pro L Roberts (0181) 977 2658
Holes 18 L 6610 yds SSS 71
V'tors U
Fees £15 (£25)
Loc 1 mile W of Kingston

Horton Park CC (1993)
Hook Road, Epsom KT19 8QG
Tel (0181) 393 8400 (Enquiries), (0181) 394 2626 (Bookings)
Fax (0181) 394 1369
Mem 410
Sec LJ Bennett (0181) 393 8400
Pro J September, H Omidiran (0181) 394 2626
Holes 18 L 5197 yds SSS 66
V'tors U SOC
Fees £11 (£13)
Loc 1 mile from A3, W of Ewell. M25 Junction 9
Mis Driving range
Arch Patrick Tallack

Hurtmore (1991)
Pay and play
Hurtmore Road, Hurtmore, Godalming GU7 2RN
Tel (01483) 426492
Fax (01483) 426121
Mem 200
Sec Maxine Burton
Pro Maxine Burton
Holes 18 L 5444 yds SSS 66
V'tors WD–U WE–booking advisable SOC
Fees £10 (£15)
Loc 5 miles S of Guildford on A3. M25 Junction 10
Arch Alliss/Clark

Kingswood (1928)
Sandy Lane, Kingswood, Tadworth KT20 6NE
Tel (01737) 833316
Fax (01737) 833920
Mem 770
Sec L Andrews (Admin) (01737) 832188
Pro J Dodds (01737) 832334
Holes 18 L 6904 yds SSS 73
Recs Am–70 P Stanford
Pro–67 R Blackie
V'tors U SOC
Fees £36 (£50)
Loc 5 miles S of Sutton on A217. M25 Junction 8, 2 miles
Mis Driving range
Arch James Braid

Laleham (1907)
Laleham Reach, Chertsey KT16 8RP
Tel (01932) 564211
Fax (01932) 564448
Mem 600
Sec Mrs PA Kennett
Pro H Stott
Holes 18 L 6203 yds SSS 70
Recs Am–65 K Archer (1995)
Pro–65 C Defoy (1986)
V'tors WD–U 9.30-4.30pm WE–M SOC–Mon–Wed
Fees £20–£27
Loc 2 miles S of Staines, opp Thorpe Park

Leatherhead (1903)
Kingston Road, Leatherhead KT22 0EE
Tel (01372) 843966
Fax (01372) 842241
Mem 600
Sec R Beswick
Pro S Norman (01372) 843956
Holes 18 L 6203 yds SSS 70
Recs Am–66 J Double (1996)
Pro–65 J Sewell (1992), S Norman (1993)
V'tors U SOC
Fees £30 (£45)
Loc On A243 to Chessington. M25 Junction 9

Limpsfield Chart (1889)
Westerham Road, Limpsfield RH8 0SL
Tel (01883) 723405/722106
Mem 300
Sec DS Adams
Pro None
Holes 9 L 5718 yds SSS 68
Recs Am–64 L Hooker
Pro–64 B Huggett
V'tors WD–U exc Thurs (Ladies Day) WE–M or by appointment SOC
Fees £18 (£20)
Loc 2 miles E of Oxted

Lingfield Park (1987)
Racecourse Road, Lingfield RH7 6PQ
Tel (01342) 834602
Fax (01342) 836077
Mem 700
Pro C Morley (01342) 832659
Holes 18 L 6500 yds SSS 72
Recs Am–70 G Sutton (1995)
Pro–69 S Defoy (1996)
V'tors WD–U WE/BH–M SOC–WD
Fees £28 (£38)
Loc Next to Lingfield racecourse. M25 Junction 6
Mis Driving range

London Scottish (1865)
Windmill Enclosure, Wimbledon Common, London SW19 5NQ
Tel (0181) 788 0135
Fax (0181) 789 7517
Mem 250
Sec S Barr (0181) 789 7517
Pro S Barr (0181) 789 1207

For list of abbreviations see page 527

Holes 18 L 5458 yds Par 68 SSS 66
Recs Am–64 A Glickberg (1975)
Pro–62 P Sefton (1996)
V'tors WD–U WE/BH–NA SOC
Fees On application
Loc Wimbledon Common
Mis Red upper garment must be worn
Arch Willie Dunn/Tom Dunn

Malden (1893)
Traps Lane, New Malden KT3 4RS
Tel (0181) 942 0654
Fax (0181) 336 2219
Mem 800
Sec Mrs A Besant (Mgr)
Pro R Hunter (Golf Mgr) (0181) 942 6009
Holes 18 L 6295 yds SSS 70
Recs Am–65 G Lashford
Pro–63 P Talbot
V'tors WD–U WE–restricted SOC–Wed–Fri
Fees On application
Loc Off A3, between Wimbledon and Kingston

Merrist Wood (1997)
Coombe Lane, Worplesdon, Guildford GU3 3PE
Tel (01483) 884045
Fax (01483) 884047
Mem 700
Sec R Penley-Martin (Gen Mgr)
Pro A Kirk (01483) 884050
Holes 18 L 6575 yds Par 72 SSS 71
Recs Am–73
Pro–69 D Griffiths
V'tors H–soft spikes only SOC–WD
Fees £35 D–£60 (£50)
Loc 2 miles W of Guildford, off A323
Arch David Williams

Milford
Station Lane, Milford GU8 5HS
Tel (01483) 419200
Fax (01483) 419199
Mem 750
Sec M Hatch (Mgr)
Pro N English (01483) 416291
Holes 18 L 5960 yds Par 69 SSS 68
Recs Am–65 D Jenkins
Pro–64 M Nicholls
V'tors WD–H WE–restricted SOC
Fees £19.50 (£35)
Loc 3 miles SW of Guildford, off A3
Arch Alliss/Clark

Mitcham (1924)
Carshalton Road, Mitcham Junction CR4 4HN
Tel (0181) 648 1508
Fax (0181) 648 4197
Mem 500
Sec WJ Dutch (0181) 648 4197
Pro JA Godfrey (0181) 640 4280
Holes 18 L 5931 yds SSS 68
Recs Am–D Wilde

V'tors WD–U WE–NA before 1.30pm SOC
Fees £13 (£13)
Loc Mitcham Junction Station

Moore Place (1926)
Public
Portsmouth Road, Esher KT10 9LN
Tel (01372) 463533
Fax (01372) 460274
Mem 80
Sec P Hirsch
Pro D Allen
Holes 9 L 4216 yds SSS 58
Recs Am–29 W Cavanagh
Pro–25 P Loxley
V'tors U
Fees £5.80 (£7.70)
Loc Centre of Esher
Arch D Allen

New Zealand (1895)
Woodham Lane, Addlestone KT15 3QD
Tel (01932) 345049
Fax (01932) 342891
Mem 300
Sec RA Marrett (01932) 342891
Pro VR Elvidge (01932) 349619
Holes 18 L 6012 yds SSS 69
Recs Am–66 P Cannings
Pro–72 A Herd
V'tors By request
Fees On application
Loc Woking 3 miles. West Byfleet 1 mile. Weybridge 5 miles
Arch Simpson/Fergusson

North Downs (1899)
Northdown Road, Woldingham CR3 7AA
Tel (01883) 653397
Fax (01883) 652832
Mem 650
Sec JAL Smith (Mgr) (01883) 652057
Pro M Homewood (01883) 653004
Holes 18 L 5843 yds SSS 68
Recs Am–66 M Smallcorn (1989), AL Smith (1996), HJ Young (1997)
Pro–65 W Humphreys (1987)
V'tors WD–U WE–M SOC–Tues/Wed/Fri
Fees £25
Loc 3 miles E of Caterham. M25 Junction 6
Arch JF Pennink

Oak Park (1984)
Heath Lane, Crondall, Farnham GU10 5PB
Tel (01252) 850880
Fax (01252) 850851
Mem 500
Sec Mrs R Smythe (Prop)
Pro S Coaker (01252) 850066
Holes Woodland 18 L 6318 yds SSS 70; Village 9 L 3279 yds Par 36
Recs Pro–66 P Simpson (1998)

V'tors H I SOC Village–U
Fees Woodland: £20 (£30) Village: £10 (£12)
Loc Off A287 Farnham-Odiham road. M3 Junction 5, 4 miles
Mis Floodlit driving range
Arch Patrick Dawson

Oaks Sports Centre (1973)
Public
Woodmansterne Road, Carshalton SM5 4AN
Tel (0181) 643 8363
Fax (0181) 770 7303
Mem 1000
Pro G Horley
Holes 18 L 6023 yds SSS 69 9 hole course
Recs Pro–66 G Horley
V'tors U
Fees 18 hole:£13 (£15) 9 hole:£6 (£7)
Loc 2 miles from Sutton on B278
Mis Floodlit driving range

Pachesham Park Golf Centre (1990)
Pay and play
Oaklawn Road, Leatherhead KT22 0BT
Tel (01372) 843453
Fax (01372) 844076
Mem 420
Sec P Taylor
Pro P Taylor
Holes 9 L 2804 yds Par 35
Recs Pro–67 W Grant (1997)
V'tors U SOC
Fees 9 holes–£7.50 (£9)
Loc NW of Leatherhead, off A244. M25 Junction 9
Mis Driving range
Arch P Taylor

Pine Ridge (1992)
Pay and play
Old Bisley Road, Frimley, Camberley GU16 5NX
Tel (01276) 20770
Fax (01276) 678837
Pro A Kelso
Holes 18 L 6458 yds SSS 71
Recs Am–65 V Phillips (1993)
Pro–67 C Montgomerie (1993)
V'tors U
Fees £16 (£20)
Loc Off Maultway, between Lightwater and Frimley. M3 Junction 3, 2 miles
Mis Floodlit driving range
Arch Clive D Smith

Purley Downs (1894)
106 Purley Downs Road, Purley, South Croydon CR2 0RB
Tel (0181) 657 8347
Fax (0181) 651 5044
Mem 700
Sec PC Gallienne

For list of abbreviations see page 527

Surrey

Pro G Wilson (0181) 651 0819
Holes 18 L 6275 yds SSS 70
Recs Am–65 MD Dawton
Pro–64 R Blackie
V'tors WD–I WE–M
SOC–Mon & Thurs
Fees On application
Loc 3 miles S of Croydon (A235)

Puttenham (1894)
Puttenham, Guildford GU3 1AL
Tel (01483) 810498
Fax (01483) 810988
Mem 500
Sec G Simmons
Pro G Simmons (01483) 810277
Holes 18 L 6212 yds SSS 71
Recs Am–67 L Boxall (1996)
V'tors WD–by prior appointment
WE/BH–M SOC–Wed & Thurs
Fees On application
Loc Between Guildford and Farnham, on Hog's Back

Pyrford (1993)
Warren Lane, Pyrford GU22 8XR
Tel (01483) 723555
Fax (01483) 729777
Mem 650
Sec D Renton
Pro N Sharratt (01483) 751070
Holes 18 L 6201 yds SSS 70
Recs Am–73 A Kikkidas
Pro–64 J Bennett
V'tors H SOC
Fees £38 (£52)
Loc 2 miles from A3 at Ripley
Arch Alliss/Clark

RAC Country Club (1913)
Woodcote Park, Epsom KT18 7EW
Tel (01372) 276211
Fax (01372) 276117
Sec K Symons
Pro I Howieson (01372) 279514
Holes Old 18 L 6709 yds SSS 72
Coronation 18 L 6223 yds SSS 70
Recs Old Am–68 GW Nielsen (1994)
Old Pro–66 M Roe (1997)
V'tors M SOC
Loc Epsom Station 1 3/4 miles
Arch Fowler/Myddleton

Redhill (1993)
Pay and play
Canada Avenue, Redhill RH1 5BF
Tel (01737) 770204
Fax (01737) 760046
Mem 90
Sec S Furlonger
Pro T Clingan
Holes 9 L 1903 yds Par 31 SSS 59
V'tors U SOC
Fees 9 holes–£4.35 (£5.25)
Loc 1 1/2 miles S of Redhill on A23. Grounds of East Surrey Hospital
Mis Floodlit driving range

Redhill & Reigate (1887)
Clarence Lodge, Pendleton Road, Redhill RH1 6LB
Tel (01737) 244626/244433
Fax (01737) 242117
Mem 500
Sec C Brown (01737) 240777
Pro W Pike (01737) 244433
Holes 18 L 5238 yds SSS 66
Recs Am–64
Pro–64
V'tors WD–U WE–phone first SOC
Fees £12 (£18)
Loc 1 mile S of Redhill on A23

Reigate Heath (1895)
The Club House, Reigate Heath RH2 8QR
Tel (01737) 242610
Fax (01737) 226793
Mem 330 80(L) 60(J)
Sec RJ Perkins (01737) 226793
Pro B Davies
Holes 9 L 5658 yds SSS 67
Recs Am–65 H Maurice (1995)
Pro–65 P Loxley (1977)
V'tors WD–U Sun/BH–M
SOC–Wed & Thurs
Fees On application
Loc W boundary of Reigate Heath

Reigate Hill
Gatton Bottom, Reigate RH2 0TU
Tel (01737) 645577
Fax (01737) 642650
Mem 650
Sec AP Barclay
Pro M Platts (01737) 646070
Holes 18 L 6175 yds Par 72 SSS 70
V'tors WD–U WE–M SOC
Fees £25
Loc 1 mile from M25 Junction 8, off A217
Arch David Williams

Richmond (1891)
Sudbrook Park, Richmond TW10 7AS
Tel (0181) 940 1463
Fax (0181) 332 7914
Mem 500
Sec RL Wilkins (0181) 940 4351
Pro N Job (0181) 940 7792
Holes 18 L 6007 yds SSS 69
Recs Am–63 A Riley, T Cowgill
Pro–63 N Price
V'tors WD–H
Fees £38
Loc Between Richmond and Kingston-upon-Thames

Richmond Park (1923)
Public
Roehampton Gate, Richmond Park, London SW15 5JR
Tel (0181) 876 3205/1795
Fax (0181) 878 1354
Sec AJ Gourvish
Pro D Bown
Holes Dukes 18 L 6036 yds SSS 68; Princes 18 L 5868 yds SSS 67
V'tors WD–U WE–booking necessary SOC–WD

Fees On application
Loc In Richmond Park
Mis Driving range
Arch Hawtree

Roehampton (1901)
Roehampton Lane, London SW15 5LR
Tel (0181) 480 4200
Fax (0181) 480 4265
Mem 1200
Sec M Yates (Chief Exec) (0181) 480 4205
JW Tucker (Mgr) (0181) 480 4206
Pro AL Scott (0181) 876 3858
Holes 18 L 6065 yds SSS 69
Recs Am–67 AL Scott, S Cooper
Pro–62 H Stott
V'tors WD/WE–Intro by member
Fees On application
Loc 1 mile W of Putney, off South Circular

Roker Park (1993)
Pay and play
Holly Lane, Aldershot Road, Guildford GU3 3PB
Tel (01483) 236677
Mem 200
Sec C Tegg
Pro K Warn (01483) 236677
Holes 9 L 3037 yds SSS 72
V'tors U SOC
Fees £7 (£8.50)
Loc 2 miles W of Guildford on A323
Mis Driving range
Arch Alan Helling

Royal Mid-Surrey (1892)
Old Deer Park, Richmond TW9 2SB
Tel (0181) 940 1894
Fax (0181) 332 2957
Mem 1250
Sec MSR Lunt
Pro D Talbot (0181) 940 0459
Holes Outer 18 L 6385 yds SSS 70
Inner 18 L 5446 yds SSS 67
Recs Outer Am–62 P Cunningham
Pro–64 R Charles, B Gallacher
V'tors WD–H or M WE/BH–M SOC
Fees £55
Loc Nr Richmond roundabout, off A316
Arch JH Taylor

Royal Wimbledon (1865)
29 Camp Road, Wimbledon Common, London SW19 4UW
Tel (0181) 946 2125
Fax (0181) 944 8652
Mem 800
Sec NI Smith
Pro H Boyle (0181) 946 4606
Holes 18 L 6362 yds SSS 71
Recs Am–66 JFM Connolly
Pro–71 R Burton
V'tors WD–H by arrangement
Loc Wimbledon Common, 2 miles S of A23 Tibbets Corner
Arch HS Colt

For list of abbreviations see page 527

Rusper (1992)
Rusper Road, Newdigate RH5 5BX
- **Tel** (01293) 871456, (01293) 871871 (Bookings)
- **Fax** (01293) 871456
- **Mem** 270
- **Sec** G Hems
- **Pro** Janice Arnold (01293) 871871
- **Holes** 9 L 6218 yds SSS 69
- **Recs** Am–72 I Tween (1996) Pro–67 R Dickman (1994)
- **V'tors** U
- **Fees** 18 holes–£11.50 (£15.50) 9 holes–£7 (£8.50)
- **Loc** 5 miles S of Dorking, off A24
- **Mis** Driving range
- **Arch** AW Blunden

St George's Hill (1912)
Golf Club Road, St George's Hill, Weybridge KT13 0NL
- **Tel** (01932) 847758
- **Fax** (01932) 821564
- **Mem** 600
- **Sec** J Robinson
- **Pro** AC Rattue (01932) 843523
- **Holes** 27 L 6097-6569 yds SSS 69-71
- **Recs** Am–65 D Swanston Pro–64 A Raitt
- **V'tors** WD–I H WE/BH–M SOC–Wed–Fri
- **Fees** £55 D–£70
- **Loc** 2 miles N of M25/A3 Junction, on B374
- **Arch** HS Colt

Sandown Park (1970)
Public
More Lane, Esher KT10 8AN
- **Tel** (01372) 461234
- **Sec** P Barriball (Mgr)
- **Pro** R Catley Smith
- **Holes** 9 L 5658 yds SSS 67 9 hole Par 3 course
- **Recs** Am–68 M Mabbott (1993)
- **V'tors** U–closed on race days
- **Fees** £6.25 (£7.75)
- **Loc** Sandown Park Racecourse
- **Mis** Floodlit driving range
- **Arch** John Jacobs

Selsdon Park Hotel (1929)
Addington Road, Sanderstead, South Croydon CR2 8YA
- **Tel** (0181) 657 8211
- **Fax** (0181) 657 3401
- **Sec** Mrs C Screene
- **Pro** M Churchill (0181) 657 4129
- **Holes** 18 L 6473 yds SSS 71
- **Recs** Am–68 M Welch Pro–64 M Job
- **V'tors** U SOC (min 12 golfers)
- **Fees** £20 (£30)
- **Loc** 3 miles S of Croydon on A2022 Purley-Addington road
- **Mis** Driving range
- **Arch** JH Taylor

Shirley Park (1914)
194 Addiscombe Road, Croydon CR0 7LB
- **Tel** (0181) 654 1143
- **Fax** (0181) 654 6733
- **Mem** 600
- **Sec** A Baird
- **Pro** P Webb (0181) 654 8767
- **Holes** 18 L 6210 yds SSS 70
- **Recs** Am–66 J Good Pro–65 J Bennett
- **V'tors** WD–U WE/BH–M SOC
- **Fees** £30
- **Loc** On A232, 1 mile E of East Croydon Station

Silvermere (1976)
Pay and play
Redhill Road, Cobham KT11 1EF
- **Tel** (01932) 867275
- **Mem** 900
- **Sec** Mrs P Devereux
- **Pro** D McClelland
- **Holes** 18 L 6333 yds SSS 71 Pro–65 S Rolley (1986)
- **V'tors** WD–U WE–NA before 1pm SOC
- **Fees** £18.50 (£25)
- **Loc** ½ mile from M25 Junction 10 on B366 to Byfleet
- **Mis** Floodlit driving range

Sunningdale (1900)
Ridgemount Road, Sunningdale, Berks SL5 9RR
- **Tel** (01344) 621681
- **Fax** (01344) 624154
- **Mem** 900
- **Sec** S Zuill
- **Pro** K Maxwell (01344) 620128
- **Holes** Old 18 L 6609 yds SSS 72 New 18 L 6703 yds SSS 72
- **Recs** Old Am–66 MC Hughesdon Pro–62 N Faldo New Am–62 C Challen Pro–64 GJ Player
- **V'tors** Mon–Thurs–I Fri/WE–M
- **Fees** Old: £105 New: £75
- **Loc** Sunningdale Station ¼ mile, off A30
- **Arch** Willie Park/HS Colt

Sunningdale Ladies (1902)
Cross Road, Sunningdale SL5 9RX
- **Tel** (01344) 20507
- **Mem** 400
- **Sec** JF Darroch
- **Holes** 18 L 3622 yds SSS 60
- **V'tors** WD/WE–by appointment. No 3 or 4 balls before 11am
- **Fees** Ladies £18 (£20) Men £22 (£27)
- **Loc** Sunningdale Station ¼ mile
- **Arch** HS Colt

Surbiton (1895)
Woodstock Lane, Chessington KT9 1UG
- **Tel** (0181) 398 3101
- **Fax** (0181) 339 0992
- **Email** Surbitongolfclub@hotmail.com

Mem 750
- **Sec** DR Crockford
- **Pro** P Milton (0181) 398 6619
- **Holes** 18 L 6055 yds SSS 69
- **Recs** Am–63 N Reilly Pro–63 C de Foy
- **V'tors** WD–H WE/BH–M
- **Fees** £30 D–£45
- **Loc** 2 miles E of Esher

Sutton Green
Sutton Green, Woking GU4 7QF
- **Tel** (01483) 747898
- **Sec** J Buchanan
- **Pro** T Dawson (01483) 766849
- **Holes** 18 L 6300 yds Par 71 SSS 70
- **V'tors** U
- **Fees** £25 (£30)
- **Loc** 2 miles S of Woking

Tandridge (1925)
Oxted RH8 9NQ
- **Tel** (01883) 712273 (Clubhouse)
- **Fax** (01883) 730537
- **Mem** 750
- **Sec** Lt Cdr SE Kennard RN (01883) 712274
- **Pro** C Evans (01883) 713701
- **Holes** 18 L 6250 yds SSS 70
- **Recs** Am–68 JC Robson Pro–69 BGC Huggett
- **V'tors** Mon/Wed/Thurs only–H SOC–Mon/Wed/Thurs
- **Fees** On application
- **Loc** 5 miles E of Redhill, off A25. M25 Junction 6
- **Arch** HS Colt

Thames Ditton & Esher (1892)
Portsmouth Road, Esher KT10 9AL
- **Tel** (0181) 398 1551
- **Mem** 300
- **Sec** D Kaye
- **Pro** M Rodbard
- **Holes** 9 L 5419 yds SSS 65
- **Recs** Am–61 T Petitt Pro–61 D Regan
- **V'tors** WD–U WE–by arrangement
- **Fees** £10 (£12)
- **Loc** Esher

Tyrrells Wood (1924)
Tyrrells Wood, Leatherhead KT22 8QP
- **Tel** (01372) 376025 (2 lines)
- **Fax** (01372) 360836
- **Mem** 744
- **Sec** CGR Kydd
- **Pro** M Taylor (01372) 375200
- **Holes** 18 L 6282 yds SSS 70
- **Recs** Am–67 P Earl (1988) Pro–65 P Hoad (1988)
- **V'tors** WD–I BH/Sat–NA Sun–NA before noon SOC
- **Fees** £34 (£44)
- **Loc** 2 miles SE of Leatherhead, off A24 nr Headley. M25 Junction 9, 1 mile

For list of abbreviations see page 527

Walton Heath (1903)
Deans Lane, Walton-on-the-Hill, Tadworth KT20 7TP
Tel (01737) 812060
Fax (01737) 814225
Mem 900
Sec N Lomas (01737) 812380
Pro K Macpherson (01737) 812152
Holes Old 18 L 6801 yds SSS 73
New 18 L 6609 yds SSS 72
Recs Old Am–68 R Revell
Pro–65 P Townsend
New Am–67 JK Tate, AJ Wells, RDH Hall
Pro–64 C Clark
Ch'ship Pro–64 I Woosnam (1987), M Harwood (1991)
V'tors WD–I H WE/BH–M SOC
Fees On application
Loc 18 miles S of London on A217/B2032. 2 miles N of M25 Junction 8
Arch WH Fowler

The Wentworth Club (1924)
Wentworth Drive, Virginia Water GU25 4LS
Tel (01344) 842201
Fax (01344) 842804
Mem 2335
Sec S Christie (Admin)
Pro D Rennie (01344) 846306
Holes West 18 L 6957 yds SSS 74
East 18 L 6176 yds SSS 70;
Edinburgh 18 L 6979 yds SSS 73; Executive 9 L 1902 yds Par 27
Recs West Am–69 N Richardson
Pro–63 W Riley
East Am–65 G Wolstenholme
Pro–62 DN Sewell, G Will
Edinburgh Pro–67 G Orr
V'tors WD–H by prior arrangement WE–M SOC–WD
Fees On application
Loc 21 miles SW of London at A30/A329 junction. M25 Junction 13, 8 miles
Mis Driving range
Arch HS Colt (East/West). Jacobs/Player (Edinburgh)

West Byfleet (1906)
Sheerwater Road, West Byfleet KT14 6AA
Tel (01932) 345230
Fax (01932) 340667
Mem 550
Sec DG Lee (Gen Mgr) (01932) 343433
Pro D Regan (01932) 346584
Holes 18 L 6211 yds SSS 70
Recs Am–66 W Calderwood
Pro–65 R Dickman, N Gorman (1994)
V'tors WD–U WE/BH–NA SOC
Fees £30 D–£38
Loc West Byfleet ½ mile on A245. M25 Junction 10 or 11
Arch CS Butchart

West Hill (1909)
Bagshot Road, Brookwood GU24 0BH
Tel (01483) 474365/472110
Fax (01483) 474252
Mem 550
Sec MC Swatton
Pro JA Clements (01483) 473172
Holes 18 L 6368 yds SSS 70
Recs Am–65 A Carter
Pro–62 G Brown
V'tors WD–H WE–M SOC
Fees £35 D–£45
Loc 5 miles W of Woking on A322

West Surrey (1910)
Enton Green, Godalming GU8 5AF
Tel (01483) 421275
Fax (01483) 415419
Mem 750
Sec RT Crabb
Pro A Tawse (01483) 417278
Holes 18 L 6259 yds SSS 70
Recs Am–66 SD Cook
Pro–65 G Orr
V'tors H SOC–Wed/Thurs/Fri
Fees £27 (£47)
Loc ½ mile SE of Milford Station
Arch Herbert Fowler

Wildwood (1992)
Horsham Road, Afold GU6 8JE
Tel (01403) 753255
Fax (01403) 752005
Sec A Hill
Pro N Parfrement
Holes 18 L 6650 yds SSS 72
Recs Pro–67 H Stott (1993)
V'tors H SOC–WD
Fees D–£25 (£37.50)
Loc 10 miles S of Guildford on A281
Mis Driving range
Arch Hawtree

Wimbledon Common (1908)
19 Camp Road, Wimbledon Common, London SW19 4UW
Tel (0181) 946 0294
Fax (0181) 947 8697
Mem 250
Sec JN Vintcent (0181) 946 7571
Pro JS Jukes
Holes 18 L 5438 yds SSS 66
Recs Am–63 MA Woodward, TP Standish; Pro–64 JS Jukes
V'tors WD–U WE–M Sun pm BH–NA SOC
Fees £10–£15
Loc Wimbledon Common
Mis Pillarbox red outer garment must be worn. London Scottish play here

Wimbledon Park (1898)
Home Park Road, London SW19 7HR
Tel (0181) 946 1002
Fax (0181) 944 8688
Mem 650
Sec PJ Dell (0181) 946 1250
Pro D Wingrove (0181) 946 4053
Holes 18 L 5492 yds SSS 66
Recs Am–60 D Braggins
Pro–60 M Gerrard
V'tors WD–H I WE/BH–after 3pm SOC
Fees D–£40 (£40)
Loc Opp All England Lawn Tennis Club

Windlemere (1978)
Pay and play
Windlesham Road, West End, Woking GU24 9QL
Tel (01276) 858727
Fax (01276) 678837
Sec CD Smith
Pro D Thomas
Holes 9 L 5346 yds SSS 66
V'tors U
Fees 9 holes–£8.50 (£10)
Loc A319 at Lightwater/West End
Mis Floodlit driving range
Arch Clive D Smith

Windlesham (1994)
Grove End, Bagshot GU19 5HY
Tel (01276) 452220
Fax (01276) 452290
Mem 800
Sec CJ Lumley
Pro L Mucklow (01276) 472323
Holes 18 L 6564 yds SSS 71
Recs Am–68 G Woodman (1996)
Pro–64 P Dwyer (1998)
V'tors H–phone first SOC–WD
Fees £40 (£50)
Loc ½ mile N of M3 Junction 3, off A30/A322
Mis Driving range
Arch Tommy Horton

The Wisley (1991)
Ripley, Woking GU23 6QU
Tel (01483) 211022
Fax (01483) 211662
Mem 700
Sec AD Lawrence (Gen Mgr)
Pro W Reid (01483) 211213
Holes 27 holes SSS 73:
Church 9 L 3356 yds;
Garden 9 L 3385 yds;
Mill 9 L 3473 yds
Recs Am–69 T Gottstein (1995)
V'tors M
Loc 1 mile S of M25 Junction 10
Arch Robert Trent Jones Jr

Woking (1893)
Pond Road, Hook Heath, Woking GU22 0JZ
Tel (01483) 760053
Fax (01483) 772441
Mem 500
Sec Lt Col IJ Holmes
Pro J Thorne (01483) 769582
Holes 18 L 6340 yds SSS 70
Recs Am–65 PJ Benka (1968)
V'tors WD–I H WE/BH–M
Fees £50
Loc W of Woking in St John's/Hook Heath area
Arch Tom Dunn

For list of abbreviations see page 527

Woodcote Park (1912)
Meadow Hill, Bridle Way, Coulsdon CR5 2QQ
Tel (0181) 660 0176
Fax (0181) 668 2788
Mem 630
Sec TJ Fensom (0181) 668 2788
Pro (0181) 668 1843
Holes 18 L 6669 yds SSS 72
Recs Am–66 D Lomas
Pro–66 C Bonner
V'tors WD–U WE–M
Fees £30 D–£40
Loc Purley 2 miles

Worplesdon (1908)
Heath House Road, Woking GU22 0RA
Tel (01483) 472277
Fax (01483) 473303
Mem 580
Sec JT Christine
Pro JT Christine (01483) 473287
Holes 18 L 6440 yds SSS 71
Recs Am–64 KG Jones (1988), AD Tillman (1991)
Pro–62
Ladies–67 W Wooldridge (1988)
V'tors WD–H WE–M
Fees On application
Loc E of Woking, off A322. 6 miles N of Guildford (A3). 6 miles S of M3 Junction 3

Sussex (East)

Ashdown Forest Golf Hotel
Chapel Lane, Forest Row RH18 5BB
Tel (01342) 824866
Fax (01342) 824869
Mem 150 (Anderida GS)
Sec LR Anderson
Pro M Landsborough (01342) 822247
Holes 18 L 5606 yds SSS 67
V'tors U SOC
Fees £16 (£21)
Loc 4 miles S of E Grinstead. 12 miles W of Tunbridge Wells
Mis Royal Ashdown Forest West Course

Brighton & Hove (1887)
Devils Dyke Road, Brighton BN1 8YJ
Tel (01273) 556482
Fax (01273) 556482
Mem 373
Sec MD Harrity
Pro P Bonsall (01273) 540560
Holes 9 L 5704 yds SSS 68
Recs Am–65 A Schofield (1992)
V'tors U SOC Sun–NA before noon
Fees £15 (£25)
Loc 4 miles N of Brighton
Arch James Braid

Cooden Beach (1912)
Cooden Beach, Bexhill-on-Sea TN39 4TR
Tel (01424) 842040
Fax (01424) 842040
Mem 700
Sec TE Hawes
Pro J Sim (01424) 843938
Holes 18 L 6470 yds SSS 71
Recs Am–68 M Harris, R Fenwick, S Graham (1998)
Pro–67 D Geall (1996)
V'tors H SOC
Fees £29 (£35)
Loc W boundary of Bexhill
Arch Herbert Fowler

Crowborough Beacon (1895)
Beacon Road, Crowborough TN6 1UJ
Tel (01892) 661511
Fax (01892) 667339
Mem 700
Sec Mrs V Harwood (01892) 661511
Pro D Newnham (01892) 653877
Holes 18 L 6273 yds SSS 70
Recs Am–67 GCD Carter, SF Robson, I McKellow (1993), G Smith (1997)
Pro–66 D Geal (1992)
V'tors I H WE/BH–M
Fees £25–£40
Loc 9 miles S of Tunbridge Wells on A26

Dale Hill Hotel (1973)
Ticehurst, Wadhurst TN5 7DQ
Tel (01580) 200112
Fax (01580) 201249
Mem 1000
Sec C Milnes
Pro A Good (01580) 201090
Holes 18 L 5856 yds SSS 69
Woosnam 18 L 6512 yds SSS 71
Recs Pro–68 K MacDonald
V'tors U SOC
Fees £20 (£30) Woosnam: £45 (£55)
Loc B2087, off A21 at Flimwell
Mis Driving range

Dewlands Manor (1992)
Pay and play
Cottage Hill, Rotherfield TN6 3JN
Tel (01892) 852266
Fax (01892) 853015
Sec T Robins
Pro N Godin
Holes 9 L 3186 yds Par 36
V'tors U–phone first
Fees 9 holes–£13.50 (£15.50)
18 holes–£25 (£29)
Loc ½ mile S of Rotherfield, off A267/B2101. 10 miles S of Tunbridge Wells. M25 Junction 5
Arch Reg Godin

The Dyke (1906)
Devil's Dyke, Devil's Dyke Road, Brighton BN1 8YJ
Tel (01273) 857296
Fax (01273) 857078
Mem 750
Sec TR White
Pro R Arnold (01273) 857260
Holes 18 L 6611 yds SSS 72
Recs Am–68 S Crooks
Pro–66 I Dryden
V'tors U exc Sun–NA
Fees £28 D–£38 (£40)
Loc 4 miles N of Brighton
Arch Fred Hawtree

East Brighton (1893)
Roedean Road, Brighton BN2 5RA
Tel (01273) 604838
Fax (01273) 680277
Mem 650
Sec DM Jackson
Pro RS Goodway (01273) 603989
Holes 18 L 6346 yds SSS 70
Recs Am–67 AW Schofield (1995)
Pro–62 D Mills (1997)
V'tors WD–U H after 9am WE–NA before 11am SOC
Fees £20 D–£27 (£24 D–£32)
Loc 1½ miles E of Town Centre, overlooking Marina
Arch James Braid

East Sussex National (1989)
Little Horsted, Uckfield TN22 5ES
Tel (01825) 880088
Fax (01825) 880066
Mem 770
Sec P Lewin (Golf Dir)
Pro I Naylor (01825) 880256
Holes East 18 L 7138 yds SSS 74
West 18 L 7154 yds SSS 74
Recs East Pro–63 S Gallagher (1998)
West Pro–64 T Bjorn (1995)
V'tors U on one course
Fees Summer–£45 Winter–£35
Loc 2 miles S of Uckfield, on A22
Mis Driving range. Golf academy
Arch Bob Cupp

Eastbourne Downs (1908)
East Dean Road, Eastbourne BN20 8ES
Tel (01323) 720827
Fax (01323) 412506
Mem 650
Sec AJ Reeves
Pro T Marshall (01323) 732264
Holes 18 L 6601 yds SSS 72
Recs Am–67 J Pullen (1988)
Pro–70 B Gallacher
V'tors WD–U WE–NA before 11am
Fees D–£20
Loc 1 mile W of Eastbourne on A259
Arch JH Taylor

For list of abbreviations see page 527

Eastbourne Golfing Park (1992)
Pay and play
Lottbridge Drove, Eastbourne BN23 6QJ
Tel (01323) 520400
Fax (01323) 520400
Mem 250
Sec G Marshall
Pro B Finch
Holes 9 L 5046 yds SSS 65
Recs Am–64 G Murray (1994)
V'tors U
Fees £8 (£12)
Loc ½ mile S of Hampden Park
Mis Floodlit driving range
Arch David Ashton

Hastings (1973)
Public
Beauport Park, Battle Road, St Leonards-on-Sea TN38 0TA
Tel (01424) 852977
Sec Mrs H Hovenden
Pro C Giddins (01424) 852981
Holes 18 L 6248 yds SSS 71
Recs Am–69 V Massarella (1981) Pro–72 S Hall (1987)
V'tors U–booking necessary SOC
Fees £10.30 (£13)
Loc 3 miles N of Hastings, off A2100 Battle road
Mis Driving range

Highwoods (1925)
Ellerslie Lane, Bexhill-on-Sea TN39 4LJ
Tel (01424) 212625
Fax (01424) 216866
Mem 800
Sec JE Osborough
Pro MJ Andrews (01424) 212770
Holes 18 L 6218 yds SSS 70 Pro–68 C Clark (1976)
V'tors WD/Sat–H Sun am–M Sun pm–H
Fees £25 (£30)
Loc 2 miles N of Bexhill
Arch JH Taylor

Hollingbury Park (1909)
Public
Ditchling Road, Brighton BN1 7HS
Tel (01273) 552010
Fax (01273) 502212
Mem 300
Sec BCL Rumary
Pro G Crompton (01273) 500086
Holes 18 L 6415 yds SSS 71
Recs Am–67 P Plant (1997) Pro–65 J Spence (1989)
V'tors U SOC
Fees £11.50 (£15.50)
Loc 1 mile NE of Brighton

Holtye (1893)
Holtye, Cowden, Edenbridge TN8 7ED
Tel (01342) 850635
Fax (01342) 850576
Mem 430

Sec JP Holmes (01342) 850576
Pro K Hinton (01342) 850957
Holes 9 L 5325 yds SSS 66
Recs Am–65 PD Scarles, JA Couling, BD Clarke, L Bridges; Pro–62 K Hinton
V'tors WD–U exc Wed/Thurs am–NA WE–NA before noon SOC–Tues & Fri
Fees D–£16 (£18)
Loc 4 miles E of E Grinstead on A264

Horam Park (1985)
Pay and play
Chiddingly Road, Horam TN21 0JJ
Tel (01435) 813477
Fax (01435) 813677
Mem 400
Sec Mrs G Lloyd
Pro M Jarvis
Holes 9 L 5864 yds SSS 70
Recs Pro–64 J Pinsent (1988)
V'tors U exc Sat–M before 4pm SOC
Fees 18 holes–£14 D–£15 9 holes–£8.50 D–£9
Loc ½ mile S of Horam towards Chiddingley. 12 miles N of Eastbourne on A267
Mis Floodlit driving range
Arch Glen Johnson

Lewes (1896)
Chapel Hill, Lewes BN7 2BB
Tel (01273) 473245
Mem 700
Sec AG Redshaw (01273) 483474
Pro P Dobson (01273) 483823
Holes 18 L 6218 yds Par 71 SSS 70
Recs Am–64 L Tremlett (1998) Pro–67 CA Burgess (1988)
V'tors WD–U WE–NA before 2pm SOC
Fees £18 (£30)
Loc ½ mile from Lewes at E end of Cliffe High Street

Mid Sussex (1995)
Spatham Lane, Ditchling BN6 8XJ
Tel (01273) 846567
Fax (01273) 845767
Mem 600
Sec J Tippett-Iles (Mgr)
Pro C Connell
Holes 18 L 6450 yds Par 71 SSS 71
Recs Pro–68 A Murray, D Mills (1996)
V'tors WD–U WE–M SOC–WD
Fees £20
Loc 1 mile E of Ditchling
Mis Driving range
Arch David Williams

Nevill (1914)
Benhall Mill Road, Tunbridge Wells TN2 5JW
Tel (01892) 525818
Fax (01892) 517861
Mem 550 142(L) 78(J)
Sec Miss KNR Pudner

Pro P Huggett (01892) 532941
Holes 18 L 6349 yds SSS 70
Recs Am–64 J Harris (1994) Pro–66 M Warner (1988)
V'tors WD–H WE/BH–M
Fees £33
Loc Tunbridge Wells 1 mile

Peacehaven (1895)
Brighton Road, Newhaven BN9 9UH
Tel (01273) 514049
Mem 290
Sec DM Jackson (01273) 512571
Pro G Williams (01273) 512602
Holes 9 L 5235 yds SSS 66
Recs Am–65 J Harris (1993)
V'tors WD–U WE/BH–after 11am SOC
Fees £11 (£17)
Loc 8 miles E of Brighton on A259
Arch James Braid

Piltdown (1904)
Piltdown, Uckfield TN22 3XB
Tel (01825) 722033
Fax (01825) 724192
Mem 400
Sec JC Duncan (Hon)
Pro J Amos (01825) 722389
Holes 18 L 6070 yds SSS 69
Recs Am–67 A Smith (1988) Pro–69 S Frost, P Lovesey
V'tors I or H exc BH/Tues am/Thurs am/Sun am SOC
Fees £27.50 D–£32
Loc 1 mile W of Maresfield, off A272 towards Isfield

Royal Ashdown Forest (1888)
Chapel Lane, Forest Row, East Grinstead RH18 5LR
Tel (01342) 822018/823014
Fax (01342) 825211
Mem 450
Sec DJ Scrivens
Pro MA Landsborough (01342) 822247
Holes Old 18 L 6477 yds SSS 71 West 18 L 5606 yds SSS 67
Recs Old Am–67 RA Darlington (1987), NJ Harrington (1996) Pro–62 HA Padgham
V'tors On application (phone first)
Fees Old: £40 (£45) West: £16 (£21)
Loc 4 miles S of E Grinstead on B2110 Hartfield road. M25 Junction 6

Royal Eastbourne (1887)
Paradise Drive, Eastbourne BN20 8BP
Tel (01323) 729738
Fax (01323) 729738
Mem 850
Sec PG White
Pro R Wooller (01323) 736986
Holes 18 L 6118 yds SSS 69 9 L 2147 yds SSS 32
Recs Am–62 J Beland (1991) Pro–62 J Pinsent (1987)

636 Sussex (East)

V'tors U H SOC
Fees 18 hole:£20 (£25) 9 hole:£12
Loc ½ mile from Town Hall

Rye (1894)
Camber, Rye TN31 7QS
Tel (01797) 225241/225460
Fax (01797) 225460
Mem 979 115(L) 125(J)
Sec Lt Col CJW Gilbert
Pro MP Lee (01797) 225218
Holes 18 L 6308 yds SSS 71
 9 L 6141 yds SSS 70
Recs Am–64 P Hurring (1988),
 G Wolstenholme (1994),
 JE Ambridge (1996)
 Pro–63 G Ralph (1994)
V'tors M
Loc 3 miles E of Rye on B2075
Arch HS Colt

Seaford (1887)
East Blatchington, Seaford BN25 2JD
Tel (01323) 892442
Fax (01323) 894113
Mem 420 110(L) 37(J)
Sec RN VandenBergh (Gen Mgr)
Pro (01323) 894160
Holes 18 L 6233 yds SSS 70
Recs Am–66 EA Snow, A Flygt
 Pro–67 H Weetman
V'tors WD–U after 10am exc Tues
 WE–M SOC
Fees £25 D–£35
Loc 1 mile N of Seaford (A259)
Arch JH Taylor

Seaford Head (1907)
Public
Southdown Road, Seaford BN25 4JS
Tel (01323) 890139
Sec JT Wass
Pro AJ Lowles
Holes 18 L 5812 yds SSS 68
Recs Am–65 D Hills
 Pro–64 M Andrews
V'tors U
Fees £12 D–£18 (£14.50 D–£20)
Loc 8 miles W of Eastbourne.
 ¾ mile S of A259

Sedlescombe (1990)
Kent Street, Sedlescombe TN33 0SD
Tel (01424) 870898
Fax (01424) 870855
Mem 380
Sec Mrs A Briggs
Pro J Andrews
Holes 18 L 6218 yds Par 72
V'tors WD–H WE–M
Fees On application
Loc 5 miles N of Hastings
Mis Floodlit driving range
Arch Glen Johnson

Sweetwoods Park (1994)
Cowden, Edenbridge TN8 7JN
Tel (01342) 850729
Fax (01342) 850866
Mem 800

Sec P Strand
Pro B Wynn
Holes 18 L 6516 yds Par 72
Recs Am–66 S Randall
 Pro–65 K Kelsall
V'tors U SOC–WD
Fees £20 (£30)
Loc 5 miles E of E Grinstead
 on A264
Mis Driving range
Arch P Strand

Waterhall (1923)
Public
Waterhall Road, Brighton BN1 8YR
Tel (01273) 508658
Mem 300
Sec LB Allen
Pro P Charman
Holes 18 L 5775 yds SSS 68
Recs Am–66 R Vance
V'tors WD–U WE–U after 8am
Fees £11.50 (£11.50)
Loc 3 miles N of Brighton between
 A23 and A27. 1 mile N of
 A2308

Wellshurst G&CC (1992)
North Street, Hellingly BN27 4EE
Tel (01435) 813636
Fax (01435) 812444
Mem 320
Sec M Adams (Man Dir)
Pro M Jarvis (01435) 813456
Holes 18 L 5771 yds SSS 68
V'tors U SOC
Fees £14 (£17.50)
Loc 2 miles N of Hailsham
 on A267
Mis Driving range

West Hove (1910)
Church Farm, Hangleton, Hove BN3 8AN
Tel (01273) 413411 (Clubhouse)
Fax (01273) 439988
Sec K Haste (Mgr)
 (01273) 419738
Pro D Cook (01273) 413494
Holes 18 L 6201 yds SSS 70 Par 70
Recs Am–69 I Poysden
 Pro–66 J Partridge
V'tors U–phone first SOC
Fees On application
Loc N of Brighton bypass. 2nd
 junction W from A23 flyover
Mis Practice driving range
Arch Hawtree

Willingdon (1898)
Southdown Road, Eastbourne BN20 9AA
Tel (01323) 410983
Mem 550
Sec Mrs J Packham
 (01323) 410981
Pro JN Debenham
 (01323) 410984
Holes 18 L 6049 yds SSS 69
Recs Am–64 DM Sewell (1986)
 Pro–62 J Sewell (1990)

V'tors WD–U H WE–MH exc Sun
 am–NA SOC–H
Fees D–£24 (£27)
Loc ½ mile N of Eastbourne,
 off A22
Arch JH Taylor/Dr A Mackenzie

Sussex (West)

Avisford Park (1990)
Pay and play
Yapton Lane, Walberton, Arundel BH18 0LS
Tel (01243) 554611
Fax (01243) 555580
Mem 75
Sec J Beach
Pro R Beach
Holes 18 L 5703 yds SSS 68
 Pro–68 R Beach (1994)
V'tors U SOC
Fees £12 (£15)
Loc 4 miles W of Arundel on A27

Bognor Regis (1892)
Downview Road, Felpham, Bognor Regis PO22 8JD
Tel (01243) 865867
Fax (01243) 860719
Mem 650
Sec BD Poston (01243) 821929
Pro S Bassil (01243) 865209
Holes 18 L 6238 yds Par 70 SSS 70
Recs Am–64 M Harris (1995)
 Pro–64 JR Day (1992),
 C Fogden (1997)
V'tors WD–I or H after 9.30am
 WE/BH–M (Apr–Sept) –I H
 (Oct–Mar) SOC–WD
Fees £25 (£30)
Loc 2 miles E of Bognor Regis,
 off A259
Arch James Braid

Burgess Hill
Pay and play
Cuckfield Road, Burgess Hill
Tel (01444) 258585
Fax (01444) 247318
Sec CJ Collins (Mgr)
Holes 9 hole Par 3 course
V'tors U
Fees On application
Loc N of Burgess Hill
Mis Floodlit driving range
Arch Steel/Collins

Chartham Park (1993)
Felcourt, East Grinstead RH19 2JT
Tel (01342) 870340
Fax (01342) 870719
Sec Denise Leech
Pro I Dryden
Holes 18 L 6688 yds Par 72 SSS 72
V'tors WD–U WE–U after 11am
Fees £27 (£40)
Loc 2 miles N of East Grinstead,
 off A22
Mis Driving range

For list of abbreviations see page 527

Chichester (1990)
Hunston Village, Chichester PO20 6AX
Tel (01243) 533833
Fax (01243) 539922
Mem 550
Pro J Slinger
Holes Cathedral 18 L 6461 yds SSS 71; Tower 18 L 6175 yds SSS 72; 9 hole Par 3 course
Recs Cathedral Am–69 P Duke Tower Pro–67 C Rota
V'tors U SOC
Fees Tower: £15 (£19.50) Cathedral: £20 (£28)
Loc 2 miles S of A27 on B2145 to Selsey
Mis Driving range
Arch Phillip Sanders

Copthorne (1892)
Borers Arm Road, Copthorne RH10 3LL
Tel (01342) 712508
Fax (01342) 717682
Mem 565
Sec DJ MacInnes (01342) 712033
Pro J Burrell (01342) 712405
Holes 18 L 6505 yds SSS 71
Recs Am–66 D Arnold Pro–66 K MacDonald
V'tors WD–U WE/BH–after 1pm SOC
Fees £30 (£35)
Loc 1 mile E of M23 Junction 10, on A264
Arch James Braid

Cottesmore (1975)
Buchan Hill, Pease Pottage, Crawley RH11 9AT
Tel (01293) 528256
Fax (01293) 522219
Mem 1200
Sec M Topper
Pro C Callan (01293) 535399
Holes Griffin 18 L 6248 yds Par 71 SSS 70; Phoenix 18 L 5514 yds Par 69 SSS 67
Recs Old Am–66 S Pardoe Pro–67 R Tinworth
V'tors U SOC
Fees Griffin: £19.50 (£25) Phoenix: £16 (£19.50)
Loc 4 miles S of Crawley, off M23 Junction 11
Arch MD Rogerson

Cowdray Park (1920)
Petworth Road, Midhurst GU29 0BB
Tel (01730) 813599
Fax (01730) 815900
Mem 700
Sec D Rodbard (Gen Mgr)
Pro R Gough (01730) 812091
Holes 18 L 6212 yds SSS 70
Recs Am–67 S Brown (1994) Pro–66 G Ralph (1989)
V'tors WD/Sat–H NA before 9.30am Sun/BH–H NA before 10am SOC–Wed & Thurs
Fees £26 (£36)
Loc 1 mile E of Midhurst on A272
Arch T Simpson

Effingham Park (1980)
West Park Road, Copthorne RH10 3EU
Tel (01342) 716528
Fax (01342) 716039
Mem 320
Sec J O'Donovan (Mgr) (01342) 712138
Pro M Root
Holes 9 L 1815 yds Par 30
Recs Am–29 Pro–26
V'tors WD–U exc Wed & Thurs before 12 noon WE–U after 11.30am
Fees £8 D–£11.50 (£9 D–£13.50)
Loc B2028/B2039. M23 Junction 10
Mis Golf academy
Arch Francisco Escario

Foxbridge (1993)
Foxbridge Lane, Plaistow RH14 0LB
Tel (01403) 753303/753343 (Bookings)
Fax (01403) 753433
Mem 300
Sec Miss K Harridge
Holes 9 L 3118 yds SSS 70
V'tors M SOC
Loc 15 miles S of Guildford, off B2133
Arch Paul Clark

Gatwick Manor (1975)
London Road, Lowfield Heath, Crawley RH10 2ST
Tel (01293) 538587
Pro C Jenkins
Holes 9 L 1246 yds SSS 28
Recs Pro–24 C Jenkins (1991)
V'tors U SOC
Fees 9 holes–£3
Loc A23 to Crawley, 1 mile past Gatwick Airport
Arch Patrick Tallack

Goodwood (1892)
Kennel Hill, Goodwood, Chichester PO18 0PN
Tel (01243) 785012 (Members)
Fax (01243) 781741
Mem 900
Sec PR Stevens (01243) 774968
Pro K MacDonald (01243) 774994
Holes 18 L 6401 yds SSS 71
Recs Am–67 C Fogden (1993) Pro–64 G Orr (1992)
V'tors WD–H after 9am WE–H after 10am SOC–Wed & Thurs
Fees £32 (£42)
Loc 3 miles NE of Chichester, on road to racecourse
Arch James Braid

Goodwood Park G&CC (1989)
Goodwood, Chichester PO18 0QB
Tel (01243) 520114
Mem 750
Sec B Geoghegan (Golf Mgr)
Pro A Wratting
Holes 18 L 6530 yds SSS 72
V'tors WD–H WE/BH–NA before noon H SOC
Fees £28 (£35)
Loc 4 miles N of Chichester
Arch Donald Steel

Ham Manor (1936)
West Drive, Angmering, Littlehampton BN16 4JE
Tel (01903) 783288
Fax (01903) 850886
Mem 860
Sec VJ Chaszczewski
Pro S Buckley (01903) 783732
Holes 18 L 6216 yds SSS 70
Recs Am–64 F Wieland (1987) Pro–62 TA Horton
V'tors WD/WE–H
Fees On application
Loc Between Worthing and Littlehampton
Arch HS Colt

Hassocks (1995)
Pay and play
London Road, Hassocks BN6 9NA
Tel (01273) 846990
Fax (01273) 846070
Mem 350
Sec Mrs J Brown (Gen Mgr) (01273) 846630
Pro C Ledger (01273) 846990
Holes 18 L 5754 yds Par 70 SSS 68
Recs Am–64 S Murray (1995) Pro–64 C Ledger (1995)
V'tors U
Fees £14.25 (£17.50)
Loc 1 mile S of Burgess Hill on A273. 7 miles N of Brighton
Arch Paul Wright

Haywards Heath (1922)
High Beech Lane, Haywards Heath RH16 1SL
Tel (01444) 414310
Fax (01444) 458319
Mem 771
Sec JE Jarman (01444) 414457
Pro M Henning (01444) 414866
Holes 18 L 6204 yds SSS 70
Recs Am–68 T Hilton Pro–66 P Sefton
V'tors WD/WE–H–restricted SOC–Wed & Thurs
Fees £26 (£36)
Loc 2 miles N of Haywards Heath, off B2112

For list of abbreviations see page 527

Hill Barn (1935)
Public
Hill Barn Lane, Worthing BN14 9QE
Tel (01903) 237301
Pro AP Higgins
Holes 18 L 6224 yds SSS 70
Recs Am–66 H Francis, B Roberts
Pro–63 J Kinsella
V'tors U
Fees £12.50 (£13.50)
Loc NE of A27 at Warren Road roundabout
Arch Hawtree

Horsham (1993)
Pay and play
Worthing Road, Horsham RH13 7AX
Tel (01403) 271525
Fax (01403) 274528
Mem 240
Sec J Ellwood (01403) 271525
Pro N Burke (Mgr)
Holes 9 L 2061 yds Par 33 SSS 30
Recs Am–60 N O'Donnell (1998)
Pro–55 J Spence (1993)
V'tors U SOC
Fees 9 holes–£6 (£7)
Loc 1 mile S of Horsham, off A24

Ifield (1927)
Rusper Road, Ifield, Crawley RH11 0LN
Tel (01293) 520222
Fax (01293) 612973
Mem 875
Sec B Gazzard
Pro J Earl (01293) 523088
Holes 18 L 6330 yds SSS 70
Recs Am–65 S Fenn
Pro–65 G Cowlishaw, P Mitchell, S Fenn
V'tors WD–H WE–M SOC
Fees £22 D–£32
Loc W of Crawley. M23 Junction 11

Littlehampton (1889)
170 Rope Walk, Littlehampton BN17 5DL
Tel (01903) 717170
Fax (01903) 726629
Mem 650
Sec KR Palmer (Sec/Mgr)
Pro G McQuitty (01903) 716369
Holes 18 L 6244 yds SSS 70
Recs Am–62 W Hawes
Pro–65 D Cook
V'tors WD–U after 9.30am WE/BH–NA before noon SOC
Fees £24 (£30)
Loc W bank of River Arun, Littlehampton
Arch Hawtree

Mannings Heath (1905)
Fullers, Hammerpond Road, Mannings Heath, Horsham RH13 6PG
Tel (01403) 210228
Fax (01403) 270974
Mem 730
Sec I Dempsey
Pro C Tucker (01403) 210228
Holes Waterfall 18 L 6378 yds SSS 70; Kingfisher 18 L 6217 yds SSS 70
Recs Am–66 J Newsome
Pro–66 R Willison
V'tors U H SOC
Fees £32 (£40)
Loc 3 miles SE of Horsham (A281). M23 Junction 11
Mis Driving range
Arch Kingfisher-David Williams

Osiers Farm (1989)
Osiers Farm, London Road, Petworth GU28 9LX
Tel (01798) 344097
Fax (01798) 342528
Mem 100
Sec A Long
Pro J Little
Holes 18 L 6191 yds Par 71 SSS 69
Recs Am–71 J Searle (1994)
V'tors U SOC
Fees 18 holes–£10 D–£12.50
9 holes–£6.50
Loc 1½ miles N of Petworth on A283
Arch C & T Duncton

Paxhill Park (1990)
East Mascalls Lane, Lindfield RH16 2QN
Tel (01444) 484467
Fax (01444) 482709
Mem 540
Sec JD Bowen
Pro S Dunkley
Holes 18 L 6196 yds SSS 68
Recs Am–67 E Pagden (1993)
V'tors WD–U WE–pm only
Fees £15 (£20)
Loc 1 mile N of Lindfield, off B2028. 4 miles NE of Haywards Heath
Mis Driving range
Arch Patrick Tallack

Pease Pottage (1986)
Horsham Road, Pease Pottage, Crawley RH11 9AP
Tel (01293) 521706
Mem 56
Sec A Venn
Pro M Root
Holes 9 L 3511 yds SSS 57
Recs Am–63 M Bolton Smith (1992)
Pro–58 S Mantel (1992)
V'tors U
Fees £8 (£11)
Loc S of Crawley, off A23
Mis Driving range

Pyecombe (1894)
Clayton Hill, Pyecombe, Brighton BN45 7FF
Tel (01273) 845372
Fax (01273) 843338
Mem 650
Sec IR Bradbery
Pro CR White (01273) 845398
Holes 18 L 6278 yds SSS 70
Recs Am–67 TM Greenfield
Pro–66 JA Brown
Ladies–68 A Greenfield
V'tors WD–U exc Tues after 9.15am WE–U after 2pm
SOC–Mon/Wed/Thurs
Fees £15 (£25)
Loc 6 miles N of Brighton on A273

Rustington (1992)
Golfers Lane, Angmering BN16 4NB
Tel (01903) 850790
Fax (01903) 850982
Pro (01903) 850790
Holes 18 L 5735 yds Par 70 SSS 68
9 hole Par 3 course
V'tors U SOC
Fees On application
Loc On A259 between Worthing and Littlehampton
Mis Floodlit driving range
Arch David Williams

Selsey (1906)
Golf Links Lane, Selsey PO20 9DR
Tel (01243) 602203
Mem 400
Sec P Carter (01243) 605176
Pro P Grindley
Holes 9 L 5834 yds SSS 68
Recs Am–64 S Gill
Pro–63 C Giddins, P Hurring
V'tors U
Fees £12 (£17)
Loc 7 miles S of Chichester

Shillinglee Park (1980)
Pay and play
Chiddingfold, Godalming GU8 4TA
Tel (01428) 653237
Fax (01428) 644391
Mem 400
Sec G Baxter (Prop)
Pro D Parkinson
Holes 9 L 2500 yds Par 32
Recs Am–65
V'tors U SOC exc Sat am
Fees £11 D–£12.50 (£13 D–£16)
9 holes–£7.50
Loc 2½ miles SE of Chiddingfold
Mis Pitch & putt course
Arch Roger Mace

Singing Hills (1992)
Pay and play
Albourne, Brighton BN6 9EB
Tel (01273) 835353
Fax (01273) 835444
Mem 400
Sec V Street
Pro W Street
Holes 27 holes SSS 69-72:
River 9 L 2826 yds
Valley 9 L 3348 yds
Lakes 9 L 3253 yds
Recs Am–67 B Anderson (1992)
Pro–66 R Frost (1993)
V'tors U SOC
Fees £18 (£26)

Slinfold Park (1993)
Stane Street, Slinfold, Horsham RH13 7RE
- **Tel** (01403) 791154 (Clubhouse)
- **Fax** (01403) 791465
- **Mem** 600
- **Sec** S Blake (Gen Mgr)
- **Pro** G McKay (01403) 791555
- **Holes** 18 L 6450 yds SSS 71
  9 hole course
- **Recs** Am–68 N Darnell
- **V'tors** U SOC
- **Fees** £25 (£25)
- **Loc** 3 miles W of Horsham (A29)
- **Mis** Driving range. Academy course
- **Arch** John Fortune

Tilgate Forest (1982)
Public
Titmus Drive, Tilgate, Crawley RH10 5EU
- **Tel** (01293) 530103
- **Fax** (01293) 523478
- **Mem** 320
- **Sec** T Reagan
- **Pro** S Trussell, D McClelland
- **Holes** 18 L 6359 yds SSS 71
  9 hole Par 3 course
- **Recs** Am–70 L Cooper (1997)
  Pro–68 J Hodgkinson (1986)
- **V'tors** U SOC–Mon–Thurs
- **Fees** 18 hole:£12 (£16)
  9 hole:£4 (£5.30)
- **Loc** 1½ miles SE of Crawley. M23 Junction 11
- **Mis** Driving range

West Chiltington (1988)
Pay and play
Broadford Bridge Road, West Chiltington RH20 2YA
- **Tel** (01798) 813574
- **Fax** (01798) 812631
- **Mem** 500
- **Sec** B Aram (Mgr)
- **Pro** C Morris (01798) 812115
- **Holes** 18 L 5969 yds Par 70 SSS 69
  9 hole Par 3 course
- **Recs** Am–66 R Ellis (1995)
  Pro–62 B Barnes (1991)
- **V'tors** U SOC
- **Fees** £15 (£17.50)
- **Loc** 2 miles E of Pulborough
- **Mis** Driving range
- **Arch** Faulkner/Barnes

West Sussex (1930)
Golf Club Lane, Wiggonholt, Pulborough RH20 2EN
- **Tel** (01798) 872563
- **Fax** (01798) 872033
- **Mem** 800
- **Sec** CP Simpson
- **Pro** T Packham
  (01798) 872426
- **Holes** 18 L 6221 yds SSS 70

- **Recs** Am–61 G Evans
- **V'tors** WD–I H after 9.30am exc Fri–M SOC–Thurs
- **Fees** On application
- **Loc** 1½ miles E of Pulborough on A283
- **Mis** Driving range
- **Arch** Campbell/Hutcheson

Worthing (1905)
Links Road, Worthing BN14 9QZ
- **Tel** (01903) 260801
- **Fax** (01903) 694664
- **Mem** 1000
- **Sec** IJ Evans
- **Pro** S Rolley (01903) 260718
- **Holes** Lower 18 L 6530 yds SSS 72
  Upper 18 L 5243 yds SSS 66
- **Recs** Lower Am–62 P Drew (1994)
  Pro–66 P Harrison (1992)
- **V'tors** WD–U H WE–confirm in advance with Pro
- **Fees** On application
- **Loc** Central Station 1½ miles (A27), nr A24 Junction
- **Arch** HS Colt

Tyne & Wear

Backworth (1937)
The Hall, Backworth, Shiremoor, Newcastle-upon-Tyne NE27 0AH
- **Tel** (0191) 268 1048
- **Mem** 400
- **Sec** D Carruthers
- **Pro** None
- **Holes** 9 L 5930 yds SSS 69
- **Recs** Am–66
- **V'tors** Mon & Fri–U Tues–Thurs–M after 5pm WE–after 12.30pm exc comp Sats–after 6pm
- **Fees** On application
- **Loc** Off Tyne Tunnel link road, Holystone roundabout

Birtley (1922)
Birtley Lane, Birtley DH3 2LR
- **Tel** (0191) 410 2207
- **Mem** 230
- **Sec** DM Dummett
- **Holes** 9 L 5660 yds SSS 67
- **Recs** Am–63 I McEntee
- **V'tors** WD–U exc Fri pm–M WE/BH–M SOC
- **Fees** £12
- **Loc** 3 miles from Birtley service area on A1(M)

Boldon (1912)
Dipe Lane, East Boldon NE36 0PQ
- **Tel** (0191) 536 4182 (Clubhouse)
- **Fax** (0191) 537 2270
- **Mem** 700
- **Sec** RW Benton
  (0191) 536 5360
- **Pro** Phipps Golf
  (0191) 536 5835
- **Holes** 18 L 6348 yds SSS 70

- **Recs** Am–67 GR Simpson (1987)
  Pro–66 M Archer (1993)
- **V'tors** WD–U WE/BH–NA before 3.30pm
- **Fees** On application
- **Loc** 8 miles SE of Newcastle

City of Newcastle (1891)
Three Mile Bridge, Gosforth, Newcastle-upon-Tyne NE3 2DR
- **Tel** (0191) 285 1775
- **Fax** (0191) 284 0700
- **Mem** 400 110(L) 60(J)
- **Sec** AJ Matthew (Mgr)
- **Pro** S McKenna
  (0191) 285 5481
- **Holes** 18 L 6528 yds SSS 71
- **Recs** Am–64 S Harrison (1995)
  Pro–66 AJ Brown (1996)
- **V'tors** U
- **Fees** £24 (£28)
- **Loc** B1318, 3 miles N of Newcastle
- **Arch** Harry Vardon

Garesfield (1922)
Chopwell NE17 7AP
- **Tel** (01207) 561278/561309
- **Fax** (01207) 561309
- **Mem** 700
- **Sec** EM Thirlwell
- **Pro** D Race (01207) 563082
- **Holes** 18 L 6196 yds SSS 70
- **Recs** Am–68 I Turner (1991)
  Pro–70 D Dunk (1978)
- **V'tors** WD–U WE/BH–NA before 4.30pm SOC
- **Fees** On application
- **Loc** 7 miles SW of Newcastle, between High Spen and Chopwell

Gosforth (1906)
Broadway East, Gosforth, Newcastle-upon-Tyne NE3 5ER
- **Tel** (0191) 285 6710
- **Mem** 380 100(L) 60(J)
- **Sec** B Pluse (0191) 285 3495
- **Pro** G Garland (0191) 285 0553
- **Holes** 18 L 6024 yds SSS 69
- **Recs** Am–65 I Potter (1992)
- **V'tors** WD–U WE–M before 4pm –U after 4pm SOC
- **Fees** £20
- **Loc** 3 miles N of Newcastle, off A6125

Heworth (1911)
Gingling Gate, Heworth, Gateshead NE10 8XY
- **Tel** (0191) 469 9832
- **Mem** 800
- **Sec** G Holbrow
- **Pro** None
- **Holes** 18 L 6404 yds SSS 71
- **Recs** Am–65 D Moralee
  Pro–69 P Highmoor
- **V'tors** WD–U WE–NA before noon
- **Fees** £15 (£15)
- **Loc** SE boundary of Gateshead

For list of abbreviations see page 527

Houghton-le-Spring (1908)
Copt Hill, Houghton-le-Spring DH5 8LU
Tel (0191) 584 1198
Mem 600
Sec N Wales (0191) 584 0048
Pro (0191) 584 7421
Holes 18 L 6416 yds Par 72 SSS 71
Recs Am–66 J Ellison
V'tors U SOC
Fees £20 (£27)
Loc 3 miles SW of Sunderland

Newcastle United (1892)
Ponteland Road, Cowgate, Newcastle-upon-Tyne NE5 3JW
Tel (0191) 286 4693 (Clubhouse)
Mem 500
Sec J Simpson
Pro (0191) 286 9998
Holes 18 L 6596 yds SSS 71
Recs Am–64 G Grant (1993)
V'tors WD–U WE/BH–M
Fees On application
Loc Nuns Moor, 2 miles W of city centre

Northumberland (1898)
High Gosforth Park, Newcastle-upon-Tyne NE3 5HT
Tel (0191) 236 2498
Fax (0191) 236 2498
Mem 500
Sec JM Forteath
Pro None
Holes 18 L 6629 yds SSS 72
Recs Am–67 W Bennett, PH Coulthard
Pro–65 A Jacklin, T Horton
V'tors WD–I BH–M
Fees £35–£45
Loc 5 miles N of Newcastle
Arch HS Colt/James Braid

Parklands (1971)
High Gosforth Park, Newcastle-upon-Tyne NE3 5HQ
Tel (0191) 236 4480/4867
Mem 770
Sec B Woof
Pro B Rumney
Holes 18 L 6060 yds Par 71 SSS 69
Recs Am–65 S Johnston, G Hewitt
Pro–65 B Rumney
V'tors U
Fees £15 (£18)
Loc 5 miles N of Newcastle
Mis 9 hole pitch & putt course. Driving range

Ravensworth (1906)
Moss Heaps, Wrekenton, Gateshead NE9 7UU
Tel (0191) 487 6014/2843
Mem 550
Sec WR Walker (0191) 416 4794
Pro S Cowell (0191) 491 3475
Holes 18 L 5872 yds SSS 68
Recs Am–63 K Kelly
Pro–64 T Horton

V'tors U H SOC
Fees £19 (£28)
Loc 3 miles S of Newcastle on B1296

Ryton (1891)
Doctor Stanners, Clara Vale, Ryton NE40 3TD
Tel (0191) 413 3253
Fax (0191) 413 1642
Mem 600
Sec S Dix
Holes 18 L 5499 metres SSS 69
Recs Am–69 P Brougham, S Dix, P Highmoor
V'tors WD–U WE–M SOC
Fees £15 (£20)
Loc 7 miles W of Newcastle, off A695

South Shields (1893)
Cleadon Hills, South Shields NE34 8EG
Tel (0191) 456 0475
Mem 700
Sec WH Loades (0191) 456 8942
Pro G Parsons (0191) 456 0110
Holes 18 L 6264 yds SSS 70
Recs Am–64 J Dryden (1993)
Pro–64 M Gregson (1978)
V'tors U SOC
Fees On application
Loc Cleadon Hills

Tynemouth (1913)
Spital Dene, Tynemouth, North Shields NE30 2ER
Tel (0191) 257 4578
Fax (0191) 259 5193
Mem 855
Sec W Storey (0191) 257 3381
Pro J McKenna (0191) 258 0728
Holes 18 L 6381 yds SSS 71
Recs Am–69 AJ Henderson
Pro–66 G Bell
V'tors WD–U 9.30am–5pm –NA before 9.30am and after 5pm WE/BH–M
Fees £16 D–£21
Loc 8 miles E of Newcastle
Arch Willie Park

Tyneside (1879)
Westfield Lane, Ryton NE40 3QE
Tel (0191) 413 2177
Fax (0191) 413 2742
Mem 660
Sec ED Stephenson (0191) 413 2742
Pro M Gunn (0191) 413 1600
Holes 18 L 6042 yds SSS 69
Recs Am–65 CW Philipson, G Lawson
Pro–65 JR Harrison
V'tors WD–U (exc 11.30–1.30pm) WE–NA before 3pm SOC
Fees (£20)
Loc 7 miles W of Newcastle. S of river, off A695
Arch HS Colt

Wallsend (1973)
Public
Rheydt Avenue, Bigges Main, Wallsend NE28 8SU
Tel (0191) 262 1973
Sec D Souter
Pro K Phillips (0191) 262 4231
Holes 18 L 6608 yds SSS 72
Recs Am–66 A Dobson (1997)
V'tors U
Fees £13 (£15)
Loc Between Newcastle and Wallsend on coast road
Mis Driving range
Arch G Showball

Washington (1980)
Stone Cellar Road, Usworth, District 12, Washington NE37 1PH
Tel (0191) 402 9988
Fax (0191) 415 1166
Mem 500
Pro W Marshall (0191) 417 8346
Holes 18 L 6604 yds SSS 72
Recs Am–68 D Godfrey (1996)
Pro–64 P Harrison (1991)
V'tors U SOC
Fees £20 (£30)
Loc Off A1(M), on A195
Mis Driving range. 9 hole pitch & putt

Wearside (1892)
Coxgreen, Sunderland SR4 9JT
Tel (0191) 534 2518
Fax (0191) 534 2518
Mem 650
Sec N Hildrew
Pro D Brolls (0191) 534 4269
Holes 18 L 6315 yds SSS 70
Par 3 course
Recs Am–64 R Walker
Pro–63 J Harrison
V'tors H SOC
Fees £25 (£32)
Loc 2 miles W of Sunderland, off A183, by A19

Westerhope (1941)
Whorlton Grange, Westerhope, Newcastle-upon-Tyne NE5 1PP
Tel (0191) 286 9125
Mem 778
Sec R Pears (0191) 286 7636
Pro N Brown (0191) 286 0594
Holes 18 L 6407 yds SSS 71
Recs Am–64 R Roper, S Phillipson
Pro–67 D Russell
V'tors WD–U
Fees £16
Loc 5 miles W of Newcastle

Whickham (1911)
Hollinside Park, Fellside Road, Whickham, Newcastle-upon-Tyne NE16 5BA
Tel (0191) 488 7309 (Clubhouse)
Fax (0191) 488 1576
Mem 650
Sec ME Pearse (0191) 488 1576

For list of abbreviations see page 527

Warwickshire

Pro G Lisle (0191) 488 8591
Holes 18 L 5878 yds Par 68 SSS 68
Recs Am–61 AJ McLure (1989)
Ladies–71 K Snell (1998)
V'tors U SOC–WD
Fees £20 (£25)
Loc 5 miles SW of Newcastle

Whitburn (1931)
*Lizard Lane, South Shields
NE34 7AF*
Tel (0191) 529 2144
Fax (0191) 529 4944
Mem 580 73(L) 85(J)
Sec Mrs V Atkinson
(0191) 529 4944
Pro D Stephenson
(0191) 529 4210
Holes 18 L 5900 yds Par 69 SSS 68
Recs Am–64 G Wilkinson (1997)
V'tors U SOC–WD exc Tues
Fees £18 (£23)
Loc 2 miles N of Sunderland on coast
Arch Colt/Alison/Morrison

Whitley Bay (1890)
*Claremont Road, Whitley Bay
NE26 3UF*
Tel (0191) 252 0180
Fax (0191) 297 0030
Mem 700
Sec B Dockar
Pro G Shipley (0191) 252 5688
Holes 18 L 6529 yds SSS 71
Recs Am–68 PB Taylor
Pro–66 J Fourie
V'tors WD–U WE–M
Fees £22 D–£30
Loc 10 miles E of Newcastle

Warwickshire

Ansty (1992)
*Brinklow Road, Ansty, Coventry
CV7 9JH*
Tel (01203) 621341/621305
Fax (01203) 602671
Mem 450
Sec R Challis
Pro J Reay
Holes 18 L 6079 yds Par 71 SSS 69
V'tors U SOC
Fees £9 (£13)
Loc Between Ansty and Brinklow (B4029). M6 Junction 2, 1 mile.
Mis Driving range
Arch D Morgan

Atherstone (1894)
*The Outwoods, Coleshill Road,
Atherstone CV9 2RL*
Tel (01827) 713110
Mem 400 40(L) 40(J)
Sec VA Walton (01827) 892568
Holes 18 L 6006 yds Par 72 SSS 70
Recs Am–68 S Brotherton, K Albrighton
V'tors WD–H WE–M SOC–WD
Fees D–£20 BH–£22
Loc ¼ mile from Atherstone on Coleshill road

The Belfry (1977)
*Public
Lichfield Road, Wishaw B76 9PR*
Tel (01675) 470301
Fax (01675) 470178
Sec R Maxfield
Pro P McGovern
Holes Brabazon 18 L 7118 yds SSS 74; Derby 18 L 6009 yds SSS 69; PGA National 18 L 7072 yds SSS 74
V'tors H SOC
Fees Brabazon: £85. Derby: £40. PGA National: £70
Loc 2 miles N of M42 Junction 9, off A446
Mis Driving range
Arch Brabazon & Derby-Alliss/Thomas; PGA National-Thomas

Bidford Grange (1992)
*Stratford Road, Bidford-on-Avon
B50 4LY*
Tel (01789) 490319
Fax (01789) 778184
Mem 310
Sec M Smith (Mgr)
Pro D Webber
Holes 18 L 7233 yds Par 72 SSS 74
Recs Am–66 D Webber
Pro–71 M Dove
V'tors U SOC
Fees £12 (£15)
Loc 5 miles W of Stratford-on-Avon on B439
Arch Swann/Tillman/Granger

Boldmere (1936)
*Public
Monmouth Drive, Sutton Coldfield,
Birmingham BJ3 6JR*
Tel (0121) 354 3379
Mem 300
Sec R Leeson
Pro T Short
Holes 18 L 4463 yds SSS 62
Recs Am–57 G Marston (1987)
Pro–57 P Weaver (1987)
V'tors U
Fees £8.50 (£9)
Loc By Sutton Park, 1 mile W of Sutton Coldfield

City of Coventry (Brandon Wood) (1977)
*Public
Brandon Lane, Coventry CV8 3GQ*
Tel (01203) 543141
Fax (01203) 545108
Mem 500
Sec C Gledhill
Pro C Gledhill
Holes 18 L 6610 yds SSS 72
Pro–68 AR Sadler
V'tors U SOC

Fees On application
Loc 6 miles SE of Coventry, off A45(S)
Mis Floodlit driving range

Copt Heath (1907)
*1220 Warwick Road, Knowle, Solihull
B93 9LN*
Tel (01564) 772650
Fax (01564) 771022
Mem 700
Sec W Lenton
Pro BJ Barton (01564) 776155
Holes 18 L 6508 yds SSS 71
Recs Am–67 JMH Mayell, PI Chalkley, G Storm
Pro–67 D Stokes
V'tors WD–H WE/BH–M SOC
Fees £35
Loc 2 miles S of Solihull on A4141

Coventry (1887)
*St Martins Road, Finham Park,
Coventry CV3 6RJ*
Tel (01203) 411123
Fax (01203) 690131
Mem 750
Sec B Fox (01203) 414152
Pro P Weaver (01203) 411298
Holes 18 L 6601 yds SSS 73
Recs Am–67 MJ Cryer
Pro–64 C Hall, A Webster (1993)
Ladies Pro–62 J Arnold (1990)
V'tors WD–H
Fees £32
Loc 2 miles S of Coventry on A444/B4113

Coventry Hearsall (1894)
*Beechwood Avenue, Coventry
CV5 6DF*
Tel (01203) 713470
Fax (01203) 691534
Mem 600
Sec Mrs ME Hudson
Pro M Tarn (01203) 713156
Holes 18 L 5983 yds SSS 69
Recs Am–64 W Nicolson (1992)
Pro–66 B Morris (1987)
V'tors WD–U WE–M
Fees D–£24
Loc 1½ miles S of Coventry, off A45

Edgbaston (1896)
*Church Road, Edgbaston, Birmingham
B15 3TB*
Tel (0121) 454 1736
Fax (0121) 454 2355
Mem 910
Sec P Heath
Pro J Cundy (0121) 454 3226
Holes 18 L 6118 yds SSS 69
Recs Am–63 P Hemphill (1998)
Pro–64 PJ Butler (1965)
V'tors H SOC
Fees £37.50 (£50)
Loc 1½ miles S of Birmingham, off A38
Arch HS Colt

For list of abbreviations see page 527

GPT (formerly Grange GC)
Copsewood, Coventry CV3 1HS
Tel (01203) 451465
Mem 350
Sec E Soutar (Hon)
Holes 9 L 6002 yds SSS 69
Recs Am–70
V'tors WD–U before 2.30pm
Sat–NA Sun–NA before noon
Fees £10 Sun–£15
Loc 2½ miles E of Coventry on A428
Arch TJ McAuley

Harborne (1893)
40 Tennal Road, Harborne, Birmingham B32 2JE
Tel (0121) 427 1728
Mem 600
Sec GA Tozer (0121) 427 3058
Pro A Quarterman (0121) 427 3512
Holes 18 L 6210 yds SSS 70
Recs Am–65 RC Ellis
Pro–65 E Cogle
V'tors WD–U WE/BH–M SOC
Fees £30 D–£35
Loc 3 miles SW of Birmingham. M5 Junction 3
Arch HS Colt

Harborne Church Farm (1926)
Public
Vicarage Road, Harborne, Birmingham B17 0SN
Tel (0121) 427 1204
Fax (0121) 428 3126
Mem 180
Sec B Flanagan
Pro P Johnson
Holes 9 L 4882 yds Par 66 SSS 64
Recs Am–62 J McAllister
V'tors U
Fees 18 holes–£8 (£8.50)
9 holes–£5 (£5.50)
Loc 3 miles SW of Birmingham

Hatchford Brook (1969)
Public
Coventry Road, Sheldon, Birmingham B26 3PY
Tel (0121) 743 9821
Fax (0121) 743 3420
Mem 500
Sec ID Thomson (0121) 779 3780
Pro M Hampton
Holes 18 L 5646 yds Par 68 SSS 67
Recs Am–69 A Allen (1987),
G Weaver (1994)
Pro–68 P Smith (1988),
J Kelly (1995)
V'tors U SOC
Fees £9 (£10)
Loc City boundary close to airport. A45/M42 Junction

Henley G&CC (1994)
Birmingham Road, Henley-in-Arden B95 5QA
Tel (01564) 793715
Fax (01564) 795754

Mem 600
Sec G Wright (Chief Exec)
Pro S Edwin
Holes 18 L 6933 yds SSS 73
9 hole Par 3 course
V'tors U–booking required SOC–H
Fees £20 D–£25 (£25 D–£30)
Loc N of Stratford-on-Avon on A3400. M40 Junction 16, 3 miles
Mis Driving range
Arch N Selwyn-Smith

Hilltop (1979)
Public
Park Lane, Handsworth, Birmingham B21 8LJ
Tel (0121) 554 4463
Pro K Highfield
Holes 18 L 6114 yds SSS 69
Recs Am–66 H Ali
Pro–65 BN Jones
V'tors U
Fees On application
Loc Sandwell Valley. M5 Junction 1

Ingon Manor (1993)
Ingon Lane, Snitterfield, Stratford-on-Avon CV37 0QE
Tel (01789) 731857
Mem 300
Pro M Reay
Holes 18 L 6554 yds Par 72 SSS 71
Recs Am–74 J Webber (1993)
Pro–74 P Broadhurst (1993)
V'tors H SOC
Fees £12 (£25)
Loc 3 miles N of Stratford-on-Avon, off A461. M40 Junction 15
Arch David Hemstock

Kenilworth (1889)
Crewe Lane, Kenilworth CV8 2EA
Tel (01926) 854296
Fax (01926) 864453
Mem 750
Sec JH McTavish (01926) 858517
Pro S Yates (01926) 512732
Holes 18 L 6413 yds SSS 71
Recs Am–62 WL Bladon (1995)
V'tors U H BH–M SOC
Fees £28 (£37)
Loc 1½ miles E of Kenilworth. 5 miles S of Coventry
Arch Hawtree

Ladbrook Park (1908)
Poolhead Lane, Tanworth-in-Arden, Solihull B94 5ED
Tel (01564) 742264
Fax (01564) 742909
Mem 700
Sec Mrs SE Burrows (Admin)
Pro R Mountford (01564) 742581
Holes 18 L 6427 yds SSS 71
Recs Am–67 PJ Sant
Pro–65 RDS Livingston
V'tors WD–U H WE/BH–M H
Fees On application

Loc 12 miles S of Birmingham. M42 Junction 3
Arch HS Colt

Leamington & County (1908)
Golf Lane, Whitnash, Leamington Spa CV31 2QA
Tel (01926) 425961
Fax (01926) 425961
Mem 650
Sec SM Cooknell
Pro I Grant (01926) 428014
Holes 18 L 6439 yds SSS 71
Recs Am–65 RG Hiatt
Pro–66 D Thomas
V'tors U SOC
Fees £25 (£40)
Loc 1½ miles S of Leamington Spa
Arch HS Colt

Marriott Forest of Arden Hotel (1970)
Maxstoke Lane, Meriden, Coventry CV7 7HR
Tel (01676) 522335
Fax (01676) 523711
Mem 650
Sec D MacLaren (Golf Dir)
Pro K Thomas (0958) 632170
Holes Arden 18 L 6718 yds Par 72 SSS 73; Aylesford 18 L 6525 yds Par 72 SSS 71
Recs Pro–63 C Montgomerie (1997)
V'tors WD–U SOC–WD
Fees Arden: £50 (£60)
Aylesford: £35 (£40)
Loc 9 miles W of Coventry, off A45. M6 Junction 4
Mis Driving range
Arch Donald Steel

Maxstoke Park (1898)
Castle Lane, Coleshill, Birmingham B46 2RD
Tel (01675) 466743
Fax (01675) 466743
Mem 600
Sec D Haywood
Pro N McEwan (01675) 464915
Holes 18 L 6442 yds SSS 71
Recs Am–64 S Walker
Pro–68 S Cronin
V'tors WD–U H WE–M
Fees £25
Loc 3 miles SE of Coleshill

Moor Hall (1932)
Moor Hall Drive, Four Oaks, Sutton Coldfield B75 6LN
Tel (0121) 308 6130
Fax (0121) 308 6130
Mem 628
Sec RV Wood
Pro A Partridge (0121) 308 5106
Holes 18 L 6249 yds SSS 70
Recs Am–65 J Cook
Pro–64 J Higgins

For list of abbreviations see page 527

V'tors WD–U H exc Thurs–U after 1pm WE/BH–M
Fees £30 D–£40
Loc 1 mile E of Sutton Coldfield

Newbold Comyn (1973)
Public
Newbold Terrace East, Leamington Spa CV32 4EW
Tel (01926) 421157
Mem 191
Sec AA Pierce
Pro D Knight
Holes 18 L 6315 yds SSS 70
Recs Am–70 G Knight
Pro–S Hutchinson (1987)
V'tors WD–U WE–booking 1 week in advance SOC
Fees £7.30 (£9.50)
Loc Off Willes Road (B4099)

North Warwickshire (1894)
Hampton Lane, Meriden, Coventry CV7 7LL
Tel (01676) 522915
Fax (01676) 522915
Mem 450
Sec EG Barnes (Hon)
Pro D Ingram (01676) 522259
Holes 9 L 6362 yds SSS 70
Recs Am–64 A Allen (1993)
V'tors WD–U WE/BH–M SOC
Fees £18
Loc 6 miles W of Coventry, off A45

Nuneaton (1906)
Golf Drive, Whitestone, Nuneaton CV11 6QF
Tel (01203) 347810
Fax (01203) 327563
Mem 650
Sec I Neale
Pro S Bainbridge (01203) 340201
Holes 18 L 6412 yds SSS 71
Recs Am–67 P Broadhurst
Pro–67 C Holmes
V'tors WD–U H WE–M SOC
Fees £25 D–£30
Loc 2 miles S of Nuneaton

Oakridge
Arley Lane, Ansley Village, Nuneaton CV10 9PH
Tel (01676) 541389
Fax (01676) 542709
Mem 500
Sec Mrs S Lovric (Admin)
Pro I Sadler
Holes 18 L 6242 yds Par 71 SSS 70
V'tors U SOC–WD
Fees £15
Loc B4112 from Nuneaton. M6 Junction 3
Arch Algie Jayes

Olton (1893)
Mirfield Road, Solihull B91 1JH
Tel (0121) 705 1083
Fax (0121) 711 2010
Mem 600

Sec BG Smith (0121) 704 1936
Pro MP Daubney
(0121) 705 7296
Holes 18 L 6232 yds SSS 71
Recs Am–63 J Berry
Pro–64 I Clark
V'tors WD–U exc Wed am WE–M
Fees £25–£35
Loc 7 miles SE of Birmingham (A41)

Purley Chase (1980)
Pipers Lane, Ridge Lane, Nuneaton CV10 0RB
Tel (01203) 393118
Mem 600
Sec Linda Jackson
Holes 18 L 6772 yds SSS 72
Recs Am–72 P Broadhurst
Pro–64 P Elson
V'tors WD/BH–U WE–U after 2.30pm SOC
Fees On application
Loc 4 miles WNW of Nuneaton on B4114 (A47) A5 Mancetter Island
Mis Driving range

Pype Hayes (1932)
Public
Eachelhurst Road, Walmley, Sutton Coldfield B76 8EP
Tel (0121) 351 1014
Fax (0121) 313 0206
Mem 320
Sec L Brogan
Pro JF Bayliss
Holes 18 L 5996 yds SSS 69
Recs Am–66 A Sheard (1992)
Pro–59 J Cawsey (1954)
V'tors U
Fees On application
Loc 5 miles NE of Birmingham

Robin Hood (1893)
St Bernards Road, Solihull B92 7DJ
Tel (0121) 706 0159
Fax (0121) 706 0806
Mem 650
Sec Mrs TA Rennie
(0121) 706 0061
Pro A Harvey
(0121) 706 0806
Holes 18 L 6635 yds SSS 72
Recs Am–68 J Draper (1988), GW Barton (1993)
V'tors WD–U WE/BH–M SOC–WD H
Fees £29 D–£35
Loc 7 miles S of Birmingham
Arch HS Colt

Rugby (1891)
Clifton Road, Rugby CV21 3RD
Tel (01788) 544637
Fax (01788) 542306
Mem 750
Sec N Towler (01788) 542306
Pro N Summers
(01788) 575134
Holes 18 L 5614 yds SSS 67

Recs Am–64 J Wilson, P Godding, S Warren
Pro–64 A Peach
V'tors WD–U WE/BH–M SOC
Fees On application
Loc 1 mile N of Rugby on B5414

Shirley (1956)
Stratford Road, Monkspath, Shirley, Solihull B90 4EW
Tel (0121) 744 6001
Fax (0121) 745 8220
Mem 570
Sec Mrs VA Duggan
Pro S Bottrill (0121) 745 4979
Holes 18 L 6510 yds SSS 71
Recs Am–67 N Burdekin
V'tors WD–U WE–M SOC
Fees £25 D–£35
Loc 8 miles S of Birmingham, nr M42 Junction 4

Sphinx (1948)
Sphinx Drive, Coventry CV3 1WA
Tel (01203) 451361
Mem 300
Sec GE Brownbridge
(01203) 597731
Holes 9 L 4262 yds SSS 60
Recs Am–61 G Mason (1994)
V'tors Fri/WE–M after 4.30pm SOC
Fees £8 (£10)
Loc Nr Binley Road, Coventry

Stoneleigh Deer Park (1992)
The Old Deer Park, Coventry Road, Stoneleigh CV8 3DR
Tel (01203) 639991
Fax (01203) 511533
Mem 850
Sec A Wild
Pro S McGuire
Holes 18 L 6083 yds SSS 71
9 hole Par 3 course
V'tors WD–U WE–NA before noon SOC–WD
Fees On application
Loc ½ mile E of Stoneleigh
Arch K Harrison

Stratford Oaks (1991)
Bearley Road, Snitterfield, Stratford-on-Avon CV37 0EZ
Tel (01789) 731982
Fax (01789) 731981
Mem 600
Sec ND Powell (Golf Dir)
Pro A Dunbar
Holes 18 L 6100 yds SSS 71
Recs Am–67 S Millington (1992)
Pro–66 D Eddiford (1992)
V'tors WD–U WE–U booking necessary
Fees £15 (£20)
Loc 4 miles NE of Stratford-on-Avon
Mis Driving range
Arch Howard Swann

644 Warwickshire

Stratford-on-Avon (1894)
Tiddington Road, Stratford-on-Avon CV37 7BA
Tel (01789) 297296
Mem 770
Sec (01789) 205749
Pro D Sutherland (01789) 205677
Holes 18 L 6311 yds SSS 70
Recs Am–63 I Roberts
Pro–64 M Gallagher
V'tors U H SOC
Fees On application
Loc ½ mile E of Stratford-on-Avon on B4086

Sutton Coldfield (1889)
110 Thornhill Road, Sutton Coldfield B74 3ER
Tel (0121) 353 2014/9633
Fax (0121) 353 5503
Mem 600
Sec RF Fletcher, K Tempest (0121) 353 9633
Pro JK Hayes (0121) 353 9633
Holes 18 L 6541 yds SSS 71
Recs Am–65 L Jacks (1986)
Pro–64 PA Elson (1978)
V'tors U H SOC
Fees £25 (£35)
Loc 9 miles N of Birmingham, off B4138

Tidbury Green (1994)
Pay and play
Tilehouse Lane, Shirley, Solihull B90 1HP
Tel (01564) 824460
Mem 300
Sec Lucy Broadhurst
Pro R Thompson
Holes 9 L 2473 yds Par 34
V'tors U SOC
Fees 18 holes–£9 (£9)
9 holes–£6 (£6)
Loc 2 miles from M42 Junction 4, nr Earlswood Lakes
Mis Driving range
Arch Derek Stevenson

Walmley (1902)
Brooks Road, Wylde Green, Sutton Coldfield B72 1HR
Tel (0121) 377 7272
Fax (0121) 377 7272
Mem 700
Sec MJ Roberts
Pro CJ Wicketts (0121) 373 7103
Holes 18 L 6537 yds SSS 72
Recs Am–66 A Carey (1998)
Pro–66 D Prosser (1997)
V'tors WD–U WE–M SOC
Fees £30 D–£35
Loc N boundary of Birmingham

Warwick (1971)
Public
Warwick Racecourse, Warwick CV34 6HW
Tel (01926) 494316
Sec Mrs R Dunkley

Pro P Sharp (01926) 491284
Holes 9 L 2682 yds SSS 66
Recs Am–67 R Buckingham
Pro–70 P Sharp
V'tors U exc while racing in progress
Fees £4 (£5)
Loc Centre of Warwick Racecourse
Mis Driving range

The Warwickshire (1993)
Leek Wootton, Warwick CV35 7QT
Tel (01926) 409409
Fax (01926) 408409
Mem 850
Sec G Ivory
Pro D Peck
Holes 18 L 7178 yds SSS 74
18 L 7154 yds SSS 74
9 hole Par 3 course
Recs Am–68 W Bladon (1996)
Pro–68 P Baker (1993)
V'tors H SOC
Fees £45 (£45)
Loc 1 mile N of Warwick, off A46. M40 Junction 15
Mis Driving range
Arch Karl Litton

Welcombe Hotel
Warwick Road, Stratford-on-Avon CV37 0NR
Tel (01789) 299012
Fax (01789) 414666
Mem 120
Sec J Moore (01789) 295252
Pro C Mason, K Hayler (01789) 299012
Holes 18 L 6294 yds SSS 70
Recs Am–67 R Fletcher (1997)
Pro–62 G Houston (1998)
V'tors U H
Fees D–£40 (D–£45)
Loc 1½ miles NE of Stratford-on-Avon on A439 towards Warwick
Mis Driving range
Arch T McAuley

Whitefields Hotel (1992)
Coventry Road, Thurlaston, Rugby CV23 9JR
Tel (01788) 521800
Fax (01788) 521695
Mem 400
Sec B Coleman
Pro M Chamberlain (01788) 817777
Holes 18 L 6223 yds Par 71 SSS 70
Recs Am–66 M McCallum
V'tors U SOC
Fees £18 (£22)
Loc 3 miles SW of Rugby at A45/M45 Junction
Mis Driving range

Widney Manor (1993)
Pay and play
Saintbury Drive, Widney Manor, Solihull B91 3SZ
Tel (0121) 711 3646
Fax (0121) 711 3691

Mem 475
Sec T Atkinson (Sec/Mgr)
Pro T Atkinson
Holes 18 L 5001 yds Par 68
V'tors U–booking 5 days in advance SOC
Fees £10 (£13)
Loc 3 miles from M42 Junction 4, off A34

Windmill Village (1990)
Birmingham Road, Allesley, Coventry CV5 9AL
Tel (01203) 404041
Fax (01203) 407016
Mem 700
Sec M Harrhy (Mgr)
Pro R Hunter (01203) 404041
Holes 18 L 5213 yds Par 70
Recs Am–68
Pro–67 R Hunter (1996)
V'tors U SOC
Fees £9.95 (£13.95)
Loc 3 miles W of Coventry on A45
Arch Hunter/Harrhy

Wishaw (1995)
Bulls Lane, Wishaw, Sutton Coldfield B76 9AA
Tel (0121) 313 2110
Sec Mrs S Wallis
Holes 18 L 5481 yds Par 72 SSS 67
V'tors U SOC
Fees £10 (£15)
Loc 3 miles NW of M42 Junction 9

Wiltshire

Bowood G&CC (1992)
Derry Hill, Calne SN11 9PQ
Tel (01249) 822228
Fax (01249) 822218
Mem 450
Sec G Elliott
Pro N Blenkarne (Golf Dir)
Holes 18 L 7317 yds Par 73 SSS 74
Recs Am–69 C Edwards (1995)
Pro–67 N Brown (1994)
V'tors U–booking required WE–M before noon SOC
Fees £32 D–£42
Loc 3 miles SE of Chippenham on A342. M4 Junction 14 (A4)
Mis Driving range. 3 Academy holes
Arch David Thomas

Bradford-on-Avon (1991)
Trowbridge Road, Bradford-on-Avon
Tel (01225) 868268
Pro G Sawyer
Holes 9 L 2100 metres SSS 61
V'tors WD–U WE–pm only
Fees 9 holes–£6.50 18 holes–£10
Loc SE of Bradford, nr River Avon

For list of abbreviations see page 527

Wiltshire

Brinkworth (1984)
Longmans Farm, Brinkworth, Chippenham SN15 5DG
Tel (01666) 510277
Mem 250
Sec J Sheppard
Holes 18 L 5900 yds SSS 69
V'tors U SOC
Fees On application
Loc 2 miles from Brinkworth (B4042). 12 miles NE of Chippenham

Broome Manor (1976)
Public
Pipers Way, Swindon SN3 1RG
Tel (01793) 532403
Fax (01793) 433255
Mem 800
Sec JE Poolman (01793) 823462
Pro B Sandry (01793) 532403
Holes 18 L 6283 yds SSS 70
9 L 2690 yds SSS 67
Recs Am–62 G Harris (1994)
Pro–66 M Bevan (1989)
V'tors U
Fees 18 hole:£10.50 9 hole:£6.50
Loc Swindon 2 miles. M4 Junction 15
Mis Floodlit driving range
Arch F Hawtree

Chippenham (1896)
Malmesbury Road, Chippenham SN15 5LT
Tel (01249) 652040
Fax (01249) 446681
Mem 650
Sec D Maddison
Pro W Creamer (01249) 655319
Holes 18 L 5540 yds SSS 67
Recs Am–64 RE Searle (1993)
Pro–64 B Sandry
V'tors U WE–M SOC
Fees £20 (£25)
Loc 1 mile N of Chippenham, off A350. M4 Junction 17

Cricklade Hotel (1992)
Common Hill, Cricklade SN6 6HA
Tel (01793) 750751
Fax (01793) 751767
Mem 140
Sec T Hooley
Pro I Bolt
Holes 9 L 1830 yds SSS 57
V'tors WD–U SOC–WD
Fees £16 D–£25
Loc ½ mile W of Cricklade on B4040. M4 Junctions 15/16
Arch Bolt/Smith

Cumberwell Park (1994)
Bradford-on-Avon BA15 2PQ
Tel (01225) 863322
Fax (01225) 868160
Mem 800
Sec R Smith (Mgr)
Pro J Jacobs
Holes 18 L 6807 yds SSS 73
Pro–63 S Little

V'tors H SOC
Fees £18 (£25)
Loc Between Bradford-on-Avon and Bath on A363. M4 Junction 18
Arch Adrian Stiff

Erlestoke Sands (1992)
Erlestoke, Devizes SN10 5UB
Tel (01380) 831069
Fax (01380) 831069
Mem 740
Sec M Pugsley
Pro A Marsh (01380) 831027
Holes 18 L 6406 yds Par 73 SSS 73
Recs Am–71 P Oakey (1993)
Pro–68 S Little (1996)
V'tors U–book with Pro SOC
Fees £16 (£25)
Loc 6 miles E of Westbury on B3098
Mis Driving area. 3 Academy holes
Arch Adrian Stiff

Hamptworth G&CC (1994)
Elmtree Farmhouse, Hamptworth Road, Landford SP5 2DU
Tel (01794) 390155
Fax (01794) 390022
Sec P Stevens
Holes 18 L 6516 yds SSS
V'tors H
Fees £25 D–£30
Loc 10 miles SE of Salisbury, off A36/B3079. M27 Junction 2, 6 miles

High Post (1922)
Great Durnford, Salisbury SP4 6AT
Tel (01722) 782231
Fax (01722) 782356
Mem 590
Sec NI Symington (01722) 782356
Pro I Welding (01722) 782219
Holes 18 L 6305 yds Par 70 SSS 70
Recs Am–64 K Weeks, RE Searle
Pro–65 P Alliss, N Sutton
V'tors WD–U WE/BH–H SOC
Fees £23 D–£28 (£35) SOC–£32
Loc 4 miles N of Salisbury on A345

Highworth (1990)
Swindon Road, Highworth SN6 7SJ
Tel (01793) 766014
Pro M Toombs
Holes 9 L 3220 yds SSS 70
V'tors U SOC
Fees £4.50 (£5)
Loc 5 miles N of Swindon (A361)
Mis 9 hole pitch & putt

Kingsdown (1880)
Kingsdown, Corsham SN13 8BS
Tel (01225) 742530
Mem 500 105(L) 45(J)
Sec J Prosser (01225) 743472
Pro A Butler (01225) 742634
Holes 18 L 6445 yds SSS 71

Recs Am–66 S Hodges (1991)
Pro–64 M Wiggett (1993)
V'tors WD–H WE–M
Fees £22
Loc 5 miles E of Bath

Manor House (1992)
Castle Combe SN14 7PL
Tel (01249) 782982
Fax (01249) 782992
Mem 400
Sec Susan Auld (Gen Mgr)
Pro C Smith (Golf Dir)
Holes 18 L 6340 yds SSS 71
Recs Am–73 M Rhodes (1995)
V'tors U H–booking necessary SOC
Fees £35 (£45)
Loc N of Castle Combe, off B4039. M4 Junction 17, 4 miles
Mis Driving range
Arch Alliss/Clarke

Marlborough (1888)
The Common, Marlborough SN8 1DU
Tel (01672) 512147
Fax (01672) 513164
Mem 750
Sec JAD Sullivan
Pro S Amor (01672) 512493
Holes 18 L 6491 yds SSS 71
Recs Am–61 G Harris
Pro–63 B Sandry
V'tors WD/WE–H SOC
Fees £22 D–£32 (£30)
Loc ½ mile N of Marlborough (A346)

Monkton Park Par Three (1975)
Pay and play
Chippenham SN15 3PP
Tel (01249) 653928
Fax (01249) 653928
Mem 100
Sec MR & BJ Dawson (Props)
Holes 9 hole Par 3 course
Recs Am–23 J Dawson (1991)
V'tors U
Fees 18 holes–£4.75 (£5)
9 holes–£3.25 (£3.50)
Loc Centre of Chippenham. M4 Junction 17
Arch M Dawson

North Wilts (1890)
Bishops' Cannings, Devizes SN10 2LP
Tel (01380) 860257
Fax (01380) 860877
Mem 625 105(L) 90(J)
Sec Mrs P Stephenson (01380) 860627
Pro GJ Laing (Golf Mgr) (01380) 860330
Holes 18 L 6333 yds SSS 70
Recs Am–65 N Williams (1996)
Pro–66 GJ Laing (1997)
Ladies–72 S Firmston (1997)
V'tors U exc Xmas Day–Jan 31–M SOC
Fees £19 (£25)
Loc 1 mile from A4, E of Calne

For list of abbreviations see page 527

Wiltshire

Oaksey Park (1991)
Pay and play
Oaksey, Malmesbury SN16 9SB
Tel (01666) 577995
Fax (01666) 577174
Holes 9 L 2900 yds SSS 68
V'tors U SOC
Fees £10 (£15)
Loc 8 miles NE of Malmesbury, off A429
Mis Driving range
Arch Chapman/Warren

Ogbourne Downs (1907)
Ogbourne St George, Marlborough SN8 1TB
Tel (01672) 841217
Mem 700
Sec DJ Knight (01672) 841327
Pro C Harraway (01672) 841287
Holes 18 L 6353 yds SSS 70
Recs Am–66 RJ Binsted, S Robertson
Pro–65 G Ryall
V'tors WD–H WE–M SOC–WD
Fees £20 (£30)
Loc 5 miles S of M4 Junction 15, on A346
Arch JH Taylor

RMCS Shrivenham (1953)
RMCS Shrivenham, Swindon SN6 8LA
Tel (01793) 785725
Mem 500
Sec R Humphrey (Mgr)
Holes 18 L 5684 yds SSS 69
Recs Am–65 M Snape
V'tors M SOC
Fees £8 (£10)
Loc Grounds of Royal Military College of Science. Entry must be arranged with Mgr

Rushmore Park
Tollard Royal, Salisbury SP5 5QB
Tel (01725) 516326
Fax (01725) 516466
Mem 300
Sec S McDonagh
Pro S McDonagh
Holes 18 hole course
V'tors U SOC
Fees £12 (£15)
Loc 8 miles SE of Shaftesbury (B3081)
Mis Driving range
Arch T Crouch

Salisbury & South Wilts (1888)
Netherhampton, Salisbury SP2 8PR
Tel (01722) 742645
Fax (01722) 742645
Mem 1100
Sec GL Pearce (Gen Mgr)
Pro J Cave (01722) 742929
Holes 18 L 6528 yds SSS 71
9 hole course Par 34
Recs Am–65 D Hutton
Pro–61 S Little

V'tors WD–U WE–H SOC–WD
Fees £25 (£40)
Loc Wilton, 3 miles SW of Salisbury on A3094
Arch Taylor/Gidman

Shrivenham Park (1967)
Pay and play
Penny Hooks, Shrivenham, Swindon SN6 8EX
Tel (01793) 783853
Fax (01793) 782999
Mem 400
Sec Mrs A Briggs
Pro B Randall
Holes 18 L 5713 yds SSS 69
V'tors U SOC
Fees £14 (£16)
Loc 4 miles E of Swindon, off A420. M4 Junction 15
Arch Glen Johnson

Thoulstone Park (1992)
Chapmanslade, Westbury BA13 4AQ
Tel (01373) 832825
Fax (01373) 832821
Sec Mrs J Pearce
Pro T Isaacs (01373) 832808
Holes 18 L 6300 yds Par 71 SSS 70
Recs Am–69 S Wilson (1994)
Pro–67 T Nash (1992)
V'tors U SOC–WD
Fees £18 (£24)
Loc 12 miles S of Bath, off A36
Mis Driving range
Arch MRM Sandow

Tidworth Garrison (1908)
Bulford Road, Tidworth SP9 7AF
Tel (01980) 842321 (Clubhouse)
Fax (01980) 842301
Mem 700
Sec T Harris (Mgr) (01980) 842301
Pro T Gosden (01980) 842393
Holes 18 L 6101 yds SSS 69
Recs Am–66 C Akrill (1992)
Pro–62 I Benson (1995)
V'tors SOC–Tues & Thurs
Fees £22
Loc 1 mile SW of Tidworth on Bulford road (A338)
Arch Donald Steel

Upavon (RAF) (1918)
Douglas Avenue, Upavon SN9 6BQ
Tel (01980) 630787
Fax (01980) 630787
Mem 550
Sec L Mitchell
Pro R Blake (01980) 630281
Holes 18 L 6415 yds SSS 71
Recs Am–71 R Greenwood (1997)
V'tors WD–U WE–M before noon –U after noon SOC–WD
Fees £16 D–£22
Loc 2 miles SE of Upavon on A342
Arch R Blake

West Wilts (1891)
Elm Hill, Warminster BA12 0AU
Tel (01985) 212702
Fax (01985) 219809
Mem 570 70(L) 70(J)
Sec DJ Spratt (01985) 213133
Pro AJ Lamb (01985) 212110
Holes 18 L 5709 yds SSS 68
Recs Am–62 CG Burton (1989)
Pro–61 I Bolt, I Harrison (1997)
V'tors WD–U H WE–U H after noon –NA before noon
Fees £15 D–£24 (£35)
Loc Off A350, on Westbury road
Arch JH Taylor

The Wiltshire
Vastern, Wootton Bassett, Swindon SN4 7PB
Tel (01793) 849999
Fax (01793) 849988
Mem 600
Sec RG Lipscombe (Gen Mgr)
Pro A Gray
Holes 18 L 6522 yds SSS 72
Recs Am–67
V'tors U SOC
Fees £30 (£30)
Loc 1 mile S of Wootton Bassett. M4 Junction 16
Arch Alliss/Clark

Wrag Barn G&CC (1990)
Shrivenham Road, Highworth, Swindon SN6 7QQ
Tel (01793) 861327
Fax (01793) 861325
Mem 500
Sec Mrs S Manners
Pro B Loughrey (01793) 766027
Holes 18 L 6600 yds SSS 71
Recs Am–71 P Poulton (1993)
Pro–66 G Clough (1992)
V'tors WD–U WE–NA before noon SOC–WD
Fees £22 (£27)
Loc 6 miles NE of Swindon on B4000. M4 Junction 15, 8 miles
Mis Driving range
Arch Hawtree

Worcestershire

Abbey Park G&CC (1985)
Dagnell End Road, Redditch B98 7BD
Tel (01527) 63918
Fax (01527) 65872
Mem 1200
Sec ME Bradley
Pro RK Cameron (01527) 68006
Holes 18 L 6411 yds SSS 71
V'tors WD–U SOC
Fees £10 (£12.50)
Loc B4101, off A441 Birmingham road
Mis Driving range
Arch Donald Steel

For list of abbreviations see page 527

Worcestershire 647

Bank House Hotel G&CC
(1992)
Bransford, Worcester WR6 5JD
Tel (01886) 833551
Fax (01886) 832461
Mem 350
Sec PAD Holmes
Pro C George
Holes 18 L 6204 yds SSS 71
Recs Am–64 T Duffy (1997)
Pro–65 G George (1997)
V'tors U SOC
Fees £15 (£25)
Loc 3 miles SW of Worcester on A4103 Hereford road. M5 Junction 7
Mis Driving range
Arch Bob Sandow

Blackwell (1893)
Blackwell, Bromsgrove, Worcestershire B60 1PY
Tel (0121) 445 1994
Fax (0121) 445 4911
Mem 300 100(L) 20(J)
Sec JT Mead
Pro N Blake (0121) 445 3113
Holes 18 L 6230 yds SSS 71
Recs Am–65 M Reynard (1994)
Pro–63 W Stephens (1994)
V'tors WD–U H WE/BH–M
Fees £50
Loc 3 miles E of Bromsgrove. M42 Junction 1 (South)

Brandhall (1946)
Public
Heron Road, Oldbury, Warley B68 8AQ
Tel (0121) 552 7475
Mem 355
Sec DJ Hart (0121) 559 9193
Pro C Yates (0121) 552 2195
Holes 18 L 5813 yds SSS 68
Recs Am–63 A Salter
V'tors U exc first 2 hrs Sat/Sun
Fees £6.60 (£8.50)
Loc 6 miles NW of Birmingham. M5 Junction 2, 1½ miles

Bromsgrove Golf Centre
(1992)
Pay and play
Stratford Road, Bromsgrove B60 1LD
Tel (01527) 575886
Mem 900
Sec D Went
Pro G Long, M Davies (01527) 575886
Holes 18 L 5869 yds SSS 68
Recs Pro–63 C Clark (1997)
V'tors U SOC–WD
Fees £12.50 (£15.50)
Loc Junction of A38/A448. M42 Junction 1. M5 Junction 4/5
Mis Driving range
Arch Hawtree

Churchill & Blakedown
(1926)
Churchill Lane, Blakedown, Kidderminster DY10 3NB
Tel (01562) 700018
Mem 350
Sec B Pendry
Pro K Wheeler (01562) 700454
Holes 9 L 6472 yds Par 72 SSS 71
Recs Am–67 R Bradshaw (1995)
V'tors WD–U WE–M
Fees £17.50
Loc 3 miles N of Kidderminster on A456

Cocks Moor Woods
(1926)
Public
Alcester Road, South King's Heath, Birmingham BK1 6ER
Tel (0121) 444 3584
Pro S Ellis
Holes 18 L 5742 yds SSS 67
Recs Am–67 A Osborne
Pro–65 G Broadbent
V'tors U
Fees On application
Loc 6 miles S of Birmingham (A435)

Droitwich G&CC (1897)
Ford Lane, Droitwich WR9 0BQ
Tel (01905) 770129
Fax (01905) 797290
Mem 782
Sec M Ashton (01905) 774344
Pro CS Thompson (01905) 770207
Holes 18 L 6058 yds SSS 69
Recs Am–62 S Braitwaite
V'tors WD–U WE/BH–M SOC–Wed & Fri
Fees £24
Loc 1 mile N of Droitwich, off A38. M5 Junction 5

Dudley (1893)
Turners Hill, Rowley Regis B65 9DP
Tel (01384) 253719
Mem 320
Sec RP Fortune (01384) 233877
Pro P Taylor (01384) 254020
Holes 18 L 5654 yds SSS 69
Recs Am–66 AA Davies
Pro–63 R Livingstone
V'tors WD–U WE–M
Fees On application
Loc 2 miles S of Dudley

Evesham (1894)
Craycombe Links, Fladbury, Pershore WR10 2QS
Tel (01386) 860395
Fax (01386) 861356
Mem 360
Sec J Dale (01386) 860436
Pro C Haynes (01386) 861144
Holes 9 L 6415 yds SSS 71
Recs Am–68
V'tors WD–H WE–M NA on comp/match days SOC
Fees D–£20
Loc Fladbury, 4 miles W of Evesham (A4538)

Fulford Heath (1933)
Tanners Green Lane, Wythall, Birmingham B47 6BH 930 pro
Tel (01564) 822806 (Clubhouse)
Fax (01564) 822629
Mem 700
Sec Mrs MA Tuckett (01564) 824758
Pro D Down (01564) 822930
Holes 18 L 6179 yds SSS 70
Recs Am–66 S Leahy
Pro–66 D Prosser
V'tors WD–H WE/BH–M SOC–Tues & Thurs
Fees On application
Loc 8 miles S of Birmingham
Arch Braid/Hawtree

Gay Hill (1913)
Hollywood Lane, Birmingham B47 5PP
Tel (0121) 430 6523/7077
Fax (0121) 436 7796
Mem 700
Sec Mrs M Adderley (0121) 430 8544
Pro A Potter (0121) 474 6001
Holes 18 L 6532 yds SSS 72
Recs Am–64 P Johnson (1993)
Pro–66 R Livingston
V'tors WD–U H WE–M SOC
Fees £28.50
Loc 7 miles S of Birmingham on A435. M42 Junction 3, 3 miles

Habberley (1924)
Trimpley Road, Kidderminster DY11 5RG
Tel (01562) 745756
Mem 250
Sec DB Lloyd
Holes 9 L 5440 yds SSS 67
Recs Am–62 M Dudley
V'tors WD–U WE–M SOC
Fees £10
Loc 3 miles NW of Kidderminster

Hagley (1980)
Wassell Grove, Hagley, Stourbridge DY9 9JW
Tel (01562) 883701
Fax (01562) 887518
Mem 700
Sec GF Yardley
Pro I Clark (01562) 883852
Holes 18 L 6353 yds SSS 72
Recs Am–66 S Hull (1995)
Pro–69 I Clark (1990)
V'tors WD–U exc Wed NA before 1.30pm WE–M after 10am SOC–WD
Fees £22 D–£28
Loc 5 miles SW of Birmingham on A456. M5 Junction 3

For list of abbreviations see page 527

Worcestershire

Halesowen (1909)
The Leasowes, Halesowen B62 8QF
Tel (0121) 550 1041
Fax (0121) 501 3606
Mem 600
Sec P Crumpton (0121) 501 3606
Pro J Nicholas (0121) 503 0593
Holes 18 L 5754 yds SSS 69
Recs Am–65 D Henn
Pro–66
V'tors WD–U WE–M SOC–WD exc Wed
Fees £18 D–£25
Loc M5 Junction 3, 2 miles

Kidderminster (1909)
Russell Road, Kidderminster DY10 3HT
Tel (01562) 822303
Fax (01562) 862041
Mem 900
Sec M Burnand
Pro NP Underwood
(01562) 740090
Holes 18 L 6405 yds SSS 71
Recs Am–66 MJ Houghton (1995)
Pro–68 F Clarke (1993)
Ladies–73 L Waring (1993)
V'tors WD–H WE–M SOC–Thurs
Fees £30 D–£40
Loc Signposted off A449 Wolverhampton-Worcester road

Kings Norton (1892)
Brockhill Lane, Weatheroak, Alvechurch, Birmingham B48 7ED
Tel (01564) 826789
Fax (01564) 826955
Mem 1050
Sec D Gutteridge (Mgr)
Pro K Hayward (01564) 822822
Holes 9 L 3382 yds SSS 36
9 L 3372 yds SSS 36
9 L 3290 yds SSS 36
V'tors WD–U WE–NA SOC
Fees £30 D–£35
Loc 7 miles S of Birmingham. 1 mile N of M42 Junction 3
Mis 12 hole short course
Arch Fred Hawtree

Lickey Hills (1927)
Public
Lickey Hills, Rednal, Birmingham B45 8RR
Tel (0121) 453 3159
Sec MR Billingham
Pro MS March
Holes 18 L 6010 yds SSS 69
Recs Am–66 S Green
Pro–72 R Livingston
V'tors U
Fees On application
Loc 10 miles SW of Birmingham. M5 Junction 4

Little Lakes (1975)
Lye Head, Bewdley, Worcester DY12 2UZ
Tel (01299) 266385
Mem 400 50(L)

Sec T Norris (01562) 67495
Pro M Laing
Holes 9 L 6247 yds SSS 72
Recs Am–70 R Dean (1990)
Pro–70 R Lane (1986)
V'tors WD–U WE–NA SOC
Fees £12 D–£15
Loc 3 miles W of Bewdley, off A456

Moseley (1892)
Springfield Road, Kings Heath, Birmingham B14 7DX
Tel (0121) 444 2115
Fax (0121) 441 4662
Mem 600
Sec RA Jowle (0121) 444 4957
Pro G Edge (0121) 444 2063
Holes 18 L 6300 yds SSS 70
Recs Am–64 C Norman (1992)
Pro–67 G Edge (1992)
Ladies–72 J Thorne (1976)
V'tors I H or M
Fees £37
Loc South Birmingham

North Worcestershire (1907)
Frankley Beeches Road, Northfield, Birmingham B31 5LP
Tel (0121) 475 1047
Fax (0121) 476 8681
Mem 550
Sec D Wilson
Pro IF Clark (0121) 475 5721
Holes 18 L 5907 yds SSS 69
Recs Am–64 DJ Russell
Pro–63 K Dickens (1988)
V'tors WD–U WE/BH–M
Fees £18 D–£25.50
Loc 7 miles SW of Birmingham, off A38
Arch James Braid

Ombersley (1991)
Bishopswood Road, Ombersley, Droitwich WR9 OLE
Tel (01905) 620747
Fax (01905) 620047
Mem 750
Sec G Glenister (Gen Mgr)
Pro G Glenister
Holes 18 L 6139 yds SSS 69
Recs Am–72
V'tors U
Fees £11.50 (£15.50)
Loc 6 miles N of Worcester, off A449
Mis Driving range
Arch David Morgan

Perdiswell Park
Pay and play
Bilford Road, Worcester WR3 8DX
Tel (01905) 754668
Fax (01905) 756608
Mem 185
Sec R Gardner
Pro M Woodward
(01905) 754668
Holes 9 L 5870 yds SSS 68

V'tors U
Fees 9 holes–£4.60 (£6)
18 holes–£7.30 (£8.50)
Loc Worcester
Mis Extension to 18 holes in 1999

Pitcheroak (1973)
Public
Plymouth Road, Redditch B97 4PB
Tel (01527) 541054
Pro D Stewart
Holes 9 L 4584 yds SSS 62
V'tors U
Fees £5.75 (£6.75)
Loc Redditch

Ravenmeadow
Hindlip Lane, Clanes, Worcester WR3 8SA
Tel (01905) 757525
Mem 120
Sec D Rodway (01905) 26815
Pro G Wheelaghan
(01905) 757525
Holes 9 L 5440 yds Par 67
V'tors U
Fees £10 (£12)
Loc 3 miles N of Worcester, off A38
Mis Driving range
Arch R Baldwin

Redditch (1913)
Lower Grinsty, Green Lane, Callow Hill, Redditch B97 5PJ
Tel (01527) 543309
Fax (01527) 543079
Mem 883
Sec WA Wells
Pro F Powell (01527) 546372
Holes 18 L 6494 yds SSS 72
Recs Am–68 RJ Stevens (1993)
Pro–68 G Mercer (1991)
V'tors WD–U SOC
Fees £27.50
Loc 3 miles SW of Redditch, off A441
Arch F Pennink

Stourbridge (1892)
Worcester Lane, Pedmore, Stourbridge DY8 2RB
Tel (01384) 393062
Mem 720
Sec Mrs MA Betts (01384) 395566
Pro M Male (01384) 393129
Holes 18 L 6231 yds SSS 70
Recs Am–65 J Fisher
Pro–63 WH Firkins
V'tors WD–U exc Wed before 4pm–M WE/BH–M
Fees £25
Loc 1 mile S of Stourbridge on Worcester road

Tolladine (1898)
The Fairway, Tolladine Road, Worcester WR4 9BA
Tel (01905) 21074 (Clubhouse)
Mem 270
Sec D Turner

For list of abbreviations see page 527

Yorkshire (East)

Holes 9 L 5174 yds SSS 67
Recs Am–65 T Sanders (1992)
Ladies–71 C George (1991)
V'tors WD–U before 4pm –M after 4pm WE/BH–M SOC
Fees On application
Loc M5 Junction 6, 1 mile

The Vale (1991)
Bishampton, Pershore WR10 2LZ
Tel (01386) 462781
Fax (01386) 462597
Mem 800
Sec D Gutteridge (Gen Mgr)
Pro Caroline Griffiths (01386) 462520
Holes 18 L 7114 yds SSS 74
9 L 2918 yds SSS 68
Recs Am–72 G Downie (1996)
V'tors WD–U H WE–U H after 1pm SOC–WD
Fees On application
Loc 6 miles NW of Evesham, off B4084. M5 Junction 6, 8 miles
Mis Driving range
Arch M Sandow

Warley (1921)
Public
Lightwoods Hill, Warley B67 5EQ
Tel (0121) 429 2440
Sec A Wooldridge
Pro D Owen
Holes 9 L 2606 yds SSS 64
Recs Am–62 M Daw
Pro–58 B Fereday
V'tors U SOC
Fees On application
Loc 5 miles W of Birmingham, off A456

Wharton Park (1992)
Longbank, Bewdley DY12 2QW
Tel (01299) 405222
Fax (01299) 405121
Mem 550
Pro A Hoare (01299) 405163
Holes 18 L 6435 yds Par 72 SSS 71
Recs Am–64 J Toman (1996)
Pro–65 D Eddiford (1996)
V'tors U SOC
Fees £20 (£25)
Loc Bewdley bypass on A456
Mis Practice ground
Arch Howard Swann

Worcester G&CC (1898)
Boughton Park, Worcester WR2 4EZ
Tel (01905) 422555
Mem 1005
Sec DG Bettsworth
Pro C Colenso (01905) 422044
Holes 18 L 6251 yds SSS 70
Recs Am–66 D Clee (1996)
Pro–67 C Colenso (1995)
V'tors WD–H WE–M SOC
Fees £25
Loc 1 mile W of Worcester on A4103
Arch Dr A Mackenzie (1926)
C Colenso (1991)

Worcestershire (1879)
Wood Farm, Malvern Wells WR14 4PP
Tel (01684) 573905
Fax (01684) 575992
Mem 770
Sec Lt Col RG Blackwell (01684) 575992
Pro RAF Lewis (01684) 564428
Holes 18 L 6449 yds SSS 71
Recs Am–67 PM Guest, MC Reynard, S Braithwaite
Pro–66 R Larratt
V'tors WD–H WE–H after 10am
Fees £32 (£37) W–£99
Loc 2 miles S of Gt Malvern, off A449/B4209

Wyre Forest Golf Centre
Pay and play
Zortech Avenue, Kidderminster DY11 7EX
Tel (01299) 822682
Fax (01299) 879433
Mem 363
Sec S Price (Mgr)
Pro S Price
Holes 18 L 5790 yds Par 70 SSS 68
V'tors U SOC
Fees £9 (£12.50)
Loc 18 miles S of Birmingham on A451, between Kidderminster and Stourport
Mis Floodlit driving range

Yorkshire (East)

Allerthorpe Park
Allerthorpe, York YO4 4RL
Tel (01759) 306686
Fax (01759) 304308
Mem 360
Pro None
Holes 13 L 5634 yds Par 68 SSS 67
V'tors U SOC
Fees £16
Loc 2 miles W of Pocklington, off A1079
Arch JG Hatcliffe

Beverley & East Riding (1889)
The Westwood, Beverley HU17 8RG
Tel (01482) 867190
Fax (01482) 868757
Mem 530
Sec B Gregory (01482) 868757
Pro I Mackie (01482) 869519
Holes 18 L 5972 yds SSS 69
Recs Am–65 N Burnley (1994)
V'tors U SOC–WD
Fees £12 (£16)
Loc Beverley-Walkington road (B1230)

Boothferry (1982)
Spaldington Lane, Spaldington, Goole DN14 7NG
Tel (01430) 430364
Fax (01430) 430567

Pro N Bundy (01430) 430364
Holes 18 L 6593 yds SSS 72
Recs Am–70 R Giles (1988)
Pro–70 M Ingham (1984),
S Rolley (1987)
Ladies–75 C Briggs (1995)
V'tors U SOC
Fees On application
Loc 3 miles N of Howden on B1288. M62 Junction 37, 2 miles
Arch Donald Steel

Bridlington (1905)
Belvedere Road, Bridlington YO15 3NA
Tel (01262) 672092/606367
Fax (01262) 606367
Mem 623
Sec C Greenwood (01262) 606367
Pro ARA Howarth (01262) 674721
Holes 18 L 6638 yds SSS 72
Recs Am–66 R Webster (1997)
Pro–69 J Healey (1996)
V'tors U exc Sun–NA
Fees £15 (£30)
Loc 1½ miles S of Bridlington, off A165
Arch James Braid

The Bridlington Links (1993)
Pay and play
Flamborough Road, Marton, Bridlington YO15 1DW
Tel (01262) 401584
Fax (01262) 401702
Mem 300
Sec PM Hancock (Gen Mgr)
Pro S Raybould
Holes 18 L 6720 yds SSS 72
9 hole course
Recs Am–69 J Smith (1995)
V'tors U
Fees £12 (£15)
Loc 2 miles N of Bridlington on B1255
Mis Floodlit driving range. 3 Academy holes
Arch Howard Swann

Brough (1893)
Cave Road, Brough HU15 1HB
Tel (01482) 667374
Fax (01482) 669873
Mem 800
Sec GW Townhill (Golf Dir) (01482) 667291
Pro GW Townhill (01482) 667483
Holes 18 L 6183 yds SSS 69
Recs Am–65 AG McKelvie (1997)
Pro–64 B Thompson (1993)
V'tors WD–U exc Wed–NA
Fees £30
Loc 10 miles W of Hull on A63

Cave Castle Hotel (1989)
South Cave, N Humberside HU15 2EU
Tel (01430) 421286/422245 (Hotel)
Fax (01430) 421118
Sec C Welton

For list of abbreviations see page 527

650 Yorkshire (East)

Pro   S MacKinder
       (01430) 421286
Holes 18 L 6409 yds SSS 71
V'tors U SOC
Fees   £12.50 (£18)
Loc   10 miles W of Hull.
       Junction of A63/M62

Cherry Burton (1993)
Pay and play
Leconfield Road, Cherry Burton, Beverley HU17 7RB
Tel   (01964) 550924
Mem   220
Sec   A Ashby (Mgr)
Pro   A Ashby
Holes 9 L 2278 yds Par 33 SSS 62
Recs   Am–62 P Killeen (1995)
V'tors U SOC
Fees   £7 (£10)
Loc   2 miles N of Beverley, off Malton road
Mis   Driving range

Cottingham
Woodhill Way, Cottingham, Hull HU16 5RZ
Tel   (01482) 842394
Fax   (01482) 845932
Mem   500
Sec   J Wiles (01482) 846030
Pro   CW Gray (01482) 842394
Holes 18 L 6459 yds Par 72 SSS 71
V'tors WD–U WE/BH–M before 11am SOC
Fees   £14 D–£20 (£20 D–£30)
Loc   3 miles N of Hull, off A164
Mis   Driving range

Driffield (1923)
Sunderlandwick, Driffield YO25 9AD
Tel   (01377) 240448 (Clubhouse), (01377) 253116 (Office)
Fax   (01377) 240599
Mem   670
Sec   PJ Mounfield
Pro   (01377) 256663
Holes 18 L 6212 yds SSS 70
Recs   Am–67 G Drewery (1985), KA Gray (1994)
V'tors H I SOC
Fees   R/D–£18 (R/D–£25)
Loc   S of Driffield on A164

Flamborough Head (1932)
Lighthouse Road, Flamborough, Bridlington YO15 1AR
Tel   (01262) 850333/850417
Fax   (01262) 850279
Mem   400
Sec   GS Thornton
       (01262) 850683
Holes 18 L 5973 yds SSS 69
Recs   Am–70 E Skaggs
V'tors U
Fees   £16 (£19) 5D–£64
Loc   5 miles NE of Bridlington

Ganstead Park (1976)
Longdales Lane, Coniston, Hull HU11 4LB
Tel   (01482) 811280 (Steward)
Fax   (01482) 817754
Mem   700
Sec   G Drewery (01482) 817754
Pro   M Smee (01482) 811121
Holes 18 L 6801 yds SSS 73
V'tors U H WE–NA before noon SOC
Fees   On application
Loc   5 miles E of Hull on A165
Arch   Peter Green

Hainsworth Park (1983)
Brandesburton, Driffield YO25 8RT
Tel   (01964) 542362
Fax   (01964) 542362
Mem   550
Sec   GF Redshaw, BW Atkin (Prop)
Pro   PR Binnington
       (01964) 542362
Holes 18 L 6027 yds SSS 69
Recs   Am–69 R Burke (1998)
V'tors U SOC
Fees   £15 (£20)
Loc   6 miles NW of Beverley, off A165 at Brandesburton roundabout

Hessle (1898)
Westfield Road, Cottingham HU16 5YL
Tel   (01482) 650171
Fax   (01482) 652679
Mem   680
Sec   RL Dorsey
Pro   G Fieldsend (01482) 650190
Holes 18 L 6604 yds SSS 72
Recs   Am–68 PM Blanshard (1997)
       Pro–69 B Thompson (1988)
       Ladies–72 E Duggleby (1994)
V'tors WD–U exc Tues 9am–1pm WE–NA before 11am
Fees   £20 (£28)
Loc   3 miles SW of Cottingham
Arch   Thomas/Alliss

Hornsea (1898)
Rolston Road, Hornsea HU18 1XG
Tel   (01964) 532020
Fax   (01964) 532020
Mem   600
Sec   BW Kirton (01964) 532020
Pro   B Thompson (01964) 534989
Holes 18 L 6685 yds SSS 72
Recs   Am–66 A Wright (1967)
       Pro–66 G Brown (1991)
V'tors WD–U WE–restricted SOC
Fees   £22 D–£30
Loc   300 yds past Hornsea Free Port
Arch   Mackenzie/Braid

Hull (1921)
The Hall, 27 Packman Lane, Kirk Ella, Hull HU10 7JT
Tel   (01482) 653026
Fax   (01482) 658919
Mem   821

Sec   R Toothill (Gen Mgr)
       (01482) 658919
Pro   D Jagger (01482) 653074
Holes 18 L 6246 yds SSS 70
Recs   Am–64 JD Dockar, R Roper
       Pro–66 AD Hill, N Hunt, S Smith, D Jagger
V'tors WD–U WE–NA
Fees   £25 D–£30
Loc   5 miles W of Hull

Kilnwick Percy (1995)
Kilnwick Percy, Pocklington YO4 2UF
Tel   (01759) 303090
Mem   350
Sec   Mrs A Clayton (Sec/Mgr)
Pro   J Townhill
Holes 18 L 6214 yds Par 70 SSS 70
V'tors U SOC
Fees   £12 (£16)
Loc   1 mile E of Pocklington, off B1246
Arch   John Day

Springhead Park (1930)
Public
Willerby Road, Hull HU5 5JE
Tel   (01482) 656309
Sec   A Farr (Hon)
       (01482) 501126
Pro   B Herrington
Holes 18 L 6402 yds SSS 71
Recs   Am–69 AD Hill, A Wright
       Pro–65 S Rolley
V'tors U SOC–phone Sec
Fees   £6 (£7.80) (1997)
Loc   4 miles W of Hull

Sutton Park (1935)
Public
Salthouse Road, Hull HU8 9HF
Tel   (01482) 374342
Fax   (01482) 701428
Mem   300
Sec   To be appointed
Pro   P Rushworth
       (01482) 711450
Holes 18 L 6251 yds SSS 70
Recs   Am–67 A Wright
       Pro–64 L Herrington
V'tors U SOC–exc Sun
Fees   £7 (£9)
Loc   3 miles E of Hull on A165

Withernsea (1907)
Chestnut Avenue, Withernsea HU19 2PG
Tel   (01964) 612258 (Clubhouse)
Mem   329 40(L) 40(J)
Sec   Mrs J Jackson
       (01964) 612078
Pro   G Harrison
       (01482) 492720
Holes 9 L 6191 yds Par 72 SSS 69
Recs   Am–BJ Hayes
V'tors WD–U WE/BH–M before 1pm SOC
Fees   £10
Loc   17 miles E of Hull on A1033. S side of Withernsea

For list of abbreviations see page 527

Yorkshire (North)

Aldwark Manor (1978)
Aldwark, Alne, York YO61 1UF
- **Tel** (01347) 838353
- **Fax** (01347) 830007
- **Sec** GF Platt (Mgr)
- **Pro** P Harrison
- **Holes** 18 L 6171 yds Par 71 SSS 70
- **Recs** Am–70 RW Smart (1994)
  Pro–69 N Squire (1992)
- **V'tors** U SOC
- **Fees** £20 D–£25 (£25 D–£30)
- **Loc** 5 miles SE of Boroughbridge, off A1. 13 miles NW of York, off A19

Ampleforth College (1962)
56 High Street, Helmsley, York YO6 5AE
- **Mem** 175
- **Sec** JE Atkinson (01439) 770678
- **Holes** 10 L 4018 yds SSS 63
- **V'tors** U exc WD 2–4pm SOC–WD
- **Fees** £8 (£12)
- **Loc** Driveway of Gilling Castle. 18 miles N of York (B1363)
- **Mis** Green fees payable at Fairfax Arms, Gilling East
- **Arch** Rev Jerome Lambert OSB

Bedale (1894)
Leyburn Road, Bedale DL8 1EZ
- **Tel** (01677) 422568
- **Mem** 600 60(J)
- **Sec** ME Leng (01677) 422451
- **Pro** AD Johnson (01677) 422343
- **Holes** 18 L 6610 yds SSS 72
- **Recs** Am–68 R Lawson (1994)
  Pro–76 N Walton (1992)
- **V'tors** U SOC
- **Fees** £20 (£30)
- **Loc** N boundary of Bedale

Bentham (1922)
Robin Lane, Bentham, Lancaster LA2 7AG
- **Tel** (015242) 61018
- **Mem** 450
- **Sec** T Tudor (015242) 62455
- **Holes** 9 L 5760 yds SSS 69
- **Recs** Am–67 CJ Carter (1992)
- **V'tors** U SOC
- **Fees** £14 (£20) W–£75
- **Loc** NE of Lancaster on B6480 towards Settle. 13 miles E of M6 Junction 34

Catterick (1930)
Leyburn Road, Catterick Garrison DL9 3QE
- **Tel** (01748) 833268
- **Fax** (01748) 833268
- **Mem** 700
- **Sec** Mrs D Hopkins (Sec/Mgr)
- **Pro** A Marshall (01748) 833671
- **Holes** 18 L 6329 yds SSS 71
  Pro–64 H Selby-Green
- **V'tors** U H SOC
- **Fees** £25 (£30)
- **Loc** 6 miles SW of Scotch Corner, via A1
- **Arch** Arthur Day

Cleveland (1887)
Queen Street, Redcar TS10 1BT
- **Tel** (01642) 483693
- **Fax** (01642) 471798
- **Mem** 800
- **Sec** P Fletcher (01642) 471798
- **Pro** S Wynn (01642) 483462
- **Holes** 18 L 6746 yds SSS 72
- **Recs** Am–66 CM Nolan (1996)
  Pro–70 B Hardcastle (1976)
- **V'tors** WD–U WE/BH–by arrangement SOC
- **Fees** £20 (£22)
- **Loc** S bank of River Tees

Cocksford (1992)
Stutton, Tadcaster LS24 9NG
- **Tel** (01937) 834253
- **Fax** (01937) 834253
- **Sec** Gill Coxon
- **Pro** G Thompson
- **Holes** 18 L 5570 yds Par 71 SSS 69
  9 L 2470 yds Par 33
- **Recs** Pro–71 M Maith (1994)
- **V'tors** WD–U WE–by arrangement SOC
- **Fees** £17 D–£21 (£23 D–26)
- **Loc** 1½ miles S of Tadcaster

Crimple Valley (1976)
Pay and play
Hookstone Wood Road, Harrogate HG2 8PN
- **Tel** (01423) 883485
- **Fax** (01423) 881018
- **Mem** 200
- **Sec** P Lumb
- **Pro** P Lumb
- **Holes** 9 L 2500 yds SSS 33
- **V'tors** U
- **Fees** 9 holes–£5 (£6)
  18 holes–£8 D–£11
- **Loc** 1 mile S of Harrogate, off A61, by Yorkshire Showground
- **Arch** R Lumb

Drax (1989)
Drax, Selby YO8 8PQ
- **Mem** 465
- **Sec** J Leedham (01757) 702247
- **Holes** 9 L 5644 yds Par 68 SSS 67
- **Recs** Am–71 GM Knights (1998)
- **V'tors** M
- **Fees** £5 (£7)
- **Loc** 5 miles S of Selby, off A1041
- **Arch** JM Scott

Easingwold (1930)
Stillington Road, Easingwold, York YO61 3ET
- **Tel** (01347) 821486
- **Fax** (01347) 822474
- **Mem** 690
- **Sec** DB Stockley (01347) 822474
- **Pro** J Hughes (01347) 821964
- **Holes** 18 L 6627 yds Par 72 SSS 72

Recs Am–67 JP Miller
  Pro–65 G Brown
- **V'tors** U
- **Fees** D–£25 D–£30 (£30)
- **Loc** 12 miles N of York on A19. S end of Easingwold
- **Arch** Hawtree/OCM

Filey (1897)
West Ave, Filey YO14 9BQ
- **Tel** (01723) 513293
- **Fax** (01723) 514952
- **Mem** 768
- **Sec** MS Scutt
- **Pro** GM Hutchinson (01723) 513134
- **Holes** 18 L 6112 yds SSS 69
- **Recs** Am–65 P Blanchard
  Pro–64 AS Murray
- **V'tors** U H SOC
- **Fees** £21 (£27) Summer
  £16 (£21) Winter
- **Loc** 1 mile S of Filey centre
- **Arch** James Braid

Forest of Galtres (1993)
Moorlands Road, Skelton, York YO3 3RF
- **Tel** (01904) 766198
- **Fax** (01904) 766198
- **Mem** 450
- **Sec** Mrs SJ Procter
- **Pro** N Suckling
- **Holes** 18 L 6312 yds Par 72 SSS 70
- **Recs** Am–72 S Spear (1997)
  Pro–67 N Suckling (1995)
- **V'tors** U SOC
- **Fees** £16 (£21)
- **Loc** Skelton, 4 miles N of York. 1½ miles off A19
- **Arch** Simon Gidman

Forest Park (1991)
Stockton-on Forest, York YO32 9UW
- **Tel** (01904) 400425
- **Mem** 650
- **Sec** N Crossley (01904) 400688
- **Pro** None
- **Holes** 18 L 6660 yds Par 71 SSS 72
  9 L 3186 yds Par 70 SSS 70
- **Recs** Am–71
- **V'tors** U SOC
- **Fees** £16 D–£22 (£21 D–£28)
  9 hole–£8 (£10)
- **Loc** 1½ miles from E end of A64 York By-pass
- **Mis** Driving range

Fulford (1906)
Heslington Lane, York YO10 5DY
- **Tel** (01904) 413579
- **Fax** (01904) 416918
- **Mem** 700
- **Sec** R Bramley BEM MIMgt
- **Pro** B Hessay (01904) 412882
- **Holes** 18 L 6775 yds SSS 72
- **Recs** Am 66 G Harland (1989)
  Pro–62 I Woosnam (1985)
- **V'tors** By arrangement with Sec
- **Fees** £35 D–£45 (£45)
- **Loc** 2 miles S of York (A64)
- **Arch** Major C McKenzie

For list of abbreviations see page 527

Ganton (1891)
Station Road, Ganton, Scarborough YO12 4PA
Tel (01944) 710329
Fax (01944) 710922
Mem 600
Sec Maj RG Woolsey
Pro G Brown (01944) 710260
Holes 18 L 6734 yds SSS 74
Recs Am–67 G Boardman
Pro–65 N Coles
V'tors By prior arrangement
Fees On application
Loc 11 miles SW of Scarborough on A64
Arch Dunn/Vardon/Braid/Colt

Harrogate (1892)
Forest Lane Head, Harrogate HG2 7TF
Tel (01423) 863158 (Clubhouse)
Fax (01423) 860073
Mem 700
Sec G Merryweather (01423) 862999
Pro P Johnson (01423) 862547
Holes 18 L 6241 yds SSS 70
Recs Am–65 NA Fegan (1995)
Pro–63 P Scott (1994)
Ladies–69 R Skaife (1993)
V'tors WD–U WE/BH–enquire first SOC–WD exc Tues
Fees £30 D–£35 (£40)
Loc 2 miles E of Harrogate on Knaresborough road (A59)
Arch Sandy Herd

Heworth (1911)
Muncaster House, Muncastergate, York YO31 9JY
Tel (01904) 424618
Fax (01904) 426156
Mem 345 80(L) 50(J)
Sec RJ Hunt (01904) 426156
Pro S Burdett (01904) 422389
Holes 12 L 6141 yds Par 70 SSS 69
V'tors U
Fees £14 (£18)
Loc NE boundary of York (A1036)

Hunley Hall (1993)
Brotton, Saltburn TS12 2QQ
Tel (01287) 676216
Fax (01287) 678250
Mem 500
Sec E Lillie
Pro A Brook (01287) 677444
Holes 27 holes:
5948-6918 yds Par/SSS 68-73
Recs Am–66 S Fox (1998)
V'tors U SOC–exc Sun
Fees £20 (£30)
Loc 15 miles SE of Middlesbrough on A174
Mis Floodlit driving range
Arch John Morgan

Kirkbymoorside (1951)
Manor Vale, Kirkbymoorside, York YO6 6EG
Tel (01751) 431215
Mem 650

Sec AR Holmes
Holes 18 L 6101 yds SSS 69
Recs Am–65 S Dunn (1995)
Ladies–69 J Brown
V'tors U between 9.30–12.30 and after 1.30pm
Fees £18 (£25)
Loc A170 between Helmsley and Pickering

Knaresborough (1920)
Boroughbridge Road, Knaresborough HG5 0QQ
Tel (01423) 863219
Fax (01423) 869345
Mem 795
Sec Gp Capt JI Barrow (Mgr) (01423) 862690
Pro GJ Vickers (01423) 864865
Holes 18 L 6433 yds SSS 71
Recs Am–68 JR McVicar (1995)
Pro–69 A Miller (1994)
V'tors U SOC
Fees £25 (£30)
Loc 1½ miles N of Knaresborough on A6055
Arch Hawtree

Malton & Norton (1910)
Welham Park, Welham Road, Norton, Malton YO17 9QE
Tel (01653) 692959
Fax (01653) 697912
Mem 820
Sec E Harrison (01653) 697912
Pro SI Robinson (01653) 693882
Holes 27 holes:
Welham L 6456 yds SSS 71
Park L 6231 yds SSS 70
Derwent L 6267 yds SSS 70
V'tors WD–U WE–restricted on match days H SOC
Fees £22 (£28)
Loc 18 miles NE of York (A64)

Masham (1895)
Burnholme, Swinton Road, Masham, Ripon HG4 4HT
Tel (01765) 689379
Fax (01765) 688054
Mem 327
Sec (01765) 688054
Holes 9 L 6068 yds SSS 69
V'tors WD–U before 5pm WE–M BH–NA
Fees £15
Loc 10 miles N of Ripon, off A6108

Middlesbrough (1908)
Brass Castle Lane, Marton, Middlesbrough TS8 9EE
Tel (01642) 311515
Fax (01642) 319607
Mem 950
Sec BC Hunt
Pro DJ Jones (01642) 311766
Holes 18 L 6215 yds SSS 70
Recs Am–64 JW Lupton (1996)
Pro–65 D Padgett (1993)

V'tors U
Fees D–£28 (£34)
Loc 3 miles S of Middlesbrough

Middlesbrough Municipal (1977)
*Public
Ladgate Lane, Middlesbrough TS5 7YZ*
Tel (01642) 315533
Fax (01642) 300726
Mem 625
Sec JC Taylor (Hon)
Pro A Hope (01642) 300720
Holes 18 L 6333 yds SSS 70
Recs Am–67 J Wharton (1995)
Pro–67 B Gallagher (1981)
V'tors U
Fees £9.80 (£12.25)
Loc 2 miles S of Middlesbrough on A174
Mis Floodlit driving range

Oakdale (1914)
Oakdale, Harrogate HG1 2LN
Tel (01423) 567162
Fax (01423) 536030
Mem 775
Sec D Rodgers
Pro C Dell (01423) 560510
Holes 18 L 6456 yds SSS 71
Recs Am–61 M Fountain (1997)
Pro–66 P Hall (1989)
V'tors WD–U 9.30–12.30 and after 2pm SOC–WD
Fees £27 D–£40
Loc ½ mile NE of Royal Hall, Harrogate
Arch Dr A Mackenzie

Pannal (1906)
Follifoot Road, Pannal, Harrogate HG3 1ES
Tel (01423) 871641
Fax (01423) 870043
Mem 780
Sec R Braddon (01423) 872628
Pro M Burgess (01423) 872620
Holes 18 L 6622 yds SSS 72
Recs Am–62 SR Macfarlane (1984)
Pro–65 A Nicholson (1993)
V'tors WD–H 9.30–12 and after 1.30pm WE–H 11–12 and after 2.30pm SOC
Fees £40 D–£50 (£50)
Loc 2½ miles S of Harrogate, on A61
Arch Herd/Mackenzie

Pike Hills (1920)
Tadcaster Road, Askham Bryan, York YO23 3UW
Tel (01904) 700797
Fax (01904) 700797
Mem 750
Sec L Hargrave
Pro I Gradwell (01904) 708756
Holes 18 L 6146 yds SSS 69
Recs Am–67 C Weir (1995)
V'tors WD–U H before 4.30pm –M after 4.30pm SOC–WD
Fees £20 D–£26
Loc 3 miles SW of York on A64

For list of abbreviations see page 527

Richmond (1892)
Bend Hagg, Richmond DL10 5EX
Tel (01748) 825319
Mem 600
Sec BD Aston (01748) 823231
Pro P Jackson (01748) 822457
Holes 18 L 5769 yds SSS 68
Recs Am–AP Jackson
Pro–64 J Harrison, P Harrison
V'tors U
Fees D–£20 (£25 D–£30)
Loc 3 miles SW of Scotch Corner
Arch Frank Pennink

Ripon City (1905)
Palace Road, Ripon HG4 3HH
Tel (01765) 603640
Mem 650 100(L) 45(J)
Pro T Davis (01765) 600411
Holes 18 L 6120 yds SSS 69
Recs Am–61
V'tors U SOC
Fees £20 (£30)
Loc 1 mile N of Ripon on A6108
Arch ADAS

Romanby (1993)
Pay and play
Yafforth Road, Northallerton DL7 0PE
Tel (01609) 779988
Fax (01609) 779084
Mem 550
Sec G McDonnell (01609) 778855
Pro T Jenkins
Holes 18 L 6663 yds SSS 72
V'tors U SOC
Fees £15 (£20)
Loc 1 mile W of Northallerton on B6271
Mis Floodlit driving range
Arch Will Adamson

Rudding Park (1995)
Pay and play
Rudding Park, Harrogate HG3 1DJ
Tel (01423) 872100
Fax (01423) 873011
Sec M Mackaness (Sec/Mgr)
Pro S Hotham (01423) 873400
Holes 18 L 6871 yds SSS 72
Recs Am–72 R Dickenson
Pro–73 P Johnson
V'tors U H SOC
Fees £19 (£21)
Loc 2 miles S of Harrogate (A658)
Mis Driving range. Golf Academy
Arch Hawtree

Saltburn (1894)
Hob Hill, Saltburn-by-the-Sea TS12 1NJ
Tel (01287) 622812
Mem 900
Sec D Becker
Pro M Nutter (01287) 624653
Holes 18 L 5846 yds SSS 68
Recs Am–66
Pro–62 D Rees
V'tors H SOC
Fees £19 (£24)
Loc 1 mile S of Saltburn

Scarborough North Cliff (1909)
North Cliff Avenue, Burniston Road, Scarborough YO12 6PP
Tel (01723) 360786
Fax (01723) 362134
Mem 860
Sec JR Freeman
Pro SN Deller (01723) 365920
Holes 18 L 6425 yds SSS 71
Recs Am–66 F Andersson
V'tors U exc Sun before 10am and comp days H SOC
Fees £20 D–£27 (£24 D–£30)
Loc 2 miles N of Scarborough on coast road
Arch James Braid

Scarborough South Cliff (1903)
Deepdale Avenue, Scarborough YO11 2UE
Tel (01723) 360522
Fax (01723) 374737
Mem 565
Sec RK Oakes (01723) 374737
Pro AR Skingle (01723) 365150
Holes 18 L 6039 yds SSS 69
Recs Am–64 J Smith (1994)
Pro–66 MJ Slater (1987)
V'tors U H
Fees £20 (£25)
Loc 1 mile S of Scarborough

Scarthingwell (1993)
Scarthingwell, Tadcaster LS24 9DG
Tel (01937) 557878
Fax (01937) 557909
Mem 400
Pro S Footman (01937) 557864
Holes 18 L 6759 yds Par 71 SSS 72
V'tors U SOC
Fees £16 (£18)
Loc 4 miles S of Tadcaster on A162

Selby (1907)
Mill Lane, Brayton, Selby YO8 9LD
Tel (01757) 228622
Mem 749
Sec JN Proctor
Pro A Smith (01757) 228785
Holes 18 L 6246 yds SSS 70
Recs Am–65 L Walker, N Ludwell
Pro–64 D Matthew
V'tors WD–H WE–NA SOC–Wed–Fri
Fees £23 D–£25
Loc 3 miles SW of Selby, off A19 at Brayton. 5 miles N of M62 Junction 34
Arch JH Taylor/Hawtree

Settle (1895)
Giggleswick, Settle BD24 ODH
Tel (01729) 825288
Mem 250
Sec RG Bannier (01729) 823596

Yorkshire (North) 653

Holes 9 L 5414 yds SSS 66
Recs Am–62 M Gray (1996)
Pro–59 L Turner (1995)
V'tors U exc Sun–restricted SOC
Fees D–£10
Loc 1 mile N of Settle on A65
Arch Tom Vardon

Skipton (1893)
Off NW Bypass, Skipton BD23 1LL
Tel (01756) 795657
Fax (01756) 796665
Mem 720
Sec EJ Paterson
Pro P Robinson (01756) 793257
Holes 18 L 6087 yds SSS 70
Recs Am–66 BJ Mallinson (1995)
V'tors U SOC
Fees £24 (£26)
Loc 1 mile N of Skipton on A59

Teesside (1901)
Acklam Road, Thornaby TS17 7JS
Tel (01642) 676249
Fax (01642) 676252
Mem 690
Sec PB Hodgson (01642) 616516
Pro K Hall (01642) 673822
Holes 18 L 6535 yds Par 72 SSS 71
Recs Am–64 G Storm
V'tors WD–U before 4.30pm WE–U after 11am BH M before 11am SOC
Fees D–£26 (£30)
Loc 2 miles S of Stockton on A1130. 1/2 mile from A19 on A1130
Arch Makepeace/Summerville

Thirsk & Northallerton (1914)
Thornton-le-Street, Thirsk YO7 4AB
Tel (01845) 522170
Mem 500
Sec J Brown (01845) 525115
Pro R Garner (01845) 526216
Holes 18 L 6495 yds SSS 71
Recs Am–68 I Richardson
Pro–68 J Harrison
V'tors WD/Sat–U H Sun–M SOC
Fees £20 D–£25 Sat/BH–£25
Loc 2 miles N of Thirsk, nr A19 and A168 roundabout
Arch ADAS

Whitby (1892)
Sandsend Road, Low Straggleton, Whitby YO21 3SR
Tel (01947) 602768
Fax (01947) 600660
Mem 900
Sec T Graham (01947) 600660
Pro R Wood (01947) 602719
Holes 18 L 6134 yds SSS 70
Recs Am–67
Pro–68
V'tors U H SOC
Fees £20 (£25)
Loc 2 miles N of Whitby on A174

For list of abbreviations see page 527

Wilton (1952)
Wilton, Redcar TS10 4QY
Tel (01642) 465265/465886
Fax (01642) 465463
Mem 863
Sec JCP Elder (01642) 465265
Pro Pat Smillie (01642) 452730
Holes 18 L 6145 yds Par 70 SSS 69
Recs Am–64 BM Christie (1991)
Pro–68 S Hunt
Ladies–75 V Duncan (1984)
V'tors WD–U after 10am Sat–NA Sun/BH–U after 10am SOC–WD exc Tues
Fees D–£18 (D–£24)
Loc 3 miles W of Redcar on A174–signs to Wilton Castle

York (1890)
Lords Moor Lane, Strensall, York YO32 5XF
Tel (01904) 491840
Fax (01904) 491852
Mem 370 123(L) 100(J)
Sec SG Watson
Pro AB Mason (01904) 490304
Holes 18 L 6301 yds SSS 70
Recs Am–66 J Miller
Pro–67 C Tyson
V'tors U–phone Sec SOC
Fees D–£34 (£38)
Loc 4 miles N of York ring road (A1237)
Arch JH Taylor

Yorkshire (South)

Abbeydale (1895)
Twentywell Lane, Dore, Sheffield S17 4QA
Tel (0114) 236 0763
Fax (0114) 236 0762
Mem 650
Sec Mrs KM Johnston
Pro N Perry (0114) 236 5633
Holes 18 L 6419 yds SSS 71
V'tors U SOC–H by arrangement
Fees £35 (£40)
Loc 5 miles S of Sheffield, off A621

Austerfield Park (1974)
Cross Lane, Austerfield, Doncaster DN10 6RF
Tel (01302) 710841/710850
Fax (01302) 710841
Mem 350 52(L) 35(J)
Sec R Whalley (01709) 719920
Pro D Roberts
Holes 18 L 6900 yds Par 73 SSS 73
9 hole Par 3 course
Recs Am–69 D Hemsworth (1995)
Pro–67 J Brennan (1988)
V'tors U SOC
Fees £14 (£18)
Loc 2 miles N of Bawtry, on A614
Mis Driving range
Arch E & M Baker

Barnsley (1925)
Public
Wakefield Road, Staincross, Barnsley S75 6JZ
Tel (01226) 382856
Sec L Lammas
Pro (01226) 380358
Holes 18 L 5951 yds Par 69 SSS 69
Recs Am–64 RI Shaw (1988)
Pro–62 M Melling (1986)
V'tors U
Fees £9 (£9.50)
Loc 4 miles N of Barnsley on A61

Beauchief Municipal (1925)
Public
Beauchief, Abbey Lane, Sheffield S8 0DB
Tel (0114) 236 7274/262 0040
Mem 450
Sec JG Pearson (0114) 230 6720
Pro A Highfield
Holes 18 L 5452 yds SSS 66
Recs Am–65 PW Hickinson
Pro–63 P Tupling
V'tors U
Fees £9
Loc A621 Sheffield

Birley Wood (1974)
Public
Birley Lane, Sheffield S12 3BP
Tel (0114) 264 7262
Mem 294
Sec M Hollis
Pro P Ball
Holes 18 L 5483 yds SSS 67
Recs Am–66 S Pearson (1991)
Pro–67 D Muscroft (1990)
V'tors U
Fees £7 (£8)
Loc 4 miles S of Sheffield on A616. M1 Junction 30

Concord Park (1952)
Public
Shiregreen Lane, Sheffield S5 6AE
Tel (0114) 257 0274/257 0053
Sec B Shepherd
Pro None
Holes 18 L 4321 yds SSS 62
Recs Am–56 S Ridal (1991)
V'tors U
Fees £5.20
Loc M1 Junction 34, 1 mile

Crookhill Park (1974)
Public
Conisborough, Doncaster DN12 2AH
Tel (01709) 862979
Mem 500
Sec C Gouldin
Pro R Swaine
Holes 18 L 5839 yds SSS 68
Recs Am–64 A Clegg, S Clegg
Pro–70
V'tors U
Fees £8.75 (£9.95)
Loc 3 miles W of Doncaster (A630)

Doncaster (1894)
Bawtry Road, Bessacarr, Doncaster DN4 7PD
Tel (01302) 865632
Fax (01302) 865994
Mem 375
Sec RJ Perkins
Pro G Bailey (01302) 868404
Holes 18 L 6230 yds SSS 70
Recs Am–66 H Green
Pro–66 H Clark
V'tors WD–U H WE/BH–NA before 11.30am SOC–WD
Fees £20 (£25)
Loc 4½ miles S of Doncaster on A638
Arch Mackenzie/Hawtree

Doncaster Town Moor (1895)
Bawtry Road, Belle Vue, Doncaster DN4 5HU
Tel (01302) 533778
Mem 540
Sec J Stoddart
Pro SC Poole (01302) 535286
Holes 18 L 6001 yds SSS 69
Recs Am–66 P Miller (1994)
Pro–63 D Shacklady (1995)
V'tors U exc Sun–NA before 11.30am SOC
Fees £14 (£16)
Loc Inside racecourse. Clubhouse on A638

Dore & Totley (1913)
Bradway Road, Bradway, Sheffield S17 4QR
Tel (0114) 236 0492
Fax (0114) 235 3436
Mem 580
Sec JR Johnson (0114) 236 9872
Pro G Roberts (0114) 236 6844
Holes 18 L 6265 yds Par 70 SSS 70
Recs Am–65 NM Parkinson
Pro–64 P Cowen
V'tors WD–U exc Wed–NA before 1pm Sat–M Sun–NA before 11am SOC–Tues & Thurs
Fees £26
Loc 5 miles SW of Sheffield, off A61

Grange Park (1972)
Pay and play
Upper Wortley Road, Kimberworth, Rotherham S61 2SJ
Tel (01709) 558884
Sec R Charity (01709) 583400
Pro E Clark (01709) 559497
Holes 18 L 6461 yds SSS 71
Recs Am–65 M Hammond
Pro–68 G Tickell
V'tors U
Fees £10
Loc 2 miles W of Rotherham on A629
Mis Driving range

For list of abbreviations see page 527

Hallamshire (1897)
Sandygate, Sheffield S10 4LA
Tel (0114) 230 1007
Fax (0114) 230 2153
Mem 600
Sec K Sharrocks (0114) 230 2153
Pro G Tickell (0114) 230 5222
Holes 18 L 6359 yds SSS 71
Recs Am–66 W Bremner, P Nelson
Pro–63 JW Wilkinson
V'tors H SOC–WD
Fees £33 (£38)
Loc W boundary of Sheffield

Hallowes (1892)
Dronfield, Sheffield S18 6UR
Tel (01246) 413734
Mem 508
Sec R Warriss
Pro P Dunn (01246) 411196
Holes 18 L 6342 yds SSS 71
Recs Am–66 S Priest (1989),
MJ Nolan (1996)
Pro–64 PL Cowen (1991)
V'tors WD–U WE–M
Fees £20 D–£27
Loc 6 miles S of Sheffield on B6057

Hickleton (1909)
Hickleton, Doncaster DN5 7BE
Tel (01709) 896081
Fax (01709) 896081
Mem 525
Sec I Wright
Pro P Shepherd (01709) 888436
Holes 18 L 6208 yds SSS 71
Recs Am–68 SJ Mason (1998)
V'tors WD–U WE–NA before noon SOC
Fees £21 (£26)
Loc 6 miles W of Doncaster on A635
Arch Huggett/Coles

Hillsborough (1920)
Worrall Road, Sheffield S6 4BE
Tel (0114) 234 3608
Fax (0114) 234 9151
Mem 533
Sec KA Dungey (0114) 234 9151
Pro G Walker (0114) 233 2666
Holes 18 L 6035 yds SSS 70
Recs Am–64 JE Laycock (1987),
MI Mackenzie (1992)
Pro–63 CW Gray (1987)
V'tors H SOC
Fees £28 (£35)
Loc Wadsley, Sheffield
Mis Driving range

Lees Hall (1907)
Hemsworth Road, Norton, Sheffield S8 8LL
Tel (0114) 255 4402
Fax (0114) 255 2900
Mem 550
Sec JW Poulson (0114) 255 2900

Pro S Berry
Holes 18 L 6171 yds SSS 70
Recs Am–64 MA Batty
Pro–63 B Hutchinson
V'tors U SOC
Fees £20 (£30)
Loc 3 miles S of Sheffield. E of A61

Lindrick (1891)
Lindrick Common, Worksop, Notts S81 8BH
Tel (01909) 485802
Fax (01909) 488685
Mem 500
Sec Lt Cdr RJM Jack RN (01909) 475282
Pro JR King (01909) 475820
Holes 18 L 6615 yds SSS 72
Recs Am–66 R Crawford (1997)
Pro–67 C Smellie (1995)
V'tors U H–by prior arrangement exc Tues SOC–WD
Fees £45 (£45)
Loc 4 miles W of Worksop on A57. M1 Junction 31

Owston Park (1988)
Public
Owston Hall, Owston, Doncaster DN6 9JF
Tel (01302) 330821
Holes 9 L 6148 yds SSS 71
V'tors U
Fees On application
Loc 5 miles N of Doncaster on A19
Arch Michael Parker

Phoenix (1932)
Pavilion Lane, Brinsworth, Rotherham S60 5PA
Tel (01709) 363788
Fax (01709) 363788
Mem 700
Sec J Burrows (01709) 370759
Pro M Roberts (01709) 382624
Holes 18 L 6145 yds SSS 69
Recs Am–65
V'tors U
Fees D–£21
Loc 2 miles S of Rotherham. M1 Junction 34
Mis Driving range
Arch H Cotton

Renishaw Park (1911)
Golf House, Mill Lane, Renishaw, Sheffield S21 3UZ
Tel (01246) 432044
Mem 450
Sec TJ Childs
Pro J Oates (01246) 435484
Holes 18 L 6262 yds SSS 70
Recs Am–64 CS Bright
Pro–66 D Dunk
V'tors H SOC
Fees £21 D–£29.50 (£34)
Loc 7 miles SE of Sheffield. 2 miles W of M1 Junction 30

Robin Hood (1996)
Owston Hall, Owston, Doncaster DN6 9JF
Tel (01302) 722800
Fax (01302) 728885
Mem 300
Sec P Hemingway
Pro S Poole (01302) 722231
Holes 18 L 6937 yds Par 72 SSS 73
Recs Pro–68 L Turner (1998)
V'tors U SOC
Fees £12 (£14)
Loc 5 miles N of Doncaster on A19 (B1220)
Arch Will Adamson

Rother Valley Golf Centre (1997)
Mansfield Road, Wales Bar, Sheffield S31 8PE
Tel (0114) 247 3000
Fax (0114) 247 6000
Mem 600
Sec MC Shattock (Mgr)
Pro JK Ripley
Holes 18 L 6602 yds Par 72 SSS 72
9 hole Par 3 course
Recs Am–71 M Armitage (1997)
Pro–71 R Wragg (1997)
V'tors U SOC
Fees £11 (£16) Mon–£7.50
Loc Rother Valley Country Park, 2 miles S of M1 Junction 31
Mis Floodlit driving range
Arch Shattock/Roe

Rotherham (1903)
Thrybergh Park, Rotherham S65 4NU
Tel (01709) 850466
Fax (01709) 855288
Mem 400
Sec G Smalley (01709) 850812
Pro S Thornhill (01709) 850480
Holes 18 L 6324 yds SSS 70
Recs Am–65 ID Garbutt (1992),
L Westwood (1993)
Pro–66 B Hutchison
V'tors WD–U SOC
Fees £26 (£35)
Loc 4 miles E of Rotherham on A630

Roundwood (1976)
Green Lane, Rawmarsh, Rotherham S62 6LA
Tel (01709) 523471
Mem 400
Sec AW Hawke (01709) 382123
Holes 9 L 5646 yds SSS 67
V'tors WE–NA before 5pm on comp days SOC–WD
Fees £12 (£15)
Loc 2 miles N of Rotherham on A633

Sandhill (1993)
Pay and play
Little Houghton, Barnsley S72 0HW
Tel (01226) 753444
Mem 275

Sec F Andrews
Holes 18 L 6250 yds SSS 70
Recs Am–69 P Kelly (1996)
V'tors U SOC
Fees £8 (£11)
Loc 6 miles E of Barnsley, off A635
Mis Driving range
Arch John Royston

Sheffield Transport
(1923)
Meadow Head, Sheffield S8 7RE
Tel (0114) 237 3216
Mem 125
Sec AE Mason
Holes 18 L 3966 yds SSS 62
Recs Am–62 VR Hutton, E Tonks, PR Pemberton
V'tors M
Loc S of Sheffield on A61

Silkstone (1893)
Field Head, Elmhirst Lane, Silkstone, Barnsley S75 4LD
Tel (01226) 790328
Mem 600
Sec J Goulding
Pro K Guy (01226) 790128
Holes 18 L 6069 yds SSS 70
Recs Am–64 D Kershaw (1995)
V'tors WD–U SOC–WD
Fees D–£26 SOC(12+)–£38
Loc 1 mile W of M1 Junction 37 on A628

Sitwell Park (1913)
Shrogs Wood Road, Rotherham S60 4BY
Tel (01709) 541046
Fax (01709) 703637
Mem 500
Sec G Simmonite
Pro N Taylor (01709) 540961
Holes 18 L 6250 yds SSS 70
Recs Am–61 R Jones (1994)
V'tors WD–U Sat-M Sun–NA before 11.30am SOC
Fees £24 D–£28 (£28)
Loc 2½ miles E of Rotherham on A631. M18 Junction 1
Arch Dr A Mackenzie

Stocksbridge & District
(1924)
30 Royd Lane, Townend, Deepcar, Sheffield S30 5RZ
Tel (0114) 288 7479
Mem 300
Sec S Marsden (0114) 288 2003
Pro T Brookes (0114) 288 2779
Holes 18 L 5200 yds Par 65 SSS 65
Recs Am–60 I Batty (1996) Pro–61 TJ Brookes (1996)
V'tors U SOC
Fees £20 (£30)
Loc 9 miles W of Sheffield (A616)

Tankersley Park (1907)
High Green, Sheffield S30 4LG
Tel (0114) 246 8247
Mem 574
Sec PA Bagshaw
Pro I Kirk (0114) 245 5583
Holes 18 L 6212 yds Par 69 SSS 70
Recs Am–65 D Platts Pro–69 W Atkinson
V'tors WD–U WE–M SOC–WD
Fees £22 D–£26 (£26)
Loc Chapeltown, 7 miles N of Sheffield. M1 Junctions 35A/36
Arch Hawtree

Thorne (1980)
Kirton Lane, Thorne, Doncaster DN8 5RJ
Tel (01405) 812054
Sec P Kitteridge (01302) 813827
Pro RD Highfield
Holes 18 L 5366 yds SSS 65
V'tors U
Fees £7.60 (£8.60)
Loc 10 miles NE of Doncaster. M18 Junction 5/6
Arch RD Highfield

Tinsley Park (1920)
Public
High Hazel Park, Darnell, Sheffield S9 4PE
Tel (0114) 203 7435
Mem 600
Sec SP Edwards
Pro AP Highfield
Holes 18 L 6103 yds SSS 69
Recs Am–68 SJ Thorpe Pro–66 D Snell
V'tors U
Fees £7.50
Loc M1 Junction 32, 1 mile

Wath-upon-Dearne
(1904)
Abdy Rawmarsh, Rotherham S62 7SJ
Tel (01709) 872149/878609
Fax (01709) 878609
Mem 680
Sec DMC Vallance (01709) 872048
Pro C Bassett (01709) 878677
Holes 18 L 5857 yds SSS 68
V'tors WD–U WE/BH–M SOC
Fees £21
Loc Abdy Farm, 1½ miles S of Wath-upon-Dearne

Wheatley (1913)
Armthorpe Road, Doncaster DN2 5QB
Tel (01302) 831655
Mem 385 100(L) 50(J)
Pro S Fox (01302) 834085
Holes 18 L 6405 yds SSS 71
Recs Am–65 D Lawrence Pro–64 I Garbutt Ladies–63 R Hudson

V'tors U SOC
Fees £24 (£30)
Loc 3 miles NE of Doncaster

Wombwell Hillies
(1989)
Public
Wentworth View, Wombwell, Barnsley S73 0LA
Tel (01226) 754433
Sec S Rolbiecki (Mgr)
Holes 9 L 2095 yds SSS 60
V'tors U
Fees On application
Loc 4 miles SE of Barnsley

Wortley (1894)
Hermit Hill Lane, Wortley, Sheffield S35 7DP
Tel (0114) 288 8469
Fax (0114) 288 8649
Mem 400
Sec WHM Hoyland
Pro I Kirk (0114) 288 6490
Holes 18 L 6033 yds SSS 69
Recs Am–65 Pro–64
V'tors WD–U WE–NA before 10am SOC
Fees £25 (£30)
Loc 2 miles W of M1 Junction 36, off A629

Yorkshire (West)

Alwoodley (1908)
Wigton Lane, Alwoodley, Leeds LS17 8SA
Tel (0113) 268 1680
Fax (0113) 293 9458
Mem 450
Sec RCW Banks
Pro JR Green (0113) 268 9603
Holes 18 L 6686 yds SSS 73
Recs Am–67 SJM Peel Pro–68 D Fitton
V'tors SOC–WD
Fees £50 (£60)
Loc 5 miles N of Leeds on A61
Arch Dr A Mackenzie

Baildon (1896)
Moorgate, Baildon, Shipley BD17 5PP
Tel (01274) 584266
Fax (01274) 530551
Mem 500
Sec JA Cooley (01274) 586299
Pro R Masters (01274) 595162
Holes 18 L 6225 yds SSS 70
Recs Am–63 I Martin Pro–64 G Brand, D Durnian
V'tors WD–U before 5pm (restricted Tues) WE/BH–restricted
Fees £16 (£20)
Loc 5 miles N of Bradford, off A6038
Arch Tom Morris/James Braid

Ben Rhydding (1947)
High Wood, Ben Rhydding, Ilkley LS9 8SB
Tel (01943) 608759
Mem 195 60(L) 36(J)
Sec A Leverton
Holes 9 L 4711 yds SSS 64
Recs Am–64 H Barker (1987)
Pro–64 GJ Brand (1984)
V'tors WD–U exc Wed pm & Thurs am WE–M
Fees £12 (£17)
Loc 2 miles SE of Ilkley

Bingley St Ives (1931)
St Ives Estate, Bingley BD16 1AT
Tel (01274) 562436
Fax (01274) 511788
Sec Mrs M Welch
Pro R Firth (01274) 562506
Holes 18 L 6480 yds SSS 71
Recs Am–64 R Jones
Pro–62 N Faldo
Ladies–69 H Butterfield
V'tors WD–U before 4pm
Fees £24 D–£27
Loc 6 miles NW of Bradford, off A650

Bracken Ghyll (1993)
Skipton Road, Addingham, Ilkley LS29 0SL
Tel (01943) 830691 (Clubhouse)
Mem 400
Sec Chloe Walker (01943) 831207
Pro None
Holes 9 L 6560 yds Par 74 SSS 71
Recs Am–63 A Emptage (1995)
V'tors WD/BH–U WE–NA before noon on comp days SOC
Fees £10 (£14)
Loc 3 miles W of Ilkley on old A65 to Addingham
Mis Indoor practice area
Arch OCM Associates

Bradford (1891)
Hawksworth Lane, Guiseley, Leeds LS20 8NP
Tel (01943) 875570
Fax (01943) 875570
Mem 550
Sec T Eagle
Pro S Weldon (01943) 873719
Holes 18 L 6259 yds SSS 71
Recs Am–66 WJ Dowsnell
V'tors WD–U WE–NA before noon SOC–WD
Fees On application
Loc 8 miles N of Bradford, off A6038. 10 miles N of Leeds on A650

Bradford Moor (1907)
Scarr Hall, Pollard Lane, Bradford BD2 4RW
Tel (01274) 771716
Mem 350
Sec CP Bedford
Pro R Hughes (01274) 771718
Holes 9 L 5854 yds SSS 68

Recs Am–65 N Bell (1997)
Pro–69 H Waller
V'tors WD–U
Fees £8–£12
Loc 2 miles N of Bradford

Bradley Park (1978)
Public
Bradley Road, Huddersfield HD2 1PZ
Tel (01484) 223772
Fax (01484) 451613
Mem 300
Sec K Blackwell
Pro PE Reilly
Holes 18 L 6202 yds SSS 70
9 hole Par 3 course
Recs Am–69 R Hall
Pro–64 P Carman
V'tors U SOC
Fees £11 (£13)
Loc 2 miles N of Huddersfield, off A6107, M62 Junction 25
Mis Floodlit driving range

Branshaw (1912)
Branshaw Moor, Oakworth, Keighley BD22 7ES
Tel (01535) 643235
Fax (01535) 647441
Mem 525
Sec T O'Hara
Pro M Tyler (01535) 647441
Holes 18 L 5858 yds SSS 69
Recs Am–65 D Eeles (1990)
Pro–64 G Moore (1997)
V'tors WD–U SOC–WD
Fees £15 (£20)
Loc 2 miles SW of Keighley on B6143
Arch James Braid/Dr A Mackenzie

Calverley (1984)
Woodhall Lane, Pudsey LS28 5JX
Tel (0113) 256 9244
Fax (0113) 256 9244
Mem 700
Sec RP Dyson
Pro D Johnson
Holes 18 L 5527 yds SSS 67
9 hole course
Recs Am–64 D Rands
V'tors WD–U WE–pm only
Fees £12 (£17)
Loc 4 miles NE of Bradford

Castle Fields (1903)
Rastrick Common, Brighouse HD6 3HL
Mem 140
Sec J Briggs (01484) 716217
Holes 6 L 2406 yds SSS 50
Recs Am–54
V'tors M
Loc 1 mile S of Brighouse

City of Wakefield (1936)
Public
Lupset Park, Horbury Road, Wakefield WF2 8QS
Tel (01924) 367442
Sec Mrs P Ambler
Pro R Holland (01924) 360582

Holes 18 L 6319 yds SSS 70
Recs Am–67 SJ Topp (1995)
Pro–67 L Turner (1995)
Ladies–71 J Oxley
V'tors U SOC–WD
Fees On application
Loc A642, 2 miles W of Wakefield. 2 miles E of M1 Junction 39/40
Arch JSF Morrison

Clayton (1906)
Thornton View Road, Clayton, Bradford BD14 6JX
Tel (01274) 880047
Mem 190 34(L) 25(J)
Sec DA Smith (01274) 572311
Holes 9 L 5515 yds SSS 67
Recs Am–65 ND Hawkins
V'tors WD–U Sat–U Sun–after 4pm
Fees £10 D–£12 (£12)
Loc 3 miles W of Bradford, off A647

Cleckheaton & District (1900)
483 Bradford Road, Cleckheaton BD19 6BU
Tel (01274) 874118 (Clubhouse)
Fax (01274) 871382
Mem 572
Sec Mrs R Newsholme (Asst Sec) (01274) 851266
Pro M Ingham (01274) 851267
Holes 18 L 5860 yds SSS 69
Recs Am–62 CA Bloice (1985)
Pro–E Wilson (1989)
V'tors U SOC
Fees £24 D–£26 (£30)
Loc Nr M62 Junction 26-A638

Cookridge Hall G&CC
Cookridge Lane, Leeds LS16 7NL
Tel (0113) 203 0002
Fax (0113) 285 7115
Mem 524
Sec J Hall (Golf Mgr) (0113) 203 0007
Pro M Pearson
Holes 18 L 6497 yds Par 72 SSS 71
V'tors WD–U WE–U after 1pm SOC
Fees £22 (£22)
Loc 5 miles NW of Leeds, via A660
Mis Driving range. Golf Academy
Arch Karl Litten

Crosland Heath (1914)
Felks Stile Road, Crosland Heath, Huddersfield HD4 7AF
Tel (01484) 653216
Mem 320
Sec D Walker (01484) 653262
Pro J Coverley (01484) 653877
Holes 18 L 6004 yds SSS 70
Recs Am–64 P Fenton (1997)
Pro–65 S Dellar
V'tors U SOC
Fees On application
Loc 3 miles W of Huddersfield, off A62

For list of abbreviations see page 527

Crow Nest Park (1994)
Pay and play
Coach Road, Hove Edge, Brighouse HD6 2LN
Tel (01484) 401121
Fax (01422) 201216
Mem 200
Sec P Knowles (01422) 201216
Pro B Parry (01484) 401121
Holes 9 L 6020 yds Par 70 SSS 69
V'tors WD–U WE–U before noon
Fees £13 (£16)
Loc 5 miles E of Halifax. M62 Junction 25
Mis Driving range
Arch Will Adamson

Dewsbury District (1891)
The Pinnacle, Sands Lane, Mirfield WF14 8HJ
Tel (01924) 492399
Mem 650
Sec CB Rhodes
Pro N Hirst (01924) 496030
Holes 18 L 6360 yds SSS 71
Recs Am–68 P Robinson (1996) Pro–67 P Cowen (1996)
V'tors WD–U WE–M –U after 4pm SOC
Fees £18 (£18)
Loc 2 miles W of Dewsbury, off A644

East Bierley (1928)
South View Road, Bierley, Bradford BD4 6PP
Tel (01274) 681023
Mem 156 47(L) 30(J)
Sec RJ Welch (01274) 683666
Holes 9 L 4692 yds SSS 63
Recs Am–59 R Watts Pro–62 B Hill
V'tors U exc Mon–NA after 4pm Sun–NA
Fees £10 (£12.50)
Loc 4 miles SE of Bradford

Elland (1910)
Hammerstones Leach Lane, Hullen Edge, Elland HX5 0TA
Tel (01422) 372505
Mem 265
Sec AD Blackburn (01422) 372014
Pro N Krzywicki (01422) 374886
Holes 9 L 2763 yds SSS 66
Recs Am–64 C Hartland
V'tors U
Fees £14 (£25)
Loc Elland 1 mile. M62 Junction 24, signpost Blackley

Fardew (1993)
Pay and play
Nursery Farm, Carr Lane, East Morton, Keighley BD20 5RY
Tel (01274) 561229
Fax (01274) 561438
Mem 100
Sec GA Richardson
Holes 9 L 3104 yds Par 72 SSS 70

Recs Am–70 R Foster (1993) Pro–66 L Turner (1994)
V'tors U SOC
Fees 9 holes–£7 (£8) 18 holes–£12 (£14)
Loc 10 miles E of Skipton on old A650. M606, 10 miles
Arch Will Adamson

Ferrybridge 'C' (1976)
PO Box 39, Stranglands Lane, Knottingley WF11 8SQ
Tel (01977) 674188
Mem 305
Sec TD Ellis
Holes 9 L 5211 yds SSS 66
Recs Am–66 L Agar (1995)
V'tors M
Fees D–£6 (D–£7)
Loc ½ mile off A1, on B6136
Arch NE Pugh

Fulneck (1892)
Fulneck, Pudsey LS28 8NT
Tel (0113) 256 5191
Mem 290
Sec J Brogden (0113) 257 4049
Holes 9 L 5456 yds SSS 67
Recs Am–64 I Holdsworth
V'tors WD–U WE/BH–M SOC
Fees £14
Loc 5 miles W of Leeds

Garforth (1913)
Long Lane, Garforth, Leeds LS25 2DS
Tel (0113) 286 2021
Fax (0113) 286 3308
Mem 550
Sec NC Brown (0113) 286 3308
Pro K Findlater (0113) 286 2063
Holes 18 L 6304 yds SSS 70
Recs Am–63 AR Gelsthorpe
V'tors WD–U H WE/BH–M SOC
Fees £26 D–£30
Loc 9 miles E of Leeds, between Garforth and Barwick-in-Elmet

Gotts Park (1933)
Public
Armley Ridge Road, Armley, Leeds LS12 2QX
Tel (0113) 234 2019
Mem 300
Sec BJ Bond (0113) 263 5557
Pro JK Simpson
Holes 18 L 4960 yds SSS 64
V'tors U
Fees On application
Loc 2 miles W of Leeds

Halifax (1895)
Union Lane, Ogden, Halifax HX2 8XR
Tel (01422) 244171
Fax (01422) 241459
Mem 450
Sec G Horrocks-Taylor
Pro M Allison (01422) 240047
Holes 18 L 6037 yds SSS 70
Recs Am–64 A Wainwright Pro–65 W Good
V'tors U WD–parties welcome SOC

Fees On application
Loc 4 miles N of Halifax on A629
Arch Alex Herd/James Braid

Halifax Bradley Hall (1907)
Holywell Green, Halifax HX4 9AN
Tel (01422) 374108
Mem 608
Sec JR Burton (01484) 715797
Pro P Wood (01422) 370231
Holes 18 L 6213 yds SSS 70
Recs Am–65 AR Whitworth
V'tors U SOC
Fees £18 (£28)
Loc S of Halifax on A6112

Halifax West End (1913)
Paddock Lane, Highroad Well, Halifax HX2 0NT
Tel (01422) 353608
Fax (01442) 341878
Mem 340 100(L) 60(J)
Sec BR Thomas (01422) 341878
Pro D Rishworth (01422) 363293
Holes 18 L 5951 yds SSS 69
Recs Am–64 SC Ingham Pro–64 AJ Bickerdike
V'tors U SOC
Fees £20 (£25)
Loc 2 miles NW of Halifax

Hanging Heaton (1922)
Whitecross Road, Bennett Lane, Dewsbury WF12 7DT
Tel (01924) 461606
Fax (01924) 430100
Mem 550
Sec SM Simpson (01924) 461729
Pro (01924) 467077
Holes 9 L 2868 yds SSS 67
Recs Am–65 J Maguire (1997) Pro–65 M Pearson (1988)
V'tors WD–U WE–M
Fees £12
Loc Dewsbury ¾ mile (A653)

Headingley (1892)
Back Church Lane, Adel, Leeds LS16 8DW
Tel (0113) 267 3052 (Clubhouse)
Fax (0113) 281 7334
Mem 675
Sec JR Burns JP (Mgr) (0113) 267 9573
Pro SA Foster (0113) 267 5100
Holes 18 L 6298 yds SSS 70
Recs Am–66 SD Mason (1995) Pro–64 S Field (1990)
V'tors WD–U before 3.30pm SOC
Fees £30 D–£35 (£40)
Loc 5 miles NW of Leeds, off A660
Arch Dr A MacKenzie

Headley (1907)
Headley Lane, Thornton, Bradford BD13 3LX
Tel (01274) 833481
Fax (01274) 670398
Mem 270 35(L) 35(J)

For list of abbreviations see page 527

Yorkshire (West)

Sec K Allan (01274) 670398
Holes 9 L 4914 yds SSS 64
Recs Am–61 A Cording (1985)
Pro–66 M Ingham (1982)
V'tors WD–U WE–M SOC
Fees On application
Loc 5 miles W of Bradford (B6145)

Hebden Bridge (1930)
Great Mount, Wadsworth, Hebden Bridge HX7 8PH
Tel (01422) 842896
Mem 300
Sec Miss S Greenwood (01422) 842732
Holes 9 L 5242 yds SSS 67
Recs Am–66 DC Astin (1998)
V'tors WD–U
Fees £12 (£15)
Loc 1 mile N of Hebden Bridge

Horsforth (1907)
Layton Rise, Layton Road, Horsforth, Leeds LS18 5EX
Tel (0113) 258 6819
Mem 365 90(L) 85(J)
Sec E Northard
Pro N Bell (0113) 258 5200
Holes 18 L 6293 yds SSS 70
Recs Am–66 SG Hurd
Pro–65 C Hislop
V'tors U SOC
Fees D–£24 (£30)
Loc 6 miles NW of Leeds

Howley Hall (1900)
Scotchman Lane, Morley, Leeds LS27 0NX
Tel (01924) 472432
Fax (01924) 478417
Mem 492
Sec K Spencer (01924) 478417
Pro G Watkinson (01924) 473852
Holes 18 L 6058 yds Par 71 SSS 69
Recs Am–66 JD Roberts (1994)
V'tors U SOC–WD/Sun before 5pm
Fees £21 D–£25 (D–£30)
Loc 4 miles SW of Leeds on B6123

Huddersfield (1891)
Fixby Hall, Lightridge Road, Huddersfield HD2 2EP
Tel (01484) 420110
Fax (01484) 424623
Mem 576
Sec JM Seatter (Gen Mgr), Mrs D Lockett (01484) 426203
Pro P Carman (01484) 426463
Holes 18 L 6432 yds SSS 71
Recs Am–64 S Hurd (1994)
Pro–64 D Padgett (1991)
V'tors U SOC–WD
Fees £33 D–£45 (£45 D–£60)
Loc 2 miles N of Huddersfield, off A6107. M62 Junction 24

Ilkley (1890)
Myddleton, Ilkley LS29 0BE
Tel (01943) 607277
Fax (01943) 816130
Mem 530
Sec AK Hatfield (01943) 600214
Pro JL Hammond (01943) 607463
Holes 18 L 6260 yds SSS 70
Recs Am–65 AC Flather (1984)
Pro–66 CS Montgomerie (1990)
V'tors U
Fees £37 (£42)
Loc NW of Ilkley, off A65

Keighley (1904)
Howden Park, Utley, Keighley BD20 6DH
Tel (01535) 603179
Fax (01535) 604778
Mem 600
Sec JP Cole (01535) 604778
Pro M Bradley (01535) 665370
Holes 18 L 6141 yds SSS 70
Recs Am–64 AW Utley (1995)
Pro–65 J Holchaks
V'tors WD–U ex Tues Sat–NA Sun/BH–NA before 2pm
Fees £24 D–£28 (£28 D–£34)
Loc 1 mile W of Keighley on A629

Leeds (1896)
Elmete Road, Roundhay, Leeds LS8 2LJ
Tel (0113) 265 8775
Fax (0113) 232 3369
Mem 545
Sec SJ Clarkson (0113) 265 9203
Pro S Longster (0113) 265 8786
Holes 18 L 6092 yds SSS 69
Recs Am–63 M Lawson
Pro–63 P Hall
V'tors WD–U WE–M SOC
Fees £25 D–£32
Loc 4 miles NE of Leeds, off A58

Leeds Golf Centre (1994)
Pay and play
Wike Ridge Lane, Shadwell, Leeds LS17 9JW
Tel (0113) 288 6000
Fax (0113) 288 6185
Mem 500
Sec D Dourambers
Pro N Harvey
Holes 18 L 6800 yds SSS 72
12 hole Par 3 course
V'tors U SOC
Fees £12.50 (£12.50)
Loc NE of Leeds, between A58 and A61
Mis Driving range. Golf Academy
Arch Donald Steel

Lightcliffe (1907)
Knowle Top Road, Lightcliffe HX3 8SW
Tel (01422) 202459
Mem 170 95(L) 84(J)

Sec IR Philp (01422) 202054
Pro R Kershaw
Holes 9 L 5368 metres SSS 68
Recs Am–66 JR Denham, CRC Denham
V'tors WD H–exc comp days Sun am–M SOC
Fees £15 (£20)
Loc 3 miles E of Halifax (A58)

Lofthouse Hill
Leeds Road, Lofthouse Hill, Wakefield WF3 3LR
Tel (01924) 823703
Fax (01924) 823703
Sec N Todd
Pro B Janes (01924) 820048
Holes 9 L 3167 yds Par 35
V'tors M SOC
Fees 18 holes–£17.50 9 holes–£10
Loc Between Leeds and Wakefield
Mis Driving range

Longley Park (1911)
Maple Street, Huddersfield HD5 9AX
Tel (01484) 426932
Mem 400
Sec D Palliser
Pro N Jones (01484) 422304
Holes 9 L 5212 yds Par 66 SSS 66
Recs Am–61 SA Martin (1997)
Pro–65 PW Bootty
V'tors WD–U exc Thurs WE–restricted
Fees £13.50 (£16)
Loc Huddersfield ½ mile

Low Laithes (1925)
Park Mill Lane, Flushdyke, Ossett WF5 9AP
Tel (01924) 273275
Fax (01924) 266067
Mem 575
Sec KN Pinder (01924) 266067
Pro P Browning (01924) 274667
Holes 18 L 6468 yds SSS 71
Recs Am–67
Pro–68
V'tors U WE–no parties SOC–WD
Fees £19 D–£23 (£32)
Loc 2 miles W of Wakefield. M1 Junction 40
Arch Dr A Mackenzie

The Manor
Bradford Road, Drighlington, Bradford BD11 1AB
Tel (0113) 285 2644
Mem 300
Sec J Crompton (Sec/Mgr)
Pro J Crompton
Holes 18 L 6508 yds Par 72 SSS 71
Recs Am–73 J Gill (1997)
Pro–67 J Crompton (1995)
V'tors U SOC–exc Sat
Fees £15 (£15)
Loc 1 mile from M62 Junction 27, off A650
Mis Floodlit driving range. 6 holes pitch & putt
Arch David Hemstock

For list of abbreviations see page 527

Marsden (1921)
Hemplow, Marsden, Huddersfield HD7 6NN
Tel (01484) 844253
Mem 200 49(L) 22(J)
Sec D Horncastle
Holes 9 L 5702 yds SSS 68
Recs Am–63 AJ Bickerdike
Pro–A Bickerdike
V'tors WD–U Sat–NA before 4pm Sun–M SOC
Fees £10
Loc 8 miles W of Huddersfield, off A62
Arch Dr A Mackenzie

Meltham (1908)
Thick Hollins Hall, Meltham, Huddersfield HD7 3DQ
Tel (01484) 850227
Fax (01484) 850227
Mem 500
Sec J Holdsworth (Hon)
Pro PF Davies (01484) 851521
Holes 18 L 6379 yds SSS 70
Recs Am–67 AG Oldham
V'tors H
Fees £20 (£25)
Loc 5 miles SW of Huddersfield (B6107)

Mid Yorkshire (1993)
Havercroft Lane, Darrington, Pontefract WF8 3BP
Tel (01977) 704522
Fax (01977) 600823
Mem 600
Sec IM Collins (Mgr)
Pro W Heywood (01977) 600844
Holes 18 L 6340 yds SSS 71
V'tors U H SOC
Fees £15 (£25)
Loc Nr A1/M62 junction
Mis Floodlit driving range
Arch Steve Marnoch

Middleton Park (1933)
Public
Ring Road, Beeston Park, Middleton LS10 3TN
Tel (0113) 270 9506
Mem 310
Sec TC Foster (0113) 252 2215
Pro S Shaw
Holes 18 L 5233 yds SSS 66
Recs Am–63 S Nicholson
V'tors U
Fees On application
Loc 3 miles S of Leeds

Moor Allerton (1923)
Coal Road, Wike, Leeds LS17 9NH
Tel (0113) 266 1154
Fax (0113) 237 1124
Mem 1200
Sec J Denton (Hon)
Pro R Lane (0113) 266 5209
Holes 27 holes: 6470–6843 yds SSS 73–74
Recs Am–65 K Wallbank (1994) Pro–65 B Waites
V'tors WD/Sat–U Sun–NA SOC
Fees £41 D–£46 (£66 D–£76)
Loc 5½ miles N of Leeds, off A61
Mis Driving range
Arch Robert Trent Jones Sr

Moortown (1909)
Harrogate Road, Leeds LS17 7DB
Tel (0113) 268 6521
Fax (0113) 268 0986
Mem 580
Sec CA Moore
Pro B Hutchinson (0113) 268 3536
Holes 18 L 6826 yds SSS 74
Recs Am–69 C Turner, R Treweek Pro–66 D McPherson
V'tors H
Fees £42 D–£50 (£47 D–£55)
Loc 5½ miles N of Leeds on A61
Arch Dr A Mackenzie

Normanton (1903)
Snydale Road, Normanton, Wakefield WF6 1PA
Tel (01924) 892943
Mem 300
Sec J McElhinney
Pro M Evans (01924) 220134
Holes 9 L 5323 yds SSS 66
Recs Am–65 R Booth (1992) Pro–65 A Wright (1991) Ladies–69 D Evans (1992)
V'tors U exc Sun–NA
Fees On application
Loc 1 mile from M62 Junction 31. A655 towards Wakefield

Northcliffe (1921)
High Bank Lane, Shipley, Bradford BD18 4LJ
Tel (01274) 584085
Fax (01274) 596731
Mem 750
Sec HR Archer (01274) 596731
Pro M Hillas (01274) 587193
Holes 18 L 6104 yds SSS 69
Recs Am–64 J Firth (1996) Pro–67 M James
V'tors U SOC
Fees £20 (£25)
Loc 3 miles NW of Bradford, off A650 Keighley road
Arch James Braid

Otley (1906)
West Busk Lane, Otley LS21 3NG
Tel (01943) 461015
Fax (01943) 850387
Mem 700
Sec (01943) 465329
Pro (01943) 463403
Holes 18 L 6225 yds SSS 70
Recs Am–65 M Wood (1966) Pro–62 GJ Brand (1988)
V'tors U exc Sat–NA SOC
Fees £26 (£33)
Loc 1 mile W of Otley, off A6038

Oulton Park (1990)
Public
Oulton, Rothwell, Leeds LS26 8EX
Tel (0113) 282 3152
Fax (0113) 282 6290
Mem 390
Sec A Booth (Mgr)
Pro S Gromett
Holes 18 L 6479 yds SSS 71 9 L 3287 yds SSS 35
Recs Am–69 A Cole (1995) Pro–65 P Wesselingh (1995)
V'tors U SOC
Fees 18 hole:£10–£20
Loc 5 miles SE of Leeds, off A642. N of M62 Junction 30
Mis Driving range
Arch Alliss/Thomas

Outlane (1906)
Slack Lane, Outlane, Huddersfield HD3 3YL
Tel (01422) 374762
Fax (01422) 311789
Mem 500
Sec A Armstrong
Pro D Chapman
Holes 18 L 6010 yds SSS 70
Recs Am–66 JJ Barrow Pro–67 D Chapman
V'tors U SOC
Fees £18 (£27)
Loc 4 miles W of Huddersfield, off A640. M62 Junction 23

Painthorpe House (1961)
Painthorpe Lane, Crigglestone, Wakefield WF4 3HE
Tel (01924) 255083
Fax (01924) 252022
Mem 180
Sec H Kershaw (01924) 274527
Holes 9 L 4520 yds SSS 62
Recs Am–62 J Turner (1998) Pro–63 (1998)
V'tors U exc Sun–NA
Fees £6 Sat–£10
Loc 1 mile SE of M1 Junction 39

Phoenix Park (1922)
Dick Lane, Thornbury, Bradford BD3 7AT
Tel (01274) 667573
Mem 180
Sec C Lally (01274) 668218
Pro None
Holes 9 L 4982 yds SSS 64
Recs Am–61 S Carey
V'tors WD/BH–U WE–NA
Fees On application
Loc Thornbury Roundabout (A647)

Pontefract & District (1900)
Park Lane, Pontefract WF8 4QS
Tel (01977) 792241
Fax (01977) 792245
Mem 841
Sec WT Smith (Mgr) (01977) 792241

For list of abbreviations see page 527

Pro NJ Newman (01977) 706806 **Holes** 18 L 6227 yds SSS 70 **Recs** Am–63 DC Rooke Pro–67 GW Townhill **V'tors** I SOC–WD exc Wed **Fees** £25 (£32) **Loc** Pontefract 1 mile on B6134. M62 Junction 32	**Pro** JA Pape (0113) 266 1686 **Holes** 9 L 5322 yds SSS 65 **Recs** Am–61 R Taylor Pro–62 M Bembridge **V'tors** U **Fees** On application **Loc** N of Leeds, off Moortown Ring Road	**Loc** 6 miles N of Bradford on A650 **Arch** Colt/Alison/Mackenzie/Braid ## Silsden (1913) *Brunthwaite, Silsden, Keighley BD20 0HN* **Tel** (01535) 652998 **Fax** (01535) 652998 **Mem** 300 **Sec** G Davey **Holes** 14 L 5018 yds SSS 65 **Recs** Am–61 **V'tors** Sat-restricted Sun–U after 1pm **Fees** On application **Loc** 5 miles N of Keighley, off A6034

Pontefract Park (1973)
Public
Park Road, Pontefract WF8
Tel (01977) 702799
Holes 18 L 4068 yds SSS 62
V'tors U
Fees On application
Loc Between Pontefract and M62 roundabout, nr racecourse

Ryburn (1910)
Norland, Sowerby Bridge, Halifax HX6 3QP
Tel (01422) 831355
Mem 200
Sec J Hoyle (01422) 843070
Holes 9 L 4907 yds SSS 64
Recs Am–64 DS Lumb (1987)
Pro–61 M Pearson (1987)
V'tors U
Fees £15 (£20)
Loc 3 miles S of Halifax

Queensbury (1923)
Brighouse Road, Queensbury, Bradford BD13 1QF
Tel (01274) 882155
Mem 230 55(L) 40(J)
Sec G Ralph
Pro J Ambler (01274) 816864
Holes 9 L 5102 yds SSS 65
Recs Am–64 S Rogers, H Wilkerson
Pro–63 P Cowan
V'tors U
Fees £15 (£30)
Loc 4 miles SW of Bradford (A647)

Sand Moor (1926)
Alwoodley Lane, Leeds LS17 7DJ
Tel (0113) 268 1685
Fax (0113) 268 5180
Mem 540
Sec BF Precious (0113) 268 5180
Pro P Tupling (0113) 268 3925
Holes 18 L 6429 yds SSS 71
Recs Am–63 SR Cage (1993)
Pro–62 S Holden (1991)
V'tors WD-H by arrangement WE–NA
Fees £32 (£40)
Loc 5 miles N of Leeds, off A61
Arch Dr A Mackenzie

South Bradford (1906)
Pearson Road, Odsal, Bradford BD6 1BH
Tel (01274) 679195
Mem 200
Pro I Marshall (01274) 673346
Holes 9 L 6004 yds SSS 69
Recs Am–65 GM Yarnold
Pro–67 S Miguel, A Caygill
V'tors WD–U WE–M
Fees On application
Loc Bradford 2 miles, nr Odsal Stadium

Rawdon (1896)
Buckstone Drive, Micklefield Lane, Rawdon LS19 6BD
Tel (0113) 250 6040
Mem 220 55(L) 50(J)
Sec RA Adams (0113) 250 6064
Pro (0113) 250 5017
Holes 9 L 5982 yds SSS 69
Recs Am–64 A Coverdale
V'tors WD–H WE/BH–M SOC
Fees £16
Loc 6 miles NW of Leeds nr A65/A658 junction

Scarcroft (1937)
Syke Lane, Leeds LS14 3BQ
Tel (0113) 289 2263
Mem 580
Sec TB Davey MBE (Gen Mgr) (0113) 289 2311
Pro D Tear (0113) 289 2780
Holes 18 L 6426 yds SSS 71
Recs Am–64 J Roberts (1995)
Pro–65 D Padgett (1990)
V'tors WD–U WE/BH–M or by arrangement SOC–WD exc Mon
Fees £28 D–£35 (£40)
Loc 7 miles N of Leeds, off A58

South Leeds (1914)
Gipsy Lane, Ring Road, Beeston, Leeds LS11 5TU
Tel (0113) 270 0479
Mem 450
Sec J Neal (0113) 277 1876
Pro M Lewis (0113) 270 2598
Holes 18 L 5865 yds SSS 68
Recs Am–63 J Law
Pro–68 J Pitts
V'tors WD–U WE–M SOC
Fees £18 (£25)
Loc 4 miles S of Leeds. 2 miles from M62 and M1

Riddlesden (1927)
Howden Rough, Riddlesden, Keighley BD20 5QN
Tel (01535) 602148
Mem 400
Sec Mrs KM Brooksbank (01535) 607246
Holes 18 L 4295 yds Par 63 SSS 61
Recs Am–60 M Mitchell (1987)
Pro–59 P Cowan (1983)
V'tors U exc Sun–NA before 2pm
Fees £15 (£20)
Loc 1 mile from Riddlesden, off Scott Lane West. 3 miles N of Keighley, off A650

Shipley (1896)
Beckfoot Lane, Cottingley Bridge, Bingley BD16 1LX
Tel (01274) 563212
Fax (01274) 568652
Email shipley.gc@btinternet.com
Mem 600
Sec GM Shaw (01274) 568652
Pro JR Parry (01274) 563674
Holes 18 L 6218 yds SSS 70
Recs Am–65 B Mallinson (1997)
Pro–64 N Bingham (1987)
V'tors WD–U exc Tues–NA before 2pm Sat–NA before 4pm
Fees £27 (£32)

Temple Newsam (1923)
Public
Temple Newsam Road, Halton, Leeds LS15 0LN
Tel (0113) 264 5624
Mem 500
Sec G Gower
Pro J Pape (0113) 264 7362
Holes Lord Irwin 18 L 6448 yds SSS 71; Lady Dorothy Wood 18 L 6029 yds SSS 70
V'tors U SOC
Fees £7.50 (£9) Summer £7 (£8.50) Winter
Loc 5 miles E of Leeds, off A63

Roundhay (1923)
Public
Park Lane, Leeds LS8 2EJ
Tel (0113) 266 2695
Mem 340
Sec RH McLauchlan

Todmorden (1894)
Rive Rocks, Cross Stone, Todmorden 0L14 8RD
Tel (01706) 812986
Mem 180 40(L) 30(J)
Sec PH Eastwood

For list of abbreviations see page 527

Holes 9 L 5878 yds SSS 68
Recs Am–67 G Morgan, J May
 Pro–68 B Hunt
V'tors WD/BH–U WE–M SOC–WD
Fees £15 (£20)
Loc 1 mile N of Todmorden, off A646

Wakefield (1891)
28 Woodthorpe Lane, Sandal, Wakefield WF2 6JH
Tel (01924) 255104
Fax (01924) 242752
Mem 500
Sec JW Wood
 (01924) 258778
Pro IM Wright
 (01924) 255380
Holes 18 L 6642 yds SSS 72
Recs Am–66 S Cage (1992)
 Pro–68 HW Muscroft (1982)
V'tors U SOC–Wed–Fri
Fees £22 (£30)
Loc 3 miles S of Wakefield on A61. M1 Junction 39

Waterton Park (1995)
The Balk, Walton, Wakefield WF2 6QL
Tel (01924) 259525
Fax (01924) 256969
Mem 650
Sec J Newton
Pro P Hall (01924) 255557
Holes 18 L 6843 yds Par 72 SSS 73
Recs Am–74 P Caddies
V'tors WD–H SOC
Fees D–£30
Loc 4 miles SE of Wakefield centre
Mis Driving range
Arch Simon Gidman

West Bowling (1898)
Newall Hall, Rooley Lane, Bradford BD5 8LB
Tel (01274) 724449
Fax (01274) 393207
Mem 500
Sec HR Archer
 (01274) 393207
Pro IA Marshall
 (01274) 728036
Holes 18 L 5769 yds SSS 68
Recs Am–65 D Chalmers (1995)
V'tors WD–U H SOC
Fees £24 (£30)
Loc Junction of M606 and Bradford Ring Road East

West Bradford (1900)
Chellow Grange, Haworth Road, Bradford BD9 6NP
Tel (01274) 542767
Fax (01274) 482079
Mem 450
Sec GA Nixon (Hon)
Pro NM Barber
 (01274) 542102
Holes 18 L 5723 yds SSS 68
Recs Am–62 P Thomas (1997)
 Pro–66
V'tors U
Fees £20 (£20)
Loc 3 miles W of Bradford (B6269)

Wetherby (1910)
Linton Lane, Linton, Wetherby LS22 4JF
Tel (01937) 580089
Fax (01937) 581915
Mem 630
Sec JR Nicholson
Pro D Padgett (01937) 583375
Holes 18 L 6235 yds SSS 70
Recs Am–63 S Dyson (1996)
 Pro–63 JR Green (1997)
V'tors WE–U after 10am SOC–WD
Fees £25 (£36)
Loc ¾ mile W of Wetherby. A1 Wetherby roundabout

Whitwood (1987)
Public
Altofts Lane, Whitwood, Castleford WF10 5PZ
Tel (01977) 512835
Sec S Hicks (Hon)
Pro R Holland
Holes 9 L 6176 yds SSS 69
V'tors WD–U WE–booking necessary
Fees On application
Loc 2 miles SW of Castleford (A655). M62 Junction 31

Willow Valley (1994)
Pay and play
Clifton, Brighouse HD6 4JB
Tel (01274) 878624
Fax (01274) 852805
Mem 200
Sec L Stone
Pro J Haworth
Holes 18 & 9 hole courses
Recs Am–75
 Pro–73

V'tors U
Fees 18 hole:£22 (£27)
 9 hole:£6.50 (£7)
Loc SW of Leeds, M62 Junction 25
Mis Driving range
Arch Jonathan Gaunt

Woodhall Hills (1905)
Woodhall Road, Calverley, Pudsey LS28 5UN
Tel (0113) 256 4771 (Clubhouse)
Mem 450
Sec ID Mackland (0113) 255 4594
Pro W Lockett (0113) 256 2857
Holes 18 L 6001 yds SSS 69
Recs Am–63 AJ Dufton
V'tors WD–U Sat–U after 4.30pm
 Sun–U after 9.30am
Fees £15 (£25 After 2pm–£15)
Loc 4 miles E of Bradford, off A647, by Calverley Golf Club

Woodsome Hall (1922)
Woodsome Hall, Fenay Bridge, Huddersfield HD8 0LQ
Tel (01484) 602971
Fax (01484) 608260
Mem 394 194(L) 103(J)
Sec AS Guest
Pro M Higginbottom
 (01484) 602034
Holes 18 L 6080 yds SSS 69
Recs Am–65 M Broadbent
 Pro–65 D Jagger
V'tors U H exc Tues–NA before 4pm SOC
Fees £27.50 (£35)
Loc 6 miles SE of Huddersfield on A629 Penistone road

Woolley Park (1995)
Woolley, Wakefield WF4 2JS
Tel (01226) 380144 (Bookings)
Fax (01226) 390295
Mem 500
Sec D Rowbottom
 (Prop) (01226) 382209
Pro J Baldwin
Holes 18 L 6471 yds Par 70 SSS 71
V'tors WD–U WE–restricted SOC
Fees £10 (£15)
Loc 5 miles S of Wakefield on A61. M1 Junction 38, 2 miles
Arch M Shattock

Ireland

Co Antrim

Antrim (1997)
Allen Park Golf Centre, 45 Castle Road, Antrim
Tel (01849) 429001
Fax (01849) 429001
Mem 235
Sec Marie Agnew (Mgr)
Pro S Hamill
Holes 18 L 6110 m Par 72 SSS 72
V'tors U
Fees £11 (£13)
Loc Antrim
Mis Driving range

Ballycastle (1890)
Cushendall Road, Ballycastle
BT64 6QP
Tel (012657) 62536
Fax (012657) 69909
Mem 920
Sec BJ Dillon (Hon)
Pro I McLaughlin (012657) 62506
Holes 18 L 5812 yds SSS 69
Recs Am–66 F Fleming (1962), J McAleese, RJ McCoy, E Hughes
Pro–64 F Daly
V'tors U H SOC
Fees £20 (£28)
Loc Between Portrush and Cushendall (A2)

Ballyclare (1923)
25 Springvale Road, Ballyclare
BT39 9JW
Tel (01960) 342352 (Clubhouse)
Fax (01960) 322696
Mem 440
Sec H McConnell (01960) 322696
Holes 18 L 5840 yds SSS 71
Recs Am–66 P Thompson
Pro–69 S Hamill
V'tors WD–U WE–NA before 4pm
Fees £16 (£22)
Loc 1½ miles N of Ballyclare. 14 miles N of Belfast
Arch T McAuley

Ballymena (1902)
128 Raceview Road, Ballymena
BT42 4HY
Tel (01266) 861207/861487
Mem 824
Sec C McAuley (Hon)
Pro K Revie
Holes 18 L 5245 m Par 68 SSS 67
Recs Am–62 D Cunning
V'tors WD/Sun–U SOC
Fees £15 (£20)
Loc 2 miles E of Ballymena on A42

Bentra
Public
Slaughterford Road, Whitehead
BT38 9TG
Tel (01960) 378996
Sec N Houston (01960) 351711
Holes 9 L 3155 yds Par 37 SSS 35
V'tors U
Fees £6.75 (£10.50)
Loc 4 miles N of Carrickfergus on A2 Larne road

Bushfoot (1890)
50 Bushfoot Road, Portballintrae
BT57 8RR
Tel (012657) 31317
Fax (012657) 31852
Mem 860
Sec J Knox Thompson (Sec/Mgr)
Holes 9 L 5876 yds SSS 67
Recs Am–63 R Sloan (1997)
V'tors U Sat–NA after noon SOC
Fees £15 (£20)
Loc 1 mile N of Bushmills. 4 miles E of Portrush

Cairndhu (1928)
192 Coast Road, Ballygally, Larne
BT40 2QC
Tel (01574) 583248
Fax (01574) 583324
Mem 875
Sec N Moore (01574) 583324
Pro R Walker (01574) 583417
Holes 18 L 6112 yds SSS 69
Recs Am–64 B McMillen, R Houston
Pro–64 D Jones, P Townsend
V'tors U exc Sat–NA
Fees £18 (£24) Mon/Wed–£15
Loc 4 miles N of Larne
Arch JSF Morrison

Carrickfergus (1926)
35 North Road, Carrickfergus
BT38 8LP
Tel (01960) 363713
Fax (01960) 363023
Mem 850
Sec RJ Campbell (Sec/Mgr)
Pro R Stevenson (01960) 351803
Holes 18 L 5752 yds SSS 68
Recs Am–64 R Donald
Pro–66 T Halpin
V'tors U
Fees £14 (£20)
Loc 8 miles E of Belfast, off A2

Cushendall (1937)
21 Shore Road, Cushendall
BT44 0QQ
Tel (012667) 71318
Mem 824

Sec S McLaughlin (012667) 58366
Holes 9 L 4834 m SSS 63
Recs Am–62 A McCallin (1995)
V'tors WE–restricted SOC
Fees £10 (£15)
Loc Cushendall, 25 miles N of Larne

Down Royal (1990)
Dungarton Road, Maze, Lisburn
BT27
Tel (01846) 621339
Fax (01846) 621339
Mem 52
Sec J Tinnion (Mgr)
Holes 18 L 6058 m Par 72 SSS 69
Recs Am–73
V'tors U
Fees £14 (£17)
Loc Lisburn
Arch Stewart Assoc

Galgorm Castle (1997)
200 Galgorm Road, Ballymena
BT42 1HL
Tel (0801) 266 650210
Fax (0801) 266 651151
Mem 400
Sec S Headley (Mgr)
Pro L Callan
Holes 18 L 6724 yds Par 72 SSS 72
V'tors U SOC
Fees £18 (£24)
Loc Ballymena

Gracehill (1995)
141 Ballinlea Road, Stranocum, Ballymoney BT53 8PX
Tel (012657) 51209
Fax (012657) 51074
Mem 320
Sec M McClure (Mgr)
Pro J Gillen, Mrs M Gillen
Holes 18 L 6600 yds Par 72
V'tors U
Fees £15–£18 (£25)
Loc 6 miles N of Ballymoney (B66)
Arch Frank Ainsworth

Greenacres (1996)
153 Ballyrobert Road, Ballyclare
BT39 9RT
Tel (01960) 354111
Fax (01960) 354166
Mem 267
Sec M Brown
Holes 18 L 6020 yds Par 71 SSS 68
V'tors U
Fees £12 Fri–£16 (£18)
Loc 3 miles from Corrs Corner on B56
Mis Floodlit driving range

For list of abbreviations see page 527

Co Antrim

Greenisland (1894)
156 Upper Road, Greenisland, Carrickfergus BT38 8RW
Tel (01232) 862236
Mem 510
Sec J Wyness (01232) 864583
Holes 9 L 5536 m Par 71 SSS 69
Recs Am–65
V'tors WD–U Sat–NA before 5pm SOC–exc Sat
Fees £12 (£18)
Loc 9 miles NE of Belfast
Arch H Middleton

Lambeg (1986)
Bells Lane, Lambeg, Lisburn BT27 4QH
Tel (01) 846 662738
Mem 200
Sec F Hazley (Hon)
Pro I Murdock
Holes 18 L 4139 m Par 66 SSS 62
Recs Am–64 A Mason (1993)
V'tors U SOC
Fees £6.70 (£7.80)
Loc SW of Belfast, off Lisburn road

Larne (1894)
54 Ferris Bay Road, Islandmagee, Larne BT40 3RJ
Tel (01) 960 382228
Mem 420
Sec KJ Hedley (Hon)
Holes 9 L 6288 yds SSS 70
Recs Am–66 IA Nesbitt, BR Hobson
Pro–68 N Drew
V'tors WD–U WE–M after 5pm SOC–WD/Sun
Fees £8 (£15)
Loc 6 miles N of Whitehead on Browns Bay road
Arch George Baillie

Lisburn (1891)
68 Eglantine Road, Lisburn BT27 5RQ
Tel (01846) 677216
Fax (01846) 603608
Mem 1421
Sec GE McVeigh (Sec/Mgr)
Pro BR Campbell (01846) 677217
Holes 18 L 6647 yds SSS 72
Recs Am–65 P Grant (1990)
Pro–64 D Feherty (1989)
V'tors WD–U WE–M SOC–Mon/Thurs/Fri
Fees £25 (£30)
Loc 3 miles S of Lisburn on A3
Arch Hawtree

Mallusk (1992)
Mallusk, Newtownabbey BT36 2RF
Mem 75
Sec J Smith (Mgr)
Holes 9 L 4444 m SSS 62
V'tors U
Fees £6.50 (£8.75)
Loc 4 miles NW of Newtownabbey (B95)

Massereene (1895)
51 Lough Road, Antrim BT41 4DQ
Tel (01849) 429293
Fax (01849) 487661
Mem 850
Sec Mrs S Greene (01849) 428096
Pro J Smyth (01849) 464074
Holes 18 L 6614 yds SSS 71
Recs Am–66 T Coulter
V'tors U SOC
Fees £20 (£25)
Loc 1 mile S of Antrim

Royal Portrush (1888)
Dunluce Road, Portrush BT56 8JQ
Tel (01265) 822311
Fax (01265) 823139
Mem 1042 256(L)
Sec Miss W Erskine
Pro DA Stevenson (01265) 823335
Holes Dunluce 18 L 6772 yds SSS 73; Valley 18 L 6273 yds SSS 70; Skerries-9 hole course
Recs Dunluce Am–67 G McGimpsey
Pro–66 J Hargreaves
Valley Am–65 MJC Hoey
V'tors WD–I H exc Wed & Fri pm–NA Sat–NA before 3pm Sun–NA before 10.30am SOC
Fees Dunluce: £60 (£70) Valley: £24 (£32)
Loc Portrush Coastal Rd ½ mile
Arch HS Colt

Whitehead (1904)
McCrae's Brae, Whitehead, Carrickfergus BT38 9NZ
Tel (01960) 353792
Fax (01960) 353631
Mem 944
Sec J Niblock (Sec/Mgr) (01960) 353631
Pro C Farr (01960) 353118
Holes 18 L 6426 yds SSS 71
Recs Am–68 A Hope
V'tors WD–U WE–M SOC–exc Sat
Fees £13 (£19)
Loc ½ mile from Whitehead, off road to Island Magee

Co Armagh

Ashfield (1990)
Freeduff, Cullyhanna, Newry BT15
Tel (01693) 868180
Mem 150
Sec J Quinn (Sec/Mgr)
Pro E Maney
Holes 18 L 5110 m Par 69 SSS 67
V'tors U
Fees On application
Loc 6 miles S of Newtownhamilton (B135)
Mis Driving range
Arch Frank Ainsworth

County Armagh (1893)
Newry Road, Armagh BT60 1EN
Tel (01861) 522501
Fax (01861) 525861
Mem 900
Sec M Grant (01861) 525861
Pro A Rankin (01861) 525864
Holes 18 L 6184 yds SSS 69
V'tors U SOC–WD
Fees £12 (£18)
Loc 40 miles SW of Belfast by M1

Edenmore (1992)
Drumnabreeze Road, Magheralin, Craigavon BT67 0RH
Tel (01846) 611310
Fax (01846) 613310
Mem 332
Sec K Logan (Sec/Mgr)
Holes 18 L 6244 yds Par 71 SSS 70
Recs Am–70 W Saunders Jr (1998)
V'tors U SOC
Fees £12 Fri–£13 Sat–£15
Loc 4 miles E of Lurgan (A3)
Arch F Ainsworth

Lurgan (1893)
The Demesne, Lurgan BT67 9BN
Tel (01762) 322087 (Clubhouse)
Fax (01762) 325306
Mem 878
Sec Mrs G Turkington
Pro D Paul (01762) 321068
Holes 18 L 5836 m SSS 70
Recs Am–65 T Cummins (1990)
Pro–65 B Todd
V'tors U SOC–Mon/Thurs/Fri am/Sun am
Fees £15 (£20)
Loc Nr Brownlow Castle, Lurgan
Arch Frank Pennink

Portadown (1906)
192 Gilford Road, Portadown BT63 5LF
Tel (01762) 355356
Mem 1004
Sec Mrs ME Holloway
Pro P Stevenson (01762) 334655
Holes 18 L 6119 yds SSS 70
Recs Am–A Poole (1996)
Pro–63
V'tors WD–U exc Tues
Fees £16 (£20)
Loc 3 miles S of Portadown, towards Gilford

Silverwood (1983)
Public
Turmoyra Lane, Silverwood, Lurgan BT66 6NG
Tel (01762) 326606
Fax (01762) 347272
Mem 250
Sec G Coupland (Sec/Mgr)
Pro D Paul (01762) 326606
Holes 18 L 6459 yds Par 72 SSS 71
V'tors U
Fees £10 (£14)
Loc Lurgan 1 mile. M1 Junction 10
Mis Floodlit driving range

For list of abbreviations see page 527

Tandragee (1922)
Markethill Road, Tandragee BT62 2ER
Tel (01762) 840727 (Clubhouse)
Fax (01762) 840664
Mem 1210
Sec B Carson (01762) 841272
Pro P Stevenson (01762) 841761
Holes 18 L 5754 m Par 71 SSS 70
Recs Am–62 P Topley
Pro–65 W Sullivan (1983)
V'tors U SOC
Fees £15 (£21)
Loc 8 miles S of Portadown on A27
Arch F Hawtree

Belfast

Ballyearl Golf Centre
Public
585 Doagh Road, Newtownabbey BT36 5RZ
Tel (01232) 848287
Fax (01232) 844896
Pro J Robinson (01232) 840899
Holes 9 L 2362 yds Par 3 course
V'tors U
Fees £4.50 (£5.30)
Loc N of Mossley on B59, via A8
Mis Floodlit driving range

Balmoral (1914)
518 Lisburn Road, Belfast BT9 6GX
Tel (01) 232 381514
Fax (01) 232 666759
Mem 925
Sec RC McConkey (Mgr)
Pro G Bleakley (01232) 667747
Holes 18 L 5909 m SSS 70
Recs Am–66 M Wilson
Pro–64 D Jones
V'tors U exc Sat SOC–Mon & Thurs
Fees £20 (£30)
Loc 2 miles S of Belfast by Kings Hall

Belvoir Park (1927)
Church Road, Newtownbreda, Belfast BT8 4AN
Tel (01232) 491693
Fax (01232) 646113
Mem 1100
Sec KH Graham (01232) 491693
Pro GM Kelly (01232) 646714
Holes 18 L 6501 yds SSS 71
Recs Am–66 TS Anderson,
JN Browne
Pro–65 G Fairweather,
P Walton (1995)
V'tors U exc Sat–NA
Fees £33 (£38)
Loc 3 miles S of Belfast centre, off Newcastle road
Arch HS Colt

Cliftonville (1911)
Westland Road, Belfast BT14 6NH
Tel (01232) 744158/746295
Mem 429
Sec JM Henderson (Hon)
Holes 9 L 6242 yds SSS 70
Recs Am–66 WRA Tennant,
IA Nesbitt, B Doherty Jr,
M Donnelly
Pro–67 S Hamill
V'tors U exc Sat
Fees £12 (£15)
Loc Belfast

Dunmurry (1905)
91 Dunmurry Lane, Dunmurry, Belfast BT17 9JS
Tel (01232) 610834
Fax (01232) 602540
Mem 493 127(L) 117(J)
Sec ID McBride (Sec/Mgr)
Pro J Dolan (01232) 621314
Holes 18 L 5832 yds SSS 68
Recs Am–64 D Flannagan
Pro–67 P Leonard
V'tors Tues & Thurs–NA after 5pm
Sat–NA before 5pm SOC
Fees £17 (£26) SOC–£16 (£20)
Loc Belfast 5 miles
Arch T McAuley

Fortwilliam (1891)
Downview Avenue, Belfast B15 4EZ
Tel (01232) 370770
Fax (01232) 781891
Mem 1100
Sec M Purdy
Pro P Hanna (01232) 770980
Holes 18 L 5973 yds SSS 69
Recs Am–67 A O'Neill
Pro–65 P Leonard
V'tors U SOC
Fees £20 (£27)
Loc 2 miles N of Belfast on A2

Gilnahirk (1983)
Public
Manns Corner, Upper Braniel Road, Belfast BT5 7TX
Tel (01232) 448477
Mem 200
Sec H Moore
Pro K Gray
Holes 9 L 2699 m SSS 68
Recs Am–65 T McIver (1993)
V'tors U
Fees On application
Loc 3 miles SE of Belfast, off A23

The Knock Club (1895)
Summerfield, Dundonald, Belfast BT16 2QX
Tel (01232) 482249
Fax (01232) 483251
Mem 900
Sec SG Managh (01232) 483251
Pro G Fairweather
(01232) 483825
Holes 18 L 6407 yds SSS 71
Recs Am–66 DT Alderdice
Pro–69 PR McGuirk
V'tors U SOC–Mon & Thurs
Fees D–£20 (£25)
Loc 4 miles E of Belfast on the Upper Newtownards Road
Arch Colt/Mackenzie/Alison

Malone (1895)
240 Upper Malone Road, Dunmurry, Belfast BT17 9LB
Tel (01232) 612695
Fax (01232) 431394
Mem 759 379(L) 211(J)
Sec JNS Agate (01232) 612758
Pro M McGee (01232) 614917
Holes 18 L 6654 yds SSS 71
9 L 3191 yds SSS 36
Pro–68 E Jones
V'tors Wed–NA after 2pm Sat–NA before 5pm SOC–Mon & Thurs
Fees £32 (£37)
Loc 6 miles S of Belfast
Arch J Harris/CK Cotton

Ormeau (1893)
50 Park Road, Belfast BT7 2EX
Tel (01232) 641069 (Members)
Fax (01232) 646250
Mem 280 70(L) 45(J)
Sec R Kirk (01232) 640700
Pro (01232) 640999
Holes 9 L 5308 yds SSS 65
Recs Am–56 E Donaldson (1995)
V'tors U SOC
Fees £12 (£14.50)
Loc 2 miles S of Belfast

Shandon Park (1926)
73 Shandon Park, Belfast BT5 6NY
Tel (01) 232 793730
Fax (01) 232 402773
Mem 1100
Sec DG Jenkins (Mgr)
(01232) 401856
Pro B Wilson (01232) 797859
Holes 18 L 6261 yds SSS 70
Recs Am–64 N Anderson
Pro–68 CP Posnett
V'tors WD–U Sat–NA before 5pm SOC
Fees £22 (£27)
Loc 3 miles E of Belfast on the Knock road

Co Carlow

Borris (1908)
Deerpark, Borris
Tel (0503) 73143
Mem 475
Sec R Long (Mgr)
Holes 9 L 6120 yds Par 70 SSS 69
Recs Am–66 D Todd (1996)
V'tors WD–U Sun–M SOC–WD/Sat
Fees £12
Loc Borris

Carlow (1899)
Deer Park, Dublin Road, Carlow
Tel (0503) 31695
Fax (0503) 40065
Mem 1300
Sec Mrs M Meaney
Pro A Gilbert (0503) 41745

For list of abbreviations see page 527

Holes 18 L 5844 m Par 70 SSS 71
Recs Am–64 J Kavanagh (1994)
Pro–68 C O'Connor
V'tors U SOC–WD
Fees £22 (£27) SOC–£20 (£25)
Loc 2 miles N of Carlow. 50 miles S of Dublin (N7)
Arch Tom Simpson

Mount Wolseley (1996)
Tullow
Tel (0503) 51674
Fax (0503) 52123
Mem 250
Sec D Morrissey (Mgr)
Pro J Bolger
Holes 18 L 6497 m Par 72 SSS 74
V'tors U
Fees £20 (£25)
Loc 15 miles E of Carlow (R275)

Co Cavan

Belturbet (1950)
Erne Hill, Belturbet
Tel (049) 22287
Mem 110
Sec PF Coffey (049) 22498
Pro None
Holes 9 L 5347 yds Par 68 SSS 65
Recs Am–64 J Costello (1982)
V'tors U SOC
Fees £10
Loc 1 mile E of Belturbet

Blacklion (1962)
Toam, Blacklion, via Sligo
Tel (072) 53024
Mem 250
Sec P Ferguson (Hon)
Holes 9 L 5544 m SSS 69
V'tors U SOC
Fees D–£8 (D–£10)
Loc 12 miles SW of Enniskillen on A4 to N16
Arch Eddie Hackett

Cabra Castle (1978)
Kingscourt
Mem 130
Holes 9 L 5308 m Par 70 SSS 68
V'tors U exc Sun–NA SOC
Fees On application
Loc 2 miles E of Kingscourt

County Cavan (1894)
Arnmore House, Drumelis, Cavan
Tel (049) 31541
Mem 800
Sec C Carroll
Holes 18 L 5519 m SSS 69
Recs Am–66 A Cafferty
Pro–65 J Purcell (1987)
V'tors U
Fees On application
Loc 2 miles W of Cavan on Killeshandra road

Slieve Russell (1994)
Ballyconnell
Tel (049) 26444
Fax (049) 26474
Mem 350
Sec PJ Creamer (049) 26458
Pro L McCool (049) 26458
Holes 18 L 7053 yds Par 72 SSS 74
9 hole Par 3 course
Recs Am–71 K Smith
Pro–68 P Walton
V'tors U SOC
Fees £28 Sat–£36
Loc 15 miles N of Cavan Town
Mis Driving range
Arch Paddy Merrigan

Virginia (1945)
Park Hotel, Virginia
Tel (049) 48066
Mem 570
Sec J Greene (Hon)
Holes 9 L 4139 m Par 64 SSS 62
Recs Am–54 PJ O'Reilly
V'tors U
Fees £8
Loc 35 miles SE of Cavan, nr Lough Ramor (N3)

Co Clare

Clonlara (1993)
Clonlara
Tel (061) 354141
Mem 85
Sec M O'Connell
Holes 12 L 5289 m Par 70 SSS 69
V'tors U
Fees £7 (£10)
Loc 8 miles NE of Limerick

Dromoland Castle (1964)
Newmarket-on-Fergus
Tel (061) 368444
Fax (061) 368498
Mem 400
Sec J O'Halloran
Pro P Murphy
Holes 18 L 6098 yds SSS 71
Recs Am–74 Dr C Hackett (1986)
V'tors U SOC
Fees D–£27 (£32) (1998)
Loc 18 miles NW of Limerick. Shannon Airport 4 miles

East Clare (1992)
Bodyke
Tel (061) 921322
Mem 450
Sec P Nesbitt (Hon)
Holes 9 L 5639 m Par 71 SSS 69
V'tors U
Fees £15
Loc 20 miles E of Ennis (R352)

Ennis (1907)
Drumbiggle Road, Ennis
Tel (065) 24074
Fax (065) 41848
Mem 860
Sec J Normoyle
Pro M Ward (065) 20690
Holes 18 L 5275 m SSS 68
Recs Am–65 L Pyne
Pro–66 P Skerritt
V'tors U exc Sun SOC
Fees £18 SOC–£13/£15
Loc 1/2 mile NW of Ennis, off N18

Kilkee (1896)
East End, Kilkee
Tel (065) 56048
Fax (065) 56977
Mem 579
Sec M Haugh
Holes 18 L 5928 m Par 71 SSS 71
Recs Am–68 D Nagle, N Cotter
V'tors U SOC
Fees £20
Loc End of Kilkee Promenade. 10 miles NW of Kilrush
Arch Eddie Hackett

Kilrush (1934)
Parknamoney, Kilrush
Tel (065) 51138
Fax (065) 52633
Mem 338
Pro J McDermott (065) 51138
Sec G Kelly (065) 59005
Holes 18 L 5986 yds Par 70 SSS 69
Recs Am–68 P King (1995)
V'tors U SOC
Fees £16 (£18)
Loc 25 miles SW of Ennis
Arch Arthur Spring

Lahinch (1892)
Lahinch
Tel (065) 81003
Fax (065) 81592
Mem 1250
Sec A Reardon (Sec/Mgr)
Pro R McCavery (065) 81408
Holes Old 18 L 6699 yds SSS 73
Castle 18 L 5620 yds SSS 69
V'tors WD–U WE–NA 9–10.30am and 1–2pm SOC
Fees Old: £45 Castle: £25
Loc 20 miles NW of Ennis on T69
Arch Morris/Gibson/Mackenzie/Harris

Shannon (1966)
Shannon Airport
Tel (061) 471020
Fax (061) 471507
Mem 1050
Sec M Corry (061) 471849
Pro A Pike (061) 471551
Holes 18 L 6515 yds Par 72 SSS 72
Recs Am–63 J Purcell
Pro–65 D Durnian
V'tors WD–U SOC
Fees £22 (£27)
Loc Shannon Airport

For list of abbreviations see page 527

Spanish Point (1915)
Spanish Point, Miltown Malbay
Tel (065) 84198
Mem 200
Sec D Fitzgerald
Holes 9 L 4624 m Par 64 SSS 63
Recs Am–27 D Twomey
Pro–23 P Skerritt
V'tors U
Fees £15
Loc 2 mile S of Miltown Malbay (N67). 20 miles W of Ennis

Woodstock (1993)
Shanagh Road, Ennis
Tel (065) 29463
Fax (065) 20204
Mem 350
Sec AM Russell (Sec/Mgr)
Holes 18 L 5879 m SSS 71
V'tors U
Fees £20 (£25)
Loc Ennis
Arch Arthur Spring

Co Cork

Bandon (1909)
Castlebernard, Bandon
Tel (023) 41111
Fax (023) 44690
Mem 800
Sec P Kehoe (Hon)
Pro P O'Boyle (023) 42224
Holes 18 L 5663 m Par 70 SSS 69
Recs Am–66 J Carroll
V'tors U
Fees On application
Loc Bandon 1½ miles. 18 miles SW of Cork

Bantry Bay (1975)
Donemark, Bantry, West Cork
Tel (027) 50579
Fax (027) 50579
Mem 580
Sec Enda J Lonergan (Mgr)
Pro F Condon
Holes 18 L 5914 m Par 71 SSS 72
Recs Am–71 B Aylmer (1997)
Pro–66 C O'Connor Jr
V'tors WD–U before 4.30 pm WE/BH–booking necessary SOC
Fees £20 (£20)
Loc 1 mile N of Bantry on Glengarriff road (N71)
Arch E Hackett/C O'Connor, Jnr

Berehaven (1902)
Millcove, Castletownbere
Tel (027) 70700
Mem 118
Sec H Barry (Sec/Mgr)
(027) 70252
Holes 9 L 2605 yds SSS 66
Recs Am–65 T Harrington (1990)
V'tors U SOC

Fees £10 (£10)
Loc 2 miles E of Castletownbere on Glengarriff road

Charleville (1909)
Charleville
Tel (063) 81257
Fax (063) 81274
Mem 650
Sec M Keane (Sec/Mgr)
Pro D Keating
Holes 18 L 6430 yds SSS 69
9 L 6750 yds SSS 72
Recs Am–65 K Carey (1995)
Ladies–68 S Keane (1990)
V'tors WD–U WE–book in advance SOC
Fees £15 (£17)
SOC–£13.50 (£15)
Loc 35 miles N of Cork on Limerick road

Cobh (1987)
Ballywilliam, Cobh
Tel (021) 812399
Fax (021) 812615
Mem 120
Sec H Cunningham
Holes 9 L 4576 m SSS 64
Recs Am–63 P McGee Jr
Pro–64 C O'Connor Sr
V'tors WD–U WE–NA
Fees £8 (£9)
Loc 1 mile N of Cobh. 16 miles SE of Cork
Arch Eddie Hackett

Coosheen (1989)
Coosheen, Schull
Tel (028) 28182
Mem 140
Sec L Morgan
Holes 9 L 4001 m Par 60 SSS 61
V'tors U
Fees £10 (£10)
Loc 20 miles S of Bantry

Cork (1888)
Little Island, Cork
Tel (021) 353451/353037
Fax (021) 353410
Mem 350 160 (L)
Sec M Sands (021) 353451
Pro P Hickey (021) 353421
Holes 18 L 6065 m SSS 72
Recs Am–66 T Cleary
Pro–67 D Smyth
V'tors WD–U H exc 12–2pm –M after 4pm Thurs–(Ladies Day)–phone in advance WE–NA before 2.30pm H
Fees £40 (£45)
Loc 5 miles E of Cork, off N25
Arch Dr A Mackenzie

Doneraile (1927)
Doneraile
Tel (022) 24137
Mem 152
Holes 9 L 5528 yds SSS 67

V'tors U
Fees On application
Loc 8 miles NW of Mallow

Douglas (1909)
Douglas, Cork
Tel (021) 891086
Fax (021) 895297
Mem 839
Sec B Barrett (Mgr) (021) 895297
Pro GS Nicholson (021) 362055
Holes 18 L 5664 m SSS 69
Recs Am–64 P Morris
Pro–64 E Darcy
V'tors WD–U exc Tues WE–NA before 2pm SOC–WD
Fees IR£19 (IR£21)
Loc Cork 3 miles

Dunmore (1967)
Dunmore House, Muckross, Clonakilty
Tel (023) 33352
Mem 163
Sec P Hogan (Hon)
Holes 9 L 4464 yds SSS 61
Recs Am–65
Pro–62
V'tors WD–U exc Wed WE–M SOC
Fees £10
Loc 3 miles S of Clonakilty
Arch Eddie Hackett

East Cork (1971)
Gortacrue, Midleton
Tel (021) 631687
Fax (021) 613695
Mem 600
Sec M Moloney (Sec/Mgr)
Pro D MacFarlane
Holes 18 L 5207 m SSS 67
Recs Am–65 G Murphy (1995)
V'tors WD–U WE–NA before noon BH–U
Fees £15
Loc 2 miles N of Midleton on L35
Arch Eddie Hackett

Fermoy (1892)
Corrin, Fermoy
Tel (025) 32694
Fax (025) 33072
Mem 800
Sec S Spillane
Pro B Moriarty (025) 31472
Holes 18 L 5795 m SSS 70
V'tors U SOC
Fees £12 (£15)
Loc 2 miles S of Fermoy, off N8

Fernhill (1994)
Carrigaline
Tel (021) 372226
Fax (021) 371011
Mem 60
Sec A Thompson (Mgr)
Holes 18 L 5602 m Par 70 SSS 68
V'tors U
Fees £12 (£14)
Loc 10 miles SE of Cork (R609)
Arch ML Bowes

For list of abbreviations see page 527

Fota Island (1993)
Carrigtwohill, Cork
Tel (021) 883710
Fax (021) 883713
Mem 400
Sec K Mulcahy (Sec/Mgr)
Pro K Morris
Holes 18 L 6986 yds Par 71 SSS 74
Recs Am–67 P Harrington
V'tors U
Fees £40 (£50)
Loc 8 miles E of Cork on N25
Mis Driving range
Arch O'Connor Jr/McEvoy/Howes

Frankfield (1984)
Frankfield, Douglas
Tel (021) 361199
Mem 280
Pro D Whyte
Holes 9 L 4621 m SSS 65
Recs Am–64
V'tors U SOC
Fees £5
Loc S of Cork
Mis Driving range

Glengarriff (1935)
Glengarriff
Tel (027) 63150
Mem 170
Sec N Deasy (Hon)
Holes 9 L 4094 m SSS 66
V'tors U
Fees D–£12
Loc 1 mile E of Glengarriff (N71)

Harbour Point (1991)
Clash, Little Island
Tel (021) 353094
Fax (021) 354408
Mem 250
Sec Ms N O'Connell (Sec/Mgr)
Holes 18 L 6063 yds SSS 72
V'tors U SOC
Fees £15–£24
Loc 5 miles E of Cork
Mis Floodlit driving range
Arch Paddy Merrigan

Kanturk (1971)
Fairy Hill, Kanturk
Tel (029) 50534
Mem 410
Sec J Pigott (029) 50588
Pro None
Holes 18 L 6262 yds Par 72 SSS 70
Recs Am–72 D O'Riordan,
 M Archdeacon (1987),
 J O'Connor (1989)
V'tors U
Fees £12 (£15)
Loc 2 miles SW of Kanturk (R579)
Arch R Barry

Kinsale Farrangalway
(1993)
Farrangalway, Kinsale
Tel (021) 774722
Fax (021) 773114

Mem 740
Sec P Murray (Sec/Mgr)
Pro G Broderick (021) 773258
Holes 18 L 6609 yds SSS 72
Recs Am–70 K McCarthy
 Pro–69 G Broderick
V'tors WD–U WE–NA SOC
Fees £20 (£25)
Loc 3 miles NW of Kinsale.
 18 miles S of Cork
Arch Jack Kenneally

Kinsale Ringenane (1912)
Ringenane, Belgooly, Kinsale
Tel (021) 772197
Mem 740
Sec C McCloskey
Pro None
Holes 9 L 5332 yds SSS 68
Recs Am–63 K McCarthy
V'tors U SOC
Fees £15
Loc 2 miles E of Kinsale (R600).
 16 miles S of Cork

Lee Valley G&CC (1993)
Clashanure, Ovens, Cork
Tel (021) 331721
Fax (021) 331695
Mem 450
Sec J O'Reilly
Pro J Savage
Holes 18 L 6800 yds SSS 72
Recs Am–71 D McFarlane (1993)
 Pro–68 F Couples (1993)
V'tors U SOC
Fees £22 (£25)
Loc 8 miles W of Cork (N22)
Mis Floodlit driving range
Arch C O'Connor Jr

Macroom (1924)
Lackaduve, Macroom
Tel (026) 41072
Fax (026) 41391
Mem 550
Sec L Gould
Pro None
Holes 18 L 5598 m SSS 70
Recs Am–66 J Mills
V'tors U H SOC
Fees D–IR£13 (IR£16)
Loc Macroom Town, through
 Castle Arch. 25 miles W of
 Cork

Mahon (1980)
Cloverhill, Blackrock, Cork
Tel (021) 294280
Mem 450
Sec B Ramsell (Hon)
Pro T O'Connor
Holes 18 L 4818 m SSS 66
V'tors U
Fees £10 (£11)
Loc SE of Cork City

Mallow (1948)
Ballyellis, Mallow
Tel (022) 21145
Fax (022) 42501

Mem 1500
Sec V Devlin
Pro S Conway
Holes 18 L 6559 yds SSS 72
Recs Am–67 J Murphy (1995)
V'tors WD–U before 5pm SOC
Fees £18 (£22)
Loc 1 mile SE of Mallow Bridge
 on Killavullen road
Arch J Harris

Mitchelstown (1908)
Mitchelstown
Tel (025) 24072
Mem 500
Sec N Brennan
Holes 15 L 5057 m SSS 67
Recs Am–65 A Spratt
V'tors U SOC
Fees £12 (£15)
Loc 30 miles NE of Cork
Arch David Jones

Monkstown (1908)
Parkgarriffe, Monkstown
Tel (021) 841376
Fax (021) 841376
Mem 900
Sec GA Finn
Pro B Murphy (021) 841686
Holes 18 L 5669 m SSS 69
Recs Am–66 J Morris Jr (1988)
 Pro–67 K Morris (1992)
V'tors U H SOC
Fees £23 (£26)
Loc 7 miles SE of Cork

Muskerry (1897)
Carrigrohane
Tel (021) 385297
Fax (021) 385297
Mem 791
Sec JJ Moynihan
Pro WM Lehane (021) 381445
Holes 18 L 5786 m SSS 71
Recs Am–64 K Bornemann
 Pro–66 J Hegerty
V'tors Restricted at certain
 times–phone first SOC
Fees £12.50–£23 (£25)
Loc 7 miles NW of Cork. 2 miles
 W of Blarney

Old Head (1997)
Kinsale
Tel (021) 778444
Fax (021) 778022
Sec R Cawley (Mgr)
Holes 18 L 7100 yds SSS 72
V'tors U SOC
Fees £50 (£60)
Loc 7 miles S of Kinsale
Arch R Kirby/J Carr

Raffeen Creek (1989)
Ringaskiddy
Tel (021) 378430
Mem 530
Holes 9 L 5098 m Par 70 SSS 67
Recs Am–67 J Hornibrook (1993)
 Pro–71 C O'Connor Sr (1989)

For list of abbreviations see page 527

Co Donegal

V'tors WD–U WE–U after noon
Fees IR£10
Loc 1 mile from Ringaskiddy Ferryport
Arch Eddie Hackett

Skibbereen (1931)
Licknavar, Skibbereen
Tel (028) 21227
Mem 580
Sec S Brett (Mgr)
Pro None
Holes 18 L 5474 m Par 71 SSS 69
Recs Am–68 J Kenneally (1993)
V'tors U SOC–Sat
Fees £12 (£16)
Loc 1 mile W of Skibbereen. 52 miles SW of Cork
Mis Driving range
Arch Eddie Hackett

Youghal (1898)
Knockaverry, Youghal
Tel (024) 92787
Fax (024) 92641
Mem 827
Sec Margaret O'Sullivan
Pro L Burns (024) 92590
Holes 18 L 5646 m SSS 69
Recs Am–67 T Kenefick (1992)
V'tors U
Fees D–IR£18 (IR£20)
Loc 30 miles E of Cork on N25 from Rosslare
Arch Cdr Harris

Co Donegal

Ballybofey & Stranorlar (1957)
The Glebe, Stranorlar
Tel (074) 31093
Mem 525
Sec A Harkin (074) 31228
Holes 18 L 5922 yds Par 68 SSS 68
Recs Am–64 E McMenamin (1992)
V'tors U SOC
Fees £15
Loc Stranorlar ¼ mile
Arch PC Carr

Ballyliffin (1947)
Inishowen, Ballyliffin
Tel (077) 76119
Fax (077) 76672
Mem 828
Sec KJ O'Doherty (Sec/Mgr)
Pro None
Holes Old 18 L 6611 yds SSS 72
Glashedy 18 L 6837 yds Par 72
Recs Old Am–
Old Pro–64 H O'Neill
Glashedy Am–
Glashedy Pro–67 G Loughery
V'tors U SOC–WD
Fees Old: IR£19 (IR£22)
Glashedy: IR£28 (IR£33)

Loc 8 miles N of Buncrana. 15 miles N of Londonderry
Arch Glashedy-Craddock/Ruddy

Buncrana (1951)
Buncrana
Tel (077) 62279
Mem 175
Sec F McGrory (Hon)
Pro NS Doherty
Holes 9 L 4250 m SSS 62
V'tors U
Fees £6
Loc 1 mile S of Buncrana, off R238

Bundoran (1894)
Bundoran
Tel (072) 41302
Fax (072) 42014
Mem 620
Sec J McGagh (Sec/Mgr)
Pro D Robinson
Holes 18 L 6159 yds Par 69 SSS 69
Recs Am–66
Pro–66
V'tors WD–U WE–restricted SOC
Fees £17 (£20)
Loc E boundary of Bundoran. 20 miles S of Donegal
Arch H Vardon

Cruit Island (1985)
Kincasslagh, Dunglow
Tel (075) 43296
Fax (075) 22439
Mem 200
Sec T Gallagher
Pro None
Holes 9 L 5297 yds Par 68 SSS 64
Recs Am–65
V'tors U SOC
Fees £7 (£10)
Loc 5 miles N of Dunglow, off R259

Donegal (1960)
Murvagh, Laghey
Tel (073) 34054
Fax (073) 34377
Mem 590
Sec J Nixon (073) 22166
J McBride (Admin)
Holes 18 L 7271 yds SSS 73
Recs Am–68 M Gannon
V'tors H SOC–exc Sun
Fees £18 (£25)
Loc 7 miles S of Donegal on N15
Arch Eddie Hackett

Dunfanaghy (1903)
Dunfanaghy, Letterkenny
Tel (074) 36335
Mem 390
Sec J Moffitt
Holes 18 L 5066 m Par 68 SSS 66
Recs Am–64 J Brogan
Pro–66 L Wallace
V'tors U SOC

Fees IR£13 (IR£15)
Loc 25 miles NW of Letterkenny on N56

Greencastle (1892)
Greencastle
Tel (077) 81013
Fax (077) 81015
Mem 600
Sec L McCafferty
Holes 18 L 5211 m SSS 67
Recs Am–67 F McCarroll (1993)
V'tors WD–U WE–restricted SOC
Fees £12 (£18)
Loc 21 miles NE of Londonderry, nr Moville
Arch Eddie Hackett

Gweedore (1926)
Magheragallon, Derrybeg, Letterkenny
Tel (075) 31140
Mem 145
Holes 9 L 6201 yds SSS 69
V'tors U
Fees £7 (£8)
Loc 3 miles N of Gweedore, off R257

Letterkenny (1913)
Barnhill, Letterkenny
Tel (074) 21150
Mem 790
Sec B Ramsay (074) 24491
Holes 18 L 6239 yds SSS 71
Recs Am–65 T Purdy (1997)
Pro–68 J Gallagher (1998)
V'tors U SOC
Fees £15
Loc 1 mile E of Letterkenny
Arch Eddie Hackett

Narin & Portnoo (1931)
Narin, Portnoo
Tel (075) 45107
Fax (074) 45107
Mem 500
Sec E Bonner (Hon)
Pro None
Holes 18 L 5950 yds Par 69 SSS 68
Recs Am–64 B McBride (1980)
Pro–63 R Browne (1980)
V'tors WD/Sat–U H Sun–NA before 2pm SOC
Fees £15 (£18) SOC–£13.50
Loc 6 miles N of Ardara. West Donegal

North West (1891)
Lisfannon, Fahan
Tel (077) 61027
Fax (077) 63284
Mem 520
Sec D Coyle (Hon)
Pro S McBriarty (077) 61715
Holes 18 L 6239 yds SSS 71
Recs Am–65 F Friel
Pro–64 M Doherty
V'tors U
Fees IR£15 (IR£20)
Loc 2 miles S of Buncrana. 12 miles N of Londonderry

For list of abbreviations see page 527

Co Donegal

Otway (1893)
Saltpans, Rathmullan, Letterkenny
Tel (074) 58319
Mem 97
Sec T Morrison (Hon)
Holes 9 L 4234 yds SSS 60
Recs Am–60 D Gallagher
V'tors U
Fees £10
Loc 15 miles NE of Letterkenny, by Lough Swilly

Portsalon (1891)
Portsalon, Fanad
Tel (074) 59459
Mem 350
Sec C Toland
Holes 18 L 5878 yds Par 69 SSS 68
Recs Am–66 K McLaughlin (1994) Pro–71 J Henderson
V'tors U
Fees £12 (£15)
Loc 20 miles N of Letterkenny

Redcastle (1983)
Redcastle, Moville
Tel (077) 82073
Mem 120
Holes 9 L 6046 yds SSS 70
V'tors U
Fees £10 (£12)
Loc 15 miles NE of Londonderry, by Lough Foyle (R238)

Rosapenna (1894)
Downings, Rosapenna
Tel (074) 55301
Fax (074) 55128
Mem 180
Sec T Diver (Hon)
Pro D Patterson
Holes 18 L 6254 yds Par 70 SSS 71
Recs Am–M McGinley, D Boyce Pro–68 F Daly
V'tors U
Fees IR£20 (IR£25)
Loc 20 miles N of Letterkenny
Mis Golf academy
Arch Morris/Vardon/Braid

Co Down

Ardglass (1896)
Castle Place, Ardglass BT30 7PP
Tel (01396) 841219
Fax (01396) 841841
Mem 841
Sec Miss D Polly
Pro P Farrell (01396) 841022
Holes 18 L 5542 m Par 70 SSS 69
Recs Am–65 D Baker Pro–64 K Morris
V'tors U SOC
Fees £15 (£21)
Loc 7 miles SE of Downpatrick on B1

Ardminnan (1995)
15 Ardminnan Road, Portaferry BT22 1QJ
Tel (01247) 771321
Fax (01247) 771321
Mem 170
Sec S McCrea (Mgr)
Pro J Peden
Holes 9 L 2766 m Par 70 SSS 69
V'tors U
Fees £10 (£15)
Loc 10 miles E of Downpatrick via ferry. 18 miles SE of Newtownards (A20)
Arch Frank Ainsworth

Banbridge (1913)
Huntly Road, Banbridge BT32 3UR
Tel (018206) 62342
Fax (018206) 69400
Mem 850
Sec H Carson (Sec/Mgr) (018206) 62211
Holes 18 L 5376 m SSS 68
Recs Am–62 R Leonard
V'tors U SOC
Fees £10 (£20)
Loc 1 mile W of Banbridge

Bangor (1903)
Broadway, Bangor BT20 4RH
Tel (01247) 270922
Fax (01247) 453394
Mem 1100
Sec DJ Ryan (Sec/Mgr)
Holes 18 L 6424 yds SSS 71
Recs Am–64 P Barry Pro–66 C O'Connor
V'tors WD–U exc –M 1–2pm Wed–U before 4.45pm Sat–NA SOC–Mon & Wed
Fees £20 Sun–£25
Loc 1 mile S of Bangor, off Donaghadee road
Arch James Braid

Blackwood (1995)
150 Crawfordsburn Road, Bangor BT19 1GB
Tel (01247) 852706
Fax (01247) 853785
Mem 330
Sec J Kennedy, Debbie Hanna
Pro R Skillen
Holes 2 x 18 hole courses
V'tors U
Fees On application
Loc W of Bangor
Mis Driving range

Bright Castle (1970)
14 Coniamstown Road, Bright, Downpatrick BT30 8LU
Tel (01) 396 841319
Mem 100
Sec J McCawl (Hon)
Holes 18 L 6810 yds Par 73 SSS 73
Recs Am–70 A Ennis
V'tors U SOC

Fees £10 (£12)
Loc 5 miles S of Downpatrick, off Killough road (B176)

Carnalea (1927)
Station Road, Bangor BT19 1EZ
Tel (01247) 465004
Fax (01247) 273989
Mem 800
Sec GY Steele (01247) 270368
Pro T Loughran (01247) 270122
Holes 18 L 5584 yds SSS 67
Recs Am–63 A Robinson (1991)
V'tors U SOC–WD
Fees £15 (£19)
Loc By Carnalea Station, Bangor

Clandeboye (1933)
Conlig, Newtownards BT23 3PN
Tel (01247) 271767/473706
Fax (01247) 473711
Mem 1291
Sec W Donald (01247) 271767
Pro P Gregory (01247) 271750
Holes Dufferin 18 L 5915 m SSS 71; Ava 18 L 5172 m SSS 68
Recs Am–65 S King Pro–68 J Heggarty, D Jones, D Feherty
V'tors WD–U WE–M SOC
Fees Dufferin: £30 Ava: £25
Loc Conlig, off A21 Bangor-Newtownards road
Arch Von Limburger/Alliss/Thomas

Crossgar (1993)
Derryboye Road, Crossgar BT30 9DL
Tel (01) 396 831523
Mem 105
Sec K Williamson (Hon)
Holes 9 L 4139 m Par 64 SSS 63
V'tors U
Fees £9 (£11)
Loc 6 miles N of Downpatrick (A7)

Donaghadee (1899)
Warren Road, Donaghadee BT21 0PQ
Tel (01247) 883624
Fax (01247) 888891
Mem 1250
Sec K Patton
Pro G Drew (01247) 882392
Holes 18 L 5570 m Par 71
Recs Am–65 J Nelson (1977), J McBurney (1994) Pro–69 E Clarke
V'tors U exc Sat–NA SOC–Mon/Wed/Fri/Sun
Fees £14 (£20)
Loc 6 miles S of Bangor on coast road. 18 miles E of Belfast

Downpatrick (1932)
Saul Road, Downpatrick BT30 6PA
Tel (01396) 612152/615947
Fax (01396) 617502
Mem 960
Sec A Vaughan (01396) 615947
Pro (01396) 615167
Holes 18 L 5702 m SSS 69

For list of abbreviations see page 527

Co Down

Recs Am–64 D Baker (1990)
V'tors U SOC
Fees £15 (£20)
Loc 25 miles SE of Belfast (A1).
Downpatrick 1½ miles
Arch Hawtree

Helen's Bay (1896)
Golf Road, Helen's Bay, Bangor BT19 1TL
Tel (01247) 852601 (Clubhouse)
Fax (01247) 852815
Sec AS Foster (01247) 852815
Holes 9 L 5181 m Par 68 SSS 67
Recs Am–67 PT Dorman (1996)
Pro–67 L Esdale
V'tors WD/Sun–U Tues/Thurs/Sat–restricted SOC–WD exc Tues
Fees On application
Loc 9 miles E of Belfast, off A2

Holywood (1904)
Nuns Walk, Demesne Road, Holywood BT18 9LE
Tel (01232) 422138
Fax (01232) 425040
Mem 800
Sec SJ Melville (Gen Mgr) (01232) 423135
Pro M Bannon (01232) 425503
Holes 18 L 5885 yds SSS 68
Recs Am–61 J Watts
Pro–64 M Bannon
V'tors WD–U exc 1.30–2.15pm
Sat–after 5pm
Fees £15 (£21)
Loc 5 miles E of Belfast on Bangor road

Kilkeel (1948)
Mourne Park, Kilkeel BT34 4LB
Tel (016937) 62296/65095
Fax (016937) 65095
Mem 672
Sec SC McBride (016937) 63787
Holes 18 L 6625 yds SSS 72
Recs Am–70 SP McVeigh (1996)
V'tors U SOC–exc BH/Sat
Fees £16 (£20)
Loc 3 miles W of Kilkeel on Newry road
Mis Driving range
Arch Eddie Hackett

Kirkistown Castle (1902)
142 Main Road, Cloughey, Newtownards BT22 1JA
Tel (012477) 71233
Fax (012477) 71699
Email kirkistown@AOL.com
Mem 948
Sec G Graham (012477) 71233
Pro J Peden (012477) 71004
Holes 18 L 5628 m SSS 70
Recs Am–68 Jas Brown
Pro–71 RJ Polley, C O'Connor
V'tors WD–U WE/BH–NA 1st tee 9.30–10.30am and 12–1.30pm SOC
Fees £13 (£20)
Loc 25 miles SE of Belfast
Arch James Braid

Mahee Island (1930)
Comber, Belfast BT23 6ET
Tel (01238) 541234
Mem 500
Sec T Reid (Hon)
Pro A McCracken
Holes 9 L 2790 yds SSS 67
Recs Am–63 W McClements (1995)
Pro–65 N Drew
V'tors U exc Sat–NA before 5pm
SOC–WD exc Mon
Fees £10 (£15)
Loc Strangford Lough, 14 miles SE of Belfast

Mount Ober G&CC
Ballymaconaghy Road, Knockbracken, Belfast BT8 4SB
Tel (01232) 792108 (Bookings)
Fax (01232) 705862
Mem 600
Sec P Laverty (Hon)
Pro G Loughrey (01232) 401811
Holes 18 L 5436 yds SSS 68
Recs Am–67
Pro–67
V'tors WD–U Sat–NA before 3pm
Sun–NA before 10.30am SOC
Fees £11.50 (£14)
Loc 2 miles SW of Belfast, nr Four Winds
Mis Floodlit driving range

Mourne (1946)
36 Golf Links Road, Newcastle BT33 0AN
Tel (013967) 23218
Mem 355
Sec T Gallagher (Hon)
Holes Play over Royal Co Down

Ringdufferin (1993)
Ringdufferin Road, Toye, Killyleagh BT30 9PH
Tel (01396) 828812
Mem 260
Holes 18 L 4652 m Par 68 SSS 66
V'tors U
Fees £9 (£10)
Loc 2 miles N of Killyleagh, off A22

Rockmount (1995)
28 Drumalig Road, Carryduff, Belfast BT8 8EQ
Tel (01232) 812279
Fax (01232) 815851
Mem 700
Sec D Patterson (Mgr)
Holes 18 L 6373 yds Par 72 SSS 71
V'tors U
Fees £18 (£22)
Loc 8 miles S of Belfast (A24)

Royal Belfast (1881)
Holywood, Craigavad BT18 0BP
Tel (01232) 428165
Fax (01232) 421404
Mem 1000
Sec Mrs SH Morrison
Pro C Spence (01232) 428586

Holes 18 L 6184 yds SSS 70
Recs Am–69 B Purdy (1991)
Pro–65 D Clark (1992)
V'tors I Sat–NA before 4.30pm
Fees £30 (£35)
Loc E of Belfast on A2

Royal County Down (1889)
Newcastle BT33 0AN
Tel (013967) 23314
Fax (013967) 26281
Email royal.co.down@virgin.net
Mem 450
Sec PE Rolph
Pro KJ Whitson (013967) 22419
Holes Ch'ship 18 L 7037 yds SSS 74
Annesley 18 L 4681 yds SSS 63
Recs Ch'ship Am–66 J Bruen,
JM Jamison, HB Smyth
Pro–67 A Compston, B Gadd
V'tors Contact Sec
Fees Ch'ship: £65 (£75)
Annesley: £15 (£20)
Loc 30 miles S of Belfast
Arch Tom Morris

Scrabo (1907)
233 Scrabo Road, Newtownards BT23 4SL
Tel (01247) 812355
Fax (01247) 822919
Mem 958
Sec Christine Hamill (Gen Mgr)
Pro P McCrystal (01247) 817848
Holes 18 L 5699 m SSS 71
Recs Am–65 J Rea (1991)
Pro–67 N Drew (1987)
V'tors WD–U WE–after 5pm SOC
Fees £15 (£20)
Loc 2 miles W of Newtownards, by Scrabo Tower

The Spa (1907)
Grove Road, Ballynahinch BT24 8BR
Tel (01) 238 562365
Mem 920
Sec TG Magee
Holes 18 L 6003 m SSS 72
Recs Am–67 R Wallace
V'tors U exc Wed–NA after 3pm
Sat–NA
Fees £15 (£20)
Loc 1 mile S of Ballynahinch.
15 miles S of Belfast

Temple G&CC (1994)
60 Church Road, Boardmills, Lisburn BT27 6UP
Tel (01846) 639213
Fax (01846) 638637
Mem 300
Sec D Kinnear (Sec/Mgr)
Holes 9 L 5451 yds Par 68 SSS 66
Recs Am–66 S Goldthorpe (1998)
V'tors U
Fees £10 (£14)
Loc 5 miles S of Belfast on Ballynahinch road

For list of abbreviations see page 527

Warrenpoint (1893)
Lower Dromore Rd, Warrenpoint BT34 3LN
Tel (016937) 52219 (Clubhouse)
Fax (016937) 52918
Mem 1265
Sec M Trainor (016937) 53695
Pro N Shaw (016937) 52371
Holes 18 L 5628 m SSS 70
Recs Am–61 P Gribben
Pro–69 S Hamill
V'tors U SOC
Fees £20 (£27)
Loc 5 miles S of Newry
Arch Tom Craddock

Co Dublin

Balbriggan (1945)
Blackhall, Balbriggan
Tel (01) 841 2173
Fax (01) 841 3927
Mem 600
Sec M O'Halloran (Sec/Mgr) (01) 841 2229
Pro None
Holes 18 L 5881 m SSS 71
V'tors WD–U WE–M SOC
Fees £16 (£18)
Loc 1 mile S of Balbriggan on N1. 18 miles N of Dublin
Arch Paramour/Stillwell/Ruddy

Balcarrick (1972)
Corballis, Donabate
Tel (01) 843 6228
Fax (01) 843 6957
Sec Joan Byrne
Holes 18 L 5940 m Par 73 SSS 71
V'tors WD–U Sat–NA before 10am Sun–NA SOC
Fees £13 (£20)
Loc 2 miles E of Donabate. 18 miles N of Dublin

Ballinascorney (1971)
Ballinascorney, Tallaght, Dublin
Tel (01) 451 6430
Mem 500
Holes 18 L 5464 m Par 71 SSS 67
V'tors WD–U
Fees On application
Loc 8 miles SW of Dublin

Beaverstown (1985)
Beaverstown, Donabate
Tel (01) 843 6439
Fax (01) 843 6721
Mem 835
Sec S Flavin (Mgr)
Holes 18 L 5855 m Par 71 SSS 70
Recs Am–72 M Perry (1987)
Pro–67 T Judd (1995)
V'tors WD–U WE/BH–M SOC
Fees £20 (£25)
Loc 4 miles N of Dublin Airport
Arch Eddie Hackett

Beech Park (1983)
Johnstown, Rathcoole
Tel (01) 458 0522/458 0100
Fax (01) 458 8365
Mem 550
Sec J Deally (Sec/Mgr)
Pro None
Holes 18 L 5730 m SSS 70
Recs Am–71 P Stapleton (1990)
Pro–67 B Todd (1989)
V'tors WD–U exc Tues/Wed–M WE–M BH–NA
Fees £22
Loc Rathcoole 1 mile on Kilteel road. SW of Dublin
Arch Eddie Hackett

City West (1994)
Saggart
Tel (01) 458 8566
Fax (01) 831 5779
Mem 270
Sec B Cooling (Mgr)
Holes 18 L 6441 yds Par 71 SSS 71
V'tors U
Fees £29 (£32)
Loc 10 miles SW of Dublin, off N7

Coldwinters (1994)
Newtown House, St Margaret's
Tel (01) 864 0324
Fax (01) 834 1400
Mem 375
Sec Mrs K Yates
Pro R Machin
Holes 18 L 5973 m SSS 71
9 L 3133 m SSS 31
V'tors U
Fees £8.50 (£12.50)
Loc NW of Dublin. Airport 2 miles
Mis Driving range. Golf Academy
Arch Martin Hawtree

Corrstown (1993)
Corrstown, Killsallaghan
Tel (01) 864 0533/4
Fax (01) 864 0537
Mem 900
Sec J Kelly
Pro P Gittens
Holes 18 L 6077 m Par 72 SSS 71
9 L 5584 m Par 70 SSS 69
Recs Am–70 C O'Connor (1997)
Pro–69 R Giles (1997)
V'tors Booking necessary
Fees £17 (£20)
Loc Dublin Airport 6 miles
Arch E Connaughton

Donabate (1925)
Balcarrick, Donabate
Tel (01) 843 6059/6346/6001
Fax (01) 843 5012
Mem 913
Sec B Judd (01) 843 6346
Pro H Jackson
Holes 18 L 6187 yds SSS 69
Recs Am–67 AJ D Hanratty
Pro–65 M Murphy
V'tors WE/BH–NA

Fees £20
Loc 8 miles N of Dublin Airport on N1

Dublin Mountain (1993)
Gortlum, Brittas
Tel (01) 458 2622
Mem 430
Sec P O'Rourke (Hon)
Holes 18 L 5433 m Par 70 SSS 69
V'tors U
Fees £7 (£9)
Loc SW of Dublin

Dun Laoghaire (1910)
Eglinton Park, Dun Laoghaire
Tel (01) 280 1055
Fax (01) 280 4868
Mem 972
Sec T Stewart (01) 280 3916
Pro O Mulhall (01) 280 1694
Holes 18 L 5478 m SSS 69
Recs Am–65 R Donnelly
Pro–65 P Skerritt
V'tors WD–U exc 12–1.30pm SOC
Fees IR£30
Loc 7 miles S of Dublin. Ferry Port 1 mile
Arch HS Colt

Finnstown
Finnstown House Hotel, Lucan
Tel (01) 628 0644
Fax (01) 628 1088
Mem 300
Sec M Doyle (01) 836 3423
Holes 9 L 5172 yds SSS 64
Recs Am–65 C Kane (1996)
V'tors H SOC
Fees £12 (£16)
Loc 7 miles W of Dublin
Arch B Browne

Forrest Little (1972)
Forrest Little, Cloghran
Tel (01) 840 1183/840 1763
Fax (01) 840 1000
Mem 900
Sec T Greany (Sec/Mgr)
Pro T Judd
Holes 18 L 5865 m SSS 70
Recs Am–67 T Judd (1984)
Pro–65 C O'Connor Jr (1984)
V'tors WD–U WE–NA
Fees IR£20
Loc Nr Dublin Airport
Arch F Hawtree

Hermitage (1905)
Lucan
Tel (01) 626 5396
Mem 1153
Sec T Spelman (01) 626 8491
Pro S Byrne (01) 626 8072
Holes 18 L 6032 m SSS 71
Recs Am–65 T Moran
Pro–65 R Davis
V'tors U SOC–WD
Fees £32 (£45)
Loc Lucan 2 miles. 8 miles W of Dublin

For list of abbreviations see page 527

Co Dublin 673

Hollywood Lakes (1992)
Ballyboughal
Tel   (01) 843 3406/7
Fax   (01) 843 3002
Mem   500
Sec   AC Brogan (Sec/Mgr)
Holes   18 L 6834 yds Par 72 SSS 72
Recs   Am–68 D Costigan Jr
V'tors   WD–U WE/BH–U after noon
Fees   £18 (£23)
Loc   10 miles N of Dublin Airport
Arch   Mel Flanagan

The Island (1890)
Corballis, Donabate
Tel   (01) 843 6104
Fax   (01) 843 6860
Mem   600
Sec   J Finn (01) 843 6462
Pro   K Kelleher (01) 843 5002
Holes   18 L 6053 m SSS 72
Recs   Am–67 T Smith (1997)
V'tors   WD–U WE–NA
Fees   £40
Loc   14 miles N of Dublin
Arch   Hawtree

Killiney (1903)
Ballinclea Road, Killiney
Tel   (01) 285 1983
Fax   (01) 285 2823
Mem   520
Sec   M O'Rourke (01) 285 2823
Pro   P O'Boyle (01) 285 6294
Holes   9 L 6220 yds SSS 70
Recs   Am–72 N Duke
          Pro–65 H Bradshaw
V'tors   U
Fees   D–£20
Loc   8 miles S of Dublin
Arch   E Connaughton

Kilternan (1987)
Kilternan
Tel   (01) 295 5559
Fax   (01) 295 5670
Mem   906
Sec   J Kinsella
Pro   G Hendley (01) 295 2986
Holes   18 L 5413 yds SSS 67
Recs   Am–69 S Foley (1991)
          Pro–68 J Hegarty (1996)
V'tors   U SOC
Fees   £16 (£20)
Loc   12 miles S of Dublin
Arch   Eddie Connaughton

Lucan (1897)
Celbridge Road, Lucan
Tel   (01) 628 0246
Fax   (01) 628 2929
Mem   740
Sec   T O'Donnell (Sec/Mgr)
          (01) 628 2106
Holes   18 L 5958 m Par 71 SSS 70
Recs   Am–68 B Dowling
V'tors   WD–U WE/BH–M SOC–WD exc Thurs
Fees   £20

Loc   14 miles W of Dublin, nr Lucan on N4
Arch   Eddie Hackett

Luttrelstown Castle (1993)
Castleknock, Dublin 15
Tel   (01) 808 9988
Fax   (01) 808 9989
Mem   400
Pro   G Campbell (Golf Dir)
Holes   18 L 6384 m Par 72 SSS 73
Recs   Am–67 J O'Brien (1996)
          Pro–66 J Young (1994)
V'tors   U SOC
Fees   £42 (£50)
Loc   7 miles W of Dublin
Mis   Driving range
Arch   Bielenberg/Connaughton

Malahide (1892)
Beechwood, The Grange, Malahide
Tel   (01) 846 1611
Fax   (01) 846 1270
Mem   850
Sec   T Gallagher (Sec/Mgr)
Pro   D Barton
Holes   27 holes: 6257-6633 yds SSS 70-72
Recs   Am–70 PA Hearne Jr
V'tors   WD–U WE–by arrangement SOC
Fees   £30 (£40)
Loc   1½ miles S of Malahide. 10 miles N of Dublin, nr airport
Arch   Eddie Hackett

Milltown (1907)
Lower Churchtown Road, Milltown, Dublin 14
Tel   (01) 497 6090
Fax   (01) 497 6008
Mem   1432
Sec   DJ Dalton (Sec/Mgr)
Pro   J Harnett (01) 497 7072
Holes   18 L 5638 m Par 71 SSS 69
Recs   Am–68 J Fanagan
          Pro–64 C Greene
V'tors   WD–U exc Tues & Wed pm Fri/WE–M BH–NA SOC–Mon & Thurs before 3.45pm
Fees   IR£35
Loc   4 miles S of Dublin centre
Arch   Freddie Davis

Portmarnock (1894)
Portmarnock
Tel   (01) 846 2794 (Clubhouse)
Fax   (01) 846 2601
Mem   971
Sec   JJ Quigley (01) 846 2968
Pro   J Purcell (01) 846 2634
Holes   27 holes: 6361-6497 m SSS 74-75
Recs   Am–68 JB Carr
          Pro–64 S Lyle (1989)
V'tors   I WE–XL
Fees   IR£70 (IR£90)
Loc   8 miles NE of Dublin

Portmarnock Hotel (1995)
Strand Road, Portmarnock
Tel   (01) 846 0611
Fax   (01) 846 1077
Sec   Moira Cassidy (Golf Dir)
          (01) 846 1800
Holes   18 L 6260 m Par 71 SSS 73
Recs   Pro–67 D Smyth (1997)
V'tors   U H
Fees   £55 Residents–£33
Loc   8 miles NE of Dublin. Airport 15 mins
Arch   Bernhard Langer

Rush (1943)
Rush
Tel   (01) 843 7548
Mem   360
Sec   BJ Clear (Sec/Mgr)
          (01) 843 8177
Holes   9 L 5598 m SSS 69
Recs   Am–68 PJ Dolan
V'tors   WD–U WE–M
Fees   £15
Loc   16 miles N of Dublin, off R127

St Margaret's G&CC (1993)
St Margaret's, Dublin
Tel   (01) 864 0400
Fax   (01) 864 0289
Mem   200
Sec   A Judge (Chief Exec)
Pro   Cobra Golf
Holes   18 L 6900 yds SSS 73
Recs   Pro–69 C Monaghan (1993)
          Ladies Pro–66 L Davies (1995)
V'tors   U SOC
Fees   £40–£45
Loc   3 miles NW of Dublin Airport, between N1/N2
Mis   Driving range
Arch   Craddock/Ruddy

Skerries (1906)
Hacketstown, Skerries
Tel   (01) 849 1204 (Clubhouse)
Fax   (01) 849 1591
Mem   1060
Sec   A Burns (01) 849 1567
Pro   J Kinsella (01) 849 0925
Holes   18 L 6081 m Par 73 SSS 72
V'tors   U SOC
Fees   IR£20 (IR£25)
Loc   20 miles N of Dublin

Slade Valley (1970)
Lynch Park, Brittas
Tel   (01) 458 2739
Fax   (01) 458 2784
Mem   800
Sec   P Maguire (01) 458 2183
Pro   J Dignam
Holes   18 L 5337 m SSS 68
Recs   Am–65
          Pro–64
V'tors   WD–U am WE–M
Fees   £17
Loc   8 miles W of Dublin, off N4
Arch   Sullivan/O'Brien

For list of abbreviations see page 527

Swords (1996)
Balheary Avenue, Swords
Tel (01) 840 9819
Fax (01) 840 9819
Mem 400
Sec O McGuinness (Mgr)
Holes 18 L 5677 m Par 71 SSS 70
V'tors U
Fees £9 (£12)
Loc 10 miles N of Dublin, nr airport
Arch T Halpin

Turvey (1994)
Turvey Avenue, Donabate
Tel (01) 843 5169
Mem 335
Sec R Martin (Mgr)
Holes 18 hole course
V'tors U
Fees £12 (£15)
Loc Donabate

Westmanstown (1988)
Clonsilla, Dublin 15
Tel (01) 820 5817
Mem 1000
Sec R Monaghan (Hon)
Holes 18 L 5819 m SSS 70
V'tors U SOC
Fees £15 (£20)
Loc 15 miles W of Dublin, nr Lucan
Arch Eddie Hackett

Woodbrook (1921)
Dublin Road, Bray
Tel (01) 282 4799
Fax (01) 282 1950
Mem 950
Sec B O'Neill (Gen Mgr)
Pro W Kinsella
Holes 18 L 6221 m SSS 72
Recs Am–L Macnamara
 Pro–D Smyth, J McHenry
 Ladies Pro–L Davies
V'tors WD–U WE–phone Sec SOC
Fees £35 (£40)
Loc 11 miles SE of Dublin on N11
Arch P McEvoy

Dublin City

Carrickmines (1900)
Golf Lane, Carrickmines, Dublin 18
Tel (01) 295 5972
Mem 500
Sec AN McEachern (Hon)
Holes 9 L 6103 yds SSS 69
Recs Am–68
 Pro–68
V'tors U exc Wed/Sat–NA
Fees £20 Sun–£23 Sat–NA
Loc 6 miles S of Dublin

Castle (1913)
Woodside Drive, Rathfarnham, Dublin 14
Tel (01) 490 4207
Fax (01) 492 0264
Mem 800
Sec LF Blackburne (Sec/Mgr)
Pro D Kinsella (01) 492 0272
Holes 18 L 6270 yds SSS 68
Recs Am–67 J Pender
 Pro–63 P Townsend
V'tors Mon/Thurs/Fri–U Wed–U before 12.30pm WE/BH–M SOC
Fees £35
Loc 5 miles S of Dublin

Clontarf (1912)
Donnycarney House, Malahide Road, Dublin 3
Tel (01) 833 1892
Fax (01) 833 1933
Mem 1035
Sec N Rooney (Mgr)
Pro J Craddock (01) 833 1877
Holes 18 L 5447 m SSS 68
Recs Am–66 R Murray
 Pro–64 H Bradshaw
V'tors WD–U WE–M SOC
Fees £26
Loc 2 miles NE of city centre
Arch HS Colt

Deer Park (1974)
Deer Park Hotel, Howth Castle, Howth
Tel (01) 8222624
Fax (01) 8392405
Mem 312
Sec JP Doran (Hon) (01) 8326039
Pro None
Holes 18 L 6781 yds Par 72 SSS 71
 18 L 6475 yds Par 72 SSS 70
 12 hole Par 3 course
Recs Am–71 P Coldrick (1995)
V'tors U SOC
Fees £8.90 (£11.50)
Loc 8 miles NE of Dublin
Arch F Hawtree

Edmondstown (1944)
Rathfarnham, Dublin 16
Tel (01) 493 2461
Fax (01) 493 3152
Mem 600
Sec S Davies (01) 493 1082
Pro A Crofton (01) 494 1049
Holes 18 L 5663 m Par 70 SSS 70
Recs Am–68 A Bernstein
V'tors WD/BH–U SOC
Fees £25 (£30) Summer
 £20 (£25) Winter
Loc 5 miles S of Dublin
Arch McAllister

Elm Green (1996)
Castleknock, Dublin 15
Tel (01) 820 0797
Fax (01) 822 6668
Sec G Carr (Sec/Mgr)
Pro A O'Connor, P McGahan
Holes 18 L 5300 m Par 71 SSS 66

Recs Am–68 B Begley
 Pro–65 E O'Connell
V'tors U
Fees £12 (£17)
Loc NW Dublin
Mis Driving range
Arch Eddie Hackett

Elm Park (1927)
Nutley House, Donnybrook, Dublin 4
Tel (01) 269 3438/269 3014
Fax (01) 269 4505
Mem 1750
Sec A McCormack (01) 269 3438
Pro S Green (01) 269 2650
Holes 18 L 5374 m SSS 68
Recs Am–63 PF Hogan
 Pro–63 P Townsend
V'tors U–phone Pro
Fees £35 (£45)
Loc 3 miles S of Dublin

Foxrock (1893)
Torquay Road, Foxrock, Dublin 18
Tel (01) 289 5668
Fax (01) 289 4943
Mem 660
Sec WM Daly (01) 289 3992
Pro D Walker (01) 289 3414
Holes 9 L 5667 m Par 70 SSS 68
Recs Am–68 D Campbell, M Sludds
 Pro–66 M Murphy
V'tors WD/BH/Sun–M Tues & Sat–NA
Fees £30
Loc 5 miles S of Dublin

Grange (1911)
Whitechurch Road, Rathfarnham, Dublin 16
Tel (01) 493 2832
Fax (01) 493 9490
Mem 1050 235(L) 210(J)
Sec JA O'Donoghue (01) 493 2889
Pro B Hamill (01) 493 2299
Holes 18 L 5517 m SSS 69
Recs Am–64 WB Buckley
 Pro–62 C O'Connor Jr
V'tors WD–U exc Tues/Wed pm–NA WE–M
Fees £35 (£40)
Loc Rathfarnham, 5 miles from centre of Dublin

Hazel Grove (1988)
Mount Seskin Road, Jobstown, Tallaght, Dublin 24
Tel (01) 452 0911
Mem 400 175(L)
Sec J Matthews
Pro None
Holes 9 L 5300 m SSS 67
Recs Am–61 H Donnelly (1996)
 Ladies–61 M O'Connell (1996)
V'tors Mon/Wed/Fri–U Sun–NA Tues/Thurs/Sat–restricted
Fees £9
Loc 3 miles from Tallaght, off Blessington road
Arch Eddie Hackett

For list of abbreviations see page 527

Howth (1916)
Carrickbrack Road, Sutton, Dublin 13
- **Tel** (01) 832 3055
- **Fax** (01) 832 1793
- **Mem** 1200
- **Sec** Ms A MacNeice
- **Pro** JF McGuirk (01) 839 3895
- **Holes** 18 L 5618 m SSS 69
- **Recs** Am–66 M Roe
  Pro–71
- **V'tors** WD–U exc Wed WE–M
- **Fees** £20 Fri–£22
- **Loc** 9 miles NE of Dublin, nr Sutton Cross

Kilmashogue (1994)
College Road, Whitechurch, Dublin 16
- **Mem** 355
- **Sec** V O'Kelly (Hon)
- **Pro** W Sullivan
- **Holes** 9 L 5320 m Par 70 SSS 70
- **Fees** £10
- **Loc** Dublin

Newlands (1926)
Clondalkin, Dublin 22
- **Tel** (01) 459 2903
- **Fax** (01) 459 3498
- **Mem** 1086
- **Sec** AT O'Neill (01) 459 3157
- **Pro** K O'Donnell (01) 459 3538
- **Holes** 18 L 6184 yds SSS 70
- **Recs** Am–66 R Burdon, P Hanley Jr
  Pro–68 C O'Connor
- **V'tors** WD–U am WE/BH–NA SOC
- **Fees** IR£32
- **Loc** 6 miles SW of Dublin at Newlands Cross (N7)
- **Arch** James Braid

Rathfarnham (1899)
Newtown, Dublin 16
- **Tel** (01) 493 1201/493 1561
- **Fax** (01) 493 1561
- **Mem** 561
- **Sec** DO Tipping (01) 493 1201
- **Pro** B O'Hara
- **Holes** 9 L 5787 m SSS 70
- **Recs** Am–69 R Hayden
- **V'tors** U exc Tues & Sat–NA
- **Fees** £22.50
- **Loc** 6 miles S of Dublin
- **Arch** John Jacobs

Royal Dublin (1885)
North Bull Island, Dollymount, Dublin 3
- **Tel** (01) 833 6346/1262
- **Fax** (01) 833 6504
- **Mem** 975
- **Sec** JA Lambe (01) 833 1262
- **Pro** L Owens (01) 833 6477 (Touring Pro C O'Connor Sr)
- **Holes** 18 L 6925 yds SSS 73
- **Recs** Am–67 G O'Donovan (1984)
  Pro–63 B Langer, G Cullen (1985)
- **V'tors** U H exc Wed Sat–NA before 4pm SOC–WD
- **Fees** IR£60 (IR£70)
- **Loc** 3 miles NE of Dublin, on coast road to Howth
- **Mis** Practice range. Indoor tuition
- **Arch** HS Colt

St Anne's (1921)
North Bull Island, Dollymount, Dublin 5
- **Tel** (01) 833 2797/6471
- **Fax** (01) 833 4618
- **Mem** 520
- **Sec** W Bornemann (01) 833 6471
- **Pro** P Skerritt
- **Holes** 18 L 5797 m Par 70 SSS 70
- **Recs** Am–67 S Rodgers
  Pro–64 P Skerritt
- **V'tors** WE/BH–NA SOC
- **Fees** £25 (£30)
- **Loc** Dublin 5 miles
- **Arch** Eddie Hackett

Stackstown (1975)
Kellystown Road, Rathfarnham, Dublin 16
- **Tel** (01) 494 1993
- **Mem** 1300
- **Sec** K Lawlor (Sec/Mgr)
- **Pro** M Kavanagh (01) 944561
- **Holes** 18 L 6494 m SSS 72
- **Recs** Am–70 P Harrington
- **V'tors** WD–U SOC
- **Fees** £16 (£20)
- **Loc** 7 miles SE of Dublin

Sutton (1890)
Cush Point, Sutton, Dublin 13
- **Tel** (01) 832 3013
- **Fax** (01) 832 1603
- **Mem** 625
- **Sec** H O'Neill
- **Pro** N Lynch
- **Holes** 9 L 5624 m Par 70 SSS 67
- **Recs** Am–64 M Hanway
  Pro–64 L Owens (1987)
- **V'tors** Tues–NA Sat–NA before 5.30pm
- **Fees** £20 (£25)
- **Loc** 7 miles E of Dublin

Co Fermanagh

Castle Hume
Belleek Road, Enniskillen BT93 7ED
- **Tel** (01) 365 327077
- **Fax** (01) 365 327076
- **Mem** 175
- **Sec** Helen Keenan (Sec/Mgr)
- **Holes** 18 L 6139 m Par 72 SSS 70
- **Recs** Am–69
- **V'tors** U
- **Fees** £12 (£18)
- **Loc** Enniskillen
- **Mis** Driving range
- **Arch** Tony Carroll

Enniskillen (1896)
Castlecoole, Enniskillen BT74 6HZ
- **Tel** (01365) 325250
- **Mem** 600
- **Sec** W McBrien
- **Pro** None
- **Holes** 18 L 5574 m SSS 70
- **Recs** Am–67 D Robinson (1992)
- **V'tors** U SOC
- **Fees** D–£15 (£18)
- **Loc** 1 mile SE of Enniskillen, on Castlecoole Estate
- **Arch** TJ McAuley

Co Galway

Athenry (1902)
Palmerstown, Oranmore
- **Tel** (091) 794466
- **Fax** (091) 794971
- **Mem** 700
- **Sec** Eileen Burke (091) 753772
- **Pro** D Cunningham (091) 790843
- **Holes** 18 L 6100 yds Par 70 SSS 70
- **Recs** Am–69 F Holland (1997)
- **V'tors** WD/Sat–U Sun–M SOC
- **Fees** £15 (£18)
- **Loc** 10 miles E of Galway on Athenry road
- **Arch** Eddie Hackett

Ballinasloe (1894)
Rosgloss, Ballinasloe
- **Tel** (0905) 42126
- **Fax** (0905) 42538
- **Mem** 835
- **Sec** Pauline Hardiman
- **Holes** 18 L 5865 m Par 72 SSS 70
- **Recs** Am–64 M Quinn
  Pro–66 C O'Connor
  Ladies–68 M Madden
- **V'tors** U SOC
- **Fees** £12
- **Loc** Ballinasloe 2 miles
- **Arch** Eddie Hackett

Bearna (1996)
Corboley, Bearna
- **Tel** (091) 592677
- **Mem** 500
- **Sec** K Cantrell (Hon)
- **Holes** 18 L 5746 m Par 72 SSS 72
- **V'tors** U
- **Fees** £15

Connemara (1973)
Ballyconnelly, Clifden
- **Tel** (095) 23502/23602
- **Fax** (095) 23662
- **Mem** 700
- **Sec** J McLaughlin (Sec/Mgr)
- **Pro** H O'Neill (095) 23502
- **Holes** 18 L 6560 m SSS 72
- **Recs** Am–67 D Mortimer (1996)
  Pro–68
- **V'tors** U H SOC
- **Fees** £25
- **Loc** 8 miles SW of Clifden
- **Arch** Eddie Hackett

Connemara Isles
Annaghvane, Lettermore, Connemara
Tel (091) 572498
Fax (091) 572214
Mem 104
Sec P O'Conghaile (Sec/Mgr)
Holes 9 L 5168 yds Par 70 SSS 67
Recs Am–PO Suilleabhain (1998)
V'tors U SOC
Fees £10–£12
Loc 3 miles W of Costello
Arch Craddock/Ruddy

Curra West (1996)
Curra, Kylebrack, Loughrea
Tel (091) 45121
Mem 60
Sec J Cunningham (Hon)
Holes 9 L 5113 m Par 70 SSS 67
V'tors U
Fees £7 (£7)

Galway (1895)
Blackrock, Salthill, Galway
Tel (091) 522033
Fax (091) 522033
Mem 1020
Sec P Fahy
Pro D Wallace (091) 523038
Holes 18 L 5828 m SSS 70
V'tors Restricted Tues & Sun
Fees £18 (£23)
Loc 3 miles W of Galway City

Galway Bay G&CC (1993)
Renville, Oranmore
Tel (091) 790500
Fax (091) 790510
Mem 425
Sec E Meagher (Mgr)
Pro E O'Connor (091) 790503
Holes 18 L 6350 m SSS 73
V'tors U H SOC
Fees £30–£35
Loc 10 miles E of Galway City (N18)
Mis Driving range. Golf Academy
Arch C O'Connor Jr

Gort (1924)
Castlequarter, Gort
Tel (091) 632244
Mem 460
Sec S Devlin (Hon) (091) 631281
Pro None
Holes 18 L 5979 m SSS 71
Recs Am–68 A Devlin
V'tors U exc Sun am SOC
Fees £12 (£12)
Loc 20 miles S of Galway
Arch C O'Connor Jr

Loughrea (1924)
Graigue, Loughrea
Tel (091) 41049
Mem 400
Sec M Hawkins (Mgr)
Holes 18 L 4987 m Par 69 SSS 66
Recs Am–67 S Glynn
V'tors U SOC

Fees On application
Loc 1 mile N of Loughrea, off Dublin–Galway road. 20 miles E of Galway
Arch Eddie Hackett

Mountbellew (1929)
Mountbellew, Ballinasloe
Tel (0905) 79259
Mem 380
Sec M Meehan (Mgr)
Holes 9 L 5143 m SSS 66
V'tors U SOC
Fees £8
Loc 50km NE of Galway on N63

Oughterard (1973)
Gortreevagh, Oughterard
Tel (091) 552131
Fax (091) 552733
Mem 850
Sec J Waters (Hon)
Pro M Ryan (Ext 226)
Holes 18 L 6150 yds SSS 69
Recs Am–67 T Hargrove (1995)
V'tors U SOC
Fees £15
Loc 15 miles NW of Galway (N59)
Arch Harris

Portumna (1907)
Ennis Road, Portumna
Tel (0509) 41059
Mem 570
Sec R Clarke (Hon)
Holes 18 L 5474 m Par 68 SSS 67
Recs Am–68 W Carty (1995), S Breen (1996)
Pro–63 H Bradshaw
V'tors U SOC
Fees £12
Loc 40 miles SE of Galway on Lough Derg

Tuam (1907)
Barnacurragh, Tuam
Tel (093) 28993
Fax (093) 26003
Mem 700
Sec V Gaffney (Sec/Mgr)
Pro L Smyth (093) 24091
Holes 18 L 5944 m SSS 71
Recs Am–68 D Williams (1996)
Pro–68 R Rafferty (1983)
V'tors Sun–NA SOC–WD
Fees £10
Loc 20 miles N of Galway
Arch Eddie Hackett

Co Kerry

Ardfert (1993)
Sackville, Ardfert, Tralee
Tel (066) 34744
Fax (066) 34744
Mem 171
Sec Sinead Maunsell
Pro N Cassidy
Holes 9 L 4754 m Par 66
V'tors U

Fees 9 holes–£9 18 holes–£14
Loc 60 miles NW of Tralee (R551)
Mis Driving range
Arch James Healy

Ballybunion (1893)
Sandhill Road, Ballybunion
Tel (068) 27146
Fax (068) 27387
Email bbgolfc@iol.ie
Mem 648
Sec J McKenna (Sec/Mgr)
Pro B O'Callaghan
Holes Old 18 L 6542 yds SSS 72
Cashen 18 L 6477 yds SSS 70
Recs Am–67 P Mulcare
V'tors U SOC
Fees Old: £60 New: £35
Old+New: D–£80
Loc 2 miles S of Ballybunion. 50 miles W of Limerick, via Tarbert

Ballyheigue Castle (1995)
Ballyheigue, Tralee
Tel (066) 33555
Fax (066) 33147
Mem 180
Sec JP Broderick (Mgr)
Holes 9 L 6292 m Par 72 SSS 74
V'tors U
Fees £17
Loc 15 miles NW of Tralee (R551)

Beaufort (1994)
Churchtown, Beaufort, Killarney
Tel (064) 44440
Fax (064) 44752
Mem 200
Sec C Kelly
Pro H Duggan
Holes 18 L 6605 yds Par 71 SSS 72
V'tors WD–H SOC
Fees £25 (£33)
Loc 7 miles W of Killarney, off N72
Arch Dr Arthur Spring

Castlegregory
Stradbally, Castlegregory
Tel (066) 39444
Mem 296
Sec M Moloney (Sec/Mgr)
Holes 9 L 5340 m SSS 68
V'tors U SOC
Fees £14 (£14)
Loc 18 miles W of Tralee
Arch Arthur Spring

Ceann Sibeal (1924)
Ballyferriter
Tel (066) 56255/56408
Fax (066) 56409
Mem 460
Sec S Fahy (Mgr)
Pro D O'Connor
Holes 18 L 6690 yds SSS 71
Recs Am–66 CG O'Sullivan
V'tors U SOC
Fees £25 D–£35
Loc Dingle Peninsula, W of Tralee
Arch Hackett/O'Connor Jr

For list of abbreviations see page 527

Dooks (1889)
Glenbeigh
Tel (066) 68205/68200
Fax (066) 68476
Mem 650
Sec M Shanahan (Sec/Mgr) (066) 67370
Holes 18 L 5346 m Par 70 SSS 68
Recs Am–72 MI McGillicuddy (1992)
V'tors WD–U H before 5pm WE/BH–phone first SOC
Fees £25 (£25)
Loc 3 miles N of Glenbeigh, on Ring of Kerry (N70)

Kenmare (1903)
Kenmare
Tel (064) 41291
Fax (064) 42061
Mem 349
Sec M MacGearailt
Pro None
Holes 18 L 5441 m SSS 69
V'tors U SOC
Fees £16
Loc 20 miles S of Killarney on Cork road
Arch Eddie Hackett

Kerries (1995)
Tralee
Tel (066) 22112
Mem 280
Sec M Barrett (Mgr)
Holes 9 L 2718 m Par 35 SSS 39
V'tors U
Fees £14
Loc Tralee

Killarney (1893)
Mahoney's Point, Killarney
Tel (064) 31034
Fax (064) 33065
Mem 1500
Sec T Prendergast
Pro T Coveney (064) 31615
Holes Mahoney's Point 18 L 6164 m SSS 72; Killeen 18 L 6475 m SSS 73
Recs Mahoney's Point Am–68 S Coyne (1968) Killeen Am–73 DF O'Sullivan Pro–65 D Feherty
V'tors H SOC
Fees £40
Loc 3 miles W of Killarney (N72)
Mis Lackabane course open May 1999
Arch Mahoney's Point: Longhurst/ Campbell; Killeen: Hackett/ O'Sullivan; Lackabane: Steel

Killorglin (1992)
Steelroe, Killorglin
Tel (066) 61979
Fax (066) 61437
Mem 230
Sec B Dodd
Pro None
Holes 18 L 6464 yds SSS 72
Recs Am–64 S Harmon (1997)
V'tors U SOC
Fees IR£14 (IR£16)
Loc 1 mile from Killorglin on Tralee road (N70). 12 miles W of Killarney
Arch Eddie Hackett

Parknasilla (1974)
Parknasilla, Sneem
Tel (064) 45122
Mem 180
Sec M Walsh
Holes 9 L 6044 yds Par 70 SSS 70
V'tors U
Fees £15
Loc Great Southern Hotel, 2 miles E of Sneem on Ring of Kerry
Mis Driving range

Ross (1995)
Ross Road, Killarney
Tel (064) 31125
Fax (064) 31860
Mem 80
Sec M Doyle (Mgr)
Pro A O'Meara
Holes 9 L 5674 m Par 72 SSS 72
V'tors U
Fees £18
Loc In Killarney
Arch Rodger Jones

Tralee (1896)
West Barrow, Ardfert
Tel (066) 36379
Fax (066) 36008
Mem 1000
Pro None
Holes 18 L 6252 m SSS 71
Recs Am–66 G O'Sullivan (1987)
V'tors WD–U H before 4.30pm exc Wed–restricted WE/BH–NA exc 11–12.30–H SOC–WD
Fees £30 (£40)
Loc 8 miles NW of Tralee on Spa/Fenit road
Arch Arnold Palmer

Waterville (1889)
Ring of Kerry, Waterville
Tel (066) 74102
Fax (066) 74482
Mem 320
Sec N Cronin
Pro L Higgins
Holes 18 L 7184 yds SSS 74
Recs Pro–65 L Higgins
V'tors U H SOC
Fees £50
Loc ¼ mile N of Waterville on Ring of Kerry
Mis Driving range
Arch Hackett/Mulcahy

Co Kildare

Athy (1906)
Geraldine, Athy
Tel (0507) 31729
Mem 450
Sec M Hogan (Hon)
Holes 18 L 6308 yds Par 71 SSS 69
V'tors WD–U Sat–M SOC
Fees £13 (£17)
Loc 1 mile N of Athy on Kildare road

Bodenstown (1983)
Bodenstown, Sallins
Tel (045) 97096
Mem 650
Sec J Sexton (Hon)
Holes Old 18 L 6132 m SSS 71 Ladyhill 18 L 5278 m SSS 68
Recs Am–69 M Kelly, W Kelly (1998)
V'tors U exc WE–NA (Old course)
Fees Old: £12 Ladyhill: £10
Loc 4 miles N of Naas on Clane road. 18 miles W of Dublin, off N7

Castlewarden G&CC (1989)
Straffan
Tel (01) 458 9254
Fax (01) 458 9254
Mem 550 225(L)
Sec J Ferriter (Hon)
Pro G Egan (01) 458 8219
Holes 18 L 6624 yds Par 72 SSS 71
V'tors WD–U WE–M SOC
Fees £17–£20 (£20)
Loc 13 miles W of Dublin, off N4
Arch Halpin/Browne

Cill Dara (1920)
Little Curragh, Kildare Town
Tel (045) 521433/521295
Mem 400
Sec P Flanagan (Hon)
Pro M O'Boyle
Holes 9 L 5842 m SSS 70
Recs Am–67 T Royce, P Doyle (1989)
V'tors WD–U before 2pm exc Wed–NA Sat–NA after noon Sun/BH–NA SOC
Fees £10 (£12)
Loc 1 mile W of Kildare town

Craddockstown (1991)
Blessington Road, Naas
Tel (045) 897610
Fax (045) 896968
Mem 580
Sec L Watson
Holes 18 L 6134 m Par 71 SSS 70
Recs Am–69 J Dempsey (1995) Ladies–75 S Lunny (1997)
V'tors U
Fees £14 (£18)
Loc Naas
Arch Arthur Spring

For list of abbreviations see page 527

Co Kildare

The Curragh (1883)
Curragh
Tel (045) 441238/441714
Fax (045) 441714
Mem 500 160(L)
Sec Ann Culleton (045) 441714
Pro G Burke (045) 441896
Holes 18 L 6035 m SSS 71
Recs Am–63 I Stewart (1997)
 Pro–63 L Walker (1997)
 Ladies–66 L Behan (1998)
V'tors WD–check with Sec
Fees On application
Loc 3 miles S of Newbridge

Highfield (1992)
Highfield House, Carbury
Tel (0405) 31021
Fax (0405) 31021
Mem 550
Sec P Duggan (Sec/Mgr)
Pro None
Holes 18 L 5707 m SSS 69
Recs Am–71 L Williams (1998)
V'tors WD–U WE–U after 12 noon
Fees £10 (£14)
Loc 32 miles W of Dublin on N4
Arch Alan Duggan

The K Club (1991)
Kildare Hotel & CC, Straffan
Tel (01) 601 7300
Fax (01) 601 7399
Mem 527
Sec P Crowe (Golf Dir)
Pro E Jones
Holes 18 L 7200 yds SSS 72
Recs Pro–64 C Montgomerie (1997)
V'tors U H SOC–WD
Fees IR£130
Loc 18 miles SW of Dublin (N7)
Mis Driving range
Arch Arnold Palmer

Killeen (1986)
Killeenbeg, Kill
Tel (045) 866003
Fax (045) 875881
Mem 170
Sec P Carey
Pro None
Holes 18 L 5815 m Par 71 SSS 71
V'tors WD–U WE–NA before 10am
Fees £17 (£20)
Loc 2 miles off N7 on Sallins road
Arch Ruddy/Craddock

Knockanally (1985)
Donadea, North Kildare
Tel (045) 869322
Fax (045) 869322
Mem 500
Sec N Lyons
Holes 18 L 6424 yds SSS 71
Recs Pro–66 K O'Donnell,
 D James (1988)
V'tors U
Fees £18 (£22)
Loc 20 miles W of Dublin on
 Galway road (M4)
Arch N Lyons

Leixlip (1994)
Leixlip
Tel (01) 624 4978
Fax (01) 624 6185
Mem 200
Sec J McKone
Holes 9 L 6030 yds Par 72 SSS 70
V'tors U
Fees £13 (£15)
Loc 10 miles W of Dublin on N4
Arch Eddie Hackett

Naas (1896)
Kerdiffstown, Naas
Tel (045) 874644
Mem 1000
Sec M Conway
Holes 18 L 5660 m SSS 70
V'tors U SOC
Fees £18 (£25)
Loc 2 miles N of Naas
Arch Arthur Spring

Newbridge (1997)
Tankardsgarden, Newbridge
Tel (045) 431289
Mem 35
Sec F Meehan (Hon)
Holes 18 L 5921 m Par Par 72 SSS 72
V'tors U
Fees £7 (£10)

Woodlands (1985)
Coolereagh, Coill Dubh
Tel (045) 860777
Mem 410
Sec T Butler (Hon)
Holes 9 L 5857 m Par 72 SSS 71
V'tors U
Fees £8 (£10)
Loc Naas

Co Kilkenny

Callan (1929)
Geraldine, Callan
Tel (056) 25136/25949
Mem 600
Sec M Duggan (Hon)
Pro J O'Dwyer
Holes 18 L 6383 yds Par 72 SSS 70
Recs Pro–69 J O'Dwyer
V'tors U SOC
Fees £11
Loc 1 mile SE of Callan. 10 miles
 SW of Kilkenny
Arch Bryan Moor

Castlecomer (1935)
Dromgoole, Castlecomer
Tel (056) 41139
Mem 450
Sec J Kelly (Hon)
Holes 9 L 5923 m Par 71 SSS 71
Recs Am–69 K Kenny (1994)
V'tors U SOC–WD
Fees £8 (£10)
Loc 11 miles N of Kilkenny on N7

Kilkenny (1896)
Glendine, Kilkenny
Tel (056) 65400
Fax (056) 65400
Mem 950
Sec S O'Neill (056) 65400
Pro N Leahy (056) 61730
Holes 18 L 6435 yds SSS 70
Recs Am–64 G Stewart
 Pro–68 B Todd
V'tors U
Fees £20 (£25)
Loc 1 mile N of Kilkenny, off N77

Mountain View
See Stop Press on page 529

Mount Juliet (1991)
Thomastown
Tel (056) 73000
Fax (056) 73019
Sec Kate MacCann
Pro M Reid
Holes 18 L 7143 yds SSS 74
Recs Pro–65 N Faldo (1993)
V'tors U
Fees £70 (£75)
Loc 10 miles S of Kilkenny, off
 Dublin–Waterford road.
Mis Driving range-residents and
 green fees. Golf Academy
Arch Jack Nicklaus

Co Laois

Abbeyleix (1895)
Rathmoyle, Abbeyleix
Tel (0502) 31450
Mem 280
Sec GP O'Hara (Hon)
Holes 9 L 5680 yds SSS 69
V'tors WD–U WE–NA SOC–WD/Sat
Fees £10
Loc 10 miles S of Portlaoise.
 60 miles SW of Dublin on
 Cork road

Heath (Portlaoise) (1930)
The Heath, Portlaoise
Tel (0502) 46533
Fax (0502) 46866
Mem 830
Sec P Carpendale (Hon)
Pro E Doyle (0502) 46622
Holes 18 L 5873 m Par 71 SSS 70
Recs Am–67 T Tyrrell (1983)
V'tors U
Fees £10 (£17)
Loc 4 miles E of Portlaoise
Mis Floodlit driving range

Mountrath (1929)
Knockanina, Mountrath
Tel (0502) 32558
Mem 500
Sec J Mulhare (0502) 32421
Holes 18 L 6020 yds Par 71 SSS 69
Recs Am–68 S Carter
V'tors U
Fees £10

For list of abbreviations see page 527

Loc 10 miles W of Portlaoise. Mountrath 2 miles

Portarlington (1909)
Garryhinch, Portarlington
Tel (0502) 23115
Fax (0502) 23044
Mem 450
Sec M Turley (Hon)
Holes 18 L 6004 m Par 72 SSS 71
Recs Am–70 M Turley (1997)
V'tors WD–U WE–restricted
Fees £14 (£17)
Loc Between Portarlington and Mountmellick on L116

Rathdowney (1931)
Coulnaboul West, Rathdowney
Tel (0505) 46170
Fax (0505) 46170
Mem 350
Sec S Bolger (Hon)
Holes 18 L 5894 m Par 71 SSS 70
Recs Am–70 P Roane
V'tors U exc Sun–NA SOC
Fees £10
Loc 1 mile S of Rathdowney. 20 miles SW of Portlaoise
Arch Hackett/Suttle

Co Leitrim

Ballinamore (1941)
Creevy, Ballinamore
Tel (078) 44346
Mem 102
Sec P Duignan (Hon)
Holes 9 L 5204 yds Par 66 SSS 63
Recs Am–68 D Gannon
V'tors U SOC
Fees £10
Loc 2 miles N of Ballinamore. 20 miles NE of Carrick-on-Shannon

Carrick-on-Shannon (1910)
Woodbrook, Carrick-on-Shannon
Tel (079) 67015
Mem 210
Sec A McNally (Sec/Mgr)
Holes 9 L 5584 yds SSS 68
V'tors U
Fees IR£12
Loc 4 miles W of Carrick-on-Shannon on N4

Co Limerick

Abbeyfeale (1993)
Dromtrasna Collins, Abbeyfeale
Tel (068) 32033
Mem 85
Sec M O'Riordan (Mgr)
Pro D Power
Holes 9 L 4004 yds Par 62 SSS 61
V'tors U
Fees £6
Loc 12 miles SW of Newcastle West

Adare Manor (1900)
Adare
Tel (061) 396204
Fax (061) 396800
Mem 400
Sec M Spillane
Pro J Coyle
Holes 18 L 5396 m SSS 69
V'tors WD–U WE–M
Fees D–£15
Loc 10 miles SW of Limerick

Castletroy (1937)
Castletroy, Limerick
Tel (061) 335261
Fax (061) 335373
Mem 940
Sec L Hayes (061) 335753
Pro (061) 330450 (Shop)
Holes 18 L 5802 m SSS 71
V'tors WD–U Sat am–U Sat pm/ Sun–M SOC–Mon/Wed/Fri
Fees £23 (£30)
Loc 2 miles N of Limerick on Dublin road

Killeline (1993)
Newcastle West
Tel (069) 61600
Fax (069) 62853
Mem 278
Sec J McCoy
Holes 18 L 6700 yds Par 72
V'tors U
Fees £12

Limerick (1891)
Ballyclough, Limerick
Tel (061) 414083
Fax (061) 415146
Mem 1325
Sec D McDonogh (061) 415146
Pro J Cassidy (061) 412492
Holes 18 L 6479 yds SSS 71
Recs Am–68 M Morrissey (1994) Pro–67 P Broadhurst (1995)
V'tors WD–U before 5pm exc Tues WE–M SOC–WD
Fees £22.50
Loc 3 miles S of Limerick

Limerick County G&CC
Ballyneety
Tel (061) 351881
Fax (061) 351384
Mem 250
Sec Vari McGreevy (Mgr)
Pro P Murphy
Holes 18 L 6137 m Par 72 SSS 74
V'tors U SOC
Fees £20 (£25)
Loc 5 miles S of Limerick (R512)
Mis Driving range
Arch Des Smyth

Newcastle West (1938)
Ardagh
Tel (069) 76500
Fax (069) 76511
Mem 450 112(L).

Sec P Lyons (Sec/Mgr)
Holes 18 L 5905 m SSS 72
Recs Am–67 A Spring (1996)
V'tors U exc Sun–U after 4pm SOC
Fees £18
Loc 6 miles N of Newcastle West, off N21
Mis Floodlit driving range
Arch Arthur Spring

Co Londonderry

Benone Par Three
53 Benone Avenue, Benone, Limavady BT49 0LQ
Tel (015047) 50555
Sec CL Smith
Holes 9 L 1427 yds Par 3 course
V'tors U
Fees On application
Loc 12 miles N of Limavady on A2 coast road

Brown Trout (1984)
209 Agivey Road, Aghadowey, Coleraine BT51 4AD
Tel (01265) 868209
Fax (01265) 868878
Mem 150
Sec B O'Hara (Sec/Mgr)
Pro K Revie
Holes 9 L 2800 yds SSS 68
Recs Am–64 D Mulholland
V'tors U SOC
Fees £10 (£15)
Loc 8 miles S of Coleraine at junction of A54/B66
Arch W O'Hara Sr

Castlerock (1901)
Circular Road, Castlerock BT51 4TJ
Tel (01265) 848314
Fax (01265) 848314
Mem 1100
Sec RG McBride
Pro R Kelly
Holes 18 L 6121 m SSS 72 9 L 2457 m SSS 34
Recs Am–67 D Mulholland
V'tors WD–U exc Fri SOC
Fees 18 hole:£25 (£35) 9 hole:£8 (£12)
Loc 5 miles W of Coleraine on A2
Arch Ben Sayers

City of Derry (1912)
49 Victoria Road, Londonderry BT47 2PU
Tel (01) 504 46369
Mem 775
Pro M Doherty (01504) 311496
Holes Prehen 18 L 6487 yds SSS 71 Dunhugh 9 L 4708 yds SSS 63
Recs Am–68 D Ballentine
V'tors WD–U before 4pm –M after 4pm WE–U H SOC
Fees On application
Loc 3 miles from E end of Craigavon Bridge towards Strabane

For list of abbreviations see page 527

Co Londonderry

Foyle (1994)
Alder Road, Londonderry BT48 8DB
Tel (01504) 352222
Fax (01504) 353967
Mem 177
Sec M Lapsley
Pro K McLaughlin
Holes 18 L 6678 m SSS 72
9 hole course
Recs Am–70 D Logue (1996)
V'tors U
Fees £12 (£15)
Loc Londonderry
Mis Driving range
Arch Frank Ainsworth

Kilrea (1920)
Drumagarner Road, Kilrea
Tel (01266) 821048
Mem 310
Sec DP Clarke
Holes 9 L 4514 yds SSS 62
Recs Am–61 R Rees (1982), T Moore (1989)
V'tors Tues & Wed–NA after 5pm Sat–NA after 12 noon
Fees £10 (£12.50)
Loc Nr Kilrea on Maghera road. 15 miles S of Coleraine

Moyola Park (1976)
15 Curran Road, Castledawson, Magherafelt BT45 8DG
Tel (01648) 468468
Fax (01648) 468468
Mem 940
Sec LWP Hastings (Hon)
Pro V Teague (01648) 468830
Holes 18 L 6062 yds Par 71
Recs Am–67 R Evans
Pro–67 J Loughrey
V'tors U SOC exc Sat
Fees £17 (£25)
Loc 40 miles NW of Belfast by M2. 35 miles S of Coleraine
Arch Don Patterson

Portstewart (1894)
117 Strand Road, Portstewart BT55 7PG
Tel (01265) 832015
Fax (01265) 834097
Mem 1524
Sec M Moss BA (01265) 833839
Pro A Hunter (01265) 832601
Holes Strand 18 L 6784 yds SSS 73
Riverside 9 L 2662 yds Par 32
Old 18 L 4733 yds SSS 62
Recs Strand Am–67 D Ballentine, M Kilgore (1997)
V'tors SOC–by arrangement
Fees Strand: £45 (£65)
Riverside: £11 (£16)
Old: £9 (£13)
Loc W boundary of Portstewart. N of Coleraine

Roe Park (1993)
Limavady BT49 9LB
Tel (01) 504 722212
Mem 300
Sec D Brockerton
Pro S Duffy
Holes 18 L 6318 yds Par 70 SSS 71
V'tors U
Fees £20 (£20)
Loc Limavady
Mis Driving range

Co Longford

County Longford (1900)
Glack, Dublin Road, Longford
Tel (043) 46310
Fax (043) 47082
Mem 327
Sec M Connellan
Pro None
Holes 18 L 6008 yds SSS 69
Recs Am–P Mitchell
V'tors U SOC
Fees On application
Loc Longford ½ mile on Dublin road
Arch Eddie Hackett

Co Louth

Ardee (1911)
Ardee
Tel (041) 53227/56283
Fax (041) 56137
Mem 650
Sec K McCarthy (Sec/Mgr) (041) 53227
Holes 18 L 6348 yds SSS 71
Recs Am–67 J Carroll
Pro–70 C O'Connor
V'tors U SOC
Fees £17 (£17)
Loc ½ mile N of Ardee
Arch Eddie Hackett

County Louth (1892)
Baltray, Drogheda
Tel (041) 982 2329
Fax (041) 982 2969
Mem 1055
Sec M Delany
Pro P McGuirk (041) 982 2444
Holes 18 L 6783 yds SSS 72
Recs Am–66 R Burns
Pro–67 P Cowen
V'tors By prior arrangement
Fees £45 (£55)
Loc 3 miles NE of Drogheda
Arch Tom Simpson

Dundalk (1905)
Blackrock, Dundalk
Tel (042) 21731
Fax (042) 22022
Mem 850
Sec J Carroll (042) 21731
Pro J Cassidy (042) 22102
Holes 18 L 6115 m SSS 72
V'tors U SOC
Fees £22 (£25)
Loc 3 miles S of Dundalk

Greenore (1896)
Greenore
Tel (042) 73212/73678
Fax (042) 73678
Mem 700
Sec R Daly (Sec/Mgr)
Holes 18 L 6506 yds Par 71 SSS 71
Recs Am–68 E McCarten
Pro–68 A Cardwell
V'tors WD–U before 5pm
WE/BH–by arrangement SOC
Fees £14 (£20)
Loc 15 miles E of Dundalk on Carlingford Lough
Arch Eddie Hackett

Killinbeg (1991)
Killin Park, Bridge a Chrin, Dundalk
Tel (042) 39303
Mem 175
Sec N Kilco (Sec/Mgr)
Pro None
Holes 18 L 4717 m Par 69 SSS 64
V'tors U SOC
Fees £10 (£14)
Loc 2 miles NW of Dundalk on Castletown road

Seapoint (1993)
Termonfeckin, Drogheda
Tel (041) 982 2333
Fax (041) 982 2331
Mem 400
Sec D Kirwan
Pro D Carroll (041) 988 1066
Holes 18 L 6184 m Par 71 SSS 72
Recs Am–72 D Branigan (1993)
Pro–68 M Bludds (1998)
V'tors U SOC
Fees £25 (£30)
Loc 5 miles NE of Drogheda (R166)
Arch Des Smyth

Towneley Hall (1994)
Tullyallen, Drogheda
Tel (041) 42229
Fax (041) 31762
Mem 125
Sec M Foley (Hon)
Holes 9 L 5221 m Par 71 SSS 69
V'tors U
Fees £6 (£7)
Loc 5 miles NW of Drogheda, off R168

Co Mayo

Achill Island (1951)
Keel, Achill
Tel (098) 43456
Mem 100
Sec E Masterson(Hon)
Holes 9 L 2689 m Par 70 SSS 67
Recs Am–69 J Lawlor (1990)
V'tors U H SOC
Fees £7
Loc 50 miles NW of Westport, on Achill Island
Arch P Skerritt

For list of abbreviations see page 527

Co Meath

Ashford Castle
Cong
Tel (092) 46003
Holes 9 L 4500 yds SSS 68
V'tors U SOC
Fees £15
Loc 25 miles N of Galway on Lough Corrib
Arch Eddie Hackett

Ballina (1910)
Mossgrove, Shanaghy, Ballina
Tel (096) 21050
Fax (096) 21050
Mem 460
Sec V Frawley (096) 21795
Holes 18 L 6103 yds SSS 69
Recs Am–69 N Dee (1996)
V'tors WD–U Sun–NA before noon SOC–WD
Fees £12 (£16)
Loc 1 mile E of Ballina

Ballinrobe (1895)
Clooncastle, Ballinrobe
Tel (092) 41118
Fax (092) 41889
Email bgcgolf@iol.ie
Mem 590
Sec Marie Jacob
Pro D Kearney
Holes 18 L 6043 m Par 73 SSS 72
Recs Am–67 P Killeen (1996)
V'tors U exc Sun–NA SOC
Fees £15–£18
Loc 2 miles NW of Ballinrobe on R331
Mis Driving range
Arch Tony O'Carroll

Ballyhaunis (1929)
Coolnaha, Ballyhaunis
Tel (0907) 30014
Mem 300
Sec T McNicholas (Hon)
Holes 9 L 5413 m Par 70 SSS 68
Recs Am–69 P Charlton (1995)
V'tors U exc Thurs (Ladies Day)–M Sun–NA SOC–WD
Fees £10
Loc 2 miles N of Ballyhaunis

Belmullet (1925)
Carne, Belmullet
Tel (097) 82292/81051
Fax (097) 81477
Mem 300
Sec A Valkenburg (097) 82292
Holes 18 L 6119 m SSS 72
V'tors U SOC
Fees £17 W–£70
Loc 2 miles W of Belmullet. 40 miles W of Ballina
Arch Eddie Hackett

Castlebar (1910)
Rocklands, Castlebar
Tel (094) 21649
Fax (094) 26088
Mem 650

Holes 18 L 6229 yds SSS 70
Recs Am–67 D Kelly
V'tors U exc Sun
Fees £12 (£15)
Loc 1 mile S of Castlebar, on Galway road

Claremorris (1917)
Castlemagarrett, Claremorris
Tel (094) 71527
Mem 300
Sec W Feeley (Hon)
Holes 18 L 6454 yds SSS 69
Recs Am–66 P Killeen
Pro–63 C O'Connor
V'tors WD–U before lunch Sat–U before noon SOC
Fees £12 (£14)
Loc 2 miles S of Claremorris (N17)
Arch Tom Craddock

Mulranny (1968)
Mulranny, Westport
Tel (098) 36262
Mem 100
Sec D Nevin (Hon)
Holes 9 L 6255 yds Par 71 SSS 69
V'tors U
Fees £8
Loc 20 miles NW of Castlebar

Swinford (1922)
Brabazon Park, Swinford
Tel (094) 51378
Mem 300
Sec T Regan (094) 51502
Holes 9 L 5901 yds SSS 68
Recs Am–70 B Finlay (1991)
V'tors U SOC–exc Sun
Fees D–£10 (£10)
Loc S of Swinford, off Kiltimagh road

Westport (1908)
Carowholly, Westport
Tel (098) 28262/27070
Fax (098) 27217
Mem 700
Sec P Smyth (Mgr)
Pro A Mealia
Holes 18 L 6653 yds SSS 72
Recs Am–65 L Halpin (1998)
V'tors U SOC
Fees £19 (£24)
Loc 2 miles W of Westport
Arch F Hawtree

Co Meath

Ashbourne (1991)
Archerstown, Ashbourne
Tel (01) 835 2005
Mem 645
Sec J Clancy
Holes 18 L 5778 m Par 71 SSS 70
V'tors WD–U WE–NA before 1pm SOC
Fees £20 (£25)
Loc 12 miles N of Dublin, off N2
Arch Des Smyth

The Black Bush (1987)
Thomastown, Dunshaughlin
Tel (01) 825 0021
Mem 950
Pro S O'Grady
Holes 18 L 6930 yds SSS 73
9 L 2800 yds SSS 35
V'tors WD–U WE–NA before 4pm SOC
Fees On application
Loc 1 mile E of Dunshaughlin, off N3. 20 miles NW of Dublin
Mis Driving range for members and green fees
Arch Robert J Browne

County Meath (1898)
Newtownmoynagh, Trim
Tel (046) 31463
Fax (046) 37554
Mem 500
Sec JJ Ennis (046) 31825
Pro None
Holes 18 L 6720 yds SSS 72
Recs Am–68 P Rayfus
V'tors WD–U exc Ladies day WE–restricted SOC–exc Sun
Fees £15 (£18)
Loc 2 miles SW of Trim. 25 miles NW of Dublin
Arch Hackett/Craddock

Gormanston College (1961)
Franciscan College, Gormanston
Tel (01) 841 2203
Fax (01) 841 2874
Mem 160
Sec Br Laurence Brady
Pro B Browne
Holes 9 L 1973 metres
Recs Am–60 G Ormsby (1992)
V'tors NA
Loc 22 miles N of Dublin

Headfort (1928)
Kells
Tel (046) 40857
Fax (046) 49282
Mem 993
Sec Enda Carroll (046) 40146
Pro B McGovern (046) 40639
Holes 18 L 6007 m SSS 71
Recs Am–66 D Sugrue (1998)
Pro–64 D Smyth (1973)
V'tors U SOC exc Sun
Fees £20 (£25)
Loc 65km NW of Dublin

Kilcock (1985)
Gallow, Kilcock
Tel (01) 628 4074
Mem 580
Sec P Delaney (Hon)
Holes 18 L 5801 m SSS 70
V'tors U
Fees £11 (£13)
Loc 20 miles W of Dublin (N4)

For list of abbreviations see page 527

Co Meath

Laytown & Bettystown (1909)
Bettystown
- **Tel** (041) 27170/27534
- **Fax** (041) 28506
- **Mem** 850
- **Sec** Helen Finnegan
- **Pro** RJ Browne (041) 28793
- **Holes** 18 L 6454 yds SSS 72
- **V'tors** U SOC–WD
- **Fees** £23 (£28)
- **Loc** 25 miles N of Dublin

Moor Park (1993)
Mooretown, Navan
- **Tel** (046) 27661
- **Mem** 180
- **Sec** M Fagan (Mgr)
- **Holes** 18 L 5600 m Par 72 SSS 69
- **V'tors** U
- **Fees** £8 (£10)
- **Loc** Navan

Royal Tara (1923)
Bellinter, Navan
- **Tel** (046) 25244/25508/25584
- **Fax** (046) 25508
- **Mem** 1000
- **Sec** P O'Brien
- **Pro** A Whiston
- **Holes** 18 L 5757 yds Par 71
  9 L 3184 yds Par 35
- **Recs** Am–66 M McQuaid
- **V'tors** U
- **Fees** £18 (£22)
- **Loc** 25 miles N of Dublin, off N3

Co Monaghan

Castleblayney (1985)
Onomy, Castleblayney
- **Tel** (042) 974 9485
- **Mem** 275
- **Sec** R Kernan (042) 974 0451
- **Holes** 9 L 2678 yds SSS 66
- **Recs** Am–70 J McCarthy (1987)
- **V'tors** U SOC
- **Fees** £8 (£10)
- **Loc** Castleblayney town centre. 18 miles SE of Monaghan
- **Arch** R Browne

Clones (1913)
Hilton Park, Clones
- **Tel** (049) 56017
- **Mem** 245
- **Sec** P McGrane (042) 42333
- **Holes** 9 L 5790 yds SSS 68
- **Recs** Am–64 D McGuigan
- **V'tors** WD–U Sun–NA before noon
- **Fees** £10
- **Loc** Hilton Park, 2½ miles from Clones

Mannan Castle (1993)
Donaghmoyne, Carrickmacross
- **Tel** (042) 63308
- **Fax** (042) 63195
- **Mem** 340
- **Sec** R Howell (042) 62531
- **Holes** 9 L 6008 m Par 72 SSS 71
- **V'tors** U
- **Fees** £10 (£10)
- **Loc** 4 miles N of Carrickmacross

Nuremore (1964)
Nuremore, Carrickmacross
- **Tel** (042) 64016
- **Mem** 120
- **Sec** M McMahon (Hon)
- **Pro** M Cassidy
- **Holes** 18 L 5870 m Par 71 SSS 69
- **V'tors** U
- **Fees** £20 (£25)
- **Loc** 1 mile S of Carrickmacross on Dublin road
- **Arch** Eddie Hackett

Rossmore (1916)
Rossmore Park, Monaghan
- **Tel** (047) 81316
- **Mem** 500
- **Sec** J McKenna (Hon)
- **Holes** 18 L 6082 yds Par 70 SSS 68
- **Recs** Am–64 R Berry
- **V'tors** WD–U WE/BH–U SOC
- **Fees** £15
- **Loc** 2 miles S of Monaghan on Cootehill road
- **Arch** Des Smyth

Co Offaly

Birr (1893)
The Glenns, Birr
- **Tel** (0509) 20082
- **Mem** 750
- **Sec** J McMenamin (Hon)
- **Holes** 18 L 6216 yds SSS 70
- **Recs** Am–62 P Lawrie
  Pro–68 RJ Browne
- **V'tors** U SOC–exc Sun–NA 11.30–12
- **Fees** £12 (£14)
- **Loc** 2 miles W of Birr
- **Mis** Driving range

Castle Barna (1992)
Castlebarnagh, Daingean
- **Tel** (0506) 53384
- **Mem** 400
- **Sec** E Mangan
- **Holes** 18 L 5595 m Par 72 SSS 69
- **V'tors** U
- **Fees** £8 (£10)
- **Loc** 12 miles E of Tullamore (R402)

Edenderry (1910)
Kishavanna, Edenderry
- **Tel** (0405) 31072
- **Mem** 750
- **Sec** N Dempsey (0405) 31575
- **Holes** 18 L 6121 m Par 72 SSS 72
- **Recs** Am–66 J Brady (1995)
- **V'tors** WD–U exc Thurs (Ladies Day) WE–restricted SOC
- **Fees** £13 (£15)
- **Loc** 1 mile E of Edenderry
- **Arch** Havers/Hackett

Tullamore (1896)
Brookfield, Tullamore
- **Tel** (0506) 21439
- **Mem** 1005
- **Sec** P Burns (Hon)
- **Pro** D McArdle (0506) 51757
- **Holes** 18 L 6322 yds SSS 70
- **Recs** Am–64 D White
  Pro–68 H Boyle, J Martin, D Jones
- **V'tors** WD–U exc Tues (Ladies Day) Sat–M 12.30–3pm Sun–NA SOC
- **Fees** £16 (£20)
- **Loc** 2½ miles S of Tullamore, off Birr road
- **Arch** James Braid

Co Roscommon

Athlone (1892)
Hodson Bay, Athlone
- **Tel** (0902) 92073/92235
- **Fax** (0902) 94080
- **Mem** 1000
- **Sec** T Corry (Hon)
- **Pro** M Quinn
- **Holes** 18 L 5854 m SSS 71
- **V'tors** U SOC
- **Fees** D–£18 (£20)
- **Loc** 3 miles N of Athlone on Roscommon road
- **Arch** F Hawtree

Ballaghaderreen (1937)
Aughalustia, Ballaghaderreen
- **Tel** (0907) 60295
- **Mem** 350
- **Sec** J Cawley (Hon)
- **Holes** 9 L 5663 yds Par 70 SSS 66
- **V'tors** U SOC
- **Fees** £10
- **Loc** Ballaghaderreen 3 miles
- **Arch** P Skerritt

Boyle (1911)
Knockadoobrusna, Roscommon Road, Boyle
- **Tel** (079) 62192
- **Mem** 145
- **Sec** D Conlon (Hon)
- **Holes** 9 L 4914 m Par 67 SSS 64
- **Recs** Am–65 A Wynne (1987)
- **V'tors** U SOC
- **Fees** £10
- **Loc** 1½ miles S of Boyle
- **Arch** Eddie Hackett

Castlerea (1905)
Clonallis, Castlerea
- **Tel** (0907) 20068/20705
- **Mem** 200
- **Sec** J Mulligan (Hon)
- **Holes** 9 L 5466 yds SSS 66

For list of abbreviations see page 527

Recs Am–63 R de Lacy Staunton
V'tors WD/Sat–U Sun–by arrangement
Fees £8 (£10)
Loc Knock Road, Castlerea

Roscommon (1904)
Moate Park, Roscommon
Tel (0903) 26382
Mem 500
Sec B Campbell (Hon)
Holes 18 L 6290 m Par 72 SSS 69
Recs Am–64 K Kearney (1992)
V'tors WD–U WE/BH–restricted SOC
Fees £15 SOC–£10
Loc 1 mile S of Roscommon
Arch Eddie Connaughton

Strokestown (1992)
Cloonfinlough, Strokestown
Mem 150
Holes 9 L 5230 m Par 68 SSS 67
V'tors U
Fees £5
Loc 15 miles N of Roscommon (R368)

Co Sligo

Ballymote (1943)
Ballinascarrow, Ballymote
Tel (071) 83158
Mem 250
Sec EJ Stagg (Hon)
Holes 9 L 5302 m SSS 67
Recs Am–67 P Mullen
V'tors U
Fees D–£7 (£7)
Loc 15 miles S of Sligo

County Sligo (1894)
Rosses Point
Tel (071) 77134/77186
Fax (071) 77460
Mem 1169
Sec RG Dunne
Pro L Robinson (071) 77171
Holes 18 L 6037 m SSS 72
Recs Am–66 F Howley (1991) Pro–67 C O'Connor Sr (1975)
V'tors U–booking required
Fees £27 (£35)
Loc 5 miles NW of Sligo
Arch Colt/Allison

Enniscrone (1931)
Ballina Road, Enniscrone
Tel (096) 36297
Fax (096) 36657
Mem 780
Sec B Casey (Hon)
Pro C McGoldrick (096) 36666
Holes 18 L 6620 yds SSS 72
Recs Am–69 D Basquil Pro–69 L Robinson

V'tors WD–U WE/BH–phone first SOC
Fees £25 (£34)
Loc S of Enniscrone. Ballina 13 km
Mis Driving range
Arch Eddie Hackett

Strandhill (1932)
Strandhill
Tel (071) 68188
Fax (071) 68811
Mem 450
Sec Sandra Corcoran
Pro Golf Shop
Holes 18 L 6032 yds Par 69 SSS 68
V'tors WD–U WE/BH–restricted SOC
Fees IR£i5 (IR£20)
Loc 6 miles W of Sligo

Tubbercurry (1990)
Ballymote Road, Tubbercurry
Tel (071) 85849
Mem 250
Sec B Kilgannon (071) 86124
Holes 9 L 5478 m SSS 69
V'tors U
Fees £10
Loc 20 miles S of Sligo
Arch Eddie Hackett

Co Tipperary

Ballykisteen G&CC (1994)
Monard
Tel (052) 51439
Mem 260
Sec Josephine Ryan
Pro D Reddan
Holes 18 L 6765 yds Par 72 SSS 73
V'tors U SOC–book in advance
Fees £20
Loc 3 miles W of Tipperary town
Mis Driving range
Arch Des Smyth

Cahir Park (1968)
Kilcommon, Cahir
Tel (052) 41474
Mem 400
Sec Imelda Dilleen
Pro D Foran
Holes 18 L 5650 m Par 71 SSS 70
Recs Am–68
V'tors U SOC–WD/Sat
Fees £12 (£15)
Loc 1 mile S of Cahir
Arch Eddie Hackett

Carrick-on-Suir (1939)
Garravoone, Carrick-on-Suir
Tel (051) 640047
Fax (051) 640558
Mem 500
Sec A Murphy (Sec/Mgr)
Holes 18 L 6061 m Par 72 SSS 70

V'tors U exc Sun–NA before 11am SOC–WD/Sat
Fees £12 (£14)
Loc 2 miles S of Carrick on Dungarvan road
Arch Eddie Hackett

Clonmel (1911)
Lyreanearla, Mountain Road, Clonmel
Tel (052) 21138/24050
Fax (052) 24050
Mem 931
Sec A Myles-Keating (052) 24050
Pro R Hayes (052) 24050
Holes 18 L 6330 yds SSS 70
Recs Am–63 M O'Neill
V'tors WD–U WE–SOC
Fees £18 (£20)
Loc 2 miles SW of Clonmel
Arch Eddie Hackett

County Tipperary (1993)
Dundrum, Cashel
Tel (062) 71116
Fax (062) 71366
Mem 200
Sec W Crowe (Mgr)
Holes 18 L 6682 yds SSS 73
V'tors U SOC
Fees £20 (£25)
Loc 6 miles W of Cashel
Arch Philip Walton

Nenagh (1929)
Beechwood, Nenagh
Tel (067) 31476
Fax (067) 34808
Mem 700
Sec PJ Hayes (Hon)
Pro G Morrison (067) 33242
Holes 18 L 5483 m Par 69 SSS 68
Recs Am–64 P Lyons (1984)
V'tors U SOC
Fees £15
Loc 3 miles NE of Nenagh on old Birr road
Arch Dr A Mackenzie/Hackett

Roscrea (1892)
Derryvale, Roscrea
Tel (0505) 21130
Mem 500
Sec N McDonnell (Hon)
Holes 18 L 5782 m SSS 71
V'tors U
Fees £12 (£15)
Loc 2 miles E of Roscrea on Dublin road (N7)
Arch Arthur Spring

Templemore (1970)
Manna South, Templemore
Tel (0504) 31400/31522
Mem 220
Sec JK Moloughney (Hon)
Holes 9 L 5442 yds SSS 67
Recs Am–68
V'tors U exc Sun SOC
Fees £5 (£10)
Loc ½ mile S of Templemore

Thurles (1909)
Turtulla, Thurles
Tel (0504) 21983
Fax (0504) 24647
Mem 850
Sec L Purcell (Admin)
Pro S Hunt
Holes 18 L 5904 m SSS 71
Recs Am–66 DF O'Sullivan
Pro–70 H Bradshaw
V'tors U
Fees £18
Loc 1 mile S of Thurles

Tipperary (1896)
Rathanny, Tipperary
Tel (062) 51119
Mem 510
Sec J Long (Hon)
Holes 9 L 5445 m Par 71 SSS 70
V'tors U SOC
Fees £12 (£14)
Loc Tipperary 1 mile

Co Tyrone

Auchnacloy (1995)
99 Tullyvar Road, Auchnacloy
Tel (01662) 557050
Mem 180
Sec S Houston
Holes 9 L 5017 m Par 70 SSS 68
V'tors U
Fees £10 (£12)
Loc 12 miles SW of Dungannon (B35)
Mis Driving range

Dungannon (1890)
34 Springfield Lane, Mullaghmore, Dungannon BT70 1QX
Tel (018687) 22098/27338
Fax (018687) 27338
Mem 830
Sec LRP Agnew
Pro None
Holes 18 L 5861 yds SSS 69
Recs Am–68 D Fitzpatrick (1993)
V'tors U
Fees £16 (£20)
Loc 1 mile NW of Dungannon on Donaghmore road

Fintona (1904)
Eccleville Desmesne, Fintona BT78 2BJ
Tel (01662) 841480/840777
Fax (01662) 841480
Mem 400
Sec D Montague (Hon)
Holes 9 L 5765 m Par 72 SSS 70
Recs Am–68 E Donnell
Pro–69 L Higgins, J Kinsella
L Robinson
V'tors U exc comp days SOC
Fees £15 (£15)
Loc 8 miles S of Omagh

Killymoon (1889)
200 Killymoon Road, Cookstown BT80 8TW
Tel (016487) 63762/62554
Fax (016487) 63762
Mem 950
Sec B Rouse (016487) 63762
Pro (016487) 63460
Holes 18 L 5488 m SSS 69
Recs Am–64 A O'Neill
Pro–65 D Smyth
V'tors U H SOC
Fees £14 (£18)
Loc 1 mile S of Cookstown, off A29

Newtownstewart (1914)
38 Golf Course Road, Newtownstewart BT78 4HU
Tel (016626) 61466
Fax (016626) 62506
Mem 700
Sec JE Mackin (016626) 71487
Pro None
Holes 18 L 5341 m Par 70 SSS 69
Recs Am–65 G Forbes, I Moore (1996)
Pro–66 J Fisher (1978)
V'tors WD–U WE–NA after noon SOC
Fees £12 (£17)
Loc 2 miles SW of Newtownstewart on B84

Omagh (1910)
83A Dublin Road, Omagh BT78 1HQ
Tel (01662) 243160/241442
Fax (01662) 243160
Mem 917
Sec JA McElholm (Hon)
Pro None
Holes 18 L 5382 m SSS 68
Recs Am–WR Barton (1993)
Ladies–61 BM Taylor (1992)
V'tors U SOC
Fees £10 (£15)
Loc 1/2 mile from Omagh on A5

Strabane (1908)
Ballycolman, Strabane BT82 9PH
Tel (01504) 382271/382007
Fax (01504) 382007
Mem 600
Sec E Kennedy (01504) 382007
Pro None
Holes 18 L 5552 m SSS 69
Recs Am–63 E Kennedy
Pro–69
V'tors WD–U WE–by arrangement SOC
Fees £10 (£12)
Loc 1/2 mile from Strabane, nr Fir Trees Hotel

Co Waterford

Dungarvan (1924)
Knocknagranagh, Dungarvan
Tel (058) 43310/41605
Fax (058) 44113
Mem 700
Sec T Whelan
Pro (058) 44707
Holes 18 L 6134 m Par 72 SSS 73
Recs Am–66 S Norris (1994)
V'tors U SOC
Fees £17 (£22)
Loc 2 miles E of Dungarvan on N25. 25 miles W of Waterford
Arch Maurice Fives

Dunmore East (1993)
Dunmore East
Tel (051) 383151
Fax (051) 383151
Mem 300
Sec M Skehan
Holes 18 L 6655 yds Par 72 SSS 70
V'tors U
Fees £10 (£14)
Loc 10 miles S of Waterford (R684)
Arch J O'Riordan

Faithlegg (1993)
Faithlegg House, Faithlegg
Tel (051) 82241
Fax (051) 82664
Mem 100
Sec J Lambe (Hon)
Pro T Higgins
Holes 18 L 6057 m SSS 72
V'tors U SOC
Fees £20
Loc 6 miles E of Waterford City on Dunmore East road
Arch Patrick Merrigan

Gold Coast (1993)
Ballinacourty, Dungarvan
Tel (058) 42249/44055
Fax (058) 43378
Mem 400
Sec T Considine (058) 44055
Pro None
Holes 18 L 6171 m Par 72 SSS 72
V'tors U SOC
Fees £18 (£20)
Loc E of Dungarvan, off R675
Arch M Fives

Lismore (1965)
Ballyin, Lismore
Tel (058) 54026
Mem 450
Sec S Hales
Holes 9 L 5291 m Par 69 SSS 67
V'tors WD–U before 5pm –M after 5pm WE–phone first SOC–exc Sun
Fees £10 (£10)
Loc 1 mile N of Lismore, off N72

Tramore (1894)
Newtown Hill, Tramore
Tel (051) 386170/381247
Fax (051) 390961
Mem 1396
Sec J Cox (Sec/Mgr)
Pro D Kiely
Holes 18 L 6055 m SSS 73
Recs Am–66 E Power
Pro–66 H Boyle
V'tors U
Fees £25 (£30)
Loc 7 miles S of Waterford
Arch Capt Tippett

Waterford (1912)
Newrath, Waterford
Tel (051) 74182
Fax (051) 53205
Mem 961
Sec J Condon (Sec/Mgr)
    (051) 76748
Pro E Condon (051) 54256
Holes 18 L 5722 m SSS 70
Recs Am–65 J Morris (1992)
V'tors U
Fees £17 (£20)
Loc 1 mile N of Waterford (N25)
Arch Willie Park/James Braid

Waterford Castle (1991)
The Island, Waterford
Tel (051) 871633
Fax (051) 871634
Mem 450
Sec D Brennan (051) 841569
Pro None
Holes 18 L 6231 m Par 72 SSS 71
Recs Am–70 J Haughey (1996)
V'tors U H SOC
Fees £25 (£29)
Loc 2 miles E of Waterford, off R683. Island in River Suir
Mis Driving range
Arch Des Smyth

West Waterford (1993)
Dungarvan
Tel (058) 43216/41475
Fax (058) 44343
Mem 150
Sec AA Spratt
Pro To be appointed
Holes 18 L 6802 yds Par 72
V'tors U SOC
Fees £18 (£22)
Loc 2 miles W of Dungarvan, off N25
Arch Eddie Hackett

Co Westmeath

Delvin Castle (1992)
Clonyn, Delvin
Tel (044) 64315
Mem 330
Sec F Dillon
Pro D Keenaghan
Holes 18 L 5818 m Par 70 SSS 68
V'tors U

Fees £10 (£12)
Loc 15 miles NE of Mullingar (N52)

Glasson G&CC
Glasson, Athlone
Tel (0902) 85120
Fax (0902) 85444
Mem 200
Sec F Reid
Pro None
Holes 18 L 7083 yds Par 72 SSS 72
Recs Pro–65 P Walton
V'tors U
Fees £27–£32
Loc 6 miles NE of Athlone (N55)
Mis Golf Academy
Arch C O'Connor Jr

Moate (1901)
Ballinagarby, Moate
Tel (0902) 81271/81270
Mem 600
Sec J Creggy (Hon)
Holes 18 L 6294 yds SSS 70
V'tors U SOC–WD
Fees £10 (£13)
Loc Moate village centre
Arch Bobby Browne

Mount Temple (1991)
Mount Temple, Moate
Tel (0902) 81841/81545
Fax (0902) 81957
Mem 150
Sec M & M Dolan (Props)
Pro None
Holes 18 L 6500 yds SSS 71
Recs Am–K Buckley (1996)
V'tors U H SOC
Fees £14 (£16)
Loc 3 miles N of N6, between Athlone and Moate
Arch Michael Dolan

Mullingar (1894)
Belvedere, Mullingar
Tel (044) 48366/48629
Fax (044) 41499
Mem 560
Sec B Kiely (Sec/Mgr)
Pro J Burns
Holes 18 L 6370 yds SSS 71
Recs Am–63 P Walton
    Pro–64
V'tors U SOC
Fees £20 (£25)
Loc 3 miles S of Mullingar (M52)
Arch James Braid

Co Wexford

Courtown (1936)
Kiltennel, Gorey
Tel (055) 25166/25432
Fax (055) 25553
Mem 800
Sec D Cleere (Mgr)

Co Wexford 685

Pro J Coone (055) 25166
Holes 18 L 6398 yds SSS 71
Recs Am–67 J McGill (1987)
    Pro–68 M Murphy (1976)
V'tors U SOC
Fees £20 (£25)
Loc 2 miles SE of Gorey
Arch Harris

Enniscorthy (1908)
Knockmarshall, Enniscorthy
Tel (054) 33191
Fax (054) 36736
Mem 830
Sec B Kenny
Pro M Sludds (054) 37600
Holes 18 L 6115 m Par 72 SSS 72
Recs Am–72 M Healy, M Coffey
    Pro–69 H O'Neill
V'tors U exc Tues & Sun–phone first SOC
Fees £15 (£18) (1998)
Loc 1½ miles SW of Enniscorthy on New Ross road
Arch Eddie Hackett

New Ross (1905)
Tinneranny, New Ross
Tel (051) 421433
Fax (051) 420098
Mem 700
Sec Kathleen Daly (Sec/Mgr)
Holes 18 L 5751 m SSS 70
Recs Am–66 M O'Brien
    Pro–65 C O'Connor
V'tors U exc Sun SOC
Fees £14 (£16)
Loc 1 mile W of New Ross

Rosslare (1905)
Rosslare Strand, Rosslare
Tel (053) 32203 (Bookings)
Fax (053) 32203
Mem 1000
Sec JF Hall (Mgr)
Pro A Skerritt (053) 32238
Holes Old 18 L 6577 yds Par 72 SSS 72; New 9 L 3153 yds Par 70 SSS 70
Recs Am–66 A Duggan (1996)
V'tors U SOC
Fees 18 hole:£22 (£30)
    9 hole:£9–£13
Loc 10 miles S of Wexford. Rosslare Ferry 6 miles
Arch Hawtree/Taylor/O'Connor Jr

St Helen's Bay (1993)
St Helen's, Kilrane, Rosslare Harbour
Tel (053) 33234/33669
Fax (053) 33803
Mem 300
Sec L Byrne
Pro None
Holes 18 L 6091 m SSS 72
V'tors U SOC
Fees £20 (£25)
Loc Nr Rosslare Ferry terminal
Arch Philip Walton

For list of abbreviations see page 527

Co Wexford

Tara Glen (1993)
Ballymoney, Gorey
Tel (055) 25413
Fax (055) 25612
Sec D Popplewell
Holes 9 L 5826 m Par 72 SSS 70
V'tors U
Fees £10
Loc 4 miles E of Gorey. 12 miles S of Arklow

Wexford (1960)
Mulgannon, Wexford
Tel (053) 42238
Mem 705
Sec P Daly (Hon)
Pro D McGrane (053) 46300
Holes 18 L 6338 yds Par 72 SSS 71
V'tors U SOC
Fees £18 (£20)
Loc Wexford ½ mile

Co Wicklow

Arklow (1927)
Abbeylands, Arklow
Tel (0402) 32492
Fax (0402) 32971
Mem 500
Sec B Timmons (Hon)
Pro None
Holes 18 L 5770 yds SSS 67
Recs Am–65 J Groomes (1994)
V'tors WD–U Sat–U after 5pm Sun–NA SOC
Fees £18
Loc 1 mile from Arklow
Arch Eddie Hackett

Baltinglass (1928)
Baltinglass
Tel (0508) 81350
Fax (0508) 81350
Mem 399
Sec F Doyle (Hon)
Pro M Murphy
Holes 9 L 6070 yds SSS 69
Recs Am–66 D Coakley Pro–70 S Hunt
V'tors U SOC
Fees £10 (£12)
Loc 38 miles S of Dublin (N81)

Blainroe (1978)
Blainroe
Tel (0404) 68168
Fax (0404) 69369
Mem 830
Sec W O'Sullivan (Sec/Mgr)
Pro J McDonald
Holes 18 L 6171 m SSS 72
Recs Am–71 L Corcoran (1996) Pro–68
V'tors U
Fees £28 (£38)
Loc 3 miles S of Wicklow on coast
Arch CW Hawtree

Bray (1897)
Ravenswell Road, Bray
Tel (01) 286 2484
Fax (01) 286 2484
Mem 530
Sec T Brennan (Sec/Mgr)
Pro M Walby
Holes 9 L 5642 m Par 70 SSS 69
Recs Am–65 K Nolan (1994)
V'tors U before 6pm SOC–WD
Fees £17
Loc 12 miles S of Dublin

Charlesland G&CC (1993)
Greystones
Tel (01) 287 6764
Fax (01) 287 3882
Mem 650
Sec L Evans (Mgr)
Pro P Heeney
Holes 18 L 6739 yds Par 72 SSS 71
V'tors U SOC
Fees IR£23 (IR£32)
Loc 18 miles SE of Dublin
Arch Eddie Hackett

Coollattin (1960)
Coollattin, Shillelagh
Tel (055) 29125
Mem 700
Sec P Cleere (Hon)
Holes 18 L 6148 yds Par 70 SSS 69
V'tors U
Fees £15 (£20)
Loc 50 miles S of Dublin in Wicklow Mountains
Arch Peter McEvoy

Delgany (1908)
Delgany
Tel (01) 287 4536
Fax (01) 287 3977
Mem 882
Sec RJ Kelly (Sec/Mgr)
Pro G Kavanagh (01) 287 4697
Holes 18 L 6025 yds SSS 69
Recs Am–63 J May (1978) Pro–61 K Morris (1997)
V'tors U exc comp days SOC–Mon/Thurs/Fri
Fees £23 (£27)
Loc 18 miles S of Dublin, nr Greystones, off N11
Arch H Vardon

Djouce Mountain (1997)
Roundwood
Tel (01) 281 8585
Fax (01) 281 8585
Mem 460
Sec D McGillycuddy (Mgr)
Pro None
Holes 9 L 5636 m Par 71 SSS 69
V'tors U SOC
Fees £10 (£12)
Loc 15 miles NW of Wicklow (R764), off N11
Arch Eddie Hackett

Druid's Glen (1995)
Newtownmountkennedy
Tel (01) 287 3600
Fax (01) 287 3699
Mem 150
Sec D Flinn (Gen Mgr)
Pro E Darcy
Holes 18 L 7026 yds Par 71 SSS 74
Recs Pro–62 C Montgomerie (1997)
V'tors U SOC
Fees £80
Loc 20 miles S of Dublin (N11)
Mis Golf Academy
Arch Craddock/Ruddy

The European Club (1989)
Brittas Bay, Wicklow
Tel (0404) 47415
Fax (0404) 47449
Mem 120
Sec P Ruddy
Pro None
Holes 18 L 6945 yds SSS 71
V'tors H SOC
Fees £45 (£45)
Loc 30 miles S of Dublin, off N11
Arch Pat Ruddy

Glenmalure (1993)
Greenane, Rathdrum
Tel (0404) 46679
Fax (0404) 46783
Mem 150
Sec A Grimes (Hon)
Holes 18 L 5237 m Par 71 SSS 66
V'tors U SOC
Fees IR£15 (IR£20)
Loc 2 miles SW of Rathdrum on Glenmalure road
Arch Suttle/McEvoy

Greystones (1895)
Greystones
Tel (01) 287 6624
Fax (01) 287 3749
Mem 850
Sec O Walsh (01) 287 4136
Holes 18 L 5322 m SSS 69
Recs Am–67 Pro–66
V'tors WD–U
Fees £25 (£30)
Loc Greystones, 18 miles S of Dublin

Kilcoole (1992)
Kilcoole
Tel (01) 287 2066
Mem 250
Email amking@iol.ie
Sec G Richardson
Holes 9 L 5506 m Par 70 SSS 69
Recs Am–71 R Mullen (1993)
V'tors WD–U WE–NA before noon SOC–WD
Fees £12 (£15)

For list of abbreviations see page 527

Old Conna (1987)
Ferndale Road, Bray
Tel (01) 282 6055
Fax (01) 282 5211
Mem 900
Sec D Diviney (Sec/Mgr)
Pro P McDaid (01) 272 0022
Holes 18 L 6551 yds SSS 72
V'tors WD–U before 4pm
WE/BH–NA SOC
Fees £27.50
Loc 2 miles N of Bray. 12 miles S of Dublin
Arch Eddie Hackett

Powerscourt (1996)
Powerscourt Estate, Enniskerry
Tel (01) 204 6033
Fax (01) 276 1303
Mem 627
Sec B Gibbons (Mgr)
Pro P Thompson
Holes 18 L 5858 m Par 72 SSS 72
V'tors U
Fees £60 (£60)
Loc Enniskerry, 5 miles W of Bray
Mis Driving range
Arch Peter McEvoy

Rathsallagh (1993)
Dunlavin
Tel (045) 403316
Fax (045) 403295
Mem 250
Sec M Bermingham (Mgr)
Holes 18 L 5943 m Par 72 SSS 72
V'tors U
Fees £35 (£45)
Loc 14 miles S of Naas (R412)
Mis Driving range
Arch Peter McEvoy

Roundwood (1995)
Newtownmountkennedy
Tel (01) 281 8488
Fax (01) 284 3642
Sec M McGuirk (Hon)
Holes 18 L 6685 yds Par 72 SSS 72
Loc 15 miles NW of Wicklow (R764)

Tulfarris (1987)
Blessington Lakes
Tel (045) 867555
Fax (045) 867561
Mem 200
Sec A Williams (Mgr)
Pro AV Williams
Holes 18 L 7172 m SSS 70
V'tors U SOC

Loc S of Kilcoole on Newcastle road, off N11
Arch Brian Williams

Fees £40
Loc 30 miles S of Dublin, off N81
Arch Patrick Merrigan

Wicklow (1904)
Dunbur Road, Wicklow
Tel (0404) 67379
Mem 450
Sec J Kelly (Hon)
Pro D Daly (0404) 66122
Holes 18 L 5695 m SSS 70
V'tors SOC–WD/Sat
Fees £18 (£20)
Loc 32 miles S of Dublin, nr Wicklow town
Arch Craddock/Ruddy

Woodenbridge (1884)
Woodenbridge, Arklow
Tel (0402) 35202
Fax (0402) 35202
Mem 550
Sec H Crummy
Holes 18 L 6344 yds Par 71 SSS 71
Recs Am–71 RJ Moran (1994)
V'tors U exc Sat & Thurs
Fees £27 (£35)
Loc 4 miles W of Arklow. 45 miles S of Dublin
Mis Practice ground
Arch Patrick Merrigan

Scotland

Aberdeenshire

Aboyne (1883)
Formaston Park, Aboyne AB34 5HP
Tel (013398) 86328
Fax (013398) 87078
Mem 725 180(J)
Sec Mrs M MacLean (013398) 87078
Pro I Wright (013398) 86328
Holes 18 L 5910 yds SSS 68
Recs Am–62 G Forbes, C Empey Pro–63 S Walker
V'tors U
Fees On application
Loc E end of Aboyne. 30 miles W of Aberdeen (A93)

Alford
Montgarrie Road, Alford AB33 8AE
Tel (019755) 62178
Fax (019755) 62178
Mem 608
Sec B Fiddes
Pro None
Holes 18 L 5483 yds Par 69 SSS 65
V'tors WD–U WE–restricted on comp days SOC
Fees £13 (£21)
Loc 25 miles W of Aberdeen on A944

Auchenblae (1894)
Public
Auchenblae, Laurencekirk AB30 1BU
Tel (01561) 320331 (Bookings)
Mem 85
Sec J McNicoll (01561) 320678
Holes 9 L 2208 yds SSS 63
Recs Am–62 AI Robertson, J McNicoll Pro–60 A Locke
V'tors U exc Wed & Fri 5.30–9pm
Fees £6 Sat–£7 Sun–£8
Loc 11 miles SW of Stonehaven. 3 miles W of Fordoun

Ballater (1892)
Victoria Road, Ballater AB35 5QX
Tel (013397) 55567
Fax (013397) 55057
Mem 670
Sec AE Barclay
Pro W Yule (013397) 55658
Holes 18 L 6094 yds SSS 69
Recs Am–61 R Damron Pro–62 K Stables
V'tors U
Fees On application
Loc 42 miles W of Aberdeen on A93

Banchory (1905)
Kinneskie, Banchory AB31 5TA
Tel (01330) 822365
Fax (01330) 822491
Mem 800
Sec Mrs A Smith (Admin)
Pro D Naylor (01330) 822447
Holes 18 L 5775 yds SSS 68
Recs Am–65 A Cowie (1998) Pro–67 C Ronald (1998)
V'tors WD–U
Fees £18 (£21)
Loc W of Banchory, off A93

Braemar (1902)
Cluniebank Road, Braemar AB35 5XX
Tel (013397) 41618
Mem 300
Sec J Pennet (01224) 704471
Holes 18 L 4916 yds SSS 64
Recs Am–58 J Crammond (1997) Pro–64 L Vannett (1988)
V'tors U SOC
Fees £12 D–£16 (£16 D–£21) W–£60
Loc Braemar ½ mile. 17 miles W of Ballater
Arch J Anderson

For list of abbreviations see page 527

Cruden Bay (1899)
Cruden Bay, Peterhead AB42 0NN
Tel (01779) 812285
Fax (01779) 812945
Mem 1070
Sec Mrs R Pittendrigh (Sec/Mgr)
Pro RG Stewart (01779) 812414
Holes 18 L 6395 yds SSS 72
9 L 5106 yds SSS 65
Recs Am–65 C Gilbert (1997)
Pro–65 L Vannet (1996),
B Marchbank (1997)
V'tors WD–U WE–H exc comp days
Fees £40 D–£60 (£50)
Loc 22 miles NE of Aberdeen (A90)
Mis Driving range
Arch Thomas Simpson

Cullen (1879)
The Links, Cullen, Buckie AB56 2UU
Tel (01542) 840685
Mem 625
Sec LIG Findlay (01542) 840174
Pro None
Holes 18 L 4610 yds Par 63 SSS 62
Recs Am–58 B Main (1979)
Ladies–62 M Seivwright (1993)
V'tors WD–U WE–restricted Jul/Aug SOC
Fees £10 D–£15
(£13 D–£18) (1998)
Loc 5 miles E of Buckie, off A98 between Aberdeen and Inverness
Arch Tom Morris

Duff House Royal (1910)
The Barnyards, Banff AB45 3SX
Tel (01261) 812062
Fax (01261) 812224
Mem 547 167(L) 132(J)
Sec Mrs J Maison
Pro RS Strachan (01261) 812075
Holes 18 L 6161 yds SSS 69
Recs Am–63 DC Clark
V'tors WD–U H WE–H 8.30–11am and 12.30–3pm
Fees £24 (£30)
Loc Moray Firth coast, between Buckie and Fraserburgh
Arch Dr A & Maj CA Mackenzie

Dunecht House (1925)
Dunecht, Skene AB3 7AX
Mem 400
Sec G Lyall (01224) 740922
Holes 9 L 3135 yds SSS 70
Recs Am–72 A Angus (1987)
V'tors M
Loc 12 miles W of Aberdeen on A944

Fraserburgh (1881)
Philorth, Fraserburgh AB4 8TL
Tel (01346) 516616
Mem 642 56(L) 119(J)
Sec AD Stewart
Holes 18 L 6278 yds SSS 70
9 L 3400 yds

Recs Am–65 BA Duthie
Pro–67 I Smith
V'tors U SOC
Fees On application
Loc 1 mile SE of Fraserburgh

Huntly (1892)
Cooper Park, Huntly AB54 4SH
Tel (01466) 792643
Mem 800
Sec EA Stott (01466) 792360
Holes 18 L 5399 yds SSS 66
Recs Am–64 S Younger
V'tors U SOC
Fees D–£18 (D–£24) W–£65
Loc N side of Huntly. 38 miles NW of Aberdeen, off A96

Insch
Golf Terrace, Insch AB52 6JY
Tel (01464) 820363
Sec B Leith (01464) 820144
Holes 18 L 5287 yds SSS 69
Recs Am–66 H McKenzie (1990), K Harper (1994)
V'tors U
Fees On application
Loc 28 miles NW of Aberdeen, off A96

Inverallochy
Public
Whitelink, Inverallochy, Fraserburgh AB43 8XY
Tel (01346) 582000
Mem 280
Sec I Watt (01346) 582096
Pro None
Holes 18 L 5244 yds SSS 65
Recs Am–57 SJ Young (1997)
V'tors U
Fees D–£10 (£15)
Loc 4 miles E of Fraserburgh, off A92

Inverurie (1923)
Blackhall Road, Inverurie AB51 5JB
Tel (01467) 620207
Fax (01467) 621051
Mem 475 120(L)
Sec B Rogerson (01467) 624080
Pro (01467) 620193
Holes 18 L 5711 yds SSS 68
Recs Am–65 R Brechin
Pro–64 B Davidson
Ladies–74 J Tough
V'tors U SOC–WD
Fees £14 D–£18 (£18 D–£24)
Loc 1 mile W of Inverurie. 16 miles NW of Aberdeen

Keith (1963)
Fife Park, Keith AB55 5DF
Tel (01542) 882469
Fax (01542) 888176
Mem 250
Sec DG Shepherd (01542) 887934 (H)
Holes 18 L 5802 yds SSS 68
Recs Am–65
Pro–64

V'tors U
Fees £12 (£14)
Loc Fife Park, W side of Keith

Kemnay (1908)
Monymusk Road, Kemnay AB51 5RA
Tel (01467) 642225 (Clubhouse), (01467) 643746 (Office)
Fax (01467) 643746
Mem 820
Sec D Imrie (01467) 643047
Pro None
Holes 18 L 5903 yds SSS 69
Recs Am–69 (1995)
Pro–72 (1996)
V'tors U
Fees £16 D–£20 (£18 D–£22)
Loc 15 miles W of Aberdeen (B993)

Kintore (1911)
Balbithan Road, Kintore AB51 0UR
Tel (01467) 632631
Fax (07070) 741588
Mem 700
Sec Mrs V Graham
Holes 18 L 6019 yds SSS 69
Recs Am–65 K Bennet (1994)
Pro–62 S McAllister (1997)
Ladies–68 S Wood (1997)
V'tors U
Fees £11 (£16)
Loc 12 miles NW of Aberdeen on A96

Longside
West End, Longside, Peterhead AB42 4XJ
Tel (01779) 821558
Mem 750
Sec S Silcock (01779) 821549
Pro None
Holes 18 L 5215 yds Par 66 SSS 66
Recs Am–69 E Brocklehurst (1996)
Ladies–71 C Thomson (1997)
V'tors U exc Sun–NA before 10.30am SOC
Fees £10 D–£14 Sat–£12 D–£16 Sun–£16 D–£20
Loc 5 miles W of Peterhead on A590

McDonald (1927)
Hospital Road, Ellon AB41 9AW
Tel (01358) 720576
Fax (01358) 720001
Mem 650
Sec G Ironside
Pro R Urquhart (01358) 722891
Holes 18 L 5986 yds SSS 69
Recs Am–65
Pro–63
V'tors U
Fees On application
Loc 15 miles N of Aberdeen, off A90

Meldrum House (1998)
Meldrum House Estate, Oldmeldrum AB51 0AE
Tel (01651) 873553 (Starter)
Fax (01651) 873635

Aberdeenshire

Mem 400
Sec C Farquharson (Gen Mgr) (01651) 873635
Pro To be appointed
Holes 18 L 6350 yds Par 70
V'tors M
Fees NA
Loc 18 miles N of Aberdeen on A947
Arch Graeme Webster

Newburgh-on-Ythan
(1888)
Newburgh, Ellon AB41 0FB
Tel (01358) 789058
Fax (01358) 789956
Mem 380 60(L) 80(J)
Sec E Leslie (01358) 789956
Pro None
Holes 18 L 6162 yds SSS 70
Recs Am–68 (1997)
V'tors U exc Tues after 3pm–NA
Fees On application
Loc 12 miles N of Aberdeen (A975)

Newmachar (1989)
Swailend, Newmachar, Aberdeen AB21 7UU
Tel (01651) 863002
Fax (01651) 863055
Mem 921
Sec G McIntosh
Pro P Smith (01651) 862127
Holes 18 L 6623 yds Par 72 SSS 74
18 L 6388 yds Par 72 SSS 71
Recs Am–67 M Vibe-Hastrup,
C Benedetti (1996),
S Young (1997),
P Strachan (1998)
Pro–65 A Tait (1995)
V'tors H SOC
Fees Hawkshill: £30 (£35)
Swaileind: £15 (£20)
Loc 12 miles N of Aberdeen on A947
Mis Driving range
Arch Dave Thomas

Oldmeldrum (1885)
Kirkbrae, Oldmeldrum AB51 0DJ
Tel (01651) 872648/873555
Fax (01651) 873555
Mem 800
Sec J Page (01651) 872315
Pro J Caven (01651) 873555
Holes 18 L 5988 yds Par 70 SSS 69
Recs Am–66 DH Clarke (1996)
V'tors WD–U before 5pm
WE–phone first
Fees £14 (£20)
Loc 17 miles N of Aberdeen on A947

Peterhead (1841)
Craigewan Links, Peterhead AB42 1LT
Tel (01779) 472149
Fax (01779) 480725
Mem 500 45(L)
Holes 18 L 6173 yds SSS 71
9 L 2237 yds SSS 62
Recs Am–64 K Buchan (1988)
Pro–64 J Farmer (1980)

V'tors U exc Sat–restricted
Fees On application
Loc 1 mile N of Peterhead
Arch Willie Park Jr/James Braid

Rosehearty
c/o Mason's Arms, Rosehearty, Fraserburgh AB4
Tel (01346) 571250 (Mem Sec)
Mem 220
Sec A Downie
Holes 9 L 2197 yds SSS 62
Recs Am–61 M Summers (1996)
V'tors U
Fees D–£7 (D–£10)
Loc 4 miles W of Fraserburgh (B9031)

Rothes (1990)
Blackhall, Rothes, Aberlour AB38 7AN
Tel (01340) 831443
Mem 270
Sec JP Tilley (01340) 831277
Pro None
Holes 9 L 2478 yds SSS 65
V'tors U
Fees £10 (£12)
Loc ½ mile SW of Rothes.
10 miles S of Elgin on A941
Arch John Souter

Royal Tarlair (1926)
Buchan Street, Macduff AB44 1TA
Tel (01261) 832897
Mem 520
Sec Mrs C Davidson
Holes 18 L 5866 yds SSS 68
Recs Am–64 A Morrison
V'tors U
Fees £10 D–£15 (£15 D–£20)
Loc Macduff, 4 miles E of Banff.
45 miles E of Aberdeen

Spey Bay (1907)
Spey Bay Hotel, Spey Bay, Fochabers IV32 7PJ
Tel (01343) 820424
Mem 180
Sec M Dann (Mgr)
Holes 18 L 6092 yds Par 70 SSS 69
Recs Am–66 M Cameron
V'tors U
Fees £10 (£13)
Loc 2 miles W of Buckie, off B9104
Mis Driving range
Arch Ben Sayers

Stonehaven (1888)
Cowie, Stonehaven AB39 3RH
Tel (01569) 762124
Fax (01569) 765973
Mem 500
Sec WA Donald
Pro None
Holes 18 L 5128 yds Par 66 SSS 65
Recs Am–61 RG Forbes (1987),
FG McCarron (1995)
V'tors Sat–NA before 3.45pm
Sun–NA before 10.45am

Fees £15 (£20)
Loc 1 mile N of Stonehaven
Arch A Simpson

Strathlene (1877)
Portessie, Buckie AB56 2DJ
Tel (01542) 831798
Mem 300
Sec D Lyon
Holes 18 L 5977 yds SSS 69
Recs Am–65 AG Ross, J Geddes
V'tors U SOC
Fees £12 (£16)
Loc ½ mile E of Buckie
Arch G Smith

Tarland (1908)
Aberdeen Road, Tarland AB34 4YN
Tel (013398) 81413
Mem 300
Sec RG Reid
Holes 9 L 5812 yds SSS 68
Recs Am–65 C Forbes (1997)
V'tors WD–U WE–enquiry advisable
SOC–WD only
Fees £14 (£18)
Loc 5 miles NW of Aboyne.
30 miles W of Aberdeen
Arch Tom Morris

Torphins (1896)
Bog Road, Torphins AB31 4JU
Tel (013398) 82115
Mem 370
Sec S MacGregor (013398) 82402
Holes 9 L 4738 yds SSS 64
Recs Am–63 J Cramond
V'tors U SOC
Fees £10 (£12)
Loc W of Torphins via Wester Beltie. 6 miles NW of Banchory

Turriff (1896)
Rosehall, Turriff AB53 4HD
Tel (01888) 562982
Fax (01888) 568050
Mem 814
Sec R Grieg
Pro R Smith (01888) 563025
Holes 18 L 6145 yds SSS 69
Recs Am–64 A Ogg (1998)
Pro–66 K Hutton (1996)
V'tors H WE–NA before 10am SOC
Fees £16 D–£20 (£21 D–£27)
Loc 35 miles N of Aberdeen (A947)
Arch GM Fraser

Aberdeen Clubs

Bon Accord (1872)
19 Golf Road, Aberdeen AB2 1QB
Tel (01224) 633464
Mem 450
Sec FN Shand
Holes Play over King's Links

For list of abbreviations see page 527

Aberdeenshire

Caledonian (1899)
20 Golf Road, Aberdeen AB2 1QB
Tel (01224) 632443
Mem 620
Sec JA Bridgeford
Holes Play over King's Links

Northern (1897)
King's Links, Aberdeen AB24 5BQ
Mem 561
Sec AW Garner
Holes Play over King's Links

Aberdeen Courses

Auchmill (1975)
Bonnyview Road, West Heatheryfold, Aberdeen AB2 7FQ
Tel (01224) 715214
Mem 300
Sec W Cameron (01464) 821217
Pro None
Holes 18 L 5883 yds Par 70 SSS 68
Recs Am–65 G McInnes (1996)
V'tors U
Fees On application
Loc 3 miles NW of Aberdeen city centre
Arch Coles/Huggett

Balnagask (1955)
Public
St Fitticks Road, Aberdeen
Tel (01224) 876407 (Starter)
Holes 18 L 5472 m SSS 69
V'tors U SOC
Fees £9 (£11.25)
Loc 1½ miles SE of Aberdeen

Deeside (1903)
Bieldside, Aberdeen AB15 9DL
Tel (01224) 869457
Fax (01224) 869457
Mem 600
Sec AG Macdonald (01224) 869457
Pro FJ Coutts (01224) 861041
Holes 18 L 5972 yds SSS 69
 9 L 3316 yds SSS 36
Recs Am–64 AK Pirie, RH Willox, DA Rennie
 Pro–63 FJ Coutts (1995)
V'tors H
Fees £25 (£30)
Loc 3 miles SW of Aberdeen on A93

Hazlehead (1927)
Public
Hazlehead Park, Aberdeen AB15 8BD
Tel (01224) 321830
Pro I Smith
Holes 18 L 5673 m SSS 70
 18 L 5303 m SSS 68
 9 L 2531 m SSS 34

Recs Am–65 D Jamieson
 Pro–67 P Oosterhuis
V'tors U
Fees £9 (£11.25)
Loc 4 miles W of Aberdeen

King's Links
Public
Golf Road, King's Links, Aberdeen AB24 5QB
Tel (01224) 632269
Pro B Davidson
Holes 18 L 5838 m SSS 71
V'tors U
Fees £9 (£11.25)
Loc 1 mile E of Aberdeen
Mis Driving range. Bon Accord, Caledonian and Northern Clubs play here

Murcar (1909)
Bridge of Don, Aberdeen AB23 8BD
Tel (01224) 704354
Fax (01224) 704354
Mem 830
Sec D Corstorphine
Pro G Forbes (01224) 704370
Holes 18 L 6287 yds SSS 71
 9 L 2680 yds SSS 35
Recs Am–65 R Grant, J Savege, E Morrison
 Pro–65 PA Smith
V'tors H Tues–NA before 12.30pm
 Wed–NA after 12 noon
 Sat–NA before 4pm Sun–NA before noon
Fees £30 D–£40 (£35 D–£45)
Loc 5 miles N of Aberdeen, off A92
Mis 9 hole course at Strabathie
Arch A Simpson

Peterculter (1989)
Oldtown, Burnside Road, Peterculter AB14 0LN
Tel (01224) 735245
Fax (01224) 735580
Mem 889
Sec K Anderson
Pro D Vannet (01224) 734994
Holes 18 L 5924 yds SSS 69
Recs Am–65 P Robb (1994)
V'tors WD–U before 4pm WE–U SOC–WD exc Mon
Fees £12–£18 (£16–£21)
Loc 8 miles W of Aberdeen on A93

Portlethen (1983)
Badentoy Road, Portlethen, Aberdeen AB12 4YA
Tel (01224) 781090
Fax (01224) 781090
Mem 1100
Pro Muriel Thomson (01224) 782571
Holes 18 L 6735 yds SSS 72
Recs Am–64 GJ Esson (1997)
 Pro–62 D Vannett (1966)
V'tors WD–U WE–NA before 11am SOC

Fees £15 D–£22 (£22)
Loc 6 miles S of Aberdeen on A90
Arch Donald Steel

Royal Aberdeen (1780)
Balgownie, Bridge of Don, Aberdeen AB23 8AT
Tel (01224) 702571
Fax (01224) 826591
Mem 350 100(J)
Sec GF Webster
Pro R MacAskill (Golf Dir) (01224) 702221
Holes 18 L 6372 yds SSS 71
 18 L 4066 yds SSS 60
Recs Am–64 J Fought
 Pro–63 A Garrido
V'tors I H SOC
Fees £55 D–£75 (£65)
Loc 2 miles N of Aberdeen, off A92 Ellon road
Arch Simpson/Braid

Westhill (1977)
Westhill Heights, Westhill AB32 6RY
Tel (01224) 742567
Fax (01224) 749124
Mem 900
Sec Amelia Burt (Admin)
Pro G Bruce (01224) 740159
Holes 18 L 5849 yds SSS 69
Recs Am–64 A Reith
 Pro–65 R McDonald
V'tors WD–U before 4.30pm Sat–M Sun–U
Fees £12 D–£18 (£16 D–£20)
Loc 8 miles W of Aberdeen, off A944
Arch Charles Lawrie

Angus

Arbroath (1903)
Public
Elliot, Arbroath DD11 2PE
Tel (01241) 872069 (Clubhouse), (01241) 875837 (Bookings)
Mem 650
Sec J Knox
Pro L Ewart (01241) 875837
Holes 18 L 6185 yds Par 70 SSS 69
Recs Am–64 G Skelly
V'tors WD–U SOC WE–NA before 10am
Fees £15 D–£20 (£20 D–£32)
Loc 1 mile SW of Arbroath on A92
Arch James Braid

Brechin (1893)
Trinity, Brechin DD9 7PD
Tel (01356) 622383
Mem 650
Sec AB May (01356) 622326
Pro S Rennie (01356) 625270
Holes 18 L 6200 yds SSS 70
Recs Am–65 G Tough
V'tors U exc Wed SOC
Fees £14 D–£19 (£18 D–£27)
Loc 1 mile N of Brechin on B90

For list of abbreviations see page 527

Angus

Caird Park (1926)
Public
Mains Loan, Caird Park, Dundee DD4 9BX
Tel	(01382) 453606, (01382) 438871 (Starter)
Mem	350
Sec	G Martin (01382) 864029
Pro	J Black (01382) 459438
Holes	18 L 6303 yds SSS 70 Yellow 9 L 1692 yds SSS 29 Red 9 L 1983 yds SSS 29
Recs	Am–67 G Lochead (1995)
V'tors	U SOC
Fees	Contact Starter
Loc	Off Kingsway bypass, N of Dundee

Camperdown (1960)
Public
Camperdown Park, Dundee DD4 9BX
Tel	(01382) 623398
Mem	330
Sec	R Gordon (01382) 814445
Pro	R Brown
Holes	18 L 6561 yds SSS 72
Recs	Am–67 G Bell
V'tors	U
Fees	£15
Loc	2 miles NW of Dundee (A923)

Downfield (1932)
Turnberry Ave, Dundee DD2 3QP
Tel	(01382) 825595
Fax	(01382) 813111
Mem	750
Sec	BD Liddle
Pro	KS Hutton (01382) 889246
Holes	18 L 6822 yds SSS 73
Recs	Am–67 P Cunningham (1997) Pro–65 A Crerar (1995)
V'tors	WD–U 9.30–noon and 2.18–3.42pm WE–limited access after 2pm
Fees	£16–£31 D–£26–£46 (£21–£36)
Loc	N of Dundee, off A923

Edzell (1895)
High St, Edzell DD9 7TF
Tel	(01356) 648235
Fax	(01356) 648094
Mem	700
Sec	IG Farquhar (01356) 647283
Pro	AJ Webster (01356) 648462
Holes	18 L 6348 yds SSS 71
Recs	Am–62 JKA Bruce (1997) Pro–67 I Young (1992)
V'tors	WD–NA 4.45–6.15pm WE–NA 7.30–10am & 12–2pm SOC
Fees	£21 D–£31 (£27 D–£41)
Loc	6 miles N of Brechin on B966
Mis	Driving range
Arch	Bob Simpson

Forfar (1871)
Cunninghill, Arbroath Road, Forfar DD8 2RL
Tel	(01307) 462120
Fax	(01307) 468495
Mem	500 140(L) 100(J)
Sec	W Baird (01307) 463773
Pro	P McNiven (01307) 465683
Holes	18 L 6052 yds Par 69 SSS 70
Recs	Am–61 KG Law (1995) Pro–65 E Brown
V'tors	U exc Sat SOC
Fees	£17 (£22)
Loc	1½ miles E of Forfar
Arch	James Braid

Kirriemuir (1908)
Northmuir, Kirriemuir DD8 4PN
Tel	(01575) 72144 (Clubhouse), (01575) 73317 (Starter/Admin)
Fax	(01575) 74608
Mem	600
Sec	A Caira (Mgr)
Pro	A Caira (01575) 73317
Holes	18 L 5510 yds SSS 67
Recs	Am–62 JL Adamson Pro–63 D Huish
V'tors	WD–U WE–NA SOC
Fees	£16 D–£22
Loc	NE outskirts of Kirriemuir. 17 miles N of Dundee
Arch	James Braid

Letham Grange (1987)
Letham Grange, Colliston, Arbroath DD11 4RL
Tel	(01241) 890377
Fax	(01241) 890414
Mem	780
Sec	E Wilson
Pro	S Moir (01241) 890377
Holes	Old 18 L 6968 yds SSS 73 New 18 L 5528 yds SSS 68
Recs	Old Am–69 D Downie (1994) New Am–62 L McLaughlin (1994) Old Pro–67 J Metcalfe, J Bickerton (1994)
V'tors	WD–U WE–U after 10.30am SOC
Fees	Old: £27.50 D–£40 (£35 D–£55) New: £15 D–£20 (£20 D–£30)
Loc	4 miles NW of Arbroath on A993
Arch	Old: Steel/Smith. New: T MacAuley

Monifieth Golf Links
Medal Starter's Box, Princes Street, Monifieth DD5 4AW
Tel	(01382) 532767 (Medal), (01382) 532967 (Ashludie)
Fax	(01382) 535553
Mem	1400
Sec	HR Nicoll (01382) 535553
Pro	I McLeod (01382) 532945
Holes	Medal 18 L 6650 yds SSS 72 Ashludie 18 L 5123 yds SSS 66
Recs	Am–63 JL Adamson Pro–64 S Sewgolum
V'tors	WD–U Sat–NA before 2pm Sun–NA before 10am SOC
Fees	Medal: £26 D–£36 (£30) Ashludie: £15 D–£21 (£16 D–£24)
Loc	6 miles E of Dundee
Mis	Abertay, Broughty, Grange/Dundee and Monifieth clubs play here

Montrose (1562)
Public
Traill Drive, Montrose DD10 8SW
Tel	(01674) 672932
Fax	(01674) 671800
Mem	1300
Sec	Mrs M Stewart
Pro	K Stables (01674) 672634
Holes	Medal 18 L 6495 yds SSS 72 Broomfield 18 L 4815 yds SSS 63
Recs	Medal Am–64 G Tough (1991) Pro–63 P Wardell (1997)
V'tors	WD–U Sat–NA before 2.30pm Sun–NA before 10am
Fees	Medal: £25 (£30) Broomfield: £10 (£14)
Loc	1 mile from Montrose, off A90
Mis	Royal Montrose, Caledonia and Mercantile clubs play here

Montrose Caledonia (1896)
Dorward Road, Montrose DD10 8SW
Tel	(01674) 672313
Sec	P McIntosh (01674) 676789
Holes	Play over Montrose courses

Montrose Mercantile
East Links, Montrose DD10 8SW
Tel	(01674) 672408
Mem	980
Sec	A Moncur (01674) 675716
Holes	Play over Montrose courses

Panmure (1845)
Barry, Carnoustie DD7 7RT
Tel	(01241) 853120
Fax	(01241) 859737
Mem	500
Sec	Maj (Retd) GW Paton (01241) 855120
Pro	N Mackintosh (01241) 852460
Holes	18 L 6317 yds Par 70 SSS 71
Recs	Am–66 I Frame (1984) Pro–62 C Moody (1990)
V'tors	WD/Sun–U Sat–NA
Fees	£32 D–£48
Loc	2 miles W of Carnoustie, off A930

Royal Montrose (1810)
Dorward Road, Montrose DD10 8SW
Tel	(01674) 672376
Mem	650
Sec	JS Richardson (01674) 676000
Holes	Play over Montrose courses

For list of abbreviations see page 527

Carnoustie Clubs

Carnoustie (1842)
3 Links Parade, Carnoustie DD7 7JE
Tel (01241) 852480
Fax (01241) 856459
Mem 900
Sec DW Curtis
Holes Play over Carnoustie courses

Carnoustie Caledonia (1887)
Links Parade, Carnoustie DD7 7JF
Tel (01241) 852115
Mem 640
Sec DC Thomson
Holes Play over Carnoustie courses

Carnoustie Ladies (1873)
12 Links Parade, Carnoustie DD7 6AZ
Tel (01241) 855252
Mem 106
Sec Mrs J Clark (01241) 859457
Holes Play over Carnoustie courses

Carnoustie Mercantile (1896)
Links Parade, Carnoustie DD7 7JE
Mem 50
Sec DG Ogilvie (01356) 647304
 Police House, Dunlappie
 Road, Edzell DD9 7UB
Holes Play over Carnoustie courses

Dalhousie (1868)
*c/o Glencoe Hotel, Links Parade,
Carnoustie DD7 7JF*
Tel (01241) 853273
Mem 150
Sec WM Osler
Holes Play over Carnoustie courses

Carnoustie Courses

Buddon Links (1981)
Public
Links Parade, Carnoustie DD7 7JE
Tel (01241) 853249 (Starter),
 (01241) 853789 (Bookings)
Fax (01241) 852720
Sec EJC Smith
Holes 18 L 5420 yds SSS 66
V'tors WD–U WE–U after 11am
Fees £16
Loc 12 miles E of Dundee, by A92
 or A930

Burnside (1914)
Public
Links Parade, Carnoustie DD7 7JE
Tel (01241) 855344 (Starter),
 (01241) 853789 (Bookings)
Fax (01241) 852720
Sec EJC Smith
Holes 18 L 6020 yds SSS 69
 Pro–62 A Tait

V'tors WD–U Sat–U after 2pm
 Sun–U after 11.30am
Fees £20
Loc 12 miles E of Dundee, by A92
 or A930

Carnoustie Championship (16th Century)
Public
Links Parade, Carnoustie DD7 7JE
Tel (01241) 853249 (Starter),
 (01241) 853789 (Bookings)
Fax (01241) 852720
Sec EJC Smith
Holes 18 L 6941 yds SSS 75
Recs Pro–64 A Tait,
 C Montgomerie
V'tors WD–H Sat–H after 2pm
 Sun–H after 11.30am
Fees £60
Loc 12 miles E of Dundee, by A92
 or A930

Argyll & Bute

Blairmore & Strone (1896)
High Road, Strone, Dunoon PA23 8JJ
Tel (01369) 840676
Mem 130
Sec JK Clark (01369) 840467
Holes 9 L 2122 yds SSS 62
Recs Am–63 JA Kirby (1987)
V'tors Mon–NA after 6pm Sat–NA
 12–4pm
Fees D–£8 (D–£10) W–£30
Loc Strone, 8 miles N of Dunoon
Arch James Braid

Bute (1888)
Kingarth, Isle of Bute PA20
Mem 234
Sec I McDougall
 (01700) 504369
Holes 9 L 2497 yds SSS 64
Recs Am–65 G McArthur (1990)
V'tors U Sat–U after 12.30pm
Fees D–£8
Loc Stravanan Bay, 6 miles S of
 Rothesay, off A845

Carradale (1906)
Carradale, Campbeltown PA28 6SA
Tel (01583) 431643
Mem 324
Sec JR Ogilvie
Pro None
Holes 9 L 2392 yds SSS 64
Recs Am–62 JW Campbell (1994)
 Pro–68 R Weir (1994)
V'tors U
Fees D–£8
Loc Carradale, 15 miles N of
 Campbeltown (B842)

Colonsay
Isle of Colonsay PA61 7YP
Tel (019512) 316
Mem 100
Sec K Byrne
Holes 18 L 4775 yds Par 72
V'tors U
Fees On application
Loc W coast of Colonsay, at
 Machrins

Cowal (1891)
Ardenslate Road, Dunoon PA23 8LT
Tel (01369) 702216
Fax (01369) 705673
Mem 900
Sec Mrs W Fraser (01369)
 705673
Pro RD Weir (01369) 702395
Holes 18 L 6063 yds SSS 70
Recs Am–64 LW Kelly (1997)
 Pro–63 RD Weir (1991)
V'tors WD–U WE–restricted SOC
Fees On application
Loc NE boundary of Dunoon
Arch James Braid (1928)

Craignure (1895)
Scallastle, Craignure, Isle of Mull PA64 5AP
Tel (01680) 812487/812416
Fax (01680) 300402
Mem 92
Sec DS Howitt
Holes 9 L 5072 yds SSS 65
Recs Am–72
V'tors U
Fees £10 D–£12
Loc 1 mile N of Craignure Ferry
 Terminal (Oban 40mins)
Mis Course re-designed 1979

Dalmally (1986)
Old Saw Mill, Dalmally PA33 1AS
Tel (01838) 200373
Mem 120
Sec AJ Burke (01838) 200370
Pro None
Holes 9 L 2277 yds Par 64 SSS 63
Recs Am–64 K MacIntyre (1994)
V'tors U
Fees R/D–£10
Loc 1 mile W of Dalmally on A85

Dunaverty (1889)
Southend, Campbeltown PA28 6RF
Tel (01586) 830677
Fax (01586) 830677
Mem 399
Sec D MacBrayne
Holes 18 L 4799 yds SSS 63
Recs Am–58
V'tors U
Fees £13
Loc 10 miles S of Campbeltown

Gigha (1992)
Isle of Gigha, Kintyre PA41 7AA
Tel (01583) 505287
Mem 30

For list of abbreviations see page 527

Argyll and Bute

Sec M Tart
Holes 9 L 5042 yds SSS 65
V'tors U
Fees D–£10
Loc Off W coast of Kintyre

Glencruitten (1905)
Glencruitten Road, Oban PA34 4PU
Tel (01631) 562868
Mem 350 105(L) 115(J)
Sec AG Brown (01631) 564604
Pro G Clark (01631) 564115
Holes 18 L 4452 yds SSS 63
Recs Am–55 JM Wilson
     Pro–60 H Bannerman,
     G Cunningham
V'tors U
Fees On application
Loc Oban 1 mile
Arch James Braid

Helensburgh (1893)
25 East Abercromby Street, Helensburgh G84 9HZ
Tel (01436) 674173
Fax (01436) 671170
Mem 825
Pro D Fotheringham
     (01436) 675505
Holes 18 L 6058 yds SSS 69
Recs Am–64 A Scott
     Pro–65 RT Drummond,
     D Chillas, B Marchbank
V'tors WD–U WE–NA
Fees On application
Loc N of Helensburgh and A814.
    8 miles W of Dumbarton
Arch Tom Morris

Innellan (1891)
Knockamillie Road, Innellan, Dunoon
Tel (01369) 830242
Mem 200
Sec A Wilson (01369) 702573
Holes 9 L 4878 yds SSS 64
Recs Am–63
V'tors U SOC
Fees £10 (£10)
Loc 4 miles S of Dunoon (A815)

Inveraray (1893)
North Cromalt, Inveraray, Argyll
Tel (01499) 302508
Mem 175
Sec R Finnan
Holes 9 L 5600 yds SSS 68
V'tors U SOC
Fees D–£10
Loc 1 mile S of Inveraray on A83

Kyles of Bute (1907)
Tighnabruaich PA21 2EE
Tel (01700) 811603
Mem 160
Sec J Thomson
Holes 9 L 2389 yds SSS 32
Recs Am–62 F McDonald (1996)
V'tors U
Fees D–£8 W–£10
Loc 26 miles W of Dunoon

Lochgilphead (1963)
Blarbuie Road, Lochgilphead PA31 8LE
Tel (01546) 602340
Mem 250
Sec N McKay (01546) 603840
Holes 9 L 4484 yds SSS 63
Recs Am–59 R Willan
     Pro–62 R Weir (1991)
V'tors U SOC
Fees D–£10 (D–£10)
Loc ½ mile N of Lochgilphead by Hospital

Machrie Hotel (1891)
Port Ellen, Isle of Islay PA42 7AN
Tel (01496) 302310
Fax (01496) 302404
Mem 332
Sec T Dunn
Holes 18 L 6226 yds SSS 70
Recs Am–66 I Middleton
     Pro–67 M Seymour
V'tors U SOC
Fees £20
Loc Machrie, 5 miles N of Port Ellen
Mis Driving range
Arch Willie Campbell

Machrihanish (1876)
Machrihanish, Campbeltown PA28 6PT
Tel (01586) 810213
Fax (01586) 810221
Mem 525 135(L) 80(J)
Sec Mrs A Anderson
Pro K Campbell (01586) 810277
Holes 18 L 6228 yds SSS 71
      9 hole course
Recs Am–65 I McLennan Jr
     Pro–64 B Lockie
V'tors U
Fees £25 D–£40 exc Sat £30
     D–£50
Loc 5 miles W of Campbeltown

Millport (1888)
Millport, Isle of Cumbrae KA28 0HB
Tel (01475) 530311
Fax (01475) 530306
Mem 288 120(L) 78(J)
Sec D Donnelly (01475) 530306
Pro K Docherty (01475) 530306
Holes 18 L 5828 yds SSS 69
Recs Am–64 AD Harrington (1981)
V'tors U SOC
Fees £14.50 D–£18.50 (£18.50
     D–£24.50) W–£51 M–£134
Loc W of Millport (Largs car ferry)
Arch James Braid

Port Bannatyne (1912)
Bannatyne Mains Road, Port Bannatyne, Isle of Bute PA20 0PH
Tel (01700) 504544
Mem 180
Sec IL MacLeod (01700) 502009
Holes 13 L 5085 yds Par 68 SSS 67
Recs Am–63 J O'Donnell
     Pro–64 W Watson
V'tors U
Fees £14 (£14)

Loc 2 miles N of Rothesay, Isle of Bute
Arch Peter Morrison

Rothesay (1892)
Canada Hill, Rothesay PA20 9HN
Tel (01700) 502244
Fax (01700) 503554
Mem 500
Sec A Shore (Hon)
Pro J Dougal (01700) 503554
Holes 18 L 5395 yds SSS 66
Recs Am–62 G Reynolds (1993)
     Pro–72 RDBM Shade (1968)
V'tors WD–U WE–book with Pro SOC
Fees On application
Loc 1 mile E of Rothesay
Mis Practice range
Arch Braid/Sayers

Tarbert (1910)
Kilberry Road, Tarbert PA29 6XX
Tel (01880) 820565
Mem 101
Sec P Cupples (01880) 820536
Holes 9 L 4460 yds SSS 63
Recs Am–62 D Lamont (1990)
     Pro–63
V'tors U SOC
Fees £5 D–£8 W–£30
Loc 1 mile W of Tarbert on B8024, off A83

Taynuilt (1987)
Taynuilt, Argyll PA35 1JH
Tel (01866) 822429
Fax (01866) 822429
Sec M Sim (Hon) Laroch,
    Taynuilt PA35 1JE
Holes 9 L 4510 yds Par 64 SSS 63
V'tors U exc Tues/WE–restricted
Fees D–£10
Loc 12 miles E of Oban on A85

Tobermory (1896)
Erray Road, Tobermory, Isle of Mull PA75 6PS
Fax (01688) 302140
Mem 180
Sec J Weir (01688) 302338
Holes 9 L 2492 yds SSS 64
Recs Am–65 G Davidson (1994)
     Ladies 72 J Jack (1993)
V'tors U
Fees D–£13 W–£50
Loc Tobermory, Isle of Mull
Mis Tickets from Western Isles Hotel, Brown's shop and Fairways Lodge
Arch David Adams

Vaul (1920)
Scarinish, Isle of Tiree PA77 6TP
Mem 100
Sec P Campbell (01879) 220334
Holes 9 L 2837 yds Par 72 SSS 68
V'tors U
Fees On application
Loc 3 miles N of Scarinish, E end of Tiree. 40 min flight from Glasgow

For list of abbreviations see page 527

Ayrshire

Annanhill (1957)
Public
Irvine Road, Kilmarnock KA3 2RT
Tel (01563) 521512 (Starter)
Mem 350
Sec T Denham
(01563) 521644/525557
Holes 18 L 6270 yds SSS 70
Recs Am–65 I McKenzie
Pro–65 J Farmer
V'tors WD/Sun–U Sat–NA SOC–exc Sat
Fees On application
Loc 1 mile N of Kilmarnock
Arch J McLean

Ardeer (1880)
Greenhead Avenue, Stevenston KA20 4JX
Tel (01294) 464542/465316
Fax (01294) 465316
Mem 500
Sec P Watson
(01294) 605243
Pro R Summerfield (Starter)
(01294) 601327
Holes 18 L 6409 yds SSS 72
Recs Am–67 J Shearer
Pro–68 A Brooks,
I Stanley, R Walker (1971)
V'tors U exc Sat–NA SOC–WD
Fees £18 D–£30 Sun–£25 D–£40
Loc ½ mile N of Stevenston, off A78
Arch H Stutt

Auchenharvie (1981)
Public
Moor Park Road, West Brewery Park, Saltcoats KA20 3HU
Mem 80
Sec A Breslin (01294) 469361
Pro R Rodgers (01292) 603103
Holes 9 L 5300 yds SSS 66
Recs Am–67 R Galloway, J Murphy, P Rodgers, A Wylie
V'tors WD–U WE–U after 9.30am
Fees £4.50 (£6.50)
Loc Low road between Saltcoats and Stevenston
Mis Driving range

Ballochmyle (1937)
Ballochmyle, Mauchline KA5 6LE
Tel (01290) 550469
Fax (01290) 550469
Mem 860
Sec A Williams
Pro None
Holes 18 L 5952 yds SSS 69
Recs Am–64 G Holland (1996)
Pro–65 A Hunter (1987)
V'tors WD/WE–U BH–M SOC exc Wed/Sat/BH
Fees On application
Loc 1 mile S of Mauchline on B705, off A76

Beith (1896)
Bigholm Road, Beith KA15 2JQ
Tel (01505) 503166
Mem 400
Sec M Murphy
Holes 18 L 5616 yds SSS 68
Recs Am–66 R Johnston; Pro–65
V'tors WD–U exc Tues–NA after 5pm Sat–NA before 2pm Sun–NA 1.30–2.30pm
Fees £15 (£20)
Loc 1 mile NE of Beith. 12 miles NE of Paisley on A737

Belleisle (1927)
Public
Bellisle Park, Doonfoot Road, Ayr KA7 4DU
Tel (01292) 441258
Fax (01292) 442632
Pro D Gemmell (01292) 441314
Holes 18 L 6477 yds SSS 72
Recs Am–63 K Gimson
Pro–64 J Farmer
Ladies–71 B Robinson
V'tors WD–U WE–H
Fees £19–£31
Loc S of Ayr in Belleisle Park
Arch James Braid

Brodick (1897)
Brodick, Isle of Arran KA27 8DL
Tel (01770) 302349
Fax (01770) 302349
Mem 640
Sec HM Macrae
Pro PS McCalla (01770) 302513
Holes 18 L 4736 yds SSS 64
Recs Am–60 A Gold
V'tors U SOC
Fees £13 D–£18 (£16 D–£25)
Loc Brodick Pier 1 mile

Brunston Castle (1992)
Golf Course Road, Dailly, Girvan KA26 9GD
Tel (01465) 811471
Fax (01465) 811545
Mem 350
Sec P McCloy (Gen Mgr)
Pro S Forbes
Holes 18 L 6792 yds SSS 72
V'tors U–booking necessary SOC
Fees £25 D–£40
Loc 4 miles E of Girvan
Arch Donald Steel

Caprington
Public
Ayr Road, Caprington, Kilmarnock KA1 4UW
Tel (01563) 521915 (Starter)
Mem 400
Sec DR Bray
Holes 18 L 5748 yds SSS 68
9 hole course
V'tors U
Fees On application
Loc 1 mile S of Kilmarnock (B7038)

Corrie (1892)
Corrie, Sannox, Isle of Arran KA27 8JD
Tel (01770) 810223
Fax (01770) 810268
Mem 200
Sec R Stevenson
(01770) 810268
Holes 9 L 1948 yds SSS 61
Recs Am–57 A Gold (1966)
V'tors U exc Thurs pm & Sat pm
Fees D–£8 W–£35
Loc 6 miles N of Brodick

Dalmilling (1961)
Public
Westwood Avenue, Ayr KA8 0QY
Tel (01292) 263893
Fax (01292) 610543
Pro P Cheyney (Golf Mgr)
Holes 18 L 5724 yds SSS 68
Recs Am–61 G McKay
V'tors U
Fees £13–£25
Loc NE boundary of Ayr, nr Ayr racecourse

Doon Valley (1927)
Hillside, Patna, Ayr KA6 7JT
Tel (01292) 531607
Mem 90
Sec J Green
Pro None
Holes 9 L 5654 yds SSS 68
V'tors U
Fees £9 (£9)
Loc 8 miles SE of Ayr (A713)

Girvan (1900)
Public
Golf Course Road, Girvan KA26 9HW
Tel (01465) 714272/714346 (Starter)
Fax (01465) 714346
Holes 18 L 5095 yds SSS 64
Recs Am–61 J Cannon
Pro–61 K Stevely
V'tors U
Fees £13–£25
Loc N side of Girvan (A77). 22 miles S of Ayr
Arch James Braid

Glasgow GC Gailes (1892)
Gailes, Irvine KA11 5AE
Tel (01294) 311258
Fax (0141) 942 0770 (Sec)
Mem 1200
Sec DW Deas (0141) 942 2011
Pro J Steven (01294) 311561
Holes 18 L 6515 yds Par 71 SSS 72
Recs Am–65 GC Sherry, LW Kelly
Pro–64 C Gillies
V'tors WD–I WE/BH–NA before 2.30pm SOC
Fees £50 D–£60 (£55)
Loc 1 mile S of Irvine, off A78
Arch Willie Park Jr

For list of abbreviations see page 527

Irvine (1887)
Bogside, Irvine KA12 8SN
Tel (01294) 275979
Mem 450
Sec W McMahon
Pro K Erskine (01294) 275626
Holes 18 L 6408 yds SSS 71
Recs Am–65 DA Roxburgh (1981)
Pro–66 R Weir (1987)
V'tors U SOC–WD
Fees On application
Loc 1 mile N of Irvine towards Kilwinning

Irvine Ravenspark (1907)
Public
Kidsneuk Lane, Irvine KA12 8SR
Tel (01294) 271193
Mem 340
Sec G Robertson
Pro P Bond (01294) 276467
Holes 18 L 6429 yds SSS 71
Recs Am–65 GJ Robertson
V'tors U
Fees £4 (£14)
Loc N side of Irvine, off A737. 7 miles N of Troon

Kilbirnie Place (1922)
Largs Road, Kilbirnie KA25 7AT
Tel (01505) 683398
Mem 450
Sec JC Walker
Pro None
Holes 18 L 5411 yds SSS 67
Recs Am–64 G McLean
V'tors WD–U
Fees On application
Loc ½ mile W of Kilbirnie, S of A760. 15 miles SW of Paisley

Kilmarnock (Barassie) (1887)
29 Hillhouse Road, Barassie, Troon KA10 6SY
Tel (01292) 311077
Fax (01292) 313920
Mem 500
Sec RL Bryce (01292) 313920
Pro G Howie (01292) 311322
Holes 18 L 6484 yds SSS 73
9 L 2888 yds SSS 34
Recs Am–68 K Fairley (1998)
V'tors WE/Wed–NA SOC–Tues & Thurs
Fees £38 D–£58
Loc Opp Barassie Railway Station
Arch Theodore Moone

Lamlash (1889)
Lamlash, Isle of Arran KA27 8JU
Tel (01770) 600296 (Clubhouse), (01770) 600196 (Starter)
Fax (01770) 600296
Mem 450
Sec J Henderson
Pro None
Holes 18 L 4640 yds SSS 64
Recs Am–60 A Young (1998)
Ladies–66 B Livingston (1992)

V'tors U SOC
Fees On application
Loc 3 miles S of Brodick on A841
Arch Auchterlonie/Fernie

Largs (1891)
Irvine Road, Largs KA30 8EU
Tel (01475) 674681 (Clubhouse)
Fax (01475) 673594
Mem 800
Sec DH Macgillivray (01475) 673594
Pro R Collinson (01475) 686192
Holes 18 L 6115 yds Par 70 SSS 71
Recs Am–64 C White (1989)
Pro–63 J Greaves (1997)
V'tors U
Fees £25 D–£35
Loc 1 mile S of Largs on A78

Lochranza (1991)
Pay and play
Lochranza, Isle of Arran KA27 8HL
Tel (0177083) 0273
Fax (0177083) 0273
Sec IM Robertson
Holes 9 L 5600 yds SSS 70
Recs Am–74 D McAllister (1993)
V'tors U SOC–May–Oct
Fees 18 holes–£8
Loc 14 miles N of Brodick
Arch IM Robertson

Loudoun Gowf (1909)
Galston, Kilmarnock KA4 8PA
Tel (01563) 821993/820551
Fax (01563) 822229
Mem 650
Sec TR Richmond (01563) 821993
Holes 18 L 6016 yds SSS 69
Recs Am–61 AG Todd
V'tors WD–U WE–M
Fees £18 D–£30 (1998)
Loc 5 miles E of Kilmarnock (A71)

Machrie Bay (1900)
Machrie Bay, Brodick, Isle of Arran KA27 8DZ
Tel (01770) 850232
Fax (01770) 850247
Mem 260
Sec J Milesi
Holes 9 L 2200 yds Par 66
Recs Am–62 A Kelso
Pro–59 W Hagen
V'tors U
Fees D–£7 W–£28
Loc 10 miles W of Brodick
Arch William Fernie

Maybole (1970)
Public
Memorial Park, Maybole KA19
Holes 9 L 2635 yds SSS 65
Recs Am–64 WW McCulloch
V'tors U
Fees £8.80–£13.50
Loc S of Maybole, off A77. 8 miles S of Ayr

Muirkirk (1991)
Pay and play
c/o 1 Cairn View, Muirkirk KA18 3QW
Tel (01290) 661556
Fax (01290) 661556
Mem 100
Sec Mrs M Casagranda
Holes 9 L 5366 yds SSS 67
V'tors U SOC
Fees £6 (£6)
Loc 12 miles W of M74 Junction 12 on A70

New Cumnock (1901)
Lochill, Cumnock Road, New Cumnock KA18 4BQ
Tel (01290) 423659
Mem 250
Sec D Scott
Holes 9 L 2588 yds SSS 65
Recs Am–62 R Hodge (1992)
V'tors U exc Sun am–NA
Fees £5 D–£8
Loc 1 mile W of New Cumnock
Arch William Fernie

Prestwick (1851)
2 Links Road, Prestwick KA9 1QG
Tel (01292) 477404
Fax (01292) 477255
Mem 580
Sec IT Bunch
Pro FC Rennie (01292) 479483
Holes 18 L 6668 yds SSS 73
Recs Am–68 PM Mayo, P Deeble, B Andrade (1987)
Pro–67 EC Brown, C O'Connor
V'tors WD–I on Application only
Fees On application
Loc Prestwick Airport 1 mile, nr railway station

Prestwick St Cuthbert (1899)
East Road, Prestwick KA9 2SX
Tel (01292) 477101
Fax (01292) 671730
Mem 865
Sec JC Rutherford
Holes 18 L 6470 yds SSS 71
Recs Am–65 S Wallace (1996)
Ladies–67 CA Gibson (1992)
V'tors WD–U WE/BH–M SOC–WD
Fees £22 D–£30
Loc ½ mile E of Prestwick

Prestwick St Nicholas (1851)
Grangemuir Road, Prestwick KA9 1SN
Tel (01292) 477608
Fax (01292) 678570
Mem 600 155(L) 68(J)
Sec GBS Thomson
Pro Shop (01292) 678559
Holes 18 L 5952 yds SSS 69
Recs Am–65 G Lawrie
Pro–63 A Johnstone
V'tors WD–U WE–NA exc Sun pm

Ayrshire

Fees £30 D–£45 Sun pm–£35
Loc Prestwick
Arch C Hunter

Routenburn (1914)
Greenock Road, Largs KA30 9AH
Tel (01475) 673230
Mem 400
Sec J Thomson (Mgr)
Pro G McQueen (01475) 687240
Holes 18 L 5650 yds SSS 68
Recs Am–64 B Moore
Pro–65 S Torrance
V'tors U SOC–WD
Fees £6.60 (£11)
Loc N of Largs, off A78
Arch James Braid

Royal Troon (1878)
Craigend Road, Troon KA10 6EP
Tel (01292) 311555
Fax (01292) 318204
Mem 800
Sec JW Chandler
Pro RB Anderson (01292) 313281
Holes Old 18 L 7097 yds SSS 74
Portland 18 L 6289 yds SSS 71
Recs Old Am–70 CW Green,
J Harkis, R Claydon,
DW Hawthorn
Pro–64 G Norman (1989),
E Woods (1997)
Portland Am–65 GS Reynolds
Pro–65 WG Cunningham
V'tors Booking required.
Mon/Tues/Thurs only–H
(max 20) WE–NA
Fees Old + Portland: D–£110
Portland: D–£70 (inc lunch)
Loc SE side of Troon (B749).
Prestwick Airport 3 miles
Mis Practice range
Arch W Fernie

Seafield (1930)
Public
Belleisle Park, Doonfoot Road, Ayr KA7 4DU
Tel (01292) 441258
Fax (01292) 442632
Pro D Gemmell (Golf Mgr)
(01292) 441314
Holes 18 L 5498 yds SSS 66
Recs Am–65 R Gibson
V'tors U
Fees £13–£25
Loc S of Ayr in Belleisle Park

Shiskine (1896)
Shiskine, Blackwaterfoot, Isle of Arran KA27 8HA
Tel (01770) 860226
Mem 550 154(L) 42(J)
Sec Mrs F Crawford
(01770) 860293
J Faulkner (01770) 860392
Holes 12 L 2990 yds SSS 42
Recs Am–39 J Melvin, J Brown
Pro–36 DH McGillivray
V'tors U SOC
Fees £12
Loc 11 miles SW of Brodick

Skelmorlie (1891)
Skelmorlie, Largs PA17 5ES
Tel (01475) 520152
Mem 390
Sec Mrs A Fahey (Hon)
Holes 13 L 5056 yds SSS 65
Recs Am–61 J McCreadie (1992)
Pro–69 J Braid, G Duncan
V'tors U exc Sat (Apr–Oct)
Fees D–£16 Sun–£18
Loc Wemyss Bay Station 1½ miles
Arch James Braid

Troon Municipal
Public
Harling Drive, Troon KA10 6NF
Tel (01292) 312464
Fax (01292) 312578
Pro G McKinlay
Holes Lochgreen 18 L 6785 yds
SSS 73; Darley 18 L 6501 yds
SSS 72; Fullarton 18 L
4822 yds SSS 63
Recs Lochgreen Am–66 R Milligan
Pro–65 J Chillas
Darley Am–66 M Rossi
Pro–66 J White
Fullarton Am–58 A McQueen
V'tors U SOC
Fees Lochgreen: £19–£31
Darley: £15–£29
Fullarton: £13–£25
Loc 4 miles N of Prestwick at
Station Brae

Troon Portland (1894)
1 Crosbie Road, Troon KA10
Tel (01292) 313488
Mem 120
Sec J Irving
Holes Play over Portland at Royal Troon

Troon St Meddans (1907)
Harling Drive, Troon KA10 6NF
Mem 200
Sec R Lamont (01294) 552878
Holes Play over Troon Municipal courses Lochgreen and Darley

Turnberry Hotel (1906)
Turnberry KA26 9LT
Tel (01655) 331000
Fax (01655) 331706
Sec E Bowman (Mgr)
Pro B Gunson
Holes Ailsa 18 L 6976 yds SSS 72
Arran 18 L 6014 yds SSS 69
Recs Ailsa Am–70 GK MacDonald
Pro–63 M Hayes,
G Norman (1986)
Arran Am–66 AP Parkin
Pro–65 E McIntosh,
C Ronald, S McGregor
V'tors On application
Fees On application
Loc 5 miles N of Girvan on A77
Arch Hutchison/Mackenzie Ross

West Kilbride (1893)
Fullerton Drive, Seamill, West Kilbride KA23 9HT
Tel (01294) 823911
Fax (01294) 823911
Mem 900
Sec H Armour
Pro G Ross (01294) 823042
Holes 18 L 6452 yds SSS 71
Recs Am–63 G Fox (1995)
Pro–63 F Mann,
J McCredie (1997)
V'tors WD–U WE–M BH–NA SOC
Fees On application
Loc West Kilbride
Arch Old Tom Morris/James Braid

Western Gailes (1897)
Gailes, Irvine KA11 5AE
Tel (01294) 311649
Fax (01294) 312312
Mem 450
Sec AM McBean
Holes 18 L 6639 yds SSS 73
Recs Am–67 RA Muscroft (1986)
Pro–65 B Gallacher (1986)
V'tors WD–H exc Thurs (booking necessary)
Fees £60 D–£90
Loc 3 miles N of Troon (A78)

Whiting Bay (1895)
Golf Course Road, Whiting Bay, Isle of Arran KA27 8PR
Tel (017707) 487
Mem 290
Sec Mrs I I'Anson
Holes 18 L 4405 yds SSS 63
Recs Am–58 N Auld
V'tors U
Fees On application
Loc 8 miles S of Brodick

Borders

Duns (1894)
Hardens Road, Duns TD11 3NR
Tel (01361) 882194
Mem 520
Sec A Campbell
(01361) 882717
Pro None
Holes 18 L 6209 yds SSS 70
Recs Am–65 I Angus
V'tors U SOC
Fees £12 (£15)
Loc 1 mile W of Duns, off A6105

Eyemouth (1894)
Gunsgreen House, Eyemouth TD14 5DX
Tel (018907) 50551
Mem 400
Sec M Gibson (018907) 50004
Pro P Terras, C Maltman
(018907) 50004
Holes 18 L 6472 yds SSS 71

For list of abbreviations see page 527

Recs Am–67 A Black, J Patterson (1998)
Pro–71 C Maltman (1997)
V'tors U SOC
Fees £15 (£20)
Loc 6 miles N of border, off A1
Arch James R Bain

Galashiels (1884)
Ladhope Recreation Ground, Galashiels TD1 2NJ
Tel **(01896) 753724**
Mem 366
Sec R Gass (01896) 755307
Holes 18 L 5309 yds SSS 67
Recs Am–61 I Frizzel
Pro–70 J Braid
V'tors U SOC
Fees £10 D–£14 (£12 D–£16)
Loc ¼ mile NE of Galashiels, off A7

Hawick (1877)
Vertish Hill, Hawick TD9 0NY
Tel **(01450) 72293**
Mem 700
Sec J Harley
Holes 18 L 5929 yds SSS 69
Recs Am–63 AJ Ballantyne
Pro–64 N Faldo
V'tors H SOC
Fees £20 D–£25
Loc ½ mile S of Hawick

The Hirsel (1948)
Kelso Road, Coldstream TD12 4NJ
Tel **(01890) 882678**
Mem 700
Sec JC Balfour (01890) 883052
Holes 18 L 6092 yds SSS 69
Recs Am–64 M Ledgerwood (1990)
V'tors U SOC
Fees £15 (£20)
Loc ½ mile W of Coldstream (A697)

Innerleithen (1886)
Leithen Water, Leithen Road, Innerleithen EH44 6NL
Tel **(01896) 830951**
Mem 175
Sec S Wyse (01896) 830071
Holes 9 L 6066 yds SSS 69
Recs Am–66 C Fraser
V'tors U
Fees £11 (£13)
Loc 1 mile N of Innerleithen on Heriot road
Arch Willie Park

Jedburgh (1892)
Dunion Road, Jedburgh TD8 6LA
Tel **(01835) 863577**
Mem 300
Sec R Strachan
Holes 9 L 5492 yds SSS 67
Recs Am–62 E Redpath (1990)
Pro–66 C Montgomerie (1992)

V'tors U
Fees £12
Loc Jedburgh 1 mile
Arch Willie Park

Kelso (1887)
Berrymoss Racecourse Road, Kelso TD5 7SL
Tel **(01573) 23009**
Mem 350
Sec JP Payne (01573) 23259
Holes 18 L 6066 yds SSS 69
Recs Am–64 JF Thomas
V'tors U SOC
Fees £15 (£18)
Loc 1 mile N of Kelso, inside racecourse
Arch James Braid

Langholm (1892)
Langholm DG13 0JR
Tel **(013873) 80673/81282**
Mem 150
Sec WJ Wilson
Holes 9 L 2872 yds SSS 68
Recs Am–63 G Davidson
V'tors U
Fees £10 (£10)
Loc 18 miles E of Lockerbie. 21 miles N of Carlisle on A7

Lauder (1896)
Galashiels Road, Lauder TD2 6QD
Tel **(01578) 722526**
Mem 250
Sec D Dickson
Holes 9 L 6002 yds SSS 70
Recs Am–66 CA Lumsden
Pro–70 W Park Jr (1905)
V'tors U SOC
Fees £10
Loc ½ mile W of Lauder
Arch W Park Jr

Melrose (1880)
Dingleton, Melrose
Tel **(0189) 682 2855**
Mem 310
Sec W MacRae (01835) 822758
Holes 9 L 5579 yds SSS 68
Recs Am–62 G Matthew (1989)
V'tors WD–U before 4pm
Fees £16 D–£20
Loc S boundary of Melrose, off A68

Minto (1928)
Denholm, Hawick TD9 8SH
Tel **(01450) 870220**
Mem 600
Sec I Todd (01835) 862611
Pro None
Holes 18 L 5460 yds SSS 67
Recs Am–65 C Kerr (1994)
V'tors U SOC
Fees £15 (£20)
Loc Denholm, 6 miles E of Hawick

Newcastleton (1894)
Holm Hill, Newcastleton TD9 0QD
Tel **(013873) 75257**
Sec FJ Ewart
Holes 9 L 5748 yds Par 70 SSS 68
V'tors U SOC
Fees D–£7 (£8) W–£35
Loc W of Newcastleton, off B6357
Arch J Shade

Peebles (1892)
Kirkland Street, Peebles EH45 8EU
Tel **(01721) 720197**
Mem 650
Sec H Gilmore
Holes 18 L 6160 yds SSS 70
Recs Am–63 C Fraser
Pro–70 RDBM Shade
V'tors H SOC
Fees £18 D–£25 (£25 D–£34)
Loc 23 miles S of Edinburgh, via A703
Arch James Braid/HS Colt

St Boswells (1899)
St Boswells, Melrose TD6 0DE
Tel **(01835) 823527**
Mem 320
Sec JG Phillips
Holes 9 L 5250 yds SSS 66
Recs Am–61 CI Ovens (1989)
V'tors U SOC
Fees £12 D–£15 (£15)
Loc Off A68 at St Boswells Green, by River Tweed
Arch Willie Park/Shade

Selkirk (1883)
The Hill, Selkirk TD7 4NW
Tel **(01750) 20621**
Mem 363
Sec A Wilson
Holes 9 L 5560 yds SSS 67
Recs Am–60 MD Cleghorn
V'tors WD–U exc Mon pm WE–phone first SOC
Fees D–£15 (£15)
Loc 1 mile S of Selkirk on A7
Arch Willie Park

Torwoodlee (1895)
Edinburgh Road, Galashiels, Torwoodlee TD1 2NE
Tel **(01896) 752260**
Mem 567
Sec A Wilson
Pro R Elliott
Holes 18 L 6200 yds Par 70 SSS 69
Recs Am–64
Pro–70
V'tors WD–U from 9.30am–1pm and after 2pm exc Thurs–NA from 4–6pm WE–by arrangement SOC
Fees £18 (£22)
Loc 1 mile N of Galashiels on A7
Arch Willie Park

For list of abbreviations see page 527

Clackmannanshire

Alloa (1891)
Schawpark, Sauchie, Alloa
FK10 3AX
Tel (01259) 722745
Mem 550 80(L) 130(J)
Sec P Ramage
Pro W Bennett
 (01259) 724476
Holes 18 L 6240 yds Par 70 SSS 71
Recs Am–63 AJ Liddle
 Pro–66 R Weir, G Harvey
V'tors U WE–no parties
Fees £16 D–£25 (£20 D–£30)
Loc Sauchie, N of Alloa on A908
Arch James Braid

Alva
Beauclerc Street, Alva FK12 5LH
Tel (01259) 760431
Mem 320
Holes 9 L 2423 yds SSS 64
Recs Am–62 (1997)
V'tors U
Fees On application
Loc Back Road, Alva, on A91
 Stirling-St Andrews road.
 Signs to Alva Glen

Braehead (1891)
Cambus, Alloa FK10 2NT
Tel (01259) 725766
Mem 800
Sec P MacMichael
Pro P Brookes
 (01259) 722078
Holes 18 L 6086 yds SSS 69
Recs Am–64 D Mackison
V'tors U–booking necessary SOC
Fees £16 D–£24 (£24 D–£32)
Loc 2 miles W of Alloa (A907)
Arch Robert Tait

Dollar (1890)
Brewlands House, Dollar
FK14 7EA
Tel (01259) 742200
Fax (01259) 743497
Mem 480
Sec JC Brown
Holes 18 L 5242 yds SSS 66
Recs Am–64 D Ross, M Davies
V'tors U SOC
Fees £12 D–£16 (£20)
Loc Dollar, off A91
Arch Ben Sayers

Tillicoultry (1899)
Alva Road, Tillicoultry FK13 6BL
Tel (01259) 750124
Fax (01259) 752934
Mem 400
Sec J Crawford
Holes 9 L 2528 yds SSS 66
Recs Am–62 J Malcolm
V'tors WD/WE–U SOC
Fees £10 (£15)
Loc 9 miles E of Stirling

Tulliallan (1902)
Kincardine, Alloa FK10 4BB
Tel (01259) 30396
Mem 525 53(L) 100(J)
Sec JS McDowall (01324) 485420
Pro S Kelly (01259) 30798
Holes 18 L 5982 yds SSS 69
Recs Am–65 A Pickles, D Johnson
 Pro–70 D Huish, S Walker,
 G Gray
V'tors U exc comp days
Fees £15 (£20)
Loc 5 miles SE of Alloa

Dumfries & Galloway

Castle Douglas (1905)
Abercromby Road, Castle Douglas
DG7 1BA
Tel (01556) 502801
Mem 510
Sec AD Millar (01556) 502099
Holes 9 L 5400 yds SSS 66
Recs Am–62 W Blayney,
 J Shepherd (1989)
V'tors U
Fees £12
Loc Off A75/A713, NE of Castle
 Douglas

Colvend (1905)
Sandyhills, Dalbeattie DG5 4PY
Tel (01556) 630398
Mem 500
Sec JB Henderson
Holes 18 L 4700 yds SSS 66
Recs Am–63 W Blayney (1990),
 S McKnight (1995)
Fees £18
Loc 6 miles S of Dalbeattie
 on A710

Crichton (1884)
Bankend Road, Dumfries DG1 4TH
Tel (01387) 247894
Fax (01387) 247894
Mem 450
Sec Mrs JD Moor (Admin),
 BC Moor
Holes 9 L 3084 yds SSS 69
Recs Am–64 W Herd Jr
 Pro–67 D Gemmell
V'tors WD–U before 3pm SOC
Fees £12
Loc 1 mile from Dumfries,
 nr Hospital

Dalbeattie (1897)
Dalbeattie, Dumfries DG5
Tel (01556) 611421
Mem 280
Sec T Moffat
Holes 9 L 4200 yds SSS 60
V'tors U
Fees On application
Loc 14 miles SW of Dumfries

Dumfries & County (1912)
Nunfield, Edinburgh Road, Dumfries
DG1 1JX
Tel (01387) 253585
Mem 600 100(L) 100(J)
Sec EC Pringle
Pro S Syme (01387) 268918
Holes 18 L 5928 yds SSS 68
Recs Am–63 IA Thomson
 Pro–63 A Thomson, F Mann,
 J McAlister
V'tors WD–U exc 12.30–2pm–NA
 Sat–NA Sun–NA before 10am
Fees £25
Loc 1 mile NE of Dumfries,
 on A701
Arch J Braid

Dumfries & Galloway (1880)
2 Laurieston Avenue, Maxwelltown,
Dumfries DG2 7NY
Tel (01387) 253582
Fax (01387) 263848
Mem 450
Sec J Donnachie (01387) 263848
Pro J Fergusson (01387) 256902
Holes 18 L 6325 yds SSS 70
V'tors U
Fees £25 (£30)
Loc Dumfries
Arch Willie Fernie

Gatehouse (1921)
Gatehouse of Fleet, Kirkcudbright DG
Tel (01557) 814766 (Clubhouse),
 (01644) 450260 (Bookings)
Mem 350
Sec JS McConchie
 (01557) 840239
Holes 9 L 2521 yds SSS 66
Recs Am–60 S Martin
V'tors U
Fees D–£10 (D–£10)
Loc ¾ mile N of Gatehouse.
 9 miles NW of Kirkcudbright

Gretna (1991)
Kirtle View, Gretna DG16 5HD
Tel (01461) 338464
Sec G & E Birnie (Props)
Holes 9 L 6430 yds SSS 71
V'tors U SOC
Fees £8 (£10)
Loc 1 mile W of Gretna, off A75
Mis Driving range
Arch Nigel Williams

Hoddom Castle (1973)
Pay and play
Hoddom Bridge, Ecclefechan DG11 1AS
Tel (01576) 300251
Fax (01576) 300757
Sec D Laycock
Holes 9 L 2274 yds SSS 33
V'tors U
Fees £7 (£9)
Loc 2 miles SW of Ecclefechan
 on B725. M74 Junction 6

For list of abbreviations see page 527

Dumfries & Galloway

Kirkcudbright (1893)
Stirling Crescent, Kirkcudbright DG6 4EZ
Tel (01557) 330314
Mem 500
Sec N Russell
Holes 18 L 5739 yds SSS 69
Recs Am–65 S McLeish (1996)
Ladies–74 M Clement (1995)
V'tors U H–phone first SOC
Fees £18 D–£23
Loc ½ mile from Kirkcudbright town centre

Lochmaben (1926)
Castlehill Gate, Lochmaben DG11 1NT
Tel (01387) 810552
Mem 650
Sec JM Dickie
Holes 18 L 5357 yds SSS 66
Recs Am–63 BJ Scott (1996)
V'tors WD–U before 5pm WE–U exc comp days SOC
Fees £16 D–£20 (£20 D–£25)
Loc 4 miles W of Lockerbie on A709. 8 miles NE of Dumfries
Arch James Braid

Lockerbie (1889)
Corrie Road, Lockerbie DG11 2ND
Tel (01576) 203363
Fax (01576) 203363
Mem 530
Sec J Thomson
Holes 18 L 5418 yds SSS 67
Recs Am–64 P Laurie (1997)
Ladies–74 W Murray (1997)
V'tors U exc Sun–NA before 11.30am
Fees £18 Sat–£22 Sun–£18
Loc ½ mile NE of Lockerbie, on Corrie road
Arch James Braid

Moffat (1884)
Coatshill, Moffat DG10 9SB
Tel (01683) 220020
Mem 350
Sec TA Rankin
Pro None
Holes 18 L 5263 yds SSS 67
Recs Am–60 GJ Rodaks (1979)
V'tors WD–restricted Wed after noon
Fees £18.50 D–£20 (£28.50 D–£31)
Loc Signposted on A701 from Beattock (A74)
Arch Ben Sayers

New Galloway (1902)
New Galloway, Dumfries DG7 3RN
Tel (01644) 450685
Mem 280
Sec NE White
Holes 9 L 5006 yds Par 68 SSS 67
Recs Am–64 M Billington (1997)
V'tors U
Fees D–£12.50
Loc S of New Galloway on A762. 20 miles N of Kirkcudbright
Arch Baillie

Newton Stewart (1981)
Kirroughtree Avenue, Minnigaff, Newton Stewart DG8 6PF
Tel (01671) 402172
Mem 380
Sec J Tait
Holes 18 L 5903 yds Par 69 SSS 70
Recs Am–66 R O'Keefe (1997)
V'tors U H
Fees £18 D–£21 (£21 D–£25)
Loc N of Newton Stewart, off A75

Portpatrick (1903)
Golf Course Road, Portpatrick DG9 8TB
Tel (01776) 810273
Fax (01776) 810811
Mem 530
Sec JA Horberry
Holes Dunskey 18 L 5908 yds SSS 68
Dinvin 9 L 1504 yds Par 27
Recs Am–63 D Gladstone (1998)
Pro–63 G Weir,
S McAllister (1997)
Ladies–71 M Wilson,
CA Malcolm
V'tors U H SOC
Fees Dunskey: £18 D–£27 (£21 D–£32) W–£100
Dinvin: £8 D–£12
Loc 8 miles SW of Stranraer
Arch CW Hunter

Powfoot (1903)
Cummertrees, Annan DG12 5QE
Tel (01461) 700276
Fax (01461) 700276
Mem 820
Sec BW Sutherland MBE (Mgr)
Pro G Dick (01461) 700327
Holes 18 L 6266 yds SSS 71
Recs Am–63 C Wright, I Thomson
Pro–67 J Stevens
V'tors WD–U Sat–NA Sun–NA before 2pm
Fees Winter £15 5D–£60 Summer D–£30 (£23) 5D–£120
Loc 4 miles W of Annan. 15 miles SE of Dumfries, off B724
Arch James Braid

St Medan (1905)
Monreith, Newton Stewart DG8 8NJ
Tel (01988) 700358
Mem 300
Sec EC Richards (01988) 500326
Holes 9 L 2277 yds SSS 63
Recs Am–60 J Grundy (1990)
V'tors U SOC
Fees £10
Loc 3 miles S of Port William, off A747

Sanquhar (1894)
Blackaddie Road, Sanquhar, Dumfries DG4 6JZ
Tel (01659) 50577
Mem 180
Sec D Hamilton (01659) 66095
Holes 9 L 5630 yds SSS 68
Recs Am–66 I Brotherston (1982)
J Copeland

V'tors U SOC
Fees £10 (£12)
Loc ½ mile W of Sanquhar (A76). 30 miles N of Dumfries

Southerness (1947)
Southerness, Dumfries DG2 8AZ
Tel (01387) 880677
Fax (01387) 880644
Mem 800
Sec WD Ramage
Pro G Gray (01387) 880677
Holes 18 L 6566 yds SSS 73
Recs Am–65 M Gronberg (1990)
Pro–71 A Crerar (1995)
V'tors H–phone first SOC
Fees D–£30 (D–£40)
Loc 16 miles S of Dumfries, off A710
Arch Mackenzie Ross

Stranraer (1905)
Creachmore, Leswalt, Stranraer DG9 0LF
Tel (01776) 870245
Fax (01776) 870445
Mem 600
Sec BC Kelly
Holes 18 L 6308 yds SSS 72
Recs Am–66 CG Findlay, J Sproule
V'tors WE–NA before 9.30am and 11.45am–1.45pm
Fees £20 (£25)
Loc 2 miles NW of Stranraer on A718
Arch James Braid

Thornhill (1893)
Blacknest, Thornhill DG3 5DW
Tel (01848) 330546
Mem 700
Sec JFK Crichton
Holes 18 L 6011 yds SSS 70
Recs Am–63 AJ Coltart (1990)
V'tors U
Fees On application
Loc 14 miles NW of Dumfries (A76)

Wigtown & Bladnoch (1960)
Lightlands Terrace, Wigtown DG8 9EF
Tel (01988) 403354
Mem 190
Sec J Bateman
Holes 9 L 2731 yds SSS 67
Recs Am–62 R Shaw (1994)
V'tors U SOC
Fees £10 (£10)
Loc Between Wigtown and Bladnoch, off A714
Arch J Muir

Wigtownshire County (1894)
Mains of Park, Glenluce, Newton Stewart DG8 0NN
Tel (01581) 300420
Mem 435

Dumfries & Galloway

Sec R McKnight
Pro None
Holes 18 L 5847 yds SSS 68
Recs Am–67 D Taylor (1995), R Shaw (1996)
V'tors U exc Wed–NA after 6pm
Fees £18 D–£23 (£20 D–£25)
Loc 8 miles E of Stranraer on A75
Arch W Gordon Cunningham

Dunbartonshire

Balmore (1906)
Balmore, Torrance G64 4AW
Tel (01360) 2120240
Mem 700
Holes 18 L 5735 yds SSS 67
Recs Am–63 A Brodie
V'tors WD–U SOC
Fees On application
Loc 4 miles N of Glasgow, off A807
Arch James Braid

Bearsden (1891)
Thorn Road, Bearsden, Glasgow G61 4BP
Tel (0141) 942 2351
Mem 500
Sec JR Mercer
Holes 9 L 6014 yds SSS 69
Recs Am–67 S Hardie (1991), P Anderson (1996)
Pro–65 R Craig (1991)
V'tors M
Loc 6 miles NW of Glasgow

Cardross (1895)
Main Road, Cardross, Dumbarton G82 5LB
Tel (01389) 841213 (Clubhouse)
Fax (01389) 841754
Mem 850
Sec IT Waugh (01389) 841754
Pro R Farrell (01389) 841350
Holes 18 L 6469 yds SSS 72
Recs Am–65 J King, JLS Kinloch (1996)
Pro–65 J White (1990)
V'tors WD–U WE–M SOC
Fees £25 D–£35
Loc 4 miles W of Dumbarton on A814
Arch Fernie (1904)/Braid (1921)

Clober (1951)
Craigton Road, Milngavie, Glasgow G62 7HP
Tel (0141) 956 1685
Mem 575
Sec TS Arthur
Pro (0141) 956 6963 (Golf Shop)
Holes 18 L 4963 yds SSS 65
Recs Am–61 PW Smith, J Graham
V'tors WD–U before 4pm WE–M BH–NA SOC–WD
Fees £15
Loc 7 miles NW of Glasgow

Clydebank & District (1905)
Hardgate, Clydebank G81 5QY
Tel (01389) 383833
Mem 780
Sec W Manson (01389) 800098
Pro D Pirie (01389) 878686
Holes 18 L 5823 yds SSS 68
Recs Am–64 D Galbraith (1965), C Barrowman Jr (1993)
Pro–64 KW Walker (1994)
Ladies–68 V Melvin (1994)
V'tors WD–H
Fees On application
Loc 2 miles N of Clydebank

Clydebank Municipal (1927)
Public
Overtoun Road, Dalmuir, Clydebank G81 3RE
Tel (0141) 952 8698 (Starter)
Fax (0141) 952 6372
Pro R Bowman (0141) 952 6372
Holes 18 L 5349 yds SSS 66
Recs Am–63 J Semple, P Semple
Pro–63 G Weir
V'tors U exc Sat–NA 11am–2.30pm
Fees On application
Loc 8 miles W of Glasgow

Dougalston (1977)
Strathblane Road, Milngavie, Glasgow G62 8HJ
Tel (0141) 956 5750
Fax (0141) 956 6480
Mem 440
Pro None
Holes 18 L 6269 yds SSS 71
Recs Am–71 J Carnegie, J McLaren (1987)
Pro–73 B Barnes
V'tors WD–U SOC
Fees £14
Loc 7 miles N of Glasgow on A81
Arch J Harris

Douglas Park (1897)
Hillfoot, Bearsden, Glasgow G61 2TJ
Tel (0141) 942 2220
Mem 470 270(L) 120(J)
Sec DN Nicolson
Pro D Scott (0141) 942 1482
Holes 18 L 5982 yds SSS 69
Recs Am–65 DJ Ward (1996), IC Bell (1997), SJ Graham (1998)
Pro–64 C Maltman (1995)
V'tors M SOC
Loc 6 miles NW of Glasgow, nr Hillfoot Station

Dullatur (1896)
Dullatur, Glasgow G68 0AR
Tel (01236) 723230
Mem 420 60(L)
Sec W Laing (01236) 727847
Pro D Sinclair
Holes 18 L 6253 yds SSS 70

Recs Am–62 D Kane Jr (1989)
Pro–68 J Farmer
V'tors WD–U WE–M SOC
Fees £25 After 1.30pm–£15
Loc 3 miles N of Cumbernauld

Dumbarton (1888)
Broadmeadow, Dumbarton G82 2BQ
Tel (01389) 32830
Mem 500
Sec WM McMonagle
Holes 18 L 5969 yds SSS 69
Recs Am–64 D Hughes
V'tors WD–U WE/BH–M
Fees D–£20
Loc 1 mile N of Dumbarton

Hayston (1926)
Campsie Road, Kirkintilloch, Glasgow G66 1RN
Tel (0141) 776 1244
Fax (0141) 775 0723
Mem 440 70(L) 60(J)
Sec JV Carmichael (0141) 775 0723
Pro S Barnett (0141) 775 0882
Holes 18 L 6042 yds SSS 70
Recs Am–62 LS Mann
Pro–64 B Moffat
V'tors WD–I before 4.30pm –M after 4.30pm WE–M
Fees £20
Loc 1 mile N of Kirkintilloch
Arch James Braid

Hilton Park (1927)
Auldmarroch Estate, Stockiemuir Road, Milngavie G62 7HB
Tel (0141) 956 5124/1215
Fax (0141) 956 4657
Mem 1200
Sec Mrs JA Warnock (0141) 956 4657
Pro W McCondichie (0141) 956 5125
Holes Hilton 18 L 6054 yds SSS 70
Allander 18 L 5487 yds SSS 67
Recs Hilton Am–65 AP McDonald, RG Fraser, B Reid
Pro–64 AF Anderson
Allander Am–66 I Weir
Pro–62 K Baxter
V'tors WD–U before 4pm
Fees On application
Loc 8 miles NW of Glasgow on A809
Arch James Braid

Kirkintilloch (1894)
Todhill, Campsie Road, Kirkintilloch G66 1RN
Tel (0141) 776 1256
Mem 420 92(L) 104(J)
Sec IM Gray (0141) 775 2387
Holes 18 L 5269 yds SSS 66
Recs Am–61 S Shaw
Pro–68 R Weir
V'tors M SOC
Fees SOC–On application
Loc 7 miles N of Glasgow

For list of abbreviations see page 527

Lenzie (1889)
19 Crosshill Road, Lenzie G66 5DA
Tel (0141) 776 1535
Mem 501 125(L) 125(J)
Sec JA Chisholm
(0141) 776 6020
Pro J McCallum
(0141) 777 7748
Holes 18 L 5984 yds SSS 69
Recs Am–64 S Lindsay
Pro–62 S Henderson (1995)
V'tors M SOC
Fees On application
Loc 6 miles NE of Glasgow

Loch Lomond
Rossdhu House, Luss G83 8NT
Tel (01436) 655555
Fax (01436) 655500
Sec K Williams (Gen Mgr)
Pro C Campbell
Holes 18 L 7060 yds Par 71
Pro–62 R Goosen
V'tors NA
Loc 20 miles NW of Glasgow on A82
Arch Weiskopf/Morrish

Milngavie (1895)
Laighpark, Milngavie, Glasgow G62 8EP
Tel (0141) 956 1619
Mem 390
Sec Mrs AJW Ness
Holes 18 L 5818 yds SSS 68
Recs Am–64 RGB McCallum, R Blair, AS McGarvie
V'tors M SOC
Fees On application
Loc 7 miles NW of Glasgow

Palacerigg (1975)
Public
Palacerigg Country Park, Cumbernauld G67 3HU
Tel (01236) 734969
Mem 360
Sec DSA Cooper
Holes 18 L 6444 yds SSS 71
Recs Am–65 G Rankin (1996)
Pro–66 J Farmer (1989)
V'tors U SOC–WD only
Fees £8
Loc 3 miles SE of Cumbernauld
Arch Henry Cotton

Vale of Leven (1907)
Northfield Road, Bonhill, Alexandria G83 9ET
Tel (01389) 752351
Mem 600
Sec J Stewart (01389) 757691
Holes 18 L 5156 yds SSS 66
Recs Am–60 G Brown (1988)
Pro–63 EC Brown (1959)
V'tors U H exc Sat (Apr–Sept) SOC (max 36 members)
Fees £18 D–£20 (£22 D–£28)
Loc Bonhill, 3 miles N of Dumbarton, off A82

Westerwood Hotel G&CC (1989)
St Andrews Drive, Cumbernauld G68 0EW
Tel (01236) 725281 (Pro)
Fax (01236) 738478
Mem 500
Pro S Killin
Holes 18 L 6616 yds SSS 72
Recs Am–67 A Forsyth (1997)
Pro–65 A Forsyth (1998)
V'tors U
Fees £22.50 (£27.50)
Loc 13 miles NE of Glasgow, off A80
Arch Thomas/Ballesteros

Windyhill (1908)
Windyhill, Bearsden G61 4QQ
Tel (0141) 942 2349
Fax (0141) 942 5874
Mem 650
Sec B Davidson
Pro G Collinson
(0141) 942 7157
Holes 18 L 6254 yds SSS 70
Recs Am–64 K Smyth (1994), A McArthur (1998)
Pro–67 G Collinson (1989)
V'tors WD–U Sun–M SOC–WD
Fees £20
Loc 8 miles NW of Glasgow
Arch James Braid

Fife

Aberdour (1896)
Seaside Place, Aberdour KY3 0TX
Tel (01383) 860688
Fax (01383) 860050
Mem 450 170(L)
Sec TH McIntyre
(01383) 860080
Pro G McCallum
(01383) 860256
Holes 18 L 5460 yds Par 67 SSS 66
Recs Am–63 S Meiklejohn (1990)
V'tors WD–book with Pro Sat–NA SOC
Fees £17 D–£28
Loc 8 miles SE of Dunfermline, on coast
Arch Robertson/Anderson

Anstruther (1890)
Marsfield Shore Road, Anstruther KY10 3DZ
Tel (01333) 310956
Fax (01333) 312283
Mem 500
Sec J Boal
Holes 9 L 4504 yds SSS 63
Recs Am–62 G Taylor (1992)
Pro–61 I Collins (1990)
V'tors U SOC
Fees £12 (£15)
Loc 9 miles S of St Andrews

Auchterderran (1904)
Public
Woodend Road, Cardenden KY5 0NH
Tel (01592) 721579
Mem 100
Holes 9 L 5400 yds SSS 66
Recs Am–66 C McRae
V'tors U SOC
Fees £9 (£12)
Loc 1 mile N of Cardenden.
6 miles W of Kirkcaldy, off A910

Balbirnie Park (1983)
Balbirnie Park, Markinch, Glenrothes KY7 6NR
Tel (01592) 612095
Fax (01592) 612383
Mem 800
Sec S Oliver
Pro DFG Scott (01592) 752006
Holes 18 L 6214 yds SSS 70
Recs Am–66 JG Wilson
Pro–65 D Orr
V'tors WE–booking essential
Fees £25 D–£33 (£30 D–£40)
Loc 2 miles E of Glenrothes
Arch Fraser Middleton

Ballingry
Pay and play
Lochore Meadows Country Park, Crosshill, Lochgelly KY5 8BA
Tel (01592) 860086
Mem 150
Holes 9 L 6482 yds SSS 71
Recs Am–68 S Meiklejohn (1990)
V'tors U
Fees On application
Loc 2 miles N of Lochgelly (B920)

Burntisland (1797)
51 Craigkennochie Terrace, Burntisland KY3 9EN
Tel (01592) 872728
Mem 100
Sec AD McPherson
Holes Play over Dodhead Course, Burntisland

Burntisland Golf House Club (1898)
Dodhead, Burntisland KY3 9EY
Tel (01592) 874093
Fax (01592) 874093
Mem 800
Sec WK Taylor (Mgr) (01592) 874093
Pro J Montgomery (01592) 872116
Holes 18 L 5965 yds SSS 70
Recs Am–65 WT Beveridge (1997)
Pro–62 D Robertson (1995)
V'tors U
Fees £15 D–£21 (£25 D–£35)
Loc 1 mile E of Burntisland on B923
Arch Willie Park Jr/James Braid

For list of abbreviations see page 527

Canmore (1897)
Venturefair Avenue, Dunfermline KY12 0PE
Tel (01383) 724969
Mem 556 77(L) 88(J)
Sec C Stuart (01383) 513604
Pro J McKinnon (01383) 728416
Holes 18 L 5437 yds SSS 66
Recs Am–61 R Wallace
Pro–65 T Bjorn (1997)
V'tors WD–U WE–restricted
Fees WD–£15 D–£20
Loc 1 mile N of Dunfermline on A823

Charleton (1994)
Pay and play
Charleton, Colinsburgh KY9 1HG
Tel (01333) 340505
Fax (01333) 340583
Sec J Pattison
Pro A Hutton (01333) 330009
Holes 18 L 6149 yds SSS 70
V'tors U SOC
Fees £18 (£22)
Loc 1 mile W of Colinsburgh, off B942
Mis Driving range. 9 holes pitch & putt
Arch John Salveson

Cowdenbeath (1991)
Public
Seco Place, Cowdenbeath KY4 8PD
Tel (01383) 511918
Mem 400
Sec D Ferguson
Holes 18 L 6100 yds SSS 69
Recs Am–68
V'tors U
Fees On application
Loc In Cowdenbeath, signposted from A909/A92

Crail Golfing Society (1786)
Balcomie Clubhouse, Fifeness, Crail KY10 3XN
Tel (01333) 450278
Fax (01333) 450416
Mem 1400
Sec JF Horsfield (Mgr) (01333) 450686
Pro G Lennie (01333) 450960
Holes Balcomie 18 L 5922 yds SSS 69; Craighead 18 L 6728 yds Par 71 SSS 72
V'tors U
Fees On application
Loc 11 miles SE of St Andrews
Arch Balcomie-Tom Morris. Craighead-Gil Hanse

Cupar (1855)
Hilltarvit, Cupar KY15 5JT
Tel (01334) 653549
Fax (01334) 653549
Mem 475
Sec JM Houston (01334) 654101

Holes 9 L 5074 yds SSS 65
Recs Am–61 TR Spence
V'tors WD–U Sat–NA SOC–WD/Sun
Fees £12 (£15)
Loc 10 miles W of St Andrews

Dunfermline (1887)
Pitfirrane, Crossford, Dunfermline KY12 8QW
Tel (01383) 723534
Mem 690
Sec R De Rose
Pro S Craig (01383) 729061
Holes 18 L 6126 yds SSS 70
Recs Am–65 RW Malcolm
Pro–65 A Brooks
V'tors WD/Sun–U 10–12 & 2–4pm Sat–M SOC–WD
Fees £20 D–£28 (£25 D–£35)
Loc 2 miles W of Dunfermline on A994
Arch JR Stutt

Dunnikier Park (1963)
Dunnikier Way, Kirkcaldy KY1 3LP
Tel (01592) 261599
Mem 600 35(L) 75(J)
Sec RA Waddell (01592) 200627
Pro G Whyte (01592) 642121
Holes 18 L 6601 yds SSS 72
Recs Am–65 S Duthie (1988)
Pro–65 A Hunter (1988)
V'tors U SOC
Fees £15 (£20)
Loc N boundary of Kirkcaldy
Arch R Stutt

Earlsferry Thistle (1875)
Melon Park, Elie KY9 1AS
Mem 60
Sec J Fyall
Holes Play over Golf House Club Course

Falkland (1976)
Public
The Myre, Falkland KY7 7AA
Tel (01337) 857404
Mem 350
Sec Mrs H Horsburgh
Holes 9 L 2384 m SSS 66
Recs Am–62 AD Morrison (1993)
V'tors U SOC
Fees On application
Loc 5 miles N of Glenrothes on A912

Glenrothes (1958)
Public
Golf Course Road, Glenrothes KY6 2LA
Tel (01592) 754561/758686
Mem 750 35(L) 50(J)
Sec Mrs PV Landells (01592) 756941
Holes 18 L 6444 yds SSS 71
Recs Am–65 C Birrell, NM Urquhart
Pro–69 R Craig, B Lawson
Ladies–70 L McKinlay (1989)

V'tors U
Fees £10 (£20)
Loc Glenrothes West, off A92. M90 Junction 29
Arch JR Stutt

Golf House Club (1875)
Elie, Leven KY9 1AS
Tel (01333) 330327
Fax (01333) 330895
Sec A Sneddon (01333) 330301
Pro R Wilson (01333) 330955
Holes 18 L 6261 yds SSS 69
9 L 2277 yds SSS 32
Recs Am–63 AW Mathers
Pro–62 K Nagle
V'tors July–Sept ballot. WE–no party bookings. WE–NA before 3pm (May–Sept)
Fees £32 D–£45 (£40 D–£50)
Loc 12 miles S of St Andrews

Kinghorn Ladies (1905)
Golf Clubhouse, McDuff Crescent, Kinghorn KY3 9RE
Tel (01592) 890345
Mem 40
Sec Miss E Douglas (01592) 890512
Holes Play over Kinghorn Municipal

Kinghorn Municipal (1887)
Public
McDuff Crescent, Kinghorn KY3 9RE
Tel (01592) 890345
Fax (01592) 55761
Sec JP Robertson (01592) 203397
Pro None
Holes 18 L 5629 yds SSS 67
Recs Am–64 G Wilkinson (1991)
V'tors U SOC
Fees £7.60 (£10)
Loc 3 miles S of Kirkcaldy (A921)
Mis Kinghorn and Kinghorn Thistle Clubs play here
Arch Tom Morris

Kirkcaldy (1904)
Balwearie Road, Kirkcaldy KY2 5LT
Tel (01592) 260370
Mem 450 100(L)
Sec AC Thomson (01592) 205240
Pro A Caira (01592) 203258
Holes 18 L 6040 yds SSS 70
Recs Am–65 R Dickson
V'tors U exc Sat–NA
Fees £16 (£22)
Loc S end of Kirkcaldy

Ladybank (1879)
Annsmuir, Ladybank KY15 7RA
Tel (01337) 830320 (Clubhouse), (01337) 830725 (Starter)
Fax (01337) 831505
Mem 900
Sec IF Sproule (01337) 830814
Pro MJ Gray (01337) 830725
Holes 18 L 6641 yds SSS 72

For list of abbreviations see page 527

Fife

Recs Am–63 P Stewart (1995)
Pro–65 M Brookes (1995)
V'tors WD–U 9.30am–4.30pm
M–after 4.30pm WE–NA
10.15am–5pm
Fees £28 (£35)
Loc 6 miles SW of Cupar

Leslie (1898)
Balsillie Laws, Leslie, Glenrothes KY6 3EZ
Tel (01592) 620040
Mem 300
Sec G Lewis
Holes 9 L 4940 yds SSS 64
Recs Am–59 R Bremer
Pro–64 J Chillas
V'tors U
Fees £5 (£8)
Loc 3 miles W of Glenrothes. M90 Junction 5/7, 11 miles

Leven Golfing Society (1820)
Links Road, Leven KY8 4HS
Tel (01333) 426096/424229
Fax (01333) 424229
Mem 635
Sec RT Wright (01333) 424229
Holes Play over Leven Links

Leven Links (1846)
The Promenade, Leven KY8 4HS
Tel (01333) 421390 (Starter)
Fax (01333) 428859
Mem 1200
Sec (01333) 428859 (Links Joint Committee)
Holes 18 L 6434 yds SSS 71
Recs Am–62 M Eliasson,
B Williams (1996)
Pro–63 P Hoad (1984)
V'tors WD–U before 5pm Sat–no parties Sun–NA before 10.30am SOC
Fees £24 (£34)
Loc E of Leven, on promenade. 12 miles SW of St Andrews

Leven Thistle (1867)
Balfour Street, Leven KY8 4JF
Tel (01333) 426397
Fax (01333) 439910
Mem 500
Sec J Scott (01333) 426333
Holes Play over Leven Links

Lochgelly (1895)
Cartmore Road, Lochgelly, Kirkcaldy KY5 9PB
Tel (01592) 780174
Mem 450
Sec RF Stuart (01383) 512238
Pro None
Holes 18 L 5454 yds SSS 66
Recs Am–65 D Sinclair (1995)
V'tors U
Fees £12 (£17)
Loc NW edge of Lochgelly.
5 miles W of Kirkcaldy

Lundin (1868)
Golf Road, Lundin Links KY8 6BA
Tel (01333) 320202
Fax (01333) 329743
Mem 800
Sec DR Thomson
Pro DK Webster
(01333) 320051
Holes 18 L 6394 yds SSS 71
Recs Am–64 C Hislop,
G MacDonald
Pro–63 AD Hare
V'tors WD–U H Sat–NA before 2.30pm Sun–M H
Fees £28 D–£36 Sat–£36
Loc 3 miles E of Leven
Arch James Braid

Lundin Ladies (1891)
Woodielea Road, Lundin Links KY8 6AR
Tel (01333) 320022 (Starter),
(01333) 320832 (Sec)
Mem 350
Holes 9 L 4730 yds SSS 67
Recs Am–67 Miss L Bennett
V'tors U
Fees On application
Loc 3 miles E of Leven

Methil (1892)
Links House, Links Road, Leven KY8 4HS
Tel (01333) 425535
Mem 50
Sec ATJ Traill
Holes Play over Leven Links

Pitreavie (1922)
Queensferry Road, Dunfermline KY11 8PR
Tel (01383) 722591
Fax (01383) 722591
Mem 700
Sec RT Mitchell MBE JP
Pro C Mitchell (01383) 723151
Holes 18 L 6031 yds SSS 69
Recs Am–65 D Manson (1990)
Pro–64 S Kennedy
V'tors U–phone Pro SOC
(Parties–max 36–must be booked in advance)
Fees £19 D–£26 (£38)
Loc 2 miles off M90 Junction 2, between Rosyth and Dunfermline
Arch Dr A Mackenzie

St Michael's (1903)
Leuchars, St Andrews KY16 0DX
Tel (01334) 839365
Fax (01334) 838666
Mem 550
Sec R Smith (01334) 838666
Holes 18 L 5802 yds SSS 68
Recs Am–68 M Aitken, J Purvis (1998)
Pro–71 J Farmer (1996)
V'tors Sun am–NA (Mar–Oct) SOC

Fees D–£18
Loc 5 miles N of St Andrews on Dundee road (A919)

Saline (1912)
Kinneddar Hill, Saline KY12 9LT
Tel (01383) 852591
Mem 400
Sec R Hutchison
(01383) 852344
Holes 9 L 5302 yds SSS 66
Recs Am–A Brown, C Mellon
V'tors U exc medal Sat
Fees £9 (£11)
Loc 5 miles NW of Dunfermline

Scoonie (1951)
Public
North Links, Leven KY8 4SP
Tel (01333) 307007
Fax (01333) 307008
Sec S Kuczerepa
Pro None
Holes 18 L 4979 m SSS 63
Recs Am–63 S Kuczerepa Jr
V'tors U SOC
Fees On application
Loc Adjoins Leven Links

Scotscraig (1817)
Golf Road, Tayport DD6 9DZ
Tel (01382) 552515
Fax (01382) 553130
Mem 750
Sec K Gourlay
Pro SJ Campbell
Holes 18 L 6550 yds SSS 72
Recs Am–69 D Landsburgh
Pro–69
V'tors WD–U WE–by prior arrangement SOC
Fees On application
Loc 10 miles N of St Andrews

Thornton (1921)
Station Road, Thornton KY1 4DW
Tel (01592) 771173 (Starter)
Fax (01592) 774955
Mem 630
Sec BSL Main (01592) 771111
Holes 18 L 6175 yds Par 70 SSS 69
Recs Am–64 A McDonaugh (1994), D Imrie (1996),
S Swan (1997)
V'tors U
Fees £15 D–£25 (£22 D–£32)
Loc 5 miles N of Kirkcaldy, off A92

St Andrews Clubs

New Golf Club (1902)
3-6 Gibson Place, St Andrews KY16 9JE
Tel (01334) 473426
Fax (01334) 477570
Mem 1550
Sec RJW Nye (Sec/Mgr)
Holes Play over St Andrews Links courses

For list of abbreviations see page 527

Royal & Ancient (1754)
St Andrews KY16 9JD
Tel (01334) 472112
Fax (01334) 477580
Mem 1800
Sec Sir MF Bonallack
Holes Play over St Andrews Links

St Andrews (1843)
Links House, The Links, St Andrews KY16 9JB
Tel (01334) 474637
Fax (01334) 479577
Mem 1909
Sec K Barber (Sec/Mgr) (0334) 73017
Holes Play over St Andrews Links

St Andrews Thistle (1817)
38 Chamberlain Street, St Andrews KY16 9JB
Mem 190
Sec DL Joy (01334) 473749
Holes Play over St Andrews Links

St Regulus Ladies'
9 Pilmour Links, St Andrews KY16 9JG
Mem 203
Sec Mrs C Nye (01334) 474520
Holes Play over St Andrews Links

The St Rule Club (1898)
12 The Links, St Andrews KY16 9JB
Tel (01334) 472988
Mem 273
Sec Mrs JM Farquhar (Golf), Mrs J Pate (Club)
Holes Play over St Andrews Links

St Andrews Courses

Balgove Course (1993)
Public
St Andrews Links Trust, St Andrews KY16 9SF
Tel (01334) 466666
Fax (01334) 477036
Sec AJR McGregor
Holes 9 L 1520 yds (Beginners course)
V'tors U
Fees £7 3D–£18 W–£36
Loc St Andrews Links, on A91
Mis Driving range
Arch Donald Steel

Duke's Course (1995)
Craigtoun Park, St Andrews KY16 9SP
Tel (01334) 474371
Fax (01334) 477668
Email oldcoursehotel@standrews.co.uk
Mem 325
Sec S Toon
Pro J Kelly

Holes 18 L 7271 yds Par 72 SSS 75
V'tors U H SOC
Fees £50 (£55)
Loc 3 miles S of St Andrews on Pitscottie road
Mis Driving range
Arch Peter Thompson CBE

Eden Course (1914)
Public
St Andrews Links Trust, St Andrews KY16 9SF
Tel (01334) 466666
Fax (01334) 477036
Sec AJR McGregor
Holes 18 L 6112 yds SSS 70
V'tors U SOC
Fees £9–£23 (£23)
Loc St Andrews Links, on A91
Mis 3D-£85 W-£175 (unlimited play over Jubilee, New, Eden, Strathtyrum and Balgove courses). Driving range
Arch HS Colt

Jubilee Course (1897)
Public
St Andrews Links Trust, St Andrews KY16 9SF
Tel (01334) 466666
Fax (01334) 477036
Sec AJR McGregor
Holes 18 L 6805 yds SSS 73
V'tors U SOC
Fees £35 (£35)
Loc St Andrews Links, on A91. Signs to West Sands
Mis 3D-£85 W-£175 (unlimited play over Jubilee, Strathtyrum, Eden & New courses). Driving range
Arch Angus/Steel

New Course (1895)
Public
St Andrews Links Trust, St Andrews KY16 9SF
Tel (01334) 466666
Fax (01334) 477036
Sec AJR McGregor
Holes 18 L 6604 yds SSS 72
Recs Am–60 O Hjartarson (1998) Pro–63 F Jowle (1955)
V'tors U SOC
Fees £35 (£35)
Loc St Andrews Links, on A91. Signs to West Sands
Mis 3D-£85 W-£175 (unlimited play over Jubilee, New, Eden, Strathtyrum and Balgove courses). Driving range
Arch Old Tom Morris

Old Course (15th Century)
Public
St Andrews Links Trust, St Andrews KY16 9SF
Tel (01334) 466666
Fax (01334) 477036
Sec AJR McGregor
Holes 18 L 6566 yds SSS 72

Recs Am–63 M Hastie (1993) Pro–65 J Leonard, J Parnevik (1997) Ladies–67 M McKay (1993)
V'tors H I No Sun play
Fees £75 (£75)
Loc St Andrews Links, on A91. Signs to West Sands
Mis Driving range

Strathtyrum Course (1993)
Public
St Andrews Links Trust, St Andrews KY16 9SF
Tel (01334) 466666
Fax (01334) 477036
Sec AJR McGregor
Holes 18 L 5094 yds Par 69 SSS 64
V'tors U SOC
Fees £17 (£17)
Loc St Andrews Links, on A91
Mis 3D-£85 W-£175 (unlimited play over Jubilee, New, Eden, Strathtyrum and Balgove courses). Driving range
Arch Donald Steel

Glasgow

Alexandra Park (1880)
Public
Alexandra Park, Dennistoun, Glasgow G31 8SE
Tel (0141) 556 1294
Mem 250
Sec G Campbell
Holes 9 L 4562 yds Par 62
V'tors U
Fees On application
Loc ½ mile E of Glasgow, nr M8
Arch Graham McArthur

Bishopbriggs (1906)
Brackenbrae Road, Bishopbriggs, Glasgow G64 2DX
Tel (0141) 772 1810
Fax (0141) 762 2532
Mem 400 100(L) 100(J)
Sec J Quin (0141) 772 8938
Holes 18 L 6041 yds SSS 69
Recs Am–63 M Loftus (1995) Pro–63 M Miller
V'tors M or I H
Fees On application
Loc 6 miles N of Glasgow on A803
Arch James Braid

Cathcart Castle (1895)
Mearns Road, Clarkston G76 7YL
Tel (0141) 638 0082
Mem 900
Sec IG Sutherland (0141) 638 9449
Pro D Naylor (0141) 638 3436
Holes 18 L 5832 yds SSS 68
Recs Am–62 S Black (1985) Pro–64 A White (1983)

Cawder (1933)
Cadder Road, Bishopbriggs, Glasgow G64 3QD
Tel (0141) 772 7101
Fax (0141) 772 4463
Mem 1200
Sec GT Stoddart (0141) 772 5167
Pro K Stevely (0141) 772 7102
Holes Cawder 18 L 6295 yds SSS 71; Keir 18 L 5877 yds SSS 68
Recs Cawder Am–68 CW Green Pro–61 I Spencer Keir Am–63 G Rodaks, GH Murray
V'tors WD–U WE–NA SOC–WD
Fees £26
Loc N of Glasgow, off A803 Kirkintilloch road
Arch Braid/Steel

Cowglen (1906)
301 Barrhead Road, Glasgow G43 1EU
Tel (0141) 632 0556
Mem 485
Sec RJG Jamieson (01292) 266600
Pro J McTear (0141) 649 9401
Holes 18 L 6006 yds SSS 69
Recs Am–63 D Barclay Howard Pro–63 S Torrance
V'tors WD–by arrangement with Sec WE–M
Fees £22.50 D–£32.50
Loc 3 miles SW of Glasgow (B762)

Glasgow (1787)
Killermont, Bearsden, Glasgow G61 2TW
Tel (0141) 942 1713
Fax (0141) 942 0770
Mem 800
Sec DW Deas (0141) 942 2011
Pro J Steven (0141) 942 8507
Holes 18 L 5982 yds Par 70 SSS 69
Recs Am–63 JS Cochran, C Barrowman Pro–65 H Weetman
V'tors M
Loc 4 miles NW of Glasgow
Arch Tom Morris Sr

Haggs Castle (1910)
70 Dumbreck Road, Dumbreck, Glasgow G41 4SN
Tel (0141) 427 0480
Fax (0141) 427 1157
Mem 970
Sec I Harvey (0141) 427 1157
Pro J McAlister (0141) 427 3355
Holes 18 L 6464 yds SSS 72
Recs Am–64 M Goggin, I Steel (1995) Pro–62 S Torrance (1984)
V'tors M SOC–Weds only
Fees SOC–£27 D–£38
Loc SW Glasgow (B768)

V'tors M SOC
Fees £17 D–£25
Loc 1 mile from Clarkston on B767

King's Park (1934)
Public
150A Croftpark Avenue, Croftfoot, Glasgow G54
Tel (0141) 630 1597
Sec PJ King
Holes 9 L 4236 yds Par 64 SSS 60
Recs Am–27 I Simpson
V'tors U
Fees On application
Loc Croftfoot, 3½ miles S of Glasgow

Knightswood (1929)
Public
Knightswood Park, Lincoln Avenue, Glasgow G13
Tel (0141) 959 6358
Mem 40
Sec J Dean (0141) 954 6495
Holes 9 L 2792 yds SSS 34
V'tors U
Fees £7
Loc 4 miles NW of Glasgow, S of A82

Lethamhill (1933)
Public
Cumbernauld Road, Glasgow G33 1AH
Tel (0141) 770 6220
Fax (0141) 770 0520
Holes 18 L 5946 yds SSS 68
Recs Am–70 R Harker
V'tors U
Fees £6.50
Loc 3 miles NE of Glasgow (A80)

Linn Park (1924)
Public
Simshill Road, Glasgow G44 5TA
Tel (0141) 637 5871
Holes 18 L 4592 yds SSS 65
Recs Am–62 J Cassidy (1989)
V'tors U
Fees £5.50
Loc 4 miles S of Glasgow, W of B766

Littlehill (1926)
Public
Auchinairn Road, Glasgow G64 1UT
Tel (0141) 772 1916
Holes 18 L 6228 yds SSS 70
Recs Am–69
V'tors U
Fees On application
Loc 3 miles NE of Glasgow, E of A803

Pollok (1892)
90 Barrhead Road, Glasgow G43 1BG
Tel (0141) 632 1080
Fax (0141) 649 1398
Mem 500
Sec I Cumming (0141) 632 4351
Pro None
Holes 18 L 6295 yds SSS 70
Recs Am–62 G Shaw Pro–62 G Cunningham

V'tors WD–I XL WE–NA SOC–WD
Fees £30 D–£40
Loc 3 miles SW of Glasgow (B762). M77 Junction 3

Ralston (1904)
Strathmore Avenue, Ralston, Paisley PA1 3DT
Tel (0141) 882 1349
Fax (0141) 883 9837
Mem 440 165(L) 100(J)
Sec J Pearson
Pro J Scott (0141) 810 4925
Holes 18 L 6100 yds SSS 69
Recs Am–62 A Forsyth Pro–62 M King
V'tors M
Loc 2 miles E of Paisley (A737)

Rouken Glen (1922)
Public
Stewarton Road, Thornliebank, Glasgow G46 7UZ
Tel (0141) 638 7044
Holes 18 L 4800 yds SSS 63
V'tors U SOC
Fees On application
Loc 5 miles S of Glasgow, W of A77
Mis Driving range

Ruchill (1928)
Public
Ruchil Park, Brassey Street, Maryhill, Glasgow G20
Mem 60
Holes 9 L 2240 yds SSS 31
V'tors U
Fees On application
Loc 2 miles N of Glasgow, W of A879

Sandyhills (1905)
223 Sandyhills Road, Glasgow G32 9NA
Tel (0141) 778 1179
Mem 700
Sec P Ward
Holes 18 L 6253 yds SSS 71
Recs Am–65 J Hay
V'tors WE–M SOC
Fees £17.50
Loc 4 miles SE of Glasgow, N of A74

Williamwood (1906)
Clarkston Road, Netherlee, Glasgow G44 3YR
Tel (0141) 637 1783
Mem 680
Sec P Laing
Pro J McTear (0141) 637 2715
Holes 18 L 5878 yds SSS 69
Recs Am–61 H Kemp (1990) Pro–61 BJ Gallacher (1974)
V'tors M
Loc 5 miles S of Glasgow
Arch James Braid

Highland

Caithness & Sutherland

Bonar Bridge, Ardgay (1904)
Bonar-Bridge, Ardgay IV24 3EJ
- **Tel** (01863) 766199
- **Fax** (01863) 766738
- **Mem** 250
- **Sec** F Mussard (01863) 766375
- **Holes** 9 L 5284 yds SSS 67
- **Recs** Am–63 M Munro (1994)
- **V'tors** U
- **Fees** D–£12 (£12)
- **Loc** ½ mile N of Bonar Bridge on A836. 12 miles W of Dornoch

Brora (1891)
Golf Road, Brora KW9 6QS
- **Tel** (01408) 621417
- **Sec** J Fraser
- **Holes** 18 L 6110 yds SSS 69
- **Recs** Am–61 J Miller
  Pro–67 D Huish
- **V'tors** U exc comp days –H for open comps SOC
- **Fees** £18 D–£24
- **Loc** 18 miles N of Dornoch (A9)
- **Arch** James Braid

The Carnegie Club (1995)
Skibo Castle, Clashmore, Dornoch IV25 3RQ
- **Tel** (01862) 894600
- **Fax** (01862) 894601
- **Sec** CA Oak
- **Pro** GJ Finlayson
- **Holes** 18 L 6671 yds Par 71 SSS 71
- **V'tors** H–booking required
- **Fees** £130 inc lunch
- **Loc** 3 miles SW of Dornoch
- **Arch** Donald Steel

Durness (1988)
Balnakeil, Durness IV27 4PN
- **Tel** (01971) 511364
- **Mem** 120
- **Sec** Mrs L Mackay (01971) 511364
- **Holes** 9 L 5555 yds SSS 69
- **Recs** Am–71 M Mackay (1996), D McIntosh (1997)
- **V'tors** U
- **Fees** D–£12 W–£50
- **Loc** 57 miles NW of Lairg on A838

Golspie (1889)
Ferry Road, Golspie KW10 6ST
- **Tel** (01408) 633266
- **Fax** (01408) 633393
- **Mem** 315
- **Sec** Mrs M MacLeod
- **Pro** None
- **Holes** 18 L 5890 yds SSS 68

- **Recs** Am–65 J Miller
  Pro–65 D Huish
- **V'tors** U SOC
- **Fees** £18 D–£20 (£20 D–£25)
- **Loc** 11 miles N of Dornoch

Helmsdale (1895)
Golf Road, Helmsdale KW8 6JA
- **Mem** 92
- **Sec** D Bishop
- **Holes** 9 L 3720 yds SSS 61
- **V'tors** U
- **Fees** £5 D–£10 W–£25
- **Loc** 30 miles N of Dornoch (A9)

Lybster (1926)
Main Street, Lybster KW1 6BL
- **Mem** 100
- **Sec** M Bowman
- **Holes** 9 L 1896 yds SSS 61
- **Recs** Am–59 D Nicholson (1991), E Larnach (1993), E Newman (1995)
- **V'tors** U SOC
- **Fees** £5
- **Loc** 13 miles S of Wick on A99

Reay (1893)
Reay, Thurso KW14 7RE
- **Tel** (01847) 811288
- **Mem** 332 56(L) 34(J)
- **Sec** Miss P Peebles (01847) 811537
- **Pro** None
- **Holes** 18 L 5865 yds SSS 68
- **Recs** Am–64 GA Dunnett (1990)
  Ladies–71 E Manson (1988)
- **V'tors** U exc comp days
- **Fees** D–£15 W–£45
- **Loc** 11 miles W of Thurso

Royal Dornoch (1877)
Golf Road, Dornoch IV25 3LW
- **Tel** (01862) 810219
- **Fax** (01862) 810792
- **Mem** 1079 198(L) 70(J)
- **Sec** JS Duncan (Sec/Mgr) (01862) 811220
- **Pro** A Skinner (01862) 810902
- **Holes** C'ship 18 L 6514 yds SSS 73
  Struie 18 L 5438 yds SSS 66
- **Recs** Am–66 CP Christy
  Pro–65 K Stables
- **V'tors** H
- **Fees** On application
- **Loc** 45 miles N of Inverness, off A9, N of Dornoch
- **Mis** Helipad by clubhouse. Airstrip nearby

Thurso (1893)
Newlands of Geise, Thurso KW14 7XD
- **Tel** (01847) 893807
- **Mem** 300
- **Sec** Capt D Phillips (01847) 895433
- **Holes** 18 L 5828 yds SSS 69
- **Recs** Am–63 G Dunnett (1989)
- **V'tors** U
- **Fees** £11
- **Loc** 2 miles SW of Thurso

Wick (1870)
Reiss, Wick KW1 5LJ
- **Tel** (01955) 602726
- **Mem** 311
- **Sec** D Shearer (01955) 602935
- **Holes** 18 L 5976 yds SSS 70
- **Recs** Am–63 R Taylor (1988), R Beames (1998)
  Pro–68 Dai Rees
- **V'tors** U
- **Fees** On application
- **Loc** 3 miles N of Wick on A99

Inverness

Abernethy (1893)
Nethy Bridge PH25 3EB
- **Tel** (01479) 821305
- **Mem** 320
- **Sec** DA Gill (01479) 821040
- **Holes** 9 L 2520 yds SSS 66
- **Recs** Am–61 I Murray
- **V'tors** U SOC
- **Fees** £12 (£16)
- **Loc** 5 miles S of Grantown (B970)

Alness (1904)
Ardross Rd, Alness, Ross-shire IV17 0QA
- **Tel** (01349) 883877
- **Mem** 300
- **Sec** Mrs E Taylor
- **Holes** 18 L 4886 yds Par 67 SSS 64
- **Recs** Am–62 C MacIver (1983), C Taylor (1989)
- **V'tors** U exc Mon–NA 5–6pm SOC
- **Fees** On application
- **Loc** ¼ mile N of Alness. 23 miles N of Inverness
- **Arch** I Scott Taylor (New holes)

Boat-of-Garten (1898)
Boat-of-Garten PH24 3BQ
- **Tel** (01479) 831282
- **Fax** (01479) 831523
- **Mem** 599
- **Sec** P Smyth
- **Holes** 18 L 5866 yds SSS 69
- **Recs** Am–67 R Beames (1998)
- **V'tors** U–booking advisable
- **Fees** £21 D–£26 (£26 D–£31)
- **Loc** 27 miles SE of Inverness (A95)
- **Arch** James Braid

Carrbridge (1980)
Carrbridge PH23 3AU
- **Tel** (01479) 841623 (Clubhouse)
- **Mem** 600
- **Sec** Mrs AT Baird
- **Holes** 9 L 2623 yds Par 71 SSS 68
- **Recs** Am–64 G Hay (1992)
- **V'tors** U exc comp days–NA
- **Fees** D–£11 (D–£13) (1998)
- **Loc** 23 miles SE of Inverness, off A9

For list of abbreviations see page 527

Highland 707

Castle Heather (1996)
Castle Heather, Inverness IV1 2AA
Tel (01463) 713334/5
Fax (01463) 712695
Mem 500
Sec GD Thompson
(01463) 713335
Pro M Piggot (01463) 713334
Holes 18 L 6700 yds Par 73 SSS 72
Recs Am–71 AG Skinner (1998)
V'tors U
Fees D–£20 (D–£25)
Loc Culduthel, SW Inverness
Mis Floodlit driving range

Fort Augustus (1930)
Markethill, Fort Augustus PH32 4AU
Mem 110
Sec H Fraser (01320) 6309
Holes 9 L 5454 yds SSS 68
Recs Am–P MacDonald (1995)
V'tors U
Fees D–£10
Loc W end of Fort Augustus

Fort William (1974)
North Road, Fort William PH33 6SW
Tel (01397) 704464
Mem 300
Sec G Bales
Holes 18 L 5686 m SSS 71
V'tors U
Fees On application
Loc 3 miles N of Fort William (A82)
Arch JR Stutt

Fortrose & Rosemarkie (1888)
Ness Road East, Fortrose IV10 8SE
Tel (01381) 620529
Mem 800
Sec Mrs M Collier
Holes 18 L 5858 yds SSS 69
Recs Am–64 G Paterson
V'tors U SOC
Fees £18 (£25)
Loc Black Isle, 12 miles N of Inverness
Arch James Braid

Grantown-on-Spey (1890)
Golf Course Road, Grantown-on-Spey PH26 3HY
Tel (01479) 872079
Fax (01479) 873725
Mem 700
Sec JA Matheson (01479) 873154
Pro B Mitchell (01479) 872398
Holes 18 L 5710 yds Par 70 SSS 68
Recs Am–60 G Bain (1984) Pro–62 D Webster
V'tors WD–U WE–U after 10am SOC
Fees D–£18 (D–£23)
Loc E side of Grantown (A95)
Arch Willie Park

Invergordon (1893)
King George Street, Invergordon IV18 0BD
Tel (01349) 852715
Mem 170 30(L) 50(J)
Sec NR Paterson (01349) 882693
Holes 18 L 6040 yds Par 69 SSS 69
V'tors U SOC
Fees £10 (£10)
Loc 15 miles NE of Dingwall (A9/B817)
Arch A Rae (1994)

Inverness (1883)
Culcabock Road, Inverness IV2 3XQ
Tel (01463) 239882
Fax (01463) 239882
Mem 1100
Sec G Thomson
Pro AP Thomson (01463) 231989
Holes 18 L 6226 yds SSS 70
Recs Am–62 ND Hampton Pro–62 N Scott-Smith
V'tors WE/BH–restricted SOC
Fees £23 D–£32 (£27 D–£35)
Loc 1 mile S of Inverness

Kingussie (1891)
Gynack Road, Kingussie PH21 1LR
Tel (01540) 661374 (Clubhouse)
Fax (01540) 662066
Mem 700
Sec ND MacWilliam (01540) 661600
Pro None
Holes 18 L 5555 yds SSS 68
Recs Am–63 ND MacWilliam (1994), B Shaw (1997) Pro–66 K Hutton (1991)
V'tors U
Fees £16 D–£20 (£18 D–£25)
Loc ½ mile N of Kingussie, off A9
Arch H Vardon

Muir of Ord (1875)
Great North Road, Muir of Ord IV6 7SX
Tel (01463) 870825
Fax (01463) 870825
Mem 700
Sec D Noble
Pro G Leggat (01463) 871311
Holes 18 L 5557 yds SSS 68
Recs Am–61 DR McIntosh (1997)
V'tors U SOC
Fees D–£12.50 (£16.50) W–£50
Loc 15 miles N of Inverness (A862)
Arch James Braid

Nairn (1887)
Seabank Road, Nairn IV12 4HB
Tel (01667) 452103
Fax (01667) 456328
Mem 938
Sec J Somerville (01667) 453208
Pro R Fyfe (01667) 452787
Holes 18 L 6722 yds SSS 74 9 hole course
Recs Am–66 S Tomisson Pro–65 D Small

V'tors U SOC
Fees On application
Loc Nairn West Shore (A96)
Arch Old Tom Morris/Braid/ Simpson

Nairn Dunbar (1899)
Lochloy Road, Nairn IV12 5AE
Tel (01667) 452741
Fax (01667) 456897
Mem 900
Sec JS Falconer
Pro To be appointed
Holes 18 L 6720 yds SSS 73
Recs Am–69 C Duffy Pro–63 RM Collinson
V'tors U
Fees £28 D–£35 (£33 D–£45)
Loc In Nairn

Newtonmore (1893)
Golf Course Road, Newtonmore PH20 1AT
Tel (01540) 673328
Fax (01540) 673878
Mem 450
Sec G Spinks
Pro R Henderson (01540) 673611
Holes 18 L 6029 yds SSS 69
Recs Am–65 TR Spence (1998) Pro–68 F Couttes (1993)
V'tors U SOC
Fees £13 D–£16 (£15 D–£21)
Loc 4 miles W of Kingussie. 46 miles S of Inverness

Spean Bridge
Spean Bridge, Fort William PH33
Mem 65
Sec AJ McLaren (Pres) (01397) 704954
Holes 9 hole course SSS 62
V'tors U
Fees On application
Loc 9 miles N of Fort William on A82

Strathpeffer Spa (1888)
Strathpeffer IV14 9AS
Tel (01997) 421011/421219
Fax (01997) 421011
Mem 350 60(L) 80(J)
Sec N Roxburgh (01997) 421396
Pro Shop (01997) 421011
Holes 18 L 4792 yds SSS 64
Recs Am–60 D Krzyzanowski Pro–66 A Herd
V'tors U SOC
Fees £14 D–£20
Loc ¼ mile N of Strathpeffer. 5 miles W of Dingwall
Arch Willie Park

Tain (1890)
Chapel Road, Tain IV19 1PA
Tel (01862) 892314
Fax (01862) 892099
Mem 500
Sec Mrs KD Ross
Pro None

For list of abbreviations see page 527

Holes 18 L 6351 yds SSS 70
Recs Am–67 M Munro (1997)
V'tors U
Fees £21 D–£27 (£25 D–£31)
Loc 35 miles N of Inverness (A9). 8 miles S of Dornoch
Arch Tom Morris

Tarbat (1909)
Portmahomack, Tain IV20 1YB
Tel (01862) 87236
Fax (01349) 853715
Mem 200
Sec D Wilson
Holes 9 L 2568 yds SSS 66
Recs Am–63 D Mackay
V'tors U H SOC
Fees D–£5 (D–£6)
Loc 10 miles E of Tain
Arch J Sutherland

Torvean (1962)
Public
Glenurquhart Road, Inverness IV3 6JN
Tel (01463) 711434 (Starter)
Fax (01463) 225651
Mem 400
Sec Mrs KM Gray (01463) 225651
Pro None
Holes 18 L 5784 yds SSS 68
Recs Am–65 DC Walker (1994)
Pro–70 R Weir (1988)
Ladies–70 C MacLeod (1995)
V'tors U
Fees £11 (£13)
Loc SW of Inverness on A82

Orkney & Shetland

Orkney (1889)
Grainbank, Kirkwall, Orkney KW15 1RD
Tel (01856) 872457
Fax (01856) 874165
Mem 415
Sec LF Howard (01856) 874165
Holes 18 L 5411 yds SSS 67
Recs Am–65 KD Peace
Pro–71 I Smith
V'tors U
Fees D–£10 W–£35
Loc 1 mile W of Kirkwall

Shetland (1891)
PO Box 18, Lerwick, Shetland ZE1 0YW
Tel (01595) 840369
Mem 450
Sec C Lobban (Mgr)
Holes 18 L 5776 yds SSS 68
Recs Am–67 MC Boxwell (1996), IG Sandison (1997)
V'tors U

Fees D–£12
Loc 3 miles N of Lerwick (A907)
Arch Fraser Middleton

Stromness (1890)
Stromness, Orkney KW16 3DU
Tel (01856) 850772
Mem 250
Sec GA Bevan (01856) 850885
Holes 18 L 4762 yds SSS 63
Recs Am–61 G Dunnet
Pro–66 R Macaskill
V'tors U
Fees D–£12
Loc Stromness, 16 miles W of Kirkwall on Hoy Sound

Whalsay (1976)
Skaw Taing, Whalsay, Shetland ZE2 9AL
Tel (01806) 566373/566450
Mem 100
Sec RP Irvine
Pro None
Holes 18 L 6009 yds Par 70 SSS 68
Recs Am–65 IG Sandison (1993)
Ladies–72 S Croy (1998)
V'tors U SOC
Fees £10
Loc 5 miles N of Symbister Ferry

West Coast

Askernish (1891)
Lochboisdale, Askernish, South Uist HS81 5SY
Tel (01878) 700301
Fax (01878) 700309
Mem 30
Sec AL Macdonald
Pro M McPhee
Holes 9 L 5114 yds SSS 67
Recs Am–66 K Robertson
V'tors U
Fees £10
Loc 5 miles NW of Lochboisdale
Arch Tom Morris Sr

Gairloch (1898)
Gairloch IV21 2BQ
Tel (01445) 712407
Mem 285
Sec A Shinkins
Holes 9 L 2281 yds SSS 64
Recs Am–63 L Chancellor (1995)
V'tors U
Fees D–£12 W–£45
Loc 60 miles W of Dingwall in Wester Ross

Isle of Harris
Scarista, Isle of Harris
Tel (01859) 520536
Mem 66
Sec A Haddow
Pro None
Holes 9 L 2442 yds Par 68 SSS 64

V'tors U
Fees £7.50 (£7.50)
Loc 13 miles S of Tarbert on W coast

Isle of Skye (1964)
Sconser, Isle of Skye IV48 8TD
Tel (01478) 650351
Mem 180
Sec M MacDonald
Holes 9 L 4798 yds Par 66 SSS 64
Recs Am–62 M Whatley
V'tors U
Fees D–£10
Loc Between Broadford and Sligachan

Lochcarron (1911)
Lochcarron, Strathcarron IV54 8YL
Mem 156
Sec Mrs K MacKenzie (01520) 722296
Holes 9 L 3578 yds Par 62 SSS 60
V'tors U exc Sat 2–5pm–NA
Fees £10 W–£40
Loc ½ mile E of Lochcarron in Wester Ross

Skeabost (1982)
Skeabost Bridge, Isle of Skye IV5 9NP
Tel (01470) 532202
Fax (01470) 532454
Mem 80
Sec DJ Matheson (01470) 532319 (Skeabost House Hotel)
Holes 9 L 3224 yds SSS 59
V'tors U
Fees D–£6
Loc 6 miles NW of Portree on Dunvegan road

Stornoway (1890)
Lady Lever Park, Stornoway, Isle of Lewis HS2 0XP
Tel (01851) 702240
Mem 400
Sec H Lloyd
Holes 18 L 5252 yds Par 68 SSS 67
Recs Am–62 C Macritchie
Pro–65 JC Farmer
V'tors U exc Sun–NA SOC
Fees D–£15 W–£45
Loc Off A857 in Lewis Castle, Isle of Lewis

Traigh (1900)
c/o Camusdarach, Arisaig PH39 4NT
Tel (01687) 450337
Mem 160
Sec A Simpson (01687) 450337
Pro None
Holes 9 L 2456 yds Par 68 SSS 65
V'tors U
Fees D–£10 (D–£12)
Loc 2 miles N of Arisaig on A830 Fort William-Mallaig road
Arch John Salveson

Lanarkshire

Airdrie (1877)
Rochsoles, Airdrie ML6 0PQ
Tel (01236) 762195
Mem 450
Sec DM Hardie
Pro G Monks (01236) 754360
Holes 18 L 6004 yds SSS 69
Recs Am–63 G Rankin
V'tors M I WE/BH–NA SOC
Fees £15 D–£25
Loc Airdrie 1 mile
Arch James Braid

Bellshill (1905)
Community Road, Orbiston, Bellshill ML4 2RZ
Tel (01698) 745124
Mem 680
Sec Mrs L Kennedy (Admin)
Holes 18 L 5900 yds Par 69 SSS 69
Recs Am–67
       Pro–70 J McCallum
V'tors WD–U Sun–NA before 1.30pm SOC
Fees D–£18 (£25)
Loc 30 miles W (A725) M74 Junction 5

Biggar (1895)
Public
The Park, Broughton Road, Biggar ML12 6AH
Tel (01899) 220618 (Clubhouse),
       (01899) 220319 (Bookings)
Mem 250
Sec WS Turnbull (01899) 220566
Pro None
Holes 18 L 5416 yds SSS 66
Recs Am–61 B Kerr (1994),
       G Venerus (1995)
       Pro–63 P Lawrie (1993)
V'tors U–booking recommended
Fees £9 (£10)
Loc 12 miles SE of Lanark (A702)
Arch Willie Park

Blairbeth (1910)
Burnside, Rutherglen, Glasgow G73 4SF
Tel (0141) 634 3355 (Clubhouse),
       (0141) 634 3325 (Office)
Mem 450
Sec FT Henderson
       (0141) 569 7266
Holes 18 L 5518 yds SSS 68
Recs Am–64 D Orr
       Pro–69 WG Cunningham
V'tors SOC–WD
Fees On application
Loc 1 mile S of Rutherglen

Bothwell Castle (1922)
Blantyre Road, Bothwell, Glasgow G71 8PS
Tel (01698) 853177
Fax (01698) 854052
Mem 1137
Pro JG Niven (01698) 852052
Holes 18 L 6243 yds SSS 70
Recs Am–62 B Howard
       Pro–61 A Crerar (1994)
V'tors WD–U 9.30–10.30am & 2.30–3.30pm
Fees £20 D–£28
Loc 3 miles N of Hamilton. M74 Junction 5

Calderbraes (1891)
57 Roundknowe Road, Uddingston G71 7TS
Tel (01698) 813425
Mem 300
Sec S McGuigan (0141) 773 2287
Holes 9 L 5046 yds Par 66 SSS 67
Recs Am–65 D Gilchrist (1986)
V'tors WD–U WE–M
Fees D–£12
Loc Start of M74

Cambuslang (1892)
30 Westburn Drive, Cambuslang G72 7NA
Tel (0141) 641 3130
Mem 200 100(L) 75(J)
Sec RM Dunlop
Holes 9 L 6072 yds SSS 69
Recs Am–62 S Gillespie (1996)
V'tors M
Fees On application
Loc Cambuslang Station 3/4 mile

Carluke (1894)
Hallcraig, Mauldslie Road, Carluke ML8 5HG
Tel (01555) 771070/770574
Mem 460 100(L)
Sec D Black (01555) 773086
Pro R Forrest (01555) 751053
Holes 18 L 5805 yds SSS 68
Recs Am–63 D Brown
       Pro–64 G Cunningham,
       R Davis, W Milne
V'tors WD–U before 4pm
       WE/BH–NA
Fees £18 D–£25
Loc 20 miles SE of Glasgow

Carnwath (1907)
Main Street, Carnwath ML11 8JX
Tel (01555) 840251
Mem 380
Sec To be appointed
Pro None
Holes 18 L 5955 yds SSS 69
Recs Am–65 B Holbrook
V'tors WD–U before 4pm Sat–NA Sun–restricted
Fees WD/Sat–D–£18
       Sun/BH–D–£22
Loc 7 miles E of Lanark

Cathkin Braes (1888)
Cathkin Road, Rutherglen, Glasgow G73 4SE
Tel (0141) 634 6605
Fax (0141) 634 6605
Mem 900
Sec H Millar
Pro S Bree (0141) 634 0650
Holes 18 L 6208 yds SSS 71
Recs Am–64 PW Jamieson (1998)
       Pro–66 C Maltman (1992)
V'tors WD–I
Fees £25
Loc 5 miles S of Glasgow (B759)
Arch James Braid

Coatbridge (1971)
Public
Townhead Road, Coatbridge ML52 2HX
Tel (01236) 28975
Mem 300
Sec O Dolan (01236) 26811
Pro G Weir (01236) 21492
Holes 18 L 6020 yds SSS 69
Recs Am–69 A Webster (1989)
V'tors U
Fees On application
Loc Townhead, E of Glasgow. 1/2 mile E of M73
Mis Driving range

Colville Park (1923)
Jerviston Estate, Motherwell ML1 4UG
Tel (01698) 263017
Fax (01698) 230418
Mem 800 64(L) 140(J)
Sec S Connacher
       (01698) 265378
Pro Golf Shop (01698) 265779
Holes 18 L 6265 yds SSS 70
Recs Am–64 S O'Hara
       Pro–66 SD Brown
V'tors M SOC–WD only
Fees D–£27
Loc 1 mile NE of Motherwell on A723
Arch James Braid

Crow Wood (1925)
Cumbernauld Road, Muirhead, Glasgow G69 9JF
Tel (0141) 799 2011
Fax (0141) 779 9148
Mem 700
Sec I McInnes (0141) 779 4954
Pro B Moffat (0141) 779 1943
Holes 18 L 6261 yds Par 71 SSS 71
Recs Am–62 D Robertson
       Pro–66 J McTear, A Oldcorn
V'tors WD–H (prior notice required) SOC
Fees £20 D–£28
Loc 5 miles NE of Glasgow, off A80
Arch James Braid

Douglas Water (1922)
Douglas Water, Lanark ML11 9NB
Tel (01555) 880361
Mem 190
Sec D Hogg
Holes 9 L 2916 yds SSS 69
Recs Am–63 P Peat
V'tors U exc Sat–restricted
Fees £7 (£10)
Loc 7 miles S of Lanark

For list of abbreviations see page 527

Lanarkshire

Drumpellier (1894)
Drumpellier Ave, Coatbridge ML5 1RX
Tel (01236) 424139/428723
Mem 500
Sec W Brownlie (01236) 428723
Pro D Ross (01236) 432971
Holes 18 L 6227 yds SSS 70
Recs Am–63 G Rankin
Pro–62 C Maltman
V'tors I
Fees £22 D–£30
Loc 8 miles E of Glasgow

East Kilbride (1900)
Chapelside Road, Nerston, East Kilbride G74 4PF
Tel (01355) 220913 (Clubhouse)
Fax (01355) 247728
Mem 834
Sec WG Gray
Pro W Walker (01355) 222192
Holes 18 L 6419 yds SSS 71
Recs Am–65 WF Bryce
Pro–64 D Ingram
V'tors M SOC
Fees On application
Loc 8 miles S of Glasgow

Easter Moffat (1922)
Mansion House, Plains, Airdrie ML6 8NP
Tel (01236) 842878
Fax (01236) 842904
Mem 450
Sec JG Timmons
(01236) 761440
Pro G King (01236) 843015
Holes 18 L 6221 yds SSS 70
Recs Am–65 B Lees (1995)
Pro–66 R Shade (1967)
V'tors WD only BH–NA
Fees On application
Loc 3 miles E of Airdrie

Hamilton (1892)
Riccarton, Ferniegair, Hamilton ML3 7UE
Tel (01698) 282872
Mem 500
Sec GM Chapman
(01698) 459537
Pro MJ Moir (01698) 282324
Holes 18 L 6255 yds SSS 71
Recs Am–62 G Hogg, B Smith
V'tors M or by arrangement with Sec
Fees On application
Loc 1½ miles S of Hamilton
Arch James Braid

Hollandbush (1954)
Public
Acre Tophead, Lesmahagow, Coalburn ML11 0JS
Tel (01555) 893484
Mem 600
Sec J Hamilton
Pro I Rae (01555) 893646
Holes 18 L 6233 yds SSS 70
Recs Am–63 G Brown, R Lynch

V'tors U
Fees £7.25 (£8.50)
Loc 10 miles SW of Lanark, off A74, between Lesmahagow and Coalburn

Kirkhill (1910)
Greenlees Road, Cambuslang, Glasgow G72 8YN
Tel (0141) 641 3083 (Clubhouse)
Fax (0141) 641 8499
Mem 570
Sec J Sweeney
(0141) 641 8499
Pro D Williamson
(0141) 641 7972
Holes 18 L 6030 yds SSS 70
Recs Am–68 S Hinshelwood (1998)
Pro–68 R Weir
V'tors WD–by prior arrangement WE/BH–NA SOC
Fees On application
Loc Cambuslang, SE Glasgow
Arch James Braid

Lanark (1851)
The Moor, Lanark ML11 7RX
Tel (01555) 663219
Fax (01555) 663219
Mem 500 130(L) 150(J)
Sec GH Cuthill
Pro A White (01555) 661456
Holes 18 L 6426 yds SSS 71
9 hole course
Recs Am–64 CV McInally
Pro–62 C Maltman
V'tors WD–U until 4pm WE–M
Fees 18 hole:£24 D–£36
9 hole:£4
Loc 30 miles S of Glasgow, off A74
Arch Tom Morris

Langlands (1985)
Langlands Road, East Kilbride G75 9DW
Tel (01355) 248173,
(01355) 224685 (Starter)
Mem 298
Sec NJ Martin (0141) 644 2623
Holes 18 L 6201 yds Par 70 SSS 70
Recs Am–64 T Hunter (1996)
V'tors U
Fees £7.90–£9.20
Loc 2 miles SE of East Kilbride, off Strathaven Road

Larkhall
Public
Burnhead Road, Larkhall, Glasgow
Tel (01698) 881113
Mem 400
Sec I Gilmour
Holes 9 L 6754 yds SSS 72
Recs Am–67 S Crolla
V'tors U exc Tues 5–8pm & Sat 7am–5pm
Fees On application
Loc SW of Larkhall on B7109. 10 miles SE of Glasgow

Leadhills (1935)
Leadhills, Biggar ML12 6XR
Tel (01659) 74222
Mem 100
Sec H Shaw
Holes 9 L 2031 yds SSS 62
V'tors U
Fees On application
Loc 6 miles S of Abington, off A74

Mount Ellen (1905)
Lochend Road, Gartcosh, Glasgow G69 9EY
Tel (01236) 872277
Mem 480
Sec WJ Dickson
Pro G Reilly
Holes 18 L 5525 yds SSS 68
V'tors WD–U from 9am–4pm WE–NA
Fees On application
Loc 8 miles NE of Glasgow, W of M73

Shotts (1895)
Blairhead, Benhar Road, Shotts ML7 5BJ
Tel (01501) 820431
Mem 700
Sec J McDermott
Pro S Strachan (01501) 822658
Holes 18 L 6205 yds SSS 70
Recs Am–65 AJ Ferguson
Pro–65 B Gunson
V'tors WD–U Sat–NA before 4.30pm
Fees D–£17 (D–£20)
Loc 18 miles E of Glasgow on B7057. M8 Junction 5, 1½ miles
Arch James Braid

Strathaven (1908)
Glasgow Road, Strathaven ML10 6NL
Tel (01357) 520421
Mem 950
Sec AW Wallace
Pro M McCrorie (01357) 521812
Holes 18 L 6226 yds SSS 70
Recs Am–65 R Scott
Pro–63 D Huish
V'tors WD–I before 4pm WE–NA
Fees On request
Loc N of Strathaven, off Glasgow road (A726)

Strathclyde Park
Public
Mote Hill, Hamilton ML3 6BY
Tel (01698) 429350
Mem 240
Sec K Will
Pro W Walker (01698) 285511
Holes 9 L 6350 yds SSS 70
Recs Am–64 JJ Smith (1993)
V'tors U exc medal days (phone booking)
Fees £3
Loc Hamilton
Mis Driving range

For list of abbreviations see page 527

Torrance House (1969)
Public
Strathaven Road, East Kilbride, Glasgow G75 0QZ
Tel (01355) 248638
Mem 650
Sec JB Asher
Pro J Dunlop (013552) 33491
Holes 18 L 6415 yds SSS 71
Recs Am–67 A Pitt
Pro–66 I Collins
V'tors U
Fees £16
Loc S of East Kilbride, off Strathaven road (A726)

Wishaw (1897)
55 Cleland Road, Wishaw ML2 7PH
Tel (01698) 372869
Mem 475 100(L)
Sec R Hutchison
Pro JG Campbell (01698) 358247
Holes 18 L 5999 yds SSS 69
Recs Am–63 G Dingwall (1996)
Pro–63 A Hunter (1989)
V'tors WD after 4pm–NA Sat–NA
Fees £13 D–£21 Sun–£26
Loc N of Wishaw town centre

Lothians

East Lothian

Aberlady (1912)
Aberlady EH32 0QD
Mem 35
Sec A Wood (01875) 870582
Holes Play over Kilspindie course

Bass Rock (1873)
6 Harperdean Cottages, Harperdean, Haddington EH41 3SQ
Mem 110
Sec SH Butterworth (01620) 822082
Holes Play over North Berwick

Castle Park
Pay and play
Gifford, Haddington EH41 4PL
Tel (01620) 810723
Mem 300
Sec S Fortune (01620) 810733
Holes L 5810 yds Par 70 SSS 68
V'tors U SOC
Fees £10 D–£15 (£12 D–£20)
Loc 2 miles S of Gifford on Longyester road
Mis Driving range

Dirleton Castle (1854)
Gullane EH31 2BB
Tel (01620) 843496
Mem 100
Sec RH Atkinson
Holes Play over Gullane courses

Dunbar (1856)
East Links, Dunbar EH42 1LT
Tel (01368) 862317
Fax (01368) 865202
Mem 998
Sec Liz Thom
Pro D Small (01368) 862086
Holes 18 L 6426 yds SSS 71
Recs Am–64 C Craig (1996)
Pro–64 R Weir (1989)
V'tors U SOC–exc Thurs
Fees £25 D–£35 (£35 D–£45)
Loc ½ mile E of Dunbar. 30 miles E of Edinburgh, off A1
Arch Tom Morris

Gifford (1904)
Edinburgh Road, Gifford EH41 4JE
Tel (01620) 810267
Mem 450
Sec G MacColl
Holes 9 L 6256 yds SSS 70
Recs Am–69 I Wilkinson (1997)
Ladies–67 S McEwan (1996)
V'tors Tues/Wed/Sat–NA after 4pm Sun–NA after noon
Fees £12 D–£15
Loc 4 miles S of Haddington. 20 miles SE of Edinburgh (B6355)
Arch Willie Watt

The Glen (1906)
East Links, North Berwick EH39 4LE
Tel (01620) 892726
Fax (01620) 895447
Mem 650
Sec DR Montgomery
Pro None
Holes 18 L 6079 yds SSS 69
Recs Am–64 A Imlah (1992)
V'tors U–booking recommended
Fees £18 D–£25 (£22 D–£30)
Loc 25 miles E of Edinburgh, off A198
Mis Golf shop (01620) 894596
Arch Mackenzie Ross

Gullane (1882)
Gullane EH31 2BB
Tel (01620) 843115 (Starter)
Fax (01620) 842327
Mem 870 300(L) 60(J)
Sec SC Owram (01620) 842255
Pro J Hume (01620) 843111
Holes No 1 18 L 6466 yds SSS 72
No 2 18 L 6244 yds SSS 70
No 3 18 L 5252 yds SSS 66
6 hole children's course
Recs No 1 Am–65 ME Lewis
Pro–65 J Hobday (1992)
No 2 Am–64 RCH Robertson
Pro–66 H Bannerman
V'tors No 1–H Nos 2/3–U
Fees No 1: £56 D–£84 (£70)
No 2: £25 D–£38 (£31)
No 3: £15 D–£23 (£20)
Children's course free
Loc 18 miles E of Edinburgh on A198
Mis Advance booking advisable

Haddington (1865)
Amisfield Park, Haddington EH41 4PT
Tel (01620) 823627
Fax (01620) 826580
Mem 650
Sec S Wilson
Pro J Sandilands (01620) 822727
Holes 18 L 6317 yds SSS 70
Recs Am–68 G Blair
V'tors WD–U WE–U 10am–12 & 2–4pm
Fees £18 (£23)
Loc 17 miles E of Edinburgh on A1. ¾ mile E of Haddington

The Honourable Company of Edinburgh Golfers (1744)
Muirfield, Gullane EH31 2EG
Tel (01620) 842123
Fax (01620) 842977
Email hceg@btinternet.com
Mem 625
Sec Gp Capt JA Prideaux
Holes 18 L 6601 yds SSS 73 (Championship L 6963 yds)
Recs Am–68 P Lyons (1995)
Pro–63 R Davis (1987)
V'tors WD–Tues & Thurs I H WE/BH–NA SOC
Fees £70 D–£95
Loc NE outskirts of Gullane, opposite sign for Greywalls Hotel on A198

Kilspindie (1867)
Aberlady, Longniddry EH32 0QD
Tel (01875) 870358
Fax (01875) 870358
Mem 460 150(L) 60(J)
Sec RM McInnes
Pro GJ Sked (01875) 870695
Holes 18 L 4957 m SSS 66
Recs Am–62 RJ Humble (1990)
Pro–59 E McIntosh (1996)
V'tors Phone Sec in advance WD–U after 9.15am WE–U after 11am SOC
Fees On application
Loc Aberlady

Longniddry (1921)
Links Road, Longniddry EH32 0NL
Tel (01875) 852141
Fax (01875) 853371
Mem 950
Sec N Robertson
Pro WJ Gray (01875) 852228
Holes 18 L 6219 yds SSS 70
Recs Am–63 C Hardin (1987)
Pro–63 P Harrison (1987)
V'tors WD–U H SOC–Mon–Thurs after 9.18am
Fees £30 D–£42 (£40)
Loc 13 miles E of Edinburgh, off A1
Arch HS Colt

For list of abbreviations see page 527

Lothians

Luffness New (1894)
Aberlady EH32 0QA
Tel (01620) 843114
Fax (01620) 842933
Mem 700
Sec Lt Col JG Tedford (01620) 843336
Pro None
Holes 18 L 6122 yds SSS 70
Recs Am–63 R Winchester
Pro–62 C O'Connor
V'tors H or I XL before 10am WE/BH–NA SOC
Fees £35 D–£50
Loc 1 mile W of Gullane (A198)
Arch Tom Morris

Musselburgh (1938)
Monktonhall, Musselburgh EH21 6SA
Tel (0131) 665 2005
Mem 800
Sec E Stoddart, G Finlay (Admin)
Pro F Mann (0131) 665 7055
Holes 18 L 6614 yds SSS 73
Recs Am–65 JM Noon
Pro–67 EC Brown, B Devlin
G Cunningham, A Jacklin
Ladies–69 J Connachan
V'tors U
Fees £18 (£25)
Loc 1 mile S of Musselburgh on B6415
Arch James Braid

Musselburgh Old Course
Public
Silver Ring Clubhouse, Millhill, Musselburgh EH21 7RG
Tel (0131) 665 6981
Mem 150
Holes 9 L 5380 yds SSS 67
Recs Am–67 P Hosie
V'tors WD/BH–U WE–U after 1pm
Fees On application
Loc 7 miles E of Edinburgh on A1

North Berwick (1832)
West Links, Beach Road, North Berwick EH39 4BB
Tel (01620) 892135
Fax (01620) 893274
Mem 324
Sec AG Flood (01620) 895040
Pro D Huish (01620) 893233
Holes 18 L 6420 yds SSS 71
Recs Am–66 G Sherry (1984)
Pro–64 N Job (1994)
V'tors U H
Fees £36 D–£54 (£54 D–£72)
Winter–£15 (£20)
Loc ½ mile W of North Berwick (A198). 24 miles E of Edinburgh

Royal Musselburgh (1774)
Prestongrange House, Prestonpans EH32 9RP
Tel (01875) 810276
Fax (01875) 810276
Mem 800
Sec TH Hardie (Sec/Mgr)
J Hanratty (Golf Sec)
Pro J Henderson (01875) 810139
Holes 18 L 6237 yds SSS 70
Recs Am–64 J Hall (1995)
V'tors U SOC
Fees £20 D–£35 (£35)
Loc 8 miles E of Edinburgh on B1361 North Berwick road
Arch James Braid

Tantallon (1853)
32 Westgate, North Berwick EH39 4AH
Tel (01620) 2114
Mem 300
Sec T Hill
Holes Play over North Berwick West Links

Thorntree (1856)
Prestongrange House, Prestonpans EH32 9RP
Mem 100
Sec J Hanratty
Holes Play over Royal Musselburgh course

Whitekirk (1995)
Whitekirk, North Berwick EH39 5PR
Tel (01620) 870300
Fax (01620) 870330
Email golf@whitekirk.u-net.com
Mem 250
Sec G Tuer
Pro D Brodie (Golf Shop)
Holes 18 L 6526 yds Par 71 SSS 72
V'tors U SOC
Fees £18 (£25)
Loc 3 miles SE of North Berwick (A198)
Mis Practice range
Arch Cameron Sinclair

Winterfield (1935)
Public
St Margarets, North Road, Dunbar EH42 1AU
Tel (01368) 862280
Mem 400
Sec M O'Donnell (01368) 862564
Pro K Phillips (01368) 863562
Holes 18 L 5053 yds SSS 65
Recs Am–61 R Walkinshaw, J Huggan
Pro–65 SWT Murray
V'tors U
Fees On application–phone Pro
Loc W side of Dunbar. 28 miles E of Edinburgh

Midlothian

Baberton (1893)
50 Baberton Avenue, Juniper Green, Edinburgh EH14 5DU
Tel (0131) 453 3361
Mem 800
Sec EW Horberry (0131) 453 4911
Pro K Kelly (0131) 453 3555
Holes 18 L 6123 yds SSS 70
Recs Am–64 RW Bradly (1989), D Beveridge Jr, BJH Tait (1991)
Pro–62 B Barnes
Ladies–67 KS Marshall (1997)
V'tors I SOC–WD
Fees £18.50 D–£28.50
Loc 5 miles SW of Edinburgh (A70)
Arch Willie Park Jr

Braid Hills (1893)
Public
Braid Hills Road, Edinburgh EH10 6JY
Tel (0131) 447 6666 (Starter)
Holes No 1 18 L 5731 yds SSS 68;
No 2 18 L 4832 yds SSS 63
Recs Am–65
V'tors U–phone starter. No 2 course closed Sun
Fees £8.80–£9.65
Loc 3 miles S of Edinburgh (A702)
Mis No 2 course open Apr–Oct

Braids United (1897)
22 Braid Hills Approach, Edinburgh EH10 6JY
Tel (0131) 452 9408
Mem 100
Sec G Hind
Holes Play over Braids 1 and 2

Broomieknowe (1906)
36 Golf Course Road, Bonnyrigg EH19 2HZ
Tel (0131) 663 9317
Fax (0131) 663 2152
Mem 500
Sec JG White
Pro M Patchett (0131) 660 2035
Holes 18 L 6200 yds Par 70
Recs Am–64 SJ Knowles (1994)
V'tors WD–U WE/BH–NA
Fees £17 D–£25 (£20)
Loc 7 miles SE of Edinburgh
Arch Braid/Hawtree

Bruntsfield Links Golfing Society (1761)
The Clubhouse, 32 Barnton Avenue, Edinburgh EH4 6JH
Tel (0131) 336 2006
Fax (0131) 336 5538
Mem 1130
Sec Cdr DM Sandford (0131) 336 1479
Pro B Mackenzie (0131) 336 4050
Holes 18 L 6407 yds SSS 71
Recs Am–67 AW Ritchie (1991)
V'tors SOC–apply to Sec–H
Fees £36 D–£50 (£42 D–£55)
Loc 3 miles NW of Edinburgh, off A90 at Davidson Mains
Arch Willie Park/Dr A Mackenzie/Hawtree

For list of abbreviations see page 527

Carrick Knowe (1930)
Public
Glendevon Park, Edinburgh EH12 5VZ
Tel (0131) 337 1096 (Starter)
Holes 18 L 6299 yds SSS 70
Recs Am–64 R Bradley
V'tors U–phone starter
Fees £8.80–£9.65
Loc 5 miles W of Edinburgh

Craigentinny (1891)
Public
Craigentinny Avenue, Edinburgh EH7
Tel (0131) 554 7501 (Starter)
Holes 18 L 5418 yds SSS 66
Recs Am–64
V'tors U–starter
Fees £8.80–£9.65
Loc 2½ miles NE of Edinburgh

Craigmillar Park (1895)
1 Observatory Road, Edinburgh EH9 3HG
Tel (0131) 667 2837
Mem 425 100(L) 70(J)
Sec T Lawson (0131) 667 0047
Pro B McGhee (0131) 667 2850
Holes 18 L 5859 yds SSS 69
Recs Am–63 D Clark (1998)
Ladies–66 M Pollock (1993)
V'tors WD–I or H before 3.30pm WE/BH–NA
Fees On application
Loc Blackford, S of Edinburgh
Arch James Braid

Duddingston (1895)
Duddingston Road West, Edinburgh EH15 3QD
Tel (0131) 661 1005
Fax (0131) 661 4301
Mem 580
Sec MGG Corsar (0131) 661 7688
Pro A McLean (0131) 661 4301
Holes 18 L 6438 yds SSS 71
Recs Am–64 G Macgregor Pro–65 S Torrance, C Maltman
V'tors WD–U SOC–Tues & Thurs
Fees £28 Soc–£25
Loc SE Edinburgh

Glencorse (1890)
Milton Bridge, Penicuik EH26 0RD
Tel (01968) 677177
Fax (01968) 674399
Mem 700
Sec W Oliver (01968) 677189
Pro C Jones (01968) 676481
Holes 18 L 5217 yds Par 64 SSS 66
Recs Am–60 N Shillinglaw (1996) Pro–60 C Brooks (1994)
V'tors WD–U SOC–Mon–Thurs/Sun pm
Fees £18.50 (£24.50)
Loc 8 miles S of Edinburgh (A701)

Kings Acre (1997)
Lasswade EH18 1AU
Tel (0131) 663 3456
Sec Lizzie King
Pro A Murdoch
Holes 18 L 5935 yds Par 70
V'tors U SOC
Fees £15 (£21)
Loc 3 miles S of Edinburgh, off A720
Arch Graeme Webster

Kingsknowe (1908)
326 Lanark Road, Edinburgh EH14 2JD
Tel (0131) 441 1144
Fax (0131) 441 2079
Mem 819
Sec R Wallace (0131) 441 1145
Pro A Marshall (0131) 441 4030
Holes 18 L 5966 yds SSS 69
Recs Am–63 JJ Little Pro–64 WB Murray
V'tors WD–U before 4pm WE–phone Pro SOC–WD before 4pm
Fees On application
Loc SW Edinburgh

Liberton (1920)
297 Gilmerton Road, Edinburgh EH16 5UJ
Tel (0131) 664 3009
Fax (0131) 666 0853
Mem 797
Sec Bernadette Giefer
Pro I Seath (0131) 664 1056
Holes 18 L 5299 yds SSS 66
Recs Am–61 RMF Jack, D Rennie Pro–63 JL Brash
V'tors WD–NA after 5pm WE–NA SOC–WD
Fees £17
Loc 3 miles S of Edinburgh

Lothianburn (1893)
106a Biggar Road, Edinburgh EH10 7DU
Tel (0131) 445 2206
Mem 600 75(L) 100(J)
Sec WFA Jardine (0131) 445 5067
Pro K Mungall (0131) 445 2288
Holes 18 L 5568 yds SSS 68
Recs Am–66 IJ Whigham (1997)
V'tors WD–U before 4.30pm –M after 4.30pm WE–NA SOC–H
Fees £16 D–£22 (£22 D–£27)
Loc S of Edinburgh, on A702. Lothianburn exit from Edinburgh by-pass
Arch James Braid (1928)

Marriott Dalmahoy Hotel & CC
Dalmahoy, Kirknewton EH27 8EB
Tel (0131) 333 4105/1845
Fax (0131) 335 3203
Sec B Anderson (Dir), Mrs JM Bryans (Sec)
Pro N Graham
Holes East 18 L 6677 yds SSS 72; West 18 L 5185 yds SSS 66
Recs East Am–65 M Backhausen, F Jacobsen Pro–62 B Barnes West Am–61 N Shillinglaw Pro–60 S Callan
V'tors WD–U H SOC–WD
Fees East: £55 (£75) West: £35 (£45)
Loc 7 miles W of Edinburgh on A71
Mis Floodlit driving range
Arch James Braid

Melville Golf Centre (1995)
Pay and play
South Melville, Lasswade EH18 1AN
Tel (0131) 654 0224 (Course)
Fax (0131) 654 0814
Mem 55
Sec Mr & Mrs MacFarlane (Props)
Pro G Carter (0131) 663 8038
Holes 9 L 4530 yds Par 66 SSS 62
V'tors U SOC
Fees £7–£12 (£9–£16)
Loc 7 miles S of Edinburgh on A7
Mis Floodlit driving range
Arch G Webster

Merchants of Edinburgh (1907)
10 Craighill Gardens, Morningside, Edinburgh EH10 5PY
Tel (0131) 447 1219
Mem 730
Sec IL Crichton
Pro NEM Colquhoun (0131) 447 8709
Holes 18 L 4889 yds SSS 64
Recs Am–59 AK Helm (1995) Ladies–66 LM Caine (1991)
V'tors WD–U before 4pm –M after 4pm WE–M SOC–WD
Fees £15
Loc SW of Edinburgh, off A701

Mortonhall (1892)
231 Braid Road, Edinburgh EH10 6PB
Tel (0131) 447 2411
Fax (0131) 447 8712
Mem 500
Sec Mrs CD Morrison (0131) 447 6974
Pro DB Horn (0131) 447 5185
Holes 18 L 6557 yds SSS 72
Recs Am–66 C Cassells Pro–68 G Cunningham
V'tors H SOC
Fees £30 (£30)
Loc 2 miles S of Edinburgh on A702
Arch James Braid/FW Hawtree

Murrayfield (1896)
43 Murrayfield Road, Edinburgh EH12 6EU
Tel (0131) 337 1009
Fax (0131) 313 0721
Mem 775

For list of abbreviations see page 527

Sec Mrs MK Hermiston (0131) 337 3478
Pro J Fisher (0131) 337 3479
Holes 18 L 5727 yds SSS 69
Recs Am–63 D Patrick
Pro–63 WB Murray
V'tors WD–I WE–M
Fees £25 D–£30
Loc 2 miles W of Edinburgh centre

Newbattle (1896)
Abbey Road, Eskbank, Dalkeith EH22 3AD
Tel (0131) 663 2123
Fax (0131) 654 1810
Mem 600
Sec HG Stanners (0131) 663 1819
Pro D Torrance (0131) 660 1631
Holes 18 L 6012 yds SSS 70
Recs Am–63 S Thorburn
Pro–61 A Oldcorn
V'tors WD–U before 4pm WE–M
Fees £17 D–£26
Loc 6 miles S of Edinburgh on A7 and A68
Arch HS Colt

Portobello (1853)
Public
Stanley Street, Portobello, Edinburgh EH15 1JJ
Tel (0131) 669 4361 (Starter)
Mem 60
Holes 9 L 2419 yds SSS 64
Recs Am–27
V'tors U–phone starter
Fees £4.50–£4.85
Loc 4 miles E of Edinburgh on A1

Prestonfield (1920)
6 Priestfield Road North, Edinburgh EH16 5HS
Tel (0131) 667 9665
Mem 800
Sec AS Robertson
Pro G MacDonald (0131) 667 8597
Holes 18 L 6212 yds SSS 70
Recs Am–66 AM Dun, MD Tummins (1997)
V'tors Sat–NA 8–10.30am and 12–1.30pm Sun–NA before 11.30am SOC
Fees £20 D–£30 (£30 D–£40)
Loc 2 miles SE of Edinburgh, off A68 Dalkeith road

Ratho Park (1928)
Ratho, Newbridge, Midlothian EH28 8NX
Tel (0131) 333 2566/1752
Fax (0131) 333 1752
Mem 550 98(L) 65(J)
Sec JS Yates (0131) 333 1752
Pro A Pate (0131) 333 1406
Holes 18 L 5900 yds SSS 68
Recs Am–61 DM Summers (1991)
Pro–64 WG Stowe
V'tors U SOC–Tues–Thurs
Fees £25 D–£35 (£35)
Loc 8 miles W of Edinburgh (A71)

Ravelston (1912)
24 Ravelston Dykes Road, Edinburgh EH4 5NZ
Tel (0131) 315 2486
Mem 610
Sec S Houston
Holes 9 L 5332 yds SSS 65
Recs Am–64 JW Fraser (1994)
Pro–67 W Murray (1987)
V'tors WD–H
Fees £15
Loc Off Queensferry Road (A90). Turn S at Blackhall
Arch James Braid

Royal Burgess Golfing Society of Edinburgh (1735)
181 Whitehouse Road, Barnton, Edinburgh EH4 6BY
Tel (0131) 339 2075
Fax (0131) 339 3712
Mem 620 50(J)
Sec JP Audis (0131) 339 2075
Pro G Yuille (0131) 339 6474
Holes 18 L 6494 yds SSS 71
Recs Am–66 J Yuille (1992)
Pro–63
V'tors I SOC
Fees On application
Loc Queensferry Road (A90)
Arch Tom Morris

Silverknowes (1947)
Public
Silverknowes, Parkway, Edinburgh EH4 5ET
Tel (0131) 336 3843 (Starter)
Mem 511
Sec DW Scobie
Holes 18 L 6202 yds SSS 70
Recs Am–65 K Reilly (1995)
V'tors U–phone starter
Fees £8.50–£9.65
Loc 4 miles N of Edinburgh

Swanston (1927)
111 Swanston Road, Fairmilehead, Edinburgh EH10 7DS
Tel (0131) 445 2239
Mem 500
Sec J Allan
Pro I Taylor (0131) 445 4002
Holes 18 L 5004 yds SSS 65
Recs Am–63 G Millar
V'tors U exc comp days–NA WE–NA after 1pm
Fees £15 D–£20 (£20 D–£25)
Loc S of Edinburgh, off Biggar road (A702)

Torphin Hill (1895)
Torphin Road, Edinburgh EH13 0PG
Tel (0131) 441 1100
Mem 450
Sec AJ Hepburn
Pro J Browne
Holes 18 L 5025 yds SSS 66
Recs Am–63 M Steven

V'tors WD–U WE–U exc comp days SOC
Fees D–£12 (D–£20)
Loc SW boundary of Edinburgh

Turnhouse (1897)
154 Turnhouse Road, Corstorphine, Edinburgh EH12 0AD
Tel (0131) 339 1014
Mem 500
Sec AB Hay (0131) 539 5937
Pro J Murray (0131) 339 7701
Holes 18 L 6171 yds SSS 70
Recs Am–62 K Weir (1998)
Pro–64 D Huish
V'tors M or by arrangement
Fees On application
Loc W of Edinburgh (A9080)

Vogrie (1990)
Pay and play
Vogrie Estate Country Park, Gorebridge EH23 4NU
Tel (01875) 821716
Holes 9 hole course Par 66
V'tors U
Fees £5.70
Loc SE of Edinburgh, off A68 (B6372)

West Lothian

Bathgate (1892)
Edinburgh Road, Bathgate EH48 1BA
Tel (01506) 652232
Fax (01506) 636775
Mem 580
Sec WA Osborne (01506) 630505
Pro S Strachan (01506) 630553
Holes 18 L 6326 yds SSS 70
Recs Am–64 J McLean
Pro–58 S Torrance (1992)
V'tors U
Fees £16 (£32)
Loc 15 miles W of Edinburgh. M8 Junction 4
Arch Wm Park Sr

Deer Park CC (1978)
Knightsridge, Livingston EH54 9PG
Tel (01506) 38843
Fax (01506) 35608
Mem 500
Sec I Thomson
Pro W Yule
Holes 18 L 6636 yds SSS 72
Recs Am–67 D Thomson (1994)
Pro–66
V'tors U SOC
Fees £16 D–£22 (£26 D–£32)
Loc N of Livingston. M8 Junction 3

Dundas Parks (1957)
South Queensferry EH30 9SS
Mem 550
Sec Mrs J Pennie (Hon) (0131) 331 3179
Holes 9 L 5510 m SSS 69

For list of abbreviations see page 527

Recs Am–65 G Lawton
V'tors M I SOC
Fees D–£10
Loc Dundas Estate (Private).
1 mile S of Queensferry
(A8000)

Greenburn (1953)
6 Greenburn Road, Fauldhouse EH47 9HG
Tel (01501) 770292
Mem 500
Sec A Stein (01501) 741967
Pro M Leighton (01501) 771187
Holes 18 L 6210 yds SSS 71
Recs Am–65 B Watson
V'tors U
Fees On application
Loc 4 miles S of M8 Junction 4 (East)/Junction 5 (West)

Harburn (1921)
West Calder EH55 8RS
Tel (01506) 871256
Fax (01506) 871131
Mem 470 80(L) 100(J)
Sec J McLinden (01506) 871131
Pro S Mills (01506) 871582
Holes 18 L 5921 yds SSS 69
Recs Am–62 M Kirk
Pro–64 A Alcorn
V'tors U
Fees £16 (£21)
Loc 2 miles S of W Calder on B7008, via A70 or A71

Linlithgow (1913)
Braehead, Linlithgow EH49 6QF
Tel (01506) 842585
Fax (01506) 842764
Mem 430
Sec D Roy
Pro S Rosie (01506) 844356
Holes 18 L 5729 yds SSS 68
Recs Am–64 J Cuddihy (1975)
Pro–65 J White (1988)
V'tors U exc Sat–NA SOC
Fees £17 D–£25 Sun–£25 D–£30
Loc SW of Linlithgow, off M9
Arch Robert Simpson

Niddry Castle (1983)
Castle Road, Winchburgh EH52 2RQ
Tel (01506) 891097
Mem 500
Sec J Thomson
Holes 9 L 5476 yds SSS 67
Recs Am–65 J Hastie (1997)
V'tors U
Fees £12 (£17)
Loc 10 miles W of Edinburgh (B9080)

Polkemmet (1981)
Public
Whitburn, Bathgate EH47 0AD
Tel (01501) 743905
Holes 9 L 2967 m SSS 37
V'tors U

Fees £4.50 (£5.25)
Loc Between Whitburn and Harthill on B7066. M8 Junctions 4/5
Mis Driving range

Pumpherston (1895)
Drumshoreland Road, Pumpherston EH53 0LF
Tel (01506) 432869
Mem 378 10(L) 54(J)
Sec I McArthur (01506) 854584
Holes 9 L 5382 yds SSS 66
Recs Am–64 P Drake (1996)
V'tors M SOC–WD
Loc 14 miles W of Edinburgh. M8 Junction 3

Uphall (1895)
Houston Mains, Uphall EH52 6JT
Tel (01506) 856404
Fax (01506) 855358
Mem 500
Sec WA Crighton
Pro G Law (01506) 855553
Holes 18 L 5588 yds Par 69 SSS 67
Recs Am–62 L Rhind (1997)
Pro–64 CJ Brooks, A Oldcorn (1992)
V'tors U
Fees £14 D–£19 (£18 D–£26)
Loc 7 miles W of Edinburgh Airport (A8). M8 Junction 3

West Linton (1890)
West Linton EH46 7HN
Tel (01968) 660463
Mem 700
Sec G Scott (01968) 660970
Pro I Wright (01968) 660256
Holes 18 L 6132 yds SSS 70
Recs Am–63 S Walker (1992)
Pro–71 B Gallacher
V'tors WD–U WE–NA before 1pm
Fees £20 D–£30 (£30) W–£75
Loc NW of Peebles on A702. 18 miles S of Edinburgh

West Lothian (1892)
Airngath Hill, Linlithgow EH49 7RH
Tel (01506) 826030
Fax (01506) 826030
Mem 850
Sec MJ Todd
Pro N Robertson (01506) 825060
Holes 18 L 6406 yds SSS 71
Recs Am–64 AG O'Neill (1990)
Pro–68 J Farmer (1980)
V'tors WD–NA after 4pm WE–by arrangement
Fees On application
Loc 1 mile N of Linlithgow, towards Bo'ness
Arch W Park Jr/Adams/Middleton

Moray

Buckpool (1933)
Barhill Road, Buckie AB56 1DU
Tel (01542) 832236
Fax (01542) 832236
Mem 500
Sec Mrs E Cowie
Holes 18 L 6257 yds SSS 70
Recs Am–65 K Buchan (1991)
Pro–64 L Vannet (1989)
Ladies–65 L Smith (1998)
V'tors U
Fees £12 D–£15 (£15 D–£20)
Loc W end of Buckpool, ½ mile off A98

Dufftown (1896)
Tomintoul Road, Dufftown AB55 4BS
Tel (01340) 820325
Fax (01340) 820325
Mem 310
Sec DM Smith
Pro None
Holes 18 L 5308 yds SSS 67
Recs Am–65 G Mercer, S Hanson, J Hanson (1996)
Pro–68 A Aird (1990)
V'tors U
Fees £10 D–£15
Loc 1 mile SW of Dufftown on Tomintoul road

Elgin (1906)
Hardhillock, Birnie Road, Elgin IV30 8SX
Tel (01343) 542338
Fax (01343) 542341
Mem 854 113(L) 150(J)
Sec DF Black
Pro I Rodger (01343) 542884
Holes 18 L 6411 yds SSS 71
Recs Am–64 NS Grant (1972)
Pro–63 K Stables (1996)
V'tors WD–U after 9.30am WE–U after 10am SOC–WD SOC–WE by arrangement
Fees £22 D–£28 (£28 D–£35)
Loc 1 mile S of Elgin on A941
Mis Driving range
Arch John MacPherson

Forres (1889)
Muiryshade, Forres IV36 0RD
Tel (01309) 672949
Mem 716 130(J)
Sec Margaret Greenaway
Pro S Aird (01309) 672250
Holes 18 L 6141 yds SSS 70
Recs Am–64 S Aird Jr
V'tors U SOC
Fees £14 (£20)
Loc 1 mile SE of Forres, off B9010

Garmouth & Kingston (1932)
Garmouth, Fochabers IV32 7NJ
Tel (01343) 870388
Fax (01343) 870388
Mem 400

For list of abbreviations see page 527

Moray

Sec A Robertson (01343) 870231
Holes 18 L 5874 yds SSS 68
Recs Am–67 C Stuart (1998)
V'tors U SOC
Fees £14 D–£16 (£16 D–£20)
Loc 8 miles NE of Elgin

Hopeman (1923)
Hopeman, Moray IV30 5YA
Tel (01343) 830578
Fax (01343) 830152
Mem 700
Sec R Johnston
Holes 18 L 5564 yds SSS 67
Recs Am–65 IS Geddes (1998)
V'tors WD–U Sat–NA before 10.30am and 12.30–2pm Sun–NA before 9.30am SOC
Fees £15 (£20)
Loc 7 miles NW of Elgin on B9012
Arch J McKenzie

Moray (1889)
Stotfield Road, Lossiemouth IV31 6QS
Tel (01343) 812018
Fax (01343) 815102
Mem 1500
Sec B Russell
Pro A Thomson (01343) 813330
Holes Old 18 L 6643 yds SSS 73
New 18 L 6005 yds SSS 69
V'tors U H SOC
Fees On application
Loc 6 miles N of Elgin

Perth & Kinross

Aberfeldy (1895)
Taybridge Road, Aberfeldy PH15 2BH
Tel (01887) 820535
Mem 260
Sec C Henderson (01887) 829509
Holes 18 L 5600 yds Par 68 SSS 66
Recs Am–65 (1997)
V'tors U
Fees £14 D–£22 W–£55
Loc 10 miles W of Ballinluig, off A9
Arch Souters

Alyth (1894)
Pitcrocknie, Alyth PH11 8HF
Tel (01828) 632268
Fax (01828) 633491
Mem 850
Sec J Docherty
Pro T Melville (01828) 632311
Holes 18 L 6205 yds SSS 70
Recs Am–65 J Cochrane Jr
Pro–64 I Young
V'tors U SOC
Fees On application
Loc 16 miles NW of Dundee (A91)
Arch Tom Morris/James Braid

Auchterarder (1892)
Ochil Road, Auchterarder PH3 1LS
Tel (01764) 662804
Fax (01764) 662804
Mem 765
Sec WM Campbell (01764) 664669
Pro G Baxter (01764) 663711
Holes 18 L 5757 yds SSS 68
Recs Am–62 M O'Brien (1997)
V'tors U SOC
Fees £18 D–£26 Sat–£24 D–£36 Sun–£36
Loc 1 mile SW of Auchterarder

Bishopshire (1903)
Pay and play
Kinnesswood, Kinross KY13
Mem 200
Sec J Proudfoot (01592) 780203
Holes 10 L 4700 m SSS 64
Recs Am–63 J Morris
V'tors U
Fees £5 (£6)
Loc 3 miles E of Kinross (A911). M90 Junction 7
Arch W Park

Blair Atholl (1896)
Invertilt Road, Blair Atholl PH18 5TG
Tel (01796) 481407
Mem 430
Sec P Turner
Holes 9 L 2855 yds SSS 68
Recs Am–65
V'tors U
Fees £14 (£17)
Loc 35 miles N of Perth, off A9

Blairgowrie (1889)
Rosemount, Blairgowrie PH10 6LG
Tel (01250) 872594
Fax (01250) 875451
Mem 1200
Sec JN Simpson (Managing Sec) (01250) 872622
Pro C Dernie (01250) 873116
Holes Rosemount 18 L 6588 yds SSS 72; Landsdowne 18 L 6895 yds SSS 73; Wee 9 L 4614 yds SSS 63
Recs Rosemount Am–64 E Giraud, W Taylor; Pro–66 G Norman Lansdowne Am–67 C Mitchell Pro–69 J McAlister
V'tors Mon/Tues/Thurs–U H 8am–12 & 2–3.30pm Wed/Fri/WE–restricted
Fees On application
Loc 1 mile S of Blairgowrie, off A93. 15 miles N of Perth
Arch Rosemount-Braid; Lansdowne-Alliss/Thomas; Wee-Old Tom Morris

Callander (1890)
Aveland Road, Callander FK17 8EN
Tel (01877) 330090
Fax (01877) 330062
Mem 700
Sec DR Allan (Mgr)
Pro W Kelly (01877) 330975

Holes 18 L 5125 yds SSS 66
Recs Am–61 B Collier
Pro–59 D Matthew
V'tors U SOC
Fees On application
Loc Off A84, E end of Callander
Arch Tom Morris

Comrie (1891)
Laggan Braes, Comrie PH6 2LR
Tel (01764) 70055
Mem 330
Sec GC Betty (01764) 670941
Holes 9 L 2983 yds SSS 70
Recs Am–65 A Philp
V'tors U
Fees £10 (£10)
Loc 7 miles W of Crieff (A85)

Craigie Hill (1909)
Cherrybank, Perth PH2 0NE
Tel (01738) 624377
Fax (01738) 620829
Mem 625
Sec DR Allan (01738) 620829
Pro S Harrier (01738) 622644
Holes 18 L 5386 yds SSS 67
Recs Am–60 G Still (1988)
Pro–63 W Murray (1986)
V'tors U exc Sat
Fees £15 (£25)
Loc W boundary of Perth
Arch Fernie/Anderson

Crieff (1891)
Perth Road, Crieff PH7 3LR
Tel (01764) 652909 (Bookings)
Fax (01764) 655096
Mem 670
Sec JS Miller (01764) 652397
Pro DJW Murchie
Holes Ferntower 18 L 6402 yds SSS 71; Dornock 9 L 4772 yds SSS 63
Recs Ferntower Am–66
Pro–66
V'tors U H NA–12–2pm or after 5pm SOC
Fees Ferntower: £21 (£28) Dornock: £12 (£15)
Loc 1 mile NE of Crieff (A85). 17 miles W of Perth

Dalmunzie (1948)
Glenshee, Blairgowrie PH10 7QG
Tel (01250) 885226
Fax (01250) 885225
Mem 52
Sec S Winton (Mgr)
Holes 9 L 2035 yds SSS 60
Recs Am–63 PD Winton
V'tors U
Fees £7 D–£10
Loc 22 miles N of Blairgowrie on A93. (Dalmunzie Hotel sign)

Dunkeld & Birnam (1892)
Fungarth, Dunkeld PH8 0HU
Tel (01350) 727524
Fax (01350) 728660
Mem 432

Perth & Kinross

Sec Mrs W Sinclair (01350) 727564
Pro None
Holes 9 L 5240 yds SSS 66
Recs Am–65 S McKendrick (1996)
V'tors WD–U WE–phone first
Fees On application
Loc Dunkeld 1 mile, off A923. 15 miles N of Perth

Dunning (1953)
Rollo Park, Dunning PH2 0QX
Tel (01764) 684747
Mem 580
Sec Mrs M Ramsay (01764) 684237
Holes L 4777 yds Par 66 SSS 63
V'tors U
Fees £12 (£14)
Loc 9 miles SW of Perth, off A9

Glenalmond
Trinity College, Glenalmond
Sec The Bursar (01738) 880275
Holes 9 L 5812 yds SSS 67
Recs Am–70 CMW Robertson Pro–72 M Dennis
V'tors U
Loc 10 miles NW of Perth
Arch James Braid

The Gleneagles Hotel
Auchterarder PH3 1NF
Tel (01764) 663543 (Golf), (01764) 662231 (Hotel)
Pro G Schofield
Holes King's 18 L 6471 yds SSS 71
Queen's 18 L 5965 yds SSS 69
Monarch 18 L 7081 SSS 74
9 hole Par 3 course
V'tors Residents & Members only
Fees NA
Loc 16 miles SW of Perth on A9
Mis Driving range. Golf Academy

Green Hotel (1900)
2 The Muirs, Kinross KY13 7AS
Tel (01577) 863407
Fax (01577) 863180
Mem 450
Sec Mrs M Smith
Holes Red 18 L 6257 yds SSS 70
Blue 18 L 6456 yds SSS 71
V'tors U
Fees £15 D–£25 (£25 D–£35)
Loc 17 miles S of Perth. M90 Junction 6/7

Kenmore (1992)
Pay and play
Mains of Taymouth, Kenmore, Aberfeldy PH15 2HN
Tel (01887) 830226
Fax (01887) 830211
Mem 120
Sec R Menzies (Mgr)
Pro None
Holes 9 L 6052 yds SSS 69
Recs Am–68 S Sutherland (1997)
V'tors U SOC

Fees 9 holes–£8 (£9) 18 holes–£11 (£12)
Loc 6 miles W of Aberfeldy on A827
Arch D Menzies & Partners

Killin (1913)
Killin FK21 8TX
Tel (01567) 820312
Mem 298
Sec J Greaves
Holes 9 L 5016 yds Par 66 SSS 65
Recs Am–61 G Smith
V'tors U SOC–Apr–Oct
Fees £12 (£12)
Loc Killin, W end of Loch Tay
Arch John Duncan

King James VI (1858)
Moncreiffe Island, Perth PH2 8NR
Tel (01738) 625170, (01738) 632460 (Starter)
Fax (01738) 445132
Mem 675
Sec Mrs H Blair (01738) 445132
Pro A Coles (01738) 632460
Holes 18 L 5664 yds SSS 69
Recs Am–63 G Clark (1976) Pro–62 W Guy (1991)
V'tors U exc Sat Sun–by reservation
Fees £18 D–£25 Sun D–£30
Loc Island in River Tay, Perth
Arch Tom Morris

Milnathort (1910)
South Street, Milnathort, Kinross KY13 7XA
Tel (01577) 864069
Mem 400
Holes 9 L 5985 yds SSS 68
Recs Am–65 D Reid (1992)
V'tors U SOC
Fees D–£10 (£15)
Loc 1 mile N of Kinross. M90 Junction 6/7

Muckhart (1908)
Muckhart, Dollar FK14 7JH
Tel (01259) 781423
Mem 550 125(L) 100(J)
Sec AB Robertson
Pro K Salmoni
Holes 18 L 6034 yds SSS 70
9 hole course
Recs Am–66 E Carnegie (1983)
V'tors U SOC
Fees 18 hole:£15 D–£22 (£22 D–£30) 9 hole:£10
Loc A91, 3 miles E of Dollar, towards Rumbling Bridge

Murrayshall (1981)
Murrayshall, New Scone, Perth PH2 7PH
Tel (01738) 551171
Fax (01738) 552595
Mem 300
Sec A Bryan (Mgr)
Pro AT Reid (01738) 552784
Holes 18 L 5877 m SSS 72

Recs Am–67 G Redford Pro–67 J Farmer
V'tors U SOC–WD/WE
Fees £22 D–£30 (£27 D–£45)
Loc 3 miles NE of Perth, off A94
Mis Driving range. Indoor Golf Centre
Arch Hamilton Stutt

Muthill (1935)
Peat Road, Muthill PH5 2AD
Tel (01764) 681523
Mem 450
Sec J Elder
Holes 9 L 2371 yds SSS 63
Recs Am–61 C MacGregor (1991) Pro–68 RM Jamieson, W Milne (1985)
V'tors U SOC
Fees £13 (£16)
Loc 3 miles S of Crieff on A822

North Inch
Public
c/o Perth & Kinross Council, 5 High Street, Perth PH1 5JS
Tel (01738) 636481 (Starter)
Sec G Harbut (01738) 475215
Holes 18 L 4340 m SSS 65
V'tors U SOC
Fees On application
Loc Nr Perth and A9, by River Tay. Signs to Bell's Sports Centre

Pitlochry (1909)
Golf Course Road, Pitlochry PH16 5QY
Tel (01796) 472792 (Bookings)
Fax (01796) 473599
Mem 498
Sec DCM McKenzie JP (01796) 472114
Pro G Hampton
Holes 18 L 5811 yds SSS 69
Recs Am–63 CP Christy, MM Niven Pro–64
V'tors U SOC
Fees D–£20 (D–£25) (1996)
Loc N side of Pitlochry (A9). 28 miles NW of Perth
Arch Fernie/Hutchison

Royal Perth Golfing Society (1833)
1/2 Atholl Crescent, Perth PH1 5NG
Tel (01738) 622265
Fax (01738) 441131
Mem 250
Sec RPJ Blake (Gen Sec) (01738) 440088, AH Anderson (Golf Sec) (01738) 637311
Holes Play over North Inch course

St Fillans (1903)
South Lochearn Rd, St Fillans PH26 2NJ
Tel (01764) 685312
Mem 400
Sec J Stanyon (01764) 685300

For list of abbreviations see page 527

718 Perth & Kinross

Holes 9 L 5796 yds SSS 67
V'tors U SOC
Fees On application
Loc 12 miles W of Crieff, on A85
Arch W Auchterlonie

Strathmore Golf Centre (1995)
Pay and play
Leroch, Alyth, Blairgowrie
PH11 8NZ
Tel (01828) 633322
Fax (01828) 633533
Mem 300
Sec P Barron (Man Dir)
Pro None
Holes 18 L 6454 yds Par 72 SSS 72
9 L 1666 yds Par 29 SSS 58
Recs Am–68 K Grant (1997)
V'tors U SOC
Fees 18 hole:£18 (£23) 9 hole:£8
Loc 5 miles E of Blairgowrie, off A926
Mis Floodlit driving range
Arch John Salvesen

Strathtay (1909)
Lyon Cottage, Strathtay, Pitlochry
PH9 0PG
Tel (01887) 840211
Mem 237
Sec IA Ramsay
Holes 9 L 4082 yds SSS 63
Recs Am–61 AM Deboys
V'tors U exc Thurs–NA after 5pm
Sat–NA 10–10.30am Sun–NA
1–4pm SOC
Fees D–£10
Loc 4 miles W of Ballinluig (A827), towards Aberfeldy

Taymouth Castle (1923)
Kenmore, Aberfeldy PH15 2NT
Tel (01887) 830228
Fax (01887) 830765
Mem 200
Sec AA MacTaggart (Golf Dir)
Pro A Marshall
Holes 18 L 6066 yds SSS 69
Recs Am–63 MM Niven
Pro–A Learmonth (1962)
V'tors U WE–booking essential SOC
Fees £16 D–£26 (£20 D–£36)
Loc 6 miles W of Aberfeldy (A827)
Arch James Braid

Whitemoss (1994)
Whitemoss Road, Dunning, Perth
PH2 0QX
Tel (01738) 730300
Mem 300
Sec V Westwood
Pro None
Holes 18 L 6200 yds Par 69 SSS 69
V'tors U SOC
Fees £15 (£15)
Loc Aberuthven, 10 miles SW of Perth, off A9

Renfrewshire

Barshaw (1920)
Public
Barshaw Park, Glasgow Road, Paisley PA2
Tel (0141) 889 2908
Fax (0141) 840 2148
Mem 103
Sec W Collins (0141) 884 2533
Holes 18 L 5703 yds SSS 67
V'tors U
Fees £6.50
Loc 1 mile E of Paisley Cross, off A737

Bonnyton (1957)
Eaglesham, Glasgow G76 0QA
Tel (01355) 302781
Fax (01355) 303151
Mem 950
Sec A Hughes
Pro K McWade (01355) 302256
Holes 18 L 6252 yds SSS 71
Recs Am–64 A Winston
Pro–68 J Wilson
V'tors I SOC–WD
Fees £31.50
Loc 2 miles W of Eaglesham. 6 miles S of Glasgow

Caldwell (1903)
Caldwell, Uplawmoor G78 4AU
Tel (01505) 850329
Fax (01505) 850604
Mem 450
Sec HIF Harper (01505) 850366
Pro S Forbes (01505) 850616
Holes 18 L 6195 yds SSS 70
Recs Am–64 JM Sharp (1974)
Pro–63 C Innes (1987),
G Collinson (1988),
C Gillies (1989)
V'tors WD–booking before 4pm–M after 4pm WE–M
Fees On application
Loc 5 miles SW of Barrhead on A736 Glasgow-Irvine road

Cochrane Castle (1895)
Scott Avenue, Craigston, Johnstone PA5 0HF
Tel (01505) 320146
Fax (01505) 325338
Mem 425
Sec JC Cowan
Pro JJ Boyd (01505) 328465
Holes 18 L 6226 yds Par 71 SSS 71
Recs Am–65 R Davidson
Pro–70 S Kelly
V'tors WD–U WE–M
Fees £17 D–£25
Loc ½ mile S of Beith Road, Johnstone
Arch Charles Hunter

East Renfrewshire (1922)
Loganswell, Pilmuir, Newton Mearns G77 6RT
Tel (013555) 500256
Mem 450

Sec AL Gillespie (0141) 333 9989
Pro GD Clarke (013555) 500206
Holes 18 L 6097 yds SSS 70
Recs Am–63 D Orr (1996)
Pro–64 CR Brooks (1989)
V'tors On application
Fees £30 D–£40
Loc 2 miles SW of Newton Mearns
Arch James Braid

Eastwood (1893)
Muirshield, Loganswell, Newton Mearns, Glasgow G77 6RX
Tel (01355) 500261
Mem 900
Sec VE Jones (01355) 500280
Pro A McGinness (01355) 500285
Holes 18 L 5864 yds SSS 69
Recs Am–61 D Orr (1996)
Pro–66 JC Farmer (1981)
V'tors M SOC
Fees £24 D–£30
Loc 9 miles SW of Glasgow
Arch Theodore Moone

Elderslie (1909)
63 Main Road, Elderslie PA5 9AZ
Tel (01505) 323956
Fax (01505) 340346
Mem 432
Sec Mrs A Anderson
Pro R Bowman (01505) 320032
Holes 18 L 6165 yds SSS 70
Recs Am–62 G Campbell (1996)
Pro–61 D Robertson (1994)
V'tors M SOC–WD
Fees £20 D–£30
Loc 2 miles SW of Paisley

Erskine (1904)
Bishopton PA7 5PH
Tel (01505) 862302
Mem 400 200(L)
Sec TA McKillop
Pro P Thomson (01505) 862108
Holes 18 L 6287 yds SSS 70
Recs Am–66 IG Riddell
Pro–63 G Collinson
V'tors WD–I WE–M
Fees £25
Loc 5 miles NW of Paisley

Fereneze (1904)
Fereneze Avenue, Barrhead G78 1HJ
Tel (0141) 881 1519
Mem 700
Sec A Johnston (0141) 887 4141
Pro (0141) 880 7058
Holes 18 L 5962 yds SSS 70
Recs Am–67 I McMillan (1995)
Pro–65 S McAllister,
A Tait (1995)
V'tors M SOC–WD
Fees D–£20
Loc 9 miles SW of Glasgow

Gleddoch (1974)
Langbank PA14 6YE
Tel (01475) 540304
Fax (01475) 540459
Mem 600

For list of abbreviations see page 527

Sec   DW Tierney
Pro   K Campbell (01475) 540704
Holes 18 L 6375 yds SSS 71
Recs   Am–64 M O'Hare
       Pro–67 J Chillas, C Gillies
V'tors WD–U WE–restricted SOC
Fees   £30
Loc   16 miles W of Glasgow
       (M8/A8)
Arch   J Hamilton Stutt

Gourock (1896)
Cowal View, Gourock PA19 1HD
Tel   (01475) 631001
Fax   (01475) 631001
Mem   538 98(L) 86(J)
Sec   AD Taylor
Pro   G Coyle (01475) 636834
Holes 18 L 6512 yds SSS 73
Recs   Am–64 N Skinner
       Pro–65 A Hunter
V'tors WD–I SOC
Fees   £18 (£22)
Loc   3 miles SW of Greenock (A770)
       7 miles W of Port Glasgow

Greenock (1890)
Forsyth Street, Greenock PA16 8RE
Tel   (01475) 720793
Mem   500 111(L) 110(J)
Sec   EJ Black
Pro   S Russell (01475) 787236
Holes 18 L 5888 yds SSS 68
       9 L 2149 yds SSS 32
Recs   Am–64 MC Mazzoni,
       C McLellan, M Carmichael
       Pro–66 H Thomson, J Panton,
       H Boyle
V'tors WD–U WE/BH–M
Fees   D–£25 (£30)
Loc   1 mile SW of Greenock on A8
Arch   James Braid

Kilmacolm (1891)
Porterfield Road, Kilmacolm PA13 4PD
Tel   (01505) 872139
Fax   (01505) 874007
Mem   776
Sec   DW Tinton
Pro   D Stewart (01505) 872695
Holes 18 L 5960 yds SSS 69
Recs   Am–64 M Stevenson
       Pro–63 R Weir, J White
V'tors WD–U WE–M
Fees   £20
Loc   10 miles W of Paisley (A761)

Lochwinnoch (1897)
Burnfoot Road, Lochwinnoch PA12 4AN
Tel   (01505) 842153
Fax   (01505) 843668
Mem   500
Sec   Mrs A Wilson
Pro   G Reilly (01505) 843029
Holes 18 L 6243 yds SSS 71
Recs   Am–63 M Beattie (1994)
       Pro–63 M Miller (1987)
V'tors WD–U before 4.30pm
       SOC–WD
Fees   £15 D–£20
Loc   9 miles SW of Paisley

Old Ranfurly (1905)
Ranfurly Place, Bridge of Weir
PA11 3DE
Tel   (01505) 613612 (Clubhouse)
Fax   (01505) 613214
Mem   375
Sec   R Mitchell (01505) 613214
Pro   None
Holes 18 L 6089 yds SSS 69
Recs   Am–62 A Hunter (1983)
       Pro–66 C Elliot (1984)
V'tors WD–I WE–M SOC
Fees   On application
Loc   7 miles W of Paisley, off A761

Paisley (1895)
Braehead, Paisley PA2 8TZ
Tel   (0141) 884 2292 (Clubhouse)
Fax   (0141) 884 3903
Mem   805
Sec   M MacPherson
       (0141) 884 3903
Pro   G Stewart (0141) 884 4114
Holes 18 L 6466 yds Par 71 SSS 72
Recs   Am–66 WB Anderson,
       S Young, M Brooke
       Pro–66 S Callan, G Collinson,
       C Gillies
V'tors WD–H SOC
Fees   £20 D–£28 (1998)
Loc   Braehead, S of Paisley
Arch   Stutt

Port Glasgow (1895)
Devol Farm, Port Glasgow PA14 5XE
Tel   (01475) 704181
Mem   375
Sec   NL Mitchell (01475) 706273
Pro   Shop (01475) 705671
Holes 18 L 5712 yds SSS 68
Recs   Am–62 M Carmichael
V'tors WD–U before 5pm –M after
       5pm WE–NA SOC
Fees   £15 D–£20
Loc   1 mile S of Port Glasgow

Ranfurly Castle (1889)
Golf Road, Bridge of Weir PA11 3HN
Tel   (01505) 612609
Fax   (01505) 612609
Mem   360 160(L) 100(J)
Sec   J Walker
Pro   T Eckford (01505) 614795
Holes 18 L 6284 yds SSS 71
Recs   Am–65 WMB Brown
       Pro–65 W Lockie (1989)
V'tors WD–H WE–M SOC–Tues
Fees   £30 D–£40
Loc   7 miles W of Paisley (A761)
Arch   Kirkcaldy/Auchterlonie

Renfrew (1894)
Blythswood Estate, Inchinnan Road,
Renfrew PA4 9EG
Tel   (0141) 886 6692
Fax   (0141) 886 1808
Mem   465 110(L) 80(J)
Sec   I Murchison
Pro   D Grant (0141) 885 1754
Holes 18 L 6818 yds SSS 73

Recs   Am–67 A Coltart (1991)
       Pro–65 J Farmer (1991)
V'tors M SOC
Fees   On application
Loc   3 miles N of Paisley,
       nr airport
Arch   Cdr JD Harris

Whinhill (1911)
Beith Road, Greenock PA16
Tel   (01475) 24694
Mem   250
Sec   R Kirkpatrick (01475) 633258
Pro   None
Holes 18 L 5504 yds SSS 68
Recs   Am–64 J Callaghan (1995)
V'tors U
Fees   On application
Loc   Upper Greenock-Largs road

Whitecraigs (1905)
72 Ayr Road, Giffnock, Glasgow
G46 6SW
Tel   (0141) 639 4530
Fax   (0141) 639 4530
Mem   1150
Sec   AG Keith CA
Pro   A Forrow (0141) 639 2140
Holes 18 L 6013 yds SSS 69
V'tors WD–I WE–M SOC–WD
Fees   On application
Loc   6 miles S of Glasgow (A77),
       nr Whitecraigs Station

Stirlingshire

Aberfoyle (1890)
Braeval, Aberfoyle FK8 3UY
Tel   (01877) 382493
Mem   600
Sec   RD Steele (01877) 382638
Holes 18 L 5218 yds SSS 66
Recs   Am–64 EJ Barnard
V'tors WD–U WE–NA before
       11.30am
Fees   £12 D–£16 (£16 D–£24)
Loc   Braeval, 18 miles NW of
       Stirling (A81)

Balfron (1992)
Kepculloch Road, Balfron G63
Mem   400
Sec   I Rubython (01360) 440915
Pro   None
Holes 9 L 5372 yds Par 68 SSS 67
V'tors WD–U before 4pm
       WE–restricted SOC
Fees   £7
Loc   18 miles NW of Glasgow,
       off A81

Bonnybridge (1924)
Larbert Road, Bonnybridge, Falkirk
FK4 1NY
Tel   (01324) 812822
Mem   425
Sec   J Mullen
Holes 9 L 6058 yds SSS 69

For list of abbreviations see page 527

Stirlingshire

Recs Am–64 S Hunter, J Maxwell
Pro–66 J McTear
V'tors WD–I SOC
Fees On application to Sec
Loc 3 miles W of Falkirk

Bridge of Allan (1895)
Sunnylaw, Bridge of Allan, Stirling
Tel (01786) 832332
Mem 471
Sec Miss M Peattie
Holes 9 L 4932 yds SSS 65
Recs Am–62 ID McFarlane
V'tors U exc Sat
Fees £10 (£15)
Loc 4 miles N of Stirling, off A9
Arch Tom Morris Sr

Buchanan Castle (1936)
Drymen G63 0HY
Tel (01360) 660307
Fax (01360) 870382
Mem 830
Sec R Kinsella
Pro K Baxter (01360) 660330
Holes 18 L 6015 yds SSS 69
Recs Am–64 C Dunan
Pro–66 D Huish, W Milne
V'tors M or by arrangement with Sec
Fees On application
Loc 18 miles NW of Glasgow.
25 miles W of Stirling,
off A811
Arch James Braid

Campsie (1897)
*Crow Road, Lennoxtown, Glasgow
G65 7HX*
Tel (01360) 310244
Mem 650
Sec D Barbour
Pro M Brennan (01360) 310920
Holes 18 L 5517 yds SSS 68
Recs Am–69 M Howat (1998)
V'tors WD–U before 4.30pm
Fees £15 (£20)
Loc N of Lennoxtown on B822
Fintry road

Dunblane New (1923)
Perth Road, Dunblane FK15 0LJ
Tel (01786) 821521
Fax (01786) 825281
Mem 700
Sec JH Dunsmore
Pro RM Jamieson
Holes 18 L 5957 yds SSS 69
Recs Am–64 GK McDonald,
AY Wilson, S Morrison
Pro–66 RM Jamieson
V'tors WD–U WE–M SOC
Fees £20 (£32)
Loc E side of Dunblane. 6 miles N
of Stirling

Falkirk (1922)
*Stirling Road, Camelon, Falkirk
FK2 7YP*
Tel (01324) 611061/612219
Fax (01324) 639573
Mem 700
Sec J Elliott
Holes 18 L 6282 yds SSS 70
Recs Am–66
Pro–66
V'tors WD–U until 4pm Sat–NA
SOC–exc Sat
Fees £15 D–£20 Sun–£30
Loc 1½ miles W of Falkirk on A9
Arch James Braid

Falkirk Tryst (1885)
*86 Burnhead Road, Larbert
FK5 4BD*
Tel (01324) 562415
Mem 800
Sec RD Wallace
(01324) 562054
Pro S Dunsmore
(01324) 562091
Holes 18 L 6053 yds SSS 69
Recs Am–62 T Gilchrist
Pro–65 J Chillas
V'tors WD–U WE–M SOC–WD
Fees £16 D–£25
Loc 3 miles NW of Falkirk on A88

Glenbervie (1932)
Stirling Road, Larbert FK5 4SJ
Tel (01324) 562605
Fax (01324) 551054
Mem 600
Sec Dr Sheila Hartley
Pro J Chillas (01324) 562725
Holes 18 L 6423 yds Par 71 SSS 70
Recs Am–64 M Retson (1997)
Pro–64 G Law, D Drysdale
V'tors WD–U before 4pm WE–M
SOC–Tues & Thurs
Fees £32 D–£47
Loc 1 mile N of Larbert on A9.
M876 Junction 2
Arch James Braid

Grangemouth (1973)
Public
Polmonthill, Polmont FK2 0YA
Tel (01324) 711500
Mem 700
Sec I Hutton (Hon)
Pro SJ Campbell
(01324) 714355
Holes 18 L 6527 yds SSS 70
Recs Am–65 LJ Blair (1996)
V'tors U–book with Pro SOC
Fees £5.50 D–£8.30 (£7.40
D–£10.20)
Loc 3 miles NE of Falkirk. M9
Junction 4

Kilsyth Lennox (1900)
*Tak-Ma-Doon Road, Kilsyth
G65 0RS*
Tel (01236) 823525 (Bookings)
Mem 250
Sec AG Stevenson
(01236) 823213
Holes 18 L 5930 yds Par 70
Recs Am–66 R Irvine (1986),
W Erskine (1987)
V'tors WD–U until 5pm –M after
5pm Sat–NA before 4pm
Sun–NA before 2pm SOC
Fees On application
Loc N of Kilsyth and A803.
12 miles NE of Glasgow

Polmont (1901)
*Manuel Rigg, Maddiston, Falkirk
FK2 0LS*
Tel (01324) 711277 (Clubhouse)
Fax (01324) 712504
Mem 300
Sec P Lees (01324) 713811
Holes 9 L 3044 yds SSS 69
Recs Am–66 C Fowler (1996)
V'tors U exc Sat–NA
Fees £8 Sun–£14
Loc 4 miles SE of Falkirk
on B805

Stirling (1869)
Queen's Road, Stirling FK8 3AA
Tel (01786) 473801
Fax (01786) 450748
Mem 1000
Sec WC McArthur
(01786) 464098
Pro I Collins
(01786) 471490
Holes 18 L 6409 yds SSS 71
Recs Am–64 KJ McArthur (1997)
Pro–66 G Everitt (1993)
V'tors WD–U SOC WE–NA
Fees On application
Loc King's Park, Stirling
Arch Braid/Cotton

Strathendrick (1901)
*Glasgow Road, Drymen
G63 0AA*
Tel (01360) 660695
Mem 480
Sec J Vickers (01360) 660675
Holes 9 L 5116 yds SSS 64
Recs Am–60 P Haggarty
Pro–64 C Dernie
V'tors WD–U SOC–WD before
5pm
Fees £10 D–£16
Loc 25 miles W of Stirling,
off A811
Arch W Fernie

Wales

Cardiganshire

Aberystwyth (1911)
Bryn-y-Mor, Aberystwyth SY23 2HY
Tel (01970) 615104
Fax (01970) 615104
Mem 390
Sec L Evans
Pro M Newson (01970) 625301
Holes 18 L 6109 yds SSS 71
Recs Am–67 P Richards
 Pro–67 P Parkin,
 G Emerson
V'tors U SOC
Fees £18.50 (£22.50)
Loc Aberystwyth 1/2 mile
Arch H Varden

Borth & Ynyslas (1885)
Borth SY24 5JS
Tel (01970) 871202
Fax (01970) 871202
Mem 550
Sec Miss S Wilson
Pro JG Lewis (01970) 871557
Holes 18 L 6100 yds SSS 70
Recs Am–65 M Stimson (1989),
 C Evans (1993)
 Pro–67 JG Lewis
 Ladies–73 K Stark
V'tors WD–U WE/BH–by prior arrangement SOC
Fees £20 (£27)
Loc 8 miles N of Aberystwyth (B4353), off A487

Cardigan (1895)
Gwbert-on-Sea, Cardigan SA43 1PR
Tel (01239) 612035/621775
Fax (01239) 621775
Mem 600
Sec JJ Jones (01239) 621775
Pro C Parsons (01239) 615359
Holes 18 L 6687 yds SSS 73
Recs Am–68 R Emanuel
V'tors H SOC
Fees D–£20 (£25) W–£70
Loc 3 miles N of Cardigan
Arch Grant Hawtree

Cilgwyn (1977)
Llangybi, Lampeter SA48 8NN
Tel (01570) 45286
Mem 290
Sec N Hill
Holes 9 L 5327 yds SSS 67
Recs Am–67 EL Jones (1991)
V'tors U SOC
Fees £10 (£15) W–£60
Loc 5 miles NE of Lampeter, off A485 at Llangybi

Penrhos G&CC (1991)
Llanrhystud, Aberystwyth SY23 5AY
Tel (01974) 202999
Fax (01974) 202100
Email Penrhosgolfclub@compuserve.com
Mem 300
Sec R Rees-Evans
Pro P Diamond
Holes 18 L 6641 yds SSS 73
 9 hole Par 3 course
Recs Am–70 I Miller (1997)
V'tors U SOC
Fees £17 (£22)
Loc 9 miles S of Aberystwyth, off A487
Mis Driving range
Arch Jim Walters

Carmarthenshire

Ashburnham (1894)
Cliffe Terrace, Burry Port SA16 0HN
Tel (01554) 832466
Fax (01554) 832466
Mem 725
Sec DK Williams (01554) 832269
Pro RA Ryder (01554) 833846
Holes 18 L 6916 yds SSS 72
Recs Am–69 Y Taylor
 Pro–71 C Evans, N Roderick
V'tors H
Fees £27 D–£32 (£32 D–£42)
Loc 5 miles W of Llanelli (A484)

Carmarthen (1907)
Blaenycoed Road, Carmarthen SA33 6EH
Tel (01267) 281214
Mem 700
Sec J Coe (01267) 281588
Pro P Gillis (01267) 281493
Holes 18 L 6245 yds SSS 71
Recs Am–68 A Smith (1998)
 Pro–69 B Barnes
V'tors H SOC
Fees £18 (£25)
Loc 4 miles NW of Carmarthen

Derllys (1993)
Derllys Court, Llysonnen Road, Carmarthen SA33 5DT
Tel (01267) 211575/211309
Fax (01267) 211575
Mem 48
Sec R Walters
Holes 9 L 2859 yds Par 70 SSS 66
V'tors U
Fees £9 D–£12 (£10 D–£13)
Loc 4 miles W of Carmarthen, off A40
Arch P Johnson

Glyn Abbey
Pay and play
Trimsaran SA17 4LB
Tel (01554) 810278
Fax (01269) 861825
Mem 240
Sec M Lane, J Smith (Mgrs)
Pro None
Holes 18 L 6173 yds Par 70 SSS 70
V'tors U SOC
Fees £10 (£12)
Loc 4 miles NW of Llanelli, between Trimsaran and Carway
Arch Hawtree

Glynhir (1909)
Glynhir Road, Llandybie, Ammanford SA18 2TF
Tel (01269) 850472
Fax (01269) 851365
Mem 700
Sec EP Rees, DB Jones (01269) 851365
Pro D Prior (01269) 851010
Holes 18 L 6006 yds SSS 70
Recs Am–66 R Collins
V'tors WD/Sat–H Sun–NA SOC–WD
Fees Winter £10 (£12) 5D–£45
 Summer £16 (£22) 5D–£70
Loc 3 1/2 miles N of Ammanford
Arch Hawtree

Conwy

Abergele (1910)
Tan-y-Gopa Road, Abergele LL22 8DS
Tel (01745) 824034
Fax (01745) 824034
Mem 1250
Sec HE Richards
Pro I Runcie (01745) 823813
Holes 18 L 6520 yds SSS 71
Recs Am–66 D Davies (1994)
 Pro–65 D Vaughan (1987)
 Ladies–71 R Brewerton (1997)
V'tors U SOC
Fees On application
Loc Abergele Castle Grounds
Arch Hawtree

Betws-y-Coed (1977)
Clubhouse, Betws-y-Coed LL24
Tel (01690) 710556
Mem 400
Sec JH Jones
Holes 9 L 4996 yds SSS 63
Recs Am–63 DWP Hughes (1990)
V'tors U SOC
Fees £15 (£20)
Loc 1/2 mile off A5, in Betws-y-Coed

For list of abbreviations see page 527

Conwy (Caernarvonshire) (1890)

Morfa, Conwy LL32 8ER
- **Tel** (01492) 593400
- **Fax** (01492) 593363
- **Mem** 750
- **Sec** DL Brown (01492) 592423
- **Pro** JP Lees (01492) 593225
- **Holes** 18 L 6936 yds SSS 74
- **Recs** Am–69 C Platt (1996)
- **V'tors** H WE–restricted SOC
- **Fees** £25 (£30)
- **Loc** ½ mile W of Conway, off A55

Llandudno (Maesdu) (1915)

Hospital Road, Llandudno LL30 1HU
- **Tel** (01492) 876450
- **Fax** (01492) 871570
- **Mem** 1109
- **Sec** G Dean
- **Pro** S Boulden (01492) 875195
- **Holes** 18 L 6513 yds SSS 72
- **Recs** Am–67 G Jones, CT Brown, M Macara; Pro–66 PJ Butler
- **V'tors** U H–recognised GC members SOC
- **Fees** £25 (£30)
- **Loc** 1 mile S of Llandudno Station, nr hospital

Llandudno (North Wales) (1894)

72 Bryniau Road, West Shore, Llandudno LL30 2DZ
- **Tel** (01492) 875325
- **Fax** (01492) 875325
- **Mem** 560
- **Sec** WR Williams
- **Pro** RA Bradbury (01492) 876878
- **Holes** 18 L 6247 yds Par 71 SSS 71
- **Recs** Am–66 L Harpin Pro–63 WS Collins
- **V'tors** U SOC–phone Sec
- **Fees** £23 (£30)
- **Loc** ¾ mile from Llandudno on West Shore

Llanfairfechan (1971)

Llannerch Road, Llanfairfechan LL33 0EB
- **Tel** (01248) 680144
- **Mem** 352
- **Sec** MJ Charlesworth (01248) 680524
- **Holes** 9 L 3119 yds SSS 57
- **Recs** Am–53 MJ Charlesworth (1983)
- **V'tors** U
- **Fees** £5 (£10)
- **Loc** 7 miles E of Bangor on A55

Old Colwyn (1907)

Woodland Avenue, Old Colwyn LL29 9NL
- **Tel** (01492) 515581
- **Mem** 250
- **Sec** DM Fisher
- **Holes** 9 L 5243 yds SSS 66
- **Recs** Am–63 C Oldham, JD Jones Roberts Pro–67 DJ Rees
- **V'tors** WD–U WE–by arrangement SOC
- **Fees** £10 (£15)
- **Loc** 2 miles E of Colwyn Bay

Penmaenmawr (1910)

Conway Old Road, Penmaenmawr LL34 6RD
- **Tel** (01492) 623330
- **Fax** (01492) 622105
- **Mem** 600
- **Sec** Mrs JE Jones
- **Holes** 9 L 5143 yds SSS 66
- **Recs** Am–63 S Wilkinson
- **V'tors** U SOC
- **Fees** £12 (£18)
- **Loc** 4 miles W of Conway

Rhos-on-Sea (1899)

Penrhyn Bay, Llandudno LL30 3PU
- **Tel** (01492) 549641
- **Mem** 600
- **Sec** G Hughes
- **Pro** M Macara
- **Holes** 18 L 6064 yds SSS 69
- **Recs** Am–69 P Knowles Pro–66 M Greenough
- **V'tors** U
- **Fees** £10 (£20)
- **Loc** On coast at Rhos-on-Sea. 4 miles E of LLandudno

Denbighshire

Bryn Morfydd Hotel (1982)

Llanrhaeadr, Denbigh LL16 4NP
- **Tel** (01745) 890280
- **Fax** (01745) 890488
- **Mem** 300
- **Pro** IP Jones
- **Holes** 18 L 5800 yds SSS 67 9 hole Par 3 course
- **V'tors** U SOC
- **Fees** £12 (£16)
- **Loc** 2½ miles SE of Denbigh on A525
- **Arch** Duchess-Alliss/Thomas. Dukes-Muirhead/Henderson

Denbigh (1922)

Henllan Road, Denbigh LL16 5AA
- **Tel** (01745) 814159
- **Fax** (01745) 814888
- **Mem** 550
- **Sec** L Jukes (01745) 816669
- **Pro** M Jones (01745) 814159
- **Holes** 18 L 5712 yds SSS 69
- **Recs** Am–65 OJ Roberts (1995) Pro–69 C Defoy (1986)
- **V'tors** U SOC
- **Fees** On application
- **Loc** 1 mile NW of Denbigh (B5382)

Kinmel Park (1989)

Pay and play
Bodelwyddan LL18 5SR
- **Tel** (01745) 833548
- **Fax** (01745) 824861
- **Sec** P Stebbings
- **Pro** P Stebbings
- **Holes** 9 L 1550 yds Par 29
- **V'tors** U
- **Fees** £3.50 (£4)
- **Loc** Off A55, between Abergele and St Asaph
- **Mis** Driving range
- **Arch** Peter Stebbings

Prestatyn (1905)

Marine Road East, Prestatyn LL19 7HS
- **Tel** (01745) 854320
- **Fax** (01745) 888353
- **Mem** 650
- **Sec** R Woodruff (Mgr) (01745) 888353
- **Pro** M Staton (01745) 852083
- **Holes** 18 L 6808 yds SSS 73
- **Recs** Am–66 RJ Edwards (1993)
- **V'tors** H SOC
- **Fees** £20 (£25)
- **Loc** 1 mile E of Prestatyn
- **Arch** S Collins

Rhuddlan (1930)

Meliden Road, Rhuddlan LL18 6LB
- **Tel** (01745) 590217
- **Fax** (01745) 590472
- **Email** www.northwales.uk.com
- **Mem** 515 155(L) 80(J)
- **Sec** D Morris
- **Pro** A Carr (01745) 590898
- **Holes** 18 L 6482 yds SSS 71
- **Recs** Am–66 D McKendrick (1995)
- **V'tors** H or I Sun–M SOC–WD
- **Fees** £18 (£30)
- **Loc** 2 miles N of St Asaph, off A55
- **Arch** F Hawtree

Rhyl (1890)

Coast Road, Rhyl LL18 3RE
- **Tel** (01745) 353171
- **Fax** (01745) 353171
- **Mem** 440
- **Sec** I StC Doig
- **Pro** T Leah
- **Holes** 9 L 6153 yds SSS 70
- **Recs** Am–L Williams (1994) Pro–67 H Cotton, C Ward, N von Nida
- **V'tors** U SOC
- **Fees** £12 (£15)
- **Loc** On A548 between Rhyl and Prestatyn
- **Arch** James Braid

Ruthin-Pwllglas (1920)

Pwllglas, Ruthin LL15 2PE
- **Tel** (01824) 702296
- **Fax** (01978) 790692
- **Mem** 360
- **Sec** Mrs BK Tremayne (Hon) (01978) 790692

Holes 10 L 5362 yds SSS 66
Recs Am–66 H Roberts
V'tors U SOC
Fees £12.50 (£18)
Loc 2½ miles S of Ruthin

St Melyd (1922)
The Paddock, Meliden Road, Prestatyn LL19 9NB
Tel (01745) 854405
Mem 400
Sec PM Storey (01745) 853574
Pro R Bradbury (01745) 888858
Holes 9 L 5857 yds SSS 68
Recs Am–65 AR Grace (1990)
Pro–66 S Wilkinson
V'tors U SOC
Fees £15 (£19)
Loc S of Prestatyn on A547

Vale of Llangollen (1908)
Holyhead Road, Llangollen LL20 7PR
Tel (01978) 860613
Fax (01978) 860906
Mem 750
Sec AD Bluck (01978) 860906
Pro DI Vaughan (01978) 860040
Holes 18 L 6656 yds Par 72 SSS 73
Recs Am–67 T Dykes (1998)
Pro–66 M Ellis (1998)
V'tors U SOC
Fees £20 (£25)
Loc 1½ miles E of Llangollen on A5

Flintshire

Caerwys (1989)
Pay and play
Caerwys, Mold CH7 5AQ
Tel (01352) 720692
Mem 200
Sec E Barlow
Pro N Lloyd
Holes 9 L 3080 yds SSS 60
Recs Am–61 T Adamson (1989)
V'tors U SOC
Fees £4.50 (£5.50)
Loc SW of Caerwys. 1½ miles S of A55 Express Way, between Holywell and St Asaph
Arch Eleanor Barlow

Flint (1966)
Cornist Park, Flint CH6 5HJ
Tel (01352) 732227, (01244) 812945
Fax (01244) 811885
Mem 390
Sec TE Owens
Holes 9 L 5953 yds SSS 69
Recs Am–65 O O'Neil, G Houston
V'tors WD–U before 5pm SOC–WD
Fees D–£10 (£10)
Loc 1 mile SW of Flint. End of M56, 8 miles

Hawarden (1911)
Groomsdale Lane, Hawarden, Deeside CH5 3EH
Tel (01244) 531447
Mem 480
Pro C Hope (01244) 520809
Holes 18 L 5842 yds SSS 68
Recs Am–64 L Hinks-Edwards
V'tors H SOC
Fees £12.50 (£15)
Loc 6 miles W of Chester, off A55

Holywell (1906)
Brynford, Holywell CH8 8LQ
Tel (01352) 710040/713937
Fax (07070) 660453
Mem 375 60(L)
Sec H Moore (01352) 713937
Pro S O'Connor (01352) 710040
Holes 18 L 6100 yds Par 70 SSS 70
Recs Am–68 PG Newton (1998)
V'tors WD–U WE–SOC
Fees £15 (£20)
Loc 2 miles S of Holywell, off A5026

Kinsale
Pay and play
Llanerchymor, Holywell CH8 9DX
Tel (01745) 561080
Fax (01745) 561079
Mem 85
Sec A Backhurst (Golf Dir)
Pro A Backhurst
Holes 9 holes Par 71 SSS 70
V'tors U
Fees 9 holes–£6 18 holes–£9
Loc 4 miles N of Holywell on A548
Mis Floodlit driving range
Arch K Smith

Mold (1909)
Pantymwyn, Mold CH7 5EH
Tel (01352) 740318/741513
Fax (01352) 741517
Mem 350 85(L) 90(J)
Sec EJ Reeves (01352) 741513
Pro M Carty (01352) 740318
Holes 18 L 5528 yds SSS 67
Recs Am–64 N Tomlinson
Pro–64 D Wills
V'tors U SOC
Fees £16 (£23)
Loc 4 miles W of Mold
Arch Hawtree

Northop Country Park (1994)
Northop, Chester CH7 6WA
Tel (01352) 840440
Fax (01352) 840445
Sec D Llewellyn
Pro M Pritchard
Holes 18 L 6735 yds Par 72
Recs Am–68
Pro–64
V'tors U–phone first
Fees £28 (£35)
Loc 3 miles S of Flint, off A55
Mis Driving range
Arch John Jacobs

Old Padeswood (1978)
Station Road, Padeswood, Mold CH7 4JL
Tel (01244) 547701 (Clubhouse)
Mem 500
Sec B Slater (Hon)
Pro A Davies (01244) 547401
Holes 18 L 6728 yds SSS 72
9 hole Par 3 course
Recs Am–66 L Lockett (1991), I Rowlands (1997)
Pro–65 I Higsby
Ladies–69 J Nicholson (1998)
V'tors U exc comp days SOC–WD
Fees £18 D–£25 (£20)
Loc 2 miles from Mold on A5118

Padeswood & Buckley (1933)
The Caia, Station Lane, Padeswood, Mold CH7 4JD
Tel (01244) 550537
Fax (01244) 541600
Mem 592
Sec GS Faulkner
Pro D Ashton (01244) 543636
Holes 18 L 5982 yds Par 70 SSS 69
Recs Am–66 SA Delves
V'tors WD–U 9am–4pm –M after 4pm Sat–U Sun–NA SOC–WD Ladies Day–Wed
Fees £20 (£25)
Loc 8 miles W of Chester, off A5118. 2nd golf club on right
Arch D Williams

Gwynedd

Aberdovey (1892)
Aberdovey LL35 0RT
Tel (01654) 767210
Fax (01654) 767027
Mem 800
Sec JM Griffiths (01654) 767493
Pro J Davies (01654) 767602
Holes 18 L 6445 yds SSS 71
Recs Am–66 BT Bell (1993)
Pro–67 J Smith
V'tors NA–8–9.30am & 1–2pm
Fees On application
Loc 3 miles W of Aberdovey (A493)

Abersoch (1907)
Golf Road, Abersoch LL53 7EY
Tel (01758) 712622
Fax (01758) 712622
Mem 700
Sec A Drosinos Jones
Pro A Drosinos Jones
Holes 18 L 5819 yds SSS 69
V'tors H SOC
Fees £18 (£20)
Loc ½ mile S of Abersoch (A55). 7 miles S of Pwllheli
Arch Harry Vardon

For list of abbreviations see page 527

Gwynedd

Bala (1973)
Penlan, Bala LL23 7BC
- **Tel** (01678) 520359
- **Fax** (01678) 521361
- **Mem** 340
- **Sec** G Rhys Jones (01678) 521361
- **Pro** T Davies
- **Holes** 10 L 4962 yds SSS 64
- **Recs** Am–63 RJ Roberts (1997) Ladies–70 G Aykroyd (1983)
- **V'tors** WD–U WE–NA pm SOC
- **Fees** £12 (£15) W–£40
- **Loc** 1 mile SW of Bala, off A494 to Dolgellau

Bala Lake Hotel
Bala LL23 7YF
- **Tel** (01678) 520344/520111
- **Fax** (01678) 521193
- **Mem** 50
- **Sec** D Pickering
- **Holes** 9 L 4280 yds SSS 61
- **V'tors** U
- **Fees** On application
- **Loc** 1½ miles S of Bala on B4403

Caernarfon (1907)
Aberforeshore, LLanfaglan, Caernarfon LL54 5RP
- **Tel** (01286) 673783/678359
- **Fax** (01286) 672535
- **Mem** 696
- **Sec** DJ Jones
- **Pro** A Owen (01286) 678359
- **Holes** 18 L 5891 yds SSS 68
- **Recs** Am–66 Pro–64
- **V'tors** U SOC
- **Fees** £18 (£24)
- **Loc** 2½ miles SW of Caernarfon

Criccieth (1905)
Ednyfed Hill, Criccieth LL52
- **Tel** (01766) 522154
- **Mem** 200
- **Sec** MG Hamilton (01766) 522697
- **Holes** 18 L 5755 yds SSS 68
- **Recs** Am–63 NJ Gore (1982) Ladies–60 F Prole (1979)
- **V'tors** U
- **Fees** £12 Sun–£15
- **Loc** 4 miles W of Portmadoc

Dolgellau (1911)
Hengwrt Estate, Pencefn Road, Dolgellau LL4 0SE
- **Tel** (01341) 422603
- **Mem** 300
- **Sec** Ms JM May
- **Pro** H Jones Davies
- **Holes** 9 L 4671 yds Par 66 SSS 63
- **Recs** Am–62 PM Smyth (1998) Pro–61 AL Williams (1937)
- **V'tors** U
- **Fees** £15 (£20)
- **Loc** ½ mile N of Dolgellau
- **Arch** J Medway

Ffestiniog (1893)
Y Cefn, Ffestiniog
- **Tel** (01766) 762637 (Clubhouse)
- **Mem** 138
- **Sec** A Roberts (01766) 831829
- **Holes** 9 L 5032 m Par 68 SSS 65
- **V'tors** U
- **Fees** On application
- **Loc** 1 mile E of Ffestiniog on Bala road (B4391)

Nefyn & District (1907)
Morfa Nefyn, Pwllheli LL53 6DA
- **Tel** (01758) 720218 (Clubhouse)
- **Fax** (01758) 720476
- **Mem** 750
- **Sec** JB Owens (01758) 720966
- **Pro** J Froom (01758) 720102
- **Holes** 18 L 6548 yds SSS 71 / 9 L 2618 yds SSS 34
- **Recs** Am–64 M Pilkington Pro–67 I Woosnam
- **V'tors** U SOC
- **Fees** £25 D–£30 (£30 D–£35)
- **Loc** 1½ miles W of Nefyn. 20 miles W of Caernarfon

Porthmadog (1905)
Morfa Bychan, Porthmadog LL49 9UU
- **Tel** (01766) 512037
- **Fax** (01766) 514638
- **Mem** 920
- **Sec** Mrs A Richardson (Office Mgr) (01766) 514124
- **Pro** P Bright (01766) 513828
- **Holes** 18 L 6330 yds Par 70 SSS 71
- **Recs** Am–63 J Morrow
- **V'tors** U H SOC
- **Fees** D–£20 (D–£26)
- **Loc** 2 miles S of Porthmadog, towards Black Rock Sands
- **Arch** James Braid

Pwllheli (1900)
Golf Road, Pwllheli LL53 5PS
- **Tel** (01758) 701644
- **Fax** (01758) 701644
- **Mem** 820
- **Sec** E Pritchard
- **Pro** J Pilkington (01758) 612520
- **Holes** 18 L 6091 yds SSS 69
- **Recs** Am–66 M Pilkington, MG Hughes Pro–65 M Macara
- **V'tors** U
- **Fees** £22 (£27)
- **Loc** ½ mile SW of Pwllheli
- **Arch** James Braid

Royal St David's (1894)
Harlech LL46 2UB
- **Tel** (01766) 780203
- **Fax** (01766) 781110
- **Mem** 870
- **Sec** DL Morkill (01766) 780361
- **Pro** J Barnett (01766) 780857
- **Holes** 18 L 6552 yds SSS 72
- **Recs** Am–64 C Platt (1992) Pro–64 K Stables (1988)
- **V'tors** U H–booking necessary SOC
- **Fees** D–£33 (D–£38)
- **Loc** W of Harlech on A496

St Deiniol (1905)
Penybryn, Bangor LL57 1PX
- **Tel** (01248) 353098
- **Mem** 500
- **Sec** EW Jones
- **Holes** 18 L 5048 m SSS 67
- **Recs** Am–61 CG Edwards (1995)
- **V'tors** U
- **Fees** £12 (£16)
- **Loc** Off A5/A55 Junction, 1 mile E of Bangor on A5122
- **Arch** James Braid

Isle of Anglesey

Anglesey (1914)
Station Road, Rhosneigr LL64 5QX
- **Tel** (01407) 811202
- **Fax** (01407) 811202
- **Mem** 450
- **Sec** K Brown (Sec/Mgr)
- **Pro** P Lovell
- **Holes** 18 L 6330 yds SSS 70
- **Recs** Am–66 M Robinson (1990) Pro–65 B Rimmer (1994)
- **V'tors** U H SOC
- **Fees** £15 (£20)
- **Loc** 8 miles SE of Holyhead, off A4080

Baron Hill (1895)
Beaumaris LL58 8YW
- **Tel** (01248) 810231
- **Mem** 360
- **Sec** A Pleming
- **Holes** 9 L 5062 m SSS 68
- **Recs** Am–65 AW Jones
- **V'tors** U exc comp days SOC–WD & Sat (apply Sec)
- **Fees** £12 W–£45
- **Loc** 1 mile SW of Beaumaris

Bull Bay (1913)
Bull Bay Road, Amlwch LL68 9RY
- **Tel** (01407) 830213
- **Fax** (01407) 832612
- **Mem** 700
- **Sec** I Furlong (Sec/Mgr) (01407) 830960
- **Pro** J Burns (01407) 831188
- **Holes** 18 L 6217 yds SSS 70
- **Recs** Am–60 T Blackwell (1996) Pro–64 A Barnett (1995)
- **V'tors** H SOC
- **Fees** £15 (£20)
- **Loc** ½ mile W of Amlwch on A5025
- **Arch** WH Fowler

Henllys Hall
Llanfaes, Beaumaris LL58 8HU
- **Tel** (01248) 810412
- **Holes** 18 L 6100 yds Par 71
- **V'tors** U SOC
- **Fees** On application
- **Loc** 2 miles N of Beaumaris (B5109)

For list of abbreviations see page 527

Holyhead (1912)
Trearddur Bay, Holyhead LL65 2YG
Tel (01407) 763279/762119
Fax (01407) 763279
Mem 484 225(L) 109(J)
Sec JA Williams
Pro S Elliott (01407) 762022
Holes 18 L 5540 m SSS 70
Recs Am–67 M Owen
Pro–69 H Gould
V'tors H SOC
Fees £17.50 D–£22
(£22.50 D–£27)
Loc 2 miles S of Holyhead
Arch James Braid

Llangefni (1983)
Public
Llangefni LL77 8YQ
Tel (01248) 722193
Pro P Lovell
Holes 9 L 1467 yds Par 28
V'tors U
Fees £3 (£3)
Loc ½ mile S of Llangefni, off A5111
Arch Hawtree

Storws Wen (1996)
Brynteg, Benllech LL78 8JY
Tel (01248) 852673
Fax (01248) 852673
Mem 300
Sec C Purves
Pro None
Holes 9 L 5002 yds Par 68 SSS 63
Recs Am–67 C Brown (1996)
Pro–69 P Lovell (1996)
V'tors U SOC
Fees £10 (£13)
Loc 2 miles from Benllech on B5108
Arch K Jones

Mid Glamorgan

Aberdare (1921)
Abernant, Aberdare CF44 0RY
Tel (01685) 871188 (Clubhouse)
Fax (01685) 872797
Mem 600
Sec (01685) 872797
Pro AW Palmer (01685) 878735
Holes 18 L 5875 yds SSS 69
Recs Am–64 N Edwards (1997)
Pro–67 AW Palmer
V'tors I or H Sat–M SOC
Fees £14 (£18)
Loc ½ mile E of Aberdare. 12 miles NW of Pontypridd

Bargoed (1912)
Heolddu, Bargoed CF8 9GF
Tel (01443) 830143
Mem 548
Sec WR Coleman (01443) 830608
Pro C Coombs (01443) 836311
Holes 18 L 6233 yds SSS 69
Recs Am–65 B Dredge

V'tors WD–U WE–M SOC–WD
Fees £10 (£15)
Loc NW boundary of Bargoed. 8 miles N of Caerphilly (A469)

Bryn Meadows Golf Hotel (1973)
The Bryn, Hengoed CF8 7SM
Tel (01495) 225590/224103
Fax (01495) 228272
Mem 550
Sec B Mayo
Pro B Hunter (01495) 221905
Holes 18 L 6156 yds SSS 69
Recs Am–69 B Dredge
Pro–68 S Price
V'tors U
Fees £17.50 (£22.50)
Loc 6 miles N of Caerphilly (A469)
Arch Mayo/Jefferies

Caerphilly (1905)
Pencapel, Mountain Road, Caerphilly CF83 1HJ
Tel (01222) 883481
Fax (01222) 863441
Mem 765
Sec (01222) 863441
Pro R Barter (01222) 869104
Holes 13 L 6039 yds SSS 71
Recs Am–65 L Absolam
Pro–68 B Huggett
V'tors WD–U H WE–M
Fees £20 W–£40
Loc 7 miles N of Cardiff, off A469
Mis Extension to 18 holes in 2000

Castell Heights (1982)
Pay and play
Blaengwynlais, Caerphilly CF8 1NG
Tel (01222) 886666 (Bookings)
Fax (01222) 869030
Mem 600
Pro S Bebb
Holes 9 L 2688 yds SSS 66
Recs Am–32 P Page (1990)
V'tors U
Fees 9 holes–£4.50 (£5.50)
Loc 4 miles from M4 Junction 32
Mis Driving range
Arch J Page

Coed-y-Mwstwr (1996)
Coychurch, Bridgend CF35 6TN
Tel (01656) 862121
Mem 260
Sec HD James (Sec/Mgr)
Holes 9 L 5834 yds Par 69 SSS 68
Recs Am–72 P Thomas, S Chilcott (1996)
V'tors UH SOC
Fees £15
Loc 2 miles W of M4 Junction 35

Creigiau (1921)
Creigiau, Cardiff CF4 8NN
Tel (01222) 890263
Fax (01222) 890263
Mem 700

Sec To be appointed
Pro I Luntz (01222) 891909
Holes 18 L 6063 yds SSS 70
Recs Am–67 MJ Harmer (1997)
Pro–66 R Dinsdale (1996)
V'tors WD–U WE/BH–M SOC–WD
Fees £30
Loc 5 miles NW of Cardiff. M4 Junction 34

Llantrisant & Pontyclun (1927)
Lanlay Road, Talbot Green, Llantrisant CF7 8HZ
Tel (01443) 222148
Mem 500
Sec JM Williams (01443) 224601
Pro N Watson (01443) 228169
Holes 12 L 5712 yds SSS 68
Recs Am–65 TJ Lewis (1974)
Pro–65 JJ Hastings (1982)
V'tors WD–U WE/BH–M SOC–WD
Fees On application
Loc 10 miles NW of Cardiff. 2 miles N of M4 Junction 34

Maesteg (1912)
Mount Pleasant, Neath Road, Maesteg CF34 9PR
Tel (01656) 732037
Fax (01656) 734106
Mem 720
Sec RK Lewis MBE (01656) 734106
Pro C Riley (01656) 735742
Holes 18 L 5929 yds SSS 69
Recs Am–69 R Jenkins (1991), M Donoghue (1992), N Hedley (1993)
Pro–64 G Ryall (1989)
V'tors WD–H SOC
Fees £17 (£20)
Loc 1 mile W of Maesteg on B4282. M4 Junctions 36 or 40

Merthyr Tydfil (1908)
Cilsanws Mountain, Cefn Coed, Merthyr Tydfil CF48 2NU
Tel (01685) 723308
Mem 200
Sec V Price
Holes 18 L 5622 yds SSS 68
Recs Am–70 C Williams, N Evans
V'tors U SOC–WD
Fees £12 (£16)
Loc 2 miles N of Merthyr Tydfil, off A470 at Cefn Coed

Morlais Castle (1900)
Pant, Dowlais, Merthyr Tydfil CF48 2UY
Tel (01685) 722822
Fax (01685) 722822
Mem 420
Sec N Powell
Pro H Jarrett (01685) 388700
Holes 18 L 6320 yds SSS 71
Recs Am–67 JP Davies (1993)
V'tors WD–U Sat–NA 12–4pm Sun–NA 8am–12noon SOC–WD

Mid Glamorgan

Fees £14 (£16)
Loc 3 miles N of Merthyr Tydfil, nr Mountain Railway

Mountain Ash (1908)
Cefnpennar, Mountain Ash CF45 4DT
Tel (01443) 472265
Mem 555
Sec G Matthews (01443) 479459
Pro M Wills (01443) 478770
Holes 18 L 5535 yds SSS 67
Recs Am–63 SJ Lewis
Pro–66 R Evans
V'tors WD–U H WE–M
Fees £15
Loc 9 miles NW of Pontypridd

Mountain Lakes (1988)
Blaengwynlais, Caerphilly CF8 1NG
Tel (01222) 861128
Fax (01222) 869030
Mem 480
Sec DC Rooney (Hon)
Pro S Bebb
Holes 18 L 6300 yds SSS 72
Recs Am–68 S Deane
Pro–68 P Price (1993)
V'tors H SOC
Fees £15 (£15)
Loc 4 miles from M4 Junction 32
Mis Driving range
Arch R Sandow

Pontypridd (1905)
Ty Gwyn Road, Pontypridd CF37 4DJ
Tel (01443) 402359
Fax (01443) 491622
Mem 850
Sec Vikki Hooley (01443) 409904
Pro W Walters (01443) 491210
Holes 18 L 5725 yds SSS 68
Recs Am–66 MC Sallam, PL Jenkins (1989)
V'tors WD–U H WE/BH–M H SOC–WD H
Fees On application
Loc E of Pontypridd, off A470. 12 miles NW of Cardiff

Pyle & Kenfig (1922)
Waun-y-Mer, Kenfig, Bridgend CF33 4PU
Tel (01656) 783093
Fax (01656) 772822
Mem 860
Sec SD Anthony (Sec/Mgr) (01656) 771613
Pro R Evans (01656) 772446
Holes 18 L 6655 yds SSS 73
Recs Am–68 R Walters
Pro–67 J Langmead, M Wootton
V'tors WD–U H WE–M SOC
Fees D–£30
Loc 2 miles NW of Porthcawl
Arch HS Colt

Rhondda (1910)
Penrhys, Ferndale, Rhondda CF43 3PW
Tel (01443) 433204
Fax (01443) 441384
Mem 500
Sec G Rees (01443) 441384
Pro R Davies (01443) 441385
Holes 18 L 6428 yds SSS 71
Recs Am–69 P Derham (1988)
Pro–67 D Ray (1991)
V'tors U H SOC
Fees £20 (£25)
Loc 6 miles W of Pontypridd

Royal Porthcawl (1891)
Rest Bay, Porthcawl CF36 3UW
Tel (01656) 782251
Fax (01656) 771687
Mem 800
Sec AW Woolcott
Pro P Evans (01656) 773702
Holes 18 L 6685 yds SSS 74
Recs Am–68 S Dodds
Pro–65 B Barnes
V'tors WD–I or H WE/BH–M SOC–H
Fees On application
Loc 22 miles W of Cardiff. M4 Junction 37

Southerndown (1905)
Ewenny, Ogmore-by-Sea, Bridgend CF32 0QP
Tel (01656) 880326
Fax (01656) 880317
Mem 700
Sec AJ Hughes (01656) 880476
Pro DG McMonagle
Holes 18 L 6417 yds SSS 72
Recs Am–65 B Lamb
Pro–64 G Hunt
V'tors U H
Fees £25 (£35)
Loc 3 miles S of Bridgend, nr Ogmore Castle ruins
Arch W Fernie

Virginia Park (1993)
Pay and play
Virginia Park, Caerphilly CF83 3SW
Tel (01222) 863919
Mem 200
Sec Mrs C Lewis
Pro R Barter (01589) 877355
Holes 9 L 4661 yds Par 66 SSS 63
V'tors U SOC
Fees On application
Loc Caerphilly, 7 miles N of Cardiff
Mis Driving range

Whitehall (1922)
The Pavilion, Nelson, Treharris CF46 6ST
Tel (01443) 740245
Mem 300
Sec M Hughes
Holes 9 L 5666 yds SSS 68

Recs Am–66 M Heames (1985)
Pro–62 I Woosnam (1980)
V'tors WD–U WE–M
Fees £15
Loc 15 miles NW of Cardiff

Monmouthshire

Alice Springs (1989)
Bettws Newydd, Usk NP5 1JY
Tel (01873) 880772 (Queens), (01873) 880708 (Kings)
Fax (01873) 880838
Mem 350
Sec KR Morgan
Pro P Williams (01873) 880914
Holes Queens 18 L 5870 yds SSS 69
Kings 18 L 6438 yds SSS 72
V'tors U SOC
Fees £15 (£18)
Loc 3 miles N of Usk on B4598
Mis Driving range
Arch Keith Morgan

Blackwood (1914)
Cwmgelli, Blackwood NP2 1EL
Tel (01495) 223152
Mem 300
Sec AD Watkins
Pro None
Holes 9 L 5304 yds SSS 66
Recs Am–64 S Erasmus
Pro–64 F Hill
V'tors WD–I SOC WE/BH–M
Fees £14
Loc ¼ mile N of Blackwood

Caerleon (1974)
Pay and play
Broadway, Caerleon NP6 1AY
Tel (01633) 420342
Mem 150
Sec P John
Pro A Campbell
Holes 9 L 3092 yds SSS
Recs Pro–66 A Campbell
V'tors U
Fees 18 holes–£5 9 holes–£3.30
Loc M4 Junction 25, 3 miles
Mis Driving range
Arch Donald Steel

Celtic Manor Hotel G&CC (1995)
Coldra Woods, Newport NP6 1JQ
Tel (01633) 413000
Fax (01633) 410284
Mem 200
Sec M Lovett
Pro K Williams (01633) 410268
Holes 18 L 7001 yds Par 70 SSS 74
18 L 4094 yds Par 61 SSS 60
V'tors H SOC
Fees On application
Loc E of Newport on A48. M4 Junction 24
Mis Golf Academy. Driving range
Arch Robert Trent Jones Sr

For list of abbreviations see page 527

Monmouthshire

Dewstow (1988)
Caerwent, Newport NP6 4AH
- **Tel** (01291) 430444
- **Fax** (01291) 425816
- **Mem** 650
- **Sec** E Tose
- **Pro** M Kedward
- **Holes** Valley 18 L 6123 yds Par 72 SSS 70; Park 18 L 6147 yds SSS 69
- **Recs** Valley Am–73 P Collins (1994)
- **V'tors** WD–U WE–by arrangement SOC
- **Fees** £11 (£15)
- **Loc** Caerwent, 5 miles W of Severn Bridge, off A48
- **Mis** Driving range

Greenmeadow (1980)
Treherbert Road, Croesyceiliog, Cwmbran NP44 2BZ
- **Tel** (01633) 369321
- **Mem** 430
- **Sec** PJ Richardson
- **Pro** C Coombs (01633) 362626
- **Holes** 15 L 5593 yds SSS 68
- **Recs** Am–66 M Challinger (1989) Pro–66 C Jenkins (1987)
- **V'tors** U SOC
- **Fees** On application
- **Loc** 4 miles N of Newport on B4042. M4 Junction 26

Llanwern (1928)
Tennyson Avenue, Llanwern, Newport NP6 2DY
- **Tel** (01633) 412380
- **Fax** (01633) 412029
- **Mem** 776
- **Sec** DJ Peak (01633) 412029
- **Pro** S Price (01633) 413233
- **Holes** 18 L 6115 yds SSS 69
- **Recs** Am–63 B Dredge (1994) Pro–64 S Dodd (1992)
- **V'tors** WD–U WE–restricted I H SOC
- **Fees** WD–£20
- **Loc** 1 mile S of M4 Junction 24

Monmouth (1896)
Leasebrook Lane, Monmouth NP5 3SN
- **Tel** (01600) 712212/772399
- **Fax** (01600) 772399
- **Mem** 600
- **Sec** Mrs E Edwards
- **Pro** None
- **Holes** 18 L 5698 yds SSS 69
- **Recs** Am–68 R Williams (1995) Ladies–70 D Hill (1995)
- **V'tors** U SOC exc BH
- **Fees** £15 (£20)
- **Loc** Signposted 1 mile along A40 Monmouth-Ross road

Monmouthshire (1892)
Llanfoist, Abergavenny NP7 9HE
- **Tel** (01873) 852606
- **Fax** (01873) 852606
- **Mem** 555 107(L) 61(J)
- **Sec** R Bradley

- **Pro** (01873) 852532
- **Holes** 18 L 5978 yds SSS 70
- **Recs** Am–64 B Dredge (1990) Pro–62 D Thomas (1962)
- **V'tors** U H SOC
- **Fees** £25 (£30)
- **Loc** 2 miles SW of Abergavenny
- **Arch** James Braid

The Newport (1903)
Great Oak, Rogerstone, Newport NP1 9FX
- **Tel** (01633) 892643/894496
- **Fax** (01633) 896676
- **Mem** 800
- **Sec** JV Dinsdale (01633) 892643
- **Pro** PM Mayo (01633) 893271
- **Holes** 18 L 6431 yds SSS 71
- **Recs** Am–64 C Mayo (1993) Pro–62 L Bond (1994)
- **V'tors** WD–U H exc WE–MH
- **Fees** £30 (£40)
- **Loc** 3 miles W of Newport on B4591. M4 Junction 27, 1 mile

Oakdale (1990)
Pay and play
Llwynon Lane, Oakdale NP2 0NF
- **Tel** (01495) 220044
- **Sec** M Lewis (Dir)
- **Pro** C Coombs
- **Holes** 9 L 1235 yds Par 28
- **V'tors** U SOC
- **Fees** On application
- **Loc** 15 miles NW of Newport via A467/B4251. M4 Junction 28
- **Mis** Driving range
- **Arch** Ian Goodenough

Parc (1990)
Pay and play
Church Lane, Coedkernew, Newport NP1 9TU
- **Tel** (01633) 680933
- **Fax** (01633) 681011
- **Mem** 450
- **Sec** C Hicks (Mgr), M Cleary (Sec)
- **Pro** J Skuse (01633) 680955
- **Holes** 18 L 5512 yds SSS 67
- **Recs** Am–68 A Skidmore
- **V'tors** U SOC
- **Fees** £11 (£13)
- **Loc** 2 miles W of Newport on A48. M4 Junction 28
- **Mis** Floodlit driving range
- **Arch** B Thomas

Pontnewydd (1875)
West Pontnewydd, Cwmbran NP44 1AB
- **Tel** (01633) 482170
- **Mem** 250
- **Sec** HR Gabe (01633) 867185
- **Holes** 10 L 5353 yds SSS 67
- **Recs** Am–62 M Hayward
- **V'tors** WD–U WE–M SOC
- **Fees** £16
- **Loc** W outskirts of Cwmbran

Pontypool (1903)
Lasgarn Lane, Trevethin, Pontypool NP4 8TR
- **Tel** (01495) 763655
- **Mem** 607 68(L) 12(J)
- **Sec** PM Jones
- **Pro** J Howard (01495) 755544
- **Holes** 18 L 5963 yds SSS 69
- **Recs** Am–64 M Hayward (1982) NR Davies (1985) Pro–64 A Sherborne, M Plummer (1995)
- **V'tors** U H SOC
- **Fees** £20
- **Loc** 1 mile N of Pontypool (A4042)

Raglan Parc
Parc Lodge, Raglan NP5 2ER
- **Tel** (01291) 690077
- **Mem** 380
- **Sec** T Lillistone
- **Pro** C Evans
- **Holes** 18 L 6604 yds Par 73
- **Recs** Am–69 R Collett (1997)
- **V'tors** U
- **Fees** £15 (£15)
- **Loc** Nr A40/A449 junction

The Rolls of Monmouth (1982)
The Hendre, Monmouth NP5 4HG
- **Tel** (01600) 715353
- **Fax** (01600) 713115
- **Mem** 200
- **Sec** Mrs SJ Orton
- **Pro** None
- **Holes** 18 L 6733 yds SSS 73
- **Recs** Am–71 A Wills Pro–68 M Thomas (1983)
- **V'tors** U SOC
- **Fees** £32 (£37)
- **Loc** 3½ miles W of Monmouth on B4233

St Pierre (1962)
St Pierre Park, Chepstow NP6 6YA
- **Tel** (01291) 625261
- **Fax** (01291) 629975
- **Mem** 840
- **Sec** TJ Cleary
- **Pro** Shop (01291) 635205
- **Holes** 18 L 6818 yds SSS 74 18 L 5732 yds SSS 68
- **Recs** Old Am–69 N Van Hootegem Pro–64 JM Olazabal New Am–63 M Bearcroft
- **V'tors** H SOC–WD
- **Fees** On application
- **Loc** 2 miles W of Chepstow (A48)
- **Mis** Driving range
- **Arch** CK Cotton

Shirenewton (1995)
Shirenewton, Chepstow NP6 6RL
- **Tel** (01291) 641642
- **Fax** (01291) 641831
- **Sec** Miss K Evans
- **Pro** R Doig
- **Holes** 18 L 6820 yds Par 72 SSS 72
- **V'tors** U SOC

For list of abbreviations see page 527

728　Monmouthshire

Fees £12 (£15)
Loc 5 miles W of Chepstow, off B4235. M4 Junction 22

Tredegar & Rhymney (1921)
Tredegar, Rhymney NP2 3BQ
Tel (01685) 840743/843400
Fax (01685) 843440
Mem 204
Sec P Kenealy
Holes 9 L 5564 yds SSS 67
Recs Am–69 J Davies
V'tors U
Fees £10 (£12.50)
Loc 1½ miles W of Tredegar (B4256)

Tredegar Park (1923)
Bassaleg Road, Newport NP9 3PX
Tel (01633) 895219
Fax (01633) 897152
Mem 800
Sec RT Howell (01633) 894433
Pro ML Morgan (01633) 894517
Holes 18 L 6097 yds SSS 70
Recs Am–67 A Wesson
V'tors H
Fees D–£25 (D–£30)
Loc W of Newport, off M4 Junction 27
Mis Relocating to new course 1999

Wernddu Golf Centre
Old Ross Road, Abergavenny NP7 8NG
Tel (01873) 856223
Fax (01873) 852177
Mem 520
Sec DG Watkins
Pro AA Ashmead
Holes 18 L 5500 yds Par 68 SSS 67
Recs Am–64 I Chivers (1997)
V'tors U
Fees 9 holes–£10 18 holes–£15
Loc 1½ miles NE of Abergavenny on B4521
Mis Floodlit driving range

West Monmouthshire (1906)
Golf Road, Pond Road, Nantyglo NP3 4QT
Tel (01495) 310233/311361
Fax (01495) 311361
Mem 600
Sec SE Williams (01495) 310233
Holes 18 L 6118 yds SSS 69
Recs Am–66 D Phillips (1994) Pro–64 C Evans (1998)
V'tors WD/Sat–U Sun–M SOC–WD
Fees £18
Loc Nr Dunlop Semtex, off Brynmawr Bypass, towards Winchestown
Arch Ben Sayers

Woodlake Park (1993)
Glascoed, Usk NP4 0TE
Tel (01291) 673933
Fax (01291) 673811
Mem 450

Sec MJ Wood
Pro A Pritchard (01291) 671043
Holes 18 L 6300 yds Par 71 SSS 72
Recs Am–67 R Price (1997) Pro–67 M Wootton (1994) Ladies–73 C Cole (1997)
V'tors H SOC
Fees Summer–£20 (£20) Winter–£15 (£20)
Loc 3 miles W of Usk, nr Llandegfedd reservoir

Pembrokeshire

Haverfordwest (1904)
Arnolds Down, Haverfordwest SA61 2XQ
Tel (01437) 763565
Fax (01437) 764143
Mem 800
Sec JH Solly (01437) 764523
Pro A Pile (01437) 768409
Holes 18 L 6005 yds SSS 69
Recs Am–63 R Scott (1997) Pro–64 AJ Pile (1995) Ladies–72 F Jones (1994)
V'tors U SOC
Fees £18 (£22)
Loc 1 mile E of Haverfordwest on A40

Milford Haven (1913)
Hubberston, Milford Haven SA72 3RX
Tel (01646) 692368
Fax (01646) 697762
Mem 380 65(L) 90(J)
Sec WS Brown
Pro (01646) 697762
Holes 18 L 6071 yds SSS 71
Recs Am–65 L Rees Pro–64 J Taylor
V'tors U SOC
Fees £15 (£20)
Loc W boundary of Milford Haven

Newport (Pembs) (1925)
Newport SA42 0NR
Tel (01239) 820244
Fax (01239) 820244
Mem 350
Sec R Dietrich
Pro C Parsons (01239) 615359
Holes 9 L 3089 yds SSS 68
Recs Am–67 A Evans
V'tors U SOC
Fees £15
Loc 2½ miles NW of Newport, towards Newport Beach
Arch James Braid

Priskilly Forest (1992)
Castle Morris, Haverfordwest SA62 5EH
Tel (01348) 840276
Sec P Evans
Holes 9 L 5712 yds Par 70 SSS 68
V'tors U SOC
Fees 9 holes–£7 18 holes–£10
Loc 2 miles off A40 at Letterston
Arch J Walters

St Davids City (1902)
Whitesands Bay, St Davids SA62 6PT
Tel (01437) 721751 (Clubhouse)
Mem 200
Sec CWJ Snushall (01437) 720312
Holes 9 L 6121 yds SSS 70
Recs Am–65 KB Walsh (1989)
V'tors U SOC
Fees D–£14
Loc 2 miles W of St Davids. 15 miles NW of Haverfordwest

South Pembrokeshire (1970)
Military Road, Pembroke Dock SA72 6SE
Tel (01646) 621453
Mem 350
Sec WD Owen (01646) 621453/621804
Pro None
Holes 18 L 5638 yds SSS 69
Recs Am–65 A Jones
V'tors U before 4.30pm SOC
Fees On application
Loc Pembroke Dock

Tenby (1888)
The Burrows, Tenby SA70 7NP
Tel (01834) 842787/842978
Mem 800
Sec JA Pearson (01834) 842978
Pro M Hawkey (01834) 844447
Holes 18 L 6450 yds SSS 71
Recs Am–65 M Peet
V'tors H SOC
Fees £25 (£30)
Loc Tenby, South Beach
Arch James Braid

Trefloyne (1996)
Trefloyne Park, Penally, Tenby SA70 7RG
Tel (01834) 842165
Mem 149
Pro S Laidler
Holes 18 L 6635 yds Par 71
V'tors U SOC
Fees £17.50 (£21.50)
Loc 1½ miles W of Tenby, off A4139 Pembroke road
Arch FH Gilman

Powys

Brecon (1902)
Newton Park, Llanfaes, Brecon LD3 8PA
Tel (01874) 622004
Mem 210
Sec DHE Roderick (01874) 625547
Holes 9 L 5256 yds SSS 66
Recs Am–61 R Dixon Pro–66 WO Moses
V'tors U SOC
Fees £10
Loc ½ mile W of Brecon on A40
Arch James Braid

For list of abbreviations see page 527

Builth Wells (1923)
Golf Club Road, Builth Wells LD2 3NF
Tel (01982) 553296
Fax (01982) 551064
Mem 425
Sec JN Jones
Pro R Truman
Holes 18 L 5376 yds SSS 67
Recs Am–65
V'tors U H SOC
Fees £15 D–£20 (£20 D–£25)
Loc W of Builth Wells on Llandovery road (A483)

Cradoc (1967)
Penoyre Park, Cradoc, Brecon LD3 9LP
Tel (01874) 623658
Fax (01874) 611711
Mem 750
Sec Mrs EG Price
Pro R Davies (01874) 625524
Holes 18 L 6331 yds SSS 72
Recs Am–65 DK Wood (1982)
V'tors U Sun–M SOC
Fees £20 (£25)
Loc 2 miles NW of Brecon, off B4520
Arch CK Cotton

Knighton (1913)
Little Ffrydd Wood, Knighton LD7 1EF
Tel (01547) 528646
Fax (01547) 529284
Mem 150
Sec AW Aspley (Hon)
Holes 9 L 5320 yds Par 68 SSS 66
Recs Am–66 M Caine, A Williams Pro–71 H Vardon
V'tors U SOC
Fees £8 (£10)
Loc SW of Knighton. 20 miles NE of Llandrindod Wells
Arch H Vardon

Llandrindod (1905)
Llandrindod Wells LD1 5NY
Tel (01597) 823873/822010
Fax (01597) 823873
Mem 420
Sec GR Harris
Pro None
Holes 18 L 5759 yds SSS 69
Recs Am–65 CJ Davies (1988)
V'tors U SOC
Fees £12 D–£15 (£18 D–£22)
Loc 1 mile E of Llandrindod Wells
Arch Harry Vardon

Machynlleth (1905)
Ffordd Drenewydd, Machynlleth SY20 8UH
Tel (01654) 702000
Mem 231
Holes 9 L 5726 yds SSS 67
Recs Am–65 Pro–65
V'tors U Sun–NA before 11.30am SOC
Fees £12 (£15)
Loc 1 mile E of Machynlleth, off A489

Rhosgoch (1991)
Rhosgoch, Builth Wells LD2 3JY
Tel (01497) 851251
Mem 150
Sec C Dance
Holes 9 L 4842 yds SSS 64
V'tors U SOC
Fees £7 (£10)
Loc 5 miles N of Hay-on-Wye

St Giles Newtown (1895)
Pool Road, Newtown SY16 3AJ
Tel (01686) 625844
Mem 350
Pro DP Owen
Holes 9 L 6012 yds SSS 70
Recs Am–67 F Costanzo Pro–64 AP Parkin
V'tors U SOC
Fees £12.50 (£15)
Loc 1 mile E of Newtown (A483). 14 miles SW of Welshpool

St Idloes (1920)
Penrhallt, Llanidloes SY18 6LG
Tel (01686) 412559
Fax (01926) 889536
Mem 292
Sec JC Green
Pro P Parkin
Holes 9 L 5510 yds SSS 66
Recs Am–63 J Davies
V'tors U H Sun–restricted SOC
Fees £10 (£12) W–£45
Loc ½ mile from Llanidloes on Trefeglwys road (B4569)

Welsh Border Golf Complex (1991)
Bulthy Farm, Bulthy, Middletown SY21 8ER
Tel (01743) 884247
Mem 200
Sec J Watt
Pro A Griffiths
Holes 9 L 3050 yds SSS 72 9 hole Par 3 course
V'tors U SOC
Fees £14
Loc Between Shrewsbury and Welshpool on A458
Mis Driving range
Arch A Griffiths

Welshpool (1929)
Golfa Hill, Welshpool SY21 9AQ
Tel (01938) 83249
Mem 500
Sec DB Pritchard (01938) 552215
Pro None
Holes 18 L 5708 yds SSS 69
Recs Am–65 DH Ryan Pro–69 S Bowen
V'tors U H
Fees £10 (£20)
Loc 4½ miles W of Welshpool, on Dolgellau road (A458)
Arch James Braid

South Glamorgan

Brynhill (1921)
Port Road, Barry CF62 8PN
Tel (01446) 735061
Mem 700
Sec P Gershenson (01446) 720277
Pro P Fountain (01446) 733660
Holes 18 L 5947 yds SSS 70
Recs Am–65 C O'Carroll, N Caulfield Ladies–62 A Phillips (1990)
V'tors WD/Sat–H Sun–NA SOC–WD
Fees £20 Sat–£25 SOC–£17
Loc A4050, 8 miles SW of Cardiff

Cardiff (1921)
Sherborne Avenue, Cyncoed, Cardiff CF2 6SJ
Tel (01222) 753067
Fax (01222) 680011
Mem 930
Sec K Lloyd (01222) 753320
Pro T Hanson (01222) 754772
Holes 18 L 6015 yds SSS 70
Recs Am–65 SP Jones
V'tors WD–H WE–M SOC–Thurs
Fees £30 (£35)
Loc 3 miles N of Cardiff. 2 miles W of Pentwyn exit of A48(M). M4 Junction 29

Cottrell Park (1996)
St Nicholas, Cardiff CF5 6JY
Tel (01446) 781781
Fax (01446) 781707
Mem 1050
Sec F McAllister
Pro M Pycroft
Holes 18 L 6606 yds Par 72 SSS 72 9 L 2807 yds Par 70 SSS 67
Recs Am–71 S Pitt (1997) Pro–67 P Mayo (1997)
V'tors U SOC–Mon & Tues
Fees 18 hole:£22.50 (£30) 9 hole:£11.25 (£15)
Loc 4 miles W of Cardiff on A48. M4 Junction 33
Mis Driving range
Arch Bob Sandow

Dinas Powis (1914)
Old Highwalls, Dinas Powis CF64 4AJ
Tel (01222) 512727
Fax (01222) 512727
Mem 490
Sec HL Williams
Pro G Bennett (01222) 513682
Holes 18 L 5486 yds SSS 67
Recs Am–65 P Davidson Pro–67 P Fountain
V'tors H SOC
Fees D–£25 (£30)
Loc 3 miles SW of Cardiff (A4055)

Glamorganshire (1890)
Lavernock Road, Penarth CF64 5UP
Tel (01222) 701185
Fax (01222) 701185

For list of abbreviations see page 527

730 South Glamorgan

Mem 700
Sec AM Reed-Gibbs
(01222) 701185
Pro A Kerr-Smith
(01222) 707401
Holes 18 L 6181 yds SSS 70
Recs Am–65 MG Mouland (1979),
N Grimmitt (1989),
B Rigby (1997)
Pro–65 A Jacklin (1969)
V'tors WD/WE–H SOC
Fees £30 (£35)
Loc 5 miles SW of Cardiff

Llanishen (1905)
Cwm, Lisvane, Cardiff CF4 5UD
Tel (01222) 752205
Fax (01222) 755078
Mem 700
Sec PH Plumb (Sec/Mgr)
(01222) 755078
Pro RA Jones (01222) 755076
Holes 18 L 5296 yds SSS 66
Recs Am–63 B Townley (1994)
Pro–63 JT Taylor
V'tors WD–U WE–M H
SOC–Thurs & Fri
Fees £24
Loc 5 miles N of Cardiff

Peterstone
Peterstone, Wentloog, Cardiff CF3 8TN
Tel (01633) 680009
Fax (01633) 680563
Email peterstone@vapro.net
Mem 700
Sec R Williams
Pro D Griffiths
Holes 18 L 6555 yds Par 72 SSS 72
Recs Am–67 A Harrhy
V'tors U SOC–WD
Fees £18
Loc 3 miles S of Castleton,
off A48. M4 Junction 28
Arch Robert Sandow

Radyr (1902)
Drysgol Road, Radyr, Cardiff CF4 8BS
Tel (01222) 842408
Fax (01222) 843914
Mem 880
Sec AM Edwards (Mgr)
Pro R Butterworth
(01222) 842476
Holes 18 L 6031 yds SSS 70
Recs Am–62 C Evans
Pro–63 PW Evans, JD Grundy
V'tors WD–H WE–M
SOC–Wed/Thurs/Fri
Fees D–£34
Loc 5 miles NW of Cardiff,
off A470. M4 Junction 32

RAF St Athan (1977)
St Athan, Barry CF62 4WA
Tel (01446) 751043
Mem 450
Sec PF Woodhouse (01446)
797186
Pro N Gillette (01446) 751043

Holes 9 L 6452 yds SSS 72
V'tors U exc Sun am–NA
Fees £10 (£15)
Loc 2 miles E of Llantwit Major.
10 miles S of Bridgend

St Andrews Major (1993)
Coldbrook Road, Cadoxton, Barry CF6 3BB
Tel (01446) 722227
Mem 350
Sec N Edmunds
Holes 9 L 2931 yds
V'tors U SOC
Fees 9 holes–£8 18 holes–£13
Loc Barry Docks Link road. M4
Junction 33
Arch MRM Leisure

St Mary's Hotel G&CC (1990)
Pay and play
St Mary's Hill, Pencoed CF35 5EA
Tel (01656) 860280/861100
Fax (01656) 863400
Mem 750
Sec Kay Brazell (01656) 861100
Pro J Peters (01656) 861599
Holes 18 L 5273 yds Par 69 SSS 68
9 L 2426 yds Par 35 SSS 34
Recs Am–63 L Janes (1996)
Pro–64 R Troake
V'tors H SOC–WD
Fees 18 hole:£14 (£16)
9 hole:£4 (£5)
Loc Off M4 Junction 35
Mis Floodlit driving range

St Mellons (1937)
St Mellons, Cardiff CF3 8XS
Tel (01633) 680401
Fax (01633) 681219
Mem 500 93(L) 70(J)
Sec Mrs K Newling
(01633) 680408
Pro B Thomas (01633) 680101
Holes 18 L 6225 yds SSS 70
Recs Am–67 S Hopkins
Pro–66 E Foster
V'tors WD–U WE–M
Fees £32
Loc 4 miles E of Cardiff on A48

Vale of Glamorgan G&CC
Hensol Park, Hensol CF7 8JY
Tel (01443) 222221
Fax (01443) 222220
Mem 900
Sec Mrs G Golding
Pro P Johnson
Holes Lake 18 L 6507 yds Par 72
Hensol L 3115 yds Par 36
Recs Pro–67 G Ryall
V'tors H SOC
Fees £25 (£30)
Loc 1 mile from M 4 Junction 34
Mis Driving range. Golf Academy
Arch Peter Johnson

Wenvoe Castle (1936)
Wenvoe, Cardiff CF5 6BE
Tel (01222) 591094
Fax (01222) 594371
Mem 540 100(L) 66(J)
Sec N Sims (01222) 594371
Pro J Harris (01222) 593649
Holes 18 L 6422 yds SSS 71
Recs Am–68 N Jones (1989)
Pro–66 PW Evans (1990)
V'tors WD–H WE/BH–M
SOC–WD
Fees £24
Loc 4 miles W of Cardiff,
off A4050

Whitchurch (1915)
Pantmawr Road, Whitchurch, Cardiff CF4 6XD
Tel (01222) 620125
Fax (01222) 529860
Mem 780
Sec JW King
(01222) 620985
Pro E Clark
(01222) 614660
Holes 18 L 6321 yds Par 71 SSS 71
Recs Am–63 B Dredge (1992)
Pro–62 I Woosnam (1986)
V'tors WD–U WE/BH–M H
SOC–Thurs
Fees £30 (£35)
Loc 3 miles NW of Cardiff
on A470. M4 Junction 32

West Glamorgan

Allt-y-Graban (1993)
Allt-y-Graban Road, Pontlliw, Swansea SA4 1DT
Tel (01792) 885757
Mem 154
Sec Mrs M Lewis (Mgr)
Pro S Rees
Holes 9 L 2210 yds Par 66 SSS 63
V'tors U SOC
Fees 18 holes–£9 (£9)
9 holes–£6 (£6)
Loc 3 miles of M4 Junction 47,
on A48
Arch FG Thomas

Clyne (1920)
120 Owls Lodge Lane, Mayals, Swansea SA3 5DP
Tel (01792) 401989
Fax (01792) 401078
Mem 850
Sec RH Thompson FCA (Mgr)
Pro M Bevan
(01792) 402094
Holes 18 L 6334 yds SSS 71
Recs Am–66 C Dickens(1982)
Pro–64 M Bevan (1990)
V'tors U H SOC
Fees £25 (£30)
Loc 3 miles SW of Swansea
Mis Driving range
Arch Colt/Harris

For list of abbreviations see page 527

Earlswood (1993)
Pay and play
Jersey Marine, Neath SA10 6JP
Tel (01792) 321578
Sec Mrs D Goatcher
 (01792) 812198
Pro M Day
Holes 18 L 5174 yds SSS 68
V'tors U SOC
Fees £8
Loc 5 miles E of Swansea (B4290)

Fairwood Park (1969)
Blackhills Lane, Upper Killay, Swansea SA2 7JN
Tel (01792) 203648
Fax (01792) 297849
Mem 650
Sec J Beer, J Pettifer (Mgr)
Pro G Hughes (01792) 299194
Holes 18 L 6741 yds SSS 72
Recs Am–69 R Maliphant,
 I Roberts (1989)
 Pro–67 J Lomas (1989),
 A Griffiths, M Wooton (1990)
V'tors U SOC
Fees £25 (£30)
Loc 4 miles W of Swansea
 (A4118)
Arch Hawtree

Glynneath (1931)
Penycraig, Pontneathvaughan, Glynneath SA11 5UH
Tel (01639) 720452
Mem 640
Sec RM Ellis (01639) 720679
Holes 18 L 5707 yds SSS 68
Recs Am–65 N Williams
 Pro–66 P Mayo
V'tors WD–U H WE–M SOC–WD
Fees £15 (£18)
Loc 2 miles NW of Glynneath
 on B4242. 15 miles NE of
 Swansea
Arch Cotton/Pennink/Lawrie

Gower
Cefn Goleu, Three Crosses, Gowerton, Swansea SA4 3HS
Tel (01792) 872480
Fax (01792) 872480
Mem 300
Holes 18 L 6450 yds Par 71 SSS 72
Recs Am–71 R Maliphant (1998)
V'tors U
Fees £15 (£17)
Loc 5 miles W of Swansea,
 off B4295
Mis Driving range
Arch Donald Steel

Inco (1965)
Clydach, Swansea SA6 5EU
Tel (01792) 844216
Mem 380
Sec DGS Murdoch
 (01792) 843336
Holes 18 L 6064 yds SSS 69
V'tors U
Fees On application
Loc N of Swansea (A4067)

Lakeside (1992)
Pay and play
Water Street, Margam, Port Talbot SA13 2PA
Tel (01639) 899959
Mem 250
Sec G Hanbury
Pro M Wootton
Holes 18 L 4390 yds Par 62 SSS 63
Recs Am–65 R Clarke (1997)
 Pro–61 M Wootton (1997)
V'tors U SOC
Fees £9.50
Loc Nr M4 Junction 38
Mis Driving range
Arch M Wootton

Langland Bay (1904)
Langland, Swansea SA3 4QR
Tel (01792) 366023
Fax (01792) 361082
Mem 700
Sec PLE Wilkins (01792) 361721
Pro M Evans (01792) 366186
Holes 18 L 5830 yds SSS 69
Recs Am–63 K Jones,
 S Dodd (1989)
 Pro–66 J Lee
V'tors U H SOC
Fees £28 (£30)
Loc 6 miles S of Swansea (A4067)

Morriston (1919)
160 Clasemont Road, Morriston, Swansea SA6 6AJ
Tel (01792) 771079
Fax (01792) 796528
Mem 425
Sec WA Jefford (Sec/Mgr),
 R Kelly (01792) 796528
Pro DA Rees (01792) 772335
Holes 18 L 5785 yds SSS 68
Recs Am–61 M Gorvett (1994)
 Pro–64 DA Rees
V'tors U H SOC–WD
Fees £21 (£30)
Loc 4 miles N of Swansea on A48.
 M4 Junction 46, 1 mile

Neath (1934)
Cadoxton, Neath SA10 8AH
Tel (01639) 643615
Mem 520
Sec DM Hughes (01639) 632759
Pro EM Bennett (01639) 633693
Holes 18 L 6500 yds SSS 72
Recs Am–66 AL Cooper (1993)
 Pro–66 F Hill
V'tors WD–U WE–M SOC
Fees £20
Loc 2 miles NE of Neath (B4434)
Arch James Braid

Palleg (1930)
Palleg Road, Lower Cwmtwrch, Swansea Valley SA9 2QQ
Tel (01639) 842193
Mem 250
Sec B Evans
Pro Sharon Roberts
 (01639) 845728
Holes 9 L 3209 yds SSS 72
Recs Am–70 J Smith (1996),
 C Evans (1997)
V'tors WD–U Sat–NA
 Sun/BH–phone first SOC
Fees On application
Loc 15 miles NE of Swansea
 (A4067). M4 Junction 45

Pennard (1896)
2 Southgate Road, Southgate, Swansea SA3 2BT
Tel (01792) 233131
Fax (01792) 234797
Email pigeon01@globalnet.co.uk
Mem 775
Sec EM Howell (01792) 233131
Pro MV Bennett (01792) 233451
Holes 18 L 6265 yds SSS 72
Recs Am–68 D Evans
 Pro–68 A Beal (1995)
V'tors U H SOC–WD only
Fees £24 (£30) W–£80
Loc 8 miles W of Swansea, by
 A4067 and B4436

Pontardawe (1924)
Cefn Llan, Pontardawe, Swansea SA8 4SH
Tel (01792) 863118
Fax (01792) 830041
Mem 610
Sec CR Hopkin (Hon),
 Mrs M Griffiths (Admin)
Pro G Hopkins (01792) 830977
Holes 18 L 6038 yds SSS 70
Recs Am–64 B Fisher (1993)
 Pro–71 D Thomas, R Brook
V'tors H SOC–WD
Fees £20
Loc 5 miles N of M4 Junction 45,
 off A4067

Swansea Bay (1892)
Jersey Marine, Neath SA10 6JP
Tel (01792) 812198
Mem 400
Sec Mrs D Goatcher
 (01792) 814153
Pro M Day (01792) 816159
Holes 18 L 6605 yds SSS 72
Recs Am–71 C Smith
V'tors U SOC
Fees £16 (£22)
Loc 5 miles E of Swansea,
 off A483

Wrexham

Chirk (1990)
Chirk, Wrexham LL14 5AD
Tel (01691) 774407
Fax (01691) 773878
Mem 850
Sec FA Barnes
Pro M Maddison
Holes 18 L 7045 yds Par 72 SSS 73
 9 hole Par 3 course
Recs Am–70 P Grimley (1997)
V'tors U after 10am SOC

For list of abbreviations see page 527

Fees £18 D–£25 (£25 D–£30)
Loc 8 miles S of Wrexham on A483
Mis Driving range

Clays Farm (1992)
Bryn Estyn Road, Wrexham LL13 9UB
Tel (01978) 661406
Mem 410
Pro D Larvin
Holes 18 L 5775 yds Par 67
V'tors U SOC
Fees £14 (£18)
Loc Wrexham, off A534

Moss Valley (1990)
Pay and play
Moss Road, Wrexham LL11 4UR
Tel (01978) 720518
Mem 100
Sec C Davies
Holes 9 L 2724 yds Par 70 SSS 66
V'tors U
Fees £4 (£5)
Loc N of Wrexham, off A541

Pen-y-Cae (1993)
Ruabon Road, Pen-y-Cae, Wrexham LL14 1TW
Tel (01978) 810108
Mem 100
Sec G Williams (Mgr)
Pro S Hubbard
Holes 9 L 4280 yds Par 64 SSS 62
V'tors U SOC–WD
Fees 9 holes–£5 (£6)
18 holes–£7.50 (£9.50)
Loc 6 miles S of Wrexham, via A483/A539
Arch John Day

Plassey (1992)
The Plassey, Eyton, Wrexham LL13 0SP
Tel (01978) 780020
Mem 100
Sec V Cliffe, G Hughes (Prop)
Holes 9 L 2308 yds Par 32
V'tors U SOC
Fees £8
Loc 2 miles SW of Wrexham, off A483
Mis Driving range. Pitch & putt
Arch K Williams

Wrexham (1906)
Holt Road, Wrexham LL13 9SB
Tel (01978) 261033
Fax (01978) 364268
Mem 650
Sec JR Scott (01978) 364268
Pro R Young (01978) 351476
Holes 18 L 6233 yds Par 70 SSS 70
Recs Am–64 M Ellis (1995)
Pro–66 SJ Edwards (1993)
V'tors H SOC–WD
Fees £25 (£30)
Loc 2 miles NE of Wrexham on A534
Arch James Braid

Clubs and Courses in Continental Europe

Austria
Innsbruck & Tirol 734
Klagenfurt & South 734
Linz & North 734
Salzburg Region 735
Steiermark 736
Vienna & East 736
Vorarlberg 738

Belgium
Antwerp Region 738
Ardennes & South 738
Brussels & Brabant 739
East 740
West & Oost Vlaanderen 740

Czech Republic 741

Denmark
Bornholm Island 741
Funen 741
Greenland 742
Jutland 742
Zealand 744

Finland
Central 745
Helsinki & South 746
North 747
South East 747
South West 748

France
Bordeaux & South West 748
Brittany 749
Burgundy & Auvergne 751
Centre 752
Channel Coast & North 753
Corsica 755
Ile de France 755
Languedoc-Roussillon 757
Loire Valley 757
Normandy 759
North East 760
Paris Region 761
Provence & Côte d'Azur 762
Rhône-Alps 764
Toulouse & Pyrenees 765

Germany
Berlin & East 766
Bremen & North West 767
Central North 767
Central South 768
Hamburg & North 769
Hanover & Weserbergland 771
Munich & South Bavaria 772
Nuremberg & North Bavaria 774
Rhineland North 775
Rhineland South 777
Saar-Pfalz 778
Stuttgart & South West 778

Greece 780

Hungary 780

Iceland 780

Italy 781
Como/Milan/Bergamo 781
Elba 782
Emilia Romagna 782
Gulf of Genoa 783
Lake Garda & Dolomites 783
Naples & South 784
Rome & Centre 784
Sardinia 784
Turin & Piemonte 785
Tuscany & Umbria 786
Venice & North East 786

Luxembourg 787

Malta 787

Netherlands 787
Amsterdam & Noord Holland 787
Breda & South West 788
East Central 788
Eindhoven & South East 789
Limburg Province 790
North 790
Rotterdam & The Hague 790
Utrecht & Hilversum 791

Norway 792

Portugal
Algarve 793
Azores 794
Lisbon & Central Portugal 794
Madeira 795
North 795

Slovenia 795

Spain
Alicante & Murcía 796
Almería 796
Badajoz & West 797
Balearic Islands 797
Barcelona & Cataluña 797
Burgos & North 799
Canary Islands 799
Córdoba 800
Galicia 800
Granada 800
Madrid Region 800
Malaga Region 801
Marbella & Estepona 801
Seville & Gulf of Cádiz 802
Valencia & Castellón 803
Valladolid 803
Zaragoza 803

Sweden
East Central 804
Far North 805
Gothenburg 806
Malmö & South Coast 807
North 808
Skane & South 809
South East 810
South West 812
Stockholm 813
West Central 815

Switzerland
Bern 816
Bernese Oberland 816
Lake Geneva & South West 816
Lugano & Ticino 817
St Moritz & Engadine 817
Zürich & North 817

Turkey 818

For list of abbreviations see page 527

Austria

Innsbruck & Tirol

Achensee (1934)
6213 Pertisau/Achensee
Tel (05243) 5377
Fax (05243) 6202
Holes 18 L 5501 m SSS 70
V'tors U H
Fees 450s (520s)
Loc Pertisau, 50 km NE of Innsbruck

Innsbruck-Igls (1935)
6074 Rinn, Oberdorf 11
Tel (05223) 78177
Fax (05223) 78243
Holes Rinn 18 L 5945 m Par 71
Lans 9 L 4657 m Par 66
V'tors H–booking necessary
Fees 480s (600s)
Loc Rinn, 10 km E of Innsbruck.
Lans, 8 km from Innsbruck

Kaiserwinkl GC Kössen (1988)
6345 Kössen, Mühlau 1
Tel (05375) 2122
Fax (05375) 2122-13
Holes 18 L 5927 m SSS 72
V'tors H
Fees 550s (600s)
Loc 30 km N of Kitzbühel,
nr German border
Arch Donald Harradine

Kitzbühel (1955)
Schloss Kaps, 6370 Kitzbühel
Tel (05356) 63007
Fax (05356) 63007-7
Holes 9 L 6044 m Par 72
V'tors H
Fees 800s
Loc Kitzbühel
Arch J Morrison

Kitzbühel-Schwarzsee (1988)
6370 Kitzbühel, Golfweg Schwarzsee 35
Tel (05356) 71645
Fax (05356) 72785
Holes 18 L 6247 m SSS 72
V'tors H–booking necessary
Fees 650–750s
Loc 4 km from Kitzbühel
Arch G Hauser

Seefeld-Wildmoos (1968)
6100 Seefeld, Postfach 22
Tel (05212) 3003-0
Fax (05212) 3722-22
Holes 18 L 5967 m SSS 72
V'tors H–booking necessary

Fees 490–730s
Loc 7 km W of Seefeld. 24 km W of Innsbruck
Arch Donald Harradine

Klagenfurt & South

Austria-Wörther See
9062 Moosburg, Golfstr 2
Tel (04272) 83486
Fax (04272) 82055
Holes 18 L 6216 m SSS 72
Fees 550s
Loc 6 km N of Wörther See
Arch G Hauser

Bad Kleinkirchheim-Reichenau (1977)
9546 Bad Kleinkirchheim, Postfach 9
Tel (04275) 594
Fax (04275) 504
Holes 18 L 6084 m SSS 72
V'tors H
Fees 600s
Loc Kleinkirchheim, 50 km NW of Klagenfurt, via Route 95
Arch Donald Harradine

Kärntner (1927)
9082 Maria Wörth, Dellach 16
Tel (04273) 2515
Fax (04273) 2606
Holes 18 L 5778 m Par 71
V'tors H
Fees 600s (700s)
Loc Dellach, S side of Wörther See. 15 km W of Klagenfurt

Klopeiner See-Turnersee (1988)
9122 St Kanzian, Grabelsdorf 94
Tel (04239) 3800-0
Fax (04239) 3800-18
Holes 18 L 6114 m Par 72
V'tors U
Fees 600s
Loc 25 km E of Klagenfurt
Arch Donald Harradine

Wörther See/Velden (1988)
9231 Köstenberg, Oberdorf 70
Tel (04274) 7045/7087
Fax (04274) 708715
Holes 18 L 6152 m SSS 72
V'tors H
Fees 600s
Loc 30 km W of Klagenfurt.
12 km from Velden
Arch Erhardt/Rossknecht

Linz & North

Amstetten-Ferschnitz (1972)
3325 Ferschnitz, Gut Edla 18
Tel (07473) 8293
Fax (07473) 82934
Holes 9 L 5948 m SSS 70
V'tors U H
Fees 350s (450s)
Loc 70 km E of Linz
Arch McIntosh

Böhmerwald GC Ulrichsberg (1990)
4161 Ulrichsberg, Seitelschlag 50
Tel (07288) 8200
Fax (07288) 8422
Holes 18 L 6240 m SSS 73
9 hole Par 3 course
V'tors U H
Fees 470s (570s)
Loc 65 km NW of Linz
Arch Rossknecht/Erhardt

Herzog Tassilo (1991)
Blankenbergerstr 30, 4540 Bad Hall
Tel (07258) 5480
Fax (07258) 5480
Holes 18 L 5710 m SSS 70
V'tors U
Fees 450s (550s)
Loc 30 km SW of Linz
Arch Peter Mayerhofer

Kremstal (1989)
Schachen 20, 4531 Kematen/Krems
Tel (07228) 7644-0
Fax (07228) 7644-7
Holes 18 L 5763 m Par 70
V'tors H
Fees 450s (550s)
Loc 20 km W of Linz
Arch Peter Mayerhofer

Linz-St Florian (1960)
4490 St Florian, Tillysburg 28
Tel (07223) 828730
Fax (07223) 828737
Holes 18 L 6091 m Par 72 SSS 72
V'tors H
Fees 600s (780s)
Loc St Florian, 15 km SE of Linz
Arch Donald Harradine

Maria Theresia (1989)
Letten 5, 4680 Haag am Hausruck
Tel (07732) 3944
Fax (07732) 3944-9
Holes 18 L 6055 m Par 72 SSS 72
V'tors H
Fees 450s (550s)
Loc Between Passau and Wels. A8 exit Haag
Arch Angst/Stärk

For list of abbreviations see page 527

Austria 735

Mühlviertel (1990)
4222 St Georgen, Am Luftenberg 1
Tel (07237) 3893
Fax (07237) 3893
Holes 18 L 5864 m Par 71 SSS 72
V'tors U H
Fees 500s (600s)
Loc 15 km NE of Linz
Arch Keith Preston

Ottenstein (1988)
3532 Niedergrünbach 60
Tel (02826) 7476
Fax (02826) 7476-4
Holes 18 L 6172 m SSS 72
V'tors U
Fees 600s (700s)
Loc 90 km NE of Linz. 100 km NW of Vienna
Arch Preston/Zinterl/Erhardt

St Oswald-Freistadt
(1988)
Promenade 22, 4271 St Oswald
Tel (07945) 7938
Fax (07945) 79384
Holes 9 L 5888 m Par 72
V'tors WD–UH WE–U H restricted
Fees 350s (450s)
Loc 40 km N of Linz
Arch Mel Flanegan

St Pölten Schloss Goldegg (1989)
3100 St Pölten Schloss Goldegg
Tel (02741) 7360/7060
Fax (02741) 73608
Holes 18 L 6249 m SSS 73
V'tors H or I
Fees 400s (500s)
Loc 8 km NW of St Pölten. 60 km W of Vienna

Schloss Ernegg (1973)
3261 Steinakirchen, Schlosshotel Ernegg
Tel (07488) 76770, (07488) 71214 (May-Oct)
Fax (07488) 76771/71171
Holes 18 L 5699 m SSS 70 9 L 2076 m SSS 62
V'tors U
Fees 450s (550s)
Loc Steinakirchen, 60 km SE of Linz. 100 km W of Vienna
Arch Tucker/Day

Traunsee
4656 Kircham, Kampesberg 38
Tel (07619) 2576
Fax (07619) 2576-11
Holes 18 L 5714 m Par 70
V'tors U
Fees 450s (550s)
Loc 10 km E of Gmunden. 50 km SW of Linz

Waldviertel
3874 Haugschlag 160
Tel (02865) 8441
Fax (02865) 8441-22
Holes 18 L 6140 m SSS 72 18 hole Par 3 course
V'tors H
Fees 490s (600s)
Loc 25 km N of Gmund. 140 km NW of Vienna

Weitra (1989)
3970 Weitra, Hausschachen
Tel (02856) 2058
Fax (02856) 2058-4
Holes 18 L 5916 m Par 72
V'tors WD–U WE–H
Fees 450s (550s)
Loc 75 km NE of Linz, nr Czech border
Arch M Gansdorfer

Wels (1981)
4616 Weisskirchen, Weyerbach 37
Tel (07243) 56038
Fax (07243) 56685
Holes 18 L 6098 m Par 72
V'tors H
Fees 500s (600s)
Loc 5 km from Salzburg-Vienna highway. 8 km SE of Wels
Arch Hauser/Hunt Hastings

Salzburg Region

Bad Gastein (1960)
5640 Bad Gastein, Golfstrasse 6
Tel (06434) 2775
Fax (06434) 2775-4
Holes 9 L 5986 m SSS 72
V'tors H
Fees 390s (500s)
Loc Bad Gastein 2 km. Salzburg 100 km
Arch B von Limburger

Goldegg
5622 Goldegg, Postfach 6
Tel (06415) 8585
Fax (06415) 8585-4
Holes 18 L 4693 m Par 70
V'tors U
Fees 560s (630s)
Loc 60 km SW of Salzburg

Gut Altentann (1989)
Hof 54, 5302 Henndorf am Wallersee
Tel (06214) 6026-0
Fax (06214) 6105-81
Holes 18 L 6223 m SSS 72
V'tors H–booking necessary
Fees 750–850s
Loc Henndorf, 16 km NE of Salzburg
Arch Jack Nicklaus

Gut Brandlhof G&CC
(1983)
5760 Saalfelden am Steinernen Meer, Hohlwegen 4
Tel (06582) 7800-555
Fax (06582) 7800-529
Holes 18 L 6218 m SSS 72
V'tors I H
Fees 550s (650s)
Loc Saalfelden, 70 km SW of Salzburg towards Zell am See
Arch Kofler

Kobernausserwald
5242 St Johann a. Walde, Strass 1
Tel (07743) 2719
Fax (07743) 2719
Holes 18 L 5963 m Par 71 SSS 71
V'tors U
Fees 200s (350s)
Loc 30 km E of Salzburg
Arch Heinz Schmidbauer

Lungau/Katschberg
(1991)
5582 St Michael, Postfach 44
Tel (06477) 7448
Fax (06477) 7448-4
Holes 18 L 6132 m Par 72 9 L 2502 m Par 56
V'tors U
Fees 520s (620s)
Loc St Michael, 120 km S of Salzburg
Arch Keith Preston

Am Mondsee (1986)
St Lorenz 400, 5310 Mondsee
Tel (06232) 3835-0
Fax (06232) 3835-83
Holes 18 L 6036 m SSS 72
V'tors H
Fees 550s (650s)
Loc Mondsee, 25 km E of Salzburg
Arch Marc Miller

Radstadt Tauerngolf
(1990)
Römerstrasse 18, 5550 Radstadt
Tel (06452) 5111
Fax (06452) 7336
Holes 18 L 6023 m Par 71 9 hole Par 3 course
V'tors U
Fees 560s (660s)
Loc 70 km NW of Salzburg

Salzburg Fuschl (1995)
5322 Hof/Salzburg
Tel (06229) 2390
Fax (06229) 2390
Holes 9 L 3650 m Par 62 9 hole Par 3 course
V'tors U
Fees 300–400s
Loc Hof, 12 km E of Salzburg

For list of abbreviations see page 527

Salzburg Klesheim (1955)
5071 Wals bei Salzburg, Schloss Klesheim
Tel (0662) 850851
Holes 9 L 5700 m SSS 70
V'tors U H
Fees 450s (450s)
Loc 5 km N of Salzburg

Salzkammergut (1933)
4820 Bad Ischl, Postfach 506
Tel (06132) 26340
Fax (06132) 26708
Holes 18 L 5890 m Par 72
V'tors U
Fees 500 (600s)
Loc 6 km W of Bad Ischl, nr Strobl. 50 km E of Salzburg

Urslautal (1991)
Schinking 1, 5760 Saalfelden
Tel (06584) 2000
Fax (06584) 7475-10
Holes 18 L 6030 m SSS 71
V'tors U H
Fees 620s (690s)
Loc 80 km SW of Salzburg
Arch Keith Preston

Zell am See-Kaprun (1983)
5700 Zell am See-Kaprun, Golfstr 25
Tel (06542) 56161
Fax (06542) 56161-16
Email gc_zellamsee_kaprun@aon.at www.golfnet.at/gczell/frames.htm
Holes 18 L 6218 m Par 72 SSS 72
       18 L 6146 m Par 73 SSS 72
V'tors H
Fees 650s (750s)
Loc Zell am See, 80 km SW of Salzburg
Arch Donald Harradine

Steiermark

Bad Gleichenberg (1984)
Am Hoffeld 3, 8344 Bad Gleichenberg
Tel (03159) 3717
Fax (03159) 3065
Holes 9 L 5904 m Par 72 SSS 72
V'tors H
Fees 350s (450s)
Loc 60 km NW of Graz
Arch Hauser

Dachstein Tauern (1990)
8967 Haus/Ennstal, Oberhaus 59
Tel (03686) 2630
Fax (03686) 2630-15
Holes 18 L 5910 m SSS 71
V'tors U
Fees 650s (750s)
Loc 2 km from Schladming. 100 km SE of Salzburg
Arch Bernhard Langer

Ennstal-Weissenbach G&LC (1978)
8940 Liezen, Postfach 193
Tel (03612) 24821
Fax (03612) 24821-4
Holes 18 L 5655 m SSS 70
V'tors U H I
Fees 450s (500s)
Loc 3 km SW of Liezen. 100 km SE of Salzburg
Arch Gert Aigner

Furstenfeld (1984)
8282 Loipersdorf, Gillersdorf 50
Tel (03382) 8533
Fax (03382) 8533-33
Holes 18 L 6192 m SSS 72
V'tors U
Fees 500s (600s)
Loc 70 km E of Graz

Graz (1989)
8051 Graz-Thal, Windhof 137
Tel (0316) 572867
Fax (0316) 572867-4
Holes 9 L 5229 m SSS 70
V'tors U
Fees 350–500s (550s)
Loc 10 km W of Graz
Arch Herwig Zisser

Gut Murstätten (1989)
8403 Lebring, Oedt 14
Tel (03182) 3555
Fax (03182) 3688
Holes 18 L 6398 m SSS 74
       9 L 3034 m SSS 72
V'tors H
Fees 550s (650s)
Loc 25 km S of Graz
Arch J Dudok van Heel

Maria Lankowitz (1992)
Puchbacher Str 109, 8591 Maria Lankowitz
Tel (03144) 6970
Fax (03144) 6970-4
Holes 18 L 6121 m SSS 72
V'tors U
Fees 430s (550s)
Loc 40 km W of Graz
Arch Herwig Zisser

Murhof (1963)
8130 Frohnleiten, Adriach 53
Tel (03126) 3010
Fax (03126) 3000-29
Holes 18 L 6198 m Par 72
V'tors U H
Fees 660s (860s)
Loc Frohnleiten, 25 km N of Graz. 150 km S of Vienna
Arch B von Limburger

Murtal (1995)
Frauenbachstr 51, 8724 Spielberg
Tel (03512) 75213
Fax (03512) 75213
Holes 18 L 6261 m Par 72

V'tors H I
Fees 480s (550s)
Loc Knittelfeld, 80 km NW of Graz, via Route S36
Arch Dietmar Allitsch

Reiting G&CC (1990)
8772 Traboch, Schulweg 7
Tel (0663) 833308/(03847) 5008
Fax (03847) 5682
Holes 9 L 6300 m Par 73 SSS 72
V'tors U
Fees 350s (390s)
Loc 60 km N of Graz

St Lorenzen (1990)
8642 St Lorenzen, Gassing 22
Tel (03864) 3961
Fax (03864) 3961-2
Holes 9 L 5374 m Par 70 SSS 70
V'tors U
Fees 300s (350s)
Loc 60 km N of Graz, nr Kapfenberg
Arch Manfred Flasch

Schloss Frauenthal (1988)
8530 Deutschlandsberg, Ulrichsberg 7
Tel (03462) 5717
Fax (03462) 5717-5
Holes 18 L 5447 m SSS 70
V'tors U H
Fees 500s (600s)
Loc 30 km SW of Graz
Arch Stephan Breisach

Schloss Pichlarn (1972)
8952 Irdning/Ennstal, Gatschen 28
Tel (03682) 24393
Fax (03682) 24393
Holes 18 L 6158 m Par 72
V'tors U
Fees 500s (650s)
Loc 2 km E of Irdning, off Salzburg-Graz road. 120 km SE of Salzburg
Arch Donald Harradine

Vienna & East

Adamstal (1994)
Gaupmannsgraben 21, 3172 Ramsal
Tel (02764) 3500
Fax (02764) 3500-15
Holes 9 L 4696-5326 m Par 70 (18 holes from July 1998)
V'tors U
Fees 400s (550s)
Loc 65 km SW of Vienna
Arch Jeff Howes

Bad Tatzmannsdorf G&CC (1991)
Am Golfplatz 2, 7431 Bad Tatzmannsdorf
Tel (03353) 8282-0
Fax (03353) 8282-735

For list of abbreviations see page 527

Holes 18 L 6304 m SSS 73
       9 L 3660 m SSS 60
V'tors U H
Fees 18 hole:520s (650s)
     9 hole:350s (400s)
Loc 120 km SE of Vienna
Arch Rossknecht/Erhardt

Brunn G&CC (1988)
2345 Brunn/Gebirge, Rennweg 50
Tel (02236) 31572/33711
Fax (02236) 33863
Holes 18 L 6138 m Par 70 SSS 70
V'tors H
Fees 550s (650s)
Loc 10 km S of Vienna
Arch G Hauser

Colony Club Gutenhof (1988)
2325 Himberg, Gutenhof
Tel (02235) 87055-0
Fax (02235) 87055-14
Holes East 18 L 6335 m SSS 73
      West 18 L 6397 m SSS 73
V'tors H
Fees 500s (750s)
Loc 7 km SE of Vienna
Arch Rossknecht/Erhardt

Danube Golf-Wien (1995)
Weingartenallee 22, 1220 Wien
Tel (0222) 25072
Fax (0222) 25072-44
Holes 18 L 6130 m SSS 72
V'tors H
Fees 550s (550s)
Loc 15 km NE of Vienna
Arch Rossknecht/Erhardt

Enzesfeld (1970)
2551 Enzesfeld
Tel (02256) 81272
Fax (02256) 81272-4
Holes 18 L 6176 m SSS 72
V'tors H
Fees 500s (750s)
Loc 32 km S of Vienna. A2
    Junction 29 (Leobersdorf)
Arch John Harris

Föhrenwald (1968)
2700 Wiener Neustadt, Postfach 105
Tel (02622) 29171
Fax (02622) 25334
Holes 18 L 6043 m SSS 72
V'tors H
Fees 400s (500s)
Loc 5 km S of Wiener Neustadt on
    Route B54

Fontana (1996)
Fontana Allee 1,
2522 Oberwaltersdorf
Tel (02253) 606401
Fax (02253) 606403
Holes 18 L 6088 m Par 72

V'tors U–booking necessary. Soft
       spikes only
Fees 1000s (1300s)
Loc 20 km S of Vienna
Arch Carrick/Erhardt

Hainburg/Donau (1977)
2410 Hainburg, Auf der Heide 762
Tel (02165) 62628
Fax (02165) 65331
Holes 18 L 6064 m SSS 72
V'tors H
Fees 400s (600s)
Loc 50 km E of Vienna
Arch G Hauser

Lechner 'BN' (1990)
Pichl 1, 2871 Zöbern
Tel (02642) 8451
Fax (02642) 8451
Holes 9 L 4088m Par 64 SSS 63
V'tors H
Fees 300s (400s)
Loc 90 km S of Vienna via A2
Arch Anton Reithofer

Lengenfeld (1995)
Am Golfplatz 1, 3552 Lengenfeld
Tel (02719) 8710
Fax (02719) 8738
Holes 18 L 6130 m Par 72
V'tors U
Fees 400s (500s)
Loc 80 km W of Vienna. Krems
    8 km

Neusiedlersee-Donnerskirchen (1988)
7082 Donnerskirchen
Tel (02683) 8171
Fax (02683) 817231
Holes 18 L 5937 m SSS 72
V'tors H
Fees 500s (500s)
Loc 45 km SE of Vienna
Arch Rossknecht-Erhardt

Schloss Ebreichsdorf (1988)
2483 Ebreichsdorf, Schlossallee 1
Tel (02254)73888
Fax (02254) 73888-13
Holes 18 L 6246 m SSS 72
V'tors WD–H WE–on request
Fees 500s (700s)
Loc 28 km S of Vienna
Arch Keith Preston

Schloss Schönborn (1987)
2013 Schönborn 4
Tel (02267) 2863/2879
Fax (02267) 2879-19
Holes 27 L 6265-6474 m
      Par 72-73

Austria 737

V'tors U H
Fees 600s (800s)
Loc 40 km N of Vienna

Schönfeld (1989)
A-2291 Schönfeld, Am Golfplatz 1
Tel (02213) 2063
Fax (02213) 20631
Holes 18 L 6175 m SSS 73
      9 hole Par 3 course
V'tors H
Fees 18 hole:500s (650s)
     9 hole:300s (400s)
Loc 35 km E of Vienna
Arch G Hauser

Semmering (1926)
2680 Semmering
Tel (02664) 8154
Fax (02664) 2114
Holes 9 L 3786 m SSS 60
V'tors H
Fees 350s (450s)
Loc 30 km SW of Vienna
    Neustadt

Thayatal Drosendorf (1994)
Autendorf 18, 2095 Drosendorf
Tel (02915) 2318
Fax (02915) 2318
Holes 18 L 4289 m Par 65
V'tors U
Fees 200s (400s)
Loc 100 km NW of Vienna,
    nr Czech border (B4)

Wien (1901)
1020 Wien, Freudenau 65a
Tel (0222) 728 9564 (Clubhouse),
    728 9667 (Caddymaster)
Fax (0222) 728 9564-20
Holes 18 L 5861 m SSS 71
V'tors WE–NA
Fees 800s
Loc 10 mins SE of Vienna

Wienerberg (1989)
1100 Wien, Gutheil Schoder 9
Tel (0222) 66123-7000
Fax (0222) 66123-7789
Holes 9 L 5710 m SSS 70
V'tors H
Fees 500s
Loc Vienna District 10
Arch G Hauser

Wienerwald (1981)
1130 Wien, Altgasse 27
Tel (0222) 877 3111 (Sec)
Holes 9 L 4652 m SSS 65
V'tors H
Fees 300s (500s)
Loc Laaben, 35 km W of Vienna
Arch Herbert Illo Holy

For list of abbreviations see page 527

Austria

Vorarlberg

Bludenz-Braz (1996)
Oberradin 60, 6751 Braz bei Bludenz
Tel (05552) 33503
Fax (05552) 33503-3
Holes 13 L 5284 m Par 70
V'tors H
Fees D–380s (D–420s)
Loc 5 km E of Bludenz
Arch Maurice O'Fives

Bregenzerwald (1997)
Unterlitten 3a, 6943 Riefensberg
Tel (05513) 8400
Fax (05513) 8400-4
Holes 18 L 5702 m Par 71
V'tors U I
Fees 460s (590s)
Loc 32 km E of Bregenz. 150 km W of Zürich
Arch Kurt Rossknecht

Montafon (1992)
6774 Tschagguns, Zelfenstrasse
Tel (05556) 77011
Fax (05556) 77011
Holes 9 L 3708 m Par 62 SSS 60
V'tors U H
Fees 300s
Loc 60 km S of Lake Constance

Belgium

Antwerp Region

Bossenstein (1989)
Moor 16, Bossenstein Kasteel, 2520 Broechem
Tel (03) 485 64 46
Fax (03) 485 78 41
Holes 18 L 6203 m SSS 72
9 hole course
V'tors H
Fees 1000fr (1500fr)
Loc 15 km E of Antwerp. 5 km N of Lier
Arch Paul Rolin

Cleydael (1988)
Kasteel Cleydael, 2630 Aartselaar
Tel (03) 887 00 79/887 18 74
Fax (03) 887 00 15
Holes 18 L 6059 m SSS 72
V'tors H WE–NA before 2pm
Fees 1500fr (2000fr)
Loc 8 km S of Antwerp. 40 km N of Brussels
Arch Paul Rolin

Inter-Mol (1984)
Goorstraat, 2400 Mol
Tel (014) 57 12 85/45 05 09
Fax (014) 58 42 73
Holes 9 L 1493 m Par 28
V'tors H
Fees 400fr (600fr)
Loc Mol, 60 km E of Antwerp

Kempense (1986)
Kiezelweg 78, 2400 Mol
Tel (014) 81 46 41 (Clubhouse)
Fax (014) 81 62 78
Holes 18 L 5904 m Par 72
V'tors H
Fees 1200fr (1700fr)
Loc 60 km E of Antwerp
Arch Marc de Keyser

Lilse (1988)
Haarlebeek 3, 2275 Lille
Tel (014) 55 19 30
Fax (014) 55 19 31
Holes 9 L 2007 m Par 64
V'tors U
Fees 600fr (800fr)
Loc Lille, 10 km SW of Turnhout, nr E7. 25 km E of Antwerp

Rinkven G&CC (1980)
Sint Jobsteenweg 120, 2970 Schilde
Tel (03) 380 12 85
Fax (03) 384 29 33
Holes 27 hole course
V'tors H–phone before visit
Fees 1500fr (2500fr)
Loc 17 km NE of Antwerp, off E19

Royal Antwerp (1888)
Georges Capiaulei 2, 2950 Kapellen
Tel (03) 666 84 56
Fax (03) 666 44 37
Holes 18 L 6140 m SSS 73
9 L 2264 m SSS 33
V'tors WD–H (phone first)
Fees 2000–2500fr
Loc Kapellen, 20 km N of Antwerp
Arch Willie Park/T Simpson (1920)

Steenhoven (1985)
Steenhoven 89, 2400 Postel-Mol
Tel (014) 37 36 61
Fax (014) 37 36 62
Holes 18 L 5950 m SSS 71
V'tors H–booking necessary
Fees 1500fr (2500fr)
Loc 30 mins W of Antwerp
Arch Pierre de Broqueville

Ternesse G&CC (1976)
Uilenbaan 15, 2160 Wommelgem
Tel (03) 355 14 30
Fax (03) 355 14 35
Holes 18 L 5876 m SSS 72
9 hole course
V'tors H–30

Fees 1500fr (2500fr)
Loc 5 km E of Antwerp on E313
Arch HJ Baker

Ardennes & South

Andenne (1988)
Ferme du Moulin 52, Stud, 5300 Andenne
Tel (085) 84 34 04
Fax (085) 84 34 04
Holes 9 L 2447 m SSS 66
V'tors U
Fees 500fr (700fr)
Loc Andenne, 20 km E of Namur
Arch C Bertier

Château Royal d'Ardenne
Tour Léopold, Ardenne 6, 5560 Houyet
Tel (082) 66 62 28
Fax (082) 66 74 53
Holes 18 L 5363 m SSS 71
V'tors H
Fees 1200fr (1800fr)
Loc 9 km SE of Dinant on Rochefort road

Falnuée (1987)
Rue E Pirson 55, 5032 Mazy
Tel (081) 63 30 90
Fax (081) 63 37 64
Holes 18 L 5700 m SSS 70
V'tors U
Fees 900fr (1400fr)
Loc 18 km NW of Namur. Mons-Liège highway Junction 13
Arch J Jottrand

Five Nations CC
Ferme du Grand Scley, 5372 Méan
Tel (086) 32 32 32
Fax (086) 32 30 11
Holes 18 L 6066 m Par 72
V'tors U
Fees 1100fr (1500fr)
Loc 30 km S of Liège
Arch Gary Player

Mont Garni (1989)
Rue du Mont Garni 3, 7331 Saint Ghislain
Tel (065) 62 27 19
Fax (065) 62 34 10
Holes 18 L 6353 m Par 74
V'tors H
Fees 1000fr (1500fr)
Loc St Ghislain, 15 km W of Mons. 65 km SW of Brussels
Arch T Macauley

Rougemont
Chemin du Beau Vallon 45, 5170 Profondeville
Tel (081) 41 14 18
Fax (081) 41 21 42
Holes 18 L 5645 m Par 72

For list of abbreviations see page 527

Belgium

V'tors U
Fees 1000fr 91500fr)
Loc Profondeville, 10 km S of Namur

Royal GC du Hainaut
(1933)
Rue de la Verrerie 2, 7050 Erbisoeul
Tel (065) 22 96 10 (Clubhouse), (065) 22 94 74 (Sec)
Fax (065) 22 51 54
Holes 9 L 3117 m Par 36
9 L 2925 m Par 36
9 L 3218 m Par 36
V'tors U H (max 36)
Fees 1500fr (2000fr) (1998)
Loc 6 km NW of Mons towards Ath on N56. Paris-Brussels motorway Junction 23
Arch Martin Hawtree

Brussels & Brabant

Bercuit (1965)
Les Gottes 3, 1390 Grez-Doiceau
Tel (010) 84 15 01
Fax (010) 84 55 95
Holes 18 L 5986 m SSS 72
V'tors U H
Fees D–1450fr (2500fr)
Loc Grez-Doiceau, 27 km SE of Brussels. Brussels-Namur highway exit 8
Arch Robert Trent Jones Sr

Brabantse (1982)
Steenwagenstraat 11, 1820 Melsbroek
Tel (02) 751 82 05
Fax (02) 751 84 25
Holes 18 L 5266 m Par 70
V'tors H
Fees 1000fr (1500fr)
Loc 10 km NE of Brussels, nr airport
Arch Paul Rolin

La Bruyère (1988)
Rue Jumerée 1, 1495 Sart-Dames-Avelines
Tel (071) 87 72 67
Fax (071) 87 72 67
Holes 18 L 5937 m SSS 71
V'tors U
Fees 900fr (1300fr)
Loc 40 km S of Brussels towards Charleroi
Arch Theys

Château de la Bawette
(1988)
Chaussée du Château de la Bawette 5, 1300 Wavre
Tel (010) 22 33 32
Fax (010) 22 90 04
Holes Parc 18 L 6076 m SSS 72
Champs 9 L 2146 m SSS 63

V'tors H–booking required
Fees Parc–1400fr (2200fr)
Champs–1000fr (1500fr)
Loc 1 km N of Wavre. 20 km SE of Brussels. E411 Exit 5
Arch Tom Macauley

Château de la Tournette
Chemin de Baudemont 23, 1400 Nivelles
Tel (067) 89 42 66/89 42 68
Fax (067) 21 95 17
Holes 18 L 6031 m Par 72
18 L 6024 m Par 71
V'tors H
Fees 1200fr (2000fr)
Loc 29 km S of Brussels (E19)
Arch Alliss/Clark

L'Empereur (1989)
Rue Emile François 9, 1474 Ways (Genappe)
Tel (067) 77 15 71
Fax (067) 77 18 33
Holes 18 L 6037 m SSS 72
9 L 1600 m Par 31
V'tors U H
Fees 18 hole:1000fr (1900fr)
9 hole:700fr (900fr)
Loc 25 km S of Brussels
Arch Marcel Vercruyce

Hulencourt (1989)
Bruyère d'Hulencourt 15, 1472 Vieux Genappe
Tel (067) 79 40 40
Fax (067) 79 40 48
Holes 18 L 6215 m Par 72
9 hole Par 3 course
V'tors H–max 28
Fees 1500fr (2500fr)
Loc 30 km S of Brussels
Arch JE Rossi

Kampenhout (1989)
Wildersedreef 56, 1910 Kampenhout
Tel (016) 65 12 16
Fax (016) 65 16 80
Holes 18 L 6142 m SSS 72
V'tors H
Fees 1000fr (1500fr)
Loc 15 km NE of Brussels (E19)
Arch R de Vooght

Keerbergen (1968)
Vlieghavelaan 50, 3140 Keerbergen
Tel (015) 23 49 61
Fax (015) 23 57 37
Holes 18 L 5503 m SSS 70
V'tors H
Fees 1100fr (1500fr)
Loc 30 km NE of Brussels
Arch Frank Pennink

Louvain-la-Neuve
Rue A Hardy 68, 1348 Louvain-la-Neuve
Tel (010) 45 05 15
Fax (010) 45 44 17
Holes 18 L 6226 m Par 72

V'tors U
Fees 1200fr (2000fr)
Loc 20 km SE of Brussels, off E411
Arch J Dudok van Heel

Overijse
Gemslaan 55, 3090 Overijse
Tel (02) 687 50 30
Fax (02) 687 37 68
Holes 9 L 5723 m Par 71
V'tors H
Fees 800fr (1500fr)
Loc 10 km S of Brussels
Arch Rossi

Pierpont (1992)
1 Grand Pierpont, 6210 Frasnes-lez-Gosselies
Tel (071) 85 17 75/85 14 19
Fax (071) 85 15 43
Holes 18 L 6257 m Par 72
5 hole Par 3 course
V'tors U
Fees 800fr (1800fr)
Loc 30 km S of Brussels via N5
Arch J Dudok van Heel

Rigenée (1981)
Rue de Châtelet 62, 1495 Villers-la-Ville
Tel (071) 87 77 65
Fax (071) 87 77 83
Holes 18 L 6031 m SSS 73
V'tors H
Fees 1100fr (1800fr)
Loc 35 km S of Brussels towards Charleroi
Arch Rolin/Descampe

Royal Amicale Anderlecht (1987)
Rue Scholle 1, 1070 Bruxelles
Tel (02) 521 16 87
Fax (02) 521 51 56
Holes 18 L 5320 m Par 71 SSS 69
V'tors H
Fees 1200fr (1800fr)
Loc SW Brussels

Royal Golf Club de Belgique (1906)
Château de Ravenstein, 3080 Tervuren
Tel (02) 767 58 01
Fax (02) 767 28 41
Holes 18 L 6075 m SSS 72
9 L 1960 m Par 32
V'tors H–max 20(men)
24(ladies)–phone first. Course closed Mon
Fees 2000fr (3000fr)
Loc Tervuren, 10 km E of Brussels
Arch Simpson

Royal Waterloo (1923)
Vieux Chemin de Wavre 50, 1380 Ohain
Tel (02) 633 18 50/633 15 97
Fax (02) 633 28 66

For list of abbreviations see page 527

Belgium

Holes 18 L 6211 m SSS 72
18 L 6224 m SSS 73
9 L 2143 m SSS 33
V'tors WD–H
Fees D–1750fr (D–2950fr)
Loc 22 km SE of Brussels
Arch Hawtree/Rolin

Sept Fontaines (1987)
1021, Chaussée d'Alsemberg,
1420 Braine l'Alleud
Tel (02) 353 02 46/353 03 46
Fax (02) 354 68 75
Holes 18 L 6047 m SSS 72
18 L 4870 m SSS 67
9 hole short course
V'tors U H
Fees 1200fr (2100fr)
Loc Braine, 15 km S of Brussels.
Motorway exit 15 (Huizingen)
Arch Rossi

Winge G&CC (1988)
Leuvensesteenweg 252, 3390 Sint Joris
Winge
Tel (016) 63 40 53
Fax (016) 63 21 40
Holes 18 L 6049 m SSS 73
V'tors H
Fees 1300–1800fr
Loc 35 km E of Brussels via Leuven
Arch P Townsend

East

Avernas
Route de Grand Hallet 19A,
4280 Hannut
Tel (019) 51 30 66
Fax (019) 51 30 66
Holes 9 L 2674 m SSS 68
V'tors H
Fees 600fr (800fr)
Loc 40 km W of Liège
Arch Hawtree/Cappart

Durbuy (1991)
Route d'Oppagne 34, 6940 Barvaux-su-
Ourthe
Tel (086) 21 44 54, (086) 21 44 49
Holes 18 L 5963 m SSS 72
9 hole Par 3 course
V'tors U
Fees 1100fr (1500fr)
Loc 45 km S of Liège
Arch Martin Hawtree

Flanders-Nippon (1988)
Vissenbroekstraat 15, 3500 Hasselt
Tel (011) 26 34 80
Fax (011) 24 34 81
Holes 18 L 5922 m SSS 72
9 L 1726 m SSS 32
V'tors U
Fees 1000fr (1500fr)
Loc Hasselt, 85 km E of Brussels
Arch Rolin/Wirtz

Henri-Chapelle (1988)
Rue du Vivier 3, 4841 Henri-Chapelle
Tel (087) 88 19 91
Fax (087) 88 36 55
Holes 18 L 6040 m SSS 72
9 L 2168 m SSS 34
Par 3 course
V'tors 18 hole:WE–H
Fees 18 hole:1200–1600fr
9 hole:900–1200fr
Loc 15 km NE of Liège. 25 km N of Maastricht
Arch Steensels/Dudok van Heel

International Gomze (1986)
Sur Counachamps 8, 4140 Gomze
Andoumont
Tel (041) 360 92 07
Fax (041) 360 92 06
Holes 18 L 5918 m SSS 72
V'tors U H
Fees On application
Loc 15 km S of Liège. Spa 20 km
Arch Paul Rolin

Limburg G&CC (1966)
Golfstraat 1, 3530 Houthalen
Tel (089) 38 35 43
Fax (089) 84 12 08
Holes 18 L 6128 m SSS 72
V'tors H
Fees 1450fr (1850fr)
Loc Houthalen, 15 km N of Hasselt
Arch Hawtree

Royal GC du Sart Tilman (1939)
Route du Condroz 541, 4031 Liège
Tel (041) 336 20 21
Fax (041) 337 20 26
Holes 18 L 6002 m SSS 72
V'tors H–booking required
Fees D–1550fr (2050fr)
Loc 10 km S of Liège on Route 620 (N35), towards Marche
Arch T Simpson

Royal Golf des Fagnes (1930)
1 Ave de l'Hippodrome, 4900 Spa
Tel (087) 79 30 30
Fax (087) 79 30 39
Holes 18 L 6010 m Par 72
V'tors H–booking required
Fees 1600fr (2000fr)
Loc 5 km N of Spa. 35 km SE of Liège
Arch T Simpson

Spiegelven GC Genk (1988)
Wiemesmeerstraat 109, 3600 Genk
Tel (089) 35 96 16
Fax (089) 36 41 84
Holes 18 L 6198 m SSS 72
9 hole Par 3 course

V'tors H
Fees 1300fr (1800fr)
Loc Genk, 18 km E of Hasselt.
20 km N of Maastricht
Arch Ron Kirby

West & Oost Vlaanderen

Damme G&CC (1987)
Doornstraat 16, 8340 Damme-Sijsele
Tel (050) 35 35 72
Fax (050) 35 89 25
Holes 18 L 6046 m SSS 72
9 hole short course
V'tors H
Fees 1450fr (1950fr)
Loc 7 km E of Bruges. Knokke 15 km
Arch J Dudok van Heel

Oudenaarde G&CC (1975)
Kasteel Petegem, Kortrykstraat 52,
9790 Wortegem-Petegem
Tel (055) 33 41 61
Fax (055) 31 98 49
Holes 18 L 6172 m Par 72
9 L 2536 m Par 34
V'tors H
Fees 1200fr (1500fr)
Loc 3 km SW of Oudenaarde
Arch HJ Baker

De Palingbeek (1991)
Eekhofstraat 14, 8902 Hollebeke-Ieper
Tel (057) 20 04 36
Fax (057) 21 89 58
Holes 18 L 6165 m Par 72
V'tors H
Fees 1200fr (1500fr)
Loc 5 km SE of Ieper, nr Hollebeke
Arch HJ Baker

Royal Latem (1909)
9830 St Martens-Latem
Tel (09) 282 54 11
Fax (09) 282 90 19
Holes 18 L 5767 m Par 70 SR 123
V'tors H
Fees 1750fr (2250fr)
Loc 10 km SW of Ghent on route N43 Ghent-Deinze

Royal Ostend (1903)
Koninklijke Baan 2, 8420 De Haan
Tel (059) 23 32 83
Fax (059) 23 37 49
Holes 18 L 5517 m SSS 70
V'tors H–36
Fees 1200–1500fr (1900–2200fr)
Loc 8 km N of Ostend towards De Haan
Arch M Hawtree (1993/4)

Royal Zoute (1899)
Caddiespad 14, 8300 Knokke-le-Zoute
Tel (050) 60 16 17 (Clubhouse),
(050) 60 37 81 (Starter)
Fax (050) 62 30 29
Holes No 1 18 L 6172 m SSS 73
No 2 18 L 3607 m SSS 60
V'tors H No 1 course–max 20
WE–restricted
Fees 2300–2500fr (2800–3500fr)
Loc Knokke-Heist
Arch HS Colt

Waregem
Bergstraat 41, 8790 Waregem
Tel (056) 60 88 08
Fax (056) 61 29 42
Holes 18 L 6038 m SSS 72
V'tors H Sun–NA before 1pm
Fees 1000fr (1600fr)
Loc 30 km SW of Ghent (E17)
Arch Paul Rolin

Czech Republic

Karlovy Vary (1904)
*Prazska 125, PO Box 60,
360 01 Karlovy Vary*
Tel (017) 333 1001-2
Fax (017) 333 1101
Email golfkv@mbox.vol.cz
www.freshnet.cz/golfresort
Holes 18 L 6226 m SSS 72
V'tors H
Fees 1100kcs (1300kcs)
Loc 8 km from Karlovy Vary
(Road 6)
Arch Noskowski

Lísnice (1928)
252 03 Lísnice
Tel (0305) 92660
Holes 9 L 5002 m SSS 67
V'tors H
Fees 400kcs
Loc 30 km from Prague towards Dobrís

Lokomotiva-Brno (1967)
c/o Chlupova 7, 602 00 Brno
Tel (05) 744615
Fax (05) 759309
Holes 9 L 4632 m SSS 68
V'tors H
Fees 100kcs (180kcs)
Loc Svratka, 80 km NW of Brno.
100 km SE of Prague
Arch Chocholac

Mariánské Lázne (1905)
PO Box 267, 353 01 Mariánské Lázne
Tel (0165) 4300
Fax (0165) 625195
Holes 18 L 6195 m SSS 72
V'tors H
Fees D–1000kcs
Loc 2 km NE of Mariánské Lázne, opposite Golf Hotel

Park GC Ostrava (1968)
747 15 Silherovice
Tel (069) 975 4144
Fax (069) 975 4144
Holes 18 L 5838 m SSS 71
V'tors H
Fees D–600kcs
Loc 15 km N of Ostrava

Podebrady (1964)
PO Box 7, 29001 Podebrady
Tel (0324) 3483
Fax (0324) 3483
Holes 9 L 6240 m SSS 72
V'tors U
Fees 300kcs (400kcs)
Loc E side of Podebrady
Arch Wagner/Havelka

Praha (1926)
Na Morani 4, 128 00 Praha 2
Tel (02) 292828/644 3828
Fax (02) 292828
Holes 9 L 5960 m SSS 72
V'tors U
Loc Prague-Motol, towards Plzen

Semily (1970)
Pod Cernym Mostem 476/1, 513 01 Semily 1
Tel (0431) 622411/622412/4428
Fax (0431) 622413
Holes 9 L 4160 m Par 64 SSS 64
V'tors WD–U WE–NA
Fees D–300kcs
Loc 2 km from Semily. 100 km NE of Prague
Arch Schovánek/Janata

Denmark

Bornholm Island

Bornholm (1972)
Plantagevej 3B, 3700 Rønne
Tel 56 95 68 54
Fax 56 95 68 53
Holes 18 L 4819 m Par 68
9 hole Par 3 course
V'tors H
Fees 160kr
Loc 4 km E of Rønne, off Route 38 towards Aakirkeby

Nexø
Dueodde Golfbane, Strandmarksvejen 14, 3730 Nexø
Tel 56 48 89 87
Fax 56 48 89 69
Email golfnexo@image.dk
www.image.dk/~golfnexo
Holes 18 L 5631 m Par 70 CR 70.4
V'tors H
Fees 180kr (180kr)
Loc 12 km S of Nexø, nr Dueodde beach
Arch Frederik Dreyer

Nordbornholm-Rø (1987)
Spellingevej 3, Rø, 3760 Gudhjem
Tel 56 48 40 50
Fax 56 48 40 52
Holes 18 L 5369 m SSS 71
V'tors WD–U WE–H
Fees D–180kr
Loc Rø, 8 km W of Gudhjem.
22 km NE of Rønne
Arch Anders Amilon

Funen

Faaborg (1989)
Dalkildegards Allee 1, 5600 Faaborg
Tel 62 61 77 43
Fax 62 61 79 34
Holes 18 L 5715 m Par 72
V'tors U H
Fees D–200kr
Loc 35 km S of Odense
Arch Frederik Dreyer

Lillebaelt (1990)
O.Hougvej 130, 5500 Middelfart
Tel 64 41 80 11
Fax 64 41 14 11
Holes 18 L 5586 m Par 71 CR 69.1
V'tors H
Fees D–180kr (D–200kr)
Loc 2 km from Middelfart. 45 km W of Odense
Arch Malling Petersen

Odense (1927)
Hestehaven 200, 5220 Odense SØ
Tel 65 95 90 00
Fax 65 95 90 88
Holes 18 L 6156 m CR 71
9 L 4154 m CR 61
V'tors U
Fees 200kr
Loc SE outskirts of Odense
Arch Jan Sederholm

Odense Eventyr (1993)
Falen 227, 5250 Odense SV
Tel 66 17 11 44
Fax 66 17 11 37
Holes 18 hole course Par 72
9 hole course
V'tors H

Fees 225kr (255kr)
Loc 5 km SW of Odense
Arch Michael Møller

SCT Knuds (1954)
Slipshavnsvej 16, 5800 Nyborg
Tel 65 31 12 12
Fax 65 30 28 04
Holes 18 L 5810 m CR 72
V'tors H
Fees 200kr D–250kr (430kr)
Loc 3 km SE of Nyborg
Arch Cotton/Dreyer

Svendborg (1970)
Tordensgaardevej 5, Sørup, 5700 Svendborg
Tel 62 22 40 77
Fax 62 20 29 77
Email Svendborg.Golf.Club.@Get2Net.DK
Holes 18 L 5490 m CR 70
V'tors U
Fees 200kr (250kr)
Loc 4 km NW of Svendborg
Arch Frederik Dreyer

Vestfyns (1974)
Rønnemosegård, Krengerupvej 27, 5620 Glamsbjerg
Tel 64 72 21 24
Fax 64 72 27 37
Holes 18 L 5629 m Par 71 CR 71
V'tors H
Fees 200kr (250kr)
Loc Glamsbjerg, 25 km SW of Odense

Greenland

Sondie Arctic Desert (1990)
Box 58, 3910 Kangerlussuaq, Greenland
Tel 29 91 14 13
Fax 29 91 11 74
Holes 18 L 5521 m SSS 72
V'tors U
Loc 2 km E of Kangerlussuaq Airport, Greenland
Arch Ulf Larson

Jutland

Aalborg (1908)
Jaegersprisvej 35, Restup Enge, 9000 Aalborg
Tel 98 34 14 76
Fax 98 34 15 84
Holes 18 L 6003 m CR 72.4
V'tors H (max 36)
Fees D–250kr (250 kr)
Loc 7 km SW of Aalborg
Arch R Harris

Aarhus (1931)
Ny Moesgaardvej 50, 8270 Hojbjerg
Tel 86 27 63 22
Fax 86 27 63 21
Holes 18 L 5725 m CR 71
V'tors H
Fees D–180kr (D–220kr)
Loc 6 km S of Aarhus, Route 451
Arch Brian Huggett

Blokhus Klit (1993)
Hunetorpvej 115, Box 230, 9490 Pandrup
Tel 98 20 95 00
Fax 98 20 95 01
Holes 18 L 5765 m CR 71
V'tors U H
Fees 200kr (250kr)
Loc 35 km NW of Aalborg
Arch Frederik Dreyer

Breinholtgård (1992)
Koksspangvej 17-19, 6710 Esbjerg V
Tel 75 11 57 00
Fax 75 11 55 12
Holes 18 L 5855 m Par 71 CR 72
V'tors U
Fees 200kr
Loc 11 km N of Esbjerg
Arch Gaunt/Trådsdahl

Brønderslev (1971)
PO Box 94, 9700 Brønderslev
Tel 98 82 32 81
Fax 98 82 45 25
Holes 18 L 5683 m CR 71
9 hole short course
V'tors H WE–booking necessary
Fees 180kr (200kr)
Loc 3 km W of Brønderslev
Arch Erik Schnack

Dejbjerg (1966)
Letagervej 1, Dejbjerg, 6900 Skjern
Tel 97 35 09 59/97 35 00 09
Holes 18 L 5275 m SSS 69
V'tors U H–max 36
Fees D–140kr (D–170kr)
Loc 6 km N of Skjern. 25 km from W coast on Skjern-Ringkøbing road (Route 28)
Arch Schnack/Dreyer

Ebeltoft (1966)
Strandgårdshøj 8a, 8400 Ebeltoft
Tel 86 34 47 87/86 36 10 64
Holes 18 L 5027 m Par 68 CR 67.6
V'tors U
Fees D–160kr
Loc 1 km N of Ebeltoft
Arch Frederik Dreyer

Esbjerg (1921)
Sønderhedevej 11, Marbaek, 6710 Esbjerg
Tel 75 26 92 19
Fax 75 26 94 19

Holes 18 L 6434 m CR 71
9 L 5520 m CR 70
V'tors U H
Fees 250kr
Loc 15 km N of Esbjerg
Arch Frederik Dreyer

Fanø Vesterhavsbad (1901)
Sdr. Banksti 2, 6720 Fanø
Tel 75 16 14 00
Fax 75 16 14 00
Holes 18 L 4450 m CR 65
V'tors U
Fees D–190kr
Loc W side of Fanø Island. Ferry from Esbjerg

Grenaa (1981)
Vestermarken 1, 8500 Grenaa
Tel (86) 32 79 29
Holes 18 L 5782 m Par 70
V'tors U
Fees 150kr
Loc 1 km W of Grenaa. 60 km NE of Aarhus
Arch Dreyer/Sommer

Gyttegård (1974)
Billundvej 43, 7250 Hejnsvig
Tel 75 33 63 82
Fax 75 33 68 20
Holes 18 L 5548 m SSS 70
V'tors H
Fees 150kr (200kr)
Loc 2 km NE of Hejnsvig. 5 km SW of Billund
Arch Amilon/Bossen

Haderslev (1971)
Simmerstedvej 151, 6100 Haderslev
Tel 74 52 83 01
Fax 74 53 36 01
Holes 18 L 5233 m CR 69
V'tors H
Fees 180kr (200kr)
Loc 2 km NW of Haderslev

Han Herreds
Starkaervej 20, 9690 Fjerritslev
Tel 98 21 26 66
Fax 98 21 24 44
Holes 18 L 5359 m CR 70.5
V'tors H
Fees 150kr
Loc 1 km N of Fjerritslev. 40 km W of Aalborg

Henne (1989)
Hennebysvej 30, 6854 Henne
Tel 75 25 56 10/40 81 39 88
Fax 75 25 56 61
Holes 18 L 6054 m Par 71
9 hole Par 3 course
V'tors U
Fees –170kr
Loc 19 km NW of Varde. 35 km N of Esbjerg
Arch Frederik Dreyer

For list of abbreviations see page 527

Herning (1964)
Golfvej 2, 7400 Herning
Tel 97 21 00 33
Fax 97 21 00 34
Holes 18 L 5571 m CR 71.8
V'tors H
Fees 150kr (200kr)
Loc 2 km E of Herning on Route 15
Arch Dreyer/Baekgaard

Himmerland G&CC (1979)
Centervej 1, Gatten, 9640 Farsö
Tel 96 49 61 00
Fax 98 66 14 56
Holes Old 18 L 5422 m SSS 69 Par 70; New 18 L 6102 m SSS 74 Par 73; 18 hole Par 3 course
V'tors H
Fees 180kr D–230kr (270kr D–320kr)
Loc Gatten, 35 km NW of Hobro towards Løgstør (Route 29)
Arch Jan Sederström

Hirtshals (1990)
Kjulvej 10, PO Box 51, 9850 Hirtshals
Tel 98 94 94 08
Fax 98 94 19 35
Holes 18 L 5620 m Par 72
V'tors U H max 48 WE–NA 10–12 noon
Fees 200kr
Loc 12 km N of Hjørring
Arch Erik Nielsen

Hjarbaek Fjord (1992)
Lynderup, 8832 Skals
Tel 86 69 62 88
Fax 86 69 62 68
Holes 27 L 8595 m SSS 72
V'tors H
Fees 225kr (260kr)
Loc 17 km NW of Viborg
Arch Henrik Jacobsen

Hjorring (1985)
Vinstrupvej, PO Box 215, 9800 Hjorring
Tel 98 91 18 28
Fax 98 90 31 00
Holes 18 L 5943 m SSS 72
V'tors H WE–NA 9–11am
Fees 180kr
Loc N of Hjorring. 50 km N of Aalborg
Arch Erik Schnack

Holmsland Klit
Klevevej 19, Søndervig, 6950 Ringkøbing
Tel 97 33 88 00
Fax 97 33 86 80
Holes 18 L 5611 m SSS 69
V'tors H
Fees 175kr
Loc 10 km W of Ringkøbing
Arch Leif Baekgaard

Holstebro (1970)
Råsted, 7570 Vemb
Tel 97 48 51 55
Holes 18 L 5853 m CR 70.8
9 L 2510 m
V'tors H
Fees 200kr (220kr)
Loc 13 km W of Holstebro (Route 16)
Arch Erik Schnack

Horsens (1972)
Silkeborgvej 44, 8700 Horsens
Tel 75 61 51 21
Holes 18 L 6020 m CR 72.4
6 hole Par 3 course
Fees 160kr
Loc 1 km W of Horsens towards Silkeborg
Arch Jan Sederholm

Hvide Klit (1972)
Hvideklitvej 28, 9982 Aalbaek
Tel 98 48 90 21/48 84 26
Fax 98 48 91 12
Holes 18 L 5875 m SSS 72
V'tors H
Fees 180kr (230kr)
Loc 3 km N of Aalbaek. 24 km N of Frederikshavn
Arch Anders Amilon

Juelsminde (1973)
Bobroholtvej 11a, 7130 Juelsminde
Tel 75 69 34 92
Fax 75 69 46 11
Holes 18 L 5680 m SSS 72
V'tors U H
Fees 170kr
Loc 20 km S of Horsens on coast. 2 km N of Juelsminde
Arch Mehlsen/Jacobsen/Møller

Kaj Lykke
Kirkebrovej 5, 6740 Bramming
Tel 75 10 22 46
Holes 18 L 5975 m Par 72
Par 3 course
V'tors H
Fees 200kr
Loc 18 km E of Esbjerg
Arch Bent Nielsen

Kalo (1992)
Aarhusvej 32, 8410 Rønde
Tel 86 37 36 00
Fax 86 37 36 46
Holes 18 L 5936 m CR 72.5
V'tors U
Fees 220kr (250kr)
Loc 20 km E of Aarhus
Arch Frederik Dreyer

Kolding (1933)
Emerholtsvej 15, 6000 Kolding
Tel 75 52 37 93
Fax 75 52 42 42
Holes 18 L 5376 m SSS 69
9 L 2065 m

V'tors U
Fees 180kr (220kr)
Loc 3 km N of Kolding
Arch Jan Sederholm

Lemvig (1986)
Søgårdevejen 6, 7620 Lemvig
Tel 97 81 09 20
Fax 97 81 09 20
Holes 18 L 5890 m CR 72
V'tors U
Fees 170kr (170kr)
Loc 2 km N of Lemvig. 35 km NE of Holsterbro
Arch Frederik Dreyer

Løkken (1990)
Vrenstedvej 226, PO Box 43, 9480 Løkken
Tel 98 99 26 57
Fax 98 99 26 58
Holes 18 L 5896 m Par 72
9 L 2964 m Par 29
V'tors U
Fees D–180kr
Loc 45 km NW of Aalborg
Arch Kaj Andersen

Nordvestjysk (1971)
Nystrupvej 19, 7700 Thisted
Tel 97 97 41 41
Holes 18 L 5675 m CR 72
V'tors H
Fees 150kr (150kr)
Loc 17 km NW of Thisted
Arch Schnack/Jacobsen

Odder (1990)
Akjaervej 200, Postbox 46, 8300 Odder
Tel 86 54 54 58
Holes 18 L 5428 m Par 70
V'tors U
Fees 160kr (200kr)
Loc 4 km SW of Odder, off Route 451
Arch Frederik Dreyer

Randers (1958)
Himmelbovej, Fladbro, 8900 Randers
Tel 86 42 88 69
Fax 86 40 88 69
Holes 18 L 5453 m SSS 70
9 hole Par 3 course
Fees 150kr (180kr)
Loc 5 km W of Randers towards Silkeborg
Arch Mogens Harbo

Ribe (1979)
Rønnehave, Snepsgårdevej 14, 6760 Ribe
Tel 30 73 65 18
Holes 18 L 5430 m CR 69
V'tors U
Fees 150kr
Loc 8 km SE of Ribe on Haderslev road
Arch Frederik Dreyer

For list of abbreviations see page 527

Rold Skov
Golfvej 1, 9520 Skørping
Tel 98 39 26 99
Fax 98 39 26 52
Holes 18 L 5850 m SSS 72
V'tors U
Fees 170kr
Loc 30 km S of Aalborg
Arch Henrik Jacobsen

Royal Oak (1992)
Golfvej, Jels, 6630 Rødding
Tel 74 55 32 94
Fax 74 55 32 95
Holes 18 L 5967 m Par 72
V'tors H–booking necessary. Soft spikes only
Fees 300kr
Loc 25 km SW of Kolding

Saeby
Vandløsvej 50, 9300 Saeby
Tel 98 46 76 77
Fax 98 46 11 24
Holes 18 L 5944 m SSS 72
V'tors U
Fees 180kr (200kr)
Loc Saeby, 12 km S of Frederikshavn
Arch Anders Amilon

Silkeborg (1966)
Sensommervej 15C, 8600 Silkeborg
Tel 86 85 33 99
Fax 86 85 35 22
Holes 18 L 5975 m SSS 72
V'tors U
Fees 225kr (275kr)
Loc 5 km E of Silkeborg
Arch Frederik Dreyer

Sønderjyllands (1968)
Uge Hedegård, 6360 Tinglev
Tel 74 68 75 25
Fax 74 68 75 05
Holes 18 L 5771 m SSS 70
V'tors H
Fees 180kr (220kr)
Loc 3 km NE of Tinglev. 15 km S of Abenrå
Arch Erik Schnack

Varde (1991)
Gellerupvej 111b, 6800 Varde
Tel 75 22 40 81
Holes 18 L 5809 m Par 71
V'tors H
Fees 150kr
Loc 20 km N of Esbjerg
Arch Erik Fauerholt

Vejle (1970)
Faellessletgard, Ibaekvej, 7100 Vejle
Tel 75 85 81 85
Fax 75 85 83 01
Holes 27 holes: 5677-6148 m Par 71-73; 9 hole Par 3 course
V'tors H
Fees 250kr (250kr)
Loc 5 km SE of Vejle
Arch J Malling Pedersen

Viborg (1973)
Moellevej 26, Overlund, 8800 Viborg
Tel 86 67 30 10
Fax 86 67 34 15
Holes 18 L 5767 m CR 72
V'tors WD–H 48 WE–H 36
Fees 170kr (200kr)
Loc 2 km E of Viborg
Arch Frederik Dreyer

Zealand

Asserbo (1946)
Bødkergaardsvej, 3300 Frederiksvaerk
Tel 47 72 14 90
Fax 47 72 14 26
Holes 18 L 5861 m Par 72
V'tors H
Fees 200kr (250kr)
Loc 3 km from Frederiksvaerk towards Liseleje
Arch Ross/Samuelsen

Copenhagen (1898)
Dyrehaven 2, 2800 Lyngby
Tel 39 63 04 83
Fax 39 63 46 83
Holes 18 L 5761 m SSS 71
V'tors WD–U WE–NA before noon
Fees 200kr (250kr)
Loc 13 km N of Copenhagen, in deer park

Dragør
Kalvebodvej 100, 2791 Dragør
Tel 32 53 89 75
Fax 32 53 88 09
Holes 18 L 5864 m SSS 71 6 hole Par 3 course
V'tors WD–U WE–U H
Fees 180kr (230kr)
Loc 15 km SE of Copenhagen centre, nr Airport
Arch Henning Jensen/Kierkegaard

Falster (1994)
Virketvej 44, 4863 Eskilstrup, Falster Island
Tel 54 43 81 43
Fax 54 43 81 23
Holes 18 L 5912 m Par 72
V'tors H
Fees 200kr (250kr)
Loc 20 km NE of Nykøbing (Route 271)
Arch Anders Amilon

Frederikssund (1974)
Egelundsgården, Skovnaesvej 9, 3630 Jaegerspris
Tel 47 31 08 77
Fax 47 31 21 88
Holes 18 L 5937 m SSS 71

Furesø (1974)
Hestkøbgård, Hestkøb Vaenge 4, 3460 Birkerød
Tel 45 81 74 44
Fax 45 82 02 24
Holes 27 holes: 5328-5641 m CR 70-71
V'tors H WD–NA before 9am WE–NA before 11am
Fees 250kr (350kr)
Loc 25 km N of Copenhagen
Arch Jan Sederholm

Gilleleje (1970)
Ferlevej 52, 3250 Gilleleje
Tel 49 71 80 56
Fax 49 71 80 86
Holes 18 L 6641 yds CR 72
V'tors H–36
Fees 250-300kr
Loc 62 km N of Copenhagen
Arch Jan Sederholm

Hedeland (1980)
Staerkendevej 232A, 2640 Hedehusene
Tel 46 13 61 88/46 13 61 69
Fax 46 13 62 78
Holes 18 L 6040 m Par 72 9 hole Par 3 course
V'tors H
Fees 160kr (200kr)
Loc 7 km SE of Roskilde. 20 km SW of Copenhagen
Arch Jan Sederholm

Helsingør
GL Hellebaekvej, 3000 Helsingør
Tel 49 21 29 70
Fax 49 21 09 70
Holes 18 L 5612 m Par 71 CR 71
V'tors U H
Fees 230–300kr (300–400kr)
Loc 2 km N of Helsingør

Hillerød (1966)
Nysøgårdsvej 9, Hammersholt, 3400 Hillerød
Tel 48 26 50 46/48 25 40 30 (Pro)
Fax 48 25 29 87
Holes 18 L 5453 m CR 71
V'tors H WE–NA before noon
Fees 200kr (250kr)
Loc 3 km S of Hillerød
Arch Sederholm/Knudsen

Holbaek (1964)
Dragerupvej 50, 4300 Holbaek
Tel 59 43 45 79
Holes 18 L 5290 m Par 70
V'tors U H
Fees 160kr (200kr)
Loc Kirsebaerholmen, 2 km E of Holbaek
Arch Dreyer/Sederholm

Rold Skov
Fees 250kr (250kr)

V'tors WD–U H WE–H 30
Fees 175kr (225kr)
Loc 3 km S of Frederikssund towards Skibby (Route 53)
Arch Dreyer/Samuelsen

Køge (1970)
Gl.Hastrupvej12, 4600 Køge
Tel 56 65 10 00
Fax 56 65 13 45
Holes 18 L 6042 m SSS 71
V'tors WE–H max 30
Fees 200kr (240kr)
Loc 3 km S of Køge. Copenhagen 38 km

Kokkedal (1971)
Kokkedal Alle 9, 2970 Horsholm
Tel 45 76 99 59
Fax 45 76 99 03
Holes 18 L 5936 m SSS 72
V'tors H–WE pm only
Fees 200kr (250kr)
Loc Hørsholm, 30 km N of Copenhagen
Arch Frank Pennink

Korsør (1964)
Tårnborgparken, Postbox 53, 4220 Korsør
Tel 53 57 18 36
Fax 53 57 18 39
Holes 18 L 5998 m CR 71.1
V'tors H WE–NA before 10am
Fees 160 (200kr)
Loc 1 km E of Korsør, on Korsør Bay

Mølleåens (1970)
Stenbaekgård, Rosenlundvej 3, 3540 Lynge
Tel 48 18 86 31/48 18 86 36 (Pro)
Fax 48 18 86 43
Holes 18 L 5494 m SSS 69
V'tors H
Fees 200kr (250kr)
Loc 32 km NW of Copenhagen
Arch Jan Sederholm

Odsherred (1967)
4573 Højby
Tel 59 30 20 76
Fax 59 30 36 76
Holes 18 L 5710 m Par 71
V'tors H
Fees 190kr (230kr)
Loc 5 km SW of Nykøbing
Arch Amilon/Dreyer

Roskilde (1973)
Gedevad, Kongemarken 34, 4000 Roskilde
Tel 46 37 01 81
Fax 46 37 01 81
Holes 18 L 5700 m CR 71
V'tors U H WE–NA before 10am
Fees 200kr (250kr)
Loc 5 km W of Roskilde
Arch Jan Sederholm

Rungsted (1937)
Vestre Stationsvej 16, 2960 Rungsted Kyst
Tel 45 86 34 44
Fax 45 86 57 70

Holes 18 L 6058 m Par 71
V'tors H WE–NA before 1pm
Fees 400kr
Loc Rungsted, 24 km N of Copenhagen
Arch Maj CA Mackenzie

Simon's Golf Club (1993)
Nybovej 5, 3490 Kvistgaard
Tel 49 19 14 78
Fax 49 19 14 70
Holes 18 L 6200 m SSS 74
V'tors H–max 36
Fees 275kr (375kr)
Loc 10 km S of Helsingør. 35 km N of Copenhagen
Arch Martin Hawtree

Skjoldenaesholm (1992)
4174 Jystrup
Tel 57 52 87 00
Fax 57 52 87 01
Holes 18 L 5974 m SSS 71
V'tors H–max 36
Fees 240kr (290kr)
Loc 10 km N of Ringsted. 60 km SW of Copenhagen
Arch Otto Bojesen

Skovlunde Herlev (1980)
Syvendehusvej 111, 2730 Herlev
Tel 44 68 90 09
Fax 44 68 90 04
Holes 18 L 4824 m Par 68 CR 66 9 hole Par 3 course
V'tors U
Fees 160kr (220kr)
Loc Herlev/Ballerup, 15 km NW of Copenhagen
Arch Torben Starup

Søllerød
Brillerne 9, 2840 Holte
Tel 45 80 17 84, 45 80 18 77
Fax 45 80 70 08
Holes 18 L 5872 m SSS 72
V'tors U
Fees 220kr (300kr)
Loc 19 km N of Copenhagen

Sorø (1979)
Suserupvej 7a, 4180 Sorø
Tel 57 84 93 95
Fax 57 84 85 58
Holes 18 L 5693 m Par 71 CR 72
V'tors H–max 48
Fees 180kr (220kr)
Loc 6 km S of Sorø. 15 km W of Ringsted
Arch Jan Sederholm

Sydsjaellands (1974)
Borupgården, Mogenstrup, 4700 Naestved
Tel 53 76 15 55
Fax 53 76 15 88
Holes 18 L 5725 m CR 70.6
V'tors H
Fees 160kr (200kr)

Loc 10 km SE of Naestved towards Praestø
Arch Dreyer/Amillon

Vallensbaek
Golfsvinget 16-20, 2625 Vallensbaek
Tel 43 62 18 99
Fax 43 62 18 33
Holes 18 L 6119 m Par 71 9 L 3130 m
V'tors H
Fees 180kr (240kr)
Loc 15 km W of Copenhagen
Arch Frederik Dreyer

Finland

Central

Etelä Pojhanmaan (1986)
P O Box 136, 60101 Seinäjoki
Tel (06) 423 4545
Fax (06) 423 4547
Holes 18 L 5804 m CR 71.9
V'tors U
Fees 170fmk
Loc 5 km E of Seinäjoki. 300 km NW of Helsinki

Karelia Golf (1987)
Vaskiportintie, 80780 Kontioniemi
Tel (013) 732411
Fax (013) 732472
Holes 18 L 5619 m CR 71
V'tors U H
Fees 185fmk
Loc 18 km N of Joensuu. 460 km NE of Helsinki
Arch Kosti Kuronen

Kokkolan (1957)
P O Box 164, 67101 Kokkola
Tel (06) 822 1636
Fax (06) 822 1630
Holes 18 L 5572 m SSS 71
V'tors U H
Fees 140fmk
Loc 3 km S of Kokkola. 500 km N of Helsinki
Arch KJ Indola

Laukaan Golf (1989)
41530 Laukaa
Tel (014) 832801
Fax (014) 832705
Holes 18 L 5547 m CR 71
V'tors U
Fees 150fmk (180fmk)
Loc 28 km NE of Jyväskylä. 300 km N of Helsinki

Finland

Tarina Golf Puijo (1988)
Golftie 135, 71800 Siilinjärvi
Tel (017) 462 5299
Fax (017) 462 5269
Holes 18 L 5779 m Par 73
V'tors U H
Fees 160fmk (180fmk)
Loc 21 km N of Kuopio (Route 5)
Arch Kosti Kuronen

Vaasan (1969)
Golfkenttätie 61, 65380 Vaasa
Tel (06) 356 9989
Fax (06) 356 9091
Holes 18 L 5602 m Par 72
V'tors H or Green card
Fees 140fmk
Loc Kraklund, 6 km SE of Vaasa on Route 724. 417 km NW of Helsinki
Arch Björn Eriksson

Helsinki & South

Alands (1978)
P O Box 111, 22101 Mariehamn
Tel (018) 43883
Fax (018) 19034
Holes 36 L 5565 m Par 71
V'tors U
Fees 160fmk (190fmk)
Loc 25 km N of Mariehamn, Aland (off SW coast of Finland)

Aura Golf (1958)
Ruissalo 85, 20100 Turku
Tel (02) 258 9201
Fax (02) 258 9121
Holes 18 L 5843 m SSS 71
V'tors H
Fees 200fmk
Loc Ruissalo Island, 9 km W of Turku
Arch Pekka Sivula

Espoo Ringside Golf (1990)
Niipperintie 20, 02920 Espoo
Tel (09) 841814
Fax (09) 841814
Holes 18 L 5855 m SSS 72
V'tors H
Fees 120fmk (200fmk)
Loc 20 km NW of Helsinki
Arch Kosti Kuronen

Espoon Golfseura (1982)
P O Box 26, 02781 Espoo
Tel (09) 819 03444
Holes 18 L 5920 m CR 72.3
V'tors H
Fees 150fmk
Loc Espoo, 24 km W of Helsinki
Arch Jan Sederholm

Helsingin Golfklubi (1932)
Talin Kartano, 00350 Helsinki
Tel (09) 550235/557899
Fax (09) 565 3596
Holes 18 L 5428 m CR 68.7
V'tors H–max 24
Fees 200fmk
Loc 7 km W of Helsinki

Hyvinkään (1989)
Golftie 63, 05880 Hyvinkää
Tel (019) 489390
Fax (019) 489392
Holes 18 L 5457 m CR 72.1
V'tors U H
Fees 170fmk
Loc 3 km N of Hyvinkää. 50 km N of Helsinki
Arch Kosti Kuronen

Keimola Golf (1988)
Kirkantie 32, 01750 Vantaa
Tel (09) 276 6650
Fax (09) 896790
Holes 27 L 5870-5924 m SSS 71-74
V'tors WD–U before 3pm –M after 3pm WE–M H
Fees 160fmk
Loc 15 km N of Helsinki
Arch Pekka Wesamaa

Kurk Golf (1985)
02550 Evitskog
Tel (09) 819 0480
Fax (09) 819 04810
Holes 18 L 5848 m Par 72
V'tors H
Fees 180fmk (200fmk)
Loc 40 km W of Helsinki
Arch Reijo Hillberg

Master Golf (1988)
Bodomintie 4, 02940 Espoo
Tel (09) 853 7002
Fax (09) 853 7027
Holes 27 L 5866-6109 m CR 70.7
V'tors U
Fees 240fmk
Loc 25 km NW of Helsinki
Arch Kuronen/Persson

Meri-Teijo (1990)
Mathildedalin Kartano, 25660 Mathildedal
Tel (02) 736 3955
Fax (02) 736 3945
Holes 18 L 5842 m CR 70.7
V'tors U
Fees 110fmk (140fmk)
Loc 20 km S of Salo. 70 km E of Turku

Messilä (1988)
Messiläntie 240, 15980 Messilä
Tel (03) 753 8171
Fax (03) 753 8174
Holes 18 L 6013 m Par 73

V'tors WD–U before 3pm
Fees D–180fmk
Loc 8 km W of Lahti. 100 km N of Helsinki
Arch Kosti Kuronen

Nevas Golf (1988)
01190 Box
Tel (09) 272 6313
Fax (09) 272 6345
Holes 18 L 5267 m CR 68.5
V'tors U
Fees 200fmk
Loc 30 km E of Helsinki
Arch Kosti Kuronen

Nordcenter G&CC (1988)
10410 Aminnefors
Tel (019) 238850
Fax (019) 238871
Holes 18 L 6375 m SSS 74
     18 L 6069 m SSS 71
V'tors H
Fees 260fmk
Loc 80 km W of Helsinki
Arch Fream/Benz

Nurmijärven (1990)
Ratasillantie, 05100 Röykkä
Tel (09) 276 6230
Fax (09) 276 62330
Email nurmijarvi@golfkeskus.inet.fi
Holes 27 L 6002-6214 m SSS 73-75
V'tors U
Fees 120–180fmk
Loc 23 km W of Klaukkala. 50 km NW of Helsinki

Peuramaa
02400 Kirkkonummi
Tel (929) 61011
Fax (929) 61114
Holes 18 L 5878 m CR 72.6
V'tors U
Fees 140fmk (160fmk)
Loc 27 km W of Helsinki

Pickala Golf (1986)
Golfkuja 5, 02580 Siuntio
Tel (09) 221 9080
Fax (09) 221 90899
Holes Seaside 18 L 5820 m SSS 72
     Park 18 L 5897 m SSS 72
V'tors H
Fees 170fmk (200fmk)
Loc 42 km W of Helsinki, on South coast
Arch Reijo Hillberg

Ruukkigolf (1986)
Brödtorp, 10420 Skuru
Tel (019) 245 4485
Fax (019) 245 4285
Holes 18 L 6165 m Par 72
V'tors U
Fees 120fmk (170fmk)
Loc 85 km W of Helsinki
Arch Lasse Heikkinen

For list of abbreviations see page 527

St Laurence (1989)
Kaivurinkatu, 08200 Lohja
Tel (019) 386603
Fax (019) 386666
Holes 18 L 6247 m Par 72
 9 L 3248 m Par 36
V'tors WD–U H before 3pm WE–U H after 1pm
Fees 200fmk (220fmk)
Loc 50 km W of Helsinki
Arch Kosti Kuronen

Sarfvik (1984)
P O Box 27, 02321 Espoo
Tel (09) 221 9000
Fax (09) 297 7134
Holes 18 L 5690 m CR 70.5
 18 L 5399 m CR 69.8
V'tors WD–U H
Fees 320fmk
Loc 20 km W of Helsinki
Arch Jan Sederholm

Sea Golf Rönnäs (1989)
Rönnäs, 07750 Isnäs
Tel (019) 634434
Fax (019) 634458
Holes 18 L 5541 m CR 70.5
V'tors U
Fees 30fmk (170fmk)
Loc 27 km SE of Porvoo. 80 km E of Helsinki

Seaside Golf (1989)
Harjattulantie 84, 20960 Turku
Tel (02) 276 2180
Fax (02) 258 7218
Holes 18 L 6348 m SSS 75
V'tors H–max 36
Fees 160–220fmk
Loc 22 km S of Turku
Arch Kosti Kuronen

Suur-Helsingin (1965)
Rinnekodintie 29, 02980 Espoo
Tel (09) 855 8687
Fax (09) 855 0648
Holes Lakisto 18 L 5551 m SSS 71
 Luukki 18 L 5085 m SSS 70
V'tors H
Fees 150fmk
Loc 25 km N of Helsinki

Golf Talma (1989)
Nygårdintie, 04240 Talma
Tel (09) 239 6166
Fax (09) 239 6131
Holes 18 L 5855 m SSS 72
 9 L 2895 m SSS 36
 9 hole Par 3 course
V'tors H
Fees 170fmk (220fmk)
Loc 35 km N of Helsinki
Arch Henrik Wartiainen

Tuusula (1983)
P O Box 178, 04301 Tuusula
Tel (09) 274 6080
Fax (09) 274 60860

Holes 18 L 5791 m CR 71
V'tors H
Fees 180fmk
Loc 30 km N of Helsinki, nr airport

Virvik Golf (1981)
Virvik, 06100 Porvoo
Tel (915) 579292
Fax (915) 579292
Holes 18 L 5855 m SSS 72
V'tors H
Fees 120fmk (140fmk)
Loc 18 km SE of Porvoo. 66 km E of Helsinki
Arch Reijo Louhimo

North

Green Zone Golf (1987)
Näräntie, 95400 Tornio
Tel (016) 431711
Fax (016) 431710
Holes 18 L 5870 m SSS 73
V'tors U
Fees 120fmk
Loc 2 km N of Tornio. 140 km N of Oulu, on Finnish/Swedish border
Arch Ake Persson

Katinkulta (1990)
88610 Vuokatti
Tel (08) 669 7488
Fax (08) 664 0710
Holes 18 L 6000 m SSS 74
V'tors H
Fees 160fmk–180fmk
Loc 36 km E of Kajaani. 600 km N of Helsinki
Arch Jan Sederholm

Oulu (1964)
Isokatu 99, 90120 Oulu
Tel (08) 371666/531 5222
Fax (08) 379728/531 5129
W'site www.infopiste.fi/ogk
Holes 18 L 6160 m SSS 73
 9 L 2990 m SSS 73
V'tors H
Fees 200–220fmk
Loc Sanginsuu, 18 km E of Oulu
Arch Ronald Fream

South East

Imatran Golf (1986)
Golftie 11, 55800 Imatra
Tel (05) 473 4954
Fax (05) 473 4953
Holes 18 L 5738 m CR 71.4
V'tors U
Fees 170fmk (170fmk)
Loc 6 km N of Imatra. 270 km E of Helsinki
Arch Kosti Kuronen

Kartano Golf (1988)
P O Box 60, 79601 Joroinen
Tel (017) 572257
Fax (017) 572263
Holes 18 L 5597 m CR 71
V'tors U
Fees 130fmk (170fmk)
Loc 20 km S of Varkaus. 330 km NE of Helsinki
Arch Ake Persson

Kerigolf (1990)
Hotellikylä Kerimaa, 58200 Kerimäki
Tel (015) 252496
Fax (015) 252124
Holes 18 L 6218 m Par 72 SSS 75
V'tors H
Fees 170fmk
Loc 15 km E of Savonlinna. 350 km NE of Helsinki
Arch Ronald Fream

Koski Golf (1987)
Eerolan Golfkeskus, 45700 Kuusankoski
Tel (05) 374 7622
Fax (05) 374 7820
Holes 18 L 6375 m Par 73
V'tors H
Fees D–120fmk (D–160fmk)
Loc 3 km E of Kuusankoski. 70 km E of Lahti
Arch Kosti Kuronen

Kymen Golf (1964)
Mussalo Golfcourse, 48310 Kotka
Tel (05) 260 5333
Fax (05) 260 5073
Holes 18 L 5651 m CR 70.6
V'tors H
Fees 160fmk
Loc 5 km W of Kotka, Mussalo Island. 130 km E of Helsinki
Arch Kosti Kuronen

Lahden Golf (1959)
P O Box 67, 15141 Lahti
Tel (03) 784 1311
Fax (03) 784 1311
Holes 18 L 5547 m CR 71.7
V'tors U H
Fees 150fmk
Loc 6 km NE of Lahti. 110 km NE of Helsinki

Porrassalmi (1989)
Annila, 50100 Mikkeli
Tel (015) 335518/335446
Fax (015) 335446
Holes 18 L 4907 m CR 65.8
V'tors H
Fees 140–160fmk
Loc 5 km S of Mikkeli

Vierumäen Golfseura (1988)
Suomen Urheiluopisto, 19120 Vierumäki
Tel (03) 842 4501
Fax (03) 842 4630
Holes 18 L 5580 m CR 71.1

V'tors U
Fees   170fmk
Loc   25 km NE of Lahti

South West

Porin Golfkerho (1939)
P O Box 25, 28601 Pori
Tel   (02) 630 3888
Fax   (02) 630 38813
Holes 18 L 6160 m SSS 74
V'tors H
Fees   160fmk
Loc   5 km NW of Pori, at Kalafornia
Arch   Reijo Louhimo

River Golf (1988)
Taivalkunta, 37120 Nokia
Tel   (03) 340 0234
Fax   (03) 340 0235
Holes 18 L 5616 m CR 70.8
V'tors U
Fees   150fmk
Loc   Nokia, 20 km W of Tampere
Arch   Kosti Kuronen

Salo Golf (1988)
Liikuntapuisto 8, 24100 Salo
Tel   (02) 731 7321
Fax   (02) 731 5600
Holes 18 L 5447 m CR 69
V'tors U
Fees   120fmk (150fmk)
Loc   110 km W of Helsinki

Tammer Golf (1965)
Toimelankatu 4, 33560 Tampere
Tel   (03) 261 3316
Fax   (03) 261 3130
Holes 18 L 5717 m CR 70
V'tors U
Fees   150fmk
Loc   Ruotula, 5 km NE of Tampere

Tawast G&CC (1987)
Tawastintie 48, 13270 Hämeenlinna
Tel   (03) 619 7502
Fax   (03) 619 7503
Holes 18 L 6063 m SSS 73
V'tors H
Fees   180fmk
Loc   5 km E of Hämeenlinna
Arch   Reijo Hillberg

Vammala (1991)
38100 Karkku
Tel   (03) 513 4070
Fax   (03) 513 90711
Holes 18 L 5522 m CR 69.2
V'tors H
Fees   120fmk (160fmk)
Loc   11 km N of Vammala. 210 km NW of Helsinki
Arch   Kosti Kuronen

Wiurila G&CC (1990)
Viurilantie 126, 24910 Halikko
Tel   (02) 737 1400
Fax   (02) 737 1404
Holes 18 L 5584 m CR 71.7
V'tors U
Fees   130fmk (160fmk)
Loc   5 km W of Salo. 115 km W of Helsinki

Yteri Golf (1988)
P O Box 230, 28101 Pori
Tel   (02) 638 0380
Fax   (02) 638 0385
Holes 18 L 5738 m SSS 72
Fees   150fmk
Loc   20 km W of Pori
Arch   Reijo Louhimo

France

Bordeaux & South West

Albret (1986)
Le Pusocq, 47230 Barbaste
Tel   05 53 65 53 69
Fax   05 53 65 61 19
Holes 18 L 5911 m SSS 71
V'tors U
Fees   140fr (170fr)
Loc   Barbaste, 30 km W of Agen
Arch   JL Pega

Arcachon (1955)
35 Bd d'Arcachon, 33260 La Teste De Buch
Tel   05 56 54 44 00
Fax   05 56 66 86 32
Holes 18 L 5930 m SSS 71
V'tors U H
Loc   60 km SW of Bordeaux
Arch   CR Blandford

Arcangues (1991)
64200 Arcangues
Tel   05 59 43 10 56
Fax   05 59 43 12 60
Holes 18 L 6142 m Par 72
V'tors U
Loc   3 km SE of Biarritz
Arch   Ronald Fream

Ardilouse (1980)
Domaine de l'Ardilouse, 33680 Lacanau-Océan
Tel   05 56 03 25 60
Fax   05 56 26 30 57
Holes 18 L 5932 m SSS 72
V'tors H

Loc   45 km W of Bordeaux
Arch   John Harris

Biarritz (1888)
Ave Edith Cavell, 64200 Biarritz
Tel   05 59 03 71 80
Fax   05 59 03 26 74
Holes 18 L 5376 m SSS 68
V'tors U
Fees   220–330fr
Loc   Biarritz
Arch   Willie Dunn

Biscarrosse (1989)
Route d'Ispe, 40600 Biscarrosse
Tel   05 58 09 84 93
Fax   05 58 09 84 50
Holes Lake 9 L 2172 m SSS 32
       Forest 9 L 3030 m SSS 36
V'tors U
Fees   160–250fr
Loc   80 km SW of Bordeaux
Arch   Brizon/Veyssieres

Blue Green-Artiguelouve (1986)
Domaine St Michel, Pau-Artiguelouve, 64230 Artiguelouve
Tel   05 59 83 09 29
Fax   05 59 83 14 05
Holes 18 L 6063 m Par 71
V'tors U
Fees   190fr (235fr)
Loc   8 km NW of Pau, off Bayonne road
Arch   J Garaialde

Blue Green-Seignosse (1989)
Avenue du Belvédère, 40510 Seignosse
Tel   05 58 41 68 30
Fax   05 58 41 68 31
Holes 18 L 6124 m Par 72
V'tors U
Fees   220–350fr
Loc   30 km N of Biarritz, nr Airport
Arch   Robert von Hagge

Bordeaux-Cameyrac (1972)
Cameyrac, 33450 St Sulpice
Tel   05 56 72 96 79
Fax   05 56 72 86 56
Holes 18 L 5927 m SSS 72
       9 L 1188 m Par 28
Loc   15 km E of Bordeaux
Arch   Jacques Quenot

Bordeaux-Lac (1977)
Avenue de Pernon, 33300 Bordeaux
Tel   05 56 50 92 72
Fax   05 56 29 01 84
Holes 18 L 6156 m SSS 72
       18 L 6159 m SSS 72
Fees   180fr (220fr)
Loc   2 km N of Bordeaux
Arch   Jean Bourret

France

Bordelais (1900)
Domaine de Kater, Rue de Kater, 33200 Bordeaux-Caudéran
Tel 05 56 28 56 04
Fax 05 56 28 59 71
Holes 18 L 4727 m SSS 67
V'tors H–restricted Tues
Fees 190fr (250fr)
Loc 3 km NW of Bordeaux

Casteljaloux (1989)
Avenue du Lac, 47700 Casteljaloux
Tel 05 53 93 51 60
Fax 05 53 93 04 10
Holes 18 L 5916 m SSS 72
V'tors U
Loc 60 km NW of Agen
Arch Michel Gayon

Castelnaud (1987)
'La Menuisière', 47290 Castelnaud de Gratecambe
Tel 05 53 01 74 64
Fax 05 53 01 78 99
Holes 18 L 6322 m SSS 73
   9 L 2184 m SSS 27
Loc 10 km N of Villeneuve on N21. 40 km N of Agen

Chantaco (1928)
Route d'Ascain, 64500 St Jean-de-Luz
Tel 05 59 26 14 22/05 59 26 19 22
Fax 05 59 26 48 37
Holes 18 L 5722 m SSS 70
V'tors U
Fees 260fr (340fr)
Loc 2 km S of St Jean-de-Luz, on Route d'Ascain
Arch HS Colt

Château des Vigiers (1990)
24240 Monestier
Tel 05 53 61 50 00
Fax 05 53 61 50 20
Holes 18 L 6003 m Par 72
   6 hole Academy course
V'tors H
Fees 205–320fr
Loc 15 km SW of Bergerac. 75 km E of Bordeaux
Arch Donald Steel

Chiberta (1926)
Boulevard des Plages, 64600 Anglet
Tel 05 59 63 83 20
Fax 05 59 63 30 56
Holes 18 L 5650 m SSS 70
V'tors H–booking required
Loc 3 km N of Biarritz. Airport 5 km
Arch T Simpson

Croix de Mortemart (1987)
St Felix de Reillac, 24260 Le Bugue
Tel 05 53 03 27 55
Holes 18 L 6222 m Par 72
V'tors U

Loc 30 km S of Perigueux, between La Douze and Le Bugue (D710)
Arch Martine Lacroix

Graves et Sauternais (1989)
St Pardon de Conques, 33210 Langon
Tel 05 56 62 25 43
Holes 18 L 5810 m SSS 71
V'tors U
Loc 5 km from Langon. 45 km SW of Bordeaux via A62

Gujan (1990)
Route de Souguinet, 33470 Gujan Mestras
Tel 05 57 52 73 73
Fax 05 56 66 10 93
Holes 18 L 6225 m SSS 72
   9 L 2635 m SSS 35
V'tors U
Fees 18 hole:200–270fr
   9 hole:140–170fr
Loc 12 km E of Arcachon on RN 250. 40 km W of Bordeaux
Arch Alain Prat

Hossegor (1930)
Ave du Golf BP#95, 40150 Hossegor
Tel 05 58 43 56 99
Fax 05 58 43 98 52
Holes 18 L 6001 m SSS 71
V'tors H
Fees 220–350fr
Loc 15 km N of Bayonne, on coast
Arch J Morrison

Makila
Route de Cambo, 64200 Bassussarry
Tel 05 59 58 42 42
Fax 05 59 58 42 48
Holes 18 L 6176 m SSS 72
V'tors H
Fees 220–300fr
Loc 5 km SE of Biarritz. Airport 2 km
Arch R Roquemore

Médoc
Chemin de Courmateau, Louens, 33290 Le Pian Médoc
Tel 05 56 70 11 90
Fax 05 56 70 11 99
Holes Chateaux 18 L 6316 m SSS 73
   Vignes 18 L 6220 m SSS 73
V'tors U
Fees 230fr (300fr)
Loc 20 km NW of Bordeaux
Arch Coore/Whitman

Moliets (1989)
Rue Mathieu Desbieys, 40660 Moliets
Tel 05 58 48 54 65
Fax 05 58 48 54 88
Holes 18 L 6172 m SSS 73
   9 hole course
V'tors U
Fees 250–320fr
Loc Moliets, 30 km N of Bayonne. 40 km W of Dax
Arch Robert Trent Jones Sr

La Nivelle (1907)
Place William Sharp, 64500 Ciboure
Tel 05 59 47 18 99/05 59 47 19 72
Holes 18 L 5570 m SSS 69
V'tors U
Loc 2 km S of St Jean-de-Luz

Pau (1856)
Rue de Golf, 64140 Pau-Billère
Tel 05 59 32 02 33
Fax 05 59 62 42 57
Holes 18 L 5312 m SSS 69
V'tors H
Fees 200fr (250fr)
Loc 2 km S of Pau. Bordeaux 200 km
Arch Willie Dunn

Périgueux (1980)
Domaine de Saltgourde, 24430 Marsac
Tel 05 53 53 02 35
Fax 05 53 09 46 29
Holes 18 L 6120 m SSS 72
V'tors U
Loc 3 km W of Périgueux, via Angoulême-Riberac road
Arch Robert Berthet

Pessac (1989)
Rue de la Princesse, 33600 Pessac
Tel 05 57 26 03 33
Fax 05 56 36 52 89
Holes 18 L 5567-5935 m SSS 72
   9 L 2911 m SSS 36
   9 hole Par 3 course
V'tors U
Fees 160fr (220fr)
Loc 4 km W of Bordeaux
Arch Olivier Brizon

Scottish Golf Aubertin (1987)
64290 Aubertin
Tel 05 59 82 70 69
Holes 18 L 4806 m Par 66
V'tors U
Loc 20 km S of Pau

Stade Montois (1993)
Pessourdat, 40090 Saint Avit
Tel 05 58 75 63 05
Fax 05 58 06 80 72
Holes 18 L 5944 m Par 71
V'tors U
Fees 180fr (180fr)
Loc Pau 80km. Biarritz 100 km
Arch J Garaialde

Brittany

Ajoncs d'Or (1976)
Kergrain Lantic, 22410 Saint-Quay Portrieux
Tel 02 96 71 90 74
Fax 02 96 71 40 83
Holes 18 L 6125 m SSS 72
V'tors U
Loc 17 km N of Saint-Brieuc. 6 km W of Étables-sur-Mer

For list of abbreviations see page 527

Baden
Kernic, 56870 Baden
Tel 02 97 57 18 96
Fax 02 97 57 22 05
Holes 18 L 6145 m SSS 73
V'tors U
Loc 12 km SW of Vannes
Arch Yves Bureau

Brest Les Abers
(1990)
Kerhoaden, 29810 Plouarzel
Tel 02 98 89 68 33
Holes 18 L 5060 m Par 71
V'tors U
Fees 200fr
Loc 15 km W 0f Brest (D5)
Arch Ch Dunoyer

Brest-Iroise (1976)
Parc de Lann-Rohou, Saint-Urbain, 29800 Landerneau
Tel 02 98 85 16 17
Fax 02 98 85 19 39
Holes 18 L 5672 m Par 71
9 L 3329 m Par 37
V'tors U
Fees 210fr (230fr)
Loc 25 km E of Brest
Arch M Fenn

Cicé-Blossac (1992)
Domaine de Cicé-Blossac, 35170 Bruz
Tel 02 99 52 79 79
Fax 02 99 57 93 60
Holes 18 L 6343 m SSS 72
V'tors U
Loc Bruz, SW of Rennes (N177)
Arch Macauley/Quenouille

Coatguelen (1987)
Château de Coatguelen, 22290 Pléhédel
Tel 02 96 55 33 40
Holes 18 hole course
V'tors U
Fees 100fr (150fr)
Loc 10 km S of Paimpol on D7.
35 km from Saint-Brieuc

Dinard (1887)
35800 St-Briac-sur-Mer
Tel 02 99 88 32 07
Fax 02 99 88 04 53
Holes 18 L 5137 m Par 68
V'tors U
Loc 8 km W of Dinard. 15 km W of Saint-Malo

La Freslonnière (1989)
Le Bois Briand, 35650 Le Rheu
Tel 02 99 14 84 09
Fax 02 99 14 94 98
Holes 18 L 5756 m SSS 72
V'tors U
Fees 200fr (250fr)
Loc 4 km SW of Rennes, off N24
Arch A du Bouexic

L'Odet (1987)
Clohars-Fouesnant, 29950 Benodet
Tel 02 98 54 87 88
Fax 02 98 54 61 40
Holes 18 L 5843 m SSS 72
9 hole Par 3 course
V'tors U H
Fees 165–260fr
Loc 6 km S of Benodet. 15 km SE of Quimper
Arch Robert Berthet

Les Ormes (1988)
Château des Ormes, Epiniac, 35120 Dol-de-Bretagne
Tel 02 99 73 54 44
Fax 02 99 73 53 65
Holes 18 L 5910 m SSS 72
V'tors H
Fees 200–260fr
Loc 8 km S of Dol, off D795
Arch A d'Ormesson

Pen Guen (1926)
22380 Saint-Cast-le-Guildo
Tel 02 96 41 91 20
Fax 02 96 41 77 62
Holes 18 L 4967m SSS 68
V'tors U
Fees 195–235fr
Loc 25 km W of Dinard. 30 km W of Saint Malo

Pléneuf-Val André
Rue de la Plage des Vallées, 22370 Pléneuf-Val André
Tel 02 96 63 01 12
Fax 02 96 63 01 06
Holes 18 L 6052 m Par 72
V'tors U
Fees 160–270fr
Loc 30 km E of St Brieuc on coast.
60 km W of St Malo
Arch Alain Prat

Ploemeur Océan
Saint-Jude, Kerham, 56270 Ploemeur
Tel 02 97 32 81 82
Fax 02 97 32 80 90
Holes 18 L 5957 m SSS 72
V'tors U H
Fees 165–255fr
Loc 10 km from Lorient-Brest road, exit Ploemeur
Arch Macauley/Quenouille

Quimper-Cornouaille (1959)
Manoir du Mesmeur, 29940 La Forêt-Fouesnant
Tel 02 98 56 97 09
Holes 18 L 5657 m SSS 71
Loc 15 km SE of Quimper
Arch F Hawtree

Rennes Saint Jacques
B P 1117, 37136 St-Jacques-de-la-Lande
Tel 02 99 30 18 18
Fax 02 99 31 51 04
Holes 18 L 6135 m Par 72
9 L 2100 m Par 32
9 hole short course
V'tors U
Fees 240fr
Loc 5 km SW of Rennes
Arch Robert Berthet

Rhuys-Kerver (1988)
Formule Golf, Domaine de Kerver, 56730 St-Gildas-de-Rhuys
Tel 02 97 45 30 09
Fax 02 97 45 36 58
Holes 18 L 6197 m SSS 73
V'tors U
Fees 230fr
Loc 30 km S of Vannes
Arch Olivier Brizon

Les Rochers (1989)
Route d'Argentré du Plessis 3, 35500 Vitré
Tel 02 99 96 52 52
Fax 02 99 96 79 34
Holes 18 L 5721 m Par 72
V'tors U
Fees 160fr (160fr)
Loc Vitré, 30 km E of Rennes
Arch JC Varro

Sables-d'Or-les-Pins
(1925)
22240 Fréhel
Tel 02 96 41 42 57
Fax 02 96 41 51 44
Holes 18 L 5586 m SSS 71
V'tors U
Fees 180–220fr
Loc 6 km SW of Fréhel. 30 km W of Dinard

St Laurent (1975)
Ploemel, 56400 Auray
Tel 02 97 56 85 18
Fax 02 97 56 89 99
Holes 18 L 6212 m SSS 72
9 L 2705 m SSS 35
V'tors U
Fees 255fr
Loc Ploemel, 16 km SW of Auray
Arch Fenn/Bureau

St Malo-Le Tronchet
(1986)
Le Tronchet, 35540 Miniac-Morvan
Tel 02 99 58 96 69
Fax 02 99 58 10 39
Holes 18 L 5936 m SSS 72
9 L 2684 m SSS 36
V'tors U
Fees D–260fr
Loc 23 km S of St Malo, off RN 137
Arch Hubert Chesneau

For list of abbreviations see page 527

St Samson (1965)
Route de Kérénoc, 22560 Pleumeur-Bodou
Tel 02 96 23 87 34
Fax 02 96 23 84 59
Holes 18 L 5807 m Par 71
V'tors U
Fees 210fr (380fr)
Loc 7 km N of Lannion on Tregastel road
Arch Hawtree

Sauzon (1987)
Les Poulins, 56360 Belle-Ile-en-Mer
Tel 02 97 31 64 65
Holes 18 L 5820 m Par 72
V'tors U
Loc Island off S coast of Brittany, near Quiberon
Arch Yves Bureau

Val Queven (1990)
Kerrousseau, 56530 Queven
Tel 02 97 05 17 96
Fax 02 97 05 19 18
Holes 18 L 6127 m SSS 72
V'tors U Sun–restricted
Fees 165–255fr
Loc 10 km W of Lorient
Arch Yves Bureau

Burgundy & Auvergne

Beaune-Levernois (1990)
21200 Levernois
Tel 03 80 24 10 29
Fax 03 80 24 03 78
Holes 18 L 6116 m Par 72
       9 hole short course
V'tors U
Fees 160fr (220fr)
Loc 5 km SE of Beaune (D470/D111)
Arch Ch Piot

Chalon-sur-Saône (1976)
Parc de Saint Nicolas, 71380 Chatenoy-en-Bresse
Tel 03 85 93 49 65
Fax 03 85 93 56 95
Holes 18 L 5859 m SSS 71
V'tors U
Fees D–145fr
Loc 3 km SE of Chalon. 125 km N of Lyon
Arch Michel Rio

Chambon-sur-Lignon (1986)
Riondet, La Pierre de la Lune, 43300 Le Chambon-sur-Lignon
Tel 04 71 59 28 10
Fax 04 71 65 87 14
Holes 18 L 6110 m Par 72

V'tors U
Fees On application
Loc 60 km NW of Saint Etienne. 120 km NW of Lyon
Arch Michel Gayon

Château d'Avoise (1992)
9 Rue de Mâcon, 71210 Montchanin
Tel 03 85 78 19 19
Fax 03 85 78 15 16
Holes 18 L 6350 m Par 72
V'tors WD–U WE–H
Loc 25 km W of Chalon
Arch Martin Hawtree

Château de Chailly
Chailly-sur-Armançon, 21320 Pouilly-en-Auxois
Tel 03 80 90 30 40
Fax 03 80 90 30 05
Holes 18 L 6146 m SSS 72
V'tors U
Loc 45 km SW of Dijon
Arch Sprecher/Watine

Château de la Salle (1989)
71260 La Salle-Mâcon Nord
Tel 03 85 36 09 71
Fax 03 85 36 06 70
Holes 18 L 6024 m SSS 71
V'tors U
Fees 160fr (220fr)
Loc 12 km NW of Mâcon. Lyon 70 km
Arch Robert Berthet

Le Coiroux (1977)
19190 Aubazine
Tel 05 55 27 25 66
Fax 05 55 27 29 33
Holes 18 L 5400 m Par 70
V'tors U
Loc 15 km E of Brive
Arch Hubert Chesneau

Dijon-Bourgogne (1972)
Bois des Norges, 21490 Norges-la-Ville
Tel 03 80 35 71 10
Fax 03 80 35 79 27
Holes 18 L 6179 m SSS 72
V'tors U
Fees 180fr (250fr)
Loc 10 km N of Dijon towards Langres
Arch Fenn/Radcliffe

Domaine de Roncemay (1989)
89110 Chassy
Tel 03 86 73 50 50
Fax 03 86 73 69 42
Holes 18 L 6401 m Par 72 SSS 73
V'tors H WE–restricted
Fees 200fr (280fr)
Loc 15 km W of Auxerre
Arch Jeremy Pern

La Fredière (1988)
La Fredière, Céron, 71110 Marcigny
Tel 03 85 25 27 40
Fax 03 85 25 06 12
Holes 18 L 4529 m SSS 68
V'tors U
Fees 150–180fr
Loc 35 km NW of Roanne
Arch Gilles Charmat

La Jonchère
Montgrenier, 23230 Gouzon
Tel 05 55 62 23 05
Holes 18 L 5858 m SSS 71
V'tors U
Loc 30 km SW of Montluçon. 100 km NE of Limoges
Arch J-L Pega

Limoges-St Lazare (1976)
Avenue du Golf, 87000 Limoges
Tel 05 55 28 30 02
Holes 18 L 6238 m SSS 73
V'tors U
Loc 2 km S of Limoges on RN20
Arch Hubert Chesneau

Mâcon La Salle (1989)
La Salle-Mâcon Nord, 71260 La Salle
Tel 03 85 36 09 71
Fax 03 85 36 06 70
Holes 18 L 6024 m Par 71
V'tors H or green card
Fees 190fr (220fr)
Loc 5 km N of Mâcon (A6)
Arch Robert Berthet

Le Nivernais
Le Bardonnay, 58470 Magny Cours
Tel 03 86 58 18 30
Fax 03 86 58 04 04
Holes 18 L 5670 m Par 71
V'tors U
Loc 12 km S of Nevers on N7. 50 km N of Moulins
Arch Alain Prat

La Porcelaine
Célicroux, 87350 Panazol
Tel 05 55 31 10 69
Fax 05 55 31 10 69
Holes 18 L 6035 m SSS 72
V'tors U
Fees 170–210fr
Loc 6 km NE of Limoges
Arch Jean Garaialde

St Junien (1997)
Les Jouberties, 87200 Saint Junien
Tel 05 55 02 96 96
Holes 18 L 5677 m Par 72
       9 hole course
V'tors U
Fees 100fr (130fr)
Loc 30 km W of Limoges (N141)

For list of abbreviations see page 527

752   France

Sporting Club de Vichy
(1907)
Allée Baugnies, 03700 Bellerive/Allier
Tel   04 70 32 39 11
Fax   04 70 32 00 54
Holes 18 L 5463 m SSS 70
V'tors H
Loc   In Vichy
Arch   Arnaud Massy

Val de Cher (1975)
03190 Nassigny
Tel   04 70 06 71 15
Holes 18 L 5450 m Par 70
V'tors U
Fees   200fr
Loc   20 km N of Montluçon on N144
Arch   Bourret/Vigand

Les Volcans (1984)
La Bruyère des Moines, 63870 Orcines
Tel   04 73 62 15 51
Fax   04 73 62 26 52
Holes 18 L 6286 m SSS 73
       9 L 1377 m SSS 29
V'tors U H
Fees   200fr (250fr)
Loc   12 km W of Clermont-Ferrand on RN 141
Arch   Lucien Roux

Centre

Les Aisses (1992)
RN20 Sud, 45240 La Ferté St Aubin
Tel   02 38 64 80 87
Fax   02 38 64 80 85
Holes 27 L 6200 m Par 72
V'tors U
Fees   180fr (250fr)
Loc   30 km S of Orléans. 140 km S of Paris
Arch   Olivier Brizon

Ardrée (1988)
37360 St Antoine-du-Rocher
Tel   02 47 56 77 38
Fax   02 47 56 79 96
Holes 18 L 5758 m Par 70
V'tors U
Loc   10 km N of Tours
Arch   Olivier Brizon

Les Bordes (1987)
41220 Saint Laurent-Nouan
Tel   02 54 87 72 13
Fax   02 54 87 78 61
Holes 18 L 6412 m Par 72
V'tors U
Fees   350fr (550fr)
Loc   30 km SW of Orléans
Arch   Robert van Hagge

Château de Cheverny
La Rousselière, 41700 Cheverny
Tel   02 54 79 24 70
Fax   02 54 79 25 52

Holes 18 L 6276 m Par 71
V'tors H
Fees   200fr (280fr)
Loc   15 km S of Blois. 200 km SW of Paris, via A10
Arch   O Van der Vinckt

Château de Maintenon
(1988)
Route de Gallardon, 28130 Maintenon
Tel   02 37 27 18 09
Fax   02 37 27 10 12
Holes 18 L 6393 m SSS 74
       9 L 1541 m SSS 30
V'tors WD–U WE–restricted
Loc   20 km W of Rambouillet (D906). 70 km SW of Paris
Arch   Michel Gayon

Château des Forges (1991)
Domaine des Forges, 79340 Menigoute
Tel   05 49 69 91 77
Holes 18 L 6400 m Par 74
       9 L 3200 m Par 37
V'tors U
Fees   200fr (250fr)
Loc   30 km W of Poitiers
Arch   Bjorn Eriksson

Château des Sept Tours
(1989)
Le Vivier des Landes, 37330 Courcelles de Touraine
Tel   02 47 24 69 75
Fax   02 47 24 23 74
Holes 18 L 6194 m Par 72
V'tors U
Fees   200fr (250fr)
Loc   35 km NW of Tours
Arch   Donald Harradine

Cognac (1987)
Saint-Brice, 16100 Cognac
Tel   05 45 32 18 17
Fax   05 45 35 10 76
Holes 18 L 6142 m SSS 72
V'tors H
Loc   5 km E of Cognac
Arch   Jean Garaialde

Le Connétable (1987)
Parc Thermal, 86270 La Roche Posay
Tel   05 49 86 25 10
Fax   05 49 19 48 40
Holes 18 L 5840 m SSS 72
V'tors U
Fees   150fr (180fr)
Loc   20 km E of Châtellerault. 40 km NE of Poitiers
Arch   JP Fourès

Domaine de Vaugouard
(1987)
Chemin des Bois, Fontenay-sur-Loing, 45210 Ferrières
Tel   02 38 95 81 52
Fax   02 38 95 79 78
Email Domaine.golf.Vaugouard@wanadoo.fr

Holes 18 L 5914 m SSS 72
V'tors U
Fees   190fr (350fr)
Loc   10 km N of Montargis. 100 km S of Paris
Arch   Fromanger/Adam

Les Dryades
36160 Pouligny-Notre-Dame
Tel   02 54 30 28 00
Holes 18 L 6120 m SSS 72
V'tors U
Loc   10 km S of La Châtre (D940). 60 km SW of Bourges
Arch   Michel Gayon

Ganay (1991)
Prieuré de Ganay, 41220 St Laurent-Nouan
Tel   02 54 87 26 24
Fax   02 54 87 72 50
Holes 27 hole course
V'tors U
Fees   100fr (140fr)
Loc   130 km S of Paris
Arch   Jim Shirley

Haut-Poitou (1987)
86130 Saint-Cyr
Tel   05 49 62 53 62
Fax   05 49 88 77 14
Holes 18 L 6590 m SSS 75
       9 L 1800 m Par 31
V'tors U
Fees   170fr Sun–200fr
Loc   20 km N of Poitiers. 70 km S of Tours
Arch   HG Baker

Loudun (1985)
Domaine St Hilaire, 86120 Roiffe
Tel   05 49 98 78 06
Fax   05 49 98 72 57
Holes 18 L 6343 m Par 72
V'tors U
Fees   130–140fr (170–180fr)
Loc   18 km N of Loudun. 15 km S of Saumur
Arch   Hubert Chesneau

Marcilly (1986)
Domaine de la Plaine, 45240 Marcilly-en-Villette
Tel   02 38 76 11 73
Fax   02 38 76 18 73
Holes 18 L 6324 m SSS 73
       9 hole course
V'tors U
Fees   130fr (170fr)
Loc   20 km SE of Orléans
Arch   Olivier Brizon

Mazières (1987)
Le Petit Chêne, 79310 Mazières-en-Gâtine
Tel   05 49 63 20 95
Fax   05 49 63 33 75
Holes 18 L 6060 m SSS 72
V'tors U

For list of abbreviations see page 527

Fees 165fr (215fr)
Loc   15 km SW of Parthenay.
      25 km NE of Niort
Arch Robert Berthet

Mignaloux Beauvoir
*Domaine de Beauvoir,
86550 Mignaloux Beauvoir*
Tel   05 49 46 70 27
Fax   05 49 55 31 95
Holes 18 L 6032 m SSS 71
V'tors WD–U WE–H
Fees 170–200fr
Loc   6 km SE of Poitiers (RN147)
Arch Olivier Brizon

Orléans Val de Loire
Château de la Touche, 45450 Donnery
Tel   02 38 59 25 15
Fax   02 38 57 01 98
Holes 18 L 5771 m SSS 71
V'tors U
Loc   16 km E of Orléans
Arch Trent Jones/Van der Vinckt

Golf du Perche (1987)
La Vallée des Aulnes, 28400 Souancé au Perche
Tel   02 37 29 17 33
Fax   02 37 29 12 88
Holes 18 L 6073 m Par 72
V'tors U
Fees 180fr (280fr)
Loc   60 km SW of Chartres (D9).
      130 km SW of Paris
Arch Laurent Heckly

La Picardière
Chemin de la Picardière, 18100 Vierzon
Tel   02 48 75 21 43
Fax   02 48 71 87 61
Holes 18 L 6077 m Par 72
V'tors U
Fees 190fr (220fr)
Loc   75 km S of Orléans, off A71
Arch JL Pega

La Prée-La Rochelle
(1990)
La Richardière, 17137 Marsilly
Tel   05 46 01 24 42
Fax   05 46 01 25 84
Holes 18 L 6012 m SSS 72
V'tors U
Fees 160–240fr
Loc   6 km N of La Rochelle
Arch Olivier Brizon

Royan (1977)
Maine-Gaudin, 17420 Saint-Palais
Tel   05 46 23 16 24
Fax   05 46 23 23 38
Holes 18 L 5970 m SSS 71
      6 hole short course
V'tors U
Fees 150–250fr
Loc   Saint-Palais, 7 km W of Royan
Arch Robert Berthet

Saintonge (1953)
Fontcouverte, 17100 Saintes
Tel   05 46 74 27 61
Fax   05 46 92 17 92
Holes 18 L 4790 m Par 68
V'tors U
Fees 150–200fr
Loc   2 km NE of Saintes
Arch Hervé Bertrand

Sancerrois (1989)
St Thibault, 18300 Sancerre
Tel   02 48 54 11 22
Fax   02 48 54 28 03
Holes 18 L 5820 m SSS 71
V'tors U
Fees 120–170fr (180–220fr)
Loc   45 km NE of Bourges
Arch Didier Fruchet

Sologne (1955)
Route de Jouy-le-Potier, 45240 La Ferté St Aubin
Tel   02 38 76 57 33
Fax   02 38 76 68 79
Holes 18 L 6400 yds SSS 72
V'tors U
Fees 120fr (170fr)
Loc   25 km S of Orléans on RN20

Sully-sur-Loire (1965)
L'Ousseau, 45600 Viglain
Tel   02 38 36 52 08
Holes 18 L 6154 m Par 72
      9 L 3155 m Par 36
Loc   3 km SW of Sully-sur-Loire

Touraine (1971)
Château de la Touche, 37510 Ballan-Miré
Tel   02 47 53 20 28
Fax   02 47 53 31 54
Holes 18 L 5671 m SSS 71
V'tors WE–H
Fees D–230fr (D–300fr)
Loc   10 km SW of Tours
Arch Michael Fenn

Val de l'Indre (1989)
Villedieu-sur-Indre, 36320 Tregonce
Tel   02 54 26 59 44
Holes 18 L 6250 m SSS 72
Fees 190fr
Loc   12 km NW of Chateauroux.
      80 km SE of Tours on RN 143
Arch Yves Bureau

Channel Coast & North

Abbeville (1989)
Route du Val, 80132 Grand-Laviers
Tel   03 22 24 98 58
Fax   03 22 24 49 61
Holes 18 L 6080 m Par 73
V'tors U

Fees 150fr (180fr)
Loc   3 km NW of Abbeville
Arch Didier Fruchet

L'Ailette
02000 Laon
Tel   03 23 24 83 99
Fax   03 23 24 84 66
Holes 18 L 6127 m Par 72
      9 hole short course
V'tors WD–H WE–H restricted
Fees 185fr (240fr)
Loc   13 km S of Laon. 45 km NW of Reims
Arch Michel Gayon

Amiens (1951)
Route d'Amiens, 80115 Querrieu
Tel   03 22 93 04 26
Fax   03 22 93 04 61
Holes 18 L 6114 m SSS 72
V'tors U
Fees 130–150fr (200–250fr)
Loc   7 km NE of Amiens (D929)
Arch Ross/Pennink

Apremont (1992)
60300 Apremont
Tel   03 44 25 61 11
Fax   03 44 25 11 72
Holes 18 L 6436 m SSS 73
V'tors H
Fees 250fr (330–480fr)
Loc   45 km N of Paris
Arch John Jacobs

Arras (1989)
Rue Briquet Taillandier, 62223 Anzin-St-Aubin
Tel   03 21 50 24 24
Fax   03 21 50 29 71
Holes 18 L 6150 m SSS 73
V'tors U
Fees 190fr (250fr)
Loc   50 km S of Lille. 110 km SE of Calais
Arch JC Cornillot

Belle Dune
Promenade de Marquenterre, 80790 Fort-Mahon-Plage
Tel   03 22 23 45 50
Fax   03 22 23 93 41
Holes 18 L 5909 m Par 72 SSS 71
V'tors H or Green card
Loc   25 km S of Le Touquet on coast
Arch JM Rossi

Blue Green-Chantilly
(1991)
Route d'Apremont, 60500 Vineuil St-Firmin
Tel   03 44 58 47 74
Fax   03 44 58 50 28
Holes 18 L 6209 m SSS 72
V'tors U
Fees 150–290fr
Loc   40 km N of Paris (A1)
Arch Huau/Nelson

Bois de Ruminghem
(1991)
1613 Rue St Antoine, 62370 Ruminghem
Tel 03 21 85 30 33
Fax 03 21 36 38 38
Holes 18 L 6115 m Par 73
V'tors U
Loc 30 km SE of Calais
Arch Bill Baker

Bondues (1968)
Château de la Vigne BP#54, 59587 Bondues Cedex
Tel 03 20 23 20 62
Fax 03 20 23 24 11
Holes 18 L 6223 m SSS 73
18 L 6000 m SSS 72
V'tors H–max 30
Fees D–200fr (D–300fr)
Loc 10 km NE of Lille
Arch Hawtree/Trent Jones

Brigode (1970)
36 Avenue de Golf, 59650 Villeneuve D'Ascq
Tel 03 20 91 17 86
Fax 03 20 05 96 36
Holes 18 L 6182 m SSS 72
V'tors WD–H
Loc 8 km NE of Lille
Arch HJ Baker

Champagne (1986)
02130 Villers-Agron
Tel 03 23 71 62 08
Fax 03 23 71 62 08
Holes 18 L 5760 m SSS 72
V'tors U
Fees 170fr (230fr)
Loc 25 km SW of Reims, via E50
Arch JC Cornillot

Chantilly (1909)
Allée de la Ménagerie, 60500 Chantilly
Tel 03 44 57 04 43
Fax 03 44 57 26 54
Holes Vineuil 18 L 6597 m SSS 71
Longeres 18 L 6378 m SSS 72
V'tors WE–NA
Fees WD–350fr
Loc 45 km N of Paris
Arch Tom Simpson

Château d'Humières
(1990)
Château d'Humières, 60113 Monchy-Humières
Tel 03 44 42 39 51
Fax 03 44 42 48 92
Holes 18 L 6176 m SSS 73
V'tors U
Fees 180fr (270fr)
Loc 80 km N of Paris. A1 Junction 11

Château de Raray
4 Rue Nicolas de Lancy, 60810 Raray
Tel 03 44 54 70 61
Fax 03 44 54 74 97
Holes 18 L 6455 m Par 72
9 L 2921 m Par 35
V'tors H
Fees 150–220fr (250–350fr)
Loc 60 km N of Paris (A1)
Arch Patrick Leglise

Chaumont-en-Vexin
(1963)
Château de Bertichère, 60240 Chaumont-en-Vexin
Tel 03 44 49 00 81
Holes 18 L 6195 m SSS 72
V'tors H
Loc 65 km NW of Paris
Arch Donald Harradine

Compiègne (1896)
Ave Royale, 60200 Compiègne
Tel 03 44 38 48 00
Fax 03 44 40 23 59
Holes 18 L 6015 m Par 71
V'tors U
Fees 150fr (250fr)
Loc 80 km NE of Paris
Arch W Freemantel

Deauville l'Amiraute
(1992)
Departementale 278, Tourgéville, 14800 Deauville
Tel 02 31 14 42 00
Fax 02 31 88 32 00
Holes 18 L 6055 m Par 73
V'tors U
Fees 220–250fr (330–350fr)
Loc 4 km S of Deauville
Arch Bill Baker

Domaine du Tilleul
(1984)
Landouzy-la-Ville, 02140 Vervins
Tel 03 23 98 48 00
Fax 03 23 98 46 46
Holes 18 L 5203 m SSS 71
V'tors Groups 10+ welcome
Fees 100–150fr (150–180fr)
Loc 7 km S of Hirson. 65 km N of Reims

Dunkerque (1991)
Fort Vallières, Coudekerque-Village, 59380 Bergues
Tel 03 28 61 07 43
Fax 03 28 60 05 93
Holes 18 L 5710 m Par 71
Fees 140fr (160fr)
Loc 5 km E of Dunkerque
Arch Robert Berthet

Hardelot Dunes Course
(1991)
Ave du Golf, 62152 Hardelot
Tel 03 21 83 73 10
Fax 03 21 83 24 33
Holes 18 L 6038 m SSS 73
V'tors U exc NA 8–9am & 1.15–2.30pm
Fees 240–300fr (350fr D–550fr)
Loc 15 km S of Boulogne
Arch Paul Rolin (1990)

Hardelot Pins Course
Ave du Golf, 62152 Hardelot
Tel 03 21 83 73 10
Fax 03 21 83 24 33
Holes 18 L 5870 m SSS 72
V'tors U
Fees 240–300fr (350fr D–550fr)
Loc 15 km S of Boulogne
Arch Tom Simpson (1931)

International Club du Lys
(1929)
Rond-Point du Grand Cerf, 60260 Lamorlaye
Tel 03 44 21 26 00
Fax 03 44 21 35 52
Holes 18 L 6022 m Par 71
18 L 4770 m Par 66
V'tors WD-H WE-H (booking necessary)
Fees WD–250fr
Loc 5 km S of Chantilly. 40 km N of Paris
Arch Tom Simpson

Morfontaine (1926)
60128 Mortefontaine
Tel 03 44 54 68 27
Fax 03 44 54 60 57
Holes 18 L 6063 m SSS 72
9 L 2550 m SSS 35
V'tors Members' guests only
Fees NA
Loc 10 km S of Senlis. N of Paris
Arch Tom Simpson

Mormal (1991)
Bois St Pierre, 59144 Preux-au-Sart
Tel 03 27 63 07 00
Fax 03 27 39 93 62
Holes 18 L 6022 m Par 72
V'tors H
Fees 170fr (220fr)
Loc 15 km E of Valenciennes, off RN49
Arch JC Cornillot

Nampont-St-Martin
(1978)
Maison Forte, 80120 Nampont-St-Martin
Tel 03 22 29 92 90/03 22 29 89 87
Fax 03 22 29 97 54
Holes Cygnes 18 L 6051 m SSS 72
Belvédère 18 L 5145 m SSS 72
V'tors U
Fees 130–150fr (200–240fr)
Loc 50 km S of Boulogne. Motorway A16 Junction 25
Arch Thomas Chatterton

Pelves (1991)
Chemin de l'Enfer, 62118 Pelves
Tel 03 21 58 95 42
Fax 03 21 24 00 04
Holes 18 L 5958 m SSS 72

For list of abbreviations see page 527

V'tors U
Loc 40 km S of Lille. 180 km N of Paris
Arch Ogama

Rebetz (1988)
Route de Noailles, 60240 Chaumont-en-Vexin
Tel 03 44 49 15 54
Fax 03 44 49 14 26
Holes 18 L 6409 m SSS 73
V'tors H
Fees 150fr (350fr)
Loc Chaumont-en-Vexin, 65 km NW of Paris, via D43
Arch J-P Fourès

Saint-Omer
Chemin des Bois, Acquin-Westbécourt, 62380 Lumbres
Tel 03 21 38 59 90
Fax 03 21 93 02 47
Holes 18 L 6400 m Par 72
9 L 2015 m Par 31
V'tors U
Fees 150–260fr (200–300fr)
Loc 10 km W of Saint-Omer. 40 km S of Calais
Arch J Dudok van Heel

Le Sart (1910)
5 Rue Jean-Jaurès, 59650 Villeneuve D'Ascq
Tel 03 20 72 02 51
Fax 03 20 98 73 28
Holes 18 L 5721 m SSS 71
V'tors U
Fees 250fr (300fr 2D–500fr)
Loc 5 km E of Lille. Motorway Lille-Gand Junction 9 (Breucq-Le Sart)
Arch Allan Macbeth

Thumeries (1935)
Bois Lenglart, 59239 Thumeries
Tel 03 20 86 58 98
Fax 03 20 86 52 66
Holes 18 L 5933 m SSS 72
V'tors U
Fees 180fr (250fr)
Loc 10 km N of Douai. 15 km S of Lille
Arch Boomer/Rossi

Le Touquet 'La Forêt' (1904)
Ave du Golf BP#41, 62520 Le Touquet
Tel 03 21 06 28 00
Fax 03 21 06 28 01
Holes 18 L 5659 m SSS 70
V'tors U H
Fees 250fr (320fr)
Loc 2 km S of Le Touquet. 30 km S of Boulogne
Arch H Hutchinson

Le Touquet 'La Mer' (1930)
Ave du Golf BP 41, 62520 Le Touquet
Tel 03 21 06 28 00
Fax 03 21 06 28 01
Holes 18 L 6275 m SSS 74
V'tors U H
Fees 270fr (350fr)
Loc As 'La Forêt'
Arch HS Colt

Le Touquet 'Le Manoir' (1994)
Ave du Golf BP#41, 62520 Le Touquet
Tel 03 21 06 28 00
Fax 03 21 06 28 01
Holes 9 L 2817 m Par 35
V'tors U
Fees 160fr (210fr)
Loc As 'La Forêt'
Arch HJ Baker

Vert Parc (1991)
3 Route d'Ecuelles, 59480 Illies
Tel 03 20 29 37 87
Fax 03 20 29 37 87
Holes 18 L 6328 m SSS 73
V'tors U
Loc 18 km SW of Lille
Arch Patrice Simon

Wimereux (1906)
Route d'Ambleteuse, 62930 Wimereux
Tel 03 21 32 43 20
Fax 03 21 33 62 21
Holes 18 L 6150 m Par 72
V'tors H
Fees 185–210fr (200–250fr)
Loc 6 km N of Boulogne on D940. 30 km S of Calais
Arch Campbell/Hutchinson

Corsica

Spérone (1990)
Domaine de Spérone, 20169 Bonifacio
Tel 04 95 73 17 13
Fax 04 95 73 17 85
Holes 18 L 6130 m SSS 73
V'tors H–max 28
Fees 330fr W–1400fr
Loc S point of Corsica, SE of Bonifacio. 25 km S of airport
Arch Robert Trent Jones Sr

Ile de France

Ableiges (1989)
95450 Ableiges
Tel 01 30 27 97 00
Fax 01 30 27 97 10
Holes 18 L 6261 m Par 72
9 L 2137 m Par 33
V'tors 18 holes:U H (max 30)
Fees 18 hole:150fr (250fr)
9 hole:120fr (150fr)
Loc 40 km NW of Paris, nr Cergy Pontoise
Arch Pern/Garaialde

Bellefontaine (1987)
95270 Bellefontaine
Tel 01 34 71 05 02
Fax 01 34 71 90 90
Holes 27 holes: 6098–6306 m Par 72
V'tors U
Fees 200fr (350fr)
Loc 27 km N of Paris
Arch Michel Gayon

Bondoufle (1990)
Departmentale 31, 91070 Bondoufle
Tel 01 60 86 41 71
Fax 01 60 86 41 56
Holes 18 L 6161 m SSS 73
V'tors U H
Loc 30 km S of Paris
Arch Michel Gayon

Bussy-St-Georges (1988)
Promenade des Golfeurs, 77600 Bussy-St-Georges
Tel 01 64 66 00 00
Fax 01 64 66 22 92
Holes 18 L 5924 m SSS 72
V'tors U
Loc 20 km E of Paris. Motorway A4 Junction 12
Arch Rolin/Cornillot

Cély (1990)
Le Château, Route de Saint-Germain, 77930 Cély-en-Bière
Tel 01 64 38 03 07
Fax 01 64 38 08 78
Holes 18 L 6026 m SSS 72
V'tors H
Loc Fontainebleau 15 km
Arch Adam/Fromanger

Cergy Pontoise (1988)
2 Allee de l'Obstacle d'Eau, 95490 Vaureal
Tel 01 34 21 03 48
Fax 01 34 21 03 34
Holes 18 L 6100 m SSS 72
V'tors WD–U WE–U H
Loc 30 km NW of Paris. A15 Junction 12
Arch Michel Gayon

Chevannes-Mennecy (1994)
91750 Chevannes
Tel 01 64 99 88 74
Fax 01 64 99 88 67
Holes 18 L 6307 m Par 72
V'tors U
Fees 120fr (200fr)
Loc 45 km S of Paris
Arch A d'Ormesson

Clement Ader (1990)
Domaine Château Pereire, 77220 Gretz
Tel 01 64 07 34 10
Fax 01 64 07 82 10
Holes 18 L 6350 m Par 72

For list of abbreviations see page 527

V'tors U
Loc 30 km SE of Paris
Arch M Saito

Coudray (1960)
Ave du Coudray, 91830 Le Coudray-Montceaux
Tel 01 64 93 81 76
Fax 01 64 93 99 95
Holes 18 L 5733 m Par 71
9 L 1500 m Par 30
V'tors H
Fees 260fr (380fr)
Loc 35 km S of Paris on A6 (Junction 11)
Arch CK Cotton

Courson Monteloup (1991)
91680 Bruyères-le-Chatel
Tel 01 64 58 80 80
Fax 01 64 58 83 06
Holes 36 hole course: 6171-6520 m SSS 72-75
V'tors WD–U WE–M exc Jul/Aug
Fees 230fr (400fr)
Loc 35 km SW of Paris, off Route D3
Arch Robert von Hagge

Crécy-la-Chapelle (1987)
Ferme de Monpichet, 77580 Crécy-la-Chapelle
Tel 01 64 04 70 75
Holes 18 L 6211 m SSS 72
V'tors U
Loc 20 km E of Paris by A4

Domaine de Belesbat (1989)
Courdimanche-sur-Essonne, 91820 Boutigny-sur-Essonne
Tel 01 69 23 19 00
Fax 01 69 23 19 01
Holes 18 L 6047 m SSS 72
V'tors H–Booking required
Fees 200fr (400fr)
Loc 50 km S of Paris, between Etampes and Fontainebleau
Arch Fromanger/Adam

Domont-Montmorency
Route de Montmorency, 95330 Domont
Tel 01 39 91 07 50
Fax 01 39 91 25 70
Holes 18 L 5775 m SSS 71
V'tors H
Fees 250fr (480fr)
Loc 18 km N of Paris
Arch Hawtree

Étiolles (1990)
Vieux Chemin de Paris, 91450 Étiolles
Tel 01 60 75 49 49
Fax 01 60 75 64 20
Holes 18 L 6239 m Par 74
9 L 2665 m SSS 36
V'tors U

Fees 260fr (390fr)
Loc 30 km S of Paris
Arch Michel Gayon

Fontainebleau (1909)
Route d'Orleans, 77300 Fontainebleau
Tel 01 64 22 22 95
Fax 01 64 22 63 76
Holes 18 L 6074 m SSS 72
V'tors WD–U WE–Jul/Aug only
Loc 1 km SW of Fontainebleau. 60 km SE of Paris
Arch Simpson/M Hawtree

Fontenailles (1991)
Domaine de Bois Boudran, 77370 Fontenailles
Tel 01 64 60 51 00
Fax 01 60 67 52 12
Holes 18 L 6256 m SSS 74
9 L 2870 m
V'tors WD–U WE–H
Fees 180–200fr (320–450fr)
Loc 60 km SE of Paris
Arch Michel Gayon

Forges-les-Bains (1989)
Rue du Général Leclerc, 91470 Forges-les-Bains
Tel 01 64 91 48 18
Fax 01 64 91 40 52
Holes 18 L 6167 m SSS 72
V'tors H or Green card
Fees 200fr (330fr)
Loc 35 km S of Paris, off A10
Arch JM Rossi

La Forteresse (1989)
Domaine de la Forteresse, 77940 Thoury-Ferrottes
Tel 01 60 96 95 10
Fax 01 60 96 01 41
Holes 18 L 6025 m Par 72
V'tors H or Green card
Fees 180fr (350fr)
Loc 25 km SE of Fontainebleau
Arch Fromanger/Adam

Greenparc (1993)
Route de Villepech, 91280 St Pierre-du-Perray
Tel 01 60 75 40 60
Fax 01 60 75 40 04
Holes 18 L 5839 m SSS 71
V'tors U
Fees 125fr (250fr)
Loc 30 km SW of Paris
Arch Robin Nelson

L'Isle Adam (1995)
1 Chemin des Vanneaux, 95290 L'Isle Adam
Tel 01 34 08 11 11
Fax 01 34 08 11 19
Holes 18 L 6230 m Par 72
V'tors U
Fees 150–250fr (250–375fr)
Loc 30 km N of Paris
Arch Ronald Fream

Marivaux (1992)
Bois de Marivaux, 91640 Janvry
Tel 01 64 90 85 85
Fax 01 64 90 82 22
Holes 18 L 6116 m Par 72
V'tors U H–max 36
Fees 150–180fr (250–350fr)
Loc 25 km SW of Paris
Arch Macauley/Quenouille

Meaux-Boutigny (1985)
Rue de Barrois, 77470 Boutigny
Tel 01 60 25 63 98
Fax 01 60 25 60 58
Holes 18 L 5981 m SSS 72
9 L 1499 m SSS 30
V'tors U
Fees 180fr (300fr)
Loc 45 km E of Paris-Highway 4
Arch Michel Gayon

Mont Griffon
BP 7, 95270 Luzarches
Tel 01 34 68 10 10
Fax 01 34 68 04 37
Holes 18 L 5905 m SSS 70
V'tors U
Fees 200fr (350fr)
Loc 27 km N of Paris
Arch Nelson/Huau/Dongradi

Ormesson (1969)
Chemin du Belvédère, 94490 Ormesson-sur-Marne
Tel 01 45 76 20 71
Fax 01 45 94 86 85
Holes 18 L 6130 m SSS 72
V'tors H
Fees 200fr (350fr)
Loc 21 km SE of Paris
Arch Harris/CK Cotton

Ozoir-la-Ferrière (1926)
Château des Agneaux, 77330 Ozoir-la-Ferrière
Tel 01 60 02 60 79
Fax 01 64 40 28 20
Holes 18 L 5859 m Par 71
9 L 2700 m Par 35
V'tors U H
Fees 18 hole:200fr (400fr)
9 hole:130fr (200fr)
Loc 25 km SE of Paris via A4 (Porte de Bercy)
Arch Sir Henry Cotton

Paris International (1991)
18 Route du Golf, 95560 Baillet-en-France
Tel 01 34 69 90 00
Fax 01 34 69 97 15
Holes 18 L 6319 m SSS 72
V'tors I or M
Loc 24 km NW of Paris
Arch Jack Nicklaus

For list of abbreviations see page 527

St Aubin (1976)
Route du Golf, 91190 St Aubin
Tel 01 69 41 25 19
Fax 01 69 41 02 25
Holes 18 L 5971 m SSS 71
9 L 1918 m SSS 31
V'tors U
Loc 30 km SW of Paris
Arch Berthet/Rio

St Germain-les-Corbeil
6 Ave du Golf, 91250 St Germain-les-Corbeil
Tel 01 60 75 81 54
Fax 01 60 75 52 89
Holes 18 L 5800 m SSS 71
Loc 30 km S of Paris

St Pierre du Perray (1974)
Melun-Sénart, St Pierre du Perray, 91100 Corbeil
Tel 01 60 75 17 47
Holes 18 L 6169 m SSS 72
Loc 30 km SE of Paris, off N6
Arch Hubert Chesneau

Seraincourt (1964)
Gaillonnet-Seraincourt, 95450 Vigny
Tel 01 34 75 47 28
Fax 01 34 75 75 47
Holes 18 L 5760 m SSS 70
V'tors WD–U WE–H
Loc 35 km NW of Paris

Villarceaux (1971)
Château du Couvent, 95710 Chaussy
Tel 01 34 67 73 83
Fax 01 34 67 72 66
Holes 18 L 6175 m Par 72
V'tors H
Fees 200–300fr
Loc 60 km NW of Paris
Arch M Backer

Languedoc-Roussillon

Cap d'Agde (1989)
4 Ave des Alizés, 34300 Cap d'Agde
Tel 04 67 26 54 40
Fax 04 67 26 97 00
Holes 18 L 6160 m SSS 72
V'tors U
Loc 25 km E of Béziers
Arch Ronald Fream

Carcassonne (1988)
Route de Ste-Hilaire, 11000 Carcassonne
Tel 04 13 20 85 43
Fax 04 68 72 57 30
Holes 18 L 5758 m Par 71
V'tors U
Fees 180fr (220fr)
Loc 2 km SW of Carcassonne
Arch J-P Basurco

Coulondres (1984)
72 Rue des Erables, 34980 Saint-Gely-du-Fesc
Tel 04 67 84 13 75
Fax 04 67 84 06 33
Holes 18 L 6175 m SSS 73
V'tors U
Fees 150fr (200fr)
Loc 10 km N of Montpellier towards Ganges
Arch Donald Harradine

Domaine de Falgos (1992)
BP 9, 66260 St Laurent-de-Cerdans
Tel 04 68 39 51 42
Fax 04 68 39 52 30
Holes 18 L 5044 m SSS 68
V'tors U
Fees 200fr (250–300fr)
Loc 60 km S of Perpignan, nr Spanish border (D115)

Fontcaude (1991)
Route de Lodève, Domaine de Fontcaude, 34990 Juvignac
Tel 04 67 03 34 30
Fax 04 67 03 34 51
Holes 18 L 6992 m SSS 72
9 hole short course
V'tors U
Fees 200–250fr
Loc 6 km W of Montpellier
Arch C Pitman

La Grande-Motte (1987)
Clubhouse du Golf, 34280 La Grande-Motte
Tel 04 67 56 05 00
Fax 04 67 29 18 84
Holes 18 L 6161 m Par 72
18 L 3076 m Par 58
6 hole short course
V'tors U
Fees 210fr (270fr)
Loc 18 km E of Montpellier
Arch Robert Trent Jones

Montpellier Massane (1988)
Domaine de Massane, 34670 Baillargues
Tel 04 67 87 87 87
Fax 04 67 87 87 90
Holes 18 L 6231 m Par 72
9 hole Par 3 course
V'tors U
Fees 200fr (260fr)
Loc 9 km E of Montpellier. A9 Junction 28
Arch Ronald Fream

Nîmes Campagne (1968)
Route de Saint Gilles, 30900 Nîmes
Tel 04 66 70 17 37
Fax 04 66 70 03 14
Holes 18 L 6135 m SSS 72
V'tors H
Fees 220fr (250fr)

Loc 7 km S of Nîmes, by Airport
Arch Morandi/Harradine

Nîmes-Vacquerolles (1990)
Route de Sauve, 30900 Nîmes
Tel 04 66 23 33 33
Fax 04 66 23 94 94
Holes 18 L 6300 m SSS 72
V'tors U
Fees 190fr (240fr)
Loc W of Nîmes centre (D999)
Arch W Baker

St Cyprien (1974)
Le Mas D'Huston, 66750 St Cyprien Plage
Tel 04 68 37 63 63
Fax 04 68 37 64 64
Holes 18 L 6480 m SSS 73
9 L 2724 m SSS 35
V'tors U H
Fees 200fr (260fr)
Loc 15 km SE of Perpignan
Arch Wright/Tomlinson

St Thomas (1992)
Route de Pézenas, 34500 Béziers
Tel 04 67 98 62 01
Fax 04 67 98 61 01
Holes 18 L 6130 m Par 72
V'tors U
Loc 7 km NE of Béziers (RN 113)
Arch Patrice Lambert

Loire Valley

Angers (1963)
Moulin de Pistrait, 49320 St Jean des Mauvrets
Tel 02 41 91 96 56
Holes 18 L 5460 m Par 70
Fees 170fr (220fr)
Loc 14 km SE of Angers. Right bank of Loire.

Anjou G&CC (1990)
Route de Cheffes, 49330 Champigné
Tel 02 41 42 01 01
Fax 02 41 42 04 37
Holes 18 L 6227 m SSS 72
6 hole short course
V'tors U H
Fees 180fr (220fr)
Loc 23 km N of Angers
Arch F Hawtree

Avrillé (1988)
Château de la Perrière, 49240 Avrillé
Tel 02 41 69 22 50
Fax 02 41 34 44 60
Holes 18 L 6116 m SSS 71
9 hole Par 3 course
V'tors U
Fees 140fr (200fr)
Loc 5 km N of Angers
Arch Robert Berthet

For list of abbreviations see page 527

Baugé-Pontigné (1994)
Route de Tours, 49150 Baugé
Tel 02 41 89 01 27
Fax 02 41 89 05 50
Holes 18 L 5558 m Par 72
V'tors U
Fees 135fr (190fr)
Loc 45 km E of Angers. 70 km SW of Tours
Arch M Prat

La Baule (1976)
44117 Saint-André-des-Eaux
Tel 02 40 60 46 18
Fax 02 40 60 41 41
Holes 18 L 6055 m CR 73.5
9 L 2881 m CR 35.2
V'tors H
Fees 190–330fr
Loc Avrillac, 3 km NE of La Baule
Arch Alliss/Thomas/Gayon

La Bretesche (1967)
Domaine de la Bretesche, 44780 Missillac
Tel 02 51 76 86 86
Fax 02 40 88 36 28
Holes 18 L 6080 m SSS 72
V'tors U
Fees 180fr (300fr)
Loc 8 km NW of Pontchâteau, between Nantes and Vannes
Arch Cotton/Baker

Cholet (1989)
Allée du Chêne Landry, 49300 Cholet
Tel 02 41 71 05 01
Fax 02 41 56 06 94
Holes 18 L 5792 m Par 71
V'tors WD–U WE–H
Loc 2 km N of Cholet. 52 km SE of Nantes
Arch Olivier Brizon

La Domangère
La Roche-sur-Yon, Route de la Rochelle, 85310 Nesmy
Tel 02 51 07 60 15
Fax 02 51 07 64 09
Holes 18 L 6480 m SSS 72
V'tors U
Loc 6 km S of La Roche-sur-Yon. 70 km S of Nantes
Arch Michel Gayon

Epinay (1991)
Boulevard de l'Epinay, 44470 Carquefou
Tel 02 40 52 73 74
Fax 02 40 52 73 20
Holes 18 L 5790 m SSS 71
V'tors U
Fees 170fr (230fr)
Loc NE of Nantes
Arch M Hawtree

Fontenelles
Saint-Gilles-Croix-de-Vie, 85220 Aiguillon-sur-Vie
Tel 02 51 54 13 94
Fax 02 51 55 45 77

Holes 18 L 6185 m Par 72
V'tors U
Loc 6 km E of St-Gilles-Croix-de-Vie. 75 km SW of Nantes
Arch Yves Bureau

Ile d'Or (1988)
BP 10, 49270 La Varenne
Tel 02 40 98 58 00
Fax 02 40 98 51 62
Holes 18 L 6292 m Par 72
9 L 1217 m Par 27
V'tors U H
Loc 30 km NE of Nantes
Arch Michel Gayon

Laval-Changé (1972)
Le Jariel, 53000 Changé-les-Laval
Tel 02 43 53 16 03
Fax 02 43 49 35 15
Holes 18 L 6068 m Par 72 SSS 72
9 L 3388 m
V'tors WD–U WE–NA
Fees 180fr (220fr)
Loc 5 km N of Laval. 60 km E of Rennes
Arch JP Foures

Le Mans Mulsanne (1961)
Route de Tours, 72230 Mulsanne
Tel 02 43 42 00 36
Fax 02 43 42 21 31
Holes 18 L 5821 m SSS 71
V'tors H
Fees 200–360fr (240–400fr)
Loc Mulsanne, 12 km S of Le Mans

Nantes
44360 Vigneux de Bretagne
Tel 02 40 63 25 82
Fax 02 40 63 64 86
Holes 18 L 5940 m SSS 72
V'tors H
Fees 170fr (250fr)
Loc 12 km NW of Nantes
Arch Frank Pennink

Nantes Erdre (1990)
Chemin du Bout des Landes, 44300 Nantes
Tel 02 40 59 21 21
Fax 02 51 84 94 50
Holes 18 L 6003 m SSS 71
V'tors U
Fees 170fr (220fr)
Loc Nantes
Arch Yves Bureau

Les Olonnes
Gazé, 85340 Olonne-sur-Mer
Tel 02 51 33 16 16
Fax 02 51 30 10 45
Holes 18 L 6127 m Par 72
V'tors U
Fees 120–250fr
Loc 3 km N of Les Sables d'Olonne
Arch Bruno Parpoil

Pornic (1912)
49 Boulevard de l'Océan, Sainte-Marie/Mer, 44210 Pornic
Tel 02 40 82 06 69
Fax 02 40 82 80 65
Holes 18 L 6119 m Par 72
V'tors U
Fees 150–250fr
Loc 1 km E of Pornic. 30 km S of La Baule
Arch Michel Gayon

Port Bourgenay (1990)
Avenue de la Mine, Port Bourgenay, 85440 Talmont-St-Hilaire
Tel 02 51 23 35 45
Fax 02 51 23 35 48
Holes 18 L 5800 m SSS 72
V'tors U
Fees 110–270fr
Loc 10 km SE of Sables d'Olonne. 100 km S of Nantes
Arch Pierre Thevenin

Sablé-Solesmes
Domaine de l'Outinière, Route de Pincé, 72300 Sablé-sur-Sarthe
Tel 02 43 95 28 78
Fax 02 43 92 39 05
Holes 27 holes SSS 72:
Forêt 9 L 3197 m
Rivière 9 L 2992 m
Cascade 9 L 3069 m
V'tors U
Fees 190–280fr
Loc 40 km SW of Le Mans
Arch Michel Gayon

Sargé-Le-Mans (1990)
Rue de Bonnétable, 72190 Sargé-les Le Mans
Tel 02 43 76 25 07
Fax 02 43 76 45 25
Holes 18 L 6054 m SSS 72
V'tors U
Fees 140fr (200fr)
Loc 6 km NE of Le Mans
Arch Antoine d'Ormesson

Savenay (1990)
44260 Savenay
Tel 02 40 56 88 05
Fax 02 40 56 89 04
Holes 18 L 6335 m Par 73
9 L 1122 m Par 30
V'tors U
Fees 150–230fr
Loc 36 km W of Nantes. 30 km E of La Baule
Arch Michel Gayon

St Jean-de-Monts (1988)
Ave des Pays de la Loire, 85160 Saint Jean-de-Monts
Tel 02 51 58 82 73
Fax 02 51 59 18 32
Holes 18 L 5962 m SSS 72
V'tors U
Loc 60 km SW of Nantes on coast

Normandy

Bellême-St-Martin
(1988)
Les Sablons, 61130 Bellême
Tel 02 33 73 00 07
Fax 02 33 73 00 17
Holes 18 L 6011 m SSS 72
V'tors U
Fees 170fr (250fr)
Loc 40 km NE of Le Mans
Arch Eric Vialatel

Beuzeval-Houlgate
(1981)
Route de Gonneville, 14510 Houlgate
Tel 02 31 24 80 49
Fax 02 31 28 04 48
Holes 18 L 5558 m SSS 72
V'tors U
Fees 130–240fr
Loc 2 km S of Houlgate. 15 km SW of Deauville
Arch Alliss/Thomas

Cabourg-Le Home
(1907)
38 Av Président Réné Coty, Le Home Varaville, 14390 Cabourg
Tel 02 31 91 25 56
Fax 02 31 91 18 30
Holes 18 L 5234 m SSS 68
V'tors H
Fees 130–260fr
Loc 4 km W of Cabourg
Arch Jackson/Brizon

Caen (1990)
Le Vallon, 14112 Bieville-Beuville
Tel 02 31 94 72 09
Fax 02 31 47 45 30
Holes 18 holes SSS 72 Par 72
9 hole course
V'tors U
Loc 5 km N of Caen (D60)
Arch F Hawtree

Champ de Bataille
Château du Champ de Bataille, 27110 Le Neubourg
Tel 02 32 35 03 72
Fax 02 32 35 83 10
Holes 18 L 6575 m SSS 72
V'tors U
Loc 28 km NW of Evreux. 45 km SW of Rouen
Arch Nelson/Huau

Clécy (1988)
Manoir de Cantelou, 14570 Clécy
Tel 02 31 69 72 72
Fax 02 31 69 70 22
Holes 18 L 5965 m Par 72
V'tors U
Fees 130–250fr
Loc 30 km S of Caen, via D562
Arch W Baker

Coutainville (1925)
Ave du Golf, 50230 Agon-Coutainville
Tel 02 33 47 03 31
Fax 02 33 47 38 42
Holes 18 L 5045 m SSS 68
V'tors H
Fees 150fr
Loc 12 km W of Coutances. 75 km S of Cherbourg

Dieppe-Pourville (1897)
51 Route de Pourville, 76200 Dieppe
Tel 02 35 84 25 05
Fax 02 35 84 97 11
Holes 18 L 5763 m Par 70
V'tors U
Fees 160–190fr (190–240fr)
Loc 2 km W of Dieppe towards Pourville
Arch Willie Park Jr

Étretat (1908)
BP No 7, Route du Havre, 76790 Étretat
Tel 02 35 27 04 89
Holes 18 L 5994 m SSS 72
V'tors H
Loc 25 km N of Le Havre. Étretat 1 km
Arch Chantepie/Fruchet

Forêt Verte
Bosc Guerard, 76710 Montville
Tel 02 35 33 62 94
Holes 18 L 7000 yds SSS 72
V'tors U
Loc 10 km N of Rouen
Arch Thierry Huau

Granville (1912)
Bréville, 50290 Bréhal
Tel 02 33 50 23 06
Fax 02 33 61 91 87
Holes 18 L 5854 m Par 71
9 L 2323 m Par 33
V'tors U
Fees 18 hole:155fr (225fr)
9 hole:100fr (130fr)
Loc 5 km N of Granville
Arch Colt/Allison/Hawtree

Le Havre (1933)
Hameau Saint-Supplix, 76930 Octeville-sur-Mer
Tel 02 35 46 36 50
Fax 02 35 46 32 66
Holes 18 L 5830 m SSS 70
V'tors H
Loc 10 km N of Le Havre

Léry Poses (1989)
BP 7, 27740 Poses
Tel 02 32 59 47 42
Holes 18 L 6242 m SSS 73
9 hole Par 3 course
V'tors U
Loc 25 km SE of Rouen
Arch J Baker

New Golf Deauville
(1929)
14 Saint Arnoult, 14800 Deauville
Tel 02 31 14 24 24
Fax 02 31 14 24 25
Holes 18 L 5933 m SSS 71
9 L 3033 m SSS 72
V'tors U–booking required
Fees 250–350fr
Loc 3 km S of Deauville
Arch Simpson/Cotton

Omaha Beach (1986)
Ferme St Sauveur, 14520 Port-en-Bessin
Tel 02 31 21 72 94
Fax 02 31 51 79 61
Holes 18 L 6229 m SSS 72
9 L 2875 m SSS 35
V'tors U H
Fees 150–220fr (260fr)
Loc 8 km N of Bayeux
Arch Yves Bureau

Parc de Brotonne (1991)
Jumièges, 76480 Duclair
Tel 02 35 05 32 97
Fax 02 35 37 99 97
Holes 18 L 6040 m SSS 72
V'tors U
Fees 100fr (165fr)
Loc 20 km W of Rouen
Arch JP Fourès

Rouen-Mont St Aignan
(1911)
Rue Francis Poulenc, 76130 Mont St Aignan
Tel 02 35 76 38 65
Fax 02 35 75 13 86
Holes 18 L 5522 m SSS 70
V'tors H WE–H after 4pm
Fees 180fr (250fr)
Loc 4 km N of Rouen

St Gatien Deauville
(1987)
14130 St Gatien-des-Bois
Tel 02 31 65 19 99
Fax 02 31 65 11 24
Holes 18 L 6272 m Par 72
9 L 3035 m Par 36
V'tors U
Fees 200fr (300fr)
Loc 8 km E of Deauville
Arch Olivier Brizon

St Julien
St Julien-sur-Calonne, 14130 Pont-l'Évêque
Tel 02 31 64 30 30
Fax 02 31 64 12 43
Holes 18 L 6290 m SSS 73
9 L 2133 m SSS 33
V'tors U
Fees 140–180fr (200–250fr)
Loc 3 km SE of Pont l'Évêque
Arch Prat/Baker

For list of abbreviations see page 527

St Saëns (1987)
Domaine du Vaudichon, 76680 St Saëns
Tel   02 35 34 25 24
Fax   02 35 34 43 33
Holes 18 L 6004 m SSS 71
V'tors U
Loc   30 km NE of Rouen
Arch   D Robinson

Le Vaudreuil (1962)
27100 Le Vaudreuil
Tel   02 32 59 02 60
Fax   02 32 59 43 88
Holes 18 L 6320 m SSS 74
V'tors H
Fees   180fr (275fr)
Loc   6 km NE of Louviers. 25 km SE of Rouen
Arch   F Hawtree

North East

Ammerschwihr
BP 19, Route des Trois Épis, 68770 Ammerschwihr
Tel   03 89 47 17 30
Fax   03 89 47 17 77
Holes 18 L 5795 m Par 70
       9 hole short course
V'tors U
Fees   200fr (250fr)
Loc   8 km W of Colmar. 70 km S of Strasbourg
Arch   Robert Berthet

Bâle G&CC (1928)
Rue de Wentzwiller, 68220 Hagenthal-le-Bas
Tel   03 89 68 50 91
Fax   03 89 68 55 66
Holes 18 L 6255 m Par 72 SSS 73
V'tors WD–H (max 32) WE–M
Fees   320fr (360fr)
Loc   15 km SW of Basle
Arch   B von Limburger

Besançon (1968)
La Chevillote, 25620 Mamirolle
Tel   03 81 55 73 54
Fax   03 81 55 88 64
Holes 18 L 6070 m SSS 73
V'tors H
Fees   200fr (250fr)
Loc   12 km E of Besançon
Arch   Michael Fenn

Bitche (1988)
Rue des Prés, 57230 Bitche
Tel   03 87 96 15 30
Fax   03 87 96 08 04
Holes 18 L 6082 m SSS 72
       9 L 2293 m SSS 34
V'tors U
Loc   75 km NW of Strasbourg. 55 km SE of Saarbrücken
Arch   Fromanger

Châlons-en-Champagne (1988)
La Grande Romanie, 51460 Courtisols
Tel   03 07 55 24 30
Fax   03 26 66 66 81
Holes 18 L 6578 m SSS 76
V'tors U
Fees   200–250fr
Loc   St Etienne au Temple, 6 km from A4 Junction 28
Arch   Alain Tribout

Château de Bournel (1990)
25680 Cubry
Tel   03 81 86 00 10
Fax   03 81 86 01 06
Holes 18 L 5985 m SSS 72
Loc   50 km NE of Besançon
Arch   Robert Berthet

Combles-en-Barrois (1948)
14 Rue Basse, 55000 Combles-en-Barrois
Tel   03 29 45 16 03
Fax   03 29 45 16 06
Holes 18 L 6100 m Par 72
V'tors U
Fees   180fr (200fr)
Loc   80 km W of Nancy, nr Bar-le-Duc
Arch   Michel Gayon

Épinal (1985)
Rue du Merle-Blanc, 88001 Épinal
Tel   03 29 34 65 97
Holes 18 L 5700 m SSS 70
V'tors H
Loc   Épinal, 70 km S of Nancy
Arch   Michel Gayon

Faulquemont-Pontpierre (1993)
Rue du Golf, 57380 Faulquemont
Tel   03 87 29 21 21
Fax   03 87 90 76 25
Holes 18 L 6000 m SSS 72
       9 hole par 3 course
V'tors U
Loc   30 km E of Metz
Arch   Flipo/Fourès

Forêt d'Orient
BP13 Rouilly-Sacey, 10220 Piney
Tel   03 25 46 37 78
Holes 18 L 6120 m Par 72
V'tors U
Loc   20 km E of Troyes
Arch   E Rossi

La Grange aux Ormes
La Grange aux Ormes, 57157 Marly
Tel   03 87 63 10 62
Fax   03 87 55 01 77
Holes 18 L 6200 m Par 72
       9 L 2001 m Par 31
V'tors U H

Fees   200fr (250fr)
Loc   3 km S of Metz
Arch   Philippe Gourdon

Kempferhof (1988)
351 Rue du Moulin, 67115 Plobsheim
Tel   03 88 98 72 72
Fax   03 88 98 74 76
Holes 18 L 6020 m SSS 72
V'tors H
Fees   350fr (500fr)
Loc   10 km S of Strasbourg
Arch   Robert von Hagge

La Largue G&CC (1988)
Chemin du Largweg, 68580 Mooslargue
Tel   03 89 07 67 67
Fax   03 89 25 62 83
Holes 18 L 6150 m SSS 72
V'tors WD–H WE–NA before noon
       H
Fees   220fr (320fr)
Loc   25 km W of Basle
Arch   Jean Garaialde

Metz-Cherisey (1963)
Château de Cherisey, 57420 Cherisey
Tel   03 87 52 70 18
Fax   03 87 52 42 44
Holes 18 L 6172 m SSS 72
V'tors H
Fees   200fr (250fr)
Loc   15 km SE of Metz
Arch   Donald Harradine

Nancy-Aingeray (1962)
Aingeray, 54460 Liverdun
Tel   03 83 24 53 87
Holes 18 L 5577 m SSS 69
V'tors H
Fees   200fr (250fr)
Loc   17 km NW of Nancy
Arch   Michael Fenn

Nancy-Pulnoy (1993)
10 Rue du Golf, 54425 Pulnoy
Tel   03 83 18 10 18
Fax   03 83 18 10 19
Holes 18 L 6000 m SSS 72
       9 hole Par 3 course
V'tors WD–U WE–H
Fees   170fr (250fr)
Loc   10 km E of Nancy
Arch   Hawtree/Flipo

Prunevelle (1930)
Ferme des Petits-Bans, 25420 Dampierre-sur-le-Doubs
Tel   03 81 98 11 77
Fax   03 81 90 28 65
Holes 18 L 6281 m SSS 73
Loc   10 km S of Montbéliard, on D126

Reims-Champagne (1928)
Château des Dames de France, 51390 Gueux
Tel   03 26 05 46 10
Fax   03 26 05 46 19

For list of abbreviations see page 527

Holes 18 L 6026 m SSS 72
V'tors U
Fees 200fr (280fr)
Loc 10 km W of Reims
Arch Michael Fenn

Rhin Mulhouse (1969)
Ile du Rhin, 68490 Chalampe
Tel 03 89 26 07 86
Fax 03 89 26 27 80
Holes 18 L 5991 m SSS 72
V'tors WE–M
Fees 240fr (330fr)
Loc 20 km E of Mulhouse
Arch Donald Harradine

Rochat (1986)
*1305 Route du Noirmont,
39220 Les Rousses*
Tel 03 84 60 06 25
Fax 03 84 60 01 73
Holes 18 L 5388 m Par 71
V'tors U
Fees 180fr (250fr)
Loc 30 km N of Geneva (N5)

Rougemont-le-Château
Route de Masevaux, 90110 Rougemont-le-Château
Tel 03 84 23 74 74
Fax 03 84 23 03 15
Holes 18 L 6002 m SSS 72
V'tors U H
Fees 180fr (300fr)
Loc 18 km NE of Belfort. 25 km NW of Mulhouse
Arch Robert Berthet

Strasbourg (1934)
Route du Rhin, 67400 Illkirch
Tel 03 88 66 17 22
Fax 03 88 65 05 67
Holes 27 holes:
6105–6138 m SSS 72–73
V'tors WD–H (max 35)
Fees WD only–230fr
Loc 10 km S of Strasbourg
Arch Donald Harradine

Metz Technopole
Rue Félix Savart, 57070 Metz Technopole 2000
Tel 03 87 39 95 95
Holes 18 L 5774 m SSS 71
6 hole Par 3 course
V'tors H or Green card
Loc SE of Metz centre
Arch Robert Berthet

Troyes-Cordelière (1957)
Château de la Cordelière, 10210 Chaource
Tel 03 25 40 18 76
Fax 03 25 40 13 66
Holes 18 L 6154 m SSS 72
V'tors H
Fees 180fr (250fr)
Loc NE of Chaource on N443. 30 km SE of Troyes
Arch P Hirigoyen

Val de Sorne
Vernantois, 39570 Lons-le-Saunier
Tel 03 84 43 04 80
Fax 03 84 47 31 21
Holes 18 L 6000 m SSS 72
V'tors U
Fees 200–250fr
Loc 4kms SE of Lons-le-Saunier, between Geneva and Lyon
Arch Hugues Lambert

La Vitarderie (1986)
Chemin de Bourdonnerie BP#41, 51700 Dormans
Tel 03 26 58 25 09
Fax 03 26 59 33 88
Holes 18 L 5969 m Par 72
V'tors U
Loc Dormans, 20 km SW of Reims
Arch Olivier Brizon

Vittel
BP 122, 88804 Vittel-Cedex
Tel 03 29 08 18 80
Holes St Jean 18 L 6326 m SSS 72
Peulin 18 L 6100 m SSS 72
9 hole course
Loc Vittel, 70 km S of Nancy
Arch Allison/Morrison/Begin

La Wantzenau (1991)
C D 302, 67610 La Wantzenau
Tel 03 88 96 37 73
Fax 03 88 96 34 71
Holes 18 L 6400 m SSS 72
V'tors H
Fees 280fr (400fr)
Loc 12 km N of Strasbourg
Arch Pern/Garaialde

Paris Region

Béthemont-Chisan CC
12 Rue du Parc de Béthemont, 78300 Poissy
Tel 01 39 75 51 13
Fax 01 39 75 49 90
Holes 18 L 6035 m SSS 72
V'tors U
Fees 250fr (500fr)
Loc 30 km W of Paris
Arch Bernhard Langer

La Boulie
La Boulie, 78000 Versailles
Tel 01 39 50 59 41
Holes 18 L 6055 m SSS 71
18 L 6206 m SSS 72
9 hole course
V'tors H WE–M
Loc 15 km SW of Paris

Disneyland Paris (1992)
1 Allee de la Mare Houleuse, 77400 Magny-le-Hongre
Tel 01 60 45 68 04
Fax 01 60 45 68 33

Holes 18 L 6221 m Par 72
9 L 2905 m Par 36
V'tors U
Fees On application
Loc 32 km E of Paris via A4
Arch Ronald Fream

Feucherolles (1992)
78810 Feucherolles
Tel 01 30 54 94 94
Fax 01 30 54 92 37
Holes 18 L 6358 m Par 72
V'tors U
Fees 300–350fr (380–490fr)
Loc 23 km W of Paris
Arch JM Poellot

Fourqueux (1963)
Rue Saint Nom 36, 78112 Fourqueux
Tel 01 34 51 41 47
Fax 01 39 21 00 70
Holes 27 holes: 5615-6025 m Par 73-74
V'tors WD–U WE–M
Loc 4 km SW of St Germain-en-Laye, W of Paris

Isabella (1969)
RN12, Sainte-Appoline, 78370 Plaisir
Tel 01 30 54 10 62
Fax 01 30 54 67 58
Holes 18 L 5629 m SSS 71
V'tors WD–H WE–NA
Loc 28 km W of Paris (RN12)
Arch Paul Rolin

Joyenval (1992)
Chemin de la Tuilerie, 78240 Chambourcy
Tel 01 39 22 27 50
Fax 01 39 79 12 90
Holes Retz 18 L 6211 m Par 72
Marly 18 L 6249 m Par 72
V'tors M
Loc 25 km N of Paris, nr St Germain-en-Laye
Arch Robert Trent Jones Sr

National Golf Club (1990)
2 Avenue du Golf, 78280 Guyancourt
Tel 01 30 43 36 00
Fax 01 30 43 85 58
Holes Albatros 18 L 6515 m Par 72
Aigle 18 L 5936 m Par 71
Oiselet 9 L 2198 m Par 32
V'tors H or Green card
Fees 150–240fr (225–360fr)
Loc St Quentin-en-Yvelines, SW of Paris (D36)
Arch Chesneau/Von Hagge

Le Prieuré (1965)
78440 Sailly
Tel 01 34 76 70 12
Fax 01 34 76 71 62
Holes Ouest 18 L 6274 m SSS 72
Est 18 L 6157 m SSS 72
V'tors WD–H
Loc Sailly, 10 km NW of Meulan (D130). 45 km NW of Paris
Arch F Hawtree

For list of abbreviations see page 527

Rochefort (1964)
78730 Rochefort-en-Yvelines
Tel 01 30 41 31 81
Fax 01 30 41 94 01
Holes 18 L 5735 m SSS 71
V'tors U
Fees 250–450fr
Loc 45 km SW of Paris
Arch Hawtree

St Cloud (1911)
60 Rue du 19 Janvier, Garches 92380
Tel 01 47 01 01 85
Fax 01 47 01 19 57
Holes 18 L 5975 m SSS 72
18 L 4867 m SSS 67
V'tors H
Fees 500fr (600fr)
Loc Porte Dauphine, 9 km W of Paris
Arch HS Colt

St Germain (1922)
Route de Poissy, 78100 St Germain-en-Laye
Tel 01 39 10 30 30
Fax 01 39 10 30 31
Holes 18 L 6117 m SSS 72
9 L 2030 m SSS 34
V'tors WD–H WE–M
Fees 400fr
Loc 20 km W of Paris
Arch HS Colt

St Nom-La-Bretêche
(1959)
Hameau Tuilerie-Bignon, 78860 St Nom-La-Bretèche
Tel 01 30 80 04 40
Fax 01 34 62 60 44
Holes 18 L 6685 yds SSS 72
18 L 6712 yds SSS 72
V'tors H
Fees WD only–500fr
Loc 24 km W of Paris on A-13
Arch F Hawtree

St Quentin-en-Yvelines
RD 912, 78190 Trappes
Tel 01 30 50 86 40
Holes 18 L 5900 m SSS 71
18 L 5753 m SSS 70
V'tors H
Loc 20 km SW of Paris
Arch Hubert Chesneau

La Vaucouleurs
(1987)
Rue de l'Eglise, 78910 Civry-la-Forêt
Tel 01 34 87 62 29
Fax 01 34 87 70 09
Holes Rivière 18 L 6298 m Par 73
Vallons 18 L 5630 m SSS 70
V'tors H or Green card
Fees 200fr (350fr)
Loc 50 km W of Paris, between Mantes and Houdan
Arch Michel Gayon

Les Yvelines
Château de la Couharde, 78940 La-Queue-les-Yvelines
Tel 01 34 86 48 89
Fax 01 34 86 50 31
Holes 18 L 6344 m Par 72
9 L 2065 m Par 31
V'tors U
Fees 170fr (290fr)
Loc Montfort-l'Amaury, 45 km W of Paris
Arch HJ Baker

Provence & Côte d'Azur

Aix Marseille (1935)
13290 Les Milles
Tel 04 42 24 40 41/04 42 24 23 01
Fax 04 42 39 97 48
Holes 18 L 6291 m SSS 73
V'tors H
Fees D–150–220fr (D–250fr)
Loc 7 km SW of Aix-en-Provence. 15 km N of Marseille

Barbaroux (1989)
Route de Cabasse, 83170 Brignoles
Tel 04 94 69 63 63
Fax 04 94 59 00 93
Holes 18 L 6367 m SSS 72
V'tors U
Fees 260fr (260fr)
Loc Brignoles, 50 km E of Aix. 40 km N of Toulon
Arch PB Dye/PD Dye

Les Baux de Provence
(1987)
Domaine de Manville, 13520 Les Baux-de-Provence
Tel 04 90 54 40 20
Fax 04 90 54 40 93
Holes 9 L 2812 m SSS 36
V'tors U H
Loc 15 km NE of Arles. 15 km S of Avignon. 80 km W of Marseilles
Arch Martin Hawtree

Beauvallon-Grimaud
Boulevard des Collines, 83120 Sainte-Maxime
Tel 04 94 96 16 98
Holes 9 L 2503 m SSS 34
V'tors H
Loc 3 km SW of Sainte Maxime

Biot (1930)
La Bastide du Roi, 06410 Biot
Tel 04 93 65 08 48
Fax 04 93 65 05 63
Holes 18 L 5054 m Par 70
V'tors U
Loc Antibes 5km. Nice 15 km

Cannes Mandelieu Riviera (1990)
Avenue des Amazones, 06210 Mandelieu
Tel 04 92 97 49 49
Fax 04 92 97 49 42
Holes 18 L 5736 m SSS 71
V'tors U H–max 36
Fees 260fr (290fr)
Loc 10 km SW of Cannes, off A8
Arch Robert Trent Jones

Cannes-Mandelieu
(1891)
Route de Golf, 06210 Mandelieu
Tel 04 93 49 55 39
Fax 04 93 49 92 90
Holes 18 L 5871 m SSS 71
9 L 2852 m SSS 33
V'tors U H
Fees 260fr (300fr)
Loc Mandelieu, 7 km W of Cannes

Cannes-Mougins
(1925)
175 Route d'Antibes, 06250 Mougins
Tel 04 93 75 79 13
Fax 04 93 75 27 60
Holes 18 L 6304 m SSS 72
V'tors H
Loc 8 km NE of Cannes (D35)
Arch Colt/Simpson (1925). Alliss/Thomas (1977)

Château L'Arc (1985)
Domaine de Château L'Arc, 13710 Fuveau
Tel 04 42 53 28 38
Fax 04 42 29 08 41
Holes 18 L 6300 m SSS 71
V'tors U
Fees 250fr (290fr)
Loc 15 km SE of Aix-en-Provence
Arch Michel Gayon

Châteaublanc
Les Plans, 84310 Morières-les-Avignon
Tel 04 90 33 39 08
Fax 04 90 33 43 24
Holes 18 L 6141 m SSS 72
9 L 1267 m Par 28
V'tors H
Fees 170fr (210fr)
Loc 5 km SE of Avignon, nr Airport
Arch Thierry Sprecher

Digne-les-Bains (1990)
St Pierre de Gaubert, 0400 Digne-les-Bains
Tel 04 92 30 58 00
Fax 04 92 30 58 39
Holes 18 L 5861 m SSS 72
V'tors U
Loc 100 km NE of Aix-en-Provence
Arch Robert Berthet

Estérel Latitudes (1989)
Ave du Golf, 83700 St Raphaël
Tel 04 94 82 47 88
Fax 04 94 44 64 61
Holes 18 L 5921 m SSS 71
9 L 1392 m Par 29
V'tors U H
Fees 285fr
Loc 6 km N of St-Raphaël
Arch Robert Trent Jones

Frégate (1992)
Domaine de Frégate RD#559, 83270 St Cyr-sur-Mer
Tel 04 94 32 50 50
Fax 04 94 29 96 94
Holes 18 L 6210 m SSS 72
9 hole short course
V'tors U H
Fees 260fr (300fr)
Loc 25 km W of Toulon on coast
Arch Ronald Fream

Gap-Bayard (1988)
Centre d'Oxygénation, 05000 Gap
Tel 04 92 50 16 83
Fax 04 92 50 17 05
Holes 18 L 6023 m SSS 72
V'tors U
Fees 185fr (200fr)
Loc 7 km N of Gap. 80 km S of Grenoble
Arch Hugues Lambert

Grand Avignon (1989)
BP 121, Les Chênes Verts, 84270 Vedene
Tel 04 90 31 49 94
Fax 04 90 31 01 21
Holes 18 L 6046 m Par 72
9 hole short course
V'tors U
Fees 210–250fr
Loc Vedene, 10 km NE of Avignon
Arch Georges Roumeas

La Grande Bastide (1990)
Chemin des Picholines, 06740 Châteauneuf de Grasse
Tel 04 93 77 70 08
Fax 04 93 77 72 36
Holes 18 L 6105 m SSS 72
V'tors U H
Fees 270fr (300fr)
Loc Grasse, 17 km N of Cannes
Arch Cabell Robinson

Grasse CC (1992)
1 Route des Trois Ponts, 06130 Grasse
Tel 04 93 60 55 44
Fax 04 93 60 55 19
Holes 18 L 6021 m SSS 72
V'tors U
Fees 280fr (300fr)
Loc 18 km N of Cannes
Arch JP Fourès

Le Lavandou
2 Ave du Cap Nègre, Cavalière, 83980 Le Lavandou
Tel 04 94 05 75 80
Holes 18 L 5649 m Par 72
V'tors U
Loc 50 km E of Toulon, between Hyères and St Tropez
Arch Yves Bureau

Miramas (1993)
Mas de Combe, 13140 Miramas
Tel 04 90 58 56 55
Fax 04 90 17 38 73
Holes 18 L 5670m Par 72
V'tors H or Green card
Fees 110–150fr (150–200fr)
Loc 50 km S of Avignon. 50 km NW of Marseilles
Arch Serge Giraud

Monte Carlo (1910)
Route du Mont-Agel, 06320 La Turbie
Tel 04 93 41 09 11
Fax 04 93 41 09 55
Holes 18 L 5679 m SSS 71
V'tors H
Fees 350fr (450fr)
Loc Mont Agel, La Turbie, 10 km N of Monte Carlo

Opio-Valbonne (1966)
Route de Roquefort-les-Pins, 06650 Opio
Tel 04 93 12 00 08
Fax 04 93 12 26 00
Holes 18 L 5892 m SSS 72
V'tors H
Fees 330fr (360fr)
Loc 15 km N of Cannes
Arch Donald Harradine

Pierrevert (1986)
La Grande Gardette, 04860 Pierrevert
Tel 04 92 72 17 19
Fax 04 92 72 59 12
Email Pierrevert.golf@wanadoo.fr
http://pro.wanadoo.fr/pierrevert.golf
Holes 18 L 6040 m SSS 72
V'tors U
Fees 200fr
Loc 5 km SW of Manosque. 45 km NE of Aix
Arch Artea

Pont Royal (1992)
Pont Royal, 13370 Mallemort
Tel 04 90 57 40 79
Fax 04 90 59 45 83
Holes 18 L 6303 m SSS 74
V'tors H
Fees 200–300fr
Loc 35 km SE of Avignon on N7, between Avignon and Aix
Arch Severiano Ballesteros

Provence G&CC (1991)
Route de Fontaine de Vaucluse, L'Isle sur la Sorgue, 84800 Saumane
Tel 04 90 20 20 65
Fax 04 90 20 32 01
Holes 18 L 6045 m SSS 72
9 hole short course
V'tors U
Loc 20 km E of Avignon
Arch Jean Garaialde

Roquebrune (1989)
CD 7, 83520 Roquebrune-sur-Argens
Tel 04 94 82 92 91
Fax 04 94 82 94 74
Holes 18 L 6031 m SSS 71
V'tors H
Fees 260fr
Loc 35 km N of Saint-Tropez. 40 km SW of Cannes
Arch Udo Barth

Royal Mougins (1993)
424 Avenue du Roi, 06250 Mougins
Tel 04 92 92 49 69
Fax 04 92 92 49 70
Holes 18 L 6004 m SSS 72
V'tors H or I
Fees 800fr (inc lunch)
Loc 5 km N of Cannes
Arch Robert von Hagge

St Endreol (1992)
Route de Bagnols-en-Fôret, 83920 La Motte
Tel 04 94 51 89 89
Fax 04 94 51 89 90
Holes 18 L 6219 m SSS 73
V'tors U H
Fees 300fr
Loc 30 km N of St Tropez. 30 km W of Cannes
Arch Michel Gayon

La Sainte-Baume (1988)
Golf Hotel, Domaine de Châteauneuf, 83860 Nans-les-Pins
Tel 04 94 78 60 12
Fax 04 94 78 63 52
Holes 18 L 6134 m SSS 72
V'tors U
Fees 210fr (260fr)
Loc 30 km S of Aix-en-Provence, via A8 (exit Saint Maximin)
Arch Robert Berthet

Sainte-Maxime
Route de Débarquement, 83120 Sainte-Maxime
Tel 04 94 49 26 60
Fax 04 94 49 00 39
Holes 18 L 6155 m SSS 71
V'tors H
Loc 15 km N of Saint Tropez. 80 km W of Nice (RN98)
Arch Donald Harradine

La Salette (1988)
Impasse des Vaudrans,
13011 La Valentine Marseille
Tel 04 91 27 12 16
Fax 04 91 27 21 33
Holes 18 L 5436 m SSS 69
V'tors U
Fees 190fr (250fr)
Loc Nr centre of Marseilles
Arch Michel Gayon

Servanes (1989)
Domaine de Servanes, 13890 Mouriès
Tel 04 90 47 59 95
Fax 04 90 47 52 58
Holes 18 L 6100m SSS 72
V'tors H
Fees 200fr (250fr)
Loc 35 km S of Avignon
Arch Sprecher/Watine

Taulane
Domaine du Château de Taulane
RN#85, 83840 La Martre
Tel 04 93 60 31 30
Fax 04 93 60 33 23
Holes 18 L 6250 m Par 72
V'tors H
Fees 200–300fr (350fr)
Loc 55 km N of Cannes on N85 (Route Napoleon)
Arch Gary Player

Valcros (1964)
Domaine de Valcros, 83250 La Londe-les-Maures
Tel 04 94 66 81 02
Fax 04 94 35 03 73
Holes 18 L 5274 m SSS 68
V'tors H
Fees 230fr (280fr)
Loc 10 km W of Le Lavandou
Arch F Hawtree

Valescure (1895)
BP 451, 83704 St-Raphaël Cedex
Tel 04 94 82 40 46
Fax 04 94 82 41 42
Holes 18 L 5067 m Par 68
V'tors U H
Fees 250fr
Loc 5 km E of St-Raphaël
Arch Lord Ashcombe

Rhône-Alps

Aix-les-Bains (1913)
Avenue du Golf, 73100 Aix-les-Bains
Tel 04 79 61 23 35
Fax 04 79 34 06 01
Holes 18 L 5597 m SSS 71
V'tors H
Loc 3 km S of Aix

Albon (1989)
Domaine de Senaud, Albon,
26140 St Rambert d'Albon
Tel 04 75 03 03 90
Fax 04 75 03 11 01

Holes 18 L 6108 m Par 72
  9 L 1260 m Par 29
V'tors U
Fees 180–240fr
Loc 60 km S of Lyon, motorway exit Chanas
Arch Antoine d'Ormesson

Annecy (1953)
Echarvines, 74290 Talloires
Tel 04 50 60 12 89
Fax 04 50 60 08 80
Holes 18 L 5017 m SSS 68
V'tors H
Loc 13 km E of Annecy
Arch Cecil Blandford

Annonay-Gourdan (1988)
Domaine de Gourdan,
07430 Saint Clair
Tel 04 75 67 03 84
Fax 04 75 67 79 50
Holes 18 L 5900 m SSS 71
V'tors U
Loc 35 km SE of St Etienne.
  50 km SW of Lyon
Arch Sprecher/Watine

Les Arcs
B P 18, 73706 Les Arcs Cedex
Tel 04 79 07 43 95
Fax 04 79 07 47 65
Holes 18 L 5547 m SSS 70
V'tors H
Loc 90 km E of Chambery on N90

Le Beaujolais (1991)
69480 Lucenay-Anse
Tel 04 74 67 04 44
Fax 04 74 67 09 60
Holes 18 L 6137 m SSS 72
V'tors U H
Loc 25 km N of Lyon

Bossey G&CC (1985)
Château de Crevin, 74160 Bossey
Tel 04 50 43 95 50
Fax 04 50 95 32 57
Holes 18 L 6022 m Par 71
V'tors WD–U WE–NA
Fees 300fr
Loc 6 km S of Geneva
Arch Robert Trent Jones Jr

La Bresse
Domaine de Mary, 01400 Condessiat
Tel 04 74 51 42 09
Fax 04 74 51 40 09
Holes 18 L 6217 m Par 72
V'tors WD–U WE–H
Loc 15 km SW of Bourg-en-Bresse, via RN73
Arch Jeremy Pern

Chamonix (1934)
BP 31, 74402 Chamonix Cedex
Tel 04 50 53 06 28
Fax 04 50 53 38 60
Holes 18 L 6087 m SSS 72

V'tors H
Loc 3 km N of Chamonix (RN 506). Geneva 80 km
Arch Robert Trent Jones Sr

Le Clou (1985)
01330 Villars-les-Dombes
Tel 04 74 98 19 65
Fax 04 74 98 15 15
Holes 18 L 5000 m SSS 67
V'tors WD–U WE–H
Loc 30 km NE of Lyon

La Commanderie (1964)
L'Aumusse-Crottet, 01290 Pont-de-Veyle
Tel 04 85 30 44 12
Fax 04 85 30 55 02
Holes 18 L 5560 m SSS 69
V'tors H
Loc 7 km E of Mâcon on RN 79

Correncon-en-Vercors (1987)
Les Ritons, 38250 Correncon-en-Vercors
Tel 04 76 95 80 42
Fax 04 76 95 84 63
Holes 18 L 5550 m Par 71
V'tors U
Loc 35 km S of Grenoble, off D531
Arch Hugues Lambert

Divonne (1931)
01220 Divonne-les-Bains
Tel 04 50 40 34 11
Fax 04 50 40 34 25
Holes 18 L 5858 m SSS 71
V'tors H–max 35
Fees 300fr (500fr)
Loc Divonne 1/2 km. 18 km N of Geneva
Arch Nakowsky

La Dombes (1986)
01390 Mionnay
Tel 04 78 91 84 84
Fax 04 78 91 02 73
Holes 18 L 6060 m SSS 71
V'tors U
Loc 20 km N of Lyon towards Bourg

Esery (1990)
Esery, 74930 Reignier
Tel 04 50 36 58 70
Fax 04 50 36 57 62
Holes 18 L 6350 m SSS 73
  9 L 2024 m SSS 31
V'tors WD–H WE–NA
Fees 280fr
Loc 10 km S of Geneva
Arch Michel Gayon

Flaine-Les-Carroz (1984)
74300 Flaine
Tel 04 50 90 85 44
Fax 04 50 90 88 21
Holes 18 L 3693 m Par 63

For list of abbreviations see page 527

V'tors U
Loc 4 km N of Flaine. 60 km SE of Geneva Airport
Arch Robert Berthet

Giez (1991)
Lac d'Annecy, 74210 Giez
Tel 04 50 44 48 41
Fax 04 50 32 55 93
Holes 18 L 5820 m Par 72
 9 L 2250 m Par 33
V'tors H or Green card
Fees 220–270fr
Loc 20 km SE of Annecy
Arch Didier Fruchet

Le Gouverneur
Château du Breuil, 01390 Monthieux
Tel 04 72 26 40 34
Fax 04 72 26 41 61
Holes 18 L 6477 m Par 72
 18 L 5959 m Par 72
 9 L 2365 m Par 34
V'tors H or green card
Fees 180fr (250fr)
Loc NE of Lyon, off A46
Arch Fruchet/Sprecher

Grenoble-Bresson (1990)
Route de Montavie, 38320 Eybens
Tel 04 76 73 65 00
Fax 04 76 73 65 51
Holes 18 L 6343 m SSS 72
V'tors U
Fees 230fr (270fr)
Loc 10 km SE of Grenoble
Arch Robert Trent Jones Jr

Grenoble-Charmeil
38210 St Quentin-sur-Isère
Tel 04 76 93 67 28
Fax 04 76 93 62 04
Holes 18 L 6200 m Par 73
V'tors U
Fees 185fr (250fr)
Loc 20 km NW of Grenoble, off A49
Arch Perl/Garaialde

Grenoble-Uriage (1921)
Les Alberges, 38410 Uriage
Tel 04 76 89 03 47
Fax 04 76 73 65 51
Holes 9 L 2005 m SSS 32
V'tors U
Fees 130fr (160fr)
Loc 15 km E of Grenoble
Arch Watine/Sprecher

Lyon (1921)
38280 Villette-d'Anthon
Tel 04 78 31 11 33
Fax 04 72 02 48 27
Holes 18 L 6229 m SSS 72
 18 L 6727 m SSS 74
V'tors U H
Fees 220fr (330fr)
Loc 20 km E of Lyon
Arch Fenn/Lambert

Lyon-Chassieu
Route de Lyon, 69680 Chassieu
Tel 04 78 90 84 77
Fax 04 78 90 88 85
Holes 18 L 5941 m Par 70
V'tors H
Loc 10 km E of Lyon
Arch Chris Pittman

Lyon-Verger (1977)
69360 Saint-Symphorien D'Ozon
Tel 04 78 02 84 20
Fax 04 78 02 08 12
Holes 18 L 5800 m SSS 69
V'tors U
Fees 180fr (250fr)
Loc 14 km S of Lyon on A7, or RN7 2 km S of Feyzin

Maison Blanche G&CC (1991)
01170 Echenevex
Tel 04 50 42 44 42
Fax 04 50 42 44 43
Holes 18 L 6246 m SSS 72
 9 L 1757 m Par 31
V'tors WD–U H (max 30)
Loc 15 km from Geneva
Arch Harradine/Dongradi

Méribel (1973)
BP 54, 73553 Méribel Cedex
Tel 04 79 00 52 67
Fax 04 79 00 38 85
Holes 18 L 5319 m SSS 70
V'tors H
Fees 270fr
Loc 15 km S of Moutiers. 35 km S of Albertville
Arch Sprecher/Watine

Mont-d'Arbois (1964)
74120 Megève
Tel 04 50 21 29 79
Fax 04 50 93 02 63
Holes 18 L 6100 m SSS 72
V'tors WE–restricted. Booking required Jul/Aug
Fees 200–300fr
Loc 3 km SE of Megève
Arch Henry Cotton

Royal Golf Club (1904)
Rive Sud du lac de Genève, 74500 Évian
Tel 04 50 75 46 66
Fax 04 50 75 65 54
Holes 18 L 6030 m SSS 72
V'tors H
Fees D–190–310fr (D–290–380fr)
Loc 2 km W of Évian. 40 km NE of Geneva Airport
Arch Cabell Robinson

St Etienne (1989)
62 Rue St Simon, 42000 St Etienne
Tel 04 77 32 14 63
Fax 04 77 33 61 23
Holes 18 L 5700 m Par 72
 6 hole Par 3 course
V'tors U
Fees 180fr (230fr)

Loc Nr centre of St Etienne. Lyon 60 km
Arch Thierry Sprecher

Salvagny
100 Rue des Granges, 69890 La Tour de Salvagny
Tel 04 78 48 83 60
Fax 04 78 48 00 16
Holes 18 L 6300 m SSS 73 Par 72
V'tors U
Loc Lyon 20 km
Arch Drancourt

La Sorelle (1991)
Domaine de Gravagnieux, 01320 Villette-sur-Ain
Tel 04 74 35 47 27
Fax 04 74 35 44 51
Holes 18 L 6100 m SSS 72
V'tors U
Loc 50 km NE of Lyon
Arch Patrick Jacquier

Tignes (1968)
Val Claret, 73320 Tignes
Tel 04 79 06 37 42
Fax 04 79 06 35 64
Holes 18 L 4810 m SSS 68
V'tors H–max 35
Fees 200fr
Loc 50 km E of Moutiers, off D902, nr Italian border. 70 km S of Chamonix

Valdaine (1989)
Domaine de la Valdaine, Montboucher/Jabron, 26740 Montelimar-Montboucher
Tel 04 75 00 71 33
Fax 04 75 01 24 49
Holes 18 L 5631 m SSS 71
V'tors U
Fees 180fr (260fr)
Loc 4 km E of Montelimar. 50 km S of Valence
Arch TJ Macauley

Valence St Didier (1983)
26300 St Didier de Charpey
Tel 04 75 59 67 01
Fax 04 75 59 68 19
Holes 18 L 5807 m SSS 71
V'tors U
Fees 160fr (210fr)
Loc 12 km E of Valence
Arch Thierry Sprecher

Toulouse & Pyrenees

Albi Lasbordes (1989)
Château de Lasbordes, 81000 Albi
Tel 05 63 54 98 07
Fax 05 63 47 21 55
Holes 18 L 6200 m SSS 72
V'tors U
Fees 170fr (230fr)
Loc 70 km NE of Toulouse
Arch Garaialde/Pern

For list of abbreviations see page 527

Ariège (1986)
09240 La Bastide-de-Serou
Tel 05 61 64 56 78
Fax 05 61 64 57 99
Holes 18 L 6000 m SSS 71
V'tors H
Loc Unjat, 17 km NW of Foix
Arch Michel Gayon

La Bigorre (1992)
Pouzac, 65200 Bagnères de Bigorre
Tel 05 62 91 06 20
Holes 18 L 5909 m SSS 72
V'tors U
Loc 18 km S of Tarbes. 150 km W of Toulouse
Arch Olivier Brizon

Château de Terrides
(1986)
Domaine de Terrides, 82100 Labourgade
Tel 05 63 95 61 07
Fax 05 63 95 64 97
Holes 18 L 6420 m SSS 71
V'tors U
Loc 45 km NW of Toulouse
Arch J-P Foures

Embats
Route de Montesquiou, 32000 Auch
Tel 05 62 05 20 80/05 62 61 10 31
Fax 05 62 05 92 55
Holes 18 L 4751 m SSS 65
V'tors U
Fees 150fr (170fr)
Loc 4 km W of Auch. 80 km W of Toulouse
Arch André Migret

Étangs de Fiac (1987)
Brazis, 81500 Fiac
Tel 05 63 70 64 70
Fax 05 63 75 32 91
Holes 18 L 5800 m SSS 71
V'tors U
Fees 150–220fr
Loc 45 km NE of Toulouse
Arch M Hawtree

Florentin-Gaillac (1990)
Le Bosc, Florentin, 81150 Marssac-sur-Tarn
Tel 05 63 55 20 50
Fax 05 63 53 26 41
Holes 18 L 6150 m SSS 71
V'tors U
Loc 10 km W of Albi. 70 km NE of Toulouse
Arch Robert Berthet

Guinlet (1986)
32800 Eauze
Tel 05 62 09 80 84
Fax 05 62 09 84 50
Holes 18 L 5565 m Par 71
V'tors U
Loc 60 km SW of Agen. 150 km SE of Bordeaux
Arch M Thevenin

Lannemezan
La Demi-Lune, 65300 Lannemezan
Tel 05 62 98 01 01
Holes 18 L 5872 m Par 70
V'tors H
Loc 38 km SE of Tarbes
Arch Hirigoyen/Laserre

Lourdes
Lac de Lourdes, 65100 Lourdes
Tel 05 62 42 02 06
Holes 18 L 5675 m SSS 72
V'tors U
Loc 4 km W of Lourdes
Arch Olivier Brizon

Luchon (1908)
BP 40, 31110 Bagnères de Luchon
Tel 05 61 79 03 27
Holes 9 L 2375 m SSS 66
V'tors H
Loc Luchon, 90 km SE of Tarbes. 145 km S of Toulouse
Arch Fenn/Hawtree

Mazamet-La Barouge
(1956)
81660 Pont de l'Arn
Tel 05 63 61 08 00/63 67 06 72
Fax 05 63 61 13 03
Holes 18 L 5623 m SSS 70
V'tors U
Fees 160fr (220fr)
Loc 2 km N of Mazamet. 80 km E of Toulouse. 80 km W of Béziers
Arch Mackenzie Ross/Hawtree

Toulouse (1951)
31320 Vieille-Toulouse
Tel 05 61 73 45 48
Fax 05 62 19 04 67
Holes 18 L 5602 m Par 69
V'tors U
Fees 250fr
Loc 8 km S of Toulouse
Arch Hawtree

Toulouse-La Ramée
Ferme Cousturier, 31170 Tournefeuille
Tel 05 61 07 09 09
Fax 05 61 07 15 93
Holes 18 L 5605 m SSS 69
9 hole short course
V'tors H
Loc SW of Toulouse
Arch Hawtree

Toulouse-Palmola (1974)
Route d'Albi, 31660 Buzet-sur-Tarn
Tel 05 61 84 20 50
Fax 05 61 84 48 92
Holes 18 L 6156 m SSS 73
V'tors U
Fees 210fr (300–350fr)
Loc 18 km NE of Toulouse. A68 Junction 4
Arch Michael Fenn

Toulouse-Seilh
Route de Grenade, 31840 Seilh
Tel 05 61 42 59 30
Fax 05 61 42 34 17
Holes Red 18 L 6122 m SSS 72
Yellow 18 L 4202 m SSS 64
V'tors H
Fees 200–250fr
Loc 15 km N of Toulouse. Blagnac Airport 5 km
Arch Jean Garaialde

Toulouse-Teoula
71 Avenue des Landes, 31830 Plaisance du Touch
Tel 05 61 91 98 80
Fax 05 61 91 49 66
Holes 18 L 5500 m Par 69
V'tors H or green card
Fees 200fr
Loc 15 km W of Toulouse
Arch Martin Hawtree

Les Tumulus (1987)
1 Rue du Bois, 65310 Laloubère
Tel 05 62 45 14 50
Fax 05 62 45 11 82
Email golf.des.tumulus@wanadoo.fr
http://perso.wanadoo.fr/tumulus
Holes 18 L 5050 m Par 70
V'tors U
Fees 150fr (180fr)
Loc 2 km S of Tarbes, towards Bagnères
Arch Charles de Ginestet

Germany

Berlin & East

Balmer See (1995)
Drewinscher Weg 1, 17429 Neppermin
Tel (038379) 28199
Fax (038379) 28222
Holes 18 L 6078 m Par 73
V'tors U H
Fees 50DM (75DM)
Loc Usedom, 50 km E of Greifswald
Arch M Skeide

Berlin G&CC Motzener See (1991)
Am Golfplatz 5, 15741 Motzen
Tel (033769) 50130
Fax (033769) 50134
Holes 18 L 6330 m SSS 73
9 L 2756 m SSS 54
V'tors H–booking required

Germany

Fees 90DM (110DM)
Loc 30 km S of Berlin
Arch Kurt Rossknecht

Berlin Wannsee (1895)
Golfweg 22, 14109 Berlin
Tel (030) 806 7060
Holes 18 L 6088 m SSS 72
9 L 4442 m SSS 64
V'tors WD–U H WE–M
Fees 100DM (120DM)
Loc 17 km SW of Berlin
Arch Harris Bros (1925)

Elbflorenz GC Dresden
(1992)
Ferdinand von Schillstr 2, 01728 Possendorf
Tel (035206) 2430
Fax (035206) 24317
Holes 18 holes Par 73
V'tors H
Fees 65DM (75DM)
Loc Dresden 12 km
Arch Dieter Sziedat

Potsdamer Tremmen
(1990)
Tremmener Landstrasse, 14641 Tremmen
Tel (033233) 80244
Fax (033233) 80957
Holes 18 L 5921 m Par 72
V'tors H
Fees 60DM (80DM)
Loc SW of Berlin

Schloss Meisdorf (1996)
Petersberger Trift 33, 06463 Meisdorf
Tel (034743) 98450
Fax (034743) 98499
Holes 18 L 6236 m Par 72
V'tors U H
Fees 40DM (60DM)
Loc 70 km S of Magdeburg
Arch Gerd Osterkamp

Semlin am See (1992)
Ferchesarerstrasse, 14715 Semlin
Tel (03385) 5540
Fax (03385) 554200
Holes 18 L 6348 m SSS 73
V'tors H
Fees 70DM (100DM)
Loc 80 km W of Berlin (B5/B188)
Arch Christoph Städler

Sporting Club Berlin
(1992)
Parkallee 3, 15526 Bad Sarrow
Tel (033631) 63300
Fax (033631) 63310
Holes 18 L 6118 m Par 72
18 L 6084 m Par 72
V'tors U
Fees 90DM (120DM)
Loc 70 km SE of Berlin
Arch Palmer/Faldo

Bremen & North West

Club Zur Vahr (1905)
Bgm-Spitta-Allee 34, 28329 Bremen
Tel Bremen (0421) 204480;
Garlstedt (04795) 417
Fax (0421) 244 9248
Holes Garlstedt 18 L 6535 m Par 74
SSS 75; Bremen 9 L 5862 m
Par 71 SSS 71
V'tors WD–H WE–M
Fees Garlstedt–70DM
Bremen–50DM
Loc Garlstedt–30 km N of
Bremen. Vahr-Bremen
Arch B von Limburger

Herzogstadt Celle
(1985)
Beukenbusch 1, 29229 Celle
Tel (05086) 395
Fax (05086) 8288
Holes 18 L 5915 m SSS 71
V'tors H
Loc 6 km NE of Celle, towards
Lüneburg. 40 km NE of
Hanover
Arch Wolfgang Siegmann

Küsten GC Hohe Klint
(1978)
Hohe Klint, 27478 Cuxhaven
Tel (04723) 2737
Fax (04723) 5022
Holes 18 L 6047 m SSS 72
V'tors U H
Fees 50DM (70DM)
Loc 12 km SW of Cuxhaven on
Route 6, nr Oxstedt

Münster-Wilkinghege
(1963)
Steinfurterstr 448, 48159 Münster
Tel (0251) 214090
Fax (0251) 261518
Holes 18 L 5990 m SSS 71
V'tors WD–H WE–I
Fees 60DM (80DM)
Loc 2 km N of Münster
Arch W Siegmann

Oldenburgischer (1964)
Am Golfplatz 1, 26180 Rastede
Tel (04402) 7240
Fax (04402) 70417
Holes 18 L 6117 m SSS 72
V'tors WD–U WE–M
Fees 50DM (60DM)
Loc 10 km N of Oldenburg,
nr Rastede
Arch Von Limburger/Schantmeyer

Ostfriesland (1980)
Postbox 1220, 26634 Wiesmoor
Tel (04944) 6440
Fax (04944) 6441

Holes 18 L 6256 m SSS 73
V'tors U
Fees 50DM (70DM)
Loc 25 km SW of Wilhelmshaven
Arch Frank Pennink

Soltau (1982)
Hof Loh, 29614 Soltau
Tel (05191) 14077
Fax (05191) 2593
Holes 18 L 6274 m SSS 73
9 L 2340 m SSS 54
V'tors H
Loc Tetendorf, S of Soltau

Syke (1989)
Schultenweg 1, 28857 Syke-Okel
Tel (04242) 8230
Fax (04242) 8255
Holes 18 L 6266 m Par 73
V'tors U H
Fees 50DM (60DM)
Loc 20 km S of Bremen

Tietlingen (1979)
29683 Fallingbostel
Tel (05162) 3889
Fax (05162) 7564
Holes 18 L 6193 m Par 72 SSS 73
V'tors H
Fees 50DM (60DM)
Loc 65 km N of Hanover, between
Walsrode and Fallingbostel
Arch Bruns/Chadwick

Verden (1988)
Holtumer Str 24, 27283 Verden
Tel (04230) 1470
Fax (04230) 1550
Holes 18 hole course Par 72 SSS 72
V'tors U
Fees 50DM (60DM)
Loc 30 km E of Bremen, nr Walle

Worpswede (1974)
Giehlermühlen, 27729 Vollersode
Tel (04763) 7313
Fax (04763) 6193
Holes 18 L 6200 m SSS 72
V'tors WD–U H WE–M H
Fees 50DM (60DM)
Loc Giehlermuhlen, 20 km N of
Bremen, off B74

Central North

Dillenburg
Auf dem Altscheid, 35687 Dillenburg
Tel (02771) 5001
Fax (02771) 5002
Holes 18 L 6115 m Par 72
V'tors U H
Fees 65DM (80DM)
Loc 30 km S of Siegen. 100 km N
of Frankfurt

Hofgut Praforst (1992)
Postfach 1137, 36081 Hünfeld
Tel   (06652) 9970
Fax   (06652) 99755
Holes   18 hole course
     9 hole course
V'tors   H–54 max
Fees   60DM (80DM)
Loc   Hünfeld, 10 km N of Fulda, off Route 27
Arch   Deutsche Golf Consult

Kassel-Wilhelmshöhe (1958)
Ehlenerstr 21, 34131 Kassel
Tel   (0561) 33509
Fax   (0561) 37729
Holes   18 L 5691 m SSS 70
V'tors   U H
Fees   60DM (80DM)
Loc   Wilhelmshöhe, 5 km W of Kassel
Arch   Donald Harradine

Kurhessischer GC Oberaula (1987)
Postfach 31, 36278 Oberaula
Tel   (06628) 1573
Fax   (06628) 1573
Holes   18 L 6050 m SSS 72
V'tors   U H
Loc   50 km S of Kassel, nr Kircheim
Arch   Deutsche Golf Consult

Licher Golf (1992)
35423 Lich
Tel   (06404) 91071
Fax   (06404) 91072
Holes   18 L 6065m SSS 72
V'tors   H–booking necessary Sun–M
Fees   80DM (100DM)
Loc   45 km N of Frankfurt
Arch   Heinz Fehring

Rhoen (1971)
Am Golfplatz, 36145 Hofbieber
Tel   (06657) 1334
Fax   (06657) 1754
Holes   18 L 5686 m SSS 70
V'tors   H
Fees   50DM (70DM)
Loc   Hofbieber, 11 km E of Fulda
Arch   Kurt Peters

Schloss Braunfels (1970)
Homburger Hof, 35619 Braunfels
Tel   (06442) 4530
Fax   (06442) 6683
Holes   18 L 6085 m Par 73
V'tors   WD–H (max 36) WE–H NA 10am–3pm
Fees   D–70DM (90DM)
Loc   70 km N of Frankfurt
Arch   Bernhard von Limburger

Schloss Sickendorf (1990)
Schloss Sickendorf, 36341 Lauterbach
Tel   (06641) 96130
Fax   (06641) 961335
Holes   18 L 6124 m SSS 72
V'tors   H
Fees   70DM
Loc   30 km W of Fulda. 120 km E of Frankfurt
Arch   Spangemacher

Winnerod
Parkstr 22, 35447 Reiskirchen
Tel   (06408) 9513-0
Fax   (06408) 9513-13
Holes   18 L 6069 m Par 72
     9 hole Par 3 course
V'tors   U H
Fees   50DM (90DM)
Loc   Hessen, 30 km N of Frankfurt/Main
Arch   Michael Pinner

Central South

Bad Kissingen (1910)
Euerdorferstr 11, 97688 Bad Kissingen
Tel   (0971) 3608
Fax   (0971) 60140
Holes   18 L 5699 m SSS 70
V'tors   U H
Fees   65DM (75DM)
Loc   Bad Kissingen 2km. 65 km N of Würzburg

Frankfurter (1913)
Golfstrasse 41, 60528 Frankfurt/Main
Tel   (069) 666 2318
Fax   (069) 666 7018
Holes   18 L 6455 yds SSS 71
V'tors   H–28 max
Fees   85DM (100DM)
Loc   6 km SW of Frankfurt, nr Airport

Hanau-Wilhelmsbad (1958)
Wilhelmsbader Allee 32, 63454 Hanau
Tel   (06181) 82071
Fax   (06181) 86967
Holes   18 L 6227 m Par 73
V'tors   WD–H WE–M H
Fees   80DM (100DM)
Loc   4 km NW of Hanau on B8-40/AB66. Frankfurt 15 km
Arch   Ernst Kothe

Homburger (1899)
Saalburgchaussee 2, 61350 Bad Homburg
Tel   (06172) 306808
Fax   (06172) 32648
Holes   10 holes Par 70 SSS 69
V'tors   H
Fees   50DM (70DM)
Loc   On B456 to Usingen

Idstein-Wörsdorf (1989)
Gut Henriettenthal, 65510 Idstein-Wörsdorf
Tel   (06126) 9322-0
Fax   (06126) 9322-22
Holes   18 L 6165 m SSS 72
V'tors   WD–H WE–M
Fees   70DM (100DM)
Loc   25 km N of Wiesbaden
Arch   Kurt Rossknecht

Kitzingen (1980)
Larson Barracks, 97318 Kitzingen
Tel   (09321) 4956
Fax   (09321) 21936
Holes   18 L 6084 m Par 72
V'tors   U
Fees   40DM (60DM)
Loc   20 km E of Würzburg

Kronberg G&LC (1954)
Schloss Friedrichshof, Hainstr 25, 61476 Kronberg/Taunus
Tel   (06173) 1426
Fax   (06173) 5953
Holes   18 L 5183 m SSS 68
V'tors   WD–U H WE–M H
Fees   70DM (90DM)
Loc   16 km NW of Frankfurt
Arch   Ernst Kothe

Main-Spessart (1990)
Postfach 1204, 97821 Marktheidenfeld-Eichenfürst
Tel   (09391) 8435
Fax   (09391) 8816
Holes   18 holes Par 72
V'tors   H–max 36
Fees   50DM (70DM)
Loc   80 km E of Frankfurt/Main
Arch   Harradine

Main-Taunus (1979)
Lange Seegewann 2, 65205 Wiesbaden
Tel   (06122) 52550/52208(Sec)
Holes   18 L 6045 m SSS 72
V'tors   H
Loc   15 km NW of Frankfurt Airport

Mannheim-Viernheim (1930)
Alte Mannheimer Str 3, 68519 Viernheim
Tel   (06204) 71313 (Clubhouse), (06204) 78737 (Sec)
Fax   (06204) 740181
Holes   9 L 6060 m SSS 72
V'tors   WD–H WE–M H (Summer)
Loc   10 km NE of Mannheim

Maria Bildhausen
Rindhof 1, 97702 Münnerstadt
Tel   (09766) 1601
Fax   (09766) 1602
Holes   18 L 6047 m Par 72
     6 hole short course
V'tors   U

Germany

Fees	60DM (70DM)
Loc	80 km NE of Wurzburg
Arch	Christian Habeck

Neuhof
Hofgut Neuhof, 63303 Dreieich

Tel	(06102) 327927/327010
Fax	(06102) 327012
Holes	18 L 6151 m SSS 72
V'tors	WD–H WE–M
Fees	100DM
Loc	Hofgut Neuhof, S of Frankfurt, off A3
Arch	Patrick Merrigan

Rhein Main (1977)
Steubenstrasse 9, 65189 Wiesbaden

Tel	(0611) 373014
Holes	18 L 6116 m SSS 71
V'tors	M
Loc	Wiesbaden 6 km

Rheinblick
Weisser Weg, 65201 Wiesbaden-Frauenstein

Tel	(0611) 420675
Fax	(0611) 941 0434
Holes	18 L 6604 yds SSS 70
V'tors	Monday play only
Loc	2 km from Wiesbaden at Hessen

Rheintal (1971)
An der Bundesstrr 291, 68723 Oftersheim

Tel	(06202) 56390
Holes	18 L 5840 m SSS 71
Fees	On application
Loc	Oftersheim, SE of Mannheim

Spessart (1972)
Golfplatz Alsberg, 63628 Bad Soden-Salmünster

Tel	(06056) 91580
Fax	(06056) 915820
Holes	18 L 6051 m SSS 72
V'tors	H
Fees	60DM (90DM) W–250DM
Loc	70 km NE of Frankfurt, via A66 towards Fulda
Arch	Elliot Rowan

St Leon-Rot (1996)
Opelstrasse 30, 68789 St Leon-Rot

Tel	(06227) 86080
Fax	(06227) 860888
Holes	18 L 6047 m Par 72
V'tors	U H
Fees	100DM (150DM)
Loc	20 km S of Heidelberg
Arch	Hannes Schreiner

Taunus Weilrod (1979)
Merzhauser Strasse, 61276 Weilrod-Altweilnau

Tel	(06083) 95200
Fax	(06083) 950215
Holes	18 L 5981 m SSS 72

V'tors	H
Fees	65DM (90DM)
Loc	25 km NW of Bad Homburg
Arch	Donald Harradine

Wiesbadener (1893)
Chausseehaus 17, 65199 Wiesbaden

Tel	(0611) 460238
Fax	(0611) 463251
Holes	9 L 5320 m SSS 68
V'tors	WD–H (max 36) WE–H (max 28)
Fees	60DM (80DM)
Loc	8 km NW of Wiesbaden, towards Schlangenbad
Arch	Hirsch

Wiesloch-Hohenhardter Hof G&LC (1983)
Hohenhardter Hof, 69168 Wiesloch-Baiertal

Tel	(06222) 72081
Fax	(06222) 71718
Holes	18 L 6080 m SSS 72
V'tors	WD–H WE–M
Fees	60DM (80DM)
Loc	17 km S of Heidelberg
Arch	Harradine/Weishaupt

Hamburg & North

Altenhof (1971)
Eckernförde, 24340 Altenhof

Tel	(04351) 41227, (04351) 45800 (Pro)
Fax	(04351) 41227
Holes	18 L 6066 m SSS 72
V'tors	H
Fees	50DM (70DM)
Loc	3 km S of Eckernförde. 25 km NW of Kiel
Arch	Donald Harradine

Berhinderten (1994)
Gustav-Delle Str 18a, 22926 Ahrensburg

Tel	(04102) 41544
Fax	(04102) 44516
Holes	18 hole course
V'tors	U
Fees	On application
Loc	20 km NE of Hamburg

Brodauer Mühle (1986)
Baumallee 14, 23730 Gut Beusloe

Tel	(04561) 8140
Fax	(04561) 407397
Holes	18 L 6113 m Par 72 SSS 72
V'tors	U H–36
Fees	50DM (80DM)
Loc	30 km N of Lübeck
Arch	Siegmann/Osterkamp

Buchholz-Nordheide
An der Rehm 25, 21244 Buchholz

Tel	(04181) 36200
Fax	(04181) 97294

Holes	18 L 6130 m SSS 72
V'tors	WD–U H WE–H I before 10am
Fees	60DM (80DM)
Loc	30 km S of Hamburg

Buxtehude (1982)
Zum Lehmfeld 1, 21614 Buxtehude

Tel	(04161) 81333
Fax	(04161) 87268
Holes	18 L 6480 m SSS 74
V'tors	WD–H WE–H before 9.30am –M H after 9.30am
Loc	30 km SW of Hamburg on Route 73 from Harburg
Arch	Wolfgang Siegmann

Deinster Mühle (1994)
Im Mühlenfeld 30, 21717 Deinste

Tel	(04149) 925112
Fax	(04149) 925111
Holes	18 L 6065 m Par 72
V'tors	U H
Fees	55DM (75DM)
Loc	50 km SW of Hamburg
Arch	David Krause

Föhr (1966)
25938 Nieblum

Tel	(04681) 580455
Fax	(04681) 580456
Holes	18 L 6089 m SSS 72
V'tors	H
Fees	60DM (70DM)
Loc	3 km SW of Wyk, by Airport

Gut Apeldör (1996)
Gut Apeldör, 25779 Hennstedt

Tel	(04836) 8408
Fax	(04836) 8409
Holes	18 L 6048 m Par 72 6 hole short course
V'tors	U H
Fees	65DM (75DM)
Loc	11 km W of Heide. 100 km N of Hamburg
Arch	DJ Krause

Gut Grambek (1981)
Schlosstr 21, 23883 Grambek

Tel	(04542) 841474
Fax	(04542) 841476
Holes	18 L 6029 m SSS 71
V'tors	H
Fees	50DM (70DM)
Loc	35 km S of Lübeck. 50 km E of Hamburg

Gut Kaden (1984)
Kadenerstrasse 9, 25486 Alveslohe

Tel	(04193) 9929-0
Fax	(04193) 992919
Holes	18 L 6076 m Par 72 9 hole course
V'tors	U H
Fees	60DM (90DM)
Loc	Alveslohe, 30 km N of Hamburg

For list of abbreviations see page 527

Germany

Gut Uhlenhorst (1989)
24229 Uhlenhorst
Tel   (04349) 91700
Fax   (04349) 919400
Email golf@gut-uhlenhorst.de
      www.gut-uhlenhorst.de
Holes 18 L 6195 m SSS 72
V'tors U
Fees   50DM (60DM)
Loc   8 km N of Kiel
Arch   Donald Harradine

Gut Waldhof (1969)
Am Waldhof, 24629 Kisdorferwohld
Tel   (04194) 99740
Fax   (04194) 1251
Holes 18 L 6044 m Par 72
V'tors WD–H WE–M
Fees   50DM (70DM)
Loc   34 km N of Hamburg via
       Autobahn A7 to
       Kaltenkirchen, or via route
       B432

Hamburg (1906)
In de Bargen 59, 22587 Hamburg
Tel   (040) 812177
Fax   (040) 817315
Holes 18 L 5925 m SSS 72
V'tors H WE–M
Fees   75DM (80DM)
Loc   Blankenese, 14 km W of
       Hamburg
Arch   Colt/Allison/Morrison

Hamburg Holm (1993)
Haverkamp 1, 25488 Holm
Tel   (04103) 91330
Fax   (04103) 913313
Holes 18 L 6170 m Par 72
V'tors WD–U WE–M
Fees   65DM (80DM)
Loc   20 km W of Hamburg
Arch   Harradine/Rossknecht

Hamburg Ahrensburg (1964)
Am Haidschlag 39-45,
22926 Ahrensburg
Tel   (04102) 51309
Fax   (04102) 81410
Holes 18 L 5782 m SSS 71
V'tors WD–U WE–M only
Loc   20 km NE of Hamburg.
       Motorway exit Ahrensburg

Hamburg Waldorfer (1960)
Schevenbarg, 22949 Ammersbek
Tel   (040) 605 1337
Fax   (040) 605 4879
Holes 18 L 6154 m SSS 72
       18 hole pitch & putt course
V'tors WD–U H WE–M H
Fees   70DM (85DM)
Loc   20 km N of Hamburg
Arch   B von Limburger

Hamburg Hittfield (1957)
Am Golfplatz 24, 21218 Seevetal
Tel   (04105) 2331
Fax   (04105) 52571
Holes 18 L 5903 m SSS 71
V'tors WD–U WE–M
Fees   60DM (80DM)
Loc   25 km S of Hamburg
Arch   Morrison/Gärtner

Hoisdorf (1977)
Hof Bornbek/Hoisdorf,
22952 Lütjensee
Tel   (04107) 7831
Fax   (04107) 9934
Holes 18 L 5958 m Par 71
V'tors WD–U WE–M only
Fees   70DM (80DM)
Loc   25 km NE of Hamburg

Jersbek
Oberteicher Weg, 22941 Jersbek
Tel   (04532) 20950
Fax   (04532) 24779
Holes 18 L 5921 m SSS 71
V'tors WD–H or I WE–M
Fees   60DM (70DM)
Loc   20 km N of Hamburg
Arch   Von Schinkel

Kieler GC Havighorst (1988)
Havighorster Weg 20,
24211 Havighorst
Tel   (04302) 965980
Fax   (04302) 965981
Holes 18 L 6242 m Par 73 SSS 73
V'tors WD–U H WE–H
Fees   50DM (60DM)
Loc   10 km S of Kiel. 85 km N of
       Hamburg
Arch   Udo Barth

Lübeck-Travemünder (1921)
Kowitzberg 41, 23570 Lübeck-
Travemünde
Tel   (04502) 74018
Fax   (04502) 72182
Holes 18 L 6071 m SSS 72
V'tors H
Loc   18 km NE of Lübeck. 70 km
       NE of Hamburg

Maritim Timmendorfer Strand (1973)
Am Golfplatz 3, 23669 Timmendorfer
Strand
Tel   (04503) 5152
Fax   (04503) 86344
Holes North 18 L 6065 m SSS 72
       South 18 L 3755 m SSS 60
V'tors WE–booking required
Fees   North D–60DM (D–90DM)
       South D–50DM (D–75DM)
Loc   15 km N of Lübeck
Arch   B von Limburger

Mittelholsteinischer Aukrug (1969)
Zum Glasberg 9, 24613 Aukrug-
Bargfeld
Tel   (04873) 595
Fax   (04873) 1698
Holes 18 L 6140 m SSS 72
V'tors WD–H WE–H booking
       necessary
Loc   10 km W of Neumunster.
       Mitte exit on Route 430

An der Pinnau (1982)
Pinnerbergerstr 81a, 25451 Quickborn
Tel   (04106) 81800
Fax   (04106) 82003
Holes 18 L 6490 m SSS 74
       18 L 6115 m SSS 72
V'tors H or I
Loc   25 km NW of Hamburg,
       nr Renzel

Am Sachsenwald (1985)
Am Riesenbett, 21521 Dassendorf
Tel   (04104) 6120
Fax   (04104) 6551
Holes 18 L 6118 m SSS 72
V'tors H
Fees   50DM (60DM)
Loc   20 km SE of Hamburg
Arch   Deutsche Golf Consult

St Dionys (1972)
Widukindweg, 21357 St Dionys
Tel   (04133) 6277
Fax   (04133) 6281
Holes 18 L 6125 m SSS 72
V'tors By appointment only
Fees   70DM (90DM)
Loc   10 km N of Lüneburg

Schloss Breitenberg
25524 Breitenberg
Tel   (04828) 8188
Fax   (04828) 8100
Holes 18 hole course
V'tors H
Fees   60DM (70DM)
Loc   50 km N of Hamburg
Arch   Gerd Osterkamp

Schloss Lüdersburg (1985)
Lüdersburger Strasse 21,
21379 Lüdersburg
Tel   (04139) 6970-0
Fax   (04139) 6970 70
Holes 18 L 6091 m SSS 73
       9 hole Par 3 course
V'tors U H
Fees   80DM (90DM)
Loc   12 km E of Lüneburg. 55 km
       SE of Hamburg
Arch   Wolfgang Siegmann

Sylt
Am Golfplatz, 25996 Wenningstedt
Tel   (04651) 45311
Fax   (04651) 45692

For list of abbreviations see page 527

Holes 18 L 6200 m SSS 72
V'tors H
Fees 100DM
Loc Sylt Island, 75 km W of Flensburg

Treudelberg G&CC
(1990)
Lemsahler Landstr 45, 22397 Hamburg
Tel (040) 608 22500
Fax (040) 608 22444
Holes 18 L 6182 m SSS 72
9 hole pitch & putt
V'tors U H
Fees 75DM (90DM)
Loc N of Hamburg centre
Arch Donald Steel

Auf der Wendlohe
Oldesloerstr 251, 22457 Hamburg
Tel (040) 550 5014/5
Fax (040) 550 3668
Holes 27 holes: 5675-6050 m SSS 72
V'tors WD–U WE–M
Loc 15 km N of Hamburg
Arch Ernst-Dietmar Hess

Wentorf-Reinbeker
(1901)
Golfstrasse 2, 21465 Wentorf
Tel (040) 729 78066
Fax (040) 729 78067
Holes 18 L 5698 m SSS 70
V'tors WD–U H WE–M
Fees 60DM (70DM)
Loc 20 km SE of Hamburg
Arch Ernst Hess

Hanover & Weserbergland

Bad Lippspringe
(1989)
Senne 1, 33173 Bad Lippspringe
Tel (05252) 53794
Fax (05252) 53811
Holes 18 L 5826 m Par 73 SSS 72
9 L 5214 m Par 68 SSS 68
V'tors H
Fees 40–50DM (50–60DM)
Loc 9 km E of Paderborn, off Route 1

Bad Salzuflen G&LC
(1956)
Schwaghof 4, 32108 Bad Salzuflen
Tel (05222) 10773
Fax (05222) 13954
Holes 18 L 6138 m Par 72
V'tors H
Fees 60DM (70DM)
Loc 3 km NE of Bad Salzuflen
Arch B von Limburger

Braunschweig (1926)
Schwartzkopffstr 10, 38126 Braunschweig
Tel (0531) 691369
Holes 18 L 5893 m SSS 71
Loc Braunschweig 5 km

Burgdorf (1970)
Waldstr 15, 31303 Burgdorf-Ehlershausen
Tel (05085) 7628
Fax (05085) 6617
Holes 18 L 6426 m SSS 74
V'tors H
Loc Burgdorf-Ehlershausen, 20 km NE of Hanover

Gifhorn (1982)
Wilscher Weg 69, 38503 Gifhorn
Tel (05371) 16737
Fax (05371) 51092
Holes 18 L 5972 m SSS 72
V'tors H
Fees 50DM (70DM)
Loc 30 km N of Braunschweig

Göttingen (1969)
Levershausen, 37154 Northeim
Tel (05551) 61915
Fax (05551) 61863
Holes 18 L 6050 m SSS 72
V'tors H
Loc 20 km N of Göttingen, towards Northeim
Arch Dr Siegmann

Hannover (1923)
Am Blauen See, 30823 Garbsen
Tel (05137) 73235
Holes 18 L 5855 m SSS 71
Loc 15 km NW of Hanover

Isernhagen (1983)
Auf Gut Lohne, 30916 Isernhagen
Tel (05139) 2998
Fax (05139) 27033
Holes 18 L 6379 m SSS 73
V'tors H–(max 34)
Loc Gut Lohne, 12 km NE of Hanover

Lipperland zu Lage
Ottenhauserstr 100, 32791 Lage/Lippe
Tel (05232) 66829
Fax (05232) 18165
Holes 18 L 6260 m SSS 73
V'tors H
Loc 22 km E of Bielefeld
Arch Heinz Wolters

Lippischer (1980)
Huxollweg 21A, 32825 Blomberg-Cappel
Tel (05231) 459
Fax (05236) 8102
Holes 18 L 6110 m SSS 72
V'tors U
Loc 12 km E of Detmold

Marienfeld (1986)
Remse 27, 33428 Marienfeld
Tel (05247) 8880
Fax (05247) 80386
Holes 18 holes Par 71
V'tors U H
Fees 50DM (60DM)
Loc Bielefeld 20 km
Arch Spangemacher

Paderborner Land (1983)
Wilseder Weg 25, 33102 Paderborn
Tel (05251) 4377
Holes 18 L 5670 m SSS 68
V'tors U
Loc Salzkotten/Thule, between B-1 and B-64

Pyrmonter (1961)
Postfach 100 828, 31758 Hameln
Tel (05281) 8196
Fax (05281) 8196
Holes 18 L 5775 m SSS 70
V'tors H
Fees 50DM (60DM)
Loc 4 km S of Bad Pyrmont. 20 km SW of Hameln
Arch Donald Harradine

RAF Gütersloh
RAF Gütersloh BFPO#47
Tel (05241) 842409
Holes 9 L 5761 yds SSS 68
Loc 5 km W of Gütersloh

Ravensberger Land
Sudstrasse 96, 32130 Enger-Pödinghausen
Tel (09224) 79751
Fax (09224) 699446
Holes 18 hole course SSS 72
6 hole pitch & putt
V'tors WD–H WE–M
Fees 40DM (50DM)
Loc 25 km NE of Bielefeld towards Herford
Arch Heinz Wolters

Schloss Schwöbber
(1985)
Schloss Schwöbber, 31855 Aerzen
Tel (05154) 9870
Fax (05154) 9871-11
Holes 18 L 6222 m Par 73
18 hole short course
Loc 10 km SW of Hameln. 60 km SW of Hanover

Senne GC Gut Welschof
Augustdorferstr 70, 33758 Schloss Holte-Stukenbrock
Tel (05207) 920936
Fax (05207) 88788
Holes 18 L 6246 m SSS 72
V'tors U H
Fees 50DM (70DM)
Loc 20 km S of Bielefeld
Arch Christoph Städler

For list of abbreviations see page 527

Sennelager (British Army) (1963)
Bad Lippspringe BFPO#16
Tel (05252) 53794
Fax (05252) 53811
Holes Old 18 L 5687 m SSS 72
New 9 L 5214 m SSS 68
V'tors U
Fees (Forces) 40DM (50DM)
(Civilians) 50DM (60DM)
Loc 9 km E of Paderborn, off Route 1

Sieben-Berge Rheden (1965)
Postfach 1152, 31021 Gronau
Tel (05182) 52336
Fax (05182) 52336
Holes 18 L 5856 m SSS 71
V'tors U H
Fees 50DM (60DM)
Loc 35 km S of Hanover
Arch B von Limburger

Weserbergland (1982)
Weissenfelder Mühle, 37647 Polle
Tel (05535) 8842
Fax (05535) 1225
Holes 18 holes SSS 72
V'tors H
Loc 35 km S of Hameln

Westfälischer Gütersloh
Gütersloher Str 127, 33397 Rietberg
Tel (05244) 2340/10528
Fax (05244) 1388
Holes 18 L 6135 m SSS 72
V'tors U H
Fees 60DM (80DM)
Loc 8 km SE of Gütersloh, nr Neuenkirchen
Arch B von Limburger

Widukind-Land (1985)
Auf dem Stickdorn 63, 32584 Löhne
Tel (05228) 7050
Fax (05228) 1039
Holes 18 hole course
V'tors U H
Fees 60DM (70DM)
Loc 30 km NE of Bielefeld
Arch Darlmeier/Brinkmeier

Munich & South Bavaria

Allgäuer G&LC (1984)
Hofgut Boschach, 87724 Ottobeuren
Tel (08332) 1310
Fax (08332) 5161
Holes 18 L 6215 m SSS 72
6 hole short course
V'tors H
Fees 60DM (80DM)
Loc 2 km S of Ottobeuren. 20 km N of Kempten

Altötting-Burghausen (1986)
Piesing 4, 84533 Haiming
Tel (08678) 986903
Fax (08678) 986905
Holes 18 L 6281 m SSS 72/73
9 L 3730 m SSS 60
9 L 3101 m SSS 71/72
V'tors U
Fees 70DM (90DM)
Loc Schloss Piesing, 4 km N of Burghausen
Arch G von Mecklenberg

Augsburg (1959)
Engelshofer Str 2, 86399 Bobingen-Burgwalden
Tel (08234) 5621
Fax (08234) 7855
Holes 18 L 6077 m Par 72 SSS 72
V'tors U
Fees 60DM (90DM)
Loc 18 km SW of Augsburg
Arch Kurt Rossknecht

Bad Tölz (1973)
83646 Wackersberg
Tel (08041) 9994
Fax (08041) 2116
Holes 9 L 2886 m SSS 71
V'tors WD-H WE-M
Fees 50DM (60DM)
Loc 5 km W of Bad Tölz. 55 km S of Munich

Bad Wörishofen
Schlingenerstr 27, 87668 Rieden
Tel (08346) 777
Holes 18 L 6318 m SSS 71
Loc 10 km S of Bad Wörishofen

Beuerberg (1982)
Gut Sterz, 82547 Beuerberg
Tel (08179) 671/728
Fax (08179) 5234
Holes 18 L 6518 m SSS 74
V'tors WD-H WE-M H
Fees 90DM (100DM)
Loc 45 km SW of Munich
Arch Donald Harradine

Im Chiemgau (1982)
Kötzing 1, 83339 Chieming-Hart
Tel (08669) 7557
Fax (08669) 78153
Holes 18 L 6200 m SSS 73
9 hole Par 3 course
V'tors WD-H
Fees D-70DM (D-100DM)
Loc 40 km W of Salzburg
Arch J Dudok van Heel

Donauwörth (1995)
See Stop Press on page 818

Ebersberg (1988)
Postfach 1351, 85554 Ebersberg
Tel (08094) 8106
Fax (08094) 8386

Holes 18 L 5907 m Par 72
6 hole Par 3 course
V'tors U H
Fees 70DM (90DM)
Loc Zaissing, 35 km E of Munich
Arch Thomas Himmel

Erding-Grünbach (1973)
Am Kellerberg, 85461 Grünbach
Tel (08122) 6465
Fax (08122) 49684
Holes 18 L 6109 m SSS 72
V'tors WD-H (max 35) WE-H (max 28)
Loc 40 km NE of Munich

Eschenried (1983)
Kurfürstenweg 10, 85232 Eschenried
Tel (08131) 87238/79650
Fax (08131) 567418
Holes 18 L 6088 m Par 72 SSS 73
V'tors U H
Fees 70DM (90DM)
Loc 8 km NW of Munich
Arch G von Mecklenburg

Feldafing (1926)
Tutzinger Str 15, 82340 Feldafing
Tel (08157) 9334-0
Fax (08157) 9334-99
Holes 18 L 5724 m SSS 71
V'tors WD-H WE-M
Fees 100DM (120DM)
Loc 32 km S of Munich
Arch B von Limburger

Garmisch-Partenkirchen (1928)
Gut Buchwies, 82496 Oberau
Tel (08824) 8344
Fax (08824) 8344
Holes 18 L 6210 m Par 72
V'tors U H
Fees 70DM (90DM)
Loc 10 km N of Garmisch-Partenkirchen

Gut Rieden
Gut Rieden, 82319 Starnberg
Tel (08151) 90770
Fax (08151) 907711
Holes 18 L 6046 yds SSS 72
V'tors H WE-M
Fees 80DM (100DM)
Loc 25 km S of Munich

Hohenpähl (1988)
82396 Pähl
Tel (08808) 1330
Fax (08808) 775
Holes 18 L 6080 m Par 71 SSS 73
18 L 5765 m Par 71 SSS 72
V'tors WD-H WE-M H
Fees 90DM (100DM)
Loc 40 km S of Munich on B2
Arch Kurt Rossknecht

Holledau
Weihern 3, 84104 Rudelzhausen
Tel (08756) 96010
Fax (08756) 815
Holes 18 L 6085 m SSS 72
9 hole course
V'tors U H
Fees 50DM (70DM)
Loc 55 km N of Munich

Höslwang im Chiemgau
(1975)
Kronberg 3, 83129 Höslwang
Tel (08075) 714
Fax (08075) 8134
Holes 18 L 8500 m Par 72
V'tors H
Fees 60DM (80DM)
Loc 80 km S of Munich
Arch Thomas Himmel

Iffeldorf
Gut Rettenberg, 82393 Iffeldorf
Tel (08856) 925555
Fax (08856) 925559
Holes 18 L 5904 m SSS 71
V'tors U
Fees 80DM (100DM)
Loc 45 km S of Munich
Arch Herv Beer

Landshut (1989)
Oberlippach 2, 84095 Furth-Landshut
Tel (08704) 8378
Fax (08704) 8379
Holes 18 L 6251 m SSS 73
V'tors H
Fees 70DM (90DM)
Loc 65 km E of Munich
Arch Kurt Rossknecht

Mangfalltal G&LC
Oed 1, 83620 Feldkirchen-Westerham
Tel (08063) 6300
Holes 18 L 5740 m SSS 72
V'tors U
Loc 40 km SE of Munich

Margarethenhof am Tegernsee (1982)
Gut Steinberg PF#1101, 83701 Gmund am Tegernsee
Tel (08022) 7506-0
Fax (08022) 74818
Holes 18 L 6056 m SSS 72
V'tors WD–H WE–before 10am
Fees 100DM (120DM)
Loc Tegernsee, 45 km S of Munich
Arch Frank Pennink

Memmingen Gut Westerhart (1994)
Westerhart 1b, 87740 Buxheim
Tel (08331) 71016
Fax (08331) 71018
Holes 18 hole course
V'tors U H
Fees 50DM (80DM)
Loc 120 km W of Munich. Memmingen 5 km

München Nord-Eichenried (1989)
Münchnerstr 57, 85452 Eichenried
Tel (08123) 93080
Fax (08123) 930893
Holes 18 L 6318 m Par 73
V'tors WD–U WE–M
Fees 90DM (110DM)
Loc 19 km NE of Munich
Arch Kurt Rossknecht

München West-Odelzhausen (1988)
Gut Todtenried, 85235 Odelzhausen
Tel (08134) 1618
Fax (08134) 7623
Holes 18 L 6169 m Par 72 SSS 72
V'tors I
Fees 60DM (90DM)
Loc 35 km NW of Munich

München-Riedhof
82544 Egling-Riedhof
Tel (08171) 7065
Fax (08171) 72452
Holes 18 L 6216 m SSS 72
V'tors WD–U H
Loc 25 km S of Münich
Arch Heinz Fehring

Münchener (1910)
Tölzerstrasse 95, 82064 Strasslach
Tel (08170) 450
Fax (08170) 611
Holes Strasslach 27 L 6177 m SSS 72; Thalkirchen 9 L 2528 m SSS 69
V'tors WD–H WE–M
Fees WD–120DM
Loc Strasslach: 10 km from Munich. Thalkirchen: Munich

Olching (1979)
Feursstrasse 89, 82140 Olching
Tel (08142) 48290
Fax (08142) 482914
Holes 18 L 6042 m Par 72
V'tors H WE–NA
Fees 80DM (100DM)
Loc 15 km W of Munich
Arch J Dudok van Heel

Pfaffing Wasserburger
München Ost, Köckmühle, 83539 Pfaffing
Tel (08076) 1718
Fax (08076) 8594
Holes 18 L 6212 m SSS 73
9 hole course
Loc 50 km E of Münich
Arch Kurt Rossknecht

Reit im Winkl-Kössen (1986)
Postfach 1101, 83237 Reit im Winkl
Tel (05375) 628535
Fax (05375) 628537
Holes 18 L 5221 m Par 70
V'tors U
Fees 60DM (80DM)
Loc 100 km SE of Munich
Arch Georg Böhm

Rottaler G&CC (1972)
Am Fischgartl 2, 84332 Herbertsfelden
Tel (08561) 5969
Fax (08561) 2646
Holes 18 L 6105 m Par 72 SSS 72
V'tors U
Fees 90DM
Loc 5 km W of Pfarrkirchen on B388. 120 km E of Munich
Arch Donald Harradine

Rottbach (1995)
Weiherhaus 5, 82216 Rottbach
Tel (08135) 93290
Fax (08135) 932911
Holes 18 L 6409 m Par 72
V'tors U
Fees 70DM (90DM)
Loc 20 km NW of Munich
Arch Thomas Himmel

Schloss Maxlrain
Freitung 14, 83104 Maxlrain-Tuntenhausen
Tel (08061) 1403
Fax (08061) 30146
Holes 18 L 6357 m Par 72 SSS 73
9 hole Par 3 course
V'tors U H
Fees 50–90DM
Loc 40 km S of Munich
Arch Paul Krings

Sonnenalp (1976)
Hotel Sonnenalp, 87527 Ofterschwang
Tel (08321) 27276 (Sec)
Fax (08321) 272242
Holes 18 L 5938 m SSS 71
Loc 4 km W of Sonthofen
Arch Donald Harradine

St Eurach G&LC (1973)
Eurach 8, 82393 Iffeldorf
Tel (08801) 1332
Fax (08801) 2523
Holes 18 L 6509 m SSS 74
V'tors H exc Wed & Fri pm–NA WE–NA
Fees 100DM
Loc 40 km S of Munich
Arch Donald Harradine

Starnberg (1986)
Uneringerstr, 82319 Starnberg
Tel (08151) 12157
Fax (08151) 29115
Holes 18 L 6057 m Par 72

Germany 773

For list of abbreviations see page 527

V'tors WD–H WE–NA
Loc 30 km S of Munich
Arch Kurt Rossknecht

Tegernseer GC Bad Wiessee (1958)
Robognerhof 1, 83707 Bad Wiessee
Tel (08022) 8769
Fax (08022) 82747
Holes 18 L 5501 m SSS 69
V'tors WD–H
Loc Tegernsee, 50 km S of Munich

Tutzing (1983)
82327 Tutzing-Deixlfurt
Tel (08158) 3600
Fax (08158) 7234
Holes 18 L 6159 m SSS 72
V'tors U H
Fees 100DM
Loc Starnberger See, 30 km SW of Munich

Waldegg-Wiggensbach (1988)
Hof Waldegg, 87487 Wiggensbach
Tel (08370) 93073
Fax (08370) 93074
Holes 18 L 5462 m SSS 69
V'tors H–max 36
Fees 60DM (80DM)
Loc 10 km W of Kempten, nr Swiss/Austrian border

Wittelsbacher GC Rohrenfeld-Neuburg (1988)
Gut Rohrenfeld, 86633 Neuburg/Donau
Tel (08431) 44118
Fax (08431) 41201
Holes 18 L 6350 m SSS 73
V'tors U H
Fees 70DM (90DM)
Loc 7 km E of Neuburg. 70 km NW of Munich
Arch J Dudok van Heel

Wörthsee (1982)
Gut Schluifeld, 82237 Wörthsee
Tel (08153) 93477-2
Fax (08153) 4280
Holes 18 L 6300 m SSS 73
V'tors WD–H WE–M
Fees 90DM (120DM)
Loc 20 km W of Munich
Arch Kurt Rossknecht

Nuremberg & North Bavaria

Abenberg (1988)
Am Golfplatz 19, 91183 Abenberg
Tel (09178) 98960
Fax (09178) 989696
Holes 18 holes Par 72 SSS 72

V'tors WD–H
Fees 70DM (90DM)
Loc 10 km S of Schwabach. 30 km S of Nuremberg

Bad Griesbach
Holzhäuser 8, 94086 Bad Griesbach
Tel (08532) 790-0
Fax (08532) 790-45
Holes Uttlau 18 L 6115 m SSS 72
Lederbach 18 L 5998 m SSS 71; Brunnwies 18 L 6029 m SSS 71
V'tors I
Fees 80DM (100DM)
Loc 28 km SW of Passau
Arch Kurt Rossknecht

Bad Windsheim (1992)
Am Weinturm 2, 91438 Bad Windsheim
Tel (09841) 5027
Fax (09841) 3448
Holes 18 L 6265 m Par 73 SSS 73
V'tors U
Fees 60DM (80DM)
Loc 40 km W of Nuremberg (B470)

Bamberg (1973)
Postfach 1525, 96006 Bamberg
Tel (09547) 7212/7109
Fax (09547) 7817
Holes 18 L 6175 m SSS 72
V'tors H
Fees 60DM (80DM)
Loc Gut Leimershof, 16 km N of Bamberg
Arch Dieter Sziedat

Donau GC Passau-Rassbach (1986)
Rassbach 8, 94136 Thyrnau-Passau
Tel (08501) 91313
Fax (08501) 91314
Holes 18 L 6165 m SSS 72
V'tors U
Fees 60DM (70DM)
Loc 10 km E of Passau
Arch Götz Mecklenburg

Fränkische Schweiz (1974)
Kanndorf 8, 91316 Ebermannstadt
Tel (09194) 4827
Fax (09194) 5410
Holes 18 L 6050 m SSS 72
V'tors H
Fees 60DM (80DM)
Loc 5 km E of Ebermannstadt. 40 km N of Nuremberg

Fürth (1951)
Vacherstrasse 261, 90768 Fürth
Tel (0911) 757522
Fax (0911) 973 2989
Holes 18 L 6478 yds SSS 71
V'tors H

Fees 50DM (80DM)
Loc 20 km W of Nuremburg
Arch C Wagner (1992)

Gäuboden (1992)
Gut Fruhstorf, 94330 Aiterhofen
Tel (09421) 72804
Fax (09421) 72804
Holes 18 L 6233 m Par 72
V'tors U H
Fees 60DM (70DM)
Loc 40 km SE of Regensburg, nr Straubing
Arch Prof Schmidt

Hof (1985)
Postfach 1324, 95012 Hof
Tel (09281) 43749
Fax (09821) 60318/709999
Holes 18 L 6040 m SSS 72
V'tors H
Fees 50DM (70DM)
Loc 2 km NE of Hof (B173)
Arch Dieter Sziedat

Lauterhofen (1987)
Ruppertslohe 18, 92283 Lauterhofen
Tel (09186) 1574
Fax (09186) 1527
Holes 18 L 6054 m SSS 72
V'tors H
Loc 25 km SE of Nuremberg
Arch Dillschnitter

Lichtenau-Weickershof (1980)
Weickershof 1, 91586 Lichtenau
Tel (09827) 92040
Fax (09827) 9204-44
Holes 18 L 6218 m SSS 72
V'tors WD–H (max 35) WE–M
Fees 60DM (80DM)
Loc 10 km E of Ansbach
Arch Dieter Sziedat

Oberfranken Thurnau (1965)
Postfach 1349, 95304 Kulmbach
Tel (09228) 319
Fax (09228) 7219
Holes 18 L 6152 m SSS 72
V'tors I H
Loc Thurnau, 18 km NW of Bayreuth. 14 km SW of Kulmbach
Arch Donald Harradine

Oberpfälzer Wald G&LC (1977)
Ödengrub, 92431 Kemnath bei Fuhrn
Tel (09439) 466
Fax (09439) 1247
Holes 18 L 5799 m SSS 71
V'tors I
Fees 50DM (60DM)
Loc 10 km E of Schwarzenfeld, towards Neunburg
Arch Max Haseneder

Oberzwieselau (1990)
94227 Lindberg
Tel (01049) 9922/2367
Fax (01049) 9922/2924
Holes 18 L 6214 yds SSS 72
V'tors H–(max 36)
Fees 70DM (90DM)
Loc 170 km NE of Munich

Regensburg G&LC
(1966)
Jagdschloss Thiergarten, 93177 Altenthann
Tel (09403) 505
Fax (09403) 4391
Holes 18 L 5785 m Par 72 SSS 71
V'tors U
Fees 60DM (90DM)
Loc 14 km E of Regensburg, nr Walhalla
Arch Donald Harradine

Regensburg-Sinzing
Minoritenhof 1, 93161 Sinzing
Tel (0941) 32504
Fax (0941) 36299
Holes 18 L 5984 m SSS 72
  6 hole short course
V'tors U H
Fees 60DM (70DM)
Loc 7 km SW of Regensburg

Am Reichswald (1960)
Schiestlstr 100, 90427 Nürnberg
Tel (0911) 305730
Fax (0911) 301200
Holes 18 L 6345 m SSS 72
V'tors U H
Fees 70DM (100DM)
Loc 10 km N of Nuremberg

Sagmühle (1984)
Golfplatz Sagmühle 1, 94086 Bad Griesbach
Tel (08532) 2038
Fax (08532) 3165
Holes 18 L 6168 m SSS 72
V'tors H
Fees 70DM (80DM)
Loc 25 km SW of Passau
Arch Kurt Rossknecht

Schloss Fahrenbach
(1993)
95709 Tröstau
Tel (09232) 882-256
Fax (09232) 882-345
Holes 18 L 5858 m Par 71
V'tors U
Loc 15 km W of Marktredwitz.
  40 km E of Bayreuth
Arch Deutsche Golf Consult

Schlossberg (1985)
Grünbach 8, 94419 Reisbach
Tel (08734) 7235
Fax (08734) 7795
Holes 18 L 6070 m SSS 72

V'tors U
Fees 70DM
Loc Sommershausen, 15 km from Dingolfing. 100 km NE of Munich, off Route 11

Schmidmühlen G&CC
(1968)
Am Theilberg, 92287 Schmidmühlen
Tel (09474) 701
Fax (09474) 8236
Holes 18 L 5946 m Par 72
Loc 35 km NW of Regensburg

Schwanhof (1994)
Klaus Conrad Allee 1, 92706 Luhe-Wildenau
Tel (09607) 92020
Fax (09607) 920248
Holes 18 hole course SSS 72
V'tors U H
Fees 70DM (90DM)
Loc 80 km N of Regensburg
Arch Pate/Weisshaupt

Rhineland North

Aachen (1927)
Schürzelter Str 300, 52074 Aachen
Tel (0241) 12501
Fax (0241) 171075
Holes 18 L 6063 m Par 72
V'tors H
Loc Seffent, 5 km NW of Aachen
Arch Murray/Morrison/Pennink

Ahaus
Schmäinghook 36, 48683 Ahaus-Alstätte
Tel (02567) 405
Fax (02567) 3524
Email info@glc-ahaus.de
  www.glc-ahaus.de
Holes 18 hole course SSS 72
  9 hole course
V'tors U H
Fees 60DM (90DM)
Loc 60 km W of Münster
Arch Deutsche Golf Consult

Am Alten Fliess (1995)
Am Alten Fliess 66, 50129 Bergheim
Tel (02238) 94410
Fax (02238) 944119
Holes 27 holes: 6050-6075 m Par 72
V'tors U H–36 max
Fees 45–100DM (60–120DM)
Loc 12 km W of Cologne
Arch Kurt Rossknecht

Artland (1988)
Westerholte 23, 49577 Ankum
Tel (05466) 301
Fax (05466) 91081
Holes 18 holes Par 72
V'tors U H

Fees 60DM (80DM)
Loc Ankum, 30 km N of Osnabrück

Bergisch-Land
Siebeneickerst 386, 42111 Wuppertal
Tel (02053) 7177
Fax (02053) 7303
Holes 18 L 6037 m SSS 72
V'tors WD–H WE–M
Fees 80DM
Loc Elberfeld, 8 km W of Wuppertal

Bochum (1982)
Im Mailand 127, 44797 Bochum
Tel (0234) 799832
Fax (0234) 795875
Holes 18 L 5300 m SSS 68
V'tors WD–H
Loc Bochum-Stiepel, 7 km S of Bochum

Castrop-Rauxel
Dortmunder Str 383, 44577 Castrop-Rauxel
Tel (02305) 62027
Fax (02305) 61410
Holes 18 L 6181 m SSS 72
V'tors U
Loc 10 km W of Dortmund

Dortmund (1956)
Reichmarkstr 12, 44265 Dortmund
Tel (0231) 774131/774609
Fax (0231) 774403
Holes 18 L 6174 m SSS 72
V'tors WE–M
Fees 60DM (80DM)
Loc 8 km S of Dortmund
Arch B von Limburger

Düsseldorf (1961)
Rommerljansweg 12, 40882 Ratingen
Tel (02102) 81092
Fax (02102) 81782
Holes 18 L 5905 m SSS 71
V'tors WD–U WE–M
Loc 11 km N of Düsseldorf

Düsseldorf Hösel
In den Höfen 32, 40883 Ratingen
Tel (02102) 68829
Holes 18 L 6160 m SSS 72
V'tors U
Loc Hösel, 15 km NE of Düsseldorf

Elfrather Mühle (1991)
An der Elfrather Mühle 145, 47802 Krefeld
Tel (02151) 4969-12-14
Fax (02151) 477359
Holes 18 L 6061 m Par 72 SSS 72
V'tors WD–H 36 WE–H 28
Fees 60DM (80DM)
Loc Krefeld 7km. Düsseldorf 25 km
Arch Ron Kirby

For list of abbreviations see page 527

Erftaue (1991)
Zur Mühlenerft 1, 41517 Grevenbroich
Tel (02181) 280637
Fax (02181) 280639
Holes 18 L 6039 m Par 72
V'tors WD–H WE–H after 1pm
Fees 60DM (80DM)
Loc 25 km SW of Düsseldorf
Arch Karl Grohs

Essen Haus Oefte (1959)
Laupendahler Landstr, 45219 Essen
Tel (02054) 83911
Holes 18 L 6100 m SSS 72
V'tors U H
Loc 14 km SW of Essen

Essen-Heidhausen
(1970)
Preutenborbeckstr 36, 45239 Essen
Tel (0201) 404111
Holes 18 L 5937 m SSS 71
V'tors U H
Loc 10 km S of Essen on B224, nr Werden

Euregio Bad Bentheim
(1987)
Postbox 1205, 48443 Bad Bentheim
Tel (05922) 6700
Fax (05922) 6701
Holes 18 L 5877 m Par 72
V'tors U exc Wed & Thurs–NA
Fees 50DM (70DM)
Loc 55 km N of Münster
Arch Prof Schmidt

Haus Bey (1992)
41334 Nettetal
Tel (02153) 9197-0
Fax (02153) 919750
Holes 18 L 6116 m SSS 72
V'tors WD–U H WE–M H
Fees 60DM (80DM)
Loc 40 km NW of Düsseldorf
Arch Paul Krings

Haus Kambach (1989)
Kambachstrasse 9-13, 52249 Eschweiler-Kinzweiler
Tel (02403) 37615
Fax (02403) 21270
Holes 18 L 6178 m SSS 72
V'tors U
Fees 60DM (70DM)
Loc 20 km NE of Aachen
Arch Dieter Sziedat

Hubbelrath (1961)
Bergische Landstr 700, 40629 Düsseldorf
Tel (02104) 72178/71848
Fax (02104) 75685
Holes East 18 L 6208 m SSS 72
       West 18 L 4325 m SSS 62
V'tors WD–U exc 12–3pm WE–M
Loc Hubbelrath, 13 km E of Düsseldorf, on Route B7
Arch B von Limburger

Hummelbachaue Neuss (1987)
Norfer Kirchstrasse, 41469 Neuss
Tel (02137) 91910
Fax (02137) 4016
Holes 18 L 6091 m Par 73
V'tors WD–H WE–H
Fees 40–80DM (80DM)
Loc 5 km W of Düsseldorf
Arch Udo Barth

Issum-Niederrhein
(1973)
Pauenweg 68, 47661 Issum 1
Tel (02835) 3626
Fax (02835) 4267
Holes 18 L 5728 m SSS 70
V'tors H
Fees 60DM (70DM)
Loc 10 km E of Geldern
Arch Harradine

Juliana (1979)
Frielinghausen 1, 45549 Sprockhövel
Tel (0202) 647070/648220
Fax (0202) 649891
Holes 18 L 6100 m SSS 71
V'tors H
Loc 30 km E of Düsseldorf
Arch De Buer

Köln G&LC
Golfplatz 2, 51429 Bergisch Gladbach
Tel (02204) 92760
Fax (02204) 927615
Holes 18 L 6090 m Par 72
V'tors WD–H WE–NA
Fees WD–100DM
Loc 15 km E of Cologne

Krefeld (1930)
Eltweg 2, 47809 Krefeld
Tel (02151) 570071/72
Holes 18 L 6082 m SSS 72
V'tors WD–U H
Fees 80DM (100DM)
Loc 7 km SE of Krefeld. Düsseldorf 16 km
Arch B von Limburger

Mühlenhof (1990)
Mühlenhof, 47546 Kalkar
Tel (02824) 924040
Fax (02824) 924093
Holes 18 L 6179 m Par 73
V'tors I
Fees 40DM (65DM)
Loc 80 km N of Düsseldorf (B67)
Arch Hans Herkberger

Nordkirchen
Am Golfplatz 6, 59394 Nordkirchen
Tel (02596) 9191
Fax (02596) 9195
Holes 18 L 6200 m SSS 71
V'tors WD–I WE–H
Fees 60DM (70DM)
Loc 30 km S of Münster
Arch Christoph Städler

Op de Niep (1995)
Bergschenweg 71, 47506 Neukirchen-Vluyn
Tel (02845) 28051
Fax (02845) 28052
Holes 18 L 6624 m Par 75 SSS 75
V'tors U H–max 36 WE–M
Fees 50DM (60DM)
Loc 20 km W of Duisburg. 30 km NW of Düsseldorf
Arch Heinz Wolters

Osnabrück (1955)
Karmannstr 1, 49084 Osnabrück
Tel (05402) 5636
Fax (05402) 5257
Holes 18 L 5881 m Par 71
V'tors U
Fees 60DM (70DM)
Loc 13 km SE of Osnabrück

RAF Germany (1956)
RAF Brüggen BFPO#25
Tel (02163) 80049
Fax (02163) 80934
Holes 18 L 6522 yds SSS 71
V'tors WD–U WE–M
Fees 40DM
Loc On B230, 1 km from Dutch/German border. 25 km W of Mönchengladbach

Ratingen Gut Grashaus
(1988)
Grevemühle, 40882 Ratingen-Homberg
Tel (02102) 9595-0
Fax (02102) 959515
Holes 18 L 5864 m Par 72
V'tors U H
Fees 70DM (90DM)
Loc 10 km N of Düsseldorf
Arch Peter Drecker

Rheine/Mesum (1998)
Winterbrockstrasse, 48432 Rheine
Tel (05975) 9490
Fax (05975) 9491
Holes 18 L 6036 m Par 72
       9 L 4442 m Par 68
V'tors U H
Fees 50DM (70DM)
Loc Gut Winterbrock, 40 km W of Münster
Arch Christoph Städler

Rittergut Birkhof
(1996)
Rittergut Birkhof, 41352 Korschenbroich
Tel (02131) 510660
Fax (02131) 510616
Holes 18 L 6037 m Par 73
       9 hole Par 3 course
V'tors U
Fees 70DM (90DM)
Loc 20 km W of Düsseldorf
Arch Kurt Rossknecht

For list of abbreviations see page 527

St Barbara's Royal Dortmund (1969)
Hesslingweg, 44309 Dortmund
Tel (0231) 202551
Fax (0231) 259183
Holes 18 L 5967 m SSS 73
V'tors H–by prior arrangement
Fees 60DM (80DM)
Loc Dortmund Brackel
Arch Brig Jones/Maj Coleman

Schloss Georghausen (1962)
Georghausen 8, 51789 Lindlar-Hommerich
Tel (02207) 4938
Fax (02207) 81230
Holes 18 L 6045 m SSS 72
V'tors H
Fees 60DM (80DM)
Loc 30 km E of Cologne

Schloss Haag (1996)
Bartelter Weg 8, 47608 Geldern
Tel (02831) 94777
Fax (02831) 94778
Holes 18 L 6193 m Par 73
V'tors H
Fees 50DM (60DM)
Loc 60 km NW of Düsseldorf (Route 9)
Arch Heinz Wolters

Schloss Myllendonk (1965)
Myllendonkerstr 113, 41352 Korschenbroich 1
Tel (02161) 641049
Fax (02161) 648806
Holes 18 L 6120 m SSS 72
V'tors H
Fees 90DM (100DM)
Loc 5 km E of Mönchengladbach

Schmitzhof (1975)
Arsbeckerstr 160, 41844 Wegberg
Tel (02436) 39090
Fax (02436) 390915
Holes 18 L 6115 m SSS 72
V'tors H
Fees 70DM (90DM)
Loc Wegberg-Merbeck, 20 km SW of Mönchengladbach

Schwarze Heide
Gahlenerstrasse 44, 46244 Bottrop-Kirchellen
Tel (02045) 82488
Fax (02045) 83077
Holes 18 L 6051 m SSS 72
V'tors I H
Fees 50DM (70DM)
Loc 55 km N of Düsseldorf
Arch Peter Drecker

Siegerland (1993)
Berghäuser Weg, 57223 Kreuztal-Mittelhees
Tel (02732) 59470
Fax (02732) 594724
Holes 18 L 6055 m Par 72
V'tors H
Fees 60DM (80DM)
Loc 15 km N of Siegen
Arch Spangemacher

Unna-Fröndenberg (1985)
Schwarzer Weg 1, 58730 Fröndenberg
Tel (02373) 70068
Fax (02373) 70069
Holes 18 L 6177 m SSS 72
9 hole Par 3 course
V'tors M H (max 34)
Fees 60DM (80DM)
Loc 25 km W of Dortmund
Arch Karl Grohs

Vechta-Welpe (1989)
Welpe 2, 49377 Vechta
Tel (04441) 5539/82168
Fax (04441) 852480
Holes 18 L 6105 m Par 72
V'tors H
Fees 50DM (70DM)
Loc 50 km SW of Bremen
Arch Rainer Preissmann

Vestischer GC Recklinghausen (1974)
Bockholterstr 475, 45659 Recklinghausen
Tel (02361) 93420
Fax (02361) 934240
Holes 18 L 6111 m SSS 72
V'tors WD–H exc Mon–NA WE–M
Fees 80DM (100DM)
Loc Nr Loemühle Airport, N of Recklinghausen
Arch Donald Harradine

Wasserburg Anholt (1972)
Am Schloss 3, 46419 Isselburg Anholt
Tel (02874) 3444
Fax (02874) 29164
Holes 18 L 6115 m SSS 72
V'tors WD–U WE–H
Loc Parkhotel, Wasserburg Anholt. 15 km W of Bocholt

Westerwald (1979)
Postfach 1231, 57621 Hachenburg
Tel (02666) 8220
Holes 18 holes SSS 72
Loc Hachenburg, 60 km E of Bonn

Rhineland South

Bad Neuenahr G&LC (1979)
Remagener Weg, 53474 Bad Neuenahr-Ahrweiler
Tel (02641) 2325
Fax (02641) 29750
Holes 18 L 6060 m SSS 72
V'tors WD–H WE–H before 10am & after 4pm
Fees 70DM (90DM)
Loc Bad Neuenahr, 40 km S of Bonn
Arch Grohs/Preissmann

Bitburger Land (1994)
Zur Weilerscheck 1, 54636 Wissmannsdorf
Tel (06527) 9272-0
Fax (0627) 9272-30
Holes 18 L 6168 m Par 72
V'tors H
Fees 70DM (90DM)
Loc 25 km NE of Trier
Arch Karl Grohs

Bonn-Godesberg in Wachtberg (1960)
Landgrabenweg, 53343 Wachtberg-Niederbachen
Tel (0228) 344003
Fax (0228) 340820
Holes 18 L 5900 m Par 71
V'tors WD–H WE–M
Fees 70DM (90DM)
Loc Niederbachem, 4 km from Bad Godesberg
Arch M Peters

Burg Overbach (1984)
Postfach 1213, 53799 Much
Tel (02245) 5550
Fax (02245) 8247
Holes 18 L 6056 m SSS 72
V'tors H
Fees 60DM (80DM)
Loc Much, 45 km E of Cologne, off A4
Arch Deutsch Golf Consult

Burg Zievel (1994)
Burg Zievel, 53894 Mechernich
Tel (02256) 1651
Fax (02256) 3479
Holes 18 L 6143 m Par 72
V'tors H
Fees 30–70DM
Loc 30 km S of Cologne
Arch G Knappertz

Eifel (1977)
Kölner Str, 54576 Hillesheim
Tel (06593) 1241
Fax (06593) 9421
Holes 18 L 6017 m Par 72
V'tors H–phone before play
Loc 70 km S of Cologne
Arch Grohs/Preissmann

Gut Heckenhof (1993)
53783 Eitorf
Tel (02243) 83137
Fax (02243) 83426
Holes 18 L 6214 m SSS 72
V'tors H
Fees On request
Loc 40 km SE of Cologne
Arch William Amick

For list of abbreviations see page 527

Internationaler Bonn
(1992)
Gut Grossenbusch, 53757 St Augustin
Tel (02241) 39880
Fax (02241) 398888
Holes 18 L 5928 m Par 72
V'tors U H
Fees 60–80DM (100DM)
Loc 6 km E of Bonn

Jakobsberg (1990)
Im Tal der Loreley, 56154 Boppard
Tel (06742) 808491
Fax (06742) 808493
Holes 18 L 6351 m Par 72 SSS 72
V'tors U
Fees 70DM (90DM)
Loc 80 km N of Mainz
Arch Wolfgang Jersombek

Mittelrheinischer Bad Ems (1938)
Denzerheide, 56130 Bad Ems
Tel (02603) 6541
Fax (02603) 13995
Holes 18 L 6050 m SSS 72
V'tors H
Fees 80DM (110DM)
Loc 13 km E of Koblenz, nr Bad Ems (6 km)
Arch Karl Hoffmann

Nahetal (1971)
Drei Buchen, 55583 Bad Münster am Stein
Tel (06708) 2145/3032
Fax (06708) 1731
Holes 18 L 6065 m SSS 72
V'tors H
Fees 60DM (80DM)
Loc 6 km S of Bad Kreuznach. 70 km SW of Frankfurt
Arch Armin Keller

Rhein Sieg (1971)
Postfach 1216, 53759 Hennef
Tel (02242) 6501
Holes 18 L 6081 m Par 72
Loc Hennef, 30 km SE of Cologne

Stromberg-Schindeldorf (1987)
Park Village Golfanlagen, Buchenring 6, 55442 Stromberg
Tel (06724) 93080
Fax (06724) 930818
Holes 18 L 5161 Par 68 SSS 68
V'tors U H–booking necessary
Fees 60DM (85DM)
Loc 5 km from A61 exit Stromberg

Wiesensee (1992)
Am Wiesensee, 56459 Westerburg-Stahlhofen
Tel (02663) 8383
Fax (02663) 8743
Holes 18 L 6092 m Par 72
 9 hole Par 3 course

V'tors H
Fees 70DM (90DM)
Loc 100 km NW of Frankfurt

Saar-Pfalz

Pfalz Neustadt (1971)
Im Lochbusch, 67435 Neustadt
Tel (06327) 97420
Fax (06327) 974218
Holes 18 L 6180 m SSS 72
V'tors U H WE–NA before 3pm
Fees 75DM (100DM)
Loc Geinsheim, 15 km SE of Neustadt towards Speyer
Arch B von Limburger

Saarbrücken (1961)
Oberlimbergerweg, 66798 Wallerfangen-Gisingen
Tel (06837) 91800/1584
Fax (06837) 91801
Holes 18 L 6231 m SSS 73
V'tors H
Fees 80DM (100DM)
Loc B406 towards Wallerfangen. 8 km N of Saarlouis
Arch Donald Harradine

Websweiler Hof (1991)
Websweiler Hof, 66424 Homburg
Tel (06841) 71111
Fax (06841) 755555
Holes 18 L 6188 m Par 72 SSS 74
V'tors U H
Fees 60DM (80DM)
Loc 35 km E of Saarbrücken

Westpfalz Schwarzbachtal (1988)
66509 Rieschweiler
Tel (06336) 6442
Fax (06336) 6408
Holes 18 L 5740 m Par 70
V'tors H
Loc 40 km E of Saarbrücken

Woodlawn
6792 Ramstein Flugplatz
Tel (06371) 476240
Fax (06371) 42158
Holes 18 L 6225 yds Par 70
V'tors Military GC–visitors restricted
Fees $13 ($16)
Loc Ramstein 3km. Kaiserlautern 10 km

Stuttgart & South West

Bad Liebenzell
Golfplatz 9, 75378 Bad Liebenzell
Tel (07052) 1574
Fax (07052) 5302
Holes 18 L 6121 m Par 72 SSS 72

V'tors H–(max 33) WE–M 10.30am–2pm
Fees 60DM (80DM)
Loc 35 km W of Stuttgart
Arch Felix Elger

Bad Rappenau (1989)
Ehrenbergstrasse 25a, 74906 Bad Rappenau
Tel (07264) 3666
Fax (07264) 3838
Holes 18 L 6103 m SSS 72
V'tors U H
Fees 60DM (80DM)
Loc 10 km NW of Heilbronn
Arch Karl Gross

Baden Hills GC Rastatt (1982)
Postfach 2, 76549 Hügelsheim
Tel (07229) 5346
Fax (07229) 5347
Holes 18 L 5906 m Par 71
V'tors H–booking necessary WD–U before 5pm WE–M before 3pm
Loc 10 km W of Badeb-Baden. 50 km N of Strasbourg

Baden-Baden (1901)
Fremersbergstr 127, 76530 Baden-Baden
Tel (07221) 23579
Fax (07221) 23528
Holes 18 L 4413 m Par 64
V'tors U
Fees 65DM (90DM)
Loc 3 km S of Baden-Baden
Arch Harry Vardon

Bodensee (1986)
Lampertsweiler 51, 88138 Weissensberg
Tel (08389) 89190
Fax (08389) 89191
Holes 18 L 6112 m SSS 72
V'tors H
Fees 75DM (90DM)
Loc 5 km NE of Lindau/Bodensee
Arch Robert Trent Jones Sr

Freiburg (1970)
Krüttweg 1, 79199 Kirchzarten
Tel (07661) 9847-0
Fax (07661) 984747
Holes 18 L 6085 m SSS 72
V'tors H
Fees 60DM (70DM)
Loc Freiburg-Kappel/Kirchzarten
Arch B von Limburger

Fürstlicher Waldsee (1998)
Hopfenweiler, 88339 Bad Waldsee
Tel (07524) 4017 200
Fax (07524) 4017 100
Holes 18 L 6474 m Par 72
 9 hole Par 3 course
V'tors U

For list of abbreviations see page 527

Germany

Fees 18 hole: 60DM (80DM)
9 hole: 25DM (40DM)
Loc 60 km SW of Ulm (Route 30)
Arch Knauss/Himmel

Hechingen Hohenzollern (1955)
Postfach 1124, 72379 Hechingen
Tel (07471) 6478
Holes 18 holes SSS 72
V'tors WE–M
Fees On application
Loc Hechingen, 50 km S of Stuttgart

Heidelberg-Lobenfeld (1968)
Biddersbacherhof, 74931 Lobbach-Lobenfeld
Tel (06226) 952110
Fax (06226) 952115
Holes 18 L 5989 m SSS 72
V'tors WD–H WE–M H
Fees 60DM (80DM)
Loc 20 km E of Heidelberg
Arch Donald Harradine

Heilbronn-Hohenlohe (1964)
Hofgasse, 74639 Zweiflingen-Friedrichsruhe
Tel (07941) 920810
Fax (07941) 920819
Holes 18 L 6039 m SSS 72
V'tors H
Fees 60DM (90DM)
Loc 25 km W of Heilbronn, nr Öhringen

Hohenstaufen (1959)
Unter dem Ramsberg, 73072 Donzdorf-Reichenbach
Tel (07162) 27171/20050
Holes 18 L 6540 yds SSS 72
Loc 15 km E of Goppingen. 45 km E of Stuttgart

Kaiserhöhe (1995)
Im Laber 4, 74747 Ravenstein-Merchingen
Tel (06297) 399
Fax (06297) 599
Holes 18 L 6049 m Par 72
9 hole Par 3 course
V'tors U H
Fees 50DM (70DM)
Loc 60 km S of Würzburg
Arch Kurt Rossknecht

Konstanz (1965)
Langenrain, Kargegg, 78476 Allensbach
Tel (07533) 5124
Fax (07533) 4897
Holes 18 L 6058 m SSS 72
V'tors WD–I WE–H max 28
Loc 15 km NW of Konstanz, nr Langenrain

Lindau-Bad Schachen (1954)
Am Schönbühl 5, 88131 Lindau
Tel (08382) 78090
Fax (08382) 78998
Holes 18 L 5871 m Par 71 SSS 71
Fees 80DM (100DM)
Loc Nr Lindau, Bodensee

Markgräflerland Kandern (1984)
Feuerbacher Str 35, 79400 Kandern
Tel (07626) 1043
Fax (07626) 1433
Holes 18 L 6044 m Par 72 SSS 71
V'tors WD–U WE–M
Loc Kandern, 10 km N of Lörrach. 14 km NW of Basle
Arch Grohs/Benz

Neckartal (1974)
Aldingerstr, Gebäude 975, 71638 Ludwigsburg-Pattonville
Tel (07141) 871319
Fax (07141) 81716
Holes 18 L 6310 m SSS 73
V'tors WD–U WE–M
Loc 5 km NE of Stuttgart, nr Kornwestheim
Arch B von Limburger

Obere Alp (1989)
Am Golfplatz 1-3, 79780 Stühlingen
Tel (07703) 9203-0
Fax (07703) 9203-18
Holes 18 L 6216 m SSS 72
9 L 3664 m SSS 60
V'tors H
Fees 18 hole:60DM (90DM)
9 hole:45DM (60DM)
Loc 40 km N of Zürich, nr Swiss border
Arch Karl Grohs

Oberschwaben-Bad Waldsee (1968)
Hofgut Hopfenweiler, 88339 Bad Waldsee
Tel (07524) 5900
Fax (07524) 6106
Holes 18 L 6148 m SSS 72
V'tors H–(max 34)
Fees 65DM (90DM)
Loc Bad Waldsee, 60 km SW of Ulm
Arch Donald Harradine

Oeschberghof L&GC (1976)
Golfplatz 1, 78166 Donaueschingen
Tel (0771) 84525
Fax (0771) 84540
Holes 18 L 6580 m SSS 74
9 L 4120 m SSS 62
V'tors H
Fees 90DM (120DM)
Loc Donaueschingen, 60 km E of Freiburg
Arch Deutsche Golf Consult

Owingen-Überlingen
Alte Owinger Str, 88696 Owingen
Tel (07551) 83040
Fax (07551) 830422
Holes 18 L 6148 m SSS 72
V'tors H
Fees 60DM (90DM)
Loc 5 km N of Überlingen, nr Lake Konstanz

Pforzheim Karlshäuser Hof
Karlshäuser Weg, 75248 Ölbronn-Dürrn
Tel (07237) 9100
Fax (07237) 5161
Holes 18 hole course SSS 72
V'tors H
Fees 60DM (80DM)
Loc 6 km N of Pforzheim. 30 km E of Karlsruhe
Arch Reinhold Weishaupt

Reutlingen-Sonnenbühl (1987)
Im Zerg, 72820 Sonnenbühl
Tel (07128) 92660
Fax (07128) 926692
Holes 18 L 6085 m SSS 72
V'tors H
Fees 60DM (80DM)
Loc 40 km S of Stuttgart

Rhein Badenweiler (1971)
79401 Badenweiler
Tel (07632) 7970
Fax (07632) 797150
Holes 18 L 6134 m SSS 72
V'tors WD–H WE–M
Loc 16 km W of Badenweiler. 30 km SW of Freiburg
Arch Donald Harradine

Rickenbach (1979)
Hennematt 20, 79736 Rickenbach
Tel (07765) 777
Fax (07765) 544
Holes 18 L 5683 m Par 70 SSS 70
V'tors WD/Sat–U H exc Tues/Thurs am Sun–NA before 3pm
Fees 65DM (85DM)
Loc 20 km N of Bad Säckingen
Arch Dudok van Heel/Himmel

Schloss Klingenburg-Günzburg (1978)
Schloss Klingenburg, 89343 Jettingen-Scheppach
Tel (08225) 3030
Fax (08225) 30350
Holes 18 L 6237 m SSS 72
V'tors H
Fees 70DM (100DM)
Loc 40 km W of Augsburg. 5 km from Stuttgart-Munich motorway, exit Burgau
Arch Harradine/Sziedat

For list of abbreviations see page 527

Germany

Schloss Langenstein
(1991)
Schloss Langenstein, 78359 Orsingen-Nenzingen
Tel (07774) 50651
Fax (07774) 50699
Holes 18 L 6389 m SSS 73
  9 hole course
V'tors WD–H WE–H (restricted)
Fees 80DM (100DM)
Loc 120 km S of Stuttgart. 75 km NE of Zürich
Arch Rod Whitman

Schloss Liebenstein (1982)
Postfach 27, 74380 Neckarwestheim
Tel (07133) 9878-0
Fax (07133) 9878-18
Holes 27 L 5890-6361 m SSS 71-73
V'tors U
Fees 60DM (80DM)
Loc 35 km N of Stuttgart
Arch Donald Harradine

Schloss Weitenburg (1984)
Sommerhalde 11, 72181 Starzach-Sulzau
Tel (07472) 8061
Fax (07472) 8062
Holes 18 L 6069 m SSS 72/73
  9 hole course
V'tors I
Fees 18 hole:70DM (90DM)
  9 hole:30DM (40DM)
Loc 50 km SW of Stuttgart in Neckar Valley
Arch Heinz Fehring

Steisslingen (1991)
Kapellenstr 4a, 78256 Steisslingen-Wiechs
Tel (07738) 7196
Fax (07738) 7196
Holes 18 L 6145 m Par 72
  6 hole course
V'tors U
Fees 65DM (95DM)
Loc 30 km N of Konstanz
Arch Dave Thomas

Stuttgarter Solitude
(1927)
71297 Mönsheim
Tel (07044) 5852
Fax (07044) 5357
Holes 18 L 6045 m Par 72 SSS 72
V'tors WD–H max 28 WE–M (phone first)
Fees 80DM (100DM)
Loc 30 km W of Stuttgart
Arch B von Limburger

Ulm/Neu-Ulm (1963)
Wochenauer Hof 2, 89186 Illerrieden
Tel (07306) 919420
Fax (07306) 919422
Holes 18 L 6076 m SSS 72
V'tors H
Fees 60DM (80DM)
Loc 15 km S of Ulm
Arch Deutsche Golf Consult

Greece

Afandou (1973)
Afandou, Rhodes
Tel (0241) 51255
Holes 18 L 6060 m Par 72
V'tors U
Loc 20 km S of Rhodes town

Corfu (1972)
PO Box 71, Ropa Valley, 49100 Corfu
Tel (0661) 94220
Fax (0661) 94220
Holes 18 L 6300 m SSS 72
V'tors U
Fees 6000–16.000dra
Loc Ermones Bay, 16 km W of Corfu town
Arch Donald Harradine

Glyfada (1962)
PO Box 70116, 166-10 Glyfada, Athens
Tel (01) 894 6459
Fax (01) 894 6834
Holes 18 L 6189 m Par 72
V'tors H
Fees 11.000dra (15.000dra)
Loc 12 km S of Athens
Arch Donald Harradine

Porto Carras G&CC
(1979)
Porto Carras, Halkidiki
Tel (0375) 71381/71221
Holes 18 L 6086 m SSS 72
V'tors U
Loc Sithonia Peninsula, 100 km SE of Thessaloniki

Hungary

Birdland G&CC
Thermal krt.10, 9740 Bükfürdo
Tel (94) 359000
Holes 18 L 6572 m Par 72
  9 hole Par 3 course
V'tors U
Fees £20 (£25)
Loc 55 km SE of Sopron (West Hungary)
Arch G Hauser

Budapest G&CC
Becsi u.5, 2024 Kisoroszi
Tel (1) 317 6025
Fax (1) 317 2749
Holes 18 L 6089 m SSS 72
V'tors U
Fees 50DM (60DM)
Loc 35 km N of Budapest via Highway 11
Arch D Hajnal

Hencse National
Kossuth u.3, 7232 Hencse
Tel (82) 481245
Fax (82) 481248
Holes 18 L 6231 m Par 72
V'tors U
Fees 55DM (65DM)
Loc 20 km from Kaposvar (SW Hungary)
Arch J Dudok van Heel

Old Lake
Toldi Miklós u.19, 2890 Tata-Remeteségpuszta
Tel (34) 380684
Fax (34) 380684
Holes 18 L 5915 m Par 72
V'tors U
Fees 80DM (100DM)
Loc Tata, 80 km W of Budapest (M1)
Arch Lázló Soproni

Pannonia G&CC
Alcsútdoboz, 8087 Mariavölgy
Tel (22) 353000
Fax (22) 353000
Holes 18 L 6170 m Par 72
V'tors U
Fees 50DM (100DM)
Loc Budapest 30 km
Arch H-G Erhardt

St Lorence G&CC
Pellérdi ut 55, 7634 Pécs
Tel (72) 252844/252142
Fax (72) 252844/252173
Holes 18 holes Par 72
V'tors U
Loc Szentlörinc, 11 km W of Pécs

Iceland

Akureyri (1935)
PO Box 317, 602 Akureyri
Tel (462) 2974
Fax (461) 1755
Holes 18 L 5783 m Par 71
V'tors U H
Fees 1500 Ikr
Loc 1 km from Akureyri (N coast)
Arch Solnes/Gudmundsson

Borgarness (1973)
Hamar, 310 Borgarnes
Tel (437) 1663
Fax (437) 2063
Holes 9 L 5548 m Par 72
V'tors U
Fees 1200 Ikr
Loc 5 km W of Borgarnes. 100 km N of Reykjavik (W coast)

For list of abbreviations see page 527

Eskifjardar (1976)
735 Eskifjördur
Holes 9 L 4418 m Par 66
Fees 1000 Ikr
Loc 3 km W of Eskifjördur
(E coast)

Húsavík (1967)
PO Box 23, Kötlum, 640 Húsavík
Tel (464) 1000
Fax (464) 1678
Holes 9 L 2460m Par 70
V'tors U
Fees 1000 Ikr
Loc 2 km from Húsavík (N coast)
Arch Nils Skjöld

Isafjardar (1978)
PO Box 367, 400 Isafjördur
Tel (456) 5081
Fax (456) 4547
Holes 9 L 4980 m Par 70
V'tors U
Fees 1000Ikr
Loc 3 km W of Isafjördur
(NW coast)

Jökull (1973)
Postholf 67, 355 Olafsvík
Tel (436) 1666
Holes 9 L 4598 m Par 68
V'tors U
Fees 1000 Ikr
Loc 5 km SE of Olafsvík (W coast)

Keilir (1967)
Box 148, 222 Hafnarfjördur
Tel (565) 3360
Fax (565) 2560
Email keilir@isholf.is
Holes 18 L 5449 m Par 71
9 L 2748 m Par 36
V'tors U
Fees 18 hole: 2000 Ikr
9 hole: 1000 Ikr
Loc Hafnarfjördur, 10 km S of Reykjavik
Arch Hannes Thorsteinsson

Kopavogs og Gardabaejar (1994)
Postholf 214, 212 Gardabaejar
Tel (565) 7373
Fax (565) 9190
Holes 18 L 5437 m Par 70
V'tors U
Fees 1700 Ikr
Loc Gardabaer, S of Reykjavis

Leynir (1965)
PO Box 9, 300 Akranes
Tel (431) 2711
Fax (431) 3711
Holes 11 L 5445 m CR 70.3
V'tors U
Fees 1500Ikr
Loc 2 km from Akranes (SW coast)
Arch H Thorsteinsson

Ness-Nesklúbburinn (1964)
PO Box 66, 172 Seltjarnarnes
Tel (561) 1930
Fax (561) 1966
Holes 9 L 5374 m Par 72
V'tors U
Fees 1500 Ikr
Loc 3 km W of Reykjavík

Oddafellowa (1990)
Urridavatnsdölum, 210 Gardabaer
Tel (565) 9094
Fax (565) 9074
Holes 18 L 5830 m Par 71
V'tors U
Fees 2000 Ikr
Loc S of Reykjavík, nr Hafnarfjördur

Olafsfjardar (1968)
Skeggjabrekku, 625 Olafsfjördur
Tel (466) 2611
Fax (466) 2611
Holes 9 L 4570 m Par 66
V'tors U
Fees 1000 IkrU
Loc 60 km NW of Akureyri
(N coast)

Reykjavíkur (1934)
PO Box 12068, 132 Reykjavík
Tel (587) 2211/2215
Fax (587) 2212
Holes 18 L 5963 m Par 71
18 L 6214 m Par 72
V'tors U
Fees 1400–2000 Ikr
Loc 8 km E of Reykjavík
Arch Nils Skjold

Saudárkróks (1970)
Hlidarendi, Postholf 56, 550 Saudárkrókur
Tel (453) 5075
Holes 9 L 5902 m Par 72
V'tors U
Fees 1000 Ikr
Loc 2 km W of Saudárkrókur
(N coast)

Sudurnesja (1964)
PO Box 112, 232 Keflavík
Tel (421) 4100
Fax (421) 5981
Holes 18 L 5861 m Par 72
V'tors U
Fees 1000–1500 Ikr
Loc N of Keflavik (SW coast).
Airport 5 km

Vestmannaeyja (1938)
Postholf 168, 902 Vestmannaeyar
Tel (481) 2363
Fax (481) 2362
Holes 18 L 5322 m Par 70
V'tors U
Fees 1500 Ikr
Loc 2 km W of Vestmannaeyar.
Island off S coast - 20 min flight from Reykjavik

Italy

Como/Milan/Bergamo

Ambrosiano (1994)
Cascina Bertacca, 20080 Bubbiano-Milan
Tel (0290) 840820
Fax (0290) 849365
Holes 18 L 6047 m Par 72
V'tors U
Fees 60.000L (90.000L)
Loc 25 km SW of Milan
Arch Cornish/Silva

Barlassina CC (1956)
Via Privata Golf 42, 20030 Birago di Camnago (MI)
Tel (0362) 560621/2/3
Fax (0362) 560934
Holes 18 L 6184 m SSS 72
V'tors WD–U
Fees 110.000L (155.000L)
Loc 22 km N of Milan
Arch J Morrison

Bergamo L'Albenza (1960)
Via Longoni 12, 24030 Almenno San Bartolomeo
Tel (035) 640028/640707
Fax (035) 640028
Holes 18 L 6198 m SSS 72
9 L 2962 m SSS 36
V'tors WD–U
Loc 13 km NW of Bergamo.
Milan 45 km
Arch Cotton/Sutton

Bogogno (1996)
See Stop Press on page 818

Brianza (1996)
Cascina Cazzo, 20040 Usmate Velate
Tel (039) 682 9089
Fax (039) 682 9059
Holes 18 L 5729 m Par 71 SSS 70
V'tors U
Fees 50.000L (80.000L)
Loc 24 km NE of Milan.
Monza 6 km
Arch Marco Croze

Carimate (1962)
Via Airoldi, 22060 Carimate
Tel (031) 790226
Fax (031) 790226
Holes 18 L 5982 m SSS 71
V'tors U H
Fees 70.000L (100.000L)
Loc 15 km S of Como. 27 km N of Milan
Arch Pier Mancinelli

Castelconturbia (1984)
Via Suno, 28010 Agrate Conturbia
Tel (0322) 832093
Fax (0322) 832428

For list of abbreviations see page 527

Holes   Red 9 L 3330 m Par 36
        Yellow 9 L 3070 m Par 36
        Blue 9 L 3210 m Par 36
V'tors WD–H WE–M H
Fees   95.000L (150.000L)
Loc   23 km N of Novara.
        Milan 60 km
Arch   Robert Trent Jones Sr

Franciacorta (1986)
Via Provinciale 34b, 25040 Nigoline di Corte Franca (Brescia)
Tel   (030) 984167
Fax   (030) 984393
Holes   18 L 6065 m SSS 72
        9 hole Par 3 course
V'tors U
Fees   70.000L (100.000L)
Loc   Nigoline, 25 km E of Bergamo.
        Autostrada A4 exit Rovato
Arch   Dye/Croze

Lanzo Intelvi (1962)
22024 Lanzo Intelvi (CO)
Tel   (031) 840169
Holes   9 L 2438 m SSS 66
V'tors U
Loc   32 km NW of Como

Menaggio & Cadenabbia (1907)
Via Golf 12, 22010 Grandola E Uniti
Tel   (0344) 32103
Fax   (0344) 30780
Holes   18 L 5455 m Par 70 SSS 69
V'tors WD–U H WE–H restricted
Fees   80.000L (110.000L)
Loc   5 km W of Menaggio. 40 km
        N of Como
Arch   John Harris

Milano (1928)
20052 Parco di Monza (MI)
Tel   (039) 303081/2/3
Fax   (039) 304427
Holes   18 L 6414 m SSS 73
        9 L 2976 m SSS 36
V'tors WD–H WE–by appointment
Fees   96.000L (144.000L)
Loc   6 km N of Monza. 18 km NE
        of Milan
Arch   Gannon/Blandford

Molinetto CC (1982)
SS Padana Superiore 11, 20063 Cernusco S/N (Ml)
Tel   (02) 9210 5128/9210 5983
Fax   (02) 9210 6235
Holes   18 L 6010 m Par 71
V'tors WD–H WE–restricted
Loc   Cernusco, 10 km E of Milan

Monticello (1975)
Via Volta 4, 22070 Cassina Rizzardi
Tel   (031) 928055
Fax   (031) 880207
Holes   18 L 6413 m SSS 72
        18 L 6056 m SSS 72
V'tors WD–H WE–NA
Fees   80.000L (100.000L)

Loc   10 km SE of Como
Arch   Jim Fazio

La Pinetina (1971)
Via al Golf 4, 22070 Appiano Gentile
Tel   (031) 933202
Fax   (031) 890342
Holes   18 L 6001 m SSS 71
V'tors WD–U WE–booking necessary
Fees   90.000L (110.000L)
Loc   12 km SW of Como. Milan
        25 km

Le Robinie (1992)
Via per Busto Arsizio 9, 21058 Solbiate Olona (VA)
Tel   (039) 331 329260
Fax   (039) 331 329266
Holes   18 L 6250 m Par 72 SSS 74
V'tors WD–U WE–H
Fees   80.000L (120.000L)
Loc   25 km NW of Milan.
        Malpensa Airport 6 km
Arch   Jack Nicklaus

La Rossera (1970)
Via Montebello 4, 24060 Chiuduno
Tel   (035) 838600
Fax   (035) 442 7047
Holes   9 L 2510 m SSS 68
V'tors U
Fees   45.000L (65.000L)
Loc   2 km from Chiuduno. 18 km
        SE of Bergamo

Le Rovedine (1978)
Via Carlo Marx, 20090 Noverasco di Opera (Ml)
Tel   (02) 5760 6420/5760 2730
Fax   (02) 5760 6405
Holes   18 L 6307 m SSS 72
V'tors U
Loc   4 km S of Milan

Royal Sant'Anna (1978)
22040 Annone di Brianza (CO)
Tel   (0341) 577551
Fax   (0341) 260143
Holes   18 L 4500 m SSS 64
V'tors U
Loc   15 km SE of Como. Milan
        40 km

Varese (1934)
Via Vittorio Veneto 32, 21020 Luvinate (VA)
Tel   (0332) 227394/229302
Fax   (0332) 222107
Holes   18 L 5936 m SSS 72
V'tors WD–U H
Fees   80.000L (120.000L)
Loc   5 km NW of Varese
Arch   Gannon/Blandford

Vigevano (1974)
Via Chitola 49, 27029 Vigevano (PV)
Tel   (0381) 346628/346077
Fax   (0381) 346091
Holes   18 L 5678 m SSS 72
Loc   25 km SE of Novara. 35 km
        SW of Milan

Villa D'Este (1926)
Via Cantù 13, 22030 Montorfano (CO)
Tel   (031) 200200
Fax   (031) 200786
Holes   18 L 5787 m SSS 71
V'tors I H
Loc   Montorfano, 7 km SE of Como
Arch   Peter Gannon

Zoate
20067 Zoate di Tribiano (MI)
Tel   (02) 9063 2183/9063 1861
Fax   (02) 9063 1861
Holes   18 L 6122 m Par 72
V'tors WD–U H
Fees   70.000L (100.000L)
Loc   Zoate, 17 km SE of Milan
Arch   Marmori

Elba

Acquabona (1971)
57037 Portoferraio, Isola di Elba (LI)
Tel   (0565) 940066
Fax   (0565) 933410
Holes   9 L 5144 m SSS 67
V'tors U
Fees   45.000L–65.000L
Loc   5 km NW of Porto Azzurro.
        6 km NW of Porto Ferraio
Arch   Gianni Albertini

Emilia Romagna

Adriatic GC Cervia (1985)
Via Jelenia Gora No 6, 48016 Cervia-Milano Marittima
Tel   (0544) 992786
Fax   (0544) 993410
Holes   18 L 6246 m SSS 72
V'tors U H
Fees   85.000L (100.000L)
Loc   20 km SE of Ravenna
Arch   Marco Croze

Bologna (1959)
Via Sabattini 69, 40050 Monte San Pietro (BO)
Tel   (051) 969100
Fax   (051) 672 0017
Holes   18 L 6171 m SSS 72
V'tors U
Fees   80.000L (100.000L)
Loc   20 km W of Bologna
Arch   Harris/Cotton

Croara (1976)
29010 Croara di Gazzola
Tel   (0523) 977105/977148
Fax   (0523) 977100
Holes   18 L 6065 m SSS 72
V'tors H
Fees   50.000L (70.000L)
Loc   16 km SW of Piacenza. 84 km
        SE of Milan
Arch   Buratti/Croze

For list of abbreviations see page 527

Matilde di Canossa
Via Casinazzo 1, 42100 San Bartolomeo
Tel (0522) 371295
Fax (0522) 371204
Holes 18 L 6231 m SSS 72
V'tors U
Fees 50.000L (80.000L)
Loc 50 km NW of Bologna
Arch Marco Croze

La Rocca (1985)
Via Campi 8, 43038 Sala Baganza (PR)
Tel (0521) 834037
Fax (0521) 834215
Holes 18 L 6076 m SSS 71
V'tors U
Fees 60.000L (80.000L)
Loc 8 km S of Parma
Arch Marco Croze

La Torre (1992)
Via Limisano 10, Riolo Terme (RA)
Tel (0546) 74035
Fax (0546) 74076
Holes 18 L 6350 m Par 72
V'tors H
Fees 40.000L (50.000L)
Loc 30 km SW of Bologna
Arch Alberto Croze

Gulf of Genoa

Degli Ulivi (1932)
Via Campo Golf 59, 18038 Sanremo
Tel (0184) 557093
Fax (0184) 557388
Holes 18 L 5203 m SSS 67
V'tors U
Loc 5 km N of Sanremo
Arch Peter Gannon

Garlenda (1965)
Via Golf 7, 17030 Garlenda
Tel (0182) 580012
Fax (0182) 580561
Holes 18 L 6047 m Par 72 SSS 71
V'tors WE–H
Fees 80.000L (130.000L)
Loc 15 km N of Alassio
Arch John Harris

Marigola (1975)
Via Vallata 5, 19032 Lerici (SP)
Tel (0187) 970193
Fax (0187) 970193
Holes 9 L 2116 m Par 49
V'tors U
Loc 6 km SE of La Spezia
Arch Franco Marmori

Pineta di Arenzano (1959)
Piazza del Golf 3, 16011 Arenzano (GE)
Tel (010) 911 1817
Fax (010) 911 1270
Holes 9 L 5527 m SSS 70
V'tors H
Fees 60.000L (85.000L)

Loc Arenzano Pineta, 20 km W of Genoa
Arch Donald Harradine

Rapallo (1930)
Via Mameli 377, 16035 Rapallo (GE)
Tel (0185) 261777
Fax (0185) 261779
Holes 18 L 5638 m Par 70
V'tors H WE–NA before noon
Fees 80.000L (120.000L)
Loc 25 km SE of Genoa. A12 motorway exit Rapallo

Versilia (1990)
Via Sipe 100, 55045 Pietrasanta (LU)
Tel (0584) 88 15 74
Fax (0584) 75 22 72
Holes 18 L 6115 m Par 72
V'tors U H
Fees 80.000L
Loc 30 km N of Pisa on coast, nr Forte dei Marmi
Arch Marco Croze

Lake Garda & Dolomites

Asiago (1967)
Via Meltar 2, 36012 Asiago (VI)
Tel (0424) 462721
Fax (0424) 462721
Holes 18 L 6005 m SSS 71
V'tors U H
Loc 3 km N of Asiago. 50 km N of Vicenza
Arch P Harradine

Bogliaco (1912)
Via Golf 11, 25088 Toscolano Maderno
Tel (0365) 643006
Fax (0365) 643006
Holes 9 L 2572 m SSS 67
V'tors H
Fees 50.000L (70.000L)
Loc Lake Garda, 40 km NE of Brescia

Ca' degli Ulivi (1988)
Via Ghiandare 2, 37010 Marciaga di Costermano (VR)
Tel (045) 725 6463/725 6485
Fax (045) 725 6876
Holes 18 L 6000 m SSS 72 9 hole course
Loc Above village of Garda. Verona Airport 35 km

Campo Carlo Magno (1922)
Golf Hotel, 38084 Madonna di Campiglio (TN)
Tel (0465) 440622
Fax (0465) 440298
Holes 9 L 5148 m SSS 67
V'tors H

Fees 75.000–100.000L
Loc Madonna di Campiglio 1 km. 74 km NW of Trento
Arch Henry Cotton

Folgaria (1987)
Loc Costa di Folgaria, 38064 Folgaria (TN)
Tel (0464) 720480
Fax (0464) 720480
Holes 9 L 2582 m SSS 70
V'tors H
Fees 60.000L (70.000L)
Loc 30 km S of Trento, off A22
Arch Marco Croze

Gardagolf CC (1985)
Via Angelo Omodeo 2, 25080 Soiano Del Lago (BS)
Tel (0365) 674707 (Sec)
Fax (0365) 674788
Holes 18 L 6505 m SSS 74 9 L 2635 m Par 35
V'tors H
Fees 85.000L (115.000L)
Loc Lake Garda, 30 km NE of Brescia.
Arch Cotton/Pennink/Steel

Karersee-Carezza
Loc Carezza 171, 39056 Welschofen-Nova Levante
Tel (0471) 612200
Fax (0471) 612200
Holes 9 L 5340 m SSS 68
V'tors U
Fees 60.000L (70.000L)
Loc 30 km S of Bolzano
Arch Marco Croze

Petersberg (1987)
Unterwinkel 5, 39040 Petersberg (BZ)
Tel (0471) 615122
Fax (0471) 615229
Holes 18 L 5100 m SSS 66
V'tors U
Fees 75.000L (95.000L)
Loc 35 km SE of Bolzano, nr Nova Ponente
Arch Marco Croze

Ponte di Legno (1980)
Corso Milano 36, 25056 Ponte di Legno (BS)
Tel (0364) 900306
Fax (0364) 900555
Holes 9 L 4803 m SSS 68
V'tors U
Fees 50.000L (70.000L)
Loc 90 km W of Trento, nr San Michele
Arch Caremoli

Verona (1963)
Ca' del Sale 15, 37066 Sommacampagna
Tel (045) 510060
Fax (045) 510242
Holes 18 L 6054 m SSS 72
V'tors H WE–M

Fees 100.000L (110.000L)
Loc 7 km W of Verona
Arch John Harris

Naples & South

Napoli (1983)
Via Campiglione 11, 80072 Arco Felice (NA)
Tel (081) 526 4296
Holes 9 L 4776 m SSS 68
V'tors M
Loc Pozzuoli, 10 km W of Naples

Porto d'Orra (1977)
PB 102, 88063 Catanzaro Lido
Tel (0961) 791045
Fax (0961) 791444
Holes 9 L 5686 m SSS 70
V'tors U
Loc 9 km N of Catanzaro Lido on coast

Riva Dei Tessali (1971)
74011 Castellaneta
Tel (099) 843 9251
Fax (099) 843 9255
Holes 18 L 5960 m SSS 71
V'tors U
Fees 60.000L
Loc 34 km SW of Taranto
Arch Marco Croze

San Michele
Loc Bosco 8/9, 87022 Cetraro (CS)
Tel (0982) 91012
Fax (0982) 91430
Holes 9 L 2760 m SSS 70
V'tors U H
Fees 30.000L (35.000L)
Loc Cetraro, 50 km N of Cosenza. 250 km SE of Naples
Arch Piero Mancinelli

Rome & Centre

Castelgandolfo (1987)
Via Santo Spirito 13, 00040 Castelgandolfo
Tel (06) 931 2301/931 3084
Fax (06) 931 2244
Holes 18 L 6025 m SSS 72
V'tors U H Sun–restricted
Fees 60.000L (100.000L)
Loc 22 km SE of Rome
Arch Robert Trent Jones

Eucalyptus (1988)
Via Cogna 5, 04011 Aprilia (Roma)
Tel (06) 92 74 62 52
Fax (06) 926 85 02
Holes 18 L 6310 m Par 72 SSS 73
V'tors WD–U WE–U H
Fees 50.000L (60.000L)
Loc 20 km S of Rome on Aprilia-Anzio road
Arch D'Onofrio/Mancinelli

Fioranello
CP 96, 00040 Santa Maria delle Mole (RM)
Tel (06) 713 8058
Fax (06) 713 8212
Holes 18 L 5417 m Par 70
V'tors U
Loc Santa Maria, 17 km SE of Rome

Fiuggi (1928)
Superstrada Anticolana 1, 03015 Fiuggi (FR)
Tel (0775) 55250
Fax (0775) 506742
Holes 9 L 5697 m SSS 70
V'tors U
Loc 60 km SE of Rome

Marco Simone (1989)
Via di Marco Simone, 00012 Guidonia (RM)
Tel (0774) 366469
Fax (0774) 366476
Holes 18 L 6317 m SSS 73
 18 hole course Par 64
V'tors U
Loc 17 km NE of Rome
Arch Fazio/Mezzacane

Nettuno
Via della Campana 18, 00048 Nettuno (RM)
Tel (06) 981 9419
Fax (06) 981 9419
Holes 18 L 6260 m SSS 72
V'tors U H
Loc 60 km S of Rome on coast
Arch Marco Croze

Olgiata (1961)
Largo Olgiata 15, 00123 Roma
Tel (06) 308 9141
Fax (06) 308 9968
Holes 18 L 6347 m SSS 73
 9 L 2947 m SSS 71
V'tors U
Fees 70.000L (120.000L)
Loc 19 km NW of Rome, nr La Storta
Arch CK Cotton

Parco de' Medici (1989)
Viale Parco de' Medici 20, 00149 Roma
Tel (06) 655 3477
Fax (06) 655 3344
Holes 18 L 6318 m SSS 73
V'tors U
Fees 90.000L
Loc 15 km SW of Rome, nr Airport
Arch P Fazio

Pescara (1992)
Contrado Cerreto 58, 66010 Miglianico (CH)
Tel (0871) 959566
Fax (0871) 950363
Holes 18 L 6184 m Par 72 SSS 72

V'tors U
Fees 50.000L (70.000L)
Loc S of Pescara (Adriatic coast)

Le Querce
San Martino, 01015 Sutri (VT)
Tel (0761) 68789
Fax (0761) 68142
Holes 18 L 6433 m SSS 72
V'tors U
Fees 70.000L
Loc 42 km N of Rome
Arch Fazio/Mezzacane

Roma (1903)
Via Appia Nuova 716A, 00178 Roma
Tel (06) 780 3407
Fax (06) 783 46219
Email golfroma@italkey.it
Holes 18 L 5854 m Par 71
V'tors WD–H WE–M H
Fees 70.000L (100.000L)
Loc 7 km SE of Rome towards Ciampino

Tarquinia
Loc Pian di Spille, Via degli Alina 271, 01016 Marina Velca/Tarquinia (VT)
Tel (0766) 812109
Holes 9 L 5442 m SSS 69
Loc 80 km N of Rome on coast

Torvaianica
Via Enna 30, 00040 Marina di Ardea
Tel (06) 913 3250
Fax (06) 913 3592
Holes 9 L 4416 m SSS 64
V'tors H
Loc 30 km S of Rome
Arch Leonardo Basili

Sardinia

Is Molas (1975)
CP 49, 09010 Pula
Tel (070) 924 1013/4
Fax (070) 924 1015
Holes 18 L 6383 m SSS 72
Fees 80.000L (100.000L)
Loc Pula, 32 km S of Cagliari
Arch Cotton/Pennink/Lurie

Pevero GC Costa Smeralda (1972)
07020 Porto Cervo
Tel (0789) 96072/96210/96211
Fax (0789) 96572
Holes 18 L 6186 m SSS 72
V'tors U H
Fees 80.000–200.000L
Loc Porto Cervo, 30 km N of Olbia, on Costa Smeralda
Arch Robert Trent Jones

For list of abbreviations see page 527

Turin & Piemonte

Alpino Di Stresa (1924)
Viale Golf Panorama 49, 28839 Vezzo (VB)
Tel (0323) 20642/20101
Fax (0323) 20642
Holes 9 L 5397 m Par 69 SSS 68
V'tors WE–U WE–restricted
Fees 18 holes–50.000L (70.000L)
9 holes–35.000L (50.000L)
Loc 7 km W of Stresa. Milan 80 km
Arch Peter Gannon

Biella Le Betulle (1958)
Valcarozza, 13887 Magnano (BI)
Tel (015) 679151
Fax (015) 679216
Holes 18 L 6427 m SSS 72
V'tors U
Fees 90.000L (120.000L)
Loc 17 km SW of Biella
Arch John Morrison

Cervino (1955)
11021 Cervinia-Breuil (AO)
Tel (0166) 949131
Fax (0116) 949131
Holes 9 L 4796 m SSS 66
V'tors U
Fees 50.000L–70.000L
Loc 53 km NE of Aosta
Arch Donald Harradine

Cherasco CC (1983)
Loc Fraschetta, Cascina Roma, 12062 Cherasco (CN)
Tel (0172) 489772/488489
Fax (0172) 488304
Holes 18 L 5947 m Par 72 SSS 71
V'tors H
Fees 60.000L (80.000L)
Loc Cherasco, 45 km S of Turin
Arch Gianmarco Croze

Claviere (1923)
Strada Nazionale 45, 10050 Claviere (TO)
Tel (0122) 878917
Holes 9 L 4650 m SSS 65
V'tors U
Loc 96 km W of Turin
Arch Luzi

Courmayeur
11013 Courmayeur (AO)
Tel (0165) 89203
Holes 9 L 2650 m SSS 67
Loc 5 km NE of Courmayeur

Le Fronde (1973)
Via Sant-Agostino 68, 10051 Avigliana (TO)
Tel (011) 932 8053/0540
Fax (011) 932 0928
Holes 18 L 5976 m SSS 71

V'tors WD–U WE–H max 34
Fees 60.000L (80.000L)
Loc Avigliana, 20 km W of Turin
Arch John Harris

I Girasoli (1991)
Via Pralormo 315, 10022 Carmagnola (TO)
Tel (011) 979 5088
Fax (011) 979 5228
Holes 18 L 4585 m Par 65
V'tors H
Fees 45.000L (60.000L)
Loc 25 km S of Turin

Iles Borromees
Loc Motta Rossa, 28833 Brovello Carpugnino (VB)
Tel (0323) 929285/929192
Fax (0323) 929190
Holes 18 L 6445 m SSS 72
V'tors U
Fees 72.000L (108.000L)
Loc 5 km S of Stresa. 80 km NW of Milan
Arch Marco Croze

Golf dei Laghi (1993)
Via Trevisani 6, 21028 Travedona Monate (VA)
Tel (0332) 978101
Fax (0332) 977532
Holes 18 L 6400 m Par 72 SSS 73
V'tors H
Fees 60.000L (100.000L)
Loc 30 km SW of Varese. 50 km NW of Milan
Arch Piero Mancinelli

Margara (1975)
Via Tenuta Margara 5, 15043 Fubine (AL)
Tel (0131) 778555
Fax (0131) 778772
Holes 18 L 6045 m SSS 72
V'tors U
Loc 15 km NW of Alessandria

La Margherita
Strada Pralormo 29, Carmagnola (TO)
Tel (011) 979 5113
Fax (011) 979 5204
Holes 18 L 6339 m SSS 73
V'tors U
Fees 50.000L (80.000L)
Loc 20 km S of Turin
Arch Croze/Ferraris

Piandisole (1964)
Via Pineta 1, 28057 Premeno (NO)
Tel (0323) 587100
Holes 9 L 2830 m SSS 67
V'tors U
Loc Premeno, 30 km N of Stresa

I Roveri (1971)
Rotta Cerbiatta 24, 10070 Fiano (TO)
Tel (011) 923 5719/923 5720
Fax (011) 923 5668

Holes 18 L 6218 m SSS 72
9 L 3107 m SSS 36
V'tors WE–NA
Loc 16 km NW of Turin. Caselle Airport 10 km
Arch Robert Trent Jones

Santa Croce
Fraz Mellana, 12012 Bóves (CN)
Tel (0171) 387041
Fax (0171) 387512
Holes 18 L 6000 m Par 72
V'tors U
Loc 80 km S of Turin, nr Cúneo
Arch Graham Cooke

La Serra (1970)
Via Astigliano 42, 15048 Valenza (AL)
Tel (0131) 954778
Fax (0131) 928294
Holes 9 L 2820 m SSS 70
V'tors H
Fees 25.000L (40.000L)
Loc 4 km W of Valenza. 7 km N of Alessandria
Arch Migliorini

Sestrieres (1932)
Piazza Agnelli 4, 10058 Sestrieres (TO)
Tel (0122) 755170/76243
Fax (0122) 76294
Holes 18 L 4598 m Par 67 SSS 65
V'tors U H
Fees 55.000L (80.000L)
Loc Sestrieres, 96 km W of Turin

Stupinigi (1972)
Corso Unione Sovietica 506, 10135 Torino
Tel (011) 347 2640
Fax (011) 397 8038
Holes 9 L 2175 m SSS 63
Loc Mirafiore, Turin

Torino (1924)
Via Grange 137, 10070 Fiano Torinese
Tel (011) 923 5440/923 5670
Fax (011) 923 5886
Holes 18 L 6216 m SSS 72
18 L 6214 m SSS 72
V'tors U H
Fees 90.000L (130.000L)
Loc 23 km NW of Turin
Arch Morrison/Croze/Cooke

Vinovo (1986)
Via Stupinigi 182, 10048 Vinovo (TO)
Tel (011) 965 3880
Fax (011) 962 3748
Holes 9 L 4278 m Par 64
V'tors U
Fees 50.000L (60.000L)
Loc Vinovo, 3 km SW of Turin
Arch Croce/Chiaravigcio

For list of abbreviations see page 527

Tuscany & Umbria

Casentino (1985)
Via Fronzola 6, Loc Il Palazzo,
52014 Poppi (Arezzo)
Tel (0575) 529810
Fax (0575) 520167
Holes 9 L 5550 m Par 72 SSS 69
V'tors WD–U WE–H
Fees 45.000L (55.000L)
Loc Poppi, 50 km SE of Florence
Arch R Brami

Castelfalfi G&CC
50050 Montaione (FI)
Tel (0571) 698093/4
Fax (0571) 698098
Holes 18 L 6095 m SSS 73
V'tors H
Loc 45 km SW of Florence
Arch Pier Mancinelli

Conero GC Sirolo (1987)
Via Betellico 6, 60020 Sirolo (AN)
Tel (071) 736 0613
Fax (071) 736 0380
Holes 18 L 6185 m Par 72
 9 hole course Par 29
V'tors U
Loc Sirolo, 20 km SE of Ancona.
 Falconara Airport 25 km
Arch Marco Croze

Cosmopolitan G&CC (1992)
Viale Pisorno 60, 56018 Tirrenia
Tel (050) 33633
Fax (050) 384707
Holes 18 L 6291 m Par 73
V'tors U
Fees 60.000L
Loc 15 km SW of Pisa
Arch David Mezzacane

Firenze Ugolino
Strada Chiantigiana 3, 50015 Grassina
Tel (055) 205 1009/203 1085
Fax (055) 230 1141
Holes 18 L 5785 m SSS 70
V'tors U
Loc Grassina, 9 km S of Florence

Lamborghini-Panicale (1992)
Loc Soderi 1, 06064 Panicale (PG)
Tel (075) 837182
Fax (075) 837582
Holes 9 L 5720 m Par 72
V'tors H
Loc 30 km W of Perugia, nr Lake Trasimeno
Arch Lamborghini Ferruccio

Montecatini (1985)
Via Dei Brogi 5, Loc Pievaccia,
51015 Monsummano Terme
Tel (0572) 62218
Fax (0572) 617435
Holes 18 L 5932 m SSS 71
V'tors WD–U H
Loc 8 km SE of Montecatini Terme.
 50 km SW of Florence (A11)
Arch Marco Croze

Le Pavoniere (1986)
Via della Fattoria 6, 50047 Prato
Tel (0574) 620855
Fax (0574) 624558
Holes 18 L 6464 m Par 72 SSS 73
V'tors U
Fees 50.000L (70.000L)
Loc Prato 10km. 25 km W of Florence
Arch Arnold Palmer

Perugia (1960)
06074 Santa Sabina-Ellera
Tel (075) 517 2204
Fax (075) 517 2370
Holes 18 L 5650 m SSS 71
V'tors U
Fees 60.000L (70.000L)
Loc 6 km NW of Perugia
Arch David Mezzacane

Poggio dei Medici
Via S Gavino 27, 50038 Scarperia Firenze
Tel (055) 843 0436
Fax (055) 843 0439
Holes 18 L 6367 m Par 73
V'tors U
Fees 60.000L (75.000L)
Loc 30 km from Florence
Arch Fioravanti/Dassù

Punta Ala (1964)
Via del Golf 1, 58040 Punta Ala (GR)
Tel (0564) 922121/922719
Fax (0564) 920182
Holes 18 L 6213 m SSS 72
V'tors U
Fees 90.000L
Loc 40 km NW of Grosseto. Siena 90km. Florence 150 km

Tirrenia (1968)
Viale San Guido, 56018 Tirrenia (PI)
Tel (050) 37518
Fax (050) 33286
Holes 9 L 3065 m SSS 72
Loc 15 km SW of Pisa on coast

Venice & North East

Albarella
Isola di Albarella, 45010 Rosolina (RO)
Tel (0426) 330124
Fax (0426) 330628
Holes 18 L 6100 m SSS 72
V'tors H
Fees 80.000L (100.000L)
Loc 80 km S of Venice
Arch Harris/Croze

Ca' della Nave (1986)
Piazza Vittoria 14,
30030 Martellago
Tel (041) 540 1555
Fax (041) 540 1926
Holes 18 L 6380 m SSS 73
 9 L 1240 m Par 28
V'tors H
Loc Martellago, 12 km NW of Venice
Arch Arnold Palmer

Cansiglio (1956)
CP 152, 31029 Vittorio Veneto
Tel (0438) 585398
Fax (0438) 585398
Holes 18 L 6007 m SSS 71
V'tors WD–U WE–H
Fees 65.000L (85.000L)
Loc 21 km NE of Vittorio Veneto. 80 km NE of Venice
Arch Trent Jones/Croze

Colli Berici (1986)
Strada Monti Comunali, 36040 Brendola (VI)
Tel (0444) 601780
Fax (0444) 400777
Holes 18 L 5798 m SSS 71
V'tors U
Fees 80.000L (100.000L)
Loc Vicenza 10km. Venice 70 km
Arch Marco Croze

Frassanelle (1990)
35030 Frassanelle di Rovolon (PD)
Tel (049) 991 0722
Fax (049) 991 0722
Holes 18 L 6180 m SSS 72
V'tors H
Fees 80.000L (100.000L)
Loc 20 km S of Padova, nr Via dei Colli
Arch Marco Croze

Lignano
Via Bonifica 3, 33054 Lignano Sabbiadoro
Tel (0431) 428025
Fax (0431) 423230
Holes 18 L 6280 m SSS 72
V'tors H
Fees 60.000L (80.000L)
Loc 90 km E of Venice on coast
Arch Marco Croze

La Montecchia (1989)
Via Montecchia 12, 35030 Selvazzano (PD)
Tel (049) 805 5550
Fax (049) 805 5737
Holes 18 L 6318 m SSS 73
 9 L 3012 m Par 36
V'tors U H
Fees 90.000L (110.000L)
Loc 8 km W of Padova. 40 km W of Venice
Arch T Macauley

Luxembourg

Clervaux (1992)
Mecherwee, 9748 Eselborn
Tel 92 93 95
Fax 92 94 51
Holes 18 L 6144 m Par 72
V'tors H
Fees 980fl (1300fl)
Loc 3 km from Clervaux in North

Gaichel
Rue de Eischen, 8469 Gaichel
Tel 39 71 08
Fax 39 00 75
Holes 9 L 5155 m Par 70
V'tors U H
Fees 700fr (900fr)
Loc 10 km W of Mersch on Belgian border

Grand-Ducal de Luxembourg (1936)
1 Route de Trèves, 2633 Senningerberg
Tel 34 00 90
Fax 34 83 91
Holes 18 L 5765 m SSS 71
V'tors H
Fees 1500fr (2000fr)
Loc 7 km N of Luxembourg
Arch Maj Simpson

Kikuoka CC Chant Val (1991)
Scheierhaff, 5412 Canach
Tel 35 61 35
Fax 35 74 50
Holes 18 L 6404 m SSS 74
V'tors H
Fees 1400fr–2060fr (2575fr)
Loc Canach, 15 km E of Luxembourg City
Arch Iwao Uematsu

Luxembourg Belenhaff (1993)
Domaine de Belenhaff, 6141 Junglinster
Tel 78 00 68-1
Fax 78 71 28
Holes 18 L 6120 m Par 72
V'tors H or Green card
Fees 1750fl (2100fl)
Loc 17 km NE of Luxembourg, nr La Rochette

Malta

Royal Malta (1888)
Marsa HMR 15, Malta
Tel (035) 23 38 51
Fax (035) 23 93 02
Holes 18 L 5020 m SSS 68
V'tors U H exc Thurs–NA before 11am Sat–NA before noon
Fees £M10
Loc Marsa, 3 miles from Valetta

The Netherlands 787

Netherlands

Amsterdam & Noord Holland

Amsterdam Old Course (1990)
Zwarte Laantje 4, 1099 CE Amsterdam
Tel (020) 694 3650
Fax (020) 663 4621
Holes 9 L 5264 m SSS 68
V'tors WE–H
Fees 90fl
Loc 5 km SE of Amsterdam

Amsterdamse (1934)
Bauduinlaan 35, 1047 HK Amsterdam
Tel (020) 497 7866
Fax (020) 497 5966
Holes 18 L 6124 m CR 73.1
V'tors WD–H WE–M
Fees 40–125fl
Loc 10 km W of Amsterdam
Arch Rolin/Jol

Haarlemmermeersche
Spieringweg, Cruquiusdijk 122, 2141 EV Vijfhuizen
Tel (023) 558 3124
Fax (023) 558 1554
Holes 9 L 6087 m SSS 72
9 hole short course
V'tors H
Fees 50fl
Loc Haarlemmermeer, W of Amsterdam
Arch C O'Connor Jr

Heemskerkse (1998)
Communicatieweg 18, 1967 PR Heemskerk
Tel (0251) 250088
Fax (0251) 241627
Holes 18 L 6167 m Par 72
Fees 65fl
Loc 25 km NW of Amsterdam

Kennemer G&CC (1910)
Kennemerweg 78, 2042 XT Zandvoort
Tel (023) 571 2836/8456
Fax (023) 571 9520
Holes 27 holes CR 71.9-72.0:
Van Hengel 9 L 2951 m
Pennink 9 L 2916 m
Colt 9 L 2942 m
V'tors H WE–NA before 3pm
Fees 125fl
Loc Zandvoort, 6 km W of Haarlem
Arch Colt/Pennink

De Noordhollandse (1982)
Sluispolderweg 6, 1817 BM Alkmaar
Tel (072) 515 6807
Fax (072) 511 6807
Holes 18 L 5865 m CR 70.6
V'tors H

Padova (1966)
35050 Valsanzibio di Galzigano
Tel (049) 913 0078
Fax (049) 913 1193
Holes 18 L 6053 m SSS 72
V'tors U
Loc Valsanzibio, 20 km S of Padua

San Floriano-Gorizia (1987)
Castello di San Floriano, 34070 San Floriano del Collio (GO)
Tel (0481) 884252/884234
Fax (0481) 884252/884052
Holes 9 L 3810 m Par 62
V'tors U
Fees 40.000L
Loc 6 km NW of Gorizia. 50 km SE of Udine, nr Slovenian border
Arch Pellicciari

Trieste (1954)
Via Padriciano 80, 34012 Trieste
Tel (040) 226159/227062
Fax (040) 226159
Holes 9 L 5826 m Par 71
Loc Padriciano, 7 km E of Trieste

Udine (1971)
Via dei Fagi 1, Località Villaverde, 33034 Fagagna (UD)
Tel (0432) 800418
Fax (0432) 800418
Holes 9 L 2944 m Par 72
V'tors H
Loc 15 km NW of Udine
Arch Marco Croze

Venezia (1928)
Via del Forte, 30011 Alberoni (Venezia)
Tel (041) 731015/731333
Fax (041) 731339
Email circologolfvenezia@ntt.it
Holes 18 L 6199 m SSS 72
V'tors U H
Fees 90.000L (100.000L)
Loc Venice Lido
Arch Cruickshank/Cotton

Villa Condulmer (1960)
Via della Croce 3, 31021 Zerman di Mogliano Veneto
Tel (041) 457062
Fax (041) 457202
Holes 18 L 5995 m SSS 71
9 hole short course
V'tors H
Fees 80.000L (Sun 100.000L)
Loc Mogliano Veneto, 17 km N of Venice
Arch Harris/Croze

For list of abbreviations see page 527

The Netherlands

Fees 80fl (105fl)
Loc   2 km N of Alkmaar
Arch Ryks/Dudok van Heel

Olympus (1973)
Abcouderstraatweg 46, 1105 AA Amsterdam Zuid-Oost
Tel   (0294) 285373
Fax   (0294) 286347
Holes 18 L 5926 m SSS 71
V'tors U–phone first
Fees 55fl
Loc   SE of Amsterdam, nr A2 and AMC Hospital
Arch Dudok van Heel/Jol

Purmer (1989)
Westerweg 60, Postbus 587, 1440 AN Purmerend
Tel   (0299) 462143
Fax   (0299) 462143
Holes 18 L 6079 m SSS 70
      9 hole course
V'tors H
Fees 55–100fl
Loc   16 km N of Amsterdam
Arch Tom McAuley

Spaarnwoude (1977)
Het Hoge Land 2, 1981 LT Velsen-Zuid
Tel   (023) 538 2708
Fax   (023) 538 7274
Holes 18 L 5668 m Par 71
      9 L 2981 m Par 36
V'tors H
Fees 45fl
Loc   14 km W of Amsterdam.
      10 km NE of Haarlem
Arch Pennink/Jol

Waterlandse (1990)
Buikslotermeerdijk 141, 1027 AC Amsterdam
Tel   (020) 632 5650
Fax   (0200 634 3506
Holes 18 L 5156 m Par 71
Fees 50fl
Loc   10 km N of Amsterdam

Zaanse (1988)
Zuiderweg 68, 1456 NH Wijdewormer
Tel   (0299) 479123
Holes 9 L 5282 m Par 70
V'tors WD–H WE–H before noon and after 3pm
Fees 60fl (70fl)
Loc   15 km NE of Amsterdam
Arch Gerard Jol

Breda & South West

Brugse Vaart (1993)
Brugse Vaart 10, 4501 NE Oostburg
Tel   (0117) 453410
Fax   (0117) 455511
Holes 18 L 6305 m SSS 72
V'tors U

Fees 55fl (65fl)
Loc   15 km N of Bruges, nr Knokke
Arch Devos/Bauwens

Domburgsche (1914)
Schelpweg 26, 4357 BP Domburg
Tel   (0118) 586106
Fax   (0118) 586109
Holes 9 L 5402 m SSS 69
V'tors H
Fees 55fl (65fl)
Loc   15 km NW of Middelburg

Efteling (1994)
Veldstraat 6, 5176 NB Kaatsheuvel
Tel   (0416) 288399
Fax   (0416) 288439
Holes 18 L 5896 m Par 72
Fees 75fl (85fl)
Loc   20 km NW of Breda

Goese (1994)
Postbus 32, 4460 AA Goes
Tel   (0113) 229556/229557
Fax   (0113) 229554
Holes 18 L 6110 m Par 72 CR 71.5
V'tors H
Fees 75fl (85fl)
Loc   25kn E of Middelburgh
Arch Donald Steel

Grevelingenhout (1988)
Oudendijk 3, 4311 NA Bruinisse
Tel   (0111) 482650
Fax   (0111) 481566
Holes 18 L 5951 m CR 70.7
      9 hole Par 3 course
V'tors WD–U H WE–NA
Fees 75fl (95fl)
Loc   55 km SW of Rotterdam
Arch Donald Harradine

Oosterhoutse (1985)
Dukaatstraat 21, 4903 RN Oosterhout
Tel   (0162) 458759
Fax   (0162) 433285
Holes 18 L 6128 m SSS 71
V'tors WD–U H WE–M
Fees 70fl (75fl)
Loc   10 km NE of Breda
Arch J Dudok van Heel

Princenbosch (1991)
Bavelseweg 153, 5126 NM Gilze
Tel   (0161) 431811
Holes 18 L 5542 m Par 70
V'tors H–max 28
Fees 60fl
Loc   10 km SW of Breda

Reymerswael (1986)
Grensweg 21, 4411 ST Rilland Bath
Tel   (0113) 551265
Fax   (0113) 551264
Holes 18 L 5986 m CR 71.4
V'tors H
Fees 45fl (55fl)

Loc   20 km W of Bergen op Zoom.
      50 km W of Breda, off A58
Arch J Dudok van Heel

Toxandria (1928)
Veenstraat 89, 5124 NC Molenschot
Tel   (0161) 411200
Fax   (0161) 411715
Holes 18 L 5974 m SSS 71
V'tors WD–I Phone first
Fees 85fl (110fl)
Loc   8 km E of Breda
Arch Morrison/Dudok van Heel

De Woeste Kop (1986)
Justaasweg 4, 4571 NB Axel
Tel   (0115) 564467/564831 (Pro)
Fax   (0115) 564467
Holes 9 L 5444 m SSS 69
V'tors U
Fees 30fl (50fl)
Loc   45 km W of Antwerp
Arch Paneels/Bosch

Wouwse Plantage (1981)
Zoomvlietweg 66, 4624 RP Bergen op Zoom
Tel   (0165) 379593
Fax   (0165) 379888
Holes 18 L 5909 m Par 72
V'tors H WE–M
Fees 70fl
Loc   10 km E of Bergen-op-Zoom, nr Roosendaal
Arch Pennink/Rolin

East Central

Breuninkhof
Bussloselaan 6, 7383 RP Bussloo
Tel   (0571) 261955
Fax   (0571) 262089
Holes 9 L 6178 m SSS 72
V'tors H
Fees 55fl (65fl)
Loc   100 km E of Amsterdam
Arch Eschauzier

Edese (1978)
Papendallaan 22, 6816 VD Arnhem
Tel   (026) 482 1985
Fax   (026) 482 1348
Holes 18 L 5740 m SSS 70
V'tors H
Fees 60fl (80fl)
Loc   National Sportcentrum Papendal. NW of Arnhem, towards Ede
Arch Pennink/Dudok van Heel

De Graafschap (1987)
Sluitdijk 4, 7241 RR Lochem
Tel   (0573) 556469
Fax   (0573) 258450
Holes 18 L 6059 m CR 71.6
V'tors H–booking required
Fees 90fl (100fl)
Loc   Lochem, 35 km NW of Arnhem

For list of abbreviations see page 527

The Netherlands

Hattemse G&CC (1930)
Veenwal 11, 8051 AS Hattem
Tel (038) 444 1909
Holes 9 L 5808 yds SSS 68
V'tors WD–H WE–M+H
Fees 40fl (50fl)
Loc Hattem, 5 km S of Zwolle
Arch Del Court van Krimpen

Keppelse (1926)
Burg Kehrerstraat 52, 7002 LD Doetinchem
Tel (0314) 343662
Fax (0314) 363200
Holes 9 L 5360 m SSS 68
Fees 60fl (65fl)
Loc Laag-Keppel, 25 km E of Arnhem
Arch JP Eschauzier

De Koepel (1983)
Postbox 88, 7640 AB Wierden
Tel (0546) 576150/574070
Fax (0546) 578109
Holes 9 L 2863 m SSS 70
V'tors WE–H
Fees 50fl (60fl)
Loc 7 km W of Almelo
Arch F Pennink

Nunspeetse G&CC (1987)
Plesmanlaan 30, 8070 AB Nunspeet
Tel (0341) 255255
Fax (0341) 261149
Holes 27 L 6100 m Par 72
V'tors U
Fees 90fl (100fl)
Loc 25 km SW of Zwolle
Arch Paul Rolin

Rosendaelsche (1895)
Apeldoornseweg 450, 6816 SN Arnhem
Tel (026) 442 1438
Fax (026) 351 1196
Holes 18 L 6057 m SSS 72
V'tors WD–H WE–NA
Fees 85fl
Loc 5 km N of Arnhem on Route N50
Arch Frank Pennink

Sallandsche De Hoek (1934)
PO Box 24, 7430 AA Diepenveen
Tel (0570) 593269
Fax (0570) 593269
Holes 18 L 5889 m SSS 71
V'tors WD–H WE–NA
Fees 90fl
Loc 6 km N of Deventer
Arch Pennink/Steel

Sybrook (1992)
Veendijk, 7525 PZ Enschede
Tel (0541) 530331
Fax (0541) 531690
Holes 18 L 5878 m Par 71
V'tors WD–H WE–M

Fees 80fl
Loc 10 km N of Enschede
Arch Rolin/Rijks

Twentsche (1926)
Almelosestraat 17, 7495 TG Ambt Delden
Tel (074) 384 1167
Fax (074) 384 1067
Holes 18 L 6208 m SSS 72
V'tors H
Fees 80fl (90fl)
Loc 4 km N of Delden
Arch TJ McAuley

Veluwse (1957)
Nr 57, 7346 AC Hoog Soeren
Tel (055) 519 1275
Fax (055) 519 1275
Holes 9 L 6264 yds SSS 70
V'tors WD–U WD–H
Fees 60fl (70fl)

Welderen (1994)
Grote Molenstraat 173, 6661 NH Elst
Tel (0481) 376591
Fax (0481) 377055
Holes 18 L 6015 m Par 72
Fees 50fl (60fl)
Loc Elst, S of Arnhem

Eindhoven & South East

De Berendonck (1985)
Weg Door de Berendonck 40, 6603 LP Wijchen
Tel (024) 642 0039
Fax (024) 641 1254
Holes 18 L 5671 m Par 71 SSS 70
V'tors WE–restricted
Fees 55fl (65fl)
Loc 5 km SW of Nijmegen
Arch J Dudok van Heel

Best G&CC
Golflaan 1, 5683 RZ Best
Tel (04993) 91443
Fax (04993) 93221
Holes 18 L 6079 m SSS 71
V'tors U
Fees 60fl (80fl)
Loc Best, 5 km NW of Eindhoven
Arch J Dudok van Heel

Crossmoor G&CC (1986)
Laurabosweg 8, 6006 VR Weert
Tel (0495) 518538
Fax (0495) 518709
Holes 18 L 6052 m Par 72
 9 hole Par 3 course
V'tors H
Fees 80fl (100fl)
Loc Weert/Altweertheide, 30 km SE of Eindhoven
Arch J Dudok van Heel

De Dommel (1928)
Zegenwerp 12, 5271 NC St Michielsgestel
Tel (07355) 12316
Fax (07355) 19168
Holes 18 L 5607 m SSS 69
V'tors WD–H WE–NA
Fees 75fl (90fl)
Loc 10 km S of Hertogenbosch
Arch Colt/Steel

Eindhovensche Golf (1930)
Eindhovenseweg 300, 5553 VB Valkenswaard
Tel (040) 201 4816
Fax (040) 204 4038
Holes 18 L 5918 m SSS 71
V'tors H
Fees 70fl (100fl)
Loc 8 km S of Eindhoven
Arch HS Colt

Gendersteyn (1994)
Locht 140, 5504 RP Veldhoven
Tel (040) 253 4444
Fax (040) 254 9747
Holes 18 L 5770 m Par 72
Fees 65fl (80fl)
Loc 10 km SW of Eindhoven

Geysteren G&CC (1974)
Het Spekt 2, 5862 AZ Geysteren
Tel (0478) 531809/532592
Fax (0478) 532963
Holes 18 L 6090 m Par 72
V'tors WD–H WE–M
Fees 80fl (100fl)
Loc Off A73 Junction 9, N270 to Wanssum. 25 km N of Venlo
Arch Pennink/Steel

Havelte (1977)
Postbus 29, Kolonieweg 2, 7970 AA Havelte
Tel (0521) 342200
Fax (0521) 343134
Holes 18 L 6243 m Par 72
Fees 65fl (75fl)
Loc 30 km SW of Assen (N371)

Haviksoord (1976)
Maarheezerweg Nrd 11, 5595 XG Leende (NB)
Tel (040) 206 1818
Fax (040) 206 2761
Holes 9 L 5880 m SSS 71
V'tors H
Fees 40fl (50fl)
Loc 10 km S of Eindhoven

Herkenbosch (1991)
Stationsweg 100, 6075 CD Herkenbosch
Tel (0475) 531458
Fax (0475) 533580
Holes 18 L 6307 m Par 71
Fees 75fl (100fl)
Loc 20 km S of Venlo, nr German border

For list of abbreviations see page 527

Het Rijk van Nijmegen
(1985)
Postweg 17, 6561 KJ Groesbeek
Tel (024) 397 6644
Fax (024) 397 6942
Holes 18 L 6010 m CR 70.6
18 L 5747 m CR 69.1
V'tors H
Fees 65fl (80fl)
Loc 5 km E of Nijmegen
Arch Paul Rolin

De Peelse Golf (1991)
Maasduinenweg 1, 5977 NP Eversoord-Sevenum
Tel (077) 467 8030
Fax (077) 467 8031
Holes 18 L 6047 m Par 72
V'tors U H
Fees 65fl (85fl)
Loc 20 km W of Venlo
Arch Alan Rijks

De Schoot (1973)
Schootsedijk 18, 5491 TD Sint Oedenrode
Tel (04134) 73011
Fax (04134) 79256
Holes 9 L 2630 m SSS 68
V'tors U
Fees 40fl (45fl)
Loc 20 km N of Eindhoven
Arch A Rijks

Tongelreep G&CC (1984)
Charles Roelslaan 15, 5644 ZX Eindhoven
Tel (040) 252 0962
Holes 9 L 5268 m Par 70
V'tors WD–H WE–H by introduction only
Fees 50fl
Loc Eindhoven
Arch J van Rooy

Welschap (1993)
Welschapsedijk 164, 5657 BB Eindhoven
Tel (040) 251 5797
Fax (040) 252 9297
Holes 18 L 5282 m Par 70
Fees 60fl (70fl)
Loc Eindhoven

Limburg Province

Brunssummerheide (1985)
Rimburgerweg 50, Brunssum
Tel (045) 527 0968
Fax (045) 527 3939
Holes 27 L 5933 m Par 72
9 hole Par 3 course
V'tors U H
Fees 70fl (90fl)
Loc 25 km NE of Maastricht

Hoenshuis G&CC (1987)
Hoensweg 17, 6367 GN Voerendaal
Tel (045) 575 3300
Fax (045) 575 0900
Holes 18 L 6074 m CR 71.2
V'tors WE–NA 10am–2pm
Fees 60fl (90fl)
Loc Limburg, 10 km NE of Maastricht
Arch Paul Rolin

De Zuid Limburgse G&CC (1956)
Dalbissenweg 22, 6281 NC Mechelen
Tel (043) 455 1397
Fax (043) 455 1576
Holes 18 L 5924 m Par 71
V'tors WD–U WE–H
Fees 60fl (90fl)
Loc Mechelen, 25 km SE of Maastricht
Arch Hawtree/Snelder/Rolin

North

Gelpenberg (1970)
Gebbeveenweg 1, 7854 TD Aalden
Tel (0591) 371784/371929
Fax (0591) 372422
Holes 18 L 6031 m Par 71
V'tors H
Fees 60fl (70fl)
Loc 16 km W of Emmen
Arch Pennink/Steel

Holthuizen (1985)
Oosteinde 7a, 9301 ZP Roden
Tel (050) 501 5103
Holes 9 L 6079 m SSS 72
V'tors H
Fees 70fl (80fl)
Loc 10 km S of Groningen
Arch A Rijks

Lauswolt G&CC (1964)
Van Harinxmaweg 8A, PO Box 36, 9244 ZN Beetsterzwaag
Tel (0512) 383590/382594
Fax (0512) 383739
Holes 18 L 6087 m CR 71.5
V'tors H
Fees 110fl (150fl)
Loc Beetsterzwaag, 5 km S of Drachten
Arch Pennink/Steel

Noord Nederlandse G&CC (1950)
Pollselaan 5, 9756 CJ Glimmen
Tel (050) 406 2004
Fax (050) 406 1922
Holes 18 L 5755 m CR 69.3
V'tors H
Fees 60fl (90fl)
Loc 12 km S of Groningen, off A28

De Semslanden (1989)
Nieuwe Dijk 1, 9514 BX Gasselternijveen
Tel (0599) 565353/564661
Fax (0599) 564661
Holes 9 L 6078 m CR 132
V'tors U
Fees 40fl (50fl)
Loc 20 km W of Assen
Arch Eschauzier/Thate

Vegilinbosschen
Legemeersterweg 18, 8527 DS Legemeer
Tel (0513) 499466
Fax (0513) 499777
Holes 18 L 5765 m SSS 71
V'tors H
Fees 60fl (80fl)
Loc 100 km N of Amsterdam
Arch Allen Rijks

Rotterdam & The Hague

Broekpolder (1981)
Watersportweg 100, 3138 HD Vlaardingen
Tel (010) 249 5566,
(010) 249 5555/249 5577
Fax (010) 249 5579
Holes 18 L 6048 m SSS 72
V'tors H
Fees 75–100fl (100–125fl)
Loc 15 km W of Rotterdam, off A20
Arch Frank Pennink

Capelle a/d IJssel (1977)
Gravenweg 311, 2905 LB Capelle a/d IJssel
Tel (010) 442 2485
Fax (010) 442 2485
Holes 18 L 5214 m SSS 68
V'tors WD–U WE–M
Fees 65fl (75fl)
Loc 5 km S of Rotterdam
Arch Donald Harradine

Cromstrijen (1989)
Veerweg 26, 3281 LX Numansdorp
Tel (0186) 654455
Fax (0186) 654681
Holes 18 L 6168 m Par 72
9 L 3710 m Par 62
V'tors WD–U H WE–M H
Fees 80fl (95fl)
Loc 30 km S of Rotterdam (A29)
Arch Tom McAuley

De Hooge Bergsche (1989)
Rottebandreef 40, 2661 JK Bergschenhoek
Tel (010) 522 0052/522 0703
Fax (010) 521 9350
Holes 18 L 5370 m Par 71 SR 112
V'tors U
Fees 60fl (75fl)

Loc Bergschenhoek, 2 km NE of Rotterdam
Arch Gerard Jol

Kleiburg (1974)
Postbus 137, 3230 AC Brielle
Tel (0181) 413390
Fax (0181) 419691
Holes 18 L 5652 m SSS 69
V'tors U
Fees 50–65fl
Loc 25 km W of Rotterdam
Arch Pennink/Jol

Koninklijke Haagsche G&CC (1893)
Groot Haesebroekeseweg 22, 2243 EC Wassenaar
Tel (070) 517 9607
Fax (070) 514 0171
Holes 18 L 5674 m SSS 71
V'tors WD–H (max 26) WE–M
Fees 150fl
Loc 6 km N of The Hague
Arch Allison/Colt

Kralingen (1982)
Kralingseweg 200, 3062 CG Rotterdam
Tel (010) 452 2283
Holes 9 L 4844 yds CR 65.5
V'tors H
Fees 35fl (45fl)
Loc 5 km from centre of Rotterdam
Arch Copijn/Cotton

Leidschendamse Leeuwenbergh (1988)
Elzenlaan 31, 2267 AT Leidschendam
Tel (070) 395 4556
Fax (070) 399 8215
Holes 18 L 5461 m Par 70
Fees 75fl (95fl)
Loc E side of The Hague

De Merwelanden (1985)
Golfbaan Crayestein, Baanhoekweg 50, 3313 LP Dordrecht
Tel (078) 621 1221
Fax (078) 616 1036
Holes 18 L 5722 m Par 71
V'tors U
Fees 50fl (70fl)
Loc 20 km SE of Rotterdam
Arch H & C Kuijsters

Noordwijkse (1915)
Randweg 25, PO Box 70, 2200 AB Noordwijk
Tel (0252) 373761
Fax (0252) 370044
Holes 18 L 5879 m CR 71.8
V'tors WD–H before noon and after 3pm
Fees 125fl
Loc 5 km N of Noordwyk. 15 km NW of Leiden
Arch Frank Pennink

Oude Maas (1975)
Veerweg 2a, 3161 EX Rhoon
Tel (010) 501 8058
Fax (010) 501 0079
Holes 18 L 5907 m Par 72
Fees 60fl (75fl)
Loc Rhoon, S of Rotterdam via A15

Rijswijkse (1987)
Delftweg 58, 2289 AL Rijswijk
Tel (070) 319 2424
Fax (070) 399 5040
Holes 18 L 6159 m Par 72 CR 70.2
V'tors U H
Fees 75fl (100fl)
Loc 5 km SE of The Hague
Arch Donald Steel

Rozenstein (1984)
Hoge Klei 1, 2242 XZ Wassenaar
Tel (070) 511 7846
Fax (070) 511 9302
Holes 18 L 5820 m SSS 70
V'tors H
Fees 60fl (90fl)
Loc 14 km NE of The Hague
Arch Dudok van Heel/Jol

Westerpark Zoetermeer (1985)
Heuvelweg 3, 2716 DZ Zoetermeer
Tel (079) 351 7283
Fax (079) 352 1335
Holes 18 L 5891 m Par 71
Fees 70fl (80fl)
Loc 10 km E of The Hague (A12)

Zeegersloot (1984)
Kromme Aarweg 5, PO Box 190, 2400 AD Alphen a/d Rijn
Tel (0172) 474567
Fax (0172) 494660
Holes 18 L 5793 m SSS 70
9 hole Par 3 course
V'tors U H
Fees 18 hole:50fl (70fl)
9 hole:25fl (35fl)
Loc Alphen, 15 km N of Gouda. 20 km S of Amsterdam
Arch Gerard Jol

Utrecht & Hilversum

Almeerderhout (1986)
Watersnipweg 19-21, 1341 AA Almere
Tel (036) 538 4444
Fax (036) 538 4435
Holes 27 L 6004-6046 m CR 71.9-72.2
9 hole Par 3 course
V'tors WD–U WE M (Max h'cap 28)
Fees 55fl (65fl)
Loc 30 km N of Hilversum
Arch Dudok van Heel/Ryks

Anderstein
Woudenbergseweg 13a, 3953 ME Maarsbergen
Tel (0343) 431330
Fax (0343) 432062
Holes 18 L 6015 m SSS 71
V'tors WD–U WE–M only
Fees 70–100fl
Loc 20 km E of Utrecht
Arch Jol/Dudok van Heel

De Batouwe (1990)
Oost Kanaalweg 1, 4011 LA Zoelen
Tel (03446) 24370
Fax (03446) 13096
Holes 18 L 5717 m Par 72 SSS 70
9 hole Par 3 course
V'tors U H–booking necessary
Fees 60fl (80fl)
Loc Tiel, 25 km SE of Utrecht
Arch Alan Rijks

Flevoland (1979)
Bosweg 98, 8231 DZ Lelystad
Tel (0320) 230077
Fax (0320) 230932
Holes 18 L 5836 m Par 71
V'tors WD–U H WE–M+H
Fees 60fl (75fl)
Loc Island of Flevoland. 1 km NW of Lelystad. 45 km N of Hilversum
Arch JS Eschauzier

De Haar (1974)
PO Box 104, Parkweg 5, 3450 AC Vleuten
Tel (030) 677 2860
Fax (030) 677 3903
Holes 9 L 6650 yds SSS 71
V'tors WD–H WE–NA
Fees 120fl (175fl)
Loc 10 km NW of Utrecht
Arch F Pennink

Hilversumsche (1910)
Soestdijkerstraatweg 172, 1213 XJ Hilversum
Tel (035) 685 7060
Fax (035) 685 3813
Holes 18 L 6098 m Par 72
V'tors Phone booking necessary
Fees 75fl (100fl)
Loc 3 km E of Hilversum, nr Baarn
Arch Burrows/Colt

De Hoge Kleij (1985)
Appelweg 4, 3832 RK Leusden
Tel (033) 461 6944
Fax (033) 465 2921
Holes 18 L 6046 m SSS 72
V'tors H
Fees 65fl (95fl)
Loc 1 km SE of Amersfoort 20 km NE of Utrecht via A28
Arch Donald Steel

For list of abbreviations see page 527

Nieuwegeinse (1985)
Postbus 486, 3437 AL Nieuwegein
Tel (030) 604 2192/0769
Fax (030) 604 2192
Holes 9 L 4630 m Par 68 SSS 65
V'tors WD–U WE–NA before 4pm
Fees 45fl
Loc 7 km S of Utrecht
Arch Paul Rolin

Utrechtse 'De Pan' (1894)
Amersfoortseweg 1, 3735 LJ Bosch en Duin
Tel (030) 695 6427
Fax (030) 696 3769
Holes 18 L 5707 m Par 72 CR 70.0
V'tors WD–H (phone first) WE–NA
Fees 125fl
Loc 10 km E of Utrecht, off A28
Arch HS Colt

Zeewolde
Golflaan 1, 3896 LL Zeewolde
Tel (036) 522 2103
Fax (036) 522 4100
Holes 27 holes Par 72
V'tors H
Fees 60fl (80fl)
Loc 20 km N of Hilversum. 60 km NE of Amsterdam
Arch A Rijks

Norway

Arendal og Omegn (1986)
Nes Verk, 4900 Tvedestrand
Tel 37 16 03 60
Fax 37 16 02 11
Holes 18 L 5528 m Par 72
V'tors U
Fees 200kr (250kr)
Loc Nes Verk, 20 km E of Arendal (E18). 95 km NE of Kristiansand

Baerum (1972)
P O Box 31, 1355 Baerum
Tel 67 56 30 85
Fax 67 56 03 87
Holes 18 L 5300 m Par 71
9 hole short course
V'tors WD–U H WE–M H between 11am–4pm. Booking advisable
Fees 250kr (250kr)
Loc 10 km W of Oslo. 10 km N of Sandvika

Bergen (1937)
Erikveien 120, 5080 Eidsvåg
Tel 05 18 20 77
Holes 9 L 4461 m Par 67
V'tors H
Fees 150kr
Loc 8 km N of Bergen

Borre (1991)
Semb Hovedgaard, 3186 Horten
Tel 33 07 32 40
Fax 33 07 32 41
Holes 18 L 6120 m Par 73
V'tors H
Fees 200kr (300kr)
Loc Horten, 50 km S of Drammen. 100 km SW of Oslo
Arch T Nordström

Borregaard (1927)
PO Box 348, 1701 Sarpsborg
Tel 69 12 15 00
Fax 69 15 74 11
Holes 9 L 4500 m SSS 65
V'tors H
Fees 150kr
Loc Opsund, 1 km N of Sarpsborg

Drøbak (1988)
Belsjøveien 50, 1440 Drøbak
Tel 64 93 16 80
Fax 64 93 39 80
Holes 18 L 5188 m Par 70
V'tors H
Fees 200kr (300kr)
Loc 40 km SE of Oslo
Arch Hauser

Elverum (1980)
PO Box 71, 2401 Elverum
Tel 62 41 35 88
Fax 62 41 55 13
Holes 18 L 5845 m Par 72
V'tors H
Fees 200kr (220kr)
Loc Starmoen Fritidspark, 10 km E of Elverum. 35 km E of Hamar. 150 km N of Oslo

Grenland (1976)
Luksefjellvn 578, 3721 Skien
Tel 35 59 07 03
Fax 35 59 06 10
Holes 18 L 5777 m Par 72
V'tors U
Fees 250kr
Loc 6 km from Skien
Arch Jan Sederholm

Groruddalen (1988)
Postboks 37, Stovner, 0913 Oslo
Tel 22 21 67 18
Holes 9 L 2520 m SSS 54
V'tors U–before 2pm
Fees 100kr
Loc 15 km N of Oslo
Arch Leif Nilsson

Hemsedal (1994)
3560 Hemsedal
Tel 32 06 23 77
Fax 32 06 23 77
Holes 9 L 4816 m Par 68
V'tors U H

Fees 150kr (190kr)
Loc 40 km N of Gol. 380 km NW of Oslo
Arch Leif Nilsson

Kjekstad (1976)
PO Box 201, 3440 Royken
Tel 31 28 58 50/31 28 53 53
Fax 31 28 91 55
Holes 18 L 5100 m SSS 67
V'tors H
Fees 200kr (250kr)
Loc 12 km SE of Drammen on Route 282. 40 km SW of Oslo
Arch Jan Sederholm

Kristiansand (1973)
PO Box 6090, Søm, 4602 Kristiansand
Tel 38 04 35 85
Fax 38 04 34 15
Holes 9 L 2485 m SSS 70
V'tors U
Fees D–150kr
Loc 8 km E of Kristiansand (E18)

Larvik (1989)
Fritzøe Gård, 3267 Larvik
Tel 33 18 33 11
Fax 33 18 76 44
Holes 18 L 6147 m Par 72
V'tors H
Fees 200kr (250kr)
Loc 3 km S of Larvik on R301 to Stavern
Arch Jan Sederholm

Narvik (1992)
PO Box 85, 8523 Elvegard
Tel 76 95 12 01
Fax 76 95 03 33
Holes 18 L 5890 m Par 72
V'tors U H
Fees 250kr
Loc 30 km S of Narvik
Arch Jan Sederholm

Nes (1988)
Rommen Golfpark, 2160 Vormsund
Tel 63 90 29 29
Fax 63 90 21 60
Holes 18 L 6081 m Par 72
V'tors H or Green card
Fees 200kr (250kr)
Loc 50 km NE of Oslo, via E6/RV2
Arch Hauser

Onsøy (1987)
Golfveien, 1626 Manstad
Tel 69 33 35 90
Fax 69 33 35 24
Holes 18 L 5600 m Par 72
V'tors U
Fees 250kr
Loc 10 km W of Fredrikstad. Oslo 80 km
Arch Andersen/Mejstedt

Oppdal (1987)
PO Box 19, 7340 Oppdal
Tel 72 42 25 10
Holes 9 L 2621 m Par 72
V'tors U
Fees 150kr
Loc 120 km S of Trondheim
Arch Jan Sederholm

Oppegård (1985)
Kongeveien 198, PO Box 50, 1416 Oppegård
Tel 66 99 18 75
Fax 66 99 18 95
Holes 18 L 5280 m Par 71
V'tors U H
Fees 200kr (250kr)
Loc 22 km S of Oslo

Oslo (1924)
Bogstad, 0757 Oslo
Tel 22 51 05 60
Fax 22 51 05 61
Holes 18 L 6719 yds SSS 72
V'tors H–Max 20 (men) 28 (ladies)
  WD–restricted before 2pm
  WE–restricted after 2pm
Fees 275kr (325kr)
Loc 8 km NW of Oslo. Signs to 'Bogstad Camping'.

Østmarka (1989)
Postboks 63, 1914 Ytre Enebakk
Tel 64 92 41 11
Fax 64 92 47 55
Holes 18 L 5640 m
V'tors H
Fees 200kr (250kr)
Loc 35 km E of Oslo

Oustoen CC (1965)
PO Box 100, 1330 Fornebu
Tel 67 53 52 95/22 56 33 54
Fax 67 53 95 44/22 59 91 83
Holes 18 L 5400m SSS 72
V'tors M
Fees 350kr
Loc Small island in Oslofjord, 10 km W of Oslo

Skjeberg (1986)
PO Box 528, 1701 Sarpsborg
Tel 69 16 63 10
Holes 18 L 5500 m Par 72
V'tors U
Fees 150kr (200kr)
Loc Hevingen, 2 km N of Sarpsborg
Arch Jan Sederholm

Sorknes
Sorknes Gaard, 2450 Rena
Tel 62 44 18 70
Fax 62 44 00 27
Holes 18 L 6150 m SSS 72
V'tors U
Fees 250kr (300kr)
Loc 170 km N of Oslo
Arch Juul Soegaard

Stavanger (1956)
Longebakke 45, 4042 Hafrsfjord
Tel 51 55 54 31
Fax 51 55 73 11
Holes 18 L 5751 m Par 71
V'tors H
Fees 250kr
Loc 6 km SW of Stavanger
Arch F Smith

Trondheim (1950)
PO Box 169, 7001 Trondheim
Tel 73 53 18 85
Fax 73 52 75 05
Holes 9 L 5632 m SSS 72
V'tors H or Green Card
Fees 200kr
Loc Trondheim 3 km

Vestfold (1958)
PO Box 64, 3173 Vear
Tel 33 36 25 00
Fax 33 36 25 01
Holes 18 L 5851 m SSS 73
V'tors H
Fees 200kr (300kr)
Loc Tønsberg 8 km
Arch F Smith

Portugal

Algarve

Alto Golf (1991)
Quinta do Alto do Poço, P O Box 1, 8500 Alvor
Tel (082) 416913/401045-7
Fax (082) 401046
Holes 18 L 6125 m SSS 73
V'tors H
Fees 9200esc
Loc 2 km W of Portimão
Arch Cotton/Dobereiner

Carvoeiro (1991)
Vale Currais, Praia do Carvoeiro, Apartado 24, 8401#Lagoa#Codex
Tel (082) 342168
Fax (082) 52649
Holes Quinta do Gramacho 18 L 5919 m Par 72 SSS 71; Vale de Pinta 18 L 5861 m Par 71 SSS 71
V'tors U
Loc 10 km E of Portimao. 60 km W of Faro, nr Lagoa
Arch Ronald Fream

Floresta Parque (1987)
Vale do Poço, Budens, 8650 Vila do Bispo
Tel (082) 695333
Fax (082) 695157

Holes 18 L 5787 m SSS 72
V'tors U
Fees 7900esc
Loc 16 km W of Lagos, nr Salema
Arch Pepe Gancedo

Palmares (1975)
Apartado 74, 8600 Lagos
Tel (082) 762961
Fax (082) 762534
Holes 18 L 5961 m Par 71 SSS 72
V'tors U
Loc Meia Praia, 5 km E of Lagos
Arch Frank Pennink

Penina (1966)
PO Box 146, Penina, 8502 Portimão
Tel (082) 415415
Fax (082) 415000
Holes Ch'ship 18 L 6343 m SSS 73
  Resort 9 L 3987 m SSS 71
  Academy 9 L 1851 m Par 30
V'tors H
Fees Ch'ship–13.500esc
  Resort–6000ecs
  Academy–5000esc
Loc 5 km W of Portimão. 12 km E of Lagos
Arch Sir Henry Cotton

Pine Cliffs G&CC (1991)
Pinhal do Concelho, 8200 Albufeira
Tel (089) 500100/501999
Fax (089) 501950
Holes 9 L 2324 m Par 66 SSS 67
V'tors U H
Fees 9 holes–5500esc
Loc 7 km W of Vilamoura
Arch Martin Hawtree

Pinheiros Altos (1992)
Quinta do Lago, 8135 Almancil
Tel (089) 359910
Fax (089) 394392
Holes 18 L 6236 m Par 72
V'tors U–phone first
Fees 15.000esc
Loc Quinta do Lago, 15 km W of Faro
Arch Ronald Fream

Quinta do Lago (1974)
Quinta Do Lago, 8135 Almancil
Tel (089) 390700/9
Fax (089) 394013
Holes Quinta do Lago 18 L 6488 m SSS 72; Ria Formosa 18 L 6205 m SSS 72
V'tors H–by prior arrangement
Fees 13.000esc
Loc 15 km W of Faro. Airport 20 km
Arch Mitchell/Lee

Salgados
Apartado 2266, Vale do Rabelho, 8200 Albufeira
Tel (089) 591111
Fax (089) 591112
Holes 18 L 6000 m Par 72

Portugal

V'tors U
Fees On application
Loc W of Albufeira
Arch P de Vasconcelos

San Lorenzo (1988)
Quinta do Lago, 8135 Almancil
Tel (089) 396522
Fax (089) 396908
Holes 18 L 6238 m SSS 73
V'tors H–restricted
Fees 18.000esc
Loc 16 km W of Faro
Arch Joseph Lee

Vale de Milho (1990)
Algar Seco, Praia do Carvoeiro, 8401 Lagoa
Tel (082) 358502
Fax (082) 358497
Holes 9 L 1845 m Par 27
V'tors U
Fees 18 holes–4000esc
 9 holes–2950esc
Loc Jorge de Lagos Village. Carvoeiro 2 km
Arch Dave Thomas

Vale do Lobo (1968)
Vale Do Lobo, 8135 Almançil
Tel (089) 394444
Fax (089) 394713
Holes Ocean 18 L 5493 m Par 71
 Royal 18 L 6175 m Par 72
V'tors H
Fees 15.000esc
Loc 19 km W of Faro. Airport 19 km
Arch Cotton/Roquemore

Vila Sol (1991)
Alto do Semino, Vilamoura, 8125 Quarteira
Tel (089) 300505
Fax (089) 300592
Holes 18 L 6189 m Par SSS 72
V'tors U H
Fees 11.000 esc
Loc 5 km E of Vilamoura. Faro Airport 10 km
Arch Donald Steel

Vilamoura Laguna (1990)
Vilamoura, 8125 Quarteira
Tel (089) 380724
Fax (089) 380726
Holes Norte 9 L 2935 m
 Este 9 L 2953 m
 Sul 9 L 3180 m
V'tors H–max 28(M) 36(L)
Fees 18 holes–10.000esc
Loc As Vilamoura Old
Arch Joseph Lee

Vilamoura Old (1969)
Vilamoura, 8125 Quarteira
Tel (089) 322650
Fax (089) 322658
Holes 18 L 5988 m Par 73 SSS 71

V'tors H–max 24(M) 28(L) Soft spikes only
Fees 18.000esc
Loc Quarteira, 25 km W of Faro
Arch Frank Pennink

Vilamoura Pinhal (1976)
Vilamoura, 8125 Quarteira
Tel (089) 321562
Fax (089) 321411
Holes 18 L 6300 m Par 72 SSS 71
V'tors H–max 28(M) 36(L)
Fees 11.000esc
Loc As Vilamoura Old
Arch Pennink/Trent Jones

Azores

Batalha (1995)
Rua do Bom Jesus, Aflitos, 9545 Fenais da Luz (Açores)
Tel (096) 498559/498560
Fax (096) 498284
Holes 18 L 6419 m SSS 72
V'tors U
Fees D–6000esc
Loc Sao Miguel Island. Ponta Delgada 10 km
Arch Cameron/Powell

Furnas (1939)
Rua do Bom Jesus, Aflitos, 9545 Fenais da Luz (Açores)
Tel (096) 498559/498560
Fax (096) 498284
Holes 18 L 6229 m SSS 72
V'tors U
Fees D–6000esc
Loc São Miguel Island. Furnas Villa 5 km
Arch Mackenzie Ross

Terceira Island (1954)
Caixa Postal 15, 9760 Praia da Victória
Tel (095) 902444
Fax (095) 902445
Holes 18 L 5790 m Par 72 SSS 70
V'tors U H
Loc 13 km NE of Angra do Heroismo

Lisbon & Central Portugal

Aroeira (1972)
Herdade da Aroeira, Fonte da Telha, 2825 Monte da Caparica
Tel (01) 297 1345
Fax (01) 297 1283
Holes 18 L 6171 m Par 71 SSS 72
V'tors U H
Fees 9000esc (12.000esc)

Loc 20 km S of Lisbon, off Setúbal/Costa da Caparica road
Arch Frank Pennink

Belas
Estrada Nacional 117, Carregueira, 2745 Queluz
Tel (01) 962 6130
Fax (01) 962 6131
Holes 18 L 6200 m Par 72
V'tors U
Loc W of Lisbon (N117)

Estoril (1945)
Avenida da República, 2765 Estoril
Tel (01) 468 0176
Fax (01) 468 2796
Holes 18 L 5210 m Par 69 SSS 68
 9 L 2350 m SSS 65
V'tors WD–U WE–M
Fees 8600esc (11.0000esc)
Loc N of Estoril on Sintra road. 30 km W of Lisbon
Arch Mackenzie Ross

Estoril-Sol Golf Academy (1976)
Quinta do Outeira, Linhó, 2710 Sintra
Tel (01) 923 2461
Fax (01) 923 2461
Holes 9 L 4118 m Par 66 SSS 66
V'tors U
Loc 7 km N of Estoril. Lisbon 35 km
Arch Harris/Fream

Lisbon Sports Club (1922)
Casal da Carregueira, 2475 Belas
Tel (01) 431 0077
Fax (01) 431 2482
Holes 18 L 5216 m Par 69 SSS 69
V'tors U
Fees D–7500esc (9500esc)
Loc Belas, 20 km NW of Lisbon
Arch Hawtree

Marvão
Estrada do Monte Pobre, Sao Salvador do d'Aramanha, 7330 Marvão
Tel (045) 93755
Fax (045) 93805
Holes 18 holes Par 72
V'tors U
Loc 25 km N of Portalegre, nr Spanish border (N118/N246)

Montado
Apartado 40, Algeruz, 2950 Palmela
Tel (065) 706775
Fax (065) 706648
Holes 18 L 6060 m SSS 72
V'tors U
Fees 8500P
Loc 5 km E of Setúbal. 40 km S of Lisbon
Arch Duarte Sottomayor

For list of abbreviations see page 527

Penha Longa (1992)
Lagoa Azul, Linhó, 2710 Sintra
Tel (01) 924 9011
Fax (01) 924 9024
Holes Atlantic 18 L 6290 m Par 72
 Monastery 9 L 2588 m Par 35
V'tors U H
Fees Atlantic: 12.000esc (17.000esc)
 Monastery: 4500esc (6500esc)
Loc 8 km N of Estoril. 17 km W of Lisbon
Arch Robert Trent Jones Jr

Quinta da Beloura
Estrada de Albarraque, 2710 Sintra
Tel (01) 910 6350
Fax (01) 910 6359
Holes 18 L 5817 m Par 73
V'tors U
Fees On application
Loc Between Estoril and Sintra, off N9
Arch R Roquemore

Quinta da Marinha (1984)
Quinta da Marinha, 2750 Cascais
Tel (01) 486 9881
Fax (01) 486 9032
Holes 18 L 6014 m Par 71 SSS 71
V'tors U
Fees 8500esc (10.500esc)
Loc 2 km W of Cascais. 32 km W of Lisbon
Arch Robert Trent Jones

Quinta do Perú
Quinta do Perú, 2830 Quinta do Conde
Tel (01) 213 4320/22
Fax (01) 213 4321
Holes 18 L 6308 m Par 72
V'tors H
Fees 10.000esc (15.000esc)
Loc E of Lisbon on EN10
Arch R Roquemore

Tróia Golf
Torralta, Tróia, 7570 Grandola
Tel (065) 494112
Fax (065) 494215
Holes 18 L 6338 m Par 72 SSS 74
V'tors U
Fees 5500esc
Loc S of Setúbal on Tróia peninsula. 50 km S of Lisbon
Arch Robert Trent Jones

Vimeiro
Praia do Porto Novo, Vimeiro, 2560 Torres Vedras
Tel (061) 984157
Fax (061) 984621
Holes 9 L 4781 m Par 68 SSS 67
V'tors U
Fees D–1500esc. Hotel guests free
Loc Vimeiro, 20 km N of Torres Vedras. 65 km N of Lisbon
Arch Frank Pennink

Madeira

Madeira (1991)
Sto Antonio da Serra, 9200 Machico
Tel (091) 552345/552356
Fax (091) 552367
Holes 18 L 6040 m Par 72
V'tors U
Fees 8000esc
Loc 25 km E of Funchal. airport 3 km
Arch Robert Trent Jones

Palheiro (1993)
Sitio do Balancal, Sao Gonçalo, 9050 Funchal
Tel (091) 792116/794411 (Bookings)
Fax (091) 792456
Holes 18 L 6022 m SSS 71
V'tors May–Sept–U Oct–April–H
Fees D–£40
Loc 5 km from Funchal, off Airport road to Camacha
Arch Cabell Robinson

North

Amarante
Quinta da Deveza, Fregim, 4600 Amarante
Tel (055) 446060
Fax (055) 446202
Holes 18 L 5085 m Par 68 SSS 68
V'tors U
Loc 50 km E of Oporto, off A4

Estela (1989)
Rio Alto, Estela, 4490 Póvoa de Varzim
Tel (052) 612400
Fax (052) 612701
Holes 18 L 6188 m Par 72 SSS 73
V'tors H
Fees 7500esc
Loc 7 km N of Póvoa de Varzim. 40 km N of Oporto (Route 13)
Arch Duarte Sottomayor

Golden Eagle G&CC
Quinta do Brincal, Arrouquelas, 2040 Rio Maior
Tel (043) 98383
Fax (043) 98167
Holes 18 L 6203 m Par 72
V'tors U
Fees On application
Loc 55 km N of Lisbon, off N1 towards Leiria
Arch R Roquemore

Miramar (1962)
Av Sacadura Cabral, Miramar, 4405 Valadares
Tel (02) 762 2067
Fax (02) 762 7859
Holes H 2477 m Par 68 SSS 67
V'tors H WE–NA after 10am
Fees 7500esc (9000esc)
Loc 8 km S of Oporto

Montebelo
Farminhão, 3510 Viseu
Tel (032) 856464
Fax (032) 856401
Holes 18 L 6300 m Par 72 SSS 72
V'tors U
Loc 75 km NE of Coimbra

Oporto (1890)
Sisto-Paramos, 4500 Espinho
Tel (02) 734 2008
Fax (02) 734 6895
Holes 18 L 5780 m Par 71 SSS 70
V'tors H WE–restricted
Fees 10.000esc
Loc Espinho, 15 km S of Oporto

Ponte de Lima
Quinta de Pias, Fornelos, 4490 Ponte de Lima
Tel (058) 43814
Fax (058) 743424
Holes 18 L 6005 m Par 71 SSS 70
V'tors U
Loc 75 km N of Oporto (N201)

Praia d'el Rey
Vale de Janelas, Apartado 2, 2510 Obidos
Tel (062) 905005
Fax (062) 905009
Holes 18 L 6467 m Par 72 SSS 72
V'tors U
Fees 7500esc (9500esc)
Loc 65 km N of Lisbon, nr Caldas da Rainha (N8)
Arch Cabell Robinson

Quinta da Barca (1997)
Barca do Lago, Gemezes, 4740 Esposende
Tel (053) 966723
Fax (053) 969068
Holes 9 L 2015 m Par 62
V'tors U
Fees 6000esc (7500esc)
Loc 25 km N of Oporto (IC1)
Arch J Santana da Silva

Vidago
Pavilhão do Golfe, 5425 Vidago
Tel (076) 907356
Fax (076) 996622
Holes 9 L 2256m Par 66 SSS 64
Loc 50 km N of Vila Real. 130 km NE of Oporto
Arch Mackenzie Ross

Slovenia

G&CC Bled (1937)
Ljublanska 5, 4260 Bled
Tel (064) 700 777
Fax (064) 718 225
Email golfbled@s5.net/Slovenija
 www.s5.net/golf-bled
Holes 18 L 6325 m SSS 73
 9 L 3092 m SSS 72
V'tors H–36 max

Fees £24 (£27)
Loc 3 km W of Bled. 50 km NW of Ljubljana, nr Austro-Italian border
Arch Donald Harradine

Castle Mokrice (1992)
Terme Catez, Topliska Cesta 35, 68250 Brezice
Tel (0608) 57000/1
Fax (0608) 57007
Holes 18 holes SSS 70
V'tors H
Fees 44DM (48DM)
Loc 30 km N of Zagreb
Arch Donald Harradine

Lipica (1989)
Lipica 5, 66210 Sezana
Tel (067) 31580
Fax (067) 72818
Holes 9 L 6240 m SSS 71
V'tors U
Fees £12 (£18)
Loc 11 km NE of Trieste. 85 km SW of Ljubljana
Arch Donald Harradine

Spain

Alicante & Murcia

Alicante (1997)
Avenida Parque, Playa San Juan, 03540 Alicante
Tel (96) 515 37 94/515 20 43
Fax (96) 516 37 07
Holes 18 L 6245 m Par 72
V'tors U H
Fees 4500P (6000P)
Loc Playa San Juan, N of Alicante
Arch Severiano Ballesteros

Altorreal (1994)
Urb Altorreal, 30500 Molina de Segura (Murcia)
Tel (968) 64 81 44
Fax (986) 64 82 48
Holes 18 L 6239 m Par 72 SSS 73
V'tors H
Fees 5000P (6000P)
Loc 10 km from Murcia on Madrid road
Arch Dave Thomas

Bonalba (1993)
Partida de Bonalba, 03110 Mutxamiel (Alicante)
Tel (96) 596 03 31
Holes 18 L 6190m Par 72 SSS 73
V'tors U

Fees 4500P (5000P)
Loc 10 km N of Alicante. A7 Junction 67
Arch Ramón Espinosa

Don Cayo (1974)
Apartado 341, 0359 Altea La Vieja (Alicante)
Tel (96) 584 80 46
Fax (96) 584 11 88
Holes 9 L 6156 m SSS 72
V'tors U H
Loc 4 km N of Altea, nr Callosa
Arch Barber/Sanz

Ifach (1974)
Crta Moraira-Calpe Km 3, Apdo 28, 03720 Benisa (Alicante)
Tel (96) 649 71 14
Fax (96) 649 71 14
Holes 9 L 3408 m SSS 59
V'tors U
Fees D–3300P
Loc 9 km N of Calpe, towards Moraira
Arch Javier Arana

Jávea (1981)
Apartado 148, 03730 Jávea (Alicante)
Tel (96) 579 25 84
Fax (96) 646 05 54
Holes 9 L 6070 m SSS 71
V'tors H
Fees D–5000P
Loc Lluca, Jávea. 90 km NE of Alicante
Arch Francisco Moreno

La Manga (1971)
Los Belones, 30385 Cartagena (Murcia)
Tel (968) 13 72 34
Fax (968) 15 72 72
Holes North 18 L 5780 m SSS 70
South 18 L 6259 m SSS 73
Princesa 18 L 5971 m SSS 72
V'tors U
Loc 30 km NE of Cartagena, nr Murcia airport
Arch RD Putman

La Marquesa (1989)
Ciudad Quesada II, 03170 Rojales (Alicante)
Tel (96) 671 42 58
Fax (96) 671 42 67
Holes 18 L 5840 m Par 72 SSS 70
V'tors U
Fees D–4200P
Loc Rojales, 40 km S of Alicante
Arch Justo Quesada

Las Ramblas (1991)
Crta Alicante-Cartagena Km48, 03189 Urb Villamartin, Orihuela (Alicante)
Tel (96) 532 20 11
Fax (96) 532 21 59
Holes 18 L 5770 m SSS 71
V'tors U H

Fees 5500P
Loc 9 km S of Torrevieja
Arch José Gancedo

Real Campoamor (1989)
Crta Cartagena-Alicante Km48, Apdo 17, 03189 Orihuela-Costa (Alicante)
Tel (96) 532 13 66
Fax (96) 532 24 54
Holes 18 L 6203 m Par 72 SSS 73
V'tors U H
Fees 5000P
Loc Torrevieja 9 km (N332)
Arch C Gracia Caselles

La Sella (1991)
Ctra La Jara-Jesús Pobre, 03749 Denia (Alicante)
Tel (96) 645 42 52/645 41 10
Fax (96) 645 42 01
Holes 18 L 6028 m SSS 71
V'tors U H
Fees 6000P
Loc Denia 5 km
Arch Juan de la Cuadra

Villamartin (1972)
Crta Alicante-Cartagena Km50, 03189 Urb Villamartin, Orihuela (Alicante)
Tel (96) 676 51 27/676 51 60
Fax (96) 676 51 70
Holes 18 L 6132 m SSS 72
V'tors U H
Fees 7000P
Loc 8 km S of Torrevieja
Arch Paul Putman

Almería

Almerimar (1976)
Urb Almerimar, 04700 El Ejido (Almería)
Tel (950) 48 02 34
Fax (950) 49 72 33
Holes 18 L 6111 m SSS 72
V'tors U
Loc 35 km W of Almería
Arch Gary Player

Cortijo Grande (1976)
Apdo 2, Cortijo Grande, 04639 Turre (Almería)
Tel (951) 47 91 76
Holes 18 L 6024 m Par 72 SSS 71
V'tors U
Loc 20 km W of Turre. 85 km N of Almería, nr Mojácar
Arch PJ Polansky

La Envia (1993)
Apdo 51, 04720 Aguadulce (Almería)
Tel (950) 55 96 41
Holes 18 L 5810 m Par 72 SSS 70
V'tors U
Loc 10 km from Almería
Arch F Mendoza

Playa Serena (1979)
Urb Playa Serena, 04740 Roquetas de Mar (Almería)
Tel (950) 33 30 55
Fax (950) 33 30 55
Holes 18 L 6301 m Par 72
V'tors H
Loc 20 km S of Almería
Arch Gallardo/Alliss

Badajoz & West

Guadiana (1992)
Crta Madrid-Lisboa Km 393, Apdo 171, 06080 Badajoz
Tel (924) 44 81 88
Holes 18 L 6381 m Par 72 SSS 73
V'tors U
Loc Badajoz
Arch Daniel Calero

Norba (1988)
Apdo 880, 10080 Cáceres
Tel (927) 23 14 41
Holes 18 L 6422 m Par 72 SSS 74
V'tors U
Loc 4 km S of Cáceres

Salamanca (1988)
Monte de Zarapicos, 37170 Zarapicos (Salamanca)
Tel (923) 32 91 02
Holes 18 L 6267 m Par 72 SSS 72
V'tors U
Loc W of Salamanca, nr Parada de Arriba (C-517)
Arch Manuel Piñero

Balearic Islands

Canyamel
Urb Canyamel, Crta de Cuevas, 07580 Capdepera (Mallorca)
Tel (971) 56 44 57
Fax (971) 56 53 80
Holes 18 L 6115 m SSS 72
V'tors H
Loc 70 km NE of Palma, nr Cala Ratjada
Arch José Gancedo

Capdepera (1989)
Apdo 6, 07580 Capdepera, Mallorca
Tel (971) 56 58 75/56 58 57
Fax (971) 56 58 74
Holes 18 L 6284 m SSS 72
V'tors U H
Loc 71 km E of Palma, between Artá and Capdepera
Arch Maples/Pape

Club Son Parc (1977)
Urb Son Parc, Mercadel (Menorca)
Tel (971) 18 88 75
Fax (971) 18 88 75
Holes 9 L 2791 m SSS 69

V'tors U H
Fees 6500P
Loc Mercadel, 18 km N of Mahón
Arch JF Martínez

Ibiza (1990)
Apdo 1270, 07840 Santa Eulalia (Ibiza)
Tel (971) 19 61 18
Fax (971) 19 60 51
Holes 18 L 6083 m SSS 72
9 L 5867 m SSS 70
V'tors H
Loc 7 km N of Ibiza town
Arch Thomas/Rivero

Pollensa (1986)
Ctra Palma-Pollensa Km 49, 07460 Pollensa (Mallorca)
Tel (971) 53 32 16
Fax (971) 53 32 65
Holes 9 L 5304 m Par 70 SSS 70
V'tors U
Fees 8000P
Loc Pollensa, 45 km N of Palma
Arch José Gancedo

Poniente (1978)
Costa de Calvia, 07181 Calvia (Mallorca)
Tel (971) 13 01 48
Fax (971) 13 01 76
Holes 18 L 6430 m SSS 72
V'tors U
Fees 8700P
Loc 12 km SW of Palma towards Cala Figuera
Arch John Harris

Pula Golf (1995)
Predio de Pula, 07550 Son Servera (Mallorca)
Tel (971) 81 70 34
Fax (971) 81 70 35
Holes 18 L 6003 m Par 71
V'tors U H
Fees 10.000P
Loc 70 km NE of Palma
Arch F López Segales

Royal Bendinat (1986)
C. Campoamor, 07015 Calviá (Mallorca)
Tel (971) 40 52 00
Fax (971) 70 07 86
Holes 18 L 5768 m SSS 71
V'tors U H
Loc 7 km W of Palma
Arch Martin Hawtree

Santa Ponsa (1976)
Santa Ponsa, 07180 Calvia (Mallorca)
Tel (971) 69 02 11/69 08 00
Fax (971) 69 33 64
Holes 18 L 6520 m SSS 74
18 L 6053 m SSS 73
V'tors No 1–U H No 2–NA
Fees 8700P
Loc 18 km W of Palma
Arch Folco Nardi

Son Antem (1993)
Apartado 102, 07620 Lluchmajor (Mallorca)
Tel (971) 66 11 24
Fax (971) 66 26 49
Holes 18 L 6325 m Par 72 SSS 72
V'tors U
Fees 8500P
Loc 20 km E of Palma (Route 717)
Arch F López Segales

Son Servera (1967)
Costa de Los Pinos, 07759 Son Servera (Mallorca)
Tel (971) 84 00 96
Fax (971) 84 01 60
Holes 9 L 5956 m SSS 72
V'tors H
Fees D–7000P
Loc Son Servera, 64 km E of Palma
Arch John Harris

Son Vida (1964)
Urb Son Vida, 07013 Palma (Mallorca)
Tel (971) 79 12 10
Fax (971) 79 11 27
Holes 18 L 5740 m SSS 71
V'tors U H
Fees 8100P
Loc 3 km NW of Palma
Arch FW Hawtree

Vall d'Or (1986)
Apdo 23, 07660 Cala D'Or (Mallorca)
Tel (971) 83 70 68/83 70 01
Fax (971) 83 72 99
Holes 18 L 5799 m SSS 71
V'tors H
Fees 7800P
Loc 60 km E of Palma, between Cala d'Or and Porto Colóm
Arch Benz/Bendly

Barcelona & Cataluña

Aro-Mas Nou (1990)
Apdo 429, 17250 Playa de Aro
Tel (972) 82 69 00
Fax (972) 82 69 06
Holes 18 L 6218 m Par 72
9 holes Par 3 course
V'tors U H
Fees 5500P (8000P)
Loc 35 km SE of Gerona on coast. A7 exit 9
Arch Ramón Espinosa

Bonmont Terres Noves (1990)
Urb Terres Noves, 43300 Montroig (Tarragona)
Tel (977) 81 81 40
Fax (977) 81 81 46
Holes 18 L 6371 m SSS 72
V'tors U H

For list of abbreviations see page 527

Fees 5500P (8000P)
Loc S of Tarragona. 130 km S of Barcelona
Arch Robert Trent Jones Jr

Caldes Internacional (1992)
Apdo 200, 08140 Caldes de Montbui (Barcelona)
Tel (93) 865 38 28
Holes 18 L 6258 m Par 72 SSS 73
V'tors U
Loc 28 km from Barcelona
Arch Ramón Espinosa

Can Bosch (1984)
Trav de les Corts 322, 08029 Barcelona
Tel (93) 405 04 22/866 25 71
Fax (93) 419 9659
Holes 9 L 3027 m SSS 71
V'tors U H
Loc 35 km NE of Barcelona
Arch Ramon Espinosa

Costa Brava (1962)
La Masia, 17246 Sta Cristina d'Aro (Gerona)
Tel (972) 83 71 50
Fax (972) 83 72 72
Holes 18 L 5573 m SSS 70
V'tors H
Fees 5500–7500P
Loc Playa de Aro 5km. 30 km SE of Gerona
Arch J Hamilton Stutt

Costa Dorada (1983)
Apartado 600, 43080 Tarragona
Tel (977) 65 33 61
Holes 18 L 6223 m SSS 73
Loc Tarragona
Arch José Gancedo

Empordà (1990)
Crta Torroella de Montgri, 17257 Gualta (Gerona)
Tel (972) 76 04 50/76 01 36
Fax (972) 75 71 00
Holes 27 L 5855-6112 m SSS 70-71
V'tors U H
Fees 5500P (8500P)
Loc 35 km E of Gerona, nr Pals. 130 km N of Barcelona
Arch Robert von Hagge

Fontanals de Cerdanya (1994)
Fontanals de Cerdanya, 17538 Soriguerola (Girona)
Tel (972) 14 43 74
Holes 18 L 6454 m Par 72 SSS 74
V'tors U
Loc 2 km from Alp de Puigcerdá

Girona (1992)
Urb Golf Girona, 17481 Sant Julià de Ramis (Girona)
Tel (972) 17 16 41
Fax (972) 17 16 82

Holes 18 L 6100 m Par 72 SSS 72
V'tors H–booking required
Fees 4500P (6000P)
Loc Sant Julià de Ramis, 4 km from Gerona
Arch Hawtree

Llavaneras (1945)
Camino del Golf, 08392 San Andres de Llavaneras (Barcelona)
Tel (93) 792 60 50
Fax (93) 795 25 58
Holes 18 L 4644 m SSS 66
V'tors U H
Fees 6000P (12.000P)
Loc 4 km N of Mataró. 34 km N of Barcelona (A19)
Arch Hawtree/Espinosa

Masia Bach (1990)
Ctra Martorell-Capelladas, 08781 Sant Esteve Sesrovires
Tel (93) 772 6310
Fax (93) 772 6356
Holes 18 L 6039 m SSS 72
9 L 3780 m SSS 60
V'tors H
Fees 7500P (20.000P)
Loc 30 km NW of Barcelona
Arch JM Olazábal

Osona Montanya (1988)
Masia L'Estanyol, 08553 El Brull (Barcelona)
Tel (93) 884 01 70
Fax (93) 884 04 07
Holes 18 L 6036 m Par 72
V'tors U H
Loc 60 km NE of Barcelona
Arch Dave Thomas

Pals (1966)
Playa de Pals, 17526 Gerona
Tel (972) 63 60 06
Fax (972) 63 70 09
Holes 18 L 6222 m Par 73
V'tors U
Loc 40 km E of Gerona. 135 km NE of Barcelona
Arch FW Hawtree

Peralada (1993)
La Garriga, 17491 Peralada, Girona
Tel (972) 53 82 87
Fax (972) 53 82 36
Holes 18 L 6128 m SSS 72
V'tors H
Fees 6000P (7500P)
Loc Costa Brava, on French border. 40 km S of Perpignan Airport, nr Llançà
Arch Jorge Soler

Real Cerdaña (1929)
Apdo 63, Puigcerdá, (Gerona)
Tel (972) 88 13 38
Holes 18 L 5735 m SSS 70
Loc Cerdaña, 1 km from Puigcerdá
Arch Javier Arana

Real Golf El Prat (1956)
Apdo 10, 08820 El Prat de Llobregat (Barcelona)
Tel (93) 379 02 78
Fax (93) 370 51 02
Holes 4 x 9 holes: 6070-6266 m SSS 73-74
V'tors H
Fees 12.135P (24.335P)
Loc El Prat, Airport 3km. 15 km S of Barcelona
Arch Arana/Thomas

Reus Aiguesverds (1989)
Crta Cambrils, Mas Guardià, 43206 Reus
Tel (977) 75 27 25
Fax (977) 75 19 38
Holes 18 L 6905 yds SSS 72
V'tors U
Fees 7000P
Loc 10 km W of Tarragona. 100 km S of Barcelona

Sant Cugat (1914)
08190 Sant Cugat del Valles
Tel (93) 674 39 08/674 39 58
Holes 18 L 5209 m SSS 68
Loc 20 km NW of Barcelona

Sant Jordi
Urb Sant Jordi d'Alfama, 43860 Ametlla de Mar (Tarragona)
Tel (977) 49 34 57
Fax (977) 49 32 77
Holes 9 L 5696 m SSS 70
V'tors U H
Loc 50 km S of Tarragona
Arch Lauresno Nomen

Terramar (1922)
Apdo 6, 08870 Sitges
Tel (93) 894 05 80/894 20 43
Fax (93) 894 70 51
Holes 18 L 5878 m Par 72
V'tors H
Fees 8500P
Loc Sitges, 37 km S of Barcelona
Arch Hawtree/Piñero/Fazio

Torremirona (1994)
Ctra N260 Km46, 17744 Navata (Girona)
Tel (972) 55 37 37
Fax (972) 55 37 16
Holes 18 L 5708 m Par 70
V'tors U
Fees 5775P (6500P)
Loc 30 km from Girona, nr Besalú, off A7

Vallromanes (1972)
C/Afveras, 08188 Vallromanes (Barcelona)
Tel (93) 572 90 64
Fax (93) 572 93 30
Holes 18 L 6038 m Par 72
V'tors H
Loc 23 km N of Barcelona between Alella and Granollers. A7 Junction 13
Arch FW Hawtree

Burgos & North

Barganiza (1982)
Apartado 277, 33080 Oviedo, Asturias
Tel (985) 74 24 68
Holes 18 L 5549 m SSS 70
Loc 12 km N of Oviedo on Gijon old road
Arch Victor García

Castillo de Gorraiz (1993)
Urb Castillo de Gorraiz, 31620 Valle de Egues (Navarra)
Tel (948) 33 70 73
Holes 18 L 6321 m Par 72 SSS 73
V'tors U
Loc 4 km from Pamplona
Arch Cabell Robinson

La Cuesta
Apdo 40, 33500 Llanes
Tel (98) 541 7084
Fax (98) 540 1973
Holes 9 L 5456 m SSS 69
V'tors U
Loc 3 km from Llanes (N-634)

Iski Golf (1992)
01119 Urturi (Alava)
Tel (945) 40 33 66
Holes 18 L 6576 m Par 73 SSS 74
V'tors U
Loc Urturi, 30 km from Logroño

Larrabea (1989)
Crta de Landa, 01170 Legutiano, (Alava)
Tel (945) 46 58 44/46 58 41
Fax (945) 46 57 25
Holes 18 L 5991 m Par 72
V'tors H
Fees 5000P (6000P)
Loc 14 km N of Vitoria, nr Villareal de Alava
Arch José Gancedo

Laukariz (1976)
Laukariz-Munguía (Viscaya)
Tel (94) 674 08 58/674 04 62
Holes 18 L 6112 m SSS 72
V'tors U
Loc 15 km N of Bilbao towards Mungía
Arch RD Putman

Lerma (1991)
Ctra Madrid-Burgos Km195, 09340 Lerma (Burgos)
Tel (947) 17 12 14/17 12 16
Fax (947) 17 12 16
Holes 18 L 6235 m SSS 72
V'tors H
Loc 30 km S of Burgos, nr Villa Ducal de Lerma
Arch Pepe Gancedo

La Llorea (1994)
Crta Nacional 632, Km 62, 33394 Lloreda (Gijón)
Tel (985) 33 31 91
Fax (985) 36 47 26
Holes 18 L 5868 m Par 71
V'tors H
Fees 5500P (6500P)
Loc 10 km E of Gijón
Arch Roland Fabret

Real Golf Castiello (1958)
Apartado de Correos 161, 33200 Gijón
Tel (985) 36 63 13
Fax (985) 13 18 00
Holes 18 L 4817 mPar 70
V'tors WE–restricted
Fees 8000P
Loc 5 km S of Gijón on Oviedo old road

Real Golf Neguri (1911)
Apdo Correos 9, 48990 Algorta
Tel (94) 469 02 00/04/08
Holes 18 L 6319 m SSS 72
6 hole Par 3 course
Loc La Galea, 20 km N of Bilbao
Arch Javier Arana

Real Golf Pedreña (1928)
Apartado 233, Santander
Tel (942) 50 00 01/50 02 66
Fax (942) 50 04 21
Holes 18 L 5745 m SSS 70
9 L 2740 m SSS 36
V'tors H
Fees 5600P (9000P)
Loc 20 km from Santander, on Bay of Santander
Arch Colt/Ballesteros

Real San Sebastián (1910)
PO Box 6, Fuenterrabia (Guipúzcoa)
Tel (943) 61 68 45/61 68 46
Fax (943) 61 14 91
Holes 18 L 6020 m SSS 71
V'tors WD–U H from 9–12 noon WE–NA
Fees 7000P
Loc Jaizubia Valley, 14 km NE of San Sebastián
Arch P Hirigoyen

Real Zarauz (1916)
Apartado 82, Zarauz, (Guipúzcoa)
Tel (943) 83 01 45
Holes 9 L 5184 m SSS 68
V'tors U
Loc Zarauz, 25 km W of San Sebastián

Ulzama (1965)
31779 Guerendiain (Navarra)
Tel (948) 30 51 62
Fax (948) 30 54 71
Holes 18 L 6246 m Par 72
V'tors U
Fees On application
Loc 20 km N of Pamplona
Arch Javier Arana

Canary Islands

Amarilla (1988)
Urb Amarilla Golf, San Miguel de Abona, 38630 Santa Cruz de Tenerife
Tel (922) 73 03 19
Fax (922) 73 00 85
Holes 18 L 6077 m Par 72
V'tors H
Fees 6875P
Loc 6 km SW of South Airport.
12 km from Playa de las Américas
Arch Donald Steel

Costa Teguise (1978)
Apdo 170, 35080 Arrecife de Lanzarote
Tel (928) 59 05 12
Fax (928) 59 04 90
Holes 18 L 5853 m SSS 72
V'tors U
Fees Summer–5400P
Winter–6900P
Loc 4 km N of Arrecife
Arch John Harris

Maspalomas (1968)
Av de Neckerman, Maspalomas, 35100 Las Palmas de Gran Canaria
Tel (928) 76 25 81/76 73 43
Fax (928) 76 82 45
Holes 18 L 6216 m SSS 72
V'tors U
Fees Summer–6000P
Winter–9000P
Loc S coast of Gran Canaria
Arch Mackenzie Ross

Real Golf Las Palmas (1891)
PO Box 93, 35310 Santa Brigida, Gran Canaria
Tel (928) 35 10 50/35 01 04
Fax (928) 35 01 10
Holes 18 L 5690 m SSS 71
V'tors WD–U WE–NA
Fees WD–9000P
Loc Bandama, Las Palmas 14 km
Arch Mackenzie Ross

Real Tenerife (1932)
El Peñón, Tacoronte, Tenerife
Tel (922) 63 66 07
Fax (922) 63 64 80
Holes 18 L 5750 m Par 71
V'tors WD–H 8am–1pm
Fees 5720P
Loc 20 km N of Santa Cruz. Puerto Cruz 15 km
Arch J Laynez

Golf del Sur (1987)
San Miguel de Abona, 38620 Tenerife (Canarias)
Tel (922) 73 81 70
Fax (922) 78 82 72
Holes North 9 L 2913 m SSS 36
Links 9 L 2469 m SSS 34
South 9 L 2957 m SSS 36

For list of abbreviations see page 527

800 Spain

V'tors H
Fees 5500–7700P
Loc Airport 3km. Playa de las Américas 12 km
Arch Pepe Gancedo

Cordoba

Córdoba (1976)
Apartado 436, 14080 Córdoba
Tel (957) 35 02 08
Holes 18 L 5964 m Par 72 SSS 73
V'tors U
Loc 9 km N of Córdoba, towards Obejo

Pozoblanco (1984)
Apdo 118, 14400 Pozoblanco (Córdoba)
Tel (957) 33 91 71
Fax (957) 33 91 71
Holes 9 L 3020 m Par 72
V'tors U
Loc Pozoblanco 3 km
Arch Carlos Luca

Galicia

Aero Club de Santiago (1976)
General Pardiñas 34, Santiago de Compostela (La Coruña)
Tel (981) 59 24 00
Holes 9 L 5816 m SSS 70
Loc Santiago Airport

Aero Club de Vigo (1951)
Reconquista 7, 36201 Vigo
Tel (986) 48 66 45/48 75 09
Holes 9 L 5622 m SSS 60
Loc Peinador Airport, 8 km from Vigo

La Coruña (1962)
Apartado 737, 15080 La Coruña
Tel (981) 28 52 00
Holes 18 L 5782 m SSS 72
Loc Arteijo, 7 km SW of La Coruña
Arch Antonio Lucena

Domaio (1993)
San Lorenzo-Domaio, 36950 Moaña (Pontevedra)
Tel (986) 32 70 50
Holes 18 L 6110 m Par 72 SSS 73
V'tors U
Arch Ramón Espinosa

La Toja (1970)
Isla de La Toja, El Grove, Pontevedra
Tel (986) 73 01 58/73 08 18
Fax (986) 73 31 22
Holes 9 L 5178 m SSS 72

V'tors H
Fees 6000–9000P
Loc La Toja island. 30 km W of Pontevedra
Arch Ramón Espinosa

Granada

Granada
Avda de los Corsarios, 18110 Las Gabias (Granada)
Tel (958) 58 44 36
Holes 18 L 6037 m Par 71 SSS 73
V'tors U
Loc Las Gabias, 8 km from Granada
Arch Ramón Espinosa

Madrid Region

Barberán (1967)
Apartado 150.239, Cuatro Vientos, 28080 Madrid
Tel (91) 509 00 59/509 11 40
Fax (91) 706 2174
Holes 9 L 6042 m SSS 72
V'tors M H
Loc 10 km SW of Madrid

La Dehesa (1991)
Calle Real 19, 28691 Villanueva La Canada
Tel (91) 815 70 22/815 70 37
Fax (91) 815 54 68
Holes 18 L 6456 m SSS 72
Loc 35 km NW of Madrid
Arch Manuel Piñero

Herreria (1966)
PO Box 28200, San Lorenzo del Escorial (Madrid)
Tel (91) 890 51 11
Holes 18 L 6050 m SSS 72
Loc Escorial, 50 km W of Madrid
Arch Antonio Lucena

Jarama R.A.C.E. (1967)
Urb Ciudalcampo, 28707 San Sebastian de los Reyes (Madrid)
Tel (91) 657 00 01
Fax (91) 657 04 62
Holes 18 L 6505 m Par 72
9 hole Par 3 course
Loc 28 km N of Madrid on Burgos road
Arch Javier Arana

Lomas-Bosque (1973)
Urb El Bosque, 28670 Villaviciosa de Odón (Madrid)
Tel (91) 616 75 00
Fax (91) 616 73 93
Holes 18 L 6075 m SSS 72
9 hole Par 3 course

V'tors WD–U H WE–M H
Fees 4400–13.000P
Loc 20 km SW of Madrid
Arch RD Putman

La Moraleja (1976)
La Moraleja, Alcobendas (Madrid)
Tel (91) 650 07 00
Holes 18 L 6016 m SSS 72
V'tors M
Loc 9 km N of Madrid on Burgos road
Arch Jack Nicklaus

Nuevo De Madrid (1972)
Las Matas (Madrid)
Tel (91) 630 08 20
Holes 18 L 5647 m SSS 70
V'tors U H
Loc 25 km NW of Madrid on La Coruña road

Olivar de la Hinojosa (1995)
Avda de Dublin, Campo de las Naciones, 28042 Madrid
Tel (91) 721 18 89
Holes 18 L 6163 m Par 72 SSS 72
V'tors U
Loc Nr Madrid Airport M40

Puerta de Hierro (1904)
Avda de Miraflores, 28035 Madrid
Tel (91) 216 1745
Fax (91) 373 8111
Holes 18 L 6347 m SSS 73
18 L 5273 m SSS 68
V'tors M only
Fees 6900P (14.950P)
Loc 4 km N of Madrid (Route VI)
Arch Harris/Simpson

Los Retamares (1991)
Crta Algete-Alalpardo Km 2300, 28130 Valdeolmos (Madrid)
Tel (91) 620 25 40
Holes 18 L 6238 m Par 72 SSS 73
9 hole Par 3 course
V'tors U
Loc 25 km N of Madrid via N-1

Somosaguas (1971)
Avda de la Cabaña, 28223 Pozuelo de Alarcón (Madrid)
Tel (91) 352 16 47
Fax (91) 352 00 30
Holes 9 L 6054 m Par 72
Loc Somosaguas
Arch John Harris

Valdeláguila (1975)
Apdo 9, Alcalá de Henares (Madrid)
Tel (91) 885 96 59
Fax (91) 885 96 59
Holes 9 L 5724 m Par 72
V'tors WD–U WE–NA
Loc Villalbilla, 10 km S of Alcalá

For list of abbreviations see page 527

Villa de Madrid CC
(1932)
Crta Castilla, 28040 Madrid
Tel (91) 357 21 32
Fax (91) 549 07 97
Holes 27 L 5900-6321 m SSS 73-74
V'tors U H
Fees 6750P (12.775P)
Loc 4 km NW of Madrid, in the Casa del Campo
Arch Javier Arana

Málaga Region

Alhaurín (1994)
Crta 426 Km15, Alhaurín el Grande
Tel (952) 59 59 70
Fax (952) 59 45 86
Holes 18 L 6221 m Par 72
18 hole Par 3 course
9 hole Par 3 course
V'tors U
Fees 6000P
Loc 6 km from Mijas
Arch Severiano Ballesteros

Añoreta (1989)
Avenida del Golf, 29730 Rincón de la Victoria (Málaga)
Tel (952) 40 40 00
Fax (952) 40 40 50
Holes 18 L 5976 m SSS 71
V'tors U
Fees 2500P (3000P)
Loc 12 km E of Málaga
Arch JM Canizares

La Cala (1991)
La Cala de Mijas, 29647 Mijas-Costa (Málaga)
Tel (952) 66 90 00, (952) 66 90 32
Fax (952) 66 90 34
Holes North 18 L 6187 m SSS 73
South 18 L 5966 m SSS 72
6 hole Par 3 course
V'tors U H
Fees 4000-8000P
Loc 6 km from Cala de Mijas, between Fuengirola and Marbella
Arch Cabell Robinson

El Candado (1965)
Urb El Candado, El Palo, 29018 Málaga
Tel (952) 29 93 40/1
Holes 9 L 4676 m SSS 66
Loc El Palo, 5 km E of Málaga on Route N340
Arch Carlos Fernández

El Chaparral
Urb El Chaparral, Mijas-Costa
Tel (952) 49 38 00
Fax (952) 49 40 51
Holes 18 L 5700 m SSS 71
V'tors U H

Loc 5 km W of Fuengirola on N340
Arch Pepe Gancedo

Guadalhorce (1988)
Crtra de Cártama Km7, Apartado 48, 29590 Campanillas (Málaga)
Tel (952) 17 93 78
Fax (952) 17 93 72
Holes 18 L 6194 m SSS 72
9 hole Par 3 course
V'tors WD–H before 1pm (booking necessary) WE–M
Fees 4000-5000P
Loc 8 km W of Málaga
Arch Kosti Kuronen

Lauro (1992)
Los Caracolillos, 29130 Alhaurín de la Torre (Málaga)
Tel (95) 241 27 67
Fax (95) 241 47 57
Holes 18 L 5971 m SSS 71
V'tors U
Fees D–5000P
Loc 15 km SW of Málaga airport on Route C-344 towards Coín
Arch Folco Nardi

Málaga Club de Campo
(1925)
Parador de Golf, Apdo 324, 29080 Málaga
Tel (952) 38 12 55
Fax (952) 38 21 41
Holes 18 L 6249 m SSS 72
V'tors U
Loc Torremolinos 4km. 12 km S of Málaga, nr Airport
Arch Tom Simpson

Mijas (1976)
Apartado 145, Fuengirola, Málaga
Tel (952) 47 68 43
Fax (952) 46 79 43
Holes Lagos 18 L 6548 m Par 71 SSS 74; Olivos 18 L 6009 m Par 72 SSS 72
V'tors H–booking required Oct–Apr
Fees 6200P
Loc 4 km NW of Fuengirola (Mijas Valley)
Arch Robert Trent Jones

Miraflores (1990)
Urb Riviera del Sol, 29647 Mijas-Costa
Tel (952) 93 19 60
Fax (952) 93 19 42
Holes 18 L 5635 m SSS 70
V'tors U
Fees 5500P
Loc 15 km E of Marbella
Arch Folco Nardi

Los Moriscos (1974)
Costa Granada, Motril (Granada)
Tel (958) 82 55 27
Fax (958) 25 52 51
Holes 9 L 5689 m SSS 72 Par 70

V'tors U
Loc 8 km W of Motril, nr Salobrena. 80 km E of Málaga
Arch Ibergolf

Torrequebrada (1976)
Apdo 120, Crta de Cadiz Km 220, 29630 Benalmadena
Tel (95) 244 27 42
Fax (95) 256 11 29
Holes 18 L 5806 m Par 72 SSS 71
V'tors H
Fees 8000P
Loc Benalmadena, 25 km S of Málaga
Arch Pepe Gancedo

Marbella & Estepona

Alcaidesa Links
CN-340 Km124.6, 11315 La Linea (Cádiz)
Tel (956) 79 10 40
Fax (956) 79 10 41
Holes 18 L 5708 m Par 71 SSS 69
V'tors U–booking advised
Fees 8500P
Loc 15 km E of Gibraltar
Arch Alliss/Clark

Aloha (1975)
Nueva Andalucia, 29660 Marbella
Tel (952) 81 37 50,
(952) 81 23 88 (Caddymaster)
Fax (952) 81 23 89
Holes 18 L 6261 m SSS 72
9 hole short course
V'tors H–booking necessary
Fees 18.000P
Loc 8 km W of Marbella, nr Puerto Banus
Arch Javier Arana

Los Arqueros (1991)
Crta de Ronda Km43, 29679 Benahavis (Málaga)
Tel (952) 78 46 00
Fax (952) 78 67 07
Holes 18 L 6130 m SSS 72
V'tors H
Fees 4500P
Loc 5 km N of San Pedro de Alcántara
Arch Severiano Ballesteros

Atalaya G&CC (1968)
Crta Benahavis 7, 29688 Málaga
Tel (952) 88 48 01
Fax (952) 88 57 35
Holes 18 L 5893 m Par 72
18 L 5123 m Par 72
V'tors U H
Loc 12 km S of Marbella. 60 km SW of Málaga
Arch B von Limburger

Las Brisas (1968)
Apdo 147, 29660 Nueva Andalucía (Málaga)
Tel (952) 81 08 75/81 30 21
Fax (952) 81 55 18
Holes 18 L 6094 m SSS 72
V'tors H–restricted
Fees 15.000P
Loc 8 km S of Marbella, nr Puerto Banus
Arch Robert Trent Jones

La Cañada (1982)
Ctra Guadiaro Km 1, 11311 Guadiaro (Cádiz)
Tel (956) 79 41 00/79 44 11
Fax (956) 79 42 41
Holes 9 L 2873 m SSS 72
V'tors U
Loc Guadiaro, 2 km from Sotogrande
Arch Robert Trent Jones

La Duquesa G&CC (1987)
Urb El Hacho, 29691 Manilva (Málaga)
Tel (952) 89 04 25/89 04 26
Fax (952) 89 00 57
Holes 18 L 6142 m SSS 72
V'tors U
Loc 10 km S of Estepona
Arch Robert Trent Jones

Estepona (1989)
Paraje Arroyo Vaquero, Apartado 274, 29680 Estepona (Málaga)
Tel (908) 65 14 99
Holes 18 L 5986 m Par 72
V'tors U
Loc 5 km W of Estepona
Arch Luis López

Guadalmina (1959)
Guadalmina Alta, San Pedro de Alcántara, 29678 Marbella (Málaga)
Tel (952) 88 65 22
Fax (952) 88 34 83
Holes North 18 L 5825 m SSS 70
South 18 L 6075 m SSS 72
9 hole Par 3 course
V'tors H (max 27M/35L)
Fees 7500P
Loc San Pedro, 12 km W of Marbella
Arch Arana/Nardi

Marbella (1994)
CN 340 Km 188, 29600 Marbella (Málaga)
Tel (952) 83 05 00
Holes 18 L 5864 m Par 71 SSS 72
V'tors U
Loc Marbella
Arch Robert Trent Jones

Monte Mayor (1992)
Crta N340 Km 165, 29660 Marbella (Málaga)
Tel (95) 211 30 88
Fax (95) 211 30 87
Holes 18 L 5593 m SSS 71
V'tors U
Fees 7500P (inc buggy)
Loc Between San Pedro and Estepona, at Cancelada
Arch Pepe Gancedo

Los Naranjos (1977)
Apdo 64, 29660 Nueva Andalucía, Marbella
Tel (952) 81 52 06/81 24 28
Fax (952) 81 14 28
Holes 18 L 6484 m SSS 72
V'tors U H
Loc 8 km S of Marbella, nr Puerto Banus
Arch Robert Trent Jones Sr

El Paraiso (1974)
Ctra Cádiz-Málaga Km 167, 29680 Estepona (Málaga)
Tel (95) 288 38 35/288 38 46
Fax (95) 288 58 27
Holes 18 L 6116 m SSS 72
V'tors U
Fees 7500P
Loc 14 km S of Marbella
Arch Player/Kirby

La Quinta G&CC (1989)
Urb La Quinta, 29660 Nueva Andalucía
Tel (952) 78 34 62
Fax (952) 78 34 66
Holes 27 L 5797-5945 m SSS 71–72
V'tors U H
Fees 7900P
Loc 3 km N of San Pedro de Alcántara
Arch Piñero/García-Garrido

Rio Real (1965)
Urb Rio Real, PO Box 82, 29600 Marbella (Málaga)
Tel (95) 277 95 09
Fax (95) 277 21 40
Holes 18 L 6130 m SSS 72
V'tors U
Loc 5 km E of Marbella. Málaga Airport 50 km
Arch Javier Arana

San Roque (1990)
CN 340 Km 126, San Roque, 11360 Cádiz
Tel (956) 61 30 30/60/90
Fax (956) 61 30 12/61 30 13
Holes 18 L 6440 m SSS 74
V'tors U H
Fees 7000P
Loc 3 km W of Sotogrande. 15 km E of Gibraltar
Arch Dave Thomas

Santa María G&CC
Coto de los Dolores, Urb Elviria, Crta N340 Km 192, 29600 Marbella (Málaga)
Tel (952) 83 03 86/83 03 88/83 10 36
Fax (952) 83 08 70
Holes 9 L 5792 m Par 71

V'tors U
Loc 10 km E of Marbella, opp Hotel Don Carlos
Arch A García Garrido

Sotogrande (1964)
Paseo del Parque, Apartado 14, Sotogrande (Cádiz)
Tel (956) 79 50 50/79 50 51
Fax (956) 79 50 29
Holes 18 L 6224 m SSS 74
9 L 1299 m Par 29
V'tors U
Loc 30 km N of Gibraltar, nr Guadiaro
Arch Robert Trent Jones

Valderrama (1985)
Apartado 1, 11310 Sotogrande (Cádiz)
Tel (956) 79 12 00
Fax (956) 79 60 28
Holes 18 L 6326 m SSS 71
9 L 1100 m SSS 27
V'tors H–12–2pm
Fees 28.000P
Loc 18 km N of Gibraltar
Arch Robert Trent Jones Sr

La Zagaleta (1994)
Crta San Pedro-Ronda Km 9, 29679 Benahavis
Tel (95) 285 54 53
Holes 18 L 6039 m Par 72 SSS 72
V'tors U
Loc S of Marbella on Ronda road
Arch Bradford Benz

Seville & Gulf of Cádiz

Bellavista (1976)
Crta Huelva-Punta Umbría, Apdo 335, Huelva
Tel (955) 31 90 17
Fax (955) 31 90 25
Holes 9 L 6270 m SSS 73
V'tors U
Loc Aljaraque, 6 km SW of Huelva, towards Punta Umbria

Costa Ballena (1997)
Crta Sta Maria-Chipiona, 11520 Rota
Tel (956) 84 70 70
Holes 18 L 6187 m Par 72 SSS 72
V'tors U
Arch J-M Olazábal

Dehesa Montenmedio (1996)
CN 340 Km42.5, 11150 Vejer-Barbate (Cádiz)
Tel (956) 23 24 40
Holes 18 L 5897 m Par 71 SSS 71
V'tors U
Loc Cádiz-Algeciras road
Arch A Maldonado

Isla Canela (1993)
Crta de la Playa, 21400 Ayamonte (Huelva)
Tel (959) 47 72 63
Holes 18 L 6248 m Par 72 SSS 73
V'tors U
Loc Ayamonte, 4 km from Portuguese border
Arch J Caterineu

Islantilla (1993)
Urb Islantilla, Apdo 52, 21410 Isla Cristina (Huelva)
Tel (959) 48 60 39/48 60 49
Fax (959) 48 61 04
Holes 27 L 5926-6142 m SSS 72-73
V'tors U H
Fees 6500P
Loc 30 km W of Huelva, nr Portuguese border
Arch Canales/Recasens

Montecastillo (1992)
Carretera de Arcos, 11406 Jérez
Tel (956) 15 12 00
Fax (956) 15 12 09
Holes 18 L 6494 m SSS 72
V'tors H
Fees 9000P
Loc 10 km NE of Jérez. 75 km S of Seville
Arch Jack Nicklaus

Novo Sancti Petri (1990)
Urb Novo Sancti Petri, Playa de la Barrosa, 11139 Chiclana de la Frontera
Tel (956) 49 40 05/49 44 50
Fax (956) 49 43 50
Holes 27 L 5197-6466 m SSS 72
V'tors U H
Fees 7500P
Loc La Barrosa, 24 km SE of Cádiz. Jérez Airport 50 km
Arch Severiano Ballesteros

Pineda De Sevilla (1939)
Apartado 1049, 41080 Sevilla
Tel (954) 61 14 00/61 33 99
Holes 18 L 6120 m SSS 72
V'tors U
Loc 3 km S of Seville on Cádiz road
Arch R & F Medina

Real Golf Sevilla (1992)
Autovía Sevilla-Utrera, 41089 Montequinto (Sevilla)
Tel (954) 12 43 01
Fax (954) 12 42 29
Holes 18 L 6321 m SSS 73
V'tors U H WE–booking necessary
Fees 6000P
Loc 3 km S of Seville
Arch José María Olazabal

Sevilla Golf (1989)
Hacienda Las Minas, Ctra de Isla Mayor, Aznalcazar (Sevilla)
Tel (955) 75 04 14
Holes 9 L 5910 m Par 71

V'tors U
Loc 15 km W of Seville
Arch A García Garrido

Vista Hermosa (1975)
Apartado 77, Urb Vista Hermosa, 11500 Puerto de Santa María, Cádiz
Tel (956) 87 56 05
Holes 9 L 5614 m Par 70
V'tors U
Loc 25 km W of Cádiz

Zaudin
Crta Mairena-Tomares, 41940 Tomares (Sevilla)
Tel (954) 15 33 44
Holes 18 L 6192 m Par 71 SSS 72
V'tors U
Fees On application
Loc Cornisa del Aljarafe, 3 km from Seville
Arch Gary Player

Valencia & Castellón

El Bosque (1989)
Crta Godelleta, 46370 Chiva-Valencia
Tel (96) 180 41 42
Fax (96) 180 40 09
Holes 18 L 6384 m SSS 74
V'tors U
Loc Nr Chiva, 24 km W of Valencia, off Madrid road
Arch Robert Trent Jones Sr

Costa de Azahar (1960)
Ctra Grao-Benicasim, Castellón de la Plana
Tel (964) 22 70 64
Holes 9 L 2724 m SSS 70
Loc 5 km NE of Castellón, on coast
Arch Angel Pérez

Escorpión (1975)
Apartado Correos 1, Betera (Valencia)
Tel (96) 160 12 11
Fax (96) 169 01 87
Holes 18 L 6345 m SSS 73
V'tors H
Fees 4000P (8000P)
Loc Betera, 20 km N of Valencia
Arch Ron Kirby

Manises (1964)
Apartado 22.029, Manises (Valencia)
Tel (96) 152 18 71
Holes 9 L 6094 m Par 73
Loc 8 km W of Valencia
Arch Javier Arana

Mediterraneo CC (1978)
Urb La Coma, Borriol (Castellón)
Tel (964) 32 12 27
Fax (964) 32 13 57
Holes 18 L 6239 m SSS 73
V'tors H

Loc Borriol, 4 km NW of Castellón
Arch Ramón Espinosa

Oliva Nova (1992)
Carretera Las Marinas, 03700 Denia
Tel (096) 285 40 00
Holes 18 L 6445m SSS 72
V'tors U
Loc 15 km N of Denia, off A7
Arch Severiano Ballesteros

Panorámica (1995)
Urb Panorámica, 12320 San Jorge (Castellón)
Tel (964) 49 30 72
Holes 18 L 6429 m Par 72 SSS 74
V'tors U
Loc A7 Junction 42 towards Vinaroz
Arch Bernhardt Langer

El Saler (1968)
Parador Luis Vives, 46012 El Saler (Valencia)
Tel (96) 161 11 86
Fax (96) 162 70 16
Holes 18 L 6485 m SSS 75
V'tors U
Loc Oliva, 18 km S of Valencia, towards Cullera
Arch Javier Arana

Valladolid

Entrepinos (1990)
Crta Pesquerela Km1.5, 47130 Simancas (Valladolid)
Tel (983) 59 05 11/59 05 61
Fax (983) 59 07 65
Holes 18 L 5208 m Par 69
V'tors U H
Fees 5000P (7000P)
Loc 15 km SW of Valladolid
Arch Manuel Piñero

Zaragoza

Aero Club de Zaragoza (1966)
Coso 34, 50004 Zaragoza
Tel (976) 21 43 78
Holes 9 L 5042 m SSS 67
Loc 12 km SW of Zaragoza, by airbase

La Penaza (1973)
Apartado 3039, Zaragoza
Tel (976) 34 28 00/34 22 48
Fax (976) 34 28 00
Holes 18 L 6122 m SSS 72
V'tors H
Loc 15 km SW of Zaragoza on Madrid road, nr airbase
Arch FW Hawtree

For list of abbreviations see page 527

Sweden

East Central

Ängsö (1979)
Björnövägen 2, 721 30 Västerås
Tel (0171) 441012
Fax (0171) 441049
Holes 18 hole course Par 72
V'tors H
Fees 160kr (230kr)
Loc 15 km E of Västerås
Arch Åke Hultström

Arboga
PO Box 263, 732 25 Arboga
Tel (0589) 70100
Holes 18 L 5890 m Par 71
V'tors U
Fees 160kr
Loc 5 km S of Arboga
Arch Sune Linde

Ärila (1951)
Nicolai, 611 92 Nyköping
Tel (0155) 214967
Fax (0155) 267657
Holes 18 L 5810 m Par 72
V'tors H
Fees 200kr (250kr)
Loc 5 km SE of Nyköping
Arch Sköld/Linde

Arlandastad
Norslunda Gård, 195 95 Rosersberg
Tel (08) 590 36515
Fax (08) 590 35518
Holes 18 L 5830 m SSS 72
9 L 1495 m SSS 29
V'tors H
Fees 250kr (320kr)
Loc 35 km N of Stockholm, nr airport
Arch Sune Linde

Askersund (1980)
Box 3002, 696 03 Ammeberg
Tel (0583) 34442
Fax (0583) 34369
Holes 18 L 5800 m SSS 72
V'tors H
Fees 180kr
Loc 10 km SE of Askersund towards Ammeberg. 1 km on road to Kärra
Arch Ronald Fream

Burvik
Burvik, 740 12 Knutby
Tel (0174) 43060
Fax (0174) 43062
Holes 18 L 5785 m SSS 72
V'tors U
Fees On application
Loc 45 km E of Uppsala. 70 km N of Stockholm
Arch Bengt Lorichs

Edenhof (1991)
740 22 Bälinge
Tel (018) 334185
Fax (018) 334186
Holes 18 L 5898 m SSS 72
V'tors H
Fees 180kr (240kr)
Loc 17 km NW of Uppsala
Arch Sune Linde

Enköping (1970)
Box 2006, 745 02 Enköping
Tel (0171) 20830
Fax (0171) 20823
Holes 18 L 5660 m Par 71
V'tors H
Fees 180kr (220kr)
Loc 1 km E of Enköping, off E18

Eskilstuna (1951)
Strängnäsvägen, 633 49 Eskilstuna
Tel (016) 142629
Fax (016) 148729
Holes 18 L 5610 m SSS 70
V'tors H
Fees 160kr (200kr)
Loc 2 km E of Eskilstuna. 20 km E of Örebro
Arch Douglas Brasier

Fagersta (1970)
Box 2051, 737 02 Fagersta
Tel (0223) 54060
Fax (0223) 54000
Holes 18 L 5775 m Par 71
V'tors U
Fees 140kr (180kr)
Loc 7 km W of Fagersta (Route 65). 70 km N of Västerås

Frösåker (1989)
Frösåker Gård, Box 17015, 720 17 Västerås
Tel (021) 25401
Fax (021) 25485
Holes 18 L 5820 m Par 72
V'tors U H
Fees 200kr (250kr)
Loc 15 km SE of Västerås
Arch Sune Linde

Fullerö (1988)
Jotsberga, 725 91 Västerås
Tel (021) 50132
Fax (021) 50431
Holes 18 L 5707 m SSS 72
V'tors H
Fees 150kr (200kr)
Loc 6 km SW of Västerås
Arch Hultström/Sjöberg

Gripsholm (1991)
Box 133, 647 32 Mariefred
Tel (0159) 13040
Fax (0159) 13345
Holes 18 holes Par 73 course
V'tors H
Fees 180kr (250kr)
Loc 1 km from Mariefred
Arch Bengt Lorichs

Grönlund (1989)
PO Box 38, 740 10 Almunge
Tel (0174) 20670
Fax (0174) 20455
Holes 18 L 5865 m SSS 71
V'tors H
Fees 200kr (260kr)
Loc 20 km E of Uppsala. 25 km NE of Arlanda Airport
Arch Åke Persson

Gustavsvik
Box 22033, 702 02 Örebro
Tel (019) 244486
Fax (019) 246490
Holes 18 holes SSS 72
V'tors H
Fees 200kr
Loc 1 km S of Örebro
Arch Turner/Wirhed

Katrineholm (1959)
Jättorp, 641 93 Katrineholm
Tel (0150) 39270
Fax (0150) 39011
Holes 18 L 5850 m SSS 72
V'tors U
Fees 200kr
Loc 7 km E of Katrineholm
Arch Nils Skjöld

Köping (1963)
Box 278, 731 26 Köping
Tel (0221) 81090
Fax (0221) 81277
Holes 18 L 5636 m Par 71
V'tors U
Fees 150kr (200kr)
Loc 5 km N of Köping (Route 250)
Arch Brasier/Sederholm

Kumla (1987)
Box 46, 692 21 Kumla
Tel (019) 577370
Fax (019) 577373
Holes 18 L 5845 m SSS 72
V'tors U
Fees 200kr
Loc 8 km E of Kumla. 20 km SE of Örebro
Arch Jan Sederholm

Linde (1984)
Dalkarlshyttan, 711 31 Lindesberg
Tel (0581) 13960
Fax (0581) 12936
Holes 18 L 5539 m Par 71
V'tors H
Fees 180kr (180kr)
Loc 42 km N of Örebro on R60. Lindesberg 2 km
Arch Jan Sederholm

Mosjö (1989)
Mosjö Gård, 705 94 Örebrö
Tel (019) 225780
Fax (019) 225045
Holes 18 L 6160 m Par 72

Sweden 805

V'tors WD–U WE–H
Fees 200kr (200kr)
Loc 10 km S of Örebrö
Arch Åke Persson

Nora (1988)
Box 108, 713 23 Nora
Tel (0587) 311660
Fax (0587) 15050
Holes 18 L 5865 m Par 72
V'tors U
Fees 160kr (200kr)
Loc 33 km N of Örebro
Arch Jeremy Turner

Örebro (1939)
Lanna, 719 93 Vintrosa
Tel (019) 291065
Fax (019) 291055
Holes 18 L 5870 m Par 71
V'tors H–(max 36)
Fees 260kr
Loc 18 km W of Örebro on Route E18
Arch Flera

Roslagen
Box 110, 761 22 Norrtälje
Tel (0176) 237194
Fax (0176) 237103
Holes 18 L 5614 m SSS 72
 9 L 2888 m SSS 36
V'tors H
Fees 18 hole:250kr 9 hole:150kr
Loc 7 km N of Norrtälje
Arch TG Oxenstierna

Sala (1970)
Fallet, Isätra, 733 92 Sala
Tel (0224) 53077/53055/53064
Fax (0224) 53143
Holes 18 L 5640 m SSS 71
V'tors U
Fees 160kr (200kr)
Loc 8 km E of Sala towards Uppsala, Route 67/72
Arch Tedrup/Linde

Sigtunabygden (1961)
Box 89, 193 22 Sigtuna
Tel (08) 592 54012
Fax (08) 592 54267
Holes 18 L 5710 m SSS 72
V'tors H
Fees 220kr (280kr)
Loc Sigtuna, 50 km N of Stockholm
Arch Nils Sköld

Södertälje (1952)
Box 91, 151 21 Södertälje
Tel (08) 550 38240
Fax (08) 550 62549
Holes 18 L 5875 m SSS 72
V'tors H WE–NA before 1pm
Fees 225kr (275kr)
Loc 4 km W of Södertälje
Arch Nils Sköld

Strängnäs (1968)
Kilenlundavägen, 645 91 Strängnäs
Tel (0152) 14731
Fax (0152) 14716
Holes 18 L 5625 m SSS 72
V'tors H
Fees 200kr (240kr)
Loc 3 km S of Strängnäs
Arch Anders Amilon

Torshälla (1960)
Box 128, 64422 Torshälla
Tel (016) 358722
Fax (016) 357491
Holes 18 L 5934 m Par 72
V'tors H
Fees 200kr (250kr)
Loc 5 km N of Eskilstuna
Arch Brasier/Linde

Tortuna
Nicktuna, Tortuna, 725 96 Västerås
Tel (021) 65300
Fax (021) 65302
Holes 18 L 5750 m SSS 72
V'tors U
Fees 150kr (180kr)
Loc 10 km N of Västerås
Arch Husell/Hultström

Trosa (1972)
Box 80, 619 22 Trosa
Tel (0156) 22458
Fax (0156) 22454
Holes 18 L 5727 m Par 72
V'tors U
Fees 200kr
Loc 5 km W of Trosa, towards Uttervik
Arch P Chamberlain

Upsala (1937)
Håmö Gård, Läby, 755 92 Uppsala
Tel (018) 460120
Fax (018) 461205
Holes 18 L 6176 m SSS 74
 9 L 1643 m SSS 56
V'tors H
Fees 240kr (300kr)
Loc 10 km W of Uppsala
Arch Greger Paulsson

Vassunda
Smedby Gård, 741 91 Knivsta
Tel (018) 381230/381235
Fax (018) 381416
Holes 18 L 6141 m Par 72
V'tors H
Fees 220kr (280kr)
Loc 45 km N of Stockholm
Arch Sune Linde

Västerås (1931)
Bjärby, 724 81 Västerås
Tel (021) 357543
Fax (021) 357573
Holes 18 L 5380 m SSS 69
V'tors U

Fees 150kr (200kr)
Loc 2 km N of Västerås
Arch Nils Sköld

Far North

Boden (1946)
Box 107, 961 21 Boden
Tel (0921) 72051
Fax (0921) 72047
Holes 18 L 5495 m SSS 72
V'tors H
Fees 160kr
Loc 7 km S of Boden
Arch Björn Eriksson

Funäsdalsfjällen (1972)
Box 66, 840 95 Funäsdalen
Tel (0684) 21100
Fax (0684) 21142
Holes 18 L 5300 m SSS 72
V'tors U
Fees 180kr
Loc Funäsdalen, nr Norwegian border
Arch Sköld/Linde

Gällivare-Malmberget (1973)
Box 35, 983 21 Malmberget
Tel (0970) 20782
Fax (0970) 20776
Holes 18 L 5620 m Par 71
V'tors H
Fees 160kr
Loc 4 km NW of Gällivare, towards Malmberget
Arch Jan Sederholm

Haparanda (1989)
Mattiu 140, 953 35 Haparanda
Tel (0922) 10660
Fax (0922) 15040
Holes 18 L 6230 m SSS 73
V'tors H
Fees 160kr
Loc 125 km E of Luleå
Arch Peter Chamberlain

Härnösand (1957)
Box 52, 871 22 Härnösand
Tel (0611) 66169
Fax (0611) 66169
Holes 18 L 5410 m SSS 70
V'tors H
Fees D–180kr
Loc Vägnön, 16 km N of Härnösand on E4, towards Hemsö Island
Arch Nils Sköld

Kalix (1990)
Box 32, 952 21 Kalix
Tel (0923) 15945/15935
Fax (0923) 77735
Holes 18 L 5700m SSS 71
V'tors U

For list of abbreviations see page 527

Sweden

Fees 160kr
Loc 80 km N of Luleå
Arch Jan Sederholm

Klövsjö-Vemdalen
Box 147, 840 32 Klövsjö
Tel (0682) 23176
Fax (0682) 23310
Holes 18 L 5732 m Par 72
9 hole course
V'tors H or Green Card
Fees 180kr (180kr)
Loc 5 km S of Klövsjö
Arch Sune Linde

Luleå (1955)
Golfbanevej 80, 975 96 Luleå
Tel (0920) 256300
Fax (0920) 256362
Holes 18 L 5675 m Par 72
V'tors H
Fees 160kr (180kr)
Loc Rutvik, 12 km E of Luleå
Arch Skjöld/Tideman

Norrmjöle (1992)
905 82 Umeå
Tel (090) 81581
Fax (090) 81565
Holes 18 L 5619 m Par 72
V'tors U
Fees 200kr
Loc 19 km S of Umeå
Arch Acke Lundgren

Östersund-Frösö (1947)
Box 40, 832 01 Frösön
Tel (063) 43001
Fax (063) 43765
Holes 18 L 6000 m Par 73
V'tors U
Fees 180kr
Loc Island of Frösö
Arch Nils Sköld

Öviks GC Puttom (1967)
Ovansjö 1970, 891 95 Arnäsvall
Tel (0660) 254001
Fax (0660) 254040
Holes 18 L 5795 m SSS 72
V'tors H
Fees 180kr
Loc 15 km N of Örnsköldsvik on E4
Arch Nils Sköld

Piteå (1960)
Nötöv 119, 941 41 Piteå
Tel (0911) 14990
Fax (0911) 14960
Holes 18 L 5325 m Par 69
V'tors H
Fees 160kr
Loc 2 km SE of Piteå
Arch Jan Sederholm

Skellefteå (1967)
Rönnbäcken, 931 92 Skellefteå
Tel (0910) 779233
Fax (0910) 779777

Holes 27 L 6135 m SSS 72
Par 3 course
V'tors U H
Fees 200kr
Loc Skellefteå 5 km
Arch Sköld/Carlsson/Larsson

Sollefteå (1970)
Box 213, 881 25 Sollefteå
Tel (0620) 21477/12670
Fax (0620) 21477/12670
Holes 18 L 5770 m SSS 72
V'tors H
Fees 180kr
Loc Österforse, 15 km SW of Sollefteå (Route 89)
Arch Nils Sköld

Sundsvall (1952)
Golfvägen 5, 862 00 Kvissleby
Tel (060) 561056
Fax (060) 561909
Holes 18 L 5885 m SSS 72
V'tors WD–H before noon WE–H after 10am
Fees 180kr (200r)
Loc Skottsund, 15 km S of Sundsvall

Timrå
Golfbanevägen 2, 860 32 Fagervik
Tel (060) 570153
Fax (060) 578136
Holes 18 L 5715 m Par 72
V'tors H
Fees 180kr (200kr)
Loc 1 km S of Sundsvall airport
Arch Sune Linde

Umeå (1954)
Lövön, 913 35 Holmsund
Tel (090) 41071/41066
Fax (090) 149120
Holes 18 L 5751 m SSS 72
9 L 2688 m SSS 70
V'tors U
Fees 200kr
Loc 16 km SE of Umeå
Arch Bo Engdahl

Gothenburg

Albatross (1973)
Lillhagsvägen, 422 50 Hisings-Backa
Tel (031) 551901/550500
Fax (031) 555900
Holes 18 L 6020 m SSS 72
Fees 220kr (250kr)
Loc 10 km N of Gothenburg on Hising Island

Chalmers
PO Box 40, 438 21 Landvetter
Tel (031) 918430
Fax (031) 916338
Holes 18 L 5560 m SSS 71
V'tors WD–U H before 4pm –M H after 4pm WE–M H before 2pm –U H after 2pm

Fees 200kr (200kr)
Loc 20 km E of Gothenburg. 2 km from Landvetter airport
Arch Gyllenhammar/Henrikson

Delsjö (1962)
Kallebäck, 412 76 Göteborg
Tel (031) 406959
Fax (031) 407130
Holes 18 L 5703 m Par 71
V'tors H WE–NA before 1pm
Fees 240kr (280kr)
Loc 5 km E of Gothenburg (Route 40)
Arch Douglas Brasier

Forsgårdens (1982)
Gamla Forsv 1, 434 47 Kungsbacka
Tel (0300) 13649
Fax (0300) 71987
Holes 18 L 6110 m SSS 72
9 L 2915 m
V'tors WD–U WE–NA before 2pm
Fees 220kr (260kr)
Loc 1 km SE of Kungsbacka. 20 km S of Gothenburg
Arch Sune Linde

Göteborg (1902)
Box 2056, 436 02 Hovås
Tel (031) 282444
Fax (031) 685333
Holes 18 L 5935 yds SSS 70
V'tors WD–U WE–M before 2pm
Fees 250kr (300kr)
Loc 11 km S of Gothenburg (Route 158)

Gullbringa (1968)
442 95 Kungälv
Tel (0303) 227161
Fax (0303) 227778
Holes 18 L 5775 m Par 70
V'tors U
Fees 220kr
Loc 14 km W of Kungälv, towards Marstrand
Arch Douglas Brasier

Kungälv-Kode
Ö Knaverstad 140, 442 97 Kode
Tel (0303) 51300
Fax (0303) 50205
Holes 18 L 5984 m Par 72
V'tors U
Fees 200kr
Loc 30 km N of Gothenburg
Arch Lars Andreasson

Kungsbacka (1971)
Hamra Gård 515, 429 44 Särö
Tel (031) 936277
Fax (031) 935085
Holes 18 L 5855 m SSS 72
9 L 2880 m SSS 36
V'tors WD–U WE–NA before 2pm
Fees 250kr (300kr)
Loc 7 km N of Kungsbacka on Route 158
Arch Pennink/Nordström

Lysegården (1966)
Box 532, 442 15 Kungälv
Tel (0303) 223426
Fax (0303) 223075
Holes 18 L 5670 m SSS 71
9 L 5444 m SSS 70
V'tors H
Fees 200kr
Loc 10 km N of Kungälv
Arch Röhss/Engström

Mölndals (1979)
Box 77, 437 21 Lindome
Tel (031) 993030
Fax (031) 994901
Holes 18 L 5625 m SSS 73
V'tors H WE–NA before 11am
Fees 200kr (240kr)
Loc Lindome, 20 km S of Gothenburg
Arch Ronald Fream

Öijared (1958)
Pl 1082, 448 92 Floda
Tel (0302) 30604
Fax (0302) 35370
Holes 18 L 5875 m Par 72
18 L 5655 m Par 71
V'tors H WE–NA before 1pm
Fees 200kr (240kr)
Loc 35 km NE of Gothenburg (E20), nr Nääs
Arch Brasier/Amilon

Partille (1986)
Box 234, 433 24 Partille
Tel (031) 987043
Fax (031) 987757
Holes 18 L 5475 m Par 70
V'tors WD–H WE–NA before 1pm
Fees 200kr (200kr)
Loc Öjersjö, 10 km E of Gothenburg
Arch Jan Sederholm

Sjögärde
430 30 Frillesås
Tel (0340) 652230
Fax (0340) 652577
Holes 18 L 5723 m SSS 72
6 hole short course
V'tors H
Fees 200kr (220kr)
Loc 20 km S of Kungsbacka
Arch Lars Andreasson

Stenungsund-Spekeröd (1993)
Lundby Pl 7480, 444 93 Spekeröd
Tel (0303) 778470
Fax (0303) 778350
Holes 18 L 6245 m Par 72
V'tors WD–H WE–NA 10–12
Fees D–220kr (D–220kr)
Loc 50 km N of Gothenburg
Arch Peter Nordwall

Stora Lundby (1983)
Torgestorp, 443 71 Grabo
Tel (0302) 44200
Fax (0302) 44125
Holes 18 L 6040 m Par 72
9 hole Par 3 course
V'tors H
Fees 180kr (220kr)
Loc 25 km NE of Gothenburg
Arch Frank Pennink

Malmö & South Coast

Barsebäck G&CC (1969)
246 55 Löddeköpinge
Tel (046) 776230
Fax (046) 772630
Holes Old 18 L 5910 m Par 72
New 18 L 6025 m Par 72
V'tors WD–H booking necessary
Fees D–320kr
Loc 35 km N of Malmö
Arch Bruce/Steel

Bokskogen (1963)
Torupsvägen 408-140, 230 40 Bara
Tel (040) 481004
Fax (040) 481081
Holes Old 18 L 6006 m Par 72
New 18 L 5542 m Par 71
V'tors H WE–after 1pm Old course
Fees 240kr (300kr)
Loc 15 km SE of Malmö, off E65
Arch Amilon/Sederholm/Lorichs

Falsterbo (1909)
Fyrvägen, 239 40 Falsterbo
Tel (040) 470078/475078
Fax (040) 472722
Holes 18 L 6577 yds Par 71
V'tors H WE–M before noon
Fees D–250–350kr
Loc 30 km SW of Malmö
Arch Gunnar Bauer

Flommens (1935)
239 40 Falsterbo
Tel (040) 475016
Fax (040) 473157
Holes 18 L 5735 m SSS 72
V'tors H WE/Jun–Aug–M before 1pm
Fees 220–260kr (260kr)
Loc 35 km SW of Malmö
Arch Bergendorff/Kristersson

Kävlinge (1991)
Box 138, 244 22 Kävlinge
Tel (046) 736270
Fax (046) 736271
Holes 18 L 5800 m SSS 72
V'tors H
Fees 160kr (220kr)
Loc 12 km N of Lund
Arch Rolf Collijn

Ljunghusen (1932)
Kinellsvag, Ljunghusen, 236 42 Höllviken
Tel (040) 450384
Fax (040) 454265
Holes 27 holes: L 5455-5895 m SSS 70-73
V'tors WD–U H WE–M before noon
Fees 220kr (280kr)
Loc Falsterbo Peninsula. 30 km SW of Malmö
Arch Douglas Brasier

Lunds Akademiska (1936)
Kungsmarken, 225 92 Lund
Tel (046) 99005
Fax (046) 99146
Holes 18 L 5780 m SSS 72
V'tors H
Fees 160kr (200kr)
Loc 5 km E of Lund
Arch Boström/Morrison

Malmö
Segesvängen, 212 27 Malmö
Tel (040) 292535
Fax (040) 292228
Holes 18 L 5720 m SSS 71
V'tors H
Fees 170kr (200kr)
Loc NE of Malmö

Örestad (1986)
Golfvägen, Habo Ljung, 234 22 Lomma
Tel (040) 410580
Fax (040) 416320
Holes 18 L 6036 m Par 73
9 L 2923 m Par 35
18 hole Par 3 course
V'tors H
Fees 170kr (200kr)
Loc 15 km N of Malmö
Arch Åke Persson

Österlen (1945)
Lilla Vik, 272 95 Simrishamn
Tel (0414) 24230
Fax (0414) 24133
Holes 18 L 5855 m SSS 72
V'tors H
Fees 120–280kr
Loc Vik, 8 km N of Simrishamn
Arch Tommy Nordström

Romeleåsen (1969)
Kvarnbrodda, 240 14 Veberöd
Tel (046) 82012
Fax (046) 82113
Holes 18 L 5783 m Par 72
V'tors U
Fees 180kr (240kr)
Loc 6 km S of Veberöd. 25 km E of Malmö
Arch Douglas Brasier

Söderslätts
Västra Grevie 19, 235 94 Vellinge
Tel (040) 443141
Fax (040) 443469
Holes 18 L 5800 m SSS 72
 9 hole Par 3 course
V'tors WD–H WE–M H before noon
Fees 200kr
Loc 15 km SE of Malmö
Arch Sune Linde

Tegelberga (1988)
Alstad Pl 140, 231 96 Trelleborg
Tel (040) 485690
Fax (040) 485691
Holes 18 L 5727 m CR 75
V'tors U
Fees 140–200kr (200–250kr)
Loc 11 km N of Trelleborg. 25 km E of Malmö
Arch Peter Chamberlain

Tomelilla
Ullstorp, 273 94 Tomelilla
Tel (0417) 13420
Fax (0417) 14455
Holes 18 L 6455 m Par 73 SSS 75
V'tors H
Fees 180kr (180kr)
Loc 15 km N of Ystad. 60 km E of Malmö
Arch Tommy Nordström

Trelleborg (1963)
Maglarp, Pl 431, 231 93 Trelleborg
Tel (0410) 330460
Fax (0410) 330281
Holes 18 L 5247 m Par 70
V'tors U H
Fees 200kr
Loc 5 km W of Trelleborg
Arch Brasier/Chamberlain

Vellinge (1991)
Toftadalsgård, 235 41 Vellinge
Tel (040) 443255
Fax (040) 443179
Holes 18 L 5766 m SSS 72
 6 hole short course
V'tors WD–U WE–NA before noon
Fees 180kr (220kr)
Loc 16 km SE of Malmö
Arch Tommy Nordström

Ystad (1930)
Långrevsvägen, 270 22 Köpingebro
Tel (0411) 550350
Fax (0411) 550392
Holes 18 L 5800 m Par 72
V'tors U
Fees 200–250kr
Loc 7 km E of Ystad, towards Simrishamn
Arch Thure Bruce

North

Alvkarleby
Västanåvägen 5, 814 94 Alvkarleby
Tel (026) 72757
Fax (026) 82307
Holes 18 holes Par 70
V'tors U
Fees On application
Loc 25 km from Gävle (Route 76)

Avesta (1963)
Åsbo, 774 01 Avesta
Tel (0226) 55913/10866/12766
Fax (0226) 12578
Holes 18 L 5560 m SSS 71
V'tors U
Fees 170kr
Loc 3 km NE of Avesta
Arch Sune Linde

Bollnäs
Norrfly 4526, 823 91 Kilafors
Tel (0278) 650540
Fax (0278) 651220
Holes 18 L 5870 m Par 72
V'tors H
Fees 180kr (200kr)
Loc 15 km S of Bollnäs (Route 83)

Dalsjö (1989)
Box 215, 781 23 Borlänge
Tel (0243) 82800/220080
Fax (0243) 220140
Holes 18 L 5715 m Par 72
V'tors H
Fees 200kr (250kr)
Loc 5 km NE of Borlänge
Arch Jeremy Turner

Falun-Borlänge (1956)
Storgarden 10, 791 93 Falun
Tel (023) 31015
Fax (023) 31072
Holes 18 L 6085 m Par 72
V'tors U
Fees 180kr (200kr)
Loc Aspeboda, 8 km N of Borlänge
Arch Nils Sköld

Gävle (1949)
Bönavägen 23, 805 95 Gävle
Tel (026) 120333/120338
Fax (026) 516468
Holes 18 L 5735 m SSS 73
Fees 200kr (250kr)
Loc 3 km N of Gävle

Hagge (1963)
Hagge, 771 90 Ludvika
Tel (0240) 28087/28513
Fax (0240) 28515
Holes 18 L 5519 m SSS 71
V'tors H
Fees D–150kr
Loc 7 km S of Ludvika
Arch Sune Linde

Hofors (1965)
Box 117, 813 22 Hofors
Tel (0290) 85125
Fax (0290) 85101
Holes 18 L 5400 m Par 70
V'tors U
Fees 180kr (200kr)
Loc 5 km SE of Hofors
Arch Sune Linde

Högbo (1962)
Daniel Tilas Väg 4, 811 92 Sandviken
Tel (026) 215015
Fax (026) 215322
Holes 18 L 5760 m Par 72
 9 L 2590 m Par 35
V'tors H
Fees 160kr
Loc 6 km N of Sandviken (Route 272)
Arch Sköld/Linde

Hudiksvall (1964)
Tjuvskär, 824 01 Hudiksvall
Tel (0650) 15930
Fax (0650) 18630
Holes 18 L 5665 m SSS 72
V'tors U
Fees 160kr
Loc 4 km SE of Hudiksvall
Arch Linde/Sköld

Leksand (1977)
Box 25, 793 21 Leksand
Tel (0247) 14640
Fax (0247) 14157
Holes 18 L 5263 m Par 70
V'tors U
Fees 120kr (180kr)
Loc 2 km N of Leksand
Arch Nils Sköld

Ljusdal (1973)
Box 151, 827 23 Ljusdal
Tel (0651) 16883
Fax (0651) 16883
Holes 18 L 5920 m Par 72
V'tors U
Fees 180kr
Loc 2 km E of Ljusdal
Arch Eriksson/Skjöld

Mora (1980)
Box 264, 792 24 Mora
Tel (0250) 10182
Fax (0250) 10306
Holes 18 L 5600 m Par 72
Fees 150kr
Loc 1 km N of Mora. 40 km NW of Rättvik
Arch Sune Linde

Rättvik (1954)
Box 29, 795 21 Rättvik
Tel (0248) 51030
Fax (0248) 12081
Holes 18 L 5350 m SSS 70
V'tors U
Fees 160–220kr
Loc 2 km N of Rättvik

Sälenfjallens (1991)
Box 20, 780 67 Sälen
Tel   (0280) 20670
Fax (0280) 20670
Holes 18 L 5035 m Par 72
V'tors U
Fees 150kr
Loc   230 km NW of Borlänge.
      400 km NW of Stockholm
Arch Sune Linde

Säter (1984)
Box 89, 783 22 Säter
Tel   (0225) 50030
Fax (0225) 51424
Holes 18 L 5781 m Par 72
V'tors U
Fees 160kr
Loc   25 km SE of Borlänge.
      180 km NW of Stockholm
Arch Sune Linde

Snöå (1990)
Snöå Bruk, 780 51 Dala-Järna
Tel   (0281) 24072
Fax (0281) 24009
Holes 18 L 5738 m SSS 73
V'tors U
Fees 160kr
Loc   80 km W of Borlänge,
      nr Dala-Järna (Route 71)
Arch Åke Persson

Söderhamn (1961)
Nygatan 5b, 826 30 Söderhamn
Tel   (0270) 281300
Fax (0270) 281003
Holes 18 L 5770 m Par 72
V'tors H
Fees 180–220kr
Loc   8 km N of Söderhamn
Arch Nils Sköld

Sollerö (1991)
Levsnäs, 79290 Sollerön
Tel   (0250) 22236
Fax (0250) 22854
Holes 18 L 7226 yds Par 72
V'tors H
Fees 160kr
Loc   14 km from Mora on Island
      of Sollerön in Siljan
Arch JR Turner

Skane & South

Allerum (1992)
Pl 7592, 260 35 Ödåkra
Tel   (042) 93051
Fax (042) 93045
Holes 18 L 6201 m SSS 73
V'tors U
Fees 130kr (200kr)
Loc   9 km NE of Helsingborg
Arch Hans Fock

Ängelholm (1973)
Box 1117, 262 22 Ängelholm
Tel   (0431) 430260/431460
Fax (0431) 431568
Holes 18 L 5760 m Par 72
V'tors H (max 36)
Fees 140–200kr
Loc   10 km E of Ängelholm on
      route 114
Arch Jan Sederholm

Araslöv
Starvägen 1, 291 75 Färlöv
Tel   (044) 71500
Fax (044) 71575
Holes 18 L 5817 m Par 72
V'tors H or Green card
Fees 160kr (220kr)
Loc   9 km NW of Kristianstad
      (Route 19)
Arch Sune Linde

Båstad (1929)
Box 1037, 269 21 Båstad
Tel   (0431) 73136
Fax (0431) 73331
Holes 18 L 5632 m Par 71
       18 L 6163 m Par 72
V'tors H
Fees 300kr
Loc   4 km W of Båstad
      (Route 115)
Arch Hawtree/Taylor/Nordström

Bedinge (1931)
Golfbanevägen,
231 76 Beddingestrand
Tel   (0410) 25514
Fax (0410) 25411
Holes 18 L 5444 m Par 70
V'tors H
Fees 120 (160kr)
Loc   Beddingestrand, 20 km E of
      Trelleborg
Arch Åke Persson

Bjäre
Salomonhög 3086, 269 93 Båstad
Tel   (0431) 361053
Fax (0431) 361764
Holes 18 L 5550 m SSS 71
V'tors H
Fees D–220–250kr
Loc   2 km E of Båstad. 60 km N
      of Helsingborg
Arch Svante Dahlgren

Bosjökloster (1974)
243 95 Höör
Tel   (0413) 25858
Fax (0413) 25895
Holes 18 L 5890 m Par 72
V'tors H
Fees 160kr (200kr)
Loc   7 km S of Höör. 40 km NE
      of Malmö
Arch Douglas Brasier

Carlskrona (1949)
PO Almö, 370 24 Nättraby
Tel   (0457) 35123
Fax (0457) 35090
Holes 18 L 5485 m Par 70
V'tors U
Fees D–200kr
Loc   18 km SW of Karlskrona
Arch Jan Sederholm

Degeberga-Widtsköfle
Box 71, 297 21 Degeberga
Tel   (044) 355035
Fax (044) 355075
Holes 18 L 6129 m SSS 72
       9 hole Par 3 course
V'tors U
Fees 100–170kr
Loc   20 km S of Kristianstad

Eslöv (1966)
Box 150, 241 22 Eslöv
Tel   (0413) 18610
Fax (0413) 18613
Holes 18 L 5630 m CR 70
V'tors H
Fees 200kr (250kr)
Loc   4 km S of Eslöv (Route 113)
Arch Thure Bruce

Hässleholm (1978)
Skyrup, 282 95 Tyringe
Tel   (0451) 53111
Fax (0451) 53138
Holes 18 L 5830 m SSS 72
V'tors U
Fees 150kr (200kr)
Loc   15 km NW of Hässleholm
Arch Persson/Bruce/Jensen

Helsingborg (1924)
260 40 Viken
Tel   (042) 236147
Holes 9 L 4578 m Par 68
V'tors U
Fees 120kr (140kr)
Loc   15 km NW of Helsingborg
Arch W Hester

Karlshamn (1962)
Box 188, 374 23 Karlshamn
Tel   (0454) 50085
Fax (0454) 50160
Holes 18 L 5861 m SSS 72
       9 holes SSS 36
V'tors H
Fees D–200kr (250kr)
Loc   Morrum, 10 km W of
      Karlshamn
Arch Douglas Brasier

Kristianstad (1924)
Box 41, 296 21 Åhus
Tel   (044) 247656
Fax (044) 247635
Holes 18 L 5810 m SSS 72
       9 L 2945 m SSS 36

For list of abbreviations see page 527

Sweden

V'tors H
Fees D–180kr (D–240kr)
Loc 18 km SE of Kristianstad. Airport 20 km
Arch Brasier/Nordström

Landskrona (1960)
Erikstorp, 261 61 Landskrona
Tel (0418) 26010
Fax (0418) 436868
Holes Old 18 L 5700 m SSS 71
New 18 L 4300 m SSS 67
V'tors U
Fees 200kr (240kr)
Loc 4 km N of Landskrona, towards Borstahusen

Mölle (1943)
260 42 Mölle
Tel (042) 347520
Fax (042) 347523
Holes 18 L 5312 m Par 70
V'tors H–max 36
Fees 260kr
Loc Mölle, 35 km NW of Helsingborg
Arch Thure Bruce

Örkelljunga
Rya 472, 286 91 Örkelljunga
Tel (0435) 53690/53640
Fax (0435) 53670
Holes 18 L 5700 m SSS 72
V'tors H
Fees 200kr (240kr)
Loc 8 km S of Örkelljunga. 40 km NE of Helsingborg (E4)
Arch Hans Fock

Östra Göinge (1981)
Box 114, 289 21 Knislinge
Tel (044) 60060
Fax (044) 69060
Holes 18 L 5898 m Par 72
V'tors H
Fees 150kr (180kr)
Loc 20 km N of Kristianstad
Arch T Nordström

Perstorp (1964)
PO Box 87, 284 22 Perstorp
Tel (0435) 35411
Fax (0435) 35959
Holes 18 L 5675 m Par 71
6 hole short course
V'tors H
Fees 150kr (200kr)
Loc 1 km S of Perstorp. 45 km E of Helsingborg
Arch Amilon/Bruce/Persson

Ronneby (1963)
Box 26, 372 21 Ronneby
Tel (0457) 10315
Fax (0457) 10412
Holes 18 L 5323 m Par 72
V'tors U
Fees 200kr
Loc 3 km S of Ronneby

Rya (1934)
PL 5500, 255 92 Helsingborg
Tel (042) 220182
Fax (042) 220394
Holes 18 L 5599 m Par 72
V'tors H
Fees 260kr
Loc 10 km S of Helsingborg
Arch Petterson/Sundblom

St Arild (1987)
Pl 1726 Fjälastorp, 260 41 Nyhamnsläge
Tel (042) 346860
Fax (042) 346042
Holes 18 L 5805 m Par 72
V'tors H
Fees 240kr (240kr)
Loc 50 km N of Helsingborg
Arch Jan Sederholm

Skepparslov (1984)
Udarpssäteri, 291 92 Kristianstad
Tel (044) 229508
Fax (044) 229503
Holes 18 L 5900 m SSS 72
V'tors U
Fees 150kr (200kr)
Loc 7 km W of Kristianstad
Arch Rolf Collijn

Söderåsen (1966)
Box 41, 260 50 Billesholm
Tel (042) 73337
Fax (042) 73963
Holes 18 L 5657 m Par 71
V'tors U
Fees 200kr
Loc 20 km E of Helsingborg
Arch Thure Bruce

Sölvesborg
Box 63, 294 22 Sölvesborg
Tel (0456) 70650
Fax (0456) 70650
Holes 18 L 5900 m Par 72
V'tors U
Fees 160kr (200kr)
Loc 30 km E of Kristianstad
Arch Sune Linde

Svalöv
Månstorp Pl 1365, 268 90 Svalöv
Tel (0418) 62462
Fax (0418) 62462
Holes 18 L 5860 m SSS 73
V'tors U
Fees 160kr (220kr)
Loc 20 km E of Landskrona

Torekov (1924)
Box 81, 260 93 Torekov
Tel (0431) 363355
Fax (0431) 364916
Holes 18 L 5701 m Par 72
V'tors Jun–Aug–H WE–M before noon
Fees 200–260kr
Loc 3 km N of Torekov
Arch Nils Sköld

Trummenas
373 02 Ramdala
Tel (0455) 60505
Fax (0455) 60571
Holes 18 L 5600 m Par 72
9 hole course
V'tors H
Fees 200kr
Loc 15 km SE of Karlskrona, off Route 22
Arch Ingmar Ericsson

Vasatorp (1973)
Box 13035, 250 13 Helsingborg
Tel (042) 235058
Fax (042) 235135
Holes 18 L 5875 m SSS 72
9 L 2940 m
V'tors H
Fees 250kr
Loc 8 km E of Helsingborg
Arch Thure Bruce

Wittsjö (1962)
Ubbaltsgården, 280 22 Vittsjö
Tel (0451) 22635
Fax (0451) 22567
Holes 18 L 5461 m Par 71
V'tors U
Fees 160kr (200kr)
Loc 2 km SE of Vittsjö
Arch Sköld/Amilon

South East

A6 Golfklubb
Centralvägen, 553 05 Jönköping
Tel (036) 308130
Fax (036) 308140
Holes 27 hole course:
9 L 3185 m Par 38
9 L 3115 m Par 37
9 L 2935 m Par 36
V'tors U H
Fees 200kr
Loc 2 km SE of Jönköping
Arch Peter Nordwall

Älmhult (1975)
Pl 1215, 343 90 Älmhult
Tel (0476) 14135
Fax (0476) 16565
Holes 18 L 5407 m SSS 71
V'tors U H
Fees D–170kr
Loc 2 km E of Älmhult on Route 120
Arch Persson/Söderberg

Åtvidaberg (1954)
Box 180, 597 24 Åtvidaberg
Tel (0120) 35425
Fax (0120) 13502
Holes 18 L 5856 m Par 72
V'tors H
Fees 180kr (220kr)
Loc 30 km SE of Linköping
Arch Douglas Brasier

For list of abbreviations see page 527

Ekerum
387 92 Borgholm, Öland
Tel (0485) 80000
Fax (0485) 80010
Holes 18 L 6045 m Par 72
9 L 2875 m Par 36
V'tors U H
Fees 220–290kr
Loc 12 km S of Borgholm. 25 km N of Öland bridge
Arch Peter Nordwall

Eksjö (1938)
Skedhult, 575 96 Eksjö
Tel (0381) 13525
Holes 18 L 5930 m SSS 72
V'tors WD–U WE–H
Fees 200kr
Loc 6 km W of Eksjö on Nässjö road
Arch Anders Amilon

Emmaboda (1976)
Kyrkogatan, 360 60 Vissefjärda
Tel (0471) 20505/20540
Fax (0471) 20440
Holes 18 L 6165 m SSS 72
V'tors H
Fees 180kr
Loc 12 km S of Emmaboda. 50 km N of Karlskrona

Finspång (1965)
Viberga Gård, 612 92 Finspång
Tel (0122) 13940
Fax (0122) 18888
Holes 18 L 5800 m SSS 72
V'tors U
Fees 160kr (240kr)
Loc 2 km E of Finspång, Route 51. Norrköping 25 km
Arch Sköld/Linde

Gotska (1986)
Box 1119, 621 22 Visby, Gotland
Tel (0498) 215545
Fax (0498) 215545
Holes 18 L 5202 m Par 69
9 L 5414 m Par 72
V'tors U H
Fees 18 hole:200kr 9 hole:100kr
Loc N outskirts of Visby
Arch Jack Wenman

Gröhögen (1996)
PL 1270, 380 65 Öland
Tel (0485) 661369
Fax (0485) 661130
Holes 18 L 3400 m Par 61
V'tors H
Fees 130 kr (130kr)
Loc 45 km S of Öland Bridge
Arch Kenneth Nilsson

Gumbalde
Box 35, 620 13 Stånga, Gotland
Tel (0498) 482880
Fax (0498) 482884
Holes 18 L 5600 m SSS 71

V'tors U
Fees 200–240kr
Loc 50 km SE of Visby, Gotland island
Arch Lars Lagergren

Hook
560 13 Hok
Tel (0393) 21420
Fax (0393) 21379
Holes 18 L 5758 m SSS 72
18 L 5750 m SSS 73
9 hole Par 3 course
V'tors H
Fees 220kr
Loc Hok, 30 km SE of Jönköping, towards Växjö
Arch Edberg/Bruce/Sederholm

Isaberg (1968)
Nissafors Bruk, 330 27 Hestra
Tel (0370) 336330
Fax (0370) 336325
Holes East 18 L 5823 m CR 71.8
West 18 L 5568 m CR 70.0
V'tors H
Fees 220kr (250–270kr)
Loc 18 km N of Gislaved, nr Nissafors. 60 km S of Jönköping
Arch Amilon/Bruce/Persson

Jönköping (1936)
Kettilstorp, 556 27 Jönköping
Tel (036) 76567
Fax (036) 76511
Holes 18 L 6370 m Par 70
V'tors WD–U H–phone in advance WE–H
Fees 200kr
Loc Kettilstorp, 3 km S of Jönköping
Arch Frederik Dreyer

Kalmar (1947)
Box 278, 391 23 Kalmar
Tel (0480) 472111
Fax (0480) 472314
Holes Blue 18 L 5700 m SSS 72
Red 18 L 5634 m SSS 72
V'tors H
Fees 250kr
Loc 9 km N of Kalmar via E22

Lagan (1966)
Box 63, 340 14 Lagan
Tel (0372) 30450/35560
Fax (0372) 35307
Holes 18 L 5600 m SSS 71
V'tors H
Fees 160kr
Loc Lagan, 10 km N of Ljungby, on Route E4
Arch Amilon/Persson/Magnusson

Landeryd (1987)
Bogestad Gård, 585 93 Linköping
Tel (013) 362200
Fax (013) 362208

Holes North 18 L 5675 m SSS 72
South 18 L 5085 m SSS 68
9 hole short course
V'tors U
Fees 220kr (240kr)
Loc 7 km SE of Linköping
Arch Nordström/Persson

Lidhems (1988)
360 14 Väckelsång
Tel (0470) 33660
Fax (0470) 33761
Holes 18 L 5755 m Par 72
V'tors H
Fees 200kr
Loc 30 km S of Växjo (Road 30)
Arch Ingmar Eriksson

Linköping (1945)
Box 10054, 580 10 Linköping
Tel (013) 120646
Fax (013) 140769
Holes 18 L 5664 m SSS 71
V'tors H
Fees 200kr (250kr)
Loc 3 km SW of Linköping
Arch Sundblom/Brasier

Mjölby (1986)
Blixberg, Miskarp, 595 92 Mjölby
Tel (0142) 12570
Fax (0142) 16553
Holes 18 L 5485 m SSS 71
V'tors H
Fees 180kr
Loc 35 km WSW of Linköping (E4)
Arch Åke Persson

Motala (1956)
PO Box 264, 591 23 Motala
Tel (0141) 50840
Fax (0141) 50864
Holes 18 L 5905 m Par 72
V'tors U
Fees 170kr (200kr)
Loc 3 km S of Motala via Route 50 or 32
Arch Sköld/Sederholm

Nässjö (1988)
Box 5, 571 21 Nässjö
Tel (0380) 10022
Fax (0380) 12082
Holes 18 L 5783 m Par 72
V'tors U
Fees 160kr
Loc 40 km E of Jönköping
Arch Bjorn Magnusson

Norrköping (1928)
Klinga Golfbana, 605 97 Norrköping
Tel (011) 335235/183654
Fax (011) 335014
Holes 18 L 5860 m SSS 73
V'tors U
Fees 160kr (200kr)
Loc Klinga, 9 km S of Norrköping on E4
Arch Nils Sköld

Sweden

Oskarshamn (1972)
Box 148, 572 23 Oskarshamn
Tel (0491) 94033
Fax (0491) 94033
Holes 18 L 5545 m SSS 71
V'tors H
Fees 170kr
Loc 10 km SW of Oskarshamn, nr Forshult
Arch Nils Sköld

Skinnarebo
Skinnarebo, 555 93 Jönköping
Tel (036) 69075
Fax (036) 362975
Holes 18 L 5686 m SSS 71
9 hole Par 3 course
V'tors H
Fees 180kr
Loc 14 km SW of Jönköping
Arch Björn Magnusson

Söderköping (1983)
Hylinge, 605 96 Norrköping
Tel (011) 70579
Holes 18 L 5730 m SSS 72
V'tors U
Fees 180kr
Loc Västra Husby, 9 km W of Söderköping
Arch Ronald Fream

Tobo (1971)
Box 101, 598 22 Vimmerby
Tel (0492) 30346
Fax (0492) 30871
Holes 18 L 5720 m Par 72
V'tors U
Fees 170kr (200kr)
Loc 10 km S of Vimmerby, nr Storebro. 60 km SW of Västervik
Arch Brasier/Jensen

Tranås (1952)
Box 430, 573 25 Tranås
Tel (0140) 311661
Fax (0140) 16161
Holes 18 L 5830 m SSS 72
V'tors U
Fees 180kr (200kr)
Loc 2 km N of Tranås

Vadstena (1957)
Hagalund, Box 122, 592 33 Vadstena
Tel (0143) 12440
Fax (0143) 12709
Holes 18 L 5486 m Par 71
V'tors U
Fees 160kr
Loc 3 km S of Vadstena, towards Vaderstad

Värnamo (1962)
Box 146, 331 21 Värnamo
Tel (0370) 23123
Fax (0370) 23216
Holes 18 L 6253 m SSS 72
V'tors U
Fees 200kr

Loc 8 km E of Värnamo on Route 127
Arch Nils Sköld

Västervik (1959)
Box 62, Ekhagen, 593 22 Västervik
Tel (0490) 32420
Fax (0490) 32421
Holes 18 L 5760 m Par 72
V'tors U
Fees 200kr (250kr)
Loc 1 km E of Västervik
Arch Sune Linde

Växjö (1959)
Box 227, 351 05 Växjö
Tel (0470) 21515
Fax (0470) 21557
Holes 18 L 5860 m Par 72
V'tors H
Fees 200kr (220kr)
Loc 5 km NW of Växjö
Arch Douglas Brasier

Vetlanda (1983)
Box 249, 574 23 Vetlanda
Tel (0383) 18310
Fax (0383) 19278
Holes 18 L 5552 m SSS 71
V'tors U
Fees 160kr
Loc Östanå, 3 km W of Vetlanda. 80 km SE of Jönköping
Arch Jan Sederholm

Visby
Kronholmen Västergarn, 620 20 Klintehamn, Gotland
Tel (0498) 245058
Fax (0498) 245240
Holes 18 L 5765 m Par 72
9 hole course
V'tors Jun–Sept–H
Fees 200–300kr
Loc Kronholmen, 25 km S of Visby, Gotland island
Arch Nordwall/Sköld

Vreta Kloster
Box 144, 590 70 Ljungsbro
Tel (013) 169700
Fax (013) 169707
Holes 18 L 5666 m Par 72
V'tors H
Fees 160kr (200kr)
Loc 15 km N of Linköping
Arch Sune Linde

South West

Alingsås (1985)
Hjälmared 4050, 441 95 Alingsås
Tel (0322) 52421
Holes 18 L 5600 m SSS 72
V'tors U
Fees 180kr (200kr)
Loc 5 km SE of Alingsås towards Borås

Bäckavattnet (1977)
Marbäck, 305 94 Halmstad
Tel (035) 44270
Fax (035) 44275
Holes 18 L 5740 m SSS 72
V'tors H
Fees 180kr
Loc 13 km E of Halmstad (RD25)

Billingen (1949)
St Kulhult, 540 17 Lerdala
Tel (0511) 80291
Fax (0511) 80244
Holes 18 L 5470 m Par 71
V'tors H
Fees 180kr
Loc 20 km NW of Skövde
Arch Douglas Brasier

Borås (1933)
Östra Vik, Kråkered, 504 95 Borås
Tel (033) 250250
Fax (033) 250176
Holes North 18 L 6005 m Par 72
South 18 L 5085 m Par 69
V'tors H–booking necessary
Fees 200kr (200kr)
Loc 6 km S of Borås, on Route 41 towards Varberg
Arch Brasier/Persson

Ekarnas (1970)
Balders Väg 12, 467 31 Grästorp
Tel (0514) 51450
Fax (0514) 51450
Holes 18 L 5501 m SSS 71
V'tors H
Fees 140kr (180kr)
Loc 25 km E of Trollhätten. Lidköping 35 km
Arch Jan Andersson

Falkenberg (1949)
Golfvägen, 311 72 Falkenberg
Tel (0346) 50287
Fax (0346) 50997
Holes 27 L 5575-5680 m SSS 72
V'tors H
Fees 200–250kr
Loc 5 km S of Falkenberg

Falköping (1965)
Box 99, 521 02 Falköping
Tel (0515) 31270
Fax (0515) 31389
Holes 18 L 5835 m Par 72
V'tors H
Fees 120kr (160kr)
Loc 7 km E of Falköping on Route 46 towards Skovde
Arch Nils Sköld

Halmstad (1930)
302 73 Halmstad
Tel (035) 30077/30280 (Starter)
Fax (035) 32308
Holes 18 L 6259 m CR 72.4
18 L 5787 m CR 69.9

For list of abbreviations see page 527

V'tors H WE–M before 1pm
Fees 400kr
Loc Tylosand, 9 km W of Halmstad
Arch Sundblom/Sköld/Pennink

Haverdals (1988)
Slingervägen 35, 31042 Haverdal
Tel (035) 59530
Fax (035) 53890
Holes 18 L 5840 m Par 72
V'tors H
Fees 220kr
Loc 11 km NW of Halmstad
Arch Anders Amilon

Hökensås (1962)
PO Box 116, 544 22 Hjo
Tel (0503) 16059
Fax (0503) 16156
Holes 18 L 5540 m Par 72
V'tors U
Fees 180kr (180kr)
Loc 8 km S of Hjo on Route 195
Arch Sune Linde

Hulta (1972)
Box 54, 517 22 Bollebygd
Tel (033) 288180
Fax (033) 288910
Holes 18 L 6000 m SSS 72
V'tors H
Fees 200kr (240kr)
Loc Bollebygd, 35 km E of Gothenburg
Arch Jan Sederholm

Knistad G&CC
541 92 Skövde
Tel (0500) 463170
Fax (0500) 463075
Holes 18 L 5790 m SSS 72
V'tors H
Fees 200kr
Loc 10 km NE of Skövde
Arch Jeremy Turner

Laholm (1964)
Box 101, 312 22 Laholm
Tel (0430) 30201
Fax (0430) 30891
Holes 18 L 5430 m SSS 70
V'tors U H
Fees 170kr (200kr)
Loc 5 miles E of Laholm on Route 24
Arch Jan Sederholm

Lidköping (1967)
Box 2029, 531 02 Lidköping
Tel (0510) 546144
Fax (0510) 546495
Holes 18 L 5382 m CR 68.6
V'tors H
Fees 180kr
Loc 5 km E of Lidköping
Arch Douglas Brasier

Mariestad (1975)
PO Box 299, 542 23 Mariestad
Tel (0501) 47147
Fax (0501) 78117
Holes 18 L 5970 m SSS 73
V'tors H
Fees 200kr
Loc 4 km W of Mariestad, at Lake Vänern

Marks (1962)
Brättingstorpsvägen 28, 511 58 Kinna
Tel (0320) 14220
Fax (0320) 12516
Holes 18 L 5530 m Par 70
V'tors H
Fees 160kr (200kr)
Loc Kinna, 30 km S of Borås
Arch Sköld/Sederholm

Onsjö (1974)
Box 6331 A, 462 42 Vänersborg
Tel (0521) 68870
Fax (0521) 17106
Email info@onsjogk.golf.se
Holes 18 L 5730 m SSS 72
V'tors U
Fees 200kr
Loc 3 km S of Vänersborg. 80 km N of Gothenburg
Arch Sköld/Linde

Ringenäs (1987)
Strandlida, 305 91 Halmstad
Tel (035) 59050
Fax (035) 59135
Holes 27 L 5395-5615 m Par 71-72
V'tors H
Fees 180–240kr (240kr)
Loc 10 km NW of Halmstad
Arch Sune Linde

Skogaby (1988)
312 93 Laholm
Tel (0430) 60190
Fax (0430) 60225
Holes 18 L 5555 m Par 71
V'tors U H
Fees 140kr (180kr)
Loc 10 km E of Laholm. 30 km SE of Halmstad
Arch J Rosengren

Töreboda (1965)
Box 18, 545 21 Töreboda
Tel (0506) 12305
Fax (0506) 12305
Holes 18 L 5355 m SSS 70
V'tors U
Fees 160kr
Loc 7 km E of Töreboda

Trollhättan (1963)
Stora Ekeskogen, 466 91 Sollebrunn
Tel (0520) 441000
Fax (0520) 441049
Holes 18 L 6200 m SSS 73
V'tors U
Fees 200kr

Loc Koberg, 20 km SE of Trollhättan
Arch Nils Sköld

Ulricehamn (1947)
523 33 Ulricehamn
Tel (0321) 10021
Fax (0321) 16004
Holes 18 L 5509 m Par 71
V'tors WD–H
Fees 160kr (200kr)
Loc Backasen, 2 km E of Ulricehamn

Vara-Bjertorp
Bjertorp, 535 91 Kvänum
Tel (0512) 20261
Fax (0512) 20261
Holes 18 L 6005 m Par 73
V'tors H
Fees 140kr (180kr)
Loc 10 km N of Vara. 110 km NE of Gothenburg (E20)
Arch Jan Sederholm

Varberg (1950)
Himle, 430 10 Tvååker
Tel (0340) 43446/37496
Fax (0340) 37440/43447
Holes East 18 L 5700 m CR 72.9
      West 18 L 6435 m CR 76.5
V'tors H
Fees 240–280kr
Loc East:15 km E of Varberg. West:8 km S of Varberg, nr E6
Arch Sköld/Nordström

Vinberg (1992)
Sannagård, 311 95 Falkenberg
Tel (0346) 19020
Fax (0346) 19042
Holes 18 L 3556 m Par 64
V'tors U
Fees 130kr (160kr)
Loc 5 km E of Falkenberg on coast
Arch Nilsson/Haglund

Stockholm

Ågesta (1958)
123 52 Farsta
Tel (08) 604 4538
Fax (08) 604 4397
Holes 18 L 5658 m SSS 72
       9 L 3404 m SSS 62
V'tors WD–U
Fees 300kr
Loc Farsta, 15 km S of Stockholm
Arch Sköld/Sederholm

Botkyrka
Malmbro Gård, 147 91 Gröding
Tel (08) 530 29650
Fax (08) 530 29409
Holes 18 holes Par 73
       9 hole Par 3 course

For list of abbreviations see page 527

V'tors WD–U H WE–H after 1pm
Fees 250kr (300kr)
Loc 30 km S of Stockholm

Bro-Bålsta (1978)
Ginnlögs Väg, 197 91 Bro
Tel (08) 582 41310
Fax (08) 582 40006
Holes 18 L 6505 m Par 73
9 L 1715 m Par 31
V'tors WD–H (max 36) WE–NA
Fees 300kr (350kr)
Loc 40 km NW of Stockholm
Arch Peter Nordwall

Djursholm (1931)
Hagbardsvägen 1, 182 63 Djursholm
Tel (08) 755 1477
Fax (08) 755 5932
Holes 18 L 5595 m SSS 71
9 L 4400 m SSS 64
V'tors WD–U H before 3pm –M
after 3pm WE–M before 3pm
–U H after 3pm
Fees 400kr
Loc 12 km N of Stockholm

Drottningholm (1958)
PO Box 183, 178 93 Drottningholm
Tel (08) 759 0085
Fax (08) 759 0851
Holes 18 L 5825 m SSS 72
V'tors WD–U H before 3pm –M
after 3pm WE–M before 3pm
–U H after 3pm
Fees 300kr
Loc 16 km W of Stockholm
Arch Sundblom/Sköld

Fågelbro G&CC
Fågelbro Säteri, 139 60 Värmdö
Tel (08) 571 40115
Fax (08) 571 40671
Holes 18 L 5445 m Par 71
V'tors WD–H WE–M
Fees 300kr (400kr)
Loc 35 km E of Stockholm
Arch Eriksson/Oredsson

Haninge (1983)
Årsta Slott, 136 91 Haninge
Tel (08) 500 32240/32270
Fax (08) 500 32340
Holes 27 L 5930 m Par 73
V'tors WD–U before 1pm –M after
1pm WE–M before 1pm –U
after 1pm
Fees 300kr
Loc 30 km S of Stockholm towards
Nynäshamn
Arch Jan Sederholm

Ingarö (1962)
Fogelvik, 134 64 Ingarö
Tel (08) 570 28244
Fax (08) 570 28379
Holes 18 L 5515 m SSS 71
18 L 5618 m SSS 72

V'tors WD–U H WE–NA before
3pm
Fees 250kr (300kr)
Loc 30 km E of Stockholm via
Route 222
Arch Sköld/Eriksson

Johannesberg G&CC
(1990)
762 95 Rimbo
Tel (08) 512 92480
Fax (08) 512 92390
Holes 18 L 6328 m SSS 74
9 hole course
V'tors H
Fees 200kr (260kr)
Loc 55 km N of Stockholm
Arch Donald Steel

Lidingö (1933)
Box 1035, 181 21 Lidingö
Tel (08) 765 7911
Fax (08) 765 5479
Holes 18 L 5770 m SSS 71
V'tors WD–U H before 3pm –NA
after 3pm Sat–NA Sun–NA
before 1pm
Fees 400kr
Loc 6 km NE of Stockholm
Arch MacDonald/Sundblom

Lindö (1978)
186 92 Vallentuna
Tel (08) 511 72260
Fax (08) 511 74122
Holes 18 L 2850 m Par 71
V'tors U
Fees 300kr (400kr)
Loc Vallentuna, 20 km N of
Stockholm
Arch Åke Persson

Lindo Park
Lindö Park, 186 92 Vallentuna
Tel (08) 511 70055 (Bookings)
Fax (08) 511 70613
Holes 18 L 5800 m SSS 72
V'tors U H–book day before play
Fees 300kr (400kr)
Loc 30 km N of Stockholm
Arch Persson/Bruce

Nynäshamn (1977)
Box 4, 148 21 Ösmo
Tel (08) 520 27190/520 38666
Fax (08) 520 38613
Holes 27 L 5690 m SSS 72
V'tors H–phone first
Fees 250kr (300kr)
Loc Ösmo, 40 km S of Stockholm
Arch Sune Linde

Österakers
Hagby 1, 184 92 Akersberga
Tel (08) 540 85165
Fax (08) 540 66832
Holes 18 L 5792 m Par 72
18 L 5780 m Par 72

V'tors WD–H WE–M before 2pm
–H after 2pm
Fees 300kr (350kr)
Loc 30 km NE of Stockholm
Arch Sederholm/Tumba

Österhaninge (1992)
Husby, 136 91 Haninge
Tel (08) 500 32077
Fax (08) 500 32293
Holes 18 L 5440 m Par 70
V'tors H
Fees 180kr (230kr)
Loc 35 km S of Stockholm
Arch Bengt Lorichs

PGA European Tour
(1992)
Box 133, 196 21 Kungsängen
Tel (08) 584 50730
Fax (08) 581 71002
Holes Kings 18 L 6200 m Par 72
Queens 18 L 5500 m Par 70
V'tors U H
Fees Kings–450kr Queens–300kr
Loc 25 km W of Stockholm via
E18 to Brunna
Arch Anders Forsbrand

Saltsjöbaden (1929)
Box 51, 133 21 Saltsjöbaden
Tel (08) 717 0125
Fax (08) 717 9713
Holes 18 L 5685 m SSS 72
9 L 3640 m SSS 60
V'tors WD–U WE–M before 2pm
Fees D–250kr
Loc 15 km E of Stockholm via
Route 228

Sollentuna (1967)
Skillingegården, 191 77 Sollentuna
Tel (08) 754 3625
Fax (08) 754 1823
Holes 18 L 5895 m SSS 72
V'tors WD–H before 3pm WE–H
after 3pm
Fees 260kr
Loc 19 km N of Stockholm. 1 km
W of E4 (Rotebro)
Arch Nils Sköld

Stockholm (1904)
Kevingestrand 20, 182 57 Danderyd
Tel (08) 544 90710
Fax (08) 544 90712
Holes 18 L 5180 m SSS 69
V'tors WD–M after 3pm WE–M
before 3pm
Fees 340kr (420kr)
Loc 7 km NE of Stockholm via
Route E18

Täby (1968)
Skålhamra Gård, 187 70 Täby
Tel (08) 510 23261
Fax (08) 510 23441
Holes 18 L 5776 m SSS 73

West Central

V'tors WD–H
Fees 300–400kr
Loc 15 km N of Stockholm
Arch Nils Sköld

Ullna (1981)
Rosenkälla, 184 92 Åkersberga
Tel (08) 510 26075
Fax (08) 510 26068
Holes 18 L 5825 m Par 72
V'tors H
Fees 425kr
Loc 20 km N of Stockholm via Route E18
Arch Sven Tumba

Ulriksdal
Box 8033, 171 08 Solna
Tel (08) 857931
Holes 18 L 3900 m SSS 61
V'tors H
Fees 130kr (160kr)
Loc 8 km N of Stockholm
Arch Alec Backhurst

Vallentuna
Box 266, 186 24 Vallentuna
Tel (08) 514 30560/1
Fax (08) 511 72370
Holes 18 L 5700 m SSS 72
V'tors WD–U WE–U after 1pm
Fees 250kr (300kr)
Loc 35 km N of Stockholm
Arch Sune Linde

Viksjö (1969)
Fjällens Gård, 175 45 Järfälla
Tel (08) 580 31300/31310
Fax (08) 580 31340
Holes 18 L 5930 m SSS 73
9 L 1830 m Par 30
V'tors U
Fees 9 hole:150kr (150kr)
18 hole:300kr (300kr)
Loc 18 km NW of Stockholm

Wäsby
Box 2017, 194 02 Upplands Väsby
Tel (08) 510 23345/23177
Fax (08) 510 23364
Holes 18 L 6170 m SSS 72
9 hole course
V'tors WD–U WE–H
Fees 170kr (220kr)
Loc 20 km N of Stockholm. 20 km S of airport
Arch Björn Eriksson

Wermdö G&CC (1966)
Torpa, 139 40 Värmdö
Tel (08) 570 20849
Fax (08) 570 20840
Holes 18 L 5577 m Par 72
V'tors H WE–NA before 2pm
Fees 300kr (350kr)
Loc 25 km E of Stockholm via Route 222
Arch Nils Sköld

Arvika (1974)
Box 197, 671 25 Arvika
Tel (0570) 54133
Fax (0570) 54233
Holes 18 L 5815 m Par 72
V'tors U
Fees 180kr
Loc 11 km E of Arvika (Route 61)
Arch Nils Sköld

Billerud (1961)
Valnäs, 660 40 Segmon
Tel (0555) 91313
Fax (0555) 91306
Holes 18 L 5874 m SSS 72
V'tors H
Fees 180kr
Loc Valnäs, 15 km N of Säffle
Arch Brasier/Sköld

Eda (1992)
Noresund, 670 40 Åmotfors
Tel (0571) 34101
Fax (0571) 34191
Holes 18 L 5575 m Par 72
V'tors U
Fees 160kr (180kr)
Loc 30 km W of Arvika
Arch Leif Nilsson

Färgelanda
Box 23, 458 21 Färgelanda
Tel (0528) 20385
Fax (0528) 20045
Holes 18 L 6000 m SSS 71
V'tors U
Fees 160kr
Loc 23 km N of Uddevalla. 100 km N of Gothenburg
Arch Åke Persson

Fjällbacka (1965)
450 71 Fjällbacka
Tel (0525) 31150
Fax (0525) 32122
Holes 18 L 5850 m SSS 72
V'tors H
Fees 180kr (240kr)
Loc 2 km N of Fjällbacka (Route 163)

Forsbacka (1969)
Box 136, 662 23 Åmål
Tel (0532) 43055
Holes 18 L 5860 m SSS 72
V'tors U
Fees 200kr
Loc 6 km W of Åmål (Route 164)

Hammarö (1991)
Sätter Tallbacken, 663 91 Hammarö
Tel (054) 521621
Fax (054) 521863
Holes 18 L 6200 m Par 72

Karlskoga (1975)
Bricketorp 647, 691 94 Karlskoga
Tel (0586) 728190
Fax (0586) 728417
Holes 18 L 5705 m Par 72
Fees 180kr
Loc Valåsen, 5 km E of Karlskoga via Route E18
Arch Sköld/Sederholm/Engdahl

Karlstad (1957)
Höja 510, 655 92 Karlstad
Tel (054) 866353
Fax (054) 866478
Holes 18 L 5970 m Par 72
9 L 2875 m Par 36
V'tors H
Fees 250kr
Loc 8 km N of Karlstad (Route 63)
Arch Sköld/Linde

Kristinehamn (1974)
Box 337, 681 26 Kristinehamn
Tel (0550) 82310
Fax (0550) 19535
Holes 18 L 5800 m SSS 72
V'tors H
Fees 200kr
Loc 3 km N of Kristinehamn
Arch Sune Linde

Lyckorna (1967)
Box 66, 459 22 Ljungskile
Tel (0522) 20176
Fax (0522) 22304
Holes 18 L 5820 m SSS 72
V'tors H
Fees 200kr
Loc 20 km S of Uddevalla
Arch Anders Amilon

Orust (1981)
Morlanda 9404, 474 93 Ellös
Tel (0304) 53170
Fax (0304) 53174
Holes 18 L 5770 m SSS 72
V'tors H
Fees 160kr (250kr)
Loc Ellös, 10 km from Henån. 80 km N of Gothenburg
Arch Lars Andreasson

Saxå (1964)
Saxån, 682 92 Filipstad
Tel (0590) 24070
Fax (0590) 24101
Holes 18 L 5680 m Par 72
V'tors U
Fees 160kr
Loc 20 km NE of Filipstad (Route 63)
Arch Sköld/Bäckman

Skaftö (1963)
Röd PL 4476, 450 34 Fiskebäckskil
Tel (0523) 23211
Fax (0523) 23215
Holes 18 L 4748 m SSS 68
V'tors WD–H
Fees 100–220kr
Loc 40 km W of Uddevalla, through Fiskebäckskil
Arch Sköld/Sederholm

Strömstad (1967)
Golfbanevägen, 452 90 Strömstad 1
Tel (0526) 61788
Fax (0526) 14766
Holes 18 L 5615 m SSS 71
V'tors H
Fees 180kr (200kr)
Loc 6 km N of Strömstad
Arch Sköld/Sederholm

Sunne (1970)
Box 108, 686 23 Sunne
Tel (0565) 14100/14210
Fax (0565) 14855
Holes 18 hole course SSS 72
V'tors H
Fees 200kr
Loc 2 km S of Sunne. 60 km N of Karlstad on Route 45
Arch Jan Sederholm

Torreby (1961)
Torreby Slott, 455 93 Munkedal
Tel (0524) 21365/21109
Fax (0524) 21351
Holes 18 L 5885 m Par 72
V'tors H
Fees 200kr
Loc Munkedal 8 km. Uddevalla 30 km
Arch Douglas Brasier

Uddeholm (1965)
Risäter 20, 683 93 Råda
Tel (0563) 60564
Fax (0563) 60017
Holes 18 L 5830 m SSS 72
V'tors U H
Fees D–160kr
Loc Lake Råda, 80 km N of Karlstad, via RD62

Switzerland

Bern

Blumisberg (1959)
3184 Wünnewil
Tel (026) 496 34 38
Fax (026) 496 35 23
Holes 18 L 6048 m SSS 73
V'tors WD–U H WE–M
Fees 80fr (80fr)
Loc Wünnewil, 16 km SW of Bern
Arch B von Limburger

Les Bois (1988)
Case Postale 26, 2336 Les Bois
Tel (032) 961 10 03
Fax (032) 961 10 17
Holes 9 L 3000 m Par 72
V'tors WD–U WE–M
Fees 75fr (90fr)
Loc 12 km NE of La Chaux-de-Fonds, on Basel road
Arch Jeremy Pern

Neuchâtel (1928)
Hameau de Voeus, 2072 Saint-Blaise
Tel (032) 753 55 50
Fax (032) 753 29 40
Holes 18 L 5944 m SSS 71
V'tors H
Fees 70fr (90fr)
Loc Voens/Saint-Blaise, 5 km E of Neuchâtel. 30 km W of Bern

Payerne (1996)
Domaine des Invouardes, 1530 Payerne
Tel (026) 660 2385
Fax (026) 660 4672
Holes 18 L 5450 m Par 70
V'tors U H
Fees 70fr (90fr)
Loc 50 km W of Bern
Arch Yves Bureau

Wallenried (1992)
1784 Wallenried
Tel (026) 684 84 80
Fax (026) 684 84 90
Holes 18 L 6000 m Par 72
V'tors WD–U H
Loc 6 km W of Fribourg
Arch Ruzzo Reuss

Wylihof (1994)
4542 Luterbach
Tel (032) 682 28 28
Fax (032) 682 65 17
Holes 18 L 6580 yds Par 73
V'tors WD–U H–max 30 WE–M H
Fees 90fr (90fr)
Loc 40 km N of Bern. 90 km W of Zürich
Arch Ruzzo Reuss von Plauen

Bernese Oberland

Interlaken-Unterseen (1964)
Postfach 110, 3800 Interlaken
Tel (033) 823 60 16
Fax (033) 823 42 03
Holes 18 L 5980 m SSS 72
V'tors H
Fees 70fr (80fr)
Loc Interlaken 3 km
Arch Donald Harradine

Riederalp (1986)
3987 Riederalp
Tel (027) 927 29 32
Fax (027) 927 29 32
Holes 9 L 3066 m SSS 55
V'tors U
Fees 45fr
Loc 10 km NE of Brig
Arch Donald Harradine

Lake Geneva & South West

Bonmont (1983)
Château de Bonmont, 1275 Chéserex
Tel (022) 369 23 45
Fax (022) 369 24 17
Holes 18 L 6165 m SSS 72
V'tors WD–restricted WE–M
Fees WD–90fr
Loc 3 km from Nyon. 30 km NE of Geneva
Arch Donald Harradine

Les Coullaux (1989)
1846 Chessel
Tel (024) 481 22 46
Fax (024) 481 22 46
Holes 9 L 2940 m Par 58
V'tors U
Fees 25–40fr (30–50fr)
Loc Chessel, between Evian and Montreux
Arch Donald Harradine

Crans-sur-Sierre (1906)
C P 112, 3963 Crans-sur-Sierre
Tel (027) 41 21 68
Fax (027) 41 95 68
Holes 18 L 6170 m SSS 72
9 L 2729 m SSS 35
9 hole Par 3 course
V'tors H
Fees On application
Loc 20 km E of Sion. Geneva 2 hrs

Domaine Impérial (1987)
Villa Prangins, 1196 Gland
Tel (022) 999 06 00
Fax (022) 999 06 06
Holes 18 L 6297 m SSS 74
V'tors WD–H exc Mon am
Fees WD–150fr
Loc Nyon, 20 km N of Geneva
Arch Pete Dye

Geneva (1923)
70 Route de la Capite, 1223 Cologny
Tel (022) 707 48 40
Fax (022) 707 48 20
Holes 18 L 6250 m Par 72
V'tors WD–am only Tues–Fri WE–M
Fees 100fr
Loc 4 km from centre of Geneva
Arch Robert Trent Jones Sr

For list of abbreviations see page 527

Lausanne (1921)
Route du Golf 3, 1000 Lausanne 25
Tel (021) 784 84 84
Fax (021) 784 84 80
Holes 18 L 6295 m SSS 74
V'tors H
Fees 90fr (110fr)
Loc 7 km N of Lausanne towards Le Mont
Arch Narbel/Harradine/Pern

Montreux (1898)
54 Route d'Evian, 1860 Aigle
Tel (024) 466 46 16
Fax (024) 466 60 47
Holes 18 L 6143 m Par 72 SSS 73
V'tors H
Fees 70fr (90fr)
Loc Aigle, 15 km S of Montreux
Arch Donald Harradine

Sion (1995)
CP 639, Rte Vissigen 150, 1951 Sion
Tel (027) 203 79 00
Fax (027) 203 79 01
Holes 9 L 2315 m Par 66
V'tors H–booking necessary
Fees 18 holes–61fr (69fr)
 9 holes–37fr (46fr)
Loc Sion, 80 km SE of Montreux
Arch JL Tronchet

Verbier (1970)
1936 Verbier
Tel (079) 412 86 48,
 (027) 771 53 14 (Season)
Fax (027) 771 60 93/771 53 14
Holes 18 L 5300 m Par 70
 18 hole Par 3 course
V'tors U
Fees 25fr (50fr)
Loc Centre of Verbier
Arch Donald Harradine

Villars (1922)
C P 152, 1884 Villars
Tel (024) 495 42 14
Fax (024) 495 42 18
Holes 18 L 4093 m SSS 61
V'tors U
Fees 50fr (65fr)
Loc 7 km E of Villars towards Les Diablerets
Arch Thierry Sprecher

Lugano & Ticino

Lugano (1923)
6983 Magliaso
Tel (091) 606 15 57/606 58 01
Fax (091) 606 65 58
Holes 18 L 5760 m SSS 71
V'tors H–(max 30)
Fees 85fr (110fr)
Loc 8 km W of Lugano towards Ponte Tresa
Arch Harradine/Robinson

Patriziale Ascona (1928)
Via al Lido 81, 6612 Ascona
Tel (091) 791 21 32
Fax (091) 791 07 06
Holes 18 L 5959 m SSS 71
V'tors H–max 30
Fees 80fr
Loc 5 km W of Locarno
Arch CK Cotton

St Moritz & Engadine

Arosa (1944)
Postfach 95, 7050 Arosa
Tel (081) 377 42 42
Fax (081) 377 46 77
Holes 9 L 4450 m Par 66 SSS 64
V'tors U
Fees 50fr
Loc 30 km S of Chur
Arch Donald Harradine

Bad Ragaz (1957)
Hans Albrecht Strasse, 7310 Bad Ragaz
Tel (081) 303 37 17
Fax (081) 303 37 27
Holes 18 L 5750 m SSS 71
V'tors H
Fees D–100fr
Loc 20 km N of Chur. 100 km SE of Zürich
Arch Donald Harradine

Davos (1929)
Postfach, 7260 Davos Dorf
Tel (081) 46 56 34
Fax (081) 46 25 55
Holes 18 L 5208 yds Par 68
V'tors WD–U
Fees On application
Loc 1 km outside Davos
Arch Donald Harradine

Engadin (1893)
7503 Samedan
Tel (081) 851 04 66
Fax (081) 851 04 67
Holes 18 L 6350 m SSS 73
V'tors H
Fees 90fr
Loc Samedan, 6 km NE of St Moritz
Arch M Verdieri

Lenzerheide Valbella (1950)
7078 Lenzerheide
Tel (081) 385 13 13
Fax (081) 385 13 19
Holes 18 L 5274 m SSS 69
V'tors H
Fees 60–80fr
Loc 20 km S of Chur towards St Moritz
Arch Donald Harradine

Vulpera (1923)
7552 Vulpera Spa
Tel (081) 864 96 88
Fax (081) 864 96 88
Holes 9 L 1982 m SSS 62
V'tors H
Fees 50fr (60fr) W–250fr
Loc Tarasp, nr Vulpera. 60 km NE of St Moritz
Arch Dell/Spencer

Zürich & North

Breitenloo (1964)
8309 Oberwil b. Bassersdorf
Tel (01) 836 40 80
Fax (01) 837 10 85
Holes 18 L 6125 m Par 72 SSS 72
V'tors WD–H by appointment
 WE–M H
Fees 100fr
Loc 10 km NE of Zürich Airport
Arch Harradine/Pennink

Bürgenstock (1927)
6363 Bürgenstock
Tel (041) 610 24 34
Fax (041) 610 76 88
Holes 9 L 2200 m Par 33
V'tors I or H
Fees 60fr (80fr)
Loc 15 km S of Lucerne
Arch Fritz Frey

Dolder (1907)
Kurhausstrasse 66, 8032 Zürich
Tel (01) 261 50 45
Fax (01) 261 53 02
Holes 9 L 1735 m SSS 58
V'tors WD–H WE–M
Fees WD–70fr
Loc Zürich

Entfelden (1988)
Postfach 230, Muhenstrasse 52, 5036 Oberentfelden
Tel (062) 723 89 84
Fax (062) 723 84 36
Holes 9 L 3960 m SSS 60
V'tors H
Fees 50fr (70fr)
Loc 50 km W of Zürich
Arch Donald Harradine

Erlen (1988)
Schlossgut Eppishausen, Schlossstr 7, 8586 Erlen
Tel (071) 648 29 30
Fax (071) 648 29 80
Holes 18 L 5913 m SSS 71
V'tors H
Fees 80fr (110fr)
Loc 30 km NW of St Gallen.
 60 km W of Zürich
Arch Deutsche Golfconsult

For list of abbreviations see page 527

818 Switzerland

Hittnau-Zürich G&CC (1964)
8335 Hittnau
Tel (01) 950 24 42
Fax (01) 951 01 66
Holes 18 L 5773 m SSS 71
V'tors WD–U WE–M
Fees WD–90fr
Loc Hittnau, 30 km E of Zürich

Küssnacht (1994)
Sekretariat/Grossarni, 6403 Küssnacht am Rigi
Tel (041) 850 70 60
Fax (041) 850 70 41
Holes 18 L 5397 m Par 68
V'tors WD–U H WE–M H
Fees 70–80fr (100fr)
Loc 20 km NE of Lucerne
Arch Peter Harradine

Lucerne (1903)
6006 Dietschiberg, 6006 Luzern
Tel (041) 420 97 87
Fax (041) 420 82 48
Holes 18 L 6082 m Par 72 SSS 71–73
V'tors H
Fees 80fr (100fr)
Loc Lucerne 2 km

Ostschweizerischer (1948)
9246 Niederbüren
Tel (071) 422 18 56
Fax (071) 422 18 25
Email www.osgc.ch
Holes 18 L 5920 m SSS 71
V'tors WD–H
Fees D–80fr (100fr)
Loc Niederbüren, 25 km NW of St Gallen
Arch Donald Harradine

Schinznach-Bad (1929)
5116 Schinznach-Bad
Tel (056) 443 12 26
Fax (056) 443 34 83
Holes 9 L 5670 m Par 71
V'tors WD–U
Fees 70fr
Loc 6 km S of Brugg, 35 km W of Zürich

Schönenberg (1967)
8824 Schönenberg
Tel (01) 788 90 40
Fax (01) 788 90 45
Holes 18 L 6340 m SSS 74
V'tors WD–H–by appointment WE–M H
Fees 90fr (150fr)
Loc 20 km S of Zürich
Arch Donald Harradine

Sempachersee (1996)
6024 Hildisrieden, Lucerne
Tel (041) 462 71 71
Fax (041) 462 71 72
Holes 18 L 6130 m Par 72 SSS 72
9 L 3950 m Par 31
V'tors U H
Fees 80fr (100fr)
Loc 13 km NW of Lucerne
Arch Kurt Rossknecht

Zürich-Zumikon (1931)
8126 Zumikon
Tel (01) 918 00 50
Fax (01) 918 00 37
Holes 18 L 6360 m SSS 74
V'tors WD–by appointment WE–M
Fees WD–100fr
Loc Zürich 10 km
Arch Donald Harradine

Turkey

Gloria Golf
Acisu Mevkii PK27 Belek, Serik, Antalya
Tel (242) 715 15 20
Fax (242) 715 15 25
Holes 18 holes Par 72
9 hole Academy course
V'tors U
Loc Antalya
Arch Michel Gayon

Kemer G&CC
Goturk Koyu Mevkii Kemerburgaz, Eyup, Istanbul
Tel (212) 239 79 13
Fax (212) 239 73 76
Holes 18 holes Par 74
V'tors U
Loc Istanbul
Arch J Dudok van Heel

Klassis G&CC
Sineklikoyu Mevkii, Silivri, Istanbul
Tel (212) 748 46 00
Fax (212) 748 46 43
Holes 18 holes Par 72
9 hole Academy course
V'tors U
Loc Istanbul
Arch Tony Jacklin

National Golf Club
Belek Turizm Merkesi, 07500 Serik, Antalya
Tel (242) 725 54 00
Fax (242) 725 55 22

Holes 18 holes Par 72
9 hole Academy course
V'tors U
Loc Antalya
Arch Feherty/Jones

Nobilis Golf
Acisu Mevkii, Belek, Antalya
Tel (242) 715 19 86/7/8
Fax (242) 715 14 79
Holes 18 holes Par 72
V'tors U
Loc Antalya
Arch Dave Thomas

Tat Golf International
Belek International Golf, Kum Tepesi Belek, 07500 Serik, Antalya
Tel (242) 725 53 03
Fax (242) 725 52 99
Holes 27 holes Par 72
V'tors U
Loc Antalya
Arch Hawtree

Stop Press

Germany – Munich & South Bavaria

Donauwörth (1995)
Lederstatt 1, 86609 Donauwörth
Tel (0906) 4044
Fax (0906) 4044
Holes 18 L 6039 m Par 72
V'tors U H
Fees 60DM (80DM)
Loc 40 km N of Augsburg
Arch Peter Harradine

Italy – Como/Milan/Bergamo

Bogogno (1996)
Via Sant'Isidoro 1, 28010 Bogogno
Tel (0322) 863339
Fax (0322) 863798
Holes 18 L 6171 m Par 72
V'tors U
Fees 100.000L (130.000L)
Loc 25 km N of Novara
Arch Robert von Hagge

PART XI

Government of the Game

The R&A and the Rules of Golf – the Background	820
The Royal and Ancient Golf Club of St Andrews – Functions	822
Other Governing Bodies	826
Championship and International Match Conditions	831
Golf Associations	835
Addresses of Golfing Organisations Worldwide	838

The R&A and the Rules of Golf – the Background

Keith Mackie

Golf was reputed to be a popular sport when St Andrews University was founded in 1413. By 1457 it had gained such a hold that able-bodied citizens were neglecting their archery practice and the sport was banned by King James II in an Act of the Scottish Parliament.

Yet no trace of written rules for playing the game has been discovered before those set down in 1744 by the Gentlemen Golfers at Leith, later to become known as the Honourable Company of Edinburgh Golfers. And for a further century and a half, each individual club or society was at liberty to play by whatever rules they chose.

Golf had been established for close on 500 years before a universally accepted code of laws was laid down to control the game wherever it was played.

In those far-off days at the dawn of golf on Scotland's east coast, each community, perhaps even each individual match, devised its own rules for coping with broken clubs and unplayable lies. By experience and tradition a broad code of conduct became accepted, and it was only when the golfers at Leith staged an open competition that it was necessary to commit those rules to paper.

Expansion of the game

It was the explosive expansion of the game at the close of the 19th century that brought the rules question to a head. Between 1886 and 1895 the number of golf clubs and societies in Britain increased from 171 to almost 1000, and prompted the editor of *Golf* magazine to speak out forcefully on the vexed rules question. In an editorial he advocated the formation of a golfers' association.

He wrote: 'Almost alone among high-class sports, Golf stands out as a conspicuous example of a difficult and intricate game played by thousands and thousands of our educated classes absolutely without any organisation, with no cohesion among the body of the players, with no code of rules made by duly accredited representatives of golf as a whole.'

It was to be five years and many anguished and angry letters in the columns of the magazine later before the leading clubs of the time asked the Royal and Ancient Golf Club of St Andrews to take responsibility for the game.

Long regarded as the spiritual leader in golf, the club had issued a set of St Andrews Rules which formed the basis of play at most clubs, but each was free to follow or ignore these laws. Any disputes had to be decided within each club.

The first Rules Committee

The R&A's first proposal proved, ironically, to be too democratic. It was suggested that seven members of the R&A and seven representatives from a well-chosen list of leading clubs around Britain should form the first rules committee. But there was a violent reaction from several old-established clubs not included in the list. Edinburgh Burgess members insisted in October of 1896 that they would not 'tolerate the supremacy of minor clubs'.

Such obduracy finally led the R&A, in September of the following year, to appoint 15 of its own members to the Rules of Golf Committee and assume control of the game from that moment on. Wisely, six members within that number were resident in England and played their golf at a variety of the leading clubs.

Apart from the United States Golf Association, which looks after its own affairs, there are now more than 100 countries, associations and unions affiliated to the R&A and submitting to its jurisdiction in the administration of the rules.

In reality the laws of the game are worldwide, any differences between America and the rest of the world having been ironed out at a meeting in a committee room at the House of Lords in 1951. The R&A and USGA consult regularly on the rules and issue a combined code which is updated on a four-yearly basis, the next review to come into effect on 1st January, 2000.

Changes

Much of the spirit of the game remains from the 13 basic laws first written down in Edinburgh in 1744, but today's golfers, accustomed as they are to velvet-smooth putting greens, would recoil in horror at Rule 1: 'You must tee your ball within a club's length of the hole'.

They might also object to a rule, which found favour for only six years in the 1850s, stipulating

that a player declaring his ball unplayable had to stand aside and let his opponent have two attempts at moving it, those two strokes counting against the original player's score if successful.

Milestones

Significant milestones in the history of the game's rules have often centred around the development of golf balls and clubs. The introduction of solid gutta percha golf balls in place of the less durable and more expensive feathery ones gave new impetus to the game, but some examples were prone to breaking up in flight. In 1850 a new rule allowed another ball to be dropped without penalty at the spot where the largest piece came to earth!

In 1904 the time allowed in searching for a ball was reduced from ten to five minutes. Five years later the first limitations were placed on the design of golf clubs. The Rules of Golf Committee would not sanction 'any substantial departure from the traditional and accepted form and make of golf clubs, which in its opinion consists of a plain shaft and a head which contains no mechanical contrivance such as springs.'

But it was not until 1921 that attempts were made to limit the distance a golf ball would travel. Two years earlier the committee had resolved to preserve the balance between power and the length of holes and to retain the special features of the game. It felt this could only be achieved by limiting the power of the ball. A maximum weight of 1.62 ounces and a minimum diameter of 1.62 inches was set.

Steel shafts were first permitted in 1929 and gave rise to a proliferation of clubs for every golf course situation, many players inflicting 20 and more on their long-suffering caddies. In 1939 a limit of 14 clubs was imposed.

Slow play, such a contentious issue in the closing years of the 20th century, was also a problem as early as 1949 and in that year club committees were empowered to disqualify players who unduly delayed others. This rule was modified in 1952 to loss of hole or a two-stroke penalty, with disqualification reserved for repeated offences.

When the R&A and the USGA agreed the first worldwide unified code of rules to come into operation in 1952 it finally sounded the deathknell for the stymie. Until that time players were forced to chip over an opponent's ball coming to rest between their own ball and the hole in matchplay.

The convention of dropping a ball over the shoulder when taking relief was changed in 1984, when players were instructed to hold the ball out at arm's length and shoulder height.

The last really significant rule change that had a resounding effect was the banning of the small 'British' ball. Its withdrawal was phased over several years in favour of the 1.68 inch American size, but was finally written out of the rule book in 1990.

No longer a minority sport

In little more than a century the game has grown out of all recognition, from a minority sport played at a handful of Scottish courses to a game enjoyed by millions in countries around the globe. To cover the almost infinite variety of situations that can occur, the original 13 rules of the game have expanded in that time to 34, many with a dozen or more sub-sections, plus definitions and appendices – and they are under constant review.

It is a credit to the lawmakers and to new generations of golfers that the game has retained its essential qualities and its integrity.

The Royal and Ancient Golf Club of St Andrews – Functions

The functions for which the Royal and Ancient Golf Club of St Andrews (the R&A) is responsible fall into three clearly defined categories: the international functions of the R&A as a governing authority for golf; the national functions of the Club as the body responsible for organising and running championships and international matches; and the functions of a private club with a wide national and international membership.

Responsibility for directing and coordinating the three functions of the R&A rests with the Club's General Committee, which controls all matters of policy. The Committee consists of 16 R&A members, eight of whom are elected by the Club; the other eight *ex officio* members are the Captain and the chairmen of the Finance, Implements and Ball, Membership, Club, Rules of Golf, Championship and Amateur Status Committees.

The execution of the decisions of the Club Committees and of the decisions taken by the members at Business Meetings is in the hands of the Secretary of the R&A, who is assisted by several senior officers and the appropriate infrastructure of secretaries and clerical staff.

International Functions

In 1897 the Royal & Ancient became the governing authority on the Rules of Golf at the suggestion of the leading golf clubs in the United Kingdom at the time. Since then an ever-increasing number of countries have sought affiliation to it, until today they number over 80, including several other unions and associations. In its negotiations with the United States Golf Association (USGA) on matters pertaining to the Rules of Golf, therefore, the R&A is not merely representing Great Britain and Ireland but these many countries as well.

Likewise, the R&A represents these countries in matters pertaining to the Rules of Amateur Status and the running of the Open and Amateur Championships, which it took over in 1919.

The R&A also supplies one of each of the two joint chairmen and joint secretaries of the World Amateur Golf Council, which is responsible for the organisation of all World Amateur Team Championships; and there is a close liaison at all times with the Professional Golfers' Association and the PGA European Tour.

The international functions of the R&A are chiefly attended to by a number of committees.

Rules of Golf Committee

The Rules of Golf Committee exists for the purpose of reviewing the Rules of Golf and of making decisions on their interpretation and publishing these decisions where necessary.

The Committee consists of 12 members elected by the Club, of whom three retire each year and are not eligible for re-election for one year (except in the case of the Chairman and Deputy Chairman), and of up to 12 additional persons invited annually to join the Committee from golf authorities at home and abroad. The bodies presently represented are:

Council of National Golf Unions
United States Golf Association
European Golf Association (2)
Australian Golf Union
New Zealand Golf Association
Royal Canadian Golf Association
South African Golf Union
Asia-Pacific Golf Confederation
South American Golf Federation
Japan Golf Association
Ladies' Golf Union

Revision of the Rules of Golf

When amendments to the Rules are under consideration, the R&A works closely with the USGA (as the only other governing authority for the Rules of Golf) for the purpose of maintaining uniformity in the Rules and their interpretation. Every four years a conference takes place with the USGA in order to discuss proposals for changes. Although the conference only takes place every four years, the Rules are under constant review and investigations as to possible improvements start not long after a revision has taken place, so that ample time can be given to consult with interested parties.

Two years after a revision, an important meeting is held with the USGA in the United States at the time of the Walker Cup to discuss progress and to start clearing the ground for the next conference.

Decisions

The Rules of Golf Committee has a Decisions Sub-Committee which answers queries from clubs and from all the Unions and Associations affiliated to the R&A. Those decisions which seem to establish important or interesting points of interpretation are published annually by the R&A and the USGA jointly and issued worldwide. This publication can be purchased directly from the R&A.

Implements and Ball Committee

The Implements and Ball Committee consists of four members elected by the Club: one member of the Rules of Golf Committee and one member of the Championship Committee, together with consultant members invited by the Committee to advise on technical matters. One of the elected Members retires each year, but the Chairman may be re-elected immediately for the sake of continuity.

The Committee works in close co-operation with its USGA counterpart committee in interpreting the Rules and Appendices relating to the control of the form and make of golf clubs and the specifications of the golf ball to ensure that the game and established golf courses are not harmed by technical developments.

Rules of Amateur Status Committee

The Rules of Amateur Status Committee consists of five members, of which four are elected by the Club and one provided by the Council of National Golf Unions. There are also Advisory Members to the Committee, representing the same Golfing Authorities as on the Rules of Golf Committee.

Revision of Rules of Amateur Status

A procedure, similar to that for the Rules of Golf, is adopted for revision of the Rules of Amateur Status and no policy changes are made without full consultation with all the affiliated Unions, the USGA and the PGA.

Decisions

The work of the Committee consists of:

(a) dealing with applications for reinstatement to amateur status;
(b) answering inquiries about the nature of prizes, conditions for tournaments etc arising out of the increased impact of commercial sponsors on amateur golf and the issue of guidelines and decisions;
(c) answering queries from individuals regarding their own position under the rules;
(d) controlling scholarships and other grants-in-aid.

National Functions

Prior to the First World War, a group of golf clubs had been responsible for the running of the Open and Amateur Championships. In 1919 a meeting of these clubs confirmed that the Royal & Ancient should be the governing authority for the game and agreed it should assume responsibility for the two championships.

The decision that the R&A should be the governing authority was endorsed at a Meeting of the English, Scottish, Irish and Welsh Unions in 1924, at which meeting what is now the Council of National Golf Unions was formed, with the object amongst others of directing the system of Standard Scratch Scores and Handicaps.

In 1948 the R&A took over the Boys' and in 1963 the Youths' Championship from the private interests which had previously run them. This was done at the request of the individuals concerned.

In 1969 the R&A itself inaugurated the British Seniors' Amateur Championship, and in 1991 it agreed to become involved in the organisation and running of the Senior British Open Championship in conjunction with the PGA European Tour.

In 1995 it replaced the Youths' Championship with the Mid-Amateur Championship.

In addition to the organisation of these five Championships, the R&A is responsible for the selection of teams to represent Great Britain and Ireland in the Walker Cup, the Eisenhower Trophy, the St Andrews Trophy and other international tournaments. It is also responsible for the organisation of such events when they are held in Great Britain and Ireland.

In its World Amateur Golf Council role it takes it in turns with the USGA to organise the World Amateur Team Championships.

These functions are exercised through the following committees:

Championship Committee

The Championship Committee is responsible for the control of the five championships and of the international matches and tournaments mentioned above.

The Committee consists of eight members elected by the Club, of whom two retire annually and are not eligible for re-election for one year. For the organisation of any particular event additional members may be co-opted where required.

The work of this Committee has greatly increased in recent years – imagine the work involved in staging the Open Championship, for which the total prize money in 1998 was £1,750,000. At the same time, the Committe must build up more substantial reserve funds to ensure the continuance of the Open Championship as a premier world event.

The Championship Committee

The remarkable development of The Open to the great occasion it is today has meant heavily increased responsibilities for the Championship Committee. The media have given it an audience of millions compared with the few thousand of the past. The R&A's determination to match the growing interest with a new attitude and astute promotion has given the event the stature and following it now enjoys. The last 26 years have seen the winner's cheque grow from £1200 to £300,000, the total prize money from £15,000 to £1,175,000 in 1998. The financial success of The Open has provided considerable sums of money for the development of junior golf and other worthy causes connected to golf.

The R&A works closely with the club of the course where the Championship is to be played, whose members take on many of the duties necessary to make it run smoothly. These include spectator control, where local clubs take charge of a hole each – usually providing three-hour shifts of up to 16 members at a time. This can involve as many as 800 people daily. Local volunteer stewards also cover such diverse duties as course control, supervision of litter collection and spectator stand control. Security, courtesy transport, car park supervision and public catering, to name but a few of the many services necessary, are provided under contract by companies expert in these fields. Close liaison with the area police authority is vital. Facilities for the Press, television crews and the vast tented village, each involving several hundred people, occupy large areas and are a major limiting factor when considering possible venues for future championships. Important for both competitors and spectators, and appreciated by both, is the radio network which provides up-to-the-minute scores and positions of the leading players which appear very quickly on the leader boards erected at strategic points round the course. The system developed over many years is as quick, informative and accurate as any in existence.

The Committee consists of eight Royal & Ancient members, who devote much time to their tasks. It has a full-time secretary who, together with the Secretary of the Club and some of his staff, is involved in the planning of The Open and other events throughout the year. Members of the Committee work long hours during Open week. From first light at about 5 am, when the Head Greenkeeper and a nominated member of the Committee tour the course deciding the pin positions on each green for the day, to dusk when the last competitor comes in, all are occupied, mostly out on the course at selected points, in two-way radio contact with the centre, ready to give a ruling when required. In the final rounds the leading players are accompanied by a member of the committee for the whole round. The many stands erected around the course, providing seats, often quite close to greens, for as many as 18,000 spectators make for special problems. A loose shot which ends under a stand will probably mean the ball may be dropped without penalty in an area nearby, which has been pre-designated by the committee; this shot should be of equal difficulty as it would have been if the stand had not been there. In these cases often an official decision is required. At the end of every round each competitor's card must be immediately checked and recorded and then, in the case of a leader, he will meet the press in the interview room.

It is the Championship Committee too which decides if any round has to be halted, postponed or cancelled due to storm and tempest. Such decisions, so difficult with so many factors consequent on a postponement to be considered, have been eased a little with improved weather forecasting and continuous contact with the local weather bureau. The work of the Committee is never ending with the myriad tasks necessary to ensure the smooth running of a championship tournament. The success of the Open is due to sound planning, the determination to move with the times and the expertise of the R&A staff who are the executive arm of the Committee.

The Open is the Championship with which all are familiar, but its Committee is equally committed to making a success of the many other events under the R&A's control which also require a great deal of planning and organisation.

The External Funds Committee

The External Funds Supervisory Committee recommends for approval to the general committee the annual donations to a number of golfing bodies, especially those concerned with the training and development of junior golf and for research on greenkeeping matters. It also make grants and loans to assist with the development of new facilities both in the UK and abroad.

Selection Committee

The Selection Committee consists of a Chairman, who is a member of the R&A, and other members, not necessarily members of the Club, appointed by the General Committee. These other members have for some years now been representative of each of the four Home Unions. Normally they hold their appointments for four years.

Club Membership

Membership of the R&A is limited to a total of 1800, of which 1050 may be resident in Great Britain and Ireland and 750 overseas.

The membership, both at home and abroad, is representative and includes many who have given or are giving great services to golf through many different unions and associations. This facilitates broad and effective representation on all the Club Committees concerned with international and national functions.

The domestic affairs of the Club are run by Committees, perhaps the most important of which is the Links Management Committee. The Royal and Ancient Golf Club of St Andrews does not own a golf course, but it is nevertheless much concerned with the maintenance and improvements of the four St Andrews golf courses. These courses are controlled by the St Andrews Links Trust and are run by the Links Management Committee. Three trustees and four members of the Management Committee are appointed by the R&A and an equal number are appointed by Fife District Council; another member of the Trust is appointed by the Secretary of State for Scotland and the incumbent MP is also a trustee. The R&A contributes an annually negotiated sum to the Trust in return for members' playing privileges.

Finance

After taking into account income derived from subscriptions to the Rules of Golf Decisions Service and the sale of official Rules publications, the net expenses of the Rules of Golf, Rules of Amateur Status and Rules for Implements and Ball are borne by an External Activities Account.

Income and expenditure of all championships run by the R&A and the expenses of teams representing Great Britain & Ireland are accounted for in separate divisions of the account.

Surpluses of all income over expenditure in the External Activities Account are held in reserve to ensure the continuance of the running of the various events at a high standard.

The Royal & Ancient Golf Club as a private members' club does not in any way benefit from the External Activities Account.

Contacts with Affiliated Golfing Authorities

In important issues, the R&A endeavours to consult all the golfing authorities that may be concerned. This covers, in particular, matters relating to Rules of Golf, Rules of Amateur Status, and the Championships.

In May 1980 the first ever International Golf Conference was held in St Andrews at which 33 countries affiliated to the R&A were represented and to which the USGA, PGA and other golfing bodies in this country sent observers. Following the great success of this event, the R&A ran similar conferences in 1985, 1989, 1993; at the last one in 1997, 60 countries were represented.

The R&A is represented at Meetings of the World Amateur Golf Council, the Council of National Golf Unions and on the CCPR.

Other Governing Bodies

Home Unions

The English Golf Union

The English Golf Union was founded in 1924 and embraces 34 County Unions with over 1,550 affiliated clubs, 23 clubs overseas, and 447 Golfing Societies and Associations. Its objects are:

(1) To further the interests of Amateur Golf in England.
(2) To assist in maintaining a uniform system of handicapping.
(3) To arrange an English Championship; an English Strokeplay Championship; an English County Championship, International and other Matches and Competitions.
(4) To cooperate with the Royal & Ancient Golf Club of St Andrews and the Council of National Golf Unions.
(5) To cooperate with other National Golf Unions and Associations in such manner as may be decided.

The Scottish Golf Union

The Scottish Golf Union was founded in 1920 and embraces 661 clubs. Subject to the stipulation and declaration that the Union recognises the Royal & Ancient Golf Club of St Andrews as the Ruling Authority in the game of golf, the objects of the Union are:

(a) To foster and maintain a high standard of Amateur Golf in Scotland and to administer and organise and generally act as the governing body of amateur golf in Scotland.
(b) To institute and thereafter carry through annually a Scottish Amateur Championship, a Scottish Open Amateur Stroke Play Championship and other such competitions and matches as they consider appropriate.
(c) To administer and apply the rules of the Standard Scratch Score and Handicapping Scheme as approved by the Council of National Golf Unions from time to time.
(d) To deal with other matters of general or local interest to amateur golfers in Scotland.

The Union's organisation consists of Area Committees covering the whole of Scotland. There are 16 Areas, each having its own Association or Committee elected by the Clubs in that particular area and each Area Association or Committee elects one delegate to serve on the Executive of the Union.

Golfing Union of Ireland

The Golfing Union of Ireland, founded in 1891, embraces 275 Clubs. Its objects are:

(1) Securing the federation of the various Clubs.
(2) Arranging Amateur Championships, Inter-Provincial and Inter-Club Competitions, and International Matches.
(3) Securing a uniform standard of handicapping.
(4) Providing for advice and assistance, other than financial, to affiliated Clubs in all matters appertaining to Golf, and generally to promote the game in every way, in which this can be better done by the Union than by individual Clubs.

Its functions include the holding of the *Close* Championship for Amateur Golfers and Tournaments for Team Matches.

Its organisation consists of Provincial Councils in each of the four Provinces elected by the Clubs in the Province – each province electing a limited number of delegates to the Central Council which meets annually.

Welsh Golfing Union

The Welsh Golfing Union was founded in 1895 and is the second oldest of the four National Unions. Unlike the other Unions it is an association of Golf Clubs and Golfing Organisations. The present membership is 127. For the purpose of electing the Executive Council, Wales is divided into ten districts which between them return 22 members. The objects of the Union are:

(a) To take any steps which may be deemed necessary to further the interests of the amateur game in Wales.

(b) To hold a Championship Meeting or Meetings each year.
(c) To encourage, financially and/or otherwise, Inter-Club, Inter-County, and International Matches, and such other events as may be authorised by the Council.
(d) To assist in setting up and maintaining a uniform system of Handicapping.
(e) To assist in the establishment and maintenance of high standards of greenkeeping.

Note: The union recognises the Royal & Ancient Golf Club of St Andrews as the ruling authority.

The Council of National Golf Unions

At a meeting of Representatives of Golf Unions and Associations in Great Britain and Ireland, called at the special request of the Scottish Golf Union, and held in York, on 14th February, 1924, resolutions were adopted from which the Council of National Golf Unions was constituted.

The Council holds an Annual Meeting in March, and such other meetings as may be necessary. Two representatives are elected from each national Home Union – England, Scotland, Ireland and Wales – and hold office until the next Annual meeting when they are eligible for re-election.

The principal function of the Council, as laid down by the York Conference, was to formulate a system of Standard Scratch Scores and Handicapping, and to co-operate with the Royal & Ancient Championship Committee in matters coming under their jurisdiction. The responsibilities undertaken by the Council at the instance of the Royal & Ancient Golf Club or the National Unions are as follows:

1. The Standard Scratch Score and Handicapping Scheme, formulated in March, 1926, approved by the Royal & Ancient, and last revised in 1989.
2. The nomination of two members on the Board of Management of The Sports Turf Research Institute, with an experimental station at St Ives, Bingley, Yorkshire.
3. The management of the Annual Amateur International Matches between the four countries – England, Scotland, Ireland and Wales.

United States Golf Association

The USGA is the national governing body of golf. Its single most important goal is preserving the integrity and values of the game.

Formed on 22nd December, 1894, a year when two clubs proclaimed different US Amateur Champions, representatives of five clubs met at a dinner at the Calumet Club in New York City. They created a central governing body to establish uniform rules, to conduct national championships and to nurture the virtues of sportsmanship in golf.

The names of the standing committees give an idea of what the USGA does: Rules of Golf, Championship, Amateur Status and Conduct, Implements and Ball, Handicap, Women's, Sectional Affairs, Green Section, Public Links, Women's Public Links, Junior Championship, Girls' Junior, Senior Championship, Senior Women's Championship, Bob Jones Award, Museum, Green Section Award, Finance, Public Information, Membership, Regional Association, Associates, Intercollegiate Relations, Mid-Amateur Championship, International Team Selection, Development, Turfgrass Research, Nominating.

The USGA, as the governing body of the game in the United States, makes and interprets the Rules of Golf in co-operation with the Royal & Ancient Golf Club of St Andrews, Scotland; developed and maintains the national system of handicapping; controls the standards of the ball and the implements of the game; works in turfgrass and turf management; and, generally speaking, preserves and promotes the game.

The Professional Golfers' Association

The Professional Golfers' Association was founded in 1901 to promote interest in the game of golf; to protect and advance the mutual and trade interests of its members; to arrange and hold meetings and tournaments periodically for the members; to institute and operate funds for the benefit of the members; to assist the members to obtain employment; and effect any other objects of a like nature as may be determined from time to time by the Association.

Classes of Membership

There shall be nine classes of membership:

(i) **Class A** Members engaged as the nominated professional on a full-time basis at a PGA Club, PGA Course or PGA Driving Range in one of the seven Regions; and members engaged as the nominated professional on a full-time basis, at an establishment in one of the seven Regions at which the public can play and/or practise which, in the opinion of the Executive Committee does not qualify as a PGA Club, Course or Driving Range but does warrant Class A status.

Note: Class A(T) – Class A members currently engaged at an establishment which has been inspected and approved as a PGA Training Establishment and currently holds

that status will be identified where appropriate by the suffix (T) after their classification.

(ii) **Class B** Members engaged by a Class A or D member to assist the nominated professional at any PGA Establishment in one of the seven Regions on a full-time basis.

(iii) **Class C** Tournament playing members (men and women).

(iv) **Class D** Members engaged as the nominated professional on a full-time basis at a PGA Establishment within the seven Regions which does not qualify as a 'Class A' establishment, or engaged on a full-time basis within the seven Regions by any other Company or any other individual designated by the Executive Committee for this purpose. (Former Class G.)

(v) **Class E** Honorary Associate Members (HAM). Those who in the opinion of the Executive Committee through their past or continuing membership justify retaining the full privileges of membership as Honorary Associate Members (HAM).

(vi) **Class F** Associate Members (AM).
(a) Those who have ceased to be eligible for other categories of membership who in the opinion of the Executive Committee through their past membership justify retaining limited privileges of membership as Associate Members; and (b) Members of the PGA European Tour or WPGET who do not qualify for Class C membership but who in the opinion of the Executive Committee justify limited privileges of membership as Associate Members.

(vii) **Class G** Honorary Life Members (HLM). Those recommended by the Board to a Special General Meeting of the Association for election as Honorary Life Members. No form of application is needed nor need reference be made to the Regional Committee concerned.

(viii) **Class H** Members who are qualified members of the Association, and ineligible for any other class of membership, engaged on a full-time basis at an establishment acceptable to the Association outside the jurisdiction of the seven Regions. (Overseas)

(ix) **Class O** Members who have not qualified at the official training centre of the Association, who are ineligible for any other class of membership, and who are current members of another PGA approved by the Association and have held such membership for not less than two years.

The Management of the Association is under the overall direction and control of a Board. The Association is divided into seven Regions each of which employs a full-time secretary and runs tournaments for the benefit of members within its Region.

The Association is responsible for arranging and obtaining sponsorship of the Ryder Cup, Club Professionals' Championship, PGA Cup matches, Seniors' Championship, PGA Assistants' Championship, Assistants' Match Play Championship and other National Championships.

Anyone who intends to become a club professional must serve a minimum of three years in registration and qualify at the PGA Training School before election as a full Member.

PGA European Tour

To be eligible to become a member of the PGA European Tour a player must possess certain minimum standards which shall be determined by the Tournament Committee. In 1976 a Qualifying School for potential new members was introduced to be held annually. The leading players are awarded cards allowing them to compete in PGA European Tour tournaments.

In 1985 the PGA European Tour became ALL EXEMPT with no more Monday pre-qualifying. Full details can be obtained from the Wentworth Headquarters.

European LPGA European Tour

The European LPGA Tour was founded in 1988 to further the development of women's professional golf throughout Europe and its membership is open to all nationalities. An amateur wishing to join the Tour must be 18 years of age, have a handicap of 1 or less and is on probation for eight rounds in tournaments, during which she must attain certain playing standards as determined by the Tournament Committee.

Government of the Amateur and Open Golf Championship

In December 1919, on the invitation of the clubs who had hitherto controlled the Amateur and Open Golf Championships, the Royal & Ancient took over the government of those events. These two championships are now controlled by a committee appointed by the Royal & Ancient Golf Club of St Andrews. The Committee is called the Royal and Ancient Golf Club Championship Committee and consists of eight members of the Club elected by the Club.

Ladies' Golf Union (LGU)

The Ladies' Golf Union was founded in 1893 with the following objectives:

(1) To promote the interests of the game of Golf.
(2) To obtain a uniformity of the rules of the game by establishing a representative legislative authority.
(3) To establish a uniform system of handicapping.
(4) To act as a tribunal and court of reference on points of uncertainty.
(5) To arrange the Annual Championship Competition and obtain the funds necessary for that purpose.

After 100 years, only the language has changed, the present Constitution defines the objectives as:

(1) To uphold the rules of the game, to advance and safeguard the interests of women's golf and to decide all doubtful and disputed points in connection therewith.
(2) To maintain, regulate and enforce the LGU Handicapping System.
(3) To employ the funds of The Union in such a manner as shall be deemed best for the interests of women's golf, with power to borrow or raise money to use for the same purpose.
(4) To maintain and regulate International events, Championships and Competitions held under the LGU regulations and to promote the interests of Great Britain and Ireland in Ladies International Golf.
(5) To make, maintain and publish such regulations as may be considered necessary for the above purposes.

The constituents of the LGU are:

Home Countries. The English Ladies' Golf Association (founded 1952), the Irish Ladies' Golf Union (founded 1893), the Scottish Ladies' Golfing Association (founded 1904), the Welsh Ladies' Golf Union (founded 1904), plus ladies' societies, girls' schools and ladies' clubs affiliated to these organisations.

Overseas. Affiliated ladies' golf unions and golf clubs in the Commonwealth and any other overseas ladies' golfing organisation affiliated to the LGU.

Individual lady members of clubs within the above categories are regarded as *members of the LGU.*

The Rules of the Game and of Amateur Status, which the LGU is bound to uphold, are those published by the Royal & Ancient Golf Club of St Andrews.

In endeavouring to fulfil its responsibilities towards advancing and safeguarding women's golf, the LGU maintains contact with other golfing organisations – the Royal & Ancient Golf Club of St Andrews, the Council of National Golf Unions, the Golf Foundation, the Central Council of Physical Recreation, the Sports Council, the Women Professional Golfers' European Tour and the Women's Committee of the United States Golf Association. This contact ensures that the LGU is informed of developments and projected developments and has an opportunity to comment upon and to influence the future of the game for women.

Either directly or through its constituent national organisations the LGU advises and is the ultimate authority on doubts or disputes which may arise in connection with the handicapping system and regulations governing competitions played under LGU conditions.

The handicapping system, together with the system for assessment of Scratch Scores, is formulated and published by the LGU. Handicap Certificates are provided by the LGU and distributed through the National Organisations and appointed club officials to every member of every affiliated club which has fulfilled the requisite conditions for obtaining an LGU handicap.

The funds of the LGU are administered by the Hon. Treasurer on the authority of the Executive Council, and the accounts are submitted annually for adoption in General Meeting.

The Women's British Open Championship, Ladies' British Amateur Championships and the Home International matches, at both senior and junior level, are organised annually by the LGU. International events involving a British or a combined British and Irish team are organised and controlled by the LGU when held in this country and the LGU acts as the coordinating body for the Commonwealth Tournament in whichever of the five participating countries it is held, four-yearly, by rotation. The LGU selects and trains the teams, provides the uniforms and pays all the expenses of participation, whether held in this country or overseas. The LGU also maintains and regulates certain competitions played under handicap, such as Medal Competitions, Coronation Foursomes, Challenge Bowls, Australian Spoons and the LGU Pendant Competition.

The day-to-day administration of certain of the LGU responsibilities in the home countries is undertaken by the National Organisations, such as that concerned with handicapping regulations, Scratch Scores, and the organisation of Challenge Bowls and Australian Spoons Competitions.

Membership subscriptions to the LGU are assessed on a per capita basis of the club membership. To save unnecessary expense and duplication of administrative work in the home countries LGU subscriptions are collected by the National Organisations along with their own, and transmitted in bulk to the LGU.

Policy is determined and control over all the LGU's activities is exercised by an Executive Council of eight members – two each elected by

the English, Irish, Scottish and Welsh national organisations. The Chairman is elected annually by the Councillors and may hold office for one year only, during which term her place on the Council is taken by her Deputy and she has no vote other than a casting vote. The President and the Hon. Treasurer of the Union also attend and take part in Council meetings but with no vote. The Council meets five times a year.

The Annual General Meeting is held in January. The formal business includes presentation of the Report of the Executive Council for the previous year and of the Accounts for the last completed financial year, the election or re-election of President, Vice-Presidents, Hon. Treasurer and Auditors, and a report of the election of Councillors and their Deputies for the ensuing year and of the European Championship Committee representative. Voting is on the following basis: Executive Council, one each (8); members in the four home countries, one per national organisation (4) and in addition one per 100 affiliated clubs or part thereof; one per overseas Commonwealth Union with a membership of 50 or more clubs, and one per 100 individually affiliated clubs.

The Lady Golfer's Handbook is published annually by the LGU and is distributed free to all affiliated clubs and organisations and to appointed Handicap Advisers. It is also available for sale to anyone interested. It contains the regulations for handicapping and Scratch Score assessment, for British Championships and international matches (with results for the past twenty years) and for LGU competitions, and sets out the Rules of the Union. It also lists every affiliated organisation, with names and addresses of officials, and every affiliated club, with Scratch Score, county of affiliation, number of members, and other useful information.

Championship and International Match Conditions

CHAMPIONSHIP CONDITIONS

Men

The Amateur Championship

The Championship, until 1982, was decided entirely by match play over 18 holes except for the final which was over 36 holes. Since 1983 the Championship has comprised two stroke play rounds of 18 holes each from which the leading 64 players and ties over the 36 holes qualify for the match play stages. Matches are over 18 holes except for the final which is over 36 holes. Full particulars can be obtained from the Championship Entries Department, Royal & Ancient Golf Club, St Andrews, Fife KY16 9JD.

The Seniors' Open Amateur Championship

The Championship consists of 18 holes on each of two days, the leading 50 players and ties over the 36 holes then playing a further 18 holes the following day. Entrants must have attained the age of 55 years prior to the first day of the Championship. Full particulars can be obtained from the Championship Entries Department, Royal & Ancient Golf Club, St Andrews, Fife KY16 9JD.

National Championships

The English, Scottish, Irish and Welsh Amateur Championships are played by holes, each match consisting of one round of 18 holes except the final which is contested over 36 holes. Full particulars of conditions of entry and method of play can be obtained from the secretaries of the respective national Unions.

English Open Amateur Strokeplay Championship

The Championship consists of one round of 18 holes on each of two days after which the leading 40 and those tying for 40th place play a further two rounds. The remainder are eliminated. Conditions for entry include: entrants must have a handicap not exceeding three; where the entries exceed 130, an 18-hole qualifying round is held the day before the Championship. Certain players are exempt from qualifying.

Full particulars of conditions of entry and method of play can be obtained from the Secretary, English Golf Union.

British Mid-Amateur Championship

The Championship comprises two stroke play rounds of 18 holes from which the leading 64 players over the 36 holes qualify for the match play stages. All matches including the final are over 18 holes. Entrants must have attained the age of 25 years prior to the first day of the Championship. Full particulars can be obtained from the Championship Entries Department, Royal & Ancient Golf Club, St Andrews, Fife KY16 9JD.

Boys

Boys' Amateur Championship

The Championship is played by matchplay, each match including the final consisting of one round of 18 holes. Entrants must be under 18 years of age at 00.00 hours on 1st January in the year of the Championship. Full particulars can be obtained from the Championship Entries Department, Royal & Ancient Golf Club, St Andrews, Fife KY16 9JD.

Ladies

Ladies' British Open Amateur Championship

The Championship consists of one 18-hole qualifying round on each of two days. The players returning the 64 lowest scores over 36 holes shall qualify for match play. Ties for 64th place shall be decided by hole-by-hole play-off.

Ladies' British Open Amateur Strokeplay Championship

The Championship consists of 72 holes stroke play; 18 holes are played on each of two days after which the first 32 and all ties for 32nd place qualify for a further 36 holes on the third day. Handicap limit is 4.

Ladies' British Open Championship

The Championship consists of 72 holes stroke play. 18 holes are played on each of four days, the field being reduced after the first 36 holes.

Entries accepted from lady amateurs with a handicap not exceeding scratch and from lady professionals. Full particulars for all three Championships can be obtained from the Administrator, LGU, The Scores, St Andrews, Fife KY16 9AT.

National Championships

Conditions of entry and method of play for the English, Scottish, Welsh and Irish Ladies' Close Championships can be obtained from the Secretaries of the respective associations.

Other championships organised by the respective national associations, from whom full particulars can be obtained, include English Ladies', Intermediate, English Ladies' Strokeplay, Scottish Girls' Open Amateur Strokeplay (under 21) and Welsh Ladies' Open Amateur Strokeplay.

Girls

Girls' British Open Amateur Championship

The Championship consists of two 18-hole qualifying rounds, followed by match play in two flights each of sixteen players.
Conditions of entry include:
Entrants must be under 18 years of age on the 1st January in the year of the Championship.
Competitors are required to hold a certified LGU international handicap not exceeding 15, or to be members of their National Junior Team for the current year.
Full particulars can be obtained from the Administrator, LGU, The Scores, St Andrews, Fife KY16 9AT.

National Championships

The English, Scottish, Irish and Welsh Girls' Close Championships are open to all girls of relevant nationality and appropriate age which may vary from country to country. A handicap limit may be set by some countries. Full particulars can be obtained via the secretaries of the respective associations.

INTERNATIONAL MATCH CONDITIONS

Men's Amateur Matches

Walker Cup – Great Britain and Ireland v United States of America

Mr GH Walker of the United States presented a Cup for international competition to be known as *The United States Golf Association International Challenge Trophy*, popularly described as *The Walker Cup*.

The Cup shall be played for by teams of amateur golfers selected from Clubs under the jurisdiction of the United States Golf Association on the one side and from England, Scotland, Wales, Northern Ireland and Eire on the other.

The International Walker Cup Match shall be held every two years in the United States of America and Great Britain and Ireland alternately.

The teams shall consist of not more than ten players and a captain.

The contest consists of four foursomes and eight singles matches over 18 holes on each of two days.

St Andrews Trophy

First staged in 1956, the St Andrews Trophy is a biennial international match played between two selected teams of amateur golfers representing Great Britain and Ireland and the Continent of Europe. Each team consists of nine players and the match is played over two consecutive days with four morning foursomes followed each afternoon by eight singles. Selection of the Great Britain and Ireland team is carried out by the Selection Committee of the Royal & Ancient Golf Club. The European Golf Association select the Continent of Europe team.

Men's World Amateur Team Championship (Eisenhower Trophy)

Founded in recognition of the need for an official world amateur team championship, the first event was played at St Andrews in 1958 and the Trophy has been played for every second year in different countries around the world.

Each country enters a team of four players who play stroke play over 72 holes, the total of the three best individual scores to be counted for each round.

European Team Championship

Founded in 1959 by the European Golf Association for competition among member countries of the Association. The Championship is held biennially and played in rotation round the countries which are grouped in four geographical zones.

Each team consists of six players who play two qualifying rounds of 18 holes, the five best scores of each round constituting the team aggregate. Flights for match play are then arranged according to qualifying round rankings. For the match play, teams consist of five players, playing two foursomes in the morning and five singles in the afternoon.

A similar championship is held every year for junior teams.

In 1990, the European Golf Association began organising the International European Championships on an annual basis.

Home Internationals *(Raymond Trophy)*

The first official International Match recorded was in 1902 at Hoylake between England and Scotland who won 32 to 25 on a holes up basis.

In 1932 International Week was inaugurated under the auspices of the British Golf Unions' Joint Advisory Council with the full approval of the four National Golf Unions. The Council of National Golf Unions is now responsible for running the matches. Teams of 11 players from England, Scotland, Ireland and Wales engage in matches consisting of 5 foursomes and 10 singles over 18 holes, the foursomes being in the morning and the singles in the afternoon. Each team plays every other team.

The eligibility of players to play for their country shall be their eligibility to play in the Amateur Championship of their country.

Men's Professional Matches

Ryder Cup

This Cup was presented by Mr Samuel Ryder, St Albans, England, (who died 2nd January, 1936) for competition between a team of British professionals and a team of American professionals. The trophy was first competed for in 1927. In 1929 the original conditions were varied to confine the British team to British-born professionals resident in Great Britain, and the American team to American-born professionals resident in the United States, in the year of the match. In 1977 the British team was extended to include European players. The matches are played biennially, in alternate continents, in accordance with the conditions as agreed between the respective PGAs.

World Cup *(formerly Canada Cup)*

Founded in America in 1953 as an International Team event for professional golfers with the intention of spreading international goodwill.

Each country is represented by two players, the best team score over 72 holes being the winners of the World Cup and the best individual score the International Trophy. It is played annually, but not in 1986.

Ladies Matches

Great Britain and Ireland *v* United States (Curtis Cup)

For a trophy presented by the late Misses Margaret and Harriot Curtis of Boston, USA, for biennial competition between teams from the United States of America and Great Britain and Ireland.

The match is sponsored jointly by the United States Golf Association and the Ladies' Golf Union who may select teams of not more than eight players.

The match consists of three foursomes and six singles of 18 holes on each of two days, the foursomes being played each morning.

Europe *v* United States (Solheim Cup)

The Solheim Cup, named after Karsten Solheim who heads the sponsoring Ping company, is the women's equivalent of the Ryder Cup. In 1990 the inaugural competition between the top women professional golfers from Europe and America took place in Florida.

The matches are played biennially in alternate continents. The format is foursomes and fourball matches on the first two days, followed by singles on the third in accordance with the conditions as agreed between the WPG European Tour and the LPGA.

Great Britain and Ireland *v* Continent of Europe (Vagliano Trophy)

For a trophy presented to the Comité des Dames de la Fédération Française de Golf and the Ladies' Golf Union by Monsieur AA Vagliano, originally for annual competition between teams of women amateur golfers from France and Great Britain and Ireland but, since 1959, by mutual agreement, for competition between teams from the Continent of Europe and Great Britain and Ireland.

The match is played biennially, alternately in Great Britain and Ireland and on the Continent of Europe, with teams of not more than nine players plus a non-playing captain. The match consists of four foursomes and eight singles, of 18 holes on each of two days. The foursomes are played each morning.

Women's World Amateur Team Championship (Espirito Santo Trophy)

Presented by Mrs Ricardo Santo of Portugal for biennial competition between teams of not more than three women amateur golfers who represent a national association affiliated to the World Amateur Golf Council. First competed for in 1964. The Championship consists of 72 holes strokeplay, 18 holes on each of four days, the two best scores in each round constituting the team aggregate.

Commonwealth Tournament (Lady Astor Trophy)

For a trophy presented by the late Viscountess Astor CH, and the Ladies' Golf Union for competition once in every four years between teams of women amateur golfers from Commonwealth countries.

The inaugural Commonwealth Tournament was played at St Andrews in 1959 between teams from Australia, Canada, New Zealand, South Africa and Great Britain and was won by the British team. The tournament is played in rotation in the competing countries, for the present Great Britain, Australia, Canada, and New Zealand, each country being entitled to nominate 6 players including a playing or non-playing captain.

Each team plays every other team and each team match consists of two foursomes and four singles over 18 holes. The foursomes are played in the morning and the singles in the afternoon.

European Ladies' Amateur Team Championship

The Championship is held biennially between teams of amateur women golfers from the European countries. Each team consists of not more than 6 players who play two qualifying rounds, the five best scores in each round constituting the team aggregate. The matchplay draw is made in flights according to the position in the qualifying rounds. The matchplay consists of two foursomes and five singles on each of three days.

A similar championship is held in alternate years for junior ladies' teams, under 21 years of age.

Home Internationals

Teams from England, Scotland, Ireland and Wales compete annually for a trophy presented to the LGU by the late Mr TH Miller. The qualifications for a player being eligible to play for her country are the same as those laid down by each country for its Close Championship.

Each team plays each other team. The matches consist of six singles and three foursomes, each of 18 holes. Each country may nominate teams of not more than eight players.

Boys Matches

Home Internationals (R&A Trophy)

Teams comprising 11 players from England, Scotland, Ireland and Wales compete against one another over three days in a single round robin format. Each fixture comprises five morning foursomes followed by ten afternoon singles.

To be eligible for selection, players must be under the age of 18 at 00.00 hours on 1st January in the year of the matches.

England v Scotland; Wales v Ireland

The International Matches between England and Scotland (10 players a side) and Wales and Ireland (10 players a side) are played on the Thursday preceding the Boys' Championship. The following day the winners of these two matches play against each other, as do the losers. To be eligible to play in these matches a boy must qualify by age to be eligible to play in the Boys' Championship.

Great Britain and Ireland v Continent of Europe (Jacques Leglise Trophy)

The Jacques Leglise Trophy is an annual international match played between two selected teams of amateur boy golfers representing Great Britain and Ireland and the Continent of Europe. Each team consists of nine players and the match is played over two consecutive days with four morning foursomes followed each afternoon by eight singles. Selection of the Great Britain and Ireland team is carried out by the Selection Committee of the Royal & Ancient Golf Club. The European Golf Association selects the Continent of Europe team

To be eligible for selection, players must be under the age of 18 at 00.00 hours on 1st January in the year of the matches.

Girls

Home Internationals

Teams from England, Scotland, Ireland and Wales compete annually for the Stroyan Cup. The qualifications for a player for the Girls' International Matches shall be the same as those laid down by each country for its Girls' Close Championship except that a player shall be under 18 years on the 1st January in the year of the Championship.

Each team, consisting of not more than eight players, plays each other team, a draw taking place to decide the order of play between the teams. The matches consist of six singles and three foursomes, each of 18 holes.

Golf Associations

The National Association of Public Golf Courses (Affiliated to English Golf Union)

1927 saw the foundation of the Association by the late FG Hawtree (Golf Course Architect) and the late JH Taylor (five times Open Champion). They were both farsighted enough to see the need for cohesion between *Private* golf, *Public* golf and the Local Councils. Up to the outbreak of World War II the Association struggled on, sustained by a small amount of very welcome financial support from the *News of the World*. This enabled the *unofficial* Championship to be staged.

After the War, the Association was revitalised and the Championship was recognised by the National Union, and so from a shaky start of 240 qualifiers, there are now some 3500 Public Course golfers trying to qualify, from a total estimated membership of 50,000. The success and importance of the *Public Courses Championship of England* prompted the commencement of the Championship for Ladies and then the Championship for Juniors – which share equal importance. Soon after the establishment of Individual Championships there came the introduction of various Club Team events, and these have now progressed to National Level with a vast following from Club members. Thus the Association now organises some 14 national events annually for the membership.

Some years ago it was realised that the Local Councils (Course Management Authorities) could not enjoy official recognition and membership of the County Unions or National Unions except through the Association. This has now been remedied and many CMA are full subscribing members of the Association, and many others permit the *Courtesy of the Course* for all our National and Zonal Tournaments. Advice is offered to CMA – when requested – on such matters as Course Construction, Club formation and integration, establishment of Standard Scratch Score and Par Values, and many other topics concerned with the management of the game of golf.

Some overseas organisations and Councils have already sought our advice and help in recent years, when forming their own Courses, Clubs and Associations.

The Constitutional aims have not changed over the years, and the Association is proud to have maintained these Aims through the activities provided by the National Executive of the Association. The aims are:

1. To unite the Clubs formed on Public Courses in England and Wales, and their Course Managements in the furtherance of the interests of Amateur Golf.
2. To promote Annual Public Courses Championships and such other matches, competitions and tournaments as shall be authorised by the executive of the Association.
3. To afford direct representation of Public Course Interests in the National Union.

The total organisation of the Association is wholly voluntary and honorary, from the President down through Vice-Presidents, Chairmen, Secretary, Treasurer and Zone Secretaries. It is quite fantastic for an unpaid Organisation to cover such an exacting *field* of work, but most gratifying to the National Executive who have secured the progress of recent years.

Association of Golf Club Secretaries

Membership is 1900, consisting of Secretaries and retired Secretaries of Clubs largely situated in Great Britain but also from Clubs in Europe and other parts of the world. The Association offers from its Headquarters at Weston-super-Mare advice on all aspects of managing a Golf Club including an extensive Information Library which has some 300 different items. Regular training courses are held for newly appointed and intending Secretaries. The Association's Journal *Golf Club Management* is circulated to all members monthly and regular business meetings are held within the 15 regions of the Association as well as National Conferences and Seminars.

The Association of Golf Writers

A group of 30 newspapermen attending the Walker Cup Match at St Andrews on 2nd June 1938 decided there was a need for an organisation to

'protect the interests of golf writers'. Their main objective was to establish a close liaison with the governing bodies and promoters of golf.

Thus was born The Association of Golf Writers, now solidly established and rightly respected as the official negotiating body of the golfing press. The Association owes much to a membership which has included many internationally recognised names who have contributed to elevating the Association to a unique level among British sports writers' associations.

Secretary: Mark Garrod, Press Association, London House, Central Park, New Lane, Leeds LS11 5DZ.

The Sports Turf Research Institute
(Bingley, West Yorkshire)

The Institute is officially recognised as the national centre for sports and amenity turf and is the official agronomist to the Championship Committee of the R&A. It is a non-profit distributing company limited by guarantee, its affairs managed by a small Executive Committee drawn from its Members Body comprising most sports controlling bodies. Golf is represented by the nominees of the R&A, the four home Golf Unions and the Council of National Golf Unions. The British Institute of Golf Course Architects, the British & International Greenkeepers Association and the PGA European Tour are represented on its Members Body and Golf Committee.

The Institute's mission is to carry out research and promote innovation; to provide advisory and consultancy services; and to provide education and publications for subscribing clubs, sports controlling bodies and the turfgrass industry at large. Activities other than research are run from its wholly owned subsidiary company, STRI Ltd.

The British Institute of Golf Course Architects

The Institute was founded in 1970 in order to establish standards of experience, knowledge and integrity in their profession. Fellowship and Membership of the Institute demonstrates that the Golf Course Architect has designed and supervised the construction throughout of a significant number of golf courses, having completed at least six full years of practical experience. Associateship is open to those with lesser degrees of experience who have also passed the Student Education Programme and satisfied the Committee that they are responsible, ethical and competent to design and direct the construction of golf courses to the high standard required. It is further required that Fellows, Members and Associates main business activity is golf course architecture.

The British Association of Golf Course Constructors

Objects: To promote the development of the golf course construction industry, to promote the adoption of policies to ensure a high quality of workmanship and working practices, to collect and disseminate information of value regarding the construction of golf courses to other members of the association, to members of the allied industries and to the public to promote the training and education of personnel within the industry and to maintain agreed standards of golf course construction by adherence to contractual procedures and codes of practice.

British and International Golf Greenkeepers' Association

The Association was formed in 1987 resulting from an amalgamation of the British, English and Scottish Associations. The Association has an official magazine, *Greenkeeping International*, which is issued free to all members.

The objects are to promote and advance all aspects of greenkeeping; to assist and encourage the proficiency of members; to arrange an International Annual Conference, educational seminars, functions and competitions; to maintain a Benevolent Fund; to act as an employment agency; to provide a magazine; to collaborate with any body or organisation which may benefit the Association or its members or with which there may be a common interest; to carry out and perform any other duties which shall be in the general interests of the Association or its members.

National Golf Clubs' Advisory Association

The National Golf Clubs' Advisory Association was founded in 1922. The objects are to protect the interests of Golf Clubs in general and to give legal advice and direction, under the opinion of Counsel, on the administrative and legal responsibilities of Golf Clubs. In cases taken to the Courts for decisions on any points which in the opinion of the Executive Committee involve principles affecting the general interests of affiliated clubs financial assistance may sometimes be given.

European Golf Association
Association Européenne de Golf

Formed at a meeting held at Luxembourg, 20th November, 1937, membership shall be restricted to European National Amateur Golf Associations or Unions. The Association shall concern itself solely with matters of an international character.

The Association shall have as its prime objects:
(a) To encourage international development of golf and strengthen bonds of friendship between the national organisations and to encourage the formation of new ones.
(b) To co-ordinate dates of the Open and Amateur Championships of its members.
(c) To arrange when such have been decided upon, European Team Championships and Matches of international character.
(d) To decide and publish the Calendar dates of the Open and Amateur Championships and Matches.

Golf Club Stewards' Association

The Golf Club Stewards' Association was founded as early as 1912. Its members are Stewards in Golf Clubs throughout the UK and Eire. It has a National Committee and Regional Branches in the South, North-West, Midlands, East Anglia, Yorkshire, Wales and the West, North-East Scotland and Ireland. The objects of the Association are to promote the interests of members; to administer a Benevolent Fund for members in need and to arrange golf competitions and matches. It also serves as an Agency for the employment of Stewards in Golf Clubs.

Addresses of Golfing Organisations Worldwide

National Associations

Great Britain & Ireland

Royal and Ancient Golf Club
Sec, Sir Michael Bonallack OBE, St Andrews, Fife KY16 9JD. *Tel* (01334) 472112 *Fax* (01334) 477580 *Website* www.RandA.org

Council of National Golf Unions
Hon Sec, A Thirlwell, 19 Birch Green, Formby, Liverpool L37 1NG. *Tel/Fax* (01704) 831800

European Ladies' Professional Golf Association
Chief Exec, T Howland, The Tytherington Club, The Old Hall, Macclesfield, Cheshire SK10 2JP. *Tel* (01625) 611444 *Fax* (01625) 610406 *Email* mail@elpga.com

Ladies' Golf Union
Sec, Mrs J Hall, The Scores, St Andrews, Fife KY16 9AT. *Tel* (01334) 475811 *Fax* (01334) 472818

The Professional Golfers' Association
Sec, DKC Wright, Centenary House, The Belfry, Sutton Coldfield, West Midlands B76 9PT. *Tel* (01675) 470333 *Fax* (01675) 477888

East Region *Sec*, S Curtis, John O'Gaunt Golf Club, Sutton Park, Sandy, Biggleswade, Beds SG19 2LY. *Tel* (01767) 261888 *Fax* (01767) 26138.

Midland Region *Sec*, A Lott, King's Norton Golf Club, Brockhill Lane, Weatheroak, Nr Alvechurch, Worcs B48 7ED. *Tel* (01564) 824909 *Fax* (01564) 822805

North Region *Sec*, J Croxton, No 2 Cottage, Bolton Golf Club, Lostock Park, Chorley New Road, Bolton, Lancs BL6 4AJ. *Tel* (01204) 496137 *Fax* (01204) 847959

South Region *Sec*, P Ward, Clandon Regis Golf Club, Epsom Road, West Clandon, Guildford, Surrey GU4 7TT. *Tel* (01483) 224200 *Fax* (01483) 223224

West Region *Sec*, R Ellis, Exeter Golf and Country Club, Topsham Road, Countess Wear, Exeter, Devon EX2 7AE. *Tel* (01392) 877657 *Fax* (01392) 876382

Irish Region *Sec*, M McCumiskey, Dundalk Golf Club, Blackrock, Dundalk, Co Louth, Eire. *Tel* (00 353) 422 1193 *Fax* (00 353) 422 1899

Scottish Region *Sec*, P Lloyd, Glenbervie Golf Club, Stirling Road, Larbert FK5 4SJ. *Tel* (01324) 562451 *Fax* (01324) 562190

PGA European Tour
Exec Dir, KD Schofield CBE, PGA European Tour, Wentworth Drive, Virginia Water, Surrey GU25 4LX. *Tel* (01344) 842881 *Fax* (01344) 842929

Artisan Golfers' Association
Hon Sec, A Everett, 51 Rose Hill Park West, Sutton, Surrey SM1 3LA. *Tel* 0181-644 7037

Association of Golf Club Secretaries
Sec, R Burniston, 7a Beaconsfield Road, Weston-super-Mare BS23 1YE. *Tel* (01934) 641166 *Fax* (01934) 644254 *Email* HQ@AGCS.org.uk

Association of Golf Writers
Sec, M Garrod, 106 Byng Drive, Potters Bar, Herts EN6 1UJ. *Tel/Fax* (01707) 654112

British Association of Golf Course Constructors
Sec, JH Franks, 37 Five Mile Drive, Wolvercote, Oxford OX2 8HT. *Tel* (01865) 516927

British Golf Collectors Society
Sec, CH Ibbetson, PO Box 13704, North Berwick, East Lothian EH39 4ZB. *Tel/Fax* (01620) 895561

The British Golf Museum
Dir, PN Lewis, *Curator*, Elinor Clark, Bruce Embankment, St Andrews, Fife KY16 9AB. *Tel* (01334) 478880 *Fax* (01334) 473306

Addresses of Golfing Organisations Worldwide 839

The British Institute of Golf Course Architects
President, H Swan, Merrist Wood House, Worplesdon, Surrey GU3 3PE.
Tel (01483) 884036 *Fax* (01483) 884037

British & International Golf Greenkeepers Association
Exec Dir, N Thomas, Bigga House, Aldwark, Alne, York Y061 1UF.
Tel (01347) 833800 *Fax* (01347) 833801

British Left-Handed Golfers' Society
Hon Sec, AC Kirkland, 7 Ingersley Road, Bollington, Cheshire SK10 5RE.
Tel (01625) 575516

British Turf & Landscape Irrigation Association
Sec, DG Halford, Myerscough College, Bilsborrow, Preston, Lancs PR3 0RY.
Tel (01995) 640611 *Fax* (01995) 640842

Golf Club Stewards' Association
Sec, G Shaw, 50 The Park, St Albans, Herts AL1 4RY. *Tel* (01727) 857334

Golf Foundation
Exec Dir, T Homer, Foundation House, Hanbury Manor, Ware, Herts SG12 0UH.
Tel (01920) 484044 *Fax* (01920) 484055
Email info@golf-foundation.org
Website www.golf-foundation.org

Golf Society of Great Britain
Sec, Miss E Mountain, Hope Point, Granville Road, St Margaret's Bay, Dover, Kent CT15 6DT. *Tel* (01304) 852229

Hole in One Golf Society
Sec, B Dickinson, PO Box 109, New Line, Greengates, Bradford, Yorkshire BD10 9UY.
Tel (01274) 618931

National Association of Public Golf Courses
Hon Sec, E Mitchell, 12 Newton Close, Redditch B98 7YR. *Tel* (01527) 542106
Fax (01527) 455320

National Golf Clubs' Advisory Association
Sec, Mrs JM Brock, 2 Angel House, Portland Square, Bakewell, Derbyshire DE45 1HB
Tel (01629) 813844 *Fax* (01629) 812614

Professional Golfers' Architects Association
Sec, NH Fletcher, Centenary House, The Belfry, Sutton Coldfield B76 9PT. *Tel* (01675) 470333
Fax (01675) 477888

Public Schools' Old Boys' Golf Association
Jt Secs: P de Pinna, Bruins, Wythwood, Haywards Heath, West Sussex RH16 4RD.

Tel 0171-265 0071. JBM Urry, Dormers, 232 Dickens Heath Road, Shirley, Solihull, West Midlands B90 1QQ. *Tel* 0121-328 5665

Public Schools' Golfing Society
Hon Sec, JNS Lowe, Flushing House, Church Road, Great Bookham, Surrey KT23 3JT.
Tel (01372) 458651 *Fax* (01372) 451361

The Society of One-Armed Golfers
Hon Sec, HF Ross, 11 Campbell Place, Torrance, Glasgow G64 4HR.
Tel (01360) 622476

Sports Turf Research Institute (STRI)
Chief Exec, Dr PM Canaway, *Marketing,* Anne Wilson, St Ives Estate, Bingley, West Yorks BD16 1AU.*Tel* (01274) 565131
Fax (01274) 561891 *Email* info@stri.org.uk
Website www.stri.org.uk

Regional Associations

England

English Golf Union
Sec, PM Baxter, National Golf Centre, The Broadway, Woodhall Spa, Lincs LN10 6PU. *Tel* (01526) 354500 *Fax* (01526) 354020
Email info@englishgolfunion.org
Website www.englishgolfunion.org

Midland Group *Sec,* RJW Baldwin, Chantry Cottage, Friar Street, Droitwich, Worcs WR9 8EQ. *Tel/Fax* (01905) 778560
Northern Group *Sec,* IG Black, 683 Chorley New Road, Lostock, Bolton BL6 4AG.
Tel (01204) 841374
South Eastern Group *Hon Sec,* MA Hobson, 22 Wye Court, Malvern Way, Ealing, London W13 8EA. *Tel* 0181-997 7466
South Western Group *Sec,* JT Lumley, 51 Roundway Park, Devizes, Wilts SN10 2EE.
Tel (01380) 723935

English Ladies' Golf Association
Sec, Mrs MJ Carr, Edgbaston Golf Club, Church Road, Birmingham B15 3TB.
Tel 0121-456 2088. *Fax* 0121-454 5542
Northern Division *Hon Sec,* Mrs L Young, 10 Cleehill Drive, North Shields, Tyne & Wear NE29 9EW. *Tel* 0191-257 6925
Midlands Division *Hon Sec,* Mrs D Harris, Ivy Cottage, Lutterworth Road, Gilmorton, Lutterworth, Leics LE17 5PN. *Tel* (01455) 556093

South-Eastern Division *Hon Sec,* Mrs R Wallis, The Bungalow, The Green, Pirbright, Woking GU24 0JE. *Tel* (01483) 476528

South-Western Division *Hon Sec,* Mrs VJ Wilde, 19 Ferndown Close, Kingsweston, Bristol BS11 0UP. *Tel* (0117) 968 3543

English Blind Golf Association
Sec, D Morris, 11 Riverside Avenue, Newquay, Cornwall TR7 1PW. *Tel/Fax* (01637) 875464

English Schools' Golf Association
Hon Sec, R Snell, 20 Dykenook Close, Whickham, Newcastle-upon-Tyne NE16 5TD. *Tel* 0191-488 3538

Bedfordshire County Golf Union
Hon Sec, C Allen, 102 Tyne Crescent, Bedford, Beds MK41 7UW. *Tel/Fax* (01234) 216835

Bedfordshire Ladies' County Golf Association
Hon Sec, Mrs H Molloy, Keepers Cottage, Beadlow, Shefford, Beds SG17 5PH. *Tel* (01525) 861202

Bedfordshire & Cambridgeshire PGA
Sec, L Scarbrow, 22 Hillcrest Road, Luton LU2 7AB. *Tel* (01582) 240197

Berks, Bucks & Oxon PGA
Hon Sec, Mrs M Green, Wayside, Aylesbury Road, Monks Risborough, Aylesbury, Bucks HP27 0JS. *Tel* (01844) 343012

Berks, Bucks & Oxon Union of Golf Clubs
Sec, R Stewart, Boston House, Grove Technology Park, Wantage, Oxon, OX12 9FF *Tel/Fax* (01235) 772797

Berkshire Ladies' County Golf Association
Hon Sec, Mrs M Shepherd, 40 Florence Road, College Town, Camberley, Surrey GU15 4QD *Tel* (01276) 35937

Buckinghamshire Ladies' County Golf Association
Hon Sec, Mrs C Hawkesworth, 22 Copthall Lane, Chalfont St Peter, Bucks SL9 0AB *Tel* (01753) 885711

Cambridgeshire Area Golf Union
Sec, RAC Blows, 2A Dukes Meadow, Stapleford, Cambridge CB2 5BH. *Tel* (01223) 842062

Cambs & Hunts Ladies' County Golf Association
Hon Sec, Mrs S Ramsay, 25 Leighton, Orton Malbourne, Peterborough PE2 5QB *Tel* (01733) 236502

Channel Islands Ladies' Golf Association
Hon Sec, c/o La Moye Golf Club, St Brelade, Jersey JE3 8GQ

Cheshire County Ladies' Golf Association
Hon Sec, Mrs B Walker, 12 Higher Downs, Knutsford, Cheshire WA16 8AW. *Tel* (01565) 634124

Cheshire PGA
Sec, J Croxton, No 2 Cottage, Bolton Golf Club, Lostock Park, Chorley New Road, Bolton BL6 4AJ. *Tel* (01204) 496137 *Fax* (01204) 847959

Cheshire Union of Golf Clubs
Hon Sec, BH Nattrass, 'Whitecliff', 6 Bryn Seiriol, Llandudno LL30 1PD. *Tel/Fax* (01492) 580518

Cornwall Golf Union
Hon Sec, JG Rowe, 8 Lydcott Crescent, Widegates, Looe, Cornwall PL13 1QG. *Tel/Fax* (01503) 240492

Cornwall Ladies' County Golf Association
Hon Sec, Mrs A Eddy, Penmester, Hain Walk, St Ives, Cornwall TR26 2AF. *Tel* (01736) 795392

Cumbria Ladies' County Golf Association
Hon Sec, Mrs V Hetherington, The Patch, Lowmoor Road, Wigton CA7 9QR. *Tel* (016973) 42403

Cumbria Union of Golf Clubs
Hon Sec, T Edmondson, Thorn Lea, Lazonby, Penrith, Cumbria CA10 1AT. *Tel* (01768) 898231

Derbyshire Ladies' County Golf Association
Hon Sec, Mrs J Morgan, Upper Burrows Farm, Brailsford, Derby DE6 3BW. *Tel* (01335) 360250

Derbyshire PGA
Sec, F McCabe, Hillside, Lower Hall Close, Holbrook, Derby DE56 0TN. *Tel* (01332) 880411

Derbyshire Union of Golf Clubs
Hon Sec, JB Kay, Tamarinda, Whitworth Road, Darley Dale, Matlock, Derbys DE4 2HH. *Tel* (01629) 734143

Devon County Golf Union
Sec, RJ Hirst, Flat 4, 27 West Street, Tavistock, Devon PL19 8JY. *Tel/Fax* (01822) 617750

Devon County Ladies' Golf Association
Hon Sec, Mrs T Philp, 2 Coastguard Road, Budleigh Salterton, Devon EX9 6HB. *Tel* (01395) 443700

Dorset County Golf Union
Hon Sec, Lt Col MD Hutchins, 38 Carlton Road, Bournemouth BH1 3TG. *Tel* (01202) 290821 *Fax* (01202) 311288

Dorset Ladies' County Golf Association
Hon Sec, Miss J Pomeroy, 10 Mill Close, East Coker, Yeovil, Somerset BA22 9LF. *Tel* (01935) 862574

Addresses of Golfing Organisations Worldwide 841

Durham County Golf Union
Hon Sec, GP Hope, 7 Merrion Close, Moorside, Sunderland SR3 2QP. *Tel* 0191-528 0421 *Fax* 0191-522 8605

Durham County Ladies' Golf Association
Sec, Mrs R Foy, Jolby Manor, Stapleton, Darlington DL2 2QS. *Tel* (01325) 377500

Essex County Amateur Golf Union
Sec/Treas, J Barbour, Suite 4, Barrack House, Barrck Square, Chelmsford CM2 0UU. *Tel* (01245) 499081 *Fax* (01245) 499091

Essex Ladies' County Golf Association
Hon Sec, Mrs M Low, 15 Rushden Road, Brentwood, Essex CM15 9ES. *Tel* (01277) 230849

Essex PGA
Sec, A Birch, 27 Curlew Crescent, Basildon, Essex SX16 5HR. *Tel* (01268) 533849

Gloucestershire & Somerset PGA
Sec, N Boland, Cotswold Hills GC, Ullenwood, Cheltenham GL53 9QT. *Tel* (01242) 515263

Gloucestershire Golf Union
Hon Sec, RF Crisp, 2 Hartley Close, Charlton Kings, Cheltenham GL53 9DN.
Tel (01242) 514024 *Fax* (01242) 221659

Gloucestershire Ladies' County Golf Association
Hon Sec, Mrs D Honey, Waterloo Corner Cottage, Cheltenham Road, Bredon, Tewkesbury GL20 7NA. *Tel* (01684) 773359

Hampshire, Isle of Wight & Channel Islands Golf Union
Sec, K Maplesden, 5 Coldharbour Wood, Rake, Liss, Hants GU33 7JJ. *Tel/Fax* (01730) 895102

Hampshire Ladies' County Golf Association
Sec, Mrs S O'Shea, 134 Carbery Avenue, Southbourne, Bournemouth BH6 3LH.
Tel (01202) 424651

Hampshire PGA
Sec, Mrs D Bryon, South Winchester Golf Club, Pitt, Winchester SO22 5QW.
Tel/Fax (01962) 860928

Hertfordshire County Ladies' Golf Association
Hon Sec, Mrs A Thomson, 13 Carleton Rise, Welwyn AL6 9RP. *Tel* (01438) 715612

Hertfordshire Golf Union
Hon Sec, JC Harkett, 5 Willow Way, Harpenden, Herts AL5 5JF. *Tel* (01582) 760841
Fax (01582) 462608

Hertfordshire PGA
Hon Sec, RA Gurney, 1 Field Lane, Letchworth, Herts SG6 3LF. *Tel* (01462) 627899

Isle of Man Golf Union
Hon Sec, AD Horne, 27 Ballahane Close, Port Erin, Isle of Man. *Tel* (01624) 834389

Isle of Wight Ladies' Golf Association
Hon Sec, Mrs JC Roberts, 416 Newport Road, Cowes, I.O.W. PO30 8PP. *Tel* (01983)293852

Kent County Golf Union
Hon Sec, JH Goby JP, St Andrew's Road, Littlestone, New Romney, Kent TN28 8RB.
Tel (01797) 367725 *Fax* (01797) 367726

Kent County Ladies' Golf Association
Hon Sec, Mrs S Daniel, 6 Wyvern Close, Dartford DA1 2NA. *Tel* (01322) 271583

Kent PGA
Sec, R Burkin, c/o West Malling Golf Club, London Road, Addington, Maidstone ME19 5AR. *Tel* (01732) 843420

Lancashire Ladies' County Golf Association
Hon Sec, Mrs SA Hampson, Highmoor Farm, Highmoor Lane, Wrightington, Wigan WN6 9PS.
Tel (01257) 252140

Lancashire PGA
Sec, J Croxton, No 2 Cottage, Bolton Golf Club, Lostock Park, Chorley New Road, Bolton BL6 4AJ. *Tel* (01204) 496137 *Fax* (01204) 847959

Lancashire Union of Golf Clubs
Sec, AV Moss, 5 Dicconson Terrace, Lytham St Annes, Lancs FY8 5JY. *Tel* (01253) 733323 *Fax* (01253) 795721

Leicestershire & Rutland Golf Union
Hon Sec, C Chamberlain, 10 Shipton Close, The Meadows, Wigston Magna, Leicester LE18 3WL. *Tel/Fax* (0116) 288 9862

Leicestershire & Rutland Ladies' County Golf Association
Hon Sec, Mrs AL Adams, 23 Fisher Close, Cossington, Leicester LE7 4US.
Tel (01509) 812869

Leicestershire PGA
Sec, D Freeman, 218 Hamilton Lane, Scraptoft LE7 9SD. *Tel* (0116) 241 4735

Lincolnshire Ladies' County Association
Hon Sec, Mrs S Gee, 17 Parksgate Avenue, Lincoln LN6 7HP. *Tel* (01522) 688778

Lincolnshire PGA
Sec, GN Hethershaw, Gainsborough GC, Thonock, Gainsborough DN21 1PZ.
Tel (01427) 848207

Lincolnshire Union of Golf Clubs
Hon Sec, GH Moore OBE, Authorpe House, 36 Horncastle Road, Woodhall Spa LN10 6UZ.
Tel (01526) 352792

Middlesex County Golf Union
Sec, PSV Cooke, 36 Grants Close, Mill Hill,
London NW7 1DD. Tel 0181-349 0414
Fax 0181-346 7565

**Middlesex Ladies' County
Golf Association**
Hon Sec, Ms B Popple, 9 Ashleigh Court, Avenue
Road, London N14 4EL. Tel 0181-886 9015

Middlesex PGA
Sec, B Eady, 8 Woodbank Drive, Chalfont
St Giles, Bucks HP8 4RP. Tel (01494) 874487

Norfolk County Golf Union
Hon Sec, RJ Trower, 12a Stanley Avenue,
Thorpe, Norwich, Norfolk NR7 0BE.
Tel/Fax (01603) 431026

Norfolk Ladies' County Association
Hon Sec, Mrs J Foad, 28 St Leonard's Close,
Wymondham, Norfolk NR18 0JF.
Tel (01953) 602692

Norfolk PGA
Hon Sec, DM Bray, 4 Bluebell Drive,
Sheringham, Norfolk NR26 8XE.
Tel (01263) 821905

North East & North West PGA
Sec, R Sentance, 7 Larch Lea, Ponteland,
Newcastle-upon-Tyne NE20 9LG.
Tel/Fax (01661) 821336

Northamptonshire Golf Union
Hon Sec, RG Halliday, 12 Edge Hill Road,
Duston, Northampton NN5 6BY.
Tel/Fax (01604) 751031

**Northamptonshire Ladies' County Golf
Association**
Hon Sec, Mrs J Ray, The Dairy, 12 Cotterstock
Road, Oundle PE8 5HA. Tel (01832) 273573

Northamptonshire PGA
Sec, S Cruickshank, 286 Birchfield Road East,
Northampton. Tel (01604) 470160

**Northumberland Ladies'
County Golf Association**
Hon Sec, Mrs PA Smith, Clonreher, Armstrong
Cottages, Bamburgh, Northumberland
NE69 7BA. Tel (01668) 214216

Northumberland Union of Golf Clubs
Hon Sec, WE Procter, 5 Oakhurst Drive, Kenton
Park, Gosforth, Newcastle-upon-Tyne NE3 4JS.
Tel/Fax 0191-285 4981

**Nottinghamshire County Ladies'
Golf Association**
Hon Sec, Mrs BA Patrick, 18 Delville Avenue,
Keyworth, Notts NG12 5JA.
Tel (0115) 937 3237

Nottinghamshire PGA
Sec, RW Futer, 52 Barden Road, Mapperley,
Nottingham NG3 5QD. Tel (0115) 952 0956

Nottinghamshire Union of Golf Clubs
Hon Sec, R Brown, 48 Weaverthorpe Road,
Woodthorpe, Notts NG5 4NB.
Tel/Fax (0115) 926 6560

Oxfordshire Ladies' County Golf Association
Hon Sec, Mrs EA Sadler, 5 Manor Farm Road,
Dorchester-on-Thames OX10 7HZ.
Tel (01865) 340018

Sheffield PGA
Sec, G Walker, Hillsborough GC, Worrall Road,
Sheffield S6 4BE. Tel (0114) 233 2666

**Shropshire & Herefordshire Union
of Golf Clubs**
Hon Sec, JR Davies, 23 Poplar Crescent,
Bayston Hill, Shrewsbury SY3 0QB.
Tel (01743) 872655

Shropshire & Hereford PGA
Sec, P Hinton, 1 Stanley Lane Cottages,
Bridgnorth, Shropshire. Tel (01746) 752045.

Shropshire Ladies' County Golf Association
Hon Sec, Mrs HF Davies, Brooklands, Oldwoods,
Bomere Heath, Shrewsbury SY4 3AX.
Tel (01939) 290427

Somerset Golf Union
Hon Sec, CF Carr, 21 Greenacre, Wembdon,
Bridgwater, Somerset TA6 7RD.
Tel/Fax (01278) 450476

Somerset Ladies' County Golf Association
Hon Sec, Mrs D Bowerman, Ridgedown,
Blagdon Hill, Taunton TA3 7SL.
Tel (01823) 42256

**Staffordshire Ladies' County Golf
Association**
Hon Sec, Mrs PM Barrow, 21 Lady Aston Park,
Little Aston Hall Drive, Sutton Coldfield
B74 3BF. Tel 0121-353 4019

Staffordshire PGA
Sec, DJ Lewis, 59 Chester Crescent, The
Westlands, Newcastle ST5 3RR. Tel/Fax (01782)
613415

Staffordshire Union of Golf Clubs
Hon Sec, BA Cox, 34 Lordswood Square,
Harborne, Birmingham B17 9BS.
Tel 0121-427 4962

Suffolk County Golf Union
Hon Sec, RA Kent, 77 Bennett Avenue, Bury St
Edmunds, Suffolk IP33 3JJ.
Tel/Fax (01284) 705765

Suffolk Ladies' County Golf Association
Hon Sec, Mrs P Dodsworth, The Beeches,
School Road, Risby, Bury St Edmunds, Suffolk
IP28 6RG. Tel (01284) 810876

Suffolk PGA
Sec, A Sleath, 21 Hasketon Road, Woodbridge,
Suffolk IP12 4LD. Tel (01394) 387014.

Addresses of Golfing Organisations Worldwide 843

Surrey County Golf Union
Hon Sec, MW Ashton, Clearglen House, 151 Frimley Road, Camberley, Surrey GU15 2PS. *Tel* (01276) 677959 *Fax* (01276) 63334

Surrey Ladies' County Golf Association
Hon Sec, Mrs D Marchant, Larchfield, Hunts Hill, Normandy, Guildford, Surrey GU3 2AH. *Tel* (01483) 810873

Surrey PGA
Sec, P Bowles, 27 Lower Wood Road, Claygate, Surrey KT10 0EU. *Tel* (01372) 463882

Sussex County Golf Union
Sec, DG Pulford, Suite 1, 216 South Coast Road, Peacehaven, East Sussex BN10 8JR. *Tel* (01273) 589791 *Fax* (01273) 585705

Sussex County Ladies' Golf Association
Hon Sec, Mrs JM Scott, Preferred Lie, Rufwood, Crawley Down, W Sussex RH10 4HD *Tel* (01342) 712213

Sussex PGA
Sec, C Pluck, 96 Cranston Avenue, Bexhill, East Sussex TN39 3NL. *Tel/Fax* (01424) 221298

Warwickshire Ladies' County Golf Association
Hon Sec, Mrs J Colley, Freshfield, Penn Lane, Tamworth-in-Arden B94 5HH. *Tel* (01564) 742543

Warwickshire PGA
Sec, J Tunnicliff, 80 Wychwood Ave, Knowle, Solihull B93 9DZ. *Tel* (01564) 773168

Warwickshire Union of Golf Clubs
Hon Sec, J Stubbings, Quaker Cottage, Wiggins Hill Road, Wishaw, Sutton Coldfield B76 9QE. *Tel* (01675) 470209

Wiltshire County Golf Union
Hon Sec, BM Townsend, 6 Whitebridge Road, Salisbury SP1 1QA. *Tel* (01722) 335792

Wiltshire Ladies' County Golf Association
Hon Sec, Mrs EM Kent, 2 Colenzo Drive, Andover, Hants SP10 1JS. *Tel* (01264) 323375

Wiltshire PGA
Sec, JAD Sullivan, Marlborough GC, The Common, Marlborough, Wilts SN8 1DU. *Tel* (01672) 512147

Worcestershire County Ladies' Golf Association
Hon Sec, Mrs S Smith, 12 Russell Road, Kidderminster DY10 3HT. *Tel* (01562) 824808

Worcestershire PGA
Sec, K Ball, 136 Alvechurch Road, West Heath, Birmingham B31 3PW. *Tel* 0121-475 7400

Worcestershire Union of Golf Clubs
Hon Sec, A Boyd, The Bears Den, Upper Street, Defford, Worcester WR8 9BG. *Tel* (01386) 750657 *Fax* (01386) 750472

Yorkshire Ladies' County Golf Association
Hon Sec, Mrs S Dennis, 2 Hesp Hills, Beckfoot Lane, Bingley BD16 1AR. *Tel* (01274) 567500

Yorkshire PGA
Sec, J Pape, 1 Summerhill Gardens, Leeds, Yorks LS8 2EL. *Tel* (0113) 266 4746

Yorkshire Union of Golf Clubs
Hon Sec, KH Dowswell, 33 George Street, Wakefield, W Yorks WF1 1LX. *Tel* (01924) 383869 *Fax* (01924) 383634

Ireland

Golfing Union of Ireland
Gen Sec, S Smith, Glencar House, 81 Eglinton Road, Donnybrook, Dublin 4. *Tel* (00 353) 1 269 4111 *Fax* (00 353) 1 269 5368 *Email* gui@iol.ie *Website* www.gui.ie

Connacht Branch *Gen Sec,* S Hosty, 31 Shantalla Road, Galway. *Tel/Fax* (00 353) 91 527072 *Fax* (00 353) 91 523224

Leinster Branch *Sec,* P Smyth, 1 Clonskeagh Square, Clonskeagh Road, Dublin 14. *Tel* (00 353) 1 269 6977 *Fax* (00 353) 1 269 3602

Munster Branch *Hon Sec,* S McMahon, 6 Town View, Mallow, Co Cork. *Tel* (00 353) 22 21026 *Fax* (00 353) 22 42373

Ulster Branch *Gen Sec,* BG Edwards, 58a High Street, Holywood, Co Down BT18 9AE. *Tel* (01232) 423708 *Fax* (01232) 426766

Irish Ladies' Golf Union
Sec, Miss MP Turvey, 1 Clonskeagh Square, Clonskeagh Road, Dublin 14. *Tel* (00 353) 1 269 6244 *Fax* (00 353) 1 283 8670

Eastern District *Hon Sec,* Miss E Foley, 10 Vale View Avenue, The Park, Cabinteely, Dublin 18. *Tel* (00 353) 1 285 6853

Midland District *Hon Sec,* Mrs N Colgan, Cloonagoose, Borris, Kilkenny. *Tel* (00 353) 503 73577

Northern District *Hon Sec,* Mrs M Nivison, 28 Downshire Road, Bangor, Co. Down BT20 3TN. *Tel* (01247) 462774

Southern District *Hon Sec,* Mrs M Power, 36 Tracton Avenue, Montenotte, Cork. *Tel* (00 353) 21 551977

Western District *Hon Sec,* Ms M Tighe, Ellison Street, Castlebar, Co Mayo. *Tel* (00 353) 94 21410

Scotland

Scottish Golf Union
Sec, H Grey, Scottish National Golf Centre, Drumoig, Leuchars, St Andrews KY16 0DW.
Tel (01382) 549500 *Fax* (01382) 549510
Email sgu@scottishgolf.com
Website www.scottishgolf.com

Area Associations:
Angus *Sec,* D Speed, 7 Eastgate, Friockheim, Arbroath DD11 4TG. *Tel* (01241) 828544 *Fax* (01241) 828455
Argyll & Bute *Sec,* G Duncanson, 2 Mount Stewart Road, Rothersay, Bute PA20 9DY. *Tel* (01700) 502468.
Ayrshire *Sec,* RL Crawford, 81 Connel Crescent, Mauchline, Ayrshire KA5 5AU. *Tel* (01290) 551434 *Fax* (01290) 551078
Borders *Sec,* RG Scott, 3 Whitebank Road, Clovenforth, Galashiels TD1 3NE. *Tel/Fax* (01896) 850570
Clackmannanshire *Sec,* T Johnson, 75 Dewar Avenue, Kincardine FK10 4RR. *Tel* (01259) 731168 (R)
Dumbartonshire *Sec,* AW Jones, 107 Larkfield Road, Lenzie, Glasgow G66 3AS. *Tel* 0141-776 7430(R)
Fife *Sec,* BR Wright, 26 East Fergus Place, Kirkcaldy, Fife KY1 1XT. *Tel* (01592) 206605 *(office)*
Glasgow *Sec,* RGJ Jamieson, 37 Eglinton Street, Beith KA21 1AZ. *Tel* (01505) 503000 *(office)*
Lanarkshire *Sec,* T Logan, 41 Woodlands Drive, Coatbridge, Lanarkshire ML5 1LB. *Tel* (01236) 428799 *Fax* (01236) 429358
Lothians *Sec,* J Wood, 28 Stoneyhill Avenue, Musselburgh EH21 6SB. *Tel/Fax* 0131-665 4813
North *Sec,* JT Jamieson, 3 Drummond Crescent, Inverness IV2 4QW. *Tel* (01463) 233624 *Fax* (01463) 710240
North-East *Sec,* G McIntosh, 41 Johnston Gardens West, Peterculter AB14 0LB. *Tel* (01651) 863002
Perth & Kinross *Sec,* DY Rae, 18 Carlownie Place, Auchterarder PH3 1BT. *Tel* (01764) 662837 *Fax* (01764) 662886
Renfrewshire *Sec,* JI McCosh, 'Muirfield', 20 Williamson Place, Johnstone, Renfrewshire PA5 9DW. *Tel* (01505) 344613
South *Sec,* JH Sommerville, Cherry Cottage, Kirkcudbright DG6 4EU. *Tel/Fax* (01557) 330445
Stirlingshire *Sec,* I Hutton, 18 Turret Drive, Polmont FK2 0QW. *Tel* (01324) 712585

Scottish Ladies' Golfing Association
Sec, Mrs S Simpson, Scottish National Golf Centre, Drumoig, Leuchars, Fife KY16 0DW
Tel (01382) 549502 *Fax* (01382) 549512

Scottish Ladies' Golfing Association – County Golf
Chairman, Mrs M Mowat, Seton Lodge, 9 Southpark Road, Ayr KA7 2TL.
Tel (01292) 268773

Aberdeen Ladies' County Golf Association
Hon Sec, Mrs M Robinson, 7 Carnegie Gardens, Aberdeen AB15 4AW. *Tel* (01224) 313582

Angus Ladies' County Golf Association
Hon Sec, Mrs A Rennie, 53 Princes Street, Monifieth, Dundee DD5 4AN.
Tel (01382) 533718

Ayrshire Ladies' County Golf Association
Hon Sec, Miss AD Cree, 19 Woodfield Road, Ayr KA8 8LZ. *Tel* (01292) 260702

Border Counties' Ladies' Golf Association
Hon Sec, Miss I Hogg, Chestnut Cottage, Bowden, Melrose TD6 0SS.
Tel (01835) 822322

Dumfriesshire Ladies' County Golf Association
Hon Sec, Miss MJ Greig, 10 Nelson Street, Dumfries DG2 9AY. *Tel* (01387) 254429

Dunbartonshire & Argyll Ladies' County Association
Hon Sec, Mrs CM Kelly, 86 Nasmyth Avenue, Bearsden, Glasgow G61 4SQ. *Tel* 0141-942 9959

East Lothian Ladies' County Association
Hon Sec, Mrs CM Campbell, Glenlair, Main Street, Gullane EH31 2HD.
Tel (01620) 842534

Fife County Ladies' Golf Association
Hon Sec, Mrs M Steele, 26 South Dewar Street, Dunfermline KY12 8AR. *Tel* (01383) 721840

Galloway Ladies' County Golf Association
Hon Sec, Ms J Maxwell, 2 Hawkes Court, Castle Douglas DG7. *Tel* (01556) 670450

Lanarkshire Ladies' County Golf Association
Hon Sec, Mrs M Heggie, 80 Weirwood Avenue, Garrowhill, Glasgow G69 6LM.
Tel 0141-771 3802

Midlothian County Ladies' Golf Association
Hon Sec, Mrs M Gammie, 4 Curriehall, Castle Drive, Balerno EH14 5AT. *Tel* 0131-449 6652

Northern Counties' Ladies' Golf Association
Hon Sec, Mrs C MacLennan, Midville, Contin, Strathpeffer IV14 9ES. *Tel* (01997) 421236

Perth & Kinross Ladies' County Golf Association
Hon Sec, Mrs P Drysdale, Annandale, Packhill Road, Rattray, Blairgowrie PH10 7DS.
Tel (01250) 873641

Renfrewshire Ladies' County Golf Association
Hon Sec, Mrs M Neilson, 47 Octavia Terrace, Greenock PA16 7SR. *Tel* (01475) 724673

Stirling & Clackmannan Ladies' Golf Association
Hon Sec, Mrs A Hunter, 22 Muirhead Road, Stenhousemuir FK5 4JA. *Tel* (01324) 554515

Scottish Golfer's Alliance
Sec/Treas, Mrs MA Caldwell, 5 Deveron Avenue, Giffnock, Glasgow G46 6NH. *Tel* 0141-638 2066

Wales

Welsh Golfing Union
Sec, R Dixon, Catsash, Newport NP6 1JQ.
Tel (01633) 430830 *Fax* (01633) 430843

Anglesey Golf Union
Hon Sec, GP Jones, 20 Gwelfor Estate, Cemaes, Anglesey LL67 0NL.
Tel (01407) 710755

Brecon & Radnor Golf Union
Hon Sec, DJ Davies, Garden House, Howey, Llandrindod Wells, Powys. *Tel* (01597) 824316

Caernarvonshire & District Golfing Union
Hon Sec, RE Jones, 23 Bryn Rhos, Rhosbodrual, Caernarfon, Gwynedd LL55 2BT.
Tel (01286) 673486

Denbighshire Golfing Union
Hon Sec, EG Howells, 10 Lon Howell, Myddleton Park, Dinbych, Clwyd CH7 3NH.

Dyfed Golfing Union
Hon Sec, A Scott, 40 Clover Park, Haverfordwest, Dyfed SA61 1UE. *Tel* (01437) 767578

Flintshire Golfing Union
Hon Sec, J Snead, 1 Cornist Cottages, Cornist Park, Flint, Clwyd CH6 5HJ. *Tel* (01352) 733461

Glamorgan County Golf Union
Hon Sec, DC Thomas, 168 North Road, Ferndale, Rhondda CF43 4RA. *Tel* (01443) 730722

Gwent Golf Union
Sec, CM Buckley, 3 Oak Court, Woodfield Park, Blackwood, Gwent NP2 0BY. *Tel* (01495) 223520

Welsh Ladies' Golf Union
Hon Sec, Mrs S Webster, Catsash, Newport NP6 1JQ. *Tel/Fax* (01633) 422911.

Caernarvonshire & Anglesey Ladies' County Golf Association
Hon Sec, Mrs M Bromley, Ty'r Ysgol, Borth Y Gest, Porthmadog LL49 9UF.
Tel (01766) 512573.

Denbighshire & Flintshire Ladies' County Golf Association
Sec, Mrs D Jones, Pyllan Clai, Bontuchel, Ruthin, Denbighshire LL15 2BW.
Tel (01824) 710674

Glamorgan Ladies' County Golf Association
Sec, Mrs S Williams, 19 Trem-y-Don, Barry, South Glamorgan CF62 6QJ. *Tel* (01446) 734865

Mid Wales Ladies' County Golf Association
Sec, Miss A James, Flat 4, Penbryn Court, Lampeter, Dyfed SA48 7EU. *Tel* (01570) 422463

Monmouthshire Ladies' County Golf Association
Hon Sec, Mrs E Davidson, Jon-Len, Goldcliff, Newport NP6 2AU. *Tel* (01633) 274477

Europe

European Golf Association
Sec, JC Storjohann, Place de la Croix Blanche 19, PO Box, 1066 Epalinges, Lausanne, Switzerland. *Tel* +41 21 784 35 32
Fax +41 21 784 35 91 *Email* asg@planet.ch

Austrian Golf Association
Sec, Mrs W Neuwirth, Haus des Sports, Prinz-Eugen-Strasse 12, 1040 Vienna.
Tel +43 1 505 3245 *Fax* +43 1 505 4962
Email oegv@magnet.at *Website* www.asn.or.at/oegv

Royal Belgian Golf Federation
Sec, E Steghers, Chausée de la Hulpe 110, 1000 Brussels. *Tel* +32 2 672 23 89
Fax +32 2 672 08 97 *Email* info@frbg.be
Website www.frbg.be

Croatian Golf Association
Sec, D Slamar, Hotel Esplanade, Mihanoviceva 1, 10000 Zagreb. *Tel* +385 1 456 66 31
Fax +385 1 457 79 07

Czech Golf Federation
Sec, Ms M Dornikova, Erpet Golf Centre, Strakonicka 510, 150 00 Prague 5, Czech Republic. *Tel/Fax* +420 2 54 45 86

Danish Golf Union
Sec, EJ Heidler, Idrattens Hus, 2605 Brondby.
Tel +45 43 26 27 00 *Fax* +45 43 26 27 01
Email info@dgu-golf.dk *Website* www.dgu-golf.dk

Finnish Golf Union
Sec, O Saarinen, Radiokatu 20, SF-00240 Helsinki.
Tel +358 9 34 81 2244 *Fax* +358 9 14 71 45.
Email osmo.saarinen@golf.slu.fi
Website www.infopiste.fi/golf

French Golf Federation
Dir, H Chesneau, 68 Rue Anatole France, 92309 Levallais Perret Cedex.
Tel +33 1 41 49 7700 *Fax* +33 1 41 49 77 01
Email ffg@ffg.org *Website* www.ffg.org

French PGA
176 Rue Jean Jaures, 92800 Puteaux.
Tel +33 1 47 72 78 23 *Fax* +33 1 42 04 41 06

German Golf Association
Postfach 2106, Victoriastr 16, 65011 Wiesbaden.
Tel +49 611 990 200 *Fax* +49 611 990 2040
Email info@dgv.golf.de *Website* www.golf.de

German PGA
Werner Haas Str 6, 86153 Augsburg.
Tel +49 821 568 710 *Fax* +49 821 568 7129

Hellenic Golf Federation
PO Box 70003, GR 16610, Glyfada, Athens.
Tel +30 1 894 1933 *Fax* +30 1 894 5162

Iceland Golf Union
Sport Center, 104 Reykjavik. *Tel* +354 568 6686
Fax +354 568 6086 *Email* gsi@toto.is
Website www.golf.is

Italian Golf Federation
Viale Tiziano 74, 00196 Rome.
Tel +39 6 323 1825 *Fax* +39 6 322 0250

Luxembourg Golf Union
c/o GC Grand-Ducal de Luxembourg,
1 Route de Trèves, 2633 Senningerberg.
Tel +352 34 00 90 *Fax* +352 34 83 91

Netherlands Golf Federation
Sec, HL Heyster, PO Box 221,
3454 ZL De Meern.*Tel* +31 30 662 1888
Fax +31 30 662 1177 *Email* golf@ngf.nl
Website www.dutchgolf.com

Netherlands PGA
Sec, Mrs R Vonk, Burg. van der Borchlaan 1,
3722 GZ Bilthoven. *Tel* +31 30 228 7018
Fax +31 30 225 0261

Norwegian Golf Federation
Sec, A Styve, Mustadvei, PO Box 163, Lilleaker,
0216 Oslo. *Tel* +47 22 73 66 20
Fax +47 22 73 66 21
Email golfforbundet@nif.idrett.no

Polish Golf Union
Sec, D Sobczynski, Ul. Foksal 18, 00-372 Warsaw.
Tel +48 22 826 44 00 *Fax* +48 22 826 85 75

Portuguese Golf Federation
Rua General Ferreira Martins 10, Miraflores,
1495 Algés. *Tel* +351 1 410 7521
Fax +351 1 410 7972
Email fpgolfe@mail.telepac.pt

Russian Golf Association
Sec, A Nikolov, 8 Luzhnetskaya Emb,
119871 Moscow. *Tel/Fax* +7 095 201 1241

Slovak Golf Union
Sec, R Ondreicka, Prievovska 14a,
82109 Bratislava. *Tel* +421 7 523 1890
Fax +421 7 521 8834

Slovenian Golf Association
Bled G&CC, Ljubljanska Cesta 7, 4260 Bled.
Tel +386 64 700 7714 *Fax* +386 64 718 225

Spanish Golf Association
Sec, L Alvarez, Capitan Haya 9-5, 28020 Madrid.
Tel +34 1 555 26 82 *Fax* +34 1 556 32 90
Email webrfeg@ibm.net
Website www.sportec.com/rfeg

Swedish Golf Federation
Sec, B Wickberg, PO Box 84, 182 11 Danderyd.
Tel +46 8 622 1500 *Fax* +46 8 755 8439
Email sgf@golf.se *Website* www.golf.se

Swedish PGA
Sec, M Sorling, Tylösand, 302 73 Halmstad.
Tel +46 35 320 30 *Fax* +46 35 320 25

Swiss Golf Association
Sec, JC Storjohann, Place de la Croix Blanche
19, 1066 Epalinges, Lausanne.
Tel +41 21 784 3531 *Fax* +41 21 784 3536
Email asg@planet.ch *Website* www.asg.ch

Swiss PGA
Sec, M Scopetta, Place de la Croix Blanche 19,
Case Postale 14, 1066 Epalinges, Lausanne.
Tel +41 21 784 3543 *Fax* +41 21 784 3536

Turkish Golf Federation
GSGM Ulus is Hani, A Blok 2-Kat205, Ulus
08050, Ankara.

North America: USA & Canada

Canadian Ladies' Golf Association
Golf House, Glen Abbey, 1333 Dorval Drive,
Oakville, Ontario L6J 4Z3. *Tel* +1 905 849 2542
Fax +1 905 849 0188

Canadian PGA
13450 Dublin Line, Acton, Ontario L7J 2W7.
Tel +1 519 853 5450 *Fax* +1 519 853 5449

Ladies' Professional Golf Association
2570 West International Speedway Blvd, Suite
B, Daytona Beach, Florida 32114.
Tel +1 904 254 8800 *Fax* +1 904 254 4755

National Golf Foundation
1150 South US Highway One, Jupiter, Florida
33477. *Tel* +1 407 744 6000

PGA of America
Box 109601, 100 Avenue of the Champions,
Palm Beach Gardens, Florida 33418.
Tel +1 407 624 8400 *Fax* +1 407 624 8448

PGA Tour
Sawgrass, Ponte Vedra, Florida 32082.
Tel +1 904 285 3700 *Fax* +1 904 285 7913

Addresses of Golfing Organisations Worldwide

Royal Canadian Golf Association
Golf House, Glen Abbey, 1333 Dorval Drive, Oakville, Ontario L6J 4Z3. *Tel* +1 905 849 9700 *Fax* +1 905 845 7040

United States Golf Association
Golf House, PO Box 708, Far Hills, New Jersey 07931. *Tel* +1 908 234 2300 *Fax* +1 908 234 2179 *Email* usga@usga.org *Website* www.usga.org

Central America

Bahamas Golf Federation
PO Box N4568, Nassau, Bahamas

Barbados Golf Association
c/o Sandy Lane Golf Club, St James, Barbados

Bermuda Golf Association
PO Box HM 433, Hamilton Bermuda HM-BX. *Tel* +1 809 298 1367

El Salvador Golf Federation
Apartado Postal 631, San Salvador

Jamaica Golf Association
Constant Spring GC, PO Box 743, Kingston 8, Jamaica. *Tel* +1 809 925 2325

Mexican Golf Association
Cincinnati, No. 40-104, Mexico 18, DF

South America

Argentine Golf Association
Corrientes 538, Piso 11, 1043 Buenos Aires. *Tel* +54 1 325 7498

Bolivian Golf Federation
Casilla 10217, La Paz

Brazilian Golf Federation
Rua 7 de Abril, 01044 São Paulo

Chilean Golf Federation
Avda Golf 266, Las Condes, Santiago

Colombian Golf Union
Carrer 7A, 72-64 Int 26, Apartado Aereo 88768, Bogotà

Ecuador Golf Federation
Casilla 08-01-15149, Guayaquil

Paraguay Golf Association
Casilla de Correo 302, Asunción

Peru Golf Federation
Casilla 5637, Lima

South American Golf Federation
Cra 7, 72-64 Int 26, Santafe de Bogota, Colombia

Uruguay Golf Association
Casilla 1484, Montevideo

Venezuela Golf Federation
Local 5, Avda. Avila, La Florida, Caracas 1050

Africa

Botswana Golf Union
PO Box 1033, Gaborone, Botswana

Ghana Golf Association
PO Box 8, Achimola, Ghana

Kenya Golf Union
PO Box 49609, Nairobi, Kenya. *Tel* +254 2 720074

Kenya Ladies' Golf Union
PO Box 45615, Nairobi, Kenya

KwaZulu - Natal Golf Union
PO Box 1939, Durban 4000, South Africa

Malawi Golf Union
PO Box 1198, Blantyre, Malawi

Malawi Ladies' Golf Union
PO Box 5319, Limbe, Malawi

Namibian Golf Union
PO Box 2989, Windhoek 9000, Namibia

Nigeria Golf Union
National Sports Commission, Surulere, PO Box 145, Lagos, Nigeria

Sierra Leone Golf Federation
Freetown Golf Club, PO Box 237, Lumley Beach, Freetown, Sierra Leone

South African Golf Association
PO Box 391994, Bramley, South Africa 2018. *Tel* +27 11 442 3723 *Fax* +27 11 442 3753

South African Ladies' Golf Union
PO Box 135, 1930 Vereenigning, Transvaal, South Africa. *Tel /Fax* +27 16 231936

South African PGA
PO Box 79432, Senderwood 2145, South Africa. *Tel* +27 11 485 2327 *Fax* +27 11 485 1799

South African Women's PGA
PO Box 781547, Sandton 2146, South Africa. *Tel* +27 11 783 3213 *Fax* +27 11 789 1367

Swaziland Golf Union
PO Box 1739, Mbabane, Swaziland

Tanzania Golf Union
PO Box 6018, Dar-es-Salaam, Tanzania. *Tel* +255 51 36415/6

Tanzania Ladies' Golf Union
PO Box 286, Dar-es-Salaam, Tanzania

Uganda Golf Union
Kitante Road, PO Box 2574, Kampala, Uganda

Zaire Golf Federation
BP 1648, Lubumbashi, Zaire

Zambian Golf Union
PO Box 71784, Ndola, Zambia

Zambia Ladies' Golf Union
PO Box 90554, Luanshya, Zambia

Zimbabwe Golf Association
PO Box 3327, Harare, Zimbabwe

Zimbabwe Ladies' Golf Union
PO Box 3814, Harare, Zimbabwe

Asia and Far East

Asia-Pacific Golf Confederation
c/o Discovery Bay Golf Club, Valley Road, Discovery Bay, Hong Kong

Asia Golf Tour Inc.
8,2A 8th Floor, Jaya Shopping Centre, Jalan Semangat, 46100 Petaling Jaya, Selangor, Malaysia. *Tel* +603 758 2784 *Fax* +603 758 2169

China Golf Associaton
9 Tiya Guan Road, Beijing, China, 100763

PGA Republic of China
No 196 Pei Ling 5th Road, Taipei, Taiwan.
Tel +886 2 8220318 *Fax* +886 2 8229684

Hong Kong Golf Association
Room 2003, Sports House, 1 Stadium Path, Son KoPo, Causeway Bay, Hong Kong.
Tel +852 2522 8804 *Fax* +852 2845 1553

Hong Kong PGA
110 Yu To Sang Building, 37 Queens Road, Central, Hong Kong HX7 3751.
Tel +852 523 3171

Indian Golf Union
Sukh Sagar Building, 25 Sarat Bose Road, Calcutta 700 020, India

Indonesian Golf Association
Rawamangun Muka Raya, Jakarta 13220, Malaysia

Japan Golf Association
606-6th Floor, Palace Building, Marunouchi, Chiyoda-ku, Tokyo. *Tel* +81 3 3215 0003 *Fax* +81 3 3214 2831

Japan Ladies PGA
7–16-3 Ginza, Chuo-ku, Tokyo 104.
Tel +81 3 3546 7801 *Fax* +81 3 3546 7805

Japan PGA
Tel +81 3 3547 0131 *Fax* +81 3 3547 1030

Korean Golf Association
13th Floor, Manhattan Bldg, 36-2, Yeo-Eui-Do-Dowg, Yeong Deung Po-Ku, Seoul.
Tel +82 2 783 4748.

Malaysian Golf Association
12a Persiaran Ampang, 55000 Kuala Lumpur.
Tel +60 3 4577931 *Fax* +60 3 4565596.

Pakistan Golf Federation
PO Box No. 1295, Rawalpindi, Pakistan

Philippines Golf Association
209 Administration Building, Rizal Memorial Sports Complex, Vito Cruz, Manila, Philippines.
Tel +63 2 588845 *Fax* +63 2 521 1587.

Republic of China Golf Association
12 F-1, 125 Nanking East Road, Section 2, Taipei, Taiwan 104, Republic of China

Singapore Golf Association
PO Box 457, Singapore 912416.
Tel +65 466 4892 *Fax* +65 466 4897.

Sri Lanka Golf Union
223 Model Farm Road, Colombo 8, Sri Lanka.

Thailand Golf Association
83 Amnuay Songkram Road, Dusit, Bangkok 10300, Thailand

Australasia

Australian Golf Union
Golf Australia House, 153–155 Cecil Street, South Melbourne, Victoria 3205.
Tel +61 3 9699 7944 *Fax* +61 3 9690 8510
Email agu@agn.org.au *Website* www.agu.org.au

Womens Golf Australia
Exec Dir, Maisie Mooney, 355 Moray Street, South Melbourne, Victoria 3205.
Tel +61 3 9690 9344 *Fax* +61 3 9696 2060
Email info@womensgolfaus.org.au
Website www.womensgolfaus.org.au

Australian PGA
4/140 George Street,
Hornsby 2077 New South Wales.
Tel +61 2 476333 *Fax* +61 2 477 7625

New Zealand Golf Association
PO Box 11842, Wellington Library,
65 Victoria Street, Wellington.
Tel +64 4 4722 967 *Fax* +64 4 4997 330
Email nzga@xtra.co.nz
Website www.nzga.co.nz

Womens Golf New Zealand
Exec Dir, Mrs J Smart, PO Box 111-87, 65 Victoria Street, Wellington. *Tel* +64 4 4726 733
Fax +64 4 4726 732 *Email* golf@globe.co.nz

New Zealand PGA
PO Box 11-934, Wellington.
Tel +64 4 4722 687 *Fax* +64 4 4712 152.

PART XII

Golf History

The Championships of Great Britain	850
Famous Players of the Past	854
Interesting Facts and Unusual Incidents	870
Record Scoring	898

The Championships of Great Britain

The Open Championship

The Open Championship was initiated by Prestwick Golf Club in 1860 and was played there each year until 1870. Players competed for the Championship Belt, the winner holding it for the year unless it was won three years in succession in which case it would become the absolute property of that player. In those days the competition consisted of three rounds of the 12 hole course Prestwick then had, all played in one day (the Open did not become a four-round contest until 1892). There were few entrants in the early years and nearly all were professionals, who were sometimes also greenkeepers and clubmakers, though there were a few amateurs.

In 1870 Young Tom Morris won the Belt outright, and the following year there was no contest.

In 1872 three clubs, Prestwick, the Royal & Ancient Golf Club of St Andrews and the Honourable Company of Golfers (who at that time played at Musselburgh), together subscribed to provide the present trophy, which was not to be won outright. Had this condition not been changed, there have been only three winners who would have earned it: Jamie Anderson and Bob Ferguson both won three times in succession in the ten years after the trophy was instituted, and Peter Thomson in 1954–56.

Also from 1872 the Championship was to be held in turn on the courses of the three subscribing clubs. So it was that Young Tom Morris was the first to win the new cup at St Andrews, though this was to be his last time for he was to die tragically in 1875 at the age of 24.

In 1890, at Prestwick, John Ball became the first amateur to win the cup. Only two other amateurs have followed him: Harold Hilton in 1892 and 1897, and Bobby Jones in 1926, 1927 and 1930. Roger Wethered tied with Jock Hutchison at St Andrews in 1921, but lost the play-off – had he not incurred a penalty stroke through treading on his ball in the third round, he may well have won.

The three courses continued to be used until 1892 when it was first played at Muirfield, where the Honourable Company had moved to. That year was also the first in which the Championship became a 72 hole contest over two days.

The Triumvirate

The year 1894 saw the first occasion the Open was played in England at Sandwich and the first English professional to win, JH Taylor. He won again the next year and for the fifth time in 1913. Harry Vardon and James Braid were the two others of the *great triumvirate* who together won sixteen Opens between 1894 and 1914. Taylor's five wins were spread over 20 years and Vardon's six over 19. Braid's wins were concentrated into ten years from 1901 to 1910, all of them in Scotland. Vardon won three times at Prestwick but never at St Andrews, where Taylor and Braid both won twice. Only Taylor managed a win at Hoylake. No other player won more than once during their supremacy. The winning scores at the time were very high by today's standards, for although the courses were marginally shorter, the equipment and clothing were primitive compared with those in use now. At Sandwich Taylor's score was 326, or 38 over an average of 4s. His 304 at Hoylake in 1913 was played in appalling weather, wearing a tweed jacket, cap and boots, and using wooden shafts and leather grips. He had no protective clothing or umbrella and won by eight strokes from Ted Ray. The last winning total over 300 was Hagen's 301 at Hoylake in 1924.

Better Standards

That improved equipment has helped combat the greater length and heavier rough of today's Championship courses is suggested by comparing the average winning scores for decades of this century.

Decade	Average winning score	Decade	Average winning score
1905–14	302	1956–65	280
1920–29	295	1966–75	280
1930–39	289	1976–85	277
1946–55	284	1986–95	273

Of the 127 Opens held so far, 21 Americans, have won, 20 Scots, 16 English, four Australians, two South Africans and one each from France, Ireland, New Zealand, Argentina, Spain and Zimbabwe.

The Scots have won 39 times but only twice since Braid in 1910 (Duncan in 1920 and Lyle in 1985), the USA 34 times, England 29, Australia nine times, South Africa seven times, Spain three times and each of the others once. Since the triumvirate's day ended, the only Englishmen to win more than once have been Sir Henry Cotton and Nick Faldo, both with three victories. The Americans have won 34 out of the last 71 Opens played.

It will be seen that certain nationalities tend to dominate for a decade or so; the Scots until 1893, then the English until 1914, the USA in the 1920s and until 1933 when the English had a short resuscitation. The Commonwealth were to the fore from 1949 to 1965 (Locke, Thomson, Nagle and Charles) with the Americans coming back again to win in 13 out of 18 years between 1966 and 1983. Equally dominating in their periods were Hagen and Jones in the twenties, Cotton in the thirties, Locke and Thomson the fifties, and thereafter Palmer, Nicklaus, Player, Trevino, Watson and Ballesteros.

Open Courses

Only 14 courses have accommodated the Open. St Andrews leads with 25, followed by Prestwick, which was discarded in 1925 as unsuitable for large crowds, with 24. The second group comprises Muirfield with 14, Royal St George's, Sandwich 12 and Hoylake with ten. Hoylake's last Open was in 1967; that it is not used now is due not to any lack of quality of the course but to lack of space. Deal appeared in 1909 and 1920, and was due again in 1949 but the sea broke across the course, and Sandwich came in for the last time until 1981. Troon and Royal Lytham and St Annes each held an Open between the wars, Carnoustie two and Princes, Sandwich, when Sarazen won in 1932, one; this course, which was used as a tank training ground during the Second World War, has not been asked again. In 1951, Portrush, the only Irish course to stage an Open, also provided the only English winner between Cotton and Jacklin in Max Faulkner. Birkdale and Turnberry are firmly established in the rota which for many years settled at four Scottish courses – St Andrews, Muirfield, Troon and Turnberry – and three in England – Royal Lytham and St Annes, Birkdale and Royal St George's, Sandwich. In 1999, however, Carnoustie will host the championship for the first time since 1975.

Traditionally the Open is only played on links courses. While there may yet be new venues by the sea capable of being stretched and groomed to be worthy of holding an Open, the many other considerations to be weighed, such as an adequate road system to carry vast crowds and nearly as many acres as the course covers to accommodate the tented village and services, it is not easy to see where the Championship Committee will turn.

Qualifying

How does one qualify to play in an Open? Since qualifying was first introduced in 1914, there have been numerous changes. Regional qualifying was tried for a year in 1926. At one of the courses used, Sunningdale, Bobby Jones (and even he had to qualify!) played what many consider the classic round of golf: a 66, all 4s and 3s, never over par, 8 birdies, 33 putts and 33 other shots.

Until 1963 all competitors, even the holder, had to play two qualifying rounds on the Open course on the Monday and Tuesday of the Open week. The qualifiers then had one round on Wednesday, one on Thursday and the leading group of between 40 and 60 players finished with two rounds on Friday. In 1963 certain exemptions from qualifying were introduced. The two rounds on the Friday were dropped in 1966 in favour of one round each on Friday and Saturday; not until 1980 was the first round played on Thursday and the last on Sunday. As the entry continued to increase, in 1970 nearby courses were used for qualifying and in 1977 regional qualifying was reintroduced in the previous week with final qualifying on nearby courses later.

There have been surprisingly few ties involving a play-off, only 14 in 127 Championships. The first should have been in 1876 involving David Strath and Bob Martin. However, Strath took umbrage over a complaint against him and refused to play again, Martin being declared the winner. Until 1963 ties were decided over 36 holes; the next two, between Nicklaus and Sanders at St Andrews in 1970 and Watson and Newton at Carnoustie in 1975, were played over 18. Later it was decided that in the event of a tie, the winner would be found immediately by a play-off over specified holes, followed by 'sudden death' if necessary. This happened in 1989 when Calcavecchia beat Norman and Grady over four holes after finishing level on 275. In 1995 there was another, John Daly beating Costantino Rocca at St Andrews, and in 1998 a third, Mark O'Meara defeating his fellow American Brian Watts at Royal Birkdale, to add the Open to the Masters title he had won three months previously.

Prize Money

In 1863 the total prize money was £10, its distribution among the 14 entrants, six of whom were amateurs, is unknown. A year later it had risen by over 50% to £16; the winner taking £6. By 1993 the total prize fund reached £1,000,000 of which the winner received £100,000. In 1998 this had risen to £300,000. Until about 1955, the winner's and leaders' rewards were very modest; even in 1939 the cheque for the first man was £100 out of a total of £500. With some justification the prestige of winning the Open then was adjudged

to be of much more value than any monetary award. The growth since the 1950s has been astonishing and is evidence that, while it is still a tremendous asset for any man to have won the Open, the authorities have recognised that it will not maintain its leading place without substantial reward.

The rapid advance of the Open to the major spectacle it has become is due to a combination of factors. Not least of these is the TV presentation of the BBC, acknowledged as the world's best in golf, the interest and enthusiasm of thousands of spectators keen to watch on the spot rather than on the box, and the Royal & Ancient's promotion of this world showpiece of golf that it has become. Behind it all has been the foresight of successive Championship Committees and, in the late 1960s and 1970s, the masterly spreading of the gospel by Keith Mackenzie, Secretary of the R&A in 1966-82, that is so ably continued by his successor, Michael Bonallack, who in June 1998 was knighted in the Queen's birthday list.

Laurence Viney

The Amateur Championship

Early History

Golf has always been a competitive game and club medals have been keenly contested since the nineteenth century. Many of the leading amateurs were members of several clubs and, aided by an excellent railway system, they competed against each other at such venues as St Andrews, Prestwick, Hoylake and Musselburgh. An embryonic *open amateur competition* was held in the late 1850s (the first being won by Robert Chambers, the publisher, in 1858) but there seems to have been little enthusiasm for such an event and it died around the time of the first Open Championship (1860). The best amateurs began to enter the Open from 1861. By the 1870s, there was renewed interest in organising a tournament for amateurs only but nothing happened, probably because no one club took a strong enough lead. A proposal in 1877 to the membership of the R&A that it sponsor a sort of Amateur Championship (involving club members and others nominated by members) was defeated.

It fell to the Hoylake golfers to set in motion the championship we now know as *The Amateur*. In 1884 the Secretary of Royal Liverpool, Thomas Potter, proposed that an event – open to all amateurs – should be organised. This original intention was not carried out until 1886 and so the winner of 1885 (AF Macfie) triumphed over a strong, but limited, field drawn from certain clubs. The clubs that were responsible for the running of the championship until the R&A took over in 1920 – and who made contributions for the purchase of the trophy – were:

Royal & Ancient
Royal Burgess Golfing Society of Edinburgh
Royal Liverpool
Royal St George's
Royal Albert, Montrose
Royal North Devon
Royal Aberdeen
Royal Blackheath
Royal Wimbledon
Royal Dublin
Alnmouth
North Berwick, New Club
Panmure, Dundee
Prestwick
Bruntsfield Links Golfing Society, Edinburgh
Dalhousie
Gullane
Formby
Honourable Company of Edinburgh Golfers
Innerleven
King James VI, Perth
Kilspindie
Luffness
Tantallon
Troon
West Lancashire

The first championship was not without its teething troubles. The format which was adopted allowed both golfers to proceed to the next round if their match was halved, so the first championship had three semi-finalists – and Macfie got a bye into the final. From 1886, the usual format was adopted.

More serious than the problem of an idiosyncratic draw, however, was the question of amateur status, raised for the first time in 1886.

The committee had to decide if it should accept the entries of John Ball III and Douglas Rolland. As a 15-year-old, Ball had finished fourth in the 1878 Open at Prestwick and on the advice of Jack Morris he accepted the prize money of 10s (50p). Rolland, a stonemason, had accepted second prize in the 1884 Open. Rolland's entry to the Amateur was refused while Ball's was accepted. Ball went on to win the championship a record eight times and the Open Championship of 1890.

The Format

After such a difficult start, the format of 18-hole matches with a 36-hole final remained until 1956. This arrangement made for many closely fought matches, as shown in 1930, the year of RT Jones' Grand Slam triumph. Jones' only victory in the event came in the right year and it is worth pointing

out that, in making his way to the final, he won in the fourth round at the 19th (by laying a stymie) against Cyril Tolley, the holder, and his victories in the sixth round and in the semi-final were by the narrowest of margins. In addition, the fact that the draw was not seeded sometimes meant early meetings between top golfers; for example, in 1926 the visiting American Walker Cup Team members, von Elm and Ouimet, met in the second round and von Elm went on to meet Jesse Sweetser in the third.

As a result of such events, there was some pressure for the introduction of seeding the draw but it was not until 1958 that the practice was officially adopted. In the 50s and 60s there were other changes in format in an attempt to satisfy large numbers of golfers who wished to play and to ensure a worthy winner.

The popularity of the championship has posed difficulties for the R&A. The mathematically ideal number of entrants to be fitted into a convenient format is 256. In 1950, 324 entered the championship causing golf to be played on the Old Course for 14 hours a day. In order to restrict the numbers turning up to the championship proper, an experiment in regional qualifying was held in 1958 (again a St Andrews year) and 488 players with handicaps of 5 and under played 36 holes of stroke play on 14 courses. This system was quickly replaced and in 1961 the handicap limit was lowered (to 3) and a balloting-out of higher handicaps was introduced so that 256 were left to play for the trophy. This method was followed until 1983 with the introduction of 36 holes of stroke play to find 64 players for match play, from which to find the eventual winner. The handicap limit in 1997 was 1.

There was also pressure for the introduction of 36-hole matches. As early as 1922 the R&A's championship committee canvassed the opinion of the 252 men who played that year. 19 of these voted in favour of 36-hole matches, seven for district qualification, 52 voted for a stroke play qualification followed by 18-hole matches and the others who replied wanted no change to the system. In 1956 and 1957 the last three rounds were played over 36 holes, in 1958 and 1959 the semi-final and final were over 36 holes and then the old format returned.

There is constant pressure on the organisers to find a format to satisfy the needs of large numbers of home and foreign players, to take into account differences in national handicapping systems, to preserve the atmosphere of the championship, to maintain match play as a central feature of top-level amateur golf and even to take into account the vagaries of the weather. The task is almost impossible.

The Winners

Any man who wins the Amateur is a considerable golfer but there are certain outstanding champions. John Ball of Royal Liverpool won the title eight times between 1888 and 1912. It is interesting to note that he never successfully defended his title. Michael Bonallack triumphed five times between 1961 and 1970, including an incredible hat-trick of victories in which he successively beat Joe Carr and Bill Hyndman twice.

Several golfers have successfully defended their title: Horace Hutchinson, Harold Hilton, Lawson Little and Peter McEvoy, while others have won twice or more – Johnny Laidlay, Freddie Tait, Bob Maxwell, Cyril Tolley, Edward Holderness, Frank Stranahan, Joe Carr and Trevor Homer.

The oldest man to win was the Hon Michael Scott, at the age of 54 in 1933. The youngest winners – John Beharrell and Bobby Cole – were both 18 years and 1 month old. Cole's victory over Ronnie Shade was achieved over 18 holes – play being affected by poor visibility. The first overseas winner was Walter Travis who won in 1904 – one consequence of his victory was the banning of the use of centre-shafted putters. The first Continental winner was the Frenchman Philippe Ploujoux, who won in 1981. A visiting Walker Cup team always made for an exciting championship and from 17 visits to Great Britain the title crossed the Atlantic 12 times.

No doubt there have been hundreds of thrilling matches played in the Championship, but few can have been as pulsating as the 1899 final at Prestwick where Johnny Ball beat Freddie Tait at the 37th hole. The victory must have been a sweet one for Ball, since Tait, the hero of Scotland, had won the previous year over Ball's home links of Hoylake. Sadly, Tait was killed in the Boer War in 1900. *The great battle*, as Jones described his fourth round tie against Tolley in 1930, rivalled the Ball-Tait final for tense excitement, but for sheer brilliance of scoring, Michael Bonallack's first round in the 1968 final must take pride of place.

The Amateur Championship has been played for over a century and in essence it has changed remarkably little. The increasing popularity of the game at home and abroad, the lure of the professional ranks with its dependence on stroke play and the increasing commercialism of all sport notwithstanding, the Championship continues to stand for all that is great in golf.

David Christie

Famous Players of the Past

In making the difficult choice of the names to be included, effort has been made to acknowledge the outstanding players and personalities of each successive era from the early pioneers to the stars of recent times.

Alliss, Percy (1897–1975)

Percy Alliss was one of Britain's most successful professionals between the wars. He was in the top six in the Open Championship seven times, his best finish being at Carnoustie in 1931 when he tied third, two strokes behind Tommy Armour. That same year he was also runner-up in the Canadian Open. He was a member of three Ryder Cup teams in 1933-35-37, an international honour also gained later by his son, Peter.

Much of his career was spent at Wansee club in Berlin, and it was during this time that he won the German Open in four successive years from 1926 and then again in 1933. He was Italian Open champion in 1927 and 1935 and won the British Matchplay Championship in 1933 and 1937. A most consistent performer, he was noted particularly for his long iron play.

Anderson, Jamie (1842–1912)

Winner of three consecutive Open Championships (1877-78-79). Born at St Andrews, he was the son of *Old Daw*, a St Andrews caddie and character. Jamie began golf when 10 years old, and rapidly developed into a fine player, noted for straight hitting and good putting. Anderson's method was to play steadily and on one occasion at St Andrews he remarked that he had played 90 consecutive holes without a bad shot or one stroke made otherwise than he had intended. He was for a period professional to Ardeer Club, but returned to St Andrews to follow his vocation of playing professional.

Anderson, Willie (1878–1910)

One of the Scottish emigrants to America, his flat swing won him the US Open in 1901, 1903, 1904 and 1905. He shares the record of four Open titles with Jones, Hogan and Nicklaus, and remains the only man to win three in a row.

Armour, Thomas D (1896–1968)

Open Champion, 1931. US Open Champion, 1927. USPGA 1930. He had a distinguished amateur career – including the French Open Amateur and tied first place in the Canadian Open. He had the unique distinction of playing in 1921 for Britain against the US as an amateur and in 1925 as a professional for the US against Britain in the unofficial international matches that preceded the inception of the Walker Cup and Ryder Cup events. When he came to the end of his tournament career he quickly gained an outstanding reputation as a coach, and books he wrote on the technique of the game were best-sellers

Auchterlonie, William (1872–1963)

Won the Open title at Prestwick at the age of 21 with a set of seven clubs which he had made himself and shortly afterwards founded the famous club-making firm in St Andrews. He never played with more than his seven clubs and was a great believer that a golfer had to be master of the half, three-quarter and full shots with each club. As professional to the Royal & Ancient Golf Club from 1935 to his death he saw one of his ambitions fulfilled – the Centenary Open at St Andrews in 1960.

Ball, John (1862–1940)

One of the greatest amateur golfers of all time. His father owned the Royal Hotel, Hoylake, prior to the formation of the golf links and when there was a small racecourse on the land later formed into the Royal Liverpool Links. The links became John Ball's playground. In 1878, when fifteen years old, he competed in the Open Championship, finished fourth, eight strokes behind the winner and ahead of many famous Scottish professionals of that time. Between 1888 and 1912 he won the Amateur Championship eight times. In 1890 he was the first amateur to win the Open Championship. He played for England against Scotland continuously from 1902 to 1911, captaining the side each year. He was Amateur Champion in 1899 when war with South Africa broke out and Ball served in that campaign with

the Cheshire Yeomanry and did not compete in the Championships of 1900-01-02. In the First World War he served in the Home Forces. He played in his last Amateur Championship in 1921, the year of the first American invasion, and he reached the fifth round although in his fifty-eighth year. Modest and retiring, he rarely spoke about his golf. On the morning of his last round in the Championship he remarked to a friend in the clubhouse, *If only a storm of wind and rain would sweep across the links from the Welsh hills I feel I could beat all of them once again.* But it was a week of torrid heat and he failed. He retired to his farm in North Wales, where he died in December 1940.

Barton, Miss Pamela (1917–43)

At the age of twenty-two when the Second World War broke out, Miss Pamela Barton had already achieved great fame in the golfing world. She won the Ladies' Championship 1936-39, was runner-up 1934-35, won the American Ladies' Championship in 1936 and the French Ladies' Championship in 1934. In 1936, at the age of nineteen, she held both the British and American Ladies' Championships, the first person to do so since 1909. Miss Barton played for England in the home internationals in 1935-36-37-38-39; for Great Britain v United States in 1934-36; v France in 1934-36-37-38-39. She was a member of the Ladies' Golf Union teams which toured Canada and America, 1934, and Australia and New Zealand in 1935. Of a charming and cheerful disposition, Miss Barton, who became a Flight Officer in the WAAF, was killed in a plane crash at an RAF airfield in Kent.

Boros, Julius (1920–94)

Of Hungarian extraction he is remembered for his long, lazy swing and quiet personality. He won two US Open Championships, the first in 1952 and the second 11 years later, at the age of 43, in a play-off against Arnold Palmer and Jackie Cupit. It made him the oldest winner of the title until overtaken by Hale Irwin (45) in 1990. He became the oldest US PGA champion – and the oldest winner of a major championship to date – at 48 in 1968, while his best finish in the US Masters was third in 1963 and his best in the Open Championship 15th at Muirfield in 1966.

Braid, James (1870–1950)

One of the greatest figures in golf of all times, James Braid, with Harry Vardon and JH Taylor, made up the Triumvirate which dominated British professional golf for twenty years before the First World War. He was the first person to win the Open Championship five times. This record was later equalled by Taylor and beaten by Vardon. Braid's achievements were remarkable for the short time in which they were accomplished. In ten years he won five times and was second on three occasions. His victories were in 1901, 1905, 1906, 1908, 1910. He won the Match Play Tournament four times, 1903-5-7-11, a record which was unequalled till 1950, and the French Open Championship in 1910. He played for Scotland v England in 1903-4-5-6-7-9-10-12 and for Great Britain against America, 1921. A joiner by trade, Braid played as an amateur in Fife and Edinburgh and in 1893 went to London and worked as a club-maker. Taylor and Vardon were well established in the golfing world before Braid turned professional in 1896 and he quickly came into prominence by finishing level with Taylor, who by that time had been Champion twice, in a challenge match. In a historic international foursomes, Braid and partner Alex Herd lost to Vardon and Taylor in a match for £400 over four courses. A tall, powerful player who lashed the ball with *divine* fury, he was famous for his imperturbability: no matter how the game was progressing he always appeared outwardly calm and it was this serenity of temperament which assisted him to his Championship victories on two occasions. A man of few words, it was once said that *Nobody could be as wise as James Braid looked.* One of the founder members of the Professional

Pam Barton   Popperfoto

Golfers' Association, Braid did much to elevate the status of the professional golfer. Braid made a major contribution to golf architecture; Gleneagles, Rosemount, Carnoustie and Dalmahoy all bear his stamp. He was admired and respected by all who knew him, as much for his modest and kindly nature as for his prowess as a golfer. He was professional at Romford for eight years and at Walton Heath for forty-five, and was for twenty-five years an honorary member of the latter club, becoming one of its directors. He was made an honorary member of the Royal & Ancient Golf Club in the last years of his life and had the distinction of being the only honorary member of the Parliamentary Golfing Society.

Bruen, Jimmy (1920–72)

Born in Belfast, but based in Cork nearly all his life, Jimmy Bruen was hailed as a teenage sensation: twice winning the Irish Amateur Championship, and in 1938, at the age of 18, becoming the youngest-ever player in the Walker Cup. In the trials at St Andrews he equalled the amateur course record of 68 (set by the great Bobby Jones), and in the match itself, playing number one, he helped Britain and Ireland record their first victory over the Americans. He and partner Harry Bentley displayed their sportsmanship during the open foursomes, refusing to claim a hole when opponent Johnny Fischer played out of turn. His career was sadly cut off in its prime by the Second World War and later by a wrist injury which forced his retirement. He died of a heart attack five days before his 52nd birthday.

Campbell, Miss Dorothy Iona (1883–1946)

Won British Ladies' Championship, 1909-11; Scottish Ladies' Championship, 1905-6-8; American Ladies' Championship, 1909-10; Canadian Ladies' Championship 1910-11-12. One of only two women golfers to win the British, American and Canadian Championships, the other being Marlene Stewart (Mrs M Stewart Streit). Played for Scotland in international matches and for British Ladies v American Ladies.

Compston, Archie (1893–1962)

One of the outstanding personalities of British golf in the years between the two World Wars who fought hard to resist the developing dominance of the American invasion. He played in three Ryder Cup matches – in 1927, 1929 and 1931. In a 72-hole challenge match he beat Hagen by 18 and 17 in 1928 at Moor Park and in the Open which followed he finished third to Hagen. He tied for second place in the Open of 1925.

Cotton, Sir Henry (1907–87)

Sir Henry Cotton bestrode the British professional golf scene as player, teacher, writer, course architect and encourager of youth from 1930 until his death in December 1987, a few days before his well-deserved knighthood was announced.

He was the only Briton to win the Open more than once in a period of 75 years, between 1914 and 1989; his three victories at Sandwich in 1934, Carnoustie in 1937 and Muirfield in 1948 were pinnacles in a dedicated, sometimes controversial, but highly successful career. All three victories contained at least one memorable round. His 65 at Sandwich (after which a golf ball was named), his last round 71 at Carnoustie in a downpour and his record 66 at Muirfield, with King George VI among the spectators, showed a style both of play and of life admired by all.

No man did more to raise the status of the professional golfer. His insistence on having Honorary Membership of clubs to which he was attached – Waterloo Brussels, Ashridge, Royal Mid-Surrey and Temple near Maidenhead – began a practice now followed by many clubs with their professionals. As Ryder Cup player and Captain, founder-member of the Golf Foundation, and his Rookie of the Year award, he led by

Henry Cotton   Popperfoto

example. His reward, which many would say came too late, was the first knighthood given for service to golf.

His many playing successes included winning eleven Continental Opens and five finals in the *News of the World* Match Play Tournament, which at the time was second only in prestige to the Open which he won twice. He was four times selected for the Ryder Cup team, being Captain in 1937 and non-playing Captain in 1953. Captain of the PGA in 1934 and 1954, he also had many other lesser tournament wins.

During the war, in which he served in the RAF, he played exhibition matches in aid of the Red Cross and encouraged his fellow professionals to do likewise. After he retired from Championship play, he devoted his time to writing articles for the golf press and several books. He was also a great supporter of the Golf Foundation and for the development of his beloved Penina in Portugal where he spent much of his last years.

He was elected to Honorary Membership of the Royal & Ancient Club in 1968 and was aware of his coming knighthood when he died a few days before it was announced.

The Curtis Sisters:
Harriet (1878–1944)
Margaret (1880–1965)

The names of Harriet Curtis and her sister Margaret will always be remembered in golf because in 1932 they donated the Curtis Cup for biennial competition between women golfers of the United States and Great Britain and Ireland. Harriet won the US Women's Amateur championship in 1906 and played her sister Margaret in the final the following year, when Margaret won the first of her three titles. Margaret competed in the event for the last time in 1947, more than 50 years after her first appearance.

Darwin, Bernard (1876–1961)

One of the most respected and widely known personalities in the game. As a graceful and authoritative writer on golf and golfers he had no equal. He knew intimately every player and every course of note throughout the world, and his phenomenal memory, fluent pen and gentle humour established him as the top historian of the game over many years. In 1937 he was awarded the CBE for his services to literature, which included journalism, books of children's stories and other sports besides golf. He was captain of the Royal & Ancient Club in 1934-35, and played internationally for England from 1902 until 1924 and in the first Walker Cup match (1922). He had travelled to the US to report the match for *The Times* and had been called in to play and captain the side when Robert Harris fell ill. During his playing career he won many amateur titles and trophies. He was a grandson of Charles Darwin.

Demaret, Jimmy (1910–83)

One of the game's most colourful characters, stemming no doubt from the fact that he was still a nightclub singer in 1940 when he won six consecutive tournaments against very strong opposition. It culminated with the Masters which he also won in 1947 and 1950, making him the first man to collect three green jackets. It was a remarkable victory because Demaret made up seven strokes on Jim Ferrier over the last six holes, winning by two after being five behind. Demaret was a co-owner of the Champions club in Houston, where the 1967 Ryder Cup and 1969 US Open were played. His record in the Ryder Cup in the years 1947-49-51 is without parallel. He won all his six matches, two of the three foursomes being in partnership with Ben Hogan.

Dickinson, Gardner (1927–98)

Known as 'The Slim Man', Gardner Dickinson played in the 1967 and 1971 Ryder Cup matches and won nine of his ten games. Five of the victories were in partnership with Arnold Palmer. His career also featured eight US Tour wins, but he never managed to finish higher than fifth in any major championship between 1953 and 1973. He went on to become a founder member of the US Senior Tour.

Duncan, George (1884–1964)

He was the last Scottish-born winner of the Open title domiciled in Britain. He won the title in 1920 and his victory was achieved after two opening rounds of 80 which left him 13 strokes behind the leader. Two years later, at Sandwich, he finished second to Hagen after one of the most exciting finishes up to that time. Hagen had finished and was already being hailed as the winner when Duncan, a very late starter, reached the 18th hole needing a 4 to tie. He failed but his round was notable as the only one under 70 in that Open and the first to break 70 in the Open since 1904. Prior to the first war, Duncan was a prominent challenger to the established Triumvirate and would probably have achieved greater fame but for the war years during which he would have been at his prime. One of the fastest players of all time, he wasted no time, especially on the greens, and his book *Golf at a Gallop* was appropriately titled.

The Dunns

The twin brothers Dunn, born at Musselburgh in 1821, were prominent in golf between 1840 and 1860. In 1849, Old Willie Dunn and Jamie Dunn

played their great match against Allan Robertson and Old Tom Morris. Willie Dunn became custodian in the Blackheath Links until 1864, and he then returned to Leith, and later to North Berwick, where he died at the age of 59. Willie Dunn was celebrated for the peculiar grace of his style and, as the longest driver of his day, he was a doughty match fighter, and one of his famous games was with Allan Robertson in 1843, when he played the St Andrews champion 20 rounds, and lost by 2 rounds and 1 to play. Another famous match was in 1852, when, partnered by Sir Robert Hay, he played Allan Robertson and Old Tom. Jamie Dunn, his twin brother, was also a fine player.

Willie's son went to America, and won the first Championship of America in 1894. He was among the first to experiment with the idea of steel shafts. About 1900 he inserted thin steel rods in split cane and lancewood shafts. He invented a coneshaped paper tee, the forerunner of the wooden tee, and was a pioneer of indoor golf schools. He died in London in 1952.

Ferguson, Bob (1848–1915)

Started to caddie on Musselburgh when aged eight. In 1866, when 18, he won the first prize in the Leith Tournament, in which all the great professionals of the day took part. The late Sir Charles Tennant put up the money for young Ferguson, who, in 1868 and 1869, beat Tom Morris six times. In 1875, at Hoylake, with young Tom Morris representing Scotland in a foursome, he beat Bob Kirk, Blackheath, and John Allan, Westward Ho!, representing England. He won the Open Championship in 1880, 1881 and 1882. In 1883 he tied with Willie Fernie, losing the 36-hole play-off by one stroke. After this Championship he became ill with typhoid, and was never able to reproduce his great form. He became the custodian of the Musselburgh links, taught the young and was widely respected in the community.

Fernie, Willie (1851–1924)

Born in St Andrews, he went to Dumfries in 1880 as greenkeeper. In 1882 he was second to Bob Ferguson in the Open Championship and after a tie with the same player he won the Open Championship in 1883 at Musselburgh after a 36-hole play-off. He became professional to Felixstowe and Ardeer and in 1887 to Troon, and was there as professional until February, 1924. He was a very stylish player and in great demand as a teacher. He played in many important stake matches, the two biggest being against Andrew Kirkaldy over Troon, Prestwick and St Andrews which he won by 4 and 3, and against Willie Park over Musselburgh and Troon which he lost by 13 and 12. He played for Scotland against England in 1904.

Hagen, Walter (1892–1969)

The first of the great golfers with star quality. People flocked to see him as much because he was a *character* as for his outstanding skill and many achievements. He did not want to be a millionaire, but merely to live like one, and this he did in dramatic style as when he used a hired Rolls-Royce as a changing room at the Open because professionals were not admitted to the clubhouse, and when he gave the whole of his first prize in the Open to his caddie. He also pioneered stylish dressing on the course. As a player he had great mastery of the recovery shot, nerves of steel beneath his debonair exterior and a fine putting touch. His best achievement was probably his four consecutive wins in the USPGA championship when the event was decided by matchplay over 36 holes. He won the US Open in 1914 and 1919 and the Open in 1922-24-28-29 and represented the US against Britain on seven occasions. His world tours with Kirkwood, his extrovert approach and the entertainment he provided on and off the course were the forerunners of the spectacular development of golf as a spectator sport. In spite of his being a contemporary of the immortal Bobby Jones, his personality was such that he was never overshadowed.

Herd, Alexander 'Sandy' (1868–1944)

His life in the forefront of the game was more prolonged than his contemporaries of the Victorian era, and when he took part in his last Open at St Andrews in 1939 he was 71 and his appearances in the Championship covered a span of 54

Walter Hagen   Popperfoto

years. A brilliant shot player, success often eluded him as he was prone to leave his putts short and to indecision. On his first appearance in the Open, at the age of 17, he possessed only four clubs and although he was frequently in contention it was not until 1902 that he won the Championship. He was the first player to win the Open using a rubber-cored ball. In 1920 at Deal and again the following year at St Andrews he was joint leader in the Open after three rounds. In 1926, aged 58, he won the PGA Match Play tournament at Royal Mid-Surrey in a 36-hole final, having played five rounds in the previous three days to reach it. Those three achievements when he was in his fifties are convincing proof of the longevity of his game. His life in golf brought him into competition with all the great Victorians – Taylor, Vardon, Kirkaldy, Braid and Park – and continued through the Jones and Hagen era up to the days of Locke, Cotton, Rees and Sarazen and others who, over 100 years after Herd's birth, were still playing Open Championship golf.

Hilton, Harold   (1869–1942)

Born at West Kirby, a few miles from Hoylake, he was one of the most scientific of golfers. He learned his game at Royal Liverpool, where he won success in boys' competitions. In 1892, the year the Open Championship was extended to 72 holes, he won, and again in 1897. He won the Amateur Championship and the Irish Open Championship four times each, the St George's Cup twice, the American Amateur Championship once and became the first player, and the only Britisher, to hold both the US and British Amateur titles at the same time. He was small, 5 feet 7 inches, but immensely powerful in build. Hilton made a major contribution to golf literature as the first editor of *Golf Monthly*.

Hogan, Ben   (1912–1997)

As one of only four golfers to date to win all four major championships – the Masters, United States Open, Open and United States PGA – Ben Hogan is assured of a place among the sport's all-time greats. He dominated the scene in America after the Second World War, playing golf of a standard few have witnessed before or since, and in 1953 came closer than anyone has ever done to achieving the Grand Slam of all four in one season. Only a clash of dates between the Open and US PGA denied him the opportunity. Yet four years earlier it had looked as if his career might be prematurely ended. Hogan and his wife were involved in a crash with a Greyhound bus in fog in Texas and there were reports that he might not survive his horrific injuries. But survive he did, and after having to learn how to walk again,

Ben Hogan   Phil Sheldon

he returned to action just under a year later and within weeks was a winner again.

Remarkably, it had taken him almost a decade as a professional to record his first victory and he was 34 when he won the first of his nine majors, the 1946 US PGA. He was 11 under par in beating Jimmy Demaret 10 and 9 in the semi-finals, and in the final, after finding himself three down to Ed Oliver, he played the next 14 holes in eight under par and won 6 and 4. He went on to win both the US Open and US PGA in 1948 and, following his crash, added six more majors in the space of four seasons.

Never fond of overseas travel, his Open Championship debut did not come until 1953, the year he won the Masters by five shots, the US Open by six and triumphed in five of the six tournaments he entered. Alien though Carnoustie must have seemed to him, he scored 73-71-70-68 to win by four strokes. It was to prove his one and only appearance in the event, but at home he continued to strive for perfection and even at the age of 54 he finished tenth in the 1967 Masters, including a round of 66 where he played the inward half in 30.

His life, dramatic from the moment his father committed suicide when Ben was nine, was made into a Hollywood film entitled *Follow the Sun*, starring Glenn Ford.

Hunter, Charles (1836–1921)

A caddie and club-maker under old Tom Morris at Prestwick, he was for three years professional at the Blackheath Club, London, and succeeded old Tom as the Prestwick Club professional in 1864. He played in the first Open Championship at Prestwick in 1860, and he was a conspicuous figure at every championship and tournament held at Prestwick, acting as starter and in charge of the house flag up till the time of his death. He did not take much part in professional competitions, preferring to attend to his club-making and his members. In fact, during one championship round, while playing a niblick shot, he received word that the Lord Ailsa wished him to come at once and pick him out a set of clubs. He put his niblick back in his bag, pocketed his ball and returned to his workshop. In 1919 he was presented with his portrait in oils by the Prestwick Club, and a replica hangs in the Club. At the Open Championship of 1914 at Prestwick, he was the recipient of a presentation from his brother professionals. As a man of fine integrity, his friendship was valued by all golfers of his time.

Hutchinson, Horace (1859–1932)

An eminent golfer from the early 80s until 1907. He was a stylish and attractive player. Won the Amateur Championship in 1886 and 1887, runner-up 1885 (the first year of the Championship), and he was in the final in 1903. He was a semi-finalist in 1896, 1901, and 1904. He represented England v Scotland 1902-3-4-6-7, and was chosen in 1905 but illness prevented him taking his place. His career in the front rank of the game extended over twenty years. He was a voluminous and pleasant writer on golf and out-door life. He was the first Englishman to captain the Royal & Ancient. In other years he was also Captain of Royal Liverpool, Royal St George's and President of Royal North Devon.

Jones, Bobby (1902–1971)

By the time he retired from competitive golf in 1930 at the age of 28, Jones had established himself as one of the greatest golfers of all time, if not the greatest. He represented America in the Walker Cup from its inauguration in 1922 until 1930, and played in the match against Great Britain in 1921. His victories included the US Open in 1923-26-29-30 (tied in 1925 and 1928 but lost the play-off; second in 1922 and 1924); US Amateur 1924-25-27-28-30 (runner-up in 1919 and 1926); Open Championship 1926-27-30; Amateur Championship 1930. In 1930, Jones reached a pinnacle which will probably never be equalled when he achieved the Grand Slam – winning in one year the Open and Amateur Championships of America and Britain. He then retired from championship golf.

Bobby Jones' stylish swing was the subject of admiration wherever he went – full, flowing, smooth, graceful and rhythmical. Yet he was of such a nervous disposition that he was frequently physically sick and unable to eat during a championship.

During his championship winning years, Jones was also a keen scholar and gained first-class honours degrees in law, English literature and mechanical engineering at three different universities. He finally settled on a legal career with his own practice in Atlanta.

It was there that he and his friend Clifford Roberts conceived and developed the idea of the great Augusta National course and the Masters tournament, now a fitting memorial to the *Master Golfer* himself.

Bobby Jones   Popperfoto

In recognition of his great skill and courage, and the esteem in which he was held in Britain and at St Andrews in particular, he was made an honorary member of the Royal & Ancient in 1956. Two years later, when in St Andrews as Captain of the US team in the inaugural competition for the Eisenhower Trophy, he was given the Freedom of the Burgh of St Andrews.

He died on 18 December, 1971 after many years of suffering from a crippling spinal disease. As a final tribute, a memorial service was held at St Andrews.

Kirkaldy, Andrew (1860–1934)

A rugged type of the old school of Scottish professionals, Andrew Kirkaldy was the last survivor of that race. After army service in Egypt and India, he was appointed professional at Winchester. He had no liking for the steady sedate life of an English professional and, after six weeks, returned to his native St Andrews, where he lived the rest of his days acting as a playing professional until he was appointed professional to the Royal and Ancient Golf Club.

A man of powerful physique, Kirkaldy was a beautiful golfer to watch, particularly his iron shots. In the Open Championship 1889 he tied with Willie Park at Musselburgh, but lost on the replay. He played in many money matches, the most notable of which was in the Open Championship at St Andrews in 1895. JH Taylor, the defending champion (also the first English professional to win the Championship), had challenged the world for £50-a-side. Kirkaldy accepted and won by a hole.

Candid and outspoken, capable of being uncouth, Kirkaldy in his old age was respected by princes and peers.

Laidlay, John Ernest (1860–1940)

Johnny Laidlay played high-quality golf for 50 years – a testimony to his technique and temperament. In all, he won more than 130 medals.

At a time when golf was booming and the opposition tough, he won the Amateur Championship twice (1889 and 1891) was runner-up three times and beaten semi-finalist three times. He was second in the 1893 Open Championship when his characteristically good putting failed. He played for Scotland every year from 1902 until 1911, when he was fifty-one.

The longevity of his very individual swing was perhaps due to his early golfing experiences at Musselburgh where he saw Young Tom Morris, knew Willie Park well and played a lot with Bob Ferguson (including a famous round by moonlight). His contribution to the game was the overlapping grip – known erroneously as the Vardon grip. Laidlay played cricket for Scotland (vs Yorkshire – taking 6 wickets for 18 runs); he was a pioneer of wildlife photography and carved beautiful furniture.

Leitch, 'Cecil' (1891–1977)

Although she had reached the semi-final of the British Ladies' Championship in 1908 at the age of 17 and had won the French Ladies' Championship in 1912, it was in 1914 that Cecil Leitch really established herself as Britain's dominant woman golfer when she won the English Ladies', the French Ladies' and the British Ladies'. She retained each of these titles when they were next held after the First World War (the English in 1919 and the British and French in 1920) and who can say how many times she might have won them in the intervening years. In all she won the French Ladies' in 1912-14-20-21-24, the English Ladies' in 1914-19, the British Ladies' in 1914-20-21-26 and the Canadian Ladies' in 1921.

Her total of four victories in the British Ladies' has never been bettered and has been equalled only by her great rival Joyce Wethered, against whom in the 1920s she had many memorable matches.

Miss Leitch was an outspoken person who occasionally battled with the golfing authorities. Her strong attacking play mirrored her personality. Aged 19, in 1910 she accepted the challenge from Harold Hilton, at his peak, to take on any woman golfer over 72 holes giving half a stroke (a stroke at every second hole). Miss Leitch won this famous challenge match by 2 and 1 and later also beat John Ball, eight times Amateur Champion. Right to the end of her life, Cecil Leitch took an active interest in golf, attending major events whenever possible.

Lema, Tony (1934–66)

'Champagne Tony', as he was called because of his habit of treating the golf writers after his victories, had much in common with Walter Hagen. He loved the 'high life' but behind it was steely resolve as well. A beautiful swinger of the club, he was a golfer of grace rather than power. His victory in the Open Championship of St Andrews in 1964 was remarkable because he had never played golf in Europe before. He had just won three American tournaments in quick succession but arrived late and had only 27 holes of practice. Aided by that famous local caddie, Tip Anderson, he quickly mastered these most revered of links and won by five strokes from Jack Nicklaus.

A player who did nothing by halves – such as losing to Gary Player in the world matchplay championship after being seven up with 17 to play – he was killed when the private aeroplane in which he was travelling crashed on a golf course in Illinois. He was only 32.

Little, Lawson (1910–68)

As an amateur he established two records in that he won both the Amateur and American Amateur Championships in 1934 and again in 1935. In the final of the 1934 Amateur he won by the margin of 14 and 13 and for the 23 holes played he was ten under 4's. He turned professional in 1936 and won the Canadian Open in the same year and in 1940, won the US Open after a play-off.

Locke, Bobby (1917–87)

The son of Northern Irish emigrants, Artur D'Arcy Locke turned professional in 1938 after a very successful amateur career, in which he won the South African Boys' Championship, the South African Amateur (twice) and Open Championship (twice) as well as finishing leading amateur in the Open Championships of 1936 and 1937. As a result of his visits to Britain, he developed a characteristic hook to increase his length and although never a long hitter, his deadly short game made him a formidable competitor. In his first year as a professional he won the Irish, Transvaal, South African and New Zealand Open Championships as well as the South African Professional title.

During the war, Locke flew Liberator bombers for nearly 2000 hours. He left the South African Air Force weighing four stones heavier and immediately resumed his winning way. Second to Snead at St Andrews in the 1946 Open, he was encouraged to visit America where he was greatly successful. He beat Snead 12–2 in a series of matches and won five tournaments in 1947, two in 1948, three in 1949 and one in 1950. Locke had bad relations with the USPGA who disliked his success and they banned him from their tournaments. Locke concentrated his efforts on Europe. He won the Open Championship four times – 1949-50-52-57 – as well as the Open Championships of Canada (1947), France (1952-53), Germany (1954), Switzerland (1954), Egypt (1954) and South Africa (six times as a professional). He also won a number of British titles including the Dunlop Masters, Spalding, the Lotus, Daks and Bowmaker Tournaments. The 1957 Open Championship was the first to be shown on television and the first in which the leaders went out last. Locke won by 3 strokes and his score of 279 was the first time 280 had been beaten at St Andrews. Locke had to mark his ball on the 72nd hole and in front of the cameras replaced it on the wrong spot. The R & A decided to let his score stand as he had derived no advantage from his technical error and disqualification would have been inequitable and against the spirit of the game.

Bobby Locke will be remembered as a beautifully dressed golfer – plus fours, white shirt and tie – with a superb temperament, especially after a disastrous hole, great self discipline, the highest standards of behaviour and a wonderful short game. He was virtually in retirement when he had a serious car crash. On recovery he continued to play golf but his competitive career was at an end. He was made an honorary member of the R & A in 1976.

Bobby Locke   Popperfoto

Longhurst, Henry (1909–78)

After leaving Cambridge University, he acquired a job as a golf writer in which he could indulge his love of the game and be paid for it. He never ceased to be amazed at his own good fortune. His regular weekly article in the *Sunday Times* became compulsory reading for the golfing cognoscenti. From writing he became involved in radio and, later, television, through which he became world famous as a commentator.

Television was the perfect medium for his talents. His humour, easy manner, gifted observation and perception, mellow voice, calm delivery and economy of word were all perfectly suited to a slow-moving sport, and from his vast knowledge and understanding of the game, he was always able to fill in any gaps in the action with an apt story or two.

Longhurst also wrote several amusing books about different periods of his life, including a brief spell as an MP. He was awarded the CBE for his

services to golf and was one of only a handful of people to be made an honorary member of the Royal & Ancient Golf Club. His own golf was good enough to have won the German Open Amateur in 1936 and to be runner-up in the French Open Amateur in 1937.

Mackenzie, Alister (1870–1934)

A prolific designer of golf courses all over the world, Dr Alexander 'Alister' Mackenzie was a family doctor and surgeon before abandoning medicine to work full-time in golf. An early design, in conjunction with Harry S Colt, was in 1907 for Alwoodley GC, Leeds, where he was a founder member and honorary secretary until 1912. He designed and redesigned dozens of courses in Britain and did outstanding work in Australia and New Zealand. But he is best remembered for designing Cypress Point in California and, with Bobby Jones, the Augusta National in Georgia, home of the US Masters.

Massy, Arnaud (1877–1958)

Born in Biarritz, France, he became, in 1907, the first overseas player to win the Open Championship. He won at Hoylake beating JH Taylor by two strokes. He also tied with Harry Vardon at St George's in 1911 but conceded the title at the 35th hole of the play-off.

Micklem, Gerald (1911–88)

As an administrator as well as a player, Gerald Micklem devoted so much of his life to the benefit of golf, amateur and professional, that he will long be remembered with respect and affection. He gave his time unsparingly to the game's development, whether locally at his favourite Sunningdale, at the R&A or on the international scene.

After becoming a pre-war Oxford Blue, he won the English Championship in 1947 and 1953, was in the Walker Cup side four times between 1947 and 1955, non-playing Captain in 1957 and 1959, and from 1947 played for 12 years in the Home Internationals. He was second in the Brabazon and also won the St George's Challenge Cup, the Berkshire Trophy, the President's Putter and several R&A Members' medals.

When he ceased to play in tournaments, his administrative responsibilities were legion. Captain of many English and British teams in European and International events, he took a leading part in the development of the Open, being Chairman of the Championship Committee of the Royal & Ancient during a key period. It was in this appointment that he made his greatest contribution to the future of the game: it is through his vision and enterprise that the Open Championship is today regarded as the most prestigious and best organised Championship anywhere in the world. He was Captain of the Royal & Ancient Club in 1968.

To the end of his life he lent his support to innumerable golf ventures and many were the amateurs and professionals whom helped and made welcome at his home.

Middlecoff, Cary (1921–98)

Qualified as a dentist, Cary Middlecoff became one of the most prolific winners on the US Tour after the Second World War. He had 37 tour victories, including the 1949 and 1956 US Opens and 1955 Masters, which he won by a then-record seven strokes from Ben Hogan. He still holds one tour record, that of the longest sudden death play-off. This was in the 1949 Motor City Open after a tie with Lloyd Mangrum. After playing 11 extra holes, and with darkness descending, it was decided that the pair should share the title.

His two US Open wins were both by a single shot, first over Sam Snead and Clayton Heafner at Medinah, and then seven years later over Julius Boros and Hogan at Inverness. A third title was denied him in 1957, when he was beaten by Dick Mayer in a play-off.

Mitchell, Abe (1897–1947)

The finest player who never won an Open Championship was the tribute paid by JH Taylor. He finished in the first six five times in the Open and was three times winner of the Match Play Championship. Along with Duncan and later Compston, he was one of the few British hopes against the American invasion of the twenties. He taught the game to St Alban's seed merchant Samuel Ryder and is the figure on top of the Ryder Cup.

Morgan, Wanda (1910–1995)

British Amateur champion in 1935, English champion three times (1931-36-37), also three times a member of the Curtis Cup teams of 1932-34-36, Wanda Morgan was one of the outstanding women players of the 1930s. She first made her mark in 1929 when, aged 19, she reached the semi-finals of the English Open and was promptly dubbed one of the 'Kent Kids', the other being Diana Fishwick (*née* Critchley). Wanda Morgan won the Kent Championship seven times and had the reputation of being a good wooden club player and outstanding with her iron play. She was less certain on the greens and changed both her putter and her method repeatedly. As a representative of the Dunlop sports company, her career was curtailed but she was a source of constant encouragement to the young.

The Morrises:
Old Tom (1821–1908)
Young Tom (1851–75)

Old Tom Morris and his son, young Tom Morris, played a prominent part in golf in the period from 1850 to 1875. The father was born at St Andrews on 16th June, 1821. At the age of eighteen, he was apprenticed to Allan Robertson in the ball-making trade. When Morris was thirty years of age, Colonel Fairlie of Coodham took him to Prestwick, and he remained there until 1865, when he returned to St Andrews and became greenkeeper to the Royal & Ancient Golf Club, a position he held until 1904.

Young Tom was born at St Andrews in 1851, and exhibited early remarkable powers as a golfer. At the age of sixteen he won the Open Professional Tournament at Montrose against the best players in the country, and he won the Championship Belt outright by scoring three successive victories in 1868-69-70. The Championship lapsed for a year, but when it was resumed in 1872, young Tom scored his fourth successive victory.

There is no doubt that young Tom was the finest golfer of his time, but the tragic death of his wife, while he was engaged playing with his father in a great golf match at North Berwick against the brothers Willie and Mungo Park, had a most depressing effect on him, and he survived his wife by only a few months. Near the finish of this match, a telegram reached North Berwick intimating that, following her confinement, young Tom's wife was dangerously ill. The telegram was held over by Provost Brodie and not handed to young Tom until the end of the match. The yacht of John Lewis, an Edinburgh golfer, was put at the service of the Morrises but before the party embarked, a second telegram brought the sad news to young Tom that his wife had died. It was a mournful party that made the voyage across the Forth to St Andrews. The brilliant young golfer never recovered from the shock, and he died on Christmas Day of the same year, 1875, at the age of twenty-four.

There was a second son, JOF Morris, who played in professional tournaments, but, although a fine golfer, he never approached the brilliant execution of his elder brother.

Old Tom competed in every Open Golf Championship up to and including 1896, the year Harry Vardon scored his first victory in the Open Championship. Old Tom died at St Andrews in 1908. He was respected throughout the golfing world for his honest, sturdy qualities. His portrait hangs in the R&A Clubhouse, and the home green at St Andrews is named in his memory. A monument, a sculpted figure of Young Tom in golfing pose, was erected by public subscription in St Andrews Cathedral Churchyard and a smaller memorial stone was placed on the grave when Old Tom died.

Ouimet, Francis (1893–1967)

He is often described as the player who started the golf boom in the US when, as a young amateur, he tied with Harry Vardon and Ted Ray for the 1913 US Open and went on to win the play-off. In an illustrious career he won the US Amateur twice and was a member of every Walker Cup team from 1922 to 1934 and was non-playing Captain from then until 1949. Ouimet was the first non-British national to be elected Captain of the R&A Golf Club in 1951. He was prominent in golf legislation and administration in America and a committee member of the USGA for many years.

The Parks

Brothers Willie and Mungo Park of Musselburgh are famous in the annals of golf for the numerous money matches they played.

Willie had the distinction of winning the very first Open Championship in 1860 and repeated his victory in 1863, 1866 and 1875. For twenty years Willie had a standing challenge in *Bell's Life*, London, to play any man in the world for £100-a-side. Willie took part in numerous matches against Tom Morris for very large stakes and in the last of these at Musselburgh in 1882, the match came to an abrupt end when Park was two up with six to play. The referee stopped play because spectators were interfering with the balls. Morris and the referee retired to Foreman's public house. Park sent a message saying if Morris did not come out and finish the match he would play the remaining holes alone and claim the stakes. This he did.

Mungo followed in his brother's footsteps by winning the Open Championship in 1874. He was for many years greenkeeper and professional at Alnmouth.

Willie's son, Willie Junior, kept up the golfing tradition of the family by winning the Open in 1887 and 1889. He designed many golf courses in Europe and America, sometimes in conjunction with property development, as at Sunningdale, and was the pioneer of the modern ideas of golf course construction. Like his forebears he took part in many private challenge matches, the one against Harry Vardon at North Berwick in 1899 being watched by the greatest crowd ever for that time and for many years afterwards. Willie Junior died in 1925 aged 61.

The third generation of this golfing family sustained a prominent golf association through Miss Doris Park (Mrs Aylmer Porter), daughter of Willie Junior, who established a distinguished record in ladies' international and championship golf.

Philp, Hugh

The master craftsman among the half-dozen clubmakers located in St Andrews in the early days of

the nineteenth century. He was especially skilled in making a wooden putter with a long head of pear-shaped design. He is believed to have made not many more than one hundred putters. The wooden putter was for centuries a favoured club at St Andrews for long approach putting. The creations of Hugh Philp are highly prized by golf club collectors. After his death in 1856 his business was carried on by Robert Forgan.

Picard, Henry (1907–97)

The disappointment of finishing only fourth in the 1935 Masters after opening with rounds of 67 and 68 for a four-stroke lead was forgotten only three years later when, back in Augusta, scores of 71-72-72-70 proved good enough for a two-shot victory. The following year he added the United States PGA championship. One down with one to play against Byron Nelson, Picard made a four-foot birdie putt to force extra holes and at the 37th he holed from seven feet for another birdie while Nelson missed from five. Winner of 27 tournaments in total, ill-health affected his career thereafter, although he continued to play in the Masters until 1969. He can also be given some of the credit for Sam Snead's success, giving him a driver in 1937 which instantly solved Snead's hooking problems and turned him into the longest straight driver in the game.

Ray, Ted (1877–1943)

Born Jersey, his early days coincided with the famous Triumvirate and it was not until 1912 that he won the Open and was runner-up the following year to Taylor. He was again runner-up in 1925 at the age of 48. In 1913 he tied for the US Open with Ouimet and Vardon, but lost the play-off. After the war he returned to America and won the US Open title in 1920 and was the last British player to hold the title until Tony Jacklin, in 1970. He and Vardon were the only British players to win both the US Open and the Open until they were joined by Jacklin. Noted for his long driving and powers of recovery, he was invariably to be seen playing with a pipe clenched between his teeth.

Rees, Dai (1913–83)

One of Britain's outstanding golfers from the 1930s to the 1960s. He played in nine Ryder Cup matches between 1937 and 1961, and was also non-playing captain in 1967. In 1957, he captained the only British team to win the Ryder Cup since 1933. He was three times a runner-up in the Open Championship and once third, won the PGA Match Play Championship four times, and the Dunlop Masters twice, in addition to numerous other tournament successes in Britain, on the Continent of Europe and in Australasia. At

Dai Rees   Popperfoto

the age of 60, he finished third in the Martini tournament. He was made an honorary member of the Royal & Ancient Golf Club in 1976.

Robertson, Allan (1815–58)

According to tradition, he was never beaten in an individual stake match on level terms. A short, thick-set man, he had a beautiful, well-timed swing, and several golfers who could recall Robertson, and who saw Harry Vardon at his best, were of the opinion that there was considerable similarity in the elegance and grace of the two players. Tom Morris, senior, worked in Allan Robertson's shop, where the principal trade was making feather balls. A disagreement occurred between Robertson and Morris on the advent of the gutta ball, because Old Tom decided to play with the invention, and Allan considered the gutta might damage his trade in featheries. Allan, through agents, endeavoured to buy up all gutta balls in order to protect his industry of feather balls. Allan Robertson and Tom Morris never seem to have come together in any single match for large stakes, but it is recorded that they never lost a foursome in which they were partners.

Ryder, Samuel (1858–1936)

Sam Ryder was a prosperous seed merchant and the Mayor of St Albans. He did not take up golf

until the age of 52 but became one of the most famous names in golf as donor of the Ryder Cup, played for in biennial competition between teams of professionals from Great Britain and Ireland (now Europe) and the United States. Ryder attended an unofficial international match between British and American professionals at Wentworth in 1926 and was greatly impressed by the chivalry and camaraderie of the two sides. He declared afterwards, 'We must do this again'. The first Ryder Cup match was played the following year at Worcester, Massachusetts, and the first in Britain in 1929 at Moortown, Yorkshire.

Sayers, Bernard (1857–1924)

Of very small stature, one of the smallest Scottish professionals, and light of build, Bernard Sayers nevertheless took a leading position in the game for over 40 years with his outstanding skill and rigid physical training. He engaged in numerous stake matches and played for Scotland against England in every match from 1903 to 1910 and in 1912 and 1913. He competed in every Open Championship from 1880 to 1923. Of a bright and sunny disposition, he contributed much to the merriment of championship and professional gatherings. He taught princes and nobles to play the game, was presented to King Edward, and received a presentation from King George, when Duke of York.

Smith, Mrs Frances (née Bunty Stephens) (1925–78)

Dominated post-war women's golf by winning the British Ladies' Championship in 1949 and 1954 (runner-up 1951-52), the English Ladies' in 1948-54-55 (runner-up 1959) and the French Ladies' in 1949. She represented Great Britain in the Curtis Cup on six consecutive occasions from 1950 to 1960. A pronounced pause at the top of her swing made her style most distinctive. She was awarded the OBE for her services to golf and was president of the English Ladies' Golf Association at the time of her death.

Smith, Horton (1908–63)

Came to notice first from Joplin, Missouri, when 20 years old, and brilliantly embarked on the professional circuit in the winter of 1929 when he won all but one of the open tournaments in which he played. He was promoted to that year's Ryder Cup team and also played in 1933 and 1935. He won the first US Masters Tournament in 1934 and again in 1936 as well as more than thirty other major events. On his 21st birthday he won the French Open. He was President of the American PGA, 1952-54, and received two national distinctions: the Ben Hogan Award for overcoming illness or injury, and the Bobby Jones Award for distinguished sportsmanship in golf. The day after the Ryder Cup match which he attended in Atlanta in 1963 he collapsed and died in a Detroit hospital.

Smith, Macdonald (1890–1949)

Born at Carnoustie, he was one of the great golfers who never won the Open Championship, in which he consistently finished in a high place, coming second in 1930 and 1932, third in 1923 and 1924, fourth in 1925 and 1934 and fifth in 1931. He went to America before he was 20. In the Open Championship at Prestwick in 1925 he entered the last round with a lead of five strokes over the field, but a wildly enthusiastic Scottish crowd of 20,000 engulfed and overwhelmed him. The sequel to these unruly scenes was the introduction of gate money the following year and Prestwick was dropped from the rota for the Open. He died in Los Angeles.

Tait, Freddie (1870–1900)

Born at 17 Drummond Place, in Edinburgh (his father PG Tait was a Professor at Edinburgh University). He joined the R&A in 1890, and that year beat all previous St Andrews' amateur records by holing the course in 77, and in 1894 he reduced the record to 72. He was first amateur in the Open Championship in 1894, 1896 and 1899 and third in 1896 and 1897. He won the Amateur Championship in 1896 at Sandwich, beating in successive rounds GC Broadwood, Charles Hutchings, JE Laidlay, John Ball, Horace Hutchinson and HH Hilton, the strongest amateurs of the day. He repeated his victory in 1898 at Hoylake, and in 1899 he fought and lost at the 37th the historic final with John Ball at Prestwick. There is a Freddie Tait Cup given annually to the best amateur in the South African Open Championship. This cup was purchased from the surplus of the fund collected during the visit of the British amateur golfers to South Africa in 1928. He was killed in the South African War at Koodoosberg Drift, aged 30.

Taylor, John Henry (1871–1963)

Last survivor of the famous Triumvirate – Taylor, Braid and Vardon – died at his Devonshire home in February, 1963, within a month of his 92nd birthday. Born at Northam, Devon, he had been professional at Burnham, Winchester and Royal Mid-Surrey. JH won the Open Championship five times – 1894-95-1900-09-13 – and also tied with Harry Vardon in 1896, but lost the replay. He was runner-up in 1904-05-06-14. His brilliant career included the French and German Open Championships and he was second in the US Open in 1900. Among the many honours he

received were honorary membership of the R&A Golf Club in 1949. He was regarded as the pioneer of British professionalism and helped to start the Professional Golfers' Association. He did much to raise the whole status of the professional and, in the words of Bernard Darwin, *turned a feckless company into a self-respecting and respected body of men.* On his retirement in 1957 the Royal North Devon Golf Club paid him their greatest compliment by electing him President.

Tolley, Cyril   (1896–1978)

A dominant figure in amateur golf in the interwar period. He won the first of two Amateur Championships in 1920 while still a student at Oxford and continued to win championships and represent England and Britain until 1938. Among other titles he won the Welsh Open (1921 and 1923) and remains the only amateur to have won the French Open (1924 and 1929). A powerful hitter with a delicate touch, Tolley was a crowd pleaser. He is remembered as much for a match he lost as for some of his victories. Having won the Amateur Championship in 1929, Tolley was a favourite to win at St Andrews in 1930. The draw was unseeded and he met Bobby Jones in the fourth round. A huge crowd turned out to watch a very exciting match which Jones won on the 19th with a stymie. Tolley was elected Captain of the R&A in 1948.

Travis, Walter   (1862–1925)

Born in Australia, Travis was the first overseas golfer to win the British Amateur, at Sandwich in 1904. He won the title using a centre-shafted putter, which was subsequently banned for many years. He won the US Amateur Championship in 1900, having taken up the game four years previously at the age of 35. He repeated his victory in 1901 and 1903 and was a semi-finalist five times between 1898 and 1914, winning also the stroke competition six times between 1900 and 1908. The *Old Man* as he was known is reckoned to have been one of the finest judges of distance who ever played golf. He died in New York.

Vardon, Harry   (1870–1937)

Born Grouville, Jersey, Vardon created a record by winning the Open Championship six times, his wins being in 1896, 1898, 1899, 1903, 1911 and 1914. He also won the American Open in 1900 and tied in 1913, subsequently losing the play-off. He had a serious illness in 1903 and it was said that he never quite regained his former dominance, particularly on the putting green.

That he was the foremost golfer of his time cannot be disputed and he innovated the modern

Harry Vardon   Popperfoto

upright swing and popularised the overlapping grip invented by JE Laidlay.

Had it not been for ill-health and the intervention of the First World War, his outstanding records both in the UK and America would almost certainly have been added to in later years. But in any event his profound influence on the game lives on. More than 100 years after his birth his achievements are still the standard of comparison with the latter-day giants of the game.

Vare, Glenna (*née* Collett)   (1903–89)

A natural all-rounder at games, her six American Amateur championships set new standards. It was only achieved however by intense study of the mechanics of the swing and concentrated practice. She attacked the ball, with both irons and woods, with uncommon verve. Sadly, perhaps, a British Amateur title eluded her, despite being in successive finals in 1929 and 1930. In the first against Joyce Wethered at St Andrews she was three under 4s for the first 11 holes and 5-up but became victim of an outstanding counter-attack by the finest woman golfer of her time. A year later she lost again, this time unexpectedly to a little-known 19-year-old, Diana (Fishwick) Critchley, at Formby. She played in five Curtis Cup matches and was also captain, proving as popular with foe as with friend.

Walker, George (1874–1953)

President of the United States Golf Association in 1920 and one of the instigators of the biennial Walker Cup matches between the leading amateurs of Great Britain and Ireland and the United States. He donated the trophy for the first match, played at Long Island, New York, on 29th August 1922, and won by the host country. Educated partly in England, at Stoneyhurst, Walker was an all-round sportsman and a good golfer, though not of international standard. His grandson, George Bush, became President of the United States.

Wethered, Joyce (Lady Heathcoat-Amory) (1899–1997)

Bobby Jones once stated that Joyce Wethered was, taking into account 'the unavoidable handicap of a woman's lesser physical strength', the finest golfer he had ever seen. Her brother Roger persuaded her into competitive golf after the First World War. She was just 18 when she entered her first English Ladies' Championship in 1920, but she won it at Sherringham by beating the holder Cecil Leitch in the final and was to remain unbeaten for the next four years, winning 33 successive matches. She also won four British Championships, equalling Leitch's record.

With her irons, her hands seldom went higher than shoulder level on either backswing or follow through and she made the game seem effortless. Jones's comment came after they played together at St Andrews. She scored 75 and he wrote: 'I had never played golf with anyone, man or woman, amateur or professional, who made me feel so utterly outclassed.' After playing in the inaugural Curtis Cup match in 1932, she forfeited her amateur status and toured America in 1935. She was reinstated as an amateur after the Second World War.

Wethered, Roger (1899–1983)

One of the outstanding amateurs of the period between the two World Wars, Roger Wethered won the Amateur Championship in 1923 and was runner-up in 1928 and 1930. He won the President's Putter of the Oxford and Cambridge GS five times (once a tie) between 1926 and 1936, played in the Walker Cup against the United States six times between 1921 and 1934, and for England against Scotland every year from 1922 to 1930. He was captain of the Royal & Ancient in 1946. But he will probably be best remembered for the fact that he tied with Jock Hutchison, a Scot who had settled in the United States, in the 1921 Open Championship at St Andrews, despite having incurred a penalty stroke by inadvertently treading on his ball. Wethered was reluctant to stay on for the 36-hole play-off the following day because of a cricket engagement in England, but was persuaded to do so, only to be beaten by nine strokes, 150 to 159. No British amateur has come so close to winning the Open Championship since.

The Whitcombe Brothers:
Ernest (1890–1971)
Charles (1895–1978)
Reginald (1898–1957)

The story of the Whitcombes is told in a limited edition publication, *The Whitcombe Brothers – A Golfing Legend*, and what a remarkable story it is. They were born in Burnham, Somerset, and won many titles between them. All three played in the 1935 Ryder Cup contest at Ridgewood, New Jersey, but only Reg, the youngest, won the Open Championship (at Sandwich in 1938). Ernest finished second to Walter Hagen in 1924 at Hoylake after leading by three strokes at one time and Charles took 76 in the final round at Muirfield in 1935 to lose by five strokes and finish third.

Wilson, Enid (1910–96)

Between the wars of 1914–18 and then 1939–45 Enid Wilson was second only to Joyce Wethered among British women golfers. She had an outstanding record which was the result of her relish for the big occasion. Her finest years were between 1931–33 when she completed a hat-trick of victories in the British Women's Championship, all of them by wide margins. In 1931 she beat Wanda Morgan by seven and six in the final at Portmarnock. The following year at Saunton she similarly despatched Clementine Montgomery, and then in 1933 she defeated Diana Plumpton by 5 and 4 at Gleneagles. She had already won the English Championship twice, in 1928 and 1930, and, before that, the British Girls' title in 1925. Twice, in 1931 and 1933, she was a semi-finalist in the American Championship, and played for Britain in the inaugural Curtis Cup match against the United States at Wentworth in 1932, beating Helen Hicks.

Enid Wilson had a sound, rather graceful, swing, and, though a hard worker on the practice ground, she never allowed golf to rule her life – indeed she retired from the game at a comparatively early age. Instead she turned to journalism, and for many years was the women's golf correspondent of the *Daily Telegraph*, her pungent views frequently ruffling the feathers of the Ladies' Golf Union. Her book, *A Gallery of Women Golfers*, was widely acclaimed. She was a familiar figure in a long tweed skirt, which she wore in all weathers, and she compiled such a valuable collection of stamps that

many of them had to be kept in the vaults of a bank. She saw out the last years of her life at her treasured Oast House at Crowborough in East Sussex.

Wood, Craig (1901–68)

Born at Lake Placid, New York, Wood was a player of 'near misses'. Like Greg Norman many years later, Wood lost play-offs for what are known now as all the major championships even if they were not then. They were the 1933 Open Championship to Densmore Shute at St Andrews, the 1934 PGA Championship to Paul Runyan at Buffalo, the 1935 Masters to Gene Sarazen at Augusta and the 1939 US Open to Byron Nelson at Philadelphia. However, success did finally come for Wood in 1941 when he won both the Masters and US Open. He was also a member of three American Ryder Cup teams.

Zaharias, Mrs George (Mildred Babe Didrikson) (1915–56)

In the 1932 Olympic Games she established three world records for women: 80 metres hurdles, javelin, and high jump. On giving up athletics she took up golf and won the Texas Women's Open in 1940-45-46; the Western Open, 1940-44-45-50; and the US National Women's Amateur, 1946. In 1947 she won the Ladies' Championship, the first American to do so. In August 1947 she turned professional and went on to win the US National Women's Open, 1948-50. In winning the Tampa Open, 1951, she set up a women's world record aggregate, for the time, of 288 for 72 holes.

She was voted Woman Athlete of the year five times in 1932-45-46-47-50, and in 1949 was voted Greatest Female Athlete of the Half-Century. The first woman to hold the post of head professional to a golf club, the *Babe* was a courageous and fighting character who left her mark in the world of sport.

Interesting Facts and Unusual Incidents

Royal Golf Clubs

- The right to the designation *Royal* is bestowed by the favour of the Sovereign or a member of the Royal House. In most cases the title is granted along with the bestowal of royal patronage on the club. The Perth Golfing Society was the first to receive the designation *Royal*. That was accorded in June 1833. King William IV bestowed the honour on the Royal & Ancient Club in 1834. The most recent Club to be so designated is the Royal Troon in 1978.

Royal and Presidential Golfers

- In the long history of the Royal and Ancient game no reigning British monarch has played in an open competition. The Duke of Windsor, when Prince of Wales in 1922, competed in the Royal & Ancient Autumn Medal at St Andrews. He also took part in competitions at Mid-Surrey, Sunningdale, Royal St George's and in the Parliamentary Handicap. He also occasionally competed in American events, sometimes partnered by a professional, and on a private visit to London in 1952 he competed in the Autumn competition of Royal St George's at Sandwich scoring 97. As Prince of Wales he had played on courses all over the world and, after his abdication, as Duke of Windsor he continued to enjoy the game for many years.
- King George VI (when Duke of York) in 1930 and the Duke of Kent in 1937 also competed in the Autumn Meeting of the Royal & Ancient, these occasions being after they had formally played themselves into the Captaincy of the Club and each returned his card in the medal round.
- King Leopold of Belgium played in the Belgian Amateur Championship at Le Zoute, the only reigning monarch ever to have played in a national championship. The Belgian King played in many competitions subsequent to his abdication. In 1949 he reached the quarter-finals of the French Amateur Championship at St Cloud, playing as Count de Rethy.
- King Baudouin of Belgium in 1958 played in the triangular match Belgium-France-Holland and won his match against a Dutch player. He also took part in the Gleneagles Hotel tournament (playing as Mr B de Rethy), partnered by Dai Rees in 1959.
- United States President George Bush accepted an invitation in 1990 to become an Honorary Member of the Royal & Ancient Golf Club of St Andrews. The honour recognised his long connection and that of his family with golf and the R&A. Both President Bush's father, Prescott Bush Sr, and his grandfather, George Herbert Walker – who donated the Walker Cup – were presidents of the United States Golf Association. Other Honorary Members of the R&A include Kel Nagle, Jack Nicklaus, Arnold Palmer, Gene Sarazen, Peter Thomson, Roberto De Vicenzo and Gary Player.
- In September 1992, the Royal & Ancient Golf Club of St Andrews announced that His Royal Highness The Duke of York had accepted the Club's invitation of Honorary Membership. The Duke of York is the third member of the Royal Family to accept membership and joins Their Royal Highnesses The Duke of Edinburgh and The Duke of Kent. In August The Duke of York visited the Club and played his first round on the Old Course, impressing the locals and caddies with his considerable skill and in particular with the length of many of his drives, said the official announcement. He has since become a single handicapper, and has appeared in a number of pro-ams, partnering Open and Masters champion Mark O'Meara to victory in the Alfred Dunhill Cup pro-am at St Andrews in 1998.

First Lady Golfer

- Mary Queen of Scots, who was beheaded on 8th February, 1587, was probably the first lady golfer so mentioned by name. As evidence of her indifference to the fate of Darnley, her husband who was murdered at Kirk o' Field, Edinburgh, she was charged at her trial with having played at golf in the fields beside Seton a few days after his death.

Record Championship Victories

- In the Amateur Championship at Muirfield, 1920, Captain Carter, an Irish golfer, defeated an American entrant by 10 and 8. This is the only

known instance where a player has won every hole in an Amateur Championship tie.
● In the final of the Canadian Ladies' Championship at Rivermead, Ottawa, 1921, Cecil Leitch defeated Mollie McBride by 17 and 15. Miss Leitch only lost 1 hole in the match, the ninth. She was 14 up at the end of the first round, and only 3 holes were necessary in the second round, Miss Leitch winning them all. She won 18 holes out of 21 played, lost 1, and halved 2.
● In the final of the French Ladies' Open Championship at Le Touquet in 1927, Mlle de la Chaume (St Cloud) defeated Mrs Alex Johnston (Moor Park) by 15 and 14, the largest victory in a European golf championship.
● At Prestwick in 1934, W Lawson Little of Presidio, San Francisco, defeated James Wallace, Troon Portland, by 14 and 13 in the final of the Amateur Championship, the record victory in the Championship. Wallace failed to win a single hole.

Players who have won Two or More Major Championships in the Same Year since 1916

(The first Masters Tournament was played in 1934.)
1922 Gene Sarazen – USPGA, US Open
1924 Walter Hagen – USPGA, Open
1926 Bobby Jones – US Open, Open
1930 Bobby Jones – US Open, Open (Bobby Jones also won the US Amateur and British Amateur in this year.)
1932 Gene Sarazen – US Open, Open
1941 Craig Wood – Masters, US Open
1948 Ben Hogan – USPGA, US Open
1949 Sam Snead – USPGA, Masters
1951 Ben Hogan – Masters, US Open
1953 Ben Hogan – Masters, US Open, Open
1956 Jack Burke – USPGA, Masters
1960 Arnold Palmer – Masters, US Open
1962 Arnold Palmer – Masters, Open
1963 Jack Nicklaus – USPGA, Masters
1966 Jack Nicklaus – Masters, Open
1971 Lee Trevino – US Open, Open
1972 Jack Nicklaus – Masters, Open
1974 Gary Player – Masters, Open
1975 Jack Nicklaus – USPGA, Masters
1977 Tom Watson – Masters, Open
1980 Jack Nicklaus – USPGA, US Open
1982 Tom Watson – US Open, Open
1990 Nick Faldo – Masters, Open
1994 Nick Price – Open, US PGA
1998 Mark O'Meara – Masters, Open

Outstanding Records in Championships, International Matches and on the Professional Circuit

● The record number of victories in the Open Championship is six, held by Harry Vardon who won in 1896-98-99-1903-11-14.

● Five-time winners of the Championship are JH Taylor in 1894-95-1900-09-13; James Braid in 1901-05-06-08-10; Peter Thomson in 1954-55-56-58-65 and Tom Watson in 1975-77-80-82-83. Thomson's 1965 win was achieved when the Championship had become a truly international event. In 1957 he finished second behind Bobby Locke. By winning again in 1958 Thomson was prevented only by Bobby Locke from winning five consecutive Open Championships.
● Four successive victories in the Open by *Young* Tom Morris is a record so far never equalled. He won in 1868-69-70-72. (The Championship was not played in 1871.) Other four-time winners are Bobby Locke in 1949-50-52-57, Walter Hagen in 1922-24-28-29, Willie Park 1860-63-66-75, and *Old* Tom Morris 1861-62-64-67.
● Since the Championship began in 1860, players who have won three times in succession are Jamie Anderson, Bob Ferguson, and Peter Thomson.
● Robert Tyre Jones won the Open three times in 1926-27-30; the Amateur in 1930; the American Open in 1923-26-29-30; and the American Amateur in 1924-25-27-28-30. In winning the four major golf titles of the world in one year (1930) he achieved a feat unlikely ever to be equalled. Jones retired from competitive golf after winning the 1930 American Open, the last of these Championships, at the age of 28.
● Jack Nicklaus has had the most wins (six) in the US Masters Tournament, followed by Arnold Palmer with four.
● In modern times there are four championships generally regarded as standing above all others – the Open, US Open, US Masters, and USPGA. Four players have held all these titles, Gene Sarazen, Ben Hogan, Gary Player and Jack Nicklaus, who in 1978 became the first player to have held each of them at least three times. His record in these events is: Open 1966-70-78; US Open 1962-67-72-80; US Masters 1963-65-66-72-75-86; USPGA 1963-71-73-75-80. His total of major championships is now 18. In 1998 at the age of 58, Nicklaus finished joint sixth in the Masters. By not playing in the Open Championship that year, he ended a run of 154 successive major championships for which he was eligible (stretching back to 1957).

The nearest approach to achieving the Grand Slam of the Open, US Open, US Masters and USPGA in one year was by Ben Hogan in 1953 when he won the first three and could not compete in the USPGA as it then overlapped with the Open Championship.
● In the 1996 English Amateur Championship at Hollinwell, Ian Richardson (50) and his son, Carl, of Burghley Park, Lincolnshire, both reached the semi-finals. Both lost.
● The record number of victories in the US Open is four, held by W Anderson, Bobby Jones, Ben Hogan and Jack Nicklaus.

- Bobby Jones (amateur), Gene Sarazen, Ben Hogan, Lee Trevino and Tom Watson are the only players to have won the Open and US Open Championships in the same year. Tony Jacklin won the Open in 1969 and the US Open in 1970 and for a few weeks was the holder of both.
- In winning the Amateur Championship in 1970 Michael Bonallack became the first player to win in three consecutive years.
- The English Amateur record number of victories is held by Michael Bonallack, who won the title five times.
- John Ball holds the record number of victories in the Amateur Championship, which he won eight times. Next comes Michael Bonallack (who was internationally known as *The Duke*) with five wins.
- Cecil Leitch and Joyce Wethered each won the British Ladies' title four times.
- The Scottish Amateur record was held by Ronnie Shade, who won five titles in successive years – 1963-64-65-66-67. His long reign as Champion ended when he was beaten in the fourth round of the 1968 Championship after winning 44 consecutive matches.
- Joyce Wethered established an unbeaten record by winning the English Ladies' in five successive years from 1920 to 1924 inclusive.
- In winning the Amateur Championships of Britain and America in 1934 and 1935 Lawson Little won 31 consecutive matches. Other dual winners of these championships in the same year are RT Jones (1930) and Bob Dickson (1967).
- Peter Thomson's victory in the 1971 New Zealand Open Championship was his ninth in that championship.
- In a four-week spell in 1971, Lee Trevino won in succession the US Open, the Canadian Open and the Open Championships.
- The finalists in the 1970 Amateur Championship, Michael Bonallack and Bill Hyndman, were the same as in 1969. This was the first time the same two players reached the final in successive years.
- On the US professional circuit the greatest number of consecutive victories is 11, achieved by Byron Nelson in 1945. Nelson also holds the record for most victories in one calendar year, again in 1945 when he won a total of 18 tournaments.
- Raymond Floyd, by winning the Doral Classic in March 1992, joined Sam Snead as the only winners of US Tour events in four different decades.
- Jack Nicklaus and the late Walter Hagen have had five wins each in the USPGA Championship. All Hagen's wins were in successive years and at match play; all Nicklaus's at stroke play.
- In 1953 Flori van Donck of Belgium had seven major victories in Europe, including the Open Championships of Switzerland, Italy, Holland, Germany and Belgium.
- Mrs Anne Sander won four major amateur titles each under a different name. She won the US Ladies' in 1958 as Miss Quast, in 1961 as Mrs Decker, in 1963 as Mrs Welts and the British Ladies' in 1980 as Mrs Sander.
- The highest number of appearances in the Ryder Cup matches is held by Nick Faldo who made his eleventh appearance in 1997.
- The greatest number of appearances in the Walker Cup matches is held by Irishman Joe Carr who made his tenth appearance in 1967.
- In the Curtis Cup Mary McKenna made her ninth consecutive appearance in 1986.
- Players who have represented their country in both Walker and Ryder Cup matches are, for the United States, Fred Haas, Ken Venturi, Gene Littler, Jack Nicklaus, Tommy Aaron, Mason Rudolph, Bob Murphy, Lanny Wadkins, Scott Simpson, Tom Kite, Jerry Pate, Craig Stadler, Jay Haas, Bill Rodgers, Hal Sutton, Curtis Strange, Davis Love III, Brad Faxon, Scott Hoch, Phil Mickelson, Corey Pavin, Justin Leonard and Tiger Woods; and for Great Britain and Ireland, Norman Drew, Peter Townsend, Clive Clark, Peter Oosterhuis, Howard Clark, Mark James, Michael King, Gordon Brand Jr, Paul Way, Ronan Rafferty, Sandy Lyle, Philip Walton, David Gilford, Colin Montgomerie and Peter Baker.

Remarkable Recoveries in Matchplay

- There have been two remarkable recoveries in the Walker Cup Matches. In 1930 at Sandwich, JA Stout, Great Britain, round in 68, was 4 up at the end of the first round against Donald Moe. Stout started in the second round, 3, 3, 3, and was 7 up. He was still 7 up with 13 to play. Moe, who went round in 67, won back the 7 holes to draw level at the 17th green. At the 18th or 36th of the match, Moe, after a long drive placed his iron shot within three feet of the hole and won the match by 1 hole.
- In 1936 at Pine Valley, George Voigt and Harry Girvan for America were 7 up with 11 to play against Alec Hill and Cecil Ewing. The British pair drew level at the 17th hole, or the 35th of the match, and the last hole was halved.
- In the 1965 Piccadilly Match Play Championship Gary Player beat Tony Lema after being 7 down with 17 to play.
- Bobby Cruickshank, the old Edinburgh player, had an extraordinary recovery in a 36-hole match in a USPGA Championship for he defeated Al Watrous after being 11 down with 12 to play.
- In a match at the Army GC, Aldershot, on 5th July, 1974, for the Gradoville Bowl, MC Smart was 8 down with 8 to play against Mike Cook. Smart succeeded in winning all the remaining holes and the 19th for victory.
- In the 1982 Suntory World Match Play Championship Sandy Lyle beat Nick Faldo after being 6 down with 18 to play.

Oldest Champions

Open Championship: Belt Tom Morris in 1867 –
46 years 99 days. *Cup* Roberto De Vicenzo,
44 years 93 days, in 1967; Harry Vardon,
44 years 42 days, in 1914; JH Taylor,
42 years 97 days, in 1913.
Amateur Championship Hon. Michael Scot, 54, at Hoylake in 1933.
British Ladies Amateur Mrs Jessie Valentine, 43, at Hunstanton in 1958.
Scottish Amateur JM Cannon, 53, at Troon in 1969.
English Amateur Terry Shingler, 41 years 11 months at Walton Heath 1977; Gerald Micklem, 41 years 8 months, at Royal Birkdale 1947.
US Open Hale Irwin, 45, at Medinah, Illinois, in 1990.
US Amateur Jack Westland, 47, at Seattle in 1952 (He had been defeated in the 1931 final, 21 years previously, by Francis Ouimet).
US Masters Jack Nicklaus, 46, in 1986.
USPGA Julius Boros, 48, in 1968. Lee Trevino, 43, in 1984.
USPGA Tour Sam Snead, 52, at Greensborough Open in 1965. Sam Snead, 61, equal second in Glen Campbell Open 1974.

Youngest Champions

Open Championship: Belt Tom Morris, Jr, 17 years 5 months, in 1868. *Cup* Willie Auchterlonie, 21 years 24 days, in 1893; Tom Morris, Jr, 21 years 5 months, in 1872; Severiano Ballesteros, 22 years 103 days, in 1979.
Amateur Championship JC Beharrell, 18 years 1 month, at Troon in 1956; R Cole (SA) 18 years 1 month, at Carnoustie in 1966.
British Ladies Amateur May Hezlett, 17, at Newcastle, Co Down, in 1899; Michelle Walker, 18, at Alwoodley in 1971.
English Amateur Nick Faldo, 18, at Lytham St Annes in 1975; Paul Downes, 18, at Birkdale in 1978; David Gilford, 18, at Woodhall Spa in 1984; Ian Garbutt, 18, at Woodhall Spa in 1990; Mark Foster, 18, at Moortown in 1994.
English Amateur Strokeplay Ronan Rafferty, 16, at Hunstanton in 1980.
British Ladies Open Strokeplay Helen Dobson, 18, at Southerness in 1989.

Disqualifications

Disqualifications are now numerous, usually for some irregularity over signing a scorecard or for late arrival at the first tee. We therefore show here only incidents in major events involving famous players or players who were in a winning position or incidents which were in themselves unusual.

● JJ McDermott, the American Open Champion 1911-12, arrived for the Open Championship at Prestwick in 1914 to discover that he had made a mistake of a week in the date the championship began. The American could not play, as the qualifying rounds were completed on the day he arrived.
● In the Amateur Championship at Sandwich in 1937, Brigadier-General Critchley, arriving at Southampton from New York on the *Queen Mary*, which had been delayed by fog, flew by specially chartered aeroplane to Sandwich. He circled over the clubhouse, so the officials knew he was nearly there, but he arrived six minutes late, and his name had been struck out. At the same championship a player, entered from Burma, who had travelled across the Pacific and the American Continent, and was also on the *Queen Mary*, travelled from Southampton by motor car and arrived four hours after his starting time to find after journeying more than halfway round the world he was *struck out*.
● An unprecedented disqualification was that of A Murray in the New Zealand Open Championship, 1937. Murray, who was New Zealand Champion in 1935, was playing with JP Hornabrook, New Zealand Amateur Champion, and at the 8th hole in the last round, while waiting for his partner to putt, Murray dropped a ball on the edge of the green and made a practice putt along the edge. Murray returned the lowest score in the championship, but he was disqualified for taking the practice putt.
● At the Open Championship at St Andrews in 1946, John Panton, Glenbervie, in the evening practised putting on a green on the New Course, which was one of the qualifying courses. He himself reported his inadvertence to the Royal & Ancient and he was disqualified.
● At the Open Championship, Sandwich, 1949, C Rotar, an American, qualified by four strokes to compete in the championship but he was disqualified because he had used a putter which did not conform to the accepted form and make of a golf club, the socket being bent over the centre of the club head. This is the only case where a player has been disqualified in the Open Championship for using an illegal club.
● In the 1957 American Women's Open Championship, Mrs Jackie Pung had the lowest score, 298 over four rounds, but lost the championship. The card she signed for the final round read *five* at the 4th hole instead of the correct *six*. Her total of 72 was correct but the error, under rigid rules, resulted in her disqualification. Betty Jameson, who partnered Mrs Pung and also returned a wrong score, was also disqualified.

Longest Match

● WR Chamberlain, a retired farmer, and George New, a postmaster at Chilton Foliat, on 1st August, 1922, met at Littlecote, the 9-hole course of Sir Ernest Wills, and they agreed to play every

Thursday afternoon over the course. This they did until New's sudden death on 13th January, 1938. An accurate record of the matches was kept giving details of each round including wind direction and playing conditions. In the elaborate system nearly two million facts were recorded. They played 814 rounds, and aggregated 86,397 strokes, of which Chamberlain took 44,008 and New 42,371. New, therefore, was 1,637 strokes up. The last round of all was halved, a suitable end to such an unusual contest.

Longest Ties

● The longest known ties in 18-hole match play rounds in major events were in an early round of the News of the World Match Play Championship at Turnberry in 1960, when WS Collins beat WJ Branch at the 31st hole and in the third round of the same tournament at Walton Heath in 1961 when Harold Henning beat Peter Alliss also at the 31st hole.
● In the 1970 Scottish Amateur Championship at Balgownie, Aberdeen, E Hammond beat J McIvor at the 29th hole in their second round tie.
● CA Palmer beat Lionel Munn at the 28th hole at Sandwich in 1908. This is the record tie of the British Amateur Championship. Munn has also been engaged in two other extended ties in the Amateur Championship. At Muirfield, in 1932, in the semi-final, he was defeated by John de Forest, the ultimate winner, at the 26th hole, and at St Andrews, in 1936, in the second round he was defeated by JL Mitchell, again at the 26th hole.

The following examples of long ties are in a different category for they occurred in competitions, either stroke play or match play, where the conditions stipulated that in the event of a tie, a further stated number of holes had to be played – in some cases 36 holes, but mostly 18. With this method a vast number of extra holes was sometimes necessary to settle ties.

● The longest known was between two American women in a tournament at Peterson (New Jersey) when 88 extra holes were required before Mrs Edwin Labaugh emerged as winner.
● In a match on the Queensland course, Australia, in October, 1933, HB Bonney and Col HCH Robertson versus BJ Canniffe and Dr Wallis Hoare required to play a further four 18-hole matches after being level at the end of the original 18 holes. In the fourth replay Hoare and Caniffe won by 3 and 2 which meant that 70 extra holes had been necessary to decide the tie.
● After finishing all square in the final of the Dudley GC's foursomes competition in 1950, FW Mannell and AG Walker played a further three 18-hole replays against T Poole and E Jones, each time finishing all square. A further 9 holes were arranged and Mannell and Walker won by 3 and 2 making a total of 61 extra holes to decide the tie.
● RA Whitcombe and Mark Seymour tied for first prize in the Penfold £750 Tournament at St Annes-on-Sea, in 1934. They had to play off over 36 holes and tied again. They were then required to play another 9 holes when Whitcombe won with 34 against 36. The tournament was over 72 holes. The first tie added 36 holes and the extra 9 holes made an aggregate of 117 holes to decide the winner. This is a record in first-class British golf but in no way compares with other long ties as it involved only two replays – one of 36 holes and one of 9.
● In the American Open Championship at Toledo, Ohio, in 1931, G Von Elm and Billy Burke tied for the title. Each returned aggregates of 292. On the first replay both finished in 149 for 36 holes but on the second replay Burke won with a score of 148 against 149. This is a record tie in a national open championship.
● Cary Middlecoff and Lloyd Mangrum were declared co-winners of the 1949 Motor City Open on the USPGA Tour after halving 11 sudden death holes.
● Australian David Graham beat American Dave Stockton at the tenth extra hole in the 1998 Royal Caribbean Classic, a record for the US Senior Tour.
● Paul Downes was beaten by Robin Davenport at the 9th extra hole in the 4th round of the 1981 English Amateur Championship, a record marathon match for the Championship.
● Severiano Ballesteros was beaten by Johnny Miller at the 9th extra hole of a sudden-death play-off at the 1982 million dollar Sun City Challenge.
● José Maria Olazabal beat Ronan Rafferty at the 9th extra hole to win the 1989 Dutch Open on the Kennemer Golf and Country Club course.

Long Drives

It is impossible to state with any certainty what is the longest ever drive. Many long drives have never been measured and many others have most likely never been brought to our attention. Then there are several outside factors which can produce freakishly long drives, such as a strong following wind, downhill terrain or bonehard ground. Where all three of these favourable conditions prevail outstandingly long drives can be achieved. Another consideration is that a long drive made during a tournament is a different proposition from one made for length alone, either on the practice ground, a long driving competition or in a game of no consequence. All this should be borne in mind when considering the long drives shown here.

● When professional Carl Hooper hit a wayward drive on the 3rd hole (456 yards) at the Oak Hills Country Club, San Antonio, during the 1992 Texas Open, he wrote himself into the record

books but out of the tournament. The ball kept bouncing and rolling on a tarmac cart path until it was stopped by a fence – 787 yards away. It took Hooper two recovery shots with a 4-iron and then an 8-iron to return to the fairway. He eventually holed out for a double bogey six and failed to survive the half-way qualifying cut.

● Tommie Campbell of Portmarnock hit a drive of 392 yards at Dun Laoghaire GC in July 1964.

● Playing in Australia, American George Bayer is reported to have driven to within chipping distance of a 589 yards hole. *It was certainly a drive of over 500 yards,* said Bayer acknowledging the strong following wind, sharp downslope where his ball landed and the bone-hard ground.

● In September, 1934, over the East Devon course, THV Haydon, Wimbledon, drove to the edge of the 9th green which was a hole of 465 yards, giving a drive of not less than 450 yards.

● EC Bliss drove 445 yards at Herne Bay in August, 1913. The drive was measured by a Government surveyor who also measured the drop in height from tee to resting place of the ball at 57 feet.

Long Carries

● At Sitwell Park, Rotherham, in 1935 the home professional, W Smithson, drove a ball which carried a dyke at 380 yards from the 2nd tee.

● George Bell, of Penrith GC, New South Wales, Australia, using a number 2 wood drove across the Nepean River, a certified carry of 309 yards in a driving contest in 1964.

● After the 1986 Irish Professional Championship at Waterville, Co. Kerry, four long-hitting professionals tried for the longest-carry record over water, across a lake in the Waterville Hotel grounds. Liam Higgins, the local professional, carried 310 yards and Paul Leonard 311, beating the previous record by 2 yards.

● In the 1972 Algarve Open at Penina, Henry Cotton vouched for a carry of 305 yards over a ditch at the 18th hole by long-hitting Spanish professional Francisco Abreu. There was virtually no wind assistance.

● At the Home International matches at Portmarnock in 1949 a driving competition was held in which all the players in all four teams competed. The actual carry was measured and the longest was 280 yards by Jimmy Bruen.

● On 6th April, 1976, Tony Jacklin hit a number of balls into Vancouver harbour, Canada, from the 495-foot high roof of a new building complex. The longest carry was measured at 389 yards.

Long Hitting

There have been numerous long hits, not on golf courses, where an outside agency has assisted the length of the shot. Such an example was a 'drive' by Liam Higgins in 1986, on the Airport runway at Baldonal, near Dublin, of 632 yards.

Longest Albatrosses

● The longest-known albatrosses (three under par) recorded at par 5 holes are:

● 647 yards-2nd hole at Guam Navy Club by Chief Petty Officer Kevin Murray of Chicago on 3rd January, 1982.

● 609 yards-15th hole at Mahaka Inn West Course, Hawaii, by John Eakin of California on 12th November, 1972.

● 602 yards-16th hole at Whiting Field Golf Course, Milton, Florida, by 27-year-old Bill Graham with a drive and a 3-wood, aided by a 25 mph tail wind.

● The longest-known albatrosses in open championships are: 580 yards 14th hole at Crans-sur-Sierre, by American Billy Casper in the 1971 Swiss Open; 558 yards 5th hole at Muirfield by American Johnny Miller in the 1972 Open Championship.

● In the 1994 German Amateur Championship at Wittelsbacher GC, Rohrenfield, Graham Rankin, a member of the visiting Scottish national team, had a two at the 592 yard 18th.

Eagles (Multiple and Consecutive)

● Wilf Jones scored three consecutive eagles at the first three holes at Moor Hall GC when playing in a competition there on August Bank Holiday Monday 1968. He scored 3, 1, 2 at holes measuring 529 yards, 176 yards and 302 yards.

● In a round of the 1980 Jubilee Cup, a mixed foursomes match play event of Colchester GC, Mrs Nora Booth and her son Brendan scored three consecutive gross eagles of 1, 3, 2 at the eighth, ninth and tenth holes.

● Three players in a four-ball match at Kington GC, Herefordshire, on 22nd July, 1948, all had eagle 2s at the 18th hole (272 yards). They were RN Bird, R Morgan and V Timson.

● Four Americans from Wisconsin on holiday at Gleneagles in 1977 scored three eagles and a birdie at the 300-yard par-4 14th hole on the King's course. The birdie was by Dr Kim Lulloff and the eagles by Dr Gordon Meiklejohn, Richard Johnson and Jack Kubitz.

● In an open competition at Glen Innes GC, Australia on 13th November, 1977, three players in a four-ball scored eagle 3s at the 9th hole (442 metres). They were Terry Marshall, Roy McHarg and Jack Rohleder.

● David McCarthy, a member of Moortown Golf Club, Leeds, had three consecutive eagles (3,3,2) on the 4th, 5th and 6th holes during a Pro-Am competition at Lucerne, Switzerland, on 7th August, 1992.

Speed of Golf Ball and Club Head and Effect of Wind and Temperature

● In *The Search for the Perfect Swing*, a scientific study of the golf swing, a first class golfer is said to have the club head travelling at 100 mph at impact. This will cause the ball to leave the club at 135 mph. An outstandingly long hitter might manage to have the club head travelling at 130 mph which would produce a ball send-off speed of 175 mph. The resultant shot would carry 280 yards.
● According to Thomas Hardman, Wilson's director of research and development, wind will reduce or increase the flight of a golf ball by approximately 1½ yards for every mile per hour of wind. Every two degrees of temperature will make a yard difference in a ball's flight.

Most Northerly Course

● The most northerly course is the Akureyri Golf Club in Iceland which is situated 65°40' North of the equator. Not far south is the Luleö course in Sweden, at 65°35' North.

Most Southerly Course

● Golf's most southerly course is Scott Base Country Club, 13° north of the South Pole. The course is run by the New Zealand Antarctic Programme and players must be kitted in full survival gear. The most difficult aspect is finding the orange golf balls which tend to get buried in the snow. Other obstacles include penguins, seals and skuas. If the ball is stolen by a skua then a penalty of one shot is incurred; but if the ball hits a skua it counts as a birdie.

Highest Golf Courses

● The highest golf course in the world is thought to be the Tuctu GC in Peru which is 14,335 feet above sea-level. High courses are also found in Bolivia with the La Paz GC being about 13,500 feet. In the Himalayas, near the border with Tibet, a 9-hole course at 12,800 feet has been laid out by keen golfers in the Indian Army.
● The highest course in Europe is at Sestriere in the Italian Alps, 6,500 feet above sea-level.
● The highest courses in Great Britain are West Monmouthshire in Wales at 1,513 feet, Leadhills in Scotland at 1,500 feet and Church Stratton in England at 1,250 feet.

Longest Courses

● The longest course in the world is Dub's Dread GC, Piper, Kansas, USA measuring 8,101 yards (par 78).

● The longest course for the Open Championship was 7,252 yards at Carnoustie in 1968.

Longest Holes

● The longest hole in the world, as far as is known, is the 6th hole measuring 782 metres (860 yards) at Koolan Island GC, Western Australia. The par of the hole is 7. There are several holes over 700 yards throughout the world.
● The longest hole for the Open Championship is the 577 yards 6th hole at Royal Troon.

Longest Tournaments

● The longest tournament held was over 144 holes in the World Open at Pinehurst, N Carolina, USA, first held in 1973. Play was over two weeks with a cut imposed at the halfway mark.
● An annual tournament is played in Germany on the longest day of the year, comprising 100 holes' medal play. The best return, in 1995, was 399 strokes.

Largest Entries

● The Open – 2,133, Royal Troon, 1997.
● The Amateur – 488, St Andrews, 1958.
● US Open – 7117 in 1998.
● The largest entry for a PGA European Tour event was 398 for the 1978 Colgate PGA Championship. Since 1985, when the all-exempt ruling was introduced, all PGA tournaments have had 144 competitors, slightly more or less.
● In 1952, Bobby Locke, the Open Champion, played a round at Wentworth, against any golfer in Britain. Cards costing 2s. 6d. each (12½p), were taken out by 24,000 golfers. The challenge was to beat the local par by more than Locke beat the par at Wentworth; 1,641 competitors, including women, succeeded in *beating* the Champion and each received a certificate signed by him. As a result of this challenge the British Golf Foundation benefited to the extent of £3,026, the proceeds from the sale of cards. A similar tournament was held in the United States and Canada when 87,094 golfers participated; 14,667 players bettered Ben Hogan's score under handicap. The fund benefited by $80,024.

Largest Prize Money

● The Machrie Tournament of 1901 was the first tournament with a first prize of £100. It was won by JH Taylor, then Open Champion, who beat James Braid in the final.
● The richest events in the world are currently the Players' Championship and the Tour Championship on the USPGA Tour. In 1998 they both offered prize money of $4 million, with a first prize of $720,000. The Andersen Consulting

World Championship and Million Dollar Challenge both have first prizes of $1 million.

(For prize money in the Open Championship see under Conditions and History of Open Championship).

Holing-in-One

Odds Against

● At the Wanderers Club, Johannesburg in January, 1951, forty-nine amateurs and professionals each played three balls at a hole 146 yards long. Of the 147 balls hit, the nearest was by Koos de Beer, professional at Reading Country Club, which finished 10½ inches from the hole. Harry Bradshaw, the Irish professional who was touring with the British team in South Africa, touched the pin with his second shot, but the ball rolled on and stopped 3 feet 2 inches from the cup.

● A competition on similar lines was held in 1951 in New York when 1,409 players who had done a hole-in-one held a competition over several days at short holes on three New York golf courses. Each player was allowed a total of five shots, giving an aggregate of 7,045 shots. No player holed-in-one, and the nearest ball finished 3½ inches from the hole.

● A further illustration of the element of luck in holing-in-one is derived from an effort by Harry Gonder, an American professional, who in 1940 stood for 16 hours 25 minutes and hit 1,817 balls trying to do a 160 yard hole-in-one. He had two official witnesses and caddies to tee and retrieve the balls and count the strokes. His 1,756th shot struck the hole but stopped an inch from the hole. This was his nearest effort.

● From this and other similar information an estimate of the odds against holing-in-one at any particular hole within the range of one shot was made at somewhere between 1,500 and 2,000 to 1 by a proficient player. Subsequently, however, statistical analysis in America has come up with the following odds: a male professional or top amateur 3,708 to 1; a female professional or top amateur 4,648 to 1; an average golfer 42,952 to 1.

Hole-in-One First Recorded

● Earliest recorded hole-in-one was in 1868 at the Open Championship with Tom Morris (Young Tom) did the 145-yard 8th hole Prestwick in one stroke. This was the first of four Open Championships won successively by Young Tom.

● The first hole-in-one recorded with the 1.66 in ball was in 1972 by John G Salvesen, a member of the R&A Championship Committee. At the time this size of ball was only experimental. Salvesen used a 7-iron for his historical feat at the 11th hole on the Old Course, St Andrews.

Holing-in-One in Important Events

Since the day of the first known hole-in-one by Tom Morris Jr, at the 8th hole (145 yards) at Prestwick in the 1868 Open Championship, holes-in-one, even in championships, have become too numerous for each to be recorded. Only where other unusual or interesting circumstances prevailed are the instances shown here.

● All hole-in-one achievements are remarkable. Many are extraordinary. Among the more amazing was that of 2-handicap Leicestershire golfer Bob Taylor, a member of the Scraptoft Club. During the final practice day for the 1974 Eastern Counties Foursomes Championship on the Hunstanton Links, he holed his tee shot with a one-iron at the 188-yard 16th. The next day, in the first round of the competition, he repeated the feat, the only difference being that because of a change of wind he used a six-iron. When he stepped on to the 16th tee the following day his partner jokingly offered him odds of 1,000,000 to one against holing-in-one for a third successive time. Taylor again used his six-iron – and holed in one!j

● 1878–Jamie Anderson, competing in the Open Championship at Prestwick, holed the 17th hole in one. Anderson was playing the next to last hole, and though it seemed then that he was winning easily, it turned out afterwards that if he had not taken this hole in one stroke he would very likely have lost. Anderson was just about to make his tee shot when Andy Stuart (winner of the first Irish Open Championship in 1892), who was acting as marker to Anderson, remarked he was standing outside the teeing ground, and that if he played the stroke from there he would be disqualified. Anderson picked up his ball and teed it in a proper place. Then he holed-in-one. He won the Championship by one stroke.

● On a Friday the 13th in 1990, Richard Allen holed-in-one at the 13th at the Barwon Heads Golf Club, Victoria, Australia, and then lost the hole. He was giving a handicap stroke to his opponent, brother-in-law Jason Ennels, who also holed-in-one.

● 1906–R Johnston, North Berwick, competing in the Open Championship, did the 14th hole at Muirfield in one. Johnston played with only one club throughout – an adjustable head club.

● 1959–The first hole-in-one in the US Women's Open Championship was recorded. It was by Patty Berg on the 7th hole (170 yards) at Churchill Valley CC, Pittsburgh.

● 1962–On 6th April, playing in the second round of the Schweppes Close Championship at Little Aston, H Middleton of Shandon Park, Belfast, holed his tee shot at the 159-yard 5th hole, winning

a prize of £1,000. Ten minutes later, playing two matches ahead of Middleton, RA Jowlc, son of the professional, Frank Jowle, holed his tee shot at the 179-yard 9th hole. As an amateur he was rewarded by the sponsors with a £30 voucher.
- 1963–By holing out in one stroke at the 18th hole (156 yards) at Moor Park on the first day of the Esso Golden round-robin tournament, HR Henning, South Africa, won the £10,000 prize offered for this feat.
- 1967–Tony Jacklin in winning the Masters tournament at St George's, Sandwich, did the 16th hole in one. His ace has an exceptional place in the records for it was seen by millions on TV, the ball in view in its flight till it went into the hole in his final round of 64.
- 1971–John Hudson, 25-year-old professional at Hendon, achieved a near miracle when he holed two consecutive holes-in-one in the Martini Tournament at Norwich. They were at the 11th and 12th holes (195 yards and 311 yards respectively) in the second round.
- 1971–In the Open Championship at Birkdale, Lionel Platts holed-in-one at the 212-yard 4th hole in the second round. This was the first instance of an Open Championship hole-in-one being recorded by television. It was incidentally Platts' seventh ace of his career.
- Nick Faldo's hole-in-one at the 14th in the 1993 Ryder Cup at The Belfry was only the second to be recorded in the history of the match. The other was by Peter Butler at Muirfield's 16th hole in 1973.
- 1973–In the 1973 Open Championship at Troon, two holes-in-one were recorded, both at the 8th hole, known as the Postage Stamp, in the first round. They were achieved by Gene Sarazen and amateur David Russell, who were by coincidence respectively the oldest and youngest competitors.
- Mrs Argea Tissies, whose husband Hermann took 15 at Royal Troon's Postage Stamp 8th hole in the 1950 Open, scored a hole-in-one at the 2nd hole at Punta Ala in the second round of the Italian Ladies' Senior Open of 1978. Exactly five years later on the same date, at the same time of day, in the same round of the same tournament at the same hole, she did it again with the same club.
- In less than two hours play in the second round of the 1989 US Open at Oak Hill Country Club, Rochester, New York, four competitors – Doug Weaver, Mark Wiebe, Jerry Pate and Nick Price – each holed the 167-yard 6th hole in one. The odds against four professionals achieving such a record in a field of 156 are reckoned at 332,000 to 1.
- On 20th May, 1998, British golf journalist Derek Lawrenson, an eight-handicapper, won a Lamborghini Diablo car, valued at over £180,000, by holing his three-iron tee shot to the 175-yard 15th hole at Mill Ride, Surrey. He was taking part in a charity day and was partnering England football stars Paul Ince and Steve McManaman.

Holing-in-One – Longest Holes

- Bob Mitera, as a 21-year-old American student, standing 5 feet 6 inches and weighing under 12 stones, claimed the world record for the longest hole-in-one. Playing over the appropriately named Miracle Hill course at Omaha, on 7th October, 1965, Bob holed his drive at the 10th hole, 447 yards long. The ground sloped sharply downhill.
- Two longer holes-in-one have been achieved, but because they were at dog-leg holes they are not generally accepted as being the longest holes-in-one. They were 496 yards (17th hole, Teign Valley) by Shaun Lynch in July 1995 and 480 yards (5th hole, Hope CC, Arkansas) by L Bruce on 15th November, 1962.
- In March, 1961, Lou Kretlow holed his tee shot at the 427-yard 16th hole at Lake Hefner course, Oklahoma City, USA.
- The longest known hole-in-one in Great Britain was the 393-yard 7th hole at West Lancashire GC, where in 1972 the assistant professional Peter Parkinson holed his tee shot.
- Other long holes-in-one recorded in Great Britain have been 380 yards (5th hole at Tankersley Park) by David Hulley in 1961; 380 yards (12th hole at White Webbs) by Danny Dunne on 30th July, 1976; 370 yards (17th hole at Chilwell Manor, distance from the forward tee) by Ray Newton in 1977; 365 yards (10th hole at Harewood Downs) by K Saunders in 1965; 365 yards (7th hole at Catterick Garrison GC) by Leslie Bruckner on 18th July, 1980.
- The longest-recorded hole-in-one by a woman was that accomplished in September, 1949 by Marie Robie – the 393-yard hole at Furnace Brook course, Wollaston, Mass, USA.
- In April 1988, Mary Anderson, a bio-chemistry student at Trinity College, Dublin, holed-in-one at the 290-yard 6th hole at the Island GC, Co Dublin.
- In January 1985 Otto Bucher from Switzerland holed-in-one at the age of 99 on La Manga's 130-yard 12th hole.
- Six-year-old Tommy Moore aced the 145-yard fourth hole at Woodbrier, West Virginia, in 1968. He had another at the same hole before his seventh birthday.
- The youngest player ever to achieve a hole in one is now believed to be Matthew Draper, who was only five when he aced the 122-yard fourth hole at Cherwell Edge, Oxfordshire, in June 1997. He used a wood.

Holing-in-One – Greatest Number by One Person

59–Amateur Norman Manley of Long Beach, California.
50–Mancil Davis, professional at the Trophy Club, Forth Worth, Texas.

31–British professional CT le Chevalier who died in 1973.
22–British amateur, Jim Hay of Kirkintilloch GC.

At One Hole

13–Joe Lucius at 15th hole of Mohawk, Ohio.
5–Left-hander, the late Fred Francis at 7th (now 16th) hole of Cardigan GC.

Holing-in-One – Greatest Frequency

● The greatest number of holes-in-one in a calendar year is 11, by JO Boydstone of California in 1962.
● John Putt of Frilford Heath GC had six holes-in-one in 1970, followed by three in 1971.
● Douglas Porteous, of Ruchill GC, Glasgow, achieved seven holes-in-one in the space of eight months. Four of them were scored in a five-day period from 26th to 30th September, 1974, in three consecutive rounds of golf. The first two were achieved at Ruchill GC in one round, the third there two days later, and the fourth at Clydebank and District GC after another two days. The following May, Porteous had three holes-in-one, the first at Linn Park GC incredibly followed by two more in the one round at Clober GC.
● Mrs Kathleen Hetherington of West Essex has holed-in-one five times, four being at the 15th hole at West Essex. Four of her five aces were within seven months in 1966.
● Mrs Dorothy Hill of Dumfries and Galloway GC holed-in-one three times in 11 days in 1977.
● James C Reid of Brodick, aged 59 and 8 handicap in 1987, achieved 14 holes-in-one, all but one on Isle of Arran courses. His success was in spite of severe physical handicaps of a stiff left knee, a damaged right ankle, two discs removed from his back and a hip replacement.
● Jean Nield, a member at Chorlton-cum-Hardy and Bramall Park, has had ten holes-in-one and her husband Nrian, who plays at Bramall Park, has had four – a husband and wife total of 14.

Holing Successive Holes-in-One

● Successive holes-in-one are rare; successive par 4 holes-in-one may be classed as near miracles. NL Manley performed the most incredible feat in September, 1964, at Del Valle Country Club, Saugus, California, USA. The par 4 7th (330 yards) and 8th (290 yards) are both slightly downhill, dog-leg holes. Manley had *aces* at both, en route to a course record of 61 (par 71).
● The first recorded example in Britain of a player holing-in-one stroke at each of two successive holes was achieved on 6th February, 1964, at the Walmer and Kingsdown course, Kent. The young assistant professional at that club, Roger Game (aged 17) holed out with a 4-wood at the 244-yard 7th hole, and repeated the feat at the 256-yard 8th hole, using a 5-iron.
● The first occasion of holing-in-one at consecutive holes in a major professional event occurred when John Hudson, 25-year-old professional at Hendon, holed-in-one at the 11th and 12th holes at Norwich during the second round of the 1971 Martini tournament. Hudson used a 4-iron at the 195-yard 11th and a driver at the 311-yard downhill 12th hole.
● Assistant professional Tom Doty (23 years), playing in a friendly match on a course near Chicago in October, 1971, had a remarkable four-hole score which included two consecutive holes-in-one, sandwiched either side by an albatross and an eagle: 4th hole (500 yards)-2; 5th hole (360 yards dog-leg)-1; 6th hole (175 yards)-1; 7th hole (375 yards)-2. Thus he was 10 under par for four consecutive holes.

Holing-in-One Twice (or More) in the Same Round by the Same Person

What might be thought to be a very rare feat indeed – that of holing-in-one twice in the same round – has in fact happened on many occasions as the following instances show. It is, nevertheless, compared to the number of golfers in the world, still something of an outstanding achievement. The first known occasion was in 1907 when J Ireland playing in a three-ball match at Worlington holed the 5th and 18th holes in one stroke and two years later in 1909 HC Josecelyne holed the 3rd (175 yards) and the 14th (115 yards) at Acton on 24th November.

● The first mention of two holes-in-one in a round by a woman is of special note in that it was followed later by a similar feat by another lady at the same club. On 19th May, 1942, Mrs W Driver, of Balgowlah Golf Club, New South Wales, holed out in one at the 3rd and 8th holes in the same round, while on 29th July, 1948, Mrs F Burke at the same club holed out in one at the second and eigth holes.
● The Rev Harold Snider, aged 75, scored his first hole-in-one on 9th June, 1976 at the 8th hole of the Ironwood course, near Phoenix. By the end of his round he had scored three holes-in-one, the other two being at the 13th (110 yards) and 14th (135 yards). Ironwood is a par-3 course, giving more opportunity of scoring holes-in-one, but, nevertheless, three holes-in-one in one round on any type of course is an outstanding achievement.
● When the Hawarden course in North Wales comprised only nine holes, Frank Mills in 1994 had two holes-in-one at the same hole in the same round. Each time, he hit a seven iron to the 134-yard 3rd and 12th.
● The youngest player to achieve two holes-in-one in the same round is thought to be Chris-

topher Anthony Jones on 14 September, 1994. At the age of 14 years and 11 months he had holes-in-one at the Sand Moor, Leeds, 137-yard 10th hole and then at the 156-yard 17th.
● The youngest woman to have performed the feat was a 17-year-old, Marjorie Merchant, playing at the Lomas Athletic GC, Argentina, at the 4th (170 yards) and 8th (130 yards) holes.
● Tony Hannam, left-handed, handicap 16 and age 71, followed a hole-in-one at the 142 yards 4th of the Bude and North Cornwall Golf Club course with another at the 143-yard 10th on Friday, 18th September, 1992.

Holes-in-One on the Same Day

● In July 1987, at the Skerries Club, Co Dublin, Rank Xerox sponsored two tournaments, a men's 18-hole four-ball with 134 pairs competing and a 9-hole mixed foursomes with 33 pairs. During the day each of the four par-3 holes on the course were holed-in-one: the 2nd by Noel Bollard, the 5th by Bart Reynolds, the 12th by Jackie Carr and the 15th by Gerry Ellis.

Two Holes-in-One at the Same Hole in the Same Game

First in World
● George Stewart and Fred Spellmeyer at the 18th hole, Forest Hills, New Jersey, USA in October 1919.

First in Great Britain
● Miss G Clutterbuck and Mrs HM Robinson at the 15th hole (120 yards), St Augustine GC, Ramsgate, on 8th May, 1925.

First in Denmark
● In a Club match in August 1987 at Himmerland, Steffan Jacobsen of Aalborg and Peter Forsberg of Himmerland halved the 15th hole in one shot, the first known occasion in Denmark.

First in Australia
● Dr & Mrs B Rankine, playing in a mixed 'Canadian foursome' event at the Osmond Club near Adelaide, South Australia in April 1987, holed-in-one in consecutive shots at the 2nd hole (162 metres), he from the men's tee with a 3-iron and his wife from the ladies' tee with a 1½ wood.

Holing-in-One – Miscellaneous Incidents

● Chemistry student Jason Bohn, aged 19, of State College, Pennsylvania, supported a charity golf event at Tuscaloosa, Alabama, in 1992 when twelve competitors were invited to try to hole-in-one at the 135-yard 2nd hole for a special prize covered by insurance. One attempt only was allowed. Bohn succeeded and was offered US$1m (paid at the rate of $5,000 a month for the next 20 years) at the cost of losing his amateur status. He took the money.
● The late Harry Vardon, who scored the greatest number of victories in the Open Championship, only once did a hole-in-one. That was in 1903 at Mundesley, Norfolk, where Vardon was convalescing from a long illness.
● Bob Hope had a hole-in-one at Palm Springs, California, at the age of 90.
● In April 1984 Joseph McCaffrey and his son, Gordon, each holed-in-one in the Spring Medal at the 164-yard 12th hole at Vale of Leven Club, Dunbartonshire.
● In a guest day at Rochford Hundred, Essex, in 1994, there were holes-in-one at all the par threes. First Paul Cairns, of Langdon Hills, holed a 4-iron at the 205-yard 15th, next Paul Francis, a member of the home club, sank a 7-iron at the 156-yard seventh and finally Jim Crabb, of Three Rivers, holed a 9-iron at the 136-yard 11th.
● In 1977, 14-year-old Gillian Field after a series of lessons holed-in-one at the 10th hole at Moor Place GC in her first round of golf.
● By holing-in-one at the 2nd hole in a match against D Graham in the 1979 Suntory World Match Play at Wentworth, Japanese professional Isao Aoki won himself a Bovis home at Gleneagles worth, inclusive of furnishings, £55,000.
● On the morning after being elected captain for 1973 of the Norwich GC, JS Murray hit his first shot as captain straight into the hole at the 169-yard 1st hole.
● Using the same club and ball, 11-handicap left-hander Christopher Smyth holed-in-one at the 2nd hole (170 yards) in two consecutive medal competitions at Headfort GC, Co Meath, in January, 1976.
● Playing over Rickmansworth course at Easter, 1960, Mrs AE (Paddy) Martin achieved a remarkable sequence of *aces*. On Good Friday she sank her tee shot at the 3rd hole (125 yards). The next day, using the same ball and the same 8-iron, at the same hole, she scored another *one*. And on the Monday (same ball, same club, same hole) she again holed out from the tee.
● Alex Evans, aged eight, holed-in-one with a 4-wood at the 136-yard 4th hole at Bromborough, Merseyside, in 1994.
● In January 1985 Otto Bucher of Switzerland, aged 99, holed-in-one at the 130-yard 12th hole at the La Manga Championship South course in Spain.
● At Barton-on-Sea in February 1989 Mrs Dorothy Huntley-Flindt, aged 91, holed-in-one at the par-3 13th. The following day Mr John Chape, a fellow member in his 80s, holed the par-3 5th in one.
● In 1995 Roy Marsland of Ratho Park, Edinburgh, had three holes in one in nine days: at Prestonfield's 5th, at Ratho Park's 3rd and at Sandilands' 2nd.

● Michael Monk, age 82, a member of Tandridge Golf Club, Surrey, waited until 1992 to record his first hole-in-one. It continued a run of rare successes for his family. In the previous 12 months, Mr Monk's daughter, Elizabeth, 52, daughter-in-law, Celia, 48, and grandson, Jeremy, 16, had all holed in one on the same course.
● Lou Holloway, a left-hander, recorded his second hole-in-one at the Mount Derby course in New Zealand 13 years after acing the same hole while playing right-handed.
● Ryan Procop, an American schoolboy, holed-in-one at a 168-yard par 3 at Glen Eagles GC, Ohio, with a putter. He confessed that he was so disgusted with himself after a 12 on the previous hole that he just grabbed his putter and hit from the tee.
● Ernie and Shirley Marsden, of Warwick Golf Club, are believed in 1993 to have equalled the record for holes-in-one by a married couple. Each has had three, as have another English couple, Mr and Mrs BE Simmonds.
● Russell Pugh, a 12-handicapper from Nottinghamshire, holed-in-one twice in three days at the 274-yard par-4 18th hole at Sidmouth in Devon in 1998. The hole has a blind tee shot.

Challenge Matches

One of the first recorded professional challenge matches was in 1843 when Allan Robertson beat Willie Dunn in a 20-round match at St Andrews over 360 holes by 2 rounds and 1 to play. Thereafter until about 1905 many matches are recorded, some for up to £200 a side – a considerable sum for the time. The Morrises, the Dunns and the Parks were the main protagonists until Vardon, Braid and Taylor took over in the 1890s. Often matches were on a home-and-away basis over 72 holes or more, with many spectators; Vardon and Willie Park Jr attracted over 10,000 at North Berwick in 1899.

Between the wars Walter Hagen, Archie Compston, Henry Cotton and Bobby Locke all played several such matches. Compston surprisingly beat Hagen by 18 up and 17 to play at Moor Park in 1928; yet typically Hagen went on to win the Open the following week at Sandwich. Cotton played classic golf at Walton Heath in 1937 when he beat Densmore Shute for £500-a-side at Walton Heath by 6 and 5 over 72 holes.

Curious and Large Wagers
(See also bets recorded under **Cross-Country Matches** *and in* **Challenge Matches***)*

● In the Royal and Ancient Club minutes an entry on 3rd November, 1870 was made in the following terms:

Sir David Moncrieffe, Bart, of Moncrieffe, backs his life against the life of John Whyte-Melville, Esq, of Strathkinnes, for a new silver club as a present to the St Andrews Golf Club, the price of the club to be paid by the survivor and the arms of the parties to be engraved on the club, and the present bet inscribed on it. No balls to be attached to it. In testimony of which this bet is subscribed by the parties thereto.

Thirteen years later, Mr Whyte-Melville, in a feeling and appropriate speech, expressed his deep regret at the lamented death of Sir Robert Moncrieffe, one of the most distinguished and zealous supporters of the club. Whyte-Melville, while lamenting the cause that led to it, had pleasure in fulfilling the duty imposed upon him by the bet, and accordingly delivered to the captain the silver putter. Whyte-Melville in 1883 was elected captain of the club a second time; he died in his eighty-sixth year in July, 1883, before he could take office and the captaincy remained vacant for a year. His portrait hangs in the Royal & Ancient clubhouse and is one of the finest and most distinguished pictures in the smoking room.
● In 1914 Francis Ouimet, who in the previous autumn had won the American Open Championship after a triangular tie with Harry Vardon and Ted Ray, came to Great Britain with Jerome D Travers, the holder of the American amateur title, to compete in the British Amateur Championship at Sandwich. An American syndicate took a bet of £30,000 to £10,000 that one or other of the two United States champions would be the winner. It only took two rounds to decide the bet against the Americans. Ouimet was beaten by a then quite unknown player, HS Tubbs, while Travers was defeated by Charles Palmer, who was 56 years of age at the time.
● 1907 John Ball for a wager undertook to go round Hoylake during a dense fog in under 90, in not more than two and a quarter hours and without losing a ball. Ball played with a black ball, went round in 81, and also beat the time.
● The late Ben Sayers, for a wager, played the 18 holes of the Burgess Society course scoring a four at every hole. Sayers was about to start against an American, when his opponent asked him what he could do the course in. *Fours* replied Sayers, meaning 72, or an average of 4s for the round. A bet was made, then the American added, *Remember a three or a five is not a four.* There were eight bogey 5s and two 3s on the Burgess course at the time Old Ben achieved his feat.

Feats of Endurance

Although golf is not a game where endurance, in the ordinary sense in which the term is employed in sport, is required, there are several instances of feats on the links which demanded great physical exertion.

● Four British golfers, Simon Gard, Nick Harley, Patrick Maxwell and his brother Alastair Maxwell, completed 14 rounds in one day at Iceland's Akureyri Golf Club, the most northern 18-hole course in the world, during June, 1991

when there was 24-hour daylight. It was claimed a record and £10,000 was raised for charity.

● In 1971 during a 24-hour period from 6 pm on 27th November until 5.15 pm on 28th November, Ian Colston completed 401 holes over the 6,061 yards Bendigo course, Victoria, Australia. Colston was a top marathon athlete but was not a golfer. However prior to his golfing marathon he took some lessons and became adept with a 6-iron, the only club he used throughout the 401 holes. The only assistance Colston had was a team of harriers to carry his 6-iron and look for his ball, and a band of motor-cyclists who provided light during the night. This is, as far as is known, the greatest number of holes played in 24 hours on foot on a full-size course.

● In 1934 Col Bill Farnham played 376 holes in 24 hours 10 minutes at the Guildford Lake Course, Guildford, Connecticut, using only a mashie and a putter.

● To raise funds for extending the Skipton GC course from 12 to 18 holes, the club professional, 24-year-old Graham Webster, played 277 holes in the hours of daylight on Monday 20th June, 1977. Playing with nothing longer than a 5-iron he averaged 81 per 18-hole round. Included in his marathon was a hole-in-one.

● Michael Moore, a 7 handicap 26-year-old member of Okehampton GC, completed on foot 15 rounds 6 holes (276 holes) there on Sunday, 25th June, 1972, in the hours of daylight. He started at 4.15 am and stopped at 9.15 pm. The distance covered was estimated at 56 miles.

● On 21st June, 1976, 5-handicapper Sandy Small played 15 rounds (270 holes) over his home course Cosby GC, length 6,128 yards, to raise money for the Society of Physically Handicapped Children. Using only a 5-iron, 9-iron and putter, Small started at 4.10 am and completed his 270th hole at 10.39 pm with the aid of car headlights. His fastest round was his first (40 minutes) and slowest his last (82 minutes). His best round of 76 was achieved in the second round.

● During the weekend of 20th-21st June, 1970, Peter Chambers of Yorkshire completed over 14 rounds of golf over the Scarborough South Cliff course. In a non-stop marathon lasting just under 24 hours, Chambers played 257 holes in 1,168 strokes, an average of 84.4 strokes per round.

● Bruce Sutherland, on the Craiglockhart Links, Edinburgh, started at 8.15 pm on 21st June, 1927, and played almost continuously until 7.30 pm on 22nd June, 1927. During the night four caddies with acetylene lamps lit the way, and lost balls were reduced to a minimum. He completed fourteen rounds. Mr Sutherland, who was a physical culture teacher, never recovered from the physical strain and died a few years later.

● Sidney Gleave, motorcycle racer, and Ernest Smith, golf professional, Davyhulme Club, Manchester, on 12th June, 1939, played five rounds of golf in five different countries – Scotland, Ireland, Isle of Man, England and Wales. Smith had to play the five rounds under 80 in one day to win the £100 wager. They travelled by plane, and the following was their programme with time taken and Smith's score:

Start 3.40 a.m. at Prestwick St Nicholas (Scotland), finished 1 hour 35 minutes later on 70.

2nd Course – Bangor, Ireland. Started at 7.15 a.m. and took 1 hour 30 minutes to finish on 76.

3rd Course – Castletown, Isle of Man. Started 10.15 am, scored 76 in 1 hour 40 minutes.

4th Course – Blackpool, Stanley Park, England. Started at 1.30 pm and scored 72 in 1 hour 55 minutes.

5th Course – Hawarden, Wales, started at 6 pma and finished 2 hours 15 minutes later with a score of 72.

● On 19th June, 1995, Ian Botham, the former England cricketer, played four rounds of golf in Ireland, Wales, Scotland and England. His playing companions were Gary Price, the professional at Branston, and Tony Wright, owner of Craythorne, Burton-on-Trent, where the last 18 holes were completed. The other courses were St Margaret's, Anglesey and Dumfries & Galloway. The first round began at 4.30 am and the last was completed at 8.30 pm.

● On Wednesday, 3rd July, 1974, ES Wilson, Whitehead, Co Antrim and Dr GW Donaldson, Newry, Co Down, played a nine-hole match in each of seven countries in the one day. The first 9 holes was at La Moye (Channel Islands) followed by Hawarden (Wales), Chester (England), Turnberry (Scotland), Castletown (Isle of Man), Dundalk (Eire) and Warrenpoint (N Ireland). They started their first round at 4.25 am and their last round at 9.25 pm. Wilson piloted his own plane throughout.

● In June 1986 to raise money for the upkeep of his medieval church, the Rector of Mark with Allerton, Somerset, the Rev Michael Pavey, played a sponsored 18 holes on 18 different courses in the Bath & Wells Diocese. With his partner, the well-known broadcaster on music, Antony Hopkins, they played the 1st at Minehead at 5.55 am and finished playing the 18th at Burnham and Berrow at 6.05 pm. They covered 240 miles in the 'round' including the distances to reach the correct tee for the 'next' hole on each course. Par for the 'round' was 70. Together the pair raised £10,500 for the church.

● To raise funds for the Marlborough Club's centenary year (1988), Laurence Ross, the Club professional, in June 1987, played eight rounds in 12 hours. Against a par of 72, he completed the 576 holes in 3 under par, playing from back tees and walking all the way.

- As part of the 1992 Centenary Celebrations of the Royal Cinque Ports Golf Club at Deal, Kent, and to support charity, a six-handicap member, John Brazell, played all 37 royal courses in Britain and Ireland in 17 days. He won 22 matches, halved three, lost 12; hit 2,834 shots for an average score of 76.6; lost 11 balls and made 62 birdies. The aim was to raise £30,000 for Leukaemia Research and the Spastics Society.
- To raise more than £500 for the Guide Dogs for the Blind charity in the summer of 1992, Mrs Cheryle Power, a member of the Langley Park Golf Club, Beckenham, Kent, played 100 holes in a day – starting at 5 am and finishing at 8.45 pm.
- David Steele, a former European Tour player, completed 17½ rounds, 315 holes, between 6 am and 9.45 pm in 1993 at the San Roque club near Gibraltar in a total of 1,291 shots. Steele was assisted by a caddie cart and raised £15,000 for charity.

Fastest Rounds

- Dick Kimbrough, 41, completed a round on foot on 8th August, 1972, at North Platte CC, Nebraska (6,068 yards) in 30 minutes 10 seconds. He carried only a 3-iron.
- At Mowbray Course, Cape Town, November 1931, Len Richardson, who had represented South Africa in the Olympic Games, played a round which measured 6,248 yards in 31 minutes 22 seconds.
- The women's all-time record for the fastest round played on a course of at least 5,600 yards is held by Sue Ledger, 20, who completed the East Berks course in 38 minutes 8 seconds, beating the previous record by 17 minutes.
- In April, 1934, after attending a wedding in Bournemouth, Hants, Captain Gerald Moxom hurried to his club, West Hill in Surrey, to play in the captain's prize competition. With daylight fading and still dressed in his morning suit, he went round in 65 minutes and won the competition with a net 71 into the bargain.
- On 14th June, 1922, Jock Hutchison and Joe Kirkwood (Australia) played round the Old Course at St Andrews in 1 hour 20 minutes. Hutchison, out in 37, led by three holes at the ninth and won by 4 and 3.
- Fastest rounds can also take another form – the time taken for a ball to be propelled round 18 holes. The fastest known round of this type is 8 minutes 53.8 seconds on 25th August, 1979 by 42 members at Ridgemount CC Rochester, New York, a course measuring 6,161 yards. The Rules of Golf were observed but a ball was available on each tee; to be driven off the instant the ball had been holed at the preceding hole.
- The fastest round with the same ball took place in January 1992 at the Paradise Golf Club, Arizona. It took only 11 minutes 24 seconds; 91 golfers being positioned around the course ready to hit the ball as soon as it came to rest and then throwing the ball from green to tee.
- In 1992 John Daly and Mark Calcavecchia were both fined by the USPGA Tour for playing the final round of the Players' Championship in Florida in 123 minutes. Daly scored 80, Calcavecchia 81.

Curious Scoring

- Tony Blackwell, playing off a handicap of four, broke the course record at Bull Bay, Anglesey, by four strokes when he had a gross 60 (net 56) in winning the club's town trophy in 1996. The course measured 6,217 yards.
- In the third round of the 1994 Volvo PGA Championship at Wentworth, Des Smyth, of Ireland, made birdie twos at each of the four short holes, the 2nd, 5th, 10th and 14th. He also had a two at the second hole in the fourth round.
- Also at Wentworth, in the 1994 World Match Play Championship, Seve Ballesteros had seven successive twos at the short holes – and still lost his quarter-final against Ernie Els.
- RH Corbett, playing in the semi-final of the Tangye Cup at Mullion in 1916, did a score of 27. The remarkable part of Corbett's score was that it was made up of nine successive 3s, bogey being 5, 3, 4, 4, 5, 3, 4, 4, 3.
- At Little Chalfont in June 1985 Adrian Donkersley played six successive holes in 6, 5, 4, 3, 2, 1 from the 9th to the 14th holes against a par of 4, 3, 4, 3, 3.
- On 2nd September, 1920, playing over Torphin, near Edinburgh, William Ingle did the first five holes in 1, 2, 3, 4, 5.
- In the summer of 1970, Keith McMillan, on holiday at Cullen, had a remarkable series of 1, 2, 3, 4, 5 at the 11th to 15th holes.
- Marc Osborne was only 14 years of age when he equalled the Betchworth Park amateur course record with a 66 in July, 1993. He was playing in the Mortimer Cup, a 36-hole medal competition, and had at the time a handicap of 6.8.
- Playing at Addington Palace, July, 1934, Ronald Jones, a member of Hendon Club, holed five consecutive holes in 5, 4, 3, 2, 1.
- Harry Dunderdale of Lincoln GC scored 5, 4, 3, 2, 1 in five consecutive holes during the first round of his club championship in 1978. The hole-in-one was the 7th, measuring 294 yards.
- At the Open Amateur Tournament of the Royal Ashdown Forest in 1936 Bobby Locke in his morning round had a score of 72, accomplishing every hole in 4.
- George Stewart of Cupar had a four at every hole over the Queen's course at Gleneagles despite forgetting to change into his golf shoes and therefore still wearing his street shoes.
- Henry Cotton told of one of the most extraordinary scoring feats ever. With some other pro-

fessionals he was at Sestrieres in the 30s for the Italian Open Championship and Joe Ezar, a colourful character in those days on both sides of the Atlantic, accepted a wager from a club official – 1,000 lira for a 66 to break the course record; 2,000 for a 65; and 4,000 for a 64. *I'll do 64*, said Ezar, and proceeded to jot down the hole-by-hole score figures he would do next day for that total. With the exception of the ninth and tenth holes where his predicted score was 3, 4 and the actual score was 4, 3, he accomplished this amazing feat exactly as nominated.

● Nick Faldo scored par figures at all 18 holes in the final round of the 1987 Open Championship at Muirfield to win the title.

● During the Colts Championship at Knowle Golf Club, Bristol, Chris Newman (Cotswold Hills) scored eight consecutive 3s with birdies at four of the holes.

● At the Toft Hotel Golf Club captain's day event L Heffernan had an ace, D Patrick a 2, R Barnett a 3 and D Heffernan a 4 at the 240 yard par-4 ninth.

● In the European Club Championship played at the Parco de Medici Club in Rome in 1998, Belgian Dimitri van Hauwaert from Royal Antwerp had an albatross 2, Norwegian Marius Bjornstad from Oslo an eagle 3 and Scotsman Andrew Hogg from Turriff a birdie 4 at the 486 metre par-5 eigth hole.

High Scores

● In the qualifying competition at Formby for the 1976 Open Championship, Maurice Flitcroft, a 46-year-old crane driver from Barrow-in-Furness, took 121 strokes for the first round and then withdrew saying, *I have no chance of qualifying*. Flitcroft entered as a professional but had never before played 18 holes. He had taken the game up 18 months previously but, as he was not a member of a club, had been limited to practising on a local beach. His round was made up thus: 7, 5, 6, 6, 6, 6, 12, 6, 7-61; 11, 5, 6, 8, 4, 9, 5, 7, 5-60, total 121. After his round Flitcroft said, 'I've made a lot of progress in the last few months and I'm sorry I did not do better. I was trying too hard at the beginning but began to put things together at the end of the round.' R&A officials, who were not amused by the bogus professional's efforts, refunded the £30 entry money to Flitcroft's two fellow-competitors. Flitcroft has since tried to qualify for the Open under assumed names: Gerard Hoppy from Switzerland and Beau Jolley (as in the wine)!

● Playing in the qualifying rounds of the 1965 Open Championship at Southport, an American self-styled professional entrant from Milwaukee, Walter Danecki, achieved the inglorious feat of scoring a total of 221 strokes for 36 holes, 81 over par. His first round over the Hillside course was 108, followed by a second round of 113. Walter, who afterwards admitted he felt *a little discouraged and sad*, declared that he entered because he was *after the money*.

● The highest individual scoring ever known in the rounds connected with the Open Championship occurred at Muirfield, 1935, when a Scottish professional started 7, 10, 5, 10, and took 65 to reach the 9th hole. Another 10 came at the 11th and the player decided to retire at the 12th hole. There he was in a bunker, and after playing four shots he had not regained the fairway.

● In 1883 in the Open Championship at Musselburgh, Willie Fernie, the winner, had a 10, the only time double figures appeared on the card of the Open Champion of the year. Fernie won after a tie with Bob Ferguson, and his score for the last hole in the tie was 2. He holed from just off the green to win by one stroke.

● In the first Open Championship at Prestwick in 1860 a competitor took 21, the highest score for one hole ever recorded in this event. The record is preserved in the archives of the Prestwick Golf Club, where the championship was founded.

● In the first round of the 1980 US Masters, Tom Weiskopf hit his ball into the water hazard in front of the par-3 12th hole five times and scored 13 for the hole.

● In the French Open at St Cloud, in 1968, Brian Barnes took 15 for the short 8th hole in the second round. After missing putts at which he hurriedly snatched while the ball was moving he penalised himself further by standing astride the line of a putt. The amazing result was that he actually took 12 strokes from about three feet from the hole. The highest scores on the European Tour were also recorded in the French Open. Philippe Porquier had a 20 at La Baule in 1978 and Ian Woosnam a 16 at La Boulie in 1986.

● US professional Dave Hill 6-putted the fifth green at Oakmont in the 1962 US Open Championship.

● Many high scores have been made at the Road Hole at St Andrews. Davie Ayton, on one occasion, was coming in a certain winner of the Open Championship when he got on the road and took 11. In 1921, at the Open Championship, one professional took 13. In 1923, competing for the Autumn Medal of the Royal & Ancient, JB Anderson required a five and a four to win the second award, but he took 13 at the Road Hole. Anderson was close to the green in two, was twice in the bunkers in the face of the green, and once on the road. In 1935, RH Oppenheimer tied for the Royal Medal (the first award) in the Autumn Meeting of the Royal & Ancient. On the play-off he was one stroke behind Captain Aitken when they stood on the 17th tee. Oppenheimer drove three balls out of bounds and eventually took 11 to the Road Hole.

● British professional Mark James scored 111 in the second round of the 1978 Italian Open. He

played the closing holes with only his right hand due to an injury to his left hand.
● In the 1927 Shawnee Open, Tommy Armour took 23 strokes to the 17th hole. Armour had won the American Open Championship a week earlier. In an effort to play the hole in a particular way, Armour hooked ball after ball out of bounds and finished with a 21 on the card. There was some doubt about the accuracy of this figure and on reaching the clubhouse Armour stated that it should be 23. This is the highest score by a professional in a tournament.

Freak Matches

● In 1912, the late Harry Dearth, an eminent vocalist, attired in a complete suit of heavy armour, played a match at Bushey Hall. He was beaten 2 and 1.
● In 1914, at the start of the First World War, JN Farrar, a native of Hoylake, was stationed at Royston, Herts. A bet was made of 10-1 that he would not go round Royston under 100 strokes, equipped in full infantry marching order, water bottle, full field kit and haversack. Farrar went round in 94. At the camp were several golfers, including professionals, who tried the same feat but failed.
● Captain Pennington took part in a match *from the air* against AJ Young, the professional at Sonning. Captain Pennington, with 80 golf balls in the locker of his machine, had to find the Sonning greens by dropping the balls as he circled over the course. The balls were covered in white cloth to ensure that they did not bounce once they struck the ground. The airman completed the course in 40 minutes, taking 29 *strokes*, while Young occupied two hours for his round of 68. Captain Pennington was eventually killed in an air crash in 1933.
● In April 1924, at Littlehampton, Harry Rowntree, an amateur golfer, played the better ball of Edward Ray and George Duncan, receiving an allowance of 150 yards to use as he required during the round. Rowntree won by 6 and 5 and had used only 50 yards 2 feet of his handicap. At one hole Duncan had a two – Rowntree, who was 25 yards from the hole, took this distance from his handicap and won the hole in one. Ray (died 1945) afterwards declared that, conceded a handicap of one yard per round, he could win every championship in the world. And he might, when reckoning is taken of the number of times a putt just stops an inch or two or how much difference to a shot three inches will make for the lie of the ball, either in a bunker or on the fairway. Many single matches on the same system have been played. An 18 handicap player opposed to a scratch player should make a close match with an allowance of 50 yards.

● The first known instance of a golf match by telephone occurred in 1957, when the Cotswold Hills Golf Club, Cheltenham, England, won a golf tournament against the Cheltenham Golf Club, Melbourne, Australia, by six strokes. A large crowd assembled at the English club to wait for the 12,000 miles telephone call from Australia. The match had been played at the suggestion of a former member of the Cotswold Hills Club, Harry Davies, and was open to every member of the two clubs. The result of the match was decided on the aggregate of the eight best scores on each side and the English club won by 564 strokes to 570.

Golf Matches Against Other Sports

● HH Hilton and Percy Ashworth, many times racket champion, contested a driving match, the former driving a golf ball with a driver, and the latter a racket ball with a racket. Best distances: Against breeze – Golfer 182 yards; Racket player 125 yards. Down wind – Golfer 230 yards; Racket player 140 yards. Afterwards Ashworth hit a golf ball with the racket and got a greater distance than with the racket ball, but was still a long way behind the ball driven by Hilton.
● In 1913, at Wellington, Shropshire, a match between a golfer and a fisherman casting a 2½ oz weight was played. The golfer, Rupert May, took 87; the fisherman JJD Mackinlay, in difficulty because of his short casts, 102. His longest cast, 105 yards, was within 12 yards of the world record at the time, held by French angler, Decautelle. When within a rod's length of a hole he ran the weight to the rod end and dropped into the hole. Five times he broke his line, and was allowed another shot without penalty.
● In December, 1913, FMA Webster, of the London Athletic Club, and Dora Roberts, with javelins, played a match with the late Harry Vardon and Mrs Gordon Robertson, who used the regulation clubs and golf balls. The golfers conceded two-thirds in the matter of distance, and they won by 5 up and 4 to play in a contest of 18 holes. The javelin throwers had a mark of two feet square in which to *hole out* while the golfers had to get their ball into the ordinary golf hole. Mr Webster's best throw was one of 160 feet.
● Several matches have taken place between a golfer on the one side and an archer on the other. The wielder of the bow and arrow has nearly always proved the victor. In 1953 at Kirkhill Golf Course, Lanarkshire, five archers beat six golfers by two games to one. There were two special rules for the match; when an archer's arrow landed six feet from the hole or the golfer's ball three feet from the hole, they were counted as holed. When the arrows landed in bunkers or in the rough, archers lifted their arrow and added a stroke. The

sixth archer in this match called off and one archer shot two arrows from each of the 18 tees.

● In 1954, at the Southbroom Club, South Africa, a match over 9 holes was played between an archer and a fisherman against two golfers. The participants were all champions of their own sphere and consisted of Vernon Adams (archer), Dennis Burd (fisherman), Jeanette Wahl (champion of Southbroom and Port Shepstone), and Ron Burd (professional at Southbroom). The conditions were that the archer had holed out when his arrows struck a small leather bag placed on the green beside the hole and in the event of his placing his approach shot within a bow's length of the pin he was deemed to have 1-putted. The fisherman, to achieve a 1-putt, had to land his sinker within a rod's length of the pin. The two golfers were ahead for brief spells, but it was the opposition who led at the deciding 9th hole where *Robin Hood* played a perfect approach for a birdie.

● An *Across England* combined match was begun on 11th October, 1965, by four golfers and two archers from Crowborough Beacon Golf Club, Sussex, accompanied by *Penny*, a white Alsatian dog, whose duty it was to find lost balls. They teed off from Carlisle Castle via Hadrian's Wall, the Pennine Way, finally holing out in the 18th hole at Newcastle United Golf Club in 612 teed shots. Casualties included 110 lost golf balls and 19 lost or broken arrows. The match took five-and-a-half days, and the distance travelled was about 60 miles. The golfers were Miss P Ward, K Meaney, K Ashdown and CA Macey; the archers were WH Hulme and T Scott. The first arrow was fired from the battlements of Carlisle Castle, a distance of nearly 300 yards, by Cumberland Champion R Willis, who also fired the second arrow right across the River Eden. R Clough, president of Newcastle United GC, holed the last two putts. The match was in aid of *Guide Dogs for the Blind* and *Friends of Crowborough Hospital*.

Cross-country Matches

● Taking 1 year, 114 days, Floyd Rood golfed his way from coast to coast across the United States. He took 114,737 shots including 3,511 penalty shots for the 3,397 mile course.

● Two Californian teenagers, Bob Aube (17) and Phil Marrone (18) went on a golfing safari in 1974 from San Francisco to Los Angeles, a trip of over 500 miles lasting 16 days. The first six days they played alongside motorways. Over 1,000 balls were used.

● In 1830, the Gold Medal winner of the Royal & Ancient backed himself for 10 sovereigns to drive from the 1st hole at St Andrews to the toll bar at Cupar, distance nine miles, in 200 teed shots. He won easily.

● In 1848, two Edinburgh golfers played a match from Bruntsfield Links to the top of Arthur's Seat – an eminence overlooking the Scottish capital, 822 feet above sea level.

● On a winter's day in 1898, Freddie Tait backed himself to play a gutta ball in 40 teed shots from Royal St George's Clubhouse, Sandwich, to the Cinque Ports Club, Deal. He was to hole out by hitting any part of the Deal Clubhouse. The distance as the crow flies was three miles. The redoubtable Tait holed out with his 32nd shot, so effectively that the ball went through a window.

● In 1900 three members of the Hackensack (NJ) Club played a game of four-and-a-half hours over an extemporised course six miles long, which stretched from Hackensack to Paterson. Despite rain, cornfields, and wide streams, the three golfers – JW Hauleebeek, Dr ER Pfaare, and Eugene Crassons – completed the round, the first and the last named taking 305 strokes each, and Dr Pfaare 327 strokes. The players used only two clubs, the mashie and the cleek.

● On 3rd December, 1920, P Rupert Phillips and W Raymond Thomas teed up on the first tee of the Radyr Golf Club and played to the last hole at Southerndown. The distance as the crow flies was 15 1/2 miles, but circumventing swamps, woods, and plough, they covered, approximately, 20 miles. The wager was that they would not do the hole in 1,000 strokes, but they holed out at their 608th stroke two days later. They carried large ordnance maps.

● On 12th March, 1921, A Stanley Turner, Macclesfield, played from his house to the Cat and Fiddle Inn, five miles distance, in 64 strokes. The route was broken and hilly with a rise of nearly 1,000 feet. Turner was allowed to tee up within two club lengths after each shot and the wagering was 6-4 against his doing the distance in 170 strokes.

● In 1919, a golfer drove a ball from Piccadilly Circus and, proceeding via the Strand, Fleet Street and Ludgate Hill, *holed out* at the Royal Exchange, London. The player drove off at 8 am on a Sunday, a time when the usually thronged thoroughfares were deserted.

● On 23rd April, 1939, Richard Sutton, a London stockbroker, played from Tower Bridge, London, to White's Club, St James's Street, in 142 strokes. The bet was he would not do *the course* in under 200 shots. Sutton used a putter, crossed the Thames at Southwark Bridge, and hit the ball short distances to keep out of trouble.

● Golfers produced the most original event in Ireland's three-week national festival of An Tostal, in 1953 – a cross-country competition with an advertised £1,000,000 for the man who could hole out in one. The 150 golfers drove off from the first tee at Kildare Club to hole out eventually on the 18th green, five miles away, on the nearby Curragh course, a distance of 8,800 yards. The unusual hazards to be negotiated included the main Dublin-Cork railway line and

highway, the Curragh Racecourse, hoofprints left by Irish thoroughbred racehorses out exercising on the plains from nearby stables, army tank tracks and about 150 telephone lines. The Golden Ball Trophy, which is played for annually – a standard size golf ball in gold, mounted on a black marble pillar beside the silver figure of a golfer on a green marble base, designed by Captain Maurice Cogan, Army GHQ, Dublin – was for the best gross. And it went to one of the longest hitters in international golf – Amateur Champion, Irish internationalist and British Walker Cup player Joe Carr, with the remarkable score of 52.

● In 1961, as a University Charities Week stunt, four Aberdeen University students set out to golf their way up Ben Nevis (4,406 feet). About halfway up, after losing 63 balls and expending 659 strokes, the quartet conceded victory to Britain's highest mountain.

● Among several cross-country golfing exploits, one of the most arduous was faced by Iain Williamson and Tony Kent, who teed off from Cained Point on the summit of Fairfield in the Lake District. With the hole cut in the lawn of the Bishop of Carlisle's home at Rydal Park, it measured 7,200 yards and passed through the summits of Great Rigg Mann, Heron Pike and Nab Scar, descending altogether 1,900 feet. Eight balls were lost and the two golfers holed out in a combined total of 303 strokes.

Long-lived Golfers

● James Priddy, aged 80, played in the Seniors' Open at his home club, Weston-super-Mare, Avon, on 27th June, 1990, and scored a gross 70 to beat his age by ten shots.

● The oldest golfer who ever lived is believed to have been Arthur Thompson of British Columbia, Canada. He equalled his age when 103 at Uplands GC, a course of over 6,000 yards. He died two years later.

● Nathaniel Vickers celebrated his 103rd birthday on Sunday, 9th October, 1949, and died the following day. He was the oldest member of the United States Senior Golf Association and until 1942 he competed regularly in their events and won many trophies in the various age divisions. When 100 years old, he apologised for being able to play only nine holes a day. Vickers predicted he would live until 103 and he died a few hours after he had celebrated his birthday.

● American George Miller, who died in 1979 aged 102, played regularly when 100 years old.

● Phyllis Tidmarsh, aged 90, won a Stableford competition at Saltford Golf Club, near Bath, when she returned 42 points. Her handicap was cut from 28 to 27.

● George Swanwick, a member of Wallasey, celebrated his 90th birthday with a luncheon at the club on 1st April, 1971. He played golf several times a week, carrying his own clubs and had holed-in-one at the ages of 75 and 85. His ambition was to complete the sequence aged 95 . . . but he died in 1973 aged 92.

● The 10th Earl of Wemyss played a round on his 92nd birthday, in 1910, at Craigielaw. At the age of 87 the Earl was partnered by Harry Vardon in a match at Kilspindie, the golf course on his East Lothian estate at Gosford. After playing his ball the venerable earl mounted a pony and rode to the next shot. He died on 30th June, 1914.

● FL Callender, aged 78, in September 1932, played nine consecutive rounds in the Jubilee Vase, St Andrews. He was defeated in the ninth, the final round, by 4 and 2. Callender's handicap was 12. This is the best known achievement of a septuagenarian in golf.

● Bernard Matthews, aged 82, of Banstead Downs Club, handicap 6, holed the course in 72 gross in August 1988. A week later he holed it in 70, twelve shots below his age. He came back in 31, finishing 4, 3, 3, 2, 3, against a par of 5, 4, 3, 3, 4. Mr Matthews's eclectic score at his Club is 37, or one over 2's.

Playing in the Dark

On numerous occasions it has been necessary to hold lamps, lighted candles, or torches at holes in order that players might finish a competition. Large entries, slow play, early darkness and an eclipse of the sun have all been causes of playing in darkness.

● Since 1972, the Whitburn Golf Club at South Shields, Tyne and Wear, has held an annual Summer Solstice Competition. All competitors, who draw lots for starting tees, must begin before 4.24 and 13 seconds am, the time the sun rises over the first hole on the longest day of the year.

● At the Open Championship in Musselburgh in November 1889 many players finished when the light had so far gone that the adjacent street lamps were lit. The cards were checked by candlelight. Several players who had no chance of the championship were paid small sums to withdraw in order to permit others who had a chance to finish in daylight. This was the last championship at Musselburgh.

● At the Southern Section of the PGA tournament on 25th September, 1907, at Burnham Beeches, several players concluded the round by the aid of torch lights placed near the holes.

● In the Irish Open Championship at Portmarnock in September, 1907, a tie in the third round between WC Pickeman and A Jeffcott was postponed owing to darkness, at the 22nd hole. The next morning Pickeman won at the 24th.

● The qualifying round of the American Amateur Championship in 1910 could not be finished in one day, and several competitors had to stop

their round on account of darkness, and complete it early in the morning of the following day.
- On 10th January, 1926, in the final of the President's Putter, at Rye, EF Storey and RH Wethered were all square at the 24th hole. It was 5 pm and so dark that, although a fair crowd was present, the balls could not be followed. The tie was abandoned and the Putter held jointly for the year. Each winner of the Putter affixes the ball he played; for 1926 there are two balls, respectively engraved with the names of the finalists.
- In the 1932 Walker Cup contest at Brooklyn, a total eclipse of the sun occurred.
- At Perth, on 14th September, 1932, a competition was in progress under good clear evening light, and a full bright moon. The moon rose at 7.10 and an hour later came under eclipse to the earth's surface. The light then became so bad that on the last three greens competitors holed out by the aid of the light from matches.
- At Carnoustie, 1932, in the competition for the *Craw's Nest* the large entry necessitated competitors being sent off in 3-ball matches. The late players had to be assisted by electric torches flashed on the greens.
- In February, 1950, Max Faulkner and his partner, R Dolman, in a Guildford Alliance event finished their round in complete darkness. A photographer's flash bulbs were used at the last hole to direct Faulkner's approach. Several of the other competitors also finished in darkness. At the last hole they had only the light from the clubhouse to aim at and one played his approach so boldly that he put his ball through the hall doorway and almost into the dressing room.
- On the second day of the 1969 Ryder Cup contest, the last 4-ball match ended in near total darkness on the 18th green at Royal Birkdale. With the help of the clubhouse lights the two American players, Lee Trevino and Miller Barber, along with Tony Jacklin for Britain each faced putts of around five feet to win their match. All missed and their game was halved.

The occasions mentioned above all occurred in competitions where it was not intended to play in the dark. There are, however, numerous instances where players set out to play in the dark either for bets or for novelty.

- On 29th November, 1878, RW Brown backed himself to go round the Hoylake links in 150 strokes, starting at 11 pm. The conditions of the match were that Mr Brown was only to be penalised *loss of distance* for a lost ball, and that no one was to help him to find it. He went round in 147 strokes, and won his bet by the narrow margin of three strokes.
- In 1876 David Strath backed himself to go round St Andrews under 100, in moonlight. He took 95, and did not lose a ball.

- In September 1928, at St Andrews, the first and last holes were illuminated by lanterns, and at 11 pm four members of the Royal and Ancient set out to play a foursome over the 2 holes. Electric lights, lanterns, and rockets were used to brighten the fairway, and the headlights of motor cars parked on Links Place formed a helpful battery. The 1st hole was won in four, and each side got a five at the 18th. About 1,000 spectators followed the freak match, which was played to celebrate the appointment of Angus Hambro to the captaincy of the club.
- In 1931, Rufus Stewart, professional, Kooyonga Club, South Australia, and former Australian Open Champion, played 18 holes of exhibition golf at night without losing a single ball over the Kooyonga course, and completed the round in 77.
- At Ashley Wood Golf Club, Blandford, Dorset, a night-time golf tournament was arranged annually with up to 180 golfers taking part over four nights. Over £6000 has been raised in four years for the Muscular Dystrophy Charity.
- At Pannal, 3rd July, 1937, RH Locke, playing in bright moonlight, holed his tee shot at the 15th hole, distance 220 yards, the only known case of holing-in-one under such conditions.

Fatal and Other Accidents on the Links

The history of golf is, unfortunately, marred by a great number of fatal accidents on or near the course. In the vast majority of such cases they have been caused either by careless swinging of the club or by an uncontrolled shot when the ball has struck a spectator or bystander. In addition to the fatal accidents there is an even larger number on record which have resulted in serious injury or blindness. We do not propose to list these accidents except where they have some unusual feature. We would remind all golfers of the tragic consequences which have so often been caused by momentary carelessness. The fatal accidents which follow have an unusual cause and other accidents given may have their humorous aspect.

- English tournament professional Richard Boxall was three shots off the lead in the third round of the 1991 Open Championship when he fractured his left leg driving from the 9th tee at Royal Birkdale. He was taken from the course to hospital by ambulance and was listed in the official results as 'retired' which entitled him to a consolation prize of £3000.

A month later, Russell Weir of Scotland, was competing in the European Teaching Professionals' Championship near Rotterdam when he also fractured his left leg driving from the 7th tee in the first round.
- In July, 1971, Rudolph Roy, aged 43, was killed at a Montreal course; in playing out of woods, the shaft of his club snapped, rebounded off a tree and the jagged edge plunged into his body.

- Harold Wallace, aged 75, playing at Lundin Links with two friends in 1950, was crossing the railway line which separates the fifth green and sixth tee, when a light engine knocked him down and he was killed instantly.
- In the summer of 1963, Harold Kalles, of Toronto, Canada, died six days after his throat had been cut by a golf club shaft, which broke against a tree as he was trying to play out of a bunker.
- At Jacksonville, Florida, on 18th March, 1952, two women golfers were instantly killed when hit simultaneously by the whirling propeller of a navy fighter plane. They were playing together when the plane with a dead engine coming in out of control, hit them from behind.
- In May, 1993, at Ponoka Community GC, Alberta, Canada, Richard McCulough hit a poor tee shot on the 13th hole and promptly smashed his driver angrily against a golf cart. The head of the driver and six inches of shaft flew through the air, piercing McCulough's throat and severing his carotoid artery. He died in hospital.
- Britain's first national open event for competitors aged over 80, at Moortown, Leeds in September, 1992, was marred when 81-year-old Frank Hart collapsed on the fourth tee and died. Play continued and Charles Mitchell, aged 80, won the Stableford competition with a gross score of 81 for 39 points.
- Playing in the 1993 Carlesburg-Tetley Cornish Festival at Tehidy Park, Ian Cornwell was struck on the leg by a wayward shot from a player two groups behind. Later, as he was leaving the 16th green, he was hit again, this time below the ear, by the same player, knocking him unconscious. This may be the first time that a player has been hit twice in the same round by the same player.

Lightning on the Links

There have been a considerable number of fatal and serious accidents through players and caddies having been struck by lightning on the course. The Royal & Ancient and the USGA have, since 1952, provided for discontinuance of play during lightning storms under the Rules of Golf (Rule 37, 6) and the United States Golf Association has given the following guide for personal safety during thunderstorms:

(a) Do not go out of doors or remain out during thunderstorms unless it is necessary. Stay inside of a building where it is dry, preferably away from fireplaces, stoves, and other metal objects.
(b) If there is any choice of shelter, choose in the following order:
 1. Large metal or metal-frame buildings.
 2. Dwellings or other buildings which are protected against lightning.
 3. Large unprotected buildings.
 4. Small unprotected buildings.
(c) If remaining out of doors is unavoidable, keep away from:
 1. Small sheds and shelters if in an exposed location.
 2. Isolated trees.
 3. Wire fences.
 4. Hilltops and wide open spaces.
(d) Seek shelter in:
 1. A cave.
 2. A depression in the ground.
 3. A deep valley or canyon.
 4. The foot of a steep or overhanging cliff.
 5. Dense woods.
 6. A grove of trees.

Note – Raising golf clubs or umbrellas above the head is dangerous.

- A serious incident with lightning involving well-known golfers was at the 1975 Western Open in Chicago when Lee Trevino, Jerry Heard and Bobby Nichols were all struck and had to be taken to hospital. At the same time Tony Jacklin had a club thrown 15 feet out of his hands.
- Two well-known competitors were struck by lightning in European events in 1977. They were Mark James of Britain in the Swiss Open and Severiano Ballesteros of Spain in the Scandinavian Open. Fortunately neither appeared to be badly injured.
- Two spectators were killed by lightning at the US Open and US PGA Championships in 1991.

Spectators Interfering with Balls

- Deliberate interference by spectators with balls in play during important money matches was not unknown in the old days when there was intense rivalry between the *schools* of Musselburgh, St Andrews, and North Berwick, and disputes arose in stake matches caused by the action of spectators in kicking the ball into either a favourable or an unfavourable position.
- Tom Morris, in his last match with Willie Park at Musselburgh, refused to go on because of interference by the spectators, and in the match on the same course about 40 years later, in 1895, between Willie Park Jr and JH Taylor, the barracking of the crowd and interference with play was so bad that when the Park-Vardon match came to be arranged in 1899, Vardon refused to accept Musselburgh as a venue.
- Even in modern times spectators have been known to interfere deliberately with players' balls, though it is usually by children. In the 1972 Penfold Tournament at Queen's Park, Bournemouth, Christy O'Connor Jr had his ball stolen by a young boy, but not being told of this at the time had to take the penalty for a lost ball. O'Connor finished in a tie for first place, but lost the play-off.
- In 1912 in the last round of the final of the Amateur Championship at Westward Ho!

between Abe Mitchell and John Ball, the drive of the former to the short 14th hit an open umbrella held by a lady protecting herself from the heavy rain, and instead of landing on the green the ball was diverted into a bunker. Mitchell, who was leading at the time by 2 holes, lost the hole and Ball won the Championship at the 38th hole.

● In the match between the professionals of Great Britain and America at Southport in 1937 a dense crowd collected round the 15th green waiting for the Sarazen-Alliss match. The American's ball landed in the lap of a woman, who picked it up and threw it so close to the hole that Sarazen got a two against Alliss' three.

● In a memorable tie between Bobby Jones and Cyril Tolley in the 1930 Amateur Championship at St Andrews, Jones's approach to the 17th green struck spectators massed at the left end of the green and led to controversy as to whether it would otherwise have gone on to the famous road. Jones himself had deliberately played for that part of the green and had requested stewards to get the crowd back. Had the ball gone on to the road, the historic Jones Quadrilateral of the year – the Open and Amateur Championships of Britain and the United States – might not have gone into the records.

● In the 1983 Suntory World Match Play Championship at Wentworth Nick Faldo hit his second shot over the green at the 16th hole into a group of spectators. To everyone's astonishment and discomfiture the ball reappeared on the green about 30 ft from the hole, propelled there by a thoroughly misguided and anonymous spectator. The referee ruled that Faldo play the ball where it lay on the green. Faldo's opponent, Graham Marsh, understandably upset by the incident, took three putts against Faldo's two, thus losing a hole he might well otherwise have won. Faldo won the match 2 and 1, but lost in the final to Marsh's fellow Australian Greg Norman by 3 and 2.

Golf Balls Killing Animals and Fish, and Incidents with Animals

● An astounding fatality to an animal through being hit by a golf ball occurred at St Margaret's-at-Cliffe Golf Club, Kent on 13th June, 1934, when WJ Robinson, the professional, killed a cow with his tee shot to the 18th hole. The cow was standing in the fairway about 100 yards from the tee, and the ball struck her on the back of the head. She fell like a log, but staggered to her feet and walked about 50 yards before dropping again. When the players reached her she was dead.

● JW Perret, of Ystrad Mynach, playing with Chas R Halliday, of Ralston, in the qualifying rounds of the Society of One Armed Golfers' Championship over the Darley course, Troon, on 27th August, 1935, killed two gulls at successive holes with his second shots. The *deadly* shots were at the 1st and 2nd holes.

● On the first day of grouse shooting of the 1975 season (12th August), 11-year-old schoolboy Willie Fraser, of Kingussie, beat all the guns when he killed a grouse with his tee shot on the local course.

● On 10th June, 1904, while playing in the Edinburgh High Constables' Competition at Kilspindie, Captain Ferguson sent a long ball into the rough at the Target hole, and on searching for it found that it had struck and killed a young hare.

● Playing in a mixed open tournament at the Waimairi Beach Golf Club in Christchurch, New Zealand, in the summer of 1961, Mrs RT Challis found her ball in fairly long spongy grass where a placing rule applied. She picked up, placed the ball and played her stroke. A young hare leaped into the air and fell dead at her feet. She had placed the ball on the leveret without seeing it and without disturbing it.

● In 1906 in the Border Championship at Hawick, a gull and a weasel were killed by balls during the afternoon's play.

● A golfer at Newark, in May, 1907, drove his ball into the river. The ball struck a trout 2lb in weight and killed it.

● On 24th April, 1975, at Scunthorpe GC, Jim Tollan's drive at the 14th hole, called *The Mallard*, struck and killed a female mallard duck in flight. The duck was stuffed and is displayed in the Scunthorpe Clubhouse.

● A Samuel, Melbourne Club, at Sandringham, was driving with an iron club from the 17th tee, when a kitten, which had been playing in the long grass, sprang suddenly at the ball. Kitten and club arrived at the objective simultaneously, with the result that the kitten took an unexpected flight through the air, landing some 20 yards away.

● As Susan Rowlands was lining up a vital putt in the closing stages of the final of the 1978 Welsh Girls' Championship at Abergele, a tiny mouse scampered up her trouser leg. After holing the putt, the mouse ran down again. Susan, who won the final, admitted that she fortunately had not known it was there.

Interference by Birds and Animals

● Crows, ravens, hawks and seagulls frequently carry off golf balls, sometimes dropping the ball actually on the green, and it is a common incident for a cow to swallow a golf ball. A plague of crows on the Liverpool course at Hoylake are addicted to golf balls – they stole 26 in one day – selecting only new balls. It was suggested that members should carry shotguns as a 15th club!

● A match was approaching a hole in a rather low-lying course, when one of the players made a crisp chip from about 30 yards from the hole. The ball trickled slowly across the green and eventually disappeared into the hole. After a momentary pause, the ball was suddenly ejected on to the green, and out jumped a large frog.

● A large black crow named Jasper which frequented the Lithgow GC in New South Wales, Australia, stole 30 golf balls in the club's 1972 Easter Tournament.

● As Mrs Molly Whitaker was playing from a bunker at Beachwood course, Natal, South Africa, a large monkey leaped from a bush and clutched her round the neck. A caddie drove it off by clipping it with an iron club.

● In Massachusetts a goose, having been hit rather hard by a golf ball which then came to rest by the side of a water hazard, took revenge by waddling over to the ball and kicking it into the water.

● In the summer of 1963, SC King had a good drive to the 10th hole at the Guernsey Club. His partner, RW Clark, was in the rough, and King helped him to search. Returning to his ball, he found a cow eating it. Next day, at the same hole, the positions were reversed, and King was in the rough. Clark placed his woollen hat over his ball, remarking, *I'll make sure the cow doesn't eat mine.* On his return he found the cow thoroughly enjoying his hat; nothing was left but the pom-pom.

Armless, One-armed, Legless and Ambidextrous Players

● In September, 1933, at Burgess Golfing Society of Edinburgh, the first championship for one-armed golfers was held. There were 43 entries and 37 of the competitors had lost an arm in the 1914-18 war. Play was over two rounds and the championship was won by WE Thomson, Eastwood, Glasgow, with a score of 169 (82 and 87) for two rounds. The Burgess course was 6,300 yards long. Thomson drove the last green, 260 yards. The championship and an international match are played annually.

● In the Boys' Amateur Championship 1923, at Dunbar and 1949 at St Andrews, there were competitors each with one arm. The competitor in 1949, RP Reid, Cupar, Fife, who lost his arm working a machine in a butcher's shop, got through to the third round.

● There have been cases of persons with no arms playing golf. One, Thomas McAuliffe, who held the club between his right shoulder and cheek, once went round Buffalo CC, USA, in 108.

● Group Captain Bader, who lost both legs in a flying accident prior to the World War 1939-45, took part in golf competitions and reached a single-figure handicap in spite of his disability.

● In 1909, Scott of Silloth, and John Haskins of Hoylake, both one-armed golfers, played a home and away match for £20-a-side. Scott finished five up at Silloth. He was seven up and 14 to play at Hoylake but Haskins played so well that Scott eventually only won by 3 and 1. This was the first match between one-armed golfers. Haskins in 1919 was challenged by Mr Mycock, of Buxton, another one-armed player. The match was 36 holes, home and away. The first half was played over the Buxton and High Peak Links, and the latter half over the Liverpool Links, and resulted in a win for Haskins by 11 and 10. Later in the same year Haskins received another challenge to play against Alexander Smart of Aberdeen. The match was 18 holes over the Balgownie Course, and ended in favour of Haskins.

● In a match, November, 1926, between the Geduld and Sub Nigel Clubs – two golf clubs connected with the South African gold mines of the same names – each club had two players minus an arm. The natural consequence was that the quartet were matched. The players were – AWP Charteris and E Mitchell, Sub Nigel; and EP Coles and J Kirby, Geduld. This is the first record of four one-armed players in a foursome.

● At Joliet Country Club, USA, a one-armed golfer named DR Anderson drove a ball 300 yards.

● Left-handedness, but playing golf right-handed, is prevalent and for a man to throw with his left hand and play golf right-handed is considered an advantage, for Bobby Jones, Jesse Sweetser, Walter Hagen, Jim Barnes, Joe Kirkwood and more recently Johnny Miller were eminent golfers who were left-handed and ambidextrous.

● In a practice round for the Open Championship in July, 1927, at St Andrews, Len Nettlefold and Joe Kirkwood changed sets of clubs at the 9th hole. Nettlefold was a left-handed golfer and Kirkwood right-handed. They played the last nine, Kirkwood with the left-handed clubs and Nettlefold with the right-handed clubs.

● The late Harry Vardon, when he was at Ganton, got tired of giving impossible odds to his members and beating them, so he collected a set of left-handed clubs, and rating himself at scratch, conceded the handicap odds to them. He won with the same monotonous regularity.

● Ernest Jones, who was professional at the Chislehurst Club, was badly wounded in the war in France in 1916 and his right leg had to be amputated below the knee. He persevered with the game, and before the end of the year he went round the Clacton course balanced on his one leg in 72. Jones later settled in the United States where he built fame and fortune as a golf teacher.

● Major Alexander McDonald Fraser of Edinburgh had the distinction of holding two handicaps simultaneously in the same club – one when he played left-handed and the other for his right-handed play. In medal competitions he had to state before teeing up which method he would use.

● Former England test cricketer Brian Close once held a handicap of 2 playing right-handed, but after retiring from cricket in 1977 decided to apply himself as a left-handed player. His left-handed handicap at the time of his retirement was 7. Close had the distinction of once beating Ted Dexter, another distinguished test cricketer and noted golfer twice in the one day, playing

Blind and Blindfolded Golf

● Major Towse, VC, whose eyes were shot out during the South African War, 1899, was probably the first blind man to play golf. His only stipulations when playing the game were that he should be allowed to touch the ball with his hands to ascertain its position, and that his caddie could ring a small bell to indicate the position of the hole. Major Towse, who played with considerable skill, was also an expert oarsman and bridge player. He died in 1945, aged 81.

● The United States Blind Golfers' Association in 1946 promoted an Invitational Golf Tournament for the blind at Country Club, Inglewood, California. This competition is held annually and in 1953 there were 24 competitors and 11 players completed the two rounds of 36 holes. The winner was Charley Boswell who lost his eyesight leading a tank unit in Germany in 1944.

● In July, 1954, at Lambton Golf and Country Club, Toronto, the first international championship for the blind was held. It resulted in a win for Joe Lazaro, of Waltham, Mass, with a score of 220 for the two rounds. He drove the 215-yard 16th hole and just missed an ace, his ball stopping 18 inches from the hole. Charley Boswell, who won the United States Blind Golfers' Association Tournament in 1953, was second. The same Charles Boswell, of Birmingham, Alabama holed the 141-yard 14th hole at the Vestavia CC in one in October, 1970.

● Another blind person to have holed-in-one was American Ben Thomas while on holiday in South Carolina in 1978.

● Rick Sorenson undertook a bet in which, playing 18 holes blindfolded at Meadowbrook Course, Minneapolis, on 25th May, 1973, he was to pay $10 for every hole over par and receive $100 for every hole in par or better. He went round in 86 losing $70 on the deal.

● Alfred Toogood played blindfolded in a match against Tindal Atkinson at Sunningdale in 1912. Toogood was beaten 8 and 7. Previously, in 1908, I Millar, Newcastle-upon-Tyne, played a match blindfolded against AT Broughton, Birkdale, at Newcastle, County Down. Blindfold putting matches have been frequently played.

● Wing-Commander *Laddie* Lucas, DSO, DFC, MP, played over Sandy Lodge golf course in Hertfordshire on 7th August, 1954, completely blindfolded and had a score of 87.

Trick Shots

● Joe Kirkwood, Australia, specialised in public exhibitions of trick and fancy shots. He played all kinds of strokes after nominating them, and among his ordinary strokes nothing was more impressive than those hit for low flight. He played a full drive from the face of a wrist watch, and the toe of a spectator's shoe, full strokes at a suspended ball, and played for slice and pull at will, and exhibited his ambidexterity by playing left-handed strokes with right-handed clubs. Holing six balls, stymieing, a full shot at a ball catching it as it descended, and hitting 12 full shots in rapid succession, with his face turned away from the ball, were shots among his repertoire. In playing the last named Kirkwood placed the balls in a row, about six inches apart, and moved quickly along the line. Kirkwood, who was born in Australia lived for many years in America. He died in November, 1970 aged 73.

● On 2nd April, 1894, a 3-ball match was played over Musselburgh course between Messrs Grant, Bowden, and Waggot, the clubmaker, the latter teeing on the face of a watch at each tee. He finished the round in 41 the watch being undamaged in any way.

● In a match at Esher on 23rd November, 1931, George Ashdown, the professional, played his tee shot for each of the 18 holes from a rubber tee strapped to the forehead of Miss Ena Shaw.

● EA Forrest, a South African professional in a music hall turn of trick golf shots, played blindfolded shots, one being from the ball teed on the chin of his recumbent partner.

● The late Paul Hahn, an American trick specialist could hit four balls with two clubs Holding a club in each hand he hit two balls, hooking one and slicing the other with the same swing. Hahn had a repertoire of 30 trick shots. In 1955 he flew round the world, exhibiting in 14 countries and on all five continents.

Balls Colliding and Touching

● Competing in the 1980 Corfu International Championship, Sharon Peachey drove from one tee and her ball collided in mid-air with one from a competitor playing another hole. Her ball ended in a pond.

● Playing in the Cornish team championship in 1973 at West Cornwall GC Tom Scott-Brown, of West Cornwall GC, and Paddy Bradley, of Tehidy GC, saw their drives from the fourth and eighth tees collide in mid-air.

● Playing in a 4-ball match at Guernsey Club in June, 1966, all four players were near the 13th green from the tee. Two of them – DG Hare and S Machin – chipped up simultaneously; the balls collided in mid-air; Machin's ball hit the green, then the flagstick, and dropped into the hole for a birdie 2.

● In May, 1926, during the meeting of the Army Golfing Society at St Andrews, Colonel Howard and Lieutenant-Colonel Buchanan Dunlop, while playing in the foursomes against J Rodger and J Mackie, hit full iron shots for the seconds to

the 16th green. Each thought he had to play his ball first, and hidden by a bunker the players struck their balls simultaneously. The balls, going towards the hole about 20 yards from the pin and five feet in the air, met with great force and dropped either side of the hole five yards apart.

● In 1972, before a luncheon celebrating the centenary year of the Ladies' Section of Royal Wimbledon GC, a 12-hole competition was held during which two competitors, Mrs L Champion and Mrs A McKendrick, driving from the eighth and ninth tees respectively, saw their balls collide in mid-air.

● In 1928, at Wentworth Falls, Australia, Dr Alcorn and EA Avery, of the Leura Club, were playing with the professional, E Barnes. The tee shots of Avery and Barnes at the 9th hole finished on opposite sides of the fairway. Unknown to each other, both players hit their seconds (chip shots) at the same time. Dr Alcorn, standing at the pin, suddenly saw two balls approaching the hole from different angles. They met in the air and then dropped into the hole.

● At Rugby, 1931, playing in a 4-ball match, H Fraser pulled his drive from the 10th tee in the direction of the ninth tee. Simultaneously a club member, driving from the ninth tee, pulled his drive. The tees were about 350 yards apart. The two balls collided in mid-air.

● Two golf balls, being played in opposite directions, collided in flight over Longniddry Golf Course on 27th June, 1953. Immediately after Stewart Elder, of Longniddry, had driven from the third tee, another ball, which had been pulled off line from the second fairway, which runs alongside the third, struck his ball about 20 feet above the ground. SJ Fleming, of Tranent, who was playing with Elder, heard a loud crack and thought Elder's ball had exploded. The balls were found undamaged about 70 yards apart.

Three and Two Balls Dislodged by One Shot

● In 1934 on the short 3rd hole (now the 13th) of Olton Course, Warwickshire, JR Horden, a scratch golfer of the club, sent his tee shot into long wet grass a few feet over the back of the green. When he played an *explosion* shot three balls dropped on to the putting green, his own and two others.

● AM Chevalier, playing at Hale, Cheshire, March, 1935, drove his ball into a grass bunker, and when he reached it there was only part of it showing. He played the shot with a niblick and to his amazement not one but three balls shot into the air. They all dropped back into the bunker and came to rest within a foot of each other. Then came another surprise. One of the *finds* was of the same manufacture and bore the same number as the ball he was playing with.

● Playing to the 9th hole, at Osborne House Club, Isle of Wight, George A Sherman lost his ball which had sunk out of sight on the sodden fairway. A few weeks later, playing from the same tee, his ball again was plugged, only the top showing. Under a local rule he lifted his ball to place it, and exactly under it lay the ball he had lost previously.

Balls in Strange Places

● Playing at the John O' Gaunt Club, Sutton, near Biggleswade (Beds), a member drove a ball which did not touch the ground until it reached London – over 40 miles away. The ball landed in a vegetable lorry which was passing the golf course and later fell out of a package of cabbages when they were unloaded at Covent Garden, London.

● In the English Open Amateur Stroke Play at Moortown in 1974, Nigel Denham, a Yorkshire County player, in the first round saw his overhit second shot to the 18th green bounce up some steps into the clubhouse. His ball went through an open door, ricocheted off a wall and came to rest in the men's bar, 20 feet from the windows. As the clubhouse was not out of bounds Denham decided to play the shot back to the green and opened a window 4 feet by 2 feet through which he pitched his ball to 12 feet from the flag. (Several weeks later the R&A declared that Denham should have been penalised two shots for opening the window. The clubhouse was an immovable obstruction and no part of it should have been moved.)

● In the Open Championship at Sandwich, 1949, Harry Bradshaw, Kilcroney, Dublin, at the 5th hole in his second round, drove into the rough and found his ball inside a beer bottle with the neck and shoulder broken off and four sharp points sticking up. Bradshaw, if he had treated the ball as in an unplayable lie might have been involved in a disqualification, so he decided to play it where it lay. With his blaster he smashed the bottle and sent the ball about 30 yards. The hole, a par 4, cost him 6.

● Kevin Sharman of Woodbridge GC hit a low, very straight drive at the club's 8th hole in 1979. After some minutes' searching, his ball was found embedded in a plastic sphere on top of the direction post.

● On the Dublin Course, 16th July, 1936, in the Irish Open Championship, AD Locke, the South African, played his tee shot at the 100-yard 12th hole, but the ball could not be found on arrival on the green. The marker removed the pin and it was discovered that the ball had been entangled in the flag. It dropped near the edge of the hole and Locke holed the short putt for a birdie two.

● While playing a round on the Geelong Golf Club Course, Australia, Easter, 1923, Captain

Charteris topped his tee shot to the short 2nd hole, which lies over a creek with deep and steep clay banks. His ball came to rest on the near slope of the creek bank. He elected to play the ball as it lay, and took his niblick. After the shot, the ball was nowhere to be seen. It was found later embedded in a mass of gluey clay stuck fast to the face of the niblick. It could not be shaken off. Charteris did what was afterwards approved by the R&A, cleaned the ball and dropped it behind without penalty.

● In October, 1929, at Blackmoor Golf Club, Bordon, Hants, a player driving from the first tee holed out his ball in the chimney of a house some 120 yards distant and some 40 yards out of bounds on the right. The owner and his wife were sitting in front of the fire when they heard a rattle in the chimney and were astonished to see a golf ball drop into the fire.

● A similar incident occurred in an inter-club match between Musselburgh and Lothianburn at Prestongrange in 1938 when a member of the former team hooked his ball at the 2nd hole and gave it up for lost. To his amazement a woman emerged from one of the houses adjacent to this part of the course and handed back the ball which she said had come down the chimney and landed on a pot which was on the fire.

● In July, 1955, J Lowrie, starter at the Eden Course, St Andrews, witnessed a freak shot. A visitor drove from the first tee just as a northbound train was passing. He sliced the shot and the ball disappeared through an open window of a passenger compartment. Almost immediately the ball emerged again, having been thrown back on to the fairway by a man in the compartment, who waved a greeting which presumably indicated that no one was hurt.

● At Coombe Wood Golf Club a player hit a ball towards the 16th green where it landed in the vertical exhaust of a tractor which was mowing the fairway. The greenkeeper was somewhat surprised to find a temporary loss of power in the tractor. When sufficient compression had built up in the exhaust system, the ball was forced out with tremendous velocity, hit the roof of a house nearby, bounced off and landed some three feet from the pin on the green.

● When carrying out an inspection of the air conditioning system at St John's Hospital, Chelmsford, in 1993, a golf ball was found in the ventilator immediately above the operating theatre. It was probably the result of a hooked drive from the first tee at Chelmsford Golf Club, which is close by, but the ball can only have entered the duct on a rebound through a three-inch gap under a ventilator hood and then descended through a series of sharp bends to its final resting place.

● There have been many occasions when misdirected shots have finished in strange places after an unusual line of flight and bounce. At Ashford, Middlesex, John Miller, aged 69, hit his tee shot out of bounds at the 12th hole (237 yards). It struck a parked car, passed through a copse, hit more cars, jumped a canopy, flew through the clubhouse kitchen window, finishing in a cooking stock-pot, without once touching the ground. Mr Miller had previously done the hole in one on four occasions.

Balls Hit To and From Great Heights

● In 1798 two Edinburgh golfers undertook to drive a ball over the spire of St Giles' Cathedral, Edinburgh, for a wager. Mr Sceales, of Leith, and Mr Smellie, a printer, were each allowed six shots and succeeded in sending the balls well over the weather-cock, a height of more than 160 feet from the ground.

● Some years later Donald McLean, an Edinburgh lawyer, won a substantial bet by driving a ball over the Melville Monument in St Andrew Square, Edinburgh – height, 154 feet.

● Tom Morris in 1860, at the famous bridge of Ballochmyle, stood in the quarry beneath and, from a stick elevated horizontally, attempted to send golf balls over the bridge. He could raise them only to the pathway, 400 feet high, which was in itself a great feat with the gutta ball.

● Captain Ernest Carter, on 28th September, 1922, drove a ball from the roadway at the 1st tee on Harlech Links against the wall of Harlech Castle. The embattlements are 200 feet over the level of the roadway, and the point where the ball struck the embattlements was 180 yards from the point where the ball was teed. Captain Carter, who was laid odds of £100 to £1, used a baffy.

● In 1896 Freddie Tait, then a subaltern in the Black Watch, drove a ball from the Rookery, the highest building on Edinburgh Castle, in a match against a brother officer to hole out in the fountain in Princes Street Gardens 350 feet below and about 300 yards distant.

● Prior to the 1977 Lancôme Tournament in Paris, Arnold Palmer hit three balls from the second stage of the Eiffel Tower, over 300 feet above ground. The longest was measured at 403 yards. One ball was hooked and hit a bus but no serious damage was done as all traffic had been stopped for safety reasons.

● Long drives have been made from mountain peaks, across the gorge at Victoria Falls, from the Pyramids, high buildings in New York, and from many other similar places. As an illustration of such freakish *drives* a member of the New York Rangers' Hockey Team from the top of Mount Edith Cavell, 11,033 feet high, drove a ball which struck the Ghost Glacier 5,000 feet below and bounced off the rocky ledge another 1,000 feet – a total drop of 2,000 yards. Later, in June, 1968, from Pikes Peak, Colorado (14,110 feet), Arthur Lynskey hit a ball which travelled 200 yards horizontally but 2 miles vertically.

Remarkable Shots

● Remarkable shots are as numerous as the grains of sand; around every 19th hole, legends are recalled of astounding shots. One shot is commemorated by a memorial tablet at the 17th hole at the Lytham and St Annes Club. It was made by Bobby Jones in the final round of the Open Championship in 1926. He was partnered by Al Watrous, another American player. They had been running neck and neck and at the end of the third round, Watrous was just leading Jones with 215 against 217. At the 16th Jones drew level then on the 17th he drove into a sandy lie in broken ground. Watrous reached the green with his second. Jones took a mashie-iron (the equivalent to a 4-iron today) and hit a magnificent shot to the green to get his 4. This remarkable recovery unnerved Watrous, who 3-putted, and Jones, getting another 4 at the last hole against 5, won his first Open Championship with 291 against Watrous' 293. The tablet is near the spot where Jones played his second shot.

● Arnold Palmer (USA), playing in the second round of the Australian Wills Masters tournament at Melbourne, in October, 1964, hooked his second shot at the 9th hole high into the fork of a gum tree. Climbing 20 feet up the tree, Palmer, with the head of his 1-iron reversed, played a hammer stroke and knocked the ball some 30 yards forward, followed by a brilliant chip to the green and a putt.

● In the foursome during the Ryder Cup at Moortown in 1929, Joe Turnesa hooked the American side's second shot at the last hole behind the marquee adjoining the clubhouse, Johnny Farrel then pitched the ball over the marquee on to the green only feet away from the pin and Turnesa holed out for a 4.

Miscellaneous Incidents and Strange Golfing Facts

● Gary Player of South Africa was honoured by his country by having his portrait on new postage stamps which were issued on 12th December, 1976. It was the first time a specific golfer had ever been depicted on any country's postage stamps. In 1981 the US Postal Service introduced stamps featuring Bobby Jones and Babe Zaharias. They are the first golfers to be thus honoured by the United States.

● Gary Harris, aged 18, became the first player to make five consecutive appearances for England in the European Boys Team Championship at Vilamoura, Portugal, in 1994.

● In February, 1971, the first ever golf shots on the moon's surface were played by Captain Alan Shepard, commander of the Apollo 14 spacecraft. Captain Shepard hit two balls with an iron head attached to a makeshift shaft. With a one-handed swing he claimed he hit the first ball 200 yards aided by the reduced force of gravity on the moon. Subsequent findings put this distance in doubt. The second was a shank. Acknowledging the occasion the R&A sent Captain Shepard the following telegram: *Warmest congratulations to all of you on your great achievement and safe return. Please refer to Rules of Golf section on etiquette, paragraph 6, quote – before leaving a bunker a player should carefully fill up all holes made by him therein, unquote.* Shepard presented the club to the USGA Museum in 1974.

● Charles (Chick) Evans competed in every US Amateur Championship held between 1907 and 1962 by which time he was 72 years old. This amounted to 50 consecutive occasions discounting the six years of the two World Wars when the championship was not held.

● In winning the 1977 US Open at Southern Hills CC, Tulsa, Oklahoma, Hubert Green had to contend with a death threat. Coming off the 14th green in the final round, he was advised by USGA officials that a phone call had been received saying that he would be killed. Green decided that play should continue and happily he went on to win, unharmed.

● It was discovered at the 1977 USPGA Championship that the clubs with which Tom Watson had won the Open Championship and the US Masters earlier in the year were illegal, having grooves which exceeded the permitted specifications. The set he used in winning the 1975 Open Championship were then flown out to him and they too were found to be illegal. No retrospective action was taken.

● Mrs Fred Daly, wife of the former Open champion, saved the clubhouse of Balmoral GC, Belfast, from destruction when three men entered the professional's shop on 5th August, 1976, and left a bag containing a bomb outside the shop beside the clubhouse when refused money. Mrs Daly carried the bag over to a hedge some distance away where the bomb exploded 15 minutes later. The only damage was broken windows. On the same day several hours afterwards, Dungannon GC in Co Tyrone suffered extensive damage to the clubhouse from terrorist bombs. Co Down GC, proposed venue of the 1979 home international matches suffered bomb damage in May that year and through fear for the safety of team members the 1979 matches were cancelled.

● The Army Golfing Society and St Andrews on 21st April, 1934, played a match 200-a-side, the largest golf match ever played. Play was by foursomes. The Army won 58, St Andrews 31 and 11 were halved.

● Jamie Ortiz-Patino, owner of the Valderrama Golf Club at Sotogrande, Spain, paid a record £84,000 (increased to £92,400 with ten per cent buyers premium) for a late seventeenth- or early eighteenth-century rake iron offered at auction in

Musselburgh in July, 1992. The iron, which had been kept in a garden shed, was bought to be exhibited in a museum being created in Valderrama.
● A Christie's golf auction during the week of the 1991 Open Championship created two world records. An American dealer bought a blacksmith-made iron club head dating from the seventeenth century for £44,000. It had been found 10 years before in a hedge near the North Berwick Golf Club in Scotland. Also, £165,000 was paid by a Japanese collector for an oil painting by Sir Francis Grant (1810–1878) of the 1823 Royal & Ancient captain, John Whyte-Melville, standing beside the Swilcan Burn at St Andrews. The same Japanese buyer successfully bid £35,200 for a rare gutty golf ball marking device from the workshops of Old Tom Morris in St Andrews, while an unused feathery golf ball by Allan Robertson fetched £11,000.
● In 1986 Alistair Risk and three colleagues on the 17th green at Brora, Sutherland, watched a cow giving birth to twin calves between the markers on the 18th tee, causing them to play their next tee shots from in front of the tee. Their application for a ruling from the R&A brought a Rules Committee reply that while technically a rule had been broken, their action was considered within the spirit of the game and there should be no penalty. The Secretary added that the Rules Committee hoped that mother and twins were doing well.
● In view of the increasing number of people crossing the road (known as Granny Clark's Wynd) which runs across the first and 18th fairways of the Old Course, St Andrews, as a right of way, the St Andrews Links committee decided in 1969 to control the flow by erecting traffic lights, with appropriate green for go, yellow for caution and red for stop. The lights are controlled from the starter's box on the first tee. Golfers on the first tee must wait until the lights turn to green before driving off and a notice has been erected at the Wynd warning pedestrians not to cross at yellow or stop.
● A traffic light for golfers was also installed in 1971 on one of Japan's most congested courses. After putting on the uphill 9th hole of the Fukuoka course in Southern Japan, players have to switch on a go-ahead signal for following golfers waiting to play their shots to the green.
● A 22-year-old professional at Brett Essex GC, Brentwood, David Moore, who was playing in the Mufulira Open in Zambia in 1976, was shot dead it is alleged by the man with whom he was staying for the duration of the tournament. It appeared his host then shot himself.
● Peggy Carrick and her daughter, Angela Uzielli, won the Mothers and Daughters Tournament at Royal Mid-Surrey in 1994 for the 21st time.
● Patricia Shepherd has won the ladies' club championship at Turriff GC Aberdeenshire 30 consecutive times from 1959 to 1988.
● Mrs Jackie Mercer won the South African Ladies' Championship in 1979, 31 years after her first victory in the event as Miss Jacqueline Smith.
● During the Royal & Ancient medal meeting on 25th September, 1907, a member of the Royal & Ancient drove a ball which struck the sharp point of a hatpin in the hat of a lady who was crossing the course. The ball was so firmly impaled that it remained in position. The lady was not hurt.
● John Cook, former English Amateur Champion, narrowly escaped death during an attempted coup against King Hassan of Morocco in July 1971. Cook had been playing in a tournament arranged by King Hassan, a keen golfer, and was at the King's birthday party in Rabat when rebels broke into the party demanding that the King give up his throne. Cook and many others present were taken hostage.
● When playing from the 9th tee at Lossiemouth golf course in June, 1971, Martin Robertson struck a Royal Navy jet aircraft which was coming in to land at the nearby airfield. The plane was not damaged.
● At a court in Inglewood, California, in 1978, Jim Brown was convicted of beating and choking an opponent during a dispute over where a ball should have been placed on the green.
● During the Northern Ireland troubles a homemade hand grenade was found in a bunker at Dungannon GC, Co Tyrone, on Sunday, 12th September, 1976.
● Tiger Woods, 18, became both the youngest and the first black golfer to win the United States Amateur Championship at Sawgrass in 1994. He went on to win the title three years in a row and then won the first major championship he played as a professional, the 1997 Masters, by a record 12 strokes and with a record low aggregate of 270, 18 under par.
● To mark the centenary of the Jersey Golf Club in 1978, the Jersey Post Office issued a set of four special stamps featuring Jersey's most famous golfer, Harry Vardon. The background of the 13p stamp was a brief biography of Vardon's career reproduced from the *Golfer's Handbook*.
● Forty-one-year-old John Mosley went for a round of golf at Delaware Park GC, Buffalo, New York, in July, 1972. He stepped on to the first tee and was challenged over a green fee by an official guard. A scuffle developed, a shot was fired and Mosley, a bullet in his chest, died on the way to hospital. His wife was awarded $131,250 in an action against the City of Buffalo and the guard. The guard was sentenced to 7½ years for second-degree manslaughter.
● When three competitors in a 1968 Pennsylvania pro-am event were about to drive from the 16th tee, two bandits (one with pistol) suddenly emerged from the bushes, struck one of the players and robbed them of wristwatches and $300.
● In the 1932 Walker Cup match at Brooklyn, Leonard Crawley succeeded in denting the cup.

An errant iron shot to the 18th green hit the cup, which was on display outside the clubhouse.
● In Johannesburg, South Africa, three golf officials appeared in court ccused of violating a 75-year-old Sunday Observance Law by staging the final round of the South African PGA championship on Sunday, 28th February, 1971. The Championship should have been completed on the Saturday but heavy rain prevented any play.
● In the Open Championship of 1876, at St Andrews, Bob Martin and David Strath tied at 176. A protest was lodged against Strath alleging he played his approach to the 17th green and struck a spectator. The Royal & Ancient ordered the replay, but Strath refused to play off the tie until a decision had been given on the protest. No decision was given and Bob Martin was declared the Champion.
● At Rose Bay, New South Wales, on 11th July, 1931, DJ Bayly MacArthur, on stepping into a bunker, began to sink. MacArthur, who weighed 14 stone, shouted for help. He was rescued when up to the armpits. He had stepped on a patch of quicksand, aggravated by excess of moisture.
● The late Bobby Cruickshank was the victim of his own jubilation in the 1934 US Open at Merion. In the 4th round while in with a chance of winning he half-topped his second shot at the 11th hole. The ball was heading for a pond in front of the green but instead of ending up in the water it hit a rock and bounced on to the green. In his delight Cruickshank threw his club into the air only to receive a resounding blow on the head as it returned to earth.
● A dog with an infallible nose for finding lost golf balls was, in 1971, given honorary membership of the Waihi GC, Hamilton, New Zealand. The dog, called Chico, was trained to search for lost balls, to be sold back to the members, the money being put into the club funds.
● By 1980 Waddy, an 11-year-old beagle belonging to Bob Inglis, the secretary of Brokenhurst Manor GC, had found over 35,000 golf balls.
● Herbert M Hepworth, Headingley, Leeds, Lord Mayor of Leeds in 1906, scored one thousand holes in 2, a feat which took him 30 years to accomplish. It was celebrated by a dinner in 1931 at the Leeds club. The first 2 of all was scored on 12th June, 1901, at Cobble Hall Course, Leeds, and the 1,000th in 1931 at Alwoodley, Leeds. Hepworth died in November, 1942.

● Fiona MacDonald was the first female to play in the Oxford and Cambridge University match at Ganton in 1986.
● Mrs Sara Gibbon won the Farnham (Surrey) Club's Grandmother's competition 48 hours after her first grand-child was born.
● At Carnoustie in the first qualifying round for the 1952 Scottish Amateur Championship a competitor drove three balls in succession out of bounds at the 1st hole and thereupon withdrew.
● In 1993, the Clark family from Hagley GC, Worcestershire, set a record for the county's three major professional events. The Worcestershire stroke play championship was won by Finlay Clark, the eldest son, who beat his father, Iain, and younger brother Cameron, who tied second. In the County Match Play it was the turn of Iain, who beat his son, Finlay, by 2 and 1 in the final. Cameron won the play-off for third place. Then in the Worcestershire Annual Pro-Am it was the turn of Cameron, with his brother, Finlay, second and father, Iain, third. To add to the achievements of the family, Cameron also won the Midland Professional Match Play Championship.
● During a Captain–Pro foursomes challenge match at Chelmsford in 1993, Club Professional Dennis Bailey, put the ball into a hole only once in all 18 holes – when he holed-in-one at the fourth.

Strange Local Rules

● The Duke of Windsor, who played on an extraordinary variety of the world's courses, once took advantage of a local rule at Jinja in Uganda and lifted his ball from a hippo's footprint without penalty.
● At the Glen Canyon course in Arizona a local rule provides that *If your ball lands within a club length of a rattlesnake you are allowed to move the ball.*
● Another local rule in Uganda read: *If a ball comes to rest in dangerous proximity to a crocodile, another ball may be dropped.*
● The 6th hole at Koolan Island GC, Western Australia also serves as a local air strip and a local rule reads: *Aircraft and vehicular traffic have right of way at all times.*
● A local rule at the RAF Waddington GC reads: *When teeing off from the 2nd, right of way must be given to taxiing aircraft.*

Record Scoring

The Open Championship

Most times champions
6 Harry Vardon, 1896-98-99-1903-11-14
5 James Braid, 1901-05-06-08-10; JH Taylor, 1894-95-1900-09-13; Peter Thomson, 1954-55-56-58-65; Tom Watson, 1975-77-80-82-83

Most times runner-up
7 Jack Nicklaus, 1964-67-68-72-76-77-79
6 JH Taylor, 1896-1904-05-06-07-14

Oldest winner
Old Tom Morris, 46 years 99 days, 1867
Roberto De Vicenzo, 44 years 93 days, 1967

Youngest winner
Young Tom Morris, 17 years 5 months 8 days, 1868
Willie Auchterlonie, 21 years 24 days, 1893
Severiano Ballesteros, 22 years 3 months 12 days, 1979

Youngest and oldest competitor
John Ball, 15 years 6 months, 1878
Gene Sarazen, 71 years 4 months 13 days, 1973

Widest margin of victory
13 strokes Old Tom Morris, 1862
12 strokes Young Tom Morris, 1870
8 strokes JH Taylor, 1900 and 1913; James Braid, 1908
6 strokes Harry Vardon, 1903; JH Taylor, 1909; Bobby Jones, 1927; Walter Hagen, 1929; Arnold Palmer, 1962; Johnny Miller, 1976

Lowest winning aggregates
267 Greg Norman, 66-68-69-64, Sandwich, 1993
268 Tom Watson, 68-70-65-65, Turnberry, 1977; Nick Price, 69-66-67-66, Turnberry, 1994
270 Nick Faldo, 67-65-67-71, St Andrews, 1990

Lowest aggregate by runner-up
269 (68-70-65-66), Jack Nicklaus, Turnberry, 1977; (69-63-70-67) Nick Faldo, Sandwich, 1993; (68-66-68-67) Jesper Parnevik, Turnberry, 1994

Lowest aggregate by an amateur
281 (68-72-70-71), Iain Pyman, Sandwich, 1993; (75, 66, 70, 70), Tiger Woods, R. Lytham, 1996

Lowest round
63 Mark Hayes, second round, Turnberry, 1977; Isao Aoki, third round, Muirfield, 1980; Greg Norman, second round, Turnberry, 1986; Paul Broadhurst, third round, St Andrews, 1990; Jodie Mudd, fourth round, Royal Birkdale, 1991; Nick Faldo, second round, Payne Stewart, fourth round, Sandwich, 1993

Lowest round by an amateur
66 Frank Stranahan, fourth round, Troon, 1950; Tiger Woods, second round, R. Lytham, 1996; Justin Rose, second round, R Birkdale, 1998

Lowest first round
64 Craig Stadler, Royal Birkdale, 1983; Christy O'Connor Jr, Royal St George's, 1985; Rodger Davis, Muirfield, 1987; Steve Pate, Ray Floyd, Muirfield, 1992

Lowest second round
63 Mark Hayes, Turnberry, 1977; Greg Norman, Turnberry, 1986; Nick Faldo, Sandwich, 1993

Lowest third round
63 Isao Aoki, Muirfield, 1980; Paul Broadhurst, St Andrews, 1990

Lowest fourth round
63 Jodie Mudd, Royal Birkdale, 1991; Payne Stewart, Sandwich, 1993

Lowest first 36 holes
130 (66-64), Nick Faldo, Muirfield, 1992
132 (67-65), Henry Cotton, Sandwich, 1934; Nick Faldo (67-65) and Greg Norman (66-66), St Andrews, 1990; Nick Faldo (69-63), Sandwich, 1993

Lowest second 36 holes
130 (65-65), Tom Watson, Turnberry, 1977 (64-66) Ian Baker-Finch, R. Birkdale, 1991; (66-64) Anders Forsbrand, Turnberry, 1994

Lowest first 54 holes
198 (67-67-64) Tom Lehman, Royal Lytham, 1996
199 (67-65-67), Nick Faldo, St Andrews, 1990; (66-64-69) Nick Faldo, Muirfield, 1992

Lowest final 54 holes
199 (66-67-66) Nick Price, Turnberry, 1994
200 (70-65-65), Tom Watson, Turnberry, 1977; (63-70-67), Nick Faldo, Sandwich, 1993 (66-64-70), Fuzzy Zoeller, Turnberry, 1994 (66-70-64), Nick Faldo, Turnberry 1994

Lowest 9 holes
28 Denis Durnian, first 9, Royal Birkdale, 1983

Champions in three decades
Harry Vardon, 1986, 1903, 1911
JH Taylor, 1894, 1900, 1913
Gary Player, 1959, 1968, 1974

Biggest span between first and last victories
19 years, JH Taylor, 1894-1913
18 years, Harry Vardon, 1896-1914
15 years, Willie Park, 1860–75
15 years, Gary Player, 1959-74
14 years, Henry Cotton, 1934-48

Successive victories
4 Young Tom Morris, 1868-72 (no championship in 1871)
3 Jamie Anderson, 1877-79; Bob Ferguson, 1880-82, Peter Thomson, 1954-56
2 Old Tom Morris, 1861-62; JH Taylor, 1894-95; Harry Vardon, 1898-99; James Braid, 1905-06; Bobby Jones, 1926-27; Walter Hagen, 1928-29; Bobby Locke, 1949-50; Arnold Palmer, 1961-62; Lee Trevino, 1971-72; Tom Watson, 1982-83

Victories by amateurs
3 Bobby Jones, 1926-27-30
2 Harold Hilton, 1892-97
1 John Ball, 1890
Roger Wethered lost a play-off in 1921

Highest number of top five finishes
16 JH Taylor and Jack Nicklaus
15 Harry Vardon and James Braid

Players with four rounds under 70
Greg Norman (66-68-69-64), Sandwich, 1993;
Ernie Els (68-69-69-68), Sandwich, 1993;
Nick Price (69-66-67-66), Turnberry, 1994;
Jesper Parnevik (68-66-68-67), Turnberry, 1994

Highest number of rounds under 70
33 Jack Nicklaus and Nick Faldo
27 Tom Watson

23 Greg Norman
21 Lee Trevino
20 Severiano Ballesteros and Nick Price

Outright leader after every round
Willie Auchterlonie, 1893; JH Taylor, 1894 and 1900; James Braid, 1908; Ted Ray, 1912; Bobby Jones, 1927; Gene Sarazen, 1932; Henry Cotton, 1934; Tom Weiskopf, 1973

Record leads (since 1892)
After 18 holes: 4 strokes, James Braid, 1908; Bobby Jones, 1927; Henry Cotton, 1934; Christy O'Connor Jr, 1985
After 36 holes: 9 strokes, Henry Cotton, 1934
After 54 holes: 10 strokes, Henry Cotton, 1934; 7 strokes, Tony Lema, 1964; 6 strokes, James Braid, 1908; Tom Lehman, 1996; 5 strokes, Arnold Palmer, 1962, Bill Rogers, 1981, Nick Faldo, 1990

Champions with each round lower than previous one
Jack White, 1904, Sandwich, 80-75-72-69
James Braid, 1906, Muirfield, 77-76-74-73
Ben Hogan, 1953, Carnoustie, 73-71-70-68
Gary Player, 1959, Muirfield, 75-71-70-68

Champion with four rounds the same
Densmore Shute, 1933, St Andrews, 73-73-73-73 (excluding the play-off)

Biggest variation between rounds of a champion
14 strokes, Henry Cotton, 1934, second round 65, fourth round 79
11 strokes, Jack White, 1904, first round 80, fourth round 69; Greg Norman, 1986, first round 74, second round 63, third round 74

Biggest variation between two rounds
18 strokes: A Tingey Jr, 1923, first round 94, second 76
17 strokes, Jack Nicklaus, 1981, first round 83, second round 66; Ian Baker-Finch, 1986, first round 86, second round 69

Best comeback by champions
After 18 holes: Harry Vardon, 1896, 11 strokes behind the leader
After 36 holes: George Duncan, 1920, 13 strokes behind leader
After 54 holes: Jim Barnes, 1925, Justin Leonard, 1997, 5 strokes behind the leader

Best comeback by non-champions
Of non-champions, Greg Norman, 1989, seven strokes behind the leader and lost in a play-off

Best finishing round by a champion
64 Greg Norman, Sandwich, 1993
65 Tom Watson, Turnberry, 1977; Severiano Ballesteros, Royal Lytham, 1988; Justin Leonard, Royal Troon, 1997

Worst finishing round by a champion since 1920
79 Henry Cotton, Sandwich, 1934
78 Reg Whitcombe, Sandwich, 1938
77 Walter Hagen, Hoylake, 1924

Best opening round by a champion
66 Peter Thomson, Royal Lytham, 1958; Nick Faldo, Muirfield, 1992; Greg Norman, Sandwich, 1993
67 Henry Cotton, Sandwich, 1934; Tom Watson, R. Birkdale, 1983; Severiano Ballesteros, R. Lytham, 1988; Nick Faldo, St Andrews, 1990; John Daly, St Andrews, 1995, Tom Lehman, R. Lytham, 1996

Worst opening round by a champion since 1919
80 George Duncan, Deal, 1920 (he also had a second round of 80)
77 Walter Hagen, Hoylake, 1924

Biggest recovery in 18 holes by a champion
George Duncan, Deal, 1920, was 13 strokes behind the leader, Abe Mitchell, after 36 holes and level after 54

Most consecutive appearances
44 Gary Player, 1955–98

Championship since 1946 with the fewest rounds under 70
St Andrews, 1946; Hoylake, 1947; Portrush, 1951; Hoylake, 1956; Carnoustie, 1968. All had only two rounds under 70

Longest course
Carnoustie, 1968, 7,252 yd (6,631m)

Largest entries
2,343 in 1998, Royal Birkdale
2,133 in 1997, Royal Troon

Courses most often used
St Andrews, 25; Prestwick, 24 (but not since 1925); Muirfield, 14; Sandwich, 12; Hoylake, 10; R. Lytham, 9; R. Birkdale, 8; R. Troon 7; Musselburgh, 6; Carnoustie, 5; Turnberry, 3; Deal, 2; R. Portrush and Prince's, 1

Attendances

Year	Attendance	Year	Attendance
1962	37,098	1981	111,987
1963	24,585	1982	133,299
1964	35,954	1983	142,892
1965	32,927	1984	193,126
1966	40,182	1985	141,619
1967	29,880	1986	134,261
1968	51,819	1987	139,189
1969	46,001	1988	191,334
1970	82,593	1989	160,639
1971	70,076	1990	207,000
1972	84,746	1991	192,154
1973	78,810	1992	150,100
1974	92,796	1993	140,100
1975	85,258	1994	128,000
1976	92,021	1995	180,000
1977	87,615	1996	170,000
1978	125,271	1997	176,797
1979	134,501	1998	180,000
1980	131,610		

Prize Money

Year	Total	First Prize £	Year	Total	First Prize £	Year	Total	First Prize £
1860	nil	nil	1958	4,850	1,000	1983	300,000	40,000
1863	10	nil	1959	5,000	1,000	1984	451,000	55,000
1864	16	6	1960	7,000	1,250	1985	530,000	65,000
1876	20	20	1961	8,500	1,400	1986	600,000	70,000
1889	22	8	1963	8,500	1,500	1987	650,000	75,000
1891	28.50	10	1965	10,000	1,750	1988	700,000	80,000
1892	110	(Am)	1966	15,000	2,100	1989	750,000	80,000
1893	100	30	1968	20,000	3,000	1990	815,000	85,000
1910	125	50	1969	30,000	4,250	1991	900,000	90,000
1920	225	75	1970	40,000	5,250	1992	950,000	95,000
1927	275	100	1971	45,000	5,500	1993	1,000,000	100,000
1930	400	100	1972	50,000	5,500	1994	1,100,000	110,000
1931	500	100	1975	75,000	7,500	1995	1,250,000	125,000
1946	1,000	150	1977	100,000	10,000	1996	1,400,000	200,000
1949	1,700	300	1978	125,000	12,500	1997	1,586,300	250,000
1953	2,450	500	1979	155,000	15,500	1998	1,774,150	300,000
1954	3,500	750	1980	200,000	25,000			
1955	3,750	1,000	1982	250,000	32,000			

US Open

Most times champion
4 Willie Anderson, 1901-03-04-05; Bobby Jones, 1923-26-29-30; Ben Hogan, 1948-50-51-53; Jack Nicklaus, 1962-67-72-80

Most times runner-up
4 Bobby Jones, 1922-24-25-28; Sam Snead, 1937-47-49-53; Arnold Palmer, 1962-63-66-67; Jack Nicklaus, 1960 (am)-68-71-82

Oldest winner
Hale Irwin, 45 years, Medinah, 1990

Youngest winner
Johnny McDermott, 19 years, Chicago, 1911

Biggest winning margin
11 strokes Willie Smith, Baltimore, 1899

Lowest winning aggregate
272 Jack Nicklaus, Baltusrol, 1980; Lee Janzen, Baltusrol, 1993

Lowest round
63 Johnny Miller, fourth round, Oakmont, 1973; Jack Nicklaus, first round, Baltusrol, 1980; Tom Weiskopf, first round, Baltusrol, 1980

Lowest 9 holes
29 Neal Lancaster, Shinnecock Hills, 1995, and Oakland Hills, 1996

Lowest first 36 holes
134 Jack Nicklaus, Baltusrol, 1980; Tze-chung Chen, Oakland Hills, 1985

Lowest final 36 holes
132 Larry Nelson, Oakmont, 1983

Most consecutive appearances
42 Jack Nicklaus 1957 to 1998

Successive victories
3 Willie Anderson, 1903-04-05

Players with four rounds under 70
Lee Trevino, 69-68-69-69, Oak Hill, 1968; Lee Janzen, 67-67-69-69, Baltusrol, 1993

Wire to wire winners
Walter Hagen, Midlothian, 1914; Jim Barnes, Columbia, 1921; Ben Hogan, Oakmont, 1953; Tony Jacklin, Hazeltine, 1970

Best opening round by a champion
63 Jack Nicklaus, Baltusrol, 1980

Worst opening round by a champion
91 Horace Rawlins, Newport, RI, 1895
Since World War II: 76 Ben Hogan, Oakland Hills, 1951

US Masters

Most times champion
6 Jack Nicklaus, 1963-65-66-72-75-86
4 Arnold Palmer, 1958-60-62-64

Most times runner-up
4 Ben Hogan, 1942-46-54-55; Jack Nicklaus, 1964-71-77-81

Oldest winner
Jack Nicklaus, 46 years, 1986

Youngest winner
Tiger Woods, 21 years, 3 months, 1997

Biggest winning margin
12 strokes Tiger Woods, 1997

Lowest winning aggregate
270 Tiger Woods, 1997

Lowest aggregate by an amateur
281 Charles Coe, 1961 (joint second)

Lowest round
63 Nick Price, 1986; Greg Norman, 1996

Lowest 9 holes
29 Mark Calcavecchia, 1992

Lowest first 36 holes
131 Raymond Floyd, 1976

Lowest final 36 holes
131 Johnny Miller, 1975

Most appearances
45 Doug Ford 1952 to 1997
44 Sam Snead 1937 to 1983

Successive victories
2 Jack Nicklaus, 1965-66; Nick Faldo, 1989-90

Players with four rounds under 70
None

Wire to wire winners
Craig Wood, 1941; Arnold Palmer, 1960; Jack Nicklaus, 1972; Raymond Floyd, 1976

Best opening round by a champion
65 Raymond Floyd, 1976

Worst opening round by a champion
75 Craig Stadler, 1982

Albatrosses
There have been three albatross twos in the Masters at Augusta National: by Gene Sarazen at the 15th, 1935; by Bruce Devlin at the eighth, 1967; and by Jeff Maggert at the 13th, 1994.

US PGA Championship

Note: The PGA was a match play event from 1916 to 1957. Since 1958 it has been played as stroke play

Most times champion
5 Walter Hagen, 1921-24-25-26-27; Jack Nicklaus 1963-71-73-75-80

Most times runner-up
4 Jack Nicklaus, 1964-65-74-83

Oldest winner
Julius Boros, 48 years 4 months 18 days, Pecan Valley, 1968

Youngest winner
Gene Sarazen, 20 years 5 months 22 days, Oakmont, 1922

Biggest winning margin
7 strokes Jack Nicklaus, Oak Hill, 1980

Lowest aggregate
267 Steve Elkington and Colin Montgomerie, Riviera, 1995 – Montgomerie lost play-off

Lowest round
63 Bruce Crampton, Firestone, 1975; Raymond Floyd, Southern Hills, 1982; Gary Player, Shoal Creek, 1984; Vijay Singh, Inverness, 1993; Michael Bradley and Brad Faxon, Riviera, 1995

Most successive victories
4 Walter Hagen, 1924-25-26-27

Lowest 9 holes
28 Brad Faxon, Riviera, 1995

Lowest first 36 holes
131 Hal Sutton, Riviera, 1983; Vijay Singh, Inverness, 1993; Ernie Els and Mark O'Meara, Riviera, 1995

Lowest final 36 holes
132 Miller Barber, Dayton, 1969; Steve Elkington and Colin Montgomerie, Riviera, 1995

Most appearances
37 Arnold Palmer

Wire to wire winners
Bobby Nichols, Columbus, 1964; Raymond Floyd, Dayton, 1969; Jack Nicklaus, PGA National, 1971; Raymond Floyd, Southern Hills, 1982; Hal Sutton, Riviera, 1983

Best opening round by a champion
63 Raymond Floyd, Southern Hills, 1982

Worst opening round by a champion
75 John Mahaffey, Oakmont, 1978

European PGA Tour

Lowest 72-hole aggregate
258 (14 under par) David Llewellyn (Wal), AGF Biarritz Open, 1988; (18 under) Ian Woosnam (Wal), Monte Carlo Open, 1990.
259 (25 under par) Mark McNulty (Zim), German Open at Frankfurt, 1987.

Lowest 9 holes
27 (9 under par) José María Canizares (Sp), Swiss Open at Crans-sur-Sierre, 1978; (7 under) Robert Lee (Eng), Johnnie Walker Monte Carlo Open at Mont Agel, 1985; (6 under) Robert Lee, Portuguese Open at Estoril, 1987; (9 under) Joakim Haeggman (Swe), Alfred Dunhill Cup at St Andrews, 1997

Lowest 18 holes
60 (11 under par) Baldovino Dassu (It), Swiss Open at Crans-sur-Sierre, 1971; David Llewellyn (Wal), AGF Biarritz Open, 1988; (9 under) Ian Woosnam (Wal), Torras Monte Carlo Open at Mont Agel, 1990; (12 under) Jamie Spence, Canon European Masters at Crans-sur-Sierre, Switzerland, 1992; (10 under) Paul Curry, Bell's Scottish Open at Gleneagles, 1992; (9 under) both Darren Clarke and Johan Rystrom, Monte Carlo Open at Mont Agel, 1992; (12 under) Bernhard Langer (Ger), Linde German Masters at Motzener See, 1997

Lowest 36 holes
124 (18 under par) Colin Montgomerie (Sco), Canon European Masters at Crans-sur-Sierre, 1996

Lowest first 36 holes
126 (12 under par) Darren Clarke (N. Ire), European Monte Carlo Open at Mont Agel, 1992

Lowest 54 holes
192 (24 under par) Anders Forbrand (Swe), Ebel European Masters Swiss Open at Crans-sur-Sierre, 1987.

Largest winning margin
17 strokes Bernhard Langer, Cacharel Under-25s' Championship in Nîmes, 1979.

Highest winning score
306 Peter Butler (Eng), Schweppes PGA Close Championship at Royal Birkdale, 1963.

Youngest winner
Dale Hayes, 18 years 290 days, Spanish Open, 1971

Oldest winner
Neil Coles, 48 years 14 days, Sanyo Open, 1982

Most wins in one season
7 Norman von Nida (Aus), 1947

US Tour

Lowest 72-hole aggregate
257 (27 under par) Mike Souchak, 60-68-64-65, Texas Open, 1955
260 (28 under par) John Huston, 63-65-66-66, Hawaiian Open, 1998

Lowest 18 holes
59 Sam Snead, third round, Greenbrier Open (Sam Snead Festival), White Sulphur Springs, West Virginia, 1959; Al Geiberger, second round, Danny Thomas Memphis Classic, Colonial CC, 1977 (when preferred lies were in operation); (13 under par) Chip Beck on the 6,914-yards Sunrise GC course, Las Vegas, third round, Las Vegas Invitational (finished third but won a bonus prize of $500,000 and another $500,000 for charities

Lowest 9 holes
27 Mike Souchak, Texas Open, 1955; Andy North, BC Open, 1975

Lowest first 36 holes
126 Tommy Bolt, 1954; Paul Azinger, 1989. (On the US mini-tour a 36-hole score of 123 was achieved by Bob Risch in the 1978 Mesa Centennial Open.)

Lowest 54 holes
189 Chandler Harper, Texas Open (last three rounds), 1954

Largest winning margin
16 strokes J Douglas Edgar, Canadian Open Championship, 1919; Bobby Locke, Chicago Victory National Championship, 1948

Youngest winner
Johnny McDermott, 19 years 10 months, US Open, 1911

Oldest winner
Sam Snead, 52 years 10 months, Greater Greensboro Open, 1965

Most wins in one season
18 Byron Nelson, 1945

National opens – excluding Europe and USA

Lowest 72-hole aggregate
255 Peter Tupling, Nigerian Open, Lagos, 1981.

Lowest 36-hole aggregate
124 (18 under par) Sandy Lyle, Nigerian Open, Ikoyi GC, Lagos, 1978 (his first year as a professional)

Lowest 18 holes
59 Gary Player, second round, Brazilian Open, Gavea GC (6,185 yards), Rio de Janeiro, 1974.

Professional events– excluding Europe and USA

Lowest 72-hole aggregate
260 Bob Charles, 66-62-69-63, Spalding Masters at Tauranga, New Zealand, 1969.

Lowest 18-hole aggregate
60 Billy Dunk (Australia), Merewether, NSW, 1970.

Lowest 9-hole aggregate
27 Bill Brask (US) at Tauranga in the New Zealand PGA in 1976.

Miscellaneous British

72-hole aggregate
Andrew Brooks recorded a 72-hole aggregate of 259 in winning the Skol (Scotland) tournament at Williamwood in 1974.

Lowest rounds
Playing on the ladies' course (4,020 yards) at Sunningdale on 26th September, 1961, Arthur Lees, the professional there, went round in 52, 10 under par. He went out in 26 (2, 3, 3, 4, 3, 3, 3, 3, 2) and came back in 26 (2, 3, 3, 3, 2, 3, 4, 3, 3).

On 1st January, 1936, AE Smith, Woolacombe Bay professional, recorded a score of 55 in a game there with a club member. The course measured 4,248 yards. Smith went out in 29 and came back in 26 finishing with a hole-in-one at the 18th.

Other low scores recorded in Britain are by CC Aylmer, an English International who went round Ranelagh in 56; George Duncan, Axenfels in 56; Harry Bannerman, Banchory in 56 in 1971; Ian Connelly, Welwyn Garden City in 56 in 1972; James Braid, Hedderwick near Dunbar in 57; H Hardman, Wirral in 58; Norman Quigley, Windermere in 58 in 1937; Robert Webster, Eaglescliffe in 58, in 1970. Harry Weetman scored 58 in a round at the 6,171 yards Croham Hurst on 30th January, 1956.

D Sewell had a round of 60 in an Alliance Meeting at Ferndown, Bournemouth, a full-size course. He scored 30 for each half and had a total of 26 putts. In September 1986, Jeffrey Burn, handicap 1, of Shrewsbury GC, scored 60 in a club competition, made up of 8 birdies, an eagle and 9 pars. He was 30 out and 30 home and no 5 on his card. Andrew Sherborne, as a 20-year-old

amateur, went round Cirencester in 60 strokes. Dennis Gray completed a round at Broome Manor, Swindon (6,906 yards, SSS 73) in the summer of 1976 in 60 (28 out, 32 in).

Playing over Aberdour on 13th June, 1936, Hector Thomson, British Amateur champion, 1936, and Jack McLean, former Scottish Amateur champion, each did 61 in the second round of an exhibition. McLean in his first round had a 63, which gave him an aggregate 124 for 36 holes.

Steve Tredinnick in a friendly match against business tycoon Joe Hyman scored a 61 over West Sussex (6,211 yards) in 1970. It included a hole-in-one at the 12th (198 yards) and a 2 at the 17th (445 yards).

Another round of 61 on a full-size course was achieved by 18-year-old Michael Jones on his home course, Worthing GC (6,274 yards), in the first round of the President's Cup in May, 1974.

In the Second City Pro-Am tournament in 1970, at Handsworth, Simon Fogarty did the second 9 holes in 27 against the par of 36.

Miscellaneous USA

Lowest rounds

The lowest known scores recorded for 18 holes in America are 55 by EF Staugaard in 1935 over the 6,419 yards Montebello Park, California, and 55 by Homero Blancas in 1962 over the 5,002 yards Premier course in Longview, Texas. Staugaard in his round had 2 eagles, 13 birdies and 3 pars.

Equally outstanding is a round of 58 (13 under par) achieved by a 13-year-old boy, Douglas Beecher, on 6th July, 1976, at Pitman CC, New Jersey. The course measured 6,180 yards from the back tees, and the middle tees, off which Douglas played, were estimated by the club professional to reduce the yardage by under 180 yards.

In 1941 at a course in Portsmouth, Virginia, measuring 6,100 yards, Chandler Harper scored 58.

Jack Nicklaus in an exhibition match at Breakers Club, Palm Beach, California, in 1973 scored 59 over the 6,200 yards course.

Ben Hogan, practising on a 7,006-yard course at Palm Beach, Florida, went round in 61 – 11 under par.

The lowest 9-hole score in America is 25, held jointly by Bill Burke over the second half of the 6,384 yards Normandie CC, St Louis in May, 1970 at the age of 29; by Daniel Cavin, who had seven 3s and two 2s on the par 36 Bill Brewer Course, Texas, in September, 1959; and by Douglas Beecher over the second half of Pitman CC, New Jersey, on 6th July, 1976, at the amazingly young age of 13. The back 9 holes of the Pitman course measured 3,150 yards (par 35) from the back tees, but even though Douglas played off the middle tees, the yardage was still over 3,000 yards for the 9 holes. He scored 8 birdies and 1 eagle.

Horton Smith scored 119 for two consecutive rounds in winning the Catalina Open in California in December, 1928. The course, however, measured only 4,700 yards.

Miscellaneous – excluding GB and USA

Tony Jacklin won the 1973 Los Lagartos Open with an aggregate of 261, 27 under par.

Henry Cotton in 1950 had a round of 56 at Monte Carlo (29 out, 27 in).

In a Pro-Am tournament prior to the 1973 Nigerian Open, British professional David Jagger went round in 59.

Max Banbury recorded a 9-hole score of 26 at Woodstock, Ontario, playing in a competition in 1952.

Women

The lowest score recorded on a full-size course by a woman is 61 by South Korean Se Ri Pak on the 6,319 yards Highland Meadows course in Ohio in July 1998 – the week after the 20-year-old became the youngest-ever winner of the US Women's Open. Pak followed her 10-under-par second round 61 with scores of 63 and 66 to set a new 72-hole record on the USLPGA of 261, 23 under. It beat the previous record by four.

The lowest 9-hole score on the US Ladies' PGA circuit is 28, first achieved by Mary Beth Zimmerman in the 1984 Rail Charity Classic and since equalled by Pat Bradley, Muffin Spencer-Devlin, Peggy Kirsch and Renee Heiken.

The lowest score for 36 holes on the USLPGA circuit is 129 by Judy Dickinson in the 1985 S&H Classic.

The lowest round on the European LPGA is 62 (11 under par) by Trish Johnson in the 1996 French Open. A 62 was also achieved by New Zealand's Janice Arnold at Coventry in 1990 during a Women's Professional Golfers' Association tournament.

The lowest 9-hole score on the European LPGA circuit is 29 by Kitrina Douglas, Regine Lautens, Laura Davies and Anne Jones.

In the Women's World Team Championship in Mexico in 1966, Mrs Belle Robertson, playing for the British team, was the only player to break 70. She scored 69 in the third round.

At Westgate-on-Sea GC (measuring 5,002 yards), Wanda Morgan scored 60 in an open tournament in 1929.

Since scores cannot properly be taken in match play no stroke records can be made in match play

events. Nevertheless we record here two outstanding examples of low scoring in the finals of national championships. Mrs Catherine Lacoste de Prado is credited with a score of 62 in the first round of the 36-hole final of the 1972 French Ladies' Open Championship at Morfontaine. She went out in 29 and came back in 33 on a course measuring 5,933 yards. In the final of the English Ladies' Championship at Woodhall Spa in 1954, Frances Stephens (later Mrs Smith) did the first nine holes against Elizabeth Price (later Mrs Fisher) in 30. It included a hole-in-one at the 5th. The nine holes measured 3,280 yards.

Amateurs

National championships

The following examples of low scoring cannot be regarded as genuine stroke play records since they took place in match play. Nevertheless they are recorded here as being worthy of note.

Michael Bonallack in beating David Kelley in the final of the English championship in 1968 at Ganton did the first 18 holes in 61 with only one putt under two feet conceded. He was out in 32 and home in 29. The par of the course was 71.

Charles McFarlane, playing in the fourth round of the Amateur Championship at Sandwich in 1914 against Charles Evans did the first nine holes in 31, winning by 6 and 5.

This score of 31 at Sandwich was equalled on several occasions in later years there. Then, in 1948, Richard Chapman of America went out in 29 in the fourth round eventually beating Hamilton McInally, Scottish Champion in 1937, 1939 and 1947, by 9 and 7.

In the fourth round of the Amateur Championship at Hoylake in 1953, Harvie Ward, the holder, did the first nine holes against Frank Stranahan in 32. The total yardage for the holes was 3,474 yards and included one hole of 527 yards and five holes over 400 yards. Ward won by one hole.

Francis Ouimet in the first round of the American Amateur Championship in 1932 against George Voigt did the first nine holes in 30. Ouimet won by 6 and 5.

Open competitions

The 1970 South African Dunlop Masters Tournament was won by an amateur, John Fourie, with a score of 266, 14 under par. He led from start to finish with rounds of 65, 68, 65, 68, finally winning by six shots from Gary Player.

Jim Ferrier, Manly, won the New South Wales championship at Sydney in 1935 with 266. His rounds were: 67, 65, 70, 64, giving an aggregate 16 strokes better than that of the runner-up. At the time he did this amazing score Ferrier was 20 years old and an amateur.

Holes below par

Most holes below par

EF Staugaard in a round of 55 over the 6,419 yards Montbello Park, California, in 1935, had two eagles, 13 birdies and three pars.

American Jim Clouette scored 14 birdies in a round at Longhills GC, Arkansas, in 1974. The course measured 6,257 yards.

Jimmy Martin in his round of 63 in the Swallow-Penfold at Stoneham in 1961 had one eagle and 11 birdies.

In the Ricarton Rose Bowl at Hamilton, Scotland, in August, 1981, Wilma Aitken, a women's amateur internationalist, had 11 birdies in a round of 64, including nine consecutive birdies from the 3rd to the 11th.

Mrs Donna Young scored nine birdies and one eagle in one round in the 1975 Colgate European Women's Open.

Consecutive holes below par

Lionel Platts had ten consecutive birdies from the 8th to 17th holes at Blairgowrie GC during a practice round for the 1973 Sumrie Better-Ball tournament.

Roberto De Vicenzo in the Argentine Centre of the Republic Championship in April, 1974 at the Cordoba GC, Villa Allende, broke par at each of the first nine holes. (By starting his round at the 10th hole they were in fact the second nine holes played by Vicenzo.) He had one eagle (at the 7th hole) and eight birdies. The par for the 3,602 yards half was 37, completed by Vicenzo in 27.

Nine consecutive holes under par have been recorded by Claude Harmon in a friendly match over Winged Foot GC, Mamaroneck, NY, in 1931; by Les Hardie at Eastern GC, Melbourne, in April, 1934; by Jimmy Smith at McCabe GC, Nashville, Tenn, in 1969; by 13-year-old Douglas Beecher, in 1976, at Pitman CC, New Jersey; by Rick Sigda at Greenfield CC, Mass, in 1979; and by Ian Jelley at Brookman Park in 1994.

TW Egan in winning the East of Ireland Championship in 1962 at Baltray had eight consecutive birdies (2nd to 9th) in the third round.

On the United States PGA tour, eight consecutive holes below par have been achieved by three players – Bob Goalby in the 1961 St Petersburg Open, Fuzzy Zoeller in the 1976 Quad Cities Open and Dewey Arnette in the 1987 Buick Open.

Fred Couples set a PGA European Tour record with 12 birdies in a round of 61 during the 1991 Scandinavian Masters on the 72-par Drottningholm course. This has since been equalled by Ernie Els (1994 Dubai Desert Classic) and by Russell Claydon and Fredrik Lindgren (1995 German Masters). Ian Woosnam, Tony Johnstone, Severiano Ballesteros, John Bickerton,

Mark O'Meara and Raymond Russell share another record with eight successive birdies.

The United States Ladies' PGA record is seven consecutive holes below par achieved by Carol Mann in the Borden Classic at Columbus, Ohio in 1975.

Miss Wilma Aitken recorded nine successive birdies (from the 3rd to the 11th) in the 1981 Ricarton Rose Bowl.

Low scoring rarities

At Standerton GC, South Africa, in May 1937, FF Bennett, playing for Standerton against Witwatersrand University, did the 2nd hole, 110 yards, in three 2s and a 1. Standerton is a 9-hole course, and in the match Bennett had to play four rounds.

In 1957 a fourball comprising HJ Marr, E Stevenson, C Bennett and WS May completed the 2nd hole (160 yards) in the grand total of six strokes. Marr and Stevenson both holed in one while Bennett and May both made 2.

The old Meadow Brook Club of Long Island, USA, had five par 3 holes and George Low in a round there in the 1950s scored two at each of them.

In a friendly match on a course near Chicago in 1971, assistant professional Tom Doty (23 years) had a remarkable low run over four consecutive holes: 4th (500 yards) 2; 5th (360 yards, dogleg) 1; 6th (175 yards) 1; 7th (375 yards) 2.

RW Bishop, playing in the Oxley Park, July medal competition in 1966, scored three consecutive 2s. They occurred at the 12th, 13th and 14th holes which measured 151, 500 and 136 yards respectively.

In the 1959 PGA Close Championship at Ashburnham, Bob Boobyer scored five 2s in one of the rounds.

American Art Wall scored three consecutive 2s in the first round of the US Masters in 1974. They were at the 4th, 5th and 6th holes, the par of which was 3, 4 and 3.

Nine consecutive 3s have been recorded by RH Corbett in 1916 in the semi-final of the Tangye Cup; by Dr James Stothers of Ralston GC over the 2,056 yards 9-hole course at Carradale, Argyll, during the summer of 1971; by Irish internationalist Brian Kissock in the Homebright Open at Carnalea GC, Bangor, in June, 1975; and by American club professional Ben Toski.

The most consecutive 3s in a British PGA event is seven by Eric Brown in the Dunlop at Gleneagles (Queen's Course) in 1960.

Hubert Green scored eight consecutive 3s in a round in the 1980 US Open.

The greatest number of 3s in one round in a British PGA event is 11 by Brian Barnes in the 1977 Skol Lager tournament at Gleneagles.

Fewest putts

The lowest known number of putts in one round is 14, achieved by Colin Collen-Smith in a round at Betchworth Park, Dorking, in June, 1947. He single-putted 14 greens and chipped into the hole on four occasions.

Professional Richard Stanwood in a round at Riverside GC, Pocatello, Idaho on 17th May, 1976 took 15 putts, chipping into the hole on five occasions.

Several instances of 16 putts in one round have been recorded in friendly games.

For 9 holes, the fewest putts is five by Ron Stutesman for the first 9 holes at Orchard Hills G&CC, Washington, USA in 1978.

Walter Hagen in nine consecutive holes on one occasion took only seven putts. He holed long putts on seven greens and chips at the other two holes.

In competitive stroke rounds in Britain and Ireland, the lowest known number of putts in one round is 18, in a medal round at Portpatrick Dunskey GC, Wilmslow GC professional Fred Taggart is reported to have taken 20 putts in one round of the 1934 Open Championship. Padraigh Hogan (Elm Park), when competing in the Junior Scratch Cup at Carlow in 1976, took only 20 putts in a round of 67.

The fewest putts in a British PGA event is believed to be 22 by Bill Large in a qualifying round over Moor Park High Course for the 1972 Benson and Hedges Match Play.

Overseas, outside the United States of America, the fewest putts is 19 achieved by Robert Wynn (GB) in a round in the 1973 Nigerian Open and by Mary Bohen (US) in the final round of the 1977 South Australian Open at Adelaide.

The USPGA record for fewest putts in one round is 18, achieved by Andy North (1990); Kenny Knox (1989); Mike McGee (1987) and Sam Trehan (1979). For 9 holes the record is eight putts by Kenny Knox (1989), Jim Colbert (1987) and Sam Trehan (1979).

The fewest putts recorded for a 72-hole US PGA Tour event is 93 by Kenny Knox in the 1989 Heritage Classic at Harbour Town Golf Links.

The fewest putts recorded by a woman is 17, by Joan Joyce in the Lady Michelob tournament, Georgia, in May, 1982.

General Index

A6 Golfklubb, 810
Aachen, 775
Aalborg, 742
Aarhus, 742
Abbeville, 753
Abbey Hill, 534
Abbey Park G&CC, 646
Abbeydale, 654
Abbeyfeale, 679
Abbeyleix, 678
Abbotsley
  Cromwell, 537
Abbotsley, 537
Abenberg, 774
Aberconwy Trophy, 265
Aberdare, 725
Aberdeenshire clubs and
  courses, 687–690
Aberdour, 701
Aberdovey, 723
Aberfeldy, 716
Aberfoyle, 719
Abergele, 721
Aberlady, 711
Abernethy, 706
Abersoch, 723
Aberystwyth, 721
Ableiges, 755
Aboyne, 687
Abridge G&CC, 559
Accrington &
  District, 585
Achensee, 734
Achill Island, 680
Acquabona, 782
Adamstal, 736
Adare Manor, 679
The Addington, 626
Addington Court, 626
Addington Palace, 626
Adriatic GC Cervia, 782
Aero Club de
  Santiago, 800
Aero Club de Vigo, 800
Aero Club de
  Zaragoza, 803
Afandou, 780
Aflac Tournament of
  Champions, 221
Ågesta, 813
Ahaus, 775
Air France Madame
  Open, 214
Airdrie, 709

Airlinks, 601
Les Aisses, 752
Aix Marseille, 762
Aix-les-Bains, 764
Ajoncs d'Or, 749
Akureyri, 780
Alands, 746
Albarella, 786
Albatross, 806
Albi Lasbordes, 765
Albon, 764
Albret, 748
Alcaidesa Links, 801
Aldeburgh, 623
Aldenham G&CC, 573
Alderley Edge, 539
Alderney, 539
Aldersley Green, 539
Aldwark Manor, 651
Aldwickbury Park, 573
Alexandra Park, 704
Alford, 687
Alfred Dunhill
  Cup, 147, 196
Alfred Dunhill South
  African PGA
  Ch'p, 133
Alfreton, 549
Alhaurín, 801
Alicante, 796
Alice Springs, 726
Alingsås, 812
Allendale, 609
Allerthorpe Park, 649
Allerton Municipal, 599
Allerum, 809
Allestree Park, 549
Allgäuer G&LC, 772
All-Ireland Inter-
  County, 264
Alloa, 698
Allt-y-Graban, 730
Almeerderhout, 791
Almerimar, 796
Älmhult, 810
Alness, 706
Alnmouth Village, 609
Alnmouth, 609
Alnwick, 609
Aloha, 801
Alpino Di Stresa, 785
Alresford, 567
Alsager G&CC, 620
Alston Moor, 547

Am Alten Fliess, 775
Altenhof, 769
Alto Golf, 793
Alton, 567
Altötting-
  Burghausen, 772
Altrincham
  Municipal, 539
Altroreal, 796
Alva, 698
Alvaston Hall, 539
Alvkarleby, 808
Alwoodley, 656
Alyth, 716
Amarante, 795
Amarilla, 799
Amateur
  Championship, 235–7
Ambrosiano, 781
Amiens, 753
Ammerschwihr, 760
Ampfield Par
  Three, 567
Ampleforth
  College, 651
Amsterdam Old Course,
  787
Amsterdamse, 787
Amstetten-
  Ferschnitz, 734
An der Pinnau, 770
Andenne, 738
Andersen Consulting
  World Championship
  of Golf, 180
Anderstein, 791
Andover, 567
Ängelholm, 809
Angers, 757
Anglesey, 724
Ängsö, 804
Angus clubs and
  courses, 690–692
Anjou G&CC, 757
Annanhill, 694
Annecy, 762
Annonay-Gourdan, 764
Añoreta, 801
Anstruther, 701
Ansty, 641
The Antlers, 265
Antrim, 663
Antrobus, 540
Appleby, 547

Apremont, 753
Aqualate, 615
Aquarius, 578
Araslöv, 809
Arboga, 804
Arbroath, 690
Arcachon, 748
Arcangues, 748
Arcot Hall, 609
Ardee, 680
Ardeer, 694
Ardfert, 676
Ardglass, 670
Ardilouse, 748
Ardminnan, 670
Ardrée, 752
Les Arcs, 764
Arendal og Omegn, 792
Argyll & Bute clubs and
  courses, 692–693
Ariège, 766
Ärila, 804
Arkley, 573
Arklow, 686
Arlandastad, 804
Army, 567
Aroeira, 794
Aro-Mas Nou, 797
Arosa, 817
Arras, 753
Arrowe Park, 599
Arscott, 616
Artland, 775
Arvika, 815
Ashbourne, 549, 681
Ashburnham, 721
Ashbury, 551
Ashby Decoy, 593
Ashdown Forest Golf
  Hotel, 634
Ashfield, 664
Ashford Castle, 681
Ashford Manor, 601
Ashford, 578
The Ashley Wood, 554
Ashridge, 573
Ashton & Lea, 585
Ashton-in-
  Makerfield, 585
Ashton-on-Mersey, 540
Ashton-under-
  Lyne, 585
Asiago, 783
Asian Tour, 175

Askernish, 708
Askersund, 804
Aspect Park, 613
Aspley Guise & Woburn Sands, 530
Asserbo, 744
Astbury, 540
Astor Salver, 314
AT&T Pebble Beach National Pro-Am, 158
Atalaya G&CC, 801
Athenry, 675
Atherstone, 641
Athlone, 682
Athy, 677
Åtvidaberg, 810
Auchenblae, 687
Auchenharvie, 694
Auchmill, 690
Auchnacloy, 684
Auchterarder, 716
Auchterderran, 701
Augsburg, 772
Aura Golf, 746
Australian Ladies' Masters, 217
Austerfield Park, 654
Austin Lodge, 579
Australasian Tour, 179
Austria clubs and courses, 734–738
Austria-Wörther See, 734
Avernas, 740
Avesta, 808
Avisford Park, 636
Avrillé, 757
Axe Cliff, 551
Aylesbury Golf Centre, 534
Aylesbury Vale, 530
Ayrshire clubs and courses, 694–696

Baberton, 712
Bäckavattnet, 812
Backworth, 639
Bacup, 585
Bad Gastein, 735
Bad Gleichenberg, 736
Bad Griesbach, 774
Bad Kissingen, 768
Bad Kleinkirchheim-Reichenau, 734
Bad Liebenzell, 778
Bad Lippspringe, 771
Bad Neuenahr G&LC, 777
Bad Ragaz, 817
Bad Rappenau, 778
Bad Salzuflen G&LC, 771
Bad Tatzmannsdorf G&CC, 736
Bad Tölz, 772
Bad Windsheim, 774
Bad Wörishofen, 772

Baden Hills GC Rastatt, 778
Baden, 750
Baden-Baden, 778
Badgemore Park, 613
Baerum, 792
Baildon, 656
Bakewell, 549
Bala Lake Hotel, 724
Bala, 724
Balbirnie Park, 701
Balbriggan, 672
Balcarrick, 672
Bâle G&CC, 760
Balfron, 719
Balgove Course, 704
Ballaghaderreen, 682
Ballards Gore G&CC, 559
Ballater, 687
Ballina, 681
Ballinamore, 679
Ballinascorney, 672
Ballinasloe, 675
Ballingry, 701
Ballinrobe, 681
Ballochmyle, 694
Ballybofey & Stranorlar, 669
Ballybunion, 676
Ballycastle, 663
Ballyclare, 663
Ballyearl Golf Centre, 665
Ballyhaunis, 681
Ballyheigue Castle, 676
Ballykisteen G&CC, 683
Ballyliffin, 669
Ballymena, 663
Ballymote, 683
Balmer See, 766
Balmoral, 665
Balmore, 700
Balnagask, 690
Baltinglass, 686
Bamberg, 774
Bamburgh Castle, 609
Banbridge, 670
Banbury Golf Centre, 613
Banchory, 687
Bandon, 667
Bangor, 670
Bank House Hotel G&CC, 647
Banstead Downs, 626
Bantry Park, 667
Barbaroux, 762
Barberán, 800
Barganiza, 799
Bargoed, 725
Barkway Park, 573
Barlassina CC, 781
Barlaston, 620
Barnard Castle, 557
Barnehurst, 579
Barnham Broom Hotel, 604

Barnsley, 654
Baron Hill, 724
Barrow Hills, 626
Barrow, 547
Barsebäck G&CC, 807
Barshaw, 718
Barton-on-Sea, 567
Basildon, 559
Basingstoke, 568
Bass Rock, 711
Båstad, 809
Batalha, 794
Batchwood Hall, 573
Batchworth Park, 573
Bath, 617
Bathgate, 714
De Batouwe, 791
Baugé-Pontigné, 758
La Baule, 758
Les Baux de Provence, 762
Bawburgh, 605
Baxenden & District, 585
Bay Hill Invitational, 159
BC Open, 163
Beacon Park, 585
Beaconsfield, 534
Beadlow Manor Hotel G&CC, 530
Beamish Park, 557
Bearna, 675
Bearsden, 700
Bearsted, 579
Bearwood Lakes, 531
Bearwood, 531
Beau Desert, 620
Beauchief Municipal, 654
Beaufort, 676
Le Beaujolais, 764
Beaune-Levernois, 751
Beauvallon-Grimaud, 762
Beaverstown, 672
Beccles, 624
Beckenham Place Park, 579
Bedale, 651
Bedford & County, 530
Bedford, 530
Bedfordshire clubs and courses, 530–531
Bedfordshire, 530
Bedinge, 809
Bedlingtonshire, 609
Beech Park, 672
Beedles Lake, 591
Beeston Fields, 611
Beith, 694
Belas, 794
Belfairs, 559
Belfast clubs and courses, 665
Belford, 609
The Belfry, 641
Belgacom Open, 146

Belgium clubs and courses, 738–741
Belhus Park, 559
Bell Canadian Open, 163
Bellavista, 802
Belle Dune, 753
Bellefontaine, 755
Belleisle, 694
Bellême-St-Martin, 759
Bellingham, 609
Bellshill, 709
BellSouth Classic, 160
Belmont Lodge, 572
Belmullet, 681
Belton Park, 593
Belton Woods Hotel, 593
Belturbet, 666
Belvoir Park, 665
Ben Rhydding, 657
Benone Par Three, 679
Benson & Hedges International Open, 137,
Bentham, 651
Bentley G&CC, 559
Benton Hall, 559
Bentra, 663
Bercuit, 739
Berehaven, 667
De Berendonck, 789
Bergamo L'Albenza, 781
Bergen, 792
Bergisch-Land, 775
Berhinderten, 769
Berkhamsted Trophy, 266
Berkhamsted, 573
The Berkshire, 532
Berkshire clubs and courses, 531–534
Berkshire Trophy, 266
Berlin G&CC Motzener, 766
Berlin Wannsee, 767
Berwick-upon-Tweed, 609
Besançon, 760
Best G&CC, 789
Betchworth Park, 626
Béthemont-Chisan CC, 761
Betws-y-Coed, 721
Beuerberg, 772
Beuzeval-Houlgate, 759
Beverley & East Riding, 649
Bexleyheath, 579
Biarritz, 748
Bidford Grange, 641
Bidston, 599
Biella Le Betulle, 785
Bigbury, 551
Biggar, 709
La Bigorre, 766
Billerud, 815

Index

Billingen, 812
Billingham, 557
Bingley St Ives, 657
Biot, 762
Birch Grove, 560
Birchwood Park Golf Centre, 579
Birchwood, 540
Bird Hills, 532
Birdland G&CC, 780
Birley Wood, 654
Birr, 682
Birstall, 591
Birtley, 639
Biscarrosse, 748
Bishop Auckland, 557
Bishopbriggs, 704
Bishop's Stortford, 573
Bishopshire, 716
Bishopswood, 568
Bitburger Land, 777
Bitche, 760
Bjäre, 809
Blaby, 591
Blackburn, 585
The Black Bush, 681
Blackley, 597
Blacklion, 666
Blackmoor, 568
Blacknest, 568
Blackpool North Shore, 585
Blackpool Park, 586
Blackwell Grange, 557
Blackwell, 647
Blackwood, 670 , 726
Blainroe, 686
Blair Atholl, 716
Blairbeth, 709
Blairgowrie, 716
Blairmore & Strone, 692
Blankney, 593
Bletchingley, 626
Blokhus Klit, 742
Bloxwich, 620
Bludenz-Braz, 738
Blue Circle, 549
Blue Green-Artiguelouve, 748
Blue Green-Chantilly Golf Hotel, 753
Blue Green-Seignosse, 748
Blue Mountain Golf Centre, 532
Blumisberg, 816
Blundells Hill, 599
Blyth, 609
BMW International Open, 144
Boat-of-Garten, 706
Bob Hope Chrysler Classic, 158
Bochum, 775
Boden, 805
Bodensee, 778
Bodenstown, 677
Bogliaco, 783

Bognor Regis, 636
Bogogno, 818
Böhmerwald GC Ulrichsberg, 734
Les Bois, 816
Bois de Ruminghem, 754
Bokskogen, 807
Boldmere, 641
Boldon, 639
Bollnäs, 808
Bologna, 782
Bolton, 586
Bolton Old Links, 586
Bolton Open Golf, 586
Bon Accord, 689
Bonalba, 796
Bonar Bridge, Ardgay, 706
Bondhay, 549
Bondoufle, 755
Bondues, 754
Bonmont, 816
Bonmont Terres Noves, 797
Bonn-Godesberg in Wachtberg, 777
Bonnybridge, 719
Bonnyton, 718
Boothferry, 649
Bootle, 599
Borås, 812
Bordeaux-Cameyrac, 748
Bordeaux-Lac, 748
Bordelais, 749
Borders clubs and courses, 696–698
Les Bordes, 752
Borgarness, 780
Bornholm, 741
Borre, 792
Borregaard, 792
Borris, 665
Borth & Ynyslas, 721
Bosjökloster, 809
El Bosque, 803
Bossenstein, 738
Bossey G&CC, 764
Boston, 594
Boston West, 594
Bothwell Castle, 709
Botkyrka, 813
Botley Park Hotel G&CC, 568
Boughton, 579
La Boulie, 761
Bourn, 612
Bournemouth & Meyrick Park, 554
Bowenhurst Golf Centre, 626
Bowood G&CC, 644
Bowood Park, 544
Bowring, 599
Boxmoor, 573
Boyce Hill, 560
Boyle, 682

Boys' Amateur Championship, 325
Boys' Home Internationals (R&A Trophy), 333
Brabantse, 739
Brabazon Trophy 239
Bracken Ghyll, 657
Brackenwood, 599
Brackley Municipal, 586
Bradford, 657
Bradford Moor, 657
Bradford-on-Avon, 644
Bradley Park, 657
Braehead, 698
Braemar, 687
Braid Hills, 712
Braids United, 712
Brailes, 613
Brailsford, 549
Braintree, 560
Bramall Park, 540
Bramhall, 540
Bramley, 626
Brampton (Talkin Tarn), 547
Brampton Heath, 607
Brampton Park, 537
Bramshaw, 568
Brancepeth Castle, 557
Brandhall, 647
Branshaw, 657
Branston G&CC, 620
Braunschweig, 771
Braxted Park, 560
Bray, 686
Brayton Park, 547
Breadsall Priory Hotel G&CC, 549
Brean, 617
Brechin, 690
Brecon, 728
Breedon Priory, 591
Bregenzerwald, 738
Breightmet, 586
Breinholtgård, 742
Breitenloo, 817
Brent Valley, 602
La Bresse, 764
Brest Les Abers, 750
Brest-Iroise, 750
La Bretesche, 758
Brett Vale, 624
Breuninkhof, 788
Brianza, 781
Brickendon Grange, 573
Brickhampton Court, 564
Bridge of Allan, 720
Bridgedowm, 573
Bridget Jackson Bowl, 314
Bridgnorth, 616
Bridlington, 649
The Bridlington Links, 649
Bridport & West Dorset, 554

Briggens House Hotel, 573
Bright Castle, 670
Brighton & Hove, 634
Brigode, 754
Brinkworth, 645
Bristol & Clifton, 565
British Mid-Amateur Ch'p, 238
British Seniors' Open Amateur Ch'p, 237
Broadstone, 555
Broadway, 565
Bro-Bålsta, 814
Brocket Hall, 574
Brocton Hall, 620
Brodauer Mühle, 769
Brodick, 694
Broekpolder, 790
Broke Hill, 579
Brokenhurst Manor, 568
Bromborough, 599
Bromley, 579
Bromsgrove Golf Centre, 647
Brønderslev, 742
Brookdale, 586
Brookmans Park, 574
Broome Manor, 645
Broome Park, 579
Broomieknowe, 712
Brora, 706
Brough, 649
Brown Trout, 679
Brugse Vaart, 788
Brunn G&CC, 737
Brunssummerheide, 790
Brunston Castle, 694
Bruntsfield Links Golfing Society, 712
La Bruyère, 739
Bryn Meadows Golf Hotel, 725
Bryn Morfydd Hotel, 722
Brynhill, 729
Buchanan Castle, 720
Buchholz-Nordheide, 769
Buckingham, 534
The Buckinghamshire, 534
Buckinghamshire clubs and courses, 534–537
Buckpool, 715
Budapest G&CC, 780
Buddon Links, 692
Bude & North Cornwall, 544
Budock Vean Hotel, 544
Buick Challenge, 163
Buick Classic, 161
Buick Invitational, 158
Buick Open, 162
Builth Wells, 729
The Bulbury Club, 555

Bull Bay, 724
Bulwell Forest, 611
Buncrana, 669
Bundoran, 669
Bungay & Waveney Valley, 624
Bunsay Downs, 560
Burford, 613
Burg Overbach, 777
Burg Zievel, 777
Burgdorf, 771
Bürgenstock, 817
Burgess Hill, 636
Burgham Park, 609
Burghill Valley, 572
Burghley Park, 594
Burhill, 626
Burhill Family Foursomes, 267
Burley, 568
Burnham & Berrow, 617
Burnham Beeches, 534
Burnham-on-Crouch, 560
Burnley, 586
Burnside, 692
Burntisland, 701
Burntisland Golf House Club, 701
Burslem, 620
The Burstead, 560
Burton-on-Trent, 549
Burvik, 804
Bury, 586
Bury St Edmunds, 624
Bush Hill Park, 602
Bushey G&CC, 574
Bushey Hall, 574
Bushfoot, 663
Bussy-St-Georges, 755
Bute, 692
Buxton & High Peak, 549

C&L Country Club, 602
Ca' degli Ulivi, 783
Ca' della Nave, 786
Cabourg-Le Home, 759
Cabra Castle, 666
Cadmore Lodge, 572
Caen, 759
Caerleon, 726
Caernarfon, 724
Caerphilly, 725
Caerwys, 723
Cahir Park, 683
Caird Park, 691
Cairndhu, 663
La Cala, 801
Calcot Park, 532
Caldecott Hall, 605
Calderbraes, 709
Calderfields, 620
Caldes International, 798
Caldwell, 718

Caldy, 599
Caledonian, 690
Callan, 678
Callander, 716
Calverley, 657
Camberley Heath, 627
Cambridge, 537
Cambridge Meridian, 537
Cambridgeshire clubs and courses, 537–538
Cambridgeshire Moat House, 537
Cambuslang, 709
Came Down, 555
Cameron Corbett Vase, 267
Camperdown, 691
Campo Carlo Magno, 783
Campsie, 720
Cams Hall Estate, 568
Can Bosch, 798
La Cañada, 802
El Candado, 801
Canford Magna, 555
Canford School, 555
Canmore, 702
Cannes Mandelieu Riviera, 762
Cannes Open, 135
Cannes-Mandelieu, 762
Cannes-Mougins, 762
Cannington, 617
Cannock Park, 620
Canon European Masters, 144
Canon Greater Hartford Open, 161
Canons Brook, 560
Canons Court, 565
Cansiglio, 786
Canterbury, 579
Canwick Park, 594
Canyamel, 797
Cap d'Agde, 757
Capdepera, 797
Cape Cornwall G&CC, 545
Capelle a/d Ijssel, 790
Caprington, 694
Carcassonne, 757
Carden Park, 540
Cardiff, 729
Cardigan, 721
Cardiganshire clubs and courses, 721
Cardross, 700
Carholme, 594
Carimate, 781
Carlisle, 547
Carlow, 665
Carlskrona, 809
Carluke, 709
Carlyon Bay, 545
Carmarthen, 721
Carmathenshire clubs and courses, 721

Carnalea, 670
The Carnegie Club, 706
Carnoustie, 692
Carnoustie Caledonia, 692
Carnoustie Championship, 692
Carnoustie Ladies, 692
Carnoustie Mercantile, 692
Carnwath, 709
Carradale, 692
Carrbridge, 706
Carrick Knowe, 713
Carrickfergus, 663
Carrickmines, 674
Carrick-on-Shannon, 679
Carrick-on-Suir, 683
Carris Trophy, 326
Carsington Water, 549
Carswell CC, 613
Carus Green, 547
Carvoeiro, 793
Casentino, 786
Castelconturbia, 781
Castelfalfi G&CC, 786
Castelgandolfo, 784
Casteljaloux, 749
Castell Heights, 725
Castelnaud, 749
Casterton, 547
Castillo de Gorriaz, 799
Castle, 674
Castle Barna, 682
Castle Douglas, 698
Castle Eden & Peterlee, 557
Castle Fields, 657
Castle Hawk, 586
Castle Heather, 707
Castle Hume, 675
Castle Mokrice, 796
Castle Park, 711
Castle Point, 560
Castle Royle, 532
Castlebar, 681
Castleblayney, 682
Castlecomer, 678
Castlegregory, 676
Castlerea, 682
Castlerock, 679
Castletown, 577
Castletroy, 679
Castlewarden G&CC, 677
Castrop-Rauxel, 775
Cathcart Castle, 704
Cathkin Braes, 709
Catterick, 651
Cave Castle Hotel, 649
Cavendish, 549
Cawder, 705
Ceann Sibeal, 676
Celtic Manor Hotel G&CC, 726
Cély, 755

Central London Golf Centre, 627
Cergy Pontoise, 755
Cervino, 785
Chadwell Springs, 574
Chalfont Park, 534
Chalgrave Manor, 530
Chalmers, 806
Châlons-en-Champagne, 760
Chalon-sur-Saône, 751
Chambon-sur-Lignon, 751
Chamonix, 764
Champ de Bataille, 759
Champagne, 754
Championship for Schools for the R&A Trophy, 343
Channel Islands clubs and courses, 539
Channels, 560
Chantaco, 749
Chantilly, 754
El Chaparral, 801
Chapel-en-le-Frith, 550
Charlesland G&CC, 686
Charleton, 702
Charleville, 667
Charnwood Forest, 591
Chart Hills, 579
Chartham Park, 636
Chartridge Park, 534
Château d'Avoise, 751
Château de Bournel, 760
Château de Chailly, 751
Château de Cheverny, 752
Château de Maintenon, 752
Château de Raray, 754
Château de Terrides, 766
Château de la Bawette, 739
Château de la Salle, 751
Château de la Tournette, 739
Château des Forges, 752
Château des Sept Tours, 752
Château des Vigiers, 749
Château d'Humièes, 754
Château l'Arc, 762
Château Royal d'Ardenne, 738
Châteaublanc, 762
Chaumont-en-Vexin, 754
Cheadle, 540
Chedington Court, 555
Chelmsford, 560

Chelsfield Lakes Golf Centre, 580
Cherasco CC, 785
Cherry Burton, 650
Cherry Lodge, 580
Cherwell Edge, 613
Chesfield Downs, 574
Chesham & Ley Hill, 534
Cheshire clubs and courses, 539–544
Cheshunt, 574
Chessington Golf Centre, 627
Chester, 540
Chesterfield, 550
Chesterfield Municipal, 550
Chester-Le-Street, 557
Chesterton Valley, 616
Chesterton, 614
Chestfield, 580
Chevannes-Mennecy, 755
Chevin, 550
Chiberta, 749
Chichester, 637
Chick-Fil-A Charity Championship, 218
Chiddingfold, 627
Im Chiemgau, 772
Chigwell, 560
Childwall, 599
Chiltern Forest, 534
Chilwell Manor, 611
Chilworth, 568
China Fleet CC, 545
Chippenham, 645
Chipping Norton, 614
Chipping Sodbury, 565
Chipstead, 627
Chirk, 731
Chislehurst, 580
Chobham, 627
Cholet, 758
Chorley, 586
Chorleywood, 574
Chorlton-cum-Hardy, 597
Christchurch, 555
Chrysler Open, 213
Chulmleigh, 551
Church Stretton, 616
Churchill & Blakedown, 647
Churston, 551
Cicé-Blossac, 750
Cilgwyn, 721
Cill Dara, 677
Cirencester, 565
Cisco World Matchplay, 147
City of Coventry (Brandon Wood), 641
City of Derry, 679
City of Hope Myrtle Beach Classic, 218
City of Newcastle, 639
City of Wakefield, 657
City West, 672
Clackmannanshire clubs and courses, 698
Clacton, 560
Clandeboye, 670
Clandon Regis, 627
Claremorris, 681
Claviere, 785
Clays Farm, 732
Clayton, 657
Cleckheaton & District, 657
Clécy, 759
Cleethorpes, 594
Cleeve Hill, 565
Clement Ader, 755
Cleobury Mortimer, 616
Clervaux, 787
Clevedon, 617
Cleveland, 651
Cleydael, 738
Cliftonville, 665
Clitheroe, 586
Clober, 700
Clones, 682
Clonlara, 666
Clonmel, 683
Clontarf, 674
Close House, 609
Le Clou, 764
Club Professionals' Championship, 197
Club Son Parc, 797
Club Zur Vahr, 767
Clydebank & District, 700
Clydebank Municipal, 700
Clyne, 730
Coatbridge, 709
Coatguelen, 750
Cobh, 667
Cobtree Manor Park, 580
Cochrane Castle, 718
Cockermouth, 547
Cocks Moor Woods, 647
Cocksford, 651
Coed-y-Mwstwr, 725
Cognac, 752
Le Coiroux, 751
Colchester, 560
Cold Ashby, 607
Coldwinters, 672
College Pines, 611
Colli Berici, 786
Collingtree Park, 607
Colmworth, 530
Colne, 586
Colne Valley, 561
Colonsay, 692
Colony Club Gutenhof, 737
Colvend, 698
Colville Park, 709
Colworth, 530
Combles-en-Barrois, 760
La Commanderie, 764
Commonwealth Tournament, 311
Compaq Open, 214
Compiègne, 754
Comrie, 716
Concord Park, 654
Conero GC Sirolo, 786
Congleton, 540
Connemara, 675
Connemara Isles, 676
Le Connétable, 752
Consett & District, 557
Continental Europe clubs and courses, 733–818
Conwy (Caernarvonshire), 722
Conwy clubs and courses, 721–722
Cooden Beach, 634
Cookridge Hall G&CC, 657
Coollattin, 686
Coombe Hill, 627
Coombe Wood, 627
Coosheen, 667
Copenhagen, 744
Copt Heath, 641
Copthorne, 637
Córdoba, 800
Corfu, 780
Corhampton, 568
Corinthian, 580
Cork, 667
Cornwall clubs and courses, 544–547
Corrençon-en-Vercors, 764
Corrie, 694
Corrstown, 672
Cortijo Grande, 796
La Coruña, 800
Cosby, 591
Cosmopolitan G&CC, 786
Costa Ballena, 802
Costa Brava, 798
Costa de Azahar, 803
Costa Dorada, 798
Costa Teguise, 799
Costessey Park, 605
Cotgrave Place G&CC, 611
Cotswold Edge, 565
Cotswold Hills, 565
Cottesmore, 637
Cottingham, 650
Cottrell Park, 729
Coudray, 756
Les Coullaux, 816
Coulondres, 757
Coulsdon Manor, 627
County Antrim clubs and courses, 663–664
County Armagh, 664
County Armagh clubs and courses, 664–665
County Carlow clubs and courses, 665–666
County Cavan, 666
County Cavan clubs and courses, 666
County Clare clubs and courses, 666–667
County Cork clubs and courses, 667–669
County Donegal clubs and courses, 669–670
County Down clubs and courses, 670–672
County Dublin clubs and courses, 672–674
County Fermanagh clubs and courses, 675
County Galway clubs and courses, 675–676
County Kerry clubs and courses, 676–677
County Kildare clubs and courses, 677–678
County Kilkenny clubs and courses, 678
County Laois clubs and courses, 678–679
County Leitrim clubs and courses, 679
County Limerick clubs and courses, 679
County Londonderry clubs and courses, 679–680
County Longford clubs and courses, 680
County Longford, 680
County Louth, 680
County Louth clubs and courses, 680
County Mayo clubs and courses, 680–681
County Meath, 681
County Meath clubs and courses, 681–682
County Monaghan clubs and courses, 682
County Offaly clubs and courses, 682
County Roscommon clubs and courses, 682–683
County Sligo, 683
County Sligo clubs and courses, 683
County Tipperary, 683
County Tipperary clubs and courses, 683–684
County Tyrone clubs and courses, 684
County Waterford clubs and courses, 684–685
County Westmeath clubs and courses, 685
County Wexford clubs and courses, 685–686

County Wicklow clubs and courses, 686–687
Courmayeur, 785
Courson Monteloup, 756
Courtown, 685
Coutainville, 759
Coventry, 641
Coventry Hearsall, 641
Cowal, 692
Cowdenbeath, 702
Cowdray Park, 637
Cowes, 578
Cowglen, 705
Coxmoor, 611
Craddockstown, 677
Cradoc, 729
Craigentinny, 713
Craigie Hill, 716
Craigmillar Park, 713
Craigmillar Park Open, 268
Craignure, 692
Crail Golfing Society, 702
Crane Valley, 555
Crans-sur-Sierre, 816
The Craythorne, 620
Cray Valley, 580
Crécy-la-Chapelle, 756
Creigiau, 725
Cretingham, 624
Crewe, 540
Crews Hill, 602
Criccieth, 724
Crichton, 698
Cricklade Hotel, 645
Crieff, 716
Crimple Valley, 651
Croara, 782
Croham Hurst, 627
Croix de Mortemart, 749
Crompton & Royton, 587
Cromstrijen, 790
Crondon Park, 561
Crook, 557
Crookhill Park, 654
Crosland Heath, 657
Crossgar, 670
Crossmoor G&CC, 789
Crow Nest Park, 658
Crow Wood, 709
Crowborough Beacon, 634
Cruden Bay, 688
Cruit Island, 669
Cuddington, 627
La Cuesta, 799
Culdrose, 545
Cullen, 688
Cumberwell Park, 645
Cumbria clubs and courses, 547–549
Cup Noodles Hawaiian Ladies' Open, 217
Cupar, 702

Curra West, 676
The Curragh, 678
Curtis Cup, 303–310
Cushendall, 663
CVS Charity Classic, 162
Czech Republic clubs and courses, 741

Dachstein Tauern, 736
Dainton Park, 551
Dalbeattie, 698
Dale Hill Hotel, 634
Dalhousie, 692
Dalmally, 692
Dalmilling, 694
Dalmunzie, 716
Dalsjö, 808
Dalston Hall, 547
Damme G&CC, 740
Danesbury Park, 574
Danube Golf-Wien, 737
Darenth Valley, 580
Darlington, 558
Dartford, 580
Dartmouth, 620
Dartmouth G&CC, 551
Darwen, 587
Datchet, 532
Davenport, 540
Daventry & District, 607
Davos, 817
Davyhulme Park, 597
De Vere Blackpool, 590
Dean Wood, 587
Deane, 587
Deangate Ridge, 580
Deanwood Park, 532
Deauville l'Amiraute, 754
Deer Park, 674
Deer Park CC, 714
Deeside, 690
Degeberga-Widtsköfle, 809
Degli Ulivi, 783
La Dehesa, 800
Dehesa Montenmedio, 802
Deinster Mühle, 769
Dejbjerg, 742
Delamere Forest, 540
Delapre, 607
Delgany, 686
Delsjö, 806
Delvin Castle, 685
Denbigh, 722
Denbighshire clubs and courses, 722–723
Denham, 534
Denmark clubs and courses, 741–745
Denton, 597
Deposit Guaranty Golf Classic, 162
Derby Sinfin, 550

Derbyshire clubs and courses, 549–551
Derbyshire Professionals', 200
Dereham, 605
Derllys, 721
Deutsche Bank– SAP Open TPC of Europe, 139
Devon clubs and courses, 551–554
Devon Open, 200
Dewlands Manor, 634
Dewsbury District, 658
Dewstow, 727
Dibden Golf Centre, 568
Didsbury, 597
Dieppe-Pourville, 759
Digne-les-Bains, 762
Dijon-Bourgogne, 751
Dillenburg, 767
Dinard, 750
Dinas Powis, 729
Dinnaton, 552
Dinsdale Spa, 558
Dirleton Castle, 711
Disley, 541
Disneyland Paris, 761
Diss, 624
Divonne, 764
Djouce Mountain, 686
Djursholm, 814
Dolder, 817
Dolgellau, 724
Dollar, 698
Domaine de Belesbat, 756
Domaine de Falgos, 757
Domaine de Roncemay, 751
Domaine de Vaugouard, 752
Domaine du Tilleul, 754
Domaine Impérial, 816
Domaio, 800
La Domangère, 758
La Dombes, 764
Domburgsche, 788
De Dommel, 789
Domont-Montmorency, 756
Don Cayo, 796
Donabate, 672
Donaghadee, 670
Donau GC Passau-Rassbach, 774
Donauwörth, 818
Doncaster, 654
Doncaster Town Moor, 654
Donegal, 669
Donegal Ladies' Irish Open, 214
Doneraile, 667
Donnington Grove CC, 532

Donnington Valley, 532
Dooks, 677
Doon Valley, 694
Doral-Ryder Open, 159
Dore & Totley, 654
Dorking, 627
Dorset clubs and courses, 554–557
Dorset Heights, 555
Dortmund, 775
Doug Sanders World Junior Ch'p, 331
Dougalston, 700
Douglas Municipal, 577
Douglas Park, 700
Douglas Water, 709
Douglas, 667
Down Royal, 663
Downes Crediton, 552
Downfield, 691
Downpatrick, 670
Downshire, 532
Dragør, 744
Drax, 651
Drayton Park, 614, 621
Driffield, 650
Drift, 628
Drøbak, 792
Droitwich G&CC, 647
Dromoland Castle, 666
Drottningholm, 814
Druid's Glen, 686
Druids Heath, 621
Drumpellier, 710
Les Dryades, 752
du Maurier Classic, 117–23, 220
Dubai Desert Classic, 134
Dublin City clubs and courses, 674–675
Dublin Mountain, 672
Duddingston, 713
Dudley, 647
Dudsbury, 555
Duff House Royal, 688
Dufftown, 715
Duke of York Trophy Winners, 343
Duke's Course, 704
Duke's Dene, 628
Dukinfield, 541
Dullatur, 700
Dulwich & Sydenham Hill, 628
Dumbarton, 700
Dumfries & County, 698
Dumfries & Galloway, 698
Dumfries & Galloway clubs and courses, 698–700
Dummer, 569
Dun Laoghaire, 672
Dunaverty, 692
Dunbar, 711

Index 913

Dunbartonshire clubs and courses, 700–701
Dunblane New, 720
Duncan Putter, 269
Dundalk, 680
Dundas Parks, 714
Dunecht House, 688
Dunfanaghy, 669
Dunfermline, 702
Dungannon, 684
Dungarvan, 684
Dunham Forest G&CC, 541
Dunham, 605
Dunkeld & Birnam, 716
Dunkerque, 754
Dunmore, 667
Dunmore East, 684
Dunmurry, 665
The Dunnerholme, 547
Dunnikier Park, 702
Dunning, 717
Duns, 696
Dunscar, 587
Dunsfold Aerodrome, 628
Dunstable Downs, 530
Dunstanburgh Castle, 609
Dunston Hall, 605
Dunwood Manor, 569
La Duquesa G&CC, 802
Durbuy, 740
Durham City, 558
Durham clubs and courses, 557–559
Durness, 706
Düsseldorf Hösel, 775
Düsseldorf, 775
Duxbury Park, 587
The Dyke, 634
Dyrham Park CC, 574

Eagles, 605
Eaglescliffe, 558
Ealing, 602
Earlsferry Thistle, 702
Earlswood, 731
Easingwold, 651
East Anglian Open, 200
East Berkshire, 532
East Bierley, 658
East Brighton, 634
East Clare, 666
East Cork, 667
East Devon, 552
East Dorset, 555
East Herts, 574
East Kilbride, 710
East Region PGA, 200
East Renfrewshire, 718
East Sussex National, 634
Eastbourne Downs, 634
Eastbourne Golfing Park, 635
Easter Moffat, 710

Eastham Lodge, 599
Eastwood, 718
Eaton, 541, 605
Ebeltoft, 742
Ebersberg, 772
Eda, 815
Eden Course, 704
Eden, 547
Edenbridge G&CC, 580
Edenderry, 682
Edenhof, 804
Edenmore, 664
Edese, 788
Edgbaston, 641
Edmondstown, 674
Edwalton, 611
Edzell, 691
Effingham, 628
Effingham Park, 637
Efteling, 788
Jacques L'Eglise Trophy, 332
Eifel, 777
Eindhovensche, 789
Eisenhower Trophy (World Amateur Team Ch'p), 259
Ekarnas, 812
Ekerum, 811
Eksjö, 811
Elbflorenz GC Dresden, 767
Elderslie, 718
Elfordleigh Hotel G&CC, 552
Elfrather Mühle, 775
Elgin, 715
Elland, 658
Ellesborough, 535
Ellesmere, 597
Ellesmere Port, 541
Elm Green, 674
Elm Park, 674
Elsenham Golf Centre, 561
Elsham, 594
Elstree, 574
Eltham Warren, 580
Elton Furze, 537
Elverum, 792
Ely City, 537
Embankment, 607
Embats, 766
Emmaboda, 811
Empordà, 798
Enderby, 591
Enfield, 602
Engadin, 817
England and Wales Ladies' County Championship, 313
England v France, 261
English Amateur Championship, 238
English Boys' County Finals, 334
English Boys' Strokeplay Ch'p, 326

English Boys' Under-16 Ch'p (McGregor Trophy), 327
English Club Championship, 263
English clubs and courses, 530–662
English County Champions' Tournament, 240
English County Championship, 263
English Girls' Championship, 336
English Ladies' Amateur Championship, 295
English Ladies' Intermediate Ch'p, 298
English Ladies' Senior Strokeplay Ch'p, 297
English Ladies' Strokeplay Ch'p, 296
English Ladies' Under-23 Ch'p, 297
English Open Amateur Strokeplay Ch'p (Brabazon Trophy), 239
English Open Mid-Amateur Ch'p (Logan Trophy), 240
English Senior Ladies' Matchplay Ch'p, 297
English Seniors' Amateur Championship, 240
Enköping, 804
Enmore Park, 618
Ennis, 666
Enniscorthy, 685
Enniscrone, 683
Enniskillen, 675
Ennstal-Weissenbach G&LC, 736
Entfelden, 817
Entrepinos, 803
Entry Hill, 618
La Envia, 796
Enville, 621
Enzesfeld, 737
Épinal, 760
Epinay, 758
Epping Forest G&CC, 561
Epsom, 628
Erding-Grünbach, 772
Erewash Valley, 550
Erftaue, 776
Erlen, 817
Erlestoke Sands, 645
Erskine, 718
Esbjerg, 742
Eschenried, 772
Escorpión, 803
Esery, 764
Eskifjardar, 781
Eskilstuna, 804
Eslöv, 809

Espoo Ringside Golf, 746
Espoon Golfseura, 746
Essen Haus Oefte, 776
Essen-Heidhausen, 776
Essex clubs and courses, 559–564
Essex G&CC, 561
The Essex Golf Complex, 561
Essex Open, 200
Essex Professionals' Ch'p, 200
Estela, 795
Estepona, 802
Estérel Latitudes, 763
Estoril, 794
Estoril-Sol Golf Academy, 794
Étangs de Fiac, 766
Etchinghill, 580
Etelä Pojhanmaan, 745
Étiolles, 756
Étretat, 759
Eucalyptus, 784
Euregio Bad Bentheim, 776
European Amateur Championship, 247
European Amateur Team Ch'p, 259
European Boys' Team Championship, 331
European Challenge Tour, 148
The European Club, 686
European Club Cup, 260
European Lady Juniors' Team Ch'p, 339
European LPGA Tour, 212
European Mid-Amateur Championship, 247
European Senior Tour, 150
European Seniors' Championship, 247
European Tour, 130–49
European Women v Senior Men, 229
European Youths' Team Ch'p, 332
Evesham, 647
Evian Masters, 213
Executive GC Cranbrook, 581
Exeter G&CC, 552
Eyemouth, 696

Faaborg, 741
Fågelbro G&CC, 814
Fagersta, 804
Fairfield Golf & Sailing Club, 597
Fairhaven, 587

Fairlop Waters, 561
Fairwood Park, 731
Faithlegg, 684
Fakenham, 605
Falkenberg, 812
Falkirk, 720
Falkirk Tryst, 720
Falkland, 702
Falköping, 812
Falmouth, 545
Falnuée, 738
Falster, 744
Falsterbo, 807
Falun-Borlänge, 808
Fanø Golf-Links, 742
Fardew, 658
Färgelanda, 815
Farnham, 628
Farnham Park, 535
Farnham Park Par Three, 628
Farrington, 618
Farthingstone Hotel, 607
Fathers and Sons Foursomes, 269
Faulquemont-Pontpierre, 760
Faversham, 581
FedEx St Jude Classic, 162
Feldafing, 772
Felixstowe Ferry, 624
Feltwell, 605
Fereneze, 718
Fermoy, 667
Ferndown, 555
Ferndown Forest, 556
Fernfell G&CC, 628
Fernhill, 667
Ferrybridge 'C', 658
Feucherolles, 761
Ffestiniog, 724
Fife clubs and courses, 701–704
Filey, 651
Filton, 565
Finchley, 602
Fingle Glen, 552
Finland clubs and courses, 745–748
Finnstown, 672
Finspång, 811
Fintona, 684
Fioranello, 784
Firenze Ugolino, 786
First Union Betsy King Classic, 221
Fishwick Hall, 587
Fiuggi, 784
Five Lakes Hotel G&CC, 561
Five Nations C C, 738
Fjällbacka, 815
Flackwell Heath, 535
Flaine-Les-Carroz, 764
Flamborough Head, 650
Flanders-Nippon, 740

Fleetlands, 569
Fleetwood, 587
Fleming Park, 569
Flempton, 624
Flevoland, 791
Flint, 723
Flintshire clubs and courses, 723
Flixton, 598
Flommens, 807
Florentin-Gaillac, 766
Floresta Parque, 793
Föhr, 769
Föhrenwald, 737
Folgaria, 783
Fontainebleau, 756
Fontana, 737
Fontanals de Credanya, 798
Fontcaude, 757
Fontenailles, 756
Fontenelles, 758
Forest Hills, 565 , 574
Forest of Dean, 565
Forest of Galtres, 651
Forest Park, 651
Forest Pines, 594
Forêt d'Orient, 760
Forêt Verte, 759
Forfar, 691
Forges-les-Bains, 756
Formby, 599
Formby Hall, 599
Formby Ladies', 600
Forres, 715
Forrest Little, 672
Forrester Park, 561
Forsbacka, 815
Forsgårdens, 806
Fort Augustus, 707
Fort William, 707
La Forteresse, 756
Fortrose & Rosemarkie, 707
Fortwilliam, 665
Fosseway CC, 618
Fota Island, 668
Fourqueux, 761
Foxbridge, 637
Foxhills, 628
Foxrock, 674
Foyle, 680
Frame Trophy, 269
France clubs and courses, 748–766
Franciacorta, 782
Frankfield, 668
Frankfurter, 768
Fränkische Schweiz, 774
Fraserburgh, 688
Frassanelle, 786
Frederikssund, 744
La Fredière, 751
Freeport-McDermott Classic, 159
Frégate, 763
Freiburg, 778

Freshwater Bay, 578
La Freslonnière, 750
Friendly's Classic, 219
Frilford Heath, 614
Frinton, 561
Frodsham, 541
Frome Golf Centre, 618
Le Fronde, 785
Frösåker, 804
Fulford, 651
Fulford Heath, 647
Fullerö, 804
Fulneck, 658
Fulwell, 602
Funäsdalsfjällen, 805
Furesø, 744
Furnas, 794
Furness, 547
Furstenfeld, 736
Fürstlicher Waldsee, 778
Fürth, 774
Furzeley, 569
Fynn Valley, 624

G&CC Golf Bled, 795
Gaichel, 787
Gainsborough, 594
Gairloch, 708
Galashiels, 697
Galgorm Castle, 663
Gällivare-Malmberget, 805
Galway, 676
Galway Bay G&CC, 676
Ganay, 752
Ganstead Park, 650
Ganton, 652
Gap-Bayard, 763
Gardagolf CC, 783
Garesfield, 639
Garforth, 658
Garlenda, 783
Garmisch-Partenkirchen, 772
Garmouth & Kingston, 715
Gatehouse, 698
Gathurst, 587
Gatley, 541
Gatton Manor Hotel G&CC, 628
Gatwick Manor, 637
Gäuboden, 774
Gävle, 808
Gay Hill, 647
Gedney Hill, 594
Gelpenberg, 790
Gendersteyn, 789
Geneva, 816
German Open, 143
Germany clubs and courses, 766–780
Gerrards Cross, 535
Geysteren G&CC, 789
Ghyll, 587

Giant Eagle LPGA Classic, 220
Giez, 765
Gifford, 711
Gifhorn, 771
Gigha, 692
Gilleleje, 744
Gillingham, 581
Gilnahirk, 665
Girls' British Open Championship, 335
Girls' Home Internationals (Stroyan Cup), 340
I Girasoli, 785
Girona, 798
Girton, 537
Girvan, 694
Glamorganshire, 729
Glasgow clubs and courses, 704–705
Glasgow GC Gailes, 694
Glasgow Matchplay Ch'p, 201
Glasgow Strokeplay Ch'p, 201
Glasgow, 705
Glasson G&CC, 685
Gleddoch, 718
The Glen, 711
Glen Gorse, 592
Glenalmond, 717
Glenbervie, 720
Glencorse, 713
Glencruitten, 693
The Gleneagles Hotel, 717
Glengarriff, 668
Glenmalure, 686
Glenrothes, 702
Gloria Golf, 818
Glossop & District, 550
Gloucester Hotel, 565
Gloucestershire clubs and courses, 564–567
Glyfada, 780
Glyn Abbey, 721
Glynhir, 721
Glynneath, 731
Goal Farm Par Three, 628
Goese, 788
The Gog Magog, 537
Gold Coast, 684
Goldegg, 735
Golden Eagle G&CC, 795
Goldenhill, 621
Golf Clubs and Courses in the British Isles, 527–732
Golf dei Laghi, 785
Golf del Sur, 799
Golf du Perche, 753
Golf Foundation Events, 341–4
Golf House Club, 702

Index 915

Golf Illustrated Gold Vase, 270
Golf Talma, 747
Golf Unions, 826–7
Golspie, 706
Goodwood Park G&CC, 637
Goodwood, 637
Goring & Streatley, 532
Gorleston, 605
Gormanston College, 681
Gort, 676
Gosfield Lake, 561
Gosforth, 639
Gosport & Stokes Bay, 569
Göteborg, 806
Gotska, 811
Göttingen, 771
Gotts Park, 658
Gourock, 719
Le Gouverneur, 765
Gower, 731
GPT (formerly Grange GC), 642
De Graafschap, 788
Gracehill, 663
Grafton Morrish Trophy, 270
Granada, 800
Grand Avignon, 763
Grand-Ducal de Luxembourg, 787
La Grande Bastide, 763
La Grande Mare, 539
La Grande-Motte, 757
La Grange aux Ormes, 760
Grange Fell, 548
Grange Park, 594, 600, 654
Grange, 674
Grangemouth, 720
Grange-over-Sands, 548
Grantown-on-Spey, 707
Granville, 759
Grasse CC, 763
Grassmoor Golf Centre, 550
Graves et Sauternais, 749
Graz, 736
Great Barr, 621
Great Britain & Ireland v Continent of Europe (Jacques L'Eglise Trophy), 332
Great Britain & Ireland v USA for the Curtis Cup, 303
Great Britain & Ireland v USA, 181
Great Hadham, 575
Great Harwood, 587
Great Lever & Farnworth, 598
Great Salterns, 569

Great Yarmouth & Caister, 605
Greater Greensboro Chrysler Classic, 160
Greater Milwaukee Open, 163
Greater Vancouver Open, 163
Greece clubs and courses, 780
Green Haworth, 587
Green Hotel, 717
Green Zone Golf, 747
Greenacres, 663
Greenburn, 715
Greencastle, 669
Greenisland, 664
Greenmeadow, 727
Greenmount, 587
Greenock, 719
Greenore, 680
Greenparc, 756
Greenway Hall, 621
Greetham Valley, 615
Grenaa, 742
Grenland, 792
Grenoble-Bresson, 765
Grenoble-Charmeil, 765
Grenoble-Uriage, 765
Gretna, 698
Grevelingenhout, 788
Greystones, 686
Griffin, 530
Grim's Dyke, 602
Grimsby, 594
Gripsholm, 804
Gröhögen, 811
Grönlund, 804
Groruddalen, 792
GTE Byron Nelson Classic, 160
Guadalhorce, 801
Guadalmina, 802
Guadiana, 797
Guildford, 628
Guinlet, 766
Gujan, 749
Gullane, 711
Gullbringa, 806
Gumbalde, 811
Gustavsvik, 804
Gut Altentann, 735
Gut Apeldör, 769
Gut Brandlhof G&CC, 735
Gut Grambek, 769
Gut Heckenhof, 777
Gut Kaden, 769
Gut Murstätten, 736
Gut Rieden, 772
Gut Uhlenhorst, 770
Gut Waldhof, 770
Gweedore, 669
Gwynedd clubs and courses, 723–724
Gyttegård, 742

De Haar, 791
Haarlemmermeersche, 787
Habberley, 647
Hadden Hill, 614
Haddington, 711
Haderslev, 742
Hadley Wood, 575
Hagge, 808
Haggs Castle, 705
Hagley, 647
Haigh Hall, 588
Hainault Forest, 562
Hainburg/Donau, 737
Hainsworth Park, 650
Hale, 541
Halesowen, 648
Halford-Hewitt Cup, 270
Halifax, 658
Halifax Bradley Hall, 658
Halifax West End, 658
Hallamshire, 655
Hallowes, 655
Halmstad, 812
Halstock, 556
Haltwhistle, 548
Ham Manor, 637
Hamburg, 770
Hamburg Hittfield, 770
Hamburg Holm, 770
Hamburg Waldorfer, 770
Hamburg-Ahrensburg, 770
Hamilton, 710
Hammarö, 815
The Hampshire, 569
Hampshire clubs and courses, 567–572
Hampshire Hog, 270
Hampshire Matchplay Ch'p, 201
Hampshire PGA Ch'p, 201
Hampshire Rose, 314
Hampshire, Isle of Wight and Channel Islands Open, 201
Hampstead, 602
Hamptworth G&CC, 645
Han Herreds, 742
Hanau-Wilhelmsbad, 768
Hanbury Manor, 575
Handsworth, 621
Hanging Heaton, 658
Haninge, 814
Hankley Common, 629
Hannover, 771
Hanover G&CC, 562
Haparanda, 805
Harborne Church Farm, 642
Harborne, 642
Harbour Point, 668

Harburn, 715
Hardelot Dunes Course, 754
Hardelot Pins Course, 754
Harewood Downs, 535
Harleyford, 535
Härnösand, 805
Harpenden, 575
Harpenden Common, 575
Harrogate, 652
Harrow School, 602
Hartland Forest G&CC, 552
Hartlepool, 558
Hartley Wintney, 569
Hartsbourne G&CC, 575
Hartswood, 562
Harwich & Dovercourt, 562
Harwood, 588
Hassan II Trophy, 180
Hässleholm, 809
Hassocks, 637
Haste Hill, 602
Hastings, 635
Hatchford Brook, 642
Hatfield London CC, 575
Hattemse G&CC, 789
Haus Bey, 776
Haus Kambach, 776
Haut-Poitou, 752
Havelte, 789
Haverdals, 813
Haverfordwest, 728
Haverhill, 624
Haviksoord, 789
Le Havre, 759
Hawarden, 723
Hawick, 697
Hawkhurst, 581
Hawkstone Park, 616
Haydock Park, 600
Hayling, 569
Hayston, 700
Haywards Heath, 637
Hazel Grove, 541, 674
Hazelwood Golf Centre, 629
Hazlehead, 690
Hazlemere G&CC, 535
Headfort, 681
Headingley, 658
Headley, 658
HealthSouth Inaugural, 217
Heath (Portlaoise), 678
Heath Park, 602
Heaton Moor, 541
Heaton Park, 598
Hebden Bridge, 659
Hechingen Hohenzollern, 779
Hedeland, 744
Heemskerske, 787

Index

Heidelberg-Lobenfeld, 779
Heilbronn-Hohenlohe, 779
Heineken Classic, 133
Hele Park Golf Centre, 552
Helen Holm Trophy, 300
Helen's Bay, 671
Helensburgh, 693
Hellidon Lakes Hotel & CC, 607
Helmsdale, 706
Helsby, 541
Helsingborg, 809
Helsingin Golfklubi, 746
Helsingør, 744
Hemingford Abbots, 537
Hemsedal, 792
Henbury, 565
Hencse National, 780
Hendon, 602
Henley G&CC, 642
Henley, 614
Henllys Hall, 724
Henne, 742
Hennerton, 532
Henri-Chapelle, 740
Hereford Municipal, 572
Herefordshire, 572
Herefordshire clubs and courses, 572
Herkenbosch, 789
Hermitage, 672
Herne Bay, 581
Herning, 743
Herreria, 800
The Hertfordshire, 575
Hertfordshire clubs and courses, 573–577
Herts Professionals' Ch'p, 201
Herzog Tassilo, 734
Herzogstadt Celle, 767
Hesketh, 600
Hessle, 650
Heswall, 600
Het Rijk van Nijmegen, 790
Hever, 581
Heworth, 639 , 652
Hexham, 609
Heydon Grange G&CC, 538
Heyrose, 541
Heysham, 588
Hickleton, 655
High Elms, 581
High Post, 645
Highcliffe Castle, 556
Highfield, 678
Highgate, 602
Highland clubs and courses, 706–708

Highwoods, 635
Highworth, 645
Hill Barn, 638
Hill Valley G&CC, 616
Hillerød, 744
Hillingdon, 603
Hills Wiltshire Pro Champ, 204
Hillsborough, 655
Hillside, 600
Hilltop, 642
Hilton Park, 700
Hilversumsche, 791
Himley Hall, 621
Himmerland G&CC, 743
Hinckley, 592
Hindhead, 629
Hindley Hall, 588
Hintlesham Hall, 624
The Hirsel, 697
Hirst Priory, 594
Hirtshals, 743
Hittnau-Zürich G&CC, 818
Hjarbaek Fjord, 743
Hjorring, 743
Hobson Municipal, 558
Hockley, 569
Hoddom Castle, 698
Hoebridge Golf Centre, 629
Hoenshuis G&CC, 790
Hof, 774
Hofgut Kolnhausen, 768
Hofors, 808
Högbo, 808
De Hoge Kleij, 791
Hohenpähl, 772
Hohenstaufen, 779
Hoisdorf, 770
Hökensås, 813
Holbaek, 744
Hollandbush, 710
Holledau, 773
Hollingbury Park, 635
Hollywood Lakes, 673
Holme Hall, 595
Holmsland Klit, 743
Holstebro, 743
Holsworthy, 552
Holthuizen, 790
Holtye, 635
Holyhead, 725
Holywell, 723
Holywood, 671
Homburger, 768
Home Internationals, 262
Home Park, 629
Honda Classic, 159
Honiton, 552
The Honourable Company of Edinburgh Golfers, 711
De Hooge Bergsche, 790

Hook, 811
Hopeman, 716
Horam Park, 635
Horncastle, 595
Hornsea, 650
Horsenden Hill, 603
Horsens, 743
Horsforth, 659
Horsham, 638
Horsley Lodge, 550
Horton Park CC, 629
Horwich, 588
Höslwang im Chiemgau, 773
Hossegor, 749
Houghton-le-Spring, 640
Houghwood, 600
Houldsworth, 541
Hounslow Heath, 603
Howley Hall, 659
Howth, 675
Hoylake Municipal, 600
Hubbelrath, 773 , 776
Huddersfield, 659
Hudiksvall, 808
Hulencourt, 739
Hull, 650
Hulta, 813
Humberston Park, 595
Humberstone Heights, 592
Hummelbachaue Neuss, 776
Hungary clubs and courses, 780
Hunley Hall, 652
Hunstanton, 605
Huntercombe, 614
Huntly, 688
Hurdwick, 552
Hurlston Hall, 588
Hurst, 532
Hurtmore, 629
Húsavík, 781
Huyton & Prescot, 600
Hvide Klit, 743
Hythe Imperial, 581
Hyvinkään, 746

Ibiza, 797
Iceland clubs and courses, 780–781
Idstein-Wörsdorf, 768
Ifach, 796
Iffeldorf, 772
Ifield, 638
Ile d'Or, 758
Iles Borromees, 785
Ilford, 562
Ilfracombe, 552
Ilkeston, 550
Ilkley, 659
Imatran Golf, 747
Immingham, 595
IMSL (Irish) Boys' Championship, 327

Inco, 731
Ingarö, 814
Ingestre Park, 621
Ingol, 588
Ingon Manor, 642
Innellan, 693
Innerleithen, 697
Innsbruck-Igls, 734
Insch, 688
Interlaken-Unterseen, 816
Inter-Mol, 738
International Club du Lys, 754
International Gomze, 740
Internationaler Bonn, 778
Inverallochy, 688
Inveraray, 693
Invergordon, 707
Inverness, 707
Inverurie, 688
Ipswich (Purdis Heath), 624
Irish Amateur Championship, 241
Irish Club Professionals' Championship, 198
Irish clubs and courses, 663–687
Irish Girls' Championship, 336
Irish Ladies' Amateur Strokeplay Ch'p, 299
Irish Ladies' Close Amateur Ch'p, 298
Irish PGA Championship, 198
Irish Senior Ladies' Amateur Ch'p, 299
Irish Seniors' Open Amateur Ch'p, 242
Irish Youth's Open Amateur Ch'p, 327
Irvine, 695
Irvine Ravenspark, 695
Is Molas, 784
Isabella, 761
Isaberg, 811
Isafjardar, 781
Isernhagen, 771
Iski Golf, 799
Isla Canela, 803
The Island, 673
Islantilla, 803
Isle of Anglesey clubs and courses, 724
Isle of Harris, 708
Isle of Man clubs and courses, 577–578
Isle of Purbeck, 556
Isle of Skye, 708
Isle of Wedmore, 618
Isle of Wight clubs and courses, 578
Isles of Scilly, 545
Issum-Niederrhein, 776

Italian Open, 136
Italy clubs and courses, 781–786
Iver, 535
Ivinghoe, 535
Izaak Walton, 621

Jakobsberg, 778
JAL Big Apple Classic, 220
Jamie Farr Kroger Classic, 220
Japan Classic, 221
Japan LPGA Tour, 223
Japan PGA Tour, 172
Jarama R.A.C.E, 800
Jávea, 796
Jedburgh, 697
Jersbek, 770
Johannesberg G&CC, 814
John Cross Bowl, 268
John O'Gaunt, 530
Johnnie Walker Classic, 133
Jökull, 781
La Jonchère, 751
Jönköping, 811
Joyenval, 761
Jubilee Course, 704
Juelsminde, 743
Juliana, 776

The K Club, 678
Kaiserhöhe, 779
Kaiserwinkl GC Kössen, 734
Kaj Lykke, 743
Kalix, 805
Kalmar, 811
Kalo, 743
Kampenhout, 739
Kanturk, 668
Karelia Golf, 745
Karersee-Carezza, 783
Karlovy Vary, 741
Karlshamn, 809
Karlskoga, 815
Karlstad, 815
Kärntner, 734
Kartano Golf, 747
Kassel-Wilhelmshöhe, 768
Katinkulta, 747
Katrineholm, 804
Kävlinge, 807
Kedleston Park, 550
Keele Golf Centre, 621
Keerbergen, 739
Keighley, 659
Keilir, 781
Keimola Golf Oy, 746
Keith, 688
Kelso, 697
Kemer G&CC, 818
Kemnay, 688

Kempense, 738
Kemper Open, 161
Kempferhof, 760
Kendal, 548
Kendleshire, 566
Kenilworth, 642
Kenmare, 677
Kenmore, 717
Kennemer G&CC, 787
Kent clubs and courses, 578–585
Kent Open, 201
Kent Professionals', 201
Kenwick Park, 595
Keppelse, 789
Kerigolf, 747
Kerries, 677
Keswick, 548
Kettering, 608
Kibworth, 592
Kidderminster, 648
Kieler GC Havighorst, 770
Kikuoka CC Chant Val, 787
Kilbirnie Place, 695
Kilcock, 681
Kilcoole, 686
Kilkee, 666
Kilkeel, 671
Kilkenny, 678
Killarney, 677
Killeen, 678
Killeline, 679
Killin, 717
Killinbeg, 680
Killiney, 673
Killiow Park, 545
Killorglin, 677
Killymoon, 684
Kilmacolm, 719
Kilmarnock (Barassie), 695
Kilmashogue, 675
Kilnwick Percy, 650
Kilrea, 680
Kilrush, 666
Kilspindie, 711
Kilsyth Lennox, 720
Kilternan, 673
Kilton Forest, 611
Kilworth Springs, 592
King Edward Bay, 577
King George V Coronation Cup, 272
King James VI, 717
Kingfisher CC, 608
Kinghorn Ladies, 702
Kinghorn Municipal, 702
Kings Acre, 713
Kings Hill, 581
King's Links, 690
King's Lynn, 605
Kings Norton, 648
King's Park, 705
Kingsdown, 645
Kingsknowe, 713

Kingsthorpe, 608
Kingsway, 595
Kingsway Golf Centre, 575
Kingswood, 629
Kington, 572
Kingussie, 707
Kingweston, 618
Kinmel Park, 722
Kinsale, 723
Kinsale Farrangalway, 668
Kinsale Ringenane, 668
Kintore, 688
Kirby Muxloe, 592
Kirkby Lonsdale, 548
Kirkbymoorside, 652
Kirkcaldy, 702
Kirkcudbright, 699
Kirkhill, 710
Kirkintilloch, 700
Kirkistown Castle, 671
Kirriemuir, 691
Kirtlington, 614
Kirton Holme, 595
Kitzbühel, 734
Kitzbühel-Schwarzsee, 734
Kitzingen, 768
Kjekstad, 792
Klassis G&CC, 818
Kleiburg, 791
Klopeiner See-Turnersee, 734
Klövsjö-Vemdalen, 806
Knaresborough, 652
Knebworth, 575
Knighton Heath, 556
Knighton, 729
Knights Grange, 541
Knightswood, 705
Knistad G&CC, 813
The Knock Club, 665
Knockanally, 678
Knole Park, 581
Knott End, 588
Knotty Hill Golf Centre, 558
Knowle, 566
Knutsford, 542
Kobernausserwald, 735
De Koepel, 789
Køge, 745
Kokkedal, 745
Kokkolan, 745
Kolding, 743
Köln G&LC, 776
Koninklijke Haagsche G&CC, 791
Konstanz, 779
Kopavogs og Gardabaejar, 781
Köping, 804
Korsør, 745
Koski Golf, 747
Kralingen, 791
Krefeld, 776
Kremstal, 734

Kristiansand, 792
Kristianstad, 809
Kristinehamn, 815
Kronberg G&LC, 768
Kumla, 804
Kungälv-Kode, 806
Kungsbacka, 806
Kurhessischer GC Oberaula, 768
Kurk Golf, 746
Küssnacht, 818
Küsten GC Hohe Klint, 767
Kyles of Bute, 693
Kymen Golf, 747

Ladbrook Park, 642
Ladies' Austrian Open, 213
Ladies' British Amateur Championship, 293
Ladies' British Open Amateur Strokeplay Championship, 295
Ladies' European Open Amateur Ch'p, 302
Ladies' German Open, 213
Ladies' Golf Union, 829–30
Ladybank, 702
Lagan, 811
Lagonda Trophy, 272
Lahden Golf, 747
Lahinch, 666
Laholm, 813
L'Ailette, 753
Lakeside Lodge, 538
Lakeside, 621, 731
Laleham, 629
Lambeg, 664
Lamberhurst, 581
Lamborghini-Panicale, 786
Lambourne, 535
Lamerwood, 575
Lamlash, 695
Lanark, 710
Lanarkshire clubs and courses, 709–711
Lancashire clubs and courses, 585–591
Lancashire Open, 201
Lancaster, 588
Landeryd, 811
Landshut, 773
Landskrona, 810
Langdon Hills, 562
Langholm, 697
Langland Bay, 731
Langlands, 710
Langley Park, 581
Langton Park G&CC, 592
Lanhydrock, 545
Lannemezan, 766
Lansdown, 618

Lansil, 588
Lanzo Intelvi, 782
Largs, 695
La Largue G&CC, 760
Larkhall, 710
Larne, 664
Larrabea, 799
Larvik, 792
Las Brisas, 802
Las Ramblas, 796
Las Vegas Invitational, 164
Lauder, 697
Laukaan Golf, 745
Laukariz, 799
Launceston, 545
Lauro, 801
Lausanne, 817
Lauswolt G&CC, 790
Lauterhofen, 774
Laval-Changé, 758
Le Lavandou, 763
Laytown & Bettystown, 682
Leadhills, 710
Leamington & County, 642
Leasowe, 600
Leatherhead, 629
Lechner "BN", 737
Leckford, 569
Lee Park, 600
Lee Valley, 603
Lee Valley G&CC, 668
Leeds Castle, 581
Leeds Golf Centre, 659
Leeds, 659
Leek, 621
Leen Valley Golf Centre, 611
Lee-on-the-Solent, 569
Lees Hall, 655
Leicestershire, 592
Leicestershire and Rutland Open, 201
Leicestershire clubs and courses, 591–593
Leicestershire Forest, 592
Leidschendamse Leeuwenbergh, 791
Leigh, 542
Leighton Buzzard, 531
Leixlip, 678
Leksand, 808
L'Empereur, 739
Lemvig, 743
Lengenfeld, 737
Lenzerheide Valbella, 817
Lenzie, 701
Leominster, 572
Lerma, 799
Léry Poses, 759
Leslie, 703
Letchworth, 575
Letham Grange, 691
Lethamhill, 705

Letterkenny, 669
Leven Gold Medal, 272
Leven Golfing Society, 703
Leven Links, 703
Leven Thistle, 703
Lewes, 635
Leyland, 588
Leynir, 781
Libbaton, 552
Liberton, 713
Licher Golf, 768
Lichtenau-Weickershof, 774
Lickey Hills, 648
Lidhems, 811
Lidingö, 814
Lidköping, 813
Lightcliffe, 659
Lignano, 786
Lillebaelt, 741
Lilleshall Hall, 616
Lilley Brook, 566
Lilse, 738
Limburg G&CC, 740
Limerick County G&CC, 679
Limerick, 679
Limoges-St Lazare, 751
Limpsfield Chart, 629
Lincoln, 595
Lincolnshire clubs and courses, 593–597
Lincolnshire Open, 201
Lindau-Bad Schachen, 779
Linde, 804
Linde German Masters, 146
Linden Hall, 610
Lindö, 814
Lindo Park, 814
Lindrick, 655
Lingdale, 592
Lingfield Park, 629
Linköping, 811
Links Country Park Hotel, 606
Links (Newmarket), 625
Linlithgow, 715
Linn Park, 705
Linz-St Florian, 734
Liphook, 569
Lipica, 796
Lipperland zu Lage, 771
Lippischer, 771
Lisbon Sports Club, 794
Lisburn, 664
L'Isle Adam, 756
Lismore, 684
Lisnice, 741
List of new entries in 1999, 529
Little Aston, 621
Little Chalfont, 535
Little Hay Golf Complex, 576
Little Lakes, 648

Littlehampton, 638
Littlehill, 705
Littlestone, 582
Liverpool Municipal, 600
Ljunghusen, 807
Ljusdal, 808
Llandrindod, 729
Llandudno (Maesdu), 722
Llandudno (North Wales), 722
Llanfairfechan, 722
Llangefni, 725
Llanishen, 730
Llantrisant & Pontyclun, 725
Llanwern, 727
Llanymynech, 616
Llavaneras, 798
La Llorea, 799
Lobden, 588
Loch Lomond, 701
Lochcarron, 708
Lochgelly, 703
Lochgilphead, 693
Lochmaben, 699
Lochranza, 695
Lochwinnoch, 719
Lockerbie, 699
L'Odet, 750
Lofthouse Hill, 659
Logan Trophy, 240
Løkken, 743
Lokomotiva-Brno, 741
Lomas-Bosque, 800
London Golf Centre, 603
The London Golf Club, 582
London Scottish, 629
London clubs, 597
Long Ashton, 566
Long Sutton, 618
Longcliffe, 592
Longhirst Hall, 610
Longley Park, 659
Longniddry, 711
Longridge, 588
Longs Drugs Challenge, 218
Longside, 688
Looe, 545
Los Angeles Championship, 217
Los Arqueros, 801
Los Moriscos, 801
Los Naranjos, 802
Los Retamares, 800
Lostwithiel G&CC, 545
Lothianburn, 713
Lothians clubs and courses, 711–715
Loudoun Gowf, 695
Loudun, 752
Loughrea, 676
Loughton, 562
Lourdes, 766

Louth, 595
Louvain-la-Neuve, 739
Low Laithes, 659
Lowes Park, 588
LPGA Corning Classic, 219
Lübeck-Travemünder, 770
Lucan, 673
Lucerne, 818
Luchon, 766
Ludlow, 616
Luffenham Heath, 615
Luffness New, 712
Lugano, 817
Luleå, 806
Lullingstone Park, 582
Lundin, 703
Lundin Ladies, 703
Lunds Akademiska, 807
Lungau/Katschberg, 735
Lurgan, 664
Lutterworth, 592
Luttrelstown Castle, 673
Luxembourg Belenhaff, 787
Luxembourg clubs and courses, 787
Lybster, 706
Lyckorna, 815
Lydd, 582
Lydney, 566
Lyme Regis, 556
Lymm, 542
Lyneham, 614
Lyon, 765
Lyon-Chassieu, 765
Lyons Gate, 556
Lyon-Verger, 765
Lysegården, 807
Lyshott Heath, 531
Lytham Green Drive, 589
Lytham Trophy, 273

Macclesfield, 542
Machrie Bay, 695
Machrie Hotel, 693
Machrihanish, 693
Machynlleth, 729
Mâcon La Salle, 751
Macroom, 668
Madeira Island Open, 139
Madeira, 795
Maesteg, 725
Magdalene Fields, 610
Mahee Island, 671
Mahon, 668
Maidenhead, 533
Main-Spessart, 768
Main-Taunus, 768
Maison Blanche G&CC, 765
Makila, 749

Málaga Club de
  Campo, 801
Malahide, 673
Malden, 630
Maldon, 562
Malkins Bank, 542
Mallow, 668
Mallusk, 664
Malmö, 807
Malone, 665
Malta clubs and
  courses, 787
Malton, 538
Malton & Norton, 652
Manchester, 598
Manchester clubs and
  courses, 597–599
La Manga, 796
Mangfalltal G&LC, 773
Mangotsfield, 566
Manises, 803
Mannan Castle, 682
Mannheim-Viernheim,
  768
Mannings Heath, 638
The Manor, 659
Manor (Kingstone), 622
Manor (Laceby), 595
Manor House, 645
Manor House Hotel,
  552
Manor of Groves
  G&CC, 576
Le Mans Mulsanne, 758
Mansfield Woodhouse,
  611
Mapledurham, 533
Mapperley, 611
Marbella, 802
March, 538
Marcilly, 752
Marco Simone, 784
Margara, 785
Margarethenhof am
  Tegernsee, 773
La Margherita, 785
Maria Bildhausen, 768
Maria Lankowitz, 736
Maria Theresia, 734
Mariánské Lázne, 741
Marienfeld, 771
Mariestad, 813
Marigola, 783
Maritim Timmendorfer
  Strand, 770
Marivaux, 756
Market Drayton, 616
Market Harborough,
  592
Market Rasen, 595
Market Rasen
  Racecourse, 595
Markgräflerland
  Kandern, 779
Marks, 813
Marland, 589
Marlborough, 645
Marple, 542

La Marquesa, 796
Marrakesh Palmeraie
  Open, 214
Marriott Dalmahoy
  Hotel & CC, 713
Marriott Forest of
  Arden Hotel, 642
Marriott Meon Valley
  Hotel, 570
Marsden, 660
Marsden Park, 589
Martin Moor, 595
Marvãa, 794
Maryport, 548
Masham, 652
Masia Bach, 798
Maspalomas, 799
Massereene, 664
Master Golf, 746
The Masters, 72–8
MasterCard
  Colonial, 160
Match conditions, 831
Matfen Hall, 610
Matilde di Canossa, 783
Matlock, 550
Mattishall, 606
Maxstoke Park, 642
Maybole, 695
Maylands, 562
Maywood, 550
Mazamet-La Barouge,
  766
Mazières, 752
McDonald, 688
McDonald's LPGA
  Ch'p, 103–9, 219
McDonald's WPGA
  Ch'p of Europe, 213
McGregor Trophy, 327
MCI Classic, 160
Meaux-Boutigny, 756
Mediterraneo CC, 803
Médoc, 749
Meldrum House, 688
Mellor &
  Townscliffe, 542
Melrose, 697
Meltham, 660
Melton Mowbray, 593
Melville Golf
  Centre, 713
Memmingen Gut
  Westhart, 773
Memorial
  Tournament, 161
Menaggio &
  Cadenabbia, 782
Mendip, 618
Mendip Spring, 618
Mentmore G&CC, 535
Meole Brace, 616
Mercedes
  Championship, 158
Merchants of
  Edinburgh, 713
Mercury Titleholders
  Championship, 218

Mere G&CC, 542
Méribel, 765
Meri-Teijo, 746
Merlin, 545
Merrist Wood, 630
Mersey Valley, 542
Merseyside clubs and
  courses, 599–601
Merthyr Tydfil, 725
De Merwelanden, 791
Messilä, 746
Methil, 703
Metz Technopole, 761
Metz-Cherisey, 760
Michelob
  Championship, 163
Michelob Light
  Classic, 219
Mickleover, 551
Mid Glamorgan clubs
  and courses, 725–726
Mid Herts, 576
Mid Kent, 582
Mid Sussex, 635
Mid Yorkshire, 660
Middlesbrough, 652
Middlesbrough
  Municipal, 652
Middlesex clubs and
  courses, 601–604
Middlesex Open, 201
Middleton Hall, 606
Middleton Park, 660
Midland Boys' Amateur
  Championship, 331
Midland Masters, 202
Midland Professionals'
  Matchplay Ch'p, 202
Midland Professionals'
  Strokeplay Ch'p, 202
Midland Seniors', 202
Les Mielles G&CC, 539
Mignaloux
  Beauvoir, 753
Mijas, 801
Milano, 782
Mile End, 616
Milford, 630
Milford Haven, 728
Mill Green, 576
Mill Hill, 603
Mill Ride, 533
Millfield, 595
Million Dollar
  Challenge, 180
Millport, 693
Milltown, 673
Milnathort, 717
Milngavie, 701
Minchinhampton, 566
Minehead & West
  Somerset, 618
Minto, 697
Miraflores, 801
Miramar, 795
Miramas, 763
Mitcham, 630
Mitchelstown, 668

Mittelholsteinischer
  Aukrug, 770
Mittelrheinischer Bad
  Ems, 778
Mjölby, 811
Moate, 685
Moatlands, 582
Moffat, 699
Mold, 723
Moliets, 749
Molinetto CC, 782
Mölle, 810
Mølleåens, 745
Mölndals, 807
Am Mondsee, 735
Monifieth Golf
  Links, 691
Monkstown, 668
Monkton Park Par
  Three, 645
Monmouth, 727
Monmouthshire, 727
Monmouthshire clubs
  and courses, 726–728
Mont Garni, 738
Mont Griffon, 756
Montado, 794
Montafon, 738
Mont-d'Arbois, 765
Monte Carlo, 763
Monte Mayor, 802
Montebelo, 795
Montecastillo, 803
Montecatini, 786
La Montecchia, 786
Monticello, 782
Montpellier
  Massane, 757
Montreux, 817
Montrose, 691
Montrose
  Caledonia, 691
Montrose
  Mercantile, 691
Moor Allerton, 660
Moor Hall, 642
Moor Park, 576 , 682
Moore Place, 630
Moors Valley, 556
Moortown, 660
Mora, 808
La Moraleja, 800
Moray, 716
Moray clubs and
  courses, 715–716
Morecambe, 589
Morfontaine, 754
Morlais Castle, 725
Mormal, 754
Moroccan Open, 134
Morpeth, 610
Morriston, 731
Mortehoe &
  Woolacombe, 553
Mortonhall, 713
Moseley, 648
Mosjö, 804
Moss Valley, 732

Mossock Hall, 589
Motala, 811
Mothers and Daughters Foursomes, 314
Motorola Western Open, 161
Mottram Hall Hotel, 542
Mount Ellen, 710
Mount Juliet, 678
Mount Murray G&CC, 578
Mount Ober G&CC, 671
Mount Oswald, 558
Mount Pleasant, 531
Mount Temple, 685
Mount Wolseley, 666
Mountain Ash, 726
Mountain Lakes, 726
Mountain View, 732
Mountbellew, 676
Mountrath, 678
Mourne, 671
Mowsbury, 531
La Moye, 539
Moyola Park, 680
Muckhart, 717
Mühlendorf, 776
Mühlviertel, 735
Muir of Ord, 707
Muirkirk, 695
Mullingar, 685
Mullion, 545
Mulrany, 681
München Nord-Eichenried, 773
München West-Odelzhausen, 773
Münchener, 773
München-Riedhof, 773
Mundesley, 606
Münster-Wilkinghege, 767
Murcar, 690
Murhof, 736
Murphy's Irish Open, 140
Murrayfield, 713
Murrayshall, 717
Murtal, 736
Muskerry, 668
Musselburgh, 712
Musselburgh Old Course, 712
Muswell Hill, 603
Muthill, 717
Mytton Fold, 589

Naas, 678
Nabisco Dinah Shore, 110–6, 218
Nahetal, 778
Nairn Dunbar, 707
Nairn, 707
Nampont-St-Martin, 754

Nancy-Aingeray, 760
Nancy-Pulnoy, 760
Nantes, 758
Nantes Erdre, 758
Napoli, 784
Narin & Portnoo, 669
Narvik, 792
Nässjö, 811
National Car Rental Classic, 164
National Car Rental English Open, 139
National Golf Club, 761, 818
Naunton Downs, 566
Nazeing, 562
Neath, 731
NEC World Series of Golf, 162
Neckartal, 779
Nefyn & District, 724–725
Nelson, 589
Nenagh, 683
Nes, 792
Ness-Nesklúbburinn, 781
Netherlands clubs and courses, 787–792
Nettuno, 784
Neuchâtel, 816
Neuhof, 769
Neusiedlersee-Donnerskirchen, 737
Nevas Golf, 746
Nevill, 635
New Course, 704
New Cumnock, 695
New Forest, 570
New Galloway, 699
New Golf Club, 703
New Golf Deauville, 759
New Mills, 551
New Ross, 685
New Zealand, 630
Newark, 612
Newbattle, 714
Newbiggin, 610
Newbold Comyn, 643
Newbridge, 678
Newburgh-on-Ythan, 689
Newbury & Crookham, 533
Newbury Racecourse, 533
Newcastle United, 640
Newcastle West, 679
Newcastleton, 697
Newcastle-under-Lyme, 622
Newlands, 675
Newmachar, 689
Newport, 578
The Newport, 727
Newport (Pembs), 728
Newquay, 545

Newton Abbot, 553
Newton Green, 625
Newton Stewart, 699
Newtonmore, 707
Newtownstewart, 684
Nexø, 741
Nick Faldo Junior Series, 331, 339
Niddry Castle, 715
Nieuwegeinse, 792
Nîmes Campagne, 757
Nîmes-Vacquerolles, 757
Nissan Open, 159
La Nivelle, 749
Le Nivernais, 751
Nizels, 582
Nobilis Golf, 818
Noord Nederlandse G&CC, 790
De Noordhollandse, 787
Noordwijkse, 791
Nora, 805
Norba, 797
Nordbornholm-Rø, 741
Nordcenter G&CC, 746
Nordkirchen, 776
Nordvestjysk, 743
Norfolk clubs and courses, 604–607
The Norfolk G&CC, 606
Norfolk Open, 202
Norfolk Professionals' Ch'p, 202
Normanby Hall, 595
Normanton, 660
Norrköping, 811
Norrmjöle, 806
North Berwick, 712
North Downs, 630
North Foreland, 582
North Hants, 570
North Inch, 717
North Manchester, 598
North Middlesex, 603
North Oxford, 614
North Shore, 596
North Warwickshire, 643
North Weald, 562
North West, 669
North Wilts, 645
North Worcestershire, 648
Northampton, 608
Northamptonshire clubs and courses, 607–608
Northamptonshire County, 608
Northcliffe, 660
Northenden, 598
Northern Open, 202
Northern Region PGA, 202
Northern, 690
Northolt, 603

Northop Country Park, 723
Northumberland, 640
Northumberland clubs and courses, 609–611
Northwood, 603
Norton, 558
Norway clubs and courses, 792–793
Nottingham City, 612
Nottinghamshire clubs and courses, 611–613
Nottinghamshire Open, 202
Notts, 612
Novo Sancti Petri, 803
Nuevo De Madrid, 800
Nuneaton, 643
Nunspeetse G&CC, 789
Nuremore, 682
Nurmijärven, 746
Nynäshamn, 814

Oadby, 593
Oak Park, 630
Oakdale, 652, 727
Oake Manor, 618
Oakleaf Golf Complex, 558
Oakmere Park, 612
Oakridge, 643
Oaks Sports Centre, 630
Oaksey Park, 646
Oastpark, 582
Obere Alp, 779
Oberfranken Thurnau, 774
Oberpfälzer Wald G&LC, 774
Oberschwaben-Bad Waldsee, 779
Oberzwieselau, 775
Oddafellowa, 781
Odder, 743
Odense Eventyr, 741
Odense, 741
Odsherred, 745
Oeschberghof L & GC, 779
The Office Depot Tournament, 217
Official World Golf Ranking, 128
Ogbourne Downs, 646
Öijared, 807
Okehampton, 553
Olafsfjordur, 781
Olching, 773
Old Colwyn, 722
Old Conna, 687
Old Course, 704
Old Fold Manor, 576
Old Head, 668
Old Lake, 780
Old Manchester, 598
Old Nene G&CC, 538
Old Padeswood, 723

Index 921

Old Ranfurly, 719
Old Thorns, 570
Oldenburgischer, 767
Oldham, 589
Oldmeldrum, 689
Oldsmobile Classic, 219
Olgiata, 784
Oliva Nova, 803
Olivar de la
 Hinojosa, 800
Les Olonnes, 758
Olton, 643
Olympus, 788
Omagh, 684
Omaha Beach, 759
Ombersley, 648
Omega (Asian PGA)
 Tour, 174
One-2-One British
 Masters, 145
Onneley, 622
Onsjö, 813
Onsøy, 792
Oosterhoutse, 788
Op de Niep, 776
The Open
 Championship, 54–63
Open Novotel
 Perrier, 148
Opio-Valbonne, 763
Oporto, 795
Oppdal, 793
Oppegård, 793
Orchardleigh, 619
Örebro, 805
Örestad, 807
Örkelljunga, 810
Orkney, 708
Orléans Val de
 Loire, 753
Ormeau, 665
Les Ormes, 539 , 750
Ormesson, 756
Ormonde Fields, 551
Ormskirk, 589
Orsett, 562
Orton Meadows, 538
Orust, 815
Osborne, 578
Osiers Farm, 638
Oskarshamn, 812
Oslo, 793
Osnabrück, 776
Osona Montanya, 798
Österakers, 814
Österhaninge, 814
Österlen, 807
Östersund-Frösö, 806
Ostfriesland, 767
Østmarka, 793
Östra Göinge, 810
Ostschweizerischer, 818
Oswestry, 616
Otley, 660
Ottenstein, 735
Otterbourne Golf
 Centre, 570
Otway, 670

Oude Mass, 791
Oudenaarde G&CC,
 740
Oughterard, 676
Oulton Park, 660
Oulu, 747
Oundle, 608
Oustoen CC, 793
Outlane, 660
Overijse, 739
Overstone Park, 608
Öviks GC Puttom, 806
Owingen-Überlingen,
 779
Owston Park, 655
Oxford and Cambridge
 Golfing Society for the
 President's
 Putter, 274
Oxford v Cambridge
 Varsity Match, 273
The Oxfordshire, 614
Oxfordshire clubs and
 courses, 613–615
Oxhey Park, 576
Oxley Park, 622
Ozoir-la-Ferrière, 756

Pachesham Park Golf
 Centre, 630
Padbrook Park, 553
Paderborner Land, 771
Padeswood & Buckley,
 723
Padova, 787
PageNet Tour
 Championship, 222
Painswick, 566
Painthorpe House, 660
Paisley, 719
Palacerigg, 701
Palheiro, 795
De Palingbeek, 740
Palleg, 731
Palmares, 793
Pals, 798
Panmure, 691
Pannal, 652
Pannonia G&CC, 780
Panorámica, 803
Panshanger Golf
 Complex, 576
El Paraíso, 802
Parc de Brotonne, 759
Parc, 727
Parco de' Medici, 784
Paris International, 756
Park, 570
Park GC Ostrava, 741
Park Hill, 593
Parkhall, 622
Parklands, 640
Parknasilla, 677
Parkstone, 556
Partille, 807
Pastures, 551
Patriziale Ascona, 817

Patshull Park Hotel
 G&CC, 622
Pau, 749
Paultons Golf
 Centre, 570
Pavenham Park, 531
Le Pavoniere, 786
Paxhill Park, 638
Payerne, 816
Peacehaven, 635
Pease Pottage, 638
Peebles, 697
Peel, 578
De Peelse Golf, 790
Pelves, 754
Pembrokeshire clubs
 and courses, 728
Pen Guen, 750
La Penaza, 803
Penha Longa, 795
Penina, 793
Penmaenmawr, 722
Penn, 622
Pennard, 731
Pennington, 732
Penrhos G&CC, 721
Penrith, 548
Penwortham, 589
Pen-y-Cae, 732
Peralada, 798
Perdiswell Park, 648
Périgueux, 749
Perivale Park, 603
Perranporth, 546
Perstorp, 810
Perth & Kinross clubs
 and courses, 716–718
Perton Park, 622
Perugia, 786
Pescara, 784
Pessac, 749
Peter McEvoy
 Trophy, 330
Peterborough
 Milton, 538
Peterculter, 690
Peterhead, 689
Petersberg, 783
Petersfield, 570
Petersfield Sussex
 Road, 570
Peterstone, 730
Peugeot Open de
 France, 140
Peugeot Open
 d'España, 135
Peuramaa, 746
Pevero GC Costa
 Smeralda, 784
Pfaffing
 Wasserburger, 773
Pfalz Neustadt, 778
Pforzheim Karlshäuser
 Hof, 779
PGA See Professional
 Golfer's Association
PGA Assistants'
 Championship, 197

PGA Cup, 191
PGA European Tour
 Trophy, 343
PGA European Tour,
 814
PGA Seniors
 Championship, 197
Phoenix Open, 158
Phoenix Park, 660
Phoenix, 655
Piandisole, 785
La Picardière, 753
Pickala Golf, 746
Pierpont, 739
Pierrevert, 763
Pike Fold, 598
Pike Hills, 652
Piltdown, 635
Pine Cliffs G&CC, 793
Pine Ridge, 630
Pineda De Sevilla, 803
Pineta di Arenzano, 783
La Pinetina, 782
Ping World
 Ranking, 211
Pinheiros Altos, 793
Pinner Hill, 603
Pitcheroak, 648
Piteå, 806
Pitlochry, 717
Pitreavie, 703
Plassey, 732
Playa Serena, 797
The Players
 Championship, 159
Pleasington, 589
Pléneuf-Val André, 750
Ploemeur Océan, 750
Podebrady, 741
Poggio dei Medici, 786
Polkemmet, 715
Pollensa, 797
Pollok, 705
Polmont, 720
Poniente, 797
Pont Royal, 763
Pontardawe, 731
Ponte de Lima, 795
Ponte di Legno, 783
Pontefract &
 District, 660
Pontefract Park, 661
Ponteland, 610
Pontnewydd, 727
Pontypool, 727
Pontypridd, 726
La Porcelaine, 751
Porin Golfkerho, 748
Pornic, 758
Porrassalmi, 747
Port Bannatyne, 693
Port Bourgenay, 758
Port Glasgow, 719
Port St Mary, 578
Portadown, 664
Portal G&CC, 542
Portal Premier, 542
Portarlington, 679

Index

Porters Park, 576
Porthmadog, 724
Portlethen, 690
Portmarnock, 673
Portmarnock Hotel, 673
Portmore Golf
 Park, 553
Porto Carras
 G&CC, 780
Porto d'Orra, 784
Portobello, 714
Portpatrick, 699
Portsalon, 670
Portsmouth, 570
Portstewart, 680
Portugal clubs and
 courses, 793–795
Portuguese Open, 134
Portumna, 676
Potsdamer Tremmen,
 767
Pottergate, 596
Potters Bar, 576
Poult Wood, 582
Poulton Park, 542
Poulton-le-Fylde, 589
Powerscourt, 687
Powfoot, 699
Powys clubs and
 courses, 728–729
Pozoblanco, 800
Praa Sands, 546
Praha, 741
Praia d'el Rey, 795
La Prée-La
 Rochelle, 753
Prenton, 600
President's Bowl, 240
President's Cup, 192
Prestatyn, 722
Prestbury, 542
Preston, 589
Prestonfield, 714
Prestwich, 598
Prestwick, 695
Prestwick St
 Cuthbert, 695
Prestwick St
 Nicholas, 695
Le Prieuré, 761
Prince of Wales
 Challenge Cup, 275
Princenbosch, 788
Princes Risborough, 535
Prince's, 582
The Priors, 562
Priors Hall, 608
Priskilly Forest, 728
Professional Golfer's
 Association, 827–8
Provence G&CC, 763
Prudhoe, 610
Prunevelle, 760
Pryors Hayes, 543
Puerta de Hierro, 800
Pula Golf, 797
Pumpherston, 715
Punta Ala, 786

Purley Chase, 643
Purley Downs, 630
Purmer, 788
Puttenham, 631
Puxton Park, 619
Pwllheli, 724
Pyecombe, 638
Pyle & Kenfig, 726
Pype Hayes, 643
Pyrford, 631
Pyrmonter, 771

Qatar Masters, 134
Quad City Classic, 161
Queens Park, 556 , 543
Queensbury, 661
Le Querce, 784
Quimper-
 Cornouaille, 750
La Quinta G&CC, 802
Quinta da Barca, 795
Quinta da Beloura, 795
Quinta da Marinha, 795
Quinta do Lago, 793
Quinta do Perú, 795

R&A *See* Royal and
 Ancient
R&A Trophy, 333, 343
RAC Country
 Club, 631
Radcliffe-on-Trent, 612
Radstadt
 Tauerngolf, 735
Radyr, 730
RAF Benson, 614
RAF Cottesmore, 615
RAF Germany, 776
RAF Gütersloh, 771
RAF Henlow, 531
RAF Marham, 606
RAF North Luffenham,
 615
RAF St Athan, 730
RAF Waddington, 596
Raffeen Creek, 668
Raglan Parc, 727
Rainbow Foods LPGA
 Classic, 220
Ralston, 705
Ramsdale Park Golf
 Centre, 612
Ramsey, 538 , 578
Ramside, 558
Randers, 743
Ranfurly Castle, 719
Rapallo, 783
Rathdowney, 679
Rathfarnham, 675
Ratho Park, 714
Rathsallagh, 687
Ratingen Gut
 Grashaus, 776
Rättvik, 808
Ravelston, 714
Ravenmeadow, 648

Ravensberger Land, 771
Ravensworth, 640
Rawdon, 661
Reading, 533
Real Campoamor, 796
Real Cerdaña, 798
Real Golf Castiello, 799
Real Golf El Prat, 798
Real Golf Las
 Palmas, 799
Real Golf Neguri, 799
Real Golf Pedreña, 799
Real Golf Sevilla, 803
Real San Sebastián, 799
Real Tenerife, 799
Real Zarauz, 799
Reaseheath, 543
Reay, 706
Rebetz, 755
Redbourn, 576
Redcastle, 670
Reddish Vale, 543
Redditch, 648
Redhill & Reigate, 631
Redhill, 631
Redlibbets, 582
Regensburg G&LC,
 775
Regensburg-
 Sinzing, 775
Regent Park
 (Bolton), 589
Regiment Way Golf
 Centre, 563
Reichswald, 775
Reigate Heath, 631
Reigate Hill, 631
Reims-Champagne, 760
Reit im Winkl-
 Kössen, 773
Reiting G&CC, 736
Renfrew, 719
Renfrewshire clubs and
 courses, 718–719
Renishaw Park, 655
Rennes Saint Jacques,
 750
Retford, 612
Reus Aiguesverds, 798
Reutlingen-
 Sonnenbühl, 779
Reykjavíkur, 781
Reymerswael, 788
Rhein Badenweiler, 779
Rhein Main, 769
Rhein Sieg, 778
Rheinblick, 769
Rheine/Mesum, 776
Rheintal, 769
Rhin Mulhouse, 761
Rhoen, 768
Rhondda, 726
Rhosgoch, 729
Rhos-on-Sea, 722
Rhuddlan, 722
Rhuys-Kerver, 750
Rhyl, 722
Ribe, 743

Richings Park
 G&CC, 536
Richmond, 631, 653
Richmond Park, 606,
 631
Rickenbach, 779
Rickmansworth, 576
Riddlesden, 661
The Ridge, 583
Riederalp, 816
Rigenée, 739
Rijswijkse, 791
Ringdufferin, 671
Ringenäs, 813
Ringway, 543
Rinkven G&CC, 738
Rio Real, 802
Ripon City, 653
Risebridge, 563
Rishton, 590
Rittergut Birkhof, 766,
 776
Riva Dei Tessali, 784
River Golf, 748
Riversmeet Par
 Three, 556
RLGC Village Play, 600
RMCS Shrivenham,
 646
Robin Hood, 643 , 655
Le Robinie, 782
La Rocca, 783
Rochat, 761
Rochdale, 590
Rochefort, 762
Les Rochers, 750
Rochester & Cobham
 Park, 583
Rochford Hundred, 563
Rockmount, 671
Rodway, 566
Roe Park, 680
Roehampton, 631
Roker Park, 631
Rold Skov, 744
The Rolls of
 Monmouth, 727
Roma, 784
Romanby, 653
Romeleåsen, 807
Romford, 563
Romiley, 543
Romney Warren, 583
Romsey, 570
Ronneby, 810
Rookery Park, 625
Roquebrune, 763
Rosapenna, 670
Roscommon, 683
Roscrea, 683
Roseberry Grange, 558
Rosebery Challenge
 Cup, 275
Rosehearty, 689
Rosendaelsche, 789
Roskilde, 745
Roslagen, 805
Ross, 677

Index 923

Rossendale, 590
La Rossera, 782
Rosslare, 685
Rossmore, 682
Ross-on-Wye, 572
Rothbury, 610
Rother Valley Golf Centre, 655
Rotherham, 655
Rothes, 689
Rothesay, 693
Rothley Park, 593
Rottaler G&CC, 773
Rottbach, 773
Rouen-Mont St Aignan, 759
Rougemont, 738
Rougemont-le-Château, 761
Rouken Glen, 705
Roundhay, 661
Roundwood, 655, 687
Routenburn, 696
Le Rovedine, 782
I Roveri, 785
Rowany, 578
Rowlands Castle, 570
Royal & Ancient, 704
Royal and Ancient Golf Club of St Andrews, 820–5; Captain of, 11
Royal Aberdeen, 690
Royal Amicale Anderlecht, 739
Royal Antwerp, 738
Royal Ascot, 533
Royal Ashdown Forest, 635
Royal Belfast, 671
Royal Bendinat, 797
Royal Birkdale, 600
Royal Blackheath, 583
Royal Burgess Golfing Society of Edinburgh, 714
Royal Cinque Ports, 583
Royal County Down, 671
Royal Cromer, 606
Royal Dornoch, 706
Royal Dublin, 675
Royal Eastbourne, 635
Royal Epping Forest, 563
Royal GC du Hainaut, 739
Royal GC du Sart Tilman, 740
Royal Golf Club de Belgique, 739
Royal Golf Club, 765
Royal Golf des Fagnes, 740
Royal Guernsey, 539
The Royal Household, 533
Royal Jersey, 539
Royal Latem, 740

Royal Liverpool, 601
Royal Lytham & St Annes, 590
Royal Malta, 787
Royal Mid-Surrey, 631
Royal Montrose, 691
Royal Mougins, 763
Royal Musselburgh, 712
Royal North Devon, 553
Royal Norwich, 606
Royal Oak, 744
Royal Ostend, 740
Royal Perth Golfing Society, 717
Royal Porthcawl, 726
Royal Portrush, 664
Royal Sant'Anna, 782
Royal St David's, 724
Royal St George's, 583
Royal Tara, 682
Royal Tarlair, 689
Royal Troon, 696
Royal Waterloo, 739
Royal West Norfolk, 606
Royal Wimbledon, 631
Royal Winchester, 571
Royal Worlington & Newmarket, 625
Royal Zoute, 741
Royan, 753
Royston, 576
Rozenstein, 791
Ruchill, 705
Rudding Park, 653
Ruddington Grange, 612
Rufford Park Golf Centre, 612
Rugby, 643
Ruislip, 603
Runcorn, 543
Rungsted, 745
Rush, 673
Rushcliffe, 612
Rushden, 608
Rushmere, 625
Rushmore Park, 646
Rusper, 632
Rustington, 638
Ruthin-Pwllglas, 722
Rutland clubs and courses, 615
Rutland County, 615
Ruukkigolf, 746
Ruxley Park, 583
Rya, 810
Ryburn, 661
Ryde, 578
The-Ryder Cup, 181
Ryder Cup– Individual Records, 187
Rye Hill, 614
Rye, 636
Ryhope, 558

Ryston Park, 606
Ryton, 640

Saarbrücken, 778
Sables-d'Or-les-Pins, 750
Sablé-Solesmes, 758
Sachsenwald, Am, 770
Saddleworth, 590
Saeby, 744
Safeco Classic, 221
Safeway LPGA, 221
Saffron Walden, 563
Sagmühle, 775
St Andrews, 704
St Andrews Links Trophy, 276
St Andrews Major, 730
St Andrews Thistle, 704
St Andrews Trophy, 260
St Anne's, 675
St Annes Old Links, 590
St Arild, 810
St Aubin, 757
St Augustines, 583
St Austell, 546
St Barbara's Royal Dortmund, 777
St Bees, 548
St Boswells, 697
St Clements, 539
St Cleres, 563
St Cloud, 762
St Cyprien, 757
St Davids City, 728
St David's Gold Cross, 276
St Deiniol, 724
St Dionys, 770
St Endreol, 763
St Enodoc, 546
St Etienne, 765
St Eurach G&LC, 773
St Fillans, 717
St Gatien Deauville, 759
St George's Grand Challenge Cup, 277
St George's Hill, 632
St Germain, 762
St Germain-les-Corbeil, 757
St Giles Newtown, 729
St Helena, 625
St Helen's Bay, 685
St Idloes, 729
St Ives, 538
St Jean-de-Monts, 758
St Julien, 759
St Junien, 751
St Kew, 546
St Laurence, 747
St Laurent, 750
St Leon-Rot, 769
St Lorence G&CC, 780

St Lorenzen, 736
St Malo-Le Tronchet, 750
St Margaret's G&CC, 673
St Mary's Hotel G&CC, 730
St Medan, 699
St Mellion Hotel G&CC, 546
St Mellons, 730
St Melyd, 723
St Michaels Jubilee, 543
St Michael's, 703
St Neot's, 538
St Nom-La-Bretêche, 762
St Oswald-Freistadt, 735
St Pierre, 727
St Pierre du Perray, 757
St Pierre Park, 539
St Pölten Schloss Goldegg, 735
St Quentin-en-Yvelines, 762
St Regulus Ladies', 704
The St Rule Club, 704
St Rule Trophy, 314
St Saëns, 760
St Samson, 751
St Thomas, 757
St Thomas's Priory, 622
Saint-Omer, 755
La Sainte-Baume, 763
Sainte-Maxime, 763
Saintonge, 753
Sala, 805
Salamanca, 797
Sale, 543
Sälenfjallens, 809
El Saler, 803
La Salette, 764
Salgados, 793
Saline, 703
Salisbury & South Wilts, 646
Sallandsche De Hoek, 789
Salo Golf, 748
Saltburn, 653
Saltford, 619
Saltsjöbaden, 814
Salvagny, 765
Salzburg Fuschl, 735
Salzburg Klesheim, 736
Salzkammergut, 736
Samsung World Championship of Women's Golf, 221
San Floriano-Gorizia, 787
San Lorenzo, 794
San Michele, 784
San Roque, 802
Sancerrois, 753
Sand Martins, 533
Sand Moor, 661

Sandbach, 543
Sandford Springs, 571
Sandhill, 655
Sandilands, 596
Sandiway, 543
Sandown Park, 632
Sandwell Park, 622
Sandy Lodge, 577
Sandyhills, 705
Sanquhar, 699
Sant Cugat, 798
Sant Jordi, 798
Santa Croce, 785
Santa María G&CC, 802
Santa Ponsa, 797
Sapey, 572
Sara Lee Classic, 218
Sarfvik, 747
Sargé-Le-Mans, 758
Le Sart, 755
Säter, 809
Saudárkróks, 781
Saunton, 553
Sauzon, 751
Savenay, 758
Saxå, 815
Scarborough North Cliff, 653
Scarborough South Cliff, 653
Scarcroft, 661
Scarthingwell, 653
Schinznach-Bad, 818
Schloss Braunfels, 768
Schloss Breitenberg, 770
Schloss Ebreichsdorf, 37
Schloss Ernegg, 735
Schloss Fahrenbach, 775
Schloss Frauenthal, 736
Schloss Georghausen, 777
Schloss Haag, 777
Schloss Klingenburg-Günzburg, 779
Schloss Langenstein, 780
Schloss Liebenstein, 780
Schloss Lüdersburg, 770
Schloss Maxlrain, 773
Schloss Meisdorf, 767
Schloss Myllendonk, 777
Schloss Pichlarn, 736
Schloss Schönborn, 737
Schloss Schwöbber, 771
Schloss Sickendorf, 768
Schloss Weitenburg, 780
Schlossberg, 775
Schmidmühlen G&CC, 775
Schmitzhof, 777
Schönenberg, 818

Schönfeld, 737
De Schoot, 790
Schwanhof, 775
Schwarze Heide, 777
Scoonie, 703
Scotland Ladies' County Ch'p, 313
Scotland Ladies' Foursomes, 313
Scotscraig, 703
Scottish Amateur Championship, 242
Scottish Area Team Championship, 264
Scottish Assistants' Championship, 199
Scottish Boys' Championship, 327
Scottish Boys' Strokeplay Ch'p, 328
Scottish Boys' Team Championship, 334
Scottish Boys' Under-16 Strokeplay Ch'p, 329
Scottish Champion of Champions, 244
Scottish Club Championship, 264
Scottish clubs and courses, 687–720
Scottish Foursomes Tournament (Glasgow Evening Times Trophy), 264
Scottish Girls' Close Championship, 338
Scottish Golf d'Aubertin, 749
Scottish Ladies' Close Amateur Ch'p, 299
Scottish Ladies' Junior Open Strokeplay Championship, 337
Scottish Ladies' Open Strokeplay Ch'p (Helen Holm Trophy), 300
Scottish Mid-Amateur Championship, 244
Scottish Open Amateur Strokeplay Ch'p, 243
Scottish PGA Matchplay Ch'p, 199
Scottish Professionals' Championship, 199
Scottish Senior Championship, 244
Scottish Senior Ladies' Amateur Ch'p, 301
Scottish Youths' Strokeplay Ch'p, 329
Scrabo, 671
Scraptoft, 593
SCT Knuds, 742
Sea Golf Rönnäs, 747
Seacroft, 596
Seafield, 696
Seaford, 636

Seaford Head, 636
Seaham, 559
Seahouses, 610
Seapoint, 680
Seascale, 548
Seaside Golf, 747
Seaton Carew, 559
Seckford, 625
Sedbergh, 548
Sedgley, 622
Sedlescombe, 636
Seedy Mill, 622
Seefeld-Wildmoos, 734
Selborne Salver, 277
Selby, 653
Selkirk, 697
La Sella, 796
Selsdon Park Hotel, 632
Selsey, 638
Semily, 741
Semlin am See, 767
Semmering, 737
Sempachersee, 818
De Semslanden, 790
Sene Valley, 583
Senior Ladies' British Amateur Strokeplay Championship, 295
Senne GC Gut Welschof, 771
Sennelager (British Army), 772
Sept Fontaines, 740
Seraincourt, 757
Serlby Park, 612
La Serra, 785
Servanes, 764
Sestrieres, 785
Settle, 653
Severn Meadows, 617
Sevilla Golf, 803
Shandon Park, 665
Shanklin & Sandown, 578
Shannon, 666
Shaw Hill Hotel G&CC, 590
Sheerness, 583
Sheffield Transport, 656
Shell Houston Open, 160
Shendish Manor, 577
Sherborne, 556
Sherdley Park Municipal, 601
Sherdons Golf Centre, 566
Sheringham, 606
Sherwood Forest, 612
Shetland, 708
Shifnal, 617
Shillinglee Park, 638
Shipley, 661
Shirehampton Park, 566
Shirenewton, 727
Shirland, 551
Shirley, 643
Shirley Park, 632

Shiskine, 696
Shooter's Hill, 583
Shoprite LPGA Classic, 219
Shortlands, 583
Shotts, 710
Shrewsbury, 617
Shrigley Hall, 543
Shrivenham Park, 646
The Shropshire, 617
Shropshire clubs and courses, 615–617
Sickleholme, 551
Sidcup, 584
Sidmouth, 553
Sieben-Berge Rheden, 772
Siegerland, 777
Sigtunabygden, 805
Silecroft, 548
Silkeborg, 744
Silkstone, 656
Silloth-on-Solway, 548
Silsden, 661
Silverdale, 548
Silverknowes, 714
Silvermere, 632
Silverstone, 536
Silverwood, 664
Simon's Golf Club, 745
Singing Hills, 638
Sion, 817
Sittingbourne & Milton Regis, 584
Sitwell Park, 656
Six Hills, 593
Sjögärde, 807
Skaftö, 816
Skeabost, 708
Skellefteå, 806
Skelmorlie, 696
Skepparslov, 810
Skerries, 673
Skibbereen, 669
Skinnarebo, 812
Skipton, 653
Skjeberg, 793
Skjoldenaesholm, 745
Skogaby, 813
Skovlunde Herlev, 745
Slade Valley, 673
Slaley Hall G&CC, 610
Sleaford, 596
Slieve Russell, 666
Slinfold Park, 639
Slovenia clubs and courses, 795–796
Smurfit European Open, 143
Snöå, 809
Söderåsen, 810
Söderhamn, 809
Söderköping, 812
Söderslätts, 808
Södertälje, 805
Solent Meads Par Three, 556
Solheim Cup, 225–9

Index

Sollefteå-Långsele, 806
Sollentuna, 814
Sollerö, 809
Søllerød, 745
Sologne, 753
Soltau, 767
Sölvesborg, 810
Somerley Park, 571
Somerset clubs and
 courses, 617–620
Somosaguas, 800
Son Antem, 797
Son Servera, 797
Son Vida, 797
Sønderjyllands, 744
Sondie Arctic
 Desert, 742
Sonnenalp, 773
Sonning, 533
La Sorelle, 765
Sorknes, 793
Sorø, 745
Sotogrande, 802
South African
 Open, 133
South American
 Tour, 178
South Beds, 531
South Bradford, 661
South Essex
 G&CC, 563
South Glamorgan clubs
 and courses, 729–730
South
 Herefordshire, 572
South Herts, 577
South Kyme, 596
South Leeds, 661
South Moor, 559
South of Scotland, 202
South
 Pembrokeshire, 728
South Shields, 640
South Staffordshire, 622
South West PGA, 202
South Winchester, 571
Southampton
 Municipal, 571
Southern Assistants'
 Matchplay Ch'p, 203
Southern Assistants'
 Ch'p, 202
Southern Professionals'
 Ch'p, 203
Southerndown, 726
Southerness, 699
Southfield, 615
Southport &
 Ainsdale, 601
Southport
 Municipal, 601
Southport Old
 Links, 601
Southwell, 612
Southwick Park, 571
Southwold, 625
Southwood, 571
The Spa, 671

Spaarnwoude, 788
Spain clubs and
 courses, 796–803
Spalding, 596
Spanish Point, 667
Sparkwell, 553
Spean Bridge, 707
Spérone, 755
Spessart, 769
Spey Bay, 689
Sphinx, 643
Spiegelven GC Genk,
 740
Sporting Club
 Berlin, 767
Sporting Club de
 Vichy, 752
Springhead Park, 650
The Springs, 615
Springwater, 613
Sprint International,
 162
Sprowston Park, 606
Stackstown, 675
Staddon Heights, 553
Stade Montois, 749
Stafford Castle, 623
Staffordshire and
 Shropshire Strokeplay
 Ch'p, 203
Staffordshire clubs and
 courses, 620–623
Staffordshire Open, 203
Stakis Puckrup Hall
 Hotel, 566
Stamford, 543
Stand, 598
Standard Life Loch
 Lomond, 141
Standard Register
 Ping, 218
Standish Court, 590
Stanedge, 551
Stanmore, 604
Stanton-on-the-
 Wolds, 613
Stapleford Abbotts, 563
Starbank LPGA
 Classic, 220
Starnberg, 773
State Farm Rail
 Classic, 221
Stavanger, 793
Staverton Park, 608
Steenhoven, 738
Steisslingen, 780
Stenungsund-Spekeröd,
 807
Stevenage, 577
Stinchcombe Hill, 567
Stirling, 720
Stirlingshire clubs and
 courses, 719–720
Stock Brook Manor,
 563
Stockholm, 814
Stockley Park, 604
Stockport, 544

Stocks Hotel
 G&CC, 577
Stocksbridge &
 District, 656
Stocksfield, 610
Stockwood Park, 531
Stockwood Vale, 619
Stoke Albany, 608
Stoke Poges, 536
Stoke Rochford, 596
Stoke-by-Nayland, 625
Stone, 623
Stoneham, 571
Stonehaven, 689
Stoneleigh Deer
 Park, 643
Stony Holme, 548
Stonyhurst Park, 590
Stora Lundby, 807
Stornoway, 708
Storws Wen, 725
Stourbridge, 648
Stowe, 536
Stowmarket, 625
Strabane, 684
Strandhill, 683
Strängnäs, 805
Stranraer, 699
Strasbourg, 761
Stratford Oaks, 643
Stratford-on-Avon, 644
Strathaven, 710
Strathclyde Park, 710
Strathendrick, 720
Strathlene, 689
Strathmore Golf
 Centre, 718
Strathpeffer Spa, 707
Strathtay, 718
Strathtyrum
 Course, 704
Strawberry Hill, 604
Stressholme, 559
Strokestown, 683
Stromberg-
 Schindeldorf, 778
Stromness, 708
Strömstad, 816
Stroyan Cup, 340
Studley Wood, 615
Stupinigi, 785
Sturminster
 Marshall, 557
Stuttgarter
 Solitude, 780
Styal, 544
Subaru Sarazen World
 Open Ch'p, 181
Sudbrook Moor, 596
Sudbury, 604
Sudurnesja, 781
Suffolk clubs and
 courses, 623–626
The Suffolk
 G&CC, 625
Suffolk Open, 203
Suffolk Professionals'
 Ch'p, 203

Sulham Valley, 533
Sully-sur-Loire, 753
Sunbury, 604
Sunderland of Scotland
 Masters, 203
Sundridge Park, 584
Sundsvall, 806
Sunne, 816
Sunningdale, 632
Sunningdale
 Foursomes, 278
Sunningdale
 Ladies, 632
Surbiton, 632
Surrey clubs and
 courses, 626–634
Sussex (East) clubs and
 courses, 634–636
Sussex (West) clubs and
 courses, 636–639
Sussex Open, 203
Sutton Bridge, 596
Sutton Coldfield, 644
Sutton Green, 632
Sutton Park, 650
Sutton, 675
Suur-Helsingin, 747
Svalöv, 810
Svendborg, 742
Swaffham, 607
Swansea Bay, 731
Swanston, 714
Swarland Hall, 610
Sweden clubs and
 courses, 804–816
Sweetwoods Park, 636
Swindon, 623
Swinford, 681
Swinley Forest, 533
Swinton Park, 598
Switzerland clubs and
 courses, 816–818
Swords, 674
Sybrook, 789
Sydsjaellands, 745
Syke, 767
Sylt, 770

Täby, 814
Tadmarton Heath, 615
Tain, 707
Tall Pines, 619
Tammer Golf, 748
Tamworth, 623
Tandragee, 665
Tandridge, 632
Tankersley Park, 656
Tantallon, 712
Tara Glen, 686
Tarbat, 708
Tarbert, 693
Tarina Golf Puijo, 746
Tarland, 689
Tarquinia, 784
Tat Golf
 Internationa, 818
Taulane, 764

926 Index

Taunton & Pickeridge, 619
Taunton Vale, 619
Taunus Weilrod, 769
Tavistock, 553
Tawast G&CC, 748
Taymouth Castle, 718
Teesside, 653
Tegelberga, 808
Tegernseer GC Bad Wiessee, 774
Tehidy Park, 546
Teign Valley, 553
Teignmouth, 553
Telford, 617
Temple G&CC, 671
Temple Newsam, 661
Temple, 533
Templemore, 683
Tenby, 728
Tennant Cup, 278
Tenterden, 584
Terceira Island, 794
Ternesse G&CC, 738
Terramar, 798
Test Valley, 571
Tewkesbury Park Hotel, 567
Thames Ditton & Esher, 632
Thaytal Drosendorf, 737
Thetford, 607
Theydon Bois, 563
Thirsk & Northallerton, 653
Thornbury Golf Centre, 567
Thorndon Park, 563
Thorne, 656
Thorney Golf Centre, 538
Thorney Park, 536
Thornhill, 699
Thornton, 703
Thorntree, 712
Thorpe Hall, 564
Thorpe Wood, 538
Thorpeness Golf Hotel, 625
Thoulstone Park, 646
Three Locks, 536
Three Rivers, 564
Thumeries, 755
Thurles, 684
Thurlestone, 554
Thurso, 706
Tickenham, 619
Tidbury Green, 644
Tidworth Garrison, 646
Tietlingen, 767
Tignes, 761
Tilgate Forest, 639
Tillicoultry, 698
Tillman Trophy, 279
Tilsworth, 531
Timrå, 806
Tinsley Park, 656

Tipperary, 684
Tirrenia, 786
Tiverton, 554
TNT Dutch Open, 142
Tobermory, 693
Tobo, 812
Todmorden, 661
Toft Hotel, 596 , 596
La Toja, 800
Tolladine, 648
Tomelilla, 808
Tongelreep G&CC, 790
Toot Hill, 564
Top Meadow, 564
Töreboda, 813
Torekov, 810
Torino, 785
Torphin Hill, 714
Torphins, 689
Torquay, 554
Torrance House, 711
La Torre, 783
Torreby, 816
Torremirona, 798
Torrequebrada, 801
Torrington, 554
Torshälla, 805
Tortuna, 805
Torvaianica, 784
Torvean, 708
Torwoodlee, 697
Toulouse, 766
Toulouse-La Ramée, 766
Toulouse-Palmola, 766
Toulouse-Seilh, 766
Toulouse-Teoula, 766
Le Touquet 'La Forêt', 755
Le Touquet 'La Mer', 755
Le Touquet 'Le Manoir', 755
The Tour Championship, 164
Touraine, 753
Tournerbury Golf Centre, 571
Towerlands, 564
Towneley Hall, 680
Towneley, 590
Toxandria, 788
Tracy Park, 567
Traigh, 708
Tralee, 677
Tramore, 685
Tranås, 812
Traunsee-Kircham, 735
Tredegar & Rhymney, 728
Tredegar Park, 728
Trefloyne, 728
Tregenna Castle Hotel, 546
Trelleborg, 808
Treloy, 546
Trent Lock Golf Centre, 613

Trent Park, 604
Trentham Park, 623
Trentham, 623
Trethorne, 546
Treudelberg G&CC, 771
Trevose, 546
Trieste, 787
Tróia Golf, 795
Trollhättan, 813
Trondheim, 793
Troon Municipal, 696
Troon Portland, 696
Troon St Meddans, 696
Trophée Lancôme, 145
Trosa, 805
Troyes-Cordelière, 761
Trubshaw Cup, 279
Trummenas, 810
Truro, 546
Tuam, 676
Tubbercurry, 683
Tucson Chrysler Classic, 159
Tudor Park Hotel, 584
Tulfarris, 687
Tullamore, 682
Tulliallan, 698
Les Tumulus, 766
Tunbridge Wells, 584
Tunshill, 590
Turespaña Masters Open Baleares, 137
Turkey clubs and courses, 818
Turnberry Hotel, 696
Turnhouse, 714
Turriff, 689
Turton, 590
Turvey, 674
Tutzing, 774
Tuusula, 747
Twentsche, 789
Twickenham, 604
Tylney Park, 571
Tyne & Wear clubs and courses, 639–641
Tynedale, 611
Tynemouth, 640
Tyneside, 640
Tyrrells Wood, 632
The Tytherington Club, 544

Uddeholm, 816
Udine, 787
Ufford Park Hotel, 625
Ullesthorpe Court Hotel, 593
Ullna, 815
Ulm/Neu-Ulm, 780
Ulricehamn, 813
Ulriksdal, 815
Ulster Professionals', 203
Ulverston, 549
Ulzama, 799

Umeå, 806
United Airlines Hawaiian Open, 158
United States v Great Britain & Ireland, 248
Unna-Fröndenberg, 777
Upavon (RAF), 646
Upchurch River Valley, 584
Uphall, 715
Upminster, 564
Upsala, 805
Upton-by-Chester, 544
Urslautal, 736
US Golf Association (USGA), 827
US LPGA Tour, 216
US Masters See Masters
US Nike Tour, 170
US Open Championship, 64–71
US PGA Championship, 79–86
US PGA Tour, 155–65
US Senior Tour, 165–9
US Women's Open, 95–102, 220
Utrechtse 'De Pan', 792
Uttoxeter, 623
Uxbridge, 604

Vaasan, 746
Vadstena, 812
Vagliano Trophy– Great Britain & Ireland v Europe, 311
Val de Cher, 752
Val de l'Indre, 753
Val de Sorne, 761
Val Queven, 751
The Vale, 649
Valcros, 764
Valdaine, 765
Valdeláguila, 800
Valderrama, 802
Vale de Milho, 794
Vale do Lobo, 794
Vale of Glamorgan G&CC, 730
Vale of Leven, 701
Vale of Llangollen, 723
Vale Royal Abbey, 544
Valence St Didier, 765
Valescure, 764
Vall d'Or, 797
Vallensbaek, 745
Vallentuna, 815
Vallromanes, 798
Vammala, 748
Vara-Bjertorp, 813
Varberg, 813
Varde, 744
Varese, 782
Värnamo, 812
Vasatorp, 810
Vassunda, 805

Index 927

Västerås, 805
Västervik, 812
La Vaucouleurs, 762
Le Vaudreuil, 760
Vaul, 693
Växjö, 812
Vechta-Welpe, 777
Vegilinbosschen, 790
Vejle, 744
Vellinge, 808
Veluwse, 789
Venezia, 787
Ventnor, 578
Verbier, 817
Verden, 767
Verona, 783
Versilia, 783
Vert Parc, 755
Verulam, 577
Vestfold, 793
Vestfyns, 742
Vestischer GC Recklinghausen, 777
Vestmannaeyja, 781
Vetlanda, 812
Viborg, 744
Vicars Cross, 544
Vidago, 795
Vierumäen Golfseura, 747
Vigevano, 782
Viksjö, 815
Vila Sol, 794
Vilamoura Laguna, 794
Vilamoura Old, 794
Vilamoura Pinhal, 794
Villa Condulmer, 787
Villa de Madrid CC, 801
Villa D'Este, 782
Villamartin, 796
Villarceaux, 757
Villars, 817
Vimeiro, 795
Vinberg, 813
Vinovo, 785
Virginia Park, 726
Virginia, 666
Virvik Golf, 747
Visby, 812
Vista Hermosa, 803
La Vitarderie, 761
Vittel, 761
Vivary, 619
Vodacom South African Tour, 176
Vogrie, 714
Les Volcans, 752
Volvo Masters, 148
Volvo PGA Championship, 137
Volvo Ranking, 130
Volvo Scandinavian Masters, 142
Vreta Kloster, 812
Vulpera, 817

Wakefield, 662
Waldegg-Wiggensbach, 774
Waldringfield Heath, 626
Waldviertel, 735
The Walker Cup, 248–58
Wallasey, 601
Wallenried, 816
Wallsend, 640
Walmer & Kingsdown, 584
Walmersley, 590
Walmley, 644
Walsall, 623
Waltham Windmill, 596
Walton Hall, 544
Walton Heath, 633
Wanstead, 564
La Wantzenau, 761
Waregem, 741
Wareham, 557
Warkworth, 611
Warley Park, 564
Warley, 649
Warren, 554, 564, 601
Warrenpoint, 672
Warrington, 544
Warwick, 644
The Warwickshire, 644
Warwickshire clubs and courses, 641–644
Warwickshire Open, 203
Warwickshire Professionals' Matchplay Ch'p, 203
Warwickshire Professionals' Strokeplay Ch'p, 203
Wäsby, 815
Washington, 640
Wasserburg Anholt, 777
Waterbridge, 554
Waterford, 685
Waterford Castle, 685
Waterhall, 636
Waterlandse, 788
Waterlooville, 571
Waterstock, 615
Waterton Park, 662
Waterville, 677
Wath-upon-Dearne, 656
Wavendon Golf Centre, 536
Weald of Kent, 584
Weald Park, 564
Wearside, 640
Websweiler Hof, 778
Weetabix Women's British Open, 88–94, 213
Wegmans Rochester International, 219
Weitra, 735
Welch's/Circle K Championship, 217

Welcombe Hotel, 644
Welderen, 789
Wellingborough, 608
Wellow, 571
Wells, 619
Wellshurst G&CC, 636
Wels, 735
Welschap, 790
Welsh Amateur Championship, 245
Welsh Amateur Strokeplay Ch'p, 246
Welsh Border Golf Complex, 729
Welsh Boys' Championship, 329
Welsh Boys' Under-15 Championship, 330
Welsh Champions of Champions, 247
Welsh clubs and courses, 721–732
Welsh Girls' Championship, 338
Welsh Inter-Counties Championship, 264
Welsh Ladies' Amateur Championship, 301
Welsh Ladies' Open Amateur Strokeplay Championship, 302
Welsh Ladies' Team Championship, 313
Welsh Mid-Amateur Championship, 246
Welsh Open Youths' Championship, 330
Welsh Professionals' Championship, 200
Welsh Senior Ladies' Championship, 302
Welsh Seniors' Amateur Championship, 246
Welshpool, 729
Welwyn Garden City, 577
Auf der Wendlohe, 771
Wensum Valley, 607
Wentorf-Reinbeker, 771
Wenvoe Castle, 730
The Wentworth Club, 633
Wergs, 623
Wermdö G&CC, 815
Wernddu Golf Centre, 728
Werneth Low, 544
Werneth, 591
Weserbergland, 772
West Berkshire, 534
West Bowling, 662
West Bradford, 662
West Byfleet, 633
West Chiltington, 639
West Cornwall, 546
West Derby, 601
West Essex, 564

West Glamorgan clubs and courses, 730–731
West Herts, 577
West Hill, 633
West Hove, 636
West Kent, 584
West Kilbride, 696
West Lancashire, 601
West Linton, 715
West Lothian, 715
West Malling, 584
West Middlesex, 604
West Monmouthshire, 728
West Region PGA, 204
West Surrey, 633
West Sussex, 639
West Waterford, 685
West Wilts, 646
Westerham, 584
Westerhope, 640
Western Gailes, 696
Western Park, 593
Westerpark Zoetmeer, 791
Westerwald, 777
Westerwood Hotel G&CC, 701
Westfälischer Gütersloh, 772
Westgate & Birchington, 584
Westhill, 690
Westhoughton, 591
Westin Texas Open, 163
Westmanstown, 674
Weston Park, 607
Weston Turville, 536
Westonbirt, 567
Weston-super-Mare, 619
Westpfalz Schwarzbachtal, 778
Westport, 681
Westwood, 623
Wetherby, 662
Wexford, 686
Wexham Park, 536
Weybrook Park, 572
Weymouth, 557
Whalley, 591
Whalsay, 708
Wharton Park, 649
Wheathill, 619
Wheatley, 656
Whetstone, 593
Whickham, 640
Whinhill, 719
Whipsnade Park, 577
Whiston Hall, 623
Whitburn, 641
Whitby, 653
Whitchurch, 730
Whitecraigs, 719
Whitefield, 598
Whitefields Hotel, 644
Whitehall, 726

Whitehead, 664
Whitehill, 577
Whitekirk, 712
Whiteleaf, 536
Whitemoss, 718
Whitewebbs, 604
Whiting Bay, 696
Whitley Bay, 641
Whitsand Bay Hotel, 547
Whitstable & Seasalter, 585
Whittaker, 591
Whittington Heath, 623
Whittlebury Park G&CC, 608
Whitwood, 662
Wick, 706
Wickham Park, 572
Wicklow, 687
Widnes, 544
Widney Manor, 644
Widukind-Land, 772
Wien, 737
Wienerberg, 737
Wienerwald, 737
Wiesbadener, 769
Wiesensee, 778
Wiesloch-Hohenhardter Hof G&LC, 769
Wigan, 591
Wigtown & Bladnoch, 699
Wigtownshire County, 699
Wildernesse, 585
Wildwood, 633
Willesley Park, 593
William Wroe, 598
Williamwood, 705
Willingdon, 636
Willow Valley, 662
Wilmslow, 544
Wilpshire, 591
Wilton, 654
The Wiltshire, 646
Wiltshire clubs and courses, 644–646

Wimbledon Common, 633
Wimbledon Park, 633
Wimereux, 755
Windermere, 549
Windlemere, 633
Windlesham, 633
Windmill Hill, 536
Windmill Village, 644
Windwhistle G&CC, 619
Windyhill, 701
Winge G&CC, 740
Winnerod, 768
Winter Hill, 534
Winterfield, 712
Wirral Ladies, 601
Wishaw, 644, 711
The Wisley, 633
Withernsea, 650
Withington, 598
Witney Lakes, 615
Wittelsbacher GC Rohrenfeld-Neuburg, 774
Wittsjö, 810
Wiurila G&CC, 748
Woburn, 536
De Woeste Kop, 788
Woking, 633
Wollaton Park, 613
Wolstanton, 623
Wombwell Hillies, 656
Women's European Amateur Team Championship, 311
Women's Home Internationals, 312
Women's Major Title Table, 124
Women's World Amateur Team Ch'p (Espirito Santo Trophy), 310
Woodbridge, 626
Woodbrook, 674

Woodbury Park, 554
Woodcote Park, 634
Woodenbridge, 687
Woodford, 564
Woodhall Hills, 662
Woodhall Spa, 596
Woodham G&CC, 559
Woodlake Park, 728
Woodlands, 678
Woodlands G&CC, 567
Woodlands Manor, 585
Woodlawn, 778
Woodsome Hall, 662
Woodspring G&CC, 567
Woodstock, 667
Woodthorpe Hall, 597
Wooler, 611
Woolley Park, 662
Woolton, 601
Worcester G&CC, 649
Worcestershire clubs and courses, 646–649
Worcestershire Open, 204
Worcestershire Strokeplay Ch'p, 204
Worcestershire, 649
Worfield, 617
Workington, 549
Worksop, 613
World Cup of Golf, 193
World Junior Team Championship, 331
Worldham Park, 572
Worlebury, 620
Worplesdon, 634
Worplesdon Mixed Foursomes, 280
Worpswede, 767
Worsley, 599
Wörther See/Velden, 734
Worthing, 639
Wörthsee, 774
Wortley, 656

Wouwse Plantage, 788
Wrag Barn G&CC, 646
Wrangaton, 554
Wrekin, 617
Wrexham, 732
Wrexham clubs and courses, 731–732
Wrotham Heath, 585
Wyboston Lakes, 531
Wycombe Heights, 536
Wyke Green, 604
Wylihof, 816
The Wynyard, 559
Wyre Forest Golf Centre, 649

Yelverton, 554
Yeovil, 620
York, 654
Yorkshire (East) clubs and courses, 649–650
Yorkshire (North) clubs and courses, 651–654
Yorkshire (South) clubs and courses, 654–656
Yorkshire (West) clubs and courses, 656–662
Yorkshire Professionals Championship', 204
Youghal, 669
Ystad, 808
Les Yvelines, 762
Yteri Golf, 748

Zaanse, 788
La Zagaleta, 802
Zaudin, 803
Zeegersloot, 791
Zeewolde, 792
Zell am See-Kaprun, 736
Zoate, 782
De Zuid Limburgse G&CC, 790
Zürich-Zumikon, 818